Best Books for Senior High Readers

Best Books for Senior High Readers™

John T. Gillespie

EDITOR

R. R. BOWKER
New Providence, New Jersey

Published by R. R. Bowker a division of Reed Publishing (U.S.A.) Inc.
Copyright © 1991 by Reed Publishing (U.S.A.) Inc.
All rights reserved
Printed and bound in the United States of America

Library of Congress Cataloging-in-Publication Data

Gillespie, John Thomas, 1928–
Best books for senior high readers / John T. Gillespie, editor.
p.   cm.
Includes index.
ISBN 0-8352-3021-X
1. Bibliography—Best books—Young adult literature.   2. High
school students—Books and reading.   3. Young adult literature—
Bibliography.   4. High school libraries—Book lists.   I. Title.
Z1037.0483   1991
[PN1009.A1]
011.62'5—dc20   91-26666
                                                          CIP

ISBN 0-8352-3021-X

9   780835   230216

Contents

Major Subjects Arranged Alphabetically   xiii

Preface   xv

Literary Forms

Fiction   **3**

Adventure and Survival Stories   3
Animal Stories   16
Classics   17
   Europe   17
     GENERAL   17
     GREAT BRITAIN AND IRELAND   18
   United States   21
Contemporary Life and Problems   23
   General   23
   Ethnic Groups and Problems   23
   Family Life and Problems   27
   Physical and Emotional Problems   33
   Personal Problems and Growing into Maturity   39
   World Affairs and Contemporary Problems   48
Fantasy   51
Historical Fiction   68
   Prehistory   68
   Ancient and Medieval History   69
     GENERAL AND MISCELLANEOUS   69
     GREECE AND ROME   69
     MIDDLE AGES   70
   Africa   70
   Asia and the Pacific   70

   Europe and the Middle East   71
   Latin America and Canada   75
   United States   76
     INDIANS OF NORTH AMERICA   76
     DISCOVERY AND EXPLORATION   76
     COLONIAL PERIOD AND FRENCH AND INDIAN WARS   77
     REVOLUTIONARY PERIOD (1775–1809)   77
     NINETEENTH CENTURY TO THE CIVIL WAR (1809–1861)   77
     THE CIVIL WAR (1861–1865)   78
     WESTERN EXPANSION AND PIONEER LIFE   78
     RECONSTRUCTION TO WORLD WAR I (1865–1914)   81
     BETWEEN WARS AND THE GREAT DEPRESSION (1919–1948)   82
   Twentieth Century Wars   82
     WORLD WAR I   82
     WORLD WAR II AND THE HOLOCAUST   83
     KOREAN WAR   85
     VIETNAM WAR   85
Horror Stories and the Supernatural   86
Humorous Stories   94
Mystery and Detective Stories   95
Romances   111
Science Fiction   116
Sports Stories   141
Short Stories and General Anthologies   142

Plays   **147**

General and Miscellaneous Collections   147
Geographical Regions   148
   Europe   148
     GENERAL   148

GREAT BRITAIN AND IRELAND   149
SHAKESPEARE   150
United States   151
Other Regions   155

Poetry   156
General and Miscellaneous Collections   156
Geographical Regions   158
  Europe   158
    GENERAL   158
    GREAT BRITAIN AND IRELAND   158
  United States   160
  Other Regions   166

Folklore and Fairy Tales   167
General and Miscellaneous   167
Geographical Regions   168
  Africa   168
  Asia and the Middle East   168
  Europe   169
  North America   170
    GENERAL AND MISCELLANEOUS   170
    INDIANS OF NORTH AMERICA   170
    UNITED STATES   171
  South and Central America   172

Mythology   173
General and Miscellaneous   173
Classical   174
Scandinavian   175

Humor and Satire   176

Speeches, Essays, and General Literary Works   179

Literary History and Criticism

General and Miscellaneous   185

Fiction   188
General and Miscellaneous   188
Europe   189
  General   189
  Great Britain and Ireland   190
United States   192
Other Regions and Countries   197

Plays   198
General and Miscellaneous   198
Europe   198
  General   198
  Great Britain and Ireland   198
    GENERAL   198
    SHAKESPEARE   199
United States   200

Poetry   201
General and Miscellaneous   201
Europe   202
  General   202
  Great Britain and Ireland   202
United States   202

Language and Communication

Signs and Symbols   207

Words and Languages   208

Writing and the Media   212
General and Miscellaneous   212
Books and Publishing   213
Newspapers, Magazines, and Journalism   213
Propaganda   214

Philosophy and Religion

Philosophy   217

Religion   219
World Religions   219
The Bible and Bible Study   222
Holidays and Holy Days   223

Society and the Individual

Government and Political Science   227
General Works   227
The United Nations and International Organizations   227
International Relations, Peace, and War   227
Various Forms of Government   230

United States Government and
Institutions 230
  General 230
  The Constitution 230
  The Presidency 232
  *Federal Government, Its Agencies, and
  Public Administration* 232
  *State and Municipal Governments and
  Agencies* 233
  The Law and the Courts 233
  Politics 235
    GENERAL 235
    ELECTIONS 236
  The Armed Forces 236
  Taxes and Public Expenditure 237

Citizenship and Civil Rights 238
Civil and Human Rights 238
Immigration 240
Ethnic Groups and Racial Prejudice 241
  General and Miscellaneous 241
  Blacks 241
  Jews 243
  Indians of North America 244
  Hispanics 244
  Other Minorities 244
Forms of Dissent 245

Social Concerns and Conflicts 246
General and Miscellaneous 246
Environmental Problems 247
  General 247
  Pollution 248
Population Problems 249
  General and Miscellaneous 249
  Aging 249
  Crime and Prisons 249
  Poverty and Homeless People 251
  Unemployment and Labor Problems 252
Public Morals 252
Sex Roles 253
Social Change and Futurism 254
Social Customs 254
Terrorism 254
Urban and Rural Life 255

Economics and Business 256
General and Miscellaneous 256
Economic Systems and Institutions 257
  General and Miscellaneous 257

Banks 258
Stock Exchanges 258
Consumerism 258
Employment and Jobs 259
Labor Unions 259
Money and Trade 259
Marketing and Advertising 259

Guidance and Personal Development

Education and the Schools 263
General and Miscellaneous 263
Development of Academic Skills 264
  Secretarial Skills 264
  Study Skills 264
  Tests and Test Taking 265
  Writing and Speaking Skills 265

Academic Guidance 269
General and Miscellaneous 269
Colleges and Universities 269
Financial Aid 273

Careers and Occupational Guidance 274
General and Miscellaneous 274
Careers 276
  General and Miscellaneous 276
  Artists and Entertainers 279
  Business Careers 281
  Construction and the Mechanical Trades .. 283
  Educators and Librarians 283
  *Lawyers, Policemen, and Other Society-
  Oriented Careers* 284
  Medical and Health Careers 285
  Scientists and Engineers 287
  Technicians and Industrial Workers 288

Personal Finances 291
Money-Making Ideas 291
  General and Miscellaneous 291
  Baby-sitting 291
Managing Money 291

Health and the Human Body 292
General and Miscellaneous 292
Aging and Death 292
Alcohol, Drugs, and Smoking 293

Bionics and Transplants 297
Diseases and Illnesses 297
Doctors, Hospitals, and Medicine 300
Genetics 302
Grooming, Personal Appearance, and
Dress 303
The Human Body 304
General and Miscellaneous 304
Brain and Nervous System 305
Senses 306
Skin and Hair 307
Teeth 307
Hygiene and Physical Fitness 307
Mental Disorders and Emotional
Problems 308
Nutrition and Diet 310
Physical Disabilities and Problems 312
Safety, Accidents, and First Aid 312
Sex Education and Reproduction 313
Sex Problems 316

Human Development and Behavior 318

General and Miscellaneous 318
Psychology and Human Behavior 318
General and Miscellaneous 318
Emotions and Emotional Behavior 320
Ethics and Ethical Behavior 320
Etiquette and Manners 321
Intelligence and Thinking 321
Measuring Human Behavior 321
Personal Guidance 322
Social Groups 324
Family and Family Problems 324

The Arts and Entertainment

General and Miscellaneous 329

Architecture and Building 330

General and Miscellaneous 330
History of Architecture 330
Regions 331
Various Types of Buildings 331

**Art, Painting, Photography, and
Sculpture** 332

General and Miscellaneous 332
History of Art 333

Regions 335
Africa 335
Asia 335
Australia and the Pacific Islands 335
Europe 335
North America 336
UNITED STATES 336

Decorative Arts 338

Music 339

General and Miscellaneous 339
History of Music 340
Jazz, Rock, and Popular Music 340
Opera and Musicals 344
Orchestra and Musical Instruments 346
Songs and Folk Songs 346

The Performing Arts 348

General and Miscellaneous 348
Ballet and the Dance 348
Circuses, Fairs, and Parades 349
Puppetry 349
Radio and Recordings 349
Television, Video, and Motion Pictures 350
Theater and Drama 355

Biography and True Adventure

Adventure and Exploration 361

Collective 361
Individual 361

The Arts and Entertainment 365

Collective 365
Artists 366
Authors 368
Composers 376
Entertainers and Performers 377
Miscellaneous Artists 384

**Contemporary and Historical
Americans** 385

Collective 385
Civil Rights Leaders 387
Presidents and Their Wives 388

Statesmen and Other Public Figures   392
Miscellaneous Historical Figures   394

Science, Medicine, Industry, and Business   **397**
Collective   397
Individual   397

Sports   **402**
Collective   402
Automobile Racing   402
Baseball   402
Basketball   404
Boxing   405
Football   405
Gymnastics and Track and Field   406
Tennis   407
Miscellaneous Sports   407

World Figures   **408**
Collective   408
Africa   408
Asia and Middle East   409
Australia and the Pacific Islands   410
Europe   411
South and Central America   415

Miscellaneous Interesting Lives   **416**

History and Geography

General History and Geography   **425**
Miscellaneous Works   425
Atlases, Maps, and Mapmaking   425

Paleontology   **426**

Anthropology and Evolution   **428**

Archaeology   **430**

World History and Geography   **432**
General   432
Ancient History   435
General and Miscellaneous   435
Egypt and Mesopotamia   435
Greece   436
Rome   437
Middle Ages through Renaissance (500–1700)   437

Eighteenth through Nineteenth Centuries (1700–1900)   438
The Twentieth Century   439
General and Miscellaneous   439
World War I   439
Between the Wars (1918–1939)   440
World War II and the Holocaust   440
Modern World History (1945–   )   448

Geographical Regions   **450**
Africa   450
General and Miscellaneous   450
Central and Eastern Africa   451
North Africa   451
South Africa   451
West Africa   452
Asia   453
General and Miscellaneous   453
China   453
India   455
Japan   455
Other Asian Lands   456
Australia and the Pacific Islands   456
Europe   457
General and Miscellaneous   457
Central Europe and the Balkans   458
France   458
Germany   459
Great Britain and Ireland   459
Greece   461
Italy   461
Scandinavia, Iceland, and Greenland   461
Spain and Portugal   462
U.S.S.R.   462
Middle East   464
General and Miscellaneous   464
Israel   464
Other Middle East Lands   465
North and South America (excluding the United States)   466
General History and Geography   466
North America   466
CANADA   466
MEXICO   466
OTHER CENTRAL AMERICAN LANDS   467
PUERTO RICO, CUBA, AND OTHER CARIBBEAN ISLANDS   468
South America   468
Polar Regions   469
United States   470
General History and Geography   470

CONTENTS

Historical Periods 475

PREHISTORY 475

INDIANS OF NORTH AMERICA 475

DISCOVERY AND EXPLORATION 477

COLONIAL PERIOD AND FRENCH AND INDIAN
WARS 477

REVOLUTIONARY PERIOD AND THE YOUNG
NATION (1775–1809) 478

NINETEENTH CENTURY TO THE CIVIL WAR
(1809–1861) 479

THE CIVIL WAR (1861–1865) 480

WESTWARD EXPANSION AND PIONEER LIFE 483

RECONSTRUCTION TO WORLD WAR I
(1865–1917) 486

BETWEEN THE WARS AND THE GREAT
DEPRESSION (1918–1941) 487

WORLD WAR II TO THE PRESENT
(EXCLUDING KOREAN AND VIETNAM WARS) 488

KOREAN AND VIETNAM WARS 491

Regions 494

MIDWEST 494

MOUNTAIN STATES 495

NORTHEAST 495

PACIFIC STATES 496

SOUTH 497

SOUTHWEST 497

Physical and Applied Sciences

General and Miscellaneous 501

Experiments and Projects 504

Astronomy and Space Science 505

General and Miscellaneous 505

Astronautics and Space Exploration 507

Comets, Meteors, and Asteroids 509

Earth and Moon 510

Sun and the Solar System 510

Stars 511

Universe 511

Biological Sciences 513

General and Miscellaneous 513

Botany 515

General and Miscellaneous 515

Foods 515

Fungi 516

Forestry and Trees 516

Plants and Flowers 516

Zoology 517

General and Miscellaneous 517

Amphibians and Reptiles 518

GENERAL AND MISCELLANEOUS 518

ALLIGATORS AND CROCODILES 518

SNAKES AND LIZARDS 518

TORTOISES AND TURTLES 518

Animal Behavior 519

GENERAL AND MISCELLANEOUS 519

COMMUNICATION 519

DEFENSES 519

REPRODUCTION 519

TRACKS 519

Animal Species 520

GENERAL AND MISCELLANEOUS 520

APE FAMILY 520

BEARS 521

BIG CATS 521

COYOTES, FOXES, AND WOLVES 521

DEER FAMILY 521

PANDAS 522

RODENTS 522

Birds 522

GENERAL AND MISCELLANEOUS 522

BEHAVIOR 523

DUCKS AND GEESE 523

EAGLES, HAWKS, AND OTHER BIRDS OF PREY 524

OWLS 524

PENGUINS 524

Conservation and Endangered Species 524

Farms and Ranches 525

GENERAL AND MISCELLANEOUS 525

ANIMALS AND CROPS 525

Insects 526

GENERAL AND MISCELLANEOUS 526

BEES AND WASPS 526

BEETLES 526

BUTTERFLIES, MOTHS, AND CATERPILLARS 526

SPIDERS 527

Land Invertebrates 527

Marine and Freshwater Life 527

GENERAL AND MISCELLANEOUS 527

CRUSTACEANS 527

DOLPHINS 527

FISH 527

SHARKS 528

SHELLS 528

WHALES, DOLPHINS, AND OTHER SEA
MAMMALS 528

Microbiology and Biotechnology 530

Pets 530
GENERAL AND MISCELLANEOUS 530
CATS 531
DOGS 532
FISH 534
GERBILS, HAMSTERS, AND GUINEA PIGS 535
HORSES 535
Zoos, Aquariums, and Animal Care Shelters 535

Chemistry 537
General and Miscellaneous 537

Geology and Geography 538
General and Miscellaneous 538
Earth and Geology 538
Earthquakes and Volcanoes 539
Icebergs and Glaciers 539
Physical Geography 539
Rocks, Minerals, and Soil 540

Mathematics 542
General and Miscellaneous 542
Algebra, Numbers, and Number Systems 543
Mathematical Games and Puzzles 543
Statistics 543
Time and Clocks 544
Weights and Measures 544

Meteorology 545
Air 545
Storms 545
Weather 545

Oceanography 546
General and Miscellaneous 546
Currents, Tides, and Waves 546
Seashores 546
Underwater Exploration and Sea Disasters 547

Physics 548
General and Miscellaneous 548
Energy and Motion 549
General and Miscellaneous 549
Nuclear Energy 549
Solar Energy 550
Light, Color, and Laser Science 550
Magnetism and Electricity 550
Nuclear Physics 550

Technology and Engineering 551
General Works and Miscellaneous Industries 551
Clothing and Textiles 552
Computers and Automation 552
Electronics 556
Machinery 557
Telegraph and Telephone 557
Television, Motion Pictures, Radio, and Recording 557
Transportation 558
General and Miscellaneous 558
Airplanes and Aeronautics 558
Automobiles and Trucks 559
Cycles 561
Railroads 561
Ships and Boats 561
Weapons, Submarines, and the Armed Forces 561

Recreation and Sports

Crafts 565
General and Miscellaneous 565
American Historical Crafts 566
Calligraphy 566
Clay, Modeling, and Ceramic Crafts 566
Costume Making and Fashion 567
Drawing and Painting 567
Masks and Mask Making 569
Paper Crafts 570
Printmaking 570
Sewing and Needle Crafts 570
Toys and Dolls 572
Woodworking and Carpentry 572

Hobbies and Pastimes 575
General and Miscellaneous 575
Cooking 576
Gardening 579
Home Repairs 580
Magic and Tricks 580
Model Making 581
Photography and Filmmaking 581
Stamp, Coin, and Other Types of Collecting 583

Health and the Human Body 292
ENTRIES 5073–5522

History and Geography 423
ENTRIES 6971–8202

Hobbies and Pastimes 575
ENTRIES 9296–9463

Human Development and Behavior 318
ENTRIES 5523–5681

Humor and Satire 176
ENTRIES 3482–3519

Jokes, Puzzles, Riddles, and Word
Games 585
ENTRIES 9464–9471

Language and Communication 205
ENTRIES 3898–3990

Literary Forms 1
ENTRIES 1–3562

Literary History and Criticism 183
ENTRIES 3563–3897

Mathematics 542
ENTRIES 8831–8865

Meteorology 545
ENTRIES 8866–8873

Music 339
ENTRIES 5813–5954

Mysteries, Curiosities, Controversial
and General Knowledge 586
ENTRIES 9472–9543

Mythology 173
ENTRIES 3448–3481

Oceanography 546
ENTRIES 8874–8898

Paleontology 426
ENTRIES 6973–6987

The Performing Arts 348
ENTRIES 5955–6116

Personal Finances 291
ENTRIES 5064–5072

Philosophy 215
ENTRIES 3991–4025

Physical and Applied Sciences 499
ENTRIES 8203–9134

Physics 548
ENTRIES 8899–8940

Plays 147
ENTRIES 2978–3145

Plays—Literary History and
Criticism 198
ENTRIES 3797–3845

Poetry 156
ENTRIES 3146–3356

Poetry—Literary History and
Criticism 201
ENTRIES 3846–3897

Recreation and Sports 563
ENTRIES 9135–9979

Religion 219
ENTRIES 4026–4122

Science, Medicine, Industry, and
Business—Biography 397
ENTRIES 6640–6704

Signs and Symbols 207
ENTRIES 3898–3902

Social Concerns and Conflicts 246
ENTRIES 4410–4560

Society and the Individual 225
ENTRIES 4123–4621

Speeches, Essays, and General
Literary Works 179
ENTRIES 3520–3562

Sports—Biography 402
ENTRIES 6705–6781

Sports and Games 591
ENTRIES 9544–9979

Technology and Engineering 551
ENTRIES 8941–9134

Words and Languages 208
ENTRIES 3903–3954

World Figures—Biography 408
ENTRIES 6782–6884

World History and Geography 432
ENTRIES 7028–7344

Writing and the Media 212
ENTRIES 3955–3990

Zoology 517
ENTRIES 8450–8779

(American Library Association, 1985), and copies of the annual *Books for the Teen Age* (New York Public Library).

Current book reviewing media were also consulted. The primary sources were *Booklist, The Book Report, School Library Journal,* and *VOYA* (*Voice of Youth Advocates*). Reviews were tabulated and drawn from journal issues beginning in January 1985 through November–December 1990, when coverage of this book ends.

Uses of This Book

Best Books for Senior High Readers was designed to help librarians and media specialists with four vital tasks: (1) to evaluate the adequacy of existing collections; (2) to build new collections or strengthen existing holdings; (3) to provide reading guidance to young adults; and (4) to prepare bibliographies and reading lists. To increase the book's usefulness, particularly when it comes to bibliographies and suggested reading, titles are arranged under broad areas of interest, or in the case of nonfiction works, by curriculum-oriented subjects rather than the Dewey Decimal classifications (suggested Dewey classification numbers are nevertheless provided within nonfiction entries).

Subject Arrangement

To help users integrate material from all three volumes in the set, we have categorized books under the same subject headings whenever possible. The junior and senior high volumes feature identical headings. These also correspond to many of the subjects used in *Best Books for Children*. Since a large part of *Best Books for Children* is devoted to picture books, complete uniformity was not possible.

Some arbitrary decisions were made concerning placement of books under specific subjects. For example, books of mathematical puzzles will be found in the Mathematics section rather than with puzzles, and books of science experiments and projects (though often dealing with a particular branch of science) are grouped under General Science—Experiments and Projects.

Arrangement

In the table of contents, subjects are arranged by the order in which they appear in the book. After the table of contents, users will find a second, alphabetical listing of major subjects, which provides entry numbers as well as page numbers for easy access. Following the main body of text are the book's three indexes. The Author Index cites authors, titles, and entry numbers (joint authors are listed separately). The Title Index gives the text's entry number. Works of fiction in both of these indexes are indicated by (F) following the title. Finally, an extensive Subject/Grade Level Index lists entries under thousands of specific subject headings and specifies grade-level suitability for each entry. The following codes are used to identify general grade levels:

JS (Junior-Senior High) grades 8 to 12
S (Senior High) grades 10 to 12

Entries

A typical entry contains the following information where applicable: (1) author, joint author, or editor; (2) title and subtitle; (3) specific grade levels given in parentheses; (4) adapter or translator; (5) indication of illustrations; (6) publication date; (7) publisher and price of hardbound edition (LB = library binding); (8) International Standard Book Number (ISBN) of hardbound edition; (9) paperback publisher (paper) and price (if no publisher is listed, it is the same as the hardbound edition); (10) ISBN of paperback edition; (11) a one- to two-line descriptive annotation (within the annotation, the phrase "for advanced readers" is often used. It refers to material that is either intellectually very challenging or sufficiently complex to require previous knowledge of the subject; whereas the phrase "for mature readers" indicates that the book contains explicit adult situations and/or language); (12) review citations; (13) Dewey Decimal classification number for nonfiction titles. Bibliographic information and prices were verified in *Books in Print 1989–1990* and some publishers' catalogs.

Review Citations

Review citations are given for books published and reviewed from 1985 through 1990. These review citations will give librarians sources from which to find more detailed information about each of the books listed. The four sources cited and their abbreviations are:

BL	*Booklist*
BR	*The Book Report*
SLJ	*School Library Journal*
VOYA	*VOYA (Voice of Youth Advocates)*

The citing of only one review does not necessarily mean that the book received only a single recommendation. It might easily also have been listed in one or more of the other bibliographies consulted. A single negative review does not preclude inclusion of a title if the other reviews are positive. Books without review citations are pre-1985 imprints or reprints of older recommended books recently brought back into print (the original publication date is indicated within the annotation whenever available).

Acknowledgments

Many people were involved in the preparation of this bibliography. I am particularly indebted to Christine Gilbert for her support and help and especially to Marion Sader, Publisher, R. R. Bowker, who inspired this book, as well as Nancy Bucenec, Bowker Production Managing Editor, whose diligent efforts brought this title to print. I thank them for their suggestions, assistance, and, above all, patience.

Literary Forms

Fiction

Adventure and Survival Stories

1 Abbey, Edward. *The Brave Cowboy: An Old Tale in a New Time* (10–12). 1977, Univ. of New Mexico Pr. paper $10.95 (0-8263-0448-6). A modern cowboy with old-fashioned ideals is in conflict with the present-day world.

2 Abrahams, Peter. *Hard Rain* (10–12). 1988, Dutton $18.95 (0-525-24581-2). A mature suspense novel about a mother's effort to locate her daughter, who has been taken by her ex-husband. (Rev: VOYA 10/88)

3 Allegretto, Michael. *Night of Reunion* (10–12). 1990, Macmillan $17.95 (0-684-19133-4). An insane killer who killed Alex's first wife and child is now after his new family. (Rev: SLJ 8/90)

4 Ambler, Eric. *The Care of Time* (10–12). 1985, Berkley paper $2.95 (0-425-08894-4). A complex novel about an ex-CIA agent in the Persian Gulf. By the same author use: *Epitaph for a Spy; The Light of Day;* and *The Schirmer Inheritance* (all 1985).

5 Ambler, Eric. *A Coffin for Dimitrios* (10–12). 1990, Carroll & Graf paper $3.95 (0-88184-619-8). One of the pioneer writers of spy thrillers at his peak. Also use: *Background to Danger; Journey into Fear; Cause for Alarm* (all 1990); and *Passage of Arms* (Berkley, 1985).

6 Anthony, Evelyn. *Albatross* (10–12). 1983, Putnam $14.95 (0-399-12773-9). Secret Intelligence Agent Davina Graham sets out to find the identity of a Russian mole who has infiltrated the Service's ranks.

7 Anthony, Evelyn. *A Place to Hide* (10–12). 1989, Jove paper $3.95 (0-515-09981-3). Through the story of an Irish family and the mysterious disappearance of a son, the author spins a fast action story about the conflict in present-day Ireland. (Rev: BL 2/15/87)

8 Anthony, Evelyn. *The Scarlet Thread* (10–12). 1990, Harper $18.95 (0-06-016100-0). In this romantic adventure, 2 lovers, accidentally separated during World War II, are reunited and face a Mafia vendetta when they try to resume their relationship. (Rev: SLJ 12/90)

9 Archer, Jeffrey. *A Matter of Honor* (10–12). 1987, Pocket paper $4.95 (0-671-64159-X). For better readers, a tense thriller about a chase across Europe to secure a priceless icon. (Rev: BL 6/15/86)

10 Archer, Jeffrey. *Shall We Tell the President?* (10–12). 1987, Pocket paper $4.50 (0-671-63305-8). Someone is out to kill the president in this exciting tale told with a dash of humor.

11 Armen, M. A. *The Hanging of Father Miguel* (10–12). 1989, Evans $14.95 (0-87131-598-X). When a wounded gunfighter is nursed back to health by the local priest, the payment asked in return is most unusual. (Rev: BL 12/15/89)

12 Babbitt, Natalie. *Herbert Rowbarge* (9–12). 1984, Farrar paper $3.95 (0-374-51852-1). A complex novel involving sets of twins and unusual relationships.

13 Ball, John. *The Kiwi Target* (10–12). 1988, Dodd $15.95 (0-396-09364-7). What starts as a business trip to New Zealand soon becomes a tale of murder and arson. (Rev: BL 11/15/88)

14 Bellow, Saul. *Henderson the Rain King* (10–12). 1984, Penguin paper $6.95 (0-14-007269-1). The challenging novel about a millionaire who

gives up his comfortable life to venture into darkest Africa.

15 Bennett, George, ed. *Great Tales of Action and Adventure* (9–12). 1978, Dell paper $2.75 (0-440-93202-5). Twelve exciting adventure stories by such writers as Edgar Allan Poe and Jack London.

16 Betancourt, Jeanne. *Between Us* (8–12). 1986, Scholastic paper $2.25 (0-590-33323-2). A high school senior discovers that her assistant is stealing drugs from the hospital pharmacy where they work. (Rev: BL 8/86; SLJ 10/86; VOYA 6/86)

17 Blum, Howard. *Wanted: The Search for Nazis in America* (10–12). 1989, Simon & Schuster paper $8.95 (0-671-67607-5). An agent for the Bureau of Immigration becomes involved in the search for Nazis in the United States.

18 Bond, Larry. *Red Phoenix* (9–12). 1989, Warner $19.95 (0-446-51433-0). In this political thriller, the 2 Koreas are once again at war. (Rev: SLJ 1/90)

19 Bond, Michael. *Monsieur Pamplemousse Aloft* (9–12). 1989, Fawcett $14.95 (0-449-90445-5). The creator of Paddington takes on the adult world by inventing a gourmand detective who, in this humorous adventure, exposes a plot to kill important French and English politicians. (Rev: BL 9/15/89)

20 Brand, Max. *The Making of a Gunman* (10–12). 1984, Warner paper $2.50 (0-446-32412-4). Young Tommy Mayo becomes the student of a famous gambler and gunslinger in this western adventure. There are approximately 100 of Brand's titles in print.

21 Brand, Max. *Thunder Moon Strikes* (10–12). 1984, Warner paper $2.50 (0-446-32074-9). In this story about a Cheyenne warrior brought up in 2 cultures, he rejoins his white family. Preceded by *Thunder Moon* (1982) and *Thunder Moon's Challenge* (1984).

22 Brand, Max. *Way of the Lawless* (10–12). 1985, Warner paper $2.50 (0-446-32665-8). In this western by the prolific writer Brand, a basically decent young man finds himself on the wrong side of the law.

23 Brenner, Barbara. *The Gorilla Signs Love* (8–12). 1984, Lothrop $11.00 (0-688-00995-6). When Maggie is sent to work in Africa on experiments in gorilla communication, she becomes involved in a series of unexpected adventures.

24 Brinkley, William. *The Last Ship* (10–12). 1988, Viking $19.95 (0-670-80981-0). A few survivors of World War III land on a tropical island to begin life anew. (Rev: BL 2/15/88; BR 1–2/89; VOYA 10/88)

25 Brown, Dale. *Day of the Cheetah* (10–12). 1989, Donald I. Fine $19.95 (1-55611-121-5). A technothriller about futuristic airplanes and a hijacking by a Russian mole. (Rev: BL 5/15/89)

26 Brown, Sam. *The Trail to Honk Ballard's Bones* (9–12). 1990, Walker $19.95 (0-8027-4101-0). In this western adventure, Honk Ballard discovers that his new trail buddy is really a bank robber. (Rev: BL 1/15/90)

27 Bryant, Will. *A Time for Heroes* (10–12). 1987, St. Martin's $17.95 (0-312-00694-2). An adventure story involving a young boy in the Old West of 1923. (Rev: BL 6/15/87)

28 Buchan, John. *The 39 Steps* (10–12). 1990, Godine paper $9.95 (0-87923-838-0). In this thriller set in Britain, Richard Hannay must clear himself of murder charges.

29 Buckley, William F. *See You Later Alligator* (10–12). 1986, Dell paper $3.95 (0-440-17682-4). For better readers, this sixth Blackford Oakes adventure takes place during the Cuban missile crisis of the 1960s. (Rev: BL 2/15/85)

30 Buckley, William F. *The Story of Henri Tod* (10–12). 1989, Dell paper $4.50 (0-440-18327-8). This spy novel takes place at the time of the building of the Berlin Wall.

31 Burroughs, Edgar Rice. *The Cave Girl* (7–12). 1975, Ruter $13.95 (0-940724-01-4). An old-fashioned adventure about a young man who must live in the primitive world of the jungle.

32 Burroughs, Edgar Rice. *Tarzan of the Apes* (9–12). 1988, Crown $9.98 (0-517-65957-3); NAL paper $2.95 (0-451-52423-3). The beginning of the famous saga of the Ape Man that contains over 20 additional titles in the series.

33 Butler, Jimmie H. *The Iskra Incident* (9–12). 1990, Dutton $18.95 (0-525-24898-6). While investigating the mysterious crash of an American-bound Soviet plane, Jack Phillips finds he is the target of a KGB plot. (Rev: BL 8/90)

34 Calvert, Patricia. *The Hour of the Wolf* (7–12). 1985, NAL paper $2.95 (0-451-13493-1). Jake, a troubled boy, finds adventure and fulfillment after he is sent to live with family friends in Alaska.

35 Camp, John. *The Fool's Run* (10–12). 1989, Henry Holt $14.95 (0-8050-0990-6). Kidd is hired by an aviation company to sabotage a rival's computer system. (Rev: BR 3–4/90)

36 Carr, Jess. *Intruder in the Wind* (10–12). 1987, Commonwealth $15.95 (0-89227-076-4); Pocket

paper $3.95 (0-671-67267-3). A disturbed Vietnam vet refuses to give back to its parents an infant he has rescued. (Rev: SLJ 4/88)

37 Carroll, James. *Family Trade* (10–12). 1983, NAL paper $4.95 (0-451-12325-5). In this suspenseful spy drama, a college freshman who is the son of a CIA official becomes involved in unexpected adventures.

38 Carroll, Lenore. *Abduction from Fort Union* (10–12). 1988, Walker $15.95 (0-8027-4080-4). A cavalry trooper goes AWOL in pursuit of his kidnapped girlfriend. (Rev: BL 5/15/88)

39 Champlin, Tim. *King of the Highbinders* (10–12). 1989, Ballantine paper $2.95 (0-345-36320-5). In San Francisco of the 1880s, young Jay McGraw is kidnapped by a gang leader in Chinatown. (Rev: BL 10/1/89)

40 Chester, William L. *Kioga of the Wilderness* (9–12). 1990, Starmont $19.95 (1-55742-046-7). An adventure story of Indian life set in a wild northern region in Siberia.

41 Childers, Erskine. *The Riddle of the Sands: A Record of Secret Service* (10–12). 1976, Amereon LB $18.95 (0-89190-240-6); Penguin paper $5.95 (0-14-000905-1). A young Englishman finds that an innocent sailing expedition is really a spying mission.

42 Childress, Mark. *V for Victor* (9–12). 1989, Knopf $16.95 (0-394-56871-1). In 1942, a 16-year-old boy living on the coast of Alabama gets involved in a spy plot. (Rev: BL 11/15/88; BR 9–10/89; SLJ 7/89; VOYA 2/90)

43 Clancy, Tom. *The Cardinal of the Kremlin* (10–12). 1988, Putnam $19.95 (0-399-13345-3); Berkley paper $5.75 (0-425-11684-0). An intense spy story involving a race for defense systems between the Soviets and Americans. (Rev: SLJ 12/88)

44 Clancy, Tom. *Clear and Present Danger* (10–12). 1989, Putnam $21.95 (0-399-13440-9). An intricate spy thriller that deals with the drug war in Colombia. (Rev: SLJ 1/90)

45 Clancy, Tom. *Patriot Games* (10–12). 1987, Putnam $19.95 (0-399-13241-4); Berkley paper $4.95 (0-425-10972-0). In this large adventure novel for better readers, hero Jack Ryan tries to prevent a terrorist plan to kidnap Princess Diana and Prince Charles. Also recommended by Clancy are *Red Storm Rising* (1986) and *The Hunt for Red October* (1984). (Rev: BL 6/1/87; SLJ 11/87)

46 Clarke, Richard. *The Arrowhead Cattle Company* (10–12). 1988, Walker $16.95 (0-8027-4079-0). A young cowhand, playing poker, wins a ranch that includes 2 abandoned boys. (Rev: BL 6/1/88)

47 Clavell, James. *Children's Story* (10–12). 1981, Delacorte $7.95 (0-385-28135-8); 1989, Dell paper $3.95 (0-440-20468-2). After a terrible war has been lost, thought control is introduced in the schools.

48 Clavell, James. *Noble House* (10–12). 1981, Delacorte $22.95 (0-385-28737-2); Dell paper $5.95 (0-440-16484-2). An action-filled story about a China trading firm in Hong Kong. Also use: *Tai-Pan* (1983).

49 Cody, Liza. *Bad Company* (9–12). 1984, Warner paper $2.95 (0-446-30738-6). In this suspense story, Anna Lee and a teenage girl are kidnapped and must escape before it is too late.

50 Collins, Larry, and Dominique Lapierre. *The Fifth Horseman* (10–12). 1981, Avon paper $4.95 (0-380-54734-1). An adventure tale involving a group of Palestinian terrorists who threaten to destroy New York City.

51 Conley, Robert J. *Go-Ahead Rider* (10–12). 1990, Evans $15.95 (0-87131-612-9). A Harvard-educated part Cherokee confronts a murder mystery when he returns to the West as a deputy. (Rev: BL 7/90)

52 Conley, Robert J. *Quitting Time* (10–12). 1990, Evans $14.95 (0-87131-586-6). A hired gun who loves Shakespeare investigates a cattle-rustling ring. (Rev: BL 1/1/90)

53 Cook, Robin. *Mortal Fear* (10–12). 1988, Putnam $17.95 (0-399-13318-6); Berkley paper $4.95 (0-425-11388-4). A doctor discovers a grisly plan to murder patients with unhealthy life-styles in this thriller for mature readers. (Rev: BL 12/1/87; VOYA 8/88)

54 Cook, Robin. *Outbreak* (10–12). 1988, Berkley paper $4.95 (0-425-10687-X). As a deadly plague strikes America, epidemiologist Marissa Blumenthal uncovers the plot behind its spread. (Rev: BL 11/1/86; SLJ 6–7/87)

55 Cook, Robin. *Sphinx* (10–12). 1983, NAL paper $4.95 (0-451-15949-7). Set in Egypt, this thriller involves a young art specialist from Boston and an antique statue in a tale of danger and romance.

56 Cook, Robin. *Vital Signs* (10–12). 1991, Putnam $21.95 (0-399-13575-8). A medical thriller that combines murder and infertility therapy. (Rev: BL 11/15/90)

57 Coonts, Stephen. *Final Flight* (10–12). 1988, Doubleday $18.95 (0-385-24555-6). An adventure story of life on an aircraft carrier that is the target of a terrorist plot. (Rev: BL 8/88)

58 Coonts, Stephen. *The Minotaur* (10–12). 1989, Doubleday $19.95 (0-385-26147-0). A new assignment for Jake Grafton of *Final Flight* (1988), this time taking the place of a man who died mysteriously while supervising the development of a stealth bomber. (Rev: BL 9/15/89)

59 Coonts, Stephen. *Under Siege* (10–12). 1990, Pocket $19.95 (0-671-72229-8). Jake Grafton becomes involved in a drug war in Washington, D.C. (Rev: BL 10/1/90)

60 Coppel, Alfred. *Show Me a Hero* (10–12). 1987, Harcourt $16.95 (0-15-182080-5); Ivy paper $3.95 (0-8041-0232-5). For better readers, a thriller about a movie crew filming in Tunisia and their attempt to free hostages. (Rev: BL 2/15/87)

61 Cormier, Robert. *After the First Death* (7–12). 1979, Pantheon LB $10.99 (0-394-94122-5). A busload of school children become the victims of a terrorist plot.

62 Crider, Bill. *Medicine Show* (9–12). 1990, Evans $15.95 (0-87131-613-7). In this western, Ray Storey sets out to avenge the death of his brother who was killed in a bank robbery. (Rev: BL 8/90)

63 Cummings, Jack. *Escape from Yuma* (10–12). 1990, Walker $19.95 (0-8027-4111-8). In the old West, an escaped convict and her 2 friends evade the law. (Rev: BL 7/90)

64 Cummings, Jack. *The Surrogate Gun* (10–12). 1990, Walker $18.95 (0-8027-4102-9). When a gunslinger humiliates some of the residents of Rosario, New Mexico, revenge is in the air. (Rev: BL 2/15/90)

65 Cussler, Clive. *Cyclops* (10–12). 1986, Pocket paper $4.95 (0-671-70464-8). A thriller involving hero Dirk Pitt and such elements as a missing blimp and a secret mission to the moon. (Rev: BL 1/15/86)

66 Cussler, Clive. *Dragon* (10–12). 1990, Simon & Schuster $21.95 (0-671-62619-1). A thriller featuring Dirk Pitt and a plot that involves extremists who placed nuclear devices in several large U.S. cities. (Rev: BL 5/1/90; SLJ 10/90)

67 Cussler, Clive. *Raise the Titanic* (10–12). 1984, Pocket paper $5.50 (0-671-66718-1). A thriller about trying to recover riches from the sunken *Titanic*.

68 Cussler, Clive. *Treasure* (10–12). 1988, Simon & Schuster $18.95 (0-671-62613-2). Adventurer Dirk Pitt combats terrorists to rescue hostages in a frozen wilderness in Greenland. (Rev: BL 3/15/88)

69 Darrell, Elizabeth. *The Flight of Flamingo* (10–12). 1989, St. Martin's $19.95 (0-312-03342-7). Two men and a woman form the eternal triangle in this English novel, which uses the airplane industry as a backdrop. (Rev: BL 12/15/89)

70 Deighton, Len. *Berlin Game* (10–12). 1989, Ballantine paper $4.95 (0-345-01071-X). Bernard Samson must investigate reports that there is a traitor operating in the British Intelligence.

71 Deighton, Len. *The Ipcress File* (10–12). 1988, Ballantine paper $3.95 (0-345-01014-0). In this spy thriller, a British agent tries to find and free a kidnapped biochemist. Also use *Funeral in Berlin* (1982) and *The Billion Dollar Brain* (1984).

72 Deighton, Len. *SS-GB: Nazi-Occupied Britain* (10–12). 1984, Ballantine paper $4.95 (0-345-31809-9). A "what if" thriller that deals with a Britain defeated and invaded by Hitler. Also use: *Catch a Falling Spy* (1984) and *Spy Story* (1985).

73 DeMille, Nelson. *Cathedral* (10–12). 1982, Dell paper $5.95 (0-440-11620-1). St. Patrick's Cathedral in New York City is seized by Irish terrorists in this thriller.

74 DeMille, Nelson. *The Charm School* (10–12). 1988, Warner $17.95 (0-446-51305-9); paper $4.95 (0-446-35320-5). An American tourist in Russia learns of a plan to infiltrate U.S. society by graduates of an Americanization program called the Charm School. (Rev: BL 3/15/88)

75 Dickey, James. *Deliverance* (10–12). 1986, Dell paper $3.95 (0-440-31868-8). For adult readers, this is the account of a hunting trip that turns into a nightmare.

76 Dickinson, Peter. *Tulku* (7–12). 1984, Ace paper $2.25 (0-441-82630-X). The son of a missionary in China joins a group of travelers on their way to Tibet.

77 Djerassi, Carl. *Cantor's Dilemma* (10–12). 1989, Doubleday $18.95 (0-385-26183-7). For better readers, this is a novel about the machinations behind research and discoveries in science. (Rev: VOYA 4/90)

78 Doyle, Arthur Conan. *When the World Screamed and Other Stories: The Professor Challenger Adventures* (9–12). 1990, Chronicle paper $8.95 (0-87701-652-6). Three stories in which the hero is Doyle's adventurer Professor Challenger. (Rev: BL 6/1/90)

79 Duncan, David James. *The River Why* (10–12). 1983, Sierra Club $12.95 (0-87156-321-5); Bantam paper $7.95 (0-553-34192-0). For better readers, a novel about fishing and the great outdoors.

80 Duncan, Robert L. *In the Enemy Camp* (9–12). 1985, Delacorte $15.95 (0-385-29388-7). In

this spy story, our ambassador to Indonesia is being trailed by a paid assassin. (Rev: SLJ 11/85)

81 Durand, Loup. *Daddy* (10–12). Trans. by J. Maxwell Brownjohn. 1989, Random $18.95 (0-394-57048-0). An 11-year-old Jewish boy is stalked by a killer because he knows a secret worth millions of dollars. (Rev: BL 10/1/88)

82 Faulkner, William. *The Reivers* (10–12). 1962, Random $17.95 (0-394-44229-6); paper $5.95 (0-394-70339-1). For better readers, this is a humorous novel of 3 young people who take a car for a joy ride into Memphis.

83 Finch, Phillip. *Trespass* (9–12). 1987, Watts $17.95 (0-531-15044-5). A group of wilderness campers fight to survive after an unexpected blizzard. (Rev: SLJ 4/88)

84 Fisher, David E., and Ralph Albertazzie. *Hostage One* (10–12). 1989, Random $18.95 (0-394-56984-9). For mature readers, an adventure novel about Quadaffi's mad plan to kidnap President Bush. (Rev: BL 5/15/89)

85 Follett, Ken. *Eye of the Needle* (10–12). 1979, NAL paper $4.95 (0-451-15524-6). A story of suspense and mounting horror involving a German spy and a family on a remote Scottish island.

86 Follett, Ken. *On the Wings of Eagles* (10–12). 1984, NAL paper $4.95 (0-451-16353-2). In this political thriller, 2 American executives are jailed illegally in Teheran. Also use by this author:*Key to Rebecca; The Man from St. Petersburg;* and *Triple* (all 1983).

87 Forbes, Colin. *Avalanche Express* (10–12). 1984, Harper paper $2.95 (0-06-080699-0). In this adventure story, a Russian who has been spying for America is fleeing for his life across Europe.

88 Forester, C. S. *The African Queen* (10–12). 1935, Little paper $8.95 (0-316-28910-8). An English spinster and a cockney male friend decide, as an act of revenge, to blow up a German boat in this novel set in Africa.

89 Forsyth, Frederick. *The Day of the Jackal* (9–12). 1971, Bantam paper $4.95 (0-553-26490-7). A rousing thriller about an attempted assassination of Charles de Gaulle.

90 Forsyth, Frederick. *The Devil's Alternative* (9–12). 1980, Viking $12.95 (0-670-27081-4); Bantam paper $4.95 (0-553-26490-7). The rescue of a man from drowning in the Mediterranean Sea begins a series of events that almost leads to nuclear disaster in this thriller.

91 Forsyth, Frederick. *The Dogs of War* (9–12). 1974, Viking $11.95 (0-670-27753-3); Bantam paper $4.95 (0-553-26868-5). An adventure story about greed and an attempt to seize power in a small West African country.

92 Forsyth, Frederick. *The Negotiator* (10–12). 1989, Bantam $19.95 (0-553-05361-2). A secret agent is dispatched to discover who is disrupting peace talks between Russia and the United States in this fast-paced thriller. (Rev: BL 3/15/89)

93 Forsyth, Frederick. *The Odessa File* (10–12). 1988, Bantam paper $4.95 (0-553-25525-8). A German reporter infiltrates an organization of former Nazis and is discovered.

94 Fowles, John. *The Collector* (10–12). 1963, Little $17.95 (0-316-29096-3); Dell paper $4.50 (0-440-31335-4). A nightmarish story about a demented man who kidnaps the girl for whom he feels an obsessive passion.

95 Freedman, Benedict, and Nancy Freedman. *Mrs. Mike* (7–12). 1968, Berkley paper $3.50 (0-425-10328-5). Based on a true story, this tells of Kathy, her love for her Mountie husband Mike, and her hard life in the Canadian Northwest.

96 French, Michael. *Soldier Boy* (8–12). 1986, Berkley paper $2.50 (0-425-09548-7). An entertaining novel about 2 teenagers undergoing basic training at Fort Ord and about their girlfriends. (Rev: SLJ 5/86; VOYA 8–10/86)

97 Galloway, Jack. *The Toothache Tree* (10–12). 1989, St. Martin's $18.95 (0-312-02659-5). Fifteen-year-old Hamilton Caine, Jr., learns about wilderness survival from his kidnapper, Bill. (Rev: SLJ 5/90)

98 Gann, Ernest K. *Fate Is the Hunter* (10–12). 1986, Simon & Schuster $10.95 (0-671-63603-0). A thrilling adventure story that was the basis of a successful movie.

99 Gardner, John. *Role of Honor* (10–12). 1984, Putnam $11.95 (0-399-12912-X); Berkley paper $4.50 (1-55773-125-X). Even though he is out of the service, James Bond cannot stay out of trouble. Also use: *License Renewed* (1985).

100 Gardner, John. *Scorpius* (10–12). 1988, Putnam $12.95 (0-399-13347-X). Is sect leader Father Valentine really an arms dealer? James Bond must find out. (Rev: BL 4/1/88)

101 Garfield, Brian. *Necessity* (10–12). 1984, St. Martin's $13.95 (0-312-56258-6). For better readers, this is the story of a woman who must assume a new identity to foil her pursuers.

102 Gilman, Dorothy. *Incident at Badamyâ* (9–12). 1989, Doubleday $16.95 (0-385-24760-5). In this adventure yarn 7 travelers are kidnapped in Burma and held for ransom. (Rev: BL 4/1/89)

103 Gilman, Dorothy. *Mrs. Pollifax and the Golden Triangle* (9–12). 1988, Doubleday $15.95 (0-385-23710-3). Mrs. Pollifax's husband is kidnapped in this thriller set in Thailand. (Rev: BL 1/15/88)

104 Gilman, Dorothy. *Mrs. Pollifax and the Hong Kong Buddha* (9–12). 1985, Fawcett paper $3.95 (0-449-20983-0). This unlikely CIA agent gets involved in a plan by terrorists to destroy Hong Kong. Another in this series is *Mrs. Pollifax on the China Station* (1983). (Rev: BL 11/1/85)

105 Gilman, Dorothy. *Mrs. Pollifax and the Whirling Dervish* (9–12). 1990, Doubleday $17.95 (0-385-41458-7). Mrs. Pollifax, a CIA agent and grandmother, finds adventure in Morocco. (Rev: BL 4/1/90; SLJ 10/90)

106 Golding, William. *Lord of the Flies* (8–12). 1962, Putnam $16.95 (0-698-10219-3). When they are marooned on a deserted island, a group of English schoolboys soon lose their civilized ways.

107 Goldman, William. *Marathon Man* (10–12). 1980, Amereon $17.95 (0-88411-653-0); Dell paper $4.95 (0-440-15502-9). There are some strong torture scenes in this adventure about a man being pursued by both government agents and a band of former Nazis.

108 Gorman, Edward. *What the Dead Men Say* (9–12). 1990, Evans $15.95 (0-87131-614-5). Set in Iowa in the 1880s, this is a revenge novel about a father who wants to punish the bank robbers who killed his daughter. (Rev: BL 8/90)

109 Greene, Graham. *Dr. Fischer of Geneva or The Bomb Party* (10–12). 1985, Viking $20.00 (0-670-27522-0). A short novel about a group of Dr. Fischer's guests who risk death to receive one of his extravagant gifts.

110 Greene, Graham. *The Human Factor* (10–12). 1988, Pocket paper $4.50 (0-318-33014-8). A challenging spy thriller involving a leak in the British intelligence network.

111 Greene, Graham. *The Portable Graham Greene* (10–12). 1977, Penguin paper $9.95 (0-14-015075-7). This generous selection includes 2 novels (*The Heart of the Matter* and *The Third Man*), plus many stories and selections from the author's autobiographical writings. [828]

112 Grey, Evelyn. *Camberleigh* (10–12). 1985, Berkley paper $3.95 (0-425-07643-1). A romantic gothic in which a gallant heroine lives through a rape and several attempts on her life. (Rev: SLJ 8/85)

113 Grove, Fred. *Deception Trail* (10–12). 1988, Doubleday $12.95 (0-385-23920-3). Three con men in the Old West make a precarious living on deception. (Rev: BL 8/88)

114 Haggard, H. Rider. *King Solomon's Mines* (9–12). 1982, Amereon LB $18.95 (0-89190-703-3). First published in 1885, this is a story of old-fashioned adventure and romance in the search for the source of King Solomon's wealth in Africa. A sequel is *Allen Quartermain* (reprinted in 1982).

115 Haggard, H. Rider. *She* (10–12). 1973, Airmont paper $1.95 (0-8049-0146-5). An exotic adventure into an African kingdom ruled by an ageless woman.

116 Hailey, Arthur. *Airport* (10–12). 1986, Dell paper $5.95 (0-440-10066-6). A multiplotted adventure novel that uses the airline industry as a background. Also use *Hotel* and *Wheels* (both 1986).

117 Hailey, Arthur. *The Evening News* (10–12). 1990, Doubleday $21.95 (0-385-23708-1). A crack news team goes to work when an anchorman's family is kidnapped in Peru. (Rev: BL 2/1/90; SLJ 9/90)

118 Hailey, Arthur. *The Moneychangers* (10–12). 1986, Dell paper $5.95 (0-440-15802-8). The world of banking and high finance is the backdrop of this lengthy adventure story.

119 Halacy, Dan. *Empire in the Dust* (F). 10–12. 1990, Walker $19.95 (0-8027-4108-8). A western that explores the conflicts between the Texas ranchers and the homesteaders. (Rev: BL 7/90)

120 Haldeman, Joe. *Tool of the Trade* (9–12). 1988, Avon paper $3.95 (0-380-70438-2). A thriller about a Russian spy being pursued by both the CIA and the KGB. (Rev: BL 4/15/87)

121 Hardy, Jon. *Biker* (8–12). 1985, Oxford Univ. Pr. $13.95 (0-19-271473-2). The story of "41," a young, restless man who tears around London delivering packages on his motorcycle. (Rev: BR 5–6/86; SLJ 5/86)

122 Hashian. *Shanidar* (9–12). 1990, Wynwood $18.95 (0-922066-38-8). A thrilling adventure story involving the president's daughter being taken as a hostage by terrorists in Iran. (Rev: BL 7/90)

123 Healy, Larry. *Angry Mountain* (7–12). 1983, Putnam $10.95 (0-396-08129-0). Sixteen-year-old Doug, in trouble with the law, is sent by his father to live on a volcanic island in Alaska.

124 Hemingway, Ernest. *The Old Man and the Sea* (10–12). 1977, Macmillan $25.00 (0-684-15363-7); paper $3.95 (0-02-051910-9). A deceptively simple novel about an old Gulf fisherman and his encounter with a giant marlin.

125 Herbert, Frank. *The White Plague* (10–12). 1987, Ace paper $4.95 (0-441-88569-1). Using as a background the current problems in Ireland, this is the story of a scientist who is seeking revenge.

126 Higgins, Jack. *Cold Harbour* (10–12). 1990, Simon & Schuster $19.95 (0-671-68425-6). A fast-paced thriller set during World War II about a submarine that takes agents to occupied France. (Rev: BL 1/1/90)

127 Higgins, Jack. *The Eagle Has Landed* (10–12). 1989, Pocket paper $4.95 (0-671-66529-4). In this thriller, a group of German paratroopers land in England during World War II to kidnap Churchill.

128 Higgins, Jack. *Night of the Fox* (10–12). 1987, Pocket paper $4.95 (0-671-64058-5). A thriller involving multiple disguises on a secret mission to the German-occupied island of Jersey during World War II. (Rev: BL 12/1/86)

129 Higgins, Jack. *Solo* (10–12). 1983, Dell paper $4.50 (0-440-18078-3). A tough Welshman sets out to find out the identity of a terrorist who has murdered his child.

130 Higgins, Jack. *Touch the Devil* (10–12). 1983, NAL paper $4.50 (0-451-16677-9). A retired agent must stop a killer whose target is Margaret Thatcher.

131 Hogan, Ray. *Solitude's Lawman* (10–12). 1988, Doubleday $12.95 (0-385-24431-2). A young horse dealer pursues a gang of bank robbers and the 16-year-old girl they have kidnapped, only to find he, too, becomes the pursued. (Rev: BL 1/1/88)

132 Holt, Victoria. *The Demon Lover* (9–12). 1983, Fawcett paper $4.95 (0-449-20098-1). This Gothic is set in England of the mid-1800s. Some others by this author are *Lord of the Far Islands* (1986), *The Judas Kiss, Menfreya in the Morning,* and *King of the Castle* (all 1982).

133 Holt, Victoria. *The Road to Paradise Island* (9–12). 1985, Fawcett paper $4.50 (0-449-20888-5). While investigating her ancestral home in England, Annalice finds a map of a Utopia-like island and a diary that reveals a murder. (Rev: BL 8/85)

134 Holt, Victoria. *Shivering Sands* (9–12). 1986, Fawcett paper $3.95 (0-449-21361-7). This is one of the author's exciting Gothic romances using historical settings and dealing with damsels in distress and dashing heroes. Others are: *The Devil on Horseback* (1987), *House of a Thou-*

sand Lanterns (1974), and *Kirkland Revels* (1962).

135 Holt, Victoria. *The Time of the Hunter's Moon* (9–12). 1984, Fawcett paper $4.95 (0-449-20511-8). In nineteenth-century England a young schoolteacher is caught up in romance, adventure, and mystery.

136 Hope, Anthony. *The Prisoner of Zenda* (10–12). 1984, Buccaneer $21.95 (0-89966-226-9); Airmont paper $1.25 (0-8049-0139-2). The original Ruritanian adventure romance. One sequel is *Rupert of Hentzau* (Penguin, 1984).

137 Household, Geoffrey. *Rogue Male* (10–12). 1985, Amereon $15.95 (0-89190-435-2). A plot to shoot a dictator fails and the hunter now becomes the hunted.

138 Houston, James. *River Runners: A Tale of Hardship and Bravery* (9–12). Illus. 1979, Macmillan $11.95 (0-689-50151-X). The action-filled story of 2 Indian boys who run a fur-trading outpost in subarctic Quebec.

139 Howatch, Susan. *Devil on Lammas Night* (9–12). 1986, Fawcett paper $2.95 (0-449-21319-6). One of the many recommended Gothic romances by this prolific author. Another is *Penmarric* (1984).

140 Hubert, Cam. *Dreamspeaker* (9–12). 1981, Avon paper $3.50 (0-380-56622-2). A boy who escapes from an institution finds friendship in a British Columbia forest.

141 Hughes, Monica. *Hunter in the Dark* (7–12). 1982, Macmillan $12.95 (0-689-30959-7); Avon paper $2.95 (0-380-67702-4). Mike tries to escape his serious illness by disappearing into the Canadian wilderness to hunt a white-tailed deer.

142 Hughes, Terence. *The Day They Stole the Queen Mary* (10–12). 1984, Jove paper $3.50 (0-515-07640-6). This thriller tells of a spy plot to kill Winston Churchill.

143 Hunsburger, H. Edward. *Crossfire* (9–12). 1985, Walker $13.95 (0-8027-4047-2). In this western, a widow and the man she has hired to help her find her missing son find murder in a corrupt Arizona town. (Rev: BL 5/1/85)

144 Hyman, Tom. *Seven Days to Petrograd* (10–12). 1988, Viking $18.95 (0-670-80865-2). A ruthless killer is hired to assassinate Lenin on his historic journey back to Russia in 1917. (Rev: BL 2/15/88)

145 Innes, Hammond. *Solomon's Seal* (10–12). 1985, Carroll & Graf paper $3.50 (0-88184-151-X). An adventure story set in New Guinea during a revolution.

146 Innes, Hammond. *The Wreck of the Mary Deare* (10–12). 1985, Carroll & Graf paper $3.50 (0-88184-152-8). Gideon Patch boards what appears to be a ghost ship and his adventures begin. Also use: *The Doomed Oasis* (1986), and *The Land God Gave to Cain* (1985).

147 Jones, Robert F. *Slade's Glacier* (10–12). 1982, Dell paper $3.25 (0-440-18441-X). Greed and revenge are 2 themes in this adventure story set in Alaska.

148 Judson, William. *Cold River* (9–12). 1976, NAL paper $3.50 (0-451-16164-5). A survival story involving a brother and sister lost in the Adirondacks.

149 Kalb, Marvin, and Ted Koppel. *In the National Interest* (10–12). 1980, Fawcett paper $2.50 (0-449-23743-5). These 2 broadcast journalists have written a taut thriller about the kidnapping of a diplomat's wife.

150 Katz, William. *After Dark* (10–12). 1988, Warner paper $3.95 (0-446-34605-5). A psychopath who believes his neighbor is a spy sets out to kill her. (Rev: VOYA 10/88)

151 Kavanaugh, Michelle. *Emerald Explosion* (9–12). 1988, Pineapple Pr. $11.95 (0-910923-46-9). Patrick refuses to believe reports of his mother's death in the Soviet Union and travels there to investigate. (Rev: BL 10/15/88; BR 11–12/88; SLJ 8/88)

152 Kaye, M. M. *Death in Zanzibar* (10–12). 1984, St. Martin's paper $3.95 (0-312-90130-5). On a trip to Zanzibar, Dany is involved in murder and a search for gold.

153 Keidel, Levi. *Caught in the Crossfire* (9–12). 1979, Herald Pr. paper $7.95 (0-8361-1888-X). A group of missionaries in Africa are caught unwillingly in the people's struggle for freedom.

154 Kelley, Leo P. *Luke Sutton: Lawman* (9–12). 1989, Doubleday $12.95 (0-385-24185-2). In this fast-moving western, a sheriff with a checkered past defends a 16-year-old boy wrongfully accused of murder. (Rev: BL 3/1/89)

155 Kennedy, William P. *Toy Soldiers* (10–12). 1988, St. Martin's $19.95 (0-312-01478-3). A chilling suspense novel for better readers about a group of American children held captive by terrorists. (Rev: BL 6/15/88; SLJ 11/88)

156 Kerr, M. E. *Fell Back* (8–12). 1989, Harper LB $11.89 (0-06-023293-5). Our young hero, John Fell, becomes involved in 2 strange deaths and a series of double-crossings in this continuation of *Fell* (1989). (Rev: BL 9/15/89; SLJ 9/89; VOYA 12/89)

157 Kerrigan, Philip. *Survival Game* (9–12). 1987, Crown $17.95 (0-517-56582-X); Avon paper $3.95 (0-380-70682-2). A simulated war game turns serious when a gunman begins picking off the participants. (Rev: SLJ 12/87)

158 Knox, Bill. *The Interface Man* (9–12). 1990, Doubleday $14.95 (0-385-41091-3). Inspector Thane is on the trail of a computer criminal in the highlands of Scotland. (Rev: BL 3/1/90)

159 Kyle, Duncan. *White Out!* (10–12). 1987, St. Martin's paper $3.95 (0-312-90918-7). Adventure on the Greenland icecap as a British engineer risks his life to save others.

160 L'Amour, Louis. *Bendigo Shafter* (9–12). 1983, Bantam paper $4.50 (0-553-26446-X). An old-fashioned western by a master of the genre. There are approximately 100 other westerns by this author available in paperback.

161 L'Amour, Louis. *The Outlaws of Mesquite* (9–12). 1990, Bantam $16.95 (0-553-05791-X). A collection of 8 action short stories about the Old West. (Rev: BL 8/90)

162 L'Amour, Louis. *Son of a Wanted Man* (10–12). 1984, Bantam paper $3.50 (0-553-24457-4). One of the many Sackett stories from this prolific author. In this episode, the son of a known criminal must decide if he wants to grow up like his father or go straight.

163 L'Amour, Louis. *The Strong Shall Live* (10–12). 1985, Bantam paper $3.50 (0-553-25200-3). Ten stories about the courageous people who survived life on the American frontier. Also use by L'Amour: *Yondering* (1989).

164 Lansdale, Joe R., ed. *The New Frontier: The Best of Today's Western Fiction* (9–12). 1989, Doubleday $12.95 (0-385-24569-6). Nineteen short stories of adventure set in the West. (Rev: BL 6/15/89)

165 Leasor, James. *Frozen Assets* (9–12). 1989, St. Martin's $17.95 (0-312-03347-8). Jason Love, part-time detective, in Afghanistan on the trail of a valuable mineral deposit in an adventure à la James Bond. (Rev: BL 7/89)

166 Le Carre, John. *The Little Drummer Girl* (10–12). 1983, Knopf $15.95 (0-394-53015-2); Bantam paper $4.95 (0-553-26757-4). A thoughtful, complex novel about attempts to infiltrate and destroy a secret Palestinian terrorist organization.

167 Le Carre, John. *A Perfect Spy* (10–12). 1986, Knopf $18.95 (0-394-55141-9); Bantam paper $4.50 (0-553-26821-X). An espionage thriller about the strange disappearance of a man considered to be "the perfect spy."

168 Le Carre, John. *The Russia House* (10–12). 1989, Knopf $19.95 (0-394-57789-2). For better readers a complex espionage novel that pits Russian intelligence moves against those of the British and Americans. (Rev: SLJ 11/89)

169 Le Carre, John. *The Spy Who Came in from the Cold* (10–12). 1984, Bantam paper $4.50 (0-553-26442-7). A spy thriller about the last assignment of a professional secret service agent.

170 Le Carre, John. *Tinker, Tailor, Soldier, Spy* (10–12). 1974, Knopf $17.45 (0-394-49219-6); Bantam paper $4.95 (0-553-26778-7). A challenging novel about George Smiley, a British agent, who comes out of retirement to unearth a Russian mole. Also use: *Smiley's People* (1972).

171 Lederer, Paul Jospeh. *North Star* (9–12). 1987, NAL paper $3.95 (0-451-14740-5). In this novel that is part of the Indian Heritage series, Richard English and a Cheyenne woman travel together into gold country via dogsled. (Rev: VOYA 2/88)

172 Lehrer, Jim. *Crown, Oklahoma* (10–12). 1989, Putnam $17.95 (0-399-13434-4). Our hero, One-Eyed Mack, sets out to break up a crime syndicate in Oklahoma in this amusing sequel to *Kick the Can* (1988). (Rev: BL 5/1/89)

173 Leib, Franklin Allen. *Fire Arrow* (10–12). 1988, Presidio $18.95 (0-89141-333-2). A thriller, for better readers, about a hijacked American airplane that is forced to land in Libya. (Rev: BL 9/15/88; SLJ 2/89)

174 Levin, Ira. *The Boys from Brazil* (10–12). 1976, Random $8.95 (0-394-40267-7). The story of a group of ex-Nazis and their diabolical plan to create a Fourth Reich.

175 Llewellyn, Caroline. *The Lady of the Labyrinth* (10–12). 1990, Macmillan $19.95 (0-684-18920-8). A brother and sister set out to find their archaeologist father in this tale of terrorism in the Mediterranean area. (Rev: BL 3/1/90; SLJ 8/90)

176 Llewellyn, Sam. *Death Roll* (10–12). 1990, Simon & Schuster $18.95 (0-671-67045-X). A novel about sailboating and a courageous hero out to win an important race. (Rev: SLJ 8/90)

177 London, Jack. *Best Short Stories of Jack London* (9–12). 1953, Amereon $15.95 (0-89190-656-8). These stories of action and adventure represent locales ranging from the South Seas to the Far North.

178 London, Jack. *The Call of the Wild, White Fang, and Other Stories* (9–12). 1981, Penguin paper $3.95 (0-14-039001-4). In addition to two complete novels, this collection contains two other stories with settings in the Arctic.

179 Lopez, Barry. *Winter Count* (10–12). 1982, Avon paper $3.95 (0-380-58107-8). This group of stories deals with survival in the wilds and man's battle with nature.

180 Lovell, Marc. *Comfort Me with Spies* (10–12). 1990, Doubleday $14.95 (0-385-26795-9). Appleton Porter, a bumbling spy, is on his first solo mission. Part of a series. (Rev: BL 6/15/90)

181 Ludlum, Robert. *The Aquitaine Progression* (10–12). 1984, Random $17.95 (0-394-53674-6); Bantam paper $5.95 (0-553-26256-4). An American lawyer gets involved against his will in a conspiracy. Also use: *The Matarese Circle* (1980), *The Matlock Paper* (1982), *The Osterman Weekend,* (1984), and *The Road to Gandolfo* (1982).

182 Ludlum, Robert. *The Bourne Identity* (9–12). 1984, Bantam paper $5.95 (0-553-26011-1). A man wakens to find that in spite of having no memory, he is the target of a killer's plot. Followed by *The Bourne Supremacy* (1986).

183 Ludlum, Robert. *The Chancellor Manuscript* (10–12). 1984, Bantam paper $5.95 (0-553-26094-4). A thriller in which the author speculates on the consequences of an assassination of J. Edgar Hoover.

184 Ludlum, Robert. *The Icarus Agenda* (10–12). 1988, Random $19.95 (0-394-54397-1). A thriller involving a heroic protagonist, a beautiful secret agent, a powerful villain, and a Middle East group of terrorists. (Rev: BL 1/1/88)

185 Ludlum, Robert. *The Matarese Circle* (10–12). 1983, Bantam paper $5.95 (0-553-25899-0). Two secret agents—one Russian, the other American—join forces to combat a terrorist group.

186 Ludlum, Robert. *The Rhinemann Exchange* (10–12). 1975, Dell paper $4.95 (0-440-15079-5). A spy thriller set during World War II involving treachery and treason.

187 Ludlum, Robert. *The Scarlatti Inheritance* (10–12). 1982, Bantam paper $4.95 (0-553-25856-7). A thriller about a secret weapon wanted by Hitler. Also use: *The Bourne Identity* (1984), *The Parsifal Mosaic* (1982), *The Gemini Contenders* (1977), and *The Holcroft Covenant* (1984).

188 Luger, Harriet. *The Elephant Tree* (7–12). 1986, Dell paper $2.25 (0-440-92394-8). Two boys forget their differences to survive in a desert where they are stranded.

189 Lyall, Gavin. *The Conduct of Major Maxim* (10–12). 1986, Penguin paper $3.50 (0-14-

009417-2). A fine spy story about a secret agent who is forced to act on his own to thwart a cold-war plot.

190 McCammon, Robert R. *Blue World* (10–12). 1990, Pocket paper $4.95 (0-671-69518-5). A powerful collection of 13 stories that combine horror and adventure. (Rev: SLJ 9/90; VOYA 8/90)

191 McCarthy, Gary. *Sodbuster* (9–12). 1988, Doubleday $12.95 (0-385-23515-1). A teenage boy and his older sister leave their Wyoming home to find their fortunes in Texas. (Rev: BL 7/88)

192 McCord, John S. *Walking Hawk* (9–12). 1989, Doubleday paper $12.95 (0-385-26263-9). A half-Indian half-white man relocates to the Montana Territory of the late 1800s when he must face murder charges. (Rev: BL 11/15/89)

193 McCunn, Ruthanne Lum. *Sole Survivor* (10–12). 1985, Design Enterprises $14.95 (0-932538-61-4). A fictionalized account of a true story involving a young Chinese ship steward who spent 133 days on a life raft. (Rev: BR 3–4/86)

194 McCutchan, Philip. *Cameron's Raid* (9–12). 1986, St. Martin's paper $3.50 (0-312-90081-3). During World War II, Lt. Com. Cameron must take his ship into Brest Harbor to destroy some U-boat shelters. (Rev: SLJ 9/85)

195 MacDonald, Patricia J. *Stranger in the House* (10–12). 1983, Dell paper $3.50 (0-440-18455-X). A hit-and-run driver suffers pangs of guilt.

196 MacInnes, Helen. *Above Suspicion* (10–12). 1954, Harcourt $24.95 (0-15-102707-2); Fawcett paper $4.95 (0-449-20858-3). This is one of the many novels of intrigue and suspense by this writer. Some others are: *The Salzburg Connection; Snare of the Hunter* (both 1985); *Decision at Delphi* (1984); *Agent in Place; Assignment in Brittany* (both 1983); *The Hidden Target;* and *The Venetian Affair* (both 1987).

197 MacLean, Alistair. *Circus* (9–12). 1984, Amereon $19.95 (0-89190-672-X); Fawcett paper $3.50 (0-449-20412-X). In this spy thriller, an aerialist is sent on a secret mission by the CIA into Eastern Europe. Other recommended adventures by MacLean include *Secret Ways* (1959), *Floodgate* (1985), and *South by Java Head* (1984).

198 MacLean, Alistair. *Partisans* (9–12). 1984, Fawcett paper $4.95 (0-449-20342-5). A World War II adventure story that takes place in Italy and Yugoslavia. Also use: *River of Death* (1984), *The Golden Gate* (1985), and *Ice Station Zebra* (1984).

199 MacLean, Alistair. *Santorini* (8–12). 1987, Doubleday $16.95 (0-385-23153-9); Fawcett paper $4.95 (0-449-20394-8). In this adventure novel a NATO ship must salvage a sunken plane carrying nuclear bombs. (Rev: BL 1/1/87)

200 Maclean, Norman. *A River Runs through It and Other Stories* (10–12). 1979, Univ. of Chicago Pr. $15.00 (0-226-50055-1); paper $7.95 (0-226-50057-8). These stories convey the grandeur of our western mountain wilderness and the ways by which man has adjusted to this environment.

201 MacLeish, Rod. *Crossing at Ivalo* (9–12). 1990, Little $18.95 (0-316-54256-3). An exciting adventure yarn about a defecting Soviet scientist and the forces that want to capture him. (Rev: BL 5/15/90)

202 McMurtry, Larry. *Horseman, Pass By* (10–12). 1979, Penguin paper $6.95 (0-14-004691-7). This sad and brutal book—about an adolescent boy, the brother he admires, and their scrupulously honest grandfather—was the basis of the film *Hud.*

203 Manguel, Alberto, ed. *Dark Arrows: Chronicles of Revenge* (9–12). 1987, Crown paper $10.95 (0-517-56259-6). From Bram Stoker to Frederick Forsyth here is a collection of stories each of which explores the theme of revenge. (Rev: BL 6/15/87; VOYA 12/87)

204 Martin, Russell, and Marc Barasch, eds. *Writers of the Purple Sage: An Anthology of Recent Western Writing* (10–12). 1984, Penguin paper $8.95 (0-14-007370-1). This collection of stories and nonfiction pieces includes selections from both white and Indian American writers.

205 Mazer, Harry. *The Island Keeper* (8–12). 1982, Dell paper $2.95 (0-440-94774-X). Sixteen-year-old Cleo escapes personal problems by fleeing to a remote Canadian island where survival is the name of the game.

206 Michener, James A. *Journey* (9–12). 1989, Random $16.95 (0-394-57826-0). An adventure story about an ill-fated expedition during the Klondike gold rush of 1897. (Rev: BL 4/1/89; SLJ 12/89)

207 Michener, James A. *Space* (10–12). Illus. 1982, Random $17.95 (0-394-50555-7). The author traces the development of the American space program beginning with characters thrown together during World War II.

208 Michener, James A. *Texas* (10–12). 1985, Random $21.95 (0-394-54154-5); Fawcett paper $5.95 (0-449-21092-8). From the conquistadors to modern oil barons, the history of Texas comes alive in this massive novel for better readers. (Rev: BL 9/15/85)

209 Moran, Richard. *Cold Sea Rising* (10–12). 1985, Berkley paper $3.95 (0-425-09558-4). Russians settle on a gigantic floating ice shelf and threaten the United States. (Rev: BL 11/15/85; VOYA 8–10/86)

210 Morrell, David. *Blood Oath* (10–12). 1983, Fawcett paper $3.95 (0-449-20391-3). Intrigue and danger follow a man who is searching for his father's grave in France.

211 Morrell, David. *The Fifth Profession* (10–12). 1990, Warner $19.95 (0-446-51562-0). A thriller that begins with a plan to rescue a beleaguered wife from a Greek island and soon involves espionage and murder. (Rev: SLJ 9/90)

212 Myers, Walter Dean. *The Nicholas Factor* (8–12). 1983, Penguin paper $11.50 (0-670-51055-6). During his first year in college, Gerald is recruited by the government to infiltrate an extremist student group.

213 Nance, John J. *Final Approach* (10–12). 1990, Crown $19.95 (0-517-57569-8). In this novel of intrigue and double-dealing, an investigator unearths some unsavory truths as he investigates a plane crash. (Rev: BL 9/1/90)

214 Nathan, Robert. *Amusement Park* (10–12). 1980, Fawcett paper $1.75 (0-449-23960-8). An adventure set in an amusement park and involving the dangerous Sky Chariot ride.

215 Noguchi, Thomas T., and Arthur Lyons. *Physical Evidence* (10–12). 1990, Putnam $19.95 (0-399-13530-8). A medical thriller about a nursing home and Freeze Time, a company that freezes bodies after death. (Rev: SLJ 7/90)

216 Nordhoff, Charles, and James N. Hall. *The Bounty Trilogy* (9–12). Illus. 1982, Little $29.95 (0-316-61161-1); paper $16.95 (0-316-61166-2). An adventure story based on fact concerning a mutiny aboard the *Bounty* and its aftermath. The three individual books are *Mutiny on the Bounty, Men against the Sea,* and *Pitcairn's Island.* These books were originally published in 1932, 1934, and 1934 respectively.

217 Paine, Lauran. *Spirit Meadow* (10–12). 1987, Walker $15.95 (0-8027-0970-2). In this western tale, Joe Bryan accidentally becomes the guardian of a 4-year-old half-Indian boy. (Rev: BL 7/87)

218 Patten, Lewis B. *Ride a Tall Horse* (10–12). 1981, NAL paper $2.75 (0-451-15322-7). In this western by the award-winning writer, a teenager tracks down a murderer. Also use *The Red Sabbath* (1987).

219 Patten, Lewis B. *Sharpshod and They Called Him a Killer* (10–12). 1990, Tor paper $3.50 (0-812-50524-7). Two previously published western adventures now released in a single volume. (Rev: VOYA 8/90)

220 Paulsen, Gary. *Murphy* (10–12). 1987, Walker $14.95 (0-8027-4068-5); paper $2.95 (0-671-64432-7). In 1889, Murphy is a sheriff in a small town in Colorado where some mysterious murders are happening. (Rev: BR 5–6/87)

221 Paulsen, Gary. *Murphy's Gold* (10–12). 1988, Walker $16.95 (0-8027-4078-2). Al Murphy, a sheriff in a run-down town, investigates the murder of a Chinese laundryman. A sequel to *Murphy* (1987). (Rev: BL 4/1/88)

222 Paulsen, Gary. *Murphy's Herd* (10–12). 1989, Walker $17.95 (0-8027-4094-4). Al Murphy, former sheriff, sets out to find the murderer of his wife. Part of a series about Murphy. (Rev: BL 6/15/89)

223 Picano, Felice. *To the Seventh Power* (9–12). 1989, Morrow $18.95 (0-688-06332-2). A thriller involving a secret government mission and 6 youngsters who are able to see into the future. (Rev: BL 1/15/89)

224 Porter, Donald. *Jubilee Jim and the Wizard of Wall Street* (10–12). 1990, Dutton $19.95 (0-525-24841-2). A novel about the days of railroad building in which such historical characters as Ulysses S. Grant appear. (Rev: BL 2/1/90)

225 Portis, Charles. *True Grit* (7–12). 1969, NAL paper $3.95 (0-451-16022-3). A 14-year-old girl in the old West sets out to avenge her father's death.

226 Poyer, David. *The Gulf* (10–12). 1990, St. Martin's $19.95 (0-312-05096-8). For mature readers, this is an action-filled adventure story set in the Persian Gulf. (Rev: BL 9/15/90)

227 Pronzini, Bill. *Firewind* (9–12). 1989, Evans $14.95 (0-87131-555-6). A 1880 northern California logging town is the setting for this tale of high adventure involving a trainload of townfolk trying to escape a forest fire. (Rev: BL 4/1/89)

228 Pronzini, Bill, ed. *More Wild Westerns* (9–12). 1989, Walker $18.95 (0-8027-4097-9). A collection of 13 western stories garnered from pulp magazines and written by such authors as Will Henry and Elmore Leonard. (Rev: BL 7/89)

229 Pronzini, Bill, and Martin H. Greenberg, eds. *Best of the West: Stories That Inspired Classic Western Films* (9–12). 1988, NAL paper $3.50 (0-451-15481-9). Nine western stories that were the basis for such films as *High Noon* and *Rio Grande.* (Rev: BL 10/15/88)

230 Pronzini, Bill, and Martin H. Greenberg, eds. *Homicidal Acts* (10–12). 1989, Ballantine

13

paper $3.50 (0-8041-0294-5). A collection of 14 murder mysteries by such authors as Norman Mailer and Donald E. Westlake. (Rev: BL 1/1/89)

231 Pullman, Philip. *Shadow in the North* (8–12). 1988, Knopf $12.95 (0-394-89453-7). Sally Lockhart, now 22, again finds adventure in Victorian England when she stalks a satanic arms manufacturer in the sequel to the much-praised *Ruby in the Smoke* (1987). (Rev: BL 4/1/88; BR 11–12/88; SLJ 5/88; VOYA 12/88)

232 Pullman, Philip. *The Tiger in the Well* (8–12). 1990, Knopf LB $16.99 (0-679-90214-7). This conclusion of the rich historical trilogy that began with *The Ruby in the Smoke* (1987) and *The Shadow in the North* (1988) completes the adventures of Victorian heroine Sally Lockhart who, in this novel, encounters a man who wants passionately to destroy her. (Rev: BL 10/15/90)

233 Puzo, Mario. *The Godfather* (10–12). 1969, Putnam $24.95 (0-399-10342-2); NAL paper $4.95 (0-451-15736-2). The story of a fictional crime family in New York led by Vito Corleone and then by his son Michael.

234 Reiss, Bob. *Saltmaker* (10–12). 1988, Viking $18.95 (0-670-80247-6). In this thriller, a U.S. president is tried for treason when he capitulates after Russian threats. (Rev: BL 5/15/88)

235 Richards, Judith. *After the Storm* (10–12). 1987, Peachtree $14.95 (0-934601-17-8). A 10-year-old boy becomes friends with a paraplegic war veteran in this episodic adventure novel set near the swamps of Lake Okeechobee. (Rev: SLJ 1/88)

236 Roderus, Frank. *Billy Ray's Forty Days* (9–12). 1989, Doubleday paper $12.95 (0-385-24750-8). The charming story of a likable new preacher in the town of Purgatory and the girl he meets. (Rev: BL 10/15/89)

237 Rovin, Jeff, and Sander Diamond. *Starik* (10–12). 1988, Dutton $17.95 (0-525-24626-6). A thriller in which the crazed leader of the Soviet Union must be stopped before he precipitates World War III. (Rev: BL 3/15/88)

238 Royce, Kenneth. *Patriots* (10–12). 1988, Crown $17.95 (0-517-56943-4). For better readers, a thriller about a terrorist coup that destroys Air Force One, killing the President. (Rev: SLJ 8/88)

239 Saint-Exupéry, Antoine de. *Night Flight* (10–12). 1932, Harcourt paper $4.95 (0-15-665605-1). This thoughtful French novel is about the adventurous early days of flying.

240 Schow, David J. *The Kill Riff* (10–12). 1988, Tor $17.95 (0-312-93065-8); paper $4.95 (0-8125-2586-8). A mentally deranged man is out to avenge his daughter's accidental death. (Rev: VOYA 10/88)

241 Scortia, Thomas, and Frank Robinson. *Blow-Out* (9–12). 1987, Watts $16.95 (0-531-15030-5); St. Martin's paper $3.95 (0-312-91040-1). A thriller set in the next century involving the construction of a tunnel to house a high-speed train. (Rev: SLJ 10/87)

242 Shaara, Michael. *The Herald* (10–12). 1981, McGraw $11.95 (0-07-056376-4). A survivor of a radiation accident tries to solve the mystery surrounding it.

243 Smith, Pauline C. *Brush Fire* (7–12). 1979, Westminster paper $8.95 (0-664-32639-0). A 17-year-old boy is responsible for saving the house in which he is living in this taut adventure story.

244 Smith, Wilbur. *A Time to Die* (10–12). 1990, Random $19.95 (0-394-58475-9). An adventure novel set in Africa about a big game hunter and an expedition into territory where 2 rival tribes are fighting. (Rev: SLJ 7/90)

245 Southall, Ivan. *The Long Night Watch* (8–12). 1984, Farrar $11.95 (0-374-34644-5). Jon and 99 other passengers leave Australia during World War II to found a new society in Tangu.

246 Spinelli, Jerry. *Night of the Whale* (9–12). 1988, Dell paper $2.95 (0-440-20071-7). With realistic language, the author tells about a week 6 senior boys spend in a beachhouse together and how they try to save a group of beached whales. (Rev: BL 12/1/85)

247 Strasser, Todd. *Beyond the Reef* (9–12). Illus. 1989, Delacorte $14.95 (0-385-29782-3). The Cooper family, including teenage son Chris, relocate to the Florida Keys where Mr. Cooper hopes to find buried treasure. (Rev: BL 8/89; BR 11–12/90; SLJ 9/89; VOYA 10/89)

248 Suyin, Han. *The Enchantress* (10–12). 1985, Bantam $16.95 (0-553-05071-0). In this novel set in China and Switzerland during the eighteenth century, twins are able to communicate through their thoughts. (Rev: SLJ 5/85)

249 Svee, Gary D. *Incident at Pishkin Creek* (9–12). 1989, Walker $18.95 (0-8027-4095-2). Max Bass exaggerated in the advertisement for a bride as poor Catherine O'Dowd discovers when she arrives in Montana. (Rev: BL 7/89)

250 Temperley, Alan. *Murdo's War* (9–12). 1989, Canongate $16.95 (0-86241-181-5). During World War II, a young Scottish lad uncovers a Nazi plot that threatens his life and the outcome of the war. (Rev: BL 10/15/89; BR 11–12/89; SLJ 12/89)

251 Thayer, J. S. *Ringer* (9–12). 1988, Crown $18.95 (0-517-56970-1). A Castro look-alike is used to collect information about a secret Soviet bomber that has been sent to Cuba. (Rev: SLJ 2/89)

252 Theroux, Paul. *The Mosquito Coast* (10–12). 1983, Avon paper $4.95 (0-380-61945-8). A novel for better readers about a discontented American who takes his unwilling family to relocate in Honduras.

253 Thomas, Craig. *Winter Hawk* (10–12). 1987, Morrow $18.95 (0-688-07091-4); Bantam paper $4.50 (0-553-28336-7). In this Mitchell Gant novel, the adventurer flies into the Soviet Union to find a scientist who can help the United States. (Rev: SLJ 11/87)

254 Thomas, Ross. *Out on the Rim* (10–12). 1987, Mysterious $17.95 (0-89296-212-7); paper $4.95 (0-445-40693-3). For better readers, a complex thriller about a struggle to possess $5 million. (Rev: BL 7/87)

255 Thompson, Julian. *A Band of Angels* (9–12). 1986, Scholastic $12.95 (0-590-33780-7); paper $2.95 (0-590-40545-4). Jordan, his suitcase of money, and 2 friends hit the road to escape government agents who are searching for them. (Rev: VOYA 6/86)

256 Thompson, Julian. *The Grounding of Group Six* (8–12). 1983, Avon paper $3.50 (0-380-83386-7). Five 16-year-olds think they are being sent to an exclusive school but actually they have been slated for murder.

257 Thompson, Julian. *The Taking of Mariasburg* (9–12). 1988, Scholastic $12.95 (0-590-41247-7). Maria buys a ghost town with her inheritance and populates it with teenagers. (Rev: BL 4/1/88; BR 9–10/88; VOYA 4/88)

258 Traven, B. *The Treasure of the Sierra Madre* (10–12). 1980, Bentley $16.00 (0-8376-0436-2); Hill & Wang paper $8.95 (0-374-52149-2). First published in 1927, this is a story of 3 American drifters and their search for gold in Mexico.

259 Trenhaile, John. *A View from the Square* (10–12). 1986, Jove paper $3.95 (0-515-08102-7). A story about espionage, betrayal, and murder.

260 Trevor, Elleston. *Deathwatch* (10–12). 1984, Beaufort $16.95 (0-8253-0237-4); Jove paper $3.50 (0-515-08337-2). A thriller about Russian and American scientists and secret agents pitted against one another during the Cold War.

261 Tryon, Thomas. *The Night of the Moonbow* (10–12). 1989, Knopf $18.95 (0-394-56006-X).

For mature readers, the story of a group of teenagers who persecute another boy who doesn't fit into the activities at their summer camp. (Rev: BL 6/15/89)

262 Uris, Leon. *Exodus* (9–12). Illus. 1958, Doubleday $21.95 (0-385-05082-8); Bantam paper $4.95 (0-553-25847-8). An adventure novel set in the days of the establishment of Israel. Also use *The Haj* (1984) and *Topaz* (1981).

263 Ustinov, Peter. *The Disinformer: Two Novellas* (10–12). 1989, Arcade $14.95 (1-55970-031-9). Two short novels—one a spy story and the other about adolescents and their parents. (Rev: SLJ 1/90)

264 Victoroff, Jeffrey Ivan. *The Wild Type* (10–12). 1989, Crown $17.95 (0-517-57127-7). Two doctors uncover a genetic plot to turn animals into killers. (Rev: SLJ 9/89)

265 Wales, Robert. *Harry* (10–12). 1986, Watts $16.95 (0-531-15017-8); Fawcett paper $2.95 (0-449-21286-6). In a wild attempt at fame and fortune, a young Australian cowboy devises an unusual cattle drive in this novel set in the 1890s. (Rev: BR 9–10/86; SLJ 11/86; VOYA 10/86)

266 Wallace, Irving. *The Seventh Secret* (9–12). 1986, NAL paper $4.95 (0-451-14557-7). Emily Ashcroft is convinced that Hitler is still alive and sets out to find him. (Rev: BL 10/15/85)

267 Washburn, L. J. *Riders of the Monte* (9–12). 1990, Evans $14.95 (0-87131-600-5). In this western, Buffalo Newcomb is out to catch the robbers who have stolen his gold and kidnapped his friend's daughter. (Rev: BL 3/1/90)

268 Watson, James. *Talking in Whispers* (8–12). 1984, Knopf LB $10.99 (0-394-96538-8); paper $10.95 (0-394-96538-3). A 16-year-old boy continues the resistance efforts of his father, who has been seized by the military government in Chile.

269 Weber, Joe. *Shadow Flight* (10–12). 1990, Presidio $19.95 (0-89141-342-1). A B-2 Stealth bomber is missing and the KGB is to blame. (Rev: BL 8/90)

270 Westlake, Donald E. *Good Behavior* (10–12). 1986, Mysterious Pr. $15.95 (0-89296-240-2); paper $3.95 (0-8125-1060-7). Professional thief John Dortmunder takes shelter in a convent and the nuns ask his help to return a young nun being held by her millionaire father. Part of a series starring Dortmunder. (Rev: SLJ 10/86)

271 White, Ellen Emerson. *Long Live the Queen* (9–12). 1989, Scholastic $13.95 (0-590-40850-X). Meg, the daughter of the U.S. president, survives a kidnapping but has difficulty recovering from the ordeal. (Rev: SLJ 3/89; VOYA 6/89)

15

272 Wilder, Thornton. *The Eighth Day* (10–12). 1987, Carroll & Graf paper $4.95 (0-88184-339-3). This novel, which takes place in both North and South America, involves complex relationships that lead to murder.

273 Wilhelm, Kate. *The Dark Door* (10–12). 1988, St. Martin's $16.95 (0-312-02182-8). Two detectives, an unbalanced arsonist, and an alien space probe are 3 elements in this thriller. (Rev: BL 10/1/88; VOYA 4/89)

274 Wilhelm, Kate. *Huysman's Pets* (10–12). 1986, Ace paper $3.50 (0-441-35441-6). When he accepts an assignment to write the biography of a famous scientist, Drew Lancaster finds he is enveloped in intrigue and mystery. For mature readers. (Rev: BL 1/1/86; SLJ 8/86; VOYA 4/86)

275 Wilkins, Kirby. *Quantum Web* (10–12). 1990, Henry Holt $19.95 (0-8050-1260-5). For mature readers, this thriller involves a young professor of physics caught in a web of intrigue in Tibet. (Rev: BL 6/15/90)

276 Wilson, F. Paul. *Black Wind* (10–12). 1989, Tor paper $5.95 (0-8125-2725-9). Parallel stories of 2 young men—one growing up in prewar Japan and the other in America—are part of this novel of intrigue, loyalty, and friendship. (Rev: VOYA 2/89)

277 Wisler, G. Clifton. *The Return of Caulfield Blake* (10–12). 1987, Evans $14.95 (0-87131-530-0). Sheriff Blake returns to his ex-wife and young son to help a community's war on a wicked rancher. (Rev: BL 1/1/88)

278 Woods, E. Z. *The Bloody Sands* (10–12). 1988, NAL paper $2.95 (0-451-15292-1). Jess McClaren sets out to stop the rustlers who are attacking the ranch of his father's friend. (Rev: BL 6/15/88)

279 Woods, Stuart. *White Cargo* (10–12). 1988, Simon & Schuster $17.95 (0-671-63333-3). The underground world in Colombia is the setting of this adventure story of a father looking for his lost daughter. (Rev: SLJ 12/88)

280 Zimmer, Michael. *Sundown* (10–12). 1988, Walker $16.95 (0-8027-4077-4). Luke Howard is hired to stop cattle rustling in this western set in Nebraska during the 1870s. (Rev: BL 3/1/88)

Animal Stories

281 Barrett, Nicholas. *Fledger* (9–12). 1985, Macmillan $13.95 (0-02-507410-5). A group of puf-

fins led by Goldie battle a pack of killer rats. (Rev: BR 1–2/86; SLJ 1/86; VOYA 4/86)

282 Bingham, Charlotte. *To Hear a Nightingale* (10–12). 1989, St. Martin's $19.95 (0-312-02991-8). A romantic story of a young widow who triumphs when her horse wins the Irish Derby. (Rev: BL 4/15/89)

283 Burnford, Sheila. *Bel Ria* (9–12). 1978, Little $12.95 (0-316-11718-8). A story about an unusual dog in Europe during World War II.

284 Caras, Roger. *Roger Caras' Treasury of Great Cat Stories* (9–12). 1987, Dutton $19.95 (0-525-24398-4); paper $12.50 (0-525-48427-2). A fine collection of short stories from internationally known writers, all about the mysterious creature, the cat. (Rev: BL 4/1/87)

285 Caras, Roger. *Roger Caras' Treasury of Great Dog Stories* (9–12). 1987, Dutton $19.95 (0-525-24399-2); paper $12.50 (0-525-48428-0). An anthology of dog stories written by great authors. (Rev: BL 4/1/87)

286 Curwood, James Oliver. *The Bear—A Novel* (8–12). 1989, Newmarket Pr. $16.95 (1-55704-054-0); paper $6.95 (1-55704-053-2). A reissue of the 1916 novel about a grizzly and an orphaned black bear cub in the wilds of British Columbia. (Rev: VOYA 4/90)

287 Getz, William. *Sam Patch: Ballad of a Jumping Man* (9–12). 1986, Watts $17.95 (0-531-15026-7). The narrator, a bear, tells how he joins a traveling troupe of players during the days of Davy Crockett. (Rev: BR 1–2/87)

288 Grey, Zane. *The Wolf Tracker and Other Animal Tales* (10–12). 1984, Santa Barbara Pr. paper $7.95 (0-915643-01-4). This collection of tales includes 4 stories about animals and the outdoors.

289 Haas, Jessie. *Working Trot* (9–12). 1983, Greenwillow $10.25 (0-688-02384-3). Instead of going to college, James decides to go to work on his uncle's Vermont horse farm.

290 Hawdon, Robin. *A Rustle in the Grass* (10–12). 1985, Dodd $13.95 (0-396-08522-9); Tor paper $3.95 (0-8125-0068-7). A group of ants lead by a young soldier ant named Dreamer defend their colony against the attack of an army of red ants. (Rev: BL 3/15/85; SLJ 8/85; VOYA 2/86)

291 Kilworth, Garry. *The Foxes of Firstdark* (9–12). 1990, Doubleday $18.95 (0-385-26427-5). A novel that brings to life the experiences of a fox clan and their struggle for survival. (Rev: BL 4/1/90)

292 Lawrence, R. D. *The White Puma* (9–12). 1990, Henry Holt $19.95 (0-8050-0685-0). An unusual story of this big cat's life in the Northwest and of the hunters who are trying to kill it. (Rev: BL 4/1/90)

293 London, Jack. *The Call of the Wild and White Fang* (7–12). 1984, Bantam paper $2.25 (0-553-21233-8). A combined edition of 2 classic animal stories and their adventures in Alaska.

294 O'Hara, Mary. *My Friend Flicka* (8–12). 1988, Harper paper $3.95 (0-06-080902-7). This story about Ken McLaughlin and the filly named Flicka is continued in *Thunderhead, Son of Flicka* and *Green Grass of Wyoming* (both 1988).

295 Peyton, K. M. *Darkling* (9–12). 1990, Delacorte $14.95 (0-385-30086-7). Jenny's unusual grandfather buys her a horse but it is her lover, Goddard, who gives her the help that this responsibility requires. (Rev: BL 5/1/90; SLJ 5/90; VOYA 6/90)

296 Popham, Melinda Worth. *Skywalker* (9–12). 1990, Graywolf $17.95 (1-55597-127-X). A charming animal tale about a group of coyotes and their search for water. (Rev: BL 4/15/90; SLJ 11/90)

297 Rawlings, Marjorie. *The Yearling* (7–12). 1962, Macmillan $24.95 (0-684-18508-3); paper $4.95 (0-02-044931-3). A young boy faces adult responsibilities in this story about a deer and life in rural Florida.

298 Schinto, Jeanne, ed. *The Literary Dog: Great Contemporary Dog Stories* (9–12). 1990, Atlantic Monthly $19.95 (0-87113-383-0). Over 30 dog stories by such present-day writers as Doris Lessing and John Updike. (Rev: BL 9/1/90)

299 Spencer, Benjamin T., and Helen Crider Smith, eds. *Memorable Dogs: An Anthology* (9–12). Illus. 1985, Harper $16.95 (0-06-015440-3). Representing both fiction and nonfiction by such authors as Hemingway and Thurber, here is a fine anthology about man's best friend. (Rev: BL 6/1/85) [820]

300 Steinbeck, John. *The Red Pony* (9–12). 1986, Viking $15.95 (0-670-81285-4); Bantam paper $2.95 (0-553-27836-3). These stories about a young boy growing up on a farm in California involve such elements as a loving family, a colt, and an old hired hand.

301 Wharton, William. *Pride* (10–12). 1987, Dell paper $4.95 (0-440-37118-X). A boy and his newfound kitten and an old war hero who has bought a lion cub cross paths in this story of love of families and animals. (Rev: BL 9/1/85)

Classics

Europe

GENERAL

302 Alain-Fournier, Henri. *The Wanderer* (10–12). 1979, NAL paper $3.95 (0-452-00754-2). For better readers, this is the classic French novel about youth and first love.

303 Balzac, Honore de. *Old Goriot* (10–12). Trans. by Marion A. Crawford. 1951, Penguin paper $3.95 (0-14-044017-8). In a squalid Parisian boarding house an old man is exploited by his selfish daughters. Originally published in 1835.

304 Cervantes, Miguel de. *The Adventures of Don Quixote de la Mancha* (8–12). 1983, Dent $15.00 (0-460-05024-9). One of several editions of this classic story of the misadventures of a knight enamored of chivalry.

305 Chekhov, Anton. *The Image of Chekhov: Forty Stories in the Order in Which They Were Written* (10–12). 1963, Knopf $15.00 (0-394-43009-3). This representative collection of Chekhov's stories covers the entire span of his output.

306 de Maupassant, Guy. *The Best Short Stories of Guy de Maupassant* (7–12). 1968, Airmont paper $2.75 (0-8049-0161-9). The French master is represented by 19 tales including "The Diamond Necklace."

307 de Maupassant, Guy. *Selected Short Stories* (10–12). 1971, Penguin paper $4.95 (0-14-044243-4). This complete collection includes all of the stories by this nineteenth-century French master of the genre.

308 Dostoevsky, Fyodor. *The Brothers Karamazov* (10–12). 1983, Buccaneer LB $31.95 (0-89966-315-X); NAL paper $3.95 (0-451-52243-5). A lengthy novel that probes into the Russian character through the story of 3 different brothers.

309 Dostoevsky, Fyodor. *Crime and Punishment* (10–12). 1950, Random $6.95 (0-394-60450-4); NAL paper $2.95 (0-451-52335-0). A psychological novel about 2 murders committed by a student and the aftermath of the murders.

310 Dostoevsky, Fyodor. *The Idiot* (10–12). 1983, Bantam paper $3.95 (0-553-21352-0). A probing novel of a man's search for nobility and perfection

311 Dumas, Alexandre. *The Count of Monte Cristo* (10–12). Illus. 1984, Putnam $13.95 (0-396-08255-6); Bantam paper $3.95 (0-553-21187-

0). This tale of imprisonment, escape, and revenge first appeared in 1844.

312 Dumas, Alexandre. *The Man in the Iron Mask* (10–12). 1976, Lightyear $26.95 (0-89968-146-8); Airmont paper $2.75 (0-8049-0150-3). This rousing French adventure story continues the exploits of the 3 Musketeers.

313 Dumas, Alexandre. *The Three Musketeers* (10–12). 1984, Buccaneer $22.95 (0-89966-486-5); Penguin paper $2.25 (0-14-035054-3). A swashbuckling novel of D'Artagnan, his friends, and their fight for justice. First published in 1844. Continued in *Twenty Years After* (1845).

314 Flaubert, Gustave. *Madame Bovary* (10–12). 1981, Random $12.95 (0-394-60460-1); paper $4.00 (0-394-60028-2). This classic of realism tells of the decline and fall of a weak woman, Emma Bovary.

315 Hugo, Victor. *The Hunchback of Notre Dame* (10–12). 1981, Buccaneer $25.95 (0-89966-382-6); NAL paper $2.95 (0-451-52222-2). The world of medieval Paris, from nobility to paupers, comes alive in this sprawling novel whose central characters are Quasimodo, a hunchback, and a gypsy named Esmeralda.

316 Hugo, Victor. *Les Miserables* (10–12). 1980, Random $16.95 (0-394-60489-X); Pocket paper $5.95 (0-671-50439-8). This lengthy novel describes the flight of Jean Valjean from the law in France during the first half of the nineteenth century. First published in 1862.

317 Stendhal. *The Red and the Black* (10–12). 1926, Modern Lib. $9.95 (0-394-605511-X); NAL paper $3.95 (0-451-51793-8). This lengthy novel chronicles the rise to power of a ruthless man named Julien Sorel.

318 Tolstoy, Leo. *Anna Karenina* (10–12). 1978, Random $12.95 (0-394-60448-2); Oxford Univ. Pr. paper $4.95 (0-19-281510-5). After an adulterous affair, a Russian married lady is so consumed with guilt she commits suicide.

319 Tolstoy, Leo. *The Death of Ivan Ilyitch: And Other Stories* (10–12). 1987, NAL paper $2.50 (0-451-52380-6). This volume contains 6 short stories including the title story about a man's thoughts before dying.

320 Tolstoy, Leo. *Great Short Works of Leo Tolstoy* (10–12). 1967, Harper paper $5.95 (0-06-083071-9). Nine stories and novellas representing the best of Tolstoy's short fiction.

321 Tolstoy, Leo. *The Portable Tolstoy* (10–12). 1978, Penguin paper $9.95 (0-14-015091-9). This sampling of Tolstoy's work includes a novella, 10 stories, plus miscellaneous other writings. [891.7]

322 Tolstoy, Leo. *War and Peace* (10–12). 1979, Random $14.95 (0-394-60475-X); NAL paper $6.95 (0-451-52326-1). The sweeping saga of the Napoleonic invasion of Russia as seen through the experience of a handful of people.

323 Turgenev, Ivan. *Fathers and Sons* (10–12). 1982, Bantam paper $2.25 (0-553-21259-1). This novel, first published in 1862, depicts intergenerational conflict in old Russia.

324 Verne, Jules. *Around the World in Eighty Days* (7–12). 1974, Dent $11.00 (0-460-05082-6); Dell paper $2.95 (0-440-90285-1). Phileas Fogg and servant Passepartout leave on a world trip, in this 1873 classic adventure.

325 Verne, Jules. *A Journey to the Center of the Earth* (7–12). Illus. 1984, Dodd $12.95 (0-396-08429-X); Penguin paper $3.95 (0-14-002265-1). A group of adventurers enter the earth through a volcano in Iceland. First published in French in 1864.

326 Verne, Jules. *Twenty Thousand Leagues under the Sea* (7–12). 1976, Dent $11.00 (0-460-05071-0); Airmont paper $1.95 (0-8049-0182-1). Evil Captain Nemo captures a group of underwater explorers. First published in 1869. A sequel is: *The Mysterious Island* (1988 Macmillan).

327 Voltaire. *Candide* (10–12). Trans. by Lowell Bair. Illus. 1985, Random paper $7.95 (0-394-60522-5). One of the many editions of this saga of the innocent who learns through experience that this is not the best of all possible worlds.

328 Voltaire. *Candide, and Other Writings* (10–12). 1985, Random $10.95 (0-394-60522-5). In addition to the novel *Candide*, this volume includes essays, poetry, and other short pieces.

329 Voltaire. *The Portable Voltaire* (10–12). 1987, Penguin paper $8.95 (0-14-015041-2). A rich selection of the works of this French novelist and philosopher. [848]

GREAT BRITAIN AND IRELAND

330 Austen, Jane. *Emma* (10–12). 1984, Bantam paper $2.50 (0-553-21273-7). Emma thinks she knows what is best for everybody, including herself. This is one of many editions of this 1815 novel. Also use: *Mansfield Park* (1983).

331 Austen, Jane. *Pride and Prejudice* (9–12). 1984, Putnam $10.95 (0-448-06032-9); paper $2.25 (0-451-52226-5). Mrs. Bennet's fondest wish is to marry off her daughters but Elizabeth won't cooperate.

332 Austen, Jane. *Sense and Sensibility* (10–12). 1969, Penguin paper $2.95 (0-14-043047-4). An edition of this 1811 novel about 2 very different sisters. Also use: *Persuasion* (1967).

333 Bennett, Arnold. *The Old Wives' Tale* (10–12). 1930, Biblio paper $3.95 (0-460-01919-8). The story of 2 sisters and their marriages.

334 Blackmore, R. D. *Lorna Doone* (10–12). 1984, Penguin paper $2.25 (0-14-035021-7). The story of a love that transcends the barriers of a family feud.

335 Brontë, Charlotte. *Jane Eyre* (8–12). 1964, Airmont paper $2.95 (0-8049-0017-5). Jane finds terror and romance when she becomes a governess for Mr. Rochester.

336 Brontë, Emily. *Wuthering Heights* (9–12). 1959, Signet paper $2.50 (0-451-52338-5). The love between Catherine and Heathcliff that even death cannot destroy.

337 Bunyan, John. *The Pilgrim's Progress* (10–12). 1978, Putnam $10.95 (0-396-07754-4); Penguin paper $2.95 (0-14-043004-0). These are 2 of many editions available of this allegory first published in 1678 about the temptation-filled journey through the life of a Christian.

338 Butler, Samuel. *The Way of All Flesh* (10–12). 1983, Buccaneer LB $17.95 (0-89966-310-9); NAL paper $4.95 (0-452-00882-4). A novel, first published in 1903, about hypocrisy and conflict in middle-class English families.

339 Chaucer, Geoffrey. *The Canterbury Tales* (10–12). Trans. by David Wright. 1965, Random paper $6.95 (0-394-70293-X). A collection of 24 stories, 22 of which are in verse. [821]

340 Chaucer, Geoffrey. *The Portable Chaucer* (10–12). 1977, Penguin paper $8.95 (0-14-015081-1). A generous sampling of Chaucer's works, most of which are from *The Canterbury Tales*. [821]

341 Collins, Wilkie. *The Moonstone* (10–12). 1977, Dent $14.95 (0-460-00979-6); paper $4.95 (0-460-01979-1). Often called the first detective story in English, this mystery story revolves around the disappearance of a diamond named the Moonstone.

342 Collins, Wilkie. *The Woman in White* (10–12). 1981, Oxford Univ. Pr. paper $3.95 (0-19-281534-2). This mystery story first appeared in 1860 and tells of a plot to illegally obtain the inheritance of the heroine of the novel.

343 Conrad, Joseph. *The Great Short Works of Joseph Conrad* (10–12). 1966, Harper paper $5.95 (0-06-083039-5). Moral and ethical problems are explored in many of this author's short stories.

344 Conrad, Joseph. *Heart of Darkness* (10–12). 1985, Bantam paper $4.95 (0-553-21263-X). A journey up the river in the Belgian Congo is also a journey into the darkest part of a man's soul.

345 Conrad, Joseph. *Lord Jim* (10–12). 1982, Buccaneer LB $19.95 (0-89966-057-6); NAL paper $2.25 (0-451-52234-6). A momentary act of cowardice changes the hero's entire life. First published in 1899.

346 Conrad, Joseph. *Nigger of the "Narcissus" and Other Stories* (10–12). 1988, Penguin paper $3.95 (0-14-043170-5). In the title story, sailors and their lives on the high seas are highlighted.

347 Conrad, Joseph. *The Portable Conrad* (10–12). 1987, Penguin paper $9.95 (0-14-015033-1). In addition to 2 novels, *The Nigger of the Narcissus* and *Typhoon*, this collection includes some short stories and examples of Conrad's nonfiction writing. [828]

348 Conrad, Joseph. *Typhoon and Other Stories* (10–12). 1984, Oxford Univ. Pr. paper $2.95 (0-19-271711-6). A fine collection of Conrad's short fiction.

349 Defoe, Daniel. *Moll Flanders* (10–12). 1983, Buccaneer LB $21.95 (0-89966-313-3); NAL paper $2.95 (0-451-52095-5). The history of a much-married tramp who had many adventures in seventeenth-century England. First published in 1722.

350 Defoe, Daniel. *Robinson Crusoe* (7–12). Illus. 1983, Macmillan $22.50 (0-684-17946-6); NAL paper $2.25 (0-451-52236-2). The classic survival story with illustrations by N. C. Wyeth.

351 Dickens, Charles. *Barnaby Rudge* (10–12). 1984, Penguin paper $5.95 (0-14-043090-3). This lengthy novel was based on the religious riots in England during 1780.

352 Dickens, Charles. *Bleak House* (10–12). 1979, Houghton paper $8.36 (0-395-05104-5). This murder mystery by Dickens is also an attack on the judicial system of the day. First published in 1853.

353 Dickens, Charles. *A Christmas Carol* (7–12). 1986, Bantam paper $1.95 (0-553-21244-3). One of many recommended editions of this tale in which Scrooge discovers the true meaning of Christmas.

354 Dickens, Charles. *David Copperfield* (10–12). 1982, Putnam $14.95 (0-396-08256-4); Airmont paper $3.75 (0-8049-0065-5). This largely autobiographical novel appeared in 1850 and has become Dickens's most popular work.

355 Dickens, Charles. *Great Expectations* (8–12). 1985, Dodd $14.95 (0-396-08687-4); paper $2.95 (0-553-21342-3). The story of Pip and his slow journey to maturity and fortune.

356 Dickens, Charles. *Hard Times* (10–12). 1986, Buccaneer LB $23.95 (0-89966-519-5); NAL paper $2.95 (0-451-52528-0). In this novel first published in 1854, a father realizes that his emphasis on the practical has robbed his children of valuable experience.

357 Dickens, Charles. *Martin Chuzzlewit* (10–12). 1982, Oxford Univ. Pr. paper $6.95 (0-19-281676-4). In order to placate his grandfather, Martin emigrates from England in this novel largely set in the United States. First published in 1844.

358 Dickens, Charles. *The Mystery of Edwin Drood* (9–12). Illus. 1980, Airmont paper $1.50 (0-8049-0114-7). The last novel of Dickens left unfinished at his death.

359 Dickens, Charles. *Nicholas Nickleby* (10–12). 1983, Bantam paper $4.95 (0-553-21265-6). The fortunes and misfortunes of Nicholas are described in this novel in which he becomes, for a time, a teacher and an actor. First published in 1839.

360 Dickens, Charles. *The Old Curiosity Shop* (10–12). 1972, Penguin paper $5.95 (0-14-043075-X). The sentimental novel of tragedy of Little Nell and her impoverished grandfather. First published in 1841.

361 Dickens, Charles. *Oliver Twist* (10–12). 1982, Buccaneer LB $28.95 (0-89966-372-9); Oxford Univ. Pr. paper $3.50 (0-19-281591-1). The rousing adventure story of a waif on the streets of Victorian England.

362 Dickens, Charles. *Tale of Two Cities* (7–12). 1985, Dodd $11.95 (0-395-08535-0); NAL paper $2.50 (0-451-52301-6). The classic novel of sacrifice during the French Revolution. A reissue.

363 Doyle, Arthur Conan. *Sherlock Holmes: The Complete Novels and Stories* (8–12). 2 vols. 1986, Bantam paper $4.95 each (Vol. 1: 0-553-21241-9; vol. 2: 0-553-21242-7). A handy collection in 2 volumes of all the writings about Holmes and Watson. (Rev: BL 3/15/87)

364 Eliot, George. *The Mill on the Floss* (10–12). 1965, NAL paper $3.95 (0-451-51922-1). The tragic story of Maggie, her brother, and the events that separated their love. First published in 1860.

365 Eliot, George. *Silas Marner* (10–12). 1983, Amereon $15.95 (0-88411-275-6); Bantam paper $1.95 (0-553-21048-3). A lonely old man, falsely accused of theft, finds salvation in the love of a young child. First published in 1861.

366 Fielding, Henry. *Tom Jones* (10–12). 1982, Buccaneer $39.95 (0-89966-398-2); NAL paper $4.95 (0-451-52334-2). The fortunes of a found-ling from rags to riches in a ribald romp. First published in 1749.

367 Goldsmith, Oliver. *The Vicar of Wakefield* (10–12). 1982, Buccaneer LB $19.95 (0-89966-373-7); Penguin paper $3.50 (0-14-043159-4). This is the story of a congenial vicar who continually endures and rises above the many misfortunes that befall him.

368 Hardy, Thomas. *Far from the Madding Crowd* (10–12). 1961, NAL paper $3.50 (0-451-52360-1). The 3 loves of Bathsheba Everdene and the tragic fate of 2 of them.

369 Hardy, Thomas. *Jude the Obscure* (10–12). 1972, Houghton paper $7.16 (0-395-05191-6). The tragic love story of Jude Fawley and his cousin Sue Bridehead. First published in 1895.

370 Hardy, Thomas. *The Mayor of Casterbridge* (10–12). n.d., Amereon LB $20.95 (0-88411-560-7); Bantam paper $2.25 (0-553-21014-6). A young hay trusser suffers the consequences of selling his wife and family while he is drunk.

371 Hardy, Thomas. *The Return of the Native* (10–12). 1983, Amereon LB $22.95 (0-88411-561-5); NAL paper $2.50 (0-451-52307-5). A young schoolteacher discovers that his wife is unfaithful. First published in 1878.

372 Hardy, Thomas. *Tess of the D'Urbervilles* (10–12). 1979, Random $8.95 (0-394-60484-9); Penguin paper $2.95 (0-14-043135-7). Through circumstances and the evil of others, a young girl suffers a series of tragedies. First published in 1891.

373 Kipling, Rudyard. *Captains Courageous* (8–12). 1984, Amereon $17.95 (0-88411-818-5); Airmont paper $1.75 (0-8049-0027-2). A spoiled young English boy learns humility and courage from some simple fishermen.

374 Kipling, Rudyard. *Kim* (10–12). 1982, Dell paper $2.25 (0-440-94500-3). Beginning in Lahore, this novel follows a young street urchin through many adventures in British-controlled India.

375 Kipling, Rudyard. *The Man Who Would Be King* (10–12). 1983, Amereon $17.95 (0-88411-995-5); Oxford Univ. Pr. paper $5.95 (0-19-281674-8). This adventure story is set in the Middle East during the British rule of India.

376 Lawrence, D. H. *The Portable D. H. Lawrence* (9–12). 1987, Penguin paper $9.95 (0-14-015028-5). This volume contains 8 stories and novellas, excerpts from novels, plus a few poems and essays. [828]

377 Lehmann, Ruth P. M., trans. *Beowulf: An Imitative Translation* (10–12). 1988, Univ. of

Texas Pr. $14.95 (0-292-70768-1); paper $5.95 (0-292-70771-1). A translation of this epic that makes it accessible to modern readers. (Rev: SLJ 3/89) [808.1]

378 Munro, H. H. *The Complete Works of Saki* (10–12). 1989, Dorset $19.95 (0-88029-259-8). As well as all the short stories of H. H. Munro, this volume includes his 3 novels. [828]

379 Shelley, Mary Wollstonecraft. *Frankenstein* (8–12). 1964, Dell paper $1.95 (0-440-92717-X). The classic novel about a scientific experiment to create a man-made human.

380 Sterne, Laurence. *Tristram Shandy* (10–12). 1979, Dent paper $4.95 (0-460-01617-2). An eccentric classic about the life of an unusual hero.

381 Stevenson, Robert Louis. *The Black Arrow* (7–12). 1963, Airmont paper $2.50 (0-8049-0020-5). Set against the War of the Roses, this is an adventure story involving a young hero, Dick Shelton. First published in 1888.

382 Stevenson, Robert Louis. *Dr. Jekyll and Mr. Hyde* (7–12). 1979, Dodd $10.95 (0-396-67758-7); paper $1.95 (0-553-21087-4). This 1886 classic of horror involves a drug-induced change of personality. One of several editions.

383 Stevenson, Robert Louis. *Kidnapped* (7–12). Illus. 1886, Putnam $11.95 (0-448-06015-9); NAL paper $1.95 (0-451-51754-7). David Balfour escapes death to claim his inheritance. One of several editions. A sequel is *Master of Ballantrae* (1914).

384 Stevenson, Robert Louis. *The Strange Case of Dr. Jekyll and Mr. Hyde* (9–12). Illus. 1990, Univ. of Nebraska Pr. $15.00 (0-8032-4212-3). An edition of this classic that includes comments by Joyce Carol Oates and engravings by Barry Moser. (Rev: BL 5/1/90)

385 Swift, Jonathan. *Gulliver's Travels* (7–12). 1975, Dent $11.00 (0-460-05018-4); NAL paper $2.95 (0-451-52219-2). The 4 fantastic voyages of Lemuel Gulliver. First published in 1726.

386 Thackeray, William Makepeace. *Vanity Fair* (10–12). 1962, NAL paper $5.95 (0-451-52041-6). The classic story of an unscrupulous heroine, Becky Sharp, and her rise to fame and fortune.

387 Trollope, Anthony. *Barchester Towers* (10–12). 1980, Oxford Univ. Pr. paper $4.95 (0-19-281507-5). This is the second in the lengthy series of novels about life in a mid-nineteenth-century cathedral town. It is preceded by *The Warden* and followed by *Doctor Thorne* (both 1980).

388 Wilde, Oscar. *The Portable Oscar Wilde* (10–12). 1981, Penguin paper $8.95 (0-14-015093-5). As well as 2 plays, this volume includes *The* *Picture of Dorian Gray,* some poems, and representative prose works. [828]

United States

389 Alcott, Louisa May. *Little Women* (7–12). 1988, Knopf $18.95 (0-394-56279-8); Penguin paper $5.95 (0-14-039069-3). The classic story of the March family whose 4 daughters are growing up in New England in the mid-1800s. There are numerous sequels, for example, *Little Men* and *Jo's Boys.*

390 Anderson, Sherwood. *The Portable Sherwood Anderson* (10–12). 1987, Penguin paper $9.95 (0-14-015076-5). A collection of fiction (including *Winesburg, Ohio*) plus a generous sampling of nonfiction pieces. [818]

391 Auchincloss, Louis, ed. *The Edith Wharton Reader* (10–12). 1989, Macmillan paper $13.95 (0-02-030300-9). A fine collection that includes excerpts from novels, short stories, novellas, and parts of Wharton's autobiography. (Rev: BL 2/1/90)

392 Cather, Willa. *Great Short Works of Willa Cather* (10–12). 1989, Harper paper $5.95 (0-06-080970-1). This is a collection of 9 short stories including the justly famous "Paul's Case." (Rev: BL 8/89)

393 Cooper, James Fenimore. *The Last of the Mohicans* (8–12). 1986, Macmillan $22.95 (0-684-18711-6); paper $2.95 (0-553-21329-6). This is the second of the classic Leatherstocking Tales. The others are *The Pioneers, The Prairie, The Pathfinder,* and *The Deerslayer* (all available in various editions).

394 Crane, Stephen. *Maggie: A Girl of the Streets* (10–12). 1985, Fawcett paper $3.50 (0-449-30024-2). A realistic novel about everyday life in New York in the 1890s.

395 Crane, Stephen. *The Red Badge of Courage* (10–12). 1980, Random $10.95 (0-394-60493-8); Penguin paper $2.25 (0-14-035055-1). The great Civil War novel about a young soldier's first taste of battle.

396 Dos Passos, John. *Manhattan Transfer* (10–12). 1980, Bentley $18.00 (0-8376-0433-8); Houghton paper $8.95 (0-395-08375-3). This novel, told from various points of view, deals with various levels of life in New York City in the early twentieth century.

397 Ehrhart, W. D., ed. *Carrying the Darkness: American Indochina—The Poetry of the Vietnam War* (10–12). 1985, Avon paper $5.95 (0-380-

89709-1). An unusual collection of poems, mostly by Vietnam War veterans, most of which have never been published before. (Rev: BL 11/1/85) [811]

398 Hale, E. E. *The Man without a Country and Other Stories* (9–12). 1968, Airmont paper $1.95 (0-8049-0185-6). The title story tells of the fate of a man who rejects his native land.

399 Harte, Bret. *The Outcasts of Poker Flat and Other Stories* (10–12). 1973, Airmont paper $1.95 (0-8049-0051-5). These famous short stories deal with the rough-and-tumble life on the American frontier.

400 Hawthorne, Nathaniel. *The House of the Seven Gables* (10–12). 1982, Buccaneer LB $21.95 (0-89966-379-6); Pocket paper $3.25 (0-671-00670-3). Hephzibah tries to shelter her brother from the evil of Judge Pyncheon in this novel set in Massachusetts.

401 Hawthorne, Nathaniel. *The Scarlet Letter* (10–12). 1984, Buccaneer LB $21.95 (0-89966-494-6); Pocket paper $3.95 (0-671-67645-8). Set in New England during Colonial times, this is a novel of adultery and expiation.

402 Hemingway, Ernest. *The Complete Short Stories of Ernest Hemingway: The Finca Vigia Edition* (10–12). 1987, Macmillan $29.95 (0-684-18668-3). There are 63 stories in this definitive collection—7 of them never published before. (Rev: BL 10/1/87)

403 Henry, O. *Forty-one Stories* (10–12). 1986, NAL paper $4.95 (0-451-52254-0). A collection by the master of the surprise ending that includes all of the favorites such as "Gift of the Magi."

404 Irving, Washington. *The Legend of Sleepy Hollow, and Other Stories* (9–12). 1964, Airmont paper $2.75 (0-8049-0050-7). The title story is the classic about Ichabod Crane and his encounter with a headless horseman.

405 James, Henry. *The Ambassadors* (10–12). 1975, Penguin paper $3.95 (0-14-003499-4). For better readers, this 1902 novel traces the conflict between old-fashioned New England values and those of Europe.

406 James, Henry. *The Portrait of a Lady* (10–12). 1983, Random $9.95 (0-394-60432-6); NAL paper 3.95 (0-451-52288-5). In this novel that first appeared in 1881, James portrays the clash of cultures when some Americans encounter Europe for the first time.

407 James, Henry. *The Turn of the Screw* (10–12). 1983, Amereon LB $16.95 (0-89190-315-1); Airmont paper $1.75 (0-8049-0155-4). In this horror story a young governess realizes that her 2

charges are controlled by ghosts. First published in 1898.

408 James, Henry. *Washington Square* (10–12). 1986, Bucanneer $17.95 (0-89966-532-2); NAL paper $3.50 (0-451-52499-3). This classic short novel of unrequited love is set in New York City. Also use by the same author *The American* (Penguin, 1981) and *The Bostonians* (NAL, 1984).

409 London, Jack. *The Call of the Wild* (7–12). Illus. 1963, Macmillan $11.95 (0-02-759510-2); NAL paper $2.50 (0-451-52390-3). In this 1903 classic, the dog Buck becomes leader of a pack of wolves.

410 London, Jack. *The Sea-Wolf* (7–12). 1958, Macmillan $15.95 (0-02-574630-8); Bantam paper $1.95 (0-553-211617-7). Wolf Larsen helps a ne'er-do-well and a female poet find their destinies in the classic that was originally published in 1904.

411 London, Jack. *White Fang* (7–12). 1972, Scholastic paper $2.50 (0-590-40523-3). A dog sacrifices himself to save his master in the classic that was first published in 1906.

412 Melville, Herman. *Billy Budd, Sailor* (10–12). 1985, Amereon $12.95 (0-89190-891-9); Pocket paper $2.50 (0-671-46716-6). The death of innocence is one of the themes in this story of a sailor who is goaded into killing a sadistic officer.

413 Melville, Herman. *Moby Dick* (10–12). Illus. 1982, Random $17.95 (0-394-60804-6); NAL paper $2.25 (0-451-52021-1). One of many editions of this novel first published in 1851 about Captain Ahab's pursuit of a ferocious white whale.

414 Melville, Herman. *Typee: A Peep at Polynesian Life* (10–12). 1982, Lib. of America $27.50 (0-940450-00-3). Three short novels by Melville all first published in the 1840s. *Omoo* is a sequel to *Typee* while *Mardi* is a complex allegory.

415 Melville, Herman. *White-Jacket: Or the World in a Man-of-War* (10–12). 1991, Oxford Univ. Pr. paper $5.95 (0-19-281828-7). Life aboard the man-of-war *Neversink* is portrayed in this realistic picture of existence in the U.S. Navy more than 100 years ago.

416 Norris, Frank. *The Octopus* (10–12). 1986, Penguin paper $5.95 (0-14-039040-5). This American classic tells of the epic struggle between the railroad and farmers on the Western frontier.

417 Poe, Edgar Allan. *The Fall of the House of Usher and Other Tales* (9–12). 1960, NAL paper $2.95 (0-451-52174-9). A collection of 14 of the best known horror stories by Poe.

418 Poe, Edgar Allan. *Selected Poetry and Prose* (10–12). 1951, Random paper $3.75 (0-394-30958-8). This volume includes a generous selection of Poe's poems, stories, and essays. [818]

419 Steinbeck, John. *The Portable Steinbeck* (10–12). 1971, Penguin paper $9.95 (0-14-015002-1). This ample anthology includes mostly fiction (some complete novels, some excerpts) plus a sampling of his nonfiction works. [818]

420 Stockton, Frank. *The Lady or the Tiger and Other Stories* (9–12). 1968, Airmont paper $1.95 (0-8049-0163-5). In the title story a life-or-death choice must be made in this classic cliffhanger.

421 Twain, Mark. *The Adventures of Huckleberry Finn* (7–12). 1959, NAL paper $1.75 (0-451-51912-4). The classic 1885 story of Huck and Jim on the Mississippi.

422 Twain, Mark. *The Adventures of Tom Sawyer* (7–12). 1982, Messner LB $14.79 (0-671-45647-4); Penguin paper $2.25 (0-14-035003-9). The story of Tom, Aunt Polly, Becky Thatcher, and the villainous Injun Joe. First published in 1876.

423 Twain, Mark. *The Complete Short Stories of Mark Twain* (9–12). 1957, Bantam paper $4.50 (0-553-21195-1). A total of 60 stories are included and arranged chronologically.

424 Twain, Mark. *A Connecticut Yankee in King Arthur's Court* (7–12). 1988, Morrow $19.95 (0-688-06346-2); NAL paper $2.25 (0-451-52353-9). Through a time travel fantasy, a swaggering Yankee is plummeted into the age of chivalry. First published in 1889.

425 Twain, Mark. *The Mysterious Stranger and Other Stories* (10–12). 1962, NAL paper $2.95 (0-451-52069-6). This is a fine collection of the most popular short stories by Mark Twain.

426 Twain, Mark. *The Prince and the Pauper* (10–12). 1982, Buccaneer $16.95 (0-89966-577-2); Penguin paper $2.25 (0-14-035017-9). Switched identities and murder are 2 of the elements in this novel set in the Midwest during the days of slavery.

427 Twain, Mark. *Pudd'nhead Wilson* (10–12). 1964, NAL paper $2.25 (0-451-52374-1). A classic detective story involving black slaves, switched identities, and murder. One of many editions.

428 Twain, Mark. *The Science Fiction of Mark Twain* (9–12). 1984, Archon Bks. LB $32.50 (0-208-02036-5). An unusual collection of stories plus an excerpt from *Connecticut Yankee* and 2 essays.

429 Twain, Mark. *Tom Sawyer Abroad and Tom Sawyer, Detective* (9–12). 1981, Univ. of California Pr. $22.50 (0-520-04560-2); paper $7.95 (0-520-04551-0). These 2 sequels are narrated by Huck Finn.

Contemporary Life and Problems

General

430 Bellow, Saul. *The Bellarosa Connection* (10–12). 1989, Penguin paper $6.95 (0-14-012686-4). A fine short novel about a Jewish man rescued from the Holocaust whose great ambition is to thank his benefactor. (Rev: BL 9/1/89)

431 Craven, Margaret. *I Heard the Owl Call My Name* (7–12). 1973, Dell paper $3.50 (0-440-34369-0). A terminally ill Anglican priest and his assignment in a coastal Indian community in British Columbia. The nonfiction story behind this book is told in *Again Calls the Owl* (1984).

432 Kalpakian, Laura. *Dark Continent and Other Stories* (10–12). 1989, Viking $17.95 (0-670-82531-X). For better readers, 6 stories that probe various kinds of human relationships. (Rev: BL 9/1/89)

433 Olshan, Joseph. *The Waterline* (10–12). 1989, Doubleday $17.95 (0-385-26505-0). A family disintegrates from feelings of guilt that they might have prevented the death of a neighbor's child. (Rev: BL 9/15/89)

Ethnic Groups and Problems

434 Aleichem, Sholom. *Holiday Tales of Sholom Aleichem* (9–12). Trans. by Aliza Shevrin. Illus. 1985, Macmillan paper $5.95 (0-689-71034-8). Jewish holidays are celebrated in this series of stories translated from the Yiddish.

435 Aleichem, Sholom. *Tevye the Dairyman and the Railroad Stories* (10–12). 1987, Schocken $19.95 (0-8052-4026-8). A collection of short stories by this Jewish master—many of the tales about Tevye are featured in *Fiddler on the Roof*. (Rev: BL 7/87)

436 Anaya, Rudolfo A. *Bless Me, Ultima* (10–12). 1976, TQS paper $12.00 (0-89229-002-1). A novel about growing up Chicano in southeastern New Mexico during the 1940s.

437 Anaya, Rudolfo A. *Heart of Aztlan* (10–12). Illus. 1988, Univ. of New Mexico Pr. $12.95 (0-

8263-1054-0); paper $7.00 (0-685-78786-9). The dramatic story of the poor Chavez family, which moves to a large city and faces unexpected problems.

438 Baldwin, James. *Evidence of Things Not Seen* (10–12). 1986, Henry Holt paper $4.95 (0-8050-0138-7). For mature readers, a novel about child murders in Atlanta that explores the racial conflicts that exist in America. (Rev: VOYA 4/86)

439 Baldwin, James. *Go Tell It on the Mountain* (10–12). 1963, Dell paper $4.95 (0-440-33007-6). The story of a teenager's conversion to religion and of the history of a black American family. A reissue.

440 Baldwin, James. *If Beale Street Could Talk* (9–12). 1986, Dell paper $4.95 (0-440-34060-8). Fonny is sent to jail for a crime he didn't commit before he can marry his pregnant girlfriend, Tish.

441 Baldwin, James. *Just above My Head* (10–12). 1990, Dell paper $5.95 (0-440-14777-8). For mature readers, this is the story of a transsexual gospel singer narrated by his younger brother.

442 Bambara, Toni Cade. *Gorilla, My Love* (10–12). 1981, Random paper $4.95 (0-394-75049-7). Fifteen stories that explore the problems of black Americans.

443 Barrett, William E. *The Lilies of the Field* (8–12). Illus. 1967, Doubleday paper $3.95 (0-385-07246-5). A young black man, Homer Smith, helps a group of German nuns to achieve their dream.

444 Baylor, Byrd. *Yes Is Better Than No* (10–12). 1972, Treasure Chest paper $6.95 (0-918080-53-3). The tragic story of a group of Papago Indians who move from their reservation to a slum in Tucson.

445 Bellow, Saul, ed. *Great Jewish Short Stories* (10–12). 1985, Dell paper $4.95 (0-440-33122-6). These stories that explore the Jewish experience at different times and in different places are by such writers as Isaac Bashevis Singer and Philip Roth.

446 Borland, Hal. *When the Legends Die* (10–12). 1963, Bantam paper $2.95 (0-553-25738-2). At the death of his parents, a young Indian boy must enter the world of the white man.

447 Bryson, Jamie S. *The War Canoe* (10–12). 1990, Alaska Northwest paper $9.95 (088240-368-0). The story of an Alaskan Indian young man, his passage into adulthood, and the building of a war canoe like the one his ancestors used. (Rev: SLJ 7/90)

448 Carter, Angela, ed. *Wayward Girls & Wicked Women* (10–12). 1988, Penguin paper

$8.95 (0-14-010371-6). A novel set in China and in the United States about several generations of immigrants and their families told from the females' point of view. (Rev: BL 3/1/89)

449 Chao, Evelina. *Gates of Grace* (9–12). 1985, Warner $15.50 (0-446-51303-2); paper $4.50 (0-446-32844-8). This novel covers 20 years in the life of the Wong family, who left China for New York's Chinatown when the communists took over. (Rev: BL 9/15/85)

450 Childress, Alice. *Rainbow Jordan* (9–12). 1982, Avon paper $2.95 (0-380-58974-5). A young black girl faces the problems and temptations of becoming a woman. Also use: *A Hero Ain't Nothin' but a Sandwich* (1977).

451 Clarke, John Henrik. *American Negro Short Stories* (10–12). 1966, Hill & Wang $9.95 (0-374-52141-7). This anthology first appeared in 1966 and contains 31 stories by and about black Americans.

452 Dorris, Michael. *A Yellow Raft in Blue Water* (10–12). 1987, Henry Holt $16.95 (0-8050-0045-3); Warner paper $7.95 (0-446-38787-8). A stirring novel dealing with 3 generations of females in an American Indian family, beginning in the present and moving back. (Rev: BL 3/1/87; BR 11–12/87; SLJ 11/87; VOYA 8–9/87)

453 Ellison, Ralph. *Invisible Man* (10–12). 1963, Random $3.95 (0-394-60338-9). The novel of a black man whose life is a path toward the complete loss of identity.

454 Erdrich, Louise. *Tracks* (10–12). 1988, Henry Holt $17.95 (0-8050-0895-0). In this third novel of a cycle, Louise Erdrich resumes the story of a group of Chippewa Indians and their culture under siege in a white man's world. For better readers. The cycle began with *Love Medicine* (1984) and continued with *The Beet Queen* (1986). (Rev: BL 7/88; VOYA 12/89)

455 Faulkner, William. *Intruder in the Dust* (10–12). 1948, Random $13.95 (0-394-43074-3). Two 16-year-old boys and an older woman try to save an elderly black man accused of murder in this Faulkner novel that is more accessible than many others.

456 Faulkner, William. *Light in August* (10–12). 1967, Random $16.95 (0-394-43335-1); paper $4.95 (0-394-71189-0). In this dense novel, Joe Christmas, part white and part black, murders his white mistress and is pursued by a mob of townspeople.

457 Fields, Jeff. *A Cry of Angels* (10–12). 1979, Ballantine paper $2.50 (0-345-28204-3). This novel, set in a black slum area in a Georgia town, tells of a young man who tries to help its residents.

458 Gaines, Ernest J. *The Autobiography of Miss Jane Pittman* (9–12). 1971, Bantam paper $3.95 (0-553-26357-9). This novel, supposedly the memoirs of a 110-year-old ex-slave, is a stirring tribute to survival and courage.

459 Gaines, Ernest J. *A Gathering of Old Men* (10–12). 1983, Knopf $17.95 (0-394-51468-8); Random paper $4.95 (0-394-72591-3). A group of old black men protect their own but assume collective guilt for a crime none of them committed.

460 Gaines, Ernest J. *In My Father's House* (10–12). 1978, Knopf $13.95 (0-394-47938-6); Norton paper $6.70 (0-393-30124-9). The life of a black minister changes when his illegitimate son suddenly appears.

461 Hale, Janet Campbell. *The Owl's Song* (10–12). 1976, Avon paper $2.50 (0-380-00605-7). An American Indian boy faces new problems when he leaves his reservation to live with a half-sister in Los Angeles.

462 Harris, Marilyn. *Hatter Fox* (9–12). 1986, Ballantine paper $3.95 (0-345-33157-5). A touching novel about a young Navaho girl and her many problems.

463 Hijuelos, Oscar. *Our House in the Last World* (10–12). 1983, Persea Books $18.95 (0-89255-069-4); Pocket paper $3.95 (0-671-50785-0). A touching novel about the Santinio family and their life in America after leaving Cuba in 1943.

464 Hughes, Langston, ed. *The Best Short Stories by Negro Writers: An Anthology from 1899 to the Present* (10–12). 1967, Little paper $9.95 (0-316-38031-8). This collection of 47 stories covers a period of Black American writing that spans almost 70 years.

465 Hurston, Zora Neale. *Their Eyes Are Watching God* (10–12). 1978, Univ. of Illinois Pr. $6.95 (0-252-00686-0). A novel about black Americans in Florida that centers on the life of Janie and her 3 marriages. First published in 1937.

466 Janus, Christopher G. *Miss 4th of July, Goodbye* (10–12). 1986, Sheffield $15.95 (0-934831-00-9). In a series of letters to Greece, a lively teenager tells about her experiences in her new home in West Virginia of 1917. (Rev: BL 1/15/86)

467 Johnston, Jennifer. *Fool's Sanctuary* (10–12). 1988, Viking $15.95 (0-670-81783-X). The tragedy of Northern Ireland is depicted in this touching story of a girl, her British soldier brother, and her rebel lover. (Rev: BL 1/15/88; VOYA 12/88)

468 Jones, Toeckey. *Go Well, Stay Well* (7–12). 1980, Harper LB $12.89 (0-06-023062-2). The story of a forbidden interracial friendship between a Zulu girl and a privileged white girl in South Africa.

469 Kadohata, Cynthia. *The Floating World* (10–12). 1989, Viking $17.95 (0-670-82680-4). For better readers, this is the story of a Japanese American girl's journey from childhood to becoming a young adult. (Rev: BL 5/15/89; SLJ 1/90; VOYA 4/90)

470 Kincaid, Jamaica. *Lucy* (10–12). 1990, Farrar $18.95 (0-374-19434-3). For mature readers, this is the story of a 19-year-old girl from Antigua and her life in a northern American city. (Rev: BL 10/1/90)

471 Lee, Harper. *To Kill a Mockingbird* (8–12). 1977, Harper $17.45 (0-397-00151-7). A small Southern town lawyer defends a black man wrongfully accused of rape.

472 Lester, Julius. *Do Lord Remember Me* (9–12). 1985, Holt $13.95 (0-03-071534-2); Pocket paper $5.95 (0-671-60707-3). A saga about a black family that spans time, from slavery to the civil rights struggle of the 1960s. (Rev: VOYA 8/85)

473 Lester, Julius. *This Strange New Feeling* (9–12). 1982, Dial $14.95 (0-8037-8491-0); Scholastic paper $2.50 (0-590-41061-4). Based on fact, this is a group of 3 short stories about slaves who react in different ways to gaining freedom.

474 Lipsyte, Robert. *The Contender* (9–12). 1967, Harper LB $12.89 (0-06-023920-4); paper $2.50 (0-06-447039-3). A black teenager hopes to get out of Harlem through a boxing career.

475 Lo, Steven C. *The Incorporation of Eric Chung* (10–12). 1989, Algonquin $14.95 (0-945575-18-1). An often humorous novel about the Americanization of a young Chinese student and his adventures in Lubbock, Texas. (Rev: SLJ 4/90)

476 McPherson, James Alan. *Hue and Cry* (10–12). 1979, Fawcett paper $2.25 (0-449-24192-0). In these 10 short stories, black and white characters explore their emotions.

477 Marzollo, Jean. *Do You Love Me, Harvey Burns?* (7–12). 1983, Dial $12.95 (0-8037-1668-0). Harvey is so concerned about being Jewish that it is about to spoil his relationship with his girlfriend.

478 Meriwether, Louise. *Daddy Was a Numbers Runner* (10–12). 1986, Feminist paper $8.95 (0-935312-57-9). The story of Frances, a black girl, growing up in Harlem during the Depression.

479 Morrison, Toni. *The Bluest Eye* (10–12). 1984, Pocket paper $3.95 (0-671-53146-8). A poor black girl wishes she could have blue eyes. For better readers.

480 Morrison, Toni. *Song of Solomon* (10–12). 1977, Knopf $14.95 (0-394-49784-8); NAL paper $4.50 (0-451-12933-4). When a young black man decides to leave his home to find his freedom, his family history is gradually revealed.

481 Morrison, Toni. *Sula* (10–12). 1973, Knopf $18.45 (0-394-48044-9); NAL paper $6.95 (0-452-26010-8). For mature readers, this is a novel about the friendship between 2 small-town black girls and the 2 different ways their lives develop.

482 Morrison, Toni. *Tar Baby* (10–12). 1981, Knopf $19.45 (0-394-42329-1); NAL paper $4.50 (0-451-15260-3). Two retired Americans, living on a Caribbean island, discover a primitive black man hiding in their home.

483 Naylor, Gloria. *Mama Day* (10–12). 1988, Ticknor $18.95 (0-89919-716-7); Random paper $7.95 (0-679-72181-9). For better readers, a love story set in a black community off the Atlantic coast of Georgia. (Rev: BL 12/15/87)

484 O'Connor, Flannery. *Everything That Rises Must Converge* (10–12). 1965, Farrar paper $7.95 (0-374-50464-4). Nine stories by this Southern writer, many of which deal with relations between blacks and whites.

485 Parks, Gordon. *The Learning Tree* (10–12). 1987, Fawcett paper $4.95 (0-449-21504-0). The story of a black boy's coming of age in a small town in Kansas in the 1920s.

486 Potok, Chaim. *The Gift of Asher Lev* (10–12). 1990, Knopf $19.95 (0-394-57212-2). Asher must return to the Brooklyn Hasidic Jewish community he left 20 years before in this sequel to the widely read *My Name is Asher Lev* (1972). (Rev: BL 2/1/90; SLJ 9/90)

487 Potok, Chaim. *The Promise* (10–12). 1969, Knopf $22.95 (0-394-44163-X); Fawcett paper $4.95 (0-449-20910-5). The friendship between 2 Jewish boys in Brooklyn becomes strained because of family problems.

488 Rios, Alberto Alvaro. *The Iguana Killer: Twelve Stories of the Heart* (10–12). 1984, Blue Moon $14.95 (0-933188-28-5); paper $7.95 (0-933188-29-3). For mature readers, this is a collection of graphic stories about Hispanics facing problems reaching maturity.

489 Rosen, Kenneth, ed. *The Man to Send Rain Clouds* (10–12). 1975, Random paper $5.95 (0-394-72016-4). Nineteen stories by American Indian writers.

490 Roth, Philip. *Goodbye, Columbus: And Five Short Stories* (10–12). 1959, Modern Lib. $7.95 (0-394-60374-5); Bantam paper $4.50 (0-553-26365-X). An early collection of stories by Philip Roth, most of which explore the theme of being Jewish in America.

491 Santiago, Danny. *Famous All Over Town* (10–12). 1983, NAL paper $7.95 (0-452-25974-0). An honest, realistic novel about a young Mexican American growing up in a California barrio.

492 Saroyan, William. *My Name Is Aram* (10–12). Illus. 1940, Harcourt $8.95 (0-15-163827-6). This is a collection of whimsical stories about Armenian Americans in general and a young boy named Aram in particular.

493 Schwartz, Delmore. *In Dreams Begin Responsibilities and Other Stories* (10–12). 1978, New Directions paper $7.95 (0-8112-0680-7). These stories explore the problems of growing up Jewish and in conflict with parental values.

494 Schwarz, Bart Andre. *The Last of the Just* (10–12). 1960, Macmillan $14.95 (0-689-70365-1). This complex, lengthy novel traces the fortunes of the Jewish Levy family through centuries of persecution.

495 Sebestyen, Ouida. *Words by Heart* (9–12). 1983, Bantam paper $2.95 (0-553-27179-2). A black girl unknowingly arouses racial conflicts in a southwestern white town at the turn of the century.

496 Shange, Ntozake. *Betsey Brown* (9–12). 1985, St. Martin's $12.95 (0-312-07727-0); paper $7.95 (0-312-07728-9). A black girl, thirteen year old Betsey, encounters racial prejudice when she attends an all-white school. (Rev: SLJ 12/85)

497 Silko, Leslie Marmon. *Ceremony* (10–12). 1986, Penguin paper $7.95 (0-14-008683-8). This story, set on an Indian reservation just after World War II, concerns the return home of a war-weary Navaho young man.

498 Singer, Isaac Bashevis. *A Crown of Feathers: And Other Stories* (10–12). 1973, Farrar paper $7.95 (0-374-51624-3). These stories with Jews as central characters range in locale from Europe and the Middle East to America.

499 Singer, Isaac Bashevis. *The Death of Methuselah* (9–12). 1988, Farrar LB $17.95 (0-374-13563-0). A collection of short stories by the Nobel Prize winner, many of which explore the Jewish experience. (Rev: BR 1–2/89)

500 Singer, Isaac Bashevis. *The Image and Other Stories* (10–12). 1985, Farrar $16.95 (0-374-17465-2). A collection of 22 new stories by this

Nobel Prize winner, many of them depicting Jewish life and customs. (Rev: BL 5/1/85)

501 Southerland, Ellease. *Let the Lion Eat Straw* (10–12). 1980, NAL paper $3.50 (0-451-14675-1). The story of a black woman's struggle to achieve a decent life for her family in present-day America.

502 Thomas, Joyce Carol. *Water Girl* (9–12). 1986, Avon paper $2.95 (0-380-89532-3). In this continuation of *Marked by Fire* (1982) and *Bright Shadow* (1983) the black girl Amber discovers that her real mother is a cousin. (Rev: BL 2/15/86; SLJ 4/86; VOYA 8–10/86)

503 Toomer, Jean. *Cane* (10–12). 1985, Peter Smith $16.50 (0-8446-6367-8); Liveright paper $4.95 (0-87140-104-5). Most of these stories deal with black life in the South.

504 Viglucci, Pat Costa. *Cassandra Robbins, Esq.* (8–12). 1987, Square One paper $4.95 (0-938961-01-2). A biracial girl being brought up in a white household meets and falls in love with a black college student. (Rev: BL 5/15/87; SLJ 5/87; VOYA 8–9/87)

505 Vilarreal, Jose Antonio. *Pocho* (10–12). 1959, Doubleday $7.95 (0-385-06118-8). For mature readers, this is a story of a Chicano boy living in California during the Depression.

506 Walker, Alice. *In Love and Trouble* (10–12). 1973, Harcourt paper $3.95 (0-15-644450-X). A group of short stories that explore the world of black women.

507 Walker, Alice. *Meridian* (10–12). 1976, Harcourt $14.95 (0-15-159265-9). The story of a southern black woman, from youth to adulthood, and her involvement in the civil rights movement.

508 Walker, Alice. *The Temple of My Familiar* (10–12). 1989, Harcourt $19.95 (0-15-188533-8). A combination of black history and contemporary social conditions is the mix in this novel for mature readers that contains scenes of sexual abuse. (Rev: BL 3/15/89)

509 Wallant, Edward L. *The Pawnbroker* (10–12). 1979, Buccaneer $16.95 (0-686-92468-1); Harcourt paper $7.95 (0-15-671422-1). A disturbing novel for better readers about a Jewish survivor of the Holocaust who runs a pawnshop in Harlem.

510 Weaver, Will. *Red Earth, White Earth* (10–12). 1986, Simon & Schuster $17.95 (0-617-61977-2). A successful computer expert comes back to his home in Minnesota and tries to resume his friendship with a Chippewa "blood brother." (Rev: SLJ 5/87)

511 Williams-Garcia, Rita. *Blue Tights* (9–12). 1987, Dutton $12.95 (0-525-67234-6). A talented black teenager has difficulty being accepted in her integrated high school. (Rev: BL 12/15/87;)

512 Wright, Richard. *Native Son* (10–12). 1969, Harper $18.45 (0-06-014762-8); paper $4.95 (0-06-083055-7). The tragic life of a black youth named Bigger Thomas who was raised in a Chicago slum.

Family Life and Problems

513 Agee, James. *A Death in the Family* (10–12). 1983, Bantam paper $4.95 (0-553-27011-7). A loving family must come to terms with the sudden death of the father.

514 Andrews, V. C. *Heaven* (10–12). 1985, Pocket paper $5.50 (0-671-52542-5). Trashy but popular fare about the trials of a girl adopted by a sadistic woman. (Rev: SLJ 1/86)

515 Arnow, Harriette. *The Dollmaker* (10–12). 1985, Univ. Pr. of Kentucky $24.00 (0-8131-1544-2); Avon paper $4.95 (0-380-00947-1). Gertie, a courageous woman, is forced to move her family to the squalor of Detroit's slums during World War II. A reissue.

516 Arnow, Harriette. *Hunter's Horn* (10–12). 1986, Univ. Pr. of Kentucky $24.00 (0-8131-1600-7). An atmospheric novel about life in the great Smokies.

517 Auster, Paul. *Moon Palace* (10–12). 1989, Viking $18.95 (0-670-82509-3). A sensitive novel about a college student and his aged companion who dictates his amazing life story to his young friend. (Rev: BL 1/15/89)

518 Bailey, Ann. *Burn Up* (9–12). 1988, Faber & Faber $11.95 (0-571-15005-5). Tough, streetwise English twin sisters are sent to live with their uncle, a minister. (Rev: BL 5/15/88)

519 Barnard, Robert. *Out of the Blackout* (10–12). 1985, Macmillan $12.95 (0-684-18282-3); Dell paper $3.95 (0-440-16761-2). In this challenging novel for better readers, a man returns to London from which he had been evacuated as a child during World War II to unravel the secrets of his past. (Rev: BL 5/1/85)

520 Barry, Lynda. *The Good Times Are Killing Me* (9–12). Illus. 1988, Real Comet $16.95 (0-941104-22-2). For better readers, the story of a seventh-grade girl growing up in a racist neighborhood during the late 1960s. (Rev: BL 10/1/88)

521 Bedford, Jean. *Sister Kate* (10–12). 1987, Penguin paper $5.95 (0-14-006496-6). A novel set in Australia about daughter Kate and her outlaw family known as the Kelly Gang. (Rev: BL 1/15/88)

522 Bennett, James Gordon. *My Father's Geisha* (10–12). 1990, Delacorte $17.95 (0-385-30097-2). The son and daughter of a career military officer dislike moving from base to base particularly when it seems their parents' marriage is breaking up. (Rev: SLJ 9/90)

523 Boissard, Janine. *Cecile* (10–12). Trans. by Mary Feeney. 1988, Little $16.95 (0-316-10103-6). The story of the youngest sister in the French Moreau family. Others in this series are: *A Matter of Feeling* (1980); *Christmas Lessons* (1984); *A Time to Choose* (1985). (Rev: BL 2/1/88; SLJ 6–7/88; VOYA 12/88)

524 Bonosky, Phillip. *A Bird in Her Hair and Other Stories* (9–12). 1987, International Pubs. paper $5.95 (0-7178-0661-8). A collection of short stories about the struggles of working people in Pennsylvania from the 1930s into the 1950s. (Rev: BL 2/15/88)

525 Bradbury, Ray. *Dandelion Wine* (9–12). 1975, Knopf $18.95 (0-394-49605-1); Bantam paper $3.95 (0-553-27553-7). A tender novel about one summer in the life of a 12-year-old boy growing up in a small Illinois town during 1928. A reissue.

526 Buechner, Frederick. *The Wizard's Tide* (9–12). 1990, Harper $13.95 (0-06-061160-X). A short novel told by an 11-year-old boy about his family's problems during the Great Depression. (Rev: BL 5/15/90; SLJ 11/90)

527 Bunting, Eve. *Will You Be My Posslq?* (9–12). 1987, Harcourt $12.95 (0-15-297399-0). Without her parents' approval freshman Kyle asks her friend Jamie to become her posslq (person of opposite sex sharing living quarters). (Rev: BL 10/1/87; SLJ 10/87; VOYA 4/88)

528 Burchard, Peter. *Sea Change* (7–12). 1984, Farrar $9.95 (0-374-36460-5). This 3-part novel deals with multigenerational mother-daughter relationships.

529 Cahill, Susan, ed. *Among Sisters* (10–12). 1989, NAL paper $4.95 (0-451-62734-2). A collection of 20 stories by well-known authors that explore the relationships between sisters. (Rev: SLJ 2/90; VOYA 4/90)

530 Capote, Truman. *Other Voices, Other Rooms* (10–12). 1968, Random $19.95 (0-394-43949-X); NAL paper $4.95 (0-451-16189-0). A 13-year-old boy finds a house full of eccentric characters when he goes to live with his father in a mansion in rural Louisiana.

531 Carter, Alden R. *Wart, Son of Toad* (9–12). 1985, Putnam $12.95 (0-448-47770-X); Berkley paper $2.50 (0-425-08885-5). After his mother and sister are killed in an accident, Steve's relations with his teacher-father (nicknamed Toad at school) steadily deteriorate. (Rev: BL 11/15/85; SLJ 2/86)

532 Casey, Dorothy. *Leaving Locke Horn* (10–12). 1986, Algonquin $15.95 (0-912697-39-3). The story of 2 families in a Maine town and the friendship of 2 women, one from each of these families. (Rev: SLJ 5/87)

533 Chavis, Geri Giebel, ed. *Family: Stories from the Interior* (10–12). 1987, Graywolf paper $11.95 (0-915308-93-2). From writers such as John Cheever and Willa Cather comes this anthology about interrelationships within the family. (Rev: BL 9/15/87)

534 Close, Jessie. *The Warping of Al* (9–12). 1990, Harper LB $13.89 (0-06-021281-0). Al tries to cope with a domineering father and a subservient mother. (Rev: SLJ 9/90)

535 Conroy, Pat. *The Great Santini* (10–12). 1987, Bantam paper $5.95 (0-553-26892-9). This novel about family discourse centers on a Marine captain who treats his family as he does his troops.

536 Conroy, Pat. *The Prince of Tides* (10–12). 1986, Houghton $19.95 (0-395-35300-9). For mature readers, a complex but rewarding novel of Southerner Tom Wingo and his family. (Rev: SLJ 4/87)

537 Cooney, Caroline B. *Don't Blame the Music* (10–12). 1986, Putnam $14.95 (0-448-47778-5). Susan, a high school senior, cannot reconcile her memories of a beloved older sister with the foul-mouthed, greedy, and selfish woman who comes back home after a failed career. (Rev: BL 8/86; BR 11–12/86; SLJ 8/86; VOYA 12/86)

538 Corcoran, Barbara. *Face the Music* (9–12). 1985, Macmillan $12.95 (0-689-31139-7). Marcie's mother is so dependent on her that it is stifling her future. (Rev: BL 11/1/85; SLJ 2/86)

539 Covington, Vicki. *Gathering Home* (10–12). 1988, Simon & Schuster $17.95 (0-671-66055-1). Whitney is a teenager who discovers that she is adopted and sets out to find her real parents. (Rev: SLJ 1/89)

540 Cunningham, Laura. *Sleeping Arrangements* (10–12). 1989, Knopf $18.95 (0-394-56112-0). When her mother dies, Lily is cared for by 2 eccentric uncles. (Rev: VOYA 4/90)

541 Dana, Barbara. *Necessary Parties* (9–12). 1986, Harper LB $14.89 (0-06-021409-0); Ban-

tam paper $3.50 (0-553-26984-4). Chris tries every trick possible to try to prevent his parents' divorce. (Rev: BL 12/15/86; BR 3–4/87; SLJ 11/86)

542 Davis, Jenny. *Sex Education* (9–12). 1988, Watts LB $12.99 (0-531-08356-X). Two high school students form an attachment to a young, pregnant housewife as part of a school assignment with unforeseen and dramatic results. (Rev: BL 9/1/88; SLJ 9/88; VOYA 8/88)

543 Dawkins, Louisa. *Chasing Shadows* (10–12). 1988, Houghton $17.95 (0-395-44143-9). A young girl copes with her broken family and a mentally unstable brother. For better readers. (Rev: BL 4/1/88)

544 Doherty, Berlie. *Granny Was a Buffer Girl* (8–12). 1988, Watts LB $13.99 (0-531-08354-3). Beginning in the 1920s this is the story of 3 generations of an English working-class family. (Rev: BL 3/1/88; BR 11–12/88; SLJ 4/88; VOYA 6/88)

545 Dunphy, Jack. *The Murderous McLaughlins* (10–12). 1988, McGraw $16.95 (0-07-018316-3). A boy grows up in an Irish immigrant home in a family dominated by a strong grandmother. For better readers. (Rev: BL 5/1/88)

546 Edmonds, Walter D. *The South African Quirt* (9–12). Illus. 1985, Little $14.95 (0-316-21153-2). Set in upstate New York in 1915, this is the story of a boy's relations with his overly critical father. (Rev: SLJ 10/85)

547 Faulkner, William. *As I Lay Dying* (10–12). 1964, Random $13.95 (0-394-41581-7); paper $2.95 (0-394-70254-9). In this difficult subjective novel, a poor white family in the South accompany the coffin of their mother to the town where she wished to be buried.

548 Faulkner, William. *The Sound and the Fury* (10–12). 1966, Random $17.95 (0-394-53241-4); paper $3.95 (0-394-70005-8). A difficult novel about the decay of a once proud and aristocratic southern white family.

549 Galsworthy, John. *The Forsyte Saga* (10–12). 1933, Macmillan $25.00 (0-684-15368-8); paper $15.95 (0-684-17653-X). This is one volume of the multivolume set that traces the fortunes of the Forsyte family. A reissue.

550 Garcia Marquez, Gabriel. *One Hundred Years of Solitude* (10–12). Trans. by Gregory Rabassa. 1970, Harper $19.45 (0-06-011418-5); Avon paper $4.95 (0-380-01503-X). Written with a technique known as magical realism, this is an imaginative account of the fortunes of the Buendia family in Colombia, South America.

551 Gardam, Jane. *The Hollow Land* (10–12). Illus. 1981, Greenwillow $10.25 (0-688-00873-9). Nine stories about a farming family in Cumbria, England, and their summer tenants from London.

552 Glover, Vivian. *The First Fig Tree* (10–12). 1988, St. Martin's $15.95 (0-312-01762-6). An elderly black woman and her great granddaughter establish bonds that help the young girl face today's realities. (Rev: BL 5/1/88)

553 Godwin, Gail. *A Mother and Two Daughters* (10–12). 1983, Avon paper $4.95 (0-380-61598-3). This adult novel tells about the gradual breakdown of a closely knit family.

554 Greber, Judith. *Mendocino* (10–12). 1988, Crown $18.95 (0-517-56761-X). A family saga for mature readers set in California about the Ross family that also deals with the treatment of minorities during our history. (Rev: BL 2/15/88)

555 Greenberg, Joanne. *Simple Gifts* (9–12). 1987, Henry Holt paper $7.95 (0-8050-0540-4). The Fleuris turn their poor Colorado ranch into a guest ranch for city folk who want local color and authenticity. (Rev: BL 6/1/86; BR 11–12/86; SLJ 9/86; VOYA 8–10/86)

556 Guest, Judith. *Ordinary People* (10–12). 1989, Ballantine paper $4.95 (0-345-33505-8). The accidental death of one of 2 sons brings a family to crisis and disintegration.

557 Hall, Lynn. *Flyaway* (9–12). 1987, Macmillan $12.95 (0-684-18888-0). Seventeen-year-old Ariel is so abused by her autocratic father that she will do anything to escape his power. (Rev: BL 9/15/87; SLJ 10/87; VOYA 12/87)

558 Hamilton, Virginia. *Junius Over Far* (9–12). 1985, Harper LB $12.89 (0-06-022195-X). Fearful that grandfather is lonely as he approaches death on a Caribbean island, 14-year-old Junius and his father go to visit him. (Rev: BL 5/15/85; BR 11–12/85; SLJ 8/85; VOYA 6/85)

559 Hamsun, Knut. *Growth of the Soil* (10–12). 1983, Random paper $7.95 (0-394-71781-3). The story of a Norwegian farming couple, their family, and their struggles.

560 Hankla, Cathryn. *A Blue Moon in Poorwater* (10–12). 1988, Ticknor & Fields $17.95 (0-89919-534-2). A coal miner's daughter from Appalachia recalls her fifth-grade year, her older brother's troubles, and her father's involvement in labor turmoils. (Rev: BL 4/15/88)

561 Harris, Mark. *Speed* (10–12). 1990, Donald I. Fine $19.95 (1-55611-180-0). A coming-of-age novel about a young man, his family, and the

special bond he had with a disabled brother. (Rev: BL 6/15/90)

562 Hassler, Jon. *Grand Opening* (9–12). 1987, Morrow $17.95 (0-688-06649-6); Ballantine paper $3.95 (0-345-35016-2). The Foster family moves to a small, unfriendly town to open up a grocery store. (Rev: BR 11–12/87; SLJ 2/88)

563 Herring, Robert. *McCampbell's War* (10–12). 1986, Viking $16.95 (0-670-80501-7). For better readers, the story of a noble Tennessee mountain man and his struggle to prevent a highway building project from destroying a family cemetery. (Rev: BR 11–12/86; SLJ 10/86; VOYA 12/86)

564 Hill, Ingrid. *Dixie Church Interstate Blues* (10–12). 1989, Viking $17.95 (0-670-82616-2). A fine collection of short stories that deal with various family situations. (Rev: BL 9/15/89)

565 Irving, John. *The World According to Garp* (10–12). 1984, Pocket paper $4.95 (0-671-52369-4). A satirical novel that spans 4 generations and 2 continents.

566 Kidd, Ronald. *Who Is Felix the Great?* (7–12). 1983, Lodestar $10.95 (0-525-66778-4). Tim still can't accept his father's death and his mother's new relationship.

567 Klein, Norma. *Going Backwards* (9–12). 1986, Scholastic $12.95 (0-590-40328-1); paper $2.50 (0-590-40329-X). A wrenching story of a boy and his grandmother, who is suffering from Alzheimer's disease, that introduces the theme of mercy killing. (Rev: BL 10/15/86; SLJ 1/87; VOYA 2/87)

568 Klein, Norma. *It's OK If You Don't Love Me* (9–12). 1976, Avon paper $2.50 (0-380-00011-3). Young people must cope with their parents' marital crises.

569 Lawrence, D. H. *Sons and Lovers* (10–12). 1982, Buccaneer LB $23.95 (0-89966-400-8); NAL paper $4.95 (0-14-043154-3). A powerful novel about Paul Morel and the destructive force of the excessive love he feels toward his mother. First published in 1913.

570 Leavitt, Caroline. *Meeting Rozzy Halfway* (9–12). 1982, Ballantine paper $2.75 (0-345-29797-0). Two very different sisters confront a series of problems in trying to understand and accept each other.

571 Leimbach, Marti. *Dying Young* (10–12). 1990, Doubleday $17.95 (0-385-26724-X). A low-key adult novel about a love triangle involving a young man dying of leukemia, his girlfriend, and another man. (Rev: BL 11/15/89)

572 L'Engle, Madeleine. *A Ring of Endless Light* (9–12). 1980, Farrar $14.95 (0-374-36299-8); Dell paper $3.50 (0-440-97232-9). In this Austin family novel, Vicky must adjust to many losses including that of her grandfather.

573 Lichtman, Wendy. *Telling Secrets* (9–12). 1986, Harper LB $13.89 (0-06-023885-2). Because her father is in jail for embezzlement and her mother has sworn her to secrecy, Toby finds it difficult to have open relationships with friends. (Rev: BL 3/15/86; BR 9–10/86; SLJ 9/86; VOYA 8–10/86)

574 Livingston, Nancy. *The Land of Our Dreams* (9–12). 1989, St. Martin's $18.95 (0-312-03374-5). This book continues the saga of the McKie family as they react to the outbreak of World War I. This is Livingston's sequel to *The Far Side of the Hill* (1988). (Rev: BL 8/89)

575 Lyons, Pam. *Love Around the Corner* (7–12). 1987, Dell paper $2.50 (0-440-94726-X). The arrival of a sick grandmother at Ronnie's house causes her to run away. (Rev: SLJ 4/87)

576 MacLeod, Alistair. *The Lost Salt Gift of Blood* (10–12). 1988, Ontario Review paper $10.95 (0-86538-063-5). Eleven short stories set in the province of Nova Scotia by one of Canada's young writers. (Rev: BL 6/15/88)

577 MacLeod, Charlotte. *Cirak's Daughter* (10–12). 1983, Macmillan paper $3.95 (0-02-044465-6). A 19-year-old girl sets out to find out about the father who deserted her years before.

578 McMurtry, Larry. *Terms of Endearment* (10–12). 1989, Simon & Schuster paper $8.95 (0-671-68208-3). The complex relationship between mother and daughter that involves adjustments to marriage and a fatal illness form the basis of this novel.

579 Marquand, John P. *The Late George Apley* (10–12). 1937, Little $15.95 (0-316-54652-6). The public and private life of a proper Bostonian.

580 Mickle, Shelly Fraser. *The Queen of October* (10–12). 1989, Algonquin $15.95 (0-945575-21-1). While her parents divorce, 13-year-old Sally is sent to a small town to live with her grandparents. (Rev: SLJ 2/90; VOYA 4/90)

581 Monninger, Joseph. *New Jersey* (10–12). 1987, Ballantine paper $3.95 (0-345-34112-0). When his father slips into insanity and abandons him, a young boy must adjust to life with an aunt and uncle. (Rev: BL 8/86)

582 Morrell, David. *Fireflies* (9–12). 1988, Dutton $16.95 (0-525-24680-0). A "nonfiction novel" about the death of the author's 15-year-old son from bone cancer. (Rev: BL 9/1/88)

583 Oates, Joyce Carol. *Them* (10–12). 1984, Fawcett paper $5.95 (0-449-20692-0). A challenging novel about a blue-collar family living in the Detroit area from the 1930s to 1967.

584 O'Connor, Sheila. *Tokens of Grace: A Novel in Stories* (9–12). Illus. 1990, Milkweed paper $9.95 (0-915943-47-6). A collection of short fiction pieces that show how a young girl, her sister, and mother weather the pain of divorce. (Rev: BL 8/90)

585 Olsen, Tillie. *Tell Me a Riddle* (10–12). 1976, Dell paper $7.95 (0-440-55010-6). Four stories about families and their intense emotional problems.

586 Park, Christine, and Caroline Heaton, eds. *Close Company: Stories of Mothers and Daughters* (10–12). 1989, Ticknor $19.95 (0-89919-832-5); paper $9.95 (0-89919-900-3). A collection of 25 stories about mother-daughter relationships all from various parts of the world. (Rev: BL 5/15/89)

587 Peck, Robert Newton. *Hallapoosa* (10–12). 1988, Walker $16.95 (0-8027-1016-6). For mature readers, the story of a 52-year-old bachelor and his brother's 2 children whom he finds he has inherited. (Rev: BR 11–12/88; VOYA 12/88)

588 Pilcher, Rosamunde. *September* (10–12). 1990, St. Martin's $22.95 (0-312-04419-4). An intergenerational novel set in Scotland with more than a touch of romance. (Rev: BL 3/15/90)

589 Plain, Belva. *Blessings* (10–12). 1989, Delacorte $19.95 (0-385-29754-8). For better readers, the story of a woman's problems when the child she put up for adoption years ago suddenly reenters her life. (Rev: BL 5/15/89)

590 Potok, Chaim. *Davita's Harp* (10–12). 1985, Knopf $16.95 (0-394-54290-8); Fawcett paper $4.50 (0-449-20775-7). A girl from a Jewish-Protestant marriage seeks her own identity. (Rev: BR 9–10/85; VOYA 8/85)

591 Pringle, Terry. *A Fine Time to Leave Me* (10–12). 1989, Algonquin $15.95 (0-945575-16-5). For mature readers this is the story of 2 young people from different backgrounds who fall in love and marry. (Rev: VOYA 2/90)

592 Rigby, Kate. *Fall of the Flamingo Circus* (10–12). 1990, Random $16.95 (0-394-58356-6). Told in diary form, this is the account of the childhood and adolescence of an English girl scarred by her abusive father. (Rev: BL 4/15/90)

593 Rubens, Bernice. *Madame Sousatzka* (10–12). 1985, Warner paper $3.95 (0-446-32898-7). For better readers the English story of a child

piano player, his mother, and his piano teacher. (Rev: BL 2/15/86)

594 Rushforth, Peter. *Kindergarten* (10–12). 1983, Avon paper $2.95 (0-380-56150-6). Jo and Corrie find love and hope through their relationship with their grandmother.

595 Sagan, Françoise. *Bonjour Tristesse* (10–12). 1961, Dutton paper $5.95 (0-525-48040-4). In this short French novel, a teenage girl uses her lover to thwart her father's remarriage. For mature readers.

596 Salinger, J. D. *Franny and Zooey* (10–12). 1961, Little $16.95 (0-316-76954-1); Bantam paper $3.50 (0-553-26360-9). A novel about the three Glass children—Franny, Zooey, and Buddy—and their various destinies.

597 Sanders, Dori. *Clover* (10–12). 1990, Algonquin $15.95 (0-945575-26-2). A 10-year-old black girl must cope with her father's death and living with a new white stepmother. (Rev: BL 3/1/90; SLJ 8/90; VOYA 8/90)

598 Santmyer, Helen Hooven. *Farewell, Summer* (8–12). 1988, Harper $12.95 (0-06-015889-1). A mature woman recalls the summer of 1905 when she was 11 and had a crush on her cousin. (Rev: BR 11–12/88)

599 Saroyan, William. *The Human Comedy* (7–12). 1973, Dell paper $3.95 (0-440-33933-2). Homer Macauley is growing up during World War II in America and becomes part of the everyday life that is the human comedy.

600 Scarbrough, George. *A Summer Ago* (10–12). 1986, St. Luke's $13.95 (0-918518-46-6). A gentle story about a teenage boy and summer spent in rural Tennessee in the early Depression years. (Rev: SLJ 2/87)

601 Segal, Harriet. *Shadow Mountain* (10–12). 1990, Donald I. Fine $19.95 (1-55611-204-1). The story of the friendship of 2 women and how it changes when each marries. (Rev: BL 5/1/90)

602 Silsbee, Peter. *The Big Way Out* (9–12). 1987, Dell paper $2.75 (0-440-90499-4). After Paul's father returns to a mental hospital and his mother leaves for New York, Paul must find a way to save his family.

603 Singer, Marilyn. *Storm Rising* (9–12). 1989, Scholastic $12.95 (0-590-42173-5). A teenage boy falls in love with a 28-year-old woman who has unusual extrasensory powers. (Rev: SLJ 10/89; VOYA 12/89)

604 Smith, Lee. *Fair and Tender Ladies* (10–12). 1988, Putnam $17.95 (0-399-13382-8). Through a series of letters, the life story of a Virginia moun-

tain girl is told from childhood to becoming a grandmother. (Rev: SLJ 3/89)

605 Steel, Danielle. *Daddy* (10–12). 1989, Delacorte $19.95 (0-385-29766-1). When a mother decides to leave her family and return to school, her 3 children and husband are left on their own. (Rev: BL 9/1/89)

606 Stegner, Wallace. *Angle of Repose* (10–12). 1985, Fawcett paper $4.95 (0-449-20988-1). A man chronicles the lives of his grandparents and their problems.

607 Steinbeck, John. *East of Eden* (10–12). 1952, Viking $24.95 (0-676-28738-5); Penguin paper $5.95 (0-14-004997-5). For better readers, this novel, set in California, involves a variation on the Cain and Abel story.

608 Steinbeck, John. *The Pearl* (9–12). Illus. 1947, Viking $15.95 (0-670-54575-9); Bantam paper $2.50 (0-553-26261-0). The lives of a poor Mexican pearl fisher and his family change dramatically after he uncovers a fabulous pearl.

609 Stirling, Jessica. *The Asking Price* (10–12). 1990, St. Martin's $17.95 (0-312-03792-9). In turn-of-the-century Glasgow, 2 newlyweds set up housekeeping. (Rev: BL 2/15/90)

610 Styron, William. *Lie Down in Darkness* (10–12). 1974, Random $24.95 (0-394-50659-6); NAL paper $9.95 (0-452-26128-7). For better readers, a novel about the South and the decline of a once-important family.

611 Sullivan, Faith. *The Cape Ann* (10–12). 1988, Crown $18.95 (0-517-56930-2). Small-town life in Minnesota prior to World War II as seen through the eyes of a young girl. (Rev: BL 5/1/88; SLJ 11/88; VOYA 12/88)

612 Thompson, Thomas. *Richie* (10–12). 1989, NAL paper $3.95 (0-451-16129-7). This story explores the alienation of a father and son and the tragic consequences.

613 Townsend, John Rowe. *Downstream* (9–12). 1987, Harper LB $12.89 (0-397-32189-9). A teenage English boy finds himself in competition with his father for the affections of an attractive divorcée. (Rev: BL 7/87; SLJ 8/87; VOYA 6/87)

614 Tyler, Anne. *Dinner at the Homesick Restaurant* (10–12). 1982, Knopf $19.45 (0-394-52381-4); Berkley paper $4.95 (0-425-09860-0). The saga of an unhappy family dominated by a mean-spirited mother.

615 Updike, John. *Rabbit, Run* (10–12). 1960, Knopf $15.95 (0-394-44206-7); Fawcett paper $4.95 (0-449-20506-1). Book one of the saga of Harry (Rabbit) Angstrom, ex-basketball star and now a car salesman. His story is continued in *Rabbit Redux* (1971), *Rabbit Is Rich* (1981), and *Rabbit at Rest* (1990).

616 Voigt, Cynthia. *The Runner* (9–12). 1985, Macmillan $12.95 (0-689-31069-2); Fawcett paper $2.50 (0-449-70154-9). The story of Bullet Tillerman, a loner who escapes a terrible home situation through his love of running and later by enlisting and going to Vietnam. Some senior high students might wish to read other stories about the Tillermans including *Dicey's Song* (1982). (Rev: BL 3/15/85; SLJ 5/85)

617 Waugh, Evelyn. *Brideshead Revisited: The Sacred and Profane Memories of Captain Charles Ryder* (10–12). 1982, Little paper $9.95 (0-316-92634-5). The story of Charles Ryder and his involvement with an aristocratic Roman Catholic English family, the Marchmains.

618 Webb, Mary. *Precious Bane* (10–12). 1974, Penguin paper $6.95 (0-14-013217-1). An English novel about the curse on the Sarn family that leads to murder.

619 Welty, Eudora. *Losing Battles* (10–12). 1970, Random $13.95 (0-394-43421-8); paper $8.95 (0-679-72882-1). A Southern novel about 2 families who have a reunion to celebrate Grandma's ninetieth birthday.

620 Welty, Eudora. *The Optimist's Daughter* (10–12). 1972, Random $13.95 (0-394-40017-1); paper $5.95 (0-394-72667-7). While tending to her dying father, a 45-year-old woman examines her life and their relationship.

621 West, Michael Lee. *Crazy Ladies* (10–12). 1990, Longstreet $18.95 (0-929264-38-X). Three generations of eccentric ladies form the focus of this novel about Gussie Hamilton and her family. (Rev: BL 9/1/90)

622 Wharton, Edith. *Ethan Frome* (9–12). 1911, Macmillan $17.50 (0-684-15326-2); Penguin paper $3.95 (0-14-039058-8). A love triangle involving Ethan, his wife Zeena, and her young cousin Mattie.

623 Whitt, Anne Hall. *The Suitcases* (10–12). 1983, NAL paper $3.95 (0-451-16322-2). Three small sisters are shuttled from one foster home to another during Depression days in this novel set in the South.

624 Wolitzer, Meg. *This Is Your Life* (10–12). 1988, Crown $17.95 (0-517-56929-9). Two daughters grow up in the shadow of a mother who is a television comedian. (Rev: SLJ 1/89)

625 Woolf, Virginia. *To the Lighthouse* (10–12). 1927, Amereon $19.95 (0-88411-849-5); Harcourt paper $5.95 (0-15-690738-0). In a novel

that stretches over several years, family conflicts and relationships are explored.

626 Zindel, Bonnie, and Paul Zindel. *A Star for the Latecomer* (9–12). 1980, Harper $12.70 (0-06-026863-6). Brooke wants to live an ordinary life but her mother, who is dying of cancer, wants her to be a star.

Physical and Emotional Problems

627 Amado, Jorge. *Gabriela, Clove and Cinnamon* (10–12). 1988, Avon paper $7.95 (0-380-75470-3). For mature readers, this novel is a love story set in a frontier Brazilian town.

628 Anaya, Rudolfo A. *Tortuga* (10–12). 1979, Editorial Justa paper $7.00 (0-915808-34-X). This is the story of a crippled Mexican boy who is placed in a body cast that resembles a giant turtle's shell.

629 Anderson, Jessica. *Tirra Lirra by the River* (10–12). 1984, Penguin paper $6.95 (0-14-006945-3). Through a series of remembrances, 70-year-old Nora re-creates her life.

630 Anderson, Sherwood. *Winesburg, Ohio* (10–12). 1987, Penguin paper $3.95 (0-14-04304-X). A portrait of the problems of small-town life as seen through the stories of several different characters.

631 Benton, John. *Lefty* (10–12). 1981, Natl. Woman's Christian Temperance Union paper $1.95 (0-318-18160-6). An 18-year-old addict from the slums of New York enters a rehabilitation program.

632 Boll, Heinrich. *The Lost Honor of Katherina Blum* (10–12). 1976, McGraw paper $6.95 (0-07-006429-6). Though brief, this is a disturbingly powerful novel for better readers about a woman who is accused of helping a political criminal in Germany.

633 Bridgers, Sue Ellen. *Sara Will* (10–12). 1985, Harper $14.95 (0-06-015385-7). For better readers, the story of how the lives of 2 reclusive sisters change when a brother-in-law and his family move in. (Rev: BL 1/1/85; VOYA 12/85)

634 Brooks, Bruce. *No Kidding* (8–12). 1989, Harper LB $13.89 (0-06-020723-X). In this novel set in the twenty-first century where alcoholism is rampant, the 14-year-old boy tries to keep his family together. (Rev: BL 3/15/89; BR 11–12/89; SLJ 3/89)

635 Bunting, Eve. *Face at the Edge of the World* (9–12). 1985, Ticknor & Fields $13.95 (0-89919-399-4); paper $3.95 (0-89919-800-7). Jed tries to find out the whys behind the suicide of his friend Charlie, a gifted black student. (Rev: BL 8/85; BR 9–10/86; SLJ 12/85; VOYA 8/85)

636 Camus, Albert. *The Fall* (10–12). Trans. by Justin O'Brien. 1957, Knopf $10.95 (0-394-42424-7); Random paper $6.95 (0-394-70223-9). In this novel for better readers, a once-successful lawyer tells of his descent into despair.

637 Camus, Albert. *The Plague* (10–12). Trans. by Stuart Gilbert. 1948, Knopf $19.45 (0-394-44061-7); Random paper $5.95 (0-394-71258-7). In this allegory, several people react to an outbreak of the bubonic plague that is ravaging their Algerian city.

638 Camus, Albert. *The Stranger* (10–12). Trans. by Stuart Gilbert. 1946, Knopf $16.45 (0-394-44748-4); Random paper $5.95 (0-679-72020-6). For better readers, this novel describes how a convicted murderer at last finds some meaning to life.

639 Carter, Alden R. *Sheila's Dying* (10–12). 1987, Putnam $13.95 (0-399-21405-4); Scholastic paper $2.75 (0-590-42045-3). Jerry discovers that his girlfriend Sheila has inoperable cancer. (Rev: BL 6/1/87; SLJ 5/87; VOYA 6/87)

640 Cary, Joyce. *The Horse's Mouth* (10–12). 1986, Amereon $19.95 (0-88411-311-6); Harper paper $5.95 (0-06-080046-1). Gulley Jimson, a most unusual English artist, is featured in this novel for better readers.

641 Childress, Alice. *Those Other People* (10–12). 1989, Putnam $14.95 (0-399-21510-7). A 17-year-old gay boy is blackmailed along with a black boy into silence over the attempted rape they have witnessed. (Rev: BL 1/1/89; SLJ 2/89; VOYA 4/89)

642 Clauser, Suzanne. *A Girl Named Sooner* (9–12). 1976, Avon paper $2.95 (0-380-00216-7). A neglected girl is given a home by a veterinarian and his wife.

643 Coetzee, J. M. *In the Heart of the Country* (10–12). 1982, Penguin paper $5.95 (0-14-006228-9). This disturbing novel for better readers is set in South Africa and tells about a lonely woman and her problems. Also use: *Waiting for the Barbarians* (1982).

644 Cole, Barbara. *Alex the Great* (8–12). 1989, Rosen $12.95 (0-8239-0941-7). The events leading up to Alex's drug overdose is told first by Alex and then by her friend, Deonna. (Rev: BR 9–10/89; VOYA 8/89)

645 Conroy, Pat. *The Water Is Wide* (10–12). 1987, Bantam paper $4.95 (0-553-26893-7). An idealistic young teacher goes to a South Carolina island to teach black children but finds he must do battle with constricting regulations.

646 Copeland, Ann. *The Golden Thread* (10–12). 1989, Viking $16.95 (0-670-82977-3). The story of a girl's career as a Catholic nun and of the problems and questions this life brings. (Rev: SLJ 2/90; VOYA 4/90)

647 Cormier, Robert. *The Bumblebee Flies Anyway* (7–12). 1983, Pantheon LB $10.99 (0-394-96120-X); Dell paper $3.25 (0-440-90871-X). A terminally ill boy and his gradual realization of his situation.

648 Cozzens, James Gould. *The Just and the Unjust* (10–12). 1965, Harcourt paper $12.95 (0-15-646578-7). This challenging adult novel takes the reader behind the scenes in a murder trial.

649 Cronin, A. J. *The Citadel* (10–12). 1983, Little $16.45 (0-316-16158-6); paper $7.95 (0-316-16183-7). An idealistic doctor finds he must battle with the establishment.

650 Cronin, A. J. *The Keys of the Kingdom* (10–12). 1984, Little $16.45 (0-316-16189-6); paper $7.95 (0-316-16184-5). An inspiring story about a young priest and his missionary work.

651 Crutcher, Chris. *Chinese Handcuffs* (10–12). 1989, Greenwillow $12.95 (0-688-08345-5). A brutal novel about basketball, a young man trying to adjust to his brother's suicide, and a sexually abused girl. (Rev: BR 9–10/89; SLJ 4/89; VOYA 6/89)

652 Dart, Iris Rainer. *Beaches* (10–12). 1986, Bantam paper $3.95 (0-553-25675-0). The story of a friendship between 2 very different women. (Rev: SLJ 10/85)

653 Degens, T. *On the Third Ward* (8–12). 1990, Harper LB $14.89 (0-06-021429-5). Set in 1951, this is the story of a group of German young people who are patients in a hospital for the treatment of tuberculosis. (Rev: BL 11/15/90)

654 Dizeno, Patricia. *Why Me? The Story of Jenny* (10–12). 1976, Avon paper $2.95 (0-380-00563-8). Jenny tries to keep her rape a secret from others.

655 Doctorow, E. L. *The Book of Daniel* (10–12). 1971, Random $14.95 (0-394-46271-8); Fawcett paper $4.50 (0-449-21430-3). This is a fictionalized account of the Rosenberg spy case and of the Rosenbergs' execution.

656 Drabble, Margaret. *The Millstone* (10–12). 1989, NAL paper $7.95 (0-452-26126-0). A mature novel by this English writer about a liberated modern woman who faces motherhood.

657 Dragonwagon, Crescent. *The Year It Rained* (10–12). 1985, Macmillan $12.95 (0-02-733110-5). A girl with severe mental problems cannot communicate with her mother who is overly dependent. For mature readers. (Rev: BL 11/15/85; BR 5–6/86; SLJ 11/85)

658 Faucher, Elizabeth. *Surviving* (9–12). 1985, Scholastic paper $2.50 (0-590-33664-9). This novel focuses on the suicide death of 2 teenagers, what caused it, and how the families cope after the tragedy. (Rev: BL 2/15/85; SLJ 9/85; VOYA 6/85)

659 Ferris, Jean. *Invincible Summer* (9–12). 1987, Farrar $12.95 (0-374-33642-3); Avon paper $2.75 (0-380-70619-9). The story of a friendship and later a love shared by 2 courageous teenagers, both suffering from leukemia. (Rev: SLJ 8/87)

660 Feuer, Elizabeth. *Paper Doll* (8–12). 1990, Farrar $13.95 (0-374-35736-6). Leslie, who lost her legs in a car accident, forms a strong loving relationship with Jeff, a cerebral palsy victim. (Rev: BL 8/90; SLJ 10/90)

661 Flanigan, Sara. *Alice* (9–12). 1988, St. Martin's $16.95 (0-312-01728-6). A teenage girl and her older brother befriend a much-abused epileptic girl in this novel set in rural Georgia. (Rev: BL 4/15/88; VOYA 2/89)

662 Gaeddert, LouAnn. *Daffodils in the Snow* (10–12). 1984, Dutton $11.95 (0-525-44150-6). When Marianne, who is involved in a religious cult, becomes pregnant, she insists that the father is God.

663 Garcia Marquez, Gabriel. *Chronicle of a Death Foretold* (10–12). 1983, Knopf $18.95 (0-394-53074-8); Ballantine paper $5.95 (0-345-31002-0). Murder upsets a wedding in this novel by the Nobel Prize winner. For better readers.

664 Golding, William. *Darkness Visible* (10–12). 1989, Farrar $14.95 (0-374-13502-9); Harcourt paper $8.95 (0-15-623931-0). A challenging novel about a mutilated man and his tragic fate.

665 Grant, Cynthia D. *Phoenix Rising: Or, How to Survive Your Life* (9–12). 1989, Macmillan $12.95 (0-689-31458-2). Jessie's inability to cope with her sister's death is so great she refuses to leave the room they once shared. (Rev: BL 3/1/89; BR 9–10/89; SLJ 2/89; VOYA 6/89)

666 Greenberg, Jan. *No Dragons to Slay* (9–12). 1984, Farrar $11.95 (0-374-35528-2); paper $3.50 (0-374-45509-0). Thomas, a 17-year-old, discovers he has cancer.

667 Greenberg, Joanne. *I Never Promised You a Rose Garden* (10–12). 1989, NAL paper $3.95

(0-451-16031-2). A 16-year-old Jewish girl sinks into schizophrenia and receives help in an asylum.

668 Greenberg, Joanne. *Of Such Small Differences* (10–12). 1988, Henry Holt $18.95 (0-8050-0902-7). A 25-year-old blind and deaf man falls in love for the first time. (Rev: BL 6/15/88; BR 3–4/89; SLJ 11/88; VOYA 12/88)

669 Greene, Graham. *The Heart of the Matter* (10–12). 1981, Amereon $18.95 (0-88411-654-9); Penguin paper $3.95 (0-14-001789-5). In a West African colony an English assistant police commissioner becomes the victim of a blackmailer.

670 Greene, Graham. *The Power and the Glory* (10–12). 1982, Viking $16.95 (0-670-56979-8); Penguin paper $3.95 (0-14-001791-7). In Mexico, a whiskey-sotted priest finds he is hunted as an outlaw.

671 Guy, Rosa. *My Love, My Love, or the Peasant Girl* (9–12). 1985, Holt $12.95 (0-03-000507-8). This, a modern retelling of the Little Mermaid story, uses a Caribbean Island as its setting and tells of the tragic love of a poor peasant girl for a rich mulatto. (Rev: BL 9/15/85; SLJ 1/86; VOYA 4/86)

672 Hassler, Jon. *Staggerford* (10–12). 1986, Ballantine paper $3.95 (0-345-33375-6). A deceptively easy story about an ordinary middle-aged English teacher and her tragic encounter with a bonewoman.

673 Hebert, Ernest. *The Dogs of March* (10–12). 1979, Ultramarine $20.00 (0-89366-144-9); Penguin paper $7.95 (0-14-005560-6). A barely literate man cracks under the pressures of society.

674 Heller, Joseph. *Something Happened* (10–12). 1989, Dell paper $5.95 (0-440-20441-0). For mature readers, this is the story of Robert Slocum—who is trapped in a middle-class existence he hates.

675 Hesse, Hermann. *Demian* (10–12). Trans. by Michael Roloff and Michael Lebeck. 1989, Buccaneer LB $21.95 (0-89966-630-2); Bantam paper $3.50 (0-553-26246-7). A psychological novel about friendship and self-discovery. First published in 1923.

676 Hoffman, Alice. *At Risk* (10–12). 1988, Putnam $17.95 (0-399-13367-4); 1989, Berkley paper $4.95 (0-425-11738-3). A small New England community is rocked when it is revealed that the young daughter of one of the families has AIDS. (Rev: BL 5/15/88; BR 11–12/89; SLJ 12/88)

677 Homes, A. M. *Jack* (9–12). 1989, Macmillan $13.95 (0-02-744831-2). Four years after his par-

ents are divorced, Jack learns that his father is gay. (Rev: BL 12/1/89; SLJ 11/89; VOYA 2/90)

678 Hooks, William H. *A Flight of Dazzle Angels* (9–12). 1988, Macmillan $13.95 (0-02-744430-9). Fifteen-year-old Annie longs to overcome her physical handicap caused by a clubfoot and live the same life others do. (Rev: SLJ 12/88; VOYA 12/88)

679 Howard, Jane. *A Different Woman* (10–12). 1982, Dutton paper $7.95 (0-525-48020-X). A novel that explores in depth the inner workings of a woman's psyche.

680 Hughes, Richard. *A High Wind in Jamaica* (10–12). 1985, Amereon $15.95 (0-88411-128-8); Harper paper $6.95 (0-06-091627-3). The amoral world of children is explored in this novel that was first published in 1929.

681 Hunter, R. Lanny, and Victor L. Hunter. *Living Dogs and Dead Lions* (10–12). 1987, Penguin paper $4.50 (0-14-010263-9). Joshua tries to rid himself of the horrible memories of the Vietnam War by visiting the widow of his commanding officer. (Rev: SLJ 12/86; VOYA 12/86)

682 Irwin, Hadley. *Abby, My Love* (9–12). 1985, Macmillan $11.95 (0-689-50323-7); NAL paper $2.50 (0-451-14501-1). After many years of friendship, Abby finally tells her boyfriend Chip that her father is sexually abusing her. (Rev: BL 3/1/85; SLJ 5/85)

683 Jarrell, Randall. *Pictures from an Institution* (10–12). 1953, Univ. of Chicago Pr. paper $7.95 (0-226-39374-7). A richly textured novel for better readers about faculty life in a progressive school for girls.

684 Kafka, Franz. *The Trial* (10–12). 1937, Knopf $16.45 (0-394-44955-X); Schocken paper $6.95 (0-8052-0416-4). A nightmarish novel in which a young man named Joseph K. is accused of an unknown crime.

685 Kata, Elizabeth. *A Patch of Blue* (10–12). 1983, Amereon $11.95 (0-89190-119-1); Warner paper $3.95 (0-446-31485-4). A blind girl finds love with a man who also has a number of personal problems.

686 Kawabata, Yasunari. *Snow Country* (10–12). 1981, Putnam paper $6.95 (0-399-50525-3). A Japanese geisha falls in love with a rich Tokyo gentleman who is not able to return her love.

687 Kerouac, Jack. *On the Road* (10–12). 1976, Buccaneer $21.95 (0-89966-134-3); Penguin paper $6.95 (0-14-004259-8). This novel about a group of drifters expresses the ideas and attitudes of the Beat Generation of the 1960s.

688 Kesey, Ken. *One Flew over the Cuckoo's Nest* (10–12). 1962, Penguin $12.95 (0-670-52604-5); paper $4.95 (0-14-004312-8). This novel deals with the power struggle between a sane inmate and the head nurse in a mental institution.

689 Keyes, Daniel. *Flowers for Algernon* (10–12). 1966, Harcourt $17.95 (0-15-131510-8); Bantam paper $3.50 (0-553-25665-3). When the I.Q. of a mentally handicapped man is changed by an operation, he faces serious problems

690 Kingsolver, Barbara. *The Bean Trees* (10–12). 1988, Harper $15.95 (0-06-015863-8). A young runaway suddenly finds herself the guardian of an abused, abandoned child. (Rev: BL 3/1/88; SLJ 12/88; VOYA 12/88)

691 Klein, Norma. *Family Secrets* (10–12). 1985, Dial $13.95 (0-8037-0221-3). Two seniors in high school become lovers and then discover that the mother of one is going to marry the father of the other. (Rev: BL 10/1/85; BR 5–6/86; SLJ 12/85)

692 Klein, Norma. *Learning How to Fall* (10–12). 1989, Bantam $14.95 (0-553-05809-6). The sudden ending of a sexual attachment brings 17-year-old Dustin to a nervous breakdown. (Rev: BL 9/1/89; BR 9–10/89; SLJ 6/89; VOYA 6/89)

693 Klein, Norma. *Sunshine* (9–12). 1976, Avon paper $3.50 (0-380-00049-0). This is the moving account of a gallant woman who died of cancer at age 20.

694 Kullman, Harry. *The Battle Horse* (9–12). 1981, Bradbury $12.95 (0-02-751240-1). After World War II, Pete returns to his teaching job at Devon, a fashionable private school.

695 La Farge, Oliver. *Laughing Boy* (9–12). 1981, Buccaneer LB $18.95 (0-89966-367-2); NAL paper $3.50 (0-451-52244-3). A touching novel first published in 1929 about 2 young Navahos and the love they feel for each other.

696 Lee, Joanna, and T. S. Cook. *Mary Jane Harper Cried Last Night* (9–12). 1978, NAL paper $2.95 (0-451-13980-1). A young inexperienced mother takes out her frustrations by abusing her baby girl.

697 Lenz, Siegfried. *The German Lesson* (10–12). 1972, New Directions paper $10.95 (0-8112-0982-2). A thoughtful German novel about duty, friendship, and conscience.

698 Leonard, Alison. *Tina's Chance* (8–12). 1988, Viking $11.95 (0-670-82430-5). A teenager traces down the cause of her mother's death and finds that she has a 50 percent chance of suffering a similar fate. (Rev: BL 10/15/88; SLJ 10/88)

699 Levenkron, Steven. *The Best Little Girl in the World* (10–12). 1989, Warner paper $4.95 (0-446-35865-7). Francessa's desire to be perfect leads her into the world of an anorexic.

700 Levenkron, Steven. *Kessa* (10–12). 1986, Popular paper $3.95 (0-445-20175-4). The author continues his story of an anorexic girl begun in *The Best Little Girl in the World* (1984). (Rev: VOYA 8–10/86)

701 Levy, Marilyn. *Putting Heather Together Again* (8–12). 1990, Ballantine paper $3.50 (0-449-70312-6). An emotionally confused girl is raped by the boy she hoped would help her. (Rev: BL 3/1/90; VOYA 8/90)

702 Levy, Marilyn. *Summer Show* (10–12). 1986, Fawcett paper $2.50 (0-449-70188-3). Through the help of the boy next door, Leslie tries to kick her drug habit. (Rev: VOYA 8–9/87; VOYA 4/87)

703 Lewis, Sinclair. *Arrowsmith* (10–12). 1982, Buccaneer LB $22.95 (0-89966-402-4); NAL paper $4.95 (0-451-52225-7). A saga of a brilliant doctor and the conflict between medical ethics and ambition.

704 Lipsyte, Robert. *One Fat Summer* (7–12). 1977, Harper LB $12.89 (0-06-023896-8); Bantam paper $2.50 (0-553-25591-6). Bobby Marks is 14, fat, and unhappy in this first novel of 3 that traces Bobby's career through his first year of college. The others are *Summer Rules* (1981) and *The Summerboy* (1982).

705 London, Jack. *Martin Eden* (10–12). 1984, Penguin paper $4.95 (0-14-039036-7). A partly autobiographical novel about an unsuccessful writer, his problems, and eventual suicide. First published in 1909.

706 Luger, Harriet. *Lauren* (10–12). 1981, Dell paper $1.50 (0-440-94700-6). A young girl faces unforseen problems when she realizes she is pregnant.

707 McCullers, Carson. *The Ballad of the Sad Cafe: The Novels and Stories of Carson McCullers* (10–12). 1987, Bantam paper $2.95 (0-553-23980-5). In addition to the title novella and six short stories, this collection includes the complete text of the novels *The Member of the Wedding* and *Reflections in a Golden Eye*.

708 McCullers, Carson. *The Heart Is a Lonely Hunter* (10–12). 1940, Houghton $16.95 (0-395-07978-0); Bantam paper $3.95 (0-553-25481-2). A deaf-mute becomes the sounding board of a number of residents in a small southern town.

709 MacLean, John. *Mac* (8–12). 1987, Houghton $13.95 (0-395-43080-1); Avon paper $2.75 (0-

380-70700-4). A high school sophomore's life falls apart after he is sexually assaulted by a doctor during a physical exam. (Rev: BL 10/1/87; SLJ 11/87)

710 McRae, Russell. *Going to the Dogs* (10–12). 1987, Viking $15.95 (0-670-81735-X). A disturbing novel only for very mature readers about a boy coming to terms with his sister's suicide. (Rev: VOYA 4/88)

711 Mahy, Margaret. *Memory* (9–12). 1988, Macmillan $13.95 (0-689-50446-2). Jonny befriends an old lady with Alzheimer's disease and from the relationship learns to accept his own past. (Rev: BL 4/15/88; BR 1–2/89; SLJ 3/88; VOYA 6/88)

712 Malmgren, Dallin. *The Whole Nine Yards* (9–12). 1986, Delacorte $14.95 (0-385-29452-2); Dell paper $2.95 (0-440-99575-2). High-schooler Storm Russell covers up his insecurities by becoming a brash, arrogant womanizer. (Rev: BL 7/86; SLJ 8/86; VOYA 6/86)

713 Manes, Stephen. *I'll Live* (9–12). 1982, Avon paper $2.25 (0-380-81737-3). Dylan is devastated when he learns that his beloved father has only 6 months to live.

714 Mann, Thomas. *Death in Venice* (10–12). 1989, Random paper $7.95 (0-679-72206-8). In this 1930 short story, a successful author finds he is infatuated with a frail boy he observes in Venice. This volume contains other short stories by Thomas Mann.

715 Maugham, W. Somerset. *The Moon and Sixpence* (10–12). 1977, Penguin paper $5.95 (0-14-000468-8). Based loosely on the life of Gauguin, this is the story of Charles Strickland and his escape to Tahiti to paint.

716 Maugham, W. Somerset. *Of Human Bondage* (10–12). Illus. 1955, Doubleday $19.95 (0-385-04899-8); Penguin paper $5.95 (0-14-001861-1). A club-footed medical student forms a disastrous attachment to a waitress named Mildred in this novel first published in 1915.

717 Maugham, W. Somerset. *The Razor's Edge* (10–12). 1978, Penguin paper $4.95 (0-14-001860-3). A confused young American after World War I seeks his salvation and personal peace in India.

718 Meyer, Carolyn. *Killing the Kudu* (9–12). 1990, Macmillan $14.95 (0-689-50508-6). With the help of a cousin and a young Irish nurse, Alex, a paraplegic teenager, begins to accept his condition. (Rev: BL 11/15/90)

719 Miklowitz, Gloria D. *Secrets Not Meant to Be Kept* (8–12). 1989, Dell paper $2.75 (0-440-

29338-8). Adrienne traces her present sexual coldness back to her preschool experiences when she was sexually abused. (Rev: BL 1/15/87; BR 5–6/87; SLJ 2/87; VOYA 2/87)

720 Myers, Walter Dean. *Sweet Illusions* (10–12). 1987, Teachers & Writers Collaborative $11.95 (0-915924-14-5); paper $4.95 (0-915924-15-3). Stories about teenage pregnancy from both male and female points of view. (Rev: BL 6/15/87; VOYA 8–9/87)

721 Nabokov, Vladimir. *Laughter in the Dark* (10–12). 1989, Random paper $8.95 (0-679-72450-8). For mature readers, the story of a blind man and his beautiful mistress.

722 Nasaw, Jonathan. *West of the Moon* (10–12). 1987, Watts $16.95 (0-531-15064-X). For mature readers, a sad novel about the death of a young boy. (Rev: BL 9/1/87)

723 Naylor, Phyllis Reynolds. *The Dark of the Tunnel* (8–12). 1985, Macmillan $12.95 (0-689-31098-6). A 17-year-old boy tries to adjust to the death of his mother from cancer. (Rev: BL 3/15/85; SLJ 5/85; VOYA 8/85)

724 O'Hara, John. *Appointment in Samarra* (10–12). 1982, Random paper $5.95 (0-394-71192-0). When his wife threatens divorce, the life of Julian English, a successful businessman, begins to fall apart.

725 Percy, Walker. *Love in the Ruins* (10–12). 1971, Farrar $22.95 (0-374-19302-9); Ivy paper $4.95 (0-8041-0378-X). A psychiatrist invents a machine to help cure emotional woes.

726 Perske, Robert. *Show Me No Mercy* (9–12). 1984, Abingdon paper $7.95 (0-687-38435-4). Andy is paralyzed in an accident that killed his wife and daughter and now he must fight to save a mentally handicapped son from an institution.

727 Pfeffer, Susan Beth. *About David* (9–12). 1982, Dell paper $2.95 (0-440-90022-0). When David kills his adoptive parents and himself, many questions are left unanswered.

728 Plath, Sylvia. *The Bell Jar* (10–12). Illus. 1971, Harper $16.95 (0-06-013356-2); Bantam paper $4.50 (0-553-26008-1). A novel about the mental illness of a brilliant 19-year-old girl and of her course of self-destruction.

729 Posner, Richard. *Sweet Pain* (9–12). 1987, Evans $11.95 (0-87131-501-7). In an act of self-destruction, Casey gives up her life and future to her boyfriend Paul who abuses her. (Rev: BL 7/87; SLJ 8/87)

730 Price, Reynolds. *A Long and Happy Life* (10–12). 1987, Macmillan $14.95 (0-689-11947-

X). After Rose becomes pregnant she wonders how much Wesley really loves her.

731 Rabinowitz, Ann. *Bethie* (8–12). 1989, Macmillan $13.95 (0-02-775661-0). Beth's friend Grace cracks under the stress of personal problems and her parents' divorce and commits suicide. (Rev: BL 4/1/89; BR 11–12/89; SLJ 5/89; VOYA 6/89)

732 Rinaldi, Ann. *Term Paper* (9–12). 1980, Walker $9.95 (0-8027-6395-2). Nicki's brother, who is her English teacher, forces her to confront her feelings about her father's death by writing a term paper about it. A sequel is *Promises Are for Keeping* (1982).

733 Rowntree, Kathleen. *The Haunting of Willow Dasset* (10–12). 1989, Little $17.95 (0-316-75975-9). A multigenerational English novel that focuses on a girl's growing up and her changing attitudes toward her family. (Rev: BL 2/15/89)

734 Rubin, Theodore Isaac. *Lisa and David's Story: Their Healing Journey from Childhood and Pain into Love and Life* (10–12). 1988, Macmillan paper $3.95 (0-02-053570-8). In this sequel to *Lisa and David* (o.p.), 2 disturbed youngsters try to cope with being in love and being separated. (Rev: BL 4/15/86)

735 Rue, Nancy. *Row This Boat Ashore* (8–12). 1986, Crossway paper $6.95 (0-89107-393-0). A bored popular senior falls in love with an idealistic physically handicapped boy. (Rev: SLJ 2/87; VOYA 4/87)

736 Samuels, Gertrude. *Run, Shelley, Run!* (9–12). 1975, NAL paper $2.50 (0-451-13987-9). Shelley, a rebellious young girl, plans on escaping from the state training school where the courts have sent her.

737 Schutz, Benjamin M. *All the Old Bargains* (10–12). 1985, Bluejay $13.95 (0-312-94014-9); Bantam paper $2.95 (0-553-26335-8). Leo tries to help a troubled teenager who has been sexually abused by her father. (Rev: SLJ 9/86)

738 Scott, Virginia M. *Belonging* (9–12). 1986, Kendall Green paper $2.95 (0-930323-33-5). A 15-year-old girl must adjust to deafness caused by an attack of meningitis. (Rev: VOYA 4/88)

739 Shannon, George. *Unlived Affections* (8–12). 1989, Harper LB $12.89 (0-06-025305-3). Through a packet of letters discovered after his grandmother's death, college-bound Willie discovers his absent father is gay. (Rev: BL 9/15/89; SLJ 9/89; VOYA 12/89)

740 Singer, Isaac Bashevis. *The Slave* (10–12). 1984, Fawcett paper $2.95 (0-449-20694-7). In this novel translated from the Yiddish, Jacob gains strength from his suffering.

741 Smith, Betty. *Tomorrow Will Be Better* (9–12). 1971, Harper paper $2.50 (0-06-080049-6). A poor young girl tries to overcome the sorrows in her marriage.

742 Smith, Lee. *Black Mountain Breakdown* (10–12). 1982, Ballantine paper $4.50 (0-345-33849-9). A girl who seems to have everything is confronted with the possibility of a mental breakdown.

743 Stewart, Edward. *Ballerina* (10–12). 1989, Dell paper $4.95 (0-440-20307-4). A novel about backstage life in the world of ballet and its hardships and rewards.

744 Synder, Anne. *Goodbye, Paper Doll* (10–12). 1980, NAL paper $2.95 (0-451-15943-8). Seventeen-year-old Rosemary must overcome anorexia nervosa as well as a multitude of other personal problems.

745 Terris, Susan. *Nell's Quilt* (9–12). 1987, Farrar $12.95 (0-374-35504-5); Scholastic paper $2.50 (0-590-41914-5). In turn-of-the-century Amherst, a young girl cracks under the strain of having to marry a man she does not like. (Rev: BL 11/1/87; SLJ 11/87)

746 Terris, Susan. *Wings and Roots* (9–12). 1982, Farrar $11.95 (0-374-38451-7). Jenny, a hospital volunteer, finds she is attracted to a bitter young man who is a polio victim.

747 Thomas, Joyce Carol. *Marked by Fire* (8–12). 1982, Avon paper $2.75 (0-380-79327-X). After she is raped a Southern black girl seems to lose her beautiful singing voice. A sequel is *Bright Shadow* (1984).

748 Updike, John. *The Poorhouse Fair* (10–12). 1959, Knopf $19.95 (0-394-41050-5); Fawcett paper $3.95 (0-449-21213-0). An unusual novel about a group of eccentrics who live in a poorhouse in New Jersey.

749 Ure, Jean. *If It Weren't for Sebastian* (9–12). 1985, Delacorte $14.95 (0-385-29380-1); Dell paper $2.95 (0-440-93996-8). An 18-year-old London girl rebelling from her family becomes involved with an emotionally unstable young man. (Rev: BL 5/1/85; BR 11–12/85; SLJ 8/85)

750 Walker, Alice. *The Color Purple* (10–12). 1982, Harcourt $12.95 (0-15-119153-0); Pocket paper $3.95 (0-671-61702-8). For better readers, the candid memoirs of Celie, her abuse, and eventual triumph.

751 Wersba, Barbara. *Fat: A Love Story* (8–12). 1987, Harper LB $11.89 (0-06-026415-2); Dell paper $3.50 (0-440-20537-9). Rita Formica, fat and unhappy, falls for rich, attractive Robert. (Rev: BL 6/1/87; SLJ 8/87; VOYA 6/87)

752 West, Nathanael. *The Day of the Locust* (10–12). 1985, Amereon $13.95 (0-88411-871-1); NAL paper $3.95 (0-451-52348-2). A classic about the sordid life behind the glamor in Hollywood.

753 Wharton, William. *Birdy* (10–12). 1979, Knopf $18.95 Avon paper $4.50 (0-380-47282-1). In a mental hospital at the end of World War II, a veteran has delusions that he is turning into a bird.

754 Wilder, Thornton. *Theophilus North* (10–12). 1988, Carroll & Graf paper $4.95 (0-88184-382-2). A 29-year-old teacher solves many of other people's problems when he spends a summer in Newport, Rhode Island.

755 Wood, Barbara. *Domina* (10–12). 1984, NAL paper $3.95 (0-451-12856-7). Set in the nineteenth century, this is the story of the problems faced by a young woman whose ambition is to become a doctor.

756 Woolf, Virginia. *Mrs. Dalloway* (10–12). 1981, Harcourt paper $5.95 (0-15-662863-5). A day in the life and thoughts of a woman during which she meets, among others, a former lover.

Personal Problems and Growing into Maturity

757 Allen, R. E. *Ozzy on the Outside* (9–12). 1989, Delacorte $14.95 (0-440-50146-6). Teenager Ozzy, still grieving after his mother's death, decides to leave home and find his fortune as a writer. (Rev: BL 6/1/89; BR 9–10/89; SLJ 6/89; VOYA 8/89)

758 Anderson, Mary. *You Can't Get There from Here* (10–12). 1983, Ace paper $2.25 (0-441-94981-9). A high school senior tries to escape her personal problems by enrolling in a theater workshop.

759 Atwood, Margaret. *Cat's Eye* (10–12). 1989, Doubleday $18.95 (0-385-26007-5). For better readers, the story of an artist's childhood and her search for fulfillment, by one of Canada's most distinguished writers. (Rev: BL 12/15/88; SLJ 7/89)

760 Babcock, Richard. *Martha Calhoun* (10–12). 1988, Random $15.95 (0-394-56542-8). A frequently humorous novel for mature readers about an unusual mother and her precocious 16-year-old daughter. (Rev: BL 3/15/88; BR 9–10/88; VOYA 8/88)

761 Beattie, Ann. *Distortions* (10–12). 1983, Warner paper $3.95 (0-446-31338-6). A collection of short stories about people of various ages and the questions they face about life and love.

762 Behrens, Michael A. *At the Edge* (10–12). 1988, Avon paper $2.50 (0-380-75610-2). On an emotional rebound from his parents' divorce, Dan has an affair with a neurotic girl. (Rev: BL 2/1/89)

763 Bell, William. *Crabbe's Journey* (9–12). 1987, Little $12.95 (0-316-08837-4). An alcoholic teenager tries to survive alone in the wilderness but finds he must rely on a girl for help. (Rev: BL 7/87; BR 11–12/87; SLJ 5/87)

764 Bellow, Saul. *The Dean's December* (10–12). 1982, Harper $14.45 (0-06-014849-7); Pocket paper $4.95 (0-671-60254-3). An introspective novel for better readers about a university administrator and his disturbing trip to Eastern Europe.

765 Benard, Robert, ed. *All Problems Are Simple and Other Stories: Nineteen Views of the College Years* (10–12). 1988, Dell paper $3.95 (0-440-20164-0). A collection of stories by such writers as Stephen King and F. Scott Fitzgerald that explore the college experience and problems older teenagers face. (Rev: BL 2/1/89; SLJ 3/89; VOYA 6/89)

766 Benard, Robert, ed. *Do You Like It Here?* (9–12). 1989, Dell paper $3.50 (0-440-20435-6). A collection of 21 adult stories about the high school years of such authors as Wright Morris, Gore Vidal, and John O'Hara. (Rev: BL 9/15/89; BR 1–2/90; SLJ 12/89; VOYA 2/90)

767 Benedict, Elizabeth. *The Beginner's Book of Dreams* (10–12). 1988, Knopf $18.95 (0-394-55157-5). A sensitive novel for mature readers about 10 years in the life of a girl who copes with the scars of her parents' divorce. (Rev: BL 4/1/88)

768 Betancourt, Jeanne. *Sweet Sixteen and Never* (9–12). 1987, Bantam paper $2.95 (0-553-25534-7). Sixteen-year-old Julie, who is facing many personal problems, has a friend who is pregnant. (Rev: SLJ 6–7/87; VOYA 8–9/87)

769 Block, Francesca Lia. *Weetzie Bat* (9–12). 1989, Harper LB $12.89 (0-06-020536-9). Four teenagers into punk culture—2 gay and a straight couple—set up housekeeping but the realities of life spoil their demi-Eden. A controversial book that received very mixed reviews. (Rev: BL 3/15/89; BR 3–4/90; SLJ 4/89; VOYA 10/89)

770 Blume, Judy. *Forever . . .* (10–12). 1975, Bradbury $12.95 (0-02-711030-3). A girl's awakening sexuality is explored in this novel that contains frank language and explicit scenes.

771 Bograd, Larry. *Travelers* (10–12). 1986, Harper LB $11.89 (0-397-32129-5). AJ, a 17-year-old boy, and his wealthy friend learn about sex and drugs on a trip to the West Coast where AJ hopes to learn about his father who died in Vietnam. (Rev: BL 3/1/86; BR 11–12/86; SLJ 8/86; VOYA 6/86)

772 Bottner, Barbara. *Let Me Tell You Everything: Memoirs of a Lovesick Intellectual* (8–12). 1989, Harper LB $12.95 (0-06-020597-0). A Brooklyn high school senior is confused about her identity—radical feminist or conventional woman. (Rev: BL 7/89; BR 9–10/89; SLJ 4/89; VOYA 6/89)

773 Bowen, Elizabeth. *The Death of the Heart* (10–12). 1986, Penguin paper $6.95 (0-14-008543-2). This adult novel for better readers tells about a homeless girl being raised in an English household in which she is not welcome.

774 Bradford, Barbara Taylor. *A Woman of Substance* (10–12). 1984, Doubleday $19.95 (0-385-12050-8); Bantam paper $5.95 (0-553-27790-1). This best-selling novel tells about the rise of a woman of substance, Emma Harte.

775 Bradford, Richard. *Red Sky at Morning* (9–12). 1968, Harper paper $8.95 (0-06-091361-4). Josh adjusts to life in a small New Mexico town when he and his mother move there during World War II.

776 Bradley, Virginia. *Who Could Forget the Mayor of Lodi?* (7–12). 1985, Putnam $11.95 (0-396-08504-0). A teacher returns to her small town for a summer and remembers her past. (Rev: BR 9–10/85)

777 Brancato, Robin F. *Facing Up* (9–12). 1984, Knopf LB $9.99 (0-394-85488-8). The friendship between Jep and Dave is strained by the attentions of Jep's girlfriend.

778 Brooks, Jerome. *Naked in Winter* (9–12). 1990, Watts LB $14.99 (0-531-08466-3). A coming-of-age novel about a sensitive, self-doubting teenager growing up in Chicago during the 1940s. (Rev: BL 4/1/90; SLJ 5/90; VOYA 6/90)

779 Buchan, Stuart. *Guys Like Us* (9–12). 1986, Delacorte $14.95 (0-385-29448-4); Dell paper $2.95 (0-440-20244-2). Two average teenager friends fall for a wealthy girl and a hidden class struggle emerges. (Rev: BL 8/86; BR 9–10/86; SLJ 9/86)

780 Bunn, Scott. *Just Hold On* (7–12). 1982, Delacorte $9.95 (0-385-28490-4). Two lonely

school students find love, friendship, and strength in each other's company.

781 Busch, Frederick. *Sometimes I Live in the Country* (10–12). 1986, Godine $15.95 (0-87923-622-1). In this frank story of a boy's growing up, an eighth-grader moves with his cop father to a small town after his parents have suffered through an ugly divorce. (Rev: BL 5/1/86)

782 Cameron, Peter. *One Way or Another* (10–12). 1986, Harper $15.95 (0-06-015569-8). For better readers, a group of subtle and touching stories about young people growing up today. (Rev: BL 5/15/86)

783 Capote, Truman. *Breakfast at Tiffany's: A Short Novel and Three Stories* (10–12). 1958, Random $13.95 (0-394-41770-4); NAL paper $3.50 (0-451-15644-7). In addition to the novella about the exploits of Holly Golightly, this volume contains *House of Flowers, A Diamond Guitar,* and *A Christmas Memory.*

784 Capote, Truman. *The Thanksgiving Visitor* (10–12). 1968, Random $19.45 (0-394-44824-3). In this tender reminiscence, a young boy learns the meaning of compassion from his spinster cousin. Also use: *A Christmas Memory* (1966).

785 Carter, Alden R. *Growing Season* (9–12). 1984, Putnam $13.95 (0-448-47749-1); Berkley paper $2.95 (0-425-08427-2). A high school senior is upset when his family decides to move to a farm.

786 Caseley, Judith. *Kisses* (9–12). 1990, Knopf LB $13.99 (0-679-90166-3). A coming-of-age novel about a talented eleventh-grade violinist and her social problems, particularly with boys. (Rev: BL 2/15/90; SLJ 2/90; VOYA 8/90)

787 Chambers, Aidan. *NIK: Now I Know* (10–12). 1988, Harper LB $13.89 (0-06-021209-8). Nik questions his religious beliefs but by a tortuous route recovers his faith. (Rev: BL 7/88; BR 5–6/89; SLJ 8/88; VOYA 10/88)

788 Clewlow, Carol. *Keeping the Faith* (10–12). 1990, Poseidon $16.95 (0-671-67117-0). A novel that deals with the effects that a strict religious upbringing can have on youngsters and how it can bring alienation in the family. (Rev: BL 2/1/90)

789 Cohen, Barbara. *Coasting* (9–12). 1985, Lothrop $11.95 (0-688-05849-3). Two friends, a Barnard college student and a young drifter from California, work out their problems in the somewhat hostile environment of New York City. (Rev: BL 11/1/85; BR 1–2/86; SLJ 11/85; VOYA 4/86)

790 Conroy, Pat. *The Lords of Discipline* (10–12). 1986, Bantam paper $5.95 (0-553-27136-9). A South Carolina military school is the setting of this novel about a young man trying to cope with a system of harsh rules and regulations.

791 Cooney, Caroline B. *Summer Nights* (7–12). 1988, Scholastic paper $2.50 (0-590-41548-4). At a farewell party, 5 high school girls look back on their school years and their friendship. (Rev: SLJ 1/89)

792 Cormier, Robert. *Beyond the Chocolate War* (9–12). 1985, Knopf LB $11.99 (0-394-97343-7); Dell paper $3.25 (0-440-90580-X). The misuse of power at Trinity High by Brother Leon and the secret society of Vigils is again explored in this sequel to *The Chocolate War* (1974). (Rev: BL 3/15/85; BR 9–10/85; SLJ 4/85)

793 Cormier, Robert. *Eight Plus One* (9–12). 1980, Pantheon $7.99 (0-394-94595-6); Bantam paper $2.75 (0-553-26815-5). These 9 stories involve such problems of growing up as coping with one's first love experience and a boy trying to grow a mustache.

794 Cormier, Robert. *I Am the Cheese* (7–12). 1977, Pantheon $12.95 (0-394-83462-3). A multi-level novel about a boy's life after his parents are forced to go underground.

795 Coyne, John. *Brothers and Sisters* (10–12). 1986, Dutton $16.95 (0-525-24385-2). A family saga about poor Irish immigrants that covers the years 1940 to 1982. (Rev: SLJ 10/86)

796 Davidson, Linda. *On the Edge* (7–12). 1988, Ivy paper $2.95 (0-8041-0243-0). Fury hits rock bottom when he loses his girl, job, and friends all in a 24-hour period. (Rev: SLJ 4/89)

797 Davies, Robertson. *Fifth Business* (10–12). 1977, Penguin paper $4.95 (0-14-004387-X). This challenging novel, the first in the Deptford trilogy, is set in Ontario and tells about the fateful results of a snowball fight. Followed by *The Manticore* (1982) and *World of Wonders* (1983).

798 Dragonwagon, Crescent, and Paul Zindel. *To Take a Dare* (9–12). 1982, Harper LB $12.89 (0-06-026859-0); Bantam paper $2.95 (0-553-26601-2). After 3 years of wandering, Chrysta must find herself.

799 Dreiser, Theodore. *An American Tragedy* (10–12). 1978, Bentley LB $26.50 (0-8376-0424-9); NAL paper $4.95 (0-451-52204-4). The tragic story of a young man whose ambition leads to murder.

800 Dreiser, Theodore. *Sister Carrie* (10–12). 1971, Bentley LB $18.00 (0-8376-0401-X); Bantam paper $2.95 (0-553-21264-8). The story of the rise of Carrie and the decline of her protector, Hurstwood. First published in 1900.

801 Eisenberg, Deborah. *Transactions in a Foreign Currency* (10–12). 1986, Knopf $15.95 (0-394-54598-2). Seven short stories each about a different woman's quest for self-understanding. (Rev: SLJ 2/87)

802 Eisenstadt, Jill. *From Rockaway* (10–12). 1987, Knopf $15.95 (0-394-55970-3); Random paper $6.95 (0-394-75761-0). A group of teens become disenchanted with the aimlessness of their existence and want more out of life. (Rev: SLJ 2/88)

803 Ellis, Bret Easton. *Less Than Zero* (10–12). 1987, Penguin paper $3.95 (0-14-010927-7). For mature readers, a novel about jaded college students one of whom has been forced into male prostitution to feed his drug habit. (Rev: VOYA 12/85)

804 Farish, Terry. *Shelter for a Seabird* (8–12). 1990, Greenwillow $12.95 (0-688-09627-1). An unmarried teenage girl who has given up her baby for adoption meets and forms a relationship with an AWOL soldier. (Rev: SLJ 11/90)

805 Farrelly, Peter. *Outside Providence* (10–12). 1988, Atlantic Monthly paper $7.95 (0-87113-222-2). For mature readers, the story of Timothy Dunphy's coming-of-age at a fancy prep school in Connecticut. (Rev: BL 4/15/88; VOYA 2/89)

806 Fast, Julius. *What Should We Do about Davey?* (10–12). 1988, St. Martin's $16.95 (0-312-00698-5). A raunchy, explicit coming-of-age story of a 16-year-old Jewish boy in New York during the Depression. (Rev: BL 2/15/88)

807 Ferris, Jean. *Across the Grain* (8–12). 1990, Farrar $13.95 (0-374-30030-5). Paige and his elder sister head to a community in the desert where they take jobs in a restaurant. (Rev: BL 11/15/90)

808 Forshay-Lunsford, Cin. *Walk through Cold Fire* (8–12). 1986, Dell paper $2.95 (0-440-99322-9). Desiree, an outsider, falls in with a gang of hoods. (Rev: BR 11–12/85; VOYA 8/85)

809 Forster, E. M. *A Room with a View* (10–12). 1987, Buccaneer $23.95 (0-89966-607-8); Bantam paper $3.95 (0-551-21323-7). A romantic novel set mainly in Florence in which a young woman overcomes her family's prejudices and marries a man beneath her station. First published in 1908.

810 Frank, Elizabeth Bales. *Cooder Cutlas* (9–12). 1987, Harper LB $13.89 (0-06-021860-6). With rock music as a backdrop, this is a novel of the enduring love shared by Cooder and his

41

girlfriend Macky. (Rev: BL 6/15/87; BR 11–12/87; SLJ 8/87; VOYA 6/87)

811 Franklin, Miles. *My Brilliant Career* (10–12). 1981, Pocket paper $3.95 (0-671-45915-5). Written in 1901, this is the story of an Australian teenager growing up in the bush country. Followed by *The End of My Career* (1983).

812 Galgut, Damon. *Sinless Season* (10–12). 1985, Penguin paper $5.95 (0-14-007077-X). A powerful, harrowing novel about teenage boys in a reform school. (Rev: SLJ 11/85)

813 Gallo, Donald R., ed. *Sixteen: Short Stories by Outstanding Writers for Young Adults* (9–12). 1984, Delacorte $16.95 (0-385-29346-1); Dell paper $3.25 (0-440-97757-6). This anthology of original short stories covers such subjects as friendship, love, and families.

814 Geary, Patricia. *Strange Toys* (10–12). 1987, Bantam paper $4.50 (0-553-26872-4). The central character is seen at 3 different ages (9, 16, and 30) in this novel about the maturation of a woman. (Rev: VOYA 6/88)

815 Gingher, Marianne. *Bobby Rex's Greatest Hit* (10–12). 1986, Macmillan $17.95 (0-689-11769-8); Ballantine paper $3.95 (0-345-34823-0). In a small North Carolina town, a young girl faces the consequences of a famous rock star writing a song about her. (Rev: SLJ 4/87)

816 Gingher, Marianne. *Teen Angel: And Other Stories of Young Love* (10–12). 1988, Macmillan $17.95 (0-689-11967-4). A collection of stories about young people that explore themes of loving and being loved. (Rev: BL 6/1/88; SLJ 12/88)

817 Glasgow, Ellen. *Barren Ground* (10–12). 1985, Amereon $22.95 (0-88411-645-X); Harcourt paper $10.95 (0-15-610685-X). This harshly realistic novel tells about the misfortunes of the daughter of a poor white farmer.

818 Godden, Rumer. *An Episode of Sparrows* (10–12). 1989, Penguin paper $4.95 (0-14-034024-6). A tender novel about children growing up in London.

819 Godden, Rumer. *Thursday's Child* (10–122). 1987, Dell paper $3.25 (0-440-98790-3). The story of a young English boy who, in spite of much opposition, aspires to a career in ballet.

820 Godwin, Gail. *The Finishing School* (10–12). 1985, Viking $16.95 (0-670-31494-3); Avon paper $4.95 (0-380-69869-2). A complex novel for better readers about the friendship through the years between 2 women separated in age by many years. (Rev: SLJ 10/85; VOYA 2/86;)

821 Gold, Ron, ed. *Stepping Stones* (9–12). 1981, Dell paper $3.25 (0-440-98269-3). This an-thology of 17 stories about adolescents and their problems is a companion volume to another book of short stories: *Point of Departure* (1981).

822 Gordon, Mary. *Final Payments* (10–12). 1986, Ballantine paper $4.95 (0-345-32973-2). For better readers, this is the story of a woman who finds her life is out of control after her father dies.

823 Greene, Graham. *The Captain and the Enemy* (10–12). 1988, Viking $17.95 (0-670-82405-4). A young man is given a new life through the kindness of a mysterious man known as the "Captain." For better readers. (Rev: BL 7/88)

824 Guernsey, JoAnn B. *Five Summers* (9–12). 1983, Houghton $10.95 (0-89919-147-9). During a 5-year period on a Minnesota farm, Mandy matures through the final years of adolescence.

825 Hailey, Elizabeth Forsythe. *A Woman of Independent Means* (10–12). 1983, Viking $17.95 (0-670-77795-1); Dell paper $4.95 (0-440-20550-6). Through a series of letters beginning in 1899, the reader follows the life of an engaging woman, Bess Garner.

826 Hall, Barbara. *Skeeball and the Secret of the Universe* (8–12). 1987, Orchard LB $12.99 (0-531-08322-5). During the summer before his senior year, Matty learns a lot about life, love, and the meaning of self-respect. (Rev: BR 5–6/88; SLJ 12/87)

827 Hall, Lynn. *The Solitary* (9–12). 1986, Macmillan $11.95 (0-684-18724-8); paper $3.95 (0-02-043315-8). A teenage victim of child abuse, now 17 and alone, returns to her parents' land to try to become self-sufficient. (Rev: BL 11/15/86; SLJ 1/87; VOYA 2/87)

828 Hamilton, Morse. *Effie's House* (9–12). 1990, Greenwillow $12.95 (0-668-09307-8). E.B. is 15 and on the road with her father, a Vietnam vet who everyone thinks was killed in action. (Rev: VOYA 6/90)

829 Hamilton, Virginia. *A White Romance* (8–12). 1987, Putnam $14.95 (0-399-21213-2); Harcourt paper $3.95 (0-15-295888-6). A formerly all-black high school becomes integrated and social values and relationships change. (Rev: SLJ 1/88; VOYA 2/88)

830 Harley, Rex. *Last Laugh* (9–12). 1988, Gollancz $17.95 (0-575-03920-5). Five short stories by this British author all dealing with teenage problems. (Rev: SLJ 2/89)

831 Harrell, Janice. *So Long, Senior Year* (7–12). 1988, Crosswinds paper $2.25 (0-373-88038-3). Four high school seniors face the problem of making choices and preparing for life after graduation. (Rev: SLJ 4/89)

832 Hart, Bruce, and Carole Hart. *Breaking Up Is Hard to Do* (10–12). 1987, Avon paper $2.95 (0-380-89970-1). Two stories about 2 young couples who fall in love, have affairs, and then break up. (Rev: BL 10/15/87; SLJ 6–7/87; VOYA 8–9/87)

833 Haseley, Dennis. *The Counterfeiter* (9–12). 1987, Macmillan $13.95 (0-02-743120-7). James is so in love with Heather that he counterfeits a $500 bill to take her on a superdate. (Rev: BL 10/15/87; SLJ 10/87; VOYA 10/87)

834 Head, Ann. *Mr. and Mrs. Bo Jo Jones* (7–12). 1973, NAL paper $2.75 (0-451-15734-6). The perennial favorite of 2 teenagers madly in love but unprepared for the responsibilities of parenthood.

835 Hemingway, Ernest. *In Our Time* (10–12). 1930, Macmillan $20.00 (0-684-16480-9); paper $7.95 (0-684-71802-2). Many of these stories explore the world of growing up in the Middle West early in this century.

836 Hesse, Hermann. *Peter Camenzind* (7–12). 1969, Farrar paper $7.95 (0-374-50784-8). Through experience—some of it bitter—a young writer grows to maturity.

837 Hesse, Hermann. *Steppenwolf* (10–12). 1983, Buccaneer LB $19.95 (0-89966-448-2); Bantam paper $4.50 (0-553-27990-4). In this novel with fantastic overtones, a young man searches for self-discovery.

838 Heyman, Anita. *Final Grades* (10–12). 1983, Putman paper $3.95 (0-396-08745-0). Conflicts with her senior English teacher force Rachel to examine her expectations.

839 Hill, Rebecca. *Blue Rise* (10–12). 1984, Penguin paper $6.95 (0-14-007132-6). Jeannine comes to terms with herself when she returns to her family home in Blue Rise, Mississippi.

840 Hobbs, Will. *Changes in Latitudes* (9–12). 1988, Macmillan $13.95 (0-689-31385-3). Teenager Travis supports his young brother's crusade to help endangered sea turtles. (Rev: BL 5/15/88; BR 9–10/88; SLJ 3/88; VOYA 6/88)

841 Hoffman, Alice. *Property Of* (10–12). 1988, Fawcett paper $3.50 (0-449-44546-1). For mature readers, this is the frank story of a middle-class girl who falls in love with the leader of a street gang.

842 Hopper, Nancy J. *Lies* (9–12). 1984, Lodestar $10.95 (0-525-67148-X). In order to attract a handsome new boy in town, Allison tells many lies and finds herself in deep trouble.

843 Horgan, Paul. *Whitewater* (10–12). 1989, Univ. of Texas Pr. paper $10.95 (0-292-79038-4). A high school senior inadvertently causes the death of 2 of his friends in this powerful novel that explores a number of values.

844 Huggan, Isabel. *The Elizabeth Stories* (9–12). 1987, Viking $15.95 (0-670-81303-6); Penguin paper $6.95 (0-14-010199-3). A beautifully written collection of interrelated short stories about a girl growing up in a small Canadian town. (Rev: BL 4/1/87; BR 11–12/87; SLJ 11/87)

845 Humphreys, Josephine. *Rich in Love* (10–12). 1987, Viking $16.95 (0-670-81810-0); Penguin paper $7.95 (0-14-010283-3). A 17-year-old girl comes of age in a family of eccentrics. (Rev: BL 8/87; BR 3–4/88; SLJ 1/88; VOYA 4/88)

846 Hyde, Elisabeth. *Her Native Colors* (10–12). 1989, Dell paper $7.95 (0-440-55014-9). The long friendship between 2 girls is tested when one prepares for marriage. (Rev: SLJ 9/86)

847 Jaspersohn, William. *Grounded* (10–12). 1988, Bantam $13.95 (0-553-05450-3). A runaway teenage boy and a rich girl who befriends him discover love and excitement on a private island. (Rev: BL 1/15/89; VOYA 2/89)

848 Jones, Adrienne. *Street Family* (9–12). 1987, Harper LB $13.89 (0-06-023050-9). A runaway girl faces life on the streets of Los Angeles. (Rev: BL 7/87; SLJ 9/87; VOYA 6/87)

849 Jones, Douglas C. *Hickory Cured* (10–12). Illus. 1987, Henry Holt $16.95 (0-8050-0383-5). A series of short stories about a boy growing up in backwater Arkansas before World War II. (Rev: SLJ 10/87; VOYA 12/87)

850 Joyce, James. *A Portrait of the Artist as a Young Man* (10–12). 1984, Amereon $17.95 (0-89190-725-4); Penguin paper $3.95 (0-14-004221-0). An autobiographical novel about the youth and early manhood of Stephen Dedalus.

851 Katz, Steve. *Florry of Washington Heights* (10–12). 1987, Sun & Moon $15.95 (0-940-65083-5); paper $10.95 (0-930-65084-5). Gang warfare in upper Manhattan about the time of the Korean War is the subject of this novel told many years later by Swanny, one of the participants. (Rev: SLJ 11/87)

852 Kauffman, M. K. *The Right Moves* (10–12). 1987, Crosswinds paper $2.25 (0-373-98014-0). Two prep school seniors decide to expose a teacher who has been holding wild drinking parties. (Rev: VOYA 4/88)

853 Kellogg, Marjorie. *Tell Me That You Love Me, Junie Moon* (10–12). 2nd ed. 1984, Farrar paper $5.95 (0-374-51825-4). After they have been released from the hospital, 3 misfits decide to live together.

854 Kerr, M. E. *Gentlehands* (7–12). 1978, Harper LB $12.89 (0-06-023177-7); Bantam paper $2.75 (0-553-26677-2). Buddy Boyle wonders if the grandfather he has recently grown to love is really a Nazi war criminal in this novel set on the eastern tip of Long Island.

855 Kerr, M. E. *Night Kites* (9–12). 1986, Harper LB $12.89 (0-06-023254-4); paper $2.50 (0-451-13208-2). Erick's life seems to be falling apart when he discovers that his older brother has AIDS and he unwillingly has an affair with his best friend's girlfriend. (Rev: BL 4/1/86; BR 1–2/87; SLJ 5/86; VOYA 6/86)

856 Kincaid, Jamaica. *Annie John* (9–12). 1985, Farrar $18.95 (0-374-10521-9); NAL paper $6.95 (0-452-26016-7). A beautifully detailed novel about a girl's childhood and adolescence on the Caribbean island of Antigua. (Rev: BL 4/1/85; SLJ 9/85)

857 Klein, Norma. *Beginners' Love* (10–12). 1983, Dial $13.95 (0-440-00626-0). Joel's relationship with Leda leads to pregnancy, abortion, and eventual separation in this novel that explores first love.

858 Klein, Norma. *Give and Take* (10–12). 1985, Viking $15.95 (0-670-80651-X). A complex novel involving many characters, their love lives, and their heartbreaks. (Rev: SLJ 9/85)

859 Klein, Norma. *My Life As a Body* (11–12). 1987, Knopf LB $13.99 (0-394-99051-X). For mature readers, the story of a love affair between a 17-year-old girl and her physically disabled classmate. (Rev: BL 10/1/87; SLJ 9/87; VOYA 4/88)

860 Klein, Norma. *No More Saturday Nights* (9–12). 1988, Knopf LB $13.99 (0-394-91944-0). Tim, an unwed father, takes his baby with him to Columbia, where he is a pre-med student. (Rev: BL 10/15/88; SLJ 11/88; VOYA 4/89)

861 Klein, Norma. *That's My Baby* (10–12). 1988, Viking $16.95 (0-670-81730-9). For mature readers, this is the story of a young playwright's affair with a married woman. (Rev: BL 5/15/88; BR 1–2/89; VOYA 4/89)

862 Knowles, John. *Peace Breaks Out* (10–12). 1982, Bantam paper $3.95 (0-553-25516-9). During the 1945–46 school year a former student who is suffering from wartime trauma returns to his private prep school as a teacher.

863 Knowles, John. *A Separate Peace* (10–12). 1987, Macmillan $25.00 (0-02-564850-0); Bantam paper $3.50 (0-553-28041-4). Life during a World

War II year in a private boys' school and a student rivalry that ends in tragedy.

864 Koertge, Ron. *The Arizona Kid* (10–12). 1988, Little $14.95 (0-316-50101-8). Teenage Billy discovers that his uncle Wes is gay. (Rev: BL 5/1/88; BR 9–10/88; SLJ 6–7/88; VOYA 10/88)

865 Koertge, Ron. *The Boy in the Moon* (9–12). 1990, Little $14.95 (0-316-50102-6). A first-person account about a high school senior's coming-of-age and exploration of his sexuality. (Rev: BL 3/1/90; SLJ 5/90; VOYA 8/90)

866 Kropp, Lloyd. *Greencastle* (10–12). 1987, Freundlich Books $17.95 (0-88191-037-6). For mature readers, a coming-of-age story about a precocious teenager and his 2 friends who are also outsiders. (Rev: BL 2/15/87)

867 Kurland, Morton L. *Our Sacred Honor* (7–12). 1987, Rosen $12.95 (0-8239-0692-2). A story from 2 points of view about a pregnant teenage girl, her boyfriend, and their decision for abortion. (Rev: SLJ 6–7/87)

868 Lehrman, Robert. *Juggling* (10–12). 1988, Berkley paper $2.50 (0-425-11128-8). An explicit novel about a teenager—his love for soccer and his first sexual encounters.

869 Levy, Marilyn. *Keeping Score* (9–12). 1987, Fawcett paper $2.50 (0-449-70266-9). A novel about a group of honor students who decide to wage their own war on drugs. (Rev: VOYA 4/88)

870 Likhanov, Albert. *Shadows across the Sun* (9–12). Trans. by Richard Lourie. 1983, Harper LB $10.89 (0-06-023869-0). In this novel set in contemporary Moscow 2 young people who live in neighboring apartments fall in love.

871 McCullers, Carson. *The Member of the Wedding* (10–12). 1963, New Directions paper $5.95 (0-8112-0093-0). A lonely young girl decides that she will accompany her brother and his wife on their honeymoon.

872 McDermott, Alice. *That Night* (10–12). 1987, Farrar $14.95 (0-374-27361-8); Harper paper $6.95 (0-06-097141-X). A pregnant young girl is separated from her boyfriend, who in turn takes revenge on the girl's family. (Rev: BL 3/15/87; SLJ 10/87)

873 McMurtry, Larry. *The Last Picture Show* (10–12). 1989, Simon & Schuster $18.95 (0-671-67604-0); Penguin paper $7.95 (0-14-005183-X). For mature readers, a coming-of-age novel set in a small Texas town during the 1950s.

874 Major, Kevin. *Thirty-six Exposures* (10–12). 1984, Delacorte $14.95 (0-385-29347-X); Dell paper $3.25 (0-440-20163-2). In brief chapters, like snapshots, a senior in high school explores moral issues and his growing sexuality.

875 Mason, Bobbie Ann. *In Country* (9–12). 1985, Harper $15.95 (0-06-015469-1); paper $7.95 (0-06-091350-8). This understated novel deals with a teenage girl and her gradual acceptance of the death of her father in the Vietnam War. (Rev: BL 8/85; SLJ 2/86)

876 Mason, Bobbie Ann. *Love Life: Stories* (10–12). 1989, Harper $17.95 (0-06-016042-X). In this collection of stories set in Kentucky, a variety of people are faced with life's pleasures and pains. (Rev: SLJ 7/89)

877 Matthews, Greg. *Little Red Rooster* (10–12). 1987, NAL $17.95 (0-453-00536-5); paper $7.95 (0-452-26078-7). In an eventful summer, adolescent Burris makes and loses a friend, falls in love, loses his virginity, and is betrayed by his love. (Rev: SLJ 12/87)

878 Maxwell, William. *The Folded Leaf* (10–12). 1981, Godine $10.95 (0-87923-351-6). The arrival of Sally Forbes disrupts the close friendship of 2 boys.

879 Mazer, Harry. *City Light* (9–12). 1988, Scholastic $12.95 (0-590-40511-X). George, a high school senior, gradually gains maturity when he learns to cope with the loss of his girlfriend and the breaking of some ties with his family. (Rev: BL 4/1/88; BR 9–10/88; SLJ 5/88; VOYA 6/88)

880 Mazer, Harry. *The Girl of His Dreams* (10–12). 1987, Harper LB $12.89 (0-690-04642-1); Avon paper $2.95 (0-380-70599-0). Willis Pierce is now 18 and into running while also being intent on his new girlfriend Sophie. Pierce was first introduced in Mazer's *The War on Villa Street* (1978). (Rev: BL 9/15/87; BR 3–4/88; SLJ 1/88; VOYA 12/87)

881 Mazer, Harry. *Hey Kid! Does She Love Me?* (9–12). 1985, Harper LB $12.89 (0-690-04276-0). Jeff is hot on the sexual trail of Mary Silver, his former girlfriend who now has a baby. (Rev: BL 5/1/85; BR 1–2/86; SLJ 5/85; VOYA 8/85)

882 Mazer, Harry. *I Love You, Stupid!* (10–12). 1981, Harper LB $12.89 (0-690-04120-9); Avon paper $2.75 (0-380-61432-4). In this sequel to *The Dollar Man* (Dell, 1988), 17-year-old Marcus and friend Wendy experiment with sex and find love.

883 Mazer, Norma Fox. *Summer Girls, Love Boys and Other Short Stories* (10–12). 1982, Delacorte $11.95 (0-385-28930-8); Dell paper $3.25 (0-440-98375-4). These 9 stories depict girls from ages 12 to 20 and the problems they face growing up.

884 Mazer, Norma Fox. *Up in Seth's Room* (8–12). 1979, Delacorte $7.95 (0-385-29058-6); Dell paper $2.95 (0-440-99190-0). Finn, age 15, tries to resist the sexual demands of 19-year-old Seth.

885 Mazer, Norma Fox, and Harry Mazer. *Heartbeat* (8–12). 1989, Bantam $13.95 (0-553-05808-8). The triangle of boy, best friend, and a girl complicated by a best friend's terminal illness. (Rev: BL 6/1/89; BR 11–12/89; SLJ 6/89; VOYA 12/89)

886 Michener, James A. *The Drifters* (10–12). 1971, Random $29.95 (0-394-46200-9). Six drifters travel the earth seeking pleasure and fulfillment.

887 Miklowitz, Gloria D. *Close to the Edge* (9–12). 1984, Dell paper $2.95 (0-440-91381-0). High-schooler Jenny learns she has inner strength when she must cope with her indifferent family and a suicidal friend.

888 Miklowitz, Gloria D. *The Day the Senior Class Got Married* (9–12). 1983, Dell paper $2.75 (0-440-92096-5). A trial marriage assignment in economics class makes 2 seniors rethink their real-life marriage plans.

889 Miller-Lachmann, Lyn. *Hiding Places* (8–12). 1987, Square One paper $4.95 (0-938961-00-4). Mark runs away from his suburban home and ends up in a shelter in New York City. (Rev: SLJ 5/87)

890 Munro, Alice. *Lives of Girls and Women* (10–12). 1990, NAL paper $7.95 (0-452-25975-4). In this adult novel by the famous Canadian writer Munro, we watch a 10-year-old girl become a young woman and trace her dreams and search for love.

891 Myers, Walter Dean. *Crystal* (9–12). 1987, Viking $12.95 (0-670-80426-6); Dell paper $3.25 (0-440-20538-7). A beautiful young black model finds success hard to handle. (Rev: BL 6/1/87; BR 9–10/87; SLJ 6–7/87; VOYA 4/88)

892 Naylor, Phyllis Reynolds. *The Year of the Gopher* (9–12). 1987, Macmillan $13.95 (0-689-31333-0); Bantam paper $2.95 (0-553-27131-8). A high school grad decides not to attend college and instead spends a year growing up. (Rev: BL 3/1/87; BR 9–10/87; SLJ 5/87; VOYA 6/87)

893 Oates, Joyce Carol. *Where Are You Going, Where Have You Been? Stories of Young America* (10–12). 1979, Fawcett paper $1.75 (0-449-30795-6). These 17 stories explore the pain of growing up in today's America.

894 Olshan, Joseph. *A Warmer Season* (10–12). 1987, McGraw $15.95 (0-07-083641-8). In this novel for mature readers, a Jewish senior in high school forms an attachment that becomes sexual with an Italian girl and becomes friendly with an older woman who is dying. (Rev: BL 5/15/87)

895 Oneal, Zibby. *In Summer Light* (9–12). 1985, Viking $12.95 (0-670-80784-2); Bantam paper $2.95 (0-553-25940-7). At odds with her successful artist father, Kate rejects him and her own artistic talents. (Rev: BL 10/15/85; SLJ 10/85)

896 Orgel, Doris. *Crack in the Heart* (9–12). 1989, Ballantine paper $2.95 (0-449-70204-9). After Zana's father dies, she and her mother move to New York City where Zana encounters many problems including a love affair. (Rev: BL 1/15/90; VOYA 4/90)

897 Paulsen, Gary. *Popcorn Days and Buttermilk Nights* (8–12). 1983, Lodestar $10.95 (0-525-66770-9); 1989, Penguin paper $3.95 (0-14-034204-4). Carley finds adventure after he is sent to his Uncle David's farm in Minnesota to sort himself out.

898 Pei, Lowry. *Family Resemblances* (9–12). 1986, Random $16.95 (0-394-55184-2); paper $6.95 (0-394-75528-6). An introspective novel about a teenage girl growing to maturity and her ambivalent feelings toward the aunt with whom she is staying. (Rev: BL 6/15/86; BR 11–12/86; SLJ 9/86; VOYA 8–10/86)

899 Piercy, Marge. *Gone to Soldiers* (10–12). 1988, Fawcett paper $5.95 (0-449-21557-1). A novel about those young people who did not go to war in 1941 and of the world that they inherited after the war. (Rev: SLJ 10/87)

900 Pliscou, Lisa. *Higher Education* (10–12). 1989, Viking $18.95 (0-670-82648-0). Miranda and her Harvard classmates make difficult choices about their lives after graduation. (Rev: VOYA 12/89)

901 Plummer, Louise. *The Romantic Obsessions and Humiliations of Annie Schlmeier* (9–12). 1987, Delacorte $14.95 (0-385-29574-X). A self-conscious Dutch girl newly arrived in the United States has a crush on the same boy as her sister. (Rev: BL 11/1/87; SLJ 12/87; VOYA 12/87)

902 Posner, Richard. *Goodnight, Cinderella* (9–12). 1989, Evans $13.95 (0-87131-587-4). Six high school students on a social merry-go-round straighten out their relationships by prom night. (Rev: BL 11/15/89; BR 3–4/90; SLJ 10/89)

903 Potok, Chaim. *My Name Is Asher Lev* (9–12). 1972, Knopf $18.95 (0-394-46137-1); Fawcett paper $3.95 (0-449-20714-5). This novel traces the conflict that a sensitive Jewish boy experiences with his strict Orthodox beliefs.

904 Powell, Padgett. *Edisto* (10–12). 1984, Farrar $11.95 (0-374-14651-9); Holt paper $5.95 (0-03-003184-2). A 12-year-old boy learns about life from his mother's lover.

905 Price, Reynolds. *The Tongues of Angels* (10–12). 1990, Macmillan $18.95 (0-689-12093-1). A middle-aged artist recalls his life as a camp counselor when he was 21 and his encounter with an unusual boy. (Rev: BL 2/15/90)

906 Raymond, Patrick. *Daniel and Esther* (9–12). 1990, Macmillan $12.95 (0-689-50504-3). In England on the verge of World War II, 2 teenagers fall completely in love. (Rev: BL 4/1/90; SLJ 3/90; VOYA 4/90)

907 Richards, Judith. *Summer Lightning* (10–12). 1987, Peachtree paper $6.95 (0-934601-18-6). In the Florida Everglades, an old man and a young boy form a friendship.

908 Robinson, Kim Stanley. *The Gold Coast* (10–12). 1988, St. Martin's $18.95 (0-312-93050-X). Jim McPherson, now in his late twenties, lives a fast life in California but lacks any purpose in his life. For better readers. (Rev: VOYA 6/88)

909 Roth, Henry. *Call It Sleep* (10–12). 1962, Avon paper $4.95 (0-380-01002-X). This novel, first published in 1934, tells of the childhood of a young Jewish boy growing up in the ghettos of New York City.

910 Ryan, Conall. *House of Cards* (10–12). 1989, Knopf $18.95 (0-394-57214-9). Several misfit high school students and their dictatorial poker instructor learn some painful personal truths. For mature readers. (Rev: BL 5/1/89)

911 Salinger, J. D. *Nine Stories* (10–12). 1953, Little $17.95 (0-316-76956-8); Bantam paper $3.50 (0-553-26360-9). This collection, which introduced the Glass family, explores the different worlds of adults and children.

912 Schieber, Phyllis. *Strictly Personal* (10–12). 1988, Ballantine paper $2.75 (0-449-70230-8). A teenage girl tries to decide if she is really ready for sex with her boyfriend. (Rev: BL 5/1/88; VOYA 6/88)

913 Schwandt, Stephen. *Holding Steady* (8–12). 1988, Henry Holt $13.95 (0-8050-0575-7). The 17-year-old boy finds solace for his father's death in the friendship of a beautiful girl. (Rev: BR 11–12/88)

914 Schwandt, Stephen. *A Risky Game* (9–12). 1986, Henry Holt $11.95 (0-8050-0091-7). When the teacher whom Julie admires asks her to participate in a class psychodrama, Julie wonders about the consequences. (Rev: BL 9/15/86; BR 5–6/87; SLJ 4/87)

915 Seidler, Tor. *Terpin* (9–12). 1982, Farrar $9.95 (0-374-37413-9). As a result of a tragedy caused by a careless lie, Terpin resolves always to tell the truth.

916 Silone, Ignazio. *Bread and Wine* (10–12). 1962, NAL paper $2.95 (0-451-51757-1). First published in 1937, this novel takes place in Fascist Italy and tells of the fearful life lived by the peasants at this time.

917 Singer, Marilyn. *The Course of True Love Never Did Run Smooth* (10–12). 1983, Harper LB $12.89 (0-06-025754-7). A gay couple "come out" during a school production of *A Midsummer Night's Dream*.

918 Smith, Betty. *Joy in the Morning* (10–12). 1963, Harper paper $3.95 (0-06-080368-1). Two young people face a number of problems when their families disown them after finding out about their marriage. Also use: *Maggie Now* (1971).

919 Smith, Mary-Ann Tirone. *The Book of Phoebe* (10–12). 1986, Dell paper $5.95 (0-440-50742-1). A pregnant Harvard senior goes to Paris to have her baby and there falls in love. (Rev: SLJ 4/86)

920 Smith, Peter J. *Highlights of the Off Season* (10–12). 1987, Penguin paper $6.95 (0-14-010292-2). Sam Grace is kicked out of his prep school and so begins an odyssey from coast to coast, where he meets some unusual characters. (Rev: SLJ 2/87)

921 Solomon, Barbara H., ed. *American Families: 28 Short Stories* (10–12). 1989, NAL paper $4.95 (0-451-16138-6). A collection of 28 stories from about 1900 to the present that deal with family relationships. (Rev: BL 10/15/89; VOYA 6/90)

922 Spark, Muriel. *The Prime of Miss Jean Brodie* (9–12). 1984, NAL paper $6.95 (0-452-26179-1). The story of an unusual teacher in a private girls' school in Edinburgh and of the changes she detects in her students.

923 Stanley, Carol. *High School Reunion* (9–12). 1986, Scholastic paper $2.25 (0-590-33579-0). Five high school friends return one year after graduation for a reunion and find changes in each of them. (Rev: BL 8/86; SLJ 3/87)

924 Stanton, Maura. *The Country I Come From* (10–12). 1988, Milkweed paper $9.95 (0-915943-33-6). Seven short stories about a teenage girl coming of age in a Midwestern Catholic family. (Rev: BL 2/1/89)

925 Strasser, Todd. *A Very Touchy Subject* (9–12). 1986, Dell paper $2.95 (0-440-98851-9). The story of a coming-of-age summer when a 17-year-old boy explores a very touchy subject—sex. (Rev: BL 3/1/85; SLJ 4/85)

926 Stretton, Barbara. *You Never Lose* (9–12). 1982, Knopf LB $9.99 (0-394-95230-8). In his senior year Jim discovers that his father, who is also his football coach, is dying of cancer.

927 Swarthout, Glendon. *Bless the Beasts and Children* (7–12). 1984, Pocket paper $2.95 (0-671-50710-9). At summer camp a group of misfits prove they have the right stuff.

928 Swindells, Robert. *Staying Up* (9–12). 1988, Oxford Univ. Pr. $13.95 (0-19-271546-1). Growing up in a working-class family in a northern England factory town. (Rev: BL 8/88; SLJ 4/88)

929 Tevis, Walter. *The Queen's Gambit* (10–12). 1983, Random $13.95 (0-394-52801-8); Dell paper $8.95 (0-440-50216-0). This is an exciting story of Beth, a brilliant chess player, and her eventual confrontation with the world champion, a Russian.

930 Thomas, Joyce Carol. *Bright Shadow* (10–12). 1983, Avon paper $2.95 (0-380-84509-1). A 20-year-old black college student's encounter with love is marred when she becomes involved in a murder.

931 Todd, Leonard. *Squaring Off* (8–12). Illus. 1990, Viking $13.95 (0-670-83377-0). Willie, who is 13, falls for his father's girlfriend Lujane, who is a stripper, in this novel that combines coming of age, humor, and the sport of boxing. (Rev: BL 11/1/90)

932 Tolan, Stephanie S. *Plague Year* (8–12). 1990, Morrow LB $12.95 (0-688-08801-5). Nonconformist Bran, whose father is a mass murderer, faces problems of acceptance at his new high school. (Rev: BL 4/1/90; SLJ 6/90)

933 Tyler, Anne. *A Slipping-Down Life* (10–12). 1983, Berkley paper $4.50 (0-425-10362-5). In this novel from 1970, Evie, a high school misfit, is drawn to a rock star she sees perform at a local club. Also use for better readers: *If Morning Ever Comes* (1987) and *Breathing Lessons* (1988).

934 Updike, David. *Out on the Marsh* (10–12). 1988, Godine $16.95 (0-87923-728-7). Thirteen stories, many about childhood and adolescence. (Rev: BR 1–2/89)

935 Ure, Jean. *The Other Side of the Fence* (9–12). 1988, Delacorte $14.95 (0-385-29627-4). Richard, a gay runaway from a wealthy British family, settles down in squatters' digs with

Bonny, an orphan who is also a drifter. (Rev: BL 2/1/88; SLJ 4/88; VOYA 4/88)

936 Voigt, Cynthia. *Tell Me If the Lovers Are Losers* (9–12). 1982, Macmillan $13.95 (0-689-30911-2); Fawcett paper $3.50 (0-449-70235-9). Three college roommates—Ann, Niki, and Hildy—gradually learn to work out their differences.

937 Walker, Paul Robert. *The Method* (8–12). 1990, Harcourt $14.95 (0-15-200528-5). A candid novel about a 15-year-old boy, his acting aspirations, and his sexual problems. (Rev: BL 8/90; SLJ 6/90)

938 Wersba, Barbara. *Beautiful Losers* (9–12). 1988, Harper LB $11.89 (0-06-026364-4). The concluding volume in the trilogy about teenaged Rita Formica and her love for Arnold, who is twice her age. Also use: *Love Is the Crooked Thing* (1987). (Rev: BL 3/15/88)

939 Wersba, Barbara. *The Farewell Kid* (9–12). 1990, Harper LB $12.89 (0-06-026379-2). Manhattan teenager Heidi Rosenbloom finds romance with Harvey Beaumont, the rich boy introduced in *Carnival of My Mind* (1982). (Rev: BL 5/15/90; SLJ 5/90)

940 Wersba, Barbara. *Wonderful Me* (9–12). 1989, Harper LB $12.89 (0-06-026362-8). Seventeen-year-old Heidi Rosenbloom spends the summer making money dog walking and coping with the worshipful attention of a mentally unstable English teacher. A sequel to *Just Be Gorgeous* (1988). (Rev: BL 5/1/89; BR 11–12/89; SLJ 4/89; VOYA 6/89)

941 West, Jessamyn. *The State of Stony Lonesome* (10–12). 1984, Harcourt $12.95 (0-15-184903-X). The story of the relationship between a lonely hard-drinking man and his young niece. (Rev: BL 1/15/85)

942 White, Edmund. *A Boy's Own Story* (10–12). 1982, Dutton $13.95 (0-525-24128-0); NAL paper $7.95 (0-452-26123-6). For mature readers, a bittersweet novel about a boy's gay adolescence.

943 Wolfe, Thomas. *Look Homeward, Angel: A Story of the Buried Life* (10–12). 1929, Macmillan paper $9.95 (0-684-17616-5). The youth of Eugene Gant in the southern town of Altamont until he leaves home to find his destiny. A sequel is *Of Time and the River* (1935).

944 Wolfe, Thomas. *The Web and the Rock* (10–12). 1939, Harper paper $10.95 (0-06-091320-7). The story of George Webber—his youth, college days, teaching career, and unhappy love life. A sequel is *You Can't Go Home Again* (1940).

945 Worth, Valerie. *Fox Hill* (10–12). 1986, Farrar $11.95 (0-374-32783-1). A hopelessly romantic girl decides to commit suicide to join the man whose portrait is hung in her aunt's country home. (Rev: BL 2/15/86; SLJ 5/86)

946 Zindel, Paul. *The Amazing and Death-Defying Diary of Eugene Dingman* (9–12). 1987, Harper LB $12.89 (0-06-026863-8); Bantam paper $2.95 (0-553-27768-5). An unhappy teenager is sent to a resort hotel to work as a busboy. (Rev: BL 10/15/87; BR 3–4/88; SLJ 10/87; VOYA 10/87)

947 Zindel, Paul. *The Girl Who Wanted a Boy* (9–12). 1981, Harper LB $12.89 (0-06-026868-9); Bantam paper $2.95 (0-553-26486-9). A 15-year-old girl suffers rejection when she sets out to develop a relationship with the boy of her dreams.

948 Zindel, Paul. *I Never Loved Your Mind* (8–12). 1970, Harper LB $12.89 (0-06-026822-0); Bantam paper $2.95 (0-553-27323-X). Two dropouts working in a hospital together suffer the pangs of love and loss.

949 Zindel, Paul. *My Darling, My Hamburger* (8–12). 1969, Harper LB $12.89 (0-06-026824-7); Bantam paper $2.95 (0-553-27324-8). Two young couples each in love face life's complications including one girl's abortion.

950 Zindel, Paul. *Pardon Me, You're Stepping on My Eyeball* (10–12). 1983, Bantam LB $12.89 (0-06-026838-7); paper $2.95 (0-553-26690-X). Marsh Mallow and Edna Shinglebox form a friendship to help solve problems caused by the adults around them. Also use: *Harry and Hortense at Hormone High* (1984).

951 Zindel, Paul. *The Pigman* (10–12). 1983, Harper LB $13.89 (0-06-26828-X); Bantam paper $3.50 (0-553-26321-8). Two teenagers must face the responsibility of causing the death of an old man they befriend. A sequel is *The Pigman's Legacy* (1984).

952 Zolotow, Charlotte, ed. *An Overpraised Season* (9–12). 1973, Harper LB $12.89 (0-06-026954-5). From such writers as John Updike, Kurt Vonnegut, and Nathaniel Benchley, this is a collection of 10 stories about adolescents and their problems relating to an older generation.

World Affairs and Contemporary Problems

953 Abe, Kobo. *The Woman in the Dunes* (10–12). 1972, Random paper $7.95 (0-394-71814-3).

For mature readers, a story about a man who is captured by a woman who lives in the sand dunes.

954 Bellow, Saul. *Mr. Sammler's Planet* (10–12). 1970, Viking $12.95 (0-670-49322-8); Penguin paper $6.95 (0-14-007317-5). Mr. Sammler, a transplanted Jew who spent time in a Nazi prison camp, looks back on his life.

955 Bellow, Saul. *The Portable Saul Bellow* (10–12). 1974, Viking $14.95 (0-670-15616-7); Penguin paper $9.95 (0-14-015079-X). In addition to the complete *Seize the Day* and *Henderson the Rain King,* this volume contains excerpts from other novels plus some stories.

956 Coetzee, J. M. *Life and Times of Michael K.* (10–12). 1985, Penguin paper $6.95 (0-14-007448-1). For better readers, this is the story of a harrowing journey through a South Africa ravaged by civil war.

957 Courtenay, Bryce. *The Power of One* (10–12). 1989, Random $18.95 (0-394-57520-2). The story of a white South African boy who tries to fight injustice in his homeland during World War II. (Rev: BR 11–12/89; VOYA 12/89)

958 Desai, Anita. *Clear Light of Day* (10–12). 1989, Penguin paper $6.95 (0-14-008670-6). This family saga takes place in New Delhi.

959 Drury, Allen. *Advise and Consent* (10–12). 1959, Doubleday $16.95 (0-385-05419-X). The Pulitzer Prize-winning novel about behind-the-scenes life in Washington, D.C. First of a lengthy series.

960 Emecheta, Buchi. *The Bride Price* (10–12). 1976, Braziller paper $6.95 (0-8076-0818-1). A love story set in Nigeria in the 1950s concerning a romance thwarted by tribal customs.

961 Gordimer, Nadine. *A Guest of Honour* (10–12). 1983, Penguin paper $6.95 (0-14-003696-2). For better readers, this is the story of a former colonist who returns to an emerging African nation. Also use *The Conservationist* (1983).

962 Gordimer, Nadine. *My Son's Story* (10–12). 1990, Farrar $19.95 (0-374-21751-3). The story of the love between a dedicated black teacher and Hannah, a white activist, set in South Africa. (Rev: BL 9/15/90)

963 Gordimer, Nadine. *Selected Stories* (10–12). 1983, Penguin paper $6.95 (0-14-00677-X). The men of the stories in this collection reflect the racial situation in South Africa.

964 Gordimer, Nadine. *A Soldier's Embrace* (10–12). 1982, Penguin paper $6.95 (0-14-005925-3). A collection of stories by this South

African writer that use various parts of Africa as locales.

965 Gordimer, Nadine. *A World of Strangers* (10–12). 1984, Penguin paper $7.95 (0-14-001704-6). Racial conflicts surface when a young Englishman befriends a bitter South African in Johannesburg. Another novel that explores this theme is *July's People* (1982).

966 Grass, Gunter. *The Tin Drum* (10–12). Trans. by Ralph Manheim. 1987, Random paper $9.95 (0-394-74560-4). This surreal novel tells of the fortunes of a dwarf in contemporary Germany with an unusual ability to relive incidents from the past.

967 Hauser, Thomas. *The Fantasy* (10–12). 1986, Richardson & Steirman $16.95 (0-931933-29-3). A behind-the-scenes novel about the publishing industry that focuses on the problems faced by a particular writer. (Rev: SLJ 4/87)

968 Hegi, Ursula. *Floating in My Mother's Palm* (10–12). 1990, Poseidon $17.95 (0-671-68947-9). An eloquent novel about growing up in a town in postwar Germany. (Rev: BL 3/15/90)

969 Hersey, John. *The Child Buyer* (10–12). 1960, Knopf $11.95 (0-394-41910-3). In this biting satire on American education, Mr. Wissey Jones tries to buy a male child to use his talents for his corporation.

970 Hoffman, Nancy, and Florence Howe, eds. *Women Working: An Anthology of Stories and Poems* (10–12). Illus. 1979, Feminist Pr. paper $9.95 (0-912670-57-6). This collection of stories and poems explores the world of work as experienced by women.

971 Jenks, Tom, ed. *Soldiers & Civilians: Americans at War and at Home* (10–12). 1986, Bantam $16.95 (0-553-05180-6); paper $8.95 (0-553-34312-2). The effects of war on people are examined using this group of stories about war, ranging from World War II to future wars. (Rev: SLJ 2/87)

972 Jones, Toeckey. *Skindeep* (10–12). 1986, Harper LB $12.89 (0-06-023052-5). In apartheid-dominated South Africa, a white girl discovers that her boyfriend is only passing as white. (Rev: BL 9/1/86; BR 3–4/87; SLJ 11/86)

973 Kazantzakis, Nikos. *Zorba the Greek* (10–12). Trans. by Carl Wildman. 1952, Simon & Schuster paper $9.95 (0-671-21132-3). The narrator of this novel takes the uninhibited Zorba, an old Greek workman, to Crete with him to help operate a mine.

974 Kemal, Yasher. *Memed, My Hawk* (10–12). 1982, Pantheon paper $6.95 (0-394-71016-9).

This tragic story, set in southern Turkey, takes place in an area where feudal conditions still exist.

975 Kiely, Benedict. *Proxopera: A Tale of Modern Ireland* (10–12). 1987, Godine $13.95 (0-87923-651-5). For better readers, a gripping tale of violence and terrorism in modern Northern Ireland. (Rev: BL 10/1/87)

976 Koestler, Arthur. *Darkness at Noon* (10–12). Trans. by Daphne Hardy. 1984, Bantam paper $4.95 (0-553-26595-4). In this 1940 novel, life in a Soviet political prison is depicted as seen through the experiences of one inmate.

977 Lederer, William J., and Eugene Burdick. *The Ugly American* (10–12). 1965, Norton $9.95 (0-393-00305-1). A group of Americans react in various ways when they are exposed to the people and culture of Southeast Asia.

978 Lewis, Sinclair. *Babbitt* (10–12). 1949, Harcourt $14.95 (0-15-110421-2); NAL paper $4.95 (0-451-52366-0). A satire on the shallow life led by members of the middle-class in an American city named Zenith.

979 Lewis, Sinclair. *Main Street* (10–12). 1950, Harcourt $14.95 (0-15-155547-8); NAL paper $4.50 (0-451-52147-1). A woman marries a small town doctor and decides to change things in Gopher Prairie, Minnesota. First published in 1920.

980 Michener, James A. *Legacy* (10–12). 1987, Random $17.95 (0-394-56432-4); Fawcett paper $4.95 (0-449-21641-1). A contemporary novel about an army officer involved with the Contras in Nicaragua. (Rev: BL 8/87)

981 Murphy, Walter F. *The Vicar of Christ* (10–12). 1988, Ballantine paper $5.95 (0-345-00939-8). A pope is chosen by destiny to reach the hearts of all humankind.

982 Murray, Sabina. *Slow Burn* (10–12). 1990, Ballantine paper $7.95 (0-345-36773-1). Set in present-day Manila, this novel tells about the spoiled lives of the children of the wealthy. (Rev: BL 6/1/90)

983 Naipaul, V. S. *A House for Mr. Biswas* (10–12). 1984, Random $9.95 (0-394-72050-4). This novel for better readers takes place in Trinidad and involves a poor Hindu living there who wishes for a better life.

984 Narayan, R. K. *The Guide* (10–12). 1988, Penguin paper $5.95 (0-14-009657-4). A man recently released from prison is mistaken for a holy man. Other novels by this Indian writer are *The Vendor of Sweets* and *The Man-Eater of Malgudi* (both 1983).

985 O'Connor, Edwin. *The Last Hurrah* (10–12). 1956, Little paper $8.95 (0-316-62659-7). An old-style politician who has been mayor of a large American city for about 40 years finds that his power is being challenged.

986 Paton, Alan. *Ah, But Your Land Is Beautiful* (10–12). 1987, Macmillan paper $6.95 (0-684-17830-3). This novel about the tragic effects of apartheid takes place in South Africa from 1952 to 1958.

987 Paton, Alan. *Cry, the Beloved Country* (10–12). 1948, Macmillan $27.50 (0-684-15559-1); paper $8.95 (0-684-71863-4). A black minister tries to save his son, accused of murder, in this touching novel set in South Africa.

988 Paulsen, Gary. *Sentries* (8–12). 1986, Bradbury $12.95 (0-02-770100-X); Penguin paper $3.95 (0-317-62279-X). The stories of 4 different young people are told. However, before their stories can be resolved, they are all wiped out by a superbomb. (Rev: BL 5/1/86; SLJ 8/86; VOYA 8–10/86)

989 Rand, Ayn. *Anthem* (10–12). NAL paper $3.95 (0-451-15993-4). A short novel set in the future about an individual fighting a powerful collective state.

990 Rand, Ayn. *Atlas Shrugged* (10–12). 1957, Random $29.45 (0-394-41576-0); NAL paper $5.95 (0-451-15748-6). In an age where everyone looks to the state for guidance and protection, one man wants to go it alone.

991 Rand, Ayn. *The Fountainhead* (10–12). 1943, Macmillan $32.50 (0-02-600910-2); NAL paper $5.95 (0-451-15823-7). The story of the careers of 2 very different men in the world of New York architecture.

992 Rochman, Hazel, ed. *Somehow Tenderness Survives: Stories of Southern Africa* (8–12). 1988, Harper LB $12.89 (0-06-025023-2). Ten stories by such writers as Nadine Gordimer about growing up in South Africa. (Rev: BL 8/88; BR 5–6/89; SLJ 12/88; VOYA 12/88)

993 Scott, Paul. *Staying On* (10–12). 1979, Avon paper $3.50 (0-380-46045-9). Mr. and Mrs. Smalley decide to stay on in India after the country gains independence.

994 Singer, Isaac Bashevis. *The Penitent* (10–12). 1983, Farrar $13.95 (0-374-23064-1); Fawcett paper $3.95 (0-449-20612-2). Higher values prevail when Joseph Shapiro decides to find his salvation in Israel.

995 Solzhenitsyn, Alexander. *One Day in the Life of Ivan Denisovich* (10–12). 1984, Bantam paper $2.95 (0-553-24777-8). A harrowing short novel about life in a Stalinist labor camp in Siberia.

996 Steinbeck, John. *Cannery Row* (10–12). 1945, Viking $16.95 (0-670-20281-9); 1989, Bantam paper $2.95 (0-553-26603-9). The adventures of a group of workers and their families who rely on a California cannery for their livelihood. Followed by *Sweet Thursday* (1954).

997 Steinbeck, John. *Tortilla Flat* (10–12). 1962, Viking $16.95 (0-670-72109-3); Penguin paper $3.95 (0-14-004240-7). The life of some poor but carefree friends in Monterey, California, during the 1930s.

998 Styron, William. *Sophie's Choice* (10–12). 1979, Random $15.95 (0-394-46109-6); Bantam paper $4.95 (0-553-25960-1). In a Jewish boarding house in Brooklyn, Sophie, a survivor of Auschwitz, meets 2 men who will change her life.

999 West, Morris L. *The Devil's Advocate* (10–12). 1959, Morrow $17.95 (0-688-01453-4). An investigation by a dying prelate of the possible sainthood of a martyred churchman forms the background of this intriguing novel.

Fantasy

1000 Aamodt, Donald. *A Name to Conjure With* (9–12). 1989, Avon paper $3.50 (0-380-75137-2). A reluctant participant embarks on a quest with a bumbling sorcerer. (Rev: BL 8/89; VOYA 10/89)

1001 Abbey, Lynn. *Unicorn & Dragon* (10–12). Illus. 1988, Avon paper $3.50 (0-380-75567-X). A fantasy set in eleventh-century England that pits Druid magic against Norman sorcery. (Rev: SLJ 6–7/87)

1002 Adams, Richard. *The Plague Dogs* (10–12). 1986, Fawcett paper $4.95 (0-499-21182-7). For better readers, this is a novel about 2 dogs that flee from a research center.

1003 Adams, Richard. *Watership Down* (7–12). 1974, Macmillan $24.50 (0-02-700030-3); Avon paper $4.95 (0-380-00293-0). In this fantasy a group of male rabbits set out to find a new home.

1004 Adams, Robert. *Castaways in Time* (10–12). 1982, NAL paper $2.95 (0-451-14099-0). In this fantasy, 8 Americans find themselves in seventeenth-century England.

1005 Adams, Robert. *Witch Goddess* (10–12). 1982, NAL paper $2.95 (0-451-14027-3). This novel is number 9 in the Hordeclan series. Many others are also published in paperback by New American Library.

1006 Alton, Andrea I. *Demon of Undoing* (10–12). 1988, Baen paper $3.50 (0-671-65413-6). After the defeat of his clan in battle, Fenobar is given the holy trust of caring for a sacred battle axe. (Rev: VOYA 2/89)

1007 Anderson, Poul. *The Shield of Time* (10–12). 1990, Tor $18.95 (0-312-85088-3). In this novel the Time Patrol travels into the past in order to protect their future. (Rev: BL 7/90)

1008 Anderson, Poul. *Three Hearts and Three Lions* (10–12). 1984, Ace paper $2.50 (0-441-80822-0). A modern soldier is transported into the past where he becomes a knight.

1009 Anderson, Poul, and Karen Anderson. *Gallicenae: The King of Ys, Book 2* (10–12). 1987, Baen paper $3.95 (0-671-65342-3). In this novel that is part of a series, Gratillonius, a Roman centurion, is sent to a mythical city-state known as Ys. (Rev: VOYA 10/87)

1010 Anthony, Piers. *Being a Green Mother* (10–12). 1987, Ballantine $16.95 (0-345-32222-3); paper $4.95 (0-345-32223-1). In this concluding part of the 5-book series Incarnations of Immortality, Orb falls in love with a man who might be Satan. (Rev: BL 10/15/87; VOYA 6/88)

1011 Anthony, Piers. *Golem in the Gears* (10–12). 1986, Ballantine paper $3.95 (0-345-31886-2). In this ninth Xanth novel, Grundy the Golem sets out to find the lost dragon of Princess Ivy. (Rev: BL 2/15/86; SLJ 5/86; VOYA 6/86)

1012 Anthony, Piers. *A Spell for Chameleon* (10–12). 1987, Ballantine paper $4.95 (0-345-34753-6). This is the introductory Xanth novel where the reader first meets the young hero Bink and his quest to find magical powers. Two others in this extensive series are: *Castle Roogna* and *The Source of Magic* (both 1987).

1013 Anthony, Piers. *Wielding a Red Sword* (10–12). 1987, Ballantine paper $4.95 (0-345-32221-5). In the fourth book of the Incarnations of Immortality series, Mym is forced to do Satan's work and finds it impossible to stop. For better readers. (Rev: BL 9/1/86)

1014 Anthony, Piers. *With a Tangled Skein* (10–12). 1985, Ballantine paper $4.95 (0-345-31885-4). In this volume in the Incarnations of Immortality series, Niobe sets out to avenge her lover's death. Earlier volumes were *On a Pale Horse* (1983) and *Bearing the Hourglass* (1984).

1015 Appel, Allen. *Twice upon a Time* (10–12). 1988, Carroll & Graf $18.95 (0-88184-384-9). A historian has an advantage over his colleagues—he can travel back in time. (Rev: VOYA 10/88)

1016 Ashley, Mike, et al., eds. *The Pendragon Chronicles* (10–12). 1990, Bedrick $18.95 (0-87226-335-5). A collection of 16 tales that explore various aspects of the Arthurian legend. (Rev: SLJ 8/90)

1017 Ashton, Francis. *The Breaking of the Seals* (10–12). 1982, Donning paper $6.95 (0-89865-200-6). In this time-travel novel, a man travels back 200,000 years.

1018 Asimov, Isaac. *Azazel* (10–12). 1988, Doubleday $16.95 (0-385-24410-X). The wishes of the demon Azazel always seem to go wrong in this collection of stories. (Rev: VOYA 4/89)

1019 Asimov, Isaac, et al., eds. *Wizards* (9–12). 1983, NAL paper $3.50 (0-451-12542-8). Ten wonderful tales featuring fascinating wizards in unusual situations.

1020 Asprin, Robert. *Little Myth Marker* (10–12). Illus. 1985, Donning $12.95 (0-89865-411-4); paper $7.95 (0-89865-413-0). In this novel that is part of the Myth Adventure series, Skeeve the wizard sets out to find the person who is sabotaging his magic business. (Rev: BL 4/1/86; VOYA 12/87)

1021 Asprin, Robert. *Myth Conception* (10–12). 1986, Ace paper $3.50 (0-441-55521-7). An apprentice magician and his friends are pitted against an army of invaders.

1022 Asprin, Robert, and Lynn Abbey, eds. *Blood Ties* (10–12). 1986, Ace paper $2.95 (0-441-80595-7). This is the ninth volume in this shared world series called Thieves World about the city of Sanctuary where sorcery and crime exist side by side. (Rev: VOYA 2/87)

1023 Asprin, Robert, and Lynn Abbey, eds. *The Face of Chaos* (10–12). 1986, Ace paper $3.95 (0-441-80587-6). In this anthology of stories by several authors, a variety of people visit the town of Santriary.

1024 Bach, Richard. *Jonathan Livingston Seagull* (10–12). 1970, Macmillan $14.95 (0-02-504540-7); Avon paper $3.95 (0-380-01286-3). Because of his unusual love of flying, Jonathan is treated as an outsider.

1025 Bailey, Robin W. *The Lake of Fire* (10–12). 1989, Bantam paper $3.95 (0-553-28185-2). In this, the fourth volume of the Dungeon series, Clive and his followers take a trip through Hell. (Rev: VOYA 6/90)

1026 Banks, Lynne Reid. *Melusine* (8–12). 1989, Harper LB $12.89 (0-06-020395-1). While staying with his family in an old French chateau, Roger discovers Melusine, a supernatural creature that is half woman and half snake. (Rev: BL 10/1/89; SLJ 11/89; VOYA 2/90)

1027 Barker, M. A. R. *The Man of Gold* (10–12). 1985, DAW paper $3.95 (0-88677-082-3). A scholar-priest is on a quest to find the legendary Man of Gold.

1028 Beagle, Peter S. *A Fine and Private Place* (10–12). 1987, Ballantine paper $3.95 (0-345-35156-8). An unusual fantasy about an old man, a graveyard, and the ghosts he befriends there.

1029 Beagle, Peter S. *The Folk of the Air* (10–12). 1988, Ballantine paper $4.95 (0-345-34699-8). For better readers, a story of how role-playing at being medieval characters leads to unleashing a power involving black magic. (Rev: BL 11/1/86)

1030 Beagle, Peter S. *The Last Unicorn* (9–12). 1968, Ballantine paper $3.95 (0-345-35167-6). A beautiful unicorn sets off to find others of her species.

1031 Bear, Greg. *The Infinity Concerto* (10–12). 1987, Ace paper $3.95 (0-441-37059-4). A 16-year-old strays into another world in this mature fantasy.

1032 Bear, Greg. *The Serpent Mage* (10–12). 1986, Berkley paper $3.50 (0-425-09337-9). Michael Perrin again goes back to the time of the Celts to help bring myth and reality together. (Rev: BL 2/1/87)

1033 Bellairs, John. *The Face in the Frost* (9–12). Illus. 1986, Ace paper $2.95 (0-441-22531-4). Two bumbling and forgetful wizards find themselves in mortal combat with an evil force.

1034 Bemmann, Hans. *The Stone and the Flute* (10–12). Trans. by Anthea Bell. 1987, Viking $19.95 (0-670-80186-0); Penguin paper $7.95 (0-14-007445-7). A lengthy book about young Listener and his quest for self-fulfillment. (Rev: BL 3/1/87)

1035 Benét, Stephen Vincent. *The Devil and Daniel Webster* (10–12). 1990, Creative Education paper $10.95 (0-88682-295-5). This classic short novel is a variation on the Faust legend, this time set in New Hampshire.

1036 Bentley-Baker, Dan. *The Paper Boat* (10–12). 1988, Pineapple $17.95 (0-910923-53-1). A novel about reincarnation and a soul that inhabits many bodies in a time span that covers ancient Egypt to the present. (Rev: BR 5–6/89)

1037 Bisson, Terry. *Fire on the Mountain* (10–12). 1988, Arbor House $15.95 (1-55710-014-4). Speculative fiction about the future where John Brown's raid on Harper's Ferry had been successful. (Rev: BL 7/88)

1038 Bisson, Terry. *Talking Man* (10–12). 1987, Avon paper $2.95 (0-380-75141-0). For better readers, this is a fantasy involving godlike creatures and their relations with humans. (Rev: BL 10/1/86)

1039 Blaylock, James P. *The Stone Giant* (10–12). 1989, Ace paper $3.95 (0-441-28702-6). Theophile Escargot's fortunes change for the worst when he steals one of his wife's pies. (Rev: VOYA 2/90)

1040 Bond, Nancy. *Another Shore* (8–12). 1988, Macmillan $15.95 (0-689-50463-2). A thoroughly modern girl time travels to Nova Scotia of 1744 and finds it impossible to return to the present. (Rev: BL 9/1/88; BR 5–6/89; SLJ 10/88; VOYA 12/88)

1041 Boyer, Elizabeth H. *The Troll's Grindstone* (10–12). 1986, Ballantine paper $3.50 (0-345-32182-0). In this quest fantasy, a human disguised as an elf incurs the wrath of a powerful sorcerer. (Rev: BL 7/86)

1042 Bradbury, Ray. *A Graveyard for Lunatics* (10–12). 1990, Knopf $18.95 (0-394-57877-5). The real and the imaginary, the past and the present, all mingle in this fantasy set in a Hollywood back lot. (Rev: SLJ 12/90)

1043 Bradbury, Ray. *The Halloween Tree* (7–12). 1972, Knopf $12.95 (0-394-82409-1); paper $3.95 (0-553-25823-0). Nine boys discover the true meaning—and horror—of the holiday, Halloween.

1044 Bradbury, Ray. *The Illustrated Man* (7–12). 1952, Bantam paper $3.50 (0-553-25483-9). A tattooed man tells a story for each of his tattoos.

1045 Bradbury, Ray. *Medicine for Melancholy* (10–12). 1990, Bantam paper $3.95 (0-553-28638-2). This is a collection of 23 tales, many with fantastic twists. Other short story collections are: *The Golden Apples of the Sun* (1971) and *I Sing the Body Electric* (1969).

1046 Bradbury, Ray. *R Is for Rocket* (10–12). 1969, Bantam paper $3.50 (0-553-25040-X). Seventeen stories that combine fantasy and science fiction.

1047 Bradbury, Ray. *Something Wicked This Way Comes* (9–12). 1983, Knopf $24.95 (0-394-53041-1); Bantam paper $4.95 (0-553-28032-5). This tale tells what happens after "The Pandemonium Shadow Show" plays in a small town.

1048 Bradbury, Ray. *The Toynbee Convector* (10–12). 1988, Knopf $17.95 (0-394-54703-9). A new collection of short stories that cover such areas as fantasy, horror, and science fiction. (Rev: BL 5/1/88; BR 1–2/89)

1049 Bradley, Marion Zimmer. *City of Sorcery* (10–12). 1984, DAW paper $4.50 (0-88677-332-6). This novel in the Darkover series traces the quest of Magdalen Loone.

1050 Bradley, Marion Zimmer. *The Colors of Space* (10–12). 1988, Donning paper $8.95 (0-318-37686-5). In this novel a young man challenges the power of the stars. Also use *Web of Stars; City of Sorcery; The Forbidden Tower; The Heritage of Hastur* (all 1984); and *Sharra's Exile* (1981).

1051 Bradley, Marion Zimmer. *The Firebrand* (10–12). 1988, Pocket paper $4.50 (0-671-67018-2). A retelling of this fantasy of events concerned with the Trojan War by the author of *Mists of Avalon* (1982). (Rev: BL 9/15/87)

1052 Bradley, Marion Zimmer. *Hawkmistress!* (10–12). 1982, DAW paper $3.95 (0-88677-239-7). A Darkover novel about Romilly, a girl who has special abilities to communicate with hawks and horses.

1053 Bradley, Marion Zimmer. *The Heirs of Hammerfell* (9–12). 1989, NAL $18.95 (0-88677-395-4). In this Darkover volume, twins of noble birth are separated in childhood and each grows up believing the other is dead. (Rev: BL 11/1/89; VOYA 6/90)

1054 Bradley, Marion Zimmer. *The House between the Worlds* (10–12). 1984, Ballantine paper $4.95 (0-345-31646-0). A tale of elves and goblins. Also use these Darkover novels: *Thendara House* (1983), *Spell Sword* (1978), *Two to Conquer* (1980), and *Winds of Darkover* (1985).

1055 Bradley, Marion Zimmer, ed. *Sword and Sorceress: An Anthology of Heroic Fantasy* (9–12). 1984, DAW paper $3.95 (0-88677-359-8). In each of these 15 fantasies the central character is a woman. There are 7 other Sword and Sorceress anthologies.

1056 Bradley, Marion Zimmer, ed. *Sword and Sorceress VII* (9–12). 1990, NAL paper $4.95 (0-88677-457-8). A further collection of stories, many by teenage writers, about women who use magic or force to achieve their goals. Also use volume II (1986) and volume IV (1987). (Rev: BL 12/1/90)

1057 Bradley, Marion Zimmer. *Sword of Chaos* (10–12). 1982, DAW paper $3.50 (0-88677-172-2). This anthology of Darkover stories contains short fantasies by Zimmer and other writers using her locale.

1058 Bradley, Marion Zimmer, et al. *Black Trillium* (10–12). 1990, Doubleday $18.95 (0-385-26185-3). This tale jointly written by Bradley, Julian May, and Andre Norton, describes the fates of 3 princesses who are separated when fleeing a coup against their parents. (Rev: BL 6/15/90)

1059 Brooks, Terry. *The Druid of Shannara* (10–12). 1991, Ballantine $19.95 (0-345-36298-5). In this, the second of the Heritage of Shannara series, the evil Shadowen continue to control the Four Lands. (Rev: BL 12/1/90)

1060 Brooks, Terry. *The Scions of Shannara* (10–12). 1990, Ballantine $19.95 (0-345-35695-0). In this, the first of a new trilogy, The Heritage of Shannara, the forces of good battle a race using evil magic. (Rev: BL 1/1/90; SLJ 9/90)

1061 Brooks, Terry. *The Wishsong of Shannara* (9–12). 1985, Ballantine $18.95 (0-345-31823-4); paper $9.95 (0-345-30833-6). In the concluding volume of the Shannara saga, a young girl finds she holds the power of the wishsong, a weapon that the Four Lands can use against their enemies. Preceded by *The Sword of Shannara* (1980) and *The Elfstones of Shannara* (1982). (Rev: BL 4/1/85; SLJ 8/85; VOYA 12/85)

1062 Brown, Mary. *The Unlikely Ones* (10–12). 1986, McGraw $15.95 (0-07-008296-0); Baen paper $3.95 (0-671-65361-X). Seven unlikely companions, including a hornless unicorn, are forced to go on a quest because of a witch's curse. (Rev: BL 10/1/86)

1063 Brust, Steven. *Brokedown Palace* (10–12). 1986, Ace paper $3.50 (0-441-07181-3). Prince Miklos must use magic to save his kingdom from an evil goddess. (Rev: VOYA 6/86)

1064 Card, Orson Scott. *Hart's Hope* (10–12). 1988, Tor paper $3.95 (0-8125-3351-8). To secure revenge, a scorned woman turns to sorcery.

1065 Card, Orson Scott. *Seventh Son* (10–12). 1987, Tor $17.95 (0-312-93019-4); paper $3.95 (0-8125-3353-4). In this the first volume of the Tales of Alvin Maker series, the author has created another world using early nineteenth-century America as a model. (Rev: BL 5/1/87; SLJ 12/87; VOYA 12/87)

1066 Carr, Terry, ed. *Fantasy Annual 4* (10–12). 1981, Pocket paper $3.50 (0-671-41273-6). This fine collection of stories is part of a series.

1067 Chalker, Jack L. *Midnight at the Well of Souls* (10–12). 1985, Ballantine paper $3.95 (0-345-32445-5). This story about Nathan Brazil is the first part of the Saga of the Well World.

Other volumes are: *Exiles at the Well of Souls* (1984), *Quest for the Well of Souls* (1985), *The Return of Nathan Brazil*, and *Twilight at the Well of Souls* (both 1986).

1068 Chalker, Jack L. *Web of the Chosen* (10–12). 1987, Ballantine paper $3.95 (0-345-33959-2). Bar Holliday finds he is changing into a subhuman creature. Also use: *A Jungle of Stars* (1988).

1069 Cherryh, C. J. *The Dreamstone* (10–12). 1983, DAW paper $2.95 (0-88677-013-0). Arafel the Sidhe is the guardian of the last magical place still not spoiled by mortals. A sequel is *The Trees of Swords and Jewels* (1983).

1070 Cherryh, C. J. *Exile's Gate* (10–12). 1988, NAL paper $3.95 (0-88677-254-0). In this fourth installment of the adventures of Morgaine, she and her liegeman continue their quest to close the disrupting Gates. The preceding volume was: *Fires of Azroth* (1979). (Rev: BL 11/1/87; VOYA 6/88)

1071 Cherryh, C. J. *Rusalka* (10–12). 1989, Ballantine $18.95 (0-345-35953-4). A reworking of the Russian folktale about the longings of the spirit of a murdered girl. (Rev: BL 9/1/89).

1072 Cherryh, C. J., and Nancy Asire. *Wizard Spawn* (9–12). 1989, Baen paper $3.50 (0-671-69838-9). Duran, a member of the ruling Ancar, leaves the court to help the oppressed Nation of the Sabirn. (Rev: VOYA 4/90)

1073 Cherryh, C. J., and Mercedes Lackey. *Reap the Whirlwind* (9–12). 1989, Baen paper $3.95 (0-671-69846-X). In this fantasy, a horde of barbarians threaten the power of the Order of the Sword of Knowledge. (Rev: VOYA 4/90)

1074 Clayton, Jo. *A Bait of Dreams* (10–12). 1985, NAL paper $3.95 (0-88677-276-1). A jewel is found that can put powerful dreams into one's mind. Also use: *The Snares of Ibex* (1984) and *Changer's Moon* (1985).

1075 Clement, Aeron. *The Cold Moons* (10–12). 1989, Doubleday $16.95 (0-385-50112-1). A group of badgers set out to find a new home when the humans around them try to exterminate them. (Rev: BL 2/1/89; BR 11–12/89; SLJ 11/89; VOYA 12/89)

1076 Cook, Glen. *Doomstalker* (10–12). 1985, Warner paper $3.50 (0-445-20062-6). A girl who survives a raid by nomads is abducted by witches who want to use her psychic powers. (Rev: BL 9/1/85; VOYA 2/86)

1077 Cook, Hugh. *The Wizards and the Warriors* (10–12). 1987, Dufour Editions $19.95 (0-86140-244-8). Enemies become allies to fight a common threat in this, the first volume of the Chronicles of an Age of Darkness series. (Rev: BL 4/15/87)

1078 Cook, Rick. *Wizardry Compiled* (9–12). 1990, Baen paper $3.95 (0-671-69856-7). In this sequel to *Wizard's Bane* (1989), Wiz becomes the target of a jealous group known as the Dark League. (Rev: VOYA 6/90)

1079 Cooke, Catherine. *Mask of the Wizard* (10–12). 1985, Tor paper $2.95 (0-8125-3384-4). A priestess tries to find allies to fight the army of the Dark. (Rev: VOYA 8/85)

1080 Cooper, Louise. *Inferno* (9–12). 1989, Tor paper $3.95 (0-812-50246-9). In this sequel to *Nemesis* (1989), Indigo must kill the demon she freed from the Tower of Regrets. (Rev: VOYA 4/90)

1081 Costello, Matthew J. *Wizard of Tizare* (9–12). 1990, Bantam paper $3.95 (0-553-28303-0). In this, the third novel in the Guardians of the Three series, the king of the mrem (beings who look like cats but act like men) is gradually losing his power to outsiders. (Rev: VOYA 8/90)

1082 Coville, Bruce. *The Dark Abyss* (10–12). 1989, Bantam paper $3.95 (0-553-27640-9). When searching for his missing twin brother, Clive is magically transported to "The Dungeon" in this second volume of this series. (Rev: VOYA 10/89)

1083 Dahl, Roald. *Two Fables* (10–12). Illus. 1987, Farrar $12.95 (0-374-28018-5). Two parables for adults involving princesses and magic kingdoms. (Rev: BL 9/1/87)

1084 Dann, Jack, and Gardner Dozois, eds. *Bestiary!* (9–12). 1985, Ace paper $2.95 (0-441-05506-0). A collection of short stories involving such exotic animals as the griffin, pegasus, centaur, and sphinx. (Rev: BL 10/1/85)

1085 David, Peter. *Knight Life* (10–12). 1987, Ace paper $2.95 (0-441-45130-6). In this witty spoof, King Arthur returns to life and visits New York City, where he plans to become mayor. (Rev: VOYA 10/87)

1086 de Camp, L. Sprague. *The Honorable Barbarian* (10–12). 1989, Ballantine $16.95 (0-345-36091-5). Young Kerin encounters sorcerers and demons on his journey to a strange land where he seeks knowledge about clocks. (Rev: BL 6/15/89; VOYA 2/90)

1087 Deitz, Tom. *Fireshaper's Doom* (9–12). 1987, Avon paper $3.50 (0-380-75329-4). Because he accidentally caused the death of a faerie boy, Sullivan faces the wrath of the boy's mother in this sequel to *Windmaster's Bane* (1984). (Rev: BL 11/15/87)

1088 Deitz, Tom. *Windmaster's Bane* (10–12). 1986, Avon paper $3.50 (0-380-75029-5). A man with second sight finds himself back in the time of legendary struggles involving the Celts. (Rev: BL 11/15/86)

1089 de Larrabeiti, Michael. *The Borribles* (10–12). 1984, Ace paper $2.50 (0-441-07024-8). The Borribles are young children growing up wild in London who fight the police and ratlike creatures called the Rumbles.

1090 De Lint, Charles. *Drink Down the Moon* (10–12). 1990, Berkley paper $3.50 (0-441-16861-2). In this fantasy set in modern Ottawa, Jackie Rowan becomes the prisoner of a wizard. This is a sequel to *Jack, the Giant Killer* (1990). (Rev: BL 5/15/90)

1091 De Lint, Charles. *Moonheart* (10–12). 1987, Ace paper $3.95 (0-317-63311-2). Various kinds of people are involved in this tale of a struggle between good and evil.

1092 Dickson, Gordon R. *The Dorsai Companion* (10–12). 1986, Ace paper $5.95 (0-441-16026-3). Four short stories that fill in the gaps in the author's extensive Dorsai series. (Rev: VOYA 12/86)

1093 Dickson, Gordon R. *The Last Dream* (9–12). 1986, Baen paper $2.95 (0-671-65559-0). Strange creatures such as witches and dragons inhabit this collection of short stories written over a period of 25 years. (Rev: VOYA 12/86)

1094 Donaldson, Stephen R. *Daughter of Regals and Other Tales* (10–12). 1985, Ballantine paper $4.95 (0-345-31443-3). Eight varying tales by the master of fantasy.

1095 Donaldson, Stephen R. *Lord Foul's Bane* (10–12). 1987, Ballantine paper $4.95 (0-345-34865-6). Thomas Covenant, a leper, finds himself in a magical world in this first volume of the Chronicles of Thomas Covenant the Unbeliever series. The others are *The Illearth War* and *The Power That Preserves* (both 1987).

1096 Donaldson, Stephen R. *A Man Rides Through* (10–12). 1987, Ballantine $19.95 (0-345-33299-7); paper $5.95 (0-345-35657-8). In the concluding volume of the fantasy begun in *The Mirror of Her Dreams* (1986), Terisa and Apt continue their struggle against the evil Mordant. (Rev: BL 10/1/87; VOYA 6/88)

1097 Donaldson, Stephen R. *The Mirror of Her Dreams* (10–12). 1986, Ballantine $19.95 (0-345-33298-9); paper $5.95 (0-345-34697-1). In this fantasy for better readers, a bumbling young sorcerer sets out to find a savior for the kingdom. (Rev: BL 8/86)

1098 Donaldson, Stephen R. *The Wounded Land* (10–12). 1987, Ballantine paper $4.95 (0-345-34868-0). This is the beginning of a second series about Thomas Covenant and his war against Lord Foul. Sequels are *The One Tree* (1987) and *White Gold Wielder* (1987).

1099 Douglas, Carole Nelson. *Keepers of Edanvant* (10–12). 1987, Tor $15.95 (0-312-93012-7); paper $3.95 (0-8125-3594-4). This volume about seeress Irissa and her lover Kendric concludes the trilogy that began with *Six of Swords* (1982) and *Exiles of the Rynth* (1984) and begins a new series. (Rev: BL 5/15/87; VOYA 12/87)

1100 Douglas, Carole Nelson. *Seven of Swords* (10–12). 1989, St. Martin's $18.95 (0-312-93142-5). Part of the Sword and Circlet series, this follows *Heir of Rengarth* (1988) and deals with 2 teenagers and their parents' struggle against the evil magician Geronfrey. (Rev: BL 2/1/89)

1101 Douglas, Carole Nelson. *Six of Swords* (10–12). 1986, Ballantine paper $3.50 (0-345-33564-3). The story of the growing love between a sorceress named Irissa and Kendric, a swordsman. Followed by *Exiles of the Rynth* (1984).

1102 Downer, Ann. *The Glass Salamander* (8–12). 1989, Macmillan $13.95 (0-689-31413-2). Caitlin sets out to find her son who has been taken to the Otherworld in this sequel to *The Spellkey* (1987). (Rev: BL 8/89; BR 3–4/90; SLJ 10/89; VOYA 12/89)

1103 Drake, David. *The Sea Hag* (9–12). 1988, Baen paper $3.95 (0-671-65424-1). This first volume in the World of Crystal Walls series is a fantasy about robots, aliens, and dragons all living together on a "home planet." (Rev: BL 8/88)

1104 Easton, M. Coleman. *The Fisherman's Curse* (10–12). 1987, Warner paper $3.50 (0-445-20332-3). A fisherman's curse brings forth a gigantic sea monster that begins ravaging the land in this sequel to *Masters of Glass* (1985). (Rev: BL 1/1/87)

1105 Eddings, David. *Demon Lord of Karanda* (10–12). 1988, Ballantine $18.95 (0-345-33004-1). This is the third quest fantasy in the planned 5 volumes of The Malloreon saga. The first 2 were *Guardians of the West* (1987) and *King of the Murgos* (1988). (Rev: BL 6/15/88; VOYA 4/89)

1106 Eddings, David. *The Diamond Throne* (10–12). 1989, Ballantine $18.95 (0-345-35691-8). In this, the first volume of a new Elenium series, the forces of good versus evil are once more in combat. For older readers. (Rev: BL 3/15/89; VOYA 12/89)

1107 Eddings, David. *Enchanters' End Game* (10–12). 1986, Ballantine paper $5.95 (0-345-33871-5). This is the fifth and last volume in the series about Garion's battle against the evil god Torak called the Belgariad Saga. The other volumes from the beginning are *The Pawn of Prophecy*, *Queen of Sorcery*, *Magician's Gambit* (all 1986), and *Castle of Wizardry* (1985).

1108 Eddings, David. *Guardians of the West* (10–12). 1987, Ballantine $16.95 (0-345-33000-5); paper $4.95 (0-345-35266-1). The beginning volume of a saga about King Garion. In this installment he sets out to save his son from an evil force. (Rev: BL 3/1/87)

1109 Eddings, David. *Sorceress of Darshiva* (10–12). 1989, Ballantine $19.95 (0-345-33005-6). In this, the fourth of a five-part series, Garion and his friends continue the search for Garion's son, stolen by Zandramas. (Rev: BL 10/1/89)

1110 Eisenstein, Phyllis. *The Sorcerer's Son* (10–12). 1989, NAL paper $3.95 (0-451-15683-8). A young man sets out to find his father, a gentle sorcerer.

1111 Ende, Michael. *Momo* (10–12). Trans. by J. Maxwell Brownjohn. Illus. 1985, Doubleday $14.95 (0-385-19093-X); Penguin paper $6.95 (0-14-007916-5). In this fantasy, a girl named Momo has the power to make people think great thoughts. (Rev: BL 1/1/85; VOYA 8/85)

1112 Ende, Michael. *The Neverending Story* (7–12). Trans. by Ralph Manheim. 1984, Penguin paper $8.95 (0-14-007431-7). An overweight boy with many problems enters the magic world of Fantastica in this charming fantasy.

1113 Estes, Rose. *Brother to the Lion* (9–12). 1988, Bantam paper $3.50 (0-553-27213-6). In the second volume of the Saga of the Lost Lands trilogy, Emri and Hawk continue their search for security in prehistoric North America. (Rev: VOYA 4/89)

1114 Farmer, Philip Jose. *A Barnstormer in Oz* (10–12). 1983, Berkley paper $2.95 (0-425-06274-0). In this variation on the Oz books, Glinda, the Good Witch, is helped by Dorothy's son.

1115 Farmer, Philip Jose. *The Lavalite World* (10–12). 1985, Berkley paper $2.95 (0-425-08625-9). Paul Janus Finnegan becomes a warrior when he moves into a new universe. This is one of many recommended books in the World of Tiers series.

1116 Feist, Raymond E. *A Darkness at Sethanon* (10–12). 1987, Bantam paper $4.50 (0-553-26328-5). Prince Arutha sets out to secure the powerful Lifestone in this sequel to *Magician* (1982) and *Silverthorn* (1985). (Rev: BL 3/1/86)

1117 Feist, Raymond E. *Prince of the Blood* (9–12). 1989, Doubleday $18.95 (0-385-23624-7). Prince Arutha sends his twin sons to Kesh to learn how to become kings in this sequel to *A Darkness at Sethanon* (1986). (Rev: BL 9/1/89; VOYA 6/90)

1118 Feist, Raymond E. *Silverthorn* (10–12). 1985, Bantam paper $3.95 (0-553-25928-8). Squire Jimmy joins Prince Arutha on a quest to find the silverthorn plant that has amazing medicinal powers in this sequel to *Magician* (1982). (Rev: BL 7/85; VOYA 12/85)

1119 Fisher, Paul R. *The Ash Staff* (10–12). 1984, Ace paper $2.25 (0-441-03116-1). Mole and his band of orphans fight an evil sorcerer. Also use: *The Hawks of Fellheath* (1984).

1120 Fisher, Paul R. *The Princess and the Thorn* (10–12). 1984, Ace paper $2.25 (0-441-67918-8). This fantasy is part of the Magic Quest series. Also use: *Mont Cant Gold* (1985).

1121 Flint, Kenneth C. *Cromm* (10–12). 1990, Doubleday $19.95 (0-385-26749-5); paper $8.95 (0-385-26750-9). A young artist finds that he is really the reincarnation of a Celtic warrior whose henchmen are out to find him. (Rev: BL 3/1/90)

1122 Flint, Kenneth C. *The Dark Druid* (10–12). 1987, Bantam paper $3.50 (0-553-26715-9). A Celtic fantasy about Finn, a legendary warrior, and his love for the beautiful Sabd. (Rev: VOYA 2/88)

1123 Foster, Alan Dean. *Spellsinger* (10–12). 1983, Warner paper $4.95 (0-446-35647-6). A young graduate student named Jonathan Meriweather is summoned to another world to lead a struggle for freedom. Others in this series are: *The Hour of the Gate, The Day of the Dissonance* (Phantasia, both 1984), and *The Moment of the Magician* (Phantasia, 1986).

1124 Friedman, Michael Jan. *The Glove of Maiden's Hair* (10–12). 1987, Warner paper $3.50 (0-445-20406-0). An elf from Norse mythology finds himself in the New York of the 1980s. (Rev: BL 3/15/87)

1125 Friedman, Michael Jan. *The Hammer and the Horn* (10–12). 1985, Warner paper $2.95 (0-445-20028-6). In this variation on Norse mythology, Vidar and Modi help recover Thor's hammer.

1126 Friesner, Esther M. *Elf Defense* (10–12). 1988, NAL paper $3.50 (0-451-15230-1). A comic fantasy involving the complications when a

mortal wants to divorce her elf husband. (Rev: BL 3/15/88)

1127 Friesner, Esther. *Hooray for Hellywood* (10–12). 1990, Berkley paper $3.50 (0-441-34281-7). In this continuation of *Here Be Demons* (1988) and *Demon Blues* (1989), demon Melisan Cardiff fights an evangelist who is really an evil spirit. (Rev: BL 2/1/90)

1128 Gardner, Craig Shaw. *A Disagreement with Death* (9–12). 1989, Ace paper $3.50 (0-441-14924-3). Wuntvor sets out to free his master, a renowned mage in this third volume of the Tehe Ballad of Wuntvor trilogy. Preceded by *A Difficulty with Dwarves* and *An Excess of Enchantment* (both 1989). (Rev: VOYA 10/89)

1129 Gardner, John. *Grendel* (10–12). 1971, Knopf $15.95 (0-394-47143-1); Random paper $4.95 (0-394-74056-4). A retelling of the Beowulf legend, from the standpoint of the monster Grendel.

1130 Garfield, Leon. *The Wedding Ghost* (9–12). Illus. 1987, Oxford Univ. Pr. $12.95 (0-19-279779-4). An unusual picture-book fantasy that re-creates a variation on the Sleeping Beauty story. (Rev: BL 4/15/87; SLJ 6–7/87)

1131 Garrett, Randall. *Lord Darcy Investigates* (10–12). 1983, Ace paper $2.75 (0-441-49142-1). This mystery involves Lord Darcy, a detective in an alternate world. Two others of his adventures are: *Murder and Magic* (1982) and *Too Many Magicians* (1983).

1132 Goldin, Stephen. *Crystals of Air and Water* (9–12). 1989, Bantam paper $3.95 (0-553-27711-1). In this, the third volume of the Parsina Saga, Prince Ahmad and his friends continue their search for the pieces of the Crystal of Oromasd. (Rev: VOYA 8/89)

1133 Goldman, William, reteller. *The Princess Bride: S. Morgenstern's Classic Tale of True Love and High Adventure* (9–12). 1982, Ballantine paper $3.95 (0-345-34803-6). A hilarious fast-paced fantasy with a hero named Westley and a heroine named Buttercup.

1134 Gray, Nicholas Stuart. *The Seventh Swan* (10–12). 1984, Ace paper $2.25 (0-441-75955-6). An imaginative continuation of the Andersen fairy tale.

1135 Greeley, Andrew M. *The Magic Cup* (10–12). 1987, Warner paper $3.95 (0-446-34903-8). Themes from ancient Irish history are cleverly woven into this fantasy.

1136 Hale, F. J. *In the Sea Nymph's Lair* (9–12). 1989, Crown paper $2.95 (0-517-00935-8). The wizard Durril, his apprentice, and an ogre fight an evil sea monster in this continuation of: *Ogre Castle* (1988). (Rev: BL 2/15/89)

1137 Hale, F. J. *Ogre Castle* (10–12). 1988, Crown paper $2.95 (0-517-99648-0). In this first volume of the Spell Wars series, a wizard and his apprentice set off to capture an ogre. (Rev: BL 9/1/88)

1138 Hambly, Barbara. *Dragonsbane* (10–12). 1986, Ballantine paper $3.95 (0-345-34939-3). In a declining empire, John Aversin sets out to kill a predatory dragon. (Rev: BL 2/15/86; SLJ 9/86; VOYA 8–10/86)

1139 Hambly, Barbara. *The Silent Tower* (10–12). 1986, Ballantine paper $3.95 (0-345-33764-6). A computer programmer leaves her world and enters a land of magic spells and sorcerers in this first volume of a trilogy. (Rev: BL 12/1/86)

1140 Hambly, Barbara. *The Silicon Mage* (10–12). 1988, Ballantine paper $3.95 (0-345-33763-8). Joanna joins her wizard lover in his battle against the Dark Mage. (Rev: BL 4/15/88)

1141 Hambly, Barbara. *The Time of the Dark* (10–12). 1984, Ballantine paper $3.50 (0-345-31965-6). In this the first part of the Darweth trilogy, a wizard and a prince flee the powers of the Dark. Followed by: *The Walls of Air* and *The Armies of Daylight* (both 1983).

1142 Hamlett, Christina. *The Enchanter* (9–12). 1990, Evans $15.95 (0-87131-610-2). A fantasy in which Merlin travels to present-day America to find his true love and rescue Excalibur from the Smithsonian. (Rev: BL 9/1/90)

1143 Hamley, Dennis. *Blood Line* (9–12). 1990, Andre Deutsch paper $7.95 (0-233-98445-3). This unusual fantasy begins when all of the channels on Roy's television set show a program that no one else at school has seen. (Rev: BL 9/1/90)

1144 Harding, Lee. *Misplaced Persons* (10–12). 1979, Harper LB $7.89 (0-06-022217-4). Three misfits find themselves in an alien world.

1145 Harris, Deborah Turner. *The Gauntlet of Malice* (10–12). 1988, Tor paper $7.95 (0-812-53952-4). The second installment of The Mages of Garrillon trilogy, about Caradoc and his fight against the evil Borthen Berigeld. Preceded by: *The Burning Stone* (1988). (Rev: BL 3/1/88)

1146 Hartwell, David G., and Kathryn Cramer, eds. *Masterpieces of Fantasy and Enchantment* (9–12). 1988, St. Martin's $19.95 (0-312-02250-6). A fine collection that might serve as a good introduction to this genre. (Rev: BL 8/88)

1147 Hawke, Simon. *The Ivanhoe Gambit* (10–12). 1987, Ace paper $2.95 (0-441-37765-3). In this time-travel novel, Sergeant Major Lucas Priest goes back to events in English history. Also use: *The Pimpernel Plot* and *The Timekeeper Conspiracy* ;(both 1987).

1148 Helprin, Mark. *Winter's Tale* (10–12). 1983, Harcourt $14.95 (0-15-197203-6); Pocket paper $4.95 (0-671-62118-1). In the year 2000 a master burglar decides to stop time in this clever fantasy.

1149 Herbert, Brian. *Sudanna, Sudanna* (10–12). 1985, Berkley paper $2.95 (0-425-08786-7). An allegorical fantasy about some docile creatures living on the planet Ut who are conquered by invaders. (Rev: BL 2/1/85)

1150 Herbert, Frank, and Bill Ransom. *The Ascension Factor* (10–12). 1989, Ace paper $4.50 (0-441-03127-7). This is the third fantasy by these authors to take place in the underwater world of Pandora. Preceded by: *The Jesus Factor* (1985) and *The Lazarus Effect* (1984). (Rev: BL 12/15/87)

1151 Hesse, Hermann. *Pictor's Metamorphoses and Other Fantasies* (10–12). 1982, Farrar $15.95 (0-374-23212-1); paper $9.95 (0-374-51723-1). A collection of pieces that fall into many categories—fantasy, fairy tales, dreams, legends.

1152 Hilton, James. *Lost Horizon* (9–12). 1983, Buccaneer $16.95 (0-89966-450-4); Pocket paper $3.95 (0-671-54148-X). This fantasy is about Shangri-la, a land where time stands still.

1153 Hindle, Lee J. *Dragon Fall* (9–12). 1984, Avon paper $2.95 (0-380-88468-2). The monsters Gabe creates for a toy company come alive and try to kill him.

1154 Hodgell, P. C. *Dark of the Moon* (10–12). 1985, Macmillan $19.95 (0-689-31171-0); Berkley paper $3.50 (0-425-09561-4). For better readers, this is a fantasy about an exiled girl and her search for her brother. (Rev: BL 11/1/85; SLJ 1/85; VOYA 4/86)

1155 Holdstock, Robert. *Lavondyss* (10–12). 1989, Morrow $18.95 (0-688-09185-7). This book tells the story of how Tallis Keeton continues her lifelong search for her brother. This is the sequel to *Mythago Wood* (1985). (Rev: BL 8/89)

1156 Holt, Tom. *Who's Afraid of Beowulf?* (9–12). 1988, St. Martin's $15.95 (0-312-02669-2). In this time-warp story, a present-day archaeologist and some ancient Vikings combat an evil wizard. (Rev: BL 1/15/89; VOYA 6/89)

1157 Hudson, W. H. *Green Mansions: A Romance of the Tropical Forest* (10–12). 1982, Buccaneer LB $19.95 (0-89966-374-5). The haunting novel of a naturalist's encounter with the bird-girl, Rima, in a South American jungle.

1158 Huff, Tanya. *Gate of Darkness, Circle of Light* (10–12). 1989, DAW paper $3.95 (0-88677-386-5). Rebecca and her friend save the Earth from the Adept of Darkness. (Rev: VOYA 4/90)

1159 Huff, Tanya. *The Last Wizard* (10–12). 1989, DAW paper $3.95 (0-88677-331-8). Crystal was formed by the merging of 7 goddesses who now want their individual freedom. (Rev: VOYA 10/89)

1160 James, Betsy. *Long Night Dance* (8–12). 1989, Dutton $12.95 (0-525-44485-8). A girl from a mixed background sorts herself out with the help of the Rigi, a tribe who live across the water from her home. (Rev: BL 7/89; BR 3–4/90; SLJ 8/89; VOYA 10/89)

1161 Jordan, Robert. *Eye of the World* (10–12). 1990, Tor $21.95 (0-312-85009-3); paper $12.95 (0-812-50048-2). In this novel, the first of a series, a group of ordinary people flee from evil magic. (Rev: BL 10/1/89; VOYA 6/90)

1162 Jordan, Robert. *The Great Hunt* (10–12). 1990, Tor $22.95 (0-312-85140-5). In this second volume of the Wheel of Time series, which began with *The Eye of the World* (1989), Rand Al Thor realizes that he is the Dragon Reporb and must lead his forces against darkness. (Rev: BL 10/15/90)

1163 Kafka, Franz. *The Metamorphosis* (10–12). 1972, Bantam paper $4.95 (0-553-21369-5). For mature readers, this is a fantastic horror story about a hapless man who is turned into an insect.

1164 Karr, Phyllis Ann. *Idylls of the Queen* (10–12). 1985, Berkley paper $2.95 (0-425-08080-3). A reworking of the Arthurian legend using as a focus a murder.

1165 Kavanaugh, James. *A Fable* (10–12). Illus. 1980, Dutton $8.95 (0-525-93154-6). This book reworks the theme of lust for gold in an ideal setting—the town of Harmony.

1166 Kay, Guy Gavriel. *The Darkest Road* (10–12). 1986, Morrow $22.95 (0-87795-822-X). For better readers, this concluding volume of a trilogy tells how Darien joins the power of Light and kills his evil father. Preceded by *The Summer Tree* and *The Wandering Fire* (both 1986). (Rev: BL 11/1/86; VOYA 4/87)

1167 Kerr, Katherine. *The Bristling Wood* (10–12). 1989, Doubleday $18.95 (0-385-24275-1). The third adventure of magician Nevynn, Prince Rhodry, and Jill in the fantasy series that began with *Daggerspell* (1987) and *Darkspell* (1987). (Rev: BL 1/15/89; SLJ 1/90)

1168 Kerr, Katherine. *Darkspell* (10–12). 1987, Doubleday $17.95 (0-385-23109-1); Ballantine pa-

per $3.95 (0-345-34431-6). Three companions combat a group of evil sorcerers in this sequel to *Daggerspell* (1987). (Rev: BL 9/1/87)

1169 Kerr, Katherine. *The Dragon Revenant* (10–12). 1990, Doubleday $18.95 (0-385-26140-3); paper $8.95 (0-385-41098-0). In this sequel to *The Bristling Wood* (1989), also set in Celtic Deverry, the ancient mage Nevynn is targeted for death. (Rev: BL 4/15/90)

1170 King, Stephen. *The Drawing of the Three* (10–12). Illus. 1989, NAL paper $12.95 (0-452-26214-3). Roland lives out the predictions of tarot cards dealt him by the man in black in the first volume in King's The Dark Tower fantasy series, *The Gunslinger* (1988). (Rev: BL 12/15/88)

1171 King, Stephen. *The Eyes of the Dragon* (9–12). 1987, Viking $18.95 (0-670-81458-X); NAL paper $4.95 (0-451-16658-2). In this tale of potions and evil magic, a king dies mysteriously and his older son is unjustly accused. (Rev: BL 11/1/86; BR 9–10/87; SLJ 6–7/87; VOYA 8–9/87)

1172 King, Stephen. *The Gunslinger* (10–12). Illus. 1988, NAL paper $10.95 (0-452-26134-1). A young marksman and a boy stalk a man in black in this, volume one of The Dark Tower series. (Rev: BL 7/88)

1173 King, Stephen, and Peter Straub. *The Talisman* (10–12). 1984, Viking $22.95 (0-670-69199-2); Berkley paper $5.95 (0-425-10533-4). For mature readers, the story of a 12-year-old boy and his search in 2 different worlds for a stone that will save his mother's life. (Rev: BL 1/15/85)

1174 Koontz, Dean R. *Lightning* (10–12). 1988, Putnam $18.95 (0-399-13319-4); Berkley paper $4.95 (0-425-11580-1). For better readers, a fast-paced novel about Laura's guardian angel who turns out to be a time-traveler from Nazi Germany. (Rev: BL 12/15/87)

1175 Kurtz, Katherine. *Camber of Culdi* (10–12). 1987, Ballantine paper $3.95 (0-345-34767-6). In this first volume of the Legends of Camber of Culdi series the Deryni, a race with unusual mental powers, revolt against their cruel masters. Others in the series are *Saint Camber* and *Camber the Heretic* (both 1987).

1176 Kurtz, Katherine. *The Deryni Archives* (10–12). 1987, Ballantine paper $3.95 (0-345-32628-4). A collection of short pieces that serve to introduce readers to the author's major creation—the Deryni. (Rev: BL 8/86; SLJ 11/86; VOYA 12/86)

1177 Kurtz, Katherine. *Deryni Rising* (10–12). 1987, Ballantine paper $3.95 (0-345-34763-3). The 14-year-old King Kelson finds his power challenged by the misuse of Deryni magic. Another in the series includes *Deryni Checkmate (1987)*.

1178 Kurtz, Katherine. *The Harrowing of Gwynedd* (10–12). 1989, Ballantine $17.95 (0-345-33259-8). For older teens the beginning of a fantasy trilogy, The Heirs of Saint Camber, which again involves the persecuted race of the Dernyi. (Rev: BL 1/1/89; SLJ 1/90; VOYA 8/89)

1179 Kurtz, Katherine. *The King's Justice* (10–12). 1985, Ballantine $16.95 (0-345-31825-0); paper $3.95 (0-345-34762-5). For better readers, this is the second novel about young King Kelson, his search for a bride, and his war against the enemies of Deryni. (Rev: BL 10/1/85; SLJ 2/86)

1180 Kurtz, Katherine. *Lammas Night* (10–12). 1983, Ballantine paper $3.95 (0-345-29516-1). In this fantasy set during World War II, a group of English witches try to contact Hitler.

1181 Kurtz, Katherine. *The Quest for Saint Camber* (10–12). 1986, Ballantine $16.95 (0-345-31826-9); paper $3.95 (0-345-30099-8). In this third novel in the Histories of King Kelson series, King Kelson, now 18, must fight the evil power of Conal who has usurped his throne. (Rev: BL 7/86; SLJ 12/86)

1182 Kushner, Ellen. *Thomas the Rhymer* (10–12). 1990, Morrow $16.95 (1-557-10046-2). Based on a folktale, this fantasy tells about a man who can only tell the truth. (Rev: BL 3/15/90)

1183 Lackey, Mercedes. *Arrow's Fall* (10–12). 1988, NAL paper $3.50 (0-88677-255-9). The last part of the Valdemar trilogy about Talia, the Queen's Own Herald. Preceded by: *Arrows of the Queen* and *Arrow's Flight* (both 1987). (Rev: BL 1/15/88)

1184 Lackey, Mercedes. *Magic's Price* (10–12). 1990, NAL paper $4.50 (0-88677-426-8). For mature teens, a fantasy in which Vanyel is pitted against the murderous Master Dark. This is the third novel of the Last Herald-Mage trilogy. Preceded by *Magic's Pawn* (1989) and *Magic's Promise* (1990). (Rev: BL 8/90)

1185 Lahey, Michael. *Quest for Apollo* (9–12). 1989, DAW paper $3.95 (0-88677-364-4). Del and Virgil travel back to ancient Rome in their search for Apollo. (Rev: VOYA 2/90)

1186 Lanier, Sterling E. *Hiero's Journey* (10–12). 1983, Ballantine paper $3.50 (0-345-30841-7). Hiero's quest leads him into conflict with the Unclean. Followed by: *The Unforsaken Hiero* (1984).

1187 Lawhead, Stephen R. *Arthur* (10–12). 1989, Crossway paper $10.95 (0-89107-475-9). The third and final volume about King Arthur and his knights. Previous books in the Pendragon Cycle were *Taliesin* (1987) and *Merlin* (1988). (Rev: BL 8/89; VOYA 2/90)

1188 Lawhead, Stephen R. *Merlin* (10–12). 1988, Crossway paper $10.95 (0-89107-436-8). The story of how Merlin prepared the world for the arrival of Arthur. (Rev: VOYA 4/89)

1189 Lee, Tanith. *Anackire* (10–12). 1983, DAW paper $3.95 (0-88677-274-5). A fantasy about a villain whose career resembles that of Richard III.

1190 Lee, Tanith. *The Storm Land* (10–12). 1976, DAW paper $3.95 (0-88677-273-7). A story about clashing empires, a hero, and a hidden goddess who helps him. A sequel is *Anackire* (1983). Some other novels by this well-liked author are: *The Dragon Hoard* (1986), *East of Midnight, The Gorgon—And Other Beastly Tales* (both 1985).

1191 Le Guin, Ursula K. *The Beginning Place* (9–12). 1980, Harper $15.45 (0-06-012573-X). Two young people who have escaped reality in a world of fantasy find there is evil in their Eden.

1192 Le Guin, Ursula K. *Very Far Away from Anywhere Else* (9–12). 1982, Bantam paper $2.50 (0-553-25396-4). An unusual girl helps a troubled teenager sort himself out.

1193 Le Guin, Ursula K. *The Wind's Twelve Quarters* (10–12). 1987, Harper paper $6.95 (0-06-091434-3). This collection includes 17 stories by Le Guin, the winner of both Hugo and Nebula awards.

1194 Lichtenberg, Jacqueline. *Dreamspy* (10–12). 1989, St. Martin's $19.95 (0-312-03327-3). In this exciting fantasy, Kyllikki and her companions struggle against the forces of an evil cousin, Zimor. (Rev: VOYA 6/90)

1195 Lillington, Kenneth. *An Ash-Blonde Witch* (9–12). 1987, Faber $10.95 (0-571-14625-2). Two very different witches compete while their villagers try to stop the strange events that result. (Rev: BL 1/15/87)

1196 Lindholm, Megan. *Luck of the Wheels* (10–12). 1989, Berkley paper $3.50 (0-441-50436-1). For older readers, an action-filled fantasy about a plot to depose an evil duke and a dislikable teenager with telepathic powers. (Rev: BL 12/1/89)

1197 Llewelyn, Morgan. *Isles of the Blest* (9–12). 1989, Berkley paper $3.95 (0-441-36610-4). Based on a Celtic legend this is the story of

Connla and his trip to the isles where there is eternal peace. (Rev: BL 5/15/89; VOYA 12/89)

1198 Macaulay, David. *Baaa* (7–12). Illus. 1985, Houghton $13.95 (0-395-38948-8); paper $4.95 (0-395-39588-7). An allegory about the world after humans have left and intelligent sheep take control. (Rev: BL 9/1/85; BR 3–4/86; SLJ 10/85)

1199 MacAvoy, R. A. *Damiano* (10–12). 1983, Bantam paper $2.95 (0-553-25347-6). The beginning of a well-received fantasy trilogy that continues in *Damiano's Lute* and *Raphael* (both 1984).

1200 MacAvoy, R. A. *The Grey Horse* (10–12). 1987, Bantam paper $3.95 (0-553-26557-1). A fantasy involving a wizard who visits nineteenth-century Ireland. (Rev: BL 7/87)

1201 MacAvoy, R. A. *Lens of the World* (10–12). 1990, Morrow $17.95 (0-688-09484-8). In this fantasy for better readers, which is also the beginning of a projected series, an orphan dwarf saves the life of a king. (Rev: BL 5/1/90)

1202 MacAvoy, R. A. *Tea with the Black Dragon* (10–12). 1984, Putnam paper $3.95 (0-553-27992-0). This novel begins realistically with a mother's search for her lost daughter in San Francisco and then enters the realm of fantasy.

1203 McCaffrey, Anne. *Nerilka's Story: A Pern Adventure* (9–12). 1986, Ballantine paper $4.95 (0-345-33949-5). A young girl leaves her Hold to help nurse the sick stricken with a terrible plague. (Rev: BL 3/1/86; SLJ 5/86)

1204 McCaffrey, Anne. *The Renegades of Pern* (9–12). 1989, Ballantine $19.95 (0-345-34096-5). The adult Dragonriders series and the juvenile Harper Hall books are brought together by mixing their characters in this fantasy that takes place in the southern part of Pern. (Rev: BL 9/15/89; VOYA 4/90)

1205 McKiernan, Dennis L. *Dragondoom* (10–12). 1990, Bantam paper $4.50 (0-553-28337-5). This quest tale about a prince and princess who are twins deals with a world where people, dragons, dwarfs, and wizards coexist. (Rev: VOYA 6/90)

1206 McKillip, Patricia A. *The Throme of the Erril of Sherill* (10–12). 1987, Ace paper $2.95 (0-441-80840-9). In a world of magic and wizards, the Crite is searching for the Throme.

1207 McKinley, Robin. *Beauty: A Retelling of the Story of Beauty and the Beast* (9–12). 1978, Harper LB $13.89 (0-06-024150-0). From the standpoint of Beauty, this is the story of her quest in the forest where she encounters Beast.

1208 McKinley, Robin, ed. *Imaginary Lands* (9–12). 1986, Greenwood $11.75 (0-688-05213-4). A collection of 9 stories about imaginary lands by such writers as Joan D. Vinge and Patricia McKillip. (Rev: BL 12/15/85; SLJ 5/86; VOYA 10/86)

1209 MacLeish, Rod. *Prince Ombra* (10–12). 1983, Tor paper $3.50 (0-8125-4550-8). The task of defeating evil Prince Ombra is given to an 8-year-old.

1210 MacLeod, Charlotte. *The Curse of the Giant Hogweed* (10–12). 1986, Avon paper $3.50 (0-380-70051-4). A humorous fantasy about an American professor suddenly adrift in medieval Wales. (Rev: BL 2/15/85)

1211 Mahy, Margaret. *The Changeover: A Supernatural Romance* (8–12). 1984, Macmillan $12.95 (0-689-50303-2). To save her brother from an evil force, Laura must use the powers of witchcraft.

1212 Mahy, Margaret. *The Tricksters* (9–12). 1987, Macmillan $13.95 (0-689-50400-4); Scholastic paper $2.95 (0-590-41513-1). The Hamilton family is torn asunder when 3 mysterious men visit their New Zealand vacation home at Christmastime. (Rev: BL 3/1/87; BR 11–12/87; SLJ 3/87; VOYA 6/87)

1213 Martin, George R. *The Armageddon Rag* (10–12). 1983, Ultramarine $20.00 (0-89366-150-3). A rock group of the 1960s is resurrected in the 1980s.

1214 Martin, George R., and Lisa Tuttle. *Windhaven* (10–12). 1980, Ultramarine $20.00 (0-671-25277-1). In this fantasy, a woman defies the conventions of her world.

1215 Marzollo, Jean. *Halfway Down Paddy Lane* (7–12). 1981, Dial $9.95 (0-8037-3329-1). A time-travel story about a girl who is transported to a New England mill town of 1850.

1216 May, Julian. *The Many-Colored Land* (10–12). 1985, Ballantine paper $4.95 (0-345-32444-7). This, the first of the Saga of Pliocene Exile, tells of the Earth in 6 million B.C. The others are: *The Golden Tore* (1985), *The Nonborn King*, and *The Adversary* (both 1987).

1217 Mayhar, Ardath. *Lords of the Triple Moons* (10–12). 1984, Ace paper $2.50 (0-441-49246-0). Johab seeks revenge on the rulers who have killed his family.

1218 Mayhar, Ardath. *Makra Choria* (7–10). 1987, Macmillan $13.95 (0-689-31326-8). The story of 2 royal sisters who are blessed (and cursed) with the amazing Gift of Power. (Rev: BR 11–12/87)

1219 Mayhar, Ardath. *Runes of the Lyre* (10–12). 1983, Ace paper $2.75 (0-441-73690-4).

Yinri finds a magic lyre and hopes to use it in a fight against evil enemies.

1220 Meaney, Dee Morrison. *Iseult: Dreams That Are Done* (10–12). 1985, Ace paper $2.95 (0-441-37387-9). A magical retelling of the Tristan and Iseult story that uses elements of fantasy. (Rev: BL 10/1/85; VOYA 4/86)

1221 Michaels, Melisa C. *Far Harbor* (9–12). 1989, Tor paper $3.95 (0-812-54580-X). A fantasy romance in which a clumsy, lanky girl meets the prince of her dreams. (Rev: VOYA 12/89)

1222 Miesel, Sandra. *Shaman* (9–12). 1989, Baen paper $3.50 (0-671-69844-3). A girl realizes that her kinship with otters will eventually help the human race. (Rev: BL 9/1/89)

1223 Moorcock, Michael. *The Jewel in the Skull* (10–12). 1990, Ace paper $3.50 (0-441-31847-9). This is the first of the History of the Runestaff series about the conquest of Europe by the Dark Empire. Also use *Elric at the End of Time* (1985).

1224 Moorcock, Michael. *The War Hound and the World's Pain* (10–12). 1981, Ultramarine $20.00 (0-671-43708-9). A fantasy set in the time of the Thirty Years' War from 1618 to 1648.

1225 Morressy, John. *Kedrigern and the Charming Couple* (10–12). 1990, Berkley paper $3.50 (0-441-43265-4). A sorcerer and his wife must race against time to prevent a princess from being turned into a wolf. (Rev: BL 12/1/89)

1226 Morressy, John. *A Voice for a Princess* (10–12). 1986, Berkley paper $2.95 (0-441-84800-1). An aged wizard leaves his guild and goes out into the world. (Rev: BL 4/1/87)

1227 Morris, Janet. *Dream Dancer* (10–12). 1984, Berkley paper $2.95 (0-425-07688-1). A bitter rivalry between 2 half-brothers is the focus of the Kerrion trilogy. The other 2 volumes are: *Cruiser Dreams* (1983) and *Earth Dreams* (1984).

1228 Murphy, Pat. *The Falling Woman: A Fantasy* (10–12). 1986, Tor $14.95 (0-312-93230-8); paper $3.95 (0-8125-4622-9). While doing archaeological work, Elizabeth Butler conjures up the ghost of a Mayan priestess. (Rev: BL 9/1/86; VOYA 4/87)

1229 Myers, John M. *Silverlock* (10–12). 1984, Ace paper $4.95 (0-441-76674-9). An allegory on the development of the human spirit that contains such characters as Don Quixote and Babe, the Blue Ox.

1230 Newman, Sharon. *Guinevere* (10–12). 1984, St. Martin's paper $5.95 (0-312-35321-9). A fantasy that re-creates the life of young Guinevere of Arthurian times.

1231 Niven, Larry, ed. *The Magic Goes Away* (10–12). 1985, Ace paper $3.95 (0-441-51554-1). The first novel in a trilogy about a land where magic is used for both good and evil. It is followed by: *The Magic May Return* (1983) and *More Magic* (1984).

1232 Norton, Andre. *Gryphon in Glory* (10–12). 1986, Ballantine paper $2.95 (0-345-34243-7). A cloven-hoofed man and his wife journey to find secrets of his past. This is a sequel to *Crystal Gryphon* (1985).

1233 Norton, Andre. *Gryphon's Eyrie* (10–12). Illus. 1989, Tor paper $3.95 (0-8125-0360-0). In this installment of the Witch World series, 2 young lovers tell, in alternating chapters, of their war against the Dark.

1234 Norton, Andre. *Lavender-Green Magic* (9–12). Illus. 1974, Harper $13.94 (0-690-00429-X); Ace paper $2.75 (0-441-47443-8). Three children move to a town where they find themselves surrounded by ancient curses and magic. Also use *Moon Called* (Tor, 1985) and *Wheel of Stars* (Tor, 1984).

1235 Norton, Andre. *Moon Mirror* (10–12). 1989, Tor $17.95 (0-312-93098-4). Nine short fantasies about such subjects as ESP, witches, magic, and quests. (Rev: BL 1/1/89; VOYA 6/89)

1236 Norton, Andre, ed. *Tales of the Witch World 2* (10–12). 1988, Tor $18.95 (0-312-93078-X). The second group of stories by various authors about Ms. Norton's famous imaginary location, Witch World. (Rev: BL 7/88)

1237 Norton, Andre. *Ware Hawk* (10–12). 1984, Ballantine paper $2.95 (0-345-31685-1). Tirtha and a Falconer battle the forces of the Dark and the Light.

1238 Norton, Andre. *Witch World* (10–12). 1986, Ace paper $3.50 (0-441-94255-5). This is the beginning of the extensive Witch World series featuring the Tregarth family. In order, some others are: *Web of the Witch World* (1986), *Year of the Unicorn* (1989), *Three against the Witch World* (1986), and *Zarsthor's Bane* (1989). Year of the Unicorn Zarsthor's Bane

1239 Norton, Andre, and Robert Adams, eds. *Magic in Ithkar II* (9–12). 1985, Tor paper $6.95 (0-812-54745-4). There are 13 fantasy stories by different writers all dealing with the Fair at Ithkar. This is a sequel to *Magic in Ithkar I* (1985). Also use: *Magic in Ithkar IV* (1987). (Rev: BL 2/1/86; VOYA 4/86)

1240 Norton, Andre, and Susan Shwartz. *Imperial Lady: A Fantasy of Han China* (10–12). 1989, Tor $17.95 (0-312-93128-X). A fantasy based on a Chinese folktale about a woman who uses her wits to save herself and husband from barbaric nomads. (Rev: BL 8/89; VOYA 6/90)

1241 Nye, Robert. *Beowulf: A New Telling* (10–12). 1982, Dell paper $2.95 (0-440-90560-5). An imaginative, sometimes humorous reworking of the ancient epic.

1242 Orgill, Douglas, and John Gribbin. *Brother Esau* (10–12). 1984, Tor paper $2.95 (0-8125-8680-8). This novel tells what happens when an abominable snowman is actually captured.

1243 Orwell, George. *Animal Farm* (9–12). Illus. 1983, Harcourt $12.95 (0-15-107252-3); NAL paper $3.50 (0-451-52230-3). A fantasy of world politics in which farm animals revolt to form a society in which everyone is meant to be equal.

1244 Palmer, David R. *Threshold* (10–12). 1985, Bantam paper $2.95 (0-553-24878-2). A would-be hero faces an unbelievably difficult set of tests. (Rev: BL 11/15/85)

1245 Pini, Richard, et al., eds. *The Blood of Ten Chiefs* (10–12). 1986, Tor paper $6.95 (0-8125-3041-1). A collection of several stories, each dealing with one of the kings of the Wolfriders made famous in the Elfquest series. (Rev: BL 2/1/87)

1246 Pini, Wendy, and Richard Pini. *Elfquest* (10–12). 1984, Berkley paper $3.50 (0-425-09039-6). The story of the wanderings of the Elf tribe, who ride wolves.

1247 Piper, H. Beam. *Federation* (10–12). 1986, Ace paper $3.50 (0-441-23191-8). A collection of 5 interrelated stories by this author. Also use: *Lord Kalvan of Otherwhere* (1984) and *Empire* (1981).

1248 Piper, H. Beam. *Fuzzies and Other People* (10–12). 1984, Ace paper $2.95 (0-441-26177-9). The last of the fuzzy trilogy that began with *Little Fuzzy* and *Fuzzy Sapiens* (both 1984).

1249 Pope, Elizabeth Marie. *The Perilous Gard* (9–12). 1984, Ace paper $2.25 (0-441-65956-X). Kate wants to save Christopher who has given himself as a sacrifice to the Fairy folk. Also use *The Sherwood Ring* (1985).

1250 Preiss, Byron, and Michael Reaves. *Dragonworld* (10–12). 1983, Bantam paper $4.95 (0-553-25857-5). Two feuding countries are menaced by a danger from without.

1251 Rabkin, Eric S., ed. *Fantastic Worlds: Myths, Tales and Stories* (10–12). 1979, Oxford Univ. Pr. $27.95 (0-19-502542-3); paper $14.95 (0-19-502541-5). A classic collection of fantasy and some science fiction from the ancient Greeks to the present. [808.8]

1252 Rawn, Melanie. *Dragon Prince* (10–12). 1988, DAW paper $3.95 (0-88677-312-1). Prince Rhoan wants to convert his land into a peaceful paradise but he is opposed by the nobleman Roelstra. (Rev: VOYA 4/89)

1253 Rawn, Melanie. *Sunrunner's Fire* (10–12). 1990, DAW paper $4.95 (0-88677-403-9). A fantasy that explores the classic struggle between good and evil. This book continues the series begun in *Dragon Prince* (1988) and *The Star Scroll* (1989)

1254 Reaves, Michael. *The Shattered World* (10–12). 1984, Baen $16.95 (0-671-49942-4). For better readers, this is a complex novel about treachery in the underworld.

1255 Reynolds, Mack, and Dean Ing. *The Other Time* (10–12). 1984, Baen paper $2.95 (0-671-55926-5). In this time-travel novel, an archaeologist visits the Aztecs.

1256 Rosenberg, Joel. *The Sleeping Dragon* (10–12). 1986, NAL paper $3.50 (0-451-15845-8). For better readers, this is the first part of the exciting Guardian of the Flame series. Others are: *Sword and the Chain* (1987); *The Silver Crown* (1985); *The Heir Apparent* (1987); and *Warrior Lives* (1988).

1257 Roth, David. *The Girl in the Grass* (10–12). n.d., Ballantine paper $2.25 (0-317-13277-6). A search is begun for a girl seen in a painting and in dreams.

1258 Ruff, Matt. *Fool on the Hill* (10–12). 1988, Atlantic Monthly $19.95 (0-87113-243-5); Warner paper $4.95 (0-446-35772-3). At Cornell University various student and town groups are being manipulated by mythological forces. (Rev: VOYA 4/89)

1259 Rush, Alison. *The Last of Danu's Children* (9–12). 1984, Tor paper $2.95 (0-8125-5250-4). Three teenagers become involved in the struggle between the forces of Good and Evil.

1260 Saberhagen, Fred. *The Fifth Book of Lost Swords: Coinspinner's Story* (10–12 6a1989). St. Martin's $16.95 (0-312-93142-5). The story of the magic sword that can both give and take away good luck continues with the evil magician Wood still trying to gain possession of it. The first 4 installments were: *The First Book of the Lost Swords: Woundhealer's Sword* (1986), *The Second Book of the Lost Swords: Sightbinder's Sword* (1987), *The Third Book of the Lost Swords: Stonecutter's Story* (1988), and *The Fourth Book of the Lost Swords: Farslayer's Story* (1989). (Rev: BL 11/1/89)

1261 Saberhagen, Fred. *Mindsword's Story* (10–12). 1990, St. Martin's paper $16.95 (0-312-

85128-6). In this, the sixth volume of the Lost Swords series, the magical Mindsword reappears and plays a part in the struggle against the Dark King. (Rev: BL 12/1/90)

1262 Saberhagen, Fred. *Pyramids* (10–12). 1987, Baen paper $3.50 (0-671-65609-0). A time traveler goes to ancient Egypt at a time when its gods were alive. (Rev: BL 12/1/86)

1263 Saha, Arthur W., ed. *The Year's Best Fantasy Stories: 14* (10–12). 1988, DAW paper $3.50 (0-88677-307-5). Each volume in this series that began in 1974 offers about a dozen top-flight stories collected from many sources.

1264 Salsitz, R. A. *Where Dragons Lie* (10–12). 1985, NAL paper $2.95 (0-451-14055-9). A princess, an old wizard, a dwarf, and a soldier's son set out to find the place where dragons go to die. (Rev: VOYA 6/86)

1265 Scarborough, Elizabeth Ann. *The Healer's War* (10–12). 1988, Doubleday $17.95 (0-385-24828-8). During the Vietnam War, an army nurse receives a magical amulet from a dying old Vietnamese man. (Rev: VOYA 6/89)

1266 Schwartz, Susan, ed. *Moonsinger's Friends* (10–12). 1985, Bluejay $16.95 (0-312-94325-3); paper $8.95 (0-312-94326-1). These 15 stories by such fantasy writers as Yolen, Cherryh, and Mc-Caffrey are all dedicated to Andre Norton and grouped according to themes often found in Norton's work. (Rev: BL 8/85; SLJ 11/85; VOYA 12/85)

1267 Sherman, Josepha. *The Shining Falcon* (10–12). 1989, Avon paper $3.95 (0-380-75436-3). A prince who is able to change shape is wounded while he is a falcon and is helped by a noblewoman. (Rev: BL 11/1/89)

1268 Shetterly, Will, and Emma Bull, eds. *Liavek* (10–12). 1985, Berkley paper $2.95 (0-441-48180-9). In this shared-world anthology the 11 stories all take place in the trading city of Liavek. This is the first of several additional compilations of stories about life in Liavek. Others in the series are: *Liavek: The Players of Luck* (1986), *Liavek: Wizard's Row* (1987), and *Liavek: Spells of Binding* (1988). (Rev: BL 8/85)

1269 Silverberg, Robert. *Dying Inside* (10–12). 1972, Ultramarine $20.00 (0-684-13083-1). David must pay the consequences when he misuses his powers to read people's minds.

1270 Simak, Clifford D. *The Fellowship of the Talisman* (10–12). n.d., Amereon $20.95 (0-89190-521-9). A questing novel set in a land in Europe during the Middle Ages. Also use: *The Visitors, Where the Evil Dwells* (both 1988), and *All the Traps of Earth* (1979).

1271 Slasitz, R. A. V. *Where Dragons Rule* (9–12). 1986, NAL paper $2.95 (0-541-14619-0). In this sequel to *Where Dragons Lie* (1985), the Princess Sharlin, friend Dar, and the golden dragon combat a force of evil. (Rev: VOYA 4/87)

1272 Springer, Nancy. *Chains of Gold* (10–12). 1988, Tor paper $2.95 (0-8125-5494-9). Two lovers escape death only to be haunted by the ghost of the person who had sacrificed himself to save them. (Rev: VOYA 12/86)

1273 Springer, Nancy. *Godbond* (9–12). 1988, Tor paper $3.95 (0-812-55496-5). Two young men and the girl they both love are trying to save the world from shrinking and dying in this climax to the Sea King trilogy. (Rev: VOYA 4/89)

1274 Springer, Nancy. *The Hex Witch of Seldom* (10–12). Illus. 1988, Baen $15.95 (0-671-65389-X). A 16-year-old girl discovers that her black stallion is really Shane, the Dark Rider. (Rev: BL 2/1/88; VOYA 10/88)

1275 Springer, Nancy. *Madbond* (9–12). 1987, Tor paper $2.95 (0-812-55486-8). In this the first of the Sea King trilogy, 2 very dissimilar friends, Dan and Kor, begin questing together. (Rev: VOYA 10/87)

1276 Stanton, Mary. *The Heavenly Horse from the Outermost West* (9–12). 1988, Baen paper $3.85 (0-671-65410-1). A horse god comes to the mortal world to save the Appaloosa line from extinction. (Rev: VOYA 2/89)

1277 Stasheff, Christopher. *Warlock Unlocked* (10–12). 1987, Ace paper $3.95 (0-441-87332-4). The forces of evil are fought by a wizard and his family.

1278 Steussy, Marti. *Forest of the Night* (10–12). 1987, Ballantine paper $2.95 (0-345-33815-4). A fantasy about a planet inhabited by very intelligent, feathered tigers. (Rev: BL 6/15/87)

1279 Stewart, Mary. *Mary Stewart's Merlin Trilogy* (9–12). Illus. 1980, Morrow $17.95 (0-688-00347-8). This fictionalized account of the story of King Arthur consists of three novels: *The Crystal Cave* (1970), *The Hollow Hills* (1973), and *The Last Enchantment* (1979). On the same subject use the author's *The Wicked Day* (1984).

1280 Stirling, S. M. *Marching through Georgia* (10–12). 1988, Baen paper $3.50 (0-671-65407-1). An alternate history epic that changes the participants and the stakes in World War II. (Rev: VOYA 12/88)

1281 Sturgeon, Theodore. *The Dreaming Jewels* (10–12). 1984, Bluejay paper $7.95 (0-312-94118-8). This prize-winning fantasy tells how love triumphs over evil. Also use: *Venus Plus X*

(1988) and *The Stars Are the Styx* (1984). (Rev: BR 3–4/86)

1282 Swigart, Rob. *Portal: A Dataspace Retrieval* (10–12). 1988, St. Martin's $18.95 (0-312-01494-5). In this complex novel, an astronaut returns to Earth after 100 years and finds it is deserted. (Rev: BL 3/1/88)

1283 Synge, Ursula. *Swan's Wing* (10–12). 1985, Ace paper $2.75 (0-441-79094-1). This fantasy, set in the Middle Ages, is a variation on Andersen's fairy tale *The Wild Swans.*

1284 Tarr, Judith. *Alamut* (10–12). 1989, Doubleday $19.95 (0-385-24720-6); paper $8.95 (0-385-26435-6). This fantasy set in the days of the Crusades involves a hero who is half human and half immortal. (Rev: VOYA 6/90)

1285 Tarr, Judith. *Ars Magica* (10–12). 1989, Bantam paper $3.95 (0-553-28145-3). The story of Pope Sylvester II and his knowledge of the magical arts. (Rev: VOYA 2/90)

1286 Tarr, Judith. *A Fall of Princes* (10–12). 1988, Tor $18.95 (0-312-93063-1); paper $4.50 (0-8125-5644-5). Two male heirs to rival empires join forces to defeat the powers of darkness in this, the concluding volume of the Avaryan Rising trilogy. (Rev: VOYA 10/88)

1287 Tarr, Judith. *The Hall of the Mountain King* (10–12). 1986, Tor $19.95 (0-312-94210-9); paper $3.95 (0-8125-5607-0). Set in a medieval-like period filled with spells and sorcery, this is the first novel about Mirain and his quests. (Rev: VOYA 2/87)

1288 Tarr, Judith. *The Hounds of God* (10–12). 1986, Bluejay $15.95 (0-312-94218-4); Tor paper $3.50 (0-8125-5605-4). The conclusion of the trilogy about the ex-monk who has magical powers that began with *The Isle of Glass* (1984) and *The Golden Horn* (1985). (Rev: BL 3/15/86)

1289 Tarr, Judith. *The Lady of Han-Gilen* (10–12). 1987, Tor paper $3.95 (0-8125-5607-0). Princess Eliane disguises herself as a boy to escape a marriage and find her own true love. (Rev: BL 5/1/87; VOYA 10/87)

1290 Tepper, Sheri S. *The Flight of Mavin Manyshaped* (10–12). 1985, Berkley paper $2.75 (0-441-24092-5). In this second Mavin Manyshaped novel, Mavin must rescue her sister who is held captive in a massive chasm. (Rev: BL 7/85)

1291 Tepper, Sheri S. *Jinian Footseer* (10–12). 1985, Tor paper $2.95 (0-812-55610-0). This is the first volume of a trilogy about Jinian, a girl who uses her unusual powers to fight evil. (Rev: BL 11/1/85; VOYA 2/86)

1292 Tepper, Sheri S. *Jinian Star-Eye* (10–12). 1986, Tor paper $2.95 (0-812-55614-3). Jinian and her lover Peter finally overcome the powerful magic of the Gamesmen in this follow-up to *Dervish Daughter* (1986). (Rev: BL 10/1/86; VOYA 2/87)

1293 Tepper, Sheri S. *Marianne, the Magus, and the Manticore* (10–12). 1985, Berkley paper $2.95 (0-441-51944-X). In this fantasy, a modern college student finds herself in an alternate world. (Rev: BL 1/1/86)

1294 Tepper, Sheri S. *The Song of Mavin Manyshaped* (10–12). 1985, Ace paper $2.75 (0-441-77523-3). In this part of the celebrated series, Mavin avoids sexual exploitation by escaping from Donderbat Keep. Others in the series are: *The Flight of Mavin Manyshaped* and *The Search for Mavin Manyshaped* (both 1985). Also use: *King's Blood Four* (1989).

1295 Tolkien, J. R. R. *The Hobbit: Or, There and Back Again* (7–12). Illus. 1938, Houghton $13.95 (0-395-07122-4); Ballantine paper $4.95 (0-345-33968-1). In this fantasy, a prelude to *The Lord of the Rings*, the reader meets Bilbo Baggins, a hobbit, in a land filled with dwarfs, elves, goblins, and dragons.

1296 Tolkien, J. R. R. *The Lord of the Rings* (9–12). 3 vols. 1967, Houghton $14.95 each (Vol. 1: 0-395-08254-4; Vol. 2: 0-395-08255-2; Vol. 3: 0-395-08256-0); Ballantine paper $4.95 each (Vol. 1: 0-345-33970-3; Vol. 2: 0-345-33971-1; Vol. 3: 0-345-33973-8). This combined volume includes all three books of the trilogy first published in 1954 and 1955. They are: *The Fellowship of the Ring, The Two Towers,* and *The Return of the King.*

1297 Tolkien, J. R. R. *The Silmarillion* (9–12). 1977, Houghton $7.95 (0-395-25730-1); Ballantine paper $3.95 (0-345-32581-8). These modern legends deal with such subjects as the creation of the world.

1298 Tolkien, J. R. R. *Unfinished Tales of Númenor and Middle-Earth* (10–12). Illus. 1980, Houghton $15.00 (0-395-29917-9); paper $8.95 (0-395-32441-6). A collection of short pieces involving the legendary creatures found in some of the author's other works.

1299 Vance, Jack. *The Green Pearl* (10–12). 1986, Berkley paper $6.95 (0-425-08746-8). For better readers, this fantasy takes place in pre-Arthurian times and involves spells and changelings. Preceded by *Lyonesse, Book I: Suldrun's Garden* (1982). (Rev: BL 3/15/86)

1300 Vance, Jack. *Lyonesse* (10–12). 1987, Berkley paper $3.95 (0-425-09595-9). This story for better readers combines elements of mythology, fairy stories, and fantasy.

1301 Vance, Jack. *Madouc* (10–12). 1990, Berkley paper $8.95 (0-441-50531-7). The courageous Princess Madouc sets out to find the identity of her father in this conclusion to a fantasy trilogy that began with *Lyonesse:* (1982) and *The Green Pearl* (1986). (Rev: BL 4/15/90)

1302 Van Scyoc, Sydney J. *Starsilk* (10–12). 1987, Berkley paper $5.95 (0-425-07207-X). This book is the concluding volume in the Brakrath trilogy that began with *Darkchild* (1987) and *Bluesong* (o.p.).

1303 Vinge, Joan D. *The Snow Queen* (10–12). 1989, Warner paper $4.95 (0-445-20529-6). When spring comes, the Snow Queen does not want to give up her throne.

1304 Volsky, Paula. *The Luck of Relian Kru* (10–12). 1987, Berkley paper $2.95 (0-441-83816-2). While fleeing from an assassin, Relian meets a sorcerer who offers safety in exchange for Relian's freedom. (Rev: BL 5/15/87)

1305 Vonnegut, Kurt. *Deadeye Dick* (10–12). 1985, Dell paper $3.95 (0-440-22765-8). An imaginative farce about the doings of the strange Waltz family of Midland City, Ohio. Also use *Mother Night* (1972).

1306 Vonnegut, Kurt. *Galapagos* (10–12). 1985, Delacorte $16.95 (0-385-29416-6); Dell paper $5.95 (0-440-12779-3). The ghost of a shipbuilder tells the story of an ill-fated cruise to the Galapagos Islands. (Rev: BL 9/1/85; BR 3–4/86; SLJ 4/86)

1307 Vonnegut, Kurt. *Slaughterhouse-Five: Or, The Children's Crusade, a Duty Dance with Death* (10–12). 1987, Dell paper $4.95 (0-440-18029-5). This is the surreal story of Billy Pilgrim who, after surviving the bombing of Dresden in World War II, spends time on the planet Trafalmador.

1308 Walsh, Jill Paton. *A Chance Child* (9–12). 1980, Avon paper $1.95 (0-380-48561-3). An orphan child travels through time and explores adolescence through the ages.

1309 Watt-Evans, Lawrence. *With a Single Spell* (9–12). 1987, Ballantine paper $3.95 (0-345-32616-4). In this humorous fantasy a wizard's apprentice decides to make it on his own. (Rev: BL 3/1/87)

1310 Waugh, Charles, and Martin H. Greenberg, eds. *Alternative Histories: Eleven Stories of the World as It Might Have Been* (10–12). 1986, Garland $19.95 (0-8240-8659-7). Eleven stories that explore such "what ifs" as what if England

had crushed the revolt of the American colonies. (Rev: BL 1/1/87)

1311 Weis, Margaret, and Tracy Hickman. *Dragon Wing* (10–12). 1990, Bantam $18.95 (0-553-05727-8). The first part of the Death Gate Cycle (to be 7 books) is a fantasy of a land inhabited by dwarfs and demons, and the ongoing struggle of good versus evil. (Rev: BL 11/15/89; BR 6/90)

1312 Weis, Margaret, and Tracy Hickman. *Dragonlance Chronicles* (9–12). 1988, TSR $16.95 (0-88038-543-X). This collection of 3 novels features as the main character Tanis, half elf and half human. The trilogy consists of *Dragons of Autumn Twilight, Dragons of Winter Night,* and *Dragons of Spring Dawning.* (Rev: VOYA 4/89)

1313 Weis, Margaret, and Tracy Hickman. *The Dragonlance Legends* (10–12). 1988, TSR $16.95 (0-88038-610-X); paper $12.95 (0-88038-653-3). This collection of 3 novels about the twins Caramon and wizard Raistlin contains *Time of the Twins, War of the Twins,* and *Test of the Twins.* (Rev: BR 9–10/89; VOYA 6/89)

1314 Weis, Margaret, and Tracy Hickman. *Elven Star* (10–12). 1990, Bantam $19.95 (0-553-07039-8). An odd assortment of elves, humans, and a dwarf are pitted against a race of giants. Part of the Deathgate series. (Rev: BL 8/90)

1315 Weis, Margaret, and Tracy Hickman. *Forging the Darksword* (10–12). 1988, Bantam paper $3.50 (0-553-26894-5). In this first volume of the Darksword trilogy, the narrative focuses on the fate of a colony of witches. Continued in *Doom of Darksword* and *Triumph of the Darksword* (both 1988). (Rev: BL 1/15/88; VOYA 8/88)

1316 Weis, Margaret, and Tracy Hickman. *The Prophet of Akhran* (10–12). 1989, Bantam paper $4.50 (0-553-28143-7). Four adventurers must cross a salt desert and try to free a nomadic tribe held captive in this third volume of the Rose of the Prophet trilogy. Others are *The Will of the Wanderer* and *The Paladin of the Night* (both 1989). (Rev: VOYA 2/90)

1317 Wellman, Manly Wade. *John the Balladeer* (10–12). 1988, Baen paper $3.50 (0-671-65418-7). The folklore and legends of the Carolinas come to life through the stories told and sung by John the Balladeer. (Rev: VOYA 2/89)

1318 Werlin, Marvin, and Mark Werlin. *The Savior* (10–12). 1979, Dell paper $2.95 (0-440-17748-0). A young boy has the power to heal or destroy in this powerful novel.

1319 White, T. H. *The Book of Merlyn: The Unpublished Conclusion to "The Once and Future King"* (9–12). 1988, Univ. of Texas Pr. paper

$8.95 (0-292-70769-X). An antiwar postscript to White's retelling of the Arthurian legend.

1320 White, T. H. *The Once and Future King* (10–12). 1958, Berkley paper $4.95 (0-425-09116-3). Beginning with *The Sword in the Stone* (1939), this omnibus includes all four of T. H. White's novels about the life and career of King Arthur. It was this version that became the basis for the musical *Camelot*.

1321 White, T. H. *The Sword in the Stone* (7–12). 1939, Putnam $11.95 (0-399-10783-5). In this, the first part of *The Once and Future King,* the career of Wart is traced until he becomes King Arthur.

1322 Wilder, Cherry. *A Princess of the Chameln* (10–12). 1985, Baen paper $2.95 (0-671-55966-4). In this the first volume of The Rulers of Hylor series, Princess Aidris flees the cruel invaders of her country but secretly prepares to lead her people to freedom.

1323 Wilder, Cherry. *The Summer's King* (9–12). 1986, Macmillan $15.95 (0-689-31118-4); Baen paper $2.95 (0-671-65617-1). King Sharn is surrounded by danger and evil magic when he sets out to find a bride. (Rev: BL 4/1/86; SLJ 5/86)

1324 Willard, Nancy. *Things Invisible to See* (10–12). 1985, Knopf $19.95 (0-394-54058-1); Bantam paper $3.95 (0-553-27652-2). For better readers, the story of twins—their love of a girl and the struggle between Death and the positive power of the Ancestress. (Rev: BR 9–10/85; SLJ 5/85)

1325 Williams, Tad. *The Dragonbone Chair* (10–12). 1988, NAL $19.95 (0-8099-0003-3). A very long fantasy, Book One of the Memory, Sorrow and Thorn series, tells the story of new King Elias and of the problems that beset his kingdom. A sequel is *Stone of Farewell* (1990). (Rev: BL 8/88; SLJ 4/89; VOYA 2/89)

1326 Williams, Tad. *Tailchaser's Song* (10–12). 1985, NAL $15.95 (0-8099-0002-5). A ginger cat sets out to find his mate in this fantasy that reminds one of Tolkien. (Rev: BL 10/15/85; SLJ 11/85)

1327 Willis, Connie. *Lincoln's Dreams* (10–12). 1987, Bantam $15.95 (0-553-05197-0); paper $3.95 (0-553-27025-7). A young researcher is troubled by unusual dreams about the outcome of our Civil War in this novel that mingles fact and fantasy. (Rev: BL 3/15/87; VOYA 10/87)

1328 Wilson, David Henry. *The Coachman Rat* (10–12). 1989, Carroll & Graf $13.95 (0-88184-508-6). A retelling of the Cinderella story by a

rat that seems almost human. (Rev: BL 9/1/89; VOYA 2/90)

1329 Windling, Terri, ed. *Faery!* (10–12). 1985, Ace paper $3.50 (0-441-22564-0). An anthology of stories about the kingdom of Faery.

1330 Windling, Terri, and Mark Alan Arnold, eds. *Elsewhere, Vol. III* (10–12). 1984, Ace paper $3.95 (0-441-20405-8). This is one volume in a series of excellent anthologies of modern fantasy.

1331 Wolfe, Gene. *The Shadow of the Torturer* (10–12). 1984, Pocket paper $3.50 (0-671-54066-1). This is the first volume of the series The Book of the New Sun, which tells about the varying fortunes of Severian the Torturer. One other is: *The Claw of the Conciliator* (1983).

1332 Wolfe, Gene. *Soldier of Arete* (10–12). 1989, Tor $17.95 (0-312-93185-9). For better readers, a historical fantasy set in the age of rivalry between Sparta and Athens. (Rev: BL 8/89)

1333 Wolfe, Gene. *Soldier of the Mist* (10–12). 1987, Tor paper $3.95 (0-8125-5815-4). A complex adventure story about an amnesiac who must read and record his life's events. (Rev: VOYA 2/87)

1334 Woolley, Persia. *Child of the Northern Spring* (10–12). 1988, Pocket paper $4.50 (0-671-62199-8). The beginning of a trilogy that sees the Arthurian story through the eyes of Guinevere. (Rev: BL 5/15/87)

1335 Wrede, Patricia C. *Caught in Crystal* (9–12). 1987, Ace paper $2.95 (0-441-76006-6). Kayl is summoned from the inn she operates to help revive the failing power of the Sisterhood of Stars. (Rev: VOYA 8–9/87)

1336 Wrede, Patricia C. *The Harp of Imach Thyssel* (10–12). 1985, Berkley paper $2.95 (0-441-31756-1). A young minstrel finds a magic harp in this fantasy that uses the same setting as the author's *Daughter of Witches* (1983). (Rev: BL 6/1/85)

1337 Wrede, Patricia C. *The Seven Towers* (10–12). 1984, Ace paper $2.95 (0-441-75976-9). A group of people join forces to prevent an evil wizard from gaining power.

1338 Wrede, Patricia C. *Snow White and Rose Red* (10–12). 1989, Tor $15.95 (0-312-93180-8). A reworking of the classic Grimm story, this is set in Elizabethan England and involves 2 sisters and exile from the Faerie kingdom. (Rev: BL 5/1/89; VOYA 12/89)

1339 Wrede, Patricia C., and Caroline Stevermer. *Sorcery and Cecilia* (10–12). 1988, Berkley paper $2.95 (0-441-77559-4). Fantasy and romance are combined in this series of letters between 2 cousins in Regency England. (Rev: BL 5/15/88; VOYA 12/88)

1340 Wurts, Janny. *Sorcerer's Legacy* (10–12). 1989, Bantam paper $3.95 (0-553-27846-0). Elienne travels through time with a sorcerer to become the consort of a prince. (Rev: VOYA 10/89)

1341 Yolen, Jane. *Sister Light, Sister Dark* (10–12). 1988, Tor $16.95 (0-312-93091-7). The first of a series about an orphaned girl brought up by the Sisterhood. (Rev: BL 10/1/88; SLJ 12/88; VOYA 4/89)

1342 Zelazny, Roger. *Blood of Amber* (9–12). 1986, Arbor House $14.95 (0-87795-829-7); Avon paper $3.95 (0-380-89636-2). Merle Corey, hero of *Trumps of Doom* (1985), escapes from prison with the help of a woman who has many shapes. This is the seventh Amber novel. (Rev: BL 9/15/86; VOYA 2/87)

1343 Zelazny, Roger. *Changeling* (10–12). 1980, Ace paper $2.95 (0-441-10264-6). An earthling is pitted against his changeling in a magical world. Also use: *The Last Defender of Camelot* (1988).

1344 Zelazny, Roger. *Nine Princes in Amber* (10–12). 1972, Avon paper $3.50 (0-380-01430-9). In this book in the Amber series, Corwin returns to Amber from Earth to seize the throne. Others in this series are: *The Guns of Avalon* (1976), *The Sign of the Unicorn, The Hand of Oberon* (both 1977), and *The Courts of Chaos* (1979).

1345 Zelazny, Roger. *This Immortal* (10–12). Rev. ed. 1989, Baen paper $3.95 (0-671-69848-6). For better readers, this story involves a plot to kill a visitor to Earth from another planet. (Rev: VOYA 6/90)

1346 Zelazny, Roger. *Trumps of Doom* (9–12). 1986, Avon paper $3.50 (0-380-89635-4). In this sixth Amber book, Merlin fights against mysterious foes from the worlds of Amber and Chaos. (Rev: BL 5/15/85)

1347 Zettner, Pat. *The Shadow Warrior* (10–12). 1989, Baen paper $3.95 (0-671-69848-6). Solgart sets out to find her brother who is pursuing goblins. (Rev: VOYA 6/89)

Historical Fiction

Prehistory

1348 Auel, Jean M. *The Mammoth Hunters* (10–12). 1985, Crown $19.95 (0-517-55627-8); Bantam paper $4.95 (0-553-26096-0). This is the third and final story set in prehistoric times about the amazing woman Ayla and her ability to survive endless hardships. The first 2 were *The Clan of the Cave Bear* (1980) and *The Valley of Horses* (1982). (Rev: BL 11/1/85)

1349 Auel, Jean M. *The Plains of Passage* (10–12). 1990, Crown $24.95 (0-517-58049-7). A sexually explicit novel for mature readers that is part of the Earth's Children series. This installment tells of Ayla and her mate Jondalar and their journey back to Jondalar's people. (Rev: BL 9/1/90)

1350 Golding, William. *The Inheritors* (10–12). 1963, Harcourt paper $6.95 (0-15-644379-1). Set in prehistoric times, this adult novel tells of encounters between Homo sapiens and Neanderthal people.

1351 Harrison, Sue. *Mother Earth, Father Sky* (10–12). 1990, Doubleday $19.95 (0-385-41159-6). The saga of an Aleutian woman of some 9,000 years ago and her search for safety and security. (Rev: BL 4/15/90)

1352 Kurten, Bjorn. *Dance of the Tiger: A Novel of the Ice Age* (10–12). 1980, Pantheon $10.95 (0-394-51267-7). This story, set in prehistoric times, tells about a young boy who is adopted by a Neanderthal clan.

1353 Raspail, Jean. *Who Will Remember the People . . .* (10–12). Trans. by Jeremy Leggatt. 1988, Mercury House $18.95 (0-916515-42-7). The history in fiction form of a primitive tribe that traveled the length of North and South America in a massive migration. (Rev: SLJ 12/89)

1354 Rosny, J. H. *Quest for Fire* (10–12). 1982, Ballantine paper $2.50 (0-345-30067-X). To ensure survival, primitive tribesmen must sustain their fire.

1355 Silverberg, Robert, et al., eds. *Neanderthals: Isaac Asimov's Wonderful World of Science Fiction #6* (10–12). 1987, NAL paper $3.95 (0-451-14716-2). Eleven stories about prehistoric people plus an informative introduction on what we really know about them. (Rev: BL 1/15/87)

1356 Tempest, John. *Vision of the Hunter* (10–12). 1989, Harper $17.95 (0-06-015684-8). A novel, set in prehistoric times, about a courageous young man and his plan to domesticate the wild reindeer. (Rev: BL 3/15/89)

1357 Thomas, Elizabeth Marshall. *The Animal Wife* (10–12). 1990, Houghton $19.95 (0-395-52453-9). A prehistoric hunter on one of his hunts captures a wife. (Rev: BL 8/90)

Ancient and Medieval History

GENERAL AND MISCELLANEOUS

1358 Gedge, Pauline. *Child of the Morning* (10–12). 1986, Buccaneer LB $20.95 (0-89966-567-5). A fictional account of the life of Hatshepsut, ancient Egypt's only female pharaoh.

1359 Holmes, Marjorie. *The Messiah* (10–12). 1987, Harper $15.95 (0-06-015808-5); paper $8.95 (0-06-064011-1). This third volume on the life of Jesus ends with the Crucifixion. (Rev: BL 9/1/87)

1360 Holmes, Marjorie. *Three from Galilee: The Young Man from Nazareth* (9–12). 1985, Harper $13.95 (0-06-015100-5); Bantam paper $3.50 (0-553-26166-5). This novelized version of the youth of Jesus Christ was preceded by the story of Mary and Joseph, *Two from Galilee* (1972). (Rev: BL 8/85)

1361 Hoover, H. M. *The Dawn Palace: The Story of Medea* (9–12). 1988, Dutton $15.95 (0-525-44388-6). A reworking of the Medea story and of her destructive love for Jason. (Rev: BL 6/1/88; BR 3–4/89; SLJ 9/88; VOYA 10/88)

1362 Norton, Andre. *Shadow Hawk* (7–12). 1987, Ballantine paper $2.95 (0-345-34366-2). A novel that centers around the struggle of the ancient Egyptians to drive out the Hyksos.

GREECE AND ROME

1363 Bradshaw, Gillian. *Imperial Purple* (9–12). 1988, Houghton $18.95 (0-395-43635-4). Set in the Roman Empire of the fifth century, this is a tale of adventure and love in Constantinople and Tyre. (Rev: BL 11/1/88; SLJ 2/89)

1364 Bradshaw, Gillian. *The Beacon at Alexandria* (9–12). 1986, Houghton $17.95 (0-395-41159-9). In the Roman Empire in the fourth century, a young girl disguises herself as a man to enter the medical school at Alexandria. (Rev: BL 9/1/86)

1365 Cash, Johnny. *Man in White* (10–12). 1986, Harper $13.95 (0-06-250132-1); paper $7.95 (0-06-250135-5). The story of St. Paul from persecu-

tor of Christians to conversion on the road to Damascus. (Rev: SLJ 12/86)

1366 Davis, Lindsey. *Silver Pigs* (10–12). 1989, Random $18.95 (0-517-57363-6). A murder mystery set in the days of ancient Rome and involving the silver mines in Britain. (Rev: BR 5–6/90; VOYA 2/90)

1367 Douglas, Lloyd C. *The Robe* (10–12). 1942, Houghton paper $8.95 (0-395-40799-0). This novel tells of the fate of a Roman soldier who won the robe of Christ at gambling. Another novel set in early Christian times is *The Big Fisherman* (1946). Also use an earlier novel of blindness and redemption, *Magnificent Obsession* (1938).

1368 Fast, Howard. *Spartacus* (9–12). 1980, Dell paper $4.50 (0-440-17649-2). The stirring story of the slave revolt in ancient Rome.

1369 Graves, Robert. *I, Claudius* (10–12). 1983, Random $9.95 (0-394-60811-9); Random paper $6.95 (0-394-72536-0). Supposedly an autobiography, this is the story of a stuttering misfit who became a Roman emperor. Followed by *Claudius, the God* (1983).

1370 Llywelyn, Morgan. *Druids* (10–12). 1991, Morrow $19.95 (0-688-08819-8). A rich historical novel that combines Druid magic and Celtic history in the time of Caesar's invasion of Gaul. (Rev: BL 12/1/90)

1371 Renault, Mary. *Fire from Heaven* (10–12). 1969, Pantheon $15.45 (0-394-42492-1); Random paper $5.95 (0-394-72291-4). This is the first volume in the powerful trilogy based on the life of Alexander the Great. The others are *The Persian Boy* (1972) and *Funeral Games* (o.p.).

1372 Renault, Mary. *The King Must Die* (10–12). 1958, Pantheon $15.45 (0-394-43195-2); Random paper $6.95 (0-394-75104-3). A historical adventure story based on the legend of Theseus. Followed by *The Bull from the Sea* (1962). Also use: *The Mask of Apollo* (1988).

1373 Renault, Mary. *The Last of the Wine* (10–12). 1975, Random paper $6.95 (0-394-71653-1). This novel contains a wonderful recreation of life in Athens during the Peloponnesian Wars.

1374 Renault, Mary. *The Praise Singer* (10–12). 1988, Random paper $6.95 (0-394-75102-7). This novel deals with the life of the poet Simonides during the sixth century in Athens.

1375 Sienkiewicz, Henryk. *Quo Vadis* (10–12). 1981, Amereon $28.95 (0-89190-484-0); Airmont paper $2.50 (0-8049-0188-0). The contrast between the hedonistic pagans and the early Christians is highlighted in this novel set in ancient Rome.

1376 Wallace, Lew. *Ben Hur* (10–12). 1987, Buccaneer LB $23.95 (0-89966-289-7); Airmont paper $2.95 (0-8049-0074-4). The story of a Jewish slave who escapes a life on the galleys and later is converted to Christianity after an encounter with Christ's healing powers.

1377 Walton, Evangeline. *The Sword Is Forged* (10–12). 1983, Ultramarine $20.00 (0-89366-161-9). For better readers, this is the first of a series of novels about the Greek hero Theseus.

MIDDLE AGES

1378 Bosse, Malcolm. *Captives of Time* (9–12). 1987, Delacorte $14.95 (0-385-29583-9); Dell paper $3.50 (0-440-20311-2). During the Middle Ages, a 17-year-old girl fights to save herself and her mentally retarded brother. (Rev: BL 1/1/88; BR 11–12/87; SLJ 11/87; VOYA 12/87)

1379 Eco, Umberto. *The Name of the Rose* (10–12). 1983, Harcourt $24.95 (0-15-144147-4); Warner paper $4.95 (0-446-34410-9). This is a complex novel for better readers about a series of murders in a troubled fourteenth-century monastery.

1380 Follett, Ken. *The Pillars of the Earth* (10–12). 1989, Morrow $22.95 (0-688-04659-2). For better readers, a massive novel of intrigue, romance, and suspense set in the Middle Ages and involving the construction of a cathedral. (Rev: BL 6/15/89)

1381 Sutcliff, Rosemary. *Blood Feud* (9–12). 1977, Dutton $7.50 (0-525-26730-1). A young Englishman in the beginning of the Middle Ages is sold into slavery to the Vikings.

1382 Tarr, Judith. *The Dagger & the Cross: A Novel of the Crusades* (10–12). 1991, Doubleday $21.95 (0-385-41181-2); paper $10.95 (0-385-41182-0). This sequel to *Alamut* (1990) takes place at the time of Saladin's victory and the fall of Jerusalem during the Crusades. (Rev: BL 12/1/90)

1383 Undset, Sigrid. *Kristin Lavransdatter* (10–12). 1935, Knopf $34.50 (0-394-43262-2). A complex trilogy about a woman's life in medieval Norway. The individual volumes—*The Bridal Wreath, The Mistress of Husaby,* and *The Cross*—are available separately in paperback from Random House.

Africa

1384 Duggan, William. *The Great Thirst* (10–12). 1985, Delacorte $16.95 (0-385-29387-9). The story of several generations of an African tribe near the Kalahari Desert and how invaders, including the whites, doom their culture. (Rev: BL 9/15/85; BR 5–6/86)

1385 Matthee, Dalene. *Fiela's Child* (9–12). 1986, Knopf $16.95 (0-394-55231-8); Ballantine paper $3.95 (0-345-33386-1). A white boy in South Africa, who has been raised by a black family, is suddenly at age 12 claimed by a white family as its own. (Rev: BL 5/1/86)

1386 Michener, James A. *The Covenant* (10–12). 1980, Random $17.95 (0-394-50505-0); Fawcett paper $5.95 (0-449-44523-2). A lengthy entertaining novel that spans 500 years of South African history.

1387 Wood, Barbara. *Green City in the Sun* (10–12). 1988, Random $19.95 (0-394-55966-5). For mature readers, the saga of the Treverton family set against the emergence of Kenya from colony to nation. (Rev: BL 2/1/88)

Asia and the Pacific

1388 Broome, Susannah. *The Pearl Pagoda* (10–12). 1982, Fawcett paper $2.95 (0-449-24469-5). In this novel set in nineteenth-century China, a young woman gets involved in the opium trade.

1389 Buck, Pearl S. *The Good Earth* (7–12). 1965, Harper $16.45 (0-381-98033-2); Pocket paper $3.95 (0-671-50086-4). The epic story of the rise from poverty of Wang Lung and his family in nineteenth-century China.

1390 Clavell, James. *Shogun* (10–12). 1983, Delacorte $21.95 (0-385-29224-4); Dell paper $5.95 (0-440-17800-2). This is an exciting novel of an English sea pilot and his crew who are cast ashore in seventeenth-century Japan.

1391 Collins, Alan. *Jacob's Ladder* (9–12). 1989, Dutton $13.95 (0-525-67272-9). A Jewish teenager's experiences in Sydney, Australia, during the Depression. (Rev: BL 6/1/89; SLJ 10/89; VOYA 8/89)

1392 Forster, E. M. *A Passage to India* (10–12). 1981, Buccaneer $21.95 (0-89966-300-1); Harcourt paper $5.95 (0-15-671142-7). The differences and conflicts of 2 races trying to live together in British-occupied India are explored in this powerful novel.

1393 Hersey, John. *A Single Pebble* (10–12). 1956, Knopf $19.95 (0-394-44562-7); Random paper $6.95 (0-394-75697-5). An American's trip up the Yangtze River reveals the differences between Eastern and Western cultures.

1394 Hesse, Hermann. *Siddhartha* (10–12). 1983, Buccaneer LB $18.95 (0-89966-447-4); Bantam paper $4.50 (0-553-27990-4). An inspiring story set in India about the journey to a state of peace and holiness by a young man. First published in 1923.

1395 Kaye, M. M. *Shadow of the Moon* (10–12). 1980, Bantam paper $4.95 (0-553-25156-2). A lengthy but rewarding novel set against a background of the India Mutiny of 1857. Also use: *The Far Pavilions* (1979).

1396 Lord, Bette Bao. *Spring Moon: A Novel of China* (10–12). 1982, Avon paper $4.95 (0-380-59923-6). In this novel about an upper-class Chinese family, the recent history of China is mirrored.

1397 McCullough, Colleen. *The Thorn Birds* (10–12). 1977, Harper $19.95 (0-06-012956-6). A family saga covering 1915 through 1969 in the lives of the Clearys of Australia.

1398 Malamud, Bernard. *The Assistant* (10–12). 1980, Avon paper $4.50 (0-380-51474-5). For better readers, this is the story of a robber who is so consumed with guilt he devotes his life to helping his victim.

1399 Malraux, André. *Man's Fate* (10–12). 1969, Random paper $8.95 (0-679-72574-1). This 1932 novel tells about a band of revolutionaries fighting in China during the Shanghai insurrection of 1927.

1400 Markandaya, Kamala. *Nectar in a Sieve* (10–12). 1955, NAL paper $3.95 (0-451-15647-1). The story of a peasant family in India and of their courage in the face of terrible disasters.

1401 Michener, James A. *Hawaii* (10–12). 1959, Random $39.50 (0-394-42797-1); Fawcett paper $6.95 (0-449-21335-8). Several historical narrative strands come together toward the end of this long, fascinating novel on Hawaiian history.

1402 Michener, James A. *Sayonara* (10–12). 1983, Fawcett paper $4.95 (0-449-20414-6). A romantic novel set in post–World War II Japan when American troops were stationed there.

1403 Namioka, Lensey. *Valley of the Broken Cherry Trees* (9–12). 1980, Delacorte $8.95 (0-440-09325-2). Two young samurai warriors solve many mysteries in sixteenth-century Japan.

1404 Verne, Jules. *Michael Strogoff* (10–12). 1964, Airmont paper $1.50 (0-8049-0048-5). This

science fiction writer turns to historical novels in this story set in Siberia at the time of the Tartars.

1405 Wonger, B. *Walg: A Novel of Australia* (10–12). 1983, Braziller paper $9.95 (0-8075-1241-3). This novel, set in Australia, tells of the aborigines and their loss of land and culture to the white man.

Europe and the Middle East

1406 Aiken, Joan. *If I Were You* (10–12). 1987, Doubleday $19.95 (0-816-14437-0). In this English historical account 2 look-alike young women decide to switch places so each can fulfill her own chosen future. (Rev: BL 5/1/87; SLJ 9/87)

1407 Belle, Pamela. *Alethea* (9–12). 1985, Berkley paper $6.95 (0-425-08397-7). The story of the Heron family in seventeenth-century England begun in *The Moon in the Water* (1984) and *The Chains of Fate* (1984) continues with young Alethea, who is determined not to marry. (Rev: SLJ 1/86)

1408 Berger, Thomas. *Arthur Rex* (10–12). 1979, Dell paper $5.95 (0-385-28005-X). A re-creation of the world of King Arthur and his knights.

1409 Carr, Philippa. *Knave of Hearts* (10–12). 1983, Putnam $13.95 (0-399-12810-7). In this historical romance set in the days of Louis XV, a young English girl must leave behind her lover when her family moves to France.

1410 Christian, Catherine. *The Pendragon* (10–12). 1984, Warner paper $3.95 (0-446-32342-X). A long but rewarding novel that is a retelling of the King Arthur legend.

1411 Cohen, Matt. *The Spanish Doctor* (10–12). 1985, Beaufort $17.95 (0-8253-0227-7). The story of a doctor caught up in the Jewish persecutions during the Inquisition in Renaissance Spain. (Rev: BL 1/15/85)

1412 Cookson, Catherine. *The Black Candle* (10–12). 1990, Simon & Schuster $19.95 (0-671-70176-2). A historical romance about families living in a small English village at the turn of the century and how events change their relationships. (Rev: SLJ 8/90)

1413 Cookson, Catherine. *The Black Velvet Gown* (10–12). 1989, Summit paper $8.95 (0-671-68253-9). A novel filled with passion and violence that is set in nineteenth-century England.

1414 Cornwell, Bernard. *Sharpe's Regiment* (9–12). 1986, Viking $16.95 (0-670-81148-3); Penguin paper $3.95 (0-14-009213-7). Further adventures of the dashing British soldier in Wellington's army. Others in the series are: *Sharpe's Eagle* (1983), *Sharpe's Gold* (1983), *Sharpe's Enemy* (1987), and *Sharpe's Revenge* (1989). (Rev: BR 1–2/87; SLJ 11/86)

1415 Cornwell, Bernard. *Sharpe's Siege* (10–12). 1987, Viking $17.95 (0-670-80866-0); Penguin paper $3.95 (0-14-008471-1). One of a series of rousing adventure stories about Major Richard Sharpe during the Napoleonic Wars. (Rev: BR 11–12/87)

1416 Crichton, Michael. *The Great Train Robbery* (10–12). 1987, Dell paper $4.95 (0-440-13099-9). This is an entertaining re-creation of a robbery that shocked Victorian England.

1417 Darcy, Clare. *Caroline and Julia* (9–12). 1982, Walker $10.95 (0-8027-0694-0). A romance set in Regency England that tells how love found an actress and a 16-year-old girl.

1418 Delderfield, R. F. *To Serve Them All My Days* (10–12). 1984, Pocket paper $5.95 (0-671-55522-7). The story of an English private school and a dedicated teacher there.

1419 di Lampedusa, Giuseppe. *The Leopard* (10–12). 1987, Pantheon paper $9.95 (0-394-75668-1). For better readers, this is the story of the decline of a wealthy Italian family in the time of Garibaldi.

1420 Doherty, P. C. *The Whyte Harte* (10–12). 1988, St. Martin's $16.95 (0-312-02318-9). A baffling mystery story set in the time of Richard II. (Rev: BL 12/1/88)

1421 Doig, Ivan. *The Sea Runners* (10–12). 1983, Penguin paper $8.95 (0-14-006780-9). The story of four indentured servants in Czarist Russia in 1853 who escape and travel to freedom by canoe.

1422 Doyle, Arthur Conan. *The White Company* (9–12). 1988, Morrow $17.00 (0-688-07817-6). This rich historical novel set in the dying days of the age of chivalry tells how lowly Alleyne achieved knighthood. (Rev: SLJ 2/88)

1423 Du Maurier, Daphne. *Jamaica Inn* (9–12). 1977, Avon paper $3.50 (0-380-0072-5). A suspenseful yarn set on the coast of England during the days of pirates. Also use *Frenchman's Creek* (1971) and *Mary Anne* (1989).

1424 Du Maurier, Daphne. *My Cousin Rachel* (9–12). 1952, Bentley LB $16.00 (0-8376-0413-3). A rich historical novel about a young man who is beginning to believe his new wife is a murderer.

1425 Dunnett, Dorothy. *The Game of Kings* (10–12). 1984, Warner paper $4.50 (0-446-31282-7).

This is the first novel in the Lymond Chronicles about Mary, Queen of Scots. Also use: *Queen's Play, The Disorderly Knights, Pawn in Frankincense, The Ringed Castle* and *Checkmate* (all 1984).

1426 Forester, C. S. *Beat to Quarters* (9–12). 1985, Little paper $7.95 (0-316-28932-9). This is the first of many novels about the gallant nineteenth-century ship captain named Hornblower. Many others in this series are published in hardcover by Amereon.

1427 Forester, C. S. *Mr. Midshipman Hornblower* (10–12). 1984, Little paper $7.95 (0-316-28912-4). This is one of a series of adventure stories about a courageous British seaman as he climbs the ranks. Some others are: *Admiral Hornblower in the West Indies* (1958), *Lieutenant Hornblower* (1952), and *Lord Hornblower* (1956).

1428 Fowles, John. *The French Lieutenant's Woman* (10–12). 1969, Little $24.95 (0-316-29099-8); NAL paper $3.95 (0-451-13598-9). A love story with deep psychological undertones set in the Devon coast during the nineteenth century.

1429 Gidley, Charles. *Armada* (10–12). 1988, Viking $19.95 (0-670-81807-0). Family and religious conflicts culminate in the fierce sea battle between Spain and England. For mature readers. (Rev: BL 1/1/88)

1430 Godwin, Parke. *Beloved Exile* (10–12). 1984, Bantam paper $3.95 (0-553-24924-X). A portrait of Queen Guenevere after King Arthur's death.

1431 Halter, Marek. *The Book of Abraham* (10–12). 1987, Dell paper $4.95 (0-440-10841-1). A lengthy novel about 100 generations of a Jewish family from the destruction of Jerusalem to the Warsaw Ghetto. (Rev: VOYA 6/86)

1432 Hardwick, Mollie. *The Merrymaid* (10–12). 1985, St. Martin's $12.95 (0-312-53019-6). Set in sixteenth-century England, this is the story of a waif who longs to run off with a traveling performer. (Rev: BL 6/1/85)

1433 Heaven, Constance. *Castle of Doves* (9–12). 1985, Putnam $16.95 (0-399-13072-1). A historical romance about 3 English people in Spain during the reign of Isabella II. (Rev: BL 7/85)

1434 Hemingway, Ernest. *For Whom the Bell Tolls* (10–12). 1977, Macmillan $30.00 (0-684-15316-5); paper $9.95 (0-684-71798-0). A love story set against the turbulence of guerrilla warfare during the Spanish Civil War.

1435 Hilton, James. *Good-bye Mr. Chips* (9–12). 1962, Little $14.45 (0-316-36420-7); Bantam paper $2.95 (0-553-25613-0). A loving tribute, in novel form, to a tough but excellent teacher in an English private school. First published in 1934.

1436 Holland, Cecelia. *The Lords of Vaumartin* (9–12). 1988, Houghton $18.95 (0-395-48828-1). A novel set in fourteenth-century France about a young knight out to claim his birthright. (Rev: BL 10/15/88; SLJ 1/89)

1437 Hylton, Sara. *My Sister Clare* (10–12). 1989, St. Martin's $19.95 (0-312-02618-8). This historical romance is set in India and England before and during World War II and deals with an unscrupulous woman and her schemes. (Rev: BL 6/1/89)

1438 Hylton, Sara. *Tomorrow's Rainbow* (10–12). 1988, St. Martin's $18.95 (0-312-01523-2). A rags-to-riches story about a young girl's rise in Britain between the 2 world wars. (Rev: BL 5/1/88)

1439 Kent, Alexander. *Colors Aloft!* (9–12). 1986, Putnam $16.95 (0-399-12988-X); Berkley paper $3.95 (0-425-10264-5). This installment of the saga of the British naval officer Bolitho takes him to the Mediterranean at the height of the Napoleonic War. Part of a long, recommended series. (Rev: BL 7/86; VOYA 12/86)

1440 Kent, Alexander. *Success to the Brave* (9–12). 1983, Putnam $13.95 (0-399-12878-6). This is the fifteenth book about Richard Bolitho of the British Navy in the late eighteenth and early nineteenth centuries. Two others are: *A Tradition of Victory* (1985) and *Enemy in Sight* (1983).

1441 Laker, Rosalind. *Circle of Pearls* (10–12). 1990, Doubleday $18.95 (0-385-26305-8). A rich historical novel set in England during the reign of the Stuarts and involving a young girl whose family are staunchly royalists. (Rev: BL 6/15/90)

1442 Livingston, Nancy. *The Far Side of the Hill* (10–12). 1988, St. Martin's $19.95 (0-312-02207-7). Two hardworking Scottish brothers seek their fortunes in England during the last days of Victoria's reign in this family saga. (Rev: BL 9/1/88)

1443 Llewellyn, Richard. *How Green Was My Valley* (9–12). 1983, Amereon LB $21.95 (0-88411-936-X); Dell paper $4.95 (0-440-33923-5). The enduring saga of a Welsh mining town and of the Morgan family who live and work there.

1444 Llywelyn, Morgan. *Lion of Ireland: The Legend of Brian Boru* (10–12). 1980, Houghton $17.95 (0-395-28588-7). This story, set in medieval Ireland, tells about the legendary deeds of Brian Boru.

1445 Llywelyn, Morgan. *Red Branch* (10–12). 1989, Morrow $19.95 (0-688-06946-0). This is a historical novel that features the fabled strong man of Irish legend Cuchulain, the Wolfhound of Cullen. (Rev: BL 1/15/89)

1446 Lofts, Norah. *Scent of Cloves* (10–12). n.d., Amereon LB $19.95 (0-89190-228-7). One of many fine historical novels from this writer, who often deals with English history in her books.

1447 Malamud, Bernard. *The Fixer* (10–12). 1982, Pocket paper $3.95 (0-671-46075-7). An innocent Jewish handyman is accused of the murder of a Christian boy in Czarist Russia.

1448 Mann, Thomas. *Buddenbrooks* (10–12). Trans. by H. T. Lowe-Porter. 1964, Knopf $30.00 (0-394-41801-8); Random paper $5.95 (0-394-72637-5). A difficult but rewarding novel about 4 generations of the Buddenbrook family in Germany.

1449 Mann, Thomas. *The Magic Mountain* (10–12). Trans. by H. T. Lowe-Porter. 1956, Knopf $30.00 (0-394-43458-7); Random paper $10.95 (0-394-70497-5). A dense philosophical novel about a tuberculosis sanitorium in Berghof before and during World War I.

1450 Michener, James A. *Poland* (10–12). 1983, Random $17.95 (0-394-53189-2); Fawcett paper $4.95 (0-449-20587-8). The history of Poland from 1200 into the 1980s is covered in a series of fictional incidents centered around a town named Bukowo. Also Use: *Iberia* (1968).

1451 Michener, James A. *The Source* (10–12). Illus. 1965, Random $34.95 (0-394-44630-5); Fawcett paper $5.95 (0-449-44525-9). Using an archaeological dig as a focal point, the author traces in fictional form thousands of years of Israeli history.

1452 Nedreaass, Torberg. *Music from a Blue Well* (10–12). Trans. by Bibbi Lee. 1988, Univ. of Nebraska Pr. $21.00 (0-8032-3315-9). Set in pre–World War I Norway, this is the story of a young girl growing up in Bergen in a family that is disintegrating. (Rev: SLJ 9/88)

1453 Newth, Mette. *The Abduction* (9–12). Trans. by Tiina Nunnally and Steve Murray. 1989, Farrar $13.95 (0-374-30008-9). A historical novel about the brutal treatment of the Greenland Inuits at the hands of the Norwegians during the seventeenth century. (Rev: BL 12/1/89; SLJ 12/89; VOYA 2/90)

1454 O'Flaherty, Liam. *The Informer* (10–12). 1980, Harcourt paper $4.95 (0-15-644356-2). During the 1920s, in Ireland, Gypo Nolan betrays a friend and must pay for it.

1455 Orczy, Emmuska. *The Scarlet Pimpernel* (10–12). 1984, Buccaneer LB $17.95 (0-89966-508-X); 1990, Penguin paper $2.95 (0-14-035056-X). An English fop is actually a leader of a group that helps aristocrats flee the French Revolution in this novel first published in 1905. Others in the series are: *The Triumph of the Scarlet Pimpernel, The Way of the Scarlet Pimpernel,* and *The Adventures of the Scarlet Pimpernel* (all reprinted in 1983).

1456 Pasternak, Boris. *Doctor Zhivago* (10–12). 1958, Pantheon $17.45 (0-394-42223-6); Ballantine paper $4.95 (0-345-34100-7). The story of an idealistic doctor in Russia during the revolutionary period.

1457 Penman, Sharon Kay. *Falls the Shadow* (10–12). 1988, Henry Holt $18.95 (0-8050-0300-2); Ballantine paper $10.95 (0-345-36033-8). An exciting novel set in medieval England during the reign of Henry III and the conflict known as the Barons' War. (Rev: BL 3/15/88; BR 5–6/88; SLJ 9/88)

1458 Penman, Sharon Kay. *Here Be Dragons* (10–12). 1987, Avon paper $4.95 (0-380-70181-2). In thirteenth-century England, a girl of noble birth falls in love with the Prince of Wales. (Rev: SLJ 9/85; VOYA 4/86)

1459 Penman, Sharon Kay. *The Sunne in Splendour* (10–12). 1990, Ballantine paper $12.95 (0-345-36313-2). A rich historical novel set in England during the fifteenth century that portrays Richard III as a kindly, misunderstood man.

1460 Plaidy, Jean. *Myself My Enemy* (10–12). 1985, Fawcett paper $3.95 (0-449-20648-3). In this, the first of a series of historical novels on the queens of England, the subject is Henriette, the wife of Charles I.

1461 Plaidy, Jean. *The Princess of Celle* (10–12). 1985, Putnam $15.95 (0-399-13070-5); Fawcett paper $3.95 (0-449-21004-9). A richly romantic novel about love and adventure that centers around the woman who for some time was the wife of England's George I. (Rev: BL 2/1/85)

1462 Plaidy, Jean. *Queen in Waiting* (9–12). 1987, Fawcett paper $3.95 (0-449-21096-0). This tale of power struggles and court intrigue is set in the reign of George I. (Rev: BL 10/1/85)

1463 Plaidy, Jean. *The Star of Lancaster* (10–12). 1982, Putnam $12.95 (0-399-12758-5). The romance and marriage of Mary of Bohun and Henry IV is the subject in this part of the Queens of England series.

1464 Plaidy, Jean. *The Vow of the Heron* (10–12). 1984, Fawcett paper $3.95 (0-449-20264-X).

This part of the author's Plantagenet series tells the story of Edward II.

1465 Porter, Jane. *The Scottish Chiefs* (10–12). Illus. 1956, Macmillan $19.95 (0-684-17620-3). A tale of love and adventure set in historical Scotland.

1466 Riley, Judith Merkle. *A Vision of Light* (10–12). 1989, Delacorte $19.95 (0-440-50109-1). A novel set in fourteenth-century England narrated by a noblewoman and her hired scribe. (Rev: BL 11/1/88; SLJ 12/89)

1467 Rutherfurd, Edward. *Sarum: The Novel of England* (10–12). 1987, Crown $19.95 (0-517-56338-X); Ivy paper $5.95. A sprawling novel that covers the history of England from the Ice Age to the present. (Rev: BL 7/87; SLJ 1/88)

1468 Salinger, J. D. *The Catcher in the Rye* (7–12). 1951, Little $17.95 (0-316-76953-3); Bantam paper $3.50 (0-553-23976-7). For mature readers, the saga of Holden Caulfield and his 3 days in New York City.

1469 Sholokhov, Mikhail. *And Quiet Flows the Don* (10–12). 1989, Random paper $10.95 (0-679-72521-0). A sprawling historical novel about a group of Cossacks living during the Russian Revolution on the banks of the Don River. Followed by *The Don Flows Home to the Sea* (1986).

1470 Singer, Isaac Bashevis. *In My Father's Court* (10–12). 1980, Fawcett paper $2.50 (0-449-24074-6). Through a series of stories set in Warsaw in the early part of the twentieth century, Singer depicts everyday Jewish life.

1471 Singer, Isaac Bashevis. *The Manor* (10–12). 1987, Farrar paper $12.95 (0-374-52080-1). This novel, originally written in Yiddish, covers a period of 40 years when Poland was being oppressed by the Russians.

1472 Singer, Isaac Bashevis. *Shosha* (10–12). 1988, Farrar paper $8.95 (0-374-52142-5). Through the stories of Aaron and Shosha, Singer describes Jewish life in Poland between the 2 world wars.

1473 Sparks, Christine. *The Elephant Man* (10–12). 1986, Ballantine paper $4.95 (0-345-34513-4). A fictionalized account of the life of the hideously deformed John Merrick and the doctor who tried to help him.

1474 Stirling, Jessica. *The Good Provider* (9–12). 1989, St. Martin's $18.95 (0-312-02580-7). A young couple in love run away from their homes in rural Scotland to find a new life in turn-of-the-century Glasgow. (Rev: BL 2/15/89)

1475 Stone, Irving. *Depths of Glory: A Biographical Novel of Camille Pissarro* (10–12).

1985, Doubleday $19.95 (0-385-12065-6); NAL paper $4.95 (0-451-14602-6). For better readers this is a long, fictionalized biography of the French impressionist painter. (Rev: BL 9/15/85)

1476 Stone, Irving. *The Greek Treasure* (10–12). 1976, NAL paper $5.95 (0-451-16173-4). A fictionalized biography of the discoverer of ancient Troy, Henry Schliemann.

1477 Stone, Irving. *Lust for Life: The Novel of Vincent van Gogh* (10–12). Illus. 1954, Doubleday $17.95 (0-385-04270-1); NAL paper $9.95 (0-452-26249-6). A lengthy fictionalized biography of the Dutch painter, Vincent van Gogh.

1478 Stone, Irving. *The Origin: A Biographical Novel of Charles Darwin* (10–12). Illus. 1980, Doubleday $17.95 (0-385-12064-8); NAL paper $4.95 (0-451-13308-0). A lengthy novel that presents a fictionalized version of the life and career of Charles Darwin.

1479 Sutcliff, Rosemary. *Bonnie Dundee* (10–12). 1984, Dutton $12.50 (0-525-44094-1). An adventure story set in Scotland during the war between King James and William and featuring a 17-year-old hero.

1480 Syrett, Netta. *Rose Cottingham* (10–12). 1977, Academy Chicago paper $5.00 (0-915864-19-3). This is the story of a girl who aspires to a writing career though this is not a popular idea in the Victorian world where she is growing up.

1481 Townsend, Guy M. *To Prove a Villain* (10–12). 1985, Perseverance Pr. paper $8.95 (0-9602676-2-X). A rich historical novel that once again investigates the question or whether of not Richard III was a villain. (Rev: BL 6/1/85)

1482 Trevor, William. *Fools of Fortune* (10–12). 1984, Penguin paper $6.95 (0-14-006982-8). For better readers, this novel covers some of the tragic events in Irish history during the early part of this century.

1483 Uris, Leon. *Trinity* (10–12). 1975, Doubleday $19.95 (0-385-03458-X); Bantam paper $4.95 (0-553-25846-X). In a novel that spans the years 1840 to 1916, the author explores the origins of the present struggle in Northern Ireland.

1484 Veryan, Patricia. *Cherished Enemy* (10–12). 1988, St. Martin's $17.95 (0-312-01746-4); Fawcett paper $3.50 (0-449-21751-5). In this, the fifth in the Golden Chronicles series, young Rosamond falls in love with a young doctor who might belong to her enemies, the Jacobites. (Rev: BL 8/88)

1485 Veryan, Patricia. *The Dedicated Villain* (10–12). 1989, St. Martin's $19.95 (0-312-02570-X). An historic romance set in England in the time of Bonnie Prince Charlie. Sixth and last of the Golden Chronicles. (Rev: BL 3/15/89)

1486 Veryan, Patricia. *Journey to Enchantment* (10–12). 1986, St. Martin's paper $3.95 (0-312-90622-6). In this second volume in the Golden Chronicle series set in the Scotland of Bonnie Prince Charlie, a mysterious person rescues Scottish rebels from capture by the English. Preceded by *Practice to Deceive* (1985). (Rev: BL 5/1/86)

1487 Veryan, Patricia. *Love Alters Not* (10–12). 1987, St. Martin's $19.95 (0-312-01062-1); Fawcett paper $3.50 (0-449-21665-9). An adventure story set in Jacobite times featuring the indomitable Dimity Cranford in this fourth Golden Chronicles series. (Rev: BL 12/15/87)

1488 Wiesel, Elie. *Dawn* (7–12). 1982, Bantam paper $2.95 (0-553-22536-7). A young survivor of the Holocaust now in Israel must execute a British officer at dawn.

1489 Woolley, Persia. *Queen of the Summer Stars* (10–12). 1990, Poseidon $19.95 (0-671-62201-3). In this part of the retelling of the Arthurian legend, Arthur marries Guinevere, who now begins to have strong feelings for Lancelot. (Rev: BL 5/1/90; SLJ 9/90)

1490 Wright, Patricia. *That Near and Distant Place* (10–12). 1988, St. Martin's $18.95 (0-312-02297-2). Three centuries of English life in the town of Furnace Green, Sussex. The second part of the series begun in *I Am England* (1987). (Rev: BL 10/1/88)

Latin America and Canada

1491 Cather, Willa. *Shadows on the Rock* (10–12). 1971, Random paper $5.95 (0-394-71680-9). A historical novel set in Quebec at the time of Frontenac and Bishop Laval.

1492 Eggleston, Edward. *Hoosier Schoolmaster* (10–12). n.d., Amereon $16.95 (0-89190-419-0). This Canadian classic is about a young schoolteacher in Canada during pioneer days.

1493 Houston, James. *Running West* (10–12). Illus. 1990, Crown $19.95 (0-517-57732-1). Both a love story and an adventure novel, this is the story of a man indentured to the Hudson Bay Company, a Dene Indian woman, and a journey into the wilderness for furs and gold. (Rev: SLJ 11/90)

1494 Michener, James A. *Caribbean* (10–12). 1989, Random $22.95 (0-394-56561-4). A sprawling novel that traces the history of the Caribbean islands and their people. (Rev: BL 9/1/89)

1495 Wilder, Thornton. *The Bridge of San Luis Rey* (10–12). 1927, Harper paper $5.95 (0-06-091341-X). This story traces the lives of 5 people who were killed when a bridge collapsed.

United States

INDIANS OF NORTH AMERICA

1496 Brown, Dee. *Creek Mary's Blood* (10–12). 1980, Pocket paper $4.95 (0-671-50709-5). The destruction of the American Indian culture by white men as seen through the experiences of Creek Mary and her 2 sons.

1497 Card, Orson Scott. *Red Prophet* (9–12). 1988, Tor $17.95 (0-312-93043-7); paper $3.95 (0-8125-3359-3). A part historical novel/part fantasy that deals with the encroachment of whites into Indian territory. (Rev: VOYA 8/88)

1498 Carter, Forrest. *Watch for Me on the Mountain* (10–12). 1990, Doubleday paper $9.95 (0-385-30082-4). A novel about the Apache leader Geronimo and his opposition to the government that tried to put his people on reservations.

1499 Clarkson, Ewan. *The Many-Forked Branch* (7–12). 1980, Dutton $10.95 (0-525-14358-0). In this story about rivalries between 2 Indian tribes, a young brave becomes caught up in this struggle.

1500 Cook-Lynn, Elizabeth. *The Power of Horses and Other Stories* (10–12). 1990, Arcade $16.95 (1-55970-050-5). A group of short stories about life on an Indian reservation at various times in the twentieth century. (Rev: SLJ 7/90)

1501 Deloria, Ella Cara. *Waterlily* (10–12). 1988, Univ. of Nebraska Pr. $18.95 (0-8032-4739-7). The story of a young Sioux girl and her growing to maturity before the white man came. (Rev: BL 4/1/88)

1502 Fuller, Iola. *The Loon Feather* (10–12). 1967, Harcourt paper $7.95 (0-15-653200-X). In this novel published in 1940, a young Indian girl named Oneta tells about the decline of her people.

1503 Jackson, Helen Hunt. *Ramona* (10–12). 1976, Lightyear $20.10 (0-89968-051-8); NAL, paper paper $3.50 (0-451-52208-7). This old-fashioned novel tells a tragic love story involving Indians in old California.

1504 Jones, Douglas C. *Season of Yellow Leaf* (10–12). 1987, Tor paper $3.95 (0-8125-8450-3). A young girl is taken captive and grows up with the Comanches.

1505 Lederer, Paul Joseph. *Cheyenne Dreams* (9–12). 1985, NAL paper $3.95 (0-451-13651-9). The story of a young Indian orphan and her adoption by a tribe of Cheyenne. Part of the Indian Heritage series. (Rev: VOYA 2/86)

1506 Lederer, Paul Joseph. *The Far Dreamer* (9–12). 1987, NAL paper $3.95 (0-451-15040-6). A fictionalized account about the Sauk Indians and of their spirit lady, Sachim. (Rev: VOYA 6/88)

1507 Lederer, Paul Joseph. *Manitou's Daughter* (10–12). 1982, NAL paper $3.95 (0-451-15429-0). This first novel in the family story about a proud Indian woman and her descendants. Followed by: *Shawnee Dawn, Seminole Skies* (both 1983), and *Cheyenne Dreams* (1989).

1508 Lesley, Craig. *River Song* (10–12). 1989, Houghton $18.95 (0-395-43083-6). The hero, Danny Kachiah, a Nez Percé Indian, faces the conflict of preserving his heritage in a white dominated culture in this sequel to *Winterkill* (1984). (Rev: BL 5/1/89)

1509 Momaday, N. Scott. *House Made of Dawn* (10–12). 1968, Harper $7.95 (0-06-091633-8). In this novel set after World War II, a young American Indian is torn between the culture of his people and that of the white man.

1510 Sanford, John. *The Song of the Meadowlark: The Story of an American Indian and the Nez Percé War* (10–12). 1986, Harper $16.95 (0-06-015546-9); Tor paper $3.95 (0-8125-8843-6). This historical novel vividly re-creates the story of Chief Joseph and the resistance of the Nez Percé Indians to government removal from their land. (Rev: BL 5/1/86)

1511 Shuler, Linda Lay. *She Who Remembers* (10–12). 1988, Arbor $18.95 (0-87795-892-0). A historical novel set in thirteenth-century America about a Pueblo Indian woman who is cast out of her tribe because she is thought to be a witch. (Rev: SLJ 8/88)

1512 Welch, James. *Fools Crow* (10–12). 1987, Penguin paper $8.95 (0-14-008937-3). A historical novel about a band of Blackfeet Indians and their struggles with neighboring tribes and white settlers. (Rev: BL 8/86; VOYA 8–9/87)

DISCOVERY AND EXPLORATION

1513 Michener, James A. *Alaska* (10–12). 1988, Random $22.50 (0-394-55154-0). Fact and fiction mingle in this mammoth historical novel about our forty-ninth state. (Rev: BL 5/15/88)

1514 Michener, James A. *Chesapeake* (10–12). 1986, Fawcett paper $5.95 (0-449-21158-4). This long multigenerational novel traces the history of the land and people of the Chesapeake Bay region from 1583 to 1978.

COLONIAL PERIOD AND FRENCH AND INDIAN WARS

1515 Farber, Norma. *Mercy Short: A Winter Journal, North Boston, 1692–93* (7–12). 1982, Dutton $11.95 (0-525-44014-3). A 17-year old Salem girl gets involved both in witchcraft and capture by Indians.

1516 Heidish, Marcy. *Witnesses* (10–12). 1983, Ballantine paper $2.50 (0-345-29742-3). This is a fictionalized biography of Anne Hutchinson, the fighter for religious freedom in colonial Massachusetts.

1517 Johnston, Mary. *To Have and to Hold* (9–12). 1976, Lightyear $18.95 (0-89968-149-2); Airmont paper $1.95 (0-8049-0160-0). In this historical novel first published in 1900, a young girl escapes an intolerable situation by fleeing to Virginia with a cargo of brides.

1518 Roberts, Kenneth. *Boon Island* (10–12). 1981, Fawcett paper $2.50 (0-449-24408-3). This novel, set in 1710, tells how a shipwrecked crew survive on the hostile Maine coast.

1519 Schurfranz, Vivian. *Danielle* (7–12). 1984, Scholastic paper $2.95 (0-590-33156-6). In this historical novel, a young girl must decide whether to become a bride or a pirate. Also use *Cassie* (1985).

REVOLUTIONARY PERIOD (1775–1809)

1520 Cornwell, Bernard. *Redcoat* (10–12). 1988, Penguin $18.95 (0-670-81681-7). A mature novel of conflicting loyalties and the time of the Revolutionary War. (Rev: VOYA 12/88)

1521 Fast, Howard. *April Morning* (9–12). 1961, Crown $8.95 (0-517-50681-5); Bantam paper $3.95 (0-553-27322-1). A short novel about the first days of the American Revolution as experienced by a 15-year-old boy.

1522 Fast, Howard. *The Immigrants* (7–12). 1987, Dell paper $4.50 (0-440-14175-3). During the early stages of the Revolutionary War, 15-year-old Adam Cooper becomes a man.

1523 Lee, Beverly Haskell. *The Secret of Van Rink's Cellar* (7–12). 1979, Lerner $8.95 (0-8225-0763-3). A young brother and sister are involved in the danger and excitement of revolutionary times in New York City.

NINTEENTH CENTURY TO THE CIVIL WAR (1809–1861)

1524 Chase-Riboud, Barbara. *Echo of Lions* (9–12). 1989, Morrow $19.95 (0-688-06407-8). A recreation in novel format of the life of Joseph Cinque, the African who led a revolt on the slave ship on which he was held and of his trial in the United States. (Rev: BL 2/15/89)

1525 Haley, Alex. *A Different Kind of Christmas* (9–12). 1988, Doubleday $15.00 (0-385-26043-1). The story of a white southerner who becomes involved in an escape via the Underground Railroad on Christmas Eve, 1855. (Rev: BL 12/15/88)

1526 Morrison, Toni. *Beloved* (10–12). 1987, Knopf $18.95 (0-394-53597-9). A complex novel for mature readers about guilt and expiation during the tragic days of slavery. (Rev: BL 7/87; SLJ 1/88)

1527 Oates, Stephen B. *The Fires of Jubilee: Nat Turner's Fierce Rebellion* (10–12). 1990, Borgo $19.95 (0-8095-9018-7); Harper paper $7.95 (0-06-091670-2). A fictionalized account of the slave rebellion led by Nat Turner in 1831 in Southampton County, Virginia.

1528 Rossner, Judith. *Emmeline* (10–12). 1984, Pocket paper $3.95 (0-671-52785-1). Based on fact, this is the story of a girl who was a mill girl in Lowell, Massachusetts, during the 1830s.

1529 Stone, Irving. *The President's Lady* (10–12). 1968, NAL paper $4.95 (0-451-15857-1). The story of the great love between Andrew Jackson and his wife, Rachel.

1530 Stowe, Harriet Beecher. *Uncle Tom's Cabin* (10–12). Illus. 1982, Lib. of America $27.50 (0-949450-01-1). The American classic about slavery and racial violence in the old South.

1531 Styron, William. *The Confessions of Nat Turner* (10–12). 1967, Random $16.95 (0-394-42099-3); Bantam paper $4.95 (0-553-26916-X). This novel re-creates the life of an amazing black leader and of the abortive slave rebellion he led in Southampton, Virginia, in 1831.

1532 Vidal, Gore. *Burr* (8–12). 1988, Ballantine paper $4.95 (0-345-00884-7). A fictionalized biography of the man who fought Alexander Hamilton and also was our third vice president.

1533 Wilson, Harriet E. *Our Nig: Sketches from the Life of a Free Black* (10–12). 1983, Random paper $8.95 (0-394-71558-6). This slave narrative is also the first published novel by a black person in America.

THE CIVIL WAR (1861–1865)

1534 Adicks, Richard. *A Court for Owls* (10–12). 1989, Pineapple Pr. $17.95 (0-910923-65-5). A novel that re-creates the conspiracy to shoot Lincoln, using one of the plotters as the central character. (Rev: BL 6/15/89)

1535 Brown, Dee. *Conspiracy of Knaves* (10–12). 1987, Henry Holt $17.45 (0-8050-0075-5); Penguin paper $4.95 (0-14-010602-2). A love story set in the Civil War that also involves a Confederate plot to free rebel prisoners held in Chicago. (Rev: BL 10/1/86; SLJ 8/87; VOYA 6/87)

1536 Herrin, Lamar. *The Unwritten Chronicles of Robert E. Lee* (10–12). Illus. 1989, St. Martin's $17.95 (0-312-03448-2). A fine historical novel that reveals the true character of Stonewall Jackson and Robert E. Lee. (Rev: SLJ 5/90)

1537 Jakes, John. *North and South* (10–12). 1985, Dell paper $5.95 (0-440-16205-X). A novel of conflict involving 2 families during the Civil War.

1538 Jones, Douglas C. *The Barefoot Brigade* (10–12). 1989, Tor paper $4.95 (0-8125-8459-7). This is the story of a group of backwoodsmen who fight for the Confederacy during the Civil War.

1539 Jones, Douglas C. *Elkhorn Tavern* (10–12). 1989, Tor paper $4.95 (0-8125-8457-0). A fictional account of the Battle of Pea Ridge in Arkansas during the Civil War as experienced by a 15-year-old boy.

1540 Kantor, MacKinlay. *Andersonville* (10–12). 1957, NAL paper $4.95 (0-451-16021-5). A lengthy novel about the terrible life led by prisoners of war during the Civil War in the Southern camp named Andersonville.

1541 King, Benjamin. *A Bullet for Stonewall* (10–12). 1990, Pelican $17.95 (0-88289-763-3). A historical novel built around the premise that Stonewall Jackson was murdered. (Rev: BL 5/1/90; VOYA 8/90)

1542 McSherry, Frank, Jr., et al., eds. *Civil War Women: American Women Shaped by Conflict in Stories* (9–12). 1988, August House paper $8.95 (0-87483-061-3). A collection of short stories mostly by well-known authors about women during the Civil War. (Rev: SLJ 9/88)

1543 Mitchell, Margaret. *Gone with the Wind* (9–12). 1936, Macmillan $29.95 (0-02-585350-3); Avon paper $5.95 (0-380-00109-8). The magnificent Civil War novel about Scarlett O'Hara and her family at Tara.

1544 Shaara, Michael. *The Killer Angels* (10–12). 1987, Ballantine paper $5.95 (0-345-34810-9). A stirring story about the Battle of Gettysburg told from several points of view.

1545 Shannon, Doris. *Cain's Daughter* (10–12). 1979, Fawcett paper $2.25 (0-449-23961-6). This novel, set in Civil War times, tells the story of three women—one black, a white from the South, and a white from the North.

1546 Skimin, Robert. *Gray Victory* (10–12). 1988, St. Martin's $19.95 (0-312-01374-4). For mature readers a novel that poses the question "What if the South had won the Civil War?" (Rev: BL 3/1/88; SLJ 12/88)

1547 Stone, Irving. *Love Is Eternal* (10–12). 1954, Doubleday $13.95 (0-385-02040-6); NAL paper $4.95 (0-451-14540-2). A lengthy, rewarding novel about Lincoln's marriage to Mary Todd.

1548 Vidal, Gore. *Lincoln: A Novel* (10–12). 1984, Random $19.45 (0-394-52895-6); Ballantine paper $4.95 (0-345-00790-5). A novel that explores Lincoln's rise to greatness during the Civil War.

1549 Walker, Margaret. *Jubilee* (9–12). 1987, Bantam paper $4.95 (0-553-25791-9). A novel often compared with *Gone with the Wind*, about blacks and poor whites living in the South before, during, and after the Civil War.

1550 West, Jessamyn. *The Friendly Persuasion* (9–12). 1982, Buccaneer LB $16.95 (0-89966-395-8). The pacifist views of the Quaker Birdwell family cause problems during the Civil War.

1551 Wicker, Tom. *Unto This Hour* (10–12). 1985, Berkley paper $4.95 (0-425-07583-4). The battle known both as Second Manassas and Second Bull Run is recreated in this novel about the Civil War.

1552 Wisler, G. Clifton. *Thunder on the Tennessee* (7–12). 1983, Lodestar $10.95 (0-525-67144-7). A 16-year-old boy joins a Texas regiment and serves in the bloody Battle of Shiloh.

1553 Woodrell, Daniel. *Woe to Live On* (10–12). 1987, Henry Holt $16.95 (0-8050-0283-9). A violent novel about the guerrilla warfare fought in Kansas and Missouri during the Civil War. (Rev: VOYA 12/87)

WESTERN EXPANSION AND PIONEER LIFE

1554 Aldrich, Bess Streeter. *A Lantern in Her Hand* (9–12). 1983, Amereon $20.95 (0-88411-260-8); NAL paper $2.95 (0-451-16168-8). This novel, originally published in 1928, tells about a young bride and her husband who are homesteaders in Nebraska in 1865. A sequel is *A White Bird Flying* (1983).

1555 Arnold, Elliott. *Blood Brother* (10–12). 1979, Univ. of Nebraska Pr. paper $9.95 (0-8032-5901-8). This novel depicts the struggle between white settlers and the Apaches, led by Cochise.

1556 Berger, Thomas. *Little Big Man* (10–12). 1985, Dell paper $5.95 (0-440-34976-1). The story of the Battle of Little Big Horn and General Custer as told by one of the survivors.

1557 Briskin, Jacqueline. *Paloverde* (10–12). 1987, Warner paper $4.50 (0-446-34889-9). For better readers, this saga traces the fortunes of the Van Vliet family in early Los Angeles.

1558 Bromfield, Louis. *The Farm* (10–12). 1976, Amereon LB $20.95 (0-88411-501-1). The story of pioneers and their struggles in the wilderness.

1559 Brown, Dee. *Killdeer Mountain* (10–12). 1984, Pocket paper $3.95 (0-671-46996-7). In 1866 Sam Morrison attends a commemoration for a Civil War hero and then begins an investigation to determine if this man was really a fraud.

1560 Cather, Willa. *Death Comes for the Archbishop* (10–12). 1967, Knopf $19.95 (0-394-42154-X); Random paper $5.95 (0-394-71679-5). A historic novel, first published in 1927, about a French priest who moved to New Mexico in the 1850s.

1561 Cather, Willa. *My Antonia* (10–12). 1983, Amereon $21.95 (0-88411-287-X); Houghton paper $5.95 (0-395-08256-7). A novel set in Nebraska about pioneering Bohemian farmers and of the courageous heroine, Antonia. First published in 1918.

1562 Cather, Willa. *O Pioneers!* (10–12). 1913, Houghton $14.95 (0-395-07516-5). This historical novel, first published in 1913, deals with the struggle for survival of a group of Swedish settlers in Nebraska.

1563 Clark, Walter Van Tilburg. *The Ox-Bow Incident* (10–12). 1989, NAL paper $4.50 (0-451-52525-6). Mob vengeance and a lynching are the focus of this novel about justice in the Old West.

1564 Doig, Ivan. *Dancing at the Rascal Fair* (10–12). 1987, Macmillan $18.95 (0-689-11764-7). The saga of 2 young Scotsmen and their struggles to homestead in the Montana of 1890. (Rev: BL 7/87)

1565 Ferber, Edna. *Cimarron* (9–12). 1930, Amereon $22.95 (0-88411-548-8). The story of the fortunes of Yancey Cravat and his wife Sabra set against the days of the land rush of 1889 in Oklahoma. Also use: *Saratoga Trunk* (Fawcett, 1980).

1566 Gloss, Molly. *The Jump-Off Creek* (9–12). 1989, Houghton $16.95 (0-395-51086-4). A realistic portrait of the struggles of a lone homesteader and her problems. (Rev: BL 9/1/89)

1567 Grey, Zane. *Riders of the Purple Sage* (10–12). 1984, Pocket paper $3.50 (0-671-52766-5). This is probably the best known of Grey's westerns, a number of which are available in paperback. This one takes place in the wilderness of Utah in 1871.

1568 Guthrie, A. B., Jr. *Fair Land, Fair Land* (10–12). 1984, Bantam paper $3.95 (0-553-26118-5). In this sequel to *The Way West* (o.p.), mountain man Dick Summers marries an Indian girl and tries to settle down.

1569 Haruf, Kent. *The Tie That Binds* (10–12). 1986, Penguin paper $6.95 (0-14-008466-5). This book spans 80 years and tells of the life of a courageous, strong-willed woman living on the high plains of Colorado.

1570 Holland, Cecelia. *The Bear Flag* (9–12). 1990, Houghton $19.95 (0-395-48886-9). A widow survives life on the American frontier in this novel about the race for settlement of California. (Rev: SLJ 8/90)

1571 Johnson, Dorothy M. *A Man Called Horse* (10–12). 1973, Ballantine paper $1.75 (0-345-29069-0). A collection of short stories about the old West that feature a rich assortment of outlaws, settlers, and Indians.

1572 Jones, Douglas C. *Come Winter* (10–12). 1989, Henry Holt $19.95 (0-8050-0944-2). In post–Civil War Arkansas, wealthy Roman Hasford tries to forget an unhappy marriage by entering politics and wielding power. The last part of a series about Roman Hasford. (Rev: BL 9/15/89)

1573 Jones, Douglas C. *Gone the Dreams and Dancing* (10–12). 1984, Tor paper $3.95 (0-8125-8453-8). A Civil War veteran moves into the West where he gains an unexpected respect and love for the Indians he encounters.

1574 Jones, Douglas C. *Roman* (10–12). 1986, Holt $16.95 (0-03-060044-8). For mature readers, this book takes its hero Roman into manhood on the American Plains after the Civil War. (Rev: BL 6/15/86; SLJ 10/86; VOYA 8–10/86)

1575 McCunn, Ruthanne Lum. *Thousand Pieces of Gold* (10–12). 1989, Beacon paper $8.95 (0-8070-8317-8). A Chinese girl is sold by her parents and brought to California during the gold rush days.

1576 McMurtry, Larry. *Anything for Billy* (10–12). 1988, Simon & Schuster $18.95 (0-671-

64268-5). A re-creation of the Billy the Kid story told through the eyes of a writer, Ben Sippy. (Rev: BL 9/1/88)

1577 Michener, James A. *Centennial* (10–12). 1988, Fawcett paper $5.95 (0-449-44522-4). A sprawling novel about trappers, traders, and settlers in the Old West.

1578 Michener, James A. *The Eagle and the Raven* (10–12). 1990, State House $19.95 (0-938349-57-0). For better readers, a novel about Sam Houston, Santa Anna, and the early history of Texas. (Rev: BL 6/15/90)

1579 Murray, Earl. *Blue Savage* (9–12). 1985, Walker $14.95 (0-8027-4048-0). A white man returns to the Indian tribe where he was raised after trying to adjust to the white man's ways. (Rev: BL 10/15/85)

1580 Nevin, David. *Dream West* (10–12). 1984, Putnam $17.95 (0-399-12742-9). A rich, lengthy novel for better readers based on the life of John Charles Fremont.

1581 Parker, F. M. *The Searcher* (10–12). 1985, NAL paper $2.95 (0-451-14126-1). The saga of a teenage boy who survives an Indian attack only to find that he must stay with a band of outlaws. (Rev: VOYA 6/86)

1582 Proctor, Geo. W. *Walks without a Soul* (10–12). 1990, Doubleday $14.95 (0-385-24470-3). In pre-Civil War Texas the wife and daughters of a slave are captured by Comanches. (Rev: BL 8/90)

1583 Richter, Conrad. *The Rawhide Knot, and Other Stories* (10–12). 1985, Univ. of Nebraska Pr. paper $6.50 (0-8032-8916-2). A collection of stories about life in the wilderness and pioneer America.

1584 Richter, Conrad. *The Trees* (10–12). 1940, Knopf $18.45 (0-394-44951-7). This is the first volume of a trilogy about the pioneer Luckett family in a wilderness close to the Ohio River. The others are *The Fields* (1946) and *The Town* (1950).

1585 Roberts, Kenneth. *Northwest Passage* (10–12). Fawcett paper $2.95 (0-449-20451-0). A lengthy historical novel about Rogers' Rangers—their battles against Indians and their search for an overland route to the Pacific.

1586 Robson, Lucia St. Clair. *Walk in My Soul* (10–12). 1987, Ballantine paper $4.95 (0-345-34701-3). For mature readers, this is the story of the love affair between Sam Houston and an Indian girl.

1587 Rølvaag, O. E. *Giants in the Earth: A Saga of the Prairie* (10–12). 1927, Harper paper $4.95

(0-06-083047-6). The stirring story of a Norwegian immigrant and his wife and their lives as pioneers on the prairies of Dakota.

1588 Schaefer, Jack. *Shane* (9–12). Illus. 1954, Houghton $13.95 (0-395-07090-2); Bantam paper $2.95 (0-553-26262-9). A stranger enters the Starret household and helps them fight an oppressive land baron.

1589 Scholefield, Alan. *The Lost Giants* (10–12). 1989, St. Martin's $18.95 (0-312-03387-7). A pioneering story about Margaret Dow from Scotland, and her family. (Rev: BL 9/1/89)

1590 Schurfranz, Vivian. *Josie* (9–12). 1988, Scholastic paper $2.75 (0-590-41207-8). In pioneer Carson City, Josie must choose between 2 men, both of whom claim to love her. (Rev: SLJ 1/89)

1591 Shura, Mary Francis. *Diana* (9–12). 1988, Scholastic paper $2.75 (0-590-41416-X). Diana is torn between the attentions of a wealthy Creole suitor and a young man who is part of the Lewis and Clarke expedition. (Rev: SLJ 1/89)

1592 Stevenson, Paul R. *Cross a Wide River* (10–12). 1989, Sunstone paper $13.95 (0-86534-117-1). A multigenerational novel that traces a family's fortune from pre-Civil War days on. (Rev: BL 1/15/89; BR 9–10/89)

1593 Swarthout, Glendon. *The Homesman* (10–12). 1990, Signet paper $4.95 (0-451-16429-6). Mary Bee agrees to accompany a group of emotionally disturbed women on a trip from the frontier back to the East where they can get help. (Rev: VOYA 8/90)

1594 Thorp, Raymond, and Robert Bunker. *Crow Killer* (10–12). 1969, Indiana Univ. Pr. paper $7.95 (0-253-20312-0). A historical novel based on fact about a man's search for revenge.

1595 Turner, Ann. *Third Girl from the Left* (9–12). 1986, Macmillan $12.95 (0-02-789510-6). A teenage mail order bride has to marry her 60-year-old correspondent in this tale set in the early West. (Rev: BL 6/1/86; SLJ 8/86; VOYA 8–10/86)

1596 West, Jessamyn. *The Massacre at Fall Creek* (10–12). 1975, Harcourt paper $6.95 (0-15-657681-3). A fictional account of the killing of nine Indians by white men in 1824 on the Indiana frontier.

1597 Wheeler, Richard. *Where the River Runs* (10–12). 1990, Evans $14.95 (0-87131-599-8). A courageous girl sets out to locate her lover who is missing in Indian territory. (Rev: BL 2/15/90)

1598 Wister, Owen. *The Virginian* (10–12). 1925, Macmillan $19.95 (0-02-630580-1). The classic novel of the American West first published in 1902 and containing the phrase "When you call me that, smile."

RECONSTRUCTION TO WORLD WAR I (1865–1914)

1599 Burns, Olive Ann. *Cold Sassy Tree* (9–12). 1984, Ticknor $16.95 (0-89919-309-9); Dell paper $8.95 (0-440-51442-8). Fourteen-year-old Will has a crush on his grandfather's young bride in this novel set in turn-of-the-century Georgia.

1600 Caldwell, Taylor. *Answer as a Man* (10–12). n.d., Amereon $24.95 (0-88411-143-1). A family saga involving Jason Garrity, the son of Irish immigrants. There are many other fine historical novels in print by Taylor Caldwell.

1601 Doctorow, E. L. *Ragtime* (10–12). 1975, Random $21.95 (0-394-46901-1); Fawcett paper $4.95 (0-449-21428-1). Three stories and several real historical people are featured in this novel set in New York City in the early twentieth century.

1602 Fast, Howard. *Freedom Road* (10–12). 1970, Amsco paper $8.25 (0-87720-752-6). A novel that is set in the Reconstruction period in the South after the Civil War. Also use another fine historical novel by Fast *Citizen Tom Paine* (Grove, 1987).

1603 Faulkner, William. *Absalom, Absalom!* (10–12). 1987, Random paper $5.95 (0-394-74775-5). A novel for better readers about a southern family and their tragedies after the Civil War.

1604 Ferber, Edna. *Show Boat* (9–12). 1979, Fawcett paper $1.95 (0-449-23191-7). The favorite novel about life on a Mississippi show boat and the romance between Magnolia and Gaylord Ravenal. Also use: *So Big* (1979) and *Ice Palace* (1980).

1605 Fitzgerald, F. Scott. *The Great Gatsby* (10–12). 1981, Macmillan $25.00 (0-684-16498-1); paper $8.95 (0-684-71760-3). The emptiness of the Jazz Age is conveyed in this novel about the mysterious Jay Gatsby and his love for Daisy.

1606 Fitzgerald, F. Scott. *Tender Is the Night* (10–12). 1977, Macmillan LB $30.00 (0-684-15151-0); paper $9.95 (0-684-71763-8). The tragic story of Dick Diver whose genius is undeveloped because of his marriage to wealthy Nicole.

1607 Fitzgerald, F. Scott. *This Side of Paradise* (10–12). 1978, Macmillan $25.00 (0-684-15601-6); paper $5.95 (0-02-019920-1). This account of the "lost generation" focuses on the life of a disillusioned wealthy and spoiled man named Amory Blaine.

1608 Freeman, Mary E. Wilkins. *Pembroke* (10–12). 1979, Academy $16.95 (0-915864-72-X); paper $8.95 (0-915864-71-1). For better readers, the story of 2 families and their children growing up in a small New England town at the turn of the century.

1609 Gourley, Catherine. *The Courtship of Joanna* (10–12). 1989, Graywolf paper $8.00 (1-55592-113-X). In the 1880s a 16-year-old girl leaves her family to work in the household of a widowed Irish coal miner and his mother. (Rev: BR 11–12/89; SLJ 10/89)

1610 Hemingway, Ernest. *The Sun Also Rises* (10–12). 1984, Macmillan $27.50 (0-684-15327-0); paper $4.95 (0-02-051870-6). A novel about some members of the "lost generation" and their futile attempts to escape reality in Spain.

1611 Hurmence, Belinda. *Tancy* (7–12). 1984, Houghton $12.95 (0-89919-228-9). After being freed from slavery at the end of the Civil War, 18-year-old Tancy sets out to find her real mother.

1612 Jones, Douglas C. *Remember Santiago* (10–12). 1988, Henry Holt $18.95 (0-8050-0776-8). Two unfortunates are in the Spanish-American War at the time of the Cuban invasion. (Rev: BL 10/15/88; VOYA 6/89)

1613 Marshall, Catherine. *Christy* (8–12). 1976, Avon paper $4.95 (0-380-00141-1). This story set in Appalachia in 1912 tells about a spunky young girl who goes there to teach.

1614 Sinclair, Upton. *The Jungle* (10–12). 1981, Buccaneer $21.95 (0-89966-415-6); NAL, paper paper $2.50 (0-451-52420-9). This frequently brutal novel tells about working in the Chicago stockyards at the turn of the century.

1615 Smith, Betty. *A Tree Grows in Brooklyn* (9–12). 1943, Buccaneer $24.95 (0-89966-303-6); Harper paper $5.50 (0-06-080126-3). The touching story of Francie Nolan growing up in a poor section of Williamsburg in Brooklyn during the early 1900s.

1616 Stone, Irving. *Adversary in the House* (10–12). 1969, NAL paper $3.50 (0-451-11165-6). A fictionalized account of the life of Eugene Debs, American labor leader. Also use the story of John Adams, *Those Who Love* (1965).

1617 Vidal, Gore. *Empire* (10–12). 1987, Random $22.50 (0-394-56123-6); Ballantine paper $4.95 (0-345-35472-9). One of a series of novels about the United States during the nineteenth century when it emerged as a world power. Others include *Burr* (1973), *1876* (1976), *Lincoln* (1984), and *Washington, D.C.* (1987). (Rev: BL 5/15/87)

1618 Vosper, Alice. *Rags to Riches* (10–12). 1983, Avon paper $2.25 (0-380-83873-7). Set in the 1880s, a poor hill girl suddenly finds she is wealthy when her father strikes it rich with a copper mine.

1619 Wharton, Edith. *The Age of Innocence* (10–12). 1920, Macmillan $35.00 (0-684-14659-2); paper $8.95 (0-684-71925-8). A picture of New York society of the 1870s and the fixed codes of behavior that must not be broken. Also use: *House of Mirth* (1976).

1620 Wilson, Dorothy Clarke. *Alice and Edith: A Biographical Novel of the Two Wives of Theodore Roosevelt* (10–12). 1989, Doubleday $18.95 (0-385-24349-9). A novel of politics, romance, and Teddy Roosevelt's 2 wives. (Rev: BL 12/1/89)

BETWEEN WARS AND THE GREAT DEPRESSION (1919–1948)

1621 Craven, Margaret. *Walk Gently This Good Earth* (10–12). 1981, Dell paper $2.25 (0-440-39484-8). The saga of an American family surviving the Depression and World War II.

1622 Doctorow, E. L. *World's Fair* (10–12). 1985, Random $17.95 (0-394-52528-0); Fawcett paper $4.95 (0-449-21237-8). For better readers, life in New York City during the 1930s is recreated through the eyes of a boy growing up. (Rev: BL 9/15/85; SLJ 2/86)

1623 Forbes, Kathryn. *Mama's Bank Account* (7–12). 1968, Harcourt paper $5.95 (0-15-656377-0). The heartwarming story of how a Norwegian family was Americanized and held together by Mama.

1624 Giardina, Denise. *Storming Heaven* (10–12). 1987, Norton $17.95 (0-393-02440-7); Ivy paper $3.95 (0-8041-0297-X). Based on fact, this is a novel set in West Virginia that tells of coal-mining labor trouble during 1921. (Rev: BL 6/15/87; SLJ 1/88)

1625 Howard, Brett. *Memphis Blues* (10–12). 1984, Holloway paper $2.25 (0-87067-048-4). The story of a mulatto growing up in the South between the wars.

1626 Kennedy, William. *Ironweed* (10–12). 1983, Penguin paper $6.95 (0-14-007020-6). This tale, set during the Depression, tells about Francis Phelan and other inhabitants of skid row in Albany, New York.

1627 Marshall, Catherine. *Julie* (9–12). 1985, Avon paper $4.50 (0-380-69891-9). During the Depression, Julie and her family move to a small town in Pennsylvania where she finds fulfillment working on her father's newspaper.

1628 Parini, Jay. *The Patch Boys* (10–12). 1988, Henry Holt paper $8.95 (0-8050-0770-9). For mature readers, this is the story of 15-year-old Sammy di Cantini growing up in a mining town in the Pennsylvania of summer 1925. (Rev: BL 10/1/86; BR 11–12/87; VOYA 12/86)

1629 Plain, Belva. *The Golden Cup* (10–12). 1987, Dell paper $5.50 (0-440-13091-3). The story of a Jewish family in New York that lives through World War I and other crises. Many characters in this novel originally appeared in the author's *Evergreen* (1978), also recommended. (Rev: BL 9/1/86)

1630 Sams, Ferrol. *Run with the Horsemen* (10–12). 1982, Peachtree $14.95 (0-931948-32-0). This novel about family life and race relations in rural Georgia during the Depression centers on Porter Osbourne, a precocious young man.

1631 Steinbeck, John. *The Grapes of Wrath* (10–12). 1939, Viking $22.95 (0-670-34791-4); Penguin paper $4.95 (0-14-004239-3). This 1939 classic tells of the odyssey of the Joad family from wind-swept Oklahoma to California.

1632 Steinbeck, John. *Of Mice and Men* (10–12). 1968, Viking $15.95 (0-670-5207-3); Penguin paper $3.95 (0-14-004891-X). The friendship between two migrant workers—one a schemer and the other mentally deficient—is the subject of this short novel.

Twentieth Century Wars

WORLD WAR I

1633 Dank, Milton. *Khaki Wings* (10–12). 1983, Dell paper $1.95 (0-317-00572-3). This is a story of the air war during the early years of World War I.

1634 Forsyth, Frederick. *The Shepherd* (10–12). n.d., Amereon $19.95 (0-88411-563-1). A pilot and his plane are saved by a mysterious World War I aircraft.

1635 Hemingway, Ernest. *A Farewell to Arms* (10–12). 1978, Macmillan $27.50 (0-684-15562-1); paper $10.95 (0-684-71797-2). First published in 1929, this is a love story set against the drama of World War I.

1636 Remarque, Erich Maria. *All Quiet on the Western Front* (10–12). 1929, Little $16.95 (0-

316-73992-8); Fawcett paper $3.95 (0-449-21394-3). The touching story of four young German boys and their army life during World War I.

WORLD WAR II AND THE HOLOCAUST

1637 Baer, Edith. *A Frost in the Night* (10–12). 1988, Schocken paper $7.95 (0-8052-0857-7). A story about Jewish family life in Germany at the time of the growth of Hitler's power.

1638 Baklanov, Grigory. *Forever Nineteen* (8–12). Trans. by Antonia W. Bouis. Illus. 1989, Harper LB $13.89 (0-397-32297-6). Drawing on personal experience, this Russian novelist tells a harrowing story of a teenager fighting in World War II. (Rev: BL 5/1/89; BR 1–2/90; SLJ 5/89; VOYA 12/89)

1639 Ballard, J. G. *Empire of the Sun* (10–12). 1984, Pocket paper $4.50 (0-671-64877-2). The saga of an 11-year-old boy separated from his parents during the World War II invasion of China by the Japanese.

1640 Bassani, Giorgio. *The Garden of the Finzi-Continis* (10–12). 1977, Harcourt paper $6.95 (0-15-634570-6). The tragic story of the fate of an Italian Jewish family under the Fascists.

1641 Benchley, Nathaniel. *A Necessary End: A Novel of World War II* (10–12). 1976, Harper $13.70 (0-06-020498-2). This story, written in the form of a journal, tells of a young signalman's adventures in the Pacific during World War II.

1642 Bienek, Horst. *Earth and Fire* (10–12). Trans. by Ralph Manheim. 1988, Macmillan $19.95 (0-689-11992-5). A novel of how the residents of a small town on the Polish-German border cope with the Russian occupation during the last days of World War II. (Rev: BL 10/1/88)

1643 Binchy, Maeve. *Light a Penny Candle* (7–12). 1989, Dell paper $5.95 (0-440-14795-6). A story of friendship and survival about 2 girls living in England during the German blitz.

1644 Bor, Josef. *The Terezin Requiem* (10–12). 1978, Avon paper $1.95 (0-380-01673-7). A group of musicians try to survive in a German concentration camp during World War II.

1645 Boulle, Pierre. *The Bridge over the River Kwai* (9–12). Trans. by Xan Fielding. 1954, Amereon $13.95 (0-89190-571-5); Bantam paper $2.95 (0-553-24850-2). The thoughtful story of life in a Japanese prisoner-of-war camp that pits a British officer against his captors.

1646 Brooks, Jerome. *Make Me a Hero* (9–12). 1980, Dutton $9.95 (0-525-34475-6). In this story set during World War II, a 12-year-old boy longs to join his older brothers who are in the service.

1647 Brown, Harry. *A Walk in the Sun* (10–12). 1970, Amereon LB $15.95 (0-88411-075-3); Carroll & Graf paper $3.95 (0-88184-117-X). A fine World War II novel about a group of American soldiers landing on a beach in Italy.

1648 Clare, George. *Last Waltz in Vienna* (10–12). 1983, Avon paper $3.95 (0-380-64709-5). The story of how the Nazi regime brought tragedy and destruction to an Austrian family.

1649 Clavell, James. *King Rat* (10–12). 1983, Delacorte $17.95 (0-385-29211-2); Dell paper $5.95 (0-440-14546-5). For mature readers, this is the brutal story of life in a Japanese prisoner of war camp.

1650 Eliach, Yaffa, ed. *Hasidic Tales of the Holocaust* (10–12). 1982, Oxford Univ. Pr. $24.95 (0-19-503199-7); Random paper $7.95 (0-679-72043-X). These are short fictional pieces written by survivors of the Holocaust.

1651 Ferry, Charles. *One More Time!* (9–12). 1985, Houghton $11.95 (0-395-36692-5). During World War II, a dance orchestra is on its last tour before being disbanded and the members question their futures. (Rev: BL 5/15/85; BR 9–10/85; SLJ 8/85)

1652 Ferry, Charles. *Raspberry One* (10–12). 1983, Houghton $11.95 (0-395-34069-1). Two friends, who are part of a torpedo squadron, experience the horrors of war firsthand in this novel set during World War II in the Pacific.

1653 Fink, Ida. *A Scrap of Time: And Other Stories* (10–12). 1987, Pantheon $15.95 (0-394-55806-5); Schocken paper $6.95 (0-8052-0869-0). These stories are about the daily life of Polish Jews during World War II written by a Holocaust survivor. (Rev: BL 6/1/87)

1654 Frank, Anne. *Anne Frank's Tales from the Secret Annex* (8–12). 1984, Doubleday $14.95 (0-385-18715-7). This is a collection of all of Anne Frank's writings—apart from the diary, that is—stories, sketches, and fairy tales. [839.3]

1655 Harris, Rosemary. *Summers of the Wild Rose* (9–12). 1988, Faber $11.95 (0-571-14702-X). In pre-war Austria and Germany, a 17-year-old English girl falls in love with a Jewish boy who becomes the victim of Hitler's anti-Semitism. (Rev: BL 3/1/88)

1656 Heggen, Thomas. *Mister Roberts* (10–12). 1983, Buccaneer LB $16.95 (0-89966-445-8). The waste of war is one of the themes of this richly comic but also touching story of life on a supply ship during World War II.

1657 Heller, Joseph. *Catch-22* (10–12). 1961, Dell paper $4.95 (0-440-11120-X). A wildly surreal novel about a group of American servicemen in the Mediterranean area during World War II.

1658 Hersey, John. *A Bell for Adano* (10–12). 1988, Random $17.95 (0-394-41660-0); paper $6.95 (0-394-75695-9). Major Jappolo and his troops try to govern justly the town of Adano in allied-occupied Italy during World War II.

1659 Hersey, John. *The Wall* (10–12). 1950, Knopf $25.00 (0-394-45092-2). Presented in the form of a diary, this novel reveals the agony within the Warsaw Ghetto during World War II.

1660 Ibuse, Masuji. *Black Rain* (9–12). 1985, Bantam paper $3.95 (0-553-24988-6). A fictional account of the effect of the bombing of Hiroshima on 3 different people. (Rev: VOYA 2/86)

1661 Jones, James. *From Here to Eternity* (10–12). 1985, Dell paper $5.95 (0-440-32770-9). This tough World War II novel uses the attack on Pearl Harbor as its climax.

1662 Keneally, Thomas. *Schindler's List* (10–12). 1983, Penguin paper $8.95 (0-14-006784-1). A mature novel that is a fictionalized treatment of the life of the German industrialist who saved the lives of many Jews during World War II.

1663 Kosinski, Jerzy. *The Painted Bird* (10–12). 1982, Random $6.95 (0-394-60433-4); Bantam paper $4.95 (0-553-26520-2). The shocking story of a stray child and his wanderings in Poland during World War II.

1664 MacLean, Alistair. *H.M.S. Ulysses* (9–12). 1985, Fawcett paper $3.50 (0-449-12929-2). This is an exciting story of a British light cruiser's treacherous voyage to Murmansk during World War II. Other adventure stories by MacLean include *Athabasca* (1986) and *Way to Dusty Death* (1985).

1665 MacLean, Alistair. *San Andreas* (9–12). 1986, Fawcett paper $4.50 (0-449-20970-9). A hospital ship becomes the target of German U-boats in this thriller set during World War II. Also use: *When Eight Bells Toll* (1984) and *Seawitch* (1986). (Rev: BL 9/1/85)

1666 Mailer, Norman. *The Naked and the Dead* (10–12). 1976, Henry Holt $18.95 (0-8050-0522-6); paper $10.95 (0-8050-0521-8). A powerful, graphic World War II novel that takes place off an island in the South Pacific.

1667 Mautner, Gabriella. *Lovers and Fugitives* (9–12). 1986, Mercury House $16.95 (0-916515-01-X). In 1940, 2 German Jews who are in love flee across Europe to escape the Nazis. (Rev: SLJ 9/86)

1668 Michener, James A. *Tales of the South Pacific* (10–12). 1947, Fawcett paper $4.95 (0-449-20652-1). Eighteen stories about life in the South Pacific during World War II. Some of them formed the basis of the Rodgers and Hammerstein musical.

1669 Monsarrat, Nicholas. *The Cruel Sea* (10–12). 1951, Knopf $24.50 (0-394-42090-X). A novel that explores in human terms the war at sea during World War II as seen through the eyes of the men of 2 British ships.

1670 Nathanson, E. M. *A Dirty Distant War* (9–12). 1987, Viking $19.95 (0-670-80334-0); Berkley paper $4.95 (0-425-12127-5). The leader of the Dirty Dozen continues his adventure in Asia during the last year of World War II. (Rev: BR 3–4/88; SLJ 4/88; VOYA 4/88)

1671 Noonan, Michael. *McKenzie's Boots* (9–12). 1988, Watts LB $13.99 (0-531-08348-9). An Australian 15 year old bluffs his way into the army during World War II and sees service in the Pacific theater. (Rev: BL 4/1/88; BR 11–12/88; SLJ 4/88; VOYA 8/88)

1672 Ramati, Alexander. *And the Violins Stopped Playing: A Story of the Gypsy Holocaust* (10–12). 1986, Watts $15.95 (0-531-15028-3). A novel based on occurrences during the Nazi Holocaust aimed at Eastern European gypsies. (Rev: BL 9/1/86; BR 11–12/86; SLJ 1/87; VOYA 2/87)

1673 Reeman, Douglas. *A Ship Must Die* (9–12). 1983, Jove paper $3.50 (0-515-07382-2). A British cruiser is on the trail of German raiders during World War II. One of the many novels by this author about World War II including *Torpedo Run*, *His Majesty's U-Boat*, and *The Pride and the Anguish* (all 1985).

1674 Remarque, Erich Maria. *Arch of Triumph* (10–12). 1929, Little $16.95 (0-316-73992-8); NAL paper $4.95 (0-316-73992-8). A novel about illegal aliens and refugees living in Paris just before the outbreak of World War II.

1675 Rudner, Lawrence. *The Magic We Do Here* (10–12). 1988, Houghton $16.95 (0-395-45034-9). The harrowing story of a Polish Jew who survives the Holocaust by pretending to be a mentally defective mute. (Rev: BL 5/15/88)

1676 Shaw, Irwin. *The Young Lions* (10–12). 1984, Dell paper $4.95 (0-440-39794-4). A lengthy novel about World War II that traces the lives of 3 combatants—2 Americans, one a Jew, and a Nazi.

1677 Shepard, Jim. *Paper Doll* (10–12). 1986, Knopf $15.95 (0-394-55519-8); Dell paper $3.95 (0-440-20076-8). For mature readers, a book about the crew of a B-17 Flying Fortress during World War II. (Rev: BR 3–4/87; VOYA 4/87)

1678 Shute, Nevil. *A Town Like Alice* (9–12). 1987, Ballantine paper $3.95 (0-345-35374-9). A novel told partly in flashbacks about a girl's search for the Australian she met in Malaya during World War II.

1679 Siegal, Aranka. *Grace in the Wilderness: After the Liberation, 1945–1948* (7–12). 1985, Farrar $13.95 (0-374-32760-2); NAL paper $2.50 (0-317-52861-0). Based on fact, this continues the story begun in *Upon the Head of a Goat* (1982) which told about 2 sisters surviving the horrors of Nazi death camps. In this sequel the girls, filled with guilt that they survived and others didn't, try to start life over. (Rev: BL 11/15/85; BR 9–10/86; SLJ 12/85; VOYA 4/86)

1680 Smith, Steven P. *American Boys* (10–12). 1984, Avon paper $4.50 (0-380-67934-5). For mature readers, the story of 4 friends and the Vietnam War.

1681 Stroup, Dorothy. *In the Autumn Wind* (10–12). 1987, Macmillan $19.95 (0-684-18642-X). A novel about the effects of the dropping of the atomic bomb on Hiroshima on a single Japanese family. (Rev: BL 2/15/87)

1682 Tanner, Janet. *Women and War* (10–12). 1988, St. Martin's $18.95 (0-312-01538-0). In this novel set in World War II Australia, 2 women vie for the love of a young doctor. (Rev: BL 4/1/88)

1683 Trew, Antony. *Yashimoto's Last Dive* (9–12). 1988, St. Martin's $16.95 (0-312-01116-4). An action-filled story of a man's revenge against the Japanese who killed his shipmates. (Rev: BL 2/1/88)

1684 Uris, Leon. *Mila 18* (10–12). 1961, Doubleday $15.95 (0-385-02076-7); Bantam paper $4.95 (0-553-24160-5). A dramatic story involving the Warsaw Ghetto freedom fighters during World War II.

1685 Watkins, Paul. *Night Over Day Over Night* (10–12). 1988, Knopf $17.95 (0-394-57047-2). In this novel for mature readers, a 17-year-old German boy enlists in the SS during the last days of World War II. (Rev: BL 3/15/88)

1686 Watkins, Yoko Kawashima. *So Far from the Bamboo Grove* (9–12). 1986, Lothrop $10.25 (0-688-06110-9). The story of a horrifying odyssey after World War II of a Japanese family from Korea back to their homeland. (Rev: BL 8/86; BR 9–10/86; SLJ 9/86; VOYA 8–10/86)

1687 Wharton, William. *A Midnight Clear* (10–12). 1983, Ballantine paper $3.95 (0-345-31291-0). In this novel set during World War II, a group

of American soldiers gain personal insights through war experience.

1688 Wouk, Herman. *The Caine Mutiny* (10–12). 1951, Doubleday $17.95 (0-385-04053-9); Pocket paper $5.95 (0-671-60425-2). The story of the men aboard the mine sweeper *Caine* and of her psychotic captain named Queeg.

1689 Wouk, Herman. *The Winds of War* (10–12). 1971, Little $24.95 (0-316-95500-0); Pocket paper $5.95 (0-671-63472-0). This novel traces the effects of the beginning of World War II on the family of Commander Pug Henry. A sequel is *War and Remembrance* (1978).

KOREAN WAR

1690 Michener, James A. *The Bridges at Toko-Ri* (9–12). 1953, Random $16.95 (0-394-41780-1); Fawcett paper $2.95 (0-449-44520-8). The story of a young navy pilot and his bombing missions over Korea during the early 1950s.

VIETNAM WAR

1691 Amos, James. *The Memorial: A Novel of the Vietnam War* (10–12). 1989, Crown $19.95 (0-517-56971-X). For mature readers, a novel in the form of an agonizing remembrance of the war in Vietnam by a survivor. (Rev: BL 6/1/89)

1692 Butler, Robert Olen. *On Distant Ground* (10–12). 1985, Knopf $14.95 (0-394-54040-9). After his tour of duty in Vietnam, an American soldier returns on the eve of Saigon's fall to find a child that might be his. (Rev: BL 2/15/85; VOYA 12/85)

1693 Currey, Richard. *Fatal Light* (10–12). 1988, Dutton $16.95 (0-525-24622-3). For better readers, this is a touching story of a young man's experience in Vietnam during the war. (Rev: BL 4/1/88)

1694 Del Vecchio, John M. *The Thirteenth Valley* (10–12). 1984, Bantam paper $5.95 (0-553-26020-0). For mature readers, this is the harrowing account of a unit during the Vietnam War.

1695 DeMille, Nelson. *Word of Honor* (10–12). 1985, Warner $17.50 (0-446-51280-X); paper $4.95 (0-446-35320-5). A compelling novel for better readers about a Vietnam veteran who is accused of wartime atrocities. (Rev: BL 10/1/85)

1696 Haldeman, Joe. *War Year* (10–12). 1984, Avon paper $2.95 (0-380-67975-2). A tough look at the everyday life of soldiers in the Vietnam War.

1697 Jones, Adrienne. *Long Time Passing* (9–12). 1990, Harper LB $14.89 (0-06-023056-8). A teenage boy comes of age in America during the years of the Vietnam War. (Rev: BL 11/15/90; SLJ 9/90)

1698 Myers, Walter Dean. *Fallen Angels* (9–12). 1988, Scholastic $12.95 (0-590-40942-5). A 17-year-old black boy and his brutal but enabling experiences in the Vietnam War. (Rev: BL 4/15/88; BR 9–10/88; SLJ 6–7/88; VOYA 8/88)

1699 O'Brien, Tim. *Going after Cacciato* (10–12). 1987, Dell paper $4.95 (0-440-32966-3). In this surreal novel, Private Cacciato's company follows him when he leaves the Vietnam War to walk to Paris. For better readers.

1700 O'Brien, Tim. *The Things They Carried* (10–12). 1990, Houghton $19.95 (0-395-51598-X). For mature readers, a group of interrelated stories involving a platoon in Vietnam. (Rev: BL 3/15/90)

1701 Proffitt, Nicholas. *Gardens of Stone* (10–12). 1987, Carroll & Graf paper $4.50 (0-88184-312-1). A career soldier faces problems and conflicts during the Vietnam War.

1702 Rostkowski, Margaret I. *The Best of Friends* (7–12). 1989, Harper LB $12.89 (0-06-025105-0). How the Vietnam War affects 3 teenaged Utah friends as each tells a part of the story. (Rev: BL 9/1/89; SLJ 9/89; VOYA 12/89)

1703 Schaeffer, Susan Fromberg. *Buffalo Afternoon* (10–12). 1989, Knopf $19.95 (0-394-57178-9). For mature readers, this is the story of a teenaged soldier's experiences in Vietnam and his inability to assimilate them back home. (Rev: BL 3/15/89)

1704 Steel, Danielle. *Message from Nam* (10–12). 1990, Delacorte $21.95 (0-385-29907-9). During the Vietnam War, a college student decides to visit that land after her fiance is killed in the war. (Rev: BL 4/1/90)

1705 Webb, James, Jr. *Fields of Fire* (10–12). 1982, Bantam paper $4.95 (0-553-25679-3). For better readers, a gripping and harrowing novel about the Vietnam War.

1706 Wright, Stephen. *Meditations in Green* (10–12). 1983, Macmillan $14.95 (0-684-18010-3); paper $8.95 (0-684-18973-9). A novel about the Vietnam War and its aftermath.

Horror Stories and the Supernatural

1707 Andrews, V. C. *Flowers in the Attic* (10–12). 1989, Pocket paper $5.50 (0-671-68287-3).

This horror story about youngsters being held prisoners in an attic is long on horror but short on quality. Continued in *Petals on the Wind; If There Be Thorns;* and *Seeds of Yesterday* (all 1989).

1708 Ansa, Tina McElroy. *Baby of the Family* (10–12). 1989, Harcourt $18.95 (0-15-110431-X). Lena McPherson was born with the magical ability to relate to ghosts. (Rev: SLJ 6/90)

1709 Anthony, Piers. *Shade of the Tree* (10–12). 1987, Tor paper $3.95 (0-8125-3103-5). The horror mounts slowly as a New York man and his 2 children move into a deserted estate in Florida. (Rev: BL 3/15/86; VOYA 8–10/86)

1710 Ashley, Mike, ed. *The Mammoth Book of Short Horror Novels* (10–12). 1988, Carroll & Graf paper $8.95 (0-88184-429-2). Ten short novels by such masters as Oliver Onions and Stephen King. (Rev: BL 9/15/88)

1711 Asimov, Isaac, et al., eds. *Devils* (9–12). 1987, NAL paper $3.50 (0-451-14865-7). A devilish collection of stories drawn from such sources as folklore and tales of horror.

1712 Asimov, Isaac, et al., eds. *Ghosts* (10–12). 1988, NAL paper $4.50 (0-451-15723-0). For better readers, a chilling collection of 14 stories, a few of which are old favorites. (Rev: BL 11/15/88)

1713 Asimov, Isaac, et al., eds. *Tales of the Occult* (9–12). 1989, Prometheus $22.95 (0-87975-506-7); paper $14.95 (0-87975-531-8). A collection of 22 stories that explore such subjects as telepathy and reincarnation. (Rev: BL 4/1/89)

1714 Barker, Clive. *Volume Three of Clive Barker's Books of Blood* (10–12). 1986, Berkley paper $3.95 (0-425-09347-6). For mature horror buffs, this is one of the many novels by Britain's answer to Stephen King. (Rev: VOYA 2/87)

1715 Bendixen, Alfred, ed. *Haunted Women: The Best Supernatural Tales by American Women Writers* (10–12). 1985, Ungar $14.95 (0-8044-2052-1). An anthology of 13 supernatural stories with a tinge of the gothic all by American women writers of the nineteenth century. (Rev: BL 1/1/85; VOYA 8–10/86)

1716 Bierce, Ambrose. *The Stories and Fables of Ambrose Bierce* (10–12). Illus. 1977, Stemmer House $14.95 (0-916144-19-4). This collection includes over 100 stories by this master of unusual and macabre subjects.

1717 Bloch, Robert. *Midnight Pleasures* (10–12). 1987, Doubleday $12.95 (0-385-19439-0). Fourteen short stories of horror by the author of *Psycho*. (Rev: VOYA 10/87)

1718 Bloch, Robert. *Psycho House* (10–12). 1990, St. Martin's $16.95 (0-312-93217-0). The Bates Motel of *Psycho* fame has been rebuilt and a knife murderer is again on the loose. (Rev: BL 1/1/90; SLJ 8/90)

1719 Boyle, Josephine. *Maiden's End* (10–12). 1989, St. Martin's $16.95 (0-312-03391-5). An unhappy teenager becomes possessed by a demon. (Rev: BL 11/1/89)

1720 Bridges, Laurie, and Paul Alexander. *Swamp Witch* (9–12). 1984, Bantam paper $2.50 (0-553-26792-2). An easily read chiller about voodoo. Also use *The Ashton Horror* and *Devil Wind* (both 1984).

1721 Brunn, Robert. *The Initiation* (9–12). 1982, Dell paper $1.95 (0-440-94047-8). Adam finds that the headmaster of his school is really a vampire.

1722 Cerf, Bennett, ed. *Famous Ghost Stories* (10–12). 1956, Amereon $21.95 (0-88411-146-6); Random paper $4.95 (0-394-70140-2). This is a superior anthology of truly scary stories.

1723 *Classic Ghost Stories* (9–12). 1975, Dover paper $5.95 (0-486-20735-8). An excellent collection featuring stories by authors like Dickens, Wilkie Collins, Bram Stoker, and Guy de Maupassant.

1724 Cook, Robin. *Coma* (10–12). 1977, NAL paper $4.95 (0-451-15953-5). A young medical student uncovers a plot to kill patients.

1725 Cook, Robin. *Mutation* (10–12). 1989, Putnam $18.95 (0-399-13402-6). A geneticist produces what he thinks is a genius for a son but there are many unexpected surprises in store for him. (Rev: BL 11/1/88; SLJ 7/89)

1726 Cooke, John Peyton. *The Lake* (10–12). 1989, Avon paper $3.95 (0-380-75768-0). Evil powers are unleashed and Stink Lake and its weird creatures begin taking over a town. (Rev: VOYA 10/89)

1727 Coville, Bruce. *Waiting Spirits* (9–12). 1984, Bantam paper $2.25 (0-553-26004-9). An old tragedy continues to produce strange happenings at the Burton home.

1728 Cox, Michael, and R. A. Gilbert, eds. *The Oxford Book of English Ghost Stories* (9–12). 1987, Oxford Univ. Pr. $22.95 (0-19-214163-5). A collection of 42 fine stories chiefly by English writers. (Rev: BL 3/1/87)

1729 Cramer, Kathryn, and David G. Hartwell, eds. *Christmas Ghosts* (10–12). 1987, Arbor House $16.95 (0-87795-873-4). Seventeen ghost stories all with a Christmas setting. (Rev: BL 9/1/87; VOYA 2/88)

1730 Cuddon, J. A., ed. *The Penguin Book of Ghost Stories* (9–12). 1985, Penguin paper $7.95 (0-14-006800-7). A collection of 33 spine tinglers by English, American, and European authors. (Rev: BL 7/85)

1731 Dahl, Roald. *Roald Dahl's Tales of the Unexpected* (10–12). 1979, Random paper $7.95 (0-394-74081-5). Included are 24 stories guaranteed to surprise and chill.

1732 Dalby, Richard, ed. *Victorian Ghost Stories by Eminent Women Writers* (9–12). 1989, Carroll & Graf $18.95 (0-88184-473-X). Twenty-one stories from the pens of such writers as Charlotte Bronte and Willa Cather. (Rev: BR 1–2/90; SLJ 11/89)

1733 Davidson, Nicole. *Crash Course* (7–12). 1990, Avon paper $2.95 (0-380-75964-0). Eight seniors in high school confront horror and death on a Thanksgiving retreat to Deep Creek Lake. (Rev: BL 9/15/90)

1734 De Lint, Charles. *Yarrow* (10–12). 1986, Ace paper $3.50 (0-441-95000-5). A fantasy novelist finds that an evil power is stealing her dreams. (Rev: VOYA 2/87)

1735 Devon, Gary. *Lost* (10–12). 1986, Knopf $17.95 (0-394-53836-6); Warner paper $4.95 (0-446-34489-3). For mature readers, a horror story about children being stalked by a psychopath. (Rev: VOYA 4/87)

1736 Dinesen, Isak. *Seven Gothic Tales* (10–12). 1939, Modern Lib. $6.95 (0-394-60496-2). The macabre and strange are featured in this collection of imaginative stories.

1737 Donaldson, D. J. *Cajun Nights* (10–12). 1988, St. Martin's $16.95 (0-312-02175-5). Voodoo and Louisiana lore combine in this horror story of murder and suicide. (Rev: BL 10/15/88)

1738 Doyle, Arthur Conan. *The Best Supernatural Tales of Arthur Conan Doyle* (10–12). 1979, Dover paper $6.50 (0-486-23725-7). A group of 15 ghost stories by this master of suspense.

1739 Du Maurier, Daphne. *Daphne du Maurier's Classics of the Macabre* (9–12). Illus. 1987, Doubleday $18.95 (0-385-24302-2). Six of the best stories by this author including "Don't Look Now" and "The Birds" all nicely illustrated with watercolors. (Rev: BL 1/1/88)

1740 Du Maurier, Daphne. *Echoes from the Macabre: Selected Stories* (9–12). 1977, Aeonian paper $20.95 (0-88411-543-7). Nine stories of suspense including the classic *The Birds*.

1741 Durst, Paul. *The Florentine Table* (10–12). 1990, Macmillan paper $4.95 (0-02-028361-X). A recently purchased table seems to be the cause of an evil presence that a family detects.

1742 Ellison, Harlan. *Deathbird Stories* (10–12). 1990, Macmillan paper $4.95 (0-02-028361-X). For mature readers, a chilling collection of stories about death and destruction.

1743 Engstrom, Elizabeth. *Black Ambrosia* (10–12). 1988, Tor paper $3.95 (0-812-51751-2). A horror novel about a female vampire and the many deaths she causes. (Rev: VOYA 8/88)

1744 Estleman, Loren D. *Sherlock Holmes vs. Dracula: Or, The Adventure of the Sanguinary Count* (10–12). 1979, Penguin paper $3.95 (0-14-005262-3). Excitement and horror are combined in this story about an encounter between Sherlock Holmes and Count Dracula.

1745 Etchison, Dennis, ed. *Masters of Darkness* (10–12). 1986, Tor paper $3.95 (0-812-51762-8). A collection of adult horror stories not for the squeamish. (Rev: VOYA 2/87)

1746 Etchison, Dennis, ed. *Masters of Darkness II* (10–12). 1988, Tor paper $3.95 (0-812-51764-4). A collection of 15 short horror stories by some of the best writers in this genre. An earlier volume, *Masters of Darkness,* appeared in 1986. (Rev: VOYA 6/88)

1747 Ferman, Edward L., and Anne Jorgan, eds. *The Best Horror Stories from the Magazine of Fantasy and Science Fiction* (10–12). 1988, St. Martin's $22.95 (0-312-01894-0). A fine collection of horror stories that spans 38 publishing years and includes such writers as Stephen King. (Rev: VOYA 12/88)

1748 Foster, Alan Dean. *Into the Out Of* (10–12). 1986, Warner $15.95 (0-446-51337-7); paper $3.95 (0-446-34559-8). In this supernatural novel, demons are infiltrating the Earth, intent on destroying humankind. (Rev: SLJ 2/87; VOYA 2/87)

1749 Fowler, Christopher. *Roofworld* (10–12). 1988, Ballantine paper $7.95 (0-345-35701-9). For mature readers, a novel about the warfare between 2 secret societies in London. (Rev: BL 9/15/88)

1750 Fowles, John. *The Magus* (10–12). Rev. ed. 1985, Dell paper $5.95 (0-440-35162-6). This story, set on a Greek island, is an elaborate tale of magic and eroticism.

1751 Gardner, Dozois, and Susan Casper, eds. *Ripper!* (10–12). 1988, Tor paper $3.95 (0-8125-1700-8). A collection of stories centered around the infamous Jack the Ripper. (Rev: VOYA 2/89)

1752 Grant, Charles L., ed. *Horrors* (10–12). 1984, Berkley paper $2.95 (0-425-09494-4). Some of the best spine tinglers are included in this anthology and its companions *Nightmares; Shadows;* and *Terrors* (all 1984).

1753 Grant, Charles L. *In a Dark Dream* (10–12). 1989, Tor $17.95 (0-312-93159-X). Events build to a horrifying climax in this novel set in an idyllic small town. (Rev: VOYA 8/89)

1754 Grant, Charles L., ed. *Midnight* (10–12). 1985, Tor paper $2.95 (0-425-11870-3). Contemporary writers from Britain, the United States, and Australia are included in this collection of 18 horror stories. Also use *Nightmare Seasons* (1985). (Rev: VOYA 8/85)

1755 Grant, Charles L., ed. *Shadows 8* (10–12). 1987, Berkley paper $2.95 (0-425-09890-7). A collection of modern horror stories many of which border on fantasy. (Rev: BL 1/1/86)

1756 Greenberg, Martin H., ed. *The Further Adventures of the Joker* (10–12). 1990, Bantam paper $4.50 (0-553-28531-9). A group of science fiction and horror stories that are for mature readers. (Rev: VOYA 6/90)

1757 Greenberg, Martin H., and Rosalind M. Greenberg, eds. *Phantoms* (9–12). 1989, DAW paper $3.95 (0-88677-348-2). A collection of page-turners that explore the world of the macabre. (Rev: VOYA 10/89)

1758 Haining, Peter, ed. *Movie Monsters: Great Horror Film Stories* (9–12). Illus. 1988, Severn House $17.95 (0-7278-1546-6). A collection of 12 stories that became the basis of such horror movies as *The Thing* and *The Fly.* (Rev: BL 1/1/89)

1759 Haining, Peter, ed. *The Mummy: Stories of the Living Corpse* (9–12). 1989, Severn House $17.95 (0-7278-1556-3). Sixteen scary stories from Poe to the moderns about mummies. (Rev: BL 7/89)

1760 Haining, Peter, ed. *Stories of the Walking Dead* (10–12). 1990, Mercedes $17.95 (0-7278-1307-2). A collection of scary fiction involving zombies. (Rev: BL 6/15/90)

1761 Hambly, Barbara. *Those Who Hunt the Night* (10–12). 1988, Del Rey $16.95 (0-345-34380-8). For mature readers, the gruesome story of a search for the man who is murdering vampires. (Rev: VOYA 4/89)

1762 Hambly, Barbara. *The Witches of Wenshar* (10–12). 1987, Ballantine paper $3.95 (0-345-32934-1). Sun Wolf travels to a witch city to improve his magic in this sequel to *The Ladies of Mandrigyn* (1984). (Rev: BL 9/1/87)

1763 Hartwell, David G., ed. *The Dark Descent* (10–12). 1987, Tor $29.95 (0-812-93035-6). A collection of 56 horror stories (many graphic in nature) by some of the best writers in the genre, of both the past and the present. (Rev: BL 1/1/88; VOYA 4/88)

1764 Herbert, James. *Haunted* (10–12). 1989, Putnam $17.95 (0-399-13486-7). David Ash, a nonbeliever in ghosts, comes to an old English estate to check on rumors that the house is haunted. (Rev: BL 11/1/89)

1765 Hill, Susan. *The Woman in Black* (10–12). Illus. 1986, Godine $15.95 (0-87923-576-4). While reviewing the papers of a deceased client, a young lawyer encounters ghosts that fill his life with horror. (Rev: BL 8/86)

1766 Hoke, Helen, ed. *Spirits, Spooks and Other Sinister Creatures* (8–12). 1984, Watts LB $12.95 (0-531-04769-5). Twelve stories of suspense, horror, and sometimes humor. Also use *Tales of Fear and Frightening Phenomena* (1982).

1767 Hoke, Helen, ed. *Uncanny Tales of Unearthly and Unexpected Horrors* (7–12). 1983, Lodestar $11.95 (0-525-66919-1). A collection of spine-tinglers by some great horror writers.

1768 Howe, Imogen. *Vicious Circle* (7–12). 1983, Dell paper $1.95 (0-440-99318-0). The children of Maple Ridge Estates are one by one coming under the spell of a wicked force.

1769 Jackson, Shirley. *The Haunting of Hill House* (9–12). 1984, Penguin paper $6.95 (0-14-007108-3). Four people decide to stay in Hill House to see if it is really haunted.

1770 Jackson, Shirley. *The Lottery* (8–12). 1949, Farrar paper $8.95 (0-374-51681-2). Macabre stories by this master that include the classic about a village and its horrifying annual tradition.

1771 James, M. R. *A Warning to the Curious* (10–12). 1989, Godine paper $10.95 (0-87923-816-X). A collection of ghost stories by a forgotten master of the art who died in the 1930s. (Rev: BL 4/15/90)

1772 James, Peter. *Possession* (10–12). 1988, Doubleday $17.95 (0-385-24705-2). A house is haunted by the ghost of a young man killed in a car crash. (Rev: BL 8/88)

1773 Jones, Stephen, and David Sutton, eds. *The Best Horror from Fantasy Tales* (10–12). Illus. 1990, Carroll & Graf $17.95 (0-88184-571-X). A collection of 20 spine-chilling tales by such authors as Clive Barker. (Rev: BL 4/1/90)

1774 Kafka, Franz. *The Complete Stories* (10–12). Illus. 1983, Schocken $22.50 (0-8052-3863-8); paper $11.95 (0-8052-0423-7). The nightmar-

ish world of Kafka is revealed in this complete collection of his short stories.

1775 Kaye, Marvin, and Saralee Kaye, eds. *Masterpieces of Terror and the Supernatural: A Treasury of Spellbinding Tales Old & New* (10–12). 1985, Doubleday $15.95 (0-385-18549-9). A gripping, chilling collection of 50 stories dating back to Shelley and Stevenson but also including modern masters. (Rev: BL 8/85)

1776 Keeping, Charles, ed. *Charles Keeping's Book of Classic Ghost Stories* (9–12). Illus. 1986, Bedrick $14.95 (0-87226-096-8). An illustrated collection of 8 classic tales by such authors as Poe, Dickens, and du Maurier. (Rev: BL 9/1/86; BR 5–6/87)

1777 Keeping, Charles, ed. *Charles Keeping's Classic Tales of the Macabre* (9–12). 1987, Bedrick $14.94 (0-87226-168-9). Eight creepy tales by such masters as Edgar Allan Poe, Arthur Conan Doyle, and Bram Stoker. (Rev: BR 3–4/88; VOYA 6/88)

1778 King, Stephen. *The Bachman Books: Four Early Novels by Stephen King* (10–12). 1986, NAL paper $5.95 (0-451-14736-7). This volume contains 4 early novels by King—*Rage, The Long Walk, Roadwork*, and *The Running Man*. (Rev: SLJ 4/86)

1779 King, Stephen. *Carrie* (10–12). 1974, Doubleday $16.95 (0-385-08695-4); NAL paper $3.95 (0-451-15071-6). Carrie, a teenager with telekenetic powers, takes horrible revenge on her tormentors.

1780 King, Stephen. *Christine* (10–12). 1983, Viking $22.95 (0-670-22026-4); NAL paper $4.95 (0-451-16044-4). Arnie buys an old Plymouth that has mystical powers to possess and destroy.

1781 King, Stephen. *Cujo* (10–12). 1981, Viking $22.95 (0-670-45193-2); NAL paper $4.95 (0-451-16135-1). This is a horror story about a huge Saint Bernard that runs amok.

1782 King, Stephen. *Cycle of the Werewolf* (10–12). 1985, NAL paper $9.95 (0-451-82119-6). A horror novel about a small Maine town under siege by a beastly killer. (Rev: VOYA 8/85)

1783 King, Stephen. *The Dark Half* (9–12). 1989, Viking $21.95 (0-670-82982-X). A fictional character supposedly put to rest by his author comes to life to seek revenge. (Rev: BL 8/89)

1784 King, Stephen. *The Dead Zone* (9–12). 1979, Viking $22.95 (0-670-26077-0); NAL paper $4.95 (0-451-15575-0). A number of men named John Smith find themselves in the strange area known as The Dead Zone.

1785 King, Stephen. *Different Seasons* (10–12). 1982, Viking $22.95 (0-670-27266-3); NAL paper $5.95 (0-451-16753-8). Four short stories by this master of suspense and mystery.

1786 King, Stephen. *Firestarter* (9–12). 1980, Viking $22.95 (0-670-31541-9); NAL paper $4.50 (0-451-15031-1). A child is born with the incredible power to start fires.

1787 King, Stephen. *Four Past Midnight* (10–12). 1990, Viking $22.95 (0-670-83538-2). For mature readers, a collection of lengthy stories by the master of horror. (Rev: BL 6/15/90)

1788 King, Stephen. *Misery* (10–12). 1987, Viking $18.95 (0-670-81364-8); NAL paper $4.95 (0-451-15353-1). For better readers, a thriller about a deranged nurse who holds her favorite author prisoner. (Rev: BR 3–4/88; VOYA 2/88)

1789 King, Stephen. *Night Shift* (10–12). 1978, Doubleday $17.95 (0-385-12991-2); paper $4.95 (0-451-16045-2). Vampires and demons inhabit these horror stories by a master of the macabre.

1790 King, Stephen. *Pet Sematary* (10–12). 1983, Doubleday $19.95 (0-385-18244-9); NAL paper $4.95 (0-451-15775-3). The frightening horror story about a family that moves next to an ancient Indian burial ground.

1791 King, Stephen. *The Shining* (10–12). 1977, Doubleday $19.95 (0-385-12167-9); NAL paper $4.95 (0-451-16091-6). The Torrances take over a deserted hotel that is haunted by the spirits of the dead.

1792 King, Stephen. *The Stand: The Complete and Uncut Edition* (10–12). Illus. 1990, Doubleday $24.95 (0-385-19957-0). This mammoth volume (over 1,100 pages) restores all the cuts made in the original 1978 edition. (Rev: BL 3/15/90)

1793 King, Stephen. *The Tommyknockers* (10–12). 1987, Putnam $19.95 (0-399-13314-3); NAL paper $5.95 (0-451-15660-9). Roberta finds a buried flying saucer and soon its evil spreads into town. (Rev: SLJ 2/88)

1794 Klause, Annette Curtis. *The Silver Kiss* (8–12). 1990, Delacorte $14.95 (0-385-30160-X). A teenage girl, beset with personal problems, meets a silver-haired boy who is a vampire in this suspenseful, sometimes gory, novel. (Rev: BL 10/15/90; SLJ 9/90)

1795 Klein, T. E. D. *Dark Gods* (10–12). 1985, Viking $16.95 (0-670-80590-4); Bantam paper $3.95 (0-553-25801-X). This volume contains 4 scary stories in which the horror is there but underplayed. (Rev: SLJ 4/86)

1796 Koontz, Dean R. *Midnight* (10–12). 1989, Putnam $18.95 (0-399-13390-9). For better read-

ers, the story of a warped scientist whose plans to form a better human society go haywire. (Rev: BL 11/1/88)

1797 Koontz, Dean R. *Phantoms* (10–12). 1983, Putnam $15.95 (0-399-12655-4); Berkley paper $4.95 (0-425-10145-2). A quiet town in California is gradually being consumed by a beast from the past in this horror story.

1798 Koontz, Dean R. *Strangers* (10–12). 1986, Putnam $17.95 (0-399-13143-4); Berkely paper $4.95 (0-425-11992-0). In this somewhat complex novel 8 unrelated characters share the same terrible fears and anxieties. (Rev: BL 3/1/86; VOYA 8–10/86)

1799 Koontz, Dean R. *Twilight Eyes* (10–12). 1987, Berkley paper $4.95 (0-425-10065-0). For mature readers, a horror tale involving a traveling carnival during the 1960s. (Rev: VOYA 2/88)

1800 Koontz, Dean R. *Watchers* (9–12). 1987, Putnam $17.95 (0-399-13263-5); Berkley paper $4.95 (0-425-10746-9). Two man-made creatures—one saintly and the other a killer—escape from the laboratory where they have been housed. (Rev: SLJ 6–7/87)

1801 Kubicek, David, and Jeff Mason, eds. *October Dreams: A Harvest of Horror* (10–12). 1989, Kubicek & Assocs. paper $9.95 (0-945881-03-7). For true horror fanatics, a group of real stomach churners. (Rev: BL 2/1/90)

1802 Levin, Ira. *Rosemary's Baby* (10–12). 1979, Dell paper $2.25 (0-440-17541-8). Rosemary is pregnant and under the increased influence of witchcraft.

1803 Lillington, Kenneth. *Full Moon* (8–12). 1986, Faber $12.95 (0-571-13792-X). The twin sister of a 17-year-old boy is possessed by an unhappy young ghost and he must straighten out these supernatural happenings. (Rev: BL 6/1/86)

1804 Lovecraft, H. P. *At the Mountains of Madness and Other Novels* (10–12). 1985, Arkham House $16.95 (0-87054-038-6). Three novels by the master of the horror novel are included plus 5 short stories. Another fine collection is *The Dunwich Horror and Others* (1985). (Rev: BL 1/1/86)

1805 Lovecraft, H. P. *The Case of Charles Dexter Ward* (10–12). 1987, Ballantine paper $3.95 (0-345-35490-7). Charles discovers he has inherited the powers of witchcraft. Also use: *At the Mountains of Madness and Other Tales of Terror* (1985).

1806 Lovecraft, H. P. *Dagon and Other Macabre Tales* (10–12). 1987, Arkham House $18.95 (0-87054-039-4). A collection of early stories by this master of horror. Other collections in this series include *The Dunwich Horror and Others* (1985) and *At the Mountains of Madness and Other Novels* (1985). (Rev: BL 1/1/87)

1807 Lovecraft, H. P. *The Tomb and Other Tales* (10–12). 1986, Ballantine paper $3.95 (0-345-33661-5). A selection of stories from this master of horror and the macabre. Also use: *The Doom That Came to Sarnath* and *The Lurking Fear* (both 1985).

1808 Lumley, Brian. *The Source* (9–12). 1989, Tor paper $4.95 (0-812-52127-7). In this, the third volume of the Necroscope series, scientists find in the Ural mountains the entrance to a world where vampires and other horrible creatures live. (Rev: VOYA 2/90)

1809 McCammon, Robert R. *Mine* (10–12). 1990, Pocket $18.95 (0-671-66486-7). A gory horror story for mature readers about a mother out to find her kidnapped child. (Rev: VOYA 6/90)

1810 McCammon, Robert R. *Swan Song* (10–12). 1987, Pocket paper $4.95 (0-671-62413-X). After World War III, the elements of good and evil in what is left of the human race fight over the spoils. (Rev: SLJ 10/87)

1811 McCauley, Kirby, ed. *Dark Forces* (10–12). 1989, NAL paper $4.95 (0-451-16221-8). A fine collection of horror and suspense stories.

1812 McNeil, W. K., comp. *Ghost Stories from the American South* (9–12). Illus. 1985, August House paper $7.95 (0-935304-84-3). A collection of blood-curdlers from locales ranging from Virginia to Texas. (Rev: SLJ 12/85)

1813 Martin, Valerie. *Mary Reilly* (9–12). 1990, Doubleday $18.95 (0-385-24968-3). A retelling of Stevenson's classic horror story from the standpoint of Dr. Jekyll's maid. (Rev: BL 12/1/89)

1814 Masterton, Graham. *Death Trance* (10–12). 1986, Tor paper $3.95 (0-812-52187-0). A grieving father wants to enter the world of the dead to visit his murdered family. (Rev: VOYA 2/87)

1815 O'Har, George M. *Psychic Fair* (8–12). 1989, Pocket paper $3.95 (0-671-67601-6). Three teenagers buy a Ouija board then make contact with a vindictive spirit. (Rev: VOYA 10/89)

1816 Olson, Paul F., and David B. Silva, eds. *Post Mortem* (9–12). 1989, St. Martin's $16.95 (0-312-02631-5). An excellent collection of 17 contemporary ghost stories. (Rev: VOYA 8/89)

1817 Page, Gerald W., ed. *The Year's Best Horror Stories* (10–12). 1990, DAW paper $4.95 (0-88677-446-2). One of a lengthy annual series of horror story collections.

1818 Paige, Richard. *The Door to December* (10–12). 1985, NAL paper $3.95 (0-451-13605-5). For mature readers, a horror story involving the investigation of a grisly mass murder. (Rev: VOYA 12/85)

1819 Peters, Elizabeth. *The Love Talker* (10–12). 1990, Tor paper $3.95 (0-8125-0727-4). Laurie and Doug wonder if someone is trying to frighten their eccentric aunt to death.

1820 Phillips, Robert, ed. *Triumph of the Night* (9–12). 1989, Carroll & Graf $18.95 (0-88184-517-5). Twenty-two ghost stories by such writers as Graham Greene, Truman Capote, and Tennessee Williams. (Rev: BL 10/1/89)

1821 Pierce, Meredith Ann. *The Darkangel* (10–12). 1984, Tor paper $2.95 (0-8215-4900-7). In this vampire story, Airiel tries to rescue the fiend's brides.

1822 Pike, Christopher. *Scavenger Hunt* (9–12). 1989, Pocket paper $2.95 (0-671-67656-3). Two groups of teenagers on a scavenger hunt encounter horror that leads to a terrifying climax. Also use: *Remember Me* (1989). (Rev: BL 9/1/89; VOYA 2/90)

1823 Poe, Edgar Allan. *The Complete Tales and Poems of Edgar Allan Poe* (9–12). 1938, Modern Lib. $12.95 (0-394-60408-3); Random paper $11.95 (0-394-71678-7). In addition to 63 stories, this volume includes 53 poems and some nonfiction works.

1824 Poe, Edgar Allan. *Tales of Terror* (7–12). Illus. 1985, Prentice $12.95 (0-13-884214-0). This is a collection of Poe's most famous stories illustrated by Neil Waldman. (Rev: BL 6/15/85; SLJ 9/85)

1825 Ramsay, Jay. *Night of the Claw* (7–12). 1985, Tor paper $3.95 (0-8125-2500-0). A horror story about a young girl beset by an evil presence in her home.

1826 Rendell, Ruth. *The New Girl Friend and Other Stories* (10–12). 1987, Ballantine paper $3.95 (0-345-32879-5). For better readers 11 stories of psychological horror by the English master. (Rev: BL 2/15/86; SLJ 1/88)

1827 Rhue, Morton. *The Wave* (9–12). 1981, Delacorte $10.95 (0-440-09822-X); Dell paper $3.25 (0-440-99371-7). What starts as an innocent experiment brings terror to a high school.

1828 Rice, Anne. *Interview with the Vampire* (10–12). 1986, Ballantine paper $5.95 (0-345-33766-2). A 200-year-old vampire reveals every horrifying detail of his life. Rice has written other horror novels involving vampires.

1829 Rice, Anne. *The Mummy: Or, Ramses the Damned* (10–12). 1989, Ballantine paper $11.95 (0-345-36000-1). For mature readers, the story of a mummy brought back to life with a curse that must be fulfilled. (Rev: BL 3/1/89)

1830 Ryan, Alan, ed. *Halloween Horrors* (9–12). 1986, Doubleday $12.95 (0-385-19558-3); Ace paper $3.50 (0-441-31607-7). A group of 13 spine tinglers, all taking place on Halloween night. (Rev: BL 9/15/86; VOYA 2/87)

1831 Ryan, Alan, ed. *Haunting Women* (9–12). 1988, Avon paper $3.95 (0-380-89881-0). Fourteen horror stories written by such women as Shirley Jackson and Ruth Rendell. (Rev: BL 11/15/88; VOYA 2/89)

1832 Salmonson, Jessica Amanda, ed. *Tales by Moonlight II* (9–12). 1989, Tor paper $3.95 (0-812-55371-3). An intriguing collection of exciting and different stories involving science fiction, horror, and fantasy. (Rev: VOYA 12/89)

1833 Salmonson, Jessica Amanda. *What Did Miss Darrington See? An Anthology of Feminist Supernatural Fiction* (10–12). 1989, Feminist Pr. $29.95 (1-55861-005-7); paper $10.95 (1-55861-006-5). A collection of 24 stories from 3 continents that spans almost 150 years of writing. (Rev: BL 9/1/89)

1834 Sarrantonio, Al. *Moonbane* (9–12). 1989, Bantam paper $3.95 (0-553-28186-0). An action-filled horror story about werewolves that arrive on Earth from meteors. (Rev: VOYA 4/90)

1835 Saul, John. *Comes the Blind Fury* (9–12). 1990, Dell paper $4.95 (0-440-11475-6). An antique doll actually contains the evil spirit of a dead girl. Also use: *Cry for the Stranger* (1986), *Suffer the Children,* and *When the Wind Blows* (both 1990).

1836 Saul, John. *Creature* (10–12). 1989, Bantam $19.95 (0-553-05354-4). Mark Tanner enters a football training program with horrifying results. (Rev: SLJ 7/89)

1837 Saul, John. *Nathaniel* (10–12). 1990, Bantam paper $4.95 (0-553-26264-5). For mature readers, a horror story about a young boy and a gruesome legend.

1838 Schiff, Stuart David, ed. *Whispers VI* (10–12). 1986, Jove paper $3.95 (0-515-10010-2). For better readers, a series of thrillers that sometimes shock, sometimes amuse. (Rev: VOYA 12/87)

1839 Schow, David J., ed. *Silver Scream* (10–12). 1988, Dark Harvest $19.95 (0-913165-27-1); Tor paper $3.95 (0-812-52555-8). An anthology of 20 horror stories all with themes involving motion pictures. (Rev: VOYA 4/89)

1840 Schwartz, Betty Ann, ed. *Great Ghost Stories* (8–12). Illus. 1985, Simon & Schuster $6.95 (0-671-60179-2). A collection of adult ghost stories suitable for young adults. Most are by well-known authors. (Rev: BL 12/15/85; SLJ 1/87)

1841 Scott, R. C. *Blood Sport* (9–12). 1984, Bantam paper $2.25 (0-553-23866-3). Bob befriends some gymnasts that he gradually believes are really vampires.

1842 Serling, Carol, et al., eds. *Rod Serling's Night Gallery Reader* (9–12). 1987, Dembner $15.95 (0-934878-93-5). A collection of wry often humorous stories that served as bases for episodes on "Night Gallery." (Rev: BL 12/15/87)

1843 Shepard, Leslie, ed. *The Dracula Book of Great Horror Stories* (10–12). 1977, Citadel $10.00 (0-8065-0565-6). Thirteen old-fashioned but still chilling horror stories.

1844 Siddons, Anne Rivers. *The House Next Door* (10–12). 1984, Ballantine paper $3.95 (0-345-32333-5). The story of a house that seems to have the power to kill its tenants.

1845 Sleator, William. *Fingers* (8–12). 1983, Atheneum $12.95 (0-689-31000-5); Bantam paper $2.50 (0-553-25004-3). Eighteen-year old Sam uses his composing talents to fool the public into thinking his pianist brother is receiving musical compositions telepathically from a dead composer.

1846 Smith, Clark Ashton. *A Rendezvous in Averoigne: Best Fantastic Tales of Clark Ashton Smith* (9–12). 1988, Arkham House $22.95 (0-87054-156-0). These 30 stories represent the nightmarish world of the master of horror. (Rev: BR 11–12/88)

1847 Smith, Martin Cruz. *Nightwing* (10–12). 1987, Hill & Co. $9.95 (0-940595-05-2); Jove paper $3.95 (0-515-08502-2). In this horror story, vampire bats bring death to a group of Hopi Indians. Also use the author's thriller about furs and murder, *Gorky Park* (1982).

1848 Sparger, Rex. *The Bargain* (9–12). 1986, Bantam paper $2.25 (0-553-25779-X). An evil force tries to control the minds of members of a rock group. Also use: *The Doll* (1987).

1849 Stanwood, Brooks. *The Glow* (10–12). 1980, Fawcett paper $4.95 (0-449-24333-8). The horror story about a horrible discovery made by 2 people while out jogging.

1850 Stoker, Bram. *Dracula* (10–12). 1985, Amereon LB $19.95 (0-88411-131-8); Dell paper $2.95 (0-440-92148-1). In epistolary form, this novel involves a baron who is a vampire and his mysterious castle in Transylvania.

1851 Straczynski, J. Michael. *Othersyde* (10–12). 1990, Dutton $18.95 (0-525-24873-0). A teenager anxious for revenge begins using an evil force to help his plans. (Rev: BL 7/90)

1852 Straub, Peter. *Ghost Story* (10–12). 1989, Pocket paper $5.95 (0-671-68563-5). This is a story of revenge about a group of New England men who confront the horror of their past lives.

1853 Strieber, Whitley. *Billy* (10–12). 1990, Putnam $19.95 (0-399-13584-7). For mature readers, a horror novel about a psychotic killer and his 12-year-old victim. (Rev: BL 6/1/90)

1854 Strieber, Whitley. *The Wolfen* (10–12). 1988, Avon paper $4.50 (0-380-70440-4). A real chiller about werewolves who are thinking, killing creatures.

1855 Tiptree, James, Jr. *Tales of the Quintana Roo* (10–12). 1986, Arkham House $11.95 (0-87054-152-8). Three ghostly tales that are set in the eastern coast of the Yucatan Peninsula and evoke the spirit of the Mayan culture. (Rev: VOYA 12/86)

1856 Trevor, Elleston. *The Theta Syndrome* (10–12). 1989, Jove paper $3.95 (0-515-10158-3). A horror story that begins when a researcher notices strange behavior patterns in the laboratory rats.

1857 Tryon, Thomas. *Harvest Home* (10–12). 1987, Dell paper $4.95 (0-440-13454-4). A young couple and their daughter discover a grisly plot when they move to a supposedly quiet New England village.

1858 Tryon, Thomas. *The Other* (10–12). 1987, Dell paper $4.95 (0-440-16736-1). A horror story set in New England involving unusual twin boys and their family.

1859 Wagner, Karl Edward, ed. *Intensive Scare* (10–12). 1990, DAW paper $3.95 (0-88677-402-0). A group of horror stories that all use doctors and the medical profession as subjects. (Rev: VOYA 6/90)

1860 Wagner, Karl Edward, ed. *The Year's Best Horror Stories: XVIII* (10–12). 1990, DAW paper $4.95 (0-88677-446-2). This is only one of an annual collection of horror stories that will give a reader goose bumps.

1861 Wagner, Karl Edward, ed. *The Year's Best Horror Stories, Volume XVII* (9–12). 1989, DAW paper $3.95 (0-88677-381-4). A collection of chilling tales that is part of a superior series published annually. (Rev: VOYA 4/90)

1862 Wakefield, H. Russell. *The Best Ghost Stories of H. Russell Wakefield* (10–12). 1982, Academy Chicago paper $7.95 (0-89733-066-8). Fourteen stories by one of this century's best writers of ghost stories.

1863 Walters, R. R. *Lily* (10–12). 1988, Tor paper $3.95 (0-812-52703-8). Sam becomes friendly with a strange woman named Lily without realizing that she is not human. (Rev: VOYA 12/88)

1864 Wescott, Earle. *Winter Wolves* (10–12). 1988, Yankee Books $13.95 (0-89909-160-1). In this novel for mature readers, a pack of ghost wolves terrorizes a Maine town. (Rev: BL 3/15/88; VOYA 12/88)

1865 Westlake, Donald E. *Tomorrow's Crimes* (10–12). 1989, Mysterious $18.95 (0-89296-299-2). Eight stories and one novella that combine mystery, suspense, and fantasy. (Rev: BL 9/15/89)

1866 Wiggins, Marianne. *John Dollar* (10–12). 1989, Harper $17.95 (0-06-016070-5). A group of girls reverts to savagery when it is marooned in a desolate place. (Rev: SLJ 7/89)

1867 Wilde, Oscar. *The Picture of Dorian Gray* (10–12). 1891, Random $6.95 (0-394-60514-4); Penguin paper $2.95 (0-14-043187-X). This fantasy involves a magical painting that mirrors the soul of a wicked man.

1868 Wilhelm, Kate. *Children of the Wind* (10–12). 1989, St. Martin's $16.95 (0-312-03303-6). A superior collection of 5 eerie short novels each involving the supernatural. (Rev: VOYA 4/90)

1869 Wilson, F. Paul. *The Tomb* (10–12). 1989, Berkley paper $4.50 (0-515-08876-5). In this thriller for mature readers, monsters emerge during a criminal investigation. Also use *The Keep* (1986).

1870 Wilson, F. Paul. *The Touch* (10–12). 1986, Jove paper $3.95 (0-515-08733-5). For mature readers, this is a horror story about a man who is able to cure people by touch. (Rev: BL 5/15/86)

1871 Wolfe, Gene. *Castleview* (10–12). 1990, St. Martin's $19.95 (0-312-85008-5). The murder of a factory manager in a small town in Illinois leads to horror involving the castle of Morgan Le Fay. (Rev: BL 1/1/90)

1872 Wright, T. M. *The Place* (10–12). 1989, Tor $17.95 (0-312-93146-8). When life becomes difficult, 8-year-old Greta retreats to "The Place" but now it too is becoming sinister and unfriendly. (Rev: VOYA 12/89)

1873 Wright, T. M. *The Playground* (10–12). 1982, Tor paper $2.95 (0-523-48046-6). In this horror novel, demonic children terrorize a community.

1874 Wright, T. M. *The School* (10–12). 1990, Tor $17.95 (0-312-85042-5). Frank and Allison Hitchcock move into an old schoolhouse they discover is haunted. (Rev: BL 8/90)

Humorous Stories

1875 Amis, Kingsley. *Lucky Jim* (10–12). 1954, Amereon $17.95 (0-89244-069-4); Penguin paper $4.95 (0-14-001648-1). A humorous novel for better readers about a junior instructor in an English college.

1876 Bodett, Tom. *The Big Garage on Clearshot: Growing Up, Growing Old, and Going Fishing at the End of the Road* (10–12). 1990, Morrow $18.95 (0-688-09525-9). Alaska's favorite storyteller continues his affectionate look at hometown life in this collection of humorous anecdotes. (Rev: BL 9/1/90)

1877 Carkeet, David. *I Been There Before* (10–12). 1985, Harper $18.95 (0-06-015426-8); Penguin paper $6.95 (0-14-009422-9). Mark Twain returns to Earth at the time of the arrival of Halley's Comet in 1985. (Rev: SLJ 9/86)

1878 DeVries, Peter. *The Tunnel of Love* (10–12). 1982, Penguin paper $6.95 (0-14-002200-7). This adult comedy tells of the problems confronted by a young couple when they try to adopt a child.

1879 Edgerton, Clyde. *Walking across Egypt* (10–12). 1987, Algonquin $14.95 (0-912697-51-2); Ballantine paper $3.95 (0-345-34649-1). A humorous story set in a small town in North Carolina about a 78-year-old woman and her friendship with a wayward teenage boy. (Rev: SLJ 6–7/87)

1880 Franzen, Bill. *Hearing from Wayne and Other Stories* (10–12). 1988, Knopf $15.95 (0-394-55501-5). A group of zany, very short stories mostly about a young man's experiences in a small town. (Rev: BL 4/1/88)

1881 Gibbons, Stella. *Cold Comfort Farm* (10–12). 1977, Penguin paper $5.95 (0-14-000140-9). A hilarious English novel for better readers about the looney Starkadder family.

1882 Greene, Constance C. *The Love Letters of J. Timothy Owen* (9–12). 1986, Harper LB $11.89 (0-06-022157-7). Tim is spurned by the object of his affections so he begins sending her anonymous love letters. (Rev: BL 10/1/86; SLJ 12/86; VOYA 12/86)

1883 Greene, Graham. *Travels with My Aunt* (10–12). 1969, Penguin paper $4.95 (0-14-003221-5). A witty, sophisticated novel about a madcap aunt in her seventies and her conservative nephew.

1884 Guareschi, Giovanni. *The Little World of Don Camillo* (10–12) 1986, Doubleday paper $5.95 (0-385-23242-X). A humorous novel about the battles between a Communist mayor and a priest in an Italian village after World War II.

1885 Kaufman, Bel. *Up the Down Staircase* (10–12). 1988, Prentice $19.95 (0-13-939158-4). A humorous, often poignant, story of a young schoolteacher in a New York high school.

1886 Koertge, Ron. *Where the Kissing Never Stops* (10–12). 1986, Atlantic Monthly $14.95 (0-87113-125-0); Dell paper $2.95 (0-440-20167-5). A candid, sometimes bawdy, story about a 17-year-old boy, his love life, and his mother who is a stripper. (Rev: BL 11/1/86; SLJ 12/86; VOYA 12/86)

1887 Korman, Gordon. *A Semester in the Life of a Garbage Bag* (9–12). 1987, Scholastic $12.95 (0-590-40694-9); paper $2.75 (0-590-40695-7). Terrible but humorous things keep happening to Jardine and he doesn't seem able to prevent them. (Rev: BL 8/87; SLJ 10/87; VOYA 8–9/87)

1888 Korman, Gordon. *Son of Interflux* (10–12). 1986, Scholastic $12.95 (0-590-40163-7); paper $2.50 (0-590-41186-1). In this humorous novel, Simon gets even with his business executive father by buying a crucial piece of property that will thwart the plans of Interflux, his father's company, to expand. (Rev: BL 11/1/86; SLJ 11/86; VOYA 12/86)

1889 Kosinski, Jerzy. *Being There* (10–12). 1985, Bantam paper $4.50 (0-553-27930-0). In this novel that contains some explicit sex, a simpleminded gardener becomes president because of a series of logical misunderstandings.

1890 Landis, J. D. *Joey and the Girls* (9–10). 1987, Bantam paper $2.95 (0-553-26415-X). Joey is having sex with 2 different girls and all is well until the 2 find out. (Rev: BL 3/15/87; SLJ 12/87; VOYA 8–9/87)

1891 McCauley, Stephen. *The Object of My Affection* (10–12). 1988, Washington Square Pr. paper $6.95 (0-671-64994-9). In this sunny novel a gay teacher decides to help his roommate who is expecting a baby. (Rev: BL 3/1/87)

1892 McClanahan, Ed. *The Natural Man* (10–12). 1983, Farrar $11.50 (0-374-21969-9); Penguin paper $5.95 (0-14-007042-7). A 15-year-old boy growing up in Needmore, Kentucky, decides to lose his virginity by his next birthday.

1893 McManus, Patrick, F. *Rubber Legs and White Tail-Hairs* (9–12). 1987, Henry Holt $14.95 (0-8050-0544-7); paper $6.95 (0-8050-0912-4). A group of short pieces that highlight human foibles in a humorous way. (Rev: SLJ 12/87)

1894 Oldham, June. *Enter Tom* (9–12). 1989, Delacorte $14.95 (0-385-29780-7). In this humorous English novel Tom and his friend Dave are feeling the pangs of unrequited love. (Rev: BL 9/15/89; SLJ 10/89)

1895 Oldham, June. *Grow Up, Cupid* (10–12). 1987, Delacorte $14.95 (0-385-29544-8). In this English comic novel the young writer of pulp romances wants to explore her own need for love. (Rev: BL 8/87; SLJ 8/87; VOYA 10/87)

1896 Oldham, June. *Moving In* (10–12). 1990, Delacorte $14.95 (0-385-30047-6). This perceptive novel tells about an English girl's humorous attempts to set up house for herself during her last year of high school. (Rev: BL 9/1/90)

1897 Powers, John R. *The Last Catholic in America* (10–12). 1982, Warner paper $3.50 (0-446-31332-7). Trauma and humor abound in these fictional recollections of attending a Catholic school in the 1950s.

1898 Pringle, Terry. *The Preacher's Kid* (10–12). 1988, Algonquin $14.95 (0-912697-77-6). In this humorous novel, a son comes to terms with the high expectations his father, a preacher, has for him. (Rev: SLJ 6–7/88; VOYA 12/88)

1899 Ross, Leonard Q. *The Education of H*Y*M*A*N K*A*P*L*A*N* (9–12). 1968, Harcourt paper $5.95 (0-15-627811-1). A series of hilarious stories about an immigrant Jew and his battle with the English language at night school.

1900 Sakai, Stan. *Usagi Yojimbo, Book One* (9–12). Illus. 1987, Fantagraphics paper $9.95 (0-930193-35-0). A humorous fantasy about a Samurai rabbit and his adventures in seventeenth-century Japan. (Rev: BL 3/15/88)

1901 Silsbee, Peter. *Love Among the Hiccups* (8–12). 1987, Macmillan $12.95 (0-02-782760-7); paper $3.95 (0-02-044983-6). A humorous mystery in which 2 teenagers are vying for the ownership of a decaying mansion. (Rev: BL 6/15/87; BR 11–12/87; SLJ 8/87; VOYA 10/87)

1902 Spark, Muriel. *The Abbess of Crewe* (10–12). 1984, Putnam paper $6.95 (0-399-50952-6). This takeoff on the Watergate affair involves some politically unscrupulous nuns in an English abbey.

1903 Stone, Bruce. *Been Clever Forever* (8–12). 1988, Harper LB $14.89 (0-06-025919-1). Ste-

phen A. Douglass, a sophomore and self-styled smartass, runs afoul of the establishment. (Rev: BL 11/15/88; BR 5–6/89; SLJ 11/88)

1904 Thompson, Julian. *Herb Seasoning* (9–12). 1990, Scholastic $12.95 (0-590-43023-8). Herbie, a teenager at loose ends, uses a counseling service to travel through time to find his destiny. (Rev: BL 5/15/90; SLJ 3/90)

1905 Thompson, Julian. *Simon Pure* (10–12). 1987, Scholastic $12.95 (0-590-40507-1); paper $2.75 (0-590-41823-8). Simon has some unusual but always hilarious adventures when he enters Riddle University. (Rev: BL 4/15/87; SLJ 3/87; VOYA 4/87)

1906 Townsend, Sue. *The Secret Diary of Adrian Mole, Age Thirteen and Three Quarters* (9–12). 1984, Avon paper $3.50 (0-380-86876-8). The trials and tribulations of a young English boy as revealed through his hilarious diary entries.

1907 Waugh, Evelyn. *The Loved One: An Anglo-American Tragedy* (10–12). 1977, Little paper $6.95 (0-316-92608-6). A sardonic, macabre novel about love in a Hollywood mortuary.

1908 Wibberley, Leonard. *The Mouse That Roared* (7–12). 1955, Bantam paper $3.50 (0-553-24969-X). To get foreign aid the tiny Duchy of Grand Fenwick declares war on the United States.

1909 Wodehouse, P. G. *Leave It to Psmith* (10–12). 1984, Amereon $16.95 (0-89190-297-X); Random paper $5.95 (0-394-72026-1). This novel is a good introduction to the many works of this English humorist.

1910 Wouk, Herman. *City Boy* (10–12). 1969, Doubleday $12.95 (0-385-04072-5). A humorous novel about the youth of Herbie Bookbinder, a Jewish kid growing up in Brooklyn.

Mystery and Detective Stories

1911 Adams, Harold. *The Man Who Met the Train* (10–12). 1988, Mysterious $15.95 (0-89296-251-8). In this Carl Wilcox mystery the hero investigates the strange deaths of a 4-year-old girl's parents. (Rev: BL 6/1/88)

1912 Alexander, Gary. *Pigeon Blood* (10–12). 1988, Walker $16.95 (0-8027-5700-6). For mature readers a novel of intrigue, murder, and humor set in a Southeast Asian country named Luong. (Rev: BL 3/1/88)

1913 Amis, Kingsley. *The Crime of the Century* (10–12). 1989, Mysterious $16.95 (0-89296-398-0). A lively whodunit with 2 endings—one by the author and the other by a contest winner. (Rev: BL 9/1/89)

1914 Asimov, Isaac. *The Best Mysteries of Isaac Asimov: The Master's Choice of His Own Favorites* (8–12). 1987, Fawcett paper $4.50 (0-449-13287-0). A collection of 31 short stories chosen by the writer as his favorites. (Rev: BL 8/86; SLJ 1/87; VOYA 2/87)

1915 Asimov, Isaac. *The Best Science Fiction of Isaac Asimov* (9–12). 1988, NAL paper $3.95 (0-451-15196-8). A collection of 28 of the stories the author thinks are his best. (Rev: BL 8/86)

1916 Asimov, Isaac, ed. *Hound Dunnit* (8–12). 1987, Carroll & Graf $17.95 (0-88184-353-9). A collection of stories involving dogs and mysteries. (Rev: VOYA 2/88)

1917 Asimov, Isaac. *Puzzles of the Black Widowers* (9–12). 1990, Doubleday $19.95 (0-385-26264-7). The fifth collection of stories about a group known as the Black Widowers who meet once a month to solve puzzles. (Rev: BL 1/15/90)

1918 Asimov, Isaac, et al., eds. *The Best Crime Stories of the Nineteenth Century* (9–12). 1988, Dembner $16.95 (0-934878-99-4). A total of 20 stories by such masters as Conan Doyle, Poe, and Twain. (Rev: BL 6/15/88)

1919 Babson, Marion. *Murder, Murder, Little Star* (10–12). 1980, Walker $9.95 (0-8027-5416-3); Bantam paper $3.50 (0-553-27478-8). A puzzler with an unexpected twist at the end.

1920 Ballard, Mignon F. *Cry at Dusk* (10–12). 1987, Dodd $15.95 (0-396-09060-5); Harlequin paper $3.50 (0-373-26025-3). A schoolteacher returning to her small-town class reunion begins investigating the mysterious death of a cousin. (Rev: BL 9/15/87)

1921 Barnard, Robert. *At Death's Door* (10–12). 1988, Macmillan $15.95 (0-684-19001-X). A celebrated actress is murdered leaving a large array of suspects. (Rev: BL 9/1/88)

1922 Barnard, Robert. *The Skeleton in the Grass* (10–12). 1988, Macmillan $15.95 (0-684-18948-8). A young governess to a pre–World War II English family encounters an unexpected case of murder. (Rev: BL 3/1/88)

1923 Barnes, Linda. *Coyote* (10–12). 1990, Delacorte $17.95 (0-385-30012-3). A mystery featuring the tough-talking, gutsy, but also vulnerable Boston detective, Carlotta Carlyle. (Rev: BL 9/1/90)

1924 Beaton, M. C. *Death of a Perfect Wife* (9–12). 1989, St. Martin's $15.95 (0-312-03322-2). A delightful mystery about some unusual characters who get involved in a murder in a quiet Scottish village. (Rev: BL 11/15/89)

1925 Beaton, M. C. *Death of an Outsider* (10–12). 1988, St. Martin's $14.95 (0-312-02188-7). The delightful Scottish detective, Hamish MacBeth, and his dog Towser get involved in a particularly gruesome murder. Also in this series: *Death of a Gossip* (1985); *Death of a Cad* (1987). (Rev: BL 12/1/88)

1926 Beck, K. K. *Peril Under the Palms* (10–12). 1989, Walker $18.95 (0-8027-5715-4). Iris Cooper, a flapper detective, solves the mystery of a double murder in the tropics. Earlier adventures of Iris were *Death in a Deck Chair* (1987) and *Murder in a Mummy Case* (1986). (Rev: SLJ 12/89)

1927 Bickham, Jack M. *Miracleworker* (10–12). 1987, Tor $16.95 (0-312-93023-2). Dr. Andra Dover discovers that the beloved local doctor has been involved in some mysterious deaths. (Rev: BL 9/1/87)

1928 Biggle, Lloyd. *The Quallsford Inheritance* (10–12). 1987, Penguin paper $3.95 (0-14-010007-5). A new Sherlock Holmes mystery narrated by Edward Porter Jones, another Baker Street Irregular. (Rev: BL 6/15/86)

1929 Blackmur, L. L. *Love Lies Slain* (10–12). 1989, St. Martin's $16.95 (0-312-03388-5). A former reporter accepts a writing assignment and finds herself involved in a double murder and a romance. (Rev: BL 9/1/89)

1930 Blain, W. Edward. *Passion Play* (10–12). 1990, Putnam $19.95 (0-399-13528-6). For better readers, the story of murder at a fashionable boarding school for boys. (Rev: BL 2/15/90; SLJ 8/90)

1931 Bleiler, E. F., ed. *A Treasury of Victorian Detective Stories* (10–12). 1982, Macmillan paper $3.95 (0-684-17640-8). This collection contains 23 classic stories by such masters as Arthur Conan Doyle, Bret Harte, and Wilkie Collins.

1932 Borthwick, J. S. *The Student Body* (10–12). 1987, St. Martin's paper $3.50 (0-312-90738-9). A graduate student helps investigate 2 murders at a small Maine college. (Rev: BL 10/1/86)

1933 Branfield, John. *The Poison Factory* (10–12). 1972, Harper LB $11.89 (0-06-020647-0). Helen tries to fathom the connection between her father's death and the factory where he worked.

1934 Braun, Lilian Jackson. *The Cat Who Lived High* (9–12). 1990, Putnam $15.95 (0-399-13554-5). Qwill and his famous Siamese Koko discover that the penthouse in which they are living was the scene of a murder-suicide. (Rev: BL 8/90)

1935 Braun, Lilian Jackson. *The Cat Who Sniffed Glue* (10–12). 1988, Putnam $15.95 (0-399-13381-X). The return of the 2 Siamese cats whose series of mysteries starring them includes *The Cat Who Knew Shakespeare* (1988). (Rev: BL 9/15/88)

1936 Braun, Lilian Jackson. *The Cat Who Talked to Ghosts* (10–12). 1990, Putnam $15.95 (0-399-13477-8). The tenth mystery about the reluctant sleuth Jim "Qwill" Qwilleran and his Siamese cat, Koko. (Rev: BL 1/1/90)

1937 Braun, Lilian Jackson. *The Cat Who Went Underground* (9–12). 1989, Putnam $14.95 (0-399-13431-X). A psychotic plumber is the target for reporter Jim Qwilleran and his ever popular 2 Siamese cats. (Rev: BL 4/15/89)

1938 Brett, Simon. *Mrs. Presumed Dead* (10–12). 1989, Macmillan $16.95 (0-684-18851-1); Dell paper $3.95 (0-440-20552-2). A rich widow decides to find out about the previous occupants of her home who disappeared mysteriously. (Rev: SLJ 8/89)

1939 Cain, James M. *Double Indemnity* (10–12). 1989, Random paper $6.95 (0-679-72322-6). A murder that is supposedly perfect is planned by an insurance salesman in this hard-boiled thriller.

1940 Cain, James M. *The Postman Always Rings Twice* (10–12). 1989, Random LB $14.95 (0-89968-234-0); paper $7.95 (0-679-72325-0). From the hard-boiled school of crime fiction comes the story of Cora and Frank who decide to kill Cora's husband and become free.

1941 Campbell, Ramsey. *The Nameless* (10–12). 1987, Tor paper $3.95 (0-8125-1664-8). A suspense story for mature readers about a mother's search for a daughter thought to be dead.

1942 Campbell, Robert. *The Cat's Meow* (10–12). 1988, NAL $16.95 (0-453-00615-9). The mysterious deaths of an old priest and his cat result in some sleuthing by Jimmy Flannery, a Chicago sewer inspector. (Rev: BL 9/1/88)

1943 Campbell, Robert. *The Gift Horse's Mouth* (10–12). 1990, Pocket $17.95 (0-671-67586-9). This, the seventh book about Jimmy Flannery, an honest Chicago precinct captain and a sewer inspector, involves murder and political intrigue. (Rev: BL 9/15/90)

1944 Campbell, Robert. *Nibbled to Death by Ducks* (10–12). 1989, Pocket $17.95 (0-671-67585-0). Jimmy Flannery investigates mysterious deaths in a nursing home. (Rev: VOYA 4/90)

1945 Chandler, Raymond. *The Big Sleep* (10–12). 1939, North Point $22.95 (0-86547-402-8); Random paper $7.95 (0-394-75828-5). This mystery classic features the sleuth Philip Marlowe. Others by this author are *Farewell, My Lovely* and *The Lady in the Lake* (both Random, 1988).

1946 Chastain, Thomas. *Perry Mason in the Case of the Burning Bequest* (9–12). 1990, Morrow $15.95 (0-688-08960-7). In this second Perry Mason novel by Chastain, the lawyer investigates a most unusual family. Preceded by: *Perry Mason in the Case of Too Many Murders* (1989). (Rev: BL 8/90)

1947 Chesterton, G. K. *Seven Suspects* (10–12). 1990, Carroll & Graf $17.95 (0-88184-578-7). Seven of the best mystery stories by the English master of the genre. (Rev: BL 5/15/90)

1948 Christie, Agatha. *Curtain* (9–12). 1975, Amereon $18.95 (0-88411-386-8); Pocket paper $3.95 (0-671-54717-8). Hercule Poirot returns to the country manor of Styles, the site of his first case (*The Mysterious Affair at Styles*), to solve another murder. This is one of many suitable titles by Christie.

1949 Christie, Agatha. *Death on the Nile* (9–12). 1969, Putnam $12.95 (0-396-08573-3); Bantam paper $3.50 (0-553-26138-X). Everyone on board the steamer sailing along the Nile envies Linnet Doyle—until she is murdered. One of many recommended mysteries involving Hercule Poirot.

1950 Christie, Agatha. *Evil under the Sun* (9–12). 1985, Putnam $12.95 (0-396-08701-9); Pocket paper $3.50 (0-671-60174-1). M. Poirot solves the mystery of the murder of beautiful Arlena Marshall. One of many suitable Poirot mysteries.

1951 Christie, Agatha. *Hercule Poirot's Casebook* (9–12). 1984, Putnam $18.95 (0-396-08417-6). Fifty short stories, each featuring the famous detective and his uncanny deductive powers.

1952 Christie, Agatha. *Miss Marple: The Complete Short Stories* (9–12). 1985, Putnam $14.95 (0-396-08747-7); Berkley paper $7.95 (0-425-09486-3). Miss Marple, the sleuth of St. Mary Mead, shines in this collection of 20 stories. (Rev: BL 12/15/85)

1953 Christie, Agatha. *The Murder at the Vicarage* (9–12). 1984, Berkley paper $3.50 (0-425-09453-7). The first Miss Marple mystery by this prolific author, who has about 100 mysteries in print.

1954 Christie, Agatha. *The Murder of Roger Ackroyd* (9–12). 1985, Putnam $12.95 (0-396-08574-1); Pocket paper $3.50 (0-671-49856-8). One of the earlier Hercule Poirot mysteries (first published in 1926), this one involving the murder of a retired businessman.

1955 Christie, Agatha. *Murder on the Orient Express* (9–12). 1985, Putnam $12.95 (0-396-08575-X); Pocket paper $3.50 (0-671-52368-6). M. Poirot in one of his most famous cases, where each of the suspects appears to have a valid motive for murder.

1956 Christie, Agatha. *Sleeping Murder* (9–12). 1976, Putnam $14.95 (0-396-08871-6); Bantam paper $3.50 (0-553-25678-5). Christie's famous female sleuth, Miss Marple, solves the mystery of a murder that occurred 18 years earlier. One of many recommended titles involving this unusual sleuth.

1957 Christie, Agatha. *Ten Little Indians* (9–12). 1983, Pocket paper $3.95 (0-671-55228-8). One of the earliest (1939) and best of this prolific writer's mysteries.

1958 Christie, Agatha. *Witness for the Prosecution* (10–12). 1987, Berkley paper $3.50 (0-425-06809-9). One of the most famous mystery tales by this very popular writer.

1959 Clarins, Dana. *The Woman Who Knew Too Much* (10–12). 1986, Bantam paper $3.95 (0-553-26100-2). When Celia tries to decipher a note she finds in a novel she is caught in the middle of a puzzling mystery. (Rev: SLJ 1/87)

1960 Clark, Mary Higgins. *The Anastasia Syndrome and Other Stories* (10–12). 1989, Simon & Schuster $19.95 (0-671-67367-X). A collection of 5 suspenseful stories (one almost book length) by this popular mystery writer. (Rev: BL 11/1/89; VOYA 4/90)

1961 Clark, Mary Higgins. *The Cradle Will Fall* (10–12). 1983, Dell paper $4.95 (0-440-11545-0). A young lawyer uncovers a conspiracy at a local hospital in this thriller.

1962 Clark, Mary Higgins. *A Cry in the Night* (10–12). 1983, Dell paper $4.95 (0-440-11065-3). Jenny finds that the home of her new husband contains a terrible secret.

1963 Clark, Mary Higgins. *Stillwatch* (9–12). 1984, Dell paper $4.95 (0-440-18305-7). A TV documentary producer finds mystery and danger when she begins investigating a vice presidential candidate in Washington.

1964 Clark, Mary Higgins. *A Stranger Is Watching* (9–12). 1978, Dell paper $4.50 (0-440-18127-5). Steve Peterson's son and girlfriend are kidnapped by a psychopath in this taut thriller.

1965 Clark, Mary Higgins. *Weep No More, My Lady* (9–12). 1987, Simon & Schuster $19.95 (0-671-55664-9). At a fashionable California spa, Elizabeth encounters the man she thinks murdered her sister in this taut mystery. (Rev: BL 5/1/87)

1966 Clark, Mary Higgins. *Where Are the Children?* (9–12). 1976, Dell paper $4.95 (0-440-19593-4). The son and daughter of Nancy Eldredge, a Cape Cod housewife, disappear and the police believe that she has murdered them.

1967 Clark, Mary Higgins. *While My Pretty One Sleeps* (9–12). 1989, Simon & Schuster $19.95 (0-671-55665-7). While investigating a murder, our heroine becomes convinced that someone has been hired to kill her. (Rev: BL 4/1/89; VOYA 4/89)

1968 Coker, Carolyn. *The Vines of Ferrara* (10–12). 1986, Dodd $14.95 (0-396-08812-0). Andrea Perkins is in Italy restoring art treasures when several people are poisoned. (Rev: BL 7/86)

1969 Cook, Robin. *Harmful Intent* (10–12). 1990, Putnam $18.95 (0-399-13481-6). Mysterious deaths in a Boston hospital cause an innocent accused man to do some private sleuthing. (Rev: BL 11/1/89)

1970 Cook, Thomas H. *Flesh and Blood* (10–12). 1989, Putnam $17.95 (0-399-13409-3). For mature readers, a hard-boiled detective yarn about a murder in the garment district of New York. (Rev: BL 1/1/89)

1971 Craig, Patricia, ed. *The Oxford Book of English Detective Stories* (9–12). 1990, Oxford Univ. Pr. paper $10.00 (0-19-214187-2). A chronologically arranged group of 33 fine detective stories that begins with the era of Arthur Conan Doyle. (Rev: BL 6/15/90)

1972 Crider, Bill. *Cursed to Death* (10–12). 1988, Walker $16.95 (0-8027-5698-0). A dentist disappears and his wife is murdered. Clearly a case for county sheriff Dan Rhodes. For mature readers. (Rev: BL 3/1/88)

1973 Crider, Bill. *One Dead Dean* (10–12). 1988, Walker $17.95 (0-8027-5711-1). An English professor decides to track down the killer of a very unpopular dean. (Rev: BL 8/88)

1974 Crider, Bill. *Ryan Rides Back* (10–12). 1988, Evans $14.95 (0-87131-542-4). A western that also involves solving the mystery of a girl's murder. (Rev: BL 6/15/88)

1975 Crisp, N. J. *In the Long Run* (10–12). 1987, Viking $16.95 (0-670-81321-4); Penguin paper

$3.95 (0-14-010950-1). A master at helping people escape from Eastern Europe finds his own life is in danger. (Rev: BL 2/1/87)

1976 Crispin, Edmund. *The Moving Toy Shop* (10–12). 1989, Penguin paper $4.95 (0-14-008817-2). This is one of the many mysteries involving an English professor from Oxford as a sleuth.

1977 Cross, Amanda. *The James Joyce Murder* (10–12). 1983, Ballantine paper $3.95 (0-345-34686-6). While working on a literary project, the English professor, Kate Fansler, must stop her work to investigate a nasty murder. There are many other entertaining mysteries with this sleuth.

1978 Cross, Amanda. *The Question of Max* (10–12). 1987, Ballantine paper $3.95 (0-345-35489-3). This mystery features Kate Fansler, an English professor, as a sleuth. Others in this series for better readers are *The Theban Mysteries* (Avon, 1979) and *Death in a Tenured Position* (1986).

1979 Davis, Kenn. *Words Can Kill* (10–12). 1984, Fawcett paper $2.50 (0-317-05464-3). For mature readers, a mystery about the investigation of the murder of a once-prominent writer.

1980 DeAndrea, William L. *Killed in Paradise* (10–12). 1988, Mysterious $15.95 (0-89296-346-8). For better readers a tale of murder aboard a cruise ship. (Rev: BL 7/88)

1981 Dickinson, Peter. *The Poison Oracle* (10–12). 1982, Pantheon paper $3.95 (0-394-71023-1). In this mystery a scientist is able to teach a chimpanzee to communicate with humans.

1982 Dickinson, Peter. *Skeleton-in-Waiting* (10–12). 1990, Pantheon $16.95 (0-394-58002-8). There is murder and mayhem in the British royal family in this somewhat slow-paced sequel to *King and Joker* (1976). (Rev: BL 11/15/89)

1983 Dodson, Susan. *Shadows across the Sand* (8–12). 1983, Fawcett paper $2.25 (0-317-13276-8). A 16-year-old girl investigates reports that her elderly retired friends are being terrorized.

1984 Doherty, P. C. *Spy in Chancery* (9–12). 1989, St. Martin's $14.95 (0-312-02984-5). This mystery is set in medieval Europe and deals with murders at the court of King Edward I of England. (Rev: BL 4/1/89)

1985 Dorner, Marjorie. *Family Closets* (10–12). 1989, McGraw $17.95 (0-07-017786-4). While Barbara visits the scene of her childhood, the skeleton of a long-lost uncle is unearthed and the murder investigation begins. (Rev: BL 6/15/89)

1986 Douglas, Arthur. *Last Rights* (10–12). 1987, St. Martin's $11.95 (0-312-00138-X). A mystery story that uses the crusade against lab use of animals as a backdrop. (Rev: BL 1/15/87)

1987 Doyle, Arthur Conan. *The Adventures of Sherlock Holmes* (9–12). 1985, Bantam paper $2.95 (0-553-26772-8). This is the first collection of stories about the master sleuth. Other collections available from various publishers are: *The Case Book of Sherlock Holmes; The Memoirs of Sherlock Holmes;* and *The Return of Sherlock Holmes.*

1988 Doyle, Arthur Conan. *The Complete Sherlock Holmes* (7–12). 1953, Doubleday $19.95 (0-385-04591-3). In 2 volumes, all the stories and novels involving Holmes and foil Watson.

1989 Doyle, Arthur Conan. *Great Stories of Sherlock Holmes* (9–12). 1962, Dell paper $1.95 (0-440-93190-8). This is a selection of 12 of Holmes's best cases.

1990 Doyle, Arthur Conan. *His Last Bow* (9–12). 1984, Berkley paper $2.50 (0-425-10491-5). This is the last full-length mystery featuring Sherlock Holmes.

1991 Doyle, Arthur Conan. *The Hound of the Baskervilles* (9–12). 1983, Buccaneer LB $14.95 (0-89966-229-3); Oxford Univ. Pr. paper $3.95 (0-19-581211-5). These are 2 of the many editions available of this Sherlock Holmes mystery about strange deaths on the moors close to the Baskerville estate.

1992 Doyle, Arthur Conan. *The Sign of the Four* (9–12). 1987, Ballantine paper $3.95 (0-345-35290-4). This is one of the 4 full-length novels featuring Sherlock Holmes.

1993 Doyle, Arthur Conan. *A Study in Scarlet* (9–12). 1982, Penguin paper $2.95 (0-14-005707-2). In this, Holmes's first appearance in a full-length novel, historical material involving the Mormons plays an important part.

1994 Doyle, Arthur Conan. *Tales of Terror and Mystery* (9–12). 1982, Buccaneer $12.95 (0-89966-429-6). From the creator of Sherlock Holmes, 13 stories of mystery and the supernatural.

1995 Du Maurier, Daphne. *Rebecca* (9–12). 1938, Doubleday $17.95 (0-385-04380-5); Avon paper $3.95 (0-380-00917-X). In this gothic romance, a timid girl marries a wealthy widower whose wife died mysteriously. Two other exciting novels by Du Maurier are *Hungry Hill* (1945) and *The Scapegoat* (1957).

1996 Dunlap, Susan. *Too Close to the Edge* (10–12). 1987, St. Martin's $14.95 (0-312-00198-3);

Dell paper $3.50 (0-440-20356-2). A wheelchair-bound activist is murdered in San Francisco and detective Jill Smith is assigned to the case. (Rev: BL 3/15/87)

1997 Eberhart, Mignon G. *Another Man's Murder* (10–12). 1983, Amereon $14.95 (0-89190-539-1); Warner paper $2.95 (0-446-34930-5). In this fast-paced mystery a young man is falsely accused of his uncle's murder. Two other recommended mysteries by this prolific author are: *Unidentified Woman* and *Witness at Large* (both 1983).

1998 Eberhart, Mignon G. *Nine O'Clock Tide* (10–12). 1980, Amereon LB $14.95 (0-88411-770-7). Meade Havelock becomes the prime suspect when her lover suddenly returns and her husband is murdered. One of many recommended mysteries by Eberhart.

1999 Eberhart, Mignon G. *Three Days for Emeralds* (10–12). 1988, Random $14.95 (0-394-56108-2). Lacy Wales finds she is a target for murder in a mystery involving her emerald engagement ring. (Rev: BL 2/15/88)

2000 Ebisch, Glen. *Lou Dunlop: Private Eye* (9–12). 1987, Crosswinds paper $2.25 (0-373-98002-7). A fast-paced mystery featuring a 17-year-old sleuth who idolizes Philip Marlowe in the Raymond Chandler novels. (Rev: VOYA 8–9/87)

2001 Elkins, Aaron J. *Murder in the Queen's Armes* (10–12). 1985, Walker $14.95 (0-8027-5626-3); paper $3.50 (0-553-26235-1). Professor Gideon Oliver and his wife Julie get involved in a murder at an archaeological dig. (Rev: BL 11/1/85)

2002 Evarts, Hal G. *Jay-Jay and the Peking Monster* (10–12). 1984, Peter Smith $15.25 (0-8446-6166-X). Two teenagers discover a box of bones they think are the remains of a prehistoric man—or are they?

2003 Farris, John. *The Uninvited* (10–12). 1987, Tor paper $3.95 (0-8125-1776-8). This story begins when a girl falls in love with a mysterious stranger.

2004 Feegel, John R. *Not a Stranger* (10–12). 1986, Warner paper $3.95 (0-87162-441-9). For the mature reader, a grim mystery about child murders in Atlanta.

2005 Fielding, Joy. *Kiss Mommy Goodbye* (10–12). 1982, NAL paper $4.50 (0-451-13230-0). A father kidnaps his 2 children from his former wife.

2006 Finch, Phillip. *In a Place Dark and Secret* (9–12). 1985, Watts $16.95 (0-531-09705-6); Jove paper $3.95 (0-515-09251-7). Sarah, a private

school student, is abducted by a deranged man. (Rev: BR 5–6/86; SLJ 2/86)

2007 Fletcher, Jessica, and Donald Bain. *Gin and Daggers: A Murder, She Wrote Mystery* (9–12). 1989, McGraw $17.95 (0-07-003239-4). Based on the television series and narrated by Jessica Fletcher, this mystery involves a murder at a writer's conference in England. (Rev: BL 6/15/89; SLJ 12/89)

2008 Fletcher, Lucille. *Mirror Image* (10–12). 1988, Morrow $16.95 (0-668-07749-8). For better readers, this is an exciting mystery about a girl's search for her long-missing sister. (Rev: BL 5/15/88)

2009 Francis, Dick. *Bolt* (10–12). 1988, Fawcett paper $4.95 (0-449-21239-4). Steeplechase jockey Kit Fielding becomes involved in a plot to sell guns to terrorists. (Rev: BL 12/1/86)

2010 Francis, Dick. *Break In* (10–12). 1986, Putnam $17.95 (0-399-13121-3); Fawcett paper $4.95 (0-317-69900-8). A jockey and family are the targets of some unfounded slurs in a gossip column in this mystery. Also use *Enquiry* (1984). (Rev: BL 1/15/86; VOYA 6/86)

2011 Francis, Dick. *The Danger* (10–12). 1984, Putnam $15.95 (0-399-12890-5); Fawcett paper $5.95 (0-449-21037-5). Multiple kidnappings and horse racing merge in this fine whodunit. Also use: *High Stakes* (1987) and *Slayride* (1984).

2012 Francis, Dick. *The Edge* (10–12). 1989, Putnam paper $18.95 (0-399-13414-X). In a mixture of horse racing and railroads, this murder mystery takes place on a transcontinental train in Canada. (Rev: BL 11/15/88)

2013 Francis, Dick. *Hot Money* (10–12). 1988, Putnam $17.95 (0-399-13349-6). Horse racing, high finance, and murder mix in this tale of greed and redemption. (Rev: BL 1/15/88; BR 11–12/88)

2014 Francis, Dick. *Longshot* (10–12). 1990, Putnam $19.95 (0-399-13581-2). A would-be writer becomes involved in a series of fatal accidents in this mystery with a racetrack setting. (Rev: BL 9/1/90)

2015 Francis, Dick. *Straight* (10–12). 1989, Putnam $18.95 (0-399-13470-0). A temporarily incapacitated jockey investigates the sudden death of his brother. (Rev: BL 9/1/89)

2016 Francis, Dick. *Trial Run* (10–12). 1987, Fawcett paper $5.95 (0-449-21273-4). A mystery involving a former steeplechase rider at the Olympics in Moscow. Also use: *Banker* (1989) and *In the Frame* (1987).

2017 Francis, Dick. *Twice Shy* (10–12). 1986, Fawcett paper $5.95 (0-449-21314-5). This English mystery about racing involves murder and a foolproof method for betting.

2018 Francis, Dick. *Whip Hand* (10–12). 1980, Fawcett paper $4.95 (0-449-21273-4). An ex-jockey turned private investigator is hired to probe into the causes of several mysterious events at a racetrack. Also use: *Proof* (1985) and *Risk* (1984).

2019 Gardner, John. *Brokenclaw* (10–12). 1990, Putnam $14.95 (0-399-13541-3). James Bond is back in the ninth of the series written by Gardner and is hot on the trail of a mastermind named Brokenclaw, who is sabotaging a secret scientific device called Lords. (Rev: BL 6/1/90)

2020 Gardner, John. *Icebreaker* (10–12). 1986, Berkley paper $3.95 (0-425-08758-1). This James Bond thriller involves an attempt to destroy a dangerous neo-Nazi movement.

2021 Gerson, Jack. *Death Squad London* (10–12). 1990, St. Martin's $17.95 (0-312-03981-6). Ernest Lohmann, a former policeman who has fled to London from Nazi Germany, investigates an apparent suicide in this chiller. Preceded by: *Death's Head Berlin* (1989). (Rev: BL 12/15/89)

2022 Giff, Patricia Reilly. *Suspect* (7–12). Illus. 1982, Dutton $8.95 (0-525-45108-0). An easily read mystery about a young man who while escaping one problem finds himself confronted with a more serious one involving murder.

2023 Gilbert, Anna. *A Walk in the Wood* (9–12). 1989, St. Martin's $16.95 (0-312-02668-4). A story of suspense and romance involving a young schoolteacher in an English village during World War II. (Rev: BL 4/1/89)

2024 Gilman, Dorothy. *The Clairvoyant Countess* (9–12). 1986, Fawcett paper $4.95 (0-449-21318-8). In this engaging novel, Madame Kartiska solves mysteries by using her psychic powers.

2025 Giroux, E. X. *A Death for a Double* (10–12). 1990, St. Martin's $15.95 (0-312-03809-7). While Robert Forsythe, the English barrister, is investigating the case of a client who has received threatening letters, murder occurs. (Rev: BL 2/15/90)

2026 Gorman, Edward, ed. *The Second Black Lizard Anthology of Crime Fiction* (10–12). 1988, Black Lizard paper $15.95 (0-88739-094-3). A collection of crime stories for mature readers that have in general a black despairing tone. (Rev: BL 12/15/88)

2027 Gorman, Edward, et al., eds. *Under the Gun: Mystery Scene Presents the Best Suspense and Mystery* (10–12). 1990, NAL $18.95 (0-453-00713-9); paper $9.95 (0-452-26406-5). A collection of superior mystery and suspense short stories that were published in 1988. (Rev: BL 2/15/90)

2028 Goulart, Ron, ed. *The Great British Detective* (9–12). 1982, NAL paper $4.95 (0-451-62562-5). An anthology of 15 stories involving such sleuths as Sherlock Holmes and Hercule Poirot.

2029 Grafton, Sue. *"G" Is for Gumshoe* (10–12). 1990, Henry Holt $16.95 (0-8050-0461-0). In this installment of the alphabet murders, Kinsey Millhone is involved in a missing persons case and a hired killer is out to get her. (Rev: BL 3/15/90; SLJ 9/90)

2030 Grant-Adamson, Lesley. *The Face of Death* (10–12). 1986, Macmillan $14.95 Fawcett paper $2.95 (0-449-21210-6). A tense psychological thriller about an amnesia victim and her new identity. (Rev: BL 6/1/86)

2031 Green, Richard Lancelyn, ed. *The Further Adventures of Sherlock Holmes, after Sir Arthur Conan Doyle* (9–12). 1986, Penguin paper $4.95 (0-14-007907-6). Many writers have tried to carry on the Holmes-Watson tradition. Here are 11 fine examples. (Rev: BL 5/15/86)

2032 Greenberg, Martin H., ed. *Masterpieces of Mystery and Suspense* (9–12). 1988, St. Martin's $19.95 (0-312-02251-4). A fine basic anthology that runs the gambit from Mark Twain to P. D. James. (Rev: BL 8/88)

2033 Greenberg, Martin H., ed. *Mummy Stories* (10–12). 1990, Ballantine paper $3.95 (0-345-36354-X). A collection of stories bound to entertain and in some cases terrify. (Rev: BL 3/15/90)

2034 Greenwood, L. B. *Sherlock Holmes and the Case of the Raleigh Legacy* (9–12). 1986, Macmillan $12.95 (0-689-11832-5). A mysterious letter sends Sherlock out on a case in this brilliant reconstruction of Doyle's characters and settings. (Rev: BL 11/15/86)

2035 Grimes, Martha. *The Anodyne Necklace* (10–12). 1983, Little $15.95 (0-316-32882-0); Dell paper $4.50 (0-440-10280-4). An unusual English mystery involving some strange characters in a seemingly ordinary village.

2036 Hall, Mary Bowen. *Emma Chizzit and the Queen Anne Killer* (10–12). 1989, Walker $18.95 (0-8027-5751-0). In this mystery set in the Sacramento area, Emma Chizzit finds the body of a baby on her veranda. (Rev: BL 11/1/89)

2037 Hall, Robert Lee. *Benjamin Franklin Takes the Case* (10–12). 1988, St. Martin's $16.95 (0-312-01735-9). Ben Franklin turns sleuth in this murder mystery set in London of 1757. (Rev: BL 5/1/88)

2038 Hammett, Dashiell. *The Maltese Falcon* (10–12). 1989, Random $7.95 (0-679-72264-5). Tough detective Sam Spade is on the trail of a valuable statuette in this mystery classic. Also use: *The Thin Man* and *The Glass Key* (both 1989).

2039 Hammett, Dashiell. *The Novels of Dashiell Hammett* (10–12). 1965, Knopf $29.50 (0-394-43860-4). Three hard-boiled mysteries (*Red Harvest; The Dain Curse;* and *The Maltese Falcon*), 2 of them featuring the detective Sam Spade.

2040 Hammett, Dashiell. *Woman in the Dark: A Novel of Dangerous Romance* (10–12). 1988, Knopf $15.95 (0-394-57269-6). A short fragment left by a master of the hard-boiled school of detective stories. (Rev: BL 9/1/88)

2041 Hardinge, George, ed. *The Mammoth Book of Modern Crime Stories* (10–12). 1987, Carroll & Graf paper $8.95 (0-88184-356-3). A collection by such contemporary British crime writers as Dick Francis, Eric Ambler, and P. D. James. (Rev: BL 10/1/87)

2042 Hardwick, Michael. *The Revenge of the Hound: The New Sherlock Holmes Novel* (9–12). Illus. 1987, Villard $18.95 (0-394-55653-4); Windsor paper $3.95 (1-55817-166-5). A collection of short stories that faithfully re-create the characters and the suspense of the original Sherlock Holmes stories. (Rev: BR 5–6/88; SLJ 4/88; VOYA 6/88)

2043 Hardwick, Molly. *Perish in July* (10–12). 1990, St. Martin's $15.95 (0-312-04402-X). The lead in a local theatrical production is murdered in this fifth novel featuring both Doran Fairweather and a rural English setting. (Rev: BL 9/1/90)

2044 Harley, Rex. *Black November* (9–12). 1990, Gollancz $17.95 (0-575-04150-1). A teenager buys a saxophone little knowing that in its case is an important murder clue. (Rev: BL 2/1/90)

2045 Harrington, Joyce. *Dreemz of the Night* (10–12). 1989, Critics Choice paper $3.50 (1-55547-291-5). A trainee cop investigates the murder of his brother, a painter of graffiti on New York subway cars. (Rev: BL 6/1/87)

2046 Harris, Thomas. *Red Dragon* (10–12). 1981, Putnam $13.95 (0-399-12442-X); Dell paper $5.95 (0-440-20615-4). A psychotic killer is

on the loose in this strong thriller for mature readers.

2047 Haynes, Conrad. *Perpetual Check* (10–12). 1988, Bantam paper $3.50 (0-553-26943-7). Harry Bishop, an unusual professor and former CIA agent, hunts down a murderer who is also a member of the board of trustees. With the same hero, use: *Bishop's Gambit Declined* (1987). (Rev: BL 4/1/88)

2048 Hebden, Mark. *Pel and the Bombers* (10–12). 1985, Walker $13.95 (0-8027-5608-5). A detective story involving the investigation of the murder of a young French boy by Inspector Pel. (Rev: BR 11–12/85)

2049 Hill, Reginald. *Ruling Passion* (10–12). 1990, Dell paper $3.95 (0-440-16889-9). A weekend house party is marred by the murder of the hosts.

2050 Hillerman, Tony. *Coyote Waits* (10–12). 1990, Harper $19.95 (0-06-016370-4). Another superior mystery involving American Indian policemen Chee and Leaphorn and the murder of another policeman. (Rev: BL 5/15/90)

2051 Hillerman, Tony. *The Ghostway* (10–12). 1985, Harper $13.45 (0-06-015396-2); Avon paper $4.95 (0-380-70024-7). Tribal detective Jim Chee solves the mystery of who murdered 3 of his fellow Navaho Indians. (Rev: BL 1/1/85)

2052 Hillerman, Tony. *The Joe Leaphorn Mysteries: Dance Hall of the Dead, Listening Woman* (9–12). 1989, Harper $16.95 (0-06-016174-4). Three novels all featuring the Navaho police lieutenant Joe Leaphorn in western settings. (Rev: BL 10/15/89)

2053 Hillerman, Tony. *People of Darkness* (10–12). 1980, Harper paper $4.95 (0-06-080950-7). Set in the Southwest, this mystery features Navajo police detective Jim Chee and gives rich background information about the culture of these Native Americans. Others in this series are *Listening Woman* (1990), *The Blessing Way, Dance Hall of the Dead* (both 1989), and *The Fly on the Wall* (1990). Listening Woman The Blessing Way Dance Hall of the Dead The Fly on the Wall

2054 Hillerman, Tony. *Talking God* (10–12). 1989, Harper $17.95 (0-06-016118-3). The 2 Navaho police officers, Jim Chee and Joe Leaphorn, featured together in the author's earlier *A Thief of Time* (1988) and *Skinwalkers* (1988) once more solve a puzzling, complex murder mystery set in New Mexico. (Rev: BL 5/1/89; SLJ 11/89; VOYA 10/89)

2055 Hoch, Edward D., ed. *The Year's Best Mystery and Suspense Stories* (10–12). 1987, Walker

$17.95 (0-8027-0983-4); paper $9.95 (0-8027-7309-5). A collection of short fiction chiefly by Americans plus a rundown of awards, and so on, in the field of mystery writing for 1987. (Rev: BL 10/1/87)

2056 Holland, Isabelle. *A Fatal Advent* (10–12). 1989, Doubleday $16.95 (0-385--24815-6). In this St. Anselm's mystery for mature readers, a visiting bishop is murdered. (Rev: BL 10/15/89)

2057 Holt, Victoria. *The Captive* (9–12). 1989, Doubleday $18.95 (0-385-26332-5). A romantic mystery involving a young heroine trapped on a desert island with a murderer. (Rev: BL 8/89; VOYA 2/90)

2058 Holt, Victoria. *Snare of Serpents* (9–12). 1990, Doubleday $19.95 (0-385-41385-8). This romantic novel, set in nineteenth-century Edinburgh, involves a young woman wrongfully accused of murder. (Rev: BL 7/90)

2059 Hornig, Doug. *The Dark Side* (10–12). 1986, Mysterious $15.95 (0-89296-168-6). In this Loren Swift novel, the investigator unravels the mystery of a death by poisonous fumes in a greenhouse. (Rev: SLJ 2/87)

2060 Howe, Melodie Johnson. *The Mother Shadow* (10–12). 1989, Viking $16.95 (0-670-82602-2). For mature readers, this is a detective story featuring Claire Conrad, an eccentric investigator, and her unraveling of the riddle of a missing codicil to an important will. (Rev: BL 6/1/89)

2061 Hunter, Mollie. *The Third Eye* (7–12). 1979, Harper LB $12.89 (0-06-022677-3). This story, set in Scotland, deals with a family curse— that the eldest son will never succeed his father.

2062 Irwin, Hadley. *So Long at the Fair* (8–12). 1988, Macmillan $12.95 (0-689-50454-3); Avon paper $2.95 (0-380-70858-2). Joel finds it impossible to adjust to the suicide of Ashley, his friend from childhood. (Rev: BL 9/15/88; BR 5–6/89; SLJ 11/88; VOYA 12/88)

2063 Jackson, Shirley. *We Have Always Lived in the Castle* (9–12). 1962, Amereon LB $17.95 (0-89190-623-1); Penguin paper $6.95 (0-14-007107-5). Two sisters have become recluses after the arsenic poisoning of 4 members of their family.

2064 James, P. D. *The Black Tower* (10–12). 1982, Warner paper $3.95 (0-446-34824-4). In this mystery for better readers, Adam Dalgliesh of Scotland Yard is confronted with a murder in a private hospital.

2065 James, P. D. *Devices and Desires* (10–12). 1990, Knopf $19.95 (0-394-58070-2). For better readers, in this novel Inspector Dalgliesh stalks a mad killer in an English coastal town near a nuclear energy plant. (Rev: BL 11/1/89)

2066 James, P. D. *Innocent Blood* (10–12). 1988, Warner paper $4.95 (0-446-31177-4). A complex puzzler about a girl who finds that her mother is the target of a terrible plot.

2067 James, P. D. *A Mind to Murder* (10–12). 1987, Warner paper $3.95 (0-446-34828-7). A challenging mystery involving detective Adam Dalgliesh, a murder, and a psychiatric clinc. James's other famous detective, Cordelia Gray, is featured in *The Skull beneath the Skin* (1988).

2068 James, P. D. *Unnatural Causes* (10–12). 1988, Warner paper $4.95 (0-446-31219-3). On what was to be a quiet vacation in Suffolk, Adam Dalgliesh encounters murder. For better readers. Also use: *Shroud for a Nightingale* (1988).

2069 James, P. D. *An Unsuitable Job for a Woman* (10–12). 1987, Warner paper $3.95 (0-446-34832-6). For better readers, this is an English mystery involving Cordelia Gray who owns a detective agency. Some other titles are *Cover Her Face* (1987) and *Death of an Expert Witness* (1988).

2070 Johnston, Velda. *Fatal Affair* (9–12). 1986, Dodd $15.95 (0-396-08873-2). Jenny sets off from New York to trace her sister who has disappeared in London. (Rev: SLJ 11/86)

2071 Johnston, Velda. *Flight to Yesterday* (10–12). 1990, St. Martin's $15.95 (0-312-03833-X). Sara dons a disguise and a new identity to find a murderer. (Rev: BL 4/1/90)

2072 Johnston, Velda. *Shadow behind the Curtain* (9–12). 1987, Warner paper $3.95 (0-446-34495-8). Deborah returns to her hometown in New Mexico to help prove her father innocent of murder. (Rev: BL 4/1/85; SLJ 5/85; VOYA 8/85)

2073 Johnston, Velda. *Voice in the Night* (10–12). 1989, Warner paper $4.95 (0-445-20202-5). Carla receives a telephone call from her husband who died 4 years before.

2074 Jordan, Cathleen, and Cynthia Manson, eds. *Tales from Alfred Hitchcock's Mystery Magazine* (8–12). 1988, Morrow $12.95 (0-688-08176-2). Twenty tales, most of which combine mystery with large doses of whimsy and comedy. (Rev: BL 11/15/88; BR 11–12/88)

2075 Kahn, Joan, ed. *Handle with Care: Frightening Stories* (9–12). 1985, Greenwillow $10.25 (0-688-04663-0). Though originally written for adults, this chilling short collection features children or teenagers as central characters. (Rev: BL 9/1/85; BR 1–2/86; SLJ 11/85; VOYA 2/86)

2076 Kallen, Lucille. *C. B. Greenfield: A Little Madness* (9–12). 1986, Random $14.95 (0-394-53090-X); Ballantine paper $3.50 (0-345-31119-1). One of the fast-paced murder mysteries that features a cranky old newspaper editor, Greenfield, and his chief reporter, Maggie. Others are *The Piano Bird* (1983), *The Tanglewood Murders* (1983), and *No Lady in the House* (1985). (Rev: BL 3/1/86)

2077 Katz, Michael J. *Last Dance in Redondo Beach* (10–12). 1989, Putnam $17.95 (0-399-13445-X). The mysterious death of a wrestler is investigated in this humorous look behind the scenes in the world of professional wrestling. (Rev: BL 3/15/89)

2078 Kaye, M. M. *Death in Berlin* (10–12). 1986, St. Martin's paper $3.95 (0-312-90103-8). In this romantic mystery set in post-World War II Berlin, a woman on vacation is falsely accused of murder. (Rev: BL 4/1/85)

2079 Kellerman, Jonathan. *Over the Edge* (10–12). 1987, Macmillan $17.95 (0-689-11635-7); NAL paper $4.95 (0-451-15219-0). The story of a teenage boy accused of 6 murders and the lawyer chosen to defend him. (Rev: SLJ 8/87)

2080 Kelly, Mary Anne. *Park Lane South, Queens* (10–12). 1990, St. Martin's $15.95 (0-312-03907-7). A child murderer is loose in New York City and somehow a young photographer who lives with her 2 sisters is involved. (Rev: BL 2/15/90)

2081 Kemelman, Harry. *Friday the Rabbi Slept Late* (10–12). 1986, Fawcett paper $3.95 (0-449-21180-0). This is one of the many well-crafted murder mysteries featuring Rabbi Small. Some others are *Saturday the Rabbi Went Hungry; Sunday the Rabbi Stayed Home; Monday the Rabbi Took Off,* (all 1987).

2082 Kemelman, Harry. *One Fine Day the Rabbi Bought a Cross* (10–12). 1987, Morrow $15.95 (0-688-05631-8); Fawcett paper $3.95 (0-449-20687-4). In this installment of the Rabbi David Small mystery series, the Rabbi becomes involved in murder while vacationing in Jerusalem. Others are *Tuesday the Rabbi Saw Red; Wednesday the Rabbi Got Wet;* and *Thursday the Rabbi Walked Out* (all 1987). (Rev: BL 2/1/87)

2083 Kemelman, Harry. *Someday the Rabbi Will Leave* (10–12). 1986, Fawcett paper $3.50 (0-449-20945-8). In this eighth mystery involving Rabbi Small, he investigates a hit-and-run accident that looks like murder. (Rev: BL 1/15/85)

2084 Kittredge, William, and Steven M. Krauzer, eds. *The Great American Detective* (10–12). 1978, NAL paper $4.95 (0-451-62462-9).

This anthology introduces such detectives as Sam Spade, Ellery Queen, and Perry Mason.

2085 Kunetka, James W. *Shadow Man* (10–12). 1988, Warner $17.95 (0-446-51358-X). For mature readers, a high-tech mystery involving murder and the theft of top secrets by a spy ring. (Rev: BL 1/1/88)

2086 Leonard, Constance. *Strange Waters* (9–12). 1985, Putnam $11.95 (0-396-08718-3). Tracy and boyfriend join a yacht crew but then strange occurrences begin. (Rev: BL 2/1/86; SLJ 11/85)

2087 Lindsay, Joan. *Picnic at Hanging Rock* (10–12). 1986, LB $17.95 (0-89966-560-8). The haunting Australian story of the disappearance of 2 schoolgirls and a governess during a picnic to celebrate Valentine's Day.

2088 Llewellyn, Caroline. *The Masks of Rome* (10–12). 1988, Macmillan $16.95 (0-684-18921-6). Using an Italian setting, this novel of murder and mystery involves a likable heroine torn between 2 men. (Rev: BL 7/88)

2089 Lovesey, Peter. *Bertie and the Seven Bodies* (10–12). 1990, Mysterious $16.95 (0-89296-399-9). An imaginative historical mystery that features Albert, Prince of Wales, as an amateur sleuth. (Rev: BL 1/15/90)

2090 Lovesey, Peter, ed. *The Black Cabinet: Superb Stories Based on Real Crimes* (9–12). 1989, Carroll & Graf $17.95 (0-88184-513-2). Fifteen stories by noted past and present writers, each one a variation on a famous actual case. (Rev: BL 12/15/89; VOYA 4/90)

2091 Lutz, John. *Better Mousetraps: The Best Mystery Stories of John Lutz* (10–12). 1988, St. Martin's $18.95 (0-312-01389-2). A collection of 35 mystery stories by a master of suspense and surprise. (Rev: BL 2/1/88)

2092 McCrumb, Sharyn. *If Ever I Return, Pretty Peggy-O* (10–12). 1990, Macmillan $17.95 (0-684-19104-0). A high school reunion becomes the scene of a murder in this taut, suspenseful tale. (Rev: BL 4/15/90; SLJ 9/90)

2093 McCrumb, Sharyn. *The Windsor Knot* (10–12). 1990, Ballantine $16.95 (0-345-36583-6). In this mystery set in Edinburgh, murder interferes with the marriage plans of an American girl, Elizabeth MacPherson, and her Scottish fiancé. Fifth in a series. (Rev: BL 9/1/90)

2094 McCullough, David, ed. *City Sleuths and Tough Guys* (9–12). 1989, Houghton $19.95 (0-395-51318-9). A collection of hard-boiled fiction from Poe to Ed McBain that includes the screenplay for *Double Indemnity*. (Rev: BL 11/1/89; SLJ 5/90)

2095 McDonald, Gregory. *Fletch and the Man Who* (10–12). 1983, Warner paper $3.95 (0-446-35560-7). Fletch is working for a presidential candidate when a series of murders occur. Part of a recommended series.

2096 McDonald, Gregory, ed. *Last Laughs: The 1986 Mystery Writers of America Anthology* (9–12). 1986, Mysterious $16.95 (0-89296-246-1). A collection of humorous mysteries, each with a surprise ending. (Rev: SLJ 3/87)

2097 McGown, Jill. *The Stalking Horse* (10–12). 1988, St. Martin's $14.95 (0-312-02291-3). After spending 16 years in prison for a crime he did not commit, Bill Holt is now free to find the real culprit. (Rev: BL 9/15/88)

2098 McInerny, Ralph. *Four on the Floor* (10–12). 1989, St. Martin's $14.95 (0-312-03345-1). Four novellas involving amateur sleuth Father Dowling and his friend Captain Phil Keegan. (Rev: BL 11/15/89)

2099 McInerny, Ralph. *Frigor Mortis* (10–12). 1989, Macmillan $18.95 (0-689-12081-8). Two murders and a missing fortune are highlights of this fast-moving whodunit. (Rev: BL 9/1/89)

2100 McInerny, Ralph. *Savings and Loan* (10–12). 1990, Macmillan $17.95 (0-689-12037-0). Andrew Broom, a small-town Indiana lawyer, investigates a murder. (Rev: BL 4/15/90)

2101 McLeave, Hugh. *Second Time Around* (10–12). 1981, Walker $9.95 (0-8027-5439-2). Two seemingly unrelated deaths occur at the beginning of this British thriller.

2102 MacLeod, Charlotte. *The Corpse in Oozak's Pond* (10–12). 1988, Mysterious paper $3.95 (0-445-40683-6). In this Peter Shandy mystery, the good professor encounters murder and a lawsuit brought by the heirs of the college founder. (Rev: SLJ 8/87)

2103 MacLeod, Charlotte. *The Gladstone Bag* (10–12). 1990, Mysterious $16.95 (0-89296-370-0). Emma Kelling encounters murder on an island where a group of artists and writers have assembled. (Rev: BL 1/15/90)

2104 MacLeod, Charlotte, ed. *Mistletoe Mysteries* (9–12). 1989, Mysterious $16.95 (0-89296-400-6). Fifteen chilling tales written especially for this collection by such masters as Mary Higgins Clark and Isaac Asimov. (Rev: BL 10/1/89)

2105 MacLeod, Charlotte. *Rest You Merry* (10–12). 1980, Avon paper $3.50 (0-380-47530-8). Murder strikes on a college campus.

2106 Marsh, Ngaio. *Artists in Crime* (10–12). 1985, Jove paper $3.50 (0-515-07534-5). For better readers, this is one of several mysteries involv-

ing Chief Inspector Roderick Alleyn. This is one of about 40 detective stories by this author currently in print.

2107 Marsh, Ngaio. *The Collected Short Fiction of Ngaio Marsh* (10–12). 1989, International Polygonics $19.95 (1-55882-050-7). A collection of mystery stories for better readers by the New Zealand writer. (Rev: BL 11/15/89)

2108 Marston, Edward. *The Queen's Head* (10–12). 1989, St. Martin's $16.95 (0-312-02970-5). A mystery thriller for mature readers dealing with murder in a theatrical troupe in Elizabethan England. (Rev: BL 6/1/89)

2109 Melville, James. *A Haiku for Hanae* (10–12). 1989, Macmillan $16.95 (0-684-19131-8). In this tenth mystery involving Japanese police superintendent Otani, the investigator explores the murder of a Christian missionary close to a Shinto shrine. (Rev: BL 12/1/89)

2110 Michaels, Barbara. *Be Buried in the Rain* (10–12). 1985, Macmillan $13.95 (0-689-11618-7); Berkley paper $3.95 (0-425-09634-3). While taking care of her grandmother, Julie finds the old house in which she is living gradually sheds some horrible family secrets. Barbara Michaels is a prolific writer of thrillers. Some other recommended ones are: *Sons of the Wolf* (1989), *Walker in the Shadows* (Fawcett, 1981), and *Wings of the Falcon* (Fawcett, 1988).

2111 Michaels, Barbara. *Into the Darkness* (10–12). 1990, Simon & Schuster $17.95 (0-671-67038-7). When Meg's grandfather dies and leaves her half of his business she returns to her New England town where she uncovers a mystery. (Rev: BL 4/1/90; SLJ 9/90)

2112 Michaels, Barbara. *Shattered Silk* (10–12). 1988, Berkley paper $4.50 (0-425-10476-1). When Karen sets up a boutique in Georgetown, she receives mysterious threats on her life. (Rev: BL 8/86; SLJ 2/87)

2113 Michaels, Barbara. *Wait for What Will Come* (10–12). 1990, Berkley paper $3.95 (0-425-12005-8). Carla's inheritance includes a frightening mansion with a strange housekeeper. Also use *Here I Stay* (1985).

2114 Mortimer, John. *Rumpole and the Age of Miracles* (10–12). 1989, Penguin paper $4.95 (0-14-011105-0). Seven stories featuring the eccentric English criminal lawyer of Old Bailey fame. (Rev: BL 10/15/89)

2115 Mortimer, John. *Rumpole of the Bailey* (10–12). 1980, Penguin paper $3.95 (0-14-004670-4). Six crime stories all solved by the 68-year-old British lawyer Horace Rumpole. Other

Rumpole stories that are also recommended for better readers are available.

2116 Moyes, Patricia. *A Six-Letter Word for Death* (10–12). 1983, Henry Holt paper $3.95 (0-8050-0244-8). A crossword puzzle is used to help solve a murder mystery in this British whodunit.

2117 Muller, Marcia. *The Shape of Dread* (10–12). 1989, Mysterious $16.95 (0-89296-271-2). Sharon McCone, a San Francisco-based private eye, solves the mystery of the missing comedian. (Rev: BL 10/15/89)

2118 Muller, Marcia, and Bill Pronzini, eds. *Kill or Cure: Suspense Stories about the World of Medicine* (9–12). 1989, Crown paper $5.98 (0-517-68135-8). Sixteen mystery tales involving medical topics that were published through the 1950s. (Rev: BL 10/15/85)

2119 Nemec, David. *Mad Blood* (10–12). 1984, Tor paper $3.50 (0-8125-0704-5). A parole officer investigates 2 horrible murders that occurred 12 years before.

2120 Nevins, Francis M., and Martin H. Greenberg, eds. *Hitchcock in Prime Time* (10–12). 1985, Avon paper $9.95 (0-380-89673-7). This is a collection of 20 stories that formed the basis of some of Hitchcock's best television shows.

2121 Nixon, Joan Lowery. *The Stalker* (9–12). 1985, Delacorte $14.95 (0-385-29376-3); Dell paper $2.95 (0-440-97753-3). In Corpus Christi, Jennifer sets out to prove the innocence of her friend, who has been accused of murder. (Rev: BR 9–10/85; SLJ 5/85; VOYA 6/85)

2122 Oliphant, B. J. *Dead in the Scrub* (10–12). 1990, Fawcett paper $3.95 (0-449-14653-7). A spunky female detective gets involved in a savings and loan swindle and murder. (Rev: SLJ 7/90)

2123 Paretsky, Sara. *Burn Marks* (10–12). 1990, Delacorte $17.95 (0-385-29892-7). Vic Warshawski, the tough female detective who is featured in many mysteries, investigates a mysterious case of arson in a hotel for the homeless. (Rev: VOYA 6/90)

2124 Parker, Robert B. *Pale Kings and Princes* (10–12). 1988, Simon & Schuster $14.95 (0-671-66073-X); Dell paper $4.50 (0-440-20004-0). One of many fine Spenser novels, this one involves the detective investigating the murder of a newspaper reporter who knew too much about a drug ring. (Rev: SLJ 11/87)

2125 Parker, Robert B. *Playmates* (10–12). 1989, Putnam $17.95 (0-399-13425-5). For mature readers, this is one of the popular Spenser novels that are a rather heady mixture of murder, humor,

and often some sexual encounters. (Rev: BL 2/1/89)

2126 Pattrick, William, ed. *Mysterious Sea Stories* (9–12). 1987, Dell paper $3.50 (0-440-16088-X). Ghost ships and pacts with the devil are frequent subjects in this fine collection of sea stories. (Rev: BL 4/1/85)

2127 Pentecost, Hugh. *Death by Fire: An Uncle George Mystery Novel* (10–12). 1986, Dodd $15.95 (0-396-08826-6). A New England town is torn by mysterious fires and a series of murders. (Rev: SLJ 4/87)

2128 Peters, Elizabeth. *The Curse of the Pharaohs* (10–12). 1988, Mysterious paper $3.95 (0-445-10648-8). A humorous mystery involving a nineteenth-century archaeological expedition. Also use: *Crocodile on the Sandbank* (1984).

2129 Peters, Elizabeth. *The Deeds of the Disturber* (10–12). 1988, Macmillan $16.95 (0-689-11907-0); Warner paper $3.95 (0-446-35333-7). Amelia Peabody Emerson, nineteenth-century English archaeologist and amateur detective, tackles the case of the mummy's curse. (Rev: BL 3/15/88; SLJ 12/88)

2130 Peters, Elizabeth. *Lion in the Valley* (9–12). 1987, Tor paper $3.95 (0-8125-0764-9). Murder and mayhem mingle in this mystery involving the Emerson family and Egypt in the settings used in earlier mysteries in this series like *Crocodile on the Sandbank* (1975). (Rev: BL 4/1/86)

2131 Peters, Ellis. *The Confession of Brother Haluin* (10–12). 1989, Mysterious $15.95 (0-89296-349-2). There are now more than a dozen mystery stories featuring Brother Cadfael, a monk who is in residence in a monastery in medieval England. (Rev: BL 2/1/89)

2132 Peters, Ellis. *Dead Man's Ransom* (10–12). 1986, Fawcett paper $3.95 (0-449-20819-2). In this ninth Brother Cadfael novel again set in twelfth-century England, the good monk gets involved in a political murder. (Rev: BL 3/15/85)

2133 Peters, Ellis. *The Heretic's Apprentice* (10–12). 1990, Mysterious $16.95 (0-89296-381-6). When a young man recently back from a pilgrimage to the Holy Land is accused of murder, Brother Cadfael steps in. (Rev: BL 2/15/90)

2134 Peters, Ellis. *A Rare Benedictine* (10–12). Illus. 1989, Mysterious $19.95 (0-89296-397-2). A collection of 3 stories featuring the medieval supersleuth Brother Cadfael. (Rev: BL 1/1/90)

2135 Peters, Ellis. *The Virgin in the Ice* (10–12). 1986, Fawcett paper $4.95 (0-449-21121-5). This is one of several mystery stories set in the Middle

Ages about Brother Cadfael. In this one he finds the murderer of a nun.

2136 Peterson, Keith. *Scarred Man* (10–12). 1990, Doubleday $18.95 (0-385-26614-6). Michael and Susannah, 2 lovers, are being followed by a scarred man who wants to kill them. (Rev: VOYA 6/90)

2137 Peyton, K. M. *A Midsummer Night's Death* (9–12). 1982, Dell paper $1.75 (0-440-95616-3). Is Jonathan's mathematics teacher involved in a colleague's suicide?

2138 Pickard, Nancy. *Bum Steer* (10–12). 1990, Pocket $16.95 (0-671-68040-4). Jenny Cain investigates the murder of a ranch owner in this follow-up to *Dead Crazy* (1988) and *No Body* (1986). (Rev: BL 1/1/90)

2139 Pike, Christopher. *Chain Letter* (9–12). 1986, Avon paper $2.95 (0-380-89968-X). Six teenagers must perform acts of repentance in connection with the hit-and-run death of a man. (Rev: VOYA 8–10/86)

2140 Pike, Christopher. *Spellbound* (10–12). 1988, Pocket paper $2.75 (0-671-64979-5). Cindy is determined to find out who murdered one of the cheerleaders at her high school. (Rev: VOYA 8/88)

2141 Pronzini, Bill. *Shackles* (10–12). 1988, St. Martin's $16.95 (0-312-01818-5). A private investigator is kidnapped and left to die in an isolated mountain cabin. (Rev: BL 6/1/88; SLJ 10/88)

2142 Pronzini, Bill. *Small Felonies: 50 Mini-Masterpieces of Crime & Detection* (10–12). 1988, St. Martin's $15.95 (0-312-02283-2). A collection of 20 short-short stories with many surprise endings. (Rev: BL 12/1/88; SLJ 3/89)

2143 Pronzini, Bill, and Martin H. Greenberg, eds. *Great Modern Police Stories* (9–12). 1986, Walker $15.95 (0-8027-0881-1); paper $11.95 (0-8027-7291-9). A rich sampling of stories about police by such writers as McBain, MacDonald, and Simenon. (Rev: BL 5/15/86)

2144 Pronzini, Bill, and Martin H. Greenberg, eds. *The Mammoth Book of Private Eye Stories* (10–12). 1988, Carroll & Graf paper $8.95 (0-88184-430-6). A collection of 26 stories about all kinds of private detectives. (Rev: BL 11/1/88)

2145 Pronzini, Bill, and Martin H. Greenberg, eds. *Prime Suspects #1* (10–12). 1987, Ballantine paper $2.95 (0-8041-0125-6). A collection of 13 stories by such masters as P. D. James and Stephen King. (Rev: BL 6/1/87)

2146 Pronzini, Bill, and Martin Greenberg, eds. *Suspicious Characters* (10–12). 1987, Ballantine paper $2.95 (0-8041-0126-4). Thirteen mystery stories by such writers as Ed McBain, John D. MacDonald, and P. D. James. (Rev: BL 12/15/87)

2147 Rae, Catherine M. *Sarah Cobb* (10–12). 1990, St. Martin's $15.95 (0-312-04579-4). A man is murdered and his 2 sisters are suspects in this mystery set in nineteenth-century New York. (Rev: BL 9/1/90)

2148 Randisi, Robert J., ed. *Justice for Hire: The Fourth Private Eye Writers of America Anthology* (10–12). 1990, Mysterious $18.95 (0-89296-371-9). A collection of 15 stories all involving private detectives. (Rev: BL 8/90)

2149 Reeves, Robert N. *Doubting Thomas* (10–12). 1985, Crown $12.95 (0-517-55616-2); Warner paper $3.95 (0-446-34156-8). After winning a small fortune by accident at the race track, an English professor finds himself involved in an underworld murder. (Rev: VOYA 8/85)

2150 Rendell, Ruth. *The Bridesmaid* (10–12). 1989, Mysterious $17.95 (0-89296-388-3). A mature psychological thriller about a sensitive young man's infatuation with a destructive woman who possibly could have committed murder. (Rev: BL 5/1/89)

2151 Rendell, Ruth. *Collected Stories* (10–12). 1988, Pantheon $19.95 (0-394-56942-3). A collection of 38 stories by a master of psychological mystery. (Rev: BL 4/1/88; SLJ 9/88)

2152 Rendell, Ruth. *The Fever Tree and Other Stories of Suspense* (10–12). 1983, Ballantine paper $2.95 (0-345-31069-1). Eleven stories by this English master of the psychological thriller.

2153 Rendell, Ruth. *Heartstones* (10–12). Illus. 1987, Harper $10.95 (0-06-015757-7); Ballantine paper $3.50 (0-345-34800-1). In this short but powerful mystery an anorexic girl believes she is guilty of murder. (Rev: BL 6/1/87; SLJ 11/87)

2154 Rendell, Ruth. *Master of the Moor* (10–12). 1988, Ballantine paper $3.95 (0-345-00870-7). For better readers, this is a novel of murder on an English moor.

2155 Rendell, Ruth. *Talking to Strange Men* (10–12). 1987, Pantheon $16.95 (0-394-56324-7); Ballantine paper $3.95 (0-345-35174-6). A group of teenagers who play espionage games and a lonely man whose wife is going to leave him are 2 of the elements in this suspenseful story. (Rev: BR 3–4/88; SLJ 5/88)

2156 Rendell, Ruth. *The Veiled One* (10–12). 1988, Pantheon $16.95 (0-394-57206-8). Inspector Wexford investigates the murder of a middle-aged housewife. (Rev: BL 6/1/88)

2157 Rinehart, Mary Roberts. *The Circular Staircase* (10–12). 1985, Carroll & Graf paper $3.50 (0-88184-106-4). This 1908 title has become a classic of murder mysteries.

2158 Robinson, Leah Ruth. *Blood Run* (10–12). 1988, NAL $17.95 (0-453-00611-6). A doctor believes that the death of her colleague is murder and not suicide as reported. (Rev: BL 9/1/88; SLJ 4/89)

2159 Robinson, Patricia. *Something to Hide* (10–12). 1990, St. Martin's $15.95 (0-312-03937-9). A murder mystery set in Charleston, South Carolina, that involves a young woman living alone in a big family mansion. (Rev: BL 2/1/90)

2160 Roosevelt, Elliott. *The Hyde Park Murder* (10–12). 1986, Avon paper $3.95 (0-380-70058-1). This is the second mystery involving Eleanor Roosevelt and murder and mayhem among the wealthy financial class. (Rev: BL 5/15/85)

2161 Roosevelt, Elliott. *Murder and the First Lady* (10–12). 1985, Avon paper $3.95 (0-380-69937-0). A mystery in which Eleanor Roosevelt serves as supersleuth.

2162 Roosevelt, Elliott. *Murder at the Palace* (10–12). 1988, St. Martin's $15.95 (0-312-01373-6). Eleanor Roosevelt again stars in this, the fifth of this series. The locale is Buckingham Palace during World War II. (Rev: BL 2/15/88)

2163 Roosevelt, Elliott. *Murder in the Blue Room* (10–12). 1990, St. Martin's $16.95 (0-312-04354-6). Another mystery involving Eleanor Roosevelt—this time about the Russian Molotov and his visit to Washington during World War II. (Rev: BL 5/15/90)

2164 Roosevelt, Elliott. *Murder in the Oval Office* (10–12). 1989, St. Martin's $16.95 (0-312-02259-X). First Lady Eleanor Roosevelt solves the murder of a congressman. (Rev: BL 12/15/88)

2165 Roosevelt, Elliott. *The White House Pantry Murder* (10–12). 1987, St. Martin's $15.95 (0-312-00202-5); Avon paper $3.95 (0-380-70404-8). This is the fourth mystery involving Eleanor Roosevelt as sleuth. In this one a body is found in a large White House refrigerator. (Rev: BL 12/15/86)

2166 Rosen, Richard. *Fadeaway* (10–12). 1986, Harper $15.95 (0-06-015599-X); NAL paper $3.95 (0-451-40148-4). A mystery featuring Harvey Blissberg on assignment to find a missing Boston Celtic star. Another mystery with Harvey is *Strike Three, You're Dead* (1984). (Rev: BL 9/1/86)

2167 St. George, Judith. *Do You See What I See?* (9–12). 1982, Putnam paper $9.95 (0-399-20912-3). Matt Runyon's suspicions concerning his neighbors on Cape Cod almost cost him his life.

2168 Satterthwait, Walter. *Miss Lizzie* (9–12). 1989, St. Martin's $17.95 (0-312-03400-8). After her acquittal, Lizzie Borden again becomes a suspect when another ax murder occurs. (Rev: BL 9/1/89)

2169 Sayers, Dorothy L. *Lord Peter* (9–12). 1987, Harper $17.95 (0-06-055039-4). The complete short stories involving England's upper-class detective, Lord Peter Wimsey.

2170 Sayers, Dorothy L. *The Nine Tailors* (10–12). 1989, Harcourt $15.95 (0-15-165897-8). A convoluted mystery for better readers involving the very English sleuth Lord Peter Wimsey. Also use *Clouds of Witness; Five Red Herrings;* and *The Unpleasantness at the Bellona Club* (all 1989).

2171 Schneider, Joyce Anne. *Darkness Falls* (10–12). 1989, Pocket $17.95 (0-671-67317-3). Dr. Amanda Hammond investigates the murder of a 17-year-old girl from an upper class Long Island community. (Rev: VOYA 10/89)

2172 Scoppettone, Sandra. *Playing Murder* (9–12). 1985, Harper LB $12.89 (0-06-025284-7); paper $2.75 (0-06-447046-6). A group of teens are playing a game called Murder when one is found fatally stabbed. (Rev: BR 9–10/85; SLJ 5/85)

2173 Sebestyen, Ouida. *The Girl in the Box* (9–12). 1988, Little $13.95 (0-316-77935-0). A high school girl is kidnapped by a masked man and kept prisoner in a damp, dark room. (Rev: BL 11/1/88; BR 1–2/89; SLJ 10/88; VOYA 2/89)

2174 Sheldon, Sidney. *The Naked Face* (10–12). 1976, Morrow $16.95 (0-688-02150-6); Warner paper $5.95 (0-446-34191-6). A psychoanalyst becomes the target for murder involving one of his patients.

2175 Shubin, Seymour. *Never Quite Dead* (10–12). 1988, St. Martin's $17.95 (0-312-02187-9). A young man continues his father's investigation into the death of an unknown youngster. (Rev: BL 12/1/88)

2176 Sierra, Patricia. *A Boy I Never Knew* (8–12). 1988, Avon paper $2.50 (0-380-75208-5). Libby sets out to find the identity of the person who murdered her boyfriend. (Rev: VOYA 6/88)

2177 Simenon, Georges. *Maigret and the Killer* (10–12). 1979, Harcourt paper $2.95 (0-15-655124-1). This is one of many psychological mysteries for better readers that feature Inspector Jules Maigret.

2178 Simpson, Dorothy. *Element of Doubt* (10–12). 1988, Macmillan $14.95 (0-684-18885-6). In this exciting whodunit a woman who has had many affairs mysteriously falls to her death. (Rev: BL 3/15/88)

2179 Sjowall, Maj, and Per Wahloo. *The Laughing Policeman* (10–12). 1977, Random paper $4.95 (0-394-72341-4). Part of a series of mysteries featuring Martin Beck, a Swedish police detective. Others are: *The Locked Room* (1980) and *Murder at the Savoy* (1977).

2180 Smith, Julie. *Tourist Trap* (10–12). 1986, Mysterious $15.95 (0-89296-162-7). In this Rebecca Schwartz novel, the lawyer takes on a maniac who is murdering innocent tourists. (Rev: SLJ 3/87)

2181 Smith, Marie, ed. *Ms. Murder* (10–12). 1989, Citadel paper $9.95 (0-8065-1139-7). For better readers, a collection of puzzlers involving female sleuths. (Rev: BL 11/15/89)

2182 Spikol, Art. *The Physalia Incident* (10–12). 1988, Viking $15.95 (0-670-81222-6). A magazine editor turns detective to investigate a mysterious death in Bermuda. (Rev: BL 3/1/88)

2183 Sprinkle, Patricia H. *Murder at Markham* (10–12). 1988, St. Martin's $15.95 (0-312-02257-3). Two ladies try to help a University of Chicago student who is falsely accused of murder. (Rev: BL 11/1/88)

2184 Stern, Madeleine, ed. *A Double Life: Newly Discovered Thrillers of Louisa May Alcott* (8–12). 1988, Little $17.95 (0-316-03101-1). This is a collection of stories that represents the other Alcott—a writer of mystery and horror stories. (Rev: BR 11–12/88)

2185 Stewart, Mary. *Thornyhold* (9–12). 1988, Morrow $15.95 (0-688-08425-7). Geillis discovers that a magic spell controls the people in her cousin's house. (Rev: BL 10/1/88)

2186 Stine, R. L. *Blind Date* (10–12). 1986, Scholastic paper $2.25 (0-590-40326-5). In this graphic horror story, Kerry realizes that his blind date is a psychopath. (Rev: BL 9/15/86; SLJ 11/86)

2187 Sucher, Dorothy. *Dead Men Don't Marry* (10–12). 1989, St. Martin's $17.95 (0-312-02900-4). Detectives Sabina Swift and Vic Newman investigate the strange death of a friend in this follow-up to *Dead Men Don't Give Seminars* (1988). (Rev: BL 6/15/89)

2188 Sullivan, Eleanor, ed. *Ellery Queen's Bad Scenes: Stories from Ellery Queen's Mystery Magazine* (9–12). 1989, Walker $19.95 (0-8027-5745-6). Starting chronologically with Baroness Orczy, this is a collection of 25 stories involving unpleasant occurrences. (Rev: BL 9/1/89; SLJ 3/90)

2189 Sullivan, Eleanor, ed. *More Murder on Cue: Stage, Screen & Radio Favorites* (9–12). 1990, Walker $19.95 (0-8027-5752-9). A group of 16 stories that have been used on TV, radio, or in the movies. (Rev: BL 2/1/90)

2190 Sullivan, Eleanor, and Cynthia Manson, eds. *Tales from Ellery Queen's Mystery Magazine: Short Stories for Young Adults* (10–12). 1986, Harcourt $13.95 (0-15-284205-5). A collection of 17 adult mystery stories that are especially suitable for young adults. (Rev: BL 11/15/86; SLJ 12/86; VOYA 4/87)

2191 Symons, Julian. *The Kentish Manor Murders* (10–12). 1988, Viking $15.95 (0-670-82142-X). For better readers, a mystery involving a plot against an eccentric recluse who is a fan of Sherlock Holmes. (Rev: BL 6/1/88)

2192 Tapply, William G. *Death at Charity's Point* (10–12). 1985, Ballantine paper $2.95 (0-345-32014-X). An adult mystery that begins with the investigation of a suicide.

2193 Tey, Josephine. *The Daughter of Time* (10–12). 1976, Buccaneer LB $21.95 (0-89966-184-X); Pocket paper $3.95 (0-671-49759-6). A hospitalized policeman spends his time unraveling the story of Richard III in this unusual mystery. Also use by the same author: *Brat Farrar* (Pocket, 1982), *Singing Sands* (Pocket, 1988), and *Miss Pym Disposes* (Pocket, 1987).

2194 Thomas, Donald. *Jekyll, Alias Hyde: A Variation* (10–12). 1989, St. Martin's $15.95 (0-312-02592-0). A retelling of the classic story with some unusual twists. (Rev: BL 1/1/89)

2195 Thompson, Julian. *Discontinued* (9–12). 1986, Scholastic paper $2.75 (0-590-40116-5). A suspenseful story about a boy investigating a cult of health-food fanatics to find the murderer of his mother and brother. (Rev: BR 1–2/86; VOYA 12/85)

2196 Truman, Margaret. *Murder at the FBI* (10–12). 1986, Fawcett paper $3.95 (0-449-20618-1). In this the sixth of her murder mysteries set in Washington, Truman poses the question, "Who murdered FBI special agent George L. Pritchard?" (Rev: BL 5/15/85)

2197 Truman, Margaret. *Murder at the Kennedy Center* (10–12). 1989, Random $17.95 (0-394-57602-0). A fund-raiser at Kennedy Center seems to be a success until the body of a murdered girl is found. (Rev: BL 6/1/89)

2198 Truman, Margaret. *Murder at the National Cathedral* (10–12). 1990, Random $18.95 (0-394-57603-9). -Mackensie Smith investigates the murder of the Episcopal priest who just married him. (Rev: BL 8/90)

2199 Truman, Margaret. *Murder in Georgetown* (10–12). 1986, Arbor House $18.95 (0-87795-797-5); Fawcett paper $4.95 (0-449-21332-3). In this continuing series, crime reporter Joe Potamos is assigned to a story involving the murder of a senator's daughter. (Rev: BL 6/1/86; VOYA 12/86)

2200 Truman, Margaret. *Murder in the White House* (10–12). 1988, Warner paper $4.95 (0-446-31488-9). In this thriller, the secretary of state is murdered in private quarters in the White House. This is one of many recommended mysteries set in Washington, D.C., that include *Murder in the Supreme Court* and *Murder in the Smithsonian* (both 1985).

2201 Truman, Margaret. *Murder on Capitol Hill* (10–12). 1988, Warner paper $4.95 (0-446-31072-7). A prominent senator is murdered at his own testimonial dinner in this mystery which is part of a series that includes *Murder on Embassy Row* (1985).

2202 Upton, Robert. *Fabergé Egg: An Amos McGuffin Mystery* (10–12). 1988, Dutton $16.95 (0-525-24692-4). An Amos McGuffin mystery in which the sleuth must solve an 18-year-old murder case which also involves the loss of a Fabergé egg. (Rev: SLJ 4/89)

2203 Van Dine, S. S. *The Canary Murder Case* (10–12). 1979, Macmillan paper $2.25 (0-684-16404-3). Philo Vance was a popular detective during the 1930s. This is one of several mysteries featuring him that is still in print.

2204 Van Thal, Herbert, ed. *The Mammoth Book of Great Detective Stories* (9–12). 1989, Carroll & Graf paper $8.95 (0-88184-530-2). A total of 26 classic stories by such writers as Sayers, Simenon, Chandler, and Chesterton. (Rev: BL 9/15/89)

2205 Vine, Barbara. *Gallowglass* (10–12). 1990, Crown $19.95 (0-517-57744-5). A young drifter falls under the spell of another man who wants help in planning a kidnapping. (Rev: SLJ 10/90)

2206 Voigt, Cynthia. *The Callender Papers* (9–12). 1983, Macmillan $13.95 (0-689-30971-6); Fawcett paper $3.50 (0-449-70184-0). A part-time position sorting out some archival papers leads to uncovering unsolved family mysteries.

2207 Wallace, Carol. *Waking Dream* (9–12). 1989, Berkley paper $3.50 (0-425-11255-1). While doing research on heiresses who marry noblemen, Sarah uncovers a murder. (Rev: SLJ 1/88)

2208 Wallace, Marilyn, ed. *Sisters in Crime 2* (10–12). 1990, Berkley paper $3.95 (0-425-11966-1). The second collection of crime stories especially written for this anthology by and about women. Preceded by *Sisters in Crime* (1989). (Rev: BL 3/15/90)

2209 Wambaugh, Joseph. *The Black Marble* (10–12). 1980, Dell paper $4.95 (0-440-10644-3). A valuable show dog is missing and Natalie Zimmerman and tough Sergeant Valnikov are assigned to the case.

2210 Westlake, Donald E. *Why Me?* (10–12). 1985, Tor paper $3.50 (0-8125-1052-6). A humorous mystery featuring a small-time thief down on his luck.

2211 Whitney, Phyllis A. *Black Amber* (9–12). 1982, Fawcett paper $3.95 (0-449-20219-4). A gothic thriller by the prolific author of such romantic mysteries as *Blue Fire* (1985), *Seven Tears for Apollo* (1985), *Spindrift* (1981), and *Window on the Square* (1983).

2212 Whitney, Phyllis A. *Dream of Orchids* (9–12). 1987, Fawcett paper $3.95 (0-449-20743-9). While visiting on the Florida Keys, Laurel becomes involved in murder. (Rev: SLJ 5/85)

2213 Whitney, Phyllis A. *Emerald* (9–12). 1983, Fawcett paper $4.95 (0-449-20099-X). When Carol and her son relocate to Palm Springs, she confronts a terrible mystery. This is one of many recommended romantic mysteries by this author that include *Golden Unicorns, Seven Tears for Apollo* (both 1985), and *Stone Bull* (1983).

2214 Whitney, Phyllis A. *Feather on the Moon* (10–12). 1988, Doubleday $17.95 (0-385-24286-7). Jennifer Blake travels to Victoria, British Columbia, in search of her daughter, kidnapped 4 years before. (Rev: BL 2/1/88)

2215 Whitney, Phyllis A. *Rainbow in the Mist* (9–12). 1989, Doubleday $18.95 (0-385-24954-3). Christy has the psychic gift of locating dead bodies—a talent that leads her to a murder mystery. (Rev: BL 11/15/88)

2216 Whitney, Phyllis A. *Rainsong* (9–12). 1984, Fawcett paper $3.95 (0-449-20510-X). Some question whether rock singer Ricky Sands's death was a suicide. Also use: *Domino* (1983) and *The Trembling Hills* (1982).

2217 Whitney, Phyllis A. *Silversword* (9–12). 1987, Doubleday $15.95 (0-385-23666-2); Fawcett paper $4.95 (0-449-21278-5). A 32-year-old woman returns to Hawaii, where her parents were mysteriously killed 26 years before. (Rev: BL 11/1/86)

2218 Whitney, Phyllis A. *The Singing Stones* (9–12). 1990, Doubleday $19.95 (0-385-41221-5). A therapist is brought in to help the disturbed daughter of her first husband in this tale of mystery and romance. (Rev: BL 12/15/89; SLJ 8/90; VOYA 6/90)

2219 Wilhelm, Kate. *Sweet, Sweet Poison* (10–12). 1990, St. Martin's $16.95 (0-312-04433-X). Mysterious events occur after a Bronx couple buys an abandoned mill in upstate New York. (Rev: BL 7/90)

2220 Wilson, Barbara Ker. *The Quade Inheritance* (9–12). 1989, St. Martin's $17.95 (0-312-02700-1). A gothic novel about a ruthless girl who will stop at nothing to secure her inheritance and of the innocent governess who becomes her victim. (Rev: BL 4/15/89; SLJ 9/89)

2221 Wilson, Gahan. *Everybody's Favorite Duck* (10–12). 1988, Mysterious $15.95 (0-89296-295-X). Enoch Bone, a detective, and his helper John Weston unravel a plot to harm the president in this wide spoof of mystery novels. (Rev: BL 10/15/88)

2222 Windsor, Patricia. *The Sandman's Eyes* (8–12). 1985, Delacorte $15.95 (0-385-29381-X); Dell paper $2.95 (0-440-97585-9). Having suffered a breakdown after witnessing a murder, 18-year-old Michael is anxious to find the murderer. (Rev: BL 4/1/85; BR 1–2/86; SLJ 5/85)

2223 Wolf, Gary. *Who Censored Roger Rabbit?* (10–12). 1982, Ballantine paper $3.50 (0-345-30325-3). In this comedy-mystery that was the basis of the famous movie, cartoon characters and live humans mix to solve an unusual problem.

2224 Zachary, Hugh. *Murder in White* (10–12). 1981, Dorchester paper $2.50 (0-8439-2298-2). A taut mystery with a hospital setting.

Romances

2225 Adler, C. S. *Roadside Valentine* (8–12). 1983, Macmillan $11.95 (0-02-700350-7); Putnam paper $2.25 (0-399-21146-2). Jamie is trying very hard to capture the affections of Louisa.

2226 Allman, Paul. *The Knot* (8–12). 1988, Rosen $12.95 (0-8239-0776-7). Told from 2 different viewpoints, this is the story of 2 high school students who fall in love and want to get married. (Rev: BR 1–2/89; SLJ 12/88; VOYA 2/89)

2227 Andrews, Kristi. *Magic Time* (8–12). 1987, Bantam paper $2.50 (0-553-26342-0). Katie makes good on a soap opera; but can she discourage the director's attentions? (Rev: SLJ 1/88)

2228 Andrews, Wendy. *Vacation Fever!* (9–12). 1984, Putnam paper $2.25 (0-399-21083-0). Sarah's summer vacation improves greatly after she meets Neal.

2229 Baldwin, Rebecca. *Arabella and the Beast* (10–12). 1988, St. Martin's $15.95 (0-312-02163-1). A Regency romance that is also a variation on the Cinderella story. (Rev: BL 12/1/88)

2230 Bennett, Jay. *I Never Said I Love You* (9–12). 1984, Avon paper $2.50 (0-380-86900-4). A boy must choose between fulfilling his father's wishes and the girl he loves.

2231 Binchy, Maeve. *Echoes* (10–12). 1986, Viking $17.95 (0-670-80938-1); Dell paper $4.50 (0-440-12209-0). A love story set in Ireland about 2 young people whose marriage is threatened by class differences. (Rev: BL 11/1/85)

2232 Blair, Alison. *Love by the Book* (8–12). 1989, Ivy paper $2.95 (0-8041-0331-3). Sam finds her life is in turmoil after her boyfriend joins her at college. Also use: *Social Studies* and *The Popcorn Project* (both 1989). (Rev: SLJ 10/89)

2233 Blake, Susan. *All-Nighter* (9–12). 1987, Ballantine paper $2.50 (0-8041-0022-5). A girl in college learns about sex and the ways of sororities. (Rev: BL 8/87; SLJ 3/88)

2234 Boissard, Janine. *A Time to Choose* (9–12). 1985, Little $15.95 (0-316-10102-8); Fawcett paper $2.50 (0-449-70160-3). Pauline Moreau is now 19, in Paris and in love with a man 12 years older than herself. (Rev: BL 10/1/85; SLJ 5/86)

2235 Brent, Madeleine. *Stormswift* (10–12). 1986, Fawcett paper $3.50 (0-449-20811-7). For better readers, this is an adventure-romance set in the late nineteenth century involving a woman who returns to England after years of slavery in Afghanistan. (Rev: BL 3/15/85)

2236 Burchard, Peter. *First Affair* (10–12). 1981, Farrar $10.95 (0-374-32336-4). A teenage boy must choose between the love he feels for a girl and an older woman.

2237 Callan, Jamie. *Just Too Cool* (9–12). 1987, NAL paper $2.50 (0-451-14663-8). A very unconventional female punk rock star falls in love with a very conventional boy whose hobby is geology. (Rev: BL 10/15/87; VOYA 8–9/87)

2238 Carr, Philippa. *The Black Swan* (10–12). 1990, Putnam $19.95 (0-399-13513-8). In this sequel to *The Changeling* (1989), our heroine, Lucie, marries an Irish terrorist in disguise in this novel set in England of Prime Minister Gladstone. (Rev: BL 2/15/90)

2239 Carr, Philippa. *The Changeling* (9–12). 1989, Putnam $18.95 (0-399-13419-0). An historical romance involving 2 babies being switched at birth. (Rev: BL 3/1/89)

2240 Carr, Philippa. *The Pool of St. Branok* (10–12). 1987, Fawcett paper $4.50 (0-449-21551-2). A long-smoldering love is rekindled when Angel and Ben meet again during the Australian gold rush. (Rev: BL 6/1/87)

2241 Carr, Philippa. *The Return of the Gypsy* (9–12). 1985, Putnam $16.95 (0-399-12064-0); Fawcett paper $3.95 (0-449-20897-4). In this light romance set in England about 100 years ago, Jessica falls in love with a man she thinks is a gypsy. (Rev: BL 2/1/85)

2242 Chatterton, Louise. *Just the Right Age* (9–12). 1984, Pocket paper $1.95 (0-671-53392-4). Linn becomes infatuated with a boy she cannot have.

2243 Chesney, Marion. *Enlightening Delilah* (9–12). 1989, St. Martin's $14.95 (0-312-02912-8). A Regency novel, third in a series, about the Tribble sisters, who run a charm school for debutantes. The first 2 are *Refining Felicity* (1988) and *Perfecting Fiona* (1989). (Rev: BL 6/15/89)

2244 Chesney, Marion. *Frederica in Fashion* (9–12). 1987, Fawcett paper $2.50 (0-317-56982-1). In this the sixth Regency romance about the 6 Armitage sisters, the youngest, Frederica, decides to run away to become a chambermaid. (Rev: BL 10/15/85)

2245 Chesney, Marion. *Marrying Harriet* (10–12). 1990, St. Martin's $15.95 (0-312-04276-0). A delightful Regency romance that is the finale to Chesney's School for Manners series. (Rev: BL 7/90)

2246 Chesney, Marion. *Rainbird's Revenge* (10–12). 1988, St. Martin's $13.95 (0-312-01506-2). A delightful Regency romance in which a group of servants decide to open up a country pub. (Rev: BL 5/15/88)

2247 Chesney, Marion. *Rake's Progress* (10–12). 1987, St. Martin's $12.95 (0-312-00674-8). In this Regency romance that is part of the House for the Season series, Lord Carlton mends his wild ways after meeting a beautiful neighbor. (Rev: BL 8/87)

2248 Chesney, Marion. *The Wicked Godmother* (9–12). 1987, St. Martin's paper $2.95 (0-317-64610-9). In this light romance, an attractive godmother faces the machinations of her wily charges, twin girls. Others in this series are *The

Miser of Mayfair* (1986) and *Plain Jane* (1986). (Rev: BL 3/1/87)

2249 Cherryh, C. J., ed. *Smuggler's Gold* (10–12). 1988, NAL paper $3.50 (0-88677-299-0). The fourth anthology by many fine writers in Cherryh's Merovingen Nights cycle of stories, the third of which was *Troubled Waters* (1988). (Rev: BL 10/15/88)

2250 Colman, Hila. *Not for Love* (9–12). 1983, Morrow $11.95 (0-688-02419-X). In this romance, Jill finds that sometimes one is forced to compromise one's ideals.

2251 Conford, Ellen. *If This Is Love, I'll Take Spaghetti* (9–12). 1983, Macmillan $11.95 (0-02-7244250-5); 1984, Scholastic paper $2.50 (0-590-41210-8). Nine stories about teenagers and variations on the love experience.

2252 Conklin, Barbara. *P.S. I Love You* (8–12). 1981, Bantam paper $2.25 (0-553-24460-4). Mariah loses her first love to cancer.

2253 Connell, Abby. *Jed and Jessie* (9–12). 1983, Warner paper $1.95 (0-446-30802-1). A teenage romance told twice—from both his and her points of view.

2254 Cookson, Catherine. *The Moth* (10–12). 1987, Pocket paper $3.95 (0-671-64478-5). In this romantic novel (set in England before World War I), a carpenter falls in love with someone above him in social station. (Rev: BL 4/1/86)

2255 Cookson, Catherine. *The Parson's Daughter* (10–12). 1987, Summit $18.95 (0-671-63293-0); Pocket paper $4.50 (0-671-64853-3). A nineteenth-century romance about the many rises and falls of a spunky heroine. (Rev: BL 3/1/87)

2256 Cooney, Linda A. *Change of Hearts* (8–12). 1985, Scholastic paper $2.50 (0-590-33390-9). The falling in and out of love of a group of high school students in Washington, D.C. (Rev: SLJ 1/86)

2257 Cooney, Linda A. *Junior* (7–12). 1988, Scholastic paper $2.50 (0-590-41677-4). Four high school girls face the pressures of preparing for college, dating, and growing self-awareness. (Rev: SLJ 1/89)

2258 Cowley, Joy. *Salmagundi* (10–12). 1985, Oxford Univ. Pr. $12.95 (0-29-558117-2). A satire on war involving 2 rival industrialists on opposite sides of town. (Rev: BR 11–12/86)

2259 Davis, Leila. *Lover Boy* (7–12). 1989, Avon paper $2.50 (0-380-75722-2). Ryan finds that his racy reputation is keeping him from the girl he really loves. (Rev: SLJ 10/89; VOYA 8/89)

2260 de France, Marie. *The Lais of Marie de France* (10–12). Trans. by Robert Hanning and Joan Ferrante. 1986, Penguin paper $6.95 (0-14-044476-9). This collection of love stories involving princes and princesses was written in the twelfth century by an unknown Frenchwoman.

2261 Dukore, Jesse. *Long Distance Love* (9–12). 1983, Bantam paper $2.25 (0-553-17853-9). Pam faces separation from her boyfriend when she goes to boarding school.

2262 Dunn, Carola. *Two Corinthians* (10–12). 1990, Walker $18.95 (0-8027-1087-5). A Regency romance about 2 attractive but seemingly unmarriageable sisters. (Rev: BL 12/15/89)

2263 Edghill, Rosemary. *The Ill-Bred Bride: Or, The Inconvenient Marriage* (10–12). 1990, St. Martin's $17.95 (0-312-03968-9). A delightful novel about a marriage of convenience in Regency England. (Rev: BL 2/15/90)

2264 Ellis, Carol. *A Kiss for Good Luck* (9–12). 1984, Warner paper $1.95 (0-446-32014-5). Two sports-minded teenagers fall in love in a story told from both points of view.

2265 French, Michael. *Lifeguards Only beyond This Point* (9–12). 1985, Berkley paper $2.25 (0-425-08408-6). Both Max and Hunter fall for the same girl, Anabelle Livingston.

2266 Gerber, Merrill Joan. *Handsome as Anything* (8–12). 1990, Scholastic $13.95 (0-590-43019-X). Rachel is attracted to 3 different boys and in making her choice learns a lot about herself. (Rev: BL 9/15/90)

2267 Gerber, Merrill Joan. *Marry Me Tomorrow* (9–12). 1987, Ballantine paper $2.50 (0-449-70182-4). Two young girls fall under the spell of an older attractive and rich bachelor. (Rev: BL 10/1/87; VOYA 12/87)

2268 Gibbons, Kaye. *A Virtuous Woman* (10–12). 1989, Algonquin $13.95 (0-945575-09-2). Told from 2 different points of view, this is the story of a happy marriage. (Rev: SLJ 8/89)

2269 Girion, Barbara. *In the Middle of a Rainbow* (9–12). 1983, Macmillan $12.95 (0-684-17885-0). Corrie believes she has met the perfect boy when she meets handsome Todd Marcus.

2270 Goldstein, Lisa. *The Dream Years* (10–12). 1989, Bantam paper $3.95 (0-553-27657-3). An unusual love story set in Paris that moves in time from the 1920s to the late 1960s. (Rev: SLJ 12/85)

2271 Goudge, Eileen. *Something Borrowed, Something Blue* (7–12). 1988, Dell paper $2.95 (0-440-20055-5). Kit agrees to marry her long-term boyfriend but then has second thoughts. (Rev: SLJ 10/88)

2272 Gould, Phillip. *Kitty Collins* (10–12). 1986, Algonquin $15.95 (0-912697-31-8); Pocket paper $3.95 (0-671-63343-0). In this romantic novel, Kitty must choose between a singing career and the husband she loves. (Rev: BL 4/15/86)

2273 Greene, Yvonne. *Little Sister* (8–12). 1981, Bantam paper $2.50 (0-553-26613-6). A teenage romance that also involves the problems of being a younger sister.

2274 Greenwald, Sheila. *Blissful Joy and the SATs: A Multiple Choice Romance* (9–12). 1982, Little $12.95 (0-316-32673-9). Events conspire to prevent Jay from making good grades on the SATs.

2275 Guest, Elissa Haden. *Handsome Man* (9–12). 1989, Macmillan paper $2.95 (0-02-043282-8). A 14-year-old girl becomes obsessed with a handsome stranger.

2276 Harrigan, Stephen. *Aransas* (10–12). 1983, Pacesetter $8.95 (0-87719-057-7). A young man falls in love with a biological researcher when he returns to his Texas gulf town to train porpoises.

2277 Hart, Bruce, and Carole Hart. *Sooner or Later* (8–12). 1978, Avon paper $2.50 (0-380-42978-0). In order to fool her 17-year-old boyfriend into thinking she is older than 13, Jessie begins an intricate pattern of lies.

2278 Hart, Nicole. *Lead on Love* (9–12). 1984, Pocket paper $1.95 (0-317-13629-1). A move to the country brings romance to Anne.

2279 Hill, Fiona. *The Country Gentleman* (10–12). 1987, St. Martin's $17.95 (0-312-01016-8); Fawcett paper $3.50 (0-449-21758-2). A breezy Regency romance about a spunky girl and a marriage of convenience. (Rev: BL 12/15/87)

2280 Hilton, James. *Random Harvest* (10–12). 1982, Buccaneer $18.95 (0-89966-414-8); Carroll & Graf paper $4.50 (0-88184-125-0). A highly romantic novel set in World War I days about an amnesia victim who has forgotten his first true love.

2281 Holland, Isabelle. *Summer of My First Love* (9–12). 1983, Fawcett paper $2.95 (0-449-0079-8). The daughter of a wealthy summer resident falls in love with a 22-year-old "townie." A sequel is *After the First Love* (1983).

2282 Holmes, Marjorie. *Saturday Night* (9–12). 1982, Dell paper $1.95 (0-440-97645-6). Carly becomes disenchanted with Danny in spite of his flattering attention.

2283 Holt, Victoria. *The Indian Fan* (9–12). 1988, Doubleday $18.95 (0-385-24600-5). The friendship between 2 young English girls, the curse of the fan made of peacock feathers, and the enchantment of India are 3 elements in this romantic novel. (Rev: BL 8/88)

2284 Holt, Victoria. *Secret for a Nightingale* (10–12). 1987, Fawcett paper $4.95 (0-449-21296-3). In this Gothic romance set in the nineteenth century, a young woman seeks revenge for the death of her son. (Rev: BL 8/86)

2285 Holt, Victoria. *The Silk Vendetta* (9–12). 1987, Doubleday $17.95 (0-385-24299-9); Fawcett paper $4.95 (0-449-21548-2). A suspenseful romance that uses the historic trade of silk weaving as its subject. (Rev: BL 8/87)

2286 Humphreys, Martha. *Side by Side* (9–12). 1984, Pocket paper $1.95 (0-671-53402-5). Carrie does not know how to handle Dan, a college student who works for her dad.

2287 Ibbotson, Eva. *A Company of Swans* (10–12). 1985, St. Martin's $14.95 (0-312-15323-6). A rebellious daughter of a pompous Englishman joins a ballet troupe headed for the Amazon. (Rev: BL 6/15/85)

2288 Jacobs, Barbara. *Stolen Kisses* (8–12). 1986, Dell paper $2.50 (0-440-97734-7). Two working English teenage girls fall in love with the same young man. (Rev: SLJ 1/87)

2289 Johnson, Maud. *I'm Christy* (9–12). 1984, Scholastic paper $9.00 (0-590-00661-4). At her new home in Virginia, Christy must overcome her shyness to make friends.

2290 Joye, Beverly. *Flight to Love* (9–12). 1983, Holloway paper $1.95 (0-317-02746-8). A black girl must decide whether she should marry.

2291 Kennedy, Kim. *In-Between Love* (9–12). 1984, Warner paper $1.95 (0-446-32006-4). Friendship turns to love told from the girl's and the boy's points of view.

2292 Klein, Norma. *French Postcards* (10–12). 1979, Fawcett paper $2.25 (0-449-14297-3). For mature readers, this book traces the love experiences of a variety of American college students spending one year in France.

2293 Klein, Norma. *Just Friends* (10–12). 1990, Knopf LB $13.99 (0-679-90213-9). Isabel finds she really loves the boy next door with whom she has grown up, in this tale of love, sex, and friendship. (Rev: BL 2/1/90; SLJ 3/90)

2294 L'Engle, Madeleine. *And Both Were Young* (9–12). 1983, Dell paper $3.50 (0-440-90229-0). Flip feels like a misfit at her Swiss school until she meets Paul.

2295 L'Engle, Madeleine. *Camilla* (10–12). 1982, Dell paper $3.50 (0-440-91171-0). A sensitive young girl experiences first love and the breakup of her family.

2296 Lenz, Jeanne R. *Do You Really Love Me?* (9–12). 1985, Ace paper $2.25 (0-441-16056-5). Jill begins work with emotionally disturbed children and encounters hostility from Bruce.

2297 Leroe, Ellen. *Confessions of a Teenage TV Addict* (9–12). 1987, Berkley paper $2.25 (0-425-10252-1). Jennifer must see her television soap operas or she cannot get through the day.

2298 Levy, Elizabeth. *Double Standard* (10–12). 1984, Avon paper $2.25 (0-380-87379-6). Two Jewish girls fall for two WASPish boys.

2299 Levy, Marilyn. *Remember to Remember Me* (9–12). 1988, Fawcett paper $2.95 (0-449-70278-2). Thea journeys from California to New York with her boyfriend to see her father, a rock star. (Rev: BL 2/1/89; SLJ 4/89; VOYA 4/89)

2300 Lindquist, Marie. *Hidden Longings* (9–12). 1987, Bantam paper $2.50 (0-553-26668-3). Charlotte takes over the family horse-breeding stables and falls in love with the man she hires as manager. (Rev: SLJ 1/88)

2301 Lindsey, Betina. *Waltz with the Lady* (10–12). 1990, Pocket paper $4.95 (0-671-67264-9). A western romance involving a college-educated woman who in the Wyoming of 1869 campaigned for women' suffrage. (Rev: VOYA 6/90)

2302 McCaffrey, Anne. *Stitch in Snow* (10–12). 1985, Tor $14.95 (0-312-93753-9); paper $3.95 (0-8125-8562-3). While away from home a children's book writer has a passionate interlude with a man she grows to love. (Rev: BL 3/15/85)

2303 McEvoy, Marjorie. *The Black Pearl* (10–12). 1988, Doubleday $12.95 (0-385-24492-4). In this romantic novel, our heroine discovers that her fiancee is a robber of ancient graves in Tunisia. (Rev: BL 6/1/88)

2304 McLeay, Alison. *Passage Home* (10–12). 1990, Simon & Schuster $19.95 (0-671-69299-2). A lengthy romance-adventure that involves a nineteenth-century woman torn between love and duty. (Rev: BL 4/1/90)

2305 Mazer, Norma Fox. *Someone to Love* (10–12). 1985, Dell paper $3.50 (0-440-98062-3). For mature readers, this is the story of a romance between a college sophomore and the dropout son of a professor.

2306 Mazer, Norma Fox. *When We First Met* (10–12). 1984, Scholastic paper $2.50 (0-590-40359-1). This story is a modern variation on the Romeo and Juliet theme.

2307 Nathan, Robert. *Portrait of Jennie* (10–12). 1940, Knopf $14.95 (0-394-44093-5). A fantasy about a young artist and the love he feels for a girl who lives outside the confines of time.

2308 Oaks, Tina. *That Cheating Sister* (7–12). 1988, Scholastic paper $2.50 (0-590-41425-9). Relations between 2 stepsisters become strained when a handsome exchange student moves in with the family. (Rev: SLJ 10/88)

2309 Plain, Belva. *Eden Burning* (10–12). 1987, Dell paper $5.95 (0-440-12135-3). This is one of several recommended family sagas by the author of the popular *Evergreen* (1982) and *Random Winds* (1983).

2310 Polcovar, Jane. *Hey, Good Looking!* (9–12). 1985, Bantam paper $2.25 (0-553-24383-7). Patty's boyfriend is not happy when she takes a job as a construction worker. (Rev: SLJ 9/85)

2311 Quin-Harkin, Janet. *Campus Cousins* (8–12). 1989, Ivy paper $2.95 (0-8041-0335-6). Four cousins endure the first 4 weeks at Colorado University. Also use: *Home Sweet Home* (1989). (Rev: SLJ 4/89)

2312 Quin-Harkin, Janet. *The Graduates* (7–12). 1986, Bantam paper $2.50 (0-553-25723-4). While attending college, Jill finds her boyfriend wants more than she is prepared to give. Also use: *The Trouble with Toni* (1986). (Rev: BL 10/1/86; SLJ 9/86; VOYA 12/86)

2313 Quin-Harkin, Janet. *The Great Boy Chase* (7–12). 1985, Bantam paper $2.50 (0-553-25071-X). Jill and a girlfriend go to Europe to visit a former exchange student. (Rev: SLJ 1/86)

2314 Quin-Harkin, Janet. *Growing Pains* (9–12). 1986, Bantam paper $2.50 (0-553-26034-0). Jill, a college freshman, does not want to give in to her boyfriend's sexual demands. (Rev: BL 2/1/87; SLJ 1/87)

2315 Ravin, Neil. *Mere Mortals* (10–12). 1989, Delacorte $18.95 (0-385-29767-X). A romance set against the grim everyday realities of hospital life. (Rev: BL 8/89)

2316 Reit, Ann. *The Bet* (9–12). 1986, Scholastic paper $2.50 (0-590-33556-1). Catherine tries to trap Zak as part of a bet, but then she finds she loves him. (Rev: BL 8/86; SLJ 10/81)

2317 Robinson, Margaret A. *Courting Emma Howe* (10–12). 1989, Ballantine paper $3.50 (0-345-35892-9). For better readers, this is a romance about a young girl from Vermont who goes to Washington state to marry a pioneering young man. (Rev: BL 12/1/87)

2318 Rosenthal, Lucy. *Great American Love Stories* (9–12). 1988, Little $24.95 (0-316-75734-9).

A collection of 28 stories and short novels that show the varied and changing faces of love. (Rev: BR 1–2/89)

2319 Rue, Nancy. *Stop in the Name of Love* (7–12). 1988, Rosen LB $12.95 (0-8239-0794-5). In this novel about love tinged with physical abuse each of 2 high school sweethearts tells the same story but from a different viewpoint. (Rev: BR 3–4/89; SLJ 11/88; VOYA 4/89)

2320 Segal, Erich. *Love Story* (10–12). 1988, Bantam paper $4.50 (0-553-27528-3). For mature readers, this is the tender love story that ends in death.

2321 Smith, Rita Pratt. *In the Forest at Midnight* (10–12). 1989, Donald I. Fine $18.95 (1-55611-131-2). Set in India of the 1940s, this is the love story of a colonial girl and a revolutionary young Indian. (Rev: BL 5/15/89)

2322 Smith, Wilbur. *Flight of the Falcon* (10–12). 1983, Fawcett paper $4.95 (0-449-20271-2). For mature readers, this is a novel set in the mid-nineteenth century about a tempestuous romance.

2323 Steel, Danielle. *The Promise* (10–12). 1978, Dell paper $5.95 (0-440-17079-6). A wealthy architect and a poor artist decide to marry in this romance by Steele. Other recommended titles are: *Once in a Lifetime* (1980), *Now and Forever* (1978), *Palomino, The Ring* (both 1982), and *Season of Passion* (1980).

2324 Stirling, Jessica. *The Wise Child* (10–12). 1990, St. Martin's $17.95 (0-312-05182-4). This romance about a woman, her husband, and their child is set in Glasgow at the turn of the century and completes the trilogy that began with *The Good Provider* (1989) and *The Asking Price* (1990). (Rev: BL 9/1/90)

2325 Thomas, Martha Lou. *Waltz with a Stranger* (9–12). 1986, Walker $15.95 (0-80270-920-6). A light Regency romance about a woman who is in love with the man who is helping her find a husband. (Rev: SLJ 5/87)

2326 Tyler, Vicky. *Danny and the Real Me* (9–12). 1987, NAL paper $2.50 (0-451-15020-1). Bored with her summer job, Jenny falls for an outrageous boy named Danny who has a purple stripe in his hair. (Rev: VOYA 6/88)

2327 Veryan, Patricia. *Logic of the Heart* (10–12). 1990, St. Martin's $18.95 (0-312-03861-5). Two supposedly mismatched people fall in love in Regency England. (Rev: BL 2/15/90)

2328 Winfield, Julia. *Only Make-Believe* (9–12). 1987, Bantam paper $2.50 (0-553-26418-4). A mock marriage in social studies class brings

Darcy close to her wedding partner—much to her boyfriend's disapproval. (Rev: SLJ 10/87)

2329 Wunsch, Josephine. *The Perfect 10* (9–10). 1986, Silhouette paper $1.95 (0-373-06182-X). Lisa sets out to capture the heart of a mysterious new boy in town. (Rev: SLJ 9/86)

2330 Zalben, Jane Breskin. *Here's Looking at You, Kid* (9–12). 1984, Farrar $11.95 (0-374-33055-7); Dell paper $2.50 (0-440-93573-3). A high school senior finds he is attracted to 2 girls.

Science Fiction

2331 Adams, Douglas. *The Hitchhiker's Guide to the Galaxy* (10–12). 1980, Crown $9.95 (0-517-54209-9); Pocket paper $3.95 (0-671-52721-5). An episodic science fiction novel that is made up of equal parts of adventure and humor. Others in the series are: *The Restaurant at the End of the Universe* (1981), *Life, the Universe, and Everything* (1982), and *So Long, Thanks for the Fish* (1985). All 4 volumes are in *The Hitchhiker's Quartet* (1986).

2332 Adams, Douglas. *The Long Dark Tea-Time of the Soul* (10–12). 1989, Simon & Schuster $16.95 (0-671-92926-7). Dirk Gently, private detective and slob first introduced in *Dirk Gently's Holistic Detective Agency* (1987), returns in another hilarious series of misadventures. (Rev: BL 1/15/89)

2333 Adams, Terry A. *Sentience* (10–12). 1986, DAW paper $3.50 (0-88677-108-0). Hanna, a telepath, is assigned to a space mission to seek out alien life. (Rev: VOYA 8–10/86)

2334 Aiken, Joan. *A Touch of Chill: Tales for Sleepless Nights* (10–12). 1980, Delacorte $9.95 (0-385-29310-0). Fifteen tales of mounting horror by a master of suspense. Also use: *A Whisper in the Night* (1984).

2335 Aldiss, Brian W. *Helliconia Winter* (10–12). 1985, Ace paper $3.95 (0-441-32629-3). For better readers, in this third volume of the trilogy, Helliconia moves into its seventh-century winter and its society continues to evolve. Preceded by *Helliconia Spring* (1982) and *Helliconia Summer* (1983). Also use: *Hothouse* (1984). (Rev: BL 3/1/85)

2336 Aldiss, Brian W. *The Year before Yesterday* (9–12). 1987, Watts $16.95 (0-531-15040-2). A reissue of the science fiction novel that explores a world after Hitler's winning World War II. (Rev: BR 9–10/87)

2337 Alexander, David M. *Fane* (10–12). 1981, Pocket paper $3.50 (0-671-83154-2). People in a medieval-like world on the planet Fane.

2338 Allen, Roger MacBride. *Rogue Powers* (10–12). 1986, Baen paper $3.50 (0-671-65584-1). The League of Planets does battle with the fascist Guardians in this sequel to *The Torch of Honor* (1985). (Rev: BL 7/86)

2339 Allen, Roger MacBride. *The Torch of Honor* (10–12). 1985, Baen paper $3.50 (0-671-55938-9). Joslyn and her husband, Terry, are sent to the planet New Finland to organize opposition to the cruel invaders who now occupy it. (Rev: BL 4/15/85; VOYA 8/85)

2340 Anderson, Poul. *The Boat of a Million Years* (10–12). 1989, St. Martin's $19.95 (0-312-93199-9). For better readers, the adventures through history of 7 people who are born immortal. (Rev: BL 9/15/89)

2341 Anderson, Poul. *Brain Wave* (7–12). 1954, Ballantine paper $2.50 (0-345-32521-4). A new age seems possible with the discovery of a mental surge that will increase the IQs of humans and animals.

2342 Anderson, Poul. *Cold Victory* (10–12). 1985, Tor paper $2.95 (0-8125-3057-8). Six stories about the Psychotechnic League. Some other books by this master are: *Conflict* (1985), *Fire Time* (1988), and *A Midsummer Tempest* (1984).

2343 Anderson, Poul. *Dialogue with Darkness* (10–12). 1985, Tor paper $2.95 (0-8125-3083-7). A collection of short stories that spans more than 30 years of this writer's career. (Rev: BL 4/15/85)

2344 Anderson, Poul. *The Long Night* (10–12). 1985, Tor paper $2.95 (0-8125-3052-7). This is a collection of 5 novellas. Also use: *The Gods Laughed* (1982) and *Broken Sword* (1988).

2345 Anderson, Poul. *New America* (10–12). 1985, Tor paper $2.95 (0-8125-3054-3). Six stories, each of which explores the topic of space colonies. Also use: *Starship* (1985).

2346 Anderson, Poul. *Past Times* (10–12). 1984, Tor paper $2.95 (0-8125-3081-0). A collection of 7 stories that use the past for settings and a nonfiction essay that uses history in science fiction. (Rev: BL 1/15/85)

2347 Anderson, Poul. *Time Patrolman* (10–12). 1983, Tor paper $2.95 (0-8125-3076-4). Time travelers want to change past history in this speculative novel by one of the great writers in this genre. Also use: *Twilight World* (1983).

2348 Anderson, Poul. *The Year of the Ransom* (9–12). 1988, Walker $15.95 (0-8027-6800-8). A time traveling patrol visits important periods in history but cannot change events. (Rev: BR 9–10/88)

2349 Anderson, Poul, and Fritz Leiber. *No Truce with Kings/Ship of Shadows* (10–12). 1989, Tor paper $2.95 (0-8125-5958-4). This double volume contains 2 classic science fiction novels, both Hugo winners from the 1960s. (Rev: VOYA 8/89)

2350 Anthony, Piers. *Chthon* (10–12). 1989, Ace paper $3.95 (0-441-11880-1). As punishment, the hero of this novel is sent to a hideous prison called Chthon.

2351 Anthony, Piers. *Cluster* (10–12). 1977, Avon paper $2.95 (0-380-01755-5). This is the first of the Cluster series. The rest, in order, are: *Chaining the Lady* and *Kirlian Quest* (both 1978); *Thousandstar* and *Viscous Circle* (both 1982).

2352 Anthony, Piers. *For Love of Evil* (10–12). 1988, Morrow $17.95 (0-688-08211-4). The penultimate volume (number 6) of the Incarnations of Immortality series. In this episode Satan is the protagonist. (Rev: BL 9/1/88)

2353 Anthony, Piers. *Ghost* (10–12). 1986, Tor $14.95 (0-312-93272-3). A deep-time ship probes the end of the universe to find a power source. (Rev: VOYA 4/87)

2354 Anthony, Piers. *Man from Mundania* (9–12). 1989, Avon paper $4.50 (0-380-75289-1). A Xanth novel that completes the trilogy begun with *Vale of the Vole* (1987) and continued in *Heaven Cent* (1988). (Rev: BL 9/89; VOYA 12/89)

2355 Anthony, Piers. *Race against Time* (7–12). 1986, Tor paper $3.50 (0-8125-3101-9). John Smith and an African girl named Ala are different from others because they are racially pure.

2356 Anthony, Piers. *Split Infinity* (10–12). 1987, Ballantine paper $4.95 (0-345-35491-5). In this first part of the Apprentice Adept series, someone is trying to kill Stile on the planet Proton. Other titles are: *Blue Adept* and *Justaposition* (both 1987).

2357 Anthony, Piers. *Total Recall* (9–12). 1989, Morrow $16.95 (0-688-05209-6). A novelization of the movie about a secret agent on Mars searching for his past. Also use *But What of Earth?* (Tor, 1989). (Rev: BL 8/89)

2358 Apostolou, John L., and Martin H. Greenberg. *The Best Japanese Science Fiction Stories* (10–12). 1989, Dembner $16.95 (0-942637-06-2). Thirteen stories by 10 of Japan's leading writers of sci-fi. (Rev: SLJ 6/89)

2359 Ardai, Charles, and Sheila Williams, eds. *Why I Left Harry's All-Night Hamburgers: And Other Stories from Isaac Asimov's Science Fiction Magazine* (8–12). 1990, Delacorte $14.95 (0-385-30044-1). A short story collection that concentrates on science fiction but also contains some fantasy. (Rev: SLJ 6/90)

2360 Asimov, Isaac. *The Bicentennial Man, and Other Stories* (10–12). 1985, Ballantine paper $3.50 (0-345-32071-9). Eleven science fiction novels about both robots and humans.

2361 Asimov, Isaac. *Caves of Steel* (10–12). 1986, Ballantine paper $4.95 (0-345-33820-0). One of this prolific author's classics of science fiction. Also use: *Pebble in the Sky* and *Naked Sun (both 1986)*.

2362 Asimov, Isaac. *Fantastic Voyage II: Destination Brain* (9–12). 1988, Bantam paper $4.95 (0-553-27327-2). An American neurophysicist and 4 Soviet scientists are miniaturized to enter the body of another scientist who is in a coma. This ia a variation of Asimov's earlier *Fantastic Voyage* (1966). (Rev: BL 8/87; VOYA 2/88)

2363 Asimov, Isaac. *Foundation and Earth* (9–12). 1986, Doubleday $16.95 (0-385-23312-4); Ballantine paper $4.95 (0-345-33996-7). In this fifth Foundation novel, a search is begun for an organism that will unite human and robot life. (Rev: BL 8/86; VOYA 4/87)

2364 Asimov, Isaac. *Foundation Trilogy* (10–12). 1982, Doubleday $17.95 (0-385-18830-7); Ballantine paper $12.95 (0-345-34088-4). A speculative science fiction series about a galactic empire facing decline and fall. The individual volumes are: *Foundation* (1980), *Foundation and Empire*, and *Second Foundation* (both 1986). A fourth volume is *Foundation's Edge* (1982).

2365 Asimov, Isaac. *I, Robot* (10–12). 1987, Ballantine paper $3.50 (0-345-33139-7). A collection about Dr. Susan Calvin and the product she produces at her factory, robots.

2366 Asimov, Isaac. *Nemesis* (9–12). 1989, Doubleday $18.95 (0-385-24792-3). A space colony arrives at a planet only to find it is slated for destruction. (Rev: BL 8/89)

2367 Asimov, Isaac. *Nightfall and Other Stories* (10–12). 1984, Ballantine paper $3.95 (0-345-31091-8). This is a collection of stories that the author calls his favorites.

2368 Asimov, Isaac. *Nine Tomorrows* (10–12). 1987, Ballantine paper $3.95 (0-345-34604-1). One of this master's finest. Also use *The Currents of Space* (1985), *End of Eternity* (1986), and *Casebook of the Black Widowers* (1985).

2369 Asimov, Isaac, ed. *One Hundred Great Science Fiction Short Short Stories* (10–12). 1988, Avon paper $3.95 (0-380-50733-1). This large collection introduces the various styles, topics, and depths of meaning in the spectrum of science fiction.

2370 Asimov, Isaac. *Prelude to Foundation* (10–12). 1988, Doubleday $18.95 (0-385-23313-2). This novel links the Empire and Foundation series and supplies a chronology of novels in these 2 series as a guide to readers. (Rev: BL 4/1/88; VOYA 10/88)

2371 Asimov, Isaac. *Robot Dreams* (7–12). 1986, Berkley paper $8.95 (0-425-09345-X). An anthology of stories by Asimov about robots, some of which date back over 30 years. (Rev: VOYA 6/87)

2372 Asimov, Isaac. *Robots and Empire* (9–12). 1985, Doubleday $16.95 (0-385-19092-1); Ballantine paper $4.50 (0-345-32894-9). The heroine of the earlier *Robots at Dawn* (1984) travels through space with a friend and 2 robots to defeat a plot against Earth. (Rev: BL 8/85)

2373 Asimov, Isaac, et al., eds. *Atlantis* (9–12). 1988, NAL paper $3.95 (0-451-15144-5). A collection of science fiction written in the last 50 years about the legendary land of Atlantis. (Rev: BL 11/15/87)

2374 Asimov, Isaac, et al., eds. *Catastrophes!* (10–12). 1981, Fawcett paper $2.50 (0-449-24425-3). An anthology of stories of catastrophes that take place in various parts of the universe.

2375 Asimov, Isaac, et al., eds. *Caught in the Organ Draft: Biology in Science Fiction* (9–12). 1983, Farrar $12.95 (0-374-31228-1). In these 12 stories biological topics such as mutants and germ warfare are explored.

2376 Asimov, Isaac, et al., eds. *Computer Crimes and Capers* (9–12). 1983, Academy Chicago $17.95 (0-89733-082-X); paper $7.95 (0-89733-087-0). A lively anthology of stories featuring computers as masters, servants, or—sometimes—arch criminals.

2377 Asimov, Isaac, et al., eds. *Great Science Fiction Stories by the World's Great Scientists* (10–12). 1985, Donald I. Fine $17.95 (0-917657-26-8). A total of 23 stories not often found in anthologies, all by scientists, known and obscure. (Rev: BL 8/85)

2378 Asimov, Isaac, et al., eds. *Hallucination Orbit: Psychology in Science Fiction* (10–12). 1983, Farrar $13.95 (0-374-32835-8). Science fiction stories that explore the mind and ask how one would react in situations are included in this anthology.

2379 Asimov, Isaac, et al., eds. *100 Great Science Fiction Short Stories* (9–12). 1984, Avon paper $3.50 (0-380-50773-0). Three masters of science fiction have chosen their favorite stories in this genre.

2380 Asimov, Isaac, et al., eds. *Robots: Isaac Asimov's Wonderful Worlds of Science Fiction, #9* (9–12). 1989, NAL paper $3.95 (0-451-15926-8). A collection of 17 stories about robots, many classic and many unavailable for some time. (Rev: BL 3/15/89)

2381 Asimov, Isaac, et al., eds. *Space Shuttles* (9–12). 1987, NAL paper $3.95 (0-451-15017-1). Fourteen stories about short-range spacecraft. (Rev: BL 10/15/87)

2382 Asimov, Isaac, and Groff Conklin, eds. *Fifty Short Science Fiction Tales* (10–12). 1963, Macmillan paper $4.95 (0-02-016390-8). For the beginning science fiction reader, this is a fine collection of very short stories.

2383 Asimov, Isaac, and Martin H. Greenberg, eds. *Amazing Stories: 60 Years of the Best Science Fiction* (10–12). 1985, TSR paper $7.95 (0-88038-216-3). A collection culled from 60 years of the magazine *Amazing Science Fiction Stories*. (Rev: BL 11/15/85; VOYA 2/86)

2384 Asimov, Isaac, and Martin H. Greenberg, eds. *Isaac Asimov Presents the Great SF Stories: 17 (1955)* (9–12). 1988, NAL paper $3.50 (0-88677-256-7). Nine stories, from 1955, by such masters as Frederik Pohl and Poul Anderson. Also use the earlier collection from 1954 that includes such authors as Arthur C. Clarke and Gordon Dickson. (Rev: BL 1/1/88; VOYA 8/88)

2385 Asimov, Isaac, and Martin H. Greenberg, eds. *Isaac Asimov Presents the Great SF Stories, 20* (9–12). 1990, NAL paper $4.95 (0-88677-405-5). This fine collection of 9 short stories covers the best published in 1958. Part of an ongoing series that includes volume 19, covering 1957. (Rev: BL 2/15/90; VOYA 8/90)

2386 Asimov, Isaac, and J. O. Jeppson, eds. *Laughing Space* (9–12). 1982, Houghton $17.95 (0-395-30519-5). A look at the humorous side of science fiction in this collection of stories, poems, and cartoons.

2387 Asimov, Isaac, and Robert Silverberg. *Nightfall* (10–12). 1990, Doubleday $19.95 (0-385-36341-4). A novel about a planet with 6 suns where night infrequently comes. (Rev: BL 10/1/90)

2388 Asimov, Janet. *Mind Transfer* (10–12). 1988, Walker $17.95 (0-8027-6748-6). The story of Seven, a robot with a human's brain. (Rev: BL 4/15/88; BR 11–12/88)

2389 Asnin, Scott. *A Cold Wind from Orion* (10–12). 1980, Ballantine paper $2.25 (0-345-29498-4). The earth faces deadly danger when a spacecraft with lethal material aboard approaches.

2390 Asprin, Robert. *Myth-nomers and Impervections* (9–12). Illus. 1987, Donning paper $7.95 (0-89865-529-3). The eighth in the zany M.Y.T.H. series that continues the misadventures of Skeeve in his battle against Queen Hemlock. (Rev: BL 2/1/88)

2391 Asprin, Robert. *Phule's Company* (10–12). 1990, Berkley paper $3.95 (0-441-66251-X). The beginning of a new series about the adventures of Captain Willard Phule, an officer in the Space Legion. (Rev: BL 6/15/90)

2392 Atwood, Margaret. *The Handmaid's Tale* (10–12). 1986, Houghton $16.95 (0-395-40425-8); Fawcett paper $5.95 (0-449-21260-2). A chilling look into the future where repression of women is rampant. For mature readers. (Rev: VOYA 12/86)

2393 Aycock, Dale. *Starspinner* (10–12). 1981, Dorchester paper $2.25 (0-8439-0973-0). A space station of the twenty-seventh century is the setting of this novel.

2394 Baen, Jim, ed. *New Destinies, Volume VIII* (10–12). 1989, Baen paper $3.50 (0-671-69839-7). This is a collection of short stories and nonfiction pieces of speculation about the future. Part of an ongoing series of paperbacks. (Rev: VOYA 6/90)

2395 Banks, Ian M. *The Player of Games* (10–12). 1989, St. Martin's $16.95 (0-312-02630-7). To repay a debt, gamesman Gurgeh must travel to the Empire of Azad where life revolves about the game of the same name. (Rev: VOYA 8/89)

2396 Bear, Greg. *Eon* (10–12). 1985, Bluejay $16.95 (0-312-94144-7); Tor paper $3.95 (0-8135-0566-2). In this novel for better readers, the world is on the brink of destruction when a strange vehicle appears. By the author of *Blood Music* (1985). (Rev: BL 7/85; BR 11–12/85; SLJ 1/86; VOYA 12/85)

2397 Bear, Greg. *Eternity* (10–12). 1988, Warner $16.95 (0-446-51402-0). An exiled girl tries to find her way back to the old Earth in this sequel to Eon (1985). (Rev: BL 9/1/88)

2398 Bear, Greg. *The Forge of God* (10–12). 1987, St. Martin's $17.95 (0-312-93021-6). Three geologists discover that Earth is about to be invaded by aliens. (Rev: BL 8/87; VOYA 2/88)

2399 Bear, Greg. *Queen of Angels* (10–12). 1990, Warner $19.95 (0-446-51400-4). In Los Angeles of 2047, murders are being committed by a poet for no plausible reason. (Rev: BL 6/1/90)

2400 Bellamy, Edward. *Looking Backward* (10–12). 1960, NAL paper $3.95 (0-451-52342-3). In 1887, a young Bostonian falls asleep and wakens in the America of year 2000 in this futuristic novel first published in 1888.

2401 Benford, Gregory. *Artifact* (10–12). 1988, Tor paper $4.50 (0-8125-3178-7). A demanding novel in which an archaeologist discovers a cube with deadly powers and touches off an international struggle. (Rev: BL 3/15/85)

2402 Benford, Gregory. *Great Sky River* (10–12). 1987, Bantam $17.95 (0-553-05238-1). On the planet Snowglade humans are fighting for survival against a mechanical enemy. (Rev: BL 10/15/87; VOYA 4/88)

2403 Benford, Gregory. *In Alien Flesh* (10–12). 1986, Tor $14.95 (0-312-93344-4); paper $3.95 (0-8125-3176-0). This collection of 13 stories explores the fringes of experience both for humans and computers. (Rev: VOYA 8–10/86)

2404 Benford, Gregory. *In the Ocean of Night* (10–12). 1987, Bantam paper $3.95 (0-553-21578-4). Earth encounters problems caused by the constellation Aquila.

2405 Benford, Gregory. *Tides of Light* (10–12). 1989, Bantam $17.95 (0-553-05322-1). Captain Killeen, fresh from adventures in *Great Sky River* (1987), tries with his people to colonize a new planet. (Rev: BL 11/15/88)

2406 Benford, Gregory. *Timescape* (10–12). 1983, Pocket paper $3.95 (0-671-50632-3). This complex Nebula award-winning novel has a sequel, *Against Infinity* (1983).

2407 Benford, Gregory, and David Brin. *Heart of the Comet* (10–12). 1986, Bantam paper $4.50 (0-553-25839-7). For better readers, a novel about a plan to explore Halley's Comet in the twenty-first century. (Rev: BL 1/15/86)

2408 Benford, Gregory, and Gordon Eklund. *If the Stars Are Gods* (10–12). 1989, Bantam paper $3.95 (0-553-27642-5). This novel contains related episodes that cover 69 years.

2409 Bester, Alfred. *The Stars My Destination* (10–12). 1987, Watts $15.95 (0-531-15050-X). A reissue of a classic science fiction novel about life in the twenty-fifth century when people travel by teleportation. (Rev: BR 11–12/87)

2410 Bickham, Jack M. *Day Seven* (10–12). 1988, Tor $17.95 (0-312-93066-6); paper $3.95 (0-8125-0581-6). The United States, Russia, and an international group are in a race to reach Mars first. (Rev: VOYA 10/88)

2411 Bischoff, David F. *The Destiny Dice* (10–12). 1985, NAL paper $3.95 (0-451-16076-2). As a result of a roll of dice, Ian Farthing is taken into the Dark Circle.

2412 Bischoff, David F., and Dennis R. Bailey. *Tin Woodman* (10–12). 1985, Ace paper $2.75 (0-441-81293-7). Because of his unusual talents with ESP, an earthling is sent to investigate an alien spaceship.

2413 Bischoff, David F., and Thomas F. Monteleone. *Day of the Dragon Star* (10–12). 1989, Ace paper $3.50 (0-441-13997-3). An ancient city is discovered by the only 2 survivors of a scientific expedition.

2414 Bishop, Michael. *Close Encounters with the Deity* (10–12). 1986, Peachtree $15.95 (0-931948-96-7); paper $8.95 (0-934601-07-0). A collection of science fiction short stories by Bishop that deal with mankind's idea of the Deity. (Rev: SLJ 1/87)

2415 Bishop, Michael, ed. *Nebula Awards 24* (10–12). 1990, Harcourt $22.95 (0-15-164932-4); paper $13.95 (0-15-665474-1). Part of an ongoing series, this recent anthology includes some of the fantasy and science fiction published in 1988. (Rev: BL 3/1/90)

2416 Bishop, Michael. *No Enemy But Time* (10–12). 1989, Bantam paper $4.95 (0-553-28187-9). This exciting Nebula Award winner is also an unusual depth-of-character study.

2417 Bisson, Terry. *Voyage to the Red Planet* (10–12). 1990, Morrow $16.95 (0-688-09495-3). A satiric novel set in the twenty-first century about a movie studio's project to make a film on Mars. (Rev: SLJ 12/90)

2418 Boulle, Pierre. *Planet of the Apes* (7–12). 1963, Vanguard $14.95 (0-8149-0064-X); NAL paper $3.95 (0-451-16016-9). Stranded on the planet Soror, Ulysse Merou discovers a civilization ruled by apes.

2419 Bova, Ben. *The Astral Mirror* (10–12). 1985, Tor paper $2.95 (0-812-53217-1). A collection of both fiction and nonfiction that demonstrates the author's wide range of interests in science. (Rev: BL 12/1/85)

2420 Bova, Ben. *Escape Plus* (10–12). 1984, Tor paper $2.95 (0-8125-3212-0). This science fiction collection contains a novella and 10 stories.

2421 Bova, Ben. *Orion* (10–12). 1989, Tor paper $3.95 (0-8125-3233-3). For better readers, this is the story of the eternal warrior Orion who once again sets out to battle. Also use: *Colony* (1988).

2422 Bova, Ben. *Out of the Sun* (10–12). 1984, Tor paper $2.95 (0-8125-3210-4). Although this is a science fiction novel, the volume also contains a long nonfiction introduction to laser technology.

2423 Bova, Ben. *Peacekeepers* (9–12). 1989, Tor paper $4.95 (0-812-50238-8). After a nuclear war a small group of peacekeepers try to capture a terrorist who has stolen some nuclear warheads. (Rev: BR 1–2/90)

2424 Bova, Ben. *Vengeance of Orion* (9–12). 1988, Tor $17.95 (0-312-93049-6); paper $3.95 (0-8125-3161-2). In this novel, Orion time travels to the time of Troy and ancient Egypt. This is a sequel to *Orion* (1986). (Rev: VOYA 6/88)

2425 Bova, Ben. *Voyagers III: Star Brothers* (10–12). 1990, Tor $18.95 (0-312-93215-4). The concluding volume of the Voyager trilogy about Keith Stoner and his attempts to keep peace on Earth. (Rev: BL 4/1/90)

2426 Bova, Ben, and Gordon R. Dickson. *Gremlins Go Home* (10–12). 1983, Tor paper $2.75 (0-8125-3221-X). A boy is recruited by gremlins to help them leave Earth.

2427 Bradbury, Ray. *Farenheit 451* (7–12). 1953, Ballantine paper $3.95 (0-345-34296-8). In this futuristic novel, book reading has become a crime.

2428 Bradbury, Ray. *The Martian Chronicles* (10–12). 1958, Doubleday $14.95 (0-385-05060-7); Bantam paper $3.50 (0-553-26363-3). These interrelated short stories tell of the colonization of Mars.

2429 Bradbury, Ray. *The October Country* (7–12). 1970, Knopf $12.00 (0-394-43892-2); paper $4.95 (0-345-25040-0). Ordinary people are caught up in unreal situations in these 19 strange stories.

2430 Bradbury, Ray. *The Stories of Ray Bradbury* (8–12). 1980, Knopf $24.50 (0-394-51335-5). An imaginative group of stories that often bridge the gap between fantasy and science fiction.

2431 Bradley, Marion Zimmer. *Four Moons of Darkover* (9–12). 1988, NAL paper $4.95 (0-88677-305-9). This is the sixth collection of stories inspired by the many tales of Darkover. (Rev: BL 10/15/88)

2432 Bradley, Marion Zimmer, et al. *Domains of Darkover* (10–12). 1990, NAL paper $3.95 (0-88677-407-1). Several authors including Bradley have written stories set in her imaginary land of Darkover. (Rev: BL 3/1/90; VOYA 8/90)

2433 Bradley, Marion Zimmer, et al. *The Other Side of the Mirror: And Other Darkover Stories* (10–12). 1987, NAL paper $3.50 (0-88677-185-4). These 5 stories (3 by Bradley) deal with events in the imaginary land of Darkover. (Rev: BL 1/1/87; VOYA 8–9/87)

2434 Bradley, Marion Zimmer, et al. *Red Sun of Darkover* (9–12). 1987, NAL paper $3.95 (0-88677-230-3). A shared world anthology of stories by many authors about Bradley's Darkover. This is the fifth such anthology. (Rev: BL 10/15/87)

2435 Brin, David. *Earth* (10–12). Illus. 1990, Bantam $19.95 (0-553-05778-2). Several people try to stop the damage caused by a man-made black hole that is eating away at the Earth's core. (Rev: BL 4/1/90; SLJ 12/90)

2436 Brin, David. *The Postman* (10–12). 1986, Bantam paper $4.95 (0-553-25704-8). After a nuclear holocaust in the United States, Gordon Krantz ventures west and assumes the identity of a postman giving hope by establishing communication among bands of survivors. (Rev: BL 9/15/85; VOYA 2/86)

2437 Brin, David. *The Practice Effect* (10–12). 1985, Bantam paper $3.95 (0-553-26981-X). A physicist finds he is a wizard in an alternate world.

2438 Brin, David. *The River of Time* (10–12). 1987, Bantam paper $3.50 (0-553-26281-5). A collection of 11 speculative short stories by a prize-winning writer of science fiction. (Rev: BL 4/1/87)

2439 Brin, David. *The Uplift War* (10–12). 1987, Phantasia $22.00 (0-932096-44-1); Bantam paper $4.50 (0-553-25121-X). Aliens occupy the planet Garth in this companion piece to *Startide Rising* (1984). (Rev: BL 9/1/87)

2440 Brooks, Terry. *Wizard at Large* (10–12). 1988, Ballantine $17.95 (0-345-43773-0). In this, the third book about the Magic Kingdom of Landover, High Lord Ben Holiday travels to Earth. Preceded by: *Magic Kingdom for Sale—Sold!* (1986); *The Black Unicorn* (1987). (Rev: BL 9/1/88; VOYA 4/89)

2441 Brunner, John. *The Best of John Brunner* (9–12). 1988, Ballantine paper $3.95 (0-345-35307-2). A collection of 15 stories by one of contemporary science fiction's finest writers. (Rev: BL 11/1/88)

2442 Brunner, John. *Stand on Zanzibar* (10–12). 1968, Bentley LB $19.50 (0-8376-0438-9); 1987, Ballantine paper $3.50 (0-345-34787-0). Two roommates—one a scientist and the other a potential killer—are the subject of this futuristic novel. Also use: *Shockwave Rider* (1984).

2443 Brust, Steven. *Cowboy Feng's Space Bar and Grille* (10–12). 1990, Ace paper $3.50 (0-441-11816-X). Cowboy Feng not only runs the best restaurant in the galaxy but also has the ability to travel through time and space. (Rev: VOYA 6/90)

2444 Bujold, Lois McMaster. *Brothers in Arms* (10–12). 1989, Baen paper $3.95 (0-671-69799-4). Our hero Miles already has 2 identities and now his enemies create a clone to complicate things further. A sequel to *The Warrior's Apprentice* (1986). (Rev: BL 12/1/88)

2445 Bujold, Lois McMaster. *Falling Free* (10–12). 1988, Baen paper $3.50 (0-671-65398-9). Leo sets out to save a group of mutants now considered obsolete and slated for destruction. (Rev: BL 3/1/88; VOYA 10/88)

2446 Bujold, Lois McMaster. *The Vor Game* (10–12). 1990, Simon & Schuster paper $4.50 (0-671-72014-7). A novel featuring Miles Vorkosigan who, as in other books in this series, confronts archenemies and has amazing madcap adventures. (Rev: BL 9/1/90)

2447 Burgess, Anthony. *A Clockwork Orange* (10–12). 1988, Norton $14.95 (0-393-02439-3); paper $7.95 (0-393-30553-8). For mature readers, a disturbing picture of a future where violence reigns.

2448 Burroughs, Edgar Rice. *At the Earth's Core* (7–12). 1980, Peter Smith $16.00 (0-8446-1778-4). David Innes travels 500 miles into the earth and finds a subterranean world. Sequels *Pellucidar* and *Tamar of Pellucidar* are also included in this volume.

2449 Burroughs, Edgar Rice. *Back to the Stone Age* (9–12). 1990, Ballantine paper $3.95 (0-345-36671-9). This is an adventure story that is part of the Pellucidar series that includes *Pellucidar* (1990), *Tarzan at the Earth's Core* (1986), *Land of Terror*, and *Savage Pellucidar* (both 1990).

2450 Burroughs, Edgar Rice. *Escape on Venus* (7–12). 1975, Ryter $13.95 (0-940724-00-6). An adventure/science fiction novel in which Duare is rescued from the terror of Venus by her lover Carson Napier. Another in this series is: *Lost on Venus* (1973).

2451 Burroughs, Edgar Rice. *The Moon Men* (7–12). 1974, Ace paper $2.75 (0-441-53757-X). Two novels, *The Moon Men* and *The Red Hawk*, about the control of Earth by a lunar force are included in this volume.

2452 Burroughs, Edgar Rice. *Pellucidar* (7–12). 1972, Ace paper $2.75 (0-441-65857-1). Part of an early science fiction series about David Innes and the hidden world he finds at the center of the Earth. Another in the series is: *Savage Pellucidar* (1973).

2453 Burroughs, Edgar Rice. *A Princess of Mars* (9–12). 1985, Ballantine paper $3.95 (0-345-33138-9). This is the beginning of a series of "space operas" involving John Carter on Mars. Some others are: *Gods of Mars, Warlord of Mars* (both 1985), and *The Chessmen of Mars* (1987).

2454 Butler, Octavia E. *Adulthood Rites* (10–12). 1988, Warner $16.95 (0-446-51422-5). A hybrid youngster learns about humans on Earth in this sequel to *Dawn* (1987). (Rev: BL 6/15/88)

2455 Caidin, Martin. *The Messiah Stone* (9–12). 1986, Baen paper $3.95 (0-671-65562-0). A mercenary is hired by a group of power brokers to locate a stone that possess magical powers. (Rev: VOYA 8–10/86)

2456 Callenbach, Ernest. *Ecotopia* (10–12). 1983, Bantam paper $4.50 (0-553-26183-5). This glimpse into the future is set in 1999. Also use: *Ecotopia Emerging* (1981).

2457 Callin, Grant. *A Lion on Tharthee* (9–12). 1987, Baen paper $3.50 (0-671-65357-1). In this sequel to *Saturnalia* (1986), humans encounter the alien Hexies. (Rev: VOYA 2/88)

2458 Card, Orson Scott. *Maps in a Mirror: The Short Fiction of Orson Scott Card* (10–12). 1990, Tor $19.95 (0-312-85047-6). For better readers, this is a mammouth collection of short stories by this writer covering science fiction, fantasy, and horror stories. (Rev: BL 9/15/90)

2459 Card, Orson Scott. *Prentice Alvin* (10–12). 1989, Tor $17.95 (0-312-93141-7). In this, the third part of the Tales of Alvin Maker series, Alvin passes successfully through his teen years and enters adulthood. (Rev: BL 12/1/88; VOYA 8/89)

2460 Card, Orson Scott. *Songmaster* (10–12). 1987, Tor paper $3.95 (0-8125-3255-4). A young boy trained as a songbird for the emperor becomes involved in court intrigue. (Rev: VOYA 4/88)

2461 Card, Orson Scott. *Speaker for the Dead* (10–12). 1986, Tor $15.95 (0-312-93738-5); paper $3.95 (0-8125-3257-0). Ender tries to prevent a war with a nonhuman intelligent race in this sequel to *Ender's Game* (1984). (Rev: BL 12/15/85; VOYA 8–10/86)

2462 Card, Orson Scott. *Treason* (9–12). 1988, St. Martin's $18.95 (0-312-02304-9). A young warrior unites his downtrodden people to fight for their liberty on the planet Treason. (Rev: BL 10/15/88)

2463 Card, Orson Scott. *Wyrms* (10–12). 1987, Arbor House $16.95 (0-87795-894-7); Tor paper $3.95 (0-8125-3357-7). For mature readers this is the story of young girl who is fated to be the leader of the kingdom of Imakulata. (Rev: BL 8/87; SLJ 12/87; VOYA 10/87)

2464 Carr, Terry, ed. *Terry Carr's Best Science Fiction of the Year* (9–12). 1985, Tor paper $3.50 (0-8125-3273-2). A fine collection of short fiction that covers the year 1984. (Rev: VOYA 2/86)

2465 Carver, Jeffrey A., and Roger Zelazny. *Clypsis* (9–12). 1987, Bantam paper $3.50 (0-553-26536-9). This novel about starship racing features a 17-year-old hero named Mike Murray. (Rev: VOYA 6/88)

2466 Chalker, Jack L. *The Labyrinth of Dreams: G.O.D., No. 1* (9–12). 1987, Tor paper $3.50 (0-8125-3306-2). Sam and Brandy Horowitz travel to alternate worlds in this fast-paced novel that is the first of a series. (Rev: VOYA 12/87)

2467 Cherryh, C. J. *Angel with the Sword* (10–12). 1985, DAW paper $3.50 (0-88677-143-9). In the city of Merovingen, a teenage girl rescues a man from drowning who turns out to have many powerful enemies. (Rev: BL 8/85)

2468 Cherryh, C. J., ed. *Divine Right* (10–12). 1989, NAL paper $3.95 (0-88677-380-6). The fifth collection of stories in the Merovingen Nights series by a number of fine science fiction writers. (Rev: BL 10/15/89)

2469 Cherryh, C. J. *Downbelow Station* (10–12). 1981, NAL paper $4.50 (0-88677-431-4). A novel about space war that is continued in *Mechanter's Luck* (1982).

2470 Cherryh, C. J., ed. *Festival Moon* (10–12). 1987, NAL paper $3.50 (0-88677-192-7). A shared-world anthology in which the stories take place in unfriendly Merovingen. (Rev: BL 4/1/87)

2471 Cherryh, C. J., ed. *Fever Season* (10–12). 1987, NAL paper $3.50 (0-88677-224-9). Tales by various authors all taking place on the planet Merovingen. (Rev: BL 9/1/87)

2472 Cherryh, C. J. *Forty Thousand in Gehenna* (10–12). 1984, DAW paper $4.50 (0-88677-429-3). The story of the colonization of a planet inhabited by lizard like creatures.

2473 Cherryh, C. J. *The Paladin* (10–12). 1988, Baen paper $3.95 (0-671-65417-9). A master samurai swordsman takes on a female student who wants to avenge her family. (Rev: BL 6/15/88)

2474 Cherryh, C. J. *The Pride of Chanur* (10–12). 1987, Phantasia $17.00 (0-932096-45-X); NAL paper $3.95 (0-88677-292-3). A human finds refuge on a spaceship operated by catlike beings. A sequel is *Chanur's Venture* (1984).

2475 Clarke, Arthur C. *Childhood's End* (7–12). 1963, Harcourt $14.95 (0-15-117205-6); Ballantine paper $3.95 (0-345-34795-1). The overlords' arrival on Earth marks the beginning of the end for mankind.

2476 Clarke, Arthur C. *The City and the Stars* (10–12). 1957, NAL paper $3.95 (0-451-16310-9). This novel is now considered a science fiction classic. Also by the same author is *Reach for Tomorrow* (1975), *Island in the Sky* (1979), *The Deep Range* (1981), and *The Sentinel* (1986).

2477 Clarke, Arthur C. *Dolphin Island* (10–12). 1987, Ace paper $2.95 (0-441-15220-1). A science fiction novel that uses the scientific study of dolphins as its focus.

2478 Clarke, Arthur C. *Imperial Earth* (10–12). 1976, Ballantine paper $3.50 (0-345-35250-5). In the year 2276, an emissary from Titan, a moon of Saturn, is sent to Earth with unforeseen results.

2479 Clarke, Arthur C. *Rendezvous with Rama* (10–12). 1988, Ballantine paper $3.50 (0-345-35056-1). Bill Norton and his crew set out to investigate a strange missile that has entered the earth's atmosphere.

2480 Clarke, Arthur C. *The Songs of Distant Earth* (9–12). 1986, Ballantine $17.95 (0-345-33219-9); paper $4.95 (0-345-32240-1). A starship fleeing a dying Earth lands on a water-covered planet. (Rev: BL 3/1/86)

2481 Clarke, Arthur C. *2001: A Space Odyssey* (9–12). 1968, NAL paper $3.95 (0-451-15580-7). This novel, based on the screenplay of the famous movie, introduces a most unusual computer named Hal.

2482 Clarke, Arthur C. *2061: Odyssey Three* (9–12). 1988, Ballantine $17.95 (0-345-35173-8); paper $4.95 (0-345-35879-1). Heywood Floyd takes part in the space mission of landing on Halley's Comet. (Rev: BL 11/1/87; BR 9–10/88)

2483 Clarke, Arthur C. *2010: Odyssey Two* (9–12). 1982, Ballantine $14.95 (0-345-30309-9); paper $3.95 (0-345-30306-7). A team of scientists try to save the deserted spaceship *Discovery*.

2484 Clarke, Arthur C. *The Wind from the Sun: Stories from the Space Age* (9–12). 1972, NAL paper $1.95 (0-451-11475-2). Eighteen science fiction stories, many with surprise endings.

2485 Clarke, Arthur C., and Gentry Lee. *Rama II* (9–12). 1989, Bantam $18.95 (0-553-05714-6). In this sequel to *Rendezvous with Rama* (1973), another spaceship like Rama I enters our solar system, its purpose again a mystery. (Rev: BL 10/1/89)

2486 Clement, Hal. *Still River* (10–12). 1989, Ballantine paper $3.95 (0-345-32917-1). Five scientists—one of whom is human—visit a strange planet named Enigma. (Rev: BL 6/1/87)

2487 Cole, Adrian. *A Place among the Fallen* (10–12). 1990, Avon paper $3.95 (0-380-70556-7). The planet Omara is threatened with destruction by the force of evil magic. (Rev: BL 7/87)

2488 Cook, Glen. *Passage at Arms* (10–12). 1985, Warner paper $2.95 (0-445-20006-5). This novel describes life aboard a Climber, a spaceship that travels through hyperspace into a new dimension. (Rev: VOYA 8/85)

2489 Cook, Paul. *Duende Meadow* (9–12). 1985, Bantam paper $2.95 (0-553-25374-3). After living for 6 centuries underground the survivors of a nuclear war emerge to find a strange new land. (Rev: BL 12/1/85)

2490 Cooper, Louise. *The Master* (9–12). 1987, Tor paper $3.50 (0-812-53396-8). In this final volume of the Time Master trilogy, Tarod must decide whether to follow the force of Order or Chaos. Previous volumes: *The Initiate* (1985) and *The Outcast* (1986). (Rev: VOYA 2/88)

2491 Cormier, Robert. *Fade* (10–12). 1988, Doubleday $15.95 (0-440-50057-5). A disturbing and sometimes terrifying novel about a 13 year old who can make himself disappear. (Rev: BL 9/1/88; BR 11–12/88; SLJ 10/88; VOYA 12/88)

2492 Cramer, John. *Twistor* (10–12). 1989, Morrow $18.95 (0-877-95967-6). A new universe is discovered in this science fiction novel with an emphasis on science. (Rev: BL 3/15/89)

2493 Crichton, Michael. *The Andromeda Strain* (9–12). 1969, Knopf $15.95 (0-394-41525-6); Dell paper $3.95 (0-440-10199-9). A mysterious capsule from space brings a threat of a deadly epidemic in this fast-paced novel.

2494 Crichton, Michael. *Jurassic Park* (10–12). 1990, Knopf $19.95 (0-394-58816-9). This thriller takes place in an amusement park on an island off Costa Rica where through genetic engineering dinosaurs live. (Rev: BL 10/1/90)

2495 Crichton, Michael. *Sphere* (9–12). 1987, Knopf $17.95 (0-394-56110-4); Ballantine paper $5.95 (0-345-35314-5). A group of scientists journey to the bottom of the sea to explore a sunken spaceship in this thriller from the author of *The Andromeda Strain* (1969). (Rev: BL 5/15/87)

2496 Crichton, Michael. *The Terminal Man* (9–12). 1972, Knopf $13.50 (0-394-44768-9); Ballantine paper $4.95 (0-345-35462-1). A man who is slipping into insanity has a computer implanted into his brain.

2497 Crispin, A. C., and Jannean Elliott. *Shadow World* (10–12). 1991, Berkley paper $3.95 (0-441-78332-5). In this StarBridge novel, Mark Kenner is given a diplomatic assignment on a warring planet. (Rev: BL 12/1/90)

2498 Crispin, A. C., and Kathleen O'Malley. *Starbridge 2: Silent Dances* (9–12). 1990, Berkley paper $3.95 (0-441-78330-9). In this Starbridge novel, a young deaf native American girl is sent into space to establish contact with a race of aliens. (Rev: BL 6/15/90)

2499 Daley, Brian. *Fall of the White Ship Avatar* (10–12). 1987, Ballantine paper $3.95 (0-345-32919-8). In this part of a series about Alacrity Fitzhugh and Hobart Floyt, these 2 heroes seek out the legendary White Ship that supposedly contains secrets of an alien race. (Rev: BL 1/15/87)

2500 Dalmas, John. *Fanglith* (9–12). 1985, Baen paper $2.95 (0-671-55988-5). Children from outer space land in medieval Europe to find their parents. (Rev: BL 12/1/85)

2501 Dalmas, John, and Carl Martin. *Touch the Stars: Emergence* (10–12). 1983, Tor paper $2.95 (0-523-48586-7). Problems occur after a faster-than-light method of transportation is discovered.

2502 Datlow, Ellen, ed. *The Fifth Omni Book of Science Fiction* (9–12). 1987, Zebra paper $3.95 (0-8217-2050-3). Such writers as Robert Silverberg and Orson Scott Card are represented in this collection from the pages of *Omni* magazine. (Rev: BL 6/15/87)

2503 De Haven, Tom. *Joe Gosh* (9–12). Illus. 1988, Walker $15.95 (0-8027-6824-5). In a world of the future, Joe Gosh has very ordinary problems involving money and his girlfriend. (Rev: BL 11/1/88; BR 3–4/89; SLJ 11/88)

2504 Dick, Philip K. *Blade Runner* (10–12). 1987, Ballantine paper $4.95 (6-345-35047-2). For better readers, this is the story of Ted Barton and his mission to find 6 rogue androids. Also use: *Clans of the Alphane Moon* (1984).

2505 Dick, Philip K. *The Collected Stories of Philip K. Dick* (10–12). 1987, Underwood-Miller $125.00 (0-88733-053-3). This expensive five-volume set covers 30 years of this author's science fiction short stories. (Rev: SLJ 4/87)

2506 Dick, Philip K. *I Hope I Shall Arrive Soon* (10–12). 1987, St. Martin's paper $3.50 (9-317-64192-1). Nine short stories dating from 1954 to 1980 by the late master of science fiction writing. (Rev: VOYA 12/85)

2507 Dick, Philip K. *The Man in the High Castle* (10–12). 1984, Berkley paper $2.95 (0-425-10143-6). This futuristic novel poses the question of what life in America would be like if we had lost World War II.

2508 Dickson, Gordon R. *The Chantry Guild* (10–12). 1988, Berkley $17.95 (0-441-10276-X). An installment in the Childe Cycle series about the Dorsai and the ongoing battle between the Younger Worlds and the Others. (Rev: BL 10/1/88)

2509 Dickson, Gordon R. *Dorsai!* (10–12). 1980, Ace paper $3.50 (0-441-16025-5). Dorsai is a world whose inhabitants are bred to be mercenary space warriors.

2510 Dickson, Gordon R. *Love Not Human* (10–12). 1981, Ace paper $2.50 (0-441-50414-0). This is a collection of stories that date from 1952 and 1976. Another collection is *The Man from Earth* (1987).

2511 Dickson, Gordon R. *Way of the Pilgrim* (10–12). 1987, Berkley $16.95 (0-441-87486-X); Ace paper $4.50 (0-441-87487-8). An intricately plotted novel about a revolt against aliens who have conquered Earth. (Rev: BL 9/1/87; VOYA 10/87)

2512 Dickson, Gordon R. *Wolf and Iron* (10–12). 1990, Tor $18.95 (0-312-93214-6). After a nuclear holocaust, a young man and his wolf companion must trek 2,000 miles across America to safety. (Rev: BL 4/1/90; SLJ 9/90)

2513 Dietz, William C. *War World* (10–12). 1986, Ace paper $2.95 (0-441-87346-4). A futuristic novel about efforts to save the Terran Empire from the hostile planet War World. (Rev: VOYA 4/87)

2514 Dillard, J. M. *The Lost Years* (9–12). 1989, Pocket $17.95 (0-671-68293-8). In this Star Trek novel, Kirk, Spock, and McCoy return to Earth after a mission of the Enterprise. (Rev: VOYA 4/90)

2515 DiSilvestro, Roger. *Living with the Reptiles* (10–12). 1990, Donald I. Fine $18.95 (1-55611-174-6). For better readers, a time travel romp that shifts quickly from the present to both the future and the past. (Rev: BL 6/1/90)

2516 Douglas, Carole Nelson. *Heir of Rengarth* (10–12). 1988, Tor $17.95 (0-312-93075-5). For mature readers, the seeress Irissa and her lover tangle with the evil Usurper Geronfrey in this sequel to *Keepers of Edanvant* (1987). (Rev: BL 5/15/88)

2517 Doyle, Arthur Conan. *The Lost World & The Poison Belt* (8–12). 1989, Chronicle paper $8.95 (0-87701-620-8). Two science fiction novels by the master of the detective story. (Rev: BL 5/15/89)

2518 Dozois, Gardner, ed. *The Year's Best Science Fiction* (10–12). 1988, St. Martin's $19.95 (0-312-01853-3); paper $12.95 (0-312-01854-1). A collection of 1987 stories from both well-known and emerging writers. This author has edited many others in this recommended series. (Rev: BL 7/88)

2519 Dozois, Gardner, ed. *The Year's Best Science Fiction: Second Annual Collection* (10–12). 1985, Bluejay paper $10.95 (0-312-94485-3). A collection of 26 stories all published in 1984. (Rev: BR 1–2/86)

2520 Dozois, Gardner, ed. *The Year's Best Science Fiction: Sixth Annual Collection* (9–12). 1989, St. Martin's $24.95 (0-312-03008-8); paper $13.95 (0-312-03009-6). This collection covers the world of science fiction for 1988 and in addition to fiction summarizes the trends and markets. (Rev: VOYA 12/89)

2521 Drake, David, ed. *Bluebloods* (10–12). 1990, Baen paper $3.50 (0-671-69866-4). The third in the Starhunters series of stories by known sci-fi masters dealing with both human and nonhuman hunters. (Rev: BL 3/1/90)

2522 Drake, David. *Bridgehead* (10–12). 1986, Tor paper $3.50 (0-812-53616-9). An action-filled adventure involving aliens who help a professor build a time machine. (Rev: BL 4/1/86)

2523 Drake, David, ed. *The Eternal City* (10–12). 1990, Baen paper $3.50 (0-671-69857-5). Thirteen science fiction stories that use the mythology and history of ancient Rome as an inspiration. (Rev: VOYA 6/90)

2524 Drake, David, and Bill Fawcett, eds. *The Fleet* (10–12). 1988, Berkley paper $3.50 (0-441-24086-0). In connected stories by several top writers, the story of how The Fleet battled evil is related. (Rev: BL 5/15/88)

2525 Duane, Diane. *Doctor's Orders* (9–12). 1990, Pocket paper $4.50 (0-671-66189-2). In this Star Trek novel, Kirk disappears and Dr. McCoy must take over the *Enterprise*. (Rev: BL 6/15/90; SLJ 12/90)

2526 Dvorkin, David. *The Captains' Honor* (9–12). 1989, Pocket paper $3.95 (0-671-68487-6). In this Star Trek novel, the Enterprise tries to help the planet Tenara after it is attacked by the M'dok. (Rev: VOYA 2/90)

2527 Dvorkin, David. *The Seekers* (10–12). 1988, Watts $16.95 (0-531-15088-7). After the decline of the interstellar Empire, a republic grew, the strength of which is now being threatened. (Rev: BR 3–4/89)

2528 Dvorkin, David. *Timetrap* (9–12). 1988, Pocket paper $3.95 (0-671-64870-5). In this Star Trek novel, Captain Kirk travels 100 years into the future. (Rev: BL 6/15/88)

2529 Egan, Doris. *The Gate of Ivory* (9–12). 1989, NAL paper $3.95 (0-88677-328-8). A refugee on a strange planet finds she must live by her wits. (Rev: BL 3/1/89; VOYA 8/89)

2530 Ellison, Harlan. *Ellison Wonderland* (10–12). 1984, St. Martin's paper $6.95 (0-312-94133-1). A collection of stories about moral problems in alien worlds.

2531 Engdahl, Sylvia Louise. *Enchantress from the Stars* (7–12). 1989, Macmillan paper $3.95 (0-02-04031-0). A dragon figures in the bringing together of a girl from a highly intelligent race and a humble woodcutter's son.

2532 Engdahl, Sylvia Louise. *The Far Side of Evil* (7–12). 1989, Macmillan paper $3.95 (0-02-043041-8). On the planet Toris, destruction from nuclear disaster seems imminent.

2533 Engh, M. J. *Wheel of the Winds* (10–12). 1988, Tor $18.95 (0-312-93095-X). A marooned earth-man must find a storehouse of hidden equipment in a hostile environment. (Rev: BL 9/15/88; VOYA 2/89)

2534 Farmer, Philip Jose. *Dayworld Breakup* (10–12). 1990, St. Martin's $18.95 (0-312-85035-2). The third volume about Dayworld, the land where overcrowding is so acute that people must spend half of their lives in suspended animation. Preceded by *Dayworld* (1984) and *Dayworld Rebel* (1987). (Rev: BL 5/1/90)

2535 Farmer, Philip Jose. *Gods of Riverworld* (10–12). 1983, Putnam $14.95 (0-399-12843-3). In this the fifth and last of the recommended Riverworld series, people who lived on Earth in the past are resurrected.

2536 Farmer, Philip Jose. *The Grand Adventure* (10–12). 1984, Berkley paper $7.95 (0-425-07211-8). This is a collection of 7 short works that can serve as an introduction to this author's work.

2537 Farmer, Philip Jose. *The Magic Labyrinth* (10–12). 1984, Berkley paper $3.50 (0-425-09550-9). This is a volume in one of the major science creations, the Riverworld saga. Some others are: *The Gods of Riverworld* (1985), *The Dark Design* (1984), and *To Your Scattered Bodies Go* (1985).

2538 Felice, Cynthia, and Connie Willis. *Water Witch* (10–12). 1984, Ace paper $2.75 (0-441-87380-4). A space adventure involving a young girl's misadventures.

2539 Ferman, Edward L., ed. *The Best from Fantasy and Science Fiction* (10–12). 1982, Ace paper $2.95 (0-441-05485-4). This is one of an extensive series of stories and contributions to the *Magazine of Fantasy and Science Fiction*.

2540 Finney, Jack. *About Time: Twelve Stories* (10–12). 1986, Simon & Schuster paper $9.95 (0-671-62887-9). Twelve stories by this popular writer about time and time travel. (Rev: BL 9/1/86)

2541 Forward, Robert L. *Dragon's Egg* (10–12). 1983, Ballantine paper $3.95 (0-345-31666-5). In this imaginative novel, life on a neutron star is depicted.

2542 Forward, Robert L. *Starquake* (10–12). 1986, Ballantine paper $3.95 (0-345-31233-3). Humans must decide whether or not to help the inhabitants of a neutron star slated for destruction in this sequel to *Dragon's Egg* (1980). (Rev: BL 10/15/85)

2543 Foster, Alan Dean. *Cyber Way* (10–12). 1990, Berkley paper $3.50 (0-441-13245-6). A Florida detective believes that aliens are responsible for a murder. (Rev: BL 5/1/90)

2544 Foster, Alan Dean. *The Deluge Drivers* (10–12). 1987, Ballantine paper $3.95 (0-345-33330-6). In this conclusion to the trilogy that began with *Icerigger* and *Mission to Moulokin* (both 1987), Ethan Fortune must foil a plot to disturb the ecological balance on his planet. (Rev: BL 5/15/87)

2545 Foster, Alan Dean. *Orphan Star* (10–12). 1985, Ballantine paper $3.50 (0-345-32449-8). Flinx is prevented from learning the truth of his origins by an archvillain. This novel is preceded by *The Tar-Aiym Krang* (1987). Others in the series are: *Nor Crystal Tears* and *For Love of Mother-Not* (both 1987).

2546 Foster, Alan Dean. *Quozl* (9–12). 1989, Berkley paper $4.50 (0-441-69454-3). An amusing science fiction novel about aliens who look like large rabbits and their visit to Earth. (Rev: BL 5/15/89; SLJ 8/89)

2547 Foster, Alan Dean. *Splinter of the Mind's Eye* (8–12). 1978, Ballantine paper $2.50 (0-345-32023-9). A novel about Luke Skywalker and Princess Leia of *Star Wars* fame and their battle against the Empire.

2548 Foster, Alan Dean. *Star Trek—Log One* (7–12). 1974, Ballantine paper $2.95 (0-345-33349-7). Captain Kirk, Spock, and the rest of the crew of the *Enterprise* explore the limits of outer space. *Star Trek—Log Two* through *Star Trek—Log Ten* are all in print.

2549 Foster, Alan Dean. *To the Vanishing Point* (9–12). 1988, Warner $15.95 (0-446-51338-5). An American family picks up a hitchhiker who later is discovered to be an alien. (Rev: BL 8/88)

2550 Fowler, Karen Joy. *Artificial Things* (10–12). 1986, Bantam paper $2.95 (0-553-26219-X). A collection of science fiction stories about women facing unusual situations. (Rev: VOYA 8–9/87)

2551 Frank, Pat. *Alas, Babylon* (10–12). 1976, Bantam paper $3.95 (0-553-26314-5). A novel about survival after World War III.

2552 Friedman, C. S. *The Madness Season* (10–12). 1990, NAL paper $4.95 (0-88677-444-6). For better readers, the adventurous tale of a hero who must save Earth from the alien Tyr. (Rev: BL 10/1/90)

2553 Gadallah, Leslie. *Cat's Gambit* (9–12). 1990, Ballantine paper $3.95 (0-345-36478-3). Two humans and 2 aliens decide to wage war on their rulers, a race of beetlelike creatures. (Rev: SLJ 7/90)

2554 Gadallah, Leslie. *Cat's Pawn* (9–12). 1987, Ballantine paper $2.95 (0-345-33742-5). Bill Anderson works on the planet Orion to help the catlike creature Talan fight the creatures of Kaz. (Rev: BL 3/15/87)

2555 Gentle, Mary. *Ancient Light* (10–12). 1989, NAL $18.95 (0-453-00644-2). Many of the inhabitants of the planet Orthe resist the changes that others feel must come in this sequel to *Golden Witchbreed* (1985). (Rev: SLJ 8/89)

2556 Gerrold, David. *Chess with a Dragon* (8–12). 1987, Walker $15.95 (0-8027-6688-9); Avon paper $3.50 (0-380-30662-8). The entire human race becomes slaves of giant slugs and Yake must save them. (Rev: BL 6/15/87; BR 11–12/87; SLJ 9/87)

2557 Gibson, William. *Burning Chrome* (10–12). 1987, Ace paper $3.95 (0-441-08934-8). An unusual collection of stories set in the future where the world is controlled by the computer manipulators. (Rev: VOYA 8–10/86)

2558 Gibson, William. *Neuromancer* (10–12). 1984, Ace paper $3.95 (0-441-56959-5). In this variation on the Faust story, a computer expert sells his soul for money.

2559 Gilliland, Alexis A. *Revolution from Rosinante* (10–12). 1981, Ballantine paper $2.25 (0-345-29265-0). Rosinante, a space colony, is helped by computers.

2560 Goldin, Stephen. *Assault on the Gods* (10–12). 1981, Fawcett paper $2.25 (0-449-24455-5). A band of space travelers try to liberate citizens of a planet governed by omnipotent gods.

2561 Goldstein, Lisa. *A Mask for the General* (10–12). 1987, Bantam $14.95 (0-553-05239-X). After an apocalypse war, the General rules America with an iron fist until the Tribes begin to organize. (Rev: BL 11/15/87)

2562 Gotlieb, Phyllis. *Son of the Morning and Other Stories* (10–12). 1983, Ace paper $2.95 (0-441-77221-8). A collection of 8 stories and 2 poems.

2563 Green, Roland. *Peace Company* (10–12). 1985, Ace paper $2.95 (0-441-65740-0). The problems of keeping interstellar peace in the twenty-fourth century are explored in this novel.

2564 Greenberg, Martin H., ed. *Amazing Science Fiction Stories: The War Years* (9–12). 1987, TSR paper $3.95 (0-88038-440-9). This collection of stories from *Amazing Stories* magazine has two companion volumes: *The Wild Years* (*1946–1955*) and *The Wonder Years* (*1926–1935*) (both 1987). (Rev: VOYA 8–9/87)

2565 Greenberg, Martin H., ed. *Amazing Stories: Visions of Other Worlds* (9–12). Illus. 1986, Random paper $7.95 (0-88038-302-X). A collection from 60 years of *Amazing Stories* magazine plus a small collection of interesting covers in color. (Rev: SLJ 4/87)

2566 Greenberg, Martin H., ed. *Foundation's Friends: Stories in Honor of Isaac Asimov* (10–12). 1989, Tor $19.95 (0-312-93174-3). A tribute to Asimov from a number of writers who have used the master's locales in these stories. (Rev: BL 10/15/89; VOYA 4/90)

2567 Gregorian, Joyce Ballou. *The Broken Citadel* (10–12). 1983, Ace paper $2.95 (0-441-08098-7). In this novel, the author has created an amazing world of the future.

2568 Haldeman, Joe. *The Forever War* (10–12). 1978, Ballantine paper $3.50 (0-345-32489-7). For mature readers, this is the story of a young warrior who returns to earth from space and finds it radically changed.

2569 Haldeman, Joe, ed. *Nebula Award Stories Seventeen* (10–12). 1983, Holt paper $3.50 (0-441-56797-5). This volume in an extensive series contains some of the best science fiction for the year 1981.

2570 Haldeman, Joe. *Worlds Apart* (10–12). 1983, Ultramarine $20.00 (0-89366-190-2). After a destructive war, Marianne must decide whether to help found a new world or stay on earth.

2571 Haldeman, Joe, and Jack C. Haldeman. *There Is No Darkness* (10–12). 1984, Ace paper $2.95 (0-441-80567-1). A young student's adventures on a spaceship are the focus of this action-filled novel.

2572 Hambly, Barbara. *Ishmael* (9–12). 1985, Pocket paper $3.50 (0-671-55427-1). In this Star Trek novel, Spock goes back in time to foil a plan to change history. (Rev: BL 7/85; VOYA 2/86)

2573 Harrison, Harry. *Bill, the Galactic Hero* (10–12). 1989, Avon paper $3.95 (0-380-75661-7). A country boy changes when he joins the emperor's military forces.

2574 Harrison, Harry. *Rebel in Time* (10–12). 1989, Tor paper $3.95 (0-8125-3967-2). History is being changed using a time machine. Also use: *Invasion: Earth* (1983).

2575 Harrison, Harry. *Return to Eden* (10–12). 1988, Bantam $18.95 (0-553-05315-9). The concluding volume in the Eden trilogy, an alternative world saga begun in *West of Eden* (1984) and *Winter in Eden* (1986). (Rev: BL 6/1/88; VOYA 4/89)

2576 Heinlein, Robert A. *Assignment in Eternity* (9–12). 1987, Baen paper $3.50 (0-671-65350-4). Two short novels, *Gulf* and *Lost Legacy,* from the pen of a master. (Rev: VOYA 2/88)

2577 Heinlein, Robert A. *The Cat Who Walks through Walls* (10–12). 1985, Putnam $17.95 (0-399-13103-5); Ace paper $4.95 (0-441-09499-6). Colonel Colin Campbell and his wife travel through time to get help solving a murder mystery. (Rev: BL 8/85)

2578 Heinlein, Robert A. *The Door into Summer* (9–12). 1986, Ballantine paper $3.95 (0-345-33012-9). An inventor has an opportunity to look into the future in this science fiction novel.

2579 Heinlein, Robert A. *Job: A Comedy of Justice* (10–12). 1985, Ballantine paper $4.95 (0-345-31650-9). A science fiction retelling of the Job story with satiric twists. Also use: *Glory Road, The Green Hills of Earth* (both 1987), *Expanded Universe* (1983), and *I Will Fear No Evil* (1987).

2580 Heinlein, Robert A. *The Moon Is a Harsh Mistress* (10–12). 1987, Ace paper $3.95 (0-441-53699-9). For better readers, the story of a penal colony on the Earth's moon.

2581 Heinlein, Robert A. *The Past through Tomorrow* (10–12). 1988, Ace paper $5.50 (0-441-65304-9). Possible future worlds are explored in this collection of short pieces.

2582 Heinlein, Robert A. *Red Planet* (8–12). 1986, Ballantine paper $3.95 (0-345-34039-6). The story of a colony of humans on Mars.

2583 Heinlein, Robert A. *Revolt in 2100* (10–12). 1986, Baen paper $3.50 (0-671-65589-2). The concept of revolution in a future civilization is explored in this novel. Also use: *Assignment in Eternity* (1987).

2584 Heinlein, Robert A. *Rocket Ship Galileo* (8–12). 1986, Ballantine paper $3.50 (0-345-33660-7). Four amateurs land on the moon. Also use: *The Rolling Stones* (1985), *Space Cadet* (1987), *Star Beast, Starman Jones* (both 1985), and *Starship Troopers* (1987).

2585 Heinlein, Robert A. *Stranger in a Strange Land* (10–12). 1961, Putnam $11.95 (0-399-10772-X); Berkley paper $3.95 (0-425-10147-9). A young man from Mars comes to Earth and must learn our strange ways.

2586 Heinlein, Robert A. *Time for the Stars* (10–12). 1990, Macmillan $14.95 (0-684-19211-X). A pair of telepathic twins become involved in a space mission. Also use: *Menace from Earth* (1987) and *Methuselah's Children* (1986).

2587 Heinlein, Robert A. *Tunnel in the Sky* (9–12). 1988, Macmillan $13.95 (0-684-18916-X). Participants find that the standard survival test becomes a life-and-death struggle. Also use: *Puppet Masters* (1986).

2588 Henderson, Zenna. *The People: No Different Flesh* (10–12). 1987, Avon paper $3.50 (0-380-01506-4). A group of aliens who look like humans infiltrate Earth's society.

2589 Herbert, Brian. *Prisoners of Arionn* (9–12). 1987, Arbor House $17.95 (0-87795-886-6). Invaders from space enclose the San Francisco area in a bubble and fly it to their home planet. (Rev: VOYA 10/87)

2590 Herbert, Frank. *Chapterhouse: Dune* (10–12). 1985, Putnam $17.95 (0-399-13027-6); Ace paper $4.95 (0-441-10267-0). In this sixth Dune book, 2 rival orders engage in a deadly duel on the planet Chapterhouse. A direct sequel to *Heretics of Dune* (1983). (Rev: BL 3/1/85; SLJ 12/85)

2591 Herbert, Frank. *Destination: Void* (10–12). 1987, Ace paper $3.95 (0-441-14302-4). A re-cently repaired computer begins causing unusual problems.

2592 Herbert, Frank. *The Dosadi Experiment* (10–12). 1987, Ace paper $3.95 (0-441-16027-1). A group of aliens are caught on a toxic planet. Also use: *The Best of Frank Herbert* (1984).

2593 Herbert, Frank. *Dune* (10–12). 1984, Putnam $19.95 (0-399-12896-4); Ace paper $4.95 (0-441-17266-0). In this, the first of a series, the Atreides family is banished to planet Dune where the ferocious Fremen live. Others in the series are: *Children of Dune* (1985), *Dune Messiah* (1976), and *God Emperor of Dune* (1981).

2594 Herbert, Frank, and Brian Herbert. *Man of Two Worlds* (10–12). 1986, Putnam $18.95 (0-399-13132-9). The human race inhabits a universe created by an alien race in this father and son collaboration. (Rev: BL 3/15/86)

2595 Hill, Douglas. *Galactic Warlord* (7–12). 1987, Dell paper $2.50 (0-440-92787-0). Keill Randor sets out to avenge the destruction of his home planet.

2596 Hoban, Russell. *Riddley Walker* (9–12). 1990, Simon & Schuster paper $8.95 (0-671-70127-4). For better readers, this is a novel set in the future after nuclear holocaust has reduced mankind to savagery.

2597 Hogan, James P. *Code of the Lifemaker* (10–12). 1984, Ballantine paper $3.95 (0-345-30549-3). In this novel for better readers, humans encounter a superior form of robot.

2598 Hogan, James P. *Endgame Enigma* (9–12). 1987, Bantam $16.95 (0-553-05169-5); paper $4.95 (0-553-27037-0). Two Americans infiltrate a Soviet space station in this suspenseful novel. (Rev: VOYA 12/87)

2599 Hogan, James P. *Inherit the Stars* (10–12). 1985, Ballantine paper $3.95 (0-345-33463-9). In this first volume of the Giants' series, a mystery surrounds the discovery of a human body on the moon. Followed by: *The Gentle Giants of Ganymede* (1984) and *Giants' Star* (1986).

2600 Hogan, James P. *Mirror Maze* (9–12). 1989, Bantam paper $4.95 (0-553-27762-6). In the year 2,000, Stephanie, a physicist, gets involved in political intrigue. (Rev: VOYA 10/89)

2601 Houston, David. *Wingmaster* (10–12). 1981, Dorchester paper $2.25 (0-8439-0945-5). This adventure story involves a fighter named Wingmaster who is struggling to free his planet, Ky.

2602 Howard, Robert E., et al. *Conan* (10–12). 1985, Ace paper $3.50 (0-441-11481-4). This is only one of the many adventure novels about this superhero.

2603 Hudson, Michael. *Thieves of Light* (9–12). 1987, Berkley paper $3.50 (0-425-09810-9). A suburban teenager is taken by spacecraft to help fight in a war against an evil force. (Rev: BL 8/87; SLJ 1/88)

2604 Huxley, Aldous. *Brave New World* (10–12). 1946, Harper LB $12.89 (0-06-012307-1); paper $4.95 (0-06-083095-6). A science fiction classic set in a future when science controls the life of mankind.

2605 Ing, Dean. *Pulling Through* (10–12). 1987, Ace paper $2.95 (0-441-69051-3). A survival story involving a group who try to find a new life after a nuclear holocaust.

2606 Ingrid, Charles. *The Marked Man* (10–12). 1989, DAW paper $3.95 (0-88677-396-2). After a nuclear war, a few human survivors adapt by growing gills and living in the oceans. (Rev: VOYA 6/90)

2607 Innes, Evan. *America 2040* (10–12). 1986, Bantam paper $3.95 (0-553-25541-X). Before the end of the world a spaceship filled with 1,000 people flies off to find an inhabitable planet. (Rev: VOYA 8–10/86)

2608 Jensen, Kris. *FreeMaster* (9–12). 1990, DAW paper $3.95 (0-88677-404-7). Sarah Anders is sent to the Ardellan planet to learn more about the inhabitants, who possess unusual powers of the mind. (Rev: VOYA 6/90)

2609 Johnson, Annabel, and Edgar Johnson. *A Memory of Dragons* (9–12). 1986, Macmillan $13.95 (0-689-31263-6). Paul takes a job as a spy to gain access to a doctor who might cure his amnesia. (Rev: BL 10/1/86; SLJ 12/86; VOYA 4/87)

2610 Johnson, James B. *Trekmaster* (10–12). 1987, NAL paper $3.50 (0-88677-221-4). A science fiction adventure yarn about a rediscovered planet and its unusual leader. (Rev: BL 9/15/87)

2611 Kagen, Janet. *Uhura's Song* (9–12). 1985, Ultramarine $20.00 (0-89366-169-4); Pocket paper $3.50 (0-671-54730-5). In this Star Trek novel, the *Enterprise* and its crew become involved with a planet where a plague has broken out. (Rev: SLJ 8/85)

2612 Karl, Jean E. *The Turning Place: Stories of a Future Past* (7–12). 1976, Dutton $9.95 (0-525-41573-4). A collection of stories that explore humankind's encounters with aliens from space.

2613 Kennealy, Patricia. *The Silver Branch: A Novel of the Keltiad* (10–12). 1988, NAL $18.95 (0-453-00627-2). Queen Aeron engages in an interstellar war to avenge the murder of her husband and parents in this prequel to *The Cop-*

per Crown (1984) and *The Throne of Scone* (1987). (Rev: BL 1/1/89)

2614 Killus, James. *Book of Shadows* (10–12). 1983, Ace paper $2.50 (0-441-07069-8). A science fiction novel noted for its suspense.

2615 King, Bernard. *Vargr-Moon* (10–12). 1988, St. Martin's $16.95 (0-312-01844-4). Using Nordic myths as a basis, this is a continuation of the adventures of Hather Lambisson, introduced in *Starkadder* (1987). (Rev: BL 6/1/88)

2616 Knight, Damon. *A for Anything* (9–12). 1990, Tor paper $3.95 (0-812-54310-6). A science fiction novel about the Gismo, a machine that reproduces everything, including people. (Rev: VOYA 8/90)

2617 Kotzwinkle, William. *E.T. The Book of the Green Planet* (9–12). 1987, Berkley paper $2.95 (0-425-08001-3). E.T. is confined to his home planet because he has become too earthly in this continuation of the novel *E. T.: The Extra Terrestrial* (1982). (Rev: BL 3/1/85)

2618 Kress, Nancy. *Trinity and Other Stories* (10–12). 1985, Bluejay $15.95 (0-312-94438-1). A collection of thought-provoking stories that pose the question "What if . . . ?" (Rev: SLJ 1/86; VOYA 2/86)

2619 Kube-McDowell, Michael P. *Empery* (10–12). 1987, Berkley paper $3.50 (0-425-09887-7). In this the last of the Trigon Disunity series which includes *Enigma* (1986), several war-happy humans plan a war against a more advanced alien race. (Rev: VOYA 10/87)

2620 Kurtz, Katherine. *The Bishop's Heir* (10–12). 1987, Ballantine paper $2.95 (0-345-34761-7). This is the beginning of a trilogy in the Deryni series, The Histories of King Kelson.

2621 Kurtz, Katherine. *The Legacy of Lehr* (8–12). Illus. 1986, Walker $15.95 (0-8027-6661-7); Avon paper $3.50 (0-380-70454-4). Mather Seton and his young wife are aboard a spaceship when a series of murders occurs. (Rev: BL 11/15/86; BR 3–4/87; VOYA 4/87)

2622 Kuttner, Henry. *The Startling Worlds of Henry Kuttner* (10–12). 1987, Warner paper $3.95 (0-445-20328-5). Three short novels by one of the great pioneers in science fiction writing. (Rev: BL 12/1/86; VOYA 8–9/87)

2623 L'Amour, Louis. *The Haunted Mesa* (9–12). 1987, Bantam $18.95 (0-553-05182-2); paper $4.95 (0-553-27022-2). When a prominent scientist disappears, his friend must travel into another dimension to find him in this novel that combines science fiction and the western. (Rev: BL 5/15/87; BR 11–12/87)

2624 Laumer, Keith. *End as a Hero* (10–12). 1985, Ace paper $2.95 (0-441-20656-5). The Gool, a total mind power, tries to control the hero of this novel.

2625 Laumer, Keith. *Galactic Odyssey* (10–12). 1987, Tor paper $2.95 (0-8125-4385-8). In search of Lady Faire, Billy Danger travels to distant planets.

2626 Laumer, Keith. *Retief to the Rescue* (10–12). 1988, Baen paper $2.95 (0-671-65376-8). This is a group of short stories dealing with the adventures of James Retief, a galactic diplomat. Others in this series include: *Retief: Diplomat at Arms* (1987) and *The Return of Retief* (1985).

2627 Laumer, Keith. *The Shape Changer* (10–12). 1984, Ace paper $2.75 (0-441-76102-X). This is one of many books about the unique Sir Lafayette O'Leary and his adventures in a new dimension.

2628 Laumer, Keith, and George Brown Rosel. *Earth Blood* (10–12). 1987, Baen paper $2.95 (0-671-65348-2). Roan Corney, a human living with aliens, tries to return to his home planet.

2629 Lee, Tanith. *Dreams of Dark and Light* (10–12). 1986, Arkham House $21.95 (0-87054-153-6). A collection of short pieces that effectively combine horror, science fiction, and often the elements of fantasy. (Rev: VOYA 8–10/86)

2630 Le Guin, Ursula K. *The Dispossessed: An Ambiguous Utopia* (10–12). 1976, Avon paper $3.95 (0-380-00382-1). A young man from a Utopian society finds a new reality when he travels to another planet.

2631 Le Guin, Ursula K. *The Eye of the Heron* (10–12). 1984, Bantam paper $2.95 (0-553-24258-X). On a distant planet, a young woman searches for her true identity.

2632 Le Guin, Ursula K. *The Lathe of Heaven* (10–12). 1982, Bentley $14.00 (0-8376-0464-8); Avon paper $2.95 (0-380-01320-7). In this novel set in the twenty-first century, a young man finds that his dreams are premonitions of events to come.

2633 Le Guin, Ursula K. *The Left Hand of Darkness* (7–12). 1969, Ace paper $3.95 (0-441-47812-3). An envoy is sent to the ice-covered planet Gethen where people can be either male or female at will.

2634 Le Guin, Ursula K. *Orsinian Tales* (10–12). 1987, Harper paper $6.95 (0-06-091433-5). A collection of short stories set in an imaginary European kingdom.

2635 Le Guin, Ursula K. *Planet of Exile* (7–12). 1974, Ace paper $1.95 (0-441-66957-3). The planet Eltanin becomes the target of ravaging barbarians.

2636 Le Guin, Ursula K. *The Wizard of Earthsea* (7–12). 1984, Bantam paper $3.95 (0-553-26250-5). Beginning when Ged is a boy wizard, this is the first volume of the Earthsea trilogy. Followed by: *The Tombs of Atuan* and *Farthest Shore* (both 1984).

2637 Leiber, Fritz. *The Big Time* (10–12). 1976, Amereon LB $15.95 (0-88411-931-9). A young girl lives outside the confines of time on a space station.

2638 Leiber, Fritz. *The Ghost Light* (10–12). 1984, Berkley paper $8.95 (0-425-06812-9). Here are 9 challenging stories by one of the great masters of science fiction.

2639 Leiber, Fritz. *Swords against Death* (7–12). 1970, Ace paper $2.95 (0-441-79193-X). In 10 stories, Fafhrd and the Gray Mouser have a series of adventures.

2640 Leiber, Fritz. *Swords and Deviltry* (7–12). 1970, Ace paper $2.95 (0-441-79197-2). Four stories of adventure and friendship featuring legendary heroes.

2641 Leiber, Fritz. *The Wanderer* (10–12). 1983, Tor paper $2.95 (0-8125-4425-0). A planet approaches Earth on a path of destruction.

2642 Lem, Stanislaw. *Cyberiad: Fables for the Cybernetic Age* (10–12). 1985, Harcourt paper $7.95 (0-15-623550-1). Each of these 13 stories deals with computers. Also use: *Tales of Pirx the Pilot* (1990).

2643 Leroe, Ellen. *Robot Romance* (7–12). 1985, Harper LB $12.89 (0-06-023746-5). In this humorous novel, Bixby disrupts both the student body and the robot faculty with his antics.

2644 Levin, Ira. *The Perfect Day* (10–12). 1979, Dell paper $2.25 (0-440-18704-4). Through the use of drugs, a computer is able to control people's lives.

2645 Lewis, C. S. *Out of the Silent Planet* (10–12). 1968, Macmillan paper $3.95 (0-02-086910-X). A philosophical science fiction novel about the kidnapping of an earthling and his adventures on Mars. The trilogy is completed with *Perelandra* and *That Hideous Strength* (both 1968).

2646 Lichtenberg, Jacqueline. *The Dushau Trilogy* (10–12). 1985, Warner paper $2.95 (0-445-20015-4). One woman goes up against the mighty Empire.

2647 Lichtenberg, Jacqueline. *Those of My Blood* (10–12). 1988, St. Martin's $19.95 (0-312-

02298-0). A race of vampires travels to the moon to explore the crash site of an alien spaceship. (Rev: SLJ 4/89)

2648 Llewellyn, Edward. *Prelude to Chaos* (10–12). 1983, DAW paper $2.95 (0-88677-008-4). In this exciting novel, Gavin and Judith must escape from their prison to prevent the production of a biological bomb.

2649 Longyear, Barry B. *The Homecoming* (8–12). Illus. 1989, Walker LB $15.95 (0-8027-6863-6). A species of lizard-like animals decides it must return to its original home—Earth. (Rev: BR 5–6/90; SLJ 9/89; VOYA 10/89)

2650 Longyear, Barry B. *Sea of Glass* (10–12). 1988, Avon paper $3.50 (0-380-70055-7). A glimpse of life in 2012 where the earth must take severe measures to ensure population control. (Rev: VOYA 6/87)

2651 Longyear, Barry B., and John Kessel. *Enemy Mine/Another Orphan* (9–12). 1989, Tor paper $2.95 (0-812-55963-0). Two enemies, a human and a Dracon, must survive together on a harsh planet. (Rev: VOYA 10/89)

2652 Lorrah, Jean. *Metamorphosis* (9–12). 1990, Pocket paper $4.95 (0-671-68402-7). In this Start Trek novel, DATA, the robot, becomes human. (Rev: VOYA 8/90)

2653 Lorrah, Jean. *The Vulcan Academy Murders* (10–12). 1987, Pocket paper $3.95 (0-671-64744-X). A Star Trek novel that involves murder on Mr. Spock's Vulcan planet. (Rev: BL 1/15/85)

2654 Lovecraft, H. P., et al. *Tales of the Cthulhu Mythos* (10–12). Illus. 1990, Arkham House $23.95 (0-87054-159-5). Several writers contributed stories about these evil extraterrestrials first created by Lovecraft. (Rev: BL 1/1/90; VOYA 4/90)

2655 Lucas, George. *Star Wars: From the Adventures of Luke Skywalker* (8–12). 1977, Ballantine paper $3.50 (0-345-34146-5). The adventures of Luke Skywalker and friends against the evil Darth Vader.

2656 Lumley, Brian. *The House of Doors* (9–12). 1990, Tor paper $4.95 (0-812-50832-7). A castle without doors or windows mysteriously appears in the Scottish highlands in this novel that combines horror with science fiction. (Rev: VOYA 8/90)

2657 MacAvoy, R. A. *The Third Eagle: Lessons along a Minor String* (10–12). 1989, Doubleday $18.95 (0-385-24919-5). A young man reaches maturity as a result of his adventures seeking his

future in outer space. (Rev: BL 1/15/89; VOYA 12/89)

2658 McCaffrey, Anne. *The Crystal Singer* (10–12). 1985, Ballantine paper $4.95 (0-345-32786-1). This novel involves a crystal singer from the Planet Ballybran and the young girl he influences.

2659 McCaffrey, Anne. *Decision at Doona* (10–12). 1979, Del Rey paper $3.50 (0-345-35377-3). A Terran colony of the planet Doona must try to coexist with a group of intelligent aliens.

2660 McCaffrey, Anne. *Dinosaur Planet Survivors* (9–12). 1984, Ballantine paper $3.95 (0-345-27246-3). After 43 years of suspended animation, the 2 central characters of the author's earlier *Dinosaur Planet* (1978) awake to find their beloved planet is again in danger. (Rev: BL 1/15/85)

2661 McCaffrey, Anne. *Dragonflight* (9–12). 1981, Ballantine $8.95 (0-345-27749-X); paper $3.95 (0-345-33546-5). This is the first volume of the author's popular Dragonriders of Pern series. It is followed by *Dragonquest* and *White Dragon*. Also use: *Moreta: Dragonlady of Pern* (all 1986).

2662 McCaffrey, Anne. *Dragonsdawn* (9–12). 1988, Ballantine $18.95 (0-345-33160-5). A novel that takes place before the Dragonriders of Pern series. This describes how the planet Pern was colonized and the origins of the deadly Threadfall. (Rev: BL 9/1/88; VOYA 4/89)

2663 McCaffrey, Anne. *Dragonsong* (7–12). 1986, Macmillan $14.95 (0-689-30507-9); Bantam paper $3.50 (0-553-23460-9). This novel, that takes place on the planet Pern, is the first volume of the Harper Hall trilogy written for younger readers. The others are *Dragonsinger* and *Dragondrums* (both 1979).

2664 McCaffrey, Anne. *Killashandra* (9–12). 1985, Ultramarine $20.00 (0-89366-187-2); Ballantine paper $4.95 (0-345-31600-2). While visiting a neighboring planet, crystal singer Killashandra is kidnapped. (Rev: SLJ 2/86)

2665 McCaffrey, Anne. *Moreta: Dragonlady of Pern* (9–12). 1984, Ballantine paper $4.95 (0-345-29873-X). The dragonriders of Pern are in danger from a mutated strain of influenza.

2666 McCaffrey, Anne. *Pegasus in Flight* (10–12). 1990, Ballantine $19.95 (0-345-36896-7). This novel takes place when people on Earth prepare to build the first space platform. (Rev: BL 11/1/90)

2667 McCaffrey, Anne. *The Rowan* (10–12). 1990, Putnam $19.95 (0-399-13570-7). This novel is set in a world where existence depends on telepathy and telekinetics. (Rev: BL 7/90)

2668 McCaffrey, Anne, and Elizabeth Moon. *Sassinak* (10–12). 1990, Baen paper $4.95 (0-671-69863-X). Volume 1 of a Planet Pirates series, which tells the story of a girl who fought against pirates while commanding a fleet cruiser. (Rev: BL 3/1/90)

2669 McCaffrey, Anne, and Jody Lynn Nye. *The Death of Sleep* (10–12). 1990, Simon & Schuster paper $4.95 (0-671-69884-2). After she awakens from a cryogenic sleep that has lasted many years, Lunzie feels alienated from the world in which she finds herself. (Rev: BL 7/90; SLJ 12/90)

2670 McCollum, Michael. *Life Probe* (10–12). 1983, Ballantine paper $3.95 (0-345-30295-8). During the twenty-first century explorers from an alien civilization land on earth.

2671 McDevitt, Jack. *A Talent for War* (9–12). 1989, Berkley paper $3.50 (0-441-79553-6). A space adventure in which a young man investigates the secret behind a legendary hero. (Rev: BL 2/15/89; VOYA 8/89)

2672 McDonough, Alex. *Scorpio* (10–12). 1990, Berkley paper $3.50 (0-441-75510-0). An alien from another planet finds himself in fourteenth-century Europe. (Rev: BL 4/1/90)

2673 MacGregor, Loren. *The Net* (9–12). 1987, Ace paper $2.95 (0-441-56941-2). Jason accepts a bet involving the theft of a huge ruby in this adventure story set in the future. (Rev: VOYA 12/87)

2674 McIntyre, Vonda N. *Dreamsnake* (10–12). 1986, Dell paper $3.95 (0-440-11729-1). In a future world, a young female healer uses the dreamsnake to ease pain and fear.

2675 McIntyre, Vonda N. *Enterprise: The First Adventure* (9–12). 1986, Pocket paper $4.50 (0-671-65912-X). A Star Trek novel that tells about the first mission of the *Enterprise*. (Rev: BL 9/15/86)

2676 McIntyre, Vonda N. *Fireflood and Other Stories* (10–12). 1979, Ultramarine $20.00 (0-395-28422-8). These 11 stories explore the problems that exist even in future utopias.

2677 McKillip, Patricia A. *Fool's Run* (10–12). 1987, Warner $15.95 (0-446-51278-8); paper $3.95 (0-445-20518-0). For better readers, the story of Aaron Fisher, his love for the Queen of Hearts, and a strange prison called the Underworld. (Rev: BL 5/15/87; BR 9–10/87; SLJ 6–7/87; VOYA 8–9/87)

2678 McKinney, Jack. *Invid Invasion* (9–12). 1987, Del Rey paper $2.95 (0-345-34143-0). Scott Bernard is battling the Invid Regis to regain Earth in this story continued in *Metamorphosis* and *Symphony of Light* (both 1987). (Rev: VOYA 4/88)

2679 McLoughlin, John. *Toolmaker Koan* (10–12). 1987, Baen $16.95 (0-671-65354-7); paper $3.50 (0-671-69779-X). In this novel of ideas, an unidentified massive object is detected in space. (Rev: VOYA 2/88)

2680 McQuay, Mike. *Suspicion* (10–12). 1987, Berkley paper $3.50 (0-441-73126-0). A human corpse turns up in a robot city and 2 humans are prime suspects. (Rev: BL 11/1/87)

2681 McRauch, Earl. *Buckaroo Banzai* (10–12). 1983, Simon & Schuster paper $4.95 (0-671-50574-2). A wild romp involving B. Banzai's battle with Dr. Lizardo.

2682 Malamud, Bernard. *God's Grace* (10–12). 1982, Farrar $13.50 (0-374-16465-7); Avon paper $3.95 (0-380-64519-X). Only Calvin Cohn survives a future war and he plus some primates must create a new and better world.

2683 Mark, Jan. *The Ennead* (10–12). 1978, Harper LB $7.89 (0-690-03873-9). The story involves Erato, a planet made of stone.

2684 Martin, George R. *Dying of the Light* (10–12). 1990, Baen paper $3.50 (0-671-69861-3). The death of a unique world is the subject of this science fiction novel.

2685 Miller, Walter M. *A Canticle for Leibowitz* (10–12). 1960, Harper paper $8.95 (0-06-091321-5). A probing novel on how human knowledge survives after an atomic holocaust.

2686 Moon, Elizabeth. *Lunar Activity* (10–12). 1990, Baen paper $3.50 (0-671-69870-2). A collection of short stories set in a time when space colonies are commonplace. (Rev: BL 4/1/90)

2687 Moore, C. L. *The Best of C. L. Moore* (10–12). 1980, Ballantine paper $2.25 (0-345-28952-8). This is a collection of stories by one of the early masters of science fiction.

2688 Moran, Daniel Keys. *The Ring* (9–12). 1988, Doubleday $19.95 (0-385-24816-4). Three races struggle for control of the Ring even though its possession brings destruction. (Rev: VOYA 4/89)

2689 Morris, Janet, ed. *Afterwar* (10–12). 1985, Baen paper $2.95 (0-671-55967-2). Each of these 11 stories deals with a different aspect of life after a nuclear war.

2690 Morris, Janet, and Chris Morris. *Threshold* (10–12). 1990, Penguin $16.95 (0-451-45022-1). Time-traveler Joe South encounters trouble at an orbital depot. (Rev: BL 7/90)

2691 Morwood, Peter. *Star Trek: Rules of Engagement* (9–12). 1990, Pocket paper $4.50 (0-671-66129-9). Kirk and the *Enterprise* are sent to evacuate personnel from a politically dangerous planet. (Rev: BL 2/15/90; VOYA 6/90)

2692 Mueller, Richard. *Jernigan's Egg* (10–12). 1986, Bluejay paper $9.95 (0-312-94246-X). A traveler in space finds his life is in danger because he possesses an enchanted egg. (Rev: SLJ 11/86; VOYA 12/86)

2693 Murphy, Pat. *The City, Not Long After* (10–12). 1989, Doubleday $17.95 (0-385-24925-X). A group of artists try to develop a new society after a plague has destroyed much of the world's population. (Rev: BL 3/15/89; VOYA 12/89)

2694 Niven, Larry. *The Integral Trees* (10–12). 1985, Ballantine paper $4.95 (0-345-32065-4). Problems arise when a new world is being prepared for humans.

2695 Niven, Larry. *Limits* (10–12). 1985, Ballantine paper $3.95 (0-345-32142-1). A collection of short science fiction without any connecting theme but all exhibiting the author's wit and style. (Rev: BL 2/1/85)

2696 Niven, Larry. *N-Space* (9–12). 1990, Tor $19.95 (0-312-85089-1). A collection of 25 of the best science fiction stories by this master. (Rev: BL 8/90)

2697 Niven, Larry. *Ringworld* (10–12). 1981, Ballantine paper $4.50 (0-345-33392-6). In this prize-winning book, 4 unique characters are sent to explore a distant place called Ringworld. A sequel is *The Ringworld Engineers* (1985).

2698 Niven, Larry, et al. *The Legacy of Heorot* (10–12). 1988, Pocket paper $4.50 (0-671-64928-0). This science fiction horror novel is a variation on the Beowulf story and takes place on a stellar colony where some unknown force is causing dogs and cattle to disappear. (Rev: BL 6/1/87; SLJ 1/89)

2699 Niven, Larry, and Steven Barnes. *The Descent of Anansi* (10–12). 1985, Tor paper $2.95 (0-8125-4700-4). In this exciting novel, a spaceship is attacked by pirates.

2700 Niven, Larry, and Jerry Pournelle. *Footfall* (10–12). 1986, Ballantine paper $4.95 (0-345-32344-0). The earth faces a terrible challenge from alien invaders from space in this novel by the authors of *Mote in God's Eye* (1975). (Rev: BL 4/15/85; SLJ 12/85; VOYA 2/86)

2701 Niven, Larry, and Jerry Pournelle. *Oath of Fealty* (10–12). 1984, Pocket paper $3.95 (0-671-53227-8). A young boy is killed as a result of a prank. Also use: *Lucifer's Hammer* (1985).

2702 Norton, Andre. *Android at Arms* (7–12). 1987, Ballantine paper $2.95 (0-345-34282-8). A double to a rightful ruler creates a duplicate world that could bring destruction to all.

2703 Norton, Andre. *The Beast Master* (10–12). 1983, Ballantine paper $2.50 (0-345-31376-3). A thriller involving telepathy between humans and animals. Also use: *Key Out of Time* (1987), *Horn Crown* (1981), and *Quag Keep* (1979). Key Out of Time Horn Crown Quag Keep

2704 Norton, Andre. *The Crystal Gryphon* (7–12). 1985, Tor paper $2.95 (0-8125-4738-1). Two young people—married by arrangement—come together when they must unite to help their people.

2705 Norton, Andre. *Dark Piper* (7–12). 1985, Ballantine paper $2.25 (0-345-31537-5). A group of survivors is trapped underground after their planet is destroyed.

2706 Norton, Andre. *Date to Go A-Hunting* (10–12). 1990, Tor $16.95 (0-312-85012-3). The hero journeys to the planet Elothian to seek his origins in this sequel to *Flight in Yiktor* (1986). (Rev: BL 11/15/89; VOYA 6/90)

2707 Norton, Andre. *Flight in Yiktor* (10–12). 1986, Tor $14.95 (0-312-93245-6). In this sequel to *Exiles to the Stars* (1971) that is also part of the Forerunner series, Maelen and Krip are joined by a refugee named Farree and enter into a quest to clear Maelen's name. (Rev: BL 3/1/86; VOYA 8–10/86)

2708 Norton, Andre. *Forerunner: The Second Venture* (10–12). 1985, Tor paper $2.95 (0-812-54747-0). In this sequel to *Forerunner* (1987), 2 young people experience unusual adventures when they crash on an unknown planet.

2709 Norton, Andre, ed. *Four from the Witch World* (10–12). 1989, Tor $16.95 (0-312-93153-0). Here are 4 stories written by different authors that take place in Andre Norton's imaginary setting, Witch World. (Rev: BL 3/1/89; VOYA 8/89)

2710 Norton, Andre. *Judgement on Janus* (7–12). 1987, Ballantine paper $2.95 (0-345-34365-4). A slave on Janus becomes a different person through a process called transformation. Also use: *Victory on Janus* (1984).

2711 Norton, Andre. *Knave of Dreams* (10–12). 1980, Ace paper $2.50 (0-441-45002-4). A fine science fiction novel from this prolific author whose works include: *Moon of Three Rings* (1987), *Star Born* (1981), and *Star Hunter/ Voodoo Planet* (1983). Star Born Star Hunter/ Voodoo Planet

2712 Norton, Andre. *Lord of Thunder* (7–12). 1987, Ballantine paper $2.50 (0-345-31396-8). A mysterious migration of the people on planet Arzor sets off an interstellar investigation.

2713 Norton, Andre. *Moon of Three Rings* (7–12). 1987, Ace paper $2.95 (0-441-53900-9). To help save him from harm, sorceress Maelen transforms Krip into an animal.

2714 Norton, Andre. *Night of Masks* (7–12). 1985, Ballantine paper $2.25 (0-345-32070-0). A disfigured man agrees to participate in a kidnapping to secure facial surgery.

2715 Norton, Andre. *Operation Time Search* (7–12). 1985, Ballantine paper $2.95 (0-345-32586-9). A young man is transported back to days when Atlantis existed.

2716 Norton, Andre. *Postmarked the Stars* (7–12). 1985, Fawcett paper $2.50 (0-345-32069-7). A spaceship, the *Solar Queen,* carries a strange cargo that seems to be the center of an intergalactic plot.

2717 Norton, Andre. *Sea Siege* (7–12). 1987, Ballantine paper $2.95 (0-345-34364-6). In a world shattered by atomic attack, a new terror arises from the ocean floor.

2718 Norton, Andre. *Sorceress of the Witch World* (7–12). 1972, Ace paper $3.50 (0-441-77558-6). Kaththena, a witch, though held captive tries to help a different race find freedom. Also use from this series *Three against the Witch World, Web of the Witch World* (both 1972), and *Year of the Unicorn* (1974).

2719 Norton, Andre, ed. *Tales of the Witch World* (10–12). 1987, St. Martin's $16.95 (0-312-94475-6); Tor paper $3.95 (0-8125-4757-8). Seventeen tales by well-known writers using Norton's creation as a locale—the Witch World. (Rev: BL 9/1/87; VOYA 2/88)

2720 Norton, Andre. *Voorloper* (10–12). 1981, Ace paper $2.75 (0-441-86611-5). On a distant planet, 2 young people search for a dangerous alien.

2721 Norton, Andre. *Wizard's Worlds* (9–12). 1989, Tor $17.95 (0-312-93191-3). Thirteen stories written over a span of 30 years that give a good sampling of the author's work. (Rev: BL 9/15/89; VOYA 2/90)

2722 Norton, Andre, and Martin H. Greenberg, eds. *Catfantastic* (9–12). 1989, NAL paper $3.95 (0-88677-355-5). A collection of 13 stories about cat-beings with unusual powers. (Rev: BL 7/89; VOYA 2/90)

2723 O'Donnell, Kevin, Jr. *Caverns—Book 1* (10–12). 1984, Berkley paper $2.75 (0-425-07469-2). This is the beginning of a series of space adventures featuring McGill Feighan. Followed by *Reefs—Book II* (1982) and *Lava— Book III* (1984).

2724 Ore, Rebecca. *Becoming Alien* (9–12). 1987, Tor paper $3.95 (0-812-54794-0). A teenager saves an alien and as a reward travels to the alien's home planet. Also use: *Being Alien* (1989). (Rev: BL 11/15/87)

2725 Orwell, George. *1984* (10–12). 1984, Harcourt $12.95 (0-15-166038-7); NAL paper $5.95 (0-452-25426-4). This prophetic novel published in 1945 tells of a future world where complete mind control is practiced.

2726 Peirce, Hayford. *Phylum Monsters* (9–12). 1989, Tor paper $3.95 (0-812-54894-9). In the twenty-fourth century, Robert Clayborn suffers a series of misfortunes. (Rev: VOYA 4/90)

2727 Perry, Steve. *The Man Who Never Missed* (10–12). 1985, Ace paper $2.95 (0-441-51916-4). Emile Khadaji decides that single-handedly he will change the future of his galaxy. (Rev: VOYA 2/86)

2728 Pike, Christopher. *The Tachyon Web* (9–12). 1986, Bantam paper $2.75 (0-553-26102-9). An Easter vacation space ride brings unexpected adventure when the spacecraft encounters an alien race. (Rev: VOYA 4/87)

2729 Pini, Richard, ed. *Winds of Change* (10–12). 1989, Tor paper $7.95 (0-812-54905-8). A part of the Elfquest saga, this is the third in a series of short story collections in the Blood of Ten Chiefs shared-world series. (Rev: BL 5/1/89)

2730 Piper, H. Beam. *Uller Uprising* (10–12). 1983, Ace paper $2.75 (0-441-84292-5). This novel is part of the author's Terran Foundation series, which also includes a volume of short stories, *The Worlds of H. Beam Piper* (1983).

2731 Pohl, Frederik. *The Annals of the Heechee* (10–12). 1988, Ballantine paper $3.95 (0-345-32566-4). In this fourth Heechee book, Robinette faces enemies who want to change the universe to satisfy their own needs. Others in this series are: *Gateway* (1977); *Beyond the Blue Event Horizon* (1980); and *Heechee Rendezvous* (1984). (Rev: BL 1/15/87)

2732 Pohl, Frederik. *Black Star Rising* (10–12). 1986, Ballantine paper $3.95 (0-345-31902-8). In this spoof for better readers, unfriendly aliens enter the solar system and create havoc. (Rev: BL 5/1/85; VOYA 12/85)

2733 Pohl, Frederik. *The Coming of the Quantum Cats* (10–12). 1986, Bantam paper $3.50 (0-553-25786-2). This novel takes place in a time when an individual can live separate parallel lives. (Rev: VOYA 8–10/86)

2734 Pohl, Frederik. *The Day the Martians Came* (10–12). 1988, St. Martin's $15.95 (0-312-02183-6). An amusing but also wise look at how a few humans react when confronted by aliens. (Rev: VOYA 4/89)

2735 Pohl, Frederik. *Gateway* (10–12). 1978, Ballantine paper $3.95 (0-345-34690-4). This prize-winning book for mature readers tells about a group of humans who travel by spaceship to an unknown but preprogrammed destination. This is the first book in the Heechee trilogy and is continued in *Beyond the Blue Event Horizon* and *Heechee Rendezvous* (both 1988). Also use: *The Annals of the Heechee* (1988).

2736 Pohl, Frederik. *Homegoing* (9–12). 1989, Ballantine $16.95 (0-345-33975-4). Sandy Washington, an earthling raised by aliens, becomes their spokesman on Earth. (Rev: BL 2/1/89)

2737 Pohl, Frederik. *Midas World* (10–12). 1984, Tor paper $2.95 (0-8125-4925-2). In this novel, the world's energy crisis is solved by using robots.

2738 Pohl, Frederik. *Narabedla Ltd.* (10–12). 1988, Ballantine $16.95 (0-345-33974-6); paper $2.95 (0-345-36026-5). Nolly Stennis is shanghaied and finds himself on a most unattractive moon called Narabedla. (Rev: VOYA 8/88)

2739 Pohl, Frederik. *The World at the End of Time* (10–12). 1990, Ballantine $17.95 (0-345-33976-2). For better readers, a sci-fi novel that stretches over millions of years. (Rev: BL 5/15/90)

2740 Pohl, Frederik, and C. M. Kornbluth. *The Space Merchants* (10–12). 1987, St. Martin's paper $3.50 (0-312-90655-2). An advertising executive tries to colonize Venus.

2741 Pohl, Frederik, and C. M. Kornbluth. *Wolfbane* (9–12). 1986, Baen paper $2.95 (0-671-65576-0). The earth is removed from its orbit by robots from a dead planet. (Rev: VOYA 12/86)

2742 Pohl, Frederik, and Jack Williamson. *Land's End* (9–12). 1988, Tor $18.95 (0-312-93071-2). A meteor shower wakens an alien asleep on the ocean bottom. (Rev: BL 8/88; VOYA 2/89)

2743 Pournelle, Jerry, ed. *Black Holes and Other Marvels* (10–12). 1978, Fawcett paper $2.50 (0-449-23962-4). An anthology of stories about unsolved mysteries of the universe including black holes. Also use: *Far Frontiers* (1988).

2744 Pournelle, Jerry. *King David's Spaceship* (10–12). 1987, Baen paper $2.95 (0-671-65616-3). A backward planet must build a spaceship. Also use: *Exiles to Glory* (1987).

2745 Pournelle, Jerry. *The Mercenary* (10–12). 1988, Watts $17.95 (0-531-15084-4). This story tells of a mercenary who travels from planet to planet trying to restore order. (Rev: BR 9–10/88; VOYA 8/88)

2746 Pournelle, Jerry, and Roland Green. *Janissaries: Clan and Crown* (10–12). 1987, Ace paper $3.95 (0-441-38298-3). Mercenaries are brought to a distant planet by flying saucers.

2747 Poyer, D. C. *Stepfather Bank* (10–12). 1988, St. Martin's paper $3.50 (0-312-91045-2). In this futuristic novel, a multinational corporation controls the world's economy. (Rev: VOYA 12/87)

2748 Preuss, Paul. *Maelstrom* (10–12). 1988, Avon paper $3.95 (0-380-75345-6). Sparta shows her courage by a plan to rescue a team of scientists in danger. (Rev: BL 10/15/88)

2749 Reamy, Tom. *San Diego Lightfoot Sue and Other Stories* (10–12). 1979, Ursus $16.95 (0-935128-00-X). A collection of stories that form a good sampling of this author's work.

2750 Reaves, Michael, and Steve Perry. *Hellstar* (10–12). 1984, Berkley paper $2.95 (0-425-07297-5). The saga of a space voyage that will take several years.

2751 Reeves-Stevens, Garfield. *Nighteyes* (10–12). 1989, Doubleday $18.95 (0-385-24755-9). An intricate novel for better readers about the abduction of humans by visiting aliens. (Rev: VOYA 6/89)

2752 Reeves-Stevens, Garfield, and Judith Reeves-Stevens. *Prime Directive* (9–12). 1990, Pocket $18.95 (0-671-70772-8). In this Star Trek novel, Captain Kirk and his officers are blamed for the destruction of a planet. (Rev: BL 9/15/90)

2753 Resnick, Mike. *The Dark Lady: A Romance of the Far Future* (9–12). 1987, Tor paper $3.50 (0-812-55116-8). In this futuristic novel, an art expert hires an alien named Leonardo to find the "Dark Lady" that has inspired men through the centuries. (Rev: VOYA 6/88)

2754 Resnick, Mike. *Ivory* (10–12). 1988, Tor $17.95 (0-312-93093-3); paper $4.95 (0-8125-0042-3). Duncan Rojas accepts an assignment to find the valuable tusks of a legendary great elephant of Africa. (Rev: VOYA 2/89)

2755 Resnick, Mike. *Santiago: A Myth of the Far Future* (9–12). 1986, Tor paper $3.50 (0-812-55112-5). The story of the elusive adventurer named Santiago and everyone's attempt to catch him. (Rev: VOYA 6/86)

2756 Resnick, Mike. *Second Contact* (10–12). 1990, Tor $17.95 (0-312-85021-0). A lawyer defending a captain who believes aliens are sabotaging a space problem becomes the target of a vicious plot. (Rev: BL 4/1/90; SLJ 8/90)

2757 Roberts, John Maddox. *Spacer: Window of the Mind* (8–12). 1988, Berkley paper $2.95 (0-441-77787-2). A 16-year-old street-smart girl flees her home planet and finds herself involved in a plan to start an intergalactic war. Also use: *The Sword, the Jewel and the Mirror* (1988). (Rev: BL 3/15/88)

2758 Robinson, Kim Stanley. *The Wide Shore* (10–12). 1984, Ace paper $3.50 (0-441-88874-7). After a nuclear holocaust, a 17-year-old boy tries to help rebuild America.

2759 Robinson, Spider. *Callahan's Crosstime Saloon* (10–12). 1989, Ace paper $3.50 (0-441-09043-5). These stories feature the seedy, coarse, but likable characters who frequent Callahan's Saloon—many are aliens, others time travelers. Some others in this series are: *Time Travelers Strictly Cash* (Berkley, 1987), and *Callahan's Lady* (1990).

2760 Robinson, Spider. *Callahan's Secret* (10–12). 1986, Berkley paper $2.95 (0-425-09082-5). Four quirky stories about time and space from the author that brought us *Callahan's Crossline Saloon* (1983) and *Callahan's Lady* (1987). (Rev: BL 9/1/86)

2761 Robinson, Spider. *Time Pressure* (9–12). 1987, Ace $16.95 (0-441-80932-4). Sam encounters a bald woman he is convinced is from outer space in a remote part of Nova Scotia. (Rev: VOYA 4/88)

2762 Robinson, Spider, and Jeanne Robinson. *Stardance* (10–12). 1984, Tor paper $2.95 (0-8125-5225-3). Beautiful Shara makes contact with intelligent aliens.

2763 Saberhagen, Fred. *Berserker: Blue Death* (9–12). 1985, Tor $6.95 (0-8125-5322-5); paper $3.50 (0-8125-5329-2). The Berserker, Old Blue, is a robot spaceship programmed to kill in this novel, which is part of the extensive Berserker series. Others are: *Berserker Man; Berserker's Planet* (both 1984); and *Berserker Throne* (1986). A Berserker story is included in the author's collection of short stories *Earth Descended* (1988). (Rev: VOYA 4/86)

2764 Saberhagen, Fred. *The Frankenstein Papers* (10–12). 1986, Baen paper $3.50 (0-671-65550-7). A reworking of the Frankenstein story in which the monster is a frightened creature unprepared to enter the world for which he was created. (Rev: BL 4/1/86; VOYA 6/86)

2765 Saberhagen, Fred. *Saberhagen: My Best* (10–12). 1987, Baen paper $2.95 (0-671-65645-7). A collection of 17 short stories that include some mythological fantasies plus science fiction. (Rev: VOYA 10/87)

2766 Sagan, Carl. *Contact* (10–12). 1986, Pocket paper $4.95 (0-671-43422-5). For better readers, a science fiction novel about Earth scientists building a space ship based on instructions that came from the star Vega. (Rev: BL 10/15/85)

2767 Saint-Exupéry, Antoine de. *The Little Prince* (7–12). Illus. 1943, Harcourt $8.95 (0-15-246503-0); paper $2.95 (0-15-652820-7). An inspirational fantasy popular with all ages about a little prince who has lived on many planets.

2768 Salmonson, Jessica Amanda, ed. *Heroic Visions* (10–12). 1987, Ace paper $2.95 (0-317-63495-X). An anthology of stories by such writers as Yolen, Leiber, Foster, and Silverberg.

2769 Salmonson, Jessica Amanda. *The Swordswoman* (10–12). 1988, Tor paper $3.50 (0-8125-5350-0). A beautiful woman from Earth battles her way through different worlds.

2770 Sanders, Scott Russell. *The Engineer of Beasts* (9–12). 1988, Watts LB $14.99 (0-531-08383-7). Mooch, a product of biological engineering, longs for the days of old when there was grass and trees. (Rev: BL 10/1/88; SLJ 11/88; VOYA 8/88)

2771 Sargent, Pamela. *Venus of Shadows* (10–12). 1988, Doubleday $19.95 (0-385-24840-7). Problems abound the Cytherian society who want to transform Venus into a peaceful democracy. (Rev: VOYA 6/89)

2772 Schmidt, Stanley. *Tweedlioop* (10–12). 1986, Bluejay paper $8.95 (0-312-94442-X). A squirrel-like alien crashes onto Earth and is held captive for technological secrets. (Rev: BL 9/1/86)

2773 Scithers, George H., and Darrell Schweitzer, eds. *Tales from the Spaceport Bar* (10–12). 1987, Avon paper $3.50 (0-380-89943-4). Twenty-two stories that take place in taverns in outer space. (Rev: BL 4/1/87)

2774 Scott, Melissa. *The Kindly Ones* (10–12). 1987, Baen paper $3.50 (0-671-65351-2). A novel about a new social system founded on the unfriendly planet of Orestes by the survivors of a shipwreck. (Rev: BL 9/1/87)

2775 Scott, Melissa. *Mighty Good Road* (10–12). 1990, Baen paper $3.95 (0-671-69873-7). Heikki is surrounded by intrigue and danger when she visits a lonely planet on a salvage operation. (Rev: BL 5/1/90)

2776 Setlowe, Richard. *The Experiment* (10–12). 1986, Zebra paper $3.95 (0-8217-1885-1). In an unusual experiment, a man has his lungs replaced with gills.

2777 Shatner, William. *Tekwar* (9–12). 1989, Putnam $18.95 (0-399-13495-6). The Captain Kirk of "Star Trek" has written a thriller set in the twenty-second century. (Rev: BL 7/89)

2778 Shaw, Bob. *The Ragged Astronauts* (10–12). 1987, Baen $15.95 (0-671-65644-9); paper $3.50 (0-671-65405-5). This novel is set in the alien worlds of Land and Overland, 2 planets locked in orbit. (Rev: VOYA 10/87)

2779 Sheffield, Charles. *Sight of Proteus* (10–12). 1988, Ballantine paper $3.95 (0-345-34433-2). In the twenty-second century, experiments with form-changing experiments could save humankind.

2780 Sheffield, Charles. *Summertide* (10–12). 1990, Del Rey $16.95 (0-345-36038-9). A group of humans and aliens visit 2 twin planets, one with gigantic tidal waves and the other with huge volcanic eruptions. This is book one of the Heritage Universe series. (Rev: VOYA 8/90)

2781 Shirley, John. *Eclipse Corona* (10–12). 1990, Warner paper $4.95 (0-445-20510-5). It is 2021 and a Fascist group has perfected a virus that will kill all non-Caucasian non-Christians on Earth. (Rev: VOYA 8/90)

2782 Silverberg, Robert. *Lord Valentine's Castle* (10–12). 1987, Bantam paper $4.50 (0-553-25097-3). A young amnesiac slowly realizes that he is the real Lord Valentine, ruler of his planet. Sequels in this series are *Majipoor Chronicles* and *Valentine Pontifex* (both 1983).

2783 Silverberg, Robert. *The New Springtime* (10–12). 1990, Warner $19.95 (0-446-51442-X). After a terrible environmental catastrophe on Earth, 2 rival city-states emerge in this sequel to *At Winter's End* (1988) (Rev: BL 4/1/90)

2784 Silverberg, Robert, ed. *Robert Silverberg's Worlds of Wonder: Exploring the Craft of Science Fiction* (9–12). 1987, Warner $17.95 (0-446-51369-5); paper $12.95 (0-446-39012-7). A collection of short science fiction plus a guide to science fiction writing. (Rev: BL 10/1/87; VOYA 2/88)

2785 Silverberg, Robert, ed. *The Science Fiction Hall of Fame* (10–12). 1976, Avon paper $5.95 (0-380-00795-9). This is volume 1 of an excellent anthology including such writers as Asimov, Clarke, and Heinlein.

2786 Silverberg, Robert. *The Secret Sharer* (10–12). 1988, Underwood $14.95 (0-88733-057-6). A reworking of Conrad's novel set in the time of starships. (Rev: BL 2/15/88)

2787 Silverberg, Robert. *Star of Gypsies* (9–12). 1986, Donald I. Fine $18.95 (0-917657-92-6); Warner paper $3.95 (0-445-20618-7). A futuristic novel about the Rom people who are destined to wander from planet to planet. (Rev: SLJ 3/87)

2788 Simak, Clifford D. *Highway of Eternity* (10–12). 1988, Ballantine paper $3.50 (0-345-32497-8). Two time-traveling humans become involved in a series of adventurous encounters. (Rev: BL 6/15/86)

2789 Simak, Clifford D. *Shakespeare's Planet* (10–12). 1988, Ballantine paper $2.95 (0-345-00762-X). A dragon caught in time is found on Shakespeare's Planet.

2790 Simak, Clifford D. *Way Station* (10–12). 1980, Ballantine LB $14.00 (0-8376-0440-0); paper $2.95 (0-345-33246-6). A way station of aliens is run by a man who seems ageless.

2791 Sloane, William. *The Edge of Running Water* (10–12). 1980, Ballantine paper $2.25 (0-345-28602-2). A machine is invented to enable people to communicate with the dead.

2792 Slonczewski, Joan. *A Door into Ocean* (9–12). 1987, Avon paper $3.95 (0-380-70150-2). Shora, an ocean world inhabited by women who can reproduce without men, is threatened with invasion. (Rev: VOYA 6/86)

2793 Smith, Dean Wesley. *Laying the Music to Rest* (9–12). 1989, Popular paper $3.95 (0-445-20934-8). This novel involves time travel into the past including a stop on the ill-fated Titanic. (Rev: VOYA 6/90)

2794 Spinrad, Norman. *Agent of Chaos* (8–12). 1988, Watts $16.95 (0-531-15072-0). Boris must decide if he should continue to fight for democracy in space or join a group of assassins. (Rev: BR 1–2/89)

2795 Sterling, Bruce, ed. *Mirrorshades: The Cyberpunk Anthology* (10–12). 1986, Ace paper $3.50 (0-441-53382-5). An anthology of hard science fiction that explores mankind's relationship to technology. (Rev: VOYA 4/87)

2796 Stewart, George R. *Earth Abides* (10–12). 1974, Archive Pr. $17.95 (0-910720-002). A classic about a group of people who survive a catastrophe that almost destroys the Earth.

2797 Strieber, Whitley, and James Kunetka. *Nature's End: The Consequences of the Twentieth Century* (10–12). 1987, Warner paper $4.95 (0-446-34355-2). In the year 2025, Earth is nearing environmental death and a false guru claims that one-third of Earth's population must die. (Rev: SLJ 10/86)

2798 Strieber, Whitley, and James Kunetka. *Warday* (10–12). 1987, Warner paper $4.95 (0-446-35035-4). A frightening novel about nuclear destruction.

2799 Swanwick, Michael. *In the Drift* (10–12). 1987, Ace paper $2.95 (0-441-37072-1). A death zone in America is caused by a nuclear meltdown.

2800 Tepper, Sheri S. *The Gate to Women's Country* (10–12). 1988, Doubleday $18.95 (0-385-24709-5); Bantam paper $4.50 (0-553-28064-3). In this thought-provoking novel women control civilization and men are relegated to either a servant or warrior class. (Rev: SLJ 12/88; VOYA 2/89)

2801 Tepper, Sheri S. *Grass* (9–12). 1989, Doubleday $18.95 (0-385-26012-1). On the planet Grass, the human inhabitants seem immune to a deadly plague. (Rev: BL 9/1/89; VOYA 2/90)

2802 Tepper, Sheri S. *Southshore* (10–12). 1987, Tor paper $3.95 (0-8125-5619-4). Thrasne in his boat visits the Southshore where he becomes embroiled in danger and intrigue in this sequel to *Northshore* (1986). (Rev: BL 4/15/87; VOYA 10/87)

2803 Terman, Douglas. *Free Flight* (10–12). 1990, Bantam paper $4.95 (0-553-28301-4). A survivor of World War III finds he has been labeled an enemy by the new government.

2804 Tevis, Walter. *The Man Who Fell to Earth* (10–12). 1989, Dell paper $7.95 (0-440-50217-9). A visit to Earth by a Martian is tinged with sadness.

2805 Thompson, Julian. *Goofbang Value Daze* (9–12). 1989, Scholastic $12.95 (0-590-41946-3). In a high school of the future, the students are being unfairly dictated to by its administrators. (Rev: BL 3/1/89; SLJ 2/89; VOYA 6/89)

2806 Thompson, W. R. *Sideshow* (10–12). 1988, Baen paper $3.50 (0-671-65375-X). In the year 2000, a group of mutant telepaths are being persecuted. (Rev: VOYA 6/88)

2807 Tiptree, James, Jr. *Brightness Falls from the Air* (10–12). 1985, Tor $14.95 (0-312-93097-6); paper $3.50 (0-812-55625-9). This novel describes the efforts to save the Dameii, a group of winged creatures on the brink of extinction. (Rev: VOYA 8–10/86)

2808 Tolkien, J. R. R. *Fellowship of the Ring* (9–12). 1986, Ballantine paper $5.95 (0-345-33970-3). This is the first part of the famous Lord of the Rings trilogy. Followed by: *The Two Towers* and *Return of the King* (both 1988).

2809 Vance, Jack. *Araminta Station* (10–12). 1988, Tor $19.95 (0-312-93044-5). A complex novel (the first of the Cadwal Chronicles) that involves a teenage hero and lots of derring-do. (Rev: BL 6/1/88)

2810 Vance, Jack. *The Dying Earth* (10–12). 1982, Pocket paper $2.25 (0-671-44184-1). On a dying earth, people seek fulfillment in many ways.

2811 Vance, Jack. *The Face* (10–12). 1980, Underwood $15.00 (0-934438-24-4). Kirth Gersen is out to avenge the death of his family in this fourth volume of the Demon Prince's novels.

2812 Vance, Jack. *The Languages of Pao* (10–12). 1989, Tor paper $3.95 (0-8125-5696-8). The planet Pao undergoes radical changes under the leadership of Beran.

2813 Varley, John. *Titan* (10–12). 1985, Berkley paper $3.95 (0-425-09846-X). In this action story, Captain Cirocco Jones and her crew are off on an expedition to Saturn.

2814 Verne, Jules. *Around the Moon* (8–12). 1968, Airmont paper $1.50 (0-8049-0182-1). An early science fiction relic about a trip to the moon. Also use: *From the Earth to the Moon* (1984)

2815 Verne, Jules. *Master of the World* (9–12). n.d., Amereon $15.95 (0-89190-518-9); $1.25 (0-8049-0073-6). A scientist who has invented an amazing machine claims he is the master of the world.

2816 Vinge, Joan D. *Catspaw* (10–12). 1988, Warner $17.95 (0-446-51396-2). Cat, the hero of Vinge's earlier young-adult novel, returns in an adult sequel again involving intrigue and danger. (Rev: BL 9/15/88)

2817 Vinge, Joan D. *Psion* (9–12). 1982, Delacorte $12.95 (0-385-28780-1); Dell paper $2.95 (0-440-50340-1). A 16-year-old boy named Cat finds the gift of telepathy a mixed blessing.

2818 Vinge, Vernor. *True Names and Other Dangers* (10–12). 1987, Baen paper $2.95 (0-671-65363-6). Artificial intelligence is the subject of this science fiction novel.

2819 Vonnegut, Kurt. *Cat's Cradle* (10–12). 1987, Dell paper $4.95 (0-440-11149-8). A mordantly humorous novel about a mythical island and the discovery of a weapon more powerful than the nuclear bomb.

2820 Vonnegut, Kurt. *Jailbird: A Novel* (10–12). 1979, Dell paper $7.95 (0-385-29280-5). A satiric look at American politics and the economic system through the misadventures of Walter F. Starbuck.

2821 Vonnegut, Kurt. *Welcome to the Monkey House: A Collection of Short Works* (10–12). 1970, Dell paper $4.95 (0-440-19478-4). The stories in this collection emphasize the bizarre, fantastic elements in contemporary life.

2822 Waugh, Charles, and Martin H. Greenberg, eds. *Space Wars* (10–12). 1988, Tor paper $3.95 (0-812-53046-2). For mature readers, a collection of military science fiction by such authors as Arthur C. Clarke and Poul Anderson. (Rev: BL 6/1/88)

2823 Waugh, Charles, and Martin H. Greenberg, eds. *Time Wars* (10–12). 1986, Tor paper $3.50 (0-812-53048-9). A collection of stories that involve war, time travel, and alternate worlds. (Rev: VOYA 4/87)

2824 Weaver, Michael D. *Mercedes Nights* (10–12). 1988, St. Martin's paper $3.50 (0-312-91223-4). A challenging novel in which clones of a very attractive woman cause problems. (Rev: VOYA 4/88)

2825 Wells, H. G. *The Complete Short Stories of H. G. Wells* (9–12). 1988, St. Martin's $19.95 (0-312-15855-6). This collection represents a number of types of stories but mainly science fiction, including such classics as *The Time Machine*.

2826 Wells, H. G. *The Door in the Wall and Other Stories* (10–12). 1980, Godine paper $6.95 (0-87923-326-5). A somewhat esoteric collection of stories that explore the limits of reality.

2827 Wells, H. G. *First Men in the Moon* (10–12). 1989, Donning paper $12.90 (0-89865-785-7). Unusual creatures are found when humans first visit the moon.

2828 Wells, H. G. *The Food of the Gods* (10–12). 1978, Pendulum paper $2.95 (0-88301-314-2). This novel is set in a land where people do not stop growing.

2829 Wells, H. G. *In the Days of the Comet* (10–12). n.d., Airmont paper $1.95 (0-8049-0111-2). The world changes as a result of gases emitted by an approaching comet.

2830 Wells, H. G. *The Invisible Man* (8–12). 1987, Buccaneer LB $16.95 (0-89966-377-X);

Bantam paper $2.95 (0-553-21353-9). Two editions of many available of the story of a scientist who finds a way to make himself invisible.

2831 Wells, H. G. *Island of Doctor Moreau* (9–12). 1983, Buccaneer LB $16.95 (0-89966-470-9); NAL paper $2.50 (0-451-52191-9). A shipwrecked sailor arrives at an island where strange experiments are taking place.

2832 Wells, H. G. *Seven Science Fiction Novels* (7–12). 1950, Dover $15.00 (0-486-20264-X). This collection includes such standard titles as *The Invisible Man* and *The War of the Worlds*.

2833 Wells, H. G. *Time Machine* (7–12). 1984, Bantam paper $2.95 (0-553-21351-2). This is one of the earliest novels to use traveling through time as its subject.

2834 Wells, H. G. *The War of the Worlds* (7–12). 1988, Bantam paper $1.95 (0-553-21338-5). In this early science fiction novel, first published in 1898, strange creatures from Mars invade England.

2835 Westall, Robert. *Futuretrack 5* (9–12). 1984, Greenwillow LB $10.25 (0-688-02598-6). In the twenty-first century, a young computer wizard and his friend dare to question the existing power structure.

2836 Weston, Susan. *Children of the Light* (10–12). 1987, St. Martin's paper $3.50 (0-312-90305-7). By a time warp, Jeremy is taken into the future after a nuclear war. (Rev: BR 3–4/86)

2837 White, James. *Code Blue: Emergency* (10–12). 1987, Ballantine paper $2.95 (0-345-34172-4). In this novel, which is part of the Sector General series, a multilegged doctor though well-meaning causes problems in a space hospital. (Rev: BL 7/87)

2838 Wilhelm, Kate. *Crazy Time* (10–12). 1988, St. Martin's $16.95 (0-312-01411-2). A romantic spoof that combines humor and science fiction in a story about a female psychologist, her anxieties, and a disappearing man. (Rev: BL 3/1/88; VOYA 6/88)

2839 Wilhelm, Kate. *Where Late the Sweet Birds Sang* (10–12). 1981, Pocket paper $2.95 (0-671-49409-0). A family can survive only if they are able to produce clones of themselves.

2840 Williams, Jon Walter. *Angel Station* (10–12). 1989, Tor $18.95 (0-312-93187-5). Maria, a witch, and her brother must steal their impounded spaceship to prevent being exiled from space forever. (Rev: VOYA 2/90)

2841 Williams, Paul O. *The Breaking of Northwall* (10–12). 1984, Ballantine paper $2.95 (0-345-32434-X). This novel is part 1 of the Pelbar cycle about life on Earth a millennium after a nuclear war. Others in print are: *The Ends of the Circle* (1986) and *Dome in the Forest* (1985).

2842 Williams, Sheila, and Charles Ardai, eds. *Why I Left Harry's All-Night Hamburgers* (7–12). 1990, Delacorte $14.95 (0-385-30044-1). A collection of 12 stories selected from *Isaac Asimov's Science Fiction Magazine*. (Rev: BL 5/15/90)

2843 Williams, Sheila, and Cynthia Manson, eds. *Tales from Isaac Asimov's Science Fiction Magazine: Short Stories for Young Adults* (9–12). 1986, Harcourt $15.95 (0-15-284209-8). In these 17 stories there is such a wide range of types and styles represented that this could serve as an introduction to science fiction for teens. (Rev: BL 1/15/87; SLJ 11/86)

2844 Williams, Walter J. *Ambassador of Progress* (10–12). 1987, Tor paper $3.95 (0-812-55791-3). A female ambassador finds she is being drawn into a conflict between city-states in this novel by the author of *Hardwired* (1987) and its sequel, *Voice of the Whirlwind* (1987). (Rev: VOYA 10/87)

2845 Williamson, Jack. *Mazeway* (10–12). 1990, Ballantine $17.95 (0-345-34032-9). Two men and a woman uncover a sinister plot when they travel through a planetary maze. (Rev: BL 2/15/90)

2846 Willis, Connie, and Cynthia Felice. *Light Raid* (10–12). 1989, Berkley $17.95 (0-441-48311-9). A 17-year-old girl must clear her mother of treason charges in this novel set in a future United States beset by another civil war. Another successful collaboration by these authors is *Water Witch* (1982). (Rev: BL 5/1/89)

2847 Wilson, F. Paul. *Dydeetown World* (10–12). 1989, Baen paper $3.50 (0-671-69828-1). A hard-boiled detective yarn with a difference—this one is set in a future time when Earth is suffering from outer space migrations. Also use a collection of short stories by this author, *Soft and Others* (1989). (Rev: BL 7/89; VOYA 2/90)

2848 Wilson, F. Paul. *The Tery* (10–12). 1990, Baen paper $3.50 (0-671-69855-9). A wounded near-human beast is nursed back to health by 2 outsiders. (Rev: BL 11/1/89; VOYA 6/90)

2849 Wilson, Robert Charles. *The Divide* (10–12). 1990, Doubleday $19.95 (0-385-24947-0); paper $8.95 (0-385-26653-3). John, unable to cope, creates a new personality for himself, Benjamin. (Rev: VOYA 6/90)

2850 Wilson, Robert Charles. *Gypsies* (9–12). 1989, Doubleday $16.95 (0-385-24933-0). A teen-

age boy discovers he has the powers to open doors and enter other places and other times. (Rev: BL 1/15/89; VOYA 12/89)

2851 Wilson, Robert Charles. *Memory Wire* (10–12). 1988, Bantam paper $3.95 (0-553-26853-8). Three people journey to Brazil to find alien transmitters that can be used as powerful weapons. (Rev: BL 12/15/87)

2852 Wingrove, David. *Chung Kuo: The Middle Kingdom* (10–12). 1990, Delacorte $19.95 (0-385-29873-0). On the overcrowded Earth 200 years from now, 7 kings rule who care for their people. (Rev: VOYA 4/90)

2853 Wolfe, Gene. *The Urth of the New Sun* (10–12). 1987, Tor $17.95 (0-312-93033-X). For better readers, this novel continues the 4-volume Book of the New Sun series and involves the continued journeys by Severian through time and space. (Rev: VOYA 4/88)

2854 Wollheim, Donald A., ed. *The World's Best SF Annual* (10–12). 1987, DAW paper $3.95 (0-88677-203-6). Part of a fine annual series, this volume contains 10 stories and one novella. (Rev: VOYA 12/87)

2855 Wurts, Janny. *Shadowfane* (10–12). 1988, Berkley paper $3.50 (0-441-76082-1). Humans and demons continue to fight in this, the concluding volume of the Cycle of Fire trilogy that began with *Stormwarden* (1984) and continued with *Keeper of the Keys* (1988). (Rev: BL 11/1/88)

2856 Wyndham, John. *The Day of the Triffids* (10–12). 1985, Ballantine paper $3.50 (0-345-32817-5). A combined science fiction and horror story about some flesh-eating plants that cause havoc on Earth.

2857 Yep, Laurence. *Shadow Lord* (9–12). 1987, Pocket paper $3.95 (0-671-66087-X). In this Star Trek novel, Prince Vikram leaves his university to rule his people.

2858 Yolen, Jane. *Cards of Grief* (10–12). 1984, Ace paper $2.75 (0-441-09167-9). A somewhat complex novel about a poet at a royal court and the process of grieving.

2859 Zahn, Timothy. *Cascade Point and Other Stories* (9–12). 1986, Bluejay $16.95 (0-312-94041-6); Baen paper $3.95 (0-671-65633-3). A collection of science fiction stories that show off the author's vivid imagination and his wild sense of humor. (Rev: VOYA 6/86)

2860 Zahn, Timothy. *A Coming of Age* (10–12). 1985, Bluejay $14.95 (0-312-94058-0); Baen paper $3.95 (0-671-65578-7). On the planet Tigris, prepubescent children have strange telekinetic powers. (Rev: BL 2/1/85)

2861 Zahn, Timothy. *Deadman Switch* (9–12). 1988, Baen paper $3.95 (0-671-69784-6). A human sacrifice is necessary to gain the precious metals that circle the planet Solitaire. Also use: *Cobra Bargain* (1988). (Rev: BL 10/15/88)

2862 Zahn, Timothy. *Spinneret* (9–12). 1985, Bluejay $15.95 (0-312-94411-X). Humans are confined to a metalless planet and discover that their metal brought from Earth is disappearing. (Rev: BL 1/1/86; VOYA 6/86)

2863 Zahn, Timothy. *Time Bomb and Zahndry Others* (9–12). 1988, Baen paper $3.50 (0-671-65431-4). A collection of short fiction by this prize-winning science fiction writer. (Rev: VOYA 2/89)

2864 Zamiatin, Eugene. *We* (10–12). 1924, Dutton paper $5.95 (0-525-47039-5). In this future where rationality reigns, people have numbers, not names.

2865 Zebrowski, George. *Sunspacer* (10–12). 1984, Harper LB $10.89 (0-06-026850-6). This novel, set on Mercury, concerns a boy attending college there.

2866 Zelazny, Roger. *A Dark Traveling* (9–12). 1987, Walker $14.95 (0-8027-6686-2); Avon paper $3.50 (0-380-70567-2). A fast-moving plot about parallel worlds highlights this Hugo Award-winning novella. (Rev: SLJ 8/87; VOYA 8–9/87)

2867 Zelazny, Roger. *Frost and Fire* (10–12). 1989, Morrow $15.95 (0-688-08942-9). Eleven short stories, one a prize winner, and 2 essays by this writer of the Amber series. Also use: *Wizard World* (Baen, 1989). (Rev: BL 7/89)

2868 Zelazny, Roger. *Knight of Shadows* (10–12). 1989, Morrow $16.95 (0-688-08726-4). This is the ninth book in the Amber series about a modern Merlin. (Rev: BL 10/15/89)

2869 Zelazny, Roger. *Signs of Chaos* (10–12). 1987, Avon paper $3.50 (0-380-89637-0). In this the eighth book in the Amber series, Merlin Corey journeys to the Keep of Four Worlds to learn a dangerous secret. (Rev: BL 9/1/87; VOYA 2/88)

2870 Zelazny, Roger, and Fred Saberhagen. *Coils* (10–12). 1988, Tor paper $3.50 (0-8125-5877-4). A young man is able to manipulate computer data through using his brain.

Sports Stories

2871 Altman, Millys N. *Racing in Her Blood* (7–12). 1980, Harper $9.89 (0-397-31895-2). A junior novel about a young girl who wants to succeed in the world of automobile racing.

2872 Butler, Bonnie. *Olympic Hopeful* (9–12). 1983, Fawcett paper $1.95 (0-449-70055-0). A shy teenager comes out of her shell through the sport of skiing.

2873 Deford, Frank. *Casey on the Loose* (10–12). Illus. 1989, Viking $15.95 (0-670-82780-0). A humorous version of the "Casey at the Bat" story that reveals the truth behind the Mudville catastrophe. (Rev: BL 5/1/89)

2874 Deuker, Carl. *On the Devil's Court* (8–12). 1988, Little $13.95 (0-316-18147-1). In this variation on the Faust legend, a senior high basketball star believes he has sold his soul to have a perfect season. (Rev: BL 12/15/88; BR 9–10/89; SLJ 1/89; VOYA 4/89)

2875 Easton, Patricia Harrison. *Rebel's Choice* (9–12). 1989, Harcourt $14.95 (0-15-200571-4). Rob, a 16-year-old boy, sorts himself out in a novel involving the world of harness racing. (Rev: BL 5/1/89; SLJ 5/89; VOYA 12/89)

2876 French, Michael. *The Throwing Season* (7–12). 1980, Delacorte $8.95 (0-440-08600-0). Henry nicknamed Indian faces a moral dilemma when he is offered a bribe to throw the track meet.

2877 Guy, David. *Football Dreams* (9–12). 1982, NAL paper $4.50 (0-451-15868-7). A story about the thoughts and actions of a freshman at Arnold Academy who wants to make the football team.

2878 Harris, Mark. *Bang the Drum Slowly* (10–12). 1981, Buccaneer $16.95 (0-89966-393-1); Univ. of Nebraska Pr. paper $6.50 (0-8032-7221-9). This is the story of a friendship between 2 baseball players—one of whom is dying of Hodgkin's disease.

2879 Kinsella, W. P. *The Iowa Baseball Confederacy* (10–12). 1986, Houghton $16.95 (0-395-38952-6); Ballantine paper $4.95 (0-345-34230-5). Like the author's earlier *Shoeless Joe* (1982) which became the movie *Field of Dreams*, this novel combines fantasy and baseball, in this case a time-travel journey to find out the truth about a critical game. (Rev: BL 4/15/86)

2880 Klinkowitz, Jerome. *Short Season and Other Stories* (10–12). 1988, Johns Hopkins Univ. Pr. $16.95 (0-8018-3614-X). A series of short stories about life in baseball's minor leagues. (Rev: BL 4/15/88)

2881 Lardner, Ring. *You Know Me Al: A Busher's Letters* (10–12). 1984, Random paper $7.95 (0-394-72634-0). This is a collection of humorous letters by a rookie in major legaue baseball many years ago.

2882 Malamud, Bernard. *The Natural* (10–12). 1961, Farrar $13.95 (0-374-21960-5); paper $8.95 (0-374-50200-5). An allegory about the strange career of an exceptional baseball pitcher who has been called "a natural."

2883 Maloney, Ray. *The Impact Zone* (10–12). 1986, Delacorte $14.95 (0-385-29447-6). Jim is grounded after his stepfather learns of his sexual experience, so he decides to run away to join his macho surfer father. (Rev: BL 5/15/86; BR 9–10/86; SLJ 8/86; VOYA 6/86)

2884 Miller, Frances A. *Losers and Winners* (9–12). 1986, Fawcett paper $2.50 (0-449-70151-4). The hero of *The Truth Trap* (1986) and *Aren't You the One Who . . .?* (Macmillan, 1983) continues to face emotional problems related to his sister's murder and escapes into the world of running. (Rev: SLJ 2/87)

2885 Plimpton, George. *The Curious Case of Sidd Finch* (9–12). 1987, Berkley paper $3.95 (1-55773-064-4). In this amusing short novel, a writer is given the assignment of finding out what makes an erratic pitcher tick. (Rev: BL 5/15/87; SLJ 3/88)

2886 Schulman, L. M., ed. *The Random House Book of Sports Stories* (7–12). 1990, Random LB $16.99 (0-394-92874-1). From a wide range of authors, past and present, comes a fine anthology of sports stories. (Rev: BL 12/1/90)

2887 Weesner, Theodore. *Winning the City* (10–12). 1990, Summit $17.95 (0-671-64241-3). For mature readers, the story of an adolescent who learns to fight back after disillusionment. (Rev: BL 7/90)

2888 Wells, Rosemary. *When No One Was Looking* (8–12). 1987, Fawcett paper $2.95 (0-449-70251-0). This story about tennis is also a mystery involving the death of the heroine's arch rival.

Short Stories and General Anthologies

2889 Abbott, Dorothy, ed. *Mississippi Writers: Reflections of Childhood and Youth* (10–12).
1985, Univ. Pr. of Mississippi $35.00 (0-87805-231-3); paper $14.95 (0-87805-232-1). This first volume of a multivolume set is a collection of stories and parts of novels by twentieth-century Mississippi writers about growing up in the South. Volume II (1986) contains nonfiction on the same subjects and volume III (1987), poetry. (Rev: BL 6/15/85)

2890 Abrahams, William, ed. *Prize Stories: The O. Henry Awards* (10–12). 1987, Doubleday $17.95 (0-385-23594-1). This is just one of the annual collections of stories by American authors.

2891 Abrahams, William, ed. *Prize Stories of the Seventies* (10–12). 1981, Pocket paper $4.95 (0-671-41866-1). This anthology includes 23 stories chosen from the O. Henry award winners.

2892 Angus, Douglas, and Sylvia Angus, eds. *Great Modern European Short Stories* (10–12). 1980, Fawcett paper $2.95 (0-449-30781-6). An excellent anthology of such writers as Camus, Chekhov, and Joyce.

2893 Auden, W. H., ed. *The Portable Greek Reader* (10–12). 1987, Penguin paper $9.95 (0-14-015039-0). This anthology introduces the wide variety and depth of the writings of the ancient Greeks. [880.8]

2894 Booth, Mark, ed. *Christian Short Stories* (10–12). 1984, Crossroads $9.95 (0-8245-0674-X). An anthology of stories by such writers as Chekhov, Dickens, and Wilde, each of which explores a Christian theme.

2895 Borges, Jorge Luis. *The Aleph and Other Stories: 1933–1969* (10–12). 1980, Dutton $8.95 (0-525-48275-X). For better readers, this is a collection of stories by the Latin American writer that spans over 30 years.

2896 Brooks, Cleanth, et al., eds. *American Literature: The Makers and the Making* (10–12). 2 vols. 1973, St. Martin's paper $19.95 ea (vol 1: 0-312-02590-4; vol. 2: 0-312-02660-9). An anthology with critical comment that spans American literature from Colonial times to the present. [810.8]

2897 Brown, Clarence, ed. *The Portable Twentieth-Century Russian Reader* (10–12). 1985, Penguin paper $9.95 (0-14-015100-1). Such authors as Gorky and Pasternak are represented in this anthology plus the full text of Yuri Olesha's novel *Envy*. (Rev: BL 5/15/85) [891.7]

2898 Burgess, Anthony. *The Devil's Mode: Stories* (10–12). 1989, Random $18.95 (0-394-57670-5). For better readers a group of 9 stories that deal with famous people in history like Attila the Hun and Shakespeare. (Rev: SLJ 6/90)

2899 Cahill, Susan, ed. *New Women and New Fiction: Short Stories Since the Sixties* (10–12). 1986, NAL paper $4.95 (0-451-62665-6). For better readers, this is a collection of short fiction by 21 important female writers from 1965 to 1985. (Rev: BL 6/1/86; SLJ 10/86)

2900 Cahill, Susan, ed. *Women and Fiction* (10–12). 1978, NAL paper $4.95 (0-451-62574-9). From various sources, here is a collection of 26 stories about and by women.

2901 Carver, Raymond, and Tom Jenks, eds. *American Short Story Masterpieces* (10–12). 1987, Delacorte $19.95 (0-385-29524-3); Dell paper $5.95 (0-440-20423-2). For better readers, here is a collection of 36 contemporary short stories by the best current practitioners. (Rev: BL 3/15/87; SLJ 8/87)

2902 Cerf, Bennett, ed. *Great Modern Short Stories* (10–12). 1955, Random paper $6.95 (0-394-70127-5). Twelve stories are included in this anthology—5 by English writers and 7 by American writers.

2903 Chapman, Abraham, ed. *Black Voices: An Anthology of Afro-American Literature* (10–12). 1968, NAL paper $5.95 (0-451-62660-5). This collection by black Americans contains all sorts of writing—fiction, poetry, criticism, and biography. [810]

2904 Cheever, John. *The Stories of John Cheever* (10–12). 1985, Ballantine paper $6.95 (0-345-33567-8). This collection represents stories written between 1946 and 1978 and won Cheever a Pulitzer prize in literature.

2905 Cofer, Judith Ortiz. *Silent Dancing: A Partial Remembrance of a Puerto Rican Childhood* (10–12). 1990, Arte Publico $8.50 (1-55885-015-5). Short stories and poems by Cofer reveal the Puerto Rican experience and the trials of growing up in 2 cultures. (Rev: BL 7/90) [818]

2906 Colette. *The Collected Stories of Colette* (10–12). 1983, Farrar $22.50 (0-374-12629-1); paper $12.95 (0-374-51865-3). Two novellas and a sampling of stories are included from the output of this prolific French writer.

2907 Crane, Milton, ed. *50 Great American Short Stories* (10–12). 1984, Bantam paper $4.95 (0-553-27294-2). This excellent anthology spans the entire history of American literature and represents the best of many authors.

2908 Dahl, Roald. *Ah, Sweet Mystery of Life* (10–12). Illus. 1990, Knopf $18.95 (0-394-58265-9). Seven early adult stories by the master of imagination and wit. (Rev: BL 3/15/90; SLJ 7/90)

2909 Davenport, Basil, ed. *The Portable Roman Reader* (10–12). 1987, Penguin paper $8.95 (0-14-015056-0). A far-reaching anthology that samples the great diversity of literature written in ancient Rome. [870.8]

2910 Eisen, Jonathan, and Stuart Troy, eds. *The Nobel Reader: Short Fiction, Poetry, and Prose by Nobel Laureates in Literature* (10–12). 1987, Crown paper $12.95 (0-517-56351-7). Selections from the works of 33 of the award recipients are included. (Rev: BL 11/15/87) [808.8]

2911 Fast, Howard. *Time and the Riddle* (10–12). 1989, Dell paper $4.95 (0-440-20517-4). A general collection of 31 stories by this prolific writer.

2912 Faulkner, William. *Collected Stories of William Faulkner* (10–12). 1950, Random $22.95 (0-394-41967-7); paper $14.95 (0-394-72257-4). A total of 42 stories that chronicle life and death in the South.

2913 Faulkner, William. *Selected Short Stories of William Faulkner* (10–12). 1961, Modern Lib. $7.95 (0-394-60456-4). This selection of 12 of Faulkner's best stories includes the now-classic "Barn Burning" and "A Rose for Emily."

2914 Faulkner, William. *Uncollected Stories of William Faulkner* (10–12). 1979, Random $17.95 (0-394-40044-5); paper $11.95 (0-394-74656-2). This posthumous collection includes some 45 stories, many of which were previously unpublished.

2915 Fitzgerald, F. Scott. *The Stories of F. Scott Fitzgerald* (10–12). 1951, Macmillan $35.00 (0-684-15366-1); paper $6.95 (0-02-019940-6). A chronologically arranged selection of Fitzgerald's stories that represent the best.

2916 Forkner, Benjamin, and Patrick Samway, eds. *A Modern Southern Reader* (10–12). 1986, Peachtree $24.95 (0-934601-01-1); paper $14.95 (0-934601-08-9). An anthology that includes both fiction and nonfiction and samples both the standard and contemporary writers from this region. (Rev: BL 1/1/87) [810]

2917 Forkner, Benjamin, and Patrick Samway, eds. *Stories of the Modern South* (10–12). 1984, Peter Smith $16.75 (0-8446-6171-6); Penguin paper $9.95 (0-14-009695-7). This anthology of 25 stories features such writers as William Faulkner, Robert Penn Warren, and Carson McCullers.

2918 Gilbert, Sandra M., and Susan Gubar, eds. *The Norton Anthology of Literature by Women: The Tradition in English* (10–12). 1985, Norton $36.95 (0-393-01940-3). This excellent 3-volume work is an anthology of English-speaking writers that begins with Queen Elizabeth and ends with Alice Walker. (Rev: BL 4/15/85) [820]

2919 Greenberg, Joanne. *Rites of Passage* (10–12). 1985, Holt paper $6.95 (0-03-003677-1). These stories deal with the lives of people who are crippled either physically or emotionally. (Rev: BR 1–2/86)

2920 Hawthorne, Nathaniel. *Tales and Sketches* (10–12). 1982, Lib. of America $27.50 (0-949450-03-8). This collection includes Hawthorne's short stories and his retelling of myths in such volumes as *Tanglewood Tales*.

2921 Hemingway, Ernest. *The Nick Adams Stories* (10–12). 1987, Macmillan $35.00 (0-02-550780-X); paper $8.95 (0-684-16940-1). These stories trace Adams's history from childhood until he becomes a parent.

2922 Hemingway, Ernest. *The Short Stories of Ernest Hemingway* (10–12). 1953, Macmillan $32.50 (0-684-15155-3); paper $10.95 (0-684-71806-5). This volume, first published in 1953, contains all the short stories written by Hemingway.

2923 Hemingway, Ernest. *The Snows of Kilimanjaro, and Other Stories* (10–12). 1987, Macmillan paper $3.95 (0-02-051830-7). This is a collection of Hemingway's best short stories.

2924 Highwater, Jamake, ed. *Words in the Blood: Contemporary Indian Writers of North and South America* (10–12). 1984, NAL paper $9.95 (0-452-00966-9). An anthology of poetry, stories, and plays by modern Indian writers. [810]

2925 Hurston, Zora Neale. *I Love Myself When I Am Laughing . . . and Then Again When I Am Looking Mean and Impressive* (10–12). 1987, Feminist Pr. paper $9.95 (0-912670-66-5). A selection of both fiction and nonfiction works by this talented black American writer with a closing essay by Alice Walker. [818]

2926 Jewett, Sarah O. *Best Stories of Sarah Orne Jewett* (10–12). Illus. 1989, Yankee paper $10.95 (0-912769-33-5). A collection of 17 short stories written by this New England writer from 1847 to 1900. (Rev: SLJ 3/89)

2927 Joyce, James. *Dubliners* (10–12). 1916, Random $6.95 (0-394-60464-4); Penguin paper $4.95 (0-14-004222-9). Catholic middle-class life in Dublin is described in this collection of stories, many of which deal with childhood and youth.

2928 Keene, Donald, ed. *Anthology of Japanese Literature from the Earliest Era to the Mid-Nineteenth Century* (10–12). Illus. 1955, Grove paper $13.95 (0-8021-5058-6). This extensive an-

thology includes excerpts from plays and novels plus stories, fairy tales, and many poems. [895.6]

2929 Keene, Donald, ed. *Modern Japanese Literature: An Anthology* (10–12). 1960, Grove paper $10.95 (0-394-17254-X). This is a collection of prose and poetry that covers Japanese literature from 1870 through the 1940s. [895.6]

2930 Kermode, Frank, and John Hollander, eds. *The Oxford Anthology of English Literature* (10–12). 2 vols. Illus. 1987, Oxford Univ. Pr. paper $21.95 each (0-19-501657-2; 0-19-501658-0). The 2 volumes in this anthology are titled: *The Middle Ages through the Eighteenth Century* and *1800 to the Present*. [820.8]

2931 Kermode, Frank, and John Hollander, eds. *The Oxford Anthology of English Literature: Major Authors Edition* (10–12). 2 vols. Illus. 1975, Oxford Univ. Pr. paper Vol. 1 $13.95; Vol. 2 $18.95 (0-19-501900-8; 0-19-501901-6). The 2 volumes in this set contain works by 30 authors. The volumes are: *From Beowulf to Johnson* and *From Blake to Auden*. [820.8]

2932 Lardner, Ring. *The Best Short Stories of Ring Lardner* (10–12). 1976, Macmillan $22.50 (0-684-14743-2); paper $7.95 (0-684-13648-1). A selection of 225 stories by this master of wry humor.

2933 Lawrence, D. H. *The Complete Short Stories* (10–12). 3 vols. 1987, Penguin paper $4.95 each (vol. 1: 0-14-004382-9; vol. 2: 0-14-004255-5; vol. 3: 0-14-004383-7). This 3 volume set includes all the stories by this writer noted for his psychological insights into human behavior.

2934 Lessing, Doris. *The Doris Lessing Reader* (10–12). 1989, Knopf $24.95 (0-394-57307-2). For mature readers here is a generous sampling of the fiction of this African writer plus a few nonfiction excerpts from her autobiographical books. (Rev: BL 2/15/89)

2935 Long, Richard A., and Eugenia W. Collier, eds. *Afro-American Writing: An Anthology of Prose and Poetry* (10–12). 2nd ed. 1985, Pennsylvania State Univ. Pr. $24.50 (0-271-00374-X). This anthology of prose and poetry by black American authors also contains critical commentary and a chronology. [810.8]

2936 McCullers, Carson. *Collected Stories* (10–12). 1987, Houghton $18.95 (0-395-44179-X); paper $11.95 (0-395-44243-5). Twenty-two stories, including "The Member of the Wedding" and "The Ballad of the Sad Cafe." (Rev: BL 6/1/87)

2937 MacDougall, Carl, ed. *The Giant Book of Scottish Short Stories* (10–12). 1989, Bedrick $29.95 (0-87226-327-4); paper $14.95 (0-87226-217-0). Fifty-one short stories by such masters as

Muriel Spark, Arthur Conan Doyle, and Saki. (Rev: BL 11/15/89; SLJ 6/90)

2938 Malamud, Bernard. *The Magic Barrel* (10–12). 1958, Farrar $14.95 (0-374-19576-5). This early collection of stories about different kinds of relationships won a National Book Award.

2939 Malamud, Bernard. *The Stories of Bernard Malamud* (10–12). 1983, Farrar $17.95 (0-374-27037-6); NAL paper $8.95 (0-452-25911-8). Each of the 25 stories included in this anthology was handpicked by the author.

2940 Malan, Robin, ed. *Ourselves in Southern Africa: An Anthology of Southern African Writing* (10–12). Illus. 1989, St. Martin's $19.95 (0-312-03194-7). Intended originally as a text, this is a collection of prose and poetry written about emotions and about social conditions in South African countries today. (Rev: BL 6/1/89) [820.9]

2941 Mancini, Pat McNees, ed. *Contemporary Latin American Short Stories* (10–12). 1979, Fawcett paper $1.95 (0-449-30844-8). This anthology includes the work of such contemporary masters as Marquez, Paz, Borges, and Fuentes.

2942 Mansfield, Katherine. *The Short Stories of Katherine Mansfield* (10–12). 1937, Knopf $22.95 (0-394-44532-5). A comprehensive collection of 88 stories by Katherine Mansfield.

2943 Markham, Beryl. *The Splendid Outcast: Beryl Markham's African Stories* (10–12). 1987, North Point $14.95 (0-86547-301-3); Dell paper $7.50 (0-440-50030-3). A collection of stories by the amazing Englishwoman Beryl Markham known during her life primarily as a daredevil aviator. (Rev: SLJ 1/88)

2944 Maugham, W. Somerset. *Collected Short Stories* (10–12). 1977, Penguin paper $4.95 (0-14-001871-9). This 4-volume collection represents the entire output of Maugham in this genre.

2945 Menton, Seymour, ed. *The Spanish American Short Story: A Critical Anthology* (10–12). 1980, Univ. of California Pr. $42.50 (0-520-03232-2); paper $12.95 (0-520-04641-1). Forty stories by such Latin American writers as Borges and Cortazar.

2946 Michie, James, ed. *The Book of Longer Short Stories* (10–12). 1975, Scarborough paper $6.95 (0-8128-1808-3). This is an anthology of such modern British writers as Huxley, Lawrence, and Maugham.

2947 Moffett, James, and Kenneth McElheny. *Points of View* (10–12). 1982, NAL paper $4.95 (0-451-62491-2). Using various fiction writing techniques as a focal point, this anthology gives examples of each.

2948 Monegal, Emir Rodríguez. *The Borzoi Anthology of Latin American Literature* (10–12). 2 vols. 1977, Knopf vol. 1 $18.95; vol. 2 $19.95 (0-394-73301-0; 0-394-73366-5). This 2-volume set begins with the writings of Columbus and the conquistadors and extends to such contemporaries as Fuentes, Borges, and Paz. [860.8]

2949 O'Connor, Flannery. *Collected Works* (10–12). 1988, Viking $30.00 (0-940450-37-2). A definitive edition of this Southern writer's work that includes short stories and novels. (Rev: SLJ 1/89)

2950 O'Connor, Flannery. *The Complete Stories* (10–12). 1971, Farrar $35.00 (0-374-12752-2); paper $9.95 (0-374-51536-0). This represents the complete output in the short story field of this southern writer.

2951 O'Connor, Frank. *Collected Stories* (10–12). 1981, Knopf $20.00 (0-394-51602-8); Random paper $2.95 (0-394-71048-7). Many of the stories in this collection reflect the boyhood of the author in County Cork, Ireland.

2952 Porter, Katherine Anne. *The Collected Stories of Katherine Anne Porter* (10–12). 1965, Harcourt paper $8.95 (0-15-618876-7). This collection includes such classics as "Pale Horse, Pale Rider," "The Leaning Tower," and "Flowering Judas."

2953 Porter, Katherine Anne. *Pale Horse, Pale Rider: Three Short Novels* (10–12). 1939, Harcourt $15.95 (0-15-170750-2). In addition to the title novella, *Noon Wine* and *Old Morality* are included.

2954 Pritchett, V. S., ed. *The Oxford Book of Short Stories* (10–12). 1981, Oxford $29.95 (0-19-214116-3); paper $11.95 (0-19-282113-X). A collection of distinguished short stories written in English during the nineteenth and twentieth centuries.

2955 Pushkin, Alexander. *Alexander Pushkin: Complete Prose Fiction* (10–12). 1983, Stanford Univ. Pr. $45.00 (0-8047-1142-9). Though most of the works collected here are fiction, such as the popular "Queen of Spades," these are also a few essays.

2956 Raffel, Burton, ed. *The Signet Classic Book of American Short Stories* (10–12). 1985, NAL paper $5.95 (0-451-52279-6). This fine anthology contains 33 stories spanning time from Washington Irving to F. Scott Fitzgerald. Also use the companion anthology *The Signet Classic Book of Contemporary Short Stories* (1982).

2957 Ravenel, Shannon, ed. *New Stories from the South: The Year's Best, 1986* (10–12). 1986, Algonquin $14.95 (0-912097-40-7); paper $9.95

(0-912697-49-0). A fine collection of 17 stories by new writers from the South. (Rev: SLJ 3/87)

2958 Saki. *The Best of Saki* (10–12). 1980, Amereon $15.95 (0-89190-115-9); Penguin paper $6.95 (0-14-004484-1). A selection of stories such as "The Open Window" that show Saki at his imaginative best.

2959 Saroyan, William. *The Man with the Heart in the Highlands & Other Early Stories* (9–12). 1989, New Directions $15.95 (0-8112-1115-0). Sixteen stories about ordinary people that usually show that innocence can triumph. (Rev: BL 10/15/89)

2960 Sillitoe, Alan. *The Loneliness of the Long-Distance Runner* (10–12). 1960, Knopf $10.95 (0-394-43389-0). Several stories in this collection explore how individuals fight the system to assert their individuality.

2961 Singer, Isaac Bashevis. *The Collected Stories of Isaac Bashevis Singer* (10–12). 1982, Farrar $19.95 (0-374-12631-3); paper $12.95 (0-374-51788-6). A collection of 47 of the best stories written by this Nobel Prize-winning author.

2962 *Six Great Modern Short Novels* (10–12). 1954, Dell paper $4.95 (0-440-37996-2). This collection includes Faulkner's *The Bear*, Melville's *Billy Budd*, Porter's *Noon Wine*, and Joyce's *The Dead*.

2963 Sohn, David A., ed. *Ten Top Stories* (9–12). 1985, Bantam paper $3.95 (0-553-26979-8). These 10 stories were chosen by teenagers as the ones that particularly interest them.

2964 Soto, Gary, ed. *California Childhood* (10–12). Illus. 1988, Creative Arts $16.95 (0-88739-062-5); paper $9.95 (0-88739-057-9). A number of writers have contributed fiction and essays on growing up in California. (Rev: SLJ 10/88) [979.4]

2965 Spencer, Elizabeth. *Jack of Diamonds* (10–12). 1988, Viking $15.95 (0-670-82261-2). For mature readers, 5 short stories that explore the inner truths that people live by. (Rev: BR 1–2/89; VOYA 2/89)

2966 Steele, Max. *The Hat of My Mother* (10–12). 1988, Algonquin $13.95 (0-912697-78-4). A group of short stories, many tinged with humor, but all dealing with poignant human experiences. (Rev: SLJ 12/88)

2967 Stegner, Wallace, and Mary Stegner, eds. *Great American Short Stories* (10–12). 1985, Dell paper $5.95 (0-440-33060-2). A useful anthology that stretches over 200 years of writing.

2968 Stones, Rosemary, ed. *More to Life Than Mr. Right: Stories for Young Feminists* (9–12). 1989, Henry Holt $12.95 (0-8050-1175-7). Eight stories by British authors about growing up female. (Rev: BL 11/1/89; BR 5–6/90; SLJ 10/89)

2969 Trevor, William, ed. *The Oxford Book of Irish Short Stories* (10–12). 1989, Oxford Univ. Pr. $24.95 (0-19-214180-5). For better readers, this is a fine cross-section of Irish writing, past and present. (Rev: BL 9/1/89; BR 10–11/89)

2970 Updike, John. *Pigeon Feathers* (10–12). 1962, Knopf $19.95 (0-394-44056-0); Fawcett paper $4.95 (0-449-21132-0). These stories cover a variety of subjects such as youth, marriage, and the family.

2971 Warren, Robert Penn, and Albert Erskine, eds. *Short Story Masterpieces* (10–12). 1954, Dell paper $6.95 (0-440-37864-8). An international collection of 36 masterpieces of short fiction.

2972 Wasserstein, Wendy. *Bachelor Girls* (10–12). 1990, Knopf $18.95 (0-394-56199-6). A collection of 29 vignettes about single life in the big city. (Rev: SLJ 8/90)

2973 Welty, Eudora. *The Collected Stories of Eudora Welty* (10–12). 1980, Harcourt $22.95 (0-15-118994-3); paper $10.95 (0-15-618921-6). This omnibus volume by one of the South's greatest writers includes stories published prior to 1980.

2974 West, Jessamyn. *Collected Stories of Jessamyn West* (10–12). 1986, Harcourt $17.95 (0-15-119010-0); paper $10.95 (0-15-618979-8). A collection of 38 previously published stories by this master storyteller. (Rev: BL 11/15/86)

2975 Wheeler, David, ed. *No, But I Saw the Movie: The Best Short Stories Ever Made into Film* (9–12). (0-14-011090-9); 1989, Penguin paper $9.95. Eighteen short stories that inspired such movies as *High Noon* and *Psycho*. (Rev: BL 7/89)

2976 Winters, Jonathan. *Winters' Tales* (10–12). 1987, Random $13.95 (0-394-56424-3). The noted comedian Jonathan Winters has written a series of short stories—some humorous and others serious. (Rev: BR 9–10/88)

2977 Woolf, Virginia. *The Virginia Woolf Reader* (10–12). 1984, Harcourt paper $10.95 (0-15-693590-2). Although some excerpts from her novels are included, this collection concentrates on the short stories, essays, letters, and diary entries of Virginia Woolf. [828]

Plays

General and Miscellaneous Collections

2978 Block, Haskell M., and Robert G. Shedd, eds. *Masters of Modern Drama* (10–12). Illus. 1962, McGraw $43.95 (0-07-553555-6). This anthology of 45 plays begins with Ibsen and ends with the 1950s. [808.82]

2979 Cerf, Bennett, and Van H. Cartmell, eds. *Thirty Famous One-Act Plays* (10–12). 1949, Modern Library $10.95 (0-394-60473-3). The playwrights range from Strindberg to Coward and Saroyan in the anthology that also includes biographical sketches. [808.82]

2980 Cerf, Bennett, and Van H. Cartmell, eds. *24 Favorite One-Act Plays* (10–12). 1958, Doubleday paper $9.95 (0-385-06617-1). An international collection of short plays—both comedies and tragedies—by such masters as Inge, Coward, and O'Neill. [808.82]

2981 Gassner, John, ed. *Twenty Best European Plays on the American Stage* (10–12). 1957, Crown $22.50 (0-517-50963-6). Some of the writers represented in this collection of twentieth-century European plays are Anouilh, Chekhov, Sartre, and Molnar. [808.82]

2982 Goldstone, Richard, and Abraham H. Lass, eds. *The Mentor Book of Short Plays* (10–12). 1989, NAL paper $4.95 (0-451-62631-1). This collection of 11 plays includes writers ranging from Chekhov to Williams. [808.2]

2983 Houghton, Norris, ed. *Romeo and Juliet and West Side Story* (10–12). 1965, Dell paper $3.95 (0-440-97483-6). This combined edition af-

fords an interesting comparison between the two versions of the same story. [808.1]

2984 Kehret, Peg. *Encore! More Winning Monologs for Young Actors* (9–12). 1988, Meriwether paper $7.95 (0-916260-54-2). A collection of 63 short pieces suitable for recitations or auditions. (Rev: SLJ 8/88) [808.85]

2985 Knee, Allan, ed. *Camelot and Idylls of the King* (10–12). 1967, Dell paper $3.50 (0-440-43948-8). Two versions of the Arthurian story: one in the poetry of Tennyson and the other in script for the Broadway musical by Alan Jay Lerner. [808.1]

2986 Nolan, Paul T. *Folk Tale Plays round the World* (9–12). 1982, Plays, Inc. $10.95 (0-8238-0253-1). This collection contains short plays based on folktales from both the Western and Eastern worlds. [808.2]

2987 Olfson, Lewy, ed. *50 Great Scenes for Student Actors* (10–12). 1970, Bantam paper $4.50 (0-553-25520-7). Scenes involving only 2 actors have been collected from such writers as Noel Coward, Anton Chekhov, and Tennessee Williams. [808.82]

2988 Shengold, Nina, ed. *The Actor's Book of Contemporary Stage Monologues* (9–12). Illus. 1987, Penguin paper $6.95 (0-14-009649-3). A splendid collection of monologues from both well-known and obscure scripts. (Rev: SLJ 1/88; VOYA 4/88) [659.1]

2989 Steffensen, James L., Jr., ed. *Great Scenes from the World Theater* (10–12). 2 vols. 1972, Avon paper $5.95 (0-380-00793-2). A collection of 180 scenes ranging from Euripides to Albee. [808.82]

Geographical Regions

Europe

GENERAL

2990 Aristophanes. *Lysistrata* (10–12). Trans. by Douglass Parker. 1970, NAL paper $3.95 (0-451-62495-5). Women decide that they have a secret weapon to end war in this ancient comedy. [882]

2991 Beckett, Samuel. *Waiting for Godot* (10–12). Illus. 1954, Grove paper $5.95 (0-8021-3034-8). The saga of 2 tramps waiting for the mysterious Godot began as a play in French and was later translated into English by the author. [842]

2992 Brecht, Bertolt. *Mother Courage and Her Children* (10–12). Ed. by Eric Bentley. 1963, Grove paper $5.95 (0-8021-3082-8). An antiwar play written at the time of Hitler's reign in Germany. [832]

2993 Brecht, Bertolt. *Two Plays* (10–12). 1983, NAL paper $4.95 (0-452-00857-3). The 2 plays included in this volume are *The Good Woman of Setzuan* and *The Caucasian Chalk Circle*. [832]

2994 Burgess, Anthony. *Cyrano de Bergerac* (9–12). 1971, Knopf $16.95 (0-394-47239-X). A new translation of the French play originally produced in 1897. [822]

2995 Chekhov, Anton. *Anton Chekhov's Plays* (10–12). Illus. 1987, Norton paper $12.95 (0-393-09163-5). In addition to the text of 4 plays (*Uncle Vanya*, *The Three Sisters*, *The Cherry Orchard*, and *The Sea Gull*), there is extensive background and critical material appended to this volume. [891.7]

2996 Chekhov, Anton. *Chekhov, The Major Plays* (10–12). 1968, NAL paper $3.50 (0-451-52270-2). The 5 plays in this collection include *The Sea Gull*, *Uncle Vanya*, and *The Three Sisters*. [891.7]

2997 Chekhov, Anton. *The Cherry Orchard* (10–12). Ed. by John Gielgud. 1963, Theatre Arts paper $3.50 (0-87830-510-6). This is a version by the actor John Gielgud of the play depicting the decline of the landed gentry in Russia at the turn of the century. [891.7]

2998 Dürrenmatt, Friedrich. *The Visit* (10–12). 1962, Grove paper $6.95 (0-394-17239-6). In this German play, a wealthy woman plans vengeance on the man who deserted her years before. [832]

2999 Fitts, Dudley, ed. *Four Greek Plays* (10–12). 1960, Harcourt paper $8.95 (0-15-632777-5). From 4 different playwrights, this anthology contains *Oedipus Rex*, *Agamemnon*, *Alcestis*, and *The Birds*. [882.08]

3000 Garcia Lorca, Federico. *Three Tragedies* (10–12). 1956, Greenwood $45.00 (0-8371-9578-0). The 3 plays included in this collection are *Blood Wedding*, *Yerma*, and *Bernarda Alba*. [862]

3001 Genet, Jean. *Blacks: A Clown Show* (10–12). Trans. by Bernard Frechtman. 1960, Grove paper $8.95 (0-394-17220-5). A surreal play in which blacks and whites exhange identities. [842]

3002 Giraudoux, Jean. *Giraudoux: Four Plays* (10–12). 1964, Hill & Wang paper $6.25 (0-8090-0712-6). The most famous play in this collection is *The Madwoman of Chaillot*, about an eccentric woman who saves Paris. [842]

3003 Gorky, Maxim. *The Lower Depths and Other Plays* (10–12). 1959, Yale Univ. Pr. paper $6.95 (0-300-00100-2). A collection of plays by the Russian playwright who often wrote about the outcasts of life. [891.7]

3004 Ibsen, Henrik. *Eight Plays* (10–12). Trans. by Eva Le Gallienne. 1981, McGraw paper $6.95 (0-07-554342-7). This collection of Ibsen's great plays includes the text of *A Doll's House* and *Hedda Gabler*. [839]

3005 Ibsen, Henrik. *An Enemy of the People* (10–12). Ed. and trans. by Arthur Miller. 1977, Penguin paper $2.95 (0-14-048140-0). This is a modern translation by Arthur Miller of the story of a doctor who cannot conform. [839]

3006 Ibsen, Henrik. *Four Great Plays* (10–12). Trans. by R. Farquharson Sharp. 1984, Bantam paper $2.95 (0-553-21280-X). The 4 plays included in this collection are *A Doll's House*, *Ghosts*, *An Enemy of the People*, and *The Wild Duck*. [808.82]

3007 Ibsen, Henrik. *Four Major Plays* (10–12). 1981, Oxford Univ. Pr. paper $4.95 (0-19-281568-7). The 4 plays included are *A Doll's House*, *Ghosts*, *Hedda Gabler*, and *The Master Builder*. [839]

3008 Ionesco, Eugene. *Four Plays* (10–12). 1988, Grove paper $8.95 (0-8021-3079-8). The 4 short plays included in this work are *The Bald Soprano*, *Jack*, *The Lesson*, and *The Chairs*. [842]

3009 Ionesco, Eugene. *Rhinoceros and Other Plays* (10–12). 1988, Grove paper $7.95 (0-8021-3098-4). The 3 satiric comedies included in this collection are *Rhinoceros*, *The Future Is in Eggs*, and *The Leader*. [842]

3010 Molière, Jean. *The Misanthrope and Other Plays* (10–12). 1989, NAL paper $3.50 (0-451-51721-0). In this classic French play, an individualist rebels against the hypocrisy around him. [842]

3011 Molière, Jean. *The Miser* (10–12). 1965, Barron's paper $4.95 (0-8120-0138-9). Greed and love are 2 subjects dealt with in this French comedy. [842]

3012 Molière, Jean. *Tartuffe, and Other Plays* (10–12). 1967, NAL paper $3.50 (0-451-52011-4). Seven of Molière's most famous plays are reprinted, including *School for Wives, School for Husbands,* and *Don Juan.* [842]

3013 Oates, Whitney J., and Eugene O'Neill Jr, eds. *Seven Famous Greek Plays* (10–12). 1955, Random paper $6.95 (0-394-70125-9). This anthology includes well-known plays by Aeschylus, Sophocles, Euripides, and Aristophanes. [882.08]

3014 Pirandello, Luigi. *Naked Masks: Five Plays* (10–12). 1957, Dutton paper $7.95 (0-525-47006-9). The plays in this collection include *Six Characters in Search of an Author, It Is So If You Think So,* and *Henry IV.* [852]

3015 Racine, Jean Baptiste. *Phaedra* (10–12). 1958, Barron's paper $4.95 (0-8120-0143-5). A reworking by this French playwright of the tragic story of a woman's love for her son. [842]

3016 Rostand, Edmond. *Cyrano de Bergerac* (10–12). 1950, Bantam paper $2.95 (0-553-21360-1). A fine translation of the play about the guardsman with the fabulous nose. [842]

3017 Sartre, Jean Paul. *No Exit, and Three Other Plays* (10–12). 1956, Vintage paper $3.95 (0-394-70016-3). The four plays by the French existential writer in this collection are *No Exit, The Flies, Dirty Hands,* and *The Respectful Prostitute.* [842]

3018 Sophocles. *Antigone* (10–12). 1973, Oxford Univ. Pr. $19.95 (0-19-501741-2). In this classic drama, Antigone defies King Creon's decree and buries the body of her dead brother. [882]

3019 Sophocles. *Electra, Antigone, Philoctetes* (10–12). 1979, Cambridge Univ. Pr. paper $7.95 (0-521-22010-6). A collection of 3 tragedies by Sophocles based on legends and myths. [882]

3020 Sophocles. *The Three Theban Plays* (10–12). 1984, Penguin paper $3.95 (0-14-044425-4). The three plays included are *Antigone, Oedipus the King,* and *Oedipus at Colonus.* [882]

3021 Strindberg, August. *The Father* (10–12). 1964, Harlan Davidson paper $4.95 (0-88295-096-7). A destructive marriage is the main subject of this tragedy. [839]

3022 Strindberg, August. *Three Plays* (10–12). 1958, Penguin paper $4.50 (0-14-044082-8). This volume contains the texts of *Miss Julie, Easter,* and *The Father.* [839]

GREAT BRITAIN AND IRELAND

3023 Besier, Rudolf. *The Barretts of Wimpole Street: A Comedy in Five Acts* (9–12). 1930, Little $14.95 (0-316-09223-1). The classic play about the courtship and marriage of Elizabeth Barrett and Robert Browning. [822]

3024 Bolt, Robert. *A Man for All Seasons* (9–12). 1962, Random $10.95 (0-394-40623-0); paper $3.50 (0-394-70321-9). The story in play form of the conflict between Sir Thomas More and Henry VIII. [822]

3025 Christie, Agatha. *The Mousetrap and Other Plays* (10–12). 1986, Bantam paper $4.95 (0-553-25902-4). Eight mystery thrillers, including *Witness for the Prosecution.* [822]

3026 Congreve, William. *The Way of the World* (10–12). 1965, Univ. of Nebraska Pr. paper $3.50 (0-8032-5354-0). This Restoration comedy of manners weaves an intricate plot that satirizes society and marriage. [822]

3027 Coward, Noel. *Three Plays* (10–12). 1981, Grove paper $7.95 (0-394-17535-2). Three of Coward's best comedies are included in this volume: *Blithe Spirit, Hay Fever,* and *Private Lives.* [822]

3028 Eliot, T. S. *The Complete Poems and Plays of T. S. Eliot, 1909–1950* (10–12). 1952, Harcourt $19.95 (0-15-121185-X). In addition to poetry, this book contains the complete text of *Murder in the Cathedral, The Family Reunion* and *The Cocktail Party.* [812]

3029 Eliot, T. S. *Murder in the Cathedral* (10–12). 1964, Harcourt paper $3.95 (0-15-663277-2). The story of the murder of Thomas à Becket as seen through the eyes of the great poet. [812]

3030 Fry, Christopher. *The Lady's Not for Burning, A Phoenix Too Frequent, and an Essay* (10–12). 1977, Oxford Univ. Pr. paper $6.95 (0-19-519916-2). The 2 most famous plays by this contemporary English playwright are included. [822]

3031 Harwood, Ronald. *The Dresser* (10–12). 1988, Grove paper $7.95 (0-394-17936-6). The last days of a faded Shakespearean actor. [822]

3032 Jonson, Ben. *Volpone* (10–12). 1962, Yale Univ. Pr. $32.50 (0-300-00622-5); paper $9.95 (0-300-00139-8). A rich man pretends to be dying to receive gifts from his friends in this early English comedy. [822]

3033 Marlowe, Christopher. *Doctor Faustus* (10–12). 1969, NAL paper $3.95 (0-451-52378-4). One of the earliest plays to deal with the story of a man who sells his soul to the devil. [822]

3034 O'Casey, Sean. *Three Plays* (10–12). 1966, St. Martin's paper $4.95 (0-312-80290-0). The 3 plays in this collection are *Juno and the Paycock, Shadow of a Gunman,* and *The Plough and the Stars.* [822]

3035 Pinter, Harold. *The Birthday Party* (10–12). 1989, Grove paper $6.95 (0-394-17232-9). Two strangers arrive at an English boarding house in this contemporary play with ambiguous meanings. [822]

3036 Shaw, George Bernard. *Caesar and Cleopatra* (10–12). 1950, Penguin paper $3.95 (0-14-048100-1). Some other individually published plays by Shaw that are suitable for this age group are *Androcles and the Lion* (1963), *Arms and the Man* (1959), and *Major Barbara* (1950). [822]

3037 Shaw, George Bernard. *Pygmalion* (10–12). 1950, Penguin paper $2.95 (0-14-048003-X). Professor Higgins takes on the challenge of changing the speech patterns of Eliza, a Cockney girl. [822]

3038 Shaw, George Bernard. *Saint Joan* (10–12). 1968, Univ. of Washington Pr., $20.00 (0-295-97885-6). In Shaw's play, Joan was killed because she was dangerous to both church and state. [822]

3039 Shaw, George Bernard. *Saint Joan, Major Barbara, Androcles and the Lion* (10–12). 1956, Random $6.95 (0-394-60480-6). In this volume, the texts of 3 of Shaw's most popular plays are given. [822]

3040 Sheridan, Richard Brinsley. *The Rivals* (10–12). Oxford Univ. Pr. paper $7.95 (0-19-831908-8). This play from 1775 is about the wooing of Lydia Languish by 2 very different suitors. [822]

3041 Sheridan, Richard Brinsley. *The School for Scandal* (10–12). 1971, Oxford Univ. Pr. paper $6.95 (0-19-911008-5). Scandalmongering and its complicated results are the subjects of this great English comedy. [822]

3042 Stoppard, Tom. *On the Razzle* (10–12). 1982, Faber paper $4.95 (0-571-11835-6). A freewheeling comedy about 2 working men on the loose in Vienna. [822]

3043 Stoppard, Tom. *Rosencrantz and Guildenstern Are Dead* (10–12). 1967, Grove paper $6.95 (0-8021-3033-X). The tragedy of Hamlet as seen through the eyes of 2 minor characters. [822]

3044 Synge, J. M. *The Playboy of the Western World* (10–12). 1968, Harper paper $6.95 (0-06-463226-1). A timid Irish peasant runs away from home because he believes he has killed his father. [822]

3045 Wilde, Oscar. *The Importance of Being Earnest* (9–12). 1976, Avon paper $2.50 (0-380-01277-4). Mistaken identities is one of the dramatic ploys used in this comedy of manners. [822]

SHAKESPEARE

3046 Armour, Richard. *Twisted Tales from Shakespeare* (9–12). 1957, McGraw paper $5.95 (0-07-002251-8). A humorous retelling of the plays of the Bard. [822.8]

3047 Chute, Marchette. *An Introduction to Shakespeare* (7–12). 1987, Scholastic paper $1.95 (0-590-30263-9). An introduction that retells the plots of his plays plus background information. [822.3]

3048 Chute, Marchette. *Stories from Shakespeare* (9–12). Illus. 1987, NAL paper $3.95 (0-451-62485-8). A clear retelling of the stories of all the plays of Shakespeare included in the first folio. [822.3]

3049 Johnston, Johanna. *Kings, Lovers, and Fools* (9–12). 1981, Scholastic paper $2.50 (0-590-41705-3). This is a simple retelling of the stories of such plays as *Hamlet, Macbeth,* and *Othello.* [822.3]

3050 Lipson, Greta Barclay, and Susan Solomon. *Romeo and Juliet: Plainspoken* (10–12). Illus. 1985, Good Apple paper $13.95 (0-86653-283-8). The book in which a modern-language version of *Romeo and Juliet* is given on one page and the Shakespeare version opposite. (Rev: SLJ 8/86) [822.3]

3051 Miles, Bernard. *Favorite Tales from Shakespeare* (7–10). Illus. 1987, Macmillan $12.95 (0-528-82100-8). A modern retelling of Shakespeare's most famous plays. [822.3]

3052 Shakespeare, William. *The Complete Works of William Shakespeare* (9–12). Illus. 1949, Doubleday paper $22.95 (0-385-00049-9). One of many editions available of the complete works of Shakespeare. [822.3]

3053 Shakespeare, William. *Four Great Comedies* (9–12). 1982, NAL paper $4.95 (0-451-52093-9). This paperback includes the full text of *The Taming of the Shrew, A Midsummer Night's Dream, Twelfth Night,* and *The Tempest.* [822.3]

3054 Shakespeare, William. *Four Great Tragedies* (9–12). 1982, NAL paper $4.95 (0-451-52318-0). The four plays included are *Hamlet, Othello, King Lear,* and *Macbeth.* [822.3]

3055 Shakespeare, William. *Hamlet* (10–12). 1981, Penguin paper $3.75 (0-14-070734-4). The classic about the melancholy prince of Denmark and his obsession with avenging his father's murder. [822.3]

3056 Shakespeare, William. *Macbeth* (10–12). 1965, Airmont paper $1.75 (0-8049-1002-2). Set in Scotland, this drama tells of the tragic results of uncontrolled ambition. [822.3]

3057 Shakespeare, William. *A Midsummer Night's Dream* (10–12). 1939, Oxford Univ. Pr. paper $5.95 (0-19-831926-2). One of many editions of this comedy about 2 pairs of lovers lost in an enchanted forest. [822.3]

3058 Shakespeare, William. *Othello* (10–12). 1958, Penguin paper $3.50 (0-14-071410-3). Unfounded jealousy brings death and downfall to a Moorish general. [822.3]

3059 Shakespeare, William. *Romeo and Juliet* (10–12). 1989, NAL paper $2.75 (0-451-52136-6). One of many editions of this play currently available. [822.3]

United States

3060 Albee, Edward. *Who's Afraid of Virginia Woolf?* (10–12). 1983, NAL paper $4.95 (0-451-15871-7). George and Martha, husband and wife, battle it out in a night to remember. Also use 2 collections of one-act plays by Albee: *American Dream and Zoo Story* (1963); *The Sandbox and Death of Bessie Smith* (1989). [812]

3061 Barnes, Clive, ed. *Best American Plays: 7th Series—1967–1973* (10–12). 1975, Crown $19.95 (0-517-51387-0). In this seventh in the *Best American Plays* series the contents include *Little Murders* and *The Price*. The eighth series, also edited by Clive Barnes, covers the years 1974 to 1982. [812.08]

3062 Blinn, William. *Brian's Song* (9–12). 1983, Bantam paper $2.95 (0-553-26618-7). This edition is the screenplay of the television movie about the doomed football player Brian Piccolo. [808.1]

3063 Cerf, Bennett, ed. *Plays of Our Time* (10–12). 1967, Random $22.95 (0-394-40661-3). There are 9 plays in this anthology, including *A Streetcar Named Desire, Mister Roberts, A Man for All Seasons,* and *A Raisin in the Sun*. [812.08]

3064 Clurman, Harold, ed. *Famous American Plays of the 1960s* (10–12). 1972, Dell paper $6.95 (0-440-32609-5). Some of the plays included are *Hogan's Goat, The Boys in the Band,* and *Benito Cereno*. [812]

3065 Clurman, Harold, ed. *Famous American Plays of the 1930s* (10–12). 1980, Dell paper

$6.95 (0-440-32478-5). The 6 plays in this collection include *Awake and Sing, Of Mice and Men,* and *The Time of Your Life*. [812]

3066 Fuller, Charles. *A Soldier's Play* (10–12). 1982, Hill & Wang paper $6.95 (0-374-52148-4). For mature readers, a powerful play involving murder in a segregated army camp during World War II. [812]

3067 Gallo, Donald R., ed. *Center Stage: One-Act Plays for Teenage Readers and Actors* (7–12). 1990, Harper LB $16.89 (0-06-022171-2). A collection of 10 one-act plays especially written for this collection by such authors as Walter Dean Myers and Ouida Sebestyen. (Rev: BL 12/1/90; SLJ 9/90) [812]

3068 Gassner, John, ed. *Best American Plays: 3d Series—1945–1951* (10–12). 1952, Crown $19.95 (0-517-50950-4). This collection includes *Death of a Salesman, A Streetcar Named Desire,* and 15 others. John Gassner also edited the fourth series (1951–1957), the fifth series (1957–1963), and the sixth series (1963–1967), as well as a supplementary volume that covers 1918 to 1958. [812.08]

3069 Gassner, John, ed. *Best Plays of the Modern American Theatre: 2nd Series* (10–12). 1947, Crown $23.95 (0-517-50948-2). The complete texts of 17 plays are given, each of which was produced during World War II (1939–1945). [812.08]

3070 Gassner, John, ed. *Twenty Best Plays of the Modern American Theatre* (10–12). 1939, Crown $22.50 (0-517-50964-4). This volume covers the best American plays of the 1930s. [812.08]

3071 Gassner, John, ed. *Twenty-Five Best Plays of the Modern American Theatre* (10–12). 1949, Crown $16.95 (0-517-50390-5). This anthology covers the years 1916 through 1929 and includes such plays as *Porgy, What Price Glory?, The Front Page,* and *Desire under the Elms*. [812.08]

3072 Gassner, John, and Mollie Gassner, eds. *Best Plays of the Early American Theatre: From the Beginning to 1916* (10–12). 1967, Crown $27.95 (0-517-50949-0). Sixteen plays are included in this anthology, including *Uncle Tom's Cabin, The Count of Monte Cristo,* and *The Octoroon*. [812.08]

3073 Geiogamah, Hanay. *New Native American Drama: Three Plays* (10–12). 1980, Univ. of Oklahoma Pr. paper $7.95 (0-8061-1586-6). Three plays that depict the problems of American Indians today. [812]

3074 Gibson, William. *The Miracle Worker: A Play for Television* (7–12). 1957, Knopf $16.95 (0-394-40630-3); Bantam paper $3.25 (0-553-

24778-6). An expanded version of the television play about Annie Sullivan and Helen Keller. [812]

3075 Goldman, James. *A Lion in Winter* (10–12). 1983, Penguin paper $4.95 (0-14-048174-5). A rich historical play about Henry II, his wife Eleanor of Aquitaine, and their 3 sons. [812]

3076 Goodrich, Frances. *The Diary of Anne Frank* (7–12). Illus. 1956, Random $12.95 (0-394-40564-1). A translation into play format of the famous diary kept by the Jewish girl hiding from the Nazis. [812]

3077 Halline, Allan G., ed. *Six Modern American Plays* (10–12). 1966, McGraw paper $6.95 (0-07-553660-9). The 6 plays in this collection are *The Glass Menagerie, Mister Roberts, Emperor Jones, The Man Who Came to Dinner, The Little Foxes,* and *Winterset.* [812]

3078 Handman, Wynn, ed. *Modern American Scenes for Student Actors* (9–12). 1978, Bantam paper $4.50 (0-553-25844-3). A total of 50 scenes are included plus information on the plot of each play and its playwright. [812.08]

3079 Hansberry, Lorraine. *A Raisin in the Sun: A Drama in Three Acts* (7–12). Illus. 1987, NAL paper $8.95 (0-452-25942-8). The drama that involves a middle-class black family in Chicago. [812]

3080 Hatch, James V., ed. *Black Theater, U.S.A. Forty-five Plays by Black Americans, 1847–1974* (10–12). 1974, Free Pr. $29.95 (0-02-914160-5). An extensive sampling of works by black American playwrights that includes works by Langston Hughes, James Baldwin, Lorraine Hansberry, and Alice Childress. [812.08]

3081 Hellman, Lillian. *Six Plays by Lillian Hellman* (9–12). 1979, Random paper $12.95 (0-394-74112-9). This collection includes *Watch on the Rhine, The Little Foxes,* and *The Children's Hour.* [812]

3082 Hewes, Henry, ed. *Famous American Plays of the 1940s* (10–12). 1960, Dell paper $6.95 (0-440-32490-4). The 6 plays in this collection include *The Skin of Our Teeth, All My Sons,* and *Member of the Wedding.* [812]

3083 Hoffman, Ted, ed. *Famous American Plays of the 1970s* (10–12). 1981, Dell paper $6.95 (0-440-32537-4). Three of the 6 plays included are *Moonchildren, Gemini,* and *Same Time Next Year.* [812]

3084 Inge, William. *Four Plays* (9–12). 1979, Grove paper $9.95 (0-394-17075-X). The 4 plays are *Bus Stop, Come Back, Little Sheba, Picnic,* and *Dark at the Top of the Stairs.* [812]

3085 Jones, Tom, and Harvey Schmidt. *The Fantasticks: The Thirtieth Anniversay Edition* (10–12). 1990, Applause $24.95 (1-55783-074-6). The text and lyrics of the long-running musical about young love and meddling fathers. [812]

3086 Kamerman, Sylvia E., ed. *Space and Science Fiction Plays for Young People* (9–12). 1983, Plays $13.95 (0-8238-0252-3). A collection of easily produced one-act plays dealing with such subjects as extraterrestrials and robots. [812]

3087 Karton, Joshua, ed. *Film Scenes for Actors, Vol. 2* (10–12). 1987, Bantam paper $5.95 (0-553-26804-X). This collection gives important excerpts from a number of important films. [812]

3088 Kesselring, Joseph. *Three Plays about Crime and Criminals* (10–12). Ed. by George Freedley. 1962, Pocket paper $3.95 (0-671-47229-1). *Arsenic and Old Lace, Kind Lady,* and *Detective Story* are the 3 plays included. [812]

3089 Lamb, Wendy, ed. *The Ground Zero Club and Other Prize-Winning Plays* (9–12). 1987, Dell paper $3.50 (0-440-93176-2). Six prize-winning plays by teenagers that are part of the Young Playwrights Festival of the Foundation of the Dramatists Guild. An earlier collection was *Meeting the Winter Bike Rider* (1986). (Rev: BL 3/1/88; SLJ 3/88) [812]

3090 Lamb, Wendy, ed. *Meeting the Winter Bike Rider and Other Prize Winning Plays* (9–12). 1986, Dell paper $3.50 (0-440-95548-3). A collection of plays by 10- to 18-year-old youngsters that represent the 1983 and 1984 winners of the Young Playwrights Festival. (Rev: BL 9/1/86; SLJ 10/86; VOYA 6/86) [812]

3091 Lamb, Wendy, ed. *Sparks in the Park and Other Prize-Winning Plays* (9–12). 1989, Dell paper $3.50 (0-440-20415-1). A stimulating collection of 7 plays written by teenagers ages 16 to 18. (Rev: BL 11/15/89; BR 1–2/90; SLJ 1/90; VOYA 2/90) [812.54]

3092 Laurents, Arthur. *West Side Story: A Musical* (7–12). Illus. 1958, Random $13.95 (0-394-40788-1). This contemporary variation on the Romeo and Juliet story contains the script and lyrics by Stephen Sondheim. [812]

3093 Lawrence, Jerome, and Robert E. Lee. *Inherit the Wind* (10–12). 1969, Bantam paper $2.95 (0-553-26915-1). A dramatic re-creation of the evolution trial that pitted Darrow against Bryan. [812]

3094 Lawrence, Jerome, and Robert E. Lee. *The Night Thoreau Spent in Jail* (9–12). 1983, Bantam paper $3.95 (0-553-27838-X). A play based on the incident when Thoreau refused to pay taxes. [812]

3095 Lerner, Alan Jay. *Camelot* (7–12). 1961, Random $13.95 (0-394-40521-8). This musical tells of the tragic love of King Arthur and Guenevere. [812]

3096 Lerner, Alan Jay. *My Fair Lady* (7–12). 1978, NAL $12.95 (0-451-13890-2). This adaptation of Shaw's *Pygmalion* contains both the script and the lyrics by Lerner. [812]

3097 Levin, Ira. *Deathtrap* (9–12). 1979, Random $9.95 (0-394-50727-4). A suspenseful mystery with interesting plot twists that keep the reader guessing. [812]

3098 Lindsay, Howard. *The Sound of Music* (7–12). Illus. 1960, Random $12.95 (0-394-40724-5). A musical version of the story of the Von Trapp family and their escape from Nazi Germany. [812]

3099 Lindsay, Howard, and Russell Crouse. *Three Comedies of American Family Life* (10–12). Ed. by Joseph E. Mersand. 1961, Pocket paper $3.95 (0-671-42886-1). The 3 comedies included in this collection are *You Can't Take It with You, I Remember Mama,* and *Life with Father.* [812]

3100 Luce, William. *The Belle of Amherst: A Play Based on the Life of Emily Dickinson* (9–12). 1978, Houghton paper $7.95 (0-395-26253-4). A one-woman play based on the life of Emily Dickinson. [812]

3101 Mcgowan, Kenneth, ed. *Famous American Plays of the 1920s* (10–12). 1950, Dell paper $6.95 (0-440-32466-1). The complete text of such plays as *What Price Glory?, Porgy and Bess,* and *Street Scene.* [812]

3102 MacLeish, Archibald. *Six Plays* (10–12). 1980, Houghton $10.00 (0-395-28419-8). Six plays in verse that date from the 1930s through the 1950s. [812]

3103 Medoff, Mark. *Children of a Lesser God* (9–12). 1980, Smith Gibbs $5.95 (0-87905-272-4). The story of the love between a teacher at a school for the deaf and one of his students. [812]

3104 Miller, Arthur. *Arthur Miller's Collected Plays* (10–12). 1987, Viking $17.95 (0-670-13598-4). This volume contains Miller's more recent plays. [812]

3105 Miller, Arthur. *The Crucible* (10–12). 1987, Penguin paper $4.95 (0-14-048138-9). A powerful play that deals with the Salem witch trials of 1692. [812]

3106 Miller, Arthur. *Death of a Salesman* (10–12). 1949, Viking $17.95 (0-670-13598-4); paper $4.50 (0-14-048134-6). The powerful drama of Willy Loman and his tragic end. [812]

3107 Miller, Arthur. *The Portable Arthur Miller* (10–12). 1987, Penguin paper $9.95 (0-14-015071-4). In addition to the complete texts of 4 of Miller's best plays, this collection contains some representative fiction and nonfiction. [818]

3108 Murray, John. *Modern Monologues for Young People* (9–12). 1982, Plays, Inc. paper $10.95 (0-8238-0255-8). This is a collection of 24 short humorous monologues on a variety of subjects. [812]

3109 Nemiroff, Robert, ed. *Lorraine Hansberry: The Collected Last Plays* (10–12). 1983, NAL paper $8.95 (0-452-25414-0). This collection of 3 plays includes *Les Blancs, The Drinking Gourd,* and *What Use Are Flowers?* [812]

3110 O'Neal, Regina. *And Then the Harvest: Three Television Plays* (10–12). 1974, Broadside Pr. paper $6.00 (0-910296-90-1). These 3 plays deal with racial prejudice as experienced by different black Americans. [812]

3111 O'Neill, Eugene. *Anna Christie, The Emperor Jones, and The Hairy Ape* (10–12). 1972, Random paper $7.95 (0-394-71855-0). These 3 early plays established O'Neill's reputation as an important American playwright. [812]

3112 O'Neill, Eugene. *The Iceman Cometh* (10–12). 1946, Vintage paper $3.95 (0-394-70018-X). A lengthy play about hopes and dreams set in a New York bar. [812]

3113 O'Neill, Eugene. *Long Day's Journey into Night* (10–12). 1956, Yale Univ. Pr. $18.50 (0-300-00807-4); paper $6.95 (0-300-04601-4). A largely autobiographical play about the tormented Tyrone family. [812]

3114 Pomerance, Bernard. *The Elephant Man* (9–12). 1987, Grove paper $6.95 (0-8021-3041-0). The touching drama of a grossly deformed man who wanted to live a normal life. [822]

3115 Richards, Stanley, ed. *The Most Popular Plays of the American Theatre: Ten of Broadway's Longest-Running Plays* (9–12). Illus. 1979, Scarborough House $24.95 (0-8128-2682-5). The 10 hits include *Life with Father, Tobacco Road, Abie's Irish Rose,* and more recent plays like *Same Time, Next Year* and *Barefoot in the Park.* [812.08]

3116 Schulman, Michael, and Eva Mekler, eds. *The Actor's Scenebook, Vol. 2* (10–12). 1987, Bantam paper $4.95 (0-553-26581-4). This is a fine collection of scenes and monologues. Also use volume I (1984). [812]

3117 Shaffer, Peter. *Amadeus* (9–12). 1981, Harper $11.45 (0-06-014032-1); paper $7.95 (0-06-090783-5). A highly subjective view in dramatic format of the relationship between Mozart and Salieri. [822]

3118 Shaffer, Peter. *Equus* (9–12). 1984, Penguin paper $4.50 (0-14-048185-0). The play about a probing confrontation between a disturbed young man and a psychiatrist. [822]

3119 Shange, Ntozake. *For Colored Girls Who Have Considered Suicide/When the Rainbow Is Enuf* (10–12). 1987, Bantam paper $3.50 (0-553-26212-2). Seven characters in a dramatic poem about being black women. [812]

3120 Shepard, Sam. *A Lie of the Mind: A Play in Three Acts* (10–12). 1987, NAL $14.95 (0-453-00530-6); paper $6.95 (0-452-25869-3). An American play that deals with complicated subjects including insanity and alienation. For mature readers. (Rev: SLJ 6–7/87) [812]

3121 Simon, Neil. *Barefoot in the Park* (9–12). Illus. 1984, Random $11.95 (0-394-40515-3). A witty play about a young married couple coping in a New York apartment. [812]

3122 Simon, Neil. *Brighton Beach Memoirs* (7–12). 1984, Random $10.95 (0-394-53739-4); NAL paper $3.95 (0-451-14765-0). The first of 3 semi-autobiographical plays about the growing pains of Brooklyn-born Eugene Jerome. The other 2 are: *Biloxi Blues* (1986); *Broadway Bound* (1988). [812]

3123 Simon, Neil. *Broadway Bound* (9–12). 1987, Random $11.95 (0-394-56395-6). The concluding semiautobiographical play in the humorous but touching trilogy that included the also-recommended *Brighton Beach Memoirs* (1984) and *Biloxi Blues* (1986). (Rev: BL 3/1/88; SLJ 5/88) [812]

3124 Simon, Neil. *The Collected Plays of Neil Simon* (9–12). 1979, Random $29.95 (0-394-50770-3); NAL paper $12.95 (0-452-25871-5). This volume includes such plays as *The Sunshine Boys* and *California Suite*. Earlier plays are found in volume one, published by NAL. [812]

3125 Simon, Neil. *The Odd Couple* (9–12). 1966, Random $10.95 (0-394-40649-4). One of Simon's earlier comedies, which later became a popular television series. [812]

3126 Simon, Neil. *They're Playing Our Song* (9–12). 1980, Random $9.95 (0-397-51069-0). The script of this show business musical contains lyrics by Carol Bayer Sager. [812]

3127 Stein, Joseph, and Sheldon Harnick. *Fiddler on the Roof: Based on Sholem Aleichem's Stories* (9–12). 1990, Limelight paper $7.95 (0-87910-136-9). The script and lyrics of this musical set in prerevolutionary Russia. [812]

3128 Strasberg, Lee, ed. *Famous American Plays of the 1950s* (10–12). 1963, Dell paper $6.95 (0-440-32491-2). The 6 plays in this collection include *Tea and Sympathy, The Zoo Story,* and *A Hatful of Rain*. [812]

3129 Thomas, Dylan. *Under Milk Wood* (10–12). 1954, New Directions paper $5.95 (0-8112-0209-7). A dream-like play about life in a small Welsh seacoast village. [822]

3130 Thompson, Ernest. *On Golden Pond* (9–12). 1981, Signet paper $3.95 (0-451-16160-2). A happily married older couple are reunited with their daughter and grandson in this touching drama. [812]

3131 Vonnegut, Kurt. *Happy Birthday, Wanda June* (10–12). 1987, Delacorte paper $9.95 (0-385-28386-5). A humorous reworking of the story of Ulysses, now named Harold Ryan and his return to his wife Penelope. [812]

3132 Warren, Robert Penn. *All the King's Men* (10–12). 1960, Harcourt $15.95 (0-394-40502-1); paper $8.95 (0-15-604762-4). An adaptation of the author's novel about the rise and fall of a Southern political despot named Willie Stark. [812]

3133 Wasserman, Dale. *Man of La Mancha* (7–12). Illus. 1966, Random $9.95 (0-394-40621-1); paper $6.95 (0-394-40619-2). Based loosely on Cervantes' novel, this is the story of the adventures of Don Quixote and his servant Sancho Panza. [812]

3134 Weintraub, Stanley, ed. *The Portable Bernard Shaw* (10–12). 1987, Penguin paper $9.95 (0-14-015090-0). A generous sampling of Shaw's work, including the complete text of such plays as *The Devil's Disciple, Pygmalion,* and *Heartbreak House*. [822]

3135 Wilder, Thornton. *Our Town* (10–12). 1960, Harper $13.45 (0-06-014645-1); paper $4.95 (0-06-080779-2). Life in the town of Grover's Corners in New Hampshire as portrayed in the prize-winning play. [812]

3136 Wilder, Thornton. *Three Plays* (10–12). 1987, Harper paper $9.95 (0-06-091293-6). This volume contains the complete scripts of *Our Town, The Skin of Our Teeth,* and *The Matchmaker*. [812]

3137 Williams, Tennessee. *Cat on a Hot Tin Roof* (10–12). 1975, New Directions paper $7.95 (0-8112-0567-3). Maggie, nicknamed the Cat, and her husband's family struggle over an inheritance in this play set on a southern plantation. [812]

3138 Williams, Tennessee. *The Glass Menagerie* (9–12). Illus. 1949, New Directions paper $4.95

(0-8112-0220-8). A tender play about a lonely girl, her collection of glass animals, and her gentleman caller. [812]

3139 Williams, Tennessee. *A Streetcar Named Desire* (10–12). 1980, New Directions paper $5.95 (0-8112-0765-X). The tragic story of Blanche, her sister Stella, and husband Stanley, set in New Orleans. [812]

3140 Wilson, August. *Fences* (10–12). 1986, NAL paper $6.95 (0-452-25842-1). The prize-winning play about a black family living in Pittsburgh in 1957 and ruled by a domineering father. (Rev: BL 9/1/86) [812]

3141 Wilson, Lanford. *Talley's Folly* (10–12). 1980, Hill & Wang paper $5.95 (0-374-52157-3). A difficult courtship is completed in a boathouse in this prize-winning play. [812]

3142 Zindel, Paul. *The Effect of Gamma Rays on Man-in-the-Moon Marigolds* (9–12). Illus. 1971, Harper $12.75 (0-06-026829-8); Bantam paper $3.95 (0-553-29028-7). This play deals with a widow and her 2 daughters, one who finds fulfillment in a science project. [812]

Other Regions

3143 Fugard, Athol. *"Master Harold" . . . and the Boys* (10–12). 1984, Penguin paper $4.95 (0-14-048187-7). In this South African play a young man raised by 2 loving black servants cannot escape feelings of prejudice. [822]

3144 Keene, Donald, ed. *Twenty Plays of the Nō Theatre* (10–12). Illus. 1970, Columbia Univ. Pr. $35.00 (0-231-03454-7); paper $17.50 (0-231-03455-5). This is a collection of representative works of the distinctly Japanese art form. [895.6]

3145 Pound, Ezra, and Ernest Fenollosa eds. *The Classic Noh Theatre of Japan* (10–12). 1959, New Directions paper $6.95 (0-8112-0152-X). A collection of classical Japanese Noh verse dramas. [895.6]

Poetry

General and Miscellaneous Collections

3146 Abse, Dannie, and Joan Abse, eds. *Voices in the Gallery: Poems & Pictures* (10–12). Illus. 1987, Salem House $24.95 (0-946590-54-0); paper $14.95 (0-946590-53-2). A collection of 75 contemporary poems matched to an equal number of artworks that complement them. (Rev: BL 9/1/87) [808.81]

3147 Aisenberg, Nadya, ed. *We Animals: Poems of Our World* (9–12). 1989, Sierra Club $22.95 (0-87156-679-6); paper $10.95 (0-87156-685-0). Classic and contemporary poets are represented in this collection of poetry about animals. (Rev: BL 9/1/89; BR 3–4/90; VOYA 2/90) [808.81]

3148 Allison, Alexander W., et al., eds. *The Norton Anthology of Poetry* (10–12). 1983, Norton paper $25.95 (0-393-95242-8). A chronologically arranged anthology of British and American poetry from Chaucer on. [821.08]

3149 Auden, W. H., ed. *The Oxford Book of Light Verse* (9–12). 1987, Oxford Univ. Pr. paper $8.95 (0-19-881331-7). Using a broad definition for light verse (not just humorous), the editor has produced an extensive anthology that has general appeal. [821.08]

3150 Baker, Russell, ed. *The Norton Book of Light Verse* (10–12). 1986, Norton $17.95 (0-393-02366-4). An amusing collection that spans centuries and a large number of past and present writers. (Rev: BL 1/1/87) [821]

3151 Blake, William. *The Complete Poetry and Prose of William Blake* (10–12). Illus. 1982, Univ. of California Pr. $45.00 (0-520-04473-8);

Anchor Bks. paper $17.95 (0-385-15213-2). This collection of prose and poetry includes Blake's letters and critical commentary from the editor. [828]

3152 Blake, William. *The Portable Blake* (10–12). Illus. 1987, Penguin paper $9.95 (0-14-015026-9). This generous collection gives a selection of prose, poetry, and drawings, plus a lengthy critical introduction. [828]

3153 Ciardi, John, and Miller Williams. *How Does a Poem Mean?* (10–12). 1975, Houghton $19.95 (0-395-18605-6). By analyzing several poems, the authors explain the value and nature of poetry. [821.08]

3154 Coleridge, Samuel Taylor. *The Portable Coleridge* (10–12). 1987, Penguin paper $9.95 (0-14-015048-X). In addition to a fine sampling of Coleridge's poetry, this compendium includes sections on his prose works. [828]

3155 Cook, Roy J., comp. *One Hundred and One Famous Poems* (7–12). 1985, Contemporary $12.95 (0-8092-5833-1). A collection of all the famous poetic masterpieces in the English language. (Rev: BR 5–6/86) [808.8]

3156 Dore, Anita, ed. *The Premier Book of Major Poets* (10–12). 1988, Fawcett paper $4.95 (0-449-44507-0). This is a collection of English and American poetry from the Middle Ages to the present. [808.1]

3157 Ellmann, Richard, and Robert O'Clair, eds. *The Norton Anthology of Modern Poetry* (10–12). 2nd ed. 1988, Norton paper $29.95 (0-393-95636-9). This collection begins with Walt Whitman and ends with James Tate. [821.08]

3158 Felleman, Hazel, ed. *Poems That Live Forever* (9–12). 1965, Doubleday $17.95 (0-385-

00358-7). A collection of familiar poems arranged under subject like love, friendship, and home. [821.08]

3159 Foss, Michael, ed. *Poetry of the World Wars* (9–12). 1990, Bedrick $18.95 (0-87226-336-3). A collection of 181 poems from 65 poets dealing with the 2 world wars. (Rev: BL 8/90) [821]

3160 Foster, John, comp. *Let's Celebrate: Festival Poems* (8–12). Illus. 1990, Oxford Univ. Pr. LB $13.95 (0-19-276083-1). With many illustrations, this handsome volume includes poems on many of the world's holidays by 41 English-speaking poets. (Rev: VOYA 8/90) [808.81]

3161 Giddings, Robert. *The War Poets* (10–12). Illus. 1988, Orion $24.95 (0-517-56804-7). In addition to describing the World War I poets and how they revolutionized the form and content of poetry, the author supplies the reader with a generous selection of examples. (Rev: SLJ 12/88) [808.1]

3162 Gordon, Ruth, sel. *Under All Silences: Shades of Love* (8–12). 1987, Harper LB $12.89 (0-06-022155-0). Sixty-six love poems, from Ancient Egypt to modern days. (Rev: BR 3–4/88; SLJ 10/87; VOYA 4/88) [808.1]

3163 Grigson, Geoffrey, ed. *The Faber Book of Nonsense Verse* (10–12). 1975, Faber $12.95 (0-571-11356-7). With emphasis on English writers, this is a wonderful collection of silly and witty poems. [808.1]

3164 Grigson, Geoffrey, ed. *The Oxford Book of Satirical Verse* (10–12). 1980, Oxford Univ. Pr. $29.95 (0-19-214110-4); paper $12.95 (0-19-281425-7). This collection of 232 satirical poems begins with the sixteenth century and extends to the present. [821.08]

3165 Harrison, Michael, and Christopher Stuart-Clark, eds. *The Oxford Book of Christmas Poems* (7–12). Illus. 1984, Oxford Univ. Pr. $12.95 (0-19-276051-3); paper $7.95 (0-19-276060-7). A total of 120 British and American poems are included. [808.81]

3166 Harrison, Michael, and Christopher Stuart-Clark, eds. *Peace and War* (7–12). Illus. 1989, Oxford Univ. Pr. $17.95 (0-19-276069-6). An anthology of war poetry in which most of the entries depict the waste and tragedy that war brings. (Rev: BL 1/1/90; VOYA 4/90) [808.81]

3167 Janeczko, Paul B., ed. *Going Over to Your Place: Poems for Each Other* (9–12). 1987, Macmillan $13.95 (0-02-747670-7). A collection of modern poems that deal with love, family, and friendship. (Rev: BL 4/1/87; SLJ 5/87; VOYA 12/87) [811]

3168 Kinsley, James, ed. *The Oxford Book of Ballads* (10–12). 1982, Oxford Univ. Pr. paper $13.95 (0-19-281330-7). The texts of 150 ballads plus 80 musical settings are included in this volume. [821.08]

3169 Koch, Kenneth, and Kate Farrell, eds. *Sleeping on the Wing: An Anthology of Modern Poetry* (7–12). 1981, Random $14.95 (0-394-50974-9); paper $7.95 (0-394-74364-4). A selection of poems from 23 poets with introductions and commentaries for each poet. [808.81]

3170 Linthwaite, Illona, ed. *Ain't I a Woman! A Book of Women's Poetry from around the World* (10–12). 1988, Bedrick $14.95 (0-87226-187-5). An international collection of poetry that expresses the varied and sensitive attitudes of women. (Rev: BR 3–4/89) [808.1]

3171 McCullough, Frances, ed. *Earth, Air, Fire, & Water* (9–12). Rev. ed. 1989, Harper LB $13.89 (0-06-024208-6). A collection of poems from many cultures that have been chosen for their specific appeal to young adults. (Rev: BL 5/15/89; SLJ 6/89; VOYA 8/89) [808.81]

3172 McCullough, Frances, ed. *Love Is Like the Lion's Tooth: An Anthology of Love Poems* (8–12). 1984, Harper LB $12.89 (0-06-024139-X). A collection of 76 poems about love that range from Sappho to the twentieth century. [808.81]

3173 Opie, Iona, and Peter Opie, eds. *The Oxford Book of Narrative Verse* (9–12). 1983, Oxford Univ. Pr. paper $9.95 (0-19-282243-8). A collection of 46 story poems chiefly by British poets with some representation from Americans. [821.08]

3174 Richman, Robert, ed. *The Direction of Poetry* (10–12). 1988, Houghton $19.95 (0-395-45426-3). A collection of poems all written since 1975 by 76 different poets, with an excellent introduction on the state of modern poetry. (Rev: BR 5–6/89) [808.1]

3175 Stallworthy, Jon, ed. *A Book of Love Poetry* (10–12). 1974, Oxford Univ. Pr. $24.95 (0-19-519774-7); paper $9.95 (0-19-504232-8). A collection of poems representing 2000 years of history arranged by subjects reflecting various aspects of love. [821.08]

3176 Stallworthy, Jon, ed. *First Lines: Poems Written in Youth from Herbert to Heaney* (10–12). 1988, Oxford Univ. Pr. paper $7.95 (0-19-282020-6). This is an interesting account of the first verse written by poets who would later become famous. (Rev: SLJ 11/87) [808.1]

3177 Stallworthy, Jon, ed. *The Oxford Book of War Poetry* (10–12). 1984, Oxford Univ. Pr. $27.95 (0-19-214125-2). This anthology covers war poetry from ancient times to Vietnam and contemporary Northern Ireland. [808.81]

3178 Swope, Mary, and Walter H. Kerr, eds. *American Classic: Car Poems for Collectors* (9–12). Illus. 1986, SCOP $8.95 (0-930526-07-4). A diverse collection of poetry that celebrates the automobile and the joys and sorrows of owning one. (Rev: BL 3/15/86) [811.5]

3179 Tomlinson, Charles, ed. *The Oxford Book of Verse in English Translation* (10–12). 1980, Oxford Univ. Pr. paper $12.95 (0-19-281426-5). A collection of verse in translation that covers many languages and historical periods. [808.81]

Geographical Regions

Europe

GENERAL

3180 Auster, Paul, ed. *The Random House Book of Twentieth-Century French Poetry* (10–12). 1987, Random paper $19.95 (0-394-71748-1). A fine bilingual collection that covers the works of 48 French poets. [841.08]

3181 El Cid Campeador. *The Poem of the Cid* (10–12). Trans. by R. Hamilton and J. Perry. 1985, Penguin paper $5.95 (0-14-044446-7). One of many editions of this epic poem about the famous Castilian warrior. [861]

3182 Garcia Lorca, Federico. *Poet in New York* (10–12). Trans. by Greg Simon and Steven F. White. Illus. 1988, Farrar $25.00 (0-374-23539-2). A collection of early Garcia Lorca poems in English and Spanish that describe the loneliness of a foreign student studying in America. (Rev: SLJ 12/88) [809.1]

3183 Homer. *The Iliad* (10–12). 1989, Doubleday $15.00 (0-385-05940-X); paper $6.50 (0-385-05941-8). One of many recommended editions of this great Greek epic about the Trojan War. [883]

3184 Homer. *The Odyssey* (10–12). 1979, Ohio Univ. Pr. $15.00 (0-8214-0433-4); Oxford Univ. Pr. paper $3.50 (0-19-281542-3). These 2 editions represent the many available of this epic poem about the wanderings of Ulysses on his way home from the Trojan War. [883]

3185 Ovid. *Metamorphoses* (10–12). 1960, NAL paper $4.95 (0-451-62622-2). One of several editions of these classic poems with mythological and historical figures connected with ancient Rome. [873]

3186 Rilke, Rainer Maria. *Selected Poems of Rainer Maria Rilke* (10–12). 1981, Harper $15.45 (0-06-010432-5). This is a bilingual selection of the most important and most popular of Rilke's poems. [831]

3187 Virgil. *The Aeneid of Virgil* (10–12). 1981, Bantam paper $2.95 (0-553-21041-6). One of several fine editions of the epic poem about the journey of Aeneas from Troy to Italy. [873]

GREAT BRITAIN AND IRELAND

3188 Amis, Kingsley, ed. *The New Oxford Book of English Light Verse* (10–12). 1978, Oxford Univ. Pr. $25.00 (0-19-221862-5). An anthology of poetry full of whimsy and laughter that includes the work of a few Americans. [821.08]

3189 Auden, W. H. *Collected Poems* (10–12). 1976, Random $39.95 (0-394-40895-0). This is the definitive collection of all the poems Auden wished to preserve. [821]

3190 Barron, W. R., ed. *Sir Gawain and the Green Knight* (10–12). 1976, Barnes & Noble paper $14.95 (0-06-490311-7). A fine edition of the medieval poem dealing with the testing of Gawain's courage. [821]

3191 *Beowulf* (10–12). Trans. by Albert W. Haley. 1978, Branden Pr. paper $7.50 (0-8283-1713-5). This is only one of many editions of the ancient epic of a hero and his dragon-slaying quest. [829]

3192 Browning, Elizabeth Barrett. *The Poetical Works of Elizabeth Barrett Browning* (10–12). 1974, Houghton $24.95 (0-395-18012-0). A volume that includes the complete poems of Elizabeth Barrett Browning, with an introduction that evaluates her output. [821]

3193 Browning, Elizabeth Barrett. *Sonnets from the Portuguese* (10–12). 1932, Harper $10.45 (0-06-010555-0). These sonnets written over a 7-year period were supposedly inspired by the poet's love for her husband. [821]

3194 Browning, Robert. *Robert Browning's Poetry: Authoritative Texts, Criticism* (10–12). 1987, Norton paper $14.95 (0-393-09092-2). A selection of poems that covers all of the poet's output, with a concentration on the major works. [821]

3195 Burns, Robert. *The Poetical Works of Burns* (10–12). 1974, Houghton $29.95 (0-395-18486-X). This volume contains the complete poems of this Scottish poet who spoke for the common man. [821]

3196 Byron, George Gordon. *The Poetical Works of Byron* (10–12). 1975, Houghton $30.00 (0-395-20431-3). A large volume that contains the complete poetic works of Byron, including "Childe Harold's Pilgrimage" and "Don Juan." [821]

3197 Carroll, Lewis. *Poems of Lewis Carroll* (9–12). Illus. 1973, Harper LB $11.89 (0-690-04540-9). The entire poetic output of Carroll is included in this volume, plus a biographical introduction. [821]

3198 Donne, John. *The Complete English Poems of John Donne* (10–12). 1985, Dent $24.50 (0-460-10091-2); paper $8.95 (0-460-11091-8). The definitive edition of Donne's poems, with extensive notes and varient readings. [821]

3199 Eliot, T. S. *Collected Poems, 1909–1962* (10–12). 1963, Harcourt $16.95 (0-15-118978-1). This volume covers all the major poems by Eliot. [811]

3200 Eliot, T. S. *Old Possum's Book of Practical Cats* (9–12). 1982, Harcourt $11.95 (0-15-168656-X); paper $4.95 (0-15-668568-X). Many of the poems in this delightful collection were used in the musical *Cats*. [811]

3201 Eliot, T. S. *The Waste Land, and Other Poems* (10–12). 1955, Harcourt paper $4.95 (0-15-694877-X). A basic collection of the most famous of this author's works. [811]

3202 Gardner, Helen, ed. *The New Oxford Book of English Verse, 1250–1950* (10–12). 1972, Oxford Univ. Pr. $35.00 (0-19-812136-9). The first edition of this anthology appeared in 1900, and it has continued to maintain its high standards in all subsequent editions. [821.08]

3203 Graves, Robert. *Collected Poems, 1975* (10–12). 1988, Oxford Univ. Pr. $29.95 (0-19-505143-2). This edition represents the complete poetic output of the English writer known also for his historical novels. [821]

3204 Grierson, H. J. C., and G. Bullough, eds. *The Oxford Book of Seventeenth Century Verse* (10–12). 1934, Oxford Univ. Pr. $49.95 (0-19-812125-3). This collection of over 600 poems represents the work of more than 100 poets. [821.08]

3205 Hardy, Thomas. *The Complete Poems of Thomas Hardy* (10–12). 1988, Macmillan $60.00 (0-02-632943-4). A fine edition of the complete poetic output of Thomas Hardy. [821]

3206 Hayward, John, ed. *The Oxford Book of Nineteenth-Century English Verse* (10–12). 1964, Oxford Univ. Pr. $45.00 (0-19-812130-X). This fine anthology covers both the Romantic and Victorian periods. [821.08]

3207 Heaney, Seamus. *Station Island* (10–12). 1985, Farrar $11.95 (0-374-26978-5); paper $6.95

(0-374-51935-8). These poems reflect the thoughts of the author during the troubled times he lived through in Ireland. [821]

3208 Hopkins, Gerard Manley. *The Poems of Gerard Manley Hopkins* (10–12). 1967, Oxford Univ. Pr. $35.00 (0-19-500164-8); paper $10.95 (0-19-281094-4). In addition to poems, this volume includes biographical material on this poet who died in 1889 at age 45. [821]

3209 Housman, A. E. *The Collected Poems of A. E. Housman* (10–12). 1965, Henry Holt paper $7.95 (0-8050-0547-1). This collection of Housman's works includes the beloved *A Shropshire Lad.* [821]

3210 Hughes, Ted. *New Selected Poems* (10–12). 1982, Harper $15.00 (0-06-011952-7). A collection of poetry by one of England's leading modern poets. [821]

3211 Keats, John. *Poems* (10–12). 1985, Penguin paper $3.95 (0-14-058500-1). The complete poetic works of the English poet who died at age 26. [821]

3212 Kennelly, Brendan, ed. *The Penguin Book of Irish Verse* (10–12). 1981, Penguin paper $8.95 (0-14-042121-1). An anthology that focuses on the more obscure and generally unknown Irish poets. [821.08]

3213 Kinsella, Thomas, ed. *The New Oxford Book of Irish Verse* (10–12). 1989, Oxford Univ. Pr. paper $9.95 (0-19-282643-3). An anthology of Irish poetry that begins in the pre-Christian era and ends in the twentieth century. [821.08]

3214 Kipling, Rudyard. *Gunga Din* (7–12). Illus. 1987, Harcourt LB $12.95 (0-15-200456-4). A splendid edition of this poem dealing with the Indian Mutiny of 1857 and the heroics of an abused water carrier. (Rev: SLJ 12/87) [821]

3215 Kipling, Rudyard. *Rudyard Kipling's Verse* (10–12). 1940, Doubleday $19.95 (0-385-04407-0). The complete poetic works, many of them narrative in nature, are included in this volume. [821]

3216 Larkin, Philip, ed. *The Oxford Book of Twentieth-Century English Verse* (10–12). 1973, Oxford Univ. Pr. $35.00 (0-19-812137-7). This is an anthology of about 600 poems from more than 200 twentieth century English poets. [821.08]

3217 Lonsdale, Roger, ed. *The New Oxford Book of Eighteenth Century Verse* (10–12). 1984, Oxford Univ. Pr. $29.95 (0-19-214122-8). An excellent collection of verse by both popular and obscure English poets of the eighteenth century. [821.08]

3218 Milton, John. *Complete Poetical Works* (10–12). 1965, Houghton $39.95 (0-395-05574-1). This edition includes all the epics, sonnets, masques, and miscellaneous poems. [821]

3219 Milton, John. *The Portable Milton* (10–12). 1987, Penguin paper $8.95 (0-14-015044-7). Many examples of Milton's prose and poetry are included, in addition to the complete texts of *Paradise Lost, Paradise Regained,* and *Samson Agonistes.* [828]

3220 Nims, John Frederick, ed. *The Harper Anthology of Poetry* (10–12). 1981, Harper $29.95 (0-06-044847-4). The entire range of English and American poetry is covered in this anthology of 700 selections. [821.08]

3221 Palgrave, Francis Turner, ed. *The Golden Treasury of the Best Songs & Lyrical Poems in the English Language* (7–12). 5th ed. 1964, Oxford Univ. Pr. $35.00 (0-19-254156-0). This famous anthology of English and Irish poetry originally appeared in 1861. [821.08]

3222 Shakespeare, William. *Sonnets* (10–12). 1963, Penguin paper $3.95 (0-14-071423-5). One of several editions of these great poems from the pen of the playwright. [821]

3223 Shakespeare, William. *The Sonnets* (10–12). 1980, St. Martin's $8.95 (0-312-74499-4). A fine edition of all of the sonnets written by Shakespeare. [821]

3224 Shelley, Percy Bysshe. *The Poetical Works of Shelley* (10–12). 1975, Houghton $24.95 (0-395-18461-4). The complete poetic output of this master of Romantic poetry. [821]

3225 Spender, Stephen. *Collected Poems, 1928–1985* (10–12). 1987, Oxford Univ. Pr. paper $12.95 (0-19-505210-2). Poems by this contemporary Englishman are grouped under such headings as War Poems and Home. [821]

3226 Tennyson, Alfred. *The Poetical Works of Tennyson* (10–12). 1974, Houghton $29.95 (0-395-18014-7). This is a collection of the poetic works of this widely loved nineteenth-century English writer. [821]

3227 Thomas, Dylan. *A Child's Christmas in Wales* (10–12). Illus. 1990, New Directions $14.95 (0-8112-1154-1); paper $4.95 (0-8112-0203-8). A poem that deals with the celebration of Christmas in a small Welsh town. [828]

3228 Thomas, Dylan. *The Collected Poems of Dylan Thomas* (10–12). 1957, New Directions paper $8.95 (0-8112-0205-4). A group of poems by this Welshman, many of which reflect his love of homeland and family. [821]

3229 Thomas, Dylan. *The Poems of Dylan Thomas* (10–12). 1971, New Directions $14.95 (0-8112-0398-0). A collection of 192 poems, some of which were published at the author's death. [821]

3230 Thwaite, Anthony, ed. *Philip Larkin: Collected Poems* (10–12). 1989, Farrar $22.50 (0-374-12623-2). A collection of poems by the man usually thought to be England's finest post-World War II poet. (Rev: BR 11–12/89) [821]

3231 Wordsworth, William. *The Poetical Works of Wordsworth* (10–12). 1982, Houghton $29.95 (0-395-18496-7). The poetry of this beloved English poet who celebrated the Lake District of England in many of his works. [821]

3232 Yeats, W. B. *Collected Poems* (10–12). 1989, Macmillan $14.95 (0-02-055650-0). A large volume that contains all the poetic works by this Irish poet and playwright. [821]

3233 Yeats, W. B. *The Collected Works of W. B. Yeats, Volume I: The Poems* (10–12). Edited by Richard J. Finneran. 1989, Macmillan $32.50 (0-02-632701-5). The poetry of one of Ireland's greatest, now collected in one volume. (Rev: BL 4/15/89) [821]

United States

3234 Adoff, Arnold, ed. *I Am the Darker Brother: An Anthology of Modern Poems by Negro Americans* (9–12). Illus. 1968, Macmillan paper $4.95 (0-02-041120-0). This anthology of 64 poems by 29 black poets of the twentieth century explores the black person's role in American life. [811.08]

3235 Adoff, Arnold, ed. *My Black Me: A Beginning Book of Black Poetry* (9–12). 1974, Dutton $12.95 (0-525-35460-3). Fifty poems about being black in America. [811.08]

3236 Adoff, Arnold, ed. *The Poetry of Black America: Anthology of the 20th Century* (10–12). 1973, Harper LB $24.89 (0-06-020090-1). In 600 poems by 145 authors, this book gives a cross-section of black American poetry writing in the twentieth century. [811.08]

3237 Angelou, Maya. *And Still I Rise* (10–12). 1978, Random $11.95 (0-394-50252-3). A highly personalized volume of poetry by the author of such companion books of poetry as *Just Give Me a Cool Drink of Water 'fore I Die* (1971), *Oh Pray My Wings Are Gonna Fit Me Well* (1975), and *Shaker, Why Don't You Sing?* (1983). [811]

3238 Angelou, Maya. *I Shall Not Be Moved* (10–12). 1990, Random $14.95 (0-394-58618-2). This slim volume is the author's fifth book of poetry and like the others conveys the richness, joy, and pain of being black. (Rev: BL 5/15/90; SLJ 9/90) [811]

3239 Ashbery, John. *Selected Poems* (10–12). 1986, Penguin paper $11.95 (0-14-058553-2). A collection of poetry by one of the most inventive and influential contemporary American poets. [811]

3240 Atwood, Margaret, ed. *The New Oxford Book of Canadian Verse in English* (9–12). 1982, Oxford Univ. Pr. $25.00 (0-19-540396-7). This selection of poetry covers the entire range of Canadian history and culture as represented in 120 different poets. [811.08]

3241 Baldwin, James. *Jimmy's Blues: Selected Poems* (10–12). 1985, St. Martin's $11.95 (0-312-44247-5); paper $9.95 (0-312-05104-2). This is the first collection of poetry by the black writer known chiefly for his novels. [811]

3242 Benét, Stephen Vincent. *John Brown's Body* (10–12). 1982, Buccaneer LB $25.95 (0-89966-405-9); Ivan R. Dee paper $11.95 (0-929587-26-X). A long narrative poem that uses the Civil War as its subject matter. [811]

3243 Berry, Wendell. *Collected Poems, 1957–1982* (10–12). 1985, North Point $16.50 (0-86547-189-4). This poetry rooted in the landscapes of rural Kentucky nevertheless has universal appeal. [811]

3244 Bly, Robert. *Selected Poems* (10–12). 1986, Harper $18.95 (0-06-015334-2); paper $9.95 (0-06-096048-5). This selection traces the various stages in the development of the author as poet. [811]

3245 Booth, Philip E. *Relations: Selected Poems, 1950–1985* (10–12). 1986, Penguin paper $12.95 (0-14-058560-5). The settings of these poems are coastal New England and many of the themes deal with family and friends. [811]

3246 Brooks, Gwendolyn. *Selected Poems* (10–12). 1963, Harper $11.45 (0-06-010535-6); paper $8.95 (0-06-090989-7). A selection of the finest poetry by this popular black American writer. [811]

3247 Bruchac, Joseph, ed. *Songs from This Earth on Turtle's Back: Contemporary American Indian Poetry* (10–12). Illus. 1983, Greenfield Review paper $9.95 (0-912678-58-5). This collection of poems is supplemented by photographs and biographical information. [811]

3248 Buchwald, Emilie, and Ruth Roston, eds. *This Sporting Life* (10–12). Illus. 1987, Milkweed Editions paper $8.50 (0-915943-14-X). An unusual collection of 100 poems by 72 American poets whose subjects are a great variety of sports. (Rev: BL 4/1/89) [808.819]

3249 Carson, Jo. *Stories I Ain't Told Nobody Yet: Selections from the People Pieces* (8–12). 1989, Watts LB $12.99 (0-531-08408-6). A group of short poems and conversations that capture the life of rural mountain people in Tennessee. (Rev: BL 2/15/89; BR 11–12/89; SLJ 3/89; VOYA 4/89) [811.54]

3250 Ciardi, John. *Selected Poems* (10–12). 1984, Univ. of Arkansas Pr. $21.00 (0-938626-29-9); paper $8.95 (0-938626-30-2). Straightforward poems on such subjects as war, family, and the problems of daily life. [811]

3251 Clifton, Lucille. *Good Woman: Poems and a Memoir, 1969–1980* (10–12). Illus. 1987, BOA Editions $25.00 (0-918526-58-2); paper $12.00 (0-918526-59-0). A retrospective collection of all this black poet's work plus a memoir in prose. (Rev: BL 4/1/88) [811]

3252 Cowley, Malcolm. *Blue Juniata: A Life, Collected and New Poems* (10–12). 1985, Penguin paper $8.95 (0-14-058556-7). These autobiographical poems trace the author's life from childhood in Pennsylvania to world traveler. [811]

3253 Crane, Stephen. *The Complete Poems of Stephen Crane* (10–12). 1972, Cornell Univ. Pr. paper $9.95 (0-8014-9130-4). This collection of 134 poems are arranged chronologically. [811]

3254 Creeley, Robert. *The Collected Poems of Robert Creeley, 1945–1975* (10–12). 1982, Univ. of California Pr. $35.00 (0-520-04243-3); paper $12.95 (0-520-04244-1). This collection by one of America's most influential poets represents 30 years of creative work. [811]

3255 Cummings, E. E. *73 Poems* (10–12). 1987, Harcourt paper $5.95 (0-15-680676-2). A collection of the poet's last works. Also use: *110 Selected Poems* (1988). [811]

3256 Day, Arthur Grove, ed. *The Sky Clears: Poetry of the American Indians* (10–12). 1983, Greenwood $35.00 (0-313-23883-9). This volume contains about 200 examples of American Indian poetry and chants. [897]

3257 Dickey, James. *The Central Motion: Poems, 1968–1979* (10–12). 1983, Wesleyan Univ. Pr. paper $12.95 (0-8195-6088-X). Three previously published collections are combined in the volume that covers the poet's output through the 1970s. [811]

3258 Dickinson, Emily. *The Complete Poems of Emily Dickinson* (10–12). 1960, Little $25.00 (0-315-18414-4); paper $12.95 (0-316-18413-6). This definitive edition contains 1,775 poems and fragments. [811]

3259 Dickinson, Emily. *Final Harvest: Emily Dickinson's Poems* (10–12). 1961, Little $17.95 (0-316-18416-0); paper $9.95 (0-316-18415-2). This selection of 575 poems gives a good cross-section of the author's work. [811]

3260 Dodge, Robert K., and Joseph B. McCullough, eds. *New and Old Voices of Wah'kontah* (10–12). 1985, International Pub. paper $4.95 (0-7178-0629-4). A valuable collection of poetry by North American Indians, most of them still alive. (Rev: BL 3/15/86) [811]

3261 Dunbar, Paul Laurence. *The Complete Poems of Paul Laurence Dunbar* (7–12). 1980, Dodd paper $5.95 (0-396-07895-8). The definitive collection first published in 1913 of this black poet's work. [811]

3262 Dunning, Stephen, et al., eds. *Reflections on a Gift of Watermelon Pickle . . . and Other Modern Verse* (7–12). Illus. 1967, Lothrop LB $13.88 (0-688-51231-3). A fine introduction to modern poetry, its forms, and its content for young adult readers. [811.08]

3263 Ellmann, Richard, ed. *The New Oxford Book of American Verse* (9–12). 1976, Oxford Univ. Pr. $35.00 (0-19-502058-8). A fine collection that begins with colonial days and ends with important contemporary poets. [811.08]

3264 Emrich, Duncan, ed. *American Folk Poetry: An Anthology* (7–12). Illus. 1974, Little $35.00 (0-316-23722-1). Folk song lyrics, ballads, and poems are included from America's past. [811.08]

3265 Ferlinghetti, Lawrence. *Endless Life: Selected Poems* (10–12). 1981, New Directions paper $9.95 (0-8112-0797-8). For this collection, the author has chosen those he thinks are his best. [811]

3266 *Fifty Years of American Poetry: Anniversary Volume for the Academy of American Poets* (10–12). Illus. 1984, Abrams $29.95 (0-8109-0934-0). This collection of poems by 126 recipients of grants from the Academy of American Poets. [811.08]

3267 Frost, Robert. *The Poetry of Robert Frost* (10–12). 1969, Henry Holt $17.50 (0-03-072535-6); paper $12.95 (0-8050-0501-3). The definitive volume of the complete poetic works of Frost. [811]

3268 Frost, Robert. *A Swinger of Birches* (7–12). Illus. 1982, Stemmer House paper $14.95 (0-916144-93-3). A nicely illustrated collection of Frost's poetry for a younger audience. [811]

3269 Ginsberg, Allen. *Collected Poems, 1947–1980* (10–12). 1984, Harper paper $15.95 (0-06-091494-7). The leader of the Beat poets in a collection of poetry that spans over 30 years. [811]

3270 Giovanni, Nikki. *Black Feeling, Black Talk, Black Judgement* (10–12). 1970, Broadside paper $3.00 (0-910296-07-3). Subjects dealt with in this collection include being black, family life, and love. Also use: *My House* (1972); *Those Who Ride the Night Winds* (1983). [811]

3271 Giovanni, Nikki. *Ego Tripping and Other Poems for Young People* (9–12). 1974, Lawrence Hill paper $7.95 (1-55652-062-X). A collection for young people by one of America's leading poets. [811]

3272 Giovanni, Nikki. *Those Who Ride the Night Winds* (10–12). 1984, Morrow paper $6.70 (0-688-02653-2). Poems about love and about people who are special to the poet like Rosa Parks and John Lennon. [811]

3273 Glenn, Mel. *Back to Class* (9–12). Illus. 1988, Clarion $13.95 (0-89919-656-X). The author creates a new series of poems—this time about teachers—in a companion volume to *Class Dismissed (1982)* and *Class Dismissed II* (1986). (Rev: BL 12/1/88; SLJ 1/89;) [811]

3274 Gould, Jean. *Modern American Women Poets* (10–12). Illus. 1985, Dodd $17.95 (0-396-08443-5). This book contains biographical information and an analysis of the work of 18 well-known contemporary women poets. (Rev: BL 1/15/85; VOYA 12/85) [811.5]

3275 Halpern, Daniel, ed. *The American Poetry Anthology* (10–12). 1976, Avon paper $9.95 (0-380-00399-6). This is a collection of poetry by 76 contemporary Americans. [811]

3276 Harmon, William, ed. *The Oxford Book of American Light Verse* (7–12). 1979, Oxford Univ. Pr. $29.95 (0-19-502509-1). In addition to poems like "A Visit from St. Nicholas," this anthology covers lyrics by Cole Porter and Stephen Sondheim. [811.08]

3277 Harris, Marie, and Kathleen Aguero, eds. *An Ear to the Ground: An Anthology of Contemporary American Poetry* (10–12). 1989, Univ. of Georgia Pr. $30.00 (0-8203-0952-4); paper $15.00 (0-8203-0953-2). For better readers, this is an excellent cross-section of the poetry being written in America today. (Rev: BL 6/1/89) [811]

3278 Hearne, Betsy. *Love Lines: Poetry in Person* (10–12). 1987, Macmillan $7.95 (0-689-50437-3). A book of poems about all types of love and of the sorrow of parting. (Rev: BL 10/15/87; SLJ 2/88; VOYA 2/88) [811]

3279 Hughes, Langston. *Selected Poems of Langston Hughes* (10–12). Illus. 1959, Knopf $22.50 (0-394-40438-6); paper $6.95 (0-394-71910-7). The author made this selection of his own poetry as being his most important. [811]

3280 Janeczko, Paul B., ed. *Don't Forget to Fly: A Cycle of Modern Poems* (7–12). 1981, Bradbury $11.95 (0-02-747780-0). Poems by 70 modern writers selected for young readers that represent a good cross-section of modern American poetry. [811.08]

3281 Janeczko, Paul B., ed. *Pocket Poems: Selected for a Journey* (9–12). 1985, Bradbury $10.95 (0-02-747820-3). There are 120 short poems by 80 poets included in this anthology arranged by subject. (Rev: BL 4/15/85; SLJ 8/85) [811]

3282 Janeczko, Paul B., ed. *Poetspeak: In Their Work, about Their Work* (7–12). Illus. 1983, Bradbury $12.95 (0-02-074770-3). The works of 60 modern American poets are represented plus comments by the poets themselves on their work. [811.08]

3283 Janeczko, Paul B., ed. *Strings: A Gathering of Family Poems* (8–12). 1984, Bradbury $11.95 (0-02-747790-8). Family life—its joys and problems—is explored in this anthology of over 100 poems by contemporary Americans. [811.08]

3284 Jarrell, Randall. *The Complete Poems* (10–12). 1969, Farrar $25.00 (0-374-12716-6); paper $12.95 (0-374-51305-8). The complete poetic works by one of America's most sensitive modern writers are reprinted in this volume. [811]

3285 Johnson, James Weldon. *God's Trombones: Seven Negro Sermons in Verse* (10–12). Illus. 1927, Viking $13.95 (0-670-34340-4); paper $5.95 (0-14-042217-X). This book consists of 7 sermons in verse similar to the one's the author heard as a child. [811]

3286 Jordan, June. *Living Room: New Poems* (10–12). 1985, Thunder's Mouth Pr. $14.95 (0-938410-27-X); paper $8.95 (0-938410-26-1). These poems deal with both personal concerns and political issues. Also use: *Things That I Do in the Dark* (1977). [811]

3287 Kumin, Maxine. *Nature: Poems* (9–12). 1989, Viking $17.95 (0-670-82438-0). A collection of poetry from the winner of the Pulitzer Prize, many of which deal with animals and humans' relations with them. (Rev: BL 2/1/89) [811]

3288 Kunitz, Stanley. *Next-to-Last Things: New Poems and Essays* (10–12). 1985, Atlantic Monthly paper $8.95 (0-87113-120-X). In addition to 13 poems, this volume contains essays about poetry and about the author's life. [811]

3289 Levertov, Denise. *Poems, 1960–1967* (10–12). 1983, New Directions $8.95 (0-8112-0859-1). A combination of 3 previously published volumes of this important poet's work. [811]

3290 Levertov, Denise. *Poems, 1968–1972* (10–12). 1987, New Directions $19.95 (0-8112-1004-9); paper $8.95 (0-8112-1005-7). A collection of poems, many of which deal with protests concerning the Vietnam War. (Rev: BL 7/87) [811]

3291 Longfellow, Henry Wadsworth. *Hiawatha* (7–12). Illus. 1983, Dial $13.89 (0-8037-0014-8). The epic narrative poem about the deeds of the famous Ojibway brave. [811]

3292 Longfellow, Henry Wadsworth. *The Poetical Works of Longfellow* (10–12). 1975, Houghton $35.00 (0-395-18487-8). The complete poetic works of Longfellow are reprinted, including such standards as "Hiawatha" and "Miles Standish." [811]

3293 Lowell, Robert. *Selected Poems* (10–12). 1987, Farrar paper $10.95 (0-374-51400-3). There are over 200 poems included in this volume, first published in 1976. [811]

3294 McKuen, Rod. *Seasons in the Sun* (10–12). 1981, Pocket paper $2.95 (0-671-44741-6). A collection of accessible poems by this writer who achieved great popularity in the 1960s. Also use: *Too Many Midnights* (1981). [811]

3295 MacLeish, Archibald. *New and Collected Poems, 1917–1982* (10–12). 1985, Houghton paper $14.95 (0-395-39569-0). This collection includes poems previously published plus those unpublished at MacLeish's death in 1982. (Rev: BL 4/1/86) [811]

3296 Marzan, Julio, ed. *Inventing a Word: An Anthology of Twentieth Century Puerto Rican Poetry* (10–12). 1980, Columbia Univ. Pr. $26.50 (0-231-05010-0); paper $14.00 (0-231-05011-9). A bilingual edition of the work of 22 poets. [811]

3297 Mason, Steve. *Johnny's Song* (10–12). 1988, Simon & Schuster paper $6.95 (0-671-66381-4). Eleven long poems about the Vietnam War written by a former army captain who is a decorated Vietnam veteran. (Rev: VOYA 8–10/86) [811]

3298 Masters, Edgar Lee. *Spoon River Anthology* (10–12). Illus. 1987, Macmillan $25.00 (0-02-

581780-9). A free-verse tribute to characters who live in an imaginary midwestern community. [811]

3299 Mazer, Norma Fox, and Marjorie Lewis, eds. *Waltzing on Water: Poetry by Women* (8–12). 1989, Dell paper $3.25 (0-440-20257-4). An anthology of poetry by women arranged chronologically by the stages of a person's life. (Rev: BL 3/15/90; SLJ 1/90) [811]

3300 Merriam, Eve. *If Only I Could Tell You: Poems for Young Lovers and Dreamers* (10–12). Illus. 1983, Knopf paper $2.95 (0-394-86043-8). A collection of poems about various facets of love by this outstanding poet. [808.1]

3301 Millay, Edna St. Vincent. *Collected Poems* (10–12). 1987, Harper paper $15.95 (0-06-090889-0). The complete edition of this popular poet's sonnets and lyrics. [811]

3302 Millay, Edna St. Vincent. *Collected Sonnets* (10–12). 1941, Harper $14.45 (0-06-012940-9); paper $6.95 (0-06-091091-7). This collection has been assembled from previously published volumes. [811]

3303 Millay, Edna St. Vincent. *Edna St. Vincent Millay's Poems Selected for Young People* (9–12). Illus. 1979, Harper paper $13.95 (0-06-024218-3). Some of this writer's more accessible poems are reprinted with accompanying woodcuts. [811]

3304 Moore, Marianne. *The Complete Poems of Marianne Moore* (10–12). 1981, Macmillan $16.95 (0-670-23505-9); Penguin paper $8.95 (0-14-042300-1). This definitive edition includes all the changes made by the author in her frequent revisions. [811]

3305 Nash, Ogden. *I Wouldn't Have Missed It: Selected Poems of Ogden Nash* (9–12). Illus. 1975, Little $19.95 (0-316-59830-5). A selection of over 400 poems chosen by the poet's daughter after his death. [811]

3306 Nash, Ogden. *The Pocket Book of Ogden Nash* (9–12). 1983, Pocket paper $3.95 (0-671-47353-0). A fine collection of this writer's wittiest and most endearing poems. [811]

3307 Niatum, Duane, ed. *Harper's Anthology of 20th Century Native American Poetry* (10–12). 1988, Harper $24.95 (0-06-250665-X); paper $14.95 (0-06-250660-8). The rich, varied work of 36 contemporary Native American poets of stature is sampled in this welcome anthology. (Rev: BL 4/1/88) [811]

3308 Owen, Guy, and Mary C. Williams, eds. *Contemporary Southern Poetry* (10–12). 1979, Louisiana State Univ. Pr. paper $12.95 (0-8071-

0578-3). Such writers as Alice Walker and James Dickey are included in this anthology. [811]

3309 Pastan, Linda. *The Imperfect Paradise* (9–12). 1988, Norton $15.95 (0-393-02565-9). A collection of mystical poems that explores the imperfect paradise the poet calls Earth. (Rev: BR 11–12/88) [811]

3310 Piercy, Marge. *Circles on the Water* (10–12). 1982, Knopf paper $14.95 (0-394-70779-6). A collection of poetry by this contemporary master that gives a sampling from various times in her career. [808.1]

3311 Plath, Sylvia. *Ariel* (10–12). 1966, Harper $13.45 (0-06-013358-9); paper $6.95 (0-06-090890-4). Refreshing poems by an American poet who died while still very young. [811]

3312 Plath, Sylvia. *The Collected Poems* (10–12). 1981, Harper $17.45 (0-06-013369-4); paper $11.95 (0-06-090900-5). This collection contains 224 poems, including a selection of her very earliest work. Also use: *Crossing the River* (1971), a volume that contains the poet's last works. [811]

3313 Poe, Edgar Allan. *Poems of Edgar Allan Poe* (8–12). Illus. 1965, Harper $12.70 (0-690-64217-2). This collection contains an introduction on Poe's poetry as well as the writer's own thoughts on the writing of poetry. [811]

3314 Pound, Ezra. *Selected Poems* (10–12). 1957, New Directions paper $6.95 (0-8112-0162-7). A sampling of this author's many-faceted poetic talents. [811]

3315 Powell, Lawrence C., ed. *Poems of Walt Whitman: Leaves of Grass* (8–12). Illus. 1986, Harper LB $11.89 (0-690-64431-0). A collection of the poems in *Leaves of Grass* that are most suited for young people. (Rev: SLJ 8/86) [811]

3316 Randall, Dudley, ed. *The Black Poets* (10–12). 1985, Bantam paper $5.95 (0-553-27563-1). An anthology of black American poetry from the days of slavery to the present. [811.08]

3317 Ray, David, ed. *From A to Z: 200 Contemporary American Poets* (7–12). Illus. 1981, Swallow Press $18.95 (0-8040-0369-6); paper $9.95 (0-8040-0370-X). A nicely illustrated collection of poetry from the twentieth century. [811.08]

3318 Rexroth, Kenneth. *Selected Poems* (10–12). 1987, New Directions paper $8.95 (0-8112-0917-2). This collection spans the author's life from his youth in the 1920s through the 1970s. [811]

3319 Rich, Adrienne. *The Fact of a Doorframe: Poems Selected and New, 1950–1984* (10–12). 1984, Norton $18.95 (0-393-01905-5); 1984, Norton paper $10.95 (0-393-30204-0). A collection that spans 34 years of the work of this controversial writer. [811]

3320 Robinson, Edwin Arlington. *Selected Poems of Edwin Arlington Robinson* (10–12). 1965, Macmillan paper $12.95 (0-02-070530-1). An introduction to this respected poet's work. [811]

3321 Roethke, Theodore. *The Collected Poems of Theodore Roethke* (10–12). 1982, Univ. of Washington Pr. $19.95 (0-295-95973-8). This is the complete output of this highly personal poet. [811]

3322 Sandburg, Carl. *The Complete Poems of Carl Sandburg* (9–12). 1970, Harcourt $27.95 (0-15-120773-9). A celebration of America and its people is found in this poet's work. Smaller collections of this author's work are: *Honey and Salt* (1963); and *The People, Yes* (1936). [811]

3323 Sandburg, Carl. *Rainbows Are Made* (7–12). 1982, Harcourt $15.95 (0-15-265480-1); paper $8.95 (0-15-265481-X). These 70 poems were chosen by Lee Bennett Hopkins because of their appeal to young people. [811]

3324 Service, Robert. *The Best of Robert Service* (9–12). 1989, Putnam paper $7.95 (0-399-55008-9). The poet of the Yukon is presented well in this collection of his most popular poems. [811]

3325 Service, Robert. *Collected Poems of Robert Service* (9–12). 1989, Putnam $21.95 (0-399-15015-3). The narrative power of this writer's work is present, particularly in his poems about the Yukon. [811]

3326 Sexton, Anne. *The Complete Poems* (10–12). 1982, Houghton paper $14.95 (0-395-32935-3). This collection by this important poet contains the complete contents of 10 previously published volumes. [811]

3327 Simpson, Louis. *People Live Here: Selected Poems, 1949–1983* (10–12). 1983, BOA Editions $25.00 (0-918526-42-6); paper $12.00 (0-918526-43-4). A collection of over 100 poems arranged by topic. [811]

3328 Smith, Dave, and David Bottoms, eds. *The Morrow Anthology of Younger American Poets* (10–12). 1985, Morrow paper $17.95 (0-688-03450-0). For better readers, this is a collection of 100 American poets all born since 1940. (Rev: BL 5/15/85) [811]

3329 Soto, Gary. *Who Will Know Us?* (10–12). 1990, Chronicle paper $8.95 (0-87701-673-9). In this recent collection Soto covers such subjects as childhood, religion, and family life. (Rev: BL 8/90) [811]

3330 Stafford, William. *A Glass Face in the Rain: New Poems* (10–12). 1987, Harper paper $7.95 (0-06-090983-8). Most of these poems deal with personal topics like family, friends, and past experiences. [811]

3331 Stetson, Erlene, ed. *Black Sister: Poetry by Black American Women, 1746–1980* (10–12). 1981, Indiana Univ. Pr. $27.50 (0-253-30512-8); paper $10.95 (0-253-20268-X). This chronologically arranged anthology covers black women poets from Wheatley to Giovanni. [811.08]

3332 Stevens, Wallace. *The Collected Works of Wallace Stevens* (10–12). 1954, Knopf $35.00 (0-394-40330-4). This collection published at the time of Stevens's 75th birthday won the Pulitzer Prize in 1955. [811]

3333 Sullivan, Charles, ed. *America in Poetry* (10–12). Illus. 1988, Abrams $40.00 (0-8109-1880-3). A collection of poetry about America by some well-known poets like Whitman and Frost with many others by newcomers. (Rev: BL 11/15/88) [811]

3334 Swanson, James W., ed. *142 Ways to Make a Poem: An Anthology of Modern Poetry* (10–12). Illus. 1978, EMC paper $6.95 (0-88436-499-2). A collection of 102 poems by contemporary Americans and well illustrated with 40 photographs. [811]

3335 Updike, John. *Facing Nature: Poems* (10–12). 1985, Knopf $13.95 (0-394-54385-8). This author, known chiefly for fiction, writes charming poems, many dealing with everyday life. [811]

3336 Vendler, Helen, ed. *The Harvard Book of Contemporary American Poetry* (10–12). 1985, Harvard Univ. Pr. $22.95 (0-674-37340-5). This anthology introduces 35 modern American poets and also gives biographical information. [811.08]

3337 Walcott, Derek. *Collected Poems, 1948–1984* (10–12). 1986, Farrar $25.00 (0-374-12626-7); paper $13.95 (0-374-52025-9). This collection by the famous black poet includes his long autobiographical poem "Another Life." [811]

3338 Warren, Robert Penn. *Being Here: Poetry, 1977–1980* (10–12). 1980, Random $10.95 (0-394-51304-5); paper $4.95 (0-394-73935-3). A collection of poems from one of the author's most productive periods. *New and Selected Poems, 1923–1985* (1985) is a work that spans a greater period but with less depth. [811]

3339 Warren, Robert Penn. *Rumor Verified* (10–12). 1981, Random paper $5.95 (0-394-74960-X). This is a collection of poems written between 1970 and 1980. [811]

3340 Weigl, Bruce. *Song of Napalm* (10–12). 1988, Atlantic Monthly $13.95 (0-87113-241-9).

Thirty-three poems by a Vietnam War veteran about war and life in general. (Rev: BL 11/1/88) [811]

3341 Whitman, Walt. *Leaves of Grass* (10–12). 1977, Doubleday $17.95 (0-385-04252-3); Random paper $10.95 (0-394-60410-5). This personalized group of poems arranged autobiographically has influenced generations of American poets. [811]

3342 Whitman, Walt. *Voyages: Poems by Walt Whitman* (7–12). Illus. 1988, Harcourt $14.95 (0-15-294495-8). After an introductory biographical sketch, there are 53 representative poems selected by Lee Bennett Hopkins. (Rev: BL 11/15/88; BR 3–4/89; SLJ 12/88; VOYA 1/89) [811.3]

3343 Whittier, John Greenleaf. *The Poetical Works of Whittier* (9–12). 1975, Houghton $29.95 (0-395-21599-4). This poet's work is characterized by his belief in people and his hatred of oppression. [811]

3344 Wilbur, Richard. *New and Collected Poems* (10–12). 1988, Harcourt $27.95 (0-15-165206-6). Six previously issued collections are combined with some new verse by one of America's foremost poets. (Rev: BL 4/15/88) [811]

3345 Williams, William Carlos. *The Collected Poems of William Carlos Williams* (10–12). 1986, New Directions $35.00 (0-8112-0999-7). This volume covers the first half of Williams's career. A second volume which was published in 1988 covers 1939 to 1962. [811]

Other Regions

3346 Carmi, T., ed. *The Penguin Book of Hebrew Verse* (10–12). 1981, Viking $25.00 (0-670-36507-6); Penguin paper $15.95 (0-14-042197-1). A bilingual anthology that covers Hebrew poetry from biblical times to the present. [892.4]

3347 Gibran, Khalil. *The Prophet* (10–12). 1923, Knopf $12.95 (0-394-40428-9). In a series of prose poems, a lofty set of ideals are presented in this popular inspirational work. [892]

3348 Henderson, Harold Gould, ed. *An Introduction to Haiku: An Anthology of Poems and Poets from Bashō to Shiki* (9–12). Illus. 1958, Doubleday paper $2.50 (0-385-09376-4). A fine

selection of these short, succinct verses from over 600 years of Japanese history. [895.6]

3349 Lin, Julia C. *Modern Chinese Poetry* (10–12). 1972, Univ. of Washington Pr. $15.00 (0-295-95145-1); paper $6.95 (0-295-95281-4). This volume supplies both an anthology of Chinese poetry written from 1919 to the early 1970s as well as a lengthy analysis. [895.1]

3350 Neruda, Pablo. *Selected Poems* (10–12). 1973, Dell paper $9.95 (0-385-28906-5). A group of poems by one of the most influential Latin American poets of the twentieth century. [861]

3351 Okpewho, Isidore, ed. *The Heritage of African Poetry: An Anthology of Oral and Written Poetry* (10–12). Illus. 1986, Longman paper $16.95 (0-582-72704-9). A textbook anthology that gives a fine overview of African poetry and valuable commentary on its styles and origins. (Rev: BL 6/15/86) [808.81]

3352 Omar Khayyam. *Rubaiyat of Omar Khayyam* (10–12). 1989, Penguin paper $4.95 (0-14-058606-7). The classic translation of the poems about the meaning of life from the Persian tentmaker, Omar. [891]

3353 *One Man's Moon: 50 Haiku* (9–12). Trans. by Cid Corman. 1984, Gnomon paper $6.50 (0-917788-26-5). A short work that offers 50 examples of haiku from several different writers. [895.6]

3354 Paz, Octavio. *Selected Poems* (10–12). 1984, New Directions $14.95 (0-8112-0903-2); paper $7.95 (0-8112-0899-0). A collection of 67 poems that demonstrates the wide diversity in the poetry of Octavio Paz. [861]

3355 Rexroth, Kenneth, ed. *One Hundred Poems from the Chinese* (10–12). 1956, New Directions $11.95 (0-8112-0370-0); paper $4.95 (0-8112-0180-5). A collection of poems by 9 ancient Chinese poets. A companion volume is *100 Poems from the Japanese* (1955). [895.1]

3356 Sato, Hiroaki, and Burton Watson, eds. *From the Country of Eight Islands: An Anthology of Japanese Poetry* (10–12). 1981, Columbia Univ. Pr. paper $15.00 (0-231-06395-4). This extensive anthology extends from poems written at the beginning of Japanese history to selections from the most famous contemporary Japanese poets. [895.6]

Folklore and Fairy Tales

General and Miscellaneous

3357 Ausubel, Nathan, ed. *A Treasury of Jewish Folklore, Stories, Traditions, Legends, Humor, Wisdom and Folk Songs of the Jewish People* (9–12). 1989, Crown $17.95 (0-517-50293-3). A treasury of Jewish wit and wisdom through the ages that also reveals a great deal about Jewish history and religion. (Rev: SLJ 6/90) [296]

3358 Bettelheim, Bruno. *The Uses of Enchantment: The Meaning and Importance of Fairy Tales* (10–12). 1976, Knopf $24.95 (0-394-49771-6); Random paper $8.95 (0-679-72393-5). A scholarly treatise on the meanings behind fairy tales and their effects on children. [398]

3359 Bierhorst, John, ed. *The Red Swan: Myths and Tales of the American Indian* (10–12). Illus. 1976, Farrar paper $10.95 (0-374-51393-7). This is a collection of 64 myths and legends from Indian cultures in both North and South America. [398.2]

3360 Briggs, Katharine. *An Encyclopedia of Fairies: Hobgoblins, Brownies, Bogies, and Other Supernatural Creatures* (10–12). 1987, Pantheon paper $12.95 (0-394-40918-3). This alphabetically arranged resource for British fairy tales covers subjects such as names of fairies and their stories as well as concepts and customs related to fairy tales. [398.03]

3361 Cavendish, Richard, ed. *Legends of the World* (10–12). Illus. 1989, Outlet paper $8.98 (0-517-68799-2). In 43 essays various legends are retold, analyzed, and placed with a certain cultural milieu. [398.2]

3362 Clarkson, Atelia, and Gilbert B. Cross, eds. *World Folktales* (10–12). 1980, Macmillan paper $14.95 (0-684-17763-3). This collection contains 66 representative folktales with extensive introductions and background material. [398.2]

3363 Cole, Joanna, ed. *Best-Loved Folktales of the World* (7–12). Illus. 1982, Doubleday paper $12.95 (0-385-18949-4). A collection of 200 tales from around the globe arranged geographically. [398.2]

3364 Dorson, Richard M., ed. *Folktales Told Around the World* (10–12). Illus. 1987, Univ. of Chicago Pr. paper $15.00 (0-226-15874-8). An international selection of folktales in authentic retellings and translations. [398.2]

3365 Huygen, Wil. *Gnomes* (10–12). Illus. 1977, Abrams $19.95 (0-8109-0965-0). Using a number of sources the author and illustrator have compiled a delightful book on gnomeology. [398]

3366 Lehane, Brendan. *Legends of Valor* (9–12). Illus. 1984, Silver Burdett $25.93 (0-8094-5221-9). In this lavishly illustrated volume, the exploits of such folk heroes as Finn MacCumal, Sigurd, and King Arthur's knights are retold. This is part of the Time-Life Enchanted World series which also includes the recommended *Fall of Camelot* and *Fabled Lands* (both 1986). [398.2]

3367 Opie, Iona, and Peter Opie, eds. *The Classic Fairy Tales* (9–12). Illus. 1987, Oxford Univ. Pr. paper $10.95 (0-19-520219-8). The definitive retelling of 24 of the most popular fairy tales of all time. [398.2]

3368 Phelps, Ethel Johnston. *The Maid of the North: Feminist Folk Tales from around the World* (10–12). 1982, Henry Holt paper $7.95 (0-8050-0679-6). A collection of folktales that highlight a number of clever heroines. [398]

3369 Sadeh, Pinhas, ed. *Jewish Folktales* (9–12). Illus. 1989, Doubleday $24.95 (0-385-19573-7); paper $12.95 (0-385-19574-5). This collection is distinguished by the worldwide coverage represented in the tales included. (Rev: BL 11/1/89) [398.2]

3370 Schwartz, Howard. *Miriam's Tambourine: Jewish Folktales from around the World* (9–12). Illus. 1987, Seth Pr. $24.95 (0-02-929260-3). A collection of 50 Jewish folktales from around the world that explores various facets of Jewish history. (Rev: BL 1/1 87) [398.2]

3371 Time-Life Books, eds. *Dragons* (9–12). Illus. 1984, Silver Burdett LB $25.94 (0-8094-5209-X). Taken from both literature and legend, this is a well-illustrated look at dragons. This is part of the Time-Life series The Enchanted World which also includes volumes on *Dwarfs, Giants and Ogres,* and *Water Spirits* (all 1985). [398.2]

3372 Time-Life Books, eds. *Fairies and Elves* (9–12). Illus. 1984, Silver Burdett LB $25.94 (0-8094-5213-8). Part of the Time-Life Enchanted World series which also contains a volume on *The Gods* (1987)—a retelling of stories about fairies and other fantastic creatures. [398.2]

3373 Time-Life Books, eds. *Magical Beasts* (9–12). Illus. 1985, Silver Burdett LB $25.93 (0-8094-5230-8). A collection of tales containing mythical animals from Greece, Egypt, and the Far East with a special chapter on unicorns. Part of the Enchanted World series from Time-Life books which also contains *Magical Justice* (1986). [398.2]

3374 Time-Life Books, eds. *Night Creatures* (9–12). Illus. 1985, Silver Burdett LB $25.93 (0-8094-5234-0). Folklores involving various monsters from Britain, Europe, and the Balkans. Also use from the same Enchanted World series: *Seekers and Saviors* (1986). [398.2]

3375 Time-Life Books, eds. *Spells and Bindings* (9–12). Illus. 1985, Silver Burdett LB $25.93 (0-8094-5242-1). Tales of magic that include Sleeping Beauty, the Pied Piper, and Pygmalion. Part of the Enchanted World series. [398.2]

3376 Yolen, Jane, ed. *Favorite Folktales from around the World* (9–12). 1986, Pantheon $19.95 (0-394-54382-3); paper $11.95 (0-394-72960-9). This collection of 160 tales represents such diverse stories as American Indian legends and others from the Brothers Grimm. (Rev: SLJ 12/86) [398]

Geographical Regions

Africa

3377 Abrahams, Roger D., ed. *African Folktales: Traditional Stories of the Black World* (7–12). Illus. 1983, Pantheon paper $12.95 (0-394-72117-9). A collection of about 100 tales from south of the Sahara. [398.2]

3378 Courlander, Harold, ed. *Treasury of African Folklore* (10–12). Illus. 1975, Crown $14.95 (0-517-51670-5). A wide and varied selection of myths from various African tribes south of the Sahara. [398.2]

3379 Dadié, Bernard Binlin. *The Black Cloth: A Collection of African Folktales* (9–12). 1987, Univ. of Massachusetts Pr. $20.00 (0-87023-556-7); paper $8.95 (0-87023-557-5). A collection of 16 retold African folktales many involving the trickster spider, Anansi. (Rev: BL 9/1/87) [843]

Asia and the Middle East

3380 *The Arabian Nights* (9–12). 1986, Crown paper $9.98 (0-517-61934-2). Sinbad and Aladdin are only 2 of the famous characters that come alive in these ancient tales. [398]

3381 Beck, Brenda E. F., et al., eds. *Folktales of India* (9–12). 1987, Univ. of Chicago Pr. $29.95 (0-226-04080-1). There are 99 tales in this collection and they represent a number of different cultures and districts. (Rev: BL 5/1/87) [398.2]

3382 Bushnaq, Inea, ed. *Arab Folktales* (10–12). 1986, Pantheon paper $11.95 (0-394-75179-5). A collection garnered from many Arab countries from Africa through the Middle East. (Rev: BL 3/1/86) [398.2]

3383 McAlpine, Helen, and William McAlpine. *Japanese Tales & Legends* (8–12). Illus. 1989, Oxford Univ. Pr. paper $7.95 (0-19-274140-3). A standard work first published in 1958 that retells Japanese creation myths, epics, and fairy tales. (Rev: BR 3–4/90) [398]

3384 Narayan, R. K. *The Ramayana: A Shortened Modern Prose Version of the Indian Epic* (7–12). 1972, Penguin paper $5.95 (0-14-004428-0). The noted Indian novelist has produced a readable translation of the epic story of Rama's quests.

3385 Roberts, Moss. *Chinese Fairy Tales and Fantasies* (10–12). 1980, Pantheon paper $11.95 (0-394-73994-9). Culled from 25 centuries of folklore, this is a collection of 100 tales. [398]

3386 Tyler, Royall, ed. *Japanese Tales* (9–12). 1987, Pantheon $19.95 (0-394-52190-0). Arranged by themes this is a mammoth collection of folktales that concentrates on those originating in the twelfth through the fourteenth centuries. (Rev: BL 5/1/87) [398.2]

3387 Yep, Laurence. *The Rainbow People* (7–10). Illus. 1989, Harper LB $13.89 (0-06-026761-5). The retelling of 20 Chinese folktales with illustrations by David Wiesner. (Rev: BL 4/1/89; BR 11–12/90) [398.2]

Europe

3388 Afanas'ev, Aleksandr. *Russian Folk Tales* (9–12). 1976, Pantheon paper $13.95 (0-394-73090-9). This is a standard collection of these traditional Russian tales. [398]

3389 Andersen, Hans Christian. *Tales and Stories* (9–12). Illus. 1980, Univ. of Washington Pr. $22.50 (0-295-95769-7); paper $14.95 (0-295-95936-3). These 27 stories are retold for an adult audience.

3390 Asbjørnsen, Peter Christen, and Jørgen Moe. *Norwegian Folk Tales* (9–12). Trans. by Pat Shaw and Carl Norman. Illus. 1982, Pantheon paper $11.95 (0-394-71054-1). From an authoritative collection that first appeared in 1845, about 25 Norwegian folktales have been reprinted. [398]

3391 Bjurstrom, C. G., ed. *French Folktales* (8–12). 1989, Pantheon $21.95 (0-394-54451-X). A fine collection of French folktales arranged by theme. (Rev: BL 9/1/89) [398.2]

3392 Calvino, Italo, reteller. *Italian Folktales* (9–12). Trans. by George Martin. 1956, Harcourt $27.50 (0-15-145770-0); Pantheon paper $14.95 (0-394-74909-4). A lively retelling of Italian folktales that include variations on such stories as "Snow White" and "Cinderella." [398]

3393 Colum, Padraic, ed. *A Treasury of Irish Folklore* (9–12). 2nd rev. ed. 1969, Crown $14.95 (0-517-50294-1). In addition to folktales this anthology includes jokes, anecdotes, and songs. [398.2]

3394 Crossley-Holland, Kevin, reteller. *British Folk Tales: New Versions* (6–12). Illus. 1987, Watts $22.50 (0-531-05733-X). A total of 55 tales—some familiar, others lesser known—are retold. (Rev: BL 1/15/88) [398.2]

3395 Crossley-Holland, Kevin, ed. *The Faber Book of Northern Folk-Tales* (10–12). 1981, Faber $11.95 (0-571-11519-5). This is considered the standard edition of the Scandinavian tales. Also use: *The Faber Book of Northern Legends* (1983). [398]

3396 Crossley-Holland, Kevin, ed. *Folk-Tales of the British Isles* (8–12). 1988, Pantheon $22.95 (0-394-56328-X); paper $11.95 (0-394-75553-7). An authoritative collection of 67 tales arranged by theme with extensive introductions to each section. (Rev: BL 5/15/88; BR 9–10/88) [398.2]

3397 Davidson, H. R. Ellis. *Scandinavian Mythology* (9–12). Illus. 1986, Bedrick $19.95 (0-87226-041-0). A fine collection of Norse legends that emphasize the role of the god Odin. (Rev: BL 12/1/86) [293]

3398 Glassie, Henry, ed. *Irish Folktales* (9–12). 1985, Pantheon $19.95 (0-394-53224-4). A collection of over 100 tales that contain all of the major themes, situations, and characters in Irish folklore. (Rev: BL 10/1/85) [398.2]

3399 Grimm, Jacob, and Wilhelm Grimm. *The Complete Grimms' Fairy Tales* (10–12). 1974, Pantheon $17.50 (0-394-49415-6). This early collection of folktales by the Grimm brothers is still considered the authoritative one. [398]

3400 Grundtvig, Svendt, ed. *Danish Fairy Tales* (10–12). 1919, Dover paper $4.95 (0-486-22891-6). Many of these stories are particularly good for storytelling. [398]

3401 Hearn, Michael Patrick, ed. *The Victorian Fairy Tale Book* (7–12). 1988, Random LB $19.95 (0-394-56594-0). A collection of fairy tales and a few poems by such writers as Browning, Barrie, and Ruskin. (Rev: BR 3–4/89) [398.2]

3402 Jacobs, Joseph, ed. *Celtic Fairy Tales* (10–12). 1968, Dover paper $4.95 (0-486-21826-0). One of the great collectors of folktales presents these from Ireland. Also use: *More Celtic Fairy Tales* (1968), *Indian Fairy Tales* (1969), and *English Fairy Tales* (Penguin, 1990). [398]

3403 McGowan, Hugh. *Leprechauns, Legends and Irish Tales* (9–12). Illus. 1990, Gollancz $24.95 (0-575-04261-3). An oversize illustrated retelling of tales and legends from Ireland. (Rev: BL 8/90) [398.2]

3404 McKinley, Robin. *The Outlaws of Sherwood* (9–12). 1988, Greenwillow $11.95 (0-688-07178-3). A reworking of the Robin Hood story in which our hero becomes a moody, self-doubting, somewhat ordinary man. (Rev: BL 12/15/88; BR 5–6/89; SLJ 1/89; VOYA 4/89) [398.2]

3405 Malory, Thomas. *King Arthur and His Knights* (10–12). 1975, Oxford Univ. Pr. paper $8.95 (0-19-501905-9). This is the classic treatment of the stories surrounding King Arthur in one of many available editions. [398]

3406 Malory, Thomas. *Le Morte d'Arthur* (10–12). 1975, Macmillan paper $16.95 (0-02-822560-1). One of many editions of this classic about King Arthur, the Round Table, and the quest for the Holy Grail. [398.2]

3407 Malory, Thomas. *Tales of King Arthur* (10–12). Illus. 1981, Schocken paper $16.95 (0-8052-0891-7). An abridged, very readable adaptation of the longer work by Sir Thomas Malory. [398.2]

3408 Matthews, John, ed. *An Arthurian Reader: Selections from Arthurian Legend, Scholarship and Story* (10–12). Illus. 1989, Aquarian Pr. $24.95 (0-85030-778-3). From medieval to contemporary sources, the 21 selections in this book and the accompanying illustrations explore the world of King Arthur and his knights. (Rev: BL 11/1/89) [398]

3409 Pyle, Howard. *Merry Adventures of Robin Hood* (10–12). 1986, NAL paper $3.50 (0-451-52284-2). One of many retellings of the stories about Robin Hood and his merry men. [398]

3410 Scott, Michael. *Irish Folk & Fairy Tales Omnibus* (9–12). 1990, Penguin paper $8.95 (0-14-012326-1). A collection of 42 of the most entertaining tales from the Emerald Isle. (Rev: BL 5/15/90) [398.2]

3411 Simpson, Jacqueline. *European Mythology* (10–12). Illus. 1987, Bedrick $19.95 (0-87226-044-5). The major stories and folklore that stem from peasant beliefs are presented. (Rev: BL 4/15/87; BR 9/10/87; SLJ 8/87) [398]

3412 Steinbeck, John. *The Acts of King Arthur and His Noble Knights* (10–12). 1986, Ballantine paper $5.95 (0-345-34512-6). Steinbeck has translated many of the old Arthurian legends into modern English. [291.1]

3413 Tolkien, J. R. R. *Sir Gawain and the Green Knight* (10–12). 1979, Ballantine paper $3.95 (0-345-27760-0). A retelling of 3 tales from the age of chivalry [398]

3414 Weinreich, Beatrice Silverman, ed. *Yiddish Folktales* (8–12). Trans. by Leonard Wolf. 1988, Pantheon $19.95 (0-394-54618-0). Over 200 folktales from Eastern Europe from the foolish men of Chelm to tales of dibbuks. (Rev: BL 10/1/88) [398.2]

3415 Zipes, Jack, ed. *Beauties, Beasts and Enchantments: Classic French Fairy Tales* (8–12). Illus. 1989, NAL $19.95 (0-453-00693-0). Using a rough chronological arrangement, this is a collection of tales from the seventeenth and eighteenth centuries. (Rev: BL 9/1/89) [398.21]

3416 Zipes, Jack, ed. *Victorian Fairy Tales: The Revolt of the Fairies and Elves* (9–12). Illus. 1987, Methuen $29.50 (0-416-42080-4). Dragons and elves abound in these 22 tales with their original illustrations. (Rev: SLJ 6–7/87) [398.2]

North America

GENERAL AND MISCELLANEOUS

3417 Abrahams, Roger D., ed. *Afro-American Folktales: Stories from Black Traditions in the New World* (9–12). 1985, Pantheon $22.45 (0-394-52755-0); paper $11.45 (0-394-72885-8). A rich collection of Afro-American folktales from South and Central America, the Caribbean, and southern United States. (Rev: BL 2/1/85; BR 11–12/85) [398.2]

3418 West, John O., ed. *Mexican-American Folklore* (9–12). Illus. 1988, August House $19.95 (0-87483-060-5); paper $9.95 (0-87483-059-1). A collection of stories, proverbs, legends, and other forms of folklore reflecting the Mexican-American culture. (Rev: BL 11/15/88) [398]

INDIANS OF NORTH AMERICA

3419 Bierhorst, John. *The Mythology of North America* (8–12). Illus. 1985, Morrow $13.00 (0-688-04145-0). A region-by-region examination of the folklore and mythology of the North American Indian. (Rev: BL 6/15/85; SLJ 8/85) [291.1]

3420 Bierhorst, John, ed. *The Sacred Path: Spells, Prayers and Power Songs of the American Indians* (10–12). 1983, Morrow $15.95 (0-688-01699-5); paper $7.95 (0-688-02647-8). This outstanding collection includes chants and prayers about such topics as birth, death, and hunting. [398]

3421 Burland, Cottie. *North American Indian Mythology* (9–12). Rev ed. Illus. 1985, Bedrick $19.95 (0-87226-016-X). The most important legends (including those of the Eskimos) are retold in this lavishly illustrated volume. (Rev: BL 1/15/86) [299]

3422 Edmonds, Margot, and Ella C. Clark. *Voices of the Wind: Native American Legends* (10–12). Illus. 1990, Facts on File $27.95 (0-8160-2067-1). A large collection of Indian legends—many lesser known and not previously in anthologies. (Rev: BL 11/15/89) [398.2]

3423 Erdoes, Richard, and Alfonso Ortiz, eds. *American Indian Myths and Legends* (10–12). Illus. 1984, Pantheon paper $12.95 (0-394-74018-1). From the entire North American continent, here is a collection of 160 tales from native American folklore. [398.2]

3424 Marriott, Alice, and Carol K. Rachlin. *American Indian Mythology* (10–12). 1972, Harper paper $4.95 (0-8152-0335-7). This is a collection of ancient and contemporary myths from 20 different tribes. [398]

3425 Marriott, Alice, and Carol K. Rachlin. *Plains Indian Mythology* (10–12). 1977, NAL paper $4.95 (0-452-00766-6). This well-written anthology includes both stories and poems from a number of different tribes that lived on the Great Plains. [291.1]

3426 Schultz, James W. *Blackfeet Tales of Glacier National Park* (9–12). 1990, Jameson paper $6.95 (0-915463-52-0). A reprint of stories collected by Schultz many years ago when he lived with the Siksika tribe of the Blackfeet. (Rev: BL 8/90) [398]

3427 Sevillano, Mando. *The Hopi Way: Tales from a Vanishing Culture* (10–12). 1986, Northland paper $9.95 (0-87358-413-9). Seven Hopi tales are retold that illustrate their love of nature and belief in magic. (Rev: BL 1/1/87) [970]

3428 Turner, Frederick W. III, ed. *The Portable North American Indian Reader* (10–12). 1974, Penguin paper $9.95 (0-14-015077-3). This fine anthology covers not only the myths and tales of the American Indian but also material on their history and present-day writers. [897]

3429 Van Etten, Teresa. *Ways of Indian Magic* (7–12). Illus. 1985, Sunstone paper $8.95 (0-86534-061-7). A fine retelling of 6 legends of the Pueblo Indians. (Rev: BR 3–4/86) [398.2]

UNITED STATES

3430 Blair, Walter. *Tall Tale America: A Legendary History of Our Humorous Heroes* (10–12). Illus. 1987, Univ. of Chicago Pr. paper $9.95 (0-226-05596-5). Mike Fink, Davy Crockett, Johnny Appleseed, and Pecos Bill are only 4 of the many tall-tale heroes the reader meets in this collection of folktales. [398.2]

3431 Botkin, B. A., ed. *A Treasury of American Folklore* (9–12). 1989, Crown $12.98 (0-517-67978-7). This collection, first published in 1944, cuts across racial and ethnic lines and represents various parts of our country. [398.2]

3432 Botkin, B. A., ed. *A Treasury of New England Folklore: Stories, Ballads, and Traditions of Yankee Folk* (10–12). 1989, Crown $12.98 (0-517-67977-9). A rich collection of songs, myths, and folktales in the Yankee tradition. [398.2]

3433 Brunvand, Jan Harold. *The Vanishing Hitchhiker: American Urban Legends and Their Meanings* (9–12). 1981, Norton $14.95 (0-393-01473-8); paper $7.95 (0-393-95169-3). This is a collection of American urban folk legends and their origins. [001.9]

3434 Coffin, Tristram P., and Hennig Cohen, eds. *Folklore in America* (10–12). Illus. 1986, Univ. Press of America paper $13.75 (0-8191-5355-9). An anthology of snippets taken from 70 years of the *Journal of American Folklore*. [398]

3435 Courlander, Harold, ed. *A Treasury of Afro-American Folklore* (10–12). Illus. 1976, Crown $14.95 (0-517-52348-5). A rich collection of folklore brought from Africa but changed with the passage of time. [398.2]

3436 Dorson, Richard M. *America in Legend* (10–12). 1974, Pantheon paper $15.95 (0-394-70926-8). This is a collection of American folklore from colonial times to the present. [598]

3437 Dorson, Richard M. *American Folklore* (10–12). 1987, Univ. of Chicago Pr. paper $4.50 (0-226-15859-4). An overview of our folklore from colonial times to the present. [398]

3438 Lee, Hector. *Heroes, Villains, and Ghosts: Folklore of Old California* (9–12). 1988, Borgo $22.95 (0-8095-4038-X). Each of these folktales has its origin in the history of California and many of them are ghost stories. (Rev: BL 2/1/85) [398]

3439 Lester, Julius. *Black Folktales* (9–12). Illus. 1987, Grove paper $7.95 (0-394-17178-0). A modern retelling with contemporary references to 12 African and Afro-American folktales. [398.2]

3440 Reader's Digest, eds. *American Folklore and Legend* (10–12). Illus. 1981, Reader's Digest $23.95 (0-89577-045-8). This illustrated account presents an interesting history of folklore as well as a retelling of famous American legends. [398.2]

3441 Smith, Jimmy Neil. *Homespun* (9–12). Illus. 1988, Crown $19.95 (0-517-56936-1). A wonderful collection of 22 favorite folktales from the country's top storytellers. (Rev: SLJ 3/89) [398.2]

3442 Steele, Phillip W. *Ozark Tales and Superstitions* (10–12). 1983, Pelican paper $4.95 (0-88289-404-8). Twenty-five tales handed down in the Ozarks through the oral tradition. [398]

3443 Zeitlin, Steven J., et al. *A Celebration of American Family Folklore* (10–12). 1982, Pantheon paper $11.95 (0-394-71223-4). A selection of American folklore taken from the collection at the Smithsonian. [398]

South and Central America

3444 Bierhorst, John. *The Mythology of South America* (9–12). Illus. 1988, Morrow $15.95 (0-688-06722-0). Region-by-region the author tells salient stories and traces themes and variations on them. (Rev: BL 9/15/88; BR 5–6/88; SLJ 5/88; VOYA 6/88) [299.8]

3445 Nicholson, Irene. *Mexican and Central American Mythology* (9–12). Rev. ed. Illus. 1985, Bedrick $19.95 (0-87226-003-8). This is a collection of myths and folklore from tribes that lived in pre-Columbian Mexico and Central America. (Rev: BL 6/15/85; BR 1–2/86) [299]

3446 Osborne, Harold. *South American Mythology* (9–12). Illus. 1986, Bedrick $19.95 (0-87226-043-7). A recounting of the myths of the pre-Columbian peoples of South America. (Rev: BL 4/15/86) [299]

3447 Paredes, Americo, ed. *Folktales of Mexico* (10–12). 1987, Univ. of Chicago Pr. paper $11.95 (0-226-64573-8). A scholarly retelling of about 80 Mexican folktales. [398.2]

Mythology

General and Miscellaneous

3448 Bierhorst, John. *The Mythology of Mexico and Central America* (9–12). Illus. 1990, Morrow $14.95 (0-688-06721-2). A collection of the 20 "basic" myths and their influence on the culture and political life of this region. (Rev: BL 10/1/90) [398.2]

3449 Bulfinch, Thomas. *Bulfinch's Mythology: The Age of Fable, The Age of Chivalry, Legends of Charlemagne* (10–12). 1913, Harper, $17.95 (0-690-57260-3); Dell paper $5.95 (0-440-30845-3). This single volume contains *The Age of Fable, The Age of Chivalry,* and *Legends of Charlemagne.* [291]

3450 Campbell, Joseph. *Myths to Live By* (10–12). 1984, Bantam paper $4.95 (0-553-27088-5). For better readers, this is an account of how myths come to be and their importance in life. [291.1]

3451 Christie, Anthony. *Chinese Mythology* (9–12). Illus. 1985, Bedrick $19.95 (0-600-34277-8). A fine collection of Chinese myths that explain such phenomena as the creation of the world. (Rev: BL 10/15/85) [299]

3452 Cotterell, Arthur. *The Macmillan Illustrated Encyclopedia of Myths & Legends* (9–12). Illus. 1989, Macmillan $29.95 (0-02-580181-3). A comprehensive guide to world mythology profusely illustrated with plenty of color. (Rev: BL 2/1/90) [291.1]

3453 Eliot, Alexander, et al. *The Universal Myths: Heroes, Gods, Tricksters and Others* (10–12). 1990, NAL paper $8.95 (0-452-01027-6). A retelling of myths that are common to many cultures, such as those dealing with the creation of the Earth. (Rev: BL 12/1/89) [291.1]

3454 Gifford, Douglas. *Warriors, Gods & Spirits from Central & South American Mythology* (7–12). Illus. by John Sibbick. 1983, Schocken $16.95 (0-8052-3857-3). Latin American mythology from Aztec tales to those reflecting Western influences. [299]

3455 Goodrich, Norma Lorre. *Ancient Myths* (10–12). 1960, NAL paper $3.95 (0-451-62361-4). This collection comes from the mythology of several ancient civilizations. Also use: *Medieval Myths* (1960). [291.1]

3456 Gray, John. *Near Eastern Mythology* (9–12). Rev. ed. Illus. 1985, Bedrick $19.95 (0-87226-004-6). A fine collection of tales that draws from the literature of the Sumerians, Jews, Babylonians, Assyrians, and Canaanites. (Rev: BL 6/15/85; BR 1–2/86) [291.1]

3457 Hamilton, Edith. *Mythology* (10–12). Illus. 1942, Little $17.95 (0-316-34114-2); NAL paper $4.95 (0-451-62523-4). In addition to Greek myths, this classic account covers the Trojan War and Norse myths. [292]

3458 Harris, Geraldine. *Gods & Pharaohs from Egyptian Mythology* (8–12). Illus. 1982, Schocken $15.95 (0-8052-3858-1). A selection of myths involving such characters as Ra, Hathor, and Isis. [299]

3459 Ions, Veronica. *Egyptian Mythology* (10–12). Rev. ed. Illus. 1983, Bedrick $19.95 (0-911745-07-6). Many of these Egyptian myths deal with the afterlife as perceived by the ancient Egyptians. [291.1]

3460 Ions, Veronica. *Indian Mythology* (10–12). Rev. ed. Illus. 1984, Bedrick $19.95 (0-911745-

55-6). This book deals primarily with myths associated with the Hindu, Buddhist, and Jain religions. [291.1]

3461 MacCana, Proinsias. *Celtic Mythology* (9–12). Rev. ed. Illus. 1985, Bedrick $19.95 (0-87226-002-X). This collection of stories about gods and mortals comes from the people who, though living in various parts of Europe, had a center of civilization in Ireland. (Rev: BL 6/15/85; BR 1–2/86) [299]

3462 Matthews, John, and Bob Stewart. *Warriors of Arthur* (10–12). Illus. 1988, Blandford $24.95 (0-7137-1900-1). An attempt to find the elements of truth in the Arthurian legends. (Rev: BL 5/1/88) [398]

3463 Parrinder, Geoffrey. *African Mythology* (10–12). Rev. ed. Illus. 1986, Bedrick $19.95 (0-87226-042-9). A lavishly illustrated book on Africa's major myths, fables, and folktales. (Rev: BL 4/15/86) [299]

3464 Perowne, Stewart. *Roman Mythology* (10–12). Rev. ed. Illus. 1984, Bedrick $19.95 (0-911745-56-4). This book covers Roman mythology and also compares the myths with those of other lands, particularly Greece and Egypt. [291.1]

3465 Piggott, Juliet. *Japanese Mythology* (10–12). Rev. ed. Illus. 1983, Bedrick $19.95 (0-911745-09-2). After a brief introduction to Japan, the myths are presented with coverage of present religions. [291.1]

3466 South, Malcolm. *Mythical and Fabulous Creatures: A Sourcebook and Research Guide* (9–12). Illus. 1988, Bedrick paper $14.95 (0-87226-208-1). This scholarly work contains 20 essays on mythical beasts and how they have been depicted in ancient and modern art and literature. (Rev: BR 5–6/89; SLJ 1/89) [291.1]

3467 Van Over, Raymond, ed. *Sun Songs: Creation Myths from Around the World* (10–12). 1980, NAL paper $4.95 (0-452-00730-5). This work of general mythology discusses creation myths from all regions of the world. [291.1]

Classical

3468 Aesop. *Aesop's Fables* (7–12). 1988, Morrow LB $13.88 (0-688-07361-1); Scholastic paper $2.25 (0-590-40569-1). This is one of many editions of the short moral tales from ancient Greece. [398.2]

3469 Aesop. *The Fables of Aesop* (9–12). Trans. by Patrick Gregory and Justina Gregory. Illus. 1975, Gambit $13.95 (0-87645-074-5); paper $8.95 (0-87645-116-4). This book, one of many available editions, covers 100 of the fables and deletes the moralizing conclusions. [398.2]

3470 Asimov, Isaac. *Words from the Myths* (9–12). Illus. 1961, Houghton $13.95 (0-395-06568-2); NAL paper $2.50 (0-451-14097-4). Many of the standard myths are retold in this account that focuses on the words derived from them. [292]

3471 Braymer, Marjorie. *Atlantis: The Biography of a Legend* (7–12). 1983, Macmillan $13.95 (0-689-50264-8). The myths surrounding Atlantis are retold plus an investigation of whether or not the present island of Thera could contain the remnents of this magical kingdom. [292]

3472 Evslin, Bernard. *The Adventures of Ulysses: The Odyssey of Homer* (8–12). 1985, Scholastic paper $2.50 (0-590-33948-6). A modern retelling of the adventures of Ulysses during the 10 years he wandered after the Trojan War. [292]

3473 Evslin, Bernard. *Heroes and Monsters of Greek Myth* (7–12). 1988, Scholastic paper $2.50 (0-590-41072-5). A simple retelling of the most famous of Greek myths. Also use: *The Greek Gods* (1988). [292]

3474 Evslin, Bernard. *Heroes, Gods and Monsters of Greek Myths* (8–12). Illus. 1984, Bantam paper $4.50 (0-553-25920-2). The most popular Greek myths are retold in modern language. [292]

3475 Evslin, Bernard. *The Trojan War: The Iliad of Homer* (8–12). 1988, Scholastic paper $2.95 (0-590-41626-X). The story of the 10-year war between the Greeks and the Trojans is retold for the modern reader. [292]

3476 Grant, Michael. *Myths of the Greeks and Romans* (9–12). 1989, NAL paper $5.95 (0-451-62693-1). This collection of stories bridges the gap between these two similar mythologies. [292]

3477 Graves, Robert. *Greek Myths* (10–12). 2 vols. 1955, Penguin paper $4.95 ea (0-14-020508-X). A scholarly but readable account that gives background information from archaeology and anthropology. [292]

3478 Pinsent, John. *Greek Mythology* (10–12). Rev. ed. Illus. 1983, Bedrick $19.95 (0-911745-08-4). An account that combines mythology with Greek history. [291.1]

3479 Usher, Kerry. *Heroes, Gods & Emperors from Roman Mythology* (8–12). Illus. 1983, Schocken $16.95 (0-8052-3880-8). The origins of

Roman mythology are given plus a generous retelling of famous myths. [292]

Scandinavian

3480 Crossley-Holland, Kevin. *The Norse Myths: Introduced and Retold* (10–12). Illus.

1980, Pantheon $16.45 (0-394-50048-2); paper $11.95 (0-394-74846-8). After a lengthy detailed introduction on background material, the important myths are retold. [293]

3481 Davidson, H. R. Ellis. *Gods and Myths of Northern Europe* (10–12). 1965, Penguin paper $6.95 (0-14-020670-1). The origins and the stories behind Scandinavian deities are given in detail. [291.1]

Humor and Satire

3482 Allen, Woody. *Without Feathers* (9–12). 1987, Ballantine paper $4.95 (0-345-33697-6). Sixteen humorous pieces plus two one-act plays are included in this collection. Also use: *Getting Even* (1971). [817]

3483 Ayres, Alex, ed. *The Wit & Wisdom of Mark Twain* (9–12). 1987, Harper $19.95 (0-06-015783-6); NAL paper $7.95 (0-452-00982-0). An alphabetically arranged collection of mostly humorous quotations by Mark Twain. (Rev: BL 8/87) [818]

3484 Barry, Lynda. *The Fun House* (10–12). 1987, Harper paper $6.95 (0-06-096228-3). Comic strips from "Ernie Pook's Comique" on the humorous but often perilous joys of childhood. (Rev: BL 6/1/88) [741.5]

3485 Bodett, Tom. *Small Comforts: More Comments and Comic Pieces* (10–12). 1987, Addison $12.95 (0-201-13417-9). Short, humorous pieces that cover such topics as chain letters, pets, being a father, and dishwashing. (Rev: BL 1/1/88) [808.7]

3486 Bombeck, Erma. *At Wit's End* (9–12). 1986, Fawcett paper $3.95 (0-449-21184-3). A fine collection of pieces by one of America's favorite humorists. Also use: *Just Wait Till You Have Children of Your Own* (1985), *If Life Is a Bowl of Cherries, What Am I Doing in the Pits?*, *I Lost Everything in the Post-Natal Depression* (both 1987), and *The Grass Is Always Greener over the Septic Tank* (1986). [808.7]

3487 Bombeck, Erma. *Family: The Ties That Bind . . . and Gag!* (9–12). 1987, McGraw $17.95 (0-07-006460-1); Fawcett paper $4.95 (0-449-21529-6). Bombeck writes humorously about family life and being a mother as she did in

Motherhood: The Second Oldest Profession (1983). (Rev: BL 8/87) [306.85]

3488 Braden, Tom. *Eight Is Enough* (9–12). 1981, Fawcett paper $2.25 (0-449-23002-3). With wit and humor, this Washington columnist tells about raising 8 children. [808.8]

3489 Brush, Stephanie. *Life: A Warning* (9–12). 1987, Simon & Schuster $12.95 (0-671-61130-5). A humorous look at the trials and tribulations life has in store for people. (Rev: SLJ 9/87) [808.7]

3490 Buchwald, Art. *I Think I Don't Remember* (10–12). Illus. 1987, Putnam $17.95 (0-399-13325-9); paper $7.95 (0-399-51482-1). Another collection of humorous pieces by the wit who takes on Washington single-handed. (Rev: BL 9/1/87) [808.7]

3491 Buchwald, Art. *While Reagan Slept* (10–12). 1983, Putnam $14.95 (0-399-12841-7); Fawcett paper $3.95 (0-449-12762-1). Humorous pieces on American politics culled from this newspaperman's columns. [808.7]

3492 Buchwald, Art. *Whose Rose Garden Is It Anyway?* (9–12). 1989, Putnam $18.95 (0-399-13480-8). The political satirist in a collection of newspaper columns mostly about the presidency of George Bush. (Rev: BL 9/1/89) [814]

3493 Buchwald, Art. *You Can Fool All of the People All the Time* (10–12). Illus. 1985, Putnam $16.95 (0-399-13104-3); Fawcett paper $7.95 (0-449-90200-5). A collection of humorous columns many of which deal with Ronald Reagan and his presidency. (Rev: BL 9/15/85) [814]

3494 Cosby, Bill. *Love and Marriage* (9–12). 1989, Doubleday $16.95 (0-385-24664-1). The comedian remembers his first attempts at love affairs and his experiences in marriage. (Rev: BL 4/15/89) [306.7]

3495 Ephron, Delia. *How to Eat Like a Child* (9–12). 1988, NAL paper $3.95 (0-451-82181-5). This is a delightful look at the behavior of children in a variety of situations. [808.7]

3496 Fulghum, Robert. *It Was on Fire When I Lay Down on It* (9–12). 1989, Villard $17.95 (0-394-58056-7). More homespun humor and wisdom from the man who gave us *All I Really Need to Know I Learned in Kindergarten* (1988). (Rev: BL 9/1/89) [814]

3497 Geist, William. *Toward a Safe and Sane Halloween and Other Tales of Suburbia* (10–12). 1985, Times Books $16.45 (0-8129-1150-4). The joys and annoyances of living in the suburbs are explored in these humorous essays by the well-known newspaper columnist. (Rev: BL 8/85) [977.3]

3498 Grizzard, Lewis. *Kathy Sue Loudermilk, I Love You* (10–12). 1984, Peachtree $11.95 (0-931948-3); Warner paper $3.95 (0-446-34299-8). A collection of humorous pieces that affectionately depict the real South. [808.7]

3499 Keillor, Garrison. *Leaving Home: A Collection of Lake Woebegon Stories* (9–12). 1990, Penguin paper $8.95 (0-14-013160-4). A collection of stories and anecdotes about Lake Woebegon culled from monologues given on American Public Radio network's *Prairie Home Companion*. (Rev: BR 1–2/88; SLJ 2/88; VOYA 4/88) [808.7]

3500 Kerr, Jean. *Please Don't Eat the Daisies* (9–12). 1979, Fawcett paper $1.95 (0-449-24099-1). This is a humorous look at bringing up a family in suburbia. [808.7]

3501 Macaulay, David. *Motel of the Mysteries* (10–12). Illus. 1979, Houghton $16.95 (0-395-28424-4); paper $8.95 (0-395-28425-2). A satire on archaeology and civilization that involves unearthing a motel in the year 4022. [817]

3502 McManus, Patrick F. *The Night the Bear Ate Goombaw* (9–12). 1989, Henry Holt $15.95 (0-8050-1033-5). McManus recalls his most misadventures as a great outdoorsman. (Rev: BL 4/15/89; BR 1–2/90; VOYA 12/89) [813]

3503 Marquis, Don. *The Lives and Times of Archy & Mehitabel* (10–12). Illus. 1950, Doubleday $10.95 (0-385-04262-0). The humorous adventures of an alley cat and a cockroach collected in one volume. [817]

3504 Muir, Frank, ed. *The Oxford Book of Humorous Prose: William Caxton to P. G.* *Wodehouse—A Conducted Tour* (10–12). 1990, Oxford Univ. Pr. $35.95 (0-19-214106-6). A fine collection of humorous writings with an emphasis on those from Britain. (Rev: BL 1/15/90) [828]

3505 Novak, William, et al., eds. *The Big Book of New American Humor: The Best of the Past 25 Years* (9–12). 1990, Harper $15.95 (0-06-096551-7). From cartoons and jokes to humorous prose pieces and television scripts, this is a fine selection of material by modern American humorists. (Rev: BL 10/15/90) [817.54]

3506 Palin, Michael. *Around the World in 80 Days with Michael Palin* (10–12). Illus. 1990, Parkwest $24.95 (0-563-20826-0). With humor and good nature, the Monty Python alumnus describes a trip that duplicates that of Phileas Fogg. (Rev: BL 8/90) [910.41]

3507 Pinkwater, Daniel. *Fish Whistle: Commentaries, Uncommentaries, and Vulgar Excesses* (9–12). 1989, Addison-Wesley $15.95 (0-201-51789-2). Seventy short humorous pieces on all sorts of subjects by the zany writer usually associated with children's books. (Rev: BL 9/1/89; BR 3–4/90; SLJ 2/90) [814]

3508 Rooney, Andrew A. *A Few Minutes with Andy Rooney* (9–12). 1982, Warner paper $4.95 (0-446-34766-3). This is a collection of short humorous pieces by the writer who gained prominence on television's "60 Minutes." Also use *And More by Andy Rooney* (1983). [808.7]

3509 Rooney, Andrew A. *The Most of Andy Rooney* (9–12). Illus. 1986, Macmillan $22.50 (0-689-11864-3). A massive volume that contains all the fun of 3 previously published works: *A Few Minutes with Andy Rooney* (1981), *And More by Andy Rooney* (1982), and *Pieces of My Mind* (1984). Pieces of My Mind (Rev: BL 2/1/87) [814]

3510 Rooney, Andrew A. *Not That You Asked. . .* (9–12). 1989, Random $15.95 (0-394-57837-6). A collection of short pieces on such topics as ladies' underwear and real estate deals. (Rev: BL 2/15/89) [814.54]

3511 Sarrantonio, Al, ed. *Fireside Treasury of Great Humor* (9–12). 1987, Simon & Schuster paper $9.95 (0-671-63283-3). Thirty-five short pieces that range from Saki and O. Henry to Woody Allen and Dorothy Parker. (Rev: BL 8/87) [814]

3512 Shalit, Gene, ed. *Laughing Matters: A Celebration of American Humor* (9–12). Illus. 1987, Doubleday $24.95 (0-385-18547-2); Ballantine paper $14.95 (0-345-36251-7). A huge collection of writings and drawings by a veritable who's who of American humor. (Rev: BL 10/1/87) [817]

3513 Smirnoff, Yakov. *America on Six Rubles a Day: Or, How to Become a Capitalist Pig* (8–12). 1987, Random paper $5.95 (0-394-75523-5). The former Soviet comedian gives humorous tips to other émigrés contemplating a move to the United States. (Rev: BL 12/1/87) [818]

3514 Thurber, James. *The Thurber Carnival* (10–12). 1945, Random $12.95 (0-394-60474-1); Harper paper $9.95 (0-06-090445-3). A collection of humorous pieces by the author taken from a number of previously published volumes, with illustrations by the author. [817]

3515 Twain, Mark. *The Innocents Abroad: Or The New Pilgrims Progress* (10–12). 1966, NAL paper $4.95 (0-451-52502-7). A humorous account of a voyage in the Mediterranean and on visits to countries in the area. [817]

3516 Twain, Mark. *Life on the Mississippi* (10–12). 1983, Buccaneer LB $23.95 (0-89966-469-5); Bantam paper $2.95 (0-553-21142-0). A nonfiction account of life on the Mississippi with many humorous passages. First published in 1874. [817]

3517 Twain, Mark. *Roughing It* (10–12). 1986, Buccaneer LB $25.95 (0-89966-524-1); Penguin paper $4.95 (0-14-039010-3). A humorous account first published in 1872 of a trip to California and Hawaii. [817]

3518 Winokur, Jon, ed. *The Portable Curmudgeon* (10–12). 1987, NAL $17.95 (0-453-00565-9). A humorous collection of insults and negative remarks from some of the greatest. (Rev: BL 10/15/87) [081]

3519 Zall, Paul M., ed. *Mark Twain Laughing: Humorous Anecdotes by and about Samuel L. Clemens* (10–12). Illus. 1987, Univ. of Tennessee Pr. paper $14.95 (0-87049-544-5). A collection of writing and anecdotes that confirm Twain's position as a great humorist. Others in this series are: *Ben Franklin Laughing* (1980) and *George Washington Laughing* (1989). (Rev: BL 12/15/85) [818]

Speeches, Essays, and General Literary Works

3520 Abbey, Edward. *One Life at a Time, Please* (10–12). 1988, Henry Holt $17.95 (0-8050-0602-8). Thought-stimulating essays on such topics as politics, free speech, travel, writing, and the nature of sin. (Rev: VOYA 8/88) [808.84]

3521 Abrams, Irwin, ed. *The Words of Peace: Selections from the Speeches of the Winners of the Nobel Peace Prize* (10–12). Illus. 1990, Newmarket $14.95 (1-55704-060-5). This volume contains selections taken from the original lectures of Nobel Prize winners from 1901 to 1989. (Rev: BL 7/90) [327.1]

3522 Baldwin, James. *The Price of the Ticket: Collected Nonfiction, 1948–1985* (10–12). 1985, St. Martin's $29.95 (0-312-64306-3). This work includes *Nobody Knows My Name, Notes of a Native Son,* and *The Fire Next Time.* [814]

3523 Berry, Wendell. *What Are People For?* (9–12). 1990, North Point $19.95 (0-86547-420-6); paper $9.95 (0-86547-437-0). A group of thoughtful essays on such diverse subjects as buying a computer and the present state of the environment. (Rev: BL 4/1/90) [081]

3524 Bly, Robert. *The Winged Voice: The Poetic Voice of Henry David Thoreau* (10–12). Illus. 1986, Random $18.95 (0-87156-762-8). A selection of prose and some poetry that are arranged under different stages of the author's developing philosophy. (Rev: SLJ 4/87) [808.84]

3525 Boller, Paul F., and John George. *They Never Said It: A Book of Fake Quotes, Misquotes, and Misleading Attributions* (10–12). 1989, Oxford Univ. Pr. $16.95 (0-19-505541-1). A dictionary of misquotes plus explanations setting the record straight arranged by the names of the

people that supposedly spoke them. (Rev: BL 2/15/89) [082]

3526 Camus, Albert. *The Myth of Sisyphus, and Other Essays* (10–12). 1959, Random paper $4.95 (0-394-70075-9). This collection of profound essays ponders the meaning of life. [844]

3527 Chatwin, Bruce. *What Am I Doing Here?* (10–12). 1989, Viking $19.95 (0-670-82508-5). A group of fine essays about traveling and the unusual people the author met on these travels. (Rev: SLJ 4/90) [808.84]

3528 Cooke, Alistair. *The Patient Has the Floor* (10–12). 1986, Knopf $16.95 (0-394-50365-1). A series of lectures on topics ranging from the American Revolution to hypochondria, from the host of Masterpiece Theater. (Rev: SLJ 11/86) [808.5]

3529 Didion, Joan. *The White Album* (10–12). 1990, Farrar paper $7.95 (0-374-52221-9). In this collection of essays, the noted author Didion describes life and general social concerns from the late 1960s to the the the late 1970s. [808.84]

3530 *Editor's Choice: Smithsonian* (10–12). Illus. 1990, Smithsonian Inst. $35.00 (0-89599-027-X). A handsome collection of 37 articles from the first 20 years of the *Smithsonian* magazine. (Rev: BL 7/90) [081]

3531 Emerson, Ralph Waldo. *Emerson's Essays* (10–12). 1981, Harper paper $6.95 (0-06-090906-4). This is one of several editions available of these famous essays. [808.84]

3532 Emerson, Ralph Waldo. *Essays, First and Second Series* (10–12). 1990, Random paper $11.50 (0-679-72612-8). This collection of Emerson's essays covers the contents of two volumes originally published in 1841 and 1844. [814]

3533 Emerson, Ralph Waldo. *The Portable Emerson* (10–12). 1981, Penguin paper $9.95 (0-14-015094-3). A generous collection of Emerson's essays plus 22 poems. [818]

3534 Giovanni, Nikki. *Sacred Cows . . . and Other Edibles* (10–12). 1988, Morrow $12.95 (0-688-04333-X). For mature readers, this renowned poet discusses such topics as baseball, censorship, and the black middle class. (Rev: BL 2/1/88) [814]

3535 Greene, Bob. *American Beat* (10–12). 1984, Penguin $7.95 (0-14-007320-5). A collection of short essays that cover a variety of personal and public problems. [808.84]

3536 Hoopes, Ned E., and Richard Peck, eds. *Edge of Awareness: Twenty-Five Contemporary Essays* (9–12). 1990, Dell paper $3.95 (0-440-92218-6). A lively collection of essays that are excellent examples of the genre. [808.7]

3537 Lindbergh, Anne Morrow. *Gift from the Sea* (10–12). 1991, Random paper $6.95 (0-679-73241-1). For better readers, this is a group of thoughtful essays addressed mainly to women. [808.8]

3538 McCarthy, Colman. *Inner Companions* (10–12). 1978, $12.50 (0-87491-054-4). In this book of essays, McCarthy describes his inner companions—the books and the thoughts that nourish his mind. [808.84]

3539 McPhee, John A. *The John McPhee Reader* (10–12). 1976, Farrar $17.50 (0-374-17992-1); paper $9.95 (0-374-51719-3). This is an excellent collection of essays culled from 12 previously published volumes. [808.84]

3540 McPhee, John A. *Table of Contents* (10–12). 1985, Farrar $15.95 (0-374-27241-7). For better readers, this is a collection of essays about such diverse subjects as bear cubs, nature study, politics, young doctors, and technology. (Rev: BL 9/1/85) [937.92]

3541 Mencken, H. L. *The American Scene: A Reader* (10–12). 1965, Knopf $20.00 (0-394-43594-X); paper $12.95 (0-394-75214-7). A selection of Mencken's essays that cover such topics as politics, journalism, religion, and literature. [818]

3542 Orwell, George. *Orwell, the Lost Writings* (10–12). 1988, Avon paper $5.95 (0-380-70118-9). This is a collection of Orwell's writings while he was a producer of programs for the BBC from 1941 through 1943. [828]

3543 Pack, Robert, and Jay Parini, eds. *The Bread Loaf Anthology of Contemporary American Essays* (10–12). 1989, Univ. Pr. of New England $25.00 (0-87451-476-2); paper $12.95 (0-87451-475-4). A collection of distinguished writing on a variety of topics, many of which are personal experiences. (Rev: BL 5/15/89) [814]

3544 Peterson, Owen, ed. *Representative American Speeches, 1988–1989* (10–12). 1989, H. W. Wilson paper $12.00. This is one of the volumes of an annual compilation of the most important speeches of the year. [815.08]

3545 Prather, Hugh. *Notes to Myself: My Struggle to Become a Person* (10–12). 1976, Bantam paper $3.95 (0-553-25765-X). These reflections on life's meaning are usually short in length and become mini-essays. [808.84]

3546 Rilke, Rainer Maria. *Where Silence Reigns: Selected Prose* (10–12). Trans. by G. Craig Houston. 1978, New Directions paper $7.95 (0-8112-0697-1). This is a sampling of letters, essays, and excerpts from Rilke's notebook that reveal his inner thoughts. [808.84]

3547 Royko, Mike. *Sez Who? Sez Me* (10–12). 1982, Dutton $13.95 (0-525-24125-6). The Chicago journalist covers a multitude of topics in this collection of short pieces. [808.94]

3548 Safire, William, and Leonard Safir, eds. *Words of Wisdom: More Good Advice* (10–12). 1989, Simon & Schuster $18.95 (0-671-67535-4). Arranged by topics from "Ability" to "Youth," this is a collection of quotations culled from many sources, each giving friendly advice. (Rev: BL 2/15/89) [082]

3549 Shapiro, James E. *Meditations from the Breakdown Lane: Running across America* (10–12). 1983, Houghton paper $6.95 (0-395-33105-6). This account explores the thoughts and experiences of a man who ran 3,000 miles from San Francisco to New York. [796.4]

3550 Synder, Gary. *The Practice of the Wild* (10–12). 1990, North Point $22.95 (0-86547-453-2); paper $10.95 (0-86547-454-0). In this challenging book, the Beat poet and student of Zen writes a series of essays about man's relation to nature and how all living things interrelate. (Rev: BL 9/15/90) [814]

3551 Thoreau, Henry David. *Walden* (10–12). 1983, Buccaneer LB $21.95 (0-89966-466-0); Doubleday paper $4.95 (0-385-09503-1). These essays on nature and life were written during the author's solitary stay at Walden Pond in Massachusetts. [818]

3552 Twain, Mark. *The Complete Essays of Mark Twain* (10–12). Illus. 1985, Doubleday paper

$15.95 (0-385-06590-6). A total of 68 essays, including some speeches, in this chronologically arranged collection. [814]

3553 Twain, Mark. *Mark Twain Speaks for Himself* (10–12). Illus. 1978, Purdue Univ. Pr. $12.95 (0-911198-49-0). Garnered from many sources, here is a collection of short pieces, many of them published for the first time. [818]

3554 Twain, Mark. *A Pen Warmed-Up in Hell: Mark Twain in Protest* (10–12). 1972, Harper $13.45 (0-06-070117-2). A collection of 23 short pieces on such subjects as war, politics, and human frailties. [818]

3555 Van Doren, Mark. *The Essays of Mark Van Doren (1924–1972)* (10–12). 1980, Greenwood LB $39.95 (0-313-22098-0). Most of these essays deal with literary criticism both on writing formats and on individual writers. [814]

3556 Vidal, Gore. *Matters of Fact and Fiction: Essays, 1973–1976* (10–12). 1977, Random $14.95 (0-394-41128-5). This collection of essays deals with such topics as writing and American politics. [808.84]

3557 Walker, Alice. *In Search of Our Mothers' Gardens: Womanist Prose* (10–12). 1983, Harcourt $16.95 (0-15-144525-7); paper $8.95 (0-15-644544-1). This is a collection of prose pieces dealing with topics like feminism, women writers, and being black in America. [818]

3558 Walker, Alice. *Living by the Word: Selected Writings, 1973–1987* (10–12). 1988, Harcourt $15.95 (0-15-152900-0). A collection of essays, talks, and journal entries mostly about her life and writing by the author of *The Color Purple*. For mature readers. (Rev: BL 3/1/88; BR 11–12/88) [813]

3559 White, E. B. *Essays of E. B. White* (10–12). 1987, Harper paper $9.95 (0-06-090662-6). Such diverse subjects as nuclear weapons and children's literature are covered in these essays. [814]

3560 White, E. B. *Poems and Sketches of E. B. White* (10–12). 1981, Harper $13.00 (0-06-014900-0); paper $5.95 (0-06-090969-2). All sorts of short pieces, including sketches, parodies, plus poems by this famous American writer. [818]

3561 Wiesel, Elie. *From the Kingdom of Memory* (10–12). 1990, Summit $19.95 (0-671-52332-5). A group of essays and speeches by the fighter for justice who won the Nobel Peace Prize. (Rev: BL 6/1/90) [815.54]

3562 Wolff, Geoffrey, ed. *The Best American Essays, 1989* (10–12). 1989, Ticknor $17.95 (0-89919-891-0); paper $8.95 (0-89919-892-9). A fine collection from many sources that includes writers such as Annie Dillard and Joan Didion. (Rev: BL 10/15/89) [814]

Literary History and Criticism

General and Miscellaneous

3563 Abrams, Meyer Howard. *A Glossary of Literary Terms* (10–12). 1981, Holt paper $11.95 (0-03-011953-7). In a series of essays, all sorts of literary terms are discussed and defined. [803]

3564 Annable, H. D. *Annable's Treasury of Literary Teasers* (10–12). 1989, Writer's Digest $10.95 (0-89879-368-8). A total of 768 questions are posed on all types of literature. (Rev: SLJ 3/90) [800]

3565 Blair, Walter, and Hamlin Hill. *America's Humor: From Poor Richard to Doonesbury* (10–12). Illus. 1987, Oxford Univ. Pr. paper $9.95 (0-19-502756-6). A survey of American humorous writing from Colonial times to the present. [817.09]

3566 Blamires, Harry. *Twentieth-Century English Literature* (10–12). Illus. 1982, Schocken $28.50 (0-8052-3827-1); paper $8.95 (0-8052-0772-4). This compact history of English literature covers writers and their works from 1900 to 1975. [820.9]

3567 Brosman, Catharine Savage. *Jean-Paul Sartre* (10–12). 1983, Twayne LB $16.95 (0-8057-6544-1). This account supplies biographical information plus an introduction and critique of his literary and philosophical writings. [848]

3568 Brown, Edward J., ed. *Major Soviet Writers* (10–12). 1973, Oxford Univ. Pr. paper $8.95 (0-19-501684-X). A collection of 17 critical essays on such writers as Pasternak and Solzhenitsyn. [891.7]

3569 Burrow, J. A. *Medieval Writers and Their Work: Middle English Literature and Its Background* (10–12). 1982, Oxford Univ. Pr. paper $9.95 (0-19-289122-7). Four hundred years of

English literature are covered in this introduction to Middle English and its writers. [820.9]

3570 Conn, Peter. *Literature in America: An Illustrated History* (10–12). Illus. 1989, Cambridge Univ. Pr. $29.95 (0-521-30373-7). For better readers, an account in text and pictures of the history of American literature. (Rev: BL 11/1/89) [810]

3571 Cooke, Michael G. *Afro-American Literature in the Twentieth Century: The Achievement of Intimacy* (10–12). 1984, Yale Univ. Pr. $29.50 (0-300-03218-8); paper $10.95 (0-300-03624-8). In a series of articles the author explores the history of black American literature and its coming of age. [810.9]

3572 Cuddon, J. A. *A Dictionary of Literary Terms* (10–12). 1977, Penguin paper $8.95 (0-14-051112-1). A comprehensive dictionary of the literary terms in use today. [803]

3573 Dover, K. J., ed. *Ancient Greek Literature* (10–12). Illus. 1980, Oxford Univ. Pr. paper $9.95 (0-19-289124-3). A historical survey of Greek literature from 700 B.C. to A.D. 500 [880.9]

3574 Downs, Robert B. *Books That Changed the World* (10–12). Rev. ed. 1978, ALA $20.00 (0-8389-0270-7); NAL paper $4.95 (0-451-62698-2). An analysis of this book by a wide range of authors—from Homer to Einstein—who have had an impact on society. [809]

3575 Drabble, Margaret, ed. *The Oxford Companion to English Literature* (10–12). 5th ed. 1985, Oxford Univ. Pr. $45.00 (0-19-866130-4). This somewhat expensive reference collection is interesting for browsers who want to learn a little bit about all of English literature and its authors. (Rev: BL 8/85) [820]

3576 Ehrlich, Eugene, and Gorton Carruth. *The Oxford Illustrated Literary Guide to the United States* (10–12). Illus. 1982, Oxford Univ. Pr. $39.95 (0-19-503186-5). Using a geographical approach, this is a guide to the literary geography of the United States with references to more than 1,500 different authors. There are 2 companion volumes from Oxford, one on Canada and the other on Great Britain and Ireland. [810.9]

3577 Elliott, Emory, et al., eds. *Columbia Literary History of the United States* (10–12). 1988, Columbia Univ. Pr. $59.95 (0-231-05812-8). A group of experts has contributed sections on all aspects of American literature from the native Indians to the present. (Rev: BL 4/1/88) [810]

3578 Emanuel, James A. *Langston Hughes* (10–12). 1967, Twayne LB $14.95 (0-8057-0388-8). An examination of this author's life and a critical examination of his work in a variety of literary formats. [818]

3579 Emerson, Everett, ed. *Major Writers of Early American Literature* (10–12). 1972, Univ. of Wisconsin Pr. paper $12.50 (0-299-06194-9). A series of essays by various authorities trace the first 200 years of American literary history. [810.9]

3580 Ford, Boris, ed. *The New Pelican Guide to English Literature* (10–12). 1988, Penguin paper $7.95 (0-14-022566-8). This paperback set on the history of English literature extends from medieval literature and Chaucer to the 1970s. [820.9]

3581 Foster, David William, and Virginia Ramos Foster, eds. *Modern Latin American Literature* (10–12). 2 vols. 1975, Ungar $120.00 (0-8044-3139-6). This anthology of critical comment includes material on 137 twentieth-century Latin American writers. [860.9]

3582 Fowler, Alastair. *A History of English Literature* (10–12). 1987, Harvard Univ. Pr. $30.00 (0-674-39665-0). From the Middle Ages through the 1980s, a well-balanced history of English literature. (Rev: BL 4/1/88) [820]

3583 Gilbar, Steven. *The Open Door: When Writers First Learned to Read* (10–12). Illus. 1989, Godine $14.95 (0-87923-809-7). Twenty-nine known writers recall their first reading experiences and their reactions. (Rev: BL 2/1/90) [028]

3584 Hammond, J. R. *An Edgar Allan Poe Companion: A Guide to the Short Stories, Romances, and Essays* (10–12). Illus. 1981, Barnes & Noble Bks. $29.50 (0-389-20172-3). After a biography, the author gives an introduction to the work of Poe in its various genres. [818]

3585 Harrison, James. *Rudyard Kipling* (10–12). 1982, Twayne LB $16.95 (0-8057-6825-4). Along with biographical information, this account gives a critical analysis of Kipling's poetry and fiction. [828]

3586 Harvey, Paul, and J. E. Heseltine, eds. *The Oxford Companion to French Literature* (10–12). 1959, Oxford Univ. Pr. $49.95 (0-19-866104-5). This reference covers French literature from earliest times to the beginning of World War II in brief articles on subjects like authors, individual works, and important places. An abridged updated version is *The Concise Oxford Dictionary of French Literature* (1976). [840.3]

3587 Highet, Gilbert. *The Classical Tradition: Greek and Roman Influences on Western Literature* (10–12). 1949, Oxford Univ. Pr. $39.95 (0-19-500578-8). This account traces how classical writers have influenced Western literature from the Middle Ages through the romantic period. [809]

3588 Holman, C. Hugh, and William Harmon. *A Handbook to Literature* (10–12). 5th ed. 1986, Macmillan $27.50 (0-02-553430-0). This book contains more than 1,500 entries on terms, movements, and groups associated with literature. [803]

3589 Howatson, M. C. *The Oxford Companion to Classical Literature* (10–12). Illus. 1989, Oxford Univ. Pr. $39.95 (0-19-866121-5). This is a useful reference work on Greek writers, their works, and related subjects. [880.3]

3590 Jackson, Blyden. *A History of Afro-American Literature, Volume I: The Long Beginning, 1746–1895* (10–12). 1989, Louisiana State Univ. Pr. $29.95 (0-8071-1511-8). In this, the first of a projected 4-volume set, 150 years of black literature is chronicled with many excerpts and examples. (Rev: BL 10/15/89) [810]

3591 Keene, Donald. *Dawn to the West: Japanese Literature of the Modern Era* (10–12). 1984, Holt paper $29.95 (0-03-062816-4). A scholarly introduction to the literature of Japan since its opening to the West in 1868. [895.6]

3592 King, Richard H. *A Southern Renaissance: The Cultural Awakening of the American South, 1930–1955* (10–12). 1980, Oxford Univ. Pr. $22.50 (0-19-502664-0). Including various types of literature, this book analyzes southern American writing and writers from 1930 to 1955. [810.9]

3593 Klein, Leonard S., ed. *African Literatures in the 20th Century: A Guide* (10–12). Rev. ed. 1986, Ungar paper $16.95 (0-8044-6362-X). A fine introduction to the major writers and their works arranged alphabetically by country. (Rev: BL 6/1/86) [809]

3594 Levi, Peter. *A Pelican History of Greek Literature* (10–12). 1985, Penguin paper $7.95 (0-14-022392-4). In narrative format, this book introduces chronologically the great writers of ancient Greece and their works. (Rev: BL 7/85) [880]

3595 Morsberger, Robert E. *James Thurber* (10–12). 1964, Twayne LB $16.95 (0-8057-0728-X); New College & Univ. Pr. paper $10.95 (0-8084-0174-2). A critical study of the American humorist and his work. [817.09]

3596 Ogilvie, R. M. *Roman Literature and Society* (10–12). 1980, Barnes & Noble $28.50 (0-389-20069-7); Penguin paper $6.95 (0-14-022081-4). This book introduces 400 years of Roman literature and also supplies historical background. [870.9]

3597 Parrington, Vernon L. *Main Currents in American Thought* (10–12). 3 vols. 1958, Harcourt paper $15.95 ea (vol 1: 0-15-655134-9; vol 2: 0-15-655135-7; vol 3: 0-15-611677-4). In 3 volumes the author traces the history of American literature from 1620 to 1920. [810.9]

3598 Plimpton, George, ed. *The Writer's Chapbook* (10–12). 1989, Viking $18.95 (0-670-81565-9). Using a subject approach, Plimpton has gleaned thoughts on a variety of topics related to life and writing from his many interviews in *The Paris Review*. (Rev: BL 11/15/89) [810]

3599 Popkin, Michael, ed. *Modern Black Writers* (10–12). 1978, Ungar $65.00 (0-8044-3258-9). An introduction to twentieth-century black writers from Africa, the Caribbean, and the United States. [809]

3600 Rhein, Phillip H. *Albert Camus* (10–12). 1989, Twayne LB $19.95 (0-8057-8253-2). In addition to a discussion of Camus' fiction, there is an introduction to his life and his non-fiction works. [848]

3601 Richter, Peyton. *Voltaire* (10–12). 1980, Twayne LB $16.95 (0-8057-6425-9). This work not only introduces Voltaire's life and works, but also discusses his influence on Western thought and literature. [848]

3602 Sampson, George. *The Concise Cambridge History of English Literature* (10–12). 1970, Cambridge $62.50 (0-521-07385-5); paper $24.95 (0-521-09581-6). This is a masterful abridgment of the massive 15-volume *Cambridge History of English Literature*. [820.9]

3603 Smith, Lucinda Irwin. *Women Who Write: From the Past and the Present to the Future* (8–12). Illus. 1989, Messner LB $14.98 (0-671-65668-6); paper $9.95 (0-671-65669-4). Interviews with living women writers and essays of famous dead ones help explore the contributions women have made to literature. (Rev: BL 10/1/89; BR 3–4/90; SLJ 10/89; VOYA 2/90) [810]

3604 Stamm, James R. *A Short History of Spanish Literature* (10–12). 1979, New York Univ. Pr. $40.00 (0-8147-7791-0); paper $17.50 (0-8147-7792-9). A general overview of Spanish literature, how it developed, and the major figures connected with it. [860.9]

3605 Strickland, Bill, ed. *On Being a Writer* (9–12). 1989, Writer's Digest $19.95 (0-89879-366-1). A collection of 31 interviews with such writers as John Steinbeck, Kurt Vonnegut, and Joseph Heller. (Rev: BL 9/1/89; SLJ 2/90) [810]

3606 Terras, Victor, ed. *Handbook of Russian Literature* (10–12). 1985, Yale Univ. Pr. $55.00 (0-300-03155-6); paper $24.95 (0-300-04868-8). This one-volume work gives entries on authors, works, periods, and related topics connected with Russian literature. [891.7]

3607 Troupe, Quincy, ed. *James Baldwin: The Legacy* (10–12). Illus. 1989, Simon & Schuster paper $10.95 (0-671-67651-2). After a series of tributes to the writer by his admirers, there is a collection of some of his essays. (Rev: BL 4/15/90) [818]

3608 Ward, Philip, ed. *The Oxford Companion to Spanish Literature* (10–12). 1978, Oxford Univ. Pr. $49.95 (0-19-866114-2). A handy reference to Spanish literature and related subjects with coverage from Roman times to the mid-1970s. [860.3]

3609 Whitlow, Roger. *Black American Literature* (10–12). 1973, Littlefield paper $8.95 (0-8226-0278-4). A survey of 45 black American writers and black folklore with an extensive bibliography on these subjects. [810.9]

3610 Wiget, Andrew. *Native American Literature* (10–12). 1985, Twayne LB $17.95 (0-8057-7408-4). A history of both Indian and Eskimo literature with particular emphasis on folklore and legends. [810.9]

3611 Yannella, Donald. *Ralph Waldo Emerson* (10–12). 1982, Twayne LB $16.95 (0-8057-7344-4). An overview of the career and literary output of this influential author and critic. [818]

Fiction

General and Miscellaneous

3612 Aldiss, Brian W. *Trillion Year Spree* (10–12). 1988, Avon paper $9.95 (0-380-70461-7). A quick overview of the history of science fiction that covers the highlights. (Rev: SLJ 9/88) [808.83]

3613 Allen, Walter. *The Short Story in English* (10–12). 1981, Oxford Univ. Pr. $29.95 (0-19-812666-2). A study of the development of the short story and its current status. [823.09]

3614 Barlowe, Wayne Douglas. *Barlowe's Guide to Extraterrestrials* (9–12). 2nd ed. Illus. 1987, Workman $12.95 (0-89480-324-7). From the world of science fiction, Barlowe has pictured in words and illustrations 50 aliens and has identified the books in which they were introduced. (Rev: VOYA 4/88) [808.83]

3615 Binyon, T. J. *Murder Will Out* (10–12). 1989, Oxford Univ. Pr. $21.95 (0-19-219223-4). Beginning with Poe's Chevalier Dysin this is a history of the detective in fiction. (Rev: SLJ 11/89) [808.83]

3616 Bleiler, E. F., ed. *Science Fiction Writers* (10–12). 1982, Macmillan LB $65.00 (0-684-16740-9). This book contains essays on 75 science fiction writers, chiefly American and English, who have written in the nineteenth and twentieth centuries. [809.3]

3617 Brownstein, Rachel M. *Becoming a Heroine: Reading about Women in Novels* (10–12). 1982, Penguin paper $7.95 (0-14-006787-6). A study of the heroine in the fiction of such writers as Jane Austen, George Eliot, and Henry James. [823.09]

3618 Cawthorn, James, and Michael Moorcock. *Fantasy: The 100 Best Books* (10–12). 1989, Carroll & Graf $15.95 (0-88184-335-0). Beginning with *Gulliver's Travels*, the authors have chosen and described both classics and contemporary works such as *Rosemary's Baby*. (Rev: BL 4/1/89) [016]

3619 Clareson, Thomas D. *Understanding Contemporary American Science Fiction: The Formative Period, 1926–1970* (10–12). 1990, Univ. of South Carolina Pr. $22.95 (0-87249-689-9). A thorough history of this great major period in the writing of science fiction. (Rev: BL 6/15/90) [813]

3620 Clarke, Arthur C. *Astounding Days: A Science Fictional Autobiography* (9–12). 1990, Bantam paper $8.95 (0-553-34822-1). A ramble through some of Clarke's ideas about stories that have appeared in *Astounding* (later named *Analog*) magazine. (Rev: BL 2/1/90) [823]

3621 Guerard, Albert J. *The Triumph of the Novel: Dickens, Dostoevsky, Faulkner* (10–12). Illus. 1976, Oxford Univ. Pr. $25.00 (0-19-502066-9); Univ. of Chicago Pr. paper $9.50 (0-226-31034-5). A critical examination of the works of 3 very different novelists who have invented their own form of realism. [809.3]

3622 Hooper, Brad. *Short Story Writers and Their Work* (10–12). 1988, American Library Assn. paper $14.95 (0-8389-0485-8). A critique of 100 writers of short stories past and present. (Rev: BL 8/88) [809.3]

3623 Jones, Stephen, and Kim Newman, eds. *Horror: 100 Best Books* (8–12). 1989, Carroll & Graf $15.95 (0-88184-417-9). Leading writers of horror stories pick and discuss their personal favorites and they include books from *Dracula* to

Stephen King's *The Shining*. (Rev: BL 3/15/89) [823]

3624 Kenney, William. *How to Read and Write about Fiction* (9–12). 1988, Arco paper $6.95 (0-13-431164-7). This book explains the various elements of a novel like character and setting and how to apply standards of excellence to increase one's appreciation of fiction. (Rev: SLJ 2/89) [808.3]

3625 Lawler, Donald L. *Approaches to Science Fiction* (10–12). 1978, Houghton $27.50 (0-395-25496-5). This book is intended to introduce science fiction to new readers and to give them standards of evaluation. [808.83]

3626 Le Guin, Ursula K. *The Language of the Night: Essays on Fantasy and Science Fiction* (10–12). 1979, Berkley paper $5.95 (0-425-07668-7). A renowned writer analyzes the importance of science fiction and fantasy writing as valid literary forms. [809.3]

3627 Lem, Stanislaw. *Microworlds: Writings on Science Fiction and Fantasy* (10–12). 1985, Harcourt paper $5.95 (0-15-659443-9). A highly critical review of science fiction writing and its literary merits. [809.3]

3628 Pearson, Carol, and Katherine Pope. *The Female Hero in American and British Literature* (10–12). 1981, Bowker $34.95 (0-8352-1402-8); paper $29.95 (0-8352-1466-4). An examination of the central female characters in several nineteenth- and twentieth-century novels. [823.09]

3629 Platt, Charles. *Dream Makers: Science Fiction and Fantasy Writers at Work* (10–12). Illus. 1987, Ungar $17.95 (0-8044-2745-3). A series of interviews with such science fiction writers as Asimov, Clarke, Dick, and Herbert. [809.3]

3630 Scholes, Robert, and Eric S. Rabkin. *Science Fiction: History, Science, Vision* (10–12). 1977, Oxford Univ. Pr. $22.50 (0-19-502173-8). A critical history of science fiction writing that pinpoints themes and scientific foundations. [809.3]

3631 Sullivan, Jack, ed. *The Penguin Encyclopedia of Horror and the Supernatural* (10–12). Illus. 1986, Viking $29.95 (0-670-80902-0). In 50 essays and 600 alphabetically arranged entries, the field of supernatural fiction is covered in relation to authors, artists, and important films. (Rev: SLJ 11/86) [809.3]

3632 Symons, Julian. *Bloody Murder: From the Detective Story to the Crime Novel* (10–12). Rev. ed. 1985, Viking $14.95 (0-670-80096-1); Penguin paper $6.95 (0-14-007263-2). This is a history of the mystery story from Poe to the present. [809.3]

3633 Woeller, Waltrand, and Bruce Cassiday. *The Literature of Crime & Detection: An Illustrated History from Antiquity to the Present* (10–12). Illus. 1988, Ungar $24.50 (0-8044-2983-9). An illustrated history of mystery and detective writing from the ancient Greeks and Romans to Agatha Christie. (Rev: BL 5/15/88; SLJ 6–7/88) [809.3]

Europe

General

3634 Alexander, Edward. *Isaac Bashevis Singer* (10–12). Illus. 1980, Twayne LB $17.95 (0-8057-6424-0). An introduction to the life and work of this writer of Yiddish literature who won the Nobel Prize. [839]

3635 Buck, Stratton. *Gustave Flaubert* (10–12). 1966, Twayne LB $17.95 (0-8057-2312-9). A detailed examination of Flaubert's novels, plus biographical information. [843.09]

3636 Durán, Manuel. *Cervantes* (10–12). 1974, Twayne LB $17.95 (0-8057-2206-8). Although concentrating on his fictional works, this study of Cervantes also includes material on his poetry and essays. [863.09]

3637 Festa-McCormick, Diana. *Honoré de Balzac* (10–12). 1979, Twayne LB $15.95 (0-8057-6383-X). Both plot summaries and critical comment are supplied for the most important Balzac novels in the Human Comedy cycle. [843.09]

3638 Field, George Wallis. *Hermann Hesse* (10–12). 1970, Twayne LB $16.95 (0-8057-2424-9). A critical and biographical study of the German writer who was a great influence on the youth of the 1960s. [833.09]

3639 Garland, Henry. *The Oxford Companion to German Literature* (10–12). 1986, Oxford Univ. Pr. $49.95 (0-19-866139-8). This one-volume reference gives entries for such subjects as titles of literary works, authors, schools of writing, and literary terms. [830.3]

3640 Jackson, Robert Louis. *Twentieth Century Interpretations of Crime and Punishment* (10–12). 1974, Prentice paper $8.95 (0-13-193086-9). A slender volume in which several international critics write their opinions and interpretations of this classic Russian novel. [891.7]

3641 Knapp, Bettina L. *Émile Zola* (10–12). 1980, Ungar $18.95 (0-8044-2482-9). After a brief biography of Zola's life, there is an analysis of his most important novels. [843.09]

3642 Robinson, Joy D. Marie. *Antoine de Saint-Exupery* (10–12). 1984, Twayne LB $17.95 (0-8057-6552-2). A biography and critical analysis of the works of this French writer and aviator. [848]

3643 Rowe, William W. *Leo Tolstoy* (10–12). 1986, Twayne LB $14.95 (0-8057-6623-5). After an introduction to the life of Tolstoy and the themes found in his work, there is a discussion of each of his novels. [891.7]

3644 Russell, P. E. *Cervantes* (10–12). 1985, Oxford Univ. Pr. $17.95 (0-19-287570-1); paper $4.95 (0-19-287569-8). A detailed study of the author's life and its relation to *Don Quixote*. [863.09]

3645 Spann, Meno. *Franz Kafka* (10–12). Illus. 1990, Twayne $18.95 (0-8057-6182-9). An introduction to the life of this unusual genius and the nightmarish world of his writings. [833.09]

Great Britain and Ireland

3646 Adelman, Gary. *Heart of Darkness: Search for the Unconscious* (10–12). 1987, Twayne $17.95 (0-8057-7953-1); paper $6.95 (0-8057-8006-8). A guide to the characters, structure, and themes in this masterpiece. (Rev: SLJ 9/87; VOYA 8–9/87) [809.3]

3647 Appignanesi, Lisa, and Sara Maitland, eds. *The Rushdie File* (10–12). 1990, Syracuse Univ. Pr. $32.50 (0-8156-2494-8); paper $12.95 (0-8156-0248-0). A variety of viewpoints are expressed concerning the pros and cons of writing and publishing *Satanic Verses,* the book that Islam found offensive. (Rev: BL 2/15/90; SLJ 8/90) [823]

3648 Benstock, Bernard, ed. *Critical Essays on James Joyce* (10–12). 1985, G. K. Hall LB $35.00 (0-8161-8751-7). A collection of 19 essays that critically examine the works of James Joyce. [823.09]

3649 Berg, Maggie. *Jane Eyre: Portrait of a Life* (10–12). 1987, Twayne $18.95 (0-8057-7955-8); paper $7.95 (0-8057-8010-6). An analysis of this novel that concentrates on its autobiographical aspects. (Rev: BL 9/15/87; SLJ 9/87; VOYA 6/88) [823]

3650 Blom, Margaret Howard. *Charlotte Brontë* (10–12). 1977, Twayne LB $16.95 (0-8057-6673-1). A critical study of the life and works of the creator of *Jane Eyre*. [823.09]

3651 Bloom, Harold, ed. *British Modernist Fiction, 1920 to 1945* (10–12). 1987, Chelsea House $49.95 (0-87754-987-7). A collection of critical pieces on British authors active between the world wars. (Rev: BL 11/15/87) [823]

3652 Bloom, Harold, ed. *George Bernard Shaw's Pygmalion* (10–12). 1988, Chelsea House $19.95 (1-555-46029-1). This is one of an extensive series from Chelsea House that, like Cliff's Notes, examines in detail great works of literature. (Rev: SLJ 8/88) [822.09]

3653 Brady, Frank, ed. *Twentieth Century Interpretations of Gulliver's Travels* (10–12). 1968, Prentice $9.95 (0-13-371575-2); paper $1.25 (0-13-371567-1). This book, part of a lengthy series, is a collection of essays that examine the structure and meanings in *Gulliver's Travels*. [823.09]

3654 Brandt, Bill. *Literary Britain* (10–12). 1987, Aperture $25.00 (0-89381-223-4). A photographic album that highlights important landmarks in the literary history of Great Britain and Ireland. (Rev: BL 2/1/87) [779]

3655 Burt, Forrest D. *W. Somerset Maugham* (10–12). 1985, Twayne LB $18.95 (0-8057-6885-8). The life of this writer is given, plus an assessment of his novels and short stories. [823.09]

3656 Costa, Richard Hauer. *H. G. Wells* (10–12). 1985, Twayne $LB $15.95 (0-8057-6887-4). A study of the entire output of H. G. Wells with particular emphasis on his speculative fiction. [823.09]

3657 Cox, Don Richard. *Arthur Conan Doyle* (10–12). 1985, Ungar $18.95 (0-8044-2146-3). In addition to discussing his mysteries, this book analyzes Doyle's adventure stories and science fiction. [823.09]

3658 Crabbe, Katharyn F. *J. R. R. Tolkien* (9–12). 1981, Ungar $18.95 (0-8044-2134-X); paper $9.95 (0-8044-6091-4). As well as biographical information, this account stresses *The Hobbit* and the *Lord of the Rings* trilogy. [823.09]

3659 Daiches, David. *The Novel and the Modern World* (10–12). Illus. 1987, Univ. of Chicago Pr. paper $13.00 (0-226-13470-9). A study of the modern novel that concentrates on the work of Conrad, Joyce, Lawrence, and Woolf. [823.09]

3660 Daiches, David, and John Flower. *Literary Landscape of the British Isles: A Narrative Atlas* (10–12). 1981, Penguin paper $9.95 (0-14-005735-8). An excellent guide, with many maps, to the places associated with the great literature of the British Isles. [820]

3661 Ermarth, Elizabeth Deeds. *George Eliot* (10–12). 1985, Twayne LB $16.95 (0-8057-6910-2). A critical study of George Eliot's works that traces her own beliefs in the themes of her novels. [823.09]

3662 Foster, Robert. *The Complete Guide to Middle-Earth: From The Hobbit to The Silmarillion* (10–12). 1985, Ballantine paper $3.95 (0-345-32436-6). An alphabetically arranged concordance to the writing of Tolkien. [808.3]

3663 Frane, Jeff. *Fritz Leiber* (10–12). 1981, Starmont House $19.95 (0-89370-039-8). This is both a biography and a critical analysis of the work of this great science fiction writer. There are many studies of other important science fiction writers available from Starmont House. [808.84]

3664 Gaiman, Neil. *Don't Panic: The Official Hitchhiker's Guide to the Galaxy Companion* (9–12). 1988, Pocket paper $7.95 (0-671-66426-3). Contains background information on this popular science fiction series that began as radio scripts. (Rev: BL 5/1/88) [791.447]

3665 Gillon, Adam. *Joseph Conrad* (10–12). 1982, Twayne LB $16.95 (0-8057-6820-3). A thorough study of the life and work of Conrad that also traces the major themes found in his writings. [823.09]

3666 Hammond, J. R. *A George Orwell Companion: A Guide to the Novels, Documentaries, and Essays* (10–12). Illus. 1982, St. Martin's $29.95 (0-312-32452-9). As well as giving plots for each of his books, this guide supplies information on themes, characters, and locations. [828]

3667 Hardwick, Michael. *The Complete Guide to Sherlock Holmes* (9–12). Illus. 1987, St. Martin's $16.95 (0-312-00580-6). A story-by-story guide to the life and times of Sherlock Holmes. (Rev: BL 5/1/87) [823]

3668 Hart, Anne. *The Life and Times of Hercule Poirot* (10–12). 1990, Putnam $19.95 (0-399-13484-0). A fictional biography of Agatha Christie's famous detective, gray cells and all. (Rev: BL 1/15/90) [823]

3669 Hornback, Bert G. *Great Expectations: A Novel of Friendship* (9–12). Illus. 1987, Twayne $17.95 (0-8057-7956-6); paper $6.95 (0-8057-8005-X). A critical analysis of this novel often studied in high school. (Rev: BL 5/15/87; SLJ 9/87) [823]

3670 Howe, Irving, ed. *1984 Revisited: Totalitarianism in Our Century* (10–12). 1983, Harper $10.53 (0-06-015158-7); paper $3.50 (0-06-080660-5). Thirteen writers analyze the themes in *1984* and their relation to the world today. [823.09]

3671 Isaacs, Neil D., and Rose A. Zimbardo, ed. *Tolkien and the Critics: Essays on J. R. R. Tol-*

kien's The Lord of the Rings (10–12). Illus. 1987, Notre Dame Pr. paper $9.95 (0-268-00279-7). This volume consists of 15 essays expressing various points of view on *The Lord of the Rings* trilogy. [823.09]

3672 Kelly, Richard. *Lewis Carroll* (9–12). 1990, Twayne LB $18.95 (0-8057-6988-9). This critical survey of Carroll's writings concentrates on the Alice books and *The Hunting of the Snark*. [828]

3673 Kirkham, Margaret. *Jane Austen, Feminism and Fiction* (10–12). 1983, Barnes & Noble $26.50 (0-389-20336-X). This critical study poses the argument that Jane Austen was really a feminist thinker. [823.09]

3674 Kobayashi, Tsukasa, et al. *Sherlock Holmes's London: Following the Footsteps of London's Master Detective* (9–12). Illus. 1986, Chronicle paper $16.95 (0-87701-380-2). A collection of old and new photographs that show the streets and places in London that Holmes knew so well. (Rev: BL 8/86) [823]

3675 Loss, Archie K. *Of Human Bondage: Coming of Age in the Novel* (10–12). 1990, Twayne paper $7.95 (0-8057-8067-X). This fine analysis of the Maugham novel gives excellent background material. Part of a series. (Rev: VOYA 6/90) [823]

3676 McConnell, Frank D. *The Science Fiction of H. G. Wells* (9–12). 1981, Oxford Univ. Pr. $25.00 (0-19-502811-2); paper $6.95 (0-19-502812-0). After a broad overview of Wells' novels, the author concentrates on 5 important novels, including *The Invisible Man* and *The War of the Worlds*. [823.09]

3677 Marcus, Steven. *Dickens: From Pickwick to Dombey* (10–12). 1987, Norton paper $6.95 (0-393-30286-5). This is a guide to the 7 novels written during Dickens' early period. [823.09]

3678 Murfin, Ross C. *Sons & Lovers: A Novel of Division & Desire* (10–12). 1987, Twayne $18.95 (0-8057-7967-1); paper $7.95 (0-8057-8007-6). A thorough critical analysis of this novel often studied in high school. (Rev: SLJ 9/87) [809.3]

3679 Murphy, Brian. *C. S. Lewis* (10–12). 1983, Starmont House $19.95 (0-89370-045-2). This is a critical evaluation of the works of the creator of Narnia and other imaginary lands. Part of a series on science fiction writers from Starmont House. [808.83]

3680 Nelson, Harland S. *Charles Dickens* (10–12). 1981, Twayne LB $16.95 (0-8057-6805-X); paper $8.95 (0-8057-6888-2). This account focuses on 5 novels, including *David Copperfield*, *Oliver Twist*, and *Great Expectations*. [823.09]

3681 Olander, Joseph D., and Martin Harry Greenberg, eds. *Arthur C. Clarke* (10–12). 1977, Taplinger $12.95 (0-8008-0402-3); paper $5.95 (0-8008-0401-5). An analysis of this science fiction writer's work that ends in the mid-1970s. [823.09]

3682 Pinion, F. B. *A George Eliot Companion: Literary Achievement and Modern Significance* (10–12). Illus. 1981, Barnes & Noble $29.50 (0-389-20208-8). Besides surveying the entire output of this prolific author, this book gives a fine introductory biography. [823.09]

3683 Riley, Dick, and Pam McAllister, eds. *The New Bedside, Bathtub & Armchair Companion to Agatha Christie* (10–12). Illus. 1986, Ungar paper $12.95 (0-8044-6725-0). Many enthusiasts of Christie have contributed articles on her novels, their plots, and characters. [823.09]

3684 Rogers, Deborah Webster. *J. R. R. Tolkien* (10–12). 1980, Twayne LB $16.95 (0-8057-6796-7). A serious discussion of the art and philosophy of Tolkien and his place in the development of fantasy literature. [823.09]

3685 Rogers, Pat, ed. *The Oxford Illustrated History of English Literature* (10–12). Illus. 1987, Oxford Univ. Pr. $35.00 (0-19-812816-9). An oversize, handsomely illustrated volume tracing the development of English literature from Anglo-Saxon times to the present. (Rev: BL 9/15/87) [820]

3686 Sagar, Keith, ed. *D. H. Lawrence Handbook* (10–12). Illus. 1982, Barnes & Noble $28.50 (0-389-20312-2); paper $12.95 (0-389-20653-9). Nine Lawrence specialists contributed essays on this author's life and writings. [823.09]

3687 Salwak, Dale. *A. J. Cronin* (10–12). 1985, Twayne LB $17.95 (0-8057-6884-X). A study of the novels of Cronin that shows how concerned he was with social issues in his fiction. [823.09]

3688 Saposnik, Irving S. *Robert Louis Stevenson* (10–12). 1974, Twayne LB $14.95 (0-8057-1517-7). Biographical information is given as well as an analysis of Stevenson's works in several genres. [828]

3689 Smyer, Richard I. *Animal Farm: Pastoralism & Politics* (9–12). 1988, Twayne $17.95 (0-8057-7980-9); paper $7.95 (0-8057-8030-0). A detailed analysis of this allegory that explains its structure and layers of meaning. (Rev: SLJ 8/88; SLJ 11/88) [823.09]

3690 Stade, George, ed. *Six Modern British Novelists* (10–12). 1974, Columbia Univ. Pr. $30.00 (0-231-03846-1); paper $17.50 (0-231-08374-2). The 6 novelists discussed are Arnold Bennett, Evelyn Waugh, Ford Madox Ford, Joseph Conrad, Virginia Woolf, and E. M. Forster. [823.09]

3691 Sutherland, James, ed. *The Oxford Book of Literary Anecdotes* (10–12). 1975, Oxford Univ. Pr. $29.95 (0-19-812139-3); paper $8.95 (0-19-281936-4). This is a fascinating collection of anecdotes about British literary figures from the seventh century to the present. [828]

3692 Tolkien, J. R. R. *The Shaping of Middle-Earth* (9–12). Illus. 1986, Houghton $16.95 (0-395-42501-8). Background notes and information on the famous fantasy written by Tolkien and edited by his son. (Rev: SLJ 3/87) [808.3]

3693 Wagoner, Mary S. *Agatha Christie* (9–12). 1986, Twayne $17.95 (0-8057-6936-6). An analysis of this mystery story writer's works with an accompanying brief biography. (Rev: BL 2/1/87) [823]

United States

3694 Asimov, Isaac. *Asimov's Galaxy: Reflections on Science Fiction* (9–12). 1989, Doubleday $17.95 (0-385-24120-8). A collection of over 50 essays on science fiction by one of the masters of the genre. (Rev: BL 1/1/89; VOYA 8/89) [809.3]

3695 Baker, Carlos. *Hemingway: The Writer as Artist* (10–12). 1972, Princeton Univ. Pr. paper $14.95 (0-691-01305-5). An analysis of both Hemingway's fiction and nonfiction. [813.09]

3696 Bakish, David. *Richard Wright* (10–12). 1973, Ungar $16.95 (0-8044-2015-7). A critical study of the black American writer that includes material on his life and politics. [813.09]

3697 Baym, Nina. *The Scarlet Letter: A Reading* (10–12). 1986, Twayne $17.95 (0-8057-7957-4); paper $6.95 (0-8057-8001-7). An analysis of this novel, often studied in high school, plus an introduction to the life of its author, Nathaniel Hawthorne. (Rev: BL 7/86; SLJ 5/87) [813]

3698 Beahm, George, ed. *The Stephen King Companion* (9–12). 1989, Andrews & McMeel paper $10.95 (0-8362-7978-6). A collection of writings about King and his work written by several hands, including his own. (Rev: BL 10/1/89; SLJ 12/89) [813]

3699 Bellamy, Joe David, ed. *The New Fiction: Interviews with Innovative American Writers* (10–12). 1974, Univ. of IIinois Pr. $22.95 (0-252-00430-2); paper $8.95 (0-252-00555-4). Interviews with 12 contemporary writers, including Tom Wolfe, Kurt Vonnegut, and Donald Barthelme. [813.09]

3700 Bishop, Rudine Sims. *Presenting Walter Dean Myers* (9–12). 1990, Twayne $19.95 (0-8057-8214-1). A profile of the life and work of this black American writer with an analysis of each of his most important books. (Rev: BL 10/15/90) [813]

3701 Bloom, Harold, ed. *American Fiction, 1914 to 1945* (10–12). 1987, Chelsea House $59.95 (0-87754-962-1). A review of the most important American authors and works written during and between the 2 world wars. (Rev: BL 11/15/87) [813]

3702 Bowden, Mary Weatherspoon. *Washington Irving* (10–12). 1981, Twayne LB $16.95 (0-8057-7314-2). An analysis of the author's major works plus a brief biography. [818]

3703 Bradbury, Ray. *Zen in the Art of Writing* (10–12). 1990, Capra $18.95 (1-877741-02-7); paper $8.95 (1-877741-01-9). In a series of essays, Bradbury discusses his career and his compulsion to write. (Rev: BL 1/1/90) [808]

3704 Brizzi, Mary T. *Anne McCaffrey* (9–12). 1986, Starmont $15.95 (0-930261-30-5); paper $7.95 (0-930261-29-1). A critical analysis of all the Pern books and the other science fiction by this popular writer. (Rev: BL 9/15/86) [813]

3705 Brooks, Cleanth. *William Faulkner: The Yoknapatawpha Country* (10–12). 1990, Louisiana State Univ. Pr. paper $16.95 (0-8071-1601-7). An analysis of the novels and stories like *Light in August* and *The Sound and the Fury* that take place in Faulkner's imaginary Yoknapatawpha county. [813.09]

3706 Buranelli, Vincent. *Edgar Allan Poe* (10–12). 1977, Twayne LB $15.95 (0-8057-7189-1); paper $4.95 (0-672-61502-9). This book analyzes the fiction as well as the poetry and nonfiction by Poe. [818]

3707 Cady, Edwin H. *Stephen Crane* (10–12). 1980, Twayne LB $14.95 (0-8057-7299-5). An analysis of the short-lived author's work and career. [813.09]

3708 Campbell, Patricia J. *Presenting Robert Cormier* (9–12). 2nd ed. Illus. 1989, Twayne $16.95 (0-8057-8212-5). A profile of this author and his work through the novel *Fade* (1989). (Rev: BL 9/15/89; BR 5–6/90; SLJ 12/89) [813.54]

3709 Chase, Richard. *The American Novel and Its Tradition* (10–12). 1978, Gordian Pr. $35.00 (0-87752-209-X); Johns Hopkins Univ. Pr. paper $10.95 (0-8018-2303-X). This is a history of the American novel from James Fenimore Cooper through William Faulkner. [813.09]

3710 Clareson, Thomas D. *Frederik Pohl* (10–12). 1987, Starmont House $17.95 (0-930261-34-8); paper $9.95 (0-930261-33-X). An analysis of the works and life of one of sci-fi's greatest writers. (Rev: BL 1/15/88) [813]

3711 Cowley, Malcolm. *A Second Flowering: Works and Days of the Lost Generation* (10–12). 1980, Penguin paper $7.95 (0-14-005498-7). This is a group of evaluative essays on the works of such writers as Hemingway, Fitzgerald, Wilder, and Wolfe. [810]

3712 Crane, Stephen. *A Collection of Critical Essays* (10–12). 1967, Prentice $12.95 (0-13-188888-9). Through a series of essays by different critics, the poetry and prose of Stephen Crane are examined. [818]

3713 Daly, Jay. *Presenting S. E. Hinton* (9–12). 2nd ed. Illus. 1989, Twayne $18.95 (0-8057-8211-7). A biography of this popular author plus an analysis of her work including *Taming the Star Runner* (1988). (Rev: BL 9/15/89; SLJ 3/90) [813.54]

3714 Detweiler, Robert. *John Updike* (10–12). 1984, Twayne LB $16.95 (0-8057-7422-X); paper $6.95 (0-8057-7429-7). A critical study of Updike and his work through the early 1980s. [813.09]

3715 Doyle, Paul A. *Pearl S. Buck* (10–12). 1980, Twayne LB $16.95 (0-8057-7325-8). A critical study of this writer that covers topics like plots, themes, and writing style. [813.09]

3716 DuPont, Denise, ed. *Women of Vision* (9–12). 1988, St. Martin's $14.95 (0-312-02321-9). Profiles of 12 female writers of science fiction including Le Guin, Vinge, and Sargent. (Rev: BL 11/15/88) [813]

3717 Dutton, Robert R. *Saul Bellow* (10–12). 1982, Twayne LB $17.95 (0-8057-7353-3). This study of Saul Bellow's fiction focuses on the symbolism used by the author. [813.09]

3718 Eble, Kenneth. *F. Scott Fitzgerald* (10–12). 1977, Twayne LB $15.95 (0-8057-7183-2); paper $6.95 (0-8057-7423-8). A fine critical biography about the writer who became a spokesman of the spirit of the jazz age. Part of an extensive series on American authors. [813.09]

3719 Evans, Elizabeth. *Thomas Wolfe* (10–12). 1984, Ungar $18.95 (0-8044-2188-9). This book reviews all of Wolfe's output, with particular emphasis on his 4 major novels. [813.09]

3720 Franklin, H. Bruce. *Robert A. Heinlein: America as Science Fiction* (10–12). Illus. 1980, Oxford Univ. Pr. $27.95 (0-19-502746-9); paper $7.95 (0-19-502747-7). This discussion of Heinlein's works ends in the late 1970s. [813.09]

3721 French, Warren. *John Steinbeck* (10–12). 1975, Twayne LB $16.95 (0-8057-0693-3); paper $7.95 (0-8057-7424-6). The novels and short stories of Steinbeck are discussed and an analysis of the reactions of literary critics is given. [813.09]

3722 Friedman, Alan Warren. *William Faulkner* (10–12). 1985, Ungar $18.95 (0-8044-2218-4). A comprehensive collection of essays that explore various facets of Faulkner's work and the degree of success he had in achieving his literary aims. [813.09]

3723 Friedman, Ellen G. *Joyce Carol Oates* (10–12). 1980, Ungar paper $7.95 (0-8044-6183-X). A series of critical essays that introduces the novels and the life of Joyce Carol Oates. [813.09]

3724 Friedman, Lenemaja. *Shirley Jackson* (10–12). 1975, Twayne LB $14.95 (0-8057-0402-7); paper $4.95 (0-672-61507-X). An evaluation and interpretation of the work of this unusual writer of novels and short stories. [813.09]

3725 Gale, Robert L. *Louis L'Amour* (10–12). 1985, Twayne LB $15.95 (0-8057-7450-5). An examination of the life and work of this prolific writer whose forte was the western novel. [813.09]

3726 Gallo, Donald R. *Presenting Richard Peck* (9–12). 1989, Twayne $18.95 (0-8057-8209-5). Part biography but chiefly an examination of Peck's works including those intended for an adult audience. (Rev: BL 11/1/89; BR 3–4/90; SLJ 12/89; VOYA 12/89) [818]

3727 Gerber, Philip. *Willa Cather* (10–12). Illus. 1975, Twayne LB $16.95 (0-8057-7155-7). Cather's fiction is examined thematically and related to her personal experiences. [813.09]

3728 Gibson, Donald B. *The Red Badge of Courage* (10–12). 1988, Twayne $17.95 (0-8057-7961-2); paper $7.95 (0-8057-8014-9). Part of an extensive series from Twayne that analyzes the great works of literature in depth. (Rev: SLJ 8/88) [813.09]

3729 Gladstein, Mimi Reisel. *The Ayn Rand Companion* (10–12). 1984, Greenwood LB $35.00 (0-313-22079-4); paper $12.95 (0-313-25737-X). A guide that analyzes the plots and characters in Rand's novels and her underlying philosophy. [813.09]

3730 Grebstein, Sheldon Norman. *Sinclair Lewis* (10–12). 1962, Twayne LB $16.95 (0-8057-0448-5); New College & Univ. Pr. paper $10.95 (0-8084-0278-1). In addition to a biography of Lewis, this account analyzes chronologically each of his novels. [813.09]

3731 Gunn, James. *Isaac Asimov: The Foundations of Science Fiction* (10–12). 1982, Oxford Univ. Pr. $24.95 (0-19-503059-1); paper $7.95 (0-19-503060-5). A study of Asimov's science fiction with emphasis on his Foundation series. [813.09]

3732 Hays, Peter L. *Ernest Hemingway* (10–12). 1990, Continuum $18.95 (0-8264-0467-7). Following a succinct biography of Hemingway, there is a critical analysis of each of his works. (Rev: BL 4/15/90) [813]

3733 Heinlein, Robert A. *Grumbles from the Grave* (9–12). Ed. by Virginia Heinlein. 1990, Ballantine $19.95 (0-345-36246-2). Letters by the famous science fiction writer that give insights into his craft and that of others in the field. (Rev: BL 12/15/89) [813]

3734 Hendrick, George. *Katherine Anne Porter* (10–12). 1988, Twayne LB $17.95 (0-8057-7513-7). An examination of the plots, themes, and characters of Porter's fiction, with special attention to *Ship of Fools*. [813.09]

3735 Hersey, John, ed. *Ralph Ellison: A Collection of Critical Essays* (10–12). 1974, Prentice $12.95 (0-13-274357-4); paper $1.95 (0-13-274340-X). A stimulating series of essays that concentrate on *The Invisible Man*. [813.09]

3736 Hillway, Tyrus. *Herman Melville* (10–12). 1979, Twayne LB $15.95 (0-8057-7526-1); paper $4.95 (0-672-61504-5). Melville's life is discussed and each of his works is critically judged. [813.09]

3737 Hipple, Ted. *Presenting Sue Ellen Bridgers* (9–12). 1990, Twayne $18.95 (0-8057-8213-3). A biography and analysis of the work of one of the major writers of young adult novels. (Rev: BL 6/1/90) [813]

3738 Hoffman, Frederick J. *William Faulkner* (10–12). 1966, Twayne LB $17.95 (0-8057-0244-X); New College & University Pr., paper $5.95 (0-8084-0326-5). After an overview of Faulkner's works, each of the novels is examined. [813.09]

3739 Holtze, Sally Holmes. *Presenting Norma Fox Mazer* (9–12). 1987, Twayne $14.95 (0-8057-8204-4); Dell paper $3.95 (0-440-20486-0). The life and work of this popular young adult novelist. (Rev: BL 9/1/87; SLJ 12/87; VOYA 10/87) [813]

3740 Hutchinson, Stuart. *Henry James: An American as Modernist* (10–12). 1983, Barnes & Noble Bks. $28.50 (0-389-20344-0). Seven of the major novels of James are examined after a general introduction to the man and his work. [813.09]

3741 Jarvis, Sharon, ed. *Inside Outer Space: Science Fiction Professionals Look at Their Craft* (10–12). 1985, Ungar $14.95 (0-8044-2411-X). Ten science fiction writers, including C. J. Cherryh and Marion Zimmer Bradley, explore various aspects of the genre. (Rev: BL 3/15/85) [809]

3742 Johnson, Charles. *Being & Race: Black Writing since 1970* (10–12). 1988, Indiana Univ. Pr. $15.95 (0-253-31165-9). A telling analysis of writers of contemporary black fiction with an introductory section on the status of black writing. (Rev: BL 2/15/88; SLJ 10/88) [810]

3743 Kazin, Alfred. *On Native Grounds: An Interpretation of Modern American Prose Literature* (10–12). 1942, Harcourt paper $9.95 (0-15-668751-8). In a brilliant series of essays, a history of American prose writing from 1890 to 1940 and its impact on society is given. [810.9]

3744 King, Stephen. *Bare Bones: Conversations on Terror with Stephen King* (9–12). 1988, Mc-Graw $16.95 (0-07-065759-9). A collection of interviews and conversations with the master of the horror novel. (Rev: BL 5/15/88) [813]

3745 Klinkowitz, Jerome. *Kurt Vonnegut* (10–12). 1982, Methuen paper $8.50 (0-416-33480-6). Biographical details of Vonnegut's life are intertwined with an examination of each of his works. [813.09]

3746 Labor, Earle. *Jack London* (10–12). Illus. 1974, Twayne LB $17.95 (0-8057-0455-8). This critical study reevaluates the position of this genius in the history of American literature. [813.09]

3747 Lane, Daryl, et al. *The Sound of Wonder: Interviews from "The Science Fiction Radio Show" Vol. 1* (9–12). Illus. 1985, Oryx paper $20.00 (0-89774-175-7). With its companion volume, number 2 (1985), there are a total of 19 in-depth interviews with science fiction luminaries such as Piers Anthony and Marion Zimmer Bradley. (Rev: BL 2/15/86; SLJ 8/86; VOYA 6/86) [813]

3748 Lehan, Richard. *The Great Gatsby: The Limits of Wonder* (10–12). 1990, Twayne $18.95 (0-8057-7960-4); paper $7.95 (0-8057-8013-0). This is an excellent analysis of this American novel plus a discussion of Fitzgerald's life. This is part of a series that, like Cliffs Notes, devotes an entire book to a single work of literature. (Rev: VOYA 6/90) [813]

3749 Lockridge, Ernest, ed. *Twentieth Century Interpretations of The Great Gatsby: A Collection of Critical Essays* (10–12). 1968, Prentice $22.50 (0-13-363820-0); paper $2.95 (0-13-363812-X). In

a series of essays and reviews this American classic is analyzed. [813.09]

3750 Lundquist, James. *J. D. Salinger* (10–12). 1979, Ungar $18.95 (0-8044-2560-4). This analysis of Salinger's work reveals the philosophical undertones in all of his work. [813.09]

3751 Lundquist, James. *Kurt Vonnegut* (10–12). 1977, Ungar paper $6.95 (0-8044-6458-8). Each of the plots of Vonnegut's novels (through *Slapstick*) is retold and analyzed. [813.09]

3752 Lundquist, James. *Sinclair Lewis* (10–12). 1972, Ungar $18.95 (0-8044-2562-0). An assessment of Lewis' output and its place in American literature. [813.09]

3753 Lundquist, James. *Theodore Dreiser* (10–12). 1974, Ungar $18.95 (0-8044-2563-9). A survey of the life and works of Dreiser and an evaluation on how he is regarded today. [813.09]

3754 McCarthy, Paul. *John Steinbeck* (10–12). 1980, Ungar $18.95 (0-8044-2606-6); paper $7.95 (0-8044-6461-8). A brief review of the author's life followed by an examination of his fiction. [813.09]

3755 McDowell, Margaret B. *Edith Wharton* (10–12). 1976, Twayne LB $17.95 (0-8057-71640-6); paper $4.95 (0-672-61509-6). An analysis and evaluation of the later fiction written from 1920 on. [813.09]

3756 Mackey, Douglas A. *Philip K. Dick* (9–12). 1988, G. K. Hall $19.95 (0-8057-7515-3). A critical assessment of this famous writer's works including posthumous publications. (Rev: BL 2/1/88) [813]

3757 McNelly, Willis E. *The Dune Encyclopedia* (10–12). 1984, Berkley paper $9.95 (0-425-10500-8). This 500-page book is a guide to the complex Dune science fiction series. [808.83]

3758 McSweeney, Kerry. *Moby-Dick: Ishmael's Mighty Book* (10–12). 1986, Twayne $17.95 (0-8057-7954-X); paper $6.95 (0-8057-8002-5). An analysis of the themes and meanings in Melville's classic, *Moby Dick*. (Rev: BL 9/15/86; SLJ 2/87) [813]

3759 Martin, Terence. *Nathaniel Hawthorne* (10–12). 1983, Twayne LB $17.95 (0-8057-7384-3); paper $7.95 (0-8057-7427-0). A critical introduction to the fiction of Hawthorne that emphasizes its underlying themes. [813.09]

3760 Merrill, Robert. *Norman Mailer* (10–12). 1978, Twayne LB $15.95 (0-8057-7254-5). A critical review of Mailer's work that ends in the mid-1970s. [813.09]

3761 Mizener, Arthur, ed. *F. Scott Fitzgerald: A Collection of Critical Essays* (10–12). 1963, Prentice $19.95 (0-13-320853-2). This collection of essays about Fitzgerald is by such distinguished writers as Lionel Trilling and Edmund Wilson. [813.09]

3762 Nilsen, Alleen Pace. *Presenting M. E. Kerr* (9–12). 1986, Twayne $13.95 (0-8057-8202-8). In addition to a biography, this account analyzes the author's work and her contributions to young adult literature. (Rev: BL 6/15/86; SLJ 5/86) [810]

3763 Nye, Jody Lynn, and Anne McCaffrey. *The Dragonlover's Guide to Pern* (9–12). Illus. 1989, Ballantine $19.95 (0-345-35424-9). A beautifully illustrated companion to the Pern series with material on such topics as geography and the care and feeding of their dragons. (Rev: BL 10/1/89; VOYA 6/90) [813]

3764 O'Connell, Nicholas. *At the Field's End: Interviews with Twenty Pacific Northwest Writers* (10–12). Illus. 1987, Madrona $21.95 (0-88089-025-8); paper $12.95 (0-88089-026-6). Twenty interviews with such writers as A. B. Guthrie, Ursula Le Guin, and Jean M. Auel. (Rev: BL 11/15/87) [810.9]

3765 Ousby, Ian. *A Reader's Guide to Fifty American Novels* (10–12). 1979, Barnes & Noble $24.50 (0-06-495318-1). An analysis of 50 novels by 24 authors that stretches from Revolutionary times to Saul Bellow's *Herzog*. [813.09]

3766 Perret, Patti. *The Faces of Science Fiction* (9–12). Illus. 1984, Bluejay $35.00 (0-312-94148-X); paper $11.95 (0-312-94147-1). Photographs of 80 major science fiction and fantasy writers are given as well as comments on their work. (Rev: BL 2/15/85) [813]

3767 Powers, Lyall H. *Faulkner's Yoknapatawpha Comedy* (10–12). 1980, Univ. of Michigan Pr. $24.95 (0-472-08727-4). An examination of 13 major novels of Faulkner that emphasizes the unity of themes and structure. [813.09]

3768 Reed, Kenneth T. *Truman Capote* (10–12). 1981, Twayne LB $16.95 (0-8057-7321-5). An introduction to the life and the writings of this author that gives detail on characterization and style. [813.09]

3769 Reino, Joseph. *Stephen King: The First Decade, Carrie to Pet Sematary* (9–12). Illus. 1988, Twayne $17.95 (0-8057-7512-9). An analysis of King's most important works published from 1973 to 1983. (Rev: BL 2/15/88) [813]

3770 Reynolds, Michaels. *The Sun Also Rises* (10–12). 1988, Twayne $18.95 (0-8057-7962-0); paper $7.95 (0-8057-8015-7). An analysis of this classic by Hemingway often read in high schools. (Rev: SLJ 11/88) [808.3]

3771 Richman, Sidney. *Bernard Malamud* (10–12). 1967, Twayne LB $16.95 (0-8057-0472-8). This book supplies a work-by-work analysis of Malamud's early works. [813.09]

3772 Root, Karen L., ed. *American Literary Almanac* (9–12). Illus. 1988, Facts on File $29.95 (0-8160-1245-8). Fact and gossip about America's literary life and its authors. (Rev: BL 8/88; BR 11–12/88) [810]

3773 Rovit, Earl H. *Ernest Hemingway* (10–12). 1963, Twayne LB $15.95 (0-8057-7455-6); paper $8.95 (0-8057-7468-9). A fine overview of Hemingway's work that touches on style, themes, and characters. [813.09]

3774 Skaggs, Peggy. *Kate Chopin* (10–12). 1985, Twayne LB $16.95 (0-8057-7439-4). An analysis of this author's two novels and short stories with emphasis on *The Awakening*. [813.09]

3775 Skillion, Anne, ed. *Introducing the Great American Novel* (10–12). 1988, Morrow $19.95 (0-688-07346-8); paper $9.95 (0-688-08065-0). A collection of essays by such writers as Sartre and T. S. Eliot on various aspects of the American novel. (Rev: BL 5/15/88) [813]

3776 Sloane, David E. *The Adventures of Huckleberry Finn: American Comic Vision* (9–12). 1988, Twayne $20.95 (0-8057-7963-9); paper $9.95 (0-8057-8016-5). This paperback gives a detailed analysis of this novel—structure, themes, and characters. (Rev: BR 9–10/88; SLJ 8/88; VOYA 2/89) [813.09]

3777 Smith, Henry Nash, ed. *Mark Twain: A Collection of Critical Essays* (10–12). 1963, Prentice $12.95 (0-13-933317-7). Many prominent writers and critics have contributed to this collection of essays, many of which deal with individual works by Twain. [813.09]

3778 Snipes, Katherine. *Robert Penn Warren* (10–12). 1984, Ungar $18.95 (0-8044-2828-X). This volume is a critical examination of Warren's novels, poetry, and nonfiction works. [818]

3779 Spivack, Charlotte. *Ursula K. Le Guin* (10–12). 1984, Twayne LB $16.95 (0-8057-7393-2); paper $7.95 (0-8057-7393-2). A critical study of the science fiction of Le Guin that discusses both adult and juvenile works. [813.09]

3780 Stevick, Philip, and Gordon Weaver, eds. *The American Short Story, 1900–1945/1945–1980* (10–12). 1983, Twayne LB $19.95 each (0-8057-9355-4; 0-8057-9350-X). This 2-volume set gives an excellent critical survey of American short fiction written during the twentieth century. [813.09]

3781 Stover, Leon. *Harry Harrison* (10–12). 1990, Twayne $18.95 (0-8057-7603-6). A critical examination of the work of this prolific author noted for his humorous science fiction. (Rev: BL 2/15/90) [813]

3782 Stover, Leon. *Robert A. Heinlein* (9–12). 1987, Twayne $17.95 (0-8057-7509-9). An in-depth study of the science fiction of this acclaimed American writer. (Rev: BL 11/15/87) [813]

3783 Sylvander, Carolyn Wedin. *James Baldwin* (10–12). 1980, Ungar $18.95 (0-8044-2484-4). A critical study of all of Baldwin's works, including fiction as well as essays and other nonfiction. [818]

3784 Touponce, William F. *Frank Herbert* (9–12). 1988, G. K. Hall $19.95 (0-8057-7514-5). A critical study of the works of the creator of *Dune* and other science fiction classics. (Rev: BL 2/1/88) [813]

3785 Underwood, Tim, and Chuck Miller, eds. *Kingdom of Fear: The World of Stephen King* (10–12). 1987, NAL paper $3.95 (0-451-14962-9). For all Stephen King enthusiasts, here is a collection of essays about his writing and the films they inspired. (Rev: SLJ 1/87; VOYA 2/87) [809.3]

3786 Voss, Arthur. *The American Short Story: A Critical Survey* (10–12). 1973, Univ. of Oklahoma Pr. paper $12.95 (0-8061-1644-7). A literary history of the short story and a discussion of the major writers in this genre. [813.09]

3787 Wagenknecht, Edward. *The Novels of Henry James* (10–12). 1983, Ungar $24.95 (0-8044-2959-6). After a short biography, each of the novels is analyzed in chronological order. [813.09]

3788 Wagenknecht, Edward. *The Tales of Henry James* (10–12). 1984, Ungar $18.95 (0-8044-2957-X). A critical survey of every one of the fiction pieces by Henry James. [813.09]

3789 Weidt, Maryann N. *Presenting Judy Blume* (9–12). Illus. 1989, Twayne $18.95 (0-8057-8208-7). A biography and a thorough analysis of Judy Blume's work with asides from both critics and Ms. Blume. (Rev: BL 11/1/89; VOYA 12/89) [813]

3790 Williamson, Jack. *Wonder's Child: My Life in Science Fiction* (9–12). Illus. 1984, Bluejay $15.95 (0-312-94454-3); paper $8.95 (0-312-94454-3). Through his experiences, Williamson traces a history of science fiction in America. [808.83]

3791 Winter, Douglas E. *Faces of Fear: Encounters with the Creators of Modern Horror* (10–12). 1985, Berkley paper $6.95 (0-425-07670-9). Interviews with 18 writers of horror and supernatural novels such as Stephen King and V. C. Andrews. (Rev: VOYA 4/86) [813]

3792 Winter, Douglas E. *Stephen King: The Art of Darkness* (10–12). Illus. 1986, NAL paper $4.95 (0-451-14612-3). A study of the novels and novellas by this master of horror fiction. [813.09]

3793 Wood, Robin, and Anne McCaffrey. *The People of Pern* (8–12). Illus. 1988, Donning $19.95 (0-89865-635-4). A companion to McCaffrey's science fiction series that describes and pictures each of the characters. (Rev: BL 1/1/89) [741.973]

3794 Zelazny, Roger, and Neil Randall. *Roger Zelazny's Visual Guide to Castle Amber* (9–12). Illus. 1988, Avon paper $8.95 (0-380-75566-1). A lavishly illustrated guide to the places and people featured in Zelazny's popular Amber series. (Rev: VOYA 2/89) [813.54]

Other Regions and Countries

3795 Meyer, Doris, ed. *Lives on the Line: The Testimony of Contemporary Latin American Authors* (10–12). 1988, Univ. of California Pr. $25.00 (0-520-06002-4). Thirty Latin American authors including Marquez, Borges, and Neruda comment on their lives and work. (Rev: BL 3/15/88) [920]

3796 Peden, Margaret Sayers, ed. *The Latin American Short Story: A Critical History* (10–12). 1983, Twayne LB $20.95 (0-8057-9351-8). A collection of critical essays that deal with the evolution of the short story in Latin America from colonial times to the present. [863.09]

Plays

General and Miscellaneous

3797 Esslin, Martin. *An Anatomy of Drama* (10–12). Illus. 1977, Hill & Wang paper $7.95 (0-8090-0550-6). An introduction to plays that explains their elements and how they are used by playwrights effectively. [808.2]

3798 Fergusson, Francis. *The Idea of a Theater: A Study of Ten Plays* (10–12). 1968, Princeton Univ. Pr. paper $10.95 (0-691-01288-1). The basic ideas in the art of drama are revealed in this examination of 10 plays. [809.2]

3799 Gilman, Richard. *The Making of Modern Drama* (10–12). 1974, Da Capo paper $10.95 (0-306-80293-1). This is a collection of critical essays on 8 playwrights that highlight the changes that have transformed the theater in the last 100 years. [809.2]

3800 Vena, Gary. *How to Read and Write about Drama* (9–12). 1988, Arco paper $6.95 (0-13-431131-0). By explaining the elements of a play, this book shows how to analyze plays and increase one's appreciation of this art form. (Rev: SLJ 2/89) [808.2]

Europe

General

3801 King, Neil. *Classical Beginnings* (10–12). Illus. 1985, Hulton paper $12.95 (0-7175-1230-4). A survey of Greek and Roman drama with critical analyses of important plays. (Rev: SLJ 3/86) [880]

3802 Kirk, Irina. *Anton Chekhov* (10–12). 1981, Twayne LB $17.95 (0-8057-6410-0). This introduction to the life and works of Chekhov discusses both his plays and his short stories. [891.7]

3803 Leatherbarrow, William J. *Fedor Dostoevsky* (10–12). 1981, Twayne LB $17.95 (0-8057-6480-1). An introduction to the life and works of Dostoevsky that analyzes each of the novels. [891.7]

3804 Melchinger, Siegfried. *Anton Chekhov* (10–12). Illus. 1972, Ungar $18.95 (0-8044-2615-5). This biographical study includes a lengthy analysis of Chekhov's plays. [891.7]

3805 Scodel, Ruth. *Sophocles* (10–12). 1984, Twayne LB $17.95 (0-8057-6578-6). A critical study of Sophocles' work, with emphasis on *Antigone, Oedipus the King,* and *Electra.* [882.09]

3806 Spatz, Lois. *Aeschylus* (10–12). 1982, Twayne LB $18.95 (0-8057-6522-0). An analysis of each of the existing plays and the problems in their interpretation. [882.09]

Great Britain and Ireland

GENERAL

3807 Adams, Douglas. *The Original Hitchhiker Radio Scripts* (9–12). 1985, Harmony paper $9.95 (0-517-55950-1). *The Hitchhiker's Guide to the Galaxy* began as a radio show in England and here are 12 of the original scripts. (Rev: BL 2/15/86) [822]

3808 Dietrich, Richard F. *British Drama 1890 to 1950* (10–12). 1989, Twayne $21.95 (0-8057-8951-0). A history of one of the golden ages of British drama that involved such luminaries as Shaw,

Wilde, Barrie, and Galsworthy. (Rev: VOYA 4/90) [822]

3809 Hinchliffe, Arnold P. *Harold Pinter* (10–12). 1981, Twayne LB $14.95 (0-8057-6784-3). An introduction to the techniques used by this playwright plus a discussion of individual plays. [822.09]

3810 King, Neil. *Elizabethan Comedy* (10–12). Illus. 1985, Hulton $12.95 (0-7175-1232-0). After an overview of the topic, individual playwrights and their work are discussed. Shakespeare is omitted. Also use the companion volume *The Elizabethan Tragedy* (1985) and a study of medieval mystery plays, *Mystery and Morality* (1985). (Rev: SLJ 3/86) [822.09]

3811 King, Neil. *The Modern Age* (10–12). Illus. 1985, Hulton $12.95 (0-7175-1236-3). A discussion of important writers and plays in the modern history of English drama. Two companion volumes are *Rakes and Rogues* (1985) on Restoration plays and *The Victorian Age* (1985). (Rev: SLJ 3/86) [822.09]

3812 *Landmarks of Modern British Drama, Vol. 1: The Plays of the Sixties* (9–12). 1986, Methuen $25.00 (0-413-59080-1); paper $8.95 (0-413-57260-9). This and its companion volume, *Landmarks of Modern British Drama, Vol. 2: The Plays of the Seventies* (1986), contain a total of 14 plays such as *Amadeus*, *Loot*, and *Equus*. (Rev: BL 5/15/86) [822]

3813 Rusinko, Susan. *Tom Stoppard* (10–12). 1986, Twayne LB $16.95 (0-8057-6909-9); paper $6.95 (0-8057-6927-7). An analysis of individual works plus an overall evaluation of Stoppard's place in the contemporary English theater. [822.09]

SHAKESPEARE

3814 Barnet, Sylvan. *A Short Guide to Shakespeare* (10–12). 1974, Harcourt paper $4.95 (0-15-681800-0). This is a brief introduction to Shakespeare, his world and his plays. [822.3]

3815 Berkoff, Steven. *I Am Hamlet* (10–12). 1990, Grove Weidenfeld $17.95 (0-8021-1175-0). A line-by-line examination of *Hamlet* from this noted actor-director's point of view. (Rev: BL 2/15/90) [822]

3816 Brown, John Russell. *Shakespeare and His Theatre* (9–12). Illus. 1982, Lothrop $14.95 (0-688-00850-X). This account describes in pictures and text what we know about Shakespeare's Globe Theatre and the nature of play production during Elizabethan times. [792.09]

3817 Fox, Levi, ed. *The Shakespeare Handbook* (10–12). Illus. 1987, G. K. Hall $29.95 (0-8161-8905-6). In addition to historical and background material plus analyses of the plays and poetry, this manual covers topics such as film treatments of the Bard's plays. (Rev: SLJ 3/88) [822.3]

3818 Frye, Northrop. *Northrop Frye on Shakespeare* (10–12). 1986, Yale Univ. Pr. $25.00 (0-300-03711-2); paper $7.95 (0-300-04208-6). The celebrated Canadian critic offers an analysis of 10 of Shakespeare's most popular plays. (Rev: BL 10/1/86) [822.3]

3819 Garfield, Leon. *Shakespeare Stories* (9–12). Illus. 1985, Schocken $18.95 (0-8052-3991-X). The stories of 12 of Shakespeare's most popular plays are retold using generous quotes from the original texts. [822.3]

3820 Gurr, Andrew, and John Orrell. *Rebuilding Shakespeare's Globe* (9–12). 1989, Routledge $25.00 (0-87830-156-9). A history of the project in London to rebuild the Globe as it was originally, from its inception in the 1890s to the present. (Rev: BR 3–4/90) [822.3]

3821 Jorgensen, Paul A. *William Shakespeare: The Tragedies* (10–12). 1985, Twayne LB $17.95 (0-8057-6906-4). A detailed analysis of each of Shakespeare's 10 tragedies. (Rev: BL 10/15/85) [822.3]

3822 Muir, Kenneth, and S. Schoenbaum, eds. *A New Companion to Shakespeare Studies* (10–12). 1987, Cambridge Univ. Pr. paper $15.95 (0-521-09645-6). Separate chapters by different Shakespearean scholars explore such subjects as his life, times, and works. [822.3]

3823 Ogburn, Charlton. *The Mysterious William Shakespeare: The Myth and Reality* (10–12). Illus. 1984, EPM Publs. $25.00 (0-939007-26-9). A fascinating study that tries to prove that Shakespeare's plays were written by the Earl of Oxford. [822.3]

3824 Onions, C. T. *A Shakespeare Glossary* (10–12). 1986, Oxford Univ. Pr. $39.95 (0-19-811199-1); paper $15.00 (0-19-871094-1). This dictionary of language used by Shakespeare is a help for readers unfamiliar with Elizabethan English. [822.3]

3825 Saccio, Peter. *Shakespeare's English Kings* (10–12). Illus. 1987, Oxford Univ. Pr. paper $9.95 (0-19-502156-8). This book discusses each of Shakespeare's historical plays and supplies valuable factual background material. [822.3]

3826 Schoenbaum, S. *Shakespeare: The Globe & The World* (10–12). Illus. 1987, Oxford Univ. Pr. paper $9.95 (0-19-502646-2). This book explores the influence Shakespeare has had on world culture. [822.3]

3827 Spevack, Marvin. *The Harvard Concordance to Shakespeare* (10–12). 1973, Harvard Univ. Pr. $76.00 (0-674-37475-4). A one-volume reference that gives entries for 29,000 different words used by Shakespeare. [822.3]

3828 Spurgeon, Caroline F. E. *Shakespeare's Imagery and What It Tells Us* (10–12). Illus. 1935, Cambridge paper $21.95 (0-521-09258-2). An analysis of Shakespeare's imagery and what this reveals about the man and his learning. [822.3]

3829 Vaughn, Jack A. *Shakespeare's Comedies* (10–12). Illus. 1980, Ungar $18.95 (0-8044-2938-3). A play-by-play analysis of each of Shakespeare's 17 comedies. [822.3]

3830 Watts, Cedric. *Hamlet* (10–12). 1988, Twayne $17.95 (0-8057-8706-2); paper $8.95 (0-8057-8710-0). One of a series of study guides that analyze the major plays of Shakespeare. (Rev: SLJ 3/89) [822.3]

3831 Wells, Stanley. *Shakespeare: An Illustrated Dictionary* (10–12). Illus. 1978, Oxford Univ. Pr. $21.95 (0-19-520054-3). Using a dictionary format, this book supplies information on Shakespeare, his plays, and their characters and people and places associated with the Bard. [822.3]

3832 Wilson, John Dover. *What Happens in Hamlet* (10–12). 1987, Cambridge paper $18.95 (0-521-09109-8). An attempt to arrive at all the hidden meanings inside *Hamlet*. [822.3]

United States

3833 Berlin, Normand. *Eugene O'Neill* (10–12). Illus. 1988, St. Martin's paper $10.95 (0-312-02125-9). This volume gives both critical and biographical material on Eugene O'Neill. [812.09]

3834 Carpenter, Frederic I. *Eugene O'Neill* (10–12). 1979, Twayne LB $15.95 (0-8057-7267-7); paper $6.95 (0-8057-7428-9). As well as background information, this book devotes single chapters to each of the greatest of O'Neill's plays. [812.09]

3835 Corrigan, Robert W., ed. *Arthur Miller: A Collection of Critical Essays* (10–12). 1969, Prentice $12.95 (0-13-582973-9). The 10 essays in this book explore the themes developed by Miller in his plays and his career as a playwright. [812.09]

3836 Falk, Signi. *Tennessee Williams* (10–12). 1978, Twayne LB $15.95 (0-8057-7202-2); paper

$6.95 (0-8057-7445-9). By using the 4 most prominent types of characters found in Williams's plays, the author analyzes this writer's major works. [812.09]

3837 Floyd, Virginia. *The Plays of Eugene O'Neill* (10–12). Illus. 1985, Ungar $24.95 (0-8044-2206-0). Through a chronological review of each of Eugene O'Neill's plays, both critical and biographical materials are covered. [812.09]

3838 Harriott, Esther. *American Voices: 5 Contemporary Playwrights in Essays & Interviews* (10–12). 1988, McFarland $24.95 (0-89950-283-0). Material is given on the works of 5 playwrights including Sam Shepard, Lanford Wilson, and David Mamet. (Rev: SLJ 4/89; VOYA 4/89) [809.5]

3839 Johnson, Robert K. *Neil Simon* (10–12). 1983, Twayne LB $18.95 (0-8057-7387-8); paper $6.95 (0-8057-7446-7). A critical study of Neil Simon's plays through 1981. [812.09]

3840 Lederer, Katherine. *Lillian Hellman* (10–12). 1979, Twayne LB $15.95 (0-8057-7275-8). After a brief biography, this volume concentrates on an analysis of Hellman's plays and her nonfiction works. [812.09]

3841 Martine, James J., ed. *Critical Essays on Arthur Miller* (10–12). 1979, G. K. Hall LB $35.00 (0-8161-8258-2). This is an anthology of reviews and critical essays about Miller's plays and his short stories. [812.09]

3842 Moss, Leonard. *Arthur Miller* (10–12). 1980, Twayne LB $16.95 (0-8057-7311-8). A thorough review of the components of each of Miller's plays, their themes, and structure. [812.09]

3843 Savran, David. *In Their Own Words: Contemporary American Playwrights* (9–12). Illus. 1988, Theatre Communications Group paper $12.95 (0-930452-70-4). Interviews with 20 modern playwrights including David Mamet, David Rabe, and Stephen Sondheim. (Rev: BL 9/1/88) [812]

3844 Vaughn, Jack A. *Early American Dramatists: From the Beginnings to 1900* (10–12). Illus. 1981, Ungar $18.91 (0-8044-2940-5). As well as a series of biographies, this book gives plot summaries and critical comment concerning important American playwrights before 1900. [812.09]

3845 Welland, Dennis. *Miller: The Playwright* (10–12). Illus. 1988, Heinemann paper $11.95 (0-413-60050-5). This is a thorough study of Miller's work for both the stage and movies. [812.09]

Poetry

General and Miscellaneous

3846 Aristotle. *Poetics* (10–12). Trans. by Gerald F. Else. 1970, Univ. of Michigan Pr. paper $8.95 (0-472-06166-6). A classic account of the elements of poetry and how to appreciate them. [808.1]

3847 Auslander, Joseph, and Frank Ernest Hill. *The Winged Horse: The Story of Poets and Their Poetry* (10–12). 1969, Haskell House LB $75.00 (0-8383-0328-5). This book first published in 1928 gives a history of world poetry from its beginning to the early twentieth century. [809.1]

3848 Barnstone, Aliki, and Willis Barnstone, eds. *A Book of Women Poets from Antiquity to Now* (10–12). 1980, Schocken $29.95 (0-8052-3693-7); paper $16.95 (0-8052-0680-9). A collection of poems by women from many cultures and time periods each with a brief biography. [808.81]

3849 Chamberlain, William. *The Policeman's Beard Is Half Constructed* (8–12). Illus. 1984, Warner $9.95 (0-446-38051-2). This is a collection of poetry generated on a microcomputer using BASIC and syntax directives plus a vocabulary. [808.1]

3850 Coffin, Charles M. *The Major Poets: English and American* (10–12). 1969, Harcourt paper $15.95 (0-15-554545-0). A fine anthology that represents poetry written in English from Chaucer to the present. [821.08]

3851 Deutsch, Babette. *Poetry Handbook: A Dictionary of Terms* (10–12). 4th ed. 1974, Harper paper $8.85 (0-06-463548-1). A handbook that defines the special vocabulary of poetry. [808.1]

3852 Doreski, Carol Kiler, and William Doreski. *How to Read and Interpret Poetry* (9–12). 1988, Arco paper $6.95 (0-13-431081-0). Through the analysis of several poems, this book tries to explain how to read and understand poetry. (Rev: SLJ 2/89) [808.1]

3853 Gordon, Bonnie Bilyeu. *Songs from Unsung Worlds: Science in Poetry* (9–12). 1985, Birkhauser Boston paper $14.95 (0-8176-3236-4). A collection from 77 contemporary poets, the subject matter of which is science and the mysteries of the universe. (Rev: BR 3–4/86) [808.81]

3854 Jerome, Judson. *The Poet's Handbook* (10–12). 1980, Writer's Digest paper $10.95 (0-89879-219-3). A handbook that covers such topics as meter, rhyme, rhythm, and the history of poetry. [808.1]

3855 Packard, William. *The Poet's Dictionary: A Handbook of Prosody and Poetic Devices* (10–12). 1989, Harper $19.95 (0-06-016130-2). The structure of poetry and techniques of poetry writing are defined and illustrated from the works of many well-known poets. (Rev: BL 7/89) [808.1]

3856 Perkins, David. *A History of Modern Poetry: Modernism and After* (10–12). 1987, Harvard Univ. Pr. $25.00 (0-674-39946-3); paper $14.95 (0-674-39947-1). A scholarly, in-depth look at poetry from the 1920s to the present. This is a companion to the author's earlier *A History of Modern Poetry: From the Eighteen Nineties to the High Modernist Mode* (1976). (Rev: SLJ 9/87) [809.1]

3857 Pritchard, William H. *Lives of the Modern Poets* (10–12). 1980, Oxford Univ. Pr. $27.50 (0-19-502690-X); paper $8.95 (0-19-502989-5). A collection of 9 essays on such poets as Yeats, Hardy, Frost, Pound, and T. S. Eliot. [821.09]

3858 Rosenthal, Macha Louis. *The Modern Poets: A Critical Introduction* (10–12). 1987, Oxford Univ. Pr. paper $8.95 (0-19-500718-2). A discussion of characteristics of modern poetry with particular emphasis on the contributions of Yeats, Eliot, and Pound. [821.09]

3859 Van Doren, Mark, ed. *An Anthology of World Poetry* (10–12). Rev. ed. 1936, Harcourt $49.95 (0-15-107665-0). A collection of poetry translated from 16 different languages. [808.81]

3860 Williams, Miller. *Patterns of Poetry: An Encyclopedia of Forms* (10–12). 1986, Louisiana State Univ. Pr. $32.50 (0-8071-1253-4); paper $14.95 (0-8071-1330-1). After a history of poetic forms, each form is described and a poem is given to illustrate it. (Rev: BL 8/86) [811]

Europe

General

3861 Dante, Alighieri. *The Portable Dante* (10–12). 1987, Penguin paper $8.95 (0-14-015032-3). Along with some short works, this collection includes *The Divine Comedy* and *The New Life.* [851]

3862 Holmes, George. *Dante* (10–12). 1987, Oxford Univ. Pr. paper $5.95 (0-19-287504-3). A study of Dante's works, his political beliefs, and his personal life. [851.09]

3863 Pasternak, Boris. *Selected Poems* (10–12). 1984, Penguin paper $7.95 (0-14-042245-5). A selection of poems by this Nobel Prize-winning writer that spans his entire creative career. [891.7]

3864 Willcock, Malcolm M. *A Companion to the Iliad* (10–12). Illus. 1976, Univ. of Chicago Pr. paper $8.95 (0-226-89855-5). A guide to the reading of *The Iliad* gives summaries, explanations of allusions, and general background material on how to appreciate this epic poem. [883]

Great Britain and Ireland

3865 Carey, John. *John Donne: Life, Mind and Art* (10–12). 1981, Oxford Univ. Pr. $25.00 (0-19-520242-2). A critical study that focuses on Donne's beliefs and how they affected his poetry. [821.09]

3866 Hirst, Wolf Z. *John Keats* (10–12). 1981, Twayne LB $15.95 (0-8057-6821-1). A critical study of Keats's works that focuses on his most popular verse. [821.09]

3867 Howard, Edwin J. *Geoffrey Chaucer* (10–12). 1964, Twayne LB $15.95 (0-8057-1088-4). In addition to a study of Chaucer's works, this study supplies details about the life and times of the subject. [821.09]

3868 Lloyd-Evans, Barbara, ed. *Five Hundred Years of English Poetry: Chaucer to Arnold* (10–12). 1989, Bedrick $39.95 (0-87226-325-8); paper $19.95 (0-87226-215-4). An excellent one-volume comprehensive collection of the major English poets. (Rev: SLJ 6/90) [821.08]

3869 MacKenzie, Norman. *A Reader's Guide to Gerard Manley Hopkins* (10–12). 1981, Cornell Univ. Pr. paper $13.95 (0-8014-9221-1). In addition to biographical details this account supplies a poem-by-poem analysis. [821.09]

3870 Peterson, Richard F. *William Butler Yeats* (10–12). 1982, Twayne LB $15.95 (0-8057-6815-7). A guide to the vast and varied output of this Irish writer. [821.09]

3871 Raffel, Burton. *T. S. Eliot* (10–12). 1982, Ungar $18.95 (0-8044-2708-9). A comprehensive look at the life and works of T. S. Eliot. [811.09]

3872 Smith, Stan. *W. H. Auden* (10–12). 1985, Blackwell $29.95 (0-631-13381-X); paper $9.95 (0-631-13515-4). A study of Auden's poetic output and its relation to political and social conditions of the time. [821.09]

3873 Thwaite, Anthony. *Six Centuries of Verse* (10–12). Illus. 1985, Methuen paper $9.95 (0-423-00960-5). Much more than an anthology, this gives critical comments for each poet represented—most are English though a few important Americans are included. (Rev: BL 8/85) [821]

3874 Wright, George T. *W. H. Auden* (10–12). 1981, Twayne LB $18.50 (0-8057-7346-0). This volume contains a detailed analysis of all of the major poems of Auden. [821.09]

United States

3875 Angelou, Maya, and Tom Feelings. *Now Sheba Sings the Song* (9–12). Illus. 1987, Dutton $18.95 (0-525-24501-4); paper $9.95 (0-525-48374-8). Drawings of 25 black women from various backgrounds by Tom Feelings are accompanied by short poems by Maya Angelou. (Rev:

BL 3/15/87; BR 11–12/87; SLJ 10/87; VOYA 10/ 87) [811]

3876 Benvenuto, Richard. *Amy Lowell* (10–12). 1985, Twayne LB $18.95 (0-8057-7436-X). An assessment of the work and influence of this poet. [811.09]

3877 Bloom, Harold, ed. *American Women Poets* (10–12). 1987, Chelsea House $49.95 (0-87754-960-5). A review of the most important female American poets and their work. (Rev: BL 11/15/ 87) [811]

3878 Breslin, James E. B. *From Modern to Contemporary: American Poetry, 1945–1965* (10–12). 1984, Univ. of Chicago Pr. $20.00 (0-226-07408-0); paper $9.95 (0-226-07409-9). This critical work discusses such poets as Richard Wilbur, Adrienne Rich, Allen Ginsberg, and Denise Levertov. [811.09]

3879 Brooks, Gwendolyn. *The World of Gwendolyn Brooks* (10–12). 1971, Harper $15.00 (0-06-010538-0). This omnibus volume includes 4 collections of poetry and a novella. [818]

3880 Calhoun, Richard J., and Robert W. Hill. *James Dickey* (10–12). Illus. 1983, Twayne LB $17.95 (0-8057-7391-6). This volume supplies an objective analysis of Dickey's work. [811.9]

3881 Cox, James M., ed. *Robert Frost: A Collection of Critical Essays* (10–12). 1962, Prentice $12.95 (0-13-331512-6). Eleven critical essays that explore various facets of Robert Frost's poetry. [811.09]

3882 Crowder, Richard. *Carl Sandburg* (10–12). 1964, Twayne LB $15.95 (0-8057-0648-8). After a biography of Sandburg, the author gives a detailed criticism of both the poetry and prose of this writer. [818]

3883 Ferlazzo, Paul J. *Emily Dickinson* (10–12). 1976, Twayne LB $16.95 (0-8057-7180-8); Macmillan paper $4.95 (0-672-61511-8). This book analyzes such subjects in Dickinson's poetry as love, death, and nature. [811.09]

3884 Frye, Northrop. *T. S. Eliot: An Introduction* (10–12). 1981, Univ. of Chicago Pr. paper $6.50 (0-226-26649-4). The celebrated Canadian critic assesses the poetry, prose, and plays of T. S. Eliot. [811.09]

3885 Gerber, Philip. *Robert Frost* (10–12). 1982, Twayne LB $16.95 (0-8057-7348-7); paper $8.95 (0-8057-7426-2). This book concentrates on an analysis of Frost's work but also gives coverage on his life and career. [811.09]

3886 Gray, Richard. *American Poetry of the Twentieth Century* (10–12). 1990, Longman $34.95 (0-582-49437-0); paper $17.95 (0-582-

49444-3). A study of schools, movements, trends, and individual poets of importance in twentieth-century American poetry. (Rev: BL 8/ 90) [811.5]

3887 Jemie, Onwuchekwa. *Langston Hughes: An Introduction to the Poetry* (10–12). 1977, Columbia Univ. Pr. paper $12.00 (0-231-06161-7). A sympathetic survey of the poetry of this black American writer. [811.09]

3888 Leary, Lewis. *John Greenleaf Whittier* (10–12). 1962, Twayne LB $13.50 (0-8057-0796-4); College & Univ. Pr. paper $10.95 (0-8084-0183-1). A discussion of the life and work of this nineteenth-century pacifist and poet. [811.09]

3889 Lourie, Dick, et al., eds. *Smart Like Me: High School-Age Writing from the Sixties to Now* (9–12). 1988, Hanging Loose Press $20.00 (0-914610-59-7); paper $10.00 (0-914610-58-9). A lively collection of almost 150 poems written by 50 teenagers over the past 20 years. (Rev: BL 11/ 1/88; SLJ 11/88) [811.54]

3890 McNeil, Helen. *Emily Dickinson* (10–12). Illus. 1986, Pantheon paper $11.95 (0-394-74766-6). Some biographical information is given but the focus of this volume is an analysis of Dickinson's poetry. (Rev: BL 10/1/86) [811]

3891 Miller, James E., Jr., and Helen Regenstein. *Walt Whitman* (10–12). 1990, Twayne LB $22.95 (0-8057-7600-1). An examination of Whitman's work under such headings as structure, language, and biographical influences. [811.09]

3892 Phillips, Elizabeth. *Marianne Moore* (10–12). 1982, Ungar $18.95 (0-8044-2698-8). After a brief biography, this work examines Moore's poetry by such subjects as structure and the influence of world events like the Vietnam War. [811.09]

3893 Sewall, Richard B., ed. *Emily Dickinson: A Collection of Critical Essays* (10–12). 1963, Prentice $12.95 (0-13-208785-5). This collection of 16 essays (many by well-known poets like Archibald MacLeish) assesses the poetry of Emily Dickinson. [811.09]

3894 Shucard, Alan. *American Poetry: The Puritans through Walt Whitman* (10–12). 1988, Twayne $21.95 (0-8057-8450-0). A fine introduction for better students to our early poetry. (Rev: BL 6/15/88) [811]

3895 Shucard, Alan, et al. *Modern American Poetry* (10–12). 1989, Twayne $21.95 (0-8057-8451-9). A study of the major American poets from 1865 to 1950, that is, from Emily Dickinson to e.e. cummings. (Rev: BL 6/15/89; VOYA 2/90) [811]

3896 Stanton, Maura. *Tales of the Supernatural* (10–12). 1988, Godine $14.95 (0-87923-749-X); paper $9.95 (0-87923-750-3). In this collection of poems the poet explores extraordinary events and surreal occurrences. (Rev: BL 1/1/89) [811]

3897 Willard, Nancy. *Water Walker* (10–12). 1989, Knopf $18.95 (0-394-57208-4); paper $9.95 (0-679-72171-1). A book of lyric poems that celebrate the wonder in ordinary things. (Rev: BL 6/15/89; BR 3–4/90) [811]

Language and Communication

Signs and Symbols

3898 Cooper, J. C. *An Illustrated Encyclopedia of Traditional Symbols* (10–12). Illus. 1978, Thames paper $12.95 (0-500-27125-9). An international collection of historical symbols taken from religions, cults, and other social institutions. [001.56]

3899 Dreyfuss, Henry. *Symbol Sourcebook: An Authoritative Guide to International Graphic Symbols* (9–12). Illus. 1972, Van Nostrand paper $26.95 (0-442-21806-0). Under 18 different languages, the functional international signs are illustrated and explained. [001.56]

3900 Fast, Julius. *Body Language* (10–12). 1970, Evans $12.95 (0-87131-039-2); Pocket paper $3.95 (0-671-63418-6). This is a study of nonverbal communication through body movements. [153.6]

3901 Modley, Rudolf. *Handbook of Pictorial Symbols: 3,250 Examples from International Sources* (9–12). Illus. 1976, Dover paper $6.95 (0-486-23357-X). All sorts of symbols are pictured and explained in this source organized by subjects. [001.56]

3902 Sternberg, Martin L. A. *American Sign Language: A Comprehensive Dictionary* (10–12). Illus. 1981, Harper paper $13.95 (0-06-091383-5). This signing dictionary contains more than 5,000 words and 8,000 diagrams. [001.56]

Words and Languages

3903 Ammer, Christine. *Fighting Words: From War, Rebellion, and Other Combative Capers* (9–12). 1989, Paragon $19.95 (1-55778-056-0); paper $10.95 (1-55778-093-5). A work about words and their stories—like jeep and fuhrer—whose origins date to periods of world conflict. (Rev: BL 3/15/89) [355]

3904 Baron, Dennis. *The English-Only Question: An Official Language for Americans?* (10–12). 1990, Yale Univ. Pr. $22.50 (0-300-04852-1). An examination of the English-only debate, its history, present status, and possible future resolution. (Rev: BL 8/90) [306]

3905 Barzun, Jacques, ed. *Modern American Usage* (10–12). 1966, Hill & Wang paper $10.95 (0-8090-0139-X). Both for browsing and as a reference book, this is a valuable guide to correct usage of the English language. [428]

3906 Bluestein, Gene. *Anglish-Yinglish: Yiddish in American Life and Literature* (9–12). 1989, Univ. of Georgia Pr. $22.50 (0-8203-1083-2); paper $9.95 (0-8203-1084-0). A dictionary of Yiddish words like "mish-mash" and "drek" that have found their way into the English language. (Rev: BL 2/15/89) [437]

3907 Bowler, Peter. *The Superior Person's Book of Words* (10–12). Illus. 1985, Godine $10.95 (0-87923-556-X). When trying to impress someone, using some of these 500 special words might help. (Rev: BL 9/15/85) [428.1]

3908 Brandreth, Gyles. *The Joy of Lex* (10–12). 1983, Morrow paper $9.95 (0-688-01397-X). A collection of word plays, tongue twisters, and other activities involving words. [413]

3909 Bryson, Bill. *The Mother Tongue: English in the World Today* (10–12). 1990, Morrow $18.95 (0-688-07895-8). A history of how English has become an international language and how it changes from one culture to another. (Rev: BL 6/1/90) [420.9]

3910 Carroll, David. *The Dictionary of Foreign Terms in the English Language* (10–12). 1979, Dutton paper $4.95 (0-8015-2053-3). This is a dictionary of about 7,000 foreign words and phrases used in English. Also use: *A Concise Dictionary of Foreign Expressions* (1984). [413]

3911 Chang, Raymond, and Margaret Scrogin Chang. *Speaking in Chinese* (10–12). 1983, Norton $12.95 (0-393-04503-X); paper $8.95 (0-393-30061-7). This book traces the history of written Chinese and explains the structure of the spoken language. [400]

3912 Chomsky, Noam. *Reflections on Language* (10–12). 1975, Pantheon paper $7.95 (0-394-73123-9). The author speculates on the origins of language and its structure. [410]

3913 Ciardi, John. *A Browser's Dictionary, and Native's Guide to the Unknown American Language* (10–12). 1980, Harper $18.95 (0-06-010766-9). This is an interesting collection of etymologies involving 1,000 English words and phrases. [427]

3914 Ciardi, John. *Good Words to You: An All-New Dictionary and Native's Guide to the Unknown American Language* (10–12). 1987, Harper $19.95 (0-06-015691-0). A delightful book about the origins of many Americanisms that is perfect for browsing. (Rev: BL 4/15/87) [422]

3915 Claiborne, Robert. *Loose Cannons & Red Herrings: A Book of Lost Metaphors* (8–12). 1988, Norton $17.95 (0-393-02578-0). The origins of many common English words and phrases in use today, e.g., funk and deep six. (Rev: BL 8/88) [422]

3916 Dunkling, Leslie, and William Gosling. *The Facts on File Dictionary of First Names* (10–12). 1984, Facts on File $22.95 (0-87196-274-8). This book discusses the origins of 4,500 first names plus 5,000 nicknames. [929.4]

3917 Ehrlich, Eugene. *Amo, Amas, Amat and More: How to Use Latin to Your Own Advantage and to the Astonishment of Others* (10–12). Illus. 1985, Harper $17.95 (0-06-181249-8); paper $7.99 (0-06-091395-9). An introduction to 1,200 Latin phrases that are used in the English language. [470]

3918 Elster, Charles Harrington. *Is There a Cow in Moscow? More Beastly Mispronunciations and Sound Advice* (9–12). 1990, Macmillan paper $8.95 (0-02-028371-7). In this sequel to *There Is No Zoo in Zoology* (1988), more frequently mispronounced words are highlighted. (Rev: BL 9/15/90) [421]

3919 Franck, Irene M., and David M. Brownstone. *Communicators* (8–12). Illus. 1986, Facts on File $14.95 (0-8160-1443-4). A history of such occupations as authors, messengers, publishers, broadcasters, and others involved in communication. (Rev: BL 4/15/87; BR 1–2/87; SLJ 3/87) [001.51]

3920 Fuller, Graham E. *How to Learn a Foreign Language* (9–12). 1987, Storm King Pr. paper $4.95 (0-394-75689-4). Written for businesspeople, this book gives many useful suggestions for mastering a language that will also help young adults. (Rev: SLJ 8/88; VOYA 8/88) [407]

3921 Gragonier, Reginald, and David Fisher, ed. *What's What: A Visual Glossary of Everyday Objects* (7–12). Illus. 1988, Ballantine paper $12.95 (0-345-30302-4). A dictionary that illustrates and names the parts of objects from a paper clip to an oil rig. (Rev: BR 1–2/90) [423]

3922 Hamalian, Leo. *Everything You Need to Know about Grammar* (10–12). 1985, Fawcett paper $3.50 (0-449-20837-0). A simple guide to the structure of English grammar. [425]

3923 Hayakawa, S. I. *Language in Thought and Action* (10–12). 4th ed. Illus. 1978, Harcourt paper $15.00 (0-15-550120-8). The author analyzes the nature of language and its relation to thinking and writing. [412]

3924 Hendrickson, Robert. *American Talk: The Words and Ways of American Dialects* (10–12). 1986, Viking $18.95 (0-670-31330-3); Penguin paper $7.95 (0-14-009421-0). From Black English to Brooklynese, this is a history of dialects in America and their present status. (Rev: BL 9/15/86) [427]

3925 Henry, Thomas. *Better English Made Easy* (10–12). 1985, Warner paper $2.95 (0-446-31190-1). This manual covers such subjects as grammar, spelling, and speech. [420]

3926 Hill-Miller, Katherine. *The Most Common Errors in English Usage and How to Avoid Them* (10–12). 1983, Arco paper $5.95 (0-668-05656-8). A usable book that explains grammar and correct usage. [428]

3927 Howard, Philip. *New Words for Old* (10–12). 1977, Oxford Univ. Pr. $14.95 (0-19-519988-X). In a series of essays the author bemoans the misuse of English words and gives many examples. [422]

3928 Jacobson, John D. *Toposaurus: A Humorous Treasury of Toponyms* (9–12). 1990, Wiley paper $10.95 (0-471-52772-6). A study of words that are related to specific places. (Rev: BL 10/15/90) [422]

3929 Johnson, Edward D. *The Washington Square Press Handbook of Good English* (10–12). 1983, Washington Square Pr. paper $4.95 (0-671-44294-5). A guide to English grammar that shows how to apply it to effective expression. [420]

3930 Katzner, Kenneth. *The Languages of the World* (10–12). 1987, Routledge paper $13.50 (0-7102-0861-8). A survey of 500 languages spoken today. [400]

3931 Kelly, Martin. *Parents Book of Baby Names* (9–12). 1985, Ballantine paper $2.95 (0-345-31428-X). This handbook consists of lists of boys' and girls' names and their derivations. (Rev: BL 10/1/85) [929.44]

3932 Lederer, Richard. *Crazy English: The Ultimate Joyride through Our Language* (10–12). Illus. 1989, Pocket $16.95 (0-671-68906-1). An enjoyable excursion into the idiosyncrasies of the English language, by the author of 2 other recommended books on the subject, *Anguished English* (1987) and *Get Thee to a Punnery* (1988). (Rev: BL 9/15/89) [427]

3933 Lerner, Sid, et al. *New Words Dictionary* (9–12). 1985, Ballantine paper $2.95 (0-345-32461-7). This little dictionary defines current words like compact disc and scuzz, many too new to be found in a regular dictionary. (Rev: BL 10/15/85) [423]

3934 Lewis, Norman. *Thirty Days to Better English* (10–12). 1985, NAL paper $4.95 (0-451-15702-8). One of several fine English handbooks by this author. This one concentrates on grammar and usage. [425]

3935 Lewis, Norman, and Wilfred Funk. *Thirty Days to a More Powerful Vocabulary* (10–12). 1989, Pocket paper $3.95 (0-671-68863-4). This is a proven program for vocabulary building. [413]

3936 Lutz, William. *Doublespeak* (9–12). 1989, Harper $17.95 (0-06-016134-5). A book about the current trend in English where, for example, potholes become pavement deficiencies. (Rev: BR 5–6/90) [420]

3937 McCrum, Robert, et al. *The Story of English* (9–12). Illus. 1986, Viking $24.95 (0-670-80467-3); Penguin paper $14.95 (0-14-009435-0). From the successful television series, this is a history of the development and rise of the English language and of its many variations around the globe. (Rev: BL 7/86; BR 9–10/87; SLJ 3/87) [420.9]

3938 Mencken, H. L. *The American Language: An Inquiry into the Development of English in the United States* (10–12). 1963, Knopf paper $22.95 (0-394-73315-0). This is the classic account of the development of American English. [427]

3939 Moore, Thurston. *The Original Word Game Dictionary* (9–12). 1983, Scarborough paper $8.95 (0-8128-6191-4). This dictionary is a help when playing over 40 word games like Scrabble. [403]

3940 *Multilingual Phrase Book* (10–12). n.d., French & European paper $3.95 (0-685-36685-5). A manual of key phrases in 8 Western European languages. [413]

3941 Newman, Edwin. *A Civil Tongue* (10–12). 1987, Warner paper $3.95 (0-446-30758-0). Various common mistakes in English language usage are pointed out with many illustrative examples. Also use by the same author and on the same subject: *Strictly Speaking* (1974). [428]

3942 Nurnberg, Maxwell W. *I Always Look Up the Word "Egregious"* (10–12). 1981, Prentice paper $7.95 (0-13-448712-5). A book about words that are often misused or confused with others. [413]

3943 Nurnberg, Maxwell W., and Morris Rosenblum. *All about Words* (10–12). 1968, NAL paper $4.95 (0-451-62598-6). A systematic approach to rapid vocabulary building. [413]

3944 Rheingold, Howard. *They Have a Word for It: A Lighthearted Lexicon of Untranslatable Words and Phrases* (10–12). 1988, Tarcher paper $7.95 (0-87477-464-0). A word book that gives interesting explanations of foreign idioms that have entered our language. (Rev: BL 3/1/88) [413]

3945 Robinson, Adam, et al. *The Princeton Review—Word Smart: Building an Educated Vocabulary* (10–12). 1988, Random paper $7.95 (0-394-75686-X). A total of 823 words that educated adults should know are introduced with frequent quizzes on their meanings. (Rev: VOYA 6/89) [413]

3946 Rosenthal, Peggy, and George Dardess. *Every Cliché in the Book* (7–12). Illus. 1987, Morrow paper $8.95 (0-688-06114-1). A guide to the most used clichés in the English language, many of which are illustrated with humorous cartoons. (Rev: BL 4/1/87) [428]

3947 Rosten, Leo. *The Joys of Yiddish* (9–12). 1970, Washington Square Pr. paper $4.95 (0-671-47349-2). An amusing dictionary of Yiddish words often encountered in English. The author continues with *Hoorah for Yiddish* (1984). [437]

3948 Safire, William. *Fumblerules: A Lighthearted Guide to Grammar and Good Usage* (10–12). 1990, Doubleday $15.00 (0-385-41301-7). In a series of short pieces, the author points out some vagaries in English grammar and usage. (Rev: BL 9/15/90) [428]

3949 Sifakis, Carl. *The Dictionary of Historic Nicknames* (10–12). 1984, Facts on File $29.95 (0-87196-561-5); paper $14.95 (0-8160-1370-5). A worldwide listing of nicknames with emphasis on current figures. [929.4]

3950 Stewart, George R. *American Given Names: Their Origin and History in the Context of the English Language* (10–12). 1979, Oxford Univ. Pr. $29.95 (0-19-502465-6); paper $7.95 (0-19-504040-6). A historical account of the origins and use of over 800 given names. [929.4]

3951 Strumpf, Michael, and Auriel Douglas. *Painless, Perfect Grammar: Tips from the Grammar Hotline* (9–12). 1985, Monarch paper $7.95 (0-671-52782-7). A practical guide not only to English grammar and its rules but also to usage and etymology. (Rev: BL 4/15/85) [425]

3952 Teleja, Tad. *Foreignisms* (9–12). 1989, Macmillan $17.95 (0-02-620420-7). A handy dictionary of foreign words and phrases and their meanings. (Rev: BL 3/15/89) [423]

3953 Webber, Elizabeth, and Mike Feinsilber. *Grand Allusions* (9–12). 1990, Farragut $21.95 (0-918535-09-3); paper $12.95 (0-918535-03-4). The origins of 500 current terms and expressions such as lounge lizard and the "Checkers" speech. (Rev: BL 7/90) [422]

3954 *Webster's Word Histories* (9–12). 1989, Merriam-Webster $14.95 (0-87779-048-5). The stories behind the origins of 1,500 words, including such recent additions to our language as yuppie. (Rev: BL 12/1/89) [422]

Writing and the Media

General and Miscellaneous

3955 Baker, Sheridan. *The Complete Stylist and Handbook* (10–12). 3rd ed. Illus. 1984, Harper $31.95 (0-06-040442-6). A book that discusses the elements of writing, grammar, and usage. [808]

3956 Bernards, Neal, ed. *The Mass Media: Opposing Viewpoints* (9–12). Illus. 1987, Greenhaven LB $15.95 (0-89908-425-7); paper $8.95 (0-89908-400-1). Through experts from various sources, viewpoints on the cultural impact of the mass media in America are explored. (Rev: BL 12/1/87) [302.2]

3957 Brown, Rita Mae. *Starting from Scratch* (10–12). 1988, Bantam $19.95 (0-553-05246-2). A prize-winning author shares her thoughts about the craft of writing and how she approaches it. (Rev: VOYA 12/88) [411]

3958 Burnett, Hallie, and Whit Burnett. *Fiction Writer's Handbook* (10–12). 1975, Harper paper $7.95 (0-06-463492-2). A guidebook that gives tips on writing and also discusses such elements as plot, character creation, and style. Also use: *On Writing the Short Story* (1983). [808.3]

3959 Elbow, Peter. *Writing with Power: Techniques for Mastering the Writing Process* (10–12). 1981, Oxford Univ. Pr. $25.00 (0-19-502912-7). A thorough teach-yourself book on the techniques of writing. [411]

3960 Franklin, Jon. *Writing for Story: Craft Secrets of Dramatic Nonfiction by a Two-Time Pulitzer Prize Winner* (10–12). 1986, Macmillan $19.95 (0-689-11785-X). A practical guide to success in writing feature articles. (Rev: BL 5/1/86) [808]

3961 Fuhrman, Candice Jacobson. *Publicity Stunt! Great Staged Events That Made the News* (10–12). Illus. 1989, Chronicle paper $12.95 (0-87701-509-0). A history of publicity stunts and the men who perpetrated them. (Rev: BL 5/1/90) [659]

3962 Giblin, James Cross. *Writing Books for Young People* (8–12). 1990, The Writer $12.00 (0-87116-158-3). A useful guide to those who would like to try their hand at creating literature for children. (Rev: BL 4/1/90) [808.06]

3963 Gleasner, Diana. *Breakthrough: Women in Writing* (10–12). 1980, Walker $9.95 (0-8027-6384-7). After an overview of women in the field of writing, Gleasner concentrates on 5 contemporary writers including Judy Blume, Erma Bombeck, and Phyllis Whitney. [411]

3964 Goldberg, Natalie. *Writing Down the Bones: Freeing the Writer Within* (10–12). 1986, Random paper $9.95 (0-87773-375-9). This writer explains something about the writing process and how to go about it. (Rev: SLJ 2/87) [411]

3965 Henderson, Kathy. *Market Guide for Young Writers* (7–12). Rev. ed. Illus. 1988, McDonald Shoe Tree paper $12.95 (0-936915-10-2). A guide for writers under age 18 on how to prepare manuscripts, where to sell them, and the kinds of material that are marketable. (Rev: BL 11/15/86) [070]

3966 Jute, Andre. *Writing a Thriller* (10–12). 1987, St. Martin's paper $10.95 (0-312-01114-8). A commonsense guide to fiction writing with emphasis on the thriller. (Rev: BL 11/15/87) [803.3]

3967 Logan, Robert K. *The Alphabet Effect* (10–12). Illus. 1986, Morrow $16.95 (0-688-06389-6);

St. Martin's paper $9.95 (0-312-00993-3). The author's thesis is that Western civilization's thought patterns emerged because of its phonetic alphabet. (Rev: BL 8/86) [411]

3968 Ogg, Oscar. *The 26 Letters* (10–12). Rev. ed. Illus. 1971, Harper $13.45 (0-690-84115-9). This book traces the history of writing from the caveman on. [411]

3969 Rusher, William A. *The Coming Battle for the Media: Curbing the Power of the Media Elite* (10–12). 1988, Morrow $16.95 (0-688-06433-7). A conservative takes on the "liberal" media establishment. (Rev: BL 4/15/88) [302.2]

3970 Sloan, William. *The Craft of Writing* (10–12). 1979, Norton paper $5.95 (0-393-30050-1). This is a series of essays on the art and craft of writing and how to master various techniques. [411]

3971 Stephens, Mitchell. *A History of News: From the Drum to the Satellite* (10–12). 1988, Viking $24.95 (0-670-81378-8). A history of news and how it is communicated from primitive societies to our present world satellite network. (Rev: BL 8/88) [070]

3972 Sternberg, Janet, ed. *The Writer on Her Work* (10–12). 1991, Norton $19.95 (0-393-02804-6); paper $10.95 (0-393-00071-0). Sixteen contemporary women writers discuss their lives and their work. [411]

3973 Swann, Alan. *How to Understand and Use Design and Layout* (10–12). Illus. 1987, North Light $22.95 (0-89134-212-5). A basic manual that explains graphic design and layout for the novice. (Rev: BL 2/1/88; SLJ 4/88) [659.13]

3974 Walson, Lillian Eichler. *The Bantam Book of Correct Letter Writing* (10–12). 1983, Bantam paper $4.95 (0-553-27086-9). A guide to writing all sorts of letters with several examples of each. [411]

Books and Publishing

3975 Burack, Sylvia K., ed. *The Writer's Handbook 1990* (10–12). 1990, Writer $27.95 (0-87116-160-5). This guide contains material on how to write well and how to sell what you have written. [808]

3976 Conrad, Barnaby. *The Complete Guide to Writing Fiction* (10–12). 1990, Writer's Digest $17.95 (0-89879-395-5). A practical guide to the major elements in novels and how to use them effectively in writing. (Rev: BL 6/1/90) [808.3]

3977 Greenfeld, Howard. *Books: From Writer to Reader* (8–12). Illus. 1989, Crown paper $19.95 (0-517-56841-1). The story of the production of a book during each stage of its development. (Rev: BL 5/15/89; SLJ 3/89; VOYA 2/90) [070.5]

3978 Holt, Robert Lawrence. *How to Publish, Promote, and Sell Your Own Book* (10–12). Illus. 1985, St. Martin's $16.95 (0-312-39618-X). A manual that covers topics related to editing, producing, and marketing books. [070.5]

3979 *The Writer's Market 1991* (10–12). 1990, Writer's Digest $24.95 (0-89879-422-6). A guide for free-lance writers on how to sell all types of writing. [808]

Newspapers, Magazines, and Journalism

3980 Black, Jim Nelson. *Managing the Student Yearbook: A Resource for Modern Yearbook Management & Design* (9–12). Illus. 1983, Taylor $19.95 (0-87833-333-9). A great organizational manual to help the production of the student yearbook. [371.8]

3981 Broder, David S. *Behind the Front Page: A Candid Look at How the News Is Made* (10–12). 1987, Simon & Schuster paper $9.95 (0-671-65721-6). A prize-winning journalist of the *Washington Post* tells how political news is reported and written. (Rev: BL 4/15/87; SLJ 9/87) [071]

3982 Brown, Alex. *In Print: Text and Type in the Age of Desktop Publishing* (10–12). Illus. 1989, Watson-Guptill $29.95 (0-8230-2544-6). A history of various kinds of printing is given plus information on the latest techniques. (Rev: SLJ 1/90) [686.2]

3983 Chancellor, John, and Walter R. Mears. *The News Business* (10–12). 1984, NAL paper $3.95 (0-451-62309-6). A glimpse at the world of news reporting plus tips on how to enter this profession. [071]

3984 Edwards, Julia. *Women of the World: The Great Foreign Correspondents* (10–12). Illus. 1988, Houghton $17.95 (0-395-44486-1). From the early days of reporters like Margaret Fuller and Nelly Bly to female correspondents in Vietnam, this is a history of women journalists. (Rev: SLJ 1/89) [070.92]

3985 Kinsella, James. *Covering the Plague: AIDS and the American Media* (10–12). Illus. 1990, Rutgers Univ. Pr. $22.95 (0-8135-1481-9). An account of how the mass media have handled, and more often mishandled, reporting on the AIDS epidemic. (Rev: BL 2/15/90) [362.1]

3986 Lee, Martin A., and Norman Solomon. *Unreliable Sources: A Guide to Detecting Bias in News Media* (10–12). Illus. 1990, Carol Publ. $19.95 (0-8184-0521-X). An account that shows that the news media are biased in favor of the Right. (Rev: BL 6/15/90) [070.1]

3987 Polking, Kirk, ed. *A Beginner's Guide to Getting Published* (10–12). 1987, Writer's Digest $11.95 (0-89879-260-6). This guide gives advice on such topics as manuscript preparation, making market contacts, and copyright laws. (Rev: BL 5/1/87) [070.52]

3988 Smith, Anthony. *Goodbye Gutenberg: The Newspaper Revolution of the 1980's* (10–12). 1980, Oxford Univ. Pr. $22.50 (0-19-502709-4). This book analyzes the changes that have recently occurred in newspapers. [070]

3989 Wainwright, Loudon. *The Great American Magazine* (10–12). Illus. 1986, Knopf $19.95 (0-394-45987-3). A history of *Life* magazine, its decline and fall, and its present resurrection. (Rev: BL 10/1/86) [051]

Propaganda

3990 Montgomery, Kathryn C. *Target: Prime Time: Advocacy Groups and Entertainment TV* (10–12). Illus. 1989, Oxford Univ. Pr. $22.95 (0-19-504964-0). An exploration of the many pressure groups that protest program content on television and of their efforts to change public image. (Rev: BL 3/15/89) [305.8]

Philosophy and Religion

Philosophy

3991 Adler, Mortimer J. *Aristotle for Everybody: Difficult Thought Made Easy* (10–12). 1983, Bantam paper $4.95 (0-553-26776-0). A logical, clear explanation of the philosophy of Aristotle. [185]

3992 Arendt, Hannah. *The Life of the Mind* (10–12). 1981, Harcourt paper $10.95 (0-15-651992-5). The author explores the nature of the mind and of thought. For better readers. [153]

3993 Aristotle. *The Basic Works of Aristotle* (10–12). 1941, Random $34.95 (0-394-41610-4). A generous selection of the writings of Aristotle that covers the major areas in his philosophical thought. [888]

3994 Aristotle. *Politics* (10–12). Trans. by Ernest Barker. 1976, Oxford Univ. Pr. paper $9.95 (0-19-500306-3). This classic on political science still has pertinence to today's problems. [320]

3995 Barnes, Jonathan. *Aristotle* (10–12). 1982, Oxford Univ. Pr. $13.95 (0-19-287582-5); paper $5.95 (0-19-287581-7). This book consists of 20 short essays on the mind and thought of Aristotle. [185]

3996 Berman, Phillip L., ed. *The Courage of Conviction* (10–12). Illus. 1985, Dodd $17.95 (0-396-08622-5). This book consists of statements of belief from 32 different people—some from organized religions, others from philosophy, sociology, science, politics, and show business. (Rev: BL 11/1/85) [158]

3997 Blackham, H. J. *Six Existentialist Thinkers* (10–12). 1983, Routledge paper $13.95 (0-7100-4611-1). For better readers, this is an explanation of existentialism and a discussion of the major figures in this philosophical movement. [142]

3998 Bronowski, Jacob. *The Western Intellectual Tradition, from Leonardo to Hegel* (10–12).

1960, Ayer $37.00 (0-8369-2448-7). This is a capsule history of Western philosophy from the Renaissance to the nineteenth century. [190]

3999 Confucius. *The Wisdom of Confucius* (10–12). 1938, Modern Lib. $8.95 (0-394-60426-1). A generous selection of the writings of the Chinese moral and ethical philosopher. [181]

4000 Creel, Herrlee Glessner. *Chinese Thought from Confucius to Mao Tse-tung* (10–12). 1953, Univ. of Chicago Pr. paper $10.95 (0-226-12030-9). An easily understood book on the history of Chinese thought and philosophy. [181]

4001 Descartes, Rene. *A Discourse on Method, and Selected Writings* (10–12). Trans. by John Veitch. 1956, Macmillan paper $3.56 (0-672-60180-X). This edition of the seventeenth-century classic also includes other important writing by Descartes. [194]

4002 Dewey, John. *Democracy and Education: An Introduction to the Philosophy of Education* (10–12). 1987, Free Pr. paper $14.95 (0-02-907370-7). An introduction to the role of education in a democratic society. [370.1]

4003 Durant, Will. *The Story of Philosophy: The Lives and Opinions of the Greater Philosophers* (10–12). 1969, Pocket paper $5.95 (0-671-49415-5). A clearly written survey of Western philosophy from Plato to John Dewey. [109]

4004 Fadiman, Clifton, ed. *Living Philosophies: The Reflections of Some Eminent Men and Women of Our Time* (10–12). 1990, Doubleday $22.50 (0-385-24880-6). Thirty-five people, including Arthur C. Clarke, Desmond Tutu, and Lewis Thomas, discuss their own philosophies of life. (Rev: BL 9/15/90) [128]

4005 Falcone, Vincent J. *Great Thinkers, Great Ideas: An Introduction to Western Thought* (10–12). 1988, North River $17.50 (0-88427-075-0). A workman-like introduction to philosophy, its terms, concepts, and great thinkers. (Rev: VOYA 2/89) [100]

4006 Fisch, Max H., ed. *Classic American Philosophers: Peirce, James, Royce, Santayana, Dewey, Whitehead* (10–12). 1951, Prentice paper $26.95 (0-13-135186-9). A selection of writings from the great American philosophers from the late nineteenth century to World War II. [191]

4007 Fulghum, Robert. *All I Really Need to Know I Learned in Kindergarten: Uncommon Thoughts on Common Things* (10–12). 1988, Random $15.95 (0-394-57102-9). A collection of essays extolling the simple things in life. (Rev: BL 10/15/88) [128]

4008 Hare, R. M. *Plato* (10–12). 1982, Oxford Univ. Pr. paper $5.95 (0-19-287585-X). A discussion of the chief ideas in the Platonic philosophy seen in relation to conditions in ancient Greece. [184]

4009 Hobbes, Thomas. *Leviathan* (10–12). 1986, Macmillan paper $5.95 (0-02-065520-7). This philosophical tract discusses the origins and uses of government. [320.1]

4010 Jaspers, Karl. *Kant* (10–12). 1966, Harcourt paper $7.95 (0-15-646685-6). An examination of the life, times, and ideas of Kant, taken from the author's *The Great Philosophers*. [109]

4011 Jaspers, Karl. *Plato & Augustine* (10–12). Trans. by Ralph Manheim. 1966, Harcourt paper $4.95 (0-15-672035-3). Taken from his book *The Great Philosophers,* this is an examination of the thoughts of Plato and Augustine. [109]

4012 Kaplan, Abraham. *The New World of Philosophy* (10–12). 1963, Random paper $3.96 (0-394-70235-2). A general introduction to the main currents and movements in modern philosophy. [100]

4013 Lavine, T. Z. *From Socrates to Sartre* (10–12). 1985, Bantam paper $5.95 (0-553-25161-9). An overview of the major movements in Western philosophy through the writings of 6 important philosophers. [100]

4014 Machiavelli, Niccolo. *The Prince* (10–12). Trans. by Robert M. Adams. 1977, Norton $19.95 (0-393-04448-3). A classic of the Renaissance about how to gain and hold political power. [320]

4015 Miller, Perry, ed. *The Transcendentalists* (10–12). 1950, Harvard Univ. Pr. paper $9.95 (0-674-90333-1). An anthology of the writings of the transcendentalists of New England that omits Thoreau and Emerson and concentrates on lesser-known figures. [141]

4016 More, Thomas. *Utopia* (10–12). Trans. by Robert M. Adams. 1976, Norton $12.95 (0-393-04397-5). This is the classic account of what constitutes an ideal state. [321]

4017 Nietzsche, Friedrich Wilhelm. *The Portable Nietzsche* (10–12). 1954, Penguin paper $8.95 (0-14-015062-5). In addition to passages from many works, entire books are reprinted including *Thus Spoke Zarathustra.* [193]

4018 Paine, Thomas. *The Rights of Man* (10–12). 1976, Citadel paper $3.95 (0-8065-0548-6). Using the French Revolution as a backdrop, this is a discussion of the basic rights of mankind. [320]

4019 Pirsig, Robert M. *Zen and the Art of Motorcycle Maintenance: An Inquiry into Values* (10–12). 1974, Morrow $22.95 (0-688-00230-7); Bantam paper $5.95 (0-553-27747-2). A number of philosophical musings are presented, all prompted by a motorcycle trip with Pirsig's young son. [191.092]

4020 Plato. *The Last Days of Socrates* (10–12). 1954, Penguin paper $3.95 (0-14-044037-2). This presentation of the last 4 dialogues of Plato tells of Socrates' trial and death. [100]

4021 Plato. *The Republic* (10–12). 1968, Basic Books paper $11.95 (0-465-06936-3). One of many editions of the series of dialogues during which Plato develops his ideas concerning the ideal state. [888]

4022 Randall, John Herman, Jr. *The Making of the Modern Mind: Fiftieth Anniversary Edition* (10–12). 1976, Columbia Univ. Pr. $55.00 (0-231-04142-X); paper $20.00 (0-231-04143-8). This is a concise history of the important ideas that have shaped the course of human civilization. [190]

4023 Russell, Bertrand. *A History of Western Philosophy* (10–12). 1945, Simon & Schuster paper $8.95 (0-04-100045-5). For advanced students, this is a survey of Western philosophy that tries to relate the thoughts of the great philosophers to social and political life. [109]

4024 Smith, John E. *The Spirit of American Philosophy* (10–12). Rev. ed. 1982, State Univ. of New York $49.50 (0-87395-650-8); paper $12.95 (0-87365-651-6). This book analyzes the contributions to philosophy of Peirce, James, Royce, Dewey, and Whitehead. [191]

4025 *Social Contract: Essays by Locke, Hume, and Rousseau* (10–12). 1980, Oxford Univ. Pr. paper $9.95 (0-19-500309-8). The book contains 3 basic writings of the social contract theory of government. [320.1]

Religion

World Religions

4026 Ahlstrom, Sydney E. *A Religious History of the American People* (10–12). 1972, Yale Univ. Pr. $55.00 (0-300-01475-9); paper $22.95 (0-300-01762-6). A history of religion in America and how it has affected culture, politics, and society. [200.9]

4027 Appel, Willa. *Cults in America: Programmed for Paradise* (10–12). 1983, Holt paper $7.95 (0-03-004997-0). This book gives a history of cults and an explanation of their types and methods used today. [289.9]

4028 Arrington, Leonard J., and Davis Bitton. *The Mormon Experience: A History of the Latter-Day Saints* (10–12). Illus. 1979, Knopf $17.50 (0-394-46566-0); paper $8.95 (0-394-74102-1). This is a history of the founding of the Mormon church and an explanation of its doctrines. [289.3]

4029 Bach, Julie S., and Thomas Modl, eds. *Religion in America: Opposing Viewpoints* (9–12). Illus. 1988, Greenhaven LB $15.95 (0-89908-437-0); paper $8.95 (0-89908-412-5). Such questions as school prayer, television evangelism, and the role of organized religion in society today are included in writings that explore a variety of viewpoints and opinions. (Rev: BL 3/1/89) [200]

4030 Backman, Milton V., Jr. *Christian Churches of America: Origins and Beliefs* (10–12). Rev. ed. 1983, Macmillan $15.95 (0-02-305090-X). This is a guide to the major Christian denominations in America, and their similarities and differences. [277.3]

4031 Bacon, Margaret Hope. *The Quiet Rebels* (7–12). 1985, New Society paper $10.95 (0-86571-057-0). An account of the history of the Quakers, their beliefs, their causes, and their affirmative action programs. (Rev: BR 3–4/86) [289.6]

4032 Ballou, Robert O., ed. *The Portable World Bible* (10–12). 1977, Penguin paper $8.95 (0-14-015005-6). This work covers the holy books of many religions including Hindu, Judeo-Christian, Islamic, and Buddhist. [200]

4033 Bancroft, Anne. *Zen: Direct Pointing to Reality* (10–12). 1987, Thames & Hudson $12.95 (0-500-81018-4). The basic concepts of Zen Buddhism are clearly presented. [294.3]

4034 Bassiouni, M. Cherif. *Introduction to Islam* (10–12). Illus. 1989, Rand McNally paper $11.95 (0-528-17900-4). A history of Islam and a discussion of the fundamental beliefs and practices of this religion. (Rev: BL 9/15/89) [297]

4035 Bedell, George C., et al. *Religion in America* (10–12). 2nd ed. 1982, Macmillan $21.84 (0-02-307810-3). A survey of various religious groups in America and how they have influenced our history. [200.9]

4036 Bentley, James. *A Calendar of Saints* (10–12). Illus. 1987, Facts on File $22.95 (0-8160-1682-8). Profiles of 365 Christian saints from various periods of history. (Rev: BR 11–12/87; SLJ 1/88) [200]

4037 Berman, Phillip L. *The Search for Meaning: Americans Talk about What They Believe and Why* (10–12). 1990, Ballantine $19.95 (0-345-33171-0). This book is the result of hundreds of interviews in which people were asked to state their religious beliefs. (Rev: BL 8/90) [200]

4038 Black, Naomi, ed. *Celebration: The Book of Jewish Festivals* (9–12). 1987, Dutton $24.95 (0-525-24512-X). Six major Jewish holidays including New Year, Sukkot, Purim, and Passover are introduced. (Rev: VOYA 10/87) [296.4]

4039 Boyer, Paul, et al. *Women in American Religion* (10–12). 1980, Univ. of Pennsylvania Pr. $36.95 (0-8122-7780-5); paper $16.95 (0-8122-1104-9). This is a historical survey of the many roles women have played in American religious life. [200.9]

4040 Carrithers, Michael. *The Buddha* (10–12). 1983, Oxford Univ. Pr. paper $5.95 (0-19-287589-2). As well as the life of the Buddha, this book tells about his teachings and the spread of Buddhism. [294.3]

4041 Chagall, Bella. *Burning Lights* (8–12). 1988, Schocken paper $6.95 (0-8052-0863-1). A recollection of growing up in a Russian Jewish town with drawings by Chagall and text by his wife. (Rev: BR 11–12/88) [947]

4042 Chidester, David. *Salvation and Suicide* (10–12). Illus. 1988, Indiana Univ. Pr. $18.95 (0-253-35056-5). An account of Jim Jones, his society, and the mass suicide at Jonestown. (Rev: BL 2/15/88) [289.9]

4043 Dimont, Max I. *Jews, God and History* (10–12). 1964, NAL paper $5.95 (0-451-16179-3). A history of the Jewish people and of their religion. [572.917]

4044 Donin, Hayim Halevy. *To Be a Jew: A Guide to Jewish Observance in Contemporary Life* (9–12). 1972, Basic Books $17.95 (0-465-08624-1). This book explains basic Jewish beliefs and tells about important religious observances. [296.4]

4045 Earhart, H. Byron. *Religions of Japan: Many Traditions within One Sacred Way* (10–12). Illus. 1984, Harper paper $6.95 (0-06-062112-5). A quick review of Japanese history and a detailed account of the country's religions. [291]

4046 *Eerdman's Handbook to the World's Religions* (10–12). Illus. 1982, Eerdmans $21.95 (0-8028-3563-5). History, practices, and beliefs are given for the world's major religions. [291]

4047 Elliot, Elizabeth. *Through Gates of Splendor* (10–12). Rev. ed. Illus. 1986, Tyndale paper $4.50 (0-8423-7151-6). The story of the lives and beliefs of five missionaries who were killed by Indians in Peru in 1956. (Rev: SLJ 4/87) [266]

4048 Frazer, James George. *The Golden Bough: A Study in Magic and Religion* (10–12). 1958, Macmillan paper $14.95 (0-02-095570-7). The origins of religion are traced back to myths, superstitions, and fable. [291]

4049 Gaer, Joseph. *What the Great Religions Believe* (7–12). 1963, NAL paper $3.95 (0-451-14320-5). The principal beliefs of 11 world religions are explained and excerpts are given from various holy books. [291]

4050 Galanter, Marc. *Cults: Faith, Healing and Coercion* (10–12). 1989, Oxford Univ. Pr. $22.95 (0-19-505631-0). An examination of various cults like the Unification Church of Mr. Moon and an exploration of why and how they exist. (Rev: SLJ 8/89) [291.9]

4051 Gaustad, Edwin Scott. *A Religious History of America* (10–12). Illus. 1966, Harper paper $10.95 (0-06-063093-0). A book that explains the beliefs and religious practices of Jews, Catholics, and Protestants and their contributions to our culture. [200.9]

4052 Goodrich, Norma Lorre. *Priestesses* (10–12). Illus. 1989, Watts $24.95 (0-531-15113-1). This is a comprehensive study of cults of revered women that have existed in various civilizations. (Rev: VOYA 6/90) [200]

4053 Hassan, Steve. *Combatting Cult Mind Control* (10–12). 1988, Harper $16.95 (0-89281-243-5). A cautionary book about the techniques used by cults with many first-person accounts by former cult members. (Rev: BR 9–10/89) [291.9]

4054 Hostetler, John A. *Amish Society* (10–12). 3rd ed. Illus. 1980, Johns Hopkins Univ. Pr. paper $9.95 (0-8018-2334-X). In addition to a history and description of this religion, this book discusses various topics, including farming practices. [289.7]

4055 *The I Ching: Or, Book of Changes* (10–12). 1968, NAL paper $6.50 (0-525-47212-6). This is one of the most important documents in Confucianism and Eastern philosophy. [299]

4056 *Jesus and His Times* (10–12). Illus. 1987, Reader's Digest $25.95 (0-89577-257-4). Jesus' life and the geography, history, and customs of his environment are revealed in text and lavish illustrations. (Rev: BL 2/1/88) [232.9]

4057 Johnson, Joan. *The Cult Movement* (9–12). Illus. 1984, Watts LB $12.90 (0-531-04767-9). This account explains the difference between organized religion and cults, gives material on how they recruit and hold members, and presents a rundown on the most important ones today. [289.9]

4058 Johnson, Paul. *A History of Christianity* (10–12). 1977, Macmillan paper $14.95 (0-689-

70591-3). A readable, well-researched volume of 2,000 years of Christian history. [270]

4059 Kertzer, Morris N. *What Is a Jew?* (10–12). 1978, Macmillan paper $5.95 (0-02-086350-0). Using a question-and-answer format, this is an explanation of Jewish customs and beliefs. [296]

4060 Laffin, John. *Holy War: Islam Fights* (10–12). 1990, Grafton paper $7.95 (0-586-06868-6). The history and present status of the Islamic concept of the jihad, or holy war, that can be waged against nonbelievers. (Rev: BL 4/1/90) [297]

4061 Levine, Saul V. *Radical Departures: Desperate Detours to Growing Up* (10–12). 1984, Harcourt paper $4.95 (0-15-675799-0). An examination of youths ages 16–26, why they are susceptible to cults, and what happens when they join cults. [306]

4062 Lewis, C. S. *The Screwtape Letters* (10–12). 1967, Amereon $14.95 (0-89190-989-3); NAL (0-451-62610-9). An experienced devil and his apprentice nephew exchange letters on religious matters in this satirical work. First published in 1943. [248]

4063 Lippman, Thomas W. *Understanding Islam: An Introduction to the Moslem World* (10–12). 1982, NAL paper $3.95 (0-451-62666-4). The life and works of Mohammed are introduced as well as a discussion of the beliefs and practices of Islam. [297]

4064 Martz, Larry, and Ginny Carroll. *Ministry of Greed: The Inside Story of the Televangelists and Their Holy Wars* (10–12). 1988, Weidenfeld & Nicolson $19.95 (1-55584-216-X). The PTL scandal involving the Bakkers is covered by 2 staff members from *Newsweek*. (Rev: BL 9/15/88) [269]

4065 Mead, Frank. *Handbook of Denominations in the United States* (10–12). 1951, Abingdon $10.95 (0-687-16571-7). This book gives a history and details of the beliefs of more than 250 different religious groups in America. [280]

4066 Melton, J. Gordon, and Robert L. Moore. *The Cult Experience: Responding to the New Religious Pluralism* (10–12). 1982, Pilgrim Pr. paper $8.95 (0-8298-0619-9). Such cults as Hare Krishna and the Unification Church are examined plus details on recruitment methods. [289.9]

4067 Morse, Flo. *The Shakers and the World's People* (10–12). 1987, Univ. Pr. of New England paper $17.95 (0-87451-426-6). A history of this unusual religious sect and its many contributions to American life. [289]

4068 Noss, John B. *Man's Religions* (10–12). Illus. 1984, Macmillan $24.50 (0-02-388478-3). An introduction to the history of the world's major religions including those no longer practiced. [291]

4069 Parrinder, Geoffrey, ed. *World Religions from Ancient History to the Present* (10–12). Rev. ed. Illus. 1985, Facts on File paper $15.95 (0-8160-1289-X). The first 12 chapters describe ancient religions and the final 9 chapters discuss the most important modern religions. (Rev: BR 9–10/86) [200]

4070 Patai, Raphael, ed. *Gates to the Old City: A Book of Jewish Legends* (10–12). Trans. by Raphael Patai. 1988, Aronson $40.00 (0-87668-958-6). A collection of religious truths, stories, and legends from 3,000 years of Jewish history. (Rev: BL 5/1/88) [296.1]

4071 Post, W. Elwood. *Saints, Signs and Symbols* (7–12). 2nd ed. Illus. 1974, Morehouse-Barlow paper $6.95 (0-8192-1171-0). A guide to the meanings behind signs and symbols of the Christian church and a listing of its saints and their contributions. [246]

4072 Powell, Andrew. *Living Buddhism* (10–12). Illus. 1989, Crown $24.95 (0-517-57266-4). A beautifully illustrated history of Buddhism over the last 2,500 years. (Rev: BL 8/89) [294.3]

4073 Rahman, Fazlur. *Islam* (10–12). 2nd ed. 1979, Univ. of Chicago Pr. paper $10.95 (0-226-70281-2). A history of Islam through the 1,400 years of its existence. [296]

4074 Randi, James. *The Faith Healer* (10–12). Illus. 1987, Prometheus $18.95 (0-87975-369-2); paper $14.95 (0-87975-535-0). After a three-year investigation of faith healing, the author turns in a negative report card but leaves the door open for a "maybe." (Rev: SLJ 3/88) [615.8]

4075 Rifkin, Paul, ed. *The God Letters* (10–12). 1986, Warner paper $5.95 (0-446-38319-8). Over 250 famous personalities from Phyllis Diller to Linus Pauling reveal their feelings about belief in God. (Rev: BL 4/15/86) [211]

4076 Rohr, Janelle, ed. *Science & Religion: Opposing Viewpoints* (9–12). Illus. 1988, Greenhaven LB $15.95 (0-89908-431-1); paper $8.95 (0-89908-406-0). The conflicts and areas of agreement between scientific truth and religious beliefs are explored from various viewpoints. (Rev: BL 5/1/88) [215]

4077 Ross, Nancy Wilson. *Buddhism: A Way of Life and Thought* (10–12). Illus. 1980, Knopf $15.95 (0-394-49286-2); paper $7.95 (0-394-47454-2). As well as telling about the teachings of Buddha, this account gives details on the several divisions in Buddhism such as Zen in Japan. [294.3]

4078 Ross, Nancy Wilson. *Three Ways of Asian Wisdom: Hinduism, Buddhism, Zen and Their Significance for the West* (10–12). Illus. 1966, Simon & Schuster paper $14.95 (0-671-24230-X). A history and detailed acccount of beliefs involving Hinduism, Buddhism, and Zen. [294]

4079 Rosten, Leo, ed. *Religions of America: Ferment and Faith in an Age of Crisis* (7–12). 1975, Simon & Schuster paper $16.95 (0-671-21971-5). An introduction to 19 religious groups plus statistics concerning their characteristics. [200.9]

4080 Sabini, John. *Islam: A Primer* (9–12). Illus. 1983, Middle East Editorial Assoc. paper $7.50 (0-918992-05-2). A concise introduction to the Islamic religion that explains such areas as culture, beliefs, and divisions. [297]

4081 Seeger, Elizabeth. *Eastern Religions* (7–12). Illus. 1973, Harper $14.70 (0-690-25342-7). A fine overview of such religions as Hinduism, Buddhism, Confucianism, and Taoism. [291]

4082 Silk, Mark. *Spiritual Politics: Religion and America since World War II* (10–12). 1988, Simon & Schuster $19.95 (0-671-43910-3). The author gives an impartial and lucid description of the status of various religions in America today. (Rev: BL 4/1/88) [261.7]

4083 Sims, Patsy. *Can Somebody Shout Amen!* (10–12). 1988, St. Martin's $15.95 (0-312-01397-3). An examination of current religious revivalists and televangelists. (Rev: BL 5/1/88) [269]

4084 Sjoo, Monica, and Barbara Mor. *The Great Cosmic Mother* (10–12). Illus. 1987, Harper paper $16.95 (0-06-250791-5). A history of the role and inspiration of women in world religions from Neolithic times on. (Rev: SLJ 5/88) [209]

4085 Smith, Huston. *The Religions of Man* (9–12). 1958, Harper paper $9.95 (0-06-090043-1). This is an introduction to 6 important world religions including Christianity, Hinduism, Islam, and Buddhism. [291]

4086 Steinberg, Milton. *Basic Judaism* (10–12). 1987, Aronson $20.00 (0-87668-975-6); Harcourt paper $4.95 (0-15-610698-1). A brief but lucid description of the religious beliefs and practices of the Jews. [296]

4087 Streiker, Lowell D. *Cults, the Continuing Threat* (10–12). 1983, Abingdon paper $3.95 (0-687-10069-0). This book reports on such cults as the Unification Church, the Children of God, and Hare Krishna. [291.9]

4088 Teresa, Mother. *Words to Love By* (7–12). 1983, Ave Maria Press paper $4.95 (0-87793-261-

1). A collection of the writing and meditations of the Nobel Prize-winning nun. [242]

4089 Wertkin, Gerard C. *The Four Seasons of Shaker Life: An Intimate Portrait of the Community at Sabbathday Lake* (10–12). Illus. 1986, Simon & Schuster paper $12.95 (0-671-61815-6). An examination of the history and way of life of the Shakers as shown through a study of the tiny community that still exists in Maine. (Rev: BL 8/86) [289]

4090 Wouk, Herman. *This Is My God* (10–12). 1959, Pocket paper $4.95 (0-671-49353-1). A declaration of faith by an orthodox Jew. [296]

The Bible and Bible Study

4091 Asimov, Isaac. *Asimov's Guide to the Bible* (7–12). 1981, Crown $12.95 (0-517-34582-X). This is a book-by-book guide to both the Old and New Testaments. [220.7]

4092 Asimov, Isaac. *Asimov's Guide to the Bible: The Old Testament* (10–12). 1976, Avon paper $10.95 (0-380-01032-1). A historical study of the Old Testament. Followed by: *Asimov's Guide to the Bible: The New Testament* (1982). [220]

4093 Barr, Robert R. *What Is the Bible?* (9–12). 1984, Harper paper $4.95 (0-86683-727-2). This is a popular introduction to the characters and stories in the Bible and their significance. [220]

4094 Berlitz, Charles. *The Lost Ship of Noah: In Search of the Ark at Ararat* (8–12). Illus. 1987, Putnam $17.95 (0-399-13182-5). Berlitz reviews the evidence concerning Noah's ark and also speculates about the end of the world. (Rev: BL 1/1/87) [222]

4095 Bishop, Jim. *The Day Christ Died* (9–12). 1957, Harper paper $4.95 (0-06-060786-6). An hour-by-hour account beginning with the Last Supper and ending with the crucifixion [232.9]

4096 Bouquet, A. C. *Everyday Life in New Testament Times* (10–12). Illus. 1954, Macmillan $30.00 (0-684-14833-1). This book gives a picture of how people lived in Palestine at the time of the Roman occupation. [225.9]

4097 Carpenter, Humphrey. *Jesus* (10–12). 1980, Oxford Univ. Pr. paper $3.95 (0-19-283016-3). This book examines closely the teachings of Jesus and their significance. [232.9]

4098 Coleman, William L. *Today's Handbook of Bible Times & Customs* (9–12). Illus. 1984, Bethany House $12.95 (0-87123-594-3). Under such headings as family life and food and drink, this is a guide to everyday life in Biblical times. [220.9]

4099 Ehrlich, Eugene, and David H. Scott. *Mene, Mene, Tekel* (9–12). Illus. 1990, Harper $18.95 (0-06-016456-5). Expressions from the King James version of the Bible such as "feet of clay" and "kiss of death" are explained in their context. (Rev: BL 8/90) [220.5]

4100 Every, George. *Christian Legends* (10–12). Illus. 1987, Bedrick $19.95 (0-87226-046-1). A collection of known and relatively obscure legends like the Creation associated with Christianity. (Rev: BL 4/15/87; BR 9–10/87; SLJ 8/87) [204]

4101 France, Peter. *An Encyclopedia of Bible Animals* (9–12). Illus. 1986, Salem House $26.95 (0-7099-3737-7). An alphabetically arranged treatment of all the animals mentioned in the Bible with references to specific passages and illustrations. (Rev: BL 11/1/86) [220]

4102 Gellman, Marc. *Does God Have a Big Toe? Stories about Stories in the Bible* (8–12). Illus. 1989, Harper LB $14.89 (0-06-022433-9). A retelling of 20 humorous stories from the Bible that explore their many meanings. (Rev: SLJ 12/89; VOYA 4/90) [220.9]

4103 Goldstein, David. *Jewish Legends* (10–12). Illus. 1987, Bedrick $19.95 (0-87226-045-3). Major figures from the Bible like Moses and Elijah plus folklore about the Torah are highlighted in this account. (Rev: BL 4/15/87; BR 9–10/87; SLJ 8/87) [296.1]

4104 Gottcent, John H. *The Bible: A Literary Study* (10–12). 1986, Twayne $17.95 (0-8057-7951-5); paper $17.95 (0-8057-8003-3). This account examines and evaluates the Bible as a piece of serious literature. (Rev: SLJ 5/87) [220]

4105 Heaton, E. W. *Everyday Life in Old Testament Times* (10–12). Illus. 1956, Macmillan $27.50 (0-684-14836-6). This book covers daily life in Israel from 1250 to 586 B.C. [221.9]

4106 Keller, Werner. *The Bible as History* (10–12). 1983, Bantam paper $5.95 (0-553-27943-2). This source weighs archaeological and historical evidence against accounts given in the Bible. [220.9]

4107 King James. *The Holy Bible: Containing the Old and New Testaments* (7–12). 1974, NAL paper $7.95 (0-452-00617-1). One of many recommended editions of the King James's version. [220.5]

4108 Metzger, Bruce, et al., eds. *Great Events of Bible Times* (9–12). Illus. 1987, Doubleday $29.95 (0-385-23678-6). Important events related to the Bible from the Great Flood and the Exodus to the conversion of St. Paul and the discovery of the Dead Sea Scrolls are covered. (Rev: SLJ 5/88) [220]

4109 Millard, Alan. *Treasures from Bible Times* (10–12). Illus. 1985, Lion $14.95 (0-85648-587-X). A general introduction to archaeological findings related to the Bible and to the antiquities that have been unearthed. (Rev: BL 5/15/85) [220]

4110 Potter, Charles Francis. *Is That in the Bible?* (9–12). 1985, Ballantine paper $3.95 (0-345-32109-X). An amazing collection of facts and trivia culled from the Bible. [220]

4111 Segal, Lore. *The Book of Adam to Moses* (7–12). Illus. 1989, Random paper $11.95 (0-8052-0961-1). A retelling of Bible stories from the Creation to the death of Moses. (Rev: BR 5–6/90) [220]

4112 Wiesel, Elie. *Messengers of God: Biblical Portraits and Legends* (10–12). 1985, Summit paper $8.95 (0-671-54134-X). For better readers, this book supplies portraits of biblical figures from Adam to Job. [220]

4113 Wilson, Edmund. *The Dead Sea Scrolls, 1947–1969* (10–12). 1969, Oxford Univ. Pr. $22.50 (0-19-500665-8). An account of the finding of these documents, their contents, and their significance. [229]

Holidays and Holy Days

4114 Cardozo, Arlene. *Jewish Family Celebrations: Shabbat, Festivals and Traditional Ceremonies* (9–12). Illus. 1982, St. Martin's $17.50 (0-312-44231-9); paper $7.95 (0-312-44232-7). This account explores the year from the standpoint of Jewish religious holidays and observances. [296.4]

4115 Charlton, Jim, and Maria Robbins. *A Christmas Companion: Recipes, Traditions and Customs from around the World* (9–12). Illus. 1989, Putnam paper $11.95 (0-399-51564-X). A handbook of how Christmas is celebrated around the world, with accompanying recipes. (Rev: BL 12/15/89) [641.5]

4116 MacArthur, John F., Jr. *God with Us: The Miracle of Christmas* (9–12). Illus. 1989, Zondervan $12.95 (0-310-28690-5). A splendidly illustrated account of the events surrounding the birth of Christ and their significance. (Rev: VOYA 4/90) [263]

4117 Muir, Frank. *Christmas Customs & Traditions* (10–12). Illus. 1977, Taplinger $7.95 (0-8008-1522-1). A history of Christmas customs in England. [394.2]

4118 Rockland, Mae Shafter. *The Hanukkah Book* (9–12). Illus. 1975, Schocken paper $9.95 (0-8052-0792-9). In addition to the observances and history associated with Hanukkah, this book gives recipes, ideas for gifts, and games. [296.4]

4119 Stewart, Martha. *Martha Stewart's Christmas* (9–12). Illus. 1989, Random $18.95 (0-517-57416-0). A how-to book on making Christmas decorations and gifts. (Rev: BR 3–4/90) [293]

4120 Time-Life Books, eds. *Christmas in America* (9–12). Illus. 1990, Silver Burdett $24.95 (0-13-133679-7). This sumptuously illustrated book about Christmas in America covers such topics as the nativity, carols, foods with recipes, stories about Christmas, and ways we celebrate the holiday. As part of their Enchanted World series, Time-Life Books also has *The Book of Christmas* (1986). (Rev: BL 12/15/87) [394.2]

4121 Trepp, Leo. *The Complete Book of Jewish Observance* (9–12). Illus. 1980, Summit (0-671-47197-5). Working from a weekly schedule to the important observances of a lifetime, Jewish rituals are explained. [296.4]

4122 Wernecke, Herbert H. *Christmas Customs Around the World* (9–12). Illus. 1959, Westminster paper $7.95 (0-664-24258-8). Using a geographical arrangement, the author describes unusual Christmas traditions around the world. [394.2]

Society and the Individual

Government and Political Science

General Works

4123 Crawford, Alan. *Thunder on the Right: The New Right and the Politics of Resentment* (10–12). 1980, Pantheon paper $3.95 (0-394-74863-X). This account examines the resurgence of right-wing political thinking in America during the 1960s and 1970s. [320.5]

The United Nations and International Organizations

4124 United Nations Dept. of Public Information. *Everyone's United Nations* (7–12). 9th ed. 1979, U.N. Publications $14.95 (92-1-100273-7); paper $9.95 (92-1-100274-5). Since its first edition in 1948, this is the standard introduction to the structure and activities of the United Nations. [341.23]

4125 *Your United Nations: The Official Guidebook* (9–12). 1985, United Nations Pubs. $9.95 (92-1-100192-7); paper $5.95 (92-1-100315-6). A guide to the United Nations buildings that also describes its structure and routines. [341.23]

International Relations, Peace, and War

4126 Allen, Thomas B., and Norman Polmar. *Merchants of Treason: America's Secrets for Sale from the Pueblo to the Present* (10–12). 1988, Delacorte $19.95 (0-385-29591-X). The story behind American traitors who stole secrets and sold them to the Russians. (Rev: BL 3/15/88) [327.1]

4127 Andrews, Elaine K. *Civil Defense in the Nuclear Age* (8–12). Illus. 1985, Watts $12.90 (0-531-04853-5). An account of the problems facing civil defense and the plight of civilians should a nuclear attack occur. (Rev: BL 5/15/85; BR 11–12/85; SLJ 8/85) [363.3]

4128 Bender, David L., and Bruno Leone, eds. *War and Human Nature: Opposing Viewpoints* (9–12). Illus. 1983, Greenhaven LB $15.95 (0-89908-341-2); paper $8.95 (0-89908-316-1). A collection of writing that offers different ideas concerning such topics as war crimes, nuclear war, and peace movements. [303.6]

4129 Bernards, Neal, and Lynn Hall, eds. *American Foreign Policy: Opposing Viewpoints* (9–12). Illus. 1987, Greenhaven $15.95 (0-89908-395-1); paper $7.95 (0-89908-370-6). The foreign policy of the United States is presented in several articles that express conflicting points of view. (Rev: BL 5/1/87; VOYA 8–9/87) [327.73]

4130 Betts, Richard. *Nuclear Blackmail and Nuclear Balance* (10–12). 1987, Brookings Institution $28.95 (0-8157-0936-6); paper $10.95 (0-8157-0935-8). A history of the international nuclear weapons situation from the late 1940s through the mid-1980s. (Rev: SLJ 1/88) [327]

4131 Bialer, Seweryn, and Michael Mandelbaum. *Global Rivals* (10–12). 1988, Knopf $18.95 (0-394-57194-0). A history of the relationship since World War II of Soviet Russia and the United States and of the various kinds of rivalries it fostered. (Rev: BR 3–4/89; SLJ 5/89) [327.73]

4132 Black, George. *The Good Neighbor* (10–12). Illus. 1988, Pantheon paper $9.95 (0-394-75965-6). A survey of the interaction between Central America and the United States through the years and how the United States has played a decisive role in the history and present condition of this Latin American area. (Rev: SLJ 4/89) [327.73]

4133 *Breakthrough: Emerging New Thinking* (10–12). Illus. 1988, Walker $19.95 (0-8027-1015-8); paper $9.95 (0-8027-1026-3). The horror of a nuclear war and ways to prevent it are discussed by American and Soviet scientists in this collection of essays. (Rev: BL 3/15/88) [327.1]

4134 Deacon, Richard. *Spyclopedia: The Comprehensive Handbook of Espionage* (10–12). Illus. 1989, Morrow $20.95 (0-688-08631-4). From 510 B.C. to the present, Deacon chronicles, spy by spy, the history of espionage. (Rev: BL 3/1/89) [327.1]

4135 Dimbleby, David, and David Reynolds. *An Ocean Apart* (10–12). Illus. 1988, Random $24.95 (0-394-56968-7). A study of the unusual relationship between the United States and Great Britain and how this has changed in the twentieth century. (Rev: BL 6/15/88) [327.73]

4136 Divine, Robert A. *Eisenhower and the Cold War* (10–12). 1981, Oxford Univ. Pr. $29.95 (0-19-502823-6); paper $7.95 (0-19-502824-4). A laudatory account of how Eisenhower handled relations with the Communist world. [327.73]

4137 Dotto, Lydia. *Planet Earth in Jeopardy: Environmental Consequences of Nuclear War* (10–12). 1986, Wiley $16.95 (0-471-99836-2). A powerful book that describes the fate of the earth after a nuclear war. (Rev: BL 4/15/86) [574.5]

4138 Dulles, Allen. *Great True Spy Stories* (9–12). 1987, Ballantine paper $5.50 (0-345-24526-6). This is a collection of thrillers about spy capers that really happened.

4139 Fairbank, John King. *The United States and China* (10–12). 4th ed. Illus. 1983, Harvard Univ. Pr. $25.00 (0-674-92437-1); paper $12.50 (0-674-92438-X). This study gives a history of China as well as details on American relations with China through 1982. [327.51]

4140 Foreign Policy Association, eds. *Cartoon History of United States Foreign Policy, 1776–1976* (9–12). Illus. 1975, Morrow $9.95 (0-317-43272-9). Through political cartoons, 200 years of American foreign policy are interpreted. [327.73]

4141 Freedman, Lawrence. *Atlas of Global Strategy* (9–12). Illus. 1985, Facts on File $24.95 (0-8160-1058-7). A collection of maps and charts about the arms race and international politics. (Rev: BL 1/15/86) [355]

4142 Goode, Stephen. *The Foreign Policy Debate: Human Rights and American Foreign Policy* (9–12). 1984, Watts LB $12.90 (0-531-04753-9). An examination of American foreign policy in relation to human rights in today's world. [323.4]

4143 Hall, Lynn, and Neal Bernards, eds. *American Foreign Policy: Opposing Viewpoints* (9–12). 1986, Greenhaven $7.95 (0-89908-370-6). Various viewpoints are expressed on topics that cover U.S. intervention in foreign affairs, foreign aid, and relations with the Soviet Union. (Rev: BR 5–6/87) [327.73]

4144 Harvard Nuclear Study Group. *Living with Nuclear Weapons* (10–12). 1983, Harvard Univ. Pr. paper $17.95 (0-674-53665-7). This sobering book examines the results of unchecked nuclear arms proliferation. [355.8]

4145 Hyland, William G. *The Cold War Is Over* (10–12). 1990, Times Books $18.95 (0-8129-1871-1). An account that shows how the West has won the cold war and its impact on the future. (Rev: BL 6/15/90) [327.73]

4146 Jones, Howard. *The Course of American Diplomacy: From the Revolution to the Present* (10–12). Illus. 1985, Watts $24.95 (0-531-09710-2). A chronologically arranged history of American diplomacy from the Revolution to Reagan. (Rev: BR 5–6/86; SLJ 2/86) [327.73]

4147 Kessler, Ronald. *The Spy in the Russian Club: How Glenn Souther Stole America's Nuclear Plans and Escaped to Moscow* (10–12). 1990, Macmillan $19.95 (0-684-19116-4). The story of the American traitor and how he spied for the Russians. (Rev: BL 4/1/90) [327]

4148 Kessler, Ronald. *Spy versus Spy: Stalking Soviet Spies in America* (10–12). Illus. 1988, Macmillan $19.95 (0-684-18945-3). A fascinating account based chiefly on interviews about counterintelligence activities in this country. (Rev: BL 6/15/88) [327.1]

4149 Kurland, Michael. *The Spy Master's Handbook* (9–12). Illus. 1988, Facts on File $18.95 (0-8160-1314-4). Basic information is given on being a spy including tools, training, and history. (Rev: BR 3–4/89; SLJ 1/89; VOYA 4/89) [327.1]

4150 Leone, Bruno, ed. *Internationalism: Opposing Viewpoints* (9–12). Rev. ed. Illus. 1986, Greenhaven LB $15.95 (0-89908-383-8); paper $8.95 (0-89908-358-7). The original sources in this volume explore conflicting viewpoints on parochial versus global interests and how they can or cannot be reconciled. (Rev: BL 8/86; SLJ 10/86) [341.2]

4151 Leone, Bruno, ed. *Nationalism: Opposing Viewpoints* (9–12). Rev. ed. Illus. 1986, Greenhaven LB $15.95 (0-89908-387-0); paper $8.95 (0-89908-362-5). A compendium of opinions on the beneficial and harmful aspects of nationalism. (Rev: BL 7/86; SLJ 10/86) [320]

4152 Lineberry, William P., ed. *Arms Control* (10–12). 1979, H. W. Wilson paper $10.00 (0-8242-0636-3). A collection of readings that explore various facets of the problems of arms control. [327.1]

4153 McGuinness, Elizabeth Ann. *People Waging Peace* (9–12). Illus. 1988, Alberti $19.95 (0-944758-10-X); paper $13.95 (0-944758-11-8). This book profiles 50 different peace workers, discusses their causes, and stresses the fact that ordinary people can change the course of history. (Rev: SLJ 11/88) [341.7]

4154 Moore, Melinda, et al. *Our Future at Stake: A Teenager's Guide to Stopping the Nuclear Arms Race* (9–12). 1984, New Society $19.95 (0-86571-055-4); paper $7.95 (0-86571-054-6). This is a guide for teenagers on how to control the growth of nuclear arms. [355.8]

4155 Morris, Charles R. *Iron Destinies, Lost Opportunities: The Arms Race between the U.S.A. and the U.S.S.R., 1945–1987* (10–12). 1988, Harper $22.95 (0-06-039082-4). The story of the confrontation between these superpowers from the end of World War II to the first missile-limitation treaties. (Rev: BL 5/15/88) [327.1]

4156 Newhouse, John. *War and Peace in the Nuclear Age* (10–12). Illus. 1989, Knopf $22.95 (0-394-56217-8). A history of the fragile peace that has been maintained since the first atomic bomb exploded and of the issues this has raised. (Rev: BL 11/15/88) [327.1]

4157 *Nuclear Winter* (9–12). Illus. 1987, GEM $11.75 (0-85596-062-3). A number of documents have been gathered here to explore different viewpoints of life after a nuclear war. Part of the Ideas in Conflict series. (Rev: BR 9–10/87) [355]

4158 Pratt, Julius W., et al. *A History of United States Foreign Policy* (10–12). 4th ed. 1980, Prentice $39.33 (0-13-392282-0). Key factors that have determined U.S. foreign policy are designated and a history of our relations with other countries is traced from the Revolution on. [327.73]

4159 Pringle, Laurence. *Nuclear War: From Hiroshima to Nuclear Winter* (7–12). Illus. 1985, Enslow $15.95 (0-89490-106-0). The author describes a wide range of atomic weapons and their

effect should a nuclear war occur. (Rev: BL 11/15/85; BR 3–4/86; SLJ 12/85; VOYA 6/86) [355]

4160 Ritchie, David. *Spacewar* (10–12). 1982, Macmillan $14.95 (0-689-11264-5). An account of what space warfare would involve and the kinds of weapons that would be employed. [358]

4161 Schell, Jonathan. *The Fate of the Earth* (10–12). 1982, Knopf $19.45 (0-394-52559-0); Avon paper $4.95 (0-380-61325-5). This sobering book describes what would happen should there be a nuclear war. [355]

4162 *The Superpowers: A New Detente* (9–12). 1989, Greenhaven LB $15.95 (0-89908-443-5); paper $7.95 (0-89908-418-4). Various points of view are represented in this account which explores such topics as arms control and armed intervention. (Rev: SLJ 3/90) [327]

4163 Szumski, Bonnie, ed. *Latin America and U.S. Foreign Policy: Opposing Viewpoints* (9–12). Illus. 1987, Greenhaven LB $15.95 (0-89908-399-4); paper $8.95 (0-89908-374-9). The blame and praise involving U.S. policies in Latin America are explored in articles by politicians, writers, and experts from both North and South America. (Rev: BL 1/1/88; SLJ 3/88) [327.7308]

4164 Szumski, Bonnie, ed. *Nuclear War: Opposing Viewpoints* (9–12). Illus. 1985, Greenhaven LB $15.95 (0-89908-378-1); paper $8.95 (0-89908-353-6). Such topics as how would a nuclear war begin and can humans survive it are discussed from a variety of viewpoints. (Rev: BL 1/1/86; SLJ 3/86) [355]

4165 Taylor, L. B., and C. L. Taylor. *Chemical and Biological Warfare* (8–12). Illus. 1985, Watts $12.90 (0-531-04925-6). Beginning with a history of chemical warfare from World War I to recent use in Afghanistan, this account raises moral questions. (Rev: BL 5/1/85; BR 9–10/85; SLJ 8/85) [358]

4166 Trager, Oliver, ed. *The Iran-Contra Arms Scandal* (9–12). 1988, Facts on File $24.95 (0-8160-1859-6). This book explores various facets of the Iran-Contra issue through a series of conflicting editorials. (Rev: BR 9–10/88) [327.73]

4167 Tuchman, Barbara W. *Stilwell and the American Experience in China, 1911–45* (10–12). Illus. 1971, Macmillan $21.95 (0-02-620290-5); Bantam paper $6.95 (0-553-25798-6). The story of Sino-American relations during the period when General Stilwell was influential. [327.73]

Various Forms of Government

4168 Arendt, Hannah. *Origins of Totalitarianism* (10–12). 1973, Peter Smith $18.75 (0-8446-5994-0); Harcourt paper $12.95 (0-15-670153-7). The author discusses anti-Semitism, totalitarianism, and imperialism. [321.9]

4169 Barber, Benjamin, and Patrick Watson. *The Struggle for Democracy* (9–12). Illus. 1989, Little $29.95 (0-316-08058-6). An examination of the nature of democracy and its problems from the ancient Greeks to the present. (Rev: BL 10/1/89) [321.8]

4170 Brezezinski, Zbigniew. *The Grand Failure: The Birth and Death of Communism in the Twentieth Century* (10–12). Illus. 1989, Macmillan $19.95 (0-684-19034-6). A history of the Communist movement, chiefly in Russia, that spans the period from Lenin through Brezhnev. (Rev: SLJ 5/90) [335.4]

4171 Brinton, Crane. *Anatomy of Revolution* (10–12). 1952, Peter Smith $16.00 (0-8446-1740-7); Vintage paper $6.95 (0-394-70044-9). This detailed account looks at 4 revolutions—the English one of the 1640s and the American, French, and Russian revolutions. [321.09]

4172 Ebenstein, William. *Today's Isms: Communism, Fascism, Capitalism, Socialism* (10–12). Illus. 1985, Prentice $34.00 (0-13-924481-6); paper $24.95 (0-13-924473-5). An account that describes the basic principles behind communism, fascism, capitalism, and socialism plus a discussion on the pros and cons of each. [335]

4173 Geller, Evelyn, ed. *Communism: End of the Monolith?* (10–12). 1978, H. W. Wilson paper $10.00 (0-8242-0624-X). Though somewhat now dated this collection of essays describes various forms of communism in existence. [335.4]

4174 McCuen, Gary E. *Militarizing Space* (8–12). Illus. 1989, GEM LB $12.95 (0-86596-070-4). In this collection of articles various aspects of the use of space for military purposes are explored. (Rev: SLJ 8/89) [358]

4175 Marx, Karl. *The Communist Manifesto of Karl Marx and Friedrich Engels* (10–12). 1976, Washington Square Pr. paper $2.95 (0-671-49952-1). A key document in the history of communism that calls on the workers of the world to overthrow the capitalist economic system that oppresses them. [335.4]

4176 Smith, David. *Marx's Kapital* for Beginners (10–12). Illus. 1983, Pantheon paper $7.95 (0-394-71265-X). A humorously illustrated introduction to the thoughts and writings of Karl Marx. [320.5]

4177 Sowell, Thomas. *Marxism: Philosophy and Economics* (10–12). 1985, Morrow $15.95 (0-688-02963-9); paper $8.95 (0-688-06426-4). A clear explanation of the ideas of Marx and Engels and how they have often been subverted in practice. (Rev: BL 3/15/85) [335.4]

United States Government and Institutions

General

4178 D'Aleo, Richard J. *FEDfind: Your Key to Finding Federal Government Information* (10–12). 1986, ICUC Pr. $17.95 (0-910205-03-5); paper $9.95 (0-910205-02-7). This book tells one how to find out about and use the important publications that come from the federal government. [353]

4179 Maddox, Robert L. *Separation of Church and State: Guarantor of Religious Freedoms* (10–12). 1987, Crossroad $17.95 (0-8245-0845-9). A historical look at the issues involved in the separation of church and state by a man who firmly believes that this separation is vital in a democracy. (Rev: BL 12/1/87) [322]

The Constitution

4180 Adler, Mortimer J. *We Hold These Truths: Understanding the Ideas and Ideals of the Constitution* (10–12). 1987, Macmillan $16.95 (0-02-500370-4); paper $6.75 (0-02-016020-8). A discussion of the ideas behind the U.S. Constitution and how they have been interpreted both in the past and at present. (Rev: BL 6/1/87) [342.73]

4181 Barbash, Fred. *The Founding: A Dramatic Account of the Writing of the Constitution* (10–12). 1987, Linden $18.95 (0-671-55256-2). A very readable account of the intrigues and outcomes of the Constitutional Convention. (Rev: BL 5/15/87) [342.73]

4182 Bartholomew, Paul C., and Joseph F. Menez. *Summaries of Leading Cases on the Constitution* (10–12). 1983, Rowman & Allanheld paper $14.95 (0-8226-8364-0). This volume summarizes the cases involving constitutional law that have come before the Supreme Court. [342]

4183 Beard, Charles A. *An Economic Interpretation of the Constitution of the United States* (10–12). 1986, Free Press $24.95 (0-02-902470-6); paper $10.95 (0-02-902030-1). An account first published in 1913 that traces the economic concerns of the writers of the Constitution and how these are reflected in the final document. [342]

4184 Bender, David L., ed. *American Government: Opposing Viewpoints* (9–12). 1987, Greenhaven $15.95 (0-89908-398-6); paper $8.95 (0-89908-373-0). An anthology of writing on the Constitution and whether or not it should be revised. (Rev: BL 2/15/88) [320.973]

4185 Bowen, Catherine Drinker. *Miracle at Philadelphia: The Story of the Constitutional Convention, May to September, 1787* (10–12). 1966, Little $18.95 (0-316-10388-8); paper $8.95 (0-316-10398-5). An authentic re-creation of the 4 months in 1787 in Philadelphia when the Constitution was written. [342]

4186 Cooke, Jacob E., ed. *The Federalist* (10–12). 1961, Wesleyan Univ. Pr. $35.00 (0-8195-3016-6); paper $12.95 (0-8195-6077-4). A series of articles about the Constitution written between 1787 and 1789 by Alexander Hamilton, James Madison, and John Jay. [342]

4187 Corwin, Edward S. *Edward S. Corwin's The Constitution and What It Means Today* (10–12). 1979, Princeton Univ. Pr. paper $16.95 (0-691-02758-7). A clause-by-clause examination of the Constitution showing how its meaning has changed through the years. [342]

4188 Cushman, Robert F. *Leading Constitutional Decisions* (10–12). 17th ed. 1987, Prentice paper $31.80 (0-13-527367-6). A survey of the landmark Supreme Court cases involving interpretation of the Constitution. [342]

4189 Friendly, Fred W., and Martha J. H. Elliott. *The Constitution: That Delicate Balance* (10–12). Illus. 1984, McGraw paper $14.50 (0-07-554612-4). Sixteen major Supreme Court cases on such topics as abortion and school prayer are discussed. [342]

4190 Garraty, John A., ed. *Quarrels That Have Shaped the Constitution* (10–12). Illus. 1987, Harper $22.95 (0-06-055062-7); paper $9.95 (0-06-096166-X). Twenty important Supreme Court decisions involving the Constitution (e.g., Roe v. Wade) are discussed. (Rev: BL 5/15/87) [342.73]

4191 Hand, Learned. *The Bill of Rights* (10–12). 1987, Macmillan paper $4.95 (0-689-70085-7). Three lectures delivered in 1958 explore the relationship between the Supreme Court and interpreting the Bill of Rights. [342]

4192 Jefferson Foundation. *Rediscovering the Constitution* (9–12). 1987, Congressional Quarterly paper $12.95 (0-87187-407-5). Each chapter focuses on a Constitutional issue and discusses various points of view concerning it. (Rev: BR 9–10/87) [342]

4193 Konvitz, Milton R., ed. *Bill of Rights Reader: Leading Constitutional Cases* (10–12). 5th ed. 1973, Cornell Univ. Pr. $47.50 (0-8014-0783-4). A survey of the most important cases to come before the Supreme Court prior to 1972 involving the Bill of Rights. [342]

4194 Landynski, Jacob W. *The Living U.S. Constitution* (9–12). 2nd rev. ed. 1982, NAL paper $4.95 (0-451-62174-3). A fine overview of the history of the Constitution, its text, major Supreme Court cases, and profiles of the signers. [342]

4195 Lieberman, Jethro K. *The Enduring Constitution: A Bicentennial Perspective* (10–12). Illus. 1987, West Publishing paper $29.00 (0-317-55978-8). In addition to a history of the U.S. Constitution, Lieberman redefined contemporary social concerns in terms of its principles. (Rev: BL 7/87) [342.73]

4196 Lomask, Milton. *The Spirit of 1787: The Making of Our Constitution* (7–12). 1980, Farrar $10.90 (0-374-37419-0); Fawcett paper $2.50 (0-317-57107-9). A clear readable introduction to the issues, events, and people behind the framing of the Constitution. [342]

4197 McGee, Dorothy H. *Framers of the Constitution* (7–12). Illus. 1987, Putnam $13.95 (0-396-09032-X). After a history of the framing of the Constitution, brief biographies on the signers as well as contributions of each state are given. (Rev: BR 9–10/87) [342]

4198 Meister, Charles. *The Founding Fathers* (9–12). 1987, McFarland $19.95 (0-89950-291-1). The author concentrates on 13 of the 35 signers of the Constitution and gives details on the contributions of each of them. (Rev: BL 1–2/88; SLJ 4/88) [973]

4199 Mitchell, Ralph. *CQ's Guide to the U.S. Constitution* (9–12). 1986, Congressional Quarterly paper $10.95 (0-87187-392-3). A detailed account of the writing of the U.S. Constitution. (Rev: BR 11–12/86) [342]

4200 Morris, Richard B. *Witnesses at the Creation: Hamilton, Madison, Jay and the Constitution* (10–12). Illus. 1989, NAL paper $4.50 (0-451-62686-9). The role of these 3 men in the formulation of the Constitution is detailed. (Rev: BL 1/1/86; BR 5–6/86; VOYA 4/86) [973.3]

4201 Peters, William. *A More Perfect Union: The Men and Events That Made the Constitution* (10–12). 1987, Crown $22.50 (0-517-56450-5). A history of the Constitution and the meaning behind each of the statements. (Rev: BL 1/1/87; SLJ 10/87) [342.73]

4202 Preiss, Byron, and David Osterlund. *The Constitution of the United States of America* (10–12). 1987, Bantam $9.95 (0-553-05202-0). A handy volume gives the text of the Constitution, how it was framed, and essays on its interpretation. (Rev: SLJ 1/88) [342]

4203 Sexton, John, and Nat Brandt. *How Free Are We? What the Constitution Says We Can and Cannot Do* (9–12). 1986, Evans $17.95 (0-87131-481-9); paper $9.95 (0-87131-474-6). A history of the Constitution and amendments plus a discussion of the rights and liberties they have established. (Rev: BL 6/1/86) [342.73]

4204 Swisher, Carl Brent. *Historic Decisions of the Supreme Court* (10–12). 2nd ed. 1979, Krieger paper $8.50 (0-88275-813-6). In chronological order, the decisions of the Supreme Court are introduced with appropriate background material. [342]

The Presidency

4205 Black, Charles L., Jr. *Impeachment: A Handbook* (10–12). 1974, Yale Univ. Pr. paper $6.95 (0-300-01819-3). A historic account of impeachment proceedings with an emphasis on explaining the process that can lead to the removal of a president. [351.9]

4206 Boller, Paul F. *Presidential Anecdotes* (10–12). 1981, Oxford Univ. Pr. $22.95 (0-19-502915-1); Penguin paper $9.95 (0-14-006349-8). Vignettes, many of them humorous, involving U.S. presidents. [353.03]

4207 Grimes, Ann. *Running Mates: The Image and Reality of the First Lady Role* (10–12). 1990, Morrow $21.95 (0-688-08532-6). Interviews with the wives of the 1988 presidential hopefuls reveal a variety of ideas concerning the role of the first lady. (Rev: BL 5/1/90) [973.928]

4208 Nelson, Michael, ed. *Guide to the Presidency* (9–12). Illus. 1989, Congressional Quarterly $145.00 (0-87187-500-4). A wonderfully complete book on the presidency that covers among other topics each president, each election, the executive branch, first ladies, presidential powers, and relations with other branches of the government. (Rev: BR 5–6/90; SLJ 3/90) [353.03]

4209 Nelson, Michael, ed. *The Presidency and the Political System* (10–12). 1984, Congressional Quarterly $14.95 (0-87187-276-5). This collection of essays explores the office of the presidency, its responsibilities, and its powers. [353.03]

4210 Nikolaieff, George A., ed. *The President and the Constitution* (10–12). 1974, Wilson $10.00 (0-8242-0523-5). In a series of essays, the powers of the president are outlined, particularly in relation to the Watergate affair. [351.9]

4211 Schlesinger, Arthur M., Jr. *The Imperial Presidency* (10–12). 1989, Houghton paper $12.95 (0-395-51561-0). The author examines presidential power and is critical of the seeming complete power the president has in foreign affairs. [353.03]

4212 Taylor, Paul. *See How They Run: Electing the President in an Age of Mediaocracy* (10–12). 1990, Knopf $22.95 (0-394-57059-6). A study of the part played by the media in the 1988 presidential election. (Rev: BL 9/15/90) [324.973]

4213 Tebbel, John, and Sarah Miles Watts. *The Press and the Presidency: From George Washington to Ronald Reagan* (10–12). 1985, Oxford Univ. Pr. $29.95 (0-19-503628-X). For better readers, an account of the relationship between the mass media and the presidency through history and an explanation of how it has changed and evolved. (Rev: BL 9/1/85) [353.03]

Federal Government, Its Agencies, and Public Administration

4214 Bisnow, Mark. *In the Shadow of the Dome: Chronicles of a Capitol Hill Aide* (10–12). 1990, Morrow $19.95 (0-688-08719-1). Memoirs about political life in Washington by a Congressional staff member of over 15 years. (Rev: BL 6/1/90) [328.73]

4215 Cline, Ray S. *Secrets, Spies, and Scholars: Blueprint of the Essential CIA* (10–12). 1978, Acropolis paper $4.95 (0-87491-268-7). A former deputy director of the CIA describes how this agency evolved and its present functions. [327.1]

4216 *Congressional Quarterly's Guide to Congress* (10–12). 3rd ed. Illus. 1982, Congressional Quarterly $110.00 (0-87187-239-0). This guide explains the origins of Congress, its powers, and its problems and tells about its membership as of 1980. [328.73]

4217 Cranford, John. *Budgeting for America* (10–12). 1989, Congressional Quarterly paper $15.95 (0-87187-441-5). A look at how the federal budget is produced and where the government spends our taxes. [353.007]

4218 Davidson, Roger H., and Walter J. Oleszek. *Congress and Its Members* (10–12). 1985, Congressional Quarterly paper $14.95 (0-87187-325-7). This book examines both the history and the functions of Congress as well as its members. (Rev: BR 11–12/85) [328.73]

4219 Freemantle, Brian. *CIA* (10–12). Illus. 1984, Scarborough $17.95 (0-8128-2947-6). A history of the CIA from its roots in World War II to the 1980s plus material on its powers and tactics. [353.007]

4220 Galloway, George B. *History of the House of Representatives* (10–12). Illus. 1976, Harper $12.45 (0-690-01101-6). This account covers the development of Congress from 1787 to Watergate. [328.73]

4221 Greider, William. *Secrets of the Temple: How the Federal Reserve Runs the Country* (10–12). 1988, Simon & Schuster paper $12.95 (0-671-67556-7). The inside story of the Federal Reserve System, its powers, and how these powers are wielded. (Rev: BL 12/15/87) [332.1]

4222 *How Congress Works* (10–12). Illus. 1983, Congressional Quarterly paper $15.95 (0-87187-254-4). A clear account of the structure and functions of Congress and the changes that were effected during the 1970s. [328.73]

4223 Koslow, Philip. *The Securities and Exchange Commission* (9–12). 1990, Chelsea House LB $14.95 (1-55546-119-0). A current rundown on the functions, history, and concerns of this agency that through its workings regulates the stock market. (Rev: SLJ 10/90) [353]

4224 McCarthy, Dennis V. N., and Philip W. Smith. *Protecting the President: The Inside Story of a Secret Service Agent* (9–12). 1987, Dell paper $3.95 (0-440-17163-6). This is the story of the Secret Service by a man who has helped protect presidents from Johnson through Reagan. (Rev: BL 11/1/85) [363.2]

4225 Malkin, Lawrence. *The National Debt* (10–12). 1988, NAL paper $4.95 (0-451-62668-0). For mature readers, this is an account of national and international finances and how our great debt has accumulated. (Rev: BL 4/15/87) [336.3]

4226 Marchetti, Victor, and John D. Marks. *The CIA and the Cult of Intelligence* (10–12). 1974, Knopf $16.95 (0-394-48239-5); Dell paper $4.95 (0-440-20336-8). Though now somewhat dated, this book gives good background information on the organization and operation of the Central Intelligence Agency. [353.007]

4227 Oleszek, Walter J. *Congressional Procedures and the Policy Process* (10–12). 1989, Congressional Quarterly $21.95 (0-87187-487-3); paper $15.95 (0-87187-477-6). A comprehensive volume that gives details on how Congress works and how it passes legislation for the nation. (Rev: SLJ 2/89) [328.73]

4228 *Powers of Congress* (10–12). 2nd ed. Illus. 1982, Congressional Quarterly paper $9.95 (0-87187-242-0). A thorough discussion of the powers of Congress that includes material on the budget, foreign affairs, commerce, and impeachment. [328.73]

4229 Redman, Eric. *The Dance of Legislation* (10–12). 1974, Simon & Schuster paper $9.95 (0-671-21746-1). A behind-the-scenes look at the U.S. Congress and the legislative process. [973]

State and Municipal Governments and Agencies

4230 Hall, George, and Thomas K. Wanstall. *Baron Wolman Presents FDNY: New York's Bravest!* (9–12). Illus. 1985, Chronicle $16.95 (0-87701-350-0). With accompanying photographs, the author describes the past and present of the New York City Fire Department, the busiest in the world. (Rev: BL 10/1/85) [363.3]

The Law and the Courts

4231 Baum, Lawrence. *The Supreme Court* (10–12). 3rd ed. 1988, Congressional Quarterly paper $17.95 (0-87187-495-4). A comprehensive report covering all aspects of the Court, its important decisions, and how an appeal reaches the Court. (Rev: BR 9–10/90; SLJ 12/89) [347]

4232 Belli, Melvin M., and Allen P. Wilkinson. *Everybody's Guide to the Law* (10–12). 1986, Harcourt $19.95 (0-15-142166-8). Written in everyday language, this is an accessible guide to the laws that affect the average citizen. (Rev: BL 11/15/86) [349.73]

4233 Brill, Steven, et al. *Trial by Jury* (10–12). 1990, Simon & Schuster $24.95 (0-671-67132-4); paper $15.95 (0-671-67133-2). Coverage is given on 16 important court cases related to social issues, such as mislabeling of products. (Rev: BL 4/15/90) [347.73]

4234 Carp, Robert A., and Ronald Stidham. *The Federal Courts* (10–12). 2nd ed. 1990, Congressional Quarterly paper $17.95 (0-87187-580-2). A clear introduction to the 3 levels of the federal judiciary system and how they evolved. (Rev: BR 5–6/86) [347.72]

4235 Coughlin, George Gordon. *Your Introduction to Law* (10–12). 4th ed. 1983, Barnes & Noble paper $6.95 (0-06-463563-5). A general introduction to the law and such legal matters as contracts, patents, libel, divorce, and wills. [340]

4236 Cox, Archibald. *Freedom of Expression* (10–12). 1981, Harvard Univ. Pr. $8.95 (0-674-31912-5); paper $3.95 (0-674-31913-3). A review of the Supreme Court actions through the 1970s concerning freedom of speech and personal privacy. [323.44]

4237 Dershowitz, Alan M. *Taking Liberties: A Compendium of Hard Cases, Legal Dilemmas, and Bum Raps* (10–12). 1988, Contemporary $19.95 (0-8092-4616-3). A collection of newspaper columns on the present status of American law as seen by a liberal Harvard law professor. (Rev: BL 5/15/88) [342.73]

4238 Faux, Marian. *Roe v. Wade* (10–12). 1988, Macmillan $22.50 (0-02-537151-7). A behind-the-scenes look at one of the most controversial decisions ever made by the Supreme Court. (Rev: BL 5/1/88) [345.73]

4239 Gorecki, Jan. *Capital Punishment: Criminal Law and Social Evolution* (10–12). 1983, Columbia Univ. Pr. $29.50 (0-231-05658-3); paper $12.50 (0-231-05659-1). The origins of the death penalty are explored and society's present-day conflicting attitudes toward it. [364.6]

4240 Guinther, John. *The Jury in America* (10–12). 1988, Facts on File $40.00 (0-8160-1772-7). A historical overview and an examination of current problems in the jury system. (Rev: BL 3/1/88; BR 9–10/88) [347.73]

4241 Gustafson, Anita. *Guilty or Innocent?* (9–12). Illus. 1985, Holt $12.95 (0-03-002927-9). An examination of the court system using as a focus 10 notorious criminal cases from that of Lizzie Borden on. (Rev: BL 11/15/85; BR 3–4/86; SLJ 9/86) [345]

4242 Headley, Lake, and William Hoffman. *The Court-Martial of Clayton Lonetree* (10–12). 1989, Henry Holt $19.95 (0-8050-0893-4). The shameful account of the trial and court martial of this American Indian accused of spying in Moscow who also became a scapegoat to protect others equally guilty. (Rev: BL 8/89) [343.73]

4243 Howell, John C. *Everyday Law for Everyone* (10–12). 1987, TAB paper $9.95 (0-8306-3011-2). This basic guide covers such topics as wills, divorce, adoption, and criminal law. (Rev: BL 4/15/88) [349.73]

4244 Hyde, Margaret O. *Juvenile Justice and Injustice* (9–12). Rev. ed. 1983, Watts LB $12.90 (0-531-04594-3). The author explores the juvenile court and correctional system particularly in relation to serious crime. [345]

4245 Joseph, Joel D. *Black Mondays: Worst Decisions of the Supreme Court* (10–12). Illus. 1987, National Pr. $17.95 (0-915765-44-6). An analysis of 24 of the worst decisions of the Supreme Court including the case involving internment of Japanese Americans during World War II. (Rev: BL 11/15/87) [347.73]

4246 Lewis, Anthony. *Gideon's Trumpet* (10–12). 1964, Random paper $8.95 (0-679-72312-9). The true story of one man's battle against injustice in the legal system in Florida. [347]

4247 Litwak, Mark. *Courtroom Crusades* (10–12). 1989, Morrow $19.95 (0-688-07486-3). Seven different types of lawyers are presented in this cross-section of the legal profession. (Rev: SLJ 5/90) [340]

4248 McArdle, Phil, and Karen McArdle. *Fatal Fascination: Where Fact Meets Fiction in Police Work* (9–12). Illus. 1988, Houghton paper $9.95 (0-395-46789-6). An inside look at the workings of a big city police department based on cases in Oakland, California. (Rev: BL 5/15/88) [363.2]

4249 O'Brien, David M. *Storm Center: The Supreme Court in American Politics* (10–12). Illus. 1986, Norton $18.95 (0-393-02330-3); paper $10.95 (0-393-95912-0). A behind-the-scenes look at how the Court operates—its caseload, the decision-making process, and the day-to-day problems. (Rev: BL 6/15/86) [347.73]

4250 Radosh, Ronald, and Joyce Milton. *The Rosenberg File: A Search for the Truth* (10–12). 1983, Random paper $8.95 (0-394-72594-8). A re-creation of the controversial espionage trial of Julius and Ethel Rosenberg. [345]

4251 Rembar, Charles. *The Law of the Land* (10–12). 1989, Simon & Schuster paper $9.95 (0-06-097219-X). A history of our legal system from its origins in medieval England to present-day America. [340]

4252 Ross, Martin J., and Jeffrey Steven Ross. *Handbook of Everyday Law* (10–12). 4th ed. 1981, Harper $15.45 (0-06-013659-6); Fawcett paper $4.95 (0-449-24516-0). A practical manual that discusses such topics as buying and selling property, contracts, insurance, and suing for damages. [340]

4253 Satter, Robert. *Doing Justice: A Trial Judge at Work* (10–12). 1990, Simon & Schuster $19.95 (0-671-69152-X). A judge who sat for 15 years on Connecticut benches tells his thoughts on the

American legal system. (Rev: BL 2/1/90) [347.97]

4254 Sloan, Irving J. *Youth and the Law* (10–12). 4th ed. 1981, Oceana $7.95 (0-379-11140-3). Topics covered include child abuse, contracts, support, child labor, and adoption. [346]

4255 Spence, Gerry. *With Justice for None: Destroying an American Myth* (10–12). 1989, Times Books $18.95 (0-8129-1696-4). For better readers, this is a hard-hitting indictment of America's present judicial system that, the author thinks, is badly in need of reform. (Rev: BL 3/1/89) [347.73]

4256 *The Supreme Court and Individual Rights* (10–12). 1988, Congressional Quarterly paper $19.95 (0-87187-465-2). This account studies the impact on American life of various decisions of the Supreme Court. [342]

4257 Van den Haag, Ernest, and John P. Conrad. *The Death Penalty: A Debate* (10–12). 1983, Plenum $19.95 (0-306-41416-3). Two authors, one for and the other against, explore arguments concerning the death penalty. [364.6]

4258 Wapner, Joseph A. *A View from the Bench* (9–12). 1987, Simon & Schuster $18.95 (0-671-63873-4); NAL paper $4.50 (0-451-82193-9). The famous judge of TV talks about his experiences on the bench and about the American judicial system. (Rev: BL 11/1/87) [347.73]

4259 Winslade, William J., and Judith Wilson Ross. *The Insanity Plea* (9–12). 1983, Macmillan $16.95 (0-684-17897-4). This controversial subject is explored by using 7 murder trials as examples including the John Hinckley case. [345]

4260 Wishman, Seymour. *Anatomy of a Jury: The System on Trial* (9–12). 1987, Penguin paper $7.95 (0-14-009851-8). Using a fictitious murder case as a framework, the author illustrates how the jury system works. (Rev: BL 6/15/86) [347.73]

4261 Woodward, Bob, and Scott Armstrong. *The Brethren: Inside the Supreme Court* (10–12). 1979, Avon paper $5.95 (0-380-52183-0). This is an account of the inner workings of the Supreme Court from 1969 through 1976. [347]

Politics

GENERAL

4262 Armstrong, Richard. *The Next Hurrah: The Changing Face of the American Political Process* (10–12). 1988, Morrow $18.95 (0-688-06783-2). A description of the current political practices in

America—warts and all. (Rev: BL 4/15/88) [324.7]

4263 Bender, David L., ed. *The Political Spectrum* (9–12). Illus. 1986, Greenhaven $15.95 (0-89908-392-7); paper $8.95 (0-89908-367-6). Through a series of articles, the terms liberal and conservative are explored and their differences highlighted. (Rev: BL 12/1/86; BR 5–6/87; SLJ 5/87) [320.5]

4264 Coffey, Wayne. *How We Choose a Congress* (10–12). 1980, St. Martin's $10.95 (0-312-39614-7). An explanation of the difficult task facing a man or woman elected to the House of Representatives or Senate. [328.73]

4265 Gottfried, Paul, and Thomas Fleming. *The Conservative Movement* (10–12). 1988, Twayne $18.95 (0-8057-9723-8); paper $7.95 (0-8057-9724-6). A history of American conservatism and the story of the resurgence of right-wing politics. (Rev: BL 2/1/88) [320.5]

4266 McCuen, Gary E. *Religion and Politics: Issues in Religious Liberty* (8–12). Illus. 1989, GEM LB $12.95 (0-86596-069-0). The question of separation of church and state is explored in a collection of writings that express various points of view. (Rev: BR 9–10/89; SLJ 8/89) [320]

4267 McCuen, Gary E. *The Religious Right* (8–12). Illus. 1989, GEM LB $12.95 (0-86596-068-2). The ways in which religious conservatism has affected American life are presented in a collection of essays expressing different points of view. (Rev: BR 9–10/89; SLJ 8/89) [320.1]

4268 Matthews, Christopher. *Hardball: How Politics Is Played—Told by One Who Knows the Game* (10–12). 1988, Summit $17.95 (0-671-63160-8). An informal account of the ploys used by various politicians to forward their careers. (Rev: BL 6/15/88) [320.973]

4269 Romney, Ronna, and Beppie Harrison. *Momentum: Women in American Politics Now* (10–12). 1988, Crown $18.95 (0-517-56890-X). An account of the increasingly important role women are playing in American politics with examples from the careers of such women as Geraldine Ferraro and Patricia Schroeder. (Rev: BL 3/15/88; SLJ 11/88; VOYA 12/88) [320]

4270 Salmore, Barbara G., and Stephen A. Salmore. *Candidates, Parties, and Campaigns: Electoral Politics in America* (10–12). 2nd ed. 1989, Congressional Quarterly paper $16.95 (0-87187-484-9). An account of how campaigns—successful and otherwise—have been and are conducted in American politics. (Rev: SLJ 11/89) [973]

4271 Seib, Philip. *Who's in Charge? How the Media Shape News and Politicians Win Votes* (10–12). 1988, Taylor $14.95 (0-87833-583-8). An account of how the media, particularly television, help shape public opinion in the political area. (Rev: BL 5/15/88) [324.4]

4272 Whitney, Sharon, and Thomas Raynor. *Women in Politics* (9–12). 1987, Watts $12.40 (0-531-10344-7). A history of the involvement of women in American politics. (Rev: BL 3/15/87; BR 5–6/87; SLJ 1/87; VOYA 4/87) [320]

4273 Wills, Gary. *Under God: Religion and American Politics* (10–12). 1990, Simon & Schuster $22.95 (0-671-65705-4). For better readers, this is a study of the relationship between religion and American politics. (Rev: BL 9/15/90) [322.1]

ELECTIONS

4274 Archer, Jules. *Winners and Losers: How Elections Work in America* (7–12). Illus. 1984, Harcourt $14.95 (0-15-297945-X). An introductory volume that explains the political process in America and how it works. [324.6]

4275 Boller, Paul F. *Presidential Campaigns* (10–12). 1984, Oxford Univ. Pr. $22.95 (0-19-503420-1); paper $8.95 (0-19-503722-7). A history of presidential campaigns with a chapter devoted to details on each campaign. [324.6]

4276 Kitman, Marvin. *The Making of the President, 1789: The Unauthorized Campaign Biography* (9–12). Illus. 1989, Harper $22.50 (0-06-015981-2). A satirical look at American elections that claims the election of George Washington was manipulated by the media. (Rev: BL 11/1/89) [324.973]

4277 Modl, Thomas, ed. *America's Elections* (8–12). Illus. 1988, Greenhaven $13.95 (0-89908-433-8); paper $6.95 (0-89908-408-7). Opposing viewpoints are presented on such topics as financing elections and the role of the media. (Rev: BL 6/15/88) [324.6973]

4278 *Presidential Elections Since 1789* (9–12). Rev. ed. Illus. 1987, Congressional Quarterly paper $14.95 (0-87187-431-8). After giving a description of the powers of the president and vice president, this account describes in detail each of the presidential elections, primary results from 1831 to 1984, and extensive material on the party conventions and Electoral College voting. (Rev: SLJ 5/88) [973]

4279 Watson, Richard. *The Presidential Contest* (9–12). 3rd ed. 1988, Congressional Quarterly paper $9.95 (0-87187-439-3). This book covers the presidency chiefly from the standpoint of the nomination process and the elections themselves. (Rev: BR 5–6/88) [324.9]

The Armed Forces

4280 Collins, Robert F. *America at Its Best: Opportunities in the National Guard* (10–12). Illus. 1989, Rosen LB $14.95 (0-8239-1024-5). Both a history of the National Guard and a guide for prospective members. (Rev: SLJ 6/90; VOYA 2/90) [355]

4281 Collins, Robert F. *Basic Training: What to Expect & How to Prepare* (9–12). 1989, Rosen $14.95 (0-8239-0833-X). This book provides information on basic training in all of the services and gives further career information for each of the services. (Rev: BL 3/1/89; BR 9–10/89) [355]

4282 da Cruz, Daniel. *Boot: The Inside Story of How a Few Good Men Became Today's Marines* (10–12). Illus. 1987, St. Martin's paper $3.95 (0-312-90060-0). The story of a Marine boot camp platoon from induction to graduation. (Rev: BL 2/15/87) [359.9]

4283 Fagan, George V. *The Air Force Academy: An Illustrated History* (10–12). Illus. 1988, Johnson Books $29.95 (1-55566-032-0). The history of the Air Force Academy in text and pictures from its origins in the 1940s to the present. (Rev: BL 8/88) [358.4]

4284 Halberstadt, Hans. *Green Berets: Unconventional Warriors* (10–12). Illus. 1988, Presidio paper $12.95 (0-89141-280-8). The history and present status of this unconventional arm of the U.S. military forces. (Rev: BL 10/15/88) [356]

4285 Marrs, Texe, and Karen Read. *Everywoman's Guide to Military Service* (10–12). Illus. 1984, Liberty paper $8.95 (0-89709-131-0). This is a fine guide for women thinking of a career in the military that covers both the problems as well as the possibilities. (Rev: BL 2/1/85) [355.348]

4286 Nalty, Bernard C. *Strength for the Fight: A History of Black Americans in the Military* (10–12). 1986, Free Pr. $22.50 (0-02-922410-1); paper $12.95 (0-02-922411-X). A history of black participation in the American armed forces from the colonial period to the present. (Rev: BL 5/15/86) [355]

4287 Polmar, Norman. *The U.S. Navy Today, Vol. 1* (10–12). Illus. 1985, Arms & Armour Pr. paper $9.95 (0-85368-718-8). An overview of the status of the U.S. Navy during the Reagan administration. (Rev: SLJ 4/86) [359]

4288 Sayer, Ian, and Douglas Botting. *America's Secret Army* (10–12). Illus. 1989, Watts $22.95 (0-531-15097-6). A history of this little-known branch of the U.S. Army known as the Counter Intelligence Corps. (Rev: VOYA 4/90) [355]

Taxes and Public Expenditure

4289 Friedman, Benjamin M. *Day of Reckoning: The Consequences of American Economic Policy in the 1980s* (10–12). 1988, Random $19.95 (0-394-56553-3). The effects of our growing national debt on the future of America. (Rev: BL 10/15/88) [336.3]

Citizenship and Civil Rights

Civil and Human Rights

4290 Bach, Julie S., ed. *Civil Liberties: Opposing Viewpoints* (8–12). Illus. 1988, Greenhaven LB $15.95 (0-89908-434-6); paper $8.95 (0-89908-409-5). Different points of view are presented on such topics as separation of church and state and the right to privacy. (Rev: BL 6/15/88) [323.4]

4291 Barker, Lucius J., and Twiley W. Barker Jr. *Civil Liberties and the Constitution: Cases and Commentaries* (10–12). 1970, Prentice $26.95 (0-13-134792-6). The problems involved in civil liberties are explored through important court cases, many with the Supreme Court. [342]

4292 Barth, Alan. *The Rights of Free Men: An Essential Guide to Civil Liberties* (10–12). 1984, Knopf $19.45 (0-394-52717-8). An eloquent plea for the upholding of civil rights by a great twentieth-century thinker. [323.4]

4293 Becker, Susan D. *The Origins of the Equal Rights Amendment: American Feminism between the Wars* (10–12). 1981, Greenwood LB $42.95 (0-313-22818-3). For better readers, a scholarly account of the equal rights amendment from the 1920s to the present. [305.4]

4294 Cohen, Marcia. *The Sisterhood: The True Story of the Women Who Changed the World* (10–12). 1988, Simon & Schuster $19.95 (0-671-49553-4). An account of the 1960s feminist movement and the work of Friedan, Steinem, Greer, and Millett. (Rev: BL 6/15/88) [305.4]

4295 Corbin, Carole Lynn. *The Right to Vote* (9–12). Illus. 1985, Watts LB $12.90 (0-531-04932-9). A history of how the right to vote was gradually extended to black Americans, women, and immigrants. [324.6]

4296 Dolan, Edward F., Jr. *Protect Your Legal Rights: A Handbook for Teenagers* (9–12). 1983, Messner $LB $11.29 (0-671-46121-4). In a question-and-answer format this book explores such topics as youth rights involving teachers, parents, employment, and the law. [346]

4297 Draper, Thomas, ed. *Human Rights* (10–12). 1982, H. W. Wilson paper $10.00 (0-8242-0665-7). A collection of articles about civil rights in foreign countries and its relation to the making of U.S. foreign policy. [323.4]

4298 Fischer, Louis, and David Schimmel. *The Rights of Students and Teachers: Resolving Conflicts in the School Community* (9–12). 1982, Harper paper $17.95 (0-06-042075-8). This book discusses the civil rights of students and teachers in relation to such topics as racial discrimination, free speech, and personal appearance. [344]

4299 Frankel, Marvin E. *Out of the Shadows of Night: The Struggle for International Human Rights* (8–12). 1989, Delacorte $16.95 (0-385-29752-1); paper $8.95 (0-385-29820-X). An international overview of the struggle for human rights around the world and the people and organizations that are helping. (Rev: BL 10/1/89; BR 11–12/89; SLJ 12/89) [323]

4300 Friedan, Betty. *The Feminine Mystique* (10–12). 1983, Dell paper $5.95 (0-440-32497-1). The classic book on how being wives and mothers has robbed American women of their identity. [305.4]

4301 Fromm, Erich. *Escape from Freedom* (10–12). 1982, Avon paper $4.95 (0-380-01167-0). This account analyzes the meaning of freedom and the individual's relationship to the state. [323.44]

4302 Gold, Maxine, ed. *Women Making History: Conversations with Fifteen New Yorkers* (10–12). Illus. 1985, N.Y.C. Commission on the Status of Women paper $4.95 (0-9610688-17). Interviews with 15 successful female New Yorkers from such fields as medicine, politics, business, and the arts. (Rev: SLJ 11/85) [305.4]

4303 Guggenheim, Martin, and Alan Sussman. *The Rights of Young People* (9–12). 1985, Southern Illinois Univ. Pr. paper $4.95 (0-8093-9959-8). In a question-and-answer format the authors discuss the legal rights of people under 18. (Rev: BL 2/1/85) [323.4]

4304 Gurko, Miriam. *The Ladies of Seneca Falls: The Birth of the Woman's Rights Movement* (10–12). Illus. 1974, Schocken paper $9.95 (0-8052-0545-4). A history of the women's civil rights movement from the 1830s to the 1920s. [323.4]

4305 Hentoff, Nat. *The First Freedom: The Tumultuous History of Free Speech in America* (9–12). 1988, Delacorte $16.95 (0-385-29643-6). A historical discussion of how the First Amendment has been interpreted in the past and the present status of freedom of speech in this country. (Rev: BR 11–12/88) [342]

4306 Hinding, Andrea, ed. *Feminism: Opposing Viewpoints* (9–12). Illus. 1986, Greenhaven, LB $15.95 (0-89908-388-9); paper $8.95 (0-89908-363-3). Women's rights are explored from various viewpoints as well as such topics as women in the workplace and women's role in marriage. (Rev: BL 6/15/86; SLJ 11/86) [305.4]

4307 Korstein, Daniel. *Thinking Under Fire* (10–12). 1987, Dodd $18.95 (0-396-08814-7). This is the story of 10 lawyers—from Andrew Hamilton to Thurgood Marshall—and their struggle to uphold the Constitution and civil liberties. (Rev: VOYA 10/87) [340.092]

4308 Larson, E. Richard, and Laughlin McDonald. *The Rights of Racial Minorities* (10–12). 1979, Avon paper $1.95 (0-380-75077-5). In a question-and-answer format, the legal rights of various racial minorities are explored. [323.4]

4309 McClellan, Grant S., ed. *The Right to Privacy* (10–12). 1976, H. W. Wilson $10.00 (0-8242-0595-2). The concept of privacy is discussed in a series of essays that explore its social, political, and philosophical aspects. [323.44]

4310 McCuen, Gary E. *Secret Democracy: Civil Liberties vs. the National Security State* (9–12). 1990, GEM LB $12.95 (0-86596-074-7). The questions raised in the conflict resulting from protecting individual rights in the face of national security problems are explored in a number of ex-

tracts that give various points of view. (Rev: SLJ 8/90) [323.4]

4311 Mitgang, Herbert. *Dangerous Dossiers* (10–12). 1988, Donald I. Fine $16.95 (1-55611-088-X). This book tells about the dossiers that federal agencies like the FBI keep on citizens and how they are used. (Rev: SLJ 6–7/88) [323.4]

4312 New Internationalist Cooperative, eds. *Women: A World Report* (10–12). Illus. 1986, Oxford Univ. Pr. $29.95 (0-19-520490-5). A report that deals with the international status of women as of the end of 1985. (Rev: BL 1/15/86) [305]

4313 Norwick, Kenneth P., ed. *Lobbying for Freedom in the 1980s: A Grass-Roots Guide to Protecting Your Rights* (10–12). 1983, Putnam paper $6.95 (0-399-50718-3). This is a guide on how to lobby for a cause with material on such issues as women's rights, abortion, and gay rights. [328]

4314 O'Neill, Terry, ed. *Censorship* (9–12). Illus. 1985, Greenhaven $15.95 (0-89908-377-3); paper $7.95 (0-89908-352-8). In a balanced collection of articles the First Amendment and censorship are explored from many viewpoints. (Rev: BL 1/1/86; SLJ 3/86) [302]

4315 Price, Janet R., et al. *The Rights of Students: The Basic ACLU Guide to a Student's Rights* (9–12). 1988, Southern Illinois Univ. Pr. paper $6.95 (0-8093-1423-1). In a question-and-answer format, the civil rights of teenage students are explored. (Rev: BL 5/15/88) [344.73]

4316 Rhoodie, Eschel M. *Discrimination against Women* (9–12). Illus. 1989, McFarland $39.95 (0-89950-448-5). An international survey of the status of women in the 1980s. (Rev: SLJ 3/90) [315.4]

4317 Rossi, Alice S., ed. *The Feminist Papers: From Adams to de Beauvoir* (10–12). 1973, Columbia Univ. Pr. $40.00 (0-231-03795-3); Northeastern Univ. paper $14.95 (1-55553-028-1). This is an anthology of writers who championed women's rights from Abigail Adams to Simone de Beauvoir. [305.4]

4318 Schultz, Bud, and Ruth Schultz. *It Did Happen Here: Recollections of Political Repression in America* (9–12). Illus. 1989, Univ. of California Pr. $22.50 (0-520-06508-5). Thirty people from various walks of life tell how their civil rights were violated by overzealous government agents. (Rev: BL 5/15/89) [323.4]

4319 Steinem, Gloria. *Outrageous Acts and Everyday Rebellions* (10–12). 1983, New American Library paper $7.95 (0-451-25579-1). A collection of writing about women's roles that spans 20 years of Gloria Steinem's writings. [305.4]

4320 Stoddard, Thomas B., et al. *The Rights of Gay People* (7–12). 1983, Bantam paper $3.95 (0-553-23136-7). Using a question-and-answer technique the authors discuss and describe the civil rights of gay people. [346]

4321 Walker, Samuel. *In Defense of American Liberties: A History of the ACLU* (10–12). Illus. 1990, Oxford Univ. Pr. $24.95 (0-19-504539-4). An excellent history of the American Civil Liberties Union, the causes they have defended in the past, and their present struggles. (Rev: BL 1/1/90) [323]

4322 Walvin, James. *Slavery and the Slave Trade: A Short Illustrated History* (9–12). Illus. 1983, Univ. Pr. of Mississippi $16.50 (0-87805-180-5); paper $9.95 (0-87805-181-3). A well-illustrated account that deals with slavery from ancient times through the nineteenth century. [326]

4323 Wandersee, Winifred D. *On the Move: American Women in the 1970s* (10–12). Illus. 1988, Twayne $18.95 (0-8057-9909-5); paper $9.95 (0-8057-9910-9). An account of a decade of the women's movement in America. (Rev: BL 3/15/88) [305.4]

4324 Williams, Juan. *Eyes on the Prize: America's Civil Rights Years, 1954–1965* (10–12). Illus. 1987, Viking $24.95 (0-670-81412-1); Penguin paper $10.95 (0-14-009653-1). A well-illustrated account of 11 very important years in the history of civil rights in this country. (Rev: BL 11/15/86; BR 9–10/87; SLJ 8/87; VOYA 8–9/87) [323.4]

Immigration

4325 Anzovin, Steven, ed. *The Problem of Immigration* (10–12). 1985, Wilson paper $10.00 (0-8242-0710-6). Various aspects of our immigration policies are presented and their impact on social and economic life. [325.73]

4326 Archdeacon, Thomas J. *Becoming American: An Ethnic History* (10–12). 1983, Free Pr. $17.95 (0-02-900830-1); paper $11.95 (0-02-900980-4). A history of immigration to this country and of our changing policies concerning opening our borders. [325.73]

4327 Bell, James B., and Richard I. Abrams. *In Search of Liberty: The Story of the Statue of Liberty and Ellis Island* (7–12). Illus. 1984, Doubleday paper $10.95 (0-385-19276-2). A richly

illustrated history of the statue and of the great period of immigration it symbolizes. [974.7]

4328 Benton, Barbara. *Ellis Island: A Pictorial History* (9–12). Illus. 1985, Facts on File $18.95 (0-8160-1124-9). This is a pictorial tribute to the entering stop for millions of would-be Americans. (Rev: BL 3/1/86; BR 11–12/86) [325]

4329 Coppa, Frank J., and Thomas J. Curran, eds. *The Immigrant Experience in America* (10–12). 1977, Twayne LB $12.50 (0-8057-8406-3). This account covers the immigration experiences of such groups as Hispanics, Germans, Jews, Africans, and Asians. [325.73]

4330 Daniels, Roger. *Coming to America: A History of Immigration and Ethnicity in American Life* (10–12). 1990, Harper $27.50 (0-06-016098-5). A history of immigration to America that concentrates on 3 periods—colonial times, 1820–1924, and modern times. (Rev: BL 10/1/90) [973]

4331 Day, Carol Olsen, and Edmund Day. *The New Immigrants* (8–12). 1985, Watts $12.90 (0-531-04929-9). A well-organized account of the new arrivals to this country and a review of our existing immigration laws. (Rev: BL 5/15/85; BR 1–2/86; SLJ 8/85) [325.73]

4332 Kennedy, John F. *A Nation of Immigrants* (10–12). Rev. ed. Illus. 1964, Harper paper $5.95 (0-06-091367-3). A history of immigration to America and of the problems each succeeding wave faced. [325.73]

4333 Knoll, Tricia. *Becoming Americans* (10–12). Illus. 1982, Coast to Coast Bks. $22.50 (0-9602664-3-7). Covering a period from 1848 through 1980, this book tells of the immigration to the United States of such groups as the Chinese, Japanese, Koreans, Filipinos, and Vietnamese. [325.73]

4334 Lacey, Dan. *The Essential Immigrant* (10–12). 1990, Hippocrene $16.95 (0-87054-610-3). A critical review of our immigration rules and regulations with suggestions on how they could and should be changed. (Rev: SLJ 7/90) [325]

4335 Morrison, Joan, and Charlotte Zabusky. *American Mosaic: The Immigrant Experience in the Words of Those Who Lived It* (9–12). 1985, Dutton $19.95 (0-525-05368-9). This is a collection of first-person accounts of immigrants to the United States. [325.73]

4336 Portes, Alejandro, and Rubén G. Rumbaut. *Immigrant America: A Portrait* (10–12). Illus. 1990, Univ. of California Pr. $35.00 (0-520-06894-7); paper $10.95 (0-520-07038-0). An overview of recent immigrants to the United States—where they came from, their backgrounds, skllls, and how they assimilate into American life. (Rev: BL 5/1/90) [304.8]

4337 Rips, Gladys Nadler. *Coming to America: Immigrants from Southern Europe* (9–12). Illus. 1981, Delacorte $9.95 (0-385-28140-4). This is a history of immigration to the United States of groups from Italy, Spain, Portugal, and Greece. [325.73]

4338 Robbins, Albert. *Coming to America: Immigrants from Northern Europe* (9–12). Illus. 1981, Delacorte $9.95 (0-385-28138-2). A historical record that uses many original sources about immigration to this country from Germany, France, the Netherlands, and Scandinavia. [325.73]

4339 Santoli, Al. *New Americans: An Oral History—Immigrants and Refugees in the U.S. Today* (10–12). 1988, Viking $19.95 (0-670-81583-7). Case studies of 18 new Americans are examined and their fascinating journeys to their new homeland are retold. (Rev: BL 9/15/88; BR 5–6/89) [325.73]

4340 Steltzer, Ulli. *The New Americans: Immigrant Life in Southern California* (7–12). Illus. 1988, NewSage $34.95 (0-939165-06-6); paper $24.95 (0-939165-07-4). Photographs of immigrants from 34 different countries and their comments about life in America are included in this fascinating chronicle. (Rev: BR 9–10/89) [305.8]

4341 Weiser, Marjorie P. K., ed. *Ethnic America* (10–12). 1978, H. W. Wilson paper $10.00 (0-8242-0623-1). A brief overview of immigrations to this country and problems facing minorities today. [305.8]

Ethnic Groups and Racial Prejudice

General and Miscellaneous

4342 Chalmers, David M. *Hooded Americanism: The History of the Ku Klux Klan* (10–12). 1987, Duke Univ. Pr. $39.95 (0-8223-0730-8); paper $16.95 (0-8223-0772-3). A history of the Klan and a statement of its beliefs. [322.4]

4343 Glazer, Nathan. *Beyond the Melting Pot: The Negroes, Puerto Ricans, Jews, Italians, and Irish of New York City* (10–12). 2nd ed. 1970, MIT Pr. paper $13.95 (0-262-57022-X). This is a classic study of various ethnic groups in New York City, their history, and social conditions through the 1960s. [305.8]

4344 Glazer, Nathan. *Ethnic Dilemmas, 1964–1982* (10–12). 1983, Harvard Univ. Pr. $20.00 (0-

674-26852-0); paper $8.95 (0-674-26853-9). A collection of essays that cover such topics as blacks, Jews, affirmative action, and bilingualism. [305.8]

4345 Leone, Bruno, ed. *Racism: Opposing Viewpoints* (9–12). Rev. ed. Illus. 1986, Greenhaven LB $15.95 (0-89908-382-X); paper $8.95 (0-89908-357-9). Various points of view on racism from writings on *Huckleberry Finn* to *Mein Kampf* are represented in this collection of extracts and articles. (Rev: BL 7/86; SLJ 11/86) [305.8]

4346 Meltzer, Milton. *The Truth about the Ku Klux Klan* (7–12). Illus. 1982, Watts LB $12.90 (0-531-04498-X). In addition to historical background, this book tells about current activities and dogma. [322.4]

4347 Pascoe, Elaine. *Racial Prejudice* (7–12). Illus. 1985, Watts $12.90 (0-531-10057-X). A history of racism in the United States, its causes and consequences, and how much exists today are all covered in this book. (Rev: BL 12/15/85; BR 5–6/86; SLJ 4/86; VOYA 4/86) [305.8]

4348 Seeger, Pete, and Bob Reiser. *Everybody Says Freedom: A History of the Civil Rights Movement in Songs and Pictures* (10–12). Illus. 1989, Norton paper $18.95 (0-393-30604-6). An account that focuses on the civil rights leaders and the songs that inspired them. (Rev: SLJ 5/90) [323.4]

4349 Sims, Patsy. *The Klan* (10–12). Illus. 1978, Scarborough House $12.50 (0-8128-2268-4); paper $10.95 (0-8128-6096-9). A well-documented history of the Klan plus material on its present membership and activities. [322.4]

Blacks

4350 Albert, Peter J., and Ronald Hoffman, eds. *We Shall Overcome: Martin Luther King, Jr., and the Black Freedom Struggle* (10–12). 1990, Pantheon $19.95 (0-394-58399-X). A collection of papers by black artists and scholars who attended a symposium on the work of Martin Luther King, Jr. (Rev: BL 8/90) [323]

4351 Anson, Robert Sam. *Best Intentions: The Education and Killing of Edmund Perry* (10–12). Illus. 1987, Random paper $6.95 (0-394-75707-6). An account of the death of a black boy who was a student at a prestigious prep school. (Rev: BL 4/15/87; BR 1–2/88; VOYA 10/87) [305.2]

4352 Baldwin, James. *The Fire Next Time* (10–12). 1963, Dell paper $4.95 (0-440-32542-0). The author expresses the anger and frustration felt by black Americans in today's America. [305.8]

4353 Baldwin, James. *No Name in the Street* (10–12). 1972, Dell paper $4.95 (0-440-36461-2). The author gives a personal view of current American social and political history as it relates to black Americans. [305.8]

4354 Baldwin, James. *Nobody Knows My Name: More Notes of a Native Son* (10–12). 1961, Dell paper $4.95 (0-440-36435-3). A series of first-person essays about the life-styles of blacks and writers in America today. [305.8]

4355 Bennett, Lerone, Jr. *Before the Mayflower: A History of Black America* (10–12). Illus. 1981, Johnson $19.95 (0-87485-029-0); Penguin paper $9.95 (0-14-007214-4). This history of black Americans begins with the ancient history of Africa and extends to contemporary social conditions. [305.8]

4356 Bennett, Lerone, Jr. *The Shaping of Black America* (10–12). Illus. 1975, Johnson $15.95 (0-87485-071-1). Black history in America from the arrival of the first Africans in 1619 to the 1970s. [305.8]

4357 Bontemps, Arna. *100 Years of Negro Freedom* (10–12). Illus. 1961, Dodd paper $2.95 (0-396-06111-7). For better readers, this is a history of black Americans from the end of slavery to the 1960s. [305.8]

4358 Cagin, Seth. *We Are Not Afraid* (10–12). Illus. 1988, Macmillan $24.95 (0-02-520260-X). The story of the murder of 3 civil rights workers in Mississippi in 1964 and its aftermath are chronicled in this account that also gives a fine history of the civil rights movement. (Rev: VOYA 4/89) [323.4]

4359 Coles, Robert. *Children of Crisis: A Study of Courage and Fear* (10–12). Illus. 1967, Little paper $19.95 (0-316-15154-8). This book about black children in America today is the first part of a monumental study of children and their problems growing up in contemporary America. Other volumes are: *Migrants, Sharecroppers, Mountaineers* (1971), *The South Goes North* (1974), *Eskimos, Chicanos, Indians* (1978), and *Privileged Ones* (1981). [305.8]

4360 Du Bois, W. E. B. *The Souls of Black Folk: Essays and Sketches* (10–12). Illus. 1979, Dodd $10.95 (0-396-07757-9); NAL paper $4.95 (0-451-52397-0). First published in 1903, this is a classic statement about the civil rights of black Americans. [305.8]

4361 Ebony, eds. *Ebony Pictorial History of Black Americans* (7–12). 3 vols. Illus. 1971, Johnson $27.95 (set) (0-87485-049-5). The 3 volumes

trace black history from slavery to today's fight for integration and equality. [305.8]

4362 Franklin, John Hope. *From Slavery to Freedom: A History of Negro Americans* (10–12). 5th ed. Illus. 1987, Knopf $35.00 (0-394-56362-X); paper $19.95 (0-394-37013-9). A history that begins with African origins and ends in the 1970s. [305.8]

4363 Griffin, John Howard. *Black Like Me* (9–12). 2nd ed. 1977, Houghton $16.95 (0-395-25102-8); NAL paper $4.95 (0-451-16317-6). A ground-breaking book about the white man who blackened his skin to experience firsthand how it feels to be a black American. [305.8]

4364 Hampton, Henry, et al. *Voices of Freedom* (9–12). 1990, Bantam $25.95 (0-553-05734-0). A compilation of interviews made for the TV series "Eyes on the Prize" that brings the civil rights struggle into sharp focus. (Rev: BL 12/15/89; SLJ 5/90) [323.1]

4365 Hoose, Phillip M. *Necessities: Racial Barriers in American Sports* (10–12). 1989, Random $15.95 (0-394-56944-X). Absorbing investigation of racism and discrimination in sports today. (Rev: BL 6/1/89) [305]

4366 Jones, Jacqueline. *Labor of Love, Labor of Sorrow: Black Women, Work, and the Family from Slavery to the Present* (10–12). Illus. 1985, Basic Books $26.95 (0-465-03756-9); Random paper $12.95 (0-394-74536-1). A history of the struggle of black women and their families from the days of slavery to the present. (Rev: BL 3/1/85) [305.4]

4367 King, Martin Luther, Jr. *Strength to Love* (10–12). 1985, Walker $11.95 (0-8027-2472-8); Fortress Pr. paper $5.95 (0-8006-1441-0). A collection of sermons against injustice and racism. [151]

4368 King, Martin Luther, Jr. *Stride Toward Freedom: The Montgomery Story* (9–12). 1987, Harper paper $8.95 (0-06-250490-8). The story of the Montgomery, Alabama, bus boycott of December 1955. [323.4]

4369 King, Martin Luther, Jr. *Where Do We Go from Here: Chaos or Community?* (10–12). 1967, Beacon paper $10.95 (0-8070-0571-1). King points out how black Americans have 3 sources of power—as consumers, voters, and workers. [323.4]

4370 King, Martin Luther, Jr. *Why We Can't Wait* (7–12). 1988, NAL paper $3.50 (0-451-62675-3). A history of the black civil rights movement to the struggle in Birmingham, Alabama. [323.4]

4371 Martin, Elmer P., and Joanne Mitchell Martin. *The Black Extended Family* (10–12). 1980, Univ. of Chicago Pr. paper $6.95 (0-226-50797-1). A study of the family structure of black Americans that evaluates its strengths and weaknesses. [305.8]

4372 Melanson, Philip H. *The Murkin Conspiracy: An Investigation of the Assassination of Dr. Martin Luther King, Jr.* (10–12). 1989, Praeger $21.95 (0-275-93029-7). A startling new theory that James Earl Ray did not act alone in the murder of Martin Luther King, Jr., and who his coconspirators were. (Rev: BL 6/1/89) [364.524]

4373 Meltzer, Milton, ed. *The Black Americans: A History in Their Own Words, 1619–1983* (9–12). 1984, Harper LB $14.89 (0-690-04418-6). A history of black people in America as revealed through letters, diaries, articles, and other documents. [305.8]

4374 Myrdal, Gunnar. *An American Dilemma* (10–12). 1975, Pantheon paper $5.95 (0-394-73042-9). This is volume one of a penetrating 2-volume study of black Americans that was originally published in 1962. [305.8]

4375 Raines, Howell. *My Soul Is Rested* (10–12). 1983, Penguin paper $8.95 (0-14-006753-1). Through a series of interviews, the civil rights movement of the 1960s is re-created. [305.8]

4376 Reynolds, Barbara. *And Still We Rise: Interviews with 50 Black Role Models* (7–12). Illus. 1988, USA Today Books paper $14.95 (0-944347-02-9). This is a collection of 50 interviews with successful black men and women from all walks of life. (Rev: SLJ 5/88) [323.4]

4377 Sitkoff, Harvard. *The Struggle for Black Equality, 1954–1980* (10–12). 1981, Hill & Wang paper $6.95 (0-8090-0144-6). A history of the modern civil rights movement. [305.8]

4378 Stampp, Kenneth M. *The Peculiar Institution: Slavery in the Antebellum South* (10–12). 1956, Knopf $17.45 (0-394-44015-3); Vintage (0-394-72307-2). A realistic portrayal of slavery in the South and of the living conditions of slaves. [326]

4379 Walker, Alice. *Good Night, Willie Lee, I'll See You in the Morning* (10–12). 1984, Harcourt paper $4.95 (0-15-636467-0). The status of black American women is explored in this collection of nonfiction writings. [305.8]

4380 Washington, James M., ed. *A Testament of Hope: The Essential Writings of Martin Luther King, Jr.* (9–12). 1986, Harper $23.95 (0-06-250931-4). A collection of the most important writings of Martin Luther King, Jr., from such

sources as sermons, speeches, essays, and interviews. (Rev: BL 3/1/86; SLJ 8/86) [323.4]

4381 Webb, Sheyann, and Rachel West Nelson. *Selma, Lord, Selma: Girlhood Memories of the Civil-Rights Days* (9–12). Illus. 1980, Univ. of Alabama Pr. $12.95 (0-8173-0031-7). Told by 2 girls in alternate chapters, this is a moving account of the civil rights struggle in Selma, Alabama. [323.4]

4382 Weisbrodt, Robert. *Freedom Bound: A History of America's Civil Rights Movement* (10–12). Illus. 1989, Norton $21.95 (0-393-02704-4). A comprehensive history of the civil rights movement from the sit-ins of 1959 through the presidency of Reagan. (Rev: BL 10/15/89; SLJ 5/90) [323.4]

4383 Woodward, C. Vann. *The Strange Career of Jim Crow* (10–12). 3rd rev. ed. 1974, Oxford Univ. Pr. paper $7.95 (0-19-501805-2). This book covers the history of segregation in the American South from 1877 through the 1960s. [305.8]

Jews

4384 Alepher, Joseph, ed. *Encyclopedia of Jewish History: Events and Eras of the Jewish People* (10–12). Illus. 1986, Facts on File $35.00 (0-8160-1220-2). In 100 entries, world Jewish history is detailed with accompanying maps, diagrams, and photographs. (Rev: BL 4/15/86) [909]

4385 Ausubel, Nathan. *Pictorial History of the Jewish People: From Bible Times to Our Own Day Throughout the World* (7–12). Rev. ed. Illus. 1984, Crown $24.95 (0-517-55283-3). Jewish history from earliest times to the present in text and illustrations. [909]

4386 Howe, Irving. *World of Our Fathers* (10–12). Illus. 1989, Harcourt $34.95 (0-15-146353-0); Schocken paper $14.95 (0-8052-0928-X). A history of the Jewish immigration to the United States from Eastern Europe in the late nineteenth and early twentieth centuries. [305.8]

4387 Lewis, Bernard. *Semites and Anti-Semites: An Inquiry into Conflict and Prejudice* (10–12). 1986, Norton $18.95 (0-393-02314-1); paper $7.95 (0-393-30420-5). An examination of anti-Semitism from historical, religious, and psychological viewpoints. (Rev: BL 6/1/86) [305.8]

4388 Meltzer, Milton, ed. *The Jewish Americans: A History in Their Own Words, 1650–1950* (7–12). Illus. 1982, Harper paper LB $13.89 (0-690-04228-0). From original sources such as diaries and letters, this is a history of Jews in America from colonial times to 1950. [305.8]

4389 Meltzer, Milton. *World of Our Fathers: The Jews of Eastern Europe* (7–12). Illus. 1974, Farrar $13.95 (0-374-38530-0). From many eyewitness accounts, the author gives a history of Jews in Eastern Europe through the massive immigrations in the earlier twentieth century. [305.8]

4390 Silberman, Charles E. *A Certain People: American Jews and Their Lives Today* (10–12). 1985, Summit $19.95 (0-671-44761-0); paper $8.95 (0-671-62877-1). A richly detailed study of the status of Jews in America today. [305.8]

Indians of North America

4391 Allen, T. D. *Navahos Have Five Fingers* (10–12). 1982, Univ. of Oklahoma Pr. paper $9.95 (0-8061-1765-6). A sympathetic account of life on a Navaho reservation in the mid-1950s. [970.004]

4392 Deloria, Vine, Jr., and Clifford M. Lytle. *The Nations Within: The Past and Future of American Indian Sovereignty* (10–12). 1984, Pantheon paper $12.95 (0-394-72566-2). A thorough study of the present political situation regarding the American Indian and self-government. [323.1]

4393 Stedman, Raymond William. *Shadows of the Indian: Stereotypes in American Culture* (10–12). 1982, Univ. of Oklahoma Pr. $29.95 (0-8061-1822-9); paper $14.95 (0-8061-1963-2). A look at the distorted view the public gets of the American Indian through stereotyped images in the media. [900.004]

4394 Taylor, Theodore W. *American Indian Policy* (10–12). 1983, Lomond $23.50 (0-912338-41-5). This account surveys the relations between American Indians and federal, state, and local governments. [323.1]

4395 White, Robert H. *Tribal Assets: The Rebirth of Native America* (10–12). 1990, Henry Holt $19.95 (0-8050-0846-2). The present status of the American Indian is explored in the context of the quiet revolution that is taking place. (Rev: BL 9/15/90) [323.1]

Hispanics

4396 Langley, Lester D. *MexAmerica: Two Countries, One Future* (10–12). 1988, Crown $19.95 (0-517-56732-6). The story of Mexican Americans, their problems and concerns, how they are treated in this country, and the immigration laws under which they live. (Rev: VOYA 10/88) [325.73]

4397 Meltzer, Milton. *The Hispanic Americans* (7–12). Illus. 1982, Harper LB $13.89 (0-690-04111-X). The story of the various Hispanic groups in America today, the conditions under which they live, and their present problems. [305.8]

Other Minorities

4398 Cateura, Linda Brandi. *Growing Up Italian* (9–12). Illus. 1987, Morrow $17.95 (0-688-06090-0). Interviews with 24 prominent Italians such as Francis Ford Coppola, Mario Cuomo, and Michael Andretti about their roots. (Rev: BL 1/15/87) [973]

4399 Chan, Sucheng. *Asian Americans: An Interpretive History* (10–12). 1990, Twayne $23.95 (0-8057-8426-8); paper $11.95 (0-8057-8437-3). A history of Asian Americans, their contributions and adversities, plus material on the prejudices they have encountered and the special problems faced by the women of this group. (Rev: BL 11/1/90) [973]

4400 Chen, Jack. *The Chinese of America* (10–12). Illus. 1980, Harper paper $15.95 (0-06-250139-9). A thoroughly documented history of Chinese Americans from 1785 to 1980. [305.8]

4401 Davis, Marilyn P. *Mexican Voices, American Dreams: An Oral History of Mexican Immigration to the United States* (10–12). 1990, Henry Holt $24.95 (0-8050-1216-8). This 15-year study by an anthropologist re-creates a history of Mexicans and Mexican Americans and their experiences from misery to hope. (Rev: BL 11/1/90) [973]

4402 Gillenkirk, Jeff, and James Motlow. *Bitter Melon* (10–12). Illus. 1988, Univ. of Washington Pr. $35.00 (0-295-96500-2); paper $19.95 (0-295-96562-2). A historical essay plus reports on many interviews are used to re-create the atmosphere of growing up in the all-Chinese town of Locke, California. (Rev: SLJ 6–7/88) [305.8]

4403 Rippley, La Vern J. *The German-Americans* (10–12). 1976, Univ. Pr. of America paper $14.25 (0-8191-2746-9). A history of Germans in America from Colonial times to the present. [305.8]

4404 Takaki, Ronald. *Strangers from a Different Shore: A History of Asian Americans* (10–12). 1989, Little $22.95 (0-316-83109-3). An account that traces the treatment (often hostile) that

Asians have received on arrival in America. (Rev: BL 6/15/89) [973]

4405 Yoors, Jan. *The Gypsies* (10–12). 1987, Waveland Pr. paper $9.50 (0-88133-305-0). The story of a Belgian boy who at age 12 ran away to live with gypsies. [305.8]

Forms of Dissent

4406 Erikson, Erik H. *Gandhi's Truth: On the Origins of Militant Nonviolence* (10–12). 1969, Norton paper $5.95 (0-393-00741-3). A psychoanalytic study of nonviolence as practiced by Gandhi. [322.4]

4407 Gandhi, Mohandas K. *Gandhi on Non-Violence* (10–12). 1965, New Directions paper $4.95 (0-8112-0097-3). Brief quotations make up most of this book which explores Gandhi's ideas on passive resistance. [322.4]

4408 Kohn, Stephen M. *Jailed for Peace: The History of American Draft Law Violators, 1658–1985* (10–12). 1986, Greenwood $29.95 (0-313-24586-X); Praeger paper $9.95 (0-275-92776-8). A 300-year history of those who for many reasons resisted military conscription. (Rev: BL 3/1/86) [355.2]

4409 Lang, Susan S. *Extremist Groups in America* (9–12). 1990, Watts LB $12.90 (0-531-10901-1). A review of hate groups in this country both from the extreme left and right. (Rev: BL 2/15/90) [305.8]

Social Concerns and Conflicts

General and Miscellaneous

4410 Arendt, Hannah. *On Revolution* (10–12). 1963, Peter Smith $16.25 (0-8446-6147-3); Penguin paper $7.95 (0-14-021681-2). A study of revolutions that focuses on the opposing characteristics of the American and French revolutions. [303.6]

4411 Bender, David L., ed. *American Values: Opposing Viewpoints* (9–12). 1989, Greenhaven LB $15.95 (0-89908-436-2); paper $8.95 (0-89908-411-7). A collection of pieces about some of the religious, social, and moral dilemmas in America today. (Rev: BL 1/1/90) [306]

4412 Cetron, Marvin, and Owen Davies. *American Renaissance: Our Life at the Turn of the 21st Century* (10–12). 1989, St. Martin's $19.95 (0-312-02860-1). After studying the social and economic indicators, these authors conclude that the United States has a bright future in the twenty-first century. (Rev: BL 8/89) [303.4]

4413 Erickson, Brad, ed. *Call to Action: Handbook for Ecology, Peace, and Justice* (10–12). 1990, Sierra Club paper $12.95 (0-87156-611-7). This collection of pieces involves such concerns as the environment, human rights, and social justice, and gives suggestions on how to act on them. (Rev: BL 7/90) [361.2]

4414 Huxley, Aldous. *Brave New World Revisited* (10–12). 1958, Harper paper $4.95 (0-06-080023-2). A nonfiction sequel to the author's *Brave New World* in which he projects into a future where thought control and chemically induced happiness are common. [303.3]

4415 Mead, Margaret. *Culture and Commitment: The New Relationships Between the Generations in the 1970s* (10–12). Rev. ed. 1978, Anchor paper $3.95 (0-385-13387-1). The author explores the conflicts in generations and how the ideas of the 1970s are causing changes in the 1980s. [305.2]

4416 Myers, Norman, ed. *Gaia: An Atlas of Planet Management* (10–12). Illus. 1984, Doubleday paper $22.95 (0-385-19072-7). This book on managing our resources concentrates on concerns involving population and the environment. (Rev: BL 2/1/85) [333.7]

4417 Naisbitt, John. *Megatrends: Ten New Directions Transforming Our Lives* (10–12). 1988, Warner paper $5.95 (0-446-35681-6). This book describes 10 important social trends that the author thinks are present today and will be very important in the future. [303.4]

4418 Rinzler, Jane. *Teens Speak Out* (9–12). 1985, Donald I. Fine paper $7.95 (0-917657-50-0). Teens voice their opinions on such subjects as careers, drugs, dating, and marriage. (Rev: BL 1/1/86) [305]

4419 Toffler, Alvin. *Future Shock* (10–12). 1970, Random $18.95 (0-394-42586-3); Bantam paper $4.95 (0-553-24649-6). The author spells out the problems that society faces in a technological age. His thoughts are continued in *The Third Wave* (1980). [303.4]

4420 Weil, Robert. *The Omni Future Almanac* (10–12). 1983, Newspaper Enterprise paper $8.95 (0-345-31034-9). In a series of articles, the author projects what life will be like a generation from now. [003]

Environmental Problems

General

4421 Bellini, James. *High Tech Holocaust* (10–12). 1989, Sierra Club paper $10.95 (0-87156-686-9). An unnerving account of how modern scientific technology has and is poisoning our world. (Rev: BL 3/15/89) [363.7]

4422 Bernards, Neal, ed. *The Environmental Crisis: Opposing Viewpoints* (9–12). Illus. 1991, Greenhaven LB $15.95 (0-89908-175-4); paper $8.95 (0-89908-150-9). A review of modern technology that is changing our environment in articles that supply various viewpoints concerning its effects. (Rev: BL 2/1/87; BR 5–6/87) [363.7]

4423 Caplan, Ruth, et al. *Our Earth, Ourselves* (9–12). Illus. 1990, Bantam paper $10.95 (0-553-34857-4). This book discusses environmental problems such as unhealthy air, global warming, and ozone depletion and gives an outline of possible solutions. (Rev: VOYA 8/90) [616.9]

4424 Carson, Rachel. *Silent Spring* (10–12). Illus. 1962, Houghton $17.95 (0-395-45389-5); paper $8.95 (0-395-45390-9). Though now over 25 years old, this book is still important as an account of how man is poisoning the environment. Also use: *Silent Spring Revisited* (1987). [632]

4425 Collins, Carol C., ed. *Our Food, Air and Water: How Safe Are They?* (9–12). Illus. 1985, Facts on File $24.95 (0-87196-967-X). A collection of editorials and cartoons that covers such environmental problems as water pollution and toxic wastes. (Rev: BL 3/15/85) [363.7]

4426 Elkington, John, et al. *The Green Consumer* (9–12). 1990, Penguin paper $8.95 (0-14-012708-9). A study of the environment and how it is being polluted by such waste products as old cars and disposable diapers. (Rev: BL 4/15/90) [363.7]

4427 Global Tomorrow Coalition. *The Global Ecology Handbook: What You Can Do about the Environmental Crisis* (10–12). 1990, Beacon $29.95 (0-8070-8500-6); paper $16.95 (0-8070-8501-4). Fourteen environmental issues are addressed in separate chapters, and current problems and possible lines of action are highlighted. (Rev: BL 5/15/90) [363.7]

4428 Goldsmith, Edward, and Nicholas Hildyard, eds. *The Earth Report: The Essential Guide to Global Ecological Issues* (10–12). Illus. 1988, Price/Stern/Sloan $19.95 (0-89586-673-0); paper $12.95 (0-89586-678-1). After 6 essays on such ecological subjects as nuclear power and acid

rain, there is an extensive glossary of terms, organizations, and events. (Rev: BL 3/15/88) [304.2]

4429 Gribbin, John. *Hothouse Earth: The Greenhouse Effect and Gaia* (10–12). 1990, Grove Weidenfeld $18.95 (0-8021-1374-5). The author explains why and how the earth is heating up and how we can slow down this process. (Rev: BL 5/15/90) [363.73]

4430 Gutnik, Martin J. *Ecology* (8–12). Illus. 1984, Watts LB $12.90 (0-531-04765-2). In a collection of projects, ecological principles are demonstrated plus material on how man and nature can upset delicate balances. [574.5]

4431 Harris, D. Mark. *Embracing the Earth: Choices for Environmentally Sound Living* (9–12). 1990, Noble Pr. paper $9.95 (0-9622683-2-1). This book explores the choices that must be made to safeguard our environment. (Rev: BL 5/15/90) [363.7]

4432 Naar, Jon. *Design for a Livable Planet* (10–12). Illus. 1990, Harper $25.95 (0-06-055165-8); paper $12.95 (0-06-096387-5). A fine overview of our environmental problems and an action manifesto. (Rev: BL 5/1/90) [363.7]

4433 National Geographic Society, eds. *Our Threatened Inheritance: National Treasures of the United States* (9–12). Illus. 1984, National Geographic $19.95 (0-87044-512-X). A guide to the American landscape and wildlife in text and stunning photographs with warnings concerning their future. [333.95]

4434 *Our Endangered Atmosphere: Global Warming and the Ozone Layer* (9–12). Illus. 1987, GEM $10.95 (0-85596-063-1). The greenhouse effect and ozone depletion are 2 topics covered in this collection of documents expressing different points of view. Part of the *Ideas in Conflict* series. (Rev: BL 9–10/87) [363.7]

4435 Palmer, Tim. *Endangered Rivers and the Conservation Movement* (10–12). Illus. 1986, Univ. of California Pr. $27.50 (0-520-05714-7). A history of the movement to save America's rivers, its present status, and how we can help today. (Rev: BL 3/15/87) [333.91]

4436 Rifkin, Jeremy, ed. *The Green Lifestyle Handbook: 1,001 Ways to Heal the Earth* (9–12). 1990, Henry Holt $16.95 (0-8050-1372-5); paper $7.95 (0-8050-1369-5). A practical guide for everyone on how we can help save the environment. (Rev: BL 5/15/90) [363.7]

4437 Roan, Sharon. *Ozone Crisis: The 15-Year Evolution of a Sudden Global Emergency* (10–12). 1989, Wiley $18.95 (0-471-61985-X). A story of how our ozone layer is being damaged and a history of the crusade to make people aware of it. (Rev: BL 7/89) [363.7]

4438 Russell, Terry, and Renny Russell. *On the Loose* (10–12). Illus. 1979, Sierra Club paper $9.95 (0-87156-264-2). In this beautifully illustrated book the authors describe the fragile beauty of America. [333.7]

4439 Schneider, Stephen H. *Global Warming: Are We Entering the Greenhouse Century?* (10–12). Illus. 1989, Sierra Club $18.95 (0-87156-693-1). A description of the greenhouse effect and the international actions it requires to prevent its growth. (Rev: SLJ 2/90) [304.2]

4440 Seymour, John, and Herbert Giradet. *Blueprint for a Green Planet* (9–12). Illus. 1987, Prentice $25.95 (0-13-079625-5); paper $17.95 (0-13-079609-3). After describing the pitiful state of our environment, the authors propose plans for citizen action groups to correct these ills. (Rev: BR 9-10/87; SLJ 8/87) [616.9]

4441 Shanks, Bernard. *This Land Is Your Land: The Struggle to Save America's Public Lands* (10–12). Illus. 1984, Sierra Club $19.95 (0-87156-822-5). An examination of the government and corporate land policies and how they often endanger our environment. [333.1]

4442 Silver, Cheryl Simon, and Ruth S. DeFries. *One Earth, One Future: Our Changing Global Environment* (10–12). 1990, National Academy Pr. $14.95 (0-309-04141-4). This is an excellent overview of the present condition of the environment and how humans have changed the earth system. (Rev: BL 9/15/90) [363.7]

4443 Sombke, Laurence. *The Solution to Pollution: 101 Things You Can Do to Clean Up Your Environment* (9–12). 1990, Master Media paper $7.95 (0-942361-19-9). A series of practical tips are given that can be used to stop the destruction of our environment. (Rev: BL 5/15/90) [363.7]

4444 Spencer, Page. *White Silk and Black Tar: A Journal of the Alaska Oil Spill* (10–12). 1990, Bergamot Books paper $9.95 (0-943127-04-1). The story of the terrible Alaskan oil spill caused by the *Exxon Valdez*. (Rev: BL 7/90) [363.73]

4445 Steger, Will, and Jon Bowermaster. *Saving the Earth: A Citizen's Guide to Environmental Action* (10–12). Illus. 1990, Knopf $19.95 (0-394-58431-7). Under the headings atmosphere, land, water, and people, the authors supply a call to action for saving our planet. (Rev: BL 5/1/90) [363.7]

4446 Wann, David. *Biologic: Environmental Protection by Design* (10–12). Illus. 1990, Johnson $19.95 (1-55566-048-7). The author presents in a commonsense manner his plan for living an environmentally safe life. (Rev: BL 9/1/90) [363.7]

4447 Weiner, Jonathan. *The Next One Hundred Years: Shaping the Fate of Our Living Earth* (10–12). 1990, Bantam $19.95 (0-553-05744-8). A sobering account about the consequences of our ecological policies that are causing the greenhouse effect. (Rev: BL 1/1/90; VOYA 8/90) [333]

4448 Wild, Russell, ed. *The Earth Care Annual 1990* (10–12). Illus. 1990, Rodale $17.95 (0-87857-875-7). A collection of essays that deal with the various environmental problems facing the earth. (Rev: BL 3/15/90) [363.7]

4449 Young, Louise B. *Sowing the Wind: Reflections on the Earth's Atmosphere* (10–12). 1990, Prentice $17.95 (0-13-083510-2). A description of our atmosphere and its present threats such as acid rain, the warming of the earth, and the destruction of the ozone layer. (Rev: BL 7/90) [363.7]

4450 Zipko, Stephen J. *Toxic Threat: How Hazardous Substances Poison Our Lives* (9–12). Illus. 1986, Messner LB $10.79 (0-671-50963-2). The environmental problems of dealing with all kinds of hazardous wastes such as pesticides, PCBs, acid rain, and air pollutants are discussed. (Rev: SLJ 11/86) [363.7]

Pollution

4451 Davidson, Art. *In the Wake of the Exxon Valdez: The Devastating Impact of the Alaska Oil Spill* (9–12). 1990, Sierra $19.95 (0-87156-614-1). The story of this country's most destructive oil spill in an account culled from many sources including dozens of interviews. (Rev: SLJ 8/90) [304.2]

4452 Epstein, Samuel S., et al. *Hazardous Waste in America* (7–12). 1982, Sierra Club paper $12.95 (0-87156-807-1). An account that explains the nature and types of hazardous wastes, the problems, and cleanups and possible solutions. [363.7]

4453 Kronenwetter, Michael. *Managing Toxic Wastes* (7–12). Illus. 1989, Messner LB $11.98 (0-671-69051-5). A description of what toxic wastes are, how they can affect our health, and methods for their storage or destruction. (Rev: BL 10/15/89; BR 3-4/90; SLJ 2/90; VOYA 4/90) [363.72]

4454 Luoma, Jon R. *Troubled Skies, Troubled Waters: The Story of Acid Rain* (10–12). 1984, Penguin paper $6.95 (0-14-008094-5). The formation of acid rain is explained and its effects on the environment. [363.7]

4455 Rousmaniere, John, ed. *The Enduring Great Lakes* (10–12). Illus. 1979, Norton $14.95 (0-393-01194-1). A book that covers the basic and most important problems facing the Great Lakes today. [574.5]

4456 Samuels, Mike, and Hal Zina Bennett. *Well Body, Well Earth: The Sierra Club Environmental Health Sourcebook* (7–12). Illus. 1983, Sierra Club paper $12.95 (0-87156-808-X). The causes and cures for the disease that is ruining our environment are explored. [616.9]

Population Problems

General and Miscellaneous

4457 Arendt, Hannah. *On Violence* (10–12). 1970, Harcourt paper $5.95 (0-15-669500-6). A study of the causes of violence and why it is so prevalent in our present culture. [303.6]

4458 Ehrlich, Paul R., and Anne H. Ehrlich. *The Population Explosion* (10–12). 1990, Simon & Schuster $18.95 (0-671-68984-3). A frightening account of the disaster that awaits humanity if the population growth is not brought under control. (Rev: BL 2/1/90) [304.6]

4459 Jones, Landon. *Great Expectations: America and the Baby Boom* (10–12). 1981, Ballantine paper $3.95 (0-345-33402-7). A firsthand account of being part of the largest generation in our history. [304.6]

4460 Langone, John. *Violence! Our Fastest-Growing Public Health Problem* (9–12). 1984, Little $14.95 (0-316-51431-4). A discussion of the causes of mob and individual violence is followed by a discussion of various kinds of violence. [303.6]

4461 McCuen, Gary E. *Inner-City Violence* (9–12). 1990, GEM LB $12.95 (0-86596-073-9). The problems of violence in our cities is covered in a series of articles that express a variety of opinions. (Rev: SLJ 8/90) [303.6]

4462 Madison, Arnold. *Runaway Teens* (9–12). 1979, Lodestar $10.95 (0-525-66636-2). An informative book that uses many case studies as examples. [362.7]

4463 Palenski, Joseph. *Kids Who Run Away* (10–12). 1984, R & E paper $12.95 (0-88247-727-7). This study focuses on interviews with more than

30 young people to determine why they ran away from home. [362.7]

4464 Rohr, Janelle, ed. *The Third World: Opposing Viewpoints* (9–12). Illus. 1989, Greenhaven LB $15.95 (0-89908-447-8); paper $7.95 (0-89908-422-2). This volume covers different opinions on the Third World in relation to such topics as poverty, human rights, and debt. (Rev: BL 1/15/90) [330]

4465 Veblen, Thorstein. *The Theory of the Leisure Class* (10–12). 1979, Penguin paper $4.95 (0-14-005363-8). In this book first published in 1899, Veblen expresses the opinion that the same social structure of the Middle Ages exists in modern society. [305.5]

4466 Wekesser, Carol, and Karin Swisher, eds. *Social Justice: Opposing Viewpoints* (9–12). Illus. 1984, Greenhaven LB $15.95 (0-89908-348-X); paper $8.95 (0-89908-323-4). In a variety of differing opinions such topics as affirmative action, women's rights, and treatment of the poor are explored. [361.1]

Aging

4467 Callahan, Daniel. *Setting Limits: Medical Goals in an Aging Society* (10–12). 1987, Simon & Schuster paper $8.95 (0-671-66831-5). The author reexamines our medical and social policies concerning the aged and makes several cogent recommendations. (Rev: BL 11/15/87) [362.1]

Crime and Prisons

4468 Blumenthal, Ralph. *Last Days of the Sicilians: The New FBI at War with the Mafia* (10–12). Illus. 1988, Times Books $18.95 (0-8129-1594-1). An account of the Mafia and the case known as the "Pizza Connection." (Rev: BL 9/15/88) [364.1]

4469 Buchanan, Edna. *The Corpse Had a Familiar Face: Covering Miami, America's Hottest Beat* (10–12). 1987, Random $17.95 (0-394-55794-8); Berkley paper $4.95 (1-55773-284-1). A crime reporter for the *Miami Herald* tells about the stories she has covered in her 15-year career. (Rev: BL 10/15/87) [070]

4470 Capote, Truman. *In Cold Blood: A True Account of a Multiple Murder and Its Consequences* (10–12). 1966, Random $19.95 (0-394-43023-9); NAL paper $4.95 (0-451-15446-0). The story of a shocking murder case where a family was killed by 2 psychotic young men. [364.1]

4471 Charriere, Henri. *Papillon* (10–12). 1988, Pocket paper $5.95 (0-88436-997-8). The life and sufferings of an innocent man in French Guiana and his eventual escape. [365]

4472 Clinard, Marshall B., and Peter C. Yeager. *Corporate Crime* (10–12). 1980, Free Pr. $17.95 (0-02-905710-8); paper $8.95 (0-02-905880-5). The authors describe various kinds of illegal corporate crime and the difficulties in controlling it. [364.1]

4473 De Sola, Ralph. *Crime Dictionary* (10–12). 1982, Facts on File $24.95 (0-87196-443-0). A dictionary of 10,000 terms related to crime and law enforcement that includes slang, drug jargon, and the names of gangs and criminals. [364.03]

4474 Dudley, William, ed. *Crime & Criminals: Opposing Viewpoints* (9–12). Illus. 1989, Greenhaven LB $15.95 (0-89908-441-9); paper $8.95 (0-89908-416-8). Conflicting points of view on causes of crime and its prevention are given through a variety of sources. (Rev: BL 11/15/89) [364]

4475 Francis, Dorothy B. *Shoplifting: The Crime Everybody Pays For* (9–12). 1980, Lodestar $11.95 (0-525-66658-3). A complete examination of the causes of shoplifting, how the courts handle it, and public attitudes toward it. [364.1]

4476 Francis, Dorothy B. *Vandalism: The Crime of Immaturity* (9–12). 1983, Lodestar $11.95 (0-525-66774-1). This examination of vandalism explores its causes, effects, and cost from the standpoints of both criminal and victim. [364]

4477 Friel, Frank, and John Guinther. *Breaking the Mob* (10–12). Illus. 1990, McGraw $19.95 (0-07-022355-6). The story set in Philadelphia of how a crime family was put behind bars. (Rev: BL 5/15/90) [364.1]

4478 Harris, Jonathan. *Super Mafia: Organized Crime Threatens America* (10–12). Illus. 1984, Messner $11.98 (0-671-49368-X). The author explores the U.S. Mafia, its organization, families, and operations. [364.1]

4479 Haskins, James. *The Guardian Angels* (8–12). Illus. 1983, Enslow LB $13.95 (0-89490-081-1). A profile of the vigilante group founded in New York City by Curtis Sliwa to fight crime. [364.4]

4480 Jones, Richard Glyn, ed. *Unsolved! Classic True Murder Cases* (9–12). Illus. 1987, Bedrick $15.95 (0-87226-047-X); paper $7.95 (0-87226-205-7). Ten unsolved murders are reported on by

such authors as Dorothy L. Sayers and James Thurber. (Rev: BL 5/1/87) [364.1]

4481 Kleiman, Dena. *A Deadly Silence: The Ordeal of Cheryl Pierson* (10–12). Illus. 1988, Atlantic Monthly $18.95 (0-87113-244-3). For mature readers, the story of the teenager who hired a classmate to murder her father. (Rev: BL 9/1/88) [364.1]

4482 Kosof, Anna. *Prison Life in America* (10–12). Illus. 1984, Watts LB $12.90 (0-531-04860-8). A study of American prisons today with suggestions for several alternatives. [365]

4483 Lewis, Craig A. *Blood Evidence: A Story of True Crime in the Suburban South* (10–12). 1990, August House $17.95 (0-87483-116-4). A true crime story of Lew Graham, a research scientist, who was convicted of murdering his wife. (Rev: BL 7/90) [345.73]

4484 McCuen, Gary E., and R. A. Baumgart. *Reviving the Death Penalty* (9–12). Illus. 1985, GEM $10.95 (0-86596-052-6). The pros and cons of this controversial topic are explored in a collection of articles and other original source material. (Rev: BL3/1/85) [364.66]

4485 Medea, Andra, and Kathleen Thompson. *Against Rape* (10–12). Illus. 1974, Farrar paper $7.95 (0-374-51119-5). An account written to help women understand rape and take necessary precautions. [364.1]

4486 Miller, Kent S., and Betty Davis Miller. *To Kill and Be Killed: Case Studies from Florida's Death Row* (10–12). 1989, Hope $16.95 (0-932727-24-7); paper $8.95 (0-932727-23-9). By using the present inhabitants of death row in Florida as case studies, the authors explore the problems posed by the death penalty. (Rev: SLJ 10/89; VOYA 10/89) [364]

4487 Mitford, Jessica. *Kind and Unusual Punishment: The Prison Business* (10–12). 1987, Vintage paper $9.95 (0-394-71093-2). An exposé of the American penal systems that points out its unnecessary cruelties and injustices. [365]

4488 Oatman, Eric F., ed. *Crime and Society* (10–12). 1979, H. W. Wilson paper $10.00 (0-8242-0632-0). In this series of articles, topics such as causes of crime, types of crime and criminals, and the criminal justice system are explored. [364]

4489 Rice, Berkeley. *Trafficking: The Boom and Bust of the Air America Cocaine Ring* (10–12). 1990, Macmillan $19.95 (0-684-19024-9). The story of how a group of middle-class American businessmen became involved in the Colombian drug trade. (Rev: BL 12/15/89) [363.4]

4490 Salerno, Joseph, and Stephen J. Rivele. *The Plumber* (10–12). Illus. 1990, Knightsbridge $19.95 (1-877961-00-0). Joe Salerno gradually became part of the Philadelphia Mafia, and when he realized his position, he decided to cooperate with the police. (Rev: BL 12/1/89) [364.1]

4491 Sands, Bill. *My Shadow Ran Fast* (10–12). 1966, NAL paper $3.95 (0-451-15249-2). A former convict's personal war against crime. [364]

4492 Silberman, Charles E. *Criminal Violence, Criminal Justice* (10–12). 1978, Random paper $4.95 (0-394-74147-1). The author explores the roots of crime in poverty, racism, and social injustice. [364]

4493 Szumski, Bonnie, ed. *America's Prisons: Opposing Viewpoints* (9–12). Illus. 1985, Greenhaven LB $15.95 (0-89908-375-7); paper $8.95 (0-89908-350-1). Three topics discussed are the nature of prisons, their types, and their effectiveness. (Rev: BL 12/15/85; BR 3–4/86; SLJ 3/86) [365]

4494 Szumski, Bonnie, ed. *Criminal Justice: Opposing Viewpoints* (9–12). Illus. 1987, Greenhaven LB $15.95 (0-89908-394-3); paper $7.95 (0-89908-369-2). In a series of articles, various viewpoints are expressed about topics like the jury system, rights of criminals, rights of victims, and legal ethics. (Rev: BL 6/1/87; SLJ 8/87; VOYA 8–9/87) [364]

4495 Szumski, Bonnie, et al., eds. *The Death Penalty* (9–12). Illus. 1986, Greenhaven LB $15.95 (0-89908-381-1); paper $8.95 (0-89908-356-0). Pros and cons of capital punishment are clearly presented in a fine collection of articles. (Rev: BL 5/15/86; SLJ 8/86) [364.6]

4496 Volkman, Ernest, and John Cummings. *The Heist* (9–12). 1988, Dell paper $3.95 (0-440-20029-6). The story of the incredible 8-million-dollar robbery at the Lufthansa terminal in New York that took place on December 11, 1978. (Rev: VOYA 4/87) [364.3]

4497 Wilkerson, David. *The Cross and the Switchblade* (10–12). 1987, Jove paper $3.50 (0-515-09025-5). A country minister works with the street gangs of New York City. [364.3]

4498 Wilson, James Q., and Richard J. Herrnstein. *Crime and Human Nature* (10–12). 1986, Simon & Schuster paper $13.95 (0-671-62810-0). For serious students, this is an examination of the factors—economic, social, and biological—that contribute to criminal behavior. (Rev: BL 9/15/85) [364.2]

4499 Wilson, Kirk. *Unsolved: Great Mysteries of the 20th Century* (10–12). 1990, Carroll & Graf $18.95 (0-88184-470-5). A collection of 10 accounts that include the deaths of John F. Kennedy, Marilyn Monroe, and Jimmy Hoffa. (Rev: BL 3/1/90) [364.1]

4500 Wright, James D., et al. *Under the Gun: Weapons, Crimes, and Violence in America* (10–12). 1983, Aldine $39.95 (0-202-30305-5); paper $19.95 (0-202-30306-3). This book discusses the distribution and use of weapons in America and their relation to violence and crime. [363.3]

Poverty and Homeless People

4501 Artenstein, Jeffrey. *Runaways: In Their Own Words* (9–12). 1990, Tor $16.95 (0-312-93132-8). Ten interviews with runaways in a shelter in Los Angeles reveal the shocking truths of life on the streets. (Rev: BL 7/90) [305.9]

4502 Brown, J. Larry, and H. F. Pizer. *Living Hungry in America* (10–12). 1987, Macmillan $18.95 (0-02-517290-5). The shameful story of the over 20 million people who are regularly hungry in America and how they are forced to live. (Rev: BL 7/87) [363.8]

4503 Conover, Ted. *Coyotes: A Journey Through the Secret World of America's Illegal Aliens* (10–12). 1987, Vintage paper $6.95 (0-394-75518-9). An account of the men smuggled across the Mexican border, their lives in the United States, and the lives of the families they have left behind. (Rev: SLJ 4/88; VOYA 2/88) [323.6]

4504 Dudley, William, ed. *Poverty* (8–12). Illus. 1988, Greenhaven LB $15.95 (0-89908-432-X); paper $8.95 (0-89908-407-9). An explanation of the causes of poverty is followed by some suggested solutions. (Rev: BL 5/15/88) [362.5]

4505 Fanning, Beverly J. *Workfare vs. Welfare* (8–12). Illus. 1989, GEM LB $12.95 (0-86596-072-0). A collection of articles that express various points of view on the welfare question. (Rev: BR 9–10/90; SLJ 8/89) [361.6]

4506 Harrington, Michael. *The New American Poverty* (10–12). 1984, Holt $17.95 (0-03-062157-7); Penguin paper $7.95 (0-14-008112-7). This account traces the roots of poverty in the 1980s to such factors as the Vietnam War and the global economy. [305.5]

4507 Harrington, Michael. *The Other America: Poverty in the United States* (10–12). 1987, Penguin paper $7.95 (0-14-021308-2). This book, first published in 1962, gives a truthful look at living conditions of poor people. [305.5]

4508 Hirsch, Kathleen. *Songs from the Alley* (10–12). 1989, Ticknor $22.95 (0-89919-488-5). A discussion of the problems of the homeless that focuses on 2 Boston women trying to cope with poverty. (Rev: BL 4/1/89) [362.8]

4509 Katz, Michael B. *In the Shadow of the Poorhouse: A Social History of Welfare in America* (10–12). 1986, Basic Books $22.95 (0-465-03225-7); paper $12.95 (0-465-03226-5). A history of the war against poverty in America and how the emphasis in tackling the problem has changed from the late eighteenth century. (Rev: BL 9/15/86) [361]

4510 Kozol, Jonathan. *Rachel and Her Children: Homeless Families in America* (10–12). 1988, Crown $17.95 (0-517-56730-X); Fawcett paper $8.95 (0-449-90339-7). By focusing on a family living in a welfare hotel in New York City, the author explores the pitiful existence of the homeless in America. (Rev: BL 1/1/88; BR 5–6/89; SLJ 3/88; VOYA 10/88) [362.5]

4511 Lappé, Frances Moore, and Joseph Collins. *World Hunger: Twelve Myths* (10–12). Illus. 1986, Grove $17.95 (0-394-55626-7); paper $7.95 (0-394-62297-9). The authors advance the position that it is a lack of democracy in the world rather than a shortage of food that causes famines. (Rev: BL 10/1/86) [363.8]

4512 Orr, Lisa, ed. *The Homeless: Opposing Viewpoints* (9–12). 1990, Greenhaven LB $15.95 (0-89908-476-1); paper $8.95 (0-89908-451-6). From a number of points of view, this collection of articles explores such facets of the homeless problem as causes and possible solutions. (Rev: BL 4/15/90; SLJ 8/90) [362.5]

4513 Sidel, Ruth. *Women and Children Last: The Plight of Poor Women in Affluent America* (10–12). 1987, Penguin paper $6.95 (0-14-010013-X). An account that shows that women and children suffer most through the current welfare process. (Rev: BL 3/1/86) [362.8]

4514 Stavsky, Lois, and I. E. Mozeson. *The Place I Call Home: Faces and Voices of Homeless Teens* (8–12). Illus. 1990, Shapolsky $14.95 (0-944007-81-3). A series of interviews with homeless teens that reveal lives of violence, poverty, and drugs. (Rev: BL 11/15/90) [362.7]

4515 Tucker, William. *The Excluded Americans: Homelessness and Housing Policies* (10–12). 1990, Regnery Gateway $24.95 (0-89526-551-6). A well-researched account of the plight of the homeless in America today. (Rev: BL 5/15/90) [363.5]

4516 Weiss, Ann E. *Welfare: Helping Hand or Trap?* (8–12). Illus. 1990, Enslow LB $15.95 (0-89490-169-9). This book not only covers the issues involved with welfare but also gives a history of public welfare from ancient Egypt through Victorian England and its poorhouses to present thinking about it from President Bush. (Rev: SLJ 6/90) [361.6]

Unemployment and Labor Problems

4517 Lens, Sidney. *Strikemakers & Strikebreakers* (7–12). Illus. 1985, Dutton $14.95 (0-525-67165-X). This history of labor unions in this country focuses on famous strikes and their resolutions. (Rev: BL 5/15/85; SLJ 9/85) [331.89]

4518 Long, Priscilla. *Where the Sun Never Shines: A History of America's Bloody Coal Industry* (10–12). Illus. 1989, Paragon $24.95 (1-55778-224-5). A history of the coal industry, particularly in regard to the formation of its labor unions. (Rev: BL 10/1/89) [338.2]

Public Morals

4519 Cook, Fred. *The Ku Klux Klan: America's Recurring Nightmare* (7–12). 1989, Messner LB $12.98 (0-671-68421-3). A history of the Ku Klux Klan, its leaders, and the messages of hate and bigotry it has spread for generations. (Rev: BR 5–6/90; BL 1/15/90; VOYA 4/90) [322.4]

4520 Everett, Melissa. *Breaking Ranks* (10–12). 1988, New Society $34.95 (0-86571-134-8); paper $12.95 (0-86571-135-6). The story of 10 men who entered government service and found that they could not compromise their values and ideals to the extent demanded of them. (Rev: BR 5–6/89; VOYA 6/89) [327.73]

4521 Glazer, Myron Peretz, and Penina Migdal Glazer. *The Whistleblowers: Exposing Corruption in Government and Industry* (10–12). 1989, Basic Books $19.95 (0-465-09173-3). Case studies of the people who often have risked everything to expose crime and corruption. (Rev: BL 3/1/89) [353]

4522 Landau, Elaine. *Surrogate Mothers* (9–12). 1988, Watts $11.90 (0-531-10603-9). In addition to an explanation of the types of surrogate parenting this volume explores the ethical and legal considerations involved. (Rev: BL 2/1/89; BR 3–4/88; SLJ 12/88; VOYA 4/89) [306.8]

4523 Lappé, Frances Moore. *Rediscovering America's Values* (10–12). 1989, Ballantine

$22.50 (0-345-32040-9). The role of government, individual social responsibility, and liberal versus conservative thought are 3 themes explored in this thoughtful account that utilizes a variety of sources and opinions. (Rev: BL 3/15/89) [320.5]

4524 McCuen, Gary E. *Pornography and Sexual Violence* (9–12). Illus. 1985, GEM $10.95 (0-86596-053-4). This book of articles, reports, and other comments explores the nature and effects of pornography. (Rev: BL 3/1/85) [364.174]

4525 Moyers, Bill. *The Secret Government: The Constitution in Crisis* (10–12). Illus. 1988, Seven Locks $16.95 (0-932020-61-5); paper $9.95 (0-932020-60-7). An exposé of the secret network of spies, profiteers, and mercenaries that is supported by the White House. (Rev: BL 11/15/88; SLJ 3/89) [973.927]

4526 Newton, David E. *Science Ethics* (8–12). Illus. 1987, Watts $11.90 (0-531-10419-2). Such topics as the use of animals in research and the participation of scientists in weapons research are addressed in this stimulating volume. (Rev: BL 12/15/87; BR 1–2/88; SLJ 2/88; VOYA 2/88) [174]

4527 Nisbet, Lee, ed. *The Gun Control Debate: You Decide* (10–12). 1990, Prometheus paper $16.95 (0-87975-618-7). From a variety of sources, this is a collection of 22 essays that explore various aspects of the gun control controversy. (Rev: BL 12/15/90) [363.3]

4528 Rohr, Janelle, ed. *Violence in America: Opposing Viewpoints* (9–12). 1990, Greenhaven LB $15.95 (0-89908-449-4); paper $8.95 (0-89908-424-9). A collection of articles that explore such topics as violence associated with the family, drugs, and teenagers. (Rev: BL 4/15/90; SLJ 8/90) [303.6]

4529 Rose, Stephen C. *Coping with a Negative World in a Positive Way* (10–12). 1987, Rosen $12.95 (0-8239-0676-0). An interesting discussion of what the really important values in life are. (Rev: VOYA 8–9/87) [170]

4530 Zimring, Franklin E., and Gordon Hawkins. *The Citizen's Guide to Gun Control* (10–12). 1987, Macmillan $17.95 (0-02-934830-7). All of the issues involving the history and present status of the gun control problem are objectively discussed. (Rev: BL 7/87; SLJ 2/89) [344.73]

Sex Roles

4531 Adams, Carol, and Rae Laurikietis. *The Gender Trap: A Closer Look at Sex Roles* (10–12). Illus. 1977, Academy Chicago paper $21.00 (0-915864-09-6). In this first of a 3-volume set, the authors explore expected behavior and accepted sex roles of women and men. [305.4]

4532 Bernards, Neal, and Terry O'Neill, eds. *Male-Female Roles: Opposing Viewpoints* (9–12). 1989, Greenhaven LB $15.95 (0-89908-446-X); paper $8.95 (0-89908-421-4). Representing a variety of points of view, this collection of pieces deals with aspects of sex roles and how and why they have changed. (Rev: BL 1/1/90; SLJ 6–7/88) [305.3]

4533 Bloom, Lynn Z., et al. *The New Assertive Women* (10–12). 1980, Dell paper $4.95 (0-440-36393-4). This book is intended to help women escape the passive sex roles that history demanded in the past. [305.4]

4534 Brownmiller, Susan. *Femininity* (10–12). 1985, Fawcett paper $8.95 (0-449-90142-4). This thoughtful book explores what is and what is not part of the condition of femininity. [155.3]

4535 de Beauvoir, Simone. *The Second Sex* (10–12). Trans. by H. M. Parshley. 1953, Knopf $25.00 (0-394-44415-9); Random paper $9.95 (0-679-72451-6). A literary treatise that explores the condition of being a woman in both the past and the present. [305.4]

4536 McNaught, Brian. *On Being Gay* (10–12). 1988, St. Martin's $13.95 (0-312-01800-2). A collection of columns by a gay Catholic journalist that gives counsel and includes a section on growing up gay. For mature readers. (Rev: BL 7/88) [306.7]

4537 O'Neill, Terry, and Neal Bernards, eds. *Male/Female Roles: Opposing Viewpoints* (9–12). Illus. 1989, Greenhaven LB $15.95 (0-89908-446-X); paper $8.95 (0-89908-421-4). Through a number of readings presenting different opinions, the problems of sex roles are explored. (Rev: SLJ 3/90) [305.3]

4538 Sidel, Ruth. *On Her Own: Growing Up in the Shadow of the American Dream* (10–12). 1990, Viking $18.95 (0-670-83154-9). Based on many interviews, Sidel examines women's role in American culture today and their opportunities as compared to men. (Rev: BL 11/15/89; SLJ 6/90) [305.4]

4539 Thom, Mary, ed. *Letters to Ms. Magazine* (10–12). 1987, Henry Holt paper $9.95 (0-8050-

0797-0). A collection of letters to *Ms. Magazine* that reflect the thoughts of women and their position in society over a 15-year period. (Rev: BR 1–2/88; SLJ 10/87; VOYA 2/88) [305.4]

Social Change and Futurism

4540 Archer, Jules. *Police State: Could It Happen Here?* (9–12). 1977, Harper LB $12.89 (0-06-020154-1). A look at the possibility of the United States becoming a police state and the events that could produce it. [973]

Social Customs

4541 Tuleja, Tad. *Curious Customs* (8–12). 1987, Harmony $15.95 (0-517-56653-2); paper $8.95 (0-517-56654-0). The amazing stories behind almost 300 popular customs and rituals in our culture. (Rev: VOYA 2/88) [390]

Terrorism

4542 Dobson, Christopher, and Ronald Payne. *The Never-Ending War: Terrorism in the 80's* (10–12). 1987, Facts on File $18.95 (0-8160-1537-6); paper $12.95 (0-8160-2056-6). A clear explanation of why terrorism grew in the 1980s, who the terrorists are, and who their targets are. (Rev: SLJ 10/87) [322.4]

4543 Dobson, Christopher, and Ronald Payne. *The Terrorists: Their Weapons, Leaders and Tactics* (10–12). Rev. ed. Illus. 1982, Facts on File $16.95 (0-87196-669-7); paper $10.95 (0-87196-668-9). A review of the various kinds of terrorism and their characteristic tactics. [303.6]

4544 Harris, Jonathan. *The New Terrorism: Politics of Violence* (9–12). Illus. 1983, Messner LB $9.97 (0-671-45807-8). After a historical survey, the author describes the international organizations that are the purveyors of today's terrorism. [303.6]

4545 Hubbard, David. *Winning Back the Sky: A Tactical Analysis of Terrorism* (10–12). 1986, Saybrook $14.95 (0-933071-04-3); paper $7.95 (0-933071-14-0). An account that stresses a get-tough attitude as a way of combating terrorism. (Rev: BL 1/1/86) [364.1]

4546 Hyde, Margaret O., and Elizabeth H. Forsyth. *Terrorism: A Special Kind of Violence* (9–12). 1987, Dodd $11.95 (0-396-08902-X). The effects of terrorist activities on the victims are highlighted in this account and ways of combating terrorism are given. (Rev: BL 4/15/87; BR 11–12/87; SLJ 5/87; VOYA 12/87) [303.6]

4547 Kronenwetter, Michael. *The War on Terrorism* (9–12). Illus. 1989, Messner LB $11.98 (0-671-69050-7). A detailed account of the forms of terrorism in the world today and of the responses that countries have developed toward it. (Rev: BL 11/15/89; BR 3–4/90; SLJ 2/90; VOYA 4/90) [909.82]

4548 Long, David E. *The Anatomy of Terrorism* (10–12). 1990, Free Press $22.95 (0-02-919345-1). A description of the roots of terrorism, who practices it, and what the civilized world can do about it. (Rev: BL 8/90) [303.6]

4549 Martin, David C., and John L. Walcott. *Best Laid Plans: America's War against Terrorism* (10–12). 1988, Harper $18.95 (0-06-015877-8). The story of America's war on terrorism based on a number of cases including the Iranian hostage crisis. (Rev: BL 7/88) [363.3]

4550 Melman, Yossi. *The Master Terrorist: The True Story behind Abu Nidal* (10–12). Illus. 1986, Watts $16.95 (0-915361-52-3). The story of the Palestinian terrorist who with his henchmen has committed over 100 acts of terrorism. (Rev: BR 11–12/86; SLJ 1/87; VOYA 4/87) [322.4]

4551 Meltzer, Milton. *The Terrorists* (9–12). Illus. 1983, Harper LB $12.89 (0-06-024194-2). A rundown of the perpetrators of international terrorism plus some background history on the subject. [303.6]

4552 O'Ballance, Edgar. *Terrorism in the 1980s* (10–12). 1989, Arms & Armour paper $19.95 (0-85368-925-3). An account that traces the roots of terrorism, its kinds and purposes, and today's leading exponents. (Rev: BL 9/1/89) [322.4]

4553 Raynor, Thomas. *Terrorism: Past, Present, Future* (9–12). Rev. ed. 1987, Watts $13.90 (0-531-10344-7). A history of terrorism that dates back to the French Revolution and a discussion of the types of terrorist activity today. (Rev: BL 4/15/87; BR 5–6/88; SLJ 5/87; VOYA 8–9/87) [303.6]

4554 Sterling, Claire. *The Terror Network* (10–12). 1984, Berkley paper $3.95 (0-425-09153-8). This is an account of the international terrorism network as it existed in the 1970s. [322.4]

4555 Szumski, Bonnie, ed. *Terrorism: Opposing Viewpoints* (9–12). Illus. 1986, Greenhaven LB $15.95 (0-89908-389-7); paper $8.95 (0-89908-364-1). This topic is explored from a variety of viewpoints and in a number of writings from different sources. (Rev: SLJ 5/87) [322.4]

Urban and Rural Life

4556 Hanmer, Trudy. *The Growth of Cities* (7–12). Illus. 1985, Watts $12.90 (0-531-10056-1). A history of cities and their distinctive characteristics and problems throughout the ages. (Rev: BL 12/1/85; BR 5–6/86; SLJ 2/86) [307.7]

4557 Haskins, James. *Street Gangs: Yesterday and Today* (9–12). 1977, Hastings paper $4.95 (0-8038-6740-9). This is a history of street gangs—how they have been formed and how they have functioned. [364.3]

4558 Jacobs, Jane. *The Death and Life of Great American Cities* (10–12). 1961, Random paper $6.95 (0-394-70241-7). A serious study of urban America and the need for creative planning and renewal of our cities. [307.7]

4559 McHarg, Ian L. *Design with Nature* (10–12). Illus. 1969, Natural History Pr. paper $15.95 (0-385-05509-9). A guide to urban planning that is allied to nature and such factors as wildlife and watersheds. [711]

4560 Mumford, Lewis. *The City in History: Its Origins, Its Transformation, and Its Prospects* (10–12). Illus. 1961, Harcourt paper $18.95 (0-15-618035-9). A study of the development of cities and of mankind as social animals. [307.7]

Economics and Business

General and Miscellaneous

4561 Consumer Reports, eds. *I'll Buy That!* (9–12). Illus. 1986, Consumer Reports $30.00 (0-89043-046-2); paper $20.00 (0-89043-032-2). The history of such innovations as the credit card, compact discs, and shopping malls. (Rev: BL 2/15/87) [303.4]

4562 Davis, Bertha. *Crisis in Industry: Can America Compete?* (9–12). Illus. 1989, Watts LB $12.90 (0-531-10659-4). A somewhat gloomy assessment of America's present economic situation internationally and its probable future. (Rev: BL 6/1/89; BR 11–12/89; SLJ 8/89; VOYA 12/89) [338]

4563 Epstein, Rachel. *Investments & the Law* (9–12). 1988, Chelsea House LB $9.95 (1-55546-632-X). This account looks at the way government controls business, like securities laws and the Federal Reserve Board. (Rev: BR 9–10/88) [332.6]

4564 Folbre, Nancy. *A Field Guide to the U.S. Economy* (9–12). 1988, Pantheon paper $10.95 (0-349-75047-0). A primer on the American economy with chapters on topics such as government spending, welfare, trade, minorities, and farming. (Rev: BR 5–6/88) [330.973]

4565 Friedman, Milton, and Rose Friedman. *Free to Choose: A Personal Statement* (10–12). 1980, Harcourt $16.95 (0-15-133481-1); Avon paper $4.95 (0-380-52548-8). A plea to free business from governmental control. [330.1]

4566 Galbraith, John Kenneth. *The Affluent Society* (10–12). 4th ed. 1984, Houghton $18.95 (0-395-36613-5); NAL paper $4.95 (0-451-62394-0). The author discusses production, distribution of wealth, and the development of sound economic and social policies. [330]

4567 Hambleton, Ronald. *The Branding of America* (9–12). Illus. 1987, Yankee Books $19.95 (0-89909-101-6). The personal stories of the people behind such products and services as Singer sewing machines, Heinz, and Saks department stories. (Rev: BL 3/1/87) [658.827]

4568 Hart, William B. *The United States and World Trade* (7–12). 1985, Watts $11.90 (0-531-10067-7). A discussion of the present conditions involving the United States and world trade and of the current high trade deficit. (Rev: BR 3–4/86; SLJ 2/86) [650]

4569 Heilbroner, Robert L. *Beyond Boom and Crash* (10–12). 1978, Norton paper $2.95 (0-393-05707-0). A short work that explores many problems facing the world economy, such as oil prices. [330.9]

4570 Heilbroner, Robert L. *The Worldly Philosophers: The Lives, Times, and Ideas of the Great Economic Thinkers* (10–12). 1980, Peter Smith $18.75 (0-8446-6291-7). This lucid account explains the ideas of economists like Adam Smith, Ricardo, Marx, and Keynes. [330.1]

4571 Heilbroner, Robert L., and Lester C. Thurow. *Economics Explained* (10–12). 1988, Peter Smith $16.25 (0-8446-6336-0); Prentice paper $6.95 (0-317-17196-8). A history of economic concepts with emphasis on those of Adam Smith, Marx, and Keynes. [330]

4572 Jennings, Diane. *Self-Made Women* (10–12). 1987, Taylor paper $9.95 (0-87833-550-1). The story of 12 successful businesswomen and how they overcame odds to get to the top. (Rev: BL 10/15/87) [338]

4573 Kroc, Ray, and Robert Anderson. *Grinding It Out: The Making of McDonalds* (9–12). 1990, St. Martin's paper $4.95 (0-312-92378-3). A history of the fast-food chain and how it grew and prospered. [650]

4574 Kronenwetter, Michael. *Capitalism vs. Socialism: Economic Policies of the USA and the USSR* (9–12). Illus. 1986, Watts LB $12.90 (0-531-10152-5). The author explains the principles behind capitalism and socialism in both theoretical and practical terms. [330.1]

4575 Lee, Susan. *Susan Lee's ABZs of Money & Finance* (10–12). 1988, Poseidon $16.95 (0-671-55712-2). In dictionary format, such terms as equity, depreciation, and sinking fund are explained. (Rev: BL 6/15/88) [332]

4576 Levi, Maurice. *Economics Deciphered: A Layman's Survival Guide* (10–12). 1981, Basic Books paper $6.95 (0-465-01795-9). Using a question-and-answer format the author explains economics in clear prose. [330]

4577 Little, Jeffrey B. *Reading the Financial Pages* (9–12). Illus. 1988, Chelsea House $9.95 (1-55546-623-0). A guide to finding out about such topics as stocks, bonds, and commodities from newspapers and other sources. (Rev: BL 10/1/88; BR 9–10/88; SLJ 10/88) [070.4]

4578 Loehr, James E., and Peter J. McLaughlin. *Mentally Tough: The Principles of Winning at Sports Applied to Winning in Business* (10–12). Illus. 1986, Evans paper $8.95 (0-87131-540-8). The authors apply the same principles and procedures that toughen athletes to the world of business and business practices. (Rev: SLJ 2/87) [650]

4579 Moore, Carl H., and Alvin E. Russell. *Money: Its Origin, Development and Modern Use* (9–10). Illus. 1987, McFarland $18.95 (0-89950-272-5). From wampum beads to credit cards this is the story of money in its many forms in America. (Rev: BL 11/15/87; VOYA 4/88) [332.4]

4580 O'Neill, Terry, ed. *Economics in America: Opposing Viewpoints* (9–12). Illus. 1986, Greenhaven LB $15.95 (0-89908-397-8); paper $8.95 (0-89908-372-2). A collection of articles that covers many points of view about American economics and its value system. (Rev: SLJ 5/87) [330]

4581 Pollard, Sidney, ed. *Wealth & Poverty: An Economic History of the Twentieth Century* (10–12). Illus. 1990, Oxford Univ. Pr. $29.95 (0-19-520821-8). An economic history of the world in this century with profiles of 100 people who were most closely involved in it. (Rev: BL 7/90) [330.9]

4582 Smith, Adam. *The Wealth of Nations* (10–12). 1936, Modern Lib. $13.95 (0-394-60409-1). The free enterprise manifesto that was first published in 1776. [330.1]

4583 Sobel, Robert, and David B. Sicilia. *The Entrepreneurs: An American Adventure* (10–12). Illus. 1986, Houghton $29.45 (0-395-42020-2). From the television series, this book explores entrepreneurship and gives biographies of innovators from many different fields. (Rev: SLJ 1/87) [650]

4584 Tong, Hsin-Min, ed. *Learning from Forty Inspiring Business Successes* (10–12). 1986, Professional Publg. paper $12.95 (0-937419-00-1). Forty profiles of individuals, companies, and products that trace their unusual success stories and why. (Rev: BL 12/15/86) [650.1]

Economic Systems and Institutions

General and Miscellaneous

4585 Birnbach, Lisa. *Going to Work: A Unique Guided Tour through Corporate America* (10–12). 1988, Random paper $15.95 (0-394-75874-9). A glimpse at 50 different American corporations, large and small, and how they operate. (Rev: BR 3–4/89) [338.7]

4586 DiBacco, Thomas V. *Made in the U.S.A. The History of American Business* (10–12). 1987, Harper $19.95 (0-06-015624-4); paper $8.95 (0-06-091466-1). An anecdotal history of American business featuring the careers of such luminaries as Ford, Carnegie, and Rockefeller. (Rev: BL 2/15/87) [338]

4587 Epstein, Rachel. *Alternative Investments* (10–12). Illus. 1988, Chelsea House $9.95 (1-55546-633-8). A slim volume that covers such topics as collectibles, gold, and savings accounts. (Rev: BL 4/1/88) [332.6]

4588 Goldstone, Nancy Bazelon. *Trading Up* (10–12). 1988, Dutton $17.95 (0-525-24621-5). A breezy account of a woman's experiences in the male-dominated business world of options trading. (Rev: SLJ 6–7/88) [332.6]

4589 Hamrin, Robert. *America's New Economy: The Basic Guide* (10–12). 1988, Watts $18.95 (0-531-15077-1). An introduction to such concepts as gross national product and the deficit plus a discussion of how these affect our lives. (Rev: BL 6/15/88) [330.973]

4590 Killen, M. Barbara. *Economics and the Consumer* (9–12). Illus. 1990, Lerner LB $14.95

(0-8225-1775-2). Such terms as *gross national product* and *resource management* are explained in this guide to consumer economics. (Rev: BL 4/15/90; SLJ 5/90) [381.3]

4591 Leone, Bruno, ed. *Capitalism: Opposing Viewpoints* (9–12). Rev. ed. Illus. 1986, Greenhaven LB $15.95 (0-89908-384-6); paper $8.95 (0-89908-359-5). A collection of primary sources that explore the history of capitalism and its vices and virtues. (Rev: BL 8/86; SLJ 10/86) [330.12]

4592 Leone, Bruno, ed. *Communism: Opposing Viewpoints* (9–12). Rev. ed. Illus. 1986, Greenhaven LB $15.95 (0-89908-385-4); paper $8.95 (0-89908-360-9). This collection of documents tries to explain the concepts involved in communism and to enumerate its successes and failures as seen from several viewpoints. (Rev: BL 8/86; SLJ 10/86) [335.43]

4593 Leone, Bruno, ed. *Socialism: Opposing Viewpoints* (9–12). Rev. ed. Illus. 1986, Greenhaven LB $15.95 (0-89908-386-2); paper $8.95 (0-89908-361-7). After a general introduction to socialism, there follows a collection of documents with many viewpoints and conflicting stands on the effectiveness of this economic and social system. (Rev: BL 8/86; SLJ 10/86) [335]

4594 Little, Jeffrey B. *Understanding a Company* (8–12). Illus. 1988, Chelsea House LB $9.95 (1-55546-622-2). The tools for analyzing companies are explained and information is given on how to apply them. (Rev: SLJ 8/88) [338.7]

4595 Mayer, Martin. *The Greatest-Ever Bank Robbery: The Collapse of the Savings and Loan Industry* (10–12). Illus. 1990, Macmillan $22.50 (0-684-19152-0). For better readers, the story of the collapse of the savings and loan industry. (Rev: BL 9/1/90) [332.3]

Banks

4596 Klebaner, Benjamin J. *American Commercial Banking: A History* (10–12). 1990, Twayne $25.95 (0-8057-9804-8); paper $12.95 (0-8057-9815-3). A 200-year history of the banking industry in America. (Rev: BL 9/1/90) [332.1]

4597 Mayer, Martin. *The Bankers* (10–12). 1980, Ballantine paper $4.95 (0-345-29569-2). A dissection of the banking business and how it operates nationally and internationally. [332.1]

Stock Exchanges

4598 Epstein, Rachel. *Investment Banking* (10–12). Illus. 1987, Chelsea House $9.95 (1-55546-630-3). An account of how a company goes public plus explanations of concepts involving mergers and takeovers. (Rev: BL 4/1/88) [332.66]

4599 Little, Jeffrey B. *Investing and Trading* (10–12). Illus. 1988, Chelsea House $9.95 (1-55546-627-3). A guide on how to invest in stocks and various allied topics such as buying on margin. (Rev: BL 4/1/88) [332.6]

4600 Little, Jeffrey B. *Stock Options* (9–12). Illus. 1988, Chelsea House $9.95 (1-55546-628-1). Such concepts as puts and calls are explained in this basic volume. Also use: *Bonds, Preferred Stocks and the Money Market* (1988) (Rev: BL 10/1/88; BR 11–12/88) [332.64]

4601 Little, Jeffrey B. *Wall Street: How It Works* (8–12). Illus. 1988, Chelsea House LB $9.95 (1-55546-621-4). Such topics as how stocks are issued and traded plus a history of the stock exchange and how it operates are covered in this brief account. (Rev: SLJ 8/88) [332.6]

4602 Little, Jeffrey B. *What Is a Share of Stock?* (10–12). Illus. 1987, Chelsea House $9.95 (1-55546-620-6). The story of how stocks come into being and what they mean to the future of a company. By the same author use: *Understanding a Company* (1987). (Rev: BL 1/15/88) [332.64]

4603 Samuelson, Paul. *The Principles of Technical Analysis* (9–12). Illus. 1988, Chelsea House LB $9.95 (1-55546-625-5). The study of stocks, their prices, and the forecasting of future prices. (Rev: BR 11–12/88) [332.6]

4604 Scott, Elaine. *Stocks and Bonds, Profits and Losses: A Quick Look at Financial Markets* (7–12). Illus. 1985, Watts $11.90 (0-531-04938-8). An excellent overview of what is involved in making stock and bond investments geared specifically to the teenage potential investor. (Rev: BL 6/15/85; BR 11–12/85; SLJ 8/85; VOYA 12/85) [332.63]

Consumerism

4605 Barach, Arnold B. *Famous American Trademarks* (9–12). Illus. 1971, Public Affairs Pr. paper $9.00 (0-8183-0165-1). The origins and history of about 100 trademarks are traced by text and pictures. [341.7]

4606 Campbell, Sally R. *The Confident Consumer* (10–12). Illus. 1988, Goodheart-Willcox $19.00 (0-87006-635-8). A well-planned and current guide to help users become wise consumers through understanding our economic system and its agencies. (Rev: BL 4/15/88) [381]

4607 Consumer Reports, eds. *Testing: Behind the Scenes at Consumer Reports, 1936–1986* (9–12). Illus. 1986, Consumer Reports $20.00 (0-89043-064-0); paper $13.00 (0-89043-056-X). How a variety of products from ballpoint pens to mattresses are tested at Consumers Union. (Rev: BL 2/15/87) [363.1]

4608 Garbarino, James. *The Future As If It Really Mattered* (10–12). 1988, Bookmakers paper $13.95 (0-917665-20-1). A book that warns us about the dangers of our consumer-oriented society. (Rev: BR 3–4/89) [640.73]

4609 Point Foundation, eds. *The Essential Whole Earth Catalog: Access to Tools and Ideas* (10–12). 1986, Doubleday paper $19.95 (0-385-23641-7). An extensive catalog of resources on various products culled from previous issues of the *Whole Earth Catalog*. (Rev: BL 11/15/86) [338.47]

Employment and Jobs

4610 Claypool, Jane. *Unemployment* (9–12). Illus. 1983, Watts LB $12.90 (0-531-04586-2). This book tells what causes unemployment, its history in this country, and its effects. [331.1]

4611 Terkel, Studs. *Working: People Talk about What They Do All Day and How They Feel about What They Do.* (10–12). 1974, Pantheon paper $7.95 (0-394-72953-6). From truck drivers to corporate presidents, this is a study based on interviews about their jobs and attitudes toward them. [331.2]

Labor Unions

4612 Brill, Steven. *The Teamsters* (10–12). 1979, Pocket paper $2.75 (0-671-82905-X). A history of the country's largest labor union, its leaders, and their power. [331.88]

4613 McKissack, Patricia, and Frederick McKissack. *A Long Hard Journey: The Story of the Pullman Porter* (9–12). 1990, Walker LB $18.95 (0-8027-6885-7). The story of the Pullman por-

ters' fight for justice and the founding of their union under A. Philip Randolph. (Rev: BR 5–6/90) [385]

4614 Meltzer, Milton. *Bread and Roses: The Struggle of American Labor* (9–12). 1990, NAL $16.95 (0-8160-2371-9); paper $3.95 (0-451-62396-7). A history of how labor organized in America. [331.88]

Money and Trade

4615 Mandell, Lewis. *The Credit Card Industry: A History* (10–12). 1990, Twayne $24.95 (0-8057-9810-2); paper $10.95 (0-8057-9816-1). From the beginning with the Diners Club card in 1949 to the present, this is a history of credit cards and their impact on society. (Rev: BL 8/90) [332.7]

Marketing and Advertising

4616 Clark, Eric. *The Want Makers: The World of Advertising—How They Make You Buy* (10–12). 1989, Viking $19.95 (0-670-82603-0). Written from a British standpoint, this book investigates the advertising industry, how campaigns are planned, and how the general populace is affected. (Rev: BL 3/1/89) [659.1]

4617 Luxenberg, Stan. *Roadside Empires: How the Chains Franchised America* (10–12). 1985, Viking $17.30 (0-670-32658-5); Penguin paper $7.95 (0-14-007734-0). This account explains carefully the inner workings of the franchising business in America. (Rev: BL 1/1/85) [381]

4618 Morgan, Hal. *Symbols of America* (9–12). Illus. 1986, Viking $40.00 (0-670-80667-6); Penguin paper $14.95 (0-14-008077-5). A collection of such trademarks as Aunt Jemima and the golden arches and the stories behind them. (Rev: BL 1/1/86) [602]

4619 Packard, Vance. *The Hidden Persuaders* (10–12). Rev. ed. 1981, Pocket paper $3.95 (0-671-42503-X). A pioneering (1957) account of motivational research and advertising. [659.1]

4620 Schudson, Michael. *Advertising, the Uneasy Persuasion: Its Dubious Impact on American Society* (10–12). 1984, Basic Books $17.95 (0-465-00078-9); paper $11.95 (0-465-00079-7). An objective account of how 3 elements—advertiser, agency, and consumer—interact to produce the world of advertising. [659.1]

4621 Tedlow, Richard S. *New and Improved: The Story of Mass Marketing in America* (9–12). Illus. 1990, Basic Books $24.95 (0-465-05023-9).

The story of how competition leads to sometimes bizarre marketing practices. (Rev: BL 4/15/90) [381]

Guidance and Personal Development

Education and the Schools

General and Miscellaneous

4622 Bergreen, Gary. *Coping with Difficult Teachers* (9–12). 1988, Rosen LB $12.95 (0-8239-0788-0). A constructive book that helps students adjust to their teachers and gives advice on creating situations of mutual help. (Rev: BR 3–4/89; SLJ 3/89; VOYA 4/89) [371.8]

4623 Boyer, Ernest L. *High School: A Report on Secondary Education in America* (10–12). 1987, Harper paper $9.95 (0-06-091224-3). An examination of several typical high schools in America with suggestions for reform. [373]

4624 Cadwalader, George. *Castaways: The Penikese Island Experiment* (9–12). 1988, Chelsea Green $17.95 (0-930031-12-1). An account of the founding of a school for juvenile delinquents on an island off the coast of Massachusetts. (Rev: BL 9/1/88; BR 11–12/88) [365]

4625 Flesch, Rudolf. *Why Johnny Still Can't Read: A New Look at the Scandal of Our Schools* (10–12). 1981, Harper paper $5.95 (0-06-091031-3). An examination of the problems in teaching reading today and how it can be done more effectively. [372.4]

4626 Franck, Irene M., and David M. Brownstone. *Scholars and Priests* (9–12). 1988, Facts on File $17.95 (0-8160-1449-3). A history that shows the interrelationship through the ages of religion and education. (Rev: BL 3/15/89; BR 3–4/89; VOYA 4/89) [371.1]

4627 Freedman, Samuel G. *Small Victories: The Real World of a Teacher, Her Students & Their High School* (10–12). 1990, Harper $22.95 (0-06-016254-6). An inspiring story about a year in the life of a New York City teacher in one of the city's worst high schools. (Rev: BL 3/15/90) [373]

4628 Gross, Beatrice, and Ronald Gross, eds. *The Great School Debate: Which Way for American Education?* (10–12). 1985, Simon & Schuster paper $14.95 (0-671-54136-6). A collection of articles and reports (including *A Nation at Risk*) that explores the current situation in American education. (Rev: BL 4/15/85) [370]

4629 Kohl, Herbert. *Thirty-Six Children* (10–12). 1988, NAL paper $7.95 (0-452-26155-4). A former teacher recalls his 2 years teaching in a school in Harlem. [371.5]

4630 Kozol, Jonathan. *Death at an Early Age* (10–12). 1987, NAL paper $7.95 (0-452-25769-7). The story of the year the author spent teaching in a predominantly black school in Boston. [370.19]

4631 Lightfoot, Sara Lawrence. *The Good High School: Portraits of Character and Culture* (10–12). 1983, Basic Books paper $12.95 (0-465-02696-6). Profiles of some of the best American high schools and what makes them superior. [373]

4632 Neill, A. S. *Summerhill: A Radical Approach to Child Rearing* (10–12). 1977, Pocket paper $4.95 (0-671-81302-1). This is a description of the famous English experimental school where freedom of action and movement is encouraged. [371]

4633 Ravitch, Diane. *The Schools We Deserve: Reflections on the Educational Crises of Our Times* (10–12). 1985, Basic Books $19.95 (0-465-07236-4); paper $10.95 (0-465-07234-8). A noted American educator looks at the present status of curriculum and goals in American schools and makes recommendations. (Rev: BL 4/15/85) [370]

4634 Rubin, Louis D., Jr., ed. *An Apple for My Teacher: Twelve Authors Tell about Teachers Who Made the Difference* (9–12). Illus. 1987, Algonquin $19.95 (0-912697-34-2); paper $10.95 (0-912697-57-1). In chapters of various lengths, 12 writers discuss their favorite teachers and what made them memorable. (Rev: SLJ 8/87) [371.1]

4635 Sizer, Theodore R. *Horace's Compromise: The Dilemma of the American High School* (10–12). 1984, Houghton paper $8.95 (0-395-37753-6). Many problems faced by capable teachers in high school today are explored with suggestions to correct these conditions. [373.1]

4636 Ware, Cindy. *Summer Options for Teenagers* (7–12). 1990, Prentice paper $16.95 (0-13-296443-0). A guide to over 1,000 summer programs for young people who want to study and learn in the summer. (Rev: BL 4/1/90) [371]

4637 Wirths, Claudine G., and Mary Bowman-Kruhm. *I Hate School: How to Hang In & When to Drop Out* (7–12). Illus. 1986, Harper LB $11.89 (0-690-04558-1); paper $7.95 (0-06-446054-1). A self-help book for those who are having trouble in school that emphasizes the importance of not dropping out. (Rev: BL 1/15/87; BR 3–4/87; SLJ 11/86; VOYA 12/86) [373.12]

Development of Academic Skills

Secretarial Skills

4638 Geffner, Andrea B. *How to Write Better Business Letters* (10–12). Illus. 1982, Barron's $8.95 (0-8120-2509-1). Techniques are outlined for all kinds of business correspondence including reports, résumés, and the standard topics involving business letters. [651.7]

4639 Hutchinson, Lois. *Standard Handbook for Secretaries* (10–12). 1969, McGraw $16.95 (0-07-031537-X). A basic reference that includes material on grammar, letter and report writing, and taking minutes of meetings. [651.02]

4640 Lindsell, Sheryl L. *The Secretary's Quick Reference Handbook* (10–12). 1983, Arco paper $3.95 (0-688-05595-2). Business English is presented plus tips on office management. [651.02]

4641 Marks, Lillian S. *Touch Typing Made Simple* (8–12). Rev. ed. Illus. 1985, Doubleday paper $7.95 (0-385-19426-9). A clear manual that gives information on specialized topics like types

of letters, tabulations, and addressing envelopes. Part of a lengthy series. (Rev: BL 2/15/86) [652.3]

4642 Schimmel, Warren T., and Stanley A. Lieberman. *Typing the Easy Way* (8–12). Illus. 1988, Barron's $10.95 (0-8120-4080-5). A well-organized manual for teaching oneself typing basics. [652.3]

4643 *Webster's Secretarial Handbook* (10–12). 2nd ed. Illus. 1983, Merriam-Webster $10.95 (0-87779-136-8). As well as the usual coverage on such topics as letter writing and bookkeeping, this manual also has a section on word processing. [651.7]

Study Skills

4644 Adler, Mortimer J., and Charles Van Doren. *How to Read a Book* (10–12). Rev. ed. 1972, Simon & Schuster paper $10.95 (0-671-21209-5). This classic explains how to approach and analyze various kinds of reading material such as stories, plays, and poetry. [028]

4645 Felknor, Bruce L. *How to Look Things Up and Find Things Out* (9–12). 1988, Morrow $22.00 (0-688-07850-8); paper $10.95 (0-688-06166-4). A very readable guide to doing basic research and the materials this involves. (Rev: BL 1/15/88) [027]

4646 Frank, Stanley D. *Remember Everything You Read: The Evelyn Wood Seven Day Speed Reading and Learning Program* (9–12). Illus. 1990, Times Books $17.95 (0-8129-1773-1). How to increase one's reading speed and still retain the content. (Rev: BL 4/15/90) [371.3]

4647 Gall, Meredith D., and Joyce P. Gall. *Study for Success* (8–12). Illus. 1985, Damien paper $7.95 (0-930539-01-X). Of value to serious junior high students through the college years, this supplies 80 excellent tips to developing specific study skills. (Rev: BL 8/85) [371.3]

4648 Hawes, Gene R., and Lynne Salop Hawes. *Hawes Guide to Successful Study Skills* (9–12). 1981, NAL paper $8.95 (0-452-26087-6). This manual contains many tips on how to improve grades through better and more organized study habits. [371.3]

4649 Kesselman-Turkel, Judi, and Franklynn Peterson. *Test Taking Strategies* (10–12). 1981, Contemporary paper $5.95 (0-8092-5850-1). A book that gives techniques and strategies for successful test taking. Also use: *Study Smarts: How to Learn More in Less Time* and *Research Shortcuts* (both 1982). [371.3]

4650 Lorayne, Harry. *How to Develop a Super-Power Memory* (10–12). 1974, NAL paper $4.95 (0-451-16149-1). Tips and techniques for increasing your ability to remember. [371.3]

4651 Maddox, Harry. *How to Study* (10–12). 1983, Fawcett paper $3.50 (0-449-30011-0). Practical tips and strategies are outlined to make studying more effective. [378]

4652 Schneider, Zola Dincin, and Phyllis B. Kalb. *Countdown to College: A Student's Guide to Getting the Most Out of High School* (9–12). 1989, College Entrance Examination Board paper $9.95 (0-87447-335-7). A guide for high school students to such topics as time management, academic planning, and extracurricular activities. (Rev: BL 12/1/89; BR 3–4/90; VOYA 2/90) [373]

4653 Todd, Alden. *Finding Facts Fast: How to Find Out What You Want and Need to Know* (10–12). 1979, Ten Speed $7.95 (0-89815-013-2); paper $5.95 (0-89815-012-4). This book describes research techniques and offers a variety of sources and methods for finding information. [001.4]

4654 Winkler, Anthony C., and Jo Ray McCuen. *Writing the Research Paper* (10–12). 2nd ed. 1985, Harcourt paper $9.00 (0-15-598292-3). A book that describes how to do research and how to transform the findings into a report or term paper. [808]

Tests and Test Taking

4655 Brownstein, Samuel C., et al. *How to Prepare for the Scholastic Aptitude Test SAT* (10–12). 1989, Barron's paper $10.95 (0-8120-4185-2). This guide gives many sample questions plus hints on how to prepare and take the SATs. Also available in a concise edition: *Barron's Basic Tips on the SAT Scholastic Aptitude Test* (1989). [378]

4656 Deptula, Edward J., ed. *Preparation for the SAT* (10–12). 1987, Arco paper $8.95 (0-13-700865-1). All kinds of tips are given for preparing for the SAT including practice exams. (Rev: BR 1–2/88) [371.2]

4657 Doster, William C., ed. *Barron's How to Prepare for the College Level Examination Program, CLEP, General Examination* (10–12). Illus. 1986, Barron's paper $9.95 (0-8120-2980-1). A guide that includes more than 4,000 test items to help improve CLEP scores. [378]

4658 Gladstone, William. *Preparation for the ACT* (10–12). 1984, Arco paper $8.95 (0-671-50220-4). A guide to the American College Testing Program, with tips on successful test taking and hints on how to write good essays. [378]

4659 Gruber, Gary R. *Inside Strategies for the SAT* (10–12). 1987, Educational Design paper $6.50 (0-87694-185-4). A proven way to improve scores on the SATs. [371.2]

4660 Kelly, John D., and Richard Rosenberg. *Lovejoy's Preparation for the SAT* (10–12). 1985, Simon & Schuster paper $8.95 (0-671-47503-7). One of the standard guides to preparing for the SATs with hints on successful test taking. [378]

4661 Lawrence, Marcia. *How to Take the SAT, Scholastic Aptitude Test* (10–12). Illus. 1979, New American Library paper $9.95 (0-452-26296-8). This is a guide in a workbook format to preparation for the SATs. [378]

4662 Lawrence, Marcia. *Test-Taking Strategies for the PSAT* (9–12). Illus. 1987, NAL paper $7.95 (0-452-25743-3). A coaching manual to help students take the PSAT successfully. (Rev: BL 9/1/87) [378]

4663 Owen, David. *None of the Above: Behind the Myth of Scholastic Aptitude* (10–12). 1986, Houghton paper $7.95 (0-395-41500-4). This well-researched account challanges the objectivity and validity of the SAT and other standardized tests that come from the Educational Testing Bureau. (Rev: BL 4/1/85) [378]

4664 Robinson, Adam, and John Katzman. *The Princeton Review—Cracking the System: The SAT and PSAT, 1990 Edition* (10–12). 1989, Random paper $10.95 (0-679-72633-0). An excellent guide to taking the SATs from the people who run the Princeton Review coaching courses. (Rev: BL 6/1/87; VOYA 4/87; VOYA 2/90) [371.2]

4665 *SAT Success* (10–12). Rev. ed. 1987, Peterson's paper $9.95 (0-87866-580-3). Three study plans are outlined—one for 18 weeks, one for 9, and one Panic Plan for crammers. (Rev: BR 1–2/88) [371.2]

4666 Weiss, John, et al. *Standing Up to the SAT* (10–12). 1989, Prentice paper $6.95 (0-13-300914-9). After a general discussion of SATs and their basic unfairness, information is given on how to prepare for each part. (Rev: BL 9/15/89) [378]

Writing and Speaking Skills

4667 Adler, Mortimer J. *How to Speak, How to Listen* (10–12). 1983, Macmillan paper $5.95 (0-

02-079590-4). The types of oral communication are discussed and tips are given on how to prepare a speech. [001.54]

4668 Allen, Steve. *How to Make a Speech* (10–12). 1986, McGraw paper $7.99 (0-07-001169-9). This book covers writing and delivery of speeches with tips on how to avoid stage fright. [808.5]

4669 Barzun, Jacques, and Henry F. Graff. *The Modern Researcher* (10–12). 4th ed. 1985, Harcourt paper $13.95 (0-15-562512-8). A manual that explains how to collect facts, organize them, and present them effectively in a report. [808]

4670 Blumenthal, Lassor A. *Successful Business Writing* (10–12). 1985, Putnam paper $5.95 (0-399-51146-6). This concise manual covers topics like résumés, speeches, letters, and proposals. [371.2]

4671 Brown, Cynthia Stokes. *Like It Was: A Complete Guide to Writing Oral History* (9–12). 1988, Teachers & Writers paper $10.95 (0-915924-12-9). A handbook that tells the reader how to conduct an oral history project, from planning it to the final transcription of the interviews. (Rev: BL 2/1/89) [907]

4672 Cash, Phyllis. *How to Develop and Write a Research Paper* (9–12). 1988, Arco paper $6.95 (0-13-404872-5). Using a 7- to 9-week time frame this book gives specifics on writing the term paper from choosing a topic to final draft. (Rev: SLJ 2/89) [808]

4673 Cool, Lisa Collier. *How to Write Irresistible Query Letters* (10–12). 1990, Writer's Digest paper $10.95 (0-89879-391-3). For would-be writers, this is a manual on how to approach publishers through letters. (Rev: SLJ 6–7/87) [808.6]

4674 Dalton, Rick, and Marianne Dalton. *The Student's Guide to Good Writing: Building Writing Skills for Success in College* (10–12). 1990, College Entrance Examination Board paper $9.95 (0-87447-353-5). A practical guide of useful tips with examples on how to improve writing skills. (Rev: BL 4/1/90; VOYA 6/90) [808]

4675 Delton, Judy. *The 29 Most Common Writing Mistakes and How to Avoid Them* (10–12). 1985, Writer's Digest $9.95 (0-89879-172-3). A guide to effective writing through an examination of common errors. [808]

4676 Fleming, Alice. *What to Say When You Don't Know What to Say* (9–12). 1982, Macmillan $11.95 (0-684-17626-2). A guide to talking in a variety of situations from conversations to public speaking. [808.5]

4677 Flesch, Rudolf. *How to Write, Speak, and Think More Effectively* (10–12). 1960, NAL paper $4.95 (0-451-14193-8). This book covers a number of ways to communicate more precisely and effectively with a concentration of writing and speaking. [808]

4678 Gardner, John. *The Art of Fiction: Notes on Craft for Young Writers* (10–12). 1984, Knopf $17.95 (0-394-50469-0); Vintage paper $5.95 (0-394-72544-1). This is a long essay on the components of fiction and how to write well. [808.3]

4679 Gordon, Karen Elizabeth. *The Well-Tempered Sentence: A Punctuation Handbook for the Innocent, the Eager and the Doomed* (9–12). 1983, Ticknor $8.85 (0-89919-170-3). An entertaining guide to punctuation with individual chapters devoted to each punctuation mark. [421]

4680 Hoff, Ron. *"I Can See You Naked": A Fearless Guide to Making Great Presentations* (9–12). Illus. 1988, Andrews & McMeel $16.95 (0-8362-7944-1); paper $8.95 (0-8362-7946-8). An often humorous guide to public speaking with sound tips for good presentations. (Rev: BL 6/1/88) [808.5]

4681 Horowitz, Lois. *Knowing Where to Look: The Ultimate Guide to Research* (10–12). 1988, Writer's Digest paper $15.95 (0-89879-329-7). A research guide that emphasizes library resources and good search strategies. [001.4]

4682 Horton, Susan R. *Thinking through Writing* (7–12). Illus. 1982, Johns Hopkins Univ. Pr. $27.50 (0-8018-2716-7); paper $8.95 (0-8018-2717-5). Fundamentals of both grammar and composition are covered plus all of the techniques necessary to write a good essay. [808]

4683 Keyworth, Cynthia. *How to Write a Term Paper* (10–12). 1982, Arco paper $5.95 (0-668-05321-6). A thorough treatment of term-paper writing from choosing a subject to the final draft. [411]

4684 Lamm, Kathryn. *10,000 Ideas for Term Papers, Projects and Reports* (8–12). 1987, Arco paper $7.95 (0-13-905209-7). Ten thousand topics for term papers arranged by subject. [808]

4685 Lewis, Norman. *Correct Spelling Made Easy* (10–12). 1987, Dell paper $4.50 (0-440-31501-8). This is a 60-day program to improve spelling skills. [421]

4686 Lieberman, Gerald F. *3,500 Good Quotes for Speakers* (10–12). 1983, Doubleday paper $4.95 (0-305-17769-0). Arranged under such subjects as courtship and magic, this is a collection of humorous quotes. [808.88]

4687 McCauley, Robie, and George Lanning. *Technique in Fiction: Second Edition Revised and Updated for a New Generation* (10–12). 1987, St. Martin's $16.95 (0-312-00692-6). A book that takes the novice writer through the basics of creating short stories or novels. (Rev: SLJ 8/87) [808.3]

4688 McMahan, Elizabeth, and Susan Day. *The Writer's Handbook* (10–12). Illus. 1980, McGraw paper $19.95 (0-07-045423-X). This account covers such topics as spelling, punctuation, grammar, and usage. [808]

4689 Means, Beth, and Lindy Lindner. *Everything You Needed to Learn about Writing in High School—But . . .* (10–12). Illus. 1989, Libraries Unlimited paper $10.95 (0-87287-711-6). Crammed full of information, this manual gives detailed instructions and practice exercises. (Rev: BL 4/1/90) [808]

4690 Meyer, Herbert E., and Jill M. Meyer. *How to Write* (8–12). 1987, Storm King Pr. paper $4.95 (0-394-75352-6). A practical guide that describes how to get organized, prepare the first draft, and polish the manuscript. (Rev: VOYA 6/87) [411]

4691 Miller, Walter James, and Elizabeth Morse-Cluley. *How to Write Book Reports: Analyzing and Evaluating Fiction, Drama, Poetry, and Non-Fiction* (9–12). 1984, Arco paper $6.95 (0-668-05909-5). Literary elements in various forms of literature are analyzed before detailed instructions on how to write the book report are given. [808]

4692 Mulkerne, Donald. *The Perfect Term Paper: Step-by-Step* (10–12). 3d rev. ed. Illus. 1983, Doubleday paper $4.95 (0-385-12380-9). A guide that begins with choosing a topic and ends with the final draft. [808]

4693 Paxson, William C. *The Mentor Guide to Writing Term Papers and Reports* (10–12). Illus. 1988, NAL paper $3.95 (0-451-62612-5). A well-organized handbook with numerous examples included in the text. (Rev: BL 5/1/88) [808.02]

4694 Peck, Robert Newton. *Fiction Is Folks: How to Create Unforgettable Characters* (10–12). 1987, Writer's Digest paper $8.95 (0-89879-266-5). In a conversational style, the author of many juvenile books discusses how to create characters in fiction. (Rev: SLJ 8/87) [808.3]

4695 Powell, David. *What Can I Write About?* (10–12). 1981, NCTE paper $9.95 (0-8141-5656-8). Seven thousand possible subjects for papers are listed. [371.3]

4696 Prochnow, Herbert V., and Herbert V. Prochnow Jr., eds. *The Public Speaker's Treasure Chest* (10–12). 4th ed. 1986, Harper $19.95 (0-06-181692-2). Besides acting as a guide on how to bring humor into a speech and providing many anecdotal examples, this book gives tips on how to prepare and deliver a speech. [808.88]

4697 Roberts, Edgar V. *Writing Themes about Literature* (10–12). 1988, Prentice paper $18.60 (0-13-970757-3). A guidebook to literary appreciation and analysis and how they can be used to effectively write about literature. [808]

4698 Schumacher, Michael. *Creative Conversations: The Writer's Guide to Conducting Interviews* (10–12). 1990, Writer's Digest paper $16.95 (0-89879-396-3). This account covers topics like preparing for the interview, kinds of interviews, how to structure them, and how to prepare the final product. (Rev: SLJ 7/90) [158]

4699 Skapura, Robert, and John Marlowe. *A Student's Guide to Research and Writing: Literature* (10–12). 1988, Libraries Unlimited $10.00 (0-87287-650-0). Both analytical and research writing are explained as well as tips on choosing topics, collecting material, and writing the final paper. (Rev: VOYA 6/89) [411]

4700 Sternberg, Patricia. *Speak Up! : A Guide to Public Speaking* (7–12). 1984, Messner LB $8.79 (0-671-47371-9). An informal, practical guide to public speaking for teenagers. [808.5]

4701 Strunk, William, Jr., and E. B. White. *The Elements of Style* (10–12). 3rd rev. ed. 1979, Macmillan $6.95 (0-02-418230-3); paper $2.25 (0-02-418220-6). A short, no-nonsense book that covers the basics of usage and composition. [808]

4702 Summers, Harrison Boyd, et al. *How to Debate: A Textbook for Beginners* (7–12). 3rd ed. 1963, Wilson $17.00 (0-8242-0019-5). An introduction to the components of a debate, their purposes, and how to debate effectively. [808.53]

4703 Tchudi, Susan, and Stephen Tchudi. *The Young Writer's Handbook* (8–12). 1984, Macmillan $13.95 (0-684-18090-1); paper $4.95 (0-689-71170-0). This book covers the elements of effective writing in such areas as fiction, poetry, letters, and school reports. [808]

4704 Teitelbaum, Harry. *How to Write Book Reports* (9–12). 1989, Simon & Schuster paper $6.95 (0-13-441403-9). An introductory guide to writing book reports and other types of literary critical evaluations. [411]

4705 Turabian, Kate L. *A Manual for Writers of Term Papers, Theses, and Dissertations* (9–12). 5th ed. 1987, Univ. of Chicago Pr. $20.00 (0-226-81624-9); paper $7.95 (0-226-81625-7). A new edition of one of the standard and most easily used manuals of style. (Rev: BL 10/1/87) [808]

4706 Vassallo, Wanda. *Speaking with Confidence: A Guide for Public Speakers* (9–12). 1990, Betterway paper $7.95 (1-55870-147-8). For anyone fearful of facing an audience this is a guide that contains sound, workable advice. (Rev: BL 8/90; SLJ 7/90) [808.5]

4707 Zinsser, William. *On Writing Well: An Informal Guide to Writing Nonfiction* (9–12). Rev. ed. 1990, Harper $19.95 (0-06-055272-7); paper $9.95 (0-06-096831-1). In this, the fourth edition, Zinsser continues to give sound general advice plus tips for special areas such as science, sports, and humor. (Rev: BL 8/90) [808]

Academic Guidance

General and Miscellaneous

4708 Bloch, Deborah Perlmutter. *How to Write a Winning Résumé* (10–12). 1989, VGM paper $7.95 (0-8442-6639-6). A guidebook that tells you how to gather pertinent information and present it in an effective résumé. (Rev: BR 3–4/90; VOYA 10/89) [331.1]

4709 Council on International Educational Exchange. *The Teenager's Guide to Study, Travel, and Adventure Abroad, 1989–1990 Edition* (7–12). 1988, St. Martin's paper $9.95 (0-312-02296-4). Over 150 different programs abroad are fully described plus general tips on travel and how to select a program. (Rev: BL 4/1/89) [370.19]

4710 Council on International Educational Exchange. *The Teenager's Guide to Study, Travel, and Adventure Abroad 1990–91* (9–12). 10th ed. 1990, St. Martin's paper $10.95 (0-312-03979-4). A fine resource for high school students who are contemplating traveling or studying abroad. (Rev: BL 3/1/87) [370.19]

4711 Greenberg, Jan. *The Teenager's Guide to the Best Summer Opportunities* (10–12). 1985, Harvard Common Pr. $16.95 (0-916782-59-X); paper $9.95 (0-916782-58-1). This guide emphasizes educational opportunities available in the summer although other enriching activities are discussed. (Rev: BL 1/1/85) [371.4]

4712 Loiry, William S. *Winning with Science: The Complete Guide to Science Research and Programs for Students* (8–12). 1986, Loiry Pub. $14.95 (0-9607654-7-6); paper $9.95 (0-9607654-8-4). This is a state-by-state guide to science programs for junior and senior high school students. [500]

4713 Melchert, John S., ed. *Work, Study, Travel Abroad: The Whole World Handbook* (10–12). 1988, St. Martin's paper $8.95 (0-312-01539-9). A handbook for travel opportunities abroad published under the auspices of the Council on International Educational Exchange. (Rev: BL 3/15/88) [370.2]

4714 Peters, Max, et al. *Barron's How to Prepare for High School Entrance Examinations (SSAT & COOP)* (8–12). 1988, Barron's paper $10.95 (0-8120-4121-6). This gives many useful tips plus a variety of sample questions. [371.2]

4715 Robinson, Jacqueline, and Dennis M. Robinson. *Arco's Complete Preparation for High School Entrance Examinations* (8–12). 1984, Arco paper $7.95 (0-668-05878-1). Review sections plus sample tests are given for high school entrance tests. [371.4]

4716 Shields, Charles J. *The College Guide for Parents* (10–12). 1988, College Board paper $12.95 (0-87447-316-0). Both parents and teenagers will find this guide informative in such areas as choosing a college, admission procedures, and financial aid. (Rev: SLJ 4/89; VOYA 6/89) [378]

4717 *Study Abroad* (10–12). 1987, UNESCO paper $16.00 (U1486-UNESCO). All kinds of educational opportunities overseas after high school are listed with details for each one. [378]

Colleges and Universities

4718 Ablow, Keith. *Medical School: Getting In, Staying In, Staying Human* (10–12). 1990, St.

Martin's paper $12.95 (0-312-04349-X). How to get into medical school is the focus of this volume with a section on what to do as early as high school. (Rev: BL 5/1/90) [610.7]

4719 *Barron's Guide to the Best, Most Popular and Most Exciting Colleges* (10–12). 1988, Barron's paper $9.95 (0-8120-3981-5). A selective guide that has a companion volume *Barron's Guide to the Most Prestigious Colleges* (1988). [378]

4720 Bauld, Harry. *On Writing the College Application Essay* (10–12). 1987, Barnes & Noble $14.95 (0-06-055076-7); paper $6.95 (0-06-463722-0). A straightforward often humorous guide to writing a successful admissions essay. (Rev: BL 9/1/87) [378]

4721 Beckham, Barry, ed. *The Black Student's Guide to Colleges* (10–12). 1982, Dutton $15.95 (0-525-93256-9); paper $8.95 (0-525-93257-7). Useful introductory chapters describe college life for black students. This is followed by a profile of 100 colleges. [378]

4722 Berger, Larry, et al. *Up Your Score: The Underground Guide to Psyching Out the SAT* (10–12). Illus. 1987, New Chapter Press paper $9.95 (0-942257-00-6). Three college students give practical tips on how to do better on SATs in a book laced with humor. (Rev: BL 12/1/87; BR 1–2/88) [378.16]

4723 Brownstein, Samuel C., and Mitchell Weiner. *Barron's Compact Guide to Colleges* (10–12). 1990, Barron's paper $5.95 (0-8120-4354-5). A useful concise guide that is an abridgement of the more extensive *Barron's Profiles of American Colleges* (1990). [378]

4724 Buckalew, M. W., and L. M. Hall. *Coping with Choosing a College* (10–12). 1990, Rosen LB $12.95 (0-8239-1079-2). Sound advice for the prospective college goer on how to make a wise academic choice. (Rev: BL 3/1/90; SLJ 12/90) [378]

4725 Caine, Clifford J. *How to Get into College: A Step-by-Step Manual* (10–12). 1985, Greene paper $10.95 (0-86616-046-9). A practical guide that even includes sample forms and letters to help the process of admission. (Rev: VOYA 12/85) [378]

4726 Collins, Robert F. *Reserve Officers Training Corps: Campus Pathways to Service Commissions* (10–12). Illus. 1986, Rosen $14.95 (0-8239-0695-7). A rundown on the ROTC programs administered on college campuses and of their content and selection processes. (Rev: BL 6/1/87; BR 3–4/87) [355]

4727 Curry, Boykin, and Brian Kasbar, eds. *Essays That Worked: 50 Essays from Successful Applications to the Nation's Top Colleges* (10–12). 1986, Mustang paper $7.95 (0-914457-14-4). A selection of admission essays that were considered superior with tips on how to write one for one's own college application. (Rev: BL 2/1/87; BR 3–4/88; SLJ 5/87; VOYA 2/87) [808]

4728 De Oliveira, Paulo, and Steve Cohen. *Getting In! The First Comprehensive Step-by-Step Strategy Guide to Acceptance at the College of Your Choice* (9–12). 1983, Workman paper $5.95 (0-89480-359-X). Beginning with students in the ninth grade and working through to campus visits and interviews, this is a complete guide to planning for successful college entrance. [378]

4729 Eberts, Marjorie, and Margaret Gisler. *How to Prepare for College* (9–12). 1990, VGM paper $7.95 (0-8442-6665-5). This account emphasizes such areas as the development of good study, speaking, and writing skills, plus how to define and reach goals. (Rev: BL 3/1/90; BR 5–6/90) [378]

4730 Edelstein, Scott. *College: A User's Manual* (10–12). 1985, Bantam paper $5.95 (0-553-34194-4). This is a practical guide to getting the most out of college for those already attending or about to register. (Rev: BL 10/1/85) [378]

4731 Ehrenhaft, George. *Write Your Way into College: Composing a Successful Application Essay* (10–12). 1987, Barron's paper $6.95 (0-8120-2997-6). A practical guide to writing essays for college admission. (Rev: BL 3/1/88; BR 5–6/88; SLJ 1/88; VOYA 4/88) [378]

4732 Farrar, Ronald T. *College 101* (10–12). 1988, Peterson's Guides paper $9.95 (0-87866-730-X). Using a question-and-answer format, this guide shows how to make your college years both profitable and pleasurable. [378]

4733 Fiske, Edward B., et al. *The Fiske Guide to Colleges* (9–12). Rev. ed. 1989, Times Books paper $11.95 (0-8129-1824-X). A guide to 300 colleges with ratings on academic programs, social life, and creature comforts. (Rev: BL 12/1/89) [378.73]

4734 Fiske, Edward B., et al. *How to Get into the Right College: The Secrets of the College Admissions Officers* (9–12). Illus. 1988, Times Books paper $7.95 (0-8129-1686-7). Based on 150 questionnaires sent to admission officers, here are tips on how to get admitted to the college of your choice. (Rev: BL 9/1/88; BR 5–6/89; SLJ 4/89; VOYA 6/89) [378]

4735 Fiske, Edward B., et al. *Selective Guide to Colleges* (10–12). 1987, Times Books paper

$10.95 (0-8129-1702-2). A guide to about 300 of the best colleges in the United States. (Rev: BL 3/1/88) [378]

4736 Fiske, Edward B., and Joseph M. Michalak. *The Best Buys in College Education* (9–12). 1985, Times Books paper $9.95 (0-8129-6345-8). A useful guide to colleges that offer quality education at affordable prices. (Rev: BL 10/1/85; SLJ 2/86) [378]

4737 Gardner, John, and A. Jerome Jewler, eds. *College Is Only the Beginning* (10–12). 1985, Wadsworth paper $12.25 (0-534-04275-9). A practical book that explains the college experience and prepares students for it. (Rev: BR 11–12/85) [378]

4738 Gelband, Scott, et al. *Your College Application* (9–12). Illus. 1986, College Entrance Examination Board paper $9.95 (0-87447-247-4). A broad discussion on the importance of the admission essay and how to master it by 3 former Harvard admission officers. (Rev: BL 3/1/87) [378]

4739 Georges, Christopher J., et al., eds. *100 Successful College Application Essays* (10–12). 1988, NAL paper $8.95 (0-452-26153-8). Sample essays are given on a variety of subjects plus an analysis of why each was considered good. (Rev: BL 12/15/88; SLJ 3/89; VOYA 2/89) [378]

4740 Greene, Howard, and Robert Minton. *Scaling the Ivy Wall* (10–12). 1987, Little paper $12.50 (0-316-32683-6). This book outlines 12 steps to ease the college admission process such as following a demanding curriculum in high school. (Rev: BR 1–2/88) [378]

4741 Hayden, Thomas C. *Peterson's Handbook for College Admissions: A Family Guide* (9–12). 3rd ed. 1989, Peterson's Guides paper $11.95 (0-87866-799-7). This is the third edition of a respected guide that covers such topics as visiting colleges, financial aid, and achievement tests. (Rev: BL 12/1/89) [378.1]

4742 Howard, Diane Wilder. *Swimming Upstream: A Complete Guide to the College Application Process for the Learning Disabled Student* (10–12). Illus. 1989, Hunt House paper $22.99 (0-9623524-0-3). A useful compendium of information and timesaving tips for the learning disabled who wish to get into college. (Rev: BL 3/1/90) [378.1]

4743 Jewler, A. Jerome, and John N. Gardner. *Step by Step to College Success* (10–12). 1987, Wadsworth paper $9.25 (0-534-07998-9). A book that concentrates on the development of the study skills necessary to succeed in college. (Rev: BL 6/1/87) [378]

4744 Kaye, Evelyn, and Janet Gardner. *College Bound* (10–12). 1988, College Board paper $9.95 (0-87447-304-7). In a casual manner, the authors tell how to get ready for college and how to function effectively when there. (Rev: BR 1–2/89; VOYA 2/89) [378]

4745 Killpatrick, Frances, and James Killpatrick. *The Winning Edge: A Complete Guide to Intercollegiate Athletic Programs* (9–12). 1989, Octameron paper $14.95 (0-945981-27-9). A guide to college programs in 35 sports and how to make the team. (Rev: BR 3/4/90) [796]

4746 Leana, Frank C. *Getting into College: A Guide for Students and Parents* (9–12). Rev. ed. 1990, Hill & Wang $17.95 (0-8090-4922-8); paper $8.95 (0-374-52242-1). The basics of looking for the right college are covered plus a thorough explanation of the application process. (Rev: BL 9/15/90) [378.1]

4747 Levin, Shirley. *Summer on Campus: College Experiences for High School Students* (10–12). Rev. ed. 1989, College Board Pub. paper $9.95 (0-87447-322-5). A total of 258 summer programs on U.S. college campuses are described with details of costs and admission requirements. (Rev: SLJ 10/89) [378]

4748 Lockerbie, D. Bruce, and Donald R. Fonseca. *College: Getting In and Staying In* (10–12). 1990, Eerdmans paper $11.95 (0-8028-0424-1). This book describes not only the admission process but also the many social, educational, and emotional changes necessary to make college life a success. (Rev: BL 9/15/90) [378.1]

4749 McGinty, Sarah. *Writing Your College Application Essay* (10–12). 1986, College Board paper $9.95 (0-87447-257-1). A step-by-step guide by a college admissions officer with sample essays included. (Rev: BL 2/1/87; BR 3–4/87) [378]

4750 McQuaid, E. Patrick, and Barbara Stahl. *How to Get into an Ivy League School* (10–12). 1985, Monarch paper $6.95 (0-671-52783-5). Profiles are given of 8 Ivy League schools plus tips on how to get into them. (Rev: VOYA 2/86) [378]

4751 Margolin, Judith B. *Financing a College Education: The Essential Guide for the 90's* (10–12). 1989, Plenum $20.95 (0-306-43071-1). A guide on how to find inexpensive quality schools and how to seek all kinds of financial aid. (Rev: BL 1/15/89) [378.38]

4752 Meiland, Jack W. *College Thinking: How to Get the Best Out of College* (10–12). 1981, NAL paper $4.95 (0-451-62655-9). Tips on how to get as much as possible from a college education by the Honors Program Director at the University of Michigan. [378]

4753 Nemko, Martin. *How to Get an Ivy League Education at a State University* (9–12). 1988, Avon paper $10.95 (0-380-75375-8). A guide to 115 public colleges judged to be the nation's best of this type. (Rev: BL 12/15/88) [378.73]

4754 Newman, Gerald, and Eleanor Weintraub Newman. *Writing Your College Admissions Essay* (10–12). Illus. 1987, Watts LB $11.90 (0-531-10428-1). Practical advice on how to organize and formulate the essay and how to write expressively and correctly. (Rev: BR 3–4/88; SLJ 1/88; VOYA 4/88) [378]

4755 Pope, Loren. *Looking beyond the Ivy League: Finding the College That's Right for You* (10–12). 1990, Penguin paper $7.95 (0-14-012209-5). An excellent beginning guide that tells the reader how to evaluate a college. (Rev: BL 3/1/90; SLJ 7/90) [378.1]

4756 Power, Helen W., and Robert DiAntonio. *The Admissions Essay: Stop Worrying and Start Writing* (10–12). 1987, Lyle Stuart paper $7.95 (0-8184-0436-1). A sound, practical guide on how to get started writing the college admissions essay. (Rev: BL 12/1/87; SLJ 11/87) [808]

4757 Reilly, Jill M., and Bonnie D. Featherstone. *College Comes Sooner Than You Think! The College Planning Guide for High School Students and Their Families* (9–12). 1987, Career Pr. paper $9.95 (0-934829-24-1). A guide that stresses a sequential preplanning process for college. (Rev: BL 6/1/88) [378.1056]

4758 Ripple, G. Gary. *Admit One! Your Guide to College Application* (10–12). Illus. 1987, Octameron paper $9.95 (0-917760-97-2). A college dean of admissions gives sound advice on getting into college. (Rev: BL 6/1/88; BR 3–4/88) [378.1058]

4759 Robertson, Adam, and John Katzman, eds. *The Princeton Review: College Admissions—Cracking the System* (10–12). 1987, Villard paper $5.95 (0-394-75189-2). How to crack even the toughest college admissions system by using some of these practical tips. (Rev: BL 12/1/87) [328]

4760 Rochester, Lois, and Judy Mandell. *The One Hour College Applicant: You Don't Need to Read a 300-Page Book to Apply to College!* (10–12). Illus. 1989, Mustang paper $8.95 (0-914457-31-4). A fast reading guide presented in outline form to applying for college admission. (Rev: BL 12/1/89; BR 1–2/90) [378.1]

4761 Roes, Nicholas A. *America's Lowest Cost Colleges* (9–12). 1989, NAR Productions paper

$9.95 (0-89780-010-9). Besides identifying hundreds of comparatively inexpensive 2- and 4-year colleges, the author discusses their facilities and programs. (Rev: BL 6/1/85) [378.73]

4762 Scheele, Adele. *Making College Pay Off* (10–12). 1983, Ballantine paper $3.50 (0-345-29837-3). A series of pointers and tips on how to productively utilize the college experience. [378]

4763 Schneider, Meg. *I Wonder What College Is Like?* (9–12). 1989, Messner LB $11.88 (0-671-65847-6); paper $5.98 (0-671-67815-9). In addition to material on the admission process, this book tells about campus life and how to earn a college degree. (Rev: SLJ 7/89; VOYA 12/89) [378]

4764 Schneider, Zola Dincin. *Campus Visits and College Interviews: A Complete Guide for College-Bound Students and Their Families* (10–12). 1987, College Entrance Examination Board paper $9.95 (0-87447-260-1). This book contains useful information and many checklists to prepare students for both visits and interviews at colleges they are investigating for possible admission. (Rev: BL 6/1/87; BR 5–6/87) [378.1]

4765 Solorzano, Lucia. *Barron's 300 Best Buys in College Education* (10–12). 1990, Barron's paper $12.95 (0-8120-4260-3). A guide to colleges where both quality education and reasonable tuition are found. (Rev: BL 12/15/90) [378]

4766 Sowell, Thomas. *Choosing a College: A Guide for Parents and Students* (9–12). 1989, Harper $17.95 (0-06-055151-8); paper $7.95 (0-06-096354-9). A practical guide that discusses various types of colleges, various types of students, and how to match them successfully. (Rev: BL 6/1/89) [378]

4767 Straughn, Charles T., and Marvelle S. Colby. *Lovejoy's College Guide for the Learning Disabled* (10–12). 1988, Simon & Schuster paper $12.95 (0-671-64717-2). A fine guide to colleges that accents students with learning disabilities. (Rev: BL 8/85) [378]

4768 Tweed, Prudence K., and Jason C. Tweed. *Colleges That Enable* (9–12). Illus. 1989, Park Avenue Pr. paper $10.95 (0-922466-12-2). A guide to 40 colleges that offer special services for the physically handicapped. (Rev: BL 12/1/89) [371.91]

4769 Ungar, Harlow G. *A Student's Guide to College Admissions: Everything Your Guidance Counselor Has No Time to Tell You* (10–12). 1986, Facts on File $19.95 (0-8160-1418-3); paper $9.95 (0-8160-1542-2). A practical guide that leads a student through each of the steps involved in college admissions. (Rev: BR 3–4/87; VOYA 2/87) [378]

4770 Utterback, Ann S. *College Admissions Face to Face* (10–12). 1989, Transemantics paper $9.95 (0-932020-72-0). This guide helps one prepare for campus visits and interviews. [378]

4771 Yale Daily News, eds. *The Insider's Guide to the Colleges: 1985–86 Edition* (10–12). 1989, St. Martin's paper $11.95 (0-312-02691-9). A refreshingly candid and often witty description of more than 200 colleges and universities from the students' point of view. (Rev: BL 8/85) [378.73]

4772 Zuker, R. Fred, and Karen Collier. *Peterson's Guide to College Admissions: Getting into the College of Your Choice* (10–12). Illus. 1987, Peterson's Guides paper $11.95 (0-87866-463-7). With profiles of more than 1,700 institutions, this guide also covers such topics as campus visits, interviews, and standardized tests. [378]

Financial Aid

4773 Blum, Laurie. *Free Money for College* (10–12). 1990, Facts on File $24.95 (0-8160-2313-1). A practical guide to funds available for undergraduates with emphasis on money from individual states. (Rev: BL 9/15/90) [378.3]

4774 Chandler, Lana J., and Michael Boggs. *The Student Loan Handbook* (10–12). Illus. 1988, Betterway paper $7.95 (0-932620-82-5). An explanation of the federally backed loans available to postsecondary school students. (Rev: BL 2/15/88; SLJ 3/88) [378]

4775 *The College Cost Book* (10–12). 1989, College Entrance Examination Board paper $13.95 (0-87467-338-1). In addition to accessing average college costs this book outlines many financial aid programs. [378]

4776 Dennis, Marguerite J. *Dollars for Scholars: Barron's Complete College Financing Guide* (9–12). 1989, Peterson's Guides paper $12.95 (0-8120-4155-0). A tabulation of educational costs today is given, plus a survey of the many different sources of financial aid available. (Rev: BL 12/1/89; VOYA 2/90) [378.3]

4777 Deutschman, Alan. *Winning Money for College* (10–12). 1987, Peterson's Guides paper $8.93 (0-87866-555-2). This guide, which is revised periodically, is a guide for high school students to many college scholarship contests. [378.3]

4778 Goeller, Priscilla S. *College Check Mate: Innovative Tuition Plans That Make You a Winner* (9–12). 1987, Octameron paper $4.50 (0-917760-94-8). A discussion of the various kinds of financing plans available to someone intent on college. (Rev: BL 6/1/88; BR 3–4/88) [378.38]

4779 Hawes, Gene R., and David M. Brownstone. *The College Money Book: How to Get a High-Quality Education at the Lowest Possible Cost* (10–12). 1984, Macmillan paper $12.95 (0-02-081040-7). This is an excellent guide to loan programs, scholarships, fellowships, and other forms of financial aid. [378]

4780 Leider, Robert. *Lovejoy's Guide to Financial Aid* (9–12). 1985, Monarch paper $9.95 (0-671-49714-6). This guide lists private and public sources of financial aid for college students, and gives points on how and when to apply. (Rev: BL 11/1/85) [378.3]

4781 Lyttle, Richard B., and Frank Farrara. *How to Pay for College or Trade School: A Dollars and Sense Guide* (9–12). 1985, Watts $11.90 (0-531-10070-7). A review of the different kinds of financial aid that are available to prospective college and trade school students. (Rev: BL 12/15/85; BR 5–6/86; SLJ 2/86; VOYA 4/86) [378.3]

Careers and Occupational Guidance

General and Miscellaneous

4782 Alexander, Sue. *Finding Your First Job* (10–12). Illus. 1980, Dutton $10.95 (0-525-29725-1). This manual for first-time job hunters covers such topics as selecting the right job, collecting proper documents, and behavior during an interview. [650.1]

4783 Amore, JoAnn, ed. *Exploring Careers* (9–12). Rev. ed. 1989, JIST $19.95 (0-942784-27-8). After a series of aptitude tests, this account describes over 300 jobs and tells what aptitudes are needed for each. (Rev: BL 3/1/90) [331.7]

4784 Beatty, Richard H. *The Resume Kit* (10–12). 1984, Wiley paper $9.95 (0-471-88148-1). With many examples, this book shows how to write various kinds of résumés for various situations. [650.1]

4785 Biegeleisen, J. I. *Job Resumes: How to Write Them, How to Present Them, Preparing for Interviews* (10–12). 1982, Putnam paper $5.95 (0-399-50822-8). This manual gives samples of résumés for more than 200 occupations. [331.1]

4786 Biegeleisen, J. I. *Make Your Job Interview a Success: A Guide for the Career-Minded Job-seeker* (10–12). Illus. 1984, Arco $11.95 (0-668-06016-6); paper $6.95 (0-668-05487-5). How to go through the interviewing process with success is the thrust of this helpful manual. [650.1]

4787 Bolles, Richard Nelson. *What Color Is Your Parachute?* (10–12). Illus. 1990, Ten Speed $16.95 (0-89815-318-2); paper $9.95 (0-89815-317-4). A new edition of the favorite book on retooling for new jobs. Though intended for adults, this has many valuable tips for teenagers. (Rev: SLJ 8/87) [331.1]

4788 Catalyst Staff, eds. *It's Your Future! Catalyst's Career Guide for High School Girls* (10–12). Illus. 1984, Peterson's Guides paper $9.95 (0-87866-280-4). A career guide specifically for girls that addresses their particular needs and concerns. [331.7]

4789 Cohen, Steve, and Paulo de Oliveira. *Getting to the Right Job: A Guide for College Graduates* (10–12). 1987, Workman paper $6.95 (0-89480-040-X). Though geared to an older audience, this account gives high school students much to think about in career planning. (Rev: SLJ 6–7/87) [650.1]

4790 Corwen, Leonard. *Your Job—Where to Find It, How to Get It* (10–12). 1981, Arco $11.95 (0-668-05129-9). From using classified ads to the interview this is a step-by-step guide to job hunting. [650.1]

4791 DuBrovin, Vivian. *Guide to Alternative Education and Training* (9–12). Illus. 1988, Watts $11.90 (0-531-10584-9). Various kinds of training programs including apprenticing are outlined. (Rev: BL 12/15/88; BR 1–2/89; SLJ 1/89; VOYA 4/89) [373.2]

4792 Elsman, Max. *How to Get Your First Job: A Field Guide for Beginners* (9–12). 1985, Crown paper $4.95 (0-517-55739-8). This guide for someone new on the labor market tells how to find out about jobs, fill out applications, and survive interviews as well as supplying many other tips. (Rev: BL 8/85; SLJ 9/85) [650.1]

4793 Figler, Howard. *The Complete Job-Search Handbook: All the Skills You Need to Get Any Job and Have a Good Time Doing It* (9–12). 1988, Henry Holt paper $11.70 (0-8050-0853-5). A practical confidence-inspiring book that offers sound solutions to many job-hunting problems. (Rev: BR 1–2/89; SLJ 11/88) [371.4]

4794 Fireside, Bryna J. *Choices: A Student Survival Guide for the 1990s* (9–12). 1989, Garrett Park paper $10.95 (0-912048-66-2). A guide to the many opportunities and options available for those who decide not to go to college. (Rev: BL 12/1/89; BR 3–4/90) [373.18]

4795 Franck, Irene M., and David M. Brownstone. *Restaurateurs & Innkeepers* (7–12). 1989, Facts on File $16.95 (0-8160-1451-5). This book contains a history of such occupations as cook, butcher, innkeeper and prostitute from ancient Greece and China to today's world. (Rev: BL 3/15/89; BR 9–10/89) [647]

4796 Fry, Ronald. *Your 1st Résumé* (10–12). 1988, Career Pr. paper $9.95 (0-934829-25-X). All the steps in writing a successful résumé from collecting appropriate material to final presentation are detailed with many examples. (Rev: BR 11–12/89) [331.1]

4797 Johnson, Barbara L. *Careers in Beauty Culture* (8–12). Illus. 1989, Rosen $10.95 (0-8239-1002-4). A career guide that discusses such topics as the beauty culture field, opportunities, preparation, working conditions, and how to advance. (Rev: BL 6/1/89; BR 9–10/89; SLJ 7/89; VOYA 10/89) [646.7]

4798 Kennedy, Joyce Lain, and Darryl Laramore. *Joyce Lain Kennedy's Career Book* (9–12). 1988, VGM $14.95 (0-8442-6680-9). Career choices and career planning are covered in this book aimed at both college-bound and noncollege-bound students. (Rev: VOYA 4/89) [371.4]

4799 Lee, Rose P. *A Real Job for You: An Employment Guide for Teens* (9–12). Illus. 1985, Betterway paper $7.95 (0-932620-45-0). This is a thorough account that covers all the basics from getting a Social Security card to getting through the interview. (Rev: BL 10/1/85; SLJ 10/85) [650.1]

4800 Lott, Catherine S., and Oscar C. Lott. *How to Land a Better Job* (10–12). Illus. 1989, VGM $7.95 (0-8442-6675-2). This volume tries to remove obstacles for the first-time job hunter. (Rev: VOYA 10/89) [371.4]

4801 Males, Carolyn, and Roberta Feigen. *Life after High School: A Career Planning Guide* (9–12). 1986, Messner $11.29 (0-671-54664-3). A commonsense guide to determining and achieving career goals after high school. (Rev: BL 9/1/86; SLJ 8/86) [331.7]

4802 Marek, Rosanne J. *Opportunities in Social Science Careers* (9–12). Illus. 1989, VGM $11.95

(0-8442-8667-2); paper $8.95 (0-8442-8668-0). Careers in all of the social sciences, for example, history, economics, geography, and sociology, are included with job descriptions and information on opportunities and working conditions. (Rev: BL 9/15/89) [300]

4803 Marks, Edith, and Adele Lewis. *Job Hunting for the Disabled* (10–12). 1983, Barron's paper $9.95 (0-8120-2487-7). In addition to standard information on job hunting this guide gives specific advice on overcoming physical barriers. [650.1]

4804 Mitchell, Joyce Slayton. *The College Board Guide to Jobs and Career Planning* (10–12). 1990, College Board paper $12.95 (0-87447-354-3). Though written for college students, this is also a valuable guide for senior high students to major career options currently available, some of which do not require higher education. (Rev: BL 11/1/90) [331.702]

4805 Mitchell, Joyce Slayton. *Stopout! Working Ways to Learn* (10–12). 1978, Garrett paper $8.95 (0-912048-18-2). This book points out how internship and volunteerism can help determine final career goals. [371.4]

4806 Myers, James, and Elizabeth Warner Scott. *Getting Skilled, Getting Ahead* (8–12). 1989, Peterson's paper $5.95 (0-87866-868-3). This book tells the reader how to choose a career that requires occupational training and how to find a private career school after high school. (Rev: BR 3–4/90) [371.4]

4807 Roesch, Roberta. *You Can Make It Without a College Degree* (10–12). Illus. 1986, Prentice $17.95 (0-13-976820-3); paper $8.95 (0-13-976812-2). This guide explains how to improve your skills and promote yourself in the job market without a college degree. (Rev: BL 6/1/86) [650.1]

4808 Segalini, Judith, and Katherine Kurtz. *The One Day Plan for Jobhunters* (10–12). 1988, Prakken paper $9.95 (0-911168-72-9). Although written for adults, this book has many good tips for teens who are looking for jobs. (Rev: BR 1–2/89) [331.1]

4809 Shanahan, William F. *College—Yes or No* (10–12). 2nd ed. 1983, Arco paper $7.95. The alternatives to college such as vocational schools, apprenticeship programs, and the armed forces are explored. [331.7]

4810 Shanahan, William F. *Guide to Apprenticeship Programs* (10–12). 1983, Arco LB $12.95 (0-668-05454-9). Apprenticeship programs in general are discussed and specific details are given on 125 of them. [331.5]

4811 Snelling, Robert O. *The Right Job* (9–12). 1987, Penguin paper $8.95 (0-14-009625-6). A practical guide to job hunting with coverage on such topics as résumés, interviews, and finding out what is the right job for you. (Rev: BL 3/15/87;) [650.1]

4812 Wagmann, Robert, and Robert Chapman. *The Right Place at the Right Time: Finding the Right Job in the New Economy* (10–12). 1987, Ten Speed paper $9.95 (0-89815-175-9). Sound advice on topics such as assessing skills and interests and how to conduct an effective, well-organized job search. (Rev: SLJ 2/88) [331.1]

4813 Wright, John W. *The American Almanac of Jobs and Salaries* (10–12). 1987, Avon $13.95 (0-380-75307-3). This periodically revised work lists and describes hundreds of jobs and gives salaries and employment advice for each. (Rev: SLJ 6–7/87) [371.4]

Careers

General and Miscellaneous

4814 Abrams, Kathleen S. *Guide to Careers without College* (9–12). Illus. 1988, Watts $11.90 (0-531-10585-7). A guide to the many occupations like selling and factory work that do not require a college education. (Rev: BL 12/15/88; BR 1–2/89; SLJ 1/89; VOYA 4/89) [331.7]

4815 Amore, JoAnn, ed. *America's Top 300 Jobs* (9–12). Illus. 1989, JIST paper $17.76 (0-942784-26-X). A description of the jobs in which over 90 percent of Americans are employed, with information on working conditions, necessary preparation, and the outlook for the future. (Rev: BL 12/1/89) [331.7]

4816 Arnold, Edwin, and Theodore Huebener. *Opportunities in Foreign Language Careers* (9–12). 1986, VGM $14.95 (0-8442-6202-X); paper $11.95 (0-8442-6204-8). A wide variety of careers including translating and teaching are described. (Rev: BR 9–10/86) [418]

4817 Baxter, Neale. *Opportunities in Federal Government Careers* (9–12). Illus. 1985, VGM $12.95 (0-8442-6207-2); paper $7.95 (0-8442-6208-0). The federal government employs more people than any other agency in the country. This is a guide to the thousands of different jobs that are available. (Rev: BL 5/15/85; VOYA 2/86) [351]

4818 Baxter, Neale. *Opportunities in State and Local Government* (9–12). Illus. 1985, VGM

$12.95 (0-8442-6193-9); paper $9.95 (0-8442-6194-7). The available positions in civil service are outlined, together with the necessary qualifications. (Rev: BR 11–12/85) [351.1]

4819 Bishop, John. *Making It in Video* (9–12). Illus. 1988, McGraw paper $12.95 (0-07-005468-1). Careers in all kinds of television—for example, cable, commercial, and educational—are discussed, plus opportunities in various other areas using video, such as industry and education. (Rev: BL 12/15/88) [384]

4820 Blake, Gary, and Robert W. Bly. *Creative Careers: Jobs in Glamour Fields* (10–12). 1985, Wiley paper $14.95 (0-471-81560-8). This guide covers such areas as publishing, show business, advertising, travel, and the media. (Rev: BL 6/15/85) [371.4]

4821 Blake, Gary, and Robert W. Bly. *Dream Jobs: A Guide to Tomorrow's Top Careers* (10–12). 1983, Wiley paper $8.95 (0-471-89204-1). Nine of the hottest areas for job hunting from advertising to telecommunications are described. [371.4]

4822 Bloch, Deborah Perlmutter. *How to Get and Get Ahead on Your First Job* (9–12). Illus. 1988, VGM paper $6.95 (0-8442-6691-4). This book gives not only hundreds of practical tips on how to get a good job but also material on how to keep it. (Rev: VOYA 6/89) [371.4]

4823 *Career Choices for Students of Communication and Journalism* (9–12). 1990, Walker paper $7.95 (0-8027-7326-5). The broad field of communication is surveyed in light of the kinds of jobs available with a concentration on the variety of branches of journalism. (Rev: BL 6/1/90) [302.2]

4824 Cassidy, William Bennett. *How to Get into U.S. Service Academies* (10–12). Illus. 1987, Prentice paper $7.95 (0-688-06596-6). A practical guide on how to gain entrance to West Point, the Naval Academy, and so on. (Rev: BL 9/1/87) [355]

4825 Catalyst Staff, eds. *What to Do with the Rest of Your Life* (10–12). 1981, Simon & Schuster paper $13.95 (0-671-25071-X). This guide is specifically aimed at young women entering the job market. [371.4]

4826 Cetron, Marvin, and Marcia Appel. *Jobs of the Future: The 500 Best Jobs—Where They'll Be and How to Get Them* (10–12). 1985, McGraw paper $6.95 (0-07-010352-6). A description of jobs, many in high tech, that the authors think will be in demand in the future. [331.7]

4827 Chmelynski, Carol Ann. *Opportunities in Restaurant Careers* (9–12). 1990, VGM $11.95 (0-8442-8662-1); paper $8.95 (0-8442-8664-8).

From fast food to haute cuisine, here is a description of a variety of restaurant-related jobs from beginning level to owning one's own eatery. (Rev: BL 12/1/89; BR 5–6/90) [647]

4828 Denny, Jon S. *Careers in Cable TV* (10–12). 1984, Harper paper $7.95 (0-06-463588-0). This career guide covers all aspects of local cable programming. [385.55]

4829 Dolber, Roslyn. *Opportunities in Fashion Careers* (9–12). Illus. 1986, VGM $10.95 (0-8442-6156-4); paper $7.95 (0-8442-6157-2). A discussion of jobs involving design, production, and merchandising fashion. (Rev: BL 12/1/86) [746]

4830 Donovan, Mary Deirdre. *Opportunities in Culinary Careers* (9–12). 1990, VGM $12.95 (0-8442-8619-2); paper $9.95 (0-8442-8620-6). This career guide lists all kinds of jobs in the food preparation area with details on training required, working conditions, and benefits. (Rev: BL 9/15/90) [647.95]

4831 Edwards, E. W. *Exploring Careers Using Foreign Languages* (9–12). 1986, Rosen LB $10.95 (0-8239-0968-9). The author describes careers using foreign languages, such as translation, business, tourism, and teaching. (Rev: BL 1/15/87; BR 3–4/87; SLJ 10/87) [371.4]

4832 Folse, Nancy McCarthy, and Marilyn Henrion. *Careers in the Fashion Industry* (10–12). 1981, Harper paper $7.95 (0-06-463510-4). This career guide to all aspects of the fashion industry was written by 2 counselors at the Fashion Institute of Technology. [391]

4833 Foote-Smith, Elizabeth. *Opportunities in Writing Careers* (9–12). 1988, VGM $12.95 (0-8442-6512-8); paper $9.95 (0-8442-6513-6). Working conditions are described plus necessary qualifications are given for a wide variety of jobs requiring writing skills. (Rev: BR 5–6/89; VOYA 4/89) [411]

4834 Fowler, Elizabeth. *The New York Times Career Planner* (10–12). Illus. 1987, Times Books paper $9.95 (0-8129-1212-8). A guide for students on how to plan for a career plus a listing of 101 job possibilities that will be in demand in the future. (Rev: SLJ 5/88) [371.4]

4835 Gearhart, Susan Wood. *Opportunities in Beauty Culture Careers* (9–12). 1988, VGM $12.95 (0-8442-6518-7); paper $9.95 (0-8442-6519-5). The entire beauty culture industry is first surveyed and then information on specific jobs within it is given. (Rev: BR 5–6/89; VOYA 6/89) [646.7]

4836 Griffith, Susan. *Work Your Way around the World* (10–12). Illus. 1989, Vacation Work paper $12.95 (0-907638-99-6). A practical guide on how to combine travel and working with tips on border formalities and suggestions for job opportunities. (Rev: SLJ 10.87) [331]

4837 Haldane, Bernard, et al. *The New Young Peoples' Job Power Now* (10–12). 1980, Acropolis $10.95 (0-87419-608-9). This book on occupational guidance is aimed at the older teen. [371.4]

4838 Hardigree, Peggy Ann. *Working Outside: A Career and Self-Employment Handbook* (10–12). 1980, Crown paper $1.98 (0-517-54008-8). For those who love the outdoors, here is a guide to over 100 jobs that involve primarily being outside. [371.4]

4839 Hawes, Gene R., and Douglass L. Brownstone. *The Outdoor Careers Guide* (9–12). 1986, Facts on File $18.95 (0-8160-1021-8); paper $9.95 (0-8160-1023-4). From tennis pro to marine biologist, here is a rundown on more than 50 careers in the outdoors. (Rev: BL 10/15/86; BR 11–12/86) [331.7]

4840 Henkin, Shepard. *Opportunities in Hotel and Motel Management* (9–12). Illus. 1985, VGM $10.95 (0-8442-6179-3). Covers the history of hotel work and enumerates each different career. (Rev: BR 11–12/85) [647]

4841 Jensen, Clayne R., and Jay H. Nayler. *Opportunities in Recreation and Leisure* (10–12). 1983, VGM $12.95 (0-8442-8585-4); paper $9.95 (0-8442-8586-2). From summer camps to fitness centers, this guide gives a thorough rundown on the types of jobs in recreation-related areas. [371.4]

4842 Johnson, Bervin, et al. *Opportunities in Photography Careers* (9–12). Illus. 1985, VGM $10.95 (0-8442-6180-7); paper $7.95 (0-8442-6181-5). As well as material on preparation for the field and a survey of the profession, the authors describe specific careers in specialized areas like industrial, scientific, and commercial photography. (Rev: BL 10/1/85; BR 11–12/85) [770.232]

4843 Jones, Ilene. *Jobs for Teenagers* (9–12). 1987, Ballantine paper $2.95 (0-345-35153-3). A step-by-step guide to securing a job and knowing how to keep it. [371.4]

4844 Krannich, Ronald L., and Caryl Rae Krannich. *The Complete Guide to Public Employment* (10–12). Illus. 1990, Impact paper $15.95 (0-942710-23-1). In addition to local, state, and federal government jobs, this guide covers such areas as associations, foundations, nonprofit organizations, and consulting firms. (Rev: BL 6/1/86) [331.119]

4845 Lee, Mary Price, and Richard S. Lee. *Opportunities in Animal and Pet Care* (10–12). 1987,

VGM $12.95 (0-8442-6244-7); paper $9.95 (0-8442-6245-5). This guide describes the many kinds of jobs available for those who wish to work with animals. [636]

4846 Lee, Richard S., and Mary Price Lee. *Careers in the Restaurant Industry* (10–12). Illus. 1988, Rosen $9.97 (0-8239-0749-X). Areas covered include jobs in restaurants, franchises, and catering. (Rev: BL 6/1/88; SLJ 1/89; VOYA 10/88) [642]

4847 Levinson, Jay Conrad. *Five Hundred Fifty-Five Ways to Earn Extra Money* (10–12). 1981, Henry Holt paper $9.95 (0-03-058671-2). Though written for adults, this guide to part-time jobs gives many tips suitable for teenagers. [371.4]

4848 Lewis, William, and Nancy Schuman. *Fast-Track Careers: A Guide to the Highest-Paying Jobs* (10–12). 1987, Wiley paper $14.95 (0-471-83801-2). A guide to high-pressure jobs in such areas as finance, real estate, the media, advertising, and sales. (Rev: SLJ 12/87) [331.1]

4849 McKay, Robert. *Opportunities in Your Own Service Business* (9–12). Illus. 1984, VGM $12.95 (0-8442-6231-5); paper $9.95 (0-8442-6232-3). A guide to small business ownership, plus how to get backing and pitfalls to avoid. (Rev: BL 6/1/85; BR 5–6/85) [650]

4850 McMillon, Bill. *Volunteer Vacations* (10–12). Illus. 1989, Chicago Review Pr. paper $11.95 (1-55652-051-4). This book contains an alphabetical listing of international service organizations and the opportunities they offer volunteers. (Rev: SLJ 10/89) [361]

4851 Martin, Molly, ed. *Hard-Hatted Women: Stories of Struggle and Success in the Trades* (10–12). 1988, Seal Pr. paper $10.95 (0-931188-66-0). Twenty-seven women from such fields as welding, mining, and carpentry tell their stories. (Rev: BL 11/15/88) [331.4]

4852 Milne, Robert Scott. *Opportunities in Travel Careers* (9–12). 1985, VGM $12.95 (0-8442-6215-3); paper $9.95 (0-8442-6216-1). A variety of jobs are discussed involving ships, airlines, travel agencies, buses, and hotels and motels. (Rev: BL 5/1/85; VOYA 8/85) [910.2]

4853 Munday, Marianne F. *Opportunities in Crafts Careers* (9–12). 1987, VGM paper $7.95 (0-8442-6017-2). Though somewhat specialized in scope, careers available to those proficient in a craft have an amazing number of job options. (Rev: BR 5–6/88) [745]

4854 Nelson, Cordner. *Careers in Pro Sports* (9–12). 1990, Rosen $12.95 (0-8239-1027-X). In addition to a discussion of the pros and cons of working in professional sports, the author talks

about qualifications for both playing and non-playing jobs. (Rev: BL 3/1/90; BR 3–4/90; SLJ 3/90; VOYA 4/90) [896]

4855 Neufeld, Rose. *Exploring Nontraditional Jobs for Women* (9–12). Illus. 1987, Rosen $9.97 (0-8239-0698-1). A review of jobs, traditionally held by men, where women should now also be entering. (Rev: BL 12/1/87; BR 1–2/88; SLJ 3/88) [331]

4856 *Newspapers Career Directory* (10–12). 1987, Career Pr. $34.95 (0-934829-21-7); paper $26.95 (0-934829-15-2). Many successful practitioners in the field describe their careers and additional information is given on contacts and opportunities in the field. (Rev: BL 5/15/87) [070]

4857 Paradis, Adrian. *Opportunities in Airline Careers* (9–12). Illus. 1986, VGM $12.95 (0-8442-6028-2); paper $9.95 (0-8442-6029-0). Careers both on the ground and in the air are outlined including air traffic controllers. (Rev: BL 6/1/87) [387.7]

4858 Paradis, Adrian. *Opportunities in Military Careers* (9–12). 1989, VGM paper $8.95 (0-8442-8649-4). The wide span of careers in the armed forces are described plus the advantages and disadvantages of life in the services. (Rev: BR 3–4/90; VOYA 12/89) [355.2]

4859 Paradis, Adrian. *Opportunities in Transportation Careers* (10–12). 1988, VGM $12.95 (0-8442-6567-5); paper $9.95 (0-8442-6568-3). This thorough account gives details on all sorts of jobs involving land, sea, and air transport. (Rev: BR 5–6/88) [910.2]

4860 Patten, Jim, and Donald Ferguson. *Opportunities in Journalism Careers* (9–12). 1989, VGM $11.95 (0-8442-8660-5); paper $8.95 (0-8442-8661-3). A history of journalism is given plus a rundown on the variety of jobs available today, qualifications necessary, and working conditions. (Rev: BR 3–4/90) [070]

4861 Perez, Dennis D. *The Enlisted Soldier's Guide* (10–12). Illus. 1986, Stackpole paper $12.95 (0-8117-2042-X). An informative guide to army life from the enlistee's point of view. (Rev: BL 6/1/87) [335]

4862 Roberson, Virginia Lee. *Careers in the Graphic Arts* (9–12). 1988, Rosen $10.95 (0-8239-0803-8). Careers involving illustration, paste-up work, layout, art, and design are described with details on job opportunities, qualifications, and working conditions. (Rev: BL 12/15/88; BR 9–10/89; VOYA 6/89) [760]

4863 Russo, Jo Ann Oritt. *Careers without College: No B.S. Necessary* (9–12). 1986, Betterway paper $7.95 (0-932620-60-4). This is a guide to 10 different careers such as restaurant management, banking, and data processing that do not require college degrees. (Rev: BL 8/86) [331.7]

4864 Sacharov, Al. *Offbeat Careers* (10–12). 1988, Ten Speed paper $6.95 (0-89815-240-2). Eighty-eight unusual careers such as becoming a symphony conductor or a belly dancer are described. (Rev: BL 6/15/88; SLJ 6–7/88) [371.4]

4865 Schefter, James L. *Telecommunications Careers* (9–12). Illus. 1988, Watts $11.90 (0-531-10426-5). An overview of careers in various fields involved with communications. (Rev: BL 6/1/88; BR 9–10/88; SLJ 5/88; VOYA 10/88) [384]

4866 Schneider, Dorothy, and Carl Schneider. *Sound Off! American Military Women Speak Out* (10–12). 1988, Dutton $18.95 (0-525-24589-8). A review based on over 300 interviews of the place of women in the armed forces. (Rev: BL 1/1/88; VOYA 8/88) [355.22]

4867 Schwartz, Lester, and Irv Brechner. *Career Finder* (10–12). 1986, Ballantine paper $9.95 (0-345-33679-8). This is a quick guide to over 1,500 careers that supplies basic information and details on opportunities. [371.4]

4868 Shields, Rhea, and Anna Williams. *Opportunities in Home Economics Careers* (9–12). 1987, VGM paper $7.95 (0-8442-6347-8). Salaries, preparation needed, and future prospects are 3 of the topics covered in this account of jobs in the home economics field. (Rev: BR 5–6/88) [640]

4869 Slappey, Mary McGowan. *Exploring Military Service for Women* (9–12). Illus. 1986, Rosen $14.95 (0-8239-0693-0). This book outlines all the military programs available for women. (Rev: BL 6/1/87; BR 3–4/87; SLJ 2/87) [355]

4870 Snelling, Robert O., and Anne M. Snelling. *Jobs! What They Are . . . Where They Are . . . What They Pay* (9–12). Rev. ed. 1989, Simon & Schuster $11.95 (0-671-50246-8). A variety of jobs in the professions, business, technology, and health-related areas are introduced with material on training necessary, work conditions, pay, and so on. (Rev: BL 3/15/89) [331.7]

4871 Weinstein, Bob. *Breaking into Communications* (9–12). Illus. 1984, Arco $12.95 (0-688-05947-8); paper $7.95 (0-668-05951-6). A guide to a variety of jobs in such areas as radio, television, and newspapers. (Rev: BL 4/15/85) [001.51]

4872 White, William C., and Donald N. Collins. *Opportunities in Agriculture Careers* (10–12). Illus. 1987, VGM $9.95 (0-8442-6554-3); paper $7.95 (0-8442-6555-1). A guide that covers standard careers plus related ones in transportation, research, and so on. (Rev: BL 6/1/88; BR 5–6/88) [630.203]

Artists and Entertainers

4873 Anderson, Marie Philomene. *Model: The Complete Guide to Becoming a Professional Model* (9–12). Illus. 1989, Doubleday paper $17.95 (0-385-26020-2). A guide to the would-be model plus chapters on such subjects as skin care, nutrition, and exercise. (Rev: BL 7/89) [659.1]

4874 Blanksteen, Jane, and Avi Odeni. *TV Careers Behind the Screen* (10–12). 1987, Wiley paper $12.95 (0-471-84815-8). From "gofers" to producers and in between, this is a guide to careers in television. (Rev: BL 9/1/87; SLJ 10/87) [791.45]

4875 Brandstein, Eve, and Joanna Lipari. *The Actor: A Practical Guide to a Professional Career* (9–12). 1987, Donald I. Fine paper $9.95 (1-55611-003-0). The authors give sound advice for someone who wishes to devote his or her life to acting. (Rev: BL 6/15/87) [792]

4876 *Career Choices for Students of Art* (9–12). 1990, Walker paper $7.95 (0-8027-7324-9). Part of a series, this volume provides current information of the many careers available for art majors. (Rev: BL 6/1/90) [702]

4877 Dearing, James. *Making Money Making Music (No Matter Where You Live)* (10–12). Illus. 1990, Writer's Digest paper $17.95 (0-89879-414-5). A guide to making money from a career in music that emphasizes opportunities at the local level. [780.42]

4878 Field, Shelly. *Career Opportunities in the Music Industry* (9–12). 1986, Facts on File $24.95 (0-8160-1126-5); paper $12.95 (0-8160-1535-X). A guide to 79 jobs in the industry with information on each. (Rev: BR 11–12/86) [780]

4879 Fridell, Squire. *Acting in Television Commercials for Fun and Profit* (9–12). Illus. 1987, Harmony $10.95 (0-517-56424-6). A thorough guide that includes writing a résumé, getting an agent, and the process of shooting a commercial. (Rev: SLJ 10/87) [791.092]

4880 Gearhart, Susan Wood. *Opportunities in Modeling Careers* (10–12). 1987, VGM $12.95 (0-8442-6236-6); paper $9.95 (0-8442-6237-4). A realistic look at what is often considered a glamorous occupation. [659.1]

4881 Gibson, James. *How to Make More in Music: A Freelance Guide* (10–12). 1984, Workbooks Pr. paper $9.95 (0-915849-00-3). Ways to make money through music. [780]

4882 Gibson, James. *Playing for Pay: How to Be a Working Musician* (9–12). 1990, Writer's Digest paper $17.95 (0-89879-403-X). A survey of the free-lance music scene—the jobs it offers and how to get them. (Rev: SLJ 8/90) [780.92]

4883 Gilbert, George. *The Complete Photography Career Handbook* (10–12). 1982, Dutton $15.95 (0-525-93238-0); paper $7.95 (0-525-93237-2). Approximately 50 career opportunities are described. [770]

4884 Gordon, Barbara, and Elliot Gordon. *Opportunities in Commercial Art and Graphic Design* (9–12). 1985, VGM $12.95 (0-8442-6293-3); paper $7.95 (0-8442-6294-3). Over 50 careers are highlighted plus background information on topics such as choosing an art school, job opportunities, and working conditions. (Rev: VOYA 2/86) [741.6]

4885 Hallstead, William F. *Broadcasting Careers for You* (9–12). 1983, Lodestar $11.95 (0-525-66767-9). A quick overview of many careers in broadcasting with material on the qualities and skills required. [384.5]

4886 Haubenstock, Susan H., and David Joselit. *Career Opportunities in Art* (9–12). 1988, Facts on File $24.95 (0-8160-1398-5). Descriptions of 75 jobs are given, from commercial art to museum administration. (Rev: BL 9/1/88; BR 1–2/89; SLJ 8/88) [702.3]

4887 Henry, Mari Lyn, and Lynne Rogers. *How to Be a Working Actor* (9–12). Illus. 1986, Evans $17.95 (0-87131-473-8). A handy, practical guide that covers such topics as how to audition, how to prepare résumés, and the types and locations of various kinds of work. (Rev: BL 6/1/86) [792]

4888 Horwin, Michael. *Careers in Film and Video Production* (10–12). Illus. 1989, Focal Press $17.95 (0-240-80049-4). An interesting presentation of the jobs available to newcomers in these fields. (Rev: BL 3/1/90) [791.43]

4889 Ito, Dee. *The School of Visual Arts Guide to Careers* (10–12). 1987, McGraw $24.95 (0-07-032117-5); paper $12.95 (0-07-032057-8). A solid career guide based on interviews with 26 people whose occupations are in the visual arts. (Rev: BL 12/1/87) [700]

4890 Laslo, Cynthia. *The Rosen Photo Guide to a Career in the Circus* (8–12). Illus. 1988, Rosen $10.95 (0-8239-0819-4). A thorough guide to all kinds of careers as performers and behind-the-scenes involvement in the circus. (Rev: BL 12/15/88) [791.3]

4891 London, Mel. *Getting into Film* (10–12). 1980, Ballantine paper $9.95 (0-345-28977-3). This book answers all kinds of questions about jobs in the film industry. [791.43]

4892 Lydon, Michael. *How to Succeed in Show Business by Really Trying* (9–12). Illus. 1985, Dodd $18.95 (0-396-08542-3). By using real life anecdotes, the author introduces material on the preparation advisable for a show business career and gives many tips on how to get started. (Rev: BL 7/85; SLJ 11/85; VOYA 2/86) [790.2]

4893 Moore, Dick. *Opportunities in Acting Careers* (9–12). 1985, VGM $12.95 (0-8442-6229-3); paper $7.95 (0-8442-6230-7). This account discusses topics such as where to find acting jobs, the role of unions, the importance of agents, and the average salaries of actors. (Rev: BL 5/1/85; VOYA 8/85) [791.4]

4894 Muench, Teri, and Susan Pomerantz. *Attn: A & R: A Step-by-Step Guide into the Recording Industry* (10–12). Illus. 1988, Alfred Publg. $14.95 (0-88284-361-3). A practical guide on how to break into the music business with many useful lists of people and addresses. (Rev: BL 6/15/88) [789.9]

4895 Pearlman, Donn. *Breaking into Broadcasting: Getting to a Good Job that Leads to the Top* (9–12). 1986, Bonus Books $15.95 (0-933893-16-7). A practical guide to many careers in radio and television broadcasting such as reporters, disk jockeys, news writers, and anchors. (Rev: BL 8/86) [791.44]

4896 Reisfeld, Randi. *So You Want to Be a Star: A Teenager's Guide to Breaking into Show Business* (7–12). Illus. 1990, Pocket paper $2.95 (0-671-70192-4). A practical guide to getting into show business that stresses talent, persistence, and luck. (Rev: BL 9/15/90) [791]

4897 Sanders, Toby. *How to Be a Compleat Clown* (10–12). Illus. 1978, Stein & Day $9.95 (0-8128-2508-X); paper $7.95 (0-8128-6090-X). This book explains how to become a clown, either as a fulfilling hobby or as a career. [791.3]

4898 Seuling, Barbara. *How to Write a Children's Book and Get It Published* (10–12). 1986, Macmillan paper $12.95 (0-684-18709-4). A step-by-step guide to writing children's books with practical tips on how to get one's efforts published. [411]

4899 Sumichrast, Michael. *Opportunities in Building Construction Trades* (9–12). 1989,

VGM $11.95 (0-8442-8633-8); paper $8.95 (0-8442-8634-6). This book is about the general aspects of this field, how to enter it, and the training and experience necessary. (Rev: BR 3–4/90) [690]

4900 Suzanne, Claudia, et al. *For Musicians Only* (9–12). 1988, Billboard paper $14.95 (0-8230-7548-6). A guide for those who would like to enter the pop music field as either instrumentalists or singers. (Rev: BL 9/1/88) [780.42]

4901 Teel, Leonard Ray, and Ron Taylor. *Into the Newsroom: An Introduction to Journalism* (9–12). 2nd ed. 1988, Globe $10.95 (0-87106-670-X). An enjoyable introduction to the world of reporting and newspaper production. [070]

4902 Williams, Randall. *The Rosen Photo Guide to a Career in Magic* (8–12). Illus. 1988, Rosen $10.95 (0-8239-0817-8). Written by a magician, this is a guide to getting started in this career, plus background information on equipment and organization. (Rev: BL 12/15/88) [792.8]

Business Careers

4903 Abbott, Marguerite, et al. *Opportunities in Occupational Therapy Careers* (9–12). 1987, VGM paper $7.95 (0-8442-6562-4). This book discusses the many areas where there is a need for occupational therapists and the working conditions in each of these areas. (Rev: BR 5–6/88) [615.8]

4904 Arpan, Jeffrey. *Opportunities in International Business Careers* (9–12). 1988, VGM $12.95 (0-8442-6516-0); paper $9.95 (0-8442-6517-9). The field of international business is introduced with the many specialized jobs this involves and how to prepare for them. (Rev: BL 3/1/89; BR 5–6/89; VOYA 6/89) [650]

4905 Banning, Kent. *Opportunities in Purchasing Careers* (9–12). 1990, VGM $11.95 (0-8442-8669-9); paper $8.95 (0-8442-8670-2). Various kinds of purchasing careers are described with a history of purchasing that describes its present-day importance. (Rev: BR 5–6/90) [650]

4906 *Career Choices for Students of Business* (9–12). 1990, Walker paper $7.95 (0-8027-7325-7). The field of business and the many kinds of careers it offers are surveyed. (Rev: BL 6/1/90) [650]

4907 *Career Choices for Students of Economics* (9–12). 1990, Walker paper $7.95 (0-8027-7328-1). A guide to careers in economics and the more theoretical aspects of business. (Rev: BL 6/1/90) [330]

4908 *Career Choices for Students of M.B.A.* (9–12). 1990, Walker paper $7.95 (0-8027-7336-2). The field of business administration is surveyed and the many jobs related to it. (Rev: BL 6/1/90) [650]

4909 Dolber, Roslyn. *Opportunities in Retailing Careers* (9–12). 1988, VGM $12.95 (0-8442-6520-9); paper $9.95 (0-8442-6521-7). From beginning clerk to manager and owner, the specializations in retailing are well introduced. (Rev: BL 3/1/89; BR 5–6/89; VOYA 6/89) [658.8]

4910 Epstein, Lawrence. *Careers in Computer Sales* (9–12). 1990, Rosen $11.95 (0-8239-0667-1). A history of computers plus a description of the hardware and software and how to get into the business of selling them. (Rev: VOYA 8/90) [001.64]

4911 Epstein, Rachel. *Careers in the Investment World* (10–12). Illus. 1987, Chelsea House $9.95 (1-55546-631-1). A basic career guide to the various positions in the investment section. (Rev: BL 3/1/88) [332.6]

4912 Ettinger, Blanche, and Estelle L. Popham. *Opportunities in Office Occupations* (10–12). 1988, VGM $12.95 (0-8442-6149-1); paper $9.95 (0-8442-6150-5). A variety of office-related jobs are described plus information on opportunities and compensation. (Rev: BR 5–6/89) [371.7]

4913 Evans, Marilyn. *Opportunities in Property Management Careers* (9–12). 1990, VGM $11.95 (0-8442-8630-0); paper $8.95 (0-8442-8631-1). The latest developments in real estate work are discussed and the variety of jobs these entail. (Rev: BR 5–6/90) [333.3]

4914 Field, Shelly. *Career Opportunities in Advertising & Public Relations* (10–12). 1990, Facts on File $29.95 (0-8160-2080-9); paper $14.95 (0-8160-2348-4). A total of 85 different careers are introduced with information on opportunities, necessary training, and work conditions. (Rev: BL 3/1/90) [659]

4915 Franck, Irene M., and David M. Brownstone. *Financiers and Traders* (9–12). Illus. 1986, Facts on File $14.95 (0-8160-1368-3). In addition to economic history, this account explains how such careers as merchant, banker, financier, and accountant evolved. (Rev: BL 9/1/86; BR 11–12/86; SLJ 10/86) [331.7]

4916 Greenberg, Jan. *Advertising Careers: The Business and the People* (10–12). 1987, Henry Holt $17.95 (0-8050-0379-7). A practical guide that gives a history of advertising and then describes the inner workings of an agency. (Rev: BL 5/15/87; BR 11–12/87; SLJ 9/87; VOYA 12/87) [659.1]

4917 Haddock, Patricia. *Careers in Banking and Finance* (10–12). 1990, Rosen $11.95 (0-8239-0962-X). In addition to an introduction to the world of banking, this account talks about many kinds of jobs, especially those found on Wall Street. (Rev: BL 3/1/90; SLJ 11/90) [332.1]

4918 Harragan, Betty Lehan. *Games Mother Never Taught You: Corporate Gamesmanship for Women* (10–12). 1989, Warner paper $5.95 (0-446-35703-0). This book explores careers in business and the special problems women face in the corporate world. [650]

4919 Henry, Fran Worden. *Toughing It Out at Harvard: The Making of a Woman MBA* (10–12). 1983, Putnam $14.95 (0-339-12799-2). The story of the education supplied by the graduate program of the Harvard Business School from a woman's point of view. [338.6]

4920 Katz, Judith A. *The Ad Game* (10–12). 1984, Harper paper $8.95 (0-06-463576-7). This introduction to the world of advertising also describes the many kinds of jobs available in it. [659.1]

4921 Koester, Pat. *Careers in Fashion Retailing* (9–12). Illus. 1990, Rosen $11.95 (0-8239-1007-5). Careers that involve retailing fashion are described, from sales clerk to store owner. (Rev: BL 6/1/90) [381]

4922 London, Mel. *Getting into Video: A Career Guide* (9–12). 1990, Ballantine paper $12.95 (0-345-35648-9). A career guide that covers such areas as public access channels, production of videos, and distribution. (Rev: BL 6/1/90) [791.45]

4923 *Marketing & Sales Career Directory* (10–12). 1987, Career Pr. $34.95 (0-934829-20-9); paper $26.95 (0-934829-14-4). A series of articles by successful marketing businessmen on how to succeed in this field. (Rev: BL 5/15/87) [380]

4924 Norback, Craig T., ed. *VGM's Handbook of Business and Management Careers* (9–12). 1989, VGM paper $12.95 (0-8442-8683-4). A brief description of 44 different jobs at various levels of business and management plus material on working conditions. (Rev: BL 9/15/89) [650]

4925 Orenstein, Vik. *How to Break into Modeling* (10–12). 1987, Writer's Digest paper $17.95 (0-89879-282-7). For both male and female would-be models this is a complete guide to such topics as kinds of modeling, how to collect a portfolio, and where to get an agent. (Rev: SLJ 1/88) [659.1]

4926 Paradis, Adrian. *Opportunities in Banking* (9–12). Rev. ed. Illus. 1986, VGM $12.95 (0-8442-6213-7); paper $7.95 (0-8442-6214-5). An

overview of the kinds of careers available in banking plus details on specific jobs such as clerks and tellers. (Rev: BL 6/1/86; BR 9–10/86; VOYA 6/86) [332.1]

4927 Pattis, S. William. *Careers in Advertising* (9–12). 1990, VGM $14.95 (0-8442-8696-6); paper $9.95 (0-8442-8697-4). The world of advertising is introduced with details on jobs in areas like sales, research, account management, media services, and production. (Rev: BL 9/15/90) [659.1]

4928 Perkins, Eric. *The Insider's Guide to Modeling: The Pros Tell You How* (9–12). Illus. 1985, Nautilus $14.95 (0-935055-12-6). How to break into the field of modeling, by a former model and photographer. (Rev: SLJ 4/86) [659.1]

4929 Perry, Robert L. *Guide to Self-Employment* (10–12). Illus. 1989, Watts LB $11.90 (0-531-10774-4). Entrepreneurship is discussed as well as the risks and rewards of owning one's own business. (Rev: BL 3/1/90; BR 3–4/90; SLJ 3/90) [650.1]

4930 Place, Irene. *Opportunities in Business Management* (9–12). 1986, VGM $12.95 (0-8442-6185-8); paper $7.95 (0-8442-6186-6). Kinds of jobs in management are discussed as well as educational requirements, job opportunities, and working conditions. (Rev: VOYA 6/86) [650]

4931 Rosenberg, Martin H. *Opportunities in Accounting Careers* (10–12). 1990, VGM $12.95 (0-8442-8577-3); paper $9.95 (0-8442-8578-1). This book examines career opportunities in public, government, management, and institutional accounting. Part of a lengthy series. (Rev: BL 12/15/90) [657]

4932 Rosenthal, Lawrence. *Exploring Careers in Accounting* (9–12). 1986, Rosen $9.97 (0-8239-0625-6). A career book that covers such basic material as types of accounting jobs, professional preparation necessary, and working conditions. (Rev: BR 1–2/87) [657]

4933 Schrayer, Robert. *Opportunities in Insurance Careers* (9–12). 1987, VGM paper $7.95 (0-8442-6009-6). This account points out the variety of jobs available in the insurance field and gives details on each of them. (Rev: BR 5–6/88) [368]

4934 Sones, Melissa. *Getting into Fashion* (9–12). 1989, Random paper $7.95 (0-345-30756-9). A career guide that includes the entire fashion industry from textile production to fashion shows and advertising. (Rev: BR 9–10/89) [746.9]

4935 Spencer, Jean. *Careers in Word Processing and Desktop Publishing* (9–12). Illus. 1990, Rosen LB $12.95 (0-8239-0994-8). This account describes the hardware and software involved in word processing and desktop publishing plus information on the jobs surrounding these activities. (Rev: BR 3–4/90; SLJ 7/90; VOYA 4/90) [001.64]

4936 Stair, Lila B., and Dorothy Domkowski. *Careers in Business* (9–12). Illus. 1986, VGM $12.95 (0-8442-6117-3); paper $9.95 (0-8442-6118-1). A wide range of areas including real estate, insurance, management, accounting, and data processing are treated in this extensive career guide. (Rev: BL 12/1/86) [650]

4937 Steinberg, Margery. *Opportunities in Marketing Careers* (9–12). 1987, VGM paper $7.95 (0-8442-6916-3). This account covers a variety of jobs and for each gives material such as education and skills necessary, possibilities for advancement, and salaries. (Rev: BR 5–6/88) [380.1]

4938 Sumichrast, Michael, and Dean A. Crist. *Opportunities in Financial Careers* (9–12). Illus. 1985, VGM $10.95 (0-8442-6209-9); paper $7.95 (0-8442-6210-2). Careers in banking, the securities market, and accounting are described along with material on training, pay, and opportunities. (Rev: BL 11/15/85; BR 11–12/85) [332.1]

4939 Tebbel, John. *Opportunities in Newspaper Publishing Careers* (9–12). 1989, VGM $11.95 (0-8442-8641-9); paper $8.95 (0-8442-8642-7). A history of newspaper careers is given followed by detailed information on careers available today, the educational qualifications necessary, and general working conditions. (Rev: BR 3–4/90; VOYA 12/89) [070]

Construction and the Mechanical Trades

4940 Fenten, D. X. *Ms. Architect* (7–12). 1977, Westminster $7.95 (0-664-32615-3). A career guide aimed at young women who are interested in architecture. [720.92]

4941 Franck, Irene M., and David M. Brownstone. *Builders* (9–12). Illus. 1986, Facts on File $14.95 (0-8160-1366-7). A historical look at what architects have done through the centuries and the relationship between their contributions and those of the building trades. (Rev: BL 9/1/86; BR 11–12/86; SLJ 10/86) [331.7]

4942 Galvin, Patrick J. *Opportunities in Plumbing and Pipe Fitting Careers* (9–12). Illus. 1988, VGM $10.95 (0-8442-6187-4); paper $7.95 (0-8442-6188-2). A clear-cut guide that tells about training, work conditions, advancement, and pay in plumbing, pipe fitting, and the heating/cooling trades. (Rev: BL 3/1/89; BR 5–6/89) [696.1]

4943 Piper, Robert J. *Opportunities in Architecture* (9–12). Rev. ed. Illus. 1984, VGM $10.95 (0-8442-6211-0); paper $7.95 (0-8442-6212-9). This book tells about a variety of jobs in the field of architecture, the training and aptitudes needed, and their rewards. (Rev: BL 6/1/85) [720.23]

4944 Sheldon, Roger. *Opportunities in Carpentry Careers* (9–12). Illus. 1986, VGM $12.95 (0-8442-6134-3); paper $9.95 (0-8442-6135-1). The advantages and disadvantages of careers in carpentry are discussed plus detailed information on apprenticeship programs. (Rev: BL 6/1/87) [694]

4945 Weber, Robert. *Opportunities in Automotive Service Careers* (9–12). 1988, VGM $12.95 (0-8442-6502-0); paper $9.95 (0-8442-6503-9). This is a practical guide that describes many different jobs and how to succeed in each with useful coverage on topics like necessary preparation, training programs, and job opportunities. (Rev: BR 5–6/89; VOYA 6/89) [629.2]

Educators and Librarians

4946 Baxter, Neale. *Opportunities in Counseling & Development Careers* (9–12). 1990, VGM $11.95 (0-8442-8656-7); paper $8.95 (0-8442-8657-5). This well-rounded account describes different counseling jobs, particularly those involving schools, and also gives a history of the field and an indication of future developments. (Rev: BR 5–6/90) [361.3]

4947 *Career Choices for Students of English* (9–12). 1990, Walker paper $7.95 (0-8027-7330-3). An account that outlines both teaching and the variety of other jobs available for English majors. Also use: *Career Choices for Students of History* (1990). (Rev: BL 6/1/90) [400]

4948 Eberts, Marjorie, and Margaret Gisler. *Careers for Bookworms and Other Literary Types* (9–12). Illus. 1990, VGM paper $8.95 (0-8442-8618-4). An imaginative look at jobs available for lovers of books and reading that naturally includes the field of librarianship. (Rev: BL 6/1/90) [381]

4949 Edelfelt, Roy A. *Careers in Education* (8–12). 1988, VGM $12.95 (0-8442-6104-1); paper $9.95 (0-8442-6114-9). This account covers not only teaching and school administration but also related careers, e.g., in continuing education. (Rev: BL 9/1/88) [371.1]

4950 Fine, Janet. *Opportunities in Teaching* (10–12). 1984, VGM $12.95 (0-8442-6504-7); paper $9.95 (0-8442-6250-1). Teaching careers at various levels are discussed and questions of suitability explored. [371.7]

4951 Heim, Kathleen, and Peggy Sullivan. *Opportunities in Library and Information Science* (9–12). Rev. ed. Illus. 1986, VGM $12.95 (0-8442-6330-3); paper $9.95 (0-8442-6146-7). A look at these careers that covers training and advancement possibilities and the place of computers in today's information centers, among other topics. (Rev: BL 12/1/86; VOYA 8–10/86) [020]

4952 Heron, Jackie. *Careers in Health and Fitness* (9–12). Illus. 1988, Rosen $9.97 (0-8239-0771-6). A great variety of careers are described from sports therapist to broadcaster. (Rev: BL 6/1/88; SLJ 6–7/88; VOYA 12/88) [613.7]

4953 Kohl, Herbert. *Growing Minds: On Becoming a Teacher* (10–12). 1984, Harper $13.95 (0-06-015257-5); paper $6.95 (0-06-091212-X). A memoir of the successes, failures, and excitement of 21 years of teaching. [371.1]

4954 Shockley, Robert J., and Glen W. Cutlip. *Careers in Teaching* (8–12). Illus. 1988, Rosen LB $9.97 (0-8239-0774-0). In addition to an overview of this profession, this book also discusses topics like advancement possibilities, salaries, and how to determine if this is a suitable profession for you. (Rev: BL 6/1/88; SLJ 9/88; VOYA 8/88) [371.1]

Lawyers, Policemen, and Other Society-Oriented Careers

4955 Belliston, Larry, and Kurt Hanks. *Extra Cash for Kids* (9–12). 1989, Wolgemuth & Hyatt paper $9.95 (0-943497-70-1). A book that outlines about 100 ways young adults can make money. [650]

4956 Berkey, Rachel L. *New Career Opportunities in the Paralegal Profession* (10–12). 1983, Arco LB $6.95 (0-668-05478-6). A useful rundown on the positions, qualifications required, and opportunities in the paralegal field. [340]

4957 *Career Choices for Students of Law* (9–12). 1990, Walker paper $7.95 (0-8027-7335-4). This account discusses many careers in law and law-related fields and gives such information as educational qualifications necessary and working conditions. (Rev: BL 6/1/90) [340]

4958 *Career Choices for Students of Political Science and Government* (9–12). 1990, Walker paper $7.95 (0-8027-7333-8). This is a current guide to job opportunities in political science and government that projects its coverage into the 1990s. (Rev: BL 6/1/90) [320]

4959 Cohen, Paul, and Shari Cohen. *Careers in Law Enforcement and Security* (9–12). 1990, Rosen $11.95 (0-8239-1026-1). In addition to jobs available in the police, this account covers detectives, investigators, and other personnel involved in law enforcement. (Rev: BL 6/1/90) [362.2]

4960 Dana, Katherine. *Opportunities in Counseling and Development* (10–12). Illus. 1985, VGM $12.95 (0-8442-6182-3); paper $9.95 (0-8442-6183-1). A wide variety of positions are described, including those in schools, industry, social agencies and private practice. (Rev: BL 2/15/86) [371.4]

4961 DeVoss, Lishka. *How to Be a Waitress (or Waiter)* (9–12). Illus. 1985, St. Martin's paper $7.95 (0-312-39537-X). A witty but informative guide to waiting on tables with tips on how to handle customers. (Rev: BL 6/15/85) [642]

4962 Eberts, Marjorie, and Margaret Gisler. *Opportunities in Fast Food Careers* (9–12). 1989, VGM $11.95 (0-8442-8643-5); paper $8.95 (0-8442-8644-3). A variety of jobs in the fast food industry are described giving both advantages and disadvantages. (Rev: BR 3–4/90; VOYA 12/89) [647]

4963 Fanning, Odom. *Opportunities in Environmental Careers* (10–12). 4th ed. Illus. 1985, VGM $10.95 (0-8442-6176-9); paper $7.95 (0-8442-6177-7). A description of a wide range of careers, preparation involved, and the working conditions in each. (Rev: BL 6/1/86) [620.8]

4964 Fins, Alice. *Opportunities in Paralegal Careers* (10–12). Rev. ed. Illus. 1984, VGM $12.95 (0-8442-6218-8); paper $9.95 (0-8442-6219-6). A thorough account of the education, training, and working conditions of a group of law-based careers. (Rev: BL 5/1/85) [340]

4965 Franck, Irene M., and David M. Brownstone. *Helpers and Aides* (7–12). 1987, Facts on File $14.95 (0-8160-1445-0). This account traces the history of such occupations as sanitation workers, fire fighters, exterminators, and undertakers. (Rev: BR 11–12/87) [630]

4966 Franck, Irene M., and David M. Brownstone. *Leaders and Lawyers* (9–12). Illus. 1986, Facts on File $14.95 (0-8160-1367-5). A historical look at how law enforcement jobs and the legal profession evolved. (Rev: BL 9/1/86; BR 11–12/86) [331.7]

4967 Fry, William R., and Roy Hoopes. *Legal Careers and the Legal System* (9–12). Illus. 1988, Enslow $12.95 (0-89490-142-7). A guide to the modern legal profession and the many and varied positions available in it. (Rev: BL 6/1/88; BR 5–6/88; SLJ 5/88) [360]

4968 Fry, William R., and Roy Hoopes. *Paralegal Careers* (9–12). Illus. 1986, Enslow $13.95 (0-89490-105-2). An introduction to the growing support field and how to enter and succeed in it. (Rev: BL 3/15/86; SLJ 5/86) [340]

4969 Gillers, Stephen, ed. *Looking at Law School: A Student Guide from the Society of American Law Teachers* (10–12). 1990, NAL paper $9.95 (0-452-01049-7). A useful career book that combines a review of legal careers with an overview of what happens in law school. [340]

4970 Gottschalk, Alfred. *To Learn and to Teach: Your Life as a Rabbi* (10–12). 1988, Rosen $12.95 (0-8239-0700-7). A guide to young people who are seriously thinking of a rabbinical career. (Rev: BL 6/1/88; VOYA 8/88) [296.6]

4971 Lee, Richard S., and Mary Price Lee. *Careers for Women in Politics* (8–12). Illus. 1989, Rosen LB $10.95 (0-8239-0966-2). An overview of the role of women today in American politics and how the imbalance with males might be corrected. (Rev: BR 3–4/90; SLJ 10/89; VOYA 12/89) [324.2]

4972 Macdonald, Robert W. *Exploring Careers in the Military Services* (9–12). 1987, Rosen $14.95 This comprehensive guide gives the positive and negative aspects of a military career, opportunities they afford, and the possibilities of career development in each of the 5 services. (Rev: VOYA 12/87) [355.1]

4973 McKay, Robert. *Planning Your Military Career* (9–12). Illus. 1984, VGM paper $6.95 (0-8442-6672-8). With a chapter devoted to each of the services, this is a fine guide to careers in the armed forces that spells out both advantages and disadvantages. [355]

4974 Munneke, Gary A. *Opportunities in Law Careers* (10–12). Illus. 1985, VGM $12.95 (0-8442-6174-2); paper $9.95 (0-8442-6175-0). This career guide describes legal positions in many different settings like business and government plus law-related jobs and how to get into law school. (Rev: BL 2/15/86; BR 9–10/86; VOYA 4/86) [340]

4975 Norback, Judith. *The Complete Computer Career Guide* (9–12). Illus. 1987, TAB $18.95 (0-8306-9554-0); paper $12.95 (0-8306-2654-9). An extremely thorough review of all sorts of positions available in the computer field. (Rev: BL 6/1/88) [004]

4976 Smith, Dennis. *Firefighters: Their Lives in Their Own Words* (10–12). Illus. 1988, Doubleday $18.95 (0-385-24121-6). A former firefighter

and his colleagues tell about all aspects of this occupation from training to action in the field. (Rev: BL 8/88) [363.3]

4977 Stern, Ron. *Law Enforcement Careers: A Complete Guide from Application to Employment* (10–12). Illus. 1988, Lawman Pr. paper $9.95 (0-944711-00-6). A former police officer describes a variety of jobs from the federal to the municipal levels. (Rev: BL 6/1/88) [363.202]

4978 Stinchcomb, James D. *Opportunities in Law Enforcement and Criminal Justice* (10–12). 1984, VGM $12.95 (0-8442-8658-3); paper $9.95 (0-8442-8659-1). This guide covers law-related careers at the federal, state, and local level. (Rev: BL 9/15/90) [340]

4979 Traynor, William. *Opportunities in Human Resources Management Careers* (9–12). 1989, VGM $11.95 (0-8442-8639-7); paper $8.95 (0-8442-8640-0). A history of the field is given followed by details concerning the variety of positions available today, qualifications necessary, and current trends. (Rev: BR 3–4/90; VOYA 12/89) [331.11]

4980 Turner, David R. *Practice for the Armed Forces Tests* (10–12). 1982, Arco LB $12.00 (0-668-05558-8). With many sample questions this guide helps prepare for tests in all branches of the Armed Forces. [355]

4981 Turow, Scott. *One L: An Inside Account of Life in the First Year of Harvard Law School* (10–12). 1978, Penguin paper $6.95 (0-14-004913-4). An account of the author's experiences during his first year at Harvard Law School. [340]

4982 Williams, Ellen. *Opportunities for Gerontology Careers* (9–12). Illus. 1986, VGM $12.95 (0-8442-6166-1); paper $9.95 (0-8442-6168-8). From investment counseling to recreation, this is a guide to all sorts of jobs working with older adults. (Rev: BL 6/1/87) [362]

4983 Wittenberg, Renee. *Opportunities in Child Care Careers* (9–12). Illus. 1986, VGM $12.95 (0-8442-6022-3); paper $9.95 (0-8442-6023-1). A comprehensive guide to a wide range of careers in the rapidly expanding area of child care. (Rev: BL 6/1/87) [362.7]

Medical and Health Careers

4984 Anastas, Lila. *Your Career in Nursing* (9–12). Illus. 1984, Natl. League for Nursing paper $10.95 (0-88737-074-8). A thorough career guide that covers such topics as the training involved, various specialties available, and how to determine whether or not you are right for nursing. (Rev: BL 2/1/85) [610.73]

4985 Anderson, Peggy. *Nurse* (10–12). 1990, Berkley paper $3.95 (0-425-12286-7). This is a day-by-day account of what is involved in being a nurse. [610.76]

4986 Brown, Margaret F. *Careers in Occupational Therapy* (9–12). Illus. 1989, Rosen LB $9.97 (0-8239-0981-6). Using many examples from the field this account covers education required, preparation, types of jobs, and the future outlook in the field of occupational therapy. (Rev: BR 9–10/89; SLJ 6/89; VOYA 10/89) [615.8]

4987 Caldwell, Carol. *Opportunities in Nutrition Careers* (9–12). 1986, VGM $10.95 (0-8442-6172-6); paper $7.95 (0-8442-6173-4). Employment conditions in a variety of jobs involving nutrition are described plus the attributes and training necessary to qualify. (Rev: BL 2/15/86; BR 9–10/86; VOYA 4/86) [641.1]

4988 *Career Choices for Students of Psychology* (9–12). 1990, Walker paper $7.95 (0-8027-7334-6). A survey of positions and their future development in the fields of both theoretical and applied psychology. (Rev: BL 6/1/90) [150]

4989 DeRidder, Margaret Djerf. *New Career Opportunities in Health and Human Services* (10–12). 1984, Arco paper $8.95 (0-668-06103-0). A number of social service occupations are described with directory information supplied. [610]

4990 Duncan, Jane Caryl. *Careers in Veterinary Medicine* (8–12). Illus. 1988, Rosen $9.97 (0-8239-0804-6). A veterinarian gives an honest description of her profession and many practical tips. (Rev: BL 9/1/88; SLJ 10/88; VOYA 10/88) [636.089]

4991 Epstein, Rachel. *Careers in Health Care* (9–12). Illus. 1989, Chelsea House $17.95 (0-7910-0081-8). All sorts of careers in medicine, dentistry, and other health-care professions are outlined. (Rev: BL 6/1/89; SLJ 8/89; VOYA 8/89) [610.69]

4992 Eskow, Dennis. *Laser Careers* (9–12). Illus. 1988, Watts $11.90 (0-531-10424-9). Laser technology is described and the fields like medicine and manufacturing where applications of this knowledge are used. (Rev: BL 6/1/88; BR 9–10/88; SLJ 5/88; VOYA 8/88) [621.36]

4993 Frederickson, Keville. *Opportunities in Nursing Careers* (9–12). 1989, VGM paper $8.95 (0-8442-8636-2). This account describes various kinds of nursing careers, the training and person-

ality necessary, and working conditions. (Rev: BR 3–4/90; VOYA 12/89) [610.73]

4994 Hammer, Arnold. *The Rosen Photo Guide to a Career in Health and Fitness* (8–12). Illus. 1988, Rosen $10.95 (0-8239-0820-8). An outline of careers in such agencies as health clubs, spas, and diet centers. (Rev: BL 12/15/88) [613.7]

4995 Heron, Jackie. *Exploring Careers in Nursing* (9–12). Illus. 1986, Rosen $10.95 (0-8239-0689-2). An introduction by an RN to the nursing profession, this account describes the psychological, physical, and educational requirements plus its rewards. (Rev: BL 12/15/86) [610.73]

4996 Ispa, Jean. *Exploring Careers in Child Care Services* (9–12). Rev. ed. Illus. 1990, Rosen LB $12.95 (0-8239-1151-9). Such careers as camp counselors, child-care center workers, and family therapists are described. (Rev: BR 1–2/87) [362.7]

4997 Jeffers, Susan. *The Rosen Photo Guide to a Career in Animal Care* (8–12). Illus. 1988, Rosen $10.95 (0-8239-0818-6). From zoos to pet shops, this is a guide to many careers involving animals. (Rev: BL 12/15/88) [636]

4998 Kacen, Alex. *Opportunities in Paramedical Careers* (9–12). Illus. 1989, VGM $12.95 (0-8442-6506-3); paper $9.95 (0-8442-6507-1). A thorough rundown on the many jobs in the medical field involving technicians and assistants and how to prepare for entrance into these fields. (Rev: BR 5–6/89; VOYA 6/89) [610.69]

4999 Kane, June Kozak. *Exploring Careers in Dietetics and Nutrition* (9–12). Illus. 1987, Rosen $11.95 (0-8239-0658-2). This book emphasizes the diversity of careers with working conditions and academic requirements outlined in each case. (Rev: BL 6/1/87; BR 11–12/87; SLJ 9/87) [613.2]

5000 Karni, Karen, and Jane Sidney Oliver. *Opportunities in Medical Technology Careers* (10–12). 1990, VGM $11.95 (0-8442-8671-0); paper $8.95 (0-8442-8672-9). A thorough introduction to the various jobs available in clinical lab work. (Rev: BL 3/1/90; BR 5–6/90) [610.69]

5001 Martin, Tony. *How to Survive Medical School* (9–12). 1984, Penguin paper $7.95 (0-14-007319-1). Sound advice is given on how to get into medical school and how to stay there successfully. [610]

5002 Schafer, R. C. *Opportunities in Chiropractic Health Care Careers* (9–12). 1986, VGM $10.95 (0-8442-6565-9); paper $7.95 (0-8442-6566-7). Schafer gives an overview of the field plus details on training and employment outlook. (Rev: BL 6/1/86; BR 9–10/86) [615.5]

5003 Seide, Diane. *Nurse Power: New Vistas in Learning* (9–12). 1985, Dutton $12.95 (0-525-67173-0). After a look at the nursing profession, the author describes career opportunities in it, the various entry points, training required, and rewards. (Rev: BL 12/1/85; BR 5–6/86; SLJ 12/85) [610.73]

5004 Seide, Diane. *Physician Power: New Vistas for Women in Medicine* (9–12). 1989, Dutton $14.95 (0-525-67276-1). Using 3 career sketches the author presents an encouraging picture of the place of women as doctors in the future. (Rev: BL 6/1/89; SLJ 6/89; VOYA 8/89) [612]

5005 Sigel, Lois Savitch. *New Careers in Hospitals* (9–12). Illus. 1988, Rosen $10.95 (0-8239-0802-X). A behind-the-scenes look at modern hospital administration and the variety of jobs it involves. (Rev: BL 12/15/88; BR 5–6/89; SLJ 4/89; VOYA 6/89) [362.1]

5006 Snook, I. Donald. *Opportunities in Hospital Administration Careers* (9–12). 1988, VGM $12.95 (0-8442-6509-8); paper $9.95 (0-8442-6510-1). The types of careers involving hospital administration are described followed by detailed information on education and experience required, job hunting tips, and a typical day on the job. (Rev: BR 5–6/89; VOYA 6/89) [362.1]

5007 Snook, I. Donald, and Leo D'Ozraio. *Opportunities in Health and Medical Careers* (10–12). 1990, VGM $12.95 (0-8442-8573-0); paper $9.95 (0-8442-8574-9). This is a fine overview of the many positions available in this expanding field. (Rev: BL 12/15/90) [610]

5008 Swanson, Barbara M. *Careers in Health Care* (9–12). 1989, VGM $14.95 (0-8442-8698-2); paper $9.95 (0-8442-8699-0). A total of 60 different careers are described plus background information on such topics as job opportunities, pay, and education needed. (Rev: BL 9/15/89; BR 3–4/90; VOYA 12/89) [610.69]

5009 Swope, Robert E. *Opportunities in Veterinary Medicine Careers* (9–12). Illus. 1987, VGM $9.95 (0-8442-6343-5); paper $7.95 (0-8442-6344-3). In addition to the usual position held by veterinarians, this guide also explores jobs in industry, government, and education. (Rev: BL 12/1/87; BR 5–6/88) [636.089]

Scientists and Engineers

5010 Basta, Nicholas. *Opportunities in Engineering Careers* (9–12). Illus. 1990, VGM $12.95 (0-8442-8583-8); paper $9.95 (0-8442-8584-6). After a general discussion of the field of engineering,

this account gives specific information on its branches and the opportunities available. (Rev: BL 6/1/90) [620]

5011 Bone, Jan. *Opportunities in Laser Technology Careers* (9–12). 1988, VGM $12.95 (0-8442-6514-4); paper $9.95 (0-8442-6512-2). After a description of what laser technology involves, the author describes in depth the many careers within this field. (Rev: BR 5–6/89) [621.36]

5012 Bone, Jan. *Opportunities in Robotics Careers* (10–12). Illus. 1987, VGM $9.95 (0-8442-6020-7); paper $7.95 (0-8442-6021-5). Although this is still a developing area, the author gives sound advice on both present opportunities and projections for the future in this field. (Rev: BL 12/1/87; BR 5–6/88) [629.892]

5013 Brown, Sheldon. *Opportunities in Biotechnology Careers* (9–12). 1989, VGM $11.95 (0-8442-8645-1); paper $8.95 (0-8442-8647-8). A history of careers in biotechnology is given plus material on how to enter them at present. (Rev: BR 3–4/90; VOYA 12/89) [575]

5014 *Career Choices for Students of Mathematics* (9–12). 1990, Walker paper $7.95 (0-8027-7331-1). In this up-to-date guide, the range of positions available to people with mathematics background is surveyed. (Rev: BL 6/1/90) [510]

5015 CEIP Fund, eds. *The Complete Guide to Environmental Careers* (10–12). 1989, Island Pr. $24.95 (0-933280-85-8); paper $14.95 (0-933280-84-X). The organization that produced this guide specializes in training for environmental careers. The book gives a well-researched, in-depth look at a variety of positions in this area. (Rev: BL 3/1/90) [363.7]

5016 Easton, Thomas A. *Careers in Science* (10–12). 1989, VGM $12.95 (0-8442-6123-8); paper $9.95 (0-8442-6124-6). An overview of the jobs available in such areas as the life and physical sciences, mathematics, computers, and related social sciences. [500]

5017 Gable, Fred B. *Opportunities in Pharmacy Careers* (9–12). Rev.ed. Illus. 1990, VGM $12.95 (0-8442-8591-9); paper $9.95 (0-8442-8592-7). A variety of pharmaceutical careers are explored with information on suitability, education necessary, and work conditions. (Rev: BL 9/15/90) [615.1]

5018 Hagerty, D., and John Heer. *Opportunities in Engineering Technology Careers* (9–12). 1987, VGM paper $7.95 (0-8442-6163-7). This book covers a specialized area of engineering and deals with subjects such as education necessary, opportunities, and the general job market. Others in this series deal with different branches of engineering such as *Opportunities in Civil Engineering Careers* (1987). (Rev: BR 5–6/88) [620]

5019 Harmon, Margaret. *Ms. Engineer* (9–12). 1979, Westminster $8.95 (0-664-32652-8). This book describes the various branches of engineering and the different roles women could play in them. [620]

5020 Heitzmann, William. *Opportunities in Marine and Maritime Careers* (9–12). 1987, VGM paper $7.95 (0-8442-6351-6). An account that gives a fine overview of this field and then gives details of the jobs in it and the prospects for the future. (Rev: BR 5–6/88) [574.92]

5021 Jones, Marilyn. *Exploring Careers as an Electrician* (9–12). 1987, Rosen $9.97 (0-8239-0686-8). Through conversations with people in the field, a girl who is considering becoming an electrician learns about this occupation. (Rev: BR 11–12/87) [621]

5022 Kantor, Elliot S., ed. *Careers in Engineering* (9–12). 1989, VGM paper $9.95 (0-8442-6312-5). An overview of the various kinds of engineering, qualifications necessary, and working conditions in each area of specialization. (Rev: VOYA 4/90) [620]

5023 Lang, Denise V. *Footsteps in the Ocean: Careers in Diving* (8–12). Illus. 1987, Dutton $13.95 (0-525-67193-5). All sorts of occupations involving underwater work and marine technology are outlined. (Rev: BL 6/1/87; SLJ 9/87) [627]

5024 Lee, Mary Price. *Ms. Veterinarian* (9–12). 1976, Westminster $8.95 (0-664-32594-7). The world of veterinary medicine as it applies to women and the careers in this field. [636.089]

5025 Marrs, Texe. *Careers with Robots* (9–12). Illus. 1988, Facts on File $21.95 (0-8160-1222-9). This guide covers a wide variety of positions in the field destined to expand in the future. (Rev: BL 9/1/88; BR 11–12/88) [629.8]

5026 Norback, Craig T., ed. *VGM's Handbook of Scientific and Technical Careers* (9–12). 1989, VGM paper $12.95 (0-8442-8684-2). A guide to 50 science-related careers in such fields as chemistry, architecture, and computers. (Rev: BL 12/1/89) [602.3]

5027 Rossbacher, Lisa A. *Career Opportunities in Geology and the Earth Sciences* (10–12). 1983, Arco paper $7.95 (0-668-05220-1). This describes a wide range of jobs, all related to the earth sciences. [550]

5028 Shapiro, Stanley Jay. *Exploring Careers in Science* (9–12). Rev. ed. Illus. 1986, Rosen $10.95 (0-8239-0725-2). A useful career guide that covers such branches as mathematical, environmental, life, and physical sciences. (Rev: BL 12/15/86; BR 3–4/87; SLJ 10/87) [502.3]

5029 Stearner, S. Phyllis. *Able Scientists—Disabled Persons* (9–12). Illus. 1984, Foundation for Science and the Handicapped paper $12.95 (0-916655-00-8). Profiles of 27 people are included in this book, all of whom have overcome such problems as being blind or deaf to reach important positions in the sciences. (Rev: BL 4/15/85) [509]

5030 Stine, Deborah. *Exploring Careers in Engineering* (9–12). 1986, Rosen $9.97 (0-8239-0660-4). An overview of the profession of engineering that tells about the different specializations in the field and the working conditions in each. (Rev: BR 1–2/87) [620]

5031 Williams, Barbara. *Breakthrough: Women in Archaeology* (9–12). 1981, Walker $9.95 (0-8027-6406-1). This book describes careers for women in archaeology and gives profiles of 6 successful women working in the field. [930.1]

5032 Winter, C. A. *Opportunities in Biological Sciences* (10–12). 1983, VGM $12.95 (0-8442-8626-5); paper $9.95 (0-8442-8628-1). This volume gives details on a variety of careers that require a background in biology. [510]

Technicians and Industrial Workers

5033 Allman, Paul. *Exploring Careers in Video* (9–12). Rev. ed. 1987, Rosen $10.95 (0-8239-1018-0). A discussion of the many jobs available in all kinds of video production including music video. (Rev: SLJ 3/88) [384.55]

5034 Bailey, David, and Laura Castoro. *Careers in Computers* (9–12). 1985, Messner $9.79 (0-671-49849-5). An overview of computer careers plus advice on how to prepare for them. (Rev: BL 4/15/85; SLJ 9/85) [001.64]

5035 Bell, John A., and Lonny D. Garvey. *Opportunities in the Machine Trades* (9–12). Rev. ed. Illus. 1986, VGM $10.95 (0-8442-6147-5); paper $7.95 (0-8442-6148-3). A guide to careers in machine shops that covers many topics including training, advancement, pay, and the role of unions. (Rev: BL 12/1/86) [621]

5036 Bone, Jan. *Opportunities in Computer Aided Design and Computer Aided Manufacturing* (9–12). Illus. 1986, VGM $10.95 (0-8442-6169-6); paper $7.95 (0-8442-6171-8). A rundown on the many jobs now available involving computer and automation applications in industry. (Rev: BL 10/15/86; VOYA 8–10/86) [620]

5037 Bone, Jan. *Opportunities in Telecommunications* (10–12). 1987, VGM $12.95 (0-8442-8654-0); paper $9.95 (0-8442-8655-9). All kinds of jobs are described plus tips on how to prepare for them. Two other guides by this author are: *Opportunities in Cable Television* (1984) and *Opportunities in Film* (1983). (Rev: BL 12/1/89; BR 5–6/90) [621.38]

5038 Borowsky, Irvin J. *Opportunities in Printing Careers* (9–12). 1985, VGM $12.95 (0-8442-6189-0); paper $7.95 (0-8442-6190-4). A history of printing is given plus a complete rundown on the jobs currently available in this industry. (Rev: VOYA 4/86) [686.2]

5039 *Career Choices for Students of Computer Science* (9–12). 1990, Walker paper $7.95 (0-8027-7327-3). After a general discussion on jobs available in the computer field, this book gives specifics on qualifications, working conditions, and so on. (Rev: BL 6/1/90) [001.64]

5040 Carter, Sharon. *Careers in Aviation* (9–12). Illus. 1990, Rosen $11.95 (0-8239-0965-4). Careers both off and on the ground related to aviation are described. (Rev: BL 6/1/90; SLJ 11/90) [629.13]

5041 Goldstein, Harold, and Bryna Shore Fraser. *Getting a Job in the Computer Age* (10–12). 1986, Peterson's Guides paper $7.96 (0-877866-440-8). This book describes the many fields in which computers are now essential tools and the kinds of training necessary in finding careers in them. (Rev: VOYA 2/87) [001.64]

5042 Golter, Gary, and Deborah Yanuch. *Opportunities in High Tech Careers* (9–12). 1987, VGM paper $7.95 (0-8442-6040-1). This account covers the new and expanding field of high technology and gives a thorough rundown on the kinds of jobs it involves and what each entails. (Rev: BR 5–6/88) [600]

5043 Hornung, D. Mark, and Richard D. Moran. *Opportunities in Microelectronics* (9–12). Illus. 1985, VGM $10.95 (0-8442-6197-1); paper $7.95 (0-8442-6199-8). A description of this field and of the importance to it of semiconductors plus a rundown on the kinds of careers it offers. (Rev: BL 12/1/85; BR 11–12/85) [621.3]

5044 Kling, Julie Lepick. *Opportunities in Computer Science Careers* (10–12). 1987, VGM $12.95 (0-8442-6238-2); paper $9.95 (0-8442-6239-0). The field of computers now offers a wide array of occupational opportunities at many levels. This guide describes each of them well. [001.64]

5045 Krueger, Gretchen Dewailly. *Opportunities in Petroleum Careers* (9–12). Illus. 1989, VGM $11.95 (0-8442-8665-6); paper $8.95 (0-8442-8666-4). The petroleum industry assimilates various skills and aptitudes in its positions. This account outlines them, provides the education needed, gives international information, and discusses working conditions. (Rev: BL 12/1/89; BR 5–6/90) [622]

5046 Laurance, Robert. *Electronic Service Careers* (10–12). Illus. 1987, Watts $11.90 (0-531-10423-0). A guide to careers in servicing and repairing the multitude of electrical products now available. (Rev: BL 3/1/88; BR 1–2/88; SLJ 3/88) [621.381]

5047 Lee, Mary Price, and Richard S. Lee. *Exploring Careers in Robotics* (9–12). Illus. 1984, Rosen $10.95 (0-8239-0620-5). After an introduction to the field of robotics, the authors describe the range of careers available in this expanding area. (Rev: BL 2/15/85) [629.8]

5048 Masterson, Richard. *Exploring Careers in Computer Graphics* (9–12). Illus. 1987, Rosen $11.95 (0-8239-0632-9). This book describes the computer graphics field, areas where technology is applied, and the kinds of jobs available. (Rev: VOYA 8–9/87) [001.64]

5049 Munday, Marianne F. *Opportunities in Word Processing* (10–12). 1987, VGM $12.95 (0-8442-6200-5); paper $9.95 (0-8442-6201-3). Word processing has become an expanding career field and this book explains the various levels and types of jobs. (Rev: VOYA 4/86) [001.64]

5050 Noerper, Norman. *Opportunities in Data Processing* (10–12). 1989, VGM $12.95 (0-8442-8637-0); paper $9.95 (0-8442-6226-9). This rapidly expanding field now offers a wide spectrum of jobs, all of which are explored in this text. (Rev: BR 3–4/90) [001.64]

5051 Paradis, Adrian. *Opportunities in Vocational & Technical Careers* (9–12). 1987, VGM $12.95 (0-8442-6018-5); paper $9.95 (0-8442-6019-3). Such subjects as necessary training, salaries, and advancement possibilities are covered for a large number of jobs. (Rev: BR 5–6/88) [600]

5052 Reed, Maxine K., and Robert Reed. *Career Opportunities in Television, Cable and Video* (9–12). 2nd ed. 1986, Facts on File $24.95 (0-8160-1285-7); paper $12.95 (0-8160-1534-1). For each job description, the authors supply much information, including duties, employment conditions, and prospects for advancement. (Rev: BR 1–2/87) [621.388]

5053 Schauer, Donald D. *Careers in Trucking* (9–12). Illus. 1987, Rosen $10.95 (0-8239-0748-1). This book discusses the many careers open for both men and women in the trucking industry and includes sample curricula on the subject from technical schools. (Rev: SLJ 3/88) [629.2]

5054 Schefter, James L. *Aerospace Careers* (10–12). Illus. 1987, Watts $11.90 (0-531-10422-2). An introduction to the aerospace industry and the many job opportunities in it. (Rev: BL 3/1/88; SLJ 2/88) [629.4]

5055 Seide, Diane. *Careers in Health Services* (9–12). 1982, Lodestar $10.50 (0-525-66768-7). This book gives a rundown on 50 different careers in the field of medicine with information on each concerning qualifications and opportunities. [613]

5056 Southworth, Scott. *Exploring High Tech Careers* (9–12). 1984, Rosen $10.95 (0-8239-0643-4). A discussion of such jobs in the computer field as engineering, programming, writing, and various kinds of manufacturing. (Rev: BL 2/15/85) [001.64]

5057 Spencer, Jean. *Exploring Careers as a Computer Technician* (9–12). Illus. 1984, Rosen $7.97 (0-8239-0626-4). In addition to aptitude and training, this book describes specific jobs and their characteristics. (Rev: BL 4/15/85) [001.64]

5058 Stone, Jack, and Stephen Roberts. *You Don't Have to Be a Genius to Land a Computer Job* (10–12). 1984, Macmillan paper $9.95 (0-672-52790-1). An informal guide to a wide range of positions available in the computer field. [001.64]

5059 Thro, Ellen. *Robotics Careers* (10–12). Illus. 1987, Watts $11.90 (0-531-10425-7). The future of robotics and the kinds of training and education needed to work in this area are discussed. (Rev: BL 3/1/88; BR 1–2/88; SLJ 3/88) [629.8]

5060 Weintraub, Joseph. *Exploring Careers in the Computer Field* (9–12). 1988, Rosen LB $11.95 (0-8239-0795-3). A fine overview of the variety of jobs available in the computer field, qualifications needed, and the nature of working conditions. [004]

5061 Winkler, Connie. *Careers in High Tech* (9–12). 1986, Arco paper $9.95 (0-668-06537-0). The jobs described are in such areas as data processing, computers, biotechnology, and artificial intelligence. (Rev: BL 10/1/86) [602]

5062 Wood, Robert. *Opportunities in Electrical Trades* (9–12). 1990, VGM $12.95 (0-8442-8587-0); paper $9.95 (0-8442-8588-9). Types of jobs, advancement opportunities, and earnings are topics in this account that gives excellent coverage on the training necessary. (Rev: BL 9/15/90) [621.3]

5063 Woodburn, John H. *Opportunities in Energy Careers* (9–12). 1985, VGM $12.95 (0-8442-6221-8); paper $7.95 (0-8442-6222-6). Careers in the coal and oil industries are covered as well as those involving solar and nuclear energy and electronic power. (Rev: VOYA 2/86) [333.79]

Personal Finances

Money-Making Ideas

General and Miscellaneous

5064 Kingstone, Brett. *The Student Entrepreneur's Guide: How to Start and Run Your Own Business* (10–12). 1989, McGraw paper $9.95 (0-07-034707-7). In a very readable style, this manual gives tips on starting your own business plus lists of types of business ventures. [338.6]

5065 Lee, Richard S., and Mary Price Lee. *Coping with Money* (9–12). 1988, Rosen $12.95 (0-8239-0783-X). This book discusses such subjects as budgeting, how to earn money, planning for college or a career, and various financial strategies. (Rev: BR 3–4/89) [332.024]

5066 Paradis, Adrian. *Opportunities in Part-Time and Summer Jobs* (9–12). Illus. 1987, VGM $12.95 (0-8442-6300-1); paper $9.95 (0-8442-6302-8). Tips on how to makret oneself plus a number of money-making ideas. (Rev: BL 9/1/87; BR 5–6/88) [331.34]

5067 Riehm, Sarah. *The Teenage Entrepreneur's Guide: 50 Money-Making Business Ideas* (9–12). 1987, Surrey Books paper $8.95 (0-940625-00-8). Though traditional jobs such as baby-sitting are discussed, the emphasis is on newer activities like home baking and making greeting cards on the computer. (Rev: BL 5/15/87) [658]

5068 Smith, Allan. *Teenage Moneymaking Guide* (9–12). 1984, Success Publg. paper $10.00 (0-931113-00-8). A roundup of suggestions for making money for the teenage entrepreneur. [371.4]

Baby-sitting

5069 Benton, Barbara. *The Babysitter's Handbook* (8–12). Illus. 1981, Morrow $13.95 (0-688-00641-8); paper $6.95 (0-688-00687-6). A handy manual that covers many practical aspects of baby-sitting and also gives material on child development. [649]

5070 James, Elizabeth, and Carol Barkin. *The Complete Babysitter's Handbook* (8–12). Illus. 1981, Messner paper $5.95 (0-671-33067-5). Topics covered include how to get baby-sitting jobs, caring for children, and emergency information. [649]

5071 Saunders, Rubie. *Baby-Sitting for Fun and Profit* (9–12). Illus. 1988, Pocket paper $2.50 (0-671-66706-8). An easy-to-follow guide manual to help both the novice and the experienced baby-sitter. [649]

Managing Money

5072 Passell, Peter. *How to Read the Financial Pages* (10–12). 1986, Warner paper $3.50 (0-446-30066-7). A slim guide on how to understand and interpret the information of the financial pages of the newspaper. (Rev: BL 2/15/86) [332.024]

Health and the Human Body

5073 *The Complete Manual of Fitness and Well-Being* (9–12). Illus. 1988, Reader's Digest $26.95 (0-88850-154-4). In addition to exercise and diet, this account covers such topics as human growth, body parts, and health. (Rev: BL 5/1/88; SLJ 6–7/88) [613]

5074 Drury, Neville, and Susan Drury. *Illustrated Dictionary of Natural Health* (10–12). Illus. 1989, Sterling paper $12.95 (0-8069-6924-5). This volume deals with alternative health information on such subjects as healing plants, diet, and exercise. (Rev: SLJ 9/89) [613]

5075 Kunz, Jeffrey R. M., ed. *The American Medical Association Family Medical Guide* (10–12). Illus. 1982, Random $29.95 (0-394-51015-1). A comprehensive guide to the human body and the meaning of various symptoms, diseases, and treatments. [616.02]

5076 Lillyquist, Michael J. *Sunlight and Health* (10–12). 1985, Dodd $15.95 (0-396-08482-6); paper $7.95 (0-396-08957-7). An overview of what sunlight is and how it affects the human body. (Rev: BL 3/15/85; SLJ 11/85) [613]

5077 McCuen, Gary E. *Poor and Minority Health Care* (9–12). Illus. 1988, GEM $12.95 (0-86596-065-8). Various viewpoints are offered on such topics as private vs. government health care, minority health care, and world health problems. (Rev: SLJ 6–7/88) [614]

5078 Mullan, Fitzhugh. *Plagues and Politics: The Story of the United States Public Health Service* (10–12). Illus. 1989, Basic Books $26.95 (0-465-05779-9). A history of the Public Health Service from its humble beginnings in 1798 as the Marine Hospital Fund to the present. (Rev: BL 9/15/89) [353]

Aging and Death

5079 Baird, Robert M., and Stuart E. Rosenbaum, eds. *Euthanasia: The Moral Issues* (10–12). 1989, Prometheus paper $11.95 (0-87975-555-5). In this collection of 19 essays, euthanasia is explained and the various legal and moral questions surrounding it are explored. (Rev: BL 3/1/90) [179.7]

5080 Bender, David L., and Richard Hagen, eds. *Death-Dying Annual, 1989* (9–12). Illus. 1989, Greenhaven paper $9.95 (0-89908-546-6). Many viewpoints are given on such subjects as the meaning of death, how to grieve, and the question of life after death. [128]

5081 Buckman, Robert. *I Don't Know What to Say: How to Help and Support Someone Who Is Dying* (10–12). 1988, Key Porter Books $19.95 (1-55013-070-6). An explanation of the dying process and how to cope with it. (Rev: BL 9/1/88) [155.9]

5082 Dolan, Edward F., Jr. *Matters of Life and Death* (9–12). 1982, Watts LB $12.90 (0-531-04497-1). This account covers controversies related to such topics as abortion and euthanasia. [179]

5083 Dychtwald, Ken, and Joe Flower. *Age Wave: The Challenges and Opportunities of an Aging America* (10–12). 1989, Tarcher $19.95 (0-87477-441-1). A book about the aging of America, how the elderly now live, and the problems they face. (Rev: SLJ 2/89) [305.2]

5084 *The Elderly* (9–12). Illus. 1990, Greenhaven LB $15.95 (0-89908-475-3); paper $7.95 (0-89908-450-8). The needs and financial problems facing this segment of the population are addressed through a series of articles expressing different viewpoints. (Rev: SLJ 8/90) [305.2]

5085 *Euthanasia: Opposing Viewpoints* (9–12). 1989, Greenhaven LB $15.95 (0-89908-442-7); paper $7.95 (0-89908-417-6). Through a collection of writings, various aspects of the subject of euthanasia are explored including the pro-life movement and the legality of living wills. (Rev: BL 11/15/89) [179]

5086 Kahn, Carol. *Beyond the Helix: DNA and the Quest for Longevity* (10–12). 1985, Times Books $17.45 (0-8129-1153-9). An inquiry that investigates the relationship between aging and DNA. (Rev: BL 10/15/85) [612]

5087 Kubler-Ross, Elisabeth. *Living with Death and Dying* (10–12). Illus. 1981, Macmillan paper $5.95 (0-02-086490-6). A frank discussion of how to care for the terminally ill. For mature readers. [128]

5088 Kubler-Ross, Elisabeth. *On Children and Death* (10–12). 1983, Macmillan $12.95 (0-02-567110-3); paper $5.95 (0-02-076670-X). From her experiences with terminally ill children, the author gives counsel and comfort to those in similar circumstances. For mature readers. [128]

5089 Kubler-Ross, Elisabeth. *To Live until We Say Good-Bye* (9–12). Illus. 1978, Prentice $12.95 (0-13-922955-8); paper $8.95 (0-13-922948-5). The process of dying as experienced by a youngster, an adult, and an elderly person. [155.9]

5090 Leder, Jane Mersky. *Dead Serious: A Book for Teenagers about Teenage Suicide* (7–12). 1987, Macmillan LB $12.95 (0-689-31262-8); Avon paper $2.95 (0-380-70661-X). This book deals specifically with the symptoms of a suicidal situation and how to cope with the aftereffects of the suicide of a relative or friend. (Rev: SLJ 8/87; VOYA 6/87) [179]

5091 Lukas, Christopher, and Henry M. Seiden. *Silent Grief: Living in the Wake of Suicide* (10–12). 1988, Macmillan $19.95 (0-684-18770-1). The various reactions to suicide are explored with liberal quotes from several case studies. (Rev: SLJ 9/88) [362.2]

5092 McCuen, Gary E., and Therese Boucher. *Terminating Life: Conflicting Values in Health Care* (9–12). Illus. 1985, GEM $11.95 (0-86596-051-8). Articles from various sources explore the complex controversies surrounding euthanasia and mercy killing. (Rev: BL 4/1/85) [174.24]

5093 Munley, Anne. *The Hospice Alternative: A New Context for Death and Dying* (10–12). 1983, Basic Books $17.50 (0-465-03060-2); paper $8.95 (0-465-03061-0). A description and evaluation of the hospice concept for the terminally ill. [362.1]

5094 O'Connor, Nancy. *Letting Go with Love: The Grieving Process* (9–12). 1985, La Mariposa $18.95 (0-9613714-1-2); paper $9.95 (0-9613714-0-4). How to cope with the death of a loved one is the subject of this self-help book. [128]

5095 Quinnett, Paul G. *Suicide: The Forever Decision* (10–12). Illus. 1987, Continuum $18.95 (0-8264-0395-6); paper $8.95 (0-8264-0391-3). From his many years' experience as a psychologist, the author explores the reasons for suicide and gives arguments for choosing life. (Rev: SLJ 3/88) [362.2]

5096 Rohr, Janelle, ed. *Death and Dying: Opposing Viewpoints* (9–12). 2nd rev. ed. 1987, Greenhaven LB $15.95 (0-89908-393-5); paper $7.95 (0-89908-368-4). A readable anthology that presents various points of view on such topics as suicide, euthanasia, and the grieving process. (Rev: BL 5/1/87) [306.9]

5097 Russell, O. Ruth. *Freedom to Die: Moral and Legal Aspects of Euthanasia* (10–12). Rev. ed. 1977, Human Sciences $44.95 (0-87705-311-1). A discussion of the pros and cons of euthanasia and how people regard it today. [174]

5098 Swisher, Karin, ed. *The Elderly: Opposing Viewpoints* (9–12). 1990, Greenhaven LB $15.95 (0-89908-475-3); paper $7.95 (0-89908-450-8). Various points of view concerning problems facing the elderly and society's responsibilities toward them are covered in a series of articles. (Rev: BL 5/15/90) [305.26]

Alcohol, Drugs, and Smoking

5099 Alibrandi, Tom. *Young Alcoholics* (9–12). 1983, CompCare paper $8.95 (0-89638-014-9). A discussion of young alcoholics followed by an analysis of drinking habits of young people in Orange County, California. [616.86]

5100 Anderson, M. A. *Tracey: A Mother's Journal of Teenage Addiction* (9–12). 1988, Black Heron paper $7.95 (0-930773-08-X). The harrowing story of one family's fight to save their 14-year-old daughter Tracey from drug addiction. (Rev: VOYA 2/89) [613.8]

5101 Avraham, Regina. *The Downside of Drugs* (8–12). Illus. 1988, Chelsea House LB $17.95 (1-55546-232-4). This account covers the effects of such drugs as nicotine, alcohol, narcotics, stimulants, and hallucinogens. (Rev: SLJ 6–7/88) [613.8]

5102 Avraham, Regina. *Substance Abuse* (8–12). 1988, Chelsea House LB $17.95 (1-55546-219-7). This account describes how drugs affect behavior and how addiction is treated. (Rev: BR 1–2/89; VOYA 4/89) [616.86]

5103 Bach, Julie S., ed. *Drug Abuse: Opposing Viewpoints* (9–12). Illus. 1987, Greenhaven LB $15.95 (0-89908-426-5); paper $8.95 (0-89908-401-X). An anthology of articles expressing different views on the causes, extent, and solutions to drug abuse. (Rev: BL 12/1/87) [362.2]

5104 Benner, Janet. *Smoking Cigarettes: The Unfiltered Truth—Understanding Why and How to Quit* (9–12). 1987, Joelle paper $10.95 (0-942723-12-7). An account that describes the physical effects of smoking on the body and outlines various methods of quitting. (Rev: BL 12/15/87) [613.85]

5105 Brecher, Edward M. *Licit and Illicit Drugs* (10–12). Illus. 1972, Little $24.95 (0-316-15340-0); paper $14.95 (0-316-10717-4). A variety of drugs are introduced with information on their specific properties and their social implications. [613.8]

5106 Claypool, Jane. *Alcohol and You* (7–12). Illus. 1988, Watts LB $12.90 (0-531-10566-0). A new edition of this introductory book on alcohol is objective but realistic in its coverage of the effects of alcohol and its place in the lives of teenagers. (Rev: SLJ 3/89; BR 3–4/89; VOYA 4/89) [613.8]

5107 Coffey, Wayne. *Straight Talk about Drinking: Teenagers Speak Out about Alcohol* (7–12). 1988, NAL paper $7.95 (0-452-26061-2). The author's experiences with alcohol plus those of 50 teenagers are combined in an account that focuses on the effects alcohol has on people. (Rev: BL 9/15/88; BR 1–2/89; SLJ 11/88; VOYA 2/89) [362.2]

5108 Cohen, Susan, and Daniel Cohen. *A Six-Pack and a Fake I.D.* (9–12). 1986, Evans $11.95 (0-87131-459-2). While acknowledging that alcohol is a part of everyday life in America, this account stresses its psychological and physical effects on the body. (Rev: BL 2/1/86; BR 5–6/86; VOYA 8–10/86) [362.292]

5109 Cohen, Susan, and Daniel Cohen. *What You Can Believe about Drugs: An Honest and Unhysterical Guide for Teens* (8–12). 1988, Evans $12.95 (0-87131-527-0). A candid look at drugs and attitudes toward them that does not evade controversial areas. (Rev: BL 9/15/88; SLJ 6–7/88) [362.2]

5110 Debner, Claudia Bialke, ed. *Chemical Dependency* (9–12). Illus. 1985, Greenhaven $15.95 (0-89908-376-5); paper $7.95 (0-89908-351-X). This book discusses such topics as alcoholism, drug abuse, nicotine addiction, and treatments for these conditions. (Rev: BL 12/1/85; SLJ 3/86) [362.2]

5111 Dolan, Edward F., Jr. *International Drug Traffic* (7–12). 1985, Watts $11.90 (0-531-04937-X). A drug-by-drug account of where they come from and how they get to the United States. (Rev: BL 5/15/85; BR 9–10/85; SLJ 9/85) [363.4]

5112 Donohoe, Tom, and Neil Johnson. *Foul Play: Drug Abuse in Sports* (10–12). Illus. 1988, Basil Blackwell paper $9.95 (0-631-14845-0). This book describes drug use in sports by examining different types of drugs and their effects. (Rev: BL 6/15/86) [362.2]

5113 Edelson, Edward. *Drugs & the Brain* (9–12). Illus. 1987, Chelsea House $18.95 (1-55546-209-X). After an explanation of how the brain works, this book explains the harm that many drugs inflict on the brain. (Rev: BL 10/1/87) [615]

5114 Engel, Joe. *Addicted: Kids Talking about Drugs in Their Own Words* (10–12). 1989, Tor $15.95 (0-312-93145-X). This book contains 10 narratives of young people involved with both alcohol and drug abuse. (Rev: SLJ 4/90) [613.8]

5115 Fishman, Ross. *Alcohol and Alcoholism* (8–12). Illus. 1986, Chelsea House $18.95 (0-87754-762-9). A history of attitudes toward alcohol in this country as well as information on its effects on the body and treatments available for alcoholics. (Rev: BL 11/15/86) [616.86]

5116 Friedland, Bruce. *Emotions & Thoughts* (8–12). 1988, Chelsea House $17.95 (1-55546-205-7). After a discussion of thinking and feeling, this book explores the effects that drugs have on the processes. (Rev: BR 1–2/89) [152.4]

5117 Glowa, John R. *Inhalants: The Toxic Fumes* (9–12). Illus. 1986, Chelsea House $18.95 (0-87754-758-0). The dangers of using such inhalants as shoe polish are described and places where help can be obtained are given. (Rev: BL 2/15/87) [616.86]

5118 *Go Ask Alice* (9–12). 1971, Simon & Schuster $11.95 (0-671-66458-1); Avon paper $3.50 (0-380-00523-9). A harrowing account in diary form of a 15-year-old girl's drug addiction and its consequences. [613.8]

5119 Golden, Sandy. *Driving the Drunk off the Road: A Handbook for Action* (10–12). 1983, Quince Mill paper $7.95 (0-914757-01-6). A practical program is outlined to reduce alcohol-related accidents. [616.86]

5120 Goodwin, Donald W. *Alcoholism: The Facts* (10–12). Illus. 1981, Oxford Univ. Pr. $17.95 (0-19-261297-2). This book covers such topics as who are at risk of becoming alcoholics, symptoms, and treatments. [613.8]

5121 Gordon, Barbara. *I'm Dancing as Fast as I Can* (10–12). 1979, Bantam paper $4.50 (0-553-23226-6). The story of how the misuse of the drug Valium created a severe mental and emotional problem for the author. [613.8]

5122 Graeber, Laurel. *Are You Dying for a Drink? Teenagers and Alcohol Abuse* (8–12). 1985, Messner $11.29 (0-671-50818-0). This book focuses on problem drinking and the teenager, how it happens, and what can be done about it. (Rev: SLJ 2/86; VOYA 6/86) [616.86]

5123 Grinspoon, Lester. *Cocaine: A Drug and Its Social Evolution* (10–12). 1983, Basic Books paper $5.95 (0-465-09372-4). A history of this drug is given and how and where it is used today. [615]

5124 Hales, Dianne. *Case Histories* (8–12). Illus. 1987, Chelsea House $18.95 (1-55546-217-0). Ten case histories of young drug addicts that concentrate on how they began taking drugs. (Rev: BL 11/1/87) [362.2]

5125 Hawley, Richard A. *Drugs and Society: Responding to an Epidemic* (8–12). Illus. 1988, Walker LB $14.85 (0-8027-6749-4). Social problems involving drugs such as drug testing, recreational use, legalization, and legal drinking age are explored and information is given on various approaches to the drug problem. (Rev: SLJ 8/88; VOYA 8/88) [616.86]

5126 Henningfield, Jack E., and Nancy Almand Ator. *Barbiturates: Sleeping Potion or Intoxicant?* (9–12). Illus. 1986, Chelsea House $18.95 (0-87754-768-8). A discussion of these drugs, why they are prescribed, their effects, and the problems in long-term use. (Rev: BL 1/1/87) [616.86]

5127 Hoobler, Thomas, and Dorothy Hoobler. *Drugs and Crime* (9–12). Illus. 1988, Chelsea House LB $17.95 (1-55546-228-6). This account tells about the heroin, cocaine, and marijuana trade and the corruption and street crime that accompany the international drug traffic. (Rev: SLJ 5/88) [616.86]

5128 Hughes, Richard, and Robert Brewin. *The Tranquilizing of America: Pill Popping and the American Way of Life* (10–12). 1987, Warner

paper $2.95 (0-446-93638-3). A horrifying account of how average people misuse prescription and nonprescription drugs. [362.2]

5129 Hyde, Margaret O., ed. *Mind Drugs* (8–12). 1986, Putnam $10.95 (0-396-08813-9). This general account introduces such drugs as cocaine, marijuana, LSD, and alcohol and describes their effects. [613.8]

5130 Johanson, Chris-Ellyn. *Cocaine: A New Epidemic* (8–12). Illus. 1986, Chelsea House $18.95 (0-87754-765-3). A history of this drug is given and information on how it is manufactured and distributed today plus extensive material on its effects. (Rev: BL 7/86) [362.2]

5131 Jorgensen, Donald G., Jr., and June A. Jorgensen. *Secrets Told by Children of Alcoholics* (8–12). Illus. 1990, TAB paper $12.95 (0-8306-5008-3). A series of interviews with young people ages 8 to 17 who tell how alcoholism affected their families. (Rev: VOYA 8/90) [661]

5132 Jussim, Daniel. *Drug Tests and Polygraphs: Essential Tools or Violations of Privacy?* (8–12). 1988, Messner LB $11.29 (0-671-64438-6); paper $5.95 (0-671-65977-4). The nature of drug testing and the controversy about its use are explored primarily through case studies. (Rev: BL 9/1/88; SLJ 5/88) [363.2]

5133 Keigley, Peggy. *Quit & Win: The War of Cigarette Withdrawal Once and for All* (9–12). 1987, PBK paper $9.95 (0-942285-00-X). A plan to quit smoking that is based on personal experience. (Rev: BL 12/15/87) [618.8]

5134 Ketcham, Katherine, and Ginny Lyford Gustafson. *Living on the Edge: A Guide to Intervention for Families with Drug and Alcohol Problems* (10–12). 1989, Bantam paper $8.95 (0-553-34606-7). Using case studies as examples, this volume discusses techniques of intervention plus sources of outside help for all parties concerned. (Rev: BL 3/1/89) [616.86]

5135 Kusinitz, Marc. *Drug Use around the World* (8–12). 1988, Chelsea House LB $17.95 (1-55545-233-2). A look at the contemporary use of drugs on an international basis. (Rev: BR 1–2/89) [616.86]

5136 Langone, John. *Bombed, Buzzed, Smashed or . . . Sober* (9–12). 1976, Little $14.95 (0-316-51424-1). Hundreds of questions are answered about teenagers and alcohol. [616.86]

5137 Lawson, John. *Friends You Can Drop: Alcohol and Drugs* (10–12). 1986, Quinlan paper $10.95 (0-933341-10-5). This account focuses on the disease of alcoholism, its treatment, and how it is often associated with drugs. (Rev: BL 10/15/86) [613.8]

5138 Lee, Essie E. *Breaking the Connection: How Young People Achieve Drug-Free Lives* (7–12). Illus. 1988, Messner LB $10.29 (0-671-63637-5); paper $5.95 (0-671-67059-X). Through several case studies the horrors of drug dependency are explored as is the hope of rehabilitation. (Rev: BR 9–10/89; SLJ 10/88; VOYA 10/88) [616.86]

5139 Leite, Evelyn, and Pamela Espeland. *Different Like Me* (7–12). Illus. 1987, Johnson Institute paper $6.95 (0-935908-34-X). This book offers help to teenagers who have parents or other members of the family abusing drugs or alcohol. (Rev: BL 10/1/87; VOYA 10/87) [362]

5140 McCuen, Gary E. *The International Drug Trade* (8–12). Illus. 1989, GEM LB $12.95 (0-86596-071-2). This collection of articles and illustrations explores various aspects of the drug trade. (Rev: BR 9–10/89; SLJ 8/89) [613.6]

5141 McFarland, Rhoda. *Coping with Substance Abuse* (7–12). 1988, Rosen $12.95 (0-8239-0733-3). Advice for those who are trying to cope with alcohol or drug abuse in the family or with friends. (Rev: BL 5/1/88; SLJ 9/88) [362.2]

5142 Mann, Marty. *Marty Mann Answers Your Questions about Drinking and Alcoholism* (10–12). 1970, National Council on Alcoholism paper $3.95 (0-318-15340-8). A former alcoholic answers questions about drinking and alcoholism. [616.86]

5143 Martin, Jo, and Kelly Clendenon. *Drugs & the Family* (8–12). Illus. 1988, Chelsea House LB $17.95 (1-55546-220-0). The case history of a family whose son spent time in a psychiatric hospital because of drug use that included LSD and harder drugs. (Rev: SLJ 6–7/88) [613.8]

5144 Morrison, Martha A. *White Rabbit: A Doctor's Story of Her Addiction and Recovery* (10–12). 1989, Crown $17.95 (0-517-56816-0). A harrowing account of a young doctor's addiction to both drugs and alcohol. (Rev: BL 1/1/89) [616.86]

5145 Nahas, Gabriel S. *Keep Off the Grass* (10–12). 1985, Eriksson paper $10.95 (0-8397-4384-X). A report on the actual hazards of using marijuana. [615]

5146 Neff, Pauline. *Tough Love: How Parents Can Deal with Drug Abuse* (10–12). 1982, Abingdon paper $7.95 (0-687-42407-0). This book outlines a 12-step program for parents and young people to deal with drug abuse. [613.8]

5147 O'Brien, Robert, and Sidney Cohen, eds. *The Encyclopedia of Drug Abuse* (10–12). 1984, Facts on File $40.00 (0-87196-690-5). All aspects of drugs and their use are discussed in this alpha-

betically arranged account with 1,000 entries. [613.8]

5148 Rodgers, Joann Ellison. *Drugs & Pain* (9–12). Illus. 1987, Chelsea House $17.95 (1-55546-212-X). A book that explores the nature of pain and its cause plus material on how drugs and other treatments can help reduce it. (Rev: BL 11/15/87) [615]

5149 Rodgers, Joann Ellison. *Drugs & Sexual Behavior* (8–12). Illus. 1988, Chelsea House LB $17.95 (1-55546-215-4). This book discusses the effects that drugs have on sexual behavior and covers related subjects like AIDS and birth control. (Rev: BR 1–2/88; SLJ 10/88; VOYA 2/89) [616.86]

5150 Ryerson, Eric. *When Your Parent Drinks Too Much: A Book for Teenagers* (7–12). 1985, Facts on File $14.95 (0-8160-1259-8); Warner paper $3.95 (0-446-34692-6). A frank, realistic book of advice for young people who have alcoholic parents that includes information on Alateen. (Rev: BL 12/1/85; BR 3–4/86; SLJ 12/85; VOYA 4/86) [362.2]

5151 Sanberg, Paul R., and Michael D. Bunsey. *Prescription Narcotics: The Addictive Painkillers* (9–12). Illus. 1986, Chelsea House $18.95 (0-87754-700-X). An overview of these helpful painkillers that can also become addictive. (Rev: BL 1/1/87) [616.86]

5152 Sandmaier, Marian. *The Invisible Alcoholics: Women and Alcohol Abuse in America* (10–12). 1980, McGraw paper $5.95 (0-07-054661-4). This book explores the problem of alcoholism in American women. [362.2]

5153 Sherman, Pecki, and Virginia Newlin. *Broken Heart Whole Heart: A Family and Addiction* (9–12). 1990, Hampshire paper $9.95 (1-877674-01-X). The story of a loving family whose well-being is shattered by the drug addiction of their teenage son. (Rev: BL 1/15/90) [362]

5154 Siegel, Ronald K. *Intoxication: Life in Pursuit of Artificial Paradise* (10–12). 1989, Dutton $19.95 (0-525-24764-5). This book deals with the reasons why humans seek intoxication and the various ways in which they have achieved it. (Rev: SLJ 9/89) [613.8]

5155 Silverstein, Alvin, and Virginia B. Silverstein. *Alcoholism* (9–12). 1975, Harper LB $12.89 (0-397-31648-8). This account written for teenagers tells about the effects of alcohol and the causes and treatment of alcoholism. [616.86]

5156 Stone, Nannette, et al. *Cocaine: Seduction and Solution* (10–12). 1984, Potter $13.95 (0-517-55175-6). As well as describing cocaine and its effects, the authors categorize the types of people who use it. [362.2]

5157 Storti, Ed, and Janet Keller. *Crisis Intervention:Acting against Addiction* (9–12). 1988, Crown $17.95 (0-517-56859-4). A series of case studies in which people have intervened to help loved ones who are addicted to drugs or alcohol. (Rev: VOYA 12/88) [616.86]

5158 Theodore, Alan. *The Origins & Sources of Drugs* (8–12). 1988, Chelsea House LB $17.95 (1-55546-234-0). A readable background book that describes where drugs come from and how they originated in history. (Rev: BR 1–2/89) [616.86]

5159 Weil, Andrew, and Winifred Rosen. *From Chocolate to Morphine: Understanding Mind-Active Drugs* (10–12). Illus. 1983, Houghton paper $9.70 (0-395-33190-0). A discussion of many commonly abused substances, their effects, and how to avoid dependence. [613.8]

5160 Williams, Terry. *The Cocaine Kids: The Inside Story of a Teenage Drug Ring* (9–12). 1989, Addison $16.95 (0-201-09360-X). The inside story of 8 teenage cocaine dealers who called themselves "the crew." (Rev: VOYA 2/90) [616.86]

5161 Winger, Gail. *Valium: The Tranquil Trap* (9–12). Illus. 1986, Chelsea House $18.95 (0-87754-759-9). A look at this popular tranquilizer and the effects of its prolonged use. (Rev: BL 1/1/87) [616.86]

5162 Zackon, Fred. *Heroin: The Street Narcotic* (9–12). Illus. 1986, Chelsea House $18.95 (0-87754-769-6). An illustrated account that tells of the production and distribution of heroin and of the effects of use and addiction. (Rev: BL 4/1/87) [616.86]

5163 Zimmerman, David R. *The Essential Guide to Non-Prescription Drugs* (10–12). 1983, Harper $27.00 (0-06-014915-9); paper $12.95 (0-06-091023-2). An examination of the ingredients in common drugs, their effectiveness, and how to use them wisely. [615]

Bionics and Transplants

5164 Dowie, Mark. *"We Have a Donor": The Bold New World of Organ Transplants* (10–12). 1989, St. Martin's $16.95 (0-312-02316-2). Using a particular case study as a focal point, the author discusses various aspects of this controversial subject. (Rev: BL 12/1/88) [617]

5165 Leinwand, Gerald. *Transplants: Today's Medical Miracles* (7–12). 1985, Watts $11.90 (0-531-04930-2). A thorough study that gives the history, problems, progress, and moral dilemmas involved in the transplanting of organs. (Rev: BL 6/1/85; BR 3–4/86; SLJ 9/85; VOYA 12/85) [617]

5166 Pekkanen, John. *Donor: How One Girl's Death Gave Life to Others* (9–12). 1986, Little $16.95 (0-316-69792-3). How 4 different people's lives were saved by organs given by a teenage accident victim. (Rev: SLJ 9/86) [617]

Diseases and Illnesses

5167 *AIDS: Opposing Viewpoints* (9–12). Illus. 1987, Greenhaven LB $15.95 (0-89908-427-3); paper $7.95 (0-89908-402-8). A variety of religious, political, and moral viewpoints are represented in this collection of articles. (Rev: SLJ 2/88) [616]

5168 *The AIDS Crisis: Conflicting Social Values* (9–12). Illus. 1987, GEM $11.95 (0-85596-061-5). The moral, social, and medical issues involving AIDS are explored in this book. Part of the Ideas in Conflict series. (Rev: BR 9–10/87) [616]

5169 American Diabetes Assn., ed. *Diabetes in the Family* (10–12). Illus. 1987, Prentice paper $9.95 (0-13-208653-0). A manual explaining diabetes and the special care required by diabetics. (Rev: BL 9/1/87) [616.4]

5170 Anku, Vincent. *What to Know about the Treatment of Cancer* (10–12). Illus. 1985, Madrona paper $7.95 (0-88089-002-9). A straightforward, honest book that describes the types of cancer and tells about current treatments and their effectiveness. (Rev: BL 1/15/85) [619.99]

5171 Balfour, Henry H., Jr., and Ralph C. Heussner. *Herpes Diseases and Your Health* (10–12). Illus. 1984, Univ. of Minnesota Pr. paper $10.95 (0-8166-1432-6). Such herpes-related diseases as chicken pox, shingles, mononucleosis, and genital herpes are discussed. [616.9]

5172 Barlow, David. *Sexually Transmitted Diseases* (10–12). 1979, Oxford Univ. Pr. paper $6.95 (0-19-261157-7). For the mature reader, this is an authoritative, well-organized account. [614.4]

5173 Blake, Jeanne. *Risky Times: How to Be AIDS-Smart & Stay Healthy* (8–12). 1990, Workman paper $5.95 (0-89480-656-4). Using many case studies as a framework this is a handbook that effectively tells teenagers how to avoid

AIDS and describes the true nature of this disease. (Rev: BL 8/90; SLJ 9/90) [616.97]

5174 Bombeck, Erma. *I Want to Grow Hair, I Want to Grow Up, I Want to Go to Boise: Children Surviving Cancer* (9–12). Illus. 1989, Harper $16.95 (0-06-016170-1). An inspirational and often funny book about children with cancer. (Rev: BL 8/89) [618.92]

5175 Brooks, Stewart. *The VD Story* (10–12). 1973, Littlefield paper $4.95 (0-8226-0252-0). The story of how medicine has fought venereal disease. [614.4]

5176 Brumberg, Joan. *Fasting Girls: The Emergence of Anorexia Nervosa as a Modern Disease* (9–12). Illus. 1988, Harvard Univ. Pr. $25.00 (0-674-29501-3). A history of this disease (back to Victorian times), its causes, and treatment. (Rev: BL 3/15/88) [616.85]

5177 Cahill, Kevin M., ed. *The AIDS Epidemic* (10–12). 1983, St. Martin's $19.95 (0-312-01499-6). These are the papers, now somewhat dated, given at an important symposium on AIDS in New York in 1983. [614.4]

5178 Check, William A. *Alzheimer's Disease* (9–12). Illus. 1989, Chelsea House $16.95 (0-7910-0056-7). A succinct explanation of what Alzheimer's disease is, its possible causes, treatments, and the personal toll it takes on families. (Rev: BL 3/1/89; BR 9–10/89; SLJ 6/89; VOYA 8/89) [618.97]

5179 Cousins, Norman. *Anatomy of an Illness as Perceived by the Patient: Reflections on Healing and Regeneration* (10–12). 1979, Norton $15.95 (0-393-01252-2); Bantam paper $7.95 (0-553-34365-3). How medicine and a therapy of laughter helped the author conquer a degenerative disease. [610]

5180 Desowitz, Robert S. *The Thorn in the Starfish: How the Human Immune System Works* (9–12). 1987, Norton paper $7.95 (0-393-30552-2). A discussion of how the human immune system works and how such factors as AIDS, tobacco, and nutrition affect it. (Rev: BL 6/15/87) [616.07]

5181 Dorris, Michael. *The Broken Cord* (10–12). 1989, Harper $18.95 (0-06-016071-3). The gifted author writes a moving memoir about his adopted son, a victim of Fetal Alcohol Syndrome, and of the condition itself. (Rev: BL 6/1/89) [362.29]

5182 Douglas, Paul Harding, and Laura Pinsky. *The Essential AIDS Fact Book* (10–12). 1987, Pocket paper $3.95 (0-671-64772-5). A short book that gives the essential facts about AIDS and preventative measures that must be taken to avoid it. (Rev: BL 10/1/87) [616.9]

5183 Fettner, Ann Giudici. *Viruses: Agents of Change* (9–12). 1990, McGraw $19.95 (0-07-020664-3). An explanation of what viruses are, the different types in existence (e.g., flu, HIV), and how they work. (Rev: BL 9/1/90) [616]

5184 Frumkin, Lyn, and John Leonard. *Questions & Answers on AIDS* (10–12). 1987, Avon paper $3.95 (0-380-75467-3). In a question-and-answer format almost 200 queries concerning all aspects of AIDS are answered. (Rev: BL 10/1/87) [616.9]

5185 Gino, Carol. *Rusty's Story* (9–12). 1986, Bantam paper $3.95 (0-553-25351-1). The true story of a woman's battle with severe epilepsy. [616.8]

5186 Gordon, Jacquie. *Give Me One Wish* (10–12). Illus. 1988, Norton $18.95 (0-393-02518-7). Told by her mother, this is the inspiring story of Christine Gordon's life (and early death) with cystic fibrosis. (Rev: BL 4/1/88) [616.37]

5187 Hall, Lynn, and Thomas Modl, eds. *AIDS* (9–12). Illus. 1987, Greenhaven $15.95 (0-89908-427-3); paper $7.95 (0-89908-402-8). A book of readings that surveys various attitudes and opinions about AIDS and the controversies that surround it. (Rev: BL 11/1/87) [362.1]

5188 Hein, Karen, and Theresa Foy Digeronimo. *AIDS, Trading Fears for Facts: A Guide for Teens* (9–12). Illus. 1989, Consumers Union paper $3.95 (0-89043-269-4). A fact-filled book about AIDS and how this disease relates to teenagers. (Rev: VOYA 2/90) [616]

5189 Holleb, Arthur I., et al., eds. *The American Cancer Society Cancer Book: Prevention, Detection, Diagnosis, Treatment, Cure* (9–12). Illus. 1986, Doubleday $24.95 (0-385-17847-6). An excellent reference book that tells what is known about cancer and also stresses early detection and prevention. (Rev: BL 6/1/86) [616.99]

5190 Hyde, Margaret O. *VD: The Silent Epidemic* (7–12). 2nd ed. Illus. 1983, McGraw $10.95 (0-07-031651-1). An introduction to various venereal diseases, their causes, effects, and treatments. [616.95]

5191 Hyde, Margaret O., and Elizabeth H. Forsyth. *AIDS: What Does It Mean to You?* (9–12). 1986, Walker LB $11.85 (0-8027-6633-1). This book, which is the first one for teenagers on the subject of AIDS, contains valuable background material although coverage ends in the mid-1980s. (Rev: BL 5/15/86; BR 11–12/86; SLJ 12/86; VOYA 6/87) [616.97]

5192 Johnson, Eric W. *VD: Venereal Disease and What You Should Do about It* (9–12). Rev ed. Illus. 1978, Harper $12.70 (0-397-31811-1). An account that concentrates on causes, symptoms, and treatment of syphilis and gonorrhea. [616.95]

5193 Kirp, David L., et al. *Learning by Heart: AIDS and Schoolchildren* (9–12). 1989, Rutgers Univ. Pr. $22.95 (0-8135-1396-0). An account of how 7 different communities coped with their schoolchildren who had AIDS. (Rev: BL 5/15/89) [362.1]

5194 Klawans, Harold L. *Toscanini's Fumble: And Other Tales of Clinical Neurology* (10–12). Illus. 1988, Contemporary $16.95 (0-8092-4727-5). Seventeen case studies that deal with such neurological problems as Parkinson's disease. (Rev: BL 3/15/88) [616.8]

5195 Kosof, Anna. *Why Me? Coping with Family Illness* (9–12). 1986, Watts LB $12.90 (0-531-10254-8). A brief account of what to do when a member of one's family is afflicted with a disease or other affliction. (Rev: BR 1–2/87; SLJ 12/86; VOYA 12/86) [362.1]

5196 Kuklin, Susan. *Fighting Back: What Some People Are Doing about AIDS* (9–12). Illus. 1989, Putnam $14.95 (0-399-21621-9). Interviews and profiles of people who individually or in organizations like the Gay Men's Health Crisis of New York City are responding positively to the AIDS problem. (Rev: BL 12/15/88; SLJ 2/89) [362.1]

5197 Lampton, Christopher. *Predicting AIDS and Other Epidemics* (9–12). Illus. 1989, Watts LB $12.90 (0-531-10785-X). This account treats the methods used in epidemiology and how they are applied to the AIDS epidemic. (Rev: SLJ 2/90) [616.9]

5198 Lance, James W. *Migraine and Other Headaches* (9–12). Illus. 1986, Macmillan paper $7.95 (0-684-18654-3). An explanation of what causes all sorts of headaches and how they can best be treated. (Rev: BL 4/15/86) [616.857]

5199 Landau, Elaine. *Sexually Transmitted Diseases* (9–12). Illus. 1986, Enslow $14.95 (0-89490-115-X). A variety of venereal diseases such as AIDS, herpes, and syphilis are discussed as well as their symptoms, causes, treatment, and prevention. (Rev: BL 8/86; BR 11–12/86; SLJ 9/86; VOYA 12/86) [616.9]

5200 Landau, Elaine. *We Have AIDs* (9–12). 1990, Watts LB $12.90 (0-531-10898-8). Nine young adults tell what it's like to have AIDS. (Rev: BL 3/1/90; SLJ 4/90; VOYA 8/90) [362.1]

5201 Langone, John. *AIDS: The Facts* (10–12). 1987, Little $17.95 (0-316-51413-6); paper $8.95 (0-316-51412-8). A thorough review of what is

known and thought to be the truth about AIDS as of 1988. (Rev: BL 2/1/88) [616.97]

5202 LeVert, Suzanne. *AIDS: In Search of a Killer* (10–12). 1987, Messner $11.98 (0-671-62840-2). Using 2 case studies to bring this trauma to life, LeVert also discusses the causes and course of this disease. (Rev: BL 8/87; SLJ 9/87; VOYA 12/87) [616]

5203 Mace, Nancy L., and Peter V. Rabins. *The Thirty-six-Hour Day* (10–12). 1984, Johns Hopkins Univ. Pr. $27.50 (0-8018-2659-4); Warner paper $5.95 (0-446-35786-3). A manual to help people caring for someone with Alzheimer's and related diseases involving mental problems in the elderly. [616]

5204 Madaras, Lynda. *Lynda Madaras Talks to Teens about AIDS: An Essential Guide for Parents, Teachers, and Young People* (9–12). Illus. 1988, Newmarket $12.95 (1-55704-010-9); paper $5.95 (1-55704-009-5). A straightforward account that tries to correct misinformation about AIDS and stresses preventive measures. (Rev: BL 11/1/88; BR 1–2/89; SLJ 11/88) [616.9]

5205 Margolies, Cynthia P., and Kenneth B. McCredie. *Understanding Leukemia* (10–12). Illus. 1983, Macmillan $16.95 (0-684-17978-4); paper $9.95 (0-317-47462-6). This book discusses leukemia from the standpoint of how it develops, various stages, methods of treatment, and how to cope with the disease. [616.99]

5206 Martelli, Leonard, et al. *When Someone You Know Has AIDS: A Practical Guide* (10–12). 1987, Crown $15.95 (0-517-56555-2); paper $9.95 (0-517-56556-0). An account aimed at those who are given responsibility for caring for a person with AIDS. (Rev: SLJ 12/87) [616]

5207 Massie, Robert, and Suzanne Massie. *Journey* (10–12). 1984, Ballantine paper $3.95 (0-345-31629-0). The true story of how the authors raised a hemophiliac son to age 18. [616.1]

5208 *Merck Manual of Diagnosis and Therapy* (10–12). 1987, Merck $21.50 (0-911918-06-7). Symptoms, diagnosis, and treatments are outlined for a number of ailments. [610.2]

5209 Miller, Caroline Adams. *My Name Is Caroline* (10–12). Illus. 1988, Doubleday $17.95 (0-385-24208-5). The amazing story of how a girl overcame bulimia with its alternating binges and purges. (Rev: BL 2/15/88; VOYA 12/88) [616.85]

5210 Morra, Marion, and Eve Potts. *Choices: Realistic Alternatives in Cancer Treatment* (10–12). 1987, Avon paper $11.95 (0-380-75308-1). In a question-and-answer format, this is a review of the many alternate treatments available for cancer plus material on risks involved and how to diagnose cancer. (Rev: BL 5/1/87; SLJ 6–7/87) [616]

5211 Mullan, Fitzhugh. *Vital Signs* (10–12). 1983, Dell $12.50 (0-374-16864-4). The story of a young doctor's struggle with cancer. [616]

5212 Nichols, Eve K., ed. *Mobilizing against AIDS* (9–12). Rev. ed. Illus. 1989, Harvard Univ. Pr. $25.00 (0-674-57763-9); paper $12.95 (0-674-57762-0). An excellent handbook that summarizes all we currently know about AIDS, related diseases, and where current research is going. (Rev: BL 2/15/89) [616.97]

5213 Nilsson, Lennart, and Jan Lindberg. *The Body Victorious* (9–12). Trans. by K. Lindquist and S. Nordfeldt. Illus. 1987, Delacorte $25.00 (0-385-29507-3). A lucid account of how the body's immune system and other defense systems operate. (Rev: SLJ 4/88) [612]

5214 Nourse, Alan E. *Herpes* (9–12). Illus. 1985, Watts $11.90 (0-531-10069-3). Various types of the herpes virus are introduced, their differences, and how their effects can be prevented and treated. (Rev: BL 10/15/85; BR 5–6/86; SLJ 12/85; VOYA 6/86) [616.95]

5215 Oyler, Chris., et al. *Go Toward the Light* (10–12). 1988, Harper $15.95 (0-06-015885-9). The touching story of the suffering and death from AIDS of a 9-year-old girl and its effects on her family. (Rev: BL 8/88) [616.97]

5216 Panger, Daniel. *Dance of the Wild Mouse* (10–12). 1979, Entwhistle $9.95 (0-9601428-4-3); paper $7.95 (0-9601428-5-1). An account of a man's tragic battle with leukemia. [616]

5217 Potts, Eve, and Marion Morra. *Understanding Your Immune System* (9–12). 1986, Avon paper $3.95 (0-380-89728-8). Using a question-and-answer format, the authors explain the immune system, how it can be strengthened, and what happens when it malfunctions. (Rev: BL 6/1/86) [612]

5218 Rosenthal, Ted. *How Could I Not Be among You?* (10–12). 1987, Persea paper $8.95 (0-89255-117-8). A young Berkeley student shares his feelings as he dies of leukemia. [616]

5219 Shilts, Randy. *And the Band Played On* (10–12). 1988, Penguin paper $12.95 (0-14-011369-X). A report on the misinformation and inaction that has surrounded the fight against AIDS in this country. (Rev: SLJ 4/88) [616]

5220 Silverstein, Alvin, and Virginia B. Silverstein. *AIDS: Deadly Threat* (10–12). Illus. 1986, Enslow $14.95 (0-89490-128-1). After a description of the immune system, this book provides information about the causes, spread, and treat-

ment of AIDS. (Rev: BL 10/1/86; SLJ 12/86; VOYA 4/87) [616.97]

5221 Strauss, Linda L. *Coping When a Parent Has Cancer* (7–12). 1988, Rosen LB $12.95 (0-8239-0785-6). In addition to discussing the types of cancer and their treatment, this book tells how a teenager can handle the crisis when a family member develops cancer. (Rev: BR 3–4/89; SLJ 2/89; VOYA 6/89) [616.99]

5222 Wachter, Oralee. *Sex, Drugs and AIDS* (9–12). 1987, Bantam paper $3.95 (0-553-34454-4). The AIDS epidemic is examined from the standpoint of the 2 chief means of contact. (Rev: VOYA 10/87) [616]

5223 Whitmore, George. *Someone Was Here: Profiles in the AIDS Epidemic* (10–12). 1988, NAL $17.95 (0-453-00601-9). A book that humanizes the AIDS scourge by giving several case studies of victims. (Rev: BL 4/1/88) [362.1]

5224 Woods, Samuel G. *Everything You Need to Know about Sexually Transmitted Disease* (7–12). Illus. 1990, Rosen LB $12.95 (0-8239-1010-5). Various kinds of venereal diseases are introduced, with their symptoms and treatments. (Rev: SLJ 9/90; VOYA 8/90) [305.4]

5225 Wurman, Richard Saul. *Medical Access* (9–12). 1985, Simon & Schuster paper $9.95 (0-671-60393-0). In addition to explaining 120 common medical tests, this book tells what goes on in an operating room and intensive care unit. (Rev: BL 11/15/85) [616]

5226 Zinner, Stephen H. *How to Protect Yourself from STDs* (10--12). 1986, Summit paper $6.95 (0-671-62876-3). An open, candid description of various venereal diseases and information on prevention. (Rev: SLJ 1/86) [616.95]

5227 Zinsser, Hans. *Rats, Lice and History* (10–12). 1935, Little $12.95 (0-316-98890-1); paper $8.95 (0-316-98896-0). The history of typhus fever and its role in human history. [616.9]

Doctors, Hospitals, and Medicine

5228 Angier, Natalie. *Natural Obsessions: The Search for the Oncogene* (10–12). Illus. 1988, Houghton $19.95 (0-395-45370-4). The day-to-day operations of 2 labs involved in cancer research. (Rev: BL 6/1/88) [616.99]

5229 Annas, George J. *Judging Medicine* (10–12). 1988, Humana Pr. $24.95 (0-89603-132-2). Such problems in medical ethics as surrogate parenting and terminal care are explored. (Rev: BL 6/15/88) [610.696]

5230 Bach, Julie S., and Susan Bursell, eds. *Biomedical Ethics: Opposing Viewpoints* (9–12). Illus. 1987, Greenhaven LB $15.95 (0-89908-396-X); paper $8.95 (0-89908-371-4). In this collection of writings, opposing points of view are expressed on such topics as genetic engineering, organ transplants, and ethical standards in medicine. (Rev: SLJ 6–7/87) [614]

5231 Bourdillon, Hilary. *Women As Healers: A History of Women and Medicine* (10–12). Illus. 1989, Cambridge Univ. Pr. paper $5.95 (0-521-31090-3). An account of the roles played by women in the history of western medicine. (Rev: BL 7/89) [610]

5232 Crichton, Michael. *Five Patients* (10–12). 1989, Ballantine paper $3.95 (0-345-33464-8). A doctor talks about some of his interesting cases. [610]

5233 Davies, Owen, ed. *The Omni Book of Medicine* (10–12). n.d., Zebra paper $3.95 (0-8217-1364-7). Topics covered in this book include cancer research, nutrition, biofeedback, and genetics. [610]

5234 Doelp, Alan. *In the Blink of an Eye: Inside a Children's Trauma Center* (10–12). 1989, Prentice $17.95 (0-13-131871-3). A glimpse into the Children's Hospital Medical Center in Washington, D.C., its patients, and the care they receive. (Rev: BL 2/1/89) [362.1]

5235 Finn, Jeffrey, and Eliot L. Marshall. *Medical Ethics* (10–12). 1990, Chelsea House $18.95 (0-7910-0086-9). This book covers issues involved in such areas as abortion, transplants, euthanasia, and genetic engineering. (Rev: VOYA 8/90) [174]

5236 Franck, Irene M., and David M. Brownstone. *Healers* (9–12). Illus. 1989, Facts on File $17.95 (0-8160-1446-9). An account with illustrations on how the modern medical profession has evolved from magic to the use of scientific principles. (Rev: SLJ 12/89; VOYA 4/90) [610]

5237 Gilbert, Susan. *Medical Fakes and Frauds* (9–12). Illus. 1989, Chelsea House $17.95 (0-7910-0090-7). A history of medical frauds plus an explanation of how these deceptions work and why people become their victims. (Rev: BL 8/89; BR 11–12/89; SLJ 9/89; VOYA 10/89) [615.8]

5238 Gutkind, Lee. *Many Sleepless Nights: The World of Organ Transplantation* (10–12). 1988, Norton $18.95 (0-393-02520-9). The world of organ transplants is explored with a particular focus on an important site, Presbyterian Univer-

sity Hospital in Pittsburgh. (Rev: BL 6/15/88) [617.95]

5239 Heintze, Carl. *Medical Ethics* (8–12). Illus. 1987, Watts $11.90 (0-531-10414-1). Various case studies are used to illustrate the many moral dilemmas facing the medical profession today. (Rev: BL 12/15/87; BR 9–10/88; SLJ 2/88) [174]

5240 Klass, Perri Elizabeth. *A Not Entirely Benign Procedure: Four Years as a Medical Student* (10–12). 1988, NAL paper $4.50 (0-451-15358-8). The process of becoming a doctor as described by a woman who spent 4 years at Harvard Medical School. (Rev: BL 4/1/87) [610.7]

5241 Kraegel, Janet, and Mary Kachoyeanos. *Just a Nurse: The Lives and Experiences of Nurses in America—In Their Own Words* (10–12). 1989, Dutton $18.95 (0-525-24760-2). Interviews with over 50 different types of nurses supply the material for a cross-section of this profession. (Rev: BL 4/15/89; SLJ 9/89) [610.73]

5242 LeBaron, Charles. *Gentle Vengeance: An Account of the First Year at Harvard Medical School* (10–12). 1982, Penguin paper $6.95 (0-14-006106-1). A fascinating account of one man's first year at Harvard Medical School. [610]

5243 Levin, Beatrice. *Women and Medicine: Pioneers Meeting the Challenge!* (10–12). 2nd ed. 1988, Media Publg. paper $9.95 (0-939644-28-2). An account of the role women have played in medicine from the ancient Greeks to the present time. (Rev: BL 10/15/88) [610]

5244 Marion, Robert. *The Boy Who Felt No Pain: Tales from the Pediatric Ward* (9–12). 1990, Addison-Wesley $17.95 (0-201-55049-0). A heartwarming collection of 14 case histories from the files of a pediatric doctor. (Rev: BL 9/1/90) [618]

5245 Marion, Robert. *The Intern Blues: The Private Ordeals of Three Young Doctors* (9–12). 1989, Morrow $18.95 (0-688-06886-3). Edited tapes made by 3 interns during an entire year form the basis of this thoughtful account. (Rev: BL 3/15/89) [610.7]

5246 Mirkin, Gabe, and Marshall Hoffman. *Sportsmedicine Book* (10–12). 1978, Little $24.95 (0-316-57434-1); $14.95 (0-316-57436-8). This book discusses sports medicine with emphasis on prevention of physical injuries and psychological problems. [616]

5247 Morantz-Sanchez, Regina Markell. *Sympathy and Science: Women Physicians in American Medicine* (10–12). 1985, Oxford Univ. Pr. paper $10.95 (0-19-504985-3). A book that explores the place of women in American medicine and how they have been treated in it. [610.69]

fitness for women of size 14 and up. (Rev: BL 11/15/89) [646.7]

5282 Hunnisett, Jean. *Period Costume for Stage & Screen: Patterns for Women's Dress, 1500–1800* (9–12). Illus. 1987, Drama Book $35.00 (0-7135-2660-2). A discussion of historic costume plus over 20 patterns are given. (Rev: BL 3/1/87) [791.43]

5283 Jackson, Carole. *Color Me Beautiful* (9–12). 1987, Ballantine paper $11.95 (0-345-34588-6). This is a collection of dress and grooming hints from a beauty consultant. [646.7]

5284 Kelly, Daniel. *The Right On! Book of Hair Care and Beauty* (9–12). 1985, Sharon paper $3.50 (0-451-82124-6). This is a guide to beauty and hair care for black women. [611]

5285 Mills, Joey. *New Classic Beauty: A Step-by-Step Guide to Naturally Glamorous Makeup* (9–12). 1987, Random $19.95 (0-394-56433-2). A beauty guide by a well-known makeup artist that is arranged by hair color. (Rev: BR 5–6/88) [646.7]

5286 Murray, Maggie Pexton. *Changing Styles in Fashion: Who, What, Why* (10–12). Illus. 1989, Fairchild $20.00 (0-87005-585-2). The world of high fashion past and present is introduced and several modern couturiers are highlighted. (Rev: BL 4/15/89) [746.92]

5287 Parks-McKay, Jane. *The Make-over: A Teen's Guide to Looking & Feeling Beautiful* (7–12). Illus. 1985, Morrow $17.95 (0-688-04155-8); paper $11.95 (0-688-04156-6). Although this book covers aspects of inner beauty involving attitudes and outlooks, most of the text and illustrations give advice on improving one's outside appearance through a number of beauty tips. (Rev: BL 11/15/85; BR 11–12/85; SLJ 11/85) [646.7]

5288 Scott, Margaret. *A Visual History of Costume: The Fourteenth & Fifteenth Centuries* (9–12). Illus. 1986, David & Charles $22.50 (0-7134-4857-1). Two hundred years of dress are covered in black-and-white reproductions of artwork and introductory chapters. (Rev: BL 1/15/87) [391]

5289 Shields, Brooke. *On Your Own* (9–12). Illus. 1985, Random $16.95 (0-394-54460-9). Brooke Shields gives advice to teens on topics like grooming, dating, and schoolwork. (Rev: BR1–2/86; SLJ 11/85; VOYA 12/85) [646.7]

5290 Tortora, Phyllis, and Keith Eubank. *A Survey of Historic Costume* (9–12). Illus. 1989, Fairchild $30.00 (0-87005-632-8). A well-illustrated history of costume and dress since ancient times. (Rev: BL 1/1/90) [391.009]

The Human Body

General and Miscellaneous

5291 Asimov, Isaac. *The Human Body: Its Structure and Operations* (9–12). Illus. 1963, Houghton paper $4.95 (0-451-62707-5). An introduction to the various systems of the human body with the exception of the nervous system. [612]

5292 Christensen, Alice. *The American Yoga Association Beginners' Manual* (10–12). Rev. ed. Illus. 1987, Simon & Schuster paper $12.95 (0-671-61935-7). A basic manual on the philosophy and practice of yoga with material on 75 postures. (Rev: BL 9/1/87) [613.7]

5293 Diagram Group. *The Healthy Body: A Maintenance Manual* (10–12). Illus. 1982, NAL paper $8.93 (0-452-25352-7). With many diagrams and charts, questions about bodily functions are answered and advice on how to stay healthy is given. [611]

5294 Dixon, Bernard, ed. *Health, Medicine, and the Human Body* (9–12). Illus. 1986, Macmillan $50.00 (0-02-908040-1). This account not only introduces the parts and systems of the body but also traces the history of important discoveries in medical history and how doctors treat disorders today. (Rev: BL 7/86) [610]

5295 Friedlander, Mark P., and Terry M. Phillips. *Winning the War Within: Understanding, Protecting, and Building Your Body's Immunity* (10–12). 1986, Rodale $19.95 (0-87857-648-7); paper $10.95 (0-87857-649-5). A discussion of our immune system, how it works, and how we can strengthen it by good nutrition, exercise, and reduction of stress. (Rev: BL 11/15/86) [616.07]

5296 Hughes, Martin. *Body Clock: The Effects of Time on Human Health* (10–12). Illus. 1989, Facts on File $24.95 (0-8160-2223-2). An explanation of the time tables that produce and regulate body growth and functions. (Rev: SLJ 6/90) [612]

5297 Landau, Terry. *About Faces* (10–12). 1989, Doubleday $29.95 (0-385-24975-6); paper $14.95 (0-385-24981-0). An account of how the human face evolved and, without words, how it can express feelings and emotions. (Rev: BL 4/15/89) [573]

5298 Miller, Jonathan. *The Human Body* (7–12). Illus. 1983, Viking $19.95 (0-670-38605-7). Based on the TV series by the same name, this is a fascinating pop-up book on body parts with accompanying text. [612]

5299 Nilsson, Lennart. *Behold Man: A Photographic Journey of Discovery inside the Body* (7–

12). Illus. 1974, Little $29.95 (0-316-60751-7); paper $19.95 (0-316-60752-5). An unusually illustrated book (many photographs represent magnifications of 45,000 times) on the body and its systems. [612]

5300 Poole, Robert M., ed. *The Incredible Machine* (9–12). Illus. 1986, National Geographic $26.95 (0-87044-620-7). Outstanding photographs and diagrams highlight this account of the parts of the human body and how they work. (Rev: BL 8/86; SLJ 11/86) [611]

5301 Powis, Raymond L. *The Human Body and Why It Works* (10–12). Illus. 1985, Prentice $17.95 (0-13-444969-X); paper $9.95 (0-13-444944-4). A somewhat technical introduction to the systems in the human body and how they operate. (Rev: SLJ 10/85) [611]

5302 Reader's Digest, eds. *ABC's of the Human Body: A Family Answer Book* (9–12). Illus. 1987, Reader's Digest $26.95 (0-89577-220-5). In a question-and-answer format, material is presented on all the systems and disorders of the human body. (Rev: BL 9/1/87) [612]

5303 Rose, Kenneth Jon. *The Body in Time* (10–12). Illus. 1988, Wiley $19.95 (0-471-85762-9). A fascinating account of how blood and tissue operate plus explanations of such common phenomena as sneezing. (Rev: BL 1/15/88; VOYA 2/89) [612]

5304 Vannini, Vanio, and Giuliano Pogliani, eds. *The Color Atlas of Human Anatomy* (9–12). Trans. by Richard T. Jolly. Illus. 1980, Harmony paper $7.95 (0-517-54514-4). Lavish illustrations give a multidimensional view of the human body and its systems. [611]

Brain and Nervous System

5305 Asimov, Isaac. *The Human Brain: Its Capacities and Functions* (9–12). Illus. 1964, NAL paper $4.95 (0-451-62363-0). This description of the brain, nervous system, and their functions incorporates scientific knowledge and current fields of research. [612]

5306 August, Paul Nordstrom. *Brain Function* (9–12). Illus. 1987, Chelsea House $17.95 (0-55546-204-9). An introduction to the nervous system that gives details on the brain and how drugs affect it. (Rev: BL 2/15/88) [612]

5307 Bergland, Richard. *The Fabric of Mind* (10–12). Illus. 1989, Penguin paper $9.95 (0-14-007460-0). A neurosurgeon explains how the brain functions and the mysteries about it not yet solved. (Rev: BL 9/1/86) [611.81]

5308 Campbell, Jeremy. *The Improbable Machine* (9–12). 1989, Simon & Schuster $19.95 (0-671-65711-9). A comparison between the human brain and how it looks with the nature of artificial intelligence. (Rev: BL 10/1/89) [153]

5309 Corrick, James A. *The Human Brain: Mind and Matter* (7–12). Illus. 1983, Arco $12.95 (0-688-05519-7). The parts of the brain, its functions, and diseases that affect it are 3 of the topics discussed. [612]

5310 Diagram Group. *The Brain: A User's Manual* (10–12). Illus. 1982, Putnam $11.95 (0-399-51379-5); Berkley paper $5.50 (0-425-06053-5). This study of the human brain is highlighted by a series of outstanding illustrations. [611]

5311 Edelson, Edward. *Nutrition and the Brain* (10–12). Illus. 1987, Chelsea House $17.95 (1-55546-210-3). An explanation of how behavior and emotion are influenced by food. (Rev: BL 2/1/88) [612]

5312 Fincher, J. *Lefties: The Origins and Consequences of Being Left-Handed* (10–12). 1980, Putnam paper $7.95 (0-399-50460-5). The causes, results, and attitudes of left-handedness. [611]

5313 Franklin, Jon. *Molecules of the Mind: The Brave New Science of Molecular Psychology* (10–12). 1987, Macmillan $18.95 (0-689-11604-7); Dell paper $5.95 (0-440-50005-2). The amazing story of the recent discovery that molecular activity in the brain actually causes thought and behavior. (Rev: BL 1/15/87) [530]

5314 Goldberg, Jeff. *Anatomy of a Scientific Discovery* (10–12). 1988, Bantam $17.95 (0-553-05261-6). The story of the discovery of endorphins, a narcotic-like substance manufactured in the brain. (Rev: SLJ 1/89) [611]

5315 Hooper, Judith, and Dick Teresi. *The Three-Pound Universe* (10–12). 1987, Dell paper $12.95 (0-440-58507-4). A tour of the human brain with special coverage of recent neurological discoveries. (Rev: BL 2/15/86) [152]

5316 Martin, Russell. *Matters Gray and White: A Neurologist, His Patients, and the Mysteries of the Brain* (10–12). 1988, Fawcett paper $4.95 (0-449-21606-3). One year in the professional life of a neurologist and how he treats such diseases as Alzheimer's and Lou Gehrig's. (Rev: BL 10/15/86) [612.8]

5317 Meltzer, Milton. *The Landscape of Memory* (8–12). 1987, Viking $12.95 (0-670-80821-0). The nature of memory is explored plus coverage of the ways we remember and causes of memory loss. (Rev: BL 4/1/87; BR 1–2/88; SLJ 4/87) [153.1]

305

5318 Metos, Thomas H. *The Human Mind: How We Think and Learn* (8–12). Illus. 1990, Watts LB $12.40 (0-531-10885-6). After an overview of the structure and basic functions of the brain, this account discusses various theories of learning. (Rev: BL 11/15/90) [153]

5319 Morgan, Brian, and Roberta Morgan. *Brainfood: Nutrition and Your Brain* (10–12). Illus. 1987, Body Pr. $18.95 (0-89586-565-3); paper $7.95 (0-89586-558-0). The authors explain in detail which foods and drugs (prescription and otherwise) affect the brain and can cause many disorders such as insomnia and stress. (Rev: SLJ 3/88) [641.1]

5320 Ornstein, Robert, and David Sobel. *The Healing Rain: Breakthrough Medical Discoveries about How the Brain Manages Health* (10–12). 1987, Simon & Schuster $19.95 (0-671-61945-4). The delicate relationship between the brain and physical well-being is explored in this intriguing account. (Rev: BL 6/15/87) [613]

5321 Pool, J. Lawrence. *Nature's Masterpiece: The Brain and How It Works* (9–12). Illus. 1986, Walker $16.95 (0-8027-0916-8); paper $9.95 (0-8027-7298-6). A brief, illustrated book that tells much of what is known about the brain's composition and functions. (Rev: BL 11/15/86) [612]

5322 Reader's Digest, eds. *ABC's of the Human Mind: A Family Answer Book* (9–12). Illus. 1990, Reader's Digest $26.95 (0-89577-345-7). A quick reference source of material on the workings of the human mind that includes many graphs and illustrations. (Rev: BL 10/15/90) [150]

5323 Restak, Richard M. *The Brain* (10–12). Illus. 1984, Bantam $27.95 (0-553-05119-9); Warner paper $5.95 (0-446-35548-2). This book outlines current information on such topics as stress, emotions, and drives. [612]

5324 Restak, Richard M. *The Mind* (10–12). Illus. 1988, Bantam $29.95 (0-553-05314-0). This book, based on the PBS series, covers 9 major topics including thinking, language, pain, and aging. (Rev: BL 10/1/88) [152]

5325 Sagan, Carl. *The Dragons of Eden: Speculations on the Evolution of Human Intelligence* (10–12). Illus. 1977, Random $10.95 (0-394-41045-9); Ballantine paper $4.95 (0-345-34629-7). A study of human intellect and the functions of the brain. [153]

5326 Silverstein, Alvin, and Virginia B. Silverstein. *World of the Brain* (9–12). 1985, Morrow $12.95 (0-688-05771-2). This work describes the brain, as well as the function of each area, and

how such influences as emotions and drugs affect the brain. (Rev: BR 5–6/86) [611]

5327 Thompson, Richard F. *The Brain* (10–12). Illus. 1985, Freeman paper $18.95 (0-7167-1462-0). For better readers, coverage on the structure of the brain and of neuroscience. (Rev: BR 1–2/86) [611]

5328 Wilson, Colin. *The Psychic Detectives: The Story of Psychometry and Paranormal Crime Detection* (9–12). 1987, Berkley paper $3.95 (0-425-10015-4). A fascinating account of how all types of psychometry are used in fighting crime. (Rev: SLJ 11/86) [133]

Senses

5329 Ackerman, Diane. *A Natural History of the Senses* (10–12). 1990, Random $19.95 (0-394-57335-8). A celebration of the senses with material on folklore, cultural values, and each individual sense. (Rev: BL 5/1/90) [612.8]

5330 Agostini, Franco. *Visual Games* (9–12). 1988, Facts on File LB $27.95 (0-8160-1979-7). An account that deals with visual perception covering illusions and Gestalt therapy. (Rev: BR 1–2/89) [617.7]

5331 Higbee, Kenneth L. *Your Memory: How It Works and How to Improve It* (10–12). 1988, Prentice paper $8.95 (0-13-973033-8). The nature of memory and techniques, chiefly mnemonic, to help retention of information. (Rev: BL 6/1/88) [153.1]

5332 Rezen, Susan V., and Carl Hausman. *Coping with Hearing Loss: A Guide for Adults and Their Families* (10–12). Illus. 1985, Dembner $15.95 (0-934878-48-X). A guide for the hearing impaired that discusses the physical causes as well as such topics as hearing aids and other possible treatments. (Rev: BL 4/15/85) [362.2]

5333 Smith, Jillyn. *Senses and Sensibilities* (10–12). Illus. 1989, Wiley $18.95 (0-471-50657-5); paper $9.95 (0-471-61839-X). An explanation of the 5 senses and how they function and dysfunction in humans and other animals. (Rev: BL 6/15/89; BR 11–12/89) [612.8]

5334 Watkins, Susan M. *Dreaming Myself, Dreaming a Town* (10–12). Illus. 1989, Kendall $21.95 (0-945512-01-5). An account of the phenomenon of dreaming and how it relates to waking experiences. (Rev: SLJ 12/89) [154.6]

Skin and Hair

5335 Flandermeyer, Kenneth L. *Clear Skin* (9–12). 1979, Little paper $8.95 (0-316-28546-3). A program is outlined to combat such problems as pimples, acne, and blackheads. [616.5]

5336 Goodman, Thomas, and Stephanie Young. *Smart Face: A Dermatologist's Guide to Cosmetics and Skin Care* (9–12). Illus. 1988, Prentice paper $9.95 (0-13-814377-3). A comprehensive guide that includes general skin care plus material on such topics as acne. (Rev: BL 9/15/88) [646.7]

5337 Lubowe, Irwin I., and Barbara Huss. *A Teen-age Guide to Healthy Skin and Hair* (9–12). Rev. ed. 1979, Dutton $12.50 (0-87690-335-9). Problems and solutions in developing and maintaining healthy skin and hair. [611]

5338 Novick, Nelson Lee. *Skin Care for Teens* (7–12). Illus. 1988, Watts $12.40 (0-531-10521-0). A no-nonsense practical guide from a well-known dermatologist. (Rev: BL 6/15/88; BR 9–10/88; SLJ 8/88; VOYA 10/88) [646.7]

5339 Reidman, Sarah R. *The Good Looks Skin Book* (9–12). 1983, Simon & Schuster (0-671-45594-X). This book attempts to answer all the questions a teenager would have about skin care. [611]

Teeth

5340 Taintor, Jerry, and Mary Jane Taintor. *The Oral Report: The Consumer's Common Sense Guide to Better Dental Care* (9–12). 1988, Facts on File $18.95 (0-8160-1392-6). All forms of dentistry are discussed with special topics such as choosing a dentist, crown and root canal work, and dentures. (Rev: BR 5–6/88) [617.6]

Hygiene and Physical Fitness

5341 Barth, Christina. *Bodywork* (10–12). Illus. 1985, Arco $12.95 (0-668-06397-1). A basic guide to the world of aerobic exercise. (Rev: BR 11–12/85) [796.4]

5342 Boston Women's Health Book Collective. *The New Our Bodies, Ourselves* (10–12). 1985, Simon & Schuster paper $16.95 (0-671-46088-9). This is now a standard handbook on the female body and how to take care of it. [613]

5343 Brody, Jane. *Jane Brody's The New York Times Guide to Personal Health* (9–12). Illus. 1982, Random $19.95 (0-686-95972-8); Avon paper $12.95 (0-380-64121-6). A popular introduction to topics related to health and medicine with emphasis on everyday concerns, prevention, and treatments. [613]

5344 Clark, Nancy. *Nancy Clark's Sports Nutrition Guidebook* (9–12). Illus. 1989, Leisure Pr. paper $12.95 (0-88011-326-X). A guide to nutrition, diet, and exercise for all, but particularly for the sports-minded. (Rev: BL 11/15/89; SLJ 3/90) [613.2]

5345 Cooke, Cynthia W., and Susan Dworkin. *The Ms. Guide to a Woman's Health* (10–12). 1984, Berkley paper $4.95 (0-425-08731-X). From this well-known magazine comes an up-to-date guide to health and well-being for women. [613]

5346 Cooper, Kenneth H. *Aerobics* (10–12). 1972, Bantam paper $4.50 (0-553-23546-X). This graded program is based on the one developed by the U.S. Air Force. [613.7]

5347 Cooper, Kenneth H. *The Aerobics Program for Total Well-Being: Exercise, Diet, Emotional Balance* (10–12). Illus. 1982, Bantam paper $11.95 (0-553-34422-6). A book on healthful living that covers nutrition, exercise, and mental health. [613.7]

5348 Creedman, Michael. *The NFL All-Pro Workout* (10–12). Illus. 1987, St. Martin's paper $12.95 (0-312-01071-0). A complete program based on National Football League drills, exercises, and ideas concerning proper nutrition. (Rev: BL 12/1/87) [613.7]

5349 Curran, Delores. *Traits of a Healthy Family* (10–12). 1984, Ballantine paper $4.95 (0-345-31750-5). This book reports on a study of 500 families and what keeps them healthy. [610]

5350 Darden, Ellington. *The Athlete's Guide to Sports Medicine* (10–12). Illus. 1981, Contemporary paper $9.95 (0-8092-7159-1). This account covers not only injuries and first aid but also conditioning and body basics. [613.7]

5351 Gardner, Robert. *The Young Athlete's Manual* (8–12). Illus. 1985, Messner $9.97 (0-671-49369-8). In addition to telling how to achieve general sports fitness, this handbook gives tips for specific sports. (Rev: BL 11/1/85; BR 11–12/86; SLJ 1/87) [613.7]

5352 Garrick, James G. *Be Your Own Personal Trainer* (10–12). Illus. 1989, Crown $19.95 (0-517-57023-8). This book tells how to assess your specific needs and find the appropriate exercises. (Rev: SLJ 10/89) [613.7]

5353 Houston, Jean. *The Possible Human: A Course in Extending Your Physical, Mental, and Creative Abilities* (10–12). 1982, J. P. Tarcher $16.95 (0-87477-219-2); paper $10.95 (0-87477-218-4). This is a guide to good health through exercising both your mind and your body. [613.7]

5354 Insel, Paul M., and Walton T. Roth. *Core Concepts in Health* (10–12). Illus. 1988, Mayfield paper $23.95 (0-87484-795-8). A textbook intended for college students that explores concepts in good health and sexuality. (Rev: BL 6/1/88) [613]

5355 Jenner, Bruce, and Bill Dobbins. *The Athletic Body: A Complete Fitness Guide for Teenagers—Sports, Strength, Health, Agility* (7–12). Illus. 1984, Simon & Schuster $17.95 (0-671-46549-X). A guide to physical fitness through sports, weight training, and good nutrition. [613.7]

5356 Jonas, Steven, and Peter Radetsky. *Pacewalking: The Balanced Way to Aerobic Health* (10–12). Illus. 1988, Crown paper $9.95 (0-517-56809-8). A book that explains the difference between walking and aerobic pacewalking and gives tips and techniques on how to practice this sport. (Rev: SLJ 8/88; VOYA 10/88) [613.7]

5357 Lyons, Pat, and Debby Burgard. *Great Shape: The First Exercise Guide for Large Women* (10–12). Illus. 1988, Arbor House $16.95 (0-87795-943-9). An exercise guide for overweight women that emphasizes aerobics, stretching, and participation in outdoor activities. (Rev: BL 2/15/88) [613.7]

5358 Mangi, Richard, et al. *Sports Fitness and Training* (9–12). 1989, Pantheon paper $17.95 (0-679-72207-6). A thorough guide to all aspects of physical training related to sports. (Rev: VOYA 2/88) [613.7]

5359 Milan, Albert R. *Breast Self-Examination* (10–12). Illus. 1980, Workman paper $3.50 (0-89480-124-4). A well-illustrated manual on how to conduct a breast examination. [613]

5360 Rosas, Debbie, and Carlos Rosas. *Non-Impact Aerobics: Introducing the NIA Technique* (9–12). Illus. 1988, Avon paper $9.95 (0-380-70522-2). A stress-free exercise system is described in this account with many photographs. (Rev: SLJ 10/88) [613.7]

5361 Schwarzenegger, Arnold, and Bill Dobbins. *Encyclopedia of Modern Bodybuilding* (9–12). Illus. 1985, Simon & Schuster $37.50 (0-671-42764-4). An expensive, heavily illustrated introduction to bodybuilding that includes training programs, exercises for various parts of the body,

a history of the sport, and other background information. (Rev: BL 10/1/85) [646.7]

5362 Shangold, Mona, and Gabe Mirkin. *The Complete Sports Medicine Book for Women* (9–12). Illus. 1985, Simon & Schuster paper $9.95 (0-671-53062-3). A discussion of health topics as they relate to women in sports. (Rev: BL 6/1/85) [613.7]

5363 Sivananda Health Center. *The Sivananda Companion to Yoga* (10–12). Illus. 1983, Simon & Schuster paper $11.95 (0-671-47088-4). Positions and techniques are described in both words and pictures. [613.7]

5364 Spence, Annette. *Exercise* (7–12). Illus. 1988, Facts on File $18.95 (0-8160-1671-2). In a question and answer format, dozens of concerns that teenagers have about exercise are addressed. (Rev: BR 9–10/89) [613.7]

5365 Spock, Benjamin, and Michael B. Rothenberg. *Baby and Child Care* (10–12). 1985, Dutton $19.95 (0-525-24312-7); Pocket paper $3.95 (0-671-43671-6). A standard manual that has been frequently revised. This is the 1985 edition. [618.92]

5366 Williams, Melvin. *Beyond Training: How Athletes Enhance Performance Legally and Illegally* (10–12). Illus. 1988, Leisure paper $10.95 (0-88011-336-7). From vitamins to steroids, all kinds of performance-enhancing drugs are described. (Rev: SLJ 1/89) [613.7]

5367 Yanker, Gary, et al. *Walking Medicine* (10–12). Illus. 1990, McGraw $24.95 (0-07-072334-X). This book explores the value of walking to one's health. (Rev: BL 6/1/90) [613.7]

Mental Disorders and Emotional Problems

5368 Abraham, Suzanne, and Derek Llewellyn-Jones. *Eating Disorders: The Facts* (9–12). 1987, Oxford Univ. Pr. $18.95 (0-19-261665-X). This account explores anorexia, bulimia, and obesity through many varied case studies. [616.8]

5369 Axline, Virginia M. *Dibs: In Search of Self* (10–12). 1964, Ballantine paper $4.95 (0-345-33925-8). A touching narrative about the play theory used to help a severely withdrawn 5-year-old boy. [616.8]

5370 Bernstein, Jane. *Loving Rachel: A Family's Journey from Grief* (9–12). 1988, Little $17.95 (0-316-09204-5). A mother's story of how she raised her second daughter who was born with learning disorders. (Rev: BL 5/1/88) [362.3]

5371 Burr, Jeanne, and Melinda Maidens, eds. *America's Troubled Children* (10–12). 1980, Facts on File $24.95 (0-87196-369-8). A collection of newspaper editorials about such youth problems as difficult family situations and juvenile crime. [362.7]

5372 Callahan, Mary. *Fighting for Tony* (10–12). Illus. 1987, Simon & Schuster $14.95 (0-671-64456-4); paper $5.95 (0-671-63265-5). The inspiring but often harrowing story of parents bringing up a child believed to be autistic. (Rev: BL 9/15/87) [618.92]

5373 Cauwels, Janice M. *Bulimia: The Binge-Purge Compulsion* (10–12). 1983, Doubleday $17.95 (0-385-18377-1). An exploration through many actual cases of the causes, characteristics, and treatment of bulimia. [616.8]

5374 Cohen, Susan, and Daniel Cohen. *Teenage Stress* (8–12). 1984, M. Evans LB $10.95 (0-87131-423-1). Causes and types of stress are explained plus hints on how to reduce it. [155.5]

5375 Craig, Eleanor. *P.S. You're Not Listening* (10–12). 1973, NAL paper $4.50 (0-451-15730-3). This is the frank account of a woman trying to help 5 emotionally disturbed youngsters. [155.4]

5376 Crook, Marion. *Teenagers Talk about Suicide* (7–12). 1988, NC Pr. paper $9.95 (1-55021-013-0). Interviews with 30 Canadian teenagers who have tried suicide are reprinted. (Rev: BR 9–10/88) [362.2]

5377 Davis, Patricia. *Suicidal Adolescents* (10–12). 1983, Thomas $22.75 (0-398-04866-5). An examination of teenage suicide, its causes, and prevention. [362.7]

5378 Dear, William. *The Dungeon Master: The Disappearance of James Dallas Egbert III* (10–12). 1984, Ballantine paper $3.95 (0-345-32695-4). The true story of a precocious teenager who mysteriously disappeared. [362.7]

5379 Flach, Frederic F. *Rickie* (10–12). 1990, Ballantine $18.95 (0-449-90349-4). The touching story of a girl's 10-year battle with schizophrenia. (Rev: BL 3/1/90) [618.92]

5380 Fynn. *Mister God, This Is Anna* (10–12). 1985, Ballantine paper $3.95 (0-345-32722-5). The haunting story of the life and death of a London waif. [155.4]

5381 Gordon, James S. *Stress Management* (9–12). Illus. 1990, Chelsea House $18.95 (0-7910-0042-7). The nature and components of stress are examined and information is given on how stress can be reduced in this book addressed to teenagers. (Rev: BL 12/15/90) [155.9]

5382 Greenberg, Harvey R. *Emotional Illness in Your Family: Helping Your Relatives, Helping Yourself* (9–12). 1989, Macmillan LB $16.95 (0-02-736921-8). Explains various types of mental illnesses. Sound advice is given on how to cope when a member of your family or a friend becomes ill. (Rev: BL 11/1/89; BR 5–6/90; SLJ 11/89; VOYA 2/90) [616.89]

5383 Hanes, Mari. *Wild Child* (10–12). 1983, Tyndale paper $3.50 (0-8423-0219-0). The true story of how a religious woman cared for an abandoned boy and brought him back to emotional health. [155.4]

5384 Hayden, Torey L. *One Child* (10–12). 1981, Avon paper $3.95 (0-380-54262-5). The story of an emotionally disturbed 6-year-old girl and the course of her treatment by the author. [155.4]

5385 Hayden, Torey L. *Somebody Else's Kids* (10–12). 1981, Avon paper $4.95 (0-380-59949-X). Case studies of a group of "special" students in a class for misfits. [371.9]

5386 Hendin, Herbert. *Suicide in America* (10–12). 1982, Norton $16.95 (0-393-01517-3); paper $9.95 (0-393-30163-X). A serious study about suicide in both young people and adults, its causes, and the latest theories about prevention. [179]

5387 Kolodny, Nancy J. *When Food's a Foe: How to Confront and Conquer Eating Disorders* (9–12). Illus. 1987, Little $15.95 (0-316-50167-0). A book about anorexia nervosa and bulimia with pointers on danger signals and how to cope with them. (Rev: BL 10/15/87; BR 3–4/88; SLJ 3/88; VOYA 2/88) [616.85]

5388 Lee, Essie E., and Richard Wortman. *Down Is Not Out: Teenagers and Depression* (8–12). 1986, Messner $11.98 (0-671-52613-8). The authors differentiate between various intensities of depression, explain causes and how to handle mood swings. (Rev: BL 3/1/86; SLJ 5/86) [616.85]

5389 Levenkron, Steven. *Treating and Overcoming Anorexia Nervosa* (10–12). 1984, Warner paper $3.95 (0-446-32743-3). Symptoms, causes, stages of development, and therapies connected with anorexia nervosa and bulimia are covered. [616.8]

5390 Levine, Mel. *Keeping a Head in School: A Student's Book about Learning Abilities and Learning Disorders* (8–12). Illus. 1990, Educators Publg. paper $14.50 (0-8388-2069-7). This account deals with all sorts of learning disorders, how they affect the learning process, and how they can be be treated. (Rev: BL 6/15/90) [371.9]

5391 MacCracken, Mary. *City Kid* (10–12). 1982, NAL paper $3.95 (0-451-14461-9). The true story of a destructive, disturbed 7-year-old boy and the teacher who tries to help him. Also use *A Circle of Children* (1975). [155.4]

5392 MacCracken, Mary. *Lovey: A Very Special Child* (8–12). 1977, NAL paper $3.50 (0-451-13364-1). The story of a remarkable teacher and how she was able to reach a troubled child. [618]

5393 MacCracken, Mary. *Turnabout Children: Overcoming Dyslexia and Other Learning Disabilities* (10–12). 1986, Little $16.95 (0-316-55540-1); NAL paper $4.50 (0-451-15876-8). Case studies of 5 children who suffered from some reading or math disability and how they were treated. (Rev: BL 12/1/86) [371.91]

5394 Marek, Elizabeth. *The Children of Santa Clara* (10–12). 1987, Viking $16.95 (0-670-81509-8); Penguin paper $2.95 (0-14-011118-2). The memoirs of a woman who worked with 14 severely disturbed children in a Santa Clara institution (Rev: BL 3/15/87; BR 11–12/87; SLJ 9/87; VOYA 8–9/87) [362.2]

5395 O'Neill, Cherry Boone. *Dear Cherry: Questions and Answers on Eating Disorders* (9–12). 1985, Continuum paper $8.95 (0-8264-0357-5). This is a collection of letters (and answers to them) that the author received after the publication of *Starving for Attention* (1982), a recommended account of her bout with anorexia nervosa. (Rev: BL 5/15/85; SLJ 9/85) [616.85]

5396 O'Neill, Cherry Boone. *Starving for Attention* (10–12). 1982, Continuum $16.95 (0-8264-0209-7); Dell paper $3.95 (0-440-17620-4). An autobiographical account of the struggle Pat Boone's daughter had with anorexia nervosa. [616.85]

5397 Palmer, R. L. *Anorexia Nervosa* (10–12). 1981, Penguin paper $4.95 (0-14-022065-8). This book is addressed both to people with this problem and those who are close to them. [616.85]

5398 Peacock, Carol A. *Hand-Me-Down Dreams* (10–12). 1987, Schocken paper $8.95 (0-8052-0678-7). A social worker's counseling of 4 teenage Boston girls in trouble with the law. [155]

5399 Polikoff, Judy. *Every Loving Gift: How a Family's Courage Saved a Special Child* (10–12). 1983, Putnam $14.95 (0-399-12783-6). The inspiring story of a family's efforts to help a brain-damaged son. [155.4]

5400 Roth, Geneen. *Feeding the Hungry Heart: The Experience of Compulsive Eating* (10–12).

1983, NAL paper $4.50 (0-451-15825-3). This book explains how one can avoid eating binges by overcoming emotional problems. [615]

5401 Rothenberg, Mira. *Children with Emerald Eyes* (10–12). 1987, Dutton paper 8.95 (0-525-48286-5). A description of a psychologist's work with autistic and schizophrenic children. [155.4]

5402 Sacker, Ira M., and Marc A. Zimmer. *Dying to Be Thin* (9–12). 1987, Warner $12.95 (0-446-38417-8). This account tells about the onset, symptoms, dangers, and treatment of various eating disorders. (Rev: VOYA 12/87) [613.2]

5403 Schreiber, Flora Rheta. *Sybil* (10–12). 1989, Warner paper $5.95 (0-446-35940-8). This is the amazing story of a woman who lived with 16 different personalities. [362.2]

5404 Sheehan, Susan. *Is There No Place on Earth for Me?* (10–12). 1982, Random $14.95 (0-395-31871-8); 1983 paper $8.95 (0-394-71378-8). The harrowing story of a schizophrenic girl. [155.4]

5405 Silverstein, Herma. *Teenage Depression* (8–12). 1990, Watts LB $12.90 (0-531-10960-7). A discussion of various types of depression giving symptoms, causes, and treatments. (Rev: BL 10/15/90) [616.85]

5406 Smith, Judie. *Coping with Suicide: A Resource Book for Teenagers and Young Adults* (10–12). 1986, Rosen $12.95 (0-8239-0670-1). This account discusses the mechanics of crisis prevention centers and their role in preventing suicide. (Rev: BL 12/1/86; BR 1–2/87; SLJ 4/87) [362.2]

5407 Young, Patrick. *Schizophrenia* (9–12). Illus. 1988, Chelsea House $17.95 (0-7910-0052-4). A look at the origins and treatment of this mysterious disease that sometimes emerges in the late teens. (Rev: BL 7/88; BR 9–10/88) [616.89]

Nutrition and Diet

5408 Arnold, Caroline. *Too Fat? Too Thin? Do You Have a Choice?* (9–12). 1984, Morrow LB $11.88 (0-688-02780-6); paper $5.25 (0-688-02779-2). This is a commonsense guide to understanding and controlling body weight. [613.2]

5409 Brody, Jane. *Jane Brody's Nutrition Book* (10–12). 1982, Bantam paper $12.95 (0-553-34421-8). A handy one-volume compendium on our knowledge of nutrition and proper eating habits. [641.1]

5410 Carper, Jean. *The Food Pharmacy: Dramatic New Evidence That Food Is Your Best Medicine* (9–12). 1988, Bantam $18.95 (0-553-05280-2). A scientific discussion on how common foods fight disease and promote good health. (Rev: BL 8/88) [615]

5411 Chilnick, Larry, et al. *The Food Book: The Complete Guide to the Most Popular Brand Name Foods* (9–12). 1987, Dell paper $9.95 (0-440-52570-5). An analysis by such topics as ingredients, calories, and amount of fat present of many brand name packaged foods found in supermarkets. (Rev: BL 5/1/87) [613.2]

5412 Edelstein, Barbara. *The Woman Doctor's Diet for Teenage Girls* (9–12). 1987, Ballantine paper $3.50 (0-345-34601-7). A cautious approach is recommended in this guide to weight loss for teenage girls. [613.2]

5413 Gershoff, Stanley, and Catherine Whitney. *The Tufts University Guide to Total Nutrition* (10–12). 1990, Harper $22.50 (0-06-015918-9). This nutrition guide covers such topics as current controversies (e.g., cholesterol), wise food purchasing, and how to read product labels. (Rev: BL 6/15/90) [613.2]

5414 Haas, Robert. *Eat to Win: The Sports Nutrition Bible* (9–12). 1983, NAL paper $4.95 (0-451-15509-2). A sports diet program that gives a 28-day menu program and recipes. [613.2]

5415 Harrington, Geri. *Real Food, Fake Food—Everything in Between: The Only Consumer's Guide to Modern Food* (10–12). 1987, Macmillan $19.95 (0-02-548420-6). A revealing, sometimes shocking examination of processed foods, additives, and preservatives. (Rev: BL 5/15/87) [613.2]

5416 *The Human Fuel Handbook: Nutrition for Peak Athletic Performance* (9–12). 1988, Health for Life paper $29.95 (0-944831-17-6). Written primarily for athletes, this is a no-nonsense guide to top performance through proper diet. (Rev: BL 3/1/89) [613.2]

5417 Jacobson, Michael F. *The Complete Eater's Digest and Nutrition Scoreboard* (9–12). Rev. ed. Illus. 1986, Doubleday paper $11.95 (0-385-18245-7). A volume that covers recent discoveries in the field of nutrition and food additives. (Rev: BL 1/15/86) [641]

5418 Lamb, Lawrence E. *The Weighting Game: The Truth about Weight Control* (9–12). Illus. 1988, Lyle Stuart $15.95 (0-8184-0487-6). A practical account of what causes fat accumulation that stresses knowing your own body and learning to live with it. (Rev: BL 1/1/89) [613.2]

5419 Largen, Velda L. *Guide to Good Food* (9–12). Illus. 1987, Goodheart-Willcox $24.00 (0-87006-602-1). A basic guide to good nutrition with many fine recipes. (Rev: BL 4/15/88) [641]

5420 Le Riche, W. Harding. *A Chemical Feast* (10–12). 1982, Facts on File $19.95 (0-87196-643-3). In this guide to food and good nutrition, topics such as pesticides, food additives, and microbiological infections are also covered. [363.1]

5421 Mott, Lawrie, and Karen Synder. *Pesticide Alert: A Guide to Pesticides in Fruit and Vegetables* (10–12). Illus. 1988, Sierra Club $15.95 (0-87156-728-8); paper $6.95 (0-87156-726-1). A guide to all the pesticides that are used in farming today, their effects, and how to remove them from fruits and vegetables. (Rev: SLJ 7/89) [668]

5422 Nix, Jan, and Linda Carlson. *Food and Fitness* (9–12). 1988, HP Books paper $9.95 (0-89586-622-6). A discussion of what constitutes a balanced diet plus many recipes and tips on exercise. (Rev: BL 4/1/88) [641.5]

5423 Peavy, Linda, and Ursula Smith. *Food, Nutrition & You* (10–12). 1982, Macmillan $12.95 (0-684-17461-8). A guide to good nutrition that is specifically aimed at adolescents and their needs. [613.2]

5424 Prevention Magazine, eds. *Natural Weight Loss* (9–12). Illus. 1985, Rodale $17.95 (0-87857-529-4). This account stresses good eating habits, some exercise, and avoidance of fad diets. (Rev: BL 9/1/85) [613.2]

5425 Reuben, David. *Everything You Always Wanted to Know about Nutrition* (9–12). 1979, Avon paper $4.50 (0-380-44370-8). Through a question-and-answer approach, basic information about foods and the food industry is given. [641.1]

5426 Rinzler, Carol Ann. *The Complete Book of Food: A Nutritional, Medical & Culinary Guide* (10–12). Illus. 1987, Pharos $24.95 (0-345-34876-1). Arranged alphabetically, individual foods are discussed under such subjects as nutrition, storage, and preparation. (Rev: BL 9/1/87) [641]

5427 Smith, Nathan J., and Bonnie Worthington-Roberts. *Food for Sport* (9–12). Rev. ed. 1989, Bull Pub. paper $9.95 (0-915950-97-9). A book on nutrition and diet for athletes that can also be used by anyone interested in his or her health. (Rev: BL 9/15/89) [613]

5428 Tver, David F., and Percy Russell. *Nutrition and Health Encyclopedia* (10–12). Illus. 1989, Van Nostrand $39.95 (0-442-23397-3). An explanation of terms and topics related to nutrition and diet arranged in a dictionary format. [613.2]

5429 Wootton, Steve. *Nutrition for Sport* (10–12). 1988, Facts on File $17.95 (0-8160-1470-1). For better readers, this account gives basic material on nutrition and on how food affects athletic performance. (Rev: BR 1–2/89) [641.1]

5430 Yudkin, John. *The Penguin Encyclopaedia of Nutrition* (9–12). Illus. 1985, Viking $20.00 (0-670-80111-9); Penguin paper $7.95 (0-14-008563-7). In handy dictionary format, the author includes entries on foods, digestion, diseases, and people connected to discoveries in the field of nutrition. (Rev: BL 7/85) [613.2]

Physical Disabilities and Problems

5431 Butterworth, Rod R., and Mickey Flodin. *The Pocket Dictionary of Signing* (9–12). Illus. 1987, Putnam paper $4.95 (0-399-51347-7). This book is a condensed version of all of the basic words and expressions found in *The Perigee Visual Dictionary of Signing* (1984). (Rev: BL 9/1/87) [419]

5432 Costello, Elaine. *Signing: How to Speak with Your Hands* (9–12). Illus. 1983, Bantam paper $15.95 (0-553-34612-1). After a history of sign language, the author explains in detail how to communicate with deaf people using today's sign language. [001.56]

5433 de Vinck, Christopher. *The Power of the Powerless: A Brother's Legacy of Love* (10–12). Illus. 1988, Doubleday $13.95 (0-385-24138-0). The story of how the handicaps of 4 different people brought their families together in more loving relationships. (Rev: BL 3/15/88; VOYA 2/89) [248.8]

5434 Forecki, Marcia Calhoun. *Speak to Me* (9–12). 1985, Gallaudet paper $12.95 (0-913580-95-3). A mother's story of how she found difficulty in accepting her son's deafness and how she was gradually able to help him. (Rev: BL 7/85) [362.4]

5435 Gilbert, Richard J. *Caffeine: The Most Popular Stimulant* (8–12). Illus. 1986, Chelsea House $18.95 (0-87754-756-4). Tea, coffee, and chocolate are covered in this account of what the author calls "the most popular drug in the world." (Rev: BL 7/86) [615]

5436 Jones, Ron. *The Acorn People* (10–12). 1977, Bantam paper $2.75 (0-553-25850-8). The story of the summer camp adventures of 5 handicapped boys. [364.5]

5437 Maloff, Chalda, and Susan Macduff Wood. *Business and Social Etiquette with Disabled People* (10–12). 1988, Charles C. Thomas $29.75 (0-398-05463-0). The dos and don'ts of getting along with disabled people. (Rev: BL 9/1/88) [395]

5438 Spradley, Thomas S., and James P. Spradley. *Deaf Like Me* (9–12). 1978, Gallaudet College Press paper $10.95 (0-930323-11-4). A touching account of how 2 parents coped with the problems of raising a deaf child. [362.4]

Safety, Accidents, and First Aid

5439 American Red Cross. *Standard First Aid and Personal Safety* (9–12). 2nd ed. Illus. 1981, Amer. Red Cross Soc. paper $5.00 (0-385-15736-3). This manual covers the essentials of first aid plus safety and preventative measures. [616.02]

5440 Auerbach, Paul S. *Medicine for the Outdoors: A Guide to Emergency Medical Procedures and First Aid* (9–12). Illus. 1986, Little $24.95 (0-316-05928-5); paper $12.95 (0-316-05929-3). A first-aid manual for the outdoor person that stresses prevention and safety measures. (Rev: BL 1/15/86) [616.02]

5441 Blair, William. *Fire! Survival and Prevention* (9–12). 1983, Harper paper $3.95 (0-06-465147-9). This book describes fires—how they start and how they can be prevented or controlled. [628.9]

5442 Garrick, James G., and Peter Radetsky. *Peak Condition* (10–12). Illus. 1987, Crown $17.95 (0-517-56246-4); Harper paper $8.95 (0-06-097133-9). A guide that identifies sports injuries, tells what causes them, and suggests treatments. (Rev: BL 10/15/86) [617]

5443 Griffith, H. Winter. *Complete Guide to Sports Injuries* (9–12). Illus. 1986, HP Books paper $12.95 (0-89586-379-0). A very thorough guide that deals not only with treatment and recovery but also with the prevention of injuries. (Rev: BL 7/86) [617.102]

5444 Peterson, Susan L. *Self-Defense for Women: How to Stay Safe and Fight Back* (10–12). Illus. 1984, Leisure Pr. paper $9.95 (0-88011-114-3). This is a guide to personal safety for women that outlines many self-defense skills. [796.8]

5445 Reader's Digest, eds. *Reader's Digest Family Safety & First Aid* (9–12). Illus. 1984, Berkley paper $4.95 (0-425-06817-X). A series of articles that stress safety in and out of the house plus material on first aid principles and techniques. [616.02]

5446 Rosenberg, Stephen N. *The Johnson & Johnson First Aid Book* (9–12). Illus. 1985, Warner paper $16.95 (0-446-38252-3). A spiral-bound handy manual that covers most emergency situations with clear text and line drawings. (Rev: BL 7/85) [616.02]

5447 Taylor, Paul, and Diane Taylor. *Conquering Athletic Injuries* (8–12). Illus. 1988, Leisure Pr. paper $19.95 (0-88011-305-7). This account identifies types of injuries and suggests treatments for physical problems in a variety of sports such as running, basketball, swimming, tennis, baseball, and soccer. (Rev: BR 11–12/88) [363.3]

5448 Williams, J. P. R., et al. *Barron's Sports Injuries* (9–12). Illus. 1988, Barron's $12.95 (0-8120-5915-8). Arranged by body parts, this handy guide identifies many types of injuries and tells how they are treated. (Rev: SLJ 10/88) [616.02]

Sex Education and Reproduction

5449 Bell, Ruth, et al. *Changing Bodies, Changing Lives* (8–12). Illus. 1988, Random paper $12.95 (0-394-75541-3). A revised edition of this now-classic teenage guide to sex and sexuality. (Rev: BL 6/1/88; SLJ 6–7/88) [306.7]

5450 Benson, Michael D. *Coping with Birth Control* (7–12). Illus. 1988, Rosen LB $12.95 (0-8239-0786-4). This book not only tells about various forms of birth control but also covers basic material on sexuality and on sexually transmitted diseases. (Rev: BR 3–4/89; SLJ 5/89; VOYA 4/89) [344]

5451 Bernards, Neal, and Lynn Hall, eds. *Teenage Sexuality: Opposing Viewpoints* (9–12). Illus. 1988, Greenhaven LB $15.95 (0-89908-430-3); paper $8.95 (0-89908-405-2). Controversial questions involving sexual activity are explored in a pro-and-con format. (Rev: BL 6/1/88) [306.7]

5452 *Better Homes and Gardens New Baby Book* (10–12). Illus. 1986, Meredith $14.95 (0-696-00022-9); Bantam paper $5.95 (0-553-26114-2). A book that covers prenatal care as well as child care to age 6. [649]

5453 Borhek, Mary V. *Coming Out to Parents* (10–12). 1983, Pilgrim Pr. paper $9.95 (0-8298-0665-2). This guide is aimed at both parents and young lesbians and gay men. [612]

5454 Boston Children's Hospital. *What Teenagers Want to Know about Sex: Questions and Answers* (8–12). Illus. 1988, Little $16.95 (0-316-25063-5). In a question-and-answer format a variety of topics like masturbation, puberty, contraception, and AIDS are explored. (Rev: BL 6/15/88; BR 9–10/88; SLJ 8/88; VOYA 8/88) [613.9]

5455 Bowe-Gutman, Sonia. *Teen Pregnancy* (8–12). Illus. 1987, Lerner LB $9.95 (0-8225-0039-6). In addition to pregnancy and available options, this book discusses general health, sex education, and contraception. (Rev: SLJ 1/88) [612]

5456 Brown, Fern G. *Teen Guide to Caring for Your Unborn Baby* (8–12). Illus. 1989, Watts LB $11.90 (0-531-10668-3). Advice to the pregnant teenager on nutrition, complaints such as nausea, and a guide to fetal development. (Rev: BL 4/15/89; BR 9–10/89; SLJ 5/89) [649.1]

5457 Brown, Fern G. *Teen Guide to Childbirth* (8–12). Illus. 1988, Watts $11.90 (0-531-10573-3). An account of the methods of assisting births, where to have children (e.g., the home, hospital), and other topics related to this subject. (Rev: BL 1/1/89; BR 3–4/89; SLJ 1/89; VOYA 4/89) [618.2]

5458 Calderone, Mary S., and Eric W. Johnson. *The Family Book about Sexuality* (10–12). Rev. ed. 1989, Harper $17.95 (0-06-016068-3). For older readers, this is a clear guide to human sexuality with new material on AIDS. (Rev: BL 4/1/89) [306.7]

5459 Cohen, Susan, and Daniel Cohen. *When Someone You Know Is Gay* (8–12). 1989, Evans $13.95 (0-87131-567-X). Written about both male and female homosexuality, this is an account for non-gays to understand a different sexual orientation. (Rev: BL 5/15/89; BR 1–2/90; SLJ 9/89) [306.7]

5460 Cohn, Anna R., and Lucinda A. Leach, eds. *Generations: A Universal Family Album* (10–12). Illus. 1987, Pantheon $35.00 (0-394-56562-2); paper $18.95 (0-394-75741-6). Customs and rituals from around the world concerning conception, birth, and infancy are collected here in text and pictures. (Rev: BL 3/1/88; BR 5–6/88; SLJ 5/88) [392]

5461 Fiedler, Jean, and Hal Fiedler. *Be Smart about Sex: Facts for Young People* (7–12). Illus. 1990, Enslow LB $17.95 (0-89490-168-0). A frank sex education manual that answers questions about masturbation, condoms, homosexuality, and sexually transmitted diseases. (Rev: SLJ 9/90) [612]

5462 Francke, Linda Bird. *The Ambivalence of Abortion* (10–12). 1978, Random $10.00 (0-394-41080-7). Interviews with a number of different people reveal the many attitudes and feelings about abortion. [179]

5463 Fricke, Aaron. *Reflections of a Rock Lobster: A Story about Growing Up Gay* (10–12). 1981, Alyson paper $5.95 (0-932870-09-0). The story of the consequences of a gay boy's inviting his male friend to the senior prom. [612]

5464 Gale, Jay. *A Young Man's Guide to Sex* (8–12). Illus. 1984, Holt $14.95 (0-03-069396-9); Price/Stern/Sloan paper $7.95 (0-89586-691-9). This practical manual about young men's sexuality covers such topics as diseases, contraception, and masturbation. [613.7]

5465 Hales, Dianne. *Pregnancy and Birth* (9–12). Illus. 1989, Chelsea House $17.95 (0-7910-0040-0). A well-illustrated book that deals with fetal development and methods of childbirth. (Rev: BL 7/89; BR 11–12/89; SLJ 1/90; VOYA 12/89) [618.2]

5466 Heron, Ann, ed. *One Teenager in Ten: Writings by Gay and Lesbian Youth* (9–12). 1983, Alyson paper $3.95 (0-932870-26-0). Twenty-eight young people—17 male and 11 female—write about growing up gay in Canada and the United States. [612]

5467 Hotchner, Tracy. *Pregnancy & Childbirth: The Complete Guide for a New Life* (10–12). Illus. 1979, Avon paper $10.95 (0-380-87635-3). A fine reference book on the pregnancy period and how to care for a young baby. [618.2]

5468 Johanson, Sue. *Talk Sex* (9–12). 1989, Penguin paper $4.50 (0-14-010377-5). In a question-and-answer format, this Canadian nurse and TV personality tackles some difficult topics. (Rev: BL 6/1/89; VOYA 4/90) [306.7]

5469 Johnson, Eric W. *Love and Sex in Plain Language* (9–12). 4th Rev. ed. Illus. 1985, Harper $15.95 (0-06-015418-7); Bantam paper $3.95 (0-553-27473-2). Because of its completeness, direct approach, and accuracy, this has become one of the standard books in the field for both young men and women. (Rev: BL 11/1/85; BL 1/15/89; VOYA 2/89) [613.9]

5470 Johnson, Eric W. *People, Love, Sex and Families* (7–12). Illus. 1985, Walker $13.95 (0-8027-6591-2). Johnson answers frank questions about sex and relationships posed by 1,000 preteens and teenagers. (Rev: BR 3–4/86) [613.9]

5471 Kelly, Gary F. *Learning about Sex: The Contemporary Guide for Young Adults* (10–12). 3rd ed. Illus. 1986, Barron's paper $6.95 (0-8120-

2432-X). In addition to supplying information about the physical and emotional aspects of sex, the author talks about sexual values. (Rev: BL 1/15/87; BR 3–4/87; VOYA 12/87) [612.6]

5472 Kitzinger, Sheila. *The Complete Book of Pregnancy and Childbirth* (9–12). Rev. ed. Illus. 1989, Knopf $18.95 (0-394-58011-7). A sensitive, thorough account of prenatal development and care and the birth experience. (Rev: BL 12/1/89) [618.2]

5473 Kurland, Adrienne. *Coping with Being Pregnant* (9–12). 1988, Rosen $12.95 (0-8239-0791-0). The author, who is a nurse, discusses prenatal care, labor, and delivery. (Rev: BR 3–4/89) [612]

5474 Landau, Elaine. *Different Drummer: Homosexuality in America* (9–12). 1986, Messner $11.29 (0-671-54997-9). An objective but sensitive look at various aspects of homosexuality, the process of accepting one's homosexuality and the homophobia that exists today. (Rev: BL 3/15/86; SLJ 5/86) [306.7]

5475 Landers, Ann. *Ann Landers Talks to Teenagers about Sex* (9–12). 1986, Fawcett paper $2.95 (0-449-70210-3). This popular columnist answers questions teenagers have about sex. [612]

5476 Lauersen, Niels H., and Eileen Stukane. *PMS: Premenstrual Syndrome and You* (9–12). Illus. 1983, Simon & Schuster paper $8.95 (0-671-47242-9). PMS is described through use of case studies and information is given on causes and cures. [618.1]

5477 Lieberman, E. James, and Ellen Peck. *Sex & Birth Control: A Guide for the Young* (8–12). Rev. ed. 1981, Schocken paper $4.95 (0-8052-0701-5). A frank discussion of puberty, teenage sex, problems, and birth control methods. [613.9]

5478 Lindsay, Jeanne Warren. *Pregnant Too Soon: Adoption Is an Option* (9–12). Rev. ed. Illus. 1987, Morning Glory $15.95 (0-930934-26-1); paper $9.95 (0-930934-25-3). An update of the 1980 volume that discusses the alternative to young mothers of adoption, including its hazards and red tape. (Rev: BL 1/1/88; BR 1–2/88) [362.7]

5479 McCoy, Kathy, and Charles Wibbelsman. *The New Teenage Body Book* (9–12). Rev. ed. 1987, HP Books $19.95 (0-89586-621-8); paper $9.95 (0-89586-619-6). A general guidance book that contains sections on dieting, sex education, and adolescent development. (Rev: BL 1/1/88; VOYA 6/88) [613]

5480 McCuen, Gary E., ed. *Children Having Children: Global Perspectives on Teenage Pregnancy* (9–12). 1988, GEM $12.95 (0-86596-064-X). Teenage pregnancy is examined from a variety of viewpoints and opinions. (Rev: BR 5–6/88) [612]

5481 McCuen, Gary E. *Hi-Tech Babies: Alternative Reproductive Technologies* (9–12). 1990, GEM LB $12.95 (0-86596-077-1). Alternate methods of reproduction are covered in a series of articles that raise interesting moral and ethical problems. (Rev: SLJ 8/90) [612]

5482 Mintz, Thomas, and Lorelie Mintz. *Threshold: Straightforward Answers to Teenagers' Questions about Sex* (10–12). 1984, Walker paper $6.95 (0-8027-7259-5). Concise and honest answers are given to the questions teenagers want to ask about sex. [612]

5483 Mohr, James C. *Abortion in America: The Origins and Evolution of National Policy, 1800–1900* (10–12). Illus. 1978, Oxford Univ. Pr. paper $9.95 (0-19-502616-0). A history of legal and social attitudes and policies concerning abortion. [179]

5484 Nilsson, Lennart. *A Child Is Born* (10–12). Rev. ed. Illus. 1989, Dell paper $19.95 (0-440-50238-1). From the meeting of egg and sperm to the birth of a baby this is an outstanding photographic record. [612]

5485 Nourse, Alan E. *Birth Control* (8–12). Illus. 1988, Watts $12.90 (0-531-10516-4). Human sex organs are described as well as a thorough discussion of the various types of birth control. (Rev: BL 5/15/88; BR 9–10/88; SLJ 6–7/88; VOYA 8/88) [613.9]

5486 Nourse, Alan E. *Teen Guide to Birth Control* (7–12). Illus. 1988, Watts $11.90 (0-531-10625-X). A concise but thorough guide written in simple terms that covers the subject in both text and many illustrations. (Rev: BL 1/15/89; BR 3–4/89; SLJ 1/89; VOYA 4/89) [613.9]

5487 Nourse, Alan E. *Teen Guide to Safe Sex* (10–12). Illus. 1988, Watts LB $11.90 (0-531-10592-X). The author describes the various sexually transmitted diseases, how they are transmitted and treated, and how to avoid them. (Rev: BL 2/1/89; SLJ 2/89; VOYA 4/89) [613.9]

5488 Orr, Lisa, ed. *Sexual Values: Opposing Viewpoints* (9–12). 1989, Greenhaven LB $15.95 (0-89908-445-1); paper $8.95 (0-89908-420-6). Different facets of such topics as pornography, AIDS, and homosexuality are covered. (Rev: BL 1/1/90) [306.7]

5489 Pomeroy, Wardell B. *Boys and Sex* (7–12). Rev. ed. 1981, Dell paper $2.95 (0-440-90753-5).

From the male's point of view, this is a basic informative account of sexual development of teenagers. A companion volume is: *Girls and Sex* (1981). [613.9]

5490 Richards, Arlene Kramer, and Irene Willis. *What to Do If You or Someone You Know Is Under 18 and Pregnant* (9–12). Illus. 1983, Lothrop $12.88 (0-688-51961-X); paper $8.95 (0-688-01044-X). A practical guide that covers such topics as abortion, adoption, marriage, sex, and birth control. [362.7]

5491 Schnell, Barry T. *The Teenage Parent's Child Support Guide* (9–12). Illus. 1989, Advocacy Center for Child Support paper $14.95 (0-910599-26-2). In this account a rundown is given on what forms of social assistance are available, pregnant students' rights, plus listings of state agencies. (Rev: BL 5/1/89; SLJ 5/89) [362.828]

5492 Shuttle, Penelope, and Peter Redgrove. *The Wise Wound: Eve's Curse and Everywoman* (10–12). 1990, Bantam paper $12.95 (0-553-34906-6). From many sources including psychology, history, and mythology, this is an account of the attitudes people have about menstruation. [612]

5493 Silverstein, Herma. *Teenage and Pregnant: What You Can Do* (7–12). 1989, Messner LB $11.98 (0-671-65221-4); paper $5.95 (0-671-65222-2). Options available to pregnant teens are discussed plus related material on such subjects as contraception and care for the expectant mother. (Rev: BL 3/15/89; BR 9–10/89; SLJ 1/89; VOYA 8/89) [306.7]

5494 Simpson, Carolyn. *Coping with an Unplanned Pregnancy* (9–12). 1990, Rosen $12.95 (0-8239-1145-4). This book discusses options available to pregnant teenagers, adjustments that have to be made, and what happens if one decides to become a mother. (Rev: VOYA 8/90) [618.2]

5495 Tapley, Donald F., and W. Duane Todd, eds. *The Columbia University College of Physicians and Surgeons Complete Guide to Pregnancy* (10–12). Illus. 1988, Crown $24.95 (0-517-57030-0). From getting advice before pregnancy to the actual birth, this is an exhaustive, authoritative work on the subject. (Rev: BL 10/15/88) [618.2]

5496 Voss, Jacqueline, and Jay Gale. *A Young Woman's Guide to Sex* (9–12). Illus. 1987, Henry Holt $15.95 (0-8050-0082-8); Price paper $7.95 (0-89586-692-7). A comprehensive, frank, and helpful discussion of all aspects of male and female sexuality. (Rev: BL 11/15/86; BR 5–6/87; SLJ 2/87; VOYA 12/86) [612]

5497 Westheimer, Ruth. *First Love: A Young People's Guide to Sexual Information* (10–12). 1986, Warner paper $3.50 (0-446-34294-7). Straightforward information about sex for teenagers given by this popular television personality and sex therapist. [612]

5498 Witt, Reni L. *PMS: What Every Woman Should Know about Premenstrual Syndrome* (9–12). Illus. 1983, Scarborough House $14.95 (0-8128-2903-4); paper $2.95 (0-8128-8078-1). A study of the days immediately before menstruation, the problems that can be encountered, plus treatments that are available. [618.1]

5499 Witt, Reni L., and Jeannine Masterson Michael. *Mom, I'm Pregnant* (7–12). 1982, Scarborough paper $6.95 (0-8128-6173-6). A discussion of the options open to a young pregnant girl plus lists of agencies that can help. [362.7]

Sex Problems [Abuse]

5500 Bass, Ellen, and Louise Thornton. *I Never Told Anyone* (10–12). 1982, Harper paper $8.95 (0-06-091050-X). A collection of writings by women who were subject to sexual abuse as children. [364.1]

5501 Benedict, Helen. *Safe, Strong, and Streetwise* (8–12). 1987, Little $14.95 (0-316-08900-4); paper $4.95 (0-316-08900-1). A rape-crisis specialist discusses sexual assault, its prevention and treatment. (Rev: BL 1/1/87; BR 1–2/87; SLJ 5/87; VOYA 2/87) [362.7]

5502 Black, Beryl. *Coping with Sexual Harassment* (9–12). 1987, Rosen $12.95 (0-8239-0732-5); paper $7.95 (0-8239-0764-3). Advice for both homosexual and heterosexual males and females on how to handle sexual harassment at school and work. (Rev: BR 11–12/87; SLJ 9/87; VOYA 10/87) [305.4]

5503 Bode, Janet. *The Voices of Rape* (9–12). Illus. 1990, Watts LB $12.90 (0-531-10959-3). The subject of rape is investigated from the viewpoints of rapists, survivors, police, and medical personnel and counselors. (Rev: BL 10/1/90) [364.1]

5504 Booher, Dianna Daniels. *Rape: What Would You Do If . . . ?* (7–12). 1981, Messner $11.29 (0-671-42201-4); paper $4.95 (0-671-49485-6). A guide on how to prevent rape and how to survive it if it occurs. [362.8]

5505 Brownmiller, Susan. *Against Our Will: Men, Women and Rape* (10–12). 1986, Bantam paper $5.95 (0-553-34516-8). For mature readers, an account of the causes and effects of rape. [364.1]

5506 Cooney, Judith. *Coping with Sexual Abuse* (9–12). 1987, Rosen $12.95 (0-8239-0684-1); paper $7.95 (0-8239-0763-5). An explicit report that concentrates on the sexual abuse that occurs in the home and how to handle it. (Rev: BL 9/1/87; BR 11–12/87; SLJ 9/87; VOYA 10/87) [362.7]

5507 Daugherty, Lynn B. *Why Me? Help for Victims of Child Sexual Abuse* (10–12). 1985, Mother Courage paper $7.95 (0-941300-01-3). A book that tries to give help to victims of child sexual abuse. [364.1]

5508 Emmens, Carol A. *The Abortion Controversy* (8–12). 1987, Messner $11.29 (0-671-62284-6); paper $5.95 (0-671-64209-X). Both pro-choice and pro-life arguments are presented fairly and objectively. (Rev: BL 6/15/87; SLJ 8/87; VOYA 12/87) [363.4]

5509 Engel, Beverly. *The Right to Innocence: Healing the Trauma of Childhood Sexual Abuse* (10–12). 1989, Jeremy P. Tarcher $17.95 (0-87477-481-0). After a fine overview of the subject, there are sections on specific help available for the victims. (Rev: SLJ 6/89) [362.7]

5510 Gallagher, Vera, and William Dodds. *Speaking Out, Fighting Back* (10–12). 1985, Madrona $14.95 (0-88089-010-X). The case studies of women who were sexually abused in their homes as children. (Rev: BR 5–6/86; VOYA 4/85) [364.1]

5511 Kosof, Anna. *Incest: Families in Crisis* (8–12). 1985, Watts $11.90 (0-531-10071-5). A definition of incest is given, its various forms explained, and advice given to anyone affected. (Rev: VOYA 4/86) [157]

5512 Landau, Elaine. *On the Streets: The Lives of Adolescent Prostitutes* (9–12). 1987, Messner $11.29 (0-671-62135-1). A sobering account on how teenage runaways of both sexes are often forced into prostitution and of the tragic results. (Rev: BL 7/87; SLJ 11/87) [306.7]

5513 Ledray, Linda E. *Recovering from Rape* (10–12). 1986, Holt paper $9.95 (0-03-064001-6). A sound, practical guide on how to handle the aftereffects of rape. (Rev: BR 11–12/86; SLJ 8/86; VOYA 12/86) [364.1]

5514 McGuire, Paula. *It Won't Happen to Me: Teenagers Talk about Pregnancy* (7–12). 1983, Dell paper $6.95 (0-385-29201-5). Fifteen pregnant teenagers tell their stories. [362.7]

5515 Owens, Carolyn, and Linda Roggow. *Pregnant and Single: Help for the Tough Choices* (9–

12). 1990, Zondervan paper $7.95 (0-310-45821-8). A guide for both teenagers and adults who are unmarried and pregnant that discusses various options. (Rev: BL 6/15/90) [362.83]

5516 Parrot, Andrea. *Coping with Date Rape & Acquaintance Rape* (9–12). 1988, Rosen $12.95 (0-8239-0784-8); paper $7.95 (0-8239-0808-9). An examination of types of rape and date rape in particular and its effects on victims of both sexes. (Rev: BL 10/15/88; SLJ 8/88; VOYA 8/88) [362.8]

5517 Shuker-Haines, Frances. *Everything You Need to Know about Date Rape* (7–12). Illus. 1989, Rosen LB $12.95 (0-8239-1013-X). The author explains how date rape occurs and what precautionary measures can be taken. (Rev: BL 1/15/90; VOYA 4/90) [362.88]

5518 Silverstein, Herma. *Teen Guide to Single Parenting* (8–12). Illus. 1989, Watts LB $11.90 (0-531-10669-1). In addition to hints on proper child care, this account tells how to cope with psychological difficulties. (Rev: BL 4/15/89; BR 9–10/89; SLJ 5/89; VOYA 10/89) [649.1]

5519 Szumski, Bonnie, ed. *Abortion* (9–12). Illus. 1986, Greenhaven $15.95 (0-89908-380-3); paper $7.95 (0-89908-355-2). A balanced presentation of both the pro-life and pro-choice arguments about abortion. (Rev: BL 5/1/86; SLJ 8/86) [363.4]

5520 Tower, Cynthia Crosson. *Secret Scars: A Guide for Survivors of Child Sexual Abuse* (10–12). 1988, Viking $16.95 (0-670-82214-0). How to overcome the trauma of sexual abuse and how to prevent future incidents. (Rev: BL 7/88; BR 1–2/89) [362.7]

5521 Tribe, Laurence H. *Abortion: The Clash of Absolutes* (10–12). 1990, Norton $18.95 (0-393-02845-3). An excellent review of all the arguments involved in the abortion debate. (Rev: BL 5/1/90) [363.4]

5522 Warshaw, Robin. *I Never Called It Rape* (10–12). 1988, Harper paper $7.95 (0-060-96276-3). Case studies of women who have been raped by friends or acquaintances. (Rev: SLJ 3/89) [364.1]

Human Development and Behavior

General and Miscellaneous

5523 Decker, Celia Anita. *Children: The Early Years* (10–12). Illus. 1988, Goodheart-Willcox $22.64 (0-87006-617-X). A book about children—how they develop and how to take care of them. (Rev: BL 4/15/88) [155.4]

5524 Hoffer, Eric. *The True Believer* (10–12). 1989, Harper paper $7.95 (0-06-091612-5). A sociological study of the various "isms" in today's society. [150]

5525 Kotre, John, and Elizabeth Hall. *Seasons of Life: Our Dramatic Journey from Birth to Death* (10–12). Illus. 1990, Little $24.95 (0-316-50252-9). This account traces human development from the biological, social, and psychological standpoints. (Rev: BL 9/1/90) [155]

5526 Morris, Desmond. *The Book of Ages* (7–12). Illus. 1983, Penguin paper $8.95 (0-14-007929-0). A book that chronicles human development from ages 0 to 100. [305.2]

Psychology and Human Behavior

General and Miscellaneous

5527 Bailey, Beth L. *From Front Porch to Back Seat: Courtship in Twentieth-Century America* (10–12). Illus. 1988, Johns Hopkins $18.95 (0-8018-3609-3). A history of courtship customs in this country from the mid-1920s to the mid-1960s. (Rev: BL 5/15/88) [392]

5528 Berne, Eric. *What Do You Say after You Say Hello? The Psychology of Human Destiny* (10–12). 1984, Bantam paper $4.95 (0-553-24822-2). A psychiatrist explores complex patterns of human behavior and how we can modify them. [193]

5529 Bettelheim, Bruno. *Freud and Man's Soul* (10–12). 1983, Knopf $11.95 (0-394-52481-0); paper $7.95 (0-394-71036-3). A sympathetic examination of Freud's thoughts and his writing. [150.19]

5530 Cosby, Bill, et al. *You Are Somebody Special* (7–12). 2nd ed. 1982, McGraw $12.95 (0-07-056511-2). Ten different specialists, including Bill Cosby, contribute articles on facing problems positively. [155.5]

5531 Dubos, Rene. *Beast or Angel? Choices That Make Us Human* (10–12). 1982, Macmillan $20.00 (0-684-17608-4). This book explores human behavior and how one can develop in various ways. [150]

5532 Evans, Christopher, ed. *Understanding Yourself* (10–12). 1980, NAL paper $5.95 (0-451-13453-2). Through a series of quizzes and games, one becomes more aware of one's own nature and personality. [150]

5533 Fancher, Raymond E. *Pioneers of Psychology* (10–12). Illus. 1979, Norton paper $11.95 (0-393-09082-5). From Descartes to Piaget and Skinner, this is a readable text on the history of psychology. [150.9]

5534 Faraday, Ann. *The Dream Game* (10–12). 1974, Harper paper $5.95 (0-06-080371-1). A manual that explains the uses of dreams and their meanings. [154.6]

5535 Freud, Sigmund. *The Basic Writings of Sigmund Freud* (10–12). Trans. by A. A. Brill. 1977, Random $19.95 (0-394-60040-8). A fine anthology that is a good introduction to the thoughts of the father of psychoanalysis. [150.19]

5536 Hagedorn, John. *People and Folks: Gangs, Crime and the Underclass in a Rustbelt City* (10–12). 1988, Lake View Pr. $29.95 (0-941702-20-0); paper $10.95 (0-941702-21-9). An examination of the big city gangs with interviews with gang members. (Rev: BL 9/1/88) [364.1]

5537 Jung, Carl Gustav. *Undiscovered Self* (10–12). Trans. by R. F. C. Hull. 1958, Little $12.95 (0-316-47693-5); NAL paper $3.95 (0-451-62539-0). A book that explores the problems of the individual and his or her relations with society. [155.2]

5538 Leahy, Michael. *Hard Lessons: Senior Year at Beverly Hills High School* (10–12). 1988, Little $16.95 (0-316-51515-8). A disturbing look at high school seniors in an affluent American community. (Rev: BL 9/1/88) [378]

5539 Marsh, Peter, ed. *Eye to Eye: How People Interact* (10–12). Illus. 1988, Salem House $24.95 (0-88162-371-7). An exploration of nonverbal behavior and its effects on other people. (Rev: BL 9/1/88; SLJ 3/89) [302.3]

5540 Nordby, Vernon J., and Calvin S. Hall. *A Guide to Psychologists and Their Concepts* (10–12). 1974, Freeman paper $11.95 (0-7167-0759-4). Arranged in alphabetical order, this book discusses the work of 40 famous psychologists. [150.9]

5541 Norman, Donald A. *The Psychology of Everyday Things* (10–12). Illus. 1988, Basic Books $19.95 (0-465-06709-3). The author explores how human cultural attitudes and knowledge influence the ways we approach technology. (Rev: SLJ 8/88) [150]

5542 Ribers, Caryl, et al. *Beyond Sugar and Spice: How Women Grow, Learn, and Thrive* (10–12). 1981, Ballantine paper $4.95 (0-345-29010-0). This account shows the differences between mothers and daughters and how the modern woman is now free to develop her own life. [305.4]

5543 Rice, F. Philip. *The Adolescent: Development, Relationships, and Culture* (10–12). Illus. 1989, Allyn & Bacon $40.00 (0-205-12310-4). A clear explanation of the kinds of maturation that take place during adolescence. [155.5]

5544 Richards, Arlene Kramer, and Irene Willis. *Boy Friends, Girl Friends, Just Friends* (7–12). 1979, Macmillan $11.95 (0-689-30695-4). The meaning of friendship is explored plus coverage on how to get and keep friends and cope with the loss of friendship. [158]

5545 Rogers, Carl R. *A Way of Being* (10–12). 1980, Houghton paper $8.95 (0-395-29915-2). A collection of papers, talks, and vignettes from one of today's great psychologists. [150.19]

5546 Shattuck, Roger. *The Forbidden Experiment: The Story of the Wild Boy of Aveyron* (10–12). Illus. 1980, Farrar $12.95 (0-374-15755-3); Washington Square Pr. paper $2.95 (0-671-42209-X). The story of the training of a feral child who was found living wild in Southern France in 1890. [155.4]

5547 Skinner, B. F. *About Behaviorism* (10–12). 1974, Knopf paper $6.95 (0-394-71618-3). An introduction to behaviorism that tries to refute criticisms of the author's theories. [150.19]

5548 Smith, Samuel. *Ideas of the Great Psychologists* (10–12). 1983, Barnes & Noble paper $7.95 (0-06-463561-9). Arranged by such concepts as personality, memory, and learning, this is an overview of the contributions of the great psychologists. [150]

5549 Solomon, Jack. *The Signs of Our Times: Semiotics* (10–12). 1988, Jeremy P. Tarcher $18.95 (0-87477-479-9). This explains the discipline of semiotics, the study of how messages of status and power are consciously and unconsciously transmitted in our culture. (Rev: SLJ 3/89) [302]

5550 Spence, Annette. *Stress & Mental Health* (7–12). Illus. 1988, Facts on File $18.95 (0-8160-1668-2). Stress, its causes and effects, and how to handle it are discussed in a question-and-answer format. (Rev: BR 9–10/89) [612]

5551 Steiner, Claude M. *Scripts People Live: Transactional Analysis of Life Scripts* (10–12). 1975, Bantam paper $4.95 (0-553-24697-6). This book suggests ways people can free themselves from the debilitating conditioning of the past. [195]

5552 Vedral, Joyce L. *I Dare You: How to Use Psychology to Get What You Want Out of Life* (10–12). 1985, Ballantine paper $3.95 (0-345-32310-6). A guide to practical psychology that gives advice on how to make the principles of human behavior work for you. [150]

5553 Watson, Robert I. *The Great Psychologists* (10–12). 4th ed. 1978, Harper paper $23.50 (0-397-47375-3). This book discusses the works of the great psychologists from Aristotle to Freud. [150.9]

5554 Wholey, Dennis. *Are You Happy? Some Answers to the Most Important Questions in Your*

Life (10–12). 1986, Houghton $16.95 (0-395-40779-6). A group of celebrities discusses what happiness is and how to attain it. (Rev: BL 10/1/86) [158]

Emotions and Emotional Behavior

5555 Agras, Stewart. *Panic: Facing Fears, Phobias and Anxiety* (9–12). 1985, W. H. Freeman paper $12.95 (0-7167-1731-X). A scholarly tome dealing with unusually intense fears, their causes, and their treatment. (Rev: BR 1–2/86) [152.4]

5556 Buscaglia, Leo. *Love* (10–12). 1985, Fawcett paper $4.95 (0-449-20846-X). This popular counselor and television personality explores the various aspects of love. Also use: *Personhood* (1986). [152.4]

5557 Curtis, Robert H. *Mind and Mood: Understanding and Controlling Your Emotions* (9–12). Illus. 1986, Macmillan $11.95 (0-684-18571-7). An explanation of what causes emotions, their effects on the human body, and how to lead a healthy emotional life. (Rev: BL 9/1/86; SLJ 10/86; VOYA 2/87) [152.4]

5558 Ephron, Delia. *Teenage Romance: Or, How to Die of Embarrassment* (10–12). 1982, Ballantine paper $5.95 (0-345-30457-8). The pangs of adolescent love are examined, often amusingly. [152.4]

5559 Fromm, Erich. *The Art of Loving* (10–12). 1956, Harper $14.45 (0-06-011375-8); paper $7.95 (0-06-090001-6). All kinds of love are analyzed with a discussion of what constitutes mature love. [152.4]

5560 Gaylin, Willard. *Feelings: Our Vital Signs* (10–12). 1979, Harper paper $6.95 (0-06-091480-7). This book describes the wide range of human feelings and how to cope with them. [152.4]

5561 Gelinas, Paul J. *Coping with Shyness* (9–12). 1987, Rosen $12.95 (0-8239-0685-X). Types of shyness are described from the harmless to severe emotional problems plus a 5-step approach to self-help. (Rev: SLJ 6–7/87; VOYA 8–9/87) [152.4]

5562 Laiken, Deidre S., and Alan J. Schneider. *Listen to Me, I'm Angry* (7–12). Illus. 1980, Lothrop LB $12.88 (0-688-51943-1). A discussion of what causes anger, how it is manifested, and how it can be controlled or directed. [152.4]

5563 Lorenz, Konrad. *On Aggression* (10–12). Trans. by Marjorie Kerr Wilson. 1966, Peter Smith $18.00 (0-8446-6213-5); Harcourt paper

$9.95 (0-15-668741-0). Using all kinds of animals as well as humans as examples, the author explores aggressive behavior. [152.4]

5564 McCoy, Kathy. *Coping with Teenage Depression* (9–12). 1985, NAL paper $4.50 (0-451-13663-2). An account that explores the causes of teenage depression and how to cope with it. [616.85]

5565 Meichenbaum, Donald. *Coping with Stress* (10–12). Illus. 1987, Facts on File $13.95 (0-8130-1103-6); paper $6.95 (0-8160-1676-3). After defining stress, the author describes its effects and what can be done about it. (Rev: SLJ 10/87) [612]

5566 Montagu, Ashley. *The Nature of Human Aggression* (10–12). Illus. 1976, Oxford Univ. Pr. paper $8.95 (0-19-502373-0). The author, unlike Konrad Lorenz, does not believe in the innate nature of human aggression and in this book attempts to prove his theories. [152.4]

5567 Rue, Nancy. *Coping with Dating Violence* (9–12). 1989, Rosen $12.95 (0-8239-0997-2). This volume tells the causes of physical abuse on dates, how to avoid it, and where to get help. (Rev: BL 5/15/89; BR 11–12/89; VOYA 10/89) [646.7]

5568 Selye, Hans. *The Stress of Life* (10–12). 1978, McGraw paper $7.95 (0-07-056212-1). The causes of stress are examined, with a discussion of how to ease the effects of stress. Also use: *Stress without Distress* (1976). [612]

5569 Smith, Manuel J. *When I Say No, I Feel Guilty* (10–12). 1985, Bantam paper $5.50 (0-553-26390-0). This is a manual on how to develop confidence and self-assertiveness. [152.4]

5570 Stefoff, Rebecca. *Friendship and Love* (9–12). Illus. 1989, Chelsea House $17.95 (0-7910-0039-7). These 2 ways that people relate to one another are described, theories on how friendship and love develop are explained, and ways of coping with these 2 feelings are explored. (Rev: BL 4/1/89; BR 11–12/89; SLJ 6/89; VOYA 8/89) [177]

5571 Wallace, Marjorie. *The Silent Twins* (10–12). Illus. 1987, Ballantine paper $3.95 (0-345-34902-8). An unusual psychological study of 2 black twins in Wales, their obsessions, and their inability to communicate. (Rev: SLJ 2/87) [157]

Ethics and Ethical Behavior

5572 Bok, Sissela. *Lying: Moral Choice in Public and Private Life* (10–12). 1979, Random paper

$6.95 (0-394-72804-1). This book considers the choices we make and the consequences of lying. [177]

5573 Johnson, Linda Carlson. *Responsibility* (8–12). Illus. 1990, Rosen LB $12.95 (0-8239-1107-1). Responsibility is defined, its types explained, and how it is related to citizenship and freedom is discussed. (Rev: SLJ 6/90) [170]

5574 Margulies, Alice. *Compassion* (8–12). Illus. 1990, Rosen LB $12.95 (0-8239-1108-X). A discussion of the different kinds of compassion and how each helps both the individual and society. (Rev: SLJ 6/90) [152.4]

5575 Martin, Judith. *Miss Manners' Guide to Excruciatingly Correct Behavior* (10–12). Illus. 1982, Macmillan $19.95 (0-689-11247-5); paper $14.95 (0-446-38632-4). A humorous but correct guide to good social behavior. [395]

5576 Post, Elizabeth L. *Emily Post's Complete Book of Wedding Etiquette* (10–12). Illus. 1982, Harper $16.95 (0-06-181681-7). Using a hypothetical couple as a model, this book covers topics from sending invitations to the honeymoon. [395]

5577 Post, Elizabeth L. *Emily Post's Etiquette* (10–12). Illus. 1984, Harper $29.95 (0-06-181684-1). This book has been considered one of the authoritative guides to etiquette since it first appeared in 1922. [395]

5578 Vanderbilt, Amy. *The Amy Vanderbilt Complete Book of Etiquette: A Guide to Contemporary Living* (10–12). Illus. 1978, Doubleday $19.95 (0-385-14238-2). An up-to-date guide to good manners that has become one of the standard books in the field. [395]

Etiquette and Manners

5579 Bride's Magazine, eds. *Bride's Book of Etiquette* (10–12). Illus. 1984, Perigee $16.95 (0-399-51096-6); paper $6.95 (0-399-51084-2). A complete book organizing the wedding ceremony and reception. [395]

5580 Carlson, Dale, and Dan Fitzgibbon. *Manners That Matter: For People under 21* (8–12). 1983, Dutton $10.95 (0-525-44008-9). A guide to acceptable behavior in a variety of settings and situations including dinners and dating. [395]

5581 De Vries, Mary A. *The New Robert's Rules of Order* (9–12). 1990, NAL paper $3.95 (0-451-16378-8). A revision of the 1893 edition with a section on pre- and post-meeting activities, such

as publicity and budgeting. (Rev: BL 4/1/90) [060.4]

5582 Ford, Charlotte. *Etiquette: Charlotte Ford's Book of Modern Manners* (9–12). 1988, Crown $25.00 (0-517-56823-3). A clear, practical guide to good manners that first appeared in 1980. (Rev: SLJ 8/88) [395]

5583 Hoving, Walter. *Tiffany's Table Manners for Teenagers* (7–12). Illus. 1989, Random $9.95 (0-394-82877-1). A practical guide to good table manners. (Rev: BR 9–10/89; SLJ 6/89) [395]

5584 Robert, Henry M. *Robert's Rules of Order* (9–12). 1989, Berkley paper $3.50 (0-425-11690-5). The authority on parliamentary procedure in a readable format. [060.4]

5585 Sternberg, Patricia. *Speak to Me: How to Put Confidence in Your Conversation* (9–12). 1984, Lothrop paper $6.50 (0-688-02694-X). A practical guide that gives pointers on how to be a good conversationalist. [808.56]

Intelligence and Thinking

5586 Cohen, Daniel. *Intelligence—What Is It?* (7–12). Illus. 1974, M. Evans $10.95 (0-87131-127-5). An easily read book on the nature of intelligence and the strengths and weaknesses of intelligence testing. [153]

5587 Fancher, Raymond E. *The Intelligence Men: Makers of the IQ Controversy* (10–12). 1985, Norton paper $5.95 (0-393-95525-7). The story of how intelligence tests evolved and of the people behind them. (Rev: BL 6/1/85) [153.9]

5588 Flesch, Rudolf. *The Art of Clear Thinking* (10–12). Illus. 1951, Harper $12.45 (0-06-001440-7); paper $6.95 (0-06-463369-1). A popular guide to what thinking is and how it can be logical. [153.4]

5589 Jastrow, Robert. *The Enchanted Loom: Mind in the Universe* (10–12). 1981, Simon & Schuster $13.95 (0-671-43308-3). An account for better readers on the evolution of the human brain and the development of thought processes. [153]

Measuring Human Behavior

5590 Asher, Herbert. *Polling and the Public: What Every Citizen Should Know* (10–12). 1988, Congressional Quarterly paper $14.95 (0-87187402-4). This volume explains how polls are taken, techniques used, and how to evaluate the validity of a poll. (Rev: BR 5–6/88; SLJ 4/88) [303.3]

5591 Greenwald, Dorothy. *Coping with Moving* (7–12). 1987, Rosen $10.97 (0-8239-0683-3). Good advice given on such practical topics as how to pack and how to fit into a new environment. (Rev: BL 3/15/88; SLJ 3/88; VOYA 6/88) [648]

Personal Guidance

5592 Armstrong, Dorinne, and Richard Armstrong. *Leaving the Nest: Mom's Guide to Living on Your Own* (10–12). Illus. 1986, Morrow paper $10.95 (0-688-05260-6). A guide for young adults on how to live independently that begins with information on how to find a room or apartment. (Rev: BL 4/15/86) [640]

5593 Ashton, Betsy. *Betsy Ashton's Guide to Living on Your Own* (10–12). 1988, Little paper $12.95 (0-316-05409-7). For the person planning to live independently, this is a guide full of useful tips and suggestions. (Rev: SLJ 11/88) [306]

5594 Atanasoff, Stevan E. *How to Survive as a Teen: When No One Understands* (7–12). 1989, Herald Pr. paper $6.95 (0-8361-3478-8). A practical handbook that covers such topics as friendship, sex, peer pressure, family conflicts, drugs, and suicide. (Rev: SLJ 4/89) [155.5]

5595 Bender, David L., ed. *Constructing a Life Philosophy: Opposing Viewpoints* (9–12). Illus. 1985, Greenhaven LB $15.95 (0-89908-379-X); paper $8.95 (0-89908-354-4). Various viewpoints concerning attitudes toward religion and society are expressed in this collection of articles. (Rev: BL 1/1/86; BR 3–4/86; SLJ 3/86) [140]

5596 Bennett, Hal Zina. *The Lens of Perception: A Field Guide to Inner Resources* (10–12). 1987, Celestial Arts paper $6.95 (0-8050-0455-6). This self-help book gives teenagers advice on how to use their inner resources to make decisions and to lead richer lives. (Rev: SLJ 5/88) [155.5]

5597 Bernstein, Joanne E. *Taking Off: Travel Tips for a Carefree Trip* (10–12). Illus. 1986, Harper $12.89 (0-397-32107-4); paper $3.95 (0-06-446047-9). A common sense guide for teenagers who want to travel without their parents that includes material on such subjects as passports, packing, and planning an itinerary. (Rev: BL 4/15/86; SLJ 10/86; VOYA 8–10/86) [910]

5598 Bode, Janet. *Different Worlds: Interracial and Cross-Cultural Dating* (8–12). 1989, Watts LB $12.90 (0-531-10663-2). A complex social problem impartially handled with data from inter-

views with social workers, teenage couples, parents, and school personnel. (Rev: BL 5/1/89; BR 9–10/89; SLJ 6/89; VOYA 10/89) [306.73]

5599 Booher, Dianna Daniels. *Love: First Aid for the Young* (9–12). 1985, Messner $11.29 (0-671-54401-2). Different kinds of love and their components are discussed with advice on how to cope with each. (Rev: BL 2/15/85; SLJ 8/85) [646.77]

5600 Cahn, Julie. *The Dating Book: A Guide to the Social Scene* (10–12). 1983, Simon & Schuster $9.29 (0-671-46742-5); paper $3.50 (0-671-46277-6). This book covers a wide number of topics for teenage girls including pregnancy and venereal disease. [306.7]

5601 Carnegie, Dale. *How to Win Friends and Influence People* (10–12). 1981, Simon & Schuster $17.95 (0-671-42517-X). This is now a classic in the field of books devoted to personal development and personality enhancement. [155.2]

5602 Chaback, Elaine, and Pat Fortunato. *The Official Kids' Survival Kit: How to Do Things on Your Own* (7–12). 1981, Little $22.95 (0-316-13532-1); paper $10.95 (0-316-13531-3). This book discusses young people's problems and tells how one can become more independent. [361.3]

5603 Cohen, Shari. *Coping with Failure* (9–12). 1988, Rosen $12.95 (0-8239-0822-4). By discussing topics such as poor grades, the author tries to give advice concerning finding and cultivating strengths. (Rev: BR 3–4/89; VOYA 4/89) [155.5]

5604 Cohen, Susan, and Daniel Cohen. *Teenage Competition: A Survival Guide* (9–12). 1987, Evans $11.95 (0-87131-487-8). A discussion of the constructive and destructive aspects of competition and how teenagers can adjust to them. (Rev: BL 6/1/87; SLJ 8/87) [155.5]

5605 Coombs, H. Samm. *Teenage Survival Manual: How to Reach 20 in One Piece (and Enjoy Every Step of the Journey)* (7–12). Rev. ed. 1989, Discovery paper $9.95 (0-925258-08-3). A new edition of a valuable guide that now includes information on suicide, stress, and AIDS. (Rev: BR 1–2/90; SLJ 12/89; VOYA 2/90) [155.5]

5606 DeVenzio, Dick. *Smart Moves: How to Succeed in School, Sports, Career, and Life* (10–12). 1989, Prometheus paper $11.95 (0-87975-546-6). A compendium of practical advice on such topics as how to do well at school, make and keep friends, and succeed in career goals. (Rev: BR 3–4/90) [155.5]

5607 Eagan, Andrea Boroff. *Why Am I So Miserable If These Are the Best Years of My Life?* (9–12). 1976, Harper $12.70 (0-397-31655-0). An updated version of this fine handbook that answers many of the questions adolescents, particularly girls, ask. (Rev: VOYA 8/88) [155.5]

5608 Gersh, Marvin J. *The Handbook of Adolescence: A Medical Guide for Parents and Teenagers* (9–12). 1983, Scarborough paper $10.95 (0-8128-6070-5). This book for both youngsters and parents deals with all adolescent health problems from acne to venereal disease. [155.5]

5609 Girodo, Michel. *Shy? (You Don't Have to Be)* (10–12). 1981, Pocket paper $2.95 (0-671-43601-0). This book explores the causes of bashfulness and tells how to overcome this problem. [152.3]

5610 Gordon, Sol. *The Teenage Survival Book* (9–12). 1981, Times Bks. $14.95 (0-8129-0972-0). This is a self-help book that gives advice on many of the problems that confront teenagers. [150]

5611 Gordon, Sol. *When Living Hurts* (9–12). Illus. 1985, Union of American Hebrew Congregations paper $8.95 (0-8074-0310-5). A guide to help those afflicted with depression and thoughts of suicide. (Rev: SLJ 8/86; VOYA 10/86) [155.5]

5612 Grosshandler, Janet. *Coping with Verbal Abuse* (8–12). 1989, Rosen LB $12.95 (0-8239-0979-4). Using principles from transactional analysis, the author gives advice on how to handle verbal abuse from various sources. (Rev: BR 3–4/90; SLJ 11/89; VOYA 12/89) [155.5]

5613 Grossvogel, David. *Dear Ann Landers: Our Intimate and Changing Dialogue with America's Best-Loved Confidante* (9–12). 1986, Berkley paper $3.95 (0-425-11627-1). A collection of columns from the writings of this popular adviser and an interview. (Rev: BL 10/1/87) [070.92]

5614 Ignoffo, Matthew. *Coping with Your Inner Critic* (8–12). 1989, Rosen LB $12.95 (0-8239-1001-6). A useful book on how to avoid being hypercritical of one's own actions. (Rev: BR 3–4/90; SLJ 9/89; VOYA 12/89) [361]

5615 Jeffers, Susan. *Feel the Fear and Do It Anyway* (10–12). 1987, Harcourt $14.95 (0-15-130559-5). The author explains how she and others can conquer fears that inhibit the fulfillment of life's possibilities. (Rev: SLJ 8/87) [152.4]

5616 Kolodny, Nancy J., et al. *Smart Choices* (10–12). Illus. 1986, Little $17.95 (0-316-50163-8). A practical manual to help teens through darkest adolescence. (Rev: BL 2/15/87; BR 5–6/87; SLJ 1/87) [305.2]

5617 Kushner, Harold. *When Bad Things Happen to Good People* (10–12). 1987, Schocken $13.95 (0-8052-3773-9); Avon paper $4.50 (0-

380-60392-6). This popular book tells how to cope with all sorts of adversity. [361.3]

5618 Lakein, Alan. *How to Get Control of Your Time and Your Life* (10–12). 1989, NAL paper $4.50 (0-451-15802-4). This book tells how to organize one's life most effectively and efficiently. [361.5]

5619 Levine, Saul V., and Kathleen Wilcox. *Dear Doctor* (7–12). 1987, Lothrop LB $12.88 (0-688-07094-9); paper $6.95 (0-688-07095-7). A selection of letters and answers from the author's self-help column for adolescents in the *Toronto Star*. (Rev: BL 6/1/87; BR 5–6/87; SLJ 5/87; VOYA 6/87) [155.5]

5620 Levinson, Nancy, and Joanne Rocklin. *Getting High in Natural Ways: An Infobook for Young People of All Ages* (10–12). 1986, Hunter House paper $6.95 (0-89793-036-3). A guide for teens on how to feel good by using such methods as meditating, exercising, and listening to music. (Rev: BL 10/1/86) [305.2]

5621 McFarland, Rhoda. *Coping through Assertiveness* (9–12). 1986, Rosen $12.95 (0-8239-0680-9). The author explains the difference between assertiveness and aggressive behavior and, among other things, how to say "no." (Rev: BL 1/15/87; BR 1–2/87; SLJ 1/87) [158.1]

5622 McFarland, Rhoda. *Coping through Self-Esteem* (8–12). 1988, Rosen LB $12.95 (0-8239-0790-2). A volume that explores the importance of feeling good about yourself and how this can be accomplished. (Rev: SLJ 8/88; VOYA 8/88) [155.2]

5623 McFarland, Rhoda. *Coping with Stigma* (9–12). 1989, Rosen $12.95 (0-8239-0998-0). A self-help manual that helps teens identify stigmas, analyze them, and get help to achieve self-acceptance. (Rev: BR 9–10/89; VOYA 12/89) [155.5]

5624 Nida, Patricia Cooney, and Wendy M. Heller. *The Teenager's Survival Guide to Moving* (7–12). 1985, Macmillan $10.95 (0-689-31077-3). Sound, practical advice for teenagers on how to cope with the moving process, deal with separation, and make new friends. (Rev: BL 4/1/85; SLJ 5/85) [648]

5625 Olney, Ross R., and Patricia J. Olney. *Imaging: Think Your Way to Success in Sports and Classroom Activities* (9–12). 1985, Macmillan $11.95 (0-689-31121-4). A self-help book for teens that advocates a strong set of positive images to motivate one to achieve goals. (Rev: BL 9/1/85; SLJ 9/86) [796]

5626 Rainer, Tristine. *The New Diary: How to Use a Journal for Self-Guidance and Expanded*

Creativity (10–12). 1979, Jeremy P. Tarcher paper $8.95 (0-87477-150-1). Rainer suggests that by keeping a journal one can discover oneself and solve problems. [194]

5627 Richards, Arlene Kramer, and Irene Willis. *Leaving Home* (9–12). 1980, Macmillan $8.95 (0-689-30757-8). A guide to success in achieving independence with many examples from case studies. [155.5]

5628 Rosenbaum, Alvin. *The Young People's Yellow Pages: A National Sourcebook for Youth* (9–12). 1983, Perigee $14.95 (0-399-50970-4); paper $8.95 (0-399-50846-5). This directory gives addresses and phone numbers where young people can get information on subjects like jobs, health, nutrition, drugs, and sex. [613.6]

5629 Schneider, Meg. *Romance! Can You Survive It? A Guide to Sticky Dating Situations* (9–12). 1984, Dell paper $2.25 (0-440-97478-X). Problems involved in dating, including those with parents and friends, are addressed in this helpful guide. [306.7]

5630 Simon, Nissa. *Don't Worry, You're Normal* (9–12). 1982, Harper LB $12.89 (0-690-04138-1); Trophy paper $4.95 (0-06-446020-7). This reassuring volume discusses concerns that trouble teenagers. [150]

5631 Sliwa, Lisa, and Keith E. Greenberg. *Attitude: Commonsense Defense for Women* (10–12). Illus. 1986, Crown paper $9.95 (0-517-56187-5). A commonsense guide for women who want to learn how to defend themselves from would-be attackers. (Rev: SLJ 5/87) [613.6]

5632 Snider, Dee, and Philip Bashe. *Dee Snider's Teenage Survival Guide* (10–12). 1987, Doubleday paper $8.95 (0-385-23900-9). Snider, a rock musician, gives sage advice on how to get through adolescence. (Rev: BL 8/87; SLJ 8/87; VOYA 12/87) [305.2]

5633 Van Buren, Abigail. *The Best of Dear Abby* (10–12). 1989, Andrews & McMeel paper $9.95 (0-8362-6241-7). This is a collection of the best of the advice columns written by this popular counselor. [361.3]

5634 Wassmer, Arthur C. *Making Contact* (10–12). 1990, Henry Holt paper $10.95 (0-8050-1348-2). A practical guide to overcoming the anxiety and inhibitions connected with bashfulness. [152.4]

5635 Weston, Carol. *Girltalk about Guys* (7–12). 1988, Harper $15.95 (0-06-055108-9). Taken from actual letters seeking advice, this is a collection of tips concerning dating, boyfriends, and sex. (Rev: BR 11–12/88) [155.5]

5636 Zimbardo, Philip G. *Shyness* (10–12). 1990, Addison paper $6.95 (0-201-55018-0). What causes shyness and how to relieve this anxiety are explored in this volume. [152.4]

Social Groups

Family and Family Problems

5637 Arnold, William V. *When Your Parents Divorce* (9–12). 1980, Westminster paper $7.95 (0-664-24294-4). A self-help book on how to cope with divorce in the family. [306.8]

5638 Bloomfield, Harold H., and Leonard Felder. *Making Peace with Your Parents* (10–12). 1984, Ballantine paper $4.95 (0-345-30904-9). For better readers, this is a manual on how to resolve differences between parents and teenagers. [306.9]

5639 Brondino, Jeanne, et al. *Raising Each Other* (7–12). Illus. 1988, Hunter House paper $7.95 (0-89793-044-4). This book, written and illustrated by a high school class, is about parent-teen relationships, problems, and solutions. (Rev: SLJ 1/89; VOYA 4/89) [306.1]

5640 Chase, Naomi Feigelson. *A Child Is Being Beaten: Violence Against Children, an American Tragedy* (10–12). 1975, McGraw paper $6.95 (0-07-010685-1). An examination of child abuse that gives historic perspective to the present-day problem. [362.7]

5641 Cline, Ruth K. J. *Focus on Families* (9–12). 1990, ABC.CLIO $28.50 (0-87436-508-2). An account that outlines problems such as single parenting and abuse that often characterize the modern family. (Rev: SLJ 9/90) [306.8]

5642 Cohen, Shari. *Coping with Being Adopted* (8–12). 1988, Rosen LB $12.95 (0-8239-0770-8). Strategies are outlined to cope with such problems as searching for one's biological parents, relations with adoptive parents, and fitting into an existing family. (Rev: SLJ 5/88; VOYA 8/88) [346.01]

5643 Cohen, Shari. *Coping with Sibling Rivalry* (8–12). 1989, Rosen $12.95 (0-8239-0977-8). How to cope with real or imaginary competition between brothers and sisters. (Rev: BL 11/1/89; SLJ 2/90) [155.5]

5644 Craven, Linda. *Stepfamilies: New Patterns in Harmony* (7–12). Illus. 1982, Messner LB $11.98 (0-671-44080-2); paper $4.95 (0-671-49486-4). This book covers stepfamilies under such topics as discipline, stepsiblings, and sexuality. [306.8]

5645 Croom, Emily Anne. *Unpuzzling Your Past: A Basic Guide to Genealogy* (9–12). Illus. 1989, Betterway paper $9.95 (1-55870-111-7). An excellent guide for someone who wishes to trace family histories, with many data-gathering tips. (Rev: SLJ 7/89) [929]

5646 D'Ambrosio, Richard. *No Language but a Cry* (10–12). 1971, Dell paper $4.50 (0-440-36457-4). The story of the gradual recovery of a battered child. [155.4]

5647 Doane, Gilbert H. *Searching for Your Ancestors* (10–12). Illus. 1980, Univ. of Minnesota Pr. $15.95 (0-8166-0934-9). An introduction to genealogy that describes the methodology used and tells how to conduct searches involving family roots outside the country. [929]

5648 Dolan, Edward F., Jr. *Child Abuse* (9–12). 1980, Watts LB $12.90 (0-531-02864-X). A history of child abuse is given plus a rundown on recent steps to give children more protection. [362.7]

5649 Edelman, Marian Wright. *Families in Peril: An Agenda for Social Change* (10–12). 1987, Harvard Univ. Pr. $15.00 (0-674-29228-6); paper $7.95 (0-674-29229-4). An examination of the American family today and the dangers that beset this institution. (Rev: BL 3/15/87) [362.8]

5650 Fletcher, William. *Recording Your Family History: A Guide to Preserving Oral History* (10–12). 1989, Ten Speed paper $11.95 (0-89815-324-7). A guide to oral history techniques that include the use of both audio and visual equipment. (Rev: BL 11/15/86; BR 5–6/87; SLJ 12/86; VOYA 6/87) [900]

5651 Fontana, Vincent J. *Somewhere a Child Is Crying: Maltreatment—Causes and Prevention* (10–12). 1973, NAL paper $4.95 (0-451-62699-0). All forms of child neglect and abuse are covered plus an action plan for treatment and prevention. [362.7]

5652 Gilbert, Sara. *How to Live with a Single Parent* (7–12). 1982, Lothrop LB $12.88 (0-688-00633-7). The author gives suggestions and practical hints on how to live successfully in a single-parent household. [306.8]

5653 Ginott, Haim. *Between Parent and Teenager* (9–12). 1982, Avon paper $4.50 (0-380-00820-3). This is a guide to developing good relations between parents and teenagers, plus solid advice about handling the problems of adolescence. [306.9]

5654 Gundlach, Julie. *My Mother Before Me: When Daughters Discover Mothers* (10–12). Illus. 1986, Carol $17.95 (0-8184-0394-2). From 80 interviews the author discusses various patterns of mother-daughter relationships. (Rev: SLJ 3/87) [306.8]

5655 Hammerslough, Jane. *Everything You Need to Know about Teen Motherhood* (7–12). Illus. 1990, Rosen LB $12.95 (0-8239-1015-6). An account of the problems that young mothers face and how to cope with them. (Rev: SLJ 9/90; VOYA 8/90) [305.4]

5656 Helmbold, F. Wilbur. *Tracing Your Ancestry* (9–12). 1978, Oxmoor House paper $7.95 (0-8487-0414-2). This is a step-by-step guide to researching one's family history. [929]

5657 Hodges, Margaret. *Making a Difference: The Story of an American Family* (9–12). Illus. 1989, Macmillan $13.95 (0-684-18979-8). Through a description of an actual family, the Sherwoods, this social institution is explored. (Rev: BL 7/89; BR 11–12/89; SLJ 5/89; VOYA 8/89) [973.71]

5658 Hook, J. N. *Family Names* (10–12). 1982, Macmillan paper $8.95 (0-02-080000-2). This account arranged by ethnic groups explains the origin of many family names. [929.4]

5659 Kalergis, Mary Motley. *Mother: A Collective Portrait* (10–12). Illus. 1987, Dutton $19.95 (0-525-24525-1); paper $12.95 (0-525-48297-0). A collection of brief essays by women on their role as mothers. (Rev: SLJ 9/87) [306.8]

5660 Kempe, C. Henry, and Ray E. Helfer, eds. *The Battered Child* (10–12). 4th ed. Illus. 1987, National Center for the Prevention of Child Abuse $37.00 (0-318-14670-3). The causes, treatment, and prevention of child abuse are covered in this sympathetic account. [362.7]

5661 Kempe, Ruth S., and C. Henry Kempe. *Child Abuse* (10–12). Illus. 1978, Harvard Univ. Pr. $15.00 (0-674-11425-6); paper $3.95 (0-674-11426-4). The authors explain the cycle of child abuse and suggest ways by which it can be broken. [362.7]

5662 Klein, David, and Marymae E. Klein. *Your Parents and Your Self: Alike/Unlike/Agreeing/Disagreeing* (10–12). 1986, Macmillan $12.95 (0-684-18684-5). The nature versus nurture argument is explored in assessing the influence of parents on their children plus a helpful guide to successful parent/child relations. (Rev: BL 4/15/87; SLJ 2/87; VOYA 2/87) [306.8]

5663 Kurzweil, Arthur. *From Generation to Generation: How to Trace Your Jewish Genealogy and Personal History* (10–12). Illus. 1982,

Schocken paper $9.95 (0-8052-0706-6). In addition to general advice on searches, the author explains how to trace Jewish family origins to Europe and Israel. [929]

5664 Lindsay, Jeanne Warren. *Teenage Marriage: Coping with Reality* (8–12). Illus. 1984, Morning Glory $14.95 (0-930934-12-1); paper $9.95 (0-930934-11-13). From interviews with 55 teenagers, mostly women, a realistic picture of the problems of teenage marriage emerges. [306.8]

5665 Lindsay, Jeanne Warren. *Teens Look at Marriage: Rainbows, Roles and Realities* (9–12). Illus. 1985, Morning Glory $15.95 (0-930934-16-4); paper $9.95 (0-930934-15-6). Using the results of 3,000 survey questionnaires sent to teens and many interviews, the author describes attitudes toward marriage by today's young adults. (Rev: BL 1/15/85; SLJ 4/85) [306.8]

5666 McGuire, Paula. *Putting It Together: Teenagers Talk about Family Breakups* (9–12). 1987, Delacorte $15.95 (0-385-29564-2). Using case studies of 18 teenagers from broken homes, the author discusses such topics as death, divorce, and abandonment. (Rev: BL 10/1/87; BR 11–12/78; SLJ 10/87; VOYA 10/87) [308.8]

5667 Marks, Jane. *HELP! My Parents Are Driving Me Crazy* (9–12). 1982, Ace paper $5.95 (0-441-32744-3). This explores conflicts between parents and children and how they can be solved or eased. [306.9]

5668 Mayer, Egon. *Love & Tradition: Marriage between Jews & Christians* (10–12). 1985, Plenum $19.95 (0-306-42043-0). This is both an historical and a sociological examination of the phenomenon of Jews and Christians marrying. (Rev: BL 9/1/85) [306.8]

5669 Miner, Jane Claypool. *Young Parents* (9–12). Illus. 1985., Messner $9.79 (0-671-49848-7). A guide to teenage pregnancy and parenting that gives much impartial advice and examines such topics as abortion, adoption, and marriage. (Rev: BL 8/85; BR 3–4/86; SLJ 10/85) [306.8]

5670 Mintz, Steven, and Susan Kellogg. *Domestic Revolutions: A Social History of American Family Life* (10–12). Illus. 1988, Free Pr. $22.50 (0-02-921290-1). A description of how changes in the American family have affected its structure and functions. (Rev: SLJ 9/88) [306.8]

5671 Owen, Ursula, ed. *Fathers: Reflections by Daughters* (10–12). Illus. 1985, Pantheon $17.95 (0-394-53913-3); paper $7.95 (0-394-72674-2). A group of distinguished American, Canadian, and British female writers were asked to contribute thoughts on their relations with their fathers in this interesting combination of both fiction and nonfiction. (Rev: BL 5/1/85) [306.8]

5672 Pruett, Kyle D. *The Nurturing Father: A Journey to the Complete Man* (10–12). 1987, Warner $18.95 (0-446-51269-9); paper $9.95 (0-446-38662-6). A child psychiatrist investigates the family situation when the father stays home and mother works. (Rev: BL 10/15/86) [306.8]

5673 Smith, Elsdon C. *New Dictionary of American Family Names* (10–12). 1973, Harper $21.45 (0-06-013933-1). This book traces the origins of the most common American surnames. [929.4]

5674 Straus, Murray A., et al. *Behind Closed Doors: Violence in the American Family* (10–12). 1980, Sage paper $12.95 (0-8039-3292-8). This comprehensive volume on all sorts of family violence is based on a survey of more than 2,000 American families. [306.8]

5675 Taylor, Paul, and Diane Taylor. *Coping with a Dysfunctional Family* (7–12). 1990, Rosen $12.95 (0-8239-1180-2). Through case studies, this account explores family problems that stem from such conditions as abuse, drugs, and neglect. (Rev: BL 11/1/90) [362.82]

5676 Towle, Alexandra, ed. *Mothers: A Celebration in Prose, Poetry, and Photographs of Mothers and Motherhood* (10–12). Illus. 1988, Simon & Schuster $17.95 (0-671-66056-X). Various aspects of motherhood are explored in snippets from writers as diverse as Queen Victoria and Oscar Wilde. (Rev: BL 5/1/88) [808.8]

5677 Vedral, Joyce L. *My Parents Are Driving Me Crazy* (8–12). 1986, Ballantine paper $2.50 (0-345-33011-0). A self-help guide on how to relate to parents and ease the problems that conflict with them cause. (Rev: BL 3/1/87; SLJ 2/87; VOYA 4/87) [306.87]

5678 Westin, Jeane Eddy. *Finding Your Roots: How Every American Can Trace His Ancestors, At Home and Abroad* (10–12). 1988, St. Martin's paper $3.50 (0-312-90539-4). A handbook on tracing one's ancestors plus information on family names, histories of famous families, and more. [929]

5679 Wholey, Dennis. *Becoming Your Own Parent* (10–12). 1988, Doubleday $17.95 (0-385-24591-2). A guide for teens who must take charge of their lives because their families are not functioning properly. (Rev: SLJ 4/89) [306.8]

5680 Winn, Marie. *Children without Childhood* (10–12). 1983, Pantheon $13.45 (0-394-51136-0). A description of how the characteristics of childhood have changed and how this reflects society's concerns. [305.2]

5681 Worth, Richard. *The American Family* (9–12). Illus. 1984, Watts LB $12.90 (0-531-04859-4). A history of the American family and how its structure has changed through the years. [306.8]

The Arts and Entertainment

General and Miscellaneous

5682 Clark, Kenneth. *Civilisation: A Personal View* (10–12). Illus. 1970, Harper $29.45 (0-06-010800-2). A history of art and human values from the seventh century to the present. [709]

5683 Feldman, Edmund Burke. *Varieties of Visual Experience* (10–12). Illus. 1987, Abrams $40.00 (0-8109-1735-1); Prentice paper $29.95 (0-13-940602-6). A comparison of images as they are presented in a number of the visual arts such as painting, sculpture, television, and architecture. (Rev: BL 7/87) [701]

5684 Franck, Irene M., and David M. Brownstone. *Artists and Artisans* (9–12). Illus. 1987, Facts on File $14.95 (0-8160-1441-8). Occupations such as glassblowing, bookbinding, and clockmaking along with the work of artists and painters are surveyed through history. (Rev: BL 9/15/87) [709]

5685 Janson, H. W. *A History of Art & Music* (10–12). Illus. 1968, Prentice paper $30.95 (0-13-389312-X). An integrated history of art and music in the Western world from primitive times to the present. [709]

Architecture and Building

General and Miscellaneous

5686 Barford, George. *Understanding Modern Architecture* (9–12). Illus. 1987, Davis $16.95 (0-87192-179-0). With illustrations on every page, this is a fine introduction to the many schools of modern architecture. (Rev: BL 4/1/87) [724.9]

5687 Giedion, Sigfried. *Space, Time and Architecture: The Growth of a New Tradition* (10–12). 5th ed. 1967, Harvard Univ. Pr. $39.95 (0-674-83040-7). A look at modern architecture and the need to integrate human needs with design and materials. [720]

5688 Hall, James. *Dictionary of Subjects and Symbols in Art* (10–12). Illus. 1974, Harper paper $12.95 (0-06-430100-1). Subjects that have inspired artists such as characters and incidents in mythology or the Bible are all explained in a dictionary format. [704.9]

5689 Murray, Peter, and Linda Murray. *The Penguin Dictionary of Art and Artists* (10–12). 5th ed. 1986, Penguin paper $7.95 (0-14-051133-4). A concise dictionary that defines terms and movement plus supplies biographical information of over 1,000 people. [703]

5690 Winters, Nathan B. *Architecture Is Elementary: Visual Thinking through Architectural Concepts* (10–12). Illus. 1986, Gibbs M. Smith paper $19.95 (0-87905-186-8). An introduction to architecture that describes different building styles and how they flourished at different periods. (Rev: SLJ 9/86) [720]

5691 Young, Michael. *Architectural and Building Design: An Introduction* (9–12). Illus. 1987, David & Charles paper $24.95 (0-434-92448-2). An interesting introduction to all sorts of building styles, external factors in planning structures, and special problems designers face. (Rev: BL 4/15/88) [721]

History of Architecture

5692 Crouch, Dora P. *History of Architecture: Stonehenge to Skyscrapers* (10–12). Illus. 1985, McGraw $38.95 (0-07-014531-8); paper $28.50 (0-07-014524-5). From ancient times to the present, architectural history is explained with many illustrations. [720.9]

5693 Hamlin, Talbot Faulkner. *Architecture through the Ages* (10–12). Rev. ed. Illus. 1953, Putnam $27.50 (0-399-30001-5). A history of architecture that relates its development to changing cultural and social conditions. [720.9]

5694 Kostof, Spiro. *A History of Architecture: Settings and Rituals* (10–12). Illus. 1985, Oxford Univ. Pr. $60.00 (0-19-503472-4); paper $35.00 (0-19-503473-0). This is an expensive volume that deals not only with architectural styles but also the social and environmental contexts in which they were developed. (Rev: BL 8/85) [720]

5695 Macaulay, David. *Great Moments in Architecture* (9–12). Illus. 1978, Houghton $15.95 (0-395-25500-7); paper $8.95 (0-395-26711-8). An amusing look at what might have been disasters in the history of world architecture. [720]

5696 Maddex, Diane, ed. *Master Builders: A Guide to Famous American Architects* (10–12). Illus. 1985, Preservation Pr. paper $9.95 (0-89133-111-5). The work of 32 individual architects and several partnerships are discussed in text and almost 400 accompanying photographs. (Rev: BL 1/15/86) [720]

5697 Yarwood, Doreen. *A Chronology of Western Architecture* (10–12). Illus. 1988, Facts on File $29.95 (0-8160-1861-8). From Bronze Age Greece to the present, this is a concise, well-illustrated history of European and North American architecture. (Rev: BL 3/15/88; BR 5–6/88) [709]

Regions

5698 Blumenson, John J. G. *Identifying American Architecture: A Pictorial Guide to Styles and Terms, 1600–1945* (10–12). 2nd ed. Illus. 1981, Norton paper $10.95 (0-399-30610-0). Through the use of pictures, various styles in the history of American architecture are identified. [720.973]

5699 Diamonstein, Barbaralee. *American Architecture Now II* (10–12). Illus. 1985, Rizzoli paper $25.00 (0-8478-0612-X). Interviews with 29 contemporary American architects plus many pictorial views of their works. (Rev: SLJ 10/86) [720.9]

5700 Kostof, Spiro. *America by Design* (10–12). Illus. 1987, Oxford Univ. Pr. $24.95 (0-19-504283-2). A history from colonial times to the present of design in America that covers such topics as buildings, highways, parks, and monuments. (Rev: SLJ 1/88) [720]

5701 Krantz, Les. *American Architects* (10–12). Illus. 1989, Facts on File $40.00 (0-8160-1420-5). The lives of 400 prominent living American architects plus a discussion of their works. (Rev: BR 1–2/90) [720.9]

5702 McAlester, Virginia, and Lee McAlester. *A Field Guide to American Houses* (10–12). Illus. 1984, Knopf $30.00 (0-394-51032-1); paper $21.95 (0-394-73969-8). This guide to domestic architecture covers the design of houses from Colonial times to the present. [728]

5703 Maddex, Diane, ed. *Built in the U.S.A.: American Buildings from Airports to Zoos* (10–12). Illus. 1985, Preservation Pr. paper $8.95 (0-89133-118-2). Arranged by their function, this is a description of illustrations of 42 types of buildings found in the United States. (Rev: BL 6/15/85) [720]

5704 Rifkind, Carole. *A Field Guide to American Architecture* (10–12). Illus. 1980, NAL paper $15.95 (0-452-26269-0). A history of American architecture as seen through the examination of various buildings. [720]

5705 Storrer, William Allin. *Architecture of Frank Lloyd Wright: A Complete Catalog* (10–12). 2nd ed. Illus. 1978, MIT Pr. paper $13.95 (0-262-69080-8). This guide covers approximately 400 buildings designed by this American master. [720.973]

5706 Wright, Frank Lloyd. *Frank Lloyd Wright: Writings and Buildings* (10–12). Illus. 1960, NAL paper $10.95 (0-452-00969-3). A sampling of this architect's writing plus sketches of many of his buildings. [720.973]

Various Types of Buildings

5707 Macaulay, David. *Castle* (9–12). Illus. 1977, Houghton $14.95 (0-395-25784-0). In excellent line drawings and text, the author describes the construction of a castle in Wales during the thirteenth century. [728.8]

5708 Macaulay, David. *Cathedral: The Story of Its Construction* (9–12). Illus. 1973, Houghton $14.95 (0-395-17513-5). The story of how an imaginary cathedral was built in France from its conception in 1252 to its completion in 1338. [726]

5709 Macaulay, David. *Unbuilding* (9–12). Illus. 1980, Houghton $15.95 (0-395-29457-6); paper $6.95 (0-395-45425-5). In this architectural spoof, the Empire State building is dismantled. [690]

5710 Sabbagh, Karl. *Skyscraper* (9–12). Illus. 1990, Viking $22.95 (0-670-83229-4). In a companion volume to the PBS series, this book tells how a high-rise building in New York City is planned, designed, and built. (Rev: BL 2/15/90) [690]

5711 Weeks, John. *The Pyramids* (10–12). Illus. 1971, Cambridge Univ. Pr. paper $5.95 (0-521-07240-9). The story of the construction of the pyramids, their uses, and contents. [726]

Art, Painting, Photography, and Sculpture

General and Miscellaneous

5712 Berger, John. *Ways of Seeing* (10–12). 1977, Peter Smith $14.75 (0-8446-6175-9); paper $5.95 (0-14-021631-6). This book, based on the television series of the same name, explains that the way we view art is often relative to our attitudes and background knowledge. [700]

5713 *The Best of Life* (7–12). Illus. 1986, Crown paper $17.95 (0-517-61940-7). A most impressive collection of photographs from pages of *Life* magazine. [779]

5714 Clark, Kenneth. *What Is a Masterpiece?* (10–12). Illus. 1983, Peter Smith $15.50 (0-8445-5991-6); Thames & Hudson paper $4.95 (0-500-27206-9). A reprint of a lecture in which the author tries to define what makes greatness in art. [701]

5715 Cumming, Robert. *Just Imagine: Ideas in Painting* (9–12). 1982, Macmillan $12.95 (0-684-17762-5). Through an examination and analysis of great paintings of the past, the various elements used by artists are explored. [741]

5716 Danziger, James, ed. *Visual Aid* (9–12). Illus. 1986, Pantheon $30.00 (0-394-55664-X). A photographic album of portraits of famous people all by equally famous photographers. (Rev: SLJ 5/87) [770]

5717 Fralin, Frances, ed. *The Indelible Image: Photographs of War—1846 to the Present* (10–12). Illus. 1985, Abrams $35.00 (0-8109-1110-8). The grim face of war from the Crimean to the present conflict in Ireland and Lebanon in an impressive but costly volume. (Rev: BL 1/1/86) [779]

5718 Gautier, Dick. *The Art of Caricature* (9–12). Illus. 1985, Putnam paper $10.95 (0-399-51132-6). This is both an instruction manual on caricature as well as a history with many examples from the past and present. (Rev: BL 11/1/85) [741.5]

5719 Hanhisalo, Judith Evans. *Enjoying Art: Painting, Sculpture, Architecture and the Decorative Arts* (10–12). 1983, Prentice paper $9.95 (0-13-281584-2). A basic guide to the appreciation of art in several formats. [701]

5720 Holme, Bryan. *Creatures of Paradise: Pictures to Grow Up With* (10–12). Illus. 1980, Oxford Univ. Pr. $18.95 (0-19-520205-8). This book explains and gives examples of how animals have been pictured by artists through the ages. [700]

5721 Hunter, Sam, and John Jacobus. *Modern Art: Painting/Sculpture/Architecture* (10–12). 2nd ed. Illus. 1985, Abrams $49.95 (0-8109-1349-6). Though expensive, this book gives up-to-date information about present developments in art along with many fine illustrations. (Rev: BL 7/85) [709]

5722 Monk, Lorraine. *Photographs That Changed the World* (8–12). Illus. 1989, Doubleday $29.95 (0-385-26195-0). From the first photograph by French inventor Niépce to the present, here is a collection of 51 outstanding photographs. (Rev: VOYA 4/90) [770]

5723 Steichen, Edward. *The Family of Man* (9–12). Illus. 1987, Simon & Schuster $25.00 (0-671-55412-3); paper $14.95 (0-671-55411-5). This is the book that resulted from the photographic exhibition created by Steichen that depicts life's similarities and differences around the world. [779]

5724 Szarkowski, John. *Photography Until Now* (10–12). Illus. 1990, Museum of Modern Art $60.00 (0-87070-573-3). An expensive but important book on the history of photography and its components. (Rev: BL 5/15/90) [770.9]

5725 Taylor, Joshua C. *Learning to Look: A Handbook for the Visual Arts* (10–12). 1981, Univ. of Chicago Pr. paper $8.95 (0-226-79154-8). A thoughtful guide to art appreciation and how to examine works of art critically. [701]

5726 Ventura, Piero. *Great Painters* (9–12). 1984, Putnam $20.95 (0-399-21115-2). This book shows many of the world's great works of art and explains how and why each was created. [759]

5727 Waldron, Ann. *True or False? Amazing Art Forgeries* (9–12). 1983, Hastings House LB $12.95 (0-8038-7220-8). The story behind some of the great art forgeries in history. [759]

5728 Whelan, Michael. *Wonderworks: Science Fiction & Fantasy Art* (9–12). Illus. 1988, Starblaze paper $12.95 (0-915442-74-4). A collection of 100 paintings by one of the foremost illustrators of fantasy and science fiction. (Rev: SLJ 2/89) [741]

History of Art

5729 Armour, Richard. *It All Started with Nudes* (9–12). 1977, McGraw paper $7.95 (0-07-002271-2). A humorous look at art history. [709]

5730 Arnason, H. H. *History of Modern Art: Painting, Sculpture, Architecture, Photography* (9–12). 3rd ed. Illus. 1986, Abrams $49.50 (0-8109-1097-7). This popular survey covers the field well from the late nineteenth century to the mid-1980s. (Rev: BL 12/15/86) [709]

5731 Ashton, Dore, ed. *Twentieth-Century Artists on Art* (10–12). 1986, Pantheon $24.95 (0-394-52276-1); paper $14.95 (0-394-73489-0). This is a collection of writing on art by the artists themselves beginning with Picasso and ending with Rothko. (Rev: BL 2/1/86) [709]

5732 Bahn, Paul G., and Jean Vertut. *Images of the Ice Age* (9–12). Illus. 1989, Facts on File $35.00 (0-8160-2130-9). An introduction to the caves of prehistoric man and to the art they contain. (Rev: BR 11–12/89) [709]

5733 Barnicoat, John. *A Concise History of Posters: 1870–1970* (9–12). Illus. 1972, Oxford Univ. Pr. paper $9.95 (0-19-520131-0). With international coverage, the author describes in text and reproductions a history of poster art from the late nineteenth century on. [741.67]

5734 Behr, Shulamith. *Women Expressionists* (10–12). Illus. 1988, Rizzoli $19.95 (0-8478-0963-3). This account describes the revolutionary work of such female artists as Käthe Kollwitz and Gabrielle Munter. (Rev: SLJ 2/89) [759.06]

5735 Branner, Robert. *Gothic Architecture* (10–12). Illus. 1961, Braziller paper $9.95 (0-8076-0332-5). An outline of the history of Gothic architecture from the twelfth through the fourteenth century with many illustrations. [723]

5736 Clark, Kenneth. *The Romantic Rebellion: Romantic versus Classic Art* (10–12). Illus. 1974, Harper paper $22.95 (0-06-430167-2). With a concentration on the French, this is a history of romantic art as seen in the work of 13 painters like David and Degas. [759.05]

5737 De la Croix, Horst, and Richard G. Tansey. *Gardner's Art Through the Ages* (7–12). 2 vols. Illus. 1970, Harcourt paper $22.00 each (Vol. 1: 0-15-503764-8; vol. 2: 0-15-503765-X). A standard adult history of art that has often been revised since its first publication in 1926. [709]

5738 Ferrier, Jean-Louis, ed. *Art of Our Century: The Chronicle of Western Art* (9–12). Trans. by Walter D. Glanze. Illus. 1989, Prentice $70.00 (0-13-011644-0). An expensive, well-illustrated volume that gives entries for each year from 1900 to 1988. (Rev: BL 5/1/90) [709.4]

5739 Gerstein, Marc S. *Impressionism: Selections from Five American Museums* (10–12). Illus. 1990, Hudson Hills paper $40.00 (0-55595-030-2). The evolution of impressionism is traced using as examples art from 5 American art galleries. (Rev: SLJ 3/90) [759.05]

5740 Getlein, Frank. *25 Impressionist Masterpieces* (10–12). Illus. 1981, Abrams $12.95 (0-8109-2247-9). An oversized volume that contains analyses of works by Manet, Renoir, Monet, Degas, Cezanne, and others. [759.05]

5741 Goffstein, M. B. *An Artists Album* (10–12). Illus. 1985, Harper LB $12.89 (0-06-021995-5). Covers the work of Vermeer, Boudin, Cezanne, Monet, and the Woodland Indians in this companion volume to *Lives of the Artist* (1981). (Rev: SLJ 10/85) [709]

5742 Gombrich, E. H. *The Story of Art* (9–12). Illus. 1985, Prentice paper $30.95 (0-13-850066-5). A standard history of art that stresses the relationships of artistic movements to social developments. [709]

5743 Grundberg, Andy, and Kathleen McCarthy Gauss. *Photography and Art: Interactions since*

1946 (10–12). Illus. 1987, Abbeville $50.00 (0-89659-683-4). The authors bridge the gap between art movements of the twentieth century like surrealism and their effects on photography. (Rev: SLJ 3/88) [770]

5744 Hamilton, George Heard. *19th and 20th Century Art: Painting, Sculpture, Architecture* (10–12). Illus. 1970, Prentice paper $34.95 (0-13-622639-6). Almost 2 centuries of art development are covered in this account that gives fullest coverage to contemporary developments. [709.04]

5745 Hartt, Frederick. *Art: A History of Painting, Sculpture, Architecture* (8–12). 3rd ed. Illus. 1989, Abrams $49.50 (0-8109-1884-6). This large, expensive volume covers art history from the Stone Age to the 1980s; stunning illustrations and clear text. (Rev: BL 4/1/89) [709]

5746 Heller, Nancy G. *Women Artists: An Illustrated History* (9–12). Illus. 1987, Abbeville $39.95 (0-89659-748-2). A history that gives information with pictures of famous women artists from the Renaissance to the present. (Rev: SLJ 5/88) [709]

5747 Hillier, Bevis. *Art Deco of the 20s and 30s* (10–12). Rev. ed. Illus. 1985, Schocken paper $9.95 (0-8052-0785-6). This book explores the lavish style of modern art and gives examples mainly from Europe. (Rev: BL 8/85) [709]

5748 Hoff, Syd. *Editorial and Political Cartooning* (9–12). Illus. 1976, Stravon Educ. Pr. $14.95 (0-87396-078-5). Using 700 examples, Hoff traces the history of political cartooning and how it has interpreted many important historical events. [741.5]

5749 Janson, H. W., and Anthony F. Janson. *History of Art for Young People* (7–12). 3rd ed. Illus. 1987, Abrams $29.95 (0-8109-1098-5). A simplification of the authors' *History of Art* (1986) written specially for junior and senior high school students. (Rev: BL 7/87) [709]

5750 Johnson, Ellen H., ed. *American Artists on Art from 1940 to 1980* (10–12). Illus. 1982, Harper paper $11.95 (0-06-430112-5). A collection of statements by contemporary artists on such developments as minimal, pop, and abstract art. [709.73]

5751 Lippard, Lucy R. *Pop Art* (10–12). Illus. 1966, Thames & Hudson paper $11.95 (0-500-20052-1). In 4 essays by art critics, the world of pop art is explored and explained. [709.04]

5752 Lynton, Norbert. *The Story of Modern Art* (10–12). 2nd ed. Illus. 1989, Prentice paper $29.95 (0-13-849860-1). The author traces the development of art in the twentieth century by

examining more than 250 representative works of art. [709.04]

5753 Moszynska, Anna. *Abstract Art* (10–12). Illus. 1990, Thames and Hudson paper $11.95 (0-500-20237-0). An international survey of abstract art from its beginnings in the early twentieth century to the present. Well illustrated. (Rev: BL 3/15/90) [709.42]

5754 *The New Yorker Album of Drawings, 1925–1975* (9–12). Illus. 1975, Penguin paper $16.95 (0-14-004968-1). A selection of 500 cartoons from the first 50 years of the history of the *New Yorker* magazine. [741.5]

5755 Newhall, Beaumont. *The History of Photography: From 1839 to the Present Day* (10–12). Rev. ed. Illus. 1982, Bulfinch Pr. $40.00 (0-87070-380-3) paper $23.50 (0-87070-381-1). A history of photography that gives many prints representing the best from the past and present. [770.9]

5756 Read, Herbert. *A Concise History of Modern Painting* (10–12). Illus. 1959, Thames & Hudson paper $11.95 (0-500-20141-2). A concise guide to twentieth-century painting that ends in the late 1950s. [759.06]

5757 Read, Herbert. *A Concise History of Modern Sculpture* (10–12). Illus. 1964, Oxford Univ. Pr. paper $9.95 (0-19-519941-3). Beginning with Rodin, this account traces the history of modern sculpture through text and many photographs. [735]

5758 Reed, Walt, and Roger Reed. *The Illustrator in America, 1880–1980: A Century of Illustration* (10–12). Illus. 1984, Madison Square Press $48.50 (0-942604-03-2). An expensive but valuable book that gives profiles of 460 artists from Frederic Remington to Maurice Sendak with 700 examples of their work. (Rev: BL 1/15/85) [741.6]

5759 Rewald, John. *The History of Impressionism* (10–12). 4th rev. ed. Illus. 1973, Museum of Modern Art $55.00 (0-87070-360-9); paper $29.95 (0-87070-369-2). A chronologically arranged history of impressionism in painting with 600 illustrations. [759.05]

5760 Rewald, John. *Post-Impressionism: From Van Gogh to Gauguin* (10–12). 3rd ed. Illus. 1978, Museum of Modern Art $60.00 (0-87070-532-6). A lavishly illustrated book that concentrates on the works of Van Gogh and Gauguin. [759.05]

5761 Reynolds, Donald M. *The Nineteenth Century* (9–12). 1985, Cambridge Univ. Pr. $22.95 (0-521-23208-2). A history of the visual arts from about 1750 to 1850 with coverage of painting, sculpture, and architecture. (Rev: BR 11–12/86) [709]

5762 Robertson, Martin. *A Shorter History of Greek Art* (10–12). Illus. 1981, Cambridge Univ. Pr. paper $23.95 (0-521-28084-2). A lucid but scholarly introduction to the evolution and characteristics of the art of ancient Greece. [709.38]

5763 Rosenblum, Robert. *19th-Century Art* (10–12). Illus. 1984, Abrams $49.50 (0-8109-1362-3). An international survey of both artistic and social developments during the nineteenth century. [709.3]

5764 Slatkin, Wendy. *Women Artists in History: From Antiquity to the 20th Century* (9–12). Illus. 1985, Prentice paper $24.60 (0-13-961821-X). A history of the role women have played in the history of art with black-and-white illustrations. (Rev: BL 3/1/85) [709]

5765 Stebbins, Theodore E., and Peter C. Sutton, eds. *Masterpiece Paintings from the Museum of Fine Arts, Boston* (9–12). Illus. 1987, Abrams $39.95 (0-8109-1424-7). Over 600 years of art history is represented in the 125 paintings highlighted. (Rev: BL 4/15/87) [750]

5766 Synder, James. *Medieval Art: Painting, Sculpture, Architecture—4th–14th Century* (10–12). Illus. 1989, Abrams $55.00 (0-8109-1532-4). Though expensive, this is an excellent guide to all forms of medieval art, including the cathedrals. (Rev: SLJ 7/89) [709.82]

Regions

Africa

5767 Willett, Frank. *African Art: An Introduction* (10–12). 1985, Thames & Hudson paper $9.95 (0-500-20103-X). A broad overview of African art that includes material on geography and culture. [709.6]

Asia

5768 Tregear, Mary. *Chinese Art* (10–12). Illus. 1980, Thames & Hudson $19.95 (0-500-18178-0). From the excellent World of Art series, this is a reliable overview of the historical art of China. [709.51]

Australia and the Pacific Islands

5769 Price, Christine. *Made in the South Pacific: Arts of the Sea People* (9–12). Illus. 1979, Dutton $11.95 (0-525-34397-0). This book shows how such items as shells, bones, and feathers are used in the South Pacific to create works of art. [707.9]

Europe

5770 Brettell, Richard R. *French Impressionists* (10–12). Illus. 1987, Art Institute of Chicago $29.95 (0-8109-0947-2); paper $18.95 (0-8109-2351-3). In addition to text on the impressionists, this volume is illustrated with examples from The Art Institute of Chicago. (Rev: BL 11/15/87) [760]

5771 Brettell, Richard R. *Post-Impressionists* (10–12). Illus. 1987, Art Institute of Chicago $29.95 (0-8109-1494-8); paper $18.95 (0-8109-2352-1). By using many color reproductions from the collection of The Art Institute of Chicago, the world of such artists as Cezanne, Manet, and Gauguin is explored. (Rev: BL 11/15/87) [760]

5772 Brown, Frank E. *Roman Architecture* (10–12). Illus. 1961, Braziller paper $9.95 (0-8076-0331-7). In text and many photographs, over 14 centuries of Roman architecture are covered. Part of the excellent Great Ages of World Architecture series. [722]

5773 Courthion, Pierre. *Manet* (10–12). Illus. 1984, Abrams $19.95 (0-8109-1318-6). Though some biographical information is included, this is essentially an examination of Manet's works. [759.4]

5774 Gowing, Lawrence. *Matisse* (10–12). Illus. 1979, Oxford Univ. Pr. paper $9.95 (0-19-520158-2). A useful examination of the work and techniques used by this prolific painter. [759.4]

5775 Gudiol, Jose. *Goya* (10–12). Illus. 1985, Abrams $19.95 (0-8109-0992-8). Along with a biography of this complex man, his art is examined and a sample of it provided in both color and black-and-white plates. [759.6]

5776 Hartt, Frederick. *Michelangelo* (10–12). Illus. 1984, Abrams $19.95 (0-8109-1335-6). This account concentrates on an examination of the paintings of Michelangelo. [759.5]

5777 Jacobus, John. *Matisse* (10–12). Illus. 1983, Abrams $19.95 (0-8109-1326-7). In addition to biographical material, Matisse's output is examined through the inclusion of 40 color plates and accompanying commentary. [759.4]

5778 Jaffe, Hans L. C. *Picasso* (10–12). Illus. 1983, Abrams $19.95 (0-8109-1480-8). The life of this influential artist is given plus over 100 illustrations, many in color. [759.6]

5779 Locher, J. L., ed. *The World of M. C. Escher* (10–12). Illus. 1972, NAL paper $9.95 (0-451-79961-5). Through several essays (one by Escher himself) and 300 illustrations, the work of this Dutch artist-mathematician is examined. [769]

5780 Lucie-Smith, Edward. *Toulouse-Lautrec* (10–12). Rev. ed. Illus. 1989, Watson-Guptill paper $19.95 (0-8230-5394-6). After a brief biography, the artist's work is analyzed by 48 color plates and accompanying text. [759.4]

5781 Munz, Ludwig. *Rembrandt* (10–12). Illus. 1984, Abrams $19.95 (0-8109-1594-4). An introduction to the work of this master through 40 color reproductions and commentary. [759.9492]

5782 Murray, Linda. *Michelangelo* (10–12). 1980, Oxford Univ. Pr. $19.95 (0-19-520163-9); paper $9.95 (0-19-520164-7). A short survey of the painting and architecture of this Renaissance master. [709.45]

5783 Pach, Walter. *Renoir* (10–12). Illus. 1983, Abrams $19.95 (0-8109-1593-6). The life and works of this Impressionist painter are covered in text and several color illustrations. [759.4]

5784 Rubin, William, ed. *Pablo Picasso: A Retrospective* (10–12). Illus. 1980, Museum of Modern Art $50.00 (0-87070-528-8). This catalog of the massive retrospective at the Museum of Modern Art in New York contains more than 900 prints of Picasso's work. [759.6]

5785 Schapiro, Meyer. *Van Gogh* (10–12). Illus. 1950, Abrams $49.50 (0-8109-0524-8). This tragic but productive life of this painter is re-created and his work analyzed. [759.9492]

5786 Scranton, Robert L. *Greek Architecture* (10–12). Illus. 1962, Braziller paper $9.95 (0-8076-0337-6). An illustrated account that emphasizes Greek temple architecture. [722]

5787 Walker, John. *Turner* (10–12). Illus. 1983, Abrams $19.95 (0-8109-1679-7). With about 100 illustrations—half in color—this is a fine introduction to the great English painter of the sea. [759.2]

5788 Wasserman, Jack. *Leonardo* (10–12). Illus. 1984, Abrams $19.95 (0-8109-1285-6). This volume includes reproductions of all of Leonardo's paintings plus many drawings and excerpts from his notebooks. [759.5]

North America

UNITED STATES

5789 Adams, Ansel. *The Portfolios of Ansel Adams* (9–12). Illus. 1977, Bulfinch $45.00 (0-8212-0723-7); paper $25.00 (0-8212-1122-6). A collection of 85 examples of this master photographer's work in black and white. [779]

5790 Baigell, Matthew. *Dictionary of American Art* (10–12). 1979, Harper paper $10.95 (0-06-430078-1). In coverage spanning the Colonial period through the 1970s, this book contains both biographical articles and material on general background topics. [709.73]

5791 Blackbeard, Bill, and Martin Williams, eds. *The Smithsonian Collection of Newspaper Comics* (9–12). Illus. 1978, Smithsonian Inst. $29.95 (0-686-77340-3); Abrams paper $24.95 (0-8109-2081-6). From 1896 to the 1970s, this is a history of the comics in America. [741.5]

5792 Craven, William, and Richard Martin, eds. *Two Hundred Years of American Art: The Munson-Williams-Proctor Institute* (10–12). Illus. 1987, Univ. of Washington Pr. paper $24.95 (0-295-96457-X). Two introductory essays and 82 artworks cover the history of American art from the mid-eighteenth to the mid-twentieth centuries. (Rev: BL 10/1/87) [759.13]

5793 Finch, Christopher. *The Art of Walt Disney: From Mickey Mouse to the Magic Kingdoms* (7–12). Illus. 1973, Abrams $39.95 (0-8109-0321-0); Crown paper $9.98 (0-517-66474-7). The life and career of Walt Disney are covered, but the main attraction in this book is a collection of almost 800 illustrations from his work. [791.43]

5794 Fine, Elsa Honig. *The Afro-American Artist: A Search for Identity* (10–12). Illus. 1973, Hacker Art $35.00 (0-87817-287-4); Brown paper $9.95 (0-317-39774-5). The development of black American art is traced from the days of slavery to the present. [709.73]

5795 Furst, Peter T., and Jill Leslie Furst. *North American Indian Art* (10–12). Illus. 1982, Rizzoli paper $25.00 (0-8478-0572-7). Using 6 major tribal areas as its focus, this book describes the visual art of each of these locations. [709.73]

5796 Goulart, Ron. *The Great Comic Book Artists, Volume 2* (7–12). Illus. 1989, St. Martin's paper $12.95 (0-312-01768-5). A wonderful browsing item that shows off the work of some of America's most famous cartoonists. Volume 1 is still available (1986). (Rev: BL 3/1/89) [741.5]

5797 Hartigan, Lynda Roscoe. *Sharing Traditions: Five Black Artists in Nineteenth-Century*

America (10–12). Illus. 1985, Smithsonian Inst. paper $17.50 (0-87474-513-6). The lives and work of 5 black American painters and sculptors of the nineteenth century are examined. [709.73]

5798 Horwitz, Elinor Lander. *Contemporary American Folk Artists* (10–12). 1975, Harper paper $3.95 (0-397-31627-5). A profile of 22 folk artists and their work. [745]

5799 Huggins, Nathan Irvin. *Harlem Renaissance* (10–12). Illus. 1971, Oxford Univ. Pr. paper $12.95 (0-19-501665-3). An excellent history of the amazing cultural life that blossomed in Harlem during the 1920s. [709.73]

5800 Kloss, William. *Treasures from the National Museum of American Art* (9–12). Illus. 1986, Smithsonian Inst. $39.95 (0-87474-594-2). This book highlights 81 color paintings (and others in black and white) and gives a good introduction to the most important artists in the history of American art. (Rev: BL 6/1/86) [709]

5801 McLanathan, Richard. *Art in America: A Brief History* (10–12). Illus. 1973, Harcourt paper $13.95 (0-15-503466-9). A concise history that includes material on painting, architecture, and sculpture. [709.73]

5802 Maddox, Jerald C. *The Pioneering Image: Celebrating 150 Years of American Photography* (9–12). 1989, Universe $29.95 (0-87663-695-4). Spanning the years 1842 through 1978, this is a well-illustrated history of American photography. (Rev: BL 9/1/89; SLJ 10/89) [770]

5803 Novak, Barbara. *American Painting of the Nineteenth Century: Realism, Idealism and the American Experience* (10–12). 2nd ed. Illus. 1979, Harper paper $15.95 (0-06-430099-4). The works of 12 American artists, including Homer, Eakins, Church, and Ryder, are introduced. [759.13]

5804 Rose, Howard. *Unexpected Eloquence: The Art in American Folk Art* (10–12). Illus. 1990, Raymond Saroff $25.00 (1-878352-00-8); paper $15.00 (1-878352-01-6). For good readers, this is a serious examination of folk art in America and how it is appreciated. (Rev: BL 3/15/90) [745]

5805 Salinger, Margaretta. *Masterpieces of American Painting in the Metropolitan Museum of Art* (9–12). Illus. 1986, Metropolitan Museum of Art $49.50 (0-394-55491-4). Historical and descriptive notes are given for reproductions of 100 paintings from the Met's collection that effectively trace a history of American art. (Rev: BL 2/1/87) [759.13]

5806 Simpson, Marc, et al. *The American Canvas: Paintings from the Collection of the Fine Arts Museums of San Francisco* (9–12). Illus. 1990, Hudson Hills $50.00 (1-55595-025-6). This volume with its 100-plus color reproductions can serve as a history of American painting. (Rev: BL 3/15/90) [759.13]

5807 Smith, Rex Alan. *The Carving of Mount Rushmore* (9–12). Illus. 1985, Abbeville $22.50 (0-89659-417-3). The story of the sculptor Gutzon Borglum and the 4 faces on Mount Rushmore. (Rev: BL 6/1/85) [730]

Decorative Arts

5808 Horwitz, Elinor Lander. *Mountain People, Mountain Crafts* (10–12). Illus. 1974, Harper $11.70 (0-397-31498-1); paper $3.95 (0-397-31499-X). A description of the folk arts of the Appalachians. [745.5]

5809 Kauffman, Henry. *Pennsylvania Dutch American Folk Art* (10–12). Rev. ed. Illus. 1964, Dover paper $5.50 (0-486-21205-X). In almost 300 photographs, Kauffman explores the origins of Pennsylvania Dutch folk art and its influence on the handicrafts of today. [745]

5810 Lucie-Smith, Edward. *Furniture: A Concise History* (10–12). 1985, Thames & Hudson $19.95 (0-500-18173-X); $11.95 (0-500-20172-2). This history of furniture reveals how people lived at various times in history. [749]

5811 Manhart, Marcia, and Tom Manhart, eds. *The Eloquent Object: The Evolution of American Art in Craft Media since 1945* (10–12). Illus. 1988, Philbrook Museum of Art $45.00 (0-86659-006-4). This handsome volume traces the application of techniques used in native crafts like weaving and potting into contemporary art forms. (Rev: BL 5/15/88) [745.0973]

5812 Porter, Norman, and Douglas Jackson. *Tiffany Glassware* (10–12). Illus. 1988, Crown $15.95 (0-517-57123-4). With lavish illustrations, this book describes Tiffany's work and life. (Rev: SLJ 5/89) [748.2]

Music

General and Miscellaneous

5813 Bebey, Francis. *African Music: A People's Art* (10–12). Trans. by Josephine Bennett. Illus. 1975, Hill paper $9.95 (0-88208-050-4). The nature of African music and its meanings are given plus a description of the instruments used. [780.9]

5814 Bernstein, Leonard. *The Joy of Music* (10–12). Illus. 1959, Simon & Schuster paper $5.95 (0-671-39721-4). This book consists of 7 scripts that the late master wrote for the "Omnibus" television series on the nature of music and how to appreciate it. [780.1]

5815 Bradley, Jack. *How to Read, Write, and Understand Music: A Practical Guide* (9–12). Illus. 1986, Hill Springs paper $19.95 (0-931856-05-1). A useful guide to the basics of music in a handy, concise treatment. (Rev: BL 3/1/87) [781]

5816 Copland, Aaron. *Music and Imagination* (10–12). 1952, Harvard Univ. Pr. paper $3.95 (0-674-58915-7). A reprint of a series of lectures on the problems facing the contemporary composer. [780.1]

5817 Copland, Aaron. *What to Listen for in Music* (10–12). 1988, McGraw $17.95 (0-07-013091-4). A reprint that explains the basic mechanics of music and how to apply them for listening pleasure. (Rev: SLJ 8/88) [780.1]

5818 Dearling, Robert, and Celia Dearling. *The Guinness Book of Music* (9–12). 3rd ed. Illus. 1987, Guinness $17.95 (0-85112-460-7). Using both chronological and alphabetical lists, the authors cover many topics such as instruments, composers, famous classical pieces, and general history. (Rev: BL 12/15/86) [780]

5819 Epstein, Helen. *Music Talks: Conversations with Working Musicians* (9–12). Illus. 1987, McGraw $17.95 (0-07-019544-7); Penguin paper $7.95 (0-14-011054-2). Short interviews with such contemporary musicians as Bernstein, Ozawa, and Previn. (Rev: BL 6/15/87) [780]

5820 Evans, Roger. *How to Read Music: For Singing, Guitar, Piano, Organ and Most Instruments* (9–12). 1979, Crown $6.95 (0-517-53897-0). A guide to reading notes and scores and an introduction to concepts involved in music notation. [780.7]

5821 Hemming, Roy. *Discovering Great Music* (9–12). 1988, Newmarket $19.95 (1-55704-027-3). A guide to classical music with introductions to 50 composers and their most important compositions. (Rev: BL 11/15/88) [789.9]

5822 Kennedy, Michael, ed. *The Concise Oxford Dictionary of Music* (7–12). 1980, Oxford Univ. Pr. paper $13.95 (0-19-311320-1). A compact guide that gives entries for compositions, composers, terms, and performers. [780.3]

5823 Kogan, Judith. *Nothing but the Best: The Struggle for Perfection at the Juilliard School* (10–12). 1987, Random $18.95 (0-394-55514-7); Limelight paper $10.95 (0-87910-122-9). Both students and faculty are highlighted in this account of what goes on at one of the country's leading schools of music. (Rev: BL 7/87; BR 1–2/88; SLJ 12/87; VOYA 12/87) [780]

5824 Kupferberg, Herbert. *The Book of Classical Music Lists* (10–12). 1985, Facts on File $19.95 (0-8160-1163-X); Penguin paper $9.95 (0-14-011188-3). A collection of trivia involving classical music, composers, the orchestra, and musical forms. (Rev: BL 2/15/86) [016.78]

5825 Machlis, Joseph. *The Enjoyment of Music: An Introduction to Perceptive Listening* (10–12). Illus. 1990, Norton $37.95 (0-393-95717-9). A guide to musical landmarks that starts with the familiar and moves to the lesser heard. [780.1]

5826 Rabin, Carol Price. *Music Festivals in America* (10–12). 1990, Berkshire Traveller paper $10.95 (0-930145-01-1). A description of 170 music festivals in Canada and the United States is given. [394.2]

5827 Randel, Don Michael, comp. *Harvard Concise Dictionary of Music* (7–12). Illus. 1978, Harvard Univ. Pr. $19.95 (0-674-37471-1); paper $8.95 (0-674-37470-3). Brief entries are given for such subjects as names of composers and musicians, musical instruments, and terms. [780.3]

5828 Schaefer, John. *New Sounds: A Listener's Guide to New Music* (10–12). 1987, Harper $22.45 (0-06-055054-6); paper $10.95 (0-06-097081-2). All kinds of modern music from minimalism to electronic jazz are described and discographies of each are provided. (Rev: BL 5/15/87) [780]

5829 Schnabel, Tom. *Stolen Moments: Conversations with Contemporary Musicians* (9–12). Illus. 1988, Acrobat $13.95 (0-918226-12-0). Through conversations with the author, readers meet such musicians as Wynton Marsalis, Philip Glass, and Joan Baez. (Rev: SLJ 2/89) [780]

5830 Wade, Graham. *The Shape of Music: An Introduction to Form in Classical Music* (7–12). 1981, Schocken $11.95 (0-8052-8109-6); paper $5.95 (0-8052-8110-X). This introduction to musical forms includes sections on such areas as the symphony and sonata. [781]

History of Music

5831 Brooks, Tilford. *America's Black Musical Heritage* (10–12). Illus. 1984, Prentice paper $29.00 (0-13-024307-8). A history of black American composers and performers from the days of slavery to the present with special emphasis on 17 important composers of yesterday and today. [781.7]

5832 Carlin, Richard. *European Classical Music 1600–1825* (9–12). Illus. 1988, Facts on File $15.95 (0-8160-1382-9). The baroque and classical periods and the emergence of the symphony and sonata forms are the principal subjects dealt with in this account. (Rev: BL 10/1/88; BR 9–10/88) [780]

5833 Copland, Aaron. *The New Music, 1900–1960* (10–12). Rev. ed. 1968, Norton paper $7.95 (0-393-00239-X). The distinguished composer gives a lucid introduction to twentieth-century music and how to approach it. [780.9]

5834 Griffin, Clive D. *Classical Music* (9–12). Illus. 1988, Dryad $17.95 (0-8521-9756-X). A briskly written overview of classical music with emphasis on the eighteenth and nineteenth centuries. (Rev: BL 2/15/89; BR 1–2/89; SLJ 12/88) [780.9]

5835 Grout, Donald Jay. *A History of Western Music* (10–12). 3rd ed. Illus. 1988, Norton $34.95 (0-393-95627-X). This is a history of Western music from ancient times to minimalism and serial music of today. [780.9]

5836 Nite, Norm N., and Charles Crespo. *Rock On: The Video Revolution* (9–12). Illus. 1985, Harper $24.50 (0-06-181644-2). A comprehensive analysis of rock video from 1979 through 1984. Preceded by *Rock On: The Solid Gold Years—Volume I* (1978) and *Rock On: The Years of Change—Volume II* (1984). (Rev: BL 10/15/85) [784.54]

5837 Pickow, Peter, and Amy Appleby. *The Billboard Book of Song Writing* (9–12). 1988, Watson-Guptill paper $16.95 (0-8230-7539-7). A useful manual that covers music-reading and lyric-writing skills, song styles and forms, and demo techniques. (Rev: BL 2/1/88) [784.5]

5838 Rushton, Julian. *Classical Music: A Concise History from Gluck to Beethoven* (10–12). Illus. 1986, Thames & Hudson paper $11.95 (0-500-20210-9). A concise, readable history that covers European music from the mid-eighteenth century to the first quarter of the nineteenth. (Rev: BL 2/1/87) [780]

5839 Southern, Eileen. *The Music of Black Americans: A History* (10–12). 2nd ed. Illus. 1983, Norton paper $16.95 (0-393-95279-7). A thorough account of black American music that begins with the seventeenth century and moves to the serious composers of today. [781.7]

Jazz, Rock, and Popular Music

5840 Aquila, Richard. *That Old Time Rock & Roll: A Chronicle of an Era, 1954–1963* (8–12). 1989, Schirmer $29.95 (0-02-870081-3); paper $22.50 (0-02-870082-1). A history complete with important biographies from the first decade of rock. (Rev: BL 9/15/89) [784.5]

5841 Ardley, Neil. *Music: An Illustrated Encyclopedia* (9–12). Illus. 1986, Facts on File $16.95 (0-8160-1543-0). Such diverse topics as opera plots, music history, and even rock are covered in brief entries. (Rev: SLJ 3/87; VOYA 6/87) [780]

5842 Berry, Jason, et al. *Up from the Cradle of Jazz: New Orleans Music since WWII* (10–12). Illus. 1986, Univ. of Georgia Pr. paper $15.95 (0-8203-0854-4). A history of jazz in New Orleans since 1950 and how it has influenced all forms of music today. (Rev: SLJ 5/87) [781]

5843 Birosik, Patti Jean. *The New Age Music Guide: Profiles and Recordings of 500 Top New Age Musicians* (10–12). 1990, Macmillan paper $12.95 (0-02-041640-7). More than 500 New Age musicians are profiled with lists of record labels and material on related musical styles. (Rev: BL 12/1/89) [016]

5844 Bonanno, Massimo. *The Rolling Stones Chronicle: The First Thirty Years* (9–12). Illus. 1990, Henry Holt paper $14.95 (0-8050-1301-6). A 30-year history of one of rock's most famous bands. (Rev: BL 6/1/90) [781.66]

5845 Brandelius, Jerilyn Lee. *Grateful Dead Family Album* (9–12). Illus. 1989, Warner $29.95 (0-446-51521-3). A history of this rock group from its founding in the 1960s to the present told in text and hundreds of photographs. (Rev: BL 1/15/90) [782]

5846 Bronson, Fred. *The Billboard Book of Number One Hits* (9–12). Illus. 1985, Billboard paper $16.95 (0-8230-7522-2). A single page is devoted to each song that was number one on the Billboard charts from July 1955 to April 1985. (Rev: SLJ 2/86) [784.5]

5847 Busnar, Gene. *It's Rock 'n' Roll* (9–12). Messner paper $4.95 (0-671-32977-4). This a comprehensive study of the music that was popular during the 1950s and 1960s. [780.42]

5848 Carlin, Richard. *Rock and Roll: 1955–1970* (7–12). Illus. 1988, Facts on File $16.95 (0-8160-1383-7). A history that begins with the pioneers like Chuck Berry and continues through Elvis, the Beatles, and other luminaries. (Rev: BL 12/15/88; BR 1–2/89; SLJ 12/88) [784.5]

5849 Carr, Ian, et al. *Jazz: The Essential Companion* (8–12). Illus. 1988, Prentice $24.95 (0-13-509274-4). A dictionary arrangement of over 1,600 entries on terms and performers. (Rev: BL 9/1/88) [785.42]

5850 Christgau, Robert. *Christgau's Record Guide: Rock Albums of the '80's* (9–12). 1990, Pantheon paper $16.95 (0-679-73015-X). This is a guide to the rock albums of the past decade with quotes from over 3,000 reviews. (Rev: BL 10/1/90) [016.78]

5851 Clayton, Peter, and Peter Gammond. *The Guinness Jazz A–Z* (9–12). Illus. 1987, Guinness $17.95 (0-85112-281-7). This comprehensive reference covers such areas in jazz as terms, people, organizations, places, and events. (Rev: BR 9–10/87) [781]

5852 Clifford, Mike, ed. *The Harmony Illustrated Encyclopedia of Rock* (8–12). Illus. 1988, Harmony paper $14.95 (0-517-57164-1). An alphabetically arranged series of illustrated biographies of important individuals and groups in the rock world. [784.5]

5853 *Country: The Music and the Musicians* (9–12). Illus. 1988, Abbeville $65.00 (0-89659-868-3). A very expensive but dazzling collection of essays and pictures that chronicle the rise of country music. (Rev: BL 1/1/89) [784.5]

5854 Crowther, Bruce, and Bruce Pinfold. *The Big Band Years* (9–12). Illus. 1988, Facts on File $24.95 (0-8160-2013-2). An account that covers the entire twentieth century (with most material on the 30s and 40s) in text and over 130 photographs. (Rev: BL 11/15/88; BR 3–4/89; SLJ 2/89) [785]

5855 Curry, Jack. *Woodstock: The Summer of Our Lives* (9–12). Illus. 1989, Weidenfeld & Nicolson $19.95 (1-55584-040-X). From interviews and other accounts, this amazing music festival and social event is re-created. (Rev: BL 4/15/89) [784.5]

5856 Damsker, Matt. *Rock Voices: The Best Lyrics of an Era* (9–12). 1980, St. Martin's paper $5.95 (0-312-68791-5). This is a collection of lyrics by such rock stars of the 1960s and 1970s as Dylan and the Beatles. [780.42]

5857 Davis, Stephen, and Peter Simon. *Reggae International* (10–12). Illus. 1983, Knopf paper $14.95 (0-394-71313-3). A collection of essays and photographs about the phenomenon of reggae music and its origins in Jamaica. [784.5]

5858 Dellar, Fred, and Alan Cackett, eds. *The Harmony Illustrated Encyclopedia of Country Music* (7–12). Illus. 1987, Harmony $22.95 (0-517-56502-1); paper $13.95 (0-517-56503-X). A well-illustrated compilation of approximately 500 biographies of country music luminaries. [784.5]

5859 Densmore, John. *Riders on the Storm: My Life with Jim Morrison and the Doors* (10–12). Illus. 1990, Delacorte $18.95 (0-385-30033-6). For mature readers, the account of 5 wild years as the drummer for the rock group, The Doors. (Rev: BL 7/90) [782]

5860 Dylan, Bob. *Lyrics, 1962–1985* (9–12). Rev. ed. Illus. 1985, Knopf paper $21.95 (0-394-54278-9). This book contains a complete set of Dylan's lyrics from 1962 through 1985. (Rev: BL 11/1/85; SLJ 3/86; VOYA 4/86) [784]

5861 Eliot, Marc. *Rockonomics: The Money behind the Music* (10–12). Illus. 1989, Watts $19.95 (0-531-15106-9). The links between big business and pop music are explored including the "payola" scandal and other similar schemes. (Rev: BL 5/1/89; BR 11–12/89; SLJ 8/89; VOYA 10/89) [784.5]

5862 Feather, Leonard. *The Encyclopedia of Jazz* (10–12). Illus. 1960, Horizon Pr. $25.00 (0-8180-1203-X); Da Capo paper $19.95 (0-306-80214-7). This volume first published in 1955 gives a brief history of jazz and more than 2,000 biographies of jazz musicians. It is followed by *The Encyclopedia of Jazz in the Sixties* (1966) and *The Encyclopedia of Jazz in the Seventies* (1976). [785.42]

5863 Flanagan, Bill. *Written in My Soul* (9–12). Illus. 1986, Contemporary $16.95 (0-8092-5153-1); paper $11.95 (0-8092-4650-3). This book contains interviews with 27 rock musicians such as Dylan, Jagger, and Sting about the process of creation and the meanings behind their work. (Rev: BL 9/15/86; SLJ 2/87) [784.5]

5864 Gans, David, and Peter Simon. *Playing in the Band: An Oral and Visual Portrait of the Grateful Dead* (9–12). Illus. 1985, St. Martin's paper $14.95 (0-312-61630-9). A book about the San Francisco rock group and their followers known as Dead Heads. (Rev: BL 6/1/85) [784.54]

5865 George, Nelson, ed. *Stop the Violence: Overcoming Self-Destruction* (10–12). Illus. 1990, Pantheon paper $7.95 (0-679-72782-5). The story of how rap musicians have banded together to fight violent crime. (Rev: BL 6/1/90) [303.6]

5866 Guralnick, Peter. *Sweet Soul Music: Rhythm and Blues and the Southern Dream of Freedom* (9–12). Illus. 1986, Harper $24.95 (0-06-015514-0); paper $14.95 (0-06-096049-3). This is the story of the rhythm-and-blues music of such performers as Ray Charles and Aretha Franklin. The author's earlier *Feel Like Goin' Home* (1971) is a history of the blues and *Lost Highway* (1979) deals with the story of rockabilly. (Rev: BL 5/1/86) [784.5]

5867 Hagan, Chet. *Grand Ole Opry: The Official History* (9–12). Illus. 1989, Henry Holt paper $19.95 (0-8050-0543-9). A chatty series of biographies and background information involving the stars and the popular radio show. (Rev: BL 5/15/89) [784.5]

5868 Hasse, John Edward, ed. *Ragtime: Its History, Composers, and Music* (10–12). Illus. 1985, Schirmer paper $18.95 (0-02-872650-2). In a series of 21 essays, musicologists discuss this American musical form that thrived around the turn of the century. [781]

5869 Helander, Brock. *The Rock Who's Who* (8–12). 1987, Macmillan paper $16.95 (0-02-871920-4). In 300 entries, biographical sketches are given for rock greats into the early 1980s. [784.5]

5870 Hentoff, Nat. *Jazz Is* (10–12). 1976, Limelight paper $8.95 (0-87910-003-6). A very personal introduction to jazz, its history, and its great musicians. [785.42]

5871 Hirshey, Gerri. *Nowhere to Run: The Story of Soul Music* (9–12). Illus. 1984, Random $17.95 (0-8129-1111-3); Penguin paper $6.95 (0-14-008149-6). A history of soul music and practitioners such as James Brown, Aretha Franklin, and Michael Jackson. [784.5]

5872 Hotchner, A. E. *Blown Away: The Rolling Stones and the Death of the Sixties* (10–12). Illus. 1990, Simon & Schuster $21.95 (0-671-69316-6). A somewhat sensational look at the Rolling Stones and the death of band member Brian Jones. (Rev: BL 9/1/90) [782.42]

5873 Javna, John, and Bob Shannon. *Behind the Hits* (9–12). 1986, Warner paper $10.95 (0-446-38171-3). True background stories behind rock and roll hits of the past 30 years. (Rev: BL 12/15/86; SLJ 1/87) [780.42]

5874 Jones, Mablen. *Getting It On: The Clothing of Rock & Roll* (8–12). Illus. 1987, Abbeville $19.98 (0-89659-686-9). A history of the costumes worn by rock stars from 1955 to 1985; includes 125 illustrations. (Rev: SLJ 6–7/88) [780.42]

5875 Josefs, Jai. *Writing Music for Hit Songs* (10–12). 1989, Writer's Digest $17.95 (0-89879-352-1). A practical guide to composing popular music for those who already know how to read music and understand its notation. (Rev: SLJ 6/90) [781]

5876 Kaplan, E. Ann. *Rocking Around the Clock: Music Television, Postmodernism & Consumer Culture* (10–12). 1987, Methuen $29.95 (0-416-33370-2); paper $11.95 (0-416-33390-7). The story behind MTV (Music Television) and rock videos, and the influence they have on today's popular culture. (Rev: BL 10/15/87) [791.45]

5877 Kienzle, Rich. *Great Guitarists: The Most Influential Players in Blues, Country Music, Jazz and Rock* (9–12). Illus. 1985, Facts on File $21.95 (0-8160-1029-3); paper $10.95 (0-8160-1033-1). Sixty guitarists are profiled from the fields of pop music, blues, country, jazz, and rock. (Rev: BR 9–10/86; SLJ 4/86) [787.6]

5878 Lees, Gene. *Meet Me at Jim and Andy's: Jazz Musicians and Their World* (9–12). 1988, Oxford Univ. Pr. $18.95 (0-19-504611-0). One of the best writers on jazz talks about a variety of performers like Artie Shaw and Duke Ellington. (Rev: BL 9/15/88) [785.42]

5879 Lewisohn, Mark. *The Beatles Live!* (9–12). Illus. 1986, Henry Holt paper $14.95 (0-8050-0158-1). A detailed history of the Beatles and their music. (Rev: BL 11/15/86; SLJ 11/86) [784.5]

5880 Liggett, Mark, and Cathy Liggett. *The Complete Handbook of Songwriting: An Insider's Guide to Making It in the Music Industry* (9–12). 1985, NAL paper $9.95 (0-452-25687-9). This manual not only outlines the techniques of songwriting but also covers such areas as royalties, contracts, and even setting up one's own music publishing firm. (Rev: BL 8/85) [784]

5881 Lyons, Len. *The One-Hundred-One Best Jazz Albums* (10–12). 1980, Morrow $14.95 (0-688-08720-5). Through a description of various phonograph albums available, a history of jazz and its greats is given. [781]

5882 Lyons, Len, and Don Perlo. *Jazz Portraits: The Lives and Music of the Essential Jazz Musicians* (10–12). Illus. 1989, Morrow $22.95 (0-688-04946-X). A summation of the styles and careers of great jazz musicians from Louis Armstrong to today's Wynton Marsalis. (Rev: BL 12/15/88) [785.42]

5883 Makower, Joel. *Woodstock: The Oral History* (9–12). Illus. 1989, Doubleday $21.95 (0-385-24716-8); paper $16.95 (0-385-24717-6). Interviews with a fascinating cross-section of attendees—from audience members and musicians to doctors and electricians—at the world's most famous rock concert. (Rev: BL 6/1/89) [784.5]

5884 Malone, Bill C. *Country Music, U.S.A.* (9–12). Rev. ed. Illus. 1985, Univ. of Texas Pr. $24.95 (0-292-71095-X); paper $14.95 (0-292-71096-8). This has become the standard guide to country music past and present and to the people behind it. (Rev: BL 10/1/85) [784.5]

5885 Marcus, Greil. *Mystery Train: Images of America in Rock 'n' Roll Music* (10–12). 1990, Dutton paper $12.95 (0-525-48556-2). An interpretation of what it is to be an American through the music of famous rock 'n' roll musicians. [780.42]

5886 Marsh, Dave, et al., eds. *The First Rock & Roll Confidential Report* (9–12). Illus. 1985, Pantheon paper $12.95 (0-394-74070-X). A thoughtful collection of pieces from *Rock & Roll Confidential* that probe such topics as payola and rating systems for records. (Rev: BR 3–4/85; SLJ 1/86; VOYA 4/86) [780.42]

5887 Marsh, Dave. *Fortunate Son: Criticism and Journalism by America's Best-Known Rock Writer* (9–12). 1985, Random paper $9.95 (0-394-72119-5). This is a collection of pieces written over a 15-year period by this well-known rock critic. (Rev: BL 6/15/85) [784.5]

5888 Marsh, Dave, and John Swenson, eds. *The New Rolling Stone Record Guide* (9–12). 1983, Random paper $13.95 (0-394-72107-1). This guide lists about 12,000 rock albums released through mid-1982. [784.5]

5889 Merrill, Hugh. *The Blues Route* (10–12). 1990, Morrow $17.95 (0-688-06611-9). Through interviews and personal observations, Hugh Merrill has tried to capture the essence of the blues. (Rev: BL 7/90) [781.643]

5890 Miller, Jim, ed. *The Rolling Stone Illustrated History of Rock & Roll* (9–12). Illus. 1980, Random $25.00 (0-394-51322-3); paper $19.95 (0-394-73938-8). A series of essays with many illustrations that trace the history of rock through the 1970s. [784.5]

5891 *The New Real Book: Jazz Classics, Choice Standards, Pop-Fusion Classics for All Instrumentalists and Vocalists* (9–12). 1988, Sher Music paper $30.00 (0-9614701-4-3). In spiral binding, musical arrangements are given for about 250 pop and jazz standards. (Rev: BL 1/1/89) [784.5]

5892 Oliver, Paul, et al. *The New Grove Gospels, Blues and Jazz with Spirituals and Ragtime* (9–12). Illus. 1988, Norton $22.95 (0-333-40785-7); paper $11.95 (0-333-40784-9). This section of the larger *Grove Dictionary* deals with basic American black musical forms. (Rev: BL 3/15/88) [783.7]

5893 Pareles, Jon, ed. *The Rolling Stone Encyclopedia of Rock & Roll* (8–12). Illus. 1983, Summit paper $14.95 (0-671-44071-3). An extremely comprehensive guide for people involved with rock music through the early 1980s. [784.5]

5894 Parkyn, Geoff. *U2: Touch the Flame—An Illustrated Documentary* (8–12). Illus. 1988, Putnam paper $12.95 (0-399-51469-4). A well-illustrated account of Ireland's famous rock group, U2. (Rev: BL 8/88) [784.5]

5895 Roberts, John S. *The Latin Tinge: The Impact of Latin American Music on the United States* (10–12). 1979, Oxford Univ. Pr. $18.95 (0-19-502564-4). This book traces the influence of

Latin American music on American music in the past few decades. [780]

5896 Rolling Stone Magazine, eds. *The Rolling Stone Interviews: The 1980s* (10–12). Illus. 1989, St. Martin's $24.95 (0-312-02973-X); paper $15.95 (0-312-02974-8). Interviews reprinted from the magazine with 34 rock musicians and actors, such as Bruce Springsteen and Joan Baez. (Rev: BL 6/15/89) [790.2]

5897 Sales, Grover. *Jazz: America's Classical Music* (10–12). 1984, Prentice $11.95 (0-13-509118-7). An introduction to this American art form and a history to the present. [781]

5898 Schaffner, Nicholas, and Elizabeth Schaffner. *Five-Hundred-Five Rock and Roll Questions Your Friends Can't Answer* (9–12). 1981, Walker $9.95 (0-8027-0674-6); paper $3.95 (0-8027-7171-8). Unusual facts and trivia about rock in a question-and-answer format. [780.42]

5899 Shestack, Melvin. *The Country Music Encyclopedia* (9–12). 1977, Harper paper $7.95 (0-690-01220-9). Though now somewhat dated, this is an interesting rundown of 200 stars of country music. [781.7]

5900 Smith, Joe. *Off the Record: An Oral History of Popular Music* (9–12). Illus. 1988, Warner $22.95 (0-446-51232-X). Over 30 years of popular music in America as culled from approximately 200 interviews with people in all areas of the business. (Rev: BL 11/15/88) [780.42]

5901 Stambler, Irwin. *Encyclopedia of Pop, Rock and Soul* (9–12). Illus. 1989, St. Martin's $35.00 (0-312-02573-4); paper $19.95 (0-312-04310-4). An alphabetically arranged guide to performers, terms and musicals in the rock world. [784.5]

5902 Swenson, John, ed. *The Rolling Stone Jazz Record Guide* (10–12). 1985, Random paper $9.95 (0-394-72643-X). Though one might disagree with some of the editor's choices, this is still considered the best guide to develop record collections in jazz. (Rev: BL 7/85) [789.9]

5903 Turner, Tony, and Barbara Aria. *All That Glittered: My Life with the Supremes* (9–12). 1990, Dutton $18.95 (0-525-24910-9). A behind-the-scenes show business saga by a young man who acted as a gofer for the Supremes. (Rev: BL 9/1/90) [782.42]

5904 Vaughan, Andrew. *Who's Who in New Country Music* (8–12). Illus. 1990, St. Martin's paper $9.95 (0-312-03953-0). A well-illustrated bio-dictionary of the newer voices and instrumentalists in country music, with a shorter concluding section on some of the old-timers. (Rev: BL 12/15/89) [781.642]

5905 Ward, Ed, et al. *Rock of Ages: The Rolling Stone History of Rock & Roll* (8–12). 1987, Summit paper $14.95 (0-671-63068-7). A 40-year history of rock that highlights the most famous personalities involved. (Rev: BL 1/1/87; SLJ 4/87) [784.5]

5906 Wenner, Jann S., ed. *20 Years of Rolling Stone: What a Long, Strange Trip It's Been* (9–12). Illus. 1987, Friendly Pr. $24.95 (0-914919-10-5). A selection of articles, interviews, and photographs from the first issue of November 9, 1967, to the end of 1987. (Rev: BL 11/15/87) [784.5]

5907 White, Timothy. *Rock Lives: Profiles and Interviews* (9–12). 1990, Henry Holt $19.95 (0-8050-1396-2). The celebrated rock critic gives a history of rock 'n' roll through interviews and profiles of important musicians. (Rev: BL 10/1/90) [782.42]

5908 Williams, Martin. *Jazz Heritage* (10–12). 1985, Oxford Univ. Pr. $21.95 (0-19-503611-5). A series of essays on the meaning of jazz which is a companion to the author's earlier *The Jazz Tradition* (1983). [785.42]

5909 Williams, Martin. *Jazz in Its Time* (9–12). 1989, Oxford Univ. Pr. $19.95 (0-19-505459-8). A collection of various incidental pieces on the history, musicians, and general topics involving the world of jazz. (Rev: BL 2/15/89) [785.42]

5910 Yelton, Geary. *The Rock Synthesizer Manual: A Revised Guide for the Electronic Musician* (10–12). 2nd ed. Illus. 1986, Rock Tech paper $11.95 (0-914283-25-1). Besides a history of synthesizers and an explanation of how they work, this manual tells the amateur how to use one. (Rev: BL 11/1/86) [789.9]

5911 Zerbey, Richard J. *Jam Plastic, Heavy Metal: Now You Can Play Lead Guitar with a Live Band* (9–12). Illus. 1986, Sound Enterprises $21.95 (0-935565-07-8); paper $15.95 (0-935565-05-1). An easily followed instruction book that gives basic chords and improvisation tips. Two companion volumes are *Jam Plastic, Punk* (1986) and *Jam Plastic, Rock* (1986). (Rev: BL 3/1/86) [787.61]

Opera and Musicals

5912 Biscardi, Cyrus Henry. *The Storybook of Opera* (7–12). Illus. 1987, Learning Publications $23.95 each (vol. I: 0-918452-93-7; vol. II: 0-918452-99-6). In 2 volumes. Included are lengthy synopses of 15 popular operas plus extensive background information. (Rev: BL 4/15/88; SLJ 3/88) [782.1]

5913 Cross, Milton. *The New Milton Cross' Complete Stories of the Great Operas* (9–12). Rev. ed. 1955, Doubleday paper $17.95 (0-385-04324-4). This book contains detailed descriptions of the action in 76 famous operas. A continuation is *The New Milton Cross' More Stories of the Great Operas* (1980). [782.1]

5914 Englander, Roger. *Opera: What's All the Screaming About?* (7–12). Illus. 1983, Walker $12.95 (0-8027-6491-6). After a general introduction to the history and conventions of opera, 50 popular operas are introduced. [782.1]

5915 Flinn, Denny Martin. *What They Did for Love: The Untold Story behind the Making of A Chorus Line* (9–12). Illus. 1989, Bantam paper $8.95 (0-553-34593-1). The story of the making of the longest running show in Broadway history. (Rev: BL 7/89) [792]

5916 Freeman, John W. *The Metropolitan Opera Stories of the Great Operas* (9–12). Illus. 1984, Norton $24.95 (0-393-01888-1). Plots are given for 150 great operas with accompanying biographical material on their composers. [782.1]

5917 Gilbert, W. S. *The Complete Plays of Gilbert and Sullivan* (10–12). Illus. 1976, Norton paper $12.95 (0-393-00828-2). This volume contains the text of all 14 of the musicals written by Gilbert with music by Sullivan. [782.81]

5918 Gottfried, Martin. *Broadway Musicals* (10–12). Illus. 1979, Abrams paper $34.95 (0-8109-8060-6). A photographic history of the Broadway musicals from 1906 to 1978. [782.81]

5919 Green, Stanley. *Encyclopaedia of the Musical Theatre* (9–12). 1976, Da Capo paper $14.95 (0-306-80113-2). A wealth of information on composers, shows, casts, plots, and songs involved in the musical theater life of London and New York. [782.81]

5920 Harewood, George H. *Definitive Kobbe's Opera Book* (10–12). Illus. 1987, Putnam $35.00 (0-399-13180-9). With detailed plots and background material for more than 300 operas, this is the most complete general guide available. [728.81]

5921 Harewood, George H. *Kobbe's Illustrated Opera Book: Twenty-six of the World's Best-Loved Operas* (9–12). Illus. 1989, Putnam $34.95 (0-399-13475-1). An introduction to the most popular operas with background material and many photographs of performers and productions. (Rev: BL 1/15/90) [782.1]

5922 Hayter, Charles. *Gilbert and Sullivan* (10–12). 1987, St. Martin's $19.95 (0-312-00446-X). In addition to an analysis of Gilbert and Sullivan's works, the author gives an introduction to Victorian theater. (Rev: BL 3/15/87) [782.81]

5923 Hines, Jerome. *Great Singers on Great Singing* (10–12). Illus. 1982, Limelight paper $12.95 (0-87910-025-7). Comments about vocal techniques and hurdles have been collected from 40 great singers for this volume. [784.9]

5924 Lerner, Alan Jay. *The Musical Theatre: A Celebration* (9–12). Illus. 1989, DaCapo paper $16.95 (0-306-80364-X). An anecdotal history of the American musical from its beginning to its maturity after World War II. (Rev: BL 11/15/86) [782.81]

5925 Perry, George. *The Complete Phantom of the Opera* (9–12). Illus. 1987, Henry Holt $24.95 (0-8050-0657-5). A lavish volume that includes the original novel, the history of the musical, and the complete script. (Rev: BL 1/15/88; BR 5–6/88; SLJ 3/88; VOYA 6/88) [782.81]

5926 Ratliff, Gerald Lee, and Suzanne Trauth. *On Stage: Producing Musical Theatre* (9–12). Illus. 1988, Rosen $14.95 (0-8239-0697-3). A guide to the structure of musicals as well as points on acting, production, choreography, and so on. (Rev: BL 9/15/88; BR 1–2/89; VOYA 12/88) [782.8]

5927 Richards, Stanley, ed. *Great Rock Musicals* (9–12). Illus. 1979, Scarborough House $19.95 (0-8128-2509-8). This book contains the scripts of 8 rock musicals, including *Grease; The Wiz; Jesus Christ, Superstar;* and *Hair.* [782.81]

5928 Rudel, Anthony J. *Tales from the Opera* (9–12). 1985, Fireside paper $9.95 (0-671-45943-0). Written as though they were short stories, the author retells the plots of 50 operas, including all of the standard ones. (Rev: BL 11/15/85) [782]

5929 Sondheim, Stephen, and James Lapine. *Into the Woods* (9–12). 1989, Theatre Communications $18.95 (0-930452-92-5); paper $8.95 (0-930452-93-3). The text and lyrics of the prize-winning musical about fairy tale characters and what happens to their "happily ever after." (Rev: BL 9/1/89) [782.81]

5930 Worth, Fred L. *Rock Facts* (7–12). Illus. 1985, Facts on File $22.95 (0-8160-1099-4); paper $14.95 (0-8160-1145-1). More than 1,500 entries, in dictionary format, about rock music and the people involved. (Rev: BR 9–10/86) [780.42]

Orchestra and Musical Instruments

5931 Crombie, David. *The Synthesizer & Electronic Keyboard Handbook* (9–12). Illus. 1984, Knopf paper $13.95 (0-394-72711-8). Beginning with the piano, this account continues to describe electronic keyboards, their use with many different musical instruments, and how to play them. (Rev: BL 4/1/85) [789.9]

5932 Del Mar, Norman. *The Anchor Companion to the Orchestra* (10–12). 1987, Doubleday $19.95 (0-385-24081-3); paper $10.95 (0-385-24082-1). In dictionary format, basic terms involving instruments, conducting, and musical practices are explained. (Rev: BL 11/15/87) [785]

5933 Denyer, Ralph. *The Guitar Handbook* (9–12). Illus. 1982, Knopf paper $22.95 (0-394-71257-9). A manual on how to play the guitar that includes material ranging from basic chords to improvisational techniques. [787.6]

5934 Diagram Group. *Musical Instruments of the World: An Illustrated Encyclopedia* (9–12). Illus. 1978, Facts on File $35.00 (0-87196-320-5); paper $14.95 (0-8160-1309-8). With more than 4,000 drawings and an extensive text, this book introduces hundreds of past and present musical instruments in a dictionary format. [781.91]

5935 Evans, Roger. *How to Play Guitar: A New Book for Everyone Interested in Guitar* (8–12). Illus. 1980, St. Martin's $10.95 (0-312-39608-2); paper $5.95 (0-312-36909-0). An easily followed basic guidebook on how to play the guitar with information on such topics as buying equipment and reading music. [787.6]

5936 Hazen, Margaret, and Robert Hazen. *The Music Men: An Illustrated History of Brass Bands in America, 1800–1920* (9–12). 1987, Smithsonian Inst. $39.95 (0-87474-546-2); paper $19.95 (0-87474-547-0). A nostalgic look at the history of the brass band, its instruments, and some of the most notable band leaders and composers. (Rev: BR 11–12/87) [785.1]

5937 Hollis, Helen Rice. *The Piano: A Pictorial Account of Its Ancestry and Development* (9–12). Rev. ed. Illus. 1985, Hippocrene paper $11.95 (0-88254-809-2). A history of the development of the piano and a discussion of famous pianists and their pianos. (Rev: BL 4/1/85) [786.2]

5938 Holmes, Thomas B. *Electronic & Experimental Music* (10–12). 1985, Macmillan paper $12.95 (0-684-18135-5). This aspect of modern music is dealt with regardless of the type of music involved; therefore, the range is from John Cage to the Talking Heads. (Rev: BL 6/15/85) [789.9]

5939 Monath, Norman. *How to Play Popular Piano in Ten Easy Lessons* (10–12). 1984, Simon & Schuster paper $10.95 (0-671-53067-4). A useful guide that requires a great deal of work on the part of the reader. [786.2]

5940 Previn, André, ed. *André Previn's Guide to the Orchestra* (7–12). Illus. 1983, Putnam $17.95 (0-399-12865-4). A brief history of music plus material on each of the sections of the orchestra. [785]

5941 Roth, Arlen. *Arlen Roth's Complete Acoustic Guitar* (9–12). Illus. 1985, Schirmer paper $11.95 (0-02-872150-0). Various styles like folk and rock are discussed and essential information on how to play each is given. (Rev: BL 4/1/86) [787.6]

5942 Wheeler, Tom. *The Guitar Book: A Handbook for Electric and Acoustic Guitarists* (9–12). Rev. ed. Illus. 1978, Harper $24.95 (0-06-014579-X). This comprehensive book on the guitar covers such topics as its history, types, manufacturers, and performers. [787.6]

5943 Wollitz, Kenneth. *The Recorder Book* (9–12). 1982, Knopf paper $12.95 (0-394-7499-5). From beginning player to expert, this book covers all levels of recorder playing. [781.91]

Songs and Folk Songs

5944 Agay, Denes, ed. *Best Loved Songs of the American People* (9–12). Illus. 1975, Doubleday $18.95 (0-385-00004-9); paper $15.95 (0-385-14006-1). With simple piano arrangements, this is an anthology of almost 400 songs that span our history and tastes. [784]

5945 Blood-Patterson, Peter, ed. *Rise Up Singing* (8–12). Illus. 1988, Sing Out $39.95 (0-86571-136-4); paper $12.95 (0-86571-138-0). Words, chords, and some background material on 1,200 songs, some folk, others pop. (Rev: BL 12/15/88; BR 3–4/89) [784.5]

5946 Carlin, Richard. *English and American Folk Music* (10–12). Illus. 1987, Facts on File $15.95 (0-8160-1381-0). Using social history as background, Carlin traces the beginnings of English and American folk music and gives many examples of both lyrics and melodies. (Rev: BL 9/1/87; BR 11–12/87) [784.4]

5947 Lax, Roger, and Frederick Smith. *The Great Song Thesaurus* (9–12). 1989, Oxford Univ. Pr. $75.00 (0-19-505488-3). A listing of more than 10,000 songs with background information on each that spans 500 years of history. [784.5]

5948 Lomax, Alan. *The Folk Songs of North America* (9–12). Illus. 1975, Doubleday paper $19.95 (0-385-03772-4). An excellent introduction to American folk songs with music and lyrics given for more than 300 of them. [784.4]

5949 Matthew-Walker, Robert. *Simon and Garfunkel* (9–12). 1990, Baton Pr. $9.95 (0-85936-244-2). A concise account of the careers and the music of these 2 stars. (Rev: BL 4/1/85) [784.54]

5950 Pankake, Marcia, and Jon Pankake. *A Prairie Home Companion Folk Song Book* (9–12). Illus. 1988, Viking $22.95 (0-670-82159-4). Folk songs and their parodies from most of these 400 selections all chosen from listeners' contributions. Most use familiar tunes as their music. (Rev: BL 11/15/88) [784.4]

5951 Reed, W. L., and M. J. Bristow, eds. *National Anthems of the World* (9–12). 1988, Blanford Pr. $70.00 (0-7137-1962-1). Though expensive for most collections, this volume contains the music and words (in the native language and English) to the national anthems of 165 different nations. [784.7]

5952 Sandburg, Carl. *The American Songbag* (7–12). Illus. 1970, Harcourt paper $12.95 (0-15-605650-X). A fine collection of all kinds of American folksongs with music and background notes from Mr. Sandburg. [784.7]

5953 Seeger, Pete. *The Incomplete Folksinger* (9–12). n.d., Simon & Schuster paper $5.95 (0-8256-0028-6). This is a handbook on folksongs and folk music in the United States. Also use: *American Favorite Ballads* (1981). [781.7]

5954 Simon, Henry W., ed. *A Treasury of Christmas Songs and Carols* (7–12). 2nd ed. Illus. 1973, Houghton paper $9.95 (0-395-17785-5). Over 100 musical compositions are highlighted with piano and guitar arrangements. [783.6]

The Performing Arts

General and Miscellaneous

5955 Franck, Irene M., and David M. Brownstone. *Performers and Players* (9–12). Illus. 1988, Facts on File $17.95 (0-8160-1448-5). A history of all sorts of performing artists such as actors, musicians, and athletes. (Rev: BL 3/15/89; BR 3–4/89; SLJ 1/89; VOYA 4/89) [790.2]

5956 Martin, Linda, and Kerry Segrave. *Women in Comedy* (9–12). Illus. 1986, Citadel $19.95 (0-8065-1000-5). Covering over 100 years of history, this volume profiles almost 70 women comedians ending with such present-day figures as Whoopi Goldberg. (Rev: BL 3/1/87) [792.2]

5957 Pomerance, Alan. *Repeal of the Blues* (9–12). Illus. 1988, Citadel $17.95 (0-8065-1105-2). A history of blacks in show business from the 30s to the early 50s and how they changed America's attitudes. (Rev: BL 11/1/88) [792]

Ballet and the Dance

5958 Anderson, Jack. *Ballet & Modern Dance: A Concise History* (10–12). Illus. 1986, Princeton Book Co. $29.95 (0-916622-42-8); paper $14.95 (0-916622-43-6). For better readers, this is a history of modern ballet from its beginnings to the mid-twentieth century. (Rev: BL 8/86; SLJ 12/86) [792.82]

5959 Balanchine, George, and Francis Mason. *101 Stories of the Great Ballets* (7–12). 1975, Doubleday paper $9.95 (0-385-03398-2). Both the classics and newer ballets are introduced plus general background material such as a brief history of ballet. [792.8]

5960 Banes, Sally. *Terpsichore in Sneakers: Post-Modern Dance* (10–12). 1987, Wesleyan Univ. Pr. $15.00 (0-8195-6160-6). The world of contemporary dance is introduced along with the important people involved. [793.3]

5961 Berger, Melvin. *The World of Dance* (9–12). Illus. 1978, Phillips $19.95 (0-87599-221-8). From early tribal dances to modern social dancing and ballet, this is a readable history of the world of dance. [793.3]

5962 Clarke, Mary, and Clement Crisp. *The Ballet Goer's Guide* (10–12). Illus. 1981, Knopf $22.50 (0-394-51307-X). As well as analyzing 143 popular ballets, this book also covers such topics as ballet history and includes biographies of famous choreographers and dancers. [792.8]

5963 Clarke, Mary, and Clement Crisp. *Dancer: Men in Dance* (9–12). 1987, Parkwest $24.95 (0-88186-076-X). The male dancer is shown from the Renaissance to the present with coverage of ballet, modern dance, and musicals. (Rev: BR 11–12/87) [793.3]

5964 De Mille, Agnes. *Portrait Gallery* (10–12). 1990, Houghton $19.95 (0-395-52809-7). A collection of profiles of people that Agnes De Mille encouraged during her years as a dancer and choreographer. (Rev: BL 7/90) [792.8]

5965 Dunning, Jennifer. *"But First a School": The First Fifty Years of the School of American Ballet* (10–12). Illus. 1985, Viking $20.00 (0-670-80407-X). This is a history of the School of American Ballet and the part that George Balanchine and Lincoln Kirstein had in its founding and operation. (Rev: BL 11/1/85) [792.8]

5966 Gordon, Suzanne. *Off Balance: The Real World of Ballet* (10–12). Illus. 1983, McGraw paper $7.95 (0-07-023770-0). A deglamorizing account of what the ballet world is really like. [792.8]

5967 Greene, Hank. *Square and Folk Dancing: A Complete Guide for Students, Teachers and Callers* (10–12). 1984, Harper paper $9.95 (0-06-464088-4). This book supplies the music, lyrics, and calls for almost 90 dances. [793.3]

5968 Gruen, John. *People Who Dance: 22 Dancers Tell Their Own Stories* (9–12). 1988, Princeton Book Co. $24.95 (0-916622-74-6). Interviews with 22 dancers from show biz, ballet, and modern dance who tell about their careers and their lives. (Rev: BL 11/15/88; SLJ 5/89) [793.32]

5969 Holiday, Ron, et al. *Cat Dancers* (9–12). Illus. 1987, Pineapple $16.95 (0-910923-35-3). The story of an unusual dancing pair and of how they train the animals they use in their act. (Rev: BL 6/1/87) [792.8]

5970 Jackson, Ellen. *Dancing: A Guide for the Dancer You Can Be* (10–12). 1983, Danceway Books $15.95 (0-937180-00-9). This is a survey of the world of dance from ballet to tap. [793.3]

5971 Long, Richard A. *The Black Tradition in American Dance* (9–12). Illus. 1989, Rizzoli $25.00 (0-8478-1092-5). An account of Afro-American dance influences and traditions in America with special emphasis on the biographies of those involved. (Rev: BL 1/1/90) [793.3]

5972 Mr. Fresh and the Supreme Rockers. *Breakdancing* (10–12). 1984, Avon paper $2.95 (0-380-88153-5). Directions are given for a number of breakdances, some of which could be dangerous if not properly executed. [793.3]

5973 Schlaich, Joan, and Betty Dupont. *Dance: The Art of Production* (9–12). Illus. 1988, Dance Horizons $24.95 (0-916622-69-X); paper $14.95 (0-916622-68-1). Every aspect of dance production is discussed, including choreography, lighting, and music. (Rev: SLJ 2/89) [793.3]

5974 Sorine, Daniel S., and Stephanie R. Sorine. *Dancershoes* (10–12). 1979, Knopf paper $8.95 (0-394-73824-1). Famous dancers reveal their secrets of success. [793.3]

5975 Thorpe, Edward. *Black Dance* (9–12). Illus. 1990, Overlook $27.50 (0-87951-379-9). An excellent history of black American dance and dancers particularly in the twentieth century with some coverage for Britain. (Rev: BL 1/1/90) [793.3]

Circuses, Fairs, and Parades

5976 Antekeier, Kristopher, and Greg Aunapu. *Ringmaster! My Year on the Road with "The Greatest Show on Earth"* (9–12). 1989, Dutton $19.95 (0-525-24757-2). A behind-the-scenes look at Ringling Bros. and Barnum & Bailey Circus from the standpoint of the ringmaster. (Rev: BL 11/1/89) [791.3]

5977 Culhane, John. *The American Circus: An Illustrated History* (9–12). Illus. 1990, Henry Holt $35.00 (0-8050-0424-6). A graphic recreation of 200 years of life under the big top. (Rev: BL 4/15/90) [791.3]

5978 Feder, Happy Jack. *Clown Skits for Everyone* (7–12). Illus. 1984, Arco paper $7.95 (0-668-06265-7). This book contains more than 30 skits for 1 or 2 clowns. [791]

5979 Fife, Bruce, et al. *Creative Clowning* (9–12). Illus. 1988, Java paper $16.95 (0-941599-03-5). All aspects of the occupation of clowning are covered, including juggling, puppetry, and magic. (Rev: BL 6/1/88; SLJ 8/88) [791.3]

5980 Jay, Ricky. *Learned Pigs & Fireproof Women* (9–12). Illus. 1986, Random $29.95 (0-394-53750-5); Warner paper $12.95 (0-446-38590-5). An unusual collection of facts about the world's most bizarre entertainers, like mind readers, daredevils, and sword swallowers. (Rev: SLJ 4/87) [791]

5981 Stolzenberg, Mark. *Be a Clown!* (7–12). Illus. 1989, Sterling paper $10.95 (0-8069-5804-9). A how-to manual that describes how to create a clown character and supplies a number of routines. (Rev: BL 1/1/90) [791.3]

Puppetry

5982 Baird, Bill. *The Art of the Puppet* (9–12). 1966, Plays $35.00 (0-8238-0067-9). A famous puppeteer gives a fascinating introduction to his art. [791.5]

Radio and Recordings

5983 Altman, Sophie, et al. *From "A" to "Z": The It's Academic Quiz Book* (9–12). 1989, Acropolis paper $9.95 (0-87491-954-1). A collection of questions and answers from the "It's Academic" quiz program. (Rev: SLJ 1/90) [384.54]

5984 Fox, Ted. *In the Groove: The Men behind the Music* (9–12). 1986, St. Martin's $18.95 (0-312-41166-9). Interviews from *Audio* magazine with the record producers who have been responsible for recording such artists as Madonna and Billy Joel. (Rev: BL 12/15/86) [780]

5985 Murrells, Joseph. *Million Selling Records from the 1900s to the 1980s: An Illustrated Directory* (9–12). Illus. 1985, Arco $35.00 (0-668-06459-5); Prentice paper $19.95 (0-668-06461-7). Though somewhat expensive, this is a fascinating guide arranged by year and international in scope to each record that has sold a million copies and the people behind them. (Rev: BL 6/1/85; SLJ 8/85) [789.9]

Television, Video, and Motion Pictures

5986 Adamson, Joe. *The Bugs Bunny Golden Jubilee: 50 Years of America's Favorite Rabbit* (9–12). Illus. 1990, Henry Holt $35.00 (0-8050-1190-0). An oversize book that is a profusely illustrated tribute to the life and times of this fabulous rabbit. (Rev: BL 2/15/90) [741.5]

5987 Adamson, Joe. *Groucho, Harpo, Chico and Sometimes Zeppo: A History of the Marx Brothers and a Satire on the Rest of the World* (10–12). Illus. 1973, Simon & Schuster paper $9.95 (0-671-47072-8). More than a biography, this is an appreciation of the unique humor and zaniness of these 3 (sometimes 4) comics. [791.43]

5988 Arlen, Michael J. *Thirty Seconds* (9–12). 1980, Farrar $9.95 (0-374-27576-9); Penguin paper $6.95 (0-14-005810-9). A detailed description of how a 30-second television commercial is made. [384.55]

5989 Benabent-Loiseau, Josee. *The Odyssey of The Bear: The Making of the Film by Jean-Jacques Annaud* (9–12). Illus. 1990, Newmarket paper $15.95 (1-55704-056-7). A diary of the making of the film *The Bear* and how those incredible animal scenes were filmed. (Rev: SLJ 7/90) [791.43]

5990 Bergan, Ronald, and Robyn Karney. *Movie Mastermind: Over 1000 Questions to Addle an Addict and Baffle a Buff* (10–12). Illus. 1984, McGraw $18.95 (0-07-004866-5); paper $8.95 (0-

07-004865-7). A series of quizzes that seriously tests one's knowledge of the movies. (Rev: BL 1/15/85) [791.43]

5991 Betrock, Alan. *The I Was a Teenage Juvenile Delinquent Rock 'n' Roll Horror Beach Party Movie Book* (9–12). Illus. 1986, St. Martin's paper $12.95 (0-312-40293-7). A humorous survey of the trashy teen exploitation movies of the 1950s and 1960s such as *Surf Party*. (Rev: BL 12/1/86) [791.43]

5992 Blacker, Irwin R. *The Elements of Screenwriting: A Guide for Film and Television Writers* (9–12). 1987, Macmillan $16.95 (0-02-511180-9); paper $4.95 (0-02-000220-3). Blacker explains the various components of a screenplay such as plot and characters and how to blend them into a well-crafted whole. (Rev: BL 1/1/87) [808]

5993 Blum, Daniel, and John Kobal. *A New Pictorial History of the Talkies* (9–12). Illus. 1982, Putnam paper $9.95 (0-399-50666-7). A history of motion pictures since the silents is given in a chronologically arranged series of pictures of stars and their films. [791.43]

5994 Bobker, Lee R. *The Elements of Film* (10–12). 1979, Harcourt paper $15.00 (0-15-522096-9). This is a splendid introduction to the technical aspects of filmmaking. [791.43]

5995 Bohn, Thomas W., and Richard L. Stromgren. *Light and Shadows: A History of Motion Pictures* (8–12). 3rd ed. Illus. 1987, Mayfield paper $29.95 (0-87484-702-8). From the silents to *Rocky* in a sumptuously illustrated volume. (Rev: BL 3/1/87) [791.43]

5996 Bookbinder, Robert. *Classics of the Gangster Film* (9–12). Illus. 1985, Citadel $19.95 (0-8065-0949-X); Carol paper $12.95 (0-8065-1053-6). From the 1930s to the present, here are 50 famous gangster movies, information about them, and stills from each. (Rev: BL 7/85) [791.43]

5997 Brady, John. *The Craft of the Screenwriter* (10–12). Illus. 1981, Simon & Schuster paper $10.95 (0-671-25230-5). A collection of interviews with 6 prominent screenwriters about their art and the obstacles they face writing in Hollywood. [808]

5998 Brouwer, Alexandra, and Thomas Lee Wright. *Working in Hollywood* (10–12). 1990, Crown $24.95 (0-517-57401-2). A description of 65 different behind-the-camera jobs that go into making movies. (Rev: BL 7/90) [384]

5999 Castleman, Harry, and Walter Podrazik. *Five-Hundred-Five Television Questions Your Friends Can't Answer* (9–12). 1983, Walker paper $3.95 (0-8027-7210-2). This is a treasure trove of trivia about television and its stars. [384.55]

6000 Chell, David. *Moviemakers at Work: Interviews* (9–12). Illus. 1987, Microsoft $19.95 (1-55615-037-7); paper $14.95 (1-55615-003-2). Behind-the-scenes interviews with special-effects people, designers, animators, and others responsible for making motion pictures. (Rev: BL 6/15/87) [791.43]

6001 Clemens, Virginia Phelps. *Behind the Filmmaking Scene* (9–12). 1982, Westminster $12.95 (0-664-32691-9). A behind-the-scenes look at the various careers that are involved in making films. [791.43]

6002 Cohen, Daniel. *Masters of Horror* (9–12). 1984, Houghton $12.95 (0-89919-221-1). Profiles of some of the great writers and stars of horror movies, including Stephen King, Steven Spielberg, and Bela Lugosi. [791.43]

6003 Cohen, Howard R., and Michael Artenstein. *Test Your Movie I.Q.* (9–12). 1989, Putnam paper $6.95 (0-399-51530-5). A movie trivia quiz book; answers are appended. (Rev: BL 4/1/89) [791]

6004 Collins, Max Allen, and John Javna. *The Best of Crime and Detective TV* (9–12). Illus. 1989, Crown paper $9.95 (0-517-57055-6). In this book, the authors profile the best TV crime and detective shows from the 1950s to the present. (Rev: SLJ 5/89) [384.55]

6005 Conner, Jeff. *Stephen King Goes to Hollywood* (9–12). Illus. 1987, NAL $19.95 (0-453-00552-7); paper $9.95 (0-452-25937-1). Numerous photos—often in color—accompany this text on a total of 13 films. (Rev: BL 2/15/88) [791.43]

6006 Cross, Donna Woolfold. *Mediaspeak* (10–12). 1984, NAL paper $4.95 (0-451-62701-6). An inquiry into how television shapes public opinion and attitudes. [384.55]

6007 Eastman, John. *Retakes: Behind the Scenes of 500 Classic Movies* (9–12). 1989, Ballantine paper $4.95 (0-345-35399-4). A collection of anecdotes about the filming of 500 important films, all of which are available on videocassettes. (Rev: BL 9/1/89) [791]

6008 Ebert, Roger. *Roger Ebert's Home Movie Companion* (9–12). 1989, Andrews, McMeel & Parker $12.95 (0-8362-6240-9). This is a guide to some of the best films available on videocassette. [791.43]

6009 Everson, William K. *American Silent Film* (9–12). Illus. 1978, Oxford Univ. Pr. $29.95 (0-19-502348-X); paper $9.95 (0-19-503208-X). An excellent readable history of American films to the advent of sound in a text illustrated with many stills. [791.43]

6010 Finler, Joel W. *The Hollywood Story* (9–12). Illus. 1988, Crown $35.00 (0-517-56576-5). An oversize volume that tells the history of American movies in text and hundreds of photographs. (Rev: SLJ 9/88) [791.43]

6011 Fraser, George MacDonald. *The Hollywood History of the World* (9–12). Illus. 1988, Morrow $18.95 (0-688-07520-7). An examination of how the movies have interpreted and misinterpreted history from ancient times to *Platoon*. (Rev: BL 9/1/88) [791.43]

6012 Fuller, John. *Prescription for Better Home Video Movies: How to Avoid the Most Common Mistakes* (8–12). Illus. 1988, Price/Stern/Sloan paper $12.95 (0-89586-676-5). This book covers topics from purchasing equipment to turning out polished home videos. (Rev: VOYA 6/89) [778.58]

6013 Gagne, Paul R. *The Zombies That Ate Pittsburgh: The Films of George A. Romero* (10–12). Illus. 1987, Dodd $14.95 (0-396-08520-2). For movie buffs, a description of the B movies of Romero that include *Night of the Living Dead*. (Rev: VOYA 10/87) [791.43]

6014 Giannetti, Louis, and Scott Eyman. *Flashback: A Brief History of Film* (9–12). Illus. 1986, Prentice paper $26.80 (0-13-322223-3). An account that details all the major films and trends in movie history illustrated with hundreds of stills. (Rev: BL 5/1/86) [791.43]

6015 Gitlin, Todd. *Inside Prime Time* (10–12). 1983, Pantheon paper $9.95 (0-394-73787-3). An inside look at television studios, production companies, and the advertising agencies that sponsor programs. [384.55]

6016 Gitlin, Todd, ed. *Watching Television: A Pantheon Guide to Popular Culture* (10–12). 1987, Pantheon paper $11.95 (0-394-74651-1). A series of thoughtful essays on how television both reflects and shapes popular culture. (Rev: BL 12/1/86) [791.45]

6017 Halliwell, Leslie. *The Dead That Walked: Dracula, Frankenstein, the Mummy, and Other Favorite Movie Monsters* (9–12). Illus. 1988, Frederick Ungar $24.95 (0-8044-2300-8). For horror movie buffs, here is a fine collection in text and pictures of creatures who return to life after death. (Rev: SLJ 1/89) [791.43]

6018 Halliwell, Leslie. *Halliwell's Film Guide* (9–12). Illus. 1990, Harper paper $19.95 (0-06-091989-2). An alphabetical critical listing of thousands of films with such background material as casts, credits, and running time. [791.4303]

6019 Helfer, Ralph. *The Beauty of the Beasts: Tales of Hollywood's Wild Animal Stars* (9–12). 1990, Tarcher $17.95 (0-87477-516-7). Written by an animal trainer, this is the story of how animals are prepared for screen appearances. (Rev: BL 4/15/90) [791.43]

6020 Hewitt, Don. *Minute by Minute* (9–12). Illus. 1985, Random $19.95 (0-394-54641-5). A behind-the-scenes view of the television show "60 Minutes." (Rev: BR 5–6/86; SLJ 4/86) [384]

6021 Javna, John. *Cult TV: A Viewer's Guide to the Shows America Can't Live Without!* (8–12). Illus. 1985, St. Martin's paper $12.95 (0-312-17848-4). A guide to the most popular TV shows ever, from "Leave It to Beaver" to "Miami Vice." (Rev: BL 5/1/86) [791.45]

6022 Kael, Pauline. *Taking It All In* (10–12). 1984, Holt $25.00 (0-03-069362-4); paper $14.95 (0-03-069361-6). From the movie critic of the *New Yorker* magazine, a collection of reviews published between 1980 and 1983. A later volume is *5001 Nights at the Movies* (1985). [791.43]

6023 Kerr, Walter. *The Silent Clowns* (10–12). Illus. 1975, Da Capo paper $19.95 (0-306-80387-9). A series of sketches about the great comedians who flourished during the days of the silent films. [791.43]

6024 Langley, Noel, et al. *The Wizard of Oz* (9–12). 1989, Dell paper $9.95 (0-385-29760-2). The final screenplay of the movie plus an interesting introduction about adapting the book for the screen. (Rev: BL 6/15/89) [791.43]

6025 MacDonald, J. Fred. *One Nation under Television: The Rise and Decline of Network TV* (10–12). 1990, Pantheon $24.95 (0-394-58018-4). A history of television that concentrates on the role the major networks played in it. (Rev: BL 6/15/90) [384]

6026 McGee, Mark Thomas. *Roger Corman: The Best of the Cheap Acts* (9–12). Illus. 1988, McFarland $24.95 (0-89950-330-6). A chronicle of the blood-and-horror movies made by the master who launched the careers of such stars as Jack Nicholson. (Rev: BL 9/1/88) [791.43]

6027 McLuhan, Marshall. *Understanding Media* (10–12). 1964, McGraw paper $8.95 (0-07-045436-1). This book states that it is the form rather than the content of a medium that determines how it communicates. [302.2]

6028 Maltin, Leonard. *Leonard Maltin's TV Movies, 1991* (9–12). 1990, NAL paper $14.95 (0-452-26522-3). This is a frequently revised

guide to motion pictures shown on television. [791.43]

6029 Maltin, Leonard, ed. *The Whole Film Sourcebook* (10–12). 1983, Universe $14.95 (0-87663-416-1); NAL paper $9.95 (0-452-25361-6). This guide includes information on programs in film study and film festivals and contains an extensive bibliography. [791.43]

6030 Markoe, Merrill, ed. *Late Night with David Letterman: The Book* (9–12). Illus. 1985, Random $8.95 (0-394-74191-9). A collection of skits, cartoons, and photos involving David Letterman's late-night television show. (Rev: SLJ 4/86) [384]

6031 Mast, Gerald. *A Short History of the Movies* (8–12). 4th ed. Illus. 1986, Macmillan $29.95 (0-02-580500-2); paper $19.96 (0-023-77060-9). A lavishly illustrated history that deals with both the creative and technical aspects of movie history. (Rev: BL 1/15/87) [791.43]

6032 Medoff, Norman J., and Tom Tanquary. *Video: ENG and EFP* (10–12). Illus. 1986, Knowledge Industry $34.95 (0-86729-147-8); paper $24.95 (0-86729-148-6). A fine basic text of portable video techniques that covers the area from planning the video to final editing. (Rev: BL 10/15/87) [778.59]

6033 Medved, Harry, and Michael Medved. *The Golden Turkey Awards* (9–12). 1980, Putnam paper $7.95 (0-399-50463-X). In an Academy Awards in reverse, the worst in the world of film is honored. Also use: *The Fifty Worst Films of All Time* (1984). [791.43]

6034 Medved, Harry, and Michael Medved. *Son of Golden Turkey Awards: More of Hollywood's Worst Achievements* (8–12). Illus. 1986, Random paper $10.95 (0-394-74341-5). In this follow-up to *The Golden Turkey Awards* (1980), the authors again supply dubious awards in such new categories as the most embarrassing nude scene and the worst performance by Ronald Reagan. (Rev: BL 5/1/86) [791.43]

6035 Mehring, Margaret. *The Screenplay: A Blending of Film Form and Film Content* (10–12). Illus. 1989, Focal $24.95 (0-240-80007-9). An explanation of the components of a screenplay and how to write one. (Rev: BL 12/15/89) [808.2]

6036 Meyer, Nicholas E. *Magic in the Dark: A Young Viewer's History of the Movies* (7–12). Illus. 1986, Facts on File $17.95 (0-8160-1256-3). A fascinating trivia-laden account that concentrates on movie history through the mid-1970s. (Rev: BL 6/15/86; BR 9–10/86; VOYA 6/86) [791.43]

6037 Meyers, Ric. *Murder on the Air* (9–12). Illus. 1989, Mysterious paper $12.95 (0-89296-977-6). A history of crime and detective series on television from "Dragnet" on. (Rev: BL 6/1/89) [791.45]

6038 Monaco, James. *How to Read a Film: The Art, Technology, Language, History, and Theory of Film and Media* (10–12). Rev. ed. Illus. 1981, Oxford Univ. Pr. $35.00 (0-19-502802-3); paper $15.95 (0-19-502806-6). A behind-the-scenes look at the social and economic factors that have shaped the movie industry over the years. [791.43]

6039 National Board of Review of Motion Pictures, eds. *The 500 Best British and Foreign Films to Buy, Rent, or Videotape* (9–12). 1988, Morrow $24.50 (0-688-07798-6); paper $15.95 (0-688-06897-9). A guide to the best American movies that gives such information as casts, plots, and an evaluation. (Rev: BL 10/15/88) [791]

6040 Norman, Barry. *The Story of Hollywood* (10–12). Illus. 1988, NAL $19.95 (0-453-00589-6). A caustic, critical view of Hollywood history from the viewpoint of a British film critic. (Rev: BL 5/1/88) [384.8]

6041 Null, Gary. *Black Hollywood: The Negro in Motion Pictures* (7–12). Illus. 1975, Citadel paper $12.95 (0-8065-0908-2). A history of black Americans in 75 years of Hollywood productions up to the mid-1970s. [791.43]

6042 O'Connor, John E. *American History/American Television: Interpreting the Video Past* (10–12). 1988, Ungar $12.95 (0-8044-2672-4). Fourteen essays on the early days of television and such performers as Milton Berle and Edward R. Murrow. [384.55]

6043 Osborne, Robert. *60 Years of the Oscar: The Official History of the Academy Awards* (7–12). Illus. 1989, Abbeville $49.95 (0-89659-952-3). A huge, well-illustrated but expensive guide to all of the awards year by year. (Rev: BL 5/15/89) [791.43]

6044 Paisner, Daniel. *The Imperfect Mirror: Inside Stories of Television Newswomen* (10–12). Illus. 1989, Morrow $18.95 (0-688-07499-5). Profiles of such personalities as Connie Chung and Jane Pauley are included in this book on TV's newswomen. (Rev: BL 3/1/89; SLJ 7/89) [070]

6045 Peary, Danny. *Cult Movies 3: 50 More of the Classics, the Sleepers, the Weird, and the Wonderful* (8–12). Illus. 1988, Simon & Schuster paper $12.95 (0-671-64810-1). This is the third collection of stills and text about movies that have achieved cult status. The earlier volumes were

Cult Movies (Doubleday, 1989) and *Cult Movies 2* (Delacorte, 1989). (Rev: SLJ 5/89) [791.43]

6046 Perry, George. *Life of Python* (10–12). 1984, Little $12.95 (0-316-70015-0). A thorough rundown on the Monty Python gang and their television programs. [384.55]

6047 Phillips, Gene D. *Alfred Hitchcock* (10–12). Illus. 1984, Twayne $18.95 (0-8057-9293-7). An analysis of Hitchcock's films and his cinematic techniques from his early silents to his last movie in 1976. [791.43]

6048 Postman, Neil. *Amusing Ourselves to Death: Public Discourse in the Age of Show Business* (10–12). 1985, Viking $14.95 (0-670-80454-1); Penguin paper $6.95 (0-14-009438-5). The author discusses the adverse effects of watching television, a medium he claims treats everything as entertainment. Postman also wrote *Teaching as a Conserving Activity* (1979). (Rev: BL 10/1/85) [302.2]

6049 Quinlan, David. *Wicked Women of the Screen* (8–12). Illus. 1988, St. Martin's $18.95 (0-312-02048-1). From Theda Bara to Joan Collins, a look at the bad ladies of movies in text and pictures. (Rev: BL 11/1/88) [791.43]

6050 Robertson, Patrick. *Guinness Film Facts and Feats* (8–12). Illus. 1985, Guinness paper $14.95 (0-85112-278-7). A volume of all the superlatives involved in motion pictures. (Rev: BL 10/15/85; SLJ 11/85) [791.43]

6051 Robinson, David. *The History of World Cinema* (10–12). 2nd ed. Illus. 1981, Scarborough Pr. $25.00 (0-8128-2747-3). A well-balanced history of world cinema that covers the United States in relation to developments elsewhere. [791.43]

6052 Robinson, Richard. *The Video Primer: Equipment, Production, and Concepts* (9–12). 1983, Perigee $10.95 (0-399-50698-5). A fine beginner's manual that covers topics such as lighting and editing. [778.59]

6053 Rosenblum, Joseph, and Robert Karen. *When the Shooting Stops . . . the Cutting Begins: A Film Editor's Story* (10–12). 1986, DaCapo paper $10.95 (0-306-80272-4). An account by a film cutter of working with such filmmakers as Woody Allen and Mel Brooks. [791.43]

6054 Rovin, Jeff. *A Pictorial History of Science Fiction Films* (9–12). Illus. 1975, Carol $12.00 (0-8065-0475-7); paper $9.95 (0-8065-0537-0). A lavishly illustrated chronicle of famous science fiction movies. [791.43]

6055 Searles, Baird. *Films of Science Fiction and Fantasy* (8–12). Illus. 1988, Abrams $39.95 (0-

8109-0922-7). Using such categories as aliens, space, and time travel, the author introduces films of science fiction and fantasy. (Rev: BL 12/1/88) [791.43]

6056 Shanks, Bob. *The Cool Fire: How to Make It in Television* (10–12). 1977, Random paper $3.95 (0-394-72285-X). A behind-the-scenes look at the business of television and how programs are made. [384.55]

6057 Shipman, David. *A Pictorial History of Science Fiction Films* (8–12). Illus. 1986, Salem House $17.95 (0-600-38520-5). From the French nineteenth century efforts to today's works by Lucas and Spielberg, this is a heavily illustrated account of science fiction and fantasy movies. (Rev: BL 2/15/86) [791.435]

6058 Sinyard, Neil. *The Films of Woody Allen* (9–12). Illus. 1987, Exeter $7.98 (0-671-08928-5). In a slim, oversize format, all but the most recent of Woody Allen's films are discussed. (Rev: BL 11/1/87) [791.43]

6059 Skal, David J. *Hollywood Gothic: The Tangled Web of Dracula from Novel to Stage to Screen* (9–12). Illus. 1990, Norton $39.95 (0-393-02904-2). Follows the trail of the many transformations of this ultimate vampire story from Bram Stoker through Bela Lugosi to the present. (Rev: BL 10/1/90) [823]

6060 Slide, Anthony, and Edward Wagenknecht. *Fifty Great American Silent Films, 1912–1920* (10–12). 1981, Dover paper $8.95 (0-486-23985-3). A pictorial survey that gives stories, stars, and background data. Also use: *Fifty Classic British Films: 1932 to 1982* (1981). [791.43]

6061 Smith, Diane G. *American Filmmakers Today* (10–12). 1983, Messner LB $9.79 (0-671-44081-0). Profiles are given of such filmmakers as Francis Coppola, Steven Spielberg, and George Lucas. [791.43]

6062 Smith, Julian. *Chaplin* (10–12). Illus. 1984, Twayne $18.95 (0-8057-9294-5). This is an appreciation of the art of this filmmaker with major attention paid to his sound films. [791.43]

6063 Smith, Marisa, and Amy Schewel, eds. *The Actor's Book of Movie Monologues* (9–12). 1986, Penguin paper $5.95 (0-14-009475-X). A collection of 80 monologues starting with *M* and ending with *The Breakfast Club*. (Rev: BL 11/1/86) [791.43]

6064 Stanley, John. *Revenge of the Creature Features Movie Guide* (9–12). Illus. 1988, Creatures at Large paper $11.95 (0-940064-04-9). A fascinating revision of *The Creature Features Movie Guide* (o.p.). (Rev: BL 6/1/88) [791.435]

6065 Taub, Eric. *Gaffers, Grips and Best Boys: An Inside Look at Who Does What in the Making of a Motion Picture* (9–12). 1987, St. Martin's paper $10.95 (0-312-01150-4). A behind-the-scenes look at making a movie that takes you through the production stage and the pre- and postproduction stages. (Rev: BL 12/15/87) [791.43]

6066 Time-Life Books, eds. *Life Goes to the Movies* (9–12). Illus. 1987, Crown $19.95 (0-517-62585-7). In a series of photographs the stars, films, studios, and personnel behind the cameras are pictured. [791.43]

6067 Trebek, Alex, and Peter Barsocchini. *The Jeopardy! Book* (8–12). Illus. 1990, Harper paper $12.95 (0-06-096511-8). As well as giving a history of this popular quiz program, this book gives many tough questions and answers that have been used in the past. (Rev: BL 9/15/90) [791.45]

6068 Utz, Peter. *Do-It-Yourself Video: A Beginner's Guide to Home Video* (9–12). Illus. 1984, Prentice $25.95 (0-13-216664-X); paper $15.95 (0-13-216656-9). A detailed manual that covers both the basic and such sophisticated advanced techniques as sound mixing and graphics. (Rev: BL 3/1/85) [621.388]

6069 Van Gelder, Peter. *That's Hollywood: A Behind-the-Scenes Look at 60 of the Greatest Films of All Time* (9–12). Illus. 1990, Harper paper $10.95 (0-06-096512-6). From *Frankenstein* to *Batman*, this is a review of Hollywood's finest and most popular movies. (Rev: BL 10/15/90) [791.43]

6070 Verna, Tony, and William T. Bode. *Live TV: An Inside Look at Directing and Producing* (9–12). 1986, Focal Pr. $24.95 (0-240-51713-X). Culled from interviews with 80 leaders in television, this is a behind-the-scenes look at the problems and rewards of live television. (Rev: BL 2/15/87) [791.45]

6071 Weaver, Tom. *Interviews with B Science Fiction and Horror Movie Makers* (9–12). Illus. 1988, McFarland $29.95 (0-89950-360-8). Interviews with 28 producers, directors, makeup people, actors, and others responsible for making grade B low-budget films. (Rev: VOYA 4/89) [791.43]

6072 Winn, Marie. *The Plug-In Drug: Television, Children, and the Family* (10–12). Rev. ed. Illus. 1985, Penguin paper $6.95 (0-14-007698-0). A discussion of the adverse effects of television viewing on children. A follow-up is *Unplugging the Plug-in Drug* (1987). (Rev: BL 1/1/85) [305.2]

6073 Winship, Michael. *Television* (9–12). Illus. 1988, Random $19.95 (0-394-56401-4). A history of this medium with information on current problems and possible future trends. Based on the PBS series. (Rev: BL 4/1/88; BR 9–10/88; SLJ 10/88; VOYA 10/88) [791.45]

6074 Withers, Robert S. *Introduction to Film* (10–12). 1983, Barnes & Noble paper $8.95 (0-06-460202-8). An introduction to the various elements and techniques used in filmmaking and how to appreciate them. [791.43]

6075 Worrell, Denise. *Icons: Intimate Portraits* (9–12). Illus. 1989, Atlantic Monthly $18.95 (0-87113-306-7). Interviews with 11 celebrities including Madonna, Steve Martin, Steven Spielberg, and Michael Jackson. (Rev: BL 4/15/89) [791.43]

Theater and Drama

6076 Adler, Stella. *The Technique of Acting* (9–12). 1988, Bantam $14.95 (0-553-05299-3). Techniques of acting from one of the foremost coaches in America. Foreword by one of her pupils, Marlon Brando. (Rev: BL 8/88) [792]

6077 Allensworth, Carl. *The Complete Play Production Handbook* (10–12). Rev. ed. Illus. 1982, Harper paper $11.95 (0-06-463558-9). In this guide to play production, the role of each member of the team—e.g., actor, director, and designer—is discussed. [792]

6078 Bartow, Arthur. *The Director's Voice: Twenty-One Interviews* (10–12). 1988, Theatre Communications Group $24.95 (0-930452-73-9); paper $14.95 (0-930452-74-7). Interviews with 21 theater directors who are currently at work in New York or regional theaters. (Rev: BL 12/15/88) [792]

6079 Blum, Daniel. *A Pictorial History of the American Theater 1860–1985* (9–12). Rev. ed. Illus. 1986, Crown $29.95 (0-517-56258-8). A new edition of this picture book of stars and scenes that traces theatrical history year by year. (Rev: SLJ 3/87) [792.73]

6080 Boleslavsky, Richard. *Acting: The First Six Lessons* (10–12). 1949, Theatre Arts Bks. $15.95 (0-87830-000-7). From the pen of an international figure in the theater come 6 essays of what is involved in the art of acting. [792]

6081 Borns, Betsy. *Comic Lives: Inside the World of American Stand-up Comedy* (10–12). 1987, Simon & Schuster paper $8.95 (0-671-

62620-5). A behind-the-scenes look at the rugged, often seedy, life that stand-up comics have to live before breaking into the big time. (Rev: BL 9/15/87) [729.2]

6082 Brockett, Oscar G. *History of the Theatre* (10–12). Illus. 1987, Allyn & Bacon $30.00 (0-205-10487-8). This is a basic history of the theater from the Egyptians to the present. [792.09]

6083 Burris-Meyer, Harold, and Edward C. Cole. *Scenery for the Theatre* (10–12). Rev. ed. Illus. 1971, Little $65.00 (0-316-11754-4). In a lucid text and more than 1,000 photographs the author explains the history and principle of stage design. [792]

6084 Corson, Richard. *Stage Makeup* (9–12). 7th ed. Illus. 1986, Prentice $42.00 (0-13-840539-5). This is the standard text on stage makeup that discusses the types of makeup and how to apply it. (Rev: BL 6/15/86) [792]

6085 Gerrold, David. *The World of Star Trek* (9–12). Rev. ed. Illus. 1984, Bluejay paper $9.95 (0-312-94463-2). The history of "Star Trek" from TV to the movies. [791.45]

6086 Gillette, A. S., and J. Michael Gillette. *Stage Scenery: Its Construction and Rigging* (10–12). 3rd ed. Illus. 1981, Harper $37.50 (0-06-042332-3). This account covers stage sets and props from their design through construction and use. [792]

6087 Grote, David. *Staging the Musical: Planning, Rehearsing, and Marketing the Amateur Production* (10–12). Illus. 1986, Prentice $16.95 (0-13-840190-X); paper $10.95 (0-13-840182-9). An excellent guide for anyone involved in amateur theatrics with tips on such topics as scenery, costumes, and sound. (Rev: BL 4/15/86) [782.81]

6088 Hagen, Uta, and Haskel Frankel. *Respect for Acting* (10–12). 1973, Macmillan $16.95 (0-02-547390-5). Guidance for the aspiring actor is given by a great actress and teacher. [791.4]

6089 Haskins, James. *Black Theater in America* (8–12). Illus. 1982, Harper $12.95 (0-690-04128-4). A history of black stage productions from after the Civil War to 1980. [792.09]

6090 Henderson, Mary C. *Theater in America: 200 Years of Plays, Players, and Productions* (9–12). Illus. 1986, Abrams $45.00 (0-8109-1084-5). Though expensive, this account gives an excellent history and a stunning collection of photographs. (Rev: BL 2/15/87) [792]

6091 Hodges, C. Walter. *Shakespeare's Theatre* (8–12). Illus. 1964, Putnam paper $5.95 (0-698-20511-1). A history of theater from religious drama to the flowering of Elizabethan plays. [792.09]

6092 Hodges, Cyril. *The Globe Restored: A Study of the Elizabethan Theatre* (10–12). Illus. 1990, Native American Book Pubs. $59.00 (1-878592-01-7); paper $39.00 (1-878592-00-9). A look at the Elizabethan theater world with emphasis on the Globe Theatre. [792.09]

6093 James, Thurston. *The Theater Props Handbook* (10–12). Illus. 1988, Betterway $29.95 (0-932620-88-4); paper $19.95 (0-932620-86-8). A guide to the building and use of a variety of stage props well illustrated by 650 photographs. (Rev: BL 2/15/88) [792]

6094 Kaminsky, Stuart M. *American Film Genres: Approaches to a Critical Theory of Popular Film* (10–12). 1984, Nelson LB $25.95 (0-8304-1048-1); paper $13.95 (0-88229-826-7). This critical study examines the artistic values in today's popular motion pictures. [791.43]

6095 Kipnis, Claude. *The Mime Book* (7–12). Illus. 1988, Meriwether paper $10.95 (0-916260-55-0). One of the world's greatest mimes explains what it is and how it is done. [792.3]

6096 Knight, Arthur. *The Liveliest Art: A Panoramic History of the Movies* (10–12). Rev. ed. 1979, NAL paper $4.95 (0-451-62652-4). Though not completely current, this book has become a standard history of the movies both here and abroad. [791.43]

6097 Koon, Helen Wickham. *How Shakespeare Won the West* (9–12). 1989, McFarland LB $24.95 (0-89950-432-9). A delightful history of the American theater during the days of the California Gold Rush. (Rev: BR 3–4/90) [792]

6098 Leacroft, Richard, and Helen Leacroft. *Theatre and Playhouse* (10–12). Illus. 1985, Methuen $39.95 (0-413-52930-4); paper $16.95 (0-413-52940-1). A history of theater design that uses specific theaters to illustrate the evolution of this form of architecture. (Rev: BL 1/1/85) [725.822]

6099 Lewis, Robert. *Advice to the Players* (10–12). 1980, Harper paper $17.95 (0-06-043967-X). A manual on the craft of acting that includes material on such topics as gesturing, voice production, and auditioning. [791.4]

6100 Maltin, Leonard. *The Disney Films* (9–12). Rev. ed. 1984, Crown paper $12.95 (0-517-55407-0). An affectionate behind-the-scenes look at the memorable Disney movies. [791.43]

6101 Mast, Gerald. *The Comic Mind: Comedy and the Movies* (10–12). 2nd ed. 1979, Univ. of Chicago Pr. paper $14.95 (0-226-50978-8). This is a study of comedy in movies, from early slapstick to today's more sophisticated humorous films. [791.43]

6102 Monaco, James. *American Film Now: The People, the Power, the Money, the Movies* (10–12). 1984, New York Zoetrope $24.95 (0-918432-64-2). An analysis of the modern film industry from a critic's point of view. [791.43]

6103 Morrow, Lee Alan, and Frank Pike. *Creating Theater: The Professionals' Approach to New Plays* (10–12). 1986, Random paper $9.95 (0-394-74279-6). Through interviews with people involved in the theater—from actors and playwrights to designers and critics—this is a collection of ideas about what makes the theater tick. (Rev: BL 11/15/86) [792]

6104 Parker, W. Oren, et al. *Scene Design and Stage Lighting* (10–12). 6th ed. Illus. 1989, Holt $39.95 (0-03-028777-4). A behind-the-scenes look at what is involved in designing and lighting a stage production. [792]

6105 Rolfe, Bari, ed. *Mimes on Miming: Writing on the Art of Mime* (10–12). Illus. 1979, Panjandrum $15.95 (0-915572-32-X); paper $8.95 (0-915572-31-1). In a series of essays the history of mime is covered as well as its applications in such areas as ballet and film. [792.3]

6106 Schindler, George. *Ventriloquism: Magic with Your Voice* (8–12). Illus. 1986, McKay paper $6.95 (0-679-14127-8). This book not only explains how to throw one's voice but also gives material on stage techniques, kinds of puppet figures, and writing routines. [793.8]

6107 Seto, Judith Roberts. *The Young Actor's Workbook* (10–12). 1988, Grove paper $10.95 (0-394-62040-2). In addition to supplying 50 scenes, this book gives many useful tips for the aspiring actor. [791.4]

6108 Spolin, Viola. *Improvisation for the Theatre: A Handbook of Teaching and Directing Techniques* (10–12). Illus. 1963, Northwestern Univ. Pr. $29.95 (0-8101-3999-5); paper $12.95 (0-8101-4000-4). An acting handbook and series of practice exercises to help directors get natural and less mechanical behavior from their actors. [792]

6109 Stanislavski, Constantin. *An Actor Prepares: Building a Character* (10–12). 1948, Theatre Arts $18.95 (0-87830-001-5). The bible of method actors, written by the Russian master. [791.4]

6110 Stein, Charles W., ed. *American Vaudeville as Seen by Its Contemporaries* (10–12). Illus. 1984, Da Capo paper $11.95 (0-306-80256-2). A history of vaudeville as found in the writings of such practitioners as the Marx Brothers, Buster Keaton, and George Burns. [792.7]

6111 Strasberg, Lee. *A Dream of Passion: The Development of the Method* (10–12). Illus. 1987, Little $16.95 (0-316-81870-4); NAL paper $8.95 (0-452-26198-8). An explanation and a history of "the method" used to train actors written by its founder. (Rev: SLJ 4/88) [791.4]

6112 Streader, Tim, and John A. Williams. *Create Your Own Stage Lighting* (9–12). 1985, Prentice $20.95 (0-13-189184-7). After a brief history of stage lighting, the British authors give a step-by-step account from the basic planning to the final production. (Rev: BR 5–6/86) [792]

6113 Thomas, Terry. *Create Your Own Stage Sets* (10–12). Illus. 1985, Prentice $18.95 (0-13-189085-9); paper $9.95 (0-13-189077-8). A profusely illustrated guide to making designs and sets for a variety of stages. (Rev: BR 11–12/85; SLJ 10/85) [792]

6114 Wickham, Glynne. *A History of the Theatre* (10–12). Illus. 1985, Cambridge Univ. Pr. $34.50 (0-521-30651-5). An amply illustrated international view of the development of the theater. (Rev: BR 9–10/86) [792]

6115 Wilk, Max. *The Golden Age of Television: Notes from the Survivors* (10–12). 1990, Moyer Bell paper $12.95 (1-55921-000-1). This is a history of the early days of television and the perils of broadcasting live. [384.55]

6116 Williams, Tennessee. *Where I Live: Selected Essays* (10–12). 1978, New Directions paper $6.95 (0-8112-8706-4). The essays in this collection deal chiefly with Williams's work and his life in the theater. [808.84]

Biography and True Adventure

Adventure and Exploration

Collective

6117 Finkelstein, Dave, and Jack London. *Greater Nowheres: A Journey through the Australian Bush* (9–12). 1988, Harper $18.95 (0-06-055108-9). An adventurous journey through remote Australia where the authors encounter strange animals and even stranger humans. (Rev: BL 7/88) [920]

6118 Green, Jonathon. *The Greatest Criminals of All Time: An Illustrated Compendium of More Than 600 Great Crooks* (10–12). Illus. 1982, Scarborough $20.00 (0-8128-2847-X). An international collection of biographies that truly constitutes a rogues' gallery. [920]

6119 LaBastille, Anne. *Women and Wilderness* (10–12). 1984, Sierra Club paper $8.95 (0-87156-828-4). This is a profile of 15 modern women who are engaged in outdoor occupations. [920]

6120 Nash, Jay Robert. *Bloodletters and Badmen: A Narrative Encyclopedia of American Criminals from the Pilgrims to the Present* (10–12). 1983, Warner paper $4.95 (0-446-32137-0). A historical encyclopedia of the worst America has produced from John Wilkes Booth and Jesse James to Capone and Lee Harvey Oswald. [920]

6121 Olds, Elizabeth Fagg. *Women of the Four Winds* (10–12). Illus. 1985, Houghton paper $9.95 (0-395-39584-4). Profiles of 4 contemporary women explorers who also represent such fields as filmmaking and anthropology. (Rev: BL 10/1/85) [920]

6122 Schullery, Paul. *The Bear Hunter's Century* (10–12). Illus. 1988, Dodd $19.95 (0-396-08923-2). A book about bears and the great bear hunt-ers (e.g., Teddy Roosevelt) of the eighteenth and nineteenth centuries. (Rev: BL 10/15/88) [920]

6123 Wilson, Derek. *The Circumnavigators* (10–12). Illus. 1989, Evans $24.95 (0-87131-601-3). From the first attempts to circle the globe to present day adventurers, this is a chronicle of travel, heroism, folly, and sometimes treachery. (Rev: SLJ 6/90) [920]

Individual

ADAMS, GRIZZLY

6124 McClung, Robert M. *The True Adventures of Grizzly Adams* (8–12). Illus. 1985, Morrow $11.95 (0-688-05794-2). An intriguing biography of this intrepid hunter, trapper, and trainer of wild animals. [921]

AMUNDSEN, ROALD

6125 Mason, Theodore K. *Two against the Ice: Amundsen and Ellsworth* (10–12). Illus. 1982, Putnam $13.95 (0-396-08092-8). A biography of Roald Amundsen, Arctic explorer, and of the American who financed and joined Amundsen's last expeditions, Lincoln Ellsworth. [921]

BORMAN, FRANK

6126 Borman, Frank, and Robert J. Serling. *Countdown: An Autobiography* (9–12). Illus. 1988, Morrow $19.95 (0-688-07929-6). An accessible biography of the astronaut and president of American Airlines. (Rev: BL 10/15/88) [921]

BRACE, ERNEST C.

6127 Brace, Ernest C. *A Code to Keep* (9–12). Illus. 1988, St. Martin's $16.95 (0-312-01403-1). The remarkable story of an ex-Marine who became a soldier of fortune in Vietnam and spent 8 years as a prisoner of war. (Rev: BL 1/1/88) [921]

BREE, MARLIN

6128 Bree, Marlin. *In the Teeth of the Northeaster: A Solo Voyage on Lake Superior* (9–12). Illus. 1988, Crown $17.95 (0-517-56449-1). An account of 3 months of sailing Lake Superior coastal waters in a 20-foot sailboat. (Rev: BL 2/1/88) [921]

CAHILL, TIM

6129 Cahill, Tim. *A Wolverine Is Eating My Leg* (9–12). 1989, Random paper $8.95 (0-679-72026-X). A fascinating travel writer tells about his adventures around the world in this continuation of *Jaguars Ripped My Flesh* (1987). (Rev: BL 2/15/89) [921]

CLARKE, THURSTON

6130 Clarke, Thurston. *Equator: A Journey* (10–12). Illus. 1988, Morrow $19.95 (0-688-06901-6). The adventurous account of a man who followed the equator around the world. (Rev: BL 10/1/88) [921]

COCHRAN, JACQUELINE

6131 Cochran, Jacqueline, and Maryann Bucknum Brinley. *Jackie Cochran: An Autobiography* (10–12). Illus. 1987, Bantam $18.95 (0-553-05211-X). The autobiography of the late aviator reconstructed from her writings and remembrances of friends and family. (Rev: BL 8/87) [921]

COLUMBUS, CHRISTOPHER

6132 Fuson, Robert Henderson. *The Log of Christopher Columbus* (9–12). Illus. 1987, International Marine $29.95 (0-87742-951-0). An introduction and epilogue give biographical details but the heart of this book is the actual log kept by Columbus from August 1492 to March 1493. (Rev: SLJ 11/88) [921]

6133 Granzotto, Gianni. *Christopher Columbus* (10–12). Trans. by Stephen Sartarelli. 1985, Univ. of Oklahoma Pr. paper $10.95 (0-8061-2100-9). A realistic portrait of the life and times of this great mariner. (Rev: BL 10/1/85) [921]

6134 Morison, Samuel Eliot. *Christopher Columbus, Mariner* (10–12). 1955, NAL paper $8.95 (0-452-00992-8). This 1955 biography is a scholarly tribute to the gallant, daring seaman. [921]

CROCKETT, DAVY

6135 Burke, James Wakefield. *David Crockett: The Man Behind the Myth* (9–12). Illus. 1984, Eakin Press $16.95 (0-89015-437-6). An engrossing biography of the wilderness scout, politician, and hero of the Alamo. (Rev: BL 4/1/85) [921]

COOK, CAPTAIN JAMES

6136 Hoobler, Dorothy, and Thomas Hoobler. *The Voyages of Captain Cook* (7–12). Illus. 1983, Putnam paper $10.95 (0-399-20975-1). This account covers in detail the 3 long sea journeys made by Cook from 1768 to 1779. [921]

DANA, RICHARD HENRY

6137 Dana, Richard Henry. *Two Years Before the Mast* (10–12). 1981, Penguin paper $4.95 (0-14-039008-1). The classic account of life on merchant ships in the early part of the nineteenth century. [910.4]

EARHART, AMELIA

6138 Earhart, Amelia. *The Fun of It: Random Records of My Own Flying and of Women in Aviation* (7–12). 1990, Omnigraphics $42.00 (1-55888-980-9); n.d., Academy paper $8.95 (0-915864-55-X). Autobiographical in part, this account is also a tribute to other woman aviation pioneers. First published in 1932. [921]

6139 Earhart, Amelia. *Last Flight* (10–12). Illus. 1988, Crown paper $12.95 (0-517-56794-6). Taken from a variety of sources like letters, this is a stirring account of Earhart's attempt to fly around the world. (Rev: BL 5/1/88) [921]

6140 Rich, Doris. *Amelia Earhart: A Biography* (9–12). 1989, Smithsonian Inst. $19.95 (0-87474-836-4). A well-crafted biography of the famous adventurer and aviator who disappeared over the Atlantic in 1928. (Rev: BL 11/1/89) [921]

6141 Lovell, Mary S. *The Sound of Wings: The Life of Amelia Earhart* (10–12). Illus. 1989, St. Martin's $22.95 (0-312-03431-8). A portrait of this fearless, headstrong pioneer of aviation and of her disappearance, which still remains a mystery. (Rev: BL 12/15/89) [921]

GRAHAM, ROBIN LEE

6142 Graham, Robin Lee, and Derek Gill. *Dove* (7–12). Illus. 1984, Bantam paper $3.95 (0-553-26629-2). A five-year solo voyage around the world and a tender romance with a girl the author met in Fiji. [921]

HALL, BRIAN

6143 Hall, Brian. *Stealing from a Deep Place: Travels in Southeastern Europe* (10–12). 1988, Hill & Wang $18.95 (0-8090-8835-5). Bicycle touring in the Balkans before the upheavals of 1989. (Rev: BL 8/88) [921]

HEYERDAHL, THOR

6144 Heyerdahl, Thor. *Kon-Tiki: Across the Pacific by Raft* (7–12). Trans. by F. H. Lyon. 1987, Pocket paper $3.95 (0-671-63789-4). The epic story of the 6-man voyage across 4,300 miles of the Pacific Ocean in an open raft. [910.4]

6145 Jenkins, Peter. *A Walk across America* (10–12). 1979, Morrow $22.45 (0-688-03427-6); Fawcett paper $5.95 (0-449-20455-3). This amazing book describes the author's trek with his dog from New York State to the Gulf of Mexico. It is followed by the account of a 3-year walk from New Orleans to Oregon in *The Walk West: A Walk across America 2* (1982). [917.3]

HILDEBRAND, JOHN

6146 Hildebrand, John. *Reading the River: A Voyage Down the Yukon* (10–12). 1988, Houghton $17.95 (0-395-42480-1). A canoe trip beginning at Whitehorse that combines history, personal observations, and geography. (Rev: BL 5/15/88) [921]

HORWITZ, TONY

6147 Horwitz, Tony. *One for the Road: Hitchhiking through the Australian Outback* (9–12). 1988, Random paper $6.95 (0-394-75817-X). A hitchhiking trip across Australia and encounters with an often hostile environment. (Rev: BL 7/88) [921]

HYNES, SAMUEL

6148 Hynes, Samuel. *Flights of Passage: Reflections of a World War II Aviator* (10–12). 1988, Naval Institute $16.95 (0-87021-215-X). For mature readers, the story of how a young man matured as a pilot of a dive-bomber during World War II. (Rev: BL 3/1/88) [921]

JOHNSON, OSA

6149 Johnson, Osa. *I Married Adventure: The Lives and Adventures of Martin and Osa Johnson* (8–12). Rev. ed. Illus. 1989, Morrow $19.95 (0-688-08687-X). First published in 1940, this is a reissue of the adventure story of 25 years spent mainly in Africa by a wildlife photographer and his wife. (Rev: BL 3/15/89) [921]

JOHNSON, WALLY

6150 Capstick, Peter Hathaway. *The Last Ivory Hunter: The Saga of Wally Johnson* (9–12). Illus. 1988, St. Martin's $18.95 (0-312-00048-0). The life story of Wally Johnson who was for 50 years a hunter and safari leader in Africa. (Rev: BL 8/88) [921]

JONES, TRISTAN

6151 Jones, Tristan. *Somewheres East of Suez* (9–12). 1988, Hearst Marine $16.95 (0-688-07750-1). This is the third installment of the solo voyages of a one-legged California adventurer in his trimaran. Preceded by *Outward Leg* (1986); *The Incredible Voyage* (1987). (Rev: BL 3/15/88) [921]

LEAST HEAT MOON, WILLIAM

6152 Least Heat Moon, William. *Blue Highways: A Journey into America* (10–12). 1983, Little $18.95 (0-316-35395-7). The author described his trip in a van across the U.S. taking only side roads. [921]

MCAULIFFE, CHRISTA

6153 Hohler, Robert T. *"I Touch the Future . . .": The Story of Christa McAuliffe* (9–12). Illus. 1986, Random $16.95 (0-394-55721-2); Berkley paper $4.50 (0-425-11054-0). A moving biography of a talented teacher who became an astronaut. (Rev: BR 5–6/87; SLJ 5/87) [921]

MARKHAM, BERYL

6154 Lovell, Mary S. *Straight on Till Morning* (10–12). Illus. 1987, St. Martin's $16.95 (0-312-01096-6); paper $10.95 (0-312-01895-9). The story of the noble-born unconventional Englishwoman, Beryl Markham, who became a famous aviator. (Rev: SLJ 1/88) [921]

PARFIT, MICHAEL

6155 Parfit, Michael. *Chasing the Glory: Travels across America* (10–12). 1988, Macmillan $17.95 (0-02-594731-1). In his own small airplane, this adventurer retraces Lindbergh's victory tour of 1927. (Rev: BL 10/1/88) [921]

POLO, MARCO

6156 Polo, Marco. *The Travels of Marco Polo* (10–12). 1958, Penguin paper $4.95 (0-14-044057-7). One of many editions of this account kept by Marco Polo of his travels in Asia in the thirteenth century. [915]

REILLY, SIDNEY

6157 Lockhart, Robin Bruce. *Reilly: Ace of Spies* (10–12). 1984, Penguin paper $4.95 (0-14-006895-3). Sidney Reilly was actually Sigmund Rosenblum, but he was also one of the most famous spies active in roughly the period around World War I. [921]

ROBERTSON FAMILY

6158 Robertson, Dougal. *Survive the Savage Sea* (7–12). 1984, Sheridan paper $13.95 (0-246-12509-8). A survival story about the Robertson family ordeal in a small raft and lifeboat. [921]

SCHIRRA, WALTER M.

6159 Schirra, Walter M., and Richard N. Billings. *Schirra's Space* (9–12). 1988, Quinlan $16.95 (1-55770-034-6). A readable autobiography by the former astronaut that gives a behind-the-scenes view of the NASA space program. (Rev: BL 2/15/89) [921]

SCOTT, ROBERT FALCON

6160 Huxley, Elspeth. *Scott of the Antarctic* (10–12). 1977, Univ. of Nebraska Pr. paper $11.95 (0-8032-7248-0). A detailed study of the life and experiences of the famed Antarctic explorer Robert Falcon Scott. [921]

SCOTT, ROBERT LEE

6161 Scott, Robert L. *The Day I Owned the Sky* (9–12). Illus. 1988, Bantam $17.95 (0-553-05248-

9). The life of the famous aviator who gained renown during World War II because of his exploits with the Flying Tigers. (Rev: BL 2/1/88) [921]

SUNQUIST, FIONA AND MEL

6162 Sunquist, Fiona, and Mel Sunquist. *Tiger Moon* (9–12). Illus. 1988, Univ. of Chicago Pr. $24.95 (0-226-78001-5). An account of 2 years spent studying the tigers of the Royal Chitwan National Park in Nepal. (Rev: BL 6/15/88) [921]

SWENDSEN, DAVID H.

6163 Swendsen, David H. *Badge in the Wilderness: My 30 Dangerous Years Combating Wildlife Violators* (9–12). Illus. 1985, Stackpole $16.95 (0-8117-0208-1). The story of a man who has devoted his life to protecting wildlife and foiling poachers. (Rev: BL 8/85) [921]

TURNER, MYLES

6164 Turner, Myles. *My Serengeti Years: The Memoirs of an African Game Warden* (10–12). Illus. 1988, Norton $17.95 (0-241-12058-6). Highlights in the life of the game warden who began his career in Serengeti National Park in 1956. (Rev: BL 6/1/88) [921]

VANDERMEERSSCHE, GASTON

6165 Mayer, Allan. *Gaston's War* (9–12). Illus. 1988, Presidio $17.95 (0-89141-291-3). The gripping story of a Belgium freedom fighter during World War II, his many exploits, capture, torture, and eventual release. (Rev: BL 1/1/88; SLJ 2/89) [921]

YEAGER, CHUCK

6166 Yeager, Chuck, and Charles Leerhsen. *Press On! Further Adventures in the Good Life* (10–12). 1988, Bantam $17.95 (0-553-05333-7). This book tells of the astronaut's life after leaving the service and is the sequel to the best-selling *Yeager* (1985). (Rev: BL 8/88) [921]

The Arts and Entertainment

Collective

6167 Backes, Clarus, ed. *Growing Up Western* (10–12). Illus. 1990, Knopf $22.95 (0-394-57393-5). Seven writers of the West like A. B. Guthrie and Dee Brown talk about their life and writing. (Rev: BL 1/15/90) [920]

6168 Brown, Peter, and Steven Gaines. *The Love You Make: The Insider's Story of the Beatles* (9–12). Illus. 1983, NAL paper $4.95 (0-451-16067-3). An honest look at the lives of the Beatles that ends in the early 1980s. [920]

6169 Canaday, John. *The Lives of the Painters* (10–12). Illus. 1969, Norton $75.00 (0-393-04231-6). In this chronologically arranged text, the lives of 450 famous painters are outlined. [920]

6170 Cross, Milton, and David Ewen. *The Milton Cross New Encyclopedia of the Great Composers and Their Music* (9–12). 1989, Doubleday $35.00 (0-385-03635-3). A 2-volume work that highlights the life and works of 67 composers. [920.03]

6171 Davies, Hunter. *The Beatles* (9–12). Illus. 1978, McGraw $14.95 (0-07-015463-5); paper $10.95 (0-07-015526-7). An in-depth look at the Beatles from childhood through the 1970s. [920]

6172 Ewen, David. *Composers of Tomorrow's Music: A Non-Technical Introduction to the Musical Avant-Garde Movement* (10–12). 1971, Greenwood LB $24.75 (0-313-22107-3). The author supplies biographical sketches of twentieth-century composers from Schoenburg and Webern to Boulez and Cage. [920]

6173 Feather, Leonard. *From Satchmo to Miles* (10–12). Illus. 1984, Da Capo $29.50 (0-306-76230-7); paper $9.95 (0-306-80302-X). A series of profiles of black jazz musicians like Count Basie, Dizzy Gillespie, Duke Ellington, and Billie Holiday. [920]

6174 Flexner, James Thomas. *America's Old Masters* (10–12). Illus. 1982, McGraw paper $9.95 (0-07-021285-6). This volume pays tribute to 4 early American painters, Benjamin West, John Singleton Copley, Charles Wilson Peale, and Gilbert Stuart. [920]

6175 Green, Stanley. *The World of Musical Comedy* (10–12). Illus. 1980, Da Capo paper $19.95 (0-306-80207-4). In several chapters, the careers of 70 individuals or groups that have been important in America's musical theater are described. [920]

6176 Hardy, Karen. *The New Breed: Actors Coming of Age* (9–12). Illus. 1988, Henry Holt paper $14.95 (0-8050-0774-1). The hopes, dreams, and techniques of 30 young actors and actresses including Patrick Swayze, Aidan Quinn, and Laura Dern. (Rev: BL 8/88; BR 3–4/88; VOYA 2/89) [791.43]

6177 Harrison, Daphne Duval. *Black Pearls: Blues Queens of the 1920s* (10–12). Illus. 1988, Rutgers Univ. Pr. $19.95 (0-8135-1279-4). Four influential black female blues singers are highlighted plus the social conditions under which they lived and performed. (Rev: BL 3/1/88) [920]

6178 Jones, Max. *Talking Jazz* (10–12). 1988, Norton $19.95 (0-393-02494-6). A collection of interviews with jazz greats of the 1930s through the 1950s. (Rev: BL 6/1/88) [920]

6179 Morley, Sheridan. *The Great Stage Stars: Distinguished Theatrical Careers of the Past and Present* (9–12). Illus. 1986, Facts on File $24.95 (0-8160-1401-9). Brief biographies are given for famous stars past and present from the United States, Britain, and Australia. (Rev: BL 4/1/86) [792]

6180 Munro, Eleanor. *Originals: American Women Artists* (10–12). Illus. 1987, Simon & Schuster paper $17.95 (0-671-42812-8). Profiles are given of 34 American women artists with emphasis on those still living and working. [920]

6181 *The New Grove Twentieth-Century American Masters* (9–12). 1987, Norton paper $13.95 (0-393-30100-1). Excerpts from the larger dictionary that deal with American composers from Ives to Bernstein. (Rev: BL 9/1/88) [920]

6182 Nichols, Janet. *American Music Makers: An Introduction to American Composers* (7–12). Illus. 1990, Walker LB $19.95 (0-8027-6958-6). An examination of the lives and careers of 10 American-born composers including George Gershwin and contemporaries such as Philip Glass and Milton Babbit. (Rev: BL 10/1/90) [920]

6183 Palmer, Robert. *Deep Blues* (10–12). 1982, Penguin paper $7.95 (0-14-006223-8). Brief biographies of the great blues musicians and performers. [920]

6184 Story, Rosalyn M. *And So I Sing* (10–12). Illus. 1990, Warner $24.95 (0-446-71016-4). Profiles of great black American female singers whose careers broke color barriers, such as Marian Anderson and Leontyne Price. (Rev: BL 1/15/90) [920]

6185 Tate, Claudia, ed. *Black Women Writers at Work* (10–12). 1983, Continuum paper $12.95 (0-8264-0243-7). Biographies of 14 contemporary black women writers like Nikki Giovanni, Alice Walker, and Toni Morrison are given. [920]

6186 Terkel, Studs. *Giants of Jazz* (10–12). Rev. ed. Illus. 1975, Harper $15.95 (0-690-00998-4). Thirteen famous jazz personalities including Benny Goodman, Louis Armstrong, Bessie Smith, and Duke Ellington are profiled. [920]

6187 Tobler, John, and Stuart Grundy. *The Guitar Greats* (9–12). Illus. 1984, St. Martin's paper $10.95 (0-312-35319-7). Interviews and general background information highlight this account of the lives of 14 famous, living electric guitarists. [920]

Artists

ADAMS, ANSEL

6188 Adams, Ansel. *Ansel Adams, an Autobiography* (10–12). Illus. 1985, Little $60.00 (0-8212-1596-5); paper $29.95 (0-8212-1787-9). This autobiography, in passing, introduces such other prominent artists as Edward Weston, Georgia O'Keeffe, Steichen, and Stieglitz. [921]

CELLINI, BENVENUTO

6189 Cellini, Benvenuto. *Autobiography* (10–12). 1956, Penguin paper $5.95 (0-14-044049-6). The candid autobiography of the great artist who was also a thief and a murderer. [921]

CÉZANNE, PAUL

6190 Rewald, John. *Cézanne: A Biography* (10–12). Illus. 1990, Abrams $29.95 (0-8109-8100-9). Through using Cézanne's autobiographical writings and memories of friends, the author has created a word picture of the painter and his works, aided by more than 250 illustrations. [921]

6191 Schapiro, Meyer. *Paul Cézanne* (9–12). Illus. 1988, Abrams $19.95 (0-8109-1043-8). Forty color plates plus a few in black and white follow a biographical sketch of the artist's life. (Rev: BL 11/15/88) [921]

CHAGALL, MARC

6192 Kagan, Andrew. *Marc Chagall* (9–12). Illus. 1989, Abbeville $29.95 (0-89659-932-9); paper $19.95 (0-89659-935-3). The life and work of this Russian Jewish painter whose faith and fantastic imagination dominated his work. (Rev: BL 12/15/89) [921]

DISNEY, WALT

6193 Schickel, Richard. *The Disney Version* (9–12). 1985, Simon & Schuster paper $10.95 (0-671-54714-3). The story of the most successful Hollywood animator, the empire he created, and the origins of his many character creations. [921]

GOGH, VINCENT VAN

6194 Bonafoux, Pascal. *Van Gogh* (10–12). Illus. 1990, Henry Holt $19.95 (0-8050-1384-9). This account traces the artist's career by using many quotes from original sources and a generous number of color illustrations. (Rev: BL 10/15/90) [921]

6195 Sweetman, David. *Van Gogh: His Life and His Art* (10–12). Illus. 1990, Crown $30.00 (0-517-57406-3). A biography that stresses van Gogh's devotion to his art and how his style gradually evolved. (Rev: BL 6/1/90) [921]

HOMER, WINSLOW

6196 Cikovsky, Nicolai. *Winslow Homer* (10–12). Illus. 1990, Abrams $39.95 (0-8109-1193-0). The life and art of one of America's finest painters accompanied by many illustrations. (Rev: BL 7/90) [921]

JONES, CHUCK

6197 Jones, Chuck. *Chuck Amuck: The Life and Times of an Animated Cartoonist* (9–12). Illus. 1989, Farrar $24.95 (0-374-12348-9). The amusing, well-illustrated biography of the man who was most responsible for the creation of Daffy Duck, Bugs Bunny, and Elmer Fudd. (Rev: BL 12/1/89) [921]

KANE, BOB

6198 Kane, Bob, and Tom Andrae. *Batman & Me* (9–12). Illus. 1989, Eclipse Books $39.95 (1-56060-016-0); paper $14.95 (1-56060-017-9). An autobiography of the creator of Batman, Robin, and other characters in the comics plus lots of illustrations. (Rev: BL 4/15/90) [921]

MICHELANGELO BUONARROTI

6199 Hibbard, Howard. *Michelangelo* (10–12). Illus. 1974, Harper $20.00 (0-06-433323-X); paper $10.95 (0-06-430148-6). A well-illustrated biography of the genius who achieved as a sculptor, painter, and architect. [921]

O'KEEFFE, GEORGIA

6200 Lisle, Laurie. *Portrait of an Artist: A Biography of Georgia O'Keeffe* (10–12). 1986, Univ. of New Mexico Pr. $29.95 (0-8263-0907-0); Pocket paper $5.95 (0-671-60040-0). The life of O'Keeffe with details on her mammoth struggle for recognition. (Rev: BR 3–4/87) [921]

6201 O'Keeffe, Georgia. *Georgia O'Keeffe* (10–12). Illus. 1977, Penguin paper $29.95 (0-14-004677-1). A handsomely illustrated autobiography of this free-spirited American artist. [921]

PICASSO, PABLO

6202 Lyttle, Richard B. *Pablo Picasso: The Man and the Image* (9–12). Illus. 1989, Macmillan $14.95 (0-689-31393-4). Picasso's unconventional life, his politics, and many loves, as well as his work, are all detailed in this fine introduction. (Rev: BL 10/1/89; BR 3–4/90; SLJ 12/89; VOYA 4/90) [921]

6203 Sommer, Robin L., and Patricia A. Mac-Donald. *Pablo Picasso* (7–12). Illus. 1990, Silver Burdett LB $17.98 (0-382-09903-6). An easily read biography that re-creates the private and public aspects of this controversial artist's life. (Rev: BL 9/15/90) [921]

REMINGTON, FREDERIC

6204 Samuels, Peggy, and Harold Samuels. *Frederic Remington: A Biography* (10–12). 1985, Univ. of Texas Pr. paper $12.95 (0-292-72451-9). This biography tells of the famous American painter of the wild West who was born in New York State in 1861 and educated at Yale. [921]

SCHULZ, CHARLES M.

6205 Johnson, Rheta Grimsley. *Good Grief: The Story of Charles M. Schulz* (9–12). Illus. 1989, Pharos $17.95 (0-88687-553-6). A biography of the creator of "Peanuts" with sidelights on his character from people who have worked with him in the past. (Rev: BL 6/15/89) [921]

SEURAT, GEORGES

6206 Courthion, Pierre. *Georges Seurat* (9–12). Illus. 1988, Abrams $19.95 (0-8109-1519-7). A biographical essay is followed by an album of reproductions. (Rev: BL 11/15/88) [921]

SUESS, DR.

6207 MacDonald, Ruth K. *Dr. Seuss* (9–12). 1988, Twayne LB $17.95 (0-8057-7524-2). A profile of the life and work of this great writer and illustrator of children's books. (Rev: SLJ 1/89) [921]

VELAZQUEZ, DIEGO

6208 Serullaz, Maurice. *Velazquez* (10–12). Illus. 1987, Abrams $19.95 (0-8190-1729-7). A lavishly illustrated biography and introduction to the work of this Spanish master. [921]

VERMEER, JAN

6209 Wheelock, Arthur K. *Jan Vermeer* (9–12). Illus. 1988, Abrams $19.95 (0-8109-1737-8). Following a critical, biographical essay and evaluation of Vermeer's paintings, there is a generous portfolio of prints. (Rev: BL 11/15/88) [921]

WRIGHT, FRANK LLOYD

6210 Murphy, Wendy Buehr. *Frank Lloyd Wright* (7–12). Illus. 1990, Silver Burdett LB $17.98 (0-382-09905-2). A brief biography of this architectural genius that uses many quotes and photographs. (Rev: BL 9/15/90) [921]

6211 Twombly, Robert C. *Frank Lloyd Wright: His Life and His Architecture* (10–12). Illus. 1979, Wiley paper $22.95 (0-471-85797-1). A biography that also contains a thoughtful assessment of this architect's work. [921]

Authors

ANGELOU, MAYA

6212 Angelou, Maya. *All God's Children Need Traveling Shoes* (10–12). 1986, Random $15.95 (0-394-52143-9); paper $5.95 (0-394-75077-2). In this fifth volume of Angelou's autobiography she tells of her 4 years in Ghana and a visit from Malcolm X. In order of publication and coverage the first 4 are: *I Know Why the Caged Bird Sings* (1970), *Gather Together in My Name* (1974), *Singin' and Swingin' and Gettin' Merry Like Christmas* (1976), and *The Heart of a Woman* (1981). (Rev: BL 2/1/86; SLJ 8/86; VOYA 8–10/86) [921]

ANTHONY, PIERS

6213 Anthony, Piers. *Bio of an Ogre: An Autobiography of Piers Anthony to Age 50* (9–12). 1988, Berkley $17.95 (0-441-06224-5). The autobiography of the prolific creator of the Incarnations of Immortality and Xanth series. (Rev: BL 7/88) [921]

AUSTEN, JANE

6214 Halperin, John. *The Life of Jane Austen* (10–12). Illus. 1984, Johns Hopkins Univ. Pr. paper $12.95 (0-8018-3410-4). In addition to a life story this account examines each of Austen's novels and relates them to her experiences. [921]

BAKER, RUSSELL

6215 Baker, Russell. *The Good Times* (10–12). Illus. 1989, Morrow $19.95 (0-688-06170-2). The newspaper reporter who so brilliantly began his autobiography with *Growing Up* (1982) continues his story to his beginning newspaper jobs and into the 1960s. (Rev: BL 4/15/89) [921]

6216 Baker, Russell. *Growing Up* (10–12). Illus. 1982, NAL paper $8.95 (0-452-25550-3). The story of the first 24 years of the life of the famous contemporary journalist. [921]

BRADBURY, RAY

6217 Mogen, David. *Ray Bradbury* (10–12). 1986, Twayne $17.95 (0-8057-7464-5). More than simply a biography, this is also a detailed analysis of each of this writer's works. (Rev: BL 1/15/87; SLJ 5/87; VOYA 4/87) [921]

BRONTË FAMILY

6218 Bentley, Phyllis. *The Brontës and Their World* (9–12). Illus. 1986, Thames & Hudson paper $9.95 (0-500-26016-8). A richly illustrated biography of the 3 Brontë sisters and their wayward brother. [921]

6219 Fraser, Rebecca. *The Brontes: Charlotte Brontë and Her Family* (10–12). Illus. 1988, Crown $25.00 (0-517-56438-6). A biography of the Brontës that links their experiences to their writing. (Rev: SLJ 5/89) [921]

6220 Pollard, Arthur. *The Landscape of the Brontës* (9–12). Illus. 1988, Dutton $22.95 (0-525-24637-1). A handsome book that recreates the lives of the Brontë sisters and the countryside where they lived. (Rev: SLJ 10/88) [921]

BRONTË, CHARLOTTE

6221 Gaskell, Elizabeth C. *The Life of Charlotte Brontë* (10–12). 1982, Dent paper $4.95 (0-460-01318-1). First published in 1857, this is a flattering look at the life of a novelist written by another successful novelist. [921]

BROOKS, GWENDOLYN

6222 Kent, George E. *A Life of Gwendolyn Brooks* (10–12). 1989, Univ. Press of Kentucky $25.00 (0-8131-1659-7). The life of the great black American poet up to 1978. (Rev: BL 8/89) [921]

BROWN, CLAUDE

6223 Brown, Claude. *Manchild in the Promised Land* (9–12). 1965, Macmillan $15.95 (0-02-517320-0); NAL paper $4.95 (0-451-15741-9). A realistic picture of growing up in Harlem in the 1950s. [921]

BROWNING, ELIZABETH BARRETT

6224 Forster, Margaret. *Elizabeth Barrett Browning: A Biography* (10–12). Illus. 1989, Doubleday $19.95 (0-385-24959-4). The story of the poet and her courage to leave her secure life to follow her true love in marriage. (Rev: SLJ 9/89) [921]

6225 Woolf, Virginia. *Flush: A Biography* (10–12). 1976, Harcourt paper $4.95 (0-15-631952-7). The life of Elizabeth Barrett Browning as seen through the experiences of her pet dog. [921]

BYRON, LORD

6226 Marchand, Leslie A. *Byron: A Portrait* (10–12). 1970, Univ. of Chicago Pr. paper $7.95 (0-226-50436-0). The story of the great Romantic poet—his work, loves, and participation in the Greek struggle for independence. [921]

CALDWELL, ERSKINE

6227 Caldwell, Erskine. *With All My Might* (10–12). Illus. 1987, Peachtree $19.95 (0-934601-11-9). This autobiography of the once-controversial American author concentrates on his youth and the many jobs he had as a young man. (Rev: SLJ 6–7/87) [921]

CAPOTE, TRUMAN

6228 Capote, Truman. *One Christmas* (9–12). 1983, Random $12.95 (0-394-53266-X). An autobiographical fragment about the author who, at age 6, spent a Christmas with his father. [921]

CATHER, WILLA

6229 Robinson, Phyllis C. *Willa: The Life of Willa Cather* (10–12). Illus. 1983, Holt paper $8.95 (0-03-071931-3). This biography of the famous writer from Nebraska draws parallels between life experiences and incidents and themes in Willa Cather's works. [921]

6230 Woodress, James. *Willa Cather: A Literary Life* (10–12). Illus. 1987, Univ. of Nebraska Pr. $35.00 (0-8032-4734-6); paper $14.95 (0-8032-9708-4). This great American writer comes to life in the pages of this biography that relates her experiences to characters and incidents in her books. (Rev: BL 10/15/87) [921]

CERVANTES, MIGUEL DE

6231 Busoni, Rafaello. *The Man Who Was Don Quixote: The Story of Miguel de Cervantes* (9–12). Illus. 1982, Prentice $9.95 (0-13-548107-4). An attractively illustrated biography of Cervantes that also introduces Spanish life during the late sixteenth and early seventeenth centuries. [921]

CHAUCER, GEOFFREY

6232 Gardner, John. *The Life and Times of Chaucer* (10–12). Illus. 1977, Random paper $9.95 (0-394-72500-X). This biography reveals the many facets of Chaucer's career as a civil servant, soldier, diplomat, but above all a writer of genius. [921]

6233 Howard, Donald R. *Chaucer: His Life, His Works, His World* (10–12). Illus. 1987, Dutton $29.95 (0-525-24400-X); Fawcett paper $12.95 (0-449-90341-9). The author has assimilated current and past research on Chaucer and produced a readable biography where his subject really comes to life. (Rev: SLJ 3/88) [921]

CHRISTIE, AGATHA

6234 Christie, Agatha. *Agatha Christie: An Autobiography* (9–12). 1985, Harper paper $7.95 (0-06-097030-8). A candid, honest self-portrait of the mystery story writer. [921]

6235 Gill, Gillian. *Agatha Christie: The Woman and Her Mysteries* (9–12). 1990, Free Pr. $22.50 (0-02-911702-X). The story of the secretive, very private woman who remains among the world's most popular writers. (Rev: BL 9/15/90) [921]

6236 Morgan, Janet. *Agatha Christie: A Biography* (10–12). 1985, Knopf $24.95 (0-394-52554-X). This officially authorized biography utilized voluminous records plus interviews with about 200 people. [921]

DAHL, ROALD

6237 Dahl, Roald. *Going Solo* (9–12). Illus. 1986, Farrar $14.95 (0-374-16503-3); Penguin paper $6.95 (0-14-010306-6). This book recounts the author's World War II activities in Africa and the Royal Air Force. For an older audience than his earlier autobiographical *Boy* (1985). (Rev: BL 9/1/86; VOYA 2/87) [921]

DICKENS, CHARLES

6238 Johnson, Edgar. *Charles Dickens: His Tragedy and Triumph* (10–12). 1986, Penguin paper $8.95 (0-14-058027-1). This biography of the novelist and social reformer tells of his public success and personal tragedy. [921]

6239 Kaplan, Fred. *Dickens: A Biography* (10–12). Illus. 1988, Morrow $24.95 (0-688-04341-0). A scholarly biography that sheds new light on the author's personal life. (Rev: BL 10/1/88) [921]

6240 MacKenzie, Norman, and Jeanne Mac-Kenzie. *Dickens: A Life* (10–12). Illus. 1979, Oxford Univ. Pr. $35.00 (0-19-211741-6). The biography of the great Victorian novelist who through his writings also fought for many worthy social causes. [921]

DICKINSON, EMILY

6241 Knapp, Bettina L. *Emily Dickinson* (10–12). 1989, Continuum $18.95 (0-8264-0441-3). A detailed biography of this writer plus an extensive review of her work and the influences that affected it. (Rev: SLJ 8/89) [921]

DILLARD, ANNIE

6242 Dillard, Annie. *An American Childhood* (10–12). 1987, Harper paper $7.95 (0-06-091518-8). The naturalist tells about growing up in Pittsburgh during the 1950s. (Rev: BL 8/87; SLJ 4/88) [921]

DOYLE, ARTHUR CONAN

6243 Symons, Julian. *Conan Doyle: Portrait of an Artist* (9–12). Illus. 1987, Mysterious $15.95 (0-89296-247-X); paper $9.95 (0-89296-926-1). A biography that points out the similarities between Doyle and his creation, Sherlock Holmes. (Rev: BL 11/1/87) [921]

ELLISON, RALPH

6244 Bishop, Jack. *Ralph Ellison* (9–12). Illus. 1987, Chelsea House $16.95 (1-55546-585-4). A biography of the writer of the acclaimed novel *Invisible Man* and his struggle for acceptance in both black and white cultures. (Rev: BL 2/15/88) [921]

FITZGERALD, ZELDA

6245 Milford, Nancy. *Zelda: A Biography* (10–12). Illus. 1970, Harper paper $8.95 (0-06-091069-0). This is the life story of F. Scott Fitzgerald's wife, Zelda, her emotional problems, and tragic death in a sanatorium fire. [921]

FRITZ, JEAN

6246 Fritz, Jean. *China Homecoming* (8–12). Illus. 1985, Putnam $13.95 (0-399-21182-9). This autobiographical account describes the return of this author to China, where she spent her childhood. (Rev: SLJ 8/85) [921]

6247 Fritz, Jean. *Homesick, My Own Story* (9–12). 1982, Putnam $13.95 (0-339-20933-6); Dell paper $3.25 (0-440-43683-4). This popular author writes about her early life in China. [921]

FROST, ROBERT

6248 Thompson, Lawrence, and R. H. Winnick. *Robert Frost* (10–12). Illus. 1982, Holt $25.00 (0-03-050921-1). An edited edition of the massive 3-volume biography of the great twentieth-century American poet. [921]

GRAVES, ROBERT

6249 Graves, Robert. *Goodbye to All That* (10–12). 1957, Doubleday paper $8.95 (0-385-09330-6). First published in 1929, this autobiography tells of Graves' childhood, World War I experiences, and his entry into the world of publishing. [921]

GUTHRIE, WOODY

6250 Guthrie, Woody. *Bound for Glory* (10–12). Illus. 1943, Peter Smith $15.75 (0-8446-6178-3); NAL paper $9.95 (0-452-26445-6). The saga of the man who grew up in poverty in the Oklahoma dust bowl and in time became one of America's most famous troubadours. [921]

GUY, ROSA

6251 Norris, Jerrie. *Presenting Rosa Guy* (9–12). 1988, Twayne LB $15.95 (0-8057-8207-9). A critical biography of the West Indian-born writer who has re-created Harlem life so vividly in her books for young adults. (Rev: BR 5–6/89; SLJ 12/88; VOYA 12/88) [921]

HANSBERRY, LORRAINE

6252 Hansberry, Lorraine. *To Be Young, Gifted and Black* (9–12). 1970, NAL paper $4.95 (0-451-15952-7). An autobiographical collection of reminiscences, letters, and quotes from Hansberry's plays. [921]

HART, MOSS

6253 Hart, Moss. *Act One: An Autobiography* (10–12). 1989, St. Martin's paper $13.95 (0-312-03272-2). An entertaining account of this playwright's youth and introduction into a life in the theater. [921]

HAWTHORNE, NATHANIEL

6254 Turner, Arlin. *Nathaniel Hawthorne* (10–12). Illus. 1980, Oxford Univ. Pr. $45.00 (0-19-

502547-4). This biography tells about Hawthorne's life and the world around him. [921]

6255 Wagenknecht, Edward. *Nathaniel Hawthorne: The Man, His Tales and Romances* (10–12). 1989, Continuum $19.95 (0-8264-0409-X). For better students, the life and a critical analysis of the work of Hawthorne. (Rev: BL 12/15/88) [921]

HELLMAN, LILLIAN

6256 Hellman, Lillian. *Three* (10–12). Illus. 1979, Little $19.95 (0-316-35514-3); paper $14.95 (0-316-35511-9). This trio of personal memoirs includes *An Unfinished Woman* (1969), *Pentimento* (1973), and *Scoundrel Time* (1976). [921]

6257 Towns, Saundra. *Lillian Hellman* (9–12). Illus. 1989, Chelsea House $16.95 (1-55546-657-5). Hellman's life is interesting not only because of her literary output but also because of her stand against blacklisting. (Rev: BL 1/15/90; BR 3–4/90; SLJ 3/90; VOYA 2/90) [921]

HEMINGWAY, ERNEST

6258 Baker, Carlos. *Ernest Hemingway: A Life Story* (10–12). Illus. 1969, Macmillan $47.50 (0-684-14740-8); paper $12.95 (0-02-001690-5). From thousands of letters and many interviews Baker has done an outstanding job of re-creating the life of Hemingway. [921]

6259 Burgess, Anthony. *Ernest Hemingway and His World* (9–12). Illus. 1978, Macmillan $10.95 (0-684-18504-0). A pictorial biography of the controversial American writer, father of the macho image. [921]

6260 Ferrell, Keith. *Ernest Hemingway: The Search for Courage* (10–12). 1984, Evans $10.95 (0-87131-431-2). A well-rounded biography of Hemingway the man, with a concluding assessment of his works. [921]

6261 Hemingway, Ernest. *Ernest Hemingway: Selected Letters, 1917–1961* (10–12). 1981, Macmillan paper $12.95 (0-684-17658-0). These 600 letters cover Hemingway's life from his youth to the eve of his suicide in 1961. [921]

6262 Hemingway, Ernest. *A Moveable Feast* (10–12). Illus. 1964, Macmillan $22.50 (0-684-17340-9); paper $4.50 (0-684-17996-2). A collection of sketches published after Hemingway's death about his life in Paris during the 1920s. [921]

6263 McDowell, Nicholas. *Hemingway* (7–12). Illus. 1989, Rourke $12.95 (0-86592-298-5). The complex life and work of Hemingway are examined with special attention paid to an analysis of his novels and stories. (Rev: BL 3/1/89) [921]

HENTOFF, NAT

6264 Hentoff, Nat. *Boston Boy* (9–12). 1986, Faber paper $7.95 (0-571-12951-X). The story of Hentoff's childhood and youth growing up in a poor Jewish neighborhood in Boston. [921]

HIMES, CHESTER

6265 Wilson, M. L. *Chester Himes* (9–12). Illus. 1988, Chelsea House $16.95 (1-55546-591-9). A biography of the black writer who began his writing career in prison. (Rev: BL 6/1/88; SLJ 5/88) [921]

HUGHES, LANGSTON

6266 Berry, Faith. *Langston Hughes: Before and beyond Harlem* (10–12). 1983, Chicago Review Pr. paper $12.95 (0-88208-157-8). This biography concentrates on the Harlem Renaissance and the writer's political activities during the 1930s. [921]

6267 Hughes, Langston. *The Big Sea: An Autobiography* (10–12). 1940, Thunders Mouth Pr. paper $11.95 (0-938410-33-4). The autobiography of the black poet and story writer up to the age of 27. Continued in *I Wonder as I Wander* (1956). [921]

6268 Rampersad, Arnold. *The Life of Langston Hughes, Volume II, 1941–1967: I Dream a World* (10–12). Illus. 1988, Oxford Univ. Pr. $22.95 (0-19-504519-X). The second and final volume of this definitive biography of one of America's finest black writers. Volume One appeared in 1986. (Rev: BL 8/88) [921]

HURSTON, ZORA NEALE

6269 Hurston, Zora Neale. *Dust Tracks on a Road* (10–12). 1984, Univ. of Illinois Pr. paper $8.95 (0-252-01047-7). The autobiography of the black anthropologist and writer of folk songs. [921]

6270 Witcover, Paul. *Zora Neale Hurston* (9–12). Illus. 1990, Chelsea House LB $17.95 (0-7910-1129-1). A biography of this black American who was a folklorist, author, and anthropologist during the Harlem renaissance. (Rev: BL 12/15/90) [921]

JAMES, WILL

6271 Bramlett, Jim. *Ride for the High Points: The Real Story of Will James* (10–12). Illus. 1987, Mountain $26.95 (0-87842-214-5). A candid look at the life of the western writer known chiefly for *Smoky the Cowhorse,* an early Newbery Award winner. (Rev: BL 3/1/88) [921]

JOHNSON, JAMES WELDON

6272 Tolbert-Rouchaleau, Jane. *James Weldon Johnson* (9–12). Illus. 1988, Chelsea House $16.95 (1-55546-596-X). The biography of the black writer who was also involved with the NAACP and the struggle for equality. (Rev: BL 6/1/88) [921]

JOHNSON, SAMUEL

6273 Boswell, James. *The Life of Samuel Johnson* (10–12). Oxford Univ. Pr. paper $14.95 (0-19-281537-7). This minute account of the life of the great eighteenth-century thinker and writer is probably the most famous biography in the English language. [921]

KAFKA, FRANZ

6274 Citati, Pietro. *Kafka* (10–12). 1990, Knopf $22.95 (0-394-56840-0). By examining the complexities of Kafka's inner thoughts, the author is able to analyze his writings. (Rev: BL 1/15/90) [921]

KEROUAC, JACK

6275 Charters, Ann. *Kerouac* (10–12). 1987, St. Martin's paper $12.95 (0-312-00617-9). The story of the brief life of Kerouac, who for a time became the spokesman of the beat generation. [921]

KERR, M. E.

6276 Kerr, M. E. *Me Me Me Me Me: Not a Novel* (7–12). 1983, Harper LB $12.89 (0-06-023193-9). A candid often hilarious account of the youth of this popular young adult novelist. [921]

KLEIN, NORMA

6277 Phy, Allene Stuart. *Presenting Norma Klein* (9–12). Illus. 1988, Twayne $15.95 (0-8057-8205-2). A biography and critical analysis of the writer, Norma Klein, who broke many taboos regarding young adult literature. (Rev: SLJ 10/88) [921]

LANE, ROSE WILDER

6278 Lane, Rose Wilder, and Roger Lea MacBride. *Rose Wilder Lane: Her Story* (9–12). 1980, Scarborough paper $7.95 (0-8128-6077-2). This is the story of the daughter of Laura Ingalls Wilder, who was also a writer as well as an ardent feminist. [921]

L'ENGLE, MADELEINE

6279 L'Engle, Madeleine. *Two-Park Invention: The Story of a Marriage* (10–12). 1988, Farrar $18.95 (0-374-28020-7). The story of the famous author's 40-year marriage to actor Hugh Franklin. (Rev: BL 9–10/89; SLJ 4/89) [921]

LEWIS, CLIVE S.

6280 Griffin, William. *Clive Staples Lewis: A Dramatic Life* (10–12). Illus. 1986, Harper $24.95 (0-06-250352-9); paper $14.95 (0-06-250353-7). A detailed scholarly biography of the Narnia creator and his life-long struggle with his religious faith. (Rev: SLJ 2/87) [921]

6281 Sibley, Brian. *C.S. Lewis: Through the Shadowlands* (10–12). Illus. 1986, Revell paper $10.95 (0-8007-1509-8). A biography of Lewis that concentrates on his relationship and marriage to Joy Davidman. (Rev: SLJ 3/87) [921]

LINDBERGH, ANNE MORROW

6282 Lindbergh, Anne Morrow. *War within and Without: Diaries and Letters of Anne Morrow Lindbergh, 1939–1944* (10–12). Illus. 1980, Harcourt $14.95 (0-15-194661-2). This is the final autobiographical collection of diary entries and letters that began with *Bring Me a Unicorn* (1972), *Hour of Gold, Hour of Lead* (1973), *Locked Rooms and Open Doors* (1974), and *The Flower Nettle* (1975). [921]

LIPPMANN, WALTER

6283 Steel, Ronald. *Walter Lippmann and the American Century* (10–12). Illus. 1980, Random paper $15.95 (0-394-74731-3). The biography of the noted journalist who knew every president from Wilson to Johnson. [921]

LONDON, JACK

6284 Perry, John. *Jack London: An American Myth* (10–12). 1981, Nelson-Hall $25.95 (0-88229-378-8); paper $14.95 (0-88229-794-5). An unflattering but intriguing portrait of this American writer and adventurer. [921]

LOWELL, JAMES RUSSELL

6285 Wagenknecht, Edward. *James Russell Lowell* (10–12). 1971, Oxford Univ. Pr $19.95 (0-19-501376-X). A biography that gives details of both the life and the complex personality of this American poet. [921]

MCCARTHY, MARY

6286 McCarthy, Mary. *How I Grew* (10–12). Illus. 1987, Harcourt $18.95 (0-15-142193-5); paper $8.95 (0-15-642185-2). In this autobiography, an unconventional author describes her unconventional youth. (Rev: SLJ 9/87) [921]

MAY, ANTOINETTE

6287 May, Antoinette. *Witness to War: A Biography of Marguerite Higgins* (10–12). 1985, Penguin paper $6.95 (0-14-007597-6). The autobiography of the foreign correspondent who covered world conflicts from World War II through the Vietnam War. [921]

MEHTA, VED

6288 Mehta, Ved. *Sound-Shadows of the New World* (10–12). Illus. 1986, Norton $17.95 (0-393-02225-0). This is the fifth autobiographical volume by the blind writer from India. He is 15, in Arkansas, and the only foreign student in a school for the blind. Preceded by *The Ledge between the Streams* (1984). (Rev: BL 1/1/86; SLJ 9/86) [921]

6289 Mehta, Ved. *The Stolen Light* (10–12). 1989, Norton $19.95 (0-393-02632-9). This is the sixth autobiographical book by the blind writer who was born in India and, in this volume, comes to California to study. (Rev: BL 3/1/89) [921]

MILLER, ARTHUR

6290 Glassman, Bruce. *Arthur Miller* (7–12). Illus. 1990, Silver Burdett LB $17.98 (0-382-09904-4). A biography for young readers of this prize-winning playwright who has been concerned with many social and political issues. (Rev: BL 9/15/90) [921]

NOLAN, CHRISTOPHER

6291 Nolan, Christopher. *Under the Eye of the Clock: The Life Story of Christopher Nolan* (9–12). 1988, St. Martin's $16.95 (0-312-01266-7). This is the autobiography told in the third person of a mute Irish boy who has become a famous poet. (Rev: SLJ 11/88) [921]

O'NEILL, EUGENE

6292 Gelb, Arthur, and Barbara Gelb. *O'Neill* (10–12). Illus. 1974, Harper paper $15.95 (0-06-090761-4). A lengthy, exhaustive study of O'Neill's life and its relation to his plays. [921]

ORWELL, GEORGE

6293 Ferrell, Keith. *George Orwell: The Political Pen* (8–12). 1985, Evans $11.95 (0-87131-444-4). The rebellious life of the author who gave us *Animal Farm* and *1984*. (Rev: BL 2/1/85; SLJ 8/85) [921]

PARKS, GORDON

6294 Parks, Gordon. *A Choice of Weapons* (10–12). 1966, Minnesota Historical Soc. paper $8.95 (0-87351-202-2). An autobiography of the photographer and novelist who fought bigotry and prejudice throughout his entire career. [921]

6295 Parks, Gordon. *Voices in the Mirror: An Autobiography* (10–12). Illus. 1990, Doubleday $22.95 (0-385-26699-5). From the pen of this well-known writer and photographer comes an autobiography of growing up poor and black in twentieth-century America. (Rev: BL 11/1/90) [921]

PLATH, SYLVIA

6296 Plath, Sylvia. *The Journals of Sylvia Plath* (10–12). Illus. 1987, Ballantine paper $4.95 (0-345-35168-1). These edited journals cover the poet's college years, her marriage, and her preparations for relocating to England with her husband in 1959. [921]

POHL, FREDERIK

6297 Pohl, Frederik. *The Way the Future Was: A Memoir* (10–12). 1979, Ballantine paper $1.95 (0-345-26059-7). The award-winning author and editor Pohl traces his lifelong involvement with science fiction. [921]

RATHER, DAN

6298 Rather, Dan. *The Camera Never Blinks: Adventures of a TV Journalist* (10–12). 1987, Ballantine paper $3.95 (0-345-35363-3). This TV journalist reviews his career and gives insights into such historical events as the civil rights movement, Kennedy's assassination, and the Vietnam War. [921]

SALINGER, J. D.

6299 French, Warren. *J. D. Salinger, Revisited* (10–12). 1988, Twayne LB $16.95 (0-8057-7522-6). An interesting, accessible introduction to this writer's life and work. (Rev: BL 10/15/88) [921]

6300 Hamilton, Ian. *J. D. Salinger: A Writing Life* (10–12). 1986, Random $17.95 (0-394-53468-9). The life of this writer until he disappeared from public life in 1965. (Rev: BL 8/86) [921]

SANDBURG, CARL

6301 Sandburg, Carl. *Always the Young Strangers* (10–12). 1953, Harcourt $12.95 (0-15-105459-2). This autobiography of the formative years of the great Swedish-American poet and biographer of Lincoln is continued in *Ever the Winds of Change* (1983). [921]

6302 Sandburg, Carl. *Prairie-Town Boy* (9–12). 1977, Harcourt paper $1.75 (0-15-673700-0). The autobiography of the poet's early years growing up in a Swedish family in the Midwest. [921]

SCHOENBRUN, DAVID

6303 Schoenbrun, David. *America Inside Out* (10–12). Illus. 1984, McGraw paper $4.95 (0-07-055477-3). The memoirs of this important journalist cover the years from World War II to the Reagan administration. [921]

SHAKESPEARE, WILLIAM

6304 Chute, Marchette. *Shakespeare of London* (9–12). 1987, Dutton paper $9.95 (0-525-48245-8). A readable biography of Shakespeare that also gives insight into each of his plays. [822.3]

6305 Levi, Peter. *The Life and Times of William Shakespeare* (10–12). Illus. 1989, Henry Holt $29.95 (0-8050-1199-4). A readable but scholarly biography that tries to answer some of the questions surrounding Shakespeare's life. (Rev: BL 10/1/89) [921]

6306 Rowse, A. L. *Shakespeare the Man* (10–12). Rev. ed. 1989, St. Martin's paper $13.95 (0-312-03425-3). An updated edition of the much-respected 1973 biography that tries to unravel many of the mysteries of Shakespeare's life. (Rev: BL 11/15/89) [921]

6307 Schoenbaum, S. *William Shakespeare: A Compact Documentary Life* (10–12). Illus. 1977, Oxford Univ. Pr. $22.50 (0-19-502211-4); paper $12.95 (0-19-502433-8). A concise, readable but scholarly account of the life of Shakespeare. [921]

SHELLEY, MARY

6308 Sunstein, Emily W. *Mary Shelley: Romance and Reality* (10–12). Illus. 1989, Little $24.95 (0-316-82246-9). For better readers, the biography of the creator of *Frankenstein*. (Rev: SLJ 1/90) [921]

SINGER, ISAAC BASHEVIS

6309 Kresh, Paul. *Isaac Bashevis Singer: The Story of a Storyteller* (7–12). Illus. 1984, Lodestar $13.95 (0-525-67156-0). The story of the Yiddish writer from his beginnings in Poland to recognition when he came to the United States. [921]

SOLZHENITSYN, ALEKSANDR

6310 Scammell, Michael. *Solzhenitsyn* (10–12). Illus. 1984, Norton $29.95 (0-393-01802-4); paper $14.95 (0-393-30378-0). This biography covers the author's life from his youth and eventual expulsion from the Soviet Union to his resettlement in Vermont. [921]

6311 Solzhenitsyn, Aleksandr. *The Oak and the Calf: Sketches of Literary Life in the Soviet Union* (10–12). 1987, Harper paper $9.95 (0-06-090869-6). This fragment about the author's life describes the repression of ideas in the Soviet Union during the 1960s. [921]

SOTO, GARY

6312 Soto, Gary. *Living Up the Street: Narrative Recollections* (10–12). 1985, Strawberry Hill paper $7.95 (0-89407-064-9). The author, known mainly for his poetry, tells about growing up a Mexican American in Fresno, California. (Rev: BL 8/85) [921]

6313 Soto, Gary. *Small Faces* (10–12). 1986, Arte Publico paper $8.00 (0-934770-49-2). The Mexican American writer is now an adult and ready for marriage and parenthood in this second installment of the autobiography begun in *Living Up the Street* (1985). (Rev: BL 7/86) [921]

6314 Soto, Gary. *A Summer Life* (10–12). 1990, Univ. Pr. of New England $16.95 (0-87451-523-8). In this collection of autobiographical essays, the poet tells about growing up Chicano in the San Joaquin Valley of California. (Rev: BL 9/1/90) [921]

STEFFENS, LINCOLN

6315 Stinson, Robert. *Lincoln Steffens* (10–12). 1979, Ungar $18.95 (0-8044-2829-8). A brief biography of this journalist who fought corruption in government and championed many reform causes. [921]

STEIN, GERTRUDE

6316 Stein, Gertrude. *The Autobiography of Alice B. Toklas* (10–12). 1990, Random paper $6.95 (0-679-72463-X). The world of Gertrude

Stein and her companion involved such luminaries as Picasso, Hemingway, and Matisse. [921]

STEVENSON, ROBERT LOUIS

6317 Calder, Jenni. *Robert Louis Stevenson: A Life Study* (10–12). Illus. 1980, Oxford Univ. Pr. $27.50 (0-19-520210-4). A portrait of this appealing author, his travels and his varied works. [921]

THURBER, JAMES

6318 Thurber, James. *My Life and Hard Times* (8–12). 1973, Harper paper $3.95 (0-06-080290-1). The famous American humorist tells about his youth in a midwestern town. [921]

TOLKIEN, J. R. R.

6319 Carpenter, Humphrey. *Tolkien* (10–12). Illus. 1977, Houghton paper $8.95 (0-395-48676-9). From a beginning in South Africa in 1892 to Tolkien's death in England in 1973, this is an enlightening biography of this important scholar and writer of fantasy. [921]

TWAIN, MARK

6320 Lauber, John. *The Making of Mark Twain* (10–12). Illus. 1988, Farrar paper $9.95 (0-374-52130-1). This account traces the childhood, youth, and young manhood of Mark Twain using many quotes from the author's own works. (Rev: BL 11/15/85) [921]

6321 Meltzer, Milton. *Mark Twain: A Writer's Life* (7–12). Illus. 1985, Watts $12.90 (0-531-10072-3). A fine portrait of this writer that uses many quotes from Twain himself to reveal specific points like his genius for comedy. (Rev: BL 10/1/85; SLJ 12/85) [921]

6322 Neider, Charles, ed. *The Autobiography of Mark Twain* (10–12). Illus. 1990, Harper paper $8.95 (0-06-092025-4). This is a well-edited version of the mass of material left by Twain to serve as his autobiography. [921]

6323 Neider, Charles, ed. *The Selected Letters of Mark Twain* (10–12). 1982, Harper $16.95 (0-06-014946-9). These letters cover Mark Twain's life from age 18 to four months before his death at 74. [921]

VONNEGUT, KURT

6324 Vonnegut, Kurt. *Palm Sunday: An Autobiographical Collage* (10–12). 1984, Dell paper $4.95 (0-440-36906-1). Through letters, speeches, reviews, and other documents, the author traces his career. [921]

WELTY, EUDORA

6325 Welty, Eudora. *One Writer's Beginnings* (10–12). Illus. 1984, Harvard Univ. Pr. $10.00 (0-674-63925-1); Warner paper $3.95 (0-446-34301-3). A reprint of a series of lectures in which the author tells about her childhood and the many influences that shaped her life. [921]

WHEATLEY, PHYLLIS

6326 Jensen, Marilyn. *Phyllis Wheatley* (9–12). 1987, Sayre $16.95 (0-87460-326-9). The story of a slave in Boston who became the first black poet in Colonial America and gained sufficient fame to be invited to England to meet the king. (Rev: BR 11–12/87; SLJ 12/87) [921]

WHITMAN, WALT

6327 Zweig, Paul. *Walt Whitman* (10–12). 1984, Basic Books $18.95 (0-465-09059-1); paper $8.95 (0-317-20657-2). A biography and an analysis of Whitman are given through key incidents in the poet's life. [921]

WILDER, LAURA INGALLS

6328 Zochert, Donald. *Laura: The Life of Laura Ingalls Wilder* (9–12). 1976, Avon paper $4.50 (0-380-01636-2). An honest, sympathetic biography of and tribute to the author of the Little House books. [921]

WOLFF, TOBIAS

6329 Wolff, Tobias. *This Boy's Life: A Memoir* (10–12). 1989, Atlantic Monthly $18.95 (0-87113-248-6). This is the story of the troubled youth of this writer who loved his mother and hated his stepfather. (Rev: BL 3/15/89; VOYA 2/90) [921]

WOOLF, VIRGINIA

6330 Lehmann, John. *Virginia Woolf and Her World* (10–12). 1987, Harcourt paper $4.95 (0-15-693581-3). A biography of the noted English writer by one of her friends. [921]

WRIGHT, RICHARD

6331 Gayle, Addison. *Richard Wright: Ordeal of a Native Son* (10–12). 1980, Peter Smith $20.00 (0-8446-6000-0). A biography of the black author who died in 1960. [921]

6332 Wright, Richard. *Black Boy: A Record of Childhood and Youth* (8–12). 1969, Harper $19.45 (0-06-014761-X). The tortured boyhood of the great black writer growing up in the South. This autobiography is continued in *American Hunger* (1977). [921]

ZINDEL, PAUL

6333 Forman, Jack Jacob. *Presenting Paul Zindel* (9–12). Illus. 1988, Twayne $16.95 (0-8057-8206-0). An analysis of both the life and works of this popular author whose trailblazing books have influenced the course of young adult literature. (Rev: SLJ 9/88; VOYA 10/88) [921]

Composers

BACH, JOHANN SEBASTIAN

6334 Arnold, Denis. *Bach* (10–12). 1984, Oxford Univ. Pr. paper $4.95 (0-19-287554-X). A biography of the great master of German baroque music and of the influence he had on the music to come. [921]

6335 Boyd, Malcolm. *Bach* (10–12). Illus. 1983, Dent $17.95 (0-460-04466-4); Random paper $9.95 (0-394-75277-5). This biography gives an extensive introduction and critique to Bach's music. [921]

6336 Felix, Warner. *Johann Sebastian Bach* (10–12). Illus. 1985, Norton $25.00 (0-393-02232-3). This 3-part volume discusses the composer's life, compositions, and his influence on the music of later centuries. [921]

BERLIOZ, HECTOR

6337 Macdonald, Hugh. *Berlioz* (10–12). Illus. 1982, Dent $17.95 (0-460-03156-2). The stormy times of this French composer are brought to life with an analysis of his music. [921]

BERNSTEIN, LEONARD

6338 Gradenwitz, Peter. *Leonard Bernstein* (10–12). Illus. 1987, Berg $28.80 (0-85496-510-6). An account that concentrates on the composer-conductor's professional life. (Rev: BL 8/87) [921]

BRITTEN, BENJAMIN

6339 Kennedy, Michael. *Britten* (10–12). Illus. 1981, Dent $17.95 (0-460-03175-9). This biography of the contemporary British composer also includes separate sections on each of his most important works. [921]

BRUCKNER, ANTON

6340 Watson, Derek. *Bruckner* (10–12). Illus. 1976, Dent $17.95 (0-460-03144-9). This biography covers the life, the struggle, triumphs, and failures of this Austrian composer's life. [921]

COPLAND, AARON

6341 Copland, Aaron, and Vivian Perlis. *Copland: 1900 through 1942* (10–12). Illus. 1984, St. Martin's paper $12.95 (0-312-01149-0). This first volume in the American composer's autobiography covers study in Paris and his early successes. Followed by *Copland since 1943* (1990). [921]

DVORAK, ANTONIN

6342 Clapham, John. *Dvorak* (10–12). Illus. 1986, Riverrun Pr. $24.95 (0-7145-4145-1). A biography of this famous Czech nationalistic composer with an account of his stay in America. [921]

ELLINGTON, DUKE

6343 Collier, James Lincoln. *Duke Ellington* (10–12). Illus. 1987, Oxford Univ. Pr. $19.95 (0-19-503770-7). An excellent biography of the bandleader and composer with excellent background material included. (Rev: BL 10/15/87) [921]

GERSHWIN, GEORGE

6344 Kendall, Alan. *George Gershwin: A Biography* (9–12). Illus. 1987, Universe $19.95 (0-87663-663-6). An accessible biography that re-creates the life of the composer and the major conflicts that dominated it. (Rev: BL 11/15/87) [921]

GRIEG, EDVARD

6345 Horton, John. *Grieg* (10–12). Illus. 1976, Dent $17.95 (0-460-03135-X). An objective biography that balances coverage on the composer's life with an analysis of his music and its importance. [921]

HANDEL, GEORGE FRIDERIC

6346 Keates, Jonathan. *Handel: The Man and His Music* (10–12). Illus. 1985, St. Martin's $19.95 (0-312-35846-6). The story of this German composer emphasizes his successful stay in England where he made his final home. [921]

6347 Young, Percy M. *Handel* (10–12). Rev. ed. Illus. 1975, Dent $17.95 (0-460-03161-9). A biography of this prolific composer who worked successfully in a variety of musical forms. [921]

HAYDN, JOSEPH

6348 Hughes, Rosemary. *Haydn* (10–12). Rev. ed. Illus. 1974, Dent $17.95 (0-460-03160-0). An account of "Papa" Haydn's long life, his music, and the tremendous influence he had on others. [921]

MAHLER, GUSTAV

6349 Kennedy, Michael. *Mahler* (10–12). 1991, Schirmer paper $13.95 (0-02-871367-2). A fine introduction to the early twentieth-century Austrian conductor and composer. [921]

MONTEVERDI, CLAUDIO

6350 Arnold, Denis. *Monteverdi* (10–12). Rev. ed. Illus. 1975, Dent $17.95 (0-460-03155-4); paper $7.95 (0-8226-0716-6). A biography that also introduces the entire field of early Italian music. [921]

MOZART, WOLFGANG AMADEUS

6351 Blom, Eric. *Mozart* (10–12). Rev. ed. Illus. 1974, Littlefield Adams paper $7.95 (0-8226-0700-X). A candid retelling of the events in Mozart's life and an assessment of his music. [921]

6352 Davenport, Marcia. *Mozart* (10–12). Illus. 1956, Macmillan $20.00 (0-684-14504-9); Avon paper $4.95 (0-380-45534-X). A sympathetic but frank study of this composer's life first published in 1932. [921]

SCHUMANN, ROBERT

6353 Chissell, Joan. *Schumann* (10–12). Rev. ed. Illus. 1967, Dent $17.95 (0-460-03170-8). This account includes a detailed examination of this German composer's work. [921]

VAUGHAN WILLIAMS, RALPH

6354 Day, James. *Vaughan Williams* (10–12). Illus. 1975, Littlefield Adams paper $7.95 (0-8226-0722-0). A brief overview of this British composer's life. [921]

WEBBER, ANDREW LLOYD

6355 Walsh, Michael. *Andrew Lloyd Webber* (9–12). Illus. 1989, Abrams $39.95 (0-8109-1275-9). An oversized volume that deals with the British musical phenomenon and composer of the music

for such hits as *Cats* and *Phantom of the Opera*. (Rev: BL 1/1/90) [921]

Entertainers and Performers

6356 Norman, Philip. *Shout! The Beatles in Their Generation* (9–12). 1983, Warner paper $4.95 (0-446-32255-5). A candid, honest portrayal of the rock group from Liverpool and of each of its 4 members. [920]

ALLEN, WOODY

6357 Brode, Douglas. *Woody Allen* (9–12). Illus. 1987, Carol paper $14.95 (0-8065-1067-6). Biographical details on this writer and comedian are given plus critical comment on his films through the mid-1980s. [921]

ARMSTRONG, LOUIS

6358 Collier, James Lincoln. *Louis Armstrong: An American Genius* (10–12). Illus. 1983, Oxford Univ. Pr. $24.95 (0-19-503377-9); paper $9.95 (0-19-503727-8). A thoroughly researched biography of this jazz great who was also a popular entertainer. [921]

6359 Pinfold, Mike. *Louis Armstrong: His Life & Times* (9–12). Illus. 1988, Universe $17.50 (0-87663-667-9); paper $10.95 (0-87663-527-3). A biography of this jazz great that stresses the social conditions that helped produce his music. (Rev: SLJ 9/88) [921]

BAEZ, JOAN

6360 Baez, Joan. *And a Voice to Sing With: A Memoir* (10–12). 1988, NAL paper $8.95 (0-452-26094-9). The biography of the folksinger associated with so many causes during the 1960s. (Rev: SLJ 8/87) [921]

BAILEY, PEARL

6361 Bailey, Pearl. *Between You and Me: A Heartfelt Memoir on Learning, Loving, and Living* (10–12). 1989, Doubleday $17.95 (0-385-26202-7). In this, the fifth book, this famous entertainer tells about her college life at Georgetown University and her graduation at age 67. (Rev: VOYA 4/90) [921]

BALANCHINE, GEORGE

6362 Taper, Bernard. *Balanchine* (10–12). Illus. 1984, Times Books $19.95 (0-8129-1136-9); Univ. of California Pr. paper $12.95 (0-520-06059-8). This updated edition of the biography that originally appeared in 1963 now includes the entire life of this master choreographer and director of the New York City Ballet Company. [921]

BARNUM, P. T.

6363 Barnum, P. T. *Barnum's Own Story* (7–12). Illus. 1962, Peter Smith $18.75 (0-8446-4001-8). The autobiography of the showman who could fool people like no one else. [921]

6364 Barnum, P. T. *Struggles and Triumphs* (10–12). 1981, Penguin paper $6.95 (0-14-0394004-9). An abridgment of the autobiography of one of America's first and greatest showmen. [921]

6365 Wallace, Irving. *The Fabulous Showman: The Lives and Times of P. T. Barnum* (10–12). 1962, NAL paper $2.95 (0-451-11385-3). A biography of a pioneer showman and circus founder. [921]

BARR, ROSEANNE

6366 Barr, Roseanne. *Roseanne: My Life as a Woman* (10–12). Illus. 1989, Harper $17.95 (0-06-015957-X). Frank language is often used in this very readable biography that concentrates on the childhood and teen years of Roseanne Barr. (Rev: BL 8/89) [921]

BARRYMORE, JOHN

6367 Fowler, Gene. *Good Night, Sweet Prince: The Life and Times of John Barrymore* (10–12). 1978, Buccaneer $24.95 (0-89966-095-9). A biography of the flamboyant but incredibly talented member of the Barrymore clan. [921]

BASIE, COUNT

6368 Basie, Count. *Good Morning Blues* (10–12). Illus. 1985, Donald I. Fine paper $10.95 (0-917657-89-6). The candid, earthy autobiography of this jazz great that was published posthumously. [921]

BEATLES

6369 DeWitt, Howard A. *The Beatles: Untold Tales* (9–12). Illus. 1985, Horizon paper $12.95 (0-938840-03-7). Based on over 50 interviews, this is a fine behind-the-scenes look at the lads from Liverpool. (Rev: SLJ 1/86) [921]

BELUSHI, JOHN

6370 Woodward, Bob. *Wired* (10–12). 1986, Pocket paper $4.95 (0-671-64077-1). For mature readers, the life of John Belushi and how it was ruined by sex and drugs. [921]

BENTLEY, TONI

6371 Bentley, Toni. *Winter Season* (10–12). 1984, Random paper $5.95 (0-394-72398-8). The biography of a young dancer that focuses on a season with the New York City Ballet. [921]

BERGEN, CANDICE

6372 Bergen, Candice. *Knock Wood* (10–12). 1985, Ballantine paper $4.95 (0-345-32137-5). For mature readers, this is the candid autobiography of the talented daughter of Edgar Bergen. [921]

BERNHARDT, SARAH

6373 Skinner, Cornelia. *Madame Sarah* (10–12). 1988, Paragon paper $9.95 (1-55778-107-9). The story of Sarah Bernhardt, the great French actress who captured the imagination of the whole theatrical world. [921]

BLAKE, EUBIE

6374 Rose, Al. *Eubie Blake* (10–12). Illus. 1979, Schirmer Bks. $13.95 (0-02-872170-5); paper $8.95 (0-02-872160-8). The story of the black composer and entertainer whose life encompassed almost a century. [921]

BOWIE, DAVID

6375 Matthew-Walker, Robert. *David Bowie: Theater of Music* (9–12). 1986, Kensal Pr. $14.00 (0-946041-34-2). A biography that concentrates on Bowie's theatrical style and the musical materials that he uses. (Rev: SLJ 8/87) [921]

BROWN, JAMES

6376 Brown, James, and Bruce Tucker. *James Brown: The Godfather of Soul* (9–12). Illus. 1990, Consortium paper $13.95 (0-938410-0). The man who influenced the soul music revolution tells about his own career and troubled personal life. (Rev: BL 6/15/90) [921]

BUFFALO BILL

6377 Yost, Nellie Snyder. *Buffalo Bill: His Family, Friends, Fame, Failures and Fortunes* (10–12). Illus. 1979, Swallow Pr. $15.00 (0-8040-

0766-7). This is a well-researched biography of the man who was at various times a wilderness scout, rancher, and lastly a showman. [921]

BURNETT, CAROL

6378 Burnett, Carol. *One More Time* (9–12). Illus. 1987, Avon paper $4.95 (0-380-70449-8). Written in letter form to her daughters, the famous performer talks about her life and rise to fame. (Rev: BR 3–4/87; SLJ 2/87) [921]

CASH, JUNE CARTER

6379 Cash, June Carter. *From the Heart* (9–12). Illus. 1987, Prentice $12.95 (0-13-530767-8). An autobiography that goes backstage in the country music scene and reveals a strength of character sustained through religious beliefs. (Rev: BL 5/1/87; BR 11–12/87) [921]

CLAPTON, ERIC

6380 Coleman, Ray. *Clapton!* (9–12). 1986, Warner paper $9.95 (0-446-38049-0). A biography of the famous rock guitarist from late adolescence to the mid-1980s. (Rev: SLJ 1/87) [921]

COLLINS, JUDY

6381 Collins, Judy. *Trust Your Heart: An Autobiography* (10–12). Illus. 1987, Houghton $18.95 (0-395-41285-4); Fawcett paper $4.95 (0-449-21662-4). A touching and candid autobiography that does not spare readers the seamy details of this star's interesting life. (Rev: SLJ 8/88) [921]

DAVIS, SAMMY

6382 Davis, Sammy, et al. *Why Me?* (9–12). Illus. 1989, Farrar $18.95 (0-374-28997-2). Autobiographical writing that emphasizes this entertainer's struggles with such enemies as bigots and alcohol. (Rev: BL 4/1/89) [921]

DE MILLE, AGNES

6383 De Mille, Agnes. *Dance to the Piper* (10–12). Illus. 1980, Da Capo LB $29.50 (0-306-79613-9). A backstage look at ballet life through the autobiography of this dancer and choreographer. Her story is continued in *And Promenade Home* (1980). [921]

DIAMOND, NEIL

6384 Wiseman, Rich. *Neil Diamond: Solitary Star* (10–12). Illus. 1987, Dodd $16.95 (0-396-08619-5). A lively account of the singer–

composer, his life, and his work. (Rev: BL 6/15/87) [921]

DUNCAN, ISADORA

6385 Kozodoy, Ruth. *Isadora Duncan* (9–12). Illus. 1987, Chelsea House $16.95 (1-55546-650-8). "The mother of modern dance" and her amazing and bizarre life and death are well portrayed. (Rev: BL 4/15/88) [921]

DYLAN, BOB

6386 Spitz, Bob. *Dylan: A Biography* (9–12). Illus. 1988, McGraw $17.95 (0-07-060330-8). The life of this reclusive artist who influenced a generation of performers and composers. (Rev: BL 11/15/88) [921]

ELLINGTON, DUKE

6387 Dance, Stanley. *The World of Duke Ellington* (10–12). Illus. 1970, Da Capo paper $10.95 (0-306-80136-1). Based on a series of interviews this is a portrait of Duke Ellington, the people around him, and the world of jazz. [921]

6388 Ellington, Duke. *Music Is My Mistress* (10–12). Illus. 1973, Da Capo paper $13.95 (0-306-80033-0). Written when Duke Ellington was 74, this is the story of the great composer and bandleader who grew up in Washington, D.C., and later became an international star. [921]

FARRELL, SUZANNE

6389 Farrell, Suzanne, and Toni Bentley. *Holding on to the Air: An Autobiography* (10–12). 1990, Summit $19.95 (0-671-68222-9). The autobiography of one of Balanchine's favorite dancers and a star of the New York City Ballet company. (Rev: BL 9/1/90) [921]

FIELDS, W. C.

6390 Fields, Ronald J. *W. C. Fields: A Life in Film* (9–12). Illus. 1984, St. Martin's paper $14.95 (0-312-85312-2). Illustrated with more than 300 photographs, this is a detailed account of W. C. Fields and his films. [921]

FONDA, JANE

6391 Davidson, Bill. *Jane Fonda: An Intimate Biography* (10–12). Illus. 1990, Dutton $18.95 (0-525-24888-9). A frank adult account of the life of this controversial actress that tells of her problems with bulimia and her radical activities. (Rev: BL 4/1/90) [921]

FRANKLIN, ARETHA

6392 Bego, Mark. *Aretha Franklin: The Queen of Soul* (9–12). Illus. 1989, St. Martin's $18.95 (0-312-02863-6). The life of the soul singer from the local Baptist church to superstardom. (Rev: BL 10/15/89) [921]

GILLESPIE, DIZZY

6393 McRae, Barry. *Dizzy Gillespie* (10–12). 1988, Universe $17.50 (0-87663-686-5). A profile of the great jazz trumpeter in words and over 70 photographs. (Rev: SLJ 5/89) [921]

GRAFFMAN, GARY

6394 Graffman, Gary. *I Really Should Be Practicing* (10–12). 1982, Avon paper $4.95 (-0-380-59873-6). The life of the concert pianist and the "pleasures and perils of playing the piano in public." [921]

GUTHRIE, WOODY

6395 Klein, Joe. *Woody Guthrie: A Life* (10–12). 1986, Ballantine paper $4.95 (0-345-33519-8). The basically tragic life of the famous folk singer and composer who spoke of and for the common man. [921]

HALEY, BILL

6396 Swenson, John. *Bill Haley: The Daddy of Rock and Roll* (10–12). Illus. 1983, Scarborough House $18.95 (0-8128-2909-3); paper $9.95 (0-8128-6177-9). The shocking story of the popular singer, his band the Comets, and his death as an alcoholic in 1981. [921]

HANFF, HELENE

6397 Hanff, Helene. *Underfoot in Show Business* (10–12). 1981, Penguin paper $4.95 (0-14-005868-0). A witty look at an unsuccessful attempt to break into the world of the theater. [921]

HAYES, HELEN

6398 Hayes, Helen, and Katherine Hatch. *My Life in Three Acts* (10–12). 1990, Harcourt $19.95 (0-15-163695-8). A lively account of the public and private life of this actress. (Rev: BL 1/1/90) [921]

HENDRIX, JIMI

6399 Hopkins, Jerry. *Hit and Run: The Jimi Hendrix Story* (9–12). Illus. 1983, Perigee Bks.

paper $8.95 (0-399-50661-6). A look at the short but spectacular career of this rock star. [921]

HEPBURN, KATHARINE

6400 Andersen, Christopher. *Young Kate* (9–12). Illus. 1988, Henry Holt $18.45 (0-8050-0709-1). The childhood of one of America's best and most feisty actresses, Katharine Hepburn. (Rev: BL 8/88; SLJ 11/88; VOYA 2/89) [921]

6401 Higham, Charles. *Kate: The Life of Katharine Hepburn* (10–12). 1981, NAL paper $4.50 (0-451-15739-7). This is the authorized biography of the amazing star whose career spanned several generations. [921]

HOLIDAY, BILLIE

6402 Deveaux, Alexis. *Don't Explain: A Song of Billie Holiday* (10–12). Illus. 1980, Harper LB $12.89 (0-06-021630-1). An honest, moving account of the tragic but fulfilling career of Lady Day. [921]

6403 Holiday, Billie. *Lady Sings the Blues* (10–12). 1956, Penguin paper $6.95 (0-14-006762-0). A candid, often brutally frank, account of what it meant to be a black entertainer in America during the 1930s, 40s, and 50s. [921]

6404 Kliment, Bud. *Billie Holiday* (8–12). Illus. 1990, Chelsea House $17.95 (1-55546-592-7). A stirring biography of one of the great ladies of song whose life ended tragically. (Rev: BL 2/15/90; SLJ 5/90; VOYA 5–6/90) [921]

6405 White, John. *Billie Holiday: Her Life & Times* (9–12). Illus. 1988, Universe $17.50 (0-87663-668-7); paper $10.95 (0-87663-528-1). The tragic life of this great blues singer is re-created as well as a picture of the times in which she lived. (Rev: SLJ 9/88) [921]

HOLLY, BUDDY

6406 Goldrosen, John, and John Beecher. *Remembering Buddy: The Definitive Biography of Buddy Holly* (9–12). Illus. 1987, Penguin paper $12.95 (0-14-010363-5). An illustrated biography of the rock and roll hero who died at age 22. (Rev: BL 10/1/87; BR 3–4/88) [921]

HORNE, LENA

6407 Haskins, James. *Lena: A Personal and Professional Biography of Lena Horne* (9–12). Illus. 1984, Scarborough House $16.95 (0-8128-2853-4); paper $3.50 (0-8128-8114-1). A thorough account of the career of this black entertainer who first came into prominence during the 1940s. [921]

HOUDINI, HARRY

6408 FitzSimons, Raymond. *Death and the Magician: The Mystery of Houdini* (9–12). Illus. 1980, Macmillan paper $7.95 (0-689-70694-4). A biography of this master showman and magician. [921]

JACKSON, MICHAEL

6409 George, Nelson. *The Michael Jackson Story* (9–12). 1987, Dell paper $3.50 (0-440-15593-2). This account traces the career of this rock phenomenon from age 5 to after the "Thriller" album. [921]

6410 Jackson, Michael. *Moonwalk* (8–12). Illus. 1988, Doubleday $15.95 (0-385-24763-X). Autobiographical writings by the rock idol accompanied by many photographs. (Rev: BL 5/15/88) [921]

6411 Marsh, Dave. *Trapped: Michael Jackson and the Crossover Dream* (10–12). 1985, Bantam paper $9.95 (0-553-34241-X). A well-written biography of Michael Jackson, his rise to stardom, and the meaning behind his success. (Rev: VOYA 8–10/86) [921]

KIRKLAND, GELSEY

6412 Kirkland, Gelsey, and Greg Lawrence. *The Shape of Love* (10–12). 1990, Doubleday $19.95 (0-385-24918-7). The story of how this dancer pieced together a failing career marred by drug abuse and made a comeback. (Rev: BL 9/1/90) [921]

KURALT, CHARLES

6413 Kuralt, Charles. *A Life on the Road* (10–12). 1990, Putnam $19.95 (0-399-13488-3). A biography of the newsman and journalist whose CBS program that explores life around the United States has been a Sunday morning favorite. (Rev: BL 9/15/90) [921]

LENNON, JOHN

6414 Baird, Julia. *John Lennon, My Brother* (9–12). Illus. 1988, Henry Holt $18.95 (0-8050-0793-8). A personalized account of the childhood and rise to stardom of John Lennon, written by his sister. (Rev: BR 3–4/89; VOYA 6/89) [921]

6415 Coleman, Ray. *Lennon* (10–12). Illus. 1985, McGraw paper $5.95 (0-07-011788-8). A lengthy, detailed biography of the rock star that

gives an interesting behind-the-scenes look at the Beatles. (Rev: BL 3/15/85) [921]

6416 Lennon, John. *Skywriting by Word of Mouth* (10–12). Illus. 1986, Harper $12.95 (0-06-015656-2). A collection of candid personal reflections by Lennon at the time he was leaving the Beatles and joining Yoko Ono. (Rev: SLJ 5/87) [921]

6417 Solt, Andrew, and Sam Egan. *Imagine: John Lennon* (9–12). 1988, Macmillan $39.95 (0-02-630910-6). A photographic tribute to John Lennon with quotes from himself and friends. (Rev: BL 9/1/88; BR 3–4/89) [921]

6418 Wiener, Jon. *Come Together: John Lennon in His Time* (9–12). 1990, Univ. of Illinois Pr. paper $13.95 (0-252-06131-4). This biography of John Lennon gives many insights into the 1960s and the important issues of that time. [921]

LYNN, LORETTA

6419 Lynn, Loretta. *Loretta Lynn: Coal Miner's Daughter* (9–12). 1976, Contemporary paper $7.95 (0-8092-5344-5). The story of the backwoods childhood of Loretta Lynn and her rise to country music stardom. [921]

MCCARTNEY, PAUL

6420 Salewicz, Chris. *McCartney: The Definitive Biography* (10–12). 1986, St. Martin's paper $4.50 (0-312-90451-7). A detailed life of the Beatle that ends in the mid-1980s. (Rev: BL 3/1/86) [921]

MACNEIL, ROBERT

6421 MacNeil, Robert. *Wordstruck: A Memoir* (10–12). Illus. 1989, Viking $18.95 (0-670-81871-2). The effects of words and reading on the TV personality as he was growing up. (Rev: BL 12/15/88) [921]

MAKEBA, MIRIAM

6422 Makeba, Miriam. *Makeba, My Story* (10–12). Illus. 1988, NAL $18.95 (0-453-00561-6). The inspiring story of the black South African singer, her efforts against apartheid, and of the country she still calls home. (Rev: BL 1/15/88; VOYA 2/89) [921]

MANDRELL, BARBARA

6423 Mandrell, Barbara, and George Vecsey. *Get to the Heart: My Story* (9–12). Illus. 1990, Bantam $19.95 (0-553-05799-5). The life and show business career of this star that focuses on the terrible car accident of 1984 and its aftermath. (Rev: BL 9/1/90) [921]

MARLEY, BOB

6424 Davis, Stephen. *Bob Marley* (10–12). Illus. 1985, Doubleday $9.95 (0-385-17956-1). A biography of a reggae star that tells a great deal about his homeland Jamaica. (Rev: BL 1/15/85) [921]

MELENDEZ, TONY

6425 Melendez, Tony, and Mel White. *A Gift of Hope: The Tony Melendez Story* (9–12). Illus. 1989, Harper $13.95 (0-06-065553-4). The autobiography of the famous guitarist who, born without arms, plays the instrument with his feet. (Rev: BL 9/15/89) [921]

OAKLEY, ANNIE

6426 Sayers, Isabelle S. *Annie Oakley and Buffalo Bill's Wild West* (9–12). Illus. 1981, Dover paper $5.95 (0-486-24120-3). Through a number of old photographs, the life of this sharp-shooter is re-created. [921]

OLIVIER, LAURENCE

6427 Olivier, Laurence. *On Acting* (10–12). Illus. 1986, Simon & Schuster $18.95 (0-671-55869-2); paper $9.95 (0-671-64562-5). An autobiography that deals with his life in the theater world and of the roles he portrayed. (Rev: SLJ 5/87) [921]

ORBISON, ROY

6428 Clayson, Alan. *Only the Lonely: Roy Orbison's Life and Legacy* (10–12). Illus. 1989, St. Martin's $17.95 (0-312-03961-1). A biography of the deceased rock star who was loved by all but who had a distressing personal life. (Rev: BL 11/15/89) [921]

POITIER, SIDNEY

6429 Poitier, Sidney. *This Life* (9–12). Illus. 1980, Ballantine paper $2.95 (0-345-29407-6). An honest, engrossing account of the actor's life through the late 1970s. [921]

PRESLEY, ELVIS

6430 Geller, Larry, et al. *If I Can Dream: Elvis' Own Story* (10–12). Illus. 1989, Simon & Schuster $19.95 (0-671-65922-7). An objective account of Elvis Presley's life written by a number of people, including his hairdresser. (Rev: SLJ 12/89) [921]

6431 Hopkins, Jerry. *Elvis: The Final Years* (9–12). 1987, Berkley paper $4.95 (0-425-09880-X). A thorough account of Presley—his career and his personal problems, from 1970 until his death. [921]

6432 Stern, Jane, and Michael Stern. *Elvis World* (9–12). Illus. 1990, Harper paper $17.95 (0-06-097290-4). A cornucopia of information about Elvis, his songs, his films, and even the recipe for his favorite snack. (Rev: SLJ 3/88) [921]

RADNER, GILDA

6433 Radner, Gilda. *It's Always Something* (10–12). 1989, Simon & Schuster $17.95 (0-671-63868-8). The biography of the comedienne and her fight against ovarian cancer, a condition that later proved to be fatal. (Rev: BL 5/15/89) [921]

ROBESON, PAUL

6434 Duberman, Martin Bauml. *Paul Robeson* (10–12). Illus. 1989, Knopf $24.95 (0-394-52780-1). For better readers, the biography of the black singer-actor who became a symbol of his people's struggle for equality. (Rev: BL 11/15/88) [921]

6435 Hamilton, Virginia. *Paul Robeson: The Life and Times of a Free Black Man* (7–12). Illus. 1974, Harper $13.95 (0-06-022188-7). A simple, easily read portrait of the multitalented black American singer and actor who suffered because of his communist beliefs. [921]

6436 Robeson, Susan. *The Whole World in His Hands* (9–12). Illus. 1981, Citadel $17.95 (0-8065-0754-3); paper $12.95 (0-8065-0977-5). An album of photographs with captions from Paul Robeson's own words that describe his life, career, and persecutions. [921]

ROBINSON, BILL

6437 Haskins, James, and N. R. Mitgang. *Mr. Bojangles: The Biography of Bill Robinson* (9–12). Illus. 1988, Morrow $17.95 (0-688-07203-8). The first biography of the world's most famous black tap dancer. (Rev: BL 5/1/88) [921]

ROBINSON, SMOKEY

6438 Robinson, Smokey, and David Ritz. *Smokey: Inside My Life* (10–12). Illus. 1989, McGraw $18.95 (0-07-053209-5). The autobiography of the Motown singer with many humorous passages about his childhood and an account of his cocaine addiction. (Rev: BL 1/1/89) [921]

RONSTADT, LINDA

6439 Bego, Mark. *Linda Ronstadt: It's So Easy!* (9–12). Illus. 1990, Eakin paper $12.95 (0-89015-775-8). A thorough review of Linda Ronstadt's life and career. (Rev: BL 9/1/90) [921]

SEEGER, PETE

6440 Dunaway, David King. *How Can I Keep from Singing: Pete Seeger* (10–12). 1990, Da Capo $13.95 (0-306-80399-2). The life story of this fine folksinger and champion of unpopular causes. [921]

SILLS, BEVERLY

6441 Sills, Beverly. *Bubbles: A Self-Portrait* (9–12). Illus. 1976, Macmillan $13.95 (0-685-73303-3). With the help of more than 200 photographs, Sills traces her life in opera. [921]

SMITH, BESSIE

6442 Albertson, Chris. *Bessie* (10–12). 1974, Scarborough House paper $8.95 (0-8128-1700-1). The life and career of one of the great blues singers of all time. [921]

SOMERS, SUZANNE

6443 Somers, Suzanne. *Keeping Secrets* (10–12). 1988, Warner $17.95 (0-446-51395-4). The autobiography of the television star that candidly tells of the devastating effects alcoholism has had on her life. (Rev: BR 3–4/89) [921]

SPRINGSTEEN, BRUCE

6444 Cross, Charles. *Backstreets: Springsteen, the Man & His Music* (7–12). Illus. 1989, Random $24.95 (0-517-57399-7). An illustrated account of Bruce Springsteen's life that concentrates on his public career. (Rev: BR 5–6/90; VOYA 4/90) [921]

6445 Marsh, Dave. *Glory Days: Bruce Springsteen in the 1980s* (10–12). Illus. 1987, Pantheon $18.95 (0-394-54668-7). In this continuation of *Born to Run* (1981), the author traces the Boss's career to the mid-1980s. (Rev: BL 4/15/87; BR 11–12/87; VOYA 10/87) [921]

STING

6446 Cohen, Barney. *Sting: Every Breath He Takes* (10–12). 1984, Berkley paper $2.95 (0-425-07638-5). A biography of this British rock star that ends in the early 1980s. [921]

STREEP, MERYL

6447 Pfaff, Eugene E., Jr., and Mark Emerson. *Meryl Streep: A Critical Biography* (10–12). Illus. 1987, McFarland $24.95 (0-89950-287-3). A serious critical biography that probes into both the public and private life of this star and gives an analysis of her work. (Rev: SLJ 5/88) [921]

TRAVIS, RANDY

6448 Cusic, Don. *Randy Travis: King of the New Country Traditionalists* (9–12). Illus. 1990, St. Martin's paper $8.95 (0-312-04412-7). A straightforward biography that traces the rise to stardom of one of country music's top performers. (Rev: BL 6/1/90) [921]

TURNER, TINA

6449 Mills, Bart. *Tina* (10–12). 1985, Warner paper $2.95 (0-446-34044-8). A well-rounded picture of Tina Turner and her career. [921]

6450 Turner, Tina, and Kurt Loder. *I, Tina* (10–12). 1987, Avon paper $4.50 (0-380-70097-2). For mature readers, these are the candid memoirs of a rock star whose career has had many problems. (Rev: BL 9/1/86; SLJ 3/87) [921]

VALENS, RITCHIE

6451 Mendheim, Beverly. *Ritchie Valens: The First Latino Rocker* (8–12). Illus. 1987, Bilingual Pr. paper $10.00 (0-916950-79-4). The story of the popular Latino rocker who died in a plane crash in 1959. (Rev: BL 12/15/87) [921]

VON TRAPP FAMILY

6452 Von Trapp, Maria. *Story of the Von Trapp Family Singers* (9–12). 1987, Cherokee $16.95 (0-87797-164-1); Doubleday paper $8.95 (0-385-02896-2). The story of the Von Trapp family, their step-mother Maria, and their escape from the Nazis. [921]

WALLER, FATS

6453 Kirkeby, Ed. *Ain't Misbehavin': The Story of Fats Waller* (10–12). Illus. 1975, Da Capo $27.50 (0-306-70683-0). Along with a biography of the great jazz pianist and composer, this account gives a good picture of Harlem after World War I. [921]

6454 Shipton, Alyn. *Fats Waller* (10–12). Illus. 1988, Universe $17.50 (0-87663-687-3). An affectionate portrait of the great jazz trumpeter, singer, and composer. (Rev: SLJ 5/89) [921]

WARNER, MALCOLM JAMAL

6455 Warner, Malcolm Jamal, and Daniel Paisner. *Theo and Me: Growing Up Okay* (9–12). 1988, Dutton $14.95 (0-525-24694-0). The story of the teenage star who plays Theo Huxtable on "The Bill Cosby Show." (Rev: BL 9/1/88; BR 5–6/89) [921]

WATERS, ETHEL

6456 Waters, Ethel. *His Eye Is on the Sparrow* (9–12). 1978, Greenwood $35.00 (0-313-20201-X). An inspiring story for mature readers of the life and career of this great black singer and actress. [921]

WEST, MAE

6457 Bergman, Carol. *Mae West* (9–12). Illus. 1987, Chelsea House $16.95 (1-55546-681-8). The story of the tough and clever performer who got her way before the days of the feminist movement. (Rev: BL 12/1/87) [921]

WESTHEIMER, RUTH

6458 Westheimer, Ruth. *All in a Lifetime* (10–12). Illus. 1987, Warner $17.95 (0-446-51376-8); paper $4.95 (0-446-34774-4). This is the autobiography of the famous sex therapist and talk show hostess. (Rev: BL 10/1/87) [921]

WONDER, STEVIE

6459 Swenson, John. *Stevie Wonder* (9–12). Illus. 1986, Harper paper $12.95 (0-06-097067-7). An engrossing biography of the poor blind black child who grew up to be a superstar. (Rev: BL 2/15/87) [921]

ZAPPA, FRANK

6460 Chevalier, Dominique. *Viva! Zappa* (9–12). Illus. 1986, St. Martin's paper $12.95 (0-312-00201-7). A biography of one of the fathers of rock, covering his career and how he has done battle against censorship. (Rev: SLJ 6–7/87) [921]

Miscellaneous Artists

MIES VAN DER ROHE, LUDWIG

6461 Schulze, Franz. *Mies van der Rohe: A Critical Biography* (10–12). Illus. 1985, Univ. of Chicago Pr. $39.95 (0-226-74059-5). An illustrated biography of the influential architect. [921]

TAYLOR, PAUL

6462 Taylor, Paul. *Private Domain: The Autobiography of Paul Taylor* (10–12). Illus. 1987, Knopf $22.95 (0-394-51683-4). The story of the influential choreographer and of his pioneering dance company. (Rev: BL 4/1/87) [921]

Contemporary and Historical Americans

Collective

6463 Boller, Paul F. *Presidential Wives* (9–12). 1988, Oxford Univ. Pr. $19.95 (0-19-503763-4). Biographical sketches and interesting anecdotes about first ladies from Martha Washington to Nancy Reagan. (Rev: BL 4/1/88) [920]

6464 Bontemps, Arna, ed. *Great Slave Narratives* (10–12). 1969, Beacon Pr. paper $14.95 (0-8070-5473-9). This is a collection of autobiographical writings by slaves. [920]

6465 Caroli, Betty Boyd. *First Ladies* (10–12). Illus. 1987, Oxford Univ. Pr. $27.95 (0-19-503768-5); paper $8.95 (0-19-505654-X). Critical biographical sketches of 36 of the nation's First Ladies. (Rev: BL 9/1/87) [920]

6466 Coulling, Mary P. *The Lee Girls* (10–12). Illus. 1987, John F. Blair $19.95 (0-89587-054-1). The story of the 4 daughters of Robert E. Lee and their devotion to him and how the family fared after the Civil War. (Rev: SLJ 2/88) [920]

6467 DeBenedetti, Charles, ed. *Peace Heroes in Twentieth-Century America* (10–12). Illus. 1986, Indiana Univ. Pr. $29.95 (0-253-34307-0); paper $9.95 (0-253-20479-8). Nine biographies, stretching from Jane Addams to Martin Luther King, of Americans who, in different ways, have fought for peace. [920]

6468 DeGregorio, William A. *The Complete Book of U.S. Presidents* (10–12). Illus. 1989, Dembner $29.95 (0-934878-17-8). A profile of each president and his administration that also supplies career highlights. [920]

6469 Franklin, John Hope, and August Meier, eds. *Black Leaders of the Twentieth Century* (7–12). Illus. 1982, Univ. of Illinois Pr. $29.95 (0-252-00870-7); paper $9.95 (0-252-00939-8). A total of 15 black Americans including W. E. B. DuBois, Marcus Garvey, and Whitney Young, Jr., are highlighted. A companion volume is: *Black Leaders of the Nineteenth Century* (1988). [920]

6470 Graff, Henry F., ed. *The Presidents: A Reference History* (10–12). 1984, Macmillan LB $65.00 (0-684-17607-6). These biographical essays explore the life and careers of each of our presidents from Washington to Carter. [920]

6471 Greene, Robert Ewell. *Black Defenders of America, 1775–1973* (10–12). Illus. 1974, Johnson $17.95 (0-87485-053-3). This book describes the careers of black Americans in the armed forces from the Revolution through the Vietnam War. [920]

6472 Haley, Alex. *Roots* (9–12). 1976, Doubleday $21.95 (0-385-03787-2); paper $5.95 (0-440-17464-3). A thoroughly researched history of a black American's family from Africa to slavery in the United States, ending with the author's own generation. [920]

6473 Hancock, Sibyl. *Famous Firsts of Black Americans* (7–12). Illus. 1983, Pelican $10.95 (0-88289-240-1). Biographies of 20 famous black Americans who have contributed in a unique way to our culture. [920]

6474 Harr, John Ensor, and Peter J. Johnson. *The Rockefeller Century* (10–12). 1988, Macmillan $29.95 (0-684-18936-4). A history of 3 generations of this influential American family. (Rev: BL 6/15/88) [920]

6475 Holland, Barbara. *Hail to the Chiefs: A Guided Tour through the Presidents* (9–12). 1990, Ballantine paper $7.95 (0-345-36273-X). A funny, often flippant, view of our presidents. (Rev: BL 6/1/90) [920]

6476 Holloway, Charles M. *Profiles in Achievement* (9–12). Illus. 1987, College Entrance Examination Board $15.95 (0-87447-291-1); paper $9.95 (0-87447-285-7). The place education played in the lives of 8 successful people from various minority groups. (Rev: BL 2/1/88; SLJ 3/88; VOYA 6/88) [920]

6477 Hook, Jason. *American Indian Warrior Chiefs: Tecumseh, Crazy Horse, Chief Joseph, Geronimo* (10–12). Illus. 1990, Firebird $24.95 (1-85314-103-8). Biographies of 4 outstanding Indian leaders complete with paintings and photographs. (Rev: BL 2/1/90; BR 5–6/90) [920]

6478 Josephson, Matthew. *The Robber Barons: The Great American Capitalists, 1861–1901* (10–12). 1987, Harcourt paper $10.95 (0-15-676790-2). A series of biographies of such capitalists as J. P. Morgan, Andrew Carnegie, and the Vanderbilts with details on how they amassed their fortunes. [920]

6479 Kennedy, John F. *Profiles in Courage* (7–12). Memorial Ed. 1964, Perennial Lib. paper $4.95 (0-06-080698-2). Sketches of several famous Americans who took unpopular stands during their lives. [920]

6480 Litwack, Leon F., and August Meier, eds. *Black Leaders of the Nineteenth Century* (10–12). Illus. 1988, Univ. of Illinois $24.95 (0-252-01506-1). Seventeen biographical sketches about such famous black Americans as Nat Turner and Harriet Tubman. (Rev: BL 4/1/88) [920]

6481 McElroy, Richard L. *American Presidents* (9–12). 1984, Daring Pr. paper $5.95 (0-938936-18-2). A pleasant collection of trivia and facts about American presidents. [920]

6482 Monroe, Sylvester, et al. *Brothers: A Story of Courage and Survival against the Odds of Today's Society* (10–12). Illus. 1988, Morrow $18.95 (0-688-07622-X). A collection of biographies of 12 black men who grew up on the South Side of Chicago. (Rev: BL 6/1/88) [977.3]

6483 Nies, Judith. *Seven Women: Portraits from the American Radical Tradition* (10–12). 1977, Penguin paper $6.95 (0-14-004792-1). Profiles of 6 American women like Harriet Tubman and Mother Jones who have had an impact on American social issues. [920]

6484 Paletta, Lu Ann. *The World Almanac of First Ladies* (9–12). Illus. 1990, St. Martin's paper $9.95 (0-88687-586-2). A collection of facts about each of our First Ladies, including such information as nicknames and astrological signs. (Rev: BL 6/1/90) [920]

6485 Parker, Thomas. *America's Foreign Policy, 1945–1976: Its Creators and Critics* (10–12). 1980, Facts on File $29.95 (0-87196-456-2). This book of biographies includes profiles of 64 presidents, advisors, secretaries of state, and other officials who have shaped American foreign policy from the end of World War II to the mid-1970s. [920.03]

6486 Peavy, Linda, and Ursula Smith. *Women Who Changed Things* (9–12). 1983, Macmillan $12.95 (0-684-17849-4). Biographies of 9 women who lived in turn-of-the-century America and changed our social history. [920]

6487 Peters, Margaret. *The Ebony Book of Black Achievement* (10–12). Illus. 1974, Johnson Pub. $8.95 (0-87485-040-1). This volume contains brief biographies of 26 black American men and women who have achieved in a number of fields. [920]

6488 Reynolds, Moira. *Nine American Women of the 19th Century: Leaders into the 20th* (9–12). Illus. 1988, McFarland $20.95 (0-89950-325-X). Brief, interesting sketches of 9 important American women such as Emma Lazarus, Louisa May Alcott, Julia Ward Howe, and Emma Willard. (Rev: BR 11–12/88; VOYA 12/88) [920]

6489 Richardson, Ben. *Great Black Americans* (10–12). Illus. 1990, Harper LB $16.87 (0-690-04791-6). An introduction to the accomplishments of 31 black Americans of both sexes who have made many unusual contributions to American life. [920]

6490 Smith, Gene. *Lee and Grant: A Dual Biography* (9–12). 1984, NAL $10.95 (0-452-00773-9). A double biography of the 2 opposing generals and their fateful clash. [921]

6491 Smith, Richard Norton, and Timothy Walch, eds. *Farewell to the Chief: Former Presidents in American Public Life* (10–12). 1990, High Plains $22.50 (0-9623333-2-8); paper $9.50 (0-9623333-3-6). A collection of biographical sketches that chronicle the lives of 14 presidents from Theodore Roosevelt to Jimmy Carter after they left office. (Rev: BL 8/90) [920]

6492 Whitney, David C. *The American Presidents* (9–12). 7th ed. Illus. 1990, Prentice $21.95 (0-13-028598-6). A profile of each president, followed by pages of statistics on topics like number of children and cabinet officials. (Rev: BL 6/1/90) [920]

Civil Rights Leaders

ABERNATHY, RALPH DAVID

6493 Abernathy, Ralph David. *And the Walls Came Tumbling Down: An Autobiography* (10–12). Illus. 1989, Harper $22.50 (0-06-016192-2). The autobiography of the civil rights leader and colleague of Martin Luther King, Jr., completed a year before his death. (Rev: BL 9/15/89) [921]

ANTHONY, SUSAN B.

6494 Barry, Kathleen. *Susan B. Anthony: A Biography of a Singular Feminist* (10–12). Illus. 1988, New York Univ. Pr. $27.95 (0-8147-1105-7). The engrossing story of one of our first feminists and her crusade for equality. (Rev: BL 9/15/88) [921]

6495 Cooper, Ilene. *Susan B. Anthony* (10–12). Illus. 1984, Watts LB $12.90 (0-531-04750-4). This is the inspiring story of one of the first American fighters for women's rights. [921]

BANNEKER, BENJAMIN

6496 Bedini, Silvio. *The Life of Benjamin Banneker* (10–12). Illus. 1984, Landmark $24.00 (0-910845-20-4). The biography of the great black American scientist and abolitionist who wrote an almanac and helped survey Washington. [921]

CHAVEZ, CESAR

6497 Levy, Jacques E. *Cesar Chavez* (10–12). Illus. 1975, Norton $19.95 (0-393-07494-3). The life story of the civil rights leader who founded La Causa, a movement to organize farm workers chiefly in California. [921]

CHESTNUT, J. L.

6498 Chestnut, J. L., and Julia Cass. *Black in Selma: The Uncommon Life of J. L. Chestnut, Jr.* (10–12). 1990, Farrar $22.95 (0-374-11404-8). The story of a black attorney who was born in Selma, Alabama, and continues the civil rights struggle there. (Rev: BL 6/1/90) [921]

CRAZY HORSE

6499 Moeller, Bill, and Jan Moeller. *Crazy Horse: His Life, His Lands: A Photographic Biography* (9–12). Illus. 1987, Beautiful America $34.95 (0-89802-493-5). Full-color photographs illustrate the places where Crazy Horse lived, fought, and died. (Rev: BL 6/15/88) [921]

CROW DOG, MARY

6500 Crow Dog, Mary, and Richard Erdoes. *Lakota Woman* (10–12). 1990, Grove Weidenfeld $17.95 (0-8021-1101-7). A moving and at times shocking autobiography of a Sioux woman's life and hardships. (Rev: BL 3/1/90; SLJ 9/90) [921]

DOUGLASS, FREDERICK

6501 Douglass, Frederick. *The Life and Times of Frederick Douglass* (10–12). 1962, Macmillan paper $14.95 (0-02-002350-2). The autobiography of the former slave who became an advisor to Presidents. [921]

6502 Huggins, Nathan Irvin. *Slave and Citizen: The Life of Frederick Douglass* (10–12). 1980, Little paper $14.95 (0-316-38001-6). An objective account of the life of the escaped slave who became a leader in the abolitionist movement. [921]

DU BOIS, W. E. B

6503 Du Bois, W. E. B. *The Autobiography of W. E. B. Du Bois* (10–12). Illus. 1976, Kraus $20.00 (0-527-25262-X). Written when he was over 90, this is both an autobiography of a distinguished black American and a history of the civil rights movement. [921]

6504 Marable, Manning. *W. E. B. Du Bois: Black Radical Democrat* (10–12). Illus. 1986, Twayne $24.95 (0-8057-7750-4); paper $10.95 (0-8057-7771-7). A compact biography of the great black intellectual, humanitarian, and civil rights leader. (Rev: BL 11/1/86) [921]

FARMER, JAMES

6505 Farmer, James. *Lay Bare the Heart: An Autobiography of the Civil Rights Movement* (10–12). 1986, NAL paper $8.95 (0-452-25803-0). Not just an autobiography of the civil rights worker and founder of CORE but also a history of the recent black struggle for equality. (Rev: BL 3/1/85) [921]

FORSTER, ARNOLD

6506 Forster, Arnold. *Square One* (10–12). 1988, Donald I. Fine $21.95 (1-55611-104-5). The memoirs of the general counsel of the Anti-Defamation League of the B'nai B'rith and his fight for civil rights. (Rev: BL 9/1/88) [921]

GARVEY, MARCUS

6507 Cronon, E. David. *Black Moses: The Story of Marcus Garvey* (10–12). Illus. 1955, Univ. of Wisconsin Pr. paper $9.95 (0-229-01214-X). A biography of the Jamaica-born black who led the civil rights movement in America during the 1920s. [921]

HAYDEN, TOM

6508 Hayden, Tom. *Reunion: A Memoir* (10–12). Illus. 1988, Random $22.50 (0-394-56533-9). The autobiography of one of the leading radicals of the 1960s. (Rev: BL 4/15/88) [921]

KING, MARTIN LUTHER, JR.

6509 Bennett, Lerone, Jr. *What Manner of Man: A Biography of Martin Luther King, Jr.* (10–12). 3rd Rev. ed. Illus. 1969, Johnson Pub. $12.95 (0-87485-027-4). This well-rounded biography covers the life of King from his childhood to tragic end. [921]

6510 Branch, Taylor. *Parting the Waters: America in the King Years, 1954–1963* (10–12). 1988, Simon & Schuster $24.95 (0-671-46097-8). A history of the civil rights movement that concentrates on the life and work of Martin Luther King, Jr. (Rev: BL 11/15/88) [921]

6511 Oates, Stephen B. *Let the Trumpet Sound: The Life of Martin Luther King, Jr.* (10–12). Illus. 1982, Harper $24.45 (0-06-014993-0); NAL paper $4.95 (0-451-62350-9). An affectionate look at the life and accomplishments of the civil rights leader who was killed in 1968. [921]

6512 Schulke, Flip, ed. *Martin Luther King, Jr.: A Documentary . . . Montgomery to Memphis* (10–12). Illus. 1976, Norton $24.95 (0-393-07487-0); paper $13.95 (0-393-07492-7). This account of the civil rights movement led by King is based on a film documentary. [921]

6513 Schulke, Flip, and Penelope McPhee. *King Remembered* (9–12). Illus. 1986, Norton $19.95 (0-393-02256-0); paper $7.95 (0-671-62016-5). A heavily illustrated biography that stresses King's work in civil rights. (Rev: BL 1/1/86) [921]

6514 Witherspoon, William R. *Martin Luther King, Jr.: To the Mountaintop* (9–12). Illus. 1985, Doubleday $24.95 (0-385-19883-3). An informal biography and history of the civil rights movement illustrated with many photographs. [921]

LAME DEER, JOHN

6515 Lame Deer, John, and Richard Erdoes. *Lame Deer, Seeker of Visions* (10–12). 1973, Simon & Schuster paper $7.95 (0-671-21535-3). The story of a Sioux Indian and the pride he has in his people and their culture. [921]

MALCOLM X

6516 Malcolm X, and Alex Haley. *The Autobiography of Malcolm X* (7–12). 1973, Ballantine paper $3.95 (0-345-33920-7). The story of the man who turned from Harlem drug pusher into a charismatic leader of his people. [921]

REDFORD, DOROTHY

6517 Redford, Dorothy, and Michael D'Orso. *Somerset Homecoming* (10–12). 1988, Doubleday $18.95 (0-385-24245-X). A black American finds her roots on a plantation in North Carolina and generates a family gathering of 2,000 people. (Rev: BL 8/88) [921]

TRUTH, SOJOURNER

6518 Ortiz, Victoria. *Sojourner Truth: A Self-Made Woman* (10–12). Illus. 1974, Harper LB $11.98 (0-397-31504-X). The inspiring story of the rise from slavery of this black woman who fought for civil rights. [921]

TUBMAN, HARRIET

6519 Bradford, Sarah. *Harriet Tubman, the Moses of Her People* (7–12). Illus. 1961, Peter Smith $12.75 (0-8446-1717-2). A biography first published in 1869 of this former slave who brought hundreds of slaves north to freedom. [921]

WASHINGTON, BOOKER T.

6520 Washington, Booker T. *Up from Slavery: An Autobiography by Booker T. Washington* (7–12). Illus. 1963, Airmont paper $1.95 (0-8049-0157-0). The story of the slave who later organized the Tuskegee Institute. [921]

Presidents and Their Wives

ADAMS, ABIGAIL

6521 Adams, Abigail. *The Book of Abigail and John: Selected Letters of the Adams Family, 1762–1784* (10–12). Illus. 1975, Harvard Univ. Pr. $27.00 (0-674-07855-1); paper $8.95 (0-674-07854-3). The correspondence between Abigail and John Adams that concentrates on the years of the Revolution. [921]

6522 Akers, Charles W. *Abigail Adams: An American Woman* (10–12). 1980, Scott, Foresman paper $13.95 (0-67339-318-6). This account of the life of the wife of one president and mother of another is based on more than 2,000 of her letters. [921]

BUSH, GEORGE

6523 Bush, George. *Looking Forward* (10–12). Illus. 1988, Bantam paper $4.95 (0-553-27791-X). A candid autobiography that deals with George Bush's career into the vice presidency. (Rev: SLJ 3/88) [921]

CARTER, JIMMY

6524 Carter, Jimmy. *Keeping Faith: Memoirs of a President* (10–12). 1983, Bantam paper $13.95 (0-553-34571-0). The story of his presidency through Carter's own recollections. [921]

CARTER, ROSALYNN

6525 Carter, Rosalynn. *First Lady from Plains* (10–12). 1988, Fawcett paper $3.95 (0-449-44529-1). A candid autobiography of the former first lady. [921]

EISENHOWER, DWIGHT D.

6526 Ambrose, Stephen E. *Eisenhower* (10–12). 1990, Simon & Schuster $29.95 (0-671-20102-X). A single-volume edition of the distinguished life story of the man who led America in both war and peace. [921]

6527 Beschloss, Michael R. *Eisenhower: A Centennial Life* (9–12). Illus. 1990, Harper $29.95 (0-06-016418-2). In honor of Eisenhower's one hundredth birthday, this lavishly illustrated biography gives an insightful overview of this important man's life. (Rev: BL 9/1/90) [921]

6528 Eisenhower, Dwight D. *The Eisenhower Diaries* (10–12). Illus. 1981, Norton $19.95 (0-393-01432-0). These diaries cover the period from 1935 to 2 years before Eisenhower's death in 1969. [921]

6529 Burk, Robert F. *Dwight D. Eisenhower: Hero & Politician* (10–12). 1986, Twayne $19.95 (0-8057-7752-0); paper $9.95 (0-8057-7773-3). A concise account that covers both Eisenhower's military and political careers equally. (Rev: BL 8/86; VOYA 4/87) [921]

GRANT, ULYSSES S.

6530 Catton, Bruce. *Grant Moves South* (10–12). 1960, Little $25.00 (0-316-13207-1). The Civil War career of General Grant that ends with the occupation of Vicksburg. Continued in *Grant Takes Command* (1969). [921]

HOOVER, HERBERT

6531 Smith, Richard Norton. *An Uncommon Man: The Triumph of Herbert Hoover* (10–12). Illus. 1984, High Plains Pr. paper $14.50 (0-9623333-1-X). An account that concentrates on Hoover's life and accomplishments after his presidency. [921]

JACKSON, ANDREW

6532 Remini, Robert V. *Andrew Jackson and the Course of American Democracy, 1833–1845* (10–12). Illus. 1984, Harper $27.50 (0-06-015279-6). The final volume of this massive 3-volume biography of Jackson. The others are: *Andrew Jackson and the Course of American Empire* (1977) and *Andrew Jackson and the Course of American Freedom* (1981). [921]

JEFFERSON, THOMAS

6533 Brodie, Fawn M. *Thomas Jefferson: An Intimate History* (10–12). Illus. 1974, Bantam paper $6.95 (0-553-27335-3). A portrait of this complex, multitalented man that describes both his public and private life. [921]

JOHNSON, LYNDON B.

6534 Conkin, Paul K. *Big Daddy from the Pedernales: Lyndon Baines Johnson* (10–12). Illus. 1986, Twayne $24.95 (0-8057-7762-8); paper $10.95 (0-8057-7772-5). An honest, unbiased look at the career and personality of this enigmatic president. (Rev: SLJ 5/87) [921]

6535 Middleton, Harry. *LBJ: The White House Years* (9–12). Illus. 1990, Abrams $45.00 (0-8109-1191-4). Brief commentary and many photographs re-create the presidency of Lyndon B. Johnson (Rev: BL 6/1/90) [921]

KENNEDY, JOHN F.

6536 Burner, David. *John F. Kennedy and a New Generation* (10–12). 1988, Little $16.95 (0-316-11724-2). An objective assessment of the presidency of John F. Kennedy and its impact on American political thinking. (Rev: BL 11/15/88) [921]

6537 Lowe, Jacques, and Wilfrid Sheed. *The Kennedy Legacy* (9–12). Illus. 1988, Viking LB $24.95 (0-670-81882-8). A beautiful book with excellent photographs that appraises the effects of the Kennedy administration on the world. (Rev: BL 5/1/88; BR 1–2/89) [921]

6538 Manchester, William. *The Death of a President, November 20–November 25, 1963* (10–12). 1967, Harper $22.95 (0-06-055136-4); paper $10.95 (0-06-091531-5). A detailed account of the last 6 days in the life of President Kennedy. [921]

6539 Manchester, William. *One Brief Shining Moment: Remembering Kennedy* (9–12). Illus. 1988, Little paper $16.95 (0-316-54511-2). A remembrance of Kennedy in 200 photographs and quotes from friends and associates. [921]

6540 Martin, Ralph G. *A Hero for Our Time: An Intimate Story of the Kennedy Years* (10–12). 1983, Fawcett paper $4.95 (0-449-20604-1). A thoroughly researched account of Kennedy's rise to power and his brief tenure as president. [921]

6541 Mills, Judie. *John F. Kennedy* (9–12). Illus. 1988, Watts $14.90 (0-531-10520-2). A detailed account that includes an evaluation of this president's term of office. (Rev: BL 6/15/88; BR 9–10/88; SLJ 5/88; VOYA 8/88) [921]

LINCOLN, ABRAHAM

6542 Bishop, Jim. *The Day Lincoln Was Shot* (9–12). Illus. 1955, Harper paper $4.95 (0-06-080005-4). An hour-by-hour account of the last day in Lincoln's life. [921]

6543 Hanchett, William. *The Lincoln Murder Conspiracies* (10–12). 1983, Univ. of Illinois Pr. $29.95 (0-252-01046-9); paper $11.95 (0-252-01361-1). A portrait of Lincoln and details on the assassination. (Rev: BR 3–4/87) [921]

6544 Handlin, Oscar, and Lilian Handlin. *Abraham Lincoln and the Union* (10–12). 1990, Scott, Foresman $17.95 (0-673-39340-2). A biography that places emphasis on Lincoln's early formative years. [921]

6545 Jennison, Keith W. *The Humorous Mr. Lincoln: A Profile in Wit, Courage and Compassion* (9–12). Illus. 1988, Countryman $8.95 (0-88150-109-3). A profile of Lincoln that explores his life through his humor. (Rev: BR 1–2/89; SLJ 2/89) [921]

6546 Oates, Stephen B. *Abraham Lincoln: The Man behind the Myths* (10–12). 1984, Harper $15.95 (0-06-015304-0); NAL paper $6.95 (0-452-00734-8). A masterful biography that re-creates the life and the world of this president and also tries to separate fact from the fiction surrounding Lincoln. [921]

6547 Oates, Stephen B. *With Malice Toward None: The Life of Abraham Lincoln* (10–12).

1978, NAL paper $4.95 (0-451-62314-2). This account probes into the personal life of Lincoln as well as his public career. [921]

6548 Reck, W. Emerson. *A. Lincoln: His Last 24 Hours* (9–12). Illus. 1987, McFarland $19.95 (0-89950-216-4). A vivid hour-by-hour recreation of the last day of Lincoln's life. (Rev: BR 11–12/87; SLJ 11/87; VOYA 12/87) [921]

6549 Sandburg, Carl. *Abraham Lincoln: The Prairie Years and the War Years* (10–12). Illus. 1970, Harcourt $49.95 (0-15-100638-5); paper $14.95 (0-15-602611-2). An abridgment of Sandburg's massive 6-volume biography of Lincoln. [921]

6550 Thomas, Benjamin P. *Abraham Lincoln: A Biography* (10–12). 1986, Gateway $11.95 (0-88296-144-6). One of the standard biographies of Lincoln that is both realistic and sympathetic in tone. [921]

NIXON, RICHARD M.

6551 Brodie, Fawn M. *Richard Nixon: The Shaping of His Character* (10–12). Illus. 1981, Norton $18.95 (0-393-01467-3). This account of the early life of Nixon ends with the Kennedy assassination in 1963. [921]

REAGAN, RONALD

6552 Barrett, Laurence I. *Gambling with History: Ronald Reagan in the White House* (10–12). 1987, Penguin paper $8.95 (0-14-007275-6). An assessment of the first 2 years of Reagan's administration. [921]

6553 Reagan, Ronald. *An American Life: The Autobiography* (10–12). Illus. 1990, Simon & Schuster $24.95 (0-671-69198-8). An informal, chatty autobiography of the former president and actor. (Rev: BL 12/1/90) [921]

6554 Sullivan, George. *Ronald Reagan* (10–12). Illus. 1985, Messner $10.98 (0-671-60168-7). The life of the former president to his second inauguration. [921]

ROOSEVELT, ELEANOR

6555 Chadakoff, Rochelle, ed. *Eleanor Roosevelt's My Day: Her Acclaimed Columns 1936–1945* (10–12). Illus. 1989, Pharos $18.95 (0-88687-407-6). A selection of the best of Eleanor Roosevelt's newspaper columns describing her day-to-day activities. (Rev: SLJ 10/89) [921]

6556 Lash, Joseph P. *Eleanor: The Years Alone* (10–12). Illus. 1972, Norton $14.95 (0-393-07361-0); NAL paper $10.95 (0-451-00771-2). The story of Eleanor Roosevelt's last 17 years, during which time she became known as the First Lady of the World. [921]

6557 Lash, Joseph P. *Eleanor and Franklin: The Story of Their Relationship Based on Eleanor Roosevelt's Private Papers* (10–12). Illus. 1971, Norton $15.95 (0-393-07459-5); NAL paper $5.95 (0-451-14076-1). The story of Eleanor and Franklin's public and private life through the death of President Roosevelt. [921]

6558 Roosevelt, Eleanor. *Eleanor Roosevelt's My Day, Volume 2: The Post-War Years* (10–12). Illus. 1990, St. Martin's $19.95 (0-88687-457-2). This collection of syndicated newspaper articles covers the years 1945–1952 and brings to life this outspoken humanitarian. Preceded by Volume One, which covers the war years. (Rev: SLJ 12/90) [921]

6559 Roosevelt, Eleanor. *This I Remember* (10–12). 1975, Greenwood $45.00 (0-8371-7702-2). This remembrance deals chiefly with life in the White House during the 1930s and early 1940s. [921]

6560 Roosevelt, Elliott. *Eleanor Roosevelt, with Love: A Centenary Remembrance* (8–12). 1984, Lodestar $12.95 (0-525-67147-1). To honor the centennial of the birth of Eleanor Roosevelt, her son wrote this easily read tribute to her and her many accomplishments. [921]

6561 Scharf, Lois. *Eleanor Roosevelt: First Lady of American Liberalism* (10–12). 1987, Twayne $24.95 (0-8057-7769-5); paper $10.95 (0-8057-7778-4). This biography is a moving tribute to Eleanor Roosevelt, who is one of the most respected people in modern history. (Rev: BR 5–6/88; SLJ 1/88) [921]

ROOSEVELT, FRANKLIN D.

6562 Freidel, Frank. *Franklin D. Roosevelt: A Rendezvous with Destiny* (10–12). Illus. 1990, Little $24.95 (0-316-29260-5). A biography that covers all aspects of this president's life, but with special emphasis on the New Deal and World War II. (Rev: BL 2/1/90) [921]

6563 Gallagher, Hugh Gregory. *FDR's Splendid Deception* (9–12). Illus. 1985, Dodd $16.95 (0-396-08521-0). The story of Roosevelt's bout with polio and how he was able to disguise its effects. (Rev: SLJ 9/85) [921]

ROOSEVELT, THEODORE

6564 McCullough, David. *Mornings on Horseback* (10–12). 1982, Simon & Schuster paper

$13.95 (0-671-44754-8). A biography of the young Teddy Roosevelt. [921]

6565 Morris, Edmund. *The Rise of Theodore Roosevelt* (10–12). Illus. 1979, Putnam $24.95 (0-698-10783-7); Ballantine paper $10.95 (0-345-33902-0). In this first part of a 2-volume biography, the author traces Roosevelt's career from birth to becoming president in 1901. [921]

TRUMAN, BESS W.

6566 Truman, Margaret. *Bess W. Truman* (10–12). 1987, Jove paper $4.50 (0-515-08973-7). An affectionate portrait of a First Lady by her devoted daughter. (Rev: BL 3/1/86) [921]

TRUMAN, HARRY S.

6567 Ferrell, Robert H. *Truman: A Centenary Remembrance* (10–12). Illus. 1984, Viking $25.00 (0-670-36196-8). A straightforward examination of the life and career of this president who guided the United States through the final days of World War II and the beginning of the postwar period. [921]

6568 Miller, Merle. *Plain Speaking: An Oral Biography of Harry S. Truman* (10–12). 1986, Berkley paper $4.95 (0-425-09499-5). An extraordinarily candid picture of the president based on tapes of interviews with Truman and his associates. [921]

6569 Pemberton, William E. *Harry S. Truman: Fair Dealer and Cold Warrior* (10–12). 1988, Twayne $24.95 (0-8057-7767-9); paper $10.95 (0-8057-7783-0). A biography that contains a highly critical assessment of Truman's policies and decisions. (Rev: BL 12/15/88; SLJ 10/89; VOYA 6/89) [921]

6570 Truman, Harry S. *The Autobiography of Harry S. Truman* (10–12). Illus. 1980, Univ. Pr. of Colorado paper $9.95 (0-87081-091-X). By careful editing of existing papers written by Truman, a chronological account of the president's life has been assembled. [921]

6571 Truman, Margaret. *Harry S. Truman* (10–12). Illus. 1984, Morrow paper $10.95 (0-688-03924-3). An affectionate view of the career of this president with many behind-the-scenes anecdotes. [921]

WASHINGTON, GEORGE

6572 Cunliffe, Marcus. *George Washington, Man and Monument* (10–12). 1982, Mentor paper $4.95 (0-451-62461-0). A scholarly biography that separates the truth from the fiction that has grown about our first president. [921]

6573 Nordham, George W. *The Age of Washington: George Washington's Presidency, 1789–1797* (10–12). Illus. 1989, Adams Pr. paper $24.95. A human portrait of our first president that concentrates on his 2 terms in office. (Rev: BL 2/1/90) [921]

6574 Schwartz, Barry. *George Washington: The Making of an American Symbol* (10–12). Illus. 1987, Free Pr. $22.50 (0-02-928141-5). An honest reappraisal of the career and accomplishments of our first president. (Rev: BL 7/87) [921]

WILSON, WOODROW

6575 Clements, Kendrick A. *Woodrow Wilson, World Statesman* (9–12). Illus. 1987, Twayne $24.95 (0-8057-7756-3); paper $10.95 (0-8057-7779-2). A readable, brief biography of the first president to make Americans think internationally. (Rev: SLJ 5/88) [921]

6576 Smith, Gene. *When the Cheering Stopped: The Last Years of Woodrow Wilson* (10–12). 1964, Morrow paper $7.95 (0-688-06011-0). The last tragic years of this president, with a focus on the impact of the U.S. rejection of the League of Nations. [921]

Statesmen and Other Public Figures

BRADLEY, OMAR

6577 Bradley, Omar, and Clay Blair. *A General's Life* (10–12). Illus. 1983, Simon & Schuster paper $15.95 (0-671-41024-5). The autobiography of this general that concentrates on his career during World War II. [921]

BRANDEIS, LOUIS

6578 Urofsky, Melvin I. *Louis D. Brandeis and the Progressive Tradition* (10–12). 1981, Scott, Foresman paper $10.95 (0-673-39354-2). A biography of the progressive Jewish Supreme Court justice who opposed both big business and big government. [921]

BRYAN, WILLIAM JENNINGS

6579 Ashby, LeRoy. *William Jennings Bryan: Champion of Democracy* (10–12). Illus. 1987, Twayne $24.95 (0-8057-7760-1); paper $10.95 (0-8057-7776-8). A biography of this outspoken American hero who took strong stands on a

variety of subjects, including the Scopes evolution question. (Rev: SLJ 1/88) [921]

CHENNAULT, CLAIRE LEE

6580 Samson, Jack. *Chennault* (10–12). Illus. 1987, Doubleday $19.95 (0-385-23171-7). The story of the indomitable air force general who became a legend during World War II. (Rev: BL 10/1/87) [921]

CUOMO, MARIO

6581 McElvaine, Robert S. *Mario Cuomo* (10–12). 1988, Macmillan $15.95 (0-684-18970-4). A highly laudatory biography of the governor of New York State. (Rev: BL 5/1/88) [921]

CUSTER, GEORGE ARMSTRONG

6582 Utley, Robert M. *Cavalier in Buckskin: George Armstrong Custer and the Western Military Frontier* (10–12). Illus. 1988, Univ. of Oklahoma Pr. $19.95 (0-8061-2150-5). The life story of the courageous, tyrannical and always controversial Civil War leader and Indian fighter. (Rev: BL 10/15/88) [921]

DARROW, CLARENCE

6583 Stone, Irving. *Clarence Darrow for the Defense: A Biography* (10–12). 1949, Doubleday $22.95 (0-385-26689-8). A somewhat novelized biography of the great defense lawyer and the causes for which he fought. [921]

DAVIS, JEFFERSON

6584 Woodworth, Steven E. *Jefferson Davis and His Generals: The Failure of the Confederate Command in the West* (10–12). Illus. 1990, Univ. Pr. of Kansas $25.00 (0-7006-0461-8). A portrait of Jefferson Davis, a courageous man, and an analysis of his military leadership. (Rev: BL 7/90) [921]

DOUGLASS, FREDERICK

6585 Douglass, Frederick. *Narrative of the Life of Frederick Douglass, an American Slave* (10–12). 1982, Penguin paper $3.95 (0-14-039012-X). An autobiography that tells of the life of this former slave and abolitionist. [921]

FRANKLIN, BENJAMIN

6586 Bowen, Catherine Drinker. *The Most Dangerous Man in America: Scenes of the Life of Benjamin Franklin* (10–12). 1986, Little paper

$8.95 (0-316-10379-9). A well-rounded portrait of this early American Renaissance man who was talented in a variety of fields including writing, science, and diplomacy. [921]

6587 Franklin, Benjamin. *The Autobiography of Benjamin Franklin* (10–12). 1986, Norton paper $8.95 (0-393-95294-0). Written between 1771 and 1788, this is more than an account of Revolutionary times; it is also an exploration of the mind of a man of varied and deep interests. [921]

6588 Lopez, Claude-Anne, and Eugenia W. Herbert. *The Private Franklin: The Man and His Family* (10–12). 1975, Norton paper $9.95 (0-393-30227-X). A portrait of Franklin that emphasizes his daily business concerns and personal life. [921]

GOLDMAN, EMMA

6589 Waldstreicher, David. *Emma Goldman* (8–12). Illus. 1990, Chelsea House $17.95 (1-55546-655-9). Biography of the great activist who held strong views on marriage, capitalism, and militarism. (Rev: BL 5/1/90; SLJ 6/90) [921]

HEARST, WILLIAM RANDOLPH

6590 Swanberg, W. A. *Citizen Hearst: A Biography of William Randolph Hearst* (10–12). Illus. 1961, Macmillan $25.00 (0-684-14503-0); paper $7.95 (0-684-17147-3). A fascinating biography of this many-faceted man known chiefly as a millionaire newspaper tycoon. [921]

HENRY, PATRICK

6591 Mayer, Henry. *A Son of Thunder: Patrick Henry and the American Republic* (10–12). 1986, Watts $22.50 (0-531-15009-7). A fine biography of the lawyer and politician who played an important role in Revolutionary times. (Rev: BR 9–10/86; SLJ 9/86) [921]

HISS, ALGER

6592 Hiss, Alger. *Recollections of a Life* (10–12). 1988, Henry Holt $19.95 (0-8050-0612-5). The autobiography of the statesman who was involved in the "pumpkin papers" scandal and spent 3 years in prison for perjury. (Rev: BR 11–12/88) [921]

HOLMES, OLIVER WENDELL

6593 Aichele, Gary J. *Oliver Wendell Holmes, Jr.* (10–12). 1989, Twayne $24.95 (0-8057-7766-0); paper $10.95 (0-8057-7784-9). A well-researched

biography of the liberal, progressive Supreme Court justice. (Rev: BL 1/15/89) [921]

HUMPHREY, HUBERT H.

6594 Cohen, Daniel. *Undefeated: The Life of Hubert H. Humphrey* (10–12). Illus. 1978, Lerner $25.00 (0-8225-9953-8). With more than 300 photographs and numerous quotes by and about Humphrey, this is a fascinating glimpse at the modern political scene. [921]

JACKSON, STONEWALL

6595 Bowers, John. *Stonewall Jackson: Portrait of a Soldier* (10–12). Illus. 1989, Morrow $19.95 (0-688-05747-0). A dramatic account of the Confederate commander who died during the Civil War. (Rev: BL 5/15/89) [921]

6596 Wheeler, Richard. *We Knew Stonewall Jackson* (10–12). Illus. 1977, Harper $11.45 (0-690-01218-7). A stirring biography of the Southern general and his untimely death at Chancellorsville. [921]

JONES, JOHN PAUL

6597 Morison, Samuel Eliot. *John Paul Jones: A Sailor's Biography* (10–12). Illus. 1990, Naval Institute Pr. $27.95 (0-87021-323-7); Northeastern Univ. Pr. paper $14.95 (0-930350-70-7). A well-documented biography of the man who has been called "the father of the U.S. Navy." [921]

KENNEDY FAMILY

6598 Collier, Peter, and David Horowitz. *The Kennedys: An American Drama* (10–12). 1985, Warner paper $4.95 (0-446-32702-6). This well-researched report presents a critical view of the Kennedy family. [921]

KISSINGER, HENRY

6599 Kissinger, Henry. *White House Years* (10–12). Illus. 1979, Little $29.95 (0-316-49661-8). This account traces Kissinger's career from 1969 to the signing of the Vietnam peace agreement in 1973. Followed by *Years of Upheaval* (1982). [921]

LONG, HUEY

6600 Williams, T. Harry. *Huey Long* (10–12). Illus. 1969, Knopf $40.00 (0-394-42954-0); Random paper $16.95 (0-394-74790-9). The prize-winning biography of the controversial Southern politician. [921]

MACARTHUR, DOUGLAS

6601 Manchester, William. *American Caesar: Douglas MacArthur, 1880–1964* (10–12). Illus. 1978, Little $29.95 (0-316-54498-1); Dell paper $12.95 (0-440-30424-5). The story of this military leader who was both admired and despised by his men. [921]

MCCARTHY, JOSEPH

6602 Ingalls, Robert P. *Point of Order: A Profile of Senator Joe McCarthy* (10–12). Illus. 1981, Putnam $9.95 (0-399-20827-5). A biography of the controversial Wisconsin senator who gained fame as a pursuer of Communists in government. [921]

6603 Reeves, Thomas C. *The Life and Times of Joe McCarthy* (10–12). 1982, Scarborough $19.95 (0-8128-2337-0); paper $14.95 (0-8128-6200-7). A well-balanced biography of the activities of this senator who was obsessed with fear of the infiltration of Communism into American life. [921]

MARSHALL, GEORGE C.

6604 Stoler, Mark A. *George C. Marshall: Soldier-Statesman of the "American Century"* (10–12). 1989, Twayne $24.95 (0-8057-7768-7); paper $10.95 (0-8057-7785-7). The life of the famous general who became an important World War II leader. (Rev: BL 1/1/89) [921]

MARSHALL, JOHN

6605 Stites, Francis N. *John Marshall: Defender of the Constitution* (10–12). 1981, Scott Foresman $19.95 (0-673-39353-4). The biography of the Chief Justice of the Supreme Court during the early days of the Republic. [921]

MATHER, COTTON

6606 Silverman, Kenneth. *The Life and Times of Cotton Mather* (10–12). Illus. 1984, Harper $29.95 (0-06-015231-1); Columbia Univ. Pr. paper $17.50 (0-231-06125-0). A biography of a man who influenced the thought and conduct of Colonial America. [921]

PATTON, GEORGE S.

6607 Blumenson, Martin. *Patton: The Man behind the Legend, 1885–1945* (10–12). Illus. 1985, Morrow $17.95 (0-688-06082-X); Berkley paper $3.95 (0-425-09703-X). A re-creation of the life and career of this army general that uses liberal quotes from Patton and his family. [921]

6608 Farago, Ladislas. *Patton: Ordeal and Triumph* (10–12). Illus. 1964, Astor-Honor $29.95 (0-8392-1084-1). A biography that stresses the many World War II campaigns that Patton led. [921]

REVERE, PAUL

6609 Forbes, Esther. *Paul Revere & the World He Lived In* (10–12). Illus. 1987, Houghton paper $9.95 (0-395-08370-2). This account not only describes the life of this silversmith and patriot but also gives a fine picture of colonial Boston. [921]

Miscellaneous Historical Figures

ADAMS, HENRY

6610 Adams, Henry. *The Education of Henry Adams* (10–12). 1981, Amereon $22.95 (0-89190-844-7); Houghton paper $7.95 (0-395-16620-9). This collection of autobiographical writings by the grandson of John Quincy Adams was first published in 1918. [921]

ADDAMS, JANE

6611 Addams, Jane. *Twenty Years at Hull House* (10–12). 1980, NAL paper $4.50 (0-451-51955-8). This autobiographical fragment consists mainly of the story of the founding of Hull House, a home for the underprivileged in Chicago. [921]

6612 Hovde, Jane. *Jane Addams* (8–12). Illus. 1989, Facts on File $16.95 (0-8160-1547-3). The life and work of this early feminist and social worker. (Rev: BL 9/15/89; BR 11–12/89; VOYA 12/89) [921]

ANTIN, MARY

6613 Antin, Mary. *The Promised Land* (10–12). 2nd ed. 1985, Princeton Univ. Pr. $35.00 (0-691-04722-7). This autobiography of a Jewish woman who immigrated to America from Russia first appeared in 1912. [921]

BECKWOURTH, JIM

6614 Wilson, Elinor. *Jim Beckwourth* (10–12). Illus. 1972, Univ. of Oklahoma Pr. paper $10.95 (0-8061-1555-6). The amazing story of the black frontiersman who was trader, prospector, war chief for the Crows, trapper, and scout. [921]

BLACK ELK, OGLALA INDIAN

6615 Black Elk. *Black Elk Speaks* (10–12). Illus. 1979, Univ. of Nebraska Pr. $19.95 (0-8032-3301-9); paper $8.95 (0-8032-8359-8). This biography first appeared in 1932 and tells the story of the amazing warrior and medicine man of the Oglala Plains Indians. [921]

BONNEY, WILLIAM

6616 Cline, Don. *Alias Billy the Kid, the Man Behind the Legend* (8–12). Illus. 1986, Sunstone $12.95 (0-86534-080-3). The real story of Billy the Kid, clearing up many misconceptions. (Rev: BR 11–12/86) [921]

BONNIE AND CLYDE

6617 Treherne, John. *The Strange History of Bonnie and Clyde* (10–12). Illus. 1985, Scarborough House $16.95 (0-8128-3030-X). The true story of Clyde, a psychopath, his girlfriend Bonnie, and their 2-year crime spree. [921]

CARSON, KIT

6618 Quaife, Milo Milton, ed. *Kit Carson's Autobiography* (10–12). 1966, Univ. of Nebraska Pr. paper $4.95 (0-8032-5031-2). This autobiography dictated in the years 1856–57 gives fascinating details of the life of this famous hunter, trapper, and Indian fighter. [921]

FREMONT, JESSIE BENTON

6619 Herr, Pamela. *Jessie Benton Fremont: A Biography* (10–12). 1987, Watts $24.95 (0-531-15011-9); Univ. of Oklahoma Pr. paper $14.95 (0-8061-2159-9). The story of the remarkable wife of John Charles Fremont and her multifaceted gifts. (Rev: BL 2/1/87) [921]

GALLAUDET, T. H.

6620 Neimark, Anne E. *A Deaf Child Listened: Thomas Gallaudet, Pioneer in American Education* (9–12). 1983, Morrow $11.95 (0-688-01719-3). The story of the great humanitarian and the founding of the first school for the deaf in America. [921]

GERONIMO

6621 Barrett, S. M., ed. *Geronimo: His Own Story* (10–12). 1983, Irvington paper $12.95 (0-8290-0658-3). The memoirs of the Apache warrior Geronimo with valuable background information about his people and their culture. [921]

6622 Debo, Angie. *Geronimo: The Man, His Time, His Place* (10–12). Illus. 1976, Univ. of Oklahoma Pr. paper $15.95 (0-8061-1828-8). The remarkable career of the Indian chief and warrior who in later life became a respected community member. [921]

GILBRETH FAMILY

6623 Gilbreth, Frank B., Jr., and Ernestine Gilbreth Carey. *Cheaper by the Dozen* (7–12). Illus. 1963, Harper $15.45 (0-690-18632-0); Bantam paper $3.50 (0-553-25018-3). The humorous exploits of the Gilbreth family dominated by a father who was an efficiency expert. Followed by: *Belles on Their Toes* (paper 1984). [921]

HICKOK, WILD BILL

6624 Rosa, Joseph G. *They Called Him Wild Bill: The Life and Adventures of James Butler Hickok* (10–12). 1979, Univ. of Oklahoma paper $16.95 (0-8061-1538-6). This is the colorful biography of an American legend—from U.S. marshall and army scout to performer in a Wild West show. [921]

ISHI

6625 Kroeber, Theodora. *Ishi: Last of His Tribe* (10–12). 1964, Bantam paper $3.50 (0-553-24898-7). The story of the last of this Indian tribe and his entry into the world of the white man. [921]

KELLER, HELEN

6626 Keller, Helen. *The Story of My Life* (7–12). Illus. 1954, Doubleday $15.95 (0-385-04453-4); Airmont paper $2.25 (0-8049-0070-1). The classic biography of the gallant lady who overcame multiple physical handicaps. [921]

6627 Lash, Joseph P. *Helen and Teacher: The Story of Helen Keller & Anne Sullivan Macy* (9–12). Illus. 1980, Dell paper $6.95 (0-440-53509-3). This is a fascinating portrait of both Helen Keller and her devoted teacher Anne Sullivan Macy. [921]

KENNEDY, ROBERT F.

6628 Schlesinger, Arthur M., Jr. *Robert Kennedy and His Times* (10–12). 1985, Houghton $19.95 (0-395-24897-3); paper $5.95 (0-345-32547-8). Biography of the combative but caring man who was assassinated while campaigning for the presidency. [921]

MERTON, THOMAS

6629 Mott, Michael. *The Seven Mountains of Thomas Merton* (10–12). Illus. 1984, Houghton paper $12.95 (0-395-40451-7). A biography of the multitalented religious thinker, with information on his many friends. [921]

MOTT, LUCRETIA

6630 Bacon, Margaret Hope. *Valiant Friend: The Life of Lucretia Mott* (10–12). 1982, Walker $12.95 (0-8027-7190-4). The exciting story of the nineteenth-century American feminist and reformer. [921]

PATTON, GEORGE

6631 Patton, George S., Jr. *War as I Knew It* (10–12). 1983, Houghton $19.95 (0-395-00074-6); paper $4.95 (0-553-24991-1). This autobiographical fragment is actually the diary kept by General Patton during World War II from July 1942 to December 1945. [921]

POCAHONTAS

6632 Woodward, Grace Steele. *Pocahontas* (10–12). Illus. 1969, Univ. of Oklahoma Pr. paper $10.95 (0-8061-1642-0). The story of the Indian woman who befriended many colonists and saved the life of Captain John Smith. [921]

ROSENBERG, ETHEL

6633 Philipson, Ilene. *Ethel Rosenberg: Beyond the Myths* (10–12). 1988, Watts $18.95 (0-531-15057-7). A well-researched biography of the woman who was executed with her husband for being Communist atomic spies. (Rev: VOYA 2/89) [921]

ROSENBERG, JULIUS AND ETHEL

6634 Meeropol, Robert, and Michael Meeropol. *We Are Your Sons: The Legacy of Julius and Ethel Rosenberg* (10–12). 1986, Univ. of Illinois

Pr. $27.50 (0-252-01263-1). The story of the imprisonment and execution for spying of Julius and Ethel Rosenberg as written by their sons. [921]

SACAJAWEA

6635 Waldo, Donna Lee. *Sacajawea* (10–12). 1979, Avon paper $5.95 (0-380-84293-9). A lengthy account of the Indian girl who accompanied the Lewis and Clark Expedition. [921]

SITTING BULL, CHIEF

6636 Vestal, Stanley. *Sitting Bull, Champion of the Sioux* (10–12). Illus. 1969, Univ. of Oklahoma Pr. paper $12.95 (0-8061-2219-6). A detailed, scholarly study of the life of the Sioux chief who lived from 1834 to 1890 [921]

STANTON, ELIZABETH CADY

6637 Banner, Lois W. *Elizabeth Cady Stanton: A Radical for Women's Rights* (10–12). 1980, Scott, Foresman paper $17.95 (0-673-39319-4). An informative biography of this early pioneer in the feminist movement and fighter for women's rights. [921]

STARR, BELLE

6638 Shirley, Glenn. *Belle Starr and Her Times: The Literature, the Facts, and the Legends* (10–12). 1990, Univ. of Oklahoma Pr. paper $11.95. This portrait of the famous female outlaw also gives a vivid picture of life in frontier America. [921]

TECUMSEH

6639 Edmunds, R. David. *Tecumseh and the Quest for Indian Leadership* (10–12). 1984, Scott Foresman paper $17.95 (0-673-39336-4). The story of this powerful Shawnee Indian and his attempts to forge a strong Indian nation during the nineteenth century. [921]

Science, Medicine, Industry, and Business

Collective

6640 Asimov, Isaac. *Asimov's Biographical Encyclopedia of Science and Technology* (9–12). 2nd Rev. ed. Illus. 1982, Doubleday paper $29.95 (0-385-17771-2). Using a chronological arrangement, Asimov outlines the accomplishments of 1,510 scientists, past and present. [920.03]

6641 De Kruif, Paul. *Microbe Hunters* (10–12). 1966, Harcourt paper $6.95 (0-15-659413-7). This account, first published in 1926, covers the work of such scientists as Leeuwenhoek, Walter Reed, and Paul Ehrlich. [920]

6642 Fucini, Joseph J., and Susan Fucini. *Entrepreneurs: The Men and Women behind Famous Brand Names* (10–12). 1985, G. K. Hall paper $9.95 (0-8161-8736-3). Biographies of such innovators as Kellogg, Sara Lee, and Calvin Klein. (Rev: BL 3/1/85) [920]

6643 Meadows, Jack. *The Great Scientists* (10–12). Illus. 1987, Oxford Univ. Pr. $35.00 (0-19-520620-7). Through the lives of 12 scientists—including Galileo, Faraday, Madame Curie, and Freud—the story of science is told. (Rev: BL 2/15/88) [920]

6644 O'Hern, Elizabeth Moot. *Profiles of Pioneer Women Scientists* (10–12). Illus. 1986, Acropolis $18.95 (0-87491-811-1). This book contains brief biographies of 20 women scientists. (Rev: SLJ 12/86) [920]

6645 Osen, Lynn M. *Women in Mathematics* (10–12). Illus. 1987, MIT Pr. paper $7.95 (0-262-65009-5). A collection of famous female mathematicians that spans 1,500 years of history. [920]

6646 Slater, Robert. *Portraits in Silicon* (10–12). Illus. 1987, MIT Pr. $24.95 (0-262-19262-4). Profiles of 31 computer pioneers who caused the remarkable growth of this industry. (Rev: BL 2/1/88) [920]

6647 Wolpert, Lewis, and Alison Richards. *A Passion for Science* (10–12). 1988, Oxford Univ. Pr. $21.95 (0-19-854213-5). A collection of profiles of important contemporary scientists who explain what science means to them and how and why they became scientists. (Rev: SLJ 2/89) [920]

6648 Wright, Robert. *Three Scientists and Their Gods: A Search for Meaning in an Age of Information* (10–12). 1988, Times Books $18.95 (0-8129-1328-0). Profiles of 3 contemporary scientists—a computer expert, a biologist, and an economist. (Rev: BL 5/1/88) [920]

Individual

ALVAREZ, LUIS W.

6649 Alvarez, Luis W. *Alvarez: The Adventures of a Physicist* (10–12). 1987, Basic Books $19.95 (0-465-00115-7); paper $9.95 (0-465-00116-6). An enthralling biography of the Nobel prize-winning physicist and his work on such projects as the development of radar and the atomic bomb. (Rev: BL 4/15/87) [921]

ARDEN, ELIZABETH

6650 Shuker, Nancy. *Elizabeth Arden: Cosmetics Entrepreneur* (8–12). Illus. 1989, Silver Burdett LB $11.98 (0-382-09587-1). The life and accomplishment of this businesswoman who turned the search for beauty into a gold mine. (Rev: BL 1/1/90; SLJ 4/90) [921]

CARNEGIE, ANDREW

6651 Wall, Joseph Frazier. *Andrew Carnegie* (10–12). Illus. 1970, Oxford Univ. Pr $39.95 (0-19-501282-8). The story of the immigrant Scottish youngster, his rise to fame and fortune, plus a picture of social and economic life of the United States in the nineteenth century. [921]

CARSON, RACHEL

6652 Gartner, Carol B. *Rachel Carson* (10–12). 1983, Ungar $18.95 (0-8044-5425-6). This is the biography of the ecologist who first warned us about pesticides and the possibility of silent springs. [921]

COUSTEAU, JACQUES

6653 Munson, Richard. *Cousteau: The Captain and His World* (9–12). Illus. 1989, Morrow $19.95 (0-688-07450-2). Cousteau's explorations, his inventions, and his life of adventure are covered in this biography. (Rev: BL 11/15/89) [921]

CRICK, FRANCIS

6654 Crick, Francis. *What Mad Pursuit* (10–12). Illus. 1988, Basic Books $16.95 (0-465-09137-7). The autobiography of the famous scientist who received a joint Nobel Prize with James Watson for the discovery of the double helix. (Rev: SLJ 2/89) [921]

CURIE, MADAME MARIE

6655 Pflaum, Rosalynd. *Grand Obsession: Madame Curie and Her World* (10–12). Illus. 1989, Doubleday $22.50 (0-385-26135-7). Not just a biography of this Polish chemist but a re-creation of the times in which she lived. [921]

DARWIN, CHARLES

6656 Clark, Ronald W. *The Survival of Charles Darwin: A Biography of a Man and an Idea* (10–12). Illus. 1985, Random $19.45 (0-394-52134-X); Avon paper $5.95 (0-380-69991-5). For better readers, the life of this famous naturalist and a discussion of his ideas in light of present-day thought. (Rev: BL 1/1/85) [921]

6657 Ralling, Christopher, comp. *The Voyage of Charles Darwin: His Autobiographical Writings* (10–12). Illus. 1986, Parkwest $18.95 (0-88186-426-9); paper $4.95 (0-88186-925-2). From his autobiography, diaries, and other writings here is a chronologically arranged account of Darwin's voyage on the HMS *Beagle*. (Rev: SLJ 10/86) [921]

DELBRUCK, MAX

6658 Fischer, Ernst, and Carol Lipson. *Thinking about Science: Max Delbruck and the Origins of Molecular Biology* (10–12). Illus. 1988, Norton $19.95 (0-393-02508-X). A readable biography about the Nobel Prize-winner who has pioneered the field of molecular biology. (Rev: SLJ 5/89) [921]

DODGE FAMILY

6659 Latham, Caroline, and David Agresta. *Dodge Dynasty: The Car and the Family That Rocked Detroit* (10–12). Illus. 1989, Harcourt $19.95 (0-15-125320-X). An entertaining profile of the family that, next to the Fords, was the best-known dynasty of the American automobile world. (Rev: BL 3/1/89) [921]

EINSTEIN, ALBERT

6660 Bernstein, Jeremy. *Einstein* (10–12). 1976, Penguin paper $4.95 (0-14-004317-9). In addition to biographical information, this account gives an explanation of Einstein's scientific theories. [921]

6661 Clark, Ronald W. *Einstein: The Life and Times* (10–12). 1979, Avon paper $5.95 (0-380-01159-X). A thoughtful biography that explores the scientist's life in relation to the important political and social events in his lifetime. [921]

6662 Sayen, Jamie. *Einstein in America* (10–12). Illus. 1985, Crown $17.95 (0-517-55604-9). This account emphasizes the personal life of this scientist and discusses the many causes he supported such as Zionism and pacifism. [921]

EMBERY, JOAN

6663 Embery, Joan. *My Wild World* (9–12). 1980, Dell paper $2.95 (0-440-15941-5). Embery describes her many years working with the San Diego Zoo and of the many animals she has encountered. [921]

FARADAY, MICHAEL

6664 Ludwig, Charles. *Michael Faraday: Father of Electronics* (9–12). 1988, Herald Pr. $6.95 (0-8361-3479-6). This is the story of the scientist who worked on such inventions as the dynamo, the generator, and the transformer. [921]

FEYNMAN, RICHARD

6665 Feynman, Richard, and Ralph Leighton. *"What Do You Care What Other People Think?": Further Adventures of a Curious Character* (10–12). 1988, Norton $17.95 (0-393-02659-0). A continuation of the biography of the Nobel Prize-winning physicist whose first book was *"Surely You're Joking, Mr. Feynman!"* (1984). (Rev: BL 10/15/88) [921]

FORD, HENRY

6666 Harris, Jacqueline L. *Henry Ford* (8–12). Illus. 1984, Watts LB $12.90 (0-531-04754-7). An easily read biography of this pioneer of the automobile industry. [921]

FOSSEY, DIAN

6667 Hayes, Harold T. P. *The Dark Romance of Dian Fossey* (10–12). Illus. 1990, Simon & Schuster $21.95 (0-671-63339-2). An absorbing account of both the private and public life of the woman who furthered research on gorilla behavior and later met a brutal end. (Rev: BL 5/1/90) [921]

6668 Mowat, Farley. *Woman in the Mists: The Story of Dian Fossey and the Mountain Gorillas of Africa* (10–12). Illus. 1987, Warner $19.95 (0-446-51360-1); Warner paper $10.95 (0-446-38720-7). A naturalist and writer has created a stirring life of the zoologist whose study of gorillas was trailblazing. (Rev: BL 9/1/87; SLJ 2/88; VOYA 4/88) [921]

FRANKLIN, ROSALIND

6669 Sayre, Anne. *Rosalind Franklin and DNA* (10–12). 1975, Norton $8.95 (0-393-07493-5); paper $7.95 (0-393-00868-1). The story of the scientist who died at age 37 before her pioneering work on DNA could be completed. [921]

FULTON, ROBERT

6670 Philip, Cynthia Owen. *Robert Fulton: A Biography* (10–12). 1985, Watts $18.95 (0-531-09756-0). This biography reveals that in addition to the steamboat, Fulton was associated with other scientific pursuits as well as being an accomplished painter of miniatures. (Rev: BL 9/15/85; BR 5–6/86) [921]

GALBRAITH, JOHN KENNETH

6671 Galbraith, John Kenneth. *A Life in Our Times: Memoirs* (10–12). 1981, Houghton $16.95 (0-395-30509-8). An autobiography of the fa-

mous statesman, economics writer, and presidential adviser. [921]

GOLDMAN, JOEL

6672 Goldman, Joel. *The Boxer Rebellion and Other Tales* (10–12). 1988, Donald I. Fine $17.95 (1-55611-105-3). A realistic, sometimes gruesome picture of a veterinarian's work and practice. (Rev: BL 9/15/88) [636.089]

HEISER, VICTOR G.

6673 Heiser, Victor G. *An American Doctor's Odyssey* (10–12). 1936, Norton $12.00 (0-393-07331-9). This 1936 autobiography deals with a doctor's travels around the world fighting disease. [921]

HERRIOT, JAMES

6674 Herriot, James. *All Creatures Great and Small* (8–12). 1972, St. Martin's $15.95 (0-312-01960-0). The first volume of Herriot's memories of being a veterinarian in Yorkshire, England, during the 1930s. Continued in *All Things Bright and Beautiful* (1974), *All Things Wise and Wonderful* (1977), and *The Lord God Made Them All* (1981). [921]

HORNEY, KAREN

6675 Jones, Constance. *Karen Horney* (9–12). Illus. 1989, Chelsea House $16.95 (1-55546-659-1). The story of the famous psychoanalyst who adjusted Freud's theories to correct a male bias. (Rev: BL 1/15/90; BR 3–4/90; SLJ 3/90) [921]

IACOCCA, LEE

6676 Iacocca, Lee. *Iacocca: An Autobiography* (10–12). Illus. 1984, Bantam $21.95 (0-553-05102-4); paper $5.50 (0-553-25147-3). A behind-the-scenes look at the automobile industry in America through the eyes of the head of Chrysler Corporation. [921]

JANNETTA, PETER

6677 Shelton, Mark L. *Working in a Very Small Place: The Making of a Neurosurgeon* (10–12). 1989, Norton $19.95 (0-393-02681-7). The biography of the Pittsburgh neurosurgeon, Peter Jannetta, whose discoveries have created dramatic pain-relieving procedures. (Rev: BL 6/1/89) [921]

JOBS, STEVEN

6678 Butcher, Lee. *Accidental Millionaire: The Rise and Fall of Steve Jobs at Apple Computer* (10–12). Illus. 1987, Paragon $19.95 (0-913729-79-5). The story of the co-founder of the Apple Co. and his downfall. (Rev: BL 9/1/87) [921]

KINGSLEY, MARY

6679 Frank, Katherine. *A Voyager Out: The Life of Mary Kingsley* (10–12). Illus. 1986, Houghton $18.95 (0-395-35317-7). The story of the brave nineteenth-century Englishwoman who ventured into Africa alone on scientific expeditions. (Rev: SLJ 3/87) [921]

KLITZMAN, ROBERT

6680 Klitzman, Robert. *A Year-Long Night: Tales of a Medical Intern* (9–12). 1989, Viking $17.95 (0-670-81777-5). A perceptive account of a doctor's internship experiences. (Rev: BL 2/1/89) [921]

KRITSICK, STEPHEN

6681 Kritsick, Stephen, and Patti Goldstein. *Creature Comforts: The Adventures of a City Vet* (9–12). 1984, Berkley paper $3.50 (0-425-06567-7). This is the story of a veterinarian's experiences in a big city pet hospital. [921]

KÜBLER-ROSS, ELISABETH

6682 Gill, Derek. *Quest: The Life of Elisabeth Kübler-Ross* (10–12). Illus. 1980, Ballantine paper $4.95 (0-345-01021-3). The biography of the Swiss psychiatrist who is famous for her work with the terminally ill. [921]

LABASTILLE, ANNE

6683 LaBastille, Anne. *Woodswoman* (10–12). 1978, Dutton $10.95 (0-525-23715-1); paper $7.95 (0-525-47504-4). A young naturalist tests her survival skills by living alone in a hand-built cabin in the Adirondacks. [921]

LANE, KENNETH

6684 Lane, Kenneth. *Diary of a Medical Nobody* (9–12). 1988, Severn House $15.95 (0-7278-0897-4). The true, heartwarming story of a doctor in rural Somerset, England, from 1929 on. (Rev: BL 2/15/88) [921]

LEAKEY, MARY

6685 Leakey, Mary. *Disclosing the Past* (10–12). 1986, McGraw paper $9.95 (0-07-036837-6). The story of the Leakey family and their devotion and accomplishments in the field of anthropology. [921]

LEAKEY, RICHARD E.

6686 Leakey, Richard E. *One Life: An Autobiography* (10–12). Illus. 1984, Salem House $18.95 (0-88162-055-6). The story of the famous anthropologist and his many adventures seeking hominid remains. [921]

LEVI-MONTALCINI, RITA

6687 Levi-Montalcini, Rita. *In Praise of Imperfection: My Life and Work* (10–12). Trans. by Luigi Attardi. 1988, Basic Books $18.95 (0-465-03217-6). The biography of a woman doctor who lived through the Nazi era in Europe, migrated to the United States, and won the Nobel Prize in 1986. (Rev: BL 3/15/88) [921]

LORENZ, KONRAD

6688 Lorenz, Konrad. *King Solomon's Ring* (10–12). 1972, NAL paper $2.95 (0-451-13229-7). This Nobel Prize winner describes his life in animal research. [921]

MEAD, MARGARET

6689 Bateson, Mary Catherine. *With a Daughter's Eye: A Memoir of Margaret Mead and Gregory Bateson* (10–12). Illus. 1984, Pocket paper $4.95 (0-671-55424-7). A reflection on the author's parents, one a British scientist and the other the anthropologist Margaret Mead. [921]

6690 Cassidy, Robert. *Margaret Mead: A Voice for the Century* (10–12). 1982, Universe paper $7.95 (0-87663-850-7). A biography that concentrates on the anthropologist's professional career and contributions. [921]

6691 Mead, Margaret. *Blackberry Winter* (10–12). 1972, Peter Smith $24.50 (0-317-60065-6). This autobiography covers the childhood of Margaret Mead, her career as an anthropologist, and her life with her family. [921]

6692 Rice, Edward. *Margaret Mead: A Portrait* (10–12). Illus. 1979, Harper LB $13.85 (0-06-025002-X). A personalized biography of this anthropologist written by a friend. [921]

MINKOW, BARRY

6693 Akst, Daniel. *Wonder Boy: Barry Minkow—The Kid Who Swindled Wall Street* (10–12). 1990, Macmillan $19.95 (0-684-18988-7). The story of the teenage multimillionaire who was eventually sentenced to 25 years in jail for various fraudulent activities. (Rev: BL 12/15/89) [921]

MORGAN, ELIZABETH

6694 Morgan, Elizabeth. *The Making of a Woman Surgeon* (10–12). 1988, Berkley paper $3.95 (0-425-10037-5). The story of a woman's 7 years of medical training. Continued in *Solo Practice* (1984). [921]

MUIR, JOHN

6695 Fox, Stephen R. *John Muir and His Legacy: The American Conservation Movement* (10–12). 1981, Little $24.95 (0-316-29110-2). A biography of the naturalist who died in 1914 and the story of the conservation movement he influenced. [921]

NEWTON, SIR ISAAC

6696 Christianson, Gale E. *In the Presence of the Creator: Isaac Newton and His Times* (10–12). Illus. 1984, Free Pr. $19.95 (0-02-905190-8). This account gives details of both Newton's life and his controversial work, as well as information on the England of his time. [921]

O'BARRY, RICHARD

6697 O'Barry, Richard, and Keith Coulbourn. *Behind the Dolphin Smile* (9–12). Illus. 1988, Algonquin $16.95 (0-912697-79-2). O'Barry has worked with dolphins throughout his entire life and tells about it in this informative memoir. (Rev: SLJ 10/88) [921]

PASTEUR, LOUIS

6698 Dubos, Rene. *Pasteur and Modern Science* (10–12). Illus. 1988, Science Tech $18.95 (0-910239-18-5). The engrossing story of one of the founders of modern microbiology and immunology. (Rev: BL 9/1/88) [921]

PAULING, LINUS

6699 Serafini, Anthony. *Linus Pauling: A Man and His Science* (10–12). Illus. 1989, Paragon $22.95 (0-913729-88-4). For better readers, here is a challenging biography of the Nobel Prize winner who has been a controversial figure. (Rev: BL 3/15/89) [921]

SLATER, CORNELIUS

6700 Slater, Cornelius. *An Apple a Day: Adventures of a Country Doctor* (9–12). 1988, Vanguard $15.95 (0-8149-0932-9). The experience—humorous, tragic, inspiring, commonplace—of a rural English doctor. (Rev: BL 1/1/88) [921]

TAYLOR, DAVID

6701 Taylor, David. *Next Panda Please! Further Adventures of a Wildlife Vet* (7–12). 1983, Scarborough $12.95 (0-8128-2857-7). Further adventures of the adventurous vet whose story began in *Zoo Vet,* now out of print. [921]

THOMAS, LEWIS

6702 Thomas, Lewis. *The Youngest Science: Notes of a Medicine-Watcher* (10–12). 1983, Viking paper $14.75 (0-670-79533-X). Autobiographical writings by the famous doctor and writer on the philosophy of science. [921]

WRIGHT, WILBUR AND ORVILLE

6703 Crouch, Tom. *The Bishop's Boys: A Life of Wilbur & Orville Wright* (9–12). Illus. 1989, Norton $22.50 (0-393-02660-4). A richly detailed, thorough account of the Wright family and the brothers' contributions to aviation history. (Rev: BR 1–2/90) [921]

6704 Walsh, John Evangelist. *One Day at Kitty Hawk: The Untold Story of the Wright Brothers and the Airplane* (10–12). Illus. 1975, Harper $12.45 (0-690-00103-7). The story of the development of the airplane, the first successful flight, and the early days of aviation. [921]

Sports

Collective

6705 Devaney, John. *Where Are They Today? Great Sport Stars of Yesteryear* (8–12). Illus. 1985, Crown $16.95 (0-517-55344-9); paper $9.95 (0-517-55345-7). Here are brief profiles of 45 famous stars of the past with information on their present activities. (Rev: BL 6/15/85) [920]

6706 Halberstam, David. *The Amateurs* (10–12). 1986, Penguin paper $6.95 (0-14-008934-9). Profiles of 4 athletes who hoped to secure a place on the 1984 U.S. Olympic rowing team. (Rev: BL 6/1/85) [920]

6707 Peary, Danny, ed. *Cult Baseball Players: The Greats, the Flakes, the Weird, and the Wonderful* (9–12). Illus. 1990, Simon & Schuster paper $9.95 (0-671-67172-3). A tribute to 59 former players like Sandy Koufax and Mickey Mantle, all of whom had colorful personalities. (Rev: BL 1/1/90) [796.357]

6708 Riley, Pat. *Show Time: Inside the Lakers Breakthrough Season* (8–12). 1988, Warner $17.95 (0-446-51427-6). The story of the Lakers' important 1986–1987 season as told by their coach. (Rev: BL 4/15/88; BR 11–12/88; VOYA 10/88) [796.32]

6709 Ritter, Lawrence S., and Donald Honig. *The 100 Greatest Baseball Players of All Time* (8–12). Rev. ed. Illus. 1986, Crown $17.95 (0-517-56181-6). As well as biographies, this volume includes pictures and statistics about each of the players considered to be baseball greats. [920]

6710 Rust, Edna, and Art Rust Jr. *Art Rust's Illustrated History of the Black Athlete* (9–12). Illus. 1985, Doubleday paper $15.95 (0-385-15140-3). From a variety of sports, this volume highlights the careers of about 100 famous black American athletes. [920]

Automobile Racing

FOYT, A. J.

6711 Foyt, A. J. *A. J.: My Life as America's Greatest Race Car Driver* (8–12). 1984, Warner paper $3.50 (0-446-32418-3). The life of the race-car driver A. J. Foyt from his first win at age 5 to the successes of the early 1980s. [921]

Baseball

ALLEN, DICK

6712 Allen, Dick, and Tim Whitaker. *Crash: The Life and Times of Dick Allen* (9–12). 1989, Ticknor $17.95 (0-89919-657-8). The life of the once controversial, now retired black baseball player that tells his side of the story. (Rev: BL 3/15/89) [921]

ANDERSON, SPARKY

6713 Anderson, Sparky, and Dan Ewald. *Sparky!* (10–12). 1990, Prentice $18.95 (0-13-109463-7). The story of one of the most successful managers in the history of baseball. (Rev: BL 3/15/90) [921]

BAYLOR, DON

6714 Baylor, Don, and Claire Smith. *Don Baylor: Baseball on the Field and in the Clubhouse* (9–12). Illus. 1989, St. Martin's $18.95 (0-312-02906-3). The World Series star currently with the Oakland A's tells his story. (Rev: BL 4/15/89) [921]

BERRA, YOGI

6715 Berra, Yogi, and Tom Horton. *Yogi: It Ain't Over . . .* (9–12). Illus. 1990, Harper paper $4.95 (0-06-100012-4). A somewhat confusing memoir by this baseball great plus tributes from his friends. (Rev: BL 4/15/89) [921]

CLEMENS, ROGER

6716 Clemens, Roger, and Peter Gammons. *Rocket Man: The Roger Clemens Story* (9–12). Illus. 1987, Viking $15.95 (0-8289-0629-7). An autobiography of the baseball player who was named Most Valuable Player in the American League in 1986. (Rev: BR 3–4/88; VOYA 4/88) [921]

DOBY, LARRY

6717 Moore, Joseph Thomas. *Pride against Prejudice: The Biography of Larry Doby* (9–12). 1988, Greenwood $35.00 (0-313-25995-X). The story of the first black player in the American League who followed Jackie Robinson's debut in the National League. (Rev: BL 3/15/88) [921]

DRAVECKY, DAVE

6718 Dravecky, Dave, and Tim Stafford. *Comeback* (9–12). 1990, Zondervan $17.95 (0-310-52880-1). The inspiring story of this baseball player's bout with cancer and his attempts to come back to the major league. (Rev: BL 4/1/90; SLJ 8/90) [921]

DRYSDALE, DON

6719 Drysdale, Don, and Bob Verdi. *Once a Bum, Always a Dodger* (9–12). Illus. 1990, St. Martin's $18.95 (0-312-03902-6). The baseball Hall of Fame pitcher who dates back to the Brooklyn Dodgers tells his story. (Rev: BL 1/1/90) [921]

GEHRIG, LOU

6720 Gehrig, Eleanor, and Joseph Durso. *My Luke and I* (9–12). 1976, Harper $11.45 (0-690-01109-1). An affectionate portrait of the famous baseball star written by his wife. [921]

6721 Robinson, Ray. *Iron Horse: Lou Gehrig in His Time* (9–12). Illus. 1990, Norton $22.95 (0-393-02857-7). A stirring life story of the quiet, dignified baseball great who inspired millions by his courage. (Rev: BL 7/90) [921]

GREENBERG, HANK

6722 Greenberg, Hank. *Hank Greenberg: The Story of My Life* (9–12). Illus. 1989, Times Books $19.95 (0-8129-1741-3). The life of the great Jewish ball player who died shortly after dictating the rough notes for this book. (Rev: BL 5/15/89) [921]

HERSHISER, OREL

6723 Hershiser, Orel, and Jerry B. Jenkins. *Out of the Blue* (8–12). Illus. 1989, Wolgemuth & Hyatt $17.95 (0-943497-57-4). The story of the incredibly talented baseball star who joined the Dodgers in 1984. (Rev: VOYA 10/89) [921]

HUNTER, CATFISH

6724 Hunter, Jim, and Armen Keteyian. *Catfish: My Life in Baseball* (8–12). Illus. 1988, McGraw $17.95 (0-07-031371-7). The story of the baseball Hall of Famer who retired in 1979. (Rev: BL 4/15/88) [921]

MANTLE, MICKEY

6725 Mantle, Mickey, and Herb Gluck. *The Mick* (10–12). 1987, Jove paper $3.95 (0-515-08599-5). For better readers, an honest autobiography that deals with Mantle's life both on and off the diamond. (Rev: BL 6/1/85) [921]

MARIS, ROGER

6726 Allen, Maury. *Roger Maris: A Man for All Seasons* (9–12). 1986, Donald I. Fine $16.95 (0-917657-94-2). A biography of the legendary batter that gives special coverage to the 1961 season when he broke Babe Ruth's record. (Rev: SLJ 1/87) [921]

MAYS, WILLIE

6727 Mays, Willie, and Lou Sahadi. *Say Hey: The Autobiography of Willie Mays* (9–12). Illus. 1988, Simon & Schuster $17.95 (0-671-63292-2). A straightforward retelling of the black baseball legend who played in the major leagues for 22 years. (Rev: BL 4/15/88) [921]

MCGRAW, JOHN

6728 Alexander, Charles C. *John McGraw* (10–12). 1988, Viking $19.95 (0-670-80730-3); Penguin paper $8.95 (0-14-009600-0). The biography of one of baseball's greats who managed the New York Giants from 1902 through 1933. (Rev: VOYA 8/88) [921]

NETTLES, GRAIG

6729 Nettles, Graig, and Peter Golenbock. *Balls* (10–12). 1984, Putnam $14.95 (0-399-12894-8). A frank autobiography by the former New York Yankee third baseman. [921]

ROBINSON, JACKIE

6730 Allen, Maury. *Jackie Robinson: A Life Remembered* (9–12). Illus. 1987, Watts $16.95 (0-531-15042-9). Using many sources including interviews with former teammates, Allen has produced a fine biography of the first black player in the major leagues. (Rev: BL 3/15/87; BR 11–12/87; SLJ 9/87; VOYA 10/87) [921]

6731 Frommer, Harvey. *Jackie Robinson* (8–12). Illus. 1984, Watts LB $12.90 (0-531-04858-6). A brief biography of the Dodger who broke the baseball color barrier. [921]

RUTH, GEORGE HERMAN ("BABE")

6732 Creamer, Robert W. *Babe: The Legend Comes to Life* (9–12). 1974, Penguin paper $8.95 (0-14-006859-7). The sports career and private life of this baseball great are discussed in this readable biography. [921]

SMITH, OZZIE

6733 Smith, Ozzie, and Rob Rains. *Wizard* (8–12). 1988, Contemporary $16.95 (0-8092-4594-9). The autobiography of the amazing shortstop of the St. Louis Cardinals. (Rev: BL 5/15/88) [921]

STENGEL, CASEY

6734 Creamer, Robert W. *Stengel: His Life and Times* (9–12). Illus. 1984, Dell paper $8.95 (0-440-57829-9). The life of the legendary baseball manager who worked at various times for both the Yankees and the Mets. [921]

WINFIELD, DAVE

6735 Winfield, Dave, and Tom Parker. *Winfield: A Player's Life* (10–12). Illus. 1988, Norton $16.95 (0-393-02467-9). An interestingly written

biography that provides unusual insights into the life and career of this New York Yankee outfielder. (Rev: BL 4/15/88) [921]

YASTRZEMSKI, CARL

6736 Yastrzemski, Carl, and Gerald Eskenazi. *Yaz: Baseball, the Wall, and Me* (9–12). Illus. 1990, Doubleday $19.95 (0-385-26769-X). The autobiography of the legendary player of the Boston Red Sox who is now a member of the Hall of Fame. (Rev: VOYA 8/90) [921]

Basketball

ABDUL-JABBAR, KAREEM

6737 Abdul-Jabbar, Kareem, and Peter Knobler. *Giant Steps* (9–12). 1985, Bantam paper $4.50 (0-553-24511-2). The autobiography of the famous basketball player that includes such interesting sidelights as the reasons for his conversion to the Islamic religion. [921]

6738 Abdul-Jabbar, Kareem, and Mignon McCarthy. *Kareem* (9–12). Illus. 1990, Random $18.95 (0-394-55927-4). A memoir of the great basketball player in the form of a diary of his last playing year. This forms a complementary volume to the player's earlier autobiography *Giant Steps* (1985). (Rev: BL 2/1/90; SLJ 8/90) [921]

AUERBACH, RED

6739 Auerbach, Red. *On and Off the Court* (9–12). 1985, Macmillan $14.95 (0-02-504390-0); Bantam paper $3.95 (0-533-26143-6). The autobiography of the man associated with leading the Boston Celtics in a variety of capacities from coach to president. [921]

BIAS, LEN

6740 Cole, Lewis. *Never Too Young to Die* (10–12). 1989, Pantheon $19.95 (0-394-56440-5). This is the story of the death by a drug overdose of the 22-year-old basketball player, Len Bias. (Rev: SLJ 1/90; VOYA 4/90) [921]

BIRD, LARRY

6741 Bird, Larry. *Drive: The Story of My Life* (9–12). Illus. 1989, Doubleday $18.95 (0-385-24821-7). The autobiography of the Boston Celtics star with insight into his personality and those of his colleagues. (Rev: BL 10/1/89) [921]

6742 Levine, Lee Daniel. *Bird: The Making of an American Sports Legend* (9–12). Illus. 1988, McGraw $17.95 (0-07-037477-5). The star of the Boston Celtics comes to life in this readable biography. (Rev: BL 10/15/88) [921]

ERVING, JULIUS

6743 Bell, Marty. *The Legend of Dr. J.: The Story of Julius Erving* (9–12). 1976, NAL paper $2.95 (0-451-12179-1). A biography of one of basketball's all-time superstars. [921]

FRAZIER, WALT

6744 Frazier, Walt. *Walt Frazier: One Magic Season & a Basketball Life* (9–12). 1988, Times Books $17.95 (0-8129-1736-7). An autobiography of the basketball star that concentrates on his first championship season during 1970. (Rev: BR 5–6/89; VOYA 6/89) [921]

JOHNSON, EARVIN "MAGIC"

6745 Johnson, Earvin "Magic," and Roy S. Johnson. *Magic's Touch* (9–12). Illus. 1989, Addison $17.95 (0-201-51794-9). An autobiography of this basketball star with many interesting sidelights about the L.A. Lakers. (Rev: BL 9/15/89) [921]

KNIGHT, BOB

6746 Mellen, Joan. *Bob Knight: His Own Man* (10–12). 1988, Donald I. Fine $18.95 (1-55611-100-2). In explicit language, the author re-created the life of the feisty coach of the Indiana University basketball team. (Rev: BL 9/1/88) [921]

Boxing

LEONARD, SUGAR RAY

6747 Haskins, James. *Sugar Ray Leonard* (7–12). Illus. 1982, Lothrop $12.95 (0-688-01436-4). A brief, heavily illustrated biography of the fighter who rose to superstardom in the boxing ring. [921]

LOUIS, JOE

6748 Barrow, Joe Louis, and Barbara Munder. *Joe Louis: 50 Years an American Hero* (9–12). Illus. 1988, McGraw $18.95 (0-07-003955-0). An estranged son re-creates the life of his father, the boxer Joe Louis. (Rev: BL 9/15/88) [921]

6749 Mead, Chris. *Champion: Joe Louis, Black Hero in White America* (10–12). Illus. 1985, Penguin paper $6.95 (0-14-009285-4). A superior biography of the black boxing champion that also gives details about attitudes of whites toward him. [921]

TYSON, MIKE

6750 Berger, Phil. *Blood Season: Tyson and the World of Boxing* (10–12). Illus. 1989, Morrow $18.95 (0-877-95962-5). A biography of the controversial heavyweight with good background information on the boxing world. (Rev: BL 7/89) [921]

Football

BLEIER, ROCKY

6751 Bleier, Rocky, and Terry O'Neil. *Fighting Back* (10–12). 1980, Scarborough $12.95 (0-8128-1767-8). The story of how Rocky Bleier overcame wounds received in Vietnam and made it to the Super Bowl. [921]

BRADSHAW, TERRY

6752 Bradshaw, Terry, and Buddy Martin. *Looking Deep* (9–12). Illus. 1989, Contemporary $17.95 (0-8092-4266-4). The story of the famous Steelers quarterback of the 1970s who led his team to the Super Bowl. (Rev: BL 9/15/89; BR 3–4/90) [921]

KNOX, CHUCK

6753 Knox, Chuck, and Bill Plaschke. *Hard Knox: The Life of an NFL Coach* (9–12). Illus. 1988, Harcourt $17.95 (0-15-133450-1). The autobiography of the man who has coached many different teams and won many different titles. (Rev: BL 10/15/88) [921]

LANDRY, TOM

6754 Landry, Tom, and Gregg Lewis. *Tom Landry: An Autobiography* (9–12). Illus. 1990, Harper $18.95 (0-310-52910-7). A story of the former Dallas Cowboys coach who was with them for 20 years. (Rev: BL 6/15/90) [921]

MADDEN, JOHN

6755 Madden, John, and Dave Anderson. *Hey, Wait a Minute, I Wrote a Book!* (9–12). 1985, Ballantine paper $4.95 (0-345-32507-9). The life of the famous sports commentator who at one time coached the Oakland Raiders. [921]

6756 Madden, John, and Dave Anderson. *One Size Doesn't Fit All* (10–12). 1988, Random $16.95 (0-394-56313-1). Memoirs of a former football coach who is now a successful television commentator. (Rev: BL 7/88; BR 3–4/89) [921]

PATERNO, JOE

6757 Paterno, Joe, and Bernard Asbell. *Paterno: By the Book* (9–12). 1989, Random $18.95 (0-394-56501-0). The autobiography of the strict Penn State football coach and the impressive record he has established. (Rev: BL 10/1/89) [921]

PICCOLO, BRIAN

6758 Morris, Jeannie. *Brian Piccolo: A Short Season* (7–12). Illus. 1972, Dell paper $3.95 (0-440-10889-6). The inspiring story of the Chicago Bears player who died of cancer at 26. [921]

REEVES, DAN

6759 Reeves, Dan, and Dick Connor. *Reeves: An Autobiography* (8–12). Illus. 1988, Bonus Books $17.95 (0-933893-64-7). The former running back of the Cowboys and now a respected coach tells his story. (Rev: BL 8/88) [921]

SCHRAMM, TEX

6760 St. John, Bob. *Tex! The Man Who Built the Dallas Cowboys* (9–12). Illus. 1988, Prentice $18.95 (0-13-911975-2). The story of Tex Schramm, team president, and "father" of the Dallas Cowboys. (Rev: BL 8/88) [921]

SMERLAS, FRED

6761 Smerlas, Fred, and Vic Carucci. *By a Nose* (9–12). Illus. 1990, Simon & Schuster $18.95 (0-671-70532-6). An up-beat biography of the football tackle who has played with the Buffalo Bills and the San Francisco 49er's. (Rev: BL 9/15/90) [921]

Gymnastics and Track and Field

BAKER, JOHN

6762 Buchanan, William. *A Shining Season* (10–12). 1987, Univ. of New Mexico Pr. paper $10.95 (0-8263-1015-X). The story of John Baker, a track star who died of cancer at age 36. [921]

BANNISTER, ROGER

6763 Bannister, Roger. *The Four-Minute Mile* (9–12). 1981, Lyons & Burford paper $9.95 (1-55821-027-X). The medical student who first broke the 4-minute mile record tells his dramatic story. [921]

BENOIT, JOAN

6764 Benoit, Joan, and Sally Baker. *Running Tide* (9–12). Illus. 1987, Knopf $16.95 (0-394-55457-4). The Olympic marathon winner and champion American distance runner tells her own story. (Rev: BL 10/1/87; BR 1–2/88; SLJ 4/88; VOYA 4/88) [921]

OWENS, JESSE

6765 Baker, William J. *Jesse Owens: An American Life* (10–12). Illus. 1986, Free Pr. $19.95 (0-02-901780-7); paper $9.95 (0-02-901760-2). The story of the black American track star whose career involved triumph at Hitler's Olympics. [921]

6766 Owens, Jesse, and Paul Neimark. *Jesse: The Man Who Outran Hitler* (10–12). 1985, Fawcett paper $3.95 (0-449-13056-8). The autobiography of the man who ran away with the 1936 Olympics. [921]

RETTON, MARY LOU

6767 Retton, Mary Lou, and Bela Karolyi. *Mary Lou: Creating an Olympic Champion* (9–12). Illus. 1985, McGraw $16.95 (0-07-051894-7). The duo-biographies of the gold medal winning gymnast at the 1984 Olympics and her coach who defected from Romania. (Rev: BL 10/15/85) [921]

THORPE, JIM

6768 Wheeler, Robert W. *Jim Thorpe: World's Greatest Athlete* (9–12). 1981, Univ. of Oklahoma Pr. paper $12.95 (0-8061-1745-1). This biography traces the amazing career of the American Indian athlete who won both the decathlon and the pentathlon in 1912. [921]

Tennis

EVERT, CHRIS

6769 Lloyd, Chris Evert, and John Lloyd. *Lloyd on Lloyd* (9–12). Illus. 1986, Beaufort $14.95 (0-8253-0374-5). An honest autobiography by the former first couple in tennis. (Rev: BL 6/1/86) [921]

NAVRATILOVA, MARTINA

6770 Navratilova, Martina. *Tennis My Way* (8–12). Illus. 1984, Penguin paper $6.95 (0-14-007183-0). Not just a biography but also a work that includes many tips on how to play tennis like the pros. [921]

6771 Navratilova, Martina, and George Vecsey. *Martina* (10–12). Illus. 1986, Fawcett paper $3.95 (0-449-20982-2). An outspoken autobiography for mature teens about this amazing tennis champion. (Rev: BL 5/1/85; BR 11–12/85; SLJ 10/85; VOYA 12/85) [921]

SHRIVER, PAM

6772 Shriver, Pam, et al. *Passing Shots: Pam Shriver on Tour* (9–12). Illus. 1988, McGraw paper $5.95 (0-07-057180-5). A candid, self-critical autobiography by one of the foremost women in tennis. (Rev: BL 9/15/86) [921]

Miscellaneous Sports

BEAL, DOUG

6773 Beal, Doug, and Marc Katz. *Spike!* (9–12). Illus. 1985, Avant paper $9.95 (0-932238-30-0). Memoirs of the coach who led the U.S. volleyball team to victory in the 1984 Olympics. (Rev: BL 1/1/86) [921]

GRETZKY, WAYNE

6774 Gretzky, Wayne, and Rick Reilly. *Gretzky: An Autobiography* (9–12). Illus. 1990, Harper $19.95 (0-06-016339-9). The autobiography of the man many consider to be the world's greatest hockey player. (Rev: BL 11/15/90) [921]

HAMILL, DOROTHY

6775 Hamill, Dorothy. *Dorothy Hamill On and Off the Ice* (9–12). Illus. 1983, Knopf LB $10.99 (0-394-95610-9). An autobiography that explains how this internationally known figure skater was able to get to the top. [921]

HAMILTON, SCOTT

6776 Steere, Michael. *Scott Hamilton* (9–12). Illus. 1985, St. Martin's $12.95 (0-312-70449-6). A candid look at the life and personality of the figure skater who won a gold medal at the 1984 Olympics. (Rev: BL 12/1/85) [921]

KING, MIKE

6777 King, Mike. *The Mike King Story* (9–12). Illus. 1985, Good Books $15.95 (0-934672-33-4). An inspiring story of a paraplegic and his amazing wheelchair ride from Alaska to Washington, D.C. (Rev: BL 2/1/86) [921]

KINMONT, JILL

6778 Valens, E. G. *The Other Side of the Mountain* (9–12). Illus. 1975, Harper paper $3.95 (0-06-080948-5). The story of the skiing champion who became a quadriplegic as a result of an accident. [921]

LEDOUX, CHRIS

6779 Brown, David G. *Gold Buckle Dreams: The Rodeo Life of Chris LeDoux* (10–12). Illus. 1987, Quinlan $16.95 (0-933341-71-7); Wolverine paper $10.95 (0-941875-08-3). The biography of a top rodeo performer who has also become a country music star. (Rev: BL 7/87) [921]

LEMOND, GREG

6780 Abt, Samuel. *LeMond: The Incredible Comeback of an American Hero* (9–12). Illus. 1990, Random $18.95 (0-394-58476-7). The story of the incredible American cyclist and his comeback after a terrible hunting accident. (Rev: BL 4/15/90) [921]

SHOEMAKER, WILLIE

6781 Shoemaker, Bill, and Barney Nagler. *Shoemaker* (10–12). Illus. 1988, Doubleday $17.95 (0-385-23945-9). The biography of the world famous jockey who spent 40 years in the sport of horse racing. (Rev: BL 3/1/88) [921]

World Figures

Collective

6782 Anderson, Christopher P. *The New Book of People* (9–12). Illus. 1986, Putnam paper $14.95 (0-399-51223-3). Capsule biographies and photographs of celebrities that might grace the pages of *People* magazine. (Rev: BL 9/1/86) [920]

6783 Attwater, Donald. *Penguin Dictionary of Saints* (10–12). 2nd ed. 1983, Penguin paper $8.95 (0-14-051123-7). An alphabetical listing of 750 saints and their accomplishments. [920.03]

6784 Forster, Margaret. *Significant Sisters: The Grassroots of Active Feminism, 1839–1939* (10–12). 1986, Oxford Univ. Pr. paper $9.95 (0-19-504014-7). Biographies of 8 early feminists from both England and the United States such as Elizabeth Blackwell and Florence Nightingale. (Rev: BL 2/1/85) [920]

6785 Fraser, Antonia. *The Warrior Queens* (10–12). Illus. 1989, Knopf $22.95 (0-394-54939-2). This book is a series of profiles of women of power from Cleopatra to Indira Gandhi and Margaret Thatcher. (Rev: BL 1/15/89; SLJ 8/89) [920]

6786 Livesey, Anthony. *Great Commanders and Their Battles* (10–12). Illus. 1987, Macmillan $39.95 (0-02-573410-5). Twenty leaders from Alexander the Great to Moshe Dayan are highlighted along with their most famous battles. (Rev: BL 3/15/88) [920]

6787 Nixon, Richard. *Leaders* (10–12). 1990, Simon & Schuster paper $12.95 (0-671-70618-7). In this collection of brief portraits, the former president profiles some important persons he has met, for example, de Gaulle, Khrushchev, and MacArthur. [920]

6788 Plutarch. *Plutarch's Lives* (10–12). 1967, Random $15.95 (0-394-60407-5). Biographies written around A.D. 120 on the lives of famous ancient Greeks and Romans. [920]

6789 Shiels, Barbara. *Winners: Women and the Nobel Prize* (10–12). Illus. 1985, Dillon $14.95 (0-87518-293-3). Biographies of 8 women who have won the Nobel Prize. [920]

6790 Wolfe, Bertram D. *Three Who Made a Revolution: A Biographical History* (10–12). Illus. 1984, Scarborough House paper $14.95 (0-8128-6212-0). Biographies of Lenin, Trotsky, and Stalin and their contributions to the Russian revolution. [920]

Africa

BIKO, STEVE

6791 Woods, Donald. *Biko* (10–12). Rev. ed. 1979, Random paper $5.95 (0-394-72654-5). In addition to being a biography of Steve Biko, the South African black leader who was murdered in 1977, this gives good background material on apartheid in South Africa. (Rev: VOYA 4/88) [921]

KENYATTA, JOMO

6792 Wepman, Dennis. *Jomo Kenyatta* (9–12). Illus. 1985, Chelsea House LB $17.95 (0-87754-575-8). A heavily illustrated biography of the first president of Kenya. [921]

MANDELA, NELSON

6793 Benson, Mary. *Nelson Mandela: The Man and the Movement* (10–12). Illus. 1986, Norton paper $8.95 (0-393-30322-5). A detailed biography with great amounts of background material that ends before the civil rights leader was released from detention. (Rev: BL 9/15/86; BR 11–12/87) [921]

6794 Meer, Fatima. *Higher Than Hope: A Biography of Nelson Mandela* (10–12). Illus. 1990, Harper $19.95 (0-06-016146-9). An authorized, up-to-date biography written by a family friend and fellow activist. (Rev: BL 3/15/90) [921]

MANDELA, WINNIE

6795 Harrison, Nancy. *Winnie Mandela* (10–12). Illus. 1985, Braziller $14.95 (0-8076-1149-2); paper $5.95 (0-8076-1173-5). The story of the civil rights leader that ends while her husband, Nelson, is still in prison. [921]

6796 Mandela, Winnie. *A Part of My Soul Went with Him* (10–12). Illus. 1985, Norton $16.95 (0-393-02215-3); paper $5.95 (0-393-30290-3). The wife of the South African civil rights leader tells her story in this account written before her husband's release. (Rev: BL 2/1/86; SLJ 11/86) [921]

MATTERA, DON

6797 Mattera, Don. *Sophiatown: Coming of Age in South Africa* (10–12). 1989, Beacon $15.95 (0-8070-0206-2). The autobiography of a young South African black who changed from street tough to political activist. (Rev: BL 2/15/89) [921]

MODISANE, BLOKE

6798 Modisane, Bloke. *Blame Me on History* (10–12). 1990, Simon & Schuster $19.95 (0-671-70794-9); paper $9.95 (0-671-70067-7). The autobiography of a black man growing up in South Africa and later facing exile for his beliefs. (Rev: BL 6/1/90) [921]

RAMUSI, MOLAPATENE COLLINS

6799 Ramusi, Molapatene Collins, and Ruth S. Turner. *Soweto, My Love* (10–12). 1989, Henry Holt $22.95 (0-8050-0263-4). The autobiography of a black man who grew up under apartheid and is now a lawyer and reformer in Johannesburg. (Rev: BL 12/1/88) [921]

TUTU, DESMOND

6800 du Boulay, Shirley. *Tutu: Voice of the Voiceless* (10–12). 1988, Eerdmans $24.95 (0-8028-3649-6). A moving biography of the archbishop and his struggle against apartheid. (Rev: BL 5/15/88) [921]

Asia and Middle East

AARONSOHN, SARAH

6801 Cowen, Ida, and Irene Gunther. *A Spy for Freedom: The Story of Sarah Aaronsohn* (8–12). Illus. 1984, Dutton $14.95 (0-525-67150-1). The touching biography of the young woman who killed herself in 1917 for the cause of Zionism in Palestine. (Rev: BL 3/1/85) [921]

AQUINO, CORAZON

6802 Komisar, Lucy. *Corazon Aquino: The Story of a Revolution* (10–12). 1987, Braziller $16.95 (0-8076-1171-9). A re-creation of this courageous fighter for justice who has become the leader of her country. (Rev: BL 5/15/87; SLJ 9/87) [921]

ARAFAT, YASSER

6803 Wallach, Janet, and John Wallach. *Arafat: In the Eyes of the Beholder* (10–12). Illus. 1990, Carol $19.95 (0-8184-0533-3). The biography of the man who is considered a saint by some and by others simply a terrorist. (Rev: BL 7/90) [921]

BHUTTO, BENAZIR

6804 Bhutto, Benazir. *Daughter of Destiny* (10–12). Illus. 1989, Simon & Schuster $19.95 (0-671-66983-4). The amazing story of the woman who fulfilled her father's destiny by becoming prime minister of Pakistan. (Rev: BL 3/1/89) [921]

GANDHI, INDIRA

6805 Currimbhoy, Nayana. *Indira Gandhi* (8–12). Illus. 1985, Watts LB $12.90 (0-531-10064-2). An easily read, heavily illustrated account of Gandhi's career in Indian politics, her assassination, and its consequences. [921]

GANDHI, MAHATMA

6806 Easwaren, Eknath. *Gandhi the Man* (10–12). 1978, Random $24.00 (0-915132-13-3); paper $12.00 (0-915132-14-1). A personal account of this great leader, teacher, and pacifist. [921]

6807 Fischer, Louis, ed. *The Essential Gandhi* (10–12). 1983, Random paper $6.95 (0-394-71466-0). This collection of writings by the great teacher and prophet reveals a great deal about his life and thoughts. [921]

6808 Fischer, Louis. *Gandhi* (10–12). 1982, NAL paper $3.95 (0-451-62742-3). An admiring biography of the man who led India through nonviolent revolt to freedom. [921]

6809 Gandhi, Mahatma. *All Men Are Brothers* (10–12). 1958, Continuum paper $9.95 (0-8264-0003-5). This collection of autobiographical writings stresses the beliefs and thoughts of Gandhi more than his personal life. [921]

GYATSO, TENZIN

6810 Gyatso, Tenzin, Dalai Lama. *Freedom in Exile: The Autobiography of the Dalai Lama* (10–12). Illus. 1990, Harper $22.95 (0-06-39116-2). In addition to covering the life of this Dalai Lama who has been in exile for more than 30 years, this account gives a brief history of Buddhism. (Rev: BL 9/1/90) [921]

HAING NGOR

6811 Haing Ngor, and Roger Warner. *A Cambodian Odyssey* (10–12). 1988, Macmillan $19.95 (0-02-589330-0). The Academy Award winning actor from *The Killing Fields* tells his own horrifying story of the war in Cambodia. (Rev: BL 2/15/88) [921]

HENG, LIANG

6812 Heng, Liang, and Judith Shapiro. *Son of the Revolution* (10–12). Illus. 1983, Random paper $8.95 (0-394-72274-4). The autobiography of a Chinese man who grew up during Mao's tenure as leader with details about the Cultural Revolution of the 1960s. [921]

MAO TSE-TUNG

6813 Poole, Frederick King. *Mao Zedong* (10–12). Illus. 1982, Watts LB $12.90 (0-531-04481-5). An interpretive biography that gives particularly fine coverage of the Cultural Revolution. [921]

6814 Terrill, Ross. *Mao: A Biography* (10–12). 1987, Harper paper $9.95 (0-06-131992-9). A well-researched biography that fairly assesses the strengths and weaknesses of this Chinese leader. [921]

MUHAMMAD

6815 Cook, Michael. *Muhammad* (10–12). 1983, Oxford Univ. Pr. paper $5.95 (0-19-287605-8). An honest treatment of the life and thoughts of the founder of Islam. [921]

SADAT, ANWAR

6816 Sadat, Anwar. *In Search of Identity: An Autobiography* (10–12). Illus. 1987, Harper paper $9.95 (0-06-132071-4). The memoirs of this Egyptian president giving details on conditions in the Middle East during the 1970s. [921]

SUNG, CH'ING-LING

6817 Chang, Jung, and Jon Halliday. *Mme Sun Yat-sen* (10–12). Illus. 1986, Penguin paper $4.95 (0-14-008455-X). The biography of the Chinese woman who long after her husband's death continued to guide the revolution that brought her country into the communist orbit. (Rev: BL 11/1/86) [921]

TURKI, FAWAZ

6818 Turki, Fawaz. *Soul in Exile* (10–12). 1988, Monthly Review Pr. $26.00 (0-85345-746-8); paper $10.00 (0-85345-747-6). A history of the Palestinian cause seen through the eyes of a leader of the revolutionists. (Rev: BL 3/15/88) [921]

YAMAMOTO, ISOROKU

6819 Hoyt, Edwin P. *Yamamoto: The Man Who Planned Pearl Harbor* (10–12). Illus. 1990, McGraw $19.95 (0-07-030626-5). The biography of the Japanese leader who rose from poverty to great power before his death in 1943. (Rev: BL 2/15/90) [921]

Australia and the Pacific Islands

CONWAY, JILL KER

6820 Conway, Jill Ker. *The Road from Coorain* (10–12). 1989, Knopf $18.95 (0-394-57456-7). The youth and adolescence in Australia of the woman who would later be the president of Smith College. (Rev: VOYA 4/90) [921]

Europe

ALEXANDER THE GREAT

6821 Arrian. *Alexander the Great* (10–12). Trans. by J. G. Lloyd. Illus. 1981, Cambridge Univ. Pr. paper $7.95 (0-521-28195-4). Four hundred years after Alexander's death, this biography was written by an officer in the army of the Roman empire. [921]

6822 Hamilton, J. R. *Alexander the Great* (10–12). 1974, Univ. of Pittsburgh Pr. paper $9.95 (0-8229-6084-2). A realistic portrait of this great statesman and soldier. [921]

6823 Renault, Mary. *The Nature of Alexander* (10–12). 1979, Ballantine paper $6.95 (0-394-73825-X). A psychological study of Alexander the Great by the writer who fictionalized his biography in a series of novels. [921]

ALFRED THE GREAT

6824 Duckett, Eleanor Shipley. *Alfred the Great* (10–12). 1956, Univ. of Chicago Pr. paper $8.95 (0-226-16779-8). A biography of this early ruler of England who was also a soldier and scholar. [921]

ARTHUR, KING

6825 Ashe, Geoffrey. *The Landscape of King Arthur* (9–12). Illus. 1988, Henry Holt $24.95 (0-8050-0711-3). Through text and photographs, the story of King Arthur is re-created. (Rev: SLJ 10/88) [921]

6826 Goodrich, Norma Lorre. *King Arthur* (10–12). 1986, Watts $24.95 (0-531-09701-3); Harper paper $10.95 (0-06-097182-7). A wealth of scholarly information that proves that King Arthur actually lived. (Rev: BR 9–10/86) [921]

ATTLEE, CLEMENT

6827 Haney, John. *Clement Attlee* (9–12). Illus. 1987, Chelsea House $16.95 (0-87754-508-1). The biography of the British political leader who led the Labour Party and helped found the post-World War II welfare state. (Rev: BL 4/15/88) [921]

BISMARCK, OTTO VON

6828 Taylor, A. J. P. *Bismarck: The Man and the Statesman* (10–12). 1987, David & Charles paper $11.95 (0-241-11565-5). The life of the Prussian leader who unified Germany is told in this detailed scholarly account. [921]

BOLEYN, ANNE, QUEEN OF ENGLAND

6829 Erickson, Carolly. *Mistress Anne* (10–12). Illus. 1984, Summit paper $10.95 (0-671-60651-4). The story of the doomed life of Henry VIII's second wife. [921]

BRANDT, WILLY

6830 Viola, Tom. *Willy Brandt* (9–12). Illus. 1987, Chelsea House $16.95 (0-87754-512-X). The story of the post-World War II mayor of West Berlin and chancellor of West Germany. (Rev: BL 4/15/88) [921]

BREZHNEV, LEONID

6831 Navazelskis, Ina. *Leonid Brezhnev* (9–12). Illus. 1988, Chelsea House LB $16.95 (0-87754-513-8). This biography of the Russian leader is part of the World Leaders Past and Present series that now contains almost 200 titles. (Rev: BR 9–10/88; VOYA 10/88) [921]

CATHERINE II, EMPRESS OF RUSSIA

6832 Alexander, John T. *Catherine the Great: Life and Legend* (10–12). 1988, Oxford Univ. Pr. $24.95 (0-19-505236-6). A fresh look at the Russian empress who ruled for 34 years. (Rev: BL 10/1/88) [921]

6833 Troyat, Henri. *Catherine the Great* (10–12). Illus. 1980, Berkley paper $4.95 (0-425-07981-3). A sympathetic portrait of the Russian Empress who began as a naive bride and ended as an internationally known despot. [921]

CROMWELL, OLIVER

6834 Fraser, Antonia. *Cromwell: The Lord Protector* (10–12). Illus. 1973, Donald I. Fine paper $11.95 (0-917657-90-X). A portrait of the English Puritan leader who led England during and after the great Civil War that deposed the Stuarts. [921]

ELIZABETH I, QUEEN OF ENGLAND

6835 Erickson, Carolly. *The First Elizabeth* (10–12). Illus. 1984, Summit paper $12.95 (0-671-50393-6). A very personal view of Elizabeth, her many appetites, and her many coups in foreign affairs. Also use by the same author: *Bloody Mary* (1985) and *Bonnie Prince Charlie* (1989). [921]

6836 Smith, Lacey Baldwin. *Elizabeth Tudor: Portrait of a Queen* (10–12). Illus. 1975, Little paper $8.95 (0-316-80153-4). An account that tells of Elizabeth's many accomplishments politically, diplomatically, and culturally. [921]

6837 Strachey, Lytton. *Elizabeth and Essex: A Tragic History* (10–12). Illus. 1928, Harcourt paper $6.95 (0-15-628310-7). The ill-fated love of a 53-year-old queen and a 20-year-old courtier told with power and drama. [921]

FRANCIS OF ASSISI

6838 Green, Julien. *God's Fool: The Life and Times of Francis of Assisi* (10–12). Trans. by Peter Heinegg. 1985, Harper $16.45 (0-06-063462-6); paper $7.95 (0-06-063461-2). An engrossing novel about the wastrel who became one of the great saints of Christendom. (Rev: BL 9/1/85) [921]

FRANK, ANNE

6839 Frank, Anne. *The Diary of Anne Frank: The Critical Edition* (7–12). Illus. 1989, Doubleday $30.00 (0-385-24023-6). The most complete version of the diary to appear in English plus a history of the volume. (Rev: BL 5/15/89) [921]

6840 Frank, Anne. *The Diary of a Young Girl* (7–12). Trans. by B. M. Mooyaart. Illus. 1967, Doubleday $21.95 (0-385-04019-9). The world-famous diary of the young Jewish girl kept while she was being hidden with her family from the Nazis. [921]

FREDERICK II, KING OF PRUSSIA

6841 Mitford, Nancy. *Frederick the Great* (10–12). Illus. 1970, Dutton paper $14.95 (0-525-48178-8). The story of the Prussian leader who excelled in such diverse areas as warfare, diplomacy, scholarship, and the arts. [921]

GARIBALDI, GIUSEPPE

6842 Mack Smith, Denis. *Garibaldi* (10–12). 1956, Greenwood LB $39.75 (0-313-23618-6). A brief account of the life of Italy's hero in the struggle for independence and unity. [921]

GORBACHEV, MIKHAIL

6843 Butson, Thomas G. *Gorbachev: A Biography* (10–12). 1985, Scarborough $14.95 (0-8128-3035-0); paper $8.95 (0-8128-6249-X). A biography of the Soviet leader that ends in the mid-1980s. [921]

HENRY VIII, KING OF ENGLAND

6844 Starkey, David. *The Reign of Henry VIII: Personalities and Politics* (9–12). 1986, Watts $17.95 (0-531-15014-3). The biography of the much-married Tudor monarch and the changes he effected in English life and religion. (Rev: VOYA 8–10/86) [921]

HITLER, ADOLF

6845 Fest, Joachim. *Hitler* (10–12). Trans. by Richard and Clara Winston. Illus. 1974, Random paper $16.95 (0-394-72023-7). A long but engrossing biography of Hitler and his times that tries to answer the question of how he was able to gain power. [921]

6846 Fuchs, Thomas. *The Hitler Fact Book* (10–12). Illus. 1990, Fountain paper $14.95 (0-9623202-9-3). This book gives all sorts of trivia about the dictator and the high German officials around him. (Rev: SLJ 6/90) [921]

6847 Harris, Nathaniel. *Hitler* (8–12). Illus. 1989, David & Charles $19.95 (0-7134-5961-1). This biography surveys the life and times of Hitler and his impact on history. (Rev: SLJ 12/89) [921]

6848 Hitler, Adolf. *Mein Kampf* (10–12). Trans. by Ralph Manheim. 1943, Houghton $17.95 (0-395-07801-6); paper $10.95 (0-395-08362-1). The beliefs and early life of Hitler as dictated to his secretary while he was in prison in 1923. [921]

6849 Toland, John. *Adolf Hitler* (10–12). 1986, Ballantine paper $5.95 (0-345-33848-0). A thoroughly researched account of the complex German leader—his rise and fall. [921]

IVAN THE TERRIBLE, CZAR OF RUSSIA

6850 Troyat, Henri. *Ivan the Terrible* (10–12). Illus. 1984, Dutton $18.95 (0-525-24246-5); Berkley paper $3.95 (0-425-08481-7). A portrait of this brutal czar who centralized authority and established relations with several European countries. [921]

JESENSKA, MILENA

6851 Buber-Neumann, Margarete. *Milena* (10–12). 1988, Henry Holt $18.95 (0-8050-0748-2). A beautiful tribute to the author's friend, Milena Jesenska, who died in a Nazi death camp. (Rev: SLJ 10/88) [921]

JOHN XXIII, POPE

6852 Hebblethwaite, Peter. *Pope John XXIII: Shepherd of the Modern World* (10–12). Illus. 1985, Doubleday paper $10.95 (0-385-23537-2). A lengthy biography of the pope who tried during his brief tenure as head of the Catholic Church to promote world peace and harmony. [921]

LENIN, VLADIMIR ILLICH

6853 Clark, Ronald W. *Lenin* (10–12). Illus. 1988, Harper $27.95 (0-06-015802-6). A balanced picture of the public and private life of the man who created Soviet communism. (Rev: BL 11/15/88) [921]

LEVCHENKO, STANISLAV

6854 Levchenko, Stanislav. *On the Wrong Side: My Life in the KGB* (10–12). 1988, Pergamon-Brassey $18.95 (0-08-034478-X); Dell paper $4.50 (0-440-20272-8). The life story of the KGB agent who defected to the United States in 1979. (Rev: BL 3/15/88) [921]

LUTHER, MARTIN

6855 Bainton, Roland H. *Here I Stand: A Life of Martin Luther* (10–12). 1950, Abingdon paper $4.95 (0-687-16894-5). A scholarly interpretation of the life, times, and contributions of this religious leader. [921]

MACBETH, KING OF SCOTLAND

6856 Stewart, Bob. *Macbeth: Scotland's Warrior King* (10–12). Illus. 1988, Sterling paper $7.95 (1-85314-000-7). The true story of the Celtic King who became the inspiration for Shakespeare's tragedy. (Rev: SLJ 10/89) [921]

MARIE ANTOINETTE

6857 Haslip, Joan. *Marie Antoinette* (10–12). Illus. 1988, Weidenfeld & Nicolson $19.95 (1-55584-183-X). A fine retelling of the tragic life of the lovely, unhappy queen. (Rev: BL 2/15/88) [921]

MARIE, QUEEN OF ROMANIA

6858 Pakula, Hannah. *The Last Romantic: A Biography of Queen Marie of Roumania* (10–12). Illus. 1984, Simon & Schuster paper $12.95 (0-671-62246-3). The story of this granddaughter of Queen Victoria who with her husband ruled in Romania between the world wars. [921]

MARX, KARL

6859 Feinberg, Barbara Silberdick. *Marx and Marxism* (10–12). 1985, Watts LB $12.90 (0-531-10065-0). A well-organized biography and appraisal of the work of this founder of the communistic political philosophy. [921]

6860 McLellan, David. *Karl Marx* (10–12). 1975, Penguin paper $4.95 (0-14-004320-9). Biographical information plus an objective explanation of Marxism. [921]

6861 Singer, Peter. *Marx* (10–12). 1980, Oxford Univ. Pr. paper $3.95 (0-19-287510-8). A brief biography that also analyzes Marx's political and economic thinking. Also use by the same author *Hegel* (1983). [921]

MARY STUART, QUEEN OF SCOTLAND

6862 Fraser, Antonia. *Mary, Queen of Scots* (10–12). Illus. 1987, Dell paper $6.95 (0-440-35476-5). A very sympathetic account of the tragic life of this Scottish queen. [921]

6863 Steel, David, and Judy Steel. *Mary Stuart's Scotland: The Landscape, Life and Legends of Mary, Queen of Scots* (9–12). Illus. 1987, Crown $19.95 (0-517-56651-6). An accurate account of this tragic queen's life with beautiful photographs of her homeland, Scotland. (Rev: SLJ 4/88) [921]

MASARYK, TOMAS

6864 Lewis, Gavin. *Tomas Masaryk* 1989, Chelsea House $17.95 (1-55546-816-0). The story of the inspiring leader who was president of Czechoslovakia from 1918 to 1934. (Rev: BR 5–6/90) [921]

MORE, SIR THOMAS

6865 Kenny, Anthony. *Thomas More* (10–12). 1983, Oxford Univ. Pr. $13.95 (0-19-287574-4); paper $5.95 (0-19-287573-6). A biography of the martyred Catholic who lived and wrote during the Tudor period of England. [921]

NAPOLEON I, EMPEROR OF THE FRENCH

6866 Weidhorn, Manfred. *Napoleon* (9–12). 1986, Macmillan $16.95 (0-689-31163-X). All of the events in Napoleon's life are retold—from Corsican background to becoming emperor and finally meeting his Waterloo. (Rev: BL 11/1/86; SLJ 2/87; VOYA 2/87) [921]

NICHOLAS II, EMPEROR OF RUSSIA

6867 Massie, Robert. *Nicholas and Alexandra* (10–12). Illus. 1967, Macmillan $29.95 (0-689-10177-5); Dell paper $6.95 (0-440-36358-6). The story of the last Czar of Russia, and his wife and family. [921]

PETER I, EMPEROR OF RUSSIA

6868 Massie, Robert. *Peter the Great: His Life and World* (10–12). 1980, Knopf $40.00 (0-394-50032-6). An account of the life of this Russian leader and reformer plus a good picture of life in Russia during the late seventeenth and early eighteenth centuries. [921]

6869 Troyat, Henri. *Peter the Great* (10–12). Illus. 1987, Dutton $22.50 (0-525-24547-2). The story of the czar who brought Russia out of its dark ages but often at a terrible cost. (Rev: BL 7/87) [921]

PHILBY, KIM

6870 Knightley, Phillip. *The Master Spy* (10–12). Illus. 1989, Knopf $19.95 (0-394-57890-2). An engrossing biography of the Englishman who became a master spy for the Russians. (Rev: BL 2/1/89) [921]

ROBERT THE BRUCE, KING OF SCOTLAND

6871 Scott, Ronald McNair. *Robert the Bruce, King of Scots* (10–12). 1989, Bedrick $24.00 (0-872-26320-7). A detailed history of the gallant king who believed in Scottish freedom and who defied England's Edward II. (Rev: BR 11–12/89; SLJ 11/89) [921]

SENESH, HANNAH

6872 Atkinson, Linda. *In Kindling Flame: The Story of Hannah Senesh, 1921–1944* (8–12). Illus. 1985, Lothrop $13.95 (0-688-02714-8). This biography tells how this courageous Jewish girl faced death during World War II to act as a resistance fighter behind enemy lines. [921]

6873 Senesh, Hannah. *Hannah Senesh—Her Life & Diary* (10–12). Trans. by Marta Cohn. Illus. 1987, Schocken paper $11.95 (0-8052-0410-5). The story of the Hungarian-born Jew who was murdered by the Nazis in 1943. [921]

STALIN, JOSEPH

6874 Caulkins, Janet. *Joseph Stalin* (7–12). Illus. 1990, Watts $13.90 (0-531-10945-3). A good summary of the history of the Soviet Union in the twentieth century that focuses on the dictator

most responsible for the course it took. (Rev: BL 11/1/90) [921]

6875 Deutscher, Isaac. *Stalin: A Political Biography* (10–12). 2nd ed. Illus. 1967, Oxford Univ. Pr. paper $16.95 (0-19-500273-3). An objective account of the life and complex personality of the Russian dictator. [921]

6876 Laqueur, Walter. *Stalin: The Glasnost Revelations* (10–12). 1990, Macmillan $24.95 (0-684-19203-9). An exposé of the horrors of the reign of Joseph Stalin during which he was responsible for the death of millions. (Rev: BL 9/15/90) [921]

VICTORIA, QUEEN OF GREAT BRITAIN

6877 Strachey, Lytton. *Queen Victoria* (10–12). Illus. 1921, Harcourt $15.95 (0-15-175695-3); paper $10.95 (0-15-675696-X). A splendid interpretive introduction to the life of Victoria and the people that surrounded her. [921]

6878 Woodham-Smith, Cecil. *Queen Victoria: From Her Birth to the Death of the Prince Consort* (10–12). Illus. 1987, Donald I. Fine paper $9.95 (0-917657-95-0). Based on letters, journals, and court documents, this is a well-researched life of this monarch from childhood to widowhood. [921]

WALLENBERG, RAOUL

6879 Smith, Danny. *Wallenberg: Lost Hero* (10–12). 1987, Templegate paper $8.95 (0-87243-155-X). The story of the courageous Swede who helped save thousands of Jews in Hungary during World War II. (Rev: BL 4/1/87) [921]

WIESENTHAL, SIMON

6880 Wiesenthal, Simon. *Justice Not Vengeance: Recollections* (10–12). Illus. 1990, Grove Weidenfeld $21.95 (1-55584-341-7). The autobiography of the famous Nazi hunter who has spent his life searching out war criminals. (Rev: BL 1/15/90) [921]

WILBERFORCE, WILLIAM

6881 Ludwig, Charles. *He Freed Britain's Slaves* (10–12). 1977, Herald Pr. $7.95 (0-8361-1822-7). A fictionized biography of William Wilberforce, who led the British war against slavery. [921]

South and Central America

CASTRO, FIDEL

6882 Bourne, Peter G. *Fidel* (10–12). 1986, Dodd $18.95 (0-396-08518-0). An objective biography of the Cuban leader with details on life inside his country. (Rev: BR 1–2/87) [921]

PERON, EVA

6883 Fraser, Nicholas. *Eva Peron* (10–12). Illus. 1981, Norton paper $8.95 (0-393-30238-5). An analysis of Eva Peron's public and private lives and of her influence on the history of Argentina. [921]

PERON, JUAN DOMINGO

6884 Page, Joseph A. *Peron* (10–12). Illus. 1983, Random $25.00 (0-394-52297-4). An exhaustive study of the life and political career of this Argentinian leader. [921]

Miscellaneous Interesting Lives

CRONKITE, KATHY

6885 Cronkite, Kathy. *On the Edge of the Spotlight* (10–12). 1982, Warner paper $3.50 (0-446-80944-6). Walter Cronkite's daughter talks about how her father's fame affected her. [921]

MILLER, ROBERT M.

6886 Miller, Robert M. *Most of My Patients Are Animals* (9–12). Illus. 1985, P. S. Eriksson $14.95 (0-8397-6037-X). The adventures of a California veterinarian who has been a doctor to all kinds of animals although his specialty is horses. (Rev: BL 8/85; SLJ 10/85) [636.089]

ABAGNALE, FRANK

6887 Abagnale, Frank W., and Stan Redding. *Catch Me If You Can* (10–12). 1989, Pocket paper $4.50 (0-671-70073-1). For mature readers, this is the autobiography of an arch swindler and con man. [921]

ALINE, COUNTESS OF ROMANONES

6888 Aline, Countess of Romanones. *The Spy Went Dancing: My Further Adventures As an Undercover Agent* (10–12). Illus. 1990, Putnam $19.95 (0-399-13509-X). One of the most glamorous spies in history helps uncover a mole in NATO headquarters in Paris in this continuation of *The Spy Wore Red* (1987). (Rev: SLJ 6/90) [921]

APPLEMAN-JURMAN, ALICIA

6889 Appleman-Jurman, Alicia. *Alicia: My Story* (9–12). 1988, Bantam $18.95 (0-553-05317-

5). The story of the Jewish survivor of the Holocaust who after the war helped smuggle refugees into Palestine. (Rev: BR 5–6/89) [921]

ARTLEY, BOB

6890 Artley, Bob. *Memories of a Former Kid* (10–12). Illus. 1978, Iowa State Univ. Pr. $9.95 (0-8138-1070-1). An autobiographical account in words and cartoons about growing up on a farm in the Midwest during the Depression. [921]

BARTOSZEWSKI, WLADYSLAW

6891 Bartoszewski, Wladyslaw. *The Warsaw Ghetto: A Christian's Testimony* (10–12). 1988, Beacon $14.95 (0-8070-5602-2). The memoirs of a man who risked death to save Jews in World War II Warsaw. (Rev: BL 2/1/88) [921]

BELCHER, WENDY

6892 Belcher, Wendy. *Honey from the Lion: An African Journey* (10–12). 1988, Dutton $16.95 (0-525-24596-0). The author tells about living and working in Ghana and the clash there between the East and the West. (Rev: BL 4/15/88) [921]

BOYCE, CHRISTOPHER

6893 Lindsey, Robert. *The Falcon and the Snowman* (10–12). 1984, Pocket paper $4.50 (0-671-54553-1). The story of two middle-class American boys whose life-styles in the 1960s led them into a life of spying for the Russians. [921]

BRAITHWAITE, E. R.

6894 Braithwaite, E. R. *To Sir, with Love* (9–12). 1960, Jove paper $2.95 (0-515-09031-X). The inspiring story of a young black teacher from British Guiana and his class in a school in London's slums. [921]

BRECHER, KENNETH

6895 Brecher, Kenneth. *Too Sad to Sing: A Memoir with Postcards* (10–12). Illus. 1988, Harcourt $22.95 (0-15-190493-6); paper $11.95 (0-15-690465-9). Through a series of postcards that evoke specific incidents, the author re-creates his life story. (Rev: SLJ 10/88) [921]

BRUCE, PRESTON

6896 Bruce, Preston. *From the Door of the White House* (9–12). 1984, Lothrop $12.95 (0-688-00883-6). The biography of the doorman at the White House who served under five presidents from Eisenhower to Ford. [921]

BURCH, JENNINGS MICHAEL

6897 Burch, Jennings Michael. *They Cage the Animals at Night* (9–12). 1984, NAL paper $4.50 (0-451-15941-1). The story of a youth from a broken home and of the many shelters and foster homes where he spent his childhood while his mother tried to cope with her mounting responsibilities. [921]

CAMPBELL, MARIA

6898 Campbell, Maria. *Halfbreed* (10–12). 1982, Univ. of Nebraska Pr. paper $5.95 (0-8032-6311-2). The candid account of the privations faced by a part Indian girl growing up in Canada. [921]

COMER FAMILY

6899 Comer, James P. *Maggie's American Dream: The Life and Times of a Black Family* (9–12). 1988, NAL $18.95 (0-453-00588-8). The well-known black educator gives an inspiring picture of his mother and her influence on her family. (Rev: BL 11/15/88) [921]

COTTELL, JOHN E.

6900 Cottell, John E. *Code Name Badger: The True Life Story of a British Secret Agent* (10–12). Illus. 1990, Morrow $19.95 (0-688-04482-4). The fantastic story of a British spy who survived both Buchenwald and Lubjanka prisons in Moscow. (Rev: BL 4/15/90) [921]

COWAN, PAUL

6901 Cowan, Paul. *An Orphan in History* (10–12). 1986, Bantam paper $3.95 (0-553-26030-8). The autobiography of a Jewish man who tried to find his true religious and cultural roots. [921]

DEFORD, ALEX

6902 Deford, Frank. *Alex: The Life of a Child* (10–12). 1984, NAL paper $3.50 (0-451-15119-4). A father recalls the life of his child who died of cystic fibrosis when she was only 8 years old. [921]

EARECKSON, JONI

6903 Eareckson, Joni, and Joe Musser. *Joni* (9–12). 1984, Bantam paper $2.95 (0-553-22886-2). A young paraplegic tells of her adjustment to this condition. [921]

ESCALANTE, JAIME

6904 Mathews, Jay. *Escalante: The Best Teacher in America* (9–12). 1988, Henry Holt $19.45 (0-8050-0450-5). The biography of the amazing teacher, Jaime Escalante, whose life was the subject of the movie *Stand and Deliver*. (Rev: SLJ 12/88; VOYA 6/89) [921]

EVANS, DALE

6905 Rogers, Dale Evans. *Angel Unaware* (10–12). 1984, Jove paper $2.95 (0-15-08952-4). Dale Evans tells about herself and her daughter's brief life in this moving autobiography. [921]

FOSTER, RORY C.

6906 Foster, Rory C. *I Never Met an Animal I Didn't Like* (8–12). Illus. 1987, Watts $15.95 (0-531-15041-0). A veterinarian who specializes in caring for wild animals and birds continues the story begun in *Dr. Wildlife: A Northwoods Veterinarian* (1985). (Rev: BL 6/1/87; SLJ 6–7/87; VOYA 8–9/87) [921]

FRIDAY, NANCY

6907 Friday, Nancy. *My Mother/My Self: The Daughter's Search for Identity* (10–12). 1987, Dell paper $5.95 (0-440-15664-5). This combination autobiography and biography probes the relationship between a daughter and her mother. [921]

GALARZA, ERNESTO

6908 Galarza, Ernesto. *Barrio Boy* (10–12). 1971, Univ. of Notre Dame Pr. paper $7.95 (0-268-00441-2). The autobiography of a Mexican boy in his new home in California. [921]

GATZOYIANNIS, ELENI

6909 Gage, Nicholas. *Eleni* (10–12). 1983, Random $19.45 (0-394-52093-9); Ballantine paper $5.95 (0-345-30122-6). The author re-creates the life of his mother in Greece during World War II and the civil war and of her unjust execution by guerrillas in 1948. [921]

GINO, CAROL

6910 Gino, Carol. *The Nurse's Story* (10–12). 1983, Bantam paper $3.95 (0-553-23667-9). The story of a girl who fought great odds to become a nurse. [921]

GISSING, VERA

6911 Gissing, Vera. *Pearls of Childhood* (10–12). Illus. 1989, St. Martin's $16.95 (0-312-02963-2). A somewhat harrowing account of a Jewish girl who left Czechoslovakia in the 1940s and relocated in England as a refugee. (Rev: BL 5/15/89) [921]

GREENE, MARILYN

6912 Greene, Marilyn, and Gary Provost. *Finder: The True Story of a Private Investigator* (10–12). 1988, Crown $18.95 (0-517-56490-4). The absorbing story of one of the few female private investigators that specialize in finding lost persons. (Rev: BL 6/15/88; SLJ 11/88; VOYA 12/88) [921]

GREENFIELD, NOAH

6913 Greenfield, Josh. *A Child Called Noah* (10–12). 1982, Harcourt paper $7.95 (0-15-616862-6). The harrowing but inspiring story of bringing up an autistic child. [921]

GUNTHER, JOHN

6914 Gunther, John. *Death Be Not Proud: A Memoir* (7–12). 1989, Harper paper $4.95 (0-06-080973-6). The moving tribute to the author's son who died at age 17 of a brain tumor. [921]

HAILEY, KENDALL

6915 Hailey, Kendall. *The Day I Became an Autodidact: And the Advice, Adventures, and* *Acrimonies That Befell Me Thereafter* (10–12). 1988, Delacorte $15.95 (0-385-29636-3). Fed up with high school, at 15 Hailey stayed home and with her parents' help, educated herself. (Rev: BL 4/15/88; SLJ 9/88; VOYA 10/88) [921]

HANNAM, CHARLES

6916 Hannam, Charles. *A Boy in That Situation: An Autobiography* (9–12). 1978, Harper $12.70 (0-06-022218-2). The story of an unattractive Jewish boy growing up as the Nazis come to power. [921]

HAYES, BILLY

6917 Hayes, Billy, and William Hoffer. *Midnight Express* (10–12). 1984, Warner paper $3.50 (0-446-31121-9). The harrowing story for mature readers of Billy Hayes's prison stay in Turkey on a drug charge. [921]

HOBBES, ANNE

6918 Hobbes, Anne, and Robert Specht. *Tisha: The Story of a Young Teacher in the Alaska Wilderness* (9–12). 1984, Bantam paper $4.95 (0-553-26596-2). This is the heartwarming biography of a young schoolteacher who at age 19 began working in the tiny Alaska town of Chicken. [921]

HOCKEN, SHEILA

6919 Hocken, Sheila. *Emma and I* (9–12). 1978, Dutton $8.95 (0-525-09780-5). In this autobiography a woman adjusts to her blindness with the help of her Seeing Eye dog. [921]

HOFFMAN, EVA

6920 Hoffman, Eva. *Lost in Translation: A Life in a New Language* (10–12). 1989, Dutton $18.95 (0-525-24601-0). The story of a Polish Jew who came to America as a teenager in the late 1950s. (Rev: BL 1/15/89) [921]

HUXLEY, ELSPETH

6921 Huxley, Elspeth. *The Flame Trees of Thika* (10–12). 1982, Penguin paper $6.95 (0-14-001715-1). An autobiographical account of growing up in Africa at the turn of the century. Followed by: *Mottled Lizard* (1982). [921]

KINGSTON, MAXINE HONG

6922 Kingston, Maxine Hong. *The Woman Warrior: Memoirs of a Girlhood among Ghosts* (10–

12). 1976, Knopf $19.95 (0-394-40067-4); Random paper $8.95 (0-394-72188-6). The memoirs of a Chinese-American woman who grew up in 2 cultures. [921]

KISOR, HENRY

6923 Kisor, Henry. *What's That Pig Outdoors? A Memoir of Deafness* (10–12). 1990, Hill & Wang $18.95 (0-8090-9689-7). The autobiography of the present book editor of the *Chicago Sun-Times* and his adjustment to the deafness which struck at age 3. (Rev: BL 3/15/90) [921]

LEONOWENS, ANNA

6924 Landon, Margaret. *Anna and the King of Siam* (7–12). Illus. 1944, Harper $16.95 (0-381-98136-3). The career of the indomitable schoolteacher whose life became the basis of a play, a musical, and 2 movies. [921]

LOOMIS, VIVIENNE

6925 Mack, John E., and Holly Hickler. *Vivienne: The Life and Suicide of an Adolescent Girl* (9–12). 1982, NAL paper $4.95 (0-451-62664-8). The powerful reconstruction of the life of an attractive young girl who committed suicide at age 14. [921]

LUND, ERIC

6926 Lund, Doris. *Eric* (9–12). 1974, Harper $16.45 (0-397-01046-X); Dell paper $2.95 (0-440-94586-0). The tragic story of a gifted young man and his fatal bout with leukemia, as told by his mother. [921]

MCFADDEN, CYRA

6927 McFadden Cyra. *Rain or Shine* (10–12). Illus. 1986, Knopf $16.95 (0-394-51937-X); Random paper $4.95 (0-394-74879-4). This biography focuses on the relationship between the author and her father, Cy Taillon, the dean of American rodeo announcers. [921]

MCMULLEN, JEANINE

6928 McMullen, Jeanine. *Wind in the Ashtree* (10–12). Illus. 1988, Norton $15.95 (0-393-02617-5). The delights and hardships of life on a small Welsh farm are told in this sequel to *My Small Country Living* (1984). (Rev: BL 10/1/88) [921]

MARKOVNA, NINA

6929 Markovna, Nina. *Nina's Journey: A Memoir of Stalin's Russia and the Second World War* (10–12). 1989, Regnery $21.95 (0-89526-550-8). A harrowing account of a Russian girl's life under Stalin's dictatorship, deportation to Germany during World War II, and eventual freedom in the United States. (Rev: BL 11/15/89) [921]

MATHABANE, MARK

6930 Mathabane, Mark. *Kaffir Boy in America: An Encounter with Apartheid* (10–12). 1989, Macmillan $19.95 (0-684-19043-5); paper $8.95 (0-02-034530-5). In a sequel to *Kaffir Boy* (1986), Mathabane describes his years in America after leaving South Africa in 1978 on a tennis scholarship. (Rev: BL 5/1/89) [921]

MECKLER, BRENDA WEISBERG

6931 Meckler, Brenda Weisberg. *Papa Was a Farmer* (10–12). Illus. 1988, Algonquin $15.95 (0-912697-95-4). An immigrant from czarist Russia who arrived in the United States in 1904 tells about her family's farming experiences in Ohio. (Rev: BL 8/88) [921]

MOHM, PHAT

6932 Sheehy, Gail. *Spirit of Survival* (10–12). 1986, Morrow $17.95 (0-688-05878-7); 1987, Bantam paper $4.95. The story of a young girl who was a refugee from the horrors of war in Cambodia and of her life in the United States. (Rev: SLJ 5/87) [921]

MOODY, ANNE

6933 Moody, Anne. *Coming of Age in Mississippi* (10–12). 1970, Dell paper $4.50 (0-440-31488-7). The story of a black girl growing up in the desperate poverty of rural Mississippi. [921]

MORGAN, SALLY

6934 Morgan, Sally. *My Place* (10–12). 1988, Seaver Books $18.95 (0-8050-0911-6). An Australian woman searches for her aboriginal family in this quest for identity. (Rev: BL 8/88; BR 3–4/89; VOYA 4/89) [921]

NJERI, ITABARI

6935 Njeri, Itabari. *Every Good-bye Ain't Gone: Family Portraits and Personal Escapades* (10–12). 1990, Times Books $17.95 (0-8129-1805-3). Through a series of autobiographical vignettes, the author describes her multiracial background and her difficult childhood and adolescence in New York City. (Rev: VOYA 8/90) [921]

NOMBERG-PRZYTYK, SARA

6936 Nomberg-Przytyk, Sara. *Auschwitz: True Tales from a Grotesque Land* (10–12). 1985, Univ. of North Carolina Pr. $17.50 (0-8078-1629-9); paper $9.95 (0-8078-4160-9). The story of the infamous concentration camp by an attendant in the hospital where Dr. Mengele performed his experiments. [921]

PAPASHVILY, GEORGE

6937 Papashvily, George, and Helen Papashvily. *Anything Can Happen* (10–12). 1985, St. Martin's $12.95 (0-312-04524-7). The humorous, heart-warming account of an immigrant from Georgia, U.S.S.R., and his adventures in America. [921]

PATTON, LARRY

6938 Kastner, Janet. *More Than an Average Guy* (9–12). Illus. 1989, Daring paper $8.95 (0-938936-25-6). An inspiring story of a boy who was born with cerebral palsy and of the family that loved him. (Rev: BL 5/15/89) [921]

POLOVCHAK, WALTER

6939 Polovchak, Walter, and Kevin Klose. *Freedom's Child* (10–12). 1988, Random $17.95 (0-394-55926-6). The story of the 12-year-old boy who refused to leave the United States to return to the U.S.S.R. with his parents. (Rev: BL 2/1/88; BR 5–6/88; VOYA 8/88) [921]

PRICE, MICHELLE

6940 Phillips, Carolyn E. *Michelle* (9–12). Illus. 1989, NAL paper $2.50 (0-451-14929-7). This is the inspiring story of a young girl's fight against bone cancer and how she never gave up, even after her leg was amputated. [921]

PRYWES, RAQUELA

6941 Gruber, Ruth. *Raquela: A Woman of Israel* (10–12). 1979, NAL paper $3.95 (0-451-13769-8). The story of an Israeli woman from the Arab riots of the 1920s to after World War II. [921]

PURL, SANDY

6942 Purl, Sandy, and Gregg Lewis. *Am I Alive? A Surviving Flight Attendant's Struggle and In-* spiring Triumph over Tragedy (10–12). 1986, Harper $13.95 (0-06-250691-9). The story of the flight attendant who saved many lives after a crash and of the psychological trauma that followed. (Rev: SLJ 9/86) [921]

RACHLIN, NAHID

6943 Rachlin, Nahid. *Foreigner* (10–12). 1979, Norton paper $8.95 (0-393-00961-0). This biography explores the nature of Islam from the standpoint of an Iranian woman. [921]

RESNICK, ROSE

6944 Resnick, Rose. *Dare to Dream: The Rose Resnick Story* (8–12). Rev. ed. Illus. 1988, Strawberry Hill paper $9.95 (0-89407-089-4). The story of the blind pianist who established many agencies to work in various ways with the blind. (Rev: BL 10/1/88) [921]

RIVERA, EDWARD

6945 Rivera, Edward. *Family Installments* (10–12). 1983, Penguin paper $8.95 (0-14-006726-4). Memories of growing up Hispanic. [921]

RODRIQUEZ, RICHARD

6946 Rodriguez, Richard. *Hunger of Memory: The Education of Richard Rodriguez* (10–12). 1983, Bantam paper $4.95 (0-553-27293-4). A series of essays that describe the life of a young boy who started school hardly able to speak English but later achieved great academic success at the British Museum. [921]

SCHARANSKY, ANATOLY

6947 Gilbert, Martin. *Scharansky: Hero of Our Time* (10–12). Illus. 1986, Viking $24.95 (0-670-81418-0). The story of a Soviet Jew's struggle to emigrate to Israel. [921]

SCHULLER, CAROL

6948 Schuller, Carol. *In the Shadow of His Wings* (9–12). 1986, Jove paper $3.95 (0-515-09802-7). The inspiring story of a girl who lost her left leg at age 13 but conquered her handicap and became a champion skier. (Rev: BL 5/15/86) [921]

SENDER, RUTH MINSKY

6949 Sender, Ruth Minsky. *To Life* (9–12). 1988, Macmillan $13.95 (0-02-781831-4). This survivor's life after being freed from the Nazi death camp described in her earlier book *The Cage*

(1986). (Rev: BL 10/15/88; BR 1–2/89; SLJ 11/88; VOYA 12/88) [921]

SHAHHAT

6950 Critchfield, Richard. *Shahhat: An Egyptian* (10–12). 1978, Syracuse Univ. Pr. $24.95 (0-8156-2202-3); Avon paper $3.50 (0-380-48405-6). This is the story of an Egyptian peasant and his family written by a man who spent 2 years with them gathering his material. [921]

SIMONIDES, CAROL

6951 Simonides, Carol, and Diane Gage. *I'll Never Walk Alone: The Inspiring Story of a Teenager's Struggle against Cancer* (7–12). Illus. 1983, Jove paper $2.95 (0-515-08067-5). The story of a teenager's futile but inspiring struggle against cancer. [921]

SOLOMON, DOROTHY A.

6952 Solomon, Dorothy Allred. *In My Father's House* (10–12). 1984, Watts $17.95 (0-531-09763-3). A harrowing biography of a woman who grew up in a multi-mothered family of Mormons. [921]

SONE, MONICA

6953 Sone, Monica. *Nisei Daughter* (9–12). 1987, Univ. of Washington Pr. paper $8.95 (0-295-95688-7). From a happy childhood in Seattle to a World War II relocation center as seen through the eyes of a Japanese American girl. [921]

STAJNER, KARLO

6954 Stajner, Karlo. *Seven Thousand Days in Siberia* (10–12). Trans. by Joel Agee. 1988, Farrar $30.00 (0-374-26126-1). An account of the author's inhumane, barbaric treatment in a Soviet prison camp for 20 years, beginning in the 1930s. (Rev: BL 1/15/88) [921]

SULLIVAN, TOM

6955 Sullivan, Tom, and Derek Gill. *If You Could See What I Hear* (8–12). 1976, NAL paper $3.95 (0-451-12735-0). The inspiring story of the blind man who excelled in sports and music. [921]

TAULBERT, CLIFTON L.

6956 Taulbert, Clifton L. *Once Upon a Time When We Were Colored* (10–12). Illus. 1989, Council Oaks $16.96 (0-933031-19-X). A touching autobiography of a black man and his family in a small Mississippi town during the 1940s and 1950s. (Rev: SLJ 12/89) [921]

TERESA, MOTHER

6957 Muggeridge, Malcolm. *Something Beautiful for God: Mother Teresa of Calcutta* (10–12). Illus. 1971, Harper $18.95 (0-06-066041-4); paper $7.95 (0-06-066043-0). This account focuses on Mother Teresa's work in Calcutta slums with her Missionaries of Charity. [921]

6958 Teresa, Mother. *My Life for the Poor* (10–12). 1985, Harper $10.95 (0-06-068237-X); Ballantine paper $4.95 (0-345-33780-8). This collection of the writings of Mother Teresa forms a type of spiritual biography of this great woman. [921]

TIBBETS, PAUL W.

6959 Tibbets, Paul W., Jr. *The Tibbets Story* (10–12). 1978, Scarborough House paper $2.95 (0-8128-7057-3). The autobiography of the pilot of the *Enola Gay,* the plane that dropped the first atomic bomb. [921]

TRULL, PATTI

6960 Trull, Patti. *On with My Life* (7–12). 1983, Putnam paper $9.95 (0-399-20977-8). The story of the author's struggle with cancer that resulted in a leg amputation and of her later work with young cancer victims. [921]

TRUMPELMAN, I. C.

6961 Epstein, Leslie. *King of the Jews* (10–12). 1989, Summit paper $8.95 (0-671-69003-5). For better readers, this is the story of I. C. Trumpelman who, in spite of criminal activities, became known as king of the Jews in the Poland of 1918. [921]

TWO TREES, JOE

6962 Kazimiroff, Theodore L. *The Last Algonquin* (10–12). 1982, Walker $18.95 (0-8027-0698-3). The story of an Algonquin who was living off the land in a park in the Bronx during the 1920s. [921]

UCHIDA, YOSHIKO

6963 Uchida, Yoshiko. *Desert Exile: The Uprooting of a Japanese American Family* (10–12). 1982, Univ. of Washington Pr. paper $8.95 (0-295-96190-2). The story of a Japanese American family from California and their internment during World War II. [921]

VAILLANCOURT, HENRI

6964 McPhee, John A. *The Survival of the Bark Canoe* (10–12). 1975, Farrar $13.95 (0-374-27207-7); paper $7.95 (0-374-51693-6). This is the story of Henri Vaillancourt and how he preserved the craft of making bark canoes. [921]

VAN DEVANTER, LYNDA

6965 Van Devanter, Lynda. *Home before Morning: The Story of an Army Nurse in Vietnam* (10–12). 1983, Warner paper $3.95 (0-446-30962-1). The story of a year spent as a surgical nurse in Vietnam and of the trauma these experiences caused on her return to America. [921]

WAZETER, MARY

6966 Wazeter, Mary, and Lewis Gregg. *Dark Marathon* (9–12). Illus. 1989, Zondervan paper $8.95 (0-310-41781-3). The inspiring story of the championship runner who used her faith to help in her struggle against anorexia nervosa, bulimia, and depression. (Rev: VOYA 10/89) [921]

WEIR, BENJAMIN

6967 Weir, Ben, et al. *Hostage Bound, Hostage Free* (10–12). 1988, Thorndike $16.95 (0-89621-842-2). The story of Benjamin Weir, an American hostage in Lebanon, and of his cruel imprisonment and eventual liberation. (Rev: BL 5/1/87) [921]

YOUNG, CATHY

6968 Young, Cathy. *Growing Up in Moscow: Memories of a Soviet Girlhood, 1963–1980* (9–12). 1989, Ticknor $18.95 (0-89919-511-3). A Russian childhood is remembered by a girl who emigrated and settled in the United States. (Rev: BL 5/15/89) [921]

ZASSENHAUS, HILTGUNT

6969 Zassenhaus, Hiltgunt. *Walls: Resisting the Third Reich—One Woman's Story* (10–12). 1974, Beacon paper $10.95 (0-8070-6389-4). Life in Nazi Germany during World War II is described by a woman who helped several political prisoners. [921]

ZELLER, FREDERIC

6970 Zeller, Frederic. *When Time Ran Out: Coming of Age in the Third Reich* (9–10). 1989, Permanent $19.95 (0-932966-89-6). Zeller, a Jew who left Germany in 1939 at the age of 15, describes his youth in Hitler's Reich. (Rev: BL 3/1/89) [921]

History and Geography

General History and Geography

Miscellaneous Works

6971 Franck, Irene M., and David M. Brownstone. *Warriors & Adventurers* (9–12). 1988, Facts on File $14.95 (0-8160-1452-3). Detailed histories are given of such occupations as flying, gambling, lawbreaking, sailing, and spying. (Rev: BR 5–6/88) [909]

Atlases, Maps, and Mapmaking

6972 Makower, Joel, ed. *The Map Catalog: Every Kind of Map and Chart on Earth and Even Some Above It* (9–12). Illus. 1986, Random $27.00 (0-394-58326-1). About 50 different maps are described and how they can be obtained. (Rev: BL 3/1/87) [912]

Paleontology

6973 Arduini, Paolo, and Giorgio Teruzzi. *Simon & Schuster's Guide to Fossils* (9–12). Illus. 1987, Simon & Schuster $22.95 (0-671-63219-1); paper $12.95 (0-671-63132-2). In addition to a detailed description of the science of paleontology, this account, through photos and text, identifies particular fossils and gives hints on how to collect them. (Rev: BL 5/1/87) [560.9]

6974 Bakker, Robert T. *The Dinosaur Heresies* (10–12). Illus. 1986, Morrow $22.95 (0-688-04287-2); Zebra paper $11.95 (0-8217-2471-1). Bakker relates his theories that dinosaurs were of the bird genus to ideas concerning their extinction. (Rev: BL 11/15/86) [567.9]

6975 Berry, R. J., and A. Hallam, eds. *The Encyclopedia of Animal Evolution* (9–12). Illus. 1987, Facts on File $24.95 (0-1860-1819-7). A stunning introduction to paleontology and how animals have evolved into present species. (Rev: BL 11/15/87) [591.3]

6976 Colbert, Edwin H. *Dinosaurs: An Illustrated History* (7–12). Illus. 1983, Hammond $30.00 (0-8437-3332-2). A description of kinds of dinosaurs, how they lived, and possible reasons for their disappearance. [567.9]

6977 Cvancara, Alan M. *Sleuthing Fossils: The Art of Investigating Past Life* (10–12). 1989, Wiley $22.95 (0-471-51046-7); paper $12.95 (0-471-62077-7). Cvancara, in a relaxed style, introduces paleontology and how the study of fossil life relates to the theory of evolution. (Rev: BL 11/15/89) [560]

6978 Czerkas, Sylvia J., and Everett C. Olson, eds. *Dinosaurs Past and Present, Volume 1* (9–12). Illus. 1987, Univ. of Washington Pr. $35.00 (0-295-96541-X); paper $22.95 (0-295-96708-0).

Famous artwork involving dinosaurs and 6 essays are the highlights of this handsome volume. Continued in Volume II (1987). (Rev: BL 11/15/87) [567.9]

6979 Dixon, Dougal. *The New Dinosaurs: An Alternative Evolution* (9–12). Illus. 1988, Salem House $19.95 (0-88162-301-6). A work that tries to answer the question of how dinosaurs would look today had they not become extinct. (Rev: BL 10/1/88; SLJ 1/89; VOYA 4/89) [567.9]

6980 Eldredge, Niles. *Life Pulse: Episodes from the Story of the Fossil Record* (10–12). Illus. 1987, Facts on File $19.95 (0-8160-1151-6). The history of life on earth as revealed by a study of the amazing record left by fossils. (Rev: BL 1/15/87; BR 11–12/87; SLJ 2/87) [560]

6981 Horner, John R., and James Gorman. *Digging Dinosaurs* (10–12). Illus. 1988, Workman $17.95 (0-89480-220-8). A famous paleontologist describes his digs in Montana that unearthed dinosaur nests and their eggs. (Rev: BL 11/1/88) [567.9]

6982 Lambert, David. *A Field Guide to Dinosaurs* (7–12). Illus. 1983, Avon paper $9.95 (0-380-83579-3). A well-illustrated guide to over 340 different dinosaurs arranged by family groups. [567.9]

6983 Lambert, David. *The Field Guide to Prehistoric Life* (10–12). Illus. 1985, Facts on File paper $21.95 (0-8160-1389-6). This book explains what fossils are, how they were formed, and their various types. (Rev: BL 6/15/85; BR 3–4/86; VOYA 12/85) [560]

6984 Paul, Gregory S. *Predatory Dinosaurs of the World* (9–12). Illus. 1988, Simon & Schuster $19.95 (0-671-61946-2). Biologist and artist Paul not only describes each of these dinosaurs but also gives material on how they lived and the reasons for their extinction. (Rev: BL 3/1/89) [567.9]

6985 Rhodes, Frank H. T., et al. *Fossils: A Guide to Prehistoric Life* (7–12). Illus. 1962, Golden paper $3.95 (0-307-24411-3). An account of how fossils are formed plus an illustrated guide to the most common plant and animal fossils. [560]

6986 Thompson, Ida. *The Audubon Society Field Guide to North American Fossils* (7–12). Illus.

1982, Knopf $14.45 (0-394-52412-8). An illustrated guide to the identification of North American fossils plus some background information on their formation. [560]

6987 Wilford, John Noble. *The Riddle of the Dinosaur* (10–12). 1986, Knopf $24.95 (0-394-52763-1); Random paper $8.95 (0-394-74392-X). This fascinating account traces a history of paleontology in relation to dinosaurs and discusses current theories concerning their extinction. (Rev: BL 1/15/86; BR 9–10/86; SLJ 8/86; VOYA 6/86) [567.9]

Anthropology and Evolution

6988 Attenborough, David. *Life on Earth: A Natural History* (9–12). Illus. 1979, Little paper $24.95 (0-316-05747-9). A pictorial introduction to the evolution of life on earth and the range of animals it has produced. [575]

6989 Benedict, Ruth. *Patterns of Culture* (10–12). 1973, Houghton paper $8.70 (0-395-08357-5). A classic in anthropology that defines culture and describes 3 different Indian cultural groups. [306]

6990 Bronowski, Jacob. *The Ascent of Man* (10–12). Illus. 1974, Little paper $24.95 (0-316-10933-9). This informal account traces man's nature and accomplishments from the use of primitive tools to the formation of the theory of relativity. [501]

6991 Cheneviere, Alain. *Vanishing Tribes* (10–12). Illus. 1987, Doubleday $35.00 (0-385-23897-5). An investigation of 20 tribes still living as primitive societies in various parts of the earth. (Rev: BL 12/1/87; SLJ 5/88) [306]

6992 Darwin, Charles. *The Essential Darwin* (10–12). Illus. 1984, Little $19.95 (0-316-45826-0); paper $12.95 (0-316-45827-9). This is an anthology of Darwin's most important writings plus a critical analysis of each. [575.01]

6993 Darwin, Charles. *The Voyage of the Beagle* (10–12). 1988, NAL paper $4.95 (0-451-62620-6). This journal records events on the 5 voyages that were responsible for the formation of the theory of evolution. [508]

6994 Dixon, Dougal. *After Man: A Zoology of the Future* (10–12). 1983, St. Martin's $10.95 (0-312-01162-8). A look at possible future paths in the evolution of various species. [573.2]

6995 Eiseley, Loren. *Darwin's Century: Evolution and the Men Who Discovered It* (10–12). 1958, Doubleday paper $6.95 (0-385-08141-3). An examination of the development of the theory of evolution from the Renaissance to the twentieth century. [573.2]

6996 Eldredge, Niles. *The Monkey Business: A Scientist Looks at Creationism* (10–12). 1984, Pocket paper $3.95 (0-671-53141-7). This volume explores arguments for and against creationism and endorses the theory of evolution. [573.2]

6997 Freeman, Derek. *Margaret Mead and Samoa: The Making and Unmaking of Anthropological Myth* (10–12). Illus. 1983, Harvard Univ. Pr. $25.00 (0-674-54830-2). A critical review of the work of Margaret Mead's study of the culture of Samoa. [306]

6998 Gallant, Roy A. *Before the Sun Dies: The Story of Evolution* (9–12). 1989, Macmillan $14.95 (0-02-735771-6). A history of the earth and life on it from its formation to the development of human beings. (Rev: BL 9/15/89; BR 3–4/90; SLJ 9/89; VOYA 10/89) [575]

6999 Hitching, Francis. *The Neck of the Giraffe: Darwin, Evolution and the New Biology* (10–12). 1983, NAL paper $7.95 (0-452-00896-4). Many questions involving the theory of evolution are explored in this provocative book. [573.2]

7000 *The Illustrated Origin of Species* (10–12). Illus. 1979, Hill & Wang $25.00 (0-8090-5735-2); paper $12.95 (0-8090-1397-5). An attractive abridgment of the original which contains all of the most important material. [575.01]

7001 Johanson, Donald, and Maitland A. Edey. *Lucy: The Beginnings of Humankind* (10–12). Illus. 1988, Warner paper $13.45 (0-446-38625-

1). The exciting account of the discovery of the bones of an extremely primitive female hominid. [573.2]

7002 Johanson, Donald, and James Shreeve. *Lucy's Child: The Discovery of a Human Ancestor* (10–12). Illus. 1989, Morrow $22.95 (0-688-06492-2). In this continuation of *Lucy: The Beginnings of Humankind* (1982), the authors find further evidence of the evolution of Homo sapiens. (Rev: SLJ 2/90) [573]

7003 Lambert, David, and Diagram Group. *The Field Guide to Early Man* (9–12). Illus. 1987, Facts on File $21.95 (0-8160-1517-1). An account of the evolution of man in the same series as *The Field Guide to Prehistoric Life* (1985). (Rev: BL 7/87; BR 1–2/88) [573.2]

7004 Leakey, Richard E., and Roger Lewin. *Origins: What New Discoveries Reveal about the Emergence of Our Species and Its Possible Future* (10–12). Illus. 1977, Dutton paper $8.95 (0-525-48246-6). A synthesis of what we know about human origins and evolution. [573.2]

7005 Leroi-Gourhan, André. *The Hunters of Prehistory* (9–12). Trans. by Claire Jacobson. Illus. 1989, Macmillan $12.95 (0-689-31293-8). A recreation of the life of prehistoric man based on excavations mainly in France. (Rev: BL 7/89; BR 11–12/89; SLJ 5/89; VOYA 8/89) [936]

7006 Lewin, Roger. *Thread of Life: The Smithsonian Looks at Evolution* (9–12). Illus. 1982, Smithsonian Books $27.50 (0-89599-010-5). A panoramic look at evolution with more than 300 color plates on animals, plants, and fossils. [575]

7007 Miller, Jonathan, and Borin Van Loon. *Darwin for Beginners* (10–12). Illus. 1982, Pantheon paper $5.95 (0-394-74847-6). A paperback in comic book format which accurately explains Darwin's theory of natural selection. [575.01]

7008 National Geographic Society, eds. *Nomads of the World* (10–12). Illus. 1971, National Geographic $7.95 (0-87044-098-5). Several scholars examine different nomadic tribes in India, the Middle East, and Africa. [306]

7009 National Geographic Society, eds. *Primitive Worlds: People Lost in Time* (10–12). Illus. 1973, National Geographic $7.95 (0-87044-127-2). The societies of several primitive peoples in Africa, New Guinea, and Central America are described. [306]

7010 *Primitive Worlds* (7–12). Illus. 1973, National Geographic $7.95 (0-87044-127-2). Anthropologists and journalists describe 6 primitive cultures found in the world today. [306]

7011 Reader, John. *The Rise of Life* (9–12). Illus. 1986, Knopf paper $19.95 (0-394-74051-3). A well-illustrated book describing the first 3.5 billion years of life on Earth. (Rev: BR 3–4/87; VOYA 4/87) [573.5]

7012 Tanner, Nancy Makepeace. *On Becoming Human* (10–12). Illus. 1981, Cambridge Univ. Pr. paper $15.95 (0-521-23554-5). An account that tries to cover the transition in human development from primate to hominid. [573.2]

7013 White, Randall. *Dark Caves, Bright Visions: Life in Ice Age Europe* (10–12). Illus. 1986, Norton $35.00 (0-393-02410-5). A beautifully illustrated account of how prehistoric humans lived that includes many examples of cave paintings. (Rev: BL 2/1/87) [930.12]

Archaeology

7014 Ceram, C. W. *Gods, Graves, and Scholars* (10–12). Illus. 1967, Knopf $30.00 (0-394-42661-4); Random paper $8.95 (0-394-74319-9). This history of archaeology covers such topics as the secret of the Rosetta Stone, the excavations at Ur, and the discovery of a great Mayan city. [930.1]

7015 Connell, Evan S. *The White Lantern* (10–12). 1989, North Point paper $9.95 (0-86547-364-1). This volume describes the great discoveries in archaeology and anthropology. [930.1]

7016 Fagan, Brian M. *The Great Journey: The Peopling of Ancient America* (10–12). Illus. 1987, Thames & Hudson $19.95 (0-500-05045-7); paper $10.95 (0-500-27515-7). An accessible account of the migrations of cave people from Siberia to both the Americas. (Rev: BL 9/1/87; SLJ 3/88) [930.1]

7017 Fagan, Brian M. *New Treasures of the Past* (10–12). Illus. 1987, Barron's $26.95 (0-8120-5866-6). After discussing new methods in archaeological research, the author gives an account of recent discoveries. (Rev: BL 11/1/87) [930.1]

7018 Gowlett, John. *Ascent to Civilization: The Archaeology of Early Man* (10–12). Illus. 1984, McGraw paper $14.95 (0-07-554724-4). This work discusses prehistoric cultures and the techniques used to find out about them. [930.1]

7019 McHargue, Georgess, and Michael Roberts. *A Field Guide to Conservation Archaeology in North America* (8–12). 1977, Harper $9.57 (0-397-31724-7); paper $4.95 (0-397-31725-5). For a beginning student, this is an introduction to archaeology and key sites in North America. [930.1]

7020 McIntosh, James. *The Practical Archaeologist* (8–12). 1988, Facts on File $18.95 (0-8160-1440-0); paper $12.95 (0-8160-1814-6). A discussion of how an archaeologist operates with particular emphasis on how sites are found and excavated. (Rev: BR 1–2/89; VOYA 10/88) [930.1]

7021 National Geographic Society, eds. *Mysteries of the Ancient World* (9–12). Illus. 1979, National Geographic LB $9.50 (0-87044-259-7). From cavemen through ancient Egypt and Greece, this is an account of the most famous archaeological excavations. [930]

7022 National Geographic Society, eds. *Splendors of the Past: Lost Cities of the Ancient World* (9–12). Illus. 1981, National Geographic $19.95 (0-87044-358-5). A lavishly illustrated volume that deals with such historical sites as Pompeii, Angkor, and those associated with the Hittite Empire. [930]

7023 Reader's Digest, eds. *Mysteries of the Ancient Americas* (9–12). Illus. 1986, Reader's Digest $28.95 (0-89577-183-7). A richly illustrated book about the first people in America and the theories about their origin and culture. (Rev: SLJ 10/86) [930.1]

7024 Robbins, Lawrence H. *Stones, Bones, and Ancient Cities* (10–12). Illus. 1990, St. Martin's $18.95 (0-312-04431-3). The personal experiences of an archaeologist as he explores lost cities, hidden burial sites, and the wonders of cave art. (Rev: BL 7/90) [930]

7025 Whitehouse, Ruth, ed. *The Facts on File Dictionary of Archaeology* (10–12). 1984, Facts on File $29.95 (0-87196-048-6). In an alphabetical arrangement, such subjects as terminology, sites, and ancient cultures are covered. [930.1]

7026 Winstone, H. V. F. *Uncovering the Ancient World* (9–12). Illus. 1986, Facts on File $24.95 (0-8160-1578-3). A history of archaeology in the Near East in the nineteenth and twentieth centuries. (Rev: BR 3–4/87) [930.1]

7027 Yadin, Yigael. *Masada: Herod's Fortress and the Zealots' Last Stand* (10–12). Illus. 1966, Random $29.95 (0-394-43542-7). An account of the archaeological excavations at the rocky fortress site of a Jewish revolt against Roman oppressors. [933]

World History and Geography

General

7028 Arnold, Guy. *Datelines of World History* (9–12). Illus. 1983, Watts LB $13.90 (0-531-09212-7). In a series of timeliness, various events that occurred simultaneously in world history are highlighted. [902]

7029 Asimov, Isaac, and Frank White. *The March of the Millennia: A Key to Looking at History* (10–12). 1990, Walker $18.95 (0-8027-1122-7). A broad millennium-by-millennium history of the development and decline of world cultures. (Rev: BL 10/15/90) [303.49]

7030 Brinton, Crane. *Ideas and Men: The Story of Western Thought* (10–12). 1963, Prentice $45.20 (0-13-449249-8). This discussion of the evolution of Western thought covers such areas as ethics, religion, politics, and science. [909]

7031 Burne, Jerome, ed. *Chronicle of the World* (9–12). Illus. 1990, ECAM $49.95 (0-13-133463-8). A giant book that covers all of world history and gives a compendium of information about every country in the world. (Rev: SLJ 8/90) [900]

7032 Carey, John, ed. *Eyewitness to History* (9–12). 1988, Harvard Univ. Pr. $24.95 (0-674-28750-9). Eyewitness accounts to important historical events extending from ancient Greece to the fall of Marcos in 1986. (Rev: BL 9/1/88; BR 3–4/89; SLJ 12/88) [909.2]

7033 Cook, Chris. *Dictionary of Historical Terms: A Guide to Names and Events of Over 1000 Years of World History* (10–12). 1983, Bedrick $22.00 (0-911745-16-5). A useful dictionary that gives entries for events, periods, places, movements, and similar terms related to world history. [903]

7034 David, Andrew. *Famous Political Trials* (9–12). 1980, Lerner LB $8.95 (0-8225-1429-X). From Joan of Arc to Soviet dissidents, this is a collection of 8 cases involving political prisoners. [364]

7035 DeFord, Miriam Allen, and Joan S. Jackson. *Who Was When? A Dictionary of Contemporaries* (7–12). 1976, H. W. Wilson $47.50 (0-8242-0532-4). In a year-by-year arrangement, the birth and death dates of important people in world history are listed by field of accomplishment. [902]

7036 Dukes, Paul. *A History of Europe 1648–1948: The Arrival, the Rise, the Fall* (10–12). 1985, Sheridan House $45.00 (0-333-28104-7); paper $24.50 (0-333-28207-8). Three hundred years of European history that concentrates on its rise and decline in world influence. (Rev: BL 4/15/86) [940.2]

7037 Duncan, David Ewing. *Pedaling to the Ends of the World* (9–12). Illus. 1986, Simon & Schuster paper $7.95 (0-671-62805-4). The story of the incredible odyssey made by David Duncan and 2 other men by bicycle through countries in Asia, the Middle East, and Africa. (Rev: SLJ 8/86) [910]

7038 Durant, Will, and Ariel Durant. *The Lessons of History* (10–12). 1968, Simon & Schuster $17.95 (0-671-41333-3). This series of essays involves a statement of conclusions reached by the authors concerning lasting values and man's place in history. [901]

7039 Dyer, Gwynne. *War* (10–12). Illus. 1985, Crown $17.95 (0-517-55615-4). This account traces the history of warfare for 9,000 years and shows how its destructive effects have adversely changed human history. (Rev: BL 12/1/85) [355]

7040 Eban, Abba. *Heritage: Civilization and the Jews* (10–12). Illus. 1984, Summit paper $16.95 (0-671-62881-X). This is not only a history of the Jews but also an account of their influence on world culture. [909]

7041 Eggenberger, David. *An Encyclopedia of Battles* (10–12). Illus. 1985, Dover paper $14.95 (0-486-24913-1). An alphabetical listing of battles that supplies valuable background information on each. [904]

7042 Franck, Irene M., and David M. Brownstone. *The Silk Road: A History* (9–12). Illus. 1986, Facts on File $24.95 (0-8160-1122-2). An account of East meeting West through the centuries that discusses the careers of such historical figures as Marco Polo, Alexander the Great, and Attila the Hun. (Rev: BR 9–10/87) [950]

7043 Freeman-Grenville, G. S. P. *Chronology of World History: A Calendar of Principal Events from 3000 B.C. to A.D. 1976* (9–12). 1978, Rowman & Littlefield $47.50 (0-8476-6040-0). Using different columns for various geographical regions, a chronology of world history is presented. [902]

7044 *Great Journeys* (9–12). Illus. 1990, Simon & Schuster $29.95 (0-671-70835-X); paper $19.95 (0-671-70834-1). Based on the PBS series, 7 adventurers describe trips to unusual parts of the world. (Rev: BL 2/15/90) [910.4]

7045 Grun, Bernard. *The Timetables of History: A Horizontal Linkage of People & Events* (9–12). 1979, Simon & Schuster $19.95 (0-671-24988-6). Important events in world history are presented in charts that begin at 5000 BC and end with AD 1978. [902]

7046 Gurney, Gene. *Kingdoms of Asia, the Middle East, and Africa* (10–12). Illus. 1986, Crown $24.95 (0-517-55256-6). This book covers past and present monarchies in the Eastern Hemisphere from Egypt to Vietnam. (Rev: BL 10/15/86) [909]

7047 Hobhouse, Henry. *Forces of Change: An Unorthodox History* (10–12). Illus. 1990, Arcade $22.95 (1-55970-087-4). A demographic history of the modern world from Columbus on, told in terms of disease, food supply, and other processes. (Rev: BL 4/15/90) [909]

7048 Hoopes, James. *Oral History: An Introduction for Students* (10–12). 1979, Univ. of North Carolina Pr. paper $7.95 (0-8078-1344-3). This work explains the methodologies used in oral history collections and gives tips on how to put them into practice. [907]

7049 *Images of the World* (9–12). Illus. 1981, National Geographic $18.95 (0-87044-394-1).

Some of the best pictures from the *National Geographic* magazine that reflect life around the world. [779]

7050 James, Naomi. *Courage at Sea: Tales of Heroic Voyages* (10–12). 1988, Salem $24.95 (0-88162-320-2). Beginning with Magellan's trip, there are 15 harrowing sea voyages reported on in this book. (Rev: VOYA 12/88) [910]

7051 Keegan, John. *The Illustrated Face of Battle: A Study of Agincourt, Waterloo and the Somme* (10–12). Rev. ed. Illus. 1989, Viking $29.95 (0-670-82703-7). This revised edition, with an expanded number of illustrations, of the 1976 title describes 3 epic battles in western history. (Rev: BL 5/1/89) [355.4]

7052 Keegan, John, and Richard Holmes. *Soldiers: A History of Men in Battle* (10–12). Illus. 1986, Viking $22.95 (0-670-80969-1). Each type of soldier is described and the origin of their specializations outlined. (Rev: BR 11–12/86; SLJ 11/86) [355]

7053 Langer, William L., ed. *An Encyclopedia of World History* (9–12). Illus. 1972, Houghton $40.00 (0-395-13592-3). Using both a geographical and chronological arrangement, the author outlines the major events in world history to 1970. [902]

7054 Lerner, Gerda. *The Majority Finds Its Past: Placing Women in History* (10–12). 1979, Oxford Univ. Pr. $21.95 (0-19-502597-0); paper $9.95 (0-19-502899-6). Through 12 illuminating essays, the role of women in history is surveyed. [909]

7055 McAllister, Pam. *You Can't Kill the Spirit* (10–12). 1988, New Society $34.95 (0-86571-130-5); paper $10.95 (0-86571-131-3). An account of how women through history have, in a nonviolent fashion, fought for justice. (Rev: BL 12/15/88; SLJ 7/89) [324.4]

7056 McClintock, Jack, and David Helgren. *Everything Is Somewhere: The Geography Quiz Book* (8–12). 1986, Morrow paper $10.95 (0-688-05873-6). A geography quiz book that has sections on the continents, countries, and U.S. states and cities. (Rev: BL 7/86) [910]

7057 MacDonald, John. *Great Battlefields of the World* (10–12). Illus. 1985, Macmillan paper $24.95 (0-02-044464-8). This account describes 30 significant battles in world history from ancient times to present times. [904]

7058 McEvedy, Colin. *The World History Factfinder* (10–12). 1989, W. H. Smith paper $15.98 (0-8317-9557-3). Eight chronologically arranged sections present world history in a series of essays, charts, and maps. [902]

7059 McNeill, William H. *A World History* (10–12). Illus. 1979, Oxford Univ. Pr. $29.95 (0-19-502554-7); paper $19.95 (0-19-502555-5). A basic world history that stresses such broad concepts as culture, communications, and geography in the development of history. [909]

7060 *Majestic Island Worlds* (10–12). Illus. 1987, National Geographic $7.95 (0-87044-625-8). The life and culture of 6 islands (e.g., Japan, Ireland and Bali) are examined. (Rev: BL 5/1/88) [910]

7061 Matthews, Rupert O. *The Atlas of Natural Wonders* (7–12). Illus. 1988, Facts on File $35.00 (0-8160-1993-2). Fifty unusual sites like Ayers Rock in Australia are described in words and pictures. (Rev: BL 11/15/88) [508]

7062 Naisbitt, John, and Patricia Aburdeen. *Megatrends 2000* (10–12). 1990, Morrow $21.95 (0-688-07224-0). A look at what this decade has in store for us in areas such as the economy, arts, religion, science, and international relations. (Rev: SLJ 4/90) [327]

7063 Newark, Tim. *Women Warlords* (10–12). Illus. 1990, Blandford $24.95 (0-713-71965-6). A history of the mighty women warriors of the early civilizations in Europe, Africa, and South America. (Rev: SLJ 6/90) [335]

7064 Perrett, Bryan. *Desert Warfare: From Its Roman Origins to the Gulf Conflict* (10–12). Illus. 1989, Sterling $24.95 (1-85059-917-2). A richly illustrated history of warfare in North Africa and the Near East that covers 2,000 years. (Rev: BL 9/1/89) [355]

7065 Poole, Robert M., ed. *Nature's Wonderlands: National Parks of the World* (9–12). Illus. 1990, National Geographic $27.95 (0-87044-766-1). A photo-text tour of the national parks of the world with fuller coverage of those that are most important. (Rev: BL 5/1/90) [363.7]

7066 Potok, Chaim. *Wanderings: Chaim Potok's History of the Jews* (10–12). Illus. 1978, Knopf $40.00 (0-394-50110-1). An informal history of the Jewish people, their wanderings, and their persecutions. [909]

7067 Potter, G. R., ed. *The Cambridge Modern History* (10–12). 1957, Macmillan $80.00 (0-521-04541-X); paper $34.50 (0-521-09974-9). This is the first volume of a 14-volume set that is considered one of the most authoritative sources of general information on world history from 1493 on. [909.08]

7068 Reader's Digest, eds. *Natural Wonders of the World* (8–12). Illus. 1981, Reader's Digest $24.95 (0-89577-087-3). From sulphur springs to natural bridges, over 500 natural phenomena are described and pictured. [910.3]

7069 Reader's Digest, eds. *Quest for the Past* (7–12). Illus. 1984, Reader's Digest $24.95 (0-89577-170-5). An introduction to world history through a series of vignettes and historical profiles from various periods. [909]

7070 Reid, Pat, and Maurice Michael. *Prisoner of War* (9–12). Illus. 1986, Beaufort $17.95 (0-8253-0372-9). A history of how prisoners of war have been treated throughout the ages plus details of famous escapes and of living conditions. (Rev: BL 4/1/86) [355.1]

7071 Russell, Jeffrey B. *A History of Witchcraft: Sorcerers, Heretics and Pagans* (9–12). Illus. 1983, Peter Smith $19.50 (0-8446-6052-3). A history of witchcraft that concentrates on Western Europe, Africa, and the United States. [133.4]

7072 Sachar, Howard M. *Diaspora: An Inquiry into the Contemporary Jewish World* (10–12). 1985, Harper $27.50 (0-06-015403-9); paper $10.95 (0-06-091347-9). The author explores Jewish communities in Europe, Australia, South America, and Africa. [909]

7073 Sedeen, Margaret, ed. *Great Rivers of the World* (7–12). Illus. 1984, National Geographic $21.95 (0-87044-537-5). In text and lavish illustrations and maps, the great waterways of the world are described. [910.2]

7074 Smith, Ronald D. *Fascinating People and Astounding Events from the History of the Western World* (10–12). 1990, ABC-CLIO $29.95 (0-87436-544-9). The history of the world is covered in a series of fact-filled essays arranged in chronological order. (Rev: SLJ 7/90) [900]

7075 *The Smithsonian Book of Inventions* (9–12). Illus. 1978, Norton $25.00 (0-89599-002-4). A history of inventions that covers such areas as technology, art, industry, and architecture. [609]

7076 Toynbee, Arnold. *A Study of History* (10–12). 1989, Crown $24.95 (0-517-17941-5). This is an abridgment of the 10-volume set that traces the causes of the rise and fall of civilizations. [909]

7077 Tuchman, Barbara W. *The March of Folly* (10–12). 1985, Ballantine paper $9.95 (0-345-30823-9). Four examples from history of government folly, including the British loss of the American colonies and the U.S. involvement in Vietnam, are explored. [909.08]

7078 Tuchman, Barbara W. *Practicing History: Selected Essays* (10–12). 1981, Knopf $16.95 (0-394-52086-6); Ballantine paper $8.95 (0-345-30363-6). A series of essays on the writing of history and the methodology used. [907]

7079 Van Loon, Hendrik Willem. *The Story of Mankind* (7–12). 1985, Liveright $27.95 (0-87140-647-0). A simple introduction to world history that was an early winner of the Newbery Medal. [909]

7080 Wetterau, Bruce. *Macmillan Concise Dictionary of World History* (10–12). 1983, Macmillan $39.95 (0-02-626110-3). In an alphabetical arrangement, the events, people, and places important in world history are introduced. [902]

7081 Winks, Robin, and Crane Brinton. *A History of Civilization: Vol. 1 Pre-History to 1765* (10–12). 1988, Prentice paper $35.00 (0-13-389884-9). This 2-volume set has become a standard introduction to world history. Volume I covers the period of prehistory to 1765, and Volume II modern history to the present. [909]

Ancient History

General and Miscellaneous

7082 Attenborough, David. *The First Eden: The Mediterranean World and Man* (10–12). Illus. 1987, Little $24.95 (0-316-05750-9). The history of the Mediterranean from its formation through its place in human history. (Rev: BL 2/15/88) [508.182]

7083 Boardman, John, et al., eds. *The Oxford History of the Classical World* (10–12). Illus. 1986, Oxford Univ. Pr. paper $18.95 (0-19-282165-2). A lavishly illustrated history of ancient Greece and Rome. (Rev: BL 1/1/87) [938]

7084 Hodges, Henry. *Technology in the Ancient World* (10–12). Illus. 1970, Knopf $13.95 (0-394-44808-1). An introduction to the tools, inventions, and scientific methods used by ancient men through to the decline of Rome. [609]

7085 Jenkins, Ian. *Greek and Roman Life* (10–12). Illus. 1986, Harvard Univ. Pr. paper $8.95 (0-674-36307-8). The dress, education, and home life are 3 topics covered in this history of everyday life in ancient Greece and Rome. (Rev: SLJ 3/87) [930]

7086 Radice, Betty. *Who's Who in the Ancient World* (10–12). Illus. 1973, Penguin paper $8.95 (0-14-051055-9). A handbook that gives identifying material on important people and places in the ancient world of Greece and Rome. [938.03]

7087 Schwartz, Max. *Machines, Buildings, Weaponry of Biblical Times* (10–12). Illus. 1990, Revell $16.95 (0-8007-1630-2); paper $9.95 (0-8007-5320-8). The story of the engineering feats of ancient peoples including an explanation of how the Tower of Babel was probably constructed. (Rev: BL 7/90) [620]

7088 Starr, Chester. *A History of the Ancient World* (10–12). 3rd ed. Illus. 1983, Oxford Univ. Pr. $35.00 (0-19-503143-1). This account covers both the western and eastern world from prehistory to fifth-century Greece. [930]

7089 Thubron, Colin. *The Ancient Mariners* (9–12). Illus. 1981, Silver Burdett $21.27 (0-8094-2739-7). The earliest sailing adventurers including the Greek and Roman periods are included in this well-illustrated volume that is part of the Time-Life series, The Seafarers. [387.5]

7090 Westwood, Jennifer, ed. *The Atlas of Mysterious Places* (9–12). Illus. 1987, Weidenfeld & Nicolson $34.95 (1-55584-130-9). A guide to such exotic places as Stonehenge and King Solomon's mines with many color and black-and-white photographs. (Rev: BL 7/87) [909]

7091 Whitehouse, Ruth, and John Wilkins. *The Making of Civilization: History Discovered through Archaeology* (10–12). Illus. 1986, Knopf paper $18.95 (0-394-72685-5). Social institutions are traced from their beginnings in the ancient civilizations of Mesopotamia through the Roman Empire. (Rev: BL 2/1/87; BR 3–4/87; VOYA 6/87) [930]

Egypt and Mesopotamia

7092 Aldred, Cyril. *The Egyptians* (10–12). Rev. ed. Illus. 1984, Thames & Hudson paper $11.95 (0-500-27345-6). The history and culture of ancient Egypt with sections on everyday life. [932]

7093 Andrews, Carol. *The British Museum Book of the Rosetta Stone* (10–12). Illus. 1986, Bedrick $12.95 (0-87226-033-X); paper $5.95 (0-87226-034-8). The story behind the slab that opened up the world of Egyptian hieroglyphics. (Rev: BL 4/15/86) [493]

7094 Bowman, Alan K. *Egypt after the Pharoahs: 332 B.C.–A.D. 642 from Alexander to the Arab Conquest* (10–12). Illus. 1986, Univ. of California Pr. $29.50 (0-520-05930-1); paper $12.95 (0-520-06665-0). A lively, well-illustrated retrospective of 300 years of Egyptian history. (Rev: BL 1/1/87) [932]

7095 David, A. Rosalie. *The Egyptian Kingdoms* (10–12). Illus. 1988, Bedrick $19.95 (0-87226-300-2). This is the story of 4,000 years of Egyptian history as revealed in archaeological finds. (Rev: BR 5–6/89; SLJ 3/89; VOYA 4/89) [932]

7096 Davidovits, Joseph, and Margie Morris. *The Pyramids: An Enigma Solved* (10–12). Illus. 1988, Hippocrene $16.95 (0-87052-559-X). New theories are espoused concerning the construction of the pyramids. (Rev: BL 11/15/88) [690]

7097 Edwards, I. E. S. *The Pyramids of Egypt* (10–12). Rev. ed. Illus. 1987, Viking $25.00 (0-670-80153-4); Penguin paper $7.95 (0-14-022549-8). A popularly written but thorough account of the structure of the pyramids, their uses and how they were built. (Rev: BL 4/15/87) [932]

7098 Romer, John. *Ancient Lives: Daily Life in Egypt of the Pharaohs* (10–12). Illus. 1984, Holt $18.95 (0-03-000733-X); paper $12.95 (0-8050-1244-3). The daily life of various strata of society in ancient Egypt is described in text with many accompanying illustrations. [932]

7099 Stead, Miriam. *Egyptian Life* (10–12). Illus. 1986, Harvard paper $8.95 (0-674-24151-7). Everyday life in ancient Egypt that covers religion, social life, and dress. (Rev: SLJ 3/87) [932]

7100 Watterson, Barbara. *The Gods of Ancient Egypt* (10–12). Illus. 1985, Facts on File $21.95 (0-8160-1111-7). A general description of the religion of ancient Egypt with detailed information on each of the gods and goddesses. (Rev: BL 7/85; SLJ 8/85) [299]

Greece

7101 Durant, Will. *The Life of Greece* (10–12). Illus. 1939, Simon & Schuster $29.95 (0-671-41800-9). A history of the world of ancient Greece from its beginning to the Roman conquest after the death of Alexander. Also use the continuation *Caesar and Christ: A History of Roman Civilization from Its Beginnings to A.D. 337* (1944). [938]

7102 Fine, John V. A. *The Ancient Greeks: A Critical History* (10–12). 1983, Belknap $40.50 (0-674-03311-6); paper $16.95 (0-674-03314-0). A history of ancient Greece that ends with the accession of Alexander the Great. [938]

7103 Grant, Michael. *The Classical Greeks* (10–12). 1989, Macmillan $27.50 (0-684-19126-1). By telling the story of 37 prominent ancient Greeks such as Plato and Aristophanes, the author traces the history of the great days of ancient Greece. The Greek history before this volume is covered in *The Rise of the Greeks* (1988) and after in *From Alexander to Cleopatra* (1983). (Rev: BL 10/1/89) [938]

7104 Green, Peter. *Ancient Greece* (10–12). Illus. 1979, Thames & Hudson paper $10.95 (0-500-27161-5). In 200 illustrations and ample text, the history of Greece is traced to the death of Alexander the Great in 323 B.C. [938]

7105 Hamilton, Edith. *The Echo of Greece* (10–12). 1987, Norton paper $6.95 (0-393-00231-4). A description of life in ancient Greece during the fourth century B.C. that gives substantial material on the famous writers of the period. [880.9]

7106 Hamilton, Edith. *The Greek Way* (10–12). 1943, Norton paper $4.95 (0-393-00230-6). Through a study of the great writers of ancient Greece, the author re-creates the life, times, and spirit of this period. [880.9]

7107 Levi, Peter. *Atlas of the Greek World* (10–12). Illus. 1981, Facts on File $40.00 (0-87196-448-1). Through maps and other kinds of illustrations, the history of ancient Greece is traced along with discussion of its lasting influence. [938]

7108 Ling, Roger. *The Greek World* (9–12). Illus. 1990, Bedrick $19.95 (0-87226-301-0). Through many illustrations and the facts revealed by archaeology, life in ancient Greece is described. (Rev: BR 5–6/89; SLJ 9/90; VOYA 4/89) [932]

7109 Pellegrino, Charles. *Unearthing Atlantis: An Archaeological Odyssey* (10–12). Illus. 1990, Random $22.95 (0-394-57550-4). The author discusses the Minoan civilization and the possibility that the island of Thera (Santorini) is actually what is left of the mythical Atlantis. (Rev: BL 6/15/90) [939]

7110 Robinson, C. E. *Everyday Life in Ancient Greece* (7–12). Illus. n.d., AMS $22.50 (0-404-14592-2). The classic account, first published in 1933, of how people lived during various periods in ancient Greek history. [938]

7111 Warren, Peter. *The Aegean Civilizations* (9–12). Illus. 1989, Bedrick $24.95 (0-87226-304-5); paper $16.95 (0-87226-213-8). An introduction to the Bronze Age civilizations of the Aegean Sea plus the Minoan and Mycenean periods. (Rev: BL 11/15/89; BR 1–2/90) [938]

7112 Wood, Michael. *In Search of the Trojan War* (10–12). Illus. 1986, Facts on File $22.95 (0-8160-1355-1); NAL paper $14.95 (0-452-26364-4). The author reconstructs what is known about Troy and the Trojan War by studying the artifacts and weeding through the discoveries and theories of others. (Rev: BL 5/1/86) [939.21]

Rome

7113 Cornell, Tim, and John Matthews. *Atlas of the Roman World* (10–12). Illus. 1982, Facts on File $40.00 (0-87196-652-2). In addition to many maps, there is an extensive text that traces the history of the Roman Empire to A.D. 565. [937]

7114 Davis, William Stearns. *A Day in Old Rome: A Picture of Roman Life* (9–12). Illus. 1959, Biblio & Tannen $18.00 (0-8196-0106-3). This account of the daily life, habits, and customs of ancient Romans first appeared in 1925. A companion volume is *A Day in Old Athens* (1959). [937]

7115 Hamilton, Edith. *The Roman Way* (10–12). 1987, Norton paper $3.95 (0-393-00232-2). By using excerpts from famous writers, the author re-creates life in ancient Rome. [870.9]

7116 Hills, C. A. R. *The Destruction of Pompeii and Herculaneum* (7–12). Illus. 1988, David & Charles LB $16.95 (0-8521-9696-2). In addition to a history of the eruption of Vesuvius in A.D. 79, this book gives general information on how the ancient Romans lived and background coverage on volcanoes and why they erupt. (Rev: SLJ 3/88) [937]

7117 Hohlfelder, Robert L., and Kenneth G. Holum. *King Herod's Dream: Caesarea on the Sea* (10–12). Illus. 1988, Norton $29.95 (0-393-02493-8). The story of this Mediterranean port built by Herod the Great that prospered for 1,200 years before it was abandoned. (Rev: BL 2/15/88) [933]

7118 Macaulay, David. *City: A Story of Roman Planning and Construction* (7–12). Illus. 1974, Houghton $14.95 (0-395-19492-X); paper $6.95 (0-395-34922-2). In text and detailed drawing, the artist explores an imaginary Roman city. [711]

7119 Tingay, Graham I. F., and John Badcock. *These Were the Romans* (10–12). Illus. 1989, Dufour paper $14.95 (0-8023-1285-3). An excellent source of all kinds of information about Rome and its empire that contains many photographs and quotes from the original documents. (Rev: BR 5–6/87; SLJ 12/89) [937]

7120 Veyne, Paul, ed. *A History of Private Life, I: From Pagan Rome to Byzantium* (10–12). Trans. by Arthur Goldhammer. Illus. 1987, Harvard Univ. Pr. $35.00 (0-674-39975-7). How people lived in the West during the days of the Roman Empire. (Rev: BL 4/15/87) [390]

7121 Vickers, Michael. *The Roman World* (9–12). Illus. 1989, Bedrick $24.95 (0-87226-302-9); paper $16.95 (0-87226-212-X). A history of the

Roman Empire and an introduction to Roman studies and archaeology. (Rev: BL 11/15/89; BR 1–2/90) [937]

Middle Ages through Renaissance (500–1700)

7122 Barber, Richard. *The Penguin Guide to Medieval Europe* (10–12). Illus. 1984, Penguin paper $12.95 (0-14-046633-9). Under such headings as church, feudal system, and politics, a history of Europe from A.D. 800 to A.D. 1400 is introduced. [940.1]

7123 Billings, Malcolm. *The Cross & the Crescent: A History of the Crusades* (10–12). Illus. 1988, Sterling $19.95 (0-8069-6904-0). A well-illustrated history of this 700-year-long war to free the Holy Land. (Rev: BL 11/1/88) [909.07]

7124 Brown, R. Allen. *The Architecture of Castles: A Visual Guide* (9–12). Illus. 1985, Facts on File $22.95 (0-8160-1146-X). The author describes the design of castles and how they were built and gives a guided tour of some of the most important ones in England. (Rev: BL 6/15/85) [725]

7125 Burckhardt, Jacob. *The Civilization of the Renaissance in Italy* (10–12). 1990, Penguin paper $8.95 (0-14-044534-X). First published in German in 1860, this is a discussion of many different facets of Renaissance life and thought. [945]

7126 Cardini, Franco. *Europe 1492: Portrait of a Continent Five Hundred Years Ago* (10–12). Illus. 1989, Facts on File $50.00 (0-8160-2188-0). The portrait of a continent emerging from the Middle Ages into the modern era. (Rev: BL 11/1/89; BR 5–6/90) [909]

7127 Durant, Will. *The Age of Faith* (10–12). Illus. 1950, Simon & Schuster $32.95 (0-671-01200-2). A history of Christian, Islamic, and Judaic cultures from A.D. 325 through A.D. 1300. [940.1]

7128 Durant, Will. *The Reformation* (10–12). Illus. 1957, Simon & Schuster $29.95 (0-671-61050-3). The careers of such people as Chaucer, Luther, Henry VIII, Calvin, and Durer are covered in this general history of Europe from 1300 to 1564. [940.2]

7129 Durant, Will, and Ariel Durant. *The Age of Louis XIV* (10–12). Illus. 1963, Simon & Schuster $29.95 (0-671-01215-0). A history of European history and civilization from 1648 to

1715 that highlights the work of such men as Molière, Peter the Great, and Cromwell. [940.2]

7130 Durant, Will, and Ariel Durant. *The Age of Reason Begins* (10–12). Illus. 1961, Simon & Schuster $29.95 (0-671-01320-3). This overview of European history and culture from 1558 through 1648 covers the careers of such personages as Galileo, Bacon, and Shakespeare. [940.2]

7131 Gies, Frances. *The Knight in History* (10–12). Illus. 1984, Harper $16.45 (0-06-015339-3); paper $9.95 (0-06-091413-0). The story of the beginnings, flowering, and decline of the institution of knighthood. [940.1]

7132 Gies, Frances, and Joseph Gies. *Life in a Medieval Village* (10–12). Illus. 1990, Harper $22.95 (0-06-016215-5). A clear, historically accurate account of everyday life in a typical English village during the Middle Ages. (Rev: BL 1/15/90; SLJ 9/90) [306]

7133 Gies, Frances, and Joseph Gies. *Women in the Middle Ages* (10–12). Illus. 1978, Barnes & Noble paper $6.95 (0-06-464037-X). The lives of 7 different women from a queen to a peasant woman are highlighted to give a cross section of the roles played by women during the Middle Ages. [305.4]

7134 Gies, Joseph, and Frances Gies. *Life in a Medieval Castle* (10–12). Illus. 1979, Harper paper $8.95 (0-06-090674-X). A Welsh castle is used as a model in this exploration of the feudal system and description of everyday life. [940.1]

7135 Goldstein, Thomas. *Dawn of Modern Science* (10–12). 1988, Houghton paper $9.95 (0-395-48924-5). An intriguing look at science during the Renaissance and how it developed. [500]

7136 Gottfried, Robert S. *The Black Death: Natural and Human Disaster in Medieval Europe* (10–12). 1983, Free Pr. $16.95 (0-02-912630-4); paper $9.95 (0-02-912370-4). The story of the terrible plague that ravaged Europe from 1347 to 1351. [616.9]

7137 Labarge, Margaret Wade. *A Small Sound of the Trumpet: Women in the Medieval Life* (10–12). Illus. 1988, Beacon paper $12.95 (0-8070-5627-8). An exploration of the role of women in life in England and continental Europe during the Middle Ages. (Rev: SLJ 3/87) [909.07]

7138 Matthew, Donald. *Atlas of Medieval Europe* (10–12). Illus. 1983, Facts on File $35.00 (0-87196-133-4). This collection of maps plus many pictures illustrate the political, social, and cultural history of Europe from the decline of the Roman Empire to the discovery of the New World. [911]

7139 Previte-Orton, C. W. *The Shorter Cambridge Medieval History* (10–12). 2 vols. Illus. 1952, Cambridge Univ. Pr. paper $23.95 each (vol. 1: 0-521-09976-5; vol. 2: 0-521-09977-3). This is a 2-volume abridgement of this standard history. Volume 1 covers the later Roman Empire to the twelfth century; volume 2, the twelfth century to the Renaissance. [940.1]

7140 Tuchman, Barbara W. *A Distant Mirror: The Calamitous 14th Century* (10–12). Illus. 1978, Knopf $45.00 (0-394-40026-7); Ballantine paper $12.95 (0-345-34957-1). The story of the fourteenth century seen principally through the experiences of a French knight who lived from 1340 to 1397. [944]

7141 Turnbull, Stephen. *The Book of the Medieval Knight* (10–12). Illus. 1985, Crown $17.95 (0-517-55863-7). A survey of knighthood in England and France as practiced during the fourteenth and fifteenth centuries. [940.1]

Eighteenth through Nineteenth Centuries (1700–1900)

7142 Brosse, Jacques. *Great Voyages of Discovery: Circumnavigators and Scientists* (10–12). Trans. by Stanley Hochman. Illus. 1985, Facts on File $35.00 (0-8160-1101-X). A well-illustrated account of the great explorers and voyaging scientists that traveled from 1764 through 1843. (Rev: BL 11/15/85; BR 5–6/86) [910.4]

7143 Durant, Will, and Ariel Durant. *The Age of Napoleon* (10–12). Illus. 1975, Simon & Schuster $29.95 (0-671-21988-X). This history of Europe covers the period from 1789 to 1815 with emphasis on the career and influence of Napoleon. [940.2]

7144 Durant, Will, and Ariel Durant. *The Age of Voltaire* (10–12). Illus. 1965, Simon & Schuster $29.95 (0-671-01325-4). A history of life and thought in Europe from 1715 to 1756. [940.2]

7145 Durant, Will, and Ariel Durant. *Rousseau and Revolution* (10–12). Illus. 1967, Simon & Schuster $32.95 (0-671-63058-X). A history of Europe during much of the eighteenth century that concentrates on the French Revolution and the beginnings of the Romantic movement. [940.2]

7146 Grant, Charles. *Waterloo* (10–12). Illus. 1990, Sterling paper $7.95 (0-8069-7326-9). A slim book that traces the military strategies used during the battle that spelled the end of Napoleon's career. (Rev: BL 6/1/90) [793.9]

7147 Nicholson, Harold. *The Congress of Vienna* (10–12). Illus. 1970, Harcourt paper $9.95 (0-15-622061-X). The history of the Congress of Vienna after the defeat of Napoleon and how the conservative decisions from this conference changed the subsequent history of Europe. [940.2]

7148 Synder, Louis L., ed. *Fifty Major Documents of the 19th Century* (10–12). 1979, Krieger paper $8.50 (0-88275-751-2). The text of 50 documents that supply excellent background information on European history during the 1800s. [940.2]

7149 Taylor, A. J. P. *The Struggle for Mastery in Europe* (10–12). 1954, Oxford Univ. Pr. $59.00 (0-19-822101-0); paper $15.95 (0-19-881270-1). A history of the beginnings of modern Europe that culminates in the outbreak of World War I. [940.2]

The Twentieth Century

General and Miscellaneous

7150 Grenville, J. A. *A World History of the Twentieth Century: Volume 1; Western Dominance, 1900–1945* (10–12). Illus. 1981, Barnes & Noble $35.00 (0-389-20171-5); Univ. Pr. of New England paper $15.00 (0-87451-315-4). This general history of the first half of the twentieth century concentrates on the role of the superpowers. [909.82]

7151 Johnson, Paul. *Modern Times: The World from the Twenties to the Eighties* (10–12). 1985, Harper $12.95 (0-06-091210-3). For better readers, this is an informal history of the mid 60 years of the twentieth century. [909]

7152 Lord, Walter. *A Night to Remember* (7–12). 1956, Bantam paper $3.95 (0-553-27827-4). A brilliant re-creation of the maiden and only voyage of the *Titanic*. [910.4]

7153 Nevin, David. *Architects of Air Power* (7–12). Illus. 1981, Silver Burdett $24.60 (0-8094-3280-3). The effect of air power on the wars fought during the twentieth century. Part of The Epic of Flight series from Time-Life Books. [358.4]

7154 Nicholls, C. S., ed. *Power: A Political History of the Twentieth Century* (10–12). Illus. 1990, Oxford Univ. Pr. $29.95 (0-19-520793-9). A brief history of this century's political life plus

brief biographies of key people involved. (Rev: BL 3/15/90) [909.82]

7155 Tuchman, Barbara W. *The Proud Tower: A Portrait of the World before the War, 1890–1914* (10–12). Illus. 1966, Macmillan $21.95 (0-02-620300-6); Bantam paper $6.95 (0-553-25602-5). This is a social history of the great powers in the 24 years leading up to World War I. [909.82]

World War I

7156 Ferrell, Robert H. *Woodrow Wilson and World War I, 1917–1921* (10–12). Illus. 1985, Harper $19.95 (0-06-011229-8); paper $9.95 (0-06-091216-2). A scholarly work about the part Wilson's decisions played in both World War I and its aftermath. [940.3]

7157 Jantzen, Steven. *Hooray for Peace, Hurrah for War: The United States during World War I* (9–12). 1990, Facts on File $16.95 (0-8160-2453-7). A brief, readable account of American policy during World War I through to the rejection of the League of Nations. [940.3]

7158 Kennedy, David M. *Over Here: The First World War and American Society* (10–12). 1980, Oxford Univ. Pr. $27.50 (0-19-502729-9); paper $9.95 (0-19-503209-8). An account of how World War I affected American society and thought. [940.3]

7159 Lawrence, T. E. *Seven Pillars of Wisdom* (10–12). 1989, Dorset $29.95 (0-88029-258-X); Penguin paper $7.95 (0-14-001696-1). A history of the Arab revolt during World War I by the man who became known as Lawrence of Arabia. [940.4]

7160 Lawson, Don. *The United States in World War I* (10–12). Illus. 1963, Harper $12.95 (0-200-71939-4). An easily read history of the 19-month period during which the United States was at war with Germany, with material on the causes and results of the war. [940.4]

7161 Simpson, Colin. *The Lusitania* (10–12). Illus. 1990, Penguin paper $5.95 (0-14-006803-1). An account of the sinking of the *Lusitania* that raises the question of whether it was deliberately planned to bring the United States into World War I. [940.4]

7162 Stokesbury, James L. *A Short History of World War I* (9–12). 1981, Morrow paper $9.95 (0-688-00129-7). A brief but penetrating history of World War I that gives both political and military perspectives. [940.3]

7163 Toland, John. *No Man's Land* (10–12). 1985, Ballantine paper $5.95 (0-345-33577-5). This is a graphic account of the events of 1918, the last year of World War I. [940.3]

7164 Tuchman, Barbara W. *The Guns of August* (10–12). Illus. 1962, Macmillan $19.95 (0-02-620311-1); Bantam paper $6.95 (0-553-25401-4). A critical history of the events leading up to World War I and of the events of the first month of the war. [940.3]

7165 Tuchman, Barbara W. *The Zimmerman Telegram* (10–12). Illus. 1966, Macmillan $14.95 (0-02-620320-0); Ballantine paper $8.95 (0-345-32425-0). The story of the German plan to bribe Mexico to attack the United States during World War I and its results. [940.3]

7166 Winter, J. M. *The Experience of World War I* (10–12). Illus. 1989, Oxford Univ. Pr. $29.95 (0-19-520776-9). A lavishly illustrated account on various aspects—military, social, economic—of World War I and its eventual effects. (Rev: BL 5/1/89) [940.3]

Between the Wars (1918–1939)

7167 Elson, Robert T. *Prelude to War* (7–12). Illus. 1977, Silver Burdett LB $25.93 (0-8094-2451-7). An account with many illustrations of the period between the two world wars. [940.53]

World War II and the Holocaust

7168 Adelson, Alan, and Robert Lapides, eds. *Lodz Ghetto: Inside a Community under Siege* (10–12). Illus. 1989, Viking $29.95 (0-670-82983-8). A history of the Lodz ghetto and the systematic extermination of its 200,000 inhabitants from 1939 to 1944. (Rev: BL 11/1/89) [305.8]

7169 Amothy, Christine. *I Am Fifteen—And I Don't Want to Die* (9–12). 1986, Scholastic paper $2.50 (0-590-40322-2). The true story of a girl during World War II and her escape first from the Nazis and then from the Russians. [940.53]

7170 Appelfeld, Aharon. *Age of Wonders* (10–12). 1989, Godine paper $11.95 (0-87923-798-8). The story of anti-Semitism in Austria immediately before World War II as experienced by an adolescent. [940.53]

7171 Appelfeld, Aharon. *For Every Sin* (10–12). Trans. by Jeffrey M. Green. 1989, Weidenfeld & Nicolson $15.95 (1-55584-318-2). The moving story of a young Jewish survivor of a Nazi death

camp and his determination to work across Europe back to his home after liberation. (Rev: BL 5/1/89)

7172 Archer, Jules. *Jungle Fighters* (8–12). Illus. 1985, Messner $9.29 (0-671-46058-7). An autobiographical account of this American's experiences during World War II and his tour of duty in the Pacific. (Rev: BL 2/1/85; BR 5–6/86; SLJ 8/85) [940.53]

7173 Arnold-Foster, Mark. *The World at War* (9–12). 1986, Scarborough $9.95 (0-8218-6202-3); paper $3.95 (0-8128-8057-9). This is a concise retelling of the major events of World War II. [940.53]

7174 Associated Press, eds. *World War II: A 50th Anniversary History* (9–12). Illus. 1989, Henry Holt $19.95 (0-8050-1095-5). Using photos from AP archives, the 5 authors have produced a readable, browsable history of the war. (Rev: BL 1/15/90; BR 5–6/90; SLJ 3/90; VOYA 6/90) [940.53]

7175 Bachrach, Deborah. *Pearl Harbor: Opposing Viewpoints* (9–12). Illus. 1989, Greenhaven $12.95 (0-89908-059-6). The events leading up to Pearl Harbor are detailed and the idea that perhaps this attack could have been prevented. (Rev: BL 4/1/89; SLJ 6/89) [940.54]

7176 Bailey, Ronald H. *The Air War in Europe* (7–12). Illus. 1979, Silver Burdett LB $25.93 (0-8094-2495-9). This account deals primarily in words and pictures with the RAF and the U.S. Air Force bombing raids and retaliation by the Luftwaffe. Part of Time-Life Books series on World War II. [940.54]

7177 Bailey, Ronald H. *Prisoners of War* (7–12). Illus. 1981, Silver Burdett LB $25.93 (0-8094-3392-3). The treatment of prisoners of war during World War II around the world is the subject of this volume from Time-Life Books. [940.54]

7178 Bar-on, Dan. *Legacy of Silence: Encounters with Children of the Third Reich* (9–12). 1989, Harvard Univ. Pr. $25.00 (0-674-52185-4). Interviews with 13 German men and women who were children during World War II telling of the roles their parents played in the Holocaust. (Rev: BL 9/15/89) [940.531]

7179 Barker, Ralph. *The RAF at War* (7–12). Illus. 1981, Silver Burdett LB $24.60 (0-8094-3292-7). The saga of the gallant airmen who held off Hitler's superior forces during the early days of World War II. From Time-Life Books Epic of Flight series. [940.54]

7180 Baudot, Marcel, et al., eds. *The Historical Encyclopedia of World War II* (10–12). 1980, Facts on File $29.95 (0-87196-401-5). In a dictionary format, the principle events, people, and places of World War II are covered, with separate chapters on the causes and consequences of the war. [940.5303]

7181 Bethell, Nicholas. *Russia Besieged* (7–12). Illus. 1977, Silver Burdett LB $25.93 (0-8094-2471-1). This volume concentrates on a history of activities of the Eastern front during the years 1941–1942. [940.54]

7182 Bickers, Richard Townshend. *The Battle of Britain* (9–12). Illus. 1990, Prentice $29.95 (0-13-083809-8). An oversized, heavily illustrated book that includes recollections from eyewitnesses. (Rev: BL 7/90) [940.54]

7183 Blumenson, Martin. *Kasserine Pass* (9–12). 1989, Jove paper $3.95 (0-515-07618-X). The story of the 1943 battle in Tunisia in which Rommel defeated the Allies. [940.53]

7184 Blumenson, Martin. *Liberation* (7–12). Illus. 1978, Silver Burdett LB $25.93 (0-8094-2511-4). The story of the freeing of Europe from German occupation during World War II. [940.54]

7185 Bosworth, Allan R. *America's Concentration Camps* (10–12). Illus. 1967, Norton $15.95 (0-393-05338-5). An account of how the Japanese American population was interned during World War II. [940.54]

7186 Botting, Douglas. *The Second Front* (7–12). Illus. 1978, Silver Burdett LB $25.93 (0-8094-2499-1). From Dieppe to D-Day in text and pictures. [940.54]

7187 Boyington, Gregory. *Baa Baa Black Sheep* (10–12). 1989, TAB $22.95 (0-8306-4008-8). This book deals with the men and exploits of the daring Flying Tigers during World War II. [940.54]

7188 Brackman, Arnold C. *The Other Nuremberg: The Untold Story of the Tokyo War Crimes Trials* (10–12). Illus. 1987, Morrow $19.95 (0-688-04783-1). The story of the trial of 28 Japanese leaders at the end of World War II. (Rev: BL 2/15/87) [341.9]

7189 Breuer, William B. *Retaking the Philippines: America's Return to Corregidor and Bataan, July 1944–March 1945* (10–12). Illus. 1987, St. Martin's paper $3.95 (0-312-90788-5). A volume on the liberation of the Philippines that concentrates on events from July 1944 through March 1945. (Rev: BL 11/15/86) [940.54]

7190 Brickhill, Paul. *The Great Escape* (9–12). Illus. 1986, Fawcett paper $3.50 (0-449-21068-5). The exciting story of the digging of 3 tunnels in a

German prisoner-of-war camp during World War II that were used to help 100 men escape. [940.54]

7191 Burgess, Alan. *The Longest Tunnel: The True Story of World War II's Great Escape* (9–12). Illus. 1990, Weidenfeld $19.95 (1-55584-033-7). The true story of the daring prisoner-of-war escape plan from a German prison camp in Poland during World War II. (Rev: BL 1/15/90) [940.54]

7192 Butterworth, Emma Macelik. *As the Waltz Was Ending* (9–12). 1985, Scholastic paper $2.50 (0-590-33210-4). An unusual perspective on World War II as it affected a student at the Vienna State Opera Ballet. [940.53]

7193 Churchill, Winston. *The Gathering Storm* (10–12). 1948, Houghton $22.95 (0-395-07537-8); paper $9.95 (0-395-41055-X). This is the first volume in Churchill's mammoth history of World War II. In chronological order the other volumes are: *Their Finest Hour* (1949), *The Grand Alliance, The Hinge of Fate* (both 1950), *Closing the Ring* (1951), and *Triumph and Tragedy* (1953). [940.53]

7194 Clayton, James D., and Anne Sharp Wells. *A Time for Giants: The Politics of the American High Command in World War II* (10–12). 1987, Watts $19.95 (0-531-15046-1). An examination of the military leaders of the United States during World War II and the roles that each played in making and carrying out decisions. (Rev: BR 5–6/88; SLJ 6–7/88) [940.53]

7195 Collier, Richard. *Fighting Words: The War Correspondents of World War Two* (10–12). Illus. 1990, St. Martin's $17.95 (0-312-03828-3). A collection of news stories written by World War II correspondents. (Rev: BL 3/15/90) [940.54]

7196 Collier, Richard. *War in the Desert* (7–12). Illus. 1977, Silver Burdett $25.95 (0-8094-2475-4). In clear prose and excellent illustrations, this is an account of the war in North Africa. [940.54]

7197 Craig, William. *Enemy at the Gates* (10–12). 1989, Bantam paper $3.95 (0-553-28267-0). This is a detailed account of the incredible 5-month siege of Leningrad. [940.53]

7198 David, Kati. *A Child's War: Fifteen Children Tell Their Story* (10–12). 1989, Four Walls Eight Windows $17.95 (0-941423-24-7). Fifteen people representing a wide range of perspectives tell of their childhoods when they were between the ages of 5 and 10 during World War II. (Rev: BL 5/1/89) [940.53]

7199 Davis, Daniel. *Behind Barbed Wire: The Imprisonment of Japanese Americans during World War II* (10–12). Illus. 1982, Dutton $12.95

(0-525-26320-9). A clear, fair account of the relocation of thousands of Japanese Americans during World War II. [940.54]

7200 Dawidowicz, Lucy S. *The War Against the Jews, 1933–1945* (10–12). 1975, Free Pr. $22.95 (0-02-908030-4); Bantam paper $10.95 (0-553-34302-5). From the roots of anti-Semitism to a country-by-country history of the fate of the Jews, this is a stirring and shocking history of the Holocaust. [940.54]

7201 Deighton, Len. *Blitzkrieg* (10–12). Illus. 1982, Ballantine paper $12.95 (0-345-29426-2). A history of the first months of World War II that ends with the fall of France and the evacuation at Dunkirk. [940.54]

7202 Dobroszycki, Lucjan, ed. *The Chronicle of the Lodz Ghetto, 1941–1944* (10–12). Illus. 1984, Yale Univ. Pr. $50.00 (0-300-03208-0). Day-by-day entries record the story of life in this Polish ghetto from January 1941 to its destruction in 1944. [943.8]

7203 Elting, John R. *Battles for Scandinavia* (7–12). Illus. 1981, Silver Burdett $25.95 (0-8094-3396-6). The story of the Russo-Finnish War and the German takeover of Scandinavia are told in this volume. [940.54]

7204 Epstein, Helen. *Children of the Holocaust: Conversations with Sons and Daughters of Survivors* (10–12). 1988, Penguin paper $7.95 (0-14-011284-7). Through a series of interviews with children of Holocaust survivors, their thoughts and scars are revealed. [940.54]

7205 Feis, Herbert. *The Road to Pearl Harbor* (10–12). 1950, Princeton Univ. Pr. paper $14.95 (0-691-01061-7). The story of the causes of the war between Japan and the United States. [940.53]

7206 Fleming, Gerald. *Hitler and the Final Solution* (10–12). Illus. 1984, Univ. of California Pr. paper $9.95 (0-520-06022-9). This account traces the blame for the decision to exterminate the Jews directly to Hitler. [943.086]

7207 Friedlander, Saul. *When Memory Comes* (10–12). Trans. by Helen R. Lane. 1980, Avon paper $3.50 (0-380-50807-9). The story of how a Jewish boy spent the war in a convent in France and of his final departure to Israel. [940.54]

7208 Garfield, Brian. *The Thousand-Mile War* (10–12). 1983, Ballantine paper $3.95 (0-345-31412-3). An account of the only military activity in North America during World War II. [940.53]

7209 Gies, Miep, and Alison Leslie Gold. *Anne Frank Remembered: The Story of Miep Gies, Who Helped to Hide the Frank Family* (8–12).

Illus. 1987, Simon & Schuster paper $7.95 (0-671-66234-1). The story of the woman who helped the Frank family during World War II and of the Resistance movement in the Netherlands. (Rev: BL 4/1/87; SLJ 11/87; VOYA 12/87) [940.53]

7210 Gilbert, Martin. *The Holocaust: A History of the Jews of Europe during the Second World War* (10–12). Illus. 1986, Henry Holt $24.45 (0-03-062416-9); paper $14.95 (0-8050-0348-7). A well-researched adult account of the plight of the Jews under the Nazis from 1933 to 1945. (Rev: SLJ 8/86) [940.53]

7211 Gilbert, Martin. *The Macmillan Atlas of the Holocaust* (10–12). Illus. 1982, Macmillan $18.99 (0-02-543380-6); Da Capo paper $13.95 (0-306-80218-X). More than 300 maps plus graphic text chronicle Hitler's war against the Jews. [940.54]

7212 Goldman, Peter, et al. *The End of the World That Was: Six Lives in the Atomic Age* (10–12). 1986, Dutton $16.95 (0-525-24428-X). An account of the lives of 6 people involved in and affected by the dropping of the atomic bomb on Hiroshima. (Rev: BL 4/15/86) [940.54]

7213 Hargrove, Hondon. *Buffalo Soldiers in Italy: Black Americans in World War II* (8–12). 1985, McFarland $22.95 (0-89950-116-8). A history of the last all-black U.S. army division and its record during World War II. (Rev: BR 9–10/85) [940.53]

7214 Hastings, Max. *Overlord: D-Day and the Battle for Normandy* (10–12). 1985, Simon & Schuster paper $8.95 (0-317-31520-X). A history of the events surrounding the Allied landings in Normandy during World War II. [940.53]

7215 Hastings, Max. *Victory in Europe: D-Day to V-E Day* (9–12). Illus. 1985, Little $25.00 (0-316-81334-6). Stills from a film by George Stevens are used to illustrate this account of the war in Europe after the Normandy invasions. (Rev: BL 6/15/85) [940.542]

7216 Hautzig, Ester. *The Endless Steppe* (10–12). 1968, Harper $13.95 (0-690-26371-6). The true story of the harrowing experiences of a family exiled to Siberia. [940.53]

7217 Hersey, John. *Hiroshima* (9–12). Illus. 1985, Knopf $13.95 (0-394-54844-2). By focusing on 6 individuals who survived, the dropping of the atomic bomb on Hiroshima is re-created. [940.54]

7218 Hersey, John. *Into the Valley: A Skirmish of the Marines* (9–12). 1989, Random $15.95 (0-8052-4078-0). A reissue of the classic account of a skirmish involving some U.S. Marines in the

Pacific during World War II. (Rev: BR 1–2/90) [940.53]

7219 Homewood, Harry. *Final Harbor* (10–12). 1984, Bantam paper $4.50 (0-553-23823-X). Life aboard a navy submarine on fleet duty during World War II. [940.53]

7220 Houston, Jeanne W., and James D. Houston. *Farewell to Manzanar* (9–12). 1983, Bantam paper $2.95 (0-553-26258-6). The story of the 3 years during World War II that Jeanne Houston, a Japanese American, and her family spent at Manzanar, an internment camp. [940.54]

7221 Howarth, Stephen. *August '39: The Last Four Weeks of Peace* (10–12). Illus. 1989, Mercury House $18.95 (0-916515-67-2). A look at the world during the fateful month preceding World War II. (Rev: BL 9/1/89) [940.53]

7222 Hoyt, Edwin P. *The GI's War: The Story of the American Soldiers in Europe in World War II* (10–12). Illus. 1988, McGraw $24.95 (0-07-030627-3). An account of the ordinary G.I. in World War II Europe. (Rev: BL 5/15/88) [940.54]

7223 Hoyt, Edwin P. *McCampbell's Heroes* (9–12). 1984, Avon paper $3.95 (0-380-68841-7). The story of the U.S. Navy's carrier fighters and their role in the Pacific area during World War II. Also use *Blue Skies and Blood: The Battle of the Coral Sea* (1989). [940.53]

7224 Hoyt, Edwin P. *The Marine Raiders* (10–12). 1989, Pocket paper $3.95 (0-671-66615-0). An inspiring account of this special unit, the role they played in the Pacific war and why they were disbanded. (Rev: BL 3/15/89) [359.96]

7225 Hoyt, Edwin P. *Men of the Gambler Bay* (10–12). 1984, Avon paper $3.50 (0-380-55806-8). This is the story of a ship and the men aboard her during World War II. Also use *Closing the Circle in the Pacific* (1984). [940.53]

7226 Hoyt, Edwin P. *U-Boats Offshore* (10–12). 1985, Jove paper $3.95 (0-515-07427-6). This writer of many books about World War II tells the story of the U-Boat and its part in the war. [940.53]

7227 Isaacson, Judith Magyar. *Seed of Sarah: Memoirs of a Girlhood* (10–12). 1990, Univ. of Illinois Pr. $18.95 (0-252-01651-3). The memoirs of a survivor of the Holocaust who was seized by the Nazis when she was 19 years old in 1944. For mature readers. (Rev: BL 11/1/89) [940.54]

7228 Jablonski, Edward. *A Pictorial History of the World War II Years* (7–12). Illus. 1977, Doubleday paper $14.95 (0-385-18553-7). In a chronological arrangement the events of the war are

retold in brief essays and many photographs. [940.53]

7229 Jungk, Robert. *Brighter Than a Thousand Suns: A Personal History of the Atomic Scientists* (10–12). 1970, Harcourt paper $5.95 (0-15-614150-7). This account of the development of the atomic bomb focuses on moral and psychological problems. [623.4]

7230 Kennett, Lee. *G.I.: The American Soldier in World War II* (10–12). Illus. 1989, Warner paper $4.50 (0-446-34895-3). A history of the enlisted man in the U.S. Army during World War II from enlistment through combat to discharge. (Rev: BL 3/15/87) [940.53]

7231 Klingaman, William K. *1941: Our Lives in a World on the Edge* (10–12). Illus. 1988, Harper $22.95 (0-06-015948-0). A world history view of the year that determined the outcome of World War II and also the history of western civilization. (Rev: BL 9/1/88) [940.53]

7232 Kurzman, Dan. *Day of the Bomb: Countdown to Hiroshima* (10–12). Illus. 1987, McGraw paper $5.95 (0-07-035688-2). The author introduces the people involved and retells the events leading up to the dropping of the first atomic bomb on Japan. (Rev: BL 10/1/85) [940.54]

7233 Lanzman, Claude. *Shoah* (10–12). 1985, Pantheon $11.95 (0-394-55142-7). This is the script of a film in which there are a series of interviews with people affected by the Holocaust, including some survivors. (Rev: VOYA 4/86) [940.53]

7234 Laska, Vera, ed. *Women in the Resistance and in the Holocaust: The Voices of Eyewitnesses* (10–12). Illus. 1983, Greenwood LB $39.95 (0-313-23457-4). This account highlights the work of the author and other women freedom fighters during World War II. [940.53]

7235 Leckie, Robert. *Helmet for My Pillow* (10–12). 1989, Bantam paper $3.95 (0-553-28265-4). A marine in World War II tells of his experiences in the Pacific. [940.54]

7236 Leitner, Isabella. *Fragments of Isabella* (10–12). 1983, Dell paper $3.95 (0-440-32453-X). A survivor of Auschwitz tells her story. Also use the continuation *Saving the Fragments* (1986). [940.53]

7237 Leonard, Thomas M. *Day by Day: The Forties* (9–12). Illus. 1977, Facts on File LB $125.00 (0-87196-375-2). Using chronological charts, the events of the 1940s are chronicled. [909.82]

7238 Lewin, Abraham. *A Cup of Tears: A Diary of the Warsaw Ghetto* (10–12). Trans. by Christopher Hutton. Illus. 1989, Basil Blackwell $19.95 (0-631-16215-1). The diary of a Jewish teacher who died with his teenage daughter in the Warsaw ghetto. (Rev: BL 2/1/89) [940.53]

7239 Lewin, Rhoda G., ed. *Witness to the Holocaust: An Oral History* (9–12). 1990, Twayne $19.95 (0-8057-9100-0). In over 50 interviews, the stories of survivors of death camps, survivors who did not go to death camps, and American liberators are told. (Rev: BR 5-6/90; VOYA 6/90) [940.53]

7240 Lewis, Nigel. *Exercise Tiger: The Dramatic True Story of a Hidden Tragedy of World War II* (9–12). Illus. 1990, Prentice $18.95 (0-13-127796-0). The story of the disastrous trial invasion of Europe and of the many casualties suffered by the Allies. (Rev: BL 7/90) [940.545]

7241 Lichter, Uri. *In the Eye of the Storm: A Memoir of Survival through the Holocaust* (9–12). Illus. 1987, Holocaust $18.95 (0-89604-088-7). The exciting story of the survival of the Lichter family, who managed to escape extermination during World War II. (Rev: SLJ 11/87) [940.53]

7242 *Life Goes to War: A Picture History of World War II* (7–12). Illus. 1981, Pocket paper $14.95 (0-671-79077-3). Sparse text but many pictures bring the war graphically to life. [940.53]

7243 Lifton, Betty Jean. *A Place Called Hiroshima* (9–12). Illus. 1985, Kodansha $24.95 (0-87011-649-5). In this album of text and photos, the author tells what has happened to Hiroshima and the survivors of the atomic attack 40 years after. (Rev: BL 10/1/85; SLJ 11/85) [940.54]

7244 Lord, Walter. *Day of Infamy* (8–12). Illus. 1987, Bantam paper $3.95 (0-553-24086-2). An hour-by-hour re-creation of the attack on Pearl Harbor with extensive background information. [940.54]

7245 Lord, Walter. *The Miracle of Dunkirk* (10–12). Illus. 1982, Viking $17.95 (0-670-28630-3); Penguin paper $7.95 (0-14-005085-X). The story of how almost 350,000 Allied troops escaped from the Germans during the evacuation of Dunkirk in 1940. [940.54]

7246 Lucas, James. *Kommando: German Special Forces of World War II* (9–12). Illus. 1987, St. Martin's paper $4.95 (0-312-90497-5). A history of the German special forces and their exploits during World War II. (Rev: SLJ 10/86) [940.53]

7247 McCombs, Don, and Fred L. Worth. *World War II Super Facts* (9–12). 1983, Warner paper $4.95 (0-446-32238-5). A collection of unusual facts about World War II usually forgotten in history books. [940.54]

7248 MacDonald, John. *Great Battles of World War II* (9–12). Illus. 1988, Macmillan paper $19.95 (0-02-044463-X). With clear illustrations and narrative, this is a chronologically arranged account of the 30 most important battles of World War II. (Rev: BL 11/15/86) [940.54]

7249 Malkin, Peter Z., and Harry Stein. *Eichmann in My Hands* (10–12). 1990, Warner $22.95 (0-446-51418-7). The story of the 12-year search for Adolf Eichmann that ended with his capture in 1960. (Rev: BL 3/15/90) [364.1]

7250 Manchester, William. *Goodbye, Darkness* (10–12). 1987, Dell paper $5.95 (0-440-32907-8). This respected author has written a personal memoir of his experiences in the Pacific during World War II. [940.53]

7251 Marrin, Albert. *Victory in the Pacific* (9–12). Illus. 1983, Macmillan $13.95 (0-689-30948-1). This account begins with the devastation of Pearl Harbor and ends with the victory over Japan in 1945. [940.54]

7252 Mee, Charles L., Jr. *Meeting at Potsdam* (10–12). Illus. 1974, Evans $10.95 (0-87131-167-4). The historic meeting of Stalin, Churchill, and Truman at Potsdam to plan post-World War II strategies is well re-created. [940.53]

7253 Meltzer, Milton. *Never to Forget: The Jews of the Holocaust* (8–12). 1976, Harper LB $14.89 (0-06-024175-6); Dell paper $3.25 (0-440-96070-3). A history of the murder of 6 million Jews and of anti-Semitism. [940.54]

7254 Messenger, Charles. *The Chronological Atlas of World War Two* (9–12). Illus. 1989, Macmillan $32.50 (0-02-584391-5). Through text and over 200 maps, the course of World War II is traced. (Rev: BL 11/1/89) [940.53]

7255 Miller, Judith. *One, by One, by One: Facing the Holocaust* (10–12). 1990, Simon & Schuster $22.95 (0-671-64472-6). An account of how the Holocaust is remembered in 6 of the countries most affected. (Rev: BL 4/1/90) [940.53]

7256 Miller, Russell. *The Commandos* (7–12). Illus. 1981, Silver Burdett LB $25.93 (0-8094-3400-8). The daring exploits of the Commandos and their many raids are chronicled in this heavily illustrated book. [940.54]

7257 Mitcham, Samuel W. *Triumphant Fox: Erwin Rommel and the Rise of the Afrika Korps* (10–12). Illus. 1984, Scarborough $18.95 (0-8128-2929-8); Jove paper $4.50 (0-505-10290-3). The story of the German World War II general with concentration on the war in North Africa. [940.54]

7258 Montagu, Ashley. *The Man Who Never Was* (10–12). 1954, Time-Life Bks. $25.00 (0-8094-8563-X). An exciting, true World War II adventure that begins with the planting of a corpse to mislead German intelligence. [940.53]

7259 Moskin, Marietta D. *I Am Rosemarie* (9–12). 1987, Scholastic paper $2.95 (0-440-94066-4). The true story of a young girl who spent 4 years in a German concentration camp. [940.53]

7260 Mosley, Leonard. *Battle of Britain* (7–12). Illus. 1977, Silver Burdett LB $25.93 (0-8094-2459-2). The story of the air war over Britain and of the civilian life during it. [940.54]

7261 Mowat, Farley. *And No Birds Sang* (10–12). 1980, Little $14.95 (0-316-58695-1); Bantam paper $3.95 (0-7704-2237-3). In this first-person narrative, the author retells his combat experiences in Italy during World War II. [940.54]

7262 Muirhead, John. *Those Who Fall* (10–12). Illus. 1987, Random $18.95 (0-394-54983-X). A moving reminiscence of a bomber pilot during World War II. (Rev: BL 1/1/87) [940.54]

7263 Müller, Filip. *Eyewitness Auschwitz: Three Years in the Gas Chambers* (10–12). Illus. 1981, Scarborough paper $7.95 (0-8128-6084-5). A history of 2 Nazi death camps written by a man who worked in the gas chambers and crematoria. [940.54]

7264 Nichols, David, ed. *Ernie's War: The Best of Ernie Pyle's World War II Dispatches* (10–12). Illus. 1986, Random $19.95 (0-394-54923-6); Simon & Schuster paper $9.95 (0-671-64452-1). A collection of war dispatches from Ernie Pyle, one of the great World War II reporters. (Rev: BR 3–4/86; SLJ 12/86) [940.53]

7265 Nir, Yehuda. *The Lost Childhood* (9–12). 1989, Harcourt $19.95 (0-15-158862-7). How 3 Polish Jews—a mother and 2 children—managed by their wits to elude their Nazi pursuers. (Rev: BL 9/1/89) [940.53]

7266 Ogburn, Charlton. *The Marauders* (10–12). 1982, Morrow paper $6.25 (0-688-01625-1). A reissue of an exciting account of exploits during World War II. [940.53]

7267 Osada, Arata, ed. *Children of Hiroshima* (10–12). 1981, Taylor & Francis $33.00 (0-85066-228-1); paper $16.00 (0-85066-216-8). This account re-creates the horrors of the Hiroshima bombing as lived by the children who survived. [940.53]

7268 Pape, Richard. *Boldness Be My Friend* (9–12). 1985, St. Martin's paper $4.50 (0-312-90515-

7). The true story of the author's exploits in Eastern Europe during World War II. (Rev: SLJ 12/85) [940.53]

7269 Parker, R. A. C. *Struggle for Survival: A History of the Second World War* (10–12). Illus. 1990, Oxford Univ. Pr. $22.50 (0-19-219126-8). A fine one-volume history that concentrates on the most significant aspects of the conflict. (Rev: BL 1/15/90) [940.53]

7270 Plant, Richard. *The Pink Triangle: The Nazi War against Homosexuals* (10–12). 1986, Henry Holt $19.95 (0-8050-0059-3); paper $9.95 (0-8050-0600-1). An account of the treatment of homosexuals in Nazi Germany and their systematic extermination in death camps. (Rev: BL 9/1/86) [306.7]

7271 Poltawska, Wanda. *And I Am Afraid of My Dreams* (10–12). Trans. by Mary Craig. Illus. 1989, Hippocrene $14.95 (0-340-40927-4). An account of a survivor of Nazi death camps who was used in experiments on humans. (Rev: SLJ 9/89) [940.53]

7272 Prager, Arthur, and Emily Prager. *World War II Resistance Stories* (7–12). 1980, Dell paper $2.25 (0-440-99800-X). Six dramatic true stories of men and women who fought behind the lines against the enemy during World War II. [940.53]

7273 Prange, Gordon W., et al. *December 7, 1941: The Day the Japanese Attacked Pearl Harbor* (9–12). 1987, McGraw $22.95 (0-07-050682-5); Warner paper $14.95 (0-446-38997-8). A re-creation of the attack on Pearl Harbor with much material from eyewitness sources. (Rev: BL 10/15/87) [940.54]

7274 Prange, Gordon W., et al. *Miracle at Midway* (10–12). 1983, Penguin paper $11.95 (0-14-006814-7). A graphic account of the battle in the Pacific that was a turning point in that theater of the war. [940.53]

7275 Rabinsky, Leatrice, and Gertrude Mann. *Journey of Conscience: Young People Respond to the Holocaust* (9–12). 1979, Anti-Defamation League of B'nai B'rith paper $1.50 (0-686-95073-9). Two teachers and 16 high school students from the United States travel to Europe to visit the site of the Holocaust. [940.54]

7276 Rashke, Richard. *Escape from Sobibor* (10–12). 1987, Avon paper $3.95 (0-380-75394-4). A re-creation of the amazing escape of prisoners from the Nazi death camp in Poland during World War II. [940.53]

7277 Read, Anthony, and David Fisher. *Kristallnacht: The Tragedy of the Nazi Night of Terror* (10–12). Illus. 1990, Times Books $19.95

(0-8129-1723-5). A chilling re-creation of the "night of broken glass" in 1938 when Nazi anti-Semitism erupted violently in Germany. (Rev: BL 11/1/89) [943.086]

7278 Reader's Digest, eds. *The World at Arms: The Reader's Digest Illustrated History of World War II* (9–12). Illus. 1989, Reader's Digest $29.95 (0-89577-333-3). An attractively organized and well-illustrated history of World War II. (Rev: BL 9/1/89; BR 1–2/90) [940.53]

7279 Reynolds, Clark G. *The Carrier War* (9–12). Illus. 1982, Silver Burdett LB $24.60 (0-8094-3305-2). This volume of the Time-Life series on World War II covers aerial warfare in the Pacific theater. Others in the series are: *The Secret War, War in the Outposts* (both 1980), and *Italy at War* (1982). [940.54]

7280 Rieul, Roland. *Escape into Espionage: The True Story of a French Patriot in World War Two* (9–12). Illus. 1987, Walker $15.95 (0-8027-0959-1); Avon paper $4.50 (0-380-70551-6). A multitime escapee from German prisoner of war camps describes World War II from his point of view. (Rev: BL 5/1/87) [940.548]

7281 Rose, Darlene Deibler. *Evidence Not Seen: A Woman's Miraculous Faith in a Japanese Prison Camp during WWII* (10–12). Illus. 1988, Harper $13.95 (0-06-067019-3). The hardships of life in a Japanese prison camp during World War II are vividly recalled by an interned missionary. (Rev: BL 9/15/88) [940.54]

7282 Ross, Bill D. *Iwo Jima: Legacy of Valor* (9–12). Illus. 1985, Random paper $9.95 (0-394-74288-5). A day-by-day account of the 1945 battle in the Pacific against the Japanese by the Marine Corps. [940.54]

7283 Rothchild, Sylvia. *Voices from the Holocaust* (10–12). 1982, NAL paper $10.95 (0-452-00860-3). This collection of memoirs of Holocaust survivors is divided into three parts—life before, during, and after World War II. [940.53]

7284 Ryan, Cornelius. *The Last Battle* (10–12). Illus. 1985, Pocket paper $5.95 (0-671-54116-1). This account re-creates the battle for Berlin during 3 fateful weeks in 1945. [940.54]

7285 Salisbury, Harrison E. *The 900 Days: The Siege of Leningrad* (10–12). Illus. 1985, Da Capo paper $15.95 (0-306-80253-8). This volume re-creates the horrifying and heroic story of the siege of Leningrad from 1941 to 1944. [940.54]

7286 Saywell, Shelley. *Women in War* (10–12). Illus. 1985, Viking $17.95 (0-670-80348-0). Stories involving women in various walks of life who contributed to the war effort during World War II are detailed. (Rev: BL 10/15/85) [940.53]

7287 Schaeffer, Susan Fromberg. *Anya* (10–12). 1976, Avon paper $4.95 (0-380-00573-5). The story of the experiences of a Russian-Jewish family in Poland during World War II. [940.53]

7288 Schultz, Duane. *The Doolittle Raid* (10–12). 1988, St. Martin's $18.95 (0-312-02195-X). The historic bombing of Tokyo in 1942 and its aftermath are vividly re-created. (Rev: BL 10/1/88) [940.54]

7289 Scott, Robert L. *God Is My Co-Pilot* (10–12). 1988, Buckeye Aviation $14.95 (0-942397-06-1); Ballantine paper $3.95 (0-345-35536-9). The inspiring story of a young pilot during World War II. [940.43]

7290 Sender, Ruth Minsky. *The Cage* (10–12). 1986, Macmillan $13.95 (0-02-781830-6). A horrifying account of a Jewish girl's experiences in Nazi death camps. (Rev: BL 9/15/86; BR 5–6/87; SLJ 11/86) [940.54]

7291 Settle, Mary Lee. *All the Brave Promises* (10–12). 1988, Macmillan paper $8.95 (0-684-18756-6). A young female American volunteer in the British Royal Air Force finds out early in World War II about the harsh realities of warfare. [940.54]

7292 Sichrovsky, Peter. *Born Guilty: Children of Nazi Families* (10–12). Trans. by Jean Steinberg. 1988, Basic Books $17.95 (0-465-00742-2). For mature readers, a series of contemporary interviews with the children and grandchildren of the Nazis responsible for the Holocaust. (Rev: BL 1/1/88) [943]

7293 Simons, Gerald. *Victory in Europe* (7–12). Illus. 1982, Silver Burdett $22.60 (0-8094-3404-0). An excellently illustrated account of the last days of the Nazi regime. Part of Time-Life Books' World War II series. [940.54]

7294 Smith, Gene. *The Dark Summer: An Intimate History of Events That Led to World War II* (10–12). 1987, Macmillan paper $9.95 (0-02-037390-2). An account that focuses on the month of 1939 preceding the declaration of war. (Rev: BL 11/1/87) [940.53]

7295 Spector, Ronald H. *Eagle against the Sun* (10–12). 1985, Random $12.95 (0-394-74101-3). This is a history of the American and Japanese conflict during World War II. [940.53]

7296 Steinberg, Rafael. *Island Fighting* (7–12). Illus. 1978, Silver Burdett $25.93 (0-8094-2487-8). The Guadalcanal campaign and the slow conquest of islands in the Pacific by U.S. forces during the last months of World War II. Part of the Time-Life series on World War II. [940.54]

7297 Steinberg, Rafael. *Return to the Philippines* (7–12). Illus. 1980, Silver Burdett $25.93 (0-8094-2515-7). A lavishly illustrated account of the liberation of the Philippines during World War II. Part of the Time-Life Books series. [940.54]

7298 Steiner, Jean Francois. *Treblinka* (10–12). 1968, NAL paper $4.50 (0-451-62566-8). The tragic and inspiring story of the death camp Treblinka and the revolt of a group of inmates. [940.54]

7299 Steinhoff, Johannes. *Voices from the Third Reich* (10–12). Illus. 1989, Regnery Gateway $24.95 (0-89526-766-7). Interviews with 150 Germans who either supported or opposed Hitler and his Third Reich. (Rev: SLJ 1/90) [940.53]

7300 Stevenson, William. *A Man Called Intrepid: The Secret War* (10–12). Illus. 1982, Ballantine paper $4.95 (0-345-31023-3). This is an amazing account of intelligence operations during World War II led by William Stevenson whose code-breaking work gained him the nickname "Intrepid." Followed by *Intrepid's Last Case* (1984). [940.54]

7301 Stiffel, Frank. *The Tale of the Ring: A Kaddish* (10–12). Illus. 1984, Pushcart $22.50 (0-916366-21-9); Bantam paper $9.95 (0-553-34214-2). The painful story of the Holocaust as seen through the eyes of a young medical student and poet who was also a Polish Jew during the time of Hitler. [940.53]

7302 Stokesbury, James L. *A Short History of World War II* (9–12). 1980, Morrow paper $9.95 (0-688-08587-3). A concise history of the war with coverage of its causes and immediate aftermath. [940.53]

7303 Sullivan, George. *Strange but True Stories of World War II* (7–12). Illus. 1983, Walker $10.95 (0-8027-6489-4). Eleven true stories of bizarre incidents during World War II. [940.53]

7304 Tapert, Annette, ed. *Lines of Battle* (10–12). Illus. 1987, Times Books $22.50 (0-8129-1316-7); Pocket paper $7.95 (0-671-66128-0). A collection of letters from American servicemen during World War II that reflect the human side of warfare. (Rev: BR 9–10/87; SLJ 10/87; VOYA 12/87) [940.53]

7305 Tateishi, John. *And Justice for All: An Oral History of the Japanese American Detention Camps* (10–12). 1984, Random $18.95 (0-394-52955-3). A few of the 115,000 Japanese Americans sent to detention camps during World War II tell their stories. [940.53]

7306 Taylor, A. J. P. *The Second World War: An Illustrated History* (10–12). Illus. 1979, Putnam paper $9.95 (0-399-50434-6). The great British historian gives a concise but penetrating history of World War II. [940.53]

7307 Ten Boom, Corrie, and John Sherrill. *The Hiding Place* (9–12). 1984, Bantam paper $3.95 (0-553-25669-6). The account of a Dutch girl growing up in Nazi-occupied Holland and her family who helped hide Jewish people. [940.54]

7308 Terkel, Studs. *"The Good War": An Oral History of World War Two* (10–12). 1984, Pantheon $19.95 (0-394-53103-5). Through a series of recorded interviews, the author traces how World War II changed the lives of a number of average Americans. [940.53]

7309 Thomas, Gordon, and Max Morgan. *Enola Gay* (10–12). 1977, Scarborough $35.00 (0-8128-2150-5). The dramatic account of the airplane and the flight to drop the atomic bomb on Hiroshima. [940.53]

7310 Time-Life Books, eds. *Across the Rhine* (9–12). Illus. 1980, Time-Life Bks. LB $25.93 (0-8094-2543-2). This part of the Time-Life series on World War II tells of the invasion of Germany and the opening of the concentration camps. Others in this series are: *The Battle of the Atlantic* (1977), *The Battle of the Bulge* (1979), *Home Front: Germany* (1982), and *The Italian Campaign* (1978). [940.54]

7311 Time-Life Books, eds. *Japan at War* (7–12). Illus. 1980, Silver Burdett LB $25.93 (0-8094-2527-0). The story of Japan's preparation for war and its role in World War II until its surrender. [940.53]

7312 Time-Life Books, eds. *WW II: Time-Life Books History of the Second World War* (8–12). Illus. 1989, Prentice $39.95 (0-13-922022-4). A lavishly illustrated account with excellent text and hundreds of maps, photographs, and diagrams. (Rev: BL 12/15/89) [940.53]

7313 Toland, John. *The Last 100 Days* (9–12). Illus. 1987, Bantam paper $10.95 (0-553-34208-8). Through interviews and use of other sources the author re-creates the last 100 days of Nazi Germany and Fascist Italy. [940.53]

7314 Vegh, Claudine. *I Didn't Say Goodbye: Interviews with Children of the Holocaust* (10–12). Trans. by Ros Schwartz. 1985, Dutton $14.95 (0-525-24308-9). A series of touching first-person accounts by survivors of the Holocaust who were only children during World War II. (Rev: SLJ 9/86) [940.53]

7315 *The Warsaw Ghetto* (10–12). Illus. 1990, Hippocrene $29.95 (0-87052-853-X). A stirring account of this ghetto and the uprising, accompanied by over 100 memorable photographs. (Rev: BL 4/1/90) [940.531]

7316 Weatherford, Doris. *American Women and World War II* (10–12). Illus. 1990, Facts on File $29.95 (0-8160-2038-8). A detailed social history of the contributions made by American women during World War II. (Rev: BL 9/1/90) [940.54]

7317 Weglyn, Michi. *Years of Infamy: The Untold Story of America's Concentration Camps* (10–12). Illus. 1978, Morrow paper $12.95 (0-688-07996-2). The injustice of the evacuation of Japanese Americans during World War II is related in this first-person account. [940.54]

7318 Wernick, Robert. *Blitzkrieg* (7–12). Illus. 1976, Silver Burdett LB $25.93 (0-8094-2455-X). The German offensive from the invasion of Poland to the evacuation at Dunkirk. From the Time-Life series on World War II. [940.54]

7319 Westall, Robert. *Children of the Blitz: Memories of a Wartime Childhood* (9–12). 1988, Penguin paper $8.95 (0-14-007404-X). A collection of anecdotes and reminiscences by people who were children during World War II in England. (Rev: BL 2/15/86) [941.084]

7320 Wheeler, Keith. *The Road to Tokyo* (9–12). Illus. 1980, Silver Burdett LB $25.93 (0-8094-2539-4). This account of the war in the Pacific includes material on the battles of Okinawa and Iwo Jima. This is part of the Time-Life series on World War II that also includes: *China-Burma-India* (1978), *War under the Pacific* (1980), *Bombers over Japan* (1982), *The Fall of Japan* (1983), and *The Aftermath: Asia* (1983). [940.54]

7321 Wheeler, Richard. *A Special Valor* (10–12). 1985, NAL paper $9.95 (0-452-00737-2). A history of the U.S. Marines during World War II in the Pacific. [940.53]

7322 Wicks, Ben. *No Time to Wave Goodbye* (10–12). Illus. 1989, St. Martin's $15.95 (0-312-03407-5). The story of the mass evacuations of children from London during World War II. (Rev: SLJ 5/90) [940.53]

7323 Wiesel, Elie. *Night* (10–12). 1982, Bantam paper $2.95 (0-553-20807-1). For mature readers, this is the story of the famous writer's experiences as a boy living through the horrors of Auschwitz and Buchenwald. [940.53]

7324 Winston, Keith. *V-Mail: Letters of a World War II Combat Medic* (9–12). Illus. 1985, Algonquin $14.95 (0-912697-28-8). A collection of letters written by a medic in Europe during World War II. (Rev: SLJ 4/86) [940.53]

7325 Winterbotham, E. W. *The Ultra Secret* (10–12). 1975, Dell paper $3.25 (0-440-19061-4). A true cloak-and-dagger story of how the British cracked the secret German radio code during World War II. [940.53]

7326 Wright, John W. *Captured on Corregidor* (9–12). 1988, McFarland LB $20.95 (0-89950-347-0). A personal reminiscence of a West Point graduate who was a prisoner of the Japanese during World War II for 3 and one-half years. (Rev: BR 1–2/89) [940.53]

7327 Wyden, Peter. *Day One: Before Hiroshima and After* (10–12). Illus. 1985, Warner paper $3.95 (0-446-84006-5). A history of the development of the first atomic bomb, the people behind it, and its use at Hiroshima. [940.54]

7328 Young, Peter, ed. *The World Almanac Book of World War II* (10–12). Illus. 1986, Pharos paper $14.95 (0-88687-275-8). This reference work includes a chronology of World War II events plus a biographical dictionary of 350 of the most important participants. [940.53]

7329 Zich, Arthur. *The Rising Sun* (7–12). Illus. 1977, Silver Burdett LB $25.93 (0-8094-2463-0). Japanese victories in World War II from Pearl Harbor to Japan's first major defeat in Midway are told in words and many illustrations. From Time-Life Books. [940.54]

7330 Ziemke, Earl F. *The Soviet Juggernaut* (9–12). Illus. 1981, Silver Burdett LB $25.93 (0-8094-3388-5). This well-illustrated account describes the war on the Russian front that culminated in the invasion of Germany. Part of the Time-Life series on World War II that also includes: *Red Army Resurgent, The Resistance* (both 1979), and *The Mediterranean* (1981). [940.54]

7331 Zyskind, Sara. *Stolen Years* (10–12). Trans. by Marganit Inbar. 1981, Lerner $11.95 (0-8225-0766-8); NAL paper $3.95 (0-451-14339-6). The story of a Holocaust survivor who was only 11 when war broke out in Europe. [940.53]

7332 Zyskind, Sara. *Struggle* (8–12). 1989, Lerner $14.95 (0-8225-0772-2). A memoir (written by his wife) of a Polish Jew and his family's story during the Holocaust, principally in Nazi death camps. (Rev: BL 7/89; SLJ 9/89) [940.53]

Modern World History (1945–)

7333 Fisher, Trevor. *The 1960s* (8–12). Illus. 1989, David & Charles $19.95 (0-7134-5603-5). Under a broad subject arrangement, the major news stories and trends of the 1960s are chronicled. (Rev: SLJ 5/89) [973.92]

7334 Hoepli, Nancy L., ed. *Aftermath of Colonialism* (10–12). 1973, H. W. Wilson paper $10.00 (0-8242-0470-0). This volume contains readings about the many world states that have gained independence since World War II. [327]

7335 Hough, Richard, and Denis Richards. *The Battle of Britain: The Greatest Air Battle of World War II* (10–12). 1989, Norton $29.95 (0-393-02766-X). A stirring account based on 300 testimonials about this great attempt to stem Hitler's invasion of Britain. (Rev: BL 11/1/89) [940.54]

7336 Merritt, Jeffrey D. *Day by Day: The Fifties* (9–12). Illus. 1979, Facts on File LB $125.00 (0-87196-383-3). This oversized volume uses charts and illustrations to trace events of the 1950s. [909.82]

7337 Mosse, George L. *Fallen Soldiers: Reshaping the Memory of the World Wars* (10–12). Illus. 1990, Oxford Univ. Pr. $19.95 (0-19-506247-7). The myths behind the glory of warfare are explored in this discussion that covers World War I through the Vietnam conflict. (Rev: BL 3/1/90) [303.6]

7338 Neuharth, Allen H. *World Power Up Close: Candid Conversations with 31 Key Leaders* (9–12). Illus. 1989, USA Today Books $12.95 (0-944347-19-3). Somewhat superficial interviews with such luminaries as Castro, Gorbachev, and Thatcher. (Rev: BL 12/1/89) [324.2]

7339 Parker, Thomas. *Day by Day: The Sixties* (9–12). Illus. 1983, Facts on File LB $125.00 (0-87196-648-4). Using a day-by-day chronology, this book, like others in the series, traces the events of a decade, in this case the 1960s. [909.82]

7340 Szulc, Tad. *Then and Now: How the World Has Changed since World War II* (10–12). 1990, Morrow $22.95 (0-688-07558-4). A decade-by-decade look at important world events and trends since 1945. (Rev: BL 5/15/90) [909.82]

7341 *The Third World* (9–12). 1989, Greenhaven LB $15.95 (0-89908-447-8); paper $7.95 (0-89908-422-2). International poverty and types of aid are discussed in this collection of pieces that represent various viewpoints. (Rev: SLJ 3/90) [796.4]

7342 Toffler, Alvin. *Powershift: Knowledge, Wealth, and Violence at the Edge of the 21st Century* (10–12). 1990, Bantam $22.95 (0-553-05776-6). A look at the world today and the methods of wielding and controlling power. (Rev: BL 9/15/90) [303.4]

7343 Vadney, T. E. *The World since 1945: A Complete History of Global Change from 1945 to the Present* (9–12). 1987, Facts on File $29.95 (0-8160-1815-4). An excellent overview of 40 years of world history that emphasizes the trouble spots and indicates trends that might influence the future. (Rev: BR 5–6/88) [909.82]

7344 Wren, Christopher S. *The End of the Line: The Failure of Communism in the Soviet Union and China* (10–12). 1990, Simon & Schuster $22.95 (0-671-63864-5). Recent changes in the Soviet Union and China are examined including Gorbachev's reforms and Tiananmen Square and their significance weighed. (Rev: BL 8/90) [335.43]

Geographical Regions

Africa

General and Miscellaneous

7345 Davidson, Basil. *Africa in History: Themes and Outlines* (10–12). 1974, Macmillan paper $10.95 (0-02-031260-1). A brief history of the entire African continent. Others in this series on African history are: *The African Genius: An Introduction to African Cultural and Social History, The African Slave Trade,* and *The Lost Cities of Africa* (all 1988). [960]

7346 Davidson, Basil. *The African Slave Trade* (10–12). Rev. ed. Illus. 1988, Little paper $10.95 (0-316-17438-6). This account gives details on the four centuries of the African slave trade, during which millions of people were cruelly forced to leave their homes. (Rev: BL 9/86) [967]

7347 Davidson, Basil. *The Lost Cities of Africa* (10–12). Rev. ed. Illus. 1988, Little paper $10.95 (0-316-17431-9). This volume attempts to reconstruct the history and culture of Africa below the Sahara before the arrival of Europeans. [960]

7348 Dostert, Pierre Etienne. *Africa* (9–12). Illus. 1988, Stryker-Post paper $6.50 (0-943448-39-5). This annual publication supplies background information on the history, economy, and culture of each of the countries in Africa. [960]

7349 Duncan, David Ewing. *From Cape to Cairo: One Man's Trek across Africa* (9–12). 1989, Weidenfeld & Nicolson $19.95 (1-55584-139-2). The land and people of central Africa as seen by a man who bicycled across the continent. (Rev: BL 8/89) [916]

7350 Harden, Blaine. *Africa: Dispatches from a Fragile Continent* (10–12). Illus. 1990, Norton $22.50 (0-393-02882-8). A collection of pieces that explore the political, social, and economic problems of Africa below the Sahara. (Rev: BL 10/1/90) [967.03]

7351 Maquet, Jacques. *Civilizations of Black Africa* (10–12). Trans. by Joan Rayfield. Illus. 1972, Oxford Univ. Pr. paper $12.95 (0-19-501464-2). This is a description of the cultures of such groups as the Bushmen, forest people, and savanna dwellers. [967]

7352 Mazrui, Ali A. *The Africans: A Triple Heritage* (10–12). Illus. 1986, Little paper $17.95 (0-316-55201-1). The history and culture of Africa is assessed in terms of 3 influences—the native civilization, Islamic, and Western. (Rev: BL 8/86) [960]

7353 Mochi, Ugo, and Dorcas MacClintock. *African Images* (8–12). Illus. 1984, Macmillan $14.95 (0-684-18089-8). An account of the many varied animals of Africa illustrated with black cutouts. (Rev: BL 1/15/85) [591.96]

7354 Moorehead, Alan. *The Blue Nile* (10–12). Rev. ed. Illus. 1983, Random paper $13.95 (0-394-71449-0). This fascinating history deals with the exploration of the Blue Nile from 1798 to 1869. [962]

7355 Murray, Jocelyn, ed. *Cultural Atlas of Africa* (9–12). Illus. 1981, Facts on File $40.00 (0-87196-558-5). With hundreds of maps and illustrations plus text, such topics as language, religion, culture, and education are covered for each country. [960]

7356 Oliver, Roland, and Michael Crowder, eds. *The Cambridge Encyclopedia of Africa* (10–12). Illus. 1981, Cambridge Univ. Pr. $49.50 (0-521-23096-9). In a series of articles, the general history and geography of Africa are covered along with profiles of each country. [960]

7357 Oliver, Roland, and J. D. Fage. *A Short History of Africa* (10–12). 1989, Facts on File $24.95 (0-8160-2089-2). A fascinating history that traces the rise and fall of African empires and of conditions today. (Rev: BR 11–12/89) [960]

7358 Rohr, Janelle, ed. *Problems of Africa: Opposing Viewpoints* (9–12). Illus. 1986, Greenhaven LB $15.95 (0-89908-390-0); paper $7.95 (0-89908-365-X). A collection of opinions from both the far left and far right on such African problems as famine and race relations. (Rev: BL 3/15/87; SLJ 2/87) [960]

7359 Rowell, Trevor. *The Scramble for Africa* (9–12). Illus. 1987, David & Charles $19.95 (0-7134-5200-5). The breakup of the continent of Africa by imperialists is documented by the key people involved. (Rev: SLJ 2/88) [960]

7360 Stevens, Stuart. *Malaria Dreams: An African Adventure* (9–12). 1989, Atlantic Monthly $18.95 (0-87113-278-8). The author and his girlfriend drive a Land Rover from central Africa to Algeria. (Rev: BL 8/89) [916.604]

7361 Ungar, Sanford J. *Africa: The People and Politics of an Emerging Continent* (10–12). 1989, Simon & Schuster paper $14.95 (0-671-67565-6). In this somewhat black narrative the author looks at Africa below the Sahara and concentrates on South Africa, Liberia, Nigeria, and Kenya. (Rev: BL 8/85) [960]

Central and Eastern Africa

7362 Dinesen, Isak. *Out of Africa and Shadows on the Grass* (10–12). 1989, Random paper $7.95 (0-679-72475-3). These 2 books re-create the author's experiences between the wars on a farm in Kenya. [967.6]

7363 Iwago, Mitsuaki. *Serengeti: Natural Order on the African Plain* (9–10). Illus. 1987, Chronicle $35.00 (0-87701-441-8); $19.95 (0-87701-432-9). Over 300 color photographs are the highlight of this sumptuous book on nature's wonders. (Rev: BL 10/1/87) [591]

7364 Smith, Anthony. *The Great Rift: Africa's Changing Valley* (9–12). Illus. 1989, Sterling $24.95 (0-8069-6907-5). A description in words and stunning photographs of the amazing section of eastern Africa that is noted for its unusual landscapes and animal life. (Rev: BL 3/1/89; BR 3–4/90) [916.76]

7365 Time-Life Books, eds. *East Africa* (9–12). Illus. 1987, Silver Burdett LB $19.45 (0-8094-5319-3). Kenya, Uganda, and Tanzania are covered in this handsome volume. (Rev: BR 3–4/88) [960]

7366 Watson, Lyall. *Lightning Bird* (10–12). 1983, Simon & Schuster paper $7.95 (0-671-47361-1). A boy's lonely journey into the African bush. [967]

North Africa

7367 Asher, Michael. *Two against the Sahara: On Camelback from Nouakchott to the Nile* (9–12). Illus. 1989, Morrow $19.95 (0-688-08926-7). The amazing story of the trip across the Sahara on camel by a man and his wife of only 5 days. (Rev: BL 12/1/89) [916.6]

7368 Hoagland, Edward. *African Calliope* (10–12). 1987, Penguin paper $7.95 (0-14-009543-8). The fascinating account of a journey through the Sudan. [962.4]

South Africa

7369 American Friends Service Committee. *South Africa: Challenge and Hope* (10–12). Rev. ed. 1987, Hill & Wang $15.95 (0-8090-8750-2); paper $7.95 (0-8090-1530-7). From an organization long against apartheid comes an account of life in a divided South Africa. (Rev: BL 2/15/87) [305.8]

7370 *Beyond the Barricades: Popular Resistance in South Africa* (10–12). Illus. 1989, Aperture paper $24.95 (0-89381-375-3). A photographic essay that reveals what words alone cannot about the anti-apartheid movement in South Africa. (Rev: SLJ 5/90) [968]

7371 Finnegan, William. *Crossing the Line: A Year in the Land of Apartheid* (10–12). 1986, Harper $22.95 (0-06-015570-1); paper $8.95 (0-06-091430-0). The moving account of an American schoolteacher in the segregated black schools of South Africa. (Rev: BL 9/1/86) [373.11]

7372 Frederikse, Julie. *South Africa: A Different Kind of War* (10–12). Illus. 1987, Beacon paper $12.95 (0-8070-0203-8). A collection of press releases, interviews, poetry, posters, and photographs from the years in South Africa when the author was a correspondent for National Public Radio. (Rev: SLJ 8/87) [968]

7373 Gordimer, Nadine, and David Goldblatt. *Lifetimes under Apartheid* (10–12). Illus. 1986, Knopf $30.00 (0-317-47546-0). Through excerpts from Gordimer's novels and 60 of Goldblatt's photographs, the agony of present-day South Africa is represented. (Rev: BL 2/1/87) [823]

7374 Holland, Heidi. *The Struggle: A History of the African National Congress* (10–12). Illus. 1990, Braziller $19.95 (0-8076-1238-3). A history of the largest anti-apartheid organization in South Africa. (Rev: BL 2/15/90) [322.4]

7375 Lapping, Brian. *Apartheid: A History* (10–12). Illus. 1987, Braziller $19.95 (0-8076-1177-8); paper $10.95 (0-8076-1232-4). A history of race relations in South Africa from the arrival of the Dutch in 1652 to the present. (Rev: BL 6/1/87) [305.8]

7376 Lauré, Jason. *South Africa: Coming of Age under Apartheid* (10–12). Illus. 1980, Farrar $15.95 (0-374-37146-6). This photojournalistic book focuses on 8 different young people growing up in South Africa. [968.06]

7377 Lelyveld, Joseph. *Move Your Shadow: South Africa, Black and White* (10–12). 1985, Times Books $18.95 (0-8129-1237-3); Penguin paper $8.95 (0-14-009326-5). Through his own experiences and those around him, the author reveals the horrors of apartheid. [968.06]

7378 Mermelstein, David, ed. *The Anti-Apartheid Reader: South Africa and the Struggle against White Racist Rule* (10–12). 1987, Grove $22.95 (0-394-55488-4); paper $12.95 (0-394-62223-5). From many sources such as speeches, articles, and interviews, this is a collection of writings about apartheid and the shameful conditions it has created. (Rev: BL 7/87) [305.8]

7379 North, James. *Freedom Rising* (10–12). Illus. 1985, NAL paper $8.95 (0-452-25805-7). The struggle for equality in South Africa through the mid-1980s. [968.06]

7380 Omer-Cooper, J. D. *History of Southern Africa* (10–12). Illus. 1987, Heinemann paper $20.00 (0-435-08010-5). Both white and black points of view are expressed in this nicely illustrated history. (Rev: BL 9/15/87) [968]

7381 Omond, Roger. *The Apartheid Handbook* (10–12). 1986, Penguin paper $6.95 (0-14-022749-0). In a question-and-answer format, details are given of life in South Africa. (Rev: BL 1/1/86) [320.56]

7382 Peace, Judy Boppell. *The Boy Child Is Dying: A South African Experience* (10–12). 1986, Harper $9.95 (0-06-066482-7). This book consists of a series of vignettes about the agony of living under apartheid. (Rev: BL 6/1/86) [320.56]

7383 Russell, Diana E. H. *Lives of Courage: Women for a New South Africa* (10–12). 1989, Basic Books $22.95 (0-465-04139-6). Interviews with 24 South African women who have actively resisted apartheid in their homeland. (Rev: BL 9/1/89) [305.4]

7384 Sparks, Allister. *The Mind of South Africa* (10–12). 1990, Knopf $24.95 (0-394-58108-3). For better readers, a history of politics in South Africa and the development of racism. (Rev: BL 2/1/90) [305.8]

7385 Tambo, Oliver. *Preparing for Power: Oliver Tambo Speaks* (10–12). Illus. 1988, Braziller $19.95 (0-8076-1194-8). The president of South Africa's African National Congress tells about apartheid and the history of the black struggles. (Rev: BL 2/15/88) [321.1]

7386 Tessendorf, K. C. *Along the Road to Soweto: A Racial History of South Africa* (9–12). Illus. 1989, Macmillan $14.95 (0-689-31401-9). An account that covers South African history from the tenth century on with emphasis on the racial problems. (Rev: BR 3–4/90; SLJ 1/90; VOYA 12/89) [320.5]

7387 Turnley, David. *Why Are They Weeping? South Africans under Apartheid* (10–12). Illus. 1988, Stewart, Tabori & Chang $35.00 (1-55670-044-X); paper $19.95 (1-55670-054-7). A pictorial work that brings to life the oppression of the blacks of South Africa. (Rev: BL 1/1/89) [968.06]

7388 Williams, Oliver F. *The Apartheid Crisis: How We Can Do Justice in a Land of Violence* (10–12). Illus. 1986, Harper paper $8.95 (0-06-250951-9). An explanation of the complex racial situation in South Africa and how it came to be. (Rev: SLJ 2/87) [968]

7389 Woods, Donald. *South African Dispatches: Letters to My Countrymen* (10–12). 1987, Henry Holt $16.95 (0-8050-0143-3). These articles were written between 1975 and 1977 just before Woods was expelled from his country for criticizing apartheid policies. (Rev: BR 5–6/87; SLJ 6–7/87; VOYA 2/87) [968]

West Africa

7390 Soyinka, Wole. *Ake: The Years of Childhood* (10–12). 1983, Random $14.95 (0-394-52807-7); paper $8.95 (0-394-72219-1). A book that tells of the author's experiences in Nigeria. [966.9]

Asia

General and Miscellaneous

7391 Durant, Will. *Our Oriental Heritage* (10–12). Illus. 1935, Simon & Schuster $29.95 (0-671-54800-X). This volume in the Durant series, The Story of Civilization, covers ancient Egypt and Mesopotamia plus the entire history of India, China, and Japan. [950]

7392 Hinton, Harold C. *East Asia and the Western Pacific* (9–12). Illus. 1988, Stryker-Post paper $6.50 (0-943448-41-7). From Australia in the south to China in the north, this annual volume gives profiles of each country in east Asia. [950]

7393 Lum, Peter. *Growth of Civilization in East Asia: China, Japan, and Korea before the 14th Century* (10–12). Illus. 1969, Phillips $25.95 (0-87599-144-0). A history of early Oriental civilizations from prehistoric times to the end of the Mongol Empire. [950]

7394 Time-Life Books, eds. *Southeast Asia* (9–12). Illus. 1987, Silver Burdett LB $19.45 (0-8094-5318-5). The countries covered in this attractive volume are Indonesia, Brunei, Singapore, Philippines, Thailand, and Malaysia. (Rev: BR 3-4/88) [954]

7395 Weiss, Julian. *The Asian Century* (10–12). 1989, Facts on File $22.95 (0-8160-1687-9). An examination of the current strengths and concerns of such countries as China, Japan, Korea, Taiwan, and Malaysia. (Rev: SLJ 6/90) [950.52]

7396 Williams, Lea E. *Southeast Asia: A History* (10–12). Illus. 1976, Oxford Univ. Pr. paper $13.95 (0-19-502000-6). A general history of Southeast Asia from prehistoric times to the 1970s. [959]

China

7397 Bloodworth, Dennis. *The Chinese Looking Glass* (10–12). Rev. ed. 1980, Farrar $15.00 (0-374-12241-5); paper $8.95 (0-374-51493-3). Over 3,000 years of Chinese history and culture are covered in this volume. [951]

7398 Bonavia, David. *The Chinese* (10–12). Illus. 1989, Penguin paper $7.95 (0-14-010479-8). An introduction to life in contemporary China. [951.05]

7399 Butterfield, Fox. *China: Alive in a Bitter Sea* (10–12). 1982, Bantam $24.95 (0-8129-0927-5); paper $12.95 (0-553-34219-3). A report on life in China at the beginning of the 1980s. [951]

7400 Chen, Yuan-trung. *The Dragon's Village* (10–12). 1981, Penguin paper $8.95 (0-14-005811-7). The Chinese Revolution as experienced by a girl in her teens. [951]

7401 Chesneaux, Jean. *China: The People's Republic, 1949–1976* (10–12). Trans. by Paul Auster and Lydia Davis. 1979, Pantheon paper $4.76 (0-394-73623-0). A history of the 27 formative years of the Communist regime in China. [951.05]

7402 Chesneaux, Jean, et al. *China from the 1911 Revolution to Liberation* (10–12). Trans. by Paul Auster and Lydia Davis. 1977, Pantheon paper $12.95 (0-394-73332-0). This is a history of China during the turbulent period 1911–1948. [951.04]

7403 Chesneaux, Jean, et al. *China from the Opium Wars to the 1911 Revolution* (10–12). Trans by Ann Destenay. 1976, Pantheon paper $11.95 (0-394-70934-9). This account of Chinese history covers the early opening up of China by the West. [951]

7404 Clayre, Alasdair. *The Heart of the Dragon* (9–12). 1986, Houghton paper $14.95 (0-395-41837-2). A well-illustrated overview of Chinese life, customs, and culture at the beginning of the 1980s. (Rev: BL 5/15/85; SLJ 10/85) [951.05]

7405 Clubb, O. Edmund. *20th Century China* (10–12). 3rd ed. Illus. 1978, Columbia Univ. Pr. paper $19.50 (0-231-04519-0). This account covers over 70 years of Chinese history from the collapse of the old order to the mid-1970s. [951]

7406 Cohen, Joan Lebold. *China Today and Her Ancient Treasures* (10–12). Illus. 1985, Abrams $49.50 (0-8109-0798-4). A lavishly illustrated history of the art of China from the Han dynasty to the twentieth century. [951]

7407 Dudley, William, and Karin Swisher, eds. *China: Opposing Viewpoints* (9–12). Illus. 1988, Greenhaven $14.95 (0-89908-439-7); paper $7.95 (0-89908-414-1). This volume, part of the Opposing Viewpoints series, presents many points of view on China's present situation including material on civil rights. (Rev: BL 2/1/89; SLJ 2/89) [951]

7408 Duke, Michael S. *The Iron House* (10–12). Illus. 1990, Gibbs Smith paper $7.95 (0-87905-225-4). An account of the events leading up to the massacre, in China at Tiananmen Square and of its aftermath. (Rev: BL 2/15/90) [951.05]

7409 Fairbank, John King. *The Great Chinese Revolution: 1800–1985* (10–12). 1986, Harper paper $7.50 (0-06-039076-X). This account covers 185 years of Chinese history from the late imperial period to the mid-1980s. [951]

7410 Hanbury-Tenison, Robin. *A Ride along the Great Wall* (10–12). 1988, Salem House $18.95 (0-88162-350-4). A true adventure of an Englishman who traveled by horseback for 3½ months following the Great Wall of China. (Rev: VOYA 8/88) [951]

7411 Hook, Brian, ed. *The Cambridge Encyclopedia of China* (10–12). Illus. 1982, Cambridge Univ. Pr. $54.50 (0-521-23099-3). Written by a number of specialists, this illustrated account describes all aspects of China and Chinese life past and present. [951]

7412 Hoyt, Edwin P. *The Rise of the Chinese Republic: From the Last Emperor to Deng Xiaoping* (10–12). Illus. 1988, McGraw $19.95 (0-07-030619-2). A complex but readable account of 80 years of Chinese history—from the Opium Wars to the mid-1980s. (Rev: BL 11/15/88) [951.04]

7413 Human Rights in China Staff. *Children of the Dragon: The Story of Tiananmen Square* (9–12). Illus. 1990, Macmillan paper $22.50 (0-02-033520-2). Eyewitness accounts, photographs, and background history produce a stirring account of the crackdown on democracy in China. (Rev: BL 6/1/90) [951]

7414 Jenkins, Peter. *Across China* (10–12). Illus. 1986, Morrow $18.95 (0-688-04223-6); Fawcett paper $4.95 (0-449-21456-7). A journey by foot across China from Tibet to Inner Mongolia. (Rev: BL 12/15/86) [915.1]

7415 Ji, Zhao, ed. *The Natural History of China* (10–12). Illus. 1990, McGraw $29.95 (0-07-010752-1). Through text, maps, and photographs, the geography, flora, and fauna of China are explored. (Rev: BL 6/1/90) [508.51]

7416 *Journey into China* (9–12). Illus. 1982, Natl. Geographic Soc. LB $23.95 (0-87044-461-1). A region-by-region description by several travelers of their journeys in China. [915.1]

7417 *June Four: A Chronicle of the Chinese Democratic Uprising* (9–12). Trans. by Zi Jin and Qin Zhou. Illus. 1989, Univ. of Arkansas Pr. paper $14.95 (1-55728-140-8). A large-format paperback with more than 230 photographs and text on the revolt in Tiananmen Square and its shocking aftermath. (Rev: BL 11/15/89) [951.05]

7418 Kaplan, Frederic M., and Julian M. Sobin, eds. *Encyclopedia of China Today* (10–12). 3rd ed. Illus. 1981, Harper $29.95 (0-06-014890-X). A fine overview of Chinese society with coverage that ends in 1979. [951.05]

7419 Kidd, David. *Peking Story* (10–12). Illus. 1988, Crown paper $11.95 (0-517-56712-1). An account of an exchange student who experienced the Chinese Communist Revolution firsthand from 1946 to 1950. (Rev: BL 1/15/88; SLJ 10/88) [951.05]

7420 Lawson, Don. *The Long March: Red China under Chairman Mao* (7–12). Illus. 1983, Harper LB $12.89 (0-690-04272-8). A lucid account of the life of Mao Tse-tung and his contribution to Chinese history. [951.04]

7421 Lin, Alice Murong Pu. *Grandmother Had No Name* (10–12). 1988, China Books & Periodicals $16.95 (0-8351-2045-7); paper $9.95 (0-8351-2034-1). Three generations of Chinese women are highlighted in this account by a member of the third generation, a Chinese American. (Rev: BL 11/15/88) [951.04]

7422 Lord, Bette Bao. *Legacies: A Chinese Mosaic* (9–12). 1990, Knopf $19.95 (0-394-58325-6). Through interviews with members of Chinese families, the author re-creates Chinese social history from 1949 to 1989. (Rev: SLJ 7/90) [951]

7423 Mahoney, Rosemary. *The Early Arrival of Dreams: A Year in China* (10–12). 1990, Ballantine $18.95 (0-449-90552-7). A bittersweet memoir by an American girl living with the Chinese while teaching English before the massacre in Tiananmen Square. (Rev: BL 9/15/90) [951]

7424 Morton, W. Scott. *China: Its History and Culture* (10–12). Illus. 1980, Harper $17.00 (0-690-01863-0); McGraw paper $9.95 (0-07-043421-2). A concise history of China from the Zhou dynasty, which began in 1027 B.C., to the succession of Deng after Mao. [951]

7425 Salisbury, Harrison E. *The Long March: The Untold Story* (10–12). Illus. 1985, Harper $22.95 (0-06-039044-1); McGraw paper $7.95 (0-07-054471-9). A lively retelling of the fateful Long March of Mao and its effects on later Chinese history. [951.04]

7426 Salisbury, Harrison E. *Tiananmen Diary: Thirteen Days in June* (9–12). 1989, Little $18.95 (0-316-80904-7); paper $10.95 (0-316-80905-5). An eyewitness account by a master correspondent of the crackdown on student protests in China. (Rev: BL 9/15/89) [951.058]

7427 Salzman, Mark. *Iron & Silk* (10–12). 1987, Random $16.95 (0-394-55156-7). An American teacher of English for 2 years in China tells about his experiences and contemporary life in China. (Rev: BL 1/15/87; BR 9–10/87; SLJ 11/87; VOYA 8–9/87) [951.05]

7428 Schwartz, Brian. *China off the Beaten Track* (10–12). Illus. 1983, St. Martin's paper $10.95 (0-312-13304-9). A guide book primarily for students who want to see China inexpensively. [915.1]

7429 Simmie, Scott, and Bob Nixon. *Tiananmen Square* (10–12). Illus. 1990, Univ. of Washington Pr. paper $14.95 (0-295-96950-4). Two Canadian journalists re-create the events leading up to the student demonstrations and the tragic events that followed. (Rev: BL 1/15/90) [951.05]

7430 Snow, Edgar. *Red Star over China* (10–12). Rev. ed. Illus. 1968, Grove $14.95 (0-8021-5093-4); Bantam paper $6.95 (0-552-26239-4). This account, first published in 1938, describes China during the fateful days of 1936 and 1937. [951.04]

7431 Spence, Jonathan D. *The Gate of Heavenly Peace* (10–12). 1982, Penguin paper $10.95 (0-14-006279-3). This book on China concentrates on the changes caused by the revolution. [951]

7432 Spence, Jonathan D. *The Search for Modern China* (10–12). Illus. 1990, Norton $29.95 (0-393-02708-2). A concise, well-illustrated history of China from the sixteenth century to 1989. (Rev: SLJ 7/90) [951]

7433 Temple, Robert. *The Genius of China: 3,000 Years of Science, Discovery, and Invention* (10–12). Illus. 1987, Simon & Schuster $19.95 (0-671-62028-2). A history of Chinese contributions to all branches of science from agriculture and astronomy to medicine and warfare. (Rev: BL 3/15/87) [509]

7434 Thubron, Colin. *Behind the Wall* (10–12). 1988, Atlantic Monthly $18.95 (0-87113-242-7). A known travel writer journeys through China from border to border with many details given on present-day life. (Rev: BL 9/15/88) [915.1]

7435 Time-Life Books, eds. *China* (7–12). Illus. 1984, Silver Burdett LB $25.93 (0-8094-5301-0). An introduction to this country with special emphasis on twentieth-century developments to the early 1980s. [951]

7436 Turnley, David, and Peter Turnley. *Beijing Spring* (10–12). Illus. 1989, Stewart, Tabori & Chang $35.00 (1-55670-130-6); paper $19.95 (1-55670-131-4). After an introductory essay by a *Newsweek* editor, the remainder of the book is devoted to photographs of the events on June 3–4 in Tiananmen Square. (Rev: BL 1/15/90) [951.05]

7437 Woodruff, John. *China in Search of Its Future: Years of Great Reform, 1982–1987* (10–12). 1989, Univ. of Washington Pr. $19.95 (0-295-96803-6). An excellent background book that explains current conditions in China in the perspective of its past. (Rev: SLJ 9/89) [951]

India

7438 Ashton, Stephen. *Indian Independence* (9–12). Illus. 1986, Batsford $19.95 (0-7134-4774-5). The story of the struggle for independence in India from 1885 through 1945, and the people involved. (Rev: SLJ 12/86) [954]

7439 Collins, Larry, and Dominique Lapierre. *Freedom at Midnight* (10–12). Illus. 1976, Avon paper $5.95 (0-380-00693-6). This covers the fateful final days of the British regime in India and the bloody riots during partition, and ends with the assassination of Gandhi in January 1948. [954.04]

7440 Mason, Philip. *The Men Who Ruled India* (10–12). Illus. 1985, Norton $27.50 (0-393-01946-2). A history of British India from 1599 to the departure of the British in 1947. [954.03]

7441 Spry-Leverton, Peter, and Peter Kornicki. *Japan* (10–12). Illus. 1988, Facts on File $22.95 (0-8160-1845-6). An overview that stresses Japan's present position in the economic world. (Rev: BL 2/15/88; BR 9–10/88) [952.03]

7442 Time-Life Books, eds. *India* (9–12). Illus. 1986, Silver Burdett LB $19.45 (0-8094-5315-0). Through lavish illustrations and many maps, the country of India and its history are introduced. [954]

7443 Traub, James. *India: The Challenge of Change* (10–12). Illus. 1985, Messner LB $10.29 (0-671-60460-0). A survey of modern India that covers such topics as religion, history, daily life, and foreign relations. (Rev: SLJ 2/86) [954]

7444 Wolpert, Stanley. *A New History of India* (10–12). 2nd ed. 1982, Oxford Univ. Pr. $29.95 (0-19-502949-6); paper $13.95 (0-19-502950-X). A comprehensive history of India that begins with prehistoric times and extends through the 1970s. [954]

Japan

7445 Bird, Isabella. *Unbeaten Tracks in Japan* (10–12). Illus. 1987, Beacon paper $9.95 (0-8070-7015-7). An account of a trek north from Tokyo by a Victorian Englishwoman in 1878. (Rev: SLJ 2/88) [952]

7446 Christopher, Robert C. *The Japanese Mind: The Goliath Explained* (10–12). 1984, Fawcett paper $7.95 (0-449-90120-3). An introduction to the Japanese people through the historical, social, and cultural forces that have shaped their behavior. [952]

7447 Dudley, William, ed. *Japan: Opposing Viewpoints* (9–12). Illus. 1989, Greenhaven LB $15.95 (0-89908-444-3); paper $7.95 (0-89908-419-2). From a number of sources different viewpoints are given, particularly on Japanese economic policies. (Rev: BL 1/15/90) [952.04]

7448 Dunn, Charles, J. *Everyday Life in Traditional Japan* (10–12). Illus. 1977, Tuttle paper $7.50 (0-8048-1384-1). A description of Japanese life during the reign of the Tokugawa shoguns, a period roughly from 1600 to 1850. [952]

7449 Ekiguchi, Kunio, and Ruth S. McCreery. *A Japanese Touch for the Seasons* (10–12). Illus. 1987, Kodansha $19.95 (0-87011-811-0). A book that explains Japanese handicrafts and gives an introduction to customs and festivals. (Rev: BL 12/15/87) [745.59]

7450 Hoyt, Edwin P. *Japan's War: The Great Pacific Conflict* (10–12). Illus. 1986, McGraw $19.95 (0-07-030612-5); DaCapo paper $14.95 (0-306-80348-8). An account of Japan's expansion efforts with emphasis on World War II. (Rev: BL 1/15/86) [940.54]

7451 Lowry, Dave. *Autumn Lightning: The Education of an American Samurai* (10–12). Illus. 1985, Shambhala paper $8.95 (0-394-73027-5). This beautifully illustrated book is part samurai history and legend and part autobiography. (Rev: VOYA 12/85) [915.2]

7452 Reischauer, Edwin O. *The Japanese* (10–12). Illus. 1977, Harvard Univ. Pr. $21.00 (0-674-47176-8). The former U.S. ambassador to Japan writes of his impressions of the people and their way of life. [952]

7453 Roberson, John R. *Japan: From Shogun to Sony, 1543–1984* (10–12). Illus. 1985, Macmillan $13.95 (0-689-31076-5). A history of Japan that begins with its opening to the West and ends with the gigantic postwar industrial development. [952]

7454 Seidensticker, Edward. *Tokyo Rising: The City since the Great Earthquake* (10–12). 1990, Knopf $24.95 (0-394-54360-2). The story of Japan's capital and its 2 rebuildings, one after the 1923 earthquake and the other after World War II. (Rev: BL 2/15/90) [952]

7455 Time-Life Books, eds. *Japan* (9–12). Illus. 1985, Silver Burdett LB $25.93 (0-8094-5121-2). The history and culture of Japan are introduced in a clear text and many attractive illustrations. [952]

Other Asian Lands

7456 Brook, Elaine. *Land of the Snow Lion: An Adventure in Tibet* (9–12). 1987, Dodd $18.95 (0-396-09100-8). An account by a British mountaineer of her 3-month journey into Tibet during 1982. (Rev: VOYA 6/88) [951]

7457 Clifford, Geoffrey, and John Balaban. *Vietnam: The Land We Never Knew* (9–12). Illus. 1989, Chronicle $29.95 (0-87701-597-X); paper $18.95 (0-87701-573-2). A book consisting of text and striking photographs about the people and life in postwar Vietnam. (Rev: BL 11/15/89) [959.704]

7458 Karnow, Stanley. *Vietnam: A History* (10–12). Illus. 1987, Penguin paper $12.95 (0-14-007324-8). This history of Vietnam concentrates on a chronicle of the war. [959.704]

7459 Lee, Ki-waik. *A New History of Korea* (10–12). Illus. 1984, Harvard Univ. Pr. $25.00 (0-674-61575-1); paper $12.95 (0-674-61576-X). A history of Korea that deemphasizes recent events and stresses those prior to the Korean War. [951.9]

7460 Mam, Teeda Butt, and Joan D. Criddle. *To Destroy You Is No Loss* (10–12). 1989, Doubleday paper $9.95 (0-385-26628-6). An eyewitness account of the incredible cruelty involved with the Khmer Rouge's control of Cambodia. (Rev: SLJ 12/87) [959.6]

7461 Matthiesson, Peter. *The Snow Leopard* (10–12). 1981, Bantam paper $3.95 (0-553-20651-6). A travel narrative about a 250-mile trek from Nepal to Tibet. [915.49]

7462 Nahm, Andrew C. *A Panorama of 5000 Years: Korean History* (8–12). 1989, Tuttle $19.95 (0-930878-68-X). A history of Korea that includes its culture and economics. [951.9]

7463 Shawcross, William. *Sideshow: Kissinger, Nixon and the Destruction of Cambodia* (10–12). 1987, Simon & Schuster paper $13.95 (0-671-64103-4). The story of the secret war the United States waged against Cambodia and its final collapse in 1975. [959.6]

Australia and the Pacific Islands

7464 Adam-Smith, Patsy, et al. *Australia: Beyond the Dreamtime* (10–12). Illus. 1989, Facts on File $24.95 (0-8160-1922-3). An excellent one-volume account of the history and culture of Australia. (Rev: BR 9–10/89) [994]

7465 Ansell, Rod, and Rachel Percy. *To Fight the Wild* (9–12). Illus. 1986, Harcourt $12.95 (0-15-289068-8). An amazing survival story about a 22-year-old man isolated in a remote part of the Australian bush country. (Rev: BL 6/15/86; SLJ 9/86) [613.6]

7466 Bligh, William. *Mutiny on Board HMS Bounty* (10–12). 1989, NAL paper $3.50 (0-451-52293-1). The story of the famous mutiny is told from the standpoint of Captain Bligh. [904]

7467 Cousteau, Jean-Michel, and Mose Richards. *Cousteau's Papua New Guinea Journey* (9–12). Illus. 1989, Abrams $39.95 (0-8109-3151-6). This is a lavishly illustrated account of an expedition through Papua New Guinea in 1988 by the son of the famous seafarer. (Rev: BL 2/1/90) [919.5]

7468 Davidson, Robyn. *Tracks* (10–12). 1983, Pantheon paper $6.95 (0-394-72167-5). For mature readers, this is the harrowing story of a courageous woman and her trek across 1,700 miles of the Australian outback. [994]

7469 Evans, Howard Ensign, and Mary Alice Evans. *Australia, a Natural History* (7–12). Illus. 1983, Smithsonian Inst. $39.95 (0-87474-418-0); paper $19.95 (0-87474-417-2). In addition to lavish coverage on plants and animals, there is information given on the aborigines and the history and geography of Australia. [574.9]

7470 Heyerdahl, Thor. *Easter Island: The Mystery Solved* (10–12). Illus. 1989, Random $24.95 (0-394-57906-2). The engrossing story of the explorer and his attempt to explain the existence of the huge monuments on Easter Island. (Rev: VOYA 6/90) [996]

7471 Irvine, Lucy. *Castaway* (10–12). 1985, Dell paper $4.50 (0-440-11069-6). For mature readers, the story of Lucy Irvine and her male companion's existence on an island off the coast of Australia. [994]

7472 Kurian, George Thomas. *Australia and New Zealand* (10–12). 1990, Facts on File $35.00 (0-8160-2350-6). In addition to the usual treatment of history and geography, this book covers such topics as foreign policy, defense, and local government. (Rev: SLJ 9/90) [990]

7473 Lawson, Don. *The New Philippines* (10–12). 2nd ed. Illus. 1986, Watts $12.90 (0-531-10269-6). In addition to background information, this account supplies details on the Marcos regime and the rise of Corazon Aquino. [959.9]

7474 Miller, James. *Koori: A Will to Win* (10–12). Illus. 1987, Salem House $16.95 (0-207-15065-6). An exploration of how conquering Europeans have exploited the Australian aborigines

and destroyed their culture. (Rev: SLJ 4/87) [994]

7475 Reader's Digest, eds. *Reader's Digest Visitor's Guide to the Great Barrier Reef* (9–12). Illus. 1989, Reader's Digest paper $19.95 (0-86438-073-9). Plant life and animal life are discussed plus a guided tour of the reef in this handsomely illustrated volume. (Rev: BL 5/15/89) [919.43]

7476 Rosca, Ninotchka. *Endgame: The Fall of Marcos* (10–12). 1987, Watts $18.95 (0-531-15038-0). A well-researched, eyewitness account of the fall of Marcos which introduces the key personalities and key events involved. (Rev: SLJ 9/88) [959.9]

7477 Terrill, Ross. *The Australians* (10–12). 1987, Simon & Schuster paper $8.95 (0-671-66239-2). A guide to the geography and history of Australia, but chiefly stresses the social life and customs of its people. (Rev: BL 9/1/87) [994]

7478 Time-Life Books, eds. *Australia* (9–12). Illus. 1985, Silver Burdett $25.93 (0-8094-5308-8). A lavishly illustrated introduction to the history, geography, people, and culture of Australia. [994]

7479 Vandenbeld, John. *Nature of Australia* (8–12). 1988, Facts on File $29.95 (0-8160-2006-X). The geography, plants, and animals of Australia are discussed in this companion volume to a television series. (Rev: BR 3–4/89) [994]

7480 Wright, Ronald. *On Fiji Islands* (10–12). 1986, Viking $19.95 (0-670-80534-X); Penguin paper $7.95 (0-14-009551-9). A history of the Fiji Islands with emphasis on how they evolved into their present condition. [996]

Europe

General and Miscellaneous

7481 Anderson, Bonnie S., and Judith P. Zinsser. *A History of Their Own: Women in Europe from Prehistory to the Present, Vol. 1* (10–12). Illus. 1988, Harper LB $27.45 (0-06-091452-1). This account reworks European history from a female perspective and defines the roles they have taken in the past. This account is completed by Volume II (1988). (Rev: SLJ 11/88) [940]

7482 *Frommer's Europe on $30.00 a Day* (10–12). 1988, Frommer paper $14.95 (0-318-32739-2). This is a guide to inexpensive travel that concentrates on the major cities in Europe.

There are many other Frommer guides as well as 2 excellent additional series for the world traveler, one from Fodor and the other Michelin. [914]

7483 Harvard Student Agencies. *Let's Go, 1990: The Budget Guide to Europe* (9–12). 1989, St. Martin's paper $12.95 (0-312-03377-X). A frequently revised guide that is up to date and budget conscious. (Rev: BL 2/1/85) [914]

7484 Holmes, George, ed. *The Oxford Illustrated History of Medieval Europe* (9–12). Illus. 1988, Oxford Univ. Pr. $35.00 (0-19-820073-0). Excellent coverage in text and illustration of about 1,000 years of European history from A.D. 500 to 1500. (Rev: BL 7/88) [940.1]

7485 McEvedy, Colin. *The Penguin Atlas of Recent History: Europe since 1815* (10–12). Illus. 1982, Penguin paper $6.95 (0-14-070834-0). A compact collection of maps that cover political and social history in Europe from 1815 to 1980. [911]

7486 Vansittart, Peter. *Voices, 1870–1914* (10–12). Illus. 1985, Watts $16.95 (0-531-09793-5). A companion to *Voices of the Great War* (1984), this volume is a collection of writings, speeches, poetry, and fiction that covers European history from 1870 to the outbreak of World War I. (Rev: SLJ 10/85) [940.2]

Central Europe and the Balkans

7487 Davies, Norman. *Heart of Europe: A Short History of Poland* (10–12). Illus. 1984, Oxford Univ. Pr. paper $10.95 (0-19-285152-7). A history of Poland with emphasis on current conditions through the early 1980s. [943.8]

7488 Michener, James A. *The Bridge at Andau* (9–12). 1957, Random $19.95 (0-394-41778-X); Fawcett paper $4.95 (0-449-21050-2). The moving story of the abortive Hungarian revolt of 1956. [943.9]

France

7489 Ash, Russell, and Bernard Higton. *Spirit of Place: Paris* (10–12). Illus. 1990, Arcade $10.45 (1-55970-009-2). In excerpts from famous writings and reproductions of paintings, the spirit of Paris is captured. (Rev: SLJ 7/90)

7490 Banfield, Susan. *The Rights of Man, the Reign of Terror: The Story of the French Revolution* (9–12). 1989, Harper LB $14.89 (0-397-

32354-9). A dramatically told account of the causes, events, and aftermath of the French Revolution. (Rev: BL 1/1/89; SLJ 4/90; VOYA 12/89) [944]

7491 Cobb, Richard, and Colin Jones, eds. *Voices of the French Revolution* (10–12). Illus. 1988, Salem House $29.95 (0-88162-338-5). Using eyewitness accounts plus additional material, this is an introduction to the major events and people involved in the French Revolution. (Rev: BL 10/15/88; VOYA 4/89) [944.04219]

7492 de Tocqueville, Alexis. *The Old Regime and the French Revolution* (10–12). 1955, Doubleday paper $7.95 (0-385-09260-1). A history that first appeared in 1856 of France before the Revolution and the conditions that caused the Revolution. [944.04]

7493 Goubert, Pierre. *The Course of French History* (10–12). Trans. by Maarten Ultee. Illus. 1988, Watts $26.95 (0-531-15054-2). For better readers, this is a stimulating overview of French history. (Rev: BL 12/15/87; BR 5–6/88) [944]

7494 Harvard Student Agencies. *Let's Go, 1990: The Budget Guide to France* (9–12). 1989, St. Martin's paper $12.95 (0-312-03378-8). Aimed mainly at student travelers, this is a practical, up-to-date guide. (Rev: BL 2/1/85) [914.4]

7495 Hibbert, Christopher. *The Days of the French Revolution* (10–12). Illus. 1980, Morrow paper $12.95 (0-688-00746-5). A history of the French Revolution that begins in 1789 and ends with the rise of Napoleon. [944.04]

7496 Horne, Alistair. *The Fall of Paris: The Siege and the Commune 1870–71* (10–12). 1981, Penguin paper $9.95 (0-14-005210-0). From letters and other personal accounts this is a reconstruction of the fall of Paris during the Franco-Prussian War of 1870–71. [944]

7497 Kirchberger, Joe H. *The French Revolution & Napoleon* (9–12). 1989, Facts on File $35.00 (0-8160-2090-6). An accurate, detailed, and scholarly account of the Revolution and the rise and fall of Napoleon. (Rev: BR 1–2/90) [944.04]

7498 Lewis, W. H. *The Splendid Century* (10–12). Illus. 1971, Morrow paper $12.95 (0-688-06009-9). A history of France during the seventeenth century under the rule of the Sun King, Louis XIV. [944]

7499 Schama, Simon. *Citizens: A Chronicle of the French Revolution* (10–12). Illus. 1989, Knopf $29.95 (0-394-55948-7). An excellent popular history of the Revolution that brings both its terror and idealism alive. (Rev: SLJ 5/90) [944.04]

7500 Time-Life Books, eds. *France* (7–12). Illus. 1985, Silver Burdett LB $19.45 (0-8094-5304-5). A portrait of the land, its people, history, and culture in words and outstanding pictures. [944]

Germany

7501 Andreas-Friedrich, Ruth. *Battleground Berlin: Diaries 1945–1948* (10–12). Trans. by Anna Boerresen. 1990, Paragon $22.95 (1-55778-191-5). The resistance fighter and journalist reprints diary entries involving the post-war agony of Berlin in this sequel to *Berlin Underground, 1938–1945* (1989). (Rev: BL 8/90) [943.1]

7502 Bornstein, Jerry. *The Wall Came Tumbling Down: The Berlin Wall and the Fall of Communism* (10–12). Illus. 1990, Arch Cape $12.99 (0-517-03306-2). A concise history with photographs of the events that led to the opening of the Berlin Wall on November 9, 1989. (Rev: BL 7/90) [335.43]

7503 Capra, Fritjof, and Charlene Spretnak. *Green Politics: The Global Promise* (10–12). 1984, Dutton $12.95 (0-525-24231-7). A history of the Green movement in Germany and their concern for the environment and nuclear disarmament. [943]

7504 Carr, William. *A History of Germany, 1815–1945* (10–12). 2nd ed. 1979, St. Martin's $25.00 (0-312-37871-8). This is a history of modern Germany from Bismarck to the end of World War II. [943]

7505 Herzstein, Robert Edwin. *The Nazis* (7–12). Illus. 1980, Silver Burdett $25.93 (0-8095-2535-1). The story of Hitler's political party with special coverage of the Holocaust. [943.086]

7506 Reichel, Sabine. *What Did You Do in the War, Daddy? Growing Up German* (10–12). 1989, Hill & Wang $19.95 (0-8090-9685-4). Through interviews with parents and others of their generation, a German-born girl tries to reconstruct what average Germans did during the Holocaust and Hitler's reign. (Rev: BL 2/15/89) [943.086]

7507 Shirer, William L. *The Rise and Fall of the Third Reich* (10–12). 1990, Simon & Schuster $35.00 (0-671-72869-5); paper $14.95 (0-671-72868-7). This lengthy account traces the history of Germany from defeat in World War I to defeat in World War II. [943.086]

7508 Speer, Albert. *Inside the Third Reich* (10–12). Illus. 1981, Macmillan paper $12.95 (0-02-037500-X). The memoirs of one of Hitler's clos-

est confidants, supplying an insider's view of the Third Reich. [943.086]

7509 Tames, Richard. *Nazi Germany* (9–12). Illus. 1986, Batsford $19.95 (0-7134-3538-0). This is a history of the Nazi period in Germany as seen through a series of portraits of people who lived through it. (Rev: SLJ 4/86) [943.08]

7510 Time-Life Books, eds. *Germany* (9–12). Illus. 1986, Silver Burdett LB $25.93 (0-8094-5305-3). This account gives fine background material on the history and peoples of Germany but ends before the fall of the Berlin Wall. [943]

Great Britain and Ireland

7511 Ackroyd, Peter. *Dickens' London: An Imaginative Vision* (9–12). Illus. 1988, Headline $24.95 (0-7472-0028-9). An introduction to the squalor and energy of Dickens' London illustrated with pictures and passages from his works. (Rev: BL 10/15/88) [823]

7512 Clarke, Amanda. *Battle of Hastings* (9–12). Illus. 1988, David & Charles $17.95 (0-8521-9755-1). The story of the important battle whose outcome ushered in the Norman period in English history. (Rev: BR 11–12/88) [941.01]

7513 Coward, Barry. *The Stuart Age: A History of England* (10–12). 1980, Longman paper $20.95 (0-582-48833-8). A history of England from James I through the reign of Queen Anne. [941.06]

7514 Delderfield, Eric R. *Kings & Queens of England and Great Britain* (10–12). Illus. 1990, Guild $24.95 (0-8160-2433-2). In one volume, coverage on monarchs and their times and dynasties from the Saxons on. (Rev: SLJ 12/90) [942]

7515 Foster, R. F., ed. *The Oxford Illustrated History of Ireland* (10–12). Illus. 1989, Oxford Univ. Pr. $35.00 (0-19-822970-4). In a beautifully illustrated volume, 6 historians re-create Irish history from early times to the present. (Rev: BL 1/15/90) [941.5]

7516 Fraser, Antonia. *The Weaker Vessel* (10–12). Illus. 1984, Random paper $9.95 (0-394-73251-0). A survey of the role played by women in seventeenth-century England. [305.4]

7517 Haigh, Christopher, ed. *The Cambridge Historical Encyclopedia of Great Britain and Ireland* (10–12). Illus. 1985, Cambridge Univ. Pr. $44.50 (0-521-25559-7); paper $16.95 (0-521-39552-6). This volume contains a series of articles that trace the history and development of the culture of England, Ireland, Scotland, and Wales. [941]

7518 Hallam, Elizabeth, ed. *The Plantagenet Chronicles* (10–12). Illus. 1986, Weidenfeld $35.00 (1-55584-018-3). This excellently illustrated volume uses quotes from many original sources to retell the lives of the Plantegenet kings from Henry II to John. (Rev: BL 11/15/86) [942.03]

7519 Harvard Student Agencies. *Let's Go, 1990: The Budget Guide to Britain and Ireland* (9–12). 1989, St. Martin's paper $12.95 (0-312-03375-3). This practical guide to budget travel in Britain and Ireland is periodically updated. (Rev: BL 2/1/85) [917.9]

7520 Hawkins, Gerald S. *Stonehenge Decoded* (10–12). 1978, Dell paper $4.50 (0-385-28974-X). The author believes that Stonehenge was once an astronomical observatory and presents facts to prove it. [941]

7521 Herriot, James. *James Herriot's Yorkshire* (9–12). Illus. 1982, Bantam paper $4.95 (0-553-25981-4). A beautifully illustrated introduction to the part of England where the famous writer practiced veterinary medicine. [914.2]

7522 Hodges, Michael. *Ireland* (9–12). 1988, David & Charles $17.95 (0-7134-5542-X). A history of Ireland that concentrates on the gaining of freedom and Irish-English relationships. (Rev: BR 9–10/89) [941.7]

7523 Howarth, David. *1066: The Year of the Conquest* (10–12). Illus. 1981, Penguin paper $6.95 (0-14-005850-8). The story of the invasion of Britain by the Normans and the triumph of William the Conqueror at the Battle of Hastings. [942.02]

7524 Jones, Christopher. *The Great Palace: The Story of Parliament* (10–12). Illus. 1985, BBC $29.95 (0-88186-150-2). The story of the British system of government and of the magnificent buildings that house its parliament. (Rev: SLJ 9/85) [941]

7525 Loomis, Roger S. *A Mirror of Chaucer's World* (10–12). Illus. 1965, Princeton Univ. Pr. paper $14.95 (0-691-01349-7). A heavily illustrated book that re-creates the world of Chaucer. [942.03]

7526 Mattingly, Garrett. *The Armada* (10–12). Illus. 1959, Houghton $29.95 (0-395-48682-3); paper $9.95 (0-395-08366-4). The story of the defeat of the Armada told chiefly from the English point of view. [942.05]

7527 Miller, Helen Hill. *Captains from Devon: The Great Elizabethan Seafarers Who Won the Oceans for England* (10–12). Illus. 1985, Algonquin $16.95 (0-912697-27-X). Along with background English historical material, this book con-

tains profiles of such men as Sir Francis Drake and Sir Walter Raleigh. (Rev: BL 10/15/85; SLJ 3/86) [942.05]

7528 Morgan, Kenneth O., ed. *The Oxford Illustrated History of Britain* (10–12). Illus. 1984, Oxford Univ. Pr. $39.95 (0-19-822684-5). Through 10 articles written by specialists, the history of Great Britain and Ireland is covered in this comprehensive one-volume work. [941]

7529 O'Brien, George. *The Village of Longing and Dancehall Days* (10–12). 1990, Viking $18.95 (0-670-82366-X). An unusual tribute to the Emerald Isle by a man who left it to relocate in America. (Rev: BL 1/1/90) [941]

7530 O'Malley, Padraig. *The Uncivil Wars: Ireland Today* (10–12). 1991, Beacon paper $14.95 (0-395-36570-8). Through a series of interviews, the current struggle in Northern Ireland is explored and its origins are traced. [941.5]

7531 Ranelagh, John O'Beirne. *A Short History of Ireland* (10–12). 1983, Cambridge Univ. Pr. $42.50 (0-521-24685-7); paper $11.95 (0-521-28889-4). A concise volume that traces the history of Ireland from earliest times to the present. [941.5]

7532 Roberts, Clayton, and David A. Roberts. *A History of England: Vol. 1: Prehistory to 1714* (10–12). 2nd ed. Illus. 1985, Prentice paper $21.95 (0-13-389966-7). This is a most enjoyable, comprehensive history of Britain that is continued from 1688 to the present in volume 2 (1985). (Rev: BL 8/85) [941]

7533 Smith, Lesley M., ed. *The Making of Britain: The Middle Ages* (10–12). Illus. 1985, Schocken $23.50 (0-8052-3957-X). A group of essays about life in Britain during the Middle Ages under such topics as government, the church, and how common people lived. (Rev: BL 7/85) [942]

7534 Time-Life Books, eds. *Britain* (9–12). Illus. 1986, Silver Burdett $25.93 (0-8094-5306-1). A history of the various regions of Great Britain and an introduction to their different peoples and places. [941]

7535 Tourtellot, Jonathan B., ed. *Discovering Britain and Ireland* (10–12). Illus. 1985, National Geographic $22.95 (0-87044-598-7). Good background information is given for the traveler as well as a description of sights to see in the British Isles and Ireland. [914.1]

7536 Trevelyan, George Macaulay. *The English Revolution, 1688–1689* (10–12). 1987, Oxford Univ. Pr. paper $6.95 (0-19-500263-6). This account traces the events that led up to the revolution, the revolution itself, and its aftermath. [942.06]

7537 Uris, Leon. *Ireland: A Terrible Beauty* (9–12). Illus. 1975, Doubleday $40.00 (0-385-07563-4); Bantam paper $14.95 (0-553-34232-0). An oversized book that captures the atmosphere and history of Ireland in text and almost 400 photographs. [941.5]

7538 Walker, Bryce. *The Armada* (7–12). Illus. 1981, Time-Life $21.27 (0-8094-2698-6). The year is 1588 and the event is the battle of the Armada that made England supreme on the high seas. [942.05]

7539 Warwick, Christopher. *Abdication* (10–12). Illus. 1986, Sidgwick & Jackson $24.95 (0-283-99351-0). A re-creation of the romance between Britain's Edward VIII and Wallis Warfield Simpson. Also by the same author: *King George VI and Queen Elizabeth* (1985). (Rev: BL 2/1/87) [941.084]

7540 Williams, Niall, and Christine Breen. *When Summer's in the Meadow* (10–12). 1989, Soho $17.95 (0-939149-23-0). The young immigrant couple in rural Ireland continue their charming story begun in *O Come Ye Back to Ireland* (1987). (Rev: BL 3/15/89) [941.9]

7541 Williamson, David. *Debrett's Kings and Queens of Britain* (9–12). Illus. 1986, Salem $27.50 (0-88162-213-3). An introduction with illustrations to each British monarch from Celtic times to the present. (Rev: BL 11/1/86) [941]

7542 Wood, Michael. *Domesday: A Search for the Roots of England* (10–12). Illus. 1988, Facts on File $24.95 (0-8160-1832-4). This handsome book explains the nature of the census taken by the Normans in Britain in 1086 and its importance in history. (Rev: SLJ 12/88) [941.02]

7543 Woodham-Smith, Cecil. *The Great Hunger: Ireland, 1845–1849* (10–12). 1980, Dutton paper $8.95 (0-525-47643-1). The story of the terrible potato famine in Ireland in the 1840s and its effect not only on Ireland but also on England and, through immigration, on the United States. [338.1]

Greece

7544 Harvard Student Agencies. *Let's Go, 1990: The Budget Guide to Greece* (9–12). 1989, St. Martin's paper $12.95 (0-312-03379-6). In addition to material on traveling cheaply in Greece, this book also includes Cyprus and Turkey. (Rev: BL 2/1/85) [915.95]

7545 Toynbee, Arnold. *The Greeks and Their Heritages* (10–12). 1981, Oxford Univ. Pr. $25.00 (0-19-215256-4). An account that deals with 3 civilizations of ancient Greece—Mycenaean, Hellenic, and Byzantine—and how each is reflected in contemporary Greek life. [949.5]

Italy

7546 Barzini, Luigi. *The Italians* (10–12). 1964, Peter Smith $19.00 (0-8446-6146-5); Macmillan paper $9.95 (0-689-70540-9). An Italian journalist probes the national character of his compatriots. [945]

7547 Durant, Will. *The Renaissance* (10–12). Illus. 1953, Simon & Schuster $29.95 (0-671-61600-5). This account discusses the cultural history of the Renaissance as well as its social and political aspects. [945]

7548 Harvard Student Agencies. *Let's Go, 1990: The Budget Guide to Italy* (9–12). 1989, St. Martin's paper $12.95 (0-312-03381-8). A practical travel guide that is oriented toward the student traveler. (Rev: BL 2/1/85) [914.5]

7549 Hibbert, Christopher. *Rome: The Biography of a City* (10–12). Illus. 1985, Norton $25.00 (0-393-01984-5); Penguin paper $14.95 (0-14-007078-8). An illustrated history of the Eternal City from pre-Roman Etruscan times to World War II. (Rev: BL 6/15/85) [945]

7550 Time-Life Books, eds. *Italy* (9–12). Illus. 1986, Silver Burdett LB $25.93 (0-8094-5311-8). This is a heavily illustrated introduction to the land, people, history, and culture of Italy. [945]

Scandinavia, Iceland, and Greenland

7551 Edwards, Ted. *Fight the Wild Island* (9–12). 1987, Salem House $18.95 (0-88162-258-3). The author brings this unusual island into sharp focus as he describes his solo walk across it. (Rev: VOYA 10/87) [949.1]

7552 Millman, Lawrence. *Last Places: A Journey in the North* (10–12). 1990, Houghton $18.95 (0-395-43615-X). For mature readers, the enthralling story of a journey across the north that duplicated the travels of the Vikings. (Rev: BL 1/1/90) [910]

7553 Time-Life Books, eds. *Scandinavia* (9–12). Illus. 1987, Silver Burdett LB $25.93 (0-8094-5310-X). A heavily illustrated volume that covers such topics as the history, economics, culture, and people of Scandinavia. [948]

Spain and Portugal

7554 Crow, John A. *Spain: The Root and the Flower* (10–12). 3rd ed. 1985, Univ. of California Pr. $37.50 (0-520-05123-8); paper $12.95 (0-520-05133-5). This is a political and cultural history of Spain that includes coverage into the post-Franco period. [946]

7555 Harvard Student Agencies. *Let's Go, 1990: The Budget Guide to Spain, Portugal, and Morocco* (9–12). 1989, St. Martin's paper $12.95 (0-312-03384-2). Aimed mainly at a student audience, this guide tells you how to see Spain, Portugal, and Morocco and appreciate their people and culture while on a tight budget. (Rev: BL 2/1/85) [914.6]

7556 Howarth, David. *The Voyage of the Armada: The Spanish Story* (10–12). Illus. 1987, Penguin paper $8.95 (0-14-006315-3). The story of the Armada written from the Spanish point of view. [946]

7557 Jackson, Gabriel. *A Concise History of the Spanish Civil War* (10–12). 1980, Thames & Hudson paper $10.95 (0-500-27180-1). An account that covers both national and international aspects of this Civil War. [946.081]

7558 McDowall, David. *The Spanish Armada* (8–12). Illus. 1988, David & Charles $17.95 (0-7134-5671-X). A British import that tells about the events surrounding this Spanish fleet and also supplies many short biographies of the people involved. (Rev: BR 11–12/88) [946]

7559 Martin, Colin, and Geoffrey Parker. *The Spanish Armada* (10–12). Illus. 1988, Norton $27.50 (0-393-02607-8). A nicely illustrated volume that celebrates the 400th birthday of this historic Spanish naval defeat. (Rev: BL 9/1/88) [946]

7560 Preston, Paul. *The Spanish Civil War, 1936–39* (10–12). Illus. 1986, Grove $20.00 (0-394-55565-1). A history of the civil war written from an anti-Franco viewpoint. (Rev: BL 9/15/86) [968]

7561 Thomas, Hugh. *The Spanish Civil War* (10–12). 3rd ed. Illus. 1986, Harper $40.00 (0-06-014278-2). This thorough account covers the war from its origins in the 1920s to the fall of Barcelona in 1939. [946.081]

7562 Time-Life Books, eds. *Spain* (9–12). Illus. 1987, Silver Burdett LB $25.93 (0-8094-5314-2).

A well-illustrated account that covers a variety of topics such as politics, history, geography, and culture. [946]

U.S.S.R.

7563 Bernards, Neal, et al., eds. *The Soviet Union: Opposing Viewpoints* (9–12). Illus. 1987, Greenhaven $13.95 (0-89908-429-X); paper $7.95 (0-89908-404-4). Pros and cons of events and policy changes effected in Russia from 1985 through 1987. (Rev: BL 2/15/88) [947]

7564 Brown, Archie, et al., eds. *The Cambridge Encyclopedia of Russia and the Soviet Union* (10–12). Illus. 1982, Cambridge Univ. Pr. $49.50 (0-521-23169-8). This handbook written by over 100 specialists covers all aspects of Soviet life in a concise format. [947]

7565 Congressional Quarterly. *The Soviet Union* (10–12). Illus. 1990, Congressional Quarterly $22.95 (0-87187-574-8). This frequently revised volume emphasizes political and economic aspects of Soviet life with special attention to foreign relations. [947.085]

7566 Conquest, Robert. *Stalin and the Kirov Murder* (10–12). 1989, Oxford Univ. Pr. $16.95 (0-19-505579-9). The story of the assassination plot that left Stalin leader of the Soviet Union. (Rev: SLJ 10/89) [947]

7567 Deriabin, Peter, and T. H. Bagley. *KGB: Masters of the Soviet Union* (10–12). 1990, Hippocrene $21.95 (0-87052-804-1). A history and analysis of the institution that helps maintain Communist control in the Soviet Union. (Rev: BL 1/15/90) [354]

7568 Gorbachev, Mikhail. *Perestroika: New Thinking for Our Country and the World* (10–12). 1988, Harper $19.95 (0-06-039085-9). The historic statement by the Russian leader of his beliefs and objectives. (Rev: BL 1/15/88; BR 11–12/88) [327]

7569 Kaiser, Robert G. *Russia from the Inside* (9–12). Illus. 1985, Dutton $20.95 (0-525-14886-8); paper $10.95 (0-525-47632-6). This collection of photographs reflects life in the Soviet Union at the beginning of the 1980s. [947]

7570 Kerblay, Basile. *Modern Soviet Society* (10–12). 1983, Pantheon paper $7.16 (0-394-71111-4). This is a study of Soviet life and structure as it existed in the late 1970s. [947.085]

7571 Klose, Kevin. *Russia and the Russians: Inside the Closed Society* (10–12). 1984, Norton paper $11.95 (0-393-30312-8). This memoir describes life in the Soviet Union as it was in the early 1980s. [947.085]

7572 Kort, Michael. *The Soviet Colossus: A History of the USSR* (10–12). 1990, Unwin paper $17.95 (0-04-445762-6). A popular history of the U.S.S.R. from the Revolution of 1917 through the pre-Gorbachev era. (Rev: BL 3/1/85) [947]

7573 Laqueur, Walter, et al. *Soviet Union 2000: Reform or Revolution?* (10–12). 1990, St. Martin's $19.95 (0-312-04425-9). A series of essays by specialists on the Soviet Union who try to predict what is in store for that country in the 1990s. (Rev: BL 8/90) [947.085]

7574 Lee, Andrea. *Russian Journal* (10–12). 1984, Random $13.50 (0-394-51891-8); paper $5.95 (-0-394-71127-0). A journal of a black American's trip to the U.S.S.R. in the early 1980s. [947]

7575 Maclean, Fitzroy. *Portrait of the Soviet Union* (10–12). Illus. 1988, Henry Holt $23.95 (0-8050-0891-8). A description of the various ethnic groups that make up the Soviet Union plus material on geography, culture, and economics. (Rev: BR 1–2/89; SLJ 9/88) [947]

7576 Mandel, William M. *Soviet but Not Russian: The "Other" Peoples of the Soviet Union* (10–12). Illus. 1985, Ramparts $20.00 (0-87867-095-5); paper $10.00 (0-87867-096-3). Sketches of the many people other than Russians who now make up almost one-half of the population of the Soviet Union. (Rev: BL 4/1/85) [305.8]

7577 Medish, Vadim. *The Soviet Union* (10–12). 4th ed. 1990, Prentice $27.80 (0-13-824020-5). A survey of Soviet life and politics through the mid-1980s. [947]

7578 Medreder, Roy A. *Let History Judge: The Origins and Consequences of Stalinism* (10–12). 1990, Columbia Univ. Pr. $19.50 (0-231-06351-2). A history of the Soviet Union during Stalin's reign of terror. [947]

7579 Pares, Bernard. *A History of Russia* (10–12). 1953, AMS Pr. $42.50 (0-404-15122-1). This broad-based book covers Russian history from the earliest times to immediately after World War II. [947]

7580 Paxton, John. *Companion to Russian History* (8–12). 1985, Facts on File $24.95 (0-87196-771-5). In 2,500 entries arranged alphabetically, the whole spectrum of Russian history from the tenth century through the Khrushchev era is covered. (Rev: BR 3–4/86) [947]

7581 Riasanovsky, Nicholas V. *A History of Russia* (10–12). 4th ed. Illus. 1984, Oxford Univ. Pr. paper $32.00 (0-19-503361-2). A fine one-volume

history that covers Russian political, social, and cultural history into the post-Stalin period. [947]

7582 Saunders, George, ed. *The October Revolution* (10–12). Illus. 1979, Columbia Univ. Pr. paper $16.00 (0-231-04591-3). A controversial retelling of the events in the early part of the Russian Revolution and of Lenin's part in shaping the course of the future. [947.084]

7583 Shipler, David K. *Russia: Broken Idols, Solemn Dreams* (10–12). 1989, Penguin paper $8.95 (0-14-012271-0). This is a report on life in Russia prior to the recent drastic changes in economics and government. [947]

7584 Shoemaker, M. Wesley. *The Soviet Union and Eastern Europe 1988* (9–12). 19th ed. Illus. 1988, Stryker-Post paper $6.50 (0-943448-44-1). An annually revised overview on political and economic life with greatest concentration on the Soviet Union. (Rev: BL 2/1/89) [947.084]

7585 Smith, Hedrick. *The Russians* (10–12). Rev. ed. Illus. 1985, Times Bks. $24.95 (0-8129-1086-9); Ballantine paper $5.95 (0-345-31746-7). An American newspaperman describes the Russian people and their attitudes during the 1970s and early 1980s. [947.085]

7586 Solzhenitsyn, Aleksandr. *The Gulag Archipelago, 1918–1956: An Experiment in Literary Investigation* (10–12). 3 vols. Illus. 1987, Harper paper $14.95 (0-06-091280-4). This is Volume 1 of a 3-volume work on the forced labor camps that were once part of the Soviet system of silencing dissidents. [365]

7587 Tessendorf, K. C. *Kill the Tsar: Youth and Terrorism in Old Russia* (8–12). 1986, Macmillan $13.95 (0-689-31124-9). A history of terrorism as practiced in czarist Russia particularly during the reign of Alexander II. (Rev: BL 8/86; SLJ 9/86; VOYA 2/87) [947.08]

7588 Time-Life Books, eds. *The Soviet Union* (8–12). 1984, Silver Burdett LB $25.93 (0-8094-5302-9). An introduction to the world's largest country with coverage on its history, geography, culture, and diversity of people. [947]

7589 Willis, David K. *Klass: How Russians Really Live* (10–12). 1985, St. Martin's $16.95 (0-312-45763-4); Avon paper $4.50 (0-380-70263-0). A candid look at life in the Soviet Union as it was during the early 1980s. [947.085]

Middle East

General and Miscellaneous

7590 Becker, Jillian. *The PLO: The Rise and Fall of the Palestine Liberation Organization* (10–12). Illus. 1984, St. Martin's paper $9.95 (0-312-59380-5). A history of the early years of the PLO that emphasizes the disastrous role it has played in the disintegration of Lebanon. [956]

7591 Cleveland, Ray L. *The Middle East and South Asia* (7–12). Illus. 1988, Stryker-Post paper $5.50 (0-943448-43-3). An annual volume for adults that gives valuable profiles of countries in the Middle East and South Asia regions. [956]

7592 Congressional Quarterly. *The Middle East* (10–12). 7th ed. Illus. 1991, Congressional Quarterly $24.95 (087-187630-2). This frequently revised volume contains a series of chapters on general topics plus coverage on each separate country and a 1991 supplement. [956]

7593 Constable, George, ed. *Arabian Peninsula* (7–12). Illus. 1985, Time-Life $13.20 (0-8094-5312-7). Topics covered in this pictorially beautiful book include an overview of the region, the rise of Islam, and the development of Saudi Arabia. (Rev: BL 3–4/86) [956]

7594 Dempsey, M. W., ed. *Atlas of the Arab World* (10–12). Illus. 1983, Facts on File paper $14.95 (0-87196-779-0). A collection of maps that highlights the geography, history, and economic development of 21 Arab countries. [909]

7595 Goldston, Robert. *The Sword of the Prophet* (10–12). Illus. 1979, Dial $11.95 (0-8037-8372-8). A history of the world of Islam from A.D. 570 to the present mid-eastern conflicts with Israel. [909]

7596 Harvard Student Agencies. *Let's Go, 1990: The Budget Guide to Israel and Egypt* (9–12). 1989, St. Martin's paper $12.95 (0-312-03380-X). For the budget-minded tourist, this is a helpful guide with many useful travel tips. (Rev: BL 2/1/85) [915.694]

7597 Haskins, James. *Leaders of the Middle East* (9–12). Illus. 1985, Enslow $16.95 (0-89490-086-2). Though some of these leaders are now dead (for example, Zia and Khomeini), these profiles give good background information to the present situation in the Middle East. (Rev: BL 7/85; BR 3–4/86; SLJ 9/85; VOYA 4/86) [956]

7598 Hillel, Shlomo. *Operation Babylon* (10–12). Trans. by Ina Friedman. 1987, Doubleday $19.95 (0-385-23597-6). The story of how 125,000 Jews from Iraq were able to flee to Israel from 1947 to 1952. (Rev: BL 11/1/87) [325]

7599 Hitti, Phillip K. *History of the Arabs, from the Earliest Times to the Present* (10–12). Illus. 1970, St. Martin's paper $19.50 (0-312-37520-4). Though not as current as possible, this is an excellent history of the Arab world from ancient times to the 1960s. [909]

7600 Laqueur, Walter, and Barry Rubin, eds. *The Israel-Arab Reader: A Documentary History of the Middle East Conflict* (10–12). 4th ed. Illus. 1985, Penguin paper $10.95 (0-14-022588-9). This is a collection of documents, letters, reports, and speeches that cover the Israeli-Arab differences from the beginnings of the Zionist movement to the mid-1980s. (Rev: BL 6/15/85) [956]

7601 Naipaul, V. S. *Among the Believers* (10–12). 1982, Random paper $9.95 (0-394-71195-5). A report circa 1980 about the author's trip through various Islamic countries. [977]

7602 Robinson, Francis. *Atlas of the Islamic World Since 1500* (10–12). Illus. 1982, Facts on File $40.00 (0-87196-629-8). A visual history of the Islamic world that covers not only politics but also economics, culture, and demographics. [909]

7603 Rohr, Janelle, ed. *The Middle East: Opposing Viewpoints* (9–12). Illus. 1987, Greenhaven LB $15.95 (0-89908-428-1); paper $7.95 (0-89908-403-6). Pros and cons are explored in issues involving Palestinians, Islamic fundamentalism, and U.S. involvement in the Middle East. (Rev: BL 1/15/88) [956.04]

Israel

7604 Anderson, Bob, and Janelle Rohr, eds. *Israel* (9–12). Illus. 1988, Greenhaven $14.95 (0-89908-435-4); paper $7.95 (0-89908-410-9). In this collection of writing, many different aspects and opinions concerning the Israeli-Palestinian conflict are explored. (Rev: BL 1/15/89) [956.94]

7605 Carroll, Raymond. *The Palestine Question* (9–12). 1983, Watts LB $12.90 (0-531-04549-8). This general introduction to the Israeli-Arab question begins in the 1940s and extends through the early 1980s. [956]

7606 Collins, Larry, and Dominique Lapierre. *O Jerusalem!* (10–12). 1980, Pocket paper $3.95 (0-671-83684-6). This is an account of the struggle for Jerusalem during the Israeli-Arab War of 1948. [956.9]

7607 Dan, Uri. *To the Promised Land: The Birth of Israel, 40th Anniversary* (9–12). Illus. 1988, Doubleday $24.95 (0-385-24597-1). An account in text and pictures of the events and people involved in the founding of Israel. (Rev: BL 4/1/88) [956.94]

7608 Dimbleby, Jonathan. *The Palestinians* (10–12). Illus. 1980, Quartet Bks. $25.00 (0-7043-2205-6). A history of the recent developments with the Arabs living in Palestine and of their many resistance movements. [956.9]

7609 Eban, Abba. *My People: The Story of the Jews* (10–12). Illus. 1987, Random paper $14.95 (0-394-72759-2). This account gives a broad historical outline of Jewish history and an assessment of their situation today, particularly in Israel. [909]

7610 Eisenberg, Dennis, et al. *The Mossad: Israel's Secret Intelligence Service—Inside Stories* (10–12). 1979, NAL paper $4.95 (0-451-15898-9). This is a history of the exploits in which Israel's secret intelligence organization has been involved since its inception in 1951. [956.9]

7611 Goldston, Robert. *Next Year in Jerusalem: A Short History of Zionism* (10–12). 1979, Fawcett paper $1.95 (0-449-24103-3). This history of Zionism supplies good background material on the present situation in the Middle East. [956.94]

7612 Hellman, Peter. *Heroes: Tales from the Israeli Wars* (10–12). 1990, Henry Holt $19.95 (0-8050-0478-5). Ten stories of ordinary men and women who have behaved heroically in time of war. (Rev: BL 4/1/90) [956.94]

7613 Herzog, Chaim. *The Arab-Israeli Wars* (10–12). Illus. 1982, Random paper $12.95 (0-394-71746-5). This account covers Arab-Israeli wars from the War of Independence in 1948 through the Yom Kippur War of 1973. [956]

7614 O'Brien, Conor Cruise. *The Siege: The Saga of Israel and Zionism* (10–12). 1986, Simon & Schuster paper $12.95 (0-671-63310-4). A history of Zionism from its beginning to post-Begin days in Israel. [956.94]

7615 Rabinovich, Abraham. *The Boats of Cherbourg* (10–12). Illus. 1988, Seaver Books $19.95 (0-8050-0680-X). The story of how 5 Israeli missile ships were successfully used against the Arabs in the Yom Kippur War. (Rev: BL 3/1/88) [956]

7616 Time-Life Books, eds. *Israel* (10–12). Illus. 1986, Silver Burdett LB $25.93 (0-8094-5313-4). An overview of Israel's history and present situation heavily illustrated with photographs. [956.94]

7617 Timerman, Jacobo. *The Longest War: Israel in Lebanon* (10–12). 1982, Knopf $11.95 (0-394-53022-5); Random paper $4.95 (0-394-71471-7). An account that is critical of Israel's role in the Lebanon disintegration and particularly of the invasion of Lebanon in 1982. [956]

7618 Wallach, John, and Janet Wallach. *Still Small Voices* (10–12). 1989, Harcourt $16.95 (0-15-184970-6). Through case studies of 12 Jews and Arabs who live on the West Bank and the Gaza Strip, the roots and present conditions of today's conflicts are explored. (Rev: BL 3/1/89) [956]

Other Middle East Lands

7619 Dodwell, Christina. *A Traveler on Horseback in Eastern Turkey and Iran* (9–12). Illus. 1989, Walker $16.95 (0-8027-1078-6). An intrepid woman describes her adventures in this inhospitable terrain. (Rev: BL 6/1/89) [915.5]

7620 Guppy, Shusha. *The Blindfold Horse: Memories of a Persian Childhood* (10–12). 1989, Beacon $17.95 (0-8070-7042-4). A fascinating account of growing up in Iran prior to the disposition of the Shah. (Rev: BL 1/15/89) [955]

7621 Mackey, Sandra. *Lebanon: Death of a Nation* (10–12). 1989, Congdon & Weed $22.95 (0-86553-204-4). A good background account of the recent history of Lebanon. (Rev: BL 7/89; BR 11–12/89; SLJ 1/90) [956]

7622 Pahlavi, R. Mohammed. *Answer to History* (10–12). 1980, Scarborough $12.95 (0-8128-2755-4); paper $7.95 (0-8128-6138-8). The late Shah of Iran tells of the revolution in the 1970s from his point of view. [955]

7623 Saikal, Amin. *Rise and Fall of the Shah* (10–12). Illus. 1980, Princeton Univ. Pr. $35.00 (0-691-03118-5). The story of the last shah's rule and his efforts to turn Iran into a world power. [955]

7624 Sick, Gary. *All Fall Down: America's Tragic Encounter with Iran* (10–12). 1985, Penguin paper $8.95 (0-14-008837-7). An advisor to President Carter on Iran tells of the hostage crisis involving Iran and the United States during 1979 and 1980. [955]

North and South America (excluding the United States)

General History and Geography

7625 Collier, Simon, et al., eds. *The Cambridge Encyclopedia of Latin America and the Caribbean* (10–12). Illus. 1985, Cambridge Univ. Pr. $49.50 (0-521-26263-1). In a series of articles and essays, such topics as geography, history, politics, culture, and economics are covered in relation to all of Latin America. [980]

7626 Crow, John A. *The Epic of Latin America* (10–12). 1980, Univ. of California Pr. $55.00 (0-520-04107-0); paper $15.95 (0-520-03776-6). A history of Latin America from the days of the Aztecs and Mayas to contemporary times. [980]

7627 Dostert, Pierre Etienne. *Latin America* (9–12). Illus. 1988, Stryker-Post paper $6.50 (0-943448-42-5). This annual publication gives general information on Central and South America plus the Caribbean as well as a country-by-country profile. [980]

7628 Gibson, Charles. *Spain in America* (10–12). Illus. 1966, Harper paper $7.95 (0-06-133077-9). This account traces the influence of Spain and Spanish culture on Latin America from colonial days to the present. [980]

7629 Needler, Martin C. *An Introduction to Latin American Politics: The Structure of Conflict* (10–12). 2nd ed. 1983, Prentice paper $27.80 (0-13-486035-7). This account of the political structure and problems of each Latin American country is current through the early 1980s. [980]

7630 Skidmore, Thomas E., and Peter H. Smith. *Modern Latin America* (10–12). 2nd ed. Illus. 1989, Oxford Univ. Pr. paper $14.95 (0-19-505534-9). This account explains the present (1989) political and economic conditions in Latin American countries and gives some predictions of possible future developments. [980]

7631 Swanson, Earl H., et al. *The Ancient Americas* (9–12). Illus. 1989, Bedrick $24.95 (0-87226-303-7); paper $16.95 (0-87226-214-6). An account that explores in words and pictures the Indian cultures of North and South America through the pre-Columbian period to the discovery of the New World. (Rev: BL 11/15/89) [970.01]

7632 Varner, John Grier, and Jeannette Johnson Varner. *Dogs of the Conquest* (10–12). 1983, Univ. of Oklahoma Pr. $22.95 (0-8061-1793-1). An unusual book that explains how dogs were used by the Spaniards to help their conquest of Latin America. [980]

North America

CANADA

7633 Berton, Pierre. *The Klondike Fever: The Life and Death of the Last Great Gold Rush* (10–12). Illus. 1959, Carroll & Graf paper $11.95 (0-88184-139-0). The story of the incredible gold stampede to the Yukon that began in 1896. [971.9]

7634 Fitzharris, Tim, and John Livingston. *Canada: A Natural History* (8–12). Illus. 1988, Viking $40.00 (0-670-82186-1). A stunning book that features both the geography and the wildlife of Canada. (Rev: BL 11/15/88) [508.71]

7635 Malcolm, Andrew H. *The Canadians* (10–12). Illus. 1985, Random $17.95 (0-8129-1158-X); Bantam paper $9.95 (0-553-34262-2). After a discussion of the geography and history of Canada, the author describes its people and how they see themselves as a national group. [971]

7636 Tanner, Ogden. *The Canadians* (7–12). Illus. 1977, Silver Burdett $25.93 (0-8094-1542-9). This book focuses its text and pictures on the early history of Canada until the end of the nineteenth century. Part of the Time-Life series on the Old West. [971]

7637 Thompson, Wayne C. *Canada 1988* (7–12). Illus. 1988, Stryker-Post paper $6.50 (0-943448-40-9). An oversize paperback that gives up-to-date information on the culture, geography, and people of Canada. (Rev: BL 2/1/86) [917.1]

7638 Time-Life Books, eds. *Canada* (9–12). Illus. 1988, Silver Burdett LB $19.45 (0-8094-5320-7). An attractive introduction to Canada covering its history, people, economy, and way of life. (Rev: BL 3–4/88) [971]

MEXICO

7639 Bazant, Jan. *A Concise History of Mexico from Hidalgo to Cardenas 1805–1940* (10–12). 1977, Cambridge Univ. Pr. paper $14.95 (0-521-29173-9). This history of modern Mexico covers all of the nineteenth century and the first half of the twentieth. [972]

7640 Coe, Michael D. *Mexico* (10–12). 3rd ed. Illus. 1986, Thames & Hudson paper $11.95 (0-550-27328-6). This is a cultural history of Mexico that ends with the arrival of the Spaniards. [972]

7641 Constable, George, ed. *Mexico* (7–12). Illus. 1985, Time-Life $13.20 (0-8094-5307-X). A clearly written, lavishly illustrated history, geography, and ethnographic survey of Mexico. (Rev: BR 3–4/86) [972]

7642 Diaz del Castillo, Bernal. *Cortez and the Conquest of Mexico by the Spaniards in 1521* (9–12). Illus. 1988, Linnet $17.50 (0-208-02221-1). In abridged form, this is the actual diary of a man who accompanied Cortez on his conquest of Mexico. (Rev: VOYA 2/89) [972]

7643 Fagan, Brian M. *The Aztecs* (10–12). Illus. 1984, W. H. Freeman paper $16.95 (0-7167-1585-6). This account covers over 200 years of Aztec culture until the destruction of their civilization by the Spaniards in the early 1500s. [972]

7644 Harvard Student Agencies. *Let's Go, 1990: The Budget Guide to Mexico* (9–12). 1989, St. Martin's paper $12.95 (0-312-03382-6). For the budget-conscious traveler, this is a practical guide to Mexico that contains material about the country and its people. (Rev: BL 2/1/85) [917.2]

7645 Lewis, Oscar. *The Children of Sanchez* (10–12). 1979, Random paper $11.95 (0-394-70280-8). Through first-person narratives, the members of a poor family in Mexico City are introduced. [972.08]

7646 Meyer, Carolyn, and Charles Gallenkamp. *The Mystery of the Ancient Maya* (10–12). Illus. 1985, Macmillan $12.95 (0-689-50319-9). The Maya Indians are introduced and what we know about their civilization is outlined. [972]

7647 Miller, Robert Ryal. *Mexico: A History* (10–12). Illus. 1985, Univ. of Oklahoma Pr. $19.95 (0-8061-1932-2); paper $12.95 (0-8061-2178-5). A multifaceted book that covers political, social, and cultural aspects of Mexican history from the early Indian civilizations to the present. (Rev: BL 9/1/85) [972]

7648 Riding, Alan. *Distant Neighbors: Portrait of the Mexicans* (10–12). 1985, Knopf $18.95 (0-394-50005-9); Random paper $8.95 (0-679-72441-9). After a brief history of Mexico, the author discusses Mexico's current problems such as overpopulation. (Rev: BL 1/1/85) [972.08]

7649 Sabloff, Jeremy A. *The Cities of Ancient Mexico: Reconstructing a Lost World* (10–12). Illus. 1989, Thames & Hudson $19.95 (0-500-05053-8). An archaeologist re-creates life in Mexico from 1000 B.C. to the coming of the Spaniards. (Rev: BL 3/15/89) [972.01]

7650 Stuart, George E., and Gene S. Stuart. *The Mysterious Maya* (10–12). Illus. 1977, National Geographic $7.95 (0-87044-233-3). An informal survey of what we know about the Mayas from their artifacts and living sites. [972]

OTHER CENTRAL AMERICAN LANDS

7651 Berryman, Phillip. *Inside Central America* (10–12). 1985, Pantheon paper $5.95 (0-394-72943-9). An account that covers developments in El Salvador, Nicaragua, Honduras, Guatemala, and Costa Rica through the mid-1980s. [972.8]

7652 Chace, James. *Endless War* (10–12). 1984, Random paper $4.95 (0-394-72779-7). Though now dated, this book gives good background information on America's changing role in the development of Central America. [972.8]

7653 Cheney, Glenn Alan. *Revolution in Central America* (10–12). Illus. 1984, Watts LB $12.90 (0-531-04761-X). This book gives coverage through the early 1980s of the conflicts in Central America. [972.8]

7654 Clements, Charles. *Witness to War: An American Doctor in El Salvador* (10–12). 1984, Bantam paper $4.50 (0-553-26779-5). A moving account of one year in the early 1980s spent by a Quaker doctor with guerrillas in El Salvador. [972.8]

7655 Gallenkamp, Charles. *Maya: The Riddle and Rediscovery of a Lost Civilization* (10–12). Illus. 1987, Penguin paper $7.95 (0-14-008831-8). This third version of the book that originally appeared in 1959 incorporates recent archaeological findings concerning the Maya. (Rev: BL 6/15/85) [972]

7656 Jenkins, Tony. *Nicaragua and the United States: Years of Conflict* (9–12). 1989, Watts LB $14.90 (0-531-10795-7). A history of U.S.-Nicaragua relations from 1853 to mid-1989, with special coverage on the Contras and the Sandinistas. (Rev: BL 12/1/89; SLJ 2/90) [327]

7657 Rolbein, Seth. *Nobel Costa Rica* (10–12). 1988, St. Martin's $16.95 (0-312-02262-X). A history of recent events in Costa Rica and how it is able to pursue its peaceful politics. (Rev: SLJ 3/89) [972.86]

7658 Wekesser, Carol, ed. *Central America: Opposing Viewpoints* (10–12). 1990, Greenhaven LB $15.95 (0-89908-484-2); paper $8.95 (0-89908-459-1). A recently revised edition of this collection of documents that express conflicting points of view about this area. [972.8]

7659 Woodward, Ralph Lee. *Central America: A Nation Divided* (10–12). 2nd ed. 1985, Oxford Univ. Pr. $32.00 (0-19-503592-5); paper $12.95 (0-19-503593-3). The story of the 5 Central American republics, their history and conflicts through 1985. [972.8]

PUERTO RICO, CUBA, AND OTHER CARIBBEAN ISLANDS

7660 Del Aguila, Juan M. *Cuba: Dilemmas of a Revolution* (10–12). Illus. 1988, Westview $35.50 (0-8133-0516-0); paper $12.95 (0-8133-0517-9). A history of Cuba, the Castro revolution, and current changes and problems. [972.91]

7661 Griffiths, John. *The Caribbean in the Twentieth Century* (8–12). Illus. 1985, Batsford $19.95 (0-7134-3839-8). A history of the Caribbean area that covers immigration, economic problems, and emerging democracies. (Rev: BL 6/15/85) [972.9]

7662 Knight, Franklin W. *The Caribbean: The Genesis of a Fragmented Nationalism* (10–12). 1990, Oxford Univ. Pr. $38.00 (0-19-505440-7); paper $14.95 (0-19-505441-5). A history of the Caribbean lands that focuses on their colonial period but also gives coverage on events before and after. [972.9]

7663 McCullough, David. *The Path between the Seas: The Creation of the Panama Canal* (10–12). Illus. 1978, Simon & Schuster paper $13.95 (0-671-24409-4). A history of the building of the canal from the first tries of de Lesseps to the opening in 1914. [972.87]

7664 Morales Carrión, Arturo. *Puerto Rico: A Political and Cultural History* (10–12). Illus. 1983, Norton paper $11.95 (0-393-30193-1). An extensive history of Puerto Rico from pre-Columbian times to 1980. [972.95]

7665 Suchlicki, Jaime. *Cuba: From Columbus to Castro* (10–12). Illus. 1990, Pergamon paper $16.95 (0-08-037450-6). A short, readable history of Cuba with extensive coverage on the events leading up to the revolution. [972.91]

7666 Wyden, Peter. *Bay of Pigs: The Untold Story* (10–12). Illus. 1980, Simon & Schuster paper $12.95 (0-671-25413-8). A behind-the-scenes look at this futile attempt to invade Cuba, and the people behind it. [972.91]

South America

7667 Allen, Benedict. *Who Goes Out in the Midday Sun? An Englishman's Trek through the Amazon Jungle* (10–12). Illus. 1986, Viking $18.95 (0-670-81032-0). An incredible adventurous odyssey through the Amazonian jungle. (Rev: BL 5/1/86; SLJ 11/86) [918.1]

7668 Bingham, Hiram. *Lost City of the Incas: The Story of Machu Picchu and Its Builders* (10–12). Illus. 1963, Macmillan paper $6.95 (0-689-70014-8). This account gives a history of Machu Picchu, its rediscovery in 1911, and how it has been excavated. [985]

7669 Cousteau, Jacques, and Mose Richards. *Jacques Cousteau's Amazon Journey* (9–12). Illus. 1984, Abrams $39.95 (0-8109-1813-7). The thrilling story of the exploration of the Amazon that took 18 months and an amazing variety of conveyances. (Rev: BL 3/15/85) [508.81]

7670 Cowell, Adrian. *The Decade of Destruction: The Crusade to Save the Amazon Rain Forest* (10–12). 1990, Henry Holt $19.95 (0-8050-1494-2). The tragedy of 10 years of government encroachment and private development that is spelling the end of the mighty Brazilian rain forest. (Rev: BL 9/15/90) [333.75]

7671 Donner, Florinda. *Shabano* (10–12). 1983, Dell paper $3.95 (0-440-38276-9). An anthropologist tells of an expedition into a remote South American jungle. [980]

7672 Garcia Marquez, Gabriel. *Clandestine in Chile: The Adventures of Miguel Littin* (10–12). Illus. 1987, Henry Holt $13.95 (0-8050-0322-3). The true story of Miguel Littin, a political exile from Chile after the death of Allende, who returned to his homeland disguised after a 12-year absence. (Rev: SLJ 8/87) [983]

7673 Hastings, Max, and Simon Jenkins. *The Battle for the Falklands* (10–12). Illus. 1983, Norton paper $10.70 (0-393-30198-2). A thorough account of the causes of the war and the military operations that ensued. [997]

7674 Hemming, John. *The Conquest of the Incas* (10–12). Illus. 1973, Harcourt paper $17.95 (0-15-622300-7). The story of the fall of the Inca Empire as caused by the Spanish conquest led by Pizarro and others. [985]

7675 Jennings, Jesse D., ed. *Ancient South Americans* (10–12). Illus. 1983, W. H. Freeman $31.95 (0-7167-1429-9). Using general geographic regions as a framework, the editor describes the early Indian cultures of South America. [980]

7676 Kane, Joe. *Running the Amazon* (9–12). Illus. 1989, Knopf $19.95 (0-394-55331-4). The story of the expedition that tried to be the first to traverse the Amazon from its source to its mouth. (Rev: BR 11–12/90; SLJ 2/90; VOYA 2/90) [981]

7677 Klein, Herbert S. *Bolivia: The Evolution of a Multi-Ethnic Society* (10–12). 1982, Oxford Univ. Pr. $29.95 (0-19-503011-7); paper $12.95 (0-19-503012-5). A history of Bolivia from 2500 B.C. to the present. [984]

7678 Lombardi, John V. *Venezuela: The Search for Order, the Dream of Progress* (10–12). Illus. 1982, Oxford Univ. Pr. $29.95 (0-19-503013-3). A scholarly history of Venezuela that points out the contrast in the agricultural and oil-related economies. [987]

7679 McIntyre, Loren. *Exploring South America* (9–12). Illus. 1990, Crown $40.00 (0-517-56134-4). A photographic journey exploring the wonders of the vast, varied continent of South America. (Rev: BL 7/90) [918]

7680 McIntyre, Loren. *The Incredible Incas and Their Timeless Land* (10–12). Illus. 1975, National Geographic LB $9.50 (0-87044-182-5). An examination of the Incas, their history and culture, and the destruction of their empire by the Spaniards. [985]

7681 Metraux, Alfred. *The History of the Incas* (10–12). Trans. by George Ordish. Illus. 1969, Schocken paper $9.95 (0-8052-0248-X). A history of the Inca empire that describes its origins, achievements, and decline. [985]

7682 Read, Piers Paul. *Alive: The Story of the Andes Survivors* (9–12). Illus. 1974, Harper $12.00 (0-397-01001-4); Avon paper $4.95 (0-380-00321-X). The harrowing story of a group of men and women who survived a plane crash in the Andes. [910.4]

7683 Rock, David. *Argentina, 1516–1982* (10–12). Illus. 1985, Univ. of California Pr. $40.00 (0-520-05189-0); paper $14.95 (0-520-06178-0). A general history of Argentina that emphasizes current history and problems. [982]

7684 Slatta, Richard W. *Cowboys of the Americas* (10–12). Illus. 1990, Yale Univ. Pr. $35.00 (0-300-04529-8). In addition to the American cowboy, Slatta looks at his counterpart in other countries such as the gaucho of Argentina. (Rev: BL 8/90) [978]

7685 Steadman, David, and Steven Zousmer. *Galapagos* (8–12). Illus. 1988, Smithsonian $24.95 (0-87474-882-8). A paleontologist follows in the footsteps of Darwin and describes life and fossils on these islands. (Rev: BR 9–10/88) [986.8]

7686 Strange, Ian J. *The Falklands: South Atlantic Islands* (7–12). Illus. 1985, Putnam LB $15.95 (0-396-08616-0). An introduction to the history and geography of the Falkland Islands with emphasis on how the people live in this severe environment. [997]

7687 Time-Life Books, eds. *Brazil* (9–12). Illus. 1987, Silver Burdett LB $19.45 (0-8094-5316-9). This well-illustrated volume covers the history, geography, and present social conditions in Brazil. [981]

7688 Timerman, Jacobo. *Prisoner without a Name, Cell without a Number* (10–12). 1981, Knopf $12.00 (0-394-51448-3); Random paper $3.95 (0-394-75131-0). The harrowing story of a political prisoner kept for 30 months in the jails of Argentina. [982]

Polar Regions

7689 Beattie, Owen, and John Geiger. *Frozen in Time: Unlocking the Secrets of the Franklin Expedition* (10–12). Illus. 1988, Dutton $18.95 (0-525-24685-1). An account of the ill-fated 1845 Arctic expedition and the strange disappearance of 2 British ships. (Rev: SLJ 3/89) [919.8]

7690 Berton, Pierre. *The Arctic Grail: The Quest for the Northwest Passage and the North Pole* (9–12). Illus. 1988, Viking $24.95 (0-670-82491-7). The story of the many adventurers who braved the unknown to explore the Arctic. (Rev: BL 10/15/88) [910]

7691 Bruemmer, Fred. *Arctic Animals: A Celebration of Survival* (9–12). Illus. 1987, North-Word $29.95 (0-942802-53-5). A beautiful volume dedicated to the fauna of the Arctic and how these animals live. (Rev: BL 9/1/87) [508.98]

7692 Bruemmer, Fred. *The Arctic World* (9–12). Illus. 1989, Crown $17.95 (0-517-67572-2). In text and photographs, this volume describes the Arctic and explains how animals, plants, and humans adjust to life here. [998]

7693 Burch, Ernest S., and Werner Forman. *The Eskimos* (9–12). Illus. 1988, Univ. of Oklahoma Pr. $22.50 (0-8061-2126-2). Color photographs highlight this account of the history, livelihood, and culture of the Eskimo. (Rev: BL 9/1/88) [306]

7694 Flegg, Jim, et al. *Poles Apart: The Natural Worlds of the Arctic and Antarctic* (9–12). Illus. 1990, Viking $29.95 (0-7207-1838-4). A lavishly illustrated guide to the 2 polar regions that covers geography as well as flora and fauna. (Rev: BL 6/15/90) [998]

7695 Freuchen, Peter. *Book of the Eskimos* (10–12). 1981, Fawcett paper $2.95 (0-449-30802-2). The author describes his life among the Eskimos. [970.004]

7696 Hosking, Eric. *Antarctic Wildlife* (10–12). Illus. 1983, Facts on File $24.95 (0-87196-679-4). This book discusses the general wildlife and ecology of Antarctica with specific details on the seabirds and seals. [591.9]

7697 Lopez, Barry. *Arctic Dreams: Imagination and Desire in a Northern Landscape* (10–12). Illus. 1986, Macmillan $22.50 (0-684-18578-4); Bantam paper $9.95 (0-553-34664-4). For better readers, an account of the history, ecology, and mystique of the arctic region. (Rev: BL 1/1/86) [508.98]

7698 Lopez, Barry. *Crossing Open Ground* (10–12). 1988, Macmillan $17.95 (0-684-18817-1). In most of these essays, the author returns to the subarctic, the scene of his highly successful *Arctic Dreams* (1986). (Rev: BL 6/1/88) [818]

7699 May, John. *The Greenpeace Book of Antarctica: A New View of the Seventh Continent* (9–12). Illus. 1989, Doubleday $24.95 (0-385-26280-9). Members of the environmental organization contributed both illustrations and text to this book, written to help preserve the continent. (Rev: BL 2/1/90) [919.8]

7700 Mickleburgh, Edwin. *Beyond the Frozen Sea: Visions of Antarctica* (10–12). Illus. 1988, St. Martin's $22.50 (0-312-01561-5). A history of the exploration of Antarctica beginning with Captain Cook's voyage 200 years ago. (Rev: BL 2/15/88) [998]

7701 Mowat, Farley. *The People of the Deer* (10–12). 1981, Bantam paper $3.50 (0-7704-2079-6). An account of the author's stay with a forgotten Eskimo tribe. A sequel is *The Desperate People* (1981). [970.004]

7702 Mowat, Farley. *The Snow Walker* (10–12). 1989, Bantam paper $3.95 (0-7704-2209-8). For better readers, this is a collection of lore, fact, and fiction about the Arctic region. [919.8]

7703 Murphy, Joseph E. *South to the Pole by Ski* (9–12). Illus. 1990, MarLor $19.95 (0-943400-49-X). A report on an 11-person skiing expedition to the South Pole. (Rev: BL 8/90) [919.8]

7704 Parfit, Michael. *South Light: A Journey to the Last Continent* (9–12). 1986, Macmillan $16.95 (0-02-594730-3). An account of the author's trip to Antarctica and of the people and animal life he encountered there. (Rev: BL 1/1/86) [919.8]

7705 Ruesch, Hans. *Top of the World* (10–12). 1986, Pocket paper $2.95 (0-671-63754-1). A story of adventure and danger among the Polar Eskimos. [970.004]

7706 Schurke, Paul. *Bering Bridge: The Soviet-American Expedition from Siberia to Alaska* (9–12). Illus. 1990, Pfeifer $17.95 (0-938586-31-9). High adventure in this account of a group of Russians and Americans (some of whom were Eskimos) and their Arctic expedition from Siberia to Alaska. (Rev: SLJ 7/90) [919.8]

7707 Senungetuk, Vivian, and Paul Tiulana. *A Place for Winter: Paul Tiulana's Story* (7–12). Illus. 1988, CIRI Foundation $15.95 (0-938227-02-5). The story of a King Island Eskimo boy, his childhood, and his people. (Rev: BL 5/15/88) [917.98]

7708 Steger, Wil, and Paul Schurke. *North to the Pole* (9–12). 1987, Times Books $19.95 (0-8129-1704-9); Ivy paper $4.95 (0-8041-0407-7). The story of the 55-day expedition by 7 men and one woman to the North Pole in 1986. (Rev: SLJ 4/88) [998]

7709 Vaughan, Norman D., and Cecil Murphey. *With Byrd at the Bottom of the World* (10–12). 1990, Stackpole $19.95 (0-8117-1904-9). A recreation of the Byrd expedition to the South Pole by the man who tended the dogs during this stressful trek. (Rev: BL 10/1/90) [919]

United States

General History and Geography

7710 Allen, Frederick L. *The Big Change: America Transforms Itself, 1900–1950* (10–12). 1983, Greenwood $35.00 (0-313-23791-3); Harper paper $7.95 (0-06-132082-X). This popular history traces some of the important movements and events in this 60-year period of American history. [973.91]

7711 Appelbaum, Diana Karter. *The Glorious Fourth: An American Holiday, an American History* (8–12). Illus. 1989, Facts on File $19.95 (0-8160-1767-0). A history of the Fourth of July celebrations from the signing of the Declaration of Independence through the centennial of the Statue of Liberty. (Rev: BR 11–12/89) [973]

7712 Ashabranner, Brent. *The Vanishing Border: A Photographic Journey Along Our Frontier with Mexico* (10–12). Illus. 1987, Dodd $14.95 (0-396-08900-3). A description in text and dramatic photos of the people and land surrounding the 2,000-mile border between the United States and Mexico. (Rev: BL 2/1/88; SLJ 2/88) [979]

7713 Baron, Robert, ed. *Soul of America* (9–12). 1989, Fulcrum $24.95 (1-55591-047-5). A fine collection of documents on American history that begins in 1492 and ends with Nixon's resignation speech of 1974. (Rev: SLJ 2/90) [973]

7714 Baxandall, Rosalyn, et al., eds. *America's Working Women* (10–12). 1987, Random paper $12.95 (0-394-72208-6). A history of working women in our country from the colonial period to the present told in excerpts from original sources. [331.4]

7715 Berth, Jack, et al. *Roadside America* (9–12). Illus. 1986, Simon & Schuster paper $10.95 (0-671-60688-3). A trivia-filled odyssey across America that tells the reader, for example, where to see the world's largest twine ball and how to locate the Lawrence Welk museum. (Rev: BL 7/86) [917.73]

7716 Boorstin, Daniel J., ed. *An American Primer* (7–12). 1968, NAL paper $7.95 (0-452-00922-7). Eighty-three documents vital to our history are reproduced plus accompanying background articles. [973]

7717 Boorstin, Daniel J. *The Americans: The Democratic Experience* (10–12). 1973, Random paper $10.95 (0-394-71011-8). This is the third volume of the author's trilogy on American civilization and how it developed. The two earlier volumes are: *The Americans: The Colonial Experience* (1959) and *The Americans: The National Experience* (1965). [973]

7718 Bruchey, Stuart. *The Wealth of the Nation: An Economic History of the United States* (10–12). 1988, Harper $16.95 (0-06-015854-9); paper $6.95 (0-06-091455-6). A popularly written economic history of the United States that begins with the Colonial period. (Rev: BL 1/15/88) [330.973]

7719 Burns, James MacGregor. *The Workshop of Democracy* (10–12). 1985, Knopf $24.95 (0-394-51275-8); paper $12.95 (0-394-74320-2). In the first volume of his history of the United States, *The Vineyard of Liberty* (1981), the author ended before the Civil War. In this volume the story is continued to the Great Depression. A striking and truly monumental work. (Rev: BL 9/1/85) [973.2]

7720 Carruth, Gorton, ed. *The Encyclopedia of American Facts and Dates* (9–12). 1987, Harper $35.00 (0-06-181143-2). In 4 parallel columns, each covering a different aspect of American life (e.g., the arts, politics), a chronology of American history is presented. [973.03]

7721 Commager, Henry Steele. *The American Mind* (10–12). 1950, Yale Univ. Pr. paper $14.95 (0-300-00046-4). In this series of essays first published in 1950, the author traces influences on the development of American society. [973]

7722 Commager, Henry Steele. *Documents of American History* (10–12). 1988, Prentice $36.00 (0-13-217274-7). This volume covers 1492 to 1898, and the second volume from 1899 to the 1970s; together they total 670 important documents, each with its own introduction. [973]

7723 Cooke, Alistair. *Alistair Cooke's America* (10–12). Illus. 1977, Knopf paper $24.95 (0-394-73449-1). In a series of essays and many accompanying pictures, an informal history of this country is given. [973]

7724 Cremin, Lawrence A. *American Education: The National Experience, 1783–1876* (10–12). 1980, Harper $34.50 (0-06-010912-2); paper $11.50 (0-06-090921-8). Defining education broadly to include the role of such institutions as the family and mass media, this is a history of American culture from 1783 to 1876. Preceded by *American Education, the American Experience: 1607–1783* (1970). [370.9]

7725 Crump, Donald J., ed. *America's Hidden Corners: Places off the Beaten Path* (9–12). Illus. 1983, National Geographic LB $9.50 (0-87044-446-8). Areas such as Chesapeake Bay and the Badlands are pictured in photographs and text in this volume devoted to unusual spots in America. [917.3]

7726 Crump, Donald J., ed. *America's Magnificent Mountains* (9–12). Illus. 1980, National Geographic LB $9.50 (0-87044-286-4). In text and impressive photographs, the wonders of America's mountain ranges are pictured. [917]

7727 Crump, Donald J., ed. *America's Majestic Canyons* (9–12). Illus. 1979, National Geographic LB $9.50 (0-87044-276-7). This lavishly illustrated volume describes the flora and fauna of some of North America's most beautiful canyons. [917]

7728 Crump, Donald J., ed. *America's Wild and Scenic Rivers* (9–12). Illus. 1983, National Geographic LB $9.50 (0-87044-445-X). A look at some of the rivers of the United States that are off the beaten track. [917.3]

7729 Current, Richard N., et al. *The Essentials of American History* (10–12). Illus. 1986, McGraw paper $17.95 (0-07-554977-8). A fine basic history of the United States by a series of specialists. [973]

7730 Davis, Kenneth C. *Don't Know Much about History: Everything You Need to Know about American History but Never Learned* (9–12). 1990, Crown $24.95 (0-517-57706-2). Basic facts about American history are given and myths and misconceptions exposed. (Rev: BL 6/15/90; SLJ 10/90) [973]

7731 DeBarr, Candice M., and Jack A. Bonkowske. *Saga of the American Flag: An Illustrated History* (8–12). Illus. 1990, Harbinger paper $9.95 (0-943173-65-5). An illustrated history of our flag that covers over 200 years. (Rev: BL 5/15/90; SLJ 9/90) [929.9]

7732 Dickson, Paul. *Library in America: A Celebration in Words and Pictures* (10–12). Illus. 1986, Facts on File $40.00 (0-8160-1365-9); paper $19.95 (0-8160-1887-1). A handsome volume on the history of libraries in the United States with an emphasis on the public library. (Rev: VOYA 4/87) [027]

7733 Evans, Sara M. *Born for Liberty: A History of Women in America* (10–12). Illus. 1989, Free Press $24.95 (0-02-902990-2). A history of the changing roles and status of women in America from the seventeenth century through the 1980s. (Rev: SLJ 4/90) [305.4]

7734 Frost, Elizabeth, ed. *The Bully Pulpit: Quotations from America's Presidents* (9–12). 1988, Facts on File $23.95 (0-8160-1247-4). Organized by subjects such as "defense" and "liberty," here is a collection of memorable quotations from our presidents. (Rev: BR 5–6/88) [973]

7735 Gardner, John W. *On Leadership* (10–12). Illus. 1989, Free Press $19.95 (0-02-911311-3). Using many examples from the past, the author outlines the qualities of leadership and the lack of proper leadership in America today. (Rev: SLJ 6/90) [973]

7736 Garraty, John A. *1,001 Things Everyone Should Know about American History* (9–12). Illus. 1989, Doubleday $19.95 (0-385-24432-0). Arranged by subjects such as politics and presidents this is a fascinating compendium of facts. (Rev: BL 4/15/89; SLJ 7/89) [973]

7737 Garreau, Joel. *The Nine Nations of North America* (10–12). 1982, Avon paper $9.95 (0-380-57885-9). This provocative book regroups the areas of North America into divisions according to economic and social resources and needs. [970]

7738 Genovese, Eugene D. *Roll, Jordan, Roll: The World the Slaves Made* (10–12). 1976, Random paper $16.95 (0-394-71652-3). This is a history of slavery in America that concentrates on the daily life and traditions of slaves. [305.8]

7739 Glackens, Ira. *Did Molly Pitcher Say That? The Men and Women Who Made American History* (9–12). Illus. 1989, Writers & Readers $18.95 (0-86316-097-2); paper $8.95 (0-86316-094-8). An informal view of American history with several amusing and fascinating sidelights. (Rev: BL 9/15/89) [973]

7740 Graham, Otis L., Jr. *The Great Campaigns: Reform and War in America, 1900–1928* (10–12). Illus. 1971, Krieger paper $9.95 (0-89464-204-9). This history covers the many dramatic changes that occurred in America during the first 3 decades of the twentieth century. [973.91]

7741 Grob, Gerald N., and George Athan Billias, eds. *Interpretations of American History: Patterns and Perspectives* (10–12). 5th ed. 1987, Free Pr. paper $13.95 ea (vol. 1: 0-02-911850-6; vol. 2: 0-02-911890-5). The first volume of this frequently updated set covers the period to 1877 and the second from that time to modern times. [973]

7742 Gutman, Herbert G. *The Black Family in Slavery and Freedom, 1750–1925* (10–12). 1977, Random paper $16.95 (0-394-72451-8). From original documents, Gutman has re-created the life of a black American family during and after slavery. [305.8]

7743 Harding, Vincent. *There Is a River: The Black Struggle for Freedom in America* (10–12). 1981, Harcourt $19.95 (0-15-189342-X); Random paper $10.00 (0-394-71148-3). This account traces the history of black Americans from their origins in Africa to freedom at the end of the Civil War. [305.8]

7744 Harvard Student Agencies. *Let's Go, 1990: The Budget Guide to the USA* (9–12). 1989, St. Martin's paper $12.95 (0-312-03385-0). Aimed at a student audience, this practical guide shows you how to see the United States on a tight budget. (Rev: BL 2/1/85) [917.3]

7745 Hawkins, Gary. *U.S.A. by Bus and Train* (10–12). 1985, Pantheon paper $9.95 (0-394-72123-2). Twenty-seven tours are outlined in this guidebook for people who have time but little money and want to see the United States. (Rev: BL 5/15/85) [917.3]

7746 Heffner, Richard D. *A Documentary History of the United States* (9–12). 1952, NAL paper $4.95 (0-451-62413-0). A basic collection of documents related to important events in American history. [973]

7747 Hofstadter, Richard. *The Age of Reform from Bryan to F.D.R.* (10–12). 1955, Knopf $16.95 (0-394-41442-X); paper $7.95 (0-394-70095-3). This prize-winning history covers the many reform movements in American history from 1890 through 1940. [973.91]

7748 Hofstadter, Richard. *The American Political Tradition, and the Men Who Made It* (10–12). 1973, Random $24.95 (0-394-48880-6); paper $9.95 (0-679-72315-3). Twelve essays are included about influential Americans from Jefferson to Franklin Delano Roosevelt. [973]

7749 Howarth, W., et al. *America's Wild Woodlands* (9–12). Illus. 1985, National Geographic LB $9.50 (0-87044-547-2). From the flowering trees of the East to the West's sequoias, this is a description of the wonders of America's forests. [917.3]

7750 Hymowitz, Carol, and Michaele Weissman. *A History of Women in America* (10–12). 1984, Bantam paper $5.95 (0-553-26914-3). This is the story of the roles played by women in American history, from the frontier to fighting in modern wars. [973]

7751 *Images of America: A Panorama of History in Photographs* (9–12). Illus. 1989, Smithsonian Inst. $39.95 (0-89599-023-7). A history of the United States as seen through the eyes of our great photographers. (Rev: BL 9/15/89) [973]

7752 Jensen, Oliver, et al. *American Album* (9–12). Illus. 1985, Houghton paper $19.95 (0-8281-3075-2). A collection of early photographs that depict life in the United States from the 1840s into the twentieth century. [917.3]

7753 Johnson, Thomas H. *The Oxford Companion to American History* (10–12). 1966, Oxford Univ. Pr. $49.95 (0-19-500597-X). This alphabetically arranged handbook contains entries for people, places, events, and movements. [973.03]

7754 Kohn, George C. *Encyclopedia of American Scandal* (9–12). 1990, Facts on File paper $19.95 (0-8160-2169-4). A source of information on the social and political scandals that have rocked the United States, including sensational murder cases, Watergate, Abscam, and the Iran Contra affair. (Rev: VOYA 8/90) [352]

7755 Kuralt, Charles. *On the Road with Charles Kuralt* (9–12). Illus. 1985, Putnam $16.95 (0-399-13087-X); Fawcett paper $5.95 (0-449-13067-3). This volume contains about 100 interviews conducted by this popular CBS commentator collected on his travels around the United States. [973.92]

7756 LaFeber, Walter. *The American Age: United States Foreign Policy at Home and Abroad since 1750* (10–12). Illus. 1989, Norton $25.00 (0-393-02629-9). A lucid account of America's developing foreign policy from before the Revolution to the present. (Rev: SLJ 9/89) [973]

7757 Levine, Michael. *The New Address Book: How to Reach Anyone Who's Anyone* (9–12). 3rd ed. 1986, Putnam paper $8.95 (0-399-51287-X). A telephone directory of famous people, organizations, and corporations. (Rev: BL 12/1/86) [973]

7758 Maddocks, Melvin. *The Atlantic Crossing* (7–12). Illus. 1981, Silver Burdett $21.72 (0-8094-2727-3). A history of the voyages to America from early history to the present. [387.5]

7759 Manchester, William. *The Glory and the Dream* (10–12). 1974, Little $35.00 (0-316-54496-5); Bantam paper $15.95 (0-553-34285-1). This volume covers 50 years of American history from the Great Depression to Richard Nixon's second term. [973.9]

7760 Matloff, Maurice. *American Wars and Heroes: Revolutionary War through Vietnam* (9–12). 1985, Arco $19.95 (0-688-06315-7). A history of the U.S. military through 9 major wars. (Rev: BR 9–10/85) [973]

7761 Mohlenbrock, Robert H. *The Field Guide to U.S. National Forests* (10–12). Illus. 1984, Congdon & Weed paper $11.95 (0-312-92206-X). A region-by-region description of our national forests that includes details on subjects like accommodations and special features. [917.3]

7762 Morison, Samuel Eliot. *The Growth of the American Republic* (10–12). Illus. 1930, Oxford Univ. Pr. $28.00 (0-19-502593-8). This is the first volume of a 2-volume set (volume two was published in 1980) that traces the political, social, and cultural history of the United States. [973]

7763 Morison, Samuel Eliot. *The Oxford History of the American People* (10–12). Illus. 1965, Oxford Univ. Pr. $39.95 (0-19-500030-7). An extremely readable history of America from prehistory to the death of President Kennedy. This book is also available in a set of 3 paperbacks published by NAL. [973]

7764 Morison, Samuel Eliot, et al. *A Concise History of the American Republic* (10–12). 2nd ed. Illus. 1983, Oxford Univ. Pr. $49.95 (0-19-503179-2); paper $24.95 (0-19-503180-6). This is a concise, authoritative history of America. [973]

7765 Morris, Richard B., ed. *Basic Documents in American History* (10–12). 1980, Krieger paper $8.50 (0-89874-202-1). These documents and their introductions cover the period from 1620 to the 1960s. [973]

7766 Morris, Richard B., ed. *Encyclopedia of American History* (9–12). Illus. 1982, Harper $29.45 (0-06-181605-1). In addition to a general chronology of American history there are also chronologies on specific subjects like science plus a brief biographical dictionary. [973.03]

7767 Mowry, George E. *The Urban Nation, 1920–1980* (10–12). 1981, Hill & Wang $17.95 (0-8090-9541-6); paper $9.95 (0-8090-0148-9). A 60-year history of modern America as seen through the growth of cities and an economy based on mass production. [973.9]

7768 National Geographic Society, eds. *Preserving America's Past* (9–12). Illus. 1983, National Geographic LB $9.50 (0-87044-420-4). This volume highlights attempts to preserve America's past by restoring buildings, relearning crafts, and similar activities. [973]

7769 National Park Foundation. *The Complete Guide to America's National Parks* (9–12). 1988, Prentice paper $9.95 (0-13-159915-5). This is the official guide to America's national parks as prepared by the National Park Foundation. [719]

7770 Nevins, Allan, and Henry Steele Commager. *A Pocket History of the United States* (9–12). 1986, Pocket paper $5.95 (0-671-63268-X). A broad overview of American history from its beginnings to the 1980s. [973]

7771 Pern, Stephen. *The Great Divide: A Walk Through America along the Continental Divide* (10–12). Illus. 1988, Viking $17.95 (0-670-82100-4). A fascinating 2,500-mile, 7-month trek from Mexico to Canada. (Rev: BL 6/1/88) [917.3]

7772 Reader's Digest, eds. *America's Historic Places: An Illustrated Guide to Our Country's Past* (9–12). Illus. 1988, Reader's Digest $26.95 (0-89577-265-5). A guided tour in words and pictures to 500 places important in our past. (Rev: BL 5/15/88) [917.3]

7773 Reader's Digest, eds. *Our National Parks: America's Spectacular Wilderness Heritage* (9–12). Illus. 1985, Reader's Digest $26.95 (0-89577-197-7). A handsome, oversized volume with splendid photographs that toasts the beauty of our national parks. (Rev: BL 6/1/85) [917.3]

7774 Reader's Digest, eds. *Reader's Digest Strange Stories, Amazing Facts of America's Past* (9–12). Illus. 1989, Reader's Digest $30.95 (0-89577-307-4). A collection of unusual facts and anecdotes about the famous and infamous in American history with a chronological index by month and year. (Rev: BL 11/1/89) [973]

7775 Schlesinger, Arthur M., Jr., ed. *The Almanac of American History* (9–12). Illus. 1983, Putnam $24.95 (0-399-12853-0); paper $10.95 (0-399-51082-6). A chronological survey of American history to 1982. [973.02]

7776 Scott, John Anthony. *The Story of America* (7–12). Illus. 1984, National Geographic LB $21.95 (0-87044-535-9). A profusely illustrated history of the United States from prehistory to after the Vietnam War. [973]

7777 Shenkman, Richard. *Legends, Lies, and Cherished Myths of American History* (8–12). 1988, Morrow $15.95 (0-688-06580-5). Hitherto believed "truths" about American history from the colonial period to President Reagan are revealed as myths. (Rev: BL 11/1/88) [973]

7778 Steinbeck, John. *Travels with Charley: In Search of America* (9–12). 1987, Penguin paper $4.95 (0-14-005320-4). This book, which first appeared in 1962, is a description of a cross-country trip by Steinbeck and his pet dog in a truck trailer. [973]

7779 Sterling, Dorothy, ed. *We Are Your Sisters: Black Women in the Nineteenth Century* (10–12). 1984, Norton paper $12.95 (0-393-30252-0). Using a variety of sources, this is an account of the experiences of black women during the nineteenth century in America. [305.4]

7780 Stewart, George R. *American Place-Names: A Concise and Selective Dictionary for the Continental United States of America* (9–12). 1985, Oxford Univ. Pr. $29.95 (0-19-503725-1); paper $9.95 (0-19-500121-4). In dictionary format, the origins of 12,000 American place-names are given with information on their location. [917.3]

7781 Tiede, Tom. *American Tapestry: Eyewitness Accounts of the Twentieth Century* (9–12). 1988, Pharos $19.95 (0-88687-359-2). An oral history collection involving many aspects of American life as recalled by people born around the turn of the century. (Rev: BL 11/1/88) [973.9]

7782 Time-Life Books, eds. *This Fabulous Century* (9–12). Illus. 1990, Silver Burdett LB $23.95 (0-8094-5758-X). Through pictures and text, this volume re-creates life in the United States during the first decade of the twentieth century. Each of the succeeding 6 volumes in this Time-Life set deals with another decade, ending with 1960–1970. Each is available through Silver Burdett at $23.95. [973.9]

7783 Time-Life Books, eds. *The United States* (8–12). Illus. 1984, Silver Burdett LB $25.93 (0-8094-5303-7). A lavishly illustrated introduction to the United States—its history, geography, and people. [917]

7784 Tindall, George Brown. *America: A Narrative History* (10–12). Illus. 1984, Norton $22.95 (0-393-95435-8). A historical narrative that traces the history of America from before Columbus to the administration of President Reagan. [973]

7785 Venion, S., et al. *Exploring America's Scenic Highways* (9–12). Illus. 1985, National Geographic LB $9.50 (0-87044-278-3). A celebration of America's colorful highways in words and pictures. [917.3]

7786 *Wilderness U.S.A.* (9–12). Illus. 1973, National Geographic $9.95 (0-87044-116-7). An overview of the nation's most important wilderness areas from the Sierra Nevadas to Alaska. [574.9]

7787 Woodward, C. Vann. *The Future of the Past* (10–12). 1989, Oxford Univ. Pr. $24.95 (0-19-505744-9). For better students, this account relates present conditions in America to the past. (Rev: SLJ 3/90) [973]

Historical Periods

PREHISTORY

7788 Chamberlain, John. *The Enterprising Americans: A Business History of the United States* (10–12). Illus. 1974, Harper $16.45 (0-06-010702-2). An exciting history of American business beginning with colonial times that includes short sketches of important figures. [330.973]

INDIANS OF NORTH AMERICA

7789 Ashabranner, Brent. *Morning Star, Black Sun: The Northern Cheyenne Indians and America's Energy Crisis* (9–12). Illus. 1982, Putnam $11.95 (0-396-08045-6). A history of the Northern Cheyenne Indians that focuses on the discovery of coal on their reservation and the conflict between gaining wealth and destroying their land. [970.004]

7790 Ashabranner, Brent. *To Live in Two Worlds: American Indian Youth Today* (7–12). Illus. 1984, Putnam LB $13.95 (0-396-08321-8). The story of the dilemma of young American Indians who are forced to live in 2 conflicting cultures. [970.004]

7791 Bancroft-Hunt, Norman, and Werner Forman. *The Indians of the Great Plains* (9–12). Illus. 1989, Bedrick $19.95 (0-87226-198-0). A history of the Plains Indians that covers their migrations, different tribes, and their treatment by the white men. (Rev: BR 3–4/90; VOYA 4/90) [940.004]

7792 Bancroft-Hunt, Norman, and Werner Forman. *People of the Totem: Indians of the Pacific Northwest* (9–12). Illus. 1989, Bedrick $19.95 (0-87226-199-9). A history of the Indians that lived from the coast of Alaska down to the mouth of the Columbia River. (Rev: BR 3–4/90; VOYA 4/90) [940.004]

7793 Beal, Merrill D. *I Will Fight No More Forever* (10–12). 1985, Ballantine paper $4.95 (0-345-32131-6). The last fighting days of Chief Joseph and the Nez Perce Indians. [970.004]

7794 Berkhofer, Robert F., Jr. *The White Man's Indian: Images of the American Indian from Co-*

lumbus to the Present (10–12). 1979, Random paper $8.76 (0-394-72794-0). A history of the stereotyping of the American Indian by whites and how it exists even today. [970.004]

7795 Brandon, William. *The American Heritage Book of Indians* (9–12). 1982, Crown $17.95 (0-517-39180-5). This handsomely illustrated volume covers the history of the American Indian from prehistoric times to the present. [970.004]

7796 Brown, Dee. *Bury My Heart at Wounded Knee: An Indian History of the American West* (10–12). 1971, Henry Holt $24.95 (0-8050-1045-9). The story of the white man's conquest of the Old West told from the Indians' point of view. [970.004]

7797 Capps, Benjamin. *The Great Chiefs* (7–12). Illus. 1975, Silver Burdett LB $25.95 (0-8094-1493-7). The lives of the great Indian chiefs of the Old West are examined in text and many illustrations. [920]

7798 Capps, Benjamin. *The Indians* (7–12). Illus. 1973, Silver Burdett LB $25.93 (0-8094-1455-4). An excellently illustrated account of the history and culture of American western Indians and their relations with white men. [970.004]

7799 Coe, Michael D., et al. *Atlas of Ancient America* (10–12). Illus. 1986, Facts on File $45.00 (0-8160-1199-0). A colorful collection of maps and other illustrations plus a comprehensive text explore the various Indian groups and their homelands. (Rev: BL 1/1/87; SLJ 3/87) [970]

7800 Coolidge, Grace. *Teepee Neighbors* (10–12). 1984, Univ. of Oklahoma Pr. paper $7.95 (0-8061-1889-X). First published in 1917, this is a collection of stories by a white missionary about the Indians of Wyoming. [970.004]

7801 Council on Interracial Books for Children. *Chronicles of American Indian Protest* (10–12). 2nd rev. ed. 1971, The Council paper $7.95 (0-930040-30-9). This collection of documents covers the struggle for freedom and land of the American Indian from 1622 to 1978. [970.004]

7802 Debo, Angie. *A History of the Indians of the United States* (10–12). Illus. 1984, Univ. of Oklahoma Pr. paper $14.95 (0-8061-1888-1). A history of native North Americans (including Eskimos) with coverage that extends into modern times. [970.004]

7803 Deloria, Vine, Jr. *Custer Died for Your Sins* (10–12). 1988, Univ. of Oklahoma Pr. paper $9.95 (0-8061-2129-7). Using history as a focus, the author writes with passion for better treatment of the American Indian. [970.004]

7804 Deloria, Vine, Jr., and Clifford M. Lytle. *American Indians, American Justice* (10–12). 1983, Univ. of Texas Pr. paper $9.95 (0-292-73834-X). A history of the U.S. government's involvement with the legal affairs of American Indians. [970.004]

7805 Dutton, Bertha P. *American Indians of the Southwest* (10–12). Rev. ed. Illus. 1983, Univ. of New Mexico Pr. paper $15.95 (0-8263-0704-3). An overview of the history and present conditions of the Pueblos, Athabascans, Utes, and other Native Americans of the Southwest. [970.004]

7806 Ehle, John. *Trail of Tears: The Rise and Fall of the Cherokee Nation* (10–12). Illus. 1988, Doubleday $19.95 (0-385-23953-X). The heartbreaking story of the forced relocation of over 18,000 Cherokee in 1838. (Rev: BL 11/15/88) [975]

7807 Fronval, George, and Daniel Dubois. *Indian Signs and Signals* (9–12). Trans. by E. W. Egan. Illus. 1985, Crown $8.98 (0-517-46612-0). In thorough text and many illustrations, this book describes the sign language of the Plains Indian. [001.56]

7808 Hagan, William T. *American Indians* (10–12). 1979, Univ. of Chicago Pr. paper $8.95 (0-226-31235-6). A broad-based history of the American Indian from first encounters with white men to the present. [970.004]

7809 Hungry Wolf, Adolf, and Beverly Hungry Wolf. *Children of the Sun: Stories by and about Indian Kids* (10–12). Illus. 1987, Morrow $13.95 (0-688-06782-4). This book is a celebration of Indian history and folklore with information on customs and traditions. (Rev: BL 1/15/87) [970]

7810 Iverson, Peter, ed. *The Plains Indians of the Twentieth Century* (10–12). Illus. 1985, Univ. of Oklahoma Pr. $22.95 (0-8061-1866-0); paper $10.95 (0-8061-1959-4). Recent developments are outlined in the present status of such tribes as the Cheyenne, Sioux, Comanche, and Crow. [970.004]

7811 Jennings, Jesse D., ed. *Ancient North Americans* (10–12). Illus. 1983, W. H. Freeman $31.95 (0-7167-1428-0). This is a 30,000-year history of the North American Indian prior to the arrival of the white man. [970.004]

7812 Josephy, Alvin M., Jr. *The Indian Heritage of America* (10–12). Illus. 1968, Knopf $27.00 (0-394-43049-2); paper $6.50 (0-394-30315-6). This is a fine survey of the cultures and history of the Native Americans of North, Central, and South America. [970.004]

7813 Josephy, Alvin M., Jr. *Now That the Buffalo's Gone* (10–12). Illus. 1982, Knopf $25.00 (0-394-46672-1). With a certain amount of necessary background history included, this is essentially an account of the present status of the American Indian. [970.004]

7814 Josephy, Alvin M., Jr. *Red Power* (10–12). 1985, Univ. of Nebraska Pr. paper $7.50 (0-8032-7563-3). This is a history of the fight for justice and freedom of the American Indian. [970.004]

7815 Katz, Jane B., ed. *I Am the Fire of Time: The Voices of Native American Women* (10–12). Illus. 1977, Dutton paper $6.95 (0-525-47475-7). An anthology of writing by American Indian women illustrated with many photographs. [970.004]

7816 Mails, Thomas E. *Fools Crow* (10–12). Illus. 1990, Univ. of Nebraska Pr. paper $9.95 (0-8032-8174-9). The ceremonial chief of the Teton Sioux Indians describes the changes imposed on his people during the twentieth century. [970.004]

7817 Marriott, Alice. *The Ten Grandmothers* (10–12). 1983, Univ. of Oklahoma Pr. paper $11.95 (0-8061-1825-3). This is a readable history of the Kiowa Indians from 1847 to 1940. [970.004]

7818 Matthiessen, Peter. *Indian Country* (10–12). 1984, Penguin paper $9.95 (0-14-013023-3). The story of 12 American Indian groups and their fight to retain their own lands. [970.004]

7819 Nabokov, Peter, ed. *Two Leggings: The Making of a Crow Warrior* (10–12). 1982, Univ. of Nebraska Pr. paper $7.95 (0-8032-8351-2). An account that describes the culture and customs of the Crow Indians. [970.004]

7820 Rawls, James. *Indians of California: The Changing Image* (10–12). Illus. 1984, Univ. of Oklahoma Pr. $26.95 (0-8061-1874-1); paper $9.95 (0-8061-2020-7). A thoughtful account that traces through history the attitudes of white people toward the native Indian tribes of California. [970.004]

7821 Reader's Digest, eds. *America's Fascinating Indian Heritage* (9–12). Illus. 1981, Reader's Digest $24.95 (0-89577-019-9). This pictorial history examines the life of American Indians from many regions and their differing cultures. [970.004]

7822 Sandoz, Mari. *Cheyenne Autumn* (10–12). Illus. 1976, Avon paper $4.95 (0-380-01094-1). The heartbreaking saga of the Cheyenne Indian trek in 1878 back to their home in Yellowstone. [970.004]

7823 Schultz, James W. *My Life as an Indian* (10–12). 1981, Fawcett paper $7.95 (0-449-

90057-6). In the 1880s, a New Englander goes to live with the Blackfeet Indians. [970.004]

7824 Spencer, Robert F. *The Native Americans* (10–12). 2nd ed. Illus. 1977, Harper $46.50 (0-06-046371-6). A history of the various groupings of American Indians and their cultural development. [970.004]

7825 Underhill, Ruth M. *The Navajos* (10–12). Illus. 1983, Univ. of Oklahoma Pr. $11.95 (0-8061-1816-4). This comprehensive history of the Navaho tribe and their humiliations at the hands of white men was first published in 1956. [970.004]

7826 Waldman, Carl. *Atlas of the North American Indian* (9–12). Illus. 1985, Facts on File $29.95 (0-87196-850-9). Maps and accompanying essays give an excellent introduction to the history, culture, and present-day status of the American Indian. (Rev: BL 1/15/86) [970]

7827 Washburn, Wilcomb E. *The Indian in America* (10–12). Illus. 1975, Harper $19.95 (0-06-014534-X); paper $8.95 (0-06-131855-8). A history that traces the change from American Indian to Indian American. [970.004]

7828 Weatherford, Jack. *Indian Givers: How the Indians of the Americas Transformed the World* (9–12). 1988, Crown $17.95 (0-517-56969-8). A discussion of the many contributions that the Indians have made to world culture and society. (Rev: BL 10/15/88; SLJ 3/89; VOYA 4/89) [970.004]

7829 White, Jon Manchip. *Everyday Life of the North American Indian* (10–12). Illus. 1979, Holmes & Meier $24.50 (0-8419-0488-X). The story of Indian civilization with separate chapters on the hunters, artists, medicine men, and other social groups and how they lived. [970.004]

7830 Yenne, Bill, and Susan Garratt. *Pictorial History of the North American Indian* (7–12). Illus. 1984, Exeter $12.98 (0-671-06988-8). A lavishly illustrated account of the various tribes of North America. [970.004]

DISCOVERY AND EXPLORATION

7831 Irwin, Constance. *Strange Footprints on the Land* (10–12). 1980, Harper LB $13.89 (0-06-022773-7). A reconstruction of what is known or thought to have happened concerning the Viking exploration of North America. [970.01]

7832 Morison, Samuel Eliot. *The European Discovery of America: The Northern Voyages* (10–12). Illus. 1971, Oxford Univ. Pr. $35.00 (0-19-501377-8). This first volume covers the northern voyages from A.D. 500 to 1600; the second vol-

ume, *The European Discovery of America: The Southern Voyages* (1974), covers the years 1492 to 1616. [973.1]

7833 Morison, Samuel Eliot. *The Great Explorers: The European Discovery of America* (10–12). Illus. 1978, Oxford Univ. Pr. $35.00 (0-19-502314-5). This is a one-volume abridgment of the author's 2-volume *The European Discovery of America.* [973.1]

COLONIAL PERIOD AND FRENCH AND INDIAN WARS

7834 Andrews, Charles M. *The Colonial Background of the American Revolution* (10–12). Rev. ed. 1961, Yale Univ. Pr. paper $9.95 (0-300-00004-9). In 4 scholarly essays, the origins of the American Revolution are traced in this examination of colonial life. [973.2]

7835 Bradford, William. *Of Plymouth Plantation, 1620–1647* (10–12). 1952, Knopf $19.95 (0-394-43895-7). This history of the Pilgrims and their colony was originally written between 1630 and 1650. [974.4]

7836 Bridenbaugh, Carl. *Jamestown, 1544–1699* (10–12). Illus. 1980, Oxford Univ. Pr. $35.00 (0-19-502650-0). A history of this English settlement in Virginia with details on the economic and social life of the community. [975.5]

7837 Bridenbaugh, Carl. *The Spirit of '76: The Growth of American Patriotism before Independence* (10–12). 1975, Oxford Univ. Pr. $16.95 (0-19-501931-8); paper $5.95 (0-19-502179-7). A history that traces the beginning of a national spirit among the colonists. [973.2]

7838 Demos, John Putnam. *Entertaining Satan: Witchcraft and the Culture of Early New England* (10–12). Illus. 1982, Oxford Univ. Pr. $35.00 (0-19-503131-8); paper $12.95 (0-19-503378-7). A scholarly examination of the Salem witchcraft hysteria and the subsequent trial, and their significance in American history. [974]

7839 Franklin, Benjamin. *Writings* (10–12). 1987, Viking $35.00 (0-940450-29-1). A collection of many pieces by Franklin that reflect the life and times of Colonial and Revolutionary America. (Rev: SLJ 12/87) [973.2]

7840 Hansen, Chadwick. *Witchcraft at Salem* (9–12). Illus. 1969, Braziller $17.95 (0-8076-0492-5); paper $8.95 (0-8076-1137-9). A readable, well-researched account of the Salem witch hunt and of colonial life in New England. [133.4]

7841 Hawke, David Freeman. *Everyday Life in Early America* (9–12). Illus. 1988, Harper $16.95 (0-06-015856-5); paper $7.95 (0-06-091251-0). A detailed account of what life was like for the average colonists in America. (Rev: BL 12/1/87; SLJ 12/88) [973.2]

7842 Hofstadter, Richard. *America at 1750: A Social Portrait* (10–12). 1971, Random paper $5.95 (0-394-71795-3). A portrait of the American people during the colonial period that explores the emerging social structure. [973.2]

7843 Reich, Jerome R. *Colonial America* (10–12). Illus. 1989, Prentice $29.95 (0-13-151176-9). A readable text that explores American history from the Norse explorations to the signing of the Declaration of Independence. [973.2]

7844 Ritchie, Robert C. *Captain Kidd and the War against the Pirates* (10–12). 1986, Harvard Univ. Pr. $22.50 (0-674-09501-4); paper $11.95 (0-674-09502-2). The true story of Captain Kidd and how he was manipulated by politics and governments. (Rev: BL 10/15/86) [364.1]

7845 Tunis, Edwin. *Colonial Craftsmen and the Beginnings of American Industry* (8–12). Illus. 1976, Harper $24.95 (0-690-01062-1). In this beautifully illustrated oversized volume, the methods and products of such colonial occupations as papermaking, shipbuilding, and glass-making are described. [670]

7846 Tunis, Edwin. *Colonial Living* (7–12). Illus. 1976, Harper $24.95 (0-590-01063-X). In over 200 detailed drawings and ample text the author describes daily life in the colonies. [973.2]

REVOLUTIONARY PERIOD AND THE YOUNG NATION (1775–1809)

7847 Birnbaum, Louis. *Red Dawn at Lexington: "If They Mean to Have a War, Let It Begin Here!"* (10–12). Illus. 1986, Houghton $18.95 (0-395-38814-7). An account of the opening years of the American Revolution that includes material on the battles of Lexington, Concord, and Bunker Hill. (Rev: BL 4/15/86; SLJ 11/86) [973.3]

7848 Canfield, Cass. *Samuel Adams's Revolution, 1765–1776* (10–12). Illus. 1976, Harper $12.45 (0-06-010619-0). The part played by Samuel Adams in the Revolution is outlined in this interesting text. [973.3]

7849 Cunliffe, Marcus. *The Nation Takes Shape, 1789–1837* (10–12). Illus. 1960, Univ. of Chicago Pr. paper $9.00 (0-226-12667-6). A history of the early years of the Republic and the establishment of national institutions. [973.4]

7850 De Pauw, Linda Grant. *Founding Mothers: Women in America in the Revolutionary Era* (10–12). Illus. 1975, Houghton $13.95 (0-395-21896-9). From a feminist point of view this is a history of the women involved in the American Revolution. [305.4]

7851 Hibbert, Christopher. *The American Revolution through British Eyes: The War for America, 1770–1781* (9–12). 1990, Norton $29.95 (0-393-02895-X). A reworking of the history of the American Revolution from the British perspective. (Rev: BL 7/90) [973.3]

7852 Lancaster, Bruce, and J. H. Plumb. *The American Heritage Book of the Revolution* (10–12). 1985, Dell paper $9.95 (0-8281-0281-3). A concise, readable account of the causes, events, and consequences of the American Revolution. [973.3]

7853 McDowell, Bart. *The Revolutionary War: America's Fight for Freedom* (9–12). Illus. 1967, National Geographic $7.95 (0-87044-047-0). With lavish illustrations, this book gives a concise picture of the causes and conflicts in the Revolution. [973.3]

7854 Miller, John C. *The Federalist Era, 1789–1801* (10–12). Illus. 1960, Harper paper $9.95 (0-06-133027-2). This account, dealing with the first years of the United States, focuses on the administrations of George Washington and John Adams. [973.4]

7855 Mitchell, Joseph B. *Decisive Battles of the American Revolution* (9–12). 1985, Fawcett paper $3.95 (0-449-30031-5). A re-creation of all the important battles in the Revolution from Lexington to Yorktown. [973.3]

7856 Morgan, Edmund S. *The Birth of the Republic, 1763–89* (10–12). 1977, Univ. of Chicago Pr. LB $16.00 (0-226-53758-7); paper $6.95 (0-226-53759-5). A clear, brief survey of the Revolutionary period that presents both American and British points of view fairly. [973.3]

7857 Morris, Richard B. *The Forging of the Union, 1781–1789* (10–12). Illus. 1987, Harper $25.00 (0-06-015733-X); paper $8.95 (0-06-091424-6). A history of the immediate events leading up to the drafting of the Constitution. (Rev: BL 4/15/87) [973.3]

7858 Paine, Thomas, and Thomas Jefferson. *Paine and Jefferson on Liberty* (10–12). 1988, Ungar paper $7.95 (0-8044-6382-4). The most important writings of these 2 key influences on the principles behind the American Revolution. (Rev: BL 8/88) [323.44]

7859 Smith, Page. *A New Age Now Begins: A People's History of the American Revolution* (10–12). Illus. 1989, Penguin paper $31.90 set (0-14-095354-X). This 2-volume work traces Revolutionary elements in American life through the

Colonial period as well as giving an unbiased account of the Revolution itself. [973.3]

7860 Smith, Page. *The Shaping of America: A People's History of the Young Republic* (10–12). Illus. 1980, Penguin paper $15.95 (0-14-012259-1). This account traces the problems of the new nation from 1783 to 1826. [973.4]

7861 Tunis, Edwin. *The Young United States, 1783 to 1830* (7–12). Illus. 1976, Harper $24.95 (0-690-01065-6). Through an interesting text and many detailed drawings, the important events and aspects of daily life of this period are pictured. [973]

7862 Wood, W. J. *Battles of the Revolutionary War, 1775–1781* (10–12). Illus. 1990, Algonquin $24.95 (0-945575-03-3). A spirited account of the battles and the leaders in the Revolutionary War complete with many maps. (Rev: BL 5/1/90) [973.3]

NINETEENTH CENTURY TO THE CIVIL WAR (1809–1861)

7863 Catton, William, and Bruce Catton. *Two Roads to Sumter* (10–12). 1963, McGraw paper $6.95 (0-07-010255-4). This account of American history during the 1850s traces the differing attitudes emerging between the South and the North. [973.6]

7864 Commager, Henry Steele, ed. *The Era of Reform, 1830–1860* (10–12). 1982, Krieger paper $8.50 (0-89874-498-9). This collection of 55 documents represents such different writers as Thomas Jefferson and Nathaniel Hawthorne. [973.5]

7865 Dangerfield, George. *The Awakening of American Nationalism, 1815–1828* (10–12). Illus. 1965, Harper paper $12.95 (0-06-133061-2). This account chronicles the conflict between opposing ideas on economic development as represented on the one hand by Henry Clay and John Quincy Adams and on the other by Andrew Jackson. [973.5]

7866 de Tocqueville, Alexis. *Democracy in America* (10–12). 2 vols. 1945, Knopf $50.00 set (0-394-42186-8); Random paper $7.95 each (vol. 1: 0-394-70110-0; vol. 2: 0-394-70111-9). This is a 2-volume edition of the author's classic treatise on democracy as inspired by his visit to America in 1831–1832. [973.5]

7867 Eisenhower, John S. D. *So Far from God: The U.S. War with Mexico, 1846–1848* (10–12). Illus. 1989, Random $24.95 (0-394-56051-5). A clear account of the war, the motives behind it, and the personalities involved. (Rev: BL 3/15/89) [973.6]

7868 Hickey, Donald R. *The War of 1812: A Forgotten Conflict* (10–12). Illus. 1989, Univ. of Illinois Pr. $32.50 (0-252-01613-0). For better readers, a well-researched account of the causes, battles, and consequences of the War of 1812. (Rev: BL 11/15/89) [973.5]

7869 Huggins, Nathan Irvin. *Black Odyssey* (10–12). 1978, Random paper $7.95 (0-394-72687-1). The story of Afro-American slavery in this country. [305.8]

7870 Hurmence, Belinda, ed. *Before Freedom, When I Just Can Remember* (10–12). Illus. 1989, John F. Blair paper $8.95 (0-89587-069-X). This is a collection of actual accounts of the lives and living conditions of 27 ex-slaves. (Rev: SLJ 9/89) [305.8]

7871 Johannsen, Robert W. *To the Halls of the Montezumas* (10–12). Illus. 1985, Oxford Univ. Pr. $29.95 (0-19-503518-6). A history of the War with Mexico and its psychological effects in the United States. [973.6]

7872 Katz, William Loren. *Breaking the Chains: African-American Slave Resistance* (9–12). Illus. 1990, Macmillan LB $14.95 (0-689-31493-0). A revealing account of American black slavery that focuses on the many uprisings and rebellions. (Rev: SLJ 11/90) [305.6]

7873 Langdon, William Chauncey. *Everyday Things in American Life, 1776–1876* (7–12). Illus. 1941, Macmillan $40.00 (0-684-17416-2). This illustrated account covers such topics as clothing, machinery, canals, bridges, and turnpikes. [973]

7874 Lincoln, Abraham. *The Lincoln-Douglas Debates of 1858* (10–12). 1965, Oxford Univ. Pr. paper $11.95 (0-19-500921-5). This book includes the actual text of the 7 debates of 1858. [973.6]

7875 Marrin, Albert. *1812: The War Nobody Won* (10–12). Illus. 1985, Macmillan $12.95 (0-689-31075-7). A history of the War of 1812 that shows the strengths and weaknesses of all combatants—American, British, and Indian. [973.5]

7876 Meltzer, Milton. *In Their Own Words: A History of the American Negro, 1619–1865* (8–12). 1964, Harper LB $10.53 (0-690-44691-8). In this the first volume of a history of black Americans through original documents, the days of slavery are re-created. The two other volumes are *In Their Own Words: A History of the American Negro 1865–1916* (1965) and *In Their Own Words: A History of the American Negro, 1916–1966* (1967). [305.8]

7877 Nevin, David. *The Mexican War* (7–12). Illus. 1978, Silver Burdett LB $25.93 (0-8094-

2301-4). A lavishly illustrated volume that highlights the causes, battles, and personalities of the war. [973.6]

7878 Paine, Ralph D. *The Fight for a Free Sea* (10–12). 1920, U.S. Pubs. Assn. $8.95 (0-911548-16-5). An account of the many naval battles and maneuvers during the War of 1812. [973.5]

7879 Potter, David M. *The Impending Crisis, 1848–1861* (10–12). Illus. 1976, Harper $12.95 (0-06-131929-5). An account of the growing tensions between North and South that finally erupted in the Civil War. [973.6]

7880 Remini, Robert V. *The Revolutionary Age of Andrew Jackson* (10–12). Illus. 1976, Harper paper $5.95 (0-06-091290-1). A history of the Jacksonian age, the people about this president, and the many struggles Old Hickory faced. [973.5]

7881 Richards, Colin. *Sheriff Pat Garrett's Last Days* (8–12). Illus. 1986, Sunstone paper $8.95 (0-86534-079-X). A history of the Wild West drawn into focus by the death of the man who shot Billy the Kid. (Rev: BR 11–12/86) [978]

7882 Schlesinger, Arthur M., Jr. *The Age of Jackson* (10–12). 1945, Little $22.50 (0-316-77344-1); paper $10.95 (0-316-77343-3). This detailed account of the Jackson era won the Pulitzer Prize for history in 1946. [973.5]

7883 Smith, Barbara Clark. *After the Revolution: The Smithsonian History of Everyday Life in the Eighteenth Century* (9–12). Illus. 1985, Pantheon $13.95 (0-394-54381-5). Using the lives of 4 Americans from different backgrounds as a framework, this illustrated volume traces everyday life during the first days of independence. (Rev: BR 5–6/86; SLJ 4/86) [973.6]

7884 Smith, Page. *The Nation Comes of Age: A People's History of the Ante-bellum Years* (10–12). 1981, Penguin paper $16.95 (0-14-012260-5). A history of the United States from the election of Andrew Jackson in 1828 to the election of Abraham Lincoln in 1860. [973.5]

7885 Van Deusen, Glyndon G. *The Jacksonian Era, 1828–1848* (10–12). Illus. 1959, Harper paper $8.95 (0-06-133028-0). In addition to the 8 years of Jackson's presidency, this account covers the 12 years that followed. [973.5]

7886 Whipple, A. B. C. *The Clipper Ships* (9–12). Illus. 1980, Silver Burdett LB $21.27 (0-8094-2678-1). Using many illustrations, this is a fine history of this period in American sea navigation. Part of the Time-Life series The Seafarers, which includes by the same author: *Fighting Sail* (1978) and *The Whalers* (1979). [387.2]

THE CIVIL WAR (1861–1865)

7887 Angle, Paul M., and William C. Davis. *A Pictorial History of the Civil War Years* (9–12). Illus. 1985, Doubleday paper $14.95 (0-385-18551-0). This pictorial history includes combat scenes, sketches by artists, and portraits of key personnel. [973.7]

7888 Bailey, Ronald H. *Battle for Atlanta: Sherman Moves East* (9–12). Illus. 1985, Time-Life Books LB $25.93 (0-8094-4773-8). In pictures and text, this account tells of the Atlanta Campaign of 1864. Others in this Time-Life series on the Civil War include: *The Assassination* (1987), *The Coastal War*, and *Confederate Ordeal* (both 1984). [973.7]

7889 Bailey, Ronald H. *The Bloodiest Day: The Battle of Antietam* (7–12). Illus. 1984, Silver Burdett LB $25.93 (0-8094-4741-X). The story of Lee's defeat in the battle that caused terrible losses on both sides. [973.7]

7890 Bailey, Ronald H. *Forward to Richmond* (9–12). Illus. 1983, Silver Burdett LB $25.93 (0-8094-4721-5). A lavishly illustrated volume that deals with the Peninsula campaign of 1862. Some others in the Time-Life series on the Civil War are: *Decoying the Yanks* (1984), *The Fight for Chattanooga* (1985), and *Pursuit to Appomattox* (1989). [973.7]

7891 Batty, Peter, and Peter Parish. *The Divided Union: The Story of the Great American War 1861–1865* (9–12). Illus. 1987, Salem House $24.95 (0-88162-234-6). A fine popular history of the Civil War notable both for its clarity and excellent illustrations. (Rev: SLJ 3/88) [973.7]

7892 Bowman, John S., ed. *The Civil War Almanac* (9–12). Illus. 1986, Newspaper Enterprise Assn. paper $14.95 (0-345-35434-6). This book consists chiefly of a detailed chronology of the war plus 133 biographical sketches of key figures. [973.7]

7893 Brandt, Nat. *The Town That Started the Civil War* (10–12). Illus. 1990, Syracuse Univ. Pr. $29.95 (0-8156-0243-X). The story of how the slavery question came into focus when a fugitive slave was saved by the town of Oberlin, Ohio, in 1858. (Rev: BL 4/15/90) [977.1]

7894 *Brother against Brother: Time-Life Books History of the Civil War* (9–12). Illus. 1990, Prentice $39.95 (0-13-921818-1). Condensed from a multivolume set, this is an excellent, well-illustrated account of the Civil War. (Rev: BL 7/90) [973.7]

7895 Catton, Bruce. *The Civil War* (7–12). Illus. 1985, Houghton paper $9.95 (0-8281-0305-4). A well-illustrated book that deals with the major events and personalities of the war. [973.7]

7896 Catton, Bruce. *Gettysburg: The Final Fury* (10–12). Illus. 1974, Doubleday $17.95 (0-385-02060-0). The story of the crucial Civil War battle that turned the balance toward the Union forces. [973.7]

7897 Catton, Bruce. *Reflections on the Civil War* (10–12). Illus. 1984, Berkley paper $4.50 (0-425-10495-8). The well-known Civil War historian reflects on the causes and consequences of this war. [973.7]

7898 Catton, Bruce. *A Stillness at Appomattox* (10–12). 1984, Pocket paper $5.95 (0-671-53143-3). This volume traces the final campaign of the Army of the Potomac from 1864 through April 1865. [973.7]

7899 Catton, Bruce. *Terrible Swift Sword* (10–12). 1963, Pocket paper $5.95 (0-671-61933-0). A highly interpretive history of the middle years of the Civil War. [973.7]

7900 Catton, Bruce. *This Hallowed Ground: The Story of the Union Side of the Civil War* (7–12). Illus. 1962, Doubleday $17.95 (0-385-04664-2); Pocket paper $4.95 (0-671-46992-4). A detailed description of the military and political aspects of the war. [973.7]

7901 Clark, Champ. *Gettysburg: The Confederate High Tide* (9–12). Illus. 1985, Silver Burdett LB $25.93 (0-8094-4757-6). This volume in the Time-Life series vividly re-creates in words and pictures the horror and glory of this important battle. The final volume in this series is *The Nation Reunited* (1987). [973.7]

7902 Commager, Henry Steele. *The Blue and the Gray, Vol. 1* (10–12). 1973, NAL paper $4.95 (0-451-62536-6). This is the first part of the noted historian's account of the Civil War and its consequences. Also use volume two (1973). [973.7]

7903 Davis, Burke. *The Civil War: Strange and Fascinating Facts* (9–12). Illus. 1982, Crown paper $5.98 (0-517-37151-0). An unusual compendium of little-known facts about the Civil War. [973.7]

7904 Davis, Burke. *The Long Surrender* (10–12). 1985, Random $19.95 (0-394-52083-1); paper $9.95 (0-679-72409-5). This account of the last days of the Civil War focuses on the capture and imprisonment of President Jefferson Davis. (Rev: BL 4/15/85) [973.7]

7905 Davis, Burke. *Sherman's March* (9–12). Illus. 1980, Random $21.95 (0-394-50739-8); paper $7.95 (0-394-74763-7). This volume deals with the destructive march of Sherman and his men through Georgia and the Carolinas. [973.7]

7906 Davis, Burke. *To Appomattox: Nine April Days, 1865* (10–12). Illus. 1959, Eastern Acorn paper $4.25 (0-915992-17-5). The dramatic story of the last 9 days of the Civil War. [973.7]

7907 Davis, William C. *Brother against Brother: The War Begins* (9–12). Illus. 1983, Silver Burdett LB $25.93 (0-8094-4701-0). This is the first volume in the Time-Life series on the Civil War (see other entries in this section). It traces the events leading up to the outbreak of war. [973.7]

7908 Davis, William C. *Death in the Trenches: Grant at Petersburg* (9–12). Illus. 1986, Silver Burdett $25.93 (0-8094-4777-0). This volume of the Time-Life series deals with the Union Army's siege of Petersburg, Virginia. [973.7]

7909 Davis, William C. *First Blood: Fort Sumter to Bull Run* (9–12). Illus. 1983, Silver Burdett LB $25.93 (0-8094-4705-3). A survey in pictures and text of such early battles of the Civil War as Bull Run and Fort Sumter. Part of the Time-Life series. [973.7]

7910 Davis, William C. *Rebels & Yankees: The Fighting Men of the Civil War* (9–12). Illus. 1989, Smith $24.98 (0-8317-3264-4). An account that tells of the training, camp life, and combat duty of average soldiers on both sides of the struggle. (Rev: BL 8/89) [973.74]

7911 Donovan, Timothy H., et al. *The American Civil War* (10–12). Illus. 1987, Avery $25.00 (0-89529-318-8); paper $18.00 (0-89529-272-6). A detailed account that covers the causes, major events, strategies, and battles of the war between the states. (Rev: BL 12/15/86) [973.7]

7912 Farwell, Byron. *Ball's Bluff* (9–12). Illus. 1990, EPM paper $12.95 (0-939009-36-6). A gripping account of the small Civil War battle of Ball's Bluff and its aftermath. (Rev: SLJ 9/90) [973.7]

7913 Foner, Eric, and Olivia Mahoney. *A House Divided: America in the Age of Lincoln* (9–12). Illus. 1990, Norton $35.00 (0-393-02755-4). A lavishly illustrated account of America after the Civil War and of the gradual healing process. (Rev: BL 6/15/90) [973.7]

7914 Fowler, William M. *Under Two Flags: The American Navy in the Civil War* (10–12). Illus. 1990, Norton $22.50 (0-393-02859-3). A well-written and well-researched account of the activities of the U.S. Navy during the Civil War, arranged geographically. (Rev: BL 8/90) [973.7]

7915 Frassanito, William A. *Grant and Lee: The Virginia Campaigns* (10–12). Illus. 1983, Macmillan $27.95 (0-684-17873-7). This pictorial volume analyzes the Virginia campaigns in a picture-by-picture treatment. [973.7]

7916 Garrison, Webb. *A Treasury of Civil War Tales* (9–12). Illus. 1988, Rutledge Hill $14.95 (0-934395-95-0). A collection of 57 stories dealing with the Civil War from the first outcries against slavery to Reconstruction. (Rev: BL 10/15/88) [973.7]

7917 Goolrick, William K. *Rebels Resurgent: Fredericksburg to Chancellorsville* (9–12). Illus. 1985, Silver Burdett LB $25.93 (0-8094-4749-5). In this volume in the Time-Life series, the early southern victories of 1862 and 1863 are reconstructed. [973.7]

7918 Gragg, Rod. *The Civil War Quiz and Fact Book* (9–12). 1985, Harper paper $9.95 (0-06-091226-X). Fascinating questions and answers involving little-known facts about the Civil War. (Rev: BL 4/15/85) [973.7]

7919 Gragg, Rod. *The Illustrated Confederate Reader* (9–12). Illus. 1989, Harper $24.95 (0-06-015798-4). A well-illustrated account of life of the Confederate prisoners in Union camps with written excerpts by the participants. (Rev: BL 5/15/89) [973.7]

7920 Hargrove, Hondon. *Black Union Soldiers in the Civil War* (10–12). 1988, McFarland LB $22.95 (0-89950-337-3). An account that describes the vital and remarkable role played by black soldiers in the Union army. (Rev: BR 3–4/89) [973.7]

7921 Hattaway, Herman. *How the North Won: A Military History of the Civil War* (10–12). Illus. 1983, Univ. of Illinois Pr. $39.95 (0-252-00918-5). An extensive review of the tactics, maneuvers, and organization that led to a victory for the North in the Civil War. [973.7]

7922 Haythornthwaite, Philip. *Uniforms of the American Civil War in Color* (9–12). Illus. 1990, Sterling paper $9.95 (0-8069-5846-4). In vivid color, this book presents over 150 Confederate and Union army uniforms. (Rev: SLJ 11/85) [973.7]

7923 Hoehling, A. A. *Damn the Torpedoes! Naval Incidents of the Civil War* (10–12). Illus. 1989, John F. Blair $19.95 (0-89587-073-8). The author re-creates the ships and the naval battles of the Civil War from a variety of sources. (Rev: BL 12/15/89) [973.7]

7924 Jackson, Donald Dale. *Twenty Million Yankees: The Northern Home Front* (9–12). Illus. 1985, Silver Burdett LB $25.93 (0-8094-4753-3). This volume in the Time-Life series deals with life in the North during the Civil War. [973.7]

7925 Jaynes, Gregory. *The Killing Ground: Wilderness to Cold Harbor* (9–12). Illus. 1986, Silver Burdett LB $25.93 (0-8094-4769-X). The story of the bloody battles in Virginia early in 1864 are retold in this volume in the Time-Life series. [973.7]

7926 Korn, Jerry. *The Fight for Chattanooga: Chickamauga to Missionary Ridge* (9–12). Illus. 1985, Silver Burdett LB $25.93 (0-8094-4817-3). In this volume in the Time-Life Civil War series, 4 battles—Chickamauga, Chattanooga, Lookout Mountain, and Missionary Ridge—are highlighted. [973.7]

7927 Leckie, Robert. *None Died in Vain: The Saga of the American Civil War* (10–12). Illus. 1990, Harper $29.95 (0-06-016280-5). A detailed study of the Civil War that contains sketches in prose of the key people involved. (Rev: BL 9/1/90) [973.7]

7928 Mitchell, Reid. *Civil War Soldiers: Their Expectations & Their Experiences* (10–12). 1988, Viking $19.95 (0-670-81742-2). Using diaries and letters as basic material the author tries to re-create the feelings of the men who fought in the Civil War. (Rev: VOYA 4/89) [973.7]

7929 Nevin, David. *The Road to Shiloh: Early Battles in the West* (9–12). Illus. 1983, Silver Burdett LB $25.93 (0-8094-4717-7). This volume of the Time-Life series deals with the early battle in Kentucky and the Battle of Shiloh in 1862. [973.7]

7930 Nevin, David. *Sherman's March: Atlanta to the Sea* (9–12). Illus. 1986, Silver Burdett LB $25.93 (0-8094-4813-0). A reconstruction of the destructive march through Georgia and the Carolinas by Sherman. Part of the Time-Life Civil War series. [973.7]

7931 Oates, Stephen B. *Our Fiery Trial: Abraham Lincoln, John Brown, and the Civil War Era* (10–12). 1983, Univ. of Massachusetts Pr. paper $9.95 (0-87023-397-1). A series of reflective essays about events and people associated with the Civil War. [973.7]

7932 Robertson, James I., Jr. *Tenting Tonight: The Soldier's Life* (7–12). Illus. 1984, Silver Burdett $14.95 (0-8094-4737-1). The daily life of the common soldiers both Union and Confederate. Part of the Time-Life Books series on the Civil War. [973.7]

7933 Rozwenc, Edwin C., ed. *The Causes of the American Civil War* (10–12). Illus. 1972, Heath paper $8.50 (0-669-82727-4). This book consists of a series of essays by historians, each of whom examines various facets of the origins of the Civil War. [973.7]

7934 Sears, Stephen W. *Landscape Turned Red: The Battle of Antietam* (10–12). Illus. 1983, Warner paper $6.95 (0-446-35503-8). This graphic account deals both with the important Battle of Antietam and the events leading up to it. [973.7]

7935 Smith, Page. *Trial by Fire* (10–12). 1982, Penguin paper $16.95 (0-14-012261-3). Using original documents from a wide spectrum of sources, the author re-creates in personal terms the nation's ordeal during the Civil War and Reconstruction. [973.7]

7936 Stampp, Kenneth M., ed. *The Causes of the Civil War* (10–12). 1986, Simon & Schuster paper $6.95 (0-671-62237-4). From eyewitness accounts and the thoughts of such contemporaries as Lincoln and Jefferson Davis, the origins of the Civil War are traced. [973.7]

7937 Stevenson, Paul R. *The American Civil War* (9–12). Illus. 1990, Sterling paper $7.95 (0-8069-7328-5). A brief volume that focuses on the military strategies used during the war. (Rev: BL 6/1/90) [973.7]

7938 Straubing, Harold Elk, ed. *Civil War Eyewitness Reports* (9–12). Illus. 1985, Shoe String $25.00 (0-208-02065-9). Drawn from diaries and other eyewitness documents, this is a series of firsthand accounts of many key events of the Civil War. (Rev: BL 4/1/85) [973.7]

7939 Street, James, Jr. *The Struggle for Tennessee: Tupelo to Stones River* (9–12). Illus. 1985, Silver Burdett LB $25.93 (0-8094-4761-4). This part of the Time-Life series deals with the important areas of Tennessee and Kentucky during the Civil War. [973.7]

7940 Symonds, Craig L. *A Battlefield Atlas of the Civil War* (10–12). Illus. 1983, Nautical & Aviation $17.95 (0-933852-49-5). Through a series of detailed maps, all of the major events and battles in the Civil War are presented. A companion volume is *Battlefield Atlas of the American Revolution* (1986). [973.7]

7941 Tapert, Annette. *The Brothers' War: Civil War Letters to Their Loved Ones from the Blue & Gray* (9–12). Illus. 1988, Random $18.95 (0-8129-1634-4). The human side of the Civil War is explored in this collection of 90 letters written by soldiers on both sides. (Rev: BR 9–10/89; VOYA 4/89) [973.7]

7942 Terdoslavich, William. *The Civil War Trivia Quiz Book* (9–12). 1985, Crown paper $4.98 (0-517-46784-4). Little-known facts about the Civil War arranged in a question-and-answer format. [973.7]

7943 Time-Life Books, eds. *The Blockade: Runners and Raiders* (9–12). Illus. 1983, Silver Burdett LB $25.93 (0-8094-4709-6). With many authentic illustrations, this volume tells of the naval events of the Civil War. Some others in this Time-Life series on the Civil War are: *War on the Mississippi* (1985), *War on the Frontier* (1986), and *The Shenandoah in Flames* (1987). [973.7]

7944 Time-Life Books, eds. *Great Battles of the Civil War* (9–12). Illus. 1990, Silver Burdett LB $32.97 (0-671-69385-9). With over 350 illustrations, this is a history of the Civil War drawn from Time-Life's extensive series. [973.7]

7945 Time-Life Books, eds. *Lee Takes Command: From Seven Days to Second Bull Run* (7–12). Illus. 1984, Silver Burdett LB $25.93 (0-8094-4805-X). A graphic account complemented with many illustrations of Lee's campaign during 1862. [973.7]

7946 Time-Life Books, eds. *Spies, Scouts, and Raiders: Irregular Operations* (9–12). Illus. 1985, Silver Burdett $25.93 (0-8094-4713-4). This pictorial volume, part of the Time-Life series, presents some of the unusual military operations of the Civil War. [973.7]

7947 Ward, Geoffrey C., et al. *The Civil War: An Illustrated History* (9–12). Illus. 1990, Knopf $50.00 (0-394-56285-2). A handsome, readable account that was prepared for the television series on the Civil War that aired in 1990. (Rev: BL 8/90) [973.7]

WESTWARD EXPANSION AND PIONEER LIFE

7948 Billington, Ray A. *The Far Western Frontier, 1830–1860* (10–12). 1962, Harper paper $9.95 (0-06-133012-4). A history of the westward movement and the different types of men and women who participated. [978]

7949 Brown, Dee. *Hear That Lonesome Whistle Blow: Railroads in the West* (9–12). Illus. 1977, Holt $13.95 (0-03-016936-4). A history of American railroads and how they helped open up the West. [385.09]

7950 Clarke, Asa Bement. *Travels in Mexico and California* (9–12). Illus. 1989, Texas A & M Univ. Pr. $17.50 (0-89096-354-1). An actual account of the perils of crossing the continent via the southern route during pioneer times. (Rev: SLJ 2/90) [973.4]

7951 Connell, Evan S. *Son of the Morning Star* (10–12). 1984, North Point Pr. $20.00 (0-86547-160-6); Harper paper $10.95 (0-06-097003-0). The story of the Battle of Little Bighorn and the defeat of General Custer. [973.8]

7952 Dary, David. *Cowboy Culture* (10–12). 1989, Avon paper $9.95 (0-7006-0390-5). A 500-year history of the American cowboy. [973]

7953 Gard, Wayne. *The Chisholm Trail* (10–12). Illus. 1984, Univ. of Oklahoma Pr. paper $12.95 (0-8061-1536-4). This is the story of the legendary trail used to transport cattle from Texas to the railroads situated in Kansas. [973.5]

7954 Gragg, Rod. *The Old West Quiz and Fact Book* (9–12). Illus. 1986, Harper $15.95 (0-06-055002-3); paper $8.95 (0-06-096077-9). A question-and-answer book about gunfighters, outlaws, cowboys, and Indians. (Rev: BL 11/1/86) [978]

7955 Hine, Robert V. *The American West: An Interpretive History* (10–12). 2nd ed. 1984, Scott, Foresman $29.95 (0-673-39341-0). This history of the American West covers topics like politics, folklore, the arts, and the role of women and minorities. [978]

7956 Horn, Huston. *The Pioneers* (7–12). Illus. 1974, Silver Burdett LB $25.93 (0-8094-1476-7). The journeys of pioneers across America are told plus the life they lived when they settled into their new homes. [978]

7957 Jackson, Donald Dale. *Gold Dust* (10–12). Illus. 1980, Knopf $17.95 (0-394-40046-1); Univ. of Nebraska Pr. paper $8.95 (0-8032-7555-2). A fascinating history of the California Gold Rush of the 1840s and 1850s and of the people it attracted. [979.4]

7958 Johnson, William Weber. *The Forty-Niners* (7–12). Illus. 1974, Silver Burdett LB $25.93 (0-8094-1471-6). The gold rushes of the 1840s and 1850s are highlighted in text and stunning illustrations. [979.4]

7959 Katz, William Loren. *The Black West* (7–12). Illus. 1987, Open Hand $24.95 (0-940880-17-2); paper $14.95 (0-940880-18-0). The opening up of the West as experienced through the lives of black Americans. (Rev: SLJ 4/88) [920]

7960 Lamar, Howard R., ed. *The Reader's Encyclopedia of the American West* (10–12). Illus. 1987, Harper $30.00 (0-06-015726-7). In over 2,400 entries the people, events, and places involved in the opening of the American West are covered. [978.03]

7961 Lavender, David. *The Great West* (9–12). Illus. 1985, Houghton paper $8.95 (0-8281-0481-6). This richly illustrated volume covers the history of the West and its development from 1763 through the beginning of the twentieth century. [978]

7962 Lavender, David. *The Rockies* (10–12). 1981, Univ. of Nebraska Pr. paper $12.95 (0-8032-7906-X). A history of the Rocky Mountain region that covers topics like exploration, mining, farming, railroads, Indians, and recent economic developments. [978]

7963 Levy, Joann. *They Saw the Elephant: Women in the California Gold Rush* (10–12). Illus. 1990, Shoe String $27.50 (0-208-02273-2). Elephant refers to Mother Lode country and this is a tribute to the women who took part in this famous gold rush. (Rev: BL 5/1/90) [979.4]

7964 Long, Jeff. *Duel of Eagles: The Mexican and U.S. Fight for the Alamo* (9–12). Illus. 1990, Morrow $22.95 (0-688-07252-6). A thoroughly researched history of the Alamo that sweeps away old myths and half-truths. (Rev: BL 7/90) [976.4]

7965 Lord, Walter. *A Time to Stand* (9–12). 1978, Univ. of Nebraska Pr. paper $5.95 (0-8032-7902-7). A gripping account of the siege and fall of the Alamo. [973.6]

7966 Marrin, Albert. *War Clouds in the West: Indians & Cavalry Men, 1860–1890* (10–12). Illus. 1984, Macmillan $14.95 (0-689-31066-8). A history of the 30 years at the end of the nineteenth century when American Indians fought for their survival against increasing numbers of white settlers. [973.8]

7967 National Geographic Society, eds. *Into the Wilderness* (9–12). Illus. 1978, National Geographic $7.95 (0-87044-252-X). A series of articles traces the exploits of important frontiersmen who opened up the West. [973]

7968 Nevin, David. *The Expressmen* (9–12). Illus. 1974, Silver Burdett LB $25.93 (0-8094-1485-6). A history with many illustrations of stagecoach service in the Old West that includes material on Wells Fargo and the Pony Express. Part of the Time-Life Old West series. [388.3]

7969 Nevin, David. *The Soldiers* (7–12). Illus. 1973, Silver Burdett LB $25.93 (0-8094-1463-5). The story of westward expansion and the Indian Wars that followed during the decade after the Civil War. [973.8]

7970 O'Neil, Paul. *The Frontiersmen* (7–12). Illus. 1977, Silver Burdett LB $25.93 (0-8094-1546-1). The life of the pioneers and events in their lives are recounted in text and many illustrations. [978]

7971 O'Neil, Paul. *The Rivermen* (9–12). Illus. 1975, Silver Burdett LB $25.93 (0-8094-1497-X). The story of the frontiersmen who traveled America's waterways in search of gold, furs, and wealth. Part of the Time-Life series, The Old West, available through Silver Burdett. [386]

7972 Parkman, Francis. *The Oregon Trail* (10–12). Illus. 1950, NAL paper $4.95 (0-451-52513-2). The authentic narrative written by Parkman about his adventures traveling west in 1846. [978]

7973 Perl, Lila. *Hunter's Stew and Hangtown Fry: What Pioneer America Ate and Why* (7–12). Illus. 1979, Houghton $13.95 (0-395-28922-X). A history of many different American ethnic groups and their foods, and how these changed and developed in America. [973.5]

7974 Poling-Kempes, Lesley. *The Harvey Girls: Women Who Opened the West* (10–12). Illus. 1989, Paragon $19.95 (1-55778-064-1). Based on research involving many interviews, this is a history of the more than 100,000 single girls who moved West to be waitresses in restaurants along the route of the Santa Fe Railroad. (Rev: BL 10/1/89) [979]

7975 Reader's Digest, eds. *Story of the Great American West* (9–12). Illus. 1981, Reader's Digest $22.95 (0-89577-039-3). An oversized volume crammed with illustrations that covers the entire history of the West from the coming of the white man to the present. [978]

7976 Reinfeld, Fred. *Pony Express* (7–12). Illus. 1973, Univ. of Nebraska Pr. paper $5.95 (0-8032-5786-4). A history of the communication system that linked the East and West and the courageous riders who manned it. [383]

7977 Rosa, Joseph G. *The Gunfighter: Man or Myth?* (10–12). 1982, Univ. of Oklahoma Pr. paper $10.95 (0-8061-1561-0). A collection of facts and myths about these rough, tough men who roamed the West during the last half of the nineteenth century. [973.5]

7978 Sandoz, Mari. *The Battle of the Little Bighorn* (10–12). 1966, Amereon $15.95 (0-89190-879-X). The story of this battle in the war against the Sioux and of the ambitions of General Custer. [973.8]

7979 Savage, William W. *The Cowboy Hero: His Image in American History and Culture* (10–12). Illus. 1987, Univ. of Oklahoma Pr. paper $8.95 (0-8061-1920-9). A history of the American cowboy with material on how he has been portrayed in the media. [973]

7980 Schlissel, Lillian. *Women's Diaries of the Westward Journey* (10–12). Illus. 1982, Schocken $16.95 (0-8052-3774-7); paper $11.95 (0-8052-0747-3). A collection of documents such as diary entries and letters that chronicle the experiences of many women as they traveled into the New West from 1840 to 1870. [978]

7981 Schlissel, Lillian, et al. *Far from Home: Families of the Westward Journey* (9–12). Illus. 1989, Schocken $19.95 (0-8052-4052-7). From a number of different sources, the authors have pieced together the stories of 4 families, their journeys west, and their lives as pioneers. (Rev: BL 4/1/89) [978]

7982 Seidman, Laurence Ivan. *Once in the Saddle: The Cowboy's Frontier, 1866–1896* (10–12). Illus. 1990, Facts on File $16.95 (0-8160-2373-5). This story of the cowboy era includes true accounts plus many photographs and illustrations. [973.8]

7983 Stewart, Elinore Pruitt. *Letters of a Woman Homesteader* (10–12). Illus. 1982, Houghton paper $7.95 (0-395-32137-9). Through a series of letters to her former employer, the young widow tells of her life as a homesteader in Wyoming. [973.5]

7984 Stone, Irving. *Men to Match My Mountains: The Opening of the Far West, 1840–1900* (10–12). Illus. 1956, Doubleday $21.95 (0-385-04662-6); Berkley paper $10.95 (0-425-10544-X). This is a history of the early settlements in California, Nevada, Utah, and Colorado. [979.1]

7985 Stratton, Joanne L. *Pioneer Women: Voices from the Kansas Frontier* (10–12). Illus. 1981, Simon & Schuster paper $11.95 (0-671-44748-3). This book is based on first-person accounts of almost 800 pioneer women who lived in Kansas between 1854 and 1890. [978.1]

7986 Tanner, Ogden. *The Ranchers* (7–12). Illus. 1977, Silver Burdett $25.93 (0-8094-1510-0). A beautifully illustrated account of the development of the ranches big and small on the western plains. Part of the Time-Life series on the Old West. [978]

7987 Time-Life Books, eds. *The Chroniclers* (9–12). Illus. 1976, Silver Burdett LB $25.93 (0-8094-1530-5). The careers of early newspapermen, writers, artists, and photographers in the old West are described with information on how they chronicled the opening up of this vast area. This is a volume in Time-Life's well-illustrated Old West series. [978]

7988 Time-Life Books, eds. *The Cowboys* (9–12). Illus. 1973, Silver Burdett LB $25.93 (0-8094-1451-1). The world of cowboys and the important role many played in the development of the old West are described and lavishly pictured in this volume in Time-Life's Old West series. [978]

7989 Time-Life Books, eds. *The Gamblers* (9–12). Illus. 1978, Silver Burdett LB $25.93 (0-8094-2309-X). The important part that various kinds of gambling played in the daily life of frontiersmen in the developing West is the topic of this nicely illustrated Time-Life volume. [978]

7990 Time-Life Books, eds. *The Miners* (9–12). Illus. 1976, Time-Life LB $25.93 (0-8094-1538-0). This part of the Time-Life Old West series deals primarily with mines and miners in the West and Alaska during the last half of the nineteenth century. [978]

7991 Time-Life Books, eds. *The Railroaders* (7–12). Illus. 1973, Silver Burdett LB $25.93 (0-8094-1467-8). The story of the building of railroads in the old West and of their effect on frontier life. [385.09]

7992 Time-Life Books, eds. *The Spanish West* (7–12). Illus. 1976, Silver Burdett LB $25.93 (0-8094-1534-8). The history of the exploration and settlement of the land north of Mexico. [979.1]

7993 Time-Life Books, eds. *The Texans* (9–12). Illus. 1975, Silver Burdett LB $25.93 (0-8094-1501-4). This volume in Time-Life's Old West series tells about the early history of Texas including the siege of the Alamo and its aftermath. [976.4]

7994 Time-Life Books, eds. *The Trailblazers* (9–12). Illus. 1973, Time-Life Books LB $25.93 (0-8094-1459-7). In this volume of the Time-Life Old West series, such men as fur trappers and mountaineers who explored the West are highlighted in a richly illustrated text. [978]

7995 Time-Life Books, eds. *The Women* (7–12). Illus. 1978, Silver Burdett LB $25.93 (0-8094-1513-5). The role that women played in the development of the American West. [305.4]

7996 Tinkle, Lon. *The Alamo* (9–12). 1960, NAL paper $2.95 (0-451-14943-2). A retelling of the events surrounding the battle and siege of the Alamo in 1836. [973.7]

7997 Trachtman, Paul. *The Gunfighters* (9–12). Illus. 1974, Silver Burdett LB $25.95 (0-8094-1480-5). A description of outlaws of the old West such as the James brothers, Butch Cassidy, and Billy the Kid. Part of the extensive Old West series from Time-Life and available through Silver Burdett. [364.3]

7998 Tunis, Edwin. *Frontier Living* (7–12). Illus. 1976, Harper $24.95 (0-690-01064-8). In interesting prose and many line drawings the author has re-created the everyday life of frontier families during the nineteenth century. [978]

7999 Turner, Frederick Jackson. *The Frontier in American History* (10–12). 1985, Univ. of Arizona Pr. paper $15.95 (0-8165-0946-8). In this series of essays first published in 1920, the noted

historian presents his ideas on the role of the frontier in shaping the American experience. [978]

8000 Wheeler, Keith. *The Scouts* (7–12). Illus. 1978, Silver Burdett LB $25.93 (0-8094-2305-7). A well-illustrated tribute to these unsung heroes who helped open up the West. Part of the Time-Life series on the Old West. [978]

8001 Wheeler, Keith. *The Townsmen* (7–12). Illus. 1975, Silver Burdett LB $25.93 (0-8094-1489-9). A description of how towns were founded in the West and how their governments and institutions evolved. From Time-Life Books. [978]

8002 Wilder, Laura Ingalls, and Rose Wilder Lane. *A Little House Sampler* (9–12). Illus. 1988, Univ. of Nebraska Pr. $15.95 (0-8032-1022-1). A collection of previously unpublished works by mother and daughter Wilder about life on the frontier. (Rev: SLJ 10/88) [973.8]

8003 Williams, John Hoyt. *A Great & Shining Road: The Epic Story of the Transcontinental Railroad* (10–12). 1988, Times Books $22.50 (0-8129-1668-9). A history of the first transcontinental railroad to the driving of the last spike in 1869. (Rev: BL 4/15/88) [385]

RECONSTRUCTION TO WORLD WAR I
(1865–1917)

8004 Ackerman, Kenneth D. *The Gold Ring: Jim Fisk, Jay Gould, and Black Friday, 1869* (10–12). 1988, Dodd $21.95 (0-396-09065-6). An engrossing retelling of one of the exploits of robber barons Jay Gould and Jim Fisk. (Rev: BL 11/1/88) [332.64]

8005 Allen, Oliver. *The Windjammers* (7–12). Illus. 1978, Time-Life $21.72 (0-8094-2704-4). A history of the many-masted ships that were important to world trade in the late nineteenth and early twentieth centuries. [387.2]

8006 Bettmann, Otto L. *The Good Old Days—They Were Terrible* (10–12). 1974, Random paper $8.95 (0-394-70941-1). A close look at everyday life in American cities from 1870 to 1900. [973.8]

8007 Cashman, Sean Dennis. *America in the Gilded Age* (10–12). 2nd ed. Illus. 1988, New York Univ. Pr. $50.00 (0-8147-1417-X); paper $16.50 (0-8147-1418-8). An account of this period in our history after the Civil War that presents the biographies of a number of key people. [973.8]

8008 Faulkner, Harold Underwood. *Politics, Reform and Expansion, 1890–1900* (10–12). Illus.

1959, Harper $17.45 (0-06-011210-7). A survey of this 10-year period during which America embarked on a course of expansion. [973.8]

8009 Franklin, John Hope. *Reconstruction: After the Civil War* (10–12). Illus. 1961, Univ. of Chicago Pr. paper $10.95 (0-226-26076-3). The period immediately after the Civil War with all its problems and challenges is well presented. [973.8]

8010 Hays, Samuel P. *The Response to Industrialism, 1885–1914* (10–12). 1957, Univ. of Chicago Pr. paper $7.00 (0-226-32162-2). This account discusses the impact of large-scale industrialization on Americans during the 30-year period before World War I. [330.973]

8011 Lawson, Don. *The United States in the Spanish-American War* (10–12). Illus. 1976, Harper LB $12.89 (0-200-00163-9). A history of the War of 1898 with special emphasis on the role of Theodore Roosevelt. [973.8]

8012 Link, Arthur S. *Woodrow Wilson and the Progressive Era, 1910–1917* (10–12). Illus. 1954, Harper paper $9.95 (0-06-133023-X). This history of the political development during this 7-year period in American history ends with our entry into World War I. [973.91]

8013 Litwack, Leon F. *Been in the Storm So Long: The Aftermath of Slavery* (10–12). 1980, Random paper $15.95 (0-394-74398-9). First-hand accounts that deal with black Americans immediately after abolition. [305.8]

8014 Mowry, George E. *The Era of Theodore Roosevelt, 1900–1912* (10–12). Illus. 1958, Harper paper $10.95 (0-06-133022-1). A readable account of the presidencies of both Theodore Roosevelt and Taft. [973.91]

8015 O'Toole, G. J. A. *The Spanish War: An American Epic—1898* (10–12). Illus. 1984, Norton paper $9.95 (0-393-30304-7). A lively reconstruction of the causes and events of the war of 1898. [973.8]

8016 Painter, Nell Irvin. *Standing at Armageddon: The United States, 1877–1919* (10–12). Illus. 1987, Norton $22.95 (0-393-02405-9). The story of the 42-year period in our history that ends with the termination of World War I. (Rev: BL 9/1/87) [973.8]

8017 Rabinowitz, Howard N., ed. *Southern Black Leaders of the Reconstruction Era* (10–12). Illus. 1982, Univ. of Illinois Pr. $27.50 (0-252-00929-0); paper $10.95 (0-252-00972-X). Profiles of the black leaders who emerged after the Civil War and of the policies they tried to implement. [975]

8018 Riis, Jacob. *How the Other Half Lives: Studies Among the Tenements of New York* (10–12). 1971, Dover paper $9.95 (0-486-22012-5). This classic account of slum conditions in New York City was first published in 1890. [305.5]

8019 Rugoff, Milton. *America's Gilded Age: Intimate Portraits from an Era of Extravagance and Chance, 1850–1890* (10–12). 1989, Henry Holt $24.95 (0-8050-0852-7). The profiles of famous Americans included range from Cornelius Vanderbilt and Jay Gould to Horatio Alger and Sojourner Truth. (Rev: BL 4/1/89; SLJ 8/89) [973.91]

8020 Smith, Gene. *High Crimes and Misdemeanors: The Impeachment and Trial of Andrew Johnson* (10–12). Illus. 1985, McGraw paper $7.95 (0-07-058478-8). A dramatic retelling of the impeachment of Johnson that ends with his death in 1875. [973.8]

8021 Smith, Page. *America Enters the World* (10–12). Illus. 1985, McGraw $29.95 (0-07-058573-3). This volume of the author's multivolume history of the United States covers the years 1901 through 1921. [973.91]

8022 Smith, Page. *The Rise of Industrial America* (10–12). Illus. 1990, Penguin $15.95 (0-14-012262-1). The story of the building of America's industrial empire and the conflict between capital and labor. [973.8]

BETWEEN THE WARS AND THE GREAT DEPRESSION (1918–1941)

8023 Agee, James, and Walker Evans. *Let Us Now Praise Famous Men* (10–12). Illus. 1960, Houghton $24.95 (0-395-48901-6); paper $12.95 (0-395-48897-4). Through photographs and thoughtful text, this volume looks at the Depression and some of the families it affected. [973.9]

8024 Allen, Frederick L. *Only Yesterday* (10–12). 1957, Harper paper $5.95 (0-06-080004-6). A popularly written informal history of American life and politics in the decade before the Crash. [973.91]

8025 Allen, Frederick L. *Since Yesterday: The Nineteen-Thirties in America* (10–12). 1986, Harper paper $8.95 (0-06-091322-3). From the stock market crash to the outbreak of war in Europe, this is a social history of America in the thirties. [973.91]

8026 Bailey, Ronald H. *The Home Front: U.S.A.* (7–12). Illus. 1977, Silver Burdett LB $25.93 (0-8094-2479-7). Life in the United States during the Depression and World War II lavishly illustrated. From Time-Life Books. [973.917]

8027 Brogan, Denis William. *The Era of Franklin D. Roosevelt* (10–12). 1950, U.S. Pubs. Assn. $8.95 (0-911548-51-3). The Roosevelt years from 1930 to his death in 1945 are re-created in this history of the Great Depression and the New Deal. [973.917]

8028 Faulkner, Harold Underwood. *From Versailles to the New Deal* (10–12). 1950, U.S. Pubs. Assn. $8.95 (0-911548-50-5). A political history of the United States during the 1920s. [973.91]

8029 Galbraith, John Kenneth. *The Great Crash, 1929* (10–12). 1988, Houghton $18.95 (0-317-66991-5); paper $8.95 (0-317-66992-3). The author describes the causes and effects of the crash and speculates on the chances of there being another one. [330.973]

8030 Goldston, Robert. *The Road between the Wars: 1918–1941* (10–12). 1978, Fawcett paper $8.95 (0-8037-7467-2). A concise history of the United States between the two world wars. [973.9]

8031 Graham, Otis L., Jr., and Meghan Robinson Wander, eds. *Franklin D. Roosevelt, His Life and Times* (10–12). Illus. 1985, G. K. Hall LB $42.00 (0-8161-8667-7). A group of specialists contributed a total of over 300 articles covering all aspects of Roosevelt's life and political career. [973.917]

8032 Karl, Barry D. *The Uneasy State: The United States from 1915–1945* (10–12). 1984, Univ. of Chicago Pr. $22.50 (0-226-42519-3). A thoughtful look at how America came of age during the 2 world wars and the period between. [973.91]

8033 Klingaman, William K. *1929: The Year of the Great Crash* (10–12). Illus. 1989, Harper $22.50 (0-06-016081-0). Through the lives of 2 dozen people, the author traces the effect of the stock market crash of 1929 on a cross-section of Americans. (Rev: BL 6/15/89; SLJ 11/89) [338.5]

8034 Lawson, Don. *FDR's New Deal* (7–12). Illus. 1979, Harper $12.95 (0-690-03953-0). A readable, well-illustrated portrayal of America between the wars. [973.917]

8035 Leuchtenburg, William E. *Franklin D. Roosevelt and the New Deal, 1932–1940* (10–12). Illus. 1963, Harper paper $8.95 (0-06-133025-6). This is a detailed account of Roosevelt's first two terms in office and the formation of domestic policies known as the New Deal. [973.917]

8036 McElvaine, Robert S. *The Great Depression: America, 1929–1941* (10–12). Illus. 1985, Random paper $10.95 (0-8129-6343-1). An account that re-creates the period of the Great Depression and gives profiles of both well-

known and common people who lived during the period. [973.91]

8037 Meltzer, Milton. *Brother, Can You Spare a Dime? The Great Depression, 1929–1933* (9–12). 1990, Facts on File $16.95 (0-8160-2372-7). A history of the Great Depression as well as material on whether it could happen again. [973.9]

8038 Nash, Gerald D. *The Great Depression and World War II: Organizing America, 1933–1945* (10–12). 1980, St. Martin's paper $12.95 (0-312-34562-3). Two momentous events in America's history—the Great Depression and World War II—are covered in this account. [973.917]

8039 Romasco, Albert U. *The Politics of Recovery: Roosevelt's New Deal* (10–12). 1983, Oxford Univ. Pr. $24.95 (0-19-503248-9). A political history of the New Deal era with emphasis on the formative years of 1933–1934. [973.917]

8040 Schraff, Anne E. *The Great Depression and the New Deal: America's Economic Collapse and Recovery* (7–12). Illus. 1990, Watts LB $12.90 (0-531-10964-X). The first half of this overview describes the collapse of our economic system and the Depression and the second half gives a picture of the New Deal and recovery. (Rev: BL 11/1/90) [973.917]

8041 Shannon, David, ed. *The Great Depression* (10–12). 1977, Peter Smith $19.50 (0-8446-2925-1). A look at how the Great Depression changed the lives of individuals. [330-973]

8042 Smith, Page. *Redeeming the Time* (10–12). 1987, McGraw $34.95 (0-07-058575-X). This, the last volume in Smith's history of the United States, covers the 1920s, the Great Depression, and the New Deal years. [973.91]

8043 Terkel, Studs. *Hard Times: An Oral History of the Great Depression* (9–12). 1970, Pantheon paper $8.95 (0-394-74691-0). This collection of first-person accounts re-creates graphically the ordeal of America during the 1930s. [973.91]

WORLD WAR II TO THE PRESENT (EXCLUDING KOREAN AND VIETNAM WARS)

8044 Abernathy, M. Glen, et al., eds. *The Carter Years: The President and Policy Making* (10–12). 1984, St. Martin's $35.00 (0-312-12286-1). A group of essays by English political specialists discussing and evaluating various aspects of the Carter administration. [973.926]

8045 Armor, John, and Peter Wright. *Manzanar* (10–12). Illus. 1988, Times Books $24.95 (0-8129-1727-8). A description of the internment camp used to house Japanese Americans during

World War II illustrated with touching photographs by Ansel Adams. (Rev: BL 11/1/88; BR 5–6/89; SLJ 5/89; VOYA 6/89) [940.5472]

8046 Arnold, Eve, et al. *The Fifties: Photographs of America* (9–12). Illus. 1985, Pantheon paper $14.95 (0-394-72720-7). From bobby soxers to the Beat Generation and the Korean War, this is a photographic record of America in the 1950s. [779]

8047 Bernstein, Carl, and Bob Woodward. *All the President's Men* (9–12). 1974, Warner paper $4.50 (0-446-32264-4). Reading like a detective story, this is the story of how the Watergate case was broken. [351.9]

8048 Bornet, Vaughn. *The Presidency of Lyndon B. Johnson* (10–12). 1984, Univ. Pr. of Kansas paper $14.95 (0-7006-0242-9). This is an assessment of both the domestic policies and foreign commitments, including the Vietnam War, that highlighted the Johnson years. [973.923]

8049 Brinkley, David. *Washington Goes to War* (10–12). Illus. 1989, Ballantine paper $4.95 (0-345-35979-8). An account of the amazing transformation in Washington during the war years, 1939–1945. (Rev: BR 1–2/90) [940.53]

8050 Broder, David S. *Changing of the Guard: Power and Leadership in America* (10–12). 1981, Penguin paper $7.95 (0-14-005940-7). This account features a series profile of politically important people who emerged during the 1970s. [973.92]

8051 Burns, Stewart. *Social Movements of the 1960s* (10–12). Illus. 1990, Twayne LB $22.95 (0-8057-9738-8); paper $9.95 (0-8057-9737-6). This book contains a history of such 1960s movements as civil rights, Vietnam War protests, women's movement, and the New Left. (Rev: SLJ 8/90) [973.9]

8052 Caputo, Philip. *A Rumor of War* (10–12). 1987, Ballantine paper $5.95 (0-345-33122-2). A first-person account of a nightmarish year spent fighting in Vietnam. [959.704]

8053 Carroll, Peter N. *It Seemed Like Nothing Happened* (10–12). 1990, Rutgers Univ. Pr. $14.95 (0-8135-1538-6). This is a history of the decade of the 1970s in the United States. [974.9]

8054 Chafe, William H. *The Unfinished Journey: America since World War II* (10–12). Illus. 1990, Oxford Univ. Pr. $35.00 (0-19-506626-X); paper $17.95 (0-19-506627-8). This is a chronicle of American history from 1945 through the 1980s. [973.92]

8055 Chancellor, John. *Peril and Promise: A Commentary on America* (10–12). 1990, Harper $17.95 (0-06-016336-4). The noted newscaster writes about the present economic and social ills of the United States and how we can cure them. (Rev: BL 3/15/90) [973.927]

8056 Divine, Robert A., ed. *Exploring the Johnson Years* (10–12). Illus. 1981, Univ. of Texas Pr. $24.95 (0-292-72031-9). A collection of essays about Johnson's presidency that covers such topics as foreign policy, civil rights, and the war on poverty. [973.923]

8057 Donovan, Robert J. *Conflict and Crisis: The Presidency of Harry S. Truman, 1945–1948* (10–12). Illus. 1977, Norton paper $11.95 (0-393-00924-6). This history details the events and decisions involved in Truman's first term in office. A similar treatment is given to the second term in *Tumultuous Years: The Presidency of Harry S. Truman, 1949–1953* (1982). [973.918]

8058 Dudley, William, and Bonnie Szumski, eds. *America's Future: Opposing Viewpoints* (9–12). Illus. 1990, Greenhaven LB $15.95 (0-89908-448-6); paper $8.95 (0-89908-423-0). A collection of different point of views on the present situation in America and where we are headed. (Rev: SLJ 8/90) [324.2]

8059 Edelstein, Andrew, and Kevin McDonough. *The Seventies: From Hotpants to Hot Tubs* (9–12). 1990, Dutton paper $12.95 (0-525-48572-4). A history of the 1970s covering politics, fashion, entertainment, and fads. (Rev: BL 7/90) [973.92]

8060 Ewing, William A. *America Worked: The 1950s Photographs of Dan Weiner* (9–12). Illus. 1989, Abrams $35.00 (0-8109-1177-9). A collection of photographs on the United States during the 1950s from the work of one of the best photojournalists of the time. (Rev: BL 9/15/89) [973]

8061 Feinberg, Barbara Silberdick. *Watergate: Scandal in the White House* (7–12). 1990, Watts LB $12.90 (0-531-10963-1). A detailed analytical examination of the Watergate Affair from the break-in to Nixon's resignation. (Rev: BL 10/1/90) [364.1]

8062 Gitlin, Todd. *The Sixties: Years of Hope, Days of Rage* (9–12). 1987, Bantam $19.95 (0-553-05233-0); paper $12.95 (0-553-34601-6). An account of all the major events, trends, and personalities of the 1960s. (Rev: BL 11/1/87) [973.933]

8063 Goldman, Eric Frederick. *The Crucial Decade—And After: America, 1945–1960* (10–12). 1982, Greenwood $35.00 (0-313-23147-8); Random paper $5.95 (0-394-70183-6). A history of these important 15 years after World War II. [973.9]

8064 Goode, Stephen. *Reaganomics: Reagan's Economic Program* (9–12). Illus. 1982, Watts LB $12.90 (0-531-04422-X). An objective account of supply side economics—the policy continued by President Bush. [338.973]

8065 Goodwin, Richard N. *Remembering America: A Voice from the Sixties* (10–12). 1988, Little $19.95 (0-316-32024-2). A former speech writer for Presidents Kennedy and Johnson looks back on a turbulent decade. (Rev: BL 9/1/88) [973.922]

8066 Halberstam, David. *The Best and the Brightest* (10–12). 1983, Penguin paper $10.95 (0-14-006983-6). An imaginative account of how the advisors to Kennedy and Johnson engineered the disasterous policies involving the war in Vietnam. [973.922]

8067 Halberstam, David. *The Next Century* (10–12). 1991, Morrow $16.95 (0-688-10391-X). A lengthy essay by this insightful writer on the major issues facing the United States today. (Rev: BL 12/15/90) [303.49]

8068 Harris, Mark Jonathan, et al., comps. *The Homefront: America during World War II* (10–12). Illus. 1984, Putnam $17.95 (0-399-12899-9). From recollections of 37 American men and women, civilian life during World War II is reconstructed. [973.917]

8069 Heath, Jim F. *Decade of Disillusionment: The Kennedy-Johnson Years* (10–12). 1975, Indiana Univ. Pr. $29.95 (0-253-31670-1); paper $9.95 (0-253-20201-9). A highly critical account of Kennedy's New Frontier and Johnson's Great Society. [973.92]

8070 Hendler, Herb. *Year by Year in the Rock Era* (7–12). 1983, Greenwood LB $36.95 (0-313-23456-6). A year-by-year chronicle of social events matched with information about artists, hits, and so on, of the rock era from 1954 through 1981. [973.92]

8071 Hurt, Henry. *Reasonable Doubt: An Investigation into the Assassination of John F. Kennedy* (10–12). 1987, Henry Holt paper $12.95 (0-8050-0360-6). A book that examines and evaluates all the works that have been written about the assassination of President Kennedy. (Rev: SLJ 8/86) [973.9]

8072 Javna, John, and Gordon Javna. *60s!* (9–12). Illus. 1983, St. Martin's paper $14.95 (0-312-01725-1). A portfolio of pictures with text about the popular culture of the 1960s. [973.92]

8073 Kahn, Albert E. *Matusow Affair: Memoir of a National Scandal* (10–12). 1987, Moyer Bell $18.95 (0-918825-38-5); paper $9.95 (0-918825-85-7). The shocking story of the paid informant

who lied to furnish the McCarthy machine with false testament during the Red Scare baiting of the 1950s. (Rev: SLJ 1/88) [973.7]

8074 Kennedy, Robert F. *Thirteen Days: A Memoir of the Cuban Missile Crisis* (10–12). 1969, NAL paper $4.95 (0-451-62794-6). A day-by-day re-creation of the events in 1962 known as the Cuban missile crisis. [973.9]

8075 Kessler, Lauren. *After All These Years: A New Look at the Sixties Generation* (10–12). 1990, Thunder's Mouth paper $13.95 (0-938410-92-X). Interviews with 51 activists of the 1960s give a rare picture of that time. (Rev: BL 5/15/90) [973.923]

8076 Ketchum, Richard M. *The Borrowed Years, 1938–1941: America on the Way to War* (9–12). 1989, Random $29.95 (0-394-56011-6). A personalized account of America on the verge of war. (Rev: BL 10/1/89) [327.73]

8077 Leuchtenburg, William E. *In the Shadow of FDR: From Harry Truman to Ronald Reagan* (10–12). 1989, Cornell Univ. Pr. $34.95 (0-8014-2341-4); paper $8.95 (0-8014-9559-8). A discussion of 8 presidents who followed FDR and how their records compared with his. [973.9]

8078 *Life: The First 50 Years, 1936–1986* (9–12). Illus. 1986, Little $50.00 (0-316-52613-4). A political and social history of America from 1936 through 1986 as seen in the pages of *Life* magazine. [779]

8079 McCoy, Donald R. *The Presidency of Harry S. Truman* (10–12). 1984, Univ. Pr. of Kansas $25.00 (0-7006-0252-6); paper $14.95 (0-7006-0255-0). An evaluation of the policies developed by Truman and the difficult decisions he made during his years in office. [973.918]

8080 MacNeil, Robert, ed. *The Way We Were: 1963—The Year Kennedy Was Shot* (9–12). Illus. 1988, Carroll & Graf $39.95 (0-88184-433-0). A book for browsing that contains over 400 photos about the year 1963 and specifically about Kennedy's assassination. (Rev: BL 10/1/88) [973.922]

8081 McQuaid, Kim. *The Anxious Years: America in the Vietnam-Watergate Era* (10–12). 1989, Basic Books $19.95 (0-465-00389-3). A readable but comprehensive account of how America changed during the years of crisis from Vietnam through Watergate. (Rev: BL 2/15/89) [973.923]

8082 Meltzer, Milton, ed. *The American Promise: Voices of a Changing Nation* (8–12). Illus. 1990, Bantam $15.95 (0-553-07020-7). In a series of excerpts from books, speeches, and interviews, the major movements affecting American life since World War II are outlined. (Rev: BL 12/15/90) [973.92]

8083 Morrison, Joan, and Robert K. Morrison. *From Camelot to Kent State: The Sixties Experience in the Words of Those Who Lived It* (9–12). Illus. 1987, Times Books paper $12.95 (0-8129-1715-1). Through the technique of oral history, the 60s are revisited through the experiences of people involved in such areas as the Vietnam War and the counterculture movement. (Rev: BL 11/1/87) [973.933]

8084 Moyers, Bill. *A World of Ideas* (10–12). Illus. 1989, Doubleday $24.95 (0-385-26278-7); paper $14.95 (0-385-26346-5). Interviews with 41 movers and shakers in American life today. (Rev: BL 4/1/89; SLJ 8/89) [973.92]

8085 O'Neil, Doris C., ed. *Life: The '60s* (9–12). Illus. 1989, Little $35.00 (0-8212-1752-6). An illustrated introduction to the 1960s through 250 photographs and connecting text. (Rev: BL 12/15/89) [973.92]

8086 O'Neill, William L. *Coming Apart: An Informal History of America in the 60's* (10–12). 1974, Times Bks. paper $9.95 (0-8129-6223-0). Under such topics as politics, war, and civil rights, this is a history of a turbulent decade, the 1960s. [973.9]

8087 Richardson, Elmo. *The Presidency of Dwight D. Eisenhower* (10–12). 1979, Univ. Pr. of Kansas $22.50 (0-7006-0183-X); paper $9.95 (0-7006-0267-4). An analysis of Eisenhower's 2 terms in office and the lasting significance of his policies. [973.921]

8088 Safire, William. *Before the Fall: An Inside View of the Pre-Watergate White House* (10–12). 1975, Da Capo paper $15.95 (0-306-80334-8). An insider's view of the White House during the Nixon years and of the events that led to the Watergate affair. [973.9]

8089 Stern, Jane, and Michael Stern. *Sixties People* (10–12). Illus. 1990, Knopf $24.95 (0-394-57050-2). A look at the various types of people that emerged during this decade when many people were caught in a search for identity. (Rev: SLJ 6/90) [973.9]

8090 Terkel, Studs. *American Dreams: Lost and Found* (10–12). 1980, Pantheon $14.95 (0-394-50793-2); Ballantine paper $4.95 (0-345-32993-7). This is a collection of impressions about present-day America from different people interviewed all across the United States. [973.9]

8091 Terkel, Studs. *The Great Divide: America at This Time* (10–12). 1988, Pantheon $18.95 (0-394-57053-7). A series of essays on the state of the United States at the end of the Reagan era. (Rev: BL 8/88; VOYA 4/89) [973.927]

8092 Unger, Irwin, and Debi Unger. *Turning Point: 1968* (9–12). Illus. 1988, Macmillan $24.95 (0-684-18696-9). The chronicle of the year 1968 complete with civil rights marches, the Vietnam War, and the heyday of the counterculture. (Rev: SLJ 3/89) [973.92]

8093 White, Theodore H. *America in Search of Itself: The Making of the President, 1956–1980* (10–12). 1982, Harper $15.95 (0-06-039007-7); Warner paper $8.95 (0-446-37559-4). The author, a noted student of American politics, interprets our political history in the years from the elections of 1956 and 1980. [973.92]

8094 White, Theodore H. *In Search of History: A Personal Adventure* (10–12). 1978, Harper $13.00 (0-06-014599-4); Warner paper $7.95 (0-446-34657-8). Through the recollections of this journalist, a 50-year history of America from the Depression to the late 1970s is traced. [973.9]

8095 White, Theodore H. *The Making of the President, 1972* (10–12). 1973, Macmillan $10.00 (0-689-10553-3). The story of the Nixon victory that also produced the Watergate affair. [324.6]

8096 Woodward, Bob, and Carl Bernstein. *The Final Days* (10–12). 1976, Simon & Schuster paper $8.95 (0-671-69087-6). This book chronicles the last 2 months of the Nixon presidency from the dismissal of John Dean to the resignation of Nixon. [973.924]

KOREAN AND VIETNAM WARS

8097 Alvarez, Everett, and Anthony S. Pitch. *Chained Eagle* (10–12). 1989, Donald I. Fine $18.95 (1-55611-167-3). The story of the 8 years of captivity of the first prisoner of war in the Vietnam War. (Rev: BL 11/1/89) [959.704]

8098 Anzenberger, Joseph. *Combat Art of the Vietnam War* (10–12). Illus. 1986, McFarland $29.95 (0-89950-197-4). Reproductions of paintings about the Vietnam War with background on each of the artists. (Rev: BR 3–4/87) [959.704]

8099 Baritz, Loren. *Backfire: American Culture and the Vietnam War* (10–12). 1985, Morrow $17.45 (0-688-04185-X); Ballantine paper $3.95 (0-345-33121-4). An account of the many bungles that characterized our involvement in this war with a warning concerning the possibility of similar disasters in the future. (Rev: BL 1/15/85) [959.704]

8100 Berry, Henry. *Hey, Mac, Where Ya Been? Living Memories of the U.S. Marines in the Korean War* (10–12). Illus. 1988, St. Martin's $22.95 (0-312-01772-3). All facets of the war and all ranks of marines are covered through carefully collected oral histories. (Rev: BL 5/15/88) [951.9]

8101 Boettcher, Thomas D. *Vietnam: The Valor and the Sorrow* (9–12). Illus. 1985, Little paper $16.95 (0-316-10081-1). An excellent popular history of the Vietnam War with many black-and-white photographs. (Rev: BL 7/85) [959.73]

8102 Bowman, John S., ed. *The Vietnam War: An Almanac* (10–12). Illus. 1985, Pharos paper $14.95 (0-88687-273-3). A chronology of both the Vietnam War and general Vietnam history. [959.704]

8103 Brady, James. *The Coldest War: A Memoir of Korea* (10–12). 1990, Crown $19.95 (0-517-57690-2). A personal history of the Korean War that is both good storytelling and a valuable account of events, places, and people. (Rev: BL 6/1/90; SLJ 11/90) [951.9]

8104 Broughton, Jack. *Going Downtown: The War against Hanoi and Washington* (10–12). Illus. 1988, Crown $18.95 (0-517-56738-5); Pocket paper $4.95 (0-671-67862-0). A Vietnam pilot writes about his many missions and of the heroism he encountered during the war. (Rev: SLJ 1/89) [959.704]

8105 Chinnery, Phil. *Air War in Vietnam* (10–12). Illus. 1987, Exeter $12.98 (0-671-08927-7). A history of aerial operations and warfare in Vietnam from the 1950s to the final airlift. (Rev: BL 1/1/88) [959.704]

8106 Coffee, Gerald. *Beyond Survival: The "Invincible Principles" for Overcoming Adversity* (10–12). 1990, Putnam $19.95 (0-399-13416-6). A POW in Vietnam for 7 years explains the principles he developed to maintain his sanity and well-being. (Rev: BL 12/1/89) [959.704]

8107 Donovan, David. *Once a Warrior King: Memories of an Officer in Vietnam* (10–12). 1986, Ballantine paper $4.95 (0-345-33316-0). For mature readers, this is a touching memoir of a caring officer at a rural outpost during the Vietnam War. (Rev: BL 6/1/85) [959.704]

8108 Dougan, Clark, et al. *The American Experience in Vietnam* (10–12). Illus. 1988, Norton $39.95 (0-393-02598-5). An account using many eyewitness narratives that describes U.S. involvement in Vietnam from Kennedy to the fall of Saigon. (Rev: BL 9/1/88) [959.70433]

8109 Dudley, William, ed. *The Vietnam War: Opposing Viewpoints* (9–12). Rev. ed. Illus. 1990, Greenhaven LB $15.95 (0-89908-478-8); paper $8.95 (0-89908-453-2). From speeches, articles, and other sources, a variety of points of view are expressed about this controversial war. (Rev: BL 1/1/85) [959.704]

8110 Edelman, Bernard, ed. *Dear America: Letters Home from Vietnam* (9–12). Illus. 1985, Norton $13.95 (0-393-01998-5). This anthology consists of 208 letters, poems, clippings, and diary entries written by American servicemen in Vietnam. [949.704]

8111 Esper, George. *The Eyewitness History of the Vietnam War: 1961–1975* (9–12). Illus. 1986, Ballantine paper $12.95 (0-345-34294-1). This book contains a simple text and hundreds of photographs, both of which trace a basic history of the war. [959.704]

8112 Fincher, E. B. *The Vietnam War* (9–12). Illus. 1980, Watts LB $12.90 (0-531-04112-3). A clear and concise history of 30 years of U.S.–Vietnam relations with fuller coverage of the course of the war. [959.704]

8113 FitzGerald, Frances. *Fire in the Lake: The Vietnamese and the Americans in Vietnam* (10–12). 1989, Random paper $9.95 (0-679-72394-3). This prize-winning book describes the effects on South Vietnam of the American intervention and entry into their civil war. [959.704]

8114 Gardner, Lloyd C. *Approaching Vietnam: From World War II through Dienbienphu, 1941–1954* (10–12). 1988, Norton $22.50 (0-393-02540-3). An account that focuses on the early days of American involvement in Southeast Asia. (Rev: BL 5/1/88) [327.730597]

8115 Goldman, Peter. *Charlie Company: What Vietnam Did to Us* (10–12). Illus. 1984, Ballantine paper $3.95 (0-345-31496-4). Interviews with the 47 survivors of Charlie Company, which fought in the Vietnam War. [959.704]

8116 Greene, Bob. *Homecoming: When the Soldiers Returned from Vietnam* (9–12). 1989, Putnam $17.95 (0-399-13386-0). A collection of letters concerning receptions received by Vietnam veterans when they returned to America. (Rev: BR 5–6/89) [959.704]

8117 Hastings, Max. *The Korean War* (9–12). Illus. 1988, Simon & Schuster paper $10.95 (0-671-66834-X). A readable, objective account of the war both in Korea and on the home front. (Rev: BL 10/15/87) [951.8]

8118 Hauptly, Denis J. *In Vietnam* (9–12). Illus. 1985, Macmillan $13.95 (0-689-31079-X). A fine basic history of the war from the early Chinese domination of the country to Vietnam's invasion of Cambodia in 1979. (Rev: BL 9/15/85; SLJ 12/85; VOYA 4/86) [959.7]

8119 Herr, Michael. *Dispatches* (10–12). 1978, Avon paper $4.50 (0-380-01976-0). A personal journal on the Vietnam War written by Herr, a correspondent. [959.704]

8120 Herring, George C. *America's Longest War: The United States and Vietnam, 1950–1975* (10–12). 1986, Temple Univ. Pr. $39.95 (0-87722-419-6); Knopf paper $13.50 (0-07-554795-3). An excellent overview of the Vietnam War that is oriented toward the American point of view. [959.704]

8121 Isaacs, Arnold R. *Without Honor: Defeat in Vietnam and Cambodia* (10–12). 1983, Johns Hopkins Univ. Pr. $35.00 (0-8018-3060-5). This history covers the end of the war in Vietnam and its eventual spread in Laos and Cambodia. [959.704]

8122 Kane, Rod. *Veteran's Day* (10–12). 1990, Orion $18.95 (0-517-56905-1). A personal memoir about the war in Vietnam and its effects on the men who fought in it. (Rev: VOYA 8/90) [959.704]

8123 Katakis, Michael. *The Vietnam Veterans Memorial* (7–12). Illus. 1988, Crown paper $15.95 (0-517-57019-X). A history of the Memorial with black-and-white photos on each page. (Rev: BL 2/1/89; SLJ 4/89; VOYA 6/89) [959.704]

8124 Kovic, Ron. *Born on the Fourth of July* (10–12). 1989, Pocket paper $4.50 (0-671-68149-4). The biography of a young marine who was physically and emotionally ruined by the Vietnam War. [959.704]

8125 Lawson, Don. *The United States in the Vietnam War* (7–12). Illus. 1981, Harper LB $12.89 (0-690-04105-5). A straightforward account of the war that also supplies excellent background information. [959.704]

8126 Mabie, Margot C. J. *Vietnam: There and Here* (9–12). Illus. 1985, Holt $11.95 (0-03-072067-2). An account of the Vietnam War that also covers its effects at home. (Rev: BL 5/1/85; SLJ 8/85) [959.704]

8127 McDonough, James. *Platoon Leader* (10–12). 1985, Presidio $15.95 (0-89141-235-2); Bantam paper $3.50 (0-553-25462-6). A vivid and compelling account of the experiences of a single platoon in Vietnam. (Rev: BL 5/15/85) [959.704]

8128 MacLear, Michael. *The Ten Thousand Day War: Vietnam 1945–1975* (10–12). 1982, Avon paper $10.95 (0-380-60970-3). This account integrates 4 points of view on the conflict—French and American as well as those of North and South Vietnam. [959.704]

8129 Marshall, Kathryn. *In the Combat Zone: An Oral History of American Women in Vietnam, 1966–1975* (10–12). 1987, Little $17.95 (0-316-54707-7); Penguin paper $7.95 (0-14-010829-7). An oral history on the important role played by women in the Vietnam conflict. (Rev: BL 1/15/87) [959.704]

8130 Mason, Robert. *Chickenhawk* (10–12). 1984, Penguin paper $4.95 (0-14-007218-7). For mature readers, the graphic story of helicopter pilots in the Vietnam War. [959.704]

8131 Maurer, Harry. *Strange Ground: Americans in Vietnam 1945–1975* (10–12). 1989, Henry Holt $29.95 (0-8050-0919-1). Interviews with 62 people who were involved in the Vietnam War in a variety of ways from diplomats to service personnel. (Rev: BR 11–12/89; SLJ 2/90; VOYA 8/89) [959.704]

8132 Millet, Allan R., ed. *A Short History of the Vietnam War* (10–12). 1978, Indiana Univ. Pr. $22.50 (0-253-35215-0); paper $6.95 (0-253-20210-8). This interesting account consists primarily of a series of articles reprinted from the *Washington Post* that trace the course of the war and its consequences. [959.704]

8133 Morrison, Wilbur H. *The Elephant & the Tiger: The Full Story of the Vietnam War* (10–12). 1990, Hippocrene $24.95 (0-87052-623-5). An extensive history of the Vietnam War written in clear prose and with a balanced point of view. (Rev: BL 4/15/90) [959.704]

8134 Norman, Geoffrey. *Bouncing Back: How a Heroic Band of POWs Survived Vietnam* (10–12). 1990, Houghton $19.95 (0-395-45186-8). The experiences of Al Stafford, a captured carrier pilot, as a prisoner of war in Vietnam. (Rev: BL 9/1/90) [959.704]

8135 Norman, Michael. *These Good Men: Friendships Forged from War* (10–12). 1990, Crown $17.95 (0-517-55984-6). A Vietnam veteran contacts the 11 members of his company that survived the war and writes of their experiences. (Rev: BL 11/1/89; VOYA 8/90) [959.704]

8136 Palmer, Laura. *Shrapnel in the Heart: Letters and Remembrances from the Vietnam Memorial* (10–12). Illus. 1987, Random $17.95 (0-394-56027-2); paper $7.95 (0-394-75988-5). A collection of poetry, letters, and other writings left at The Wall. (Rev: BL 11/15/87; BR 3–4/88; SLJ 3/88; VOYA 4/88) [959.704]

8137 *Reflections on the Wall: The Vietnam Veterans Memorial* (9–12). Illus. 1987, Stackpole $16.95 (0-8117-1846-8). Using black-and-white photographs, this book depicts events since 1982 in which America's Vietnam veterans have honored the memory of their fallen comrades in ceremonies in Washington, D.C. (Rev: BL 7/87) [975.3]

8138 Safer, Morley. *Flashbacks: On Returning to Vietnam* (10–12). Illus. 1990, Random $18.95 (0-

394-58374-4). On a return trip to Vietnam, this veteran newsman recalls his experiences there during the war. (Rev: BL 2/1/90; SLJ 8/90) [959.704]

8139 Salisbury, Harrison E., ed. *Vietnam Reconsidered: Lessons from a War* (10–12). 1984, Harper paper $9.95 (0-06-132052-8). This assessment of the results of the Vietnam War is the result of a 1983 symposium that involved such experts as Seymour Hersh and Frances Fitzgerald. [959.704]

8140 Santoli, Al. *Everything We Had* (10–12). 1982, Ballantine paper $3.95 (0-345-32279-7). Interviews with 33 veterans of the Vietnam War on the war and its impact on their lives. [959.704]

8141 Santoli, Al. *To Bear Any Burden* (10–12). Illus. 1985, Dutton $18.95 (0-525-24327-5); Ballantine paper $3.95 (0-345-33188-5). The war in Vietnam is reconstructed in the words of soldiers, advisers, refugees, government officials, and civilians from both sides. (Rev: BL 4/15/85; SLJ 9/85) [959.704]

8142 Sevy, Grace, ed. *The American Experience in Vietnam: A Reader* (10–12). 1989, Univ. of Oklahoma Pr. $24.95 (0-8061-2211-0). A collection of 30 speeches, essays, and interviews dealing with various aspects of the war. (Rev: BL 10/1/89) [959.704]

8143 Shafer, D. Michael, ed. *The Legacy: The Vietnam War in the American Imagination* (10–12). 1990, Farrar $24.95 (0-8070-5400-3). Eleven academicians write about the effects of the Vietnam War on America and the changing attitudes toward it. (Rev: BL 9/1/90) [959.704]

8144 Stokesbury, James L. *A Short History of the Korean War* (10–12). Illus. 1988, Morrow $18.95 (0-688-06377-2). A clearly written, thorough account of this war that traces its origins back to 1945. (Rev: BL 9/1/88) [951.9]

8145 Summers, Harry G., Jr. *Vietnam War Almanac* (9–12). Illus. 1985, Facts on File paper $12.95 (0-8160-1813-8). This work includes a brief history of the war, a chronology, and entries for 500 topics related to the war. [959.704]

8146 Terry, Wallace, ed. *Bloods: An Oral History of the Vietnam War by Black Veterans* (10–12). Illus. 1985, Ballantine paper $5.95 (0-345-31197-3). This volume consists of 20 narratives that survey the contributions of black servicemen in the Vietnam War. [959.704]

8147 Time-Life Books, eds. *A War Remembered* (10–12). Illus. 1986, Silver Burdett LB $14.95 (0-939526-20-4). This is one volume of an extensive 25-volume set from Time-Life Books that chroni-

cles in text and many pictures the Vietnam War. [959.704]

8148 Wheeler, John. *Touched with Fire: The Future of the Vietnam Generation* (10–12). 1984, Watts $16.95 (0-531-09832-X). This account concentrates on the adjustments made by veterans after the Vietnam War. [959.704]

8149 Whelan, Richard. *Drawing the Line: The Korean War, 1950–1953* (10–12). Illus. 1990, Little $24.95 (0-316-93403-8). A history of the Korean War that stresses the political aspects. (Rev: BL 3/15/90) [951.904]

8150 Wilcox, Fred A. *Waiting for an Army to Die: The Tragedy of Agent Orange* (10–12). 1983, Random paper $6.95 (0-394-71518-7). An account of the fate of those serving in Vietnam who were exposed to the defoliant Agent Orange. [355.1]

8151 Willenson, Kim, et al. *The Bad War: An Oral History of the Vietnam War* (10–12). 1988, NAL paper $8.95 (0-452-26063-9). This book is the result of a series of interviews conducted by *Newsweek* reporters with both Vietnamese and Americans involved in this war. (Rev: SLJ 12/87) [959.704]

8152 Williams, William Appleman, et al., eds. *America in Vietnam: A Documentary History* (10–12). 1985, Doubleday $19.95 (0-385-19752-7); paper $10.95 (0-385-19201-0). This work is a combination of documents and original essays that surveys America's role in Asia in the past with particular emphasis on the Vietnam War. (Rev: BL 2/1/85) [959.704]

Regions

MIDWEST

8153 Nelson, Barney. *Voices & Visions of the American West* (9–10). Illus. 1986, Texas Monthly $35.00 (0-87719-049-6). A photographic study of the life and work of cowboys and cowgirls in the American West. (Rev: BL 11/15/86) [978]

8154 Rydjord, John. *Indian Place-Names* (9–12). 1982, Univ. of Oklahoma Pr. paper $12.95 (0-8061-1763-4). This book, organized by tribes and linguistic families, tells the stories behind Kansas place names originated by American Indians. [910]

8155 Worster, Donald. *Dust Bowl: The Southern Plains in the 1930s* (10–12). Illus. 1979, Oxford Univ. Pr. paper $9.95 (0-19-503212-8). The story of the ecological disaster in Oklahoma and Kansas, its historical importance, the efforts during the New Deal to handle this situation, and the present situation. [978]

MOUNTAIN STATES

8156 Annerino, John. *Hiking the Grand Canyon* (10–12). Illus. 1986, Sierra Club paper $10.95 (0-87156-755-5). This is a guidebook to the Grand Canyon for the person who is serious about exploring it thoroughly. (Rev: BL 4/15/86) [917.91]

8157 Beasley, Conger, Jr., et al. *The Sierra Club Guides to the National Parks of the Rocky Mountains and the Great Plains* (7–12). Illus. 1984, Stewart, Tabori & Chang paper $14.95 (0-394-72754-1). A history and detailed description is given for each park. [917.8]

8158 Simpson, Ross W. *The Fires of '88: Yellowstone Park & Montana in Flames* (9–12). Illus. 1989, American Geographic paper $9.95 (0-938314-66-1). An account of the severe forest fires that destroyed over one million acres of timber. (Rev: BL 6/1/89) [917.87]

8159 Wallace, Robert. *The Grand Canyon* (8–12). Illus. 1985, Time-Life $13.95 (0-8094-1144-X). The history and the unique natural life of the Grand Canyon are covered in this lavishly illustrated volume. [574.9]

NORTHEAST

8160 Anderson, Jervis. *This Was Harlem* (10–12). Illus. 1982, Farrar paper $14.95 (0-374-51717-6). A 50-year history of Harlem that notes its gradual change from a white to a black community and how it became the center of black culture during the 1920s. [974.7]

8161 Bigler, Philip. *Washington in Focus: The Photo History of the Nation's Capital* (9–12). Illus. 1988, Vandemere paper $8.95 (0-918339-07-3). A history in pictures and text of Washington, D.C., from its beginnings to the Metro and the Vietnam Memorial. (Rev: BL 12/15/88) [975.3]

8162 Blanchet, Christian. *The Statue of Liberty* (10–12). Illus. 1985, Houghton $29.95 (0-8281-1189-8). This book tells of the beginnings of the statue in France, its opening in 1886, and its subsequent history. [947.7]

8163 Burchard, Sue. *The Statue of Liberty* (9–12). Illus. 1985, Harcourt $13.95 (0-15-279969-9). Through the events surrounding this landmark, the author re-creates important events in over 100 years of American history. [974.7]

8164 Durham, Michael S. *The Mid-Atlantic States* (8–12). Illus. 1989, Stewart, Tabori & Chang $24.95 (1-55670-060-1); paper $17.95 (1-55670-050-4). A sumptuously illustrated guide to the historic spots and museums in the middle Atlantic states. (Rev: BL 4/1/89) [917.4]

8165 Fox, Nancy Jo. *Liberties with Liberty: The Fascinating History of America's Proudest Symbol* (9–12). Illus. 1986, Dutton $22.50 (0-525-24377-1); paper $14.95 (0-525-48192-3). This book is really a gallery of illustrations, from cartoons to intricate paintings, that tell the story of the Statue of Liberty. (Rev: BL 9/1/86) [704.9]

8166 Hayden, Richard Seth, and Thierry W. Despont. *Restoring the Statue of Liberty: Sculpture, Structure, Symbol* (10–12). Illus. 1986, McGraw $39.95 (0-07-027327-8); paper $14.95 (0-07-027326-X). The story of how the statue was restored in time for its hundredth birthday. (Rev: BL 5/15/86) [974.7]

8167 Kulik, Stephen, et al., eds. *The Audubon Society Field Guide to the Natural Places of the Northeast* (10–12). Illus. 1984, Pantheon paper $12.95 (0-394-72282-5). This is a guide to the flora and fauna of preserves from Long Island north to the Canadian border. The area of southern Virginia to New York State is covered in *The Audubon Society Field Guide to the Natural Places of the Mid-Atlantic States* (1984). [917.4]

8168 LaBastille, Anne. *Beyond Black Bear Lake* (10–12). 1987, Norton $15.95 (0-393-02388-5); paper $7.95 (0-393-30538-2). LaBastille continues to tell about her life in the Adirondack wilderness and of her commitment to ecology in this sequel to *Woodswoman* (1974). (Rev: BL 12/15/86) [333.7]

8169 Lewis, David L. *When Harlem Was in Vogue* (10–12). 1989, Oxford Univ. Pr. paper $11.95 (0-19-505969-7). A history of Harlem from 1904 to 1935 with emphasis on its prominence during the 1920s. [947.7]

8170 McPhee, John A. *In Suspect Terrain* (10–12). 1983, Farrar $12.95 (0-374-17650-7); paper $7.95 (0-374-51794-0). This is an exploration of the Appalachian system as conducted by the author and geologist Anita Harris. [974]

8171 Peters, James Edward. *Arlington National Cemetery: Shrine to America's Heroes* (10–12). Illus. 1986, Woodbine $16.95 (0-933149-23-9); paper $12.95 (0-933149-04-2). The history of the national cemetery that is the last resting place of some 200,000 Americans. (Rev: BL 12/1/86) [917]

8172 Smith, Howard. *A Naturalist's Guide to the Year* (10–12). Illus. 1985, Dutton $18.95 (0-525-

24297-X). A guide to the many changes in nature that occur during a year in the Northeast. (Rev: SLJ 9/85) [507]

8173 Spiering, Frank. *Bearer of a Million Dreams: The Biography of the Statue of Liberty* (10–12). Illus. 1986, Jameson Books $16.95 (0-915463-35-0). The history of the Statue of Liberty from the standpoint of 5 lives that were most responsible for her, such as sculptor Bartholdi, publisher Pulitzer, and poet Emma Lazarus. (Rev: BL 7/86) [974.1]

8174 White House Historical Association, Washington, D.C. *The White House* (9–12). Illus. 1962, The Association $12.95 (0-912308-35-4); paper $9.50 (0-912308-11-7). This is a guided tour of the White House with many pictures and historical explanations. [975.3]

8175 Wiencek, Henry. *Southern New England* (8–12). Illus. 1989, Stewart, Tabori & Chang $24.95 (1-55670-059-8); paper $17.95 (1-55670-051-2). A beautifully illustrated guide to museums and historical sites in Connecticut, Rhode Island, and Massachusetts. (Rev: BL 4/1/89) [917.4]

PACIFIC STATES

8176 Arnold, Thomas A. *The Adventure Guide to the Pacific Northwest* (9–12). Illus. 1988, Hunter paper $12.95 (1-55650-034-3). A travel guide with maps and pictures that highlights outdoor activities available from Northern California through Washington State. (Rev: BL 9/1/88) [917.95]

8177 Boessenecker, John. *Badge and Buckshot: Lawlessness in Old California* (10–12). Illus. 1988, Univ. of Oklahoma Pr. $22.95 (0-8061-2097-5). A profile of 10 of California's most famous lawmen and infamous outlaws. (Rev: BL 2/15/88) [979.4]

8178 Brown, Joseph E., et al. *The Sierra Club Guides to the National Parks of the Pacific Southwest and Hawaii* (7–12). Illus. 1984, Stewart, Tabori & Chang paper $14.95 (0-394-72490-9). Many color photographs and maps enhance the detailed description of each park. Also use companion volumes on the parks of the East and Middle West (1986), the Desert Southwest (1984), and the Pacific Southwest and Hawaii (1984). [917.9]

8179 Carter, Frances. *Hawaii for Free: Hundreds of Free Things to Do in Hawaii* (10–12). Illus. 1988, Mustang paper $6.95 (0-914457-21-7). A guide for the frugal tourist who wants to see Hawaii inexpensively and to those who simply

wish to learn more about these islands. (Rev: BL 10/15/88) [919.69]

8180 Haines, John. *The Stars, the Snow, the Fire: Twenty-five Years in the Northern Wilderness* (10–12). 1989, Graywolf $16.00 (1-55597-117-2). A collection of essays about life in the interior wilderness of Alaska by a poet who went there to forget modern life. (Rev: BL 5/15/89) [818.5403]

8181 Harvard Student Agencies. *Let's Go, 1990: The Budget Guide to California and Hawaii* (9–12). 1989, St. Martin's paper $12.95 (0-312-03376-1). This book tells about these 2 states and offers inexpensive travel tips. Also use: *Let's Go, 1990: The Budget Guide to the Pacific Northwest, Western Canada and Alaska* (1989). (Rev: BL 2/1/85) [917.9]

8182 McConnaughey, Bayard, and Evelyn McConnaughey. *Pacific Coast* (9–12). Illus. 1985, Knopf paper $15.95 (0-394-73130-1). A nature guide to the ecology of the Pacific states with emphasis on the bird life. (Rev: SLJ 9/85) [979]

8183 McGinniss, Joe. *Going to Extremes* (10–12). Illus. 1980, NAL paper $8.95 (0-452-26301-8). A descriptive tour of the state of Alaska and of recent developments, some of which cause concern for the author. [979.8]

8184 McPhee, John A. *Coming into the Country* (10–12). 1982, Bantam paper $4.95 (0-553-25527-4). The author describes his trip by canoe and kayak through an Alaskan wilderness. [917.98]

8185 Murray, John A., ed. *A Republic of Rivers: Three Centuries of Nature Writing from Alaska and the Yukon* (10–12). Illus. 1990, Oxford Univ. Pr. $19.95 (0-19-506102-0). From the Bering expedition of 1741 to the present time of environmentalism, this is a collection of writings about Alaska by about 50 authors. (Rev: BL 9/1/90) [508.798]

8186 Nelson, Richard. *The Island Within* (10–12). 1989, North Point $18.95 (0-86547-404-4). An anthropologist investigates an uninhabited island in the Haida Strait. (Rev: BL 9/15/89) [306]

8187 Palmer, Tim. *The Sierra Nevada: A Mountain Journey* (10–12). Illus. 1988, Island Pr. $31.95 (0-933280-54-8); paper $19.95 (0-933280-53-X). A thoughtful account of 9 months spent following the Sierra Nevada mountains of California and Nevada. (Rev: BL 11/15/88) [333.78]

8188 Scott, Alastair. *Tracks across Alaska: A Dog Sled Journey* (9–12). Illus. 1990, Atlantic Monthly $19.95 (0-87113-389-X). The story of an

800-mile trek through Alaskan tundra by dog-sled. (Rev: BL 9/15/90) [917.980]

8189 Shane, Scott. *Discovering Mount St. Helens! : A Guide to the National Volcanic Monument* (10–12). 1985, Univ. of Washington Pr. paper $8.95 (0-295-96222-4). This is a guide to the Mount St. Helen's area and a description of its eruptions. [979.7]

8190 Sullivan, William L. *Listening for Coyote: A Walk across Oregon's Wilderness* (10–12). Illus. 1988, Morrow $18.95 (0-688-07880-X). A 2-month, 1,360-mile hike, the terrain, wildlife, and the people the author meets in his journey through the wilderness area of Oregon. (Rev: BL 9/15/88) [917.95]

8191 Walker, Tom. *Shadows on the Tundra: Alaskan Tales of Predators, Prey and Man* (10–12). Illus. 1989, Stackpole $19.95 (0-8117-1724-0). In short narrative pieces and photographs such animals as grizzlies and wolves are introduced. (Rev: SLJ 5/90) [979.8]

8192 Wheeler, Keith. *The Alaskans* (7–12). Illus. 1977, Silver Burdett LB $25.93 (0-8094-1505-4). The history of Alaska from purchase to before World War I. Part of the Time-Life Books series on the Old West. [979.8]

8193 Wright, Sam. *Koviashuvik: A Time and Place of Joy* (10–12). 1989, Sierra Club $17.95 (0-87156-688-5). A graceful, eloquently written tribute to Alaska and to Eskimos by a man who with his wife spent many years there. (Rev: BL 3/15/89) [128.4]

SOUTH

8194 Abbott, Shirley. *Womenfolks: Growing Up down South* (10–12). 1983, Ticknor paper $8.95 (0-89919-283-1). An account of a girl's youth in Arkansas and the lives of her female relatives. [975]

8195 Haley, James L. *Texas: An Album of History* (9–12). Illus. 1985, Doubleday $24.95 (0-385-17307-5). This history that concentrates on key events and people contains over 200 photographs. (Rev: BL 10/1/85) [976.4]

8196 Wiencek, Henry. *Virginia and the Capital Region* (8–12). Illus. 1989, Stewart, Tabori & Chang $24.95 (1-55670-058-X); paper $17.95 (1-55670-048-2). Historical sites and museums are described and illustrated in this guide to Washington, D.C., and Virginia. (Rev: BL 4/1/89) [917.4]

8197 Wigginton, Eliot, ed. *Foxfire* (9–12). Illus. 1972, Doubleday $15.95 (0-385-07350-X); paper $13.95 (0-385-07353-4). There are now over 10 of these guides to handcrafts and various country activities that started as a chronicle of change in an Appalachian village. [975.8]

SOUTHWEST

8198 Beasley, Conger, Jr., et al. *The Sierra Club Guides to the National Parks of the Desert Southwest* (7–12). Illus. 1984, Stewart, Tabori & Chang paper $14.95 (0-394-72488-7). In addition to a description of the parks there is also a rundown on the flora and fauna in the region. [917.9]

8199 Fishbein, Seymour L. *Yellowstone Country: The Enduring Wonder* (9–12). Illus. 1989, National Geographic $9.50 (0-87044-718-1). A profile of the world's oldest national park with particularly good coverage on its flora and fauna. (Rev: BL 11/1/89; SLJ 1/90) [917.87]

8200 La Farge, Oliver, and Arthur N. Morgan. *Santa Fe: The Autobiography of a Southwestern Town* (10–12). Illus. 1985, Univ. of Oklahoma Pr. paper $15.95 (0-8061-1696-X). In excerpts from newspaper articles, the history of the city of Santa Fe is given from 1849 to 1953. [978.9]

8201 Lavender, David. *The Southwest* (10–12). 1984, Univ. of New Mexico Pr. paper $15.95 (0-8263-0736-1). The history of the entire Southwest is given, with emphasis on New Mexico and Arizona. [979.1]

8202 McCarry, Charles. *The Great Southwest* (10–12). Illus. 1980, National Geographic LB $9.50 (0-87044-288-0). This introduction to the Southwest covers the history but also emphasizes the geography of the region. [979.1]

Physical and Applied Sciences

General and Miscellaneous

8203 Alic, Margaret. *Hypatia's Heritage* (10–12). Illus. 1986, Beacon paper $10.95 (0-8070-6731-8). A clearly written account of women's many contributions to science. (Rev: BL 9/15/86) [509]

8204 Asimov, Isaac. *Asimov on Science: A 30-Year Retrospective* (9–12). 1989, Doubleday $17.95 (0-385-26345-7). A collection of magazine columns on various aspects of science. Also use: *The Tyrannosaurus Prescription and 100 Other Essays* (1989). (Rev: BL 9/1/89) [500]

8205 Asimov, Isaac. *Asimov's Chronology of Science and Discovery* (9–12). Illus. 1989, Harper $29.95 (0-06-015612-0). From 4 million B.C. to the present, Asimov gives entries on major scientific breakthroughs in chronological order. (Rev: BL 10/15/89) [509]

8206 Asimov, Isaac. *Asimov's New Guide to Science* (9–12). Illus. 1984, Basic Books $29.95 (0-465-00473-3). A 2-part work that introduces such areas as physics, chemistry, astronomy, the earth, and the human body. [500]

8207 Asimov, Isaac. *The Beginning and the End* (10–12). 1977, Pocket paper $3.50 (0-671-47644-0). A general work on science that covers such topics as gravitation, water, the moon, and the earth in A.D. 2176. [500]

8208 Asimov, Isaac. *Far As Human Eye Could See* (10–12). 1987, Doubleday $15.95 (0-385-23514-3); Windsor paper $3.95 (1-55817-107-4). A collection of pieces mostly on astronomy and chemistry by the prolific writer. (Rev: BL 2/1/87; VOYA 8–9/87) [500]

8209 Asimov, Isaac. *Frontiers: New Discoveries about Man and His Planet, Outer Space and the Universe* (9–12). 1990, Dutton $19.95 (0-525-24662-2). A collection of essays, each dealing with a new advance in science. (Rev: BL 12/15/89) [500]

8210 Asimov, Isaac. *Out of the Everywhere* (10–12). 1990, Doubleday $17.95 (0-385-26201-9). A collection of essays on a variety of scientific topics written in 1987 and 1988. (Rev: BL 5/15/90) [500]

8211 Asimov, Isaac. *The Planet That Wasn't* (10–12). 1976, Doubleday paper $7.95 (0-385-11687-X). This is a collection of essays covering a number of topics in science. Also use *The Tragedy of the Moon* (1978). [500]

8212 Asimov, Isaac. *The Subatomic Monster* (9–12). 1985, NAL paper $3.95 (0-451-62530-7). This is a collection of essays dealing with such topics as relativity, biology, and the stars. (Rev: BL 8/85) [500]

8213 Bodanis, David. *The Secret House* (10–12). Illus. 1988, Simon & Schuster paper $12.95 (0-671-65718-6). The author describes scientifically the many common occurrences that happen in a house on a typical day, for example, dust being distributed by air currents. (Rev: BL 9/15/86) [500]

8214 Bruno, Leonard. *The Landmarks of Science* (9–12). Illus. 1989, Facts on File $40.00 (0-8160-2137-6). Using the actual writings of famous scientists like Galileo, Darwin, and Freud, the author traces the history of science. (Rev: BR 5–6/90) [500]

8215 Calder, Nigel, and John Newell, eds. *On the Frontiers of Science* (9–12). Illus. 1989, Facts on File $35.00 (0-8160-2205-4). A compilation of writings by contemporary scientists about current work being accomplished in many different branches of science. (Rev: BR 5–6/90) [500]

8216 Curtis, Will, ed. *The Nature of Things* (10–12). Illus. 1985, Countryman $15.95 (0-88150-028-3); Ecco paper $10.95 (0-88001-207-2). Over 200 short science essays on such subjects as planets, space, plants, and diet. (Rev: SLJ 9/85) [500]

8217 de Camp, L. Sprague. *The Fringe of the Unknown* (10–12). 1983, Prometheus paper $14.95 (0-87975-217-3). A collection of unusual information about various branches of science. [500]

8218 Flanagan, Dennis. *Flanagan's Version: A Spectator's Guide to Science on the Eve of the Twenty-First Century* (10–12). 1988, Knopf $18.95 (0-394-55547-3); Random paper $8.95 (0-679-72156-8). The founder of *Scientific American* discusses the various branches of science and how they overlap. (Rev: BL 4/15/88; BR 11–12/88; SLJ 10/88; VOYA 12/88) [500]

8219 Franck, Irene M., and David M. Brownstone. *Scientists and Technologists* (9–12). Illus. 1988, Facts on File $14.95 (0-8160-1450-7). A history of an amazing array of careers in science and technology and how they have changed through the centuries. (Rev: BR 5–6/88; SLJ 6–7/88; VOYA 8/88) [500]

8220 Gardner, Martin. *Gardner's Whys and Wherefores* (10–12). 1989, Univ. of Chicago Pr. $19.95 (0-226-28245-7). A collection of essays and book reviews on a variety of science topics by this writer associated with the magazine *Scientific American*. (Rev: SLJ 11/89) [500]

8221 Gornick, Vivian. *Women in Science: Portraits from a World in Transition* (10–12). 1983, Simon & Schuster paper $8.95 (0-671-69592-4). This is a survey account of women in various branches of science and the particular problems they face. [509]

8222 Hofstadter, Douglas R. *Gödel, Escher, Bach: An Eternal Golden Braid* (10–12). 1979, Basic $34.95 (0-465-02685-0); Random paper $14.95 (0-394-75682-7). For better readers, this is an exploration of technology and human intelligence that mixes science and art. [500]

8223 Krishtalka, Leonard. *Dinosaur Plots & Other Intrigues in Natural History* (10–12). Illus. 1989, Morrow $17.95 (0-688-07116-3). In a most entertaining fashion, this noted paleontologist writes about many scientific subjects, many related to his field. (Rev: BL 3/15/89) [560]

8224 Metos, Thomas H. *The New Eyes of the Scientist* (9–12). Illus. 1988, Watts $12.90 (0-531-10609-8). For better readers, a history and description of the many new telescopes, microscopes, and allied tools that allow us to probe scientific mysteries deeper than before. (Rev:

BL 1/15/89; BR 1–2/89; SLJ 1/89; VOYA 4/89) [502]

8225 Morrison, Philip, and Phylis Morrison. *The Ring of Truth* (10–12). Illus. 1989, Random paper $15.95 (0-679-72130-4). This volume tells much about what scientific truths are known and also about the methods used to uncover them. (Rev: BR 3–4/88; SLJ 2/88) [501]

8226 Nicholls, Peter, ed. *The Science in Science Fiction* (7–12). Illus. 1983, Knopf $25.00 (0-394-53010-1); paper $14.95 (0-394-71364-8). Such subjects common in science fiction as space travel, aliens, and UFOs are examined for scientific truth. [500]

8227 *On the Brink of Tomorrow: Frontiers of Science* (10–12). Illus. 1982, National Geographic Soc. $7.95 (0-87044-414-X). A collection of articles about recent scientific developments in such areas of science as medicine, brain research, and astrophysics. [500]

8228 Papacosta, Pangratios. *The Splendid Voyage: An Introduction to New Sciences and New Technologies* (9–12). Illus. 1987, Prentice paper $10.95 (0-13-835380-8). A clear explanation of such recent scientific breakthroughs as CAT scans, microchips, and laser science. (Rev: BL 4/1/87) [500]

8229 Rensberger, Boyce. *How the World Works: A Guide to Science's Greatest Discoveries* (9–12). Illus. 1986, Morrow $18.95 (0-688-05398-X); paper $7.95 (0-688-07293-3). For the layman, an explanation of the important theories in science from big bang to evolution. (Rev: BL 3/15/86) [500]

8230 Roberts, Royston M. *Serendipity: Accidental Discoveries in Science* (9–12). Illus. 1989, Wiley $18.95 (0-471-50658-3); paper $12.95 (0-471-60203-5). An entertaining collection of anecdotes concerning the unusual circumstances surrounding some scientific discoveries. (Rev: BR 1–2/90; SLJ 11/89) [500]

8231 Ronan, Colin A. *Science: Its History and Development Among the World's Cultures* (10–12). Illus. 1983, Facts on File $29.95 (0-87196-745-6); paper $14.95 (0-8160-1165-6). A history of science from ancient civilizations to the present. [509]

8232 Sagan, Carl. *Broca's Brain: Reflections on the Romance of Science* (10–12). 1979, Ballantine paper $4.95 (0-345-33689-5). A collection of essays on new scientific developments such as the search for extraterrestrial life. [500]

8233 Shapiro, Gilbert. *A Skeleton in the Darkroom: Stories of Serendipity in Science* (10–12). Illus. 1986, Harper $13.95 (0-06-250778-8). The story of seven scientific discoveries of importance that occurred by accident. (Rev: SLJ 4/87) [509]

8234 Shropshire, Walter, ed. *The Joys of Research* (10–12). 1982, Smithsonian Inst. paper $7.95 (0-87474-857-7). Eight scientists, including 4 Nobel prize winners, write about scientific research and what it means to them. [001.4]

8235 Snow, C. P. *Two Cultures: And a Second Look* (10–12). 1969, Cambridge Univ. Pr. paper $9.95 (0-521-09576-X). This study by the famous novelist describes the rifts between science and art. [500]

8236 Vare, Ethlie Ann, and Greg Ptacek. *Mothers of Invention* (10–12). Illus. 1988, Morrow $17.95 (0-688-06464-7). A rundown on women inventors through history, some important and some less so, like the inventor of the chocolate chip cookie. (Rev: SLJ 5/88) [500]

8237 Weller, Tom. *Science Made Stupid: How to Discomprehend the World Around Us* (9–12). Illus. 1985, Houghton paper $7.95 (0-395-36646-1). A humorous takeoff on science texts and lab manuals. (Rev: SLJ 8/85) [500]

8238 WGBH/Boston. *Nova: Adventures in Science* (9–12). Illus. 1983, Addison paper $16.95 (0-201-05359-4). A collection of material from various Nova television shows that covers a wide variety of scientific topics. [500]

Experiments and Projects

8239 Adams, Richard C. *Science with Computers* (9–12). 1987, Watts $12.90 (0-531-10324-2). How to improve science projects by using the computer to produce graphs, databases, simulations, and so on. (Rev: BR 1–2/88) [507]

8240 Apfel, Necia H. *Astronomy Projects for Young Scientists* (9–12). 1984, Prentice paper $7.95 (0-668-06006-9). This book outlines clearly a series of science fair projects using astronomy as a focus. [523]

8241 Gutnik, Martin J. *Genetics* (9–12). Illus. 1985, Watts $12.90 (0-531-04936-1). Many of these projects are complicated but all explore principles in heredity, genetics, and evolution. (Rev: BL 12/1/85; BR 5–6/86) [595.1]

8242 Harre, Rom. *Great Scientific Experiments: Twenty Experiments That Changed Our View of the World* (10–12). Illus. 1984, Oxford Univ. Pr. $24.95 (0-19-520436-0); paper $9.95 (0-19-286036-4). Good background material is given on 20 discoveries and their importance in scientific history. [509]

8243 Iritz, Maxine Haren. *Science Fair: Developing a Successful and Fun Project* (8–12). Illus. 1987, TAB $14.95 (0-8306-0936-9); paper $9.95 (0-8306-2936-X). A thorough step-by-step introduction to doing a science project. (Rev: BL 4/15/88) [507]

8244 Schaaf, Fred. *Seeing the Sky: 100 Projects, Activities & Explorations in Astronomy* (9–12). Illus. 1990, Wiley paper $12.95 (0-471-51067-X). In addition to many activities, from the simple to the complex, this informative work gives background facts about sky phenomena. (Rev: BL 10/15/90) [523]

8245 Stine, G. Harry. *On the Frontiers of Science: Strange Machines You Can Build* (10–12). Illus. 1985, Macmillan paper $9.95 (0-689-11562-8). This book tells you how to make a number of unusual gadgets and contraptions such as a detecting rod and a wishing machine. (Rev: BL 6/15/85) [621.8]

8246 Tocci, Salvatore. *Biology Projects for Young Scientists* (10–12). Illus. 1987, Watts LB $12.90 (0-531-10429-X). This advanced project book requires some background knowledge of science and access to a well-equipped laboratory. (Rev: BL 12/15/87; BR 1–2/88; SLJ 3/88; VOYA 2/88) [507]

Astronomy and Space Science

General and Miscellaneous

8247 Berry, Richard. *Discover the Stars* (9–12). Illus. 1987, Crown paper $12.95 (0-517-56529-3). A beginner's guide to exploring stars, planets, and the moon with hints on how to use a telescope. (Rev: SLJ 4/88; VOYA 4/88) [523]

8248 Brecher, Kenneth, and Michael Feirtag, eds. *Astronomy of the Ancients* (10–12). Illus. 1987, MIT Pr. paper $9.95 (0-262-52070-2). A history of the role played in ancient civilizations by astronomy and its influence in such areas as agriculture, religion, and mythology. [520]

8249 Brown, Peter Lancaster. *Star and Planet Spotting: A Field Guide to the Night Sky* (10–12). Illus. 1990, Sterling paper $8.95 (0-8069-7268-8). As well as providing a history of star-gazing, this volume supplies a guided tour of the sky at night. (Rev: BL 6/1/90) [523.8]

8250 Calder, Nigel. *Timescale: An Atlas of the Fourth Dimension* (10–12). Illus. 1983, Penguin paper $8.95 (0-14-006342-0). From the big bang theory through time and space to the year 2000. [529]

8251 Chaisson, Eric. *Relatively Speaking: Relativity, Black Holes, and the Fate of the Universe* (10–12). Illus. 1988, Norton $18.95 (0-393-02536-5). For advanced students this is a brief account of Einstein's life and a detailed explanation of his theory. (Rev: BL 9/15/88) [530.1]

8252 Chaple, Glenn. *Exploring with a Telescope* (8–12). Illus. 1988, Watts LB $11.90 (0-531-10581-4). In addition to tips on buying and operating a telescope, this book describes how to use one and become an amateur astronomer. (Rev: BR 3–4/89) [523]

8253 Chartrand, Mark R. *Skyguide: A Field Guide for Amateur Astronomers* (7–12). Illus. 1982, Golden paper $9.95 (0-307-13667-1). A guide for sky watchers who have only binoculars or a simple telescope. [523]

8254 Clark, David H. *The Cosmos from Space: Astronomical Breakthroughs—The View from Beyond Earth's Atmosphere* (10–12). 1987, Crown $14.95 (0-517-56245-6). A review of the part astronautics can play in developing astronomy. (Rev: BL 6/1/87; VOYA 12/87) [520]

8255 Cohen, Martin. *In Darkness Born* (10–12). 1988, Cambridge Univ. Pr. $19.95 (0-521-26270-4). For better readers with a science background, this account delves into theories about the birth of stars and the universe. (Rev: BR 9–10/88) [523]

8256 DeVorkin, David H. *Practical Astronomy* (9–12). 1986, Smithsonian paper $12.95 (0-87474-359-1). A collection of lecture notes with problems and exercises. (Rev: BR 5–6/87) [523]

8257 Dickinson, Terence. *Nightwatch: An Equinox Guide to Viewing the Universe* (9–12). Rev. ed. Illus. 1989, Camden House $34.95 (0-920656-91-9); paper $24.95 (0-920656-89-7). A popular manual on the various bodies visible in the sky and the equipment needed to view them. (Rev: BL 11/1/89) [520]

8258 Eicher, David. *The Universe from Your Backyard* (10–12). 1988, Cambridge Univ. Pr. $24.95 (0-521-36229-7). Directions are given on how to find almost 700 celestial bodies in this anthology taken from the pages of *Astronomy* magazine. (Rev: BR 5–6/89) [523]

8259 Field, George, and Donald Goldsmith. *The Space Telescope: Eyes above the Atmosphere* (9–12). 1989, Contemporary $18.95 (0-8092-4495-

0). The history, structure, and capabilities of the Hubble Space Telescope are described in this volume published several months before the actual launching. (Rev: BL 11/1/89) [522]

8260 Fjermedal, Grant. *New Horizons in Amateur Astronomy* (9–12). Illus. 1989, Putnam paper $10.95 (0-399-51486-4). An introduction to astronomy, telescopes, and how to contact fellow enthusiasts. (Rev: BL 2/1/89) [523]

8261 Friedman, Herbert. *The Astronomer's Universe: Stars, Galaxies, and Cosmos* (10–12). 1990, Norton $24.95 (0-393-02818-6). A view of the past history of astronomy and material on present challenges and findings. (Rev: BL 5/15/90) [520]

8262 Gallant, Roy A. *Once Around the Galaxy* (10–12). Illus. 1983, Watts LB $12.90 (0-531-04681-8). A history of astronomy in relation to what we have learned about the Milky Way galaxy. [523]

8263 Goldsmith, Donald. *Supernova! The Exploding Star of 1987* (10–12). Illus. 1989, St. Martin's $15.95 (0-312-02647-1). Current theories in astronomy are explained through the observations of a supernova. (Rev: BR 3–4/90; SLJ 6/90) [523]

8264 Graham-Smith, Francis, and Bernard Lovell. *Pathways to the Universe* (9–12). Illus. 1989, Cambridge Univ. Pr. $24.95 (0-521-32004-6). A readable, well-organized introduction to astronomy that can be used both for reference and for recreational reading. (Rev: BR 9–10/89) [523]

8265 Jastrow, Robert. *Red Giants and White Dwarfs* (10–12). Illus. 1990, Norton $11.90 (0-393-85004-8). This book describes the birth of stars, the evolution of life on earth, and the possibility of life elsewhere. [523.1]

8266 Lederman, Leon M., and David N. Schramm. *From Quarks to the Cosmos: Tools of Discovery* (10–12). Illus. 1989, Scientific American $32.95 (0-7167-5052-X). Through a discussion of particles and the amazing tools used to explore them, the authors introduce current thinking about space and time. (Rev: BL 11/15/89) [520]

8267 Little, Robert T. *Astrophotography: A Step-by-Step Approach* (10–12). Illus. 1986, Macmillan $20.95 (0-02-948980-6). For the amateur astronomer, here is a clear explanation of the equipment necessary and techniques to use in photographing the sky. (Rev: BL 3/15/86) [522]

8268 McAleer, Neil. *The Cosmic Mind-Boggling Book* (9–12). 1982, Warner $11.95 (0-446-39046-1). A fascinating collection of unusual facts about the planets, stars, and universe. [523]

8269 McAleer, Neil. *The Mind-Boggling Universe: A Dazzling Scientific Journey through Distant Space and Time* (10–12). Illus. 1987, Doubleday paper $8.95 (0-385-23039-7). A tour of our universe from our own Milky Way to the farthest reaches of space. (Rev: BL 2/15/87) [523]

8270 Makower, Joel, ed. *The Air & Space Catalog* (10–12). Illus. 1989, Random $27.50 (0-394-58327-2); paper $16.95 (0-679-72038-3). A directory of organizations, materials, and activities connected with aeronautics, space exploration, aviation, and meteorology. (Rev: BL 12/15/89; SLJ 5/90; VOYA 8/90) [500.5]

8271 Mayall, Newton, et al. *The Sky Observer's Guide* (10–12). Illus. 1985, Western paper $2.95 (0-307-24007-6). A guide for the amateur astronomer that supplies many maps of the sky at various times of the year. [523]

8272 Mitton, Simon, and Jacqueline Mitton. *Invitation to Astronomy* (10–12). Illus. 1986, Basil Blackwell $29.95 (0-631-14699-7); paper $9.95 (0-631-14695-4). A description of the science of astronomy, the tools of the trade, and recent discoveries in the field. (Rev: SLJ 11/86) [523]

8273 Moore, Patrick. *Astronomers' Stars* (10–12). Illus. 1989, Norton $17.95 (0-393-02663-9). Sixteen different kinds of stars are introduced in this overview of astronomy. (Rev: BL 7/89; SLJ 4/90) [523]

8274 Moore, Patrick. *Exploring the Night Sky with Binoculars* (9–12). 1986, Cambridge Univ. Pr. $24.95 (0-521-30756-2). A book that covers such topics as the history of astronomy, stellar maps, facts about the stars, and how to use binoculars. (Rev: BR 5–6/87) [523]

8275 Moore, Patrick. *The Guinness Book of Astronomy* (9–12). Illus. 1988, Sterling $19.95 (0-85112-375-9). A fact-crammed book that introduces both the solar system and the universe. (Rev: SLJ 1/89) [523]

8276 Moore, Patrick. *The New Atlas of the Universe* (7–12). Illus. 1984, Crown $24.95 (0-517-55500-X). A detailed series of maps that introduce our solar system and the universe beyond. [523]

8277 Moore, Patrick. *Pocket Guide to Astronomy* (9–12). 1980, Simon & Schuster paper $7.95 (0-671-25309-3). A handy guide to this science, suitable for the beginner. [523]

8278 Muirden, James. *The Amateur Astronomer's Handbook* (10–12). 3rd ed. Illus. 1983, Harper paper $10.95 (0-317-65074-2). A guide for the beginner that includes material on equipment and its use, stars, and the solar system. [523]

8279 Muirden, James. *The Astronomy Handbook* (10–12). Illus. 1982, Arco paper $10.95 (0-688-06235-5). A fine guide for the amateur astronomer to identify stars, planets, and other heavenly bodies. [523]

8280 Muirden, James. *Astronomy with a Small Telescope* (10–12). Illus. 1986, Prentice $18.95 (0-13-049941-2). A compact instructive guide to what one can see in the sky using a telescope. (Rev: BL 8/86) [520.2]

8281 Preston, Richard. *First Light: The Search for the Edge of the Universe* (10–12). 1987, Atlantic Monthly $18.95 (0-87113-200-1); NAL paper $8.95 (0-452-26170-8). An account of current astrological research with focus on the work being done at the Palomar Observatory in California. (Rev: BL 12/15/87; SLJ 5/88) [522.19]

8282 Raymo, Chet. *The Soul of the Night: An Astronomical Pilgrimage* (10–12). Illus. 1989, Prentice paper $8.95 (0-13-824004-3). A philosophical introduction to astronomy that calls on literature, mythology, religion, and other areas for meaning and insight. (Rev: SLJ 1/86) [523]

8283 Ridpath, Ian. *Star Tales* (10–12). Illus. 1989, Universe $19.95 (0-87663-694-6). An illustrated history of star gazing, and the various constellations that have been found. (Rev: SLJ 6/89) [523]

8284 Ronan, Colin A. *The Skywatcher's Handbook* (8–12). Illus. 1989, Crown paper $13.95 (0-517-57326-1). An excellent handbook that describes and explains a wide range of phenomena that occur in both the day and night skies. (Rev: BR 3–4/90; VOYA 2/90) [523]

8285 Sagan, Carl. *The Cosmic Connection: An Extraterrestrial Perspective* (10–12). Illus. 1987, Anchor Pr. paper $10.95 (0-385-17365-2). An introduction to our galaxy, to other galaxies, and to the study of extraterrestrial intelligence. [523.1]

8286 Sagan, Carl. *Cosmos* (9–12). Illus. 1980, Random paper $5.95 (0-345-33135-4). A chronological account of how and what we have learned about our universe. [520]

8287 Sanford, John. *Observing the Constellations* (9–12). Illus. 1990, Simon & Schuster $26.95 (0-671-68927-4); paper $16.95 (0-671-68924-X). A how-to guide for observing the 88 constellations, aimed at both the beginning sky watcher and those with some experience. (Rev: BL 12/15/89) [523.8]

8288 Schaaf, Fred. *The Starry Room: Naked Eye Astronomy in the Intimate Universe* (10–12). Illus. 1988, Wiley $19.95 (0-471-62088-2). The author recounts his experience of sky watching for 10 years without a telescope. (Rev: BL 12/15/88) [523]

8289 Snow, Theodore P. *The Cosmic Cycle* (9–12). Illus. 1985, Darwin $14.95 (0-87850-041-3). A fine introduction to astronomy complete with 34 excellent color plates. (Rev: SLJ 3/86) [523]

8290 Trefil, James. *Space, Time, Infinity: The Smithsonian Views and Universe* (9–12). Illus. 1985, Pantheon $16.95 (0-394-54843-4). An easy-to-understand introduction to astronomy with many attractive color illustrations. (Rev: BL 10/15/85) [520]

8291 Tucker, Wallace, and Karen Tucker. *The Dark Matter* (10–12). Illus. 1988, Morrow $16.95 (0-688-06112-5). A popularization that describes the search for dark matter in the universe. (Rev: SLJ 10/88) [523]

8292 Tyson, Neil De Grasse. *Merlin's Tour of the Universe* (9–12). Illus. 1989, Columbia Univ. Pr. $29.95 (0-231-06924-3). In a question-and-answer format, an astronomer answers queries on such topics as the moon, black holes, and the universe. (Rev: BL 9/15/89) [520]

8293 Whitney, Charles A. *Whitney's Star Finder: A Field Guide to the Heavens* (9–12). Rev. ed. Illus. 1985, Random paper $16.95 (0-679-72582-2). A simple guide to stars that is geared for use by the amateur without complex equipment. (Rev: BL 1/1/86; SLJ 4/86) [523]

Astronautics and Space Exploration

8294 Aldrin, Buzz, and Malcolm McConnell. *Men from Earth* (10–12). Illus. 1989, Bantam $19.95 (0-553-05374-4). Former astronaut Buzz Aldrin reviews the history of our space program and its future possibilities. (Rev: BL 5/15/89) [629.45]

8295 Alexander, Kent. *Countdown to Glory: NASA's Trials and Triumphs in Space* (9–12). Illus. 1989, Price/Stern/Sloan $29.95 (0-89586-787-7). A richly illustrated history of the American space program. (Rev: BL 9/15/89) [353]

8296 Angelo, Joseph A., Jr. *Dictionary of Space Technology* (10–12). Illus. 1982, Facts on File $35.00 (0-87196-583-6). An extensive dictionary that covers more than 1,500 words and terms connected with astronautics and space. [629.4]

8297 Benford, Timothy B., and Brian Wilkes. *The Space Program Quiz and Fact Book* (9–12). Illus. 1984, Harper $15.45 (0-06-015454-3); paper $9.95 (0-06-096005-1). Using a question-and-answer format and many photographs, this book reviews both the American and the Russian space programs. [629.4]

8298 Caes, Charles J. *Studies in Starlight: Understanding Our Universe* (10–12). Illus. 1988, TAB $18.95 (0-8306-0946-6); paper $12.95 (0-8306-2946-7). A brief history of astronomy plus a discussion of the present status of astrophysics. (Rev: BL 5/15/88) [523.01]

8299 Davies, Owen, ed. *The Omni Book of Space* (10–12). 1983, Zebra paper $3.95 (0-8217-1275-6). From the pages of *Omni* magazine, this is a collection of articles related to space and space exploration. [629.4]

8300 Davis, Joel. *Flyby: The Interplanetary Odyssey of Voyager 2* (9–12). 1987, Macmillan $19.95 (0-689-11657-8). A detailed account of the space probe by *Voyager 2* of the planet Uranus. (Rev: BL 5/1/87) [629.46]

8301 Ferris, Timothy. *Spaceshots: The Beauty of Nature Beyond Earth* (10–12). Illus. 1985, Pantheon paper $15.95 (0-394-53890-0). An outstanding collection of photographs that show various planetary and lunar characteristics. [778.3]

8302 Furniss, Tim. *Space Rocket* (10–12). Illus. 1988, Gloucester LB $11.90 (0-531-17099-3). A handsomely illustrated book that concentrates on rocket technology and its uses in space launches and space exploration. (Rev: SLJ 4/89) [629.133]

8303 Hurt, Harry. *For All Mankind* (9–12). 1988, Atlantic Monthly $22.95 (0-87113-170-6). An extremely readable history of the space program of the United States from its beginning to the Apollo moon mission. (Rev: BL 11/1/88) [629.45]

8304 Jackson, Francis, and Patrick Moore. *Life in the Universe* (10–12). Illus. 1989, Norton $18.95 (0-393-02664-7). For advanced students, this is a fascinating approach to the possibility of life beyond Earth; a revision of the authors' 1962 title. (Rev: BL 5/1/89) [574.999]

8305 Lewis, Richard S. *Challenger: The Final Voyage* (9–12). Illus. 1988, Columbia $29.95 (0-231-06490-X). An engrossing re-creation of the tragedy of the 1986 crash of the *Challenger* space shuttle. (Rev: BL 5/15/88) [363.1]

8306 Logsden, Tom. *Space, Inc. Your Guide to Investing in Space Exploration* (10–12). 1988, Crown $22.50 (0-517-56812-8). This book explains how space exploration may affect our lives in the future in such ways as supplying rare materials, helping predict weather, and assisting in detecting petroleum deposits. (Rev: SLJ 1/89; VOYA 12/88) [629.4]

8307 McAleer, Neil. *The Omni Space Almanac: A Complete Guide to the Space Age* (9–12). Illus. 1987, Pharos paper $14.95 (0-88687-406-8). A nicely illustrated volume that traces the accomplishments in space exploration and what are the probable future developments. (Rev: BL 7/87) [629.4]

8308 McDonough, Thomas R. *Space: The Next Twenty-Five Years* (10–12). 1987, Wiley $17.95 (0-471-85671-1). A clearly written indication of what will be the salient developments in space exploration in the next 25 years. (Rev: BL 7/87) [500.5]

8309 Moche, Dinah L. *Astronomy Today* (7–12). Illus. 1982, Random $11.99 (0-394-94423-2). An overview of astronomy that includes material on space probes and the planned space stations of the future. [523]

8310 Moore, Patrick. *The Unfolding Universe* (7–12). Illus. 1982, Crown $17.95 (0-517-54836-4). A rundown of space exploration through the *Voyager* probe. [520]

8311 Murray, Bruce. *Journey into Space: The First Three Decades of Space Exploration* (10–12). Illus. 1989, Norton $19.95 (0-393-02675-2). A history of American space programs that is critical of NASA and the deployment of space shuttles. (Rev: BL 6/15/89) [919.9]

8312 Needell, Allan A., ed. *The First 25 Years in Space: A Symposium* (10–12). Illus. 1983, Smithsonian Inst. $17.95 (0-87474-688-X); paper $12.95 (0-87474-713-9). The results of a symposium on the status of space exploration 25 years after the launching of *Sputnik I*. [629.4]

8313 Oberg, James E. *The New Race for Space: The U.S. and Russia Leap to the Challenge for Unlimited Rewards* (10–12). Illus. 1984, Stackpole paper $14.95 (0-8117-2177-9). A history of the space race from *Sputnik* to the early 1980s with projections to 2000. [629.4]

8314 Oberg, James E., and Alcestis R. Oberg. *Pioneering Space: Living on the Next Threshold* (9–12). Illus. 1986, McGraw $16.95 (0-07-048034-6). A futuristic account of how people will live on a day-to-day basis in space. (Rev: BL 1/1/86) [919.7]

8315 Osman, Tony. *Space History* (7–12). Illus. 1983, St. Martin's $16.95 (0-312-74945-7). An account that tells of mankind's attempts to conquer space from ancient times to the *Voyager* expeditions. [629.4]

8316 Pogue, William R. *How Do You Go to the Bathroom in Space?* (7–12). 1985, Tor paper $4.95 (0-812-54910-4). In a question-and-answer format, the author, who spent 84 days in space, discusses the practical aspects of space travel. (Rev: VOYA 12/85) [629.47]

8317 Ride, Sally, and Susan Okie. *To Space and Back* (8–12). Illus. 1986, Lothrop $16.95 (0-688-06159-1); paper $9.95 (0-688-09112-1). A photojourney that begins 4 hours before launch and ends after landing. (Rev: BR 11–12/86; VOYA 12/86) [629]

8318 Riva, Peter, and Barbara Hitchcock, comps. *Sightseeing: A Space Panorama* (8–12). Illus. 1985, Knopf $24.95 (0-394-54243-6). A spectacular view of space as pictured in 84 captioned photographs from NASA's archives. (Rev: SLJ 5/86) [629.4]

8319 Schick, Ron, and Julia Van Haaften. *The View from Space: American Astronaut Photography, 1962–1972* (9–12). Illus. 1988, Crown $30.00 (0-517-56082-8). A collection of stunning photographs taken during the Mercury, Gemini, and Apollo space probes. (Rev: BL 7/88; SLJ 10/88) [779]

8320 Shapland, David, and Michael Rycroft. *Spacelab: Research in Earth Orbit* (10–12). Illus. 1984, Cambridge Univ. Pr. $34.50 (0-521-26077-9). A behind-the-scenes look at the development of Spacelab from its inception to launching in 1983. [629.44]

8321 Shayler, David. *Shuttle Challenger* (9–12). Illus. 1987, Prentice $12.95 (0-13-125147-3). A well-illustrated history of the space shuttle *Challenger,* of its many missions, and of the people who were aboard. (Rev: BL 10/15/87; BR 5–6/88) [629]

8322 Shipman, Harry L. *Humans in Space: 21st Century Frontiers* (10–12). Illus. 1989, Plenum $22.95 (0-306-43171-8). This account explores the problems of humans living in space and suggests possible solutions. (Rev: SLJ 1/90) [629]

8323 Spangenburg, Ray, and Diane Moser. *Opening the Space Frontier* (8–12). Illus. 1989, Facts on File $22.95 (0-8160-1848-0). A history of space exploration from the fiction of Jules Verne to the realities of today. (Rev: BR 5–6/90; SLJ 4/90; VOYA 4/90) [500.5]

8324 Swift, David W. *SETI Pioneers: Scientists Talk about Their Search for Extraterrestrial Intelligence* (10–12). 1990, Univ. of Arizona Pr. $35.00 (0-8165-1119-5). This book consists of interviews with 16 scientists who are involved in searching for extraterrestrial intelligence. (Rev: BL 4/15/90) [574]

8325 Time-Life Books, eds. *Life in Space* (7–12). Illus. 1983, Little paper $19.95 (0-316-85063-2). Twenty-five years of America's exploration of space ending in the early 1980s. [629.4]

8326 Vogt, Gregory. *A Twenty-fifth Anniversary Album of NASA* (7–12). Illus. 1983, Watts LB $12.90 (0-531-04655-9). A history of the National Aeronautics and Space Administration, its achievements and failures. [629.4]

8327 Von Braun, Wernher, and Frederick I. Ordway III. *Space Travel: A History* (10–12). Illus. 1985, Harper $29.95 (0-06-181898-4). A review of man's attempts to conquer space from a history of astronomy in ancient Greece to the *Voyager* missions. [629.4]

8328 Whitby, Max. *Space Technology* (10–12). Illus. 1987, Parkwest $24.95 (0-563-20380-3); paper $12.95 (0-563-20378-1). An international view of current events in space and possible future developments. (Rev: BL 6/1/88; BR 9–10/88) [500.5]

8329 Wolfe, Tom. *The Right Stuff* (10–12). 1983, Farrar $15.95 (0-374-25033-2); Bantam paper $4.95 (0-553-25596-7). Profiles of the early astronauts such as Glenn, Schirra, and Shepard. [629.45]

Comets, Meteors, and Asteroids

8330 Dodd, Robert T. *Thunderstones and Shooting Stars: The Meaning of Meteorites* (10–12). Illus. 1986, Harvard Univ. Pr. $24.95 (0-674-89137-6). An account that traces the origin and characteristics of meteorites and what they can tell us about outer space. (Rev: BL 11/1/86; SLJ 5/87) [523.5]

8331 Hall, Louis Brewer. *Searching for Comets: Deciphering the Secrets of Our Cosmic Past* (10–12). Illus. 1989, McGraw $17.95 (0-07-025633-0). Using the missions to explore the phenomenon of Halley's Comet, the author gives us a look at the science of the study of comets. (Rev: BL 12/15/89) [523.6]

8332 Moore, Patrick, and John Mason. *The Return of Halley's Comet* (9–12). Illus. 1984, Norton $15.95 (0-393-01872-5); Warner paper $6.95 (0-446-38303-1). This book discusses the characteristics of comets in general with particular emphasis on Halley's Comet. [523.6]

8333 Sagan, Carl, and Ann Druyan. *Comet* (9–12). Illus. 1985, Random $27.95 (0-394-54908-2). A richly illustrated book about all kinds of comets, but Halley's in particular. (Rev: BL 10/1/85; BR 11–12/86; VOYA 8–10/86) [523.6]

8334 Vogt, Gregory. *Halley's Comet: What We've Learned* (9–12). Illus. 1987, Watts LB $10.40 (0-

531-10304-8). This account incorporates material garnered by scientists from the return of the comet in 1986. (Rev: SLJ 2/88) [523.6]

8335 Whipple, Fred L. *The Mystery of Comets* (10–12). Illus. 1985, Smithsonian $24.95 (0-87474-968-9); paper $13.95 (0-87474-971-9). For better students, a history of our knowledge of comets with chapters on current theories about their existence. (Rev: BR 3–4/86; SLJ 3/86) [523.6]

Earth and the Moon

8336 Bova, Ben. *Welcome to Moonbase* (10–12). 1987, Ballantine paper $9.95 (0-345-32859-0). An on-the-spot account of what a lunar community in the twenty-first century will look like and how it will function. (Rev: BL 1/15/88) [629.45]

8337 Erickson, Jon. *Exploring Earth from Space* (8–12). Illus. 1989, TAB paper $15.95 (0-8306-3242-5). Beginning with the history of space exploration, this account also covers how we on Earth profit from the use of space. (Rev: BR 1–2/90) [500.5]

8338 Fisher, David E. *The Birth of the Earth: A Wanderlied through Space, Time, and the Human Imagination* (10–12). Illus. 1987, Columbia Univ. Pr. $30.00 (0-231-06042-4); paper $16.00 (0-231-06043-2). An account of how the solar system came into being and how Earth evolved. (Rev: BL 3/15/87) [523.2]

8339 Hockey, Thomas A. *The Book of the Moon* (10–12). Illus. 1986, Prentice $19.95 (0-13-079971-8); paper $9.95 (0-13-079963-7). Although mainly about the moon, this book also furnishes information on space exploration and astronomy. (Rev: BL 10/15/86) [523.3]

8340 Kelley, Kevin W., ed. *The Home Planet* (8–12). Illus. 1988, Addison $39.95 (0-201-15197-9). An extraordinary collection of 150 color photographs of our earth taken by Russian and American astronauts. (Rev: BL 10/1/88) [525]

Sun and the Solar System

8341 Burgess, Eric. *Uranus & Neptune: The Distant Giants* (10–12). Illus. 1988, Columbia Univ. Pr. $29.95 (0-231-06492-6). An account that incorporates recent findings about these 2 planets. (Rev: SLJ 10/88) [523.4]

8342 Couper, Heather, and Nigel Henbest. *New Worlds: In Search of the Planets* (10–12). Illus. 1986, Addison paper $12.95 (0-201-11316-3). An introduction to each of the planets with outstanding photographs as illustrations. (Rev: BL 11/15/86) [523.4]

8343 Elliot, James, and Richard Kerr. *Rings: Discoveries from Galileo to Voyager* (10–12). Illus. 1987, MIT Pr. paper $8.95 (0-262-55013-X). A description of how we found out about the rings that circle large planets. [523.4]

8344 Frazier, Kendrick. *Solar Systems* (9–12). Illus. 1985, Silver Burdett $24.60 (0-8094-4530-1). A well-illustrated account that describes what we know about our solar system. [523.2]

8345 Gallant, Roy A. *The Planets: Exploring the Solar System* (9–12). Illus. 1982, Macmillan $15.95 (0-02-736930-7). A guide to the planets in our solar system that incorporates material from recent space probes. [523.4]

8346 Jackson, Joseph H., and John H. Baumert. *Pictorial Guide to the Planets* (10–12). 3rd ed. Illus. 1981, Harper $22.50 (0-06-014869-1). In addition to discussing the solar system this book includes material on rockets, space probes, and the possibility of extraterrestrial life. [523]

8347 Preiss, Byron, ed. *The Planets* (9–12). Illus. 1985, Bantam $24.95 (0-553-05109-1); paper $16.95 (0-553-34783-7). Science fiction, essays, and stunning illustrations are used to provide a guided tour of the planets. (Rev: BL 1/15/86; SLJ 9/86; VOYA 6/86) [813]

8348 Ripley, S. Dillon. *Fire of Life: The Smithsonian Book of the Sun* (10–12). Illus. 1981, Norton $24.95 (0-393-80006-7). This book describes what we know about the sun and its effects on the environments of planets including the earth. [523.7]

8349 Roop, Peter, and Connie Roop. *The Solar System* (8–12). Illus. 1988, Greenhaven LB $12.95 (0-89908-053-8). This account brings in opposing viewpoints about such subjects as life on Mars, the formation of the Earth and our Moon, and the behavior of comets. (Rev: SLJ 1/89) [523.2]

8350 Wilford, John Noble. *Mars Beckons* (10–12). Illus. 1990, Knopf $24.95 (0-394-58359-0). The story of what we know about Mars and what we are learning through data collected from the *Viking* probe. (Rev: BL 5/15/90) [523.4]

Stars

8351 Cooke, Donald A. *The Life & Death of Stars* (9–12). Illus. 1985, Crown $29.95 (0-517-55268-X). The life cycle of stars is explained in simple language with stunning photographs. (Rev: BL 8/85) [523.8]

8352 Engelbrektson, Sune. *Stars, Planets and Galaxies* (10–12). 1975, Bantam paper $4.95 (0-553-26441-9). A guide to the various bodies of matter found in the universe. [523.8]

8353 Hartmann, William K., et al. *Cycles of Fire: Stars, Galaxies and the Wonders of Deep Space* (9–12). Illus. 1987, Workman $27.50 (0-89480-510-X); paper $14.95 (0-89480-502-9). A stunningly illustrated guide to the stars with photographs, charts, and more than 100 paintings. (Rev: BL 12/15/87; SLJ 4/88; VOYA 6/88) [523.8]

8354 Marschall, Laurence A. *The Supernova Story* (10–12). Illus. 1988, Plenum $22.95 (0-306-42955-1). An astronomer looks at this celestial phenomenon from the star of Bethlehem to the present. (Rev: BL 9/1/88) [523.8]

8355 Menzel, Donald H., and Jay M. Pasachoff. *A Field Guide to the Stars and Planets* (7–12). 2nd ed. Illus. 1983, Houghton $19.95 (0-395-34641-X); paper $12.95 (0-395-34835-8). Photographs, sky maps, charts, and timetables are features of this volume in the Peterson Field Guide series. [523]

8356 Peltier, Leslie. *Leslie Peltier's Guide to the Stars* (10–12). Illus. 1986, Kalmbach paper $11.95 (0-317-61675-7). A guide to star gazing using only a pair of binoculars. (Rev: BL 2/1/87) [523]

8357 Zim, Herbert, and Robert Baker. *Stars* (7–12). 1985, Western paper $3.95 (0-307-24493-8). A fine little paperback guide to stars and the solar system. [523.8]

Universe

8358 Asimov, Isaac. *The Collapsing Universe* (10–12). 1983, Pocket paper $3.95 (0-671-63233-7). A well-organized tour of the universe that explains such phenomena as quasars, pulsars, and black holes. [523]

8359 Asimov, Isaac. *The Exploding Suns: The Secrets of the Supernovas* (9–12). Illus. 1986, NAL paper $4.50 (0-451-62481-5). A popularization that covers such topics as black holes, types of novas, and the makeup of our universe. (Rev: SLJ 10/85) [523.8]

8360 Close, Frank. *Apocalypse When? Cosmic Catastrophe and the Fate of the Universe* (10–12). Illus. 1989, Morrow $17.95 (0-688-08413-3). In sometimes technical language, Close explores the ongoing changes in our universe and the possible causes of its end. (Rev: BL 5/1/89) [523.1]

8361 Cohen, Nathan. *Gravity's Lens: Views of the New Cosmology* (10–12). Illus. 1988, Wiley $19.95 (0-471-63282-1). A history of the theories about the universe and current thinking in this area. (Rev: BL 8/88) [523.1]

8362 Darling, David. *Deep Time* (10–12). 1989, Delacorte $17.95 (0-385-29757-2). Following a single proton through time and space, the author traces the history of our universe. (Rev: BL 8/89) [523.1]

8363 Dickinson, Terence. *The Universe . . . and Beyond* (10–12). Illus. 1986, Camden House $29.95 (0-920656-50-1); paper $19.95 (0-920656-48-X). A space tour beginning with our moon then extending to the planets, other galaxies, and beyond. (Rev: BL 11/15/86) [523.1]

8364 Ferris, Timothy. *The Red Limit: The Search for the Edge of the Universe* (10–12). Rev. ed. 1983, Morrow paper $12.95 (0-688-01836-X). A review of the important facts we know about the universe. [523]

8365 Friedman, Herbert. *The Amazing Universe* (10–12). Illus. 1975, National Geographic Soc. LB $9.50 (0-87044-184-1). A review of theories concerning the sun, stars, black holes, quasars, and so on. [523.1]

8366 Hawking, Stephen W. *A Brief History of Time: From the Big Bang to Black Holes* (10–12). Illus. 1988, Bantam $17.95 (0-553-05243-8). For better readers, a proposed theory of the nature and creation of the universe. (Rev: BL 4/1/88; VOYA 8/88) [523.1]

8367 Jastrow, Robert. *God and the Astronomers* (10–12). Illus. 1978, Norton $9.95 (0-393-85000-5). A review of the big bang theory of the creation of the universe. [523.1]

8368 Jastrow, Robert. *Until the Sun Dies* (10–12). Illus. 1977, Norton $12.95 (0-393-06415-8); Warner paper $3.95 (0-446-32195-8). This is a reflection by the author on the origin of life and of the universe. [577]

8369 Jespersen, James, and Jane Fitz-Randolph. *From Quarks to Quasars: A Tour of the Universe*

(9–12). Illus. 1987, Macmillan $16.95 (0-689-31270-9). For students with some physics background, this is a review of what we know or theorize about the universe. (Rev: BL 7/87; BR 11–12/87; SLJ 3/87; VOYA 6/87) [523.1]

8370 Preiss, Byron, ed. *The Universe* (10–12). Illus. 1987, Bantam $27.95 (0-553-05227-6). A collection of nonfiction articles on various extrasolar subjects such as black holes, each followed by a science fiction selection on the same topic. (Rev: BL 1/15/88; VOYA 4/88) [523.1]

8371 Trefil, James. *The Dark Side of the Universe: A Scientist Explores the Mysteries of the Cosmos* (10–12). Illus. 1988, Macmillan $17.95 (0-684-18795-7). Theories about the creation of the universe and the galaxies are fascinatingly explored. (Rev: BL 9/1/88) [523.1]

Biological Sciences

General and Miscellaneous

8372 Abbey, Edward. *Beyond the Wall* (10–12). 1984, Henry Holt $14.95 (0-03-069299-7); paper $7.95 (0-8050-0820-9). A collection of essays about the beauty and wonder of nature. [507]

8373 *ABC's of Nature: A Family Answer Book* (7–12). Illus. 1984, Reader's Digest $24.95 (0-89577-169-1). An easily read question-and-answer introduction to natural history. [500]

8374 Adler, Irving. *How Life Began* (8–12). Rev. ed. Illus. 1977, Day $12.95 (0-381-99603-4). An examination of molecular structure and theories on how life began at that level. [577]

8375 Amos, William H., and Stephen H. Amos. *Atlantic & Gulf Coasts* (9–12). Illus. 1985, Knopf paper $16.95 (0-394-73109-3). This volume describes the habitat thoroughly and then identifies the species that live there. (Rev: BL 7/85; SLJ 9/85) [574.5]

8376 Asimov, Isaac. *The Relativity of Wrong* (9–12). 1988, Doubleday $17.95 (0-385-24473-8). A collection of entertaining columns that explore many facets of science including scientific ethics. (Rev: BL 4/15/88) [520]

8377 Attenborough, David. *The Living Planet: A Portrait of the Earth* (9–12). Illus. 1985, Little $25.00 (0-316-05748-7); paper $17.95 (0-316-05749-5). This book discusses and pictures life in various environments such as deserts, grasslands, oceans, and the sky. [574]

8378 Berrill, Michael, and Deborah Berrill. *A Sierra Club Naturalist's Guide to the North Atlantic Coast: Cape Cod to Newfoundland* (10–12). Illus. 1981, Sierra Club $24.95 (0-87156-242-1); paper $12.95 (0-87156-243-X). As well as the general geology and climate of this region, there is extensive coverage on the marine habitats for animal and plant life that these coastlines contain. [574.9]

8379 Brown, Tom, Jr., and William Owen. *The Search* (10–12). 1982, Berkley paper $7.95 (0-425-10251-3). Interesting writing on nature by a survival expert. Also use: *The Tracker* (1984). [507]

8380 Brown, Vinson. *The Amateur Naturalist's Handbook* (10–12). 1980, Prentice paper $11.95 (0-13-023721-3). For the nonscientist, this is a guide to the wonders of nature. [507]

8381 Burroughs, John. *Deep Woods* (10–12). Illus. 1990, Gibbs Smith paper $9.95 (0-87905-030-6). A collection of natural history essays culled from 7 of his best-known books. (Rev: BL 9/1/90) [814]

8382 Camazine, Scott. *The Naturalist's Year* (10–12). Illus. 1987, Wiley paper $14.95 (0-471-84845-X). Twenty-four chapters, each dealing with a different natural occurrence like the growth of skunk cabbage, an avalanche, and the phenomenon of pollination. (Rev: SLJ 11/87) [507]

8383 Carrighar, Sally. *One Day at Teton Marsh* (10–12). 1979, Univ. of Nebraska Pr. paper $7.95 (0-8032-6302-3). This 1945 book introduces the flora and fauna of the swamp with chapters on 14 different species. [507]

8384 Catton, Chris, and James Gray. *Sex in Nature* (10–12). Illus. 1985, Facts on File $19.95 (0-8160-1294-6). From the single-celled plant to mankind the role of sex in nature and its many variations are discussed with many illustrations. (Rev: BL 2/15/86) [574.1]

8385 Dillard, Annie. *Pilgrim at Tinker Creek* (10–12). 1988, Harper paper $8.95 (0-06-091545-5). This is a collection of thoughtful pieces about nature and man's relation to it. [507]

8386 Durrell, Gerald. *The Amateur Naturalist* (10–12). Illus. 1983, Knopf $29.45 (0-394-53390-9); McKay paper $18.95 (0-679-72837-6). An introduction to nature by studying various environments such as grasslands, marshlands, and sea shores. [500]

8387 Durrell, Gerald. *My Family & Other Animals* (10–12). 1983, Peter Smith $14.95 (0-8446-6073-6); Penguin paper $5.95 (0-14-001399-7). A memoir about the life of the Durrell family on Corfu and of the wildlife observed by their son, young Gerald. A sequel is *Birds, Beasts and Relatives* (1983). [574.9]

8388 Elia, Irene. *The Female Animal* (10–12). 1988, Henry Holt $21.95 (0-8050-0702-4). The characteristics of the female of the species—be it fish, bird, or mammal—are explored in this well-researched account. (Rev: VOYA 2/89) [574]

8389 Finch, Robert, and John Elder, eds. *The Norton Book of Nature Writing* (10–12). 1990, Norton $24.95 (0-393-02799-6). From Charles Darwin to Annie Dillard, this is a grand selection of fine writing about nature. (Rev: BL 5/15/90) [508]

8390 Fletcher, Colin. *The Secret Worlds of Colin Fletcher* (10–12). Illus. 1989, Knopf $19.95 (0-394-56283-6). A collection of essays on nature including such subjects as California's redwoods, Alaska's wilderness, ecology, and unusual animals. Fletcher is also the author of *The Man Who Walked through Time* (1968). (Rev: BL 5/1/89) [796.5]

8391 Forward, Robert L. *Future Magic* (10–12). 1988, Avon paper $3.95 (0-380-89814-4). The author, a physicist, explores some of the remote and not-so-remote possible developments in physics from space elevators to time travel. (Rev: BL 7/88) [609]

8392 Gorman, James. *The Man with No Endorphins and Other Reflections on Science* (10–12). 1988, Viking $15.95 (0-670-81842-9). An amusing collection of pieces about the marvels and shortcomings of science in everyday life. (Rev: BL 4/15/88; BR 1–2/89) [500]

8393 Gould, Stephen Jay. *The Flamingo's Smile: Reflections in Natural History* (10–12). 1985, Norton $17.95 (0-393-02228-5); paper $8.95 (0-393-30375-6). Another collection of essays on the wonders of nature study. Also from the same author: *Ever Since Darwin* (1977), and *Hen's Teeth and Horse's Toes* (1983). [500]

8394 Gould, Stephen Jay. *The Panda's Thumb: More Reflections in Natural History* (10–12). 1982, Norton paper $5.95 (0-393-01380-4). For better science students, this is a collection of 31 essays on natural history. [507]

8395 Hubbell, Sue. *A Country Year: Living the Questions* (10–12). Illus. 1986, Random $17.95 (0-394-55146-X); Harper paper $7.95 (0-06-097086-3). In short chapters, Hubbell takes us through a year out-of-doors in the Ozark Mountains. (Rev: SLJ 10/86) [500]

8396 Joseph, Lawrence E. *Gaia: The Growth of an Idea* (10–12). 1990, St. Martin's $19.95 (0-312-04318-X). This theory that accepts the living systems of the Earth as a single changing unit is explored. (Rev: BL 5/15/90) [550]

8397 Miller, Debbie. *Midnight Wilderness: Journeys in the Arctic National Wildlife Refuge* (10–12). Illus. 1990, Sierra Club $25.00 (0-87156-715-6). An account of 14 years studying the wildlife of Alaska and of the feelings of wonder and awe it continues to produce. (Rev: BL 2/15/90) [508]

8398 Palmer, E. Laurence. *Fieldbook of Natural History* (9–12). 2nd ed. Illus. 1975, McGraw $32.95 (0-07-048425-2). About 2,000 plants and animals are identified and described in this well-organized sourcebook. [500]

8399 Pepi, David. *Thoreau's Method: A Handbook for Nature Study* (10–12). Illus. 1985, Prentice $13.95 (0-13-919887-3). This is a handbook on how to study nature using the principles of Thoreau. (Rev: BL 4/15/85) [574]

8400 Perry, Donald. *Kingdom in the Sky: A Field Biologist's Adventures in the Jungle Canopy* (10–12). 1986, Simon & Schuster $16.95 (0-671-55454-3). An unsual scientific study of the life above ground in the trees and vines in a tropical rain forest. (Rev: BL 9/15/86) [574]

8401 Quammen, David. *Natural Acts: A Sidelong View of Science and Nature* (10–12). 1985, Lyons $16.95 (0-8052-3967-7); Dell paper $6.95 (0-440-55696-1). A collection of witty and thoughtful articles on a variety of topics in natural history. (Rev: BL 3/15/85; SLJ 9/85) [508]

8402 Reader's Digest, eds. *Reader's Digest North American Wildlife* (7–12). Illus. 1982, Reader's Digest $22.45 (0-89577-102-0). In text and illustrations, over 2,000 North American plants and animals are described. [574.9]

8403 Seff, Philip, and Nancy R. Seff. *Our Fascinating Earth* (10–12). 1990, Contemporary paper $12.95 (0-8092-4185-4). A cornucopia of unusual bits of scientific facts and myths about Earth. (Rev: BL 5/15/90) [508]

8404 Sherwood, Martin, and Christine Sutton, eds. *The Physical World* (10–12). Illus. 1988, Oxford Univ. Pr. $35.00 (0-19-520632-0). In this nicely illustrated volume, an introduction is given to physics and chemistry and their roles in our everyday life in such areas as sound, light, and electricity. (Rev: BL 7/88) [530]

8405 Storer, John H. *The Web of Life* (10–12). 1982, NAL paper $3.50 (0-451-62472-6). A basic book on ecology that introduces the subject in nonscientific terms. [574.5]

8406 Teale, Edwin Way. *Journey into Summer* (10–12). 1990, St. Martin's paper $12.95 (0-312-04456-9). This famous naturalist writes about the glories of summer. Also use: *North with the Spring, Autumn across America,* and *Wandering through Winter* (all 1990). [507]

8407 Thomas, Lewis. *The Lives of a Cell: Notes of a Biology Watcher* (10–12). 1984, Bantam paper $5.95 (0-553-27580-1). A collection of brilliant essays on various topics from tiny microorganisms to life in outer space. [574]

8408 Thomas, Lewis. *The Medusa and the Snail* (10–12). 1983, Bantam paper $3.95 (0-553-25913-X). For better readers, a group of thoughtful essays about the mysteries and wonders of nature. [507]

8409 Wagner, Frederic H. *Wildlife of the Deserts* (9–12). Illus. 1980, Abrams $19.95 (0-8109-1764-5). A well-illustrated account of life in 21 of the world's major desert areas. [574.5]

8410 Wallace, David Rains. *Idle Weeds: The Life of a Sandstone Ridge* (10–12). Illus. 1980, Sierra Club $12.95 (0-87156-271-5). A description of the wild plants and other living things found on a sandstone ridge. [574]

Botany

General and Miscellaneous

8411 *America's Wildlife Hideaways* (9–12). Illus. 1989, National Wildlife Federation $29.95 (0-945051-08-5). An impressive work of photographs, text, and maps that illustrate the flora and fauna found in our national parks and wildlife sanctuaries. (Rev: BL 1/1/90) [508.73]

8412 Bellamy, David. *Bellamy's New World: A Botanical History of America* (10–12). Illus. 1985, Parkwest $24.95 (0-88186-025-5). By examining plants across our country, the author is able to trace how plants developed their characteris-

tics and adapted to various habitats. (Rev: BL 8/85; SLJ 9/85) [333.95]

8413 Prance, Ghillean Tolmie. *Leaves* (9–12). Illus. 1985, Crown $35.00 (0-517-55152-7). All aspects of leaves are explored from their fossilized forms to their uses today. (Rev: BL 4/15/85) [582.01]

Foods

8414 Benarde, Melvin A. *The Food Additives Dictionary* (10–12). 1987, Pocket paper $4.95 (0-671-42837-3). This book describes in dictionary format the additives in our food and the functions they perform. [641.3]

8415 Bonar, Ann. *The Macmillan Treasury of Herbs* (10–12). Illus. 1985, Macmillan $15.95 (0-02-513470-1). In addition to a history of herbs and their uses, this volume describes individual herbs, tells how to cultivate and harvest them, and gives many suggestions for use. (Rev: BL 8/85) [635.7]

8416 Igoe, Robert S. *Dictionary of Food Ingredients* (10–12). 1989, Van Nostrand $31.95 (0-442-31927-4). A dictionary of the approximately 1,000 food ingredients approved by the Food and Drug Administration. [664]

8417 Jacobson, Michael F., and Sarah Fritschner. *The Fast-Food Guide: What's Good, What's Bad, and How to Tell the Difference* (8–12). Illus. 1986, Workman paper $5.95 (0-89480-351-4). This guide analyzes the contents of convenience foods and then compares one product to another. (Rev: BL 11/15/86; SLJ 3/87) [647]

8418 Kowalchik, Claire, and William H. Hylton, eds. *Rodale's Illustrated Encyclopedia of Herbs* (9–12). Illus. 1987, Rodale $24.95 (0-87857-699-1). In addition to an alphabetically arranged description of each herb, this lavishly illustrated volume contains background historical material, plus coverage of such subjects as medicinal uses, cooking, and gardening. (Rev: BL 10/15/87) [635]

8419 Mindell, Earl. *Unsafe at Any Meal* (9–12). 1987, Warner $16.95 (0-446-51235-4); paper $4.95 (0-446-34670-5). The author, a proponent of natural foods, discusses caffeine, sweeteners, livestock drugs, and other food topics. (Rev: SLJ 9/87) [641.4]

8420 Morton, Julia F. *Herbs and Spices* (10–12). Illus. 1977, Western paper $2.95 (0-307-24364-8). With copious illustrations, over 370 species edible herbs and spices are identified and described. [635]

8421 Visser, Margaret. *Much Depends on Dinner: The Extraordinary History and Mythology, Allure and Obsessions, Perils and Taboos, of an Ordinary Meal* (10–12). 1988, Grove $18.95 (0-802-10023-6). Background facts and myths about such common foods as corn, chicken, and ice cream are given in this analysis of a simple meal. (Rev: BL 1/15/88) [394.1]

Fungi

8422 Lincoff, Gary. *The Audubon Society Field Guide to North American Mushrooms* (7–12). Illus. 1981, Knopf LB $14.45 (0-394-51992-2). Over 700 species are introduced and pictured in color photographs. [589.2]

Forestry and Trees

8423 Brockman, C. Frank. *Trees of North America* (7–12). Illus. 1968, Golden paper $9.95 (0-307-63658-5). This handy guide identifies 594 different trees that grow north of Mexico. [582.16]

8424 Collingwood, G. H., and Warren D. Brush. *Knowing Your Trees* (10–12). Rev. ed. Illus. 1984, American Forestry Assn. $9.50 (0-686-26731-1). About 200 trees in the United States are identified and details given on such subjects as their bark, leaves, flowers, and fruit. [582.16]

8425 Elias, Thomas S. *The Complete Trees of North America* (10–12). Illus. 1987, Crown $14.89 (0-517-64104-6). A detailed, comprehensive guide to North American trees that identifies them and gives characteristics. [582.16]

8426 Line, Les, et al. *The Audubon Society Book of Trees* (7–12). Illus. 1981, Abrams $35.00 (0-8109-0673-2). Using various environments as chapter headings (for example, tropical rain forest), this is a worldwide introduction to trees. [582.16]

8427 Little, Elbert L. *The Audubon Society Field Guide to North American Trees: Eastern Region* (7–12). Illus. 1980, Knopf $14.45 (0-394-50760-6). This volume describes through text and pictures of leaves, needles, and so on, the trees found east of the Rocky Mountains. [582.16]

8428 Little, Elbert L. *The Audubon Society Field Guide to North American Trees: Western Region* (7–12). Illus. 1980, Knopf $14.45 (0-394-50761-4). Trees east of the Rockies are identified and pictured in photos and drawings. [582.16]

8429 Petrides, George A. *A Field Guide to Trees and Shrubs* (7–12). Illus. 1972, Houghton paper $13.95 (0-395-17579-8). A total of 646 varieties found in northern United States and southern Canada are described and illustrated. [582.1]

8430 Time-Life Books, eds. *The Loggers* (7–12). Illus. 1976, Time-Life $19.94 (0-8094-1527-5). A history of logging in America's West and of the men who tamed the forests. [634.9]

8431 Zim, Herbert, and Alexander C. Martin. *Trees* (7–12). 1952, Western paper $3.95 (0-307-24056-8). A description of 143 species of North American trees. [582.16]

Plants and Flowers

8432 Angier, Bradford. *Field Guide to Medicinal Wild Plants* (10–12). Illus. 1978, Stackpole paper $16.95 (0-8117-2076-4). With many color illustrations the author introduces more than 100 wild medicinal plants, many of them originally used by primitive tribes. [581.6]

8433 Buckles, Mary Parker. *The Flowers Around Us: A Photographic Essay on their Reproductive Structures* (10–12). Illus. 1985, Univ. of Missouri Pr. $29.95 (0-8262-0402-3). Through photographs and text, the author shows the reproductive parts of various flowers and how they function in the production of seeds. (Rev: BL 12/1/85) [582]

8434 Hemphill, John, and Rosemary Hemphill. *Herbs: Their Cultivation and Usage* (10–12). Illus. 1987, Borgo Pr. $28.95 (0-7137-1451-4). A description of 30 different herbs with additional material on how to grow them. [635]

8435 Johnson, Lady Bird, and Carlton B. Lees. *Wildflowers across America* (9–12). Illus. 1988, Abbeville $39.95 (0-89659-770-9). A beautifully illustrated book (with photographs in color) of our various wildflowers. (Rev: BL 6/15/88) [582.13]

8436 MacFarlane, Ruth B. *Collecting and Preserving Plants for Science and Pleasure* (9–12). Illus. 1985, Arco $13.95 (0-688-06009-3); paper $8.95 (0-688-06013-1). In addition to describing the various ways to preserve plants, the author gives material on identification and displaying techniques. (Rev: BL 6/1/85; BR 9–10/85) [579]

8437 Martin, Alexander C. *Weeds* (7–12). 1973, Western paper $3.95 (0-307-24353-2). A compact guide to many different varieties of weeds, how to identify them, and their characteristics. [632]

8438 Martin, Alexander C., and Herbert Zim. *Flowers* (7–12). 1987, Western paper $3.95 (0-307-24054-1). An introduction to many flowers with material on how to identify and grow them. [582.13]

8439 Niehaus, Theodore F. *A Field Guide to Pacific States Wildflowers* (7–12). Illus. 1976, Houghton paper $12.95 (0-395-31662-6). About 1,500 wildflowers from the Pacific states are highlighted in this volume of the Peterson Field Guide series. [582.13]

8440 Niering, William A., and Nancy C. Olmstead. *The Audubon Society Field Guide to North American Wildflowers: Eastern Region* (7–12). Illus. 1979, Knopf $14.95 (0-394-50432-1). From the Rockies to the Atlantic this guide identifies, describes, and pictures the most common wildflowers. [582.13]

8441 Peterson, Roger Tory, and Margaret McKenny. *A Field Guide to Wildflowers of North-Eastern and North-Central North America* (7–12). Illus. 1968, Houghton $19.95 (0-395-08086-X); paper $14.95 (0-395-18325-1). A guide to more than 1,300 wildflowers in the region with an equal number of accompanying illustrations. [582.13]

8442 Prince, J. H. *Plants That Eat Animals* (7–12). Illus. 1979, Elsevier $8.95 (0-525-66599-4). A general, easily read introduction to such plants as the venus flytrap and sundew. [583]

8443 Reader's Digest, eds. *Magic and Medicine of Plants* (9–12). Illus. 1986, Random $26.95 (0-89577-221-3). Information about medicinal plants that covers fields like pharmacolognosy, myth, botany, and folklore. (Rev: SLJ 5/87) [581.6]

8444 Richardson, P. Mick. *Flowering Plants: Magic in Bloom* (9–12). Illus. 1986, Chelsea House $18.95 (0-87754-757-2). The story of plant-derived hallucinogenic substances is given plus information on their effects and their role in world folklore and religion. (Rev: BL 4/15/87) [398]

8445 Schnell, Donald E. *Carnivorous Plants of the United States and Canada* (10–12). Illus. 1976, Blair $19.95 (0-910244-90-1). A description of 45 species, their characteristics, and where they are found. [583]

8446 Spellenberg, Richard. *The Audubon Society Field Guide to North American Wildflowers: Western Region* (7–12). Illus. 1979, Knopf $14.95 (0-394-50431-3). From California to Alaska this is a guide to more than 600 western wildflowers. [582.13]

8447 Stokes, Donald, and Lillian Stokes. *A Guide to Enjoying Wildflowers* (9–12). Illus.

1985, Little $18.95 (0-316-81728-7). A guide to 50 wildflowers found in the United States with an accompanying painting for each. (Rev: BL 2/15/85) [582.13]

8448 Venning, Frank D. *Wildflowers of North America* (7–12). Illus. 1984, Western paper $3.95 (0-307-13664-7). A concise guide that describes in text and illustrations hundreds of wildflowers that grow in North America. [582.13]

8449 Wilkins, Malcolm. *Plant Watching: How Plants Remember, Tell Time, Form Partnerships and More* (10–12). 1988, Facts on File $29.95 (0-8160-1736-0). A technical but readable account of the importance of plants and how they grow. (Rev: BR 1–2/89) [581]

Zoology

General and Miscellaneous

8450 Alexander, R. McNeill, ed. *The Encyclopedia of Animal Biology* (9–12). Illus. 1987, Facts on File $24.95 (0-8160-1817-0). An introduction to zoology with lavish illustrations and clear text. (Rev: BL 11/15/87; VOYA 8/88) [591]

8451 *Animal Rights: Opposing Viewpoints* (9–12). 1989, Greenhaven LB $15.95 (0-89908-440-0); paper $7.95 (0-89908-415-X). An anthology of writings that explore such questions as do animals have rights and to what extent should laboratory research involving animals be allowed. (Rev: BL 11/15/89) [174]

8452 Bale, Peter. *Wildlife Through the Camera* (9–12). Illus. 1985, Parkwest $24.95 (0-88186-452-8). An introduction to all kinds of animals, great and small, both in text and with many photographs. (Rev: BL 7/85) [597.6]

8453 Berman, William. *How to Dissect: Exploring with Probe and Scalpel* (10–12). 4th ed. Illus. 1984, Arco paper $7.95 (O-688-05941-9). A description of how to dissect 12 different organisms. [591.4028]

8454 Hoffmeister, Donald, and Herbert Zim. *Mammals* (7–12). 1987, Western paper $3.95 (0-307-24058-4). This book identifies 218 species and gives details on the habitats of each. [559]

8455 Moore, Peter D., ed. *The Encyclopedia of Animal Ecology* (9–12). Illus. 1987, Facts on File $24.95 (0-8160-1818-9). After a discussion of the ecological regions of the world, there is coverage on how the animal kingdom has adapted to them. (Rev: BL 11/15/87) [591.5]

8456 Muir, John. *Muir Among the Animals: The Wildlife Writings of John Muir* (10–12). Illus. 1986, Sierra Club $17.95 (0-87156-769-5). A collection of the best writings by this astounding nineteenth-century naturalist. (Rev: BL 11/15/86) [590]

8457 Quammen, David. *The Flight of the Iguana: A Sidelong View of Science and Nature* (10–12). 1988, Delacorte $17.95 (0-385-29592-8). A fine writer tackles a number of nature subjects (e.g., the iguana) plus one or 2 topics involving humans. (Rev: BL 8/88) [508]

8458 Savage, R. J. G. *Mammal Evolution: An Illustrated Guide* (9–12). Illus. 1986, Facts on File $40.00 (0-8160-1194-X). A lavishly illustrated book that traces the evolution of various common animals. (Rev: BR 3–4/87; SLJ 5/87) [559]

8459 Wallace, David Rains. *The Dark Range: A Naturalist's Night Notebook* (10–12). Illus. 1978, Sierra Club paper $8.95 (0-87156-251-0). This book looks at the varieties of nocturnal wildlife that exist in many different habitats. [590]

8460 Whitfield, Philip, ed. *Macmillan Illustrated Animal Encyclopedia* (7–12). Illus. 1984, Macmillan $35.00 (0-02-627680-1). Worldwide coverage is given for about 2,000 species, each described in the text and in a color illustration. [591.03]

Amphibians and Reptiles

GENERAL AND MISCELLANEOUS

8461 Behler, John L., and F. W. King. *The Audubon Society Field Guide to North American Reptiles and Amphibians* (9–12). Illus. 1979, Knopf $15.95 (0-394-50824-6). This comprehensive account covers reptiles and amphibians found in continental United States, Canada, and Hawaii. [597.6]

8462 Conant, Roger. *A Field Guide to Reptiles and Amphibians of Eastern and Central North America* (9–12). 2nd ed. Illus. 1975, Houghton $18.95 (0-395-19979-4); paper $13.95 (0-395-19977-8). Using both photographs and hundreds of maps, 574 species and subspecies are identified and described. A companion volume is *A Field Guide to Western Reptiles and Amphibians* (1985). [597.6]

8463 Gibbons, Whit. *Their Blood Runs Cold: Adventures with Reptiles and Amphibians* (7–12). Illus. 1983, Univ. of Alabama Pr. paper $9.95 (0-8173-0133-X). An informal guide, geo-graphically arranged, to snakes, crocodiles, turtles, salamanders, and toads. [597.6]

8464 Halliday, Tim R., and Kraig Adler, eds. *The Encyclopedia of Reptiles and Amphibians* (9–12). Illus. 1986, Facts on File $24.95 (0-8160-1359-4). A lavishly illustrated book that gives both general information and specific details on each species. (Rev: BL 6/1/86) [597.6]

8465 Mattison, Chris. *The Care of Reptiles and Amphibians in Captivity* (9–12). Rev. ed. Illus. 1987, Blandford $17.95 (0-7137-1826-9). A comprehensive guide to housing and raising such reptiles and amphibians as snakes, frogs, turtles, newts, and salamanders. (Rev: BL 6/15/87) [639.3]

8466 Smith, Hobart M., and Edmund Brodie, Jr. *Reptiles of North America* (7–10). Illus. 1982, Western $9.95 (0-307-13666-3). This book identifies many reptiles, gives pictures of them, and describes their habitats. [597.9]

8467 Smith, Hobart M., and Herbert Zim. *Reptiles and Amphibians* (7–12). Illus. 1987, Western paper $3.95 (0-307-24057-6). A concise well-illustrated guide to 212 American species. [597.9]

8468 Stebbins, Robert C. *A Field Guide to Western Reptiles and Amphibians* (9–12). Rev. ed. Illus. 1985, Houghton $17.95 (0-395-08211-0); paper $12.95 (0-395-19421-0). A fine field guide that identifies species, gives a picture of each, and describes both habits and habitats. (Rev: BL 8/85) [597.6]

ALLIGATORS AND CROCODILES

8469 Ross, Charles A., ed. *Crocodiles and Alligators* (9–12). Illus. 1989, Facts on File $35.00 (0-8160-2174-0). A richly illustrated volume that tells about the origins, structure, habitats, and behavior of these amphibians. (Rev: BL 11/1/89) [597.98]

SNAKES AND LIZARDS

8470 Mattison, Chris. *Snakes of the World* (9–12). Illus. 1986, Facts on File $21.95 (0-8160-1082-X). A richly illustrated account that covers diet, defense behavior, and the mythology of the snake. (Rev: BL 5/15/86) [597]

TORTOISES AND TURTLES

8471 Alderton, David. *Turtles & Tortoises of the World* (9–12). Illus. 1988, Facts on File $22.95 (0-8160-1733-6). This thorough introduction covers such topics as structure, anatomy, reproduction, and origin and distribution. (Rev: BR 5–6/89) [598.92]

8472 Rudloe, Jack. *Time of the Turtle* (10–12). 1989, Dutton paper $9.95 (0-525-48487-6). This book explores the structure and habits of the turtle. [597.9]

Animal Behavior

GENERAL AND MISCELLANEOUS

8473 Bardens, Dennis. *Psychic Animals: A Fascinating Investigation of Paranormal Behavior* (9–12). Illus. 1989, Henry Holt $16.95 (0-8050-0730-X); paper $9.95 (0-8050-0731-8). The author, a researcher in animal behavior, presents evidence that animals possess psychic abilities such as telepathy and clairvoyance. (Rev: SLJ 9/89; VOYA 2/89) [591.51]

8474 Downer, John. *Supersense: Perception in the Animal World* (9–12). Illus. 1989, Henry Holt $24.95 (0-8050-1087-4). A description of the senses of animals plus a discussion of the "sixth sense" some seem to possess. (Rev: BL 9/15/89; VOYA 4/90) [591]

8475 Freedman, Russell. *Can Bears Predict Earthquakes? Unsolved Mysteries of Animal Behavior* (9–12). 1982, Prentice $10.95 (0-13-114009-4). Many mysteries are explored involving the significance of types of animal behavior. [591.51]

8476 Griffin, Donald R. *Animal Thinking* (10–12). 1984, Harvard Univ. Pr. paper $9.95 (0-674-03713-8). From the lowliest of creatures to communication between chimps, this is a thorough description of what we know about animal intelligence. [591.5]

8477 Maxwell, Gavin. *Ring of Bright Water* (9–12). 1987, Penguin paper $6.95 (0-14-003923-6). The author describes the wildlife on the northwest coast of Scotland and particularly the otters he befriended. [589.74]

8478 Mortenson, Joseph. *Whale Songs and Wasp Maps: The Mystery of Animal Thinking* (10–12). Illus. 1987, Dutton $17.95 (0-525-24442-5). A discussion of animal intelligence and if they possess the power of consciousness. (Rev: BL 1/15/87) [156]

8479 *Remarkable Animals: A Unique Encyclopaedia of Wildlife Wonders* (8–12). Illus. 1987, Guinness $19.95 (0-85112-867-X). The Guinness records people have produced an engrossing look at oddities in animal life. (Rev: BL 11/1/87; BR 11–12/87) [591]

8480 Slater, Peter J., ed. *The Encyclopedia of Animal Behavior* (9–12). Illus. 1987, Facts on File $24.95 (0-8160-1816-2). A handsome edition that explores behavioral patterns of animals chiefly through many color photographs. (Rev: BL 11/15/87) [591.9]

COMMUNICATION

8481 Cole, Jacci. *Animal Communication: Opposing Viewpoints* (9–12). Illus. 1989, Greenhaven $12.90 (0-89908-062-6). The various ways by which animals communicate with each other and with humans are explained with separate chapters on such animals as wolves, whales, and pets. (Rev: BL 4/1/89) [591.59]

8482 Evans, Peter, and Gerald Durrell. *Ourselves and Other Animals* (9–12). Illus. 1987, Pantheon $24.95 (0-394-55962-2). A book that discusses how animals communicate and the interesting parallels between these and human methods of communication. (Rev: BL 11/1/87; SLJ 4/88; VOYA 2/88) [591.59]

8483 Nollman, Jim. *Animal Dreaming: The Art and Science of Interspecies Communication* (10–12). Illus. 1987, Bantam paper $8.95 (0-553-34427-7). An account of how Nollman has been able to communicate with a wide variety of animals through music. (Rev: BL 6/1/87) [591.59]

DEFENSES

8484 Freedman, Russell. *How Animals Defend Their Young* (9–12). 1978, Dutton $8.95 (0-525-32282-1). This book explains the various ways animals defend themselves and their young, such as by building shelters and using camouflage. [591.51]

8485 Nichol, John. *Bites and Stings: The World of Venomous Animals* (9–12). Illus. 1989, Facts on File $19.95 (0-8160-2233-X). A guide to the animal life like wasps and jellyfish that can cause bodily harm if disturbed plus information on how to handle such injuries. (Rev: BL 7/89; BR 5–6/90) [591.6]

REPRODUCTION

8486 Walters, Mark Jerome. *The Dance of Life: Courtship in the Animal Kingdom* (10–12). Illus. 1988, Arbor House $16.95 (0-87795-934-X). The courtship habits and sex lives of a variety of animals from the lowly horseshoe crab to the chimpanzee are explained and discussed. (Rev: BL 1/1/88) [591.56]

TRACKS

8487 Murie, Olaus J. *A Field Guide to Animal Tracks* (7–12). 2nd ed. Illus. 1974, Houghton

$17.95 (0-395-19978-6); paper $12.95 (0-395-18323-5). This important volume in the Peterson Field Guide series first appeared in 1954 and now has become a classic in the area of identifying animal tracks and droppings. [591.5]

Animal Species

GENERAL AND MISCELLANEOUS

8488 Alden, Peter. *Peterson First Guide to Mammals of North America* (8–12). Illus. 1987, Houghton paper $3.95 (0-395-42767-3). An uncluttered basic guide to mammal identification with many illustrations and useful background material. (Rev: BL 5/15/87) [599]

8489 Anderson, Sydney, ed. *Simon and Schuster's Guide to Mammals* (9–12). Illus. 1984, Simon & Schuster paper $12.95 (0-671-42805-5). This guide, originally published in Italy, introduces the orders of mammals and highlights 426 species. [599]

8490 Burt, William Henry. *A Field Guide to the Mammals* (7–12). 3rd ed. Illus. 1976, Houghton $18.95 (0-395-24082-4); paper $13.95 (0-395-24084-0). An identification guide to 380 species of mammals found in North America. [599]

8491 Forsyth, Adrian. *Mammals of the American North* (9–12). Illus. 1985, Camden House $29.95 (0-920656-42-0). In addition to being an attractive picture book, this volume gives extensive and accurate information on mammals in northern United States and southern Canada. (Rev: BL 2/1/86) [599.007]

8492 Holmgren, Virginia C. *Raccoons: In Folklore, History & Today's Backyards* (9–12). Illus. 1990, Capra paper $10.95 (0-88496-312-8). The habits of raccoons are explored as well as an account of how they figure in American folklore and legends. (Rev: BL 4/1/90) [599.74]

8493 Leslie, Robert Franklin. *Ringo, the Robber Raccoon: The True Story of a Northwoods Rogue* (9–12). Illus. 1984, Putnam $10.95 (0-396-08323-4). The story of a friendship between a young man and a wild raccoon in a provincial park in British Columbia. [599.74]

8494 MacDonald, David, ed. *The Encyclopedia of Mammals* (7–12). Illus. 1984, Facts on File $65.00 (0-87196-871-1). Almost 200 animal species are compiled in this volume on living mammals, which is illustrated with both photographs and drawings. [599]

8495 Whitaker, John O., Jr. *The Audubon Society Field Guide to North American Mammals* (7–

12). Illus. 1980, Knopf $15.95 (0-394-50762-2). This excellent guide contains almost 200 pages of color photographs. [599]

8496 *Wild Animals of North America* (7–12). Illus. 1979, National Geographic $29.95 (0-87044-294-5). A superbly illustrated guide to the common species of animals found on our continent. [599]

APE FAMILY

8497 Fossey, Dian. *Gorillas in the Mist* (9–12). Illus. 1983, Houghton paper $11.95 (0-395-36638-0). The results of many years of field study of gorillas are reported on by this outstanding naturalist. [599.88]

8498 Goodall, Jane. *In the Shadow of Man* (8–12). Rev. ed. 1988, Houghton paper $9.95 (0-395-33145-5). The story of a scientist's observations of chimpanzees at the Gombe Stream Chimpanzee Reserve in Tanzania. (Rev: BR 11–12/88) [599.8]

8499 Goodall, Jane. *Through a Window: My Thirty Years with the Chimpanzees of Gombe* (10–12). 1990, Houghton $21.95 (0-395-50081-8). Goodall continues her story of the study of chimpanzees and their society in the Gombe Stream National Park in Tanzania. Goodall's first 10 years at Gombe is covered in the celebrated *In the Shadow of Man* (1972). (Rev: BL 8/90) [591]

8500 Kevles, Bettyann. *Thinking Gorillas: Testing and Teaching the Greatest Ape* (9–12). 1980, Dutton $10.95 (0-525-41074-0). This fascinating book describes the attempts to teach and test a group of captured gorillas. [599.88]

8501 Koebner, Linda. *Forgotten Animals: The Rehabilitation of Laboratory Primates* (8–12). 1984, Lodestar $12.95 (0-525-66773-3). The author describes how chimpanzees no longer needed for lab experimentation are saved and cared for. [599.8]

8502 Morris, Desmond. *The Illustrated Naked Ape: A Zoologist's Study of the Human Animal* (9–12). Illus. 1986, Crown $19.95 (0-517-56320-7). A richly illustrated edition that describes humans and their relation to the rest of the animal kingdom. [599]

8503 Strum, Shirley C. *Almost Human: A Journey into the World of Baboons* (9–12). Illus. 1987, Random $22.50 (0-394-54724-1). A description of the life and habits of the Pumphouse Gang, a group of baboons living in Kenya. (Rev: BL 11/15/87) [599.8]

8504 Terrace, Herbert S. *Nim: A Chimpanzee Who Learned Sign Language* (9–12). 1986, Columbia Univ. Pr. $30.00 (0-231-06340-7). The story of how a chimpanzee was taught to communicate with humans by using sign language. [599.8]

BEARS

8505 Craighead, Frank C., Jr. *Track of the Grizzly* (10–12). Illus. 1979, Sierra Club $10.95 (0-87156-223-5); paper $9.95 (0-87156-322-3). This introduction to the grizzly bear is a result of the 13-year study in Yellowstone National Park. [599.74]

8506 Mills, William. *Bears and Men* (9–12). Illus. 1986, Algonquin $24.95 (0-912697-41-5). The pictorial account and text of an expedition to observe and photograph polar bears on western Hudson Bay. (Rev: SLJ 2/87) [599.74]

8507 Olsen, Jack. *Night of the Grizzlies* (10–12). 1971, NAL paper $3.95 (0-451-15687-0). The relations between mankind and animals are explored in this account of a fatal attack of grizzlies in Glacier National Park. [599.74]

8508 Peacock, Doug. *Grizzly Years: In Search of the American Wilderness* (10–12). Illus. 1990, Henry Holt $19.95 (0-8050-0448-3). A Vietnam vet, still suffering from the shock of his experiences, traces and studies the grizzly bears of Wyoming and Montana. (Rev: BL 9/1/90) [599.74]

BIG CATS

8509 Adamson, Joy. *Born Free: A Lioness of Two Worlds* (7–12). 1987, Pantheon $11.95 (0-394-56161-4); paper $4.95 (0-394-71263-3). First published in 1960, this is an account of a young lionesss growing up in captivity in Kenya. [599.74]

8510 Hillard, Darla. *Vanishing Tracks: Four Years among the Snow Leopards of Nepal* (9–12). Illus. 1989, Arbor House $22.95 (0-877-95972-2). The story of an expedition in which Hillard, a nature-loving secretary (like Jane Goodall), participated to help save the elusive snow leopard of the Himalayas. (Rev: BL 5/15/89) [599.74]

8511 Thapar, Valmik. *Tiger: Portrait of a Predator* (7–12). Illus. 1986, Facts on File $24.95 (0-8160-1238-5). Thapar has studied tigers in India and gives a fascinating account of their habits and declining population. (Rev: BR 11–12/86) [599.74]

COYOTES, FOXES, AND WOLVES

8512 Brandenburg, Jim. *White Wolf: Living with an Arctic Legend* (10–12). Illus. 1988, NorthWord $40.00 (0-942802-95-0). In stunning photos and sparse text, an introduction to the Arctic wolf. (Rev: BL 12/15/88) [599.744]

8513 Hyde, Dayton O. *Don Coyote* (10–12). 1986, Arbor House $16.95 (0-87795-783-5); Ballantine paper $3.95 (0-345-34704-8). A book that explores the great outdoors and balances in nature by focusing on the coyote and its habitat. (Rev: BL 6/15/86; VOYA 8–10/86) [599.74]

8514 Lawrence, R. D. *In Praise of Wolves* (10–12). 1986, Holt $16.45 (0-03-001597-9); Ballantine paper $3.95 (0-345-34916-4). A book that resulted from the author's many years studying the habits and behavior of wolves. (Rev: VOYA 6/86) [599.74]

8515 Lawrence, R. D. *Secret Go the Wolves* (9–12). 1985, Ballantine paper $3.50 (0-345-33200-8). The story of how Lawrence and his wife raised a pair of wolf pups. [599.7]

8516 Leslie, Robert Franklin. *In the Shadow of a Rainbow* (10–12). 1986, Norton paper $6.95 (0-393-30392-6). The story of an unusual friendship between man and wolf. [599.74]

8517 Lopez, Barry. *Of Wolves and Men* (9–12). 1978, Macmillan $15.95 (0-684-16322-5). An account that contrasts the wolf of folklore with the true nature of this caring social creature. [599.74]

8518 MacDonald, David. *Running with the Fox* (9–12). Illus. 1988, Facts on File $23.95 (0-8160-1880-3). With 120 photographs, the author explores the behavior and habits of foxes. (Rev: BR 9–10/88; VOYA 8/88) [599.7]

8519 Mech, L. David. *The Arctic Wolf: Living with the Pack* (9–12). Illus. 1988, Voyageur $24.95 (0-89658-099-7). A detailed account of the life and habits of wolves by a man who lived among them. (Rev: BL 11/15/88) [599.744]

8520 Mowat, Farley. *Never Cry Wolf* (10–12). 1983, Bantam paper $3.50 (0-553-26624-1). The true story of a man's adventures living with a pack of wolves and learning about their ways. [599.74]

8521 Savage, Candace. *Wolves* (9–12). Illus. 1989, Sierra Club $29.95 (0-87156-689-3). A fascinating account of wolf behavior accompanied by 97 color photographs. (Rev: BL 12/1/89) [599.74]

DEER FAMILY

8522 Cox, Daniel, and John Ozoga. *Whitetail Country* (8–12). Illus. 1988, Willow Creek Pr.

$39.00 (0-932558-43-7). Wonderful photographs complement this account of the life and living habits of the deer. (Rev: BR 3–4/89) [599.73]

8523 Hoshino, Michio. *Moose* (10–12). Illus. 1988, Chronicle $18.95 (0-87701-503-1); paper $9.95 (0-87701-494-9). A photographic essay on this animal took photographer Hoshino 8 years to assemble. (Rev: BL 12/1/88) [599.73]

PANDAS

8524 MacClintock, Dorcas. *Red Pandas: A Natural History* (8–12). Illus. 1988, Macmillan $LB $13.95 (0-684-18677-2). This is a detailed scientific study of the Red Panda in its natural habitats and in zoos. (Rev: SLJ 10/88) [599.74]

RODENTS

8525 Fenton, M. Brock. *Just Bats* (7–12). Illus. 1983, Univ. of Toronto Pr. paper $12.95 (0-8020-6464-7). An introduction to this frequently misunderstood and very useful flying rodent. [599.4]

8526 Ryden, Hope. *Lily Pond: Four Years with a Family of Beavers* (10–12). Illus. 1989, Morrow $17.95 (0-877-95979-X). A fascinating account of beaver-watching over a 4-year period. (Rev: BL 11/15/89) [599.32]

8527 Tuttle, Merlin D. *America's Neighborhood Bats* (9–12). Illus. 1988, Univ. of Texas Pr. $19.95 (0-292-70403-8); paper $9.95 (0-292-70406-2). A brief account filled with amazing photographs that helps clarify misunderstandings about this very useful animal. (Rev: BL 3/1/89) [599.4]

Birds

GENERAL AND MISCELLANEOUS

8528 Audubon, John James. *The Birds of America* (7–12). Illus. 1985, Macmillan $39.95 (0-02-504450-8). A total of 435 plates are reproduced in this handsome volume. [598]

8529 Austin, Oliver L., Jr. *Families of Birds* (7–12). Illus. 1985, Western paper $2.95 (0-307-24015-0). A simple guide to bird identification with many colorful illustrations. [598]

8530 *Book of North American Birds* (9–12). 1990, Random $32.95 (0-89577-351-1). About 600 U.S. and Canadian birds are pictured in color paintings and described in a lucid text. (Rev: BL 9/1/90) [598]

8531 Brooks, Bruce. *On the Wing* (9–12). Illus. 1989, Macmillan $35.00 (0-684-19119-9). An introduction to the physiology of birds and their habits complete with 150 stunning photographs. (Rev: BL 9/15/89) [598]

8532 Bull, John, et al. *Birds of North America, Eastern Region: A Quick Identification Guide to Common Birds* (9–12). Illus. 1985, Macmillan $16.95 (0-02-518230-7); paper $9.95 (0-02-079660-9). A picture guide to 253 species of birds found in the eastern part of Canada and the United States. Also use: *Birds of North America, Western Region* (1989). (Rev: BL 8/85) [598]

8533 Burton, Robert. *Eggs: Nature's Perfect Package* (9–12). Illus. 1987, Facts on File $22.95 (0-8160-1384-5). A survey covering egg development from fertilization to hatching in text and more than 300 color photographs. (Rev: BL 9/1/87) [591.1]

8534 Cronin, Edward W. *Getting Started in Bird Watching* (10–12). Illus. 1986, Houghton paper $5.95 (0-395-34397-6). Handy tips and checklists for 9 different regions of the United States highlight this beginner's manual. (Rev: BL 6/1/86) [598]

8535 Ehrlich, Paul R., et al. *The Birder's Handbook: A Field Guide to the Natural History of North American Birds* (9–12). Illus. 1988, Simon & Schuster $24.95 (0-671-62133-5); paper $14.95 (0-671-65989-8). An extremely comprehensive guide to the 646 birds native to North America. (Rev: BL 10/1/88) [598.297]

8536 Farrand, John. *How to Identify Birds* (10–12). Illus. 1987, McGraw paper $13.50 (0-07-019975-2). A noted bird watcher tells how to identify birds by such characteristics as size, habitat, and voice. For more specific information see the author's *Eastern Birds* and *Western Birds* (both 1987). (Rev: BL 11/15/87) [598]

8537 Fuller, Errol. *Extinct Birds* (9–12). Illus. 1988, Facts on File $35.00 (0-8160-1833-2). A lavishly illustrated account of birds that have become extinct. (Rev: BL 2/1/88; BR 9–10/88) [598]

8538 Hosking, Eric. *Seabirds of the World* (7–12). Illus. 1983, Facts on File $24.95 (0-87196-249-7). All kinds of sea birds from penguins to gulls are described. [598]

8539 Jones, John Oliver. *Where the Birds Are: A Guide to All 50 States and Canada* (10–12). Illus. 1990, Morrow $24.95 (0-688-09609-3); paper $15.95 (0-688-05178-2). A state-by-state guide to bird watching plus material on individual species. (Rev: BL 5/15/90) [598.7]

8540 Lentz, Joan Easton, and Judith Young. *Birdwatching: A Guide for Beginners* (10–12). Illus. 1985, Capra paper $8.95 (0-88496-231-8). After identifying bird families and their habitats in the United States, the authors give tips on how to watch them and where. (Rev: BL 9/15/85) [598]

8541 Perrins, Christopher M., and Alex L. A. Middleton, eds. *The Encyclopedia of Birds* (9–12). Illus. 1985, Facts on File $45.00 (0-8160-1150-8). This expensive fully illustrated volume gives excellent information on all kinds of birds arranged by their general size. (Rev: BL 8/85) [598]

8542 Peterson, Roger Tory. *A Field Guide to the Birds* (7–12). 4th ed. Illus. 1980, Houghton $19.95 (0-395-26621-1); paper $14.95 (0-395-26619-X). An exhaustive guide to the birds found east of the Rockies. [598]

8543 Peterson, Roger Tory. *A Field Guide to Western Birds* (9–12). 3rd ed. Illus. 1990, Houghton $22.95 (0-395-51749-4); paper $15.95 (0-395-51424-X). This book covers the birds found in the Rockies and West plus a section on the Hawaiian Islands. [598]

8544 Peterson, Roger Tory. *How to Know the Birds* (9–12). 1949, NAL paper $4.50 (0-451-12939-3). A basic bird identification guide by one of this country's most respected naturalists. [598]

8545 Robbins, Chandler S., et al., eds. *Birds of North America* (7–12). Rev. ed. Illus. 1983, Golden Press $12.95 (0-307-37002-X); paper $9.95 (0-307-33656-5). A handy compact guide arranged into 2 main sections—water birds and land birds. [598]

8546 Scott, Shirley L., ed. *Field Guide to the Birds of North America* (7–12). Illus. 1983, National Geographic paper $14.95 (0-87044-472-7). A guide to over 800 species (each with a color print) arranged by families. [598]

8547 Socha, Laura O'Biso. *A Birdwatcher's Handbook: Field Ornithology for Backyard Naturalists* (10–12). Illus. 1987, Dodd paper $7.95 (0-396-09074-5). A basic guide with tips on the methods used to identify birds and the equipment to use. (Rev: BL 10/1/87) [598]

8548 Soper, Tony. *Oceans of Birds* (9–12). Illus. 1990, David & Charles $19.95 (0-7153-9199-2). A worldwide survey of sea birds with many pages of color photographs and maps. (Rev: BL 3/15/90) [598.29]

8549 Stap, Don. *A Parrot without a Name: The Search for the Last Unknown Birds on Earth* (10–12). Illus. 1990, Knopf $19.95 (0-394-55596-1). An account of an expedition into the jungles of Peru to locate and identify as many birds as possible. (Rev: BL 5/15/90) [598]

8550 Stokes, Donald. *A Guide to the Behavior of Common Birds* (7–12). Illus. 1979, Little $16.95 (0-316-81722-8); paper $9.95 (0-316-81725-2). The first of 3 volumes, each of which describes the behavior of 25 different birds. Volume 2 is: *A Guide to Bird Behavior: In the Wild and at Your Feeder* (1985); volume 3 is: *A Guide to Bird Behavior* (1989). [598]

8551 Stokes, Donald, and Lillian Stokes. *The Bird Feeder Book: An Easy Guide to Attracting, Identifying, and Understanding Your Feeder Birds* (8–12). Illus. 1987, Little paper $8.95 (0-316-81733-3). A manual that describes, with color photographs, 72 backyard birds, plus tips on how to attract and feed them. (Rev: BL 2/1/88) [598]

8552 Stokes, Donald, and Lillian Stokes. *The Complete Birdhouse Book: The Easy Guide to Attracting Nesting Birds* (9–12). Illus. 1990, Little paper $9.95 (0-316-81714-7). Plans for various birdhouses are given plus instructions on how to build them. (Rev: BL 9/15/90) [598]

8553 Whitfield, Philip, ed. *The Macmillan Illustrated Encyclopedia of Birds: A Visual Who's Who in the World of Birds* (7–12). Illus. 1988, Macmillan paper $19.95 (0-02-044462-1). Descriptions of appearances and habits plus hundreds of color drawings highlight this coverage of approximately 600 species of birds. (Rev: BL 3/1/89) [598]

8554 Zim, Herbert, and Ira Gabrielson. *Birds* (7–12). 1956, Western paper $3.95 (0-307-24053-3). A handy field guide to the identification of about 120 common birds. [598]

BEHAVIOR

8555 Burton, Robert. *Bird Behavior* (9–12). Illus. 1985, Knopf $18.95 (0-394-53957-5). With profuse illustrations, this is an explanation of bird behavior under such headings as migration, flight, and communication. (Rev: BL 9/1/85) [598.2]

8556 Heinrich, Bernd. *Ravens in Winter: A Zoological Detective Story* (10–12). 1989, Summit $19.95 (0-671-67809-4). An exploration of the behavior of ravens and their social instincts. (Rev: BL 9/1/89) [598.8]

DUCKS AND GEESE

8557 Soothill, Eric, and Peter Whitehead. *Wildfowl of the World* (9–12). 1989, Blandford paper $17.95 (0-7137-2110-3). A description of 128 species of waterfowl and a description of their habitats. (Rev: BL 9/1/89) [598.4]

EAGLES, HAWKS, AND OTHER BIRDS OF PREY

8558 Clark, William S. *A Field Guide to Hawks: North America* (9–12). Illus. 1987, Houghton $19.95 (0-395-36001-3); paper $13.95 (0-395-44112-9). An extensively illustrated guide to 39 species of hawks. (Rev: BL 10/1/87) [598]

8559 Dunne, Pete, et al. *Hawks in Flight: The Flight Identification of North American Migrant Raptors* (10–12). Illus. 1988, Houghton $17.95 (0-395-42388-0). A field guide to 23 species of North American birds of prey. (Rev: BL 3/15/88) [598]

8560 Haley, Neale. *Birds for Pets and Pleasure* (9–12). Illus. 1981, Delacorte LB $8.95 (0-385-28053-X); paper $4.95 (0-440-00475-6). This account focuses on the problems of the breeding of eagles in captivity. [598]

8561 Hosking, Eric, et al. *Eric Hosking's Birds of Prey of the World* (10–12). Illus. 1988, Stephen Greene $19.95 (0-8289-0653-X). From one of the great bird photographers comes an intense, beautiful look at these predators. (Rev: BL 9/1/88) [598]

8562 True, Dan. *Flying Free* (9–12). 1990, Wynwood Pr. paper $8.95 (0-922066-12-4). This is the true story of how a television producer found himself caring for a newborn baby eagle. [598]

OWLS

8563 Alcorn, Gordon Dee. *Owls: An Introduction for the Amateur Naturalist* (9–12). Illus. 1986, Prentice paper $9.95 (0-13-647504-3). An attractively illustrated introduction to the 18 North American owl species. (Rev: BL 6/1/86) [598.9]

8564 Burton, John A., ed. *Owls of the World: Their Evolution, Structure and Ecology* (9–12). Rev. ed. Illus. 1985, Tanager $29.95 (0-88072-060-3). Since its first edition in 1874, this has become the standard work on owls that covers in a well-illustrated text such topics as anatomy, conservation, and species. (Rev: BL 3/15/85) [598]

8565 Sparks, John, and Tony Soper. *Owls: Their Natural & Unnatural History* (8–12). Illus. 1989, Facts on File $22.95 (0-8160-2154-6). As well as information on all kinds of owls, their anatomy, and habits, this account covers folklore and superstitions surrounding the owl. (Rev: BR 5–6/90) [598]

PENGUINS

8566 Kaehler, Wolfgang. *Penguins* (9–12). Illus. 1989, Chronicle $22.95 (0-87701-649-6); paper $12.95 (0-87701-637-2). An inviting glimpse into the varieties of penguins and how and where they live. (Rev: BL 11/1/89) [598.4]

8567 Peterson, Roger Tory. *Penguins* (10–12). Illus. 1979, Houghton $40.00 (0-394-27092-8). A richly illustrated narrative about the 16 different kinds of penguins and how they live. [598]

Conservation and Endangered Species

8568 Adams, Douglas, and Mark Carwardine. *Last Chance to See* (10–12). Illus. 1991, Crown $19.95 (0-517-57195-1). The noted science fiction writer examines the plight of many of the earth's endangered species. (Rev: BL 12/1/90) [591.52]

8569 Bergman, Charles. *Wild Echoes: Encounters with the Most Endangered Species in North America* (10–12). Illus. 1989, McGraw $19.95 (0-07-004922-X). Using such species as wolves, panthers, and whales as examples, Bergman questions mankind's relationship with nature. (Rev: BL 11/15/89) [591.52]

8570 DiSilvestro, Roger. *The Endangered Kingdom: The Struggle to Save America's Wildlife* (9–12). 1989, Wiley $19.95 (0-471-60600-6). The author describes the changes in America's wildlife since the Europeans arrived and their effects on specific species. (Rev: BL 11–12/89) [591]

8571 DiSilvestro, Roger. *Fight for Survival* (10–12). Illus. 1990, Wiley $29.95 (0-471-50835-7). The story of such endangered species as wolves, sharks, sea turtles, dolphins, and cranes. (Rev: BL 6/1/90) [333.95]

8572 Ehrlich, Paul R., and Anne H. Ehrlich. *Extinction* (10–12). 1981, Random $16.95 (0-394-51312-6). A book that explores questions of how and why species become extinct and how each disappearance affects the earth. [560]

8573 Fitzgerald, Sarah. *International Wildlife Trade: Whose Business Is It Anyway?* (10–12). Illus. 1989, World Wildlife $40.00 (0-942635-13-2); paper $25.00 (0-942635-10-8). The international import and export business in wildlife and its effect on endangered species are explored. (Rev: BL 6/1/90) [333.95]

8574 Fraser, Laura, et al. *The Animal Rights Handbook: Everyday Ways to Save Animal Lives* (10–12). 1990, Living Planet paper $4.95 (0-9626072-0-7). This guide to animals' rights includes sections on uses of animals, their treatment in various situations, important addresses, and suggestions for change. (Rev: BL 10/1/90) [179.3]

8575 LaBastille, Anne. *Mama Poc: An Eyewitness Account of the Extinction of a Species* (10–12). 1990, Norton $19.95 (0-393-02830-5). The story of one woman's fight to save the giant grebe, the flightless water fowl, of Guatemala. (Rev: BL 6/1/90) [598.443]

8576 Matthiessen, Peter. *Wildlife in America* (10–12). Rev. ed. Illus. 1987, Viking $29.95 (0-670-81906-9). An account of the wildlife of North America that have become extinct or have seriously declining populations as a result of intervention of the white race. (Rev: BL 11/15/87) [591.97]

8577 Mowat, Farley. *Sea of Slaughter* (10–12). 1985, Bantam paper $9.95 (0-553-34269-X). An account of how man's greed and brutality have affected the wildlife along the northern Atlantic seaboard. (Rev: BL 4/15/85) [639.9]

8578 Penny, Malcolm. *Rhinos: Endangered Species* (9–12). 1988, Facts on File $19.95 (0-8160-1882-0). The shocking story of how humans have depleted the stock of rhinoceros to such an extent it seems headed for extinction. (Rev: SLJ 5/88) [591]

8579 Schreiber, Rudolf L., et al., eds. *Save the Birds* (9–12). Illus. 1989, Houghton $39.95 (0-395-51172-0). An oversized, beautifully illustrated book that describes our wasting the environment and endangering the welfare of the bird population. (Rev: BL 12/1/89) [639.9]

8580 Stouffer, Marty. *Marty Stouffer's Wild America* (8–12). 1988, Times Books $24.95 (0-8129-1610-7). A wildlife documentary maker discusses his career and the importance of conservation. (Rev: BR 3–4/89; VOYA 4/89) [320.5]

Farms and Ranches

GENERAL AND MISCELLANEOUS

8581 Brown, Bruce. *Lone Tree* (9–12). 1989, Crown $17.95 (0-517-56987-6). This story of a triple murder and suicide highlights the plight of many farmers in America today. (Rev: VOYA 4/90)

8582 Franck, Irene M., and David M. Brownstone. *Harvesters* (7–12). 1987, Facts on File $17.95 (0-8160-1444-2). Although this book concentrates on the history of farming, it also covers topics such as whaling, hunting, fishing, and bee keeping. (Rev: BR 11–12/87) [630]

8583 Hasselstrom, Linda. *Windbreak: A Woman Rancher on the Northern Plains* (10–12). 1987, Barn Owl paper $12.95 (0-9609626-3-8). Using a diary format, the author describes a year on a South Dakota cattle ranch and such everyday activities as haying, mending fences, and branding cattle. (Rev: SLJ 12/87) [307.7]

8584 Kline, David. *Great Possessions: An Amish Farmer's Journal* (10–12). 1990, North Point $16.95 (0-86547-405-2). A series of essays about the love of nature and its wonders, and the joys of farming the old-fashioned way. (Rev: BL 4/15/90) [508]

8585 Rhodes, Richard. *Farm: A Year in the Life of an American Farmer* (10–12). 1989, Simon & Schuster $19.95 (0-671-63647-2). The everyday trials and triumphs of a Missouri farmer and his family. (Rev: BL 9/1/89; SLJ 5/90) [630]

8586 Solkoff, Joel. *The Politics of Food: The Decline of Agriculture and the Rise of Agribusiness in America* (10–12). 1985, Sierra Club $17.95 (0-87156-846-2). A history of agriculture in this country and of the Department of Agriculture from 1862 to Reagan. (Rev: SLJ 2/86) [630]

8587 Staten, Jay, and Pat Staten. *The Embattled Farmer* (10–12). 1987, Fulcrum $15.95 (1-55591-011-4). A general survey of the present economic factors and government programs that are changing the conditions of our embattled farmers. (Rev: BL 4/1/88) [338.1]

ANIMALS AND CROPS

8588 Coats, C. David. *Old MacDonald's Factory Farm* (10–12). 1989, Continuum $17.95 (0-8264-0439-1). An account of modern agricultural methods as applied to the raising of farm animals and the shocking cruelties that have resulted. (Rev: BL 7/89) [179.3]

8589 Haynes, Cynthia. *Raising Turkeys, Ducks, Geese, Pigeons, and Guineas* (10–12). Illus. 1987, TAB $24.95 (0-8306-0803-6); paper $16.95 (0-8306-2803-7). A general guide to the breeding and raising of a variety of poultry species. (Rev: BL 4/1/88) [636.5]

8590 Rath, Sara. *About Cows* (10–12). Illus. 1987, NorthWord paper $14.95 (0-942802-75-6). A wide array of information about cows including profiles of such famous bovines as Elsie. (Rev: BL 4/1/88) [636.2142]

8591 Schwab, Jim. *Raising Less Corn and More Hell: Midwestern Farmers Speak Out* (10–12). 1988, Univ. of Illinois Pr. $24.95 (0-252-01398-0). The current problems facing farmers in the Midwest are graphically introduced through a number of interviews. (Rev: BL 4/15/89) [338.1]

Insects

GENERAL AND MISCELLANEOUS

8592 Borror, Donald J., and Richard E. White. *A Field Guide to the Insects of America North of Mexico* (9–12). Illus. 1970, Houghton paper $12.95 (0-395-18523-8). In addition to an identification manual, this book explains how to observe insects and how to collect and preserve them. [595.7]

8593 Cottam, Clarence, and Herbert Zim. *Insects* (7–12). 1987, Western paper $3.95 (0-307-24055-X). A handy field guide that gives identification material of 218 common species. [595.7]

8594 Evans, Howard Ensign. *The Pleasures of Entomology: Portraits of Insects and the People Who Study Them* (10–12). Illus. 1985, Smithsonian Inst. paper $14.95 (0-87474-421-0). An enjoyable personal look at the study of insects plus information on many species and their habits. (Rev: BL 8/85) [595.7]

8595 Fichter, George S. *Insect Pests* (7–12). 1966, Western paper $3.95 (0-307-24016-9). A handy field guide to 350 insect pests found in North America. [595.7]

8596 Klausnitzer, Bernhard. *Insects: Their Biology and Cultural History* (10–12). Illus. 1988, Universe $40.00 (0-87663-666-0). A well-illustrated guide to 35 common orders of insects. (Rev: BL 3/15/88) [595.7]

8597 Leahy, Christopher. *Peterson First Guide to Insects of North America* (8–12). Illus. 1987, Houghton paper $3.95 (0-395-35640-7). This simplified guide supplies basics on identification, anatomy, and life stages. (Rev: BL 5/15/87) [599]

8598 Milne, Lorus, and Margery Milne. *The Audubon Society Field Book of Insects* (9–12). Illus. 1983, Abrams $35.00 (0-8109-1806-4). A beautifully illustrated look at our most common insects and their habits. [595.7]

8599 Milne, Lorus, and Margery Milne. *The Audubon Society Field Guide to North American Insects and Spiders* (7–12). Illus. 1980, Knopf $14.45 (0-394-50763-0). An extensive use of color photographs makes this a fine guide for identifying insects. [595.7]

8600 O'Toole, Christopher, ed. *The Encyclopedia of Insects* (9–12). Illus. 1986, Facts on File $24.95 (0-8160-1358-6). A large format book with stunning illustrations that gives general information and detailed facts about individual species. (Rev: BL 6/1/86; BR 11–12/86) [595.7]

8601 O'Toole, Christopher. *Insects in Camera: A Photographic Essay on Behaviour* (9–12). Illus.

1985, Oxford Univ. Pr. $29.95 (0-19-217694-3). In chapters organized under such headings as defense, mating, and egg laying, the author presents 287 amazing color photographs of insect life. (Rev: BL 9/1/85) [595.7]

8602 Wootton, Anthony. *Insects of the World* (9–12). Illus. 1984, Facts on File $24.95 (0-87196-991-2). This nicely illustrated volume describes how insects evolved, their characteristics, and how to identify them. [595.7]

BEES AND WASPS

8603 Gould, James L., and Carol Grant Gould. *The Honey Bee* (10–12). Illus. 1988, Scientific American $32.95 (0-7167-5023-6). A thorough study in interesting text and unusual photographs of this amazing insect. (Rev: BL 12/1/88; BR 3–4/89) [595.79]

8604 von Frisch, Karl. *Bees: Their Vision, Chemical Senses, and Language* (10–12). Rev. ed. Illus. 1971, Cornell Univ. Pr. paper $10.95 (0-8014-9126-6). A classic account first published in 1950 that explores the complex behavior of bees. [595.7]

BEETLES

8605 White, Richard E. *A Field Guide to the Beetles of North America* (9–12). Illus. 1983, Houghton $17.95 (0-395-31808-4); paper $12.95 (0-395-33953-7). An identification guide that also covers such topics as the habits and structure of beetles and how to collect them. [595.7]

BUTTERFLIES, MOTHS, AND CATERPILLARS

8606 Klots, Alexander B. *A Field Guide to the Butterflies of North America, East of the Great Plains . . .* (9–12). Illus. 1951, Houghton $17.95 (0-395-07865-2); paper 9.95 (0-395-25859-6). Eastern butterflies from Greenland to Mexico are identified and their behavior explored. [595.7]

8607 Mitchell, Robert T., and Herbert Zim. *Butterflies and Moths* (7–12). 1964, Western paper $3.95 (0-307-24052-5). This compact guide identifies and describes hundreds of varieties of butterflies and moths. [595.7]

8608 Preston-Mafham, Rod, and Ken Preston-Mafham. *Butterflies of the World* (8–12). Illus. 1988, Facts on File $22.95 (0-8160-1601-1). An attractively illustrated book that introduces butterflies and moths and gives facts about their evolution, structure, types, and life cycles. (Rev: BR 3–4/89) [595.78]

8609 Pyle, Robert Michael. *The Audubon Society Field Guide to North American Butterflies* (7–12). Illus. 1981, Knopf $14.45 (0-394-51914-0). An introduction to over 600 species of butterflies in about 1,000 color photographs and text. [595.7]

8610 Pyle, Robert Michael. *The Audubon Society Handbook for Butterfly Watchers* (10–12). Illus. 1984, Macmillan $17.95 (0-684-18151-7). A book that explains how to observe butterflies in an organized fashion while also covering such topics as their behavioral characteristics and how to photograph them. [595.7]

8611 Tekulsky, Mathew. *The Butterfly Garden* (10–12). Illus. 1985, Harvard Common $16.95 (0-916782-70-0); paper $8.95 (0-916782-69-7). A handbook for those who wish to attract and study butterflies. (Rev: BL 12/1/85) [638]

SPIDERS

8612 Jones, Dick. *Spider* (7–12). Illus. 1986, Facts on File $12.95 (0-8160-1578-2). A lavishly illustrated volume that describes many species of spiders and all facets of their lives. (Rev: BR 1–2/87; VOYA 2/87) [595.4]

8613 Levi, Herbert, and Lorna R. Levi. *Spiders and Their Kin* (7–12). Illus. 1969, Western paper $3.95 (0-307-24021-5). A handy identification guide to many kinds of spiders with illustrations for each. [595.4]

Land Invertebrates

8614 Buchsbaum, Ralph. *Animals without Backbones: An Introduction to the Invertebrates* (10–12). Rev. ed. Illus. 1948, Univ. of Chicago Pr. $25.00 (0-226-07869-8); paper $17.00 (0-226-07870-1). A thorough introduction of the structure and characteristics of the main groups of invertebrate animals. [592]

Marine and Freshwater Life

GENERAL AND MISCELLANEOUS

8615 Banister, Keith, and Andrew Campbell, eds. *The Encyclopedia of Aquatic Life* (9–12). Illus. 1986, Facts on File $45.00 (0-8160-1257-1). Thousands of species are covered in text and illustrations under 3 headings: fish, aquatic invertebrates, and aquatic mammals. (Rev: BL 2/1/86) [591.92]

8616 Boschung, Herbert T., Jr., et al. *The Audubon Society Field Guide to North American Fishes, Whales, and Dolphins* (7–12). Illus. 1983, Knopf $15.95 (0-394-53405-0). About 600 marine and freshwater fish and aquatic mammals are identified and described. [597]

8617 Colin, Patrick. *Marine Invertebrates & Plants of the Living Reef* (10–12). Illus. 1988, TFH $29.95 (0-86622-875-6). With over 430 color photographs, this account helps identify the animals and plants found around the reefs in the Caribbean. (Rev: BR 1–2/89) [574.94]

8618 Meinkoth, Norman A. *The Audubon Society Field Guide to North American Seashore Creatures* (7–12). Illus. 1981, Knopf $14.95 (0-394-51993-0). This is a guide to such invertebrates as sponges, corals, urchins, and anemones. [592]

8619 Reid, George K. *Pond Life* (7–12). Illus. 1967, Golden Press paper $3.95 (0-307-24017-7). Text and illustrations present the plants, animals, fish, and insects found in and around ponds. [574.92]

8620 Thompson, Gerald, and Jennifer Coldrey. *The Pond* (7–12). Illus. 1984, MIT $35.00 (0-262-20049-X). In a series of excellent photos and clear text, the animal and plant life of ponds is explored. [574.92]

8621 Warner, William W. *Distant Water: The Fate of the North Atlantic Fisherman* (10–12). 1984, Penguin paper $8.95 (0-14-006967-4). This account tells of the last days of the factory trawlers that fished for cod and herring in the North Atlantic. [639.3]

CRUSTACEANS

8622 Warner, William W. *Beautiful Swimmers: Watermen, Crabs and the Chesapeake Bay* (10–12). Illus. 1976, Little $22.50 (0-316-92326-5). In addition to the life cycle of the crab, this book also describes the watermen who catch them in Chesapeake Bay. [565]

DOLPHINS

8623 Robson, Frank. *Pictures in the Dolphin Mind* (10–12). 1988, Sheridan $14.95 (0-911378-78-2). This is an account of the author's career studying and communicating with dolphins and whales in the wild. (Rev: VOYA 12/88) [599.5]

FISH

8624 Eschmeyer, William N., and Earl S. Herald. *A Field Guide to Pacific Coast Fishes of North America: Fish the Gulf of Alaska to Baja California* (7–12). Illus. 1983, Houghton $19.95

(0-395-26873-7); paper $12.95 (0-395-33188-9). In this volume in the Peterson Field Guide series, about 500 fish are described and illustrated. [597]

8625 Filisky, Michael. *Peterson First Guide to Fishes of North America* (7–12). Illus. 1989, Houghton paper $4.95 (0-395-50219-5). This is a concise version of the parent Peterson guide that gives basic material on common fish but with less detail. (Rev: BL 6/1/89) [597]

8626 Haig-Brown, Roderick. *Silver: The Life Story of an Atlantic Salmon* (9–12). Illus. 1989, Lyons & Burford $15.95 (1-55821-051-2). From one of Canada's finest nature writers, a reprint of the 1931 book that is the life story of an Atlantic salmon. (Rev: BL 12/15/89) [597]

8627 Robins, C. Richard, and G. Carleton Ray. *A Field Guide to Atlantic Coast Fishes of North America* (9–122). Illus. 1986, Houghton $20.95 (0-395-31852-1); paper $14.95 (0-395-39198-9). An excellent field guide that describes almost 1,100 species of fish that are found between the Arctic and the Caribbean. (Rev: BL 6/1/86) [597]

8628 Shoemaker, Hurst, and Herbert Zim. *Fishes* (7–12). Illus. 1987, Western paper $3.95 (0-307-24059-2). A compact, colorfully illustrated guide to 278 of the most common fish of North America. [597]

SHARKS

8629 Moss, Sanford A. *Sharks: An Introduction for the Amateur Naturalist* (9–12). Illus. 1984, Prentice $21.95 (0-13-808312-6); paper $10.95 (0-13-808304-5). A profile of the shark that highlights its unique features and capabilities. (Rev: BL 2/15/85) [597]

8630 Reader's Digest, eds. *Sharks: Silent Hunters of the Deep* (8–12). Illus. 1987, Reader's Digest $19.95 (0-86438-014-3). This handsomely illustrated account describes the ways of sharks, gives material on famous encounters, and identifies all 344 species. (Rev: BL 5/15/87; BR 11–12/87; SLJ 1/88; VOYA 8–9/87) [597]

8631 Springer, Victor G., and Joy P. Gold. *Sharks in Question: The Smithsonian Answer Book* (9–12). Illus. 1989, Smithsonian Institution $39.95 (0-87474-878-X); paper $15.95 (0-87474-877-1). Using a question-and-answer format plus stunning photographs, the authors tell all and explode myths about this sea creature. (Rev: BL 6/1/89; SLJ 8/89) [597]

8632 Stafford-Deitsch, Jeremy. *Shark: A Photographer's Story* (10–12). Illus. 1987, Sierra Club $19.95 (0-87156-776-8); paper $16.95 (0-87156-733-4). After a discussion of shark anatomy and behavior, the author takes you on a well-

illustrated global exploration of their haunts. (Rev: BL 11/15/87; BR 3–4/88; VOYA 2/89) [597]

8633 Steel, Rodney. *Sharks of the World* (9–12). Illus. 1985, Facts on File $22.95 (0-8160-1086-2). Straightforward information is given on sharks plus intriguing photographs. (Rev: BL 2/1/86) [597]

8634 Stevens, John D., ed. *Sharks* (9–12). Illus. 1987, Facts on File $29.95 (0-8160-1800-6). An oversize book with stunning photographs on each page and 17 chapters each written by a shark specialist. (Rev: BL 9/15/87) [591]

SHELLS

8635 Abbott, R. Tucker. *Seashells of North America: A Guide to Field Identification* (7–12). Illus. 1968, Golden paper $9.95 (0-307-13657-4). This handy volume identifies 850 species found on either or both of our coasts. [594]

8636 Abbott, R. Tucker. *Seashells of the World* (7–12). Rev. ed. Illus. 1985, Western paper $3.95 (0-307-24410-5). A concise guide that identifies in text and color pictures 850 common shells. [564]

8637 Douglass, Jackie Leatherby. *Peterson First Guide to Shells of North America* (7–12). Illus. 1989, Houghton paper $4.95 (0-395-48297-6). This is an abridged edition of the complete field guide that is more accessible and less forbidding than the parent volume. (Rev: BL 6/1/89) [594]

8638 Morris, Percy A. *A Field Guide to Pacific Coast Shells, Including Shells of Hawaii and the Gulf of California* (7–12). 2nd rev. ed. Illus. 1966, Houghton $17.95 (0-395-08029-0); paper $12.95 (0-395-18322-7). A total of 945 species are described and illustrated in this Peterson Field Guide. A companion volume is: *A Field Guide to Shells of the Atlantic and Gulf Coasts and the West Indies* (1973). [594]

8639 Morris, Percy A. *A Field Guide to Shells of the Atlantic and Gulf Coasts and the West Indies* (7–12). 3rd ed. Illus. 1973, Houghton $17.95 (0-395-16809-0); paper $12.95 (0-395-17170-9). A standard guide to the shells of these coasts with many illustrations and detailed descriptions. [594]

WHALES, DOLPHINS, AND OTHER SEA MAMMALS

8640 Bonner, Nigel. *Whales of the World* (9–12). Illus. 1989, Facts on File $22.95 (0-8160-1734-4). A description of various kinds of whales and behavioral patterns, plus a discussion of the possible extinction that many species now face. (Rev: BL 10/1/89; BR 1–2/90) [599.5]

8641 Bruemmer, Fred, and Brian Davies. *Seasons of the Seal* (9–12). Illus. 1988, NorthWord $29.95 (0-942802-93-4). This book, written to commemorate the end of the legalized killing of harp seals, is a well-illustrated account on the life history of this species. (Rev: BL 9/15/88) [599.74]

8642 Darling, James. *Wild Whales* (8–12). Illus. 1988, Summer Wild Productions paper $14.95 (0-9692807-2-6). The killer, humpback, and gray whales are highlighted in this picture album. (Rev: BL 11/15/88) [599.5]

8643 Day, David. *The Whale War* (10–12). Illus. 1987, Sierra Club $19.95 (0-87156-775-X); paper $9.95 (0-87156-778-4). A chronicle of the international crusade to save the whale. (Rev: BL 9/1/87) [639.9]

8644 Doak, Wade. *Encounters with Whales and Dolphins* (10–12). Illus. 1989, Sheridan $29.95 (0-911378-86-3). A book that grew out of the author's involvement with Project Interlock, the purpose of which was to study the needs of whales and dolphins. (Rev: VOYA 2/90) [599.5]

8645 Ellis, Richard. *The Book of Whales* (9–12). Illus. 1980, Knopf paper $24.95 (0-394-73371-1). A beautifully illustrated book that describes how whales evolved, various species, and their behavior. [599.5]

8646 Ellis, Richard. *Dolphins and Porpoises* (10–12). Illus. 1989, Random paper $24.95 (0-679-72286-6). A detailed account of each of the 43 different species and of the characteristics of each. (Rev: BR 11–12/89; VOYA 2/90) [599.5]

8647 Evans, Peter G. *The Natural History of Whales and Dolphins* (10–12). Illus. 1987, Facts on File $21.95 (0-8160-1732-8). This book covers such topics as evolution, diet, social organization, and current research on whales and dolphins. (Rev: VOYA 10/88) [599.5]

8648 Gardner, Robert. *The Whale Watchers' Guide* (9–12). 1984, Messner LB $10.98 (0-671-45811-6); paper $5.95 (0-671-49807-X). This guide to an increasingly popular pastime helps one identify 26 different species of whales. [599.5]

8649 Gormley, Gerard. *A Dolphin Summer* (9–12). 1985, Taplinger $14.95 (0-8008-2264-1). The story of the first 8 months of a female dolphin's life. (Rev: BL 9/1/85; SLJ 4/86) [599.5]

8650 Gormley, Gerard. *Orcas of the Gulf: A Natural History* (9–12). Illus. 1990, Sierra Club $24.95 (0-87156-601-X); paper $10.95 (0-87156-624-9). In a beautifully illustrated volume, the

life and habits of the killer whale are revealed. (Rev: BL 4/15/90) [599.5]

8651 Haley, Delphine, ed. *Marine Mammals of Eastern North Pacific and Arctic Waters* (10–12). 2nd ed. Illus. 1986, Pacific Search $32.95 (0-931397-11-1); paper $22.95 (0-931397-11-1). Separate articles written by 21 experts are given on each animal. Good illustrations. (Rev: BL 10/1/86) [599.09]

8652 Harrison, Richard, and M. M. Bryden, eds. *Whales, Dolphins and Porpoises* (9–12). Illus. 1988, Facts on File $35.00 (0-8160-1977-0). A handsome oversize volume with lucid text and copious illustrations. (Rev: BL 1/1/89; BR 3–4/89) [599.5]

8653 Hoyt, Erich. *The Whale-Watcher's Handbook* (10–12). Illus. 1984, Doubleday paper $12.95 (0-385-19036-0). As well as describing species of whales, dolphins, and porpoises, this book tells where they can be observed and how to whale-watch effectively. [599.5]

8654 Leatherwood, Stephen, and Randall R. Reeves. *The Sierra Club Handbook of Whales and Dolphins* (9–12). Illus. 1983, Sierra Club $25.00 (0-87156-340-X); paper $14.95 (0-87156-340-1). Through color and black-and-white pictures and an extensive text, 76 species are described. [599.5]

8655 Mowat, Farley. *A Whale for the Killing* (10–12). 1972, Amereon $16.95 (0-89190-822-6); paper $3.95 (0-553-26752-3). The author makes a plea for whales in this description of the horrible death inflicted on one trapped in a bay in Newfoundland. [599.5]

8656 Stonehouse, Bernard. *Sea Mammals of the World* (9–12). Illus. 1985, Penguin $8.95 (0-14-007081-8). A guide to a wide range of aquatic mammals in an illustrated pocket-size format. (Rev: BL 2/15/86) [599.09]

8657 Whitehead, Hal. *Voyage to the Whales* (9–12). Illus. 1990, Chelsea House $22.50 (0-9300-3125-3). A detailed, informative account of the author's research into sperm whales and their behavior conducted from his sloop in the Indian Ocean. (Rev: SLJ 7/90) [599.5]

8658 Williams, Heathcote. *Whale Nation* (10–12). Illus. 1988, Harmony $25.00 (0-517-56932-9). In free verse, generous quotes from other writers, and many illustrations this book explores the life of whales, their characteristics, and how they have been slaughtered for profit. (Rev: SLJ 1/89; VOYA 2/89) [599.5]

Microbiology and Biotechnology

8659 Pines, Maya. *Inside the Cell: The New Frontier of Medical Science* (10–12). Illus. 1980, Enslow $12.95 (0-89490-031-5). A description of the components of the human cell and how such agents as drugs and disease affect it. [574.87]

8660 Sagan, Dorion, and Lynn Margulis. *Garden of Microbial Delights: A Practical Guide to the Subvisible World* (10–12). Illus. 1988, Harcourt $24.95 (0-15-134290-3). A guide to microscopic organisms and how they affect our lives. (Rev: BL 9/1/88; SLJ 1/89) [576]

Pets

GENERAL AND MISCELLANEOUS

8661 Alderton, David. *A Birdkeeper's Guide to Pet Birds* (8–12). Illus. 1987, Tetra $9.95 (3-923880-70-7). A general guide that tells how to choose a pet bird, the varieties available, and how to care for and feed your pet. By the same author: *A Birdkeeper's Guide to Budgies* (1988); *A Birdkeeper's Guide to Finches* (1988). (Rev: BL 9/1/88) [636.686]

8662 Alderton, David. *Looking After Cage Birds: Keep and Care* (9–12). Illus. 1989, Ward Lock paper $11.95 (0-7063-6524-0). A handbook of care and feeding of cage birds plus a survey of the various species. (Rev: BL 3/15/89) [636.6]

8663 Ames, Felicia. *The Bird You Care For* (9–12). 1970, NAL paper $1.75 (0-451-07527-7). A concise manual for bird lovers that emphasizes good care and proper feeding. [598]

8664 Anderson, Robert. *A Step-by-Step Book about Snakes* (9–12). Illus. 1987, TFH $9.95 (0-86622-914-0). A view of snakes as house pets with pointers on their care and feeding. (Rev: BL 5/1/88) [636.14]

8665 Axelson, R. Dean. *Caring for Your Pet Bird* (10–12). 1989, Borgo $28.50 (0-8095-7538-8); Sterling paper $12.95 (0-8069-6986-5). Four topics discussed are care, feeding, housing, and disease treatment. (Rev: BL 5/15/85) [598]

8666 Barrie, Anmarie. *A Step-by-Step Book about Canaries* (9–12). Illus. 1987, TFH $9.95 (0-86622-922-1). A well-illustrated guide to caring for canaries in the home. (Rev: BL 5/1/88) [636.686]

8667 Barrie, Anmarie. *A Step-by-Step Book about Rabbits* (9–12). Illus. 1987, TFH paper $2.95 (0-86622-475-0). After a discussion of types of rabbits, this book tells how to feed and care for them. (Rev: BL 11/15/87) [636.9]

8668 Birmelin, Immanuel, and Annette Wolter. *The New Parakeet Handbook* (9–12). Illus. 1986, Barron's paper $6.50 (0-8120-2985-2). A manual on selecting and caring for parakeets, also known as budgerigars. (Rev: BL 5/15/86) [636.6]

8669 Corbo, Margarete Sigi, and Diane Marie Barras. *Arnie, the Darling Starling* (9–12). 1985, Fawcett paper $2.95 (0-449-20654-8). A delightful memoir of bringing up a starling as a pet. [598]

8670 Curtis, Patricia. *Animal Partners: Training Animals to Help People* (8–12). 1982, Lodestar $10.95 (0-525-66791-1). This account outlines how various species of animals, such as dogs and horses, can be used to help handicapped people. Also use the author's: *The Animal Shelter* (1984). [636.08]

8671 Fogle, Bruce. *Games Pets Play: Or How Not to be Manipulated by Your Pet* (9–12). Illus. 1987, Viking $16.95 (0-670-80892-X). An examination of both the behavior of pets and of their owners. (Rev: BL 11/15/86) [636.08]

8672 Garisto, Leslie, and Peg Streep. *The Best-Ever Book of Dog & Cat Names* (7–12). 1989, Henry Holt paper $7.95 (0-8050-0775-X). Over 1,000 names for dogs and cats taken from history and literature are listed and explained. (Rev: BR 9–10/89) [636.08]

8673 Gerstenfeld, Sheldon L. *The Bird Care Book: All You Need to Know to Keep Your Bird Healthy and Happy* (8–12). Rev. ed. Illus. 1989, Addison paper $10.95 (0-201-09559-9). A basic handbook on the choosing, care, and feeding of both pet and wild birds. (Rev: BL 9/15/89) [636.6]

8674 Jahn, Johannes. *A Step-by-Step Book about Turtles* (9–12). Illus. 1987, TFH $9.95 (0-86622-913-2). Clear text and fine photographs help the reader who wishes to keep turtles as pets. (Rev: BL 5/1/88) [639.392]

8675 Lantermann, Werner. *The New Parrot Handbook: Everything about Purchase, Acclimation, Care, Diet, Disease, and Behavior of Parrots* (9–12). Illus. 1986, Barron's paper $6.50 (0-8120-3729-4). A complete handbook that covers choosing and caring for a bird with information about species, breeding, and behavior. (Rev: BL 11/1/86) [636.6]

8676 Leeds, Robert X. *All the Comforts of Home: The Story of the First Pet Motel* (9–12). Illus. 1987, Dodd $17.95 (0-396-08881-3). A humorous account of the first hotel for pets, which was established in Chicago in 1973. (Rev: BL 3/15/87) [636]

8677 Low, Rosemary. *The Complete Book of Parrots* (9–12). Illus. 1989, Barron's $16.95 (0-8120-5971-9). A stunning book on the various kinds of parrots and how to take care of them. (Rev: BL 5/15/89) [636.6]

8678 Low, Rosemary. *Keeping Parrots* (10–12). Illus. 1986, Blandford paper $9.95 (0-7137-1695-9). This brief volume contains a wealth of information about everyday care, feeding, and housing of parrots and related species. (Rev: BL 4/1/86) [636.6]

8679 Randolph, Elizabeth. *The Basic Bird Book* (9–12). 1989, Ballantine paper $3.50 (0-449-21597-0). A basic book that discusses how to choose and care for pet birds. (Rev: BL 6/15/89) [636.68]

8680 Rosenfeld, Arthur. *Exotic Animals as Pets* (8–12). Illus. 1987, Simon & Schuster $21.95 (0-671-63690-1); paper $12.95 (0-671-47654-8). This account tells of the habits of such animals as lizards, parrots, and snakes and how to take care of them. (Rev: BL 4/15/87) [636.08]

8681 Serpell, James. *In the Company of Animals* (10–12). 1986, Basil Blackwell $19.95 (0-631-14536-2). The author explores the different attitudes society has toward pets as opposed to other domesticated animals like pigs and cattle. (Rev: SLJ 12/86) [636.08]

8682 Stevens, Paul Drew. *Real Animal Heroes: True Stories of Courage, Devotion and Sacrifice* (9–12). 1990, NAL paper $8.95 (0-452-26366-2). Fifty-three short, true stories about how various animals saved the day. (Rev: BL 12/1/89) [636]

8683 Vriends, Matthew M. *Pigeons* (7–12). Illus. 1988, Barron's paper $4.50 (0-8120-4044-9). A brief but thorough guide to raising pigeons plus material on their behavior and how to breed them. (Rev: BL 2/1/89) [636.5]

8684 Vriends, Matthew M. *Simon and Schuster's Guide to Pet Birds* (9–12). Illus. 1985, Simon & Schuster $11.95 (0-671-50695-1). This illustrated book covers the care and feeding of 206 different birds. [598]

8685 Weber, William J. *Care of Uncommon Pets* (9–12). Illus. 1979, Henry Holt $10.95 (0-8050-0294-4); paper $5.95 (0-8050-8320-7). This book explains how to take care of such pets as salamanders, snakes, hamsters, and parakeets. [636.08]

8686 Wood, Gerald L. *Guinness Book of Pet Records* (8–12). Illus. 1985, Sterling paper $12.95 (0-85112-295-7). Arranged by type of pet such as dogs and cats, this is a rundown on the fattest, biggest, fastest, and so on, plus a lot of photographs. (Rev: BL 5/1/85; SLJ 8/85) [636.08]

CATS

8687 Ames, Felicia. *The Cat You Care For* (9–12). 1968, NAL paper $3.50 (0-451-13041-3). A brief but thorough manual on basic cat care. [636.8]

8688 Amory, Cleveland. *The Cat and the Curmudgeon* (9–12). 1990, Little $17.95 (0-316-03739-7). The further adventures of the author's cat, Polar Bear, first begun in *The Cat Who Came for Christmas* (1987). (Rev: BL 7/90) [818]

8689 Brown, Philip. *Uncle Whiskers* (9–12). Illus. 1980, Warner paper $2.95 (0-446-87108-7). The true story of a remarkable cat that was crippled in an accident. [636.8]

8690 Burton, Jane, and Kim Taylor. *Your Cat's First Year* (9–12). Illus. 1985, Simon & Schuster $12.95 (0-671-60090-7). From birth to producing a first litter, this is the story of a group of kittens all wonderfully photographed in color. (Rev: BL 12/15/85) [599.74]

8691 Caras, Roger. *A Celebration of Cats* (9–12). Illus. 1987, Simon & Schuster paper $7.95 (0-671-64576-2). A tribute to the cat that explores its history, various breeds, and its place in world folklore. (Rev: BL 1/1/87) [636.8]

8692 Caras, Roger, ed. *Harper's Illustrated Handbook of Cats* (9–12). Illus. 1985, Harper paper $9.95 (0-06-091199-0). Every cat breed recognized in the United States is described plus copious material on cat care. (Rev: BL 12/1/85) [636.8]

8693 Gerstenfeld, Sheldon L. *The Cat Care Book: All You Need to Know to Keep Your Cat Healthy and Happy* (8–12). Rev. ed. Illus. 1989, Addison paper $10.95 (0-201-09569-6). Tips on how to choose a cat and detailed information on taking care of cats as pets. (Rev: BL 9/15/89) [636.8]

8694 Gruber, Terry Deroy. *Working Cats* (9–12). 1979, Harper $11.95 (0-397-01376-0); paper $9.95 (0-690-01951-3). This unusual book shows how cats are used to perform a number of useful tasks. [636.8]

8695 Gurney, Eric. *How to Live with a Calculating Cat* (9–12). 1981, Pocket paper $2.50 (0-671-44140-X). An often humorous examination of cat behavior. [636.8]

8696 Loeb, Jo, and Paul Loeb. *You Can Train Your Cat* (10–12). Illus. 1989, Pocket paper $4.50 (0-671-67182-0). Topics like walking on a lead, scratching, chewing, and performing tricks are covered. [636.8]

8697 Morris, Desmond. *Catlore* (7–12). 1987, Crown $12.95 (0-517-56903-5). A rich collection of facts about cats and cat behavior that even analyzes the sounds cats make. (Rev: VOYA 10/88) [599.74]

8698 Morris, Desmond. *Catwatching* (8–12). 1987, Crown $9.95 (0-517-56518-6). Using a question-and-answer approach, the author explores many facets of cat behavior. (Rev: BL 4/1/87) [636.8]

8699 Moyes, Patricia. *How to Talk to Your Cat* (9–12). Illus. 1979, NAL paper $3.95 (0-451-12835-4). This book explains how one can communicate with a cat. [636.8]

8700 Muller, Ulrike. *Long-Haired Cats* (10–12). 1984, Barron's paper $4.95 (0-8120-2803-1). A specialized book on the types of long-haired cats and how to care for them with a special chapter on cat psychology. [636.8]

8701 Pugnetti, Gino. *Simon and Schuster's Guide to Cats* (9–12). 1983, Simon & Schuster $23.95 (0-671-49167-9); paper $10.95 (0-671-49170-9). A guide to the different breeds of cats and how to care for them with additional material on the history of cats and their personality. [636.8]

8702 Richards, Dorothy Silkstone. *How to Choose & Care for Your Cat* (7–12). Illus. 1982, HP paper $9.95 (0-89586-173-9). After an introduction to various breeds, this guide gives pointers on caring for your cat. [636.8]

8703 Shelley, Purrey B. *Cat-a-Log* (9–12). 1983, Putnam paper $6.95 (0-448-18959-3). An anthology of poems, stories, and nonfiction pieces about cats and their history. [636.8]

8704 Steneman, Shep. *Garfield: The Complete Cat Book* (7–10). 1981, Random LB $7.99 (0-394-94893-9). Information about cats is conveyed with the help of the cartoon character Garfield. [599.74]

8705 Taylor, David. *You & Your Cat* (9–12). Illus. 1986, Knopf paper $12.95 (0-394-72984-6). Historical and anatomical information is followed by material on each breed and on the care and grooming of your cat. (Rev: BL 7/86; BR 11–12/86) [636.8]

8706 Warner, Matt. *Cats of the World* (9–12). Illus. 1976, Bantam paper $4.95 (0-553-26476-1). This is an illustrated guide to various breeds and their origins. [636.8]

8707 Wester, Thomas. *Cats* (8–12). Illus. 1987, Simon & Schuster paper $9.95 (0-671-63433-X).

A stunning collection of photographs of cats plus a few poems about felines. (Rev: BL 5/15/87) [779]

8708 Widmer, Patricia P. *Pat Widmer's Cat Book* (9–12). 1984, NAL paper $3.95 (0-451-12904-0). This book on cat care is aimed at owners in an urban or suburban setting. [636.8]

DOGS

8709 American Kennel Club Staff. *The Complete Dog Book* (7–12). 17th ed. Illus. 1985, Howell Book House $19.95 (0-87605-463-7). This is the standard work on descriptions of each of the dog breeds currently recognized by the American Kennel Club. (Rev: BL 6/15/85) [636.7]

8710 Barton, Bob. *All about Puppies—Your Dog's First Year* (9–12). 1980, NAL paper $3.50 (0-451-14389-2). A guide to the care and feeding of dogs during the first 12 months of their lives. [636.7]

8711 Barton, Bob. *The Dog for You* (9–12). 1980, NAL paper $3.50 (0-451-14727-8). A book that identifies and describes 50 of the favorite breeds of dogs. [636.7]

8712 Belfield, Wendall, and Martin Zucher. *How to Have a Healthier Dog* (9–12). 1982, NAL paper $4.95 (0-451-16027-4). Dog care is made simple in this handy volume. [636.7]

8713 Benjamin, Carol Lea. *The Chosen Puppy: How to Select and Raise a Great Puppy from an Animal Shelter* (10–12). Illus. 1990, Howell Book House paper $6.95 (0-87605-417-3). This is an informal guide to selecting and training a dog from an animal shelter; many humorous illustrations. (Rev: BL 9/1/90) [636.7]

8714 Burton, Jane, and Michael Allaby. *A Dog's Life: A Year in the Life of a Dog* (9–12). Illus. 1986, Howell Book House $14.95 (0-87605-401-7). One year in the life of a litter of collies told in text and wonderful photographs. (Rev: BL 12/15/86) [636.7]

8715 Caras, Roger, ed. *Harper's Illustrated Handbook of Dogs* (9–12). Illus. 1985, Harper paper $9.95 (0-06-091198-0). Every breed recognized by the American Kennel Club (and some that are not) is described with sections on care and training. (Rev: BL 12/1/85) [636.7]

8716 Delmar, Diana. *The Guilt-Free Dog Owner's Guide: Caring for a Dog When You're Short on Time and Space* (10–12). Illus. 1990, Storey paper $7.95 (0-88266-575-8). A manual on how to keep a dog happy and well trained when you have to be away for hours each day. (Rev: BL 4/1/90) [636.7]

8717 Edney, Andrew, and Roger Mugford. *The Practical Guide to Dog and Puppy Care* (8–12). Illus. 1987, Tetra $9.95 (3-923880-65-0). The authors describe how one can have both a healthy and well-trained dog as a perfect pet. (Rev: BL 4/1/88) [636.7]

8718 Fletcher, Walter. *Dogs of the World* (9–12). 1977, Bantam paper $4.95 (0-553-26440-0). This handbook is a worldwide guide to dog breeds and their identifying traits and characteristics. [636.7]

8719 Gerstenfeld, Sheldon L. *The Dog Care Book: All You Need to Know to Keep Your Dog Healthy and Happy* (8–12). Rev. ed. Illus. 1989, Addison paper $10.95 (0-201-09667-6). Tips on selecting a dog plus extensive material on care and feeding. (Rev: BL 9/15/89) [636.7]

8720 Hart, Benjamin, and Lynette Hart. *The Perfect Puppy: How to Choose Your Dog by Its Behavior* (9–12). 1988, Freeman paper $9.95 (0-7167-1829-4). A guide to choosing the right dog that outlines the characteristics of 56 different breeds. (Rev: BR 5–6/88) [599.74]

8721 Herriot, James. *James Herriot's Dog Stories* (9–12). Illus. 1986, St. Martin's $19.95 (0-312-43968-7). The famous veterinarian tells some of his favorite anecdotes about his 50 years working with dogs. (Rev: BL 4/15/86; SLJ 9/86) [636.7]

8722 Howe, John. *Choosing the Right Dog: A Buyer's Guide to All the AKC Breeds Plus . . .* (10–12). Rev. ed. Illus. 1980, Harper $14.95 (0-06-012014-2). This book prepares the reader for dog ownership by discussing such topics as types of breeds, special skills, illnesses, and price. [636.7]

8723 Kay, William J., and Elizabeth Randolph, eds. *The Complete Book of Dog Health* (9–12). Illus. 1985, Macmillan $19.18 (0-02-600930-7); Howell paper $14.95 (0-87605-455-6). This is a comprehensive account that covers all topics from diagnosing symptoms to choosing a veterinarian. (Rev: BL 6/1/85) [636.7]

8724 Klever, Ulrich. *The Complete Book of Dog Care: How to Raise a Happy and Healthy Dog* (9–12). Illus. 1989, Barron's paper $8.95 (0-8120-4158-5). The kinds of purebred dogs are profiled, plus information on how to select a dog and how to train and care for it. (Rev: BL 1/15/90) [636.7]

8725 MacDonald, David, ed. *The Complete Book of the Dog* (9–12). Illus. 1989, Smith $12.98 (0-8317-1545-6). Complete with hundreds of illustrations, this book traces the history of the dog and covers such topics as training, anatomy,

and tips on care and feeding. (Rev: BL 10/15/85; SLJ 4/86; VOYA 2/86) [636.7]

8726 Margolis, Matthew, and Catherine Swan. *The Dog in Your Life* (9–12). 1982, Random $10.95 (0-394-71174-2). This book covers selection, care, and training of dogs. [636.7]

8727 Miller, Harry. *Common Sense Book of Puppy and Dog Care* (9–12). Illus. 1987, Bantam paper $3.95 (0-553-26414-1). With several photographs as illustrations, this is a straightforward guide to dog care. [636.7]

8728 Morris, Desmond. *Dogwatching* (8–12). 1987, Crown $9.95 (0-517-56519-6). Why dogs act the way they do is explored in a question-and-answer format. (Rev: BL 4/1/87) [636.8]

8729 Mowat, Farley. *The Dog Who Wouldn't Be* (7–12). Illus. 1957, Little $16.95 (0-316-58636-6); Bantam paper $2.75 (0-553-26244-0). A humorous reminiscence of the author's dog, who thought he was a human. [818]

8730 Palmer, Joan. *A Dog Owner's Guide to Training Your Dog* (8–12). Illus. 1987, Tetra $9.95 (3-923880-76-6). Instructions are given in a clear, practical manner on all levels of dog training. (Rev: BL 4/1/88) [636.7]

8731 Palmer, Joan. *A Practical Guide to Selecting a Small Dog* (8–12). Illus. 1987, Tetra $9.95 (3-923880-79-0). A guide to the basic breeds of small dogs highlighting good and bad points related to such areas as training and suitability as house pets. (Rev: BL 4/1/88) [636.7]

8732 Poortvliet, Rien. *Dogs* (7–12). Illus. 1983, Abrams $29.95 (0-8109-0809-3). Drawings and paintings of dogs interspersed with dog lore. [636.7]

8733 Pugnetti, Gino. *Simon & Schuster's Guide to Dogs* (9–12). Illus. 1989, Simon & Schuster paper $12.50 (0-918367-29-8). A handbook that gives information on 324 breeds. [636.7]

8734 Reader's Digest, eds. *The Reader's Digest Illustrated Book of Dogs* (8–12). Rev. ed. Illus. 1989, Reader's Digest $24.95 (0-89577-340-6). Not just a dog care manual but an introduction to their history, social habits, psychology, and contributions to civilization. (Rev: BL 1/1/90; BR 3–4/90) [636.7]

8735 Siegal, Mordecai. *The Good Dog Book: Loving Care* (9–12). 1978, NAL paper $3.50 (8-451-13232-7). This book provides information about the care of both puppies and adult dogs. [636.5]

8736 Siegal, Mordecai, and Matthew Margolis. *Good Dog, Bad Dog* (7–12). Illus. 1973, NAL paper $4.95 (0-451-15521-1). A practical manual for training dogs at home. [636.7]

8737 Smith, Ernie. *Warm Hearts & Cold Noses: A Common Sense Guide to Understanding the Family Dog* (9–12). 1987, Sunstone paper $10.95 (0-86534-109-5). A pet-care manual that covers topics such as feeding, housebreaking, and leash training. (Rev: BR 5–6/88) [636.7]

8738 Taylor, David. *The Ultimate Dog Book* (9–12). Illus. 1990, Simon & Schuster $29.95 (0-671-70988-7). An oversize book that discusses such topics as history, anatomy, breeds, and dog care. (Rev: BL 9/15/90) [636.7]

8739 Taylor, David, and Peter Scott. *You & Your Dog* (9–12). Illus. 1986, Knopf paper $12.95 (0-394-72983-8). Practical suggestions on choosing and caring for your dog are given along with information on history, anatomy, and a description of various breeds. (Rev: BL 7/86; BR 11–12/86; SLJ 9/86; VOYA 8–10/86) [636.7]

8740 Ullman, H. J., and E. Ullman. *Poodles* (8–12). 1984, Barron's paper $4.95 (0-8120-2812-0). A slim volume on one of the most intelligent breeds of dogs. Part of an extensive series on various kinds of pets. [636.7]

8741 Vine, Louis L. *The Total Dog Book: The Breeders' and Pet Owners' Complete Guide to Better Dog Care* (9–12). 1988, Warner paper $5.95 (0-446-31483-8). This complete handbook on maintaining healthy dogs stresses prevention of problems. [636.5]

8742 Wayne, Kyra Petrovskaya. *Max, the Dog That Refused to Die* (9–12). Illus. 1979, Alpine paper $6.98 (0-931866-02-2). This is the engrossing story of a 3-year-old Doberman and his fight for survival in the High Sierras after getting lost on a camping trip. [636.7]

8743 Widmer, Patricia P. *Pat Widmer's Dog Training Book* (9–12). 1980, NAL paper $3.95 (0-451-14468-6). A thorough manual on the care and training of a dog. [636.7]

8744 Woodhouse, Barbara. *Dog Training My Way* (10–12). 1985, Berkley paper $3.95 (0-425-08108-7). This is a print version of the television series on dog training given by the renowned British pet specialist. [636.7]

8745 Woodhouse, Barbara. *Encyclopedia of Dogs and Puppies* (9–12). 1987, Berkley paper $3.50 (0-425-08469-8). From her years of experience working with dogs, this specialist answers many questions about dogs and their care. [636.7]

8746 Yates, Elizabeth. *Sound Friendships: The Story of Hearing Ear Dogs* (9–12). 1987, Coun-

tryman paper $7.95 (0-88150-081-X). A description of how dogs are trained to help the deaf or hearing impaired. (Rev: BL 4/1/87; SLJ 6–7/87) [636.7]

FISH

8747 Andrews, Chris. *A Fishkeeper's Guide to Fancy Goldfishes* (9–12). Illus. 1988, Tetra $9.95 (3-923880-69-3). A handbook that first explains the various kinds of goldfish and then gives useful tips on their care and feeding. A companion volume is: *A Fishkeeper's Guide to Fish Breeding* (1988). (Rev: BL 6/15/88) [639.3752]

8748 Axelrod, Herbert R., and Leonard P. Schultz. *Handbook of Tropical Aquarium Fishes* (9–12). Rev. ed. Illus. 1983, TFH $9.95 (0-87666-491-5). An illustrated guide to more than 400 different tropical fish and how to care for them. [639.3]

8749 Axelrod, Herbert R., and William Vorderwinkler. *Encyclopedia of Tropical Fish: With Special Emphasis on the Techniques of Breeding* (7–12). 2nd ed. Illus. 1975, TFH $17.95 (0-86622-110-7). A standard reference work on tropical fish, how to care for them and breed them. [639.3]

8750 Braemer, Helga, and Ines Scheurmann. *Tropical Fish* (8–12). 1983, Barron's paper $4.95 (0-8120-2686-1). A concise, well-illustrated book on selecting and caring for tropical fish with material on how to operate a freshwater aquarium. Part of an extensive series on pets from Barron's. [597]

8751 Emmens, Cliff W. *A Step-by-Step Book about Tropical Fish* (8–12). Illus. 1988, TFH paper $2.95 (0-86622-471-8). A brief, brightly illustrated introduction to various types of tropical fish, their care, and housing. (Rev: BL 1/1/89) [639.34]

8752 Halstead, Bruce W., and Bonnie L. Landa. *Tropical Fish: A Guide for Setting Up and Maintaining an Aquarium for Tropical Fish and Other Animals* (7–12). Illus. 1975, Golden paper $3.95 (0-307-24361-3). A handy guide to the various species of tropical fish plus some material on caring for them. [639.3]

8753 Harris, Jack C. *A Step-by-Step Book about Goldfish* (9–12). Illus. 1987, TFH $9.95 (0-86622-917-5). Topics covered in this guide include varieties, feeding, and health problems. (Rev: BL 5/1/88) [639.344]

8754 Harris, Jack C. *A Step-by-Step Book about Guppies* (8–12). Illus. 1988, TFH paper $2.95 (0-86622-464-5). The world of the guppy is introduced along with details on how to care for them and breed them. (Rev: BL 1/1/89; BR 3–4/89) [639.37]

8755 Keller, Gunter. *A Step-by-Step Book about Discus* (8–12). Illus. 1988, TFH paper $2.95 (0-86622-465-3). This small paperback tells how to house, feed, and care for the popular discus fish. (Rev: BL 1/1/89) [639.37]

GERBILS, HAMSTERS, AND GUINEA PIGS

8756 Barrie, Anmarie. *A Step-by-Step Book about Guinea Pigs* (9–12). Illus. 1987, TFH $9.95 (0-86622-916-7). A clear, concise text plus many illustrations highlight this book on how to house and care for guinea pigs. (Rev: BL 5/1/88) [636.9]

8757 Barrie, Anmarie. *A Step-by-Step Book about Hamsters* (9–12). Illus. 1987, TFH $9.95 (0-86622-915-9). Grooming and showing of these animals are 2 of the many topics covered. (Rev: BL 5/1/88) [636.9]

8758 Bielfeld, Horst. *Guinea Pigs: Everything about Purchase, Care, Nutrition, and Diseases* (7–12). Illus. 1983, Barron's paper $4.50 (0-8120-2629-2). A nicely illustrated guide to choosing and caring for guinea pigs. [636.08]

HORSES

8759 Burt, Olive W. *The Horse in America* (9–12). Illus. 1975, Day $12.45 (0-381-99630-1). A history of horses in America and how they have changed our history. [636.1]

8760 Chapple, Judy. *Your Horse: A Step-by-Step Guide to Horse Ownership* (10–12). Illus. 1984, Garden Way paper $9.95 (0-88266-353-4). Starting with how to choose a horse, this guide supplies all kinds of information on caring for and training horses. [636.1]

8761 Dakin, Janet Wilder. *Jeffy's Journal: Raising a Morgan Horse* (10–12). Illus. 1990, Stephen Greene $16.95 (0-8289-0767-6). For people interested in horses and horse training this is a case study of how the author raised a Morgan horse named Jeffy. (Rev: BL 7/90) [636.1]

8762 Edwards, Elwyn Hartley, and Candida Geddes, eds. *The Complete Horse Book* (9–12). Illus. 1988, David & Charles $22.95 (0-943955-00-9). A wonderful source of general information on all aspects of the horse from history to care and breeding. Well illustrated. (Rev: BL 3/1/88) [636.1]

8763 Gordon-Watson, Mary. *The Handbook of Riding* (10–12). Illus. 1982, Knopf $22.50 (0-394-52110-2). A well-illustrated guide to horsemanship by an Olympic gold medalist. [636.1]

8764 Mills, Bruce, and Barbara Carne. *A Basic Guide to Horse Care and Management* (9–12). Rev. ed. Illus. 1988, Howell $17.95 (0-87605-871-3). This is a lucid, complete guide to the care of saddle horses. (Rev: BL 4/15/89) [636.1]

8765 Morris, Desmond. *Horsewatching* (10–12). Illus. 1989, Crown $12.95 (0-517-57267-2). Extensive answers are given to questions concerning the anatomy, habits, history, and behavior of the horse. (Rev: BL 5/1/89) [636.1]

8766 Solomon, Diane S. *Teaching Riding: Step-by-Step Schooling for Horses and Rider* (10–12). Illus. 1982, Univ. of Oklahoma Pr. $19.95 (0-8061-1580-7). This step-by-step guide to horsemanship covers such topics as training, handling, and equipment. [794.4]

8767 Spaulding, Jackie. *The Family Horse: How to Choose, Care for, Train and Work Your Horse* (10–12). 1982, Hartley & Marks paper $9.95 (0-88179-007-9). A first-time owner's guide to keeping and training a horse. [636.1]

8768 Twelveponies, Mary. *There Are No Problem Horses—Only Problem Riders* (10–12). 1982, Houghton paper $9.95 (0-395-33194-3). A book on horsemanship that stresses how horses think and how riders can communicate with them. [636.1]

8769 Young, John Richard. *The Schooling of the Horse* (10–12). 1982, Univ. of Oklahoma Pr. $29.95 (0-8061-1787-7). This is a basic handbook on how to train riding horses. [798.2]

Zoos, Aquariums, and Animal Care Shelters

8770 Axelrod, Herbert R., et al. *Dr. Axelrod's Mini-Atlas of Freshwater Aquarium Fishes* (10–12). Illus. 1987, TFH $29.95 (0-86622-385-1). This large volume not only identifies freshwater aquarium fish but also covers setting up and maintaining an aquarium. (Rev: BL 12/1/87) [639]

8771 Barrie, Anmarie. *A Step-by-Step Book about Our First Aquarium* (9–12). Illus. 1987, TFH paper $2.95 (0-86622-454-8). This introductory guide covers all topics from choosing a tank to maintaining a balanced habitat. (Rev: BL 11/15/87) [639.34]

8772 Catala, Rene. *Treasures of the Tropic Seas* (9–12). Illus. 1986, Facts on File $50.00 (0-8160-1590-2). An expensive but excellently illustrated book on the marine life in the New Caledonia

Aquarium of Noumea. (Rev: BL 2/15/87) [574.92]

8773 Hanna, Jack, and John Stravinsky. *Monkeys on the Interstate and Other Tales from America's Favorite Zookeeper* (9–12). Illus. 1989, Doubleday $18.95 (0-385-24731-1). Entertaining stories of the unusual exploits of "America's favorite zookeeper." (Rev: BL 5/15/89) [636.08]

8774 Mills, Dick. *You & Your Aquarium* (9–12). Illus. 1986, Knopf paper $12.95 (0-394-72985-4). In addition to material on setting up an aquarium, this account features material on fish anatomy, feeding, and breeding. (Rev: BL 7/86; BR 11–12/86; SLJ 11/86) [639.4]

8775 Rudloe, Jack. *The Living Dock* (8–12). 1988, Fulcrum $24.95 (1-55591-036-X). The author describes the marine biological supply company he operates and the many organisms he collects off his dock in the swamplands of Florida. (Rev: BR 9–10/89) [574.92]

8776 Schaffer, Moselle. *Camel Lot: The True Story of a Zoo-Illogical Farm* (9–12). 1990, Vi-

king $16.95 (0-670-82884-X). Stories, most of them very funny, about the weird and wonderful animals that the author has cared for. (Rev: BL 3/15/90) [636]

8777 Sedgwick, John. *The Peaceable Kingdom: A Year in the Life of America's Oldest Zoo* (9–12). 1988, Morrow $19.95 (0-688-06367-5). A disillusioned man recaptures a love of life during a year spent at the Philadelphia Zoo. (Rev: BL 1/15/88) [590]

8778 Sterba, Gunther, ed. *The Aquarium Encyclopedia* (10–12). Illus. 1983, MIT Pr. $45.00 (0-262-19207-1). An alphabetically arranged compendium of information on home aquariums and their upkeep. [639.3]

8779 Tongren, Sally. *To Keep Them Alive: Wild Animal Breeding* (9–12). Illus. 1985, Dembner $19.95 (0-934878-66-8). This book tells how zoos are helping to preserve endangered species by breeding them in captivity. (Rev: BL 11/1/85) [636.08]

Chemistry

General and Miscellaneous

8780 Asimov, Isaac. *A Short History of Chemistry* (9–12). Illus. 1965, Greenwood LB $35.00 (0-313-20769-0). This is a readable account that stresses progress from the eighteenth century on to the modern age. [540.9]

8781 Atkins, P. W. *Molecules* (10–12). Illus. 1987, Scientific American $32.95 (0-7167-5019-8). Molecules are described and 160 chemical compounds from simple to complex are analyzed. (Rev: BL 6/15/88) [547.1]

8782 Bickel, Leonard. *The Deadly Element: The Story of Uranium* (10–12). 1980, Scarborough paper $7.95 (0-8128-6089-6). This book explores the element uranium and discusses how its manipulation has caused many problems as well as scientific opportunities. [669]

8783 Faraday, Michael. *Faraday's Chemical History of a Candle: Twenty-Two Experiments and Six Classic Lectures* (7–10). Illus. 1988, Chicago Review paper $9.95 (1-55652-035-2). A collection of lectures on the basics of chemistry plus some simple experiments, all from the pen of the nineteenth-century chemist. (Rev: BL 11/15/88; BR 3–4/89; SLJ 1/89) [540.2]

8784 Hess, Fred C. *Chemistry Made Simple* (10–12). Rev. ed. Illus. 1984, Doubleday paper $8.95 (0-385-18850-1). An easily understood presentation of the basic concepts and facts in the area of chemistry. One of a large Made Simple series that covers many academic subjects. [540]

Geology and Geography

General and Miscellaneous

8785 Ballard, Robert D. *Exploring Our Living Planet* (10–12). Illus. 1983, National Geographic LB $21.95 (0-87044-397-6). After a general introduction on how the earth has evolved, this book discusses the many forces at work changing its surface. [551.1]

8786 Menard, H. W. *Islands* (10–12). Illus. 1987, Scientific American $32.95 (0-7167-5017-1). An account of how islands are formed, how they evolved and, in some cases, died. (Rev: BL 11/15/87) [551.2]

8787 *Powers of Nature* (9–12). Illus. 1978, National Geographic Soc. LB $9.50 (0-87044-239-2). A richly illustrated book that describes such phenomena as earthquakes, floods, droughts, and volcanoes. [550]

8788 Redfern, Ron. *The Making of a Continent* (10–12). Illus. 1983, Times Books paper $19.95 (0-8129-1617-4). The geologic history of North America is given with special emphasis on the role of plate tectonics. [551.1]

8789 Rhodes, Frank H. T. *Geology* (7–12). Illus. 1972, Golden paper $3.95 (0-307-24349-4). A well-illustrated introduction to such topics as the earth's composition, earthquakes, oceans, winds, and the formation of mountains. [551]

8790 Trefil, James. *Meditations at 10,000 Feet: A Scientist in the Mountains* (10–12). 1987, Macmillan paper $8.95 (0-02-025890-9). Viewing the world from the top of mountains, the author gives a great deal of information about geology, rocks, glaciers, and related topics. (Rev: BL 4/1/86) [551]

8791 Watson, Lyall. *The Water Planet: A Celebration of the Wonder of Water* (10–12). Illus. 1988, Crown $30.00 (0-517-56504-8). In this beautifully illustrated volume, the wonders of water are explored in relation to the earth, science, life, and history. (Rev: SLJ 10/88) [551.4]

8792 Young, Louise B. *The Blue Planet* (10–12). Illus. 1983, Little $18.45 (0-316-97707-1). The evolution of our planet and how such forces as oceans and volcanoes have changed its shape. [550]

Earth and Geology

8793 Brown, Bruce, and Lane Morgan. *The Miracle Planet* (9–12). Illus. 1990, W. H. Smith $29.98 (0-8317-5999-2). A stunningly illustrated account of the Earth, its interior, its climate, regions, and the life it supports. (Rev: BL 1/15/90) [550]

8794 Cvancara, Alan M. *A Field Manual for the Amateur Geologist: Tools and Activities for Exploring Our Planet* (10–12). Illus. 1985, Prentice paper $12.95 (0-13-316522-1). This handbook explains all kinds of land formations and how to study them and also contains a section on rock and fossil identification. (Rev: BL 8/85) [550]

8795 Francis, Peter, and Pat Jones. *Images of Earth* (9–12). Illus. 1985, Prentice $24.95 (0-13-451394-0). A stunningly beautiful collection of aerial photographs of the earth taken from a variety of vantage points. (Rev: BL 4/15/85) [550]

8796 Harrington, John W. *Dance of the Continents: Adventures with Rocks and Time* (10–12).

1983, Houghton paper $9.95 (0-87477-168-4). This geological study explores the concept of continental drift. [551.1]

8797 Headstrom, Richard. *Suburban Geology* (9–12). Illus. 1985, Prentice paper $8.95 (0-13-859232-2). This beginner's manual starts with a definition of what rocks and minerals are and continues into the areas of identification and description of various rocks and minerals. (Rev: BL 8/85) [550]

8798 Lambert, David, and The Diagram Group. *The Field Guide to Geology* (10–12). Illus. 1988, Facts on File $21.95 (0-8160-1697-6). A general account that covers such subjects as how the earth was formed, rocks, and plate tectonics. (Rev: BL 5/15/88; BR 3–4/89) [551]

8799 Milne, Antony. *Our Drowning World* (10–12). 1988, Prism Pr. $19.95 (1-85327-004-0). A grim picture of the future where our land surfaces will decrease because of the rise of the oceans. (Rev: BL 3/1/88; SLJ 9/88) [551.4]

Earthquakes and Volcanoes

8800 Carson, Rob. *Mount St. Helens: The Eruption and Recovery of a Volcano* (9–12). Illus. 1990, Sasquatch $28.00 (0-912365-33-1); paper $19.95 (0-912365-32-3). With excellent photographs, this is the story of the Mount St. Helens eruption, its aftermath, and the condition today. (Rev: BL 6/15/90) [508.79]

8801 Erickson, Jon. *Volcanoes and Earthquakes* (10–12). Illus. 1988, TAB $22.95 (0-8306-1942-9); paper $12.95 (0-8306-2842-8). In addition to general information on volcanoes and earthquakes the author gives a valuable introduction to plate tectonics and how planets were formed. (Rev: BL 1/1/89) [551.2]

8802 Golden, Frederic. *The Trembling Earth: Probing & Predicting Quakes* (10–12). Illus. 1983, Macmillan $13.95 (0-684-17884-2). An explanation of what causes earthquakes with material on plate tectonics. [551.2]

8803 Heppenheimer, T. A. *The Coming Quake: Science and Trembling on the California Earthquake Frontier* (10–12). Illus. 1988, Times Books $17.95 (0-8129-1616-6). A pre-1989 look at the probability of earthquakes in California that is still valid today. (Rev: BL 9/1/88) [551.22]

8804 Kohler, Pierre. *Volcanoes, Earthquakes, and the Formation of Continents* (9–12). Trans. by A. V. Carozzi and M. Carozzi. Illus. 1988,

Barron's paper $4.95 (0-8120-3832-0). A brief, illustrated account that gives current general information on such topics as the theory of drifting continents, types of volcanic eruptions, causes of earthquakes, and the Richter Scale. (Rev: BL 5/15/88; SLJ 4/88) [551]

8805 Lambert, M. B. *Volcanoes* (10–12). Illus. 1980, Univ. of Washington Pr. paper $8.95 (0-295-95783-2). A varied account that covers many aspects of volcanoes including lava, magma, volcanic landforms, and the lore of volcanoes. [551.2]

8806 Ritchie, David. *Superquake! The Last Days of Los Angeles* (10–12). 1988, Crown $18.95 (0-517-56699-0); paper $8.95 (0-517-57850-6). After a discussion of plate tectonics, the author describes the worst possible earthquake that could hit Los Angeles. (Rev: BL 11/15/87) [551.2]

8807 Time-Life Books, eds. *Volcano* (8–12). Illus. 1982, Silver Burdett $24.60 (0-8094-4305-8). A profusely illustrated account on famous eruptions and a rundown on what we know about volcanoes. From the Planet Earth series from Time-Life Books. [551.2]

8808 Walker, Bryce. *Earthquake* (7–12). Illus. 1982, Silver Burdett LB $24.60 (0-8094-4301-5). The history of the world's most famous earthquakes is given plus coverage on what causes them. Part of the Time-Life Books Series on the Earth. [551.2]

Icebergs and Glaciers

8809 Bailey, Ronald H. *Glacier* (8–12). Illus. 1982, Silver Burdett LB $24.60 (0-8094-4317-1). A nicely illustrated book on what we know about glaciers. From the Planet Earth series from Time-Life Books. [551.3]

Physical Geography

8810 Berger, Bruce. *The Telling Distance: Conversations with the American Desert* (10–12). 1990, Breitenbush $19.95 (0-932576-74-5). Berger recounts his experiences hiking, camping, and exploring the wonders of the deserts of the Southwest. (Rev: BL 7/90) [917.904]

8811 Brown, Lauren. *Grasslands* (9–12). Illus. 1985, Knopf paper $15.95 (0-394-73121-2). This volume describes grasslands in the United States and then identifies the species found there. (Rev: BL 7/85; SLJ 9/85) [574.5]

8812 Fuller, Margaret. *Mountains: A Natural History and Hiking Guide* (10–12). Illus. 1989, Wiley paper $12.95 (0-471-62080-7). A guide to the mountains of the world; also a mountaineering handbook. (Rev: BL 4/15/89) [508.314]

8813 Jackson, Donald Dale. *Underground Worlds* (7–12). Illus. 1982, Silver Burdett LB $24.60 (0-8094-4321-X). General information on caves is given, specific caves are described, and an introduction is given to spelunking. From Time-Life Books. [551.4]

8814 Levenson, Thomas. *Ice Time: Climate, Science, & Life on Earth* (10–12). 1989, Harper $18.95 (0-06-016063-2). A description of how climate science has evolved and how man's intervention in the environment is affecting climate. (Rev: SLJ 9/89) [551.6]

8815 MacMahon, James A. *Deserts* (9–12). Illus. 1985, Knopf paper $15.95 (0-394-73139-5). This volume not only describes the desert habitat but also, with pictures, describes the various species that live there. (Rev: BL 7/85; SLJ 9/85) [574.5]

8816 Newman, Arnold. *The Tropical Rainforest: A World Survey of Our Most Valuable Endangered Habitat* (10–12). Illus. 1990, Facts on File $40.00 (0-8160-1944-4). An examination of the ecology of the world's rain forests and why it is essential that they not be destroyed. (Rev: BL 9/15/90) [574.5]

8817 Nichol, John. *The Mighty Rain Forest* (10–12). Illus. 1990, Sterling $29.95 (0-7153-9461-4). An overview of the life in a rain forest and what is happening internationally to this habitat. (Rev: BL 6/1/90) [574.5]

8818 Niering, William A. *Wetlands* (9–12). Illus. 1985, Knopf paper $15.95 (0-394-73147-6). After identifying and describing the wetlands of North America, this account identifies each species living there. (Rev: BL 7/85; SLJ 9/85) [574.5]

8819 Page, Jake. *Arid Lands* (7–12). Illus. 1984, Silver Burdett LB $24.60 (0-8094-4513-1). An introduction to deserts and how man has adapted to this hostile environment. [551.4]

8820 Page, Jake. *Forest* (9–12). Illus. 1983, Silver Burdett $24.60 (0-8095-4347-7). A description in pictures and text of the flora and fauna of the world's forests. Part of the Planet Earth series from Time-Life. [634.9]

8821 Sutton, Ann, and Myron Sutton. *Eastern Forests* (9–12). Illus. 1985, Knopf paper $15.95 (0-394-73126-3). Although this book chiefly aims

to identify species living in eastern forests, it also describes this habitat and their locations. (Rev: BL 7/85; SLJ 9/85) [574.5]

8822 Sutton, Ann, and Myron Sutton. *Wildlife of the Forests* (7–12). Illus. 1979, Abrams $19.95 (0-8109-1759-9). Through text and excellent illustrations, this account introduces the forests of the world and the life they support. [574.5]

8823 Time-Life Books, eds. *Grasslands and Tundra* (8–12). Illus. 1985, Silver Burdett $24.60 (0-8094-4521-2). In this lavishly illustrated book from Time-Life, the ecology of grasslands and tundra is introduced and man's relation to them. [574.5]

8824 Whitney, Stephen. *Western Forests* (9–12). Illus. 1985, Knopf paper $15.95 (0-394-73127-1). A description of each species, color illustrations, and a general introduction to this type of habitat are the highlights of this field guide. (Rev: BL 7/85; SLJ 9/85) [574.5]

Rocks, Minerals, and Soil

8825 Chesterman, Charles W., and Kurt E. Lowe. *The Audubon Society Field Guide to North American Rocks and Minerals* (7–12). Illus. 1978, Knopf $14.45 (0-394-50269-8). A key by color arrangement plus color illustrations of each rock and mineral are two features of this basic guide. [549]

8826 Dietrich, R. V., and Reed Wicander. *Minerals, Rocks and Fossils* (9–12). 1983, Wiley paper $9.95 (0-471-89883-X). For the amateur geologist, this is a guide to identifying and collecting rocks, minerals, and fossils. [552]

8827 Pellant, Chris, and Roger Phillips. *Rocks, Minerals & Fossils of the World* (9–12). Illus. 1990, Little paper $17.95 (0-316-69796-6). An identification manual that contains photographs and data in three sections—one each on rocks, minerals, and fossils. (Rev: BL 6/15/90) [552]

8828 Pough, Frederick H. *A Field Guide to Rocks and Minerals* (7–12). 4th ed. Illus. 1976, Houghton $17.95 (0-395-24047-6); paper $13.95 (0-395-24049-2). Part of the Peterson Field Guide series, this book contains photographs of 270 specimens to help identification. [549]

8829 Sorrell, Charles A. *Rocks and Minerals* (7–12). Illus. 1974, Western $9.95 (0-307-47005-9). A basic compact guide that identifies hundreds of mineral varieties with color illustrations. [552]

8830 Zim, Herbert, and Paul R. Shaffer. *Rocks and Minerals: A Guide to Familiar Minerals, Gems, Ores, and Rocks* (7–12). Rev. ed. Illus. 1960, Western paper $3.95 (0-307-24499-7). A quick identification guide to 400 rocks and minerals plus background information on formation and uses. [549]

Mathematics

General and Miscellaneous

8831 Albers, Donald J., and G. L. Alexanderson, eds. *Mathematical People: Profiles and Interviews* (10–12). Illus. 1985, Birkhauser $26.95 (0-8176-3191-7); Contemporary paper $12.95 (0-8092-4976-6). This is a collection of sketches on the century's leading mathematicians and an explanation of why they are important. (Rev: BL 6/15/85) [510]

8832 Castellano, Carmine, and Clifford B. Seitz. *Basic Mathematics Skills* (10–12). 1982, Arco paper $6.95 (0-668-05126-4). This is a general introduction to mathematics plus techniques on how to master basic operations. [510]

8833 Collins, A. Frederick. *Rapid Math without a Calculator* (9–12). Rev. ed. 1987, Citadel paper $4.95 (0-8065-1058-7). A manual that helps you cut calculation time in multiplication, division, and other mathematical operations. (Rev: BL 2/1/88) [513.2]

8834 *For All Practical Purposes: Introduction to Contemporary Mathematics* (10–12). Illus. 1987, Freeman $28.95 (0-7167-1830-8). An explanation of how mathematics affects every aspect of our daily life. Based on a PBS series. (Rev: BL 4/1/88) [510]

8835 Gardner, Martin. *Knotted Doughnuts and Other Mathematical Entertainments* (10–12). Illus. 1986, W. H. Freeman $16.95 (0-7167-1794-8); paper $10.95 (0-7167-1799-9). A collection of puzzles, brain teasers, and games from the author's column in *Scientific American*. (Rev: BL 12/15/86; BR 3–4/87) [793.7]

8836 Hershey, Robert L. *How to Think with Numbers* (10–12). 1987, William Kaufmann paper $7.95 (0-939765-14-4). A good remedial mathematics course that reviews basic concepts and their applications. [510]

8837 Hoffman, Paul. *Archimedes' Revenge: The Joys and Perils of Mathematics* (10–12). Illus. 1988, Norton $17.95 (0-393-02522-5). In this collection of columns, the author tells what we know and do not know in the field of mathematics. (Rev: BL 7/88; SLJ 7/89) [510]

8838 Hogben, Lancelot. *Mathematics for the Million* (10–12). 4th ed. Illus. 1968, Norton $22.50 (0-343-06361-5); paper $10.98 (0-393-30035-8). This is a popular introduction to mathematics and its everyday applications. [510]

8839 Kogelman, Stanley, and Joseph Warren. *Mind over Math* (10–12). Illus. 1978, McGraw paper $6.95 (0-07-035281-X). Based on the authors' many workshops, this is a course on how to overcome math anxiety. [510]

8840 Lieberthal, Edwin M., and Bernadette Lieberthal. *The Complete Book of Fingermath* (7–12). Illus. 1979, McGraw $21.96 (0-07-037680-8). How hands and fingers can be turned into primitive computers. [513]

8841 Peterson, Ivers. *The Mathematical Tourist: Snapshots of Modern Mathematics* (10–12). Illus. 1988, Freeman $17.95 (0-7167-1953-3). A somewhat technical book that explains concepts in mathematics from both the present and the past. (Rev: BR 3–4/89) [510]

8842 Sperling, Abraham, and Monroe Stuart. *Mathematics Made Simple* (10–12). Rev. ed. Illus. 1981, Doubleday paper $7.95 (0-385-17481-0). The basic principles of mathematics are explained with many examples. This is part of an extensive series that covers many academic subjects. [510]

8843 Steinhaus, Hugo. *One Hundred Problems in Elementary Mathematics* (9–12). 1979, Dover paper $3.95 (0-486-23875-X). These are problems that illustrate basic operations in mathematics. [510]

8844 Tobias, Sheila. *Overcoming Math Anxiety* (10–12). Illus. 1978, Norton $16.95 (0-393-06439-5); Houghton paper $8.95 (0-395-29088-0). The author explains how to conquer a fear and avoidance of mathematics. [510]

8845 Tobias, Sheila. *Succeed with Math: Every Student's Guide to Conquering Math Anxiety* (10–12). Illus. 1987, College Entrance Examination Board paper $12.95 (0-87447-259-8). A book that helps readers develop problem-solving techniques as well as understand mathematical concepts. (Rev: BL 2/1/88; BR 3–4/88; VOYA 4/88) [510]

Algebra, Numbers, and Number Systems

8846 Asimov, Isaac. *Asimov on Numbers* (10–12). Illus. 1987, Pocket paper $3.95 (0-671-49404-X). A collection of 17 essays on the history and present status of numbers and numbering systems. [512]

8847 Asimov, Isaac. *Realm of Numbers* (7–12). Illus. 1981, Fawcett paper $2.50 (0-449-24399-0). Basic concepts about numbers from zero to infinity are introduced and explained. [510]

8848 Ifrah, Georges. *From One to Zero: A Universal History of Numbers* (9–12). Trans. by Lowell Bair. Illus. 1987, Penguin paper $14.95 (0-14-009919-0). A history of how numbering systems evolved including the concept of zero. (Rev: BL 7/85) [513.5]

Mathematical Games and Puzzles

8849 Agostini, Franco. *Math and Logic Games* (9–12). Illus. 1986, Harper paper $14.95 (0-06-097021-9). A collection of games, tricks, and puzzles using mathematical concerns and knowledge. [793.7]

8850 Agostini, Franco, and Nicola Alberto De Carlo. *Intelligence Games* (10–12). Illus. 1987, Simon & Schuster paper $13.95 (0-671-53201-9).

A collection of games testing various kinds of intelligence. (Rev: BL 9/1/87) [793.7]

8851 Fixx, James F. *Games for the Superintelligent* (9–12). 1988, Doubleday paper $3.98 (0-385-23400-7). A collection of brain teasers involving mathematics, logic, and language. Also use: *More Games for the Superintelligent* (1982). [793]

8852 Gardner, Martin. *Aha! Gotcha: Paradoxes to Puzzle and Delight* (7–12). Illus. 1982, W. H. Freeman paper $10.95 (0-7167-1361-6). A book of puzzles from *Scientific American* that involve mathematics and logic. [793.7]

8853 Gardner, Martin. *Hexaflexagons and Other Mathematical Diversions* (10–12). 1988, Univ. of Chicago Pr. paper $10.95 (0-226-28254-6). A collection of brain teasers and mathematical puzzles from the pages of *Scientific American*. (Rev: SLJ 5/89) [793.7]

8854 Gardner, Martin. *Puzzles from Other Worlds* (10–12). 1984, Random paper $5.95 (0-394-72140-3). One of many collections of mathematical puzzles from this author. Also use: *Mathematical Carnival* (1977). [793.7]

8855 Gardner, Martin. *Time Travel and Other Mathematical Bewilderments* (10–12). Illus. 1987, W. H. Freeman $17.95 (0-7167-1924-X); paper $12.95 (0-7167-1925-8). Another collection of puzzles and explanatory descriptions from *Scientific American*. (Rev: BL 1/15/88) [793.7]

8856 Studio D. *Picture Puzzles for the Super Smart* (9–12). Illus. 1985, Sterling paper $4.95 (0-8069-7956-6). This is a collection of picture puzzles similar to those on standardized tests that test ability to detect relationships. (Rev: SLJ 2/86) [793.7]

8857 Thomas, David A. *Math Projects for Young Scientists* (9–12). Illus. 1988, Watts $11.90 (0-531-10523-7). A practical guide to designing, planning, and carrying out various research projects in mathematics. (Rev: BL 4/15/88; BR 11–12/88; SLJ 9/88; VOYA 8/88) [510]

Statistics

8858 Huff, Darrell. *How to Lie with Statistics* (10–12). Illus. 1954, Norton paper $3.95 (0-393-09426-X). A now classic account of how numbers can be manipulated to produce desired results. [519.5]

8859 Siskin, Bernard, et al. *What Are the Chances? Risks, Odds, and Likelihood in Every-*

day Life (10–12). 1989, Crown $16.95 (0-517-57260-5). A fascinating look at topics like sports, disasters, and health from the statistician's point of view. (Rev: SLJ 8/89; VOYA 8/89) [310]

Time and Clocks

8860 Howse, Derek. *Greenwich Time and the Discovery of the Longitude* (10–12). Illus. 1980, Oxford Univ. Pr. $32.95 (0-19-215948-8). The story behind the concept of longitude and how Greenwich becomes the world's timekeeper. [529]

8861 Macvey, John W. *Time Travel* (10–12). 1990, Scarborough House $16.95 (0-8128-3107-1). A serious study about the possibility of time travel and what could happen if it occurred. (Rev: BL 6/1/90) [530.1]

8862 Zerubavel, Eviator. *The Seven Day Circle: The History and Meaning of the Week* (9–12). Illus. 1985, Macmillan $19.95 (0-02-934680-0); Univ. of Chicago Pr. paper $9.95 (0-226-98165-

7). A detailed account of the historical and religious origins of our week. (Rev: SLJ 12/85) [529]

Weights and Measures

8863 Asimov, Isaac. *The Measure of the Universe* (10–12). Illus. 1983, Harper $15.45 (0-06-015129-3). The author describes concepts of measurement as related to such areas as speed, length, mass, and volume. [530.8]

8864 Blocksma, Mary. *Reading the Numbers* (10–12). 1989, Viking $18.95 (0-670-82682-0); Penguin paper $7.95 (0-14-010654-5). A wonderful browsing book that explains such measurements as wattages, lumber sizes, ISBNs (International Standard Book Numbers), and bar codes. (Rev: BL 5/1/89) [530.8]

8865 Diagram Group. *Comparisons* (10–12) Illus. 1982, St. Martin's paper $9.95 (0-312-15485-2). This illustrated volume studies units of measurement for various aspects of our environment. [389]

Meteorology

Air

8866 Allen, Oliver. *Atmosphere* (7–12). Illus. 1983, Silver Burdett LB $24.60 (0-8094-4337-6). A well-illustrated introduction to the earth's atmosphere, its properties, and how man is changing it. From Time-Life Books. [551.5]

Storms

8867 Erickson, Jon. *Violent Storms* (10–12). Illus. 1988, TAB $24.95 (0-8306-9042-5); paper $16.95 (0-8306-2942-4). In addition to a description of the nature and causes of storms, the author gives a general introduction to weather and such topics as the greenhouse effect and acid rain. (Rev: BL 1/1/89; VOYA 4/89) [551.5]

8868 Whipple, A. B. C. *Storm* (8–12). Illus. 1982, Silver Burdett LB $24.60 (0-8094-4313-9). This well-illustrated book from Time-Life describes various kinds of storms and their causes. [551.5]

Weather

8869 Gribbin, John, ed. *The Breathing Planet* (10–12). Illus. 1986, Basil Blackwell $39.95 (0-631-14288-6); paper $12.95 (0-631-14289-4). A collection of essays and articles about the world's changing atmosphere and climate. (Rev: BL 4/1/86) [551.5]

8870 Lockhart, Gary. *The Weather Companion: An Album of Meteorological History, Science, Legend, & Folklore* (9–12). 1988, Wiley paper $12.95 (0-471-62079-3). From ancient myths to modern research, this book covers the lore and facts concerning the weather. (Rev: BR 3–4/89) [551.5]

8871 Ludlum, David M. *The American Weather Book* (10–12). 1990, American Meteorological Soc. paper $14.95 (0-933876-97-1). A collection of facts, myths, and figures all involving the weather. [551.6]

8872 Ramsey, Dan. *Weather Forecasting: A Young Meteorologist's Guide* (8–12). Illus. 1990, TAB $19.95 (0-8306-8338-0); paper $10.95 (0-8306-3338-3). A detailed and often technical examination of the techniques of weather forecasting with many tables, charts, and diagrams. (Rev: BL 10/15/90) [551.6]

8873 Zim, Herbert, et al. *Weather* (7–12). Illus. 1987, Western paper $3.95 (0-307-24051-7). A nicely illustrated handy guide to all kinds of weather and what causes them. [551.6]

Oceanography

General and Miscellaneous

8874 Bartlett, Jonathan, ed. *The Ocean Environment* (10–12). 1977, H. W. Wilson paper $10.00 (0-8242-0600-2). In this collection of articles, such topics as marine farms, ocean energy resources, and extracting minerals from the seas are discussed. [333.91]

8875 Carson, Rachel. *The Sea around Us* (7–12). Rev. ed. Illus. 1961, Oxford Univ. Pr. $19.95 (0-19-506186-1). First published in 1951, this volume describes the origins of oceans, how they are explored, and the life that exists in them. [551.46]

8876 Erickson, Jon. *The Mysterious Oceans* (9–12). Illus. 1988, TAB $22.95 (0-8306-9342-4). After discussing how oceans were formed, the author explores such topics as deep sea life, waves, food resources, and pollution. (Rev: VOYA 2/89) [551.46]

8877 Groves, Don. *The Oceans: A Book of Questions and Answers* (9–12). Illus. 1989, Wiley paper $12.95 (0-471-60712-6). Information is given on the oceans and their exploration in a question-and-answer format. (Rev: BL 4/15/89; BR 11–12/90) [551.46]

8878 Rehder, Harald A. *The Audubon Society Field Guide to North American Seashells* (7–12). Illus. 1981, Knopf paper $14.45 (0-394-51913-2). Seven hundred of the most common seashells from our coasts are pictured in color photographs and described in the text. [594]

8879 Whipple, A. B. C. *Restless Oceans* (7–12). Illus. 1983, Silver Burdett LB $24.60 (0-8094-4341-4). A lavishly illustrated introduction to oceans and marine life from Time-Life Books. [551.46]

Currents, Tides, and Waves

8880 Bascom, Willard. *Waves and Beaches: The Dynamics of the Ocean Surface* (7–12). Rev. ed. Illus. 1980, Anchor $9.95 (0-385-14844-5). A primer on waves—their power and beauty and how they shape the shorelines of the world. [551.46]

Seashores

8881 *America's Seashore Wonderlands* (9–12). Illus. 1985, National Geographic $9.50 (0-87044-548-0); paper $7.95 (0-87044-543-X). Beginning with the northwest coast and ending with New England, this is an illustrated tour of our seashores. (Rev: BL 5/1/86) [574.5]

8882 Carson, Rachel. *The Edge of the Sea* (7–12). Illus. 1955, Houghton paper $9.95 (0-395-28519-4). The author describes the 3 basic types of seashores and gives examples of each on the Atlantic coast of the United States. [574.92]

8883 Sackett, Russell. *Edge of the Sea* (7–12). Illus. 1983, Silver Burdett LB $22.60 (0-8094-4333-3). Coastal areas are described and the life that these areas support are introduced in text and many illustrations. [574.5]

8884 Trefil, James. *Scientist at the Seashore* (10–12). Illus. 1987, Macmillan paper $8.95 (0-02-025920-4). This account covers such topics as tides, waves, and surf. [530]

8885 Zim, Herbert, and Lester Ingle. *Seashores* (7–12). 1955, Western paper $3.95 (0-307-24496-6). About 500 species of plants, shells, animals, and birds that are found on seashores are identified. [551.4]

Underwater Exploration and Sea Disasters

8886 Ballard, Robert D., and Rick Archbold. *The Discovery of the Titanic* (9–12). Illus. 1987, Warner $35.00 (0-446-51385-7); paper $17.95 (0-446-38912-9). An account of the complex, often frustrating but eventually successful quest for the wreck of the *Titanic*. (Rev: BL 12/1/87; VOYA 4/88) [622]

8887 Callahan, Steven. *Adrift: Seventy-Six Days Lost at Sea* (9–12). Illus. 1986, Ballantine paper $4.95 (0-345-34083-3). The incredible saga of a shipwrecked man who lived for 76 days on a rubber raft in the Atlantic Ocean. (Rev: BL 1/1/86; SLJ 9/86) [910]

8888 Cousteau, Jacques, and Frederic Dumas. *The Silent World* (7–12). Illus. 1987, Lyons & Burford paper $12.95 (0-941130-45-2). A description of how the aqualung was developed and how it has opened up the exploration of oceans and their sunken treasures. [551.46]

8889 Cousteau, Jacques, and Alexis Sivirine. *Jacques Cousteau's Calypso* (7–12). Illus. 1983, Abrams $39.95 (0-8109-0788-7). The story of Cousteau's ship and of the techniques he uses to explore the oceans of the world. [551.46]

8890 Davie, Michael. *Titanic: The Death and Life of a Legend* (10–12). Illus. 1987, Knopf $19.95 (0-317-58565-7); Henry Holt paper $10.95 (0-8050-0909-4). A re-creation of the sinking of

the *Titanic* that highlights the mysteries surrounding it that have not yet been solved. (Rev: BL 6/1/87) [363.1]

8891 Davies, Eryl. *Ocean Frontiers* (10–12). Illus. 1980, Viking $11.50 (0-670-52026-8). A guide to both the development of undersea exploration and to the many uses of oceans and the life they contain. [551.46]

8892 Earle, Sylvia A., and Al Giddings. *Exploring the Deep Frontier: The Adventure of Man in the Sea* (9–12). Illus. 1980, National Geographic $14.95 (0-87044-343-7). A history of underwater exploration with coverage on the evolution of machines and techniques. [551.4]

8893 Lord, Walter. *The Night Lives On* (8–12). Illus. 1986, Morrow $15.95 (0-688-04939-7). The author reviews the facts in light of new evidence about the sinking of the *Titanic* in this sequel to *A Night to Remember* (1955). (Rev: BL 8/86; BR 1–2/87; SLJ 2/87) [810]

8894 Mowat, Farley. *Grey Seas Under* (10–12). 1989, Bantam paper $3.50 (0-7704-2214-4). The story of a North Atlantic salvage tug during the 1940s and 1950s. [386]

8895 National Geographic Society, eds. *Undersea Treasures* (9–12). Illus. 1974, National Geographic $7.95 (0-87044-147-7). Several divers describe their adventure seeking underwater treasures from sunken ships. [910.4]

8896 *The Ocean Realm* (9–12). Illus. 1978, National Geographic Soc. LB $9.50 (0-87044-256-2). This book presents in illustrated format several accounts of underwater exploration. [551.46]

8897 Pringle, Laurence. *Rivers and Lakes* (10–12). 1985, Silver Burdett LB $24.60 (0-8094-4509-3). A general description of the lakes and rivers of the United States and of the animal and plant life they contain. From Time-Life Books. [551.48]

8898 Wade, Wyn Craig. *The Titanic: End of a Dream* (9–12). Illus. 1986, Penguin paper $4.95 (0-14-009635-3). An account of the sinking of the *Titanic* and the expedition that located it in 1985. [910.4]

Physics

General and Miscellaneous

8899 Abbott, Edwin A. *Flatland: A Romance of Many Dimensions* (10–12). 1982, Enslow $12.95 (0-87523-199-3); NAL paper $3.50 (0-451-52290-7). Using humor to make points, the author examines such concepts as space, time, and dimension. [530]

8900 Asimov, Isaac. *Asimov on Physics* (10–12). 1979, Avon paper $4.95 (0-380-41848-7). A collection of previously published essays on various branches of physics. [530]

8901 Aveni, Anthony. *Empires of Time: Calendars, Clocks, and Cultures* (10–12). 1989, Basic Books $24.95 (0-465-01950-1). The concept of time is explored as it is viewed and measured in various cultures. (Rev: BL 10/1/89) [529]

8902 Barnett, Lincoln. *The Universe of Dr. Einstein* (8–12). 1980, Amereon $16.95 (0-8488-0146-6). A lucid explanation of Einstein's theory of relativity and how it is changing our ideas of the universe. [530.1]

8903 Calder, Nigel. *Einstein's Universe* (10–12). 1980, Penguin paper $7.95 (0-14-005499-5). Without using mathematics, the theory of relativity is explained. [530.1]

8904 Close, Frank, et al. *The Particle Explosion* (10–12). Illus. 1987, Oxford Univ. Pr. $39.95 (0-19-851965-6). Types of particles are discussed and their behavior plus a history of particle physics from X-rays on. (Rev: BL 6/1/87) [539.7]

8905 Cohen, I. Bernard. *The Birth of a New Physics* (10–12). Rev. ed. Illus. 1985, Norton $19.95 (0-393-01994-2); paper $7.95 (0-393-30045-5). For better science students, this ac-

count traces the development of modern physics and explains current theories and their applications. (Rev: BL 10/1/85) [530]

8906 Crease, Robert P., and Charles C. Mann. *The Second Creation: Makers of the Revolution in Twentieth-Century Physics* (10–12). 1986, Macmillan paper $11.95 (0-02-084550-2). A history of twentieth-century physics with profiles of the men behind the discoveries. (Rev: BL 5/1/86) [539]

8907 Einstein, Albert. *The Meaning of Relativity* (10–12). 5th ed. 1956, Princeton Univ. Pr. $30.00 (0-691-08007-0). A difficult but rewarding series of lectures on relativity that requires a knowledge of mathematics. [530.1]

8908 Gribbin, John. *In Search of Schrodinger's Cat: Quantum Physics and Reality* (10–12). 1984, Bantam $10.95 (0-553-34253-3). For better science students, this is an introduction to and explanation of quantum physics. [530]

8909 Gribbin, John. *In Search of the Big Bang: Quantum Physics and Cosmology* (10–12). Illus. 1986, Bantam paper $9.95 (0-553-34258-4). In clear prose the author introduces quantum physics and the theories devised to explain the creation of the universe. (Rev: BL 6/1/86) [523.1]

8910 Gribbin, John. *Timewarps* (10–12). 1980, Dell paper $4.95 (0-385-29078-0). An examination of the concept of time and its relation to the mind. [530]

8911 Motz, Lloyd, and Jefferson Hane Weaver. *The Story of Physics* (10–12). Illus. 1989, Plenum $24.50 (0-306-43076-2). A clearly written history of physics that explores such topics as Newton's contributions, optics, relativity, and quantum mechanics. (Rev: BL 5/1/89) [530]

8912 Noddy, Tom. *Bubble Magic* (9–12). 1988, Running Pr. LB $15.90 (0-89471-660-3); paper $8.95 (0-89471-659-X). This book supplies information on the physics of bubbles as well as many projects involving soap bubbles of various sizes and shapes. (Rev: SLJ 2/89) [668]

8913 Parker, Barry. *Einstein's Dream: The Search for a Unified Theory of the Universe* (10–12). 1986, Plenum $19.95 (0-306-42343-X). The story of the 30-year search since Einstein's death to uncover a unified theory to explain the universe. (Rev: BL 9/1/86) [523.1]

8914 Peat, F. David. *Cold Fusion: The Making of a Scientific Discovery* (10–12). 1989, Contemporary $16.95 (0-8092-4243-5). A behind-the-scenes look at scientific research that focuses on the discovery of cold fusion at the University of Utah in 1989. (Rev: SLJ 2/90) [530]

8915 Spielberg, Nathan, and Bryon D. Anderson. *Seven Ideas That Shook the Universe* (10–12). Illus. 1987, Wiley $22.95 (0-471-85974-5); paper $14.95 (0-471-84816-6). From Copernicus to Einstein here is a readable account of the development of the great concepts in physics. (Rev: BL 5/15/87; SLJ 11/87) [500.2]

Energy and Motion

General and Miscellaneous

8916 Gunston, Bill, et al. *Guinness Book of Speed Facts and Feats* (8–12). Illus. 1985, Sterling $17.95 (0-85112-267-1). A book of speed records involving animals, humans, plants, sports, and the like. (Rev: SLJ 8/85) [531]

8917 Goldin, Augusta. *Oceans of Energy: Reservoir of Power for the Future* (10–12). Illus. 1980, Harcourt $9.95 (0-15-257688-6). The many possibilities of using the energy in oceans to generate power are explored. [333.91]

8918 Oatman, Eric F., ed. *Prospects for Energy in America* (10–12). 1980, H. W. Wilson paper $10.00 (0-8242-0646-0). In this collection of articles, America's energy problems are discussed and possible solutions are proposed. [333.79]

8919 Stobaugh, Robert, et al., eds. *Energy Future* (10–12). 1983, Random paper $6.95 (0-394-71063-0). A report on the energy crisis and possible solutions. [333.79]

Nuclear Energy

8920 Croall, Stephen. *Nuclear Power for Beginners* (10–12). Illus. 1983, Pantheon paper $3.95 (0-394-71539-X). In a witty text and humorous illustrations, the facts and concerns surrounding nuclear energy are explored. [539.7]

8921 Deutsch, Robert W. *Nuclear Power: A Rational Approach* (10–12). 4th ed. Illus. 1986, GP Courseware paper $4.95 (0-87683-831-X). A proponent of the use of nuclear energy explains how it can be done safely. (Rev: BL 3/15/87) [363.1]

8922 Gale, Robert Peter, and Thomas Hauser. *Final Warning: The Legacy of Chernobyl* (10–12). 1988, Warner $18.95 (0-446-51409-8). A discretionary tale about the nuclear disaster in the U.S.S.R. and its lessons concerning nuclear energy. (Rev: BL 3/1/88) [363.1]

8923 Kaku, Michio, and Jennifer Trainer, eds. *Nuclear Power* (10–12). Illus. 1982, Norton paper $8.95 (0-393-30128-1). In 20 challenging essays, power specialists discuss the pros and cons of nuclear technology. [621.48]

8924 Kiefer, Irene. *Nuclear Energy at the Crossroads* (10–12). Illus. 1982, Macmillan $14.95 (0-689-30926-0). As well as an introduction to peaceful uses of nuclear power, this book discusses nuclear accidents and what causes them. [333.79]

8925 Lampton, Christopher. *Predicting Nuclear and Other Technological Disasters* (9–12). Illus. 1989, Watts LB $12.90 (0-531-10784-1). This book discusses the possibility and probability of nuclear accidents and what they could involve. (Rev: BL 11/15/89; BR 5–6/90; SLJ 2/90; VOYA 4/90) [363.1]

8926 League of Women Voters Education Fund. *The Nuclear Waste Primer: A Handbook for Citizens* (10–12). 1985, Nick Lyons $11.95 (0-8052-6007-2); paper $5.95 (0-8052-6006-4). This concise handbook explains what nuclear wastes are, how they are presently being handled, and how to participate in making decisions involving them. (Rev: BL 12/15/85) [363.7]

8927 Lerager, Jim. *In the Shadow of the Cloud: Photographs & Histories of America's Atomic Veterans* (10–12). Illus. 1988, Fulcrum $23.95 (1-55591-030-0). This is the story of the thousands of servicemen who were exposed to nuclear weapons testing and how it has affected their health. (Rev: BR 1–2/89) [612]

8928 McCuen, Gary E. *Nuclear Waste: The Biggest Clean-Up in History* (9–12). 1990, GEM LB $12.95 (0-86596-076-3). From many different sources, this is a collection of points of view concerning one of the great environmental problems. (Rev: SLJ 8/90) [333.79]

8929 Robinson, Mark Aaron. *100 Grams of Uranium Equal 290 Tons of Coal* (10–12). Illus. 1988, R & D Engineering paper $12.95 (0-945318-00-6). The author makes a telling case for the use of nuclear energy and minimizes the possibility of nuclear disasters. (Rev: BL 12/1/88) [621.483]

Solar Energy

8930 Buckley, Shawn. *Sun Up to Sun Down* (10–12). 1979, McGraw paper $6.95 (0-07-008790-3). This is a book about solar energy and how it can be captured and used. [621.47]

8931 Kaufman, Allan. *Exploring Solar Energy: Principles & Projects* (9–12). 1989, Prakken paper $8.95 (0-911168-60-5). An account that explains the 3 aspects of solar energy and gives 8 projects of varying difficulty and sophistication. (Rev: BR 5–6/90) [621.47]

Light, Color, and Laser Science

8932 Burkig, Valerie. *Photonics: The New Science of Light* (8–12). Illus. 1986, Enslow $15.95 (0-89490-107-9). A solid introduction to modern optics and its branches involving lasers, fiber optics, and new optical instruments. (Rev: BL 8/86; SLJ 9/86; VOYA 8–10/86) [621.36]

8933 Chijiiwa, Hideaki. *Color Harmony: A Guide to Creative Color Combinations* (10–12). Illus. 1987, Writer's Digest paper $15.95 (0-935603-06-9). This book on color shows how colors can be combined effectively and the effects on viewers. (Rev: SLJ 9/87) [752]

8934 Heckman, Philip. *The Magic of Holography* (9–12). Illus. 1986, Macmillan $19.95 (0-689-31168-0). A history and description of uses of this science in which an object can be seen from many viewpoints at the same time. (Rev: BL 12/1/86; SLJ 11/86; VOYA 12/86) [621]

8935 Laurence, Clifford L. *The Laser Book: A New Technology of Light* (9–12). Illus. 1986, Prentice $19.95 (0-13-523622-3). For the layperson here is a history of laser science, its many uses in today's world, and a guide to careers in the field. (Rev: BL 11/15/86) [621.36]

Magnetism and Electricity

8936 Hazen, Robert M. *The Breakthrough: The Race for the Superconductor* (10–12). Illus. 1988, Summit $18.95 (0-671-65829-8). Accessible science writing about the drama and suspense involved in the search for the best superconductor. (Rev: BL 5/15/88) [537.623]

8937 Langone, John. *Superconductivity: The New Alchemy* (10–12). 1989, Contemporary $19.95 (0-8092-4581-7). Beginning with elementary explanations of electricity basics, the author moves to the recent developments in the area of superconductors. (Rev: BL 6/15/89) [621.3]

8938 Mayo, Jonathan L. *Superconductivity: The Threshold of a New Technology* (10–12). Illus. 1988, TAB $18.95 (0-8306-9122-7); paper $12.95 (0-8306-9322-X). This highly technical subject is introduced simply and with excellent illustrations. (Rev: BL 4/15/89) [621.3]

Nuclear Physics

8939 Fritzsch, Harald. *Quarks: The Stuff of Matter* (10–12). Illus. 1983, Basic Books $19.95 (0-465-06781-6); paper $9.95 (0-465-06784-0). An explanation of the theory of this member of the family of subparticles. [539.7]

8940 Rhodes, Richard. *The Making of the Atomic Bomb* (10–12). Illus. 1987, Simon & Schuster paper $12.95 (0-6716-5719-4). For better readers, a detailed history of the atomic bomb and the men behind the scenes. (Rev: BL 1/15/87) [358.39]

Technology and Engineering

General Works and Miscellaneous Industries

8941 Brennan, Richard P. *Levitating Trains and Kamikaze Genes: Technological Literacy for the 1990s* (10–12). 1990, Wiley paper $18.95 (0-471-62295-8). An account of the moral issues involving such technological advances as artificial intelligence. (Rev: BL 3/1/90) [600]

8942 Brown, Kenneth A. *Inventors at Work: Interviews* (10–12). 1987, Microsoft $17.95 (1-55615-123-3); paper $9.95 (1-55615-042-3). Interviews with 16 contemporary inventors who work in the areas of computers and laser technology. (Rev: BL 12/15/87) [609.2]

8943 Fox, Roy. *Technology* (9–12). 1985, David & Charles $19.95 (0-7134-3710-3). A survey of the developments in technology from the Industrial Revolution to today's frontiers in computers and atomic energy. (Rev: SLJ 11/85) [600]

8944 Franck, Irene M., and David M. Brownstone. *Manufacturers and Miners* (9–12). Illus. 1989, Facts on File $17.95 (0-8160-1447-7). An historical account of how factories, mines, and the jobs they need performed evolved through history. (Rev: BL 3/15/89; BR 11–12/89) [331.7]

8945 French, Thomas E. *Mechanical Drawing* (10–12). Illus. 1985, McGraw $33.96 (0-07-022333-5). A textbook that introduces drafting techniques and methods. [604.2]

8946 Hawke, David Freeman. *Nuts and Bolts of the Past: A History of American Technology, 1776–1860* (10–12). 1988, Harper $17.95 (0-06-015901-4). A history of the men and the ideas

that produced our factories, industry, and transportation systems. (Rev: BL 8/88) [609]

8947 *Inventors and Discoverers: Changing Our World* (9–12). Illus. 1988, National Geographic $19.95 (0-87044-751-3). A capsule history of modern technology in words and pictures that highlights major inventions like the steam engine, cameras, and computers. (Rev: BL 3/15/89) [609]

8948 Jackson, Albert E., and David Day. *Tools and How to Use Them* (10–12). Illus. 1978, Knopf paper $13.95 (0-394-73542-0). Tools for every kind of work including plumbing, woodwork, and home maintenance are pictured and their uses described. [621.9]

8949 Lasson, Kenneth. *Mouse Traps and Muffling Cups: One Hundred Brilliant and Bizarre United States Patents* (9–12). Illus. 1986, Arbor House paper $9.95 (0-87795-786-X). In illustrations and text from the Patent Office, the patents for such diverse items as the Wright Brothers' airplane and a diaper for birds. (Rev: BL 10/1/86) [608.77]

8950 Macaulay, David. *The Way Things Work* (7–12). Illus. 1988, Houghton $24.95 (0-395-42857-2). From the zipper to the computer, the author through his text and masterful drawings explains the wonders of technology. (Rev: BL 1/15/89; BR 5–6/89; SLJ 12/88; VOYA 4/89) [600]

8951 Seymour, Richard D., et al. *Exploring Communications* (9–12). Illus. 1987, Goodheart-Willcox $16.40 (0-87006-539-4). An easily read textbook that introduces the entire communications field and suggests many interesting activities. (Rev: BL 10/15/87) [001.516]

8952 Sutton, Caroline, and Duncan M. Anderson. *How Do They Do That?* (10–12). 1982, Morrow paper $8.95 (0-688-01111-X). An explanation is given for a variety of present-day achievements. [600]

8953 Wright, R. Thomas. *Processes of Manufacturing* (10–12). Illus. 1987, Goodheart-Willcox $22.00 (0-87006-633-1). An advanced textbook that introduces the various methods of processing a variety of materials. (Rev: BL 10/15/87) [670]

8954 Yankee Magazine, eds. *The Inventive Yankee: From Rockets to Roller Skates, 200 Years of Yankee Inventors and Inventions* (9–12). 1989, Yankee Books $24.95 (0-89909-172-5). In a series of informal articles (some humorous) on inventions, this is a tribute to American ingenuity, success, and some failures. (Rev: BL 3/15/89) [609]

8955 Zerwick, Chloe. *A Short History of Glass* (10–12). Rev. ed. Illus. 1990, Abrams $19.95 (0-8109-3801-4). Using the exhibits at the Corning Museum in New York State as a focus, this well-illustrated account traces the history and importance of glass. (Rev: BL 6/1/90) [666.1]

Clothing and Textiles

8956 Macaulay, David. *Mill* (8–12). Illus. 1983, Houghton $15.95 (0-395-34830-7); paper $7.95 (0-395-52019-3). In a text that uses original sources and many excellent diagrams, 4 different nineteenth-century New England cotton mills are described. [690]

Computers and Automation

8957 Ahl, David. *BASIC Computer Games* (9–12). 1978, Workman paper $8.95 (0-89480-052-3). This is a collection of challenging microcomputer games using BASIC. Also use *More BASIC Computer Games* (1980). [001.64]

8958 Asimov, Isaac, and Karen A. Frenkel. *Robots, Machines in Man's Image* (10–12). Illus. 1985, Robotic Industries $21.95 (0-317-39396-0). A readable history of robots from mythology to current research on artificial intelligence. [629.8]

8959 Barrett, Judy. *The Joys of Computer Networking: The Personal Connection Handbook* (10–12). 1984, McGraw paper $9.95 (0-07-003768-X). How to use your computer and a

modem to establish networks and tap informational data bases. [001.64]

8960 Bradbeer, Robin, et al. *The Beginner's Guide to Computers* (9–12). 1982, Addison paper $9.95 (0-201-11209-4). A beginner's guide to computer technology presented in a concise, elementary fashion. [001.64]

8961 Bradley, David J. *Assembly Language Programming for the IBM Personal Computer* (10–12). 1984, Prentice $43.20 (0-13-049189-6); paper $30.95 (0-13-049171-3). For advanced computer students, this account covers all aspects of using the Assembly computer language in the IBM personal computer. [005]

8962 Burnham, David. *The Rise of the Computer State* (10–12). 1984, Random paper $6.95 (0-394-72375-9). This account probes the effects of computers on society, particularly in relation to the right to privacy. [001.64]

8963 Curran, Susan, and Ray Curnow. *Overcoming Computer Illiteracy: A Friendly Introduction to Computers* (9–12). 1984, Penguin $12.95 (0-14-007159-8). A user-friendly guide to computers—how they work and how they can work for you. [001.64]

8964 Darcy, Laura, and Louise Boston, comps. *Webster's New World Dictionary of Computer Terms* (7–12). 1983, Simon & Schuster paper $5.95 (0-671-46866-9). Definitions and explanations are given for over 2,500 words, terms, and abbreviations. [001.64]

8965 Davies, Owen. *The Omni Book of Computers and Robots* (10–12). 1983, Zebra paper $3.95 (0-8217-1276-4). This is a collection of articles from *Omni* magazine that deal with computer technology and robotics and their present and future applications. [001.64]

8966 Dewdney, A. K. *The Armchair Universe: An Exploration of Computer Worlds* (10–12). Illus. 1988, Freeman $19.95 (0-716-71938-X); paper $13.95 (0-716-71939-8). A collection of columns named "Computer Recreations" from *Scientific American* magazine. (Rev: BL 4/15/88; BR 9–10/88) [005.26]

8967 Dewey, Patrick R. *Interactive Fiction and Adventure Games for Microcomputers: An Annotated Directory, 1988* (9–12). Illus. 1987, Meckler paper $39.50 (0-88736-170-6). Detailed information including cost and difficulty level is given on interactive games all arranged by title. (Rev: BL 4/15/88) [016.7948]

8968 D'Ignazio, Fred. *Small Computers: Exploring Their Technology and Future* (9–12). Illus. 1981, Watts $11.90 (0-531-04269-3). The author explains the parts and functions of the small computer, gives hints on purchasing one, and discusses possible future developments. [004]

8969 D'Ignazio, Fred. *Working Robots* (7–12). Illus. 1982, Elsevier $12.50 (0-525-66740-7). A survey of the kinds of robots in use today with a look into the future. [629.8]

8970 Ditlea, Steve, ed. *Digital Deli* (9–12). Illus. 1984, Workman paper $12.95 (0-89480-591-6). A collection of short pieces about the varied world of the computer that cover such topics as computer camps for children, the Moog synthesizer, and artificial intelligence. (Rev: BL 1/1/85) [001.64]

8971 Dock, V. Thomas. *Structured COBOL: American National Standard* (10–12). 2nd ed. 1984, West $34.25 (0-314-77896-9). This is a comprehensive introduction to COBOL and how to program using it. [001.64]

8972 Evans, Christopher. *The Micro Millenium* (10–12). 1982, Pocket paper $3.95 (0-671-46212-1). This book explores the ways computers have changed our society and methods of communication. [001.64]

8973 Fenton, Erfert, and Christine Morrissett. *Canned Art: Clip Art for the MacIntosh* (10–12). Illus. 1990, Peachpit Pr. paper $29.95 (0-938151-16-9). A catalog of MacIntosh clip art from 37 different companies. (Rev: SLJ 9/90) [001.64]

8974 Freedman, Alan. *The Computer Glossary for Everyone: It's Not Just a Glossary!* (9–12). 4th ed. Illus. 1987, Amacom paper $26.95 (0-8144-7709-7). This dictionary gives easily understood entries for terms, abbreviations, and acronyms. [004]

8975 Freiberger, Paul, and Michael Swaine. *Fire in the Valley: The Making of the Personal Computer* (10–12). 1984, McGraw paper $11.95 (0-07-881121-X). A fascinating history of the computer industry and the people involved in it. [001.64]

8976 Gader, Bertram, and Manuel V. Nodar. *Apple Software for Pennies* (9–12). 1985, Warner paper $9.95 (0-446-38206-X). A guide to free or inexpensive software for Apple computers. [001.64]

8977 Galanter, Eugene. *Advanced Programming Handbook* (10–12). 1984, Putnam $14.95 (0-399-50975-5); paper $8.95 (0-399-50976-3). A programming book for computer enthusiasts who have mastered the basics. [001.64]

8978 Glossbrenner, Alfred. *The Complete Handbook of Personal Computer Communications: Everything You Need to Go Online with the World* (8–12). Rev. ed. 1989, St. Martin's paper $18.95 (0-312-03312-5). A guide that explains how a modem can open up a new world through your microcomputer. (Rev: BL 3/1/86) [384]

8979 Goldstein, Larry Joel. *IBM PC Introduction, BASIC Programming and Applications* (10–12). 1989, Prentice $24.95 (0-13-449531-7). An introduction to this popular personal computer plus material on how to use it and begin programming using BASIC. [001.64]

8980 Gookin, Dan, and Andy Townsend. *Hard Disk Management with MS-DOS and PC-DOS* (10–12). Illus. 1987, TAB $26.95 (0-8306-0697-1); paper $18.60 (0-8306-2897-5). A guide to MS-DOS management for people with some background knowledge and experience. (Rev: BL 4/15/88) [005.74]

8981 Graham, Lyle J. *Your IBM PC: A Guide to the IBM Personal Computer* (9–12) Illus. 1984, Osborne paper $18.95 (0-88134-120-7). This introduction to the IBM PC covers such topics as software, graphics, and sound. [004]

8982 Hartnell, Tim. *Tim Hartnell's Giant Book of Computer Games* (8–12). 1984, Ballantine paper $9.95 (0-345-35207-6). Simple programs are given for more than 40 computer games. Followed by *Tim Hartnell's Second Giant Book of Computer Games* (1984). Also use *Creating Adventure Games for Your Computer* (1984). [001.64]

8983 Heiserman, David L. *Build Your Own Working Robot: The Second Generation* (10–12). Illus. 1987, TAB $18.95 (0-8306-1181-9); paper $12.95 (0-8306-2781-2). Detailed but complex plans on how to build Buster, a 14-inch-tall robot. (Rev: BL 12/1/87) [629.8]

8984 Hordeski, Michael F. *Microcomputer Local Area Networks: Network Design and Implementation* (10–12). Illus. 1987, TAB $26.95 (0-8306-2888-6). A thorough discussion of networking from using simple modems to complex systems. (Rev: BL 4/15/88) [004.6]

8985 Jankel, Annabel, and Rocky Morton. *Creative Computer Graphics* (10–12). Illus. 1984, Cambridge Univ. Pr. $34.50 (0-521-26251-8). This account explains how computer graphics are used in such areas as motion pictures, video games, advertising, and NASA space simulations. [006.6]

8986 Jeffries, Ron, and Glen Fisher. *Commodore 64 Fun and Games: Volume 2* (8–12). 1984, Warner paper $12.95 (0-446-38183-7). This book contains 35 programs for pastimes using the Commodore 64 computer. [001.64]

8987 Jensen, Craig. *The Craft of Computer Programming* (10–12). Illus. 1985, Warner paper

$12.50 (0-446-38147-0). A clearly written introduction to programming that covers principles and gives summaries on each of the languages. (Rev: BL 9/1/85) [001.64]

8988 Jespersen, James, and Jane Fitz-Randolph. *RAMS, ROMS & Robots: The Inside Story of Computers* (9–12). Illus. 1984, Macmillan LB $13.95 (0-689-31063-3). The text covers such topics as analog and digital computers, storage methods, memory, and artificial intelligence. [004]

8989 Kelly, Kevin, ed. *Signal: Communication Tools for the Information Age—A Whole Earth Catalog* (9–12). Illus. 1988, Harmony paper $16.95 (0-517-57084-X). This is an excellent sourcebook for material on subjects involving computers and such related devices as TV satellites, FAX publishing, and desktop publishing. (Rev: BL 3/1/89) [621.38]

8990 Kidder, Tracy. *The Soul of a New Machine* (10–12). 1981, Little $19.95 (0-316-49170-5); paper $4.95 (0-380-59931-7). The story of the design and production of the minicomputer. [001.64]

8991 Lampton, Christopher. *BASIC for Beginners* (9–12). 1984, Watts LB $11.90 (0-531-04745-8). After an introduction to the computer the author explains BASIC computer vocabulary and suggests many projects. Continued in *Advanced BASIC* (1984). [005]

8992 Lampton, Christopher. *CD ROMs* (8–12). 1987, Watts $10.40 (0-531-10378-1). For the person who has some knowledge of computers, this is a discussion of the operation of CD ROMs and optical information storage systems. (Rev: BR 1–2/88) [001.64]

8993 Lampton, Christopher. *FORTRAN for Beginners* (9–12). 1984, Watts LB $11.90 (0-531-04747-4). An introduction to both computers and this computer language, with many examples of applications. [005]

8994 Lampton, Christopher. *Graphics and Animation on the Commodore 64* (10–12). Illus. 1985, Watts $10.90 (0-531-10058-8). For the advanced computer user, a course on creating and animating computer images. Part of a series which includes: *Graphics and Animation on the Apple II* (1985), *Graphics and Animation on the Atari* (1986), and *Graphics and Animation on the TRS-80* (1985). (Rev: BL 12/15/85) [001.64]

8995 Ledgard, Henry. *Elementary BASIC* (9–12). Illus. 1982, Science Research paper $20.95 (0-574-21385-6). By introducing several problems and suggesting solutions, the author introduces the language of BASIC. [005]

8996 Ledgard, Henry. *Elementary PASCAL* (9–12). Illus. 1982, Random paper $19.95 (0-394-52424-1). The basics of PASCAL are introduced by using a problem-solving technique. [005]

8997 Lien, David A. *Learning IBM BASIC for the Personal Computer* (10–12). 1984, CompuSoft paper $19.95 (0-932760-13-9). This is a fine introduction to programming the IBM personal computer using BASIC. [001.64]

8998 Lundell, Allan. *Virus! The Secret World of Computer Invaders That Breed and Destroy* (10–12). 1989, Contemporary paper $9.95 (0-8092-4437-3). The story of how destructive computer programs can ruin the world of information and what can and cannot be done about it. (Rev: BL 11/1/89) [005.8]

8999 McAfee, J., and Colin Haynes. *Computer Viruses, Worms, Data Diddlers, Killer Programs and Other Threats to Your System* (10–12). Illus. 1989, St. Martin's $24.95 (0-312-03064-9); paper $16.95 (0-312-02889-X). This account includes a description of various computer viruses, their causes, and consequences. (Rev: SLJ 12/89) [001.64]

9000 McComb, Gordon. *The Robot Builder's Bonanza: 99 Inexpensive Robotics Projects* (10–12). Illus. 1987, TAB $23.95 (0-8306-0800-1); paper $14.95 (0-8306-2800-2). For advanced students, an introduction to robotics plus projects involving many practical applications. (Rev: BL 12/1/87) [629.8]

9001 McWilliams, Peter A. *The Personal Computer Book* (9–12). Illus. 1984, Quantum Pr. paper $9.95 (0-385-19683-0). An excellent book for the beginner who needs an introduction to personal computers. [004]

9002 Math, Irwin. *Bits and Pieces: Understanding and Building Computing Devices* (10–12). 1984, Macmillan $13.95 (0-684-17879-6). For experienced computer users here is a manual on how to build computer devices that actually work. [001.64]

9003 Moravec, Hans. *Mind Children: The Future of Robot and Human Intelligence* (10–12). 1988, Harvard Univ. Pr. $18.95 (0-674-57616-0). A discussion of the human mind versus the robot's and how these 2 elements can coexist in the future. (Rev: BL 10/1/88) [006.3]

9004 Morrison, Chris, and Teresa S. Stover. *PC Care Manual: Diagnosing and Maintaining Your MS-DOS, CP/M or Macintosh System* (10–12). Illus. 1987, TAB $24.95 (0-8306-0991-1); paper $16.60 (0-8306-2991-2). A troubleshooter's manual that lists potential problems and suggests solutions. (Rev: BL 4/15/88) [621.391]

9005 Nelson, Ted. *Computer Lib/Dream Machines* (8–12). Illus. 1987, Microsoft paper $18.95 (0-914845-49-7). All kinds of odd bits of computer information in a catalog-type format. A revision of the 1974 title. (Rev: BL 4/15/88) [001.64]

9006 Norton, Peter. *Inside the IBM PC: Access to Advanced Features and Programming* (10–12). 1985, Brady paper $19.95 (0-317-37784-1). This manual goes beyond the basic texts and supplies information on the more sophisticated aspects of the IBM personal computer. [001.64]

9007 Olsen, Gary. *Getting Started in Computer Graphics* (10–12). Illus. 1990, North Light $27.95 (0-89134-330-X). A thorough guide that covers topics on software packages, the basics of design, and drawing and painting with various programs. (Rev: BL 7/90) [006.6]

9008 Owen, Jan. *Getting the Most from Your Computer* (9–12). Illus. 1984, McGraw paper $10.95 (0-07-047953-4). This basic book covers such topics as word processing, software selection, and database management. (Rev: BL 1/1/85) [001.64]

9009 Porter, Kent. *The New American Computer Dictionary* (9–12). 1983, NAL $4.50 (0-451-13794-9). A handy volume that defines and describes over 2,000 computer terms and expressions. [001.64]

9010 Price, Robert V., and Jerry Willis. *How to Use the Apple II and IIe* (9–12). 1984, Weber paper $9.95 (0-88056-139-4). A guide to these 2 models plus information on how to choose software for them. [001.64]

9011 Rose, Frank. *Into the Heart of the Mind* (10–12). 1984, Harper $15.45 (0-06-015306-7). The quest by American scientists to create artificial intelligence. [001.53]

9012 Ruane, Pat, and Jane Hyman. *LOGO Activities for the Computer* (10–12). Illus. 1984, Messner LB $9.79 (0-671-50634-X). An introduction to LOGO computer language that includes basic commands and techniques of file storage. [005]

9013 Shane, June Grant. *Programming for Microcomputers: Apple II BASIC* (10–12). 1983, Houghton paper $29.16 (0-395-35207-X). A basic introduction to this Apple computer and to elementary programming of it using BASIC. [001.64]

9014 Spencer, Donald D. *Problem Solving with BASIC* (8–12). 1983, Camelot paper $3.95 (0-89218-075-7). An easily understood guide to beginning programming using BASIC. [001.64]

9015 Spencer, Donald D. *What Computers Can Do* (8–12). 1982, Camelot paper $6.95 (0-89218-043-9). This book, by a prolific author in the area of computers, describes the functions of computers and how they have changed our lives. Also use: *Understanding Computers* (1988) and *BASIC Programming* (1983). [001.64]

9016 Stoll, Cliff. *The Cuckoo's Egg: Tracking a Spy through the Maze of Computer Espionage* (10–12). 1989, Doubleday $18.95 (0-385-24946-2). A fascinating account of tracking a computer hacker who was selling secrets to the Soviets. (Rev: BL 9/15/89; VOYA 6/90) [364.1]

9017 Stultz, Russell Allen. *The Illustrated Word Processing Dictionary* (9–12). Illus. 1983, Prentice paper $24.95 (0-13-450718-5). A glossary of terms involved with word and data processing, defined in diagrams and text. [001.64]

9018 Tatchell, Judy, and Nick Cutler. *Practical Things to Do with a Microcomputer* (10–12). Illus. 1983, EDC LB $9.96 (0-8811-0-140-0); paper $2.95 (0-86020-731-5). This book outlines all sorts of activities possible on a home computer including word processing, graphics, and games. [001.64]

9019 Time-Life Books, eds. *Artificial Intelligence* (9–12). Illus. 1986, Silver Burdett $25.83 (0-8094-5676-1). A survey of artificial thinking machines is given in an excellently illustrated book. Others in this recommended Understanding Computers series are: *Robotics* (1986), *Memory and Storage* (1987), *The Military Frontier* (1988), and *The Software Challenge* (1989). [006.3]

9020 Time-Life Books, eds. *The Personal Computer* (9–12). Illus. 1989, Silver Burdett $25.83 (0-8094-6067-X). In oversize format and excellent illustrations the basics of the personal computer are explained. This is part of a 23-volume set called Understanding Computers available through Silver Burdett. Some other titles are: *Computer Basics* (1985), *The Computerized Society* (1987), *Computers and the Cosmos* (1988), *Alternate Computers* (1989), and *The Chipmakers* (1988). [006.3]

9021 Time-Life Books, eds. *Software* (9–12). Illus. 1985, Silver Burdett $25.93 (0-8094-7554-5). A lavishly illustrated introduction to software packages and utility programs. This is part of the Understanding Computers series that also includes these recommended titles: *Computer Images, Input-Output, Computer Security,* and *Computer Languages* (all 1986). [005]

9022 Time-Life Books, eds. *Understanding Computers* (10–12). 1985, Silver Burdett LB $19.45

(0-8094-5655-9). This is one of the introductory volumes in this extensive 23-volume series on computers that also includes a volume called *The Personal Computer* (1989). [001.65]

9023 Tracton, Ken. *The BASIC Cookbook* (10–12). 1985, TAB paper $7.95 (0-8306-1855-4). This book serves as both a reference work and a guide to programming using BASIC. [001.64]

9024 Trainor, Timothy N. *Computer Concepts and Applications* (9–12). Rev. ed. Illus. 1987, Mitchell $20.00 (0-394-39052-0). An overview of the world of computers that explains how they work and their history and gives examples of some popular microcomputers. (Rev: BL 4/15/88) [004]

9025 Turkle, Sherry. *The Second Self: Computers and the Human Spirit* (10–12). 1984, Simon & Schuster paper $10.95 (0-671-60602-6). This account examines reactions of both children and adults to computers and their technology. [004]

9026 Waldrop, M. Mitchell. *Man-Made Minds: The Promise of Artificial Intelligence* (10–12). 1987, Walker $22.95 (0-8027-0899-4); paper $14.95 (0-8027-7297-8). After a history of the research, the author describes the future of artificial intelligence and the issues involved. (Rev: BL 2/15/87) [006.3]

9027 Weber, Jack. *Computers: The Next Generation* (9–12). Illus. 1985, Arco $11.95 (0-668-06339-4). This work concentrates on what tomorrow's computers will be like and what their new uses will involve. (Rev: BL 9/1/85; BR 9–10/85; SLJ 4/85) [001.64]

9028 Whiteside, Thomas. *Computer Capers: Tales of Electronic Thievery, Embezzlement, and Fraud* (10–12). 1978, Harper $13.00 (0-690-01743-X). This book shows how computers have been used to perform outlandish crimes. [364.1]

9029 Willis, Jerry. *How to Use the Coleco Adam* (9–12). 1984, Weber paper $9.95 (0-88056-149-1). This is part of a series on how to use various models of home computers. Another is: *How to Use the Vic 20* (1983). [001.64]

9030 Willis, Jerry, and Merl K. Miller. *Computers for Everybody* (8–12). 1983, Weber paper $15.95 (0-88056-131-9). An introductory work aimed at reducing computer anxiety. [001.64]

9031 Wold, Allen L. *Computer Science* (9–12). Illus. 1984, Watts LB $12.90 (0-531-04764-4). This is a guide for students who want to use their computer in their science projects. [004]

9032 Wolverton, Van. *Running MS DOS* (9–12). 1988, Microsoft $35.00 (1-55615-116-0); paper

$22.95 (1-55615-115-2). An updated guide that takes beginners through the steps to master MS DOS. (Rev: SLJ 10/88) [001.64]

9033 Wulforst, Harry. *Breakthrough to the Computer Age* (9–12). 1982, Macmillan $12.95 (0-684-17499-5). This is a history of the development and evolution of the modern computer. [001.64]

Electronics

9034 Blumenthal, Howard J. *The Electronic Home Advisor* (10–12). 1988, Andrews & McMeel paper $9.95 (0-8362-2525-2). A buying guide to such household gadgets as VCRs, stereos, and compact disc players. (Rev: BL 12/15/88) [683.8]

9035 Grob, Bernard. *Basic Electronics* (10–12). 6th ed. 1988, McGraw $44.95 (0-07-025119-3). An introduction to the principles of electronics and their applications in radio, television, and other industrial areas. [621.38]

9036 Guzman, Andres. *33 Fun-and-Easy Weekend Electronics Projects* (10–12). Illus. 1987, TAB $14.95 (0-8306-0261-5); paper $8.95 (0-8306-2861-4). Using fairly simple circuitry, this is a good book for the novice electrician. (Rev: BL 4/15/88) [621.381]

9037 Haynie, W. J. *Electricity and Electronics Today* (10–12). Illus. 1988, EMC $17.95 (0-8219-0179-6). A useful introduction to electronics though some background knowledge is sometimes necessary. (Rev: BL 4/15/88) [621.3]

9038 Malcolm, Douglas R. *How to Build Electronic Projects* (10–12). 1980, McGraw $11.10 (0-07-039760-0). This book explains the basics of electronics and introduces a number of interesting projects. [621.381]

9039 Matt, Stephen R. *Electricity and Basic Electronics* (10–12). Illus. 1989, Goodheart-Willcox $20.40 (0-87006-680-3). A text that covers a vocationally oriented approach to electronics and basic electricity. (Rev: BL 4/15/89) [621.3]

9040 Schechter, Bruce. *The Path of No Resistance: The Story of the Revolution in Superconductivity* (10–12). 1989, Simon & Schuster $19.95 (0-671-65785-2). A well-researched and clear story of the discovery of superconductors and of their amazing potential today. (Rev: BL 4/15/89) [537.6]

9041 Time-Life Books, eds. *Basic Writing* (8–12). Illus. 1989, Silver Burdett $20.60 (0-8094-7363-1). Part of the Home Repair and Improvement series from Time-Life Books, this well illustrated volume covers basic topics in home wiring such as adding outlets and rewiring lamps. [621.319]

9042 Traister, John E., and Robert J. Traister. *Encyclopedic Dictionary of Electronic Terms* (7–12). Illus. 1984, Prentice paper $18.95 (0-13-276981-6). All of the basic terms in electronics are explained, usually in fairly simple terms. [621.381]

Machinery

9043 Time-Life Books, eds. *How Things Work in Your Home: And What to Do When They Don't* (9–12). Illus. 1985, Henry Holt paper $16.95 (0-8050-0126-3). After a description of how common machines around the house operate, this book tells how to keep them working properly. (Rev: SLJ 9/85) [621.8]

9044 Toboldt, Bill. *Diesel: Fundamentals, Service, Repair* (10–12). Illus. 1983, Goodheart-Willcox $19.00 (0-87006-424-X). This is an introduction to diesel engines that includes material on design, maintenance, and structure. [621.43]

Telegraph and Telephone

9045 Thomas, Ronald R. *Understanding Telecommunications* (10–12). Illus. 1989, TAB $17.95 (0-8306-3229-8). A fairly technical introduction to such subjects as electronics, radio systems, computer communications, and telemarketing. (Rev: VOYA 4/90) [384]

Television, Motion Pictures, Radio, and Recording

9046 *The ARRL Handbook, 1990* (10–12). Illus. 1989, American Radio Relay League $23.00 (0-87259-167-0). A guide to ham radio equipment and activities from the American Radio Relay League. For many editions this was called *The Radio Amateur's Handbook.* [621.3841]

9047 Brewer, Bryan, and Edd Key. *The Compact Disc Book: A Complete Guide to the Digital Sound of the Future* (9–12). Illus. 1987, Harcourt paper $12.95 (0-15-620050-3). A popularly written guide to the history, technology, and future of the compact disc. (Rev: BL 3/15/88) [621.389]

9048 Browne, Steven E. *Videotape Editing: A Postproduction Primer* (10–12). Illus. 1988, Focal Pr. $21.95 (0-240-51791-1). After a general introduction to videotaping, the author describes different kinds of editing and how they can be done. (Rev: BL 1/1/89) [778.59]

9049 Dearborn, Laura. *Good Sound: An Uncomplicated Guide to Choosing and Using Audio Equipment* (9–12). Illus. 1987, Morrow paper $12.95 (0-688-06424-8). A commonsense guide to components and sound systems that compares various brands and makes recommendations. (Rev: BL 12/1/87) [621.389]

9050 Harwood, Don. *Everything You Always Wanted to Know about Portable Video Tape Recording* (10–12). Illus. 1982, VTR Publg. paper $9.95 (0-915146-05-3). Though somewhat dated in equipment coverage, this gives good background material on production and editing techniques. [778.59]

9051 Kybett, Harry. *The Complete Handbook of Videocassette Recorders* (10–12). 1986, TAB paper $14.95 (0-8306-0731-5). A tour inside a video recorder with an explanation of parts, functions, and circuitry. [778.59]

9052 Porter, Martin. *The Complete Guide to Making Home Video Movies* (9–12). Rev. ed. Illus. 1987, Pocket paper $3.95 (0-671-63922-6). A revision of the 1984 title that gives guidance in purchase and use of equipment and techniques and advice on home video recording. (Rev: BL 1/1/88) [778.59]

9053 Sweeney, Daniel. *Demystifying Compact Discs: A Guide to Digital Audio* (9–12). Illus. 1986, TAB paper $9.95 (0-8306-2728-6). An explanation of CDs, how they work, plus a guide to the necessary equipment. (Rev: BL 1/1/87) [621.389]

9054 Utz, Peter. *Video User's Handbook* (10–12). 3rd. ed. Illus. 1988, Prentice paper $19.95 (0-13-941899-7). A practical guide to the use of video recorders that also covers such related topics as lighting and film production. [621.388]

Transportation

General and Miscellaneous

9055 Patton, Phil. *Open Road: A Celebration of the American Highway* (9–12). 1986, Simon & Schuster $17.95 (0-671-52021-6); Touchstone paper $7.95 (0-317-59998-4). A history of American highways and how the call of the open road has influenced America. (Rev: BL 7/86) [388.1]

Airplanes and Aeronautics

9056 Allen, Oliver. *The Airline Builders* (9–12). Illus. 1981, Silver Burdett LB $24.60 (0-8094-3284-1). With many illustrations, this is a history of the development of commercial airlines in this country. [387.7]

9057 Angelucci, Enzo, ed. *World Encyclopedia of Civil Aircraft: From Leonardo da Vinci to the Present* (9–12). Illus. 1982, Crown $29.95 (0-517-54724-4). This richly illustrated volume traces the history of airplanes from da Vinci to the space shuttle. [629.133]

9058 Apostolo, Giorgio. *The Illustrated Encyclopedia of Helicopters* (7–12). Illus. 1984, Bonanza $12.98 (0-517-43935-2). Besides describing helicopters and how they work, Apostolo gives a brief history of this mode of aviation. [629.133]

9059 Bilstein, Roger E. *Flight in America, 1900–1983: From the Wrights to the Astronauts* (10–12). Illus. 1984, Johns Hopkins Univ. Pr. paper $14.95 (0-8018-3561-5). A history of flight in America and how it has affected our lives and culture. [629.13]

9060 Botting, Douglas. *The Giant Airships* (7–12). Illus. 1980, Silver Burdett LB $24.60 (0-8094-3271-4). From the recommended Epic of Flight series from Time-Life Books, this volume deals with the history of Zeppelins, dirigibles, and other airships. [629.133]

9061 Boyne, Walter J. *The Leading Edge* (10–12). Illus. 1986, Stewart, Tabori & Chang $29.95 (0-941434-93-1); paper $18.95 (1-55670-016-4). A history of flight that concentrates on the contributions of both test pilots and engineers. (Rev: SLJ 2/87) [629.13]

9062 Boyne, Walter J. *The Smithsonian Book of Flight* (9–12). Illus. 1987, Smithsonian Inst. $35.00 (0-517-56614-1). An engrossing history of flight impressively illustrated with historic photographs. (Rev: BL 11/15/87) [629.13]

9063 Bryan, C. D. B. *The National Air and Space Museum* (10–12). Illus. 1988, Abrams $65.00 (0-8109-1380-1). A history of aeronautics and the airplane as reflected in the collection of the National Air and Space Museum. [629.13]

9064 Gunston, Bill. *Jane's Aerospace Dictionary* (10–12). 1989, Jane's Information Group $45.00 (0-7106-0580-3). A total of 20,000 entries of terms, equations, acronyms, and so on, involved with aerospace. (Rev: SLJ 4/87) [629.13]

9065 Hoffer, William, and Marilyn Hoffer. *Freefall* (10–12). 1989, St. Martin's $17.95 (0-312-02919-5). The true story of the Air Canada flight in 1983 that crashed without casualties. (Rev: BL 5/15/89) [363.1]

9066 Hooper, Meredith. *Cleared for Take-Off: International Flight Beyond the Passenger Cabin* (7–12). Illus. 1987, Salem House $14.95 (0-207-15474-0). A behind-the-scenes look at a Qantas flight from Australia to London. (Rev: SLJ 4/87) [338.4]

9067 Jackson, Donald Dale. *The Aeronauts* (9–12). Illus. 1980, Silver Burdett LB $24.60 (0-8094-3267-6). A history of ballooning that is part of the Epic of Flight series from Time-Life Books. [629.133]

9068 *Jane's All the World's Aircraft, 1990–1991* (10–12). Illus. 1990, Jane's Information Group $185.00 (0-7106-0908-6). This expensive large volume published annually identifies all the aircraft of various countries of the world. [629.133]

9069 Lightbody, Andy, and Joe Poyer. *The Illustrated History of Helicopters* (9–12). Illus. 1990, Publications Intl. $24.95 (0-88176-652-6). A lavishly illustrated history of helicopters with a fair amount of technical data. (Rev: BL 9/1/90) [623.746]

9070 Lindbergh, Charles A. *The Spirit of St. Louis* (10–12). 1975, Macmillan $50.00 (0-684-14421-2). An autobiographical account first published in 1954 on the first solo transatlantic flight. [629.13]

9071 Lomax, Judy. *Women of the Air* (9–12). Illus. 1987, Dodd $15.95 (0-369-08980-1); Ivy paper $3.95 (0-8041-0311-9). An account of how women have participated in the history of aviation from ballooning in the eighteenth century to present-day astronauts. (Rev: SLJ 10/87; VOYA 10/87) [629.13]

9072 Moolman, Valerie. *Women Aloft* (7–12). Illus. 1981, Silver Burdett LB $24.60 (0-8094-3288-9). A tribute to women in aeronautics from balloonists in the nineteenth century to today. [629.13]

9073 Nevin, David. *The Pathfinders* (9–12). Illus. 1980, Silver Burdett LB $24.60 (0-8095-3255-2). A history of long-distance air flights from 1909 to 1938 is part of the Epic of Flight series from Time-Life Books. A few others in the series that deal with the history of airplanes are: *The Bush Pilots, The Explorers* (both 1983), and *The Road to Kitty Hawk* (1981). [629.13]

9074 Prendergast, Curtis. *The First Aviators* (9–12). Illus. 1981, Silver Burdett LB $24.60 (0-8095-3263-3). This volume from the Time-Life series on flight traces the history of the airplane from after the Wright brothers to the beginning of World War I. Others in this series include: *Barnstormers and Speed Kings* (1980), *Flying the Mail* (1982), and *Knights of the Air* (1980). [629.13]

9075 Saint-Exupéry, Antoine de. *Wind, Sand, and Stars* (10–12). Trans. by Lewis Galantiere. Illus. 1987, Harcourt paper $3.95 (0-15-697090-2). Philosophical essays about flight first published in 1940 by the French author-aviator. [629.13]

9076 Seo, Hiroshi. *Boeing 747* (10–12). Illus. 1984, Jane's Information Group $10.95 (0-7106-0304-5). For better readers, this is a history and profile of the Boeing 747 jumbo jet airplane. (Rev: BL 4/1/85) [629.133]

9077 Stewart, Stanley. *Flying the Big Jets* (9–12). 1985, Arco $16.95 (0-668-06346-7). An experienced pilot tells what it is like to fly jumbo jets. (Rev: BR 9–10/85) [629.133]

Automobiles and Trucks

9078 *Automotive Encyclopedia* (9–12). Illus. 1989, Goodheart-Willcox $30.00 (0-87006-691-9). A frequently revised text on the basics of auto mechanics. [629.2]

9079 Billiet, Walter E. *Do-It-Yourself Automotive Maintenance and Repair* (9–12). 1979, Prentice $17.95 (0-13-217190-2); paper $7.95 (0-13-217182-1). A beginner's guide to basic automobile repair and maintenance techniques. [629.28]

9080 Black, Naomi, and Mark Smith. *America on Wheels: Tales and Trivia of the Automobile* (9–12). Illus. 1986, Morrow $15.95 (0-688-05948-1). A collection of trivia about automobiles and the men behind them. (Rev: BL 5/1/86) [629.2]

9081 Bohr, Peter, ed. *Road & Track's Used Car Classics: A Guide to Affordable Exciting Cars* (9–12). Illus. 1985, John Muir paper $12.95 (0-912528-69-9). A review of the most popular used domestic and foreign cars and why they are in demand. (Rev: BL 1/1/86) [629]

9082 Burnham, Colin. *Customizing Cars* (10–12). Illus. 1980, Arco $12.95 (0-688-04888-3); paper $8.95 (0-688-04892-1). A volume that tells how to customize ordinary cars, hot rods, and low riders. [629.28]

9083 Carley, Larry W. *Do-It-Yourself Car Care* (9–12). Illus. 1987, TAB $17.95 (0-8306-0843-5); paper $11.95 (0-8306-2143-1). A useful guide that includes tips on maintenance, tune-ups, and trouble shooting. (Rev: BL 6/15/88) [629.28]

9084 *Chilton's Auto Repair Manual, 1987–91* (7–12). Illus. 1990, Chilton $25.75 (0-8019-8032-1). A standard work that is revised frequently and covers cars built from 1987 to 1991. [629.28]

9085 Christy, Joe, and Clay Johnson. *Your Pilot's License* (10–12). 1988, TAB paper $12.95 (0-8306-2477-5). This manual covers all the skills it is necessary to master to get a pilot's license. [629.133]

9086 Consumer Guide, eds. *Consumer Guide Automobile Book: All New 1990 Edition* (9–12). Illus. 1989, NAL paper $8.95 (0-451-82214-5). This is an annual publication that gives material on models, prices, ratings, and overall value. (Rev: BL 5/1/90) [629.282]

9087 Consumer Guide, eds. *Consumer Guide to Cars, 1990* (9–12). 1990, NAL paper $4.95 (0-451-16415-6). This annual volume rates models of cars currently on the market. [629.2]

9088 Consumer Guide, eds. *Corvette: America's Sports Car* (9–12). Illus. 1989, Publications International $100.00 (0-88176-599-6). From 1953 to the present, an illustrated history of this American sports car. (Rev: BL 2/1/90) [629.222]

9089 *50 Years of American Automobiles, 1939–1989* (9–12). Illus. 1989, Publications International $49.95 (0-88176-592-9). An expensive but stunning review of automobile history that covers all makes and models plus comparative tables that deal with body styles, weight, price, and so on. (Rev: BL 11/1/89) [338.7]

9090 Flammang, James. *The Great Book of Dream Cars* (9–12). Illus. 1990, Publications International $29.95 (0-88176-685-2). Forty recent-vintage cars from both America and abroad are described and pictured. (Rev: BL 7/90) [629.22]

9091 Freeman, Kerry A., ed. *Chilton's Easy Car Care* (10–12). Illus. 1985, Chilton paper $13.95 (0-8019-7553-0). This basic volume explains how various kinds of engines work and how to maintain them. Chilton also publishes repair manuals on individual makes of cars, e.g., Datsun, Nissan. [629.28]

9092 Freeman, Kerry A., ed. *Chilton's Guide to Auto Tune-Ups and Troubleshooting* (9–12). Illus. 1983, Chilton $13.50 (0-8019-7376-7). A guide to the major automobile systems and how to keep them in good working order. [629.28]

9093 Gillis, Jack. *The Car Book* (9–12). 1990, Harper paper $9.95 (0-06-096548-7). This annual publication evaluates new car models. [629.2]

9094 Gillis, Jack. *How to Make Your Car Last Almost Forever* (9–12). Illus. 1987, Putnam paper $6.95 (0-399-51336-1). A beginner's book on car maintenance. [629.28]

9095 Gillis, Jack. *The Used Car Book 1991* (9–12). 1990, Harper paper $9.95 (0-06-096549-5). An annual guide to buying safe and reliable used cars. [629.2]

9096 Goulter, Vic, and Barbara Goulter. *How to Keep Your Car Mechanic Honest* (9–12). Illus. 1987, Stein & Day $16.95 (0-8128-3110-1); paper $7.95 (0-8128-6260-0). A guide to how a car works, what constitutes basic maintenance, and what major repairs involve. (Rev: BL 7/87) [629.28]

9097 Hensel, George. *Learn to Drive* (9–12). Illus. 1987, Warner paper $4.95 (0-446-34493-1). In addition to coverage on how to drive, this book gives pointers on how to pass the road test and tips on difficult situations such as night driving. (Rev: BL 7/87) [629.283]

9098 Hoffman, Jeffrey. *Corvette: America's Supercar* (9–12). 1990, Running Pr. $14.98 (0-89471-830-4). A slim volume about this classic car that first appeared in 1952. [629.2]

9099 Huntington, Roger. *American Supercar* (9–12). Illus. 1990, Motorbooks paper $12.95 (0-87938-464-6). This large-format book uses text and many illustrations to explore the world of the high-performance automobile. [629.2]

9100 Lyons, Pete, et al. *Ferrari: The Man and His Machines* (9–12). Illus. 1989, Publications International $15.98 (0-88176-526-0). This is the story of the famous manufacturer of automobiles and of his illustrious product. (Rev: BL 4/1/90) [629.222]

9101 McCarthy, Laura Flynn. *Your Quick & Easy Car Care and Safe Driving Handbook* (9–12). Illus. 1990, Doubleday paper $9.95 (0-385-40003-9). A concise manual on how to maintain a car, plus driving tips on how to avoid accidents. (Rev: BL 5/1/90) [629.287]

9102 Makower, Joel. *How to Buy a Used Car/ How to Sell a Used Car* (9–12). Illus. 1988, Putnam paper $7.95 (0-399-51443-0). A practical no-nonsense guide to acquiring or disposing of a used car. (Rev: BL 3/15/88) [629.222]

9103 Mateja, Jim. *Used Cars: Finding the Best Buy* (9–12). Illus. 1987, Bonus Books paper $5.95 (0-933893-27-2). A guide to locating and testing quality used cars with tips on financing and car care. (Rev: BL 3/15/87) [629.2]

9104 Murphy, Jim. *Custom Car: A Nuts-and-Bolts Guide to Creating One* (9–12). Illus. 1989, Clarion $14.95 (0-89919-272-6). Through many photographs, this book shows how a wrecked automobile was transformed into a custom car. (Rev: BR 11–12/89; SLJ 7/89) [629.2]

9105 Nader, Ralph, and Clarence Ditlow. *Lemon Book: Auto Rights* (9–12). 1990, Moyer Bell $22.50 (1-55921-020-6); paper $12.95 (1-55921-019-2). A book on how to get satisfaction after purchasing a car. (Rev: BL 3/15/90) [629.222]

9106 Neely, William, and John S. F. McCormick. *Five-Hundred-Five Automobile Questions Your Friends Can't Answer* (9–12). 1984, Walker paper $3.95 (0-8027-7212-9). A question-and-answer trivia book about famous cars and models. [629.2]

9107 Petersen Publishing Co., eds. *Petersen's Basic How to Tune Your Car* (9–12). 7th rev. ed. 1985, Green Hill paper $9.95 (0-89803-126-5). A car-care book that covers basic maintenance techniques. [629.2]

9108 Porazik, Juraj. *Old Time Classic Cars, 1885–1940* (9–12). Illus. 1985, Prentice $8.95 (0-668-06307-6). An international history of the automobile plus a detailed description of the outstanding models. (Rev: BL 3/15/85) [629.222]

9109 Ross, James R. *How to Buy a Car, 1989: A Former Car Salesman Tells All* (9–12). 1988, St. Martin's paper $3.95 (0-312-91368-8). A guide that covers all aspects of car buying from choosing a dealer to negotiating a service contract. [629.2]

9110 Sclar, Deanna. *Auto Repair for Dummies* (8–12). Rev. ed. Illus. 1988, McGraw paper $14.95 (0-07-055878-7). A basic manual now in its third edition that is noted for its clarity and completeness. (Rev: BL 3/15/89) [629.28]

9111 Sears, Brad. *Last Chance Garage* (10–12). 1984, Harper $14.95 (0-06-015309-1). This guide tells you about a car's systems—how they operate and what to do if they do not function properly. [629.2]

9112 Sports Illustrated, eds. *Sports Illustrated Safe Driving* (9–12). Illus. 1974, Harper paper $5.95 (0-397-00991-7). Through drawings and text, the basic dos and don'ts of safe driving are covered. [629.2]

9113 Stockel, Martin W., and Martin T. Stockel. *Auto Mechanics Fundamentals* (10–12). Illus. 1990, Goodheart-Willcox $24.00 (0-87006-770-2). The various systems in an automobile are discussed and their parts analyzed. [629.2]

9114 Stockel, Martin W., and Martin T. Stockel. *Auto Service and Repair* (10–12). Illus. 1984, Goodheart-Willcox $28.60 (0-87006-466-5). A guide to locating and correcting maintenance and repair problems in automobiles. [629.28]

9115 Toboldt, Bill. *Auto Body Repairing and Repainting* (10–12). Illus. 1982, Goodheart-Willcox $16.00 (0-87006-423-1). This specialized book covers auto body repairs and repainting in a step-by-step set of procedures. [629.28]

9116 Toboldt, Bill, et al., eds. *Goodheart-Willcox Automotive Encyclopedia: Fundamental Principles, Operation, Construction, Service, Repair* (9–12). Illus. 1989, Goodheart-Willcox $28.00 (0-87006-691-9). This comprehensive volume includes material on car construction and servicing. (Rev: BL 4/15/89) [629.2]

9117 Weissler, Paul. *Weekend Mechanic's Handbook: Complete Auto Repairs You Can Make* (9–12). 2nd ed. Illus. 1988, Prentice paper $16.95 (0-13-948100-1). Basic instructions are given for such procedures as tune-ups, brake jobs, and body repairs. (Rev: BL 9/15/88) [629.28]

9118 Wright, J. Patrick. *On a Clear Day You Can See General Motors: John Z. De Lorean's Look inside the Automotive Giant* (10–12). 1980, Avon paper $4.95 (0-380-51722-1). An interesting account of how one of the most important corporations in America was really managed in the 1970s. [388.3]

Cycles

9119 Jaspersohn, William. *Motorcycle: The Making of a Harley-Davidson* (9–12). 1984, Little $14.95 (0-316-45817-1). An account that tells how a motorcycle is made—from its initial design to manufacture at the plant. [629.2]

Railroads

9120 Marshall, John. *Rail—The Records* (9–12). Illus. 1989, Borgo $24.95 (0-8095-7519-1). All kinds of records are reported here on the history

and development of the world's railroads. (Rev: SLJ 4/86) [385]

Ships and Boats

9121 Greenhill, Basil. *The Evolution of the Wooden Ship* (10–12). Illus. 1989, Facts on File $24.95 (0-8160-2121-X). A history of wooden ships that concentrates on the schooners used in the mid-1850s. (Rev: BR 11–12/90; SLJ 11/89) [387.2]

9122 van der Meer, Ron, and Alan McGowan. *Sailing Ships* (8–12). Illus. 1984, Viking $18.95 (0-670-61529-3). A history of sailing ships spanning 5,000 years in many 3-dimensional illustrations and text. [623.8]

Weapons, Submarines, and the Armed Forces

9123 Angelucci, Enzo, and Peter Bowers. *The American Fighter* (10–12). Illus. 1987, Crown $40.00 (0-517-56588-9). An oversized volume that tells in text and pictures the history of U.S. fighter planes to 1985. (Rev: BL 1/1/88) [358.4]

9124 Brown, Ashley, ed. *The Green Berets: U.S. Special Forces from Vietnam to Delta Force* (10–12). Illus. 1986, Random paper $4.95 (0-394-74403-9). A history of this special service force with emphasis on its role in the Vietnam War. (Rev: VOYA 4/87) [355.3]

9125 Diagram Group. *Weapons, an International Encyclopedia from 5000 BC to 2000 AD* (9–12). 1990, St. Martin's $24.95 (0-312-03952-4); paper $16.95 (0-312-03950-6). From the clubs of cavemen to nuclear weapons, this account describes them all in pictures and text. [623.4]

9126 Gething, Michael J. *F-15 Eagle* (7–12). Illus. 1983, Arco $12.95 (0-668-05902-8). A history of the development of this unusual jet fighter plane. [623.74]

9127 Gunston, Bill. *F-111* (7–12). Illus. 1983, Arco $11.95 (0-668-05904-4). The story of the designing and building of this controversial fighter bomber. [623.74]

9128 Heatley, C. J. *Forged in Steel: U.S. Marine Corps Aviation* (10–12). Illus. 1987, Howell Pr. $37.00 (0-943231-00-0). A compilation of photos and captions of marine planes and activities associated with the Marine Corps. (Rev: BL 2/15/88) [359.96]

9129 Jordan, John. *An Illustrated Guide to the Modern US Navy* (10–12). Illus. 1983, Prentice $10.95 (0-668-85505-7). All major warships from aircraft carriers to supply vessels are covered in text and pictures. A comparison volume is: *An Illustrated Guide to the U.S. Air Force* (1982). [359.3]

9130 Kirk, John, and Aaron Klein. *Ships of the U.S. Navy* (10–12). Illus. 1987, Exeter $14.98 (0-671-08913-7). A well-illustrated account that tells about various types of ships, weapons, and the aircraft entailed. (Rev: BL 1/1/88) [359.31]

9131 Lyon, Hugh. *An Illustrated Guide to Modern Warships* (10–12). Illus. 1985, Prentice $10.95 (0-668-84966-9). A compact guide to to-

day's fighting ships with accompanying photographs. [359.3]

9132 MacPherson, Malcolm C. *Time Bomb: Fermi, Heisenberg and the Race for the Atomic Bomb* (9–12). 1987, Berkley paper $3.95 (0-425-10423-0). The story of the race on both sides of the Atlantic during World War II to develop the atomic bomb. (Rev: BR 11–12/86; VOYA 10/86) [623.4]

9133 Polmar, Norman. *Ships and Aircraft of the U.S. Fleet* (10–12). Illus. 1987, Naval Institute $29.95 (0-87021-649-X). A complete, well-illustrated volume on the present status of the U.S. Navy. (Rev: BL 4/1/88) [623.8]

9134 Walter, John. *Handgun* (10–12). Illus. 1988, David & Charles $19.95 (0-7153-9172-0). A history of handguns, the most famous models and their creators. (Rev: BL 10/15/88) [683.43]

Recreation and Sports

Crafts

General and Miscellaneous

9135 Beard, D. C. *The American Boys Handy Book: What to Do and How to Do It* (9–12). 1966, Tuttle $14.50 (0-8048-0006-5). This collection of projects and activities, though first published in 1882, still supplies lots of valuable ideas. [745]

9136 *Better Homes and Gardens Blue Ribbon Bazaar Crafts* (10–12). Illus. 1987, Meredith $21.95 (0-696-01495-5). Over 90 designs for various crafts plus information about running a bazaar. (Rev: BL 9/1/87) [745.5]

9137 *Better Homes and Gardens Country Bazaar Crafts* (9–12). Illus. 1986, Meredith paper $6.95 (0-696-01562-5). A fine collection of over 45 patterns and instructions involving such objects as toys, pillows, afghans, and other gifts. (Rev: BL 1/1/87) [745.5]

9138 Black, Penny. *The Book of Potpourri: Fragrant Flower Mixes for Scenting and Decorating the Home* (9–12). Illus. 1989, Simon & Schuster $19.95 (0-671-68210-5). How to make scented fragrances using either dry or moist methods, complete with 40 recipes and directions. (Rev: BL 10/1/89) [745.92]

9139 Black, Penny. *The Book of Pressed Flowers* (10–12). Illus. 1988, Simon & Schuster $17.95 (0-671-66071-3). A fine craft book on pressing and arranging dried flowers and other plants. (Rev: BL 6/1/88) [745.92]

9140 Brown, Rachel. *The Weaving, Spinning, and Dyeing Book* (10–12). Rev. ed. Illus. 1983, Knopf $29.95 (0-394-71595-0). Various kinds of weaving techniques and patterns are introduced through 50 different projects. [746.1]

9141 Cherry, Raymond. *Leathercrafting: Procedures and Projects* (10–12). 5th ed. Illus. 1979, Glencoe paper $13.28 (0-02-672700-5). A how-to book that explains the basics of leather work with many sample projects. [745.53]

9142 Coles, Janet, and Robert Budwig. *The Book of Beads* (9–12). Illus. 1990, Simon & Schuster $19.95 (0-671-70525-3). An excellent book with many color illustrations on the kinds and nature of various beads and techniques of beadwork. (Rev: BL 8/90) [745.58]

9143 Fife, Bruce. *Dr. Dropo's Balloon Sculpturing for Beginners* (8–12). Illus. 1988, Java paper $5.50 (0-941599-01-9). How to create all sorts of shapes using inflated balloons. (Rev: BL 9/1/88) [745.594]

9144 Jacobs, Betty E. M. *Flowers That Last Forever: Growing, Harvesting, and Preserving* (9–12). Illus. 1988, Storey Communications $21.95 (0-88266-540-5); paper $9.95 (0-88266-518-9). An extensive guide to drying flowers and making tasteful arrangements of the finished product. (Rev: BL 11/15/88) [635.9]

9145 Johnson, Kay. *Canework* (9–12). Illus. 1987, Dryad $19.95 (0-8521-9606-7). Arranged from the simple to the more complex, this guide gives instructions on how to make such items as placemats and baskets. (Rev: BL 2/1/87) [746.41]

9146 MacLennan, Jennifer. *Simple Puppets You Can Make* (8–12). Illus. 1988, Sterling $17.95 (0-8069-6816-8). Instructions are given on how to make 3 different kinds of puppets with easily found materials. (Rev: BL 5/1/88) [745.592]

9147 Meilach, Dona Z. *Contemporary Batik and Tie-Dye: Methods, Inspiration, Dyes* (10–12). Illus. 1973, Crown paper $7.95 (0-517-50089-2).

Design ideas and techniques are both presented in this guide to batik and tie dyeing. [746.6]

9148 Musheno, Elizabeth J. *Fast and Easy Home Decorating* (10–12). Illus. 1986, St. Martin's paper $11.95 (0-312-28469-1). Using a dictionary approach, this is a useful guide to decorating a new home or remodeling an old one. (Rev: BL 8/86) [645]

9149 Oster, Maggie. *Gifts and Crafts from the Garden* (9–12). Illus. 1988, Rodale $19.95 (0-87857-775-0). Over 100 projects like wreathmaking, all involving the use of dried plants and flowers. (Rev: BL 11/15/88) [745.92]

9150 Reader's Digest, eds. *Reader's Digest Crafts & Hobbies* (9–12). Illus. 1979, Reader's Digest $23.95 (0-89577-063-6). Information on 37 popular crafts including leatherwork, jewelry making, and bookbinding. [745.5]

9151 Thompson, George L. *Rubber Stamps and How to Make Them* (9–12). 1982, Pantheon paper $5.95 (0-394-71124-6). This unusual hobby of rubber stamp making is well introduced with many interesting examples. [745.5]

9152 Time-Life Books, eds. *Working with Metal* (10–12). Illus. 1990, Silver Burdett LB $20.60 (0-8094-7388-7). With many illustrations and clear text, this volume covers the basic terms, tools, and practices in metalworking. Part of Time-Life's Home Repair and Improvement series. [684]

9153 Tomalin, Stefany. *Beads! Make Your Own Unique Jewelry* (9–12). Illus. 1989, David & Charles $19.95 (0-7153-9105-4). A guide to all sorts of stones and how to use them in making jewelry. (Rev: BL 6/15/89) [745.594]

9154 von Bornstedt, Marianne, and Ulla Prytz. *Folding Table Napkins* (10–12). Illus. 1979, Sterling paper $6.95 (0-8069-8974-2). This short book gives many examples of distinctive ways to fold both cloth and paper napkins. [642]

9155 Wiley, Jack, and Suzanne L. Cheatle. *Dynamite Kites: 30 Plans to Build and Fly* (8–12). Illus. 1988, TAB paper $8.95 (0-8306-2969-6). From very easy to more complex, there are full directions to create 30 kites. (Rev: BL 9/1/88) [629.133]

American Historical Crafts

9156 Yeager, Carole. *Yankee Folk Crafts* (9–12). Illus. 1988, Yankee Books $19.95 (0-89909-164-4). A series of 60 designs and detailed instruc-

tions for many objects first made by settlers in New England. (Rev: BL 1/15/89) [745]

Calligraphy

9157 Biegeleisen, J. I. *The ABC of Lettering* (10–12). 5th ed. Illus. 1976, Harper paper $7.95 (0-06-464079-5). This book shows many different alphabets and gives advice on supplies and techniques. [745.6]

9158 Butterworth, Emma Macalik. *The Complete Book of Calligraphy* (10–12). Illus. 1980, Harper $15.00 (0-690-01852-5); paper $6.95 (0-06-463595-3). The author begins with materials needed and moves on to basic techniques. [745.6]

9159 Lawther, Gail, and Christopher Lawther. *You Can Learn Lettering and Calligraphy* (10–12). Illus. 1987, North Light $15.95 (0-89134-215-X). An easily followed guide for the beginner that gives 11 alphabets plus many other examples. (Rev: BL 1/15/88) [745.6]

9160 Sassoon, Rosemary. *The Practical Guide to Calligraphy* (10–12). 1982, Norton paper $9.25 (0-500-27251-4). A useful guide to calligraphy, from England. [745.6]

9161 Shepherd, Margaret. *Learning Calligraphy: A Book of Lettering, Design and History* (10–12). Illus. 1978, Macmillan paper $11.95 (0-02-015550-6). Basic material on calligraphy is logically presented in this volume that is continued in *Using Calligraphy* (1979). [745.6]

Clay, Modeling, and Ceramic Crafts

9162 Cosentino, Peter. *The Encyclopedia of Pottery Techniques* (10–12). Illus. 1990, Running Pr. $24.95 (0-89471-892-4). Through many color illustrations, both the finished product and step-by-step instructions on how to create pottery are covered. (Rev: BL 9/15/90) [738]

9163 Frith, Donald E. *Mold Making for Ceramics* (10–12). Illus. 1985, Chilton $60.00 (0-8019-7359-7). A very expensive book covering the entire field of mold making in ceramics, complete with many line drawings and color photographs. (Rev: BR 3–4/86) [666]

9164 Hopper, Robin. *The Ceramic Spectrum: A Simplified Approach to Glaze & Color Development* (10–12). Illus. 1984, Chilton $42.00 (0-8019-7275-2). This is a complete guide to the glazing process in ceramic making. [738.1]

9165 Kenny, John B. *The Complete Book of Pottery Making* (7–12). 2nd ed. Illus. 1976, Chilton paper $17.95 (0-8019-5933-0). In easily followed instructions with many photographs, the steps in pottery making are outlined. [738.1]

9166 Nelson, Glenn C. *Ceramics: A Potter's Handbook* (10–12). Illus. 1984, Holt paper $25.50 (0-03-063227-7). A basic how-to guide for both the beginning and experienced potter. [738.1]

Costume Making, Dress, and Fashion

9167 Bond, David. *Guinness Guide to 20th Century Fashion* (10–12). Illus. 1988, Sterling $24.95 (0-85112-356-2). A chronological guide to clothing and hairdos from 1900 through the 1980s. (Rev: SLJ 7/89) [391]

9168 Jackson, Sheila. *Costumes for the Stage: A Complete Handbook for Every Type of Play* (9–12). Illus. 1988, New Amsterdam paper $11.95 (0-941533-36-0). A manual for junior and senior high students on creating costumes for their productions. [792]

9169 Lister, Margot. *Costume: An Illustrated Survey from Ancient Times to the Twentieth Century* (9–12). Illus. 1968, Plays $24.95 (0-8238-0096-2). A survey of dress from ancient times to 1914 with hints on how to make many of these costumes. [391]

9170 Molloy, John T. *Dress for Success* (10–12). 1984, Warner paper $7.95 (0-446-38263-9). A guide to creating a wardrobe that will help you succeed in life. [646]

9171 Nunn, Joan. *Fashion in Costume, 1200–1980* (10–12). Illus. 1984, Schocken $20.95 (0-8052-3905-7). A description in text and pictures to what people wore in Europe and America from the late Middle Ages to the present. [391]

9172 O'Donnol, Shirley Miles. *American Costume, 1915–1970: A Source Book for the Stage Costumer* (9–12). Illus. 1982, Indiana Univ. Pr. $35.00 (0-253-30589-6); paper $15.00 (0-253-20543-3). A nicely illustrated guide to twentieth-century fashion that emphasizes women's clothes. [792]

9173 Wallach, Janet. *Working Wardrobe: Affordable Clothes That Work for You* (10–12). Illus. 1987, Warner paper $11.95 (0-446-38757-6). A practical guide for girls on how to build an attractive and affordable wardrobe. [646]

9174 Wilcox, R. Turner. *The Dictionary of Costume* (7–12). Illus. 1969, Macmillan LB $50.00 (0-684-15150-2). First published in 1969, this book describes in words and drawings over 3,000 articles of clothing. [391]

9175 Wilcox, R. Turner. *Five Centuries of American Costume* (9–12). Illus. 1963, Macmillan $27.50 (0-684-15161-8). Arranged in chronological order, this is a description of what people wore in America from the Vikings to 1960. [391]

9176 Wilcox, R. Turner. *Folk and Festival Costume of the World* (9–12). Illus. 1965, Macmillan $50.00 (0-684-15379-3). An illustrated survey of folk costumes around the world. [391]

9177 Worrell, Estelle A. *Children's Costume in America, 1607–1910* (9–12). Illus. 1980, Macmillan $30.00 (0-684-16645-3). All forms of children's attire and accessories are described and illustrated in this account that covers 300 years of our history. [391]

9178 Yarwood, Doreen. *The Encyclopedia of World Costume* (9–12). Illus. 1986, Crown $14.98 (0-517-61943-1). A guide to dress from ancient times to the present in text and more than 2,000 drawings. [391]

9179 Zamkoff, Bernard, and Jeanne Price. *Basic Pattern Skills for Fashion Design* (10–12). Illus. 1987, Fairchild $17.50 (0-87005-570-4). For beginning fashion design students this is a fine introduction to pattern design. (Rev: BL 4/15/88) [746.9]

Drawing and Painting

9180 Abling, Bina. *Fashion Sketchbook* (10–12). Illus. 1987, Fairchild $16.50 (0-87005-562-3). An excellent beginner's guide to both fashion design and fashion illustration. (Rev: BL 3/15/88) [741.672]

9181 Bagnall, Brian. *Creative Drawing and Painting* (9–12). Illus. 1987, Writer's Digest $29.95 (0-89134-177-3). An illustrated basic guide to the media used in art and the components like composition and perspective that are found in drawings and paintings. (Rev: BL 5/15/87; SLJ 9/87) [741.2]

9182 Bolognese, Don, and Elaine Raphael. *Pencil* (7–12). Illus. 1986, Watts LB $10.90 (0-531-10134-7). For the better artist, a manual that describes the tools and techniques used in pencil drawing. Also use: *Pen & Ink* and *Charcoal & Pastel* (both 1986). (Rev: BR 9–10/86; SLJ 10/86) [741.2]

9183 Bro, Lu. *Drawing: A Studio Guide* (10–12). Illus. 1979, Norton paper $14.95 (0-393-95018-2). A practical guide to the techniques of drawing in a studio setting. [741.2]

9184 Browning, Colleen. *Working Out a Painting* (9–12). Illus. 1988, Watson-Guptill $27.50 (0-8230-2994-8). Using many examples from her own art, the author supplies a fine introduction to painting figures in oils. (Rev: BL 1/1/89) [751.45]

9185 Clark, Roberta C. *How to Paint Living Portraits* (10–12). Illus. 1990, North Light $27.95 (0-89134-326-1). A guide with many illustrations on how to do portraits in various media such as watercolor, oil, and charcoal. (Rev: BL 9/1/90) [751.45]

9186 Couch, Tony. *Watercolor: You Can Do It!* (9–12). Illus. 1987, North Light $25.95 (0-89134-188-9). A lucid step-by-step manual on the materials and techniques involved in watercolor painting. (Rev: BL 6/15/87) [751.42]

9187 Crespo, Michael. *Watercolor Day by Day* (9–12). Illus. 1987, Watson-Guptill $27.50 (0-8230-5668-6). Organized like a daily course, this manual starts with the basics and moves to more advanced material. (Rev: BL 5/15/87) [751.42]

9188 De Reyna, Rudy. *How to Draw What You See* (10–12). Illus. 1972, Watson-Guptill $16.95 (0-8230-1460-6). Using basic shapes such as the cube and cone, the author shows how to draw using various media. [741.2]

9189 Gerberg, Mort. *The Arbor House Book of Cartooning* (7–12). Illus. 1983, Arbor $16.95 (0-87795-372-4); paper $8.95 (0-87795-399-6). In addition to instructions on how to cartoon, this guide tells you how to submit and sell your product to a variety of sources. [741.5]

9190 Gerberg, Mort. *Cartooning: The Art and the Business* (9–12). Rev. ed. Illus. 1989, Morrow paper $14.45 (1-557-10017-9). In addition to basic techniques, this book shows how styles differ within the medium (e.g., comics, children's books) and how to sell the finished product. (Rev: BL 3/15/89) [741.5]

9191 Gordon, Louise. *How to Draw the Human Figure: An Anatomical Approach* (7–10). Illus. 1979, Penguin paper $8.95 (0-14-046477-8). This

is both a short course on anatomy and a fine manual on how to draw the human body. [743]

9192 Graves, Douglas R. *Drawing Portraits* (10–12). Illus. 1974, Watson-Guptill paper $14.95 (0-8230-1431-2). An excellent guide to portraiture that covers such topics as posing positions, lighting, and drawing faces and hands. [743]

9193 Hayes, Colin. *The Complete Guide to Painting and Drawing* (10–12). Illus. 1979, Mayflower $15.98 (0-8137-1615-0). Using more than 600 illustrations, the author describes drawing and painting from the basic materials and stretching the canvas to the final framing. [741.2]

9194 Hebblewhite, Ian. *Northlight Handbook of Artists' Materials* (10–12). Illus. 1986, Writer's Digest $24.95 (0-89134-176-5). An exhaustive compilation of material on the quality of such artists' tools as paints, inks, brushes, pens, and other instruments. (Rev: SLJ 5/87) [741.2]

9195 Henning, Fritz. *Drawing & Painting with Ink* (10–12). Illus. 1986, North Light $24.95 (0-89134-175-7). Following a discussion of materials, the author gives detailed information and illustrations on a variety of techniques and skills. (Rev: BL 4/15/87) [760]

9196 Hill, Adrian. *The Beginner's Book of Oil Painting* (9–12). 1986, Blandford paper $7.95 (0-7137-1743-2). A practical manual that deals with such areas as faces, landscapes, animals, and buildings. Also use *The Beginner's Book of Watercolour Painting* (1986). (Rev: BR 11–12/86) [741]

9197 Hoff, Syd. *The Art of Cartooning* (9–12). Illus. 1973, Stravon Educ. Pr. $16.95 (0-87396--072-6). A helpful guide for the novice cartoonist by a master. [741.5]

9198 Hutton-Jamieson, Iain. *Colored Pencil Drawing Techniques* (9–12). Illus. 1986, North Light $22.95 (0-89134-147-1). An excellent how-to guide that covers such subjects as materials, composition, pencil strokes, and blending of colors. (Rev: BL 1/15/87; SLJ 3/87) [741.24]

9199 Johnson, Cathy. *Drawing and Painting from Nature* (10–12). Illus. 1989, TAB $27.95 (0-8306-5502-6). After a general discussion of media and use of different surfaces, the author has separate chapters on such subjects as trees and flowers. (Rev: BR 1–2/90; VOYA 2/90) [741]

9200 Lee, Stan, and John Buscema. *How to Draw Comics the Marvel Way* (9–12). 1984, Simon & Schuster paper $10.95 (0-671-53077-1). Step-by-step instructions are given for drawing cartoons like the Hulk and the Thing. [741.5]

9201 McKenzie, Alan. *How to Draw and Sell Comic Strips for Newspapers and Comic Books* (9–12). Illus. 1987, Writer's Digest $18.95 (0-89134-214-1). In addition to giving detailed instructions with examples on how to draw comics, the author gives a history of comics and tells students how to sell their products. (Rev: SLJ 4/88) [741.5]

9202 Magnus, Günter Hugo. *Graphic Techniques for Designers and Illustrators* (10–12). Illus. 1986, Barron's $21.95 (0-8120-5466-0). With many illustrations, Magnus supplies an excellent guide to commercial art and design. (Rev: BL 1/1/87) [741.6]

9203 Maiotti, Etorri. *The Pastel Handbook* (9–12). Illus. 1988, Crown $11.95 (0-517-56306-1). The materials and techniques for producing portraits, figure studies, still lifes, and landscapes are all included in this book. (Rev: SLJ 2/89; VOYA 2/89) [741.2]

9204 Meyer, Susan E., and Martim Avillez. *How to Draw in Pen and Ink* (9–12). Illus. 1985, Macmillan paper $12.95 (0-02-011920-8). A beginner's book that starts with materials and basic exercises and then moves into more complicated subjects like composition and perspective. (Rev: BL 11/15/85) [741.26]

9205 Morgan, Jacqui. *Watercolor for Illustration* (10–12). Illus. 1986, Watson-Guptill $24.95 (0-8230-5658-9). A commercial watercolorist shows techniques for those who want to become professionals. (Rev: BL 12/1/86) [751.42]

9206 Nicolaides, Kimon. *The Natural Way to Draw: A Working Plan for Art Study* (10–12). Illus. 1990, Houghton paper $8.95 (0-395-53007-5). Using illustrations from both old masters and students, this book demonstrates drawing basics. [741.2]

9207 Petrie, Ferdinand, and John Shaw. *The Big Book of Painting Nature in Watercolor* (10–12). Illus. 1990, Watson-Guptill paper $29.95 (0-8230-0499-6). This book contains 135 separate lessons on techniques of painting subjects from nature using watercolors. (Rev: BL 9/1/90) [751.42]

9208 Ranson, Ron. *Water-Color Painting* (10–12). Illus. 1985, Sterling $14.95 (0-7137-1096-8). A simple introduction to water-color painting that conveys enthusiasm and love for this art form. (Rev: BR 5–6/86) [741]

9209 Richardson, John Adkins. *The Complete Book of Cartooning* (9–12). Illus. 1977, Prentice paper $12.95 (0-13-157586-4). An introduction to the art of cartooning, its styles, and techniques. [741.5]

9210 Robb, Tom. *Pack Up and Sketch* (9–12). Illus. 1987, Knopf $7.95 (0-394-74971-5). A practical handbook that explains the elements of drawing using a variety of media. (Rev: VOYA 6/87) [741]

9211 Ross, Al. *Cartooning Fundamentals* (9–10). Illus. 1977, Stravon Educ. Pr. $16.95 (0-87396-080-7). Using his own cartoons as examples, Ross explains the fundamentals of cartooning. [741.5]

9212 Sarnoff, Bob. *Cartoons and Comics: Ideas and Techniques* (9–12). Illus. 1988, Davis $18.95 (0-87192-202-9). A basic handbook with plenty of examples to help the novice. (Rev: BL 3/15/89) [741.5]

9213 Smith, Ray. *The Artist's Handbook* (10–12). Illus. 1987, Knopf $24.95 (0-394-55585-6). A basic manual and guide to all forms of art techniques from etching to oil painting. (Rev: BL 3/15/88) [760]

9214 Smith, Ray. *How to Draw and Paint What You See* (10–12). Illus. 1984, Knopf $24.95 (0-394-72484-4). A comprehensive volume that covers drawing and painting in a variety of media including oil, acrylic, and watercolor. [750]

9215 Tate, Elizabeth. *The North Light Illustrated Book of Painting Techniques* (9–12). Illus. 1986, Writer's Digest $27.95 (0-89134-148-X). An alphabetically arranged guide to over 40 painting techniques explained in both text and illustrations. (Rev: BL 4/1/87; SLJ 3/87) [708]

9216 Vallejo, Boris. *Fantasy Art Techniques* (9–12). Illus. 1985, Arco $21.95 (0-668-06234-7). A portfolio of color reproductions of paintings created by Vallejo to illustrate works of fantasy plus a description of the techniques used. (Rev: SLJ 5/86) [070.5]

9217 Woods, Michael. *Starting Pencil Drawing* (9–12). Illus. 1988, Dryad $19.95 (0-8521-9679-2). A beginner's guide that covers all aspects of drawing with excellent illustrative examples. (Rev: BL 4/15/88) [741.2]

Masks and Mask Making

9218 Sivin, Carole. *Maskmaking* (9–12). Illus. 1987, Davis $18.95 (0-87192-178-2). A history of maskmaking plus the techniques and materials needed to create your own. (Rev: BL 3/1/87) [731.75]

9219 Smith, Dick. *Dick Smith's Do-It-Yourself Monster Make-Up Handbook* (9–12). Illus. 1985,

Imagine, Inc. paper $10.95 (0-911137-02-5). An Academy Award-winning makeup artist tells how to create several monster disguises and supplies photographs of the finished products. (Rev: BL 11/1/85) [792.027]

Paper Crafts

9220 Ayture-Scheele, Zulal. *The Great Origami Book* (9–12). Illus. 1987, Sterling $19.95 (0-8069-6060-9); paper $10.95 (0-8069-6640-8). In easy-to-follow instructions and many illustrations, directions for folding 8 basic forms and 40 figures are given. (Rev: BL 11/15/87) [736]

9221 Bodger, Lorraine. *Gift Wraps* (9–12). Illus. 1985, Harper paper $5.95 (0-06-091240-5). In addition to material on how to create bows and wrap presents effectively, this book tells how to make one's own wraps. (Rev: BL 1/15/86) [745.54]

9222 Hawcock, David. *Paper Dinosaurs* (8–12). Illus. 1988, Sterling paper $12.95 (0-8069-6890-7). How to make a total of 20 of the most popular dinosaurs from paper. (Rev: BL 12/1/88; SLJ 1/89) [745.592]

9223 Kitagawa, Yoshiko. *Creative Cards: Wrap a Message with a Personal Touch* (8–12). Illus. 1987, Kodansha $14.95 (0-87011-818-8). A guide to production of one's own greeting cards from 48 easily followed designs. (Rev: BL 1/15/88) [745.594]

9224 Kline, Richard. *The Ultimate Paper Airplane* (9–12). Illus. 1985, Simon & Schuster paper $8.85 (0-671-55551-0). A new concept in airplane design is shown in this paper airplane and 7 variations. (Rev: BL 9/1/85) [745.592]

Printmaking

9225 Ross, John, et al. *The Complete Printmaker: Techniques, Traditions, Innovations* (9–12). Rev. ed. Illus. 1989, Free Pr. $45.00 (0-02-927371-4). A thorough introduction to various kinds of printmaking, necessary techniques, and the printmaking business—all well illustrated. (Rev: BL 1/15/90) [760]

Sewing and Needle Crafts

9226 *The Arco Guide to Knitting Stitches* (9–12). Illus. 1985, Arco $12.95 (0-668-06389-0). More than 500 stitches from the basic to the esoteric are described in words and pictures with details on when to use them. (Rev: BL 5/1/85) [746.43]

9227 *Basic Guide to Dressmaking: How to Sew Successful Clothes* (10–12). Illus. 1985, Arco $12.95 (0-668-06298-3). A basic guide that begins with understanding patterns and continues into such techniques as putting in fasteners. [646.4]

9228 *Better Homes and Gardens American Patchwork & Quilting* (9–12). Illus. 1985, Meredith $24.95 (0-696-01015-1). An excellent handbook on both patchwork and quilting with easy instructions and over 160 designs. (Rev: BL 11/1/85) [746.46]

9229 *Better Homes and Gardens America's Best Cross-Stitch* (10–12). Illus. 1988, Meredith $21.95 (0-696-01625-7). A fine handbook with well-illustrated projects at a variety of difficulty levels. (Rev: BL 6/1/88) [746.44]

9230 *Better Homes and Gardens Knitting & Crocheting* (9–12). Illus. 1986, Meredith $24.95 (0-696-01445-9). A collection of 100 standard patterns with clear instructions and color photographs. (Rev: BL 8/86) [746.43]

9231 *Better Homes and Gardens Patchwork & Quilting* (7–12). Illus. 1977, Meredith $6.95 (0-696-00175-6). Such patchwork projects as placemats, tablecloths, and quilts are outlined in a step-by-step approach. [746.46]

9232 *Better Homes and Gardens Traditional American Crafts* (8–12). Illus. 1988, Meredith $19.95 (0-696-01530-7). Over 120 projects using such crafts as rugmaking, crocheting, and patchwork are outlined plus an overview of the nature of traditional crafts. (Rev: BL 1/1/89) [745.5]

9233 Colton, Virginia, ed. *Reader's Digest Complete Guide to Needlework* (10–12). Illus. 1979, Reader's Digest $24.95 (0-89577-059-8). From applique to rug making, 10 different needlecrafts are presented. [746.4]

9234 *The Complete Book of Needlecrafts* (9–12). Illus. 1990, Chilton paper $25.00 (0-8019-8081-X). All kinds of needlecrafts are featured, from rug hooking to embroidery, and many different projects are outlined from easy to difficult. (Rev: BL 6/1/90) [746.44]

9235 Curl, Sue, and Erika Knight. *Knit 4 Seasons* (10–12). Illus. 1987, Macmillan $22.50 (0-684-18791-4). A total of 36 patterns are given and rated for difficulty with each related to a season. (Rev: BL 3/1/88) [746.9]

9236 Dodson, Jackie. *Know Your Sewing Machine* (9–12). Illus. 1988, Chilton paper $12.95 (0-8019-7810-6). In addition to explaining the parts and the uses of the sewing machine, this book outlines many projects using the techniques described. (Rev: SLJ 2/89) [646.2]

9237 Don, Sarah. *Traditional Samplers* (9–12). Illus. 1986, Viking $16.95 (0-670-80732-X). After giving a general history of sampler art, the author gives 22 designs based on old patterns. (Rev: BL 9/15/85) [746.44]

9238 Erickson, Mary Anne, and Eve Cohen. *Knitting by Design: A Step-by-Step Guide to Designing and Knitting Your Own Clothes* (9–12). Illus. 1986, Bantam paper $14.95 (0-553-34271-1). An easy-to-understand guide to knitting basics—from needles to finished product—plus 31 patterns. (Rev: BL 1/1/87) [746.9]

9239 Frank, Agnes, and Linda Stokes. *Quilting for Beginners: Patchwork & Appliqué Projects for all Ages* (10–12). Illus. 1986, Main Street $22.50 (0-915590-73-5); paper $14.95 (0-915590-72-7). Complete with 20 projects, this is an excellent step-by-step guide for the novice. (Rev: BL 4/15/86) [746.46]

9240 Goldsworthy, Maureen. *Mend It!* (10–12). 1980, Scarborough $10.95 (0-8128-2695-7); paper $5.95 (0-8128-6046-2). This is a simple-to-use guide to clothes repair. [646]

9241 Hiatt, June Hemmons. *The Principles of Knitting: Methods and Techniques of Hand Knitting* (10–12). Illus. 1989, Simon & Schuster $29.95 (0-671-55233-3). A comprehensive overview of all sorts of knitting techniques with many explanatory drawings. (Rev: BL 4/1/89) [746.9]

9242 Ladbury, Ann. *The Sewing Book: A Complete Practical Guide* (9–12). Illus. 1985, Exeter $12.98 (0-671-07577-2). Everything that a beginner needs to know including how to run a sewing machine and details of dressmaking. (Rev: BL 3/1/86) [646.2]

9243 Leinhauser, Jean, and Rita Weiss. *The 7-Day Afghan Book* (9–12). Illus. 1985, Sterling $19.95 (0-8069-5708-5). Fifty designs are presented, any one of which the authors claim can be knitted in 7 days. (Rev: BL 10/15/85) [746.43]

9244 Ligon, Linda, ed. *Homespun, Handknit: Caps, Socks, Mittens, and Gloves* (10–12). Illus. 1987, Interweave paper $15.00 (0-934026-26-2). Simple enough for the beginner, this includes many styles for various age groups. (Rev: BL 2/15/88) [746.9]

9245 McClun, Diana, and Laura Nownes. *Quilts! Quilts! Quilts! The Complete Guide to Quiltmaking* (10–12). Illus. 1988, Quilt Digest paper $19.95 (0-913327-16-6). A very practical, uncomplicated guide to quilting that gives both basic and advanced information. (Rev: BL 2/1/89) [746.9]

9246 Martin, Peigi, and Susan Young. *Patchwork Made Easy* (9–12). Illus. 1988, Sterling $19.95 (0-8069-6882-6); paper $9.95 (0-8069-6860-5). Twenty designs are introduced with their use to create such objects as aprons, quilts, and tea cozies. (Rev: BL 12/1/88) [746.46]

9247 Matthews, Anne. *Vogue Dictionary of Knitting Stitches* (10–12). Illus. 1985, Morrow $17.95 (0-688-04687-8); paper $14.95 (0-688-04688-6). With excellent illustrations and text, the author gives explanations for every stitch used by needleworkers. (Rev: BL 9/1/85) [746.432]

9248 Ormrod, Audrey. *Exploring Cross-Stitch* (9–12). Illus. 1988, Wallace-Homestead paper $16.95 (0-87069-515-0). Dozens of patterns are introduced from variations on the cross-stitch. (Rev: BL 9/15/88) [746.44]

9249 Reader's Digest, eds. *Reader's Digest Complete Guide to Sewing* (7–12). Illus. 1976, Reader's Digest $23.95 (0-89577-026-1). Basic techniques in sewing are introduced plus a number of projects. [646.2]

9250 Ryan, Mildred Graves. *The Complete Encyclopedia of Stitchery* (7–12). Illus. 1979, NAL paper $9.95 (0-452-25384-5). "Stitchery" involves 7 types including crocheting, needlepoint, embroidery, knitting, and rugmaking. [746.4]

9251 *Sew It Yourself Home Decorating: Creative Ideas for Beautiful Interiors* (9–12). 1986, Prentice paper $14.95. A helpful guide with more than 40 designs to craft projects for every room in the house. (Rev: BL 6/1/85) [646.2]

9252 Seward, Linda. *The Complete Book of Patchwork, Quilting and Appliqué* (8–12). Illus. 1989, Prentice paper $18.95 (0-13-157694-1). A comprehensive guide to the basics of these needle crafts; includes excellent illustrations. (Rev: BL 8/89) [746.46]

9253 Seward, Linda. *Small Quilting Projects* (10–12). Illus. 1988, Sterling $19.95 (0-8069-6740-4). A guide to 21 quilting projects that are basic enough for even a beginner. (Rev: BL 4/1/88) [746.46]

9254 Shaeffer, Claire B. *Sew a Beautiful Gift* (9–12). Illus. 1986, Sterling paper $12.95 (0-8069-6314-X). Simple directions are given for making 150 different gifts, most of which can be made in less than 2 hours. (Rev: BR 1–2/87; SLJ 12/86) [646]

9255 Singer Sewing Company. *Sewing for Style: Details and Techniques beyond the Basics* (10–12). Illus. 1985, Cy De Cosse $16.95 (0-86573-207-8); paper $12.95 (0-86573-208-6). In this continuation of *Sewing Essentials* (1984), more difficult techniques like making pockets and linings are discussed in text and shown in many photographs. (Rev: BR 9–10/86; SLJ 2/86) [646.2]

9256 Stiles, Phyllis, ed. *Not Just Another Embroidery Book* (10–12). Illus. 1988, Lark Books paper $19.95 (0-937274-23-2). An introduction to embroidery that stresses creativity. (Rev: BL 12/1/88) [746.44]

9257 *Timesaving Sewing* (10–12). Illus. 1987, Contemporary $14.95 (0-86573-215-9); paper $11.95 (0-86573-216-7). A fine guide to time-saving techniques from shopping for fabrics to producing dresses, draperies, and place mats. (Rev: BL 1/15/88) [646.2]

9258 Vogue and Butterick Patterns, eds. *The Vogue/Butterick Step-by-Step Guide to Sewing Techniques* (9–12). Illus. 1989, Prentice $24.95 (0-13-944125-5). A complete handbook that covers topics from appliqués to zippers in 47 illustrated separate sections. (Rev: BL 11/1/89) [646.2]

9259 *The Vogue Sewing Book* (9–12). Illus. 1987, Wehman Bros. $34.95 (0-685-70732-6). An easily understood manual with coverage for both the novice and the expert. [646.4]

9260 Zieman, Nancy, and Robbie Fanning. *The Busy Woman's Sewing Book* (9–12). Rev. ed. Illus. 1988, Open Chain $16.25 (0-932086-02-0); paper $9.95 (0-932086-03-9). Sewing basics are covered in a time-efficient mode. Well-illustrated. (Rev: BL 5/1/88) [646.2]

Toys and Dolls

9261 Forde, Terry. *Fun-to-Make Wooden Toys* (10–12). Illus. 1986, Sterling paper $9.95 (0-8069-6378-6). For the woodworking hobbyist, here is a clearly written, easy-to-follow set of projects. (Rev: BL 10/15/87) [694]

9262 *101 Soft Toys: Fun to Make Toys for Children & Babies* (9–12). Illus. 1985, Arco $18.95 (0-668-06248-7). Clear instructions and fine diagrams characterize this manual on how to make some lovable toys. (Rev: BL 6/1/85; BR 9–10/85) [745.592]

9263 Taylor, E. J. *Dollmaking* (9–12). Illus. 1988, Workman paper $9.95 (0-89480-311-5). Using basic materials and simple techniques, the reader is instructed on how to create 7 basic types of dolls. (Rev: BL 3/1/88) [745.592]

9264 Wakefield, David. *How to Make Animated Toys* (9–12). Illus. 1987, Sterling paper $12.95 (0-943822-94-7). A how-to guide to making toys with movable parts such as a hopping kangaroo. (Rev: BL 2/1/87) [745.592]

Woodworking and Carpentry

9265 *Better Homes and Gardens Woodworking Projects You Can Build* (10–12). 1980, Meredith paper $6.95 (0-696-01385-1). With simple instructions, this manual offers 60 projects including tables, cabinets, and chairs. [684]

9266 Blandford, Percy W. *24 Table Saw Projects* (10–12). Illus. 1988, TAB paper $6.95 (0-8306-2964-5). Step-by-step instructions on how to make such items as cabinets and benches. (Rev: BL 5/1/88) [684]

9267 Brann, Donald R. *How to Build Outdoor Projects* (10–12). 1981, Easi-Bild paper $9.95 (0-87733-807-8). Easily followed directions are given to build all sorts of outdoor furniture. [684]

9268 Capotosto, Rosario. *Woodworking Projects for the Home Workshop* (9–12). Illus. 1988, Sterling paper $16.95 (0-8069-6888-5). Techniques in woodworking are introduced along with several projects that range from the simple to complicated. (Rev: SLJ 5/89) [684]

9269 Chaffin, Casey, and Nick Engler. *Projects for the Router* (10–12). Illus. 1988, Sterling paper $9.95 (0-8069-6680-7). About 20 projects, such as cabinet-making, that use the router are detailed. (Rev: BL 6/1/88) [684]

9270 Cliffe, Roger W. *Woodworker's Handbook* (9–12). Illus. 1990, Sterling paper $19.95 (0-8069-7238-6). A basic introduction to woodworking techniques and tools as well as instructions for 25 different projects. (Rev: BL 4/15/90) [684]

9271 Crabb, Tom. *Band Saw Projects* (8–12). Illus. 1988, Sterling paper $9.95 (0-8069-6718-8). An introduction to the band saw plus 25 projects from chests to wind chimes. (Rev: BL 9/1/88) [684]

9272 De Cristoforo, R. J. *The Table Saw Book* (10–12). Illus. 1988, TAB $23.95 (0-8306-7789-5); paper $15.95 (0-8306-2789-8). An introduction to the table saw, the various types of cuts it can produce, and how to select and use one. (Rev: BL 5/1/88) [684]

9273 Demske, Dick. *Carpentry and Woodworking* (10–12). 1984, Creative Homeowner paper $8.95 (0-932944-62-0). An introduction to woodworking is given plus directions for 20 projects. [684]

9274 Erickson, Jon. *Build Your Own Kit House* (10–12). Illus. 1988, TAB $22.95 (0-8306-7873-5); paper $14.95 (0-8306-7873-8). A step-by-step manual on how to prepare sites, construct prefab houses, and subcontract for specialized work. (Rev: BL 4/15/89) [690]

9275 Higginbotham, Bill. *Whittling* (10–12). 1982, Sterling paper $9.95 (0-8069-7598-9). An introduction to this folk art is given plus 32 patterns for projects. [684]

9276 Jacobson, James A. *Making Small Wooden Boxes* (7–12). Illus. 1986, Sterling paper $10.95 (0-8069-6290-9). This book gives detailed instructions for 42 projects at various levels of difficulty. (Rev: BR 11–12/86) [687]

9277 Jones, Bernard E., ed. *The Complete Woodworker* (10–12). Illus. 1980, Ten Speed $14.95 (0-89815-034-5); paper $8.95 (0-89815-022-1). In this classic (1917) book, hand tools only are used to create a number of useful objects. [684]

9278 Key, Ray. *Woodturning: A Designer's Notebook* (9–12). Illus. 1987, Sterling paper $12.95 (0-8069-6566-5). A beginner's manual on the machines and techniques of woodturning with many projects on how to make useful objects. (Rev: BL 10/15/87) [745.51]

9279 Maguire, Byron W. *Cabinetmaking: From Design to Finish* (10–12). Illus. 1986, Prentice $35.00 (0-13-109794-6). Written for shop classes, this is a manual that explains all the procedures one must master to build a cabinet. (Rev: BL 5/15/86) [684.1]

9280 Marlow, A. W. *Classic Furniture Projects* (10–12). 1979, Scarborough paper $9.95 (0-8128-6034-9). A step-by-step approach is outlined for a number of interesting projects for craftsmen with some experience in woodworking. [684]

9281 Marlow, A. W. *Fine Furniture for the Amateur Cabinetmaker* (10–12). Illus. 1990, Scarborough paper $12.95 (0-8128-2250-1). For the advanced woodworking student, this is a fine collection of projects. [684]

9282 Miller, Wilbur R., et al. *Woodworking* (10–12). Illus. 1978, Glencoe paper $7.72 (0-02-672800-1). A guide that covers basic tools, techniques, and materials in woodworking. [684]

9283 Pierce, Sharon. *Making Holiday Folk Toys & Figures* (10–12). Illus. 1988, Sterling paper $9.95 (0-8069-6604-1). For the woodworker, detailed plans on how to make 25 toys and gifts. (Rev: BL 12/1/87; BR 5–6/88) [745.592]

9284 Practical Homeowner, eds. *Build-It-Better-Yourself Storage Around the House* (9–12). Illus. 1988, Rodale $19.95 (0-87857-753-X). Clear directions to make 70 different items involving shelving and other home storage methods. (Rev: BL 4/15/88) [684.1]

9285 Reid, John. *From One Sheet of Plywood* (7–12). Illus. 1987, Sterling $19.95 (0-8069-6650-2); paper $12.95 (0-8069-6652-1). A beginner's guide to basic furniture construction and other useful projects. (Rev: BL 4/15/88) [684]

9286 Roszkiewicz, Ron, and Phyllis Straw. *The Woodturner's Companion* (10–12). Illus. 1985, Sterling $14.95 (0-8069-7940-2). A practical manual of projects involving such items as bowls, plates, and furniture. (Rev: BL 1/1/85) [684]

9287 Scott, Ernest. *Working in Wood* (10–12). Illus. 1980, Putnam $25.00 (0-399-12550-7). A comprehensive lavishly illustrated manual that covers the traditional skills of the woodworker. [684]

9288 Self, Charles R. *Making Birdhouses and Feeders* (9–12). Illus. 1986, Sterling paper $9.95 (0-8069-6244-5). Over 40 projects are described that even a beginner with few tools can accomplish. (Rev: SLJ 5/86) [684]

9289 Self, Charles R. *Making Fancy Birdhouses & Feeders* (10–12). Illus. 1988, Sterling paper $9.95 (0-8069-6690-4). In addition to specific projects, the author discusses materials, tools, types of joints, and finishing methods. (Rev: BL 5/15/86) [690]

9290 Spielman, Patrick, and Patricia Spielman. *Scroll Saw Puzzle Patterns* (9–12). Illus. 1989, Sterling paper $12.95 (0-8069-6586-X). A total of 80 plans are included for puzzles involving the alphabet, animals, robots, and so on. (Rev: BL 1/15/89) [688.7]

9291 Tangerman, Elmer J. *Complete Guide to Wood Carving* (9–12). Illus. 1985, Sterling $29.95 (0-8069-5532-5); paper $13.95 (0-8069-7922-4). This beginner's guide describes the tools and materials needed plus details on how to carve faces, animals, and figures. (Rev: BL 2/15/85; BR 1–2/86) [731.4]

9292 Tangerman, Elmer J. *Whittling and Woodcarving* (10–12). 1936, Dover paper $4.95 (0-486-20965-2). This is a beginner's guide to these ancient crafts. [684]

9293 Taylor, Stephen. *A Place of Your Own Making: How to Build a One-Room Cabin, Studio, Shack or Shed* (10–12). Illus. 1988, Henry Holt paper $14.45 (0-8050-0364-9). A clear how-to book that explains construction from the foundation to the finished product. (Rev: SLJ 12/88) [684]

9294 Time-Life Books, eds. *Working with Wood* (10–12). Illus. 1979, Silver Burdett LB $20.60 (0-8094-2427-4). Basic woodworking skills, tools, and techniques are introduced in this volume from the Time-Life Home Repair and Improvement series. [694]

9295 Wagner, Willis H. *Woodworking* (7–12). Illus. 1981, Goodheart-Willcox $7.96 (0-97006-503-3). An introduction to woodworking that stresses care and safety. [684]

Hobbies and Pastimes

General and Miscellaneous

9296 *Better Homes and Gardens 1990 Decorating and Remodeling Book* (10–12). Illus. 1990, Meredith $19.95 (0-696-01890-4). A basic guide to interior decorating that covers such topics as walls, lighting, and furniture arrangements. [747]

9297 Billy, Christopher. *Summer Opportunities for Kids and Teenagers* (7–12). 1984, Peterson's Guides paper $10.95 (0-87866-370-3). Activities such as summer camps, travel, and advanced schooling are described. [790.1]

9298 Cook, Hal. *Arranging: The Basics of Contemporary Floral Design* (10–12). Illus. 1985, Morrow $19.95 (0-688-02572-2). Treating flower arranging as an art form, the author discusses such concepts as form, color, line, and space. Many fine color photographs are included. (Rev: BL 9/1/85) [745.922]

9299 Finnigan, Dave. *The Complete Juggler* (9–12). Illus. 1987, Random paper $10.95 (0-394-74678-3). A simply written manual that starts with basics and works gradually into more advanced techniques and stunts. (Rev: BL 4/1/87) [793.8]

9300 Francome, Colin, and Charlie Holland. *Juggling for All* (9–12). Illus. 1987, David & Charles paper $9.95 (0-7153-8897-5). A brief paperback that tells the beginner how to juggle balls, boxes, clubs, and so on. (Rev: BL 12/15/87) [793.8]

9301 Newman, Frederick. *Mouthsounds* (10–12). 1980, Workman paper $6.95 (0-89480-128-7). This is a guide to making all sorts of interesting sounds including tips on how to be a master at whistling. [620.2]

9302 Olson, Beverly, and Judy Lazzara. *Country Flower Drying* (8–12). 1988, Sterling $19.95 (0-8069-6747-1); paper $9.95 (0-8069-6746-3). A concise manual on raising and drying flowers plus tips on creating arrangements and other uses of dried flowers. (Rev: BR 11–12/88) [745.92]

9303 Owens, Tom. *Collecting Sports Autographs* (9–12). 1989, Bonus paper $6.95 (0-933893-79-5). A thorough introduction to this hobby that covers topics such as hobby shows, techniques of soliciting, autographing, and organizing collections. (Rev: BL 5/1/89) [929.99]

9304 Pratt, Douglas R. *The Beginner's Guide to Radio Control Sport Flying* (10–12). Illus. 1988, TAB $9.95 (0-8306-9320-3). A guide to the hobby of flying radio-controlled sport planes, complete with many helpful tips, descriptions of components, and advice on assembling models. (Rev: VOYA 12/88) [629.133]

9305 Ritchard, Dan, and Kathleen Moloney. *Ventriloquism for the Total Dummy* (9–12). Illus. 1987, Random paper $7.95 (0-394-75638-X). This is a basic guide for the beginner that outlines successful practice techniques. (Rev: BL 3/15/88) [793.8]

9306 Summers, Kit. *Juggling with Finesse* (9–12). Illus. 1987, Finesse Pr. paper $14.95 (0-938981-00-5). Simple instructions profusely illustrated on how to juggle a variety of objects. (Rev: BL 10/1/87) [793.8]

9307 Time-Life Books, eds. *Time-Life Complete Fix-It-Yourself Manual* (9–12). Illus. 1989, Prentice paper $24.95 (0-13-921651-0). Drawn from the Time-Life extensive Fix-It-Yourself series, this volume covers repairs to all kinds of appliances, furniture, autos, and sound equipment. [620]

9308 Time-Life Books, eds. *Time-Life Complete Home Repair Manual* (9–12). Illus. 1989, Silver Burdett $18.72 (0-13-921636-7). This manual on home improvement covers such subjects as lighting, plumbing, roofs, basements, floors, stairs, and doors. [643]

Cooking

9309 Anderson, Jean, and Elaine Hanna. *The New Doubleday Cookbook* (9–12). 1985, Doubleday $16.95 (0-385-19577-X). An updated edition of a staple cookbook that now contains more than 4,000 recipes. (Rev: BL 1/1/86) [641.5]

9310 Appleby, Amy, and Jerald B. Stone. *Celebrate the Bounty* (9–12). 1990, Ballantine paper $8.95 (0-345-36129-6). An unusual cookbook in which each recipe is for a food mentioned in the Bible. (Rev: BL 2/15/90) [641.5]

9311 Axcell, Claudia, et al. *Simple Foods for the Pack* (10–12). Rev. ed. Illus. 1986, Sierra Club paper $8.95 (0-87156-757-1). For the outdoor person, here is a collection of recipes and food suggestions that can be either prepared beforehand or cooked over a campfire. [641.5]

9312 Baggett, Nancy. *The International Cookie Cookbook* (9–12). Illus. 1988, Stewart, Tabori & Chang $24.95 (1-55670-041-5). An oversize volume of recipes from around the world, many pictured in lovely color photographs. (Rev: BL 3/15/89) [641.8]

9313 Bayless, Rick, and Deann Groen Bayless. *Authentic Mexican: Regional Cooking from the Heart of Mexico* (10–12). Illus. 1987, Morrow $24.95 (0-688-04394-1). A thorough guide to genuine Mexican cooking that also features bits of history and information about the country's culture. (Rev: BL 4/15/87) [641]

9314 *Better Homes and Gardens Cooking for Two* (9–12). Illus. 1982, Meredith $7.95 (0-696-00452-6). A useful cookbook that describes small-scale meal preparation and gives about 190 recipes. [641.5]

9315 *Better Homes and Gardens New Cook Book* (9–12). Illus. 1990, Meredith $19.95 (0-693-00891-2); paper $6.95 (0-553-26766-3). A fine basic cookbook with easy-to-follow instructions and ample illustrations. (Rev: BL 11/1/89; BR 1–2/90) [641.5]

9316 *Betty Crocker's Microwave Cookbook* (9–12). Rev. ed. Illus. 1990, Prentice $19.95 (0-13-073859-X). A how-to manual that explains the

dos and don'ts of microwave cooking and gives more than 500 recipes. (Rev: BL 10/15/90) [641.5]

9317 *Betty Crocker's Smart Cook: The Essential Everyday Cookbook* (9–12). Illus. 1988, Prentice $16.95 (0-13-074311-9). An up-to-date cookbook with modern recipes, most of which take less than an hour to prepare, plus plenty of color photographs. (Rev: BL 1/15/89; BR 1–2/89) [641.5]

9318 *Betty Crocker's Step-by-Step Cookbook* (9–12). Illus. 1988, Prentice $14.95 (0-13-074345-3). Over 350 basic recipes with basic instructions and often pictures for each stage in the food's preparation. (Rev: BL 3/15/89) [641.5]

9319 Branson, Ann, ed. *The Good Housekeeping Illustrated Cookbook* (9–12). Rev. ed. Illus. 1988, Hearst $24.95 (0-688-08074-X). A fine basic cookbook that contains about 1,500 recipes and many illustrations and drawings. (Rev: BL 1/15/89) [641.5]

9320 Brown, Sarah, ed. *Microwave Cooking* (9–12). Illus. 1990, Reader's Digest paper $14.95 (0-89577-348-1). Besides giving a number of excellent recipes, this colorfully illustrated book gives a great deal of background information on microwave cooking. (Rev: BL 9/1/90) [641.5]

9321 Child, Julia. *The French Chef Cookbook* (10–12). Illus. 1968, Knopf $15.50 (0-394-40135-2); Bantam paper $5.95 (0-553-26434-6). Based on the highly successful TV series of over 100 programs, this is an excellent introduction to traditional French cooking. The author's *The Way to Cook* (1989) is a more general introduction to French cooking with more standard recipes. [641.5]

9322 Claiborne, Craig. *Craig Claiborne's Kitchen Primer* (9–12). 1972, Knopf $12.95 (0-394-42071-3); paper $6.95 (0-394-71854-2). In this handy manual, the well-known chef explains basic cooking techniques and describes important utensils and their uses. [641.5]

9323 Claiborne, Craig. *Craig Claiborne's The New York Times Food Encyclopedia* (10–12). Illus. 1985, Random $24.95 (0-8129-1271-3). In dictionary format with more than 1,000 entries, the author discusses all sorts of topics about and related to food and food preparation. [641.03]

9324 Claiborne, Craig. *The New York Times Cook Book* (10–12). Rev. ed. 1990, Harper $25.00 (0-06-01610-1). The fourth edition of this standard cookbook that concentrates on recipes rather than cooking techniques. Also use: *The New York Times International Cook Book* (1990). (Rev: BL 4/1/90) [641.59]

9325 Cooley, Denton, and Carolyn Moore. *Eat Smart for a Healthy Heart* (10–12). Illus. 1987, Barron's $19.95 (0-8120-5745-7). This book consists of menus and recipes designed for people who suffer from heart disease, diabetes, or obesity. (Rev: SLJ 9/87) [641.5]

9326 Crocker, Betty. *Betty Crocker's Cookbook* (9–12). Illus. 1990, Western $19.95 (0-13-084732-1); 1990, Western paper $9.95 (0-307-09813-3). A fine general cookbook that is part of a series of more specialized ones issued under the authorship of Betty Crocker. Also use: *Betty Crocker's New International Cookbook* (1989). [641.5]

9327 Crocker, Betty. *Betty Crocker's Microwave Cooking* (9–12). Rev. ed. Illus. 1984, Golden Pr. $6.95 (0-307-09941-5). A book of basic standard recipes all of which have been adapted for the microwave oven. [641.5]

9328 Crocker, Betty, eds. *Betty Crocker's New International Cookbook* (9–12). Illus. 1989, Prentice $18.95 (0-13-074378-X). A new edition of this classic cookbook with 450 recipes, 40 percent of them new. (Rev: BL 10/1/89) [641.59]

9329 Cunningham, Marion. *The Fannie Farmer Cookbook* (9–12). 13th ed. Illus. 1990, Knopf $22.95 (0-394-56788-9). The latest edition of this classic cookbook has been strengthened in the areas of microwave and outdoor cooking. (Rev: BL 8/90) [641.5]

9330 Delmar, Charles. *The Essential Cook* (9–12). Illus. 1989, Hill House $24.95 (0-929694-00-7). An excellent handbook on food preparation that includes such subjects as methods of cooking, equipment needed, and shopping tips. (Rev: BR 11–12/90; SLJ 7/89) [641.5]

9331 Diamond, Marilyn. *The American Vegetarian Cookbook: From the Fit for Life Kitchen* (9–12). 1990, Warner $24.95 (0-446-51561-2). As well as many tempting recipes, this book contains much information on nutrition and health. (Rev: BL 8/90) [641]

9332 Dwyer, Karen Kangas. *Easy Livin' Microwave Cooking: The New Microwave Primer* (9–12). Illus. 1989, St. Martin's paper $9.95 (0-312-02910-1). A basic work on how to use the microwave oven plus 200 easy-to-follow recipes. (Rev: BL 6/15/89) [641.5]

9333 Dyer, Ceil. *Best Recipes from the Backs of Boxes, Bottles and Jars* (10–12). 1989, Galahad paper $9.95 (0-88365-737-6). Easy-to-prepare foods using recommended recipes from various product manufacturers. [641.5]

9334 Dyer, Ceil. *Wok Cookery* (10–12). 1981, Dell paper $4.95 (0-440-19663-9). This is a good guide to Oriental cooking with a fine selection of basic recipes. Followed by *More Wok Cookery* (1982). [641.5]

9335 Eshleman, Ruthe, and Mary Winston, comps. *The American Heart Association Cookbook* (10–12). 3rd rev. ed. Illus. 1979, Ballantine paper $12.95 (0-345-32819-1). A cookbook that emphasizes low-cholesterol recipes and those that promote weight control. [641.5]

9336 Family Circle, eds. *The Best of Family Circle Cookbook* (9–12). Illus. 1985, Family Circle $19.95 (0-933585-4). From the food editors of this well-known supermarket magazine comes a collection of 300 illustrated recipes. [641.5]

9337 Farm Journal, eds. *Farm Journal's Country Cookbook* (10–12). 1981, Ballantine paper $4.95 (0-345-29781-4). From the pages of *Farm Journal,* this is a collection of favorite recipes. [641.5]

9338 Good Housekeeping. *The Good Housekeeping All-American Cookbook* (9–12). Illus. 1987, Hearst $24.95 (0-688-06333-0). A new cookbook that concentrates on basic recipes enhanced by careful step-by-step directions and many color illustrations. (Rev: BL 1/1/88) [641.5]

9339 *Great Cooking: The Best Recipes from Time-Life Books* (9–12). Illus. 1986, Henry Holt $29.95 (0-8050-0147-6). An anthology of 450 dishes culled from the famous Time-Life series with 170 color photographs. (Rev: BL 11/15/86) [641.5]

9340 Greene, Janet, et al. *Putting Food By* (10–12). Illus. 1988, Stephen Greene $22.95 (0-8289-0645-9); paper $9.95 (0-8289-0644-0). This is the fourth edition of this manual on such techniques as canning and freezing. (Rev: BL 9/1/88) [641.4]

9341 Hadamuscin, John. *Special Occasions: Holiday Entertaining All Year Round* (10–12). 1988, Harmony $22.50 (0-517-57005-X). A collection of menus involving notable annual events plus interesting background information on the foods associated with them. (Rev: BL 7/88) [642]

9342 Hansen, Barbara. *Mexican Cookery* (10–12). Illus. 1988, Price/Stern/Sloan $12.95 (0-89586-589-0). Easily followed recipes and many illustrations highlight this guide to the food of many different regions of Mexico. [641.5]

9343 Heatter, Maida. *Maida Heatter's Best Dessert Book Ever* (9–12). Illus. 1990, Random $24.95 (0-394-57832-5). A wonderful collection of dessert recipes that are easy to follow. (Rev: BL 8/90) [641.8]

9344 Hill, Barbara. *The Cook's Book of Indispensable Ideas: A Kitchen Sourcebook* (10–12). 1988, Summer House paper $9.95 (0-940367-11-4). Helpful tips and plenty of good advice in this companion to *Cook's Book of Essential Information* (1987). (Rev: BL 9/1/88) [641.5]

9345 Hultman, Tami, ed. *The Africa News Cookbook: African Cooking for Western Kitchens* (10–12). Illus. 1986, Penguin paper $14.95 (0-14-046751-3). Many African cuisines are represented in this collection of recipes, most of which use fairly accessible ingredients. (Rev: BL 5/15/86) [641.596]

9346 Hurley, Judith Benn. *Healthy Microwave Cooking: Better Nutrition in Half the Time!* (9–12). Illus. 1988, Rodale $21.95 (0-87857-771-8). A basic guide to microwave cooking with plenty of recipes from appetizers to desserts. (Rev: BL 11/15/88) [641.5]

9347 Jones, Evan. *American Food: The Gastronomic Story* (10–12). 1990, Viking $25.00 (0-87951-354-3). This book contains a generous sampling of American traditional and regional foods. [641.5]

9348 Kenneally, Joyce A. *The Good Housekeeping Illustrated Microwave Cookbook* (9–12). Illus. 1989, Hearst $25.00 (0-688-08473-7). A stunningly illustrated guide to microwave cooking complete with a host of recipes. (Rev: BL 2/1/90) [641]

9349 Kreschollek, Margie. *The Guaranteed Goof-Proof Microwave Cookbook* (9–12). 1988, Bantam paper $7.95 (0-553-34457-9). A simply followed microwave cookbook that stresses ease of preparation and commonly found ingredients. (Rev: BL 12/15/87) [641.5]

9350 Lemlin, Jeanne. *Vegetarian Pleasures: A Menu Cookbook* (9–12). Illus. 1986, Knopf $22.95 (0-394-54117-0); paper $16.95 (0-394-74302-4). From breakfast to dinner, here is a collection of 250 vegetarian recipes that are simple to prepare. (Rev: BL 5/1/86) [641.5]

9351 Martin, Pol. *Easy Cooking for Today* (8–12). Illus. 1988, Brimar $29.95 (2-920845-07-1). A simple guide for the beginning cook that contains a section on microwave cooking. (Rev: BL 9/1/88) [641.5]

9352 Nidetch, Jean. *Weight Watchers New International Cookbook* (9–12). 1987, NAL paper $10.95 (0-452-25951-7). A collection of tasty recipes aimed at the weight conscious. [641.5]

9353 Nidetch, Jean. *Weight Watchers Quick Success Program Cookbook* (9–12). Illus. 1989, NAL $18.95 (0-453-01016-4). A cookbook that involves the Quick Success weight control program of the Weight Watchers foundation. (Rev: BL 1/15/89) [613.2]

9354 Pruess, Joanna. *The Supermarket Epicure: The Cookbook for Gourmet Food at Supermarket Prices* (9–12). Illus. 1988, Morrow $19.95 (0-688-08070-7). A cookbook and cornucopia of shopping tips using the supermarket as a home base. (Rev: BL 8/88) [641.5]

9355 Roden, Claudia. *Mediterranean Cookery* (10–12). Illus. 1987, Knopf $24.95 (0-394-54434-X); McKay paper $18.95 (0-679-72835-X). This book is particularly noteworthy for its recipes from Turkey, Lebanon, and Morocco as well as the usual Mediterranean countries. (Rev: BL 10/15/87) [641.59]

9356 Rombauer, Irma S., and Marion Rombauer Becker. *Joy of Cooking* (7–12). Illus. 1986, Macmillan $16.95 (0-02-604570-2); NAL paper $11.95 (0-452-26189-9). First published in 1931, this has through several editions become one of the standard basic American cookbooks. [641.5]

9357 Rosenberg, Lawrence M. *Cake Decorating Simplified: The Roth Method* (9–12). Illus. 1990, Bragdon paper $14.95 (0-916410-53-6). A lusciously illustrated book on cake decorating plus 63 cake recipes. (Rev: BL 3/1/86) [641.8]

9358 Rosso, Julee, and Sheila Lukins. *The New Basics Cookbook* (10–12). Illus. 1989, Workman $29.95 (0-89480-392-1); paper $18.95 (0-89480-341-7). A beautifully designed cookbook that contains outstanding basic recipes plus many cooking tips. (Rev: BL 3/1/90) [641.5]

9359 Spencer, Colin. *The New Vegetarian: Cooking with Style the Vegetarian Way* (10–12). Illus. 1986, Viking $19.95 (0-670-81271-4). An introduction to vegetarianism plus a collection of outstanding recipes. (Rev: BL 4/1/87) [641.5]

9360 Sunset Books, eds. *Oriental Cookbook* (9–12). 1984, Lane paper $7.95 (0-376-02534-4). With 150 recipes, this book is a guide to the cuisine of 11 different countries. [641.5]

9361 Time-Life Books, eds. *Beef and Veal* (10–12). Illus. 1979, Silver Burdett LB $25.93 (0-8094-2855-5). Techniques of cooking beef and veal are given plus many fine recipes. Others in this series include: *Fish* (1979), *Lamb* (1981), *Pork* (1980), *Poultry* (1979), and *Shellfish* (1982). [641.8]

9362 Time-Life Books, eds. *Breads* (10–12). Illus. 1981, Silver Burdett $25.93 (0-8094-291-2). From the Good Cook series this book gives illustrated directions on how to make a variety of breads. Some others in the series are: *Cakes*, *Candy* (both 1981), *Cookies and Crackers* (1982), and *Pies and Pastries* (1981). [641.8]

9363 Time-Life Books, eds. *Pasta* (10–12). Illus. 1980, Silver Burdett $25.93 (0-8094-2892-X). As well as many recipes involving various kinds of pasta, this account tells how to make one's own pasta. Some others in this series on the Good Cook are: *Fruits* (1983), *Vegetables* (1979), and *Outdoor Cooking* (1982). [641.8]

9364 Time-Life Books, eds. *Salads* (10–12). Illus. 1980, Silver Burdett LB $25.93 (0-8094-2880-6). A lavishly illustrated book on how to make a variety of salads and dressings. In the same series are *Sauces* (1983) and *Eggs and Cheese* (1980). [641.8]

9365 Time-Life Books, eds. *Soups* (10–12). Illus. 1979, Silver Burdett LB $25.93 (0-8094-2862-9). In addition to many fine recipes, this book includes a well-illustrated section on techniques of making soups. [641.8]

9366 Tracy, Lisa. *The Gradual Vegetarian* (10–12). 1986, Dell paper $8.95 (0-440-53124-1). This book offers a 3-stage program on how to eliminate meat from one's diet. (Rev: BL 4/1/85) [613.2]

9367 Wood, Jacqueline, and Joclyn Scott Gilchrist. *The Campus Survival Cookbook #2* (10–12). 1981, Morrow paper $8.95 (0-688-00568-3). Aimed at the college student who must cook, this is also a good cooking primer for high school students. [641.5]

9368 Ying, Mildred, et al., eds. *The New Good Housekeeping Cookbook* (8–12). Illus. 1986, Hearst $19.95 (0-688-03897-2). A thorough revision of this basic cookbook that now contains over 2,000 recipes plus menus and information on microwave cooking. (Rev: BL 1/1/87) [641.5]

9369 Zisman, Honey, and Larry Zisman. *The Burger Book* (9–12). 1987, St. Martin's paper $7.95 (0-312-00084-7). Almost 100 recipes for different kinds of hamburgers are given plus material on suitable side dishes. (Rev: BL 3/15/87) [641.6]

Gardening

9370 Beard, Henry, and Roy McKie. *Gardening* (10–12). 1982, Workman paper $5.95 (0-89480-200-3). This is a humorous but instructive guide to this pastime. [635]

9371 *Better Homes and Gardens Complete Guide to Gardening* (9–12). Illus. 1979, Meredith $24.95 (0-696-00041-5). A complete guide to both indoor and outdoor gardening. Also use: *Better Homes and Gardens Successful Gardening* (1987). [635]

9372 *Better Homes and Gardens New Garden Book* (9–12). Illus. 1990, Meredith $24.95 (0-696-00042-3). Forty years after its first edition, this remains one of the best general gardening books available. (Rev: BL 4/1/90) [635]

9373 Bremness, Lesley. *The Complete Book of Herbs: A Practical Guide to Growing & Using Herbs* (10–12). 1988, Viking $24.95 (0-670-81894-1). This is a directory of over 100 herbs, their characteristics, and cultivation plus 80 recipes for their use. (Rev: BL 1/1/89) [635.7]

9374 Chiusoli, Alessandro, and Maria Luisa Boriani. *Simon & Schuster's Guide to House Plants* (9–12). Illus. 1987, Simon & Schuster $22.95 (0-671-63218-3); paper $12.95 (0-671-63131-4). This guide gives information on 243 plants and how to care for them. (Rev: BL 5/15/87) [635.9]

9375 Cox, Jeff, et al. *How to Grow Vegetables Organically* (10–12). Illus. 1988, Rodale $21.95 (0-87857-683-5). A manual on organic gardening with information on raising over 60 varieties of vegetables. (Rev: BL 3/1/88) [635]

9376 Creasy, Rosalind. *The Gardener's Handbook of Edible Plants* (9–12). Illus. 1986, Sierra Club $25.00 (0-87156-758-X); paper $12.95 (0-87156-759-8). More than 100 plants are listed alphabetically with information on ease of cultivation and tips on use. (Rev: BL 10/15/86) [635]

9377 Damrosch, Barbara. *The Garden Primer* (9–12). Illus. 1988, Workman $22.95 (0-89480-317-4); paper $16.95 (0-89480-316-6). A multitude of facts and advice on all kinds of plants, including houseplants, with detailed information on about 300 specific varieties. (Rev: BL 11/15/88) [635]

9378 Foster, Catharine Osgood. *The Organic Gardener* (10–12). Illus. 1972, Knopf paper $8.95 (0-394-71785-6). A manual on organic gardening that includes material on mulching, types of plants, and controlling weeds and insect pests. [635]

9379 Graf, Alfred Byrd. *Exotic Plant Manual* (10–12). 5th ed. Illus. 1978, Roehrs $37.50 (0-911266-13-5). A handbook on exotic plants that can be grown in the home, garden, or greenhouse. [635.9]

9380 Hessayon, D. G. *The House Plant Expert* (10–12). 1990, Sterling paper $8.95 (0-903505-13-4). This is a practical book that identifies major house plants and tells how to care for them. [635]

9381 *Illustrated Guide to Gardening* (7–12). Illus. 1978, Reader's Digest Assn. $26.95 (0-

89577-046-6). An extensive guide that covers all kinds of gardening including greenhouses. [635]

9382 Lammers, Susan M. *All about Houseplants* (10–12). Rev. ed. Illus. 1982, Ortho paper $7.95 (0-89721-002-6). A comprehensive guide to all kinds of houseplants and how to cultivate them. [635.9]

9383 Moggi, Guido, and Luciano Giugnolini. *Simon and Schuster's Guide to Garden Flowers* (10–12). Illus. 1983, Simon & Schuster paper $12.95 (0-671-46678-X). With many color illustrations, this is a guide to 369 flowering plants. [635.9]

9384 Newcomb, Duane, and Karen Newcomb. *The Complete Vegetable Gardener's Sourcebook* (10–12). 1989, Prentice paper $14.95 (0-13-612110-1). This thorough handbook covers all aspects of vegetable gardening. [635]

9385 Reader's Digest, eds. *Reader's Digest Guide to Creative Gardening* (9–12). Illus. 1987, Reader's Digest $28.95 (0-276-35223-8). A comprehensive, richly illustrated volume that identifies individual plants and gives their growing requirements. [635]

9386 Rich, Libby. *Odyssey Book of Houseplants* (9–12). Illus. 1990, Plant Odyssey paper $21.95 (0-9625702-0-6). A guide to the characteristics and care of 150 different houseplants. (Rev: BL 3/15/90) [635.965]

9387 *Taylor's Guide to Ground Covers, Vines & Grasses* (10–12). Illus. 1987, Houghton paper $14.95 (0-395-43094-1). Taken from the larger encyclopedia, this paperback covers general botanical information, nature of species, and how to grow healthy plants. In the same series are: *Taylor's Guide to Houseplants; Taylor's Guide to Shrubs;* and *Taylor's Guide to Vegetables and Herbs* (all 1987). (Rev: BL 5/1/87) [635.9]

9388 Wright, Michael. *The Complete Book of Gardening* (10–12). 1979, Harper $20.00 (0-397-01292-6); Warner paper $16.95 (0-446-39116-6). A basic handbook for cultivating all kinds of plants and trees in various climates. Also use: *Complete Indoor Gardener* (1979). [635.9]

Home Repairs

9389 Brimer, John B. *Homeowner's Complete Outdoor Building Book: Wood and Masonry Construction* (10–12). Illus. 1989, Sterling paper $16.95 (0-8069-5796-4). The first part of this book deals with woodwork projects such as

decks and fences and the second part with concrete and cement constructions such as steps and driveways. [690]

9390 Gladstone, Bernard. *The Simon & Schuster Complete Guide to Home Repair and Maintenance* (9–12). Illus. 1987, Simon & Schuster paper $12.95 (0-671-63940-4). Many topics are covered including carpentry, plumbing, furniture repair, and electrical systems. [643]

9391 Powell, Evan. *Complete Guide to Home Appliance Repair* (9–12). 2nd ed. Illus. 1984, Popular Science $24.45 (0-06-013384-8); paper $14.95 (0-06-091190-5). Plenty of photographs and step-by-step instructions highlight this basic guide to repairing appliances. [643]

9392 Time-Life Books, eds. *The Home Workshop* (10–12). Illus. 1989, Silver Burdett LB $23.27 (0-8094-6281-8). A basic guide to setting up and maintaining a practical home workshop. This is part of a 36-volume set from Time-Life Books called the Home Repair and Improvement series that covers all sorts of projects from kitchens and bathrooms to porches and patios. [684]

Magic and Tricks

9393 Blackstone, Harry, et al. *The Blackstone Book of Magic & Illusion* (9–12). Illus. 1985, Newmarket $22.95 (0-937858-45-5). This volume combines a history of magic, the life story of magician Harry Blackstone, and tips and tricks for the amateur. (Rev: BL 5/15/85; SLJ 9/85) [793.8]

9394 Christopher, Milbourne. *Milbourne Christopher's Magic Book* (9–12). Illus. 1985, Harper paper $5.95 (0-06-463708-5). This book describes more than 100 magic tricks, most of which require no special equipment. [793.8]

9395 Fisher, John. *Body Magic* (10–12). Illus. 1979, Scarborough $10.00 (0-8128-2330-3); paper $6.95 (0-8128-6088-8). This book presents more than 100 tricks using the powers we have in our hands, eyes, and nervous sytems. [793.8]

9396 Frederick, Guy. *One-Hundred-One Best Magic Tricks* (9–12). 1985, NAL paper $3.50 (0-451-15859-8). A step-by-step explanation of these tricks with directions on how to perform them. [793.8]

9397 Hay, Henry. *The Amateur Magician's Handbook* (7–12). 4th ed. 1982, NAL paper $4.95 (0-

451-15502-5). Tricks for magicians of all ages are given and at various levels of difficulty. [793.8]

9398 Kaye, Marvin. *The Stein and Day Handbook of Magic* (9–12). Illus. 1973, Scarborough $10.00 (0-8128-1628-5); paper $8.95 (0-8128-6203-1). Good background material on magic and magicians is given as well as a wide variety of magic tricks. [793.8]

9399 Paulsen, Kathryn. *The Complete Book of Magic and Witchcraft* (10–12). Rev. ed. 1970, NAL paper $4.50 (0-451-15515-7). A history of magic and witchcraft through the ages. [793.8]

9400 Scarne, John. *Scarne on Card Tricks* (9–12). 1986, NAL paper $4.50 (0-451-15864-4). A description and explanation of 150 card tricks. [795.4]

9401 Schindler, George. *Magic with Everyday Objects* (10–12). Illus. 1980, Scarborough House paper $7.95 (0-8128-6030-6). This book describes more than 150 tricks, many hundreds of years old. [793.8]

9402 Severn, Bill. *Bill Severn's Best Magic: 50 Top Tricks to Entertain and Amaze Your Friends on All Occasions* (9–12). 1990, Stackpole $12.95 (0-8117-2229-5). Instructions on how to perform over 50 tricks are given so simply that even the beginner can master them. (Rev: BL 3/15/90) [793.8]

Model Making

9403 Botermans, Jack. *Paper Flight* (9–12). 1984, Henry Holt paper $12.95 (0-8050-0500-5). Simple directions are given on how to build 48 paper airplane models. [629.133]

9404 Schleicher, Robert. *Building and Flying Model Aircraft* (9–12). Illus. 1988, Dover paper $5.95 (0-486-25801-7). A comprehensive guide to model aircraft construction. [629.133]

9405 Schleicher, Robert. *The HO Model Railroading Handbook* (9–12). Rev. ed. Illus. 1983, Chilton paper $13.95 (0-8019-7384-8). This guide introduces the beginner to railroad modeling using HO products. [625.1]

9406 Smeed, Vic, ed. *Complete Railway Modelling* (9–12). Illus. 1982, Ebury Pr. $60.00 (0-85223-196-2). A beginner's guide to enhancing and expanding a commercially made railroad set. [625.1]

9407 Stine, G. Harry. *Handbook of Model Rocketry* (10–12). 1983, Prentice paper $12.95 (0-668-

05360-7). An excellent handbook on model rockets that includes the use of computers in this hobby. [629.133]

Photography and Filmmaking

9408 *The Art of Photography, 1839–1989* (9–12). Illus. 1989, Yale Univ. Pr. $50.00 (0-300-04457-7). This huge, expensive book is an appropriate tribute to 150 years of photography. (Rev: BL 5/15/89) [799]

9409 Bailey, Adrian, and Adrian Holloway. *The Book of Color Photography* (10–12). Rev. ed. Illus. 1984, Knopf paper $15.95 (0-394-72467-4). In addition to basic skills and techniques, this book contains separate chapters on such subjects as people, landscapes, and wildlife. [778.6]

9410 Busselle, Michael. *The Complete 35mm Sourcebook* (9–12). Illus. 1988, Amphoto $27.50 (0-8174-3702-9); paper $19.95 (0-8174-3703-7). A handbook that begins with selecting a camera and proceeds to mounting and exhibiting the final product. (Rev: BL 2/1/89) [770]

9411 Canavor, Natalie. *Sell Your Photographs: The Complete Marketing Strategy for the Freelancer* (10–12). 1982, NAL paper $7.95 (0-452-25638-0). This book gives practical advice on how freelancers can sell their photographs. [770]

9412 Carver, George T., and Eugene E. Lee. *Beginning Photography* (9–12). Illus. 1985, Prentice paper $20.00 (0-13-071440-2). This textbook can be read independently as a fine introduction to the basics of black-and-white photography. (Rev: BL 8/85) [770]

9413 *The Complete Kodak Book of Photography* (9–12). Illus. 1986, Crown $29.95 (0-517-56243-X). An introduction to photography that includes material on lighting, darkroom techniques, equipment, and related topics. [770.2]

9414 Curtin & London, eds. *The Book of 35mm Photography* (9–12). Illus. 1983, Focal Pr. paper $15.95 (0-240-51763-6). Aimed at the beginner, this is a concise guide to equipment and procedures involved in 35mm photography. [770.28]

9415 Eastman Kodak Company, eds. *The New Joy of Photography* (9–12). Illus. 1985, Addison paper $16.95 (0-201-11692-8). An updated edition of this book, which covers the latest equipment developments plus all the basics. (Rev: SLJ 5/86) [770]

9416 Farndon, John. *Mastering Color Photography* (9–12). Illus. 1985, Silver Burdett LB $19.27

(0-86706-244-4). A richly illustrated guide to color photography that is part of the Kodak Library of Creative Photography series from Time-Life Books. Some others are: *Making Color Work for You* (1983), *Creating Special Effects* (1984), and *How to Catch the Action* (1983). [778.6]

9417 Grimm, Tom. *The Basic Book of Photography* (10–12). Rev. ed. Illus. 1985, NAL paper $10.95 (0-452-26096-5). A complete, well-illustrated guide to modern photography. [770]

9418 Grimm, Tom, et al. *The Basic Darkroom Book* (9–12). Rev. ed. Illus. 1986, NAL paper $9.95 (0-452-25892-8). A useful manual on techniques and skills involved in successful development of film in the darkroom. (Rev: BL 12/15/86) [770]

9419 Grimm, Tom, and Michele Grimm. *The Good Guide for Bad Photographers* (9–12). 1982, NAL paper $7.95. This is a practical guide on how to avoid mistakes in taking pictures. [770]

9420 Grundberg, Andy. *Grundberg's Goof-Proof Photography Guide* (9–12). Illus. 1989, Simon & Schuster paper $8.95 (0-671-67291-6). A practical guide that stresses aspects of good picture taking. (Rev: BL 12/15/89) [771]

9421 Hattersley, Ralph. *Beginner's Guide to Photography* (9–12). 1982, Doubleday paper $6.95 (0-385-17705-4). This is a useful guide for the beginner on how to take better pictures. [770]

9422 Hedgecoe, John. *The Book of Photography: How to See and Take Better Pictures* (10–12). Illus. 1984, Knopf paper $16.95 (0-394-72466-6). An introduction to fine picture taking by a prolific writer in the field who has several other recommended titles in print on photography. [770.2]

9423 Hedgecoe, John. *John Hedgecoe's Darkroom Techniques* (10–12). Illus. 1985, Simon & Schuster paper $9.95 (0-671-66442-5). With a richly illustrated text, the author includes material on developing both color and black-and-white film. [770.28]

9424 Horenstein, Henry. *Black and White Photography: A Basic Manual* (10–12). 2nd rev. ed. Illus. 1983, Little $24.95 (0-316-37313-3); paper $14.95 (0-316-37314-1). A manual that explores varieties of cameras, composition, film developing, and related topics. [770.2]

9425 Hoy, Frank P. *Photojournalism: The Visual Approach* (10–12). Illus. 1986, Prentice $41.00 (0-13-665548-3). This is a fine overview of the field that emphasizes daily newspaper types of photojournalism. (Rev: BL 5/15/86) [778.9]

9426 Jacobs, Mark. *Photography in Focus* (10–12). Illus. 1985, National Textbook $19.95 (0-8442-5483-5); paper $16.95 (0-8442-5484-3). Using the latest information on techniques and equipment, this report covers all aspects of photography from the camera, lenses, and light to film development and printmaking. (Rev: BL 6/1/85; BR 9–10/85) [770]

9427 Langford, Michael. *The Darkroom Handbook* (10–12). Illus. 1981, Knopf paper $19.95 (0-394-72468-2). A very useful guide to developing color and black-and-white film plus allied processes. [770.28]

9428 Langford, Michael. *Michael Langford's 35mm Handbook* (9–12). Rev. ed. Illus. 1987, Knopf paper $15.95 (0-394-75547-2). A concise but thorough guide on how to be an excellent 35mm photographer. (Rev: BL 10/15/87) [770]

9429 *The Magic of Black-and-White* (9–12). Illus. 1985, Silver Burdett LB $19.27 (0-86706-352-1). A richly illustrated account that covers all aspects of black-and-white photography and also gives a history of the medium. This is part of the Time-Life series the Kodak Library of Creative Photography. Some other titles include: *Mastering Composition and Light* (1984), *Print Your Own Pictures* and *Taking Better Travel Photos* (both 1983). [770.28]

9430 *Make Color Work for You* (7–12). Illus. 1983, Silver Burdett LB $19.27 (0-86706-204-5). A guide to color photography that stresses its use creatively. [778.6]

9431 Moeller, Susan. *Shooting War* (9–12). Illus. 1989, Basic Books $25.95 (0-465-07777-3). From the Spanish American War through Vietnam, this is a collection of the most famous war photographs with information about the photographers. (Rev: SLJ 12/89) [778]

9432 *More Joy of Photography* (9–12). Illus. 1988, Addison-Wesley paper $16.95 (0-201-14559-6). An update of the 1979 volume, again edited at Eastman Kodak, this gives an introduction to both photographic techniques and to the work of some famous photographers. (Rev: BL 12/1/88) [770]

9433 Pfeiffer, C. Boyd. *The Orvis Guide to Outdoor Photography* (9–12). Illus. 1986, Winchester $18.95 (0-8329-0433-3); paper $13.95 (0-8329-0434-1). A concise, practical guide to taking better pictures while enjoying the outdoors. (Rev: BL 7/86) [778.7]

9434 *Photographing the Drama of Daily Life* (9–12). Illus. 1984, Silver Burdett LB $19.27 (0-86706-225-8). A guide on how to shoot effective news photographs. This is part of the Kodak

Library of Creative Photography series from Time-Life Books that contains 16 other titles including *Photographing Buildings and Cityscapes* (1984), *Photographing Friends and Family* (1983), and *Set Up Your Home Studio* (1985). [770.28]

9435 Pinkard, Bruce. *The Photographer's Bible: An Encyclopedic Reference Manual* (9–12). Illus. 1983, Arco $24.95 (0-688-05781-5). A wide range of topics and terms related to photography are covered in this alphabetically arranged book. [770.3]

9436 Platt, Richard. *The Photographer's Idea Book: How to See and Take Better Pictures* (9–12). Illus. 1985, Amphoto $24.50 (0-8174-5415-2); paper $16.95 (0-8174-5416-0). Instead of basics this book goes into some of the finer points in picture taking. Illustrated with many color examples. (Rev: BL 2/1/86) [770.28]

9437 Rothstein, Arthur. *Documentary Photography* (10–12). Illus. 1985, Focal Pr. $24.95 (0-240-51754-7). From Matthew Brady's Civil War photographs to the present, this account describes documentary photography and its techniques with many examples. (Rev: BL 3/1/86) [778.9]

9438 Van Wormer, Joe. *How to Be a Wildlife Photographer* (7–12). Illus. 1982, Lodestar $10.95 (0-525-66772-5). Calling on 20 years of experience, Van Wormer gives many pointers on how to find wildlife and how to photograph it successfully. [770]

9439 Vestal, David. *The Art of Black and White Enlarging* (10–12). Illus. 1984, Harper $24.95 (0-06-181896-8). Specifically aimed at one past the beginner level, this book gives many details of producing fine black-and-white prints. [770.28]

9440 Wignall, Jeff. *Landscape Photography* (9–12). Illus. 1988, McGraw paper $12.95 (0-07-070299-3). Lots of practical advice is given plus many photographs as examples. (Rev: BL 6/15/88) [778.9]

Stamp, Coin, and Other Types of Collecting

9441 Andrews, Charles J. *Fell's United States Coin Book* (7–12). Illus. 1983, Fell $11.95 (0-8119-0595-0); paper $7.95 (0-8119-0588-8). Every coin minted in the United States is listed with material about value and the history of coins. [737.4]

9442 Benjamin, Christopher. *Most Valuable Baseball Cards* (9–12). Illus. 1990, Putnam paper $10.95 (0-399-51592-5). A history of baseball cards that gives special emphasis to the most famous. (Rev: BL 5/1/90) [769.497]

9443 Brecka, Jon, ed. *Baseball Cards: Questions & Answers* (9–12). Illus. 1990, Krause paper $5.95 (0-87341-144-7). Over 500 frequently asked questions about this popular hobby are answered in this book. (Rev: BL 9/15/90) [359]

9444 Cribb, Joe, et al. *The Coin Atlas* (9–12). Illus. 1990, Facts on File $40.00 (0-8160-2097-3). This account tells about the history and geography of countries as revealed in their coins and also gives a history of the world's coinage system. (Rev: SLJ 9/90) [737.4]

9445 Friedberg, Robert. *Paper Money of the United States: A Complete Illustrated Guide with Valuations* (10–12). Illus. 1989, Coin & Currency Inst. $21.50 (0-87184-512-1). This is a complete catalog of American paper money from its first use in 1861 to the present. [769.5]

9446 Ganz, David L. *The World of Coins and Coin Collecting* (9–12). 1985, Macmillan $22.50 (0-684-18238-6). A basic guide on how to begin a coin collection and how to develop and display it. [737.4]

9447 Green, Paul M., and Donn Pearlman. *Making Money with Baseball Cards: A Handbook of Insider Secrets and Strategies* (8–12). Illus. 1989, Bonus paper $7.95 (0-933893-77-9). A guide to the hobby that can be an investment for the future or simply a pleasant extension of one's love of baseball. (Rev: BL 3/15/89) [796.357]

9448 Hegenberger, John. *Collector's Guide to Comic Books* (9–12). Illus. 1990, Chilton paper $12.95 (0-87069-548-7). This account covers the history of comic books, types of comic books, and how to get into the hobby of collecting them. (Rev: BL 8/90; SLJ 9/90) [741.5]

9449 Hobson, Burton. *Coin Collecting as a Hobby* (9–12). Rev. ed. Illus. 1986, Sterling LB $13.29 (0-8069-4749-7). A fine guide on how to begin and maintain a coin collection. [737.4]

9450 Hobson, Burton. *Coin Collecting for Beginners* (9–12). 1982, Wilshire paper $5.00 (0-87980-022-4). This account supplies solid basic information on how to begin and organize a coin collection. [737]

9451 Hudgeons, Marc, ed. *The Official Blackbook Price Guide of U.S. Coins* (9–12). 1990, Ballantine paper $5.95 (0-87637-823-8). A listing of the current prices of coins in various conditions. [737.4]

9452 Hughes, Stephen. *Pop Culture Mania* (10–12). 1984, McGraw $17.95 (0-07-031114-5); paper $8.95 (0-07-031113-7). This is a guide to collecting items that reflect the pop culture of the twentieth century. [790.1]

9453 Ilma, Viola. *Funk & Wagnalls Guide to the World of Stamp Collecting* (9–12). Illus. 1978, Funk & Wagnalls $15.45 (0-308-10330-0). This is both a practical guide to stamp collecting and an interesting history of stamps. [769.56]

9454 Kirk, Troy. *Collector's Guide to Baseball Cards* (9–12). Illus. 1990, Chilton paper $16.95 (0-87069-533-9). A guide to collecting baseball cards that covers a history of the hobby, a guide to the most valuable cards, and tips on how to build a fine collection. (Rev: BL 6/15/90) [769.49]

9455 Kronnick, Buck. *The Baseball Fan's Complete Guide to Collecting Autographs* (8–12). Illus. 1990, Betterway paper $9.95 (1-55870-153-2). A basic guide to this hobby that includes over 100 pages of addresses of players. (Rev: SLJ 8/90) [929.2]

9456 Mackay, James. *The Guinness Book of Stamps, Facts and Feats* (7–12). Illus. 1989, Guinness paper $17.95 (0-85112-351-1). All sorts of curiosities about postage stamps such as the most valuable, the largest, and so on. (Rev: BL 4/15/89) [769.56]

9457 Obojski, Robert. *Coin Collector's Price Guide* (9–12). Illus. 1990, Sterling paper $6.95 (0-8069-6864-8). In this catalog prices are given for both U.S. and Canadian coins minted from the eighteenth century to the present. [737.4]

9458 Pelton, Robert W. *Collecting Autographs for Fun and Profit* (9–12). Illus. 1987, Betterway paper $9.95 (0-932620-80-9). A guide to acquiring and organizing not only autographs but also such other types of primary sources as diaries, manuscripts, and musical scores. (Rev: BL 12/1/87) [928.8]

9459 *Postal Service Guide to U.S. Stamps* (7–12). Illus. 1988, U.S. Postal Service paper $5.00 (0-9604756-8-0). A well-illustrated history of U.S. postage stamps. [769.56]

9460 Reinfeld, Fred. *A Catalogue of the World's Most Popular Coins* (7–12). Illus. 1987, Sterling $29.95 (0-8069-4738-1); paper $19.95 (0-8069-4740-3). For both modern and ancient coins, histories are given plus current values. [737.4]

9461 Schwarz, Ted. *Beginner's Guide to Stamp Collecting* (9–12). 1983, Prentice paper $10.95 (0-668-05551-0). A well-illustrated guide to the basics of stamp collecting. [759.56]

9462 *Scott Standard Postage Stamp Catalogue* (7–12). 4 vols. Illus. 1989, Scott paper $20.00 each (vol. 1: 0-685-70738-5; vol. 2: 0-685-70739-3; vol. 3: 0-685-70740-7; vol. 4: 0-685-70741-5). This is the most comprehensive stamp catalog in print. Volume 1 deals with stamps from the English-speaking world; the other 3 volumes cover alphabetically the other countries of the world. [769.56]

9463 Yeoman, R. S. *A Guide Book of United States Coins* (9–12). Illus. 1991, Western $8.95 (0-307-19892-8). In this annual publication the prices of coins from A.D. 1616 to the present are given. [737.4]

Jokes, Puzzles, Riddles, and Word Games

Jokes and Riddles

9464 Asimov, Isaac. *Isaac Asimov's Treasury of Humor* (8–12). 1979, Houghton paper $10.95 (0-395-28412-0). This is a collection of Asimov's all-time favorite jokes and riddles. [808.7]

9465 Phillips, Louis, comp. *The Latin Riddle Book* (10–12). Trans. by Stan Schechter. Illus. 1988, Harmony $9.95 (0-517-56975-2). For Latin students a book of riddles that will keep them guessing. (Rev: SLJ 4/89) [470]

Puzzles

9466 Botermans, Jack. *Paper Capers: An Amazing Array of Games, Puzzles, and Tricks* (9–12). Illus. (0-8050-0139-5); 1986, Henry Holt paper $9.95. A collection of 40 different puzzles that can be made from paper or cardboard. (Rev: BL 12/1/86; SLJ 11/86) [745.54]

9467 Gleason, Norma. *Cryptograms and Spygrams* (10–12). 1981, Dover paper $3.50 (0-486-24036-3). This is a collection of over 100 puzzles and problems to solve. [793.7]

9468 Smullyan, Raymond. *To Mock a Mockingbird* (7–12). 1985, Knopf $14.95 (0-394-53491-3). A book of 200 puzzles—some fairly easy, others very difficult—but all with solutions given. (Rev: VOYA 12/85) [793.7]

9469 Townsend, Charles B. *The World's Most Challenging Puzzles* (9–12). Illus. 1988, Sterling $10.95 (0-8069-6730-7). All kinds of classic tricks and problems are included with answers in the back. (Rev: SLJ 2/89) [793.7]

9470 Treat, Lawrence. *You're the Detective! 24 Solve-Them-Yourself Picture Mysteries* (7–12). Illus. 1983, Godine paper $6.95 (0-87923-478-4). By observing clues given in pictures, readers can solve a group of mysteries. [793.7]

Word Games

9471 Salny, Abbie, and Burke Lewis Frumkes. *The Mensa Think Smart Book* (9–12). Illus. 1986, Harper paper $7.95 (0-06-091255-3). A collection of word games, puzzles, and quizzes that are mind benders. (Rev: BL 4/1/86) [153]

Mysteries, Curiosities, Controversial and General Knowledge

9472 Arvey, Michael. *ESP: Opposing Viewpoints* (9–12). Illus. 1989, Greenhaven $13.95 (0-89908-057-X). Pros and cons are given with many illustrations and quotes on this controversial subject. (Rev: BL 3/1/89; SLJ 6/89) [133.8]

9473 Arvey, Michael. *Reincarnation: Opposing Viewpoints* (9–12). Illus. 1989, Greenhaven LB $13.95 (0-89908-067-7). The pros and cons of believing in reincarnation are presented in this interesting account. (Rev: BL 3/1/90) [133.9]

9474 Arvey, Michael. *UFOs: Opposing Viewpoints* (9–12). Illus. 1989, Greenhaven LB $13.95 (0-89908-060-X). This volume explores both sides of the UFO controversy. (Rev: BL 12/15/89; SLJ 3/90) [001.9]

9475 Ashley, Leonard R. N. *The Wonderful World of Magic and Witchcraft* (9–12). Illus. 1986, Dembner $17.50 (0-934878-71-4); paper $10.95 (0-934878-72-2). A compendium of information on magic and witchcraft arranged by such subjects as witchcraft trials and recipes and formulas. By the author of *The Wonderful World of Superstition, Prophecy and Luck* (1984). (Rev: BL 4/15/86) [133.4]

9476 Berlitz, Charles. *The Bermuda Triangle* (9–12). Illus. 1987, Avon paper $4.95 (0-380-00465-8). An account that discusses the various mysterious disappearances of planes and ships that have occurred in this stretch of the Atlantic Ocean. [001.9]

9477 Bradbury, Will, ed. *Into the Unknown* (8–12). Illus. 1981, Reader's Digest $22.95 (0-89577-098-9). A collection of accounts about the

unexplained mysteries of the Earth such as Stonehenge and UFOs. [001.9]

9478 Burnam, Tom. *More Misinformation* (9–12). Illus. 1980, Harper $16.45 (0-690-01685-9); Ballantine paper $2.50 (0-345-29251-0). An entertaining book that debunks popularly held beliefs. A sequel to *Dictionary of Misinformation* (1975). [001.9]

9479 Caraceau, Jean-Luc, and Cecile Donner. *The Dictionary of Superstitions* (9–12). Illus. 1987, Granada paper $7.95 (0-8050-0366-5). Arranged by topic, here is a rundown on superstitions involved with 153 different subjects. (Rev: SLJ 6–7/87) [001.9]

9480 Cohen, Daniel. *The Encyclopedia of Ghosts* (9–12). Illus. 1984, Dodd $14.95 (0-396-08308-0); paper $7.95 (0-396-09050-8). In 105 entries, the author describes famous and infamous spirits. [133.1]

9481 Cohen, Daniel. *The Encyclopedia of Monsters* (9–12). 1990, Dorset $17.95 (0-88029-442-6). A guide to all sorts of monsters, including the vampire, abominable snowman, and giant sea creatures. [398]

9482 Cohen, Daniel. *The Encyclopedia of the Strange* (9–12). Illus. 1985, Dodd $16.95 (0-396-08656-X); Avon paper $3.95 (0-380-70268-1). A collection of weird and often bizarre information on such topics as Atlantis, Jack the Ripper, levitation, and King Tut's tomb. (Rev: SLJ 11/85) [001.9]

9483 Cohen, Daniel. *The Great Airship Mystery: A UFO of the 1890s* (9–12). Illus. 1981, Dodd $10.95 (0-396-07990-3). This is an account of the sightings of a mysterious airship in the United States during the 1890s. [001.9]

9484 Cohen, Daniel. *Greatest Monsters in the World* (7–12). 1986, Pocket paper $2.50 (0-671-62672-8). An easily read book that describes such monsters as the one supposedly in Loch Ness. [398]

9485 Cohen, Daniel. *Supermonsters* (7–12). 1986, Pocket paper $2.50 (0-671-62219-6). Such creatures as vampires, zombies, and werewolves are described. [398]

9486 Cohen, Daniel. *UFOs: The Third Wave* (10–12). 1988, Evans $12.95 (0-87131-541-6). Starting with the 1940s, Cohen reviews the sightings of UFOs with emphasis on current material. (Rev: BL 12/15/88; SLJ 12/88) [001.9]

9487 Cohen, Daniel. *The World of UFOs* (9–12). Illus. 1978, Harper $13.95 (0-397-31780-8). A history of the many sightings of UFOs from 1947 to the mid-1970s. [001.9]

9488 Curran, Douglas. *In Advance of the Landing: Folk Concepts of Outer Space* (10–12). Illus. 1986, Abbeville paper $16.95 (0-89659-523-4). About the people who believe in UFOs and aliens from outer space. (Rev: BL 5/1/86) [001.9]

9489 Curran, Robert, et al. *The Haunted: One Family's Nightmare* (10–12). 1988, St. Martin's $16.95 (0-312-01440-6). The Smurl family's duplex is possessed by 4 spirits, one of whom is a murderer and another a demon. (Rev: BL 4/1/88) [133.426]

9490 Daniken, Erich von. *Chariots of the Gods? Unsolved Mysteries of the Past* (9–12). Trans. by Michael Heron. Illus. 1970, Putnam $42.50 (0-317-19961-7); Berkley paper $3.50 (0-425-07481-1). A fascinating argument for the belief that the earth was visited long ago by people from other planets. [001.9]

9491 Dinsdale, Tim. *Loch Ness Monster* (9–12). 4th ed. Illus. 1982, Routledge paper $14.95 (0-7100-9022-6). An account of the search for Nessie, the monster that supposedly lives in this picturesque lake in the Scottish Highlands. [001.9]

9492 Dunkling, Leslie. *Guinness Book of Names* (8–12). 1989, Sterling paper $12.95 (0-85112-327-9). A fascinating collection of all kinds of personal and place names with emphasis on the unusual. (Rev: BL 11/1/86; SLJ 12/86) [929.4]

9493 Fairley, John, and Simon Welfare. *Arthur C. Clarke's World of Strange Powers* (8–12). 1984, Putnam $19.95 (0-399-13066-7). A collection of stories about unusual phenomena such as ghosts and reincarnation. [001.9]

9494 Feldman, David. *When Do Fish Sleep? And Other Imponderables of Everyday Life* (9–12). 1989, Harper $15.95 (0-06-016161-2). Part of a series that answers such questions as "Why is bubble gum pink?" Other books in this series are: *Imponderables* (1986) and *Why Do Clocks Run Clockwise?* (1987). (Rev: BL 10/1/89) [031.02]

9495 Feldman, David. *Why Do Clocks Run Clockwise? and Other Imponderables: Mysteries of Everyday Life Explained by David Feldman* (9–12). Illus. 1987, Harper $14.95 (0-06-015781-X). The author answers questions such as "Why do ketchup bottles have narrow necks?" and "Why do nurses wear white?" A sequel to: *Imponderables* (Morrow, 1986). (Rev: BL 1/15/88) [031]

9496 Feldman, David. *Why Do Dogs Have Wet Noses? And Other Imponderables of Everyday Life* (9–12). Illus. 1990, Harper $17.95 (0-06-016293-7). One of a series of books of imponderables—e.g., *When Do Fish Sleep?* (1989)—that answer such questions as "How did the football get its shape?" (Rev: BL 9/15/90) [031.02]

9497 Floyd, E. Randall. *Great Southern Mysteries* (9–12). 1989, August House $16.95 (0-87483-097-4). A collection of oddities about the past and present that leaves many unanswered questions. (Rev: BL 10/15/89; SLJ 5/90) [002]

9498 Forbes, Malcolm, and Jeff Bloch. *What a Way to Go* (10–12). Illus. 1988, Simon & Schuster $16.95 (0-671-65709-7). Unusual stories involving the deaths of 175 famous people. (Rev: BL 6/1/88) [920]

9499 Gardner, Martin. *The New Age: Notes of a Fringe-Watcher* (10–12). Illus. 1988, Prometheus $19.95 (0-87975-432-X). A skeptic takes on spiritualists and psychics and tries to debunk them. (Rev: BL 4/1/88) [133]

9500 Gittelson, Bernard, and Laura Torbet. *Intangible Evidence* (9–12). Illus. 1987, Simon & Schuster $24.95 (0-671-64800-1); paper $14.95 (0-671-62541-0). A review of psychic phenomena that includes sections of palmistry and astrology. (Rev: BL 10/15/87) [133.8]

9501 Goldberg, M. Hirsh. *The Book of Lies* (9–12). Illus. 1990, Morrow $15.95 (0-688-08443-5). A fascinating collection of facts about such skulduggery as Watergate and the dyed hair of Elvis Presley. (Rev: BL 4/15/90) [177.3]

9502 Good, Timothy. *Above Top Secret: The Worldwide U.F.O. Cover-Up* (10–12). Illus. 1988, Morrow $18.95 (0-688-07860-5). A thorough investigation of the UFO phenomenon,

587

international in scope, and supplying history dating back to the 1930s. (Rev: BL 6/1/88) [001.9]

9503 *Guinness Book of Answers* (9–12). Illus. 1989, Sterling $17.95 (0-85112-334-1). A wealth of general information is contained in this volume arranged by subject. (Rev: BR 9–10/86; SLJ 4/86) [310]

9504 Haislip, Barbara. *Stars, Spells, Secrets, and Sorcery: A Do-It-Yourself Book of the Occult* (7–12). Illus. 1978, Dell paper $1.75 (0-440-98454-8). This book is a rundown on such subjects as I Ching, tarot cards, and astrology. [133.5]

9505 Heymann, Tom. *On an Average Day . . .* (9–12). 1989, Ballantine paper $6.95 (0-449-90453-9). A collection of trivia and statistics about everyday life in America. (Rev: BL 9/1/89) [031]

9506 Holzer, Hans. *Best True Ghost Stories* (10–12). 1986, Prentice paper $6.95 (0-13-071928-5). A psychic investigator tells about some of his recent cases. [133.1]

9507 Hopkins, Budd. *Intruders: The Incredible Visitations at Copley Woods* (10–12). Illus. 1987, Random $17.95 (0-394-56076-0). For better readers, the story of people who claim to have been abducted by aliens from UFOs. (Rev: BL 4/1/87; VOYA 10/87) [001.9]

9508 Jarvis, Sharon, ed. *The Uninvited: True Tales of the Unknown, Vol. II* (9–12). 1989, Bantam paper $3.95 (0-553-28251-4). A collection of 13 true tales that involve such phenomena as UFOs, vampires, and Bigfoot. (Rev: VOYA 4/90) [133]

9509 Kennedy, Crawford Q. *The Divination Handbook* (9–12). 1990, Signet paper $4.50 (0-451-16366-4). This unusual book tells the reader how to forecast the future through such media as tea leaves and coffee grounds. (Rev: VOYA 6/90) [133.3]

9510 Klass, Philip J. *UFOs Explained* (9–12). Illus. 1975, Random paper $6.95 (0-394-72106-3). Using many sightings as examples, the author tries to sort out fact from fancy. [001.9]

9511 Lessem, Don. *The Worst of Everything* (9–12). 1988, McGraw paper $6.95 (0-07-037473-2). An unusual book of lists that deals with the worst of everything, e.g., the world's dullest people. (Rev: BL 5/1/88) [031]

9512 Long, Greg. *Examining the Earthlight Theory: The Yakima UFO Microcosm* (9–12). Illus. 1990, Center for UFO Studies $17.95 (0-929343-57-3). An investigation of the many sightings of UFOs on the Yakima Indian Reservation in Washington State. (Rev: BL 7/90) [001.942]

9513 MacDonald, Hope. *When Angels Appear* (10–12). 1982, Zondervan paper $6.95 (0-310-28531-3). A series of eyewitness accounts of supernatural phenomena. [133]

9514 McFarlan, Donald, ed. *Guinness Book of World Records 1990–91* (7–12). 1990, Bantam paper $5.95 (0-553-28452-5). The ultimate listing of superlatives in every field. [032]

9515 Mackal, Roy P. *The Monsters of Loch Ness* (9–12). Illus. 1976, Swallow paper $9.95. The story of the author's search for the Loch Ness monster from 1965 through 1970. [001.9]

9516 McWhirter, Norris, et al., eds. *Guinness Book of World Records* (6–12). Illus. 1989, Sterling LB $21.49 (0-8069-0276-0); Bantam paper $4.95 (0-27926-2). The one and only Guinness and its collection of famous facts. [032]

9517 Marsden, Simon. *The Haunted Realm: Ghosts, Spirits and Their Uncanny Abodes* (10–12). Illus. 1987, Dutton $19.95 (0-525-24498-0). Photographs of some of the stately homes of England and stories of the ghosts that inhabit them. (Rev: BL 6/1/87) [133.1]

9518 Myers, Arthur. *The Ghostly Register* (9–12). Illus. 1986, Contemporary paper $9.95 (0-8092-5081-0). A guide to 64 houses that are reputedly haunted. (Rev: SLJ 3/87) [133.1]

9519 Nerys, Dee. *Fortune-Telling by Playing Cards* (9–12). 1982, Sterling paper $7.95 (0-85030-266-8). How to see into the future through a deck of playing cards. [133.3]

9520 Nickell, Joe, and John F. Fischer. *Secrets of the Supernatural: Investigating the World's Occult Mysteries* (9–12). Illus. 1988, Prometheus $18.95 (0-87975-461-3). The scientific investigation of 10 supernatural occurrences. (Rev: BL 9/1/88) [133]

9521 Page, Michael. *Encyclopedia of Things That Never Were: Creatures, Places, and People* (8–12). Illus. 1987, Viking $25.00 (0-670-81607-8). In addition to covering folklore and mythology, this book covers strange places and creatures from literature, science, magic, and history. (Rev: BR 9–10/87) [398]

9522 Pelton, Robert W. *Loony Laws: That You Never Knew You Were Breaking* (9–12). 1990, Walker paper $8.95 (0-8027-7339-7). A rundown on such unusual laws as the illegality of falling asleep in a barber's chair in Erie, Pennsylvania. (Rev: BL 7/90) [349.73]

9523 Picknett, Lynn. *Flights of Fancy? 100 Years of Paranormal Experiences* (9–12). Illus. 1988, Ward Lock $29.95 (0-7063-6526-7). An exploration of the paranormal from metal bending to fairies. (Rev: BL 9/1/88) [133]

9524 Pollack, Rachel. *Teach Yourself Fortune Telling: Palmistry, the Crystal Ball, Runes, Tea Leaves, the Tarot* (9–12). Illus. 1986, Henry Holt paper $10.95 (0-8050-0125-5). This book describes how one can become an amateur fortune-teller and concentrates on the tarot cards and what they mean. (Rev: BL 12/15/86) [133.3]

9525 Reader's Digest, eds. *Mysteries of the Unexplained* (9–12). Illus. 1983, Reader's Digest $24.95 (0-89577-146-2). In this large, well-illustrated book, such topics as prophecies and UFOs are explored. [001.9]

9526 Riccio, Dolores, and Joan Bingham. *Haunted Houses, U.S.A.* (10–12). Illus. 1989, Pocket paper $8.95 (0-671-66258-9). A travel guide to haunted houses that gives background information and is arranged geographically. (Rev: VOYA 12/89) [133.1]

9527 Roberts, Nancy. *Haunted Houses: Tales from 30 American Homes* (10–12). Illus. 1988, Globe Pequot $15.95 (0-87106-775-7); paper $9.95 (0-87106-768-4). Eerie tales of hauntings in homes including the one where the "Rosemary's baby" story originated. (Rev: BL 7/88) [133.1]

9528 Rovin, Jeff. *The Encyclopedia of Monsters* (8–12). Illus. 1989, Facts on File $29.95 (0-8160-1824-3). A collection of monsters from such diverse fields as folklore, movies, advertising, religion, and bubble-gum cards. (Rev: VOYA 4/90) [398]

9529 Rovin, Jeff. *The Encyclopedia of Superheroes* (9–12). Illus. 1985, Facts on File $29.95 (0-8160-1168-0); paper $19.95 (0-8160-1679-8). Here is a dictionary of more than 1,000 superheroes culled from mythology, TV, movies, literature, and (chiefly) comic books. (Rev: BL 11/1/85) [001.51]

9530 Schultz, Ted, ed. *Fringes of Reason: A Whole Earth Catalog* (10–12). Illus. 1989, Crown paper $14.95 (0-517-57165-X). An account of contemporary people who live by unusual beliefs like Channeling, Apocalypse psychology, and a knowledge of Spontaneous Human Combustion. (Rev: VOYA 8/89) [133]

9531 Scott, Beth, and Michael Norman. *Haunted Heartland* (10–12). 1985, Northword $19.95 (0-942802-96-9); Warner paper $4.95 (0-446-35725-1). This is a scary collection of supposedly true ghost stories all from the Midwest. (Rev: BL 11/15/85; SLJ 3/86) [133]

9532 Spencer, John, and Hilary Evans, eds. *Phenomenon: Forty Years of Flying Saucers* (10–12). 1989, Avon paper $4.50 (0-380-70654-7). A serious collection of essays and reports from many sources that tries to separate fact from imagination. (Rev: BL 3/15/89) [001.9]

9533 Stein, Wendy. *Atlantis: Opposing Viewpoints* (9–12). Illus. 1989, Greenhaven $12.95 (0-89908-056-1). The possibility of the existence of the ancient site and its possible location are explored. (Rev: BL 3/1/89; SLJ 6/89) [398.2]

9534 Stern, Jane, and Michael Stern. *The Encyclopedia of Bad Taste* (9–12). Illus. 1990, Harper $29.95 (0-06-016470-0). The whole world of bad taste from polyester to fuzzy dice is explored in this witty catalog, a tribute to pop culture. (Rev: BL 9/1/90) [031.02]

9535 Strieber, Whitley. *Communion: A True Story* (9–12). 1987, Morrow $17.95 (0-688-07086-8); Avon paper $4.95 (0-380-70388-2). The author describes the many visits he has had from nonhuman aliens. (Rev: SLJ 8/87) [574.999]

9536 Time-Life Books, eds. *Ghosts* (9–12). Illus. 1984, Silver Burdett LB $25.93 (0-8094-5217-0). A lavishly illustrated book about ghosts, their habits, their haunts, and the power of exorcism. Part of the Enchanted World series available through Silver Burdett that includes these titles: *Lore of Love, The Secret Arts,* and *Tales of Terror* (all 1987). [133.1]

9537 Tyndall, Carolyn, et al. *And the Lucky Winner Is . . .* (9–12). 1986, St. Martin's paper $3.95 (0-312-90025-2). This manual is a guide to entering and winning all sorts of contests and sweepstakes. [914]

9538 Vallee, Jacques. *Confrontations: A Scientist's Search for Alien Contact* (9–12). 1990, Ballantine $19.95 (0-345-36453-8). A scientist looks at the UFO phenomenon and poses some explanations and further questions. (Rev: BL 4/15/90) [001.9]

9539 Varasdi, J. Allen. *Myth Information* (8–12). 1989, Ballantine paper $3.95 (0-345-35985-2). A fascinating collection of facts that challenge some popular beliefs such as the belief that the American buffalo is really a bison. (Rev: BL 11/1/89) [001.9]

9540 Walters, Ed, and Frances Walters. *The Gulf Breeze Sightings: The Most Astounding Multiple Sightings of UFOs in U.S. History* (10–12). Illus. 1990, Morrow $19.95 (0-688-09087-7). An account of many sightings of UFOs—in a readable account that adds to the controversy. (Rev: BL 1/1/90) [001.9]

9541 Wambach, Helen. *Reliving Past Lives* (10–12). 1984, Harper paper $6.95 (0-06-464080-9). These are case studies, collected by a psychologist, of people who claim to have lived previous lives. [127]

9542 Warren, William E. *The Screaming Skull* (9–12). 1987, Prentice $10.95 (0-13-796699-7). This is a collection of true stories of unexplained phenomena such as ghosts and strange disappearances. (Rev: VOYA 12/87) [152.2]

9543 Wilson, Colin. *Poltergeist: A Study in Destructive Haunting* (9–12). 1983, Putnam paper $6.95 (0-399-50732-9). Several cases of poltergeist intervention are cited in this fascinating book. [133.1]

Sports and Games

General and Miscellaneous

9544 Allsen, Phillip E., and Alan R. Witbeck. *Racquetball* (10–12). 1988, W. C. Brown paper $6.20 (0-318-35056-4). From the simple to the complex, this manual covers the techniques and strategies used in racquetball. [796.34]

9545 Alvarez, A. *Feeding the Rat: Profile of a Climber* (10–12). 1989, Atlantic Monthly $17.95 (0-87113-307-5). Through a profile of the Welshman Mo Anthoine, the author gives a fine introduction to mountaineering around the world. (Rev: BL 6/15/89) [796.522]

9546 Anderson, Dave, ed. *The Red Smith Reader* (9–12). 1982, Random paper $7.95 (0-394-71750-3). A collection of pieces by the famous sportscaster on such topics as fishing and the Olympics. [796]

9547 Anderson, Harry, and Turk Pipkin. *Harry Anderson's Games You Can't Lose: A Guide for Suckers* (9–12). Illus. 1989, Pocket paper $6.95 (0-671-64727-X). Anderson, a TV entertainer, unmasks the secrets of gamblers and con artists. (Rev: BL 3/15/89) [795]

9548 Banks, Mike. *Mountain Climbing for Beginners* (10–12). Illus. 1978, Scarborough $8.95 (0-8128-2448-2); paper $3.95 (0-8128-2447-4). This is a guide for those who are interested in basic knowledge of this sport. [796.5]

9549 Barash, David P. *The Great Outdoors* (10–12). 1989, Lyle Stuart $17.95 (0-8184-0496-5). Outdoor pursuits such as horseback riding, backpacking, cross-country skiing, and stargazing are discussed. (Rev: BL 5/1/89) [796.5]

9550 Berkow, Ira. *Pitchers Do Get Lonely and Other Sports Stories* (8–12). 1988, Macmillan $17.95 (0-689-11964-X). *New York Times* columnist Berkow writes entertainingly about people in sports. (Rev: BL 4/15/88) [796]

9551 Blum, Arlene. *Annapurna: A Woman's Place* (10–12). 1980, Sierra $19.95 (0-87156-236-7); paper $10.95 (0-87156-806-3). An account of an all-women mountaineering team and their ascent of Annapurna. [796.5]

9552 Boehm, David A., et al., eds. *Guinness Sports Record Book, 1990–91* (7–12). Illus. 1990, Sterling $17.95 (0-8069-7304-8); paper $11.95 (0-8069-7305-6). From archery to yachting, this book gives records set in over 60 sports. [796.03]

9553 Charlton, James, et al. *Croquet: Its History, Strategy, Rules, and Records* (9–12). Rev. ed. Illus. 1988, Greene paper $11.95 (0-8289-0666-1). An introduction to this historic and interesting lawn game is written with humor and charm. (Rev: BL 9/1/88) [796.35]

9554 Cobb, Sue. *The Edge of Everest: A Woman Challenges the Mountain* (9–12). Illus. 1989, Stackpole $16.95 (0-8117-1681-3). An account of the grueling almost successful attempt to scale Mount Everest by an American expedition that included the author, a 51-year-old attorney. (Rev: BL 11/1/89) [796.5]

9555 Cook, Sam. *Quiet Magic* (10–12). Illus. 1988, Pfeifer-Hamilton $16.95 (0-938586-17-3). A selection of the author's newspaper columns on outdoor life, hunting, fishing, and winter sports. (Rev: BL 12/15/88) [796.5]

9556 Davis, Mac. *Great Sports Humor* (9–12). 1982, Putnam paper $4.95 (0-448-12327-4). True humorous stories from a variety of sources are retold in this volume. [796]

9557 Davis, Mac. *Strange and Incredible Sports Happenings* (9–12). 1982, Putnam paper $4.95 (0-448-12326-6). Weird and wonderful stories from a number of sources. [796]

9558 Diagram Group. *The Rule Book* (9–12). Illus. 1987, St. Martin's paper $9.95 (0-312-00677-2). This book gives a little history of 55 sports plus an outline of the rules and regulations of each of them. [796]

9559 Dintiman, George B., and Robert D. Ward. *Sport Speed* (9–12). Illus. 1988, Leisure Pr. paper $11.95 (0-88011-325-1). A discussion of speed in sports and how athletes can improve or correct their performance in this area. (Rev: BL 9/15/88) [613.7]

9560 Edwards, Sally. *Triathlon: A Triple Fitness Sport* (10–12). Illus. 1983, Contemporary paper $10.95 (0-8092-5555-3). A guide to this grueling sports event that combines swimming, running, and cycling. [796.4]

9561 Egbert, Barbara. *Action Cheerleading* (9–12). Illus. 1985, Sterling paper $9.95 (0-8069-7886-4). A manual that is as enthusiastic as its subject and covers both basic and complicated routines. (Rev: BL 6/15/85; SLJ 5/85) [791]

9562 Egbert, Barbara. *Cheerleading and Songleading* (10–12). Illus. 1980, Sterling paper $9.95 (0-8069-8950-5). An introduction to cheerleading with 20 stunts described plus an extensive section on how to be an effective song leader. [791]

9563 Feminist Press Staff. *Out of the Bleachers* (10–12). 1979, McGraw $14.04 (0-07-020429-2). An anthology of articles dealing with women in sports. [798]

9564 Figler, Stephen, and Howard Figler. *The Athlete's Game Plan for College and Career* (10–12). 1984, Peterson's Guides paper $9.95 (0-87866-266-9). Advice for student athletes on how to combine sports, academic studies, and a possible career in sports. [796]

9565 Fixx, James F., et al. *Maximum Sports Performance* (10–12). Illus. 1985, Random $17.95 (0-394-53682-7). A book for coaches as well as players on how to improve such areas as coordination, speed, agility, and endurance. (Rev: BR 11–12/85; SLJ 2/86) [796]

9566 Fluegelman, Andrew. *More New Games! And Playful Ideas from the New Games Foundation* (7–12). Illus. 1981, Doubleday paper $9.95 (0-385-17514-0). A collection of 60 games usually requiring no special equipment and graded for amount of activity required. [790.1]

9567 Frommer, Harvey. *Sports Date Book* (8–12). 1981, Ace paper $2.50 (0-448-17214-3). Using a calendar approach, this is a listing of great sports events. [796]

9568 Gardiner, Steve. *Why I Climb: Personal Insights of Top Climbers* (10–12). Illus. 1990, Stackpole paper $12.95 (0-8117-2321-6). The pleasure in and need for mountaineering is revealed in a series of sketches about famous mountaineers. (Rev: BL 5/1/90) [796.5]

9569 Glowacz, Stefan, and Uli Wiesmeier. *Rocks around the World* (9–12). Trans. by Martin Boysen. Illus. 1989, Sierra Club $24.95 (0-87156-677-X). The thrilling experiences of Glowacz, an internationally known rock climber, are captured in his text and the impressive photographs of Wiesmeier. (Rev: BL 3/15/89) [796.5]

9570 Goldman, William, and Mike Lupica. *Wait till Next Year* (10–12). 1988, Bantam $19.95 (0-553-05319-1). Two writers combine their talents to produce an overview of the New York sports scene of 1987. (Rev: BL 12/15/88) [796]

9571 Gross, Albert C. *Endurance: The Events, the Athletes, the Attitude* (10–12). Illus. 1986, Dodd paper $8.95 (0-396-08393-5). The concept of endurance in sports and an exploration of whether limitations in this area exist are discussed. (Rev: SLJ 5/87) [796]

9572 *Guinness Sports Record Book, 1989–90* (7–12). Illus. 1989, Sterling $17.95 (0-8069-6711-2); paper $11.95 (0-8069-6711-0). After background material, each sport is handled separately in alphabetical order including Olympic competitions and such games as chess and scrabble. (Rev: BR 3–4/90) [796]

9573 Hogan, Marty, and Ken Wong. *High-Performance Racquetball* (9–12). Illus. 1985, HP Books paper $8.95 (0-89586-356-1). A professional player explains the rules of racquetball plus techniques and tips to help ensure success on the court. (Rev: BL 10/15/85) [798.343]

9574 Hollander, Zander, and David Schulz. *The Illustrated Sports Record Book* (9–12). 1987, NAL paper $3.95 (0-451-15743-5). A well-illustrated volume of facts and figures on several sports. [796]

9575 Horowitz, Judy, and Billy Bloom. *The Frisbee Book* (9–12). 1984, Macmillan paper $9.95 (0-88011-105-4). A thorough, informative, and often humorous guide to every facet of Frisbee use. [796]

9576 Iooss, Walter, and Frank Deford. *Sports People* (10–12). Illus. 1988, Abrams $35.00 (0-8109-1520-0). A photo album with captions of

100 sports personalities in action. (Rev: BL 12/15/88) [779]

9577 Krakauer, Jon. *Eiger Dreams: Ventures among Men and Mountains* (9–12). 1990, Lyons $17.95 (1-55821-057-1). The author writes in 12 different short pieces about the dangers and thrills of mountaineering. (Rev: SLJ 8/90) [795.5]

9578 Kuntzleman, Charles T. *The Complete Book of Walking* (10–12). 1989, Pocket paper $4.95 (0-671-70074-X). Tips on how to get the most out of walking are given plus good information on training. [796.4]

9579 Liss, Howard. *The Giant Book of More Strange But True Sports Stories* (9–12). Illus. 1983, Random paper $7.95 (0-394-85633-3). This is a collection of 150 short pieces about unusual happenings in baseball, football, boxing, golf, and auto racing. [797]

9580 Long, John. *How to Rock Climb!* (9–12). Illus. 1989, Chockstone paper $9.95 (0-934641-20-X). A fine handbook that will serve as both an introduction to the sport as well as a manual for the expert. (Rev: BL 9/1/89) [796.5]

9581 Loughman, Michael. *Learning to Rock Climb* (10–12). Illus. 1981, Sierra Club paper $10.95 (0-87156-281-2). A guide to mountaineering that stresses safety and sound techniques. [796.5]

9582 Lupica, Mike. *Shooting from the Lip* (8–12). 1988, Bonus Books $15.95 (0-933893-60-4). Fun mixed with pathos in the short pieces by the sports columnist of the New York *Daily News*. (Rev: BL 4/15/88) [796]

9583 McIntyre, Thomas. *The Way of the Hunter: The Art and Spirit of Modern Hunting* (9–12). Illus. 1988, Dutton $18.95 (0-525-24718-1). This book covers various kinds of hunting in various locales using a number of different kinds of weapons. (Rev: BL 11/15/88) [799.2]

9584 Michener, James A. *Sports in America* (10–12). 1987, Fawcett paper $4.95 (0-449-21450-8). A review of sports today that points up the excesses of the industry. [796]

9585 Mizerak, Steve, and Joel Cohen. *Steve Mizerak's Pocket Billiards: Tips and Trick Shots* (10–12). 1982, Contemporary paper $8.95 (0-8092-5779-3). An introduction to billiards and tips on how to build one's skills. Also use: *Inside Pocket Billiards* (1973). [794.7]

9586 Nash, Bruce, and Allan Zullo. *The Sports Hall of Shame* (9–12). Illus. 1987, Pocket paper $8.95 (0-671-63387-2). From the authors who have already covered baseball and football, here

are terrible moments from a number of other sports. (Rev: BL 10/1/87) [796.02]

9587 Neil, Randy L. *The Official Pompon Girl's Handbook* (7–12). Illus. 1983, St. Martin's paper $6.95 (0-312-58222-6). Various routines are introduced in text and pictures plus all sorts of background material. [791]

9588 Neil, Randy L., and Elaine Hart. *The All-New Official Cheerleader's Handbook* (10–12). Illus. 1986, Simon & Schuster paper $14.95 (0-671-61210-7). This guide covers cheerleading from basic movements to complex stunts. [791]

9589 Nuwer, Hank. *Recruiting in Sports* (9–12). 1989, Watts LB $12.90 (0-531-10796-5). A guide to the sports recruitment program of colleges and universities with greatest emphasis on football and basketball. (Rev: BL 10/1/89; BR 3–4/90; SLJ 12/89; VOYA 4/90) [796]

9590 Orlick, Terry. *Cooperative Sports and Games Book* (10–12). 1975, Pantheon paper $9.95 (0-318-17035-3). This book describes 100 games that depend on cooperation, rather than competition, for success. [798]

9591 Parker, Donald, and David Hewitt. *Table Tennis* (9–12). Illus. 1990, Ward Lock paper $6.95 (0-7063-6775-8). Two English coaches give concise but thorough information about this sport, which now has a place in Olympic competition. (Rev: BL 10/1/90) [796.346]

9592 Phillips, Betty Lou. *Go! Fight! Win! The National Cheerleaders Association Guide for Cheerleaders* (10–12). Illus. 1981, Delacorte LB $11.80 (0-440-02957-0); paper $9.95 (0-440-02956-2). An introduction to cheerleading with many photographs that covers stunts, formations, and cheers. [791]

9593 Rice, Wayne, and Mike Yaconelli. *Play It! Over 400 Great Games for Groups* (8–12). Illus. 1986, Zondervan paper $10.95 (0-310-35191-X). All kinds of games—indoor, outdoor, active, cerebral, and those involving few or more players—are described. (Rev: BL 1/15/87) [790.1]

9594 Schrier, Eric W., and William F. Allman, eds. *Newton at the Bat: The Science in Sports* (9–12). 1984, Macmillan paper $7.95 (0-684-18820-1). This account covers physical and physiological aspects of a number of sports including golf, skiing, sailing, and wrestling. [797]

9595 Scott, Dave, and Liz Barrett. *Dave Scott's Triathlon Training* (10–12). Illus. 1986, Simon & Schuster paper $10.95 (0-671-60473-2). A thorough training program for those who want to enter the combination swimming, cycling, and running event. (Rev: BL 12/1/86) [796.4]

9596 Sherwonit, Bill. *To the Top of Denali: Climbing Adventures on North America's Highest Peak* (9–12). Illus. 1990, Alaska Northwest paper $10.95 (0-88240-402-4). This book gives details of the major mountain climbing expeditions that have been associated with Mount Denali, also known as Mount McKinley. (Rev: BL 9/15/90) [796.5]

9597 Silverman, Ruth, ed. *Athletes: Photographs, 1860–1986* (8–12). Illus. 1987, Knopf $35.00 (0-394-55104-4). A collection of 139 sports photographs that cover the history of the medium and reveal inner aspects of the sports world. (Rev: BL 1/15/88) [796]

9598 Siner, Howard, ed. *Sports Classics: American Writers Choose Their Best* (10–12). 1983, Putnam $16.95 (0-698-11248-2). In this anthology culled from a variety of newspapers and magazines, sport writers have chosen their favorite pieces. [796]

9599 Sloan, Dave, ed. *Best Sports Stories: The Anthology That Honors 1989's Top Sports Writing and Photography* (9–12). Illus. 1990, Sporting News paper $10.95 (0-89204-353-9). An anthology of the best sports journalism and photography of 1989. (Rev: BL 8/90) [796.058]

9600 Smith, Susan Rogerson. *Cheerleader-Baton Twirler: Try Out and Win* (8–12). Illus. 1985, Tor paper $2.50 (0-812-59470-3). All kinds of tips not only on cheerleading and baton twirling but also on fitness, beauty, and diet. (Rev: BL 6/15/85) [796.46]

9601 Sporting News, eds. *Best Sport Stories* (9–12). 1990, Sporting News paper $10.95 (0-89204-353-9). This is one of the annual compilations of best sports articles from the pages of *Sporting News*. [798]

9602 Sports Illustrated, eds. *Sports Illustrated Handball* (9–12). Illus. 1976, Harper paper $2.95 (0-397-01095-8). This is a fine introduction to handball with many accompanying pictures to illustrate moves and techniques. [976.31]

9603 Sports Illustrated, eds. *Sports Illustrated Squash* (9–12). Illus. 1971, Harper paper $2.95 (0-397-00838-4). A concise, well-illustrated guide to this indoor sport. [796.31]

9604 Vecsey, George. *A Year in the Sun: The Life & Times of a Sports Columnist* (10–12). 1989, Random $19.95 (0-8129-1678-6). In diary format, the author tells of a year of his sports writing that included covering the World Soccer Cup and the Good Will Games in Moscow. (Rev: BR 9–10/89; SLJ 9/89; VOYA 10/89) [796]

9605 Walker, David A., and James Haskins. *Double Dutch* (7–12). 1986, Enslow $13.95 (0-89490-096-X). A history of jumping rope with old rhymes plus tips on basic skills. (Rev: BR 11–12/86) [793]

9606 Whittingham, Richard, ed. *Life in Sports* (9–12). Illus. 1985, Harper paper $14.95 (0-06-091475-0). A group of eloquent sports photographs from the pages of *Life* magazine. [796]

9607 Williams, John C., and Glenn Helgeland. *Archery for Beginners* (9–12). Rev. ed. Illus. 1985, Contemporary paper $8.95 (0-8092-5256-2). From an Olympic archer and coach comes a book that covers all introductory material from equipment to shooting techniques and applications in such other sports as hunting and fishing. (Rev: BL 8/85) [799.32]

9608 Wiswell, Phil. *Kids' Games: Traditional Indoor and Outdoor Activities for Children of All Ages* (8–12). Illus. 1987, Doubleday paper $12.95 (0-385-23405-8). A description with rules of many outdoor games plus some board games and indoor activities. (Rev: BL 3/15/87) [793.4]

9609 Woods, Karl Morrow. *The Sports Success Book: The Athlete's Guide to Sports Achievement* (9–12). Illus. 1985, Copperfield Pr. $17.95 (0-933857-00-4); paper $12.95 (0-933857-01-2). A guide to becoming a successful athlete from junior high through the Olympics to the pros. (Rev: BL 10/15/85; SLJ 4/86; VOYA 12/85) [796]

Air Games and Sports

9610 Coombs, Charles. *Soaring: Where the Hawks and Eagles Fly* (9–12). Illus. 1988, Henry Holt $13.95 (0-8050-0496-3). Through the experiences of a fictitious student, the author explains the basics of the sport of soaring. (Rev: VOYA 2/89) [797.5]

9611 Dean, Anabel. *Wind Sports* (7–12). 1982, Westminster $12.95 (0-664-32696-X). An introduction to sports that rely on the wind, such as gliding, hang gliding, parachuting, and ice boating. [797.5]

9612 Fair, Erik. *Right Stuff for New Hang Glider Pilots* (9–12). Illus. 1987, Publitec Editions paper $7.95 (0-913581-00-3). A collection of articles by Fair exploring many topics related to hang gliding. (Rev: BL 4/1/87) [797.5]

9613 Wirth, Dick. *Ballooning: The Complete Guide to Riding the Winds* (10–12). Illus. 1984, Random paper $12.95 (0-394-72796-7). The parts of the balloon are fully described as well as navigational tips. [797.5]

Automobile Racing

9614 Fox, Jack C. *The Illustrated History of the Indianapolis 500* (9–12). 3rd ed. Illus. 1985, Carl Hungness $69.95 (0-915088-05-3). This is an expensive but handsomely illustrated volume that covers each race and gives additional information on drivers, records, and prizes. (Rev: BL 9/1/85) [796.7]

9615 Henry, Alan. *Fifty Famous Motor Races* (9–12). Illus. 1988, Patrick Stephens $29.95 (0-85059-937-7). Such great races as Daytona, Grand Prix, and Le Mans are highlighted. (Rev: BL 9/15/88) [796.7]

9616 Morrison, Ian. *The Guinness Guide to Formula One* (9–12). Illus. 1989, Sterling $24.95 (0-85112-348-1). A thorough account of the past and present of the Formula One Grand Prix automobile race. (Rev: BL 10/15/89) [796.7]

9617 Nye, Doug. *Famous Racing Cars: Fifty of the Greatest, from Panhard to Williams-Honda* (10–12). Illus. 1989, Patrick Stephens $29.95 (0-85260-036-5). In 5 to 10 pages per car, 50 racing greats are discussed in pictures and a text that includes information on design, performance, and engineering. (Rev: BL 5/1/89) [629.2]

9618 Roebuck, Nigel. *Grand Prix Greats: A Personal Appreciation of 25 Famous Formula 1 Drivers* (9–12). Illus. 1987, Stevens $24.95 (0-85059-792-7). A lively book about the Grand Prix and of 25 race car drivers who participated in it. (Rev: BL 5/15/87) [796.7]

9619 Stambler, Irwin. *Off-Roading: Racing and Riding* (9–12). 1984, Putnam $10.95 (0-399-21144-6). This is a guide to driving and racing such 4-wheel drive vehicles as jeeps, vans, and dune buggies. [796.7]

Baseball

9620 Adair, Robert K. *The Physics of Baseball* (10–12). Illus. 1990, Harper $16.95 (0-06-055188-7); paper $7.95 (0-06-096461-8). This account describes the physical principles behind such baseball elements as pitching and batting. (Rev: SLJ 7/90) [796.357]

9621 Angell, Roger. *Five Seasons: A Baseball Companion* (9–12). 1988, Simon & Schuster paper $8.95 (0-671-65692-9). A history of the game of baseball in America from 1972 to 1979. [796.357]

9622 Angell, Roger. *Season Ticket: A Baseball Companion* (10–12). 1988, Houghton $18.95 (0-395-38165-7). A further collection of columns on baseball culled from *New Yorker* articles that appeared from 1983 through 1987. Preceded by: *Late Innings* (Ballantine, 1988). (Rev: BL 1/15/88) [796]

9623 Ashburn, Richie, and Allen Lewis. *Richie Ashburn's Phillies Trivia* (9–12). 1983, Running Pr. LB $15.90 (0-89471-220-9). Fans of the Philadelphia baseball team will find 312 questions on their team in this trivia book. [796.357]

9624 Asinof, Eliot. *Eight Men Out* (9–12). 1981, Holtzman $24.95 (0-941372-00-6); Henry Holt paper $9.95 (0-8050-0346-0). The story of a shameful incident in baseball history when 8 Chicago White Sox players in 1919 were bribed into losing the World Series. [796.357]

9625 Astor, Gerald, et al. *The Baseball Hall of Fame 50th Anniversary Book* (8–12). Illus. 1988, Prentice $40.00 (0-13-056573-3). A readable history of baseball plus profiles of 9 all-time greats. (Rev: BL 9/1/88) [796.357]

9626 Boggs, Wade, and David Brisson. *The Techniques of Modern Hitting* (9–12). Illus. 1990, Putnam paper $12.95 (0-399-51595-X). The ace slugger reveals some of his secrets. (Rev: BL 5/1/90) [796.357]

9627 Boswell, Thomas. *The Heart of the Order* (10–12). Illus. 1989, Doubleday $18.95 (0-385-19967-8). A collection of articles and essays by one of America's best contemporary writers about baseball. (Rev: BL 3/1/89) [796.357]

9628 Boswell, Thomas. *How Life Imitates the World Series* (10–12). 1983, Penguin paper $7.95 (0-14-006469-9). An analysis of the spirit and tempo of baseball as it changes during the months from the beginning of a season to the World Series. [796.357]

9629 Bouton, Jim. *Ball Four* (9–12). Illus. 1990, Macmillan $21.95 (0-02-513980-0); paper $12.95 (0-02-030665-2). A behind-the-scenes look at big league baseball that openly criticizes many aspects of the game. [796.357]

9630 Breslin, Jimmy. *Can't Anybody Here Play This Game?* (9–12). 1982, Penguin paper $5.95 (0-14-006217-3). A humorous look at the first season of the Mets in 1962 and how they became known as the Hitless Wonders. [796.357]

9631 Brosnan, Jim. *The Long Season* (9–12). 1983, Penguin paper $6.95 (0-14-006754-X). A baseball diary on what it is like to play the long season. [796.357]

9632 Bryan, Mike. *Baseball Lives* (9–12). 1989, Pantheon $19.95 (0-394-56467-7). A series of interviews with all sorts of people connected with baseball including coaches, team doctors, vendors, and player agents. (Rev: BL 4/15/89) [796.357]

9633 Canseco, Jose, and Dave McKay. *Strength Training for Baseball* (9–12). Illus. 1990, Putnam paper $13.95 (0-399-51596-8). How to gain greater skill and strength in sports through exercise and weight training. (Rev: BL 5/1/90) [613.7]

9634 Carew, Rod, et al. *Rod Carew's Art and Science of Hitting* (9–12). Illus. 1986, Viking $17.95 (0-670-80905-5); Penguin paper $7.95 (0-14-008516-5). An ace batter covers the basics of hitting with examples of his and other players' experiences. (Rev: BL 7/86) [796.357]

9635 Carter, Craig, ed. *The Complete Baseball Record Book, 1990* (7–12). Illus. 1990, Sporting News paper $12.95 (0-89204-338-5). An excellent book that covers hitting, fielding, and pitching in both regular and championship seasons. [796.357]

9636 Coberly, Rich. *The No-Hit Hall of Fame: No-Hitters of the 20th Century* (9–12). Illus. 1985, Triple Play paper $13.95 (0-934289-00-X). This is the story of the 177 no-hit games played in the major leagues from 1900 to 1984. (Rev: BL 11/1/85) [796.357]

9637 Cohen, Stanley. *A Magic Summer* (8–12). 1988, Harcourt $16.95 (0-15-155096-4). A detailed look at the fateful 1969 baseball season when the Mets became the world's champions. (Rev: BL 4/15/88) [796.357]

9638 Dickey, Glenn. *The History of National League Baseball since 1876* (9–12). 1982, Scarborough House paper $9.95 (0-8128-6101-9). A history of how baseball has evolved over the years with plenty of background statistics. [796.357]

9639 Dickey, Glenn. *The History of the World Series since 1903* (8–12). Illus. 1984, Scarborough House $18.95 (0-8128-2951-4). The most memorable and important World Series are described in detail in this book. [796.357]

9640 Einstein, Charles, ed. *The Fireside Book of Baseball* (9–12). 4th ed. Illus. 1987, Simon & Schuster paper $10.95 (0-671-63812-2). An anthology of both fiction, nonfiction, and poetry about our national pastime. (Rev: BL 10/1/87) [796.357]

9641 Falkner, David. *The Nine Sides of the Diamond: Baseball's Great Glove Men on the Fine Art of Defense* (9–12). 1990, Times Books $18.95 (0-8129-1806-1). This is a discussion of each of the fielding positions as well as some of the superstars that filled these positions. (Rev: BL 4/1/90) [796.357]

9642 Falls, Joe. *The Detroit Tigers: An Illustrated History* (9–12). Illus. 1989, Walker $24.95 (0-8027-1082-4). A history of this team, its glories and defeats plus interviews with players past and present. (Rev: SLJ 9/89) [796.357]

9643 Fiffer, Steve. *How to Watch Baseball: A Fan's Guide to Savoring the Fine Points of the Game* (9–12). Illus. 1987, Facts on File $16.95 (0-8160-1354-3); paper $9.95 (0-8160-2001-9). A guide for spectators on how to enjoy the subtleties of baseball. (Rev: BL 3/15/87) [796.357]

9644 Fleming, G. H. *The Unforgettable Season* (9–12). 1982, Penguin paper $5.95 (0-14-006273-4). A re-creation of the 1908 baseball season. [796.357]

9645 Garagiola, Joe. *Baseball Is a Funny Game* (9–12). 1990, Harper paper $7.95 (0-06-091672-9). These are personal remembrances of Garagiola's days in baseball and growing up with Yogi Berra. [796.357]

9646 Goldis, Al, and Rick Wolff. *Breaking into the Big Leagues* (9–12). Illus. 1988, Leisure Pr. paper $10.95 (0-88011-298-0). A practical guide for those fledgling baseball players with eyes on the major leagues. (Rev: BL 4/1/88; BR 5–6/88) [796.357]

9647 Golenbock, Peter. *The Forever Boys* (10–12). Illus. 1991, Birch Lane Pr. $19.95 (1-55972-034-4). An examination of the Sun Belt Senior League in which many of the players are former big leaguers. (Rev: BL 12/15/90) [796.357]

9648 Gordon, Peter H., et al., eds. *Diamonds Are Forever: Artists and Writers on Baseball* (9–12). Illus. 1987, Chronicle $35.00 (0-87701-475-2); paper $18.95 (0-87701-468-X). An oversized book on all forms of art—prose, painting, photographs—inspired by baseball. (Rev: BL 2/15/88) [796.357]

9649 Grossinger, Richard, and Kevin Kerrane, eds. *Into the Temple of Baseball* (9–12). Illus. 1990, Celestial Arts paper $17.95 (0-89087-598-7). A delightful collection of poems, essays, and general pieces about baseball. (Rev: BL 5/1/90) [796.357]

9650 Gutman, Dan. *It Ain't Cheatin' If You Don't Get Caught* (9–12). 1990, Penguin paper $7.95 (0-14-011652-4). A history of cheating in baseball told with wit and humor. (Rev: BL 3/1/90) [796.357]

9651 Hargrove, Sharon, and Richard Hauer Costa. *Safe at Home: A Baseball Wife's Story* (10–12). Illus. 1989, Texas A & M Univ. Pr.

$16.95 (0-89096-376-2). The wife of a former major league player reveals another facet of the sport of baseball. (Rev: BL 6/1/89) [796.357]

9652 Hollander, Zander. *The Complete Handbook of Baseball* (7–12). 1989, NAL paper $5.95 (0-451-16449-0). An annual compilation of baseball statistics and other interesting facts. [796.357]

9653 Honig, Donald. *The American League: An Illustrated History* (9–12). Illus. 1987, Crown $22.50 (0-517-56685-0). This is a history of the American League from its inception in 1903 to the mid-1980s. Also use the companion volume *The National League: An Illustrated History* (1983). [796.357]

9654 Honig, Donald. *The Greatest First Basemen of All Times* (9–12). Illus. 1988, Crown $18.95 (0-517-56842-X). The author chooses his best first basemen and then explains why he made each choice. (Rev: SLJ 10/88) [796.357]

9655 Honig, Donald. *The Greatest Pitchers of All Time* (9–12). Illus. 1988, Crown $18.95 (0-517-56887-X). Profiles and portraits are given for each of the 22 pitchers featured in this book. (Rev: SLJ 2/89) [796.357]

9656 Honig, Donald. *The Power Hitters* (9–12). Illus. 1989, Sporting News $19.95 (0-89204-302-4). A profile of the 26 all-time best home-run hitters, beginning with Babe Ruth and ending with Mike Schmidt. (Rev: BL 7/89) [796.357]

9657 Honig, Donald. *The World Series: An Illustrated History from 1903 to the Present* (8–12). Illus. 1986, Crown $19.95 (0-517-56182-4). A history of the World Series that is distinguished by its amazing photographs. (Rev: SLJ 2/87) [796.357]

9658 Hoppel, Joe. *The Series* (8–12). Illus. 1988, Sporting News paper $12.95 (0-89204-272-9). Coverage of every World Series from 1903 to 1987 from the pages of *The Sporting News*. (Rev: BL 7/88) [796.357]

9659 Houk, Ralph, and Robert W. Creamer. *Season of Glory: The Amazing Saga of the 1961 New York Yankees* (9–12). 1988, Putnam $18.95 (0-399-13260-0). A chronicle of the amazing season of the Bronx Bombers and the home run records they set. (Rev: BL 3/15/88) [796.357]

9660 House, Tom. *The Winning Pitcher: Baseball's Top Pitchers Demonstrate What It Takes to Be an Ace* (7–12). Illus. 1987, Contemporary paper $10.95 (0-8092-4878-6). A discussion of the elements of good pitching and those players who have mastered them. (Rev: BL 6/1/87) [796.357]

9661 James, Bill. *The Baseball Book* (9–12). 1990, Random paper $12.95 (0-679-72411-7). An annual that focuses on current players and an analysis of last year's season. (Rev: BL 6/15/90) [796.357]

9662 James, Bill, and Mary A. Wirth. *The Bill James Historical Baseball Abstract* (9–12). 1988, Random $29.95 (0-394-53713-0); paper $15.95 (0-394-75805-6). This volume provides historical statistics and commentary on baseball. (Rev: BR 11–12/88; SLJ 8/88; VOYA 12/88) [796.357]

9663 Jarrett, William. *Timelines of Sports History: Baseball* (7–12). Illus. 1989, Facts on File $17.95 (0-8160-1918-5). A chronology of baseball events from 1903 through 1988. (Rev: BL 8/89; VOYA 2/90) [796.357]

9664 Johnstone, Jay. *Over the Edge: Baseball's Uncensored Exploits from Way Out in Left Field* (9–12). Illus. 1988, Bantam paper $3.95 (0-553-27285-3). A collection of humorous anecdotes about baseball that is a continuation of the author's *Temporary Insanity* (1985). (Rev: BL 4/15/87) [796.357]

9665 Johnstone, Jay, and Rick Talley. *Some of My Best Friends Are Crazy: Baseball's Favorite Lunatic Goes in Search of His Peers* (9–12). 1990, Macmillan $18.95 (0-02-559560-1). A collection of unusual, mostly humorous bits of trivia about baseball. (Rev: BL 5/15/90) [796.357]

9666 Jordan, Pat. *Sports Illustrated Pitching* (7–12). Rev. ed. Illus. 1988, NAL paper $9.95 (0-452-26101-5). Basic pitching skills are covered plus how to throw such pitches as the fastball and curveball. (Rev: BL 7/85) [796.357]

9667 Kahn, Roger. *The Boys of Summer* (10–12). Illus. 1987, Harper paper $9.95 (0-06-091416-5). An account of a boy growing up in Brooklyn and of his devotion to the Dodgers. [796.357]

9668 Kaplan, Jim. *Playing the Field: Why Defense Is the Most Fascinating Art in Major League Baseball* (9–12). Illus. 1987, Algonquin paper $13.95 (0-912697-36-9). An entertaining account of defensive baseball at various positions with many examples from games of the past. (Rev: SLJ 10/87) [796.357]

9669 Kindall, Jerry. *Sports Illustrated Baseball* (9–12). Illus. 1983, Harper $11.95 (0-06-015079-3); paper $9.95 (0-06-091055-0). Through diagrams, drawings, and photos plus text, the basics of baseball are explained. [796.357]

9670 Kingston, John. *Five-Hundred-Five Baseball Questions Your Friends Can't Answer* (8–12). 1981, Walker paper $3.95 (0-8027-7189-0). Questions like "How many stitches are there on a baseball?" are included in this collection of trivia. [796.357]

9671 Lee, Bill, and Dick Lally. *The Wrong Stuff* (10–12). 1985, Penguin paper $4.95 (0-14-007941-6). With much salty language, the former major-league pitcher talks about baseball during his career. [796.357]

9672 Lemke, Bob, and Dan Albaugh. *Sports Collector's Digest Baseball Card Price Guide* (9–12). Illus. 1988, Krause paper $12.95 (0-87341-105-6). A thorough guide to collectible baseball cards and their current prices. (Rev: BL 6/15/88) [769.49]

9673 Lenburg, Jeff. *Baseball's All-Star Game: A Game-by-Game Guide* (8–12). Illus. 1986, McFarland $18.95 (0-89950-231-8). From 1933 through 1986, here is an account of each of the baseball All-Star games and the important players. (Rev: BL 2/1/87; SLJ 2/87) [796.357]

9674 Luciano, Ron, and David Fisher. *The Fall of the Roman Umpire* (9–12). 1986, Bantam $15.95 (0-553-05136-9); paper $3.95 (0-553-26133-9). Another collection of random reflections about baseball. Some others are *Strike Two* (1985), *The Umpire Strikes Back* (1984), and *Remembrance of Swings Past* (1988). (Rev: BL 5/15/86) [796.333]

9675 Luciano, Ron, and David Fisher. *Remembrance of Swings Past* (10–12). 1988, Bantam $16.95 (0-553-05262-4). The third collection of humorous baseball pieces by the former umpire. (Rev: BL 5/15/88) [796.357]

9676 McCaffrey, Eugene, and Roger A. McCaffrey. *Players' Choice: Major League Baseball Players Vote on the All-Time Greats* (9–12). Illus. 1987, Facts on File $16.95 (0-8160-1362-4). Over 600 players were polled to find out who and what were "the best" in a variety of categories. (Rev: BL 3/15/87) [796.357]

9677 McCarver, Tim, and Ray Robinson. *Oh, Baby, I Love It!* (9–12). 1987, Random $16.95 (0-394-55691-7); Dell paper $4.95 (0-440-20083-0). McCarver, a former catcher and current announcer, tells of his 28 love affairs with baseball. (Rev: BR 11–12/87; SLJ 10/87; VOYA 10/87) [796.357]

9678 Major League Baseball Training Staff, and Lee Lowenfish. *The Professional Baseball Trainers' Fitness Book* (10–12). 1988, Warner paper $12.95 (0-446-38752-5). Trainers from the major league teams give advice on topics like exercise, diet, and fitness. (Rev: VOYA 8/88) [796.357]

9679 Marazzi, Rich, and Len Fiorito. *Aaron to Zuverink* (10–12). 1984, Avon paper $4.50 (0-

380-68445-4). More than 1,000 major league players of the 1950s are profiled. [796.357]

9680 Meyer, Gladys C. *Softball for Girls & Women* (10–12). Illus. 1982, Macmillan $15.95 (0-684-17458-8); paper $9.95 (0-684-18140-1). All facets of softball are explored in this guide geared to the specific needs of women. [796.357]

9681 Mlyn, Scott. *Before the Game* (9–12). Illus. 1988, Taylor paper $13.95 (0-87833-605-2). Various forms of pregame rituals and activities are explored in text and photographs. (Rev: BL 6/15/88) [796.357]

9682 Nash, Bruce, and Allan Zullo. *The Baseball Hall of Shame: Young Fan's Edition* (7–12). 1990, Pocket paper $2.95 (0-671-69354-9). Some of the darker moments in baseball history are retold under a variety of subjects. [796.357]

9683 Nash, Bruce, and Allan Zullo. *The Baseball Hall of Shame 4* (8–12). 1990, Pocket paper $7.95 (0-671-69172-4). The fourth collection of boo-boos involving our national pastime. Others are: Volume 1 (1986), Volume 2 (1986), and Volume 3 (1987). (Rev: BL 4/15/90) [796.357]

9684 Nelson, Kevin, ed. *Baseball's Greatest Quotes* (9–12). 1982, Simon & Schuster paper $7.95 (0-671-43474-8). A collection of wit and wisdom from people involved in baseball. Also use: *Baseball's Greatest Insults* (1984). [796.357]

9685 Nelson, Kevin. *The Greatest Stories Ever Told (about Baseball)* (8–12). 1986, Putnam paper $7.95 (0-399-51227-6). A topically arranged collection of anecdotes by the author of *Baseball's Greatest Quotes* (1984) and *Baseball's Greatest Insults* (1984). (Rev: BL 4/1/86; VOYA 8–10/86) [796.357]

9686 Nemec, David. *Great Baseball Feats, Facts & Firsts* (9–12). 1989, NAL paper $4.95 (0-451-16124-6). A well-organized compendium of fascinating baseball trivia. (Rev: BL 7/87) [796.357]

9687 Obojski, Robert. *Baseball's Strangest Moments* (7–12). Illus. 1988, Sterling LB $12.49 (0-8069-4195-2). A collection of tales about weird, usually funny, events in baseball. (Rev: BR 11–12/88) [796.357]

9688 Okrent, Daniel, and Steve Wulf. *Baseball Anecdotes* (9–12). 1989, Oxford Univ. Pr. $18.95 (0-19-504396-0). A colorful collection of facts and figures about the history and present status of baseball. (Rev: SLJ 9/89) [796.357]

9689 Pearlman, Donn. *Collecting Baseball Cards: Dimes to Dollars* (9–12). Illus. 1987, Bonus Books paper $6.95 (0-933893-30-2). A guide to this hobby that covers such topics as how to evaluate cards, where to locate cards, and how to organize a collection. (Rev: BL 4/1/87) [796.357]

9690 Phillips, Louis, and Arnie Markoe. *Baseball Rules Illustrated* (7–12). Illus. 1982, Simon & Schuster paper $7.95 (0-671-61136-4). Definitions of terms are included plus rules as they affect each position. [796.357]

9691 Rappoport, Ken. *Double Header* (9–12). 1982, Ace paper $2.25 (0-448-16843-X). The history of both the New York Yankees and the Los Angeles Dodgers. [796.357]

9692 Reichler, Joseph L., ed. *The Baseball Encyclopedia: The Complete and Official Record of Major League Baseball* (7–12). 6th ed. 1985, Macmillan $39.95 (0-02-601930-2). This has become the standard reference work on baseball and contains information through 1984. (Rev: BL 8/85) [796.357]

9693 Reidenbaugh, Lowell. *The Sporting News Selects Baseball's 50 Greatest Games* (9–12). Illus. 1986, Sporting News $19.95 (0-89204-224-9). A you-are-there account of 50 of the greatest moments in baseball history. (Rev: BL 11/15/86) [796.357]

9694 Reidenbaugh, Lowell. *The Sporting News Selects Baseball's 25 Greatest Pennant Races* (9–12). Illus. 1987, Sporting News $19.95 (0-89204-256-7). A description of baseball's best and most exciting pennant races. Companion volumes are *The Sporting News Selects Baseball's 50 Great Games* and *The Sporting News Selects Baseball's 25 Greatest Teams* (both 1988). (Rev: BL 12/1/87; BR 1–2/88) [796.357]

9695 Ritter, Lawrence S. *The Story of Baseball* (9–12). Rev. ed. 1990, Morrow $13.95 (0-688-09056-7); paper $8.95 (0-688-09057-5). This history of baseball also includes biographies of some of its greatest players. [796.357]

9696 Seaver, Tom, and Lee Lowenfish. *The Art of Pitching* (9–12). Illus. 1984, Morrow $16.95 (0-688-02663-X). A book on the pitching style of Seaver and 4 other major league players. [796.357]

9697 Shannon, Mike, ed. *The Best of Spitball: The Literary Baseball Magazine* (10–12). Illus. 1988, Pocket paper $5.95 (0-671-64983-3). A collection of articles, poems, and stories that have appeared in this magazine devoted to baseball. (Rev: BL 5/15/88) [796.357]

9698 Shlain, Bruce. *Oddballs* (8–12). 1989, Penguin paper $7.95 (0-14-011128-X). A humorous introduction to some of the unusual personalities that have inhabited professional baseball. (Rev: BL 4/1/89) [796.357]

9699 Thorn, John, ed. *The Armchair Book of Baseball* (9–12). Illus. 1985, Macmillan $19.95 (0-684-18482-6). A fine collection of writings on baseball—some by players and coaches, others by sports writers or others who have a passion for the game. (Rev: BL 11/1/85) [796.357]

9700 Thorn, John, ed. *The Armchair Book of Baseball II* (10–12). Illus. 1987, Macmillan $19.95 (0-684-18772-8). A collection of writing on baseball by such writers as Philip Roth, Garrison Keillor, and Russell Baker. (Rev: BL 9/1/87) [796.357]

9701 Thorn, John. *The Game for All America* (9–12). Illus. 1988, Sporting News $35.00 (0-89204-279-6). A collection of color photographs that capture the essence of America's national sport. (Rev: BL 6/15/88) [796.357]

9702 Thorn, John, et al., eds. *The Whole Baseball Catalogue* (9–12). 1990, Simon & Schuster paper $17.95 (0-671-68347-0). An assortment of articles on all aspects of baseball, from lists of best books to team mascots. (Rev: BL 3/1/90) [796.357]

9703 Tullis, John. *I'd Rather Be a Yankee* (9–12). 1987, Jove paper $3.95 (0-515-09073-5). From dozens of interviews, the author has re-created a history of Yankee baseball from 1903 to the mid-1980s. (Rev: BL 11/1/86) [798.357]

9704 Tygiel, Jules. *Baseball's Great Experiment* (9–12). 1984, Random paper $9.95 (0-394-72593-X). The story of Jackie Robinson's entry into major league baseball and its effects. [796.357]

9705 Uecker, Bob, and Mickey Herskowitz. *Catcher in the Wry* (9–12). 1987, Jove paper $3.95 (0-515-09029-8). A humorous look at baseball by a former player now an announcer. [798.357]

9706 Wheeler, Lonnie. *Bleachers: A Summer in Wrigley Field* (8–12). 1988, Contemporary $16.95 (0-8092-4641-4). Life in the bleachers watching the Chicago Cubs during the summer of 1987. (Rev: BL 5/15/88) [796.357]

9707 Williams, Ted, and John Underwood. *The Science of Hitting* (9–12). Rev. ed. Illus. 1986, Simon & Schuster paper $9.95 (0-671-62103-3). From one of the great hitters of all time, advice is given on the fundamentals as well as comments on great batters of the past and present. (Rev: BL 7/86) [796.357]

9708 Wimmer, Dick. *Baseball Fathers, Baseball Sons* (9–12). 1988, Morrow $15.95 (0-688-07634-3). The results of interviews with baseball players concerning their relationships with their fathers. (Rev: BL 6/15/88) [796.357]

9709 Winegardner, Mark. *Prophet of the Sandlots: Journeys with a Major League Scout* (9–12). 1990, Atlantic Monthly $18.95 (0-87113-336-9). The author tells of his experiences traveling with Tony Lucadello, a major league scout, during his last season. (Rev: BL 2/1/90; VOYA 6/90) [796.357]

9710 Wood, Robert. *Dodger Dogs to Fenway Franks: The Ultimate Guide to America's Top Baseball Parks* (8–12). Illus. 1988, McGraw $16.95 (0-07-071696-X). In 1985, Wood visited all 26 major league parks and graded them on everything from their food to their atmosphere. (Rev: BL 8/88) [796.357]

9711 Zolna, Ed, and Mike Conklin. *Mastering Softball* (9–12). Illus. 1981, Contemporary paper $6.95 (0-8092-7183-4). A team manager and a sportswriter present a well-illustrated guide to softball. [796.357]

Basketball

9712 Beard, Butch, et al. *Butch Beard's Basic Basketball* (9–12). Illus. 1985, Michael Kesend paper $12.95 (0-935576-14-2). A basic handbook on the techniques it is necessary to master to become a fine basketball player. (Rev: SLJ 5/86) [796.32]

9713 Bird, Larry. *Bird on Basketball: How-to Strategies from the Great Celtics Champion* (8–12). Rev. ed. Illus. 1988, Addison paper $9.95 (0-201-14209-0). The basketball star associated with the Boston Celtics gives advice to young players on basics. [796.32]

9714 Campbell, Nelson, ed. *Grass Roots & Schoolyards: A High School Basketball Anthology* (10–12). 1988, Greene $16.95 (0-8289-0640-8). A collection of 36 articles about high school teams, games, and players. (Rev: BL 1/15/88; VOYA 10/88) [796.32]

9715 Coombs, Charles. *BMX: A Guide to Bicycle Motocross* (9–12). 1983, Morrow $13.95 (0-688-01867-X). An easily read introduction to this special bicycle that gives information about choosing and caring for the equipment plus guidance on how to perform stunts. [796.6]

9716 Cousy, Bob, and Frank G. Power Jr. *Basketball: Concepts and Techniques* (10–12). Illus. 1983, Wm. Brown $32.95 (0-697-06835-8). Team and individual strategies are given for both offensive and defensive basketball. [796.32]

9717 Cousy, Bob, and Bob Ryan. *Cousy on the Celtic Mystique* (9–12). Illus. 1988, McGraw $17.95 (0-07-013332-8). The legendary Celtic player analyzes what makes that team tick. (Rev: BL 1/15/89) [796.32]

9718 Feinstein, John. *Forever's Team* (10–12). 1990, Villard $18.95 (0-394-56892-3). The story of the remarkable Duke University basketball team of 1977–1978 and what has happened to its members. (Rev: SLJ 4/90; VOYA 8/90) [796.32]

9719 Feinstein, John. *A Season Inside: One Year in College Basketball* (9–12). 1988, Random $18.95 (0-394-56891-5). An overview of the 1987–1988 college basketball season with insight into various programs and players. (Rev: BL 11/15/88; BR 5–6/89) [796.32]

9720 Gandolfi, Giorgio, and Gerald Secor Couzens. *Hoops! The Official National Basketball Players Association Guide to Playing Basketball* (9–12). Illus. 1987, McGraw paper $10.95 (0-07-013276-3). A well-illustrated guide to individual offensive basketball skills. [796.32]

9721 Gergen, Joe. *The Final Four* (9–12). Illus. 1987, Sporting News paper $19.95 (0-89204-257-5). From 1939 through 1987, a description of each of the final NCAA basketball tournaments. (Rev: BL 4/1/88) [796.323]

9722 Goldaper, Sam, and Arthur Pincus. *How to Talk Basketball* (7–12). Illus. 1983, Dembner paper $8.95 (0-934878-38-2). An illustrated dictionary of terms plus entries on key personalities in basketball. [796.32]

9723 Golenbock, Peter. *Personal Fouls* (9–12). 1989, Carroll & Graf $18.95 (0-88184-526-4). A critical look at the coach and the basketball program at North Carolina State. (Rev: BL 9/1/89) [796.323]

9724 Halberstam, David. *The Breaks of the Game* (10–12). 1983, Ballantine paper $4.95 (0-345-29625-7). This prize-winning book offers an incisive look into the world of professional basketball. [796.32]

9725 Heeren, Dave. *The Basketball Abstract* (8–12). Illus. 1989, Prentice paper $12.95 (0-13-069170-4). A new method of evaluating performance is applied to the NBA teams with some surprising results. (Rev: BL 2/1/89) [796.32]

9726 Hollander, Zander. *The Complete Handbook of Pro-Basketball* (9–12). 1989, NAL paper $5.95 (0-451-16283-8). An annual publication that gives vital statistics on teams and players. [796.32]

9727 Hoose, Phillip M. *Hoosiers: The Fabulous Basketball Life of Indiana* (7–12). 1986, Random paper $7.95 (0-394-74778-X). The people, places, and great moments of Indiana high school basketball are covered. (Rev: BR 3–4/87; VOYA 4/87) [796.32]

9728 Isaacs, Neil D., and Dick Motta. *Sports Illustrated Basketball* (7–12). Illus. 1988, NAL paper $9.95 (0-452-26207-0). A thorough guide that includes coverage on plays, positions, offense and defense playing plus a chapter on how to enjoy the game as a spectator. [796.32]

9729 Jeremiah, Maryalyce. *Basketball: The Woman's Game* (7–12). Illus. 1983, Athletic Inst. paper $7.95 (0-87670-069-5). The fundamentals of basketball as seen through the specific needs of female players. [796.32]

9730 Mikes, Jay. *Basketball Fundamentals* (9–12). 1987, Human Kinetics $17.95 (0-88011-281-6). A self-help book that emphasizes the psychology of the game as well as practical skills. (Rev: BR 5–6/87) [796.32]

9731 Montieth, Mark. *Passion Play: A Season with the Purdue Boilermakers and Coach Gene Keady* (9–12). Illus. 1988, Bonus $15.95 (0-933893-73-6). The 1987–1988 college basketball season as seen from the perspective of a fairly successful season with the Boilermakers. (Rev: BL 11/15/88) [796.323]

9732 Packer, Billy, and Roland Lazenby. *College Basketball's 25 Greatest Teams* (9–12). Illus. 1989, Sporting News $19.95 (0-89204-314-8). Two veteran sportsmen select the best college teams and tell why they were selected. (Rev: BL 1/1/90) [796.323]

9733 Packer, Billy, and Roland Lazenby. *Fifty Years of the Final Four: Golden Moments of the NCAA Basketball Tournament* (9–12). Illus. 1987, Taylor $19.95 (0-87833-592-7). A summary of each of the first 50 National Collegiate Athletic Association Final Four tournaments complete with many interviews. (Rev: BL 1/1/88) [796.32]

9734 Ryna, Bob. *The Boston Celtics: The History, Legends, and Images of America's Most Celebrated Team* (9–12). Illus. 1989, Addison-Wesley $23.95 (0-201-15326-2). Both fans and detractors of the Celtics will find this behind-the-scenes account absorbing. (Rev: BL 11/15/89) [796.323]

9735 Salzberg, Charles. *From Set Shot to Slam Dunk* (10–12). 1987, Dutton $17.95 (0-525-24555-3). An entertaining history of professional basketball from the beginning in the 1930s through the 1960s. (Rev: VOYA 8/88) [796.32]

9736 Shaughnessy, Dan. *Ever Green: The Boston Celtics* (9–12). Illus. 1990, St. Martin's $18.95 (0-

312-05083-6). A year-by-year history of this basketball team with profiles of coaches and players from 1946 to the present. (Rev: BL 10/1/90) [796.323]

9737 Stauth, Cameron. *The Franchise* (9–12). Illus. 1990, Morrow $19.95 (0-688-09573-9). An account of the 1989–1990 season of the Detroit Pistons, nicknamed the bad boys of baseball. (Rev: BL 4/15/90) [796.324]

9738 Telander, Rick. *Heaven Is a Playground* (10–12). 1988, Simon & Schuster paper $7.95 (0-671-66650-9). This is a book about basketball and working with inner-city youth. [796.32]

9739 Young, Faye, and Wayne Coffey. *Winning Basketball for Girls* (9–12). Illus. 1984, Facts on File $18.95 (0-87196-833-9); paper $9.95 (0-87196-843-6). The game's fundamentals are explained with special emphasis on the needs of young female players. [796.32]

Bicycles and Cycling

9740 Berto, Frank J. *Bicycling Magazine's Complete Guide to Upgrading Your Bike* (10–12). Illus. 1988, Rodale $19.95 (0-87857-750-5); paper $14.95 (0-87857-751-3). A series of articles that help the reader evaluate bicycles and give hints on selecting and installing new equipment. (Rev: BL 4/1/88) [629.2]

9741 Bicycling Magazine, eds. *All-Terrain Bikes* (9–12). Illus. 1985, Rodale paper $4.95 (0-87857-546-4). A description of the rugged bicycles developed in California plus a buying guide and usage tips. (Rev: BL 10/1/85) [629]

9742 Bicycling Magazine, eds. *Bicycle Repair* (9–12). Illus. 1985, Rodale paper $4.95 (0-87857-543-X). This is a quick course on the tools and techniques used in bicycle repairs. Also use: *Easy Bicycle Maintenance* (1985). (Rev: BL 10/1/85) [629]

9743 Bicycling Magazine, eds. *Bicycle Touring* (10–12). Illus. 1985, Rodale paper $4.95 (0-87857-547-2). A practical guide on how to plan successful and safe road trips. [796.6]

9744 Bicycling Magazine, eds. *Bicycling Magazine's Complete Guide to Bicycle Maintenance and Repair* (9–12). Illus. 1986, Rodale $19.95 (0-87857-603-7); paper $14.95 (0-87857-604-5). A guide that tells how to make any necessary repairs and how to keep your bike in good working order. (Rev: BL 4/15/86) [629.28]

9745 Bicycling Magazine, eds. *Cycling for Women* (9–12). Illus. 1989, Rodale paper $4.95 (0-87857-811-0). General tips for both sexes are interspersed with those specifically aimed at women's abilities and endurance levels. (Rev: BL 3/15/89) [796.6]

9746 Bicycling Magazine, eds. *Fitness through Cycling* (10–12). 1985, Rodale paper $4.95 (0-87857-548-0). This book explains how the sport of bicycling can be used as a tool in ensuring good health. [796.6]

9747 *Chilton's Motorcycle and ATV Repair Manual, 1945–85* (10–12). Illus. 1986, Chilton $29.95 (0-8019-7635-9). A frequently revised guide to tune-ups, maintenance, and repairs of major makes of motorcycles. [629.28]

9748 Coello, Dennis. *The Complete Mountain Biker* (9–12). Illus. 1989, Lyons & Burford paper $12.95 (1-55821-021-0). The thorough guide to this sport that covers buying a bicycle and accessories plus tips on safe, enjoyable riding. (Rev: BL 7/89) [796.6]

9749 Coello, Dennis. *The Mountain Bike Repair Handbook* (9–12). Illus. 1990, Lyons & Burford paper $12.95 (1-55821-064-4). Both simple and complex repairs are described clearly in text and many diagrams. (Rev: BL 7/90) [629.28]

9750 Coello, Dennis. *Touring on Two Wheels: The Bicycle Traveler's Handbook* (9–12). Illus. 1988, Lyons & Burford paper $12.95 (0-941130-79-7). A manual that covers such topics as planning the trip, equipment, riding techniques, and repairs. (Rev: BL 1/15/89) [796.6]

9751 Coles, Clarence W., and Harold T. Glenn. *Glenn's New Complete Bicycle Manual* (10–12). 1987, Crown $19.95 (0-517-54313-3). An excellent collection of information on topics such as bicycle models, equipment, maintenance, and safe riding techniques. (Rev: VOYA 4/88) [796.6]

9752 Cuthbertson, Tom. *Anybody's Bike Book* (9–12). 4th rev. ed. 1990, Ten Speed paper $8.95 (0-89815-392-1). This is an introduction to bikes and their parts plus coverage of repair and maintenance. [796.6]

9753 Dolan, Edward F., Jr. *Bicycle Touring and Camping* (7–12). Illus. 1982, Wanderer paper $5.95 (0-671-44544-8). In addition to details on how to plan a trip and the gear necessary, material is given on safe and comfortable biking techniques. [796.6]

9754 Grant, Richard, and Nigel Thomas. *BMX Action Bike Book* (7–12). Illus. 1985, Arco paper $3.95 (0-668-06376-6). Techniques, equip-ment, and the language of BMX are included in this useful volume. [796.6]

9755 Honig, Daniel. *How to Bike Better* (9–12). 1985, Ballantine paper $2.50 (0-345-31846-3). This book explains such biking techniques as use of gears and braking. [796.6]

9756 Lehrer, John. *The Complete Guide to Choosing a Performance Bicycle* (9–12). Illus. 1988, Running Pr. $24.95 (0-89471-588-7); paper $14.95 (0-89471-587-9). A guide to quality bicycles that covers such topics as types of frames, models, and components. (Rev: BL 5/1/88) [629.2]

9757 LeMond, Greg. *Greg LeMond's Pocket Guide to Bicycle Maintenance and Repair* (9–12). Illus. 1990, Putnam paper $8.95 (0-399-51511-9). The Tour de France winner tells how to keep your bicycle in fine working order and how to do repair work when necessary. (Rev: BL 3/15/90) [629.28]

9758 LeMond, Greg, and Kent Gordis. *Greg LeMond's Complete Book of Bicycling* (9–12). Illus. 1987, Putnam $22.95 (0-399-13229-5); paper $9.95 (0-399-51594-1). For both the beginner and specialist, this book covers equipment, techniques, and training. (Rev: BL 10/1/87) [796.6]

9759 McGurn, James. *On Your Bicycle: An Illustrated History of Cycling* (9–12). Illus. 1988, Facts on File $21.95 (0-8160-1748-4). A nicely illustrated account of bicycles from the times of da Vinci to the present. (Rev: BL 12/15/87) [629.2]

9760 Marino, John, et al. *John Marino's Bicycling Book* (7–12). Illus. 1981, Tarcher paper $7.95 (0-87477-245-1). An interesting compilation of information that includes topics such as choosing bikes and equipment, touring tips, riding skills, and first aid. [796.6]

9761 Matheny, Fred. *Beginning Bicycle Racing* (9–12). Illus. 1987, Countryman paper $14.95 (0-941950-14-X). A guide to this popular sport that involves coverage of equipment, techniques, and training programs. (Rev: SLJ 12/87) [796.6]

9762 Matheny, Fred. *Bicycling Magazine's Complete Guide to Riding and Racing Techniques* (9–12). Illus. 1989, Rodale $19.95 (0-87857-804-8); paper $14.95 (0-87857-805-6). Using over 150 photographs this is a guide that starts with basics and expands into such areas as specific types of competition. (Rev: BL 3/15/89) [796.6]

9763 Nye, Peter. *Hearts of Lions: The History of American Bicycle Racing* (8–12). 1988, Norton $19.95 (0-393-02543-8). A history of a once very popular sport and how it has had a comeback in the 80s and 90s. (Rev: BR 5–6/89) [796.6]

9764 Osborn, Bob. *The Complete Book of BMX* (7–12). Illus. 1984, Harper paper $13.95 (0-06-091135-2). Information for both beginner and experienced rider is well illustrated with photos, diagrams, and cartoons. [796.6]

9765 Sloane, Eugene A. *The Complete Book of Bicycling* (9–12). Illus. 1988, Simon & Schuster paper $15.95 (0-671-65802-6). A basic guide that covers such topics as the history of the bicycle, types of races, repairs, and maintenance. [629.2]

9766 Van der Plas, Rob. *The Bicycle Repair Book* (9–12). Rev. ed. 1989, Bicycle Books paper $7.95 (0-933201-11-7). This manual describes how to keep a bicycle in good condition and how to perform repairs when necessary. (Rev: BL 9/1/85) [796.6]

9767 Van der Plas, Rob. *The Bicycle Touring Manual: Using the Bicycle for Touring and Camping* (9–12). Illus. 1987, Bicycle Books paper $9.95 (0-933201-15-X). For those who will be taking medium or long trips via bicycle, this is a guide to equipment, gear, riding techniques, and safety measures. Also use the author's *Roadside Bicycle Repairs: The Simple Guide to Fixing Your Bike* (1987). (Rev: BL 10/15/87) [796.6]

9768 Van der Plas, Rob. *The Mountain Bike Book: Choosing, Riding and Maintaining the Off-Road Bicycle* (9–12). Illus. 1988, Bicycle Books paper $8.95 (0-933201-18-4). In a revision of the 1984 title, here is a compendium of information about flat-tire bicycles (Rev: BL 9/1/88) [796.6]

Bodybuilding

9769 Columbu, Franco, and Dick Tyler. *Weight Training and Body Building for Young Athletes* (10–12). 1979, Simon & Schuster paper $6.95 (0-671-33006-3). A former Mr. Universe gives tips and programs for body development. [796.4]

9770 Fahey, Thomas D. *Basic Weight Training* (9–12). Illus. 1989, Mayfield paper $10.95 (0-87484-875-X). A college instructor gives valuable advice on how to design a weight-training program and how to carry it out sensibly. (Rev: BL 4/15/89) [613.7]

9771 Hatfield, Frederick C. *Powerlifting: A Scientific Approach* (10–12). 1981, Contemporary paper $9.95 (0-8029-7001-3). This introduction to weight lifting gives basic rules and information on training schedules. [796.4]

9772 Parker, Robert B., and John R. Marsh. *Sports Illustrated Training with Weights* (10–12). Illus. 1990, Dutton paper $9.95 (0-452-26334-4). A well-illustrated guide to weight lifting that stresses caution and safety. [796.4]

9773 Pearl, Bill, and Gary T. Moran. *Getting Stronger: Weight Training for Men & Women* (9–12). Illus. 1986, Random paper $14.95 (0-936070-04-8). A comprehensive account that begins with programs for the novice and continues through high levels and also covers topics like equipment, exercise, and nutrition. (Rev: SLJ 5/87) [796.4]

9774 Portugues, Gladys, and Joyce L. Vedral. *Hard Bodies* (10–12). Illus. 1986, Dell paper $12.95 (0-440-53424-0). A bodybuilding manual for women that stresses weight training. (Rev: BL 2/15/86) [796.41]

9775 Schwarzenegger, Arnold. *Arnold's Bodybuilding for Men* (10–12). Illus. 1981, Simon & Schuster paper $14.95 (0-671-53163-8). A guide to exercise and weight lifting that stresses a total fitness program. [613.7]

9776 Wayne, Rick. *Muscle Wars* (9–12). Illus. 1985, St. Martin's $18.95 (0-312-55353-6). A candid behind-the-scenes look at the infighting in the world of bodybuilding. (Rev: BL 12/1/85) [646.7]

9777 Weider, Ben, and Robert Kennedy. *Pumping Up! Super Shaping the Feminine Physique* (10–12). 1989, Borgo LB $24.95 (0-8095-7529-9). A basic introduction to bodybuilding for women. [796.4]

9778 Weider, Joe. *Bodybuilding: The Weider Approach* (10–12). 1981, Contemporary $17.50 (0-8092-5909-5); paper $12.95 (0-8092-5908-7). From the man who trained Schwarzenegger and Ferrigno comes an easy-to-follow manual on bodybuilding. [796.4]

Bowling

9779 Borden, Fred, and Jay Elias. *Bowling: Knowledge Is the Key* (9–12). Illus. 1987, Bowling Concepts paper $19.95 (0-9619177-0-9). A straightforward instructional program that is simple to follow and thorough. (Rev: BL 6/15/87) [794.6]

9780 Holman, Marshall, and Roy G. Nelson. *Marshall Holman's Bowling Tips and Techniques* (9–12). Illus. 1985, Contemporary paper $8.95 (0-8092-5324-0). An informative collection of tips and techniques by a former Bowler of the Year. (Rev: BL 2/1/86) [764.6]

9781 Salvino, Carmen, and Frederick C. Klein. *Fast Lanes* (10–12). Illus. 1988, Bonus Books paper $9.95 (0-933893-46-9). Biography mixed with instruction by an important professional bowler. (Rev: BL 5/15/88) [794.6]

9782 Sports Illustrated, eds. *Sports Illustrated Bowling* (9–12). Illus. 1987, NAL paper $9.95 (0-452-26038-8). Useful tips plus basic information on how to bowl are given in this guide illustrated with many drawings. [794.6]

Boxing and Wrestling

9783 Combs, Steve. *Winning Wrestling* (10–12). Illus. 1980, Contemporary paper $9.95 (0-8092-7086-2). Aimed at a high school and college audience, this book covers all the basic skills and gives coverage to such topics as weight control and exercise. [796.8]

9784 Hellickson, Russ, and Andrew Baggott. *An Instructional Guide to Amateur Wrestling* (9–12). Illus. 1987, Putnam paper $10.95 (0-399-51269-1). An introduction to wrestling that includes information about strategies and holds plus 200 photographs. (Rev: BL 10/1/87) [796.8]

9785 Jarman, Tom, and Reid Hanley. *Wrestling for Beginners* (10–12). 1983, Contemporary paper $9.95 (0-8092-5656-8). A well-organized manual that includes background information on wrestling. [796.8]

9786 Plummer, William. *Buttercups and Strong Boys: A Sojourn at the Golden Gloves* (9–12). 1989, Viking $17.95 (0-670-80321-9). A professional sportswriter studied the preparations for the Golden Glove competition for 1983–1984 and describes them in detail. (Rev: BL 2/1/89) [796.8]

9787 Sugar, Bert, and John Grasso. *Five-Hundred-Five Boxing Questions Your Friends Can't Answer* (10–12). 1982, Walker $10.95 (0-8027-0689-4); paper $3.95 (0-8027-7180-7). A trivia book that will test the knowledge of every boxing fan. [796.8]

9788 Valentine, Tom. *Inside Wrestling* (10–12). 1972, Contemporary paper $7.95 (0-8092-8852-4). A behind-the-scenes look at the amazing world of wrestling. [796.8]

Camping, Hiking, and Backpacking

9789 Angier, Bradford. *How to Stay Alive in the Woods* (10–12). 1962, Macmillan paper $5.95 (0-02-028050-5). An excellent manual on the outdoors and wilderness survival. [613.6]

9790 Boy Scouts of America. *Fieldbook* (9–12). 3rd ed. Illus. 1984, Boy Scouts of America paper $7.95 (0-8395-3200-8). This Boy Scout manual gives information on the outdoors and how to appreciate our environment. [369.43]

9791 Carra, Andrew J. *Camping* (10–12). 1978, Scarborough paper $4.95 (0-8128-2117-3). A complete guide on how and where to go camping. [613.6]

9792 Doan, Marilyn. *Hiking Light* (9–12). 1983, Peter Smith $14.50 (0-8446-6046-9). A manual on hiking, plus information on how to take care of the natural environment. [613.6]

9793 Elman, Robert. *The Hiker's Bible* (9–12). 1982, Doubleday paper $4.95 (0-385-17505-1). This thorough guide covers both hiking and backpacking. [613.6]

9794 Fletcher, Colin. *The Complete Walker III: The Joys and Techniques of Hiking and Backpacking* (10–12). Illus. 1984, Knopf $22.95 (0-394-51962-0); paper $16.95 (0-394-72264-7). This readable, thorough guide to hiking and backpacking first appeared in 1969 and is in its third edition. [796.5]

9795 Fry, Alan. *Wilderness Survival Handbook* (10–12). Illus. 1982, St. Martin's paper $10.95 (0-312-87952-0). A manual on survival techniques for hikers, backpackers, and other kinds of outdoors people. [613.6]

9796 Hart, John. *Walking Softly in the Wilderness* (10–12). Rev. ed. Illus. 1984, Sierra Club paper $9.95 (0-87156-813-6). This account is both a guide to backpacking and an enumeration of many environmental concerns. [796.5]

9797 Lehmberg, Paul. *In the Strong Woods* (10–12). 1981, St. Martin's paper $4.95 (0-312-41173-1). The story of the author's sojourn alone in the North Woods. [613.6]

9798 McManus, Patrick F. *They Shoot Canoes, Don't They?* (10–12). 1981, Holt $12.95 (0-03-058646-1). A collection of anecdotes, many of them humorous, about the author's experiences camping, hiking, and hunting. [613.6]

9799 McNeish, Cameron. *The Backpacker's Manual* (9–12). Illus. 1984, Random paper $12.95 (0-

8129-6338-5). A complete guide for the back-packer that includes such topics as equipment, walking techniques, campsite preparation, and simple cooking tips. (Rev: BL 3/1/85) [688.7]

9800 Manning, Harvey. *Backpacking One Step at a Time* (9–12). Rev. ed. Illus. 1986, Random paper $8.95 (0-394-72939-0). In addition to information on equipment and techniques, this book tells how to get the most enjoyment possible out of backpacking. (Rev: SLJ 9/86; VOYA 8–10/86) [796.5]

9801 Olsen, Larry Dean. *Outdoor Survival Skills* (9–12). Illus. 1990, Chicago Review paper $11.95 (1-55652-084-0). This practical guide on how to live off the land includes material on building a shelter and finding food. (Rev: BL 5/15/90) [613.6]

9802 Randolph, John. *Backpacking Basics* (7–12). Illus. 1982, Prentice LB $9.95 (0-13-055798-6). Such basics as preparing for a hike; finding directions, safety, and comfort concerns; and camping out are treated. [796.5]

9803 Riviere, Bill. *The L. L. Bean Guide to the Outdoors* (10–12). Illus. 1981, Random $15.50 (0-394-51928-0). In addition to hiking, camping, and backpacking this general account includes some material on skiing and canoeing. [796.5]

9804 Sandi, Michael. *Sports Illustrated Backpacking* (9–12). Illus. 1989, NAL paper $9.95 (0-452-26270-4). This guide for the beginner gives many useful tips and suggestions in a well-illustrated format. [796.5]

9805 Shanks, Bernard. *Wilderness Survival* (10–12). Rev. ed. n.d., Universe $19.95 (0-87663-655-5). Current information is given on how to survive in a wilderness. [613.6]

Chess, Checkers, and Other Board and Card Games

9806 De Satnick, Shelly. *Bridge for Everyone: A Step-by-Step Text and Workbook* (10–12). 1982, Avon paper $9.95 (0-380-81083-2). An elementary but excellent introduction to bridge. [795.4]

9807 Frey, Richard. *According to Hoyle* (9–12). 1985, Fawcett paper $3.95 (0-449-21112-6). This handbook supplies instructions, rules, and regulations for over 200 games. [795.4]

9808 Gibson, Walter B. *Hoyle's Modern Encyclopedia of Card Games: Rules of All the Basic Games and Popular Variations* (10–12). Illus.

1974, Dolphin Books paper $9.95 (0-385-07680-0). The master of "according to Hoyle" fame describes a number of card games including poker and solitaire. [795.4]

9809 Goren, Charles H. *Fundamentals of Contract Bridge* (10–12). 1982, Pocket paper $2.75 (0-671-43998-7). One of the masters supplies a fine introduction to this card game. [795.4]

9810 Goren, Charles H. *Goren's New Bridge Complete* (10–12). Rev. ed. Illus. 1985, Doubleday $21.95 (0-385-23324-8). From advice and explanations aimed at beginners to tournament-winning techniques, this is a fine all-around guide to bridge. [795.41]

9811 Gunther, Noel, and Richard Hutton. *Beyond Boardwalk and Park Place* (9–12). Illus. 1986, Bantam paper $5.95 (0-553-34341-6). For Monopoly enthusiasts, here is a variation on the game that makes it faster and more exciting. (Rev: SLJ 5/87) [794]

9812 Haig-Brown, Roderick. *A Primer of Fly-Fishing* (10–12). 1982, Univ. of Washington Pr. paper $8.95 (0-295-95932-0). This Canadian writer and sportsman gives basic advice on fly-fishing. [799.1]

9813 Holland, Tim. *Beginning Backgammon* (9–12). 1974, McKay paper $4.95 (0-679-14038-7). An elementary guide for the beginner in this board game that combines chance with skill. [794]

9814 Mason, Bill. *Sports Illustrated Fly Fishing: Learn from a Master* (10–12). Illus. 1988, NAL paper $11.95 (0-452-26097-3). This illustrated guide covers topics like types of flies and casting techniques. [799.1]

9815 Morehead, Albert H., and Geoffrey Mott-Smith, eds. *Hoyle's Rules of Games* (9–12). 2nd rev. ed. 1983, NAL paper $7.95 (0-452-26049-3). This is a guide on how to play over 200 card and parlor games. [794.4]

9816 Pandolfini, Bruce, ed. *The Best of Chess Life and Review, Volume I, 1933–1960* (9–12). 1988, Simon & Schuster paper $10.95 (0-671-62984-2). A collection of articles, model games, and problems from these periodicals. Followed by: *The Best of Chess Life and Review, Volume II, 1960–1988* (1988). (Rev: BL 6/1/88) [794.1]

9817 Parlett, David. *Oxford Guide to Card Games* (9–12). 1990, Oxford Univ. Pr. $19.95 (0-19-214165-1). This authoritative guide supplies directions on how to play over 300 card games.

9818 Pritchard, D. B. *Begin Chess* (9–12). 1987, NAL paper $2.95 (0-451-14723-5). A fine introduction to this game with clear instructions for the beginner. [794.1]

9819 Redman, Tim, ed. *U.S. Chess Federation's Official Rules of Chess* (10–12). 1987, McKay paper $7.95 (0-679-14154-5). This is the official book of international chess rules and their interpretation. [794.1]

9820 Reese, Terence. *Begin Bridge with Reese* (9–12). 1979, NAL paper $4.50 (0-451-16292-7). Basic techniques and strategies are outlined for the beginning bridge player. [168]

9821 Reinfeld, Fred. *Be a Winner at Chess* (9–12). 1986, Fawcett paper $3.50 (0-449-21257-2). This book presumes a basic knowledge of chess and describes many interesting strategies. Also use by this author: *Beginner's Guide to Winning Chess* (1982), *Chess in a Nutshell* (1989), *The Complete Chessplay* (1982), and *Win at Chess* (1945). [794.1]

9822 Reinfeld, Fred. *How to Win at Checkers* (9–12). 1982, Wilshire paper $5.00 (0-87980-068-2). A guide to this board game and popular pastime. [794]

9823 Walker, J. N. *Chess for Tomorrow's Champions* (10–12). 1983, Oxford Univ. Pr. paper $8.95 (0-19-217804-0). A guide to help players who know the basics improve their game. [794.1]

Fishing and Hunting

9824 Brykcznski, Terry, and David Reuther, eds. *The Armchair Angler* (10–12). Illus. 1986, Macmillan $22.50 (0-684-18565-2). A collection of articles and essays about the legend and lore of fishing. [799.1]

9825 Capstick, Peter Hathaway. *Last Horizons: Hunting, Fishing & Shooting on Five Continents* (10–12). Illus. 1989, St. Martin's $19.95 (0-312-02535-1). A collection of entertaining short pieces about the author's hunting and fishing experiences in many different locales. (Rev: BL 1/1/89) [799]

9826 Cook, Sam. *Up North* (10–12). Illus. 1986, Pfeifer-Hamilton $14.95 (0-938586-09-2). A book about outdoor recreation such as hunting, fishing, and camping. (Rev: BL 9/1/87) [796.5]

9827 Fichter, George S., and Phil Frances. *Fishing* (7–12). 1987, Western paper $3.95 (0-307-

24050-9). This guide not only identifies many fish but also tells how they can be caught. [799.1]

9828 Gierach, John. *The View from Rat Lake* (10–12). 1988, Pruett $18.95 (0-87108-743-X). Witty essays about nature in general and fishing in particular. (Rev: BL 3/1/88) [799.1]

9829 Lee, David. *A Basic Guide to Fishing: For Freshwater Anglers of All Ages* (10–12). 1983, Prentice paper $9.95 (0-13-062307-5). For the beginning fisherman, this is a readable and helpful guide. [799.1]

9830 Ovington, Ray. *Basic Bait Fishing* (7–12). Illus. 1984, Stackpole paper $9.95 (0-8117-2173-6). Both salt and freshwater fishing are covered in this account that covers such topics as tackle, bait, and fishing skills. [799.1]

9831 Ovington, Ray. *Basic Fishing* (9–12). 1982, Stackpole paper $10.95 (0-8117-2141-8). This basic guide covers topics like equipment, techniques, and types of fish. [799.1]

9832 Pfeiffer, C. Boyd, and Irv Swope. *The Practical Fisherman* (7–12). Illus. 1982, Winchester Press paper $12.95 (0-87691-348-6). A fine overview of fishing in both salt and freshwater locales plus sections on boats and boat maintenance. [799.1]

9833 Schultz, Ken, and Dan D. Gapen. *The Complete Book of Freshwater Fishing* (9–12). Illus. 1989, Stephen Greene paper $21.95 (0-8289-0678-5). A readable guide to this sport written by 2 experts who have arranged the contents by species of fish. (Rev: BL 5/15/89) [799.1]

9834 Sparano, Vin T., ed. *Classic Hunting Tales* (10–12). 1987, Beaufort $18.95 (0-8253-0345-1). This editor has again produced a fine anthology of true hunting stories in this sequel to *The Greatest Hunting Stories Ever Told* (1983). (Rev: BL 2/15/87) [799.2]

9835 Swainbank, Todd, and Eric Seidler, eds. *Taking Freshwater Game Fish: A Treasury of Expert Advice* (9–12). Illus. 1989, Countryman paper $14.95 (0-88150-113-1). An informal guide with separate chapters on each of various species of fish. (Rev: BL 2/1/89) [799.1]

9836 Zern, Ed. *Hunting and Fishing from "A" to Zern* (9–12). Illus. 1985, Lyons & Burford $17.95 (0-941130-97-5). A collection of humorous pieces about hunting and fishing by a respected writer about the outdoors. (Rev: BL 11/1/85) [799.1]

Football

9837 Anderson, Dave. *The Story of Football* (9–12). Illus. 1985, Morrow $13.95 (0-688-05634-2); paper $8.95 (0-688-05635-0). After a brief history of the sport, each position is explained and its functions and moves detailed. [796.332]

9838 Anderson, Ken. *The Art of Quarterbacking* (10–12). Illus. 1984, Linden Pr. paper $10.95 (0-671-50724-9). A book that emphasizes the psychological aspects of football and being a successful quarterback. [796.332]

9839 Brock, Ted, and Jim Campbell. *The Super Official NFL Trivia Book* (9–12). 1985, NAL paper $3.95 (0-451-13822-8). A collection of strange but true facts about football. [796.33]

9840 Brock, Ted, and Larry Eldridge. *25 Years: The NFL since 1960* (8–12). Illus. 1985, Fireside $22.50 (0-671-60441-4); paper $14.95 (0-671-60440-6). A history of the National Football League that is made outstanding because of its photographs. (Rev: BL 2/1/86) [796]

9841 DeLuca, Sam. *Football Made Easy* (10–12). 1983, Jonathan David paper $6.95 (0-8246-0296-X). A former Jets player gives both basic and advanced information on playing football. [796.33]

9842 Foehr, Donna. *Football for Women and Men Who Want to Learn the Game* (9–12). 1988, National Pr. paper $9.95 (0-915765-49-7). A complete guide for both sexes to participate either as players or as spectators in the sport of football. (Rev: BL 10/15/88) [796.332]

9843 *Football Register* (7–12). Illus. 1989, Sporting News paper $9.95 (0-89204-217-6). Biographical information for each player and coach in the National Football League is given in this annual publication. [796.332]

9844 Garber, Angus. *End Zone: A Photographic Celebration of Football* (8–12). Illus. 1987, Henry Holt $15.95 (0-8050-0556-0). An introduction to the many aspects of football through stunning color photographs. (Rev: BR 5-6/88; VOYA 2/88) [796.332]

9845 Greenberg, Martin H., and Mark J. Sabljak. *Who's Who in the Super Bowls* (8–12). Illus. 1986, Dembner $22.50 (0-934878-80-3); paper $14.95 (0-934878-81-1). An alphabetical listing with identification of all the players in the first 20 Super Bowls. (Rev: BL 11/15//86) [796.332]

9846 Gunther, Marc, and Bill Carter. *Monday Night Mayhem: The Inside Story of ABC's Monday Night Football* (8–12). Illus. 1988, Morrow $18.95 (0-688-07553-3). A behind-the-scenes look at the television show that starred such luminaries as Howard Cosell and Frank Gifford. (Rev: BL 10/1/88) [791.45]

9847 Herskowitz, Mickey. *The Quarterbacks: The Uncensored Truth about Men in the Pocket* (9–12). Illus. 1990, Morrow $19.95 (0-688-07387-5). Through anecdotes and interviews, the professional football careers of some 29 NFL quarterbacks are reviewed. (Rev: BL 10/1/90) [799.332]

9848 Hollander, Zander. *The Complete Handbook of Pro-Football* (9–12). 1989, NAL paper $5.95 (0-451-16117-3). This is an annual compilation of facts and statistics on players and teams. [796.33]

9849 Hoppel, Joe, et al., eds. *College Football's Twenty-five Greatest Teams* (7–12). Illus. 1988, Sporting News paper $14.95 (0-89204-281-8). The results of 2 polls conducted by *The Sporting News* will surprise many readers. (Rev: BL 1/15/89) [796.332]

9850 Jarrett, William. *Timelines of Sports History: Football* (7–12). Illus. 1989, Facts on File $17.95 (0-8160-1919-3). A chronology of famous events connected with the history of football from 1865 through 1988. (Rev: BL 8/89; BR 5-6/90) [796.332]

9851 Jennings, David, et al. *The Art of Place-Kicking and Punting* (9–12). Illus. 1985, Linden paper $10.95 (0-671-55721-1). Three experts in the field, such as Jennings of the Giants, discuss the importance of kicking in football and give many tips on techniques. (Rev: BL 9/1/85) [796.332]

9852 Kramer, Jerry. *Instant Replay: The Green Bay Diary of Jerry Kramer* (10–12). 1968, Holtzman $24.95 (0-941372-05-7). An insider's look at football and a great team. [796.33]

9853 Lorimer, Lawrence T., and John Devaney. *The Football Book* (9–12). 1977, Random LB $7.99 (0-394-93574-8); paper $2.44 (0-394-83574-3). Rules, terms, teams, history, and personalities are all covered in this encyclopedia of football. [796.33]

9854 Madden, John, and Dave Anderson. *One Knee Equals Two Feet: (And Everything Else You Need to Know about Football)* (10–12). 1986, Random $16.95 (0-394-55328-4); Jove paper $4.50 (0-515-09193-6). A former coach and a sportswriter assess the strengths and weaknesses of a number of football players. (Rev: BL 8/86; BR 5-6/87; SLJ 12/86; VOYA 4/87) [796.332]

9855 Namath, Joe. *Football for Young Players and Parents* (5–12). Illus. 1986, Simon &

Schuster paper $10.95 (0-671-63953-6). In addition to tips on technique, equipment, and training, Namath speaks about the philosophy of the sport. (Rev: BL 12/15/86) [796.332]

9856 Nash, Bruce, and Allan Zullo. *The Football Hall of Shame* (9–12). 1990, Pocket paper $7.95 (0-671-69413-8). A recent collection that continues to bring into focus some of the low points of the game. (Rev: BL 9/15/90) [796.33]

9857 Peck, Richard E. *Something for Joey* (9–12). 1978, Bantam paper $2.75 (0-553-25532-0). The touching story of the relationship between the football star John Cappelletti and his younger brother, who died of leukemia. [796.332]

9858 Perrin, Tom. *Football: A College History* (7–12). 1987, McFarland $29.95 (0-89950-294-6). A thorough historical account that mentions 4,600 players and coaches that have played in the last 100 years. (Rev: VOYA 8/88) [796.332]

9859 Pincus, Arthur. *How to Talk Football* (9–12). 1984, Norton paper $8.95 (0-934878-83-8). With wit and humor, the author presents a dictionary of football terms and profiles of some players. [796.33]

9860 Plimpton, George. *Paper Lion* (10–12). 1966, Harper paper $8.95 (0-06-091540-4). The "professional" amateur tries his hand at big league football and tells all. [796.33]

9861 Riffenburgh, Beau, and David Boss. *Great Ones: NFL Quarterbacks from Baugh to Montana* (9–12). Illus. 1989, Viking $22.95 (0-670-82979-X). An attractively packaged tribute in text and pictures to the noteworthy quarterbacks of the National Football League. (Rev: BL 1/1/90; VOYA 4/90) [796.332]

9862 Rowe, Peter. *American Football: The Records* (7–12). Illus. 1989, Sterling paper $14.95 (0-85112-350-3). This comprehensive guide covers subjects like the history of the sport, its variations, famous coaches and players, and important statistics. Many illustrations. (Rev: SLJ 12/86) [796.332]

9863 Telander, Rick. *The Hundred Yard Lie: The Corruption of College Football and What We Can Do to Stop It* (9–12). 1989, Simon & Schuster $17.95 (0-671-68095-1). The author believes that in its present state, college football helps neither the student nor the sport. (Rev: BL 10/15/89) [796.332]

9864 Whittingham, Richard. *Saturday Afternoon: College Football and the Men Who Made the Day* (9–12). Illus. 1986, Workman paper $11.95 (0-89480-933-4). A history of college football from its beginnings in the 1800s to today. (Rev: BL 3/1/86) [796.332]

9865 Wilkinson, Bud. *Sports Illustrated Football: Defense* (9–12). Rev. ed. Illus. 1986, Harper paper $8.95 (0-06-055007-4). Using all kinds of illustrations the author explains team and individual defensive moves and techniques. Also use: *Sports Illustrated Football: Offense* (1986). [796.332]

9866 Wood, Bob. *Big Ten Country: A Journey through One Football Season* (9–12). Illus. 1989, Morrow $17.95 (0-688-08922-4). A tour of the facilities and ambience and a look into the personalities of the employees at each of the Big Ten football stadiums. (Rev: BL 9/15/89) [796.332]

Golf

9867 Boswell, Thomas. *Strokes of Genius* (10–12). Illus. 1987, Doubleday $19.95 (0-385-19968-6); Penguin paper $7.95 (0-121-011386-1). A collection of pieces by Boswell about golf, famous players, and unusual golf courses. (Rev: BL 4/15/87) [796.352]

9868 Grout, Jack. *On the Lesson Tee: Basic Golf Fundamentals* (9–12). 1982, Sterling paper $7.95 (0-87670-064-4). An informal guide to golf basics that is particularly good for the beginner. [796.352]

9869 Hogan, Ben. *Power Golf* (10–12). 1989, Pocket paper $4.50 (0-671-68246-6). Expert advice for people already familiar with the basics of golf. [796.352]

9870 Kaskie, Shirli. *A Woman's Golf Game* (10–12). 1983, Contemporary paper $9.95 (0-8092-5756-4). For both the beginner and the experienced female golfer, this is a fine guide. [796.352]

9871 Lopez, Nancy. *The Complete Golfer* (9–12). Illus. 1989, Contemporary paper $11.95 (0-8092-4711-9). This well-known golf professional gives her tips on the sport for both men and women. (Rev: BR 11–12/89) [796.352]

9872 Miller, Johnny, and Desmond Tolhurst. *Johnny Miller's Golf for Juniors* (8–12). Illus. 1987, Doubleday paper $13.95 (0-385-27944-2). With many illustrations, this is a basic guide for beginners that concentrates on fundamental skills. (Rev: BL 3/15/87; SLJ 9/87) [796.352]

9873 Mulvoy, Mark. *Sports Illustrated Golf* (9–12). Illus. 1983, Harper $12.95 (0-06-014871-3); paper $8.95 (0-06-090868-8). This book for the beginning golfer covers swings, equipment, and other basics. [796.352]

9874 Nash, Bruce, and Allan Zullo. *The Golf Hall of Shame* (9–12). 1989, Pocket paper $7.95 (0-671-68488-9). Golfing goofs from the caddies to the pros. (Rev: BL 11/15/89) [796.352]

9875 Nicklaus, Jack, and Ken Bowden. *Play Better Golf: Vol. I, The Swing from A to Z* (10–12). 1985, Pocket paper $6.95 (0-671-55651-7). This book on how to improve your golf swing is continued in *Play Better Golf: Vol II, The Short Game and Scoring* (1986). [796.352]

9876 Palmer, Arnold. *Play Great Golf: Mastering the Fundamentals of Your Game* (9–12). Illus. 1987, Doubleday $24.95 (0-385-24301-4). Plenty of pointers are given in text and pictures on the fundamentals of golf with emphasis on the swing. (Rev: BL 2/1/88) [796.352]

9877 Saunders, Vivien. *The Complete Book of Golf Practice* (9–12). Illus. 1989, Stanley Paul $29.95 (0-09-173672-2). A collection of tips on how to improve one's golf techniques. (Rev: BL 5/15/89) [796.352]

9878 United States Golf Assn. *Golf Rules in Pictures* (9–12). Rev. ed. Illus. 1984, Putnam paper $6.96 (0-399-50984-4). This guide explains and illustrates golf rules and also gives definitions of terms. [796.352]

9879 Watson, Tom, and Frank Hannigan. *The New Rules of Golf* (10–12). 1988, Random paper $9.95 (0-394-75632-0). This handbook gives a complete rundown of golf rules and regulations. [796.352]

9880 Whitworth, Kathy, and Rhonda Glenn. *Golf for Women* (10–12). Illus. 1990, St. Martin's $19.95 (0-312-04013-X). A useful manual that contains tips and techniques for both the beginner and experienced female golfer. (Rev: BL 4/15/90) [796.352]

Gymnastics

9881 Aykroyd, Peter. *Modern Gymnastics* (8–12). Illus. 1986, Prentice paper $9.95 (0-668-06462-5). A fine book on women's gynmastics that covers the basics and devotes a separate chapter to each piece of equipment. (Rev: BR 11–12/85; VOYA 2/86) [796.4]

9882 Sands, Bill. *Modern Women's Gymnastics for Both Teacher and Gymnast* (10–12). 1982, Sterling paper $7.95 (0-87670-065-2). This is a guide to 4 gymnastic events for women. [796.4]

9883 Sands, Bill, and Mike Conklin. *Everybody's Gymnastics Book* (10–12). Illus. 1984, Macmillan $19.95 (0-684-18091-X). This book gives both a history of gymnastics and an explanation of both men's and women's events. [796.4]

Horsemanship

9884 Hirsch, Joe, and Jim Bolus. *Kentucky Derby: The Chance of a Lifetime* (10–12). Illus. 1988, McGraw $39.95 (0-07-029069-5). A history that covers over 100 years of America's most famous horse race. (Rev: BL 6/15/88) [798.4]

9885 Pervier, Evelyn. *Horsemanship* (7–12). 3 vols. Illus. 1984, Messner LB $9.29 each (vol. 1: 0-671-45519-2; vol. 2: 0-671-45520-6; vol. 3: 0-671-45521-4); paper $5.95 each (vol. 1: 0-688-05935-4; vol. 2: 0-688-05942-7; vol. 3: 0-688-05950-8). The three volumes in this set are *Basics for Beginners; Basics for Intermediate Riders;* and *Basics for More Advanced Riders.* [798.2]

Ice Hockey

9886 Fischler, Stan, and Shirley Fischler. *Everybody's Hockey Book* (7–12). Illus. 1983, Macmillan $22.50 (0-684-18022-7). After an interesting history of the sport, this account tells about training, equipment, and individual plays. [796.96]

9887 Plimpton, George. *Open Net* (10–12). 1987, Penguin paper $6.95 (0-14-009709-0). The author becomes a trial goaltender for the Boston Bruins to find out what the world of hockey is really like. (Rev: BL 11/1/85) [796.96]

9888 Wolfe, Bernie, and Mitch Henkin. *How to Watch Ice Hockey* (9–12). Illus. 1985, National Pr. paper $6.95 (0-915765-09-8). All of the rules of a hockey match are carefully explained plus a description of each position and the kinds of action one can expect at a typical game. (Rev: BL 12/15/85) [796.96]

Ice Skating

9889 Fassi, Carlo. *Figure Skating with Carlo Fassi* (9–12). Illus. 1980, Macmillan paper $12.95 (0-684-17644-0). An excellent book for both beginner and expert with clear text and many illustrations. [796.91]

9890 Petkevich, John Misha. *Sports Illustrated Figure Skating* (9–12). Illus. 1988, NAL paper $10.95 (0-452-26209-7). Written for the beginner, this is a heavily illustrated guide to figure skating basics. [796.91]

9891 Whedon, Julia. *The Fine Art of Ice Skating: An Illustrated History and Portfolio of Stars* (9–12). Illus. 1988, Abrams $29.95 (0-8109-1127-2). A beautifully illustrated history of ice skating plus an introduction to over 30 contemporary masters of this pastime. (Rev: BL 12/1/88) [796.91]

Kite Making and Flying

9892 Eden, Maxwell. *Kiteworks: Explorations in Kite Building and Flying* (10–12). Illus. 1989, Sterling $19.95 (0-8069-6712-9). A thorough discussion of the types of kite construction, a history of kites, and instructions on how to construct different kites. (Rev: BL 3/15/90; SLJ 4/90) [796.1]

Martial Arts

9893 Crompton, Paul. *The Complete Martial Arts* (9–12). Illus. 1989, McGraw $24.95 (0-07-014450-8). The author explores 25 different forms of martial arts from karate and judo to the more obscure disciplines. (Rev: BL 10/15/89) [796.8]

9894 Kozuki, Russell. *Karate for Young People* (8–12). 1982, Sterling paper $4.95 (0-8069-7560-1). A good manual for the beginner that adapts basics for this audience. Also use *Junior Karate* (1971). [796.8]

9895 Oyama, Mas. *Mas Oyama's Essential Karate* (9–12). 1979, Sterling paper $12.95 (0-8069-8844-4). An easily understood guide for the beginner on the basics of karate. [796.8]

9896 Parulski, George R., Jr. *The Complete Book of Judo* (10–12). Illus. 1984, Contemporary paper $9.95 (0-8092-5450-6). A guide that covers such topics as history, conditioning, postures, and nutrition. [796.8]

9897 Ribner, Susan, and Richard Chin. *The Martial Arts* (9–12). Illus. 1978, Harper LB $12.89

(0-06-025000-3). This oversize, heavily illustrated book gives a basic introduction to such martial arts as karate, kung fu, and judo. [796.8]

9898 Tegner, Bruce. *Bruce Tegner's Complete Book of Jujitsu* (7–12). Illus. 1977, Thor $14.95 (0-87407-516-5); paper $7.95 (0-87407-027-0). A master in the martial arts introduces this ancient Japanese form of self-defense and gives basic information on stances and routines. [796.8]

9899 Tegner, Bruce. *Bruce Tegner's Complete Book of Self-Defense* (7–12). New ed. Illus. 1975, Thor $14.95 (0-87407-510-6); paper $7.95 (0-87407-030-9). A basic primer on ways to defend oneself including hand blows and restraints. [796.8]

9900 Tegner, Bruce. *Judo: Beginner to Black Belt* (10–12). 2nd rev. ed. Illus. 1982, Thor $14.95 (0-87407-521-1). An introduction to the techniques of modern judo and their applications plus a short section on traditional judo. [796.8]

9901 Tegner, Bruce. *Karate: Beginner to Black Belt* (7–12). Illus. 1982, Thor $14.95 (0-87407-520-3); paper $7.95 (0-87407-040-6). In an account that stresses safety and fitness, techniques for both the novice and the experienced are explained. [796.8]

9902 Tegner, Bruce. *Self-Defense: A Basic Course* (10–12). 1979, Thor paper $5.95 (0-87407-031-7). This volume is intended for young adult men and covers a variety of ways to protect oneself. [796.8]

9903 Tegner, Bruce, and Alice McGrath. *Self-Defense & Assault Prevention for Girls & Women* (7–12). Illus. 1977, Thor $5.95 (0-87407-026-0). Various defensive and offensive techniques are introduced in situations where they would be appropriate. [796.8]

9904 Tegner, Bruce, and Alice McGrath. *Solo Forms of Karate, Tai Chi, Aikido & Kung Fu* (9–12). Illus. 1981, Thor $5.95 (0-87407-034-1). Routines are described in copious pictures plus text that emphasize exercise and good training. [796.8]

9905 Van Clief, Ron. *The Ron Van Clief Green & Purple Belt Guide Book* (10–12). Illus. 1985, Crown paper $9.95 (0-517-55183-7). This handbook guides one through the exercises and activities associated with 2 of the 5 belts. Also use: *The Ron Van Clief White Belt Guide Book* (1985). (Rev: SLJ 4/85) [796.8]

Olympic Games

9906 Greenberg, Stan. *The Guinness Book of Olympics Records* (7–12). Illus. 1988, Bantam paper $3.95 (0-553-27194-6). A thorough history of each Olympiad from 1896 to the present with lists of winners in each sport and current records. [796.4]

9907 Hart-Davis, Duff. *Hitler's Games: The 1936 Olympics* (10–12). Illus. 1986, Harper $16.95 (0-06-015554-X). In addition to a description of the Olympic games of 1936, this book explores their social and political importance. [796.4]

9908 Wallechinsky, David. *The Complete Book of the Olympics* (9–12). Rev. ed. Illus. 1988, Viking $35.00 (0-670-82110-1); Penguin paper $12.95 (0-14-010771-1). A hefty text that includes historical information on all past winners in both the summer and winter games. (Rev: BL 2/15/88) [796.4]

Running and Jogging

9909 Fixx, James F. *The Complete Book of Running* (10–12). Illus. 1977, Random $18.95 (0-394-41159-5). This book answers all kinds of questions one might have about running. A follow-up is *Jim Fixx's Second Book of Running* (1980). [796.4]

9910 Glover, Bob, and Pete Schuder. *The Competitive Runner's Handbook* (10–12). 1983, Penguin paper $7.95 (0-14-046565-0). A series of fitness programs are outlined for various kinds of races. [796.4]

9911 Glover, Bob, and Jack Shepherd. *The Runner's Handbook* (10–12). 1985, Penguin paper $8.95 (0-14-046713-0). This basic book covers running for both men and women. [796.4]

9912 Heinonen, Janet. *Sports Illustrated Running for Women* (9–12). Illus. 1989, NAL paper $9.95 (0-452-26271-2). Through copious illustrations and text, the basics of running for women are covered. [796.4]

9913 Honig, Daniel. *How to Run Better* (10–12). 1985, Ballantine paper $2.50 (0-345-31845-5). Skill development and training schedules are topics covered in this thorough manual. [796.4]

9914 Kardong, Don. *Thirty Phone Booths to Boston: Tales of a Wayward Runner* (9–12). 1987, Greene paper $7.95 (0-8289-0627-0). An internationally known runner writes entertainingly about different aspects of his sport. (Rev: BL 11/15/85) [796.4]

9915 Kostrubala, Thaddeus. *The Joy of Running* (10–12). 1982, Pocket paper $3.50 (0-671-54340-7). This is both a manual and a pep talk for runners. [796.4]

9916 Ullyot, Joan L. *Running Free: A Book for Women Runners and Their Friends* (10–12). Illus. 1980, Putnam paper $7.95 (0-399-50580-6). A book, for women, on the benefits of running and how to engage in this pastime safely. [796.4]

Sailing and Boating

9917 Adkins, Jan. *The Craft of Sail* (10–12). 1973, Walker $11.95 (0-8027-0401-8); paper $10.95 (0-8027-7214-5). A respected manual on small-boat craftsmanship. [797.1]

9918 Aebi, Tania, and Bernadette Brennan. *Maiden Voyage* (9–12). 1989, Simon & Schuster $19.95 (0-671-66653-3). The story of a sailboat and the youngest person and the only American woman to circle the globe. (Rev: BL 8/89) [910.41]

9919 Bangs, Richard, and Christian Kallen. *Riding the Dragon's Back: The Race to Raft the Upper Yangtze* (9–12). Illus. 1989, Macmillan $22.95 (0-689-11932-1). The story of a group of Americans and Chinese and their raft and kayak trip through the dangerous waters of the Yangtze. (Rev: BL 9/15/89; SLJ 6/90) [915]

9920 Barta, Ernie. *Sailing "the Annapolis Way"* (10–12). 1984, Stackpole paper $10.95 (0-8117-2262-7). From the nation's famous sailing school comes this manual on all types of sailing. [797.1]

9921 Bavier, Robert N., Jr. *Keys to Racing Success* (10–12). Illus. 1982, Putnam $19.95 (0-396-08064-2). A clear, informal guide to successful sailing in general and racing in particular. [623.88]

9922 *Boat Owner's Manual* (9–12). Illus. 1985, Intertec paper $4.95 (0-87288-184-9). This short paperback gives a wealth of information on small boats and their safe operation. (Rev: BL 9/1/85) [623.823]

9923 Bond, Bob, and Steve Sleight. *Small Boat Sailing: The Basic Guide* (10–12). Illus. 1983, Knopf $15.95 (0-394-52446-2). For beginning sailors, this account covers equipment and gear as well as advice on sailing small crafts. [797.1]

9924 Caswell, Christopher. *The Illustrated Book of Basic Boating* (9–12). Illus. 1990, Hearst paper $9.95 (0-688-08931-3). A step-by-step guide to power boating, from launching to tying up to a dock. (Rev: BL 7/90) [796.125]

9925 Franzel, Dave. *Sailing: The Basics* (9–12). Illus. 1985, International Marine paper $14.95 (0-87742-201-X). A fine manual for the novice that not only discusses basics but also more complicated maneuvering. (Rev: BL 3/1/86) [797.1]

9926 George, M. B. *Basic Sailing* (7–12). Rev. ed. Illus. 1984, Morrow paper $8.95 (0-688-03567-1). A long-respected basic teaching manual that begins with parts of the boat and moves on to complex sailing skills and techniques. [797.1]

9927 Greenwald, Michael. *Survivor* (9–12). Illus. 1989, Blue Horizons $34.95 (0-931297-03-8); paper $26.95 (0-931297-02-6). A manual that tells true tales of marine survival and gives hundreds of safety tips. (Rev: BL 1/15/90) [613.69]

9928 Harrison, Dave. *Sports Illustrated Canoeing* (9–12). Illus. 1988, NAL paper $9.95 (0-452-26109-0). Using nontechnical language this is a well-illustrated guide to canoe basics. [797.1]

9929 Johnson, Peter. *The Sail Magazine Book of Sailing* (9–12). Illus. 1989, Knopf $40.00 (0-394-57457-5). After giving a brief history of sailing, the author covers all of today's major races. (Rev: BL 10/1/89) [796.323]

9930 Mason, Bill. *Path of the Paddle: An Illustrated Guide to the Art of Canoeing* (9–12). Illus. 1989, NorthWord paper $19.95 (1-55971-004-7). A thorough series of lessons, from beginning to advanced techniques, all illustrated with photographs. (Rev: BL 5/15/89) [797.1]

9931 Morgan, Dodge. *The Voyage of American Promise* (10–12). Illus. 1989, Houghton $19.95 (0-395-44096-3). The story of the building of the *American Promise* and of the man who used it to circumnavigate the globe in only 150 days. (Rev: BL 6/15/89) [797.1]

9932 Mowat, Farley. *The Boat Who Wouldn't Float* (10–12). 1981, Bantam paper $2.95 (0-553-24552-X). True adventures, many humorous, aboard a leaky schooner in the North Atlantic. [797.1]

9933 Riviere, Bill. *The Open Canoe* (9–12). Illus. 1985, Little $12.95 (0-316-74768-8). A fine handbook that is organized by different kinds of canoeing such as recreational and competitive. (Rev: BL 8/85) [797.1]

9934 Robinson, Bill, ed. *80 Years of Yachting* (9–12). Illus. 1987, Dodd $19.95 (0-396-08958-5). A fascinating collection of articles about yachting from the magazine of the same name. (Rev: BL 5/15/87) [797.1]

9935 Rousmaniere, John. *The Annapolis Book of Seamanship* (9–12). Rev. ed. Illus. 1989, Simon & Schuster $29.95 (0-671-67447-1). An extensive text that covers such topics as boat structures, "rules of the road," boating techniques, and safety procedures. (Rev: BL 9/15/89) [623.88]

9936 Rousmaniere, John. *The Sailing Lifestyle: A Guide to Sailing and Cruising for Pleasure* (9–12). 1988, Simon & Schuster paper $9.95 (0-671-65944-8). Basic boating skills are covered including steering, tacking, and general navigation. (Rev: BL 5/15/85) [797.1]

9937 Schryver, Doug. *Sailing School* (9–12). Illus. 1987, Barrons $19.95 (0-8120-5813-5). In addition to material on sailing theory and practice, this how-to guide gives material on this history of sailing. (Rev: SLJ 9/87) [797.1]

9938 Starkell, Don. *Paddle to the Amazon* (10–12). Illus. 1989, Prima $19.95 (0-914629-91-3). An adventure-filled account of a 2-year canoe trip of a father and son from Winnipeg to the heart of Brazil. (Rev: BL 7/89)

9939 Toghill, Jeff. *Sailing for Beginners* (9–12). 1986, Norton paper $6.95 (0-393-30299-7). A basic guide that covers all sizes and classes of sailboats. [797.1]

9940 White, Rick. *Catamaran Racing: Solutions, Secrets, Speed* (10–12). Illus. 1983, Putnam paper $12.95 (0-396-08201-7). A useful introduction to catamaran racing with clear instructions and many diagrams. [797.1]

9941 Zadig, Ernest A. *The Complete Book of Boating* (9–12). 3rd ed. Illus. 1985, Prentice $24.95 (0-13-157496-5). This guide to both powerboats and sailboats covers such subjects as types of pleasure boats, motors, maintenance, navigation, and repairs. (Rev: BL 9/1/85) [623]

Skiing

9942 Althen, K. C. *The Complete Book of Snowboarding* (10–12). Illus. 1990, Tuttle paper $15.95 (0-8048-7035-7). This basic guide to this sport, which is a variation on skiing, includes material on equipment, kinds of terrain, racing, and various maneuvers. (Rev: BL 10/1/90) [799.93]

9943 Campbell, Stu, et al. *The Way to Ski! The Official Method* (9–12). Illus. 1986, HP $19.95 (0-89586-485-1); paper $12.95 (0-89586-444-4). An easily followed handbook on the basics of skiing. (Rev: BL 1/1/87) [769.93]

9944 Petrick, Tim. *Sports Illustrated Skiing* (9–12). Illus. 1987, NAL paper $9.95 (0-452-26039-6). From the basic to the advanced, this illustrated account covers skiing techniques and provides information on topics like equipment. (Rev: BL 3/15/86) [797.93]

9945 Sheahan, Casey. *Sports Illustrated Cross-Country Skiing* (9–12). Illus. 1988, NAL paper $9.95 (0-452-26208-9). Techniques and skills are outlined plus advice on buying equipment and adjustments to various terrains. [796.93]

9946 Tanler, Bill, ed. *Ski Tech's Guide to Equipment, Skiwear, and Accessories* (9–12). Illus. 1990, John Muir paper $11.95 (0-945465-45-9). From the pages of *Ski Tech* magazine a complete guide to selecting ski equipment and accessories. (Rev: BL 2/1/90) [796.93]

9947 Yacenda, John. *High Performance Skiing* (9–12). Illus. 1987, Leisure Pr. paper $12.95 (0-88011-288-3). An instructional manual that concentrates on improving downhill skiing techniques. (Rev: BL 12/1/87) [796]

Soccer

9948 Brown, Michael. *Soccer Rules in Pictures* (9–12). Illus. 1986, Putnam paper $6.95 (0-399-51267-5). Organized by subject, this guide explains in text and drawings the rules that apply in various situations. (Rev: BL 12/15/86) [796.334]

9949 Chyzowych, Walter. *The Official Soccer Book of the United States Soccer Federation* (10–12). n.d., U.S. Soccer Federation paper $7.00 (0-318-16830-8). This manual covers topics such as training, physical fitness, and strategies. [796.334]

9950 Crow, Tatu, and Kevin Crow. *Championship Soccer* (7–12). Illus. 1989, Contemporary paper $10.95 (0-8092-4614-7). With over 100 diagrams, this book emphasizes the basic skills for beginners. (Rev: BR 9–10/89) [796.334]

9951 Herbst, Dan. *Sports Illustrated Soccer: The Complete Player* (7–12). Illus. 1988, NAL paper $9.95 (0-452-26026-2). Basic and advanced skills are explained plus a variety of game strategies. [796.334]

9952 Rosenthal, Gary. *Soccer Skills and Drills* (10–12). 1978, Macmillan paper $10.95 (0-87460-

258-0). In addition to a rundown on techniques, this manual includes a glossary and the official rules. [796.334]

Surfing, Water Skiing, and Other Water Sports

9953 Armstead, Lloyd D. *Whitewater Rafting in Eastern America* (10–12). 1989, East Woods paper $9.95 (0-87106-603-3). A guide to the sport of rafting plus an outline of 35 river journeys. [797.1]

9954 Evans, Jeremy. *The Complete Guide to Short Board Sailing* (9–12). Illus. 1987, International Marine paper $12.95 (0-87742-245-1). An excellent guide to this special form of windsurfing. (Rev: BL 7/87) [797.3]

9955 Grubb, Jake, et al. *The New Sailboard Book* (9–12). Illus. 1990, Norton paper $16.95 (0-393-30682-8). This guide to a fast-growing sport contains information on equipment, basic techniques, and types of competitions. (Rev: BL 5/1/85) [797.124]

9956 Ketels, Hank, and Jack McDowell. *Sports Illustrated Scuba Diving* (7–12). Illus. 1988, NAL paper $9.95 (0-452-26108-2). A useful manual that discusses such topics as fitness, equipment, kinds of dives, and safety measures. [797.2]

9957 Winans, Chip, et al. *Boardsailing Made Easy: Teaching and Techniques* (9–12). Rev. ed. Illus. 1985, Chip Winans paper $14.95 (0-9613234-0-X). A complete guide to a growing sport also known as windsurfing that even includes material on physical conditioning. (Rev: BL 7/85; VOYA 12/85) [797.3]

Swimming and Diving

9958 Brems, Marianne. *The Fit Swimmer: 120 Workouts & Training Tips* (10–12). Illus. 1984, Contemporary paper $7.95 (0-8092-5454-9). For a person who has chosen swimming as a way of keeping fit, this book describes 120 workouts. [797.2]

9959 Chambliss, Daniel F. *Champions: The Making of Olympic Swimmers* (9–12). Illus. 1988, Morrow $14.95 (0-688-07618-1). Using one actual team as an example, the author explores the world of championship swimming. (Rev: 7/88) [797.2]

9960 Counsilman, James E. *The Complete Book of Swimming* (9–12). 1979, Macmillan paper $7.95 (0-689-70583-2). This book for both the novice and the expert gives material on strokes, drills, and advanced techniques. [797.2]

9961 Lee, Owen. *The Skin Diver's Bible* (9–12). Rev. ed. Illus. 1986, Doubleday paper $9.95 (0-385-13543-2). A thorough introduction to both snorkeling and scuba diving that covers such topics as equipment and safety. (Rev: BL 2/1/86) [797.2]

9962 *On the Guard: The YMCA Lifeguard Manual* (10–12). Illus. 1986, Human Kinetics paper $12.00 (0-87322-059-5). This thorough guide covers such topics as the stages of drowning, rescue techniques, special problems such as heart attacks and cramps, and lifeguarding in different situations such as pools and oceans. (Rev: BL 8/86) [797]

9963 Vaz, Katherine, et al. *Swim Swim: A Complete Handbook for Fitness Swimmers* (10–12). Illus. 1986, Contemporary paper $7.95 (0-8092-5134-5). This is a fine guide for people who use swimming to keep fit. It details training tips, kinds of strokes, and more. (Rev: BL 4/15/86) [797.2]

Tennis and Other Racquet Games

9964 Ashe, Arthur. *Arthur Ashe's Tennis Clinic* (9–12). Illus. 1981, Simon & Schuster $12.95 (0-914178-44-X). Fundamentals of tennis plus information on exercise and equipment are given in this book. [796.342]

9965 Burwash, Peter, and John Tullius. *Total Tennis* (9–12). Illus. 1989, Macmillan $22.50 (0-02-620401-0). Two tennis experts present a book on tennis techniques that concentrates on perfecting one's strokes. (Rev: BL 9/1/89) [796.342]

9966 Collins, Bud. *My Life with the Pros* (10–12). Illus. 1989, Dutton $19.95 (0-525-24659-2). A celebrated tennis commentator and journalist recalls his experiences with the greats of tennis. (Rev: BL 5/1/89) [796.342]

9967 Douglas, Paul. *The Handbook of Tennis* (9–12). Illus. 1982, Knopf $25.00 (0-394-52373-3). A comprehensive guide to tennis that covers such topics as history, strokes, strategies, injuries, and equipment. [796.342]

9968 King, Billie Jean, and Cynthia Starr. *We Have Come a Long Way: The Story of Women's Tennis* (9–12). Illus. 1988, McGraw $24.95 (0-07-034625-9). A history of women's tennis by one of this sport's greatest players. (Rev: BL 12/15/88) [796.342]

9969 Lendl, Ivan, and George Mendoza. *Hitting Hot* (9–12). Illus. 1986, Random $14.95 (0-394-55407-8). A 14-day tennis clinic with a specific skill covered on each day. (Rev: BR 5–6/87; VOYA 2/87) [796.342]

9970 MacCurdy, Doug, and Shawn Tully. *Sports Illustrated Tennis* (9–12). Illus. 1988, NAL paper $9.95 (0-452-26103-1). With many illustrations such topics as kinds of strokes and different kinds of competitions are covered. [796.342]

9971 Strandemo, Steve, and Bill Bruns. *Strategic Racquetball* (10–12). Illus. 1985, Pocket paper $7.95 (0-617-54745-3). For the experienced player, a guide to winning at racquetball. (Rev: BL 1/1/86) [796.343]

9972 Turner, Ed, and Marty Hogan. *Skills & Strategies for Winning Racquetball* (9–12). Illus. 1987, Leisure Pr. paper $12.95 (0-88011-289-1). A thorough guide that covers not only techniques and strategies but also equipment and warm-up exercises. (Rev: BL 12/1/87) [796.34]

9973 Yandell, John. *Visual Tennis: Mental Imagery and the Quest for the Winning Edge* (9–12). Illus. 1990, Doubleday $16.95 (0-385-26422-4). Using over 400 photographs, key techniques in tennis are illustrated. (Rev: BL 6/1/90) [796.342]

Track and Field

9974 Jonas, Steven. *Triathloning for Ordinary Mortals* (10–12). Illus. 1986, Norton $19.95 (0-393-02251-X); paper $12.95 (0-393-30279-2). A practical guide that is aimed at the average person's capabilities. (Rev: BL 5/1/86) [796.4]

9975 Rosen, Mel, and Karen Rosen. *Sports Illustrated Track: Championship Running* (9–12). Illus. 1988, NAL paper $9.95 (0-452-26105-8). A heavily illustrated account of various kinds of competitive events and how to compete in them. [796.4]

9976 Santos, Jim, and Ken Shannon. *Sports Illustrated Track: Championship Field Events* (7–12). Illus. 1988, NAL $9.95 (0-452-26273-9). A nicely illustrated guide to such events as the pole vault, the shot put, and the javelin. [796.4]

9977 Weatherby, W. J., et al. *Chariots of Fire & a Christian Message for Today* (10–12). 1983,

Harper paper $5.95 (0-06-069282-0). This story about 2 British athletes during the 1924 Olympics is based on the prize-winning film. [798]

Northwest $19.95 (0-9615088-2-5); paper $12.95 (0-9615088-3-3). A guide for players who want to improve their volleyball skills. (Rev: BL 11/15/88) [796.32]

Volleyball

9978 Lucas, Jeff. *Pass, Set, Crush: Volleyball Illustrated* (9–12). 2nd ed. Illus. 1988, Euclid

9979 Rosenthal, Gary. *Volleyball: The Game and How to Play It* (9–12). 1983, Macmillan paper $9.95 (0-684-17908-3). This guide is aimed at both players and coaches. [793.32]

Author Index

Authors are arranged alphabetically by last name. Authors' and joint authors' names are followed by book titles—which are also arranged alphabetically—and the text entry number. Book Titles may refer to those that appear as a main entry or as an internal entry in the text. All fiction titles are indicated by (F), following the entry number.

Aamodt, Donald. *A Name to Conjure With,* 1000(F)

Abagnale, Frank W. *Catch Me If You Can,* 6887

Abbey, Edward. *Beyond the Wall,* 8372
The Brave Cowboy, 1(F)
One Life at a Time, Please, 3520

Abbey, Lynn. *Unicorn & Dragon,* 1001(F)

Abbey, Lynn (jt. author). *Blood Ties,* 1022(F)
The Face of Chaos, 1023(F)

Abbott, Dorothy, ed. *Mississippi Writers,* 2889(F)

Abbott, Edwin A. *Flatland,* 8899

Abbott, Marguerite, et al. *Opportunities in Occupational Therapy Careers,* 4903

Abbott, R. Tucker. *Seashells of North America,* 8635
Seashells of the World, 8636

Abbott, Shirley. *Womenfolks,* 8194

Abdul-Jabbar, Kareem. *Giant Steps,* 6737
Kareem, 6738

Abe, Kobo. *The Woman in the Dunes,* 953(F)

Abernathy, M. Glen, et al., eds. *The Carter Years,* 8044

Abernathy, Ralph David. *And the Walls Came Tumbling Down,* 6493

Abling, Bina. *Fashion Sketchbook,* 9180

Ablow, Keith. *Medical School,* 4718

Abraham, Suzanne. *Eating Disorders,* 5368

Abrahams, Peter. *Hard Rain,* 2(F)

Abrahams, Roger D., ed. *African Folktales,* 3377
Afro-American Folktales, 3417

Abrahams, William, ed. *Prize Stories,* 2890(F)
Prize Stories of the Seventies, 2891(F)

Abrams, Irwin, ed. *The Words of Peace,* 3521

Abrams, Kathleen S. *Guide to Careers without College,* 4814

Abrams, Meyer Howard. *A Glossary of Literary Terms,* 3563

Abrams, Richard I. (jt. author). *In Search of Liberty,* 4327

Abse, Dannie, ed. *Voices in the Gallery,* 3146

Abse, Joan, (jt. author). *Voices in the Gallery,* 3146

Abt, Samuel. *LeMond,* 6780

Aburdeen, Patricia (jt. author). *Megatrends 2000,* 7062

Ackerman, Diane. *A Natural History of the Senses,* 5329

Ackerman, Kenneth D. *The Gold Ring,* 8004

Ackroyd, Peter. *Dickens' London,* 7511

Adair, Robert K. *The Physics of Baseball,* 9620

Adam-Smith, Patsy, et al. *Australia,* 7464

Adams, Abigail. *The Book of Abigail and John,* 6521

Adams, Ansel. *Ansel Adams, an Autobiography,* 6188
The Portfolios of Ansel Adams, 5789

Adams, Carol. *The Gender Trap,* 4531

Adams, Douglas. *Dirk Gently's Holistic Detective Agency,* 2332(F)
The Hitchhiker's Guide to the Galaxy, 2331(F)
The Hitchhiker's Quartet, 2331(F)
Last Chance to See, 8568
Life, the Universe, and Everything, 2331(F)
The Long Dark Tea-Time of the Soul, 2332(F)
The Original Hitchhiker Radio Scripts, 3807
The Restaurant at the End of the Universe, 2331(F)
So Long, Thanks for the Fish, 2331(F)

Adams, Harold. *The Man Who Met the Train,* 1911(F)

Adams, Henry. *The Education of Henry Adams,* 6610

Adams, Richard. *The Plague Dogs,* 1002(F)
Watership Down, 1003(F)

Adams, Richard C. *Science with Computers,* 8239

Adams, Robert. *Castaways in Time,* 1004(F)
  Witch Goddess, 1005(F)
Adams, Robert (jt. author). *Magic in Ithkar I,*
  1239(F)
  Magic in Ithkar II, 1239(F)
  Magic in Ithkar IV, 1239(F)
Adams, Terry A. *Sentience,* 2333(F)
Adamson, Joe. *The Bugs Bunny Golden Jubilee,*
  5986
  Groucho, Harpo, Chico and Sometimes Zeppo,
  5987
Adamson, Joy. *Born Free,* 8509
Addams, Jane. *Twenty Years at Hull House,* 6611
Adelman, Gary. *Heart of Darkness,* 3646
Adelson, Alan, ed. *Lodz Ghetto,* 7168
Adicks, Richard. *A Court for Owls,* 1534(F)
Adkins, Jan. *The Craft of Sail,* 9917
Adler, C. S. *Roadside Valentine,* 2225(F)
Adler, Irving. *How Life Began,* 8374
Adler, Kraig (jt. author). *The Encyclopedia of*
  Reptiles and Amphibians, 8464
Adler, Mortimer J. *Aristotle for Everybody,* 3991
  How to Read a Book, 4644
  How to Speak, How to Listen, 4667
  We Hold These Truths, 4180
Adler, Stella. *The Technique of Acting,* 6076
Adoff, Arnold, ed. *I Am the Darker Brother,* 3234
  My Black Me, 3235
  The Poetry of Black America, 3236
Aebi, Tania. *Maiden Voyage,* 9918
Aesop. *Aesop's Fables,* 3468
  The Fables of Aesop, 3469
Afanas'ev, Aleksandr. *Russian Folk Tales,* 3388
Agay, Denes, ed. *Best Loved Songs of the Ameri-*
  can People, 5944
Agee, James. *A Death in the Family,* 513(F)
  Let Us Now Praise Famous Men, 8023
Agostini, Franco. *Intelligence Games,* 8850
  Math and Logic Games, 8849
  Visual Games, 5330
Agras, Stewart. *Panic,* 5555
Agresta, David (jt. author). *Dodge Dynasty,*
  6659
Aguero, Kathleen (jt. author). *An Ear to the*
  Ground, 3277
Ahl, David. *BASIC Computer Games,* 8957
  More BASIC Computer Games, 8957
Ahlstrom, Sydney E. *A Religious History of the*
  American People, 4026
Aichele, Gary J. *Oliver Wendell Holmes, Jr,* 6593
Aiken, Joan. *If I Were You,* 1406(F)
  A Touch of Chill, 2334(F)
  A Whisper in the Night, 2334(F)
Aisenberg, Nadya, ed. *We Animals,* 3147
Akers, Charles W. *Abigail Adams,* 6522
Akst, Daniel. *Wonder Boy,* 6693
Alain-Fournier, Henri. *The Wanderer,* 302(F)
Albaugh, Dan (jt. author). *Sports Collector's Di-*
  gest Baseball Card Price Guide, 9672

Albee, Edward. *American Dream and Zoo*
  Story, 3060
  The Sandbox and Death of Bessie Smith, 3060
  Who's Afraid of Virginia Woolf? 3060
Albers, Donald J., ed. *Mathematical People,*
  8831
Albert, Peter J., ed. *We Shall Overcome,* 4350
Albertazzie, Ralph (jt. author). *Hostage One,*
  84(F)
Albertson, Chris. *Bessie,* 6442
Alcorn, Gordon Dee. *Owls,* 8563
Alcott, Louisa May. *Jo's Boys,* 389(F)
  Little Men, 389(F)
  Little Women, 389(F)
Alden, Peter. *Peterson First Guide to Mammals*
  of North America, 8488
Alderton, David. *A Birdkeeper's Guide to Bud-*
  gies, 8661
  A Birdkeeper's Guide to Finches, 8661
  A Birdkeeper's Guide to Pet Birds, 8661
  Looking After Cage Birds, 8662
  Turtles & Tortoises of the World, 8471
Aldiss, Brian W. *Helliconia Spring,* 2335(F)
  Helliconia Summer, 2335(F)
  Helliconia Winter, 2335(F)
  Hothouse, 2335(F)
  Trillion Year Spree, 3612
  The Year before Yesterday, 2336(F)
Aldred, Cyril. *The Egyptians,* 7092
Aldrich, Bess Streeter. *A Lantern in Her Hand,*
  1554(F)
  A White Bird Flying, 1554(F)
Aldrin, Buzz. *Men from Earth,* 8294
Aleichem, Sholom. *Holiday Tales of Sholom Alei-*
  chem, 434(F)
  Tevye the Dairyman and the Railroad Stories,
  435(F)
Alepher, Joseph, ed. *Encyclopedia of Jewish His-*
  tory, 4384
Alexander, Charles C. *John McGraw,* 6728
Alexander, David M. *Fane,* 2337(F)
Alexander, Edward. *Isaac Bashevis Singer,* 3634
Alexander, Gary. *Pigeon Blood,* 1912(F)
Alexander, John T. *Catherine the Great,* 6832
Alexander, Kent. *Countdown to Glory,* 8295
Alexander, Paul (jt. author). *The Ashton Hor-*
  ror, 1720(F)
  Devil Wind, 1720(F)
  Swamp Witch, 1720(F)
Alexander, R. McNeill, ed. *The Encyclopedia of*
  Animal Biology, 8450
Alexander, Sue. *Finding Your First Job,* 4782
Alexanderson, G. L. (jt. author). *Mathematical*
  People, 8831
Alibrandi, Tom. *Young Alcoholics,* 5099
Alic, Margaret. *Hypatia's Heritage,* 8203
Aline, Countess of Romanones. *The Spy Went*
  Dancing, 6888
  The Spy Wore Red, 6888

Allaby, Michael (jt. author). *A Dog's Life*, 8714

Allegretto, Michael. *Night of Reunion*, 3(F)

Allen, Benedict. *Who Goes Out in the Midday Sun?* 7667

Allen, Dick. *Crash*, 6712

Allen, Frederick L. *The Big Change*, 7710
Only Yesterday, 8024
Since Yesterday, 8025

Allen, Maury. *Jackie Robinson*, 6730
Roger Maris, 6726

Allen, Oliver. *The Airline Builders*, 9056
Atmosphere, 8866
The Windjammers, 8005

Allen, R. E. *Ozzy on the Outside*, 757(F)

Allen, Roger MacBride. *Rogue Powers*, 2338(F)
The Torch of Honor, 2339(F)

Allen, Steve. *How to Make a Speech*, 4668

Allen, T. D. *Navahos Have Five Fingers*, 4391

Allen, Thomas B. *Merchants of Treason*, 4126

Allen, Walter. *The Short Story in English*, 3613

Allen, Woody. *Getting Even*, 3482
Without Feathers, 3482

Allensworth, Carl. *The Complete Play Production Handbook*, 6077

Allison, Alexander W., et al., eds. *The Norton Anthology of Poetry*, 3148

Allman, Paul. *Exploring Careers in Video*, 5033
The Knot, 2226(F)

Allman, William F. (jt. author). *Newton at the Bat*, 9594

Allsen, Phillip E. *Racquetball*, 9544

Althen, K. C. *The Complete Book of Snowboarding*, 9942

Altman, Millys N. *Racing in Her Blood*, 2871(F)

Altman, Sophie, et al. *From "A" to "Z,"* 5983

Alton, Andrea I. *Demon of Undoing*, 1006(F)

Alvarez, A. *Feeding the Rat*, 9545

Alvarez, Everett. *Chained Eagle*, 8097

Alvarez, Luis W. *Alvarez*, 6649

Amado, Jorge. *Gabriela, Clove and Cinnamon*, 627(F)

Ambler, Eric. *Background to Danger*, 5(F)
The Care of Time, 4(F)
Cause for Alarm, 5(F)
A Coffin for Dimitrios, 5(F)
Epitaph for a Spy, 4(F)
Journey into Fear, 5(F)
The Light of Day, 4(F)
Passage of Arms, 5(F)
The Schirmer Inheritance, 4(F)

Ambrose, Stephen E. *Eisenhower*, 6526

American Diabetes Assn., ed. *Diabetes in the Family*, 5169

American Friends Service Committee. *South Africa*, 7369

American Kennel Club Staff. *The Complete Dog Book*, 8709

American Red Cross. *Standard First Aid and Personal Safety*, 5439

Ames, Felicia. *The Bird You Care For*, 8663
The Cat You Care For, 8687

Amis, Kingsley. *The Crime of the Century*, 1913(F)
Lucky Jim, 1875(F)

Amis, Kingsley, ed. *The New Oxford Book of English Light Verse*, 3188

Ammer, Christine. *Fighting Words*, 3903

Amore, JoAnn, ed. *America's Top 300 Jobs*, 4815
Exploring Careers, 4783

Amory, Cleveland. *The Cat and the Curmudgeon*, 8688
The Cat Who Came for Christmas, 8688

Amos, James. *The Memorial*, 1691(F)

Amos, Stephen H. (jt. author). *Atlantic & Gulf Coasts*, 8375

Amos, William H. *Atlantic & Gulf Coasts*, 8375

Amothy, Christine. *I Am Fifteen—And I Don't Want to Die*, 7169

Anastas, Lila. *Your Career in Nursing*, 4984

Anaya, Rudolfo A. *Bless Me, Ultima*, 436(F)
Heart of Aztlan, 437(F)
Tortuga, 628(F)

Andersen, Christopher. *Young Kate*, 6400

Andersen, Hans Christian. *Tales and Stories*, 3389(F)

Anderson, Bob, ed. *Israel*, 7604

Anderson, Bonnie S. *A History of Their Own*, 7481

Anderson, Bryon D. (jt. author). *Seven Ideas That Shook the Universe*, 8915

Anderson, Christopher P. *The New Book of People*, 6782

Anderson, Dave. *The Story of Football*, 9837

Anderson, Dave (jt. author). *Hey, Wait a Minute, I Wrote a Book!* 6755
One Knee Equals Two Feet, 9854
One Size Doesn't Fit All, 6756

Anderson, Dave, ed. *The Red Smith Reader*, 9546

Anderson, Duncan M. (jt. author). *How Do They Do That?* 8952

Anderson, Harry. *Harry Anderson's Games You Can't Lose*, 9547

Anderson, Jack. *Ballet & Modern Dance*, 5958

Anderson, Jean. *The New Doubleday Cookbook*, 9309

Anderson, Jervis. *This Was Harlem*, 8160

Anderson, Jessica. *Tirra Lirra by the River*, 629(F)

Anderson, Karen (jt. author). *Gallicenae*, 1009(F)

Anderson, Ken. *The Art of Quarterbacking*, 9838

Anderson, M. A. *Tracey*, 5100

Anderson, Marie Philomene. *Model*, 4873

Anderson, Mary. *You Can't Get There from Here*, 758(F)

Anderson, Peggy. *Nurse*, 4985

Anderson, Poul. *The Boat of a Million Years*, 2340(F)
Brain Wave, 2341(F)
Broken Sword, 2344(F)
Cold Victory, 2342(F)
Conflict, 2342(F)
Dialogue with Darkness, 2343(F)
Fire Time, 2342(F)
Gallicenae, 1009(F)
The Gods Laughed, 2344(F)
The Long Night, 2344(F)
A Midsummer Tempest, 2342(F)
New America, 2345(F)
No Truce with Kings/Ship of Shadows, 2349(F)
Past Times, 2346(F)
The Shield of Time, 1007(F)
Starship, 2345(F)
Three Hearts and Three Lions, 1008(F)
Time Patrolman, 2347(F)
Twilight World, 2347(F)
The Year of the Ransom, 2348(F)
Anderson, Robert. *A Step-by-Step Book about Snakes*, 8664
Anderson, Robert (jt. author). *Grinding It Out*, 4573
Anderson, Sherwood. *The Portable Sherwood Anderson*, 390
Winesburg, Ohio, 630(F)
Anderson, Sparky. *Sparky!* 6713
Anderson, Sydney, ed. *Simon and Schuster's Guide to Mammals*, 8489
Andrae, Tom (jt. author). *Batman & Me*, 6198
Andreas-Friedrich, Ruth. *Battleground Berlin*, 7501
Berlin Underground, 1938–1945, 7501
Andrews, Carol. *The British Museum Book of the Rosetta Stone*, 7093
Andrews, Charles J. *Fell's United States Coin Book*, 9441
Andrews, Charles M. *The Colonial Background of the American Revolution*, 7834
Andrews, Chris. *A Fishkeeper's Guide to Fancy Goldfishes*, 8747
A Fishkeeper's Guide to Fish Breeding, 8747
Andrews, Elaine K. *Civil Defense in the Nuclear Age*, 4127
Andrews, Kristi. *Magic Time*, 2227(F)
Andrews, V. C. *Flowers in the Attic*, 1707(F)
Heaven, 514(F)
If There Be Thorns, 1707(F)
Petals on the Wind, 1707(F)
Seeds of Yesterday, 1707(F)
Andrews, Wendy. *Vacation Fever!* 2228(F)
Angell, Roger. *Five Seasons*, 9621
Late Innings, 9622
Season Ticket, 9622
Angelo, Joseph A., Jr. *Dictionary of Space Technology*, 8296

Angelou, Maya. *All God's Children Need Traveling Shoes*, 6212
And Still I Rise, 3237
Gather Together in My Name, 6212
The Heart of a Woman, 6212
I Know Why the Caged Bird Sings, 6212
I Shall Not Be Moved, 3238
Just Give Me a Cool Drink of Water 'fore I Die, 3237
Now Sheba Sings the Song, 3875
Oh Pray My Wings Are Gonna Fit Me Well, 3237
Shaker, Why Don't You Sing? 3237
Singin' and Swingin' and Gettin' Merry Like Christmas, 6212
Angelucci, Enzo. *The American Fighter*, 9123
Angelucci, Enzo, ed. *World Encyclopedia of Civil Aircraft*, 9057
Angier, Bradford. *Field Guide to Medicinal Wild Plants*, 8432
How to Stay Alive in the Woods, 9789
Angier, Natalie. *Natural Obsessions*, 5228
Angle, Paul M. *A Pictorial History of the Civil War Years*, 7887
Angus, Douglas, ed. *Great Modern European Short Stories*, 2892(F)
Angus, Sylvia (jt. author). *Great Modern European Short Stories*, 2892(F)
Anku, Vincent. *What to Know about the Treatment of Cancer*, 5170
Annable, H. D. *Annable's Treasury of Literary Teasers*, 3564
Annas, George J. *Judging Medicine*, 5229
Annerino, John. *Hiking the Grand Canyon*, 8156
Ansa, Tina McElroy. *Baby of the Family*, 1708(F)
Ansell, Rod. *To Fight the Wild*, 7465
Anson, Robert Sam. *Best Intentions*, 4351
Antekeier, Kristopher. *Ringmaster!* 5976
Anthony, Evelyn. *Albatross*, 6(F)
A Place to Hide, 7(F)
The Scarlet Thread, 8(F)
Anthony, Piers. *Bearing the Hourglass*, 1014(F)
Being a Green Mother, 1010(F)
Bio of an Ogre, 6213
Blue Adept, 2356(F)
But What of Earth? 2357(F)
Castle Roogna, 1012(F)
Chaining the Lady, 2351(F)
Chthon, 2350(F)
Cluster, 2351(F)
For Love of Evil, 2352(F)
Ghost, 2353(F)
Golem in the Gears, 1011(F)
Heaven Cent, 2354(F)
Justaposition, 2356(F)
Kirlian Quest, 2351(F)
Man from Mundania, 2354(F)
On a Pale Horse, 1014(F)

Race against Time, 2355(F)
Shade of the Tree, 1709(F)
The Source of Magic, 1012(F)
A Spell for Chameleon, 1012(F)
Split Infinity, 2356(F)
Thousandstar, 2351(F)
Total Recall, 2357(F)
Vale of the Vole, 2354(F)
Viscous Circle, 2351(F)
Wielding a Red Sword, 1013(F)
With a Tangled Skein, 1014(F)
Antin, Mary. *The Promised Land*, 6613
Anzenberger, Joseph. *Combat Art of the Vietnam War*, 8098
Anzovin, Steven, ed. *The Problem of Immigration*, 4325
Apfel, Necia H. *Astronomy Projects for Young Scientists*, 8240
Apostolo, Giorgio. *The Illustrated Encyclopedia of Helicopters*, 9058
Apostolou, John L. *The Best Japanese Science Fiction Stories*, 2358(F)
Appel, Allen. *Twice upon a Time*, 1015(F)
Appel, Marcia (jt. author). *Jobs of the Future*, 4826
Appel, Willa. *Cults in America*, 4027
Appelbaum, Diana Karter. *The Glorious Fourth*, 7711
Appelfeld, Aharon. *Age of Wonders*, 7170
For Every Sin, 7171(F)
Appignanesi, Lisa, ed. *The Rushdie File*, 3647
Appleby, Amy. *Celebrate the Bounty*, 9310
Appleby, Amy (jt. author). *The Billboard Book of Song Writing*, 5837
Appleman-Jurman, Alicia. *Alicia*, 6889
Aquila, Richard. *That Old Time Rock & Roll*, 5840
Archbold, Rick (jt. author). *The Discovery of the Titanic*, 8886
Archdeacon, Thomas J. *Becoming American*, 4326
Archer, Jeffrey. *A Matter of Honor*, 9(F)
Shall We Tell the President? 10(F)
Archer, Jules. *Jungle Fighters*, 7172
Police State, 4540
Winners and Losers, 4274
Ardai, Charles, ed. *Why I Left Harry's All-Night Hamburgers*, 2359(F)
Ardley, Neil. *Music*, 5841
Arduini, Paolo. *Simon & Schuster's Guide to Fossils*, 6973
Arendt, Hannah. *The Life of the Mind*, 3992
On Revolution, 4410
On Violence, 4457
Origins of Totalitarianism, 4168
Aria, Barbara (jt. author). *All That Glittered*, 5903
Aristophanes. *Lysistrata*, 2990
Aristotle. *The Basic Works of Aristotle*, 3993

Poetics, 3846
Politics, 3994
Arlen, Michael J. *Thirty Seconds*, 5988
Armen, M. A. *The Hanging of Father Miguel*, 11(F)
Armor, John. *Manzanar*, 8045
Armour, Richard. *It All Started with Nudes*, 5729
Twisted Tales from Shakespeare, 3046
Armstead, Lloyd D. *Whitewater Rafting in Eastern America*, 9953
Armstrong, Dorinne. *Leaving the Nest*, 5592
Armstrong, Richard. *The Next Hurrah*, 4262
Armstrong, Richard (jt. author). *Leaving the Nest*, 5592
Armstrong, Scott (jt. author). *The Brethren*, 4261
Arnason, H. H. *History of Modern Art*, 5730
Arnold, Caroline. *Too Fat? Too Thin? Do You Have a Choice?* 5408
Arnold, Denis. *Bach*, 6334
Monteverdi, 6350
Arnold, Edwin. *Opportunities in Foreign Language Careers*, 4816
Arnold, Elliott. *Blood Brother*, 1555(F)
Arnold, Eve, et al. *The Fifties*, 8046
Arnold, Guy. *Datelines of World History*, 7028
Arnold, Mark Alan (jt. author). *Elsewhere, Vol. III*, 1330(F)
Arnold, Thomas A. *The Adventure Guide to the Pacific Northwest*, 8176
Arnold, William V. *When Your Parents Divorce*, 5637
Arnold-Foster, Mark. *The World at War*, 7173
Arnow, Harriette. *The Dollmaker*, 515(F)
Hunter's Horn, 516(F)
Arpan, Jeffrey. *Opportunities in International Business Careers*, 4904
Arrian. *Alexander the Great*, 6821
Arrington, Leonard J. *The Mormon Experience*, 4028
Artenstein, Jeffrey. *Runaways*, 4501
Artenstein, Michael (jt. author). *Test Your Movie I.Q*, 6003
Artley, Bob. *Memories of a Former Kid*, 6890
Arvey, Michael. *ESP*, 9472
Reincarnation, 9473
UFOs, 9474
Asbell, Bernard (jt. author). *Paterno*, 6757
Asbjørnsen, Peter Christen. *Norwegian Folk Tales*, 3390
Ash, Russell. *Spirit of Place*, 7489(F)
Ashabranner, Brent. *Morning Star, Black Sun*, 7789
To Live in Two Worlds, 7790
The Vanishing Border, 7712
Ashbery, John. *Selected Poems*, 3239
Ashburn, Richie. *Richie Ashburn's Phillies Trivia*, 9623
Ashby, LeRoy. *William Jennings Bryan*, 6579

Ashe, Arthur. *Arthur Ashe's Tennis Clinic*, 9964
Ashe, Geoffrey. *The Landscape of King Arthur*, 6825
Asher, Herbert. *Polling and the Public*, 5590
Asher, Michael. *Two against the Sahara*, 7367
Ashley, Leonard R. N. *The Wonderful World of Magic and Witchcraft*, 9475
The Wonderful World of Superstition, Prophecy and Luck, 9475
Ashley, Mike, ed. *The Mammoth Book of Short Horror Novels*, 1710(F)
Ashley, Mike, et al., eds. *The Pendragon Chronicles*, 1016(F)
Ashton, Betsy. *Betsy Ashton's Guide to Living on Your Own*, 5593
Ashton, Dore, ed. *Twentieth-Century Artists on Art*, 5731
Ashton, Francis. *The Breaking of the Seals*, 1017(F)
Ashton, Stephen. *Indian Independence*, 7438
Asimov, Isaac. *Asimov on Numbers*, 8846
Asimov on Physics, 8900
Asimov on Science, 8204
Asimov's Biographical Encyclopedia of Science and Technology, 6640
Asimov's Chronology of Science and Discovery, 8205
Asimov's Galaxy, 3694
Asimov's Guide to the Bible, 4091, 4092
Asimov's New Guide to Science, 8206
Azazel, 1018(F)
The Beginning and the End, 8207
The Best Mysteries of Isaac Asimov, 1914(F)
The Best Science Fiction of Isaac Asimov, 1915(F)
The Bicentennial Man, and Other Stories, 2360(F)
Casebook of the Black Widowers, 2368(F)
Caves of Steel, 2361(F)
The Collapsing Universe, 8358
The Currents of Space, 2368(F)
End of Eternity, 2368(F)
The Exploding Suns, 8359
Fantastic Voyage, 2362(F)
Fantastic Voyage II, 2362(F)
Far As Human Eye Could See, 8208
Foundation, 2364(F)
Foundation and Earth, 2363(F)
Foundation and Empire, 2364(F)
Foundation Trilogy, 2364(F)
Foundation's Edge, 2364(F)
Frontiers, 8209
The Human Body, 5291
The Human Brain, 5305
I, Robot, 2365(F)
Isaac Asimov's Treasury of Humor, 9464
The March of the Millennia, 7029
The Measure of the Universe, 8863
Naked Sun, 2361(F)
Nemesis, 2366(F)
Nightfall, 2387(F)
Nightfall and Other Stories, 2367(F)
Nine Tomorrows, 2368(F)
Out of the Everywhere, 8210
Pebble in the Sky, 2361(F)
The Planet That Wasn't, 8211
Prelude to Foundation, 2370(F)
Puzzles of the Black Widowers, 1917(F)
Realm of Numbers, 8847
The Relativity of Wrong, 8376
Robot Dreams, 2371(F)
Robots and Empire, 2372(F)
Robots at Dawn, 2372(F)
Robots, Machines in Man's Image, 8958
Second Foundation, 2364(F)
A Short History of Chemistry, 8780
The Subatomic Monster, 8212
The Tragedy of the Moon, 8211
The Tyrannosaurus Prescription and 100 Other Essays, 8204
Words from the Myths, 3470
Asimov, Isaac, ed. *Amazing Stories*, 2383(F)
Fifty Short Science Fiction Tales, 2382(F)
Hound Dunnit, 1916(F)
Isaac Asimov Presents the Great SF Stories, 2384(F)
Isaac Asimov Presents the Great SF Stories, 20, 2385(F)
Laughing Space, 2386(F)
One Hundred Great Science Fiction Short Short Stories, 2369(F)
Asimov, Isaac, et al., eds. *Atlantis*, 2373(F)
The Best Crime Stories of the Nineteenth Century, 1918(F)
Catastrophes! 2374(F)
Caught in the Organ Draft, 2375(F)
Computer Crimes and Capers, 2376(F)
Devils, 1711(F)
Ghosts, 1712(F)
Great Science Fiction Stories by the World's Great Scientists, 2377(F)
Hallucination Orbit, 2378(F)
100 Great Science Fiction Short Stories, 2379(F)
Robots, 2380(F)
Space Shuttles, 2381(F)
Tales of the Occult, 1713(F)
Wizards, 1019(F)
Asimov, Janet. *Mind Transfer*, 2388(F)
Asinof, Eliot. *Eight Men Out*, 9624
Asire, Nancy (jt. author). *Wizard Spawn*, 1072(F)
Asnin, Scott. *A Cold Wind from Orion*, 2389(F)
Asprin, Robert. *Little Myth Marker*, 1020(F)
Myth Conception, 1021(F)
Myth-nomers and Im-pervections, 2390(F)
Phule's Company, 2391(F)
Asprin, Robert, ed. *Blood Ties*, 1022(F)
The Face of Chaos, 1023(F)

Associated Press, ed. *World War II*, 7174

Astor, Gerald, et al. *The Baseball Hall of Fame 50th Anniversary Book*, 9625

Atanasoff, Stevan E. *How to Survive as a Teen*, 5594

Atkins, P. W. *Molecules*, 8781

Atkinson, Linda. *In Kindling Flame*, 6872

Ator, Nancy Almand (jt. author). *Barbiturates*, 5126

Attenborough, David. *The First Eden*, 7082
Life on Earth, 6988
The Living Planet, 8377

Attwater, Donald. *Penguin Dictionary of Saints*, 6783

Atwood, Margaret. *Cat's Eye*, 759(F)
The Handmaid's Tale, 2392(F)

Atwood, Margaret, ed. *The New Oxford Book of Canadian Verse in English*, 3240

Auchincloss, Louis, ed. *The Edith Wharton Reader*, 391(F)

Auden, W. H. *Collected Poems*, 3189

Auden, W. H., ed. *The Oxford Book of Light Verse*, 3149
The Portable Greek Reader, 2893

Audubon, John James. *The Birds of America*, 8528

Auel, Jean M. *The Clan of the Cave Bear*, 1348(F)
The Mammoth Hunters, 1348(F)
The Plains of Passage, 1349(F)
The Valley of Horses, 1348(F)

Auerbach, Paul S. *Medicine for the Outdoors*, 5440

Auerbach, Red. *On and Off the Court*, 6739

August, Paul Nordstrom. *Brain Function*, 5306

Aunapu, Greg (jt. author). *Ringmaster!* 5976

Auslander, Joseph. *The Winged Horse*, 3847

Austen, Jane. *Emma*, 330(F)
Mansfield Park, 330(F)
Persuasion, 332(F)
Pride and Prejudice, 331(F)
Sense and Sensibility, 332(F)

Auster, Paul. *Moon Palace*, 517(F)

Auster, Paul, ed. *The Random House Book of Twentieth-Century French Poetry*, 3180

Austin, Oliver L., Jr. *Families of Birds*, 8529

Ausubel, Nathan. *Pictorial History of the Jewish People*, 4385

Ausubel, Nathan, ed. *A Treasury of Jewish Folklore, Stories, Traditions, Legends, Humor, Wisdom and Folk Songs of the Jewish People*, 3357

Aveni, Anthony. *Empires of Time*, 8901

Avery, James. *The Right Jewelry for You*, 5271

Avillez, Martim (jt. author). *How to Draw in Pen and Ink*, 9204

Avraham, Regina. *The Downside of Drugs*, 5101
Substance Abuse, 5102

Axcell, Claudia, et al. *Simple Foods for the Pack*, 9311

Axelrod, Herbert R. *Encyclopedia of Tropical Fish*, 8749
Handbook of Tropical Aquarium Fishes, 8748

Axelrod, Herbert R., et al. *Dr. Axelrod's Mini-Atlas of Freshwater Aquarium Fishes*, 8770

Axelson, R. Dean. *Caring for Your Pet Bird*, 8665

Axline, Virginia M. *Dibs*, 5369

Aycock, Dale. *Starspinner*, 2393(F)

Aykroyd, Peter. *Modern Gymnastics*, 9881

Ayres, Alex, ed. *The Wit & Wisdom of Mark Twain*, 3483

Ayture-Scheele, Zulal. *The Great Origami Book*, 9220

Babbitt, Natalie. *Herbert Rowbarge*, 12(F)

Babcock, Richard. *Martha Calhoun*, 760(F)

Babson, Marion. *Murder, Murder, Little Star*, 1919(F)

Bach, Julie S., ed. *Biomedical Ethics*, 5230
Religion in America, 4029

Bach, Julie S., ed. *Civil Liberties*, 4290
Drug Abuse, 5103

Bach, Richard. *Jonathan Livingston Seagull*, 1024(F)

Bachrach, Deborah. *Pearl Harbor*, 7175

Backes, Clarus, ed. *Growing Up Western*, 6167

Backman, Milton V., Jr. *Christian Churches of America*, 4030

Bacon, Margaret Hope. *The Quiet Rebels*, 4031
Valiant Friend, 6630

Badcock, John (jt. author). *These Were the Romans*, 7119

Baen, Jim, ed. *New Destinies, Volume VIII*, 2394(F)

Baer, Edith. *A Frost in the Night*, 1637(F)

Baez, Joan. *And a Voice to Sing With*, 6360

Baggett, Nancy. *The International Cookie Cookbook*, 9312

Baggott, Andrew (jt. author). *An Instructional Guide to Amateur Wrestling*, 9784

Bagley, T. H. (jt. author). *KGB*, 7567

Bagnall, Brian. *Creative Drawing and Painting*, 9181

Bahn, Paul G. *Images of the Ice Age*, 5732

Baigell, Matthew. *Dictionary of American Art*, 5790

Bailey, Adrian. *The Book of Color Photography*, 9409

Bailey, Ann. *Burn Up*, 518(F)

Bailey, Beth L. *From Front Porch to Back Seat*, 5527

Bailey, David. *Careers in Computers*, 5034

Bailey, Dennis R. (jt. author). *Tin Woodman*, 2412(F)

Bailey, Pearl. *Between You and Me*, 6361

Bailey, Robin W. *The Lake of Fire*, 1025(F)

Bailey, Ronald H. *The Air War in Europe*, 7176
The Assassination, 7888

Battle for Atlanta, 7888
The Bloodiest Day, 7889
The Coastal War, 7888
Confederate Ordeal, 7888
Decoying the Yanks, 7890
The Fight for Chattanooga, 7890
Forward to Richmond, 7890
Glacier, 8809
The Home Front, 8026
Prisoners of War, 7177
Pursuit to Appomattox, 7890
Bain, Donald (jt. author). *Gin and Daggers*, 2007(F)
Bainton, Roland H. *Here I Stand*, 6855
Baird, Bill. *The Art of the Puppet*, 5982
Baird, Julia. *John Lennon, My Brother*, 6414
Baird, Robert M., ed. *Euthanasia*, 5079
Baker, Carlos. *Ernest Hemingway*, 6258
Hemingway, 3695
Baker, Robert (jt. author). *Stars*, 8357
Baker, Russell. *The Good Times*, 6215
Growing Up, 6216
Baker, Russell, ed. *The Norton Book of Light Verse*, 3150
Baker, Sally (jt. author). *Running Tide*, 6764
Baker, Sheridan. *The Complete Stylist and Handbook*, 3955
Baker, William J. *Jesse Owens*, 6765
Bakish, David. *Richard Wright*, 3696
Bakker, Robert T. *The Dinosaur Heresies*, 6974
Baklanov, Grigory. *Forever Nineteen*, 1638(F)
Balaban, John (jt. author). *Vietnam*, 7457
Balanchine, George. *101 Stories of the Great Ballets*, 5959
Baldwin, James. *Evidence of Things Not Seen*, 438(F)
The Fire Next Time, 4352
Go Tell It on the Mountain, 439(F)
If Beale Street Could Talk, 440(F)
Jimmy's Blues, 3241
Just above My Head, 441(F)
No Name in the Street, 4353
Nobody Knows My Name, 4354
The Price of the Ticket, 3522
Baldwin, Rebecca. *Arabella and the Beast*, 2229(F)
Bale, Peter. *Wildlife Through the Camera*, 8452
Balfour, Henry H., Jr. *Herpes Diseases and Your Health*, 5171
Ball, John. *The Kiwi Target*, 13(F)
Ballard, J. G. *Empire of the Sun*, 1639(F)
Ballard, Mignon F. *Cry at Dusk*, 1920(F)
Ballard, Robert D. *The Discovery of the Titanic*, 8886
Exploring Our Living Planet, 8785
Ballou, Robert O., ed. *The Portable World Bible*, 4032
Balzac, Honore de. *Old Goriot*, 303(F)
Bambara, Toni Cade. *Gorilla, My Love*, 442(F)

Bancroft, Anne. *Zen*, 4033
Bancroft-Hunt, Norman. *The Indians of the Great Plains*, 7791
People of the Totem, 7792
Banes, Sally. *Terpsichore in Sneakers*, 5960
Banfield, Susan. *The Rights of Man, the Reign of Terror*, 7490
Bangs, Richard. *Riding the Dragon's Back*, 9919
Banister, Keith, ed. *The Encyclopedia of Aquatic Life*, 8615
Banks, Ian M. *The Player of Games*, 2395(F)
Banks, Lynne Reid. *Melusine*, 1026(F)
Banks, Mike. *Mountain Climbing for Beginners*, 9548
Banner, Lois W. *Elizabeth Cady Stanton*, 6637
Banning, Kent. *Opportunities in Purchasing Careers*, 4905
Bannister, Roger. *The Four-Minute Mile*, 6763
Bar-on, Dan. *Legacy of Silence*, 7178
Barach, Arnold B. *Famous American Trademarks*, 4605
Barasch, Marc (jt. author). *Writers of the Purple Sage*, 204(F)
Barash, David P. *The Great Outdoors*, 9549
Barbash, Fred. *The Founding*, 4181
Barber, Benjamin. *Struggle for Democracy*, 4169
Barber, Richard. *The Penguin Guide to Medieval Europe*, 7122
Bardens, Dennis. *Psychic Animals*, 8473
Barford, George. *Understanding Modern Architecture*, 5686
Baritz, Loren. *Backfire*, 8099
Barker, Clive. *Volume Three of Clive Barker's Books of Blood*, 1714(F)
Barker, Lucius J. *Civil Liberties and the Constitution*, 4291
Barker, M. A. R. *The Man of Gold*, 1027(F)
Barker, Ralph. *The RAF at War*, 7179
Barker, Twiley W., Jr. (jt. author). *Civil Liberties and the Constitution*, 4291
Barkin, Carol (jt. author). *The Complete Babysitter's Handbook*, 5070
Barlow, David. *Sexually Transmitted Diseases*, 5172
Barlowe, Wayne Douglas. *Barlowe's Guide to Extraterrestrials*, 3614
Barnard, Robert. *At Death's Door*, 1921(F)
Out of the Blackout, 519(F)
The Skeleton in the Grass, 1922(F)
Barnes, Clive, ed. *Best American Plays*, 3061
Barnes, Jonathan. *Aristotle*, 3995
Barnes, Linda. *Coyote*, 1923(F)
Barnes, Steven (jt. author). *The Descent of Anansi*, 2699(F)
Barnet, Sylvan. *A Short Guide to Shakespeare*, 3814
Barnett, Lincoln. *The Universe of Dr. Einstein*, 8902
Barnicoat, John. *A Concise History of Posters*, 5733

Barnstone, Aliki, ed. *A Book of Women Poets from Antiquity to Now,* 3848

Barnstone, Willis (jt. author). *A Book of Women Poets from Antiquity to Now,* 3848

Barnum, P. T. *Barnum's Own Story,* 6363
Struggles and Triumphs, 6364

Baron, Dennis. *The English-Only Question,* 3904

Baron, Robert, ed. *Soul of America,* 7713

Barr, Robert R. *What Is the Bible?* 4093

Barr, Roseanne. *Roseanne,* 6366

Barras, Diane Marie (jt. author). *Arnie, the Darling Starling,* 8669

Barrett, Judy. *The Joys of Computer Networking,* 8959

Barrett, Laurence I. *Gambling with History,* 6552

Barrett, Liz (jt. author). *Dave Scott's Triathlon Training,* 9595

Barrett, Nicholas. *Fledger,* 281(F)

Barrett, S. M., ed. *Geronimo,* 6621

Barrett, William E. *The Lilies of the Field,* 443(F)

Barrie, Anmarie. *A Step-by-Step Book about Canaries,* 8666
A Step-by-Step Book about Guinea Pigs, 8756
A Step-by-Step Book about Hamsters, 8757
A Step-by-Step Book about Our First Aquarium, 8771
A Step-by-Step Book about Rabbits, 8667

Barron, W. R., ed. *Sir Gawain and the Green Knight,* 3190

Barrow, Joe Louis. *Joe Louis,* 6748

Barry, Kathleen. *Susan B. Anthony,* 6494

Barry, Lynda. *The Fun House,* 3484
The Good Times Are Killing Me, 520(F)

Barsocchini, Peter (jt. author). *The Jeopardy! Book,* 6067

Barta, Ernie. *Sailing "the Annapolis Way,"* 9920

Barth, Alan. *The Rights of Free Men,* 4292

Barth, Christina. *Bodywork,* 5341

Bartholomew, Paul C. *Summaries of Leading Cases on the Constitution,* 4182

Bartlett, Jonathan, ed. *The Ocean Environment,* 8874

Barton, Bob. *All about Puppies—Your Dog's First Year,* 8710
The Dog for You, 8711

Bartoszewski, Wladyslaw. *The Warsaw Ghetto,* 6891

Bartow, Arthur. *The Director's Voice,* 6078

Barwell, Barbara. *Becoming a Beauty Queen,* 5272

Barzini, Luigi. *The Italians,* 7546

Barzun, Jacques. *The Modern Researcher,* 4669

Barzun, Jacques, ed. *Modern American Usage,* 3905

Bascom, Willard. *Waves and Beaches,* 8880

Bashe, Philip (jt. author). *Dee Snider's Teenage Survival Guide,* 5632

Basie, Count. *Good Morning Blues,* 6368

Bass, Ellen. *I Never Told Anyone,* 5500

Bassani, Giorgio. *The Garden of the Finzi-Continis,* 1640(F)

Bassiouni, M. Cherif. *Introduction to Islam,* 4034

Basta, Nicholas. *Opportunities in Engineering Careers,* 5010

Bateson, Mary Catherine. *With a Daughter's Eye,* 6689

Batty, Peter. *The Divided Union,* 7891

Baudot, Marcel, et al., eds. *The Historical Encyclopedia of World War II,* 7180

Bauld, Harry. *On Writing the College Application Essay,* 4720

Baum, Lawrence. *The Supreme Court,* 4231

Baumert, John H. (jt. author). *Pictorial Guide to the Planets,* 8346

Baumgart, R. A. (jt. author). *Reviving the Death Penalty,* 4484

Bavier, Robert N., Jr. *Keys to Racing Success,* 9921

Baxandall, Rosalyn, et al., eds. *America's Working Women,* 7714

Baxter, Neale. *Opportunities in Counseling & Development Careers,* 4946
Opportunities in Federal Government Careers, 4817
Opportunities in State and Local Government, 4818

Bayless, Deann Groen (jt. author). *Authentic Mexican,* 9313

Bayless, Rick. *Authentic Mexican,* 9313

Baylor, Byrd. *Yes Is Better Than No,* 444(F)

Baylor, Don. *Don Baylor,* 6714

Baym, Nina. *The Scarlet Letter,* 3697

Bazant, Jan. *A Concise History of Mexico from Hidalgo to Cardenas 1805–1940,* 7639

Beagle, Peter S. *A Fine and Private Place,* 1028(F)
The Folk of the Air, 1029(F)
The Last Unicorn, 1030(F)

Beahm, George, ed. *The Stephen King Companion,* 3698

Beal, Doug. *Spike!* 6773

Beal, Merrill D. *I Will Fight No More Forever,* 7793

Bear, Greg. *Blood Music,* 2396(F)
Eon, 2396(F)
Eternity, 2397(F)
The Forge of God, 2398(F)
The Infinity Concerto, 1031(F)
Queen of Angels, 2399(F)
The Serpent Mage, 1032(F)

Beard, Butch, et al. *Butch Beard's Basic Basketball,* 9712

Beard, Charles A. *An Economic Interpretation of the Constitution of the United States,* 4183

Beard, D. C. *The American Boys Handy Book,* 9135

Beard, Henry. *Gardening,* 9370

Beasley, Conger, Jr., et al. *The Sierra Club Guides to the National Parks of the Desert Southwest,* 8198

The Sierra Club Guides to the National Parks of the Rocky Mountains and the Great Plains, 8157

Beaton, M. C. *Death of a Cad,* 1925(F)

Death of a Gossip, 1925(F)

Death of a Perfect Wife, 1924(F)

Death of an Outsider, 1925(F)

Beattie, Ann. *Distortions,* 761(F)

Beattie, Owen. *Frozen in Time,* 7689

Beatty, Richard H. *The Resume Kit,* 4784

Bebey, Francis. *African Music,* 5813

Beck, Brenda E. F., et al., eds. *Folktales of India,* 3381

Beck, K. K. *Death in a Deck Chair,* 1926(F)

Murder in a Mummy Case, 1926(F)

Peril Under the Palms, 1926(F)

Becker, Jillian. *The PLO,* 7590

Becker, Marion Rombauer (jt. author). *Joy of Cooking,* 9356

Becker, Susan D. *The Origins of the Equal Rights Amendment,* 4293

Beckett, Samuel. *Waiting for Godot,* 2991

Beckham, Barry, ed. *The Black Student's Guide to Colleges,* 4721

Bedell, George C., et al. *Religion in America,* 4035

Bedford, Jean. *Sister Kate,* 521(F)

Bedini, Silvio. *The Life of Benjamin Banneker,* 6496

Beecher, John (jt. author). *Remembering Buddy,* 6406

Bego, Mark. *Aretha Franklin,* 6392

Linda Ronstadt, 6439

Behler, John L. *The Audubon Society Field Guide to North American Reptiles and Amphibians,* 8461

Behr, Shulamith. *Women Expressionists,* 5734

Behrens, Michael A. *At the Edge,* 762(F)

Belcher, Wendy. *Honey from the Lion,* 6892

Belfield, Wendall. *How to Have a Healthier Dog,* 8712

Bell, James B. *In Search of Liberty,* 4327

Bell, John A. *Opportunities in the Machine Trades,* 5035

Bell, Marty. *The Legend of Dr. J.,* 6743

Bell, Ruth, et al. *Changing Bodies, Changing Lives,* 5449

Bell, William. *Crabbe's Journey,* 763(F)

Bellairs, John. *The Face in the Frost,* 1033(F)

Bellamy, David. *Bellamy's New World,* 8412

Bellamy, Edward. *Looking Backward,* 2400(F)

Bellamy, Joe David, ed. *The New Fiction,* 3699

Belle, Pamela. *Alethea,* 1407(F)

The Chains of Fate, 1407(F)

The Moon in the Water, 1407(F)

Belli, Melvin M. *Everybody's Guide to the Law,* 4232

Bellini, James. *High Tech Holocaust,* 4421

Belliston, Larry. *Extra Cash for Kids,* 4955

Bellow, Saul. *The Bellarosa Connection,* 430(F)

The Dean's December, 764(F)

Henderson the Rain King, 14(F)

Mr. Sammler's Planet, 954(F)

The Portable Saul Bellow, 955(F)

Bellow, Saul, ed. *Great Jewish Short Stories,* 445(F)

Bemmann, Hans. *The Stone and the Flute,* 1034(F)

Benabent-Loiseau, Josee. *The Odyssey of The Bear,* 5989

Benard, Robert, ed. *All Problems Are Simple and Other Stories,* 765(F)

Do You Like It Here? 766(F)

Benarde, Melvin A. *The Food Additives Dictionary,* 8414

Benchley, Nathaniel. *A Necessary End,* 1641(F)

Bender, David L., ed. *American Government,* 4184

Death-Dying Annual, 1989, 5080

War and Human Nature, 4128

American Values, 4411

Constructing a Life Philosophy, 5595

The Political Spectrum, 4263

Bendixen, Alfred, ed. *Haunted Women,* 1715(F)

Benedict, Elizabeth. *The Beginner's Book of Dreams,* 767(F)

Benedict, Helen. *Safe, Strong, and Streetwise,* 5501

Benedict, Ruth. *Patterns of Culture,* 6989

Benford, Gregory. *Against Infinity,* 2406(F)

Artifact, 2401(F)

Great Sky River, 2402(F), 2405(F)

Heart of the Comet, 2407(F)

If the Stars Are Gods, 2408(F)

In Alien Flesh, 2403(F)

In the Ocean of Night, 2404(F)

Tides of Light, 2405(F)

Timescape, 2406(F)

Benford, Timothy B. *The Space Program Quiz and Fact Book,* 8297

Benjamin, Carol Lea. *The Chosen Puppy,* 8713

Benjamin, Christopher. *Most Valuable Baseball Cards,* 9442

Benner, Janet. *Smoking Cigarettes,* 5104

Bennett, Arnold. *The Old Wives' Tale,* 333(F)

Bennett, George, ed. *Great Tales of Action and Adventure,* 15(F)

Bennett, Hal Zina. *The Lens of Perception,* 5596

Bennett, Hal Zina (jt. author). *Well Body, Well Earth,* 4456

Bennett, James Gordon. *My Father's Geisha,* 522(F)

Bennett, Jay. *I Never Said I Love You,* 2230(F)

Bennett, Lerone, Jr. *Before the Mayflower,* 4355

The Shaping of Black America, 4356
What Manner of Man, 6509
Benoit, Joan. *Running Tide,* 6764
Benson, Mary. *Nelson Mandela,* 6793
Benson, Michael D. *Coping with Birth Control,* 5450
Benstock, Bernard, ed. *Critical Essays on James Joyce,* 3648
Bentley, James. *A Calendar of Saints,* 4036
Bentley, Phyllis. *The Brontës and Their World,* 6218
Bentley, Toni. *Winter Season,* 6371
Bentley, Toni (jt. author). *Holding on to the Air,* 6389
Bentley-Baker, Dan. *The Paper Boat,* 1036(F)
Benton, Barbara. *The Babysitter's Handbook,* 5069
Ellis Island, 4328
Benton, John. *Lefty,* 631(F)
Benvenuto, Richard. *Amy Lowell,* 3876
Benét, Stephen Vincent. *The Devil and Daniel Webster,* 1035(F)
John Brown's Body, 3242
Berg, Maggie. *Jane Eyre,* 3649
Bergan, Ronald. *Movie Mastermind,* 5990
Bergen, Candice. *Knock Wood,* 6372
Berger, Bruce. *The Telling Distance,* 8810
Berger, John. *Ways of Seeing,* 5712
Berger, Larry, et al. *Up Your Score,* 4722
Berger, Melvin. *The World of Dance,* 5961
Berger, Phil. *Blood Season,* 6750
Berger, Thomas. *Arthur Rex,* 1408(F)
Little Big Man, 1556(F)
Bergland, Richard. *The Fabric of Mind,* 5307
Bergman, Carol. *Mae West,* 6457
Bergman, Charles. *Wild Echoes,* 8569
Bergreen, Gary. *Coping with Difficult Teachers,* 4622
Berkey, Rachel L. *New Career Opportunities in the Paralegal Profession,* 4956
Berkhofer, Robert F., Jr. *The White Man's Indian,* 7794
Berkoff, Steven. *I Am Hamlet,* 3815
Berkow, Ira. *Pitchers Do Get Lonely and Other Sports Stories,* 9550
Berlin, Normand. *Eugene O'Neill,* 3833
Berlitz, Charles. *The Bermuda Triangle,* 9476
The Lost Ship of Noah, 4094
Berman, Phillip L. *The Search for Meaning,* 4037
Berman, Phillip L., ed. *The Courage of Conviction,* 3996
Berman, William. *How to Dissect,* 8453
Bernards, Neal, ed. *American Foreign Policy,* 4129
The Environmental Crisis, 4422
Male-Female Roles, 4532
The Mass Media, 3956
Teenage Sexuality, 5451
Bernards, Neal, et al., eds. *The Soviet Union,* 7563

Berne, Eric. *What Do You Say after You Say Hello?* 5528
Bernstein, Carl. *All the President's Men,* 8047
Bernstein, Carl (jt. author). *The Final Days,* 8096
Bernstein, Jane. *Loving Rachel,* 5370
Bernstein, Jeremy. *Einstein,* 6660
Bernstein, Joanne E. *Taking Off,* 5597
Bernstein, Leonard. *The Joy of Music,* 5814
Berra, Yogi. *Yogi,* 6715
Berrill, Deborah (jt. author). *A Sierra Club Naturalist's Guide to the North Atlantic Coast,* 8378
Berrill, Michael. *A Sierra Club Naturalist's Guide to the North Atlantic Coast,* 8378
Berry, Faith. *Langston Hughes,* 6266
Berry, Henry. *Hey, Mac, Where Ya Been?* 8100
Berry, Jason, et al. *Up from the Cradle of Jazz,* 5842
Berry, R. J., ed. *The Encyclopedia of Animal Evolution,* 6975
Berry, Richard. *Discover the Stars,* 8247
Berry, Wendell. *Collected Poems, 1957–1982,* 3243
What Are People For? 3523
Berryman, Phillip. *Inside Central America,* 7651
Berth, Jack, et al. *Roadside America,* 7715
Berto, Frank J. *Bicycling Magazine's Complete Guide to Upgrading Your Bike,* 9740
Berton, Pierre. *The Arctic Grail,* 7690
The Klondike Fever, 7633
Beschloss, Michael R. *Eisenhower,* 6527
Besier, Rudolf. *The Barretts of Wimpole Street,* 3023
Bester, Alfred. *The Stars My Destination,* 2409(F)
Betancourt, Jeanne. *Between Us,* 16(F)
Sweet Sixteen and Never, 768(F)
Bethell, Nicholas. *Russia Besieged,* 7181
Betrock, Alan. *The I Was a Teenage Juvenile Delinquent Rock 'n' Roll Horror Beach Party Movie Book,* 5991
Bettelheim, Bruno. *Freud and Man's Soul,* 5529
The Uses of Enchantment, 3358
Bettmann, Otto L. *The Good Old Days—They Were Terrible,* 8006
Betts, Richard. *Nuclear Blackmail and Nuclear Balance,* 4130
Bhutto, Benazir. *Daughter of Destiny,* 6804
Bialer, Seweryn. *Global Rivals,* 4131
Bickel, Leonard. *The Deadly Element,* 8782
Bickers, Richard Townshend. *The Battle of Britain,* 7182
Bickham, Jack M. *Day Seven,* 2410(F)
Miracleworker, 1927(F)
Bicycling Magazine, ed. *All-Terrain Bikes,* 9741
Bicycle Repair, 9742
Bicycle Touring, 9743
Bicycling's Complete Guide to Bicycle Maintenance and Repair, 9744

Cycling for Women, 9745
Easy Bicycle Maintenance, 9742
Fitness through Cycling, 9746
Biegeleisen, J. I. *The ABC of Lettering,* 9157
Job Resumes, 4785
Make Your Job Interview a Success, 4786
Bielfeld, Horst. *Guinea Pigs,* 8758
Bienek, Horst. *Earth and Fire,* 1642(F)
Bierce, Ambrose. *The Stories and Fables of Ambrose Bierce,* 1716(F)
Bierhorst, John. *The Mythology of Mexico and Central America,* 3448
The Mythology of North America, 3419
The Mythology of South America, 3444
Bierhorst, John, ed. *The Red Swan,* 3359
The Sacred Path, 3420
Biggle, Lloyd. *The Quallsford Inheritance,* 1928(F)
Bigler, Philip. *Washington in Focus,* 8161
Billias, George Athan (jt. author). *Interpretations of American History,* 7741
Billiet, Walter E. *Do-It-Yourself Automotive Maintenance and Repair,* 9079
Billings, Malcolm. *The Cross & the Crescent,* 7123
Billings, Richard N. (jt. author). *Schirra's Space,* 6159
Billington, Ray A. *The Far Western Frontier, 1830–1860,* 7948
Billy, Christopher. *Summer Opportunities for Kids and Teenagers,* 9297
Bilstein, Roger E. *Flight in America, 1900–1983,* 9059
Binchy, Maeve. *Echoes,* 2231(F)
Light a Penny Candle, 1643(F)
Bingham, Charlotte. *To Hear a Nightingale,* 282(F)
Bingham, Hiram. *Lost City of the Incas,* 7668
Bingham, Joan (jt. author). *Haunted Houses, U.S.A,* 9526
Binyon, T. J. *Murder Will Out,* 3615
Bird, Isabella. *Unbeaten Tracks in Japan,* 7445
Bird, Larry. *Bird on Basketball,* 9713
Drive, 6741
Birmelin, Immanuel. *The New Parakeet Handbook,* 8668
Birnbach, Lisa. *Going to Work,* 4585
Birnbaum, Louis. *Red Dawn at Lexington,* 7847
Birosik, Patti Jean. *The New Age Music Guide,* 5843
Biscardi, Cyrus Henry. *The Storybook of Opera,* 5912
Bischoff, David F. *Day of the Dragon Star,* 2413(F)
The Destiny Dice, 2411(F)
Tin Woodman, 2412(F)
Bishop, Jack. *Ralph Ellison,* 6244
Bishop, Jim. *The Day Christ Died,* 4095
The Day Lincoln Was Shot, 6542

Bishop, John. *Making It in Video,* 4819
Bishop, Michael. *Close Encounters with the Deity,* 2414(F)
No Enemy But Time, 2416(F)
Bishop, Michael, ed. *Nebula Awards 24,* 2415(F)
Bishop, Rudine Sims. *Presenting Walter Dean Myers,* 3700
Bisnow, Mark. *In the Shadow of the Dome,* 4214
Bisson, Terry. *Fire on the Mountain,* 1037(F)
Talking Man, 1038(F)
Voyage to the Red Planet, 2417(F)
Bitton, Davis (jt. author). *The Mormon Experience,* 4028
Bjurstrom, C. G., ed. *French Folktales,* 3391
Black, Beryl. *Coping with Sexual Harassment,* 5502
Black, Charles L., Jr. *Impeachment,* 4205
Black Elk. *Black Elk Speaks,* 6615
Black, George. *The Good Neighbor,* 4132
Black, Jim Nelson. *Managing the Student Yearbook,* 3980
Black, Naomi. *America on Wheels,* 9080
Black, Naomi, ed. *Celebration,* 4038
Black, Penny. *The Book of Potpourri,* 9138
The Book of Pressed Flowers, 9139
Blackbeard, Bill, ed. *The Smithsonian Collection of Newspaper Comics,* 5791
Blacker, Irwin R. *The Elements of Screenwriting,* 5992
Blackham, H. J. *Six Existentialist Thinkers,* 3997
Blackmore, R. D. *Lorna Doone,* 334(F)
Blackmur, L. L. *Love Lies Slain,* 1929(F)
Blackstone, Harry, et al. *The Blackstone Book of Magic & Illusion,* 9393
Blain, W. Edward. *Passion Play,* 1930(F)
Blair, Alison. *Love by the Book,* 2232(F)
The Popcorn Project, 2232(F)
Social Studies, 2232(F)
Blair, Clay (jt. author). *A General's Life,* 6577
Blair, Walter. *America's Humor,* 3565
Tall Tale America, 3430
Blair, William. *Fire!* 5441
Blake, Gary. *Creative Careers,* 4820
Dream Jobs, 4821
Blake, Jeanne. *Risky Times,* 5173
Blake, Susan. *All-Nighter,* 2233(F)
Blake, William. *The Complete Poetry and Prose of William Blake,* 3151
The Portable Blake, 3152
Blamires, Harry. *Twentieth-Century English Literature,* 3566
Blanchet, Christian. *The Statue of Liberty,* 8162
Blandford, Percy W. *24 Table Saw Projects,* 9266
Blanksteen, Jane. *TV Careers Behind the Screen,* 4874
Blaylock, James P. *The Stone Giant,* 1039(F)
Bleier, Rocky. *Fighting Back,* 6751
Bleiler, E. F., ed. *Science Fiction Writers,* 3616

A Treasury of Victorian Detective Stories, 1931(F)

Bligh, William. *Mutiny on Board HMS Bounty*, 7466

Blinn, William. *Brian's Song*, 3062

Bloch, Deborah Perlmutter. *How to Get and Get Ahead on Your First Job*, 4822
How to Write a Winning Résumé, 4708

Bloch, Jeff (jt. author). *What a Way to Go*, 9498

Bloch, Robert. *Midnight Pleasures*, 1717(F)
Psycho House, 1718(F)

Block, Francesca Lia. *Weetzie Bat*, 769(F)

Block, Haskell M., ed. *Masters of Modern Drama*, 2978

Blocksma, Mary. *Reading the Numbers*, 8864

Blom, Eric. *Mozart*, 6351

Blom, Margaret Howard. *Charlotte Brontë*, 3650

Blood-Patterson, Peter, ed. *Rise Up Singing*, 5945

Bloodworth, Dennis. *The Chinese Looking Glass*, 7397

Bloom, Billy (jt. author). *The Frisbee Book*, 9575

Bloom, Harold, ed. *American Fiction, 1914 to 1945*, 3701
American Women Poets, 3877
British Modernist Fiction, 1920 to 1945, 3651
George Bernard Shaw's Pygmalion, 3652

Bloom, Lynn Z., et al. *The New Assertive Women*, 4533

Bloomfield, Harold H. *Making Peace with Your Parents*, 5638

Bluestein, Gene. *Anglish-Yinglish*, 3906

Blum, Arlene. *Annapurna*, 9551

Blum, Daniel. *A New Pictorial History of the Talkies*, 5993
A Pictorial History of the American Theater 1860–1985, 6079

Blum, Howard. *Wanted*, 17(F)

Blum, Laurie. *Free Money for College*, 4773

Blume, Judy. *Forever . . ,* 770(F)

Blumenson, John J. G. *Identifying American Architecture*, 5698

Blumenson, Martin. *Kasserine Pass*, 7183
Liberation, 7184
Patton, 6607

Blumenthal, Howard J. *The Electronic Home Advisor*, 9034

Blumenthal, Lassor A. *Successful Business Writing*, 4670

Blumenthal, Ralph. *Last Days of the Sicilians*, 4468

Bly, Robert. *Selected Poems*, 3244
The Winged Voice, 3524

Bly, Robert W. (jt. author). *Creative Careers*, 4820
Dream Jobs, 4821

Boardman, John, et al., eds. *The Oxford History of the Classical World*, 7083

Bobker, Lee R. *The Elements of Film*, 5994

Bodanis, David. *The Secret House*, 8213

Bode, Janet. *Different Worlds*, 5598
The Voices of Rape, 5503

Bode, William T. (jt. author). *Live TV*, 6070

Bodett, Tom. *The Big Garage on Clearshot*, 1876(F)
Small Comforts, 3485

Bodger, Lorraine. *Gift Wraps*, 9221

Boehm, David A., et al., eds. *Guinness Sports Record Book, 1990–91*, 9552

Boessenecker, John. *Badge and Buckshot*, 8177

Boettcher, Thomas D. *Vietnam*, 8101

Boggs, Michael (jt. author). *The Student Loan Handbook*, 4774

Boggs, Wade. *The Techniques of Modern Hitting*, 9626

Bograd, Larry. *Travelers*, 771(F)

Bohn, Thomas W. *Light and Shadows*, 5995

Bohr, Peter, ed. *Road & Track's Used Car Classics*, 9081

Boissard, Janine. *Cecile*, 523(F)
Christmas Lessons, 523(F)
A Matter of Feeling, 523(F)
A Time to Choose, 2234(F)

Bok, Sissela. *Lying*, 5572

Boleslavsky, Richard. *Acting*, 6080

Boll, Heinrich. *The Lost Honor of Katherina Blum*, 632(F)

Boller, Paul F. *Presidential Anecdotes*, 4206
Presidential Campaigns, 4275
Presidential Wives, 6463
They Never Said It, 3525

Bolles, Richard Nelson. *What Color Is Your Parachute?* 4787

Bolognese, Don. *Charcoal & Pastel*, 9182
Pen & Ink, 9182
Pencil, 9182

Bolt, Robert. *A Man for All Seasons*, 3024

Bolus, Jim (jt. author). *Kentucky Derby*, 9884

Bombeck, Erma. *At Wit's End*, 3486
Family, 3487(F)
The Grass Is Always Greener over the Septic Tank, 3486
I Lost Everything in the Post-Natal Depression, 3486
I Want to Grow Hair, I Want to Grow Up, I Want to Go to Boise, 5174
If Life Is a Bowl of Cherries, What Am I Doing in the Pits? 3486
Just Wait Till You Have Children of Your Own, 3486
Motherhood, 3487(F)

Bonafoux, Pascal. *Van Gogh*, 6194

Bonanno, Massimo. *The Rolling Stones Chronicle*, 5844

Bonar, Ann. *The Macmillan Treasury of Herbs*, 8415

Bonavia, David. *The Chinese*, 7398

Bond, Bob. *Small Boat Sailing*, 9923

Bond, David. *Guinness Guide to 20th Century Fashion*, 9167

Bond, Larry. *Red Phoenix*, 18(F)

Bond, Michael. *Monsieur Pamplemousse Aloft*, 19(F)

Bond, Nancy. *Another Shore*, 1040(F)

Bone, Jan. *Opportunities in Cable Television*, 5037

Opportunities in Computer Aided Design and Computer Aided Manufacturing, 5036

Opportunities in Film, 5037

Opportunities in Laser Technology Careers, 5011

Opportunities in Robotics Careers, 5012

Opportunities in Telecommunications, 5037

Bonkowske, Jack A. (jt. author). *Saga of the American Flag*, 7731

Bonner, Nigel. *Whales of the World*, 8640

Bonosky, Phillip. *A Bird in Her Hair and Other Stories*, 524(F)

Bontemps, Arna. *100 Years of Negro Freedom*, 4357

Bontemps, Arna, ed. *Great Slave Narratives*, 6464

Booher, Dianna Daniels. *Love*, 5599

Rape, 5504

Bookbinder, Robert. *Classics of the Gangster Film*, 5996

Boorstin, Daniel J. *The Americans*, 7717

Boorstin, Daniel J., ed. *An American Primer*, 7716

Booth, Mark, ed. *Christian Short Stories*, 2894(F)

Booth, Philip E. *Relations*, 3245

Bor, Josef. *The Terezin Requiem*, 1644(F)

Borden, Fred. *Bowling*, 9779

Borges, Jorge Luis. *The Aleph and Other Stories*, 2895(F)

Borhek, Mary V. *Coming Out to Parents*, 5453

Boriani, Maria Luisa (jt. author). *Simon & Schuster's Guide to House Plants*, 9374

Borland, Hal. *When the Legends Die*, 446(F)

Borman, Frank. *Countdown*, 6126

Bornet, Vaughn. *The Presidency of Lyndon B. Johnson*, 8048

Borns, Betsy. *Comic Lives*, 6081

Bornstein, Jerry. *The Wall Came Tumbling Down*, 7502

Bornstein, Jerry (jt. author). *New Frontiers in Genetics*, 5259

Bornstein, Sandy. *New Frontiers in Genetics*, 5259

Borowsky, Irvin J. *Opportunities in Printing Careers*, 5038

Borror, Donald J. *A Field Guide to the Insects of America North of Mexico*, 8592

Borthwick, J. S. *The Student Body*, 1932(F)

Boschung, Herbert T., Jr., et al. *The Audubon Society Field Guide to North American Fishes, Whales, and Dolphins*, 8616

Boss, David (jt. author). *Great Ones*, 9861

Bosse, Malcolm. *Captives of Time*, 1378(F)

Boston Children's Hospital. *What Teenagers Want to Know about Sex*, 5454

Boston, Louise (jt. author). *Webster's New World Dictionary of Computer Terms*, 8964

Boston Women's Health Book Collective. *The New Our Bodies, Ourselves*, 5342

Boswell, James. *The Life of Samuel Johnson*, 6273

Boswell, Thomas. *The Heart of the Order*, 9627

How Life Imitates the World Series, 9628

Strokes of Genius, 9867

Bosworth, Allan R. *America's Concentration Camps*, 7185

Botermans, Jack. *Paper Capers*, 9466

Paper Flight, 9403

Botkin, B. A., ed. *A Treasury of American Folklore*, 3431

A Treasury of New England Folklore, 3432

Botting, Douglas. *The Giant Airships*, 9060

The Second Front, 7186

Botting, Douglas (jt. author). *America's Secret Army*, 4288

Bottner, Barbara. *Let Me Tell You Everything*, 772(F)

Bottoms, David (jt. author). *The Morrow Anthology of Younger American Poets*, 3328

Boucher, François. *20,000 Years of Fashion*, 5273

Boucher, Therese (jt. author). *Terminating Life*, 5092

Boulle, Pierre. *The Bridge over the River Kwai*, 1645(F)

Planet of the Apes, 2418(F)

Bouquet, A. C. *Everyday Life in New Testament Times*, 4096

Bourdillon, Hilary. *Women As Healers*, 5231

Bourne, Peter G. *Fidel*, 6882

Bouton, Jim. *Ball Four*, 9629

Bova, Ben. *The Astral Mirror*, 2419(F)

Colony, 2421(F)

Escape Plus, 2420(F)

Gremlins Go Home, 2426(F)

Orion, 2421(F)

Out of the Sun, 2422(F)

Peacekeepers, 2423(F)

Vengeance of Orion, 2424(F)

Voyagers III, 2425(F)

Welcome to Moonbase, 8336

Bowden, Ken (jt. author). *Play Better Golf*, 9875

Bowden, Mary Weatherspoon. *Washington Irving*, 3702

Bowe-Gutman, Sonia. *Teen Pregnancy*, 5455

Bowen, Catherine Drinker. *Miracle at Philadelphia*, 4185

The Most Dangerous Man in America, 6586

Bowen, Elizabeth. *The Death of the Heart*, 773(F)

Bowermaster, Jon (jt. author). *Saving the Earth*, 4445

Bowers, John. *Stonewall Jackson*, 6595

Bowers, Peter (jt. author). *The American Fighter*, 9123

Bowler, Peter. *The Superior Person's Book of Words*, 3907

Bowles, Polly (jt. author). *Becoming a Beauty Queen*, 5272

Bowman, Alan K. *Egypt after the Pharoahs*, 7094

Bowman, John S., ed. *The Civil War Almanac*, 7892

The Vietnam War, 8102

Bowman-Kruhm, Mary (jt. author). *I Hate School*, 4637

Boy Scouts of America. *Fieldbook*, 9790

Boyd, Malcolm. *Bach*, 6335

Boyer, Elizabeth H. *The Troll's Grindstone*, 1041(F)

Boyer, Ernest L. *High School*, 4623

Boyer, Paul, et al. *Women in American Religion*, 4039

Boyington, Gregory. *Baa Baa Black Sheep*, 7187

Boyle, Josephine. *Maiden's End*, 1719(F)

Boyne, Walter J. *The Leading Edge*, 9061

The Smithsonian Book of Flight, 9062

Brace, Ernest C. *A Code to Keep*, 6127

Brackman, Arnold C. *The Other Nuremberg*, 7188

Bradbeer, Robin, et al. *The Beginner's Guide to Computers*, 8960

Bradbury, Ray. *Dandelion Wine*, 525(F)

Farenheit 451, 2427(F)

The Golden Apples of the Sun, 1045(F)

A Graveyard for Lunatics, 1042(F)

The Halloween Tree, 1043(F)

I Sing the Body Electric, 1045(F)

The Illustrated Man, 1044(F)

The Martian Chronicles, 2428(F)

Medicine for Melancholy, 1045(F)

The October Country, 2429(F)

R Is for Rocket, 1046(F)

Something Wicked This Way Comes, 1047(F)

The Stories of Ray Bradbury, 2430(F)

The Toynbee Convector, 1048(F)

Zen in the Art of Writing, 3703

Bradbury, Will, ed. *Into the Unknown*, 9477

Braden, Tom. *Eight Is Enough*, 3488

Bradford, Barbara Taylor. *A Woman of Substance*, 774(F)

Bradford, Richard. *Red Sky at Morning*, 775(F)

Bradford, Sarah. *Harriet Tubman, the Moses of Her People*, 6519

Bradford, William. *Of Plymouth Plantation, 1620–1647*, 7835

Bradley, David J. *Assembly Language Programming for the IBM Personal Computer*, 8961

Bradley, Jack. *How to Read, Write, and Understand Music*, 5815

Bradley, Marion Zimmer. *City of Sorcery*, 1049(F), 1050(F)

The Colors of Space, 1050(F)

The Firebrand, 1051(F)

The Forbidden Tower, 1050(F)

Four Moons of Darkover, 2431(F)

Hawkmistress! 1052(F)

The Heirs of Hammerfell, 1053(F)

The Heritage of Hastur, 1050(F)

The House between the Worlds, 1054(F)

Mists of Avalon, 1051(F)

Sharra's Exile, 1050(F)

Spell Sword, 1054(F)

Sword of Chaos, 1057(F)

Thendara House, 1054(F)

Two to Conquer, 1054(F)

Web of Stars, 1050(F)

Winds of Darkover, 1054(F)

Bradley, Marion Zimmer, ed. *Sword and Sorceress*, 1055(F)

Sword and Sorceress VII, 1056(F)

Bradley, Marion Zimmer, et al. *Black Trillium*, 1058(F)

Domains of Darkover, 2432(F)

The Other Side of the Mirror, 2433(F)

Red Sun of Darkover, 2434(F)

Bradley, Omar. *A General's Life*, 6577

Bradley, Virginia. *Who Could Forget the Mayor of Lodi?* 776(F)

Bradshaw, Gillian. *Imperial Purple*, 1363(F)

Th Beacon at Alexandria, 1364(F)

Bradshaw, Terry. *Looking Deep*, 6752

Brady, Frank, ed. *Twentieth Century Interpretations of Gulliver's Travels*, 3653

Brady, James. *The Coldest War*, 8103

Brady, John. *The Craft of the Screenwriter*, 5997

Braemer, Helga. *Tropical Fish*, 8750

Braithwaite, E. R. *To Sir, with Love*, 6894

Bramlett, Jim. *Ride for the High Points*, 6271

Brancato, Robin F. *Facing Up*, 777(F)

Branch, Taylor. *Parting the Waters*, 6510

Brand, Max. *The Making of a Gunman*, 20(F)

Thunder Moon, 21(F)

Thunder Moon Strikes, 21(F)

Thunder Moon's Challenge, 21(F)

Way of the Lawless, 22(F)

Brandelius, Jerilyn Lee. *Grateful Dead Family Album*, 5845

Brandenburg, Jim. *White Wolf*, 8512

Brandon, William. *The American Heritage Book of Indians*, 7795

Brandreth, Gyles. *The Joy of Lex*, 3908

Brandstein, Eve. *The Actor*, 4875

Brandt, Bill. *Literary Britain*, 3654

Brandt, Nat. *The Town That Started the Civil War*, 7893

Brandt, Nat (jt. author). *How Free Are We?* 4203

Branfield, John. *The Poison Factory,* 1933(F)

Brann, Donald R. *How to Build Outdoor Projects,* 9267

Branner, Robert. *Gothic Architecture,* 5735

Branson, Ann, ed. *The Good Housekeeping Illustrated Cookbook,* 9319

Braun, Lilian Jackson. *The Cat Who Knew Shakespeare,* 1935(F)
The Cat Who Lived High, 1934(F)
The Cat Who Sniffed Glue, 1935(F)
The Cat Who Talked to Ghosts, 1936(F)
The Cat Who Went Underground, 1937(F)

Braymer, Marjorie. *Atlantis,* 3471

Brecher, Edward M. *Licit and Illicit Drugs,* 5105

Brecher, Kenneth. *Too Sad to Sing,* 6895

Brecher, Kenneth, ed. *Astronomy of the Ancients,* 8248

Brechner, Irv (jt. author). *Career Finder,* 4867

Brecht, Bertolt. *Mother Courage and Her Children,* 2992
Two Plays, 2993

Brecka, Jon, ed. *Baseball Cards,* 9443

Bree, Marlin. *In the Teeth of the Northeaster,* 6128

Breen, Christine (jt. author). *O Come Ye Back to Ireland,* 7540
When Summer's in the Meadow, 7540

Bremness, Lesley. *The Complete Book of Herbs,* 9373

Brems, Marianne. *The Fit Swimmer,* 9958

Brennan, Bernadette (jt. author). *Maiden Voyage,* 9918

Brennan, Richard P. *Levitating Trains and Kamikaze Genes,* 8941

Brenner, Barbara. *The Gorilla Signs Love,* 23(F)

Brent, Madeleine. *Stormswift,* 2235(F)

Breslin, James E. B. *From Modern to Contemporary,* 3878

Breslin, Jimmy. *Can't Anybody Here Play This Game?* 9630

Brett, Simon. *Mrs. Presumed Dead,* 1938(F)

Brettell, Richard R. *French Impressionists,* 5770
Post-Impressionists, 5771

Breuer, William B. *Retaking the Philippines,* 7189

Brewer, Bryan. *The Compact Disc Book,* 9047

Brewin, Robert (jt. author). *The Tranquilizing of America,* 5128

Brezezinski, Zbigniew. *The Grand Failure,* 4170

Brickhill, Paul. *The Great Escape,* 7190

Bridenbaugh, Carl. *Jamestown, 1544–1699,* 7836
The Spirit of '76, 7837

Bride's Magazine, eds. *Bride's Book of Etiquette,* 5579

Bridgers, Sue Ellen. *Sara Will,* 633(F)

Bridges, Laurie. *The Ashton Horror,* 1720(F)
Devil Wind, 1720(F)
Swamp Witch, 1720(F)

Briggs, Katharine. *An Encyclopedia of Fairies,* 3360

Brill, Steven. *The Teamsters,* 4612

Brill, Steven, et al. *Trial by Jury,* 4233

Brimer, John B. *Homeowner's Complete Outdoor Building Book,* 9389

Brin, David. *Earth,* 2435(F)
The Postman, 2436(F)
The Practice Effect, 2437(F)
The River of Time, 2438(F)
Startide Rising, 2439(F)
The Uplift War, 2439(F)

Brin, David (jt. author). *Heart of the Comet,* 2407(F)

Brinkley, David. *Washington Goes to War,* 8049

Brinkley, William. *The Last Ship,* 24(F)

Brinley, Maryann Bucknum (jt. author). *Jackie Cochran,* 6131

Brinton, Crane. *Anatomy of Revolution,* 4171
Ideas and Men, 7030

Brinton, Crane (jt. author). *A History of Civilization,* 7081

Briskin, Jacqueline. *Paloverde,* 1557(F)

Brisson, David (jt. author). *The Techniques of Modern Hitting,* 9626

Bristow, M. J. (jt. author). *National Anthems of the World,* 5951

Brizzi, Mary T. *Anne McCaffrey,* 3704

Bro, Lu. *Drawing,* 9183

Brock, Ted. *The Super Official NFL Trivia Book,* 9839
25 Years, 9840

Brockett, Oscar G. *History of the Theatre,* 6082

Brockman, C. Frank. *Trees of North America,* 8423

Brode, Douglas. *Woody Allen,* 6357

Broder, David S. *Behind the Front Page,* 3981
Changing of the Guard, 8050

Brodie, Edmund, Jr. (jt. author). *Reptiles of North America,* 8466

Brodie, Fawn M. *Richard Nixon,* 6551
Thomas Jefferson, 6533

Brody, Jane. *Jane Brody's Nutrition Book,* 5409
Jane Brody's The New York Times Guide to Personal Health, 5343

Brogan, Denis William. *The Era of Franklin D. Roosevelt,* 8027

Bromfield, Louis. *The Farm,* 1558(F)

Brondino, Jeanne, et al. *Raising Each Other,* 5639

Bronowski, Jacob. *The Ascent of Man,* 6990
The Western Intellectual Tradition, from Leonardo to Hegel, 3998

Bronson, Fred. *The Billboard Book of Number One Hits,* 5846

Brontë, Charlotte. *Jane Eyre,* 335(F)

Brontë, Emily. *Wuthering Heights,* 336(F)

Brook, Elaine. *Land of the Snow Lion,* 7456

Brooks, Bruce. *No Kidding*, 634(F)
  On the Wing, 8531
Brooks, Cleanth. *William Faulkner*, 3705
Brooks, Cleanth, et al., eds. *American Literature*, 2896
Brooks, Gwendolyn. *Selected Poems*, 3246
  The World of Gwendolyn Brooks, 3879
Brooks, Jerome. *Make Me a Hero*, 1646(F)
  Naked in Winter, 778(F)
Brooks, Stewart. *The VD Story*, 5175
Brooks, Terry. *The Black Unicorn*, 2440(F)
  The Druid of Shannara, 1059(F)
  The Elfstones of Shannara, 1061(F)
  Magic Kingdom for Sale—Sold! 2440(F)
  The Scions of Shannara, 1060(F)
  The Sword of Shannara, 1061(F)
  The Wishsong of Shannara, 1061(F)
  Wizard at Large, 2440(F)
Brooks, Tilford. *America's Black Musical Heritage*, 5831
Broome, Susannah. *The Pearl Pagoda*, 1388(F)
Brosman, Catharine Savage. *Jean-Paul Sartre*, 3567
Brosnan, Jim. *The Long Season*, 9631
Brosse, Jacques. *Great Voyages of Discovery*, 7142
Broughton, Jack. *Going Downtown*, 8104
Brouwer, Alexandra. *Working in Hollywood*, 5998
Brown, Alex. *In Print*, 3982
Brown, Archie, et al., eds. *The Cambridge Encyclopedia of Russia and the Soviet Union*, 7564
Brown, Ashley, ed. *The Green Berets*, 9124
Brown, Bruce. *Lone Tree*, 8581
  The Miracle Planet, 8793
Brown, Clarence, ed. *The Portable Twentieth-Century Russian Reader*, 2897
Brown, Claude. *Manchild in the Promised Land*, 6223
Brown, Cynthia Stokes. *Like It Was*, 4671
Brown, Dale. *Day of the Cheetah*, 25(F)
Brown, David G. *Gold Buckle Dreams*, 6779
Brown, Dee. *Bury My Heart at Wounded Knee*, 7796
  Conspiracy of Knaves, 1535(F)
  Creek Mary's Blood, 1496(F)
  Hear That Lonesome Whistle Blow, 7949
  Killdeer Mountain, 1559(F)
Brown, Edward J., ed. *Major Soviet Writers*, 3568
Brown, Fern G. *Teen Guide to Caring for Your Unborn Baby*, 5456
  Teen Guide to Childbirth, 5457
Brown, Frank E. *Roman Architecture*, 5772
Brown, Harry. *A Walk in the Sun*, 1647(F)
Brown, J. Larry. *Living Hungry in America*, 4502
Brown, James. *James Brown*, 6376
Brown, John Russell. *Shakespeare and His Theatre*, 3816

Brown, Joseph E., et al. *The Sierra Club Guides to the National Parks of the Pacific Southwest and Hawaii*, 8178
Brown, Kenneth A. *Inventors at Work*, 8942
Brown, Lauren. *Grasslands*, 8811
Brown, Margaret F. *Careers in Occupational Therapy*, 4986
Brown, Mary. *The Unlikely Ones*, 1062(F)
Brown, Michael. *Soccer Rules in Pictures*, 9948
Brown, Peter. *The Love You Make*, 6168
Brown, Peter Lancaster. *Star and Planet Spotting*, 8249
Brown, Philip. *Uncle Whiskers*, 8689
Brown, R. Allen. *The Architecture of Castles*, 7124
Brown, Rachel. *The Weaving, Spinning, and Dyeing Book*, 9140
Brown, Rita Mae. *Starting from Scratch*, 3957
Brown, Sam. *The Trail to Honk Ballard's Bones*, 26(F)
Brown, Sarah, ed. *Microwave Cooking*, 9320
Brown, Sheldon. *Opportunities in Biotechnology Careers*, 5013
Brown, Tom, Jr. *The Search*, 8379
  The Tracker, 8379
Brown, Vinson. *The Amateur Naturalist's Handbook*, 8380
Browne, Steven E. *Videotape Editing*, 9048
Browning, Colleen. *Working Out a Painting*, 9184
Browning, Elizabeth Barrett. *The Poetical Works of Elizabeth Barrett Browning*, 3192
  Sonnets from the Portuguese, 3193
Browning, Robert. *Robert Browning's Poetry*, 3194
Brownmiller, Susan. *Against Our Will*, 5505
  Femininity, 4534
Brownstein, Rachel M. *Becoming a Heroine*, 3617
Brownstein, Samuel C. *Barron's Compact Guide to Colleges*, 4723
  Barron's Profiles of American Colleges, 4723
Brownstein, Samuel C., et al. *Barron's Basic Tips of the SAT Scholastic Aptitude Test*, 4655
  How to Prepare for the Scholastic Aptitude Test SAT, 4655
Brownstone, David M. (jt. author). *Artists and Artisans*, 5684
  Builders, 4941
  Clothiers, 5280
  The College Money Book, 4779
  Communicators, 3919
  Financiers and Traders, 4915
  Harvesters, 8582
  Healers, 5236
  Helpers and Aides, 4965
  Leaders and Lawyers, 4966
  Manufacturers and Miners, 8944

Performers and Players, 5955
Restaurateurs & Innkeepers, 4795
Scholars and Priests, 4626
Scientists and Technologists, 8219
The Silk Road, 7042
Warriors & Adventurers, 6971
Brownstone, Douglass L. (jt. author). *The Outdoor Careers Guide*, 4839
Bruce, Preston. *From the Door of the White House*, 6896
Bruchac, Joseph, ed. *Songs from This Earth on Turtle's Back*, 3247
Bruchey, Stuart. *The Wealth of the Nation*, 7718
Bruemmer, Fred. *Arctic Animals*, 7691
The Arctic World, 7692
Seasons of the Seal, 8641
Brumberg, Joan. *Fasting Girls*, 5176
Brunn, Robert. *The Initiation*, 1721(F)
Brunner, John. *The Best of John Brunner*, 2441(F)
Shockwave Rider, 2442(F)
Stand on Zanzibar, 2442(F)
Bruno, Leonard. *The Landmarks of Science*, 8214
Bruns, Bill (jt. author). *Strategic Racquetball*, 9971
Brunvand, Jan Harold. *The Vanishing Hitchhiker*, 3433
Brush, Stephanie. *Life*, 3489
Brush, Warren D. (jt. author). *Knowing Your Trees*, 8424
Brust, Steven. *Brokedown Palace*, 1063(F)
Cowboy Feng's Space Bar and Grille, 2443(F)
Bryan, C. D. B. *The National Air and Space Museum*, 9063
Bryan, Mike. *Baseball Lives*, 9632
Bryant, Will. *A Time for Heroes*, 27(F)
Bryden, M. M. (jt. author). *Whales, Dolphins and Porpoises*, 8652
Brykcznski, Terry, ed. *The Armchair Angler*, 9824
Bryson, Bill. *The Mother Tongue*, 3909
Bryson, Jamie S. *The War Canoe*, 447(F)
Buber-Neumann, Margarete. *Milena*, 6851
Buchan, John. *The 39 Steps*, 28(F)
Buchan, Stuart. *Guys Like Us*, 779(F)
Buchanan, Edna. *The Corpse Had a Familiar Face*, 4469
Buchanan, William. *A Shining Season*, 6762
Buchsbaum, Ralph. *Animals without Backbones*, 8614
Buchwald, Art. *I Think I Don't Remember*, 3490
While Reagan Slept, 3491
Whose Rose Garden Is It Anyway? 3492
You Can Fool All of the People All the Time, 3493
Buchwald, Emilie, ed. *This Sporting Life*, 3248
Buck, Pearl S. *The Good Earth*, 1389(F)
Buck, Stratton. *Gustave Flaubert*, 3635

Buckalew, M. W. *Coping with Choosing a College*, 4724
Buckles, Mary Parker. *The Flowers Around Us*, 8433
Buckley, Shawn. *Sun Up to Sun Down*, 8930
Buckley, William F. *See You Later Alligator*, 29(F)
The Story of Henri Tod, 30(F)
Buckman, Robert. *I Don't Know What to Say*, 5081
Budwig, Robert (jt. author). *The Book of Beads*, 9142
Buechner, Frederick. *The Wizard's Tide*, 526(F)
Bujold, Lois McMaster. *Brothers in Arms*, 2444(F)
Falling Free, 2445(F)
The Vor Game, 2446(F)
The Warrior's Apprentice, 2444(F)
Bulfinch, Thomas. *Bulfinch's Mythology*, 3449
Bull, Emma (jt. author). *Liavek*, 1268(F)
Bull, John, et al. *Birds of North America, Eastern Region*, 8532
Birds of North America, Western Region, 8532
Bullough, G. (jt. author). *The Oxford Book of Seventeenth Century Verse*, 3204
Bunker, Robert (jt. author). *Crow Killer*, 1594(F)
Bunn, Scott. *Just Hold On*, 780(F)
Bunsey, Michael D. (jt. author). *Prescription Narcotics*, 5151
Bunting, Eve. *Face at the Edge of the World*, 635(F)
Will You Be My Posslq? 527(F)
Bunyan, John. *The Pilgrim's Progress*, 337(F)
Burack, Sylvia K., ed. *The Writer's Handbook 1990*, 3975
Buranelli, Vincent. *Edgar Allan Poe*, 3706
Burch, Ernest S. *The Eskimos*, 7693
Burch, Jennings Michael. *They Cage the Animals at Night*, 6897
Burchard, Peter. *First Affair*, 2236(F)
Sea Change, 528(F)
Burchard, Sue. *The Statue of Liberty*, 8163
Burckhardt, Jacob. *The Civilization of the Renaissance in Italy*, 7125
Burdick, Eugene (jt. author). *The Ugly American*, 977(F)
Burgard, Debby (jt. author). *Great Shape*, 5357
Burgess, Alan. *The Longest Tunnel*, 7191
Burgess, Anthony. *A Clockwork Orange*, 2447(F)
Cyrano de Bergerac, 2994
The Devil's Mode, 2898(F)
Ernest Hemingway and His World, 6259
Burgess, Eric. *Uranus & Neptune*, 8341
Burk, Robert F. *Dwight D. Eisenhower*, 6529
Burke, James Wakefield. *David Crockett*, 6135
Burkig, Valerie. *Photonics*, 8932
Burland, Cottie. *North American Indian Mythology*, 3421

Burnam, Tom. *Dictionary of Misinformation,* 9478

More Misinformation, 9478

Burne, Jerome, ed. *Chronicle of the World,* 7031

Burner, David. *John F. Kennedy and a New Generation,* 6536

Burnett, Carol. *One More Time,* 6378

Burnett, Hallie. *Fiction Writer's Handbook,* 3958

On Writing the Short Story, 3958

Burnett, Whit (jt. author). *Fiction Writer's Handbook,* 3958

On Writing the Short Story, 3958

Burnford, Sheila. *Bel Ria,* 283(F)

Burnham, Colin. *Customizing Cars,* 9082

Burnham, David. *The Rise of the Computer State,* 8962

Burns, James MacGregor. *The Vineyard of Liberty,* 7719

The Workshop of Democracy, 7719

Burns, Olive Ann. *Cold Sassy Tree,* 1599(F)

Burns, Robert. *The Poetical Works of Burns,* 3195

Burns, Stewart. *Social Movements of the 1960s,* 8051

Burr, Jeanne, ed. *America's Troubled Children,* 5371

Burris-Meyer, Harold. *Scenery for the Theatre,* 6083

Burroughs, Edgar Rice. *At the Earth's Core,* 2448(F)

Back to the Stone Age, 2449(F)

The Cave Girl, 31(F)

The Chessmen of Mars, 2453(F)

Escape on Venus, 2450(F)

Gods of Mars, 2453(F)

Land of Terror, 2449(F)

Lost on Venus, 2450(F)

The Moon Men, 2451(F)

Pellucidar, 2449(F), 2452(F)

A Princess of Mars, 2453(F)

Savage Pellucidar, 2449(F), 2452(F)

Tarzan at the Earth's Core, 2449(F)

Tarzan of the Apes, 32

Warlord of Mars, 2453(F)

Burroughs, John. *Deep Woods,* 8381

Burrow, J. A. *Medieval Writers and Their Work,* 3569

Bursell, Susan (jt. author). *Biomedical Ethics,* 5230

Burt, Forrest D. *W. Somerset Maugham,* 3655

Burt, Olive W. *The Horse in America,* 8759

Burt, William Henry. *A Field Guide to the Mammals,* 8490

Burton, Jane. *A Dog's Life,* 8714

Your Cat's First Year, 8690

Burton, John A., ed. *Owls of the World,* 8564

Burton, Robert. *Bird Behavior,* 8555

Eggs, 8533

Burwash, Peter. *Total Tennis,* 9965

Buscaglia, Leo. *Love,* 5556

Personhood, 5556

Buscema, John (jt. author). *How to Draw Comics the Marvel Way,* 9200

Busch, Frederick. *Sometimes I Live in the Country,* 781(F)

Bush, George. *Looking Forward,* 6523

Bushnaq, Inea, ed. *Arab Folktales,* 3382

Busnar, Gene. *It's Rock 'n' Roll,* 5847

Busoni, Rafaello. *The Man Who Was Don Quixote,* 6231

Busselle, Michael. *The Complete 35mm Sourcebook,* 9410

Butcher, Lee. *Accidental Millionaire,* 6678

Butler, Bonnie. *Olympic Hopeful,* 2872(F)

Butler, Jimmie H. *The Iskra Incident,* 33(F)

Butler, Octavia E. *Adulthood Rites,* 2454(F)

Dawn, 2454(F)

Butler, Robert Olen. *On Distant Ground,* 1692(F)

Butler, Samuel. *The Way of All Flesh,* 338(F)

Butson, Thomas G. *Gorbachev,* 6843

Butterfield, Fox. *China,* 7399

Butterworth, Emma M. *As the Waltz Was Ending,* 7192

The Complete Book of Calligraphy, 9158

Butterworth, Rod R. *The Perigee Visual Dictionary of Signing,* 5431

The Pocket Dictionary of Signing, 5431

Byrde, Penelope. *A Visual History of Costume,* 5274

Byron, George Gordon. *The Poetical Works of Byron,* 3196

Cackett, Alan (jt. author). *The Harmony Illustrated Encyclopedia of Country Music,* 5858

Cadwalader, George. *Castaways,* 4624

Cady, Edwin H. *Stephen Crane,* 3707

Caes, Charles J. *Studies in Starlight,* 8298

Cagin, Seth. *We Are Not Afraid,* 4358

Cahill, Kevin M., ed. *The AIDS Epidemic,* 5177

Cahill, Susan, ed. *Among Sisters,* 529(F)

New Women and New Fiction, 2899(F)

Women and Fiction, 2900(F)

Cahill, Tim. *Jaguars Ripped My Flesh,* 6129

A Wolverine Is Eating My Leg, 6129

Cahn, Julie. *The Dating Book,* 5600

Caidin, Martin. *The Messiah Stone,* 2455(F)

Cain, James M. *Double Indemnity,* 1939(F)

The Postman Always Rings Twice, 1940(F)

Caine, Clifford J. *How to Get into College,* 4725

Calder, Jenni. *Robert Louis Stevenson,* 6317

Calder, Nigel. *Einstein's Universe,* 8903

Timescale, 8250

Calder, Nigel, ed. *On the Frontiers of Science,* 8215

Calderone, Mary S. *The Family Book about Sexuality,* 5458

Caldwell, Carol. *Opportunities in Nutrition Careers,* 4987

Caldwell, Erskine. *With All My Might,* 6227

Caldwell, Taylor. *Answer as a Man,* 1600(F)

Calhoun, Richard J. *James Dickey,* 3880

Callahan, Daniel. *Setting Limits,* 4467

Callahan, Mary. *Fighting for Tony,* 5372

Callahan, Steven. *Adrift,* 8887

Callan, Jamie. *Just Too Cool,* 2237(F)

Callenbach, Ernest. *Ecotopia,* 2456(F)
Ecotopia Emerging, 2456(F)

Callin, Grant. *A Lion on Tharthee,* 2457(F)
Saturnalia, 2457(F)

Calvert, Patricia. *The Hour of the Wolf,* 34(F)

Calvino, Italo, reteller. *Italian Folktales,* 3392

Camazine, Scott. *The Naturalist's Year,* 8382

Cameron, Peter. *One Way or Another,* 782(F)

Camp, John. *The Fool's Run,* 35(F)

Campbell, Andrew (jt. author). *The Encyclopedia of Aquatic Life,* 8615

Campbell, Jeremy. *The Improbable Machine,* 5308

Campbell, Jim (jt. author). *The Super Official NFL Trivia Book,* 9839

Campbell, Joseph. *Myths to Live By,* 3450

Campbell, Maria. *Halfbreed,* 6898

Campbell, Nelson, ed. *Grass Roots & Schoolyards,* 9714

Campbell, Patricia J. *Fade,* 3708
Presenting Robert Cormier, 3708

Campbell, Ramsey. *The Nameless,* 1941(F)

Campbell, Robert. *The Cat's Meow,* 1942(F)
The Gift Horse's Mouth, 1943(F)
Nibbled to Death by Ducks, 1944(F)

Campbell, Sally R. *The Confident Consumer,* 4606

Campbell, Stu, et al. *The Way to Ski!* 9943

Camus, Albert. *The Fall,* 636(F)
The Myth of Sisyphus, and Other Essays, 3526
The Plague, 637(F)
The Stranger, 638(F)

Canaday, John. *The Lives of the Painters,* 6169

Canavor, Natalie. *Sell Your Photographs,* 9411

Canfield, Cass. *Samuel Adams's Revolution, 1765–1776,* 7848

Canseco, Jose. *Strength Training for Baseball,* 9633

Caplan, Ruth, et al. *Our Earth, Ourselves,* 4423

Capote, Truman. *Breakfast at Tiffany's,* 783(F)
A Christmas Memory, 784(F)
In Cold Blood, 4470
One Christmas, 6228
Other Voices, Other Rooms, 530(F)
The Thanksgiving Visitor, 784(F)

Capotosto, Rosario. *Woodworking Projects for the Home Workshop,* 9268

Capps, Benjamin. *The Great Chiefs,* 7797
The Indians, 7798

Capra, Fritjof. *Green Politics,* 7503

Capstick, Peter Hathaway. *Last Horizons,* 9825
The Last Ivory Hunter, 6150

Caputo, Philip. *A Rumor of War,* 8052

Caraceau, Jean-Luc. *The Dictionary of Superstitions,* 9479

Caras, Roger. *A Celebration of Cats,* 8691
Roger Caras' Treasury of Great Cat Stories, 284(F)
Roger Caras' Treasury of Great Dog Stories, 285(F)

Caras, Roger, ed. *Harper's Illustrated Handbook of Cats,* 8692
Harper's Illustrated Handbook of Dogs, 8715

Card, Orson Scott. *Ender's Game,* 2461(F)
Hart's Hope, 1064(F)
Maps in a Mirror, 2458(F)
Prentice Alvin, 2459(F)
Red Prophet, 1497(F)
Seventh Son, 1065(F)
Songmaster, 2460(F)
Speaker for the Dead, 2461(F)
Treason, 2462(F)
Wyrms, 2463(F)

Cardini, Franco. *Europe 1492,* 7126

Cardozo, Arlene. *Jewish Family Celebrations,* 4114

Carew, Rod, et al. *Rod Carew's Art and Science of Hitting,* 9634

Carey, Ernestine Gilbreth (jt. author). *Belles on Their Toes,* 6623
Cheaper by the Dozen, 6623

Carey, John. *John Donne,* 3865

Carey, John, ed. *Eyewitness to History,* 7032

Carkeet, David. *I Been There Before,* 1877(F)

Carley, Larry W. *Do-It-Yourself Car Care,* 9083

Carlin, Richard. *English and American Folk Music,* 5946
European Classical Music 1600–1825, 5832
Rock and Roll, 5848

Carlo, Nicola Alberto De (jt. author). *Intelligence Games,* 8850

Carlson, Dale. *Manners That Matter,* 5580

Carlson, Linda (jt. author). *Food and Fitness,* 5422

Carmi, T., ed. *The Penguin Book of Hebrew Verse,* 3346

Carne, Barbara (jt. author). *A Basic Guide to Horse Care and Management,* 8764

Carnegie, Dale. *How to Win Friends and Influence People,* 5601

Caroli, Betty Boyd. *First Ladies,* 6465

Carp, Robert A. *The Federal Courts,* 4234

Carpenter, Frederic I. *Eugene O'Neill,* 3834

Carpenter, Humphrey. *Jesus,* 4097
Tolkien, 6319

Carper, Jean. *The Food Pharmacy,* 5410

Carr, Ian, et al. *Jazz,* 5849

Carr, Jess. *Intruder in the Wind,* 36(F)

Carr, Philippa. *The Black Swan,* 2238(F)

The Changeling, 2239(F)
Knave of Hearts, 1409(F)
The Pool of St. Branok, 2240(F)
The Return of the Gypsy, 2241(F)
Carr, Terry, ed. *Fantasy Annual 4*, 1066(F)
Terry Carr's Best Science Fiction of the Year, 2464(F)
Carr, William. *A History of Germany, 1815–1945*, 7504
Carra, Andrew J. *Camping*, 9791
Carrighar, Sally. *One Day at Teton Marsh*, 8383
Carrithers, Michael. *The Buddha*, 4040
Carroll, David. *A Concise Dictionary of Foreign Expressions*, 3910
The Dictionary of Foreign Terms in the English Language, 3910
Carroll, Ginny (jt. author). *Ministry of Greed*, 4064
Carroll, James. *Family Trade*, 37(F)
Carroll, Lenore. *Abduction from Fort Union*, 38(F)
Carroll, Lewis. *Poems of Lewis Carroll*, 3197
Carroll, Peter N. *It Seemed Like Nothing Happened*, 8053
Carroll, Raymond. *The Palestine Question*, 7605
Carruth, Gorton (jt. author). *The Oxford Illustrated Literary Guide to the United States*, 3576
Carruth, Gorton, ed. *The Encyclopedia of American Facts and Dates*, 7720
Carson, Jo. *Stories I Ain't Told Nobody Yet*, 3249(F)
Carson, Rachel. *The Edge of the Sea*, 8882
The Sea around Us, 8875
Silent Spring, 4424
Silent Spring Revisited, 4424
Carson, Rob. *Mount St. Helens*, 8800
Carter, Alden R. *Growing Season*, 785(F)
Sheila's Dying, 639(F)
Wart, Son of Toad, 531(F)
Carter, Angela, ed. *Wayward Girls & Wicked Women*, 448(F)
Carter, Bill (jt. author). *Monday Night Mayhem*, 9846
Carter, Craig, ed. *The Complete Baseball Record Book, 1990*, 9635
Carter, Forrest. *Watch for Me on the Mountain*, 1498(F)
Carter, Frances. *Hawaii for Free*, 8179
Carter, Jimmy. *Keeping Faith*, 6524
Carter, Rosalynn. *First Lady from Plains*, 6525
Carter, Sharon. *Careers in Aviation*, 5040
Cartmell, Van H. (jt. author). *Thirty Famous One-Act Plays*, 2979
24 Favorite One-Act Plays, 2980
Carucci, Vic (jt. author). *By a Nose*, 6761
Carver, George T. *Beginning Photography*, 9412
Carver, Jeffrey A. *Clypsis*, 2465(F)
Carver, Raymond, ed. *American Short Story Masterpieces*, 2901(F)

Carwardine, Mark (jt. author). *Last Chance to See*, 8568
Cary, Joyce. *The Horse's Mouth*, 640(F)
Caseley, Judith. *Kisses*, 786(F)
Casey, Dorothy. *Leaving Locke Horn*, 532(F)
Cash, Johnny. *Man in White*, 1365(F)
Cash, June Carter. *From the Heart*, 6379
Cash, Phyllis. *How to Develop and Write a Research Paper*, 4672
Cashman, Sean Dennis. *America in the Gilded Age*, 8007
Casper, Susan (jt. author). *Ripper!* 1751(F)
Cass, Julia (jt. author). *Black in Selma*, 6498
Cassiday, Bruce (jt. author). *The Literature of Crime & Detection*, 3633
Cassidy, Robert. *Margaret Mead*, 6690
Cassidy, William Bennett. *How to Get into U.S. Service Academies*, 4824
Castellano, Carmine. *Basic Mathematics Skills*, 8832
Castleman, Harry. *Five-Hundred-Five Television Questions Your Friends Can't Answer*, 5999
Castoro, Laura (jt. author). *Careers in Computers*, 5034
Caswell, Christopher. *The Illustrated Book of Basic Boating*, 9924
Catala, Rene. *Treasures of the Tropic Seas*, 8772
Catalyst Staff, eds. *It's Your Future!* 4788
What to Do with the Rest of Your Life, 4825
Cateura, Linda Brandi. *Growing Up Italian*, 4398
Cather, Willa. *Death Comes for the Archbishop*, 1560(F)
Great Short Works of Willa Cather, 392(F)
My Antonia, 1561(F)
O Pioneers! 1562(F)
Shadows on the Rock, 1491(F)
Catton, Bruce. *The Civil War*, 7895
Gettysburg, 7896
Grant Moves South, 6530
Grant Takes Command, 6530
Reflections on the Civil War, 7897
A Stillness at Appomattox, 7898
Terrible Swift Sword, 7899
This Hallowed Ground, 7900
Catton, Bruce (jt. author). *Two Roads to Sumter*, 7863
Catton, Chris. *Sex in Nature*, 8384
Catton, William. *Two Roads to Sumter*, 7863
Caulkins, Janet. *Joseph Stalin*, 6874
Cauwels, Janice M. *Bulimia*, 5373
Cavendish, Richard, ed. *Legends of the World*, 3361
Cawthorn, James. *Fantasy*, 3618
CEIP Fund, ed. *The Complete Guide to Environmental Careers*, 5015
Cellini, Benvenuto. *Autobiography*, 6189
Ceram, C. W. *Gods, Graves, and Scholars*, 7014

Cerf, Bennett, ed. *Famous Ghost Stories,* 1722(F)
Great Modern Short Stories, 2902(F)
Plays of Our Time, 3063
Thirty Famous One-Act Plays, 2979
24 Favorite One-Act Plays, 2980
Cervantes, Miguel de. *The Adventures of Don Quixote de la Mancha,* 304(F)
Cetron, Marvin. *American Renaissance,* 4412
Jobs of the Future, 4826
Chaback, Elaine. *The Official Kids' Survival Kit,* 5602
Chace, James. *Endless War,* 7652
Chadakoff, Rochelle, ed. *Eleanor Roosevelt's My Day,* 6555
Chafe, William H. *The Unfinished Journey,* 8054
Chaffin, Casey. *Projects for the Router,* 9269
Chagall, Bella. *Burning Lights,* 4041
Chaisson, Eric. *Relatively Speaking,* 8251
Chalker, Jack L. *Exiles at the Well of Souls,* 1067(F)
A Jungle of Stars, 1068(F)
The Labyrinth of Dreams, 2466(F)
Midnight at the Well of Souls, 1067(F)
Quest for the Well of Souls, 1067(F)
The Return of Nathan Brazil, 1067(F)
Twilight at the Well of Souls, 1067(F)
Web of the Chosen, 1068(F)
Chalmers, David M. *Hooded Americanism,* 4342
Chamberlain, John. *The Enterprising Americans,* 7788
Chamberlain, William. *The Policeman's Beard Is Half Constructed,* 3849
Chambers, Aidan. *NIK,* 787(F)
Chambliss, Daniel F. *Champions,* 9959
Champlin, Tim. *King of the Highbinders,* 39(F)
Chan, Sucheng. *Asian Americans,* 4399
Chancellor, John. *The News Business,* 3983
Peril and Promise, 8055
Chandler, Lana J. *The Student Loan Handbook,* 4774
Chandler, Raymond. *The Big Sleep,* 1945(F)
Farewell, My Lovely, 1945(F)
The Lady in the Lake, 1945(F)
Chang, Jung. *Mme Sun Yat-sen,* 6817
Chang, Margaret Scrogin (jt. author). *Speaking in Chinese,* 3911
Chang, Raymond. *Speaking in Chinese,* 3911
Chao, Evelina. *Gates of Grace,* 449(F)
Chaple, Glenn. *Exploring with a Telescope,* 8252
Chapman, Abraham, ed. *Black Voices,* 2903
Chapman, Robert (jt. author). *The Right Place at the Right Time,* 4812
Chapple, Judy. *Your Horse,* 8760
Charlton, James, et al. *Croquet,* 9553
Charlton, Jim. *A Christmas Companion,* 4115
Charriere, Henri. *Papillon,* 4471
Charters, Ann. *Kerouac,* 6275

Chartrand, Mark R. *Skyguide,* 8253
Chase, Deborah. *The New Medically Based No-Nonsense Beauty Book,* 5275
Chase, Naomi Feigelson. *A Child Is Being Beaten,* 5640
Chase, Richard. *The American Novel and Its Tradition,* 3709
Chase-Riboud, Barbara. *Echo of Lions,* 1524(F)
Chastain, Thomas. *Perry Mason in the Case of the Burning Bequest,* 1946(F)
Perry Mason in the Case of Too Many Murders, 1946(F)
Chatterton, Louise. *Just the Right Age,* 2242(F)
Chatwin, Bruce. *What Am I Doing Here?* 3527
Chaucer, Geoffrey. *The Canterbury Tales,* 339
The Portable Chaucer, 340
Chavis, Geri Giebel, ed. *Family,* 533(F)
Cheatle, Suzanne L. (jt. author). *Dynamite Kites,* 9155
Check, William A. *Alzheimer's Disease,* 5178
Cheever, John. *The Stories of John Cheever,* 2904(F)
Chekhov, Anton. *Anton Chekhov's Plays,* 2995
Chekhov, The Major Plays, 2996
The Cherry Orchard, 2997
The Image of Chekhov, 305(F)
Chell, David. *Moviemakers at Work,* 6000
Chen, Jack. *The Chinese of America,* 4400
Chen, Yuan-trung. *The Dragon's Village,* 7400
Cheneviere, Alain. *Vanishing Tribes,* 6991
Cheney, Glenn Alan. *Revolution in Central America,* 7653
Cherry, Raymond. *Leathercrafting,* 9141
Cherryh, C. J. *Angel with the Sword,* 2467(F)
Chanur's Venture, 2474(F)
Downbelow Station, 2469(F)
The Dreamstone, 1069(F)
Exile's Gate, 1070(F)
Fires of Azroth, 1070(F)
Forty Thousand in Gehenna, 2472(F)
Mechanter's Luck, 2469(F)
The Paladin, 2473(F)
The Pride of Chanur, 2474(F)
Reap the Whirlwind, 1073(F)
Rusalka, 1071(F)
The Trees of Swords and Jewels, 1069(F)
Wizard Spawn, 1072(F)
Cherryh, C. J., ed. *Divine Right,* 2468(F)
Festival Moon, 2470(F)
Fever Season, 2471(F)
Smuggler's Gold, 2249(F)
Troubled Waters, 2249(F)
Chesneaux, Jean. *China,* 7401
Chesneaux, Jean, et al. *China from the 1911 Revolution to Liberation,* 7402
China from the Opium Wars to the 1911 Revolution, 7403
Chesney, Marion. *Enlightening Delilah,* 2243(F)
Frederica in Fashion, 2244(F)

Marrying Harriet, 2245(F)
The Miser of Mayfair, 2248(F)
Perfecting Fiona, 2243(F)
Plain Jane, 2248(F)
Rainbird's Revenge, 2246(F)
Rake's Progress, 2247(F)
Refining Felicity, 2243(F)
The Wicked Godmother, 2248(F)
Chester, William L. *Kioga of the Wilderness,*
    40(F)
Chesterman, Charles W. *The Audubon Society
    Field Guide to North American Rocks and
    Minerals,* 8825
Chesterton, G. K. *Seven Suspects,* 1947(F)
Chestnut, J. L. *Black in Selma,* 6498
Chevalier, Dominique. *Viva! Zappa,* 6460
Chidester, David. *Salvation and Suicide,* 4042
Chijiiwa, Hideaki. *Color Harmony,* 8933
Child, Julia. *The French Chef Cookbook,* 9321
    The Way to Cook, 9321
Childers, Erskine. *The Riddle of the Sands,*
    41(F)
Childress, Alice. *A Hero Ain't Nothin' but a
    Sandwich,* 450(F)
    Rainbow Jordan, 450(F)
    Those Other People, 641(F)
Childress, Mark. *V for Victor,* 42(F)
Chilnick, Larry, et al. *The Food Book,* 5411
Chin, Richard (jt. author). *The Martial Arts,*
    9897
Chinnery, Phil. *Air War in Vietnam,* 8105
Chissell, Joan. *Schumann,* 6353
Chiusoli, Alessandro. *Simon & Schuster's Guide
    to House Plants,* 9374
Chmelynski, Carol Ann. *Opportunities in Restau-
    rant Careers,* 4827
Chomsky, Noam. *Reflections on Language,* 3912
Christensen, Alice. *The American Yoga Associa-
    tion Beginners' Manual,* 5292
Christgau, Robert. *Christgau's Record Guide,* 5850
Christian, Catherine. *The Pendragon,* 1410(F)
Christianson, Gale E. *In the Presence of the Cre-
    ator,* 6696
Christie, Agatha. *Agatha Christie,* 6234
    Curtain, 1948(F)
    Death on the Nile, 1949(F)
    Evil under the Sun, 1950(F)
    Hercule Poirot's Casebook, 1951(F)
    Miss Marple, 1952(F)
    The Mousetrap and Other Plays, 3025
    The Murder at the Vicarage, 1953(F)
    The Murder of Roger Ackroyd, 1954(F)
    Murder on the Orient Express, 1955(F)
    Sleeping Murder, 1956(F)
    Ten Little Indians, 1957(F)
    Witness for the Prosecution, 1958(F)
Christie, Anthony. *Chinese Mythology,* 3451
Christopher, Milbourne. *Milbourne Christopher's
    Magic Book,* 9394

Christopher, Robert C. *The Japanese Mind,* 7446
Christy, Joe. *Your Pilot's License,* 9085
Churchill, Winston. *Closing the Ring,* 7193
    The Gathering Storm, 7193
    The Grand Alliance, 7193
    The Hinge of Fate, 7193
    Their Finest Hour, 7193
    Triumph and Tragedy, 7193
Chute, Marchette. *An Introduction to Shake-
    speare,* 3047
    Shakespeare of London, 6304
    Stories from Shakespeare, 3048
Chyzowych, Walter. *The Official Soccer Book of
    the United States Soccer Federation,* 9949
Ciardi, John. *A Browser's Dictionary, and Na-
    tive's Guide to the Unknown American Lan-
    guage,* 3913
    Good Words to You, 3914
    How Does a Poem Mean? 3153
    Selected Poems, 3250
Cikovsky, Nicolai. *Winslow Homer,* 6196
Citati, Pietro. *Kafka,* 6274
Claiborne, Craig. *Craig Claiborne's Kitchen
    Primer,* 9322
    *Craig Claiborne's The New York Times Food
    Encyclopedia,* 9323
    The New York Times Cook Book, 9324
    The New York Times International Cook Book,
    9324
Claiborne, Robert. *Loose Cannons & Red Her-
    rings,* 3915
Clancy, Tom. *The Cardinal of the Kremlin,* 43(F)
    Clear and Present Danger, 44(F)
    The Hunt for Red October, 45(F)
    Patriot Games, 45(F)
    Red Storm Rising, 45(F)
Clapham, John. *Dvorak,* 6342
Clare, George. *Last Waltz in Vienna,* 1648(F)
Clareson, Thomas D. *Frederik Pohl,* 3710
    *Understanding Contemporary American Science
    Fiction,* 3619
Clarins, Dana. *The Woman Who Knew Too
    Much,* 1959(F)
Clark, Champ. *Gettysburg,* 7901
    The Nation Reunited, 7901
Clark, David H. *The Cosmos from Space,* 8254
Clark, Ella C. (jt. author). *Voices of the Wind,*
    3422
Clark, Eric. *The Want Makers,* 4616
Clark, Kenneth. *Civilisation,* 5682
    The Romantic Rebellion, 5736
    What Is a Masterpiece? 5714
Clark, Mary Higgins. *The Anastasia Syndrome
    and Other Stories,* 1960(F)
    The Cradle Will Fall, 1961(F)
    A Cry in the Night, 1962(F)
    Stillwatch, 1963(F)
    A Stranger Is Watching, 1964(F)
    Weep No More, My Lady, 1965(F)

Where Are the Children? 1966(F)
While My Pretty One Sleeps, 1967(F)
Clark, Nancy. *Nancy Clark's Sports Nutrition Guidebook,* 5344
Clark, Roberta C. *How to Paint Living Portraits,* 9185
Clark, Ronald W. *Einstein,* 6661
Lenin, 6853
The Survival of Charles Darwin, 6656
Clark, Walter Van Tilburg. *The Ox-Bow Incident,* 1563(F)
Clark, William S. *A Field Guide to Hawks,* 8558
Clarke, Amanda. *Battle of Hastings,* 7512
Clarke, Arthur C. *Astounding Days,* 3620
Childhood's End, 2475(F)
The City and the Stars, 2476(F)
The Deep Range, 2476(F)
Dolphin Island, 2477(F)
Imperial Earth, 2478(F)
Island in the Sky, 2476(F)
Rama II, 2485(F)
Reach for Tomorrow, 2476(F)
Rendezvous with Rama, 2479(F)
The Sentinel, 2476(F)
The Songs of Distant Earth, 2480(F)
2001: A Space Odyssey, 2481(F)
2061, 2482(F)
2010: Odyssey Two, 2483(F)
The Wind from the Sun, 2484(F)
Clarke, Asa Bement. *Travels in Mexico and California,* 7950
Clarke, John Henrik. *American Negro Short Stories,* 451(F)
Clarke, Mary. *The Ballet Goer's Guide,* 5962
Dancer, 5963
Clarke, Richard. *The Arrowhead Cattle Company,* 46(F)
Clarke, Thurston. *Equator,* 6130
Clarkson, Atelia, ed. *World Folktales,* 3362
Clarkson, Ewan. *The Many-Forked Branch,* 1499(F)
Clauser, Suzanne. *A Girl Named Sooner,* 642(F)
Clavell, James. *Children's Story,* 47(F)
King Rat, 1649(F)
Noble House, 48(F)
Shogun, 1390(F)
Tai-Pan, 48(F)
Claypool, Jane. *Alcohol and You,* 5106
Unemployment, 4610
Clayre, Alasdair. *The Heart of the Dragon,* 7404
Clayson, Alan. *Only the Lonely,* 6428
Clayton, James D. *A Time for Giants,* 7194
Clayton, Jo. *A Bait of Dreams,* 1074(F)
Changer's Moon, 1074(F)
The Snares of Ibex, 1074(F)
Clayton, Peter. *The Guinness Jazz A–Z,* 5851
Clemens, Roger. *Rocket Man,* 6716
Clemens, Virginia Phelps. *Behind the Filmmaking Scene,* 6001

Clement, Aeron. *The Cold Moons,* 1075(F)
Clement, Hal. *Still River,* 2486(F)
Clements, Charles. *Witness to War,* 7654
Clements, Kendrick A. *Woodrow Wilson, World Statesman,* 6575
Clendenon, Kelly (jt. author). *Drugs & the Family,* 5143
Cleveland, Ray L. *The Middle East and South Asia,* 7591
Clewlow, Carol. *Keeping the Faith,* 788(F)
Cliffe, Roger W. *Woodworker's Handbook,* 9270
Clifford, Geoffrey. *Vietnam,* 7457
Clifford, Mike, ed. *The Harmony Illustrated Encyclopedia of Rock,* 5852
Clifton, Lucille. *Good Woman,* 3251
Clinard, Marshall B. *Corporate Crime,* 4472
Cline, Don. *Alias Billy the Kid, the Man Behind the Legend,* 6616
Cline, Ray S. *Secrets, Spies, and Scholars,* 4215
Cline, Ruth K. J. *Focus on Families,* 5641
Close, Frank. *Apocalypse When?* 8360
Close, Frank, et al. *The Particle Explosion,* 8904
Close, Jessie. *The Warping of Al,* 534(F)
Clubb, O. Edmund. *20th Century China,* 7405
Clurman, Harold, ed. *Famous American Plays of the 1960s,* 3064
Famous American Plays of the 1930s, 3065
Coats, C. David. *Old MacDonald's Factory Farm,* 8588
Cobb, Richard, ed. *Voices of the French Revolution,* 7491
Cobb, Sue. *The Edge of Everest,* 9554
Coberly, Rich. *The No-Hit Hall of Fame,* 9636
Cochran, Jacqueline. *Jackie Cochran,* 6131
Cody, Liza. *Bad Company,* 49(F)
Coe, Michael D. *Mexico,* 7640
Coe, Michael D., et al. *Atlas of Ancient America,* 7799
Coello, Dennis. *The Complete Mountain Biker,* 9748
The Mountain Bike Repair Handbook, 9749
Touring on Two Wheels, 9750
Coen, Patricia. *Beautiful Braids,* 5277
Coetzee, J. M. *In the Heart of the Country,* 643(F)
Life and Times of Michael K, 956(F)
Waiting for the Barbarians, 643(F)
Cofer, Judith Ortiz. *Silent Dancing,* 2905
Coffee, Gerald. *Beyond Survival,* 8106
Coffey, Wayne. *How We Choose a Congress,* 4264
Straight Talk about Drinking, 5107
Coffey, Wayne (jt. author). *Winning Basketball for Girls,* 9739
Coffin, Charles M. *The Major Poets,* 3850
Coffin, Tristram P., ed. *Folklore in America,* 3434
Cohen, Barbara. *Coasting,* 789(F)
Cohen, Barney. *Sting,* 6446

Cohen, Daniel. *The Encyclopedia of Ghosts*, 9480

The Encyclopedia of Monsters, 9481
The Encyclopedia of the Strange, 9482
The Great Airship Mystery, 9483
Greatest Monsters in the World, 9484
Intelligence—What Is It? 5586
Masters of Horror, 6002
Supermonsters, 9485
UFOs, 9486
Undefeated, 6594
The World of UFOs, 9487
Cohen, Daniel (jt. author). *A Six-Pack and a Fake I.D*, 5108
Teenage Competition, 5604
Teenage Stress, 5374
What You Can Believe about Drugs, 5109
When Someone You Know Is Gay, 5459
Cohen, Eve (jt. author). *Knitting by Design*, 9238
Cohen, Hennig (jt. author). *Folklore in America*, 3434
Cohen, Howard R. *Test Your Movie I.Q*, 6003
Cohen, I. Bernard. *The Birth of a New Physics*, 8905
Cohen, Joan Lebold. *China Today and Her Ancient Treasures*, 7406
Cohen, Joel (jt. author). *Inside Pocket Billiards*, 9585
Steve Mizerak's Pocket Billiards, 9585
Cohen, Marcia. *The Sisterhood*, 4294
Cohen, Martin. *In Darkness Born*, 8255
Cohen, Matt. *The Spanish Doctor*, 1411(F)
Cohen, Nathan. *Gravity's Lens*, 8361
Cohen, Paul. *Careers in Law Enforcement and Security*, 4959
Cohen, Shari. *Coping with Being Adopted*, 5642
Coping with Failure, 5603
Coping with Sibling Rivalry, 5643
Cohen, Shari (jt. author). *Careers in Law Enforcement and Security*, 4959
Cohen, Sidney (jt. author). *The Encyclopedia of Drug Abuse*, 5147
Cohen, Stanley. *A Magic Summer*, 9637
Cohen, Steve. *Getting to the Right Job*, 4789
Cohen, Steve (jt. author). *Getting In!* 4728
Cohen, Susan. *A Six-Pack and a Fake I.D*, 5108
Teenage Competition, 5604
Teenage Stress, 5374
What You Can Believe about Drugs, 5109
When Someone You Know Is Gay, 5459
Cohn, Anna R., ed. *Generations*, 5460
Coker, Carolyn. *The Vines of Ferrara*, 1968(F)
Colbert, Edwin H. *Dinosaurs*, 6976
Colby, Marvelle S. (jt. author). *Lovejoy's College Guide for the Learning Disabled*, 4767
Coldrey, Jennifer (jt. author). *The Pond*, 8620
Cole, Adrian. *A Place among the Fallen*, 2487(F)
Cole, Barbara. *Alex the Great*, 644(F)

Cole, Edward C. (jt. author). *Scenery for the Theatre*, 6083
Cole, Jacci. *Animal Communication*, 8481
Cole, Joanna, ed. *Best-Loved Folktales of the World*, 3363
Cole, Lewis. *Never Too Young to Die*, 6740
Coleman, Ray. *Clapton!* 6380
Lennon, 6415
Coleman, William L. *Today's Handbook of Bible Times & Customs*, 4098
Coleridge, Samuel Taylor. *The Portable Coleridge*, 3154
Coles, Clarence W. *Glenn's New Complete Bicycle Manual*, 9751
Coles, Janet. *The Book of Beads*, 9142
Coles, Robert. *Children of Crisis*, 4359
Eskimos, Chicanos, Indians, 4359
Migrants, Sharecroppers, Mountaineers, 4359
Privileged Ones, 4359
The South Goes North, 4359
Colette. *The Collected Stories of Colette*, 2906(F)
Colin, Patrick. *Marine Invertebrates & Plants of the Living Reef*, 8617
Collier, Eugenia W. (jt. author). *Afro-American Writing*, 2935
Collier, James Lincoln. *Duke Ellington*, 6343
Louis Armstrong, 6358
Collier, Karen (jt. author). *Peterson's Guide to College Admissions*, 4772
Collier, Peter. *The Kennedys*, 6598
Collier, Richard. *Fighting Words*, 7195
War in the Desert, 7196
Collier, Simon, et al., eds. *The Cambridge Encyclopedia of Latin America and the Caribbean*, 7625
Collingwood, G. H. *Knowing Your Trees*, 8424
Collins, A. Frederick. *Rapid Math without a Calculator*, 8833
Collins, Alan. *Jacob's Ladder*, 1391(F)
Collins, Bud. *My Life with the Pros*, 9966
Collins, Carol C., ed. *Our Food, Air and Water*, 4425
Collins, Donald N. (jt. author). *Opportunities in Agriculture Careers*, 4872
Collins, Joseph (jt. author). *World Hunger*, 4511
Collins, Judy. *Trust Your Heart*, 6381
Collins, Larry. *The Fifth Horseman*, 50(F)
Freedom at Midnight, 7439
O Jerusalem! 7606
Collins, Max Allen. *The Best of Crime and Detective TV*, 6004
Collins, Robert F. *America at Its Best*, 4280
Basic Training, 4281
Reserve Officers Training Corps, 4726
Collins, Wilkie. *The Moonstone*, 341(F)
The Woman in White, 342(F)
Colman, Hila. *Not for Love*, 2250(F)
Colton, Virginia, ed. *Reader's Digest Complete Guide to Needlework*, 9233

Colum, Padraic, ed. *A Treasury of Irish Folklore*, 3393

Columbu, Franco. *Weight Training and Body Building for Young Athletes*, 9769

Combs, Steve. *Winning Wrestling*, 9783

Comer, James P. *Maggie's American Dream*, 6899

Commager, Henry Steele. *The American Mind*, 7721

  The Blue and the Gray, Vol. 1, 7902

  Documents of American History, 7722

Commager, Henry Steele (jt. author). *A Pocket History of the United States*, 7770

Commager, Henry Steele, ed. *The Era of Reform, 1830–1860*, 7864

Conant, Roger. *A Field Guide to Reptiles and Amphibians of Eastern and Central North America*, 8462

  A Field Guide to Western Reptiles and Amphibians, 8462

Conford, Ellen. *If This Is Love, I'll Take Spaghetti*, 2251(F)

Confucius. *The Wisdom of Confucius*, 3999

Congressional Quarterly. *The Middle East*, 7592

  The Soviet Union, 7565

Congreve, William. *The Way of the World*, 3026

Conkin, Paul K. *Big Daddy from the Pedernales*, 6534

Conklin, Barbara. *P.S. I Love You*, 2252(F)

Conklin, Groff (jt. author). *Fifty Short Science Fiction Tales*, 2382(F)

Conklin, Mike (jt. author). *Everybody's Gymnastics Book*, 9883

  Mastering Softball, 9711

Conley, Robert J. *Go-Ahead Rider*, 51(F)

  Quitting Time, 52(F)

Conn, Peter. *Literature in America*, 3570

Connell, Abby. *Jed and Jessie*, 2253(F)

Connell, Evan S. *Son of the Morning Star*, 7951

  The White Lantern, 7015

Conner, Jeff. *Stephen King Goes to Hollywood*, 6005

Connor, Dick (jt. author). *Reeves*, 6759

Conover, Ted. *Coyotes*, 4503

Conquest, Robert. *Stalin and the Kirov Murder*, 7566

Conrad, Barnaby. *The Complete Guide to Writing Fiction*, 3976

Conrad, John P. (jt. author). *The Death Penalty*, 4257

Conrad, Joseph. *The Great Short Works of Joseph Conrad*, 343(F)

  Heart of Darkness, 344(F)

  Lord Jim, 345(F)

  Nigger of the "Narcissus" and Other Stories, 346(F)

  The Portable Conrad, 347

  Typhoon and Other Stories, 348(F)

Conroy, Pat. *The Great Santini*, 535(F)

  The Lords of Discipline, 790(F)

  The Prince of Tides, 536(F)

  The Water Is Wide, 645(F)

Constable, George, ed. *Arabian Peninsula*, 7593

  Mexico, 7641

Consumer Guide, eds. *Consumer Guide Automobile Book*, 9086

  Consumer Guide to Cars, 1990, 9087

  Corvette, 9088

Consumer Reports, eds. *I'll Buy That!* 4561

  Testing, 4607

Conway, Jill Ker. *The Road from Coorain*, 6820

Cook, Chris. *Dictionary of Historical Terms*, 7033

Cook, Fred. *The Ku Klux Klan*, 4519

Cook, Glen. *Doomstalker*, 1076(F)

  Passage at Arms, 2488(F)

Cook, Hal. *Arranging*, 9298

Cook, Hugh. *The Wizards and the Warriors*, 1077(F)

Cook, Michael. *Muhammad*, 6815

Cook, Paul. *Duende Meadow*, 2489(F)

Cook, Rick. *Wizardry Compiled*, 1078(F)

Cook, Robin. *Coma*, 1724(F)

  Harmful Intent, 1969(F)

  Mortal Fear, 53(F)

  Mutation, 1725(F)

  Outbreak, 54(F)

  Sphinx, 55(F)

  Vital Signs, 56(F)

Cook, Roy J., comp. *One Hundred and One Famous Poems*, 3155

Cook, Sam. *Quiet Magic*, 9555

  Up North, 9826

Cook, T. S. (jt. author). *Mary Jane Harper Cried Last Night*, 696(F)

Cook, Thomas H. *Flesh and Blood*, 1970(F)

Cook-Lynn, Elizabeth. *The Power of Horses and Other Stories*, 1500(F)

Cooke, Alistair. *Alistair Cooke's America*, 7723

  The Patient Has the Floor, 3528

Cooke, Catherine. *Mask of the Wizard*, 1079(F)

Cooke, Cynthia W. *The Ms. Guide to a Woman's Health*, 5345

Cooke, Donald A. *The Life & Death of Stars*, 8351

Cooke, Jacob E., ed. *The Federalist*, 4186

Cooke, John Peyton. *The Lake*, 1726(F)

Cooke, Michael G. *Afro-American Literature in the Twentieth Century*, 3571

Cookson, Catherine. *The Black Candle*, 1412(F)

  The Black Velvet Gown, 1413(F)

  The Moth, 2254(F)

  The Parson's Daughter, 2255(F)

Cool, Lisa Collier. *How to Write Irresistible Query Letters*, 4673

Cooley, Denton. *Eat Smart for a Healthy Heart*, 9325

Coolidge, Grace. *Teepee Neighbors*, 7800

Coombs, Charles. *BMX*, 9715
  Soaring, 9610
Coombs, H. Samm. *Teenage Survival Manual*,
  5605
Cooney, Caroline B. *Don't Blame the Music*,
  537(F)
  Summer Nights, 791(F)
Cooney, Judith. *Coping with Sexual Abuse*, 5506
Cooney, Linda A. *Change of Hearts*, 2256(F)
  Junior, 2257(F)
Coonts, Stephen. *Final Flight*, 57(F)
  The Minotaur, 58(F)
  Under Siege, 59(F)
Cooper, Ilene. *Susan B. Anthony*, 6495
Cooper, J. C. *An Illustrated Encyclopedia of Tra-
  ditional Symbols*, 3898
Cooper, James Fenimore. *The Deerslayer*, 393(F)
  The Last of the Mohicans, 393(F)
  The Pathfinder, 393(F)
  The Pioneers, 393(F)
  The Prairie, 393(F)
Cooper, Kenneth H. *Aerobics*, 5346
  The Aerobics Program for Total Well-Being,
  5347
Cooper, Louise. *Inferno*, 1080(F)
  The Initiate, 2490(F)
  The Master, 2490(F)
  Nemesis, 1080(F)
  The Outcast, 2490(F)
Copeland, Ann. *The Golden Thread*, 646(F)
Copland, Aaron. *Copland*, 6341
  Copland since 1943, 6341
  Music and Imagination, 5816
  The New Music, 1900–1960, 5833
  What to Listen for in Music, 5817
Coppa, Frank J., ed. *The Immigrant Experience
  in America*, 4329
Coppel, Alfred. *Show Me a Hero*, 60(F)
Corbin, Carole Lynn. *The Right to Vote*, 4295
Corbo, Margarete Sigi. *Arnie, the Darling Star-
  ling*, 8669
Corcoran, Barbara. *Face the Music*, 538(F)
Cormier, Robert. *After the First Death*, 61(F)
  Beyond the Chocolate War, 792(F)
  The Bumblebee Flies Anyway, 647(F)
  The Chocolate War, 792(F)
  Eight Plus One, 793(F)
  Fade, 2491(F)
  I Am the Cheese, 794(F)
Cornell, Tim. *Atlas of the Roman World*, 7113
Cornwell, Bernard. *Redcoat*, 1520(F)
  Sharpe's Eagle, 1414(F)
  Sharpe's Enemy, 1414(F)
  Sharpe's Gold, 1414(F)
  Sharpe's Regiment, 1414(F)
  Sharpe's Revenge, 1414(F)
  Sharpe's Siege, 1415(F)
Corrick, James A. *The Human Brain*, 5309
Corrigan, Robert W., ed. *Arthur Miller*, 3835

Corson, Richard. *Stage Makeup*, 6084
Corwen, Leonard. *Your Job—Where to Find It,
  How to Get It*, 4790
Corwin, Edward S. *Edward S. Corwin's The Con-
  stitution and What It Means Today*, 4187
Cosby, Bill. *Love and Marriage*, 3494
Cosby, Bill, et al. *You Are Somebody Special*,
  5530
Cosentino, Peter. *The Encyclopedia of Pottery
  Techniques*, 9162
Costa, Richard Hauer. *H. G. Wells*, 3656
Costa, Richard Hauer (jt. author). *Safe at
  Home*, 9651
Costello, Elaine. *Signing*, 5432
Costello, Matthew J. *Wizard of Tizare*, 1081(F)
Cottam, Clarence. *Insects*, 8593
Cottell, John E. *Code Name Badger*, 6900
Cotterell, Arthur. *The Macmillan Illustrated En-
  cyclopedia of Myths & Legends*, 3452
Couch, Tony. *Watercolor*, 9186
Coughlin, George Gordon. *Your Introduction to
  Law*, 4235
Coulbourn, Keith (jt. author). *Behind the Dol-
  phin Smile*, 6697
Coulling, Mary P. *The Lee Girls*, 6466
Council on International Educational Exchange.
  *The Teenager's Guide to Study, Travel, and
  Adventure Abroad, 1989–1990 Edition*, 4709
  *The Teenager's Guide to Study, Travel, and Ad-
  venture Abroad 1990–91*, 4710
Council on Interracial Books for Children.
  Chronicles of American Indian Protest, 7801
Counsilman, James E. *The Complete Book of
  Swimming*, 9960
Couper, Heather. *New Worlds*, 8342
Courlander, Harold, ed. *Treasury of African Folk-
  lore*, 3378
  A Treasury of Afro-American Folklore, 3435
Courtenay, Bryce. *The Power of One*, 957(F)
Courthion, Pierre. *Georges Seurat*, 6206
  Manet, 5773
Cousins, Norman. *Anatomy of an Illness as Per-
  ceived by the Patient*, 5179
Cousteau, Jacques. *Jacques Cousteau's Amazon
  Journey*, 7669
  Jacques Cousteau's Calypso, 8889
  The Silent World, 8888
Cousteau, Jean-Michel. *Cousteau's Papua New
  Guinea Journey*, 7467
Cousy, Bob. *Basketball*, 9716
  Cousy on the Celtic Mystique, 9717
Couzens, Gerald Secor (jt. author). *Hoops!* 9720
Coville, Bruce. *The Dark Abyss*, 1082(F)
  Waiting Spirits, 1727(F)
Covington, Vicki. *Gathering Home*, 539(F)
Cowan, Paul. *An Orphan in History*, 6901
Coward, Barry. *The Stuart Age*, 7513
Coward, Noel. *Three Plays*, 3027
Cowell, Adrian. *The Decade of Destruction*, 7670

Cowen, Ida. *A Spy for Freedom*, 6801
Cowley, Joy. *Salmagundi*, 2258(F)
Cowley, Malcolm. *Blue Juniata*, 3252
  A Second Flowering, 3711
Cox, Archibald. *Freedom of Expression*, 4236
Cox, Daniel. *Whitetail Country*, 8522
Cox, Don Richard. *Arthur Conan Doyle*, 3657
Cox, James M., ed. *Robert Frost*, 3881
Cox, Jeff, et al. *How to Grow Vegetables Organically*, 9375
Cox, Michael, ed. *The Oxford Book of English Ghost Stories*, 1728(F)
Coyne, John. *Brothers and Sisters*, 795(F)
Cozzens, James Gould. *The Just and the Unjust*, 648(F)
Crabb, Tom. *Band Saw Projects*, 9271
Crabbe, Katharyn F. *J. R. R. Tolkien*, 3658
Craig, Eleanor. *P.S. You're Not Listening*, 5375
Craig, Patricia, ed. *The Oxford Book of English Detective Stories*, 1971(F)
Craig, William. *Enemy at the Gates*, 7197
Craighead, Frank C., Jr. *Track of the Grizzly*, 8505
Cramer, John. *Twistor*, 2492(F)
Cramer, Kathryn, ed. *Christmas Ghosts*, 1729(F)
Cramer, Kathryn (jt. author). *Masterpieces of Fantasy and Enchantment*, 1146(F)
Crane, Milton, ed. *50 Great American Short Stories*, 2907(F)
Crane, Stephen. *A Collection of Critical Essays*, 3712
  The Complete Poems of Stephen Crane, 3253
  Maggie, 394(F)
  The Red Badge of Courage, 395(F)
Cranford, John. *Budgeting for America*, 4217
Craven, Linda. *Stepfamilies*, 5644
Craven, Margaret. *Again Calls the Owl*, 431(F)
  I Heard the Owl Call My Name, 431(F)
  Walk Gently This Good Earth, 1621(F)
Craven, William, ed. *Two Hundred Years of American Art*, 5792
Crawford, Alan. *Thunder on the Right*, 4123
Creamer, Robert W. *Babe*, 6732
  Stengel, 6734
Creamer, Robert W. (jt. author). *Season of Glory*, 9659
Crease, Robert P. *The Second Creation*, 8906
Creasy, Rosalind. *The Gardener's Handbook of Edible Plants*, 9376
Creedman, Michael. *The NFL All-Pro Workout*, 5348
Creel, Herrlee Glessner. *Chinese Thought from Confucius to Mao Tse-tung*, 4000
Creeley, Robert. *The Collected Poems of Robert Creeley, 1945–1975*, 3254
Cremin, Lawrence A. *American Education*, 7724
  American Education, the American Experience, 7724
Crespo, Charles (jt. author). *Rock On*, 5836, 5836

Crespo, Michael. *Watercolor Day by Day*, 9187
Cribb, Joe, et al. *The Coin Atlas*, 9444
Crichton, Michael. *The Andromeda Strain*, 2493(F)
  Five Patients, 5232
  The Great Train Robbery, 1416(F)
  Jurassic Park, 2494(F)
  Sphere, 2495(F)
  The Terminal Man, 2496(F)
Crick, Francis. *What Mad Pursuit*, 6654
Criddle, Joan D. (jt. author). *To Destroy You Is No Loss*, 7460
Crider, Bill. *Cursed to Death*, 1972(F)
  Medicine Show, 62(F)
  One Dead Dean, 1973(F)
  Ryan Rides Back, 1974(F)
Crisp, Clement (jt. author). *The Ballet Goer's Guide*, 5962
  Dancer, 5963
Crisp, N. J. *In the Long Run*, 1975(F)
Crispin, A. C. *Shadow World*, 2497(F)
  Starbridge 2, 2498
Crispin, Edmund. *The Moving Toy Shop*, 1976(F)
Crist, Dean A. (jt. author). *Opportunities in Financial Careers*, 4938
Critchfield, Richard. *Shahhat*, 6950
Croall, Stephen. *Nuclear Power for Beginners*, 8920
Crocker, Betty. *Betty Crocker's Cookbook*, 9326
  Betty Crocker's Microwave Cooking, 9327
  Betty Crocker's New International Cookbook, 9326
Crocker, Betty, ed. *Betty Crocker's New International Cookbook*, 9328
Crombie, David. *The Synthesizer & Electronic Keyboard Handbook*, 5931
Crompton, Paul. *The Complete Martial Arts*, 9893
Cronin, A. J. *The Citadel*, 649(F)
  The Keys of the Kingdom, 650(F)
Cronin, Edward W. *Getting Started in Bird Watching*, 8534
Cronkite, Kathy. *On the Edge of the Spotlight*, 6885
Cronon, E. David. *Black Moses*, 6507
Crook, Marion. *Teenagers Talk about Suicide*, 5376
Croom, Emily Anne. *Unpuzzling Your Past*, 5645
Cross, Amanda. *Death in a Tenured Position*, 1978(F)
  The James Joyce Murder, 1977(F)
  The Question of Max, 1978(F)
  The Theban Mysteries, 1978(F)
Cross, Charles. *Backstreets*, 6444
Cross, Donna Woolfold. *Mediaspeak*, 6006
Cross, Gilbert B. (jt. author). *World Folktales*, 3362

Cross, Milton. *The Milton Cross New Encyclopedia of the Great Composers and Their Music*, 6170

The New Milton Cross' Complete Stories of the Great Operas, 5913

The New Milton Cross' More Stories of the Great Operas, 5913

Crossley-Holland, Kevin. *The Norse Myths*, 3480

Crossley-Holland, Kevin, ed. *The Faber Book of Northern Folk-Tales*, 3395

The Faber Book of Northern Legends, 3395

Folk-Tales of the British Isles, 3396

Crossley-Holland, Kevin, reteller. *British Folk Tales*, 3394

Crouch, Dora P. *History of Architecture*, 5692

Crouch, Tom. *The Bishop's Boys*, 6703

Crouse, Russell (jt. author). *Three Comedies of American Family Life*, 3099

Crow Dog, Mary. *Lakota Woman*, 6500

Crow, John A. *The Epic of Latin America*, 7626

Spain, 7554

Crow, Kevin (jt. author). *Championship Soccer*, 9950

Crow, Tatu. *Championship Soccer*, 9950

Crowder, Michael (jt. author). *The Cambridge Encyclopedia of Africa*, 7356

Crowder, Richard. *Carl Sandburg*, 3882

Crowther, Bruce. *The Big Band Years*, 5854

Crump, Donald J., ed. *America's Hidden Corners*, 7725

America's Magnificent Mountains, 7726

America's Majestic Canyons, 7727

America's Wild and Scenic Rivers, 7728

Crutcher, Chris. *Chinese Handcuffs*, 651(F)

Cuddon, J. A. *A Dictionary of Literary Terms*, 3572

Cuddon, J. A., ed. *The Penguin Book of Ghost Stories*, 1730(F)

Culhane, John. *The American Circus*, 5977

Cumming, Robert. *Just Imagine*, 5715

Cummings, E. E. *110 Selected Poems*, 3255

73 Poems, 3255

Cummings, Jack. *Escape from Yuma*, 63(F)

The Surrogate Gun, 64(F)

Cummings, John (jt. author). *The Heist*, 4496

Cunliffe, Marcus. *George Washington, Man and Monument*, 6572

The Nation Takes Shape, 1789–1837, 7849

Cunningham, Laura. *Sleeping Arrangements*, 540(F)

Cunningham, Marion. *The Fannie Farmer Cookbook*, 9329

Curl, Sue. *Knit 4 Seasons*, 9235

Curnow, Ray (jt. author). *Overcoming Computer Illiteracy*, 8963

Curran, Delores. *Traits of a Healthy Family*, 5349

Curran, Douglas. *In Advance of the Landing*, 9488

Curran, Robert, et al. *The Haunted*, 9489

Curran, Susan. *Overcoming Computer Illiteracy*, 8963

Curran, Thomas J. (jt. author). *The Immigrant Experience in America*, 4329

Current, Richard N., et al. *The Essentials of American History*, 7729

Currey, Richard. *Fatal Light*, 1693(F)

Currimbhoy, Nayana. *Indira Gandhi*, 6805

Curry, Boykin, ed. *Essays That Worked*, 4727

Curry, Jack. *Woodstock*, 5855

Curtin & London, eds. *The Book of 35mm Photography*, 9414

Curtis, Patricia. *Animal Partners*, 8670

The Animal Shelter, 8670

Curtis, Robert H. *Mind and Mood*, 5557

Curtis, Will, ed. *The Nature of Things*, 8216

Curwood, James Oliver. *The Bear—A Novel*, 286(F)

Cushman, Robert F. *Leading Constitutional Decisions*, 4188

Cusic, Don. *Randy Travis*, 6448

Cussler, Clive. *Cyclops*, 65(F)

Dragon, 66(F)

Raise the Titanic, 67(F)

Treasure, 68(F)

Cuthbertson, Tom. *Anybody's Bike Book*, 9752

Cutler, Nick (jt. author). *Practical Things to Do with a Microcomputer*, 9018

Cutlip, Glen W. (jt. author). *Careers in Teaching*, 4954

Cvancara, Alan M. *A Field Manual for the Amateur Geologist*, 8794

Sleuthing Fossils, 6977

Czerkas, Sylvia J., ed. *Dinosaurs Past and Present, Volume 1*, 6978

da Cruz, Daniel. *Boot*, 4282

Dadié, Bernard Binlin. *The Black Cloth*, 3379

Dahl, Roald. *Ah, Sweet Mystery of Life*, 2908(F)

Boy, 6237

Going Solo, 6237

Roald Dahl's Tales of the Unexpected, 1731(F)

Two Fables, 1083(F)

Daiches, David. *Literary Landscape of the British Isles*, 3660

The Novel and the Modern World, 3659

Dakin, Janet Wilder. *Jeffy's Journal*, 8761

Dalby, Richard, ed. *Victorian Ghost Stories by Eminent Women Writers*, 1732(F)

D'Aleo, Richard J. *FEDfind*, 4178

Daley, Brian. *Fall of the White Ship Avatar*, 2499(F)

Dalmas, John. *Fanglith*, 2500(F)

Touch the Stars, 2501(F)

Dalton, Marianne (jt. author). *The Student's Guide to Good Writing*, 4674

Dalton, Rick. *The Student's Guide to Good Writing*, 4674

Daly, Jay. *Presenting S. E. Hinton*, 3713

D'Ambrosio, Richard. *No Language but a Cry*, 5646

Damrosch, Barbara. *The Garden Primer*, 9377

Damsker, Matt. *Rock Voices*, 5856

Dan, Uri. *To the Promised Land*, 7607

Dana, Barbara. *Necessary Parties*, 541(F)

Dana, Katherine. *Opportunities in Counseling and Development*, 4960

Dana, Richard Henry. *Two Years Before the Mast*, 6137

Dance, Stanley. *The World of Duke Ellington*, 6387

Dangerfield, George. *The Awakening of American Nationalism, 1815–1828*, 7865

Daniels, Roger. *Coming to America*, 4330

Daniken, Erich von. *Chariots of the Gods?* 9490

Dank, Milton. *Khaki Wings*, 1633(F)

Dann, Jack, ed. *Bestiary!* 1084(F)

Dante, Alighieri. *The Portable Dante*, 3861

Danziger, James, ed. *Visual Aid*, 5716

Darcy, Clare. *Caroline and Julia*, 1417(F)

Darcy, Laura, comp. *Webster's New World Dictionary of Computer Terms*, 8964

Darden, Ellington. *The Athlete's Guide to Sports Medicine*, 5350

Dardess, George (jt. author). *Every Cliché in the Book*, 3946

Darling, David. *Deep Time*, 8362

Darling, James. *Wild Whales*, 8642

Darrell, Elizabeth. *The Flight of Flamingo*, 69(F)

Dart, Iris Rainer. *Beaches*, 652(F)

Darwin, Charles. *The Essential Darwin*, 6992
The Voyage of the Beagle, 6993

Dary, David. *Cowboy Culture*, 7952

Datlow, Ellen, ed. *The Fifth Omni Book of Science Fiction*, 2502(F)

Daugherty, Lynn B. *Why Me?* 5507

Davenport, Basil, ed. *The Portable Roman Reader*, 2909

Davenport, Marcia. *Mozart*, 6352

David, A. Rosalie. *The Egyptian Kingdoms*, 7095

David, Andrew. *Famous Political Trials*, 7034

David, Kati. *A Child's War*, 7198

David, Peter. *Knight Life*, 1085(F)

Davidovits, Joseph. *The Pyramids*, 7096

Davidson, Art. *In the Wake of the Exxon Valdez*, 4451

Davidson, Basil. *Africa in History*, 7345
The African Genius, 7345
The African Slave Trade, 7345, 7346
The Lost Cities of Africa, 7345, 7347

Davidson, Bill. *Jane Fonda*, 6391

Davidson, H. R. Ellis. *Gods and Myths of Northern Europe*, 3481
Scandinavian Mythology, 3397

Davidson, Linda. *On the Edge*, 796(F)

Davidson, Nicole. *Crash Course*, 1733(F)

Davidson, Robyn. *Tracks*, 7468

Davidson, Roger H. *Congress and Its Members*, 4218

Davie, Michael. *Titanic*, 8890

Davies, Brian (jt. author). *Seasons of the Seal*, 8641

Davies, Eryl. *Ocean Frontiers*, 8891

Davies, Hunter. *The Beatles*, 6171

Davies, Norman. *Heart of Europe*, 7487

Davies, Owen. *The Omni Book of Computers and Robots*, 8965

Davies, Owen (jt. author). *American Renaissance*, 4412

Davies, Owen, ed. *The Omni Book of Medicine*, 5233
The Omni Book of Space, 8299

Davies, Robertson. *Fifth Business*, 797(F)
The Manticore, 797(F)
World of Wonders, 797(F)

Davis, Bertha. *Crisis in Industry*, 4562

Davis, Burke. *The Civil War*, 7903
The Long Surrender, 7904
Sherman's March, 7905
To Appomattox, 7906

Davis, Daniel. *Behind Barbed Wire*, 7199

Davis, Jenny. *Sex Education*, 542(F)

Davis, Joel. *Flyby*, 8300

Davis, Kenn. *Words Can Kill*, 1979(F)

Davis, Kenneth C. *Don't Know Much about History*, 7730

Davis, Leila. *Lover Boy*, 2259(F)

Davis, Lindsey. *Silver Pigs*, 1366(F)

Davis, Mac. *Great Sports Humor*, 9556
Strange and Incredible Sports Happenings, 9557

Davis, Marilyn P. *Mexican Voices, American Dreams*, 4401

Davis, Patricia. *Suicidal Adolescents*, 5377

Davis, Sammy, et al. *Why Me?* 6382

Davis, Stephen. *Bob Marley*, 6424
Reggae International, 5857

Davis, William C. *Brother against Brother*, 7907
Death in the Trenches, 7908
First Blood, 7909
Rebels & Yankees, 7910

Davis, William C. (jt. author). *A Pictorial History of the Civil War Years*, 7887

Davis, William Stearns. *A Day in Old Athens*, 7114
A Day in Old Rome, 7114

Dawidowicz, Lucy S. *The War Against the Jews, 1933–1945*, 7200

Dawkins, Louisa. *Chasing Shadows*, 543(F)

Day, Arthur Grove, ed. *The Sky Clears*, 3256

Day, Carol Olsen. *The New Immigrants*, 4331

Day, David. *The Whale War*, 8643

Day, David (jt. author). *Tools and How to Use Them*, 8948

Day, Edmund (jt. author). *The New Immigrants*, 4331

Day, James. *Vaughan Williams*, 6354

Day, Susan (jt. author). *The Writer's Handbook*, 4688

de Beauvoir, Simone. *The Second Sex*, 4535

de Camp, L. Sprague. *The Fringe of the Unknown*, 8217

The Honorable Barbarian, 1086(F)

De Cristoforo, R. J. *The Table Saw Book*, 9272

de France, Marie. *The Lais of Marie de France*, 2260(F)

De Haven, Tom. *Joe Gosh*, 2503(F)

De Kruif, Paul. *Microbe Hunters*, 6641

De la Croix, Horst. *Gardner's Art Through the Ages*, 5737

de Larrabeiti, Michael. *The Borribles*, 1089(F)

De Lint, Charles. *Drink Down the Moon*, 1090(F)

Jack, the Giant Killer, 1090(F)

Moonheart, 1091(F)

Yarrow, 1734(F)

de Maupassant, Guy. *The Best Short Stories of Guy de Maupassant*, 306(F)

Selected Short Stories, 307(F)

De Mille, Agnes. *And Promenade Home*, 6383

Dance to the Piper, 6383

Portrait Gallery, 5964

De Oliveira, Paulo. *Getting In!* 4728

De Pauw, Linda Grant. *Founding Mothers*, 7850

De Reyna, Rudy. *How to Draw What You See*, 9188

De Satnick, Shelly. *Bridge for Everyone*, 9806

De Sola, Ralph. *Crime Dictionary*, 4473

de Tocqueville, Alexis. *Democracy in America*, 7866

The Old Regime and the French Revolution, 7492

de Vinck, Christopher. *The Power of the Powerless*, 5433

De Vries, Mary A. *The New Robert's Rules of Order*, 5581

Deacon, Richard. *Spyclopedia*, 4134

Dean, Anabel. *Wind Sports*, 9611

DeAndrea, William L. *Killed in Paradise*, 1980(F)

Dear, William. *The Dungeon Master*, 5378

Dearborn, Laura. *Good Sound*, 9049

Dearing, James. *Making Money Making Music (No Matter Where You Live)*, 4877

Dearling, Celia (jt. author). *The Guinness Book of Music*, 5818

Dearling, Robert. *The Guinness Book of Music*, 5818

DeBarr, Candice M. *Saga of the American Flag*, 7731

DeBenedetti, Charles, ed. *Peace Heroes in Twentieth-Century America*, 6467

Debner, Claudia Bialke, ed. *Chemical Dependency*, 5110

Debo, Angie. *Geronimo*, 6622

A History of the Indians of the United States, 7802

Decker, Celia Anita. *Children*, 5523

Defoe, Daniel. *Moll Flanders*, 349(F)

Robinson Crusoe, 350(F)

Deford, Frank. *Alex*, 6902

Casey on the Loose, 2873(F)

Deford, Frank (jt. author). *Sports People*, 9576

DeFord, Miriam Allen. *Who Was When?* 7035

DeFries, Ruth S. (jt. author). *One Earth, One Future*, 4442

Degens, T. *On the Third Ward*, 653(F)

DeGregorio, William A. *The Complete Book of U.S. Presidents*, 6468

Deighton, Len. *Berlin Game*, 70(F)

The Billion Dollar Brain, 71(F)

Blitzkrieg, 7201

Catch a Falling Spy, 72(F)

Funeral in Berlin, 71(F)

The Ipcress File, 71(F)

Spy Story, 72(F)

SS-GB, 72(F)

Deitz, Tom. *Fireshaper's Doom*, 1087(F)

Windmaster's Bane, 1088(F)

Del Aguila, Juan M. *Cuba*, 7660

Del Mar, Norman. *The Anchor Companion to the Orchestra*, 5932

Del Vecchio, John M. *The Thirteenth Valley*, 1694(F)

Delderfield, Eric R. *Kings & Queens of England and Great Britain*, 7514

Delderfield, R. F. *To Serve Them All My Days*, 1418(F)

Dellar, Fred, ed. *The Harmony Illustrated Encyclopedia of Country Music*, 5858

Delmar, Charles. *The Essential Cook*, 9330

Delmar, Diana. *The Guilt-Free Dog Owner's Guide*, 8716

Deloria, Ella Cara. *Waterlily*, 1501(F)

Deloria, Vine, Jr. *American Indians, American Justice*, 7804

Custer Died for Your Sins, 7803

The Nations Within, 4392

Delton, Judy. *The 29 Most Common Writing Mistakes and How to Avoid Them*, 4675

DeLuca, Sam. *Football Made Easy*, 9841

DeMille, Nelson. *Cathedral*, 73(F)

The Charm School, 74(F)

Word of Honor, 1695(F)

Demos, John Putnam. *Entertaining Satan*, 7838

Dempsey, M. W., ed. *Atlas of the Arab World*, 7594

Demske, Dick. *Carpentry and Woodworking*, 9273

Dennis, Marguerite J. *Dollars for Scholars*, 4776

Denny, Jon S. *Careers in Cable TV*, 4828

Densmore, John. *Riders on the Storm*, 5859

Denyer, Ralph. *The Guitar Handbook*, 5933

Deptula, Edward J., ed. *Preparation for the SAT*, 4656

Deriabin, Peter. *KGB*, 7567

DeRidder, Margaret Djerf. *New Career Opportunities in Health and Human Services*, 4989

Dershowitz, Alan M. *Taking Liberties*, 4237

Desai, Anita. *Clear Light of Day*, 958(F)

Descartes, Rene. *A Discourse on Method, and Selected Writings*, 4001

Deslandres, Yvonne (jt. author). *20,000 Years of Fashion*, 5273

Desowitz, Robert S. *Thorn in the Starfish*, 5180

Despont, Thierry W. (jt. author). *Restoring the Statue of Liberty*, 8166

Detweiler, Robert. *John Updike*, 3714

Deuker, Carl. *On the Devil's Court*, 2874(F)

Deutsch, Babette. *Poetry Handbook*, 3851

Deutsch, Robert W. *Nuclear Power*, 8921

Deutscher, Isaac. *Stalin*, 6875

Deutschman, Alan. *Winning Money for College*, 4777

Devaney, John. *Where Are They Today?* 6705

Devaney, John (jt. author). *The Football Book*, 9853

Deveaux, Alexis. *Don't Explain*, 6402

DeVenzio, Dick. *Smart Moves*, 5606

Devon, Gary. *Lost*, 1735(F)

DeVorkin, David H. *Practical Astronomy*, 8256

DeVoss, Lishka. *How to Be a Waitress (or Waiter)*, 4961

DeVries, Peter. *The Tunnel of Love*, 1878(F)

Dewdney, A. K. *The Armchair Universe*, 8966

Dewey, John. *Democracy and Education*, 4002

Dewey, Patrick R. *Interactive Fiction and Adventure Games for Microcomputers*, 8967

DeWitt, Howard A. *The Beatles*, 6369

di Lampedusa, Giuseppe. *The Leopard*, 1419(F)

Diagram Group. *The Brain*, 5310

Comparisons, 8865

The Healthy Body, 5293

Musical Instruments of the World, 5934

The Rule Book, 9558

Weapons, an International Encyclopedia from 5000 BC to 2000 AD, 9125

Diagram Group (jt. author). *The Field Guide to Early Man*, 7003

The Field Guide to Geology, 8798

The Field Guide to Prehistoric Life, 7003

Diamond, Marilyn. *The American Vegetarian Cookbook*, 9331

Diamond, Sander (jt. author). *Starik*, 237(F)

Diamonstein, Barbaralee. *American Architecture Now II*, 5699

DiAntonio, Robert (jt. author). *The Admissions Essay*, 4756

Diaz del Castillo, Bernal. *Cortez and the Conquest of Mexico by the Spaniards in 1521*, 7642

DiBacco, Thomas V. *Made in the U.S.A*, 4586

Dick, Philip K. *Blade Runner*, 2504(F)

Clans of the Alphane Moon, 2504(F)

The Collected Stories of Philip K. Dick, 2505(F)

I Hope I Shall Arrive Soon, 2506(F)

The Man in the High Castle, 2507(F)

Dickens, Charles. *Barnaby Rudge*, 351(F)

Bleak House, 352(F)

A Christmas Carol, 353(F)

David Copperfield, 354(F)

Great Expectations, 355(F)

Hard Times, 356(F)

Martin Chuzzlewit, 357(F)

The Mystery of Edwin Drood, 358(F)

Nicholas Nickleby, 359(F)

The Old Curiosity Shop, 360(F)

Oliver Twist, 361(F)

Tale of Two Cities, 362(F)

Dickey, Glenn. *The History of National League Baseball since 1876*, 9638

The History of the World Series since 1903, 9639

Dickey, James. *The Central Motion*, 3257

Deliverance, 75(F)

Dickinson, Emily. *The Complete Poems of Emily Dickinson*, 3258

Final Harvest, 3259

Dickinson, Peter. *King and Joker*, 1982(F)

The Poison Oracle, 1981(F)

Skeleton-in-Waiting, 1982(F)

Tulku, 76(F)

Dickinson, Terence. *Nightwatch*, 8257

The Universe . . . and Beyond, 8363

Dickson, Gordon R. *The Chantry Guild*, 2508(F)

Dorsai! 2509(F)

The Dorsai Companion, 1092(F)

The Last Dream, 1093(F)

Love Not Human, 2510(F)

The Man from Earth, 2510(F)

Way of the Pilgrim, 2511(F)

Wolf and Iron, 2512(F)

Dickson, Gordon R. (jt. author). *Gremlins Go Home*, 2426(F)

Dickson, Paul. *Library in America*, 7732

Didion, Joan. *The White Album*, 3529

Dietrich, R. V. *Minerals, Rocks and Fossils*, 8826

Dietrich, Richard F. *British Drama 1890 to 1950*, 3808

Dietz, William C. *War World*, 2513(F)

Digeronimo, Theresa Foy (jt. author). *AIDS, Trading Fears for Facts*, 5188

D'Ignazio, Fred. *Small Computers*, 8968

Working Robots, 8969

Dillard, Annie. *An American Childhood*, 6242

Pilgrim at Tinker Creek, 8385

Dillard, J. M. *The Lost Years*, 2514(F)

Dimbleby, David. *An Ocean Apart*, 4135

Dimbleby, Jonathan. *The Palestinians*, 7608

Dimont, Max I. *Jews, God and History*, 4043

Dinesen, Isak. *Out of Africa and Shadows on the Grass*, 7362

Seven Gothic Tales, 1736(F)

Dinsdale, Tim. *Loch Ness Monster*, 9491

Dintiman, George B. *Sport Speed*, 9559

DiSilvestro, Roger. *The Endangered Kingdom*, 8570

Fight for Survival, 8571

Living with the Reptiles, 2515(F)

Ditlea, Steve, ed. *Digital Deli*, 8970

Ditlow, Clarence (jt. author). *Lemon Book*, 9105

Divine, Robert A. *Eisenhower and the Cold War*, 4136

Divine, Robert A., ed. *Exploring the Johnson Years*, 8056

Dixon, Bernard, ed. *Health, Medicine, and the Human Body*, 5294

Dixon, Dougal. *After Man*, 6994

The New Dinosaurs, 6979

Dizeno, Patricia. *Why Me?* 654(F)

Djerassi, Carl. *Cantor's Dilemma*, 77(F)

Doak, Wade. *Encounters with Whales and Dolphins*, 8644

Doan, Marilyn. *Hiking Light*, 9792

Doane, Gilbert H. *Searching for Your Ancestors*, 5647

Dobbins, Bill (jt. author). *The Athletic Body*, 5355

Encyclopedia of Modern Bodybuilding, 5361

Dobroszycki, Lucjan, ed. *The Chronicle of the Lodz Ghetto, 1941–1944*, 7202

Dobson, Christopher. *The Never-Ending War*, 4542

The Terrorists, 4543

Dock, V. Thomas. *Structured COBOL*, 8971

Doctorow, E. L. *The Book of Daniel*, 655(F)

Ragtime, 1601(F)

World's Fair, 1622(F)

Dodd, Robert T. *Thunderstones and Shooting Stars*, 8330

Dodds, William (jt. author). *Speaking Out, Fighting Back*, 5510

Dodge, Robert K., ed. *New and Old Voices of Wah'kon-tah*, 3260

Dodson, Jackie. *Know Your Sewing Machine*, 9236

Dodson, Susan. *Shadows across the Sand*, 1983(F)

Dodwell, Christina. *A Traveler on Horseback in Eastern Turkey and Iran*, 7619

Doelp, Alan. *In the Blink of an Eye*, 5234

Doherty, Berlie. *Granny Was a Buffer Girl*, 544(F)

Doherty, P. C. *Spy in Chancery*, 1984(F)

The Whyte Harte, 1420(F)

Doig, Ivan. *Dancing at the Rascal Fair*, 1564(F)

The Sea Runners, 1421(F)

Dolan, Edward F., Jr. *Bicycle Touring and Camping*, 9753

Child Abuse, 5648

International Drug Traffic, 5111

Matters of Life and Death, 5082

Protect Your Legal Rights, 4296

Dolber, Roslyn. *Opportunities in Fashion Careers*, 4829

Opportunities in Retailing Careers, 4909

Domkowski, Dorothy (jt. author). *Careers in Business*, 4936

Don, Sarah. *Traditional Samplers*, 9237

Donaldson, D. J. *Cajun Nights*, 1737(F)

Donaldson, Stephen R. *Daughter of Regals and Other Tales*, 1094(F)

The Illearth War, 1095(F)

Lord Foul's Bane, 1095(F)

A Man Rides Through, 1096(F)

The Mirror of Her Dreams, 1097(F)

The One Tree, 1098(F)

The Power That Preserves, 1095(F)

White Gold Wielder, 1098(F)

The Wounded Land, 1098(F)

Donin, Hayim Halevy. *To Be a Jew*, 4044

Donne, John. *The Complete English Poems of John Donne*, 3198

Donner, Cecile (jt. author). *The Dictionary of Superstitions*, 9479

Donner, Florinda. *Shabano*, 7671

Donohoe, Tom. *Foul Play*, 5112

Donovan, David. *Once a Warrior King*, 8107

Donovan, Mary Deirdre. *Opportunities in Culinary Careers*, 4830

Donovan, Robert J. *Conflict and Crisis*, 8057

Tumultuous Years, 8057

Donovan, Timothy H., et al. *The American Civil War*, 7911

Dore, Anita, ed. *The Premier Book of Major Poets*, 3156

Doren, Charles Van (jt. author). *How to Read a Book*, 4644

Doreski, Carol Kiler. *How to Read and Interpret Poetry*, 3852

Doreski, William (jt. author). *How to Read and Interpret Poetry*, 3852

Dorner, Marjorie. *Family Closets*, 1985(F)

Dorris, Michael. *The Broken Cord*, 5181

A Yellow Raft in Blue Water, 452(F)

D'Orso, Michael (jt. author). *Somerset Homecoming*, 6517

Dorson, Richard M. *America in Legend*, 3436

American Folklore, 3437

Dorson, Richard M., ed. *Folktales Told Around the World*, 3364

Dos Passos, John. *Manhattan Transfer*, 396(F)

Doster, William C., ed. *Barron's How to Prepare for the College Level Examination Program, CLEP, General Examination*, 4657

Dostert, Pierre Etienne. *Africa*, 7348

Latin America, 7627

Dostoevsky, Fyodor. *The Brothers Karamazov*, 308(F)

Crime and Punishment, 309(F)

The Idiot, 310(F)

Dotto, Lydia. *Planet Earth in Jeopardy*, 4137

Dougan, Clark, et al. *The American Experience in Vietnam*, 8108

Douglas, Arthur. *Last Rights,* 1986(F)

Douglas, Auriel (jt. author). *Painless, Perfect Grammar,* 3951

Douglas, Carole Nelson. *Exiles of the Rynth,* 1101(F)
Heir of Rengarth, 2516(F)
Keepers of Edanvant, 1099(F)
Seven of Swords, 1100(F)
Six of Swords, 1101(F)

Douglas, Lloyd C. *The Big Fisherman,* 1367(F)
Magnificent Obsession, 1367(F)
The Robe, 1367(F)

Douglas, Paul. *The Handbook of Tennis,* 9967

Douglas, Paul Harding. *The Essential AIDS Fact Book,* 5182

Douglass, Frederick. *The Life and Times of Frederick Douglass,* 6501
Narrative of the Life of Frederick Douglass, an American Slave, 6585

Douglass, Jackie Leatherby. *Peterson First Guide to Shells of North America,* 8637

Dover, K. J., ed. *Ancient Greek Literature,* 3573

Dowie, Mark. *"We Have a Donor,"* 5164

Downer, Ann. *The Glass Salamander,* 1102(F)
The Spellkey, 1102(F)

Downer, John. *Supersense,* 8474

Downs, Robert B. *Books That Changed the World,* 3574

Doyle, Arthur Conan. *The Adventures of Sherlock Holmes,* 1987(F)
The Best Supernatural Tales of Arthur Conan Doyle, 1738(F)
The Case Book of Sherlock Holmes, 1987(F)
The Complete Sherlock Holmes, 1988(F)
Great Stories of Sherlock Holmes, 1989(F)
His Last Bow, 1990(F)
The Hound of the Baskervilles, 1991(F)
The Lost World & The Poison Belt, 2517(F)
The Memoirs of Sherlock Holmes, 1987(F)
The Return of Sherlock Holmes, 1987(F)
Sherlock Holmes, 363(F)
The Sign of the Four, 1992(F)
A Study in Scarlet, 1993(F)
Tales of Terror and Mystery, 1994(F)
When the World Screamed and Other Stories, 78(F)
The White Company, 1422(F)

Doyle, Paul A. *Pearl S. Buck,* 3715

Dozois, Gardner, ed. *The Year's Best Science Fiction,* 2518(F), 2519(F), 2520(F)

Dozois, Gardner (jt. author). *Bestiary!* 1084(F)

D'Ozraio, Leo (jt. author). *Opportunities in Health and Medical Careers,* 5007

Drabble, Margaret. *The Millstone,* 656(F)

Drabble, Margaret, ed. *The Oxford Companion to English Literature,* 3575

Dragonwagon, Crescent. *To Take a Dare,* 798(F)
The Year It Rained, 657(F)

Drake, David. *Bridgehead,* 2522(F)

The Sea Hag, 1103(F)

Drake, David, ed. *Bluebloods,* 2521(F)
The Eternal City, 2523(F)

Drake, David, ed. *The Fleet,* 2524(F)

Draper, Thomas, ed. *Human Rights,* 4297

Dravecky, Dave. *Comeback,* 6718

Dreiser, Theodore. *An American Tragedy,* 799(F)
Sister Carrie, 800(F)

Dreyfuss, Henry. *Symbol Sourcebook,* 3899

Drury, Allen. *Advise and Consent,* 959(F)

Drury, Neville. *Illustrated Dictionary of Natural Health,* 5074

Drury, Susan (jt. author). *Illustrated Dictionary of Natural Health,* 5074

Druyan, Ann (jt. author). *Comet,* 8333

Drysdale, Don. *Once a Bum, Always a Dodger,* 6719

Du Bois, W. E. B. *The Autobiography of W. E. B. Du Bois,* 6503
The Souls of Black Folk, 4360

du Boulay, Shirley. *Tutu,* 6800

Du Maurier, Daphne. *Daphne du Maurier's Classics of the Macabre,* 1739(F)
Echoes from the Macabre, 1740(F)
Frenchman's Creek, 1423(F)
Hungry Hill, 1995(F)
Jamaica Inn, 1423(F)
Mary Anne, 1423(F)
My Cousin Rachel, 1424(F)
Rebecca, 1995(F)
The Scapegoat, 1995(F)

Duane, Diane. *Doctor's Orders,* 2525(F)

Duberman, Martin Bauml. *Paul Robeson,* 6434

Dubois, Daniel (jt. author). *Indian Signs and Signals,* 7807

Dubos, Rene. *Beast or Angel?* 5531
Pasteur and Modern Science, 6698

DuBrovin, Vivian. *Guide to Alternative Education and Training,* 4791

Duckett, Eleanor Shipley. *Alfred the Great,* 6824

Dudley, William, ed. *America's Future,* 8058
Crime & Criminals, 4474
China, 7407
Genetic Engineering, 5260
Japan, 7447
Poverty, 4504
The Vietnam War, 8109

Duggan, William. *The Great Thirst,* 1384(F)

Duke, Michael S. *The Iron House,* 7408

Dukes, Paul. *A History of Europe 1648–1948,* 7036

Dukore, Jesse. *Long Distance Love,* 2261(F)

Dulles, Allen. *Great True Spy Stories,* 4138(F)

Dumas, Alexandre. *The Count of Monte Cristo,* 311(F)
The Man in the Iron Mask, 312(F)
The Three Musketeers, 313(F)
Twenty Years After, 313(F)

Dumas, Frederic (jt. author). *The Silent World*, 8888

Dunaway, David King. *How Can I Keep from Singing*, 6440

Dunbar, Paul Laurence. *The Complete Poems of Paul Laurence Dunbar*, 3261

Duncan, David Ewing. *From Cape to Cairo*, 7349
Pedaling to the Ends of the World, 7037

Duncan, David James. *The River Why*, 79(F)

Duncan, Jane Caryl. *Careers in Veterinary Medicine*, 4990

Duncan, Robert L. *In the Enemy Camp*, 80(F)

Dunkling, Leslie. *The Facts on File Dictionary of First Names*, 3916
Guinness Book of Names, 9492

Dunlap, Susan. *Too Close to the Edge*, 1996(F)

Dunn, Carola. *Two Corinthians*, 2262(F)

Dunn, Charles, J. *Everyday Life in Traditional Japan*, 7448

Dunne, Pete, et al. *Hawks in Flight*, 8559

Dunnett, Dorothy. *Checkmate*, 1425(F)
The Disorderly Knights, 1425(F)
The Game of Kings, 1425(F)
Pawn in Frankincense, 1425(F)
Queen's Play, 1425(F)
The Ringed Castle, 1425(F)

Dunning, Jennifer. *"But First a School"*, 5965

Dunning, Stephen, et al., eds. *Reflections on a Gift of Watermelon Pickle . . . and Other Modern Verse*, 3262

Dunphy, Jack. *The Murderous McLaughlins*, 545(F)

Dupont, Betty (jt. author). *Dance*, 5973

DuPont, Denise, ed. *Women of Vision*, 3716

Durand, Loup. *Daddy*, 81(F)

Durant, Ariel (jt. author). *The Age of Louis XIV*, 7129
The Age of Napoleon, 7143
The Age of Reason Begins, 7130
The Age of Voltaire, 7144
The Lessons of History, 7038
Rousseau and Revolution, 7145

Durant, Will. *The Age of Faith*, 7127
The Age of Louis XIV, 7129
The Age of Napoleon, 7143
The Age of Reason Begins, 7130
The Age of Voltaire, 7144
Caesar and Christ, 7101
The Lessons of History, 7038
The Life of Greece, 7101
Our Oriental Heritage, 7391
The Reformation, 7128
The Renaissance, 7547
Rousseau and Revolution, 7145
The Story of Philosophy, 4003

Durham, Michael S. *The Mid-Atlantic States*, 8164

Durrell, Gerald. *The Amateur Naturalist*, 8386
Birds, Beasts and Relatives, 8387
My Family & Other Animals, 8387

Durrell, Gerald (jt. author). *Ourselves and Other Animals*, 8482

Dürrenmatt, Friedrich. *The Visit*, 2998

Durso, Joseph (jt. author). *My Luke and I*, 6720

Durst, Paul. *The Florentine Table*, 1741(F)

Durán, Manuel. *Cervantes*, 3636

Dutton, Bertha P. *American Indians of the Southwest*, 7805

Dutton, Robert R. *Saul Bellow*, 3717

Dvorkin, David. *The Captains' Honor*, 2526(F)
The Seekers, 2527(F)
Timetrap, 2528(F)

Dworkin, Susan (jt. author). *The Ms. Guide to a Woman's Health*, 5345

Dwyer, Karen Kangas. *Easy Livin' Microwave Cooking*, 9332

Dychtwald, Ken. *Age Wave*, 5083

Dyer, Ceil. *Best Recipes from the Backs of Boxes, Bottles and Jars*, 9333
More Wok Cookery, 9334
Wok Cookery, 9334

Dyer, Gwynne. *War*, 7039

Dylan, Bob. *Lyrics, 1962–1985*, 5860

Eagan, Andrea Boroff. *Why Am I So Miserable If These Are the Best Years of My Life?* 5607

Eareckson, Joni. *Joni*, 6903

Earhart, Amelia. *The Fun of It*, 6138
Last Flight, 6139

Earhart, H. Byron. *Religions of Japan*, 4045

Earle, Sylvia A. *Exploring the Deep Frontier*, 8892

Eastman, John. *Retakes*, 6007

Eastman Kodak Company, eds. *The New Joy of Photography*, 9415

Easton, M. Coleman. *The Fisherman's Curse*, 1104(F)
Masters of Glass, 1104(F)

Easton, Patricia Harrison. *Rebel's Choice*, 2875(F)

Easton, Thomas A. *Careers in Science*, 5016

Easwaren, Eknath. *Gandhi the Man*, 6806

Eban, Abba. *Heritage*, 7040
My People, 7609

Ebenstein, William. *Today's Isms*, 4172

Eberhart, Mignon G. *Another Man's Murder*, 1997(F)
Nine O'Clock Tide, 1998(F)
Three Days for Emeralds, 1999(F)
Unidentified Woman, 1997(F)
Witness at Large, 1997(F)

Ebert, Roger. *Roger Ebert's Home Movie Companion*, 6008

Eberts, Marjorie. *Careers for Bookworms and Other Literary Types*, 4948
How to Prepare for College, 4729
Opportunities in Fast Food Careers, 4962

Ebisch, Glen. *Lou Dunlop*, 2000(F)

Eble, Kenneth. *F. Scott Fitzgerald*, 3718

Ebony, eds. *Ebony Pictorial History of Black Americans*, 4361

Eco, Umberto. *The Name of the Rose*, 1379(F)

Eddings, David. *Castle of Wizardry*, 1107(F)
Demon Lord of Karanda, 1105(F)
The Diamond Throne, 1106(F)
Enchanters' End Game, 1107(F)
Guardians of the West, 1108(F)
King of the Murgos, 1105(F)
Magician's Gambit, 1107(F)
The Pawn of Prophecy, 1107(F)
Queen of Sorcery, 1107(F)
Sorceress of Darshiva, 1109(F)

Edelfelt, Roy A. *Careers in Education*, 4949

Edelman, Bernard, ed. *Dear America*, 8110

Edelman, Marian Wright. *Families in Peril*, 5649

Edelson, Edward. *Drugs & the Brain*, 5113
Nutrition and the Brain, 5311

Edelstein, Andrew. *The Seventies*, 8059

Edelstein, Barbara. *The Woman Doctor's Diet for Teenage Girls*, 5412

Edelstein, Scott. *College*, 4730

Eden, Maxwell. *Kiteworks*, 9892

Edey, Maitland A. (jt. author). *Lucy*, 7001

Edgerton, Clyde. *Walking across Egypt*, 1879(F)

Edghill, Rosemary. *The Ill-Bred Bride*, 2263(F)

Edmonds, Margot. *Voices of the Wind*, 3422

Edmonds, Walter D. *The South African Quirt*, 546(F)

Edmunds, R. David. *Tecumseh and the Quest for Indian Leadership*, 6639

Edney, Andrew. *The Practical Guide to Dog and Puppy Care*, 8717

Edwards, E. W. *Exploring Careers Using Foreign Languages*, 4831

Edwards, Elwyn Hartley, ed. *The Complete Horse Book*, 8762

Edwards, I. E. S. *The Pyramids of Egypt*, 7097

Edwards, Julia. *Women of the World*, 3984

Edwards, Sally. *Triathlon*, 9560

Edwards, Ted. *Fight the Wild Island*, 7551

Egan, Doris. *The Gate of Ivory*, 2529(F)

Egan, Sam (jt. author). *Imagine*, 6417

Egbert, Barbara. *Action Cheerleading*, 9561
Cheerleading and Songleading, 9562

Eggenberger, David. *An Encyclopedia of Battles*, 7041

Eggleston, Edward. *Hoosier Schoolmaster*, 1492(F)

Ehle, John. *Trail of Tears*, 7806

Ehrenhaft, George. *Write Your Way into College*, 4731

Ehrhart, W. D., ed. *Carrying the Darkness*, 397

Ehrlich, Anne H. (jt. author). *Extinction*, 8572
The Population Explosion, 4458

Ehrlich, Eugene. *Amo, Amas, Amat and More*, 3917

Mene, Mene, Tekel, 4099

The Oxford Illustrated Literary Guide to the United States, 3576

Ehrlich, Paul R. *Extinction*, 8572
The Population Explosion, 4458

Ehrlich, Paul R., et al. *The Birder's Handbook*, 8535

Eicher, David. *The Universe from Your Backyard*, 8258

Einstein, Albert. *The Meaning of Relativity*, 8907

Einstein, Charles, ed. *The Fireside Book of Baseball*, 9640

Eiseley, Loren. *Darwin's Century*, 6995

Eisen, Jonathan, ed. *The Nobel Reader*, 2910

Eisenberg, Deborah. *Transactions in a Foreign Currency*, 801(F)

Eisenberg, Dennis, et al. *The Mossad*, 7610

Eisenhower, Dwight D. *The Eisenhower Diaries*, 6528

Eisenhower, John S. D. *So Far from God*, 7867

Eisenstadt, Jill. *From Rockaway*, 802(F)

Eisenstein, Phyllis. *The Sorcerer's Son*, 1110(F)

Ekiguchi, Kunio. *A Japanese Touch for the Seasons*, 7449

Eklund, Gordon (jt. author). *If the Stars Are Gods*, 2408(F)

El Cid Campeador. *The Poem of the Cid*, 3181

Elbow, Peter. *Writing with Power*, 3959

Elder, John (jt. author). *The Norton Book of Nature Writing*, 8389

Eldredge, Niles. *Life Pulse*, 6980
The Monkey Business, 6996

Eldridge, Larry (jt. author). *25 Years*, 9840

Elia, Irene. *The Female Animal*, 8388

Eliach, Yaffa, ed. *Hasidic Tales of the Holocaust*, 1650(F)

Elias, Jay (jt. author). *Bowling*, 9779

Elias, Thomas S. *The Complete Trees of North America*, 8425

Eliot, Alexander, et al. *The Universal Myths*, 3453

Eliot, George. *The Mill on the Floss*, 364(F)
Silas Marner, 365(F)

Eliot, Marc. *Rockonomics*, 5861

Eliot, T. S. *Collected Poems, 1909–1962*, 3199
The Complete Poems and Plays of T. S. Eliot, 1909–1950, 3028
Murder in the Cathedral, 3029
Old Possum's Book of Practical Cats, 3200
The Waste Land, and Other Poems, 3201

Elkington, John, et al. *The Green Consumer*, 4426

Elkins, Aaron J. *Murder in the Queen's Armes*, 2001(F)

Ellington, Duke. *Music Is My Mistress*, 6388

Elliot, Elizabeth. *Through Gates of Splendor*, 4047

Elliot, James. *Rings*, 8343

Elliott, Emory, et al., eds. *Columbia Literary History of the United States*, 3577

Elliott, Jannean (jt. author). *Shadow World,* 2497(F)

Elliott, Martha J. H. (jt. author). *The Constitution,* 4189

Ellis, Bret Easton. *Less Than Zero,* 803(F)

Ellis, Carol. *A Kiss for Good Luck,* 2264(F)

Ellis, Richard. *The Book of Whales,* 8645
Dolphins and Porpoises, 8646

Ellison, Harlan. *Deathbird Stories,* 1742(F)
Ellison Wonderland, 2530(F)

Ellison, Ralph. *Invisible Man,* 453(F)

Ellmann, Richard, ed. *The New Oxford Book of American Verse,* 3263
The Norton Anthology of Modern Poetry, 3157

Elman, Robert. *The Hiker's Bible,* 9793

Elsman, Max. *How to Get Your First Job,* 4792

Elson, Robert T. *Prelude to War,* 7167

Elster, Charles Harrington. *Is There a Cow in Moscow?* 3918
There Is No Zoo in Zoology, 3918

Elting, John R. *Battles for Scandinavia,* 7203

Emanuel, James A. *Langston Hughes,* 3578

Embery, Joan. *My Wild World,* 6663

Emecheta, Buchi. *The Bride Price,* 960(F)

Emerson, Everett, ed. *Major Writers of Early American Literature,* 3579

Emerson, Mark (jt. author). *Meryl Streep,* 6447

Emerson, Ralph Waldo. *Emerson's Essays,* 3531
Essays, First and Second Series, 3532
The Portable Emerson, 3533

Emmens, Carol A. *The Abortion Controversy,* 5508

Emmens, Cliff W. *A Step-by-Step Book about Tropical Fish,* 8751

Emrich, Duncan, ed. *American Folk Poetry,* 3264

Ende, Michael. *Momo,* 1111(F)
The Neverending Story, 1112(F)

Engdahl, Sylvia Louise. *Enchantress from the Stars,* 2531(F)
The Far Side of Evil, 2532(F)

Engel, Beverly. *The Right to Innocence,* 5509

Engel, Joe. *Addicted,* 5114

Engelbrektson, Sune. *Stars, Planets and Galaxies,* 8352

Engh, M. J. *Wheel of the Winds,* 2533(F)

Englander, Roger. *Opera,* 5914

Engler, Nick (jt. author). *Projects for the Router,* 9269

Engstrom, Elizabeth. *Black Ambrosia,* 1743(F)

Ephron, Delia. *How to Eat Like a Child,* 3495
Teenage Romance, 5558

Epstein, Helen. *Children of the Holocaust,* 7204
Music Talks, 5819

Epstein, Lawrence. *Careers in Computer Sales,* 4910

Epstein, Leslie. *King of the Jews,* 6961

Epstein, Rachel. *Alternative Investments,* 4587
Careers in Health Care, 4991
Careers in the Investment World, 4911
Investment Banking, 4598
Investments & the Law, 4563

Epstein, Samuel S., et al. *Hazardous Waste in America,* 4452

Erdoes, Richard (jt. author). *Lakota Woman,* 6500
Lame Deer, Seeker of Visions, 6515

Erdoes, Richard, ed. *American Indian Myths and Legends,* 3423

Erdrich, Louise. *The Beet Queen,* 454(F)
Love Medicine, 454(F)
Tracks, 454(F)

Erickson, Brad, ed. *Call to Action,* 4413

Erickson, Carolly. *Bloody Mary,* 6835
Bonnie Prince Charlie, 6835
The First Elizabeth, 6835
Mistress Anne, 6829

Erickson, Jon. *Build Your Own Kit House,* 9274
Exploring Earth from Space, 8337
The Mysterious Oceans, 8876
Violent Storms, 8867
Volcanoes and Earthquakes, 8801

Erickson, Mary Anne. *Knitting by Design,* 9238

Erikson, Erik H. *Gandhi's Truth,* 4406

Ermarth, Elizabeth Deeds. *George Eliot,* 3661

Erskine, Albert (jt. author). *Short Story Masterpieces,* 2971(F)

Eschmeyer, William N. *A Field Guide to Pacific Coast Fishes of North America,* 8624

Eshleman, Ruthe, comp. *The American Heart Association Cookbook,* 9335

Eskenazi, Gerald (jt. author). *Yaz,* 6736

Eskow, Dennis. *Laser Careers,* 4992

Espeland, Pamela (jt. author). *Different Like Me,* 5139

Esper, George. *The Eyewitness History of the Vietnam War: 1961–1975,* 8111

Esslin, Martin. *An Anatomy of Drama,* 3797

Estes, Rose. *Brother to the Lion,* 1113(F)

Estleman, Loren D. *Sherlock Holmes vs. Dracula,* 1744(F)

Etchison, Dennis, ed. *Masters of Darkness,* 1745(F), 1746(F)
Masters of Darkness II, 1746(F)

Ettinger, Blanche. *Opportunities in Office Occupations,* 4912

Eubank, Keith (jt. author). *A Survey of Historic Costume,* 5290

Evans, Christopher. *The Micro Millenium,* 8972

Evans, Christopher, ed. *Understanding Yourself,* 5532

Evans, Elizabeth. *Thomas Wolfe,* 3719

Evans, Hilary (jt. author). *Phenomenon,* 9532

Evans, Howard Ensign. *Australia, a Natural History,* 7469
The Pleasures of Entomology, 8594

Evans, Jeremy. *The Complete Guide to Short Board Sailing*, 9954

Evans, Marilyn. *Opportunities in Property Management Careers*, 4913

Evans, Mary Alice (jt. author). *Australia, a Natural History*, 7469

Evans, Peter. *Ourselves and Other Animals*, 8482

Evans, Peter G. *The Natural History of Whales and Dolphins*, 8647

Evans, Roger. *How to Play Guitar*, 5935
How to Read Music, 5820

Evans, Sara M. *Born for Liberty*, 7733

Evans, Walker (jt. author). *Let Us Now Praise Famous Men*, 8023

Evarts, Hal G. *Jay-Jay and the Peking Monster*, 2002(F)

Everett, Melissa. *Breaking Ranks*, 4520

Everson, William K. *American Silent Film*, 6009

Every, George. *Christian Legends*, 4100

Evslin, Bernard. *The Adventures of Ulysses*, 3472
The Greek Gods, 3473
Heroes and Monsters of Greek Myth, 3473
Heroes, Gods and Monsters of Greek Myths, 3474
The Trojan War, 3475

Ewald, Dan (jt. author). *Sparky!* 6713

Ewen, David. *Composers of Tomorrow's Music*, 6172

Ewen, David (jt. author). *The Milton Cross New Encyclopedia of the Great Composers and Their Music*, 6170

Ewing, Elizabeth. *History of Twentieth Century Fashion*, 5278

Ewing, William A. *America Worked*, 8060

Eyman, Scott (jt. author). *Flashback*, 6014

Fadiman, Clifton, ed. *Living Philosophies*, 4004

Fagan, Brian M. *The Aztecs*, 7643
The Great Journey, 7016
New Treasures of the Past, 7017

Fagan, George V. *The Air Force Academy*, 4283

Fage, J. D. (jt. author). *A Short History of Africa*, 7357

Fahey, Thomas D. *Basic Weight Training*, 9770

Fair, Erik. *Right Stuff for New Hang Glider Pilots*, 9612

Fairbank, John King. *The Great Chinese Revolution*, 7409
The United States and China, 4139

Fairley, John. *Arthur C. Clarke's World of Strange Powers*, 9493

Falcone, Vincent J. *Great Thinkers, Great Ideas*, 4005

Falk, Signi. *Tennessee Williams*, 3836

Falkner, David. *The Nine Sides of the Diamond*, 9641

Falls, Joe. *The Detroit Tigers*, 9642

Family Circle, eds. *The Best of Family Circle Cookbook*, 9336

Fancher, Raymond E. *The Intelligence Men*, 5587
Pioneers of Psychology, 5533

Fanning, Beverly J. *Workfare vs. Welfare*, 4505

Fanning, Odom. *Opportunities in Environmental Careers*, 4963

Fanning, Robbie (jt. author). *The Busy Woman's Sewing Book*, 9260

Faraday, Ann. *The Dream Game*, 5534

Faraday, Michael. *Faraday's Chemical History of a Candle*, 8783

Farago, Ladislas. *Patton*, 6608

Farber, Norma. *Mercy Short*, 1515(F)

Farish, Terry. *Shelter for a Seabird*, 804(F)

Farm Journal, eds. *Farm Journal's Country Cookbook*, 9337

Farmer, James. *Lay Bare the Heart*, 6505

Farmer, Philip Jose. *A Barnstormer in Oz*, 1114(F)
The Dark Design, 2537(F)
Dayworld, 2534(F)
Dayworld Breakup, 2534(F)
Dayworld Rebel, 2534(F)
Gods of Riverworld, 2535(F)
The Grand Adventure, 2536(F)
The Lavalite World, 1115(F)
The Magic Labyrinth, 2537(F)
To Your Scattered Bodies Go, 2537(F)

Farndon, John. *Creating Special Effects*, 9416
How to Catch the Action, 9416
Making Color Work for You, 9416
Mastering Color Photography, 9416

Farrand, John. *Eastern Birds*, 8536
How to Identify Birds, 8536
Western Birds, 8536

Farrar, Ronald T. *College 101*, 4732

Farrara, Frank (jt. author). *How to Pay for College or Trade School*, 4781

Farrell, Kate (jt. author). *Sleeping on the Wing*, 3169

Farrell, Suzanne. *Holding on to the Air*, 6389

Farrelly, Peter. *Outside Providence*, 805(F)

Farris, John. *The Uninvited*, 2003(F)

Farwell, Byron. *Ball's Bluff*, 7912

Fassi, Carlo. *Figure Skating with Carlo Fassi*, 9889

Fast, Howard. *April Morning*, 1521(F)
Citizen Tom Paine, 1602(F)
Freedom Road, 1602(F)
The Immigrants, 1522(F)
Spartacus, 1368(F)
Time and the Riddle, 2911(F)

Fast, Julius. *Body Language*, 3900
What Should We Do about Davey? 806(F)

Faucher, Elizabeth. *Surviving*, 658(F)

Faulkner, Harold Underwood. *From Versailles to the New Deal*, 8028
Politics, Reform and Expansion, 1890–1900, 8008

Faulkner, William. *Absalom, Absalom!* 1603(F)
As I Lay Dying, 547(F)
Collected Stories of William Faulkner, 2912(F)
Intruder in the Dust, 455(F)
Light in August, 456(F)
The Reivers, 82(F)
Selected Short Stories of William Faulkner, 2913(F)
The Sound and the Fury, 548
Uncollected Stories of William Faulkner, 2914(F)
Faux, Marian. *Roe v. Wade*, 4238
Fawcett, Bill (jt. author). *The Fleet*, 2524(F)
Feather, Leonard. *The Encyclopedia of Jazz*, 5862
The Encyclopedia of Jazz in the Seventies, 5862
The Encyclopedia of Jazz in the Sixties, 5862
From Satchmo to Miles, 6173
Featherstone, Bonnie D. (jt. author). *College Comes Sooner Than You Think!* 4757
Feder, Happy Jack. *Clown Skits for Everyone*, 5978
Feegel, John R. *Not a Stranger*, 2004(F)
Feelings, Tom (jt. author). *Now Sheba Sings the Song*, 3875
Feigen, Roberta (jt. author). *Life after High School*, 4801
Feinberg, Barbara Silberdick. *Marx and Marxism*, 6859
Watergate, 8061
Feinsilber, Mike (jt. author). *Grand Allusions*, 3953
Feinstein, John. *Forever's Team*, 9718
A Season Inside, 9719
Feirtag, Michael (jt. author). *Astronomy of the Ancients*, 8248
Feis, Herbert. *The Road to Pearl Harbor*, 7205
Feist, Raymond E. *A Darkness at Sethanon*, 1116(F)
Magician, 1118(F)
Prince of the Blood, 1117(F)
Silverthorn, 1118(F)
Felder, Leonard (jt. author). *Making Peace with Your Parents*, 5638
Feldman, David. *Imponderables*, 9495
When Do Fish Sleep? 9494 9496
Why Do Clocks Run Clockwise? and Other Imponderables, 9495
Why Do Dogs Have Wet Noses? 9496
Feldman, Edmund Burke. *Varieties of Visual Experience*, 5683
Felice, Cynthia. *Water Witch*, 2538(F)
Felice, Cynthia (jt. author). *Light Raid*, 2846(F)
Water Witch, 2846(F)
Felix, Warner. *Johann Sebastian Bach*, 6336
Felknor, Bruce L. *How to Look Things Up and Find Things Out*, 4645
Felleman, Hazel, ed. *Poems That Live Forever*, 3158

Feminist Press Staff. *Out of the Bleachers*, 9563
Fenollosa, Ernest (jt. author). *The Classic Noh Theatre of Japan*, 3145
Fenten, D. X. *Ms. Architect*, 4940
Fenton, Erfert. *Canned Art*, 8973
Fenton, M. Brock. *Just Bats*, 8525
Ferber, Edna. *Cimarron*, 1565(F)
Ice Palace, 1604(F)
Saratoga Trunk, 1565(F)
Show Boat, 1604(F)
So Big, 1604(F)
Ferguson, Donald (jt. author). *Opportunities in Journalism Careers*, 4860
Fergusson, Francis. *The Idea of a Theater*, 3798
Ferlazzo, Paul J. *Emily Dickinson*, 3883
Ferlinghetti, Lawrence. *Endless Life*, 3265
Ferman, Edward L., ed. *The Best from Fantasy and Science Fiction*, 2539(F)
The Best Horror Stories from the Magazine of Fantasy and Science Fiction, 1747(F)
Ferrell, Keith. *Ernest Hemingway*, 6260
George Orwell, 6293
Ferrell, Robert H. *Truman*, 6567
Woodrow Wilson and World War I, 1917–1921, 7156
Ferri, Elisa. *Finger Tips*, 5279
Ferrier, Jean-Louis, ed. *Art of Our Century*, 5738
Ferris, Jean. *Across the Grain*, 807(F)
Invincible Summer, 659(F)
Ferris, Timothy. *The Red Limit*, 8364
Spaceshots, 8301
Ferry, Charles. *One More Time!* 1651(F)
Raspberry One, 1652(F)
Fest, Joachim. *Hitler*, 6845
Festa-McCormick, Diana. *Honoré de Balzac*, 3637
Fettner, Ann Giudici. *Viruses*, 5183
Feuer, Elizabeth. *Paper Doll*, 660(F)
Feynman, Richard. *Surely You're Joking, Mr. Feynman!* 6665
"What Do You Care What Other People Think?" 6665
Fichter, George S. *Fishing*, 9827
Insect Pests, 8595
Fiedler, Hal (jt. author). *Be Smart about Sex*, 5461
Fiedler, Jean. *Be Smart about Sex*, 5461
Field, George. *The Space Telescope*, 8259
Field, George Wallis. *Hermann Hesse*, 3638
Field, Shelly. *Career Opportunities in Advertising & Public Relations*, 4914
Career Opportunities in the Music Industry, 4878
Fielding, Henry. *Tom Jones*, 366(F)
Fielding, Joy. *Kiss Mommy Goodbye*, 2005(F)
Fields, Jeff. *A Cry of Angels*, 457(F)
Fields, Ronald J. *W. C. Fields*, 6390
Fife, Bruce. *Dr. Dropo's Balloon Sculpturing for Beginners*, 9143

Fife, Bruce, et al. *Creative Clowning*, 5979

Fiffer, Steve. *How to Watch Baseball*, 9643

Figler, Howard. *The Complete Job-Search Handbook*, 4793

Figler, Howard (jt. author). *The Athlete's Game Plan for College and Career*, 9564

Figler, Stephen. *The Athlete's Game Plan for College and Career*, 9564

Filisky, Michael. *Peterson First Guide to Fishes of North America*, 8625

Finch, Christopher. *The Art of Walt Disney*, 5793

Finch, Phillip. *In a Place Dark and Secret*, 2006(F)

Trespass, 83(F)

Finch, Robert, ed. *The Norton Book of Nature Writing*, 8389

Fincher, E. B. *The Vietnam War*, 8112

Fincher, J. *Lefties*, 5312

Fine, Elsa Honig. *The Afro-American Artist*, 5794

Fine, Janet. *Opportunities in Teaching*, 4950

Fine, John V. A. *The Ancient Greeks*, 7102

Fink, Ida. *A Scrap of Time*, 1653(F)

Finkelstein, Dave. *Greater Nowheres*, 6117

Finler, Joel W. *The Hollywood Story*, 6010

Finn, Jeffrey. *Medical Ethics*, 5235

Finnegan, William. *Crossing the Line*, 7371

Finney, Jack. *About Time*, 2540(F)

Finnigan, Dave. *The Complete Juggler*, 9299

Fins, Alice. *Opportunities in Paralegal Careers*, 4964

Fiorito, Len (jt. author). *Aaron to Zuverink*, 9679

Fireside, Bryna J. *Choices*, 4794

Fisch, Max H., ed. *Classic American Philosophers*, 4006

Fischer, Ernst. *Thinking about Science*, 6658

Fischer, John F. (jt. author). *Secrets of the Supernatural*, 9520

Fischer, Louis. *Gandhi*, 6808

The Rights of Students and Teachers, 4298

Fischer, Louis, ed. *The Essential Gandhi*, 6807

Fischler, Shirley (jt. author). *Everybody's Hockey Book*, 9886

Fischler, Stan. *Everybody's Hockey Book*, 9886

Fishbein, Seymour L. *Yellowstone Country*, 8199

Fisher, David (jt. author). *The Fall of the Roman Umpire*, 9674

Kristallnacht, 7277

Remembrance of Swings Past, 9674, 9675

Strike Two, 9674

The Umpire Strikes Back, 9674

Fisher, David (jt. author). *What's What*, 3921

Fisher, David E. *The Birth of the Earth*, 8338

Hostage One, 84(F)

Fisher, Glen (jt. author). *Commodore 64 Fun and Games*, 8986

Fisher, John. *Body Magic*, 9395

Fisher, Paul R. *The Ash Staff*, 1119(F)

The Hawks of Fellheath, 1119(F)

Mont Cant Gold, 1120(F)

The Princess and the Thorn, 1120(F)

Fisher, Trevor. *The 1960s*, 7333

Fishman, Ross. *Alcohol and Alcoholism*, 5115

Fiske, Edward B. *The Best Buys in College Education*, 4736

Fiske, Edward B., et al. *The Fiske Guide to Colleges*, 4733

How to Get into the Right College, 4734

Selective Guide to Colleges, 4735

Fitts, Dudley, ed. *Four Greek Plays*, 2999

Fitz-Randolph, Jane (jt. author). *From Quarks to Quasars*, 8369

RAMS, ROMS & Robots, 8988

Fitzgerald, F. Scott. *The Great Gatsby*, 1605(F)

The Stories of F. Scott Fitzgerald, 2915(F)

Tender Is the Night, 1606(F)

This Side of Paradise, 1607(F)

FitzGerald, Frances. *Fire in the Lake*, 8113

Fitzgerald, Sarah. *International Wildlife Trade*, 8573

Fitzgibbon, Dan (jt. author). *Manners That Matter*, 5580

Fitzharris, Tim. *Canada*, 7634

FitzSimons, Raymond. *Death and the Magician*, 6408

Fixx, James F. *The Complete Book of Running*, 9909

Games for the Superintelligent, 8851

Jim Fixx's Second Book of Running, 9909

More Games for the Superintelligent, 8851

Fixx, James F., et al. *Maximum Sports Performance*, 9565

Fjermedal, Grant. *New Horizons in Amateur Astronomy*, 8260

Flach, Frederic F. *Rickie*, 5379

Flammang, James. *The Great Book of Dream Cars*, 9090

Flanagan, Bill. *Written in My Soul*, 5863

Flanagan, Dennis. *Flanagan's Version*, 8218

Flandermeyer, Kenneth L. *Clear Skin*, 5335

Flanigan, Sara. *Alice*, 661(F)

Flaubert, Gustave. *Madame Bovary*, 314(F)

Flegg, Jim, et al. *Poles Apart*, 7694

Fleming, Alice. *What to Say When You Don't Know What to Say*, 4676

Fleming, G. H. *The Unforgettable Season*, 9644

Fleming, Gerald. *Hitler and the Final Solution*, 7206

Fleming, Thomas (jt. author). *The Conservative Movement*, 4265

Flesch, Rudolf. *The Art of Clear Thinking*, 5588

How to Write, Speak, and Think More Effectively, 4677

Why Johnny Still Can't Read, 4625

Fletcher, Colin. *The Complete Walker III*, 9794

The Man Who Walked through Time, 8390

The Secret Worlds of Colin Fletcher, 8390

Fletcher, Jessica. *Gin and Daggers*, 2007(F)

Fletcher, Lucille. *Mirror Image*, 2008(F)

Fletcher, Walter. *Dogs of the World*, 8718

Fletcher, William. *Recording Your Family History*, 5650

Flexner, James Thomas. *America's Old Masters*, 6174

Flinn, Denny Martin. *What They Did for Love*, 5915

Flint, Kenneth C. *Cromm*, 1121(F)
The Dark Druid, 1122(F)

Flodin, Mickey (jt. author). *The Perigee Visual Dictionary of Signing*, 5431
The Pocket Dictionary of Signing, 5431

Flower, Joe (jt. author). *Age Wave*, 5083

Flower, John (jt. author). *Literary Landscape of the British Isles*, 3660

Floyd, E. Randall. *Great Southern Mysteries*, 9497

Floyd, Virginia. *The Plays of Eugene O'Neill*, 3837

Fluegelman, Andrew. *More New Games!* 9566

Foehr, Donna. *Football for Women and Men Who Want to Learn the Game*, 9842

Fogle, Bruce. *Games Pets Play*, 8671

Folbre, Nancy. *A Field Guide to the U.S. Economy*, 4564

Follett, Ken. *Eye of the Needle*, 85(F)
Key to Rebecca, 86(F)
The Man from St. Petersburg, 86(F)
On the Wings of Eagles, 86(F)
The Pillars of the Earth, 1380(F)
Triple, 86(F)

Folse, Nancy McCarthy. *Careers in the Fashion Industry*, 4832

Foner, Eric. *A House Divided*, 7913

Fonseca, Donald R. (jt. author). *College*, 4748

Fontana, Vincent J. *Somewhere a Child Is Crying*, 5651

Foote-Smith, Elizabeth. *Opportunities in Writing Careers*, 4833

Forbes, Colin. *Avalanche Express*, 87(F)

Forbes, Esther. *Paul Revere & the World He Lived In*, 6609

Forbes, Kathryn. *Mama's Bank Account*, 1623(F)

Forbes, Malcolm. *What a Way to Go*, 9498

Ford, Boris, ed. *The New Pelican Guide to English Literature*, 3580

Ford, Charlotte. *Etiquette*, 5582

Forde, Terry. *Fun-to-Make Wooden Toys*, 9261

Forecki, Marcia Calhoun. *Speak to Me*, 5434

Foreign Policy Association, eds. *Cartoon History of United States Foreign Policy, 1776–1976*, 4140

Forester, C. S. *Admiral Hornblower in the West Indies*, 1427(F)
The African Queen, 88(F)
Beat to Quarters, 1426(F)

Lieutenant Hornblower, 1427(F)
Lord Hornblower, 1427(F)
Mr. Midshipman Hornblower, 1427(F)

Forkner, Benjamin, ed. *A Modern Southern Reader*, 2916
Stories of the Modern South, 2917(F)

Forman, Jack Jacob. *Presenting Paul Zindel*, 6333

Forman, Werner (jt. author). *The Eskimos*, 7693
The Indians of the Great Plains, 7791
People of the Totem, 7792

Forshay-Lunsford, Cin. *Walk through Cold Fire*, 808(F)

Forster, Arnold. *Square One*, 6506

Forster, E. M. *A Passage to India*, 1392(F)
A Room with a View, 809(F)

Forster, Margaret. *Elizabeth Barrett Browning*, 6224
Significant Sisters, 6784

Forsyth, Adrian. *Mammals of the American North*, 8491

Forsyth, Elizabeth H. (jt. author). *AIDS*, 5191
Terrorism, 4546

Forsyth, Frederick. *The Day of the Jackal*, 89(F)
The Devil's Alternative, 90(F)
The Dogs of War, 91(F)
The Negotiator, 92(F)
The Odessa File, 93(F)
The Shepherd, 1634(F)

Fortunato, Pat (jt. author). *The Official Kids' Survival Kit*, 5602

Forward, Robert L. *Dragon's Egg*, 2541(F), 2542(F)
Future Magic, 8391
Starquake, 2542(F)

Foss, Michael, ed. *Poetry of the World Wars*, 3159

Fossey, Dian. *Gorillas in the Mist*, 8497

Foster, Alan Dean. *Cyber Way*, 2543(F)
The Day of the Dissonance, 1123(F)
The Deluge Drivers, 2544(F)
For Love of Mother-Not, 2545(F)
The Hour of the Gate, 1123(F)
Icerigger, 2544(F)
Into the Out Of, 1748(F)
Mission to Moulokin, 2544(F)
The Moment of the Magician, 1123(F)
Nor Crystal Tears, 2545(F)
Orphan Star, 2545(F)
Quozl, 2546(F)
Spellsinger, 1123(F)
Splinter of the Mind's Eye, 2547(F)
Star Trek—Log One, 2548(F)
The Tar-Aiym Krang, 2545(F)
To the Vanishing Point, 2549(F)

Foster, Catharine Osgood. *The Organic Gardener*, 9378

Foster, David William, ed. *Modern Latin American Literature*, 3581

Foster, John, comp. *Let's Celebrate*, 3160
Foster, R. F., ed. *The Oxford Illustrated History of Ireland*, 7515
Foster, Robert. *The Complete Guide to Middle-Earth*, 3662
Foster, Rory C. *Dr. Wildlife*, 6906
I Never Met an Animal I Didn't Like, 6906
Foster, Virginia Ramos (jt. author). *Modern Latin American Literature*, 3581
Fowler, Alastair. *A History of English Literature*, 3582
Fowler, Christopher. *Roofworld*, 1749(F)
Fowler, Elizabeth. *The New York Times Career Planner*, 4834
Fowler, Gene. *Good Night, Sweet Prince*, 6367
Fowler, Karen Joy. *Artificial Things*, 2550(F)
Fowler, William M. *Under Two Flags*, 7914
Fowles, John. *The Collector*, 94(F)
The French Lieutenant's Woman, 1428(F)
The Magus, 1750(F)
Fox, Jack C. *The Illustrated History of the Indianapolis 500*, 9614
Fox, Levi, ed. *The Shakespeare Handbook*, 3817
Fox, Nancy Jo. *Liberties with Liberty*, 8165
Fox, Roy. *Technology*, 8943
Fox, Stephen R. *John Muir and His Legacy*, 6695
Fox, Ted. *In the Groove*, 5984
Foyt, A. J. *A. J.*, 6711
Fralin, Frances, ed. *The Indelible Image*, 5717
France, Peter. *An Encyclopedia of Bible Animals*, 4101
Frances, Phil (jt. author). *Fishing*, 9827
Francis, Dick. *Banker*, 2016(F)
Bolt, 2009(F)
Break In, 2010(F)
The Danger, 2011(F)
The Edge, 2012(F)
Enquiry, 2010(F)
High Stakes, 2011(F)
Hot Money, 2013(F)
In the Frame, 2016(F)
Longshot, 2014(F)
Proof, 2018(F)
Risk, 2018(F)
Slayride, 2011(F)
Straight, 2015(F)
Trial Run, 2016(F)
Twice Shy, 2017(F)
Whip Hand, 2018(F)
Francis, Dorothy B. *Shoplifting*, 4475
Vandalism, 4476
Francis, Peter. *Images of Earth*, 8795
Franck, Irene M. *Artists and Artisans*, 5684
Builders, 4941
Clothiers, 5280
Communicators, 3919
Financiers and Traders, 4915
Harvesters, 8582
Healers, 5236
Helpers and Aides, 4965
Leaders and Lawyers, 4966
Manufacturers and Miners, 8944
Performers and Players, 5955
Restaurateurs & Innkeepers, 4795
Scholars and Priests, 4626
Scientists and Technologists, 8219
The Silk Road, 7042
Warriors & Adventurers, 6971
Francke, Linda Bird. *The Ambivalence of Abortion*, 5462
Francome, Colin. *Juggling for All*, 9300
Frane, Jeff. *Fritz Leiber*, 3663
Frank, Agnes. *Quilting for Beginners*, 9239
Frank, Anne. *Anne Frank's Tales from the Secret Annex*, 1654
The Diary of a Young Girl, 6840
The Diary of Anne Frank, 6839
Frank, Elizabeth Bales. *Cooder Cutlas*, 810(F)
Frank, Katherine. *A Voyager Out*, 6679
Frank, Pat. *Alas, Babylon*, 2551(F)
Frank, Stanley D. *Remember Everything You Read*, 4646
Frankel, Haskel (jt. author). *Respect for Acting*, 6088
Frankel, Marvin E. *Out of the Shadows of Night*, 4299
Franklin, Benjamin. *The Autobiography of Benjamin Franklin*, 6587
Writings, 7839
Franklin, H. Bruce. *Robert A. Heinlein*, 3720
Franklin, John Hope. *From Slavery to Freedom*, 4362
Reconstruction, 8009
Franklin, John Hope, ed. *Black Leaders of the Nineteenth Century*, 6469
Black Leaders of the Twentieth Century, 6469
Franklin, Jon. *Molecules of the Mind*, 5313
Writing for Story, 3960
Franklin, Miles. *The End of My Career*, 811(F)
My Brilliant Career, 811(F)
Franzel, Dave. *Sailing*, 9925
Franzen, Bill. *Hearing from Wayne and Other Stories*, 1880(F)
Fraser, Antonia. *Cromwell*, 6834
Mary, Queen of Scots, 6862
The Warrior Queens, 6785
The Weaker Vessel, 7516
Fraser, Bryna Shore (jt. author). *Getting a Job in the Computer Age*, 5041
Fraser, George MacDonald. *The Hollywood History of the World*, 6011
Fraser, Laura, et al. *The Animal Rights Handbook*, 8574
Fraser, Nicholas. *Eva Peron*, 6883
Fraser, Rebecca. *The Brontes*, 6219
Frassanito, William A. *Grant and Lee*, 7915
Frazer, James George. *The Golden Bough*, 4048

Frazier, Kendrick. *Solar Systems*, 8344

Frazier, Walt. *Walt Frazier*, 6744

Frederick, Guy. *One-Hundred-One Best Magic Tricks*, 9396

Frederickson, Keville. *Opportunities in Nursing Careers*, 4993

Frederikse, Julie. *South Africa*, 7372

Freedman, Alan. *The Computer Glossary for Everyone*, 8974

Freedman, Benedict. *Mrs. Mike*, 95(F)

Freedman, Lawrence. *Atlas of Global Strategy*, 4141

Freedman, Nancy (jt. author). *Mrs. Mike*, 95(F)

Freedman, Russell. *Can Bears Predict Earthquakes?* 8475

How Animals Defend Their Young, 8484

Freedman, Samuel G. *Small Victories*, 4627

Freeman, Derek. *Margaret Mead and Samoa*, 6997

Freeman, John W. *The Metropolitan Opera Stories of the Great Operas*, 5916

Freeman, Kerry A., ed. *Chilton's Easy Car Care*, 9091

Chilton's Guide to Auto Tune-Ups and Troubleshooting, 9092

Freeman, Mary E. Wilkins. *Pembroke*, 1608(F)

Freeman-Grenville, G. S. P. *Chronology of World History*, 7043

Freemantle, Brian. *CIA*, 4219

Freiberger, Paul. *Fire in the Valley*, 8975

Freidel, Frank. *Franklin D. Roosevelt*, 6562

French, Michael. *Lifeguards Only beyond This Point*, 2265(F)

Soldier Boy, 96(F)

The Throwing Season, 2876(F)

French, Thomas E. *Mechanical Drawing*, 8945

French, Warren. *J. D. Salinger, Revisited*, 6299

John Steinbeck, 3721

Frenkel, Karen A. (jt. author). *Robots, Machines in Man's Image*, 8958

Freuchen, Peter. *Book of the Eskimos*, 7695

Freud, Sigmund. *The Basic Writings of Sigmund Freud*, 5535

Frey, Richard. *According to Hoyle*, 9807

Fricke, Aaron. *Reflections of a Rock Lobster*, 5463

Friday, Nancy. *My Mother/My Self*, 6907

Fridell, Squire. *Acting in Television Commercials for Fun and Profit*, 4879

Friedan, Betty. *The Feminine Mystique*, 4300

Friedberg, Robert. *Paper Money of the United States*, 9445

Friedland, Bruce. *Emotions & Thoughts*, 5116

Friedlander, Mark P. *Winning the War Within*, 5295

Friedlander, Saul. *When Memory Comes*, 7207

Friedman, Alan Warren. *William Faulkner*, 3722

Friedman, Benjamin M. *Day of Reckoning*, 4289

Friedman, C. S. *The Madness Season*, 2552(F)

Friedman, Ellen G. *Joyce Carol Oates*, 3723

Friedman, Herbert. *The Amazing Universe*, 8365

The Astronomer's Universe, 8261

Friedman, Lenemaja. *Shirley Jackson*, 3724

Friedman, Michael Jan. *The Glove of Maiden's Hair*, 1124(F)

The Hammer and the Horn, 1125(F)

Friedman, Milton. *Free to Choose*, 4565

Friedman, Rose (jt. author). *Free to Choose*, 4565

Friel, Frank. *Breaking the Mob*, 4477

Friendly, Fred W. *The Constitution*, 4189

Friesner, Esther. *Demon Blues*, 1127(F)

Here Be Demons, 1127(F)

Hooray for Hellywood, 1127(F)

Friesner, Esther M. *Elf Defense*, 1126(F)

Frith, Donald E. *Mold Making for Ceramics*, 9163

Fritschner, Sarah (jt. author). *The Fast-Food Guide*, 8417

Fritz, Jean. *China Homecoming*, 6246

Homesick, My Own Story, 6247

Fritzsch, Harald. *Quarks*, 8939

Fromm, Erich. *The Art of Loving*, 5559

Escape from Freedom, 4301

Frommer, Harvey. *Jackie Robinson*, 6731

Sports Date Book, 9567

Fronval, George. *Indian Signs and Signals*, 7807

Frost, Elizabeth, ed. *The Bully Pulpit*, 7734

Frost, Robert. *The Poetry of Robert Frost*, 3267

A Swinger of Birches, 3268

Frumkes, Burke Lewis (jt. author). *The Mensa Think Smart Book*, 9471

Frumkin, Lyn. *Questions & Answers on AIDS*, 5184

Fry, Alan. *Wilderness Survival Handbook*, 9795

Fry, Christopher. *The Lady's Not for Burning, A Phoenix Too Frequent, and an Essay*, 3030

Fry, Ronald. *Your 1st Résumé*, 4796

Fry, William R. *Legal Careers and the Legal System*, 4967

Paralegal Careers, 4968

Frye, Northrop. *Northrop Frye on Shakespeare*, 3818

T. S. Eliot, 3884

Fuchs, Thomas. *The Hitler Fact Book*, 6846

Fucini, Joseph J. *Entrepreneurs*, 6642

Fucini, Susan (jt. author). *Entrepreneurs*, 6642

Fugard, Athol. *"Master Harold" . . . and the Boys*, 3143

Fuhrman, Candice Jacobson. *Publicity Stunt!* 3961

Fulghum, Robert. *All I Really Need to Know I Learned in Kindergarten*, 4007

It Was on Fire When I Lay Down on It, 3496

Fuller, Charles. *A Soldier's Play*, 3066

Fuller, Errol. *Extinct Birds*, 8537

Fuller, Graham E. *How to Learn a Foreign Language*, 3920

Fuller, Iola. *The Loon Feather,* 1502(F)

Fuller, John. *Prescription for Better Home Video Movies,* 6012

Fuller, Margaret. *Mountains,* 8812

Funk, Wilfred (jt. author). *Thirty Days to a More Powerful Vocabulary,* 3935

Furniss, Tim. *Space Rocket,* 8302

Furst, Jill Leslie (jt. author). *North American Indian Art,* 5795

Furst, Peter T. *North American Indian Art,* 5795

Fuson, Robert Henderson. *The Log of Christopher Columbus,* 6132

Fynn. *Mister God, This Is Anna,* 5380

Gable, Fred B. *Opportunities in Pharmacy Careers,* 5017

Gabrielson, Ira (jt. author). *Birds,* 8554

Gadallah, Leslie. *Cat's Gambit,* 2553(F)
Cat's Pawn, 2554(F)

Gader, Bertram. *Apple Software for Pennies,* 8976

Gaeddert, LouAnn. *Daffodils in the Snow,* 662(F)

Gaer, Joseph. *What the Great Religions Believe,* 4049

Gage, Diane (jt. author). *I'll Never Walk Alone,* 6951

Gage, Nicholas. *Eleni,* 6909

Gagne, Paul R. *The Zombies That Ate Pittsburgh,* 6013

Gaiman, Neil. *Don't Panic,* 3664

Gaines, Ernest J. *The Autobiography of Miss Jane Pittman,* 458(F)
A Gathering of Old Men, 459(F)
In My Father's House, 460(F)

Gaines, Steven (jt. author). *The Love You Make,* 6168

Galanter, Eugene. *Advanced Programming Handbook,* 8977

Galanter, Marc. *Cults,* 4050

Galarza, Ernesto. *Barrio Boy,* 6908

Galbraith, John Kenneth. *The Affluent Society,* 4566
The Great Crash, 1929, 8029
A Life in Our Times, 6671

Gale, Jay. *A Young Man's Guide to Sex,* 5464

Gale, Jay (jt. author). *A Young Woman's Guide to Sex,* 5496

Gale, Robert L. *Louis L'Amour,* 3725

Gale, Robert Peter. *Final Warning,* 8922

Galgut, Damon. *Sinless Season,* 812(F)

Gall, Joyce P. (jt. author). *Study for Success,* 4647

Gall, Meredith D. *Study for Success,* 4647

Gallagher, Hugh Gregory. *FDR's Splendid Deception,* 6563

Gallagher, Vera. *Speaking Out, Fighting Back,* 5510

Gallant, Roy A. *Before the Sun Dies,* 6998
Once Around the Galaxy, 8262
The Planets, 8345

Gallenkamp, Charles. *Maya,* 7655

Gallenkamp, Charles (jt. author). *The Mystery of the Ancient Maya,* 7646

Gallo, Donald R. *Presenting Richard Peck,* 3726

Gallo, Donald R., ed. *Center Stage,* 3067
Sixteen, 813(F)

Galloway, George B. *History of the House of Representatives,* 4220

Galloway, Jack. *The Toothache Tree,* 97(F)

Galsworthy, John. *The Forsyte Saga,* 549(F)

Galvin, Patrick J. *Opportunities in Plumbing and Pipe Fitting Careers,* 4942

Gammond, Peter (jt. author). *The Guinness Jazz A–Z,* 5851

Gammons, Peter (jt. author). *Rocket Man,* 6716

Gandhi, Mahatma. *All Men Are Brothers,* 6809

Gandhi, Mohandas K. *Gandhi on Non-Violence,* 4407

Gandolfi, Giorgio. *Hoops!* 9720

Gann, Ernest K. *Fate Is the Hunter,* 98(F)

Gans, David. *Playing in the Band,* 5864

Ganz, David L. *The World of Coins and Coin Collecting,* 9446

Gapen, Dan D. (jt. author). *The Complete Book of Freshwater Fishing,* 9833

Garagiola, Joe. *Baseball Is a Funny Game,* 9645

Garbarino, James. *The Future As If It Really Mattered,* 4608

Garber, Angus. *End Zone,* 9844

Garcia Lorca, Federico. *Poet in New York,* 3182
Three Tragedies, 3000

Garcia Marquez, Gabriel. *Chronicle of a Death Foretold,* 663(F)
Clandestine in Chile, 7672
One Hundred Years of Solitude, 550(F)

Gard, Wayne. *The Chisholm Trail,* 7953

Gardam, Jane. *The Hollow Land,* 551(F)

Gardiner, Steve. *Why I Climb,* 9568

Gardner, Craig Shaw. *A Difficulty with Dwarves,* 1128(F)
A Disagreement with Death, 1128(F)
An Excess of Enchantment, 1128(F)

Gardner, Dozois, ed. *Ripper!* 1751(F)

Gardner, Helen, ed. *The New Oxford Book of English Verse, 1250–1950,* 3202

Gardner, Janet (jt. author). *College Bound,* 4744

Gardner, John. *The Art of Fiction,* 4678
Brokenclaw, 2019(F)
Grendel, 1129(F)
Icebreaker, 2020(F)
License Renewed, 99(F)
The Life and Times of Chaucer, 6232
Role of Honor, 99(F)
Scorpius, 100(F)

Gardner, John, ed. *College Is Only the Beginning,* 4737

Gardner, John N. (jt. author). *Step by Step to College Success*, 4743

Gardner, John W. *On Leadership*, 7735

Gardner, Lloyd C. *Approaching Vietnam*, 8114

Gardner, Martin. *Aha! Gotcha*, 8852

Gardner's Whys and Wherefores, 8220

Hexaflexagons and Other Mathematical Diversions, 8853

Knotted Doughnuts and Other Mathematical Entertainments, 8835

Mathematical Carnival, 8854

The New Age, 9499

Puzzles from Other Worlds, 8854

Time Travel and Other Mathematical Bewilderments, 8855

Gardner, Robert. *The Whale Watchers' Guide*, 8648

The Young Athlete's Manual, 5351

Garfield, Brian. *Necessity*, 101(F)

The Thousand-Mile War, 7208

Garfield, Leon. *Shakespeare Stories*, 3819

The Wedding Ghost, 1130(F)

Garisto, Leslie. *The Best-Ever Book of Dog & Cat Names*, 8672

Garland, Henry. *The Oxford Companion to German Literature*, 3639

Garratt, Susan (jt. author). *Pictorial History of the North American Indian*, 7830

Garraty, John A. *1,001 Things Everyone Should Know about American History*, 7736

Garraty, John A., ed. *Quarrels That Have Shaped the Constitution*, 4190

Garreau, Joel. *The Nine Nations of North America*, 7737

Garrett, Randall. *Lord Darcy Investigates*, 1131(F)

Murder and Magic, 1131(F)

Too Many Magicians, 1131(F)

Garrick, James G. *Be Your Own Personal Trainer*, 5352

Peak Condition, 5442

Garrison, Webb. *A Treasury of Civil War Tales*, 7916

Gartner, Carol B. *Rachel Carson*, 6652

Garvey, Lonny D. (jt. author). *Opportunities in the Machine Trades*, 5035

Gaskell, Elizabeth C. *The Life of Charlotte Brontë*, 6221

Gassner, John, ed. *Best American Plays*, 3068

Best Plays of the Early American Theatre, 3072

Best Plays of the Modern American Theatre, 3069

Twenty Best European Plays on the American Stage, 2981

Twenty Best Plays of the Modern American Theatre, 3070

Twenty-Five Best Plays of the Modern American Theatre, 3071

Gassner, Mollie (jt. author). *Best Plays of the Early American Theatre*, 3072

Gauss, Kathleen McCarthy (jt. author). *Photography and Art*, 5743

Gaustad, Edwin Scott. *A Religious History of America*, 4051

Gautier, Dick. *The Art of Caricature*, 5718

Gayle, Addison. *Richard Wright*, 6331

Gaylin, Willard. *Feelings*, 5560

Gearhart, Susan Wood. *Opportunities in Beauty Culture Careers*, 4835

Opportunities in Modeling Careers, 4880

Geary, Patricia. *Strange Toys*, 814(F)

Geddes, Candida (jt. author). *The Complete Horse Book*, 8762

Gedge, Pauline. *Child of the Morning*, 1358(F)

Geffner, Andrea B. *How to Write Better Business Letters*, 4638

Gehrig, Eleanor. *My Luke and I*, 6720

Geiger, John (jt. author). *Frozen in Time*, 7689

Geiogamah, Hanay. *New Native American Drama*, 3073

Geist, William. *Toward a Safe and Sane Halloween and Other Tales of Suburbia*, 3497

Gelb, Arthur. *O'Neill*, 6292

Gelb, Barbara (jt. author). *O'Neill*, 6292

Gelband, Scott, et al. *Your College Application*, 4738

Gelinas, Paul J. *Coping with Shyness*, 5561

Geller, Evelyn, ed. *Communism*, 4173

Geller, Larry, et al. *If I Can Dream*, 6430

Gellman, Marc. *Does God Have a Big Toe?* 4102

Genet, Jean. *Blacks*, 3001

Genovese, Eugene D. *Roll, Jordan, Roll*, 7738

Gentle, Mary. *Ancient Light*, 2555(F)

Golden Witchbreed, 2555(F)

George, John (jt. author). *They Never Said It*, 3525

George, M. B. *Basic Sailing*, 9926

George, Nelson. *The Michael Jackson Story*, 6409

George, Nelson, ed. *Stop the Violence*, 5865

Georges, Christopher J., et al., eds. *100 Successful College Application Essays*, 4739

Gerber, Merrill Joan. *Handsome as Anything*, 2266(F)

Marry Me Tomorrow, 2267(F)

Gerber, Philip. *Robert Frost*, 3885

Willa Cather, 3727

Gerberg, Mort. *The Arbor House Book of Cartooning*, 9189

Cartooning, 9190

Gergen, Joe. *The Final Four*, 9721

Gerrold, David. *Chess with a Dragon*, 2556(F)

The World of Star Trek, 6085

Gersh, Marvin J. *The Handbook of Adolescence*, 5608

Gershoff, Stanley. *The Tufts University Guide to Total Nutrition*, 5413

Gerson, Jack. *Death Squad London*, 2021(F)

Death's Head Berlin, 2021(F)

Gerstein, Marc S. *Impressionism*, 5739

Gerstenfeld, Sheldon L. *The Bird Care Book*, 8673
The Cat Care Book, 8693
The Dog Care Book, 8719

Gething, Michael J. *F-15 Eagle*, 9126

Getlein, Frank. *25 Impressionist Masterpieces*, 5740

Getz, William. *Sam Patch*, 287(F)

Giannetti, Louis. *Flashback*, 6014

Giardina, Denise. *Storming Heaven*, 1624(F)

Gibbons, Kaye. *A Virtuous Woman*, 2268(F)

Gibbons, Stella. *Cold Comfort Farm*, 1881(F)

Gibbons, Whit. *Their Blood Runs Cold*, 8463

Giblin, James Cross. *Writing Books for Young People*, 3962

Gibran, Khalil. *The Prophet*, 3347

Gibson, Charles. *Spain in America*, 7628

Gibson, Donald B. *The Red Badge of Courage*, 3728

Gibson, James. *How to Make More in Music*, 4881
Playing for Pay, 4882

Gibson, Walter B. *Hoyle's Modern Encyclopedia of Card Games*, 9808

Gibson, William. *Burning Chrome*, 2557(F)
The Miracle Worker, 3074
Neuromancer, 2558(F)

Giddings, Al (jt. author). *Exploring the Deep Frontier*, 8892

Giddings, Robert. *The War Poets*, 3161

Gidley, Charles. *Armada*, 1429(F)

Giedion, Sigfried. *Space, Time and Architecture*, 5687

Gierach, John. *The View from Rat Lake*, 9828

Gies, Frances. *The Knight in History*, 7131
Life in a Medieval Village, 7132
Women in the Middle Ages, 7133

Gies, Frances (jt. author). *Life in a Medieval Castle*, 7134

Gies, Joseph. *Life in a Medieval Castle*, 7134

Gies, Joseph (jt. author). *Life in a Medieval Village*, 7132
Women in the Middle Ages, 7133

Gies, Miep. *Anne Frank Remembered*, 7209

Giff, Patricia Reilly. *Suspect*, 2022(F)

Gifford, Douglas. *Warriors, Gods & Spirits from Central & South American Mythology*, 3454

Gilbar, Steven. *The Open Door*, 3583

Gilbert, Anna. *A Walk in the Wood*, 2023(F)

Gilbert, George. *The Complete Photography Career Handbook*, 4883

Gilbert, Martin. *The Holocaust*, 7210
The Macmillan Atlas of the Holocaust, 7211
Scharansky, 6947

Gilbert, R. A. (jt. author). *The Oxford Book of English Ghost Stories*, 1728(F)

Gilbert, Richard J. *Caffeine*, 5435

Gilbert, Sandra M., ed. *The Norton Anthology of Literature by Women*, 2918

Gilbert, Sara. *How to Live with a Single Parent*, 5652

Gilbert, Susan. *Medical Fakes and Frauds*, 5237

Gilbert, W. S. *The Complete Plays of Gilbert and Sullivan*, 5917

Gilbreth, Frank B., Jr. *Belles on Their Toes*, 6623
Cheaper by the Dozen, 6623

Gilchrist, Joclyn Scott (jt. author). *The Campus Survival Cookbook #2*, 9367

Gill, Derek. *Quest*, 6682

Gill, Derek (jt. author). *Dove*, 6142
If You Could See What I Hear, 6955

Gill, Gillian. *Agatha Christie*, 6235

Gillenkirk, Jeff. *Bitter Melon*, 4402

Gillers, Stephen, ed. *Looking at Law School*, 4969

Gillette, A. S. *Stage Scenery*, 6086

Gillette, J. Michael (jt. author). *Stage Scenery*, 6086

Gilliland, Alexis A. *Revolution from Rosinante*, 2559(F)

Gillis, Jack. *The Car Book*, 9093
How to Make Your Car Last Almost Forever, 9094
The Used Car Book 1991, 9095

Gillon, Adam. *Joseph Conrad*, 3665

Gilman, Dorothy. *The Clairvoyant Countess*, 2024(F)
Incident at Badamyâ, 102(F)
Mrs. Pollifax and the Golden Triangle, 103(F)
Mrs. Pollifax and the Hong Kong Buddha, 104(F)
Mrs. Pollifax and the Whirling Dervish, 105(F)
Mrs. Pollifax on the China Station, 104(F)

Gilman, Richard. *The Making of Modern Drama*, 3799

Gingher, Marianne. *Bobby Rex's Greatest Hit*, 815(F)
Teen Angel, 816(F)

Gino, Carol. *The Nurse's Story*, 6910
Rusty's Story, 5185

Ginott, Haim. *Between Parent and Teenager*, 5653

Ginsberg, Allen. *Collected Poems, 1947–1980*, 3269

Giovanni, Nikki. *Black Feeling, Black Talk, Black Judgement*, 3270
Ego Tripping and Other Poems for Young People, 3271
My House, 3270
Sacred Cows . . . and Other Edibles, 3534
Those Who Ride the Night Winds, 3270, 3272

Giradet, Herbert (jt. author). *Blueprint for a Green Planet*, 4440

Giraudoux, Jean. *Giraudoux*, 3002

Girion, Barbara. *In the Middle of a Rainbow*, 2269(F)

Girodo, Michel. *Shy? (You Don't Have to Be)*, 5609

Giroux, E. X. *A Death for a Double,* 2025(F)

Gisler, Margaret (jt. author). *Careers for Book-worms and Other Literary Types,* 4948
How to Prepare for College, 4729
Opportunities in Fast Food Careers, 4962

Gissing, Vera. *Pearls of Childhood,* 6911

Gitlin, Todd. *Inside Prime Time,* 6015
The Sixties, 8062

Gitlin, Todd, ed. *Watching Television,* 6016

Gittelson, Bernard. *Intangible Evidence,* 9500

Giugnolini, Luciano (jt. author). *Simon and Schuster's Guide to Garden Flowers,* 9383

Glackens, Ira. *Did Molly Pitcher Say That?* 7739

Gladstein, Mimi Reisel. *The Ayn Rand Companion,* 3729

Gladstone, Bernard. *The Simon & Schuster Complete Guide to Home Repair and Maintenance,* 9390

Gladstone, William. *Preparation for the ACT,* 4658

Glasgow, Ellen. *Barren Ground,* 817(F)

Glassie, Henry, ed. *Irish Folktales,* 3398

Glassman, Bruce. *Arthur Miller,* 6290

Glazer, Myron Peretz. *The Whistleblowers,* 4521

Glazer, Nathan. *Beyond the Melting Pot,* 4343
Ethnic Dilemmas, 1964–1982, 4344

Glazer, Penina Migdal (jt. author). *The Whistleblowers,* 4521

Gleasner, Diana. *Breakthrough,* 3963

Gleason, Norma. *Cryptograms and Spygrams,* 9467

Glenn, Harold T. (jt. author). *Glenn's New Complete Bicycle Manual,* 9751

Glenn, Mel. *Back to Class,* 3273
Class Dismissed, 3273
Class Dismissed II, 3273

Glenn, Rhonda (jt. author). *Golf for Women,* 9880

Global Tomorrow Coalition. *The Global Ecology Handbook,* 4427

Gloss, Molly. *The Jump-Off Creek,* 1566(F)

Glossbrenner, Alfred. *The Complete Handbook of Personal Computer Communications,* 8978

Glover, Bob. *The Competitive Runner's Handbook,* 9910
The Runner's Handbook, 9911

Glover, Vivian. *The First Fig Tree,* 552(F)

Glowa, John R. *Inhalants,* 5117

Glowacz, Stefan. *Rocks around the World,* 9569

Gluck, Herb (jt. author). *The Mick,* 6725

Godden, Rumer. *An Episode of Sparrows,* 818(F)
Thursday's Child, 819(F)

Godwin, Gail. *The Finishing School,* 820(F)
A Mother and Two Daughters, 553(F)

Godwin, Parke. *Beloved Exile,* 1430(F)

Goeller, Priscilla S. *College Check Mate,* 4778

Goffstein, M. B. *An Artists Album,* 5741
Lives of the Artist, 5741

Gold, Alison Leslie (jt. author). *Anne Frank Remembered,* 7209

Gold, Joy P. (jt. author). *Sharks in Question,* 8631

Gold, Maxine, ed. *Women Making History,* 4302

Gold, Ron, ed. *Point of Departure,* 821(F)
Stepping Stones, 821(F)

Goldaper, Sam. *How to Talk Basketball,* 9722

Goldberg, Jeff. *Anatomy of a Scientific Discovery,* 5314

Goldberg, M. Hirsh. *The Book of Lies,* 9501

Goldberg, Natalie. *Writing Down the Bones,* 3964

Goldblatt, David (jt. author). *Lifetimes under Apartheid,* 7373

Golden, Frederic. *The Trembling Earth,* 8802

Golden, Sandy. *Driving the Drunk off the Road,* 5119

Goldin, Augusta. *Oceans of Energy,* 8917

Goldin, Stephen. *Assault on the Gods,* 2560(F)
Crystals of Air and Water, 1132(F)

Golding, William. *Darkness Visible,* 664(F)
The Inheritors, 1350(F)
Lord of the Flies, 106(F)

Goldis, Al. *Breaking into the Big Leagues,* 9646

Goldman, Eric Frederick. *The Crucial Decade—And After,* 8063

Goldman, James. *A Lion in Winter,* 3075

Goldman, Joel. *The Boxer Rebellion and Other Tales,* 6672

Goldman, Peter. *Charlie Company,* 8115

Goldman, Peter, et al. *The End of the World That Was,* 7212

Goldman, William. *Marathon Man,* 107(F)
Wait till Next Year, 9570

Goldman, William, reteller. *The Princess Bride,* 1133(F)

Goldrosen, John. *Remembering Buddy,* 6406

Goldsmith, Donald. *Supernova!* 8263

Goldsmith, Donald (jt. author). *The Space Telescope,* 8259

Goldsmith, Edward, ed. *The Earth Report,* 4428

Goldsmith, Oliver. *The Vicar of Wakefield,* 367(F)

Goldstein, David. *Jewish Legends,* 4103

Goldstein, Harold. *Getting a Job in the Computer Age,* 5041

Goldstein, Larry Joel. *IBM PC Introduction, BASIC Programming and Applications,* 8979

Goldstein, Lisa. *The Dream Years,* 2270(F)
A Mask for the General, 2561(F)

Goldstein, Patti (jt. author). *Creature Comforts,* 6681

Goldstein, Thomas. *Dawn of Modern Science,* 7135

Goldston, Robert. *Next Year in Jerusalem,* 7611
The Road between the Wars, 8030
The Sword of the Prophet, 7595

Goldstone, Nancy Bazelon. *Trading Up,* 4588

Goldstone, Richard, ed. *The Mentor Book of Short Plays,* 2982

Goldsworthy, Maureen. *Mend It!* 9240

Golenbock, Peter. *The Forever Boys,* 9647
Personal Fouls, 9723

Golenbock, Peter (jt. author). *Balls,* 6729

Golter, Gary. *Opportunities in High Tech Careers,* 5042

Gombrich, E. H. *The Story of Art,* 5742

Good Housekeeping. *The Good Housekeeping All-American Cookbook,* 9338

Good, Timothy. *Above Top Secret,* 9502

Goodall, Jane. *In the Shadow of Man,* 8498
Through a Window, 8499

Goode, Stephen. *The Foreign Policy Debate,* 4142
Reaganomics, 8064

Goodman, Thomas. *Smart Face,* 5336

Goodrich, Frances. *The Diary of Anne Frank,* 3076

Goodrich, Norma Lorre. *Ancient Myths,* 3455
King Arthur, 6826
Medieval Myths, 3455
Priestesses, 4052

Goodwin, Donald W. *Alcoholism,* 5120

Goodwin, Richard N. *Remembering America,* 8065

Gookin, Dan. *Hard Disk Management with MS-DOS and PC-DOS,* 8980

Goolrick, William K. *Rebels Resurgent,* 7917

Gorbachev, Mikhail. *Perestroika,* 7568

Gordimer, Nadine. *The Conservationist,* 961(F)
A Guest of Honour, 961(F)
July's People, 965(F)
Lifetimes under Apartheid, 7373
My Son's Story, 962(F)
Selected Stories, 963(F)
A Soldier's Embrace, 964(F)
A World of Strangers, 965(F)

Gordis, Kent (jt. author). *Greg LeMond's Complete Book of Bicycling,* 9758

Gordon, Barbara. *I'm Dancing as Fast as I Can,* 5121
Opportunities in Commercial Art and Graphic Design, 4884

Gordon, Bonnie Bilyeu. *Songs from Unsung Worlds,* 3853

Gordon, Elliot (jt. author). *Opportunities in Commercial Art and Graphic Design,* 4884

Gordon, Jacquie. *Give Me One Wish,* 5186

Gordon, James S. *Stress Management,* 5381

Gordon, Karen Elizabeth. *The Well-Tempered Sentence,* 4679

Gordon, Louise. *How to Draw the Human Figure,* 9191

Gordon, Mary. *Final Payments,* 822(F)

Gordon, Peter H., et al., eds. *Diamonds Are Forever,* 9648

Gordon, Ruth, sel. *Under All Silences,* 3162

Gordon, Sol. *The Teenage Survival Book,* 5610
When Living Hurts, 5611

Gordon, Suzanne. *Off Balance,* 5966

Gordon-Watson, Mary. *The Handbook of Riding,* 8763

Gorecki, Jan. *Capital Punishment,* 4239

Goren, Charles H. *Fundamentals of Contract Bridge,* 9809
Goren's New Bridge Complete, 9810

Gorky, Maxim. *The Lower Depths and Other Plays,* 3003

Gorman, Edward. *What the Dead Men Say,* 108(F)

Gorman, Edward, ed. *The Second Black Lizard Anthology of Crime Fiction,* 2026(F)

Gorman, Edward, et al., eds. *Under the Gun,* 2027(F)

Gorman, James. *The Man with No Endorphins and Other Reflections on Science,* 8392

Gorman, James (jt. author). *Digging Dinosaurs,* 6981

Gormley, Gerard. *A Dolphin Summer,* 8649
Orcas of the Gulf, 8650

Gornick, Vivian. *Women in Science,* 8221

Gosling, William (jt. author). *The Facts on File Dictionary of First Names,* 3916

Gotlieb, Phyllis. *Son of the Morning and Other Stories,* 2562(F)

Gottcent, John H. *The Bible,* 4104

Gottfried, Martin. *Broadway Musicals,* 5918

Gottfried, Paul. *The Conservative Movement,* 4265

Gottfried, Robert S. *The Black Death,* 7136

Gottschalk, Alfred. *To Learn and to Teach,* 4970

Goubert, Pierre. *The Course of French History,* 7493

Goudge, Eileen. *Something Borrowed, Something Blue,* 2271(F)

Goulart, Ron. *The Great Comic Book Artists, Volume 2,* 5796

Goulart, Ron, ed. *The Great British Detective,* 2028(F)

Gould, Carol Grant (jt. author). *The Honey Bee,* 8603

Gould, James L. *The Honey Bee,* 8603

Gould, Jean. *Modern American Women Poets,* 3274

Gould, Phillip. *Kitty Collins,* 2272(F)

Gould, Stephen Jay. *Ever Since Darwin,* 8393
The Flamingo's Smile, 8393
Hen's Teeth and Horse's Toes, 8393
The Panda's Thumb, 8394

Goulter, Barbara (jt. author). *How to Keep Your Car Mechanic Honest,* 9096

Goulter, Vic. *How to Keep Your Car Mechanic Honest,* 9096

Gourley, Catherine. *The Courtship of Joanna,* 1609(F)

Gowing, Lawrence. *Matisse,* 5774

Gowlett, John. *Ascent to Civilization*, 7018

Gradenwitz, Peter. *Leonard Bernstein*, 6338

Graeber, Laurel. *Are You Dying for a Drink?* 5122

Graf, Alfred Byrd. *Exotic Plant Manual*, 9379

Graff, Henry F. (jt. author). *The Modern Researcher*, 4669

Graff, Henry F., ed. *The Presidents*, 6470

Graffman, Gary. *I Really Should Be Practicing*, 6394

Grafton, Sue. *"G" Is for Gumshoe*, 2029(F)

Gragg, Rod. *The Civil War Quiz and Fact Book*, 7918

   The Illustrated Confederate Reader, 7919

   The Old West Quiz and Fact Book, 7954

Gragonier, Reginald, ed. *What's What*, 3921

Graham, Lyle J. *Your IBM PC*, 8981

Graham, Otis L., Jr. *The Great Campaigns*, 7740

Graham, Otis L., Jr., ed. *Franklin D. Roosevelt, His Life and Times*, 8031

Graham, Robin Lee. *Dove*, 6142

Graham-Smith, Francis. *Pathways to the Universe*, 8264

Grant, Charles. *Waterloo*, 7146

Grant, Charles L. *In a Dark Dream*, 1753(F)

Grant, Charles L., ed. *Horrors*, 1752(F)

   Midnight, 1754(F)

   Nightmare Seasons, 1754(F)

   Nightmares, 1752(F)

   Shadows, 1752(F)

   Shadows 8, 1755(F)

   Terrors, 1752(F)

Grant, Cynthia D. *Phoenix Rising*, 665(F)

Grant, Michael. *The Classical Greeks*, 7103

   From Alexander to Cleopatra, 7103

   Myths of the Greeks and Romans, 3476

   The Rise of the Greeks, 7103

Grant, Richard. *BMX Action Bike Book*, 9754

Grant-Adamson, Lesley. *The Face of Death*, 2030(F)

Granzotto, Gianni. *Christopher Columbus*, 6133

Grass, Gunter. *The Tin Drum*, 966(F)

Grasso, John (jt. author). *Five-Hundred-Five Boxing Questions Your Friends Can't Answer*, 9787

Graves, Douglas R. *Drawing Portraits*, 9192

Graves, Robert. *Claudius, the God*, 1369(F)

   Collected Poems, 1975, 3203

   Goodbye to All That, 6249

   Greek Myths, 3477

   I, Claudius, 1369(F)

Gray, James (jt. author). *Sex in Nature*, 8384

Gray, John. *Near Eastern Mythology*, 3456

Gray, Nicholas Stuart. *The Seventh Swan*, 1134(F)

Gray, Richard. *American Poetry of the Twentieth Century*, 3886

Greber, Judith. *Mendocino*, 554(F)

Grebstein, Sheldon Norman. *Sinclair Lewis*, 3730

Greeley, Andrew M. *The Magic Cup*, 1135(F)

Green, Jonathon. *The Greatest Criminals of All Time*, 6118

Green, Julien. *God's Fool*, 6838

Green, Paul M. *Making Money with Baseball Cards*, 9447

Green, Peter. *Ancient Greece*, 7104

Green, Richard Lancelyn, ed. *The Further Adventures of Sherlock Holmes, after Sir Arthur Conan Doyle*, 2031(F)

Green, Roland. *Peace Company*, 2563(F)

Green, Roland (jt. author). *Janissaries*, 2746(F)

Green, Stanley. *Encyclopaedia of the Musical Theatre*, 5919

   The World of Musical Comedy, 6175

Greenberg, Hank. *Hank Greenberg*, 6722

Greenberg, Harvey R. *Emotional Illness in Your Family*, 5382

Greenberg, Jan. *Advertising Careers*, 4916

   No Dragons to Slay, 666(F)

   The Teenager's Guide to the Best Summer Opportunities, 4711

Greenberg, Joanne. *I Never Promised You a Rose Garden*, 667(F)

   Of Such Small Differences, 668(F)

   Rites of Passage, 2919(F)

   Simple Gifts, 555(F)

Greenberg, Keith E. (jt. author). *Attitude*, 5631

Greenberg, Martin H. *Who's Who in the Super Bowls*, 9845

Greenberg, Martin H., ed. *Amazing Science Fiction Stories*, 2564(F)

   Amazing Stories, 2565(F)

   Foundation's Friends, 2566(F)

   The Further Adventures of the Joker, 1756(F)

   Masterpieces of Mystery and Suspense, 2032(F)

   Mummy Stories, 2033(F)

   Phantoms, 1757(F)

   The Wild Years (1946–1955), 2564(F)

   The Wonder Years (1926–1935), 2564(F)

Greenberg, Martin H. (jt. author). *Alternative Histories*, 1310(F)

   Amazing Stories, 2383(F)

   Arthur C. Clarke, 3681

   The Best Japanese Science Fiction Stories, 2358(F)

   Best of the West, 229(F)

   Catfantastic, 2722(F)

   Great Modern Police Stories, 2143(F)

   Hitchcock in Prime Time, 2120(F)

   Homicidal Acts, 230(F)

   Isaac Asimov Presents the Great SF Stories, 2384(F)

   Isaac Asimov Presents the Great SF Stories, 20, 2385(F)

   The Mammoth Book of Private Eye Stories, 2144(F)

Prime Suspects #1, 2145(F)
Space Wars, 2822(F)
Suspicious Characters, 2146(F)
Time Wars, 2823(F)
Greenberg, Rosalind M. (jt. author). *Phantoms,* 1757(F)
Greenberg, Stan. *The Guinness Book of Olympics Records,* 9906
Greene, Bob. *American Beat,* 3535
Homecoming, 8116
Greene, Constance C. *The Love Letters of J. Timothy Owen,* 1882(F)
Greene, Graham. *The Captain and the Enemy,* 823(F)
Dr. Fischer of Geneva or The Bomb Party, 109(F)
The Heart of the Matter, 669(F)
The Human Factor, 110(F)
The Portable Graham Greene, 111
The Power and the Glory, 670(F)
Travels with My Aunt, 1883(F)
Greene, Hank. *Square and Folk Dancing,* 5967
Greene, Howard. *Scaling the Ivy Wall,* 4740
Greene, Janet, et al. *Putting Food By,* 9340
Greene, Marilyn. *Finder,* 6912
Greene, Robert Ewell. *Black Defenders of America,* 6471
Greene, Yvonne. *Little Sister,* 2273(F)
Greenfeld, Howard. *Books,* 3977
Greenfield, Josh. *A Child Called Noah,* 6913
Greenhill, Basil. *The Evolution of the Wooden Ship,* 9121
Greenwald, Dorothy. *Coping with Moving,* 5591
Greenwald, Michael. *Survivor,* 9927
Greenwald, Sheila. *Blissful Joy and the SATs,* 2274(F)
Greenwood, L. B. *Sherlock Holmes and the Case of the Raleigh Legacy,* 2034(F)
Gregg, Lewis (jt. author). *Dark Marathon,* 6966
Gregorian, Joyce Ballou. *The Broken Citadel,* 2567(F)
Greider, William. *Secrets of the Temple,* 4221
Grenville, J. A. *A World History of the Twentieth Century,* 7150
Gretzky, Wayne. *Gretzky,* 6774
Grey, Evelyn. *Camberleigh,* 112(F)
Grey, Zane. *Riders of the Purple Sage,* 1567(F)
The Wolf Tracker and Other Animal Tales, 288(F)
Gribbin, John. *Hothouse Earth,* 4429
In Search of Schrodinger's Cat, 8908
In Search of the Big Bang, 8909
Timewarps, 8910
Gribbin, John (jt. author). *Brother Esau,* 1242(F)
Gribbin, John, ed. *The Breathing Planet,* 8869
Grierson, H. J. C., ed. *The Oxford Book of Seventeenth Century Verse,* 3204
Griffin, Clive D. *Classical Music,* 5834

Griffin, Donald R. *Animal Thinking,* 8476
Griffin, John Howard. *Black Like Me,* 4363
Griffin, William. *Clive Staples Lewis,* 6280
Griffith, H. Winter. *Complete Guide to Sports Injuries,* 5443
Griffith, Susan. *Work Your Way around the World,* 4836
Griffiths, John. *The Caribbean in the Twentieth Century,* 7661
Grigson, Geoffrey, ed. *The Faber Book of Nonsense Verse,* 3163
The Oxford Book of Satirical Verse, 3164
Grimes, Ann. *Running Mates,* 4207
Grimes, Martha. *The Anodyne Necklace,* 2035(F)
Grimm, Jacob. *The Complete Grimms' Fairy Tales,* 3399
Grimm, Michele (jt. author). *The Good Guide for Bad Photographers,* 9419
Grimm, Tom. *The Basic Book of Photography,* 9417
The Good Guide for Bad Photographers, 9419
Grimm, Tom, et al. *The Basic Darkroom Book,* 9418
Grimm, Wilhelm (jt. author). *The Complete Grimms' Fairy Tales,* 3399
Grinspoon, Lester. *Cocaine,* 5123
Grizzard, Lewis. *Kathy Sue Loudermilk, I Love You,* 3498
Grob, Bernard. *Basic Electronics,* 9035
Grob, Gerald N., ed. *Interpretations of American History,* 7741
Gross, Albert C. *Endurance,* 9571
Gross, Beatrice, ed. *The Great School Debate,* 4628
Gross, Ronald (jt. author). *The Great School Debate,* 4628
Grosshandler, Janet. *Coping with Verbal Abuse,* 5612
Grossinger, Richard, ed. *Into the Temple of Baseball,* 9649
Grossvogel, David. *Dear Ann Landers,* 5613
Grote, David. *Staging the Musical,* 6087
Grout, Donald Jay. *A History of Western Music,* 5835
Grout, Jack. *On the Lesson Tee,* 9868
Grove, Fred. *Deception Trail,* 113(F)
Groves, Don. *The Oceans,* 8877
Grubb, Jake, et al. *The New Sailboard Book,* 9955
Gruber, Gary R. *Inside Strategies for the SAT,* 4659
Gruber, Ruth. *Raquela,* 6941
Gruber, Terry Deroy. *Working Cats,* 8694
Gruen, John. *People Who Dance,* 5968
Grun, Bernard. *The Timetables of History,* 7045
Grundberg, Andy. *Grundberg's Goof-Proof Photography Guide,* 9420

Photography and Art, 5743

Grundtvig, Svendt, ed. *Danish Fairy Tales,* 3400

Grundy, Stuart (jt. author). *The Guitar Greats,* 6187

Guareschi, Giovanni. *The Little World of Don Camillo,* 1884(F)

Gubar, Susan (jt. author). *The Norton Anthology of Literature by Women,* 2918

Gudiol, Jose. *Goya,* 5775

Guerard, Albert J. *The Triumph of the Novel,* 3621

Guernsey, JoAnn B. *Five Summers,* 824(F)

Guest, Elissa Haden. *Handsome Man,* 2275(F)

Guest, Judith. *Ordinary People,* 556(F)

Guggenheim, Martin. *The Rights of Young People,* 4303

Guinther, John. *The Jury in America,* 4240

Guinther, John (jt. author). *Breaking the Mob,* 4477

Gundlach, Julie. *My Mother Before Me,* 5654

Gunn, James. *Isaac Asimov,* 3731

Gunston, Bill. *F-111,* 9127

Jane's Aerospace Dictionary, 9064

Gunston, Bill, et al. *Guinness Book of Speed Facts and Feats,* 8916

Gunther, Irene (jt. author). *A Spy for Freedom,* 6801

Gunther, John. *Death Be Not Proud,* 6914

Gunther, Marc. *Monday Night Mayhem,* 9846

Gunther, Noel. *Beyond Boardwalk and Park Place,* 9811

Guppy, Shusha. *The Blindfold Horse,* 7620

Guralnick, Peter. *Feel Like Goin' Home,* 5866

Lost Highway, 5866

Sweet Soul Music, 5866

Gurko, Miriam. *The Ladies of Seneca Falls,* 4304

Gurney, Eric. *How to Live with a Calculating Cat,* 8695

Gurney, Gene. *Kingdoms of Asia, the Middle East, and Africa,* 7046

Gurr, Andrew. *Rebuilding Shakespeare's Globe,* 3820

Gustafson, Anita. *Guilty or Innocent?* 4241

Gustafson, Ginny Lyford (jt. author). *Living on the Edge,* 5134

Guthrie, A. B., Jr. *Fair Land, Fair Land,* 1568(F)

Guthrie, Woody. *Bound for Glory,* 6250

Gutkind, Lee. *Many Sleepless Nights,* 5238

Gutman, Dan. *It Ain't Cheatin' If You Don't Get Caught,* 9650

Gutman, Herbert G. *The Black Family in Slavery and Freedom, 1750–1925,* 7742

Gutnik, Martin J. *Ecology,* 4430

Genetics, 8241

Guy, David. *Football Dreams,* 2877(F)

Guy, Rosa. *My Love, My Love, or the Peasant Girl,* 671(F)

Guzman, Andres. *33 Fun-and-Easy Weekend Electronics Projects,* 9036

Gyatso, Tenzin, Dalai Lama. *Freedom in Exile,* 6810

Haaften, Julia Van (jt. author). *The View from Space,* 8319

Haas, Jessie. *Working Trot,* 289(F)

Haas, Robert. *Eat to Win,* 5414

Hadamuscin, John. *Special Occasions,* 9341

Haddock, Patricia. *Careers in Banking and Finance,* 4917

Hagan, Chet. *Grand Ole Opry,* 5867

Hagan, William T. *American Indians,* 7808

Hagedorn, John. *People and Folks,* 5536

Hagen, Richard (jt. author). *Death-Dying Annual, 1989,* 5080

Hagen, Uta. *Respect for Acting,* 6088

Hagerty, D. *Opportunities in Civil Engineering Careers,* 5018

Opportunities in Engineering Technology Careers, 5018

Haggard, H. Rider. *Allen Quartermain,* 114(F)

King Solomon's Mines, 114(F)

She, 115(F)

Haig-Brown, Roderick. *A Primer of Fly-Fishing,* 9812

Silver, 8626

Haigh, Christopher, ed. *The Cambridge Historical Encyclopedia of Great Britain and Ireland,* 7517

Hailey, Arthur. *Airport,* 116(F)

The Evening News, 117(F)

Hotel, 116(F)

The Moneychangers, 118(F)

Wheels, 116(F)

Hailey, Elizabeth Forsythe. *A Woman of Independent Means,* 825(F)

Hailey, Kendall. *The Day I Became an Autodidact,* 6915

Haines, John. *The Stars, the Snow, the Fire,* 8180

Haing Ngor. *A Cambodian Odyssey,* 6811

Haining, Peter, ed. *Movie Monsters,* 1758(F)

The Mummy, 1759(F)

Stories of the Walking Dead, 1760(F)

Haislip, Barbara. *Stars, Spells, Secrets, and Sorcery,* 9504

Halacy, Dan. *Empire in the Dust,* 119

Halberstadt, Hans. *Green Berets,* 4284

Halberstam, David. *The Amateurs,* 6706

The Best and the Brightest, 8066

The Breaks of the Game, 9724

The Next Century, 8067

Haldane, Bernard, et al. *The New Young Peoples' Job Power Now,* 4837

Haldeman, Jack C. (jt. author). *There Is No Darkness,* 2571(F)

Haldeman, Joe. *The Forever War,* 2568(F)

There Is No Darkness, 2571(F)
Tool of the Trade, 120(F)
War Year, 1696(F)
Worlds Apart, 2570(F)
Haldeman, Joe, ed. *Nebula Award Stories Seventeen*, 2569(F)
Hale, E. E. *The Man without a Country and Other Stories*, 398(F)
Hale, F. J. *In the Sea Nymph's Lair*, 1136(F)
Ogre Castle, 1137(F)
Hale, Janet Campbell. *The Owl's Song*, 461(F)
Hales, Dianne. *Case Histories*, 5124
Pregnancy and Birth, 5465
Haley, Alex. *A Different Kind of Christmas*, 1525(F)
Roots, 6472
Haley, Alex (jt. author). *The Autobiography of Malcolm X*, 6516
Haley, Delphine, ed. *Marine Mammals of Eastern North Pacific and Arctic Waters*, 8651
Haley, James L. *Texas*, 8195
Haley, Neale. *Birds for Pets and Pleasure*, 8560
Hall, Barbara. *Skeeball and the Secret of the Universe*, 826(F)
Hall, Brian. *Stealing from a Deep Place*, 6143
Hall, Calvin S. (jt. author). *A Guide to Psychologists and Their Concepts*, 5540
Hall, Elizabeth (jt. author). *Seasons of Life*, 5525
Hall, George. *Baron Wolman Presents FDNY*, 4230
Hall, James. *Dictionary of Subjects and Symbols in Art*, 5688
Hall, James N. (jt. author). *The Bounty Trilogy*, 216(F)
Hall, L. M. (jt. author). *Coping with Choosing a College*, 4724
Hall, Louis Brewer. *Searching for Comets*, 8331
Hall, Lynn. *Flyaway*, 557(F)
The Solitary, 827(F)
Hall, Lynn, ed. *AIDS*, 5187
Hall, Lynn (jt. author). *American Foreign Policy*, 4129
Teenage Sexuality, 5451
Hall, Mary Bowen. *Emma Chizzit and the Queen Anne Killer*, 2036(F)
Hall, Robert Lee. *Benjamin Franklin Takes the Case*, 2037(F)
Hallam, A. (jt. author). *The Encyclopedia of Animal Evolution*, 6975
Hallam, Elizabeth, ed. *The Plantagenet Chronicles*, 7518
Halliday, Jon (jt. author). *Mme Sun Yat-sen*, 6817
Halliday, Tim R., ed. *The Encyclopedia of Reptiles and Amphibians*, 8464
Halline, Allan G., ed. *Six Modern American Plays*, 3077

Halliwell, Leslie. *The Dead That Walked*, 6017
Halliwell's Film Guide, 6018
Hallstead, William F. *Broadcasting Careers for You*, 4885
Halperin, John. *The Life of Jane Austen*, 6214
Halpern, Daniel, ed. *The American Poetry Anthology*, 3275
Halstead, Bruce W. *Tropical Fish*, 8752
Halter, Marek. *The Book of Abraham*, 1431(F)
Hamalian, Leo. *Everything You Need to Know about Grammar*, 3922
Hambleton, Ronald. *The Branding of America*, 4567
Hambly, Barbara. *The Armies of Daylight*, 1141(F)
Dragonsbane, 1138(F)
Ishmael, 2572(F)
The Ladies of Mandrigyn, 1762(F)
The Silent Tower, 1139(F)
The Silicon Mage, 1140(F)
Those Who Hunt the Night, 1761(F)
The Time of the Dark, 1141(F)
The Walls of Air, 1141(F)
The Witches of Wenshar, 1762(F)
Hamill, Dorothy. *Dorothy Hamill On and Off the Ice*, 6775
Hamilton, Edith. *The Echo of Greece*, 7105
The Greek Way, 7106
Mythology, 3457
The Roman Way, 7115
Hamilton, George Heard. *19th and 20th Century Art*, 5744
Hamilton, Ian. *J. D. Salinger*, 6300
Hamilton, J. R. *Alexander the Great*, 6822
Hamilton, Morse. *Effie's House*, 828(F)
Hamilton, Virginia. *Junius Over Far*, 558(F)
Paul Robeson, 6435
A White Romance, 829(F)
Hamlett, Christina. *The Enchanter*, 1142(F)
Hamley, Dennis. *Blood Line*, 1143(F)
Hamlin, Talbot Faulkner. *Architecture through the Ages*, 5693
Hammer, Arnold. *The Rosen Photo Guide to a Career in Health and Fitness*, 4994
Hammerslough, Jane. *Everything You Need to Know about Teen Motherhood*, 5655
Hammett, Dashiell. *The Glass Key*, 2038(F)
The Maltese Falcon, 2038(F)
The Novels of Dashiell Hammett, 2039(F)
The Thin Man, 2038(F)
Woman in the Dark, 2040(F)
Hammond, J. R. *An Edgar Allan Poe Companion*, 3584
A George Orwell Companion, 3666
Hampton, Henry, et al. *Voices of Freedom*, 4364
Hamrin, Robert. *America's New Economy*, 4589
Hamsun, Knut. *Growth of the Soil*, 559(F)
Hanbury-Tenison, Robin. *A Ride along the Great Wall*, 7410

Hanchett, William. *The Lincoln Murder Conspiracies*, 6543

Hancock, Sibyl. *Famous Firsts of Black Americans*, 6473

Hand, Learned. *The Bill of Rights*, 4191

Handlin, Lilian (jt. author). *Abraham Lincoln and the Union*, 6544

Handlin, Oscar. *Abraham Lincoln and the Union*, 6544

Handman, Wynn, ed. *Modern American Scenes for Student Actors*, 3078

Hanes, Mari. *Wild Child*, 5383

Haney, John. *Clement Attlee*, 6827

Hanff, Helene. *Underfoot in Show Business*, 6397

Hanhisalo, Judith Evans. *Enjoying Art*, 5719

Hankla, Cathryn. *A Blue Moon in Poorwater*, 560(F)

Hanks, Kurt (jt. author). *Extra Cash for Kids*, 4955

Hanley, Reid (jt. author). *Wrestling for Beginners*, 9785

Hanmer, Trudy. *The Growth of Cities*, 4556

Hanna, Elaine (jt. author). *The New Doubleday Cookbook*, 9309

Hanna, Jack. *Monkeys on the Interstate and Other Tales from America's Favorite Zookeeper*, 8773

Hannam, Charles. *A Boy in That Situation*, 6916

Hannigan, Frank (jt. author). *The New Rules of Golf*, 9879

Hansberry, Lorraine. *A Raisin in the Sun*, 3079
To Be Young, Gifted and Black, 6252

Hansen, Barbara. *Mexican Cookery*, 9342

Hansen, Chadwick. *Witchcraft at Salem*, 7840

Harden, Blaine. *Africa*, 7350

Hardigree, Peggy Ann. *Working Outside*, 4838

Harding, Lee. *Misplaced Persons*, 1144(F)

Harding, Vincent. *There Is a River*, 7743

Hardinge, George, ed. *The Mammoth Book of Modern Crime Stories*, 2041(F)

Hardwick, Michael. *The Complete Guide to Sherlock Holmes*, 3667
The Revenge of the Hound, 2042(F)

Hardwick, Mollie. *The Merrymaid*, 1432(F)

Hardwick, Molly. *Perish in July*, 2043(F)

Hardy, Jon. *Biker*, 121(F)

Hardy, Karen. *The New Breed*, 6176

Hardy, Thomas. *The Complete Poems of Thomas Hardy*, 3205
Far from the Madding Crowd, 368(F)
Jude the Obscure, 369(F)
The Mayor of Casterbridge, 370(F)
The Return of the Native, 371(F)
Tess of the D'Urbervilles, 372(F)

Hare, R. M. *Plato*, 4008

Harewood, George H. *Definitive Kobbe's Opera Book*, 5920
Kobbe's Illustrated Opera Book, 5921

Hargrove, Hondon. *Black Union Soldiers in the Civil War*, 7920
Buffalo Soldiers in Italy, 7213

Hargrove, Sharon. *Safe at Home*, 9651

Harley, Rex. *Black November*, 2044(F)
Last Laugh, 830(F)

Harmon, Margaret. *Ms. Engineer*, 5019

Harmon, William (jt. author). *A Handbook to Literature*, 3588

Harmon, William, ed. *The Oxford Book of American Light Verse*, 3276

Harnick, Sheldon (jt. author). *Fiddler on the Roof*, 3127

Harr, John Ensor. *The Rockefeller Century*, 6474

Harragan, Betty Lehan. *Games Mother Never Taught You*, 4918

Harre, Rom. *Great Scientific Experiments*, 8242

Harrell, Janice. *So Long, Senior Year*, 831(F)

Harrigan, Stephen. *Aransas*, 2276(F)

Harrington, Geri. *Real Food, Fake Food—Everything in Between*, 5415

Harrington, John W. *Dance of the Continents*, 8796

Harrington, Joyce. *Dreemz of the Night*, 2045(F)

Harrington, Michael. *The New American Poverty*, 4506
The Other America, 4507

Harriott, Esther. *American Voices*, 3838

Harris, D. Mark. *Embracing the Earth*, 4431

Harris, Deborah Turner. *The Burning Stone*, 1145(F)
The Gauntlet of Malice, 1145(F)

Harris, Geraldine. *Gods & Pharaohs from Egyptian Mythology*, 3458

Harris, Jack C. *A Step-by-Step Book about Goldfish*, 8753
A Step-by-Step Book about Guppies, 8754

Harris, Jacqueline L. *Henry Ford*, 6666

Harris, Jonathan. *The New Terrorism*, 4544
Super Mafia, 4478

Harris, Marie, ed. *An Ear to the Ground*, 3277

Harris, Marilyn. *Hatter Fox*, 462(F)

Harris, Mark. *Bang the Drum Slowly*, 2878(F)
Speed, 561(F)

Harris, Mark Jonathan, et al., comps. *The Homefront*, 8068

Harris, Nathaniel. *Hitler*, 6847

Harris, Rosemary. *Summers of the Wild Rose*, 1655(F)

Harris, Thomas. *Red Dragon*, 2046(F)

Harrison, Beppie (jt. author). *Momentum*, 4269

Harrison, Daphne Duval. *Black Pearls*, 6177

Harrison, Dave. *Sports Illustrated Canoeing*, 9928

Harrison, Harry. *Bill, the Galactic Hero*, 2573(F)
Invasion, 2574(F)
Rebel in Time, 2574(F)
Return to Eden, 2575(F)
West of Eden, 2575(F)

Winter in Eden, 2575(F)

Harrison, James. *Rudyard Kipling,* 3585

Harrison, Michael, ed. *The Oxford Book of Christmas Poems,* 3165
Peace and War, 3166

Harrison, Nancy. *Winnie Mandela,* 6795

Harrison, Richard, ed. *Whales, Dolphins and Porpoises,* 8652

Harrison, Sue. *Mother Earth Father Sky,* 1351(F)

Hart, Anne. *The Life and Times of Hercule Poirot,* 3668

Hart, Benjamin. *The Perfect Puppy,* 8720

Hart, Bruce. *Breaking Up Is Hard to Do,* 832(F)
Sooner or Later, 2277(F)

Hart, Carole (jt. author). *Breaking Up Is Hard to Do,* 832(F)
Sooner or Later, 2277(F)

Hart, Elaine (jt. author). *The All-New Official Cheerleader's Handbook,* 9588

Hart, John. *Walking Softly in the Wilderness,* 9796

Hart, Lynette (jt. author). *The Perfect Puppy,* 8720

Hart, Moss. *Act One,* 6253

Hart, Nicole. *Lead on Love,* 2278(F)

Hart, William B. *The United States and World Trade,* 4568

Hart-Davis, Duff. *Hitler's Games,* 9907

Harte, Bret. *The Outcasts of Poker Flat and Other Stories,* 399(F)

Hartigan, Lynda Roscoe. *Sharing Traditions,* 5797

Hartmann, William K., et al. *Cycles of Fire,* 8353

Hartnell, Tim. *Creating Adventure Games for Your Computer,* 8982
Tim Hartnell's Giant Book of Computer Games, 8982
Tim Hartnell's Second Giant Book of Computer Games, 8982

Hartt, Frederick. *Art,* 5745
Michelangelo, 5776

Hartwell, David G., ed. *The Dark Descent,* 1763(F)
Masterpieces of Fantasy and Enchantment, 1146(F)

Hartwell, David G. (jt. author). *Christmas Ghosts,* 1729(F)

Haruf, Kent. *The Tie That Binds,* 1569(F)

Harvard Nuclear Study Group. *Living with Nuclear Weapons,* 4144

Harvard Student Agencies. *Let's Go, 1990,* 7483, 7494, 7519, 7544, 7548, 7555, 7596, 7644, 7744, 8181, 8181

Harvey, Paul, ed. *The Concise Oxford Dictionary of French Literature,* 3586
The Oxford Companion to French Literature, 3586

Harwood, Don. *Everything You Always Wanted to Know about Portable Video Tape Recording,* 9050

Harwood, Ronald. *The Dresser,* 3031

Haseley, Dennis. *The Counterfeiter,* 833(F)

Hashian. *Shanidar,* 122(F)

Haskins, James. *Black Theater in America,* 6089
The Guardian Angels, 4479
Leaders of the Middle East, 7597
Lena, 6407
Mr. Bojangles, 6437
Street Gangs, 4557
Sugar Ray Leonard, 6747

Haskins, James (jt. author). *Double Dutch,* 9605

Haslip, Joan. *Marie Antoinette,* 6857

Hassan, Steve. *Combatting Cult Mind Control,* 4053

Hasse, John Edward, ed. *Ragtime,* 5868

Hasselstrom, Linda. *Windbreak,* 8583

Hassler, Jon. *Grand Opening,* 562(F)
Staggerford, 672(F)

Hastings, Max. *The Battle for the Falklands,* 7673
The Korean War, 8117
Overlord, 7214
Victory in Europe, 7215

Hatch, James V., ed. *Black Theater, U.S.A,* 3080

Hatch, Katherine (jt. author). *My Life in Three Acts,* 6398

Hatfield, Frederick C. *Powerlifting,* 9771

Hattaway, Herman. *How the North Won,* 7921

Hattersley, Ralph. *Beginner's Guide to Photography,* 9421

Haubenstock, Susan H. *Career Opportunities in Art,* 4886

Hauptly, Denis J. *In Vietnam,* 8118

Hauser, Thomas. *The Fantasy,* 967(F)

Hauser, Thomas (jt. author). *Final Warning,* 8922

Hausman, Carl (jt. author). *Coping with Hearing Loss,* 5332

Hautzig, Ester. *The Endless Steppe,* 7216

Hawcock, David. *Paper Dinosaurs,* 9222

Hawdon, Robin. *A Rustle in the Grass,* 290(F)

Hawes, Gene R. *The College Money Book,* 4779
Hawes Guide to Successful Study Skills, 4648
The Outdoor Careers Guide, 4839

Hawes, Lynne Salop (jt. author). *Hawes Guide to Successful Study Skills,* 4648

Hawke, David Freeman. *Everyday Life in Early America,* 7841
Nuts and Bolts of the Past, 8946

Hawke, Simon. *The Ivanhoe Gambit,* 1147(F)
The Pimpernel Plot, 1147(F)
The Timekeeper Conspiracy, 1147(F)

Hawking, Stephen W. *A Brief History of Time,* 8366

Hawkins, Gary. *U.S.A. by Bus and Train,* 7745

Hawkins, Gerald S. *Stonehenge Decoded,* 7520

Hawkins, Gordon (jt. author). *The Citizen's Guide to Gun Control,* 4530

Hawley, Richard A. *Drugs and Society,* 5125

Hawthorne, Nathaniel. *The House of the Seven Gables,* 400(F)
The Scarlet Letter, 401(F)
Tales and Sketches, 2920(F)

Hay, Henry. *The Amateur Magician's Handbook,* 9397

Hayakawa, S. I. *Language in Thought and Action,* 3923

Hayden, Richard Seth. *Restoring the Statue of Liberty,* 8166

Hayden, Thomas C. *Peterson's Handbook for College Admissions,* 4741

Hayden, Tom. *Reunion,* 6508

Hayden, Torey L. *One Child,* 5384
Somebody Else's Kids, 5385

Hayes, Billy. *Midnight Express,* 6917

Hayes, Colin. *The Complete Guide to Painting and Drawing,* 9193

Hayes, Harold T. P. *The Dark Romance of Dian Fossey,* 6667

Hayes, Helen. *My Life in Three Acts,* 6398

Haynes, Colin (jt. author). *Computer Viruses, Worms, Data Diddlers, Killer Programs and Other Threats to Your System,* 8999

Haynes, Conrad. *Bishop's Gambit Declined,* 2047(F)
Perpetual Check, 2047(F)

Haynes, Cynthia. *Raising Turkeys, Ducks, Geese, Pigeons, and Guineas,* 8589

Haynie, W. J. *Electricity and Electronics Today,* 9037

Hays, Peter L. *Ernest Hemingway,* 3732

Hays, Samuel P. *The Response to Industrialism, 1885–1914,* 8010

Hayter, Charles. *Gilbert and Sullivan,* 5922

Haythornthwaite, Philip. *Uniforms of the American Civil War in Color,* 7922

Hayward, John, ed. *The Oxford Book of Nineteenth-Century English Verse,* 3206

Hazen, Margaret. *The Music Men,* 5936

Hazen, Robert (jt. author). *The Music Men,* 5936

Hazen, Robert M. *The Breakthrough,* 8936

Head, Ann. *Mr. and Mrs. Bo Jo Jones,* 834(F)

Head, Sandy Summers. *Sizing Up,* 5281

Headley, Lake. *The Court-Martial of Clayton Lonetree,* 4242

Headstrom, Richard. *Suburban Geology,* 8797

Healy, Larry. *Angry Mountain,* 123(F)

Heaney, Seamus. *Station Island,* 3207

Hearn, Michael Patrick, ed. *The Victorian Fairy Tale Book,* 3401

Hearne, Betsy. *Love Lines,* 3278

Heath, Jim F. *Decade of Disillusionment,* 8069

Heatley, C. J. *Forged in Steel,* 9128

Heaton, Caroline (jt. author). *Close Company,* 586(F)

Heaton, E. W. *Everyday Life in Old Testament Times,* 4105

Heatter, Maida. *Maida Heatter's Best Dessert Book Ever,* 9343

Heaven, Constance. *Castle of Doves,* 1433(F)

Hebblethwaite, Peter. *Pope John XXIII,* 6852

Hebblewhite, Ian. *Northlight Handbook of Artists' Materials,* 9194

Hebden, Mark. *Pel and the Bombers,* 2048(F)

Hebert, Ernest. *The Dogs of March,* 673(F)

Heckman, Philip. *The Magic of Holography,* 8934

Hedgecoe, John. *The Book of Photography,* 9422
John Hedgecoe's Darkroom Techniques, 9423

Heer, John (jt. author). *Opportunities in Civil Engineering Careers,* 5018
Opportunities in Engineering Technology Careers, 5018

Heeren, Dave. *The Basketball Abstract,* 9725

Heffner, Richard D. *A Documentary History of the United States,* 7746

Hegenberger, John. *Collector's Guide to Comic Books,* 9448

Heggen, Thomas. *Mister Roberts,* 1656(F)

Hegi, Ursula. *Floating in My Mother's Palm,* 968(F)

Heidish, Marcy. *Witnesses,* 1516(F)

Heilbroner, Robert L. *Beyond Boom and Crash,* 4569
Economics Explained, 4571
The Worldly Philosophers, 4570

Heim, Kathleen. *Opportunities in Library and Information Science,* 4951

Hein, Karen. *AIDS, Trading Fears for Facts,* 5188

Heinlein, Robert A. *Assignment in Eternity,* 2576(F)
The Cat Who Walks through Walls, 2577(F)
The Door into Summer, 2578(F)
Expanded Universe, 2579(F)
Glory Road, 2579(F)
The Green Hills of Earth, 2579(F)
Grumbles from the Grave, 3733
I Will Fear No Evil, 2579(F)
Job, 2579(F)
Menace from Earth, 2586(F)
Methuselah's Children, 2586(F)
The Moon Is a Harsh Mistress, 2580(F)
The Past through Tomorrow, 2581(F)
Puppet Masters, 2587(F)
Red Planet, 2582(F)
Revolt in 2100, 2583(F)
Rocket Ship Galileo, 2584(F)
The Rolling Stones, 2584(F)
Space Cadet, 2584(F)
Star Beast, 2584(F)
Starman Jones, 2584(F)
Starship Troopers, 2584(F)
Stranger in a Strange Land, 2585(F)
Time for the Stars, 2586(F)
Tunnel in the Sky, 2587(F)

Heinonen, Janet. *Sports Illustrated Running for Women*, 9912

Heinrich, Bernd. *Ravens in Winter*, 8556

Heintze, Carl. *Medical Ethics*, 5239

Heiser, Victor G. *An American Doctor's Odyssey*, 6673

Heiserman, David L. *Build Your Own Working Robot*, 8983

Heitzmann, William. *Opportunities in Marine and Maritime Careers*, 5020

Helander, Brock. *The Rock Who's Who*, 5869

Helfer, Ralph. *The Beauty of the Beasts*, 6019

Helfer, Ray E. (jt. author). *The Battered Child*, 5660

Helgeland, Glenn (jt. author). *Archery for Beginners*, 9607

Helgren, David (jt. author). *Everything Is Somewhere*, 7056

Heller, Joseph. *Catch-22*, 1657(F)
  Something Happened, 674(F)

Heller, Nancy G. *Women Artists*, 5746

Heller, Wendy M. (jt. author). *The Teenager's Survival Guide to Moving*, 5624

Hellickson, Russ. *An Instructional Guide to Amateur Wrestling*, 9784

Hellman, Lillian. *Pentimento*, 6256
  Scoundrel Time, 6256
  Six Plays by Lillian Hellman, 3081
  Three, 6256
  An Unfinished Woman, 6256

Hellman, Peter. *Heroes*, 7612

Helmbold, F. Wilbur. *Tracing Your Ancestry*, 5656

Helprin, Mark. *Winter's Tale*, 1148(F)

Hemingway, Ernest. *The Complete Short Stories of Ernest Hemingway*, 402(F)
  Ernest Hemingway, 6261
  A Farewell to Arms, 1635(F)
  For Whom the Bell Tolls, 1434(F)
  In Our Time, 835(F)
  A Moveable Feast, 6262
  The Nick Adams Stories, 2921(F)
  The Old Man and the Sea, 124(F)
  The Short Stories of Ernest Hemingway, 2922(F)
  The Snows of Kilimanjaro, and Other Stories, 2923(F)
  The Sun Also Rises, 1610(F)

Hemming, John. *The Conquest of the Incas*, 7674

Hemming, Roy. *Discovering Great Music*, 5821

Hemphill, John. *Herbs*, 8434

Hemphill, Rosemary (jt. author). *Herbs*, 8434

Henbest, Nigel (jt. author). *New Worlds*, 8342

Henderson, Harold Gould, ed. *An Introduction to Haiku*, 3348

Henderson, Kathy. *Market Guide for Young Writers*, 3965

Henderson, Mary C. *Theater in America*, 6090

Henderson, Zenna. *The People*, 2588(F)

Hendin, Herbert. *Suicide in America*, 5386

Hendler, Herb. *Year by Year in the Rock Era*, 8070

Hendrick, George. *Katherine Anne Porter*, 3734

Hendrickson, Robert. *American Talk*, 3924

Heng, Liang. *Son of the Revolution*, 6812

Henkin, Mitch (jt. author). *How to Watch Ice Hockey*, 9888

Henkin, Shepard. *Opportunities in Hotel and Motel Management*, 4840

Henning, Fritz. *Drawing & Painting with Ink*, 9195

Henningfield, Jack E. *Barbiturates*, 5126

Henrion, Marilyn (jt. author). *Careers in the Fashion Industry*, 4832

Henry, Alan. *Fifty Famous Motor Races*, 9615

Henry, Fran Worden. *Toughing It Out at Harvard*, 4919

Henry, Mari Lyn. *How to Be a Working Actor*, 4887

Henry, O. *Forty-one Stories*, 403(F)

Henry, Thomas. *Better English Made Easy*, 3925

Hensel, George. *Learn to Drive*, 9097

Hentoff, Nat. *Boston Boy*, 6264
  The First Freedom, 4305
  Jazz Is, 5870

Heppenheimer, T. A. *The Coming Quake*, 8803

Herald, Earl S. (jt. author). *A Field Guide to Pacific Coast Fishes of North America*, 8624

Herbert, Brian. *Prisoners of Arionn*, 2589(F)
  Sudanna, Sudanna, 1149(F)

Herbert, Brian (jt. author). *Man of Two Worlds*, 2594(F)

Herbert, Eugenia W. (jt. author). *The Private Franklin*, 6588

Herbert, Frank. *The Ascension Factor*, 1150(F)
  The Best of Frank Herbert, 2592(F)
  Chapterhouse, 2590(F)
  Children of Dune, 2593(F)
  Destination, 2591(F)
  The Dosadi Experiment, 2592(F)
  Dune, 2593(F)
  Dune Messiah, 2593(F)
  God Emperor of Dune, 2593(F)
  Heretics of Dune, 2590(F)
  The Jesus Factor, 1150(F)
  The Lazarus Effect, 1150(F)
  Man of Two Worlds, 2594(F)
  The White Plague, 125(F)

Herbert, James. *Haunted*, 1764(F)

Herbst, Dan. *Sports Illustrated Soccer*, 9951

Heron, Ann, ed. *One Teenager in Ten*, 5466

Heron, Jackie. *Careers in Health and Fitness*, 4952
  Exploring Careers in Nursing, 4995

Herr, Michael. *Dispatches*, 8119

Herr, Pamela. *Jessie Benton Fremont*, 6619

Herrin, Lamar. *The Unwritten Chronicles of Robert E. Lee*, 1536(F)

Herring, George C. *America's Longest War*, 8120
Herring, Robert. *McCampbell's War*, 563(F)
Herriot, James. *All Creatures Great and Small*, 6674
All Things Bright and Beautiful, 6674
All Things Wise and Wonderful, 6674
James Herriot's Dog Stories, 8721
James Herriot's Yorkshire, 7521
The Lord God Made Them All, 6674
Herrnstein, Richard J. (jt. author). *Crime and Human Nature*, 4498
Hersey, John. *A Bell for Adano*, 1658(F)
The Child Buyer, 969(F)
Hiroshima, 7217
Into the Valley, 7218
A Single Pebble, 1393(F)
The Wall, 1659(F)
Hersey, John, ed. *Ralph Ellison*, 3735
Hershey, Robert L. *How to Think with Numbers*, 8836
Hershiser, Orel. *Out of the Blue*, 6723
Herskowitz, Mickey. *The Quarterbacks*, 9847
Herskowitz, Mickey (jt. author). *Catcher in the Wry*, 9705
Herzog, Chaim. *The Arab-Israeli Wars*, 7613
Herzstein, Robert Edwin. *The Nazis*, 7505
Heseltine, J. E. (jt. author). *The Concise Oxford Dictionary of French Literature*, 3586
The Oxford Companion to French Literature, 3586
Hess, Fred C. *Chemistry Made Simple*, 8784
Hessayon, D. G. *The House Plant Expert*, 9380
Hesse, Hermann. *Demian*, 675(F)
Peter Camenzind, 836(F)
Pictor's Metamorphoses and Other Fantasies, 1151(F)
Siddhartha, 1394(F)
Steppenwolf, 837(F)
Heussner, Ralph C. (jt. author). *Herpes Diseases and Your Health*, 5171
Hewes, Henry, ed. *Famous American Plays of the 1940s*, 3082
Hewitt, David (jt. author). *Table Tennis*, 9591
Hewitt, Don. *Minute by Minute*, 6020
Heyerdahl, Thor. *Easter Island*, 7470
Kon-Tiki, 6144
Heyman, Anita. *Final Grades*, 838(F)
Heymann, Tom. *On an Average Day . . ,* 9505
Hiatt, June Hemmons. *The Principles of Knitting*, 9241
Hibbard, Howard. *Michelangelo*, 6199
Hibbert, Christopher. *The American Revolution through British Eyes*, 7851
The Days of the French Revolution, 7495
Rome, 7549
Hickey, Donald R. *The War of 1812*, 7868
Hickler, Holly (jt. author). *Vivienne*, 6925
Hickman, Tracy (jt. author). *Doom of the Darksword*, 1315(F)

Dragon Wing, 1311(F)
Dragonlance Chronicles, 1312(F)
The Dragonlance Legends, 1313(F)
Dragons of Autumn Twilight, 1312(F)
Dragons of Spring Dawning, 1312(F)
Dragons of Winter Night, 1312(F)
Elven Star, 1314(F)
Forging the Darksword, 1315(F)
The Paladin of the Night, 1316(F)
The Prophet of Akhran, 1316(F)
Test of the Twins, 1313(F)
Time of the Twins, 1313(F)
Triumph of the Darksword, 1315(F)
War of the Twins, 1313(F)
The Will of the Wanderer, 1316(F)
Higbee, Kenneth L. *Your Memory*, 5331
Higginbotham, Bill. *Whittling*, 9275
Higgins, Jack. *Cold Harbour*, 126(F)
The Eagle Has Landed, 127(F)
Night of the Fox, 128(F)
Solo, 129(F)
Touch the Devil, 130(F)
Higham, Charles. *Kate*, 6401
Highet, Gilbert. *The Classical Tradition*, 3587
Highwater, Jamake, ed. *Words in the Blood*, 2924
Higton, Bernard (jt. author). *Spirit of Place*, 7489(F)
Hijuelos, Oscar. *Our House in the Last World*, 463(F)
Hildebrand, John. *Reading the River*, 6146
Hildyard, Nicholas (jt. author). *The Earth Report*, 4428
Hill, Adrian. *The Beginner's Book of Oil Painting*, 9196
The Beginner's Book of Watercolour Painting, 9196
Hill, Barbara. *Cook's Book of Essential Information*, 9344
The Cook's Book of Indispensable Ideas, 9344
Hill, Douglas. *Galactic Warlord*, 2595(F)
Hill, Fiona. *The Country Gentleman*, 2279(F)
Hill, Frank Ernest (jt. author). *The Winged Horse*, 3847
Hill, Hamlin (jt. author). *America's Humor*, 3565
Hill, Ingrid. *Dixie Church Interstate Blues*, 564(F)
Hill, Rebecca. *Blue Rise*, 839(F)
Hill, Reginald. *Ruling Passion*, 2049(F)
Hill, Robert W. (jt. author). *James Dickey*, 3880
Hill, Susan. *The Woman in Black*, 1765(F)
Hill-Miller, Katherine. *The Most Common Errors in English Usage and How to Avoid Them*, 3926
Hillard, Darla. *Vanishing Tracks*, 8510
Hillel, Shlomo. *Operation Babylon*, 7598
Hillerman, Tony. *The Blessing Way*, 2053(F)
Coyote Waits, 2050(F)

Dance Hall of the Dead, 2053(F)
The Fly on the Wall, 2053(F)
The Ghostway, 2051(F)
The Joe Leaphorn Mysteries, 2052(F)
Listening Woman, 2053(F)
People of Darkness, 2053(F)
Skinwalkers, 2054(F)
Talking God, 2054(F)
A Thief of Time, 2054(F)
Hillier, Bevis. *Art Deco of the 20s and 30s,* 5747
Hills, C. A. R. *The Destruction of Pompeii and Herculaneum,* 7116
Hillway, Tyrus. *Herman Melville,* 3736
Hilton, James. *Good-bye Mr. Chips,* 1435(F)
Lost Horizon, 1152(F)
Random Harvest, 2280(F)
Hinchliffe, Arnold P. *Harold Pinter,* 3809
Hinding, Andrea, ed. *Feminism,* 4306
Hindle, Lee J. *Dragon Fall,* 1153(F)
Hine, Robert V. *The American West,* 7955
Hines, Jerome. *Great Singers on Great Singing,* 5923
Hinton, Harold C. *East Asia and the Western Pacific,* 7392
Hipple, Ted. *Presenting Sue Ellen Bridgers,* 3737
Hirsch, Joe. *Kentucky Derby,* 9884
Hirsch, Kathleen. *Songs from the Alley,* 4508
Hirshey, Gerri. *Nowhere to Run,* 5871
Hirst, Wolf Z. *John Keats,* 3866
Hiss, Alger. *Recollections of a Life,* 6592
Hitchcock, Barbara (jt. author). *Sightseeing,* 8318
Hitching, Francis. *The Neck of the Giraffe,* 6999
Hitler, Adolf. *Mein Kampf,* 6848
Hitti, Phillip K. *History of the Arabs, from the Earliest Times to the Present,* 7599
Hoagland, Edward. *African Calliope,* 7368
Hoban, Russell. *Riddley Walker,* 2596(F)
Hobbes, Anne. *Tisha,* 6918
Hobbes, Thomas. *Leviathan,* 4009
Hobbs, Will. *Changes in Latitudes,* 840(F)
Hobhouse, Henry. *Forces of Change,* 7047
Hobson, Burton. *Coin Collecting as a Hobby,* 9449
Coin Collecting for Beginners, 9450
Hoch, Edward D., ed. *The Year's Best Mystery and Suspense Stories,* 2055(F)
Hocken, Sheila. *Emma and I,* 6919
Hockey, Thomas A. *The Book of the Moon,* 8339
Hodgell, P. C. *Dark of the Moon,* 1154(F)
Hodges, C. Walter. *Shakespeare's Theatre,* 6091
Hodges, Cyril. *The Globe Restored,* 6092
Hodges, Henry. *Technology in the Ancient World,* 7084
Hodges, Margaret. *Making a Difference,* 5657
Hodges, Michael. *Ireland,* 7522
Hoehling, A. A. *Damn the Torpedoes!* 7923
Hoepli, Nancy L., ed. *Aftermath of Colonialism,* 7334

Hoff, Ron. *"I Can See You Naked,"* 4680
Hoff, Syd. *The Art of Cartooning,* 9197
Editorial and Political Cartooning, 5748
Hoffer, Eric. *The True Believer,* 5524
Hoffer, Marilyn (jt. author). *Freefall,* 9065
Hoffer, William. *Freefall,* 9065
Hoffer, William (jt. author). *Midnight Express,* 6917
Hoffman, Alice. *At Risk,* 676(F)
Property Of, 841(F)
Hoffman, Eva. *Lost in Translation,* 6920
Hoffman, Frederick J. *William Faulkner,* 3738
Hoffman, Jeffrey. *Corvette,* 9098
Hoffman, Marshall (jt. author). *Sportsmedicine Book,* 5246
Hoffman, Nancy, ed. *Women Working,* 970(F)
Hoffman, Paul. *Archimedes' Revenge,* 8837
Hoffman, Ronald (jt. author). *We Shall Overcome,* 4350
Hoffman, Ted, ed. *Famous American Plays of the 1970s,* 3083
Hoffman, William (jt. author). *The Court-Martial of Clayton Lonetree,* 4242
Hoffmeister, Donald. *Mammals,* 8454
Hofstadter, Douglas R. *Gödel, Escher, Bach,* 8222
Hofstadter, Richard. *The Age of Reform from Bryan to F.D.R,* 7747
America at 1750, 7842
The American Political Tradition, and the Men Who Made It, 7748
Hogan, Ben. *Power Golf,* 9869
Hogan, James P. *Code of the Lifemaker,* 2597(F)
Endgame Enigma, 2598(F)
The Gentle Giants of Ganymede, 2599(F)
Giants' Star, 2599(F)
Inherit the Stars, 2599(F)
Mirror Maze, 2600(F)
Hogan, Marty. *High-Performance Racquetball,* 9573
Hogan, Marty (jt. author). *Skills & Strategies for Winning Racquetball,* 9972
Hogan, Ray. *Solitude's Lawman,* 131(F)
Hogben, Lancelot. *Mathematics for the Million,* 8838
Hohler, Robert T. *"I Touch the Future . . .",* 6153
Hohlfelder, Robert L. *King Herod's Dream,* 7117
Hoke, Helen, ed. *Spirits, Spooks and Other Sinister Creatures,* 1766(F)
Tales of Fear and Frightening Phenomena, 1766(F)
Uncanny Tales of Unearthly and Unexpected Horrors, 1767(F)
Holdstock, Robert. *Lavondyss,* 1155(F)
Mythago Wood, 1155(F)
Holiday, Billie. *Lady Sings the Blues,* 6403
Holiday, Ron, et al. *Cat Dancers,* 5969

Holland, Barbara. *Hail to the Chiefs*, 6475
Holland, Cecelia. *The Bear Flag*, 1570(F)
  The Lords of Vaumartin, 1436(F)
Holland, Charlie (jt. author). *Juggling for All*, 9300
Holland, Heidi. *The Struggle*, 7374
Holland, Isabelle. *After the First Love*, 2281(F)
  A Fatal Advent, 2056(F)
  Summer of My First Love, 2281(F)
Holland, Tim. *Beginning Backgammon*, 9813
Hollander, John (jt. author). *The Oxford Anthology of English Literature*, 2930, 2931
Hollander, Zander. *The Complete Handbook of Baseball*, 9652
  The Complete Handbook of Pro-Basketball, 9726
  The Complete Handbook of Pro-Football, 9848
  The Illustrated Sports Record Book, 9574
Holleb, Arthur I., et al., eds. *The American Cancer Society Cancer Book*, 5189
Hollis, Helen Rice. *The Piano*, 5937
Holloway, Adrian (jt. author). *The Book of Color Photography*, 9409
Holloway, Charles M. *Profiles in Achievement*, 6476
Holman, C. Hugh. *A Handbook to Literature*, 3588
Holman, Marshall. *Marshall Holman's Bowling Tips and Techniques*, 9780
Holme, Bryan. *Creatures of Paradise*, 5720
Holmes, George. *Dante*, 3862
Holmes, George, ed. *The Oxford Illustrated History of Medieval Europe*, 7484
Holmes, Marjorie. *The Messiah*, 1359(F)
  Saturday Night, 2282(F)
  Three from Galilee, 1360(F)
  Two from Galilee, 1360(F)
Holmes, Richard (jt. author). *Soldiers*, 7052
Holmes, Thomas B. *Electronic & Experimental Music*, 5938
Holmgren, Virginia C. *Raccoons*, 8492
Holt, Robert Lawrence. *How to Publish, Promote, and Sell Your Own Book*, 3978
Holt, Tom. *Who's Afraid of Beowulf?* 1156(F)
Holt, Victoria. *The Captive*, 2057(F)
  The Demon Lover, 132(F)
  The Devil on Horseback, 134(F)
  House of a Thousand Lanterns, 134(F)
  The Indian Fan, 2283(F)
  The Judas Kiss, 132(F)
  King of the Castle, 132(F)
  Kirkland Revels, 134(F)
  Lord of the Far Islands, 132(F)
  Menfreya in the Morning, 132(F)
  The Road to Paradise Island, 133(F)
  Secret for a Nightingale, 2284(F)
  Shivering Sands, 134(F)
  The Silk Vendetta, 2285(F)
  Snare of Serpents, 2058(F)
  The Time of the Hunter's Moon, 135(F)

Holtze, Sally Holmes. *Presenting Norma Fox Mazer*, 3739
Holum, Kenneth G. (jt. author). *King Herod's Dream*, 7117
Holzer, Hans. *Best True Ghost Stories*, 9506
Homer. *The Iliad*, 3183
  The Odyssey, 3184
Homes, A. M. *Jack*, 677(F)
Homewood, Harry. *Final Harbor*, 7219
Honig, Daniel. *How to Bike Better*, 9755
  How to Run Better, 9913
Honig, Donald. *The American League*, 9653
  The Greatest First Basemen of All Times, 9654
  The Greatest Pitchers of All Time, 9655
  The National League, 9653
  The Power Hitters, 9656
  The World Series, 9657
Honig, Donald (jt. author). *The 100 Greatest Baseball Players of All Time*, 6709
Hoobler, Dorothy. *The Voyages of Captain Cook*, 6136
Hoobler, Dorothy (jt. author). *Drugs and Crime*, 5127
Hoobler, Thomas. *Drugs and Crime*, 5127
Hoobler, Thomas (jt. author). *The Voyages of Captain Cook*, 6136
Hook, Brian, ed. *The Cambridge Encyclopedia of China*, 7411
Hook, J. N. *Family Names*, 5658
Hook, Jason. *American Indian Warrior Chiefs*, 6477
Hooks, William H. *A Flight of Dazzle Angels*, 678(F)
Hooper, Brad. *Short Story Writers and Their Work*, 3622
Hooper, Judith. *The Three-Pound Universe*, 5315
Hooper, Meredith. *Cleared for Take-Off*, 9066
Hoopes, James. *Oral History*, 7048
Hoopes, Ned E., ed. *Edge of Awareness*, 3536
Hoopes, Roy (jt. author). *Legal Careers and the Legal System*, 4967
  Paralegal Careers, 4968
Hoose, Phillip M. *Hoosiers*, 9727
  Necessities, 4365
Hoover, H. M. *The Dawn Palace*, 1361(F)
Hope, Anthony. *The Prisoner of Zenda*, 136(F)
  Rupert of Hentzau, 136(F)
Hopkins, Budd. *Intruders*, 9507
Hopkins, Gerard Manley. *The Poems of Gerard Manley Hopkins*, 3208
Hopkins, Jerry. *Elvis*, 6431
  Hit and Run, 6399
Hoppel, Joe. *The Series*, 9658
Hoppel, Joe, et al., eds. *College Football's Twenty-five Greatest Teams*, 9849
Hopper, Nancy J. *Lies*, 842(F)
Hopper, Robin. *The Ceramic Spectrum*, 9164
Hordeski, Michael F. *Microcomputer Local Area Networks*, 8984

Horenstein, Henry. *Black and White Photography*, 9424

Horgan, Paul. *Whitewater*, 843(F)

Horn, Huston. *The Pioneers*, 7956

Hornback, Bert G. *Great Expectations*, 3669

Horne, Alistair. *The Fall of Paris*, 7496

Horner, John R. *Digging Dinosaurs*, 6981

Hornig, Doug. *The Dark Side*, 2059(F)

Hornung, D. Mark. *Opportunities in Microelectronics*, 5043

Horowitz, David (jt. author). *The Kennedys*, 6598

Horowitz, Judy. *The Frisbee Book*, 9575

Horowitz, Lois. *Knowing Where to Look*, 4681

Horton, John. *Grieg*, 6345

Horton, Susan R. *Thinking through Writing*, 4682

Horton, Tom (jt. author). *Yogi*, 6715

Horwin, Michael. *Careers in Film and Video Production*, 4888

Horwitz, Elinor Lander. *Contemporary American Folk Artists*, 5798

Mountain People, Mountain Crafts, 5808

Horwitz, Tony. *One for the Road*, 6147

Hoshino, Michio. *Moose*, 8523

Hosking, Eric. *Antarctic Wildlife*, 7696

Seabirds of the World, 8538

Hosking, Eric, et al. *Eric Hosking's Birds of Prey of the World*, 8561

Hostetler, John A. *Amish Society*, 4054

Hotchner, A. E. *Blown Away*, 5872

Hotchner, Tracy. *Pregnancy & Childbirth*, 5467

Hough, Richard. *The Battle of Britain*, 7335

Houghton, Norris, ed. *Romeo and Juliet and West Side Story*, 2983

Houk, Ralph. *Season of Glory*, 9659

House, Tom. *The Winning Pitcher*, 9660

Household, Geoffrey. *Rogue Male*, 137(F)

Housman, A. E. *The Collected Poems of A. E. Housman*, 3209

Houston, David. *Wingmaster*, 2601(F)

Houston, James. *River Runners*, 138(F)

Running West, 1493(F)

Houston, James D. (jt. author). *Farewell to Manzanar*, 7220

Houston, Jean. *The Possible Human*, 5353

Houston, Jeanne W. *Farewell to Manzanar*, 7220

Hovde, Jane. *Jane Addams*, 6612

Hoving, Walter. *Tiffany's Table Manners for Teenagers*, 5583

Howard, Brett. *Memphis Blues*, 1625(F)

Howard, Diane Wilder. *Swimming Upstream*, 4742

Howard, Donald R. *Chaucer*, 6233

Howard, Edwin J. *Geoffrey Chaucer*, 3867

Howard, Jane. *A Different Woman*, 679(F)

Howard, Philip. *New Words for Old*, 3927

Howard, Robert E., et al. *Conan*, 2602(F)

Howard, Ted. *Who Should Play God?* 5262

Howarth, David. *1066*, 7523

The Voyage of the Armada, 7556

Howarth, Stephen. *August '39*, 7221

Howarth, W., et al. *America's Wild Woodlands*, 7749

Howatch, Susan. *Devil on Lammas Night*, 139(F)

Penmarric, 139(F)

Howatson, M. C. *The Oxford Companion to Classical Literature*, 3589

Howe, Florence (jt. author). *Women Working*, 970(F)

Howe, Imogen. *Vicious Circle*, 1768(F)

Howe, Irving. *World of Our Fathers*, 4386

Howe, Irving, ed. *1984 Revisited*, 3670

Howe, John. *Choosing the Right Dog*, 8722

Howe, Melodie Johnson. *The Mother Shadow*, 2060(F)

Howell, John C. *Everyday Law for Everyone*, 4243

Howse, Derek. *Greenwich Time and the Discovery of the Longitude*, 8860

Hoy, Frank P. *Photojournalism*, 9425

Hoyt, Edwin P. *Blue Skies and Blood*, 7223

Closing the Circle in the Pacific, 7225

The GI's War, 7222

Japan's War, 7450

The Marine Raiders, 7224

McCampbell's Heroes, 7223

Men of the Gambler Bay, 7225

The Rise of the Chinese Republic, 7412

U-Boats Offshore, 7226

Yamamoto, 6819

Hoyt, Erich. *The Whale-Watcher's Handbook*, 8653

Hubbard, David. *Winning Back the Sky*, 4545

Hubbell, Sue. *A Country Year*, 8395

Hubert, Cam. *Dreamspeaker*, 140(F)

Hudgeons, Marc, ed. *The Official Blackbook Price Guide of U.S. Coins*, 9451

Hudson, Michael. *Thieves of Light*, 2603(F)

Hudson, W. H. *Green Mansions*, 1157(F)

Huebener, Theodore (jt. author). *Opportunities in Foreign Language Careers*, 4816

Huff, Darrell. *How to Lie with Statistics*, 8858

Huff, Tanya. *Gate of Darkness, Circle of Light*, 1158(F)

The Last Wizard, 1159(F)

Huggan, Isabel. *The Elizabeth Stories*, 844(F)

Huggins, Nathan Irvin. *Black Odyssey*, 7869

Harlem Renaissance, 5799

Slave and Citizen, 6502

Hughes, Langston. *The Big Sea*, 6267

I Wonder as I Wander, 6267

Selected Poems of Langston Hughes, 3279

Hughes, Langston, ed. *The Best Short Stories by Negro Writers*, 464(F)

Hughes, Martin. *Body Clock*, 5296

Hughes, Monica. *Hunter in the Dark*, 141(F)

Hughes, Richard. *A High Wind in Jamaica*, 680(F)
The Tranquilizing of America, 5128
Hughes, Rosemary. *Haydn*, 6348
Hughes, Stephen. *Pop Culture Mania*, 9452
Hughes, Ted. *New Selected Poems*, 3210
Hughes, Terence. *The Day They Stole the Queen Mary*, 142(F)
Hugo, Victor. *The Hunchback of Notre Dame*, 315(F)
Les Miserables, 316(F)
Hultman, Tami, ed. *The Africa News Cookbook*, 9345
Human Rights in China Staff. *Children of the Dragon*, 7413
Humphreys, Josephine. *Rich in Love*, 845(F)
Humphreys, Martha. *Side by Side*, 2286(F)
Hungry Wolf, Adolf. *Children of the Sun*, 7809
Hunnisett, Jean. *Period Costume for Stage & Screen*, 5282
Hunsburger, H. Edward. *Crossfire*, 143(F)
Hunter, Jim. *Catfish*, 6724
Hunter, Mollie. *The Third Eye*, 2061(F)
Hunter, R. Lanny. *Living Dogs and Dead Lions*, 681(F)
Hunter, Sam. *Modern Art*, 5721
Hunter, Victor L. (jt. author). *Living Dogs and Dead Lions*, 681(F)
Huntington, Roger. *American Supercar*, 9099
Hurley, Judith Benn. *Healthy Microwave Cooking*, 9346
Hurmence, Belinda. *Tancy*, 1611(F)
Hurmence, Belinda, ed. *Before Freedom, When I Just Can Remember*, 7870
Hurston, Zora Neale. *Dust Tracks on a Road*, 6269
I Love Myself When I Am Laughing . . . and Then Again When I Am Looking Mean and Impressive, 2925
Their Eyes Are Watching God, 465(F)
Hurt, Harry. *For All Mankind*, 8303
Hurt, Henry. *Reasonable Doubt*, 8071
Huss, Barbara (jt. author). *A Teen-age Guide to Healthy Skin and Hair*, 5337
Hutchinson, Lois. *Standard Handbook for Secretaries*, 4639
Hutchinson, Stuart. *Henry James*, 3740
Hutton, Richard (jt. author). *Beyond Boardwalk and Park Place*, 9811
Hutton-Jamieson, Iain. *Colored Pencil Drawing Techniques*, 9198
Huxley, Aldous. *Brave New World*, 2604(F)
Brave New World Revisited, 4414
Huxley, Elspeth. *The Flame Trees of Thika*, 6921
Mottled Lizard, 6921
Scott of the Antarctic, 6160
Huygen, Wil. *Gnomes*, 3365
Hyde, Dayton O. *Don Coyote*, 8513
Hyde, Elisabeth. *Her Native Colors*, 846(F)

Hyde, Lawrence E. (jt. author). *Cloning and the New Genetics*, 5263
Hyde, Margaret O. *AIDS*, 5191
Cloning and the New Genetics, 5263
Juvenile Justice and Injustice, 4244
Terrorism, 4546
VD, 5190
Hyde, Margaret O., ed. *Mind Drugs*, 5129
Hyland, William G. *The Cold War Is Over*, 4145
Hylton, Sara. *My Sister Clare*, 1437(F)
Tomorrow's Rainbow, 1438(F)
Hylton, William H. (jt. author). *Rodale's Illustrated Encyclopedia of Herbs*, 8418
Hyman, Jane (jt. author). *LOGO Activites for the Computer*, 9012
Hyman, Tom. *Seven Days to Petrograd*, 144(F)
Hymowitz, Carol. *A History of Women in America*, 7750
Hynes, Samuel. *Flights of Passage*, 6148

Iacocca, Lee. *Iacocca*, 6676
Ibbotson, Eva. *A Company of Swans*, 2287(F)
Ibsen, Henrik. *Eight Plays*, 3004
An Enemy of the People, 3005
Four Great Plays, 3006
Four Major Plays, 3007
Ibuse, Masuji. *Black Rain*, 1660(F)
Ifrah, Georges. *From One to Zero*, 8848
Ignoffo, Matthew. *Coping with Your Inner Critic*, 5614
Igoe, Robert S. *Dictionary of Food Ingredients*, 8416
Ordway, Frederick I., III (jt. author). *Space Travel*, 8327
Ilma, Viola. *Funk & Wagnalls Guide to the World of Stamp Collecting*, 9453
Ing, Dean. *Pulling Through*, 2605(F)
Ing, Dean (jt. author). *The Other Time*, 1255(F)
Ingalls, Robert P. *Point of Order*, 6602
Inge, William. *Four Plays*, 3084
Ingle, Lester (jt. author). *Seashores*, 8885
Ingrid, Charles. *The Marked Man*, 2606(F)
Innes, Evan. *America 2040*, 2607(F)
Innes, Hammond. *The Doomed Oasis*, 146(F)
The Land God Gave to Cain, 146(F)
Solomon's Seal, 145(F)
The Wreck of the Mary Deare, 146(F)
Insel, Paul M. *Core Concepts in Health*, 5354
Ionesco, Eugene. *Four Plays*, 3008
Rhinoceros and Other Plays, 3009
Ions, Veronica. *Egyptian Mythology*, 3459
Indian Mythology, 3460
Iooss, Walter. *Sports People*, 9576
Iritz, Maxine Haren. *Science Fair*, 8243
Irvine, Lucy. *Castaway*, 7471
Irving, John. *The World According to Garp*, 565(F)
Irving, Washington. *The Legend of Sleepy Hollow, and Other Stories*, 404(F)

Irwin, Constance. *Strange Footprints on the Land*, 7831
Irwin, Hadley. *Abby, My Love*, 682(F)
So Long at the Fair, 2062(F)
Isaacs, Arnold R. *Without Honor*, 8121
Isaacs, Neil D. *Sports Illustrated Basketball*, 9728
Isaacs, Neil D, ed. *Tolkien and the Critics*, 3671
Isaacson, Judith Magyar. *Seed of Sarah*, 7227
Ispa, Jean. *Exploring Careers in Child Care Services*, 4996
Ito, Dee. *The School of Visual Arts Guide to Careers*, 4889
Iverson, Peter, ed. *The Plains Indians of the Twentieth Century*, 7810
Iwago, Mitsuaki. *Serengeti*, 7363

Jablonski, Edward. *A Pictorial History of the World War II Years*, 7228
Jackson, Albert E. *Tools and How to Use Them*, 8948
Jackson, Blyden. *A History of Afro-American Literature, Volume I*, 3590
Jackson, Carole. *Color Me Beautiful*, 5283
Jackson, Donald Dale. *The Aeronauts*, 9067
Gold Dust, 7957
Twenty Million Yankees, 7924
Underground Worlds, 8813
Jackson, Douglas (jt. author). *Tiffany Glassware*, 5812
Jackson, Ellen. *Dancing*, 5970
Jackson, Francis. *Life in the Universe*, 8304
Jackson, Gabriel. *A Concise History of the Spanish Civil War*, 7557
Jackson, Helen Hunt. *Ramona*, 1503(F)
Jackson, Joan S. (jt. author). *Who Was When?* 7035
Jackson, Joseph H. *Pictorial Guide to the Planets*, 8346
Jackson, Karen (jt. author). *The Right Jewelry for You*, 5271
Jackson, Michael. *Moonwalk*, 6410
Jackson, Robert Louis. *Twentieth Century Interpretations of Crime and Punishment*, 3640
Jackson, Sheila. *Costumes for the Stage*, 9168
Jackson, Shirley. *The Haunting of Hill House*, 1769(F)
The Lottery, 1770(F)
We Have Always Lived in the Castle, 2063(F)
Jacobs, Barbara. *Stolen Kisses*, 2288(F)
Jacobs, Betty E. M. *Flowers That Last Forever*, 9144
Jacobs, Jane. *The Death and Life of Great American Cities*, 4558
Jacobs, Joseph, ed. *Celtic Fairy Tales*, 3402
English Fairy Tales, 3402
Indian Fairy Tales, 3402
More Celtic Fairy Tales, 3402
Jacobs, Mark. *Photography in Focus*, 9426

Jacobson, James A. *Making Small Wooden Boxes*, 9276
Jacobson, John D. *Toposaurus*, 3928
Jacobson, Michael F. *The Complete Eater's Digest and Nutrition Scoreboard*, 5417
The Fast-Food Guide, 8417
Jacobus, John. *Matisse*, 5777
Jacobus, John (jt. author). *Modern Art*, 5721
Jaffe, Hans L. C. *Picasso*, 5778
Jahn, Johannes. *A Step-by-Step Book about Turtles*, 8674
Jakes, John. *North and South*, 1537(F)
James, Betsy. *Long Night Dance*, 1160(F)
James, Bill. *The Baseball Book*, 9661
The Bill James Historical Baseball Abstract, 9662
James, Elizabeth. *The Complete Babysitter's Handbook*, 5070
James, Henry. *The Ambassadors*, 405(F)
The American, 408(F)
The Bostonians, 408(F)
The Portrait of a Lady, 406(F)
The Turn of the Screw, 407(F)
Washington Square, 408(F)
James, M. R. *A Warning to the Curious*, 1771(F)
James, Naomi. *Courage at Sea*, 7050
James, P. D. *The Black Tower*, 2064(F)
Cover Her Face, 2069(F)
Death of an Expert Witness, 2069(F)
Devices and Desires, 2065(F)
Innocent Blood, 2066(F)
A Mind to Murder, 2067(F)
Shroud for a Nightingale, 2068(F)
The Skull beneath the Skin, 2067(F)
Unnatural Causes, 2068(F)
An Unsuitable Job for a Woman, 2069(F)
James, Peter. *Possession*, 1772(F)
James, Thurston. *The Theater Props Handbook*, 6093
Janeczko, Paul B., ed. *Don't Forget to Fly*, 3280
Going Over to Your Place, 3167
Pocket Poems, 3281
Poetspeak, 3282
Strings, 3283
Jankel, Annabel. *Creative Computer Graphics*, 8985
Janson, Anthony F. (jt. author). *History of Art*, 5749
History of Art for Young People, 5749
Janson, H. W. *History of Art*, 5749
A History of Art & Music, 5685
History of Art for Young People, 5749
Jantzen, Steven. *Hooray for Peace, Hurrah for War*, 7157
Janus, Christopher G. *Miss 4th of July, Goodbye*, 466(F)
Jarman, Tom. *Wrestling for Beginners*, 9785
Jarrell, Randall. *The Complete Poems*, 3284
Pictures from an Institution, 683(F)

Jarrett, William. *Timelines of Sports History,* 9663, 9850

Jarvis, Sharon, ed. *Inside Outer Space,* 3741
The Uninvited, 9508

Jaspers, Karl. *Kant,* 4010
Plato & Augustine, 4011

Jaspersohn, William. *Grounded,* 847(F)
Motorcycle, 9119

Jastrow, Robert. *The Enchanted Loom,* 5589
God and the Astronomers, 8367
Red Giants and White Dwarfs, 8265
Until the Sun Dies, 8368

Javna, Gordon (jt. author). *60s!* 8072

Javna, John. *Behind the Hits,* 5873
Cult TV, 6021
60s! 8072

Javna, John (jt. author). *The Best of Crime and Detective TV,* 6004

Jay, Ricky. *Learned Pigs & Fireproof Women,* 5980

Jaynes, Gregory. *The Killing Ground,* 7925

Jeffers, Susan. *Feel the Fear and Do It Anyway,* 5615
The Rosen Photo Guide to a Career in Animal Care, 4997

Jefferson Foundation. *Rediscovering the Constitution,* 4192

Jefferson, Thomas (jt. author). *Paine and Jefferson on Liberty,* 7858

Jeffries, Ron. *Commodore 64 Fun and Games,* 8986

Jemie, Onwuchekwa. *Langston Hughes,* 3887

Jenkins, Ian. *Greek and Roman Life,* 7085

Jenkins, Jerry B. (jt. author). *Out of the Blue,* 6723

Jenkins, Peter. *Across China,* 7414
A Walk across America, 6145
The Walk West, 6145

Jenkins, Simon (jt. author). *The Battle for the Falklands,* 7673

Jenkins, Tony. *Nicaragua and the United States,* 7656

Jenks, Tom, ed. *Soldiers & Civilians,* 971(F)

Jenks, Tom (jt. author). *American Short Story Masterpieces,* 2901(F)

Jenner, Bruce. *The Athletic Body,* 5355

Jennings, David, et al. *The Art of Place-Kicking and Punting,* 9851

Jennings, Diane. *Self-Made Women,* 4572

Jennings, Jesse D., ed. *Ancient North Americans,* 7811
Ancient South Americans, 7675

Jennison, Keith W. *The Humorous Mr. Lincoln,* 6545

Jensen, Clayne R. *Opportunities in Recreation and Leisure,* 4841

Jensen, Craig. *The Craft of Computer Programming,* 8987

Jensen, Kris. *FreeMaster,* 2608(F)

Jensen, Marilyn. *Phyllis Wheatley,* 6326

Jensen, Oliver, et al. *American Album,* 7752

Jeppson, J. O. (jt. author). *Laughing Space,* 2386(F)

Jeremiah, Maryalyce. *Basketball,* 9729

Jerome, Judson. *The Poet's Handbook,* 3854

Jespersen, James. *From Quarks to Quasars,* 8369
RAMS, ROMS & Robots, 8988

Jewett, Sarah O. *Best Stories of Sarah Orne Jewett,* 2926(F)

Jewler, A. Jerome. *Step by Step to College Success,* 4743

Jewler, A. Jerome (jt. author). *College Is Only the Beginning,* 4737

Ji, Zhao, ed. *The Natural History of China,* 7415

Johannsen, Robert W. *To the Halls of the Montezumas,* 7871

Johanson, Chris-Ellyn. *Cocaine,* 5130

Johanson, Donald. *Lucy,* 7001
Lucy's Child, 7002

Johanson, Sue. *Talk Sex,* 5468

Johnson, Annabel. *A Memory of Dragons,* 2609(F)

Johnson, Barbara L. *Careers in Beauty Culture,* 4797

Johnson, Bervin, et al. *Opportunities in Photography Careers,* 4842

Johnson, Cathy. *Drawing and Painting from Nature,* 9199

Johnson, Charles. *Being & Race,* 3742

Johnson, Clay (jt. author). *Your Pilot's License,* 9085

Johnson, Dorothy M. *A Man Called Horse,* 1571(F)

Johnson, Earvin "Magic." *Magic's Touch,* 6745

Johnson, Edgar. *Charles Dickens,* 6238

Johnson, Edgar (jt. author). *A Memory of Dragons,* 2609(F)

Johnson, Edward D. *The Washington Square Press Handbook of Good English,* 3929

Johnson, Ellen H., ed. *American Artists on Art from 1940 to 1980,* 5750

Johnson, Eric W. *Love and Sex in Plain Language,* 5469
People, Love, Sex and Families, 5470
VD, 5192

Johnson, Eric W. (jt. author). *The Family Book about Sexuality,* 5458

Johnson, James B. *Trekmaster,* 2610(F)

Johnson, James Weldon. *God's Trombones,* 3285

Johnson, Joan. *The Cult Movement,* 4057

Johnson, Kay. *Canework,* 9145

Johnson, Lady Bird. *Wildflowers across America,* 8435

Johnson, Linda Carlson. *Responsibility,* 5573

Johnson, Maud. *I'm Christy,* 2289(F)

Johnson, Neil (jt. author). *Foul Play,* 5112

Johnson, Osa. *I Married Adventure,* 6149

Johnson, Paul. *A History of Christianity,* 4058

Modern Times, 7151

Johnson, Peter. *The Sail Magazine Book of Sailing*, 9929

Johnson, Peter J. (jt. author). *The Rockefeller Century*, 6474

Johnson, Rheta Grimsley. *Good Grief*, 6205

Johnson, Robert K. *Neil Simon*, 3839

Johnson, Roy S. (jt. author). *Magic's Touch*, 6745

Johnson, Thomas H. *The Oxford Companion to American History*, 7753

Johnson, William Weber. *The Forty-Niners*, 7958

Johnston, Jennifer. *Fool's Sanctuary*, 467(F)

Johnston, Johanna. *Kings, Lovers, and Fools*, 3049

Johnston, Mary. *To Have and to Hold*, 1517(F)

Johnston, Velda. *Fatal Affair*, 2070(F)
Flight to Yesterday, 2071(F)
Shadow behind the Curtain, 2072(F)
Voice in the Night, 2073(F)

Johnstone, Jay. *Over the Edge*, 9664
Some of My Best Friends Are Crazy, 9665
Temporary Insanity, 9664

Jonas, Steven. *Pacewalking*, 5356
Triathloning for Ordinary Mortals, 9974

Jones, Adrienne. *Long Time Passing*, 1697(F)
Street Family, 848(F)

Jones, Bernard E., ed. *The Complete Woodworker*, 9277

Jones, Christopher. *The Great Palace*, 7524

Jones, Chuck. *Chuck Amuck*, 6197

Jones, Colin, eds (jt. author). *Voices of the French Revolution*, 7491

Jones, Constance. *Karen Horney*, 6675

Jones, Dick. *Spider*, 8612

Jones, Douglas C. *The Barefoot Brigade*, 1538(F)
Come Winter, 1572(F)
Elkhorn Tavern, 1539(F)
Gone the Dreams and Dancing, 1573(F)
Hickory Cured, 849(F)
Remember Santiago, 1612(F)
Roman, 1574(F)
Season of Yellow Leaf, 1504(F)

Jones, Evan. *American Food*, 9347

Jones, Howard. *The Course of American Diplomacy*, 4146

Jones, Ilene. *Jobs for Teenagers*, 4843

Jones, Jacqueline. *Labor of Love, Labor of Sorrow*, 4366

Jones, James. *From Here to Eternity*, 1661(F)

Jones, John Oliver. *Where the Birds Are*, 8539

Jones, Landon. *Great Expectations*, 4459

Jones, Mablen. *Getting It On*, 5874

Jones, Marilyn. *Exploring Careers as an Electrician*, 5021

Jones, Max. *Talking Jazz*, 6178

Jones, Pat (jt. author). *Images of Earth*, 8795

Jones, Richard Glyn, ed. *Unsolved!* 4480

Jones, Robert F. *Slade's Glacier*, 147(F)

Jones, Ron. *The Acorn People*, 5436

Jones, Stephen, ed. *The Best Horror from Fantasy Tales*, 1773(F)
Horror, 3623

Jones, Toeckey. *Go Well, Stay Well*, 468(F)
Skindeep, 972(F)

Jones, Tom. *The Fantasticks*, 3085

Jones, Tristan. *The Incredible Voyage*, 6151
Outward Leg, 6151
Somewheres East of Suez, 6151

Jonson, Ben. *Volpone*, 3032

Jordan, Cathleen, ed. *Tales from Alfred Hitchcock's Mystery Magazine*, 2074(F)

Jordan, John. *An Illustrated Guide to the Modern US Navy*, 9129
An Illustrated Guide to the U.S. Air Force, 9129

Jordan, June. *Living Room*, 3286
Things That I Do in the Dark, 3286

Jordan, Pat. *Sports Illustrated Pitching*, 9666

Jordan, Robert. *Eye of the World*, 1161(F)
The Great Hunt, 1162(F)

Jorgan, Anne (jt. author). *The Best Horror Stories from the Magazine of Fantasy and Science Fiction*, 1747(F)

Jorgensen, Donald G., Jr. *Secrets Told by Children of Alcoholics*, 5131

Jorgensen, June A. (jt. author). *Secrets Told by Children of Alcoholics*, 5131

Jorgensen, Paul A. *William Shakespeare*, 3821

Josefs, Jai. *Writing Music for Hit Songs*, 5875

Joselit, David (jt. author). *Career Opportunities in Art*, 4886

Joseph, Joel D. *Black Mondays*, 4245

Joseph, Lawrence E. *Gaia*, 8396

Josephson, Matthew. *The Robber Barons*, 6478

Josephy, Alvin M., Jr. *The Indian Heritage of America*, 7812
Now That the Buffalo's Gone, 7813
Red Power, 7814

Joyce, James. *Dubliners*, 2927(F)
A Portrait of the Artist as a Young Man, 850(F)

Joye, Beverly. *Flight to Love*, 2290(F)

Judson, William. *Cold River*, 148(F)

Jung, Carl Gustav. *Undiscovered Self*, 5537

Jungk, Robert. *Brighter Than a Thousand Suns*, 7229

Jussim, Daniel. *Drug Tests and Polygraphs*, 5132

Jute, Andre. *Writing a Thriller*, 3966

Kacen, Alex. *Opportunities in Paramedical Careers*, 4998

Kachoyeanos, Mary (jt. author). *Just a Nurse*, 5241

Kadohata, Cynthia. *The Floating World*, 469(F)

Kaehler, Wolfgang. *Penguins*, 8566

Kael, Pauline. *5001 Nights at the Movies*, 6022
Taking It All In, 6022

Kafka, Franz. *The Complete Stories*, 1774(F)
The Metamorphosis, 1163(F)
The Trial, 684(F)

Kagan, Andrew. *Marc Chagall*, 6192

Kagen, Janet. *Uhura's Song*, 2611(F)

Kahn, Albert E. *Matusow Affair*, 8073

Kahn, Carol. *Beyond the Helix*, 5086

Kahn, Joan, ed. *Handle with Care*, 2075(F)

Kahn, Roger. *The Boys of Summer*, 9667

Kaiser, Robert G. *Russia from the Inside*, 7569

Kaku, Michio, ed. *Nuclear Power*, 8923

Kalb, Marvin. *In the National Interest*, 149(F)

Kalb, Phyllis B. (jt. author). *Countdown to College*, 4652

Kalergis, Mary Motley. *Mother*, 5659

Kallen, Christian (jt. author). *Riding the Dragon's Back*, 9919

Kallen, Lucille. *C. B. Greenfield*, 2076(F)
No Lady in the House, 2076(F)
The Piano Bird, 2076(F)
The Tanglewood Murders, 2076(F)

Kalpakian, Laura. *Dark Continent and Other Stories*, 432(F)

Kamerman, Sylvia E., ed. *Space and Science Fiction Plays for Young People*, 3086

Kaminsky, Stuart M. *American Film Genres*, 6094

Kane, Bob. *Batman & Me*, 6198

Kane, Joe. *Running the Amazon*, 7676

Kane, June Kozak. *Exploring Careers in Dietetics and Nutrition*, 4999

Kane, Rod. *Veteran's Day*, 8122

Kantor, Elliot S., ed. *Careers in Engineering*, 5022

Kantor, MacKinlay. *Andersonville*, 1540(F)

Kaplan, Abraham. *The New World of Philosophy*, 4012

Kaplan, E. Ann. *Rocking Around the Clock*, 5876

Kaplan, Fred. *Dickens*, 6239

Kaplan, Frederic M., ed. *Encyclopedia of China Today*, 7418

Kaplan, Jim. *Playing the Field*, 9668

Kardong, Don. *Thirty Phone Booths to Boston*, 9914

Karen, Robert (jt. author). *When the Shooting Stops . . . the Cutting Begins*, 6053

Karl, Barry D. *The Uneasy State*, 8032

Karl, Jean E. *The Turning Place*, 2612(F)

Karney, Robyn (jt. author). *Movie Mastermind*, 5990

Karni, Karen. *Opportunities in Medical Technology Careers*, 5000

Karnow, Stanley. *Vietnam*, 7458

Karolyi, Bela (jt. author). *Mary Lou*, 6767

Karr, Phyllis Ann. *Idylls of the Queen*, 1164(F)

Karton, Joshua, ed. *Film Scenes for Actors, Vol. 2*, 3087

Kasbar, Brian (jt. author). *Essays That Worked*, 4727

Kaskie, Shirli. *A Woman's Golf Game*, 9870

Kastner, Janet. *More Than an Average Guy*, 6938

Kata, Elizabeth. *A Patch of Blue*, 685(F)

Katakis, Michael. *The Vietnam Veterans Memorial*, 8123

Katz, Jane B., ed. *I Am the Fire of Time*, 7815

Katz, Judith A. *The Ad Game*, 4920

Katz, Marc (jt. author). *Spike!* 6773

Katz, Michael B. *In the Shadow of the Poorhouse*, 4509

Katz, Michael J. *Last Dance in Redondo Beach*, 2077(F)

Katz, Steve. *Florry of Washington Heights*, 851(F)

Katz, William. *After Dark*, 150(F)

Katz, William Loren. *The Black West*, 7959
Breaking the Chains, 7872

Katzman, John (jt. author). *The Princeton Review—Cracking the System*, 4664

Katzman, John (jt. author). *The Princeton Review*, 4759

Katzner, Kenneth. *The Languages of the World*, 3930

Kauffman, Henry. *Pennsylvania Dutch American Folk Art*, 5809

Kauffman, M. K. *The Right Moves*, 852(F)

Kaufman, Allan. *Exploring Solar Energy*, 8931

Kaufman, Bel. *Up the Down Staircase*, 1885(F)

Kavanaugh, James. *A Fable*, 1165(F)

Kavanaugh, Michelle. *Emerald Explosion*, 151(F)

Kawabata, Yasunari. *Snow Country*, 686(F)

Kay, Guy Gavriel. *The Darkest Road*, 1166(F)
The Summer Tree, 1166(F)
The Wandering Fire, 1166(F)

Kay, William J., ed. *The Complete Book of Dog Health*, 8723

Kaye, Evelyn. *College Bound*, 4744

Kaye, M. M. *Death in Berlin*, 2078(F)
Death in Zanzibar, 152(F)
The Far Pavilions, 1395(F)
Shadow of the Moon, 1395(F)

Kaye, Marvin. *The Stein and Day Handbook of Magic*, 9398

Kaye, Marvin, ed. *Masterpieces of Terror and the Supernatural*, 1775(F)

Kaye, Saralee (jt. author). *Masterpieces of Terror and the Supernatural*, 1775(F)

Kazantzakis, Nikos. *Zorba the Greek*, 973(F)

Kazimiroff, Theodore L. *The Last Algonquin*, 6962

Kazin, Alfred. *On Native Grounds*, 3743
Keates, Jonathan. *Handel*, 6346
Keats, John. *Poems*, 3211
Keegan, John. *The Illustrated Face of Battle*, 7051
Soldiers, 7052
Keene, Donald. *Dawn to the West*, 3591
Keene, Donald, ed. *Anthology of Japanese Literature from the Earliest Era to the Mid-Nineteenth Century*, 2928
Modern Japanese Literature, 2929
Twenty Plays of the Nō Theatre, 3144
Keeping, Charles, ed. *Charles Keeping's Book of Classic Ghost Stories*, 1776(F)
Charles Keeping's Classic Tales of the Macabre, 1777(F)
Kehret, Peg. *Encore!* 2984
Keidel, Levi. *Caught in the Crossfire*, 153(F)
Keigley, Peggy. *Quit & Win*, 5133
Keillor, Garrison. *Leaving Home*, 3499
Keller, Gunter. *A Step-by-Step Book about Discus*, 8755
Keller, Helen. *The Story of My Life*, 6626
Keller, Janet (jt. author). *Crisis Intervention*, 5157
Keller, Werner. *The Bible as History*, 4106
Kellerman, Jonathan. *Over the Edge*, 2079(F)
Kelley, Kevin W., ed. *The Home Planet*, 8340
Kelley, Leo P. *Luke Sutton*, 154(F)
Kellogg, Marjorie. *Tell Me That You Love Me, Junie Moon*, 853(F)
Kellogg, Susan (jt. author). *Domestic Revolutions*, 5670
Kelly, Daniel. *The Right On! Book of Hair Care and Beauty*, 5284
Kelly, Gary F. *Learning about Sex*, 5471
Kelly, John D. *Lovejoy's Preparation for the SAT*, 4660
Kelly, Kevin, ed. *Signal*, 8991
Kelly, Martin. *Parents Book of Baby Names*, 3931
Kelly, Mary Anne. *Park Lane South, Queens*, 2080(F)
Kelly, Richard. *Lewis Carroll*, 3672
Kemal, Yasher. *Memed, My Hawk*, 974(F)
Kemelman, Harry. *Friday the Rabbi Slept Late*, 2081(F)
Monday the Rabbi Took Off, 2081(F)
One Fine Day the Rabbi Bought a Cross, 2082(F)
Saturday the Rabbi Went Hungry, 2081(F)
Someday the Rabbi Will Leave, 2083(F)
Sunday the Rabbi Stayed Home, 2081(F)
Thursday the Rabbi Walked Out, 2082(F)
Tuesday the Rabbi Saw Red, 2082(F)
Wednesday the Rabbi Got Wet, 2082(F)
Kempe, C. Henry (jt. author). *Child Abuse*, 5661
Kempe, C. Henry, ed. *The Battered Child*, 5660

Kempe, Ruth S. *Child Abuse*, 5661
Kendall, Alan. *George Gershwin*, 6344
Keneally, Thomas. *Schindler's List*, 1662(F)
Kenneally, Joyce A. *The Good Housekeeping Illustrated Microwave Cookbook*, 9348
Kennealy, Patricia. *The Copper Crown*, 2613(F)
The Silver Branch, 2613(F)
The Throne of Scone, 2613(F)
Kennedy, Crawford Q. *The Divination Handbook*, 9509
Kennedy, David M. *Over Here*, 7158
Kennedy, John F. *A Nation of Immigrants*, 4332
Profiles in Courage, 6479
Kennedy, Joyce Lain. *Joyce Lain Kennedy's Career Book*, 4798
Kennedy, Kim. *In-Between Love*, 2291(F)
Kennedy, Michael. *Britten*, 6339
Mahler, 6349
Kennedy, Michael, ed. *The Concise Oxford Dictionary of Music*, 5822
Kennedy, Robert (jt. author). *Pumping Up!* 9777
Kennedy, Robert F. *Thirteen Days*, 8074
Kennedy, William. *Ironweed*, 1626(F)
Kennedy, William P. *Toy Soldiers*, 155(F)
Kennelly, Brendan, ed. *The Penguin Book of Irish Verse*, 3212
Kennett, Lee. *G.I.*, 7230
Kenney, William. *How to Read and Write about Fiction*, 3624
Kenny, Anthony. *Thomas More*, 6865
Kenny, John B. *The Complete Book of Pottery Making*, 9165
Kent, Alexander. *Colors Aloft!* 1439(F)
Enemy in Sight, 1440(F)
Success to the Brave, 1440(F)
A Tradition of Victory, 1440(F)
Kent, George E. *A Life of Gwendolyn Brooks*, 6222
Kerblay, Basile. *Modern Soviet Society*, 7570
Kermode, Frank, ed. *The Oxford Anthology of English Literature*, 2930, 2931
Kerouac, Jack. *On the Road*, 687(F)
Kerr, Jean. *Please Don't Eat the Daisies*, 3500
Kerr, Katherine. *The Bristling Wood*, 1167(F)
Darkspell, 1168(F)
The Dragon Revenant, 1169(F)
Kerr, M. E. *Fell*, 156(F)
Fell Back, 156(F)
Gentlehands, 854(F)
Me Me Me Me Me, 6276
Night Kites, 855(F)
Kerr, Richard (jt. author). *Rings*, 8343
Kerr, Walter. *The Silent Clowns*, 6023
Kerr, Walter H. (jt. author). *American Classic*, 3178
Kerrane, Kevin (jt. author). *Into the Temple of Baseball*, 9649
Kerrigan, Philip. *Survival Game*, 157(F)
Kertzer, Morris N. *What Is a Jew?* 4059

Kesey, Ken. *One Flew over the Cuckoo's Nest,* 688(F)

Kessel, John (jt. author). *Enemy Mine/Another Orphan,* 2651(F)

Kesselman-Turkel, Judi. *Research Shortcuts,* 4649
Study Smarts, 4649
Test Taking Strategies, 4649

Kesselring, Joseph. *Three Plays about Crime and Criminals,* 3088

Kessler, Lauren. *After All These Years,* 8075

Kessler, Ronald. *The Spy in the Russian Club,* 4147
Spy versus Spy, 4148

Ketcham, Katherine. *Living on the Edge,* 5134

Ketchum, Richard M. *The Borrowed Years, 1938–1941,* 8076

Ketels, Hank. *Sports Illustrated Scuba Diving,* 9956

Keteyian, Armen (jt. author). *Catfish,* 6724

Kevles, Bettyann. *Thinking Gorillas,* 8500

Key, Edd (jt. author). *The Compact Disc Book,* 9047

Key, Ray. *Woodturning,* 9278

Keyes, Daniel. *Flowers for Algernon,* 689(F)

Keyworth, Cynthia. *How to Write a Term Paper,* 4683

Kidd, David. *Peking Story,* 7419

Kidd, Ronald. *Who Is Felix the Great?* 566(F)

Kidder, Tracy. *The Soul of a New Machine,* 8992

Kiefer, Irene. *Nuclear Energy at the Crossroads,* 8924

Kiely, Benedict. *Proxopera,* 975(F)

Kienzle, Rich. *Great Guitarists,* 5877

Killen, M. Barbara. *Economics and the Consumer,* 4590

Killpatrick, Frances. *The Winning Edge,* 4745

Killpatrick, James (jt. author). *The Winning Edge,* 4745

Killus, James. *Book of Shadows,* 2614(F)

Kilworth, Garry. *The Foxes of Firstdark,* 291(F)

Kincaid, Jamaica. *Annie John,* 856(F)
Lucy, 470(F)

Kindall, Jerry. *Sports Illustrated Baseball,* 9669

King, Benjamin. *A Bullet for Stonewall,* 1541(F)

King, Bernard. *Starkadder,* 2615(F)
Vargr-Moon, 2615(F)

King, Billie Jean. *We Have Come a Long Way,* 9968

King, F. W. (jt. author). *The Audubon Society Field Guide to North American Reptiles and Amphibians,* 8461

King James. *The Holy Bible,* 4107

King, Martin Luther, Jr. *Strength to Love,* 4367
Stride Toward Freedom, 4368
Where Do We Go from Here, 4369
Why We Can't Wait, 4370

King, Mike. *The Mike King Story,* 6777

King, Neil. *Classical Beginnings,* 3801
Elizabethan Comedy, 3810

Elizabethan Tragedy, 3810
The Modern Age, 3811
Mystery and Morality, 3810
Rakes and Rogues, 3811
The Victorian Age, 3811

King, Richard H. *A Southern Renaissance,* 3592

King, Stephen. *The Bachman Books,* 1778(F)
Bare Bones, 3744
Carrie, 1779(F)
Christine, 1780(F)
Cujo, 1781(F)
Cycle of the Werewolf, 1782(F)
The Dark Half, 1783(F)
The Dead Zone, 1784(F)
Different Seasons, 1785(F)
The Drawing of the Three, 1170(F)
The Eyes of the Dragon, 1171(F)
Firestarter, 1786(F)
Four Past Midnight, 1787(F)
The Gunslinger, 1172(F)
Misery, 1788(F)
Night Shift, 1789(F)
Pet Sematary, 1790(F)
The Shining, 1791(F)
The Stand, 1792(F)
The Talisman, 1173(F)
The Tommyknockers, 1793(F)

Kingsolver, Barbara. *The Bean Trees,* 690(F)

Kingston, John. *Five-Hundred-Five Baseball Questions Your Friends Can't Answer,* 9670

Kingston, Maxine Hong. *The Woman Warrior,* 6922

Kingstone, Brett. *The Student Entrepreneur's Guide,* 5064

Kinsella, James. *Covering the Plague,* 3985

Kinsella, Thomas, ed. *The New Oxford Book of Irish Verse,* 3213

Kinsella, W. P. *The Iowa Baseball Confederacy,* 2879(F)
Shoeless Joe, 2879(F)

Kinsley, James, ed. *The Oxford Book of Ballads,* 3168

Kipling, Rudyard. *Captains Courageous,* 373(F)
Gunga Din, 3214
Kim, 374(F)
The Man Who Would Be King, 375(F)
Rudyard Kipling's Verse, 3215

Kipnis, Claude. *The Mime Book,* 6095

Kirchberger, Joe H. *The French Revolution & Napoleon,* 7497

Kirk, Irina. *Anton Chekhov,* 3802

Kirk, John. *Ships of the U.S. Navy,* 9130

Kirk, Troy. *Collector's Guide to Baseball Cards,* 9454

Kirkeby, Ed. *Ain't Misbehavin',* 6453

Kirkham, Margaret. *Jane Austen, Feminism and Fiction,* 3673

Kirkland, Gelsey. *The Shape of Love,* 6412

Kirp, David L., et al. *Learning by Heart,* 5193

Kisor, Henry. *What's That Pig Outdoors?* 6923
Kissinger, Henry. *White House Years,* 6599
Years of Upheaval, 6599
Kitagawa, Yoshiko. *Creative Cards,* 9223
Kitman, Marvin. *The Making of the President, 1789,* 4276
Kittredge, William, ed. *The Great American Detective,* 2084(F)
Kitzinger, Sheila. *The Complete Book of Pregnancy and Childbirth,* 5472
Klass, Perri Elizabeth. *A Not Entirely Benign Procedure,* 5240
Klass, Philip J. *UFOs Explained,* 9510
Klause, Annette Curtis. *The Silver Kiss,* 1794(F)
Klausnitzer, Bernhard. *Insects,* 8596
Klawans, Harold L. *Toscanini's Fumble,* 5194
Klebaner, Benjamin J. *American Commercial Banking,* 4596
Kleiman, Dena. *A Deadly Silence,* 4481
Klein, Aaron (jt. author). *Ships of the U.S. Navy,* 9130
Klein, David. *Your Parents and Your Self,* 5662
Klein. Frederick C. (jt. author). *Fast Lanes,* 9781
Klein, Herbert S. *Bolivia,* 7677
Klein, Joe. *Woody Guthrie,* 6395
Klein, Leonard S., ed. *African Literatures in the 20th Century,* 3593
Klein, Marymae E. (jt. author). *Your Parents and Your Self,* 5662
Klein, Norma. *Beginners' Love,* 857(F)
Family Secrets, 691(F)
French Postcards, 2292(F)
Give and Take, 858(F)
Going Backwards, 567(F)
It's OK If You Don't Love Me, 568(F)
Just Friends, 2293(F)
Learning How to Fall, 692(F)
My Life As a Body, 859(F)
No More Saturday Nights, 860(F)
Sunshine, 693(F)
That's My Baby, 861(F)
Klein, T. E. D. *Dark Gods,* 1795(F)
Klever, Ulrich. *The Complete Book of Dog Care,* 8724
Kliment, Bud. *Billie Holiday,* 6404
Kline, David. *Great Possessions,* 8584
Kline, Richard. *The Ultimate Paper Airplane,* 9224
Kling, Julie Lepick. *Opportunities in Computer Science Careers,* 5044
Klingaman, William K. *1941,* 7231
1929, 8033
Klinkowitz, Jerome. *Kurt Vonnegut,* 3745
Short Season and Other Stories, 2880(F)
Klitzman, Robert. *A Year-Long Night,* 6680
Klose, Kevin. *Russia and the Russians,* 7571
Klose, Kevin (jt. author). *Freedom's Child,* 6939
Kloss, William. *Treasures from the National Museum of American Art,* 5800

Klots, Alexander B. *A Field Guide to the Butterflies of North America, East of the Great Plains . . ,* 8606
Knapp, Bettina L. *Emily Dickinson,* 6241
Émile Zola, 3641
Knee, Allan, ed. *Camelot and Idylls of the King,* 2985
Knight, Arthur. *The Liveliest Art,* 6096
Knight, Damon. *A for Anything,* 2616(F)
Knight, Erika (jt. author). *Knit 4 Seasons,* 9235
Knight, Franklin W. *The Caribbean,* 7662
Knightley, Phillip. *The Master Spy,* 6870
Knobler, Peter (jt. author). *Giant Steps,* 6737
Knoll, Tricia. *Becoming Americans,* 4333
Knowles, John. *Peace Breaks Out,* 862(F)
A Separate Peace, 863(F)
Knox, Bill. *The Interface Man,* 158(F)
Knox, Chuck. *Hard Knox,* 6753
Knudtson, Peter (jt. author). *Genethics,* 5267
Kobal, John (jt. author). *A New Pictorial History of the Talkies,* 5993
Kobayashi, Tsukasa, et al. *Sherlock Holmes's London,* 3674
Koch, Kenneth, ed. *Sleeping on the Wing,* 3169
Koebner, Linda. *Forgotten Animals,* 8501
Koertge, Ron. *The Arizona Kid,* 864(F)
The Boy in the Moon, 865(F)
Where the Kissing Never Stops, 1886(F)
Koester, Pat. *Careers in Fashion Retailing,* 4921
Koestler, Arthur. *Darkness at Noon,* 976(F)
Kogan, Judith. *Nothing but the Best,* 5823
Kogelman, Stanley. *Mind over Math,* 8839
Kohl, Herbert. *Growing Minds,* 4953
Thirty-Six Children, 4629
Kohler, Pierre. *Volcanoes, Earthquakes, and the Formation of Continents,* 8804
Kohn, George C. *Encyclopedia of American Scandal,* 7754
Kohn, Stephen M. *Jailed for Peace,* 4408
Kolodny, Nancy J. *When Food's a Foe,* 5387
Kolodny, Nancy J., et al. *Smart Choices,* 5616
Komisar, Lucy. *Corazon Aquino,* 6802
Konvitz, Milton R., ed. *Bill of Rights Reader,* 4193
Koon, Helen Wickham. *How Shakespeare Won the West,* 6097
Koontz, Dean R. *Lightning,* 1174(F)
Midnight, 1796(F)
Phantoms, 1797(F)
Strangers, 1798(F)
Twilight Eyes, 1799(F)
Watchers, 1800(F)
Koppel, Ted (jt. author). *In the National Interest,* 149(F)
Korman, Gordon. *A Semester in the Life of a Garbage Bag,* 1887(F)
Son of Interflux, 1888(F)
Korn, Jerry. *The Fight for Chattanooga,* 7926
Kornbluth, C. M. (jt. author). *The Space Merchants,* 2740(F)

Wolfbane, 2741(F)
Kornicki, Peter (jt. author). *Japan,* 7441
Korstein, Daniel. *Thinking Under Fire,* 4307
Kort, Michael. *The Soviet Colossus,* 7572
Kosinski, Jerzy. *Being There,* 1889(F)
The Painted Bird, 1663(F)
Koslow, Philip. *The Securities and Exchange
   Commission,* 4223
Kosof, Anna. *Incest,* 5511
Prison Life in America, 4482
Why Me? 5195
Kostof, Spiro. *America by Design,* 5700
A History of Architecture, 5694
Kostrubala, Thaddeus. *The Joy of Running,* 9915
Kotre, John. *Seasons of Life,* 5525
Kotzwinkle, William. *E.T,* 2617(F), 2617(F)
Kovic, Ron. *Born on the Fourth of July,* 8124
Kowalchik, Claire, ed. *Rodale's Illustrated Ency-
   clopedia of Herbs,* 8418
Kozodoy, Ruth. *Isadora Duncan,* 6385
Kozol, Jonathan. *Death at an Early Age,* 4630
Rachel and Her Children, 4510
Kozuki, Russell. *Junior Karate,* 9894
Karate for Young People, 9894
Kraegel, Janet. *Just a Nurse,* 5241
Krakauer, Jon. *Eiger Dreams,* 9577
Kramer, Jerry. *Instant Replay,* 9852
Krannich, Caryl Rae (jt. author). *The Complete
   Guide to Public Employment,* 4844
Krannich, Ronald L. *The Complete Guide to
   Public Employment,* 4844
Krantz, Les. *American Architects,* 5701
Krauzer, Steven M. (jt. author). *The Great
   American Detective,* 2084(F)
Kreschollek, Margie. *The Guaranteed Goof-
   Proof Microwave Cookbook,* 9349
Kresh, Paul. *Isaac Bashevis Singer,* 6309
Kress, Nancy. *Trinity and Other Stories,* 2618(F)
Krishtalka, Leonard. *Dinosaur Plots & Other In-
   trigues in Natural History,* 8223
Kritsick, Stephen. *Creature Comforts,* 6681
Kroc, Ray. *Grinding It Out,* 4573
Kroeber, Theodora. *Ishi,* 6625
Kronenwetter, Michael. *Capitalism vs. Socialism,*
   4574
Managing Toxic Wastes, 4453
The War on Terrorism, 4547
Kronnick, Buck. *The Baseball Fan's Complete
   Guide to Collecting Autographs,* 9455
Kropp, Lloyd. *Greencastle,* 866(F)
Krueger, Gretchen Dewailly. *Opportunities in Pe-
   troleum Careers,* 5045
Kube-McDowell, Michael P. *Empery,* 2619(F)
Enigma, 2619(F)
Kubicek, David, ed. *October Dreams,* 1801(F)
Kubler-Ross, Elisabeth. *Living with Death and
   Dying,* 5087
On Children and Death, 5088
To Live until We Say Good-Bye, 5089

Kuklin, Susan. *Fighting Back,* 5196
Kulik, Stephen, et al., eds. *The Audubon Society
   Field Guide to the Natural Places in Mid-
   Atlantic States,* 8167
*The Audubon Society Field Guide to the Natu-
   ral Places of the Northeast,* 8167
Kullman, Harry. *The Battle Horse,* 694(F)
Kumin, Maxine. *Nature,* 3287
Kunetka, James (jt. author). *Nature's End,*
   2797(F)
Warday, 2798(F)
Kunetka, James W. *Shadow Man,* 2085(F)
Kunitz, Stanley. *Next-to-Last Things,* 3288
Kuntzleman, Charles T. *The Complete Book of
   Walking,* 9578
Kunz, Jeffrey R. M., ed. *The American Medical
   Association Family Medical Guide,* 5075
Kupferberg, Herbert. *The Book of Classical Mu-
   sic Lists,* 5824
Kuralt, Charles. *A Life on the Road,* 6413
On the Road with Charles Kuralt, 7755
Kurian, George Thomas. *Australia and New Zea-
   land,* 7472
Kurland, Adrienne. *Coping with Being Pregnant,*
   5473
Kurland, Michael. *The Spy Master's Handbook,*
   4149
Kurland, Morton L. *Our Sacred Honor,* 867(F)
Kurten, Bjorn. *Dance of the Tiger,* 1352(F)
Kurtz, Katherine. *The Bishop's Heir,* 2620(F)
Camber of Culdi, 1175(F)
Camber the Heretic, 1175(F)
The Deryni Archives, 1176(F)
Deryni Checkmate, 1177(F)
Deryni Rising, 1177(F)
The Harrowing of Gwynedd, 1178(F)
The King's Justice, 1179(F)
Lammas Night, 1180(F)
The Legacy of Lehr, 2621(F)
The Quest for Saint Camber, 1181(F)
Saint Camber, 1175(F)
Kurtz, Katherine (jt. author). *The One Day Plan
   for Jobhunters,* 4808
Kurzman, Dan. *Day of the Bomb,* 7232
Kurzweil, Arthur. *From Generation to Genera-
   tion,* 5663
Kushner, Ellen. *Thomas the Rhymer,* 1182(F)
Kushner, Harold. *When Bad Things Happen to
   Good People,* 5617
Kusinitz, Marc. *Drug Use around the World,*
   5135
Kuttner, Henry. *The Startling Worlds of Henry
   Kuttner,* 2622(F)
Kybett, Harry. *The Complete Handbook of
   Videocassette Recorders,* 9051
Kyle, Duncan. *White Out!* 159(F)

La Farge, Oliver. *Laughing Boy,* 695(F)
Santa Fe, 8200

Labarge, Margaret Wade. *A Small Sound of the Trumpet*, 7137

LaBastille, Anne. *Beyond Black Bear Lake*, 8168

Mama Poc, 8575

Women and Wilderness, 6119

Woodswoman, 6683

Labor, Earle. *Jack London*, 3746

Lacey, Dan. *The Essential Immigrant*, 4334

Lackey, Mercedes. *Arrow's Fall*, 1183(F)

Arrow's Flight, 1183(F)

Arrows of the Queen, 1183(F)

Magic's Pawn, 1184

Magic's Price, 1184

Magic's Promise, 1184

Lackey, Mercedes (jt. author). *Reap the Whirlwind*, 1073(F)

Ladbury, Ann. *The Sewing Book*, 9242

LaFeber, Walter. *The American Age*, 7756

Laffin, John. *Holy War*, 4060

Lahey, Michael. *Quest for Apollo*, 1185(F)

Laiken, Deidre S. *Listen to Me, I'm Angry*, 5562

Lakein, Alan. *How to Get Control of Your Time and Your Life*, 5618

Laker, Rosalind. *Circle of Pearls*, 1441(F)

Lally, Dick (jt. author). *The Wrong Stuff*, 9671

Lamar, Howard R., ed. *The Reader's Encyclopedia of the American West*, 7960

Lamb, Lawrence E. *The Weighting Game*, 5418

Lamb, Wendy, ed. *The Ground Zero Club and Other Prize-Winning Plays*, 3089

Meeting the Winter Bike Rider, 3089

Meeting the Winter Bike Rider and Other Prize Winning Plays, 3090

Sparks in the Park and Other Prize-Winning Plays, 3091

Lambert, David. *A Field Guide to Dinosaurs*, 6982

The Field Guide to Early Man, 7003

The Field Guide to Geology, 8798

The Field Guide to Prehistoric Life, 6983, 7003

Lambert, M. B. *Volcanoes*, 8805

Lame Deer, John. *Lame Deer, Seeker of Visions*, 6515

Lamm, Kathryn. *10,000 Ideas for Term Papers, Projects and Reports*, 4684

Lammers, Susan M. *All about Houseplants*, 9382

L'Amour, Louis. *Bendigo Shafter*, 160(F)

The Haunted Mesa, 2623(F)

The Outlaws of Mesquite, 161(F)

Son of a Wanted Man, 162(F)

The Strong Shall Live, 163(F)

Yondering, 163(F)

Lampton, Christopher. *Advanced BASIC*, 8989

BASIC for Beginners, 8989

CD ROMs, 8993

FORTRAN for Beginners, 8990

Graphics and Animation on the Apple II, 8994

Graphics and Animation on the Atari, 8994

Graphics and Animation on the Commodore 64, 8994

Graphics and Animation on the TRS-80, 8994

Predicting AIDS and Other Epidemics, 5197

Predicting Nuclear and Other Technological Disasters, 8925

Lancaster, Bruce. *The American Heritage Book of the Revolution*, 7852

Lance, James W. *Migraine and Other Headaches*, 5198

Landa, Bonnie L. (jt. author). *Tropical Fish*, 8752

Landau, Elaine. *Different Drummer*, 5474

On the Streets, 5512

Sexually Transmitted Diseases, 5199

Surrogate Mothers, 4522

We Have AIDs, 5200

Landau, Terry. *About Faces*, 5297

Landers, Ann. *Ann Landers Talks to Teenagers about Sex*, 5475

Landis, J. D. *Joey and the Girls*, 1890(F)

Landon, Margaret. *Anna and the King of Siam*, 6924

Landry, Tom. *Tom Landry*, 6751

Landynski, Jacob W. *The Living U.S. Constitution*, 4194

Lane, Daryl, et al. *The Sound of Wonder*, 3747

Lane, Kenneth. *Diary of a Medical Nobody*, 6684

Lane, Rose Wilder. *Rose Wilder Lane*, 6278

Lane, Rose Wilder (jt. author). *A Little House Sampler*, 8002

Lang, Denise V. *Footsteps in the Ocean*, 5023

Lang, Susan S. *Extremist Groups in America*, 4409

Langdon, William Chauncey. *Everyday Things in American Life, 1776–1876*, 7873

Langer, William L., ed. *An Encyclopedia of World History*, 7053

Langford, Michael. *The Darkroom Handbook*, 9427

Michael Langford's 35mm Handbook, 9428

Langley, Lester D. *MexAmerica*, 4396

Langley, Noel, et al. *The Wizard of Oz*, 6024

Langone, John. *AIDS*, 5201

Bombed, Buzzed, Smashed or . . . Sober, 5136

Superconductivity, 8937

Violence! 4460

Lanier, Sterling E. *Hiero's Journey*, 1186(F)

The Unforsaken Hiero, 1186(F)

Lanning, George (jt. author). *Technique in Fiction*, 4687

Lansdale, Joe R., ed. *The New Frontier*, 164(F)

Lantermann, Werner. *The New Parrot Handbook*, 8675

Lanzman, Claude. *Shoah*, 7233

Lapides, Robert (jt. author). *Lodz Ghetto*, 7168

Lapierre, Dominique (jt. author). *The Fifth Horseman*, 50(F)

Freedom at Midnight, 7439

O Jerusalem! 7606

Lapine, James (jt. author). *Into the Woods,* 5929

Lapping, Brian. *Apartheid,* 7375

Lappé, Frances Moore. *Rediscovering America's Values,* 4523

World Hunger, 4511

Laqueur, Walter. *Stalin,* 6876

Laqueur, Walter, ed. *The Israel-Arab Reader,* 7600

Laqueur, Walter, et al. *Soviet Union 2000,* 7573

Laramore, Darryl (jt. author). *Joyce Lain Kennedy's Career Book,* 4798

Lardner, Ring. *The Best Short Stories of Ring Lardner,* 2932(F)

You Know Me Al, 2881(F)

Largen, Velda L. *Guide to Good Food,* 5419

Larkin, Philip, ed. *The Oxford Book of Twentieth-Century English Verse,* 3216

Larson, E. Richard. *The Rights of Racial Minorities,* 4308

Lash, Joseph P. *Eleanor,* 6556

Eleanor and Franklin, 6557

Helen and Teacher, 6627

Laska, Vera, ed. *Women in the Resistance and in the Holocaust,* 7234

Laslo, Cynthia. *The Rosen Photo Guide to a Career in the Circus,* 4890

Lass, Abraham H., eds (jt. author). *The Mentor Book of Short Plays,* 2982

Lasson, Kenneth. *Mouse Traps and Muffling Cups,* 8949

Latham, Caroline. *Dodge Dynasty,* 6659

Lauber, John. *The Making of Mark Twain,* 6320

Lauersen, Niels H. *PMS,* 5476

Laumer, Keith. *Earth Blood,* 2628(F)

End as a Hero, 2624(F)

Galactic Odyssey, 2625(F)

Retief, 2626(F)

Retief to the Rescue, 2626(F)

The Return of Retief, 2626(F)

The Shape Changer, 2627(F)

Laurance, Robert. *Electronic Service Careers,* 5046

Laurence, Clifford L. *The Laser Book,* 8935

Laurents, Arthur. *West Side Story,* 3092

Laurikietis, Rae (jt. author). *The Gender Trap,* 4531

Lauré, Jason. *South Africa,* 7376

Lavender, David. *The Great West,* 7961

The Rockies, 7962

The Southwest, 8201

Lavine, T. Z. *From Socrates to Sartre,* 4013

Lawhead, Stephen R. *Arthur,* 1187(F)

Merlin, 1187(F), 1188(F)

Taliesin, 1187(F)

Lawler, Donald L. *Approaches to Science Fiction,* 3625

Lawrence, D. H. *The Complete Short Stories,* 2933(F)

The Portable D. H. Lawrence, 376

Sons and Lovers, 569(F)

Lawrence, Greg (jt. author). *The Shape of Love,* 6412

Lawrence, Jerome. *Inherit the Wind,* 3093

The Night Thoreau Spent in Jail, 3094

Lawrence, Marcia. *How to Take the SAT, Scholastic Aptitude Test,* 4661

Test-Taking Strategies for the PSAT, 4662

Lawrence, R. D. *In Praise of Wolves,* 8514

Secret Go the Wolves, 8515

The White Puma, 292(F)

Lawrence, T. E. *Seven Pillars of Wisdom,* 7159

Lawson, Don. *FDR's New Deal,* 8034

The Long March, 7420

The New Philippines, 7473

The United States in the Spanish-American War, 8011

The United States in the Vietnam War, 8125

The United States in World War I, 7160

Lawson, John. *Friends You Can Drop,* 5137

Lawther, Christopher (jt. author). *You Can Learn Lettering and Calligraphy,* 9159

Lawther, Gail. *You Can Learn Lettering and Calligraphy,* 9159

Lax, Roger. *The Great Song Thesaurus,* 5947

Lazenby, Roland (jt. author). *College Basketball's 25 Greatest Teams,* 9732

Fifty Years of the Final Four, 9733

Lazzara, Judy (jt. author). *Country Flower Drying,* 9302

Le Carre, John. *The Little Drummer Girl,* 166(F)

A Perfect Spy, 167(F)

The Russia House, 168(F)

Smiley's People, 170(F)

The Spy Who Came in from the Cold, 169(F)

Tinker, Tailor, Soldier, Spy, 170(F)

Le Guin, Ursula K. *The Beginning Place,* 1191(F)

The Dispossessed, 2630(F)

The Eye of the Heron, 2631(F)

Farthest Shore, 2636(F)

The Language of the Night, 3626

The Lathe of Heaven, 2632(F)

The Left Hand of Darkness, 2633(F)

Orsinian Tales, 2634(F)

Planet of Exile, 2635(F)

The Tombs of Atuan, 2636(F)

Very Far Away from Anywhere Else, 1192(F)

The Wind's Twelve Quarters, 1193(F)

The Wizard of Earthsea, 2636(F)

Le Riche, W. Harding. *A Chemical Feast,* 5420

Leach, Lucinda A. (jt. author). *Generations,* 5460

Leacroft, Helen (jt. author). *Theatre and Playhouse,* 6098

Leacroft, Richard. *Theatre and Playhouse,* 6098

League of Women Voters Education Fund. *The Nuclear Waste Primer*, 8926

Leahy, Christopher. *Peterson First Guide to Insects of North America*, 8597

Leahy, Michael. *Hard Lessons*, 5538

Leakey, Mary. *Disclosing the Past*, 6685

Leakey, Richard E. *One Life*, 6686
Origins, 7004

Leana, Frank C. *Getting into College*, 4746

Leary, Lewis. *John Greenleaf Whittier*, 3888

Leasor, James. *Frozen Assets*, 165(F)

Least Heat Moon, William. *Blue Highways*, 6152

Leatherbarrow, William J. *Fedor Dostoevsky*, 3803

Leatherwood, Stephen. *The Sierra Club Handbook of Whales and Dolphins*, 8654

Leavitt, Caroline. *Meeting Rozzy Halfway*, 570(F)

LeBaron, Charles. *Gentle Vengeance*, 5242

Leckie, Robert. *Helmet for My Pillow*, 7235
None Died in Vain, 7927

Leder, Jane Mersky. *Dead Serious*, 5090

Lederer, Katherine. *Lillian Hellman*, 3840

Lederer, Paul Joseph. *Cheyenne Dreams*, 1505(F), 1507(F)
The Far Dreamer, 1506(F)
Manitou's Daughter, 1507(F)
Seminole Skies, 1507(F)
Shawnee Dawn, 1507(F)

Lederer, Paul Jospeh. *North Star*, 171(F)

Lederer, Richard. *Anguished English*, 3932
Crazy English, 3932
Get Thee to a Punnery, 3932

Lederer, William J. *The Ugly American*, 977(F)

Lederman, Leon M. *From Quarks to the Cosmos*, 8266

Ledgard, Henry. *Elementary BASIC*, 8995
Elementary PASCAL, 8996

Ledray, Linda E. *Recovering from Rape*, 5513

Lee, Andrea. *Russian Journal*, 7574

Lee, Beverly Haskell. *The Secret of Van Rink's Cellar*, 1523(F)

Lee, Bill. *The Wrong Stuff*, 9671

Lee, David. *A Basic Guide to Fishing*, 9829

Lee, Essie E. *Breaking the Connection*, 5138
Down Is Not Out, 5388

Lee, Eugene E. (jt. author). *Beginning Photography*, 9412

Lee, Gentry (jt. author). *Rama II*, 2485(F)

Lee, Harper. *To Kill a Mockingbird*, 471(F)

Lee, Hector. *Heroes, Villains, and Ghosts*, 3438

Lee, Joanna. *Mary Jane Harper Cried Last Night*, 696(F)

Lee, Ki-waik. *A New History of Korea*, 7459

Lee, Martin A. *Unreliable Sources*, 3986

Lee, Mary Price. *Exploring Careers in Robotics*, 5047
Ms. Veterinarian, 5024
Opportunities in Animal and Pet Care, 4845

Lee, Mary Price (jt. author). *Careers for Women in Politics*, 4971
Careers in the Restaurant Industry, 4846
Coping with Money, 5065

Lee, Owen. *The Skin Diver's Bible*, 9961

Lee, Richard S. *Careers for Women in Politics*, 4971
Careers in the Restaurant Industry, 4846
Coping with Money, 5065

Lee, Richard S. (jt. author). *Exploring Careers in Robotics*, 5047
Opportunities in Animal and Pet Care, 4845

Lee, Robert E. (jt. author). *Inherit the Wind*, 3093
The Night Thoreau Spent in Jail, 3094

Lee, Rose P. *A Real Job for You*, 4799

Lee, Stan. *How to Draw Comics the Marvel Way*, 9200

Lee, Susan. *Susan Lee's ABZs of Money & Finance*, 4575

Lee, Tanith. *Anackire*, 1189(F)
The Dragon Hoard, 1190(F)
Dreams of Dark and Light, 2629(F)
East of Midnight, 1190(F)
The Gorgon—And other Beastly Tales, 1190(F)
The Storm Land, 1190(F)

Leeds, Robert X. *All the Comforts of Home*, 8676

Leerhsen, Charles (jt. author). *Press On!* 6166
Yeager, 6166

Lees, Carlton B. (jt. author). *Wildflowers across America*, 8435

Lees, Gene. *Meet Me at Jim and Andy's*, 5878

Lehan, Richard. *The Great Gatsby*, 3748

Lehane, Brendan. *Fabled Lands*, 3366
Fall of Camelot, 3366
Legends of Valor, 3366

Lehmann, John. *Virginia Woolf and Her World*, 6330

Lehmann, Ruth P. M., trans. *Beowulf*, 377

Lehmberg, Paul. *In the Strong Woods*, 9797

Lehrer, Jim. *Crown, Oklahoma*, 172(F)
Kick the Can, 172(F)

Lehrer, John. *The Complete Guide to Choosing a Performance Bicycle*, 9756

Lehrman, Robert. *Juggling*, 868(F)

Leib, Franklin Allen. *Fire Arrow*, 173(F)

Leiber, Fritz. *The Big Time*, 2637(F)
The Ghost Light, 2638(F)
Swords against Death, 2639(F)
Swords and Deviltry, 2640(F)
The Wanderer, 2641(F)

Leiber, Fritz (jt. author). *No Truce with Kings/ Ship of Shadows*, 2349(F)

Leider, Robert. *Lovejoy's Guide to Financial Aid*, 4780

Leighton, Ralph (jt. author). *Surely You're Joking, Mr. Feynman!* 6665
"What Do You Care What Other People Think?" 6665

Leimbach, Marti. *Dying Young,* 571(F)
Leinhauser, Jean. *The 7-Day Afghan Book,* 9243
Leinwand, Gerald. *Transplants,* 5165
Leite, Evelyn. *Different Like Me,* 5139
Leitner, Isabella. *Fragments of Isabella,* 7236
  Saving the Fragments, 7236
Lelyveld, Joseph. *Move Your Shadow,* 7377
Lem, Stanislaw. *Cyberiad,* 2642(F)
  Microworlds, 3627
  Tales of Pirx the Pilot, 2642(F)
Lemke, Bob. *Sports Collectors Digest Baseball Card Price Guide,* 9672
Lemlin, Jeanne. *Vegetarian Pleasures,* 9350
LeMond, Greg. *Greg LeMond's Complete Book of Bicycling,* 9758
  Greg LeMond's Pocket Guide to Bicycle Maintenance and Repair, 9757
Lenburg, Jeff. *Baseball's All-Star Game,* 9673
Lendl, Ivan. *Hitting Hot,* 9969
L'Engle, Madeleine. *And Both Were Young,* 2294(F)
  Camilla, 2295(F)
  A Ring of Endless Light, 572(F)
  Two-Park Invention, 6279
Lennon, John. *Skywriting by Word of Mouth,* 6416
Lens, Sidney. *Strikemakers & Strikebreakers,* 4517
Lentz, Joan Easton. *Birdwatching,* 8540
Lenz, Jeanne R. *Do You Really Love Me?* 2296(F)
Lenz, Siegfried. *The German Lesson,* 697(F)
Leonard, Alison. *Tina's Chance,* 698(F)
Leonard, Constance. *Strange Waters,* 2086(F)
Leonard, John (jt. author). *Questions & Answers on AIDS,* 5184
Leonard, Thomas M. *Day by Day,* 7237
Leone, Bruno, ed. *Capitalism,* 4591
  Communism, 4592
  Huckleberry Finn, 4345
  Internationalism, 4150
  Mein Kampf, 4345
  Nationalism, 4151
  Racism, 4345
  Socialism, 4593
Leone, Bruno, eds (jt. author). *War and Human Nature,* 4128
Lerager, Jim. *In the Shadow of the Cloud,* 8927
Lerner, Alan Jay. *Camelot,* 3095
  The Musical Theatre, 5924
  My Fair Lady, 3096
Lerner, Gerda. *The Majority Finds Its Past,* 7054
Lerner, Sid, et al. *New Words Dictionary,* 3933
Leroe, Ellen. *Confessions of a Teenage TV Addict,* 2297(F)
  Robot Romance, 2643(F)
Leroi-Gourhan, André. *The Hunters of Prehistory,* 7005
Lesley, Craig. *River Song,* 1508(F)
  Winterkill, 1508(F)
Leslie, Robert Franklin. *In the Shadow of a Rainbow,* 8516
  Ringo, the Robber Raccoon, 8493
Lessem, Don. *The Worst of Everything,* 9511
Lessing, Doris. *The Doris Lessing Reader,* 2934(F)
Lester, Julius. *Black Folktales,* 3439
  Do Lord Remember Me, 472(F)
  This Strange New Feeling, 473(F)
Leuchtenburg, William E. *Franklin D. Roosevelt and the New Deal, 1932–1940,* 8035
  In the Shadow of FDR, 8077
Levchenko, Stanislav. *On the Wrong Side,* 6854
Levenkron, Steven. *The Best Little Girl in the World,* 699(F)
  Kessa, 700(F)
  Treating and Overcoming Anorexia Nervosa, 5389
Levenson, Thomas. *Ice Time,* 8814
LeVert, Suzanne. *AIDS,* 5202
Levertov, Denise. *Poems, 1960–1967,* 3289
  Poems, 1968–1972, 3290
Levi, Herbert. *Spiders and Their Kin,* 8613
Levi, Lorna R. (jt. author). *Spiders and Their Kin,* 8613
Levi, Maurice. *Economics Deciphered,* 4576
Levi, Peter. *Atlas of the Greek World,* 7107
  The Life and Times of William Shakespeare, 6305
  A Pelican History of Greek Literature, 3594
Levi-Montalcini, Rita. *In Praise of Imperfection,* 6687
Levin, Beatrice. *Women and Medicine,* 5243
Levin, Ira. *The Boys from Brazil,* 174(F)
  Deathtrap, 3097
  The Perfect Day, 2644(F)
  Rosemary's Baby, 1802(F)
Levin, Shirley. *Summer on Campus,* 4747
Levine, Lee Daniel. *Bird,* 6742
Levine, Mel. *Keeping a Head in School,* 5390
Levine, Michael. *The New Address Book,* 7757
Levine, Saul V. *Dear Doctor,* 5619
  Radical Departures, 4061
Levinson, Jay Conrad. *Five Hundred Fifty-Five Ways to Earn Extra Money,* 4847
Levinson, Nancy. *Getting High in Natural Ways,* 5620
Levy, Elizabeth. *Double Standard,* 2298(F)
Levy, Jacques E. *Cesar Chavez,* 6497
Levy, Joann. *They Saw the Elephant,* 7963
Levy, Marilyn. *Keeping Score,* 869(F)
  Putting Heather Together Again, 701(F)
  Remember to Remember Me, 2299(F)
  Summer Show, 702(F)
Lewin, Abraham. *A Cup of Tears,* 7238
Lewin, Rhoda G., ed. *Witness to the Holocaust,* 7239
Lewin, Roger. *Thread of Life,* 7006

Lewin, Roger (jt. author). *Origins,* 7004

Lewis, Adele (jt. author). *Job Hunting for the Disabled,* 4803

Lewis, Allen (jt. author). *Richie Ashburn's Phillies Trivia,* 9623

Lewis, Anthony. *Gideon's Trumpet,* 4246

Lewis, Bernard. *Semites and Anti-Semites,* 4387

Lewis, C. S. *Out of the Silent Planet,* 2645(F)
Perelandra, 2645(F)
The Screwtape Letters, 4062
That Hideous Strength, 2645(F)

Lewis, Craig A. *Blood Evidence,* 4483

Lewis, David L. *When Harlem Was in Vogue,* 8169

Lewis, Gavin. *Tomas Masaryk,* 6864

Lewis, Gregg (jt. author). *Am I Alive?* 6942
Tom Landry, 6751

Lewis, Marjorie (jt. author). *Waltzing on Water,* 3299

Lewis, Nigel. *Exercise Tiger,* 7240

Lewis, Norman. *Correct Spelling Made Easy,* 4685
Thirty Days to a More Powerful Vocabulary, 3935
Thirty Days to Better English, 3934

Lewis, Oscar. *The Children of Sanchez,* 7645

Lewis, Richard S. *Challenger,* 8305

Lewis, Robert. *Advice to the Players,* 6099

Lewis, Sinclair. *Arrowsmith,* 703(F)
Babbitt, 978(F)
Main Street, 979(F)

Lewis, W. H. *The Splendid Century,* 7498

Lewis, William. *Fast-Track Careers,* 4848

Lewisohn, Mark. *The Beatles Live!* 5879

Lichtenberg, Jacqueline. *Dreamspy,* 1194(F)
The Dushau Trilogy, 2646(F)
Those of My Blood, 2647(F)

Lichter, Uri. *In the Eye of the Storm,* 7241

Lichtman, Wendy. *Telling Secrets,* 573(F)

Lieberman, E. James. *Sex & Birth Control,* 5477

Lieberman, Gerald F. *3,500 Good Quotes for Speakers,* 4686

Lieberman, Jethro K. *The Enduring Constitu-·tion,* 4195

Lieberman, Stanley A. (jt. author). *Typing the Easy Way,* 4642

Lieberthal, Bernadette (jt. author). *The Complete Book of Fingermath,* 8840

Lieberthal, Edwin M. *The Complete Book of Fingermath,* 8840

Lien, David A. *Learning IBM BASIC for the Personal Computer,* 8997

Lifton, Betty Jean. *A Place Called Hiroshima,* 7243

Liggett, Cathy (jt. author). *The Complete Handbook of Songwriting,* 5880

Liggett, Mark. *The Complete Handbook of Songwriting,* 5880

Lightbody, Andy. *The Illustrated History of Helicopters,* 9069

Lightfoot, Sara Lawrence. *The Good High School,* 4631

Ligon, Linda, ed. *Homespun, Handknit,* 9244

Likhanov, Albert. *Shadows across the Sun,* 870(F)

Lillington, Kenneth. *An Ash-Blonde Witch,* 1195(F)
Full Moon, 1803(F)

Lillyquist, Michael J. *Sunlight and Health,* 5076

Lin, Alice Murong Pu. *Grandmother Had No Name,* 7421

Lin, Julia C. *Modern Chinese Poetry,* 3349

Lincoff, Gary. *The Audubon Society Field Guide to North American Mushrooms,* 8422

Lincoln, Abraham. *The Lincoln-Douglas Debates of 1858,* 7874

Lindberg, Jan (jt. author). *The Body Victorious,* 5213

Lindbergh, Anne Morrow. *Bring Me a Unicorn,* 6282
The Flower Nettle, 6282
Gift from the Sea, 3537
Hour of Gold, Hour of Lead, 6282
Locked Rooms and Open Doors, 6282
War within and Without, 6282

Lindbergh, Charles A. *The Spirit of St. Louis,* 9070

Lindholm, Megan. *Luck of the Wheels,* 1196(F)

Lindner, Lindy (jt. author). *Everything You Needed to Learn about Writing in High School—But . . ,* 4689

Lindquist, Marie. *Hidden Longings,* 2300(F)

Lindsay, Howard. *The Sound of Music,* 3098
Three Comedies of American Family Life, 3099

Lindsay, Jeanne Warren. *Pregnant Too Soon,* 5478
Teenage Marriage, 5664
Teens Look at Marriage, 5665

Lindsay, Joan. *Picnic at Hanging Rock,* 2087(F)

Lindsell, Sheryl L. *The Secretary's Quick Reference Handbook,* 4640

Lindsey, Betina. *Waltz with the Lady,* 2301(F)

Lindsey, Robert. *The Falcon and the Snowman,* 6893

Line, Les, et al. *The Audubon Society Book of Trees,* 8426

Lineberry, William P., ed. *Arms Control,* 4152

Ling, Roger. *The Greek World,* 7108

Link, Arthur S. *Woodrow Wilson and the Progressive Era, 1910–1917,* 8012

Linthwaite, Illona, ed. *Ain't I a Woman!* 3170

Lipari, Joanna (jt. author). *The Actor,* 4875

Lippard, Lucy R. *Pop Art,* 5751

Lippman, Thomas W. *Understanding Islam,* 4063

Lipson, Carol (jt. author). *Thinking about Science,* 6658

Lipson, Greta Barclay. *Romeo and Juliet,* 3050

Lipsyte, Robert. *The Contender,* 474(F)
One Fat Summer, 704(F)

Summer Rules, 704(F)

The Summerboy, 704(F)

Lisle, Laurie. *Portrait of an Artist,* 6200

Liss, Howard. *The Giant Book of More Strange But True Sports Stories,* 9579

Lister, Margot. *Costume,* 9169

Little, Elbert L. *The Audubon Society Field Guide to North American Trees,* 8427, 8428

Little, Jeffrey B. *Bonds, Preferred Stocks and the Money Market,* 4600

Investing and Trading, 4599

Reading the Financial Pages, 4577

Stock Options, 4600

Understanding a Company, 4594, 4602

Wall Street, 4601

What Is a Share of Stock? 4602

Little, Robert T. *Astrophotography,* 8267

Litwack, Leon F. *Been in the Storm So Long,* 8013

Litwack, Leon F., ed. *Black Leaders of the Nineteenth Century,* 6480

Litwak, Mark. *Courtroom Crusades,* 4247

Livesey, Anthony. *Great Commanders and Their Battles,* 6786

Livingston, John (jt. author). *Canada,* 7634

Livingston, Nancy. *The Far Side of the Hill,* 574(F), 1442(F)

The Land of Our Dreams, 574(F)

Llewellyn, Caroline. *The Lady of the Labyrinth,* 175(F)

The Masks of Rome, 2088(F)

Llewellyn, Edward. *Prelude to Chaos,* 2648(F)

Llewellyn, Richard. *How Green Was My Valley,* 1443(F)

Llewellyn, Sam. *Death Roll,* 176(F)

Llewellyn-Jones, Derek (jt. author). *Eating Disorders,* 5368

Lloyd, Chris Evert. *Lloyd on Lloyd,* 6769

Lloyd, John (jt. author). *Lloyd on Lloyd,* 6769

Lloyd-Evans, Barbara, ed. *Five Hundred Years of English Poetry,* 3868

Llywelyn, Morgan. *Druids,* 1370(F)

Isles of the Blest, 1197(F)

Lion of Ireland, 1444(F)

Red Branch, 1445(F)

Lo, Steven C. *The Incorporation of Eric Chung,* 475(F)

Locher, J. L., ed. *The World of M. C. Escher,* 5779

Lockerbie, D. Bruce. *College,* 4748

Lockhart, Gary. *The Weather Companion,* 8870

Lockhart, Robin Bruce. *Reilly,* 6157

Lockridge, Ernest, ed. *Twentieth Century Interpretations of The Great Gatsby,* 3749

Loder, Kurt (jt. author). *I, Tina,* 6450

Loeb, Jo. *You Can Train Your Cat,* 8696

Loeb, Paul (jt. author). *You Can Train Your Cat,* 8696

Loehr, James E. *Mentally Tough,* 4578

Lofts, Norah. *Scent of Cloves,* 1446(F)

Logan, Robert K. *The Alphabet Effect,* 3967

Logsden, Tom. *Space, Inc,* 8306

Loiry, William S. *Winning with Science,* 4712

Lomask, Milton. *The Spirit of 1787,* 4196

Lomax, Alan. *The Folk Songs of North America,* 5948

Lomax, Judy. *Women of the Air,* 9071

Lombardi, John V. *Venezuela,* 7678

London, Jack. *Best Short Stories of Jack London,* 177(F)

The Call of the Wild, 409(F)

The Call of the Wild and White Fang, 293(F)

The Call of the Wild, White Fang, and Other Stories, 178(F)

Martin Eden, 705(F)

The Sea-Wolf, 410(F)

White Fang, 411(F)

London, Jack (jt. author). *Greater Nowheres,* 6117

London, Mel. *Getting into Film,* 4891

Getting into Video, 4922

Long, David E. *The Anatomy of Terrorism,* 4548

Long, Greg. *Examining the Earthlight Theory,* 9512

Long, Jeff. *Duel of Eagles,* 7964

Long, John. *How to Rock Climb!* 9580

Long, Priscilla. *Where the Sun Never Shines,* 4518

Long, Richard A. *The Black Tradition in American Dance,* 5971

Long, Richard A., ed. *Afro-American Writing,* 2935

Longfellow, Henry Wadsworth. *Hiawatha,* 3291

The Poetical Works of Longfellow, 3292

Longyear, Barry B. *Enemy Mine/Another Orphan,* 2651(F)

The Homecoming, 2649(F)

Sea of Glass, 2650(F)

Lonsdale, Roger, ed. *The New Oxford Book of Eighteenth Century Verse,* 3217

Loomis, Roger S. *A Mirror of Chaucer's World,* 7525

Loon, Borin Van (jt. author). *Darwin for Beginners,* 7007

Lopez, Barry. *Arctic Dreams,* 7697

Crossing Open Ground, 7698

Of Wolves and Men, 8517

Winter Count, 179(F)

Lopez, Claude-Anne. *The Private Franklin,* 6588

Lopez, Nancy. *The Complete Golfer,* 9871

Lorayne, Harry. *How to Develop a Super-Power Memory,* 4650

Lord, Bette Bao. *Legacies,* 7422

Spring Moon, 1396(F)

Lord, Walter. *Day of Infamy,* 7244

The Miracle of Dunkirk, 7245

The Night Lives On, 8893

A Night to Remember, 7152, 8893

A Time to Stand, 7965

Lorenz, Konrad. *King Solomon's Ring,* 6688
On Aggression, 5563

Lorimer, Lawrence T. *The Football Book,* 9853

Loring, Ann (jt. author). *Emergency!* 5251

Lorrah, Jean. *Metamorphosis,* 2652(F)
The Vulcan Academy Murders, 2653(F)

Loss, Archie K. *Of Human Bondage,* 3675

Lott, Catherine S. *How to Land a Better Job,* 4800

Lott, Oscar C. (jt. author). *How to Land a Better Job,* 4800

Loughman, Michael. *Learning to Rock Climb,* 9581

Lourie, Dick, et al., eds. *Smart Like Me,* 3889

Lovecraft, H. P. *At the Mountains of Madness and Other Novels,* 1804(F), 1806(F)
At the Mountains of Madness and Other Tales of Terror, 1805(F)
The Case of Charles Dexter Ward, 1805(F)
Dagon and Other Macabre Tales, 1806(F)
The Doom That Came to Sarnath, 1807(F)
The Dunwich Horror and Others, 1804(F), 1806(F)
The Lurking Fear, 1807(F)
The Tomb and Other Tales, 1807(F)

Lovecraft, H. P., et al. *Tales of the Cthulhu Mythos,* 2654(F)

Lovell, Bernard (jt. author). *Pathways to the Universe,* 8264

Lovell, Marc. *Comfort Me with Spies,* 180(F)

Lovell, Mary S. *The Sound of Wings,* 6141
Straight on Till Morning, 6154

Lovesey, Peter. *Bertie and the Seven Bodies,* 2089(F)

Lovesey, Peter, ed. *The Black Cabinet,* 2090(F)

Low, Rosemary. *The Complete Book of Parrots,* 8677
Keeping Parrots, 8678

Lowe, Jacques. *The Kennedy Legacy,* 6537

Lowe, Kurt E. (jt. author). *The Audubon Society Field Guide to North American Rocks and Minerals,* 8825

Lowell, Robert. *Selected Poems,* 3293

Lowenfish, Lee (jt. author). *The Art of Pitching,* 9696
The Professional Baseball Trainers' Fitness Book, 9678

Lowry, Dave. *Autumn Lightning,* 7451

Lubowe, Irwin I. *A Teen-age Guide to Healthy Skin and Hair,* 5337

Lucas, George. *Star Wars,* 2655(F)

Lucas, James. *Kommando,* 7246

Lucas, Jeff. *Pass, Set, Crush,* 9978

Luce, William. *The Belle of Amherst,* 3100

Luciano, Ron. *The Fall of the Roman Umpire,* 9674
Remembrance of Swings Past, 9674, 9675
Strike Two, 9674

The Umpire Strikes Back, 9674

Lucie-Smith, Edward. *Furniture,* 5810
Toulouse-Lautrec, 5780

Ludlum, David M. *The American Weather Book,* 8871

Ludlum, Robert. *The Aquitaine Progression,* 181(F)
The Bourne Identity, 187(F), 182(F)
The Bourne Supremacy, 182(F)
The Chancellor Manuscript, 183(F)
The Gemini Contenders, 187(F)
The Holcroft Covenant, 187(F)
The Icarus Agenda, 184(F)
The Matarese Circle, 185(F), 181(F)
The Matlock Paper, 181(F)
The Osterman Weekend, 181(F)
The Parsifal Mosaic, 187(F)
The Rhinemann Exchange, 186(F)
The Road to Gandolfo, 181(F)
The Scarlatti Inheritance, 187(F)

Ludwig, Charles. *He Freed Britain's Slaves,* 6881
Michael Faraday, 6664

Luger, Harriet. *The Elephant Tree,* 188(F)
Lauren, 706(F)

Lukas, Christopher. *Silent Grief,* 5091

Lukins, Sheila (jt. author). *The New Basics Cookbook,* 9358

Lum, Peter. *Growth of Civilization in East Asia,* 7393

Lumley, Brian. *The House of Doors,* 2656(F)
The Source, 1808(F)

Lund, Doris. *Eric,* 6926

Lundell, Allan. *Virus!* 8998

Lundquist, James. *J. D. Salinger,* 3750
Kurt Vonnegut, 3751
Sinclair Lewis, 3752
Theodore Dreiser, 3753

Luoma, Jon R. *Troubled Skies, Troubled Waters,* 4454

Lupica, Mike. *Shooting from the Lip,* 9582

Lupica, Mike (jt. author). *Wait till Next Year,* 9570

Lutz, John. *Better Mousetraps,* 2091(F)

Lutz, William. *Doublespeak,* 3936

Luxenberg, Stan. *Roadside Empires,* 4617

Lyall, Gavin. *The Conduct of Major Maxim,* 189(F)

Lydon, Michael. *How to Succeed in Show Business by Really Trying,* 4892

Lynn, Loretta. *Loretta Lynn,* 6419

Lynton, Norbert. *The Story of Modern Art,* 5752

Lyon, Hugh. *An Illustrated Guide to Modern Warships,* 9131

Lyons, Arthur (jt. author). *Physical Evidence,* 215(F)

Lyons, Len. *Jazz Portraits,* 5882
The One-Hundred-One Best Jazz Albums, 5881

Lyons, Pam. *Love Around the Corner,* 575(F)

Lyons, Pat. *Great Shape,* 5357

Lyons, Pete, et al. *Ferrari*, 9100

Lytle, Clifford M. (jt. author). *American Indians, American Justice*, 7804
The Nations Within, 4392

Lyttle, Richard B. *How to Pay for College or Trade School*, 4781
Pablo Picasso, 6202

Mabie, Margot C. J. *Vietnam*, 8126

McAfee, J. *Computer Viruses, Worms, Data Diddlers, Killer Programs and Other Threats to Your System*, 8999

McAleer, Neil. *The Cosmic Mind-Boggling Book*, 8268
The Mind-Boggling Universe, 8269
The Omni Space Almanac, 8307

McAlester, Lee (jt. author). *A Field Guide to American Houses*, 5702

McAlester, Virginia. *A Field Guide to American Houses*, 5702

McAllister, Pam. *You Can't Kill the Spirit*, 7055

McAllister, Pam (jt. author). *The New Bedside, Bathtub & Armchair Companion to Agatha Christie*, 3683

McAlpine, Helen. *Japanese Tales & Legends*, 3383

McAlpine, William (jt. author). *Japanese Tales & Legends*, 3383

McArdle, Karen (jt. author). *Fatal Fascination*, 4248

McArdle, Phil. *Fatal Fascination*, 4248

MacArthur, John F., Jr. *God with Us*, 4116

Macaulay, David. *Baaa*, 1198(F)
Castle, 5707
Cathedral, 5708
City, 7118
Great Moments in Architecture, 5695
Mill, 8956
Motel of the Mysteries, 3501
Unbuilding, 5709
The Way Things Work, 8950

MacAvoy, R. A. *Damiano*, 1199(F)
Damiano's Lute, 1199(F)
The Grey Horse, 1200(F)
Lens of the World, 1201(F)
Raphael, 1199(F)
Tea with the Black Dragon, 1202(F)
The Third Eagle, 2657(F)

MacBride, Roger Lea (jt. author). *Rose Wilder Lane*, 6278

McCaffrey, Anne. *The Crystal Singer*, 2658(F)
The Death of Sleep, 2669(F)
Decision at Doona, 2659(F)
Dinosaur Planet, 2660(F)
Dinosaur Planet Survivors, 2660(F)
Dragondrums, 2663(F)
Dragonflight, 2661(F)
Dragonquest, 2661(F)

Dragonsdawn, 2662(F)
Dragonsinger, 2663(F)
Dragonsong, 2663(F)
Killashandra, 2664(F)
Moreta, 2661(F), 2665(F)
Nerilka's Story, 1203(F)
Pegasus in Flight, 2666(F)
The Renegades of Pern, 1204(F)
The Rowan, 2667(F)
Sassinak, 2668(F)
Stitch in Snow, 2302(F)
White Dragon, 2661(F)

McCaffrey, Anne (jt. author). *The Dragonlover's Guide to Pern*, 3763
The People of Pern, 3793

McCaffrey, Eugene. *Players' Choice*, 9676

McCaffrey, Roger A. (jt. author). *Players' Choice*, 9676

McCammon, Robert R. *Blue World*, 190(F)
Mine, 1809(F)
Swan Song, 1810(F)

MacCana, Proinsias. *Celtic Mythology*, 3461

McCarry, Charles. *The Great Southwest*, 8202

McCarthy, Colman. *Inner Companions*, 3538

McCarthy, Dennis V. N. *Protecting the President*, 4224

McCarthy, Gary. *Sodbuster*, 191(F)

McCarthy, Laura Flynn. *Your Quick & Easy Car Care and Safe Driving Handbook*, 9101

McCarthy, Mary. *How I Grew*, 6286

McCarthy, Mignon (jt. author). *Kareem*, 6738

McCarthy, Paul. *John Steinbeck*, 3754

McCarver, Tim. *Oh, Baby, I Love It!* 9677

McCauley, Kirby, ed. *Dark Forces*, 1811(F)

McCauley, Robie. *Technique in Fiction*, 4687

McCauley, Stephen. *The Object of My Affection*, 1891(F)

McClanahan, Ed. *The Natural Man*, 1892(F)

McClellan, Grant S., ed. *The Right to Privacy*, 4309

MacClintock, Dorcas. *Red Pandas*, 8524

MacClintock, Dorcas (jt. author). *African Images*, 7353

McClintock, Jack. *Everything Is Somewhere*, 7056

McClun, Diana. *Quilts! Quilts! Quilts!* 9245

McClung, Robert M. *The True Adventures of Grizzly Adams*, 6124

McCollum, Michael. *Life Probe*, 2670(F)

McComb, Gordon. *The Robot Builder's Bonanza*, 9000

McCombs, Don. *World War II Super Facts*, 7247

McConnaughey, Bayard. *Pacific Coast*, 8182

McConnaughey, Evelyn (jt. author). *Pacific Coast*, 8182

McConnell, Frank D. *The Science Fiction of H. G. Wells*, 3676

McConnell, Malcolm (jt. author). *Men from Earth*, 8294

McCord, John S. *Walking Hawk,* 192(F)

McCormick, John S. F. (jt. author). *Five-Hundred-Five Automobile Questions Your Friends Can't Answer,* 9106

McCoy, Donald R. *The Presidency of Harry S. Truman,* 8079

McCoy, Kathy. *Coping with Teenage Depression,* 5564

The New Teenage Body Book, 5479

MacCracken, Mary. *A Circle of Children,* 5391

City Kid, 5391

Lovey, 5392

Turnabout Children, 5393

McCredie, Kenneth B. (jt. author). *Understanding Leukemia,* 5205

McCreery, Ruth S. (jt. author). *A Japanese Touch for the Seasons,* 7449

McCrum, Robert, et al. *The Story of English,* 3937

McCrumb, Sharyn. *If Ever I Return, Pretty Peggy-O,* 2092(F)

The Windsor Knot, 2093(F)

McCuen, Gary E. *Hi-Tech Babies,* 5481

Inner-City Violence, 4461

The International Drug Trade, 5140

Manipulating Life, 5264

Militarizing Space, 4174

Nuclear Waste, 8928

Poor and Minority Health Care, 5077

Pornography and Sexual Violence, 4524

Religion and Politics, 4266

The Religious Right, 4267

Reviving the Death Penalty, 4484

Secret Democracy, 4310

Terminating Life, 5092

McCuen, Gary E., ed. *Children Having Children,* 5480

McCuen, Jo Ray (jt. author). *Writing the Research Paper,* 4654

McCullers, Carson. *The Ballad of the Sad Cafe,* 707(F)

Collected Stories, 2936(F)

The Heart Is a Lonely Hunter, 708(F)

The Member of the Wedding, 871(F)

McCullough, Colleen. *The Thorn Birds,* 1397(F)

McCullough, David. *Mornings on Horseback,* 6564

The Path between the Seas, 7663

McCullough, David, ed. *City Sleuths and Tough Guys,* 2094(F)

McCullough, Frances, ed. *Earth, Air, Fire, & Water,* 3171

Love Is Like the Lion's Tooth, 3172

McCullough, Joseph B. (jt. author). *New and Old Voices of Wah'kon-tah,* 3260

McCunn, Ruthanne Lum. *Sole Survivor,* 193(F)

Thousand Pieces of Gold, 1575(F)

MacCurdy, Doug. *Sports Illustrated Tennis,* 9970

McCutchan, Philip. *Cameron's Raid,* 194(F)

McDermott, Alice. *That Night,* 872(F)

McDevitt, Jack. *A Talent for War,* 2671(F)

MacDonald, David. *Running with the Fox,* 8518

MacDonald, David, ed. *The Complete Book of the Dog,* 8725

The Encyclopedia of Mammals, 8494

McDonald, Gregory. *Fletch and the Man Who,* 2095(F)

MacDonald, Gregory, ed. *Last Laughs,* 2096(F)

MacDonald, Hope. *When Angels Appear,* 9513

Macdonald, Hugh. *Berlioz,* 6337

MacDonald, J. Fred. *One Nation under Television,* 6025

MacDonald, John. *Great Battlefields of the World,* 7057

Great Battles of World War II, 7248

McDonald, Laughlin (jt. author). *The Rights of Racial Minorities,* 4308

MacDonald, Patricia A. (jt. author). *Pablo Picasso,* 6203

MacDonald, Patricia J. *Stranger in the House,* 195(F)

Macdonald, Robert W. *Exploring Careers in the Military Services,* 4972

MacDonald, Ruth K. *Dr. Seuss,* 6207

McDonough, Alex. *Scorpio,* 2672(F)

McDonough, James. *Platoon Leader,* 8127

McDonough, Kevin (jt. author). *The Seventies,* 8059

McDonough, Thomas R. *Space,* 8308

MacDougall, Carl, ed. *The Giant Book of Scottish Short Stories,* 2937(F)

McDowall, David. *The Spanish Armada,* 7558

McDowell, Bart. *The Revolutionary War,* 7853

McDowell, Jack (jt. author). *Sports Illustrated Scuba Diving,* 9956

McDowell, Margaret B. *Edith Wharton,* 3755

McDowell, Nicholas. *Hemingway,* 6263

Mace, Nancy L. *The Thirty-six-Hour Day,* 5203

McElheny, Kenneth (jt. author). *Points of View,* 2947(F)

McElroy, Richard L. *American Presidents,* 6481

McElvaine, Robert S. *The Great Depression,* 8036

Mario Cuomo, 6581

McEvedy, Colin. *The Penguin Atlas of Recent History,* 7485

The World History Factfinder, 7058

McEvoy, Marjorie. *The Black Pearl,* 2303(F)

McFadden Cyra. *Rain or Shine,* 6927

McFarlan, Donald, ed. *Guinness Book of World Records 1990–91,* 9514

McFarland, Rhoda. *Coping through Assertiveness,* 5621

Coping through Self-Esteem, 5622

Coping with Stigma, 5623

Coping with Substance Abuse, 5141

MacFarlane, Ruth B. *Collecting and Preserving Plants for Science and Pleasure,* 8436

McGee, Dorothy H. *Framers of the Constitution,* 4197

McGee, Mark Thomas. *Roger Corman,* 6026

McGinniss, Joe. *Going to Extremes,* 8183

McGinty, Sarah. *Writing Your College Application Essay,* 4749

McGowan, Alan (jt. author). *Sailing Ships,* 9122

McGowan, Hugh. *Leprechauns, Legends and Irish Tales,* 3403

Mcgowan, Kenneth, ed. *Famous American Plays of the 1920s,* 3101

McGown, Jill. *The Stalking Horse,* 2097(F)

McGrath, Alice (jt. author). *Self-Defense & Assault Prevention for Girls & Women,* 9903

Solo Forms of Karate, Tai Chi, Aikido & Kung Fu, 9904

MacGregor, Loren. *The Net,* 2673(F)

McGuinness, Elizabeth Ann. *People Waging Peace,* 4153

McGuire, Paula. *It Won't Happen to Me,* 5514

Putting It Together, 5666

McGurn, James. *On Your Bicycle,* 9759

McHarg, Ian L. *Design with Nature,* 4559

McHargue, Georgess. *A Field Guide to Conservation Archaeology in North America,* 7019

Machiavelli, Niccolo. *The Prince,* 4014

Machlis, Joseph. *The Enjoyment of Music,* 5825

McInerny, Ralph. *Four on the Floor,* 2098(F)

Frigor Mortis, 2099(F)

Savings and Loan, 2100(F)

MacInnes, Helen. *Above Suspicion,* 196(F)

Agent in Place, 196(F)

Assignment in Brittany, 196(F)

Decision at Delphi, 196(F)

The Salzburg Connection, 196(F)

Snare of the Hunter, 196(F)

McIntosh, James. *The Practical Archaeologist,* 7020

McIntyre, Loren. *Exploring South America,* 7679

The Incredible Incas and Their Timeless Land, 7680

McIntyre, Thomas. *The Way of the Hunter,* 9583

McIntyre, Vonda N. *Dreamsnake,* 2674(F)

Enterprise, 2675(F)

Fireflood and Other Stories, 2676(F)

Mack, John E. *Vivienne,* 6925

Mack Smith, Denis. *Garibaldi,* 6842

Mackal, Roy P. *The Monsters of Loch Ness,* 9515

McKay, Dave (jt. author). *Strength Training for Baseball,* 9633

Mackay, James. *The Guinness Book of Stamps, Facts and Feats,* 9456

McKay, Robert. *Opportunities in Your Own Service Business,* 4849

Planning Your Military Career, 4973

McKenny, Margaret (jt. author). *A Field Guide to Wildflowers of North-Eastern and North-Central North America,* 8441

McKenzie, Alan. *How to Draw and Sell Comic Strips for Newspapers and Comic Books,* 9201

MacKenzie, Jeanne (jt. author). *Dickens,* 6240

MacKenzie, Norman. *Dickens,* 6240

A Reader's Guide to Gerard Manley Hopkins, 3869

Mackey, Douglas A. *Philip K. Dick,* 3756

Mackey, Sandra. *Lebanon,* 7621

McKie, Roy (jt. author). *Gardening,* 9370

McKiernan, Dennis L. *Dragondoom,* 1205(F)

McKillip, Patricia A. *Fool's Run,* 2677(F)

The Throme of the Erril of Sherill, 1206(F)

McKinley, Robin. *Beauty,* 1207(F)

The Outlaws of Sherwood, 3404

McKinley, Robin, ed. *Imaginary Lands,* 1208(F)

McKinney, Jack. *Invid Invasion,* 2678(F)

Metamorphosis, 2678(F)

Symphony of Light, 2678(F)

McKissack, Frederick (jt. author). *A Long Hard Journey,* 4613

McKissack, Patricia. *A Long Hard Journey,* 4613

McKuen, Rod. *Seasons in the Sun,* 3294

Too Many Midnights, 3294

McLanathan, Richard. *Art in America,* 5801

McLaughlin, Peter J. (jt. author). *Mentally Tough,* 4578

MacLean, Alistair. *Athabasca,* 1664(F)

Circus, 197(F)

Floodgate, 197(F)

The Golden Gate, 198(F)

H.M.S. Ulysses, 1664(F)

Ice Station Zebra, 198(F)

Partisans, 198(F)

River of Death, 198(F)

San Andreas, 1665(F)

Santorini, 199(F)

Seawitch, 1665(F)

Secret Ways, 197(F)

South by Java Head, 197(F)

Way to Dusty Death, 1664(F)

When Eight Bells Toll, 1665(F)

Maclean, Fitzroy. *Portrait of the Soviet Union,* 7575

MacLean, John. *Mac,* 709(F)

Maclean, Norman. *A River Runs through It and Other Stories,* 200(F)

MacLear, Michael. *The Ten Thousand Day War,* 8128

McLeave, Hugh. *Second Time Around,* 2101(F)

McLeay, Alison. *Passage Home,* 2304(F)

MacLeish, Archibald. *New and Collected Poems, 1917–1982,* 3295

Six Plays, 3102

MacLeish, Rod. *Crossing at Ivalo,* 201(F)

Prince Ombra, 1209(F)

McLellan, David. *Karl Marx,* 6860

MacLennan, Jennifer. *Simple Puppets You Can Make,* 9146

MacLeod, Alistair. *The Lost Salt Gift of Blood,* 576(F)

MacLeod, Charlotte. *Cirak's Daughter*, 577(F)
The Corpse in Oozak's Pond, 2102(F)
The Curse of the Giant Hogweed, 1210(F)
The Gladstone Bag, 2103(F)
Rest You Merry, 2105(F)
MacLeod, Charlotte, ed. *Mistletoe Mysteries*, 2104(F)
McLoughlin, John. *Toolmaker Koan*, 2679(F)
McLuhan, Marshall. *Understanding Media*, 6027
McMahan, Elizabeth. *The Writer's Handbook*, 4688
MacMahon, James A. *Deserts*, 8815
McManus, Patrick F. *The Night the Bear Ate Goombaw*, 3502
Rubber Legs and White Tail-Hairs, 1893(F)
They Shoot Canoes, Don't They? 9798
McMillon, Bill. *Volunteer Vacations*, 4850
McMullen, Jeanine. *My Small Country Living*, 6928
Wind in the Ashtree, 6928
McMurtry, Larry. *Anything for Billy*, 1576(F)
Horseman, Pass By, 202(F)
The Last Picture Show, 873(F)
Terms of Endearment, 578(F)
McNaught, Brian. *On Being Gay*, 4536
McNeil, Helen. *Emily Dickinson*, 3890
MacNeil, Robert. *Wordstruck*, 6421
MacNeil, Robert, ed. *The Way We Were*, 8080
McNeil, W. K., comp. *Ghost Stories from the American South*, 1812(F)
McNeill, William H. *A World History*, 7059
McNeish, Cameron. *The Backpacker's Manual*, 9799
McNelly, Willis E. *The Dune Encyclopedia*, 3757
McPhee, John A. *Coming into the Country*, 8184
In Suspect Terrain, 8170
The John McPhee Reader, 3539
The Survival of the Bark Canoe, 6964
Table of Contents, 3540
McPhee, Penelope (jt. author). *King Remembered*, 6513
McPherson, James Alan. *Hue and Cry*, 476(F)
MacPherson, Malcolm C. *Time Bomb*, 9132
McQuaid, E. Patrick. *How to Get into an Ivy League School*, 4750
McQuaid, Kim. *The Anxious Years*, 8081
McQuay, Mike. *Suspicion*, 2680(F)
McRae, Barry. *Dizzy Gillespie*, 6393
McRae, Russell. *Going to the Dogs*, 710(F)
McRauch, Earl. *Buckaroo Banzai*, 2681(F)
McSherry, Frank, Jr., et al., eds. *Civil War Women*, 1542(F)
McSweeney, Kerry. *Moby-Dick*, 3758
Macvey, John W. *Time Travel*, 8861
McWhirter, Norris, et al., eds. *Guinness Book of World Records*, 9516
McWilliams, Peter A. *The Personal Computer Book*, 9001
Madaras, Lynda. *Lynda Madaras Talks to Teens about AIDS*, 5204

Madden, John. *Hey, Wait a Minute, I Wrote a Book!* 6755
One Knee Equals Two Feet, 9854
One Size Doesn't Fit All, 6756
Maddex, Diane, ed. *Built in the U.S.A.*, 5703
Master Builders, 5696
Maddocks, Melvin. *The Atlantic Crossing*, 7758
Maddox, Harry. *How to Study*, 4651
Maddox, Jerald C. *The Pioneering Image*, 5802
Maddox, Robert L. *Separation of Church and State*, 4179
Madison, Arnold. *Runaway Teens*, 4462
Magnus, Günter Hugo. *Graphic Techniques for Designers and Illustrators*, 9202
Maguire, Byron W. *Cabinetmaking*, 9279
Mahoney, Olivia (jt. author). *A House Divided*, 7913
Mahoney, Rosemary. *The Early Arrival of Dreams*, 7423
Mahy, Margaret. *The Changeover*, 1211(F)
Memory, 711(F)
The Tricksters, 1212(F)
Maidens, Melinda, eds (jt. author). *America's Troubled Children*, 5371
Mailer, Norman. *The Naked and the Dead*, 1666(F)
Mails, Thomas E. *Fools Crow*, 7816
Maiotti, Etorri. *The Pastel Handbook*, 9203
Maitland, Sara (jt. author). *The Rushdie File*, 3647
Major, Kevin. *Thirty-six Exposures*, 874(F)
Major League Baseball Training Staff. *The Professional Baseball Trainers' Fitness Book*, 9678
Makeba, Miriam. *Makeba, My Story*, 6422
Makower, Joel. *How to Buy a Used Car/How to Sell a Used Car*, 9102
Woodstock, 5883
Makower, Joel, ed. *The Air & Space Catalog*, 8270
The Map Catalog, 6972
Malamud, Bernard. *The Assistant*, 1398(F)
The Fixer, 1447(F)
God's Grace, 2682(F)
The Magic Barrel, 2938(F)
The Natural, 2882(F)
The Stories of Bernard Malamud, 2939(F)
Malan, Robin, ed. *Ourselves in Southern Africa*, 2940
Malcolm, Andrew H. *The Canadians*, 7635
Malcolm, Douglas R. *How to Build Electronic Projects*, 9038
Malcolm X. *The Autobiography of Malcolm X*, 6516
Males, Carolyn. *Life after High School*, 4801
Malkin, Lawrence. *The National Debt*, 4225
Malkin, Peter Z. *Eichmann in My Hands*, 7249
Malmgren, Dallin. *The Whole Nine Yards*, 712(F)

Maloff, Chalda. *Business and Social Etiquette with Disabled People,* 5437

Malone, Bill C. *Country Music, U.S.A,* 5884

Maloney, Ray. *The Impact Zone,* 2883(F)

Malory, Thomas. *King Arthur and His Knights,* 3405
Le Morte d'Arthur, 3406
Tales of King Arthur, 3407

Malraux, André. *Man's Fate,* 1399(F)

Maltin, Leonard. *The Disney Films,* 6100
Leonard Maltin's TV Movies, 1991, 6028

Maltin, Leonard, ed. *The Whole Film Sourcebook,* 6029

Mam, Teeda Butt. *To Destroy You Is No Loss,* 7460

Manchester, William. *American Caesar,* 6601
The Death of a President, November 20–November 25, 1963, 6538
The Glory and the Dream, 7759
Goodbye, Darkness, 7250
One Brief Shining Moment, 6539

Mancini, Pat McNees, ed. *Contemporary Latin American Short Stories,* 2941(F)

Mandel, William M. *Soviet but Not Russian,* 7576

Mandela, Winnie. *A Part of My Soul Went with Him,* 6796

Mandelbaum, Michael (jt. author). *Global Rivals,* 4131

Mandell, Judy (jt. author). *The One Hour College Applicant,* 4760

Mandell, Lewis. *The Credit Card Industry,* 4615

Mandrell, Barbara. *Get to the Heart,* 6423

Manes, Stephen. *I'll Live,* 713(F)

Mangi, Richard, et al. *Sports Fitness and Training,* 5358

Manguel, Alberto, ed. *Dark Arrows,* 203(F)

Manhart, Marcia, ed. *The Eloquent Object,* 5811

Manhart, Tom (jt. author). *The Eloquent Object,* 5811

Mann, Charles C. (jt. author). *The Second Creation,* 8906

Mann, Gertrude (jt. author). *Journey of Conscience,* 7275

Mann, Marty. *Marty Mann Answers Your Questions about Drinking and Alcoholism,* 5142

Mann, Thomas. *Buddenbrooks,* 1448(F)
Death in Venice, 714(F)
The Magic Mountain, 1449(F)

Manning, Harvey. *Backpacking One Step at a Time,* 9800

Mansfield, Katherine. *The Short Stories of Katherine Mansfield,* 2942(F)

Manson, Cynthia (jt. author). *Tales from Alfred Hitchcock's Mystery Magazine,* 2074(F)
Tales from Ellery Queen's Mystery Magazine, 2190(F)
Tales from Isaac Asimov's Science Fiction Magazine, 2843(F)

Mantle, Mickey. *The Mick,* 6725

Maquet, Jacques. *Civilizations of Black Africa,* 7351

Marable, Manning. *W. E. B. Du Bois,* 6504

Marazzi, Rich. *Aaron to Zuverink,* 9679

Marchand, Leslie A. *Byron,* 6226

Marchetti, Victor. *The CIA and the Cult of Intelligence,* 4226

Marcus, Greil. *Mystery Train,* 5885

Marcus, Steven. *Dickens,* 3677

Marek, Elizabeth. *The Children of Santa Clara,* 5394

Marek, Rosanne J. *Opportunities in Social Science Careers,* 4802

Margolies, Cynthia P. *Understanding Leukemia,* 5205

Margolin, Judith B. *Financing a College Education,* 4751

Margolis, Matthew. *The Dog in Your Life,* 8726

Margolis, Matthew (jt. author). *Good Dog, Bad Dog,* 8736

Margulies, Alice. *Compassion,* 5574

Margulis, Lynn (jt. author). *Garden of Microbial Delights,* 8660

Marino, John, et al. *John Marino's Bicycling Book,* 9760

Marion, Robert. *The Boy Who Felt No Pain,* 5244
The Intern Blues, 5245

Mark, Jan. *The Ennead,* 2683(F)

Markandaya, Kamala. *Nectar in a Sieve,* 1400(F)

Markham, Beryl. *The Splendid Outcast,* 2943(F)

Markoe, Arnie (jt. author). *Baseball Rules Illustrated,* 9690

Markoe, Merrill, ed. *Late Night with David Letterman,* 6030

Markovna, Nina. *Nina's Journey,* 6929

Marks, Edith. *Job Hunting for the Disabled,* 4803

Marks, Jane. *HELP! My Parents Are Driving Me Crazy,* 5667

Marks, John D. (jt. author). *The CIA and the Cult of Intelligence,* 4226

Marks, Lillian S. *Touch Typing Made Simple,* 4641

Marlow, A. W. *Classic Furniture Projects,* 9280
Fine Furniture for the Amateur Cabinetmaker, 9281

Marlowe, Christopher. *Doctor Faustus,* 3033

Marlowe, John (jt. author). *A Student's Guide to Research and Writing,* 4699

Marquand, John P. *The Late George Apley,* 579(F)

Marquis, Don. *The Lives and Times of Archy & Mehitabel,* 3503

Marrin, Albert. *1812,* 7875
Victory in the Pacific, 7251
War Clouds in the West, 7966

Marriott, Alice. *American Indian Mythology,* 3424

Plains Indian Mythology, 3425

The Ten Grandmothers, 7817

Marrs, Texe. *Careers with Robots*, 5025

Everywoman's Guide to Military Service, 4285

Marschall, Laurence A. *The Supernova Story*, 8354

Marsden, Simon. *The Haunted Realm*, 9517

Marsh, Dave. *Born to Run*, 6445

Fortunate Son, 5887

Glory Days, 6445

Trapped, 6411

Marsh, Dave, ed. *The New Rolling Stone Record Guide*, 5888

Marsh, Dave, et al., eds. *The First Rock & Roll Confidential Report*, 5886

Marsh, John R. (jt. author). *Sports Illustrated Training with Weights*, 9772

Marsh, Ngaio. *Artists in Crime*, 2106(F)

The Collected Short Fiction of Ngaio Marsh, 2107(F)

Marsh, Peter, ed. *Eye to Eye*, 5539

Marshall, Catherine. *Christy*, 1613(F)

Julie, 1627(F)

Marshall, Eliot L. (jt. author). *Medical Ethics*, 5235

Marshall, John. *Rail—The Records*, 9120

Marshall, Kathryn. *In the Combat Zone*, 8129

Marston, Edward. *The Queen's Head*, 2108(F)

Martelli, Leonard, et al. *When Someone You Know Has AIDS*, 5206

Martin, Alexander C. *Flowers*, 8438

Weeds, 8437

Martin, Alexander C. (jt. author). *Trees*, 8431

Martin, Buddy (jt. author). *Looking Deep*, 6752

Martin, Carl (jt. author). *Touch the Stars*, 2501(F)

Martin, Colin. *The Spanish Armada*, 7559

Martin, David C. *Best Laid Plans*, 4549

Martin, Elmer P. *The Black Extended Family*, 4371

Martin, George R. *The Armageddon Rag*, 1213(F)

Dying of the Light, 2684(F)

Windhaven, 1214(F)

Martin, Jo. *Drugs & the Family*, 5143

Martin, Joanne Mitchell (jt. author). *The Black Extended Family*, 4371

Martin, Judith. *Miss Manners' Guide to Excruciatingly Correct Behavior*, 5575

Martin, Linda. *Women in Comedy*, 5956

Martin, Molly, ed. *Hard-Hatted Women*, 4851

Martin, Peigi. *Patchwork Made Easy*, 9246

Martin, Pol. *Easy Cooking for Today*, 9351

Martin, Ralph G. *A Hero for Our Time*, 6540

Martin, Richard (jt. author). *Two Hundred Years of American Art*, 5792

Martin, Russell. *Matters Gray and White*, 5316

Martin, Russell, ed. *Writers of the Purple Sage*, 204(F)

Martin, Terence. *Nathaniel Hawthorne*, 3759

Martin, Tony. *How to Survive Medical School*, 5001

Martin, Valerie. *Mary Reilly*, 1813(F)

Martine, James J., ed. *Critical Essays on Arthur Miller*, 3841

Martz, Larry. *Ministry of Greed*, 4064

Marx, Karl. *The Communist Manifesto of Karl Marx and Friedrich Engels*, 4175

Marzan, Julio, ed. *Inventing a Word*, 3296

Marzollo, Jean. *Do You Love Me, Harvey Burns?* 477(F)

Halfway Down Paddy Lane, 1215(F)

Mason, Bill. *Path of the Paddle*, 9930

Sports Illustrated Fly Fishing, 9814

Mason, Bobbie Ann. *In Country*, 875(F)

Love Life, 876(F)

Mason, Francis (jt. author). *101 Stories of the Great Ballets*, 5959

Mason, Jeff (jt. author). *October Dreams*, 1801(F)

Mason, John (jt. author). *The Return of Halley's Comet*, 8332

Mason, Philip. *The Men Who Ruled India*, 7440

Mason, Robert. *Chickenhawk*, 8130

Mason, Steve. *Johnny's Song*, 3297

Mason, Theodore K. *Two against the Ice*, 6125

Massie, Robert. *Journey*, 5207

Nicholas and Alexandra, 6867

Peter the Great, 6868

Massie, Suzanne (jt. author). *Journey*, 5207

Mast, Gerald. *The Comic Mind*, 6101

A Short History of the Movies, 6031

Masters, Edgar Lee. *Spoon River Anthology*, 3298

Masterson, Richard. *Exploring Careers in Computer Graphics*, 5048

Masterton, Graham. *Death Trance*, 1814(F)

Mateja, Jim. *Used Cars*, 9103

Math, Irwin. *Bits and Pieces*, 9002

Mathabane, Mark. *Kaffir Boy*, 6930

Kaffir Boy in America, 6930

Matheny, Fred. *Beginning Bicycle Racing*, 9761

Bicycling Magazine's Complete Guide to Riding and Racing Techniques, 9762

Mathews, Jay. *Escalante*, 6904

Matloff, Maurice. *American Wars and Heroes*, 7760

Matt, Stephen R. *Electricity and Basic Electronics*, 9039

Mattera, Don. *Sophiatown*, 6797

Matthee, Dalene. *Fiela's Child*, 1385(F)

Matthew, Donald. *Atlas of Medieval Europe*, 7138

Matthew-Walker, Robert. *David Bowie*, 6375

Simon and Garfunkel, 5949

Matthews, Anne. *Vogue Dictionary of Knitting Stitches*, 9247

Matthews, Christopher. *Hardball*, 4268

Matthews, Greg. *Little Red Rooster,* 877(F)

Matthews, John. *Warriors of Arthur,* 3462

Matthews, John (jt. author). *Atlas of the Roman World,* 7113

Matthews, John, ed. *An Arthurian Reader,* 3408

Matthews, Rupert O. *The Atlas of Natural Wonders,* 7061

Matthiessen, Peter. *Indian Country,* 7818
Wildlife in America, 8576

Matthiesson, Peter. *The Snow Leopard,* 7461

Mattingly, Garrett. *The Armada,* 7526

Mattison, Chris. *The Care of Reptiles and Amphibians in Captivity,* 8465
Snakes of the World, 8470

Maugham, W. Somerset. *Collected Short Stories,* 2944(F)
The Moon and Sixpence, 715(F)
Of Human Bondage, 716(F)
The Razor's Edge, 717(F)

Maurer, Harry. *Strange Ground,* 8131

Mautner, Gabriella. *Lovers and Fugitives,* 1667(F)

Maxwell, Gavin. *Ring of Bright Water,* 8477

Maxwell, Joe (jt. author). *Beautiful Braids,* 5277

Maxwell, William. *The Folded Leaf,* 878(F)

May, Antoinette. *Witness to War,* 6287

May, John. *The Greenpeace Book of Antarctica,* 7699

May, Julian. *The Adversary,* 1216(F)
The Golden Tore, 1216(F)
The Many-Colored Land, 1216(F)
The Nonborn King, 1216(F)

Mayall, Newton, et al. *The Sky Observer's Guide,* 8271

Mayer, Allan. *Gaston's War,* 6165

Mayer, Egon. *Love & Tradition,* 5668

Mayer, Henry. *A Son of Thunder,* 6591

Mayer, Martin. *The Bankers,* 4597
The Greatest-Ever Bank Robbery, 4595

Mayhar, Ardath. *Lords of the Triple Moons,* 1217(F)
Makra Choria, 1218(F)
Runes of the Lyre, 1219(F)

Mayo, Jonathan L. *Superconductivity,* 8938

Mays, Willie. *Say Hey,* 6727

Mazer, Harry. *City Light,* 879(F)
The Dollar Man, 882(F)
The Girl of His Dreams, 880(F)
Hey Kid! Does She Love Me? 881(F)
I Love You, Stupid! 882(F)
The Island Keeper, 205(F)
The War on Villa Street, 880(F)

Mazer, Harry (jt. author). *Heartbeat,* 885(F)

Mazer, Norma Fox. *Heartbeat,* 885(F)
Someone to Love, 2305(F)
Summer Girls, Love Boys and Other Short Stories, 883(F)
Up in Seth's Room, 884(F)
When We First Met, 2306(F)

Mazer, Norma Fox, eds. *Waltzing on Water,* 3299

Mazrui, Ali A. *The Africans,* 7352

Mead, Chris. *Champion,* 6749

Mead, Frank. *Handbook of Denominations in the United States,* 4065

Mead, Margaret. *Blackberry Winter,* 6691
Culture and Commitment, 4415

Meadows, Jack. *The Great Scientists,* 6643

Meaney, Dee Morrison. *Iseult,* 1220(F)

Means, Beth. *Everything You Needed to Learn about Writing in High School—But . . ,* 4689

Mears, Walter R. (jt. author). *The News Business,* 3983

Mech, L. David. *The Arctic Wolf,* 8519

Meckler, Brenda Weisberg. *Papa Was a Farmer,* 6931

Medea, Andra. *Against Rape,* 4485

Medish, Vadim. *The Soviet Union,* 7577

Medoff, Mark. *Children of a Lesser God,* 3103

Medoff, Norman J. *Video,* 6032

Medreder, Roy A. *Let History Judge,* 7578

Medved, Harry. *The Fifty Worst Films of All Time,* 6033
The Golden Turkey Awards, 6033
Son of Golden Turkey Awards, 6034

Medved, Michael (jt. author). *The Fifty Worst Films of All Time,* 6033
The Golden Turkey Awards, 6033
Son of Golden Turkey Awards, 6034

Mee, Charles L., Jr. *Meeting at Potsdam,* 7252

Meer, Fatima. *Higher Than Hope,* 6794

Meeropol, Michael (jt. author). *We Are Your Sons,* 6634

Meeropol, Robert. *We Are Your Sons,* 6634

Mehring, Margaret. *The Screenplay,* 6035

Mehta, Ved. *The Ledge between the Streams,* 6288
Sound-Shadows of the New World, 6288
The Stolen Light, 6289

Meichenbaum, Donald. *Coping with Stress,* 5565

Meier, August (jt. author). *Black Leaders of the Nineteenth Century,* 6480
Black Leaders of the Twentieth Century, 6469

Meilach, Dona Z. *Contemporary Batik and Tie-Dye,* 9147

Meiland, Jack W. *College Thinking,* 4752

Meinkoth, Norman A. *The Audubon Society Field Guide to North American Seashore Creatures,* 8618

Meister, Charles. *The Founding Fathers,* 4198

Mekler, Eva (jt. author). *The Actor's Scenebook, Vol. 2,* 3116

Melanson, Philip H. *The Murkin Conspiracy,* 4372

Melchert, John S., ed. *Work, Study, Travel Abroad,* 4713

Melchinger, Siegfried. *Anton Chekhov,* 3804

Melendez, Tony. *A Gift of Hope,* 6425

Mellen, Joan. *Bob Knight,* 6746

Melman, Yossi. *The Master Terrorist*, 4550

Melton, J. Gordon. *The Cult Experience*, 4066

Meltzer, Milton. *Bread and Roses*, 4614
Brother, Can You Spare a Dime? 8037
The Hispanic Americans, 4397
In Their Own Words, 7876, 7876
The Landscape of Memory, 5317
Mark Twain, 6321
Never to Forget, 7253
The Terrorists, 4551
The Truth about the Ku Klux Klan, 4346
World of Our Fathers, 4389

Meltzer, Milton, ed. *The American Promise*, 8082
The Black Americans, 4373
The Jewish Americans, 4388

Melville, Herman. *Billy Budd, Sailor*, 412(F)
Moby Dick, 413(F)
Typee, 414(F)
White-Jacket, 415(F)

Melville, James. *A Haiku for Hanae*, 2109(F)

Menard, H. W. *Islands*, 8786

Mencken, H. L. *The American Language*, 3938
The American Scene, 3541

Mendheim, Beverly. *Ritchie Valens*, 6451

Mendoza, George (jt. author). *Hitting Hot*, 9969

Menez, Joseph F. (jt. author). *Summaries of Leading Cases on the Constitution*, 4182

Menton, Seymour, ed. *The Spanish American Short Story*, 2945(F)

Menzel, Donald H. *A Field Guide to the Stars and Planets*, 8355

Meriwether, Louise. *Daddy Was a Numbers Runner*, 478(F)

Mermelstein, David, ed. *The Anti-Apartheid Reader*, 7378

Merriam, Eve. *If Only I Could Tell You*, 3300

Merrill, Hugh. *The Blues Route*, 5889

Merrill, Robert. *Norman Mailer*, 3760

Merritt, Jeffrey D. *Day by Day*, 7336

Messenger, Charles. *The Chronological Atlas of World War Two*, 7254

Metos, Thomas H. *The Human Mind*, 5318
The New Eyes of the Scientist, 8224

Metraux, Alfred. *The History of the Incas*, 7681

Metzger, Bruce, et al., eds. *Great Events of Bible Times*, 4108

Meyer, Carolyn. *Killing the Kudu*, 718(F)
The Mystery of the Ancient Maya, 7646

Meyer, Doris, ed. *Lives on the Line*, 3795

Meyer, Gladys C. *Softball for Girls & Women*, 9680

Meyer, Herbert E. *How to Write*, 4690

Meyer, Jill M. (jt. author). *How to Write*, 4690

Meyer, Nicholas E. *Magic in the Dark*, 6036

Meyer, Susan E. *How to Draw in Pen and Ink*, 9204

Meyers, Ric. *Murder on the Air*, 6037

Michael, Jeannine Masterson (jt. author). *Mom, I'm Pregnant*, 5499

Michael, Maurice (jt. author). *Prisoner of War*, 7070

Michaels, Barbara. *Be Buried in the Rain*, 2110(F)
Here I Stay, 2113(F)
Into the Darkness, 2111(F)
Shattered Silk, 2112(F)
Sons of the Wolf, 2110(F)
Wait for What Will Come, 2113(F)
Walker in the Shadows, 2110(F)
Wings of the Falcon, 2110(F)

Michaels, Melisa C. *Far Harbor*, 1221(F)

Michalak, Joseph M. (jt. author). *The Best Buys in College Education*, 4736

Michener, James A. *Alaska*, 1513(F)
The Bridge at Andau, 7488
The Bridges at Toko-Ri, 1690(F)
Caribbean, 1494(F)
Centennial, 1577(F)
Chesapeake, 1514(F)
The Covenant, 1386(F)
The Drifters, 886(F)
The Eagle and the Raven, 1578(F)
Hawaii, 1401(F)
Iberia, 1450(F)
Journey, 206(F)
Legacy, 980(F)
Poland, 1450(F)
Sayonara, 1402(F)
The Source, 1451(F)
Space, 207(F)
Sports in America, 9584
Tales of the South Pacific, 1668(F)
Texas, 208(F)

Michie, James, ed. *The Book of Longer Short Stories*, 2946(F)

Mickle, Shelly Fraser. *The Queen of October*, 580(F)

Mickleburgh, Edwin. *Beyond the Frozen Sea*, 7700

Middleton, Alex L. A. (jt. author). *The Encyclopedia of Birds*, 8541

Middleton, Harry. *LBJ*, 6535

Miesel, Sandra. *Shaman*, 1222(F)

Mikes, Jay. *Basketball Fundamentals*, 9730

Miklowitz, Gloria D. *Close to the Edge*, 887(F)
The Day the Senior Class Got Married, 888(F)
Secrets Not Meant to Be Kept, 719(F)

Milan, Albert R. *Breast Self-Examination*, 5359

Miles, Bernard. *Favorite Tales from Shakespeare*, 3051

Milford, Nancy. *Zelda*, 6245

Millard, Alan. *Treasures from Bible Times*, 4109

Millay, Edna St. Vincent. *Collected Poems*, 3301
Collected Sonnets, 3302
Edna St. Vincent Millay's Poems Selected for Young People, 3303

Miller, Arthur. *Arthur Miller's Collected Plays*, 3104

The Crucible, 3105
Death of a Salesman, 3106
The Portable Arthur Miller, 3107
Miller, Betty Davis (jt. author). *To Kill and Be Killed,* 4486
Miller, Caroline Adams. *My Name Is Caroline,* 5209
Miller, Chuck (jt. author). *Kingdom of Fear,* 3785
Miller, Debbie. *Midnight Wilderness,* 8397
Miller, Frances A. *Aren't You the One Who . . .?* 2884(F)
  Losers and Winners, 2884(F)
  The Truth Trap, 2884(F)
Miller, Harry. *Common Sense Book of Puppy and Dog Care,* 8727
Miller, Helen Hill. *Captains from Devon,* 7527
Miller, James. *Koori,* 7474
Miller, James E., Jr. *Walt Whitman,* 3891
Miller, Jim, ed. *The Rolling Stone Illustrated History of Rock & Roll,* 5890
Miller, John C. *The Federalist Era, 1789–1801,* 7854
Miller, Johnny. *Johnny Miller's Golf for Juniors,* 9872
Miller, Jonathan. *Darwin for Beginners,* 7007
  The Human Body, 5298
Miller, Judith. *One, by One, by One,* 7255
Miller, Kent S. *To Kill and Be Killed,* 4486
Miller, Merl K. (jt. author). *Computers for Everybody,* 9030
Miller, Merle. *Plain Speaking,* 6568
Miller, Perry, ed. *The Transcendentalists,* 4015
Miller, Robert M. *Most of My Patients Are Animals,* 6886
Miller, Robert Ryal. *Mexico,* 7647
Miller, Russell. *The Commandos,* 7256
Miller, Walter James. *How to Write Book Reports,* 4691
Miller, Walter M. *A Canticle for Leibowitz,* 2685(F)
Miller, Wilbur R., et al. *Woodworking,* 9282
Miller-Lachmann, Lyn. *Hiding Places,* 889(F)
Millet, Allan R., ed. *A Short History of the Vietnam War,* 8132
Millman, Lawrence. *Last Places,* 7552
Mills, Bart. *Tina,* 6449
Mills, Bruce. *A Basic Guide to Horse Care and Management,* 8764
Mills, Dick. *You & Your Aquarium,* 8774
Mills, Joey. *New Classic Beauty,* 5285
Mills, Judie. *John F. Kennedy,* 6541
Mills, William. *Bears and Men,* 8506
Milne, Antony. *Our Drowning World,* 8799
Milne, Lorus. *The Audubon Society Field Book of Insects,* 8598
  The Audubon Society Field Guide to North American Insects and Spiders, 8599

Milne, Margery (jt. author). *The Audubon Society Field Book of Insects,* 8598
  The Audubon Society Field Guide to North American Insects and Spiders, 8599
Milne, Robert Scott. *Opportunities in Travel Careers,* 4852
Milton, John. *Complete Poetical Works,* 3218
  The Portable Milton, 3219
Milton, Joyce (jt. author). *The Rosenberg File,* 4250
Mindell, Earl. *Unsafe at Any Meal,* 8419
Miner, Jane Claypool. *Young Parents,* 5669
Minton, Robert (jt. author). *Scaling the Ivy Wall,* 4740
Mintz, Lorelie (jt. author). *Threshold,* 5482
Mintz, Steven. *Domestic Revolutions,* 5670
Mintz, Thomas. *Threshold,* 5482
Mirkin, Gabe. *Sportsmedicine Book,* 5246
Mirkin, Gabe (jt. author). *The Complete Sports Medicine Book for Women,* 5362
Mitcham, Samuel W. *Triumphant Fox,* 7257
Mitchell, Joseph B. *Decisive Battles of the American Revolution,* 7855
Mitchell, Joyce Slayton. *The College Board Guide to Jobs and Career Planning,* 4804
  Stopout! Working Ways to Learn, 4805
Mitchell, Margaret. *Gone with the Wind,* 1543(F)
Mitchell, Ralph. *CQ's Guide to the U.S. Constitution,* 4199
Mitchell, Reid. *Civil War Soldiers,* 7928
Mitchell, Robert T. *Butterflies and Moths,* 8607
Mitford, Jessica. *Kind and Unusual Punishment,* 4487
Mitford, Nancy. *Frederick the Great,* 6841
Mitgang, Herbert. *Dangerous Dossiers,* 4311
Mitgang, N. R. (jt. author). *Mr. Bojangles,* 6437
Mitton, Jacqueline (jt. author). *Invitation to Astronomy,* 8272
Mitton, Simon. *Invitation to Astronomy,* 8272
Mizener, Arthur, ed. *F. Scott Fitzgerald,* 3761
Mizerak, Steve. *Inside Pocket Billiards,* 9585
  Steve Mizerak's Pocket Billiards, 9585
Mlyn, Scott. *Before the Game,* 9681
Moche, Dinah L. *Astronomy Today,* 8309
Mochi, Ugo. *African Images,* 7353
Modisane, Bloke. *Blame Me on History,* 6798
Modl, Thomas, ed. *America's Elections,* 4277
Modl, Thomas (jt. author). *AIDS,* 5187
  Religion in America, 4029
Modley, Rudolf. *Handbook of Pictorial Symbols,* 3901
Moe, Jørgen (jt. author). *Norwegian Folk Tales,* 3390
Moeller, Bill. *Crazy Horse: His Life, His Lands,* 6499
Moeller, Jan (jt. author). *Crazy Horse: His Life, His Lands,* 6499
Moeller, Susan. *Shooting War,* 9431
Moffett, James. *Points of View,* 2947(F)

Mogen, David. *Ray Bradbury*, 6217

Moggi, Guido. *Simon and Schuster's Guide to Garden Flowers*, 9383

Mohlenbrock, Robert H. *The Field Guide to U.S. National Forests*, 7761

Mohr, James C. *Abortion in America*, 5483

Molière, Jean. *The Misanthrope and Other Plays*, 3010

The Miser, 3011

Tartuffe, and Other Plays, 3012

Molloy, John T. *Dress for Success*, 9170

Moloney, Kathleen (jt. author). *Ventriloquism for the Total Dummy*, 9305

Momaday, N. Scott. *House Made of Dawn*, 1509(F)

Monaco, James. *American Film Now*, 6102

How to Read a Film, 6038

Monath, Norman. *How to Play Popular Piano in Ten Easy Lessons*, 5939

Monegal, Emir Rodríguez. *The Borzoi Anthology of Latin American Literature*, 2948

Monk, Lorraine. *Photographs That Changed the World*, 5722

Monninger, Joseph. *New Jersey*, 581(F)

Monroe, Sylvester, et al. *Brothers*, 6482

Monsarrat, Nicholas. *The Cruel Sea*, 1669(F)

Montagu, Ashley. *The Man Who Never Was*, 7258

The Nature of Human Aggression, 5566

Monteleone, Thomas F. (jt. author). *Day of the Dragon Star*, 2413(F)

Montgomery, Kathryn C. *Target: Prime Time*, 3990

Montieth, Mark. *Passion Play*, 9731

Moody, Anne. *Coming of Age in Mississippi*, 6933

Moolman, Valerie. *Women Aloft*, 9072

Moon, Elizabeth. *Lunar Activity*, 2686(F)

Moon, Elizabeth (jt. author). *Sassinak*, 2668(F)

Moorcock, Michael. *Elric at the End of Time*, 1223(F)

The Jewel in the Skull, 1223(F)

The War Hound and the World's Pain, 1224(F)

Moorcock, Michael (jt. author). *Fantasy*, 3618

Moore, C. L. *The Best of C. L. Moore*, 2687(F)

Moore, Carl H. *Money*, 4579

Moore, Carolyn (jt. author). *Eat Smart for a Healthy Heart*, 9325

Moore, Dick. *Opportunities in Acting Careers*, 4893

Moore, Joseph Thomas. *Pride against Prejudice*, 6717

Moore, Marianne. *The Complete Poems of Marianne Moore*, 3304

Moore, Melinda, et al. *Our Future at Stake*, 4154

Moore, Patrick. *Astronomers' Stars*, 8273

Exploring the Night Sky with Binoculars, 8274

The Guinness Book of Astronomy, 8275

The New Atlas of the Universe, 8276

Pocket Guide to Astronomy, 8277

The Return of Halley's Comet, 8332

The Unfolding Universe, 8310

Moore, Patrick (jt. author). *Life in the Universe*, 8304

Moore, Peter D., ed. *The Encyclopedia of Animal Ecology*, 8455

Moore, Robert L. (jt. author). *The Cult Experience*, 4066

Moore, Thurston. *The Original Word Game Dictionary*, 3939

Moorehead, Alan. *The Blue Nile*, 7354

Mor, Barbara (jt. author). *The Great Cosmic Mother*, 4084

Morales Carrión, Arturo. *Puerto Rico*, 7664

Moran, Daniel Keys. *The Ring*, 2688(F)

Moran, Gary T. (jt. author). *Getting Stronger*, 9773

Moran, Richard. *Cold Sea Rising*, 209(F)

Moran, Richard D. (jt. author). *Opportunities in Microelectronics*, 5043

Morantz-Sanchez, Regina Markell. *Sympathy and Science*, 5247

Moravec, Hans. *Mind Children*, 9003

More, Thomas. *Utopia*, 4016

Morehead, Albert H., ed. *Hoyle's Rules of Games*, 9815

Morgan, Arthur N. (jt. author). *Santa Fe*, 8200

Morgan, Brian. *Brainfood*, 5319

Morgan, Dodge. *The Voyage of American Promise*, 9931

Morgan, Edmund S. *The Birth of the Republic, 1763–89*, 7856

Morgan, Elizabeth. *The Making of a Woman Surgeon*, 6694

Solo Practice, 6694

Morgan, Hal. *Symbols of America*, 4618

Morgan, Jacqui. *Watercolor for Illustration*, 9205

Morgan, Janet. *Agatha Christie*, 6236

Morgan, Kenneth O., ed. *The Oxford Illustrated History of Britain*, 7528

Morgan, Lane (jt. author). *The Miracle Planet*, 8793

Morgan, Max (jt. author). *Enola Gay*, 7309

Morgan, Roberta (jt. author). *Brainfood*, 5319

Morgan, Sally. *My Place*, 6934

Morison, Samuel Eliot. *Christopher Columbus, Mariner*, 6134

The European Discovery of America, 7832, 7832

The Great Explorers, 7833

The Growth of the American Republic, 7762

John Paul Jones, 6597

The Oxford History of the American People, 7763

Morison, Samuel Eliot, et al. *A Concise History of the American Republic*, 7764

Morley, Sheridan. *The Great Stage Stars*, 6179

Morra, Marion. *Choices*, 5210

Morra, Marion (jt. author). *Understanding Your Immune System*, 5217

Morrell, David. *Blood Oath*, 210(F)
The Fifth Profession, 211(FF)
Fireflies, 582(F)

Morressy, John. *Kedrigern and the Charming Couple*, 1225(F)
A Voice for a Princess, 1226(F)

Morris, Charles R. *Iron Destinies, Lost Opportunities*, 4155

Morris, Chris (jt. author). *Threshold*, 2690(F)

Morris, Desmond. *The Book of Ages*, 5526
Catlore, 8697
Catwatching, 8698
Dogwatching, 8728
Horsewatching, 8765
The Illustrated Naked Ape, 8502

Morris, Edmund. *The Rise of Theodore Roosevelt*, 6565

Morris, Janet. *Cruiser Dreams*, 1227(F)
Dream Dancer, 1227(F)
Earth Dreams, 1227(F)
Threshold, 2690(F)

Morris, Janet, ed. *Afterwar*, 2689(F)

Morris, Jeannie. *Brian Piccolo*, 6758

Morris, Margie (jt. author). *The Pyramids*, 7096

Morris, Percy A. *A Field Guide to Pacific Coast Shells, Including Shells of Hawaii and the Gulf of California*, 8638
A Field Guide to Shells of the Atlantic and Gulf Coasts and the West Indies, 8639

Morris, Richard B. *The Forging of the Union, 1781–1789*, 7857
Witnesses at the Creation, 4200

Morris, Richard B., ed. *Basic Documents in American History*, 7765
Encyclopedia of American History, 7766

Morrison, Chris. *PC Care Manual*, 9004

Morrison, Ian. *The Guinness Guide to Formula One*, 9616

Morrison, Joan. *American Mosaic*, 4335
From Camelot to Kent State, 8083

Morrison, Martha A. *White Rabbit*, 5144

Morrison, Philip. *The Ring of Truth*, 8225

Morrison, Phylis (jt. author). *The Ring of Truth*, 8225

Morrison, Robert K. (jt. author). *From Camelot to Kent State*, 8083

Morrison, Toni. *Beloved*, 1526(F)
The Bluest Eye, 479(F)
Song of Solomon, 480(F)
Sula, 481(F)
Tar Baby, 482(F)

Morrison, Wilbur H. *The Elephant & the Tiger*, 8133

Morrissett, Christine (jt. author). *Canned Art*, 8973

Morrow, Lee Alan. *Creating Theater*, 6103

Morsberger, Robert E. *James Thurber*, 3595

Morse, Flo. *The Shakers and the World's People*, 4067

Morse-Cluley, Elizabeth (jt. author). *How to Write Book Reports*, 4691

Mortenson, Joseph. *Whale Songs and Wasp Maps*, 8478

Mortimer, John. *Rumpole and the Age of Miracles*, 2114(F)
Rumpole of the Bailey, 2115(F)

Morton, Julia F. *Herbs and Spices*, 8420

Morton, Rocky (jt. author). *Creative Computer Graphics*, 8985

Morton, W. Scott. *China*, 7424

Morwood, Peter. *Star Trek*, 2691(F)

Moser, Diane (jt. author). *Opening the Space Frontier*, 8323

Moskin, Marietta D. *I Am Rosemarie*, 7259

Mosley, Leonard. *Battle of Britain*, 7260

Moss, Leonard. *Arthur Miller*, 3842

Moss, Sanford A. *Sharks*, 8629

Mosse, George L. *Fallen Soldiers*, 7337

Moszynska, Anna. *Abstract Art*, 5753

Motlow, James (jt. author). *Bitter Melon*, 4402

Mott, Lawrie. *Pesticide Alert*, 5421

Mott, Michael. *The Seven Mountains of Thomas Merton*, 6629

Mott-Smith, Geoffrey (jt. author). *Hoyle's Rules of Games*, 9815

Motta, Dick (jt. author). *Sports Illustrated Basketball*, 9728

Motz, Lloyd. *The Story of Physics*, 8911

Mowat, Farley. *And No Birds Sang*, 7261
The Boat Who Wouldn't Float, 9932
The Desperate People, 7701
The Dog Who Wouldn't Be, 8729
Grey Seas Under, 8894
Never Cry Wolf, 8520
The People of the Deer, 7701
Sea of Slaughter, 8577
The Snow Walker, 7702
A Whale for the Killing, 8655
Woman in the Mists, 6668

Mowry, George E. *The Era of Theodore Roosevelt, 1900–1912*, 8014
The Urban Nation, 1920–1980, 7767

Moyers, Bill. *The Secret Government*, 4525
A World of Ideas, 8084

Moyes, Patricia. *How to Talk to Your Cat*, 8699
A Six-Letter Word for Death, 2116(F)

Mozeson, I. E. (jt. author). *The Place I Call Home*, 4514

Mr. Fresh and the Supreme Rockers. *Breakdancing*, 5972

Mueller, Richard. *Jernigan's Egg*, 2692(F)

Muench, Teri. *Attn: A & R*, 4894

Mugford, Roger (jt. author). *The Practical Guide to Dog and Puppy Care*, 8717

Muggeridge, Malcolm. *Something Beautiful for God*, 6957

Muir, Frank. *Christmas Customs & Traditions*, 4117

Muir, Frank, ed. *The Oxford Book of Humorous Prose*, 3504

Muir, John. *Muir Among the Animals*, 8456

Muir, Kenneth, ed. *A New Companion to Shakespeare Studies*, 3822

Muirden, James. *The Amateur Astronomer's Handbook*, 8278
The Astronomy Handbook, 8279
Astronomy with a Small Telescope, 8280

Muirhead, John. *Those Who Fall*, 7262

Mulkerne, Donald. *The Perfect Term Paper*, 4692

Mullan, Fitzhugh. *Plagues and Politics*, 5078
Vital Signs, 5211

Müller, Filip. *Eyewitness Auschwitz*, 7263

Muller, Marcia. *The Shape of Dread*, 2117(F)

Muller, Marcia, ed. *Kill or Cure*, 2118(F)

Muller, Ulrike. *Long-Haired Cats*, 8700

Mulvoy, Mark. *Sports Illustrated Golf*, 9873

Mumford, Lewis. *The City in History*, 4560

Munday, Marianne F. *Opportunities in Crafts Careers*, 4853
Opportunities in Word Processing, 5049

Munder, Barbara (jt. author). *Joe Louis*, 6748

Munley, Anne. *The Hospice Alternative*, 5093

Munneke, Gary A. *Opportunities in Law Careers*, 4974

Munro, Alice. *Lives of Girls and Women*, 890(F)

Munro, Eleanor. *Originals*, 6180

Munro, H. H. *The Complete Works of Saki*, 378

Munson, Richard. *Cousteau*, 6653

Munz, Ludwig. *Rembrandt*, 5781

Murfin, Ross C. *Sons & Lovers*, 3678

Murie, Olaus J. *A Field Guide to Animal Tracks*, 8487

Murphey, Cecil (jt. author). *With Byrd at the Bottom of the World*, 7709

Murphy, Brian. *C. S. Lewis*, 3679

Murphy, Jim. *Custom Car*, 9104

Murphy, Joseph E. *South to the Pole by Ski*, 7703

Murphy, Pat. *The City, Not Long After*, 2693(F)
The Falling Woman, 1228(F)

Murphy, Walter F. *The Vicar of Christ*, 981(F)

Murphy, Wendy Buehr. *Frank Lloyd Wright*, 6210

Murray, Bruce. *Journey into Space*, 8311

Murray, Earl. *Blue Savage*, 1579(F)

Murray, Jocelyn, ed. *Cultural Atlas of Africa*, 7355

Murray, John. *Modern Monologues for Young People*, 3108

Murray, John A., ed. *A Republic of Rivers*, 8185

Murray, Linda. *Michelangelo*, 5782

Murray, Linda (jt. author). *The Penguin Dictionary of Art and Artists*, 5689

Murray, Maggie Pexton. *Changing Styles in Fashion*, 5286

Murray, Peter. *The Penguin Dictionary of Art and Artists*, 5689

Murray, Sabina. *Slow Burn*, 982(F)

Murrells, Joseph. *Million Selling Records from the 1900s to the 1980s*, 5985

Musheno, Elizabeth J. *Fast and Easy Home Decorating*, 9148

Musser, Joe (jt. author). *Joni*, 6903

Myers, Arthur. *The Ghostly Register*, 9518

Myers, James. *Getting Skilled, Getting Ahead*, 4806

Myers, John M. *Silverlock*, 1229(F)

Myers, Norman, ed. *Gaia*, 4416

Myers, Walter Dean. *Crystal*, 891(F)
Fallen Angels, 1698(F)
The Nicholas Factor, 212(F)
Sweet Illusions, 720(F)

Myrdal, Gunnar. *An American Dilemma*, 4374

Naar, Jon. *Design for a Livable Planet*, 4432

Nabokov, Peter, ed. *Two Leggings*, 7819

Nabokov, Vladimir. *Laughter in the Dark*, 721(F)

Nader, Ralph. *Lemon Book*, 9105

Nagler, Barney (jt. author). *Shoemaker*, 6781

Nahas, Gabriel S. *Keep Off the Grass*, 5145

Nahm, Andrew C. *A Panorama of 5000 Years*, 7462

Naipaul, V. S. *Among the Believers*, 7601
House for Mr. Biswas, 983(F)

Naisbitt, John. *Megatrends*, 4417
Megatrends 2000, 7062

Nalty, Bernard C. *Strength for the Fight*, 4286

Namath, Joe. *Football for Young Players and Parents*, 9855

Namioka, Lensey. *Valley of the Broken Cherry Trees*, 1403(F)

Nance, John J. *Final Approach*, 213(F)

Narayan, R. K. *The Guide*, 984(F)
The Man-Eater of Malgudi, 984(F)
The Ramayana, 3384(FF)
The Vendor of Sweets, 984(F)

Nasaw, Jonathan. *West of the Moon*, 722(F)

Nash, Bruce. *The Baseball Hall of Shame*, 9682
The Baseball Hall of Shame 4, 9683
The Football Hall of Shame, 9856
The Golf Hall of Shame, 9874
The Sports Hall of Shame, 9586

Nash, Gerald D. *The Great Depression and World War II*, 8038

Nash, Jay Robert. *Bloodletters and Badmen*, 6120

Nash, Ogden. *I Wouldn't Have Missed It*, 3305
The Pocket Book of Ogden Nash, 3306

Nathan, Robert. *Amusement Park*, 214(F)
Portrait of Jennie, 2307(F)

Nathanson, E. M. *A Dirty Distant War*, 1670(F)

National Board of Review of Motion Pictures, eds. *The 500 Best British and Foreign Films to Buy, Rent, or Videotape*, 6039

National Geographic Society, eds. *Into the Wilderness*, 7967

Mysteries of the Ancient World, 7021

Nomads of the World, 7008

Our Threatened Inheritance, 4433

Preserving America's Past, 7768

Primitive Worlds, 7009

Splendors of the Past, 7022

Undersea Treasures, 8895

National Park Foundation. *The Complete Guide to America's National Parks*, 7769

Navazelskis, Ina. *Leonid Breznev*, 6831

Navratilova, Martina. *Martina*, 6771

Tennis My Way, 6770

Nayler, Jay H. (jt. author). *Opportunities in Recreation and Leisure*, 4841

Naylor, Gloria. *Mama Day*, 483(F)

Naylor, Phyllis Reynolds. *The Dark of the Tunnel*, 723(F)

The Year of the Gopher, 892(F)

Nedreaass, Torberg. *Music from a Blue Well*, 1452(F)

Needell, Allan A., ed. *The First 25 Years in Space*, 8312

Needler, Martin C. *An Introduction to Latin American Politics*, 7629

Neely, William. *Five-Hundred-Five Automobile Questions Your Friends Can't Answer*, 9106

Neff, Pauline. *Tough Love*, 5146

Neider, Charles, ed. *The Autobiography of Mark Twain*, 6322

The Selected Letters of Mark Twain, 6323

Neil, Randy L. *The All-New Official Cheerleader's Handbook*, 9588

The Official Pompon Girl's Handbook, 9587

Neill, A. S. *Summerhill*, 4632

Neimark, Anne E. *A Deaf Child Listened*, 6620

Neimark, Paul (jt. author). *Jesse*, 6766

Nelson, Barney. *Voices & Visions of the American West*, 8153

Nelson, Cordner. *Careers in Pro Sports*, 4854

Nelson, Glenn C. *Ceramics*, 9166

Nelson, Harland S. *Charles Dickens*, 3680

Nelson, Kevin. *The Greatest Stories Ever Told (about Baseball)*, 9685

Nelson, Kevin, ed. *Baseball's Greatest Insults*, 9684

Baseball's Greatest Quotes, 9684

Nelson, Michael, ed. *Guide to the Presidency*, 4208

The Presidency and the Political System, 4209

Nelson, Rachel West (jt. author). *Selma, Lord, Selma*, 4381

Nelson, Richard. *The Island Within*, 8186

Nelson, Roy G. (jt. author). *Marshall Holman's Bowling Tips and Techniques*, 9780

Nelson, Ted. *Computer Lib/Dream Machines*, 9005

Nemec, David. *Great Baseball Feats, Facts & Firsts*, 9686

Mad Blood, 2119(F)

Nemiroff, Robert, ed. *Lorraine Hansberry*, 3109

Nemko, Martin. *How to Get an Ivy League Education at a State University*, 4753

Neruda, Pablo. *Selected Poems*, 3350

Nerys, Dee. *Fortune-Telling by Playing Cards*, 9519

Nettles, Graig. *Balls*, 6729

Neufeld, Rose. *Exploring Nontraditional Jobs for Women*, 4855

Neuharth, Allen H. *World Power Up Close*, 7338

Nevin, David. *Architects of Air Power*, 7153

The Bush Pilots, 9073

Dream West, 1580(F)

The Explorers, 9073

The Expressmen, 7968

The Mexican War, 7877

The Pathfinders, 9073

The Road to Kitty Hawk, 9073

The Road to Shiloh, 7929

Sherman's March, 7930

The Soldiers, 7969

Nevins, Allan. *A Pocket History of the United States*, 7770

Nevins, Francis M., eds. *Hitchcock in Prime Time*, 2120(F)

New Internationalist Cooperative, eds. *Women*, 4312

Newark, Tim. *Women Warlords*, 7063

Newcomb, Duane. *The Complete Vegetable Gardener's Sourcebook*, 9384

Newcomb, Karen (jt. author). *The Complete Vegetable Gardener's Sourcebook*, 9384

Newell, John (jt. author). *On the Frontiers of Science*, 8215

Newhall, Beaumont. *The History of Photography*, 5755

Newhouse, John. *War and Peace in the Nuclear Age*, 4156

Newlin, Virginia (jt. author). *Broken Heart Whole Heart*, 5153

Newman, Arnold. *The Tropical Rainforest*, 8816

Newman, Edwin. *A Civil Tongue*, 3941

Strictly Speaking, 3941

Newman, Eleanor Weintraub (jt. author). *Writing Your College Admissions Essay*, 4754

Newman, Frederick. *Mouthsounds*, 9301

Newman, Gerald. *Writing Your College Admissions Essay*, 4754

Newman, Kim (jt. author). *Horror*, 3623

Newman, Sharon. *Guinevere*, 1230(F)

Newth, Mette. *The Abduction*, 1453(F)

Newton, David E. *Science Ethics*, 4526

Niatum, Duane, ed. *Harper's Anthology of 20th Century Native American Poetry*, 3307

Nichol, John. *Bites and Stings*, 8485

The Mighty Rain Forest, 8817

Nicholls, C. S., ed. *Power*, 7154

Nicholls, Peter, ed. *The Science in Science Fiction*, 8226

Nichols, David, ed. *Ernie's War*, 7264

Nichols, Eve K., ed. *Mobilizing against AIDS*, 5212

Nichols, Janet. *American Music Makers*, 6182

Nicholson, Harold. *The Congress of Vienna*, 7147

Nicholson, Irene. *Mexican and Central American Mythology*, 3445

Nickell, Joe. *Secrets of the Supernatural*, 9520

Nicklaus, Jack. *Play Better Golf*, 9875

Nicolaides, Kimon. *The Natural Way to Draw*, 9206

Nida, Patricia Cooney. *The Teenager's Survival Guide to Moving*, 5624

Nidetch, Jean. *Weight Watchers New International Cookbook*, 9352
  Weight Watchers Quick Success Program Cookbook, 9353

Niehaus, Theodore F. *A Field Guide to Pacific States Wildflowers*, 8439

Niering, William A. *The Audubon Society Field Guide to North American Wildflowers*, 8440
  Wetlands, 8818

Nies, Judith. *Seven Women*, 6483

Nietzsche, Friedrich Wilhelm. *The Portable Nietzsche*, 4017

Nikolaieff, George A., ed. *The President and the Constitution*, 4210

Nilsen, Alleen Pace. *Presenting M. E. Kerr*, 3762

Nilsson, Lennart. *Behold Man*, 5299
  The Body Victorious, 5213
  A Child Is Born, 5484

Nims, John Frederick, ed. *The Harper Anthology of Poetry*, 3220

Nir, Yehuda. *The Lost Childhood*, 7265

Nisbet, Lee, ed. *The Gun Control Debate*, 4527

Nite, Norm N. *Rock On*, 5836, 5836

Niven, Larry. *The Descent of Anansi*, 2699(F)
  Footfall, 2700(F)
  The Integral Trees, 2694(F)
  Limits, 2695(F)
  Lucifer's Hammer, 2701(F)
  Mote in God's Eye, 2700(F)
  N-Space, 2696(F)
  Oath of Fealty, 2701(F)
  Ringworld, 2697(F)
  The Ringworld Engineers, 2697(F)

Niven, Larry, ed. *The Magic Goes Away*, 1231(F)
  The Magic May Return, 1231(F)
  More Magic, 1231(F)

Niven, Larry, et al. *The Legacy of Heurot*, 2698(F)

Nix, Jan. *Food and Fitness*, 5422

Nixon, Bob (jt. author). *Tiananmen Square*, 7429

Nixon, Joan Lowery. *The Stalker*, 2121(F)

Nixon, Richard. *Leaders*, 6787

Njeri, Itabari. *Every Good-bye Ain't Gone*, 6935

Nodar, Manuel V. (jt. author). *Apple Software for Pennies*, 8976

Noddy, Tom. *Bubble Magic*, 8912

Noerper, Norman. *Opportunities in Data Processing*, 5050

Noguchi, Thomas T. *Physical Evidence*, 215(F)

Nolan, Christopher. *Under the Eye of the Clock*, 6291

Nolan, Paul T. *Folk Tale Plays round the World*, 2986

Nollman, Jim. *Animal Dreaming*, 8483

Nomberg-Przytyk, Sara. *Auschwitz*, 6936

Noonan, Michael. *McKenzie's Boots*, 1671(F)

Norback, Craig T., ed. *VGM's Handbook of Business and Management Careers*, 4924
  VGM's Handbook of Scientific and Technical Careers, 5026

Norback, Judith. *The Complete Computer Career Guide*, 4975

Nordby, Vernon J. *A Guide to Psychologists and Their Concepts*, 5540

Nordham, George W. *The Age of Washington*, 6573

Nordhoff, Charles. *The Bounty Trilogy*, 216(F)

Norman, Barry. *The Story of Hollywood*, 6040

Norman, Donald A. *The Psychology of Everyday Things*, 5541

Norman, Geoffrey. *Bouncing Back*, 8134

Norman, Michael. *These Good Men*, 8135

Norman, Michael (jt. author). *Haunted Heartland*, 9531

Norman, Philip. *Shout!* 6356

Norris, Frank. *The Octopus*, 416(F)

Norris, Jerrie. *Presenting Rosa Guy*, 6251

North, James. *Freedom Rising*, 7379

Norton, Andre. *Android at Arms*, 2702(F)
  The Beast Master, 2703(F)
  The Crystal Gryphon, 2704(F)
  Dark Piper, 2705(F)
  Date to Go A-Hunting, 2706(F)
  Exiles to the Stars, 2707(F)
  Flight in Yiktor, 2707(F)
  Forerunner, 2708(F)
  Gryphon in Glory, 1232(F)
  Gryphon's Eyrie, 1233(F)
  Horn Crown, 2703(F)
  Imperial Lady, 1240(F)
  Judgement on Janus, 2710(F)
  Key Out of Time, 2703(F)
  Knave of Dreams, 2711(F)
  Lavender-Green Magic, 1234(F)
  Lord of Thunder, 2712(F)
  Moon Called, 1234(F)
  Moon Mirror, 1235(F)
  Moon of Three Rings, 2713(F)
  Night of Masks, 2714(F)

Operation Time Search, 2715(F)
Postmarked the Stars, 2716(F)
Quag Keep, 2703(F)
Sea Siege, 2717(F)
Shadow Hawk, 1362(F)
Sorceress of the Witch World, 2718(F)
Star Born, 2711(F)
Star Hunter/Voodoo Planet, 2711(F)
Three against the Witch World, 2718(F)
Victory on Janus, 2710(F)
Voorloper, 2720(F)
Ware Hawk, 1237(F)
Web of the Witch World, 2718(F)
Wheel of Stars, 1234(F)
Witch World, 1238(F)
Wizard's Worlds, 2721(F)
Year of the Unicorn, 2718(F), 1238(F)
Zarsthor's Bane, 1238(F)
Norton, Andre, ed. *Catfantastic,* 2722(F)
Four from the Witch World, 2709(F)
Magic in Ithkar I, 1239(F)
Magic in Ithkar II, 1239(F)
Magic in Ithkar IV, 1239(F)
Tales of the Witch World, 2719(F)
Tales of the Witch World 2, 1236(F)
Norton, Peter. *Inside the IBM PC,* 9006
Norwick, Kenneth P., ed. *Lobbying for Freedom in the 1980s,* 4313
Noss, John B. *Man's Religions,* 4068
Nourse, Alan E. *Birth Control,* 5485
Herpes, 5214
Teen Guide to Birth Control, 5486
Teen Guide to Safe Sex, 5487
Novak, Barbara. *American Painting of the Nineteenth Century,* 5803
Novak, William, et al., eds. *The Big Book of New American Humor,* 3505
Novick, Nelson Lee. *Skin Care for Teens,* 5338
Nownes, Laura (jt. author). *Quilts! Quilts! Quilts!* 9245
Null, Gary. *Black Hollywood,* 6041
Nunn, Joan. *Fashion in Costume, 1200–1980,* 9171
Nurnberg, Maxwell W. *All about Words,* 3943
I Always Look Up the Word "Egregious", 3942
Nuwer, Hank. *Recruiting in Sports,* 9589
Nye, Doug. *Famous Racing Cars,* 9617
Nye, Jody Lynn. *The Dragonlover's Guide to Pern,* 3763
Nye, Jody Lynn (jt. author). *The Death of Sleep,* 2669(F)
Nye, Peter. *Hearts of Lions,* 9763
Nye, Robert. *Beowulf,* 1241(F)

Oaks, Tina. *That Cheating Sister,* 2308(F)
Oates, Joyce Carol. *Them,* 583(F)
Where Are You Going, Where Have You Been? 893(F)

Oates, Stephen B. *Abraham Lincoln,* 6546
The Fires of Jubilee, 1527(F)
Let the Trumpet Sound, 6511
Our Fiery Trial, 7931
With Malice Toward None, 6547
Oates, Whitney J., ed. *Seven Famous Greek Plays,* 3013
Oatman, Eric F., ed. *Crime and Society,* 4488
Prospects for Energy in America, 8918
O'Ballance, Edgar. *Terrorism in the 1980s,* 4552
O'Barry, Richard. *Behind the Dolphin Smile,* 6697
Oberg, Alcestis R. (jt. author). *Pioneering Space,* 8314
Oberg, James E. *The New Race for Space,* 8313
Pioneering Space, 8314
Obojski, Robert. *Baseball's Strangest Moments,* 9687
Coin Collector's Price Guide, 9457
O'Brien, Conor Cruise. *The Siege,* 7614
O'Brien, David M. *Storm Center,* 4249
O'Brien, George. *The Village of Longing and Dancehall Days,* 7529
O'Brien, Robert, ed. *The Encyclopedia of Drug Abuse,* 5147
O'Brien, Tim. *Going after Cacciato,* 1699(F)
The Things They Carried, 1700(F)
O'Casey, Sean. *Three Plays,* 3034
O'Clair, Robert (jt. author). *The Norton Anthology of Modern Poetry,* 3157
O'Connell, Nicholas. *At the Field's End,* 3764
O'Connor, Edwin. *The Last Hurrah,* 985(F)
O'Connor, Flannery. *Collected Works,* 2949(F)
The Complete Stories, 2950(F)
Everything That Rises Must Converge, 484(F)
O'Connor, Frank. *Collected Stories,* 2951(F)
O'Connor, John E. *American History/American Television,* 6042
O'Connor, Nancy. *Letting Go with Love,* 5094
O'Connor, Sheila. *Tokens of Grace,* 584(F)
Odeni, Avi (jt. author). *TV Careers Behind the Screen,* 4874
O'Donnell, Kevin, Jr. *Caverns—Book 1,* 2723(F)
Lava—Book III, 2723(F)
Reefs—Book II, 2723(F)
O'Donnol, Shirley Miles. *American Costume, 1915–1970,* 9172
O'Flaherty, Liam. *The Informer,* 1454(F)
Ogburn, Charlton. *The Marauders,* 7266
The Mysterious William Shakespeare, 3823
Ogg, Oscar. *The 26 Letters,* 3968
Ogilvie, R. M. *Roman Literature and Society,* 3596
O'Har, George M. *Psychic Fair,* 1815(F)
O'Hara, John. *Appointment in Samarra,* 724(F)
O'Hara, Mary. *Green Grass of Wyoming,* 294(F)
My Friend Flicka, 294(F)
Thunderhead, Son of Flicka, 294(F)

O'Hern, Elizabeth Moot. *Profiles of Pioneer Women Scientists*, 6644

O'Keeffe, Georgia. *Georgia O'Keeffe*, 6201

Okie, Susan (jt. author). *To Space and Back*, 8317

Okpewho, Isidore, ed. *The Heritage of African Poetry*, 3351

Okrent, Daniel. *Baseball Anecdotes*, 9688

Olander, Joseph D., ed. *Arthur C. Clarke*, 3681

Oldham, June. *Enter Tom*, 1894(F)
 Grow Up, Cupid, 1895(F)
 Moving In, 1896(F)

Olds, Elizabeth Fagg. *Women of the Four Winds*, 6121

Oleszek, Walter J. *Congressional Procedures and the Policy Process*, 4227

Oleszek, Walter J. (jt. author). *Congress and Its Members*, 4218

Olfson, Lewy, ed. *50 Great Scenes for Student Actors*, 2987

Oliphant, B. J. *Dead in the Scrub*, 2122(F)

Oliveira, Paulo de (jt. author). *Getting to the Right Job*, 4789

Oliver, Jane Sidney (jt. author). *Opportunities in Medical Technology Careers*, 5000

Oliver, Paul, et al. *The New Grove Gospels, Blues and Jazz with Spirituals and Ragtime*, 5892

Oliver, Roland. *A Short History of Africa*, 7357

Oliver, Roland, ed. *The Cambridge Encyclopedia of Africa*, 7356

Olivier, Laurence. *On Acting*, 6427

Olmstead, Nancy C. (jt. author). *The Audubon Society Field Guide to North American Wildflowers*, 8440

Olney, Patricia J. (jt. author). *Imaging*, 5625

Olney, Ross R. *Imaging*, 5625

Olsen, Gary. *Getting Started in Computer Graphics*, 9007

Olsen, Jack. *Night of the Grizzlies*, 8507

Olsen, Larry Dean. *Outdoor Survival Skills*, 9801

Olsen, Tillie. *Tell Me a Riddle*, 585(F)

Olshan, Joseph. *A Warmer Season*, 894(F)
 The Waterline, 433(F)

Olson, Beverly. *Country Flower Drying*, 9302

Olson, Everett C. (jt. author). *Dinosaurs Past and Present, Volume 1*, 6978

Olson, Paul F., ed. *Post Mortem*, 1816(F)

O'Malley, Kathleen (jt. author). *Starbridge 2*, 2498

O'Malley, Padraig. *The Uncivil Wars*, 7530

Omar Khayyam. *Rubaiyat of Omar Khayyam*, 3352

Omer-Cooper, J. D. *History of Southern Africa*, 7380

Omond, Roger. *The Apartheid Handbook*, 7381

O'Neal, Regina. *And Then the Harvest*, 3110

Oneal, Zibby. *In Summer Light*, 895(F)

O'Neil, Doris C., ed. *Life*, 8085

O'Neil, Paul. *The Frontiersmen*, 7970
 The Rivermen, 7971

O'Neil, Terry (jt. author). *Fighting Back*, 6751

O'Neill, Cherry Boone. *Dear Cherry*, 5395
 Starving for Attention, 5396

O'Neill, Eugene. *Anna Christie, The Emperor Jones, and The Hairy Ape*, 3111
 The Iceman Cometh, 3112
 Long Day's Journey into Night, 3113

O'Neill, Eugene, Jr. (jt. author). *Seven Famous Greek Plays*, 3013

O'Neill, Terry, ed. *Censorship*, 4314
 Economics in America, 4580
 Male/Female Roles, 4537

O'Neill, William L. *Coming Apart*, 8086

Onions, C. T. *A Shakespeare Glossary*, 3824

Opie, Iona, ed. *The Classic Fairy Tales*, 3367
 The Oxford Book of Narrative Verse, 3173

Opie, Peter (jt. author). *The Classic Fairy Tales*, 3367
 The Oxford Book of Narrative Verse, 3173

Orczy, Emmuska. *The Adventures of the Scarlet Pimpernel*, 1455(F)
 The Scarlet Pimpernel, 1455(F)
 The Triumph of the Scarlet Pimpernel, 1455(F)
 The Way of the Scarlet Pimpernel, 1455(F)

Ore, Rebecca. *Becoming Alien*, 2724(F)
 Being Alien, 2724(F)

Orenstein, Vik. *How to Break into Modeling*, 4925

Orgel, Doris. *Crack in the Heart*, 896(F)

Orgill, Douglas. *Brother Esau*, 1242(F)

Orlick, Terry. *Cooperative Sports and Games Book*, 9590

Ormrod, Audrey. *Exploring Cross-Stitch*, 9248

Ornstein, Robert. *The Healing Rain*, 5320

Orr, Lisa, ed. *The Homeless*, 4512
 Sexual Values, 5488

Orrell, John (jt. author). *Rebuilding Shakespeare's Globe*, 3820

Ortiz, Alfonso (jt. author). *American Indian Myths and Legends*, 3423

Ortiz, Victoria. *Sojourner Truth*, 6518

Orwell, George. *Animal Farm*, 1243(F)
 1984, 2725(F)
 Orwell, the Lost Writings, 3542

Osada, Arata, ed. *Children of Hiroshima*, 7267

Osborn, Bob. *The Complete Book of BMX*, 9764

Osborne, Harold. *South American Mythology*, 3446

Osborne, Robert. *60 Years of the Oscar*, 6043

Osen, Lynn M. *Women in Mathematics*, 6645

Osman, Tony. *Space History*, 8315

Oster, Maggie. *Gifts and Crafts from the Garden*, 9149

Osterlund, David (jt. author). *The Constitution of the United States of America*, 4202

O'Toole, Christopher. *Insects in Camera*, 8601

O'Toole, Christopher, ed. *The Encyclopedia of Insects*, 8600

O'Toole, G. J. A. *The Spanish War*, 8015

Ousby, Ian. *A Reader's Guide to Fifty American Novels*, 3765

Ovid. *Metamorphoses*, 3185

Ovington, Ray. *Basic Bait Fishing*, 9830
Basic Fishing, 9831

Owen, David. *None of the Above*, 4663

Owen, Guy, ed. *Contemporary Southern Poetry*, 3308

Owen, Jan. *Getting the Most from Your Computer*, 9008

Owen, Ursula, ed. *Fathers*, 5671

Owen, William (jt. author). *The Search*, 8379
The Tracker, 8379

Owens, Carolyn. *Pregnant and Single*, 5515

Owens, Jesse. *Jesse*, 6766

Owens, Tom. *Collecting Sports Autographs*, 9303

Oyama, Mas. *Mas Oyama's Essential Karate*, 9895

Oyler, Chris., et al. *Go Toward the Light*, 5215

Ozoga, John (jt. author). *Whitetail Country*, 8522

Pach, Walter. *Renoir*, 5783

Pack, Robert, ed. *The Bread Loaf Anthology of Contemporary American Essays*, 3543

Packard, Vance. *The Hidden Persuaders*, 4619

Packard, William. *The Poet's Dictionary*, 3855

Packer, Billy. *College Basketball's 25 Greatest Teams*, 9732
Fifty Years of the Final Four, 9733

Page, Gerald W., ed. *The Year's Best Horror Stories*, 1817(F)

Page, Jake. *Arid Lands*, 8819
Forest, 8820

Page, Joseph A. *Peron*, 6884

Page, Michael. *Encyclopedia of Things That Never Were*, 9521

Pahlavi, R. Mohammed. *Answer to History*, 7622

Paige, Richard. *The Door to December*, 1818(F)

Paine, Lauran. *Spirit Meadow*, 217(F)

Paine, Ralph D. *The Fight for a Free Sea*, 7878

Paine, Thomas. *Paine and Jefferson on Liberty*, 7858
The Rights of Man, 4018

Painter, Nell Irvin. *Standing at Armageddon*, 8016

Paisner, Daniel. *The Imperfect Mirror*, 6044

Paisner, Daniel (jt. author). *Theo and Me*, 6455

Pakula, Hannah. *The Last Romantic*, 6858

Palenski, Joseph. *Kids Who Run Away*, 4463

Paletta, Lu Ann. *The World Almanac of First Ladies*, 6484

Palgrave, Francis Turner, ed. *The Golden Treasury of the Best Songs & Lyrical Poems in the English Language*, 3221

Palin, Michael. *Around the World in 80 Days with Michael Palin*, 3506

Palmer, Arnold. *Play Great Golf*, 9876

Palmer, David R. *Threshold*, 1244(F)

Palmer, E. Laurence. *Fieldbook of Natural History*, 8398

Palmer, Joan. *A Dog Owner's Guide to Training Your Dog*, 8730
A Practical Guide to Selecting a Small Dog, 8731

Palmer, Larry I. *Law, Medicine, and Social Justice*, 5248

Palmer, Laura. *Shrapnel in the Heart*, 8136

Palmer, R. L. *Anorexia Nervosa*, 5397

Palmer, Robert. *Deep Blues*, 6183

Palmer, Tim. *Endangered Rivers and the Conservation Movement*, 4435
The Sierra Nevada, 8187

Pandolfini, Bruce, ed. *The Best of Chess Life and Review, Volume I, 1933–1960*, 9816
The Best of Chess Life and Review, Volume II, 1960–1988, 9816

Panger, Daniel. *Dance of the Wild Mouse*, 5216

Pankake, Jon (jt. author). *A Prairie Home Companion Folk Song Book*, 5950

Pankake, Marcia. *A Prairie Home Companion Folk Song Book*, 5950

Papacosta, Pangratios. *The Splendid Voyage*, 8228

Papashvily, George. *Anything Can Happen*, 6937

Papashvily, Helen (jt. author). *Anything Can Happen*, 6937

Pape, Richard. *Boldness Be My Friend*, 7268

Paradis, Adrian. *Opportunities in Airline Careers*, 4857
Opportunities in Banking, 4926
Opportunities in Military Careers, 4858
Opportunities in Part-Time and Summer Jobs, 5066
Opportunities in Transportation Careers, 4859
Opportunities in Vocational & Technical Careers, 5051

Paredes, Americo, ed. *Folktales of Mexico*, 3447

Pareles, Jon, ed. *The Rolling Stone Encyclopedia of Rock & Roll*, 5893

Pares, Bernard. *A History of Russia*, 7579

Paretsky, Sara. *Burn Marks*, 2123(F)

Parfit, Michael. *Chasing the Glory*, 6155
South Light, 7704

Parini, Jay. *The Patch Boys*, 1628(F)

Parini, Jay (jt. author). *The Bread Loaf Anthology of Contemporary American Essays*, 3543

Parish, Peter (jt. author). *The Divided Union*, 7891

Park, Christine, ed. *Close Company*, 586(F)

Parker, Barry. *Einstein's Dream*, 8913

Parker, Donald. *Table Tennis*, 9591

Parker, F. M. *The Searcher*, 1581(F)

Parker, Geoffrey (jt. author). *The Spanish Armada*, 7559

Parker, R. A. C. *Struggle for Survival*, 7269

Parker, Robert B. *Pale Kings and Princes*, 2124(F)

Playmates, 2125(F)

Sports Illustrated Training with Weights, 9772

Parker, Thomas. *America's Foreign Policy, 1945–1976*, 6485

Day by Day, 7339

Parker, Tom (jt. author). *Winfield*, 6735

Parker, W. Oren, et al. *Scene Design and Stage Lighting*, 6104

Parkman, Francis. *The Oregon Trail*, 7972

Parks, Gordon. *A Choice of Weapons*, 6294

The Learning Tree, 485(F)

Voices in the Mirror, 6295

Parks-McKay, Jane. *The Make-over*, 5287

Parkyn, Geoff. *U2*, 5894

Parlett, David. *Oxford Guide to Card Games*, 9817

Parrinder, Geoffrey. *African Mythology*, 3463

Parrinder, Geoffrey, ed. *World Religions from Ancient History to the Present*, 4069

Parrington, Vernon L. *Main Currents in American Thought*, 3597

Parrot, Andrea. *Coping with Date Rape & Acquaintance Rape*, 5516

Parulski, George R., Jr. *The Complete Book of Judo*, 9896

Pasachoff, Jay M. (jt. author). *A Field Guide to the Stars and Planets*, 8355

Pascoe, Elaine. *Racial Prejudice*, 4347

Passell, Peter. *How to Read the Financial Pages*, 5072

Pastan, Linda. *The Imperfect Paradise*, 3309

Pasternak, Boris. *Doctor Zhivago*, 1456(F)

Selected Poems, 3863

Patai, Raphael, ed. *Gates to the Old City*, 4070

Paterno, Joe. *Paterno*, 6757

Paton, Alan. *Ah, But Your Land Is Beautiful*, 986(F)

Cry, the Beloved Country, 987(F)

Patten, Jim. *Opportunities in Journalism Careers*, 4860

Patten, Lewis B. *The Red Sabbath*, 218(F)

Ride a Tall Horse, 218(F)

Sharpshod and They Called Him a Killer, 219(F)

Pattis, S. William. *Careers in Advertising*, 4927

Patton, George S., Jr. *War as I Knew It*, 6631

Patton, Phil. *Open Road*, 9055

Pattrick, William, ed. *Mysterious Sea Stories*, 2126(F)

Paul, Gregory S. *Predatory Dinosaurs of the World*, 6984

Paulsen, Gary. *Murphy*, 220(F), 221(F)

Murphy's Gold, 221(F)

Murphy's Herd, 222(F)

Popcorn Days and Buttermilk Nights, 897(F)

Sentries, 988(F)

Paulsen, Kathryn. *The Complete Book of Magic and Witchcraft*, 9399

Paxson, William C. *The Mentor Guide to Writing Term Papers and Reports*, 4693

Paxton, John. *Companion to Russian History*, 7580

Payne, Ronald (jt. author). *The Never-Ending War*, 4542

The Terrorists, 4543

Paz, Octavio. *Selected Poems*, 3354

Peace, Judy Boppell. *The Boy Child Is Dying*, 7382

Peacock, Carol A. *Hand-Me-Down Dreams*, 5398

Peacock, Doug. *Grizzly Years*, 8508

Pearl, Bill. *Getting Stronger*, 9773

Pearlman, Donn. *Breaking into Broadcasting*, 4895

Collecting Baseball Cards, 9689

Pearlman, Donn (jt. author). *Making Money with Baseball Cards*, 9447

Pearson, Carol. *The Female Hero in American and British Literature*, 3628

Peary, Danny. *Cult Movies*, 6045

Cult Movies 3, 6045

Cult Movies 2, 6045

Peary, Danny, ed. *Cult Baseball Players*, 6707

Peat, F. David. *Cold Fusion*, 8914

Peavy, Linda. *Food, Nutrition & You*, 5423

Women Who Changed Things, 6486

Peck, Ellen (jt. author). *Sex & Birth Control*, 5477

Peck, Richard (jt. author). *Edge of Awareness*, 3536

Peck, Richard E. *Something for Joey*, 9857

Peck, Robert Newton. *Fiction Is Folks*, 4694

Hallapoosa, 587(F)

Peden, Margaret Sayers, ed. *The Latin American Short Story*, 3796

Pei, Lowry. *Family Resemblances*, 898(F)

Peirce, Hayford. *Phylum Monsters*, 2726(F)

Pekkanen, John. *Donor*, 5166

M.D, 5249

Pellant, Chris. *Rocks, Minerals & Fossils of the World*, 8827

Pellegrino, Charles. *Unearthing Atlantis*, 7109

Peltier, Leslie. *Leslie Peltier's Guide to the Stars*, 8356

Pelton, Robert W. *Collecting Autographs for Fun and Profit*, 9458

Loony Laws, 9522

Pemberton, William E. *Harry S. Truman*, 6569

Penman, Sharon Kay. *Falls the Shadow*, 1457(F)

Here Be Dragons, 1458(F)

The Sunne in Splendour, 1459(F)

Penny, Malcolm. *Rhinos*, 8578

Pentecost, Hugh. *Death by Fire*, 2127(F)

Pepi, David. *Thoreau's Method*, 8399

Percy, Rachel (jt. author). *To Fight the Wild*, 7465

Percy, Walker. *Love in the Ruins*, 725(F)

Perez, Dennis D. *The Enlisted Soldier's Guide*, 4861

Perkins, David. *A History of Modern Poetry*, 3856, 3856

Perkins, Eric. *The Insider's Guide to Modeling*, 4928

Perl, Lila. *Hunter's Stew and Hangtown Fry*, 7973

Perlis, Vivian (jt. author). *Copland*, 6341
Copland since 1943, 6341

Perlo, Don (jt. author). *Jazz Portraits*, 5882

Pern, Stephen. *The Great Divide*, 7771

Perowne, Stewart. *Roman Mythology*, 3464

Perret, Patti. *The Faces of Science Fiction*, 3766

Perrett, Bryan. *Desert Warfare*, 7064

Perrin, Tom. *Football*, 9858

Perrins, Christopher M., ed. *The Encyclopedia of Birds*, 8541

Perry, Donald. *Kingdom in the Sky*, 8400

Perry, George. *The Complete Phantom of the Opera*, 5925
Life of Python, 6046

Perry, John. *Jack London*, 6284

Perry, Robert L. *Guide to Self-Employment*, 4929

Perry, Steve. *The Man Who Never Missed*, 2727(F)

Perry, Steve (jt. author). *Hellstar*, 2750(F)

Perske, Robert. *Show Me No Mercy*, 726(F)

Pervier, Evelyn. *Horsemanship*, 9885

Peters, Elizabeth. *Crocodile on the Sandbank*, 2128(F), 2130(F)
The Curse of the Pharaohs, 2128(F)
The Deeds of the Disturber, 2129(F)
Lion in the Valley, 2130(F)
The Love Talker, 1819(F)

Peters, Ellis. *The Confession of Brother Haluin*, 2131(F)
Dead Man's Ransom, 2132(F)
The Heretic's Apprentice, 2133(F)
A Rare Benedictine, 2134(F)
The Virgin in the Ice, 2135(F)

Peters, James Edward. *Arlington National Cemetery*, 8171

Peters, Margaret. *The Ebony Book of Black Achievement*, 6487

Peters, Max, et al. *Barron's How to Prepare for High School Entrance Examinations (SSAT & COOP)*, 4714

Peters, William. *A More Perfect Union*, 4201

Petersen Publishing Co., eds. *Petersen's Basic How to Tune Your Car*, 9107

Peterson, Franklyn (jt. author). *Research Shortcuts*, 4649
Study Smarts, 4649
Test Taking Strategies, 4649

Peterson, Ivers. *The Mathematical Tourist*, 8841

Peterson, Keith. *Scarred Man*, 2136(F)

Peterson, Owen, ed. *Representative American Speeches, 1988–1989*, 3544

Peterson, Richard F. *William Butler Yeats*, 3870

Peterson, Roger Tory. *A Field Guide to the Birds*, 8542
A Field Guide to Western Birds, 8543
A Field Guide to Wildflowers of North-Eastern and North-Central North America, 8441
How to Know the Birds, 8544
Penguins, 8567

Peterson, Susan L. *Self-Defense for Women*, 5444

Petkevich, John Misha. *Sports Illustrated Figure Skating*, 9890

Petrick, Tim. *Sports Illustrated Skiing*, 9944

Petrides, George A. *A Field Guide to Trees and Shrubs*, 8429

Petrie, Ferdinand. *The Big Book of Painting Nature in Watercolor*, 9207

Peyton, K. M. *Darkling*, 295(F)
A Midsummer Night's Death, 2137(F)

Pfaff, Eugene E., Jr. *Meryl Streep*, 6447

Pfeffer, Susan Beth. *About David*, 727(F)

Pfeiffer, C. Boyd. *The Orvis Guide to Outdoor Photography*, 9433
The Practical Fisherman, 9832

Pflaum, Rosalynd. *Grand Obsession*, 6655

Phelps, Ethel Johnston. *The Maid of the North*, 3368

Philip, Cynthia Owen. *Robert Fulton*, 6670

Philipson, Ilene. *Ethel Rosenberg*, 6633

Phillips, Betty Lou. *Go! Fight! Win!* 9592

Phillips, Carolyn E. *Michelle*, 6940

Phillips, Elizabeth. *Marianne Moore*, 3892

Phillips, Gene D. *Alfred Hitchcock*, 6047

Phillips, Louis. *Baseball Rules Illustrated*, 9690

Phillips, Louis, comp. *The Latin Riddle Book*, 9465

Phillips, Robert, ed. *Triumph of the Night*, 1820(F)

Phillips, Roger (jt. author). *Rocks, Minerals & Fossils of the World*, 8827

Phillips, Terry M. (jt. author). *Winning the War Within*, 5295

Phy, Allene Stuart. *Presenting Norma Klein*, 6277

Picano, Felice. *To the Seventh Power*, 223(F)

Pickard, Nancy. *Bum Steer*, 2138(F)
Dead Crazy, 2138(F)
No Body, 2138(F)

Picknett, Lynn. *Flights of Fancy?* 9523

Pickow, Peter. *The Billboard Book of Song Writing*, 5837

Pierce, Meredith Ann. *The Darkangel*, 1821(F)

Pierce, Sharon. *Making Holiday Folk Toys & Figures*, 9283

Piercy, Marge. *Circles on the Water*, 3310
Gone to Soldiers, 899(F)

Piggott, Juliet. *Japanese Mythology*, 3465

Pike, Christopher. *Chain Letter*, 2139(F)
Remember Me, 1822(F)
Scavenger Hunt, 1822(F)
Spellbound, 2140(F)

The Tachyon Web, 2728(F)
Pike, Frank (jt. author). *Creating Theater,* 6103
Pilcher, Rosamunde. *September,* 588(F)
Pincus, Arthur. *How to Talk Football,* 9859
Pincus, Arthur (jt. author). *How to Talk Basketball,* 9722
Pines, Maya. *Inside the Cell,* 8659
Pinfold, Bruce (jt. author). *The Big Band Years,* 5854
Pinfold, Mike. *Louis Armstrong,* 6359
Pini, Richard (jt. author). *Elfquest,* 1246(F)
Pini, Richard, ed. *Winds of Change,* 2729(F)
Pini, Richard, et al., eds. *The Blood of Ten Chiefs,* 1245(F)
Pini, Wendy. *Elfquest,* 1246(F)
Pinion, F. B. *A George Eliot Companion,* 3682
Pinkard, Bruce. *The Photographer's Bible,* 9435
Pinkwater, Daniel. *Fish Whistle,* 3507
Pinsent, John. *Greek Mythology,* 3478
Pinsky, Laura (jt. author). *The Essential AIDS Fact Book,* 5182
Pinter, Harold. *The Birthday Party,* 3035
Piper, H. Beam. *Empire,* 1247(F)
Federation, 1247(F)
Fuzzies and Other People, 1248(F)
Fuzzy Sapiens, 1248(F)
Little Fuzzy, 1248(F)
Lord Kalvan of Otherwhere, 1247(F)
Uller Uprising, 2730(F)
The Worlds of H. Beam Piper, 2730(F)
Piper, Robert J. *Opportunities in Architecture,* 4943
Pipkin, Turk (jt. author). *Harry Anderson's Games You Can't Lose,* 9547
Pirandello, Luigi. *Naked Masks,* 3014
Pirsig, Robert M. *Zen and the Art of Motorcycle Maintenance,* 4019
Pitch, Anthony S. (jt. author). *Chained Eagle,* 8097
Pizer, H. F. (jt. author). *Living Hungry in America,* 4502
Place, Irene. *Opportunities in Business Management,* 4930
Plaidy, Jean. *Myself My Enemy,* 1460(F)
The Princess of Celle, 1461(F)
Queen in Waiting, 1462(F)
The Star of Lancaster, 1463(F)
The Vow of the Heron, 1464(F)
Plain, Belva. *Blessings,* 589(F)
Eden Burning, 2309(F)
Evergreen, 2309(F), 1629(F)
The Golden Cup, 1629(F)
Random Winds, 2309(F)
Plant, Richard. *The Pink Triangle,* 7270
Plaschke, Bill (jt. author). *Hard Knox,* 6753
Plath, Sylvia. *Ariel,* 3311
The Bell Jar, 728(F)
The Collected Poems, 3312
Crossing the River, 3312
The Journals of Sylvia Plath, 6296

Plato. *The Last Days of Socrates,* 4020
The Republic, 4021
Platt, Charles. *Dream Makers,* 3629
Platt, Richard. *The Photographer's Idea Book,* 9436
Plimpton, George. *The Curious Case of Sidd Finch,* 2885(F)
Open Net, 9887
Paper Lion, 9860
Plimpton, George, ed. *The Writer's Chapbook,* 3598
Pliscou, Lisa. *Higher Education,* 900(F)
Plumb, J. H. (jt. author). *The American Heritage Book of the Revolution,* 7852
Plummer, Louise. *The Romantic Obsessions and Humiliations of Annie Schlmeier,* 901(F)
Plummer, William. *Buttercups and Strong Boys,* 9786
Plutarch. *Plutarch's Lives,* 6788
Podrazik, Walter (jt. author). *Five-Hundred-Five Television Questions Your Friends Can't Answer,* 5999
Poe, Edgar Allan. *The Complete Tales and Poems of Edgar Allan Poe,* 1823(F)
The Fall of the House of Usher and Other Tales, 417(F)
Poems of Edgar Allan Poe, 3313
Selected Poetry and Prose, 418
Tales of Terror, 1824(F)
Pogliani, Giuliano (jt. author). *The Color Atlas of Human Anatomy,* 5304
Pogue, William R. *How Do You Go to the Bathroom in Space?* 8316
Pohl, Frederik. *The Annals of the Heechee,* 2731(F)
Beyond the Blue Event Horizon, 2731(F)
Black Star Rising, 2732(F)
The Coming of the Quantum Cats, 2733(F)
The Day the Martians Came, 2734(F)
Gateway, 2731(F), 2735(F)
Heechee Rendezvous, 2731(F)
Homegoing, 2736(F)
Land's End, 2742(F)
Midas World, 2737(F)
Narabedla Ltd, 2738(F)
The Space Merchants, 2740(F)
The Way the Future Was, 6297
Wolfbane, 2741(F)
The World at the End of Time, 2739(F)
Point Foundation, ed. *The Essential Whole Earth Catalog,* 4609
Poitier, Sidney. *This Life,* 6429
Polcovar, Jane. *Hey, Good Looking!* 2310(F)
Polikoff, Judy. *Every Loving Gift,* 5399
Poling-Kempes, Lesley. *The Harvey Girls,* 7974
Polking, Kirk, ed. *A Beginner's Guide to Getting Published,* 3987
Pollack, Rachel. *Teach Yourself Fortune Telling,* 9524

Pollard, Arthur. *The Landscape of the Brontës*, 6220

Pollard, Sidney, ed. *Wealth & Poverty*, 4581

Polmar, Norman. *Ships and Aircraft of the U.S. Fleet*, 9133

The U.S. Navy Today, Vol. 1, 4287

Polmar, Norman (jt. author). *Merchants of Treason*, 4126

Polo, Marco. *The Travels of Marco Polo*, 6156

Polovchak, Walter. *Freedom's Child*, 6939

Poltawska, Wanda. *And I Am Afraid of My Dreams*, 7271

Pomerance, Alan. *Repeal of the Blues*, 5957

Pomerance, Bernard. *The Elephant Man*, 3114

Pomerantz, Susan (jt. author). *Attn: A & R*, 4894

Pomeroy, Wardell B. *Boys and Sex*, 5489

Girls and Sex, 5489

Pool, J. Lawrence. *Nature's Masterpiece*, 5321

Poole, Frederick King. *Mao Zedong*, 6813

Poole, Robert M., ed. *The Incredible Machine*, 5300

Nature's Wonderlands, 7065

Poortvliet, Rien. *Dogs*, 8732

Pope, Elizabeth Marie. *The Perilous Gard*, 1249(F)

The Sherwood Ring, 1249(F)

Pope, Katherine (jt. author). *The Female Hero in American and British Literature*, 3628

Pope, Loren. *Looking beyond the Ivy League*, 4755

Popham, Estelle L. (jt. author). *Opportunities in Office Occupations*, 4912

Popham, Melinda Worth. *Skywalker*, 296(F)

Popkin, Michael, ed. *Modern Black Writers*, 3599

Porazik, Juraj. *Old Time Classic Cars, 1885–1940*, 9108

Porter, Donald. *Jubilee Jim and the Wizard of Wall Street*, 224(F)

Porter, Jane. *The Scottish Chiefs*, 1465(F)

Porter, Katherine Anne. *The Collected Stories of Katherine Anne Porter*, 2952(F)

Pale Horse, Pale Rider, 2953(F)

Porter, Kent. *The New American Computer Dictionary*, 9009

Porter, Martin. *The Complete Guide to Making Home Video Movies*, 9052

Porter, Norman. *Tiffany Glassware*, 5812

Portes, Alejandro. *Immigrant America*, 4336

Portis, Charles. *True Grit*, 225(F)

Portugues, Gladys. *Hard Bodies*, 9774

Posner, Richard. *Goodnight, Cinderella*, 902(F)

Sweet Pain, 729(F)

Post, Elizabeth L. *Emily Post's Complete Book of Wedding Etiquette*, 5576

Emily Post's Etiquette, 5577

Post, W. Elwood. *Saints, Signs and Symbols*, 4071

Postman, Neil. *Amusing Ourselves to Death*, 6048

Teaching as a Conserving Activity, 6048

Potok, Chaim. *Davita's Harp*, 590(F)

The Gift of Asher Lev, 486(F)

My Name Is Asher Lev, 903(F)

The Promise, 487(F)

Wanderings, 7066

Potter, Charles Francis. *Is That in the Bible?* 4110

Potter, David M. *The Impending Crisis, 1848–1861*, 7879

Potter, G. R., ed. *The Cambridge Modern History*, 7067

Potts, Eve. *Understanding Your Immune System*, 5217

Potts, Eve (jt. author). *Choices*, 5210

Pough, Frederick H. *A Field Guide to Rocks and Minerals*, 8828

Pound, Ezra. *Selected Poems*, 3314

Pound, Ezra, ed. *The Classic Noh Theatre of Japan*, 3145

Pournelle, Jerry. *Exiles to Glory*, 2744(F)

Janissaries, 2746(F)

King David's Spaceship, 2744(F)

The Mercenary, 2745(F)

Pournelle, Jerry (jt. author). *Footfall*, 2700(F)

Lucifer's Hammer, 2701(F)

Mote in God's Eye, 2700(F)

Oath of Fealty, 2701(F)

Pournelle, Jerry, ed. *Black Holes and Other Marvels*, 2743(F)

Far Frontiers, 2743(F)

Powell, Andrew. *Living Buddhism*, 4072

Powell, David. *What Can I Write About?* 4695

Powell, Evan. *Complete Guide to Home Appliance Repair*, 9391

Powell, Lawrence C., ed. *Poems of Walt Whitman*, 3315

Powell, Padgett. *Edisto*, 904(F)

Power, Frank G., Jr. (jt. author). *Basketball*, 9716

Power, Helen W. *The Admissions Essay*, 4756

Powers, John R. *The Last Catholic in America*, 1897(F)

Powers, Lyall H. *Faulkner's Yoknapatawpha Comedy*, 3767

Powis, Raymond L. *The Human Body and Why It Works*, 5301

Poyer, D. C. *Stepfather Bank*, 2747(F)

Poyer, David. *The Gulf*, 226(F)

Poyer, Joe (jt. author). *The Illustrated History of Helicopters*, 9069

Practical Homeowner, eds. *Build-It-Better-Yourself Storage Around the House*, 9284

Prager, Arthur. *World War II Resistance Stories*, 7272

Prager, Emily (jt. author). *World War II Resistance Stories*, 7272

Prance, Ghillean Tolmie. *Leaves*, 8413

Prange, Gordon W., et al. *December 7, 1941*, 7273

Miracle at Midway, 7274

Prather, Hugh. *Notes to Myself,* 3545

Pratt, Douglas R. *The Beginner's Guide to Radio Control Sport Flying,* 9304

Pratt, Julius W., et al. *A History of United States Foreign Policy,* 4158

Preiss, Byron. *The Constitution of the United States of America,* 4202
Dragonworld, 1250(F)

Preiss, Byron, ed. *The Planets,* 8347
The Universe, 8370

Prendergast, Curtis. *Barnstormers and Speed Kings,* 9074
The First Aviators, 9074
Flying the Mail, 9074
Knights of the Air, 9074

Preston, Paul. *The Spanish Civil War, 1936–39,* 7560

Preston, Richard. *First Light,* 8281

Preston-Mafham, Ken (jt. author). *Butterflies of the World,* 8608

Preston-Mafham, Rod. *Butterflies of the World,* 8608

Preuss, Paul. *Maelstrom,* 2748(F)

Prevention Magazine, ed. *Natural Weight Loss,* 5424

Previn, André, ed. *André Previn's Guide to the Orchestra,* 5940

Previte-Orton, C. W. *The Shorter Cambridge Medieval History,* 7139

Price, Christine. *Made in the South Pacific,* 5769

Price, Janet R., et al. *The Rights of Students,* 4315

Price, Jeanne (jt. author). *Basic Pattern Skills for Fashion Design,* 9179

Price, Reynolds. *A Long and Happy Life,* 730(F)
The Tongues of Angels, 905(F)

Price, Robert V. *How to Use the Apple II and IIe,* 9010

Prince, J. H. *Plants That Eat Animals,* 8442

Pringle, Laurence. *Nuclear War,* 4159
Rivers and Lakes, 8897

Pringle, Terry. *A Fine Time to Leave Me,* 591(F)
The Preacher's Kid, 1898(F)

Pritchard, D. B. *Begin Chess,* 9818

Pritchard, William H. *Lives of the Modern Poets,* 3857

Pritchett, V. S., ed. *The Oxford Book of Short Stories,* 2954(F)

Prochnow, Herbert V., ed. *The Public Speaker's Treasure Chest,* 4696

Prochnow, Herbert V., Jr. (jt. author). *The Public Speaker's Treasure Chest,* 4696

Proctor, Geo. W. *Walks without a Soul,* 1582(F)

Proffitt, Nicholas. *Gardens of Stone,* 1701(F)

Pronzini, Bill. *Firewind,* 227(F)
Shackles, 2141(F)
Small Felonies, 2142(F)

Pronzini, Bill, ed. *Best of the West,* 229(F)
Great Modern Police Stories, 2143(F)

Homicidal Acts, 230(F)
The Mammoth Book of Private Eye Stories, 2144(F)
More Wild Westerns, 228(F)
Prime Suspects #1, 2145(F)
Suspicious Characters, 2146(F)

Pronzini, Bill (jt. author). *Kill or Cure,* 2118(F)

Provost, Gary (jt. author). *Finder,* 6912

Pruess, Joanna. *The Supermarket Epicure,* 9354

Pruett, Kyle D. *The Nurturing Father,* 5672

Prytz, Ulla (jt. author). *Folding Table Napkins,* 9154

Ptacek, Greg (jt. author). *Mothers of Invention,* 8236

Pugnetti, Gino. *Simon and Schuster's Guide to Cats,* 8701
Simon & Schuster's Guide to Dogs, 8733

Pullman, Philip. *Ruby in the Smoke,* 231(F)
The Ruby in the Smoke, 232(F)
Shadow in the North, 231(F)
The Shadow in the North, 232(F)
The Tiger in the Well, 232(F)

Purl, Sandy. *Am I Alive?* 6942

Pushkin, Alexander. *Alexander Pushkin,* 2955(F)

Puzo, Mario. *The Godfather,* 233(F)

Pyle, Howard. *Merry Adventures of Robin Hood,* 3409

Pyle, Robert Michael. *The Audubon Society Field Guide to North American Butterflies,* 8609
The Audubon Society Handbook for Butterfly Watchers, 8610

Quaife, Milo Milton, ed. *Kit Carson's Autobiography,* 6618

Quammen, David. *The Flight of the Iguana,* 8457
Natural Acts, 8401

Quin-Harkin, Janet. *Campus Cousins,* 2311(F)
The Graduates, 2312(F)
The Great Boy Chase, 2313(F)
Growing Pains, 2314(F)
Home Sweet Home, 2311(F)
The Trouble with Toni, 2312(F)

Quinlan, David. *Wicked Women of the Screen,* 6049

Quinnett, Paul G. *Suicide,* 5095

Rabin, Carol Price. *Music Festivals in America,* 5826

Rabinovich, Abraham. *The Boats of Cherbourg,* 7615

Rabinowitz, Ann. *Bethie,* 731(F)

Rabinowitz, Howard N., ed. *Southern Black Leaders of the Reconstruction Era,* 8017

Rabins, Peter V. (jt. author). *The Thirty-six-Hour Day,* 5203

Rabinsky, Leatrice. *Journey of Conscience,* 7275

Rabkin, Eric S. (jt. author). *Science Fiction,* 3630

Rabkin, Eric S., ed. *Fantastic Worlds*, 1251
Rachlin, Carol K. (jt. author). *American Indian Mythology*, 3424
Plains Indian Mythology, 3425
Rachlin, Nahid. *Foreigner*, 6943
Racine, Jean Baptiste. *Phaedra*, 3015
Radetsky, Peter (jt. author). *Pacewalking*, 5356
Peak Condition, 5442
Radice, Betty. *Who's Who in the Ancient World*, 7086
Radner, Gilda. *It's Always Something*, 6433
Radosh, Ronald. *The Rosenberg File*, 4250
Rae, Catherine M. *Sarah Cobb*, 2147(F)
Raffel, Burton. *T. S. Eliot*, 3871
Raffel, Burton, ed. *The Signet Classic Book of American Short Stories*, 2956(F)
The Signet Classic Book of Contemporary Short Stories, 2956(F)
Rahman, Fazlur. *Islam*, 4073
Rainer, Tristine. *The New Diary*, 5626
Raines, Howell. *My Soul Is Rested*, 4375
Rains, Rob (jt. author). *Wizard*, 6733
Ralling, Christopher, comp. *The Voyage of Charles Darwin*, 6657
Ramati, Alexander. *And the Violins Stopped Playing*, 1672(F)
Rampersad, Arnold. *The Life of Langston Hughes, Volume II, 1941–1967*, 6268
Ramsay, Jay. *Night of the Claw*, 1825(F)
Ramsey, Dan. *Weather Forecasting*, 8872
Ramusi, Molapatene Collins. *Soweto, My Love*, 6799
Rand, Ayn. *Anthem*, 989(F)
Atlas Shrugged, 990(F)
The Fountainhead, 991(F)
Randall, Dudley, ed. *The Black Poets*, 3316
Randall, John Herman, Jr. *The Making of the Modern Mind*, 4022
Randall, Neil (jt. author). *Roger Zelazny's Visual Guide to Castle Amber*, 3794(F)
Randel, Don Michael, comp. *Harvard Concise Dictionary of Music*, 5827
Randi, James. *The Faith Healer*, 4074
Randisi, Robert J., ed. *Justice for Hire*, 2148(F)
Randolph, Elizabeth. *The Basic Bird Book*, 8679
Randolph, Elizabeth (jt. author). *The Complete Book of Dog Health*, 8723
Randolph, John. *Backpacking Basics*, 9802
Ranelagh, John O'Beirne. *A Short History of Ireland*, 7531
Ransom, Bill (jt. author). *The Ascension Factor*, 1150(F)
The Jesus Factor, 1150(F)
The Lazarus Effect, 1150(F)
Ranson, Ron. *Water-Color Painting*, 9208
Raphael, Elaine (jt. author). *Charcoal & Pastel*, 9182
Pen & Ink, 9182
Pencil, 9182

Rappoport, Ken. *Double Header*, 9691
Rashke, Richard. *Escape from Sobibor*, 7276
Raspail, Jean. *Who Will Remember the People . . ,* 1353(F)
Rath, Sara. *About Cows*, 8590
Rather, Dan. *The Camera Never Blinks*, 6298
Ratliff, Gerald Lee. *On Stage*, 5926
Ravenel, Shannon, ed. *New Stories from the South*, 2957(F)
Ravin, Neil. *Mere Mortals*, 2315(F)
Ravitch, Diane. *The Schools We Deserve*, 4633
Rawlings, Marjorie. *The Yearling*, 297(F)
Rawls, James. *Indians of California*, 7820
Rawn, Melanie. *Dragon Prince*, 1252(F), 1253(F)
The Star Scroll, 1253(F)
Sunrunner's Fire, 1253(F)
Ray, David, ed. *From A to Z*, 3317
Ray, G. Carleton (jt. author). *A Field Guide to Atlantic Coast Fishes of North America*, 8627
Raymo, Chet. *The Soul of the Night*, 8282
Raymond, Patrick. *Daniel and Esther*, 906(F)
Raynor, Thomas. *Terrorism*, 4553
Raynor, Thomas (jt. author). *Women in Politics*, 4272
Read, Anthony. *Kristallnacht*, 7277
Read, Herbert. *A Concise History of Modern Painting*, 5756
A Concise History of Modern Sculpture, 5757
Read, Karen (jt. author). *Everywoman's Guide to Military Service*, 4285
Read, Piers Paul. *Alive*, 7682
Reader, John. *The Rise of Life*, 7011
Reader's Digest, eds. *ABC's of the Human Body*, 5302
ABC's of the Human Mind, 5322
American Folklore and Legend, 3440
America's Fascinating Indian Heritage, 7821
America's Historic Places, 7772
Magic and Medicine of Plants, 8443
Mysteries of the Ancient Americas, 7023
Mysteries of the Unexplained, 9525
Natural Wonders of the World, 7068
Our National Parks, 7773
Quest for the Past, 7069
Reader's Digest Complete Guide to Sewing, 9249
Reader's Digest Crafts & Hobbies, 9150
Reader's Digest Family Safety & First Aid, 5445
Reader's Digest Guide to Creative Gardening, 9385
The Reader's Digest Illustrated Book of Dogs, 8734
Reader's Digest North American Wildlife, 8402
Reader's Digest Strange Stories, Amazing Facts of America's Past, 7774
Reader's Digest Visitor's Guide to the Great Barrier Reef, 7475
Sharks, 8630

Story of the Great American West, 7975
The World at Arms: The Reader's Digest Illustrated History of World War II, 7278
Reagan, Ronald. *An American Life*, 6553
Reamy, Tom. *San Diego Lightfoot Sue and Other Stories*, 2749(F)
Reaves, Michael. *Hellstar*, 2750(F)
The Shattered World, 1254(F)
Reaves, Michael (jt. author). *Dragonworld*, 1250(F)
Reck, W. Emerson. *A. Lincoln*, 6548
Redding, Stan (jt. author). *Catch Me If You Can*, 6887
Redfern, Ron. *The Making of a Continent*, 8788
Redford, Dorothy. *Somerset Homecoming*, 6517
Redgrove, Peter (jt. author). *The Wise Wound*, 5492
Redman, Eric. *The Dance of Legislation*, 4229
Redman, Tim, ed. *U.S. Chess Federation's Official Rules of Chess*, 9819
Reed, Kenneth T. *Truman Capote*, 3768
Reed, Maxine K. *Career Opportunities in Television, Cable and Video*, 5052
Reed, Robert (jt. author). *Career Opportunities in Television, Cable and Video*, 5052
Reed, Roger (jt. author). *The Illustrator in America, 1880–1980*, 5758
Reed, W. L., ed. *National Anthems of the World*, 5951
Reed, Walt. *The Illustrator in America, 1880–1980*, 5758
Reeman, Douglas. *His Majesty's U-Boat*, 1673(F)
The Pride and the Anguish, 1673(F)
A Ship Must Die, 1673(F)
Torpedo Run, 1673(F)
Reese, Terence. *Begin Bridge with Reese*, 9820
Reeves, Dan. *Reeves*, 6759
Reeves, Randall R. (jt. author). *The Sierra Club Handbook of Whales and Dolphins*, 8654
Reeves, Robert N. *Doubting Thomas*, 2149(F)
Reeves, Thomas C. *The Life and Times of Joe McCarthy*, 6603
Reeves-Stevens, Garfield. *Nighteyes*, 2751(F)
Prime Directive, 2752(F)
Reeves-Stevens, Judith (jt. author). *Prime Directive*, 2752(F)
Regenstein, Helen (jt. author). *Walt Whitman*, 3891
Rehder, Harald A. *The Audubon Society Field Guide to North American Seashells*, 8878
Reich, Jerome R. *Colonial America*, 7843
Reichel, Sabine. *What Did You Do in the War, Daddy?* 7506
Reichler, Joseph L., ed. *The Baseball Encyclopedia*, 9692
Reid, George K. *Pond Life*, 8619
Reid, John. *From One Sheet of Plywood*, 9285
Reid, Pat. *Prisoner of War*, 7070

Reidenbaugh, Lowell. *The Sporting News Selects Baseball's 50 Great Games*, 9694
The Sporting News Selects Baseball's 50 Greatest Games, 9693
The Sporting News Selects Baseball's 25 Greatest Pennant Races, 9694
The Sporting News Selects Baseball's 25 Greatest Teams, 9694
Reidman, Sarah R. *The Good Looks Skin Book*, 5339
Reilly, Jill M. *College Comes Sooner Than You Think!* 4757
Reilly, Rick (jt. author). *Gretzky*, 6774
Reinfeld, Fred. *Be a Winner at Chess*, 9821
Beginner's Guide to Winning Chess, 9821
A Catalogue of the World's Most Popular Coins, 9460
Chess in a Nutshell, 9821
The Complete Chessplay, 9821
How to Win at Checkers, 9822
Pony Express, 7976
Win at Chess, 9821
Reino, Joseph. *Stephen King*, 3769
Reischauer, Edwin O. *The Japanese*, 7452
Reiser, Bob (jt. author). *Everybody Says Freedom*, 4348
Reisfeld, Randi. *So You Want to Be a Star*, 4896
Reiss, Bob. *Saltmaker*, 234(F)
Reit, Ann. *The Bet*, 2316(F)
Remarque, Erich Maria. *All Quiet on the Western Front*, 1636(F)
Arch of Triumph, 1674(F)
Rembar, Charles. *The Law of the Land*, 4251
Remini, Robert V. *Andrew Jackson and the Course of American Democracy, 1833–1845*, 6532
Andrew Jackson and the Course of American Empire, 6532
Andrew Jackson and the Course of American Freedom, 6532
The Revolutionary Age of Andrew Jackson, 7880
Renault, Mary. *The Bull from the Sea*, 1372(F)
Fire from Heaven, 1371(F)
The King Must Die, 1372(F)
The Last of the Wine, 1373(F)
The Mask of Apollo, 1372(F)
The Nature of Alexander, 6823
The Persian Boy, 1371(F)
The Praise Singer, 1374(F)
Rendell, Ruth. *The Bridesmaid*, 2150(F)
Collected Stories, 2151(F)
The Fever Tree and Other Stories of Suspense, 2152(F)
Heartstones, 2153(F)
Master of the Moor, 2154(F)
The New Girl Friend and Other Stories, 1826(F)
Talking to Strange Men, 2155(F)
The Veiled One, 2156(F)

Rensberger, Boyce. *How the World Works*, 8229

Resnick, Mike. *The Dark Lady*, 2753(F)
Ivory, 2754(F)
Santiago, 2755(F)
Second Contact, 2756(F)

Resnick, Rose. *Dare to Dream*, 6944

Restak, Richard M. *The Brain*, 5323
The Mind, 5324

Retton, Mary Lou. *Mary Lou*, 6767

Reuben, David. *Everything You Always Wanted to Know about Nutrition*, 5425

Reuther, David (jt. author). *The Armchair Angler*, 9824

Rewald, John. *Cézanne*, 6190
The History of Impressionism, 5759
Post-Impressionism, 5760

Rexroth, Kenneth. *Selected Poems*, 3318

Rexroth, Kenneth, ed. *One Hundred Poems from the Chinese*, 3355
100 Poems from the Japanese, 3355

Reynolds, Barbara. *And Still We Rise*, 4376

Reynolds, Clark G. *The Carrier War*, 7279
Italy at War, 7279
The Secret War, 7279
War in the Outposts, 7279

Reynolds, David (jt. author). *An Ocean Apart*, 4135

Reynolds, Donald M. *The Nineteenth Century*, 5761

Reynolds, Mack. *The Other Time*, 1255(F)

Reynolds, Michaels. *The Sun Also Rises*, 3770

Reynolds, Moira. *Nine American Women of the 19th Century*, 6488

Rezen, Susan V. *Coping with Hearing Loss*, 5332

Rhein, Phillip H. *Albert Camus*, 3600

Rheingold, Howard. *They Have a Word for It*, 3944

Rhodes, Frank H. T. *Geology*, 8789

Rhodes, Frank H. T., et al. *Fossils*, 6985

Rhodes, Richard. *Farm*, 8585
The Making of the Atomic Bomb, 8940

Rhoodie, Eschel M. *Discrimination against Women*, 4316

Rhue, Morton. *The Wave*, 1827(F)

Riasanovsky, Nicholas V. *A History of Russia*, 7581

Ribers, Caryl, et al. *Beyond Sugar and Spice*, 5542

Ribner, Susan. *The Martial Arts*, 9897

Riccio, Dolores. *Haunted Houses, U.S.A*, 9526

Rice, Anne. *Interview with the Vampire*, 1828(F)
The Mummy, 1829(F)

Rice, Berkeley. *Trafficking*, 4489

Rice, Edward. *Margaret Mead*, 6692

Rice, F. Philip. *The Adolescent*, 5543

Rice, Wayne. *Play It!* 9593

Rich, Adrienne. *The Fact of a Doorframe*, 3319

Rich, Doris. *Amelia Earhart*, 6140

Rich, Libby. *Odyssey Book of Houseplants*, 9386

Richards, Alison (jt. author). *A Passion for Science*, 6647

Richards, Arlene Kramer. *Boy Friends, Girl Friends, Just Friends*, 5544
Leaving Home, 5627
What to Do If You or Someone You Know Is Under 18 and Pregnant, 5490

Richards, Colin. *Sheriff Pat Garrett's Last Days*, 7881

Richards, Denis (jt. author). *The Battle of Britain*, 7335

Richards, Dorothy Silkstone. *How to Choose & Care for Your Cat*, 8702

Richards, Judith. *After the Storm*, 235(F)
Summer Lightning, 907(F)

Richards, Mose (jt. author). *Cousteau's Papua New Guinea Journey*, 7467
Jacques Cousteau's Amazon Journey, 7669

Richards, Stanley, ed. *Great Rock Musicals*, 5927
The Most Popular Plays of the American Theatre, 3115

Richardson, Ben. *Great Black Americans*, 6489

Richardson, Elmo. *The Presidency of Dwight D. Eisenhower*, 8087

Richardson, John Adkins. *The Complete Book of Cartooning*, 9209

Richardson, P. Mick. *Flowering Plants*, 8444

Richman, Robert, ed. *The Direction of Poetry*, 3174

Richman, Sidney. *Bernard Malamud*, 3771

Richter, Conrad. *The Fields*, 1584(F)
The Rawhide Knot, and Other Stories, 1583(F)
The Town, 1584(F)
The Trees, 1584(F)

Richter, Peyton. *Voltaire*, 3601

Ride, Sally. *To Space and Back*, 8317

Riding, Alan. *Distant Neighbors*, 7648

Ridpath, Ian. *Star Tales*, 8283

Riehm, Sarah. *The Teenage Entrepreneur's Guide*, 5067

Rieul, Roland. *Escape into Espionage*, 7280

Riffenburgh, Beau. *Great Ones*, 9861

Rifkin, Jeremy (jt. author). *Who Should Play God?* 5262

Rifkin, Jeremy, ed. *The Green Lifestyle Handbook*, 4436

Rifkin, Paul, ed. *The God Letters*, 4075

Rifkind, Carole. *A Field Guide to American Architecture*, 5704

Rigby, Kate. *Fall of the Flamingo Circus*, 592(F)

Riis, Jacob. *How the Other Half Lives*, 8018

Riley, Dick, ed. *The New Bedside, Bathtub & Armchair Companion to Agatha Christie*, 3683

Riley, Judith Merkle. *A Vision of Light*, 1466(F)

Riley, Pat. *Show Time*, 6708

Rilke, Rainer Maria. *Selected Poems of Rainer Maria Rilke*, 3186
Where Silence Reigns, 3546

Rinaldi, Ann. *Promises Are for Keeping,* 732(F)
Term Paper, 732(F)
Rinehart, Mary Roberts. *The Circular Staircase,* 2157(F)
Rinzler, Carol Ann. *The Complete Book of Food,* 5426
Rinzler, Jane. *Teens Speak Out,* 4418
Rios, Alberto Alvaro. *The Iguana Killer,* 488(F)
Ripley, S. Dillon. *Fire of Life,* 8348
Ripple, G. Gary. *Admit One!* 4758
Rippley, La Vern J. *The German-Americans,* 4403
Rips, Gladys Nadler. *Coming to America,* 4337
Ritchard, Dan. *Ventriloquism for the Total Dummy,* 9305
Ritchie, David. *Spacewar,* 4160
Superquake! 8806
Ritchie, Robert C. *Captain Kidd and the War against the Pirates,* 7844
Ritter, Lawrence S. *The 100 Greatest Baseball Players of All Time,* 6709
The Story of Baseball, 9695
Ritz, David (jt. author). *Smokey,* 6438
Riva, Peter, comp. *Sightseeing,* 8318
Rivele, Stephen J. (jt. author). *The Plumber,* 4490
Rivera, Edward. *Family Installments,* 6945
Riviere, Bill. *The L. L. Bean Guide to the Outdoors,* 9803
The Open Canoe, 9933
Roan, Sharon. *Ozone Crisis,* 4437
Robb, Tom. *Pack Up and Sketch,* 9210
Robbins, Albert. *Coming to America,* 4338
Robbins, Chandler S., et al., eds. *Birds of North America,* 8545
Robbins, Lawrence H. *Stones, Bones, and Ancient Cities,* 7024
Robbins, Maria (jt. author). *A Christmas Companion,* 4115
Roberson, John R. *Japan,* 7453
Roberson, Virginia Lee. *Careers in the Graphic Arts,* 4862
Robert, Henry M. *Robert's Rules of Order,* 5584
Roberts, Clayton. *A History of England,* 7532
Roberts, David A. (jt. author). *A History of England,* 7532
Roberts, Edgar V. *Writing Themes about Literature,* 4697
Roberts, John Maddox. *Spacer,* 2757(F)
The Sword, the Jewel and the Mirror, 2757(F)
Roberts, John S. *The Latin Tinge,* 5895
Roberts, Kenneth. *Boon Island,* 1518(F)
Northwest Passage, 1585(F)
Roberts, Michael (jt. author). *A Field Guide to Conservation Archaeology in North America,* 7019
Roberts, Moss. *Chinese Fairy Tales and Fantasies,* 3385
Roberts, Nancy. *Haunted Houses,* 9527

Roberts, Royston M. *Serendipity,* 8230
Roberts, Stephen (jt. author). *You Don't Have to Be a Genius to Land a Computer Job,* 5058
Robertson, Adam, ed. *The Princeton Review,* 4759
Robertson, Dougal. *Survive the Savage Sea,* 6158
Robertson, James I., Jr. *Tenting Tonight,* 7932
Robertson, Martin. *A Shorter History of Greek Art,* 5762
Robertson, Patrick. *Guinness Film Facts and Feats,* 6050
Robeson, Susan. *The Whole World in His Hands,* 6436
Robins, C. Richard. *A Field Guide to Atlantic Coast Fishes of North America,* 8627
Robinson, Adam. *The Princeton Review— Cracking the System,* 4664
Robinson, Adam, et al. *The Princeton Review— Word Smart,* 3945
Robinson, Bill, ed. *80 Years of Yachting,* 9934
Robinson, C. E. *Everyday Life in Ancient Greece,* 7110
Robinson, David. *The History of World Cinema,* 6051
Robinson, Dennis M. (jt. author). *Arco's Complete Preparation for High School Entrance Examinations,* 4715
Robinson, Edwin Arlington. *Selected Poems of Edwin Arlington Robinson,* 3320
Robinson, Francis. *Atlas of the Islamic World Since 1500,* 7602
Robinson, Frank (jt. author). *Blow-Out,* 241(F)
Robinson, Jacqueline. *Arco's Complete Preparation for High School Entrance Examinations,* 4715
Robinson, Jeanne (jt. author). *Stardance,* 2762(F)
Robinson, Joy D. Marie. *Antoine de Saint-Exupery,* 3642
Robinson, Kim Stanley. *The Gold Coast,* 908(F)
The Wide Shore, 2758(F)
Robinson, Leah Ruth. *Blood Run,* 2158(F)
Robinson, Margaret A. *Courting Emma Howe,* 2317(F)
Robinson, Mark Aaron. *100 Grams of Uranium Equal 290 Tons of Coal,* 8929
Robinson, Patricia. *Something to Hide,* 2159(F)
Robinson, Phyllis C. *Willa,* 6229
Robinson, Ray. *Iron Horse,* 6721
Robinson, Ray (jt. author). *Oh, Baby, I Love It!* 9677
Robinson, Richard. *The Video Primer,* 6052
Robinson, Smokey. *Smokey,* 6438
Robinson, Spider. *Callahan's Crosstime Saloon,* 2759(F)
Callahan's Lady, 2759(F)
Callahan's Secret, 2759(F), 2760(F)
Stardance, 2762(F)

Time Pressure, 2761(F)
Time Travelers Strictly Cash, 2759(F)
Robson, Frank. *Pictures in the Dolphin Mind,* 8623
Robson, Lucia St. Clair. *Walk in My Soul,* 1586(F)
Rochester, Lois. *The One Hour College Applicant,* 4760
Rochman, Hazel, ed. *Somehow Tenderness Survives,* 992(F)
Rock, David. *Argentina, 1516–1982,* 7683
Rockland, Mae Shafter. *The Hanukkah Book,* 4118
Rocklin, Joanne (jt. author). *Getting High in Natural Ways,* 5620
Roden, Claudia. *Mediterranean Cookery,* 9355
Roderus, Frank. *Billy Ray's Forty Days,* 236(F)
Rodgers, Joann Ellison. *Drugs & Pain,* 5148
Drugs & Sexual Behavior, 5149
Rodriguez, Richard. *Hunger of Memory,* 6946
Roebuck, Nigel. *Grand Prix Greats,* 9618
Roes, Nicholas A. *America's Lowest Cost Colleges,* 4761
Roesch, Roberta. *You Can Make It Without a College Degree,* 4807
Roethke, Theodore. *The Collected Poems of Theodore Roethke,* 3321
Rogers, Carl R. *A Way of Being,* 5545
Rogers, Dale Evans. *Angel Unaware,* 6905
Rogers, Deborah Webster. *J. R. R. Tolkien,* 3684
Rogers, Lynne (jt. author). *How to Be a Working Actor,* 4887
Rogers, Pat, ed. *The Oxford Illustrated History of English Literature,* 3685
Roggow, Linda (jt. author). *Pregnant and Single,* 5515
Rohr, Janelle, ed. *Death and Dying,* 5096
The Middle East, 7603
Problems of Africa, 7358
Science & Religion, 4076
The Third World, 4464
Violence in America, 4528
Rohr, Janelle (jt. author). *Israel,* 7604
Rolbein, Seth. *Nobel Costa Rica,* 7657
Rolfe, Bari, ed. *Mimes on Miming,* 6105
Rolling Stone Magazine, ed. *The Rolling Stone Interviews,* 5896
Romasco, Albert U. *The Politics of Recovery,* 8039
Rombauer, Irma S. *Joy of Cooking,* 9356
Romer, John. *Ancient Lives,* 7098
Romney, Ronna. *Momentum,* 4269
Ronan, Colin A. *Science,* 8231
The Skywatcher's Handbook, 8284
Rooney, Andrew A. *And More by Andy Rooney,* 3508
A Few Minutes with Andy Rooney, 3508
The Most of Andy Rooney, 3509
Not That You Asked. . ., 3510

Pieces of My Mind, 3509
Roop, Connie (jt. author). *The Solar System,* 8349
Roop, Peter. *The Solar System,* 8349
Roosevelt, Eleanor. *Eleanor Roosevelt's My Day, Volume 2,* 6558
This I Remember, 6559
Roosevelt, Elliott. *Eleanor Roosevelt, with Love,* 6560
The Hyde Park Murder, 2160(F)
Murder and the First Lady, 2161(F)
Murder at the Palace, 2162(F)
Murder in the Blue Room, 2163(F)
Murder in the Oval Office, 2164(F)
The White House Pantry Murder, 2165(F)
Root, Karen L., ed. *American Literary Almanac,* 3772
Rosa, Joseph G. *The Gunfighter,* 7977
They Called Him Wild Bill, 6624
Rosas, Carlos (jt. author). *Non-Impact Aerobics,* 5360
Rosas, Debbie. *Non-Impact Aerobics,* 5360
Rosca, Ninotchka. *Endgame,* 7476
Rose, Al. *Eubie Blake,* 6374
Rose, Darlene Deibler. *Evidence Not Seen,* 7281
Rose, Frank. *Into the Heart of the Mind,* 9011
Rose, Howard. *Unexpected Eloquence,* 5804
Rose, Kenneth Jon. *The Body in Time,* 5303
Rose, Stephen C. *Coping with a Negative World in a Positive Way,* 4529
Rosel, George Brown (jt. author). *Earth Blood,* 2628(F)
Rosen, Karen (jt. author). *Sports Illustrated Track,* 9975
Rosen, Kenneth, ed. *The Man to Send Rain Clouds,* 489(F)
Rosen, Mel. *Sports Illustrated Track,* 9975
Rosen, Richard. *Fadeaway,* 2166(F)
Strike Three, You're Dead, 2166(F)
Rosen, Winifred (jt. author). *From Chocolate to Morphine,* 5159
Rosenbaum, Alvin. *The Young People's Yellow Pages,* 5628
Rosenbaum, Stuart E. (jt. author). *Euthanasia,* 5079
Rosenberg, Joel. *The Heir Apparent,* 1256(F)
The Silver Crown, 1256(F)
The Sleeping Dragon, 1256(F)
Sword and the Chain, 1256(F)
Warrior Lives, 1256(F)
Rosenberg, Lawrence M. *Cake Decorating Simplified,* 9357
Rosenberg, Martin H. *Opportunities in Accounting Careers,* 4931
Rosenberg, Richard (jt. author). *Lovejoy's Preparation for the SAT,* 4660
Rosenberg, Stephen N. *The Johnson & Johnson First Aid Book,* 5446
Rosenblum, Joseph. *When the Shooting Stops . . . the Cutting Begins,* 6053

Rosenblum, Morris (jt. author). *All about Words*, 3943

Rosenblum, Robert. *19th-Century Art*, 5763

Rosenfeld, Arthur. *Exotic Animals as Pets*, 8680

Rosenfield, Israel, et al. *DNA for Beginners*, 5265

Rosenthal, Gary. *Soccer Skills and Drills*, 9952
Volleyball, 9979

Rosenthal, Lawrence. *Exploring Careers in Accounting*, 4932

Rosenthal, Lucy. *Great American Love Stories*, 2318(F)

Rosenthal, Macha Louis. *The Modern Poets*, 3858

Rosenthal, Peggy. *Every Cliché in the Book*, 3946

Rosenthal, Ted. *How Could I Not Be among You?* 5218

Rosny, J. H. *Quest for Fire*, 1354(F)

Ross, Al. *Cartooning Fundamentals*, 9211

Ross, Bill D. *Iwo Jima*, 7282

Ross, Charles A., ed. *Crocodiles and Alligators*, 8469

Ross, James R. *How to Buy a Car, 1989*, 9109

Ross, Jeffrey Steven (jt. author). *Handbook of Everyday Law*, 4252

Ross, John, et al. *The Complete Printmaker*, 9225

Ross, Judith Wilson (jt. author). *The Insanity Plea*, 4259

Ross, Leonard Q. *The Education of H*Y*M*A*N K*A*P*L*A*N*, 1899(F)

Ross, Martin J. *Handbook of Everyday Law*, 4252

Ross, Nancy Wilson. *Buddhism*, 4077
Three Ways of Asian Wisdom, 4078

Rossbacher, Lisa A. *Career Opportunities in Geology and the Earth Sciences*, 5027

Rossi, Alice S., ed. *The Feminist Papers*, 4317

Rossner, Judith. *Emmeline*, 1528(F)

Rosso, Julee. *The New Basics Cookbook*, 9358

Rostand, Edmond. *Cyrano de Bergerac*, 3016

Rosten, Leo. *Hoorah for Yiddish*, 3947
The Joys of Yiddish, 3947

Rosten, Leo, ed. *Religions of America*, 4079

Rostkowski, Margaret I. *The Best of Friends*, 1702(F)

Roston, Ruth (jt. author). *This Sporting Life*, 3248

Roszkiewicz, Ron. *The Woodturner's Companion*, 9286

Roth, Arlen. *Arlen Roth's Complete Acoustic Guitar*, 5941

Roth, David. *The Girl in the Grass*, 1257(F)

Roth, Geneen. *Feeding the Hungry Heart*, 5400

Roth, Henry. *Call It Sleep*, 909(F)

Roth, Philip. *Goodbye, Columbus*, 490(F)

Roth, Walton T. (jt. author). *Core Concepts in Health*, 5354

Rothchild, Sylvia. *Voices from the Holocaust*, 7283

Rothenberg, Michael B. (jt. author). *Baby and Child Care*, 5365

Rothenberg, Mira. *Children with Emerald Eyes*, 5401

Rothstein, Arthur. *Documentary Photography*, 9437

Rouché, Berton. *The Medical Detectives*, 5250

Rousmaniere, John. *The Annapolis Book of Seamanship*, 9935
The Sailing Lifestyle, 9936

Rousmaniere, John, ed. *The Enduring Great Lakes*, 4455

Rovin, Jeff. *The Encyclopedia of Monsters*, 9528
The Encyclopedia of Superheroes, 9529
A Pictorial History of Science Fiction Films, 6054
Starik, 237(F)

Rovit, Earl H. *Ernest Hemingway*, 3773

Rowe, Peter. *American Football*, 9862

Rowe, William W. *Leo Tolstoy*, 3643

Rowell, Trevor. *The Scramble for Africa*, 7359

Rowntree, Kathleen. *The Haunting of Willow Dasset*, 733(F)

Rowse, A. L. *Shakespeare the Man*, 6306

Royce, Kenneth. *Patriots*, 238(F)

Royko, Mike. *Sez Who? Sez Me*, 3547

Rozwenc, Edwin C., ed. *The Causes of the American Civil War*, 7933

Ruane, Pat. *LOGO Activites for the Computer*, 9012

Rubens, Bernice. *Madame Sousatzka*, 593(F)

Rubin, Barry (jt. author). *The Israel-Arab Reader*, 7600

Rubin, Louis D., Jr., ed. *An Apple for My Teacher*, 4634

Rubin, Theodore Isaac. *Lisa and David's Story*, 734(F)

Rubin, William, ed. *Pablo Picasso*, 5784

Rudel, Anthony J. *Tales from the Opera*, 5928

Rudloe, Jack. *The Living Dock*, 8775
Time of the Turtle, 8472

Rudner, Lawrence. *The Magic We Do Here*, 1675(F)

Rue, Nancy. *Coping with Dating Violence*, 5567
Row This Boat Ashore, 735(F)
Stop in the Name of Love, 2319(F)

Ruesch, Hans. *Top of the World*, 7705

Ruff, Matt. *Fool on the Hill*, 1258(F)

Rugoff, Milton. *America's Gilded Age*, 8019

Rumbaut, Rubén G. (jt. author). *Immigrant America*, 4336

Rush, Alison. *The Last of Danu's Children*, 1259(F)

Rusher, William A. *The Coming Battle for the Media*, 3969

Rushforth, Peter. *Kindergarten*, 594(F)

Rushton, Julian. *Classical Music*, 5838

Rusinko, Susan. *Tom Stoppard*, 3813
Russell, Alvin E. (jt. author). *Money*, 4579
Russell, Bertrand. *A History of Western Philosophy*, 4023
Russell, Diana E. H. *Lives of Courage*, 7383
Russell, Jeffrey B. *A History of Witchcraft*, 7071
Russell, O. Ruth. *Freedom to Die*, 5097
Russell, P. E. *Cervantes*, 3644
Russell, Percy (jt. author). *Nutrition and Health Encyclopedia*, 5428
Russell, Renny (jt. author). *On the Loose*, 4438
Russell, Terry. *On the Loose*, 4438
Russo, Jo Ann Oritt. *Careers without College*, 4863
Rust, Art, Jr. (jt. author). *Art Rust's Illustrated History of the Black Athlete*, 6710
Rust, Edna. *Art Rust's Illustrated History of the Black Athlete*, 6710
Rutherfurd, Edward. *Sarum*, 1467(F)
Ryan, Alan, ed. *Halloween Horrors*, 1830(F)
Haunting Women, 1831(F)
Ryan, Bob (jt. author). *Cousy on the Celtic Mystique*, 9717
Ryan, Conall. *House of Cards*, 910(F)
Ryan, Cornelius. *The Last Battle*, 7284
Ryan, Mildred Graves. *The Complete Encyclopedia of Stitchery*, 9250
Rycroft, Michael (jt. author). *Spacelab*, 8320
Ryden, Hope. *Lily Pond*, 8526
Rydjord, John. *Indian Place-Names*, 8154
Ryerson, Eric. *When Your Parent Drinks Too Much*, 5150
Ryna, Bob. *The Boston Celtics*, 9734
Rølvaag, O. E. *Giants in the Earth*, 1587(F)

Sabbagh, Karl. *Skyscraper*, 5710
Saberhagen, Fred. *Berserker*, 2763(F)
Berserker Man, 2763(F)
Berserker Throne, 2763(F)
Berserker's Planet, 2763(F)
Earth Descended, 2763(F)
The Fifth Book of Lost Swords, 1260(F)
The First Book of the Lost Swords, 1260(F)
The Fourth Book of the Lost Swords, 1260(F)
The Frankenstein Papers, 2764(F)
Mindsword's Story, 1261(F)
Pyramids, 1262(F)
Saberhagen, 2765(F)
The Second Book of the Lost Swords, 1260(F)
The Third Book of the Lost Swords, 1260(F)
Saberhagen, Fred (jt. author). *Coils*, 2870(F)
Sabini, John. *Islam*, 4080
Sabljak, Mark J. (jt. author). *Who's Who in the Super Bowls*, 9845
Sabloff, Jeremy A. *The Cities of Ancient Mexico*, 7649
Saccio, Peter. *Shakespeare's English Kings*, 3825
Sachar, Howard M. *Diaspora*, 7072
Sacharov, Al. *Offbeat Careers*, 4864

Sacker, Ira M. *Dying to Be Thin*, 5402
Sackett, Russell. *Edge of the Sea*, 8883
Sadat, Anwar. *In Search of Identity*, 6816
Sadeh, Pinhas, ed. *Jewish Folktales*, 3369
Safer, Morley. *Flashbacks*, 8138
Safir, Leonard (jt. author). *Words of Wisdom*, 3548
Safire, William. *Before the Fall*, 8088
Fumblerules, 3948
Safire, William, ed. *Words of Wisdom*, 3548
Sagan, Carl. *Broca's Brain*, 8232
Comet, 8333
Contact, 2766(F)
The Cosmic Connection, 8285
Cosmos, 8286
The Dragons of Eden, 5325
Sagan, Dorion. *Garden of Microbial Delights*, 8660
Sagan, Françoise. *Bonjour Tristesse*, 595(F)
Sagar, Keith, ed. *D. H. Lawrence Handbook*, 3686
Saha, Arthur W., ed. *The Year's Best Fantasy Stories*, 1263(F)
Sahadi, Lou (jt. author). *Say Hey*, 6727
Saikal, Amin. *Rise and Fall of the Shah*, 7623
Saint-Exupéry, Antoine de. *The Little Prince*, 2767(F)
Night Flight, 239(F)
Wind, Sand, and Stars, 9075
Sakai, Stan. *Usagi Yojimbo, Book One*, 1900(F)
Saki. *The Best of Saki*, 2958(F)
Salerno, Joseph. *The Plumber*, 4490
Sales, Grover. *Jazz*, 5897
Salewicz, Chris. *McCartney*, 6420
Salinger, J. D. *The Catcher in the Rye*, 1468(F)
Franny and Zooey, 596(F)
Nine Stories, 911(F)
Salinger, Margaretta. *Masterpieces of American Painting in the Metropolitan Museum of Art*, 5805
Salisbury, Harrison E. *The Long March*, 7425
The 900 Days, 7285
Tiananmen Diary, 7426
Salisbury, Harrison E., ed. *Vietnam Reconsidered*, 8139
Salmonson, Jessica Amanda. *The Swordswoman*, 2769(F)
What Did Miss Darrington See? 1833(F)
Salmonson, Jessica Amanda, ed. *Heroic Visions*, 2768(F)
Tales by Moonlight II, 1832(F)
Salmore, Barbara G. *Candidates, Parties, and Campaigns*, 4270
Salmore, Stephen A. (jt. author). *Candidates, Parties, and Campaigns*, 4270
Salny, Abbie. *The Mensa Think Smart Book*, 9471
Salsitz, R. A. *Where Dragons Lie*, 1264(F)
Salvino, Carmen. *Fast Lanes*, 9781
Salwak, Dale. *A. J. Cronin*, 3687

Salzberg, Charles. *From Set Shot to Slam Dunk*, 9735

Salzman, Mark. *Iron & Silk*, 7427

Sampson, George. *The Concise Cambridge History of English Literature*, 3602

Sams, Ferrol. *Run with the Horsemen*, 1630(F)

Samson, Jack. *Chennault*, 6580

Samuels, Gertrude. *Run, Shelley, Run!* 736(F)

Samuels, Harold (jt. author). *Frederic Remington*, 6204

Samuels, Mike. *Well Body, Well Earth*, 4456

Samuels, Peggy. *Frederic Remington*, 6204

Samuelson, Paul. *The Principles of Technical Analysis*, 4603

Samway, Patrick (jt. author). *A Modern Southern Reader*, 2916
Stories of the Modern South, 2917(F)

Sanberg, Paul R. *Prescription Narcotics*, 5151

Sandburg, Carl. *Abraham Lincoln*, 6549
Always the Young Strangers, 6301
The American Songbag, 5952
The Complete Poems of Carl Sandburg, 3322
Ever the Winds of Change, 6301
Honey and Salt, 3322
The People, Yes, 3322
Prairie-Town Boy, 6302
Rainbows Are Made, 3323

Sanders, Dori. *Clover*, 597(F)

Sanders, Scott Russell. *The Engineer of Beasts*, 2770(F)

Sanders, Toby. *How to Be a Compleat Clown*, 4897

Sandi, Michael. *Sports Illustrated Backpacking*, 9804

Sandmaier, Marian. *The Invisible Alcoholics*, 5152

Sandoz, Mari. *The Battle of the Little Bighorn*, 7978
Cheyenne Autumn, 7822

Sands, Bill. *Everybody's Gymnastics Book*, 9883
Modern Women's Gymnastics for Both Teacher and Gymnast, 9882
My Shadow Ran Fast, 4491

Sanford, John. *Observing the Constellations*, 8287
The Song of the Meadowlark, 1510(F)

Santiago, Danny. *Famous All Over Town*, 491(F)

Santmyer, Helen Hooven. *Farewell, Summer*, 598(F)

Santoli, Al. *Everything We Had*, 8140
New Americans, 4339
To Bear Any Burden, 8141

Santos, Jim. *Sports Illustrated Track*, 9976

Saposnik, Irving S. *Robert Louis Stevenson*, 3688

Sargent, Pamela. *Venus of Shadows*, 2771(F)

Sarnoff, Bob. *Cartoons and Comics*, 9212

Saroyan, William. *The Human Comedy*, 599(F)
The Man with the Heart in the Highlands & Other Early Stories, 2959(F)
My Name Is Aram, 492(F)

Sarrantonio, Al. *Moonbane*, 1834(F)

Sarrantonio, Al, ed. *Fireside Treasury of Great Humor*, 3511

Sartre, Jean Paul. *No Exit, and Three Other Plays*, 3017

Sassoon, Rosemary. *The Practical Guide to Calligraphy*, 9160

Sato, Hiroaki, ed. *From the Country of Eight Islands*, 3356

Satter, Robert. *Doing Justice*, 4253

Satterthwait, Walter. *Miss Lizzie*, 2168(F)

Saul, John. *Comes the Blind Fury*, 1835(F)
Creature, 1836(F)
Nathaniel, 1837(F)

Saunders, George, ed. *The October Revolution*, 7582

Saunders, Rubie. *Baby-Sitting for Fun and Profit*, 5071

Saunders, Vivien. *The Complete Book of Golf Practice*, 9877

Savage, Candace. *Wolves*, 8521

Savage, R. J. G. *Mammal Evolution*, 8458

Savage, William W. *The Cowboy Hero*, 7979

Savran, David. *In Their Own Words*, 3843

Sayen, Jamie. *Einstein in America*, 6662

Sayer, Ian. *America's Secret Army*, 4288

Sayers, Dorothy L. *Clouds of Witness*, 2170(F)
Five Red Herrings, 2170(F)
Lord Peter, 2169(F)
The Nine Tailors, 2170(F)
The Unpleasantness at the Bellona Club, 2170(F)

Sayers, Isabelle S. *Annie Oakley and Buffalo Bill's Wild West*, 6426

Sayre, Anne. *Rosalind Franklin and DNA*, 6669

Saywell, Shelley. *Women in War*, 7286

Scammell, Michael. *Solzhenitsyn*, 6310

Scarborough, Elizabeth Ann. *The Healer's War*, 1265(F)

Scarbrough, George. *A Summer Ago*, 600(F)

Scarne, John. *Scarne on Card Tricks*, 9400

Schaaf, Fred. *Seeing the Sky*, 8244
The Starry Room, 8288

Schaefer, Jack. *Shane*, 1588(F)

Schaefer, John. *New Sounds*, 5828

Schaeffer, Susan Fromberg. *Anya*, 7287
Buffalo Afternoon, 1703(F)

Schafer, R. C. *Opportunities in Chiropractic Health Care Careers*, 5002

Schaffer, Moselle. *Camel Lot*, 8776

Schaffner, Elizabeth (jt. author). *Five-Hundred-Five Rock and Roll Questions Your Friends Can't Answer*, 5898

Schaffner, Nicholas. *Five-Hundred-Five Rock and Roll Questions Your Friends Can't Answer*, 5898

Schama, Simon. *Citizens*, 7499

Schapiro, Meyer. *Paul Cézanne*, 6191
Van Gogh, 5785

Scharf, Lois. *Eleanor Roosevelt,* 6561

Schauer, Donald D. *Careers in Trucking,* 5053

Schechter, Bruce. *The Path of No Resistance,* 9040

Scheele, Adele. *Making College Pay Off,* 4762

Schefter, James L. *Aerospace Careers,* 5054
Telecommunications Careers, 4865

Schell, Jonathan. *The Fate of the Earth,* 4161

Scheurmann, Ines (jt. author). *Tropical Fish,* 8750

Schewel, Amy (jt. author). *The Actor's Book of Movie Monologues,* 6063

Schick, Ron. *The View from Space,* 8319

Schickel, Richard. *The Disney Version,* 6193

Schieber, Phyllis. *Strictly Personal,* 912(F)

Schiff, Stuart David, ed. *Whispers VI,* 1838(F)

Schimmel, David (jt. author). *The Rights of Students and Teachers,* 4298

Schimmel, Warren T. *Typing the Easy Way,* 4642

Schindler, George. *Magic with Everyday Objects,* 9401
Ventriloquism, 6106

Schinto, Jeanne, ed. *The Literary Dog,* 298(F)

Schirra, Walter M. *Schirra's Space,* 6159

Schlaich, Joan. *Dance,* 5973

Schleicher, Robert. *Building and Flying Model Aircraft,* 9404
The HO Model Railroading Handbook, 9405

Schlesinger, Arthur M., Jr. *The Age of Jackson,* 7882
The Imperial Presidency, 4211
Robert Kennedy and His Times, 6628

Schlesinger, Arthur M., Jr., ed. *The Almanac of American History,* 7775

Schlissel, Lillian. *Women's Diaries of the Westward Journey,* 7980

Schlissel, Lillian, et al. *Far from Home,* 7981

Schmidt, Harvey (jt. author). *The Fantasticks,* 3085

Schmidt, Stanley. *Tweedlioop,* 2772(F)

Schnabel, Tom. *Stolen Moments,* 5829

Schneider, Alan J. (jt. author). *Listen to Me, I'm Angry,* 5562

Schneider, Carl (jt. author). *Sound Off!* 4866

Schneider, Dorothy. *Sound Off!* 4866

Schneider, Joyce Anne. *Darkness Falls,* 2171(F)

Schneider, Meg. *I Wonder What College Is Like?* 4763
Romance! Can You Survive It? 5629

Schneider, Stephen H. *Global Warming,* 4439

Schneider, Zola Dincin. *Campus Visits and College Interviews,* 4764
Countdown to College, 4652

Schnell, Barry T. *The Teenage Parent's Child Support Guide,* 5491

Schnell, Donald E. *Carnivorous Plants of the United States and Canada,* 8445

Schoenbaum, S. *Shakespeare,* 3826
William Shakespeare, 6307

Schoenbaum, S. (jt. author). *A New Companion to Shakespeare Studies,* 3822

Schoenbrun, David. *America Inside Out,* 6303

Scholefield, Alan. *The Lost Giants,* 1589(F)

Scholes, Robert. *Science Fiction,* 3630

Schow, David J. *The Kill Riff,* 240(F)

Schow, David J., ed. *Silver Scream,* 1839(F)

Schraff, Anne E. *The Great Depression and the New Deal,* 8040

Schramm, David N. (jt. author). *From Quarks to the Cosmos,* 8266

Schrayer, Robert. *Opportunities in Insurance Careers,* 4933

Schreiber, Flora Rheta. *Sybil,* 5403

Schreiber, Rudolf L., et al., eds. *Save the Birds,* 8579

Schrier, Eric W., ed. *Newton at the Bat,* 9594

Schryver, Doug. *Sailing School,* 9937

Schuder, Pete (jt. author). *The Competitive Runner's Handbook,* 9910

Schudson, Michael. *Advertising, the Uneasy Persuasion,* 4620

Schulke, Flip. *King Remembered,* 6513

Schulke, Flip, ed. *Martin Luther King, Jr.* 6512

Schuller, Carol. *In the Shadow of His Wings,* 6948

Schullery, Paul. *The Bear Hunter's Century,* 6122

Schulman, L. M., ed. *The Random House Book of Sports Stories,* 2886(F)

Schulman, Michael, ed. *The Actor's Scenebook, Vol. 2,* 3116

Schultz, Bud. *It Did Happen Here,* 4318

Schultz, Duane. *The Doolittle Raid,* 7288

Schultz, James W. *Blackfeet Tales of Glacier National Park,* 3426
My Life as an Indian, 7823

Schultz, Ken. *The Complete Book of Freshwater Fishing,* 9833

Schultz, Leonard P. (jt. author). *Handbook of Tropical Aquarium Fishes,* 8748

Schultz, Ruth (jt. author). *It Did Happen Here,* 4318

Schultz, Ted, ed. *Fringes of Reason,* 9530

Schulz, David (jt. author). *The Illustrated Sports Record Book,* 9574

Schulze, Franz. *Mies van der Rohe,* 6461

Schumacher, Michael. *Creative Conversations,* 4698

Schuman, Nancy (jt. author). *Fast-Track Careers,* 4848

Schurfranz, Vivian. *Cassie,* 1519(F)
Danielle, 1519(F)
Josie, 1590(F)

Schurke, Paul. *Bering Bridge,* 7706

Schurke, Paul (jt. author). *North to the Pole,* 7708

Schutz, Benjamin M. *All the Old Bargains,* 737(F)

Schwab, Jim. *Raising Less Corn and More Hell,* 8591

Schwandt, Stephen. *Holding Steady*, 913(F)
A Risky Game, 914(F)
Schwartz, Barry. *George Washington*, 6574
Schwartz, Betty Ann, ed. *Great Ghost Stories*, 1840(F)
Schwartz, Brian. *China off the Beaten Track*, 7428
Schwartz, Delmore. *In Dreams Begin Responsibilities and Other Stories*, 493(F)
Schwartz, Howard. *Miriam's Tambourine*, 3370
Schwartz, Lester. *Career Finder*, 4867
Schwartz, Max. *Machines, Buildings, Weaponry of Biblical Times*, 7087
Schwartz, Susan, ed. *Moonsinger's Friends*, 1266(F)
Schwarz, Bart Andre. *The Last of the Just*, 494(F)
Schwarz, Ted. *Beginner's Guide to Stamp Collecting*, 9461
Schwarzenegger, Arnold. *Arnold's Bodybuilding for Men*, 9775
Encyclopedia of Modern Bodybuilding, 5361
Schweitzer, Darrell (jt. author). *Tales from the Spaceport Bar*, 2773(F)
Scithers, George H., ed. *Tales from the Spaceport Bar*, 2773(F)
Sclar, Deanna. *Auto Repair for Dummies*, 9110
Scodel, Ruth. *Sophocles*, 3805
Scoppettone, Sandra. *Playing Murder*, 2172(F)
Scortia, Thomas. *Blow-Out*, 241(F)
Scott, Alastair. *Tracks across Alaska*, 8188
Scott, Beth. *Haunted Heartland*, 9531
Scott, Dave. *Dave Scott's Triathlon Training*, 9595
Scott, David H. (jt. author). *Mene, Mene, Tekel*, 4099
Scott, Elaine. *Stocks and Bonds, Profits and Losses*, 4604
Scott, Elizabeth Warner (jt. author). *Getting Skilled, Getting Ahead*, 4806
Scott, Ernest. *Working in Wood*, 9287
Scott, John Anthony. *The Story of America*, 7776
Scott, Margaret. *A Visual History of Costume*, 5288
Scott, Melissa. *The Kindly Ones*, 2774(F)
Mighty Good Road, 2775(F)
Scott, Michael. *Irish Folk & Fairy Tales Omnibus*, 3410
Scott, Paul. *Staying On*, 993(F)
Scott, Peter (jt. author). *You & Your Dog*, 8739
Scott, R. C. *Blood Sport*, 1841(F)
Scott, Robert L. *The Day I Owned the Sky*, 6161
God Is My Co-Pilot, 7289
Scott, Ronald McNair. *Robert the Bruce, King of Scots*, 6871
Scott, Shirley L., ed. *Field Guide to the Birds of North America*, 8546
Scott, Virginia M. *Belonging*, 738(F)
Scranton, Robert L. *Greek Architecture*, 5786

Searles, Baird. *Films of Science Fiction and Fantasy*, 6055
Sears, Brad. *Last Chance Garage*, 9111
Sears, Stephen W. *Landscape Turned Red*, 7934
Seaver, Tom. *The Art of Pitching*, 9696
Sebestyen, Ouida. *The Girl in the Box*, 2173(F)
Words by Heart, 495(F)
Sedeen, Margaret, ed. *Great Rivers of the World*, 7073
Sedgwick, John. *The Peaceable Kingdom*, 8777
Seeger, Elizabeth. *Eastern Religions*, 4081
Seeger, Pete. *American Favorite Ballads*, 5953
Everybody Says Freedom, 4348
The Incomplete Folksinger, 5953
Seff, Nancy R. (jt. author). *Our Fascinating Earth*, 8403
Seff, Philip. *Our Fascinating Earth*, 8403
Segal, Erich. *Love Story*, 2320(F)
Segal, Harriet. *Shadow Mountain*, 601(F)
Segal, Lore. *The Book of Adam to Moses*, 4111
Segalini, Judith. *The One Day Plan for Jobhunters*, 4808
Segrave, Kerry (jt. author). *Women in Comedy*, 5956
Seib, Philip. *Who's in Charge?* 4271
Seide, Diane. *Careers in Health Services*, 5055
Nurse Power, 5003
Physician Power, 5004
Seiden, Henry M. (jt. author). *Silent Grief*, 5091
Seidensticker, Edward. *Tokyo Rising*, 7454
Seidler, Eric (jt. author). *Taking Freshwater Game Fish*, 9835
Seidler, Tor. *Terpin*, 915(F)
Seidman, Laurence Ivan. *Once in the Saddle*, 7982
Seitz, Clifford B. (jt. author). *Basic Mathematics Skills*, 8832
Self, Charles R. *Making Birdhouses and Feeders*, 9288
Making Fancy Birdhouses & Feeders, 9289
Selye, Hans. *The Stress of Life*, 5568
Stress without Distress, 5568
Sender, Ruth Minsky. *The Cage*, 7290
To Life, 6949
Senesh, Hannah. *Hannah Senesh—Her Life & Diary*, 6873
Senungetuk, Vivian. *A Place for Winter*, 7707
Seo, Hiroshi. *Boeing 747*, 9076
Serafini, Anthony. *Linus Pauling*, 6699
Serling, Carol, et al., eds. *Rod Serling's Night Gallery Reader*, 1842(F)
Serling, Robert J. (jt. author). *Countdown*, 6126
Serpell, James. *In the Company of Animals*, 8681
Serullaz, Maurice. *Velazquez*, 6208
Service, Robert. *The Best of Robert Service*, 3324
Collected Poems of Robert Service, 3325
Setlowe, Richard. *The Experiment*, 2776(F)
Seto, Judith Roberts. *The Young Actor's Workbook*, 6107

Settle, Mary Lee. *All the Brave Promises*, 7291

Seuling, Barbara. *How to Write a Children's Book and Get It Published*, 4898

Severn, Bill. *Bill Severn's Best Magic*, 9402

Sevillano, Mando. *The Hopi Way*, 3427

Sevy, Grace, ed. *The American Experience in Vietnam*, 8142

Sewall, Richard B., ed. *Emily Dickinson*, 3893

Seward, Linda. *The Complete Book of Patchwork, Quilting and Appliqué*, 9252
Small Quilting Projects, 9253

Sexton, Anne. *The Complete Poems*, 3326

Sexton, John. *How Free Are We?* 4203

Seymour, John. *Blueprint for a Green Planet*, 4440

Seymour, Richard D., et al. *Exploring Communications*, 8951

Shaara, Michael. *The Herald*, 242(F)
The Killer Angels, 1544(F)

Shaeffer, Claire B. *Sew a Beautiful Gift*, 9254

Shafer, D. Michael, ed. *The Legacy*, 8143

Shaffer, Paul R. (jt. author). *Rocks and Minerals*, 8830

Shaffer, Peter. *Amadeus*, 3117
Equus, 3118

Shakespeare, William. *The Complete Works of William Shakespeare*, 3052
Four Great Comedies, 3053
Four Great Tragedies, 3054
Hamlet, 3055
Macbeth, 3056
A Midsummer Night's Dream, 3057
Othello, 3058
Romeo and Juliet, 3059
Sonnets, 3222
The Sonnets, 3223

Shalit, Gene, ed. *Laughing Matters*, 3512

Shanahan, William F. *College—Yes or No*, 4809
Guide to Apprenticeship Programs, 4810

Shane, June Grant. *Programming for Microcomputers*, 9013

Shane, Scott. *Discovering Mount St. Helens!* 8189

Shange, Ntozake. *Betsey Brown*, 496(F)
For Colored Girls Who Have Considered Suicide/When the Rainbow Is Enuf, 3119

Shangold, Mona. *The Complete Sports Medicine Book for Women*, 5362

Shanks, Bernard. *This Land Is Your Land*, 4441
Wilderness Survival, 9805

Shanks, Bob. *The Cool Fire*, 6056

Shannon, Bob (jt. author). *Behind the Hits*, 5873

Shannon, David, ed. *The Great Depression*, 8041

Shannon, Doris. *Cain's Daughter*, 1545(F)

Shannon, George. *Unlived Affections*, 739(F)

Shannon, Ken (jt. author). *Sports Illustrated Track*, 9976

Shannon, Mike, ed. *The Best of Spitball*, 9697

Shapiro, Gilbert. *A Skeleton in the Darkroom*, 8233

Shapiro, James E. *Meditations from the Breakdown Lane*, 3549

Shapiro, Judith (jt. author). *Son of the Revolution*, 6812

Shapiro, Stanley Jay. *Exploring Careers in Science*, 5028

Shapland, David. *Spacelab*, 8320

Shatner, William. *Tekwar*, 2777(F)

Shattuck, Roger. *The Forbidden Experiment*, 5546

Shaughnessy, Dan. *Ever Green*, 9736

Shaw, Bob. *The Ragged Astronauts*, 2778(F)

Shaw, George Bernard. *Androcles and the Lion*, 3036
Arms and the Man, 3036
Caesar and Cleopatra, 3036
Major Barbara, 3036
Pygmalion, 3037
Saint Joan, 3038
Saint Joan, Major Barbara, Androcles and the Lion, 3039

Shaw, Irwin. *The Young Lions*, 1676(F)

Shaw, John (jt. author). *The Big Book of Painting Nature in Watercolor*, 9207

Shawcross, William. *Sideshow*, 7463

Shayler, David. *Shuttle Challenger*, 8321

Sheahan, Casey. *Sports Illustrated Cross-Country Skiing*, 9945

Shedd, Robert G. (jt. author). *Masters of Modern Drama*, 2978

Sheed, Wilfrid (jt. author). *The Kennedy Legacy*, 6537

Sheehan, Susan. *Is There No Place on Earth for Me?* 5404

Sheehy, Gail. *Spirit of Survival*, 6932

Sheffield, Charles. *Sight of Proteus*, 2779(F)
Summertide, 2780(F)

Sheldon, Roger. *Opportunities in Carpentry Careers*, 4944

Sheldon, Sidney. *The Naked Face*, 2174(F)

Shelley, Mary Wollstonecraft. *Frankenstein*, 379(F)

Shelley, Percy Bysshe. *The Poetical Works of Shelley*, 3224

Shelley, Purrey B. *Cat-a-Log*, 8703

Shelton, Mark L. *Working in a Very Small Place*, 6677

Shengold, Nina, ed. *The Actor's Book of Contemporary Stage Monologues*, 2988

Shenkman, Richard. *Legends, Lies, and Cherished Myths of American History*, 7777

Shepard, Jim. *Paper Doll*, 1677(F)

Shepard, Leslie, ed. *The Dracula Book of Great Horror Stories*, 1843(F)

Shepard, Sam. *A Lie of the Mind*, 3120

Shepherd, Jack (jt. author). *The Runner's Handbook*, 9911

Shepherd, Margaret. *Learning Calligraphy*, 9161
Using Calligraphy, 9161

Sheridan, Richard Brinsley. *The Rivals,* 3040
The School for Scandal, 3041
Sherman, Josepha. *The Shining Falcon,* 1267(F)
Sherman, Pecki. *Broken Heart Whole Heart,* 5153
Sherrill, John (jt. author). *The Hiding Place,* 7307
Sherwonit, Bill. *To the Top of Denali,* 9596
Sherwood, Martin, ed. *The Physical World,* 8404
Shestack, Melvin. *The Country Music Encyclopedia,* 5899
Shetterly, Will, ed. *Liavek,* 1268(F)
Shields, Brooke. *On Your Own,* 5289
Shields, Charles J. *The College Guide for Parents,* 4716
Shields, Rhea. *Opportunities in Home Economics Careers,* 4868
Shiels, Barbara. *Winners,* 6789
Shilts, Randy. *And the Band Played On,* 5219
Shipler, David K. *Russia,* 7583
Shipman, David. *A Pictorial History of Science Fiction Films,* 6057
Shipman, Harry L. *Humans in Space,* 8322
Shipton, Alyn. *Fats Waller,* 6454
Shirer, William L. *The Rise and Fall of the Third Reich,* 7507
Shirley, Glenn. *Belle Starr and Her Times,* 6638
Shirley, John. *Eclipse Corona,* 2781(F)
Shlain, Bruce. *Oddballs,* 9698
Shockley, Robert J. *Careers in Teaching,* 4954
Shoemaker, Bill. *Shoemaker,* 6781
Shoemaker, Hurst. *Fishes,* 8628
Shoemaker, M. Wesley. *The Soviet Union and Eastern Europe 1988,* 7584
Shohen, Saundra. *Emergency!* 5251
Sholokhov, Mikhail. *And Quiet Flows the Don,* 1469(F)
The Don Flows Home to the Sea, 1469(F)
Shreeve, James (jt. author). *Lucy's Child,* 7002
Shriver, Pam, et al. *Passing Shots,* 6772
Shropshire, Walter, ed. *The Joys of Research,* 8234
Shubin, Seymour. *Never Quite Dead,* 2175(F)
Shucard, Alan. *American Poetry,* 3894
Shucard, Alan, et al. *Modern American Poetry,* 3895
Shuker, Nancy. *Elizabeth Arden,* 6650
Shuker-Haines, Frances. *Everything You Need to Know about Date Rape,* 5517
Shuler, Linda Lay. *She Who Remembers,* 1511(F)
Shura, Mary Francis. *Diana,* 1591(F)
Shute, Nevil. *A Town Like Alice,* 1678(F)
Shuttle, Penelope. *The Wise Wound,* 5492
Shwartz, Susan (jt. author). *Imperial Lady,* 1240(F)
Sibley, Brian. *C.S. Lewis,* 6281
Sichrovsky, Peter. *Born Guilty,* 7292

Sicilia, David B. (jt. author). *The Entrepreneurs,* 4583
Sick, Gary. *All Fall Down,* 7624
Siddons, Anne Rivers. *The House Next Door,* 1844(F)
Sidel, Ruth. *On Her Own,* 4538
Women and Children Last, 4513
Siegal, Aranka. *Grace in the Wilderness,* 1679(F)
Upon the Head of a Goat, 1679(F)
Siegal, Mordecai. *Good Dog, Bad Dog,* 8736
The Good Dog Book, 8735
Siegel, Mary-Ellen (jt. author). *Finger Tips,* 5279
Siegel, Ronald K. *Intoxication,* 5154
Sienkiewicz, Henryk. *Quo Vadis,* 1375(F)
Sierra, Patricia. *A Boy I Never Knew,* 2176(F)
Sifakis, Carl. *The Dictionary of Historic Nicknames,* 3949
Sigel, Lois Savitch. *New Careers in Hospitals,* 5005
Silberman, Charles E. *A Certain People,* 4390
Criminal Violence, Criminal Justice, 4492
Silk, Mark. *Spiritual Politics,* 4082
Silko, Leslie Marmon. *Ceremony,* 497(F)
Sillitoe, Alan. *The Loneliness of the Long-Distance Runner,* 2960(F)
Sills, Beverly. *Bubbles,* 6441
Silone, Ignazio. *Bread and Wine,* 916(F)
Silsbee, Peter. *The Big Way Out,* 602(F)
Love Among the Hiccups, 1901(F)
Silva, David B. (jt. author). *Post Mortem,* 1816(F)
Silver, Cheryl Simon. *One Earth, One Future,* 4442
Silverberg, Robert. *At Winter's End,* 2783(F)
Dying Inside, 1269(F)
Lord Valentine's Castle, 2782(F)
Majipoor Chronicles, 2782(F)
The New Springtime, 2783(F)
The Secret Sharer, 2786(F)
Star of Gypsies, 2787(F)
Valentine Pontifex, 2782(F)
Silverberg, Robert (jt. author). *Nightfall,* 2387(F)
Silverberg, Robert, ed. *Robert Silverberg's Worlds of Wonder,* 2784
The Science Fiction Hall of Fame, 2785(F)
Silverberg, Robert, et al., eds. *Neanderthals,* 1355(F)
Silverman, Kenneth. *The Life and Times of Cotton Mather,* 6606
Silverman, Ruth, ed. *Athletes,* 9597
Silverstein, Alvin. *AIDS,* 5220
Alcoholism, 5155
Futurelife, 5252
World of the Brain, 5326
Silverstein, Herma. *Teen Guide to Single Parenting,* 5518
Teenage and Pregnant, 5493

Teenage Depression, 5405
Silverstein, Virginia B. (jt. author). *AIDS*, 5220
Alcoholism, 5155
Futurelife, 5252
World of the Brain, 5326
Simak, Clifford D. *All the Traps of Earth*, 1270(F)
The Fellowship of the Talisman, 1270(F)
Highway of Eternity, 2788(F)
Shakespeare's Planet, 2789(F)
The Visitors, 1270(F)
Way Station, 2790(F)
Where the Evil Dwells, 1270(F)
Simenon, Georges. *Maigret and the Killer*, 2177(F)
Simmie, Scott. *Tiananmen Square*, 7429
Simon, Henry W., ed. *A Treasury of Christmas Songs and Carols*, 5954
Simon, Neil. *Barefoot in the Park*, 3121
Biloxi Blues, 3122, 3123
Brighton Beach Memoirs, 3122, 3123
Broadway Bound, 3122, 3123
The Collected Plays of Neil Simon, 3124
The Collected Plays of Neil Simon, Volume I, 3125
The Odd Couple, 3125
They're Playing Our Song, 3126
Simon, Nissa. *Don't Worry, You're Normal*, 5630
Simon, Peter (jt. author). *Playing in the Band*, 5864
Reggae International, 5857
Simonides, Carol. *I'll Never Walk Alone*, 6951
Simons, Gerald. *Victory in Europe*, 7293
Simpson, Carolyn. *Coping with an Unplanned Pregnancy*, 5494
Simpson, Colin. *The Lusitania*, 7161
Simpson, Dorothy. *Element of Doubt*, 2178(F)
Simpson, Jacqueline. *European Mythology*, 3411
Simpson, Louis. *People Live Here*, 3327
Simpson, Marc, et al. *The American Canvas*, 5806
Simpson, Ross W. *The Fires of '88*, 8158
Sims, Patsy. *Can Somebody Shout Amen!* 4083
The Klan, 4349
Sinclair, Upton. *The Jungle*, 1614(F)
Siner, Howard, ed. *Sports Classics*, 9598
Singer, Isaac Bashevis. *The Collected Stories of Isaac Bashevis Singer*, 2961(F)
A Crown of Feathers, 498(F)
The Death of Methuselah, 499(F)
The Image and Other Stories, 500(F)
In My Father's Court, 1470(F)
The Manor, 1471(F)
The Penitent, 994(F)
Shosha, 1472(F)
The Slave, 740(F)
Singer, Marilyn. *The Course of True Love Never Did Run Smooth*, 917(F)
Storm Rising, 603(F)
Singer, Peter. *Hegel*, 6861
Marx, 6861
Singer Sewing Company. *Sewing Essentials*, 9255
Sewing for Style, 9255
Sinyard, Neil. *The Films of Woody Allen*, 6058
Siskin, Bernard, et al. *What Are the Chances?* 8859
Sitkoff, Harvard. *The Struggle for Black Equality, 1954–1980*, 4377
Sivananda Health Center. *The Sivananda Companion to Yoga*, 5363
Sivin, Carole. *Maskmaking*, 9218
Sivirine, Alexis (jt. author). *Jacques Cousteau's Calypso*, 8889
Sizer, Theodore R. *Horace's Compromise*, 4635
Sjoo, Monica. *The Great Cosmic Mother*, 4084
Sjowall, Maj. *The Laughing Policeman*, 2179(F)
The Locked Room, 2179(F)
Murder at the Savoy, 2179(F)
Skaggs, Peggy. *Kate Chopin*, 3774
Skal, David J. *Hollywood Gothic*, 6059
Skapura, Robert. *A Student's Guide to Research and Writing*, 4699
Skidmore, Thomas E. *Modern Latin America*, 7630
Skillion, Anne, ed. *Introducing the Great American Novel*, 3775
Skimin, Robert. *Gray Victory*, 1546(F)
Skinner, B. F. *About Behaviorism*, 5547
Skinner, Cornelia. *Madame Sarah*, 6373
Slappey, Mary McGowan. *Exploring Military Service for Women*, 4869
Slasitz, R. A. V. *Where Dragons Lie*, 1271(F)
Where Dragons Rule, 1271(F)
Slater, Cornelius. *An Apple a Day*, 6700
Slater, Peter J., ed. *The Encyclopedia of Animal Behavior*, 8480
Slater, Robert. *Portraits in Silicon*, 6646
Slatkin, Wendy. *Women Artists in History*, 5764
Slatta, Richard W. *Cowboys of the Americas*, 7684
Sleator, William. *Fingers*, 1845(F)
Sleight, Steve (jt. author). *Small Boat Sailing*, 9923
Slide, Anthony. *Fifty Classic British Films*, 6060
Fifty Great American Silent Films, 1912–1920, 6060
Sliwa, Lisa. *Attitude*, 5631
Sloan, Dave, ed. *Best Sports Stories*, 9599
Sloan, Irving J. *Youth and the Law*, 4254
Sloan, William. *The Craft of Writing*, 3970
Sloane, David E. *The Adventures of Huckleberry Finn*, 3776
Sloane, Eugene A. *The Complete Book of Bicycling*, 9765
Sloane, William. *The Edge of Running Water*, 2791(F)
Slonczewski, Joan. *A Door into Ocean*, 2792(F)
Smeed, Vic, ed. *Complete Railway Modelling*, 9406

Smerlas, Fred. *By a Nose*, 6761

Smirnoff, Yakov. *America on Six Rubles a Day*, 3513

Smith, Adam. *The Wealth of Nations*, 4582

Smith, Allan. *Teenage Moneymaking Guide*, 5068

Smith, Anthony. *Goodbye Gutenberg*, 3988
The Great Rift, 7364

Smith, Barbara Clark. *After the Revolution*, 7883

Smith, Betty. *Joy in the Morning*, 918(F)
Maggie Now, 918(F)
Tomorrow Will Be Better, 741(F)
A Tree Grows in Brooklyn, 1615(F)

Smith, Claire (jt. author). *Don Baylor*, 6714

Smith, Clark Ashton. *A Rendezvous in Averoigne*, 1846(F)

Smith, Danny. *Wallenberg*, 6879

Smith, Dave, ed. *The Morrow Anthology of Younger American Poets*, 3328

Smith, David. *Marx's Kapital* for Beginners, 4176

Smith, Dean Wesley. *Laying the Music to Rest*, 2793(F)

Smith, Dennis. *Firefighters*, 4976

Smith, Diane G. *American Filmmakers Today*, 6061

Smith, Dick. *Dick Smith's Do-It-Yourself Monster Make-Up Handbook*, 9219

Smith, Elsdon C. *New Dictionary of American Family Names*, 5673

Smith, Ernie. *Warm Hearts & Cold Noses*, 8737

Smith, Frederick (jt. author). *The Great Song Thesaurus*, 5947

Smith, Gene. *The Dark Summer*, 7294
High Crimes and Misdemeanors, 8020
Lee and Grant, 6490
When the Cheering Stopped, 6576

Smith, Hedrick. *The Russians*, 7585

Smith, Helen Crider (jt. author). *Memorable Dogs*, 299

Smith, Henry Nash, ed. *Mark Twain*, 3777

Smith, Hobart M. *Reptiles and Amphibians*, 8467
Reptiles of North America, 8466

Smith, Howard. *A Naturalist's Guide to the Year*, 8172

Smith, Huston. *The Religions of Man*, 4085

Smith, Jillyn. *Senses and Sensibilities*, 5333

Smith, Jimmy Neil. *Homespun*, 3441

Smith, Joe. *Off the Record*, 5900

Smith, John E. *The Spirit of American Philosophy*, 4024

Smith, Judie. *Coping with Suicide*, 5406

Smith, Julian. *Chaplin*, 6062

Smith, Julie. *Tourist Trap*, 2180(F)

Smith, Lacey Baldwin. *Elizabeth Tudor*, 6836

Smith, Lee. *Black Mountain Breakdown*, 742(F)
Fair and Tender Ladies, 604(F)

Smith, Lesley M., ed. *The Making of Britain*, 7533

Smith, Lucinda Irwin. *Women Who Write*, 3603

Smith, Manuel J. *When I Say No, I Feel Guilty*, 5569

Smith, Marie, ed. *Ms. Murder*, 2181(F)

Smith, Marisa, ed. *The Actor's Book of Movie Monologues*, 6063

Smith, Mark (jt. author). *America on Wheels*, 9080

Smith, Martin Cruz. *Gorky Park*, 1847(F)
Nightwing, 1847(F)

Smith, Mary-Ann Tirone. *The Book of Phoebe*, 919(F)

Smith, Nathan J. *Food for Sport*, 5427

Smith, Ozzie. *Wizard*, 6733

Smith, Page. *America Enters the World*, 8021
The Nation Comes of Age, 7884
A New Age Now Begins, 7859
Redeeming the Time, 8042
The Rise of Industrial America, 8022
The Shaping of America, 7860
Trial by Fire, 7935

Smith, Pauline C. *Brush Fire*, 243(F)

Smith, Peter H. (jt. author). *Modern Latin America*, 7630

Smith, Peter J. *Highlights of the Off Season*, 920(F)

Smith, Philip W. (jt. author). *Protecting the President*, 4224

Smith, Ray. *The Artist's Handbook*, 9213
How to Draw and Paint What You See, 9214

Smith, Rex Alan. *The Carving of Mount Rushmore*, 5807

Smith, Richard Norton. *An Uncommon Man*, 6531

Smith, Richard Norton, ed. *Farewell to the Chief*, 6491

Smith, Rita Pratt. *In the Forest at Midnight*, 2321(F)

Smith, Ronald D. *Fascinating People and Astounding Events from the History of the Western World*, 7074

Smith, Samuel. *Ideas of the Great Psychologists*, 5548

Smith, Stan. *W. H. Auden*, 3872

Smith, Steven P. *American Boys*, 1680(F)

Smith, Susan Rogerson. *Cheerleader-Baton Twirler*, 9600

Smith, Ursula (jt. author). *Food, Nutrition & You*, 5423
Women Who Changed Things, 6486

Smith, Wilbur. *Flight of the Falcon*, 2322(F)
A Time to Die, 244(F)

Smullyan, Raymond. *To Mock a Mockingbird*, 9468

Smyer, Richard I. *Animal Farm*, 3689

Snelling, Anne M. (jt. author). *Jobs!* 4870

Snelling, Robert O. *Jobs!* 4870
The Right Job, 4811

Snider, Dee. *Dee Snider's Teenage Survival Guide*, 5632

Snipes, Katherine. *Robert Penn Warren*, 3778

Snook, I. Donald. *Opportunities in Health and Medical Careers*, 5007

Opportunities in Hospital Administration Careers, 5006

Snow, C. P. *Two Cultures*, 8235

Snow, Edgar. *Red Star over China*, 7430

Snow, Theodore P. *The Cosmic Cycle*, 8289

Sobel, David (jt. author). *The Healing Rain*, 5320

Sobel, Robert. *The Entrepreneurs*, 4583

Sobin, Julian M. (jt. author). *Encyclopedia of China Today*, 7418

Socha, Laura O'Biso. *A Birdwatcher's Handbook*, 8547

Sohn, David A., ed. *Ten Top Stories*, 2963(F)

Solkoff, Joel. *The Politics of Food*, 8586

Solomon, Barbara H., ed. *American Families*, 921(F)

Solomon, Diane S. *Teaching Riding*, 8766

Solomon, Dorothy Allred. *In My Father's House*, 6952

Solomon, Jack. *The Signs of Our Times*, 5549

Solomon, Norman (jt. author). *Unreliable Sources*, 3986

Solomon, Susan (jt. author). *Romeo and Juliet*, 3050

Solorzano, Lucia. *Barron's 300 Best Buys in College Education*, 4765

Solt, Andrew. *Imagine*, 6417

Solzhenitsyn, Aleksandr. *The Gulag Archipelago, 1918–1956*, 7586

The Oak and the Calf, 6311

Solzhenitsyn, Alexander. *One Day in the Life of Ivan Denisovich*, 995(F)

Sombke, Laurence. *The Solution to Pollution*, 4443

Somers, Suzanne. *Keeping Secrets*, 6443

Sommer, Robin L. *Pablo Picasso*, 6203

Sondheim, Stephen. *Into the Woods*, 5929

Sone, Monica. *Nisei Daughter*, 6953

Sones, Melissa. *Getting into Fashion*, 4934

Soothill, Eric. *Wildfowl of the World*, 8557

Soper, Tony. *Oceans of Birds*, 8548

Soper, Tony (jt. author). *Owls*, 8565

Sophocles. *Antigone*, 3018

Electra, Antigone, Philoctetes, 3019

The Three Theban Plays, 3020

Sorine, Daniel S. *Dancershoes*, 5974

Sorine, Stephanie R. (jt. author). *Dancershoes*, 5974

Sorrell, Charles A. *Rocks and Minerals*, 8829

Soto, Gary. *Living Up the Street*, 6312

Small Faces, 6313

A Summer Life, 6314

Who Will Know Us? 3329

Soto, Gary, ed. *California Childhood*, 2964

South, Malcolm. *Mythical and Fabulous Creatures*, 3466

Southall, Ivan. *The Long Night Watch*, 245(F)

Southerland, Ellease. *Let the Lion Eat Straw*, 501(F)

Southern, Eileen. *The Music of Black Americans*, 5839

Southworth, Scott. *Exploring High Tech Careers*, 5056

Sowell, Thomas. *Choosing a College*, 4766

Marxism, 4177

Soyinka, Wole. *Ake*, 7390

Spangenburg, Ray. *Opening the Space Frontier*, 8323

Spann, Meno. *Franz Kafka*, 3645

Sparano, Vin T., ed. *Classic Hunting Tales*, 9834

The Greatest Hunting Stories Ever Told, 9834

Sparger, Rex. *The Bargain*, 1848(F)

The Doll, 1848(F)

Spark, Muriel. *The Abbess of Crewe*, 1902(F)

The Prime of Miss Jean Brodie, 922(F)

Sparks, Allister. *The Mind of South Africa*, 7384

Sparks, Christine. *The Elephant Man*, 1473(F)

Sparks, John. *Owls*, 8565

Spatz, Lois. *Aeschylus*, 3806

Spaulding, Jackie. *The Family Horse*, 8767

Specht, Robert (jt. author). *Tisha*, 6918

Spector, Ronald H. *Eagle against the Sun*, 7295

Speer, Albert. *Inside the Third Reich*, 7508

Spellenberg, Richard. *The Audubon Society Field Guide to North American Wildflowers*, 8446

Spence, Annette. *Exercise*, 5364

Stress & Mental Health, 5550

Spence, Gerry. *With Justice for None*, 4255

Spence, Jonathan D. *The Gate of Heavenly Peace*, 7431

The Search for Modern China, 7432

Spencer, Benjamin T., ed. *Memorable Dogs*, 299

Spencer, Colin. *The New Vegetarian*, 9359

Spencer, Donald D. *BASIC Programming*, 9015

Problem Solving with BASIC, 9014

Understanding Computers, 9015

What Computers Can Do, 9015

Spencer, Elizabeth. *Jack of Diamonds*, 2965(F)

Spencer, Jean. *Careers in Word Processing and Desktop Publishing*, 4935

Exploring Careers as a Computer Technician, 5057

Spencer, John, ed. *Phenomenon*, 9532

Spencer, Page. *White Silk and Black Tar*, 4444

Spencer, Robert F. *The Native Americans*, 7824

Spender, Stephen. *Collected Poems, 1928–1985*, 3225

Sperling, Abraham. *Mathematics Made Simple*, 8842

Spevack, Marvin. *The Harvard Concordance to Shakespeare*, 3827

Spielberg, Nathan. *Seven Ideas That Shook the Universe*, 8915

Spielman, Patricia (jt. author). *Scroll Saw Puzzle Patterns*, 9290

Spielman, Patrick. *Scroll Saw Puzzle Patterns,* 9290

Spiering, Frank. *Bearer of a Million Dreams,* 8173

Spikol, Art. *The Physalia Incident,* 2182(F)

Spinelli, Jerry. *Night of the Whale,* 246(F)

Spinrad, Norman. *Agent of Chaos,* 2794(F)

Spitz, Bob. *Dylan,* 6386

Spivack, Charlotte. *Ursula K. Le Guin,* 3779

Spock, Benjamin. *Baby and Child Care,* 5365

Spolin, Viola. *Improvisation for the Theatre,* 6108

Sporting News, ed. *Best Sport Stories,* 9601

Sports Illustrated, ed. *Sports Illustrated Bowling,* 9782

Sports Illustrated Handball, 9602

Sports Illustrated Safe Driving, 9112

Sports Illustrated Squash, 9603

Spradley, James P. (jt. author). *Deaf Like Me,* 5438

Spradley, Thomas S. *Deaf Like Me,* 5438

Spretnak, Charlene (jt. author). *Green Politics,* 7503

Springer, Nancy. *Chains of Gold,* 1272(F)

Godbond, 1273(F)

The Hex Witch of Seldom, 1274(F)

Madbond, 1275(F)

Springer, Victor G. *Sharks in Question,* 8631

Sprinkle, Patricia H. *Murder at Markham,* 2183(F)

Spry-Leverton, Peter. *Japan,* 7441

Spurgeon, Caroline F. E. *Shakespeare's Imagery and What It Tells Us,* 3828

St. George, Judith. *Do You See What I See?* 2167(F)

St. John, Bob. *Tex!* 6760

Stade, George, ed. *Six Modern British Novelists,* 3690

Stafford, Tim (jt. author). *Comeback,* 6718

Stafford, William. *A Glass Face in the Rain,* 3330

Stafford-Deitsch, Jeremy. *Shark,* 8632

Stahl, Barbara (jt. author). *How to Get into an Ivy League School,* 4750

Stair, Lila B. *Careers in Business,* 4936

Stajner, Karlo. *Seven Thousand Days in Siberia,* 6954

Stallworthy, Jon, ed. *A Book of Love Poetry,* 3175

First Lines, 3176

The Oxford Book of War Poetry, 3177

Stambler, Irwin. *Encyclopedia of Pop, Rock and Soul,* 5901

Off-Roading, 9619

Stamm, James R. *A Short History of Spanish Literature,* 3604

Stampp, Kenneth M. *The Peculiar Institution,* 4378

Stampp, Kenneth M., ed. *The Causes of the Civil War,* 7936

Stanislavski, Constantin. *An Actor Prepares,* 6109

Stanley, Carol. *High School Reunion,* 923(F)

Stanley, John. *Revenge of the Creature Features Movie Guide,* 6064

Stanton, Mary. *The Heavenly Horse from the Outermost West,* 1276(F)

Stanton, Maura. *The Country I Come From,* 924(F)

Tales of the Supernatural, 3896

Stanwood, Brooks. *The Glow,* 1849(F)

Stap, Don. *A Parrot without a Name,* 8549

Starkell, Don. *Paddle to the Amazon,* 9938

Starkey, David. *The Reign of Henry VIII,* 6844

Starr, Chester. *A History of the Ancient World,* 7088

Starr, Cynthia (jt. author). *We Have Come a Long Way,* 9968

Stasheff, Christopher. *Warlock Unlocked,* 1277(F)

Staten, Jay. *The Embattled Farmer,* 8587

Staten, Pat (jt. author). *The Embattled Farmer,* 8587

Stauth, Cameron. *The Franchise,* 9737

Stavsky, Lois. *The Place I Call Home,* 4514

Stead, Miriam. *Egyptian Life,* 7099

Steadman, David. *Galapagos,* 7685

Stearner, S. Phyllis. *Able Scientists—Disabled Persons,* 5029

Stebbins, Robert C. *A Field Guide to Western Reptiles and Amphibians,* 8468

Stebbins, Theodore E., ed. *Masterpiece Paintings from the Museum of Fine Arts, Boston,* 5765

Stedman, Raymond William. *Shadows of the Indian,* 4393

Steel, Danielle. *Daddy,* 605(F)

Message from Nam, 1704(F)

Now and Forever, 2323(F)

Once in a Lifetime, 2323(F)

Palomino, 2323(F)

The Promise, 2323(F)

The Ring, 2323(F)

Season of Passion, 2323(F)

Steel, David. *Mary Stuart's Scotland,* 6863

Steel, Judy (jt. author). *Mary Stuart's Scotland,* 6863

Steel, Rodney. *Sharks of the World,* 8633

Steel, Ronald. *Walter Lippmann and the American Century,* 6283

Steele, Max. *The Hat of My Mother,* 2966(F)

Steele, Phillip W. *Ozark Tales and Superstitions,* 3442

Steere, Michael. *Scott Hamilton,* 6776

Steffensen, James L., Jr., ed. *Great Scenes from the World Theater,* 2989

Stefoff, Rebecca. *Friendship and Love,* 5570

Steger, Wil. *North to the Pole,* 7708

Steger, Will. *Saving the Earth,* 4445

Stegner, Mary (jt. author). *Great American Short Stories,* 2967(F)

Stegner, Wallace. *Angle of Repose,* 606(F)
Stegner, Wallace, ed. *Great American Short Stories,* 2967(F)
Steichen, Edward. *The Family of Man,* 5723
Stein, Charles W., ed. *American Vaudeville as Seen by Its Contemporaries,* 6110
Stein, Gertrude. *The Autobiography of Alice B. Toklas,* 6316
Stein, Harry (jt. author). *Eichmann in My Hands,* 7249
Stein, Joseph. *Fiddler on the Roof,* 3127
Stein, Wendy. *Atlantis,* 9533
Steinbeck, John. *The Acts of King Arthur and His Noble Knights,* 3412
Cannery Row, 996(F)
East of Eden, 607(F)
The Grapes of Wrath, 1631(F)
Of Mice and Men, 1632(F)
The Pearl, 608(F)
The Portable Steinbeck, 419
The Red Pony, 300(F)
Sweet Thursday, 996(F)
Tortilla Flat, 997(F)
Travels with Charley, 7778
Steinberg, Margery. *Opportunities in Marketing Careers,* 4937
Steinberg, Milton. *Basic Judaism,* 4086
Steinberg, Rafael. *Island Fighting,* 7296
Return to the Philippines, 7297
Steinem, Gloria. *Outrageous Acts and Everyday Rebellions,* 4319
Steiner, Claude M. *Scripts People Live,* 5551
Steiner, Jean Francois. *Treblinka,* 7298
Steinhaus, Hugo. *One Hundred Problems in Elementary Mathematics,* 8843
Steinhoff, Johannes. *Voices from the Third Reich,* 7299
Steltzer, Ulli. *The New Americans,* 4340
Stendhal. *The Red and the Black,* 317(F)
Steneman, Shep. *Garfield,* 8704
Stephens, Mitchell. *A History of News,* 3971
Sterba, Gunther, ed. *The Aquarium Encyclopedia,* 8778
Sterling, Bruce, ed. *Mirrorshades,* 2795(F)
Sterling, Claire. *The Terror Network,* 4554
Sterling, Dorothy, ed. *We Are Your Sisters,* 7779
Stern, Jane. *Elvis World,* 6432
The Encyclopedia of Bad Taste, 9534
Sixties People, 8089
Stern, Madeleine, ed. *A Double Life,* 2184(F)
Stern, Michael (jt. author). *Elvis World,* 6432
The Encyclopedia of Bad Taste, 9534
Sixties People, 8089
Stern, Ron. *Law Enforcement Careers,* 4977
Sternberg, Janet, ed. *The Writer on Her Work,* 3972
Sternberg, Martin L. A. *American Sign Language,* 3902
Sternberg, Patricia. *Speak to Me,* 5585

Speak Up! 4700
Sterne, Laurence. *Tristram Shandy,* 380(F)
Stetson, Erlene, ed. *Black Sister,* 3331
Steussy, Marti. *Forest of the Night,* 1278(F)
Stevens, John D., ed. *Sharks,* 8634
Stevens, Paul Drew. *Real Animal Heroes,* 8682
Stevens, Stuart. *Malaria Dreams,* 7360
Stevens, Wallace. *The Collected Works of Wallace Stevens,* 3332
Stevenson, Paul R. *The American Civil War,* 7937
Cross a Wide River, 1592(F)
Stevenson, Robert Louis. *The Black Arrow,* 381(F)
Dr. Jekyll and Mr. Hyde, 382(F)
Kidnapped, 383(F)
Master of Ballantrae, 383(F)
The Strange Case of Dr. Jekyll and Mr. Hyde, 384(F)
Stevenson, William. *Intrepid's Last Case,* 7300
A Man Called Intrepid, 7300
Stevermer, Caroline (jt. author). *Sorcery and Cecilia,* 1339(F)
Stevick, Philip, ed. *The American Short Story, 1900–1945/1945–1980,* 3780
Stewart, Bob. *Macbeth,* 6856
Stewart, Bob (jt. author). *Warriors of Arthur,* 3462
Stewart, Edward. *Ballerina,* 743(F)
Stewart, Elinore Pruitt. *Letters of a Woman Homesteader,* 7983
Stewart, George R. *American Given Names,* 3950
American Place-Names, 7780
Earth Abides, 2796(F)
Stewart, Martha. *Martha Stewart's Christmas,* 4119
Stewart, Mary. *The Crystal Cave,* 1279(F)
The Hollow Hills, 1279(F)
The Last Enchantment, 1279(F)
Mary Stewart's Merlin Trilogy, 1279(F)
Thornyhold, 2185(F)
The Wicked Day, 1279(F)
Stewart, Stanley. *Flying the Big Jets,* 9077
Stidham, Ronald (jt. author). *The Federal Courts,* 4234
Stiffel, Frank. *The Tale of the Ring,* 7301
Stiles, Phyllis, ed. *Not Just Another Embroidery Book,* 9256
Stinchcomb, James D. *Opportunities in Law Enforcement and Criminal Justice,* 4978
Stine, Deborah. *Exploring Careers in Engineering,* 5030
Stine, G. Harry. *Handbook of Model Rocketry,* 9407
On the Frontiers of Science, 8245
Stine, R. L. *Blind Date,* 2186(F)
Stinson, Robert. *Lincoln Steffens,* 6315
Stirling, Jessica. *The Asking Price,* 609(F)

The Good Provider, 1474(F)
The Wise Child, 2324(F)
Stirling, S. M. *Marching through Georgia,*
    1280(F)
Stites, Francis N. *John Marshall,* 6605
Stobaugh, Robert, et al., eds. *Energy Future,*
    8919
Stockel, Martin T. (jt. author). *Auto Mechanics
    Fundamentals,* 9113
    Auto Service and Repair, 9114
Stockel, Martin W. *Auto Mechanics Fundamen-
    tals,* 9113
    Auto Service and Repair, 9114
Stockton, Frank. *The Lady or the Tiger and
    Other Stories,* 420(F)
Stoddard, Thomas B., et al. *The Rights of Gay
    People,* 4320
Stoker, Bram. *Dracula,* 1850(F)
Stokes, Donald. *The Bird Feeder Book,* 8551
    The Complete Birdhouse Book, 8552
    A Guide to Bird Behavior, 8550
    A Guide to Enjoying Wildflowers, 8447
    A Guide to the Behavior of Common Birds,
    8550
Stokes, Lillian (jt. author). *The Bird Feeder
    Book,* 8551
    The Complete Birdhouse Book, 8552
    A Guide to Enjoying Wildflowers, 8447
Stokes, Linda (jt. author). *Quilting for Begin-
    ners,* 9239
Stokesbury, James L. *A Short History of the Ko-
    rean War,* 8144
    A Short History of World War I, 7162
    A Short History of World War II, 7302
Stoler, Mark A. *George C. Marshall,* 6604
Stoll, Cliff. *The Cuckoo's Egg,* 9016
Stolzenberg, Mark. *Be a Clown!* 5981
Stone, Bruce. *Been Clever Forever,* 1903(F)
Stone, Irving. *Adversary in the House,* 1616(F)
    Clarence Darrow for the Defense, 6583
    Depths of Glory, 1475(F)
    The Greek Treasure, 1476(F)
    Love Is Eternal, 1547(F)
    Lust for Life, 1477(F)
    Men to Match My Mountains, 7984
    The Origin, 1478(F)
    The President's Lady, 1529(F)
    Those Who Love, 1616(F)
Stone, Jack. *You Don't Have to Be a Genius to
    Land a Computer Job,* 5058
Stone, Jerald B. (jt. author). *Celebrate the
    Bounty,* 9310
Stone, Nannette, et al. *Cocaine,* 5156
Stonehouse, Bernard. *Sea Mammals of the
    World,* 8656
Stones, Rosemary, ed. *More to Life Than Mr.
    Right,* 2968(F)
Stoppard, Tom. *On the Razzle,* 3042
    Rosencrantz and Guildenstern Are Dead, 3043

Storer, John H. *The Web of Life,* 8405
Storrer, William Allin. *Architecture of Frank
    Lloyd Wright,* 5705
Storti, Ed. *Crisis Intervention,* 5157
Story, Rosalyn M. *And So I Sing,* 6184
Stouffer, Marty. *Marty Stouffer's Wild America,*
    8580
Stover, Leon. *Harry Harrison,* 3781
    Robert A. Heinlein, 3782
Stover, Teresa S. (jt. author). *PC Care Manual,*
    9004
Stowe, Harriet Beecher. *Uncle Tom's Cabin,*
    1530(F)
Strachey, Lytton. *Elizabeth and Essex,* 6837
    Queen Victoria, 6877
Straczynski, J. Michael. *Othersyde,* 1851(F)
Strandemo, Steve. *Strategic Racquetball,* 9971
Strange, Ian J. *The Falklands,* 7686
Strasberg, Lee. *A Dream of Passion,* 6111
Strasberg, Lee, ed. *Famous American Plays of
    the 1950s,* 3128
Strasser, Todd. *Beyond the Reef,* 247(F)
    A Very Touchy Subject, 925(F)
Stratton, Joanne L. *Pioneer Women,* 7985
Straub, Peter. *Ghost Story,* 1852(F)
Straub, Peter (jt. author). *The Talisman,* 1173(F)
Straubing, Harold Elk, ed. *Civil War Eyewitness
    Reports,* 7938
Straughn, Charles T. *Lovejoy's College Guide for
    the Learning Disabled,* 4767
Straus, Murray A., et al. *Behind Closed Doors,*
    5674
Strauss, Linda L. *Coping When a Parent Has
    Cancer,* 5221
Stravinsky, John (jt. author). *Monkeys on the In-
    terstate and Other Tales from America's Fa-
    vorite Zookeeper,* 8773
Straw, Phyllis (jt. author). *The Woodturner's
    Companion,* 9286
Streader, Tim. *Create Your Own Stage Lighting,*
    6112
Streep, Peg (jt. author). *The Best-Ever Book of
    Dog & Cat Names,* 8672
Street, James, Jr. *The Struggle for Tennessee,*
    7939
Streiker, Lowell D. *Cults, the Continuing Threat,*
    4087
Stretton, Barbara. *You Never Lose,* 926(F)
Strickland, Bill, ed. *On Being a Writer,* 3605
Strieber, Whitley. *Billy,* 1853(F)
    Communion, 9535
    Nature's End, 2797(F)
    Warday, 2798(F)
    The Wolfen, 1854(F)
Strindberg, August. *The Father,* 3021
    Three Plays, 3022
Stromgren, Richard L. (jt. author). *Light and
    Shadows,* 5995
Stroup, Dorothy. *In the Autumn Wind,* 1681(F)

Strum, Shirley C. *Almost Human,* 8503
Strumpf, Michael. *Painless, Perfect Grammar,* 3951
Strunk, William, Jr. *The Elements of Style,* 4701
Stuart, Gene S. (jt. author). *The Mysterious Maya,* 7650
Stuart, George E. *The Mysterious Maya,* 7650
Stuart, Monroe (jt. author). *Mathematics Made Simple,* 8842
Stuart-Clark, Christopher (jt. author). *The Oxford Book of Christmas Poems,* 3165
Peace and War, 3166
Studio D. *Picture Puzzles for the Super Smart,* 8856
Stukane, Eileen (jt. author). *PMS,* 5476
Stultz, Russell Allen. *The Illustrated Word Processing Dictionary,* 9017
Sturgeon, Theodore. *The Dreaming Jewels,* 1281(F)
The Stars Are the Styx, 1281(F)
Venus Plus X, 1281(F)
Stwertka, Albert (jt. author). *Genetic Engineering,* 5266
Stwertka, Eve. *Genetic Engineering,* 5266
Styron, William. *The Confessions of Nat Turner,* 1531(F)
Lie Down in Darkness, 610(F)
Sophie's Choice, 998(F)
Sucher, Dorothy. *Dead Men Don't Give Seminars,* 2187(F)
Dead Men Don't Marry, 2187(F)
Suchlicki, Jaime. *Cuba,* 7665
Sugar, Bert. *Five-Hundred-Five Boxing Questions Your Friends Can't Answer,* 9787
Sullivan, Charles, ed. *America in Poetry,* 3333
Sullivan, Eleanor, ed. *Ellery Queen's Bad Scenes,* 2188(F)
More Murder on Cue, 2189(F)
Tales from Ellery Queen's Mystery Magazine, 2190(F)
Sullivan, Faith. *The Cape Ann,* 611(F)
Sullivan, George. *Ronald Reagan,* 6554
Strange but True Stories of World War II, 7303
Sullivan, Jack, ed. *The Penguin Encyclopedia of Horror and the Supernatural,* 3631
Sullivan, Peggy (jt. author). *Opportunities in Library and Information Science,* 4951
Sullivan, Tom. *If You Could See What I Hear,* 6955
Sullivan, William L. *Listening for Coyote,* 8190
Sumichrast, Michael. *Opportunities in Building Construction Trades,* 4899
Opportunities in Financial Careers, 4938
Summers, Harrison Boyd, et al. *How to Debate,* 4702
Summers, Harry G., Jr. *Vietnam War Almanac,* 8145
Summers, Kit. *Juggling with Finesse,* 9306
Sunquist, Fiona. *Tiger Moon,* 6162

Sunquist, Mel (jt. author). *Tiger Moon,* 6162
Sunset Books, eds. *Oriental Cookbook,* 9360
Sunstein, Emily W. *Mary Shelley,* 6308
Sussman, Alan (jt. author). *The Rights of Young People,* 4303
Sutcliff, Rosemary. *Blood Feud,* 1381(F)
Bonnie Dundee, 1479(F)
Sutherland, James, ed. *The Oxford Book of Literary Anecdotes,* 3691
Sutton, Ann. *Eastern Forests,* 8821
Wildlife of the Forests, 8822
Sutton, Caroline. *How Do They Do That?* 8952
Sutton, Christine (jt. author). *The Physical World,* 8404
Sutton, David (jt. author). *The Best Horror from Fantasy Tales,* 1773(F)
Sutton, Myron (jt. author). *Eastern Forests,* 8821
Wildlife of the Forests, 8822
Sutton, Peter C. (jt. author). *Masterpiece Paintings from the Museum of Fine Arts, Boston,* 5765
Suyin, Han. *The Enchantress,* 248(F)
Suzanne, Claudia, et al. *For Musicians Only,* 4900
Suzuki, David. *Genethics,* 5267
Svee, Gary D. *Incident at Pishkin Creek,* 249(F)
Swainbank, Todd, ed. *Taking Freshwater Game Fish,* 9835
Swaine, Michael (jt. author). *Fire in the Valley,* 8975
Swan, Catherine (jt. author). *The Dog in Your Life,* 8726
Swanberg, W. A. *Citizen Hearst,* 6590
Swann, Alan. *How to Understand and Use Design and Layout,* 3973
Swanson, Barbara M. *Careers in Health Care,* 5008
Swanson, Earl H., et al. *The Ancient Americas,* 7631
Swanson, James W., ed. *142 Ways to Make a Poem,* 3334
Swanwick, Michael. *In the Drift,* 2799(F)
Swarthout, Glendon. *Bless the Beasts and Children,* 927(F)
The Homesman, 1593(F)
Sweeney, Daniel. *Demystifying Compact Discs,* 9053
Sweetman, David. *Van Gogh,* 6195
Swendsen, David H. *Badge in the Wilderness,* 6163
Swenson, John. *Bill Haley,* 6396
Stevie Wonder, 6459
Swenson, John, ed. *The Rolling Stone Jazz Record Guide,* 5902
Swenson, John (jt. author). *The New Rolling Stone Record Guide,* 5888
Swift, David W. *SETI Pioneers,* 8324
Swift, Jonathan. *Gulliver's Travels,* 385(F)
Swigart, Rob. *Portal,* 1282(F)

Swindells, Robert. *Staying Up*, 928(F)

Swisher, Carl Brent. *Historic Decisions of the Supreme Court*, 4204

Swisher, Karin, ed. *The Elderly*, 5098

Swisher, Karin (jt. author). *China*, 7407
Social Justice, 4466

Swope, Irv (jt. author). *The Practical Fisherman*, 9832

Swope, Mary, ed. *American Classic*, 3178

Swope, Robert E. *Opportunities in Veterinary Medicine Careers*, 5009

Sylvander, Carolyn Wedin. *James Baldwin*, 3783

Symonds, Craig L. *Battlefield Atlas of the American Revolution*, 7940
A Battlefield Atlas of the Civil War, 7940

Symons, Julian. *Bloody Murder*, 3632
Conan Doyle, 6243
The Kentish Manor Murders, 2191(F)

Synder, Anne. *Goodbye, Paper Doll*, 744(F)

Synder, Gary. *The Practice of the Wild*, 3550

Synder, James. *Medieval Art*, 5766

Synder, Karen (jt. author). *Pesticide Alert*, 5421

Synder, Louis L., ed. *Fifty Major Documents of the 19th Century*, 7148

Synge, J. M. *The Playboy of the Western World*, 3044

Synge, Ursula. *Swan's Wing*, 1283(F)

Syrett, Netta. *Rose Cottingham*, 1480(F)

Szarkowski, John. *Photography Until Now*, 5724

Szulc, Tad. *Then and Now*, 7340

Szumski, Bonnie, ed. *Abortion*, 5519
America's Prisons, 4493
Criminal Justice, 4494
The Health Crisis, 5253
Latin America and U.S. Foreign Policy, 4163
Nuclear War, 4164
Terrorism, 4555

Szumski, Bonnie, eds (jt. author). *America's Future*, 8058

Szumski, Bonnie, et al., eds. *The Death Penalty*, 4495

Taintor, Jerry. *The Oral Report*, 5340

Taintor, Mary Jane (jt. author). *The Oral Report*, 5340

Takaki, Ronald. *Strangers from a Different Shore*, 4404

Talley, Rick (jt. author). *Some of My Best Friends Are Crazy*, 9665

Tambo, Oliver. *Preparing for Power*, 7385

Tames, Richard. *Nazi Germany*, 7509

Tangerman, Elmer J. *Complete Guide to Wood Carving*, 9291
Whittling and Woodcarving, 9292

Tanler, Bill, ed. *Ski Tech's Guide to Equipment, Skiwear, and Accessories*, 9946

Tanner, Janet. *Women and War*, 1682(F)

Tanner, Nancy Makepeace. *On Becoming Human*, 7012

Tanner, Ogden. *The Canadians*, 7636
The Ranchers, 7986

Tanquary, Tom (jt. author). *Video*, 6032

Tansey, Richard G. (jt. author). *Gardner's Art Through the Ages*, 5737

Taper, Bernard. *Balanchine*, 6362

Tapert, Annette. *The Brothers' War*, 7941

Tapert, Annette, ed. *Lines of Battle*, 7304

Tapley, Donald F., ed. *The Columbia University College of Physicians and Surgeons Complete Guide to Pregnancy*, 5495

Tapply, William G. *Death at Charity's Point*, 2192(F)

Tarr, Judith. *Alamut*, 1284(F)
Ars Magica, 1285(F)
The Dagger & the Cross, 1382(F)
A Fall of Princes, 1286(F)
The Golden Horn, 1288(F)
The Hall of the Mountain King, 1287(F)
The Hounds of God, 1288(F)
The Isle of Glass, 1288(F)
The Lady of Han-Gilen, 1289(F)

Tatchell, Judy. *Practical Things to Do with a Microcomputer*, 9018

Tate, Claudia, ed. *Black Women Writers at Work*, 6185

Tate, Elizabeth. *The North Light Illustrated Book of Painting Techniques*, 9215

Tateishi, John. *And Justice for All*, 7305

Taub, Eric. *Gaffers, Grips and Best Boys*, 6065

Taulbert, Clifton L. *Once Upon a Time When We Were Colored*, 6956

Taylor, A. J. P. *Bismarck*, 6828
The Second World War, 7306
The Struggle for Mastery in Europe, 7149

Taylor, C. L. (jt. author). *Chemical and Biological Warfare*, 4165

Taylor, David. *Next Panda Please!* 6701
The Ultimate Dog Book, 8738
You & Your Cat, 8705
You & Your Dog, 8739

Taylor, Diane (jt. author). *Conquering Athletic Injuries*, 5447
Coping with a Dysfunctional Family, 5675

Taylor, E. J. *Dollmaking*, 9263

Taylor, Joshua C. *Learning to Look*, 5725

Taylor, Kim (jt. author). *Your Cat's First Year*, 8690

Taylor, L. B. *Chemical and Biological Warfare*, 4165

Taylor, Paul. *Conquering Athletic Injuries*, 5447
Coping with a Dysfunctional Family, 5675
Private Domain, 6462
See How They Run, 4212

Taylor, Ron (jt. author). *Into the Newsroom*, 4901

Taylor, Stephen. *A Place of Your Own Making*, 9293

Taylor, Theodore W. *American Indian Policy*, 4394

Tchudi, Stephen (jt. author). *The Young Writer's Handbook*, 4703

Tchudi, Susan. *The Young Writer's Handbook*, 4703

Teale, Edwin Way. *Autumn across America*, 8406
Journey into Summer, 8406
North with the Spring, 8406
Wandering through Winter, 8406

Tebbel, John. *Opportunities in Newspaper Publishing Careers*, 4939
The Press and the Presidency, 4213

Tedlow, Richard S. *New and Improved*, 4621

Teel, Leonard Ray. *Into the Newsroom*, 4901

Tegner, Bruce. *Bruce Tegner's Complete Book of Jujitsu*, 9898
Bruce Tegner's Complete Book of Self-Defense, 9899
Judo, 9900
Karate, 9901
Self-Defense, 9902
Self-Defense & Assault Prevention for Girls & Women, 9903
Solo Forms of Karate, Tai Chi, Aikido & Kung Fu, 9904

Teitelbaum, Harry. *How to Write Book Reports*, 4704

Tekulsky, Mathew. *The Butterfly Garden*, 8611

Telander, Rick. *Heaven Is a Playground*, 9738
The Hundred Yard Lie, 9863

Teleja, Tad. *Foreignisms*, 3952

Temperley, Alan. *Murdo's War*, 250(F)

Tempest, John. *Vision of the Hunter*, 1356(F)

Temple, Robert. *The Genius of China*, 7433

Ten Boom, Corrie. *The Hiding Place*, 7307

Tennyson, Alfred. *The Poetical Works of Tennyson*, 3226

Tepper, Sheri S. *Dervish Daughter*, 1292(F)
The Flight of Mavin Manyshaped, 1290(F)
The Gate to Women's Country, 2800(F)
Grass, 2801(F)
Jinian Footseer, 1291(F)
Jinian Star-Eye, 1292(F)
King's Blood Four, 1294(F)
Marianne, the Magus, and the Manticore, 1293(F)
Northshore, 2802(F)
The Search for Mavin Manyshaped, 1294(F)
The Song of Mavin Manyshaped, 1294(F)
Southshore, 2802(F)

Terdoslavich, William. *The Civil War Trivia Quiz Book*, 7942

Teresa, Mother. *My Life for the Poor*, 6958
Words to Love By, 4088

Teresi, Dick (jt. author). *The Three-Pound Universe*, 5315

Terkel, Studs. *American Dreams*, 8090
Giants of Jazz, 6186

"The Good War," 7308
The Great Divide, 8091
Hard Times, 8043
Working, 4611

Terman, Douglas. *Free Flight*, 2803(F)

Terrace, Herbert S. *Nim*, 8504

Terras, Victor, ed. *Handbook of Russian Literature*, 3606

Terrill, Ross. *The Australians*, 7477
Mao, 6814

Terris, Susan. *Nell's Quilt*, 745(F)
Wings and Roots, 746(F)

Terry, Wallace, ed. *Bloods*, 8146

Teruzzi, Giorgio (jt. author). *Simon & Schuster's Guide to Fossils*, 6973

Tessendorf, K. C. *Along the Road to Soweto*, 7386
Kill the Tsar, 7587

Tevis, Walter. *The Man Who Fell to Earth*, 2804(F)
The Queen's Gambit, 929(F)

Tey, Josephine. *Brat Farrar*, 2193(F)
The Daughter of Time, 2193(F)
Miss Pym Disposes, 2193(F)
Singing Sands, 2193(F)

Thackeray, William Makepeace. *Vanity Fair*, 386(F)

Thapar, Valmik. *Tiger*, 8511

Thayer, J. S. *Ringer*, 251(F)

Theodore, Alan. *The Origins & Sources of Drugs*, 5158

Theroux, Paul. *The Mosquito Coast*, 252(F)

Thom, Mary, ed. *Letters to Ms. Magazine*, 4539

Thomas, Benjamin P. *Abraham Lincoln*, 6550

Thomas, Craig. *Winter Hawk*, 253(F)

Thomas, David A. *Math Projects for Young Scientists*, 8857

Thomas, Donald. *Jekyll, Alias Hyde*, 2194(F)

Thomas, Dylan. *A Child's Christmas in Wales*, 3227
The Collected Poems of Dylan Thomas, 3228
The Poems of Dylan Thomas, 3229
Under Milk Wood, 3129

Thomas, Elizabeth Marshall. *The Animal Wife*, 1357(F)

Thomas, Gordon. *Enola Gay*, 7309

Thomas, Hugh. *The Spanish Civil War*, 7561

Thomas, Joyce Carol. *Bright Shadow*, 930(F)
Marked by Fire, 747(F)
Water Girl, 502(F)

Thomas, Lewis. *The Lives of a Cell*, 8407
The Medusa and the Snail, 8408
The Youngest Science, 6702

Thomas, Martha Lou. *Waltz with a Stranger*, 2325(F)

Thomas, Nigel (jt. author). *BMX Action Bike Book*, 9754

Thomas, Ronald R. *Understanding Telecommunications*, 9045

Thomas, Ross. *Out on the Rim*, 254(F)

Thomas, Terry. *Create Your Own Stage Sets*, 6113

Thompson, Ernest. *On Golden Pond*, 3130

Thompson, George L. *Rubber Stamps and How to Make Them*, 9151

Thompson, Gerald. *The Pond*, 8620

Thompson, Ida. *The Audubon Society Field Guide to North American Fossils*, 6986

Thompson, Julian. *A Band of Angels*, 255(F)
  Discontinued, 2195(F)
  Goofbang Value Daze, 2805(F)
  The Grounding of Group Six, 256(F)
  Herb Seasoning, 1904(F)
  Simon Pure, 1905(F)
  The Taking of Mariasburg, 257(F)

Thompson, Kathleen (jt. author). *Against Rape*, 4485

Thompson, Lawrence. *Robert Frost*, 6248

Thompson, Richard F. *The Brain*, 5327

Thompson, Thomas. *Richie*, 612(F)

Thompson, W. R. *Sideshow*, 2806(F)

Thompson, Wayne C. *Canada 1988*, 7637

Thoreau, Henry David. *Walden*, 3551

Thorn, John. *The Game for All America*, 9701

Thorn, John, ed. *The Armchair Book of Baseball*, 9699
  The Armchair Book of Baseball II, 9700

Thorn, John, et al., eds. *The Whole Baseball Catalogue*, 9702

Thornton, Louise (jt. author). *I Never Told Anyone*, 5500

Thorp, Raymond. *Crow Killer*, 1594(F)

Thorpe, Edward. *Black Dance*, 5975

Thro, Ellen. *Robotics Careers*, 5059

Thubron, Colin. *The Ancient Mariners*, 7089
  Behind the Wall, 7434

Thurber, James. *My Life and Hard Times*, 6318
  The Thurber Carnival, 3514

Thurow, Lester C. (jt. author). *Economics Explained*, 4571

Thwaite, Anthony. *Six Centuries of Verse*, 3873

Thwaite, Anthony, ed. *Philip Larkin*, 3230

Tibbets, Paul W., Jr. *The Tibbets Story*, 6959

Tiede, Tom. *American Tapestry*, 7781

Time-Life Books, eds. *Across the Rhine*, 7310
  Alternate Computers, 9020
  Artificial Intelligence, 9019
  Australia, 7478
  Basic Writing, 9041
  The Battle of the Atlantic, 7310
  The Battle of the Bulge, 7310
  Beef and Veal, 9361
  The Blockade, 7943
  The Book of Christmas, 4120
  Brazil, 7687
  Breads, 9362
  Britain, 7534
  Cakes, 9362
  Canada, 7638
  Candy, 9362
  China, 7435
  The Chipmakers, 9020
  Christmas in America, 4120
  The Chroniclers, 7987
  Computer Basics, 9020
  Computer Images, 9021
  Computer Languages, 9021
  Computer Security, 9021
  The Computerized Society, 9020
  Computers and the Cosmos, 9020
  Cookies and Crackers, 9362
  The Cowboys, 7988
  Dragons, 3371
  Dwarfs, 3371
  East Africa, 7365
  Eggs and Cheese, 9364
  Fairies and Elves, 3372
  Fish, 9361
  France, 7500
  Fruits, 9363
  The Gamblers, 7989
  Germany, 7510
  Ghosts, 9536
  Giants and Ogres, 3371
  The Gods, 3372
  Grasslands and Tundra, 8823
  Great Battles of the Civil War, 7944
  Home Front, 7310
  The Home Workshop, 9392
  How Things Work in Your Home, 9043
  India, 7442
  Input-Output, 9021
  Israel, 7616
  The Italian Campaign, 7310
  Italy, 7550
  Japan, 7455
  Japan at War, 7311
  Lamb, 9361
  Lee Takes Command, 7945
  Life Goes to the Movies, 6066
  Life in Space, 8325
  The Loggers, 8430
  Lore of Love, 9536
  Magical Beasts, 3373
  Magical Justice, 3373
  Memory and Storage, 9019
  The Military Frontier, 9019
  The Miners, 7990
  Night Creatures, 3374
  Outdoor Cooking, 9363
  Pasta, 9363
  The Personal Computer, 9020
  Pies and Pastries, 9362
  Pork, 9361
  Poultry, 9361
  The Railroaders, 7991
  Robotics, 9019

Salads, 9364
Sauces, 9364
Scandinavia, 7553
The Secret Arts, 9536
Seekers and Saviors, 3374
Shellfish, 9361
The Shenandoah in Flames, 7943
Software, 9021
The Software Challenge, 9019
Soups, 9365
Southeast Asia, 7394
The Soviet Union, 7588
Spain, 7562
The Spanish West, 7992
Spells and Bindings, 3375
Spies, Scouts, and Raiders, 7946
Tales of Terror, 9536
The Texans, 7993
This Fabulous Century, 7782
Time-Life Complete Fix-It-Yourself Manual, 9307
Time-Life Complete Home Repair Manual, 9308
The Trailblazers, 7994
Understanding Computers, 9022
The United States, 7783
Vegetables, 9363
Volcano, 8807
War on the Frontier, 7943
War on the Mississippi, 7943
A War Remembered, 8147
Water Spirits, 3371
The Women, 7995
Working with Metal, 9152
Working with Wood, 9294
WW II, 7312
Timerman, Jacobo. *The Longest War,* 7617
Prisoner without a Name, Cell without a Number, 7688
Tindall, George Brown. *America,* 7784
Tingay, Graham I. F. *These Were the Romans,* 7119
Tinkle, Lon. *The Alamo,* 7996
Tiptree, James, Jr. *Brightness Falls from the Air,* 2807(F)
Tales of the Quintana Roo, 1855(F)
Tiulana, Paul (jt. author). *A Place for Winter,* 7707
Tobias, Sheila. *Overcoming Math Anxiety,* 8844
Succeed with Math, 8845
Tobler, John. *The Guitar Greats,* 6187
Toboldt, Bill. *Auto Body Repairing and Repainting,* 9115
Diesel, 9044
Toboldt, Bill, et al., eds. *Goodheart-Willcox Automotive Encyclopedia,* 9116
Tocci, Salvatore. *Biology Projects for Young Scientists,* 8246
Todd, Alden. *Finding Facts Fast,* 4653

Todd, Leonard. *Squaring Off,* 931(F)
Todd, W. Duane (jt. author). *The Columbia University College of Physicians and Surgeons Complete Guide to Pregnancy,* 5495
Toffler, Alvin. *Future Shock,* 4419
Powershift, 7342
The Third Wave, 4419
Toghill, Jeff. *Sailing for Beginners,* 9939
Tolan, Stephanie S. *Plague Year,* 932(F)
Toland, John. *Adolf Hitler,* 6849
The Last 100 Days, 7313
No Man's Land, 7163
Tolbert-Rouchaleau, Jane. *James Weldon Johnson,* 6272
Tolhurst, Desmond (jt. author). *Johnny Miller's Golf for Juniors,* 9872
Tolkien, J. R. R. *Fellowship of the Ring,* 2808(F)
The Hobbit, 1295(F)
The Lord of the Rings, 1296(F)
Return of the King, 2808(F)
The Shaping of Middle-Earth, 3692
The Silmarillion, 1297(F)
Sir Gawain and the Green Knight, 3413
The Two Towers, 2808(F)
Unfinished Tales of Númenor and Middle-Earth, 1298(F)
Tolstoy, Leo. *Anna Karenina,* 318(F)
The Death of Ivan Ilyitch, 319(F)
Great Short Works of Leo Tolstoy, 320(F)
The Portable Tolstoy, 321
War and Peace, 322(F)
Tomalin, Stefany. *Beads!* 9153
Tomlinson, Charles, ed. *The Oxford Book of Verse in English Translation,* 3179
Tong, Hsin-Min, ed. *Learning from Forty Inspiring Business Successes,* 4584
Tongren, Sally. *To Keep Them Alive,* 8779
Toomer, Jean. *Cane,* 503(F)
Torbet, Laura (jt. author). *Intangible Evidence,* 9500
Tortora, Phyllis. *A Survey of Historic Costume,* 5290
Touponce, William F. *Frank Herbert,* 3784
Tourtellot, Jonathan B., ed. *Discovering Britain and Ireland,* 7535
Tower, Cynthia Crosson. *Secret Scars,* 5520
Towle, Alexandra, ed. *Mothers,* 5676
Towns, Saundra. *Lillian Hellman,* 6257
Townsend, Andy (jt. author). *Hard Disk Management with MS-DOS and PC-DOS,* 8980
Townsend, Charles B. *The World's Most Challenging Puzzles,* 9469
Townsend, Guy M. *To Prove a Villain,* 1481(F)
Townsend, John Rowe. *Downstream,* 613(F)
Townsend, Sue. *The Secret Diary of Adrian Mole, Age Thirteen and Three Quarters,* 1906(F)
Toynbee, Arnold. *The Greeks and Their Heritages,* 7545

A Study of History, 7076
Trachtman, Paul. *The Gunfighters,* 7997
Tracton, Ken. *The BASIC Cookbook,* 9023
Tracy, Lisa. *The Gradual Vegetarian,* 9366
Trager, Oliver, ed. *The Iran-Contra Arms Scandal,* 4166
Trainer, Jennifer (jt. author). *Nuclear Power,* 8923
Trainor, Timothy N. *Computer Concepts and Applications,* 9024
Traister, John E. *Encyclopedic Dictionary of Electronic Terms,* 9042
Traister, Robert J. (jt. author). *Encyclopedic Dictionary of Electronic Terms,* 9042
Traub, James. *India,* 7443
Trauth, Suzanne (jt. author). *On Stage,* 5926
Traven, B. *The Treasure of the Sierra Madre,* 258(F)
Traynor, William. *Opportunities in Human Resources Management Careers,* 4979
Treat, Lawrence. *You're the Detective!* 9470
Trebek, Alex. *The Jeopardy! Book,* 6067
Trefil, James. *The Dark Side of the Universe,* 8371
  Meditations at 10,000 Feet, 8790
  Scientist at the Seashore, 8884
  Space, Time, Infinity, 8290
Tregear, Mary. *Chinese Art,* 5768
Treherne, John. *The Strange History of Bonnie and Clyde,* 6617
Trenhaile, John. *A View from the Square,* 259(F)
Trepp, Leo. *The Complete Book of Jewish Observance,* 4121
Trevelyan, George Macaulay. *The English Revolution, 1688–1689,* 7536
Trevor, Elleston. *Deathwatch,* 260(F)
  The Theta Syndrome, 1856(F)
Trevor, William. *Fools of Fortune,* 1482(F)
Trevor, William, ed. *The Oxford Book of Irish Short Stories,* 2969(F)
Trew, Antony. *Yashimoto's Last Dive,* 1683(F)
Tribe, Laurence H. *Abortion,* 5521
Trollope, Anthony. *Barchester Towers,* 387(F)
  Doctor Thorne, 387(F)
  The Warden, 387(F)
Troupe, Quincy, ed. *James Baldwin,* 3607
Troy, Stuart (jt. author). *The Nobel Reader,* 2910
Troyat, Henri. *Catherine the Great,* 6833
  Ivan the Terrible, 6850
  Peter the Great, 6869
True, Dan. *Flying Free,* 8562
Trull, Patti. *On with My Life,* 6960
Truman, Harry S. *The Autobiography of Harry S. Truman,* 6570
Truman, Margaret. *Bess W. Truman,* 6566
  Harry S. Truman, 6571
  Murder at the FBI, 2196(F)
  Murder at the Kennedy Center, 2197(F)
  Murder at the National Cathedral, 2198(F)
Murder in Georgetown, 2199(F)
Murder in the Smithsonian, 2200(F)
Murder in the Supreme Court, 2200(F)
Murder in the White House, 2200(F)
Murder on Capitol Hill, 2201(F)
Murder on Embassy Row, 2201(F)
Tryon, Thomas. *Harvest Home,* 1857(F)
  The Night of the Moonbow, 261(F)
  The Other, 1858(F)
Tuchman, Barbara W. *A Distant Mirror,* 7140
  The Guns of August, 7164
  The March of Folly, 7077
  Practicing History, 7078
  The Proud Tower, 7155
  Stilwell and the American Experience in China, 1911–45, 4167
  The Zimmerman Telegram, 7165
Tucker, Bruce (jt. author). *James Brown,* 6376
Tucker, Karen (jt. author). *The Dark Matter,* 8291
Tucker, Wallace. *The Dark Matter,* 8291
Tucker, William. *The Excluded Americans,* 4515
Tuleja, Tad. *Curious Customs,* 4541
Tullis, John. *I'd Rather Be a Yankee,* 9703
Tullius, John (jt. author). *Total Tennis,* 9965
Tully, Shawn (jt. author). *Sports Illustrated Tennis,* 9970
Tunis, Edwin. *Colonial Craftsmen and the Beginnings of American Industry,* 7845
  Colonial Living, 7846
  Frontier Living, 7998
  The Young United States, 1783 to 1830, 7861
Turabian, Kate L. *A Manual for Writers of Term Papers, Theses, and Dissertations,* 4705
Turgenev, Ivan. *Fathers and Sons,* 323(F)
Turki, Fawaz. *Soul in Exile,* 6818
Turkle, Sherry. *The Second Self,* 9025
Turnbull, Stephen. *The Book of the Medieval Knight,* 7141
Turner, Ann. *Third Girl from the Left,* 1595(F)
Turner, Arlin. *Nathaniel Hawthorne,* 6254
Turner, David R. *Practice for the Armed Forces Tests,* 4980
Turner, Ed. *Skills & Strategies for Winning Racquetball,* 9972
Turner, Frederick Jackson. *The Frontier in American History,* 7999
Turner, Frederick W. III, ed. *The Portable North American Indian Reader,* 3428
Turner, Myles. *My Serengeti Years,* 6164
Turner, Ruth S. (jt. author). *Soweto, My Love,* 6799
Turner, Tina. *I, Tina,* 6450
Turner, Tony. *All That Glittered,* 5903
Turnley, David. *Beijing Spring,* 7436
  Why Are They Weeping? 7387
Turnley, Peter (jt. author). *Beijing Spring,* 7436
Turow, Scott. *One L,* 4981
Tuttle, Lisa (jt. author). *Windhaven,* 1214(F)

738

Tuttle, Merlin D. *America's Neighborhood Bats,* 8527

Tver, David F. *Nutrition and Health Encyclopedia,* 5428

Twain, Mark. *The Adventures of Huckleberry Finn,* 421(F)
The Adventures of Tom Sawyer, 422(F)
The Complete Essays of Mark Twain, 3552
The Complete Short Stories of Mark Twain, 423(F)
A Connecticut Yankee in King Arthur's Court, 424(F)
The Innocents Abroad, 3515
Life on the Mississippi, 3516
Mark Twain Speaks for Himself, 3553
The Mysterious Stranger and Other Stories, 425(F)
A Pen Warmed-Up in Hell, 3554
The Prince and the Pauper, 426(F)
Pudd'nhead Wilson, 427(F)
Roughing It, 3517
The Science Fiction of Mark Twain, 428(F)
Tom Sawyer Abroad and Tom Sawyer, Detective, 429(F)

Tweed, Jason C. (jt. author). *Colleges That Enable,* 4768

Tweed, Prudence K. *Colleges That Enable,* 4768

Twelveponies, Mary. *There Are No Problem Horses—Only Problem Riders,* 8768

Twombly, Robert C. *Frank Lloyd Wright,* 6211

Tygiel, Jules. *Baseball's Great Experiment,* 9704

Tyler, Anne. *Breathing Lessons,* 933(F)
Dinner at the Homesick Restaurant, 614(F)
If Morning Ever Comes, 933(F)
A Slipping-Down Life, 933(F)

Tyler, Dick (jt. author). *Weight Training and Body Building for Young Athletes,* 9769

Tyler, Royall, ed. *Japanese Tales,* 3386

Tyler, Vicky. *Danny and the Real Me,* 2326(F)

Tyndall, Carolyn, et al. *And the Lucky Winner Is . . . ,* 9537

Tyson, Neil De Grasse. *Merlin's Tour of the Universe,* 8292

Uchida, Yoshiko. *Desert Exile,* 6963

Uecker, Bob. *Catcher in the Wry,* 9705

Ullman, E. (jt. author). *Poodles,* 8740

Ullman, H. J. *Poodles,* 8740

Ullyot, Joan L. *Running Free,* 9916

Underhill, Ruth M. *The Navajos,* 7825

Underwood, John (jt. author). *The Science of Hitting,* 9707

Underwood, Tim, ed. *Kingdom of Fear,* 3785

Undset, Sigrid. *Kristin Lavransdatter,* 1383(F)

Ungar, Harlow G. *A Student's Guide to College Admissions,* 4769

Ungar, Sanford J. *Africa,* 7361

Unger, Debi (jt. author). *Turning Point,* 8092

Unger, Irwin. *Turning Point,* 8092

United Nations Dept. of Public Information. *Everyone's United Nations,* 4124

United States Golf Assn. *Golf Rules in Pictures,* 9878

Updike, David. *Out on the Marsh,* 934(F)

Updike, John. *Facing Nature,* 3335
Pigeon Feathers, 2970(F)
The Poorhouse Fair, 748(F)
Rabbit at Rest, 615(F)
Rabbit Is Rich, 615(F)
Rabbit Redux, 615(F)
Rabbit, Run, 615(F)

Upton, Robert. *Fabergé Egg,* 2202(F)

Ure, Jean. *If It Weren't for Sebastian,* 749(F)
The Other Side of the Fence, 935(F)

Uris, Leon. *Exodus,* 262(F)
The Haj, 262(F)
Ireland, 7537
Mila 18, 1684(F)
Topaz, 262(F)
Trinity, 1483(F)

Urofsky, Melvin I. *Louis D. Brandeis and the Progressive Tradition,* 6578

Usher, Kerry. *Heroes, Gods & Emperors from Roman Mythology,* 3479

Ustinov, Peter. *The Disinformer,* 263(F)

Utley, Robert M. *Cavalier in Buckskin,* 6582

Utterback, Ann S. *College Admissions Face to Face,* 4770

Utz, Peter. *Do-It-Yourself Video,* 6068
Video User's Handbook, 9054

Vadney, T. E. *The World since 1945,* 7343

Valens, E. G. *The Other Side of the Mountain,* 6778

Valentine, Tom. *Inside Wrestling,* 9788

Vallee, Jacques. *Confrontations,* 9538

Vallejo, Boris. *Fantasy Art Techniques,* 9216

Van Buren, Abigail. *The Best of Dear Abby,* 5633

Van Clief, Ron. *The Ron Van Clief Green & Purple Belt Guide Book,* 9905
The Ron Van Clief White Belt Guide Book, 9905

Van den Haag, Ernest. *The Death Penalty,* 4257

van der Meer, Ron. *Sailing Ships,* 9122

Van der Plas, Rob. *The Bicycle Repair Book,* 9766
The Bicycle Touring Manual, 9767
The Mountain Bike Book, 9768
Roadside Bicycle Repairs, 9767

Van Deusen, Glyndon G. *The Jacksonian Era, 1828–1848,* 7885

Van Devanter, Lynda. *Home before Morning,* 6965

Van Dine, S. S. *The Canary Murder Case,* 2203(F)

Van Doren, Mark. *The Essays of Mark Van Doren (1924–1972)*, 3555

Van Doren, Mark, ed. *An Anthology of World Poetry*, 3859

Van Etten, Teresa. *Ways of Indian Magic*, 3429

Van Gelder, Peter. *That's Hollywood*, 6069

Van Loon, Hendrik Willem. *The Story of Mankind*, 7079

Van Over, Raymond, ed. *Sun Songs*, 3467

Van Scyoc, Sydney J. *Darkchild*, 1302(F)
Starsilk, 1302(F)

Van Thal, Herbert, ed. *The Mammoth Book of Great Detective Stories*, 2204(F)

Van Wormer, Joe. *How to Be a Wildlife Photographer*, 9438

Vance, Jack. *Araminta Station*, 2809(F)
The Dying Earth, 2810(F)
The Face, 2811(F)
The Green Pearl, 1299(F)
The Languages of Pao, 2812(F)
Lyonesse, 1300(F)
Lyonesse, Book I, 1299(F)
Madouc, 1301(F)

Vandenbeld, John. *Nature of Australia*, 7479

Vanderbilt, Amy. *The Amy Vanderbilt Complete Book of Etiquette*, 5578

Vannini, Vanio, ed. *The Color Atlas of Human Anatomy*, 5304

Vansittart, Peter. *Voices, 1870–1914*, 7486
Voices of the Great War, 7486

Varasdi, J. Allen. *Myth Information*, 9539

Vare, Ethlie Ann. *Mothers of Invention*, 8236

Varley, John. *Titan*, 2813(F)

Varner, Jeannette Johnson (jt. author). *Dogs of the Conquest*, 7632

Varner, John Grier. *Dogs of the Conquest*, 7632

Vassallo, Wanda. *Speaking with Confidence*, 4706

Vaughan, Andrew. *Who's Who in New Country Music*, 5904

Vaughan, Norman D. *With Byrd at the Bottom of the World*, 7709

Vaughn, Jack A. *Early American Dramatists*, 3844
Shakespeare's Comedies, 3829

Vaz, Katherine, et al. *Swim Swim*, 9963

Veblen, Thorstein. *The Theory of the Leisure Class*, 4465

Vecsey, George. *A Year in the Sun*, 9604

Vecsey, George (jt. author). *Get to the Heart*, 6423
Martina, 6771

Vedral, Joyce L. *I Dare You*, 5552
My Parents Are Driving Me Crazy, 5677

Vedral, Joyce L. (jt. author). *Hard Bodies*, 9774

Vegh, Claudine. *I Didn't Say Goodbye*, 7314

Vena, Gary. *How to Read and Write about Drama*, 3800

Vendler, Helen, ed. *The Harvard Book of Contemporary American Poetry*, 3336

Venion, S., et al. *Exploring America's Scenic Highways*, 7785

Venning, Frank D. *Wildflowers of North America*, 8448

Ventura, Piero. *Great Painters*, 5726

Verdi, Bob (jt. author). *Once a Bum, Always a Dodger*, 6719

Verna, Tony. *Live TV*, 6070

Verne, Jules. *Around the Moon*, 2814(F)
Around the World in Eighty Days, 324(F)
From the Earth to the Moon, 2814(F)
A Journey to the Center of the Earth, 325(F)
Master of the World, 2815(F)
Michael Strogoff, 1404(F)
The Mysterious Island, 326(F)
Twenty Thousand Leagues under the Sea, 326(F)

Vertut, Jean (jt. author). *Images of the Ice Age*, 5732

Veryan, Patricia. *Cherished Enemy*, 1484(F)
The Dedicated Villain, 1485(F)
Journey to Enchantment, 1486(F)
Logic of the Heart, 2327(F)
Love Alters Not, 1487(F)
Practice to Deceive, 1486(F)

Vestal, David. *The Art of Black and White Enlarging*, 9439

Vestal, Stanley. *Sitting Bull, Champion of the Sioux*, 6636

Veyne, Paul, ed. *A History of Private Life, I*, 7120

Vickers, Michael. *The Roman World*, 7121

Victoroff, Jeffrey Ivan. *The Wild Type*, 264(F)

Vidal, Gore. *Burr*, 1532(F)
1876, 1617(F)
Empire, 1617(F)
Lincoln, 1548(F), 1617(F)
Matters of Fact and Fiction, 3556
Washington, D.C., 1617(F)

Viglucci, Pat Costa. *Cassandra Robbins, Esq*, 504(F)

Vilarreal, Jose Antonio. *Pocho*, 505(F)

Vine, Barbara. *Gallowglass*, 2205(F)

Vine, Louis L. *The Total Dog Book*, 8741

Vinge, Joan D. *Catspaw*, 2816(F)
Psion, 2817(F)
The Snow Queen, 1303(F)

Vinge, Vernor. *True Names and Other Dangers*, 2818(F)

Viola, Tom. *Willy Brandt*, 6830

Virgil. *The Aeneid of Virgil*, 3187

Visser, Margaret. *Much Depends on Dinner*, 8421

Vogt, Gregory. *Halley's Comet*, 8334
A Twenty-fifth Anniversary Album of NASA, 8326

Vogue and Butterick Patterns, eds. *The Vogue/ Butterick Step-by-Step Guide to Sewing Techniques*, 9258

Voigt, Cynthia. *The Callender Papers*, 2206(F)
Dicey's Song, 616(F)
The Runner, 616(F)
Tell Me If the Lovers Are Losers, 936(F)
Volkman, Ernest. *The Heist*, 4496
Volsky, Paula. *The Luck of Relian Kru*, 1304(F)
Voltaire. *Candide*, 327(F)
Candide, and Other Writings, 328(F)
The Portable Voltaire, 329
von Bornstedt, Marianne. *Folding Table Napkins*, 9154
Von Braun, Wernher. *Space Travel*, 8327
von Frisch, Karl. *Bees*, 8604
Von Trapp, Maria. *Story of the Von Trapp Family Singers*, 6452
Vonnegut, Kurt. *Cat's Cradle*, 2819(F)
Deadeye Dick, 1305(F)
Galapagos, 1306(F)
Happy Birthday, Wanda June, 3131
Jailbird, 2820(F)
Mother Night, 1305(F)
Palm Sunday, 6324
Slaughterhouse-Five, 1307(F)
Welcome to the Monkey House, 2821(F)
Vorderwinkler, William (jt. author). *Encyclopedia of Tropical Fish*, 8749
Vosper, Alice. *Rags to Riches*, 1618(F)
Voss, Arthur. *The American Short Story*, 3786
Voss, Jacqueline. *A Young Woman's Guide to Sex*, 5496
Vriends, Matthew M. *Pigeons*, 8683
Simon and Schuster's Guide to Pet Birds, 8684

Wachter, Oralee. *Sex, Drugs and AIDS*, 5222
Wade, Graham. *The Shape of Music*, 5830
Wade, Wyn Craig. *The Titanic*, 8898
Wagenknecht, Edward. *James Russell Lowell*, 6285
Nathaniel Hawthorne, 6255
The Novels of Henry James, 3787
The Tales of Henry James, 3788
Wagenknecht, Edward (jt. author). *Fifty Classic British Films*, 6060
Fifty Great American Silent Films, 1912–1920, 6060
Wagmann, Robert. *The Right Place at the Right Time*, 4812
Wagner, Frederic H. *Wildlife of the Deserts*, 8409
Wagner, Karl Edward, ed. *Intensive Scare*, 1859(F)
The Year's Best Horror Stories, 1860(F)
The Year's Best Horror Stories, Volume XVII, 1861(F)
Wagner, Willis H. *Woodworking*, 9295
Wagoner, Mary S. *Agatha Christie*, 3693
Wahloo, Per (jt. author). *The Laughing Policeman*, 2179(F)
The Locked Room, 2179(F)

Murder at the Savoy, 2179(F)
Wainwright, Loudon. *The Great American Magazine*, 3989
Wakefield, David. *How to Make Animated Toys*, 9264
Wakefield, H. Russell. *The Best Ghost Stories of H. Russell Wakefield*, 1862(F)
Walch, Timothy (jt. author). *Farewell to the Chief*, 6491
Walcott, Derek. *Collected Poems, 1948–1984*, 3337
Walcott, John L. (jt. author). *Best Laid Plans*, 4549
Waldman, Carl. *Atlas of the North American Indian*, 7826
Waldo, Donna Lee. *Sacajawea*, 6635
Waldron, Ann. *True or False?* 5727
Waldrop, M. Mitchell. *Man-Made Minds*, 9026
Waldstreicher, David. *Emma Goldman*, 6589
Wales, Robert. *Harry*, 265(F)
Walker, Alice. *The Color Purple*, 750(F)
Good Night, Willie Lee, I'll See You in the Morning, 4379
In Love and Trouble, 506(F)
In Search of Our Mothers' Gardens, 3557
Living by the Word, 3558
Meridian, 507(F)
The Temple of My Familiar, 508(F)
Walker, Bryce. *The Armada*, 7538
Earthquake, 8808
Walker, David A. *Double Dutch*, 9605
Walker, J. N. *Chess for Tomorrow's Champions*, 9823
Walker, John. *Turner*, 5787
Walker, Margaret. *Jubilee*, 1549(F)
Walker, Paul Robert. *The Method*, 937(F)
Walker, Samuel. *In Defense of American Liberties*, 4321
Walker, Tom. *Shadows on the Tundra*, 8191
Wall, Joseph Frazier. *Andrew Carnegie*, 6651
Wallace, Carol. *Waking Dream*, 2207(F)
Wallace, David Rains. *The Dark Range*, 8459
Idle Weeds, 8410
Wallace, Irving. *The Fabulous Showman*, 6365
The Seventh Secret, 266(F)
Wallace, Lew. *Ben Hur*, 1376(F)
Wallace, Marilyn, ed. *Sisters in Crime*, 2208(F)
Sisters in Crime 2, 2208(F)
Wallace, Marjorie. *The Silent Twins*, 5571
Wallace, Robert. *The Grand Canyon*, 8159
Wallach, Janet. *Arafat*, 6803
Working Wardrobe, 9173
Wallach, Janet (jt. author). *Still Small Voices*, 7618
Wallach, John. *Still Small Voices*, 7618
Wallach, John (jt. author). *Arafat*, 6803
Wallant, Edward L. *The Pawnbroker*, 509(F)
Wallechinsky, David. *The Complete Book of the Olympics*, 9908

Walsh, Jill Paton. *A Chance Child*, 1308(F)

Walsh, John Evangelist. *One Day at Kitty Hawk*, 6704

Walsh, Michael. *Andrew Lloyd Webber*, 6355

Walson, Lillian Eichler. *The Bantam Book of Correct Letter Writing*, 3974

Walter, John. *Handgun*, 9134

Walters, Ed. *The Gulf Breeze Sightings*, 9540

Walters, Frances (jt. author). *The Gulf Breeze Sightings*, 9540

Walters, Mark Jerome. *The Dance of Life*, 8486

Walters, R. R. *Lily*, 1863(F)

Walton, Evangeline. *The Sword Is Forged*, 1377(F)

Walvin, James. *Slavery and the Slave Trade*, 4322

Wambach, Helen. *Reliving Past Lives*, 9541

Wambaugh, Joseph. *The Black Marble*, 2209(F)

Wander, Meghan Robinson (jt. author). *Franklin D. Roosevelt, His Life and Times*, 8031

Wandersee, Winifred D. *On the Move*, 4323

Wann, David. *Biologic*, 4446

Wanstall, Thomas K. (jt. author). *Baron Wolman Presents FDNY*, 4230

Wapner, Joseph A. *A View from the Bench*, 4258

Ward, Ed, et al. *Rock of Ages*, 5905

Ward, Geoffrey C., et al. *The Civil War*, 7947

Ward, Philip, ed. *The Oxford Companion to Spanish Literature*, 3608

Ward, Robert D. (jt. author). *Sport Speed*, 9559

Ware, Cindy. *Summer Options for Teenagers*, 4636

Warner, Malcolm Jamal. *Theo and Me*, 6455

Warner, Matt. *Cats of the World*, 8706

Warner, Roger (jt. author). *A Cambodian Odyssey*, 6811

Warner, William W. *Beautiful Swimmers*, 8622
Distant Water, 8621

Warren, Joseph (jt. author). *Mind over Math*, 8839

Warren, Peter. *The Aegean Civilizations*, 7111

Warren, Robert Penn. *All the King's Men*, 3132
Being Here, 3338
New and Selected Poems, 1923–1985, 3338
Rumor Verified, 3339

Warren, Robert Penn, ed. *Short Story Masterpieces*, 2971(F)

Warren, William E. *The Screaming Skull*, 9542

Warshaw, Robin. *I Never Called It Rape*, 5522

Warwick, Christopher. *Abdication*, 7539
King George VI and Queen Elizabeth, 7539

Washburn, L. J. *Riders of the Monte*, 267(F)

Washburn, Wilcomb E. *The Indian in America*, 7827

Washington, Booker T. *Up from Slavery*, 6520

Washington, James M., ed. *A Testament of Hope*, 4380

Wasserman, Dale. *Man of La Mancha*, 3133

Wasserman, Jack. *Leonardo*, 5788

Wasserstein, Wendy. *Bachelor Girls*, 2972(F)

Wassmer, Arthur C. *Making Contact*, 5634

Waters, Ethel. *His Eye Is on the Sparrow*, 6456

Watkins, Paul. *Night Over Day Over Night*, 1685(F)

Watkins, Susan M. *Dreaming Myself, Dreaming a Town*, 5334

Watkins, Yoko Kawashima. *So Far from the Bamboo Grove*, 1686(F)

Watson, Burton (jt. author). *From the Country of Eight Islands*, 3356

Watson, Derek. *Bruckner*, 6340

Watson, James. *Talking in Whispers*, 268(F)

Watson, James D. *The Double Helix*, 5268

Watson, Lyall. *Lightning Bird*, 7366
The Water Planet, 8791

Watson, Patrick (jt. author). *The Struggle for Democracy*, 4169

Watson, Richard. *The Presidential Contest*, 4279

Watson, Robert I. *The Great Psychologists*, 5553

Watson, Tom. *The New Rules of Golf*, 9879

Watt-Evans, Lawrence. *With a Single Spell*, 1309(F)

Watterson, Barbara. *The Gods of Ancient Egypt*, 7100

Watts, Cedric. *Hamlet*, 3830

Watts, Sarah Miles (jt. author). *The Press and the Presidency*, 4213

Waugh, Charles, ed. *Alternative Histories*, 1310(F)
Space Wars, 2822(F)
Time Wars, 2823(F)

Waugh, Evelyn. *Brideshead Revisited*, 617(F)
The Loved One, 1907(F)

Wayne, Kyra Petrovskaya. *Max, the Dog That Refused to Die*, 8742

Wayne, Rick. *Muscle Wars*, 9776

Wazeter, Mary. *Dark Marathon*, 6966

Weatherby, W. J., et al. *Chariots of Fire & a Christian Message for Today*, 9977

Weatherford, Doris. *American Women and World War II*, 7316

Weatherford, Jack. *Indian Givers*, 7828

Weaver, Gordon (jt. author). *The American Short Story, 1900–1945/1945–1980*, 3780

Weaver, Jefferson Hane (jt. author). *The Story of Physics*, 8911

Weaver, Michael D. *Mercedes Nights*, 2824(F)

Weaver, Tom. *Interviews with B Science Fiction and Horror Movie Makers*, 6071

Weaver, Will. *Red Earth, White Earth*, 510(F)

Webb, James, Jr. *Fields of Fire*, 1705(F)

Webb, Mary. *Precious Bane*, 618(F)

Webb, Sheyann. *Selma, Lord, Selma*, 4381

Webber, Elizabeth. *Grand Allusions*, 3953

Weber, Jack. *Computers*, 9027

Weber, Joe. *Shadow Flight*, 269(F)

Weber, Robert. *Opportunities in Automotive Service Careers*, 4945

Weber, William J. *Care of Uncommon Pets*, 8685

Weeder, Richard S. *Surgeon,* 5254
Weeks, John. *The Pyramids,* 5711
Weesner, Theodore. *Winning the City,* 2887(F)
Weglyn, Michi. *Years of Infamy,* 7317
Weider, Ben. *Pumping Up!* 9777
Weider, Joe. *Bodybuilding,* 9778
Weidhorn, Manfred. *Napoleon,* 6866
Weidt, Maryann N. *Presenting Judy Blume,* 3789
Weigl, Bruce. *Song of Napalm,* 3340
Weil, Andrew. *From Chocolate to Morphine,* 5159
Weil, Robert. *The Omni Future Almanac,* 4420
Weiner, Jonathan. *The Next One Hundred Years,* 4447
Weiner, Mitchell (jt. author). *Barron's Compact Guide to Colleges,* 4723
Barron's Profiles of American Colleges, 4723
Weinreich, Beatrice Silverman, ed. *Yiddish Folktales,* 3414
Weinstein, Bob. *Breaking into Communications,* 4871
Weintraub, Joseph. *Exploring Careers in the Computer Field,* 5060
Weintraub, Stanley, ed. *The Portable Bernard Shaw,* 3134
Weir, Ben, et al. *Hostage Bound, Hostage Free,* 6967
Weis, Margaret. *Doom of the Darksword,* 1315(F)
Dragon Wing, 1311(F)
Dragonlance Chronicles, 1312(F)
The Dragonlance Legends, 1313(F)
Dragons of Autumn Twilight, 1312(F)
Dragons of Spring Dawning, 1312(F)
Dragons of Winter Night, 1312(F)
Elven Star, 1314(F)
Forging the Darksword, 1315(F)
The Paladin of the Night, 1316(F)
The Prophet of Akhran, 1316(F)
Test of the Twins, 1313(F)
Time of the Twins, 1313(F)
Triumph of the Darksword, 1315(F)
War of the Twins, 1313(F)
The Will of the Wanderer, 1316(F)
Weisbrodt, Robert. *Freedom Bound,* 4382
Weiser, Marjorie P. K., ed. *Ethnic America,* 4341
Weiss, Ann E. *Bioethics,* 5255
Welfare, 4516
Weiss, John, et al. *Standing Up to the SAT,* 4666
Weiss, Julian. *The Asian Century,* 7395
Weiss, Rita (jt. author). *The 7-Day Afghan Book,* 9243
Weissler, Paul. *Weekend Mechanic's Handbook,* 9117
Weissman, Michaele (jt. author). *A History of Women in America,* 7750
Wekesser, Carol, ed. *Central America,* 7658
Social Justice, 4466
Welch, James. *Fools Crow,* 1512(F)

Welfare, Simon (jt. author). *Arthur C. Clarke's World of Strange Powers,* 9493
Welland, Dennis. *Miller,* 3845
Weller, Tom. *Science Made Stupid,* 8237
Wellman, Manly Wade. *John the Balladeer,* 1317(F)
Wells, Anne Sharp (jt. author). *A Time for Giants,* 7194
Wells, H. G. *The Complete Short Stories of H. G. Wells,* 2825(F)
The Door in the Wall and Other Stories, 2826(F)
First Men in the Moon, 2827(F)
The Food of the Gods, 2828(F)
In the Days of the Comet, 2829(F)
The Invisible Man, 2830(F)
Island of Doctor Moreau, 2831(F)
Seven Science Fiction Novels, 2832(F)
Time Machine, 2833(F)
The War of the Worlds, 2834(F)
Wells, Rosemary. *When No One Was Looking,* 2888(F)
Wells, Stanley. *Shakespeare,* 3831
Welty, Eudora. *The Collected Stories of Eudora Welty,* 2973(F)
Losing Battles, 619(F)
One Writer's Beginnings, 6325
The Optimist's Daughter, 620(F)
Wenner, Jann S., ed. *20 Years of Rolling Stone,* 5906
Wepman, Dennis. *Jomo Kenyatta,* 6792
Werlin, Mark (jt. author). *The Savior,* 1318(F)
Werlin, Marvin. *The Savior,* 1318(F)
Wernecke, Herbert H. *Christmas Customs Around the World,* 4122
Wernick, Robert. *Blitzkrieg,* 7318
Wersba, Barbara. *Beautiful Losers,* 938(F)
Carnival of My Mind, 939(F)
The Farewell Kid, 939(F)
Fat, 751(F)
Just Be Gorgeous, 940(F)
Love Is the Crooked Thing, 938(F)
Wonderful Me, 940(F)
Wertkin, Gerard C. *The Four Seasons of Shaker Life,* 4089
Wescott, Earle. *Winter Wolves,* 1864(F)
West, Jessamyn. *Collected Stories of Jessamyn West,* 2974(F)
The Friendly Persuasion, 1550(F)
The Massacre at Fall Creek, 1596(F)
The State of Stony Lonesome, 941(F)
West, John O., ed. *Mexican-American Folklore,* 3418
West, Michael Lee. *Crazy Ladies,* 621(F)
West, Morris L. *The Devil's Advocate,* 999(F)
West, Nathanael. *The Day of the Locust,* 752(F)
Westall, Robert. *Children of the Blitz,* 7319
Futuretrack 5, 2835(F)
Wester, Thomas. *Cats,* 8707

Westheimer, Ruth. *All in a Lifetime*, 6458
First Love, 5497
Westin, Jeane Eddy. *Finding Your Roots*, 5678
Westlake, Donald E. *Good Behavior*, 270(F)
Tomorrow's Crimes, 1865(F)
Why Me? 2210(F)
Weston, Carol. *Girltalk about Guys*, 5635
Weston, Susan. *Children of the Light*, 2836(F)
Westwood, Jennifer, ed. *The Atlas of Mysterious Places*, 7090
Wetterau, Bruce. *Macmillan Concise Dictionary of World History*, 7080
WGBH/Boston. *Nova*, 8238
Wharton, Edith. *The Age of Innocence*, 1619(F)
Ethan Frome, 622(F)
House of Mirth, 1619(F)
Wharton, William. *Birdy*, 753(F)
A Midnight Clear, 1687(F)
Pride, 301(F)
Whedon, Julia. *The Fine Art of Ice Skating*, 9891
Wheeler, David, ed. *No, But I Saw the Movie*, 2975(F)
Wheeler, John. *Touched with Fire*, 8148
Wheeler, Keith. *The Aftermath*, 7320
The Alaskans, 8192
Bombers over Japan, 7320
China-Burma-India, 7320
The Fall of Japan, 7320
The Road to Tokyo, 7320
The Scouts, 8000
The Townsmen, 8001
War under the Pacific, 7320
Wheeler, Lonnie. *Bleachers*, 9706
Wheeler, Richard. *A Special Valor*, 7321
We Knew Stonewall Jackson, 6596
Where the River Runs, 1597(F)
Wheeler, Robert W. *Jim Thorpe*, 6768
Wheeler, Tom. *The Guitar Book*, 5942
Wheelock, Arthur K. *Jan Vermeer*, 6209
Whelan, Michael. *Wonderworks*, 5728
Whelan, Richard. *Drawing the Line*, 8149
Whipple, A. B. C. *The Clipper Ships*, 7886
Fighting Sail, 7886
Restless Oceans, 8879
Storm, 8868
The Whalers, 7886
Whipple, Fred L. *The Mystery of Comets*, 8335
Whitaker, John O., Jr. *The Audubon Society Field Guide to North American Mammals*, 8495
Whitaker, Tim (jt. author). *Crash*, 6712
Whitby, Max. *Space Technology*, 8328
White, E. B. *Essays of E. B. White*, 3559
Poems and Sketches of E. B. White, 3560
White, E. B. (jt. author). *The Elements of Style*, 4701
White, Edmund. *A Boy's Own Story*, 942(F)
White, Ellen Emerson. *Long Live the Queen*, 271(F)

White, Frank (jt. author). *The March of the Millennia*, 7029
White House Historical Association, Washington, D.C. *The White House*, 8174
White, James. *Code Blue*, 2837(F)
White, John. *Billie Holiday*, 6405
White, Jon Manchip. *Everyday Life of the North American Indian*, 7829
White, Mel (jt. author). *A Gift of Hope*, 6425
White, Randall. *Dark Caves, Bright Visions*, 7013
White, Richard E. *A Field Guide to the Beetles of North America*, 8605
White, Richard E. (jt. author). *A Field Guide to the Insects of America North of Mexico*, 8592
White, Rick. *Catamaran Racing*, 9940
White, Robert H. *Tribal Assets*, 4395
White, T. H. *The Book of Merlyn*, 1319(F)
The Once and Future King, 1320(F)
The Sword in the Stone, 1321(F)
White, Theodore H. *America in Search of Itself*, 8093
In Search of History, 8094
The Making of the President, 1972, 8095
White, Timothy. *Rock Lives*, 5907
White, William C. *Opportunities in Agriculture Careers*, 4872
Whitehead, Hal. *Voyage to the Whales*, 8657
Whitehead, Peter (jt. author). *Wildfowl of the World*, 8557
Whitehouse, Ruth. *The Making of Civilization*, 7091
Whitehouse, Ruth, ed. *The Facts on File Dictionary of Archaeology*, 7025
Whiteside, Thomas. *Computer Capers*, 9028
Whitfield, Philip, ed. *Macmillan Illustrated Animal Encyclopedia*, 8460
The Macmillan Illustrated Encyclopedia of Birds, 8553
Whitlow, Roger. *Black American Literature*, 3609
Whitman, Walt. *Leaves of Grass*, 3341
Voyages, 3342
Whitmore, George. *Someone Was Here*, 5223
Whitney, Catherine (jt. author). *The Tufts University Guide to Total Nutrition*, 5413
Whitney, Charles A. *Whitney's Star Finder*, 8293
Whitney, David C. *The American Presidents*, 6492
Whitney, Phyllis A. *Black Amber*, 2211(F)
Blue Fire, 2211(F)
Domino, 2216(F)
Dream of Orchids, 2212(F)
Emerald, 2213(F)
Feather on the Moon, 2214(F)
Golden Unicorns, 2213(F)
Rainbow in the Mist, 2215(F)
Rainsong, 2216(F)
Seven Tears for Apollo, 2211(F), 2213(F)

Silversword, 2217(F)
The Singing Stones, 2218(F)
Spindrift, 2211(F)
Stone Bull, 2213(F)
The Trembling Hills, 2216(F)
Window on the Square, 2211(F)
Whitney, Sharon. *Women in Politics,* 4272
Whitney, Stephen. *Western Forests,* 8824
Whitt, Anne Hall. *The Suitcases,* 623(F)
Whittier, John Greenleaf. *The Poetical Works of Whittier,* 3343
Whittingham, Richard. *Saturday Afternoon,* 9864
Whittingham, Richard, ed. *Life in Sports,* 9606
Whitworth, Kathy. *Golf for Women,* 9880
Wholey, Dennis. *Are You Happy?* 5554
Becoming Your Own Parent, 5679
Wibbelsman, Charles (jt. author). *The New Teen-age Body Book,* 5479
Wibberley, Leonard. *The Mouse That Roared,* 1908(F)
Wicander, Reed (jt. author). *Minerals, Rocks and Fossils,* 8826
Wicker, Tom. *Unto This Hour,* 1551(F)
Wickham, Glynne. *A History of the Theatre,* 6114
Wicks, Ben. *No Time to Wave Goodbye,* 7322
Widmer, Patricia P. *Pat Widmer's Cat Book,* 8708
Pat Widmer's Dog Training Book, 8743
Wiencek, Henry. *Southern New England,* 8175
Virginia and the Capital Region, 8196
Wiener, Jon. *Come Together,* 6418
Wiesel, Elie. *Dawn,* 1488(F)
From the Kingdom of Memory, 3561
Messengers of God, 4112
Night, 7323
Wiesenthal, Simon. *Justice Not Vengeance,* 6880
Wiesmeier, Uli (jt. author). *Rocks around the World,* 9569
Wiget, Andrew. *Native American Literature,* 3610
Wiggins, Marianne. *John Dollar,* 1866(F)
Wigginton, Eliot, ed. *Foxfire,* 8197
Wignall, Jeff. *Landscape Photography,* 9440
Wilbur, Richard. *New and Collected Poems,* 3344
Wilcox, Fred A. *Waiting for an Army to Die,* 8150
Wilcox, Kathleen (jt. author). *Dear Doctor,* 5619
Wilcox, R. Turner. *The Dictionary of Costume,* 9174
Five Centuries of American Costume, 9175
Folk and Festival Costume of the World, 9176
Wild, Russell, ed. *The Earth Care Annual 1990,* 4448
Wilde, Oscar. *The Importance of Being Earnest,* 3045
The Picture of Dorian Gray, 1867(F)
The Portable Oscar Wilde, 388
Wilder, Cherry. *A Princess of the Chameln,* 1322(F)

The Summer's King, 1323(F)
Wilder, Laura Ingalls. *A Little House Sampler,* 8002
Wilder, Thornton. *The Bridge of San Luis Rey,* 1495(F)
The Eighth Day, 272(F)
Our Town, 3135
Theophilus North, 754(F)
Three Plays, 3136
Wiley, Jack. *Dynamite Kites,* 9155
Wilford, John Noble. *Mars Beckons,* 8350
The Riddle of the Dinosaur, 6987
Wilhelm, Kate. *Children of the Wind,* 1868(F)
Crazy Time, 2838(F)
The Dark Door, 273(F)
Huysman's Pets, 274(F)
Sweet, Sweet Poison, 2219(F)
Where Late the Sweet Birds Sang, 2839(F)
Wilk, Max. *The Golden Age of Television,* 6115
Wilkerson, David. *The Cross and the Switch-blade,* 4497
Wilkes, Brian (jt. author). *The Space Program Quiz and Fact Book,* 8297
Wilkins, John (jt. author). *The Making of Civilization,* 7091
Wilkins, Kirby. *Quantum Web,* 275(F)
Wilkins, Malcolm. *Plant Watching,* 8449
Wilkinson, Allen P. (jt. author). *Everybody's Guide to the Law,* 4232
Wilkinson, Bud. *Sports Illustrated Football,* 9865
Willard, Nancy. *Things Invisible to See,* 1324(F)
Water Walker, 3897
Willcock, Malcolm M. *A Companion to the Iliad,* 3864
Willenson, Kim, et al. *The Bad War,* 8151
Willett, Frank. *African Art,* 5767
Williams, Anna (jt. author). *Opportunities in Home Economics Careers,* 4868
Williams, Barbara. *Breakthrough,* 5031
Williams, Ellen. *Opportunities for Gerontology Careers,* 4982
Williams, Heathcote. *Whale Nation,* 8658
Williams, J. P. R., et al. *Barron's Sports Injuries,* 5448
Williams, John A. (jt. author). *Create Your Own Stage Lighting,* 6112
Williams, John C. *Archery for Beginners,* 9607
Williams, John Hoyt. *A Great & Shining Road,* 8003
Williams, Jon Walter. *Angel Station,* 2840(F)
Williams, Juan. *Eyes on the Prize,* 4324
Williams, Lea E. *Southeast Asia,* 7396
Williams, Martin. *Jazz Heritage,* 5908
Jazz in Its Time, 5909
The Jazz Tradition, 5908
Williams, Martin (jt. author). *The Smithsonian Collection of Newspaper Comics,* 5791
Williams, Mary C. (jt. author). *Contemporary Southern Poetry,* 3308

Williams, Melvin. *Beyond Training,* 5366

Williams, Miller. *Patterns of Poetry,* 3860

Williams, Miller (jt. author). *How Does a Poem Mean?* 3153

Williams, Niall. *O Come Ye Back to Ireland,* 7540

When Summer's in the Meadow, 7540

Williams, Oliver F. *The Apartheid Crisis,* 7388

Williams, Paul O. *The Breaking of Northwall,* 2841(F)

Dome in the Forest, 2841(F)

The Ends of the Circle, 2841(F)

Williams, Randall. *The Rosen Photo Guide to a Career in Magic,* 4902

Williams, Sheila, ed. *Tales from Isaac Asimov's Science Fiction Magazine,* 2843(F)

Why I Left Harry's All-Night Hamburgers, 2842(F)

Williams, T. Harry. *Huey Long,* 6600

Williams, Tad. *The Dragonbone Chair,* 1325(F)

Stone of Farewell, 1325(F)

Tailchaser's Song, 1326(F)

Williams, Ted. *The Science of Hitting,* 9707

Williams, Tennessee. *Cat on a Hot Tin Roof,* 3137

The Glass Menagerie, 3138

A Streetcar Named Desire, 3139

Where I Live, 6116

Williams, Terry. *The Cocaine Kids,* 5160

Williams, Walter J. *Ambassador of Progress,* 2844(F)

Hardwired, 2844(F)

Voice of the Whirlwind, 2844(F)

Williams, William Appleman, et al., eds. *America in Vietnam,* 8152

Williams, William Carlos. *The Collected Poems of William Carlos Williams,* 3345

Williams-Garcia, Rita. *Blue Tights,* 511(F)

Williamson, David. *Debrett's Kings and Queens of Britain,* 7541

Williamson, Jack. *Mazeway,* 2845(F)

Wonder's Child, 3790

Williamson, Jack (jt. author). *Land's End,* 2742(F)

Willis, Connie. *Light Raid,* 2846(F)

Lincoln's Dreams, 1327(F)

Water Witch, 2846(F)

Willis, Connie (jt. author). *Water Witch,* 2538(F)

Willis, David K. *Klass,* 7589

Willis, Irene (jt. author). *Boy Friends, Girl Friends, Just Friends,* 5544

Leaving Home, 5627

What to Do If You or Someone You Know Is Under 18 and Pregnant, 5490

Willis, Jerry. *Computers for Everybody,* 9030

How to Use the Coleco Adam, 9029

How to Use the Vic 20, 9029

Willis, Jerry (jt. author). *How to Use the Apple II and IIe,* 9010

Wills, Gary. *Under God,* 4273

Wilson, August. *Fences,* 3140

Wilson, Barbara Ker. *The Quade Inheritance,* 2220(F)

Wilson, Colin. *Poltergeist,* 9543

The Psychic Detectives, 5328

Wilson, David Henry. *The Coachman Rat,* 1328(F)

Wilson, Derek. *The Circumnavigators,* 6123

Wilson, Dorothy Clarke. *Alice and Edith,* 1620(F)

Wilson, Edmund. *The Dead Sea Scrolls, 1947–1969,* 4113

Wilson, Elinor. *Jim Beckwourth,* 6614

Wilson, F. Paul. *Black Wind,* 276(F)

Dydeetown World, 2847(F)

The Keep, 1869(F)

Soft and Others, 2847(F)

The Tery, 2848(F)

The Tomb, 1869(F)

The Touch, 1870(F)

Wilson, Gahan. *Everybody's Favorite Duck,* 2221(F)

Wilson, Harriet E. *Our Nig,* 1533(F)

Wilson, James Q. *Crime and Human Nature,* 4498

Wilson, John Dover. *What Happens in Hamlet,* 3832

Wilson, Kirk. *Unsolved,* 4499

Wilson, Lanford. *Talley's Folly,* 3141

Wilson, M. L. *Chester Himes,* 6265

Wilson, Robert Charles. *The Divide,* 2849(F)

Gypsies, 2850(F)

Memory Wire, 2851(F)

Wimmer, Dick. *Baseball Fathers, Baseball Sons,* 9708

Winans, Chip, et al. *Boardsailing Made Easy,* 9957

Windling, Terri, ed. *Elsewhere, Vol. III,* 1330(F)

Faery! 1329(F)

Windsor, Patricia. *The Sandman's Eyes,* 2222(F)

Winegardner, Mark. *Prophet of the Sandlots,* 9709

Winfield, Dave. *Winfield,* 6735

Winfield, Julia. *Only Make-Believe,* 2328(F)

Winger, Gail. *Valium,* 5161

Wingerson, Lois. *Mapping Our Genes,* 5269

Wingrove, David. *Chung Kuo,* 2852(F)

Winkler, Anthony C. *Writing the Research Paper,* 4654

Winkler, Connie. *Careers in High Tech,* 5061

Winks, Robin. *A History of Civilization,* 7081

Winn, Marie. *Children without Childhood,* 5680

The Plug-In Drug, 6072

Unplugging the Plug-in Drug, 6072

Winnick, R. H. (jt. author). *Robert Frost,* 6248

Winokur, Jon, ed. *The Portable Curmudgeon,* 3518

Winship, Michael. *Television,* 6073

Winslade, William J. *The Insanity Plea,* 4259

Winston, Keith. *V-Mail,* 7324

Winston, Mary (jt. author). *The American Heart Association Cookbook,* 9335

Winstone, H. V. F. *Uncovering the Ancient World,* 7026

Winter, C. A. *Opportunities in Biological Sciences,* 5032

Winter, Douglas E. *Faces of Fear,* 3791
Stephen King, 3792

Winter, J. M. *The Experience of World War I,* 7166

Winterbotham, E. W. *The Ultra Secret,* 7325

Winters, Jonathan. *Winters' Tales,* 2976(F)

Winters, Nathan B. *Architecture Is Elementary,* 5690

Wirth, Dick. *Ballooning,* 9613

Wirth, Mary A. (jt. author). *The Bill James Historical Baseball Abstract,* 9662

Wirths, Claudine G. *I Hate School,* 4637

Wiseman, Rich. *Neil Diamond,* 6384

Wishman, Seymour. *Anatomy of a Jury,* 4260

Wisler, G. Clifton. *The Return of Caulfield Blake,* 277(F)
Thunder on the Tennessee, 1552(F)

Wister, Owen. *The Virginian,* 1598(F)

Wiswell, Phil. *Kids' Games,* 9608

Witbeck, Alan R. (jt. author). *Racquetball,* 9544

Witcover, Paul. *Zora Neale Hurston,* 6270

Withers, Robert S. *Introduction to Film,* 6074

Witherspoon, William R. *Martin Luther King, Jr.* 6514

Witt, Reni L. *Mom, I'm Pregnant,* 5499
PMS, 5498

Wittenberg, Renee. *Opportunities in Child Care Careers,* 4983

Wodehouse, P. G. *Leave It to Psmith,* 1909(F)

Woeller, Waltrand. *The Literature of Crime & Detection,* 3633

Wold, Allen L. *Computer Science,* 9031

Wolf, Beverly Hungry (jt. author). *Children of the Sun,* 7809

Wolf, Gary. *Who Censored Roger Rabbit?* 2223(F)

Wolfe, Bernie. *How to Watch Ice Hockey,* 9888

Wolfe, Bertram D. *Three Who Made a Revolution,* 6790

Wolfe, Gene. *Castleview,* 1871(F)
The Claw of the Conciliator, 1331(F)
The Shadow of the Torturer, 1331(F)
Soldier of Arete, 1332(F)
Soldier of the Mist, 1333(F)
The Urth of the New Sun, 2853(F)

Wolfe, Thomas. *Look Homeward, Angel,* 943(F)
Of Time and the River, 943(F)
The Web and the Rock, 944(F)
You Can't Go Home Again, 944(F)

Wolfe, Tom. *The Right Stuff,* 8329

Wolff, Geoffrey, ed. *The Best American Essays, 1989,* 3562

Wolff, Rick (jt. author). *Breaking into the Big Leagues,* 9646

Wolff, Tobias. *This Boy's Life,* 6329

Wolitzer, Meg. *This Is Your Life,* 624(F)

Wollheim, Donald A., ed. *The World's Best SF Annual,* 2854(F)

Wollitz, Kenneth. *The Recorder Book,* 5943

Wolpert, Lewis. *A Passion for Science,* 6647

Wolpert, Stanley. *A New History of India,* 7444

Wolter, Annette (jt. author). *The New Parakeet Handbook,* 8668

Wolverton, Van. *Running MS DOS,* 9032

Wong, Ken (jt. author). *High-Performance Racquetball,* 9573

Wonger, B. *Walg,* 1405(F)

Wood, Barbara. *Domina,* 755(F)
Green City in the Sun, 1387(F)

Wood, Bob. *Big Ten Country,* 9866

Wood, Gerald L. *Guinness Book of Pet Records,* 8686

Wood, Jacqueline. *The Campus Survival Cookbook #2,* 9367

Wood, Michael. *Domesday,* 7542
In Search of the Trojan War, 7112

Wood, Robert. *Dodger Dogs to Fenway Franks,* 9710
Opportunities in Electrical Trades, 5062

Wood, Robin. *The People of Pern,* 3793

Wood, Susan Macduff (jt. author). *Business and Social Etiquette with Disabled People,* 5437

Wood, W. J. *Battles of the Revolutionary War, 1775–1781,* 7862

Woodburn, John H. *Opportunities in Energy Careers,* 5063

Woodham-Smith, Cecil. *The Great Hunger,* 7543
Queen Victoria, 6878

Woodhouse, Barbara. *Dog Training My Way,* 8744
Encyclopedia of Dogs and Puppies, 8745

Woodrell, Daniel. *Woe to Live On,* 1553(F)

Woodress, James. *Willa Cather,* 6230

Woodruff, John. *China in Search of Its Future,* 7437

Woods, Donald. *Biko,* 6791
South African Dispatches, 7389

Woods, E. Z. *The Bloody Sands,* 278(F)

Woods, Karl Morrow. *The Sports Success Book,* 9609

Woods, Michael. *Starting Pencil Drawing,* 9217

Woods, Samuel G. *Everything You Need to Know about Sexually Transmitted Disease,* 5224

Woods, Stuart. *White Cargo,* 279(F)

Woodward, Bob. *The Brethren,* 4261
The Final Days, 8096
Wired, 6370

Woodward, Bob (jt. author). *All the President's Men,* 8047

Woodward, C. Vann. *The Future of the Past,* 7787

The Strange Career of Jim Crow, 4383

Woodward, Grace Steele. *Pocahontas*, 6632

Woodward, Ralph Lee. *Central America*, 7659

Woodworth, Steven E. *Jefferson Davis and His Generals*, 6584

Woolf, Virginia. *Flush*, 6225
Mrs. Dalloway, 756(F)
To the Lighthouse, 625(F)
The Virginia Woolf Reader, 2977

Woolley, Persia. *Child of the Northern Spring*, 1334(F)
Queen of the Summer Stars, 1489(F)

Wootton, Anthony. *Insects of the World*, 8602

Wootton, Steve. *Nutrition for Sport*, 5429

Wordsworth, William. *The Poetical Works of Wordsworth*, 3231

Worrell, Denise. *Icons*, 6075

Worrell, Estelle A. *Children's Costume in America, 1607–1910*, 9177

Worster, Donald. *Dust Bowl*, 8155

Worth, Fred L. *Rock Facts*, 5930

Worth, Fred L. (jt. author). *World War II Super Facts*, 7247

Worth, Richard. *The American Family*, 5681

Worth, Valerie. *Fox Hill*, 945(F)

Worthington-Roberts, Bonnie (jt. author). *Food for Sport*, 5427

Wortman, Richard (jt. author). *Down Is Not Out*, 5388

Wouk, Herman. *The Caine Mutiny*, 1688(F)
City Boy, 1910(F)
This Is My God, 4090
War and Remembrance, 1689(F)
The Winds of War, 1689(F)

Wrede, Patricia C. *Caught in Crystal*, 1335(F)
Daughter of Witches, 1336(F)
The Harp of Imach Thyssel, 1336(F)
The Seven Towers, 1337(F)
Snow White and Rose Red, 1338(F)
Sorcery and Cecilia, 1339(F)

Wren, Christopher S. *The End of the Line*, 7344

Wright, Frank Lloyd. *Frank Lloyd Wright*, 5706

Wright, George T. *W. H. Auden*, 3874

Wright, J. Patrick. *On a Clear Day You Can See General Motors*, 9118

Wright, James D., et al. *Under the Gun*, 4500

Wright, John W. *The American Almanac of Jobs and Salaries*, 4813
Captured on Corregidor, 7326

Wright, Michael. *The Complete Book of Gardening*, 9388
Complete Indoor Gardener, 9388

Wright, Patricia. *I Am England*, 1490(F)
That Near and Distant Place, 1490(F)

Wright, Peter (jt. author). *Manzanar*, 8045

Wright, R. Thomas. *Processes of Manufacturing*, 8953

Wright, Richard. *American Hunger*, 6332
Black Boy, 6332

Native Son, 512(F)

Wright, Robert. *Three Scientists and Their Gods*, 6648

Wright, Ronald. *On Fiji Islands*, 7480

Wright, Sam. *Koviashuvik*, 8193

Wright, Stephen. *Meditations in Green*, 1706(F)

Wright, T. M. *The Place*, 1872(F)
The Playground, 1873(F)
The School, 1874(F)

Wright, Thomas Lee (jt. author). *Working in Hollywood*, 5998

Wulf, Steve (jt. author). *Baseball Anecdotes*, 9688

Wulforst, Harry. *Breakthrough to the Computer Age*, 9033

Wunsch, Josephine. *The Perfect 10*, 2329(F)

Wurman, Richard Saul. *Medical Access*, 5225

Wurts, Janny. *Keeper of the Keys*, 2855(F)
Shadowfane, 2855(F)
Sorcerer's Legacy, 1340(F)
Stormwarden, 2855(F)

Wyden, Peter. *Bay of Pigs*, 7666
Day One, 7327

Wyndham, John. *The Day of the Triffids*, 2856(F)

Yacenda, John. *High Performance Skiing*, 9947

Yaconelli, Mike (jt. author). *Play It!* 9593

Yadin, Yigael. *Masada*, 7027

Yale Daily News, eds. *The Insider's Guide to the Colleges*, 4771

Yalof, Ina. *Life and Death*, 5256

Yandell, John. *Visual Tennis*, 9973

Yankee Magazine, eds. *The Inventive Yankee*, 8954

Yanker, Gary, et al. *Walking Medicine*, 5367

Yannella, Donald. *Ralph Waldo Emerson*, 3611

Yanuch, Deborah (jt. author). *Opportunities in High Tech Careers*, 5042

Yarwood, Doreen. *A Chronology of Western Architecture*, 5697
The Encyclopedia of World Costume, 9178

Yastrzemski, Carl. *Yaz*, 6736

Yates, Elizabeth. *Sound Friendships*, 8746

Yeager, Carole. *Yankee Folk Crafts*, 9156

Yeager, Chuck. *Press On!* 6166
Yeager, 6166

Yeager, Peter C. (jt. author). *Corporate Crime*, 4472

Yeats, W. B. *Collected Poems*, 3232
The Collected Works of W. B. Yeats, Volume I, 3233

Yelton, Geary. *The Rock Synthesizer Manual*, 5910

Yenne, Bill. *Pictorial History of the North American Indian*, 7830

Yeoman, R. S. *A Guide Book of United States Coins*, 9463

Yep, Laurence. *The Rainbow People*, 3387
  Shadow Lord, 2857(F)
Ying, Mildred, et al., eds. *The New Good House-keeping Cookbook*, 9368
Yolen, Jane. *Cards of Grief*, 2858(F)
  Sister Light, Sister Dark, 1341(F)
Yolen, Jane, ed. *Favorite Folktales from around the World*, 3376
Yoors, Jan. *The Gypsies*, 4405
Yost, Nellie Snyder. *Buffalo Bill*, 6377
Young, Cathy. *Growing Up in Moscow*, 6968
Young, Ernie. *Alpha & Omega*, 5257
Young, Faye. *Winning Basketball for Girls*, 9739
Young, John Richard. *The Schooling of the Horse*, 8769
Young, Judith (jt. author). *Birdwatching*, 8540
Young, Louise B. *The Blue Planet*, 8792
  Sowing the Wind, 4449
Young, Michael. *Architectural and Building Design*, 5691
Young, Patrick. *Schizophrenia*, 5407
Young, Percy M. *Handel*, 6347
Young, Peter, ed. *The World Almanac Book of World War II*, 7328
Young, Stephanie (jt. author). *Smart Face*, 5336
Young, Susan (jt. author). *Patchwork Made Easy*, 9246
Yoxen, Edward. *The Gene Business*, 5270
Yudkin, John. *The Penguin Encyclopaedia of Nutrition*, 5430

Zabusky, Charlotte (jt. author). *American Mosaic*, 4335
Zachary, Hugh. *Murder in White*, 2224(F)
Zackon, Fred. *Heroin*, 5162
Zadig, Ernest A. *The Complete Book of Boating*, 9941
Zahn, Timothy. *Cascade Point and Other Stories*, 2859(F)
  Cobra Bargain, 2861(F)
  A Coming of Age, 2860(F)
  Deadman Switch, 2861(F)
  Spinneret, 2862(F)
  Time Bomb and Zahndry Others, 2863(F)
Zalben, Jane Breskin. *Here's Looking at You, Kid*, 2330(F)
Zall, Paul M., ed. *Ben Franklin Laughing*, 3519
  George Washington Laughing, 3519
  Mark Twain Laughing, 3519
Zamiatin, Eugene. *We*, 2864(F)
Zamkoff, Bernard. *Basic Pattern Skills for Fashion Design*, 9179
Zassenhaus, Hiltgunt. *Walls*, 6969
Zebrowski, George. *Sunspacer*, 2865(F)
Zeitlin, Steven J., et al. *A Celebration of American Family Folklore*, 3443
Zelazny, Roger. *Blood of Amber*, 1342(F)
  Changeling, 1343(F)
  Coils, 2870(F)
  The Courts of Chaos, 1344(F)
  A Dark Traveling, 2866(F)
  Frost and Fire, 2867(F)
  The Guns of Avalon, 1344(F)
  The Hand of Oberon, 1344(F)
  Knight of Shadows, 2868(F)
  The Last Defender of Camelot, 1343(F)
  Nine Princes in Amber, 1344(F)
  Roger Zelazny's Visual Guide to Castle Amber, 3794(F)
  The Sign of the Unicorn, 1344(F)
  Signs of Chaos, 2869(F)
  This Immortal, 1345(F)
  Trumps of Doom, 1342(F), 1346(F)
  Wizard World, 2867(F)
Zelazny, Roger (jt. author). *Clypsis*, 2465(F)
Zeller, Frederic. *When Time Ran Out*, 6970
Zerbey, Richard J. *Jam Plastic, Heavy Metal*, 5911
  Jam Plastic, Punk, 5911
  Jam Plastic, Rock, 5911
Zern, Ed. *Hunting and Fishing from "A" to Zern*, 9836
Zerubavel, Eviator. *The Seven Day Circle*, 8862
Zerwick, Chloe. *A Short History of Glass*, 8955
Zettner, Pat. *The Shadow Warrior*, 1347(F)
Zich, Arthur. *The Rising Sun*, 7329
Ziegler, Edward. *Emergency Doctor*, 5258
Zieman, Nancy. *The Busy Woman's Sewing Book*, 9260
Ziemke, Earl F. *The Mediterranean*, 7330
  Red Army Resurgent, 7330
  The Resistance, 7330
  The Soviet Juggernaut, 7330
Zim, Herbert. *Birds*, 8554
  Rocks and Minerals, 8830
  Seashores, 8885
  Stars, 8357
  Trees, 8431
Zim, Herbert (jt. author). *Butterflies and Moths*, 8607
  Fishes, 8628
  Flowers, 8438
  Insects, 8593
  Mammals, 8454
  Reptiles and Amphibians, 8467
Zim, Herbert, et al. *Weather*, 8873
Zimbardo, Philip G. *Shyness*, 5636
Zimbardo, Rose A. (jt. author). *Tolkien and the Critics*, 3671
Zimmer, Marc A. (jt. author). *Dying to Be Thin*, 5402
Zimmer, Michael. *Sundown*, 280(F)
Zimmerman, David R. *The Essential Guide to Non-Prescription Drugs*, 5163
Zimring, Franklin E. *The Citizen's Guide to Gun Control*, 4530
Zindel, Bonnie. *A Star for the Latecomer*, 626(F)

Zindel, Paul. *The Amazing and Death-Defying Diary of Eugene Dingman*, 946(F)
The Effect of Gamma Rays on Man-in-the-Moon Marigolds, 3142
The Girl Who Wanted a Boy, 947(F)
Harry and Hortense at Hormone High, 950(F)
I Never Loved Your Mind, 948(F)
My Darling, My Hamburger, 949(F)
Pardon Me, You're Stepping on My Eyeball, 950(F)
The Pigman, 951(F)
Zindel, Paul (jt. author). *A Star for the Latecomer*, 626(F)
To Take a Dare, 798(F)
Zinner, Stephen H. *How to Protect Yourself from STDs*, 5226
Zinsser, Hans. *Rats, Lice and History*, 5227
Zinsser, Judith P. (jt. author). *A History of Their Own*, 7481
Zinsser, William. *On Writing Well*, 4707
Zipes, Jack, ed. *Beauties, Beasts and Enchantments*, 3415
Victorian Fairy Tales, 3416

Zipko, Stephen J. *Toxic Threat*, 4450
Zisman, Honey. *The Burger Book*, 9369
Zisman, Larry (jt. author). *The Burger Book*, 9369
Zochert, Donald. *Laura*, 6328
Zolna, Ed. *Mastering Softball*, 9711
Zolotow, Charlotte, ed. *An Overpraised Season*, 952(F)
Zousmer, Steven (jt. author). *Galapagos*, 7685
Zucher, Martin (jt. author). *How to Have a Healthier Dog*, 8712
Zuker, R. Fred. *Peterson's Guide to College Admissions*, 4772
Zullo, Allan (jt. author). *The Baseball Hall of Shame*, 9682
The Baseball Hall of Shame 4, 9683
The Football Hall of Shame, 9856
The Golf Hall of Shame, 9874
The Sports Hall of Shame, 9586
Zweig, Paul. *Walt Whitman*, 6327
Zyskind, Sara. *Stolen Years*, 7331
Struggle, 7332

Title Index

This index contains both main entry titles and internal titles cited in the entries. References are to entry numbers, not page numbers. All fiction titles are indicated by (F), following the entry number.

A for Anything, 2616(F)
A. J.: My Life as America's Greatest Race Car Driver, 6711
A. J. Cronin, 3687
A. Lincoln: His Last 24 Hours, 6548
Aaron to Zuverink, 9679
The Abbess of Crewe, 1902(F)
Abby, My Love, 682(F)
The ABC of Lettering, 9157
ABC's of Nature: A Family Answer Book, 8373
ABC's of the Human Body: A Family Answer Book, 5302
ABC's of the Human Mind: A Family Answer Book, 5322
Abdication, 7539
The Abduction, 1453(F)
Abduction from Fort Union, 38(F)
Abigail Adams: An American Woman, 6522
Able Scientists—Disabled Persons, 5029
Abortion, 5519
Abortion: The Clash of Absolutes, 5521
The Abortion Controversy, 5508
Abortion in America: The Origins and Evolution of National Policy, 1800–1900, 5483
About Behaviorism, 5547
About Cows, 8590
About David, 727(F)
About Faces, 5297
About Time: Twelve Stories, 2540(F)
Above Suspicion, 196(F)

Above Top Secret: The Worldwide U.F.O. Cover-Up, 9502
Abraham Lincoln: A Biography, 6550
Abraham Lincoln: The Man behind the Myths, 6546
Abraham Lincoln: The Prairie Years and the War Years, 6549
Abraham Lincoln and the Union, 6544
Absalom, Absalom! 1603(F)
Abstract Art, 5753
Accidental Millionaire: The Rise and Fall of Steve Jobs at Apple Computer, 6678
According to Hoyle, 9807
The Acorn People, 5436
Across China, 7414
Across the Grain, 807(F)
Across the Rhine, 7310
Act One: An Autobiography, 6253
Acting: The First Six Lessons, 6080
Acting in Television Commercials for Fun and Profit, 4879
Action Cheerleading, 9561
The Actor: A Practical Guide to a Professional Career, 4875
An Actor Prepares: Building a Character, 6109
The Actor's Book of Contemporary Stage Monologues, 2988
The Actor's Book of Movie Monologues, 6063
The Actor's Scenebook, Vol. 2, 3116
The Acts of King Arthur and His Noble Knights, 3412

The Ad Game, 4920
Addicted: Kids Talking about Drugs in Their Own Words, 5114
Admiral Hornblower in the West Indies, 1427(F)
The Admissions Essay: Stop Worrying and Start Writing, 4756
Admit One! Your Guide to College Application, 4758
The Adolescent: Development, Relationships, and Culture, 5543
Adolf Hitler, 6849
Adrift: Seventy-Six Days Lost at Sea, 8887
Adulthood Rites, 2454(F)
Advanced BASIC, 8989
Advanced Programming Handbook, 8977
The Adventure Guide to the Pacific Northwest, 8176
The Adventures of Don Quixote de la Mancha, 304(F)
The Adventures of Huckleberry Finn, 421(F)
The Adventures of Huckleberry Finn: American Comic Vision, 3776
The Adventures of Sherlock Holmes, 1987(F)
The Adventures of the Scarlet Pimpernel, 1455(F)
The Adventures of Tom Sawyer, 422(F)
The Adventures of Ulysses: The Odyssey of Homer, 3472
The Adversary, 1216(F)
Adversary in the House, 1616(F)

Advertising Careers: The Business and the People, 4916

Advertising, the Uneasy Persuasion: Its Dubious Impact on American Society, 4620

Advice to the Players, 6099

Advise and Consent, 959(F)

The Aegean Civilizations, 7111

The Aeneid of Virgil, 3187

Aerobics, 5346

The Aerobics Program for Total Well-Being: Exercise, Diet, Emotional Balance, 5347

The Aeronauts, 9067

Aerospace Careers, 5054

Aeschylus, 3806

Aesop's Fables, 3468

The Affluent Society, 4566

Africa, 7348

Africa: Dispatches from a Fragile Continent, 7350

Africa: The People and Politics of an Emerging Continent, 7361

Africa in History: Themes and Outlines, 7345

The Africa News Cookbook: African Art: An Introduction, 5767

African Calliope, 7368

African Cooking for Western Kitchens, 9345

African Folktales: Traditional Stories of the Black World, 3377

The African Genius: An Introduction to African Cultural and Social History, 7345

African Images, 7353

African Literatures in the 20th Century: A Guide, 3593

African Music: A People's Art, 5813

African Mythology, 3463

The African Queen, 88(F)

The African Slave Trade, 7346

The Africans: A Triple Heritage, 7352

The Afro-American Artist: A Search for Identity, 5794

Afro-American Folktales: Stories from Black Traditions in the New World, 3417

Afro-American Literature in the Twentieth Century: The Achievement of Intimacy, 3571

Afro-American Writing: An Anthology of Prose and Poetry, 2935

After All These Years: A New Look at the Sixties Generation, 8075

After Dark, 150(F)

After Man: A Zoology of the Future, 6994

After the First Death, 61(F)

After the First Love, 2281(F)

After the Revolution: The Smithsonian History of Everyday Life in the Eighteenth Century, 7883

After the Storm, 235(F)

The Aftermath: Asia, 7320

Aftermath of Colonialism, 7334

Afterwar, 2689(F)

Again Calls the Owl, 431(F)

Against Infinity, 2406(F)

Against Our Will: Men, Women and Rape, 5505

Against Rape, 4485

Agatha Christie, 3693

Agatha Christie: A Biography, 6236

Agatha Christie: An Autobiography, 6234

Agatha Christie: The Woman and Her Mysteries, 6235

The Age of Faith, 7127

The Age of Innocence, 1619(F)

The Age of Jackson, 7882

The Age of Louis XIV, 7129

The Age of Napoleon, 7143

The Age of Reason Begins, 7130

The Age of Reform from Bryan to F.D.R. 7747

The Age of Voltaire, 7144

The Age of Washington: George Washington's Presidency, 1789–1797, 6573

Age of Wonders, 7170

Age Wave: The Challenges and Opportunities of an Aging America, 5083

Agent in Place, 196(F)

Agent of Chaos, 2794(F)

Ah, But Your Land Is Beautiful, 986(F)

Ah, Sweet Mystery of Life, 2908(F)

Aha! Gotcha: Paradoxes to Puzzle and Delight, 8852

AIDS, 5187

AIDS: Deadly Threat, 5220

AIDS: In Search of a Killer, 5202

AIDS: Opposing Viewpoints, 5167

AIDS: The Facts, 5201

AIDS: What Does It Mean to You? 5191

The AIDS Crisis: Conflicting Social Values, 5168

The AIDS Epidemic, 5177

AIDS, Trading Fears for Facts: A Guide for Teens, 5188

Ain't I a Woman! A Book of Women's Poetry from around the World, 3170

Ain't Misbehavin': The Story of Fats Waller, 6453

The Air & Space Catalog, 8270

The Air Force Academy: An Illustrated History, 4283

The Air War in Europe, 7176

Air War in Vietnam, 8105

The Airline Builders, 9056

Airport, 116(F)

Ake: The Years of Childhood, 7390

The Alamo, 7996

Alamut, 1284(F)

Alas, Babylon, 2551(F)

Alaska, 1513(F)

The Alaskans, 8192

Albatross, 6(F)

Albert Camus, 3600

Alcohol and Alcoholism, 5115

Alcohol and You, 5106

Alcoholism, 5155

Alcoholism: The Facts, 5120

The Aleph and Other Stories: 1933–1969, 2895(F)

Alethea, 1407(F)

Alex: The Life of a Child, 6902

Alex the Great, 644(F)

Alexander Pushkin: Complete Prose Fiction, 2955(F)

Alexander the Great, 6821, 6822

Alfred Hitchcock, 6047

Alfred the Great, 6824

Alias Billy the Kid, the Man Behind the Legend, 6616

Alice, 661(F)

Alice and Edith: A Biographical Novel of the Two Wives of Theodore Roosevelt, 1620(F)

Alicia: My Story, 6889

Alistair Cooke's America, 7723

Alive: The Story of the Andes Survivors, 7682

All about Houseplants, 9382

All about Puppies—Your Dog's First Year, 8710

All about Words, 3943

All Creatures Great and Small, 6674

All Fall Down: America's Tragic Encounter with Iran, 7624

All God's Children Need Traveling Shoes, 6212

All I Really Need to Know I Learned in Kindergarten: Uncommon Thoughts on Common Things, 4007

All in a Lifetime, 6458

All Men Are Brothers, 6809

The All-New Official Cheerleader's Handbook, 9588

All-Nighter, 2233(F)

All Problems Are Simple and Other Stories: Nineteen Views of the College Years, 765(F)

All Quiet on the Western Front, 1636(F)

All-Terrain Bikes, 9741

All That Glittered: My Life with the Supremes, 5903

All the Brave Promises, 7291

All the Comforts of Home: The Story of the First Pet Motel, 8676

All the King's Men, 3132

All the Old Bargains, 737(F)

All the President's Men, 8047

All the Traps of Earth, 1270(F)

All Things Bright and Beautiful, 6674

All Things Wise and Wonderful, 6674

Allen Quartermain, 114(F)

The Almanac of American History, 7775

Almost Human: A Journey into the World of Baboons, 8503

Along the Road to Soweto: A Racial History of South Africa, 7386

Alpha & Omega: Ethics at the

Frontiers of Life and Death, 5257

The Alphabet Effect, 3967

Alternate Computers, 9020

Alternative Histories: Eleven Stories of the World as It Might Have Been, 1310(F)

Alternative Investments, 4587

Alvarez: The Adventures of a Physicist, 6649

Always the Young Strangers, 6301

Alzheimer's Disease, 5178

Am I Alive? A Surviving Flight Attendant's Struggle and Inspiring Triumph over Tragedy, 6942

Amadeus, 3117

The Amateur Astronomer's Handbook, 8278

The Amateur Magician's Handbook, 9397

The Amateur Naturalist, 8386

The Amateur Naturalist's Handbook, 8380

The Amateurs, 6706

The Amazing and Death-Defying Diary of Eugene Dingman, 946(F)

Amazing Science Fiction Stories: The War Years, 2564(F)

Amazing Stories: 60 Years of the Best Science Fiction, 2383(F)

Amazing Stories: Visions of Other Worlds, 2565(F)

The Amazing Universe, 8365

Ambassador of Progress, 2844(F)

The Ambassadors, 405(F)

The Ambivalence of Abortion, 5462

Amelia Earhart: A Biography, 6140

America: A Narrative History, 7784

America at Its Best: Opportunities in the National Guard, 4280

America at 1750: A Social Portrait, 7842

America by Design, 5700

America Enters the World, 8021

America in Legend, 3436

America in Poetry, 3333

America in Search of Itself: The Making of the President, 1956–1980, 8093

America in the Gilded Age, 8007

America in Vietnam: A Documentary History, 8152

America Inside Out, 6303

America on Six Rubles a Day: Or, How to Become a Capitalist Pig, 3513

America on Wheels: Tales and Trivia of the Automobile, 9080

America 2040, 2607(F)

America Worked: The 1950s Photographs of Dan Weiner, 8060

The American, 408(F)

The American Age: United States Foreign Policy at Home and Abroad since 1750, 7756

American Album, 7752

The American Almanac of Jobs and Salaries, 4813

American Architects, 5701

American Architecture Now II, 5699

American Artists on Art from 1940 to 1980, 5750

American Beat, 3535

American Boys, 1680(F)

The American Boys Handy Book: What to Do and How to Do It, 9135

American Caesar: Douglas MacArthur, 1880–1964, 6601

The American Cancer Society Cancer Book: Prevention, Detection, Diagnosis, Treatment, Cure, 5189

The American Canvas: Paintings from the Collection of the Fine Arts Museums of San Francisco, 5806

An American Childhood, 6242

The American Circus: An Illustrated History, 5977

The American Civil War, 7911, 7937

American Classic: Car Poems for Collectors, 3178

American Commercial Banking: A History, 4596

American Costume, 1915–1970: A Source Book for the Stage Costumer, 9172

An American Dilemma, 4374

An American Doctor's Odyssey, 6673

American Dream and Zoo Story, 3060

American Dreams: Lost and Found, 8090

American Education: The National Experience, 1783–1876, 7724

American Education, the American Experience: 1607–1783, 7724

The American Experience in Vietnam, 8108

The American Experience in Vietnam: A Reader, 8142

American Families: 28 Short Stories, 921(F)

The American Family, 5681

American Favorite Ballads, 5953

American Fiction, 1914 to 1945, 3701

The American Fighter, 9123

American Film Genres: Approaches to a Critical Theory of Popular Film, 6094

American Film Now: The People, the Power, the Money, the Movies, 6102

American Filmmakers Today, 6061

American Folk Poetry: An Anthology, 3264

American Folklore, 3437

American Folklore and Legend, 3440

American Food: The Gastronomic Story, 9347

American Football: The Records, 9862

American Foreign Policy: Opposing Viewpoints, 4129

American Given Names: Their Origin and History in the Context of the English Language, 3950

American Government: Opposing Viewpoints, 4184

The American Heart Association Cookbook, 9335

The American Heritage Book of Indians, 7795

The American Heritage Book of the Revolution, 7852

American History/American Television: Interpreting the Video Past, 6042

American Hunger, 6332

American Indian Mythology, 3424

American Indian Myths and Legends, 3423

American Indian Policy, 4394

American Indian Warrior Chiefs: Tecumseh, Crazy Horse, Chief Joseph, Geronimo, 6477

American Indians, 7808

American Indians, American Justice, 7804

American Indians of the Southwest, 7805

The American Language: An Inquiry into the Development of English in the United States, 3938

The American League: An Illustrated History, 9653

An American Life: The Autobiography, 6553

American Literary Almanac, 3772

American Literature: The Makers and the Making, 2896

The American Medical Association Family Medical Guide, 5075

The American Mind, 7721

American Mosaic: The Immigrant Experience in the Words of Those Who Lived It, 4335

American Music Makers: An Introduction to American Composers, 6182

American Negro Short Stories, 451(F)

The American Novel and Its Tradition, 3709

American Painting of the Nineteenth Century: Realism, Idealism and the American Experience, 5803

American Place-Names: A Concise and Selective Dictionary for the Continental United States of America, 7780

American Poetry: The Puritans through Walt Whitman, 3894

The American Poetry Anthology, 3275

American Poetry of the Twentieth Century, 3886

The American Political Tradition, and the Men Who Made It, 7748

American Presidents, 6481

The American Presidents, 6492

An American Primer, 7716

The American Promise: Voices of a Changing Nation, 8082

American Renaissance: Our Life at the Turn of the 21st Century, 4412

The American Revolution through British Eyes: The War for America, 1770–1781, 7851

The American Scene: A Reader, 3541

The American Short Story: A Critical Survey, 3786

American Short Story Masterpieces, 2901(F)

The American Short Story, 1900–1945/1945–1980, 3780

American Sign Language: A Comprehensive Dictionary, 3902

American Silent Film, 6009

The American Songbag, 5952

American Supercar, 9099

American Talk: The Words and Ways of American Dialects, 3924

American Tapestry: Eyewitness Accounts of the Twentieth Century, 7781

An American Tragedy, 799(F)

American Values: Opposing Viewpoints, 4411

American Vaudeville as Seen by Its Contemporaries, 6110

The American Vegetarian Cookbook: From the Fit for Life Kitchen, 9331

American Voices: 5 Contemporary Playwrights in Essays & Interviews, 3838

American Wars and Heroes: Revolutionary War through Vietnam, 7760

The American Weather Book, 8871

The American West: An Interpretive History, 7955

American Women and World War II, 7316

American Women Poets, 3877

The American Yoga Association Beginners' Manual, 5292

The Americans: The Colonial Experience, 7717

The Americans: The Democratic Experience, 7717

The Americans: The National Experience, 7717

America's Black Musical Heritage, 5831

America's Concentration Camps, 7185

America's Elections, 4277

America's Fascinating Indian Heritage, 7821

America's Foreign Policy, 1945–1976: Its Creators and Critics, 6485

America's Future: Opposing Viewpoints, 8058

America's Gilded Age: Intimate Portraits from an Era of Extravagance and Chance, 1850–1890, 8019

America's Hidden Corners: Places off the Beaten Path, 7725

America's Historic Places: An Illustrated Guide to Our Country's Past, 7772

America's Humor: From Poor Richard to Doonesbury, 3565

America's Longest War: The United States and Vietnam, 1950–1975, 8120

America's Lowest Cost Colleges, 4761

America's Magnificent Mountains, 7726

America's Majestic Canyons, 7727

America's Neighborhood Bats, 8527

America's New Economy: The Basic Guide, 4589

America's Old Masters, 6174

America's Prisons: Opposing Viewpoints, 4493

America's Seashore Wonderlands, 8881

America's Secret Army, 4288

America's Top 300 Jobs, 4815

America's Troubled Children, 5371

America's Wild and Scenic Rivers, 7728

America's Wild Woodlands, 7749

America's Wildlife Hideaways, 8411

America's Working Women, 7714

Amish Society, 4054

Amo, Amas, Amat and More: How to Use Latin to Your Own Advantage and to the Astonishment of Others, 3917

Among Sisters, 529(F)

Among the Believers, 7601

Amusement Park, 214(F)

Amusing Ourselves to Death: Public Discourse in the Age of Show Business, 6048

Amy Lowell, 3876

The Amy Vanderbilt Complete Book of Etiquette: A Guide to Contemporary Living, 5578

Anackire, 1189(F)

The Anastasia Syndrome and Other Stories, 1960(F)

Anatomy of a Jury: The System on Trial, 4260

Anatomy of a Scientific Discovery, 5314

Anatomy of an Illness as Perceived by the Patient: Reflections on Healing and Regeneration, 5179

An Anatomy of Drama, 3797

Anatomy of Revolution, 4171

The Anatomy of Terrorism, 4548

The Anchor Companion to the Orchestra, 5932

The Ancient Americas, 7631

Ancient Greece, 7104

Ancient Greek Literature, 3573

The Ancient Greeks: A Critical History, 7102

Ancient Light, 2555(F)

Ancient Lives: Daily Life in Egypt of the Pharaohs, 7098

The Ancient Mariners, 7089

Ancient Myths, 3455

Ancient North Americans, 7811

Ancient South Americans, 7675

And a Voice to Sing With: A Memoir, 6360

And Both Were Young, 2294(F)

And I Am Afraid of My Dreams, 7271

And Justice for All: An Oral History of the Japanese American Detention Camps, 7305

And More by Andy Rooney, 3508

And No Birds Sang, 7261

And Promenade Home, 6383

And Quiet Flows the Don, 1469(F)

And So I Sing, 6184

And Still I Rise, 3237

And Still We Rise: Interviews with 50 Black Role Models, 4376

And the Band Played On, 5219

And the Lucky Winner Is . . . 9537

And the Violins Stopped Playing: A Story of the Gypsy Holocaust, 1672(F)

And the Walls Came Tumbling Down: An Autobiography, 6493

And Then the Harvest: Three Television Plays, 3110

Andersonville, 1540(F)

Andrew Carnegie, 6651

Andrew Jackson and the Course of American Democracy, 1833–1845, 6532

Andrew Jackson and the Course of American Empire, 6532

Andrew Jackson and the Course of American Freedom, 6532

Andrew Lloyd Webber, 6355

Androcles and the Lion, 3036

Android at Arms, 2702(F)

The Andromeda Strain, 2493(F), 2495(F)

André Previn's Guide to the Orchestra, 5940

Angel Station, 2840(F)

Angel Unaware, 6905

Angel with the Sword, 2467(F)

Angle of Repose, 606(F)

Anglish-Yinglish: Yiddish in American Life and Literature, 3906

Angry Mountain, 123(F)

Anguished English, 3932

Animal Communication: Opposing Viewpoints, 8481

Animal Dreaming: The Art and Science of Interspecies Communication, 8483

Animal Farm, 1243(F)

Animal Farm: Pastoralism & Politics, 3689

Animal Partners: Training Animals to Help People, 8670

Animal Rights: Opposing Viewpoints, 8451

The Animal Rights Handbook: Everyday Ways to Save Animal Lives, 8574

The Animal Shelter, 8670

Animal Thinking, 8476

The Animal Wife, 1357(F)

Animals without Backbones: An Introduction to the Invertebrates, 8614

Ann Landers Talks to Teenagers about Sex, 5475

Anna and the King of Siam, 6924

Anna Christie, The Emperor Jones, and The Hairy Ape, 3111

Anna Karenina, 318(F)

Annable's Treasury of Literary Teasers, 3564

The Annals of the Heechee, 2731(F), 2735(F)

The Annapolis Book of Seamanship, 9935

Annapurna: A Woman's Place, 9551

Anne Frank Remembered: The Story of Miep Gies, Who Helped to Hide the Frank Family, 7209

Anne Frank's Tales from the Secret Annex, 1654

Anne McCaffrey, 3704

Annie John, 856(F)

Annie Oakley and Buffalo Bill's Wild West, 6426

The Anodyne Necklace, 2035(F)

Anorexia Nervosa, 5397

Another Man's Murder, 1997(F)

Another Shore, 1040(F)

Ansel Adams, an Autobiography, 6188

Answer as a Man, 1600(F)

Answer to History, 7622

Antarctic Wildlife, 7696

Anthem, 989(F)

Anthology of Japanese Literature from the Earliest Era to the Mid-Nineteenth Century, 2928

An Anthology of World Poetry, 3859

The Anti-Apartheid Reader: South Africa and the Struggle against White Racist Rule, 7378

Antigone, 3018

Antoine de Saint-Exupery, 3642

Anton Chekhov, 3802, 3804

Anton Chekhov's Plays, 2995

The Anxious Years: America in the Vietnam-Watergate Era, 8081

Anya, 7287

Anybody's Bike Book, 9752

Anything Can Happen, 6937

Anything for Billy, 1576(F)

Apartheid: A History, 7375

The Apartheid Crisis: How We Can Do Justice in a Land of Violence, 7388

The Apartheid Handbook, 7381

Apocalypse When? Cosmic Catastrophe and the Fate of the Universe, 8360

An Apple a Day: Adventures of a Country Doctor, 6700

An Apple for My Teacher: Twelve Authors Tell about Teachers Who Made the Difference, 4634

Apple Software for Pennies, 8976

Appointment in Samarra, 724(F)

Approaches to Science Fiction, 3625

Approaching Vietnam: From World War II through Dienbienphu, 1941–1954, 8114

April Morning, 1521(F)

The Aquarium Encyclopedia, 8778

The Aquitaine Progression, 181(F)

Arab Folktales, 3382

The Arab-Israeli Wars, 7613

Arabella and the Beast, 2229(F)

The Arabian Nights, 3380

Arabian Peninsula, 7593

Arafat: In the Eyes of the Beholder, 6803

Araminta Station, 2809(F)

Aransas, 2276(F)

The Arbor House Book of Cartooning, 9189

Arch of Triumph, 1674(F)

Archery for Beginners, 9607

Archimedes' Revenge: The Joys and Perils of Mathematics, 8837

Architects of Air Power, 7153

Architectural and Building Design: An Introduction, 5691

Architecture Is Elementary: Visual Thinking through Architectural Concepts, 5690

The Architecture of Castles: A Visual Guide, 7124

Architecture of Frank Lloyd Wright: A Complete Catalog, 5705

Architecture through the Ages, 5693

The Arco Guide to Knitting Stitches, 9226

Arco's Complete Preparation for High School Entrance Examinations, 4715

Arctic Animals: A Celebration of Survival, 7691

Arctic Dreams: Imagination and Desire in a Northern Landscape, 7697

The Arctic Grail: The Quest for the Northwest Passage and the North Pole, 7690

The Arctic Wolf: Living with the Pack, 8519

The Arctic World, 7692

Are You Dying for a Drink? Teenagers and Alcohol Abuse, 5122

Are You Happy? Some Answers to the Most Important Questions in Your Life, 5554

Aren't You the One Who . . .? 2884(F)

Aretha Franklin: The Queen of Soul, 6392

Argentina, 1516–1982, 7683

Arid Lands, 8819

Ariel, 3311

Aristotle, 3995

Aristotle for Everybody: Difficult Thought Made Easy, 3991

The Arizona Kid, 864(F)

Arlen Roth's Complete Acoustic Guitar, 5941

Arlington National Cemetery: Shrine to America's Heroes, 8171

Armada, 1429(F)

The Armada, 7526, 7538

The Armageddon Rag, 1213(F)

The Armchair Angler, 9824

The Armchair Book of Baseball, 9699

The Armchair Book of Baseball II, 9700

The Armchair Universe: An Exploration of Computer Worlds, 8966

The Armies of Daylight, 1141(F)

Arms and the Man, 3036

Arms Control, 4152

Arnie, the Darling Starling, 8669

Arnold's Bodybuilding for Men, 9775

Around the Moon, 2814(F)

Around the World in Eighty Days, 324(F)

Around the World in 80 Days with Michael Palin, 3506

Arranging: The Basics of Contemporary Floral Design, 9298

The ARRL Handbook, 1990, 9046

The Arrowhead Cattle Company, 46(F)

Arrow's Fall, 1183(F)

Arrow's Flight, 1183(F)

Arrows of the Queen, 1183(F)

Arrowsmith, 703(F)

Ars Magica, 1285(F)

Art: A History of Painting, Sculpture, Architecture, 5745

Art Deco of the 20s and 30s, 5747

Art in America: A Brief History, 5801

The Art of Black and White Enlarging, 9439

The Art of Caricature, 5718

The Art of Cartooning, 9197

The Art of Clear Thinking, 5588

The Art of Fiction: Notes on Craft for Young Writers, 4678

The Art of Loving, 5559

Art of Our Century: The Chronicle of Western Art, 5738

The Art of Photography, 1839–1989, 9408

The Art of Pitching, 9696

The Art of Place-Kicking and Punting, 9851

The Art of Quarterbacking, 9838

The Art of the Puppet, 5982

The Art of Walt Disney: From Mickey Mouse to the Magic Kingdoms, 5793

Art Rust's Illustrated History of the Black Athelete, 6710

Arthur, 1187(F)

Arthur Ashe's Tennis Clinic, 9964

Arthur C. Clarke, 3681

Arthur C. Clarke's World of Strange Powers, 9493

Arthur Conan Doyle, 3657

Arthur Miller, 3842, 6290

Arthur Miller: A Collection of Critical Essays, 3835

Arthur Miller's Collected Plays, 3104

Arthur Rex, 1408(F)

An Arthurian Reader: Selections from Arthurian Legend, Scholarship and Story, 3408

Artifact, 2401(F)

Artificial Intelligence, 9019

Artificial Things, 2550(F)

An Artists Album, 5741

Artists and Artisans, 5684

The Artist's Handbook, 9213

Artists in Crime, 2106(F)

As I Lay Dying, 547(F)

As the Waltz Was Ending, 7192

The Ascension Factor, 1150(F)

The Ascent of Man, 6990

Ascent to Civilization: The Archaeology of Early Man, 7018

An Ash-Blonde Witch, 1195(F)

The Ash Staff, 1119(F)

The Ashton Horror, 1720(F)

Asian Americans: An Interpretive History, 4399

The Asian Century, 7395

Asimov on Numbers, 8846

Asimov on Physics, 8900

Asimov on Science: A 30-Year Retrospective, 8204

Asimov's Biographical Encyclopedia of Science and Technology, 6640

Asimov's Chronology of Science and Discovery, 8205

Asimov's Galaxy: Reflections on Science Fiction, 3694

Asimov's Guide to the Bible, 4091

Asimov's Guide to the Bible: The New Testament, 4092

Asimov's Guide to the Bible: The Old Testament, 4092

Asimov's New Guide to Science, 8206

The Asking Price, 609(F)

The Assassination, 7888

Assault on the Gods, 2560(F)

Assembly Language Programming for the IBM Personal Computer, 8961

Assignment in Brittany, 196(F)

Assignment in Eternity, 2576(F), 2583(F)

The Assistant, 1398(F)

Astounding Days: A Science Fictional Autobiography, 3620

The Astral Mirror, 2419(F)

Astronomers' Stars, 8273

The Astronomer's Universe: Stars, Galaxies, and Cosmos, 8261

The Astronomy Handbook, 8279

Astronomy of the Ancients, 8248

Astronomy Projects for Young Scientists, 8240

Astronomy Today, 8309

Astronomy with a Small Telescope, 8280

Astrophotography: A Step-by-Step Approach, 8267

At Death's Door, 1921(F)

At Risk, 676(F)

At the Earth's Core, 2448(F)

At the Edge, 762(F)

At the Field's End: Interviews with Twenty Pacific Northwest Writers, 3764

At the Mountains of Madness and Other Novels, 1804(F), 1806(F)

At the Mountains of Madness and Other Tales of Terror, 1805(F)

At Winter's End, 2783(F)

At Wit's End, 3486

Athabasca, 1664(F)

Athletes: Photographs, 1860–1986, 9597

The Athlete's Game Plan for College and Career, 9564

The Athlete's Guide to Sports Medicine, 5350

The Athletic Body: A Complete Fitness Guide for Teenagers—Sports, Strength, Health, Agility, 5355

Atlantic & Gulf Coasts, 8375

The Atlantic Crossing, 7758

Atlantis, 2373(F)

Atlantis: Opposing Viewpoints, 9533

Atlantis: The Biography of a Legend, 3471

Atlas of Ancient America, 7799

Atlas of Global Strategy, 4141

Atlas of Medieval Europe, 7138

The Atlas of Mysterious Places, 7090

The Atlas of Natural Wonders, 7061

Atlas of the Arab World, 7594

Atlas of the Greek World, 7107

Atlas of the Islamic World Since 1500, 7602

Atlas of the North American Indian, 7826

Atlas of the Roman World, 7113

Atlas Shrugged, 990(F)

Atmosphere, 8866

Attitude: Commonsense Defense for Women, 5631

Attn: A & R: A Step-by-Step Guide into the Recording Industry, 4894

The Audubon Society Book of Trees, 8426

The Audubon Society Field Book of Insects, 8598

The Audubon Society Field Guide to North American Butterflies, 8609

The Audubon Society Field Guide to North American Fishes, Whales, and Dolphins, 8616

The Audubon Society Field Guide to North American Fossils, 6986

The Audubon Society Field Guide to North American Insects and Spiders, 8599

The Audubon Society Field Guide to North American Mammals, 8495

The Audubon Society Field Guide to North American Mushrooms, 8422

The Audubon Society Field Guide to North American Reptiles and Amphibians, 8461

The Audubon Society Field Guide to North American Rocks and Minerals, 8825

The Audubon Society Field Guide to North American Seashells, 8878

The Audubon Society Field Guide to North American Seashore Creatures, 8618

The Audubon Society Field Guide to North American Trees: Eastern Region, 8427

The Audubon Society Field Guide to North American Trees: Western Region, 8428

The Audubon Society Field Guide to North American Wildflowers: Eastern Region, 8440

The Audubon Society Field Guide to North American Wildflowers: Western Region, 8446

The Audubon Society Field Guide to the Natural Places in Mid-Atlantic States, 8167

The Audubon Society Field Guide to the Natural Places of the Northeast, 8167

The Audubon Society Handbook for Butterfly Watchers, 8610

August '39: The Last Four Weeks of Peace, 7221

Auschwitz: True Tales from a Grotesque Land, 6936

Australia, 7478

Australia: Beyond the Dreamtime, 7464

Australia, a Natural History, 7469

Australia and New Zealand, 7472

The Australians, 7477

Authentic Mexican: Regional Cooking from the Heart of Mexico, 9313

Auto Body Repairing and Repainting, 9115

Auto Mechanics Fundamentals, 9113

Auto Repair for Dummies, 9110

Auto Service and Repair, 9114

Autobiography, 6189

The Autobiography of Alice B. Toklas, 6316

The Autobiography of Benjamin Franklin, 6587

The Autobiography of Harry S. Truman, 6570

The Autobiography of Malcolm X, 6516

The Autobiography of Mark Twain, 6322

The Autobiography of Miss Jane Pittman, 458(F)

The Autobiography of W. E. B. Du Bois, 6503

Automotive Encyclopedia, 9078

Autumn across America, 8406

Autumn Lightning: The Education of an American Samurai, 7451

Avalanche Express, 87(F)

The Awakening of American Nationalism, 1815–1828, 7865

The Ayn Rand Companion, 3729

Azazel, 1018(F)

The Aztecs, 7643

Baa Baa Black Sheep, 7187

Baaa, 1198(F)

Babbitt, 978(F)

Babe: The Legend Comes to Life, 6732

Baby and Child Care, 5365

Baby of the Family, 1708(F)

Baby-Sitting for Fun and Profit, 5071

The Babysitter's Handbook, 5069

Bach, 6334, 6335

Bachelor Girls, 2972(F)

The Bachman Books: Four Early Novels by Stephen King, 1778(F)

Back to Class, 3273

Back to the Stone Age, 2449(F)

Backfire: American Culture and the Vietnam War, 8099

Background to Danger, 5(F)

The Backpacker's Manual, 9799

Backpacking Basics, 9802

Backpacking One Step at a Time, 9800

Backstreets: Springsteen, the Man & His Music, 6444

Bad Company, 49(F)

The Bad War: An Oral History of the Vietnam War, 8151

Badge and Buckshot: Lawlessness in Old California, 8177

Badge in the Wilderness: My 30 Dangerous Years Combating Wildlife Violators, 6163

A Bait of Dreams, 1074(F)

Balanchine, 6362
Ball Four, 9629
The Ballad of the Sad Cafe: The Novels and Stories of Carson McCullers, 707(F)
Ballerina, 743(F)
Ballet & Modern Dance: A Concise History, 5958
The Ballet Goer's Guide, 5962
Ballooning: The Complete Guide to Riding the Winds, 9613
Balls, 6729
Ball's Bluff, 7912
A Band of Angels, 255(F)
Band Saw Projects, 9271
Bang the Drum Slowly, 2878(F)
Banker, 2016(F)
The Bankers, 4597
The Bantam Book of Correct Letter Writing, 3974
Barbiturates: Sleeping Potion or Intoxicant? 5126
Barchester Towers, 387(F)
Bare Bones: Conversations on Terror with Stephen King, 3744
The Barefoot Brigade, 1538(F)
Barefoot in the Park, 3121
The Bargain, 1848(F)
Barlowe's Guide to Extraterrestrials, 3614
Barnaby Rudge, 351(F)
A Barnstormer in Oz, 1114(F)
Barnstormers and Speed Kings, 9074
Barnum's Own Story, 6363
Baron Wolman Presents FDNY: New York's Bravest! 4230
Barren Ground, 817(F)
The Barretts of Wimpole Street: A Comedy in Five Acts, 3023
Barrio Boy, 6908
Barron's Basic Tips on the SAT Scholastic Aptitude Test, 4655
Barron's Compact Guide to Colleges, 4723
Barron's Guide to the Best, Most Popular and Most Exciting Colleges, 4719
Barron's Guide to the Most Prestigious Colleges, 4719
Barron's How to Prepare for High School Entrance Examinations (SSAT & COOP), 4714

Barron's How to Prepare for the College Level Examination Program, CLEP, General Examination, 4657
Barron's Profiles of American Colleges, 4723
Barron's Sports Injuries, 5448
Barron's 300 Best Buys in College Education, 4765
Baseball Anecdotes, 9688
The Baseball Book, 9661
Baseball Cards: Questions & Answers, 9443
The Baseball Encyclopedia: The Complete and Official Record of Major League Baseball, 9692
The Baseball Fan's Complete Guide to Collecting Autographs, 9455
Baseball Fathers, Baseball Sons, 9708
The Baseball Hall of Fame 50th Anniversary Book, 9625
The Baseball Hall of Shame 4, 9683
The Baseball Hall of Shame: Young Fan's Edition, 9682
Baseball Is a Funny Game, 9645
Baseball Lives, 9632
Baseball Rules Illustrated, 9690
Baseball's All-Star Game: A Game-by-Game Guide, 9673
Baseball's Great Experiment, 9704
Baseball's Greatest Insults, 9684
Baseball's Greatest Quotes, 9684
Baseball's Strangest Moments, 9687
Basic Bait Fishing, 9830
The Basic Bird Book, 8679
The Basic Book of Photography, 9417
BASIC Computer Games, 8957
The BASIC Cookbook, 9023
The Basic Darkroom Book, 9418
Basic Documents in American History, 7765
Basic Electronics, 9035
Basic Fishing, 9831
BASIC for Beginners, 8989
Basic Guide to Dressmaking:

How to Sew Successful Clothes, 9227
A Basic Guide to Fishing: For Freshwater Anglers of All Ages, 9829
A Basic Guide to Horse Care and Management, 8764
Basic Judaism, 4086
Basic Mathematics Skills, 8832
Basic Pattern Skills for Fashion Design, 9179
BASIC Programming, 9015
Basic Sailing, 9926
Basic Training: What to Expect & How to Prepare, 4281
Basic Weight Training, 9770
The Basic Works of Aristotle, 3993
Basic Writing, 9041
The Basic Writings of Sigmund Freud, 5535
Basketball: Concepts and Techniques, 9716
Basketball: The Woman's Game, 9729
The Basketball Abstract, 9725
Basketball Fundamentals, 9730
Batman & Me, 6198
The Battered Child, 5660
Battle for Atlanta: Sherman Moves East, 7888
The Battle for the Falklands, 7673
The Battle Horse, 694(F)
The Battle of Britain, 7182
Battle of Britain, 7260
The Battle of Britain: The Greatest Air Battle of World War II, 7335
Battle of Hastings, 7512
The Battle of the Atlantic, 7310
The Battle of the Bulge, 7310
The Battle of the Little Bighorn, 7978
Battlefield Atlas of the American Revolution, 7940
A Battlefield Atlas of the Civil War, 7940
Battleground Berlin: Diaries 1945–1948, 7501
Battles for Scandinavia, 7203
Battles of the Revolutionary War, 1775–1781, 7862
Bay of Pigs: The Untold Story, 7666
Be a Clown! 5981
Be a Winner at Chess, 9821

Be Buried in the Rain, 2110(F)
Be Smart about Sex: Facts for Young People, 5461
Be Your Own Personal Trainer, 5352
Beaches, 652(F)
The Beacon at Alexandria, 1364(F)
Beads! Make Your Own Unique Jewelry, 9153
The Bean Trees, 690(F)
The Bear Flag, 1570(F)
The Bear Hunter's Century, 6122
The Bear—A Novel, 286(F)
Bearer of a Million Dreams: The Biography of the Statue of Liberty, 8173
Bearing the Hourglass, 1014(F)
Bears and Men, 8506
The Beast Master, 2703(F)
Beast or Angel? Choices That Make Us Human, 5531
Beat to Quarters, 1426(F)
The Beatles, 6171
The Beatles: Untold Tales, 6369
The Beatles Live! 5879
Beauties, Beasts and Enchantments: Classic French Fairy Tales, 3415
Beautiful Braids, 5277
Beautiful Losers, 938(F)
Beautiful Swimmers: Watermen, Crabs and the Chesapeake Bay, 8622
Beauty: A Retelling of the Story of Beauty and the Beast, 1207(F)
The Beauty of the Beasts: Tales of Hollywood's Wild Animal Stars, 6019
Becoming a Beauty Queen: The Complete Guide, 5272
Becoming a Heroine: Reading about Women in Novels, 3617
Becoming Alien, 2724(F)
Becoming American: An Ethnic History, 4326
Becoming Americans, 4333
Becoming Your Own Parent, 5679
Beef and Veal, 9361
Been Clever Forever, 1903(F)
Been in the Storm So Long:

The Aftermath of Slavery, 8013
Bees: Their Vision, Chemical Senses, and Language, 8604
The Beet Queen, 454(F)
Before Freedom, When I Just Can Remember, 7870
Before the Fall: An Inside View of the Pre-Watergate White House, 8088
Before the Game, 9681
Before the Mayflower: A History of Black America, 4355
Before the Sun Dies: The Story of Evolution, 6998
Begin Bridge with Reese, 9820
Begin Chess, 9818
The Beginner's Book of Dreams, 767(F)
The Beginner's Book of Oil Painting, 9196
The Beginner's Book of Watercolour Painting, 9196
The Beginner's Guide to Computers, 8960
A Beginner's Guide to Getting Published, 3987
Beginner's Guide to Photography, 9421
The Beginner's Guide to Radio Control Sport Flying, 9304
Beginner's Guide to Stamp Collecting, 9461
Beginner's Guide to Winning Chess, 9821
Beginners' Love, 857(F)
The Beginning and the End, 8207
Beginning Backgammon, 9813
Beginning Bicycle Racing, 9761
Beginning Photography, 9412
The Beginning Place, 1191(F)
Behind Barbed Wire: The Imprisonment of Japanese Americans during World War II, 7199
Behind Closed Doors: Violence in the American Family, 5674
Behind the Dolphin Smile, 6697
Behind the Filmmaking Scene, 6001
Behind the Front Page: A Candid Look at How the News Is Made, 3981
Behind the Hits, 5873

Behind the Wall, 7434
Behold Man: A Photographic Journey of Discovery inside the Body, 5299
Beijing Spring, 7436
Being a Green Mother, 1010(F)
Being Alien, 2724(F)
Being & Race: Black Writing since 1970, 3742
Being Here: Poetry, 1977–1980, 3338
Being There, 1889(F)
Bel Ria, 283(F)
A Bell for Adano, 1658(F)
The Bell Jar, 728(F)
Bellamy's New World: A Botanical History of America, 8412
The Bellarosa Connection, 430(F)
The Belle of Amherst: A Play Based on the Life of Emily Dickinson, 3100
Belle Starr and Her Times: The Literature, the Facts, and the Legends, 6638
Belles on Their Toes, 6623
Belonging, 738(F)
Beloved, 1526(F)
Beloved Exile, 1430(F)
Ben Franklin Laughing, 3519
Ben Hur, 1376(F)
Bendigo Shafter, 160(F)
Benjamin Franklin Takes the Case, 2037(F)
Beowulf, 3191
Beowulf: A New Telling, 1241(F)
Beowulf: An Imitative Translation, 377
Bering Bridge: The Soviet-American Expedition from Siberia to Alaska, 7706
Berlin Game, 70(F)
Berlin Underground, 1938–1945, 7501
Berlioz, 6337
The Bermuda Triangle, 9476
Bernard Malamud, 3771
Berserker: Blue Death, 2763(F)
Berserker Man, 2763(F)
Berserker Throne, 2763(F)
Berserker's Planet, 2763(F)
Bertie and the Seven Bodies, 2089(F)
Bess W. Truman, 6566
Bessie, 6442

The Best American Essays, 1989, 3562

Best American Plays: 7th Series—1967–1973, 3061

Best American Plays: 3d Series—1945–1951, 3068

The Best and the Brightest, 8066

The Best Buys in College Education, 4736

The Best Crime Stories of the Nineteenth Century, 1918(F)

The Best from Fantasy and Science Fiction, 2539(F)

The Best Ghost Stories of H. Russell Wakefield, 1862(F)

The Best Horror from Fantasy Tales, 1773(F)

The Best Horror Stories from the Magazine of Fantasy and Science Fiction, 1747(F)

Best Intentions: The Education and Killing of Edmund Perry, 4351

The Best Japanese Science Fiction Stories, 2358(F)

Best Laid Plans: America's War against Terrorism, 4549

The Best Little Girl in the World, 699(F)

Best Loved Songs of the American People, 5944

The Best Mysteries of Isaac Asimov: The Master's Choice of His Own Favorites, 1914(F)

The Best of C. L. Moore, 2687(F)

The Best of Chess Life and Review, Volume I, 1933–1960, 9816

The Best of Chess Life and Review, Volume II, 1960–1988, 9816

The Best of Crime and Detective TV, 6004

The Best of Dear Abby, 5633

The Best of Family Circle Cookbook, 9336

The Best of Frank Herbert, 2592(F)

The Best of Friends, 1702(F)

The Best of John Brunner, 2441(F)

The Best of Life, 5713

The Best of Robert Service, 3324

The Best of Saki, 2958(F)

The Best of Spitball: The Literary Baseball Magazine, 9697

Best of the West: Stories That Inspired Classic Western Films, 229(F)

Best Plays of the Early American Theatre: From the Beginning to 1916, 3072

Best Plays of the Modern American Theatre: 2nd Series, 3069

Best Recipes from the Backs of Boxes, Bottles and Jars, 9333

The Best Science Fiction of Isaac Asimov, 1915(F)

The Best Short Stories by Negro Writers: An Anthology from 1899 to the Present, 464(F)

The Best Short Stories of Guy de Maupassant, 306(F)

Best Short Stories of Jack London, 177(F)

The Best Short Stories of Ring Lardner, 2932(F)

Best Sport Stories, 9601

Best Sports Stories: The Anthology That Honors 1989's Top Sports Writing and Photography, 9599

Best Stories of Sarah Orne Jewett, 2926(F)

The Best Supernatural Tales of Arthur Conan Doyle, 1738(F)

The Best-Ever Book of Dog & Cat Names, 8672

Best-Loved Folktales of the World, 3363

Best True Ghost Stories, 9506

Bestiary! 1084(F)

The Bet, 2316(F)

Bethie, 731(F)

Betsey Brown, 496(F)

Betsy Ashton's Guide to Living on Your Own, 5593

Better English Made Easy, 3925

Better Homes and Gardens American Patchwork & Quilting, 9228

Better Homes and Gardens America's Best Cross-Stitch, 9229

Better Homes and Gardens Blue Ribbon Bazaar Crafts, 9136

Better Homes and Gardens Complete Guide to Gardening, 9371

Better Homes and Gardens Cooking for Two, 9314

Better Homes and Gardens Country Bazaar Crafts, 9137

Better Homes and Gardens Knitting & Crocheting, 9230

Better Homes and Gardens New Baby Book, 5452

Better Homes and Gardens New Cook Book, 9315

Better Homes and Gardens New Garden Book, 9372

Better Homes and Gardens 1990 Decorating and Remodeling Book, 9296

Better Homes and Gardens Patchwork & Quilting, 9231

Better Homes and Gardens Successful Gardening, 9371

Better Homes and Gardens Traditional American Crafts, 9232

Better Homes and Gardens Woodworking Projects You Can Build, 9265

Better Mousetraps: The Best Mystery Stories of John Lutz, 2091(F)

Betty Crocker's Cookbook, 9326

Betty Crocker's Microwave Cookbook, 9316

Betty Crocker's Microwave Cooking, 9327

Betty Crocker's New International Cookbook, 9326, 9328

Betty Crocker's Smart Cook: The Essential Everyday Cookbook, 9317

Betty Crocker's Step-by-Step Cookbook, 9318

Between Parent and Teenager, 5653

Between Us, 16(F)

Between You and Me: A Heartfelt Memoir on Learning, Loving, and Living, 6361

Beyond Black Bear Lake, 8168

Beyond Boardwalk and Park Place, 9811

Beyond Boom and Crash, 4569

Beyond Sugar and Spice: How Women Grow, Learn, and Thrive, 5542

Beyond Survival: The "Invincible Principles" for Overcoming Adversity, 8106

Beyond the Barricades: Popular Resistance in South Africa, 7370

Beyond the Blue Event Horizon, 2731(F), 2735(F)

Beyond the Chocolate War, 792(F)

Beyond the Frozen Sea: Visions of Antarctica, 7700

Beyond the Helix: DNA and the Quest for Longevity, 5086

Beyond the Melting Pot: The Negroes, Puerto Ricans, Jews, Italians, and Irish of New York City, 4343

Beyond the Reef, 247(F)

Beyond the Wall, 8372

Beyond Training: How Athletes Enhance Performance Legally and Illegally, 5366

The Bible: A Literary Study, 4104

The Bible as History, 4106

The Bicentennial Man, and Other Stories, 2360(F)

Bicycle Repair, 9742

The Bicycle Repair Book, 9766

Bicycle Touring, 9743

Bicycle Touring and Camping, 9753

The Bicycle Touring Manual: Using the Bicycle for Touring and Camping, 9767

Bicycling Magazine's Complete Guide to Riding and Racing Techniques, 9762

Bicycling Magazine's Complete Guide to Upgrading Your Bike, 9740

Bicycling Magazine's Complete Guide to Bicycle Maintenance and Repair, 9744

The Big Band Years, 5854

The Big Book of New American Humor: The Best of the Past 25 Years, 3505

The Big Book of Painting Nature in Watercolor, 9207

The Big Change: America Transforms Itself, 1900–1950, 7710

Big Daddy from the Pedernales: Lyndon Baines Johnson, 6534

The Big Fisherman, 1367(F)

The Big Garage on Clearshot: Growing Up, Growing Old, and Going Fishing at the End of the Road, 1876(F)

The Big Sea: An Autobiography, 6267

The Big Sleep, 1945(F)

Big Ten Country: A Journey through One Football Season, 9866

The Big Time, 2637(F)

The Big Way Out, 602(F)

Biker, 121(F)

Biko, 6791

Bill Haley: The Daddy of Rock and Roll, 6396

The Bill James Historical Baseball Abstract, 9662

The Bill of Rights, 4191

Bill of Rights Reader: Leading Constitutional Cases, 4193

Bill Severn's Best Magic: 50 Top Tricks to Entertain and Amaze Your Friends on All Occasions, 9402

Bill, the Galactic Hero, 2573(F)

The Billboard Book of Number One Hits, 5846

The Billboard Book of Song Writing, 5837

Billie Holiday, 6404

Billie Holiday: Her Life & Times, 6405

The Billion Dollar Brain, 71(F)

Billy, 1853(F)

Billy Budd, Sailor, 412(F)

Billy Ray's Forty Days, 236(F)

Biloxi Blues, 3122

Bio of an Ogre: An Autobiography of Piers Anthony to Age 50, 6213

Bioethics: Dilemmas in Modern Medicine, 5255

Biologic: Environmental Protection by Design, 4446

Biology Projects for Young Scientists, 8246

Biomedical Ethics: Opposing Viewpoints, 5230

Bird: The Making of an American Sports Legend, 6742

Bird Behavior, 8555

The Bird Care Book: All You Need to Know to Keep Your Bird Healthy and Happy, 8673

The Bird Feeder Book: An

Easy Guide to Attracting, Identifying, and Understanding Your Feeder Birds, 8551

A Bird in Her Hair and Other Stories, 524(F)

Bird on Basketball: How-to Strategies from the Great Celtics Champion, 9713

The Bird You Care For, 8663

The Birder's Handbook: A Field Guide to the Natural History of North American Birds, 8535

A Birdkeeper's Guide to Budgies, 8661

A Birdkeeper's Guide to Finches, 8661

A Birdkeeper's Guide to Pet Birds, 8661

Birds, 8554

Birds, Beasts and Relatives, 8387

Birds for Pets and Pleasure, 8560

The Birds of America, 8528

Birds of North America, ;e n8545

Birds of North America, Eastern Region: A Quick Identification Guide to Common Birds, 8532

Birds of North America, Western Region, 8532

A Birdwatcher's Handbook: Field Ornithology for Backyard Naturalists, 8547

Birdwatching: A Guide for Beginners, 8540

Birdy, 753(F)

Birth Control, 5485

The Birth of a New Physics, 8905

The Birth of the Earth: A Wanderlied through Space, Time, and the Human Imagination, 8338

The Birth of the Republic, 1763–89, 7856

The Birthday Party, 3035

The Bishop's Boys: A Life of Wilbur & Orville Wright, 6703

Bishop's Gambit Declined, 2047(F)

The Bishop's Heir, 2620(F)

Bismarck: The Man and the Statesman, 6828

Bites and Stings: The World of Venomous Animals, 8485

Bits and Pieces: Understanding and Building Computing Devices, 9002
Bitter Melon, 4402
Black Amber, 2211(F)
Black Ambrosia, 1743(F)
Black American Literature, 3609
The Black Americans: A History in Their Own Words, 1619–1983, 4373
Black and White Photography: A Basic Manual, 9424
The Black Arrow, 381(F)
Black Boy: A Record of Childhood and Youth, 6332
The Black Cabinet: Superb Stories Based on Real Crimes, 2090(F)
The Black Candle, 1412(F)
The Black Cloth: A Collection of African Folktales, 3379
Black Dance, 5975
The Black Death: Natural and Human Disaster in Medieval Europe, 7136
Black Defenders of America, 6471
Black Elk Speaks, 6615
The Black Extended Family, 4371
The Black Family in Slavery and Freedom, 1750–1925, 7742
Black Feeling, Black Talk, Black Judgement, 3270
Black Folktales, 3439
Black Holes and Other Marvels, 2743(F)
Black Hollywood: The Negro in Motion Pictures, 6041
Black in Selma: The Uncommon Life of J. L. Chestnut, Jr. 6498
Black Leaders of the Nineteenth Century, 6480
Black Leaders of the Twentieth Century, 6469
Black Like Me, 4363
The Black Marble, 2209(F)
Black Mondays: Worst Decisions of the Supreme Court, 4245
Black Moses: The Story of Marcus Garvey, 6507
Black Mountain Breakdown, 742(F)
Black November, 2044(F)
Black Odyssey, 7869

The Black Pearl, 2303(F)
Black Pearls: Blues Queens of the 1920s, 6177
The Black Poets, 3316
Black Rain, 1660(F)
Black Sister: Poetry by Black American Women, 1746–1980, 3331
Black Star Rising, 2732(F)
The Black Student's Guide to Colleges, 4721
The Black Swan, 2238(F)
Black Theater in America, 6089
Black Theater, U.S.A. Forty-five Plays by Black Americans, 1847–1974, 3080
The Black Tower, 2064(F)
The Black Tradition in American Dance, 5971
Black Trillium, 1058(F)
The Black Unicorn, 2440(F)
Black Union Soldiers in the Civil War, 7920
The Black Velvet Gown, 1413(F)
Black Voices: An Anthology of Afro-American Literature, 2903
The Black West, 7959
Black Wind, 276(F)
Black Women Writers at Work, 6185
Blackberry Winter, 6691
Blackfeet Tales of Glacier National Park, 3426
Blacks: A Clown Show, 3001
The Blackstone Book of Magic & Illusion, 9393
Blade Runner, 2504(F)
Blame Me on History, 6798
Bleachers: A Summer in Wrigley Field, 9706
Bleak House, 352(F)
Bless Me, Ultima, 436(F)
Bless the Beasts and Children, 927(F)
The Blessing Way, 2053(F)
Blessings, 589(F)
Blind Date, 2186(F)
The Blindfold Horse: Memories of a Persian Childhood, 7620
Blissful Joy and the SATs: A Multiple Choice Romance, 2274(F)
Blitzkrieg, 7201, 7318
The Blockade: Runners and Raiders, 7943
Blood Brother, 1555(F)

Blood Evidence: A Story of True Crime in the Suburban South, 4483
Blood Feud, 1381(F)
Blood Line, 1143(F)
Blood Music, 2396(F)
Blood Oath, 210(F)
Blood of Amber, 1342(F)
The Blood of Ten Chiefs, 1245(F)
Blood Run, 2158(F)
Blood Season: Tyson and the World of Boxing, 6750
Blood Sport, 1841(F)
Blood Ties, 1022(F)
The Bloodiest Day: The Battle of Antietam, 7889
Bloodletters and Badmen: A Narrative Encyclopedia of American Criminals from the Pilgrims to the Present, 6120
Bloods: An Oral History of the Vietnam War by Black Veterans, 8146
Bloody Mary, 6835
Bloody Murder: From the Detective Story to the Crime Novel, 3632
The Bloody Sands, 278(F)
Blow-Out, 241(F)
Blown Away: The Rolling Stones and the Death of the Sixties, 5872
Blue Adept, 2356(F)
The Blue and the Gray, Vol. 1, 7902
Blue Fire, 2211(F)
Blue Highways: A Journey into America, 6152
Blue Juniata: A Life, Collected and New Poems, 3252
A Blue Moon in Poorwater, 560(F)
The Blue Nile, 7354
The Blue Planet, 8792
Blue Rise, 839(F)
Blue Savage, 1579(F)
Blue Skies and Blood: The Battle of the Coral Sea, 7223
Blue Tights, 511(F)
Blue World, 190(F)
Bluebloods, 2521(F)
Blueprint for a Green Planet, 4440
The Blues Route, 5889
The Bluest Eye, 479(F)
BMX: A Guide to Bicycle Motocross, 9715
BMX Action Bike Book, 9754

Boardsailing Made Easy: Teaching and Techniques, 9957

The Boat of a Million Years, 2340(F)

Boat Owner's Manual, 9922

The Boat Who Wouldn't Float, 9932

The Boats of Cherbourg, 7615

Bob Knight: His Own Man, 6746

Bob Marley, 6424

Bobby Rex's Greatest Hit, 815(F)

Body Clock: The Effects of Time on Human Health, 5296

The Body in Time, 5303

Body Language, 3900

Body Magic, 9395

The Body Victorious, 5213

Bodybuilding: The Weider Approach, 9778

Bodywork, 5341

Boeing 747, 9076

Boldness Be My Friend, 7268

Bolivia: The Evolution of a Multi-Ethnic Society, 7677

Bolt, 2009(F)

Bombed, Buzzed, Smashed or . . . Sober, 5136

Bombers over Japan, 7320

Bonds, Preferred Stocks and the Money Market, 4600

Bonjour Tristesse, 595(F)

Bonnie Dundee, 1479(F)

Bonnie Prince Charlie, 6835

The Book of Abigail and John: Selected Letters of the Adams Family, 1762–1784, 6521

The Book of Abraham, 1431(F)

The Book of Adam to Moses, 4111

The Book of Ages, 5526

The Book of Beads, 9142

The Book of Christmas, 4120

The Book of Classical Music Lists, 5824

The Book of Color Photography, 9409

The Book of Daniel, 655(F)

The Book of Lies, 9501

The Book of Longer Short Stories, 2946(F)

A Book of Love Poetry, 3175

The Book of Merlyn: The Unpublished Conclusion to

"The Once and Future King", 1319(F)

Book of North American Birds, 8530

The Book of Phoebe, 919(F)

The Book of Photography: How to See and Take Better Pictures, 9422

The Book of Potpourri: Fragrant Flower Mixes for Scenting and Decorating the Home, 9138

The Book of Pressed Flowers, 9139

Book of Shadows, 2614(F)

Book of the Eskimos, 7695

The Book of the Medieval Knight, 7141

The Book of the Moon, 8339

The Book of 35mm Photography, 9414

The Book of Whales, 8645

A Book of Women Poets from Antiquity to Now, 3848

Books: From Writer to Reader, 3977

Books That Changed the World, 3574

Boon Island, 1518(F)

Boot: The Inside Story of How a Few Good Men Became Today's Marines, 4282

Born for Liberty: A History of Women in America, 7733

Born Free: A Lioness of Two Worlds, 8509

Born Guilty: Children of Nazi Families, 7292

Born on the Fourth of July, 8124

Born to Run, 6445

The Borribles, 1089(F)

The Borrowed Years, 1938–1941: America on the Way to War, 8076

The Borzoi Anthology of Latin American Literature, 2948

Boston Boy, 6264

The Boston Celtics: The History, Legends, and Images of America's Most Celebrated Team, 9734

The Bostonians, 408(F)

Bouncing Back: How a Heroic Band of POWs Survived Vietnam, 8134

Bound for Glory, 6250

The Bounty Trilogy, 216(F)

The Bourne Identity, 182(F), 187(F)

The Bourne Supremacy, 182(F)

Bowling: Knowledge Is the Key, 9779

The Boxer Rebellion and Other Tales, 6672

Boy, 6237

The Boy Child Is Dying: A South African Experience, 7382

Boy Friends, Girl Friends, Just Friends, 5544

A Boy I Never Knew, 2176(F)

A Boy in That Situation: An Autobiography, 6916

The Boy in the Moon, 865(F)

The Boy Who Felt No Pain: Tales from the Pediatric Ward, 5244

Boys and Sex, 5489

The Boys from Brazil, 174(F)

The Boys of Summer, 9667

A Boy's Own Story, 942(F)

The Brain, 5323, 5327

The Brain: A User's Manual, 5310

Brain Function, 5306

Brain Wave, 2341(F)

Brainfood: Nutrition and Your Brain, 5319

The Branding of America, 4567

Brat Farrar, 2193(F)

The Brave Cowboy: An Old Tale in a New Time, 1(F)

Brave New World, 2604(F)

Brave New World Revisited, 4414

Brazil, 7687

Bread and Roses: The Struggle of American Labor, 4614

Bread and Wine, 916(F)

The Bread Loaf Anthology of Contemporary American Essays, 3543

Breads, 9362

Break In, 2010(F)

Breakdancing, 5972

Breakfast at Tiffany's: A Short Novel and Three Stories, 783(F)

Breaking into Broadcasting: Getting to a Good Job that Leads to the Top, 4895

Breaking into Communications, 4871

Breaking into the Big Leagues, 9646

The Breaking of Northwall, 2841(F)

The Breaking of the Seals, 1017(F)

Breaking Ranks, 4520

Breaking the Chains: African-American Slave Resistance, 7872

Breaking the Connection: How Young People Achieve Drug-Free Lives, 5138

Breaking the Mob, 4477

Breaking Up Is Hard to Do, 832(F)

The Breaks of the Game, 9724

Breakthrough: Emerging New Thinking, 4133

The Breakthrough: The Race for the Superconductor, 8936

Breakthrough: Women in Archaeology, 5031

Breakthrough: Women in Writing, 3963

Breakthrough to the Computer Age, 9033

Breast Self-Examination, 5359

Breathing Lessons, 933(F)

The Breathing Planet, 8869

The Brethren: Inside the Supreme Court, 4261

Brian Piccolo: A Short Season, 6758

Brian's Song, 3062

The Bride Price, 960(F)

Bride's Book of Etiquette, 5579

Brideshead Revisited: The Sacred and Profane Memories of Captain Charles Ryder, 617(F)

The Bridesmaid, 2150(F)

The Bridge at Andau, 7488

Bridge for Everyone: A Step-by-Step Text and Workbook, 9806

The Bridge of San Luis Rey, 1495(F)

The Bridge over the River Kwai, 1645(F)

Bridgehead, 2522(F)

The Bridges at Toko-Ri, 1690(F)

A Brief History of Time: From the Big Bang to Black Holes, 8366

Bright Shadow, 930(F)

Brighter Than a Thousand Suns: A Personal History of the Atomic Scientists, 7229

Brightness Falls from the Air, 2807(F)

Brighton Beach Memoirs, 3122, 3123

Bring Me a Unicorn, 6282

The Bristling Wood, 1167(F)

Britain, 7534

British Drama 1890 to 1950, 3808

British Folk Tales: New Versions, 3394

British Modernist Fiction, 1920 to 1945, 3651

The British Museum Book of the Rosetta Stone, 7093

Britten, 6339

Broadcasting Careers for You, 4885

Broadway Bound, 3122, 3123

Broadway Musicals, 5918

Broca's Brain: Reflections on the Romance of Science, 8232

Brokedown Palace, 1063(F)

The Broken Citadel, 2567(F)

The Broken Cord, 5181

Broken Heart Whole Heart: A Family and Addiction, 5153

Broken Sword, 2344(F)

Brokenclaw, 2019(F)

The Brontes: Charlotte Brontë and Her Family, 6219

The Brontës and Their World, 6218

Brother against Brother: The War Begins, 7907

Brother against Brother: Time-Life Books History of the Civil War, 7894

Brother, Can You Spare a Dime? The Great Depression, 1929–1933, 8037

Brother Esau, 1242(F)

Brother to the Lion, 1113(F)

Brothers: A Story of Courage and Survival against the Odds of Today's Society, 6482

Brothers and Sisters, 795(F)

Brothers in Arms, 2444(F)

The Brothers Karamazov, 308(F)

The Brothers' War: Civil War Letters to Their Loved Ones from the Blue & Gray, 7941

A Browser's Dictionary, and Native's Guide to the Un-known American Language, 3913

Bruce Tegner's Complete Book of Jujitsu, 9898

Bruce Tegner's Complete Book of Self-Defense, 9899

Bruckner, 6340

Brush Fire, 243(F)

Bubble Magic, 8912

Bubbles: A Self-Portrait, 6441

Buckaroo Banzai, 2681(F)

Buddenbrooks, 1448(F)

The Buddha, 4040

Buddhism: A Way of Life and Thought, 4077

Budgeting for America, 4217

Buffalo Afternoon, 1703(F)

Buffalo Bill: His Family, Friends, Fame, Failures and Fortunes, 6377

Buffalo Soldiers in Italy: Black Americans in World War II, 7213

The Bugs Bunny Golden Jubilee: 50 Years of America's Favorite Rabbit, 5986

Build-It-Better-Yourself Storage Around the House, 9284

Build Your Own Kit House, 9274

Build Your Own Working Robot: The Second Generation, 8983

Builders, 4941

Building and Flying Model Aircraft, 9404

Built in the U.S.A. American Buildings from Airports to Zoos, 5703

Bulfinch's Mythology: The Age of Fable, The Age of Chivalry, Legends of Charlemagne, 3449

Bulimia: The Binge-Purge Compulsion, 5373

The Bull from the Sea, 1372(F)

A Bullet for Stonewall, 1541(F)

The Bully Pulpit: Quotations from America's Presidents, 7734

Bum Steer, 2138(F)

The Bumblebee Flies Anyway, 647(F)

The Burger Book, 9369

Burn Marks, 2123(F)

Burn Up, 518(F)

Burning Chrome, 2557(F)

Burning Lights, 4041
The Burning Stone, 1145(F)
Burr, 1532(F)
Bury My Heart at Wounded Knee: An Indian History of the American West, 7796
The Bush Pilots, 9073
Business and Social Etiquette with Disabled People, 5437
The Busy Woman's Sewing Book, 9260
"But First a School": The First Fifty Years of the School of American Ballet, 5965
But What of Earth? 2357(F)
Butch Beard's Basic Basketball, 9712
Buttercups and Strong Boys: A Sojourn at the Golden Gloves, 9786
Butterflies and Moths, 8607
Butterflies of the World, 8608
The Butterfly Garden, 8611
By a Nose, 6761
Byron: A Portrait, 6226

C. B. Greenfield: A Little Madness, 2076(F)
C. S. Lewis, 3679
C.S. Lewis: Through the Shadowlands, 6281
Cabinetmaking: From Design to Finish, 9279
Caesar and Christ: A History of Roman Civilization from Its Beginnings to A.D. 337, 7101
Caesar and Cleopatra, 3036
Caffeine: The Most Popular Stimulant, 5435
The Cage, 7290
The Caine Mutiny, 1688(F)
Cain's Daughter, 1545(F)
Cajun Nights, 1737(F)
Cake Decorating Simplified: The Roth Method, 9357
Cakes, 9362
A Calendar of Saints, 4036
California Childhood, 2964
Call It Sleep, 909(F)
The Call of the Wild, 409(F)
The Call of the Wild and White Fang, 293(F)
The Call of the Wild, White Fang, and Other Stories, 178(F)
Call to Action: Handbook for Ecology, Peace, and Justice, 4413

Callahan's Crosstime Saloon, 2759(F)
Callahan's Lady, 2759(F)
Callahan's Secret, 2759(F), 2760(F)
The Callender Papers, 2206(F)
Camber of Culdi, 1175(F)
Camber the Heretic, 1175(F)
Camberleigh, 112(F)
A Cambodian Odyssey, 6811
The Cambridge Encyclopedia of Africa, 7356
The Cambridge Encyclopedia of China, 7411
The Cambridge Encyclopedia of Latin America and the Caribbean, 7625
The Cambridge Encyclopedia of Russia and the Soviet Union, 7564
The Cambridge Historical Encyclopedia of Great Britain and Ireland, 7517
The Cambridge Modern History, 7067
Camel Lot: The True Story of a Zoo-Illogical Farm, 8776
Camelot, 3095
Camelot and Idylls of the King, 2985
The Camera Never Blinks: Adventures of a TV Journalist, 6298
Cameron's Raid, 194(F)
Camilla, 2295(F)
Camping, 9791
Campus Cousins, 2311(F)
The Campus Survival Cookbook #2, 9367
Campus Visits and College Interviews: A Complete Guide for College-Bound Students and Their Families, 4764
Can Bears Predict Earthquakes? Unsolved Mysteries of Animal Behavior, 8475
Can Somebody Shout Amen! 4083
Canada, 7638
Canada: A Natural History, 7634
Canada 1988, 7637
The Canadians, 7635, 7636
The Canary Murder Case, 2203(F)
Candidates, Parties, and Campaigns: Electoral Politics in America, 4270
Candide, 327(F)

Candide, and Other Writings, 328(F)
Candy, 9362
Cane, 503(F)
Canework, 9145
Canned Art: Clip Art for the MacIntosh, 8973
Cannery Row, 996(F)
Can't Anybody Here Play This Game? 9630
The Canterbury Tales, 339
A Canticle for Leibowitz, 2685(F)
Cantor's Dilemma, 77(F)
The Cape Ann, 611(F)
Capital Punishment: Criminal Law and Social Evolution, 4239
Capitalism: Opposing Viewpoints, 4591
Capitalism vs. Socialism: Economic Policies of the USA and the USSR, 4574
The Captain and the Enemy, 823(F)
Captain Kidd and the War against the Pirates, 7844
Captains Courageous, 373(F)
Captains from Devon: The Great Elizabethan Seafarers Who Won the Oceans for England, 7527
The Captains' Honor, 2526(F)
The Captive, 2057(F)
Captives of Time, 1378(F)
Captured on Corregidor, 7326
The Car Book, 9093
The Cardinal of the Kremlin, 43(F)
Cards of Grief, 2858(F)
The Care of Reptiles and Amphibians in Captivity, 8465
The Care of Time, 4(F)
Care of Uncommon Pets, 8685
Career Choices for Students of Art, 4876
Career Choices for Students of Business, 4906
Career Choices for Students of Communication and Journalism, 4823
Career Choices for Students of Computer Science, 5039
Career Choices for Students of Economics, 4907
Career Choices for Students of English, 4947
Career Choices for Students of History, 4947

Career Choices for Students of Law, 4957
Career Choices for Students of M.B.A. 4908
Career Choices for Students of Mathematics, 5014
Career Choices for Students of Political Science and Government, 4958
Career Choices for Students of Psychology, 4988
Career Finder, 4867
Career Opportunities in Advertising & Public Relations, 4914
Career Opportunities in Art, 4886
Career Opportunities in Geology and the Earth Sciences, 5027
Career Opportunities in Television, Cable and Video, 5052
Career Opportunities in the Music Industry, 4878
Careers for Bookworms and Other Literary Types, 4948
Careers for Women in Politics, 4971
Careers in Advertising, 4927
Careers in Aviation, 5040
Careers in Banking and Finance, 4917
Careers in Beauty Culture, 4797
Careers in Business, 4936
Careers in Cable TV, 4828
Careers in Computer Sales, 4910
Careers in Computers, 5034
Careers in Education, 4949
Careers in Engineering, 5022
Careers in Fashion Retailing, 4921
Careers in Film and Video Production, 4888
Careers in Health and Fitness, 4952
Careers in Health Care, 4991, 5008
Careers in Health Services, 5055
Careers in High Tech, 5061
Careers in Law Enforcement and Security, 4959
Careers in Occupational Therapy, 4986
Careers in Pro Sports, 4854
Careers in Science, 5016
Careers in Teaching, 4954

Careers in the Fashion Industry, 4832
Careers in the Graphic Arts, 4862
Careers in the Investment World, 4911
Careers in the Restaurant Industry, 4846
Careers in Trucking, 5053
Careers in Veterinary Medicine, 4990
Careers in Word Processing and Desktop Publishing, 4935
Careers with Robots, 5025
Careers without College: No B.S. Necessary, 4863
Caribbean, 1494(F)
The Caribbean: The Genesis of a Fragmented Nationalism, 7662
The Caribbean in the Twentieth Century, 7661
Caring for Your Pet Bird, 8665
Carl Sandburg, 3882
Carnival of My Mind, 939(F)
Carnivorous Plants of the United States and Canada, 8445
Caroline and Julia, 1417(F)
Carpentry and Woodworking, 9273
Carrie, 1779(F)
The Carrier War, 7279
Carrying the Darkness: American Indochina—The Poetry of the Vietnam War, 397
The Carter Years: The President and Policy Making, 8044
Cartoon History of United States Foreign Policy, 1776–1976, 4140
Cartooning: The Art and the Business, 9190
Cartooning Fundamentals, 9211
Cartoons and Comics: Ideas and Techniques, 9212
The Carving of Mount Rushmore, 5807
Cascade Point and Other Stories, 2859(F)
The Case Book of Sherlock Holmes, 1987(F)
Case Histories, 5124
The Case of Charles Dexter Ward, 1805(F)
Casebook of the Black Widowers, 2368(F)
Casey on the Loose, 2873(F)

Cassandra Robbins, Esq. 504(F)
Cassie, 1519(F)
Castaway, 7471
Castaways: The Penikese Island Experiment, 4624
Castaways in Time, 1004(F)
Castle, 5707
Castle of Doves, 1433(F)
Castle of Wizardry, 1107(F)
Castle Roogna, 1012(F)
Castleview, 1871(F)
Cat-a-Log, 8703
The Cat and the Curmudgeon, 8688
The Cat Care Book: All You Need to Know to Keep Your Cat Healthy and Happy, 8693
Cat Dancers, 5969
Cat on a Hot Tin Roof, 3137
The Cat Who Came for Christmas, 8688
The Cat Who Knew Shakespeare, 1935(F)
The Cat Who Lived High, 1934(F)
The Cat Who Sniffed Glue, 1935(F)
The Cat Who Talked to Ghosts, 1936(F)
The Cat Who Walks through Walls, 2577(F)
The Cat Who Went Underground, 1937(F)
The Cat You Care For, 8687
A Catalogue of the World's Most Popular Coins, 9460
Catamaran Racing: Solutions, Secrets, Speed, 9940
Catastrophes! 2374(F)
Catch a Falling Spy, 72(F)
Catch Me If You Can, 6887
Catch-22, 1657(F)
The Catcher in the Rye, 1468(F)
Catcher in the Wry, 9705
Catfantastic, 2722(F)
Catfish: My Life in Baseball, 6724
Cathedral, 73(F)
Cathedral: The Story of Its Construction, 5708
Catherine the Great, 6833
Catherine the Great: Life and Legend, 6832
Catlore, 8697
Cats, 8707
Cat's Cradle, 2819(F)

Cat's Eye, 759(F)
Cat's Gambit, 2553(F)
The Cat's Meow, 1942(F)
Cats of the World, 8706
Cat's Pawn, 2554(F)
Catspaw, 2816(F)
Catwatching, 8698
Caught in Crystal, 1335(F)
Caught in the Crossfire, 153(F)
Caught in the Organ Draft: Biology in Science Fiction, 2375(F)
Cause for Alarm, 5(F)
The Causes of the American Civil War, 7933
The Causes of the Civil War, 7936
Cavalier in Buckskin: George Armstrong Custer and the Western Military Frontier, 6582
The Cave Girl, 31(F)
Caverns—Book 1, 2723(F)
Caves of Steel, 2361(F)
CD ROMs, 8993
Cecile, 523(F)
Celebrate the Bounty, 9310
Celebration: The Book of Jewish Festivals, 4038
A Celebration of American Family Folklore, 3443
A Celebration of Cats, 8691
Celtic Fairy Tales, 3402
Celtic Mythology, 3461
Censorship, 4314
Centennial, 1577(F)
Center Stage: One-Act Plays for Teenage Readers and Actors, 3067
Central America: A Nation Divided, 7659
Central America: Opposing Viewpoints, 7658
The Central Motion: Poems, 1968–1979, 3257
The Ceramic Spectrum: A Simplified Approach to Glaze & Color Development, 9164
Ceramics: A Potter's Handbook, 9166
Ceremony, 497(F)
A Certain People: American Jews and Their Lives Today, 4390
Cervantes, 3636, 3644
Cesar Chavez, 6497
Cézanne: A Biography, 6190
Chain Letter, 2139(F)

Chained Eagle, 8097
Chaining the Lady, 2351(F)
The Chains of Fate, 1407(F)
Chains of Gold, 1272(F)
Challenger: The Final Voyage, 8305
Champion: Joe Louis, Black Hero in White America, 6749
Champions: The Making of Olympic Swimmers, 9959
Championship Soccer, 9950
A Chance Child, 1308(F)
The Chancellor Manuscript, 183(F)
Change of Hearts, 2256(F)
Changeling, 1343(F)
The Changeling, 2239(F)
The Changeover: A Supernatural Romance, 1211(F)
Changer's Moon, 1074(F)
Changes in Latitudes, 840(F)
Changing Bodies, Changing Lives, 5449
Changing of the Guard: Power and Leadership in America, 8050
Changing Styles in Fashion: Who, What, Why, 5286
The Chantry Guild, 2508(F)
Chanur's Venture, 2474(F)
Chaplin, 6062
Chapterhouse: Dune, 2590(F)
Charcoal & Pastel, 9182
Chariots of Fire & a Christian Message for Today, 9977
Chariots of the Gods? Unsolved Mysteries of the Past, 9490
Charles Dickens, 3680
Charles Dickens: His Tragedy and Triumph, 6238
Charles Keeping's Book of Classic Ghost Stories, 1776(F)
Charles Keeping's Classic Tales of the Macabre, 1777(F)
Charlie Company: What Vietnam Did to Us, 8115
Charlotte Brontë, 3650
The Charm School, 74(F)
Chasing Shadows, 543(F)
Chasing the Glory: Travels across America, 6155
Chaucer: His Life, His Works, His World, 6233
Cheaper by the Dozen, 6623
Checkmate, 1425(F)

Cheerleader-Baton Twirler: Try Out and Win, 9600
Cheerleading and Songleading, 9562
Chekhov, The Major Plays, 2996
Chemical and Biological Warfare, 4165
Chemical Dependency, 5110
A Chemical Feast, 5420
Chemistry Made Simple, 8784
Chennault, 6580
Cherished Enemy, 1484(F)
The Cherry Orchard, 2997
Chesapeake, 1514(F)
Chess for Tomorrow's Champions, 9823
Chess in a Nutshell, 9821
Chess with a Dragon, 2556(F)
The Chessmen of Mars, 2453(F)
Chester Himes, 6265
Cheyenne Autumn, 7822
Cheyenne Dreams, 1505(F), 1507(F)
Chickenhawk, 8130
Child Abuse, 5648, 5661
The Child Buyer, 969(F)
A Child Called Noah, 6913
A Child Is Being Beaten: Violence Against Children, an American Tragedy, 5640
A Child Is Born, 5484
Child of the Morning, 1358(F)
Child of the Northern Spring, 1334(F)
Childhood's End, 2475(F)
Children: The Early Years, 5523
Children Having Children: Global Perspectives on Teenage Pregnancy, 5480
Children of a Lesser God, 3103
Children of Crisis: A Study of Courage and Fear, 4359
Children of Dune, 2593(F)
Children of Hiroshima, 7267
The Children of Sanchez, 7645
The Children of Santa Clara, 5394
Children of the Blitz: Memories of a Wartime Childhood, 7319
Children of the Dragon: The Story of Tiananmen Square, 7413
Children of the Holocaust: Conversations with Sons and Daughters of Survivors, 7204

Children of the Light, 2836(F)
Children of the Sun: Stories by and about Indian Kids, 7809
Children of the Wind, 1868(F)
Children with Emerald Eyes, 5401
Children without Childhood, 5680
Children's Costume in America, 1607–1910, 9177
Children's Story, 47(F)
A Child's Christmas in Wales, 3227
A Child's War: Fifteen Children Tell Their Story, 7198
Chilton's Auto Repair Manual, 1987–91, 9084
Chilton's Easy Car Care, 9091
Chilton's Guide to Auto Tune-Ups and Troubleshooting, 9092
Chilton's Motorcycle and ATV Repair Manual, 1945–85, 9747
China, 7435
China: Alive in a Bitter Sea, 7399
China: Its History and Culture, 7424
China: Opposing Viewpoints, 7407
China: The People's Republic, 1949–1976, 7401
China-Burma-India, 7320
China from the 1911 Revolution to Liberation, 7402
China from the Opium Wars to the 1911 Revolution, 7403
China Homecoming, 6246
China in Search of Its Future: Years of Great Reform, 1982–1987, 7437
China off the Beaten Track, 7428
China Today and Her Ancient Treasures, 7406
The Chinese, 7398
Chinese Art, 5768
Chinese Fairy Tales and Fantasies, 3385
Chinese Handcuffs, 651(F)
The Chinese Looking Glass, 7397
Chinese Mythology, 3451
The Chinese of America, 4400
Chinese Thought from Confucius to Mao Tse-tung, 4000
The Chipmakers, 9020

The Chisholm Trail, 7953
The Chocolate War, 792(F)
A Choice of Weapons, 6294
Choices: A Student Survival Guide for the 1990s, 4794
Choices: Realistic Alternatives in Cancer Treatment, 5210
Choosing a College: A Guide for Parents and Students, 4766
Choosing the Right Dog: A Buyer's Guide to All the AKC Breeds Plus . . . 8722
The Chosen Puppy: How to Select and Raise a Great Puppy from an Animal Shelter, 8713
Christgau's Record Guide: Rock Albums of the '80's, 5850
Christian Churches of America: Origins and Beliefs, 4030
Christian Legends, 4100
Christian Short Stories, 2894(F)
Christine, 1780(F)
A Christmas Carol, 353(F)
A Christmas Companion: Recipes, Traditions and Customs from around the World, 4115
Christmas Customs & Traditions, 4117
Christmas Customs Around the World, 4122
Christmas Ghosts, 1729(F)
Christmas in America, 4120
Christmas Lessons, 523(F)
A Christmas Memory, 784(F)
Christopher Columbus, 6133
Christopher Columbus, Mariner, 6134
Christy, 1613(F)
Chronicle of a Death Foretold, 663(F)
The Chronicle of the Lodz Ghetto, 1941–1944, 7202
Chronicle of the World, 7031
The Chroniclers, 7987
Chronicles of American Indian Protest, 7801
The Chronological Atlas of World War Two, 7254
A Chronology of Western Architecture, 5697
Chronology of World History: A Calendar of Principal Events from 3000 B.C. to A.D. 1976, 7043
Chthon, 2350(F)

Chuck Amuck: The Life and Times of an Animated Cartoonist, 6197
Chung Kuo: The Middle Kingdom, 2852(F)
CIA, 4219
The CIA and the Cult of Intelligence, 4226
Cimarron, 1565(F)
Cirak's Daughter, 577(F)
A Circle of Children, 5391
Circle of Pearls, 1441(F)
Circles on the Water, 3310
The Circular Staircase, 2157(F)
The Circumnavigators, 6123
Circus, 197(F)
The Citadel, 649(F)
The Cities of Ancient Mexico: Reconstructing a Lost World, 7649
Citizen Hearst: A Biography of William Randolph Hearst, 6590
Citizen Tom Paine, 1602(F)
Citizens: A Chronicle of the French Revolution, 7499
The Citizen's Guide to Gun Control, 4530
City: A Story of Roman Planning and Construction, 7118
The City and the Stars, 2476(F)
City Boy, 1910(F)
The City in History: Its Origins, Its Transformation, and Its Prospects, 4560
City Kid, 5391
City Light, 879(F)
The City, Not Long After, 2693(F)
City of Sorcery, 1049(F), 1050(F)
City Sleuths and Tough Guys, 2094(F)
Civil Defense in the Nuclear Age, 4127
Civil Liberties: Opposing Viewpoints, 4290
Civil Liberties and the Constitution: Cases and Commentaries, 4291
A Civil Tongue, 3941
The Civil War, 7895
The Civil War: An Illustrated History, 7947
The Civil War: Strange and Fascinating Facts, 7903
The Civil War Almanac, 7892

Civil War Eyewitness Reports, 7938

The Civil War Quiz and Fact Book, 7918

Civil War Soldiers: Their Expectations & Their Experiences, 7928

The Civil War Trivia Quiz Book, 7942

Civil War Women: American Women Shaped by Conflict in Stories, 1542(F)

Civilisation: A Personal View, 5682

The Civilization of the Renaissance in Italy, 7125

Civilizations of Black Africa, 7351

The Clairvoyant Countess, 2024(F)

The Clan of the Cave Bear, 1348(F)

Clandestine in Chile: The Adventures of Miguel Littin, 7672

Clans of the Alphane Moon, 2504(F)

Clapton! 6380

Clarence Darrow for the Defense: A Biography, 6583

Class Dismissed, 3273

Class Dismissed II, 3273

Classic American Philosophers: Peirce, James, Royce, Santayana, Dewey, Whitehead, 4006

The Classic Fairy Tales, 3367

Classic Furniture Projects, 9280

Classic Ghost Stories, 1723(F)

Classic Hunting Tales, 9834

The Classic Noh Theatre of Japan, 3145

Classical Beginnings, 3801

The Classical Greeks, 7103

Classical Music: A Concise History from Gluck to Beethoven, 5838

Classical Music, 5834

The Classical Tradition: Greek and Roman Influences on Western Literature, 3587

Classics of the Gangster Film, 5996

Claudius, the God, 1369(F)

The Claw of the Conciliator, 1331(F)

Clear and Present Danger, 44(F)

Clear Light of Day, 958(F)

Clear Skin, 5335

Cleared for Take-Off: International Flight Beyond the Passenger Cabin, 9066

Clement Attlee, 6827

The Clipper Ships, 7886

Clive Staples Lewis: A Dramatic Life, 6280

A Clockwork Orange, 2447(F)

Cloning and the New Genetics, 5263

Close Company: Stories of Mothers and Daughters, 586(F)

Close Encounters with the Deity, 2414(F)

Close to the Edge, 887(F)

Closing the Circle in the Pacific, 7225

Closing the Ring, 7193

Clothiers, 5280

Clothing Care & Repair, 5276

Clouds of Witness, 2170(F)

Clover, 597(F)

Clown Skits for Everyone, 5978

Cluster, 2351(F)

Clypsis, 2465(F)

The Coachman Rat, 1328(F)

The Coastal War, 7888

Coasting, 789(F)

Cobra Bargain, 2861(F)

Cocaine: A Drug and Its Social Evolution, 5123

Cocaine: A New Epidemic, 5130

Cocaine: Seduction and Solution, 5156

The Cocaine Kids: The Inside Story of a Teenage Drug Ring, 5160

Code Blue: Emergency, 2837(F)

Code Name Badger: The True Life Story of a British Secret Agent, 6900

Code of the Lifemaker, 2597(F)

A Code to Keep, 6127

A Coffin for Dimitrios, 5(F)

Coils, 2870(F)

The Coin Atlas, 9444

Coin Collecting as a Hobby, 9449

Coin Collecting for Beginners, 9450

Coin Collector's Price Guide, 9457

Cold Comfort Farm, 1881(F)

Cold Fusion: The Making of a Scientific Discovery, 8914

Cold Harbour, 126(F)

The Cold Moons, 1075(F)

Cold River, 148(F)

Cold Sassy Tree, 1599(F)

Cold Sea Rising, 209(F)

Cold Victory, 2342(F)

The Cold War Is Over, 4145

A Cold Wind from Orion, 2389(F)

The Coldest War: A Memoir of Korea, 8103

The Collapsing Universe, 8358

The Collected Plays of Neil Simon, 3124

The Collected Plays of Neil Simon, Volume I, 3125

Collected Poems, 3189, 3232, 3301

The Collected Poems, 3312

Collected Poems, 1957–1982, 3243

Collected Poems, 1948–1984, 3337

Collected Poems, 1947–1980, 3269

Collected Poems, 1909–1962, 3199

Collected Poems, 1975, 3203

Collected Poems, 1928–1985, 3225

The Collected Poems of A. E. Housman, 3209

The Collected Poems of Dylan Thomas, 3228

The Collected Poems of Robert Creeley, 1945–1975, 3254

Collected Poems of Robert Service, 3325

The Collected Poems of Theodore Roethke, 3321

The Collected Poems of William Carlos Williams, 3345

The Collected Short Fiction of Ngaio Marsh, 2107(F)

Collected Short Stories, 2944(F)

Collected Sonnets, 3302

Collected Stories, 2151(F), 2936(F), 2951(F)

The Collected Stories of Colette, 2906(F)

The Collected Stories of Eudora Welty, 2973(F)

The Collected Stories of Isaac Bashevis Singer, 2961(F)

Collected Stories of Jessamyn West, 2974(F)

The Collected Stories of Katherine Anne Porter, 2952(F)

The Collected Stories of Philip K. Dick, 2505(F)

Collected Stories of William Faulkner, 2912(F)

Collected Works, 2949(F)

The Collected Works of W. B. Yeats, Volume I: The Poems, 3233

The Collected Works of Wallace Stevens, 3332

Collecting and Preserving Plants for Science and Pleasure, 8436

Collecting Autographs for Fun and Profit, 9458

Collecting Baseball Cards: Dimes to Dollars, 9689

Collecting Sports Autographs, 9303

A Collection of Critical Essays, 3712

The Collector, 94(F)

Collector's Guide to Baseball Cards, 9454

Collector's Guide to Comic Books, 9448

College: A User's Manual, 4730

College: Getting In and Staying In, 4748

College Admissions Face to Face, 4770

College Basketball's 25 Greatest Teams, 9732

The College Board Guide to Jobs and Career Planning, 4804

College Bound, 4744

College Check Mate: Innovative Tuition Plans That Make You a Winner, 4778

College Comes Sooner Than You Think! The College Planning Guide for High School Students and Their Families, 4757

The College Cost Book, 4775

College Football's Twenty-five Greatest Teams, 9849

The College Guide for Parents, 4716

College Is Only the Beginning, 4737

The College Money Book: How to Get a High-Quality Education at the Lowest Possible Cost, 4779

College 101, 4732

College Thinking: How to Get the Best Out of College, 4752

College—Yes or No, 4809

Colleges That Enable, 4768

Colonial America, 7843

The Colonial Background of the American Revolution, 7834

Colonial Craftsmen and the Beginnings of American Industry, 7845

Colonial Living, 7846

Colony, 2421(F)

The Color Atlas of Human Anatomy, 5304

Color Harmony: A Guide to Creative Color Combinations, 8933

Color Me Beautiful, 5283

The Color Purple, 750(F)

Colored Pencil Drawing Techniques, 9198

Colors Aloft! 1439(F)

The Colors of Space, 1050(F)

Columbia Literary History of the United States, 3577

The Columbia University College of Physicians and Surgeons Complete Guide to Pregnancy, 5495

Coma, 1724(F)

Combat Art of the Vietnam War, 8098

Combatting Cult Mind Control, 4053

Come Together: John Lennon in His Time, 6418

Come Winter, 1572(F)

Comeback, 6718

Comes the Blind Fury, 1835(F)

Comet, 8333

Comfort Me with Spies, 180(F)

Comic Lives: Inside the World of American Stand-up Comedy, 6081

The Comic Mind: Comedy and the Movies, 6101

Coming Apart: An Informal History of America in the 60's, 8086

The Coming Battle for the Media: Curbing the Power of the Media Elite, 3969

Coming into the Country, 8184

A Coming of Age, 2860(F)

Coming of Age in Mississippi, 6933

The Coming of the Quantum Cats, 2733(F)

Coming Out to Parents, 5453

The Coming Quake: Science and Trembling on the California Earthquake Frontier, 8803

Coming to America: A History of Immigration and Ethnicity in American Life, 4330

Coming to America: Immigrants from Northern Europe, 4338

Coming to America: Immigrants from Southern Europe, 4337

The Commandos, 7256

Commodore 64 Fun and Games: Volume 2, 8986

Common Sense Book of Puppy and Dog Care, 8727

Communicators, 3919

Communion: A True Story, 9535

Communism: End of the Monolith? 4173

Communism: Opposing Viewpoints, 4592

The Communist Manifesto of Karl Marx and Friedrich Engels, 4175

The Compact Disc Book: A Complete Guide to the Digital Sound of the Future, 9047

Companion to Russian History, 7580

A Companion to the Iliad, 3864

A Company of Swans, 2287(F)

Comparisons, 8865

Compassion, 5574

The Competitive Runner's Handbook, 9910

The Complete Babysitter's Handbook, 5070

The Complete Baseball Record Book, 1990, 9635

The Complete Birdhouse Book: The Easy Guide to Attracting Nesting Birds, 8552

The Complete Book of Bicycling, 9765

The Complete Book of BMX, 9764

The Complete Book of Boating, 9941

The Complete Book of Calligraphy, 9158

The Complete Book of Cartooning, 9209

The Complete Book of Dog Care: How to Raise a Happy and Healthy Dog, 8724

The Complete Book of Dog Health, 8723

The Complete Book of Fingermath, 8840

The Complete Book of Food: A Nutritional, Medical & Culinary Guide, 5426

The Complete Book of Freshwater Fishing, 9833

The Complete Book of Gardening, 9388

The Complete Book of Golf Practice, 9877

The Complete Book of Herbs: A Practical Guide to Growing & Using Herbs, 9373

The Complete Book of Jewish Observance, 4121

The Complete Book of Judo, 9896

The Complete Book of Magic and Witchcraft, 9399

The Complete Book of Needlecrafts, 9234

The Complete Book of Parrots, 8677

The Complete Book of Patchwork, Quilting and Appliqué, 9252

The Complete Book of Pottery Making, 9165

The Complete Book of Pregnancy and Childbirth, 5472

The Complete Book of Running, 9909

The Complete Book of Snowboarding, 9942

The Complete Book of Swimming, 9960

The Complete Book of the Dog, 8725

The Complete Book of the Olympics, 9908

The Complete Book of U.S. Presidents, 6468

The Complete Book of Walking, 9578

The Complete Chessplay, 9821

The Complete Computer Career Guide, 4975

The Complete Dog Book, 8709

The Complete Eater's Digest and Nutrition Scoreboard, 5417

The Complete Encyclopedia of Stitchery, 9250

The Complete English Poems of John Donne, 3198

The Complete Essays of Mark Twain, 3552

The Complete Golfer, 9871

The Complete Grimms' Fairy Tales, 3399

The Complete Guide to America's National Parks, 7769

The Complete Guide to Choosing a Performance Bicycle, 9756

The Complete Guide to Environmental Careers, 5015

Complete Guide to Home Appliance Repair, 9391

The Complete Guide to Making Home Video Movies, 9052

The Complete Guide to Middle-Earth: From The Hobbit to The Silmarillion, 3662

The Complete Guide to Painting and Drawing, 9193

The Complete Guide to Public Employment, 4844

The Complete Guide to Sherlock Holmes, 3667

The Complete Guide to Short Board Sailing, 9954

Complete Guide to Sports Injuries, 5443

Complete Guide to Wood Carving, 9291

The Complete Guide to Writing Fiction, 3976

The Complete Handbook of Baseball, 9652

The Complete Handbook of Personal Computer Communications: Everything You Need to Go Online with the World, 8978

The Complete Handbook of Pro-Basketball, 9726

The Complete Handbook of Pro-Football, 9848

The Complete Handbook of Songwriting: An Insider's Guide to Making It in the Music Industry, 5880

The Complete Handbook of Videocassette Recorders, 9051

The Complete Horse Book, 8762

Complete Indoor Gardener, 9388

The Complete Job-Search Handbook: All the Skills You Need to Get Any Job and Have a Good Time Doing It, 4793

The Complete Juggler, 9299

The Complete Kodak Book of Photography, 9413

The Complete Manual of Fitness and Well-Being, 5073

The Complete Martial Arts, 9893

The Complete Mountain Biker, 9748

The Complete Phantom of the Opera, 5925

The Complete Photography Career Handbook, 4883

The Complete Play Production Handbook, 6077

The Complete Plays of Gilbert and Sullivan, 5917

The Complete Poems, 3284, 3326

The Complete Poems and Plays of T. S. Eliot, 1909–1950, 3028

The Complete Poems of Carl Sandburg, 3322

The Complete Poems of Emily Dickinson, 3258

The Complete Poems of Marianne Moore, 3304

The Complete Poems of Paul Laurence Dunbar, 3261

The Complete Poems of Stephen Crane, 3253

The Complete Poems of Thomas Hardy, 3205

Complete Poetical Works, 3218

The Complete Poetry and Prose of William Blake, 3151

The Complete Printmaker: Techniques, Traditions, Innovations, 9225

Complete Railway Modelling, 9406

The Complete Sherlock Holmes, 1988(F)

The Complete Short Stories, 2933(F)

The Complete Short Stories of Ernest Hemingway: The Finca Vigia Edition, 402(F)

The Complete Short Stories of H. G. Wells, 2825(F)

The Complete Short Stories of Mark Twain, 423(F)

The Complete Sports Medicine Book for Women, 5362

The Complete Stories, 1774(F), 2950(F)

The Complete Stylist and Handbook, 3955

The Complete Tales and Poems of Edgar Allan Poe, 1823(F)

The Complete 35mm Sourcebook, 9410

The Complete Trees of North America, 8425

The Complete Vegetable Gardener's Sourcebook, 9384

The Complete Walker III: The Joys and Techniques of Hiking and Backpacking, 9794

The Complete Woodworker, 9277

The Complete Works of Saki, 378

The Complete Works of William Shakespeare, 3052

Composers of Tomorrow's Music: A Non-Technical Introduction to the Musical Avant-Garde Movement, 6172

Computer Basics, 9020

Computer Capers: Tales of Electronic Thievery, Embezzlement, and Fraud, 9028

Computer Concepts and Applications, 9024

Computer Crimes and Capers, 2376(F)

The Computer Glossary for Everyone: It's Not Just a Glossary! 8974

Computer Images, 9021

Computer Languages, 9021

Computer Lib/Dream Machines, 9005

Computer Science, 9031

Computer Security, 9021

Computer Viruses, Worms, Data Diddlers, Killer Programs and Other Threats to Your System, 8999

The Computerized Society, 9020

Computers: The Next Generation, 9027

Computers and the Cosmos, 9020

Computers for Everybody, 9030

Conan, 2602(F)

Conan Doyle: Portrait of an Artist, 6243

The Concise Cambridge History of English Literature, 3602

A Concise Dictionary of Foreign Expressions, 3910

A Concise History of Mexico from Hidalgo to Cardenas 1805–1940, 7639

A Concise History of Modern Painting, 5756

A Concise History of Modern Sculpture, 5757

A Concise History of Posters: 1870–1970, 5733

A Concise History of the American Republic, 7764

A Concise History of the Spanish Civil War, 7557

The Concise Oxford Dictionary of French Literature, 3586

The Concise Oxford Dictionary of Music, 5822

The Conduct of Major Maxim, 189(F)

Confederate Ordeal, 7888

The Confession of Brother Haluin, 2131(F)

Confessions of a Teenage TV Addict, 2297(F)

The Confessions of Nat Turner, 1531(F)

The Confident Consumer, 4606

Conflict, 2342(F)

Conflict and Crisis: The Presidency of Harry S. Truman, 1945–1948, 8057

Confrontations: A Scientist's Search for Alien Contact, 9538

Congress and Its Members, 4218

The Congress of Vienna, 7147

Congressional Procedures and the Policy Process, 4227

Congressional Quarterly's Guide to Congress, 4216

A Connecticut Yankee in King Arthur's Court, 424(F)

Conquering Athletic Injuries, 5447

The Conquest of the Incas, 7674

The Conservationist, 961(F)

The Conservative Movement, 4265

Conspiracy of Knaves, 1535(F)

The Constitution: That Delicate Balance, 4189

The Constitution of the United States of America, 4202

Constructing a Life Philosophy: Opposing Viewpoints, 5595

Consumer Guide Automobile Book: All New 1990 Edition, 9086

Consumer Guide to Cars, 1990, 9087

Contact, 2766(F)

Contemporary American Folk Artists, 5798

Contemporary Batik and Tie-Dye: Methods, Inspiration, Dyes, 9147

Contemporary Latin American Short Stories, 2941(F)

Contemporary Southern Poetry, 3308

The Contender, 474(F)

Cooder Cutlas, 810(F)

Cookies and Crackers, 9362

Cook's Book of Essential Information, 9344

The Cook's Book of Indispensable Ideas: A Kitchen Sourcebook, 9344

The Cool Fire: How to Make It in Television, 6056

Cooperative Sports and Games Book, 9590

Coping through Assertiveness, 5621

Coping through Self-Esteem, 5622

Coping When a Parent Has Cancer, 5221

Coping with a Dysfunctional Family, 5675

Coping with a Negative World in a Positive Way, 4529

Coping with an Unplanned Pregnancy, 5494

Coping with Being Adopted, 5642

Coping with Being Pregnant, 5473

Coping with Birth Control, 5450

Coping with Choosing a College, 4724
Coping with Date Rape & Acquaintance Rape, 5516
Coping with Dating Violence, 5567
Coping with Difficult Teachers, 4622
Coping with Failure, 5603
Coping with Hearing Loss: A Guide for Adults and Their Families, 5332
Coping with Money, 5065
Coping with Moving, 5591
Coping with Sexual Abuse, 5506
Coping with Sexual Harassment, 5502
Coping with Shyness, 5561
Coping with Sibling Rivalry, 5643
Coping with Stigma, 5623
Coping with Stress, 5565
Coping with Substance Abuse, 5141
Coping with Suicide: A Resource Book for Teenagers and Young Adults, 5406
Coping with Teenage Depression, 5564
Coping with Verbal Abuse, 5612
Coping with Your Inner Critic, 5614
Copland: 1900 through 1942, 6341
Copland since 1943, 6341
The Copper Crown, 2613(F)
Corazon Aquino: The Story of a Revolution, 6802
Core Concepts in Health, 5354
Corporate Crime, 4472
The Corpse Had a Familiar Face: Covering Miami, America's Hottest Beat, 4469
The Corpse in Oozak's Pond, 2102(F)
Correct Spelling Made Easy, 4685
Cortez and the Conquest of Mexico by the Spaniards in 1521, 7642
Corvette: America's Sports Car, 9088
Corvette: America's Supercar, 9098
The Cosmic Connection: An Extraterrestrial Perspective, 8285

The Cosmic Cycle, 8289
The Cosmic Mind-Boggling Book, 8268
Cosmos, 8286
The Cosmos from Space: Astronomical Breakthroughs—The View from Beyond Earth's Atmosphere, 8254
Costume: An Illustrated Survey from Ancient Times to the Twentieth Century, 9169
Costumes for the Stage: A Complete Handbook for Every Type of Play, 9168
The Count of Monte Cristo, 311(F)
Countdown: An Autobiography, 6126
Countdown to College: A Student's Guide to Getting the Most Out of High School, 4652
Countdown to Glory: NASA's Trials and Triumphs in Space, 8295
The Counterfeiter, 833(F)
Country: The Music and the Musicians, 5853
Country Flower Drying, 9302
The Country Gentleman, 2279(F)
The Country I Come From, 924(F)
The Country Music Encyclopedia, 5899
Country Music, U.S.A. 5884
A Country Year: Living the Questions, 8395
Courage at Sea: Tales of Heroic Voyages, 7050
The Courage of Conviction, 3996
The Course of American Diplomacy: From the Revolution to the Present, 4146
The Course of French History, 7493
The Course of True Love Never Did Run Smooth, 917(F)
A Court for Owls, 1534(F)
The Court-Martial of Clayton Lonetree, 4242
Courting Emma Howe, 2317(F)
Courtroom Crusades, 4247
The Courts of Chaos, 1344(F)
The Courtship of Joanna, 1609(F)

Cousteau: The Captain and His World, 6653
Cousteau's Papua New Guinea Journey, 7467
Cousy on the Celtic Mystique, 9717
The Covenant, 1386(F)
Cover Her Face, 2069(F)
Covering the Plague: AIDS and the American Media, 3985
Cowboy Culture, 7952
Cowboy Feng's Space Bar and Grille, 2443(F)
The Cowboy Hero: His Image in American History and Culture, 7979
The Cowboys, 7988
Cowboys of the Americas, 7684
Coyote, 1923(F)
Coyote Waits, 2050(F)
Coyotes: A Journey Through the Secret World of America's Illegal Aliens, 4503
CQ's Guide to the U.S. Constitution, 4199
Crabbe's Journey, 763(F)
Crack in the Heart, 896(F)
The Cradle Will Fall, 1961(F)
The Craft of Computer Programming, 8987
The Craft of Sail, 9917
The Craft of the Screenwriter, 5997
The Craft of Writing, 3970
Craig Claiborne's Kitchen Primer, 9322
Craig Claiborne's The New York Times Food Encyclopedia, 9323
Crash: The Life and Times of Dick Allen, 6712
Crash Course, 1733(F)
Crazy English: The Ultimate Joyride through Our Language, 3932
Crazy Horse: His Life, His Lands: A Photographic Biography, 6499
Crazy Ladies, 621(F)
Crazy Time, 2838(F)
Create Your Own Stage Lighting, 6112
Create Your Own Stage Sets, 6113
Creating Adventure Games for Your Computer, 8982
Creating Special Effects, 9416

Creating Theater: The Professionals' Approach to New Plays, 6103

Creative Cards: Wrap a Message with a Personal Touch, 9223

Creative Careers: Jobs in Glamour Fields, 4820

Creative Clowning, 5979

Creative Computer Graphics, 8985

Creative Conversations: The Writer's Guide to Conducting Interviews, 4698

Creative Drawing and Painting, 9181

Creature, 1836(F)

Creature Comforts: The Adventures of a City Vet, 6681

Creatures of Paradise: Pictures to Grow Up With, 5720

The Credit Card Industry: A History, 4615

Creek Mary's Blood, 1496(F)

Crime & Criminals: Opposing Viewpoints, 4474

Crime and Human Nature, 4498

Crime and Punishment, 309(F)

Crime and Society, 4488

Crime Dictionary, 4473

The Crime of the Century, 1913(F)

Criminal Justice: Opposing Viewpoints, 4494

Criminal Violence, Criminal Justice, 4492

Crisis in Industry: Can America Compete? 4562

Crisis Intervention: Acting against Addiction, 5157

Critical Essays on Arthur Miller, 3841

Critical Essays on James Joyce, 3648

Crocodile on the Sandbank, 2128(F), 2130(F)

Crocodiles and Alligators, 8469

Cromm, 1121(F)

Cromwell: The Lord Protector, 6834

Croquet: Its History, Strategy, Rules, and Records, 9553

Cross a Wide River, 1592(F)

The Cross & the Crescent: A History of the Crusades, 7123

The Cross and the Switchblade, 4497

Crossfire, 143(F)

Crossing at Ivalo, 201(F)

Crossing Open Ground, 7698

Crossing the Line: A Year in the Land of Apartheid, 7371

Crossing the River, 3312

Crow Killer, 1594(F)

A Crown of Feathers: And Other Stories, 498(F)

Crown, Oklahoma, 172(F)

The Crucial Decade—And After: America, 1945–1960, 8063

The Crucible, 3105

The Cruel Sea, 1669(F)

Cruiser Dreams, 1227(F)

Cry at Dusk, 1920(F)

A Cry in the Night, 1962(F)

A Cry of Angels, 457(F)

Cry, the Beloved Country, 987(F)

Cryptograms and Spygrams, 9467

Crystal, 891(F)

The Crystal Cave, 1279(F)

The Crystal Gryphon, 2704(F)

The Crystal Singer, 2658(F)

Crystals of Air and Water, 1132(F)

Cuba: Dilemmas of a Revolution, 7660

Cuba: From Columbus to Castro, 7665

The Cuckoo's Egg: Tracking a Spy through the Maze of Computer Espionage, 9016

Cujo, 1781(F)

Cult Baseball Players: The Greats, the Flakes, the Weird, and the Wonderful, 6707

The Cult Experience: Responding to the New Religious Pluralism, 4066

The Cult Movement, 4057

Cult Movies, 6045

Cult Movies 3: 50 More of the Classics, the Sleepers, the Weird, and the Wonderful, 6045

Cult Movies 2, 6045

Cult TV: A Viewer's Guide to the Shows America Can't Live Without! 6021

Cults: Faith, Healing and Coercion, 4050

Cults in America: Programmed for Paradise, 4027

Cults, the Continuing Threat, 4087

Cultural Atlas of Africa, 7355

Culture and Commitment: The New Relationships Between the Generations in the 1970s, 4415

A Cup of Tears: A Diary of the Warsaw Ghetto, 7238

The Curious Case of Sidd Finch, 2885(F)

Curious Customs, 4541

The Currents of Space, 2368(F)

The Curse of the Giant Hogweed, 1210(F)

The Curse of the Pharaohs, 2128(F)

Cursed to Death, 1972(F)

Curtain, 1948(F)

Custer Died for Your Sins, 7803

Custom Car: A Nuts-and-Bolts Guide to Creating One, 9104

Customizing Cars, 9082

Cyber Way, 2543(F)

Cyberiad: Fables for the Cybernetic Age, 2642(F)

Cycle of the Werewolf, 1782(F)

Cycles of Fire: Stars, Galaxies and the Wonders of Deep Space, 8353

Cycling for Women, 9745

Cyclops, 65(F)

Cyrano de Bergerac, 2994, 3016

D. H. Lawrence Handbook, 3686

Daddy, 605(F), 81(F)

Daddy Was a Numbers Runner, 478(F)

Daffodils in the Snow, 662(F)

The Dagger & the Cross: A Novel of the Crusades, 1382(F)

Dagon and Other Macabre Tales, 1806(F)

Damiano, 1199(F)

Damiano's Lute, 1199(F)

Damn the Torpedoes! Naval Incidents of the Civil War, 7923

Dance: The Art of Production, 5973

Dance Hall of the Dead, 2053(F)

The Dance of Legislation, 4229

The Dance of Life: Courtship in the Animal Kingdom, 8486

Dance of the Continents: Adventures with Rocks and Time, 8796

Dance of the Tiger: A Novel of the Ice Age, 1352(F)

Dance of the Wild Mouse, 5216

Dance to the Piper, 6383

Dancer: Men in Dance, 5963

Dancershoes, 5974

Dancing: A Guide for the Dancer You Can Be, 5970

Dancing at the Rascal Fair, 1564(F)

Dandelion Wine, 525(F)

The Danger, 2011(F)

Dangerous Dossiers, 4311

Daniel and Esther, 906(F)

Danielle, 1519(F)

Danish Fairy Tales, 3400

Danny and the Real Me, 2326(F)

Dante, 3862

Daphne du Maurier's Classics of the Macabre, 1739(F)

Dare to Dream: The Rose Resnick Story, 6944

The Dark Abyss, 1082(F)

Dark Arrows: Chronicles of Revenge, 203(F)

Dark Caves, Bright Visions: Life in Ice Age Europe, 7013

Dark Continent and Other Stories, 432(F)

The Dark Descent, 1763(F)

The Dark Design, 2537(F)

The Dark Door, 273(F)

The Dark Druid, 1122(F)

Dark Forces, 1811(F)

Dark Gods, 1795(F)

The Dark Half, 1783(F)

The Dark Lady: A Romance of the Far Future, 2753(F)

Dark Marathon, 6966

The Dark Matter, 8291

Dark of the Moon, 1154(F)

The Dark of the Tunnel, 723(F)

Dark Piper, 2705(F)

The Dark Range: A Naturalist's Night Notebook, 8459

The Dark Romance of Dian Fossey, 6667

The Dark Side, 2059(F)

The Dark Side of the Universe: A Scientist Explores the Mysteries of the Cosmos, 8371

The Dark Summer: An Intimate History of Events That Led to World War II, 7294

A Dark Traveling, 2866(F)

The Darkangel, 1821(F)

Darkchild, 1302(F)

The Darkest Road, 1166(F)

Darkling, 295(F)

Darkness at Noon, 976(F)

A Darkness at Sethanon, 1116(F)

Darkness Falls, 2171(F)

Darkness Visible, 664(F)

The Darkroom Handbook, 9427

Darkspell, 1168(F)

Darwin for Beginners, 7007

Darwin's Century: Evolution and the Men Who Discovered It, 6995

Date to Go A-Hunting, 2706(F)

Datelines of World History, 7028

The Dating Book: A Guide to the Social Scene, 5600

Daughter of Destiny, 6804

Daughter of Regals and Other Tales, 1094(F)

The Daughter of Time, 2193(F)

Daughter of Witches, 1336(F)

Dave Scott's Triathlon Training, 9595

David Bowie: Theater of Music, 6375

David Copperfield, 354(F)

David Crockett: The Man Behind the Myth, 6135

Davita's Harp, 590(F)

Dawn, 1488(F), 2454(F)

Dawn of Modern Science, 7135

The Dawn Palace: The Story of Medea, 1361(F)

Dawn to the West: Japanese Literature of the Modern Era, 3591

Day by Day: The Fifties, 7336

Day by Day: The Forties, 7237

Day by Day: The Sixties, 7339

The Day Christ Died, 4095

The Day I Became an Autodidact: And the Advice, Adventures, and Acrimonies That Befell Me Thereafter, 6915

The Day I Owned the Sky, 6161

A Day in Old Athens, 7114

A Day in Old Rome: A Picture of Roman Life, 7114

The Day Lincoln Was Shot, 6542

Day of Infamy, 7244

Day of Reckoning: The Consequences of American Economic Policy in the 1980s, 4289

Day of the Bomb: Countdown to Hiroshima, 7232

Day of the Cheetah, 25(F)

The Day of the Dissonance, 1123(F)

Day of the Dragon Star, 2413(F)

The Day of the Jackal, 89(F)

The Day of the Locust, 752(F)

The Day of the Triffids, 2856(F)

Day One: Before Hiroshima and After, 7327

Day Seven, 2410(F)

The Day the Martians Came, 2734(F)

The Day the Senior Class Got Married, 888(F)

The Day They Stole the Queen Mary, 142(F)

The Days of the French Revolution, 7495

Dayworld, 2534(F)

Dayworld Breakup, 2534(F)

Dayworld Rebel, 2534(F)

Dead Crazy, 2138(F)

Dead in the Scrub, 2122(F)

Dead Man's Ransom, 2132(F)

Dead Men Don't Give Seminars, 2187(F)

Dead Men Don't Marry, 2187(F)

The Dead Sea Scrolls, 1947–1969, 4113

Dead Serious: A Book for Teenagers about Teenage Suicide, 5090

The Dead That Walked: Dracula, Frankenstein, the Mummy, and Other Favorite Movie Monsters, 6017

The Dead Zone, 1784(F)

Deadeye Dick, 1305(F)

The Deadly Element: The Story of Uranium, 8782

A Deadly Silence: The Ordeal of Cheryl Pierson, 4481
Deadman Switch, 2861(F)
A Deaf Child Listened: Thomas Gallaudet, Pioneer in American Education, 6620
Deaf Like Me, 5438
The Dean's December, 764(F)
Dear America: Letters Home from Vietnam, 8110
Dear Ann Landers: Our Intimate and Changing Dialogue with America's Best-Loved Confidante, 5613
Dear Cherry: Questions and Answers on Eating Disorders, 5395
Dear Doctor, 5619
Death and Dying: Opposing Viewpoints, 5096
The Death and Life of Great American Cities, 4558
Death and the Magician: The Mystery of Houdini, 6408
Death at an Early Age, 4630
Death at Charity's Point, 2192(F)
Death Be Not Proud: A Memoir, 6914
Death by Fire: An Uncle George Mystery Novel, 2127(F)
Death Comes for the Archbishop, 1560(F)
Death-Dying Annual, 1989, 5080
A Death for a Double, 2025(F)
Death in a Deck Chair, 1926(F)
Death in a Tenured Position, 1978(F)
Death in Berlin, 2078(F)
A Death in the Family, 513(F)
Death in the Trenches: Grant at Petersburg, 7908
Death in Venice, 714(F)
Death in Zanzibar, 152(F)
Death of a Cad, 1925(F)
Death of a Gossip, 1925(F)
Death of a Perfect Wife, 1924(F)
The Death of a President, November 20–November 25, 1963, 6538
Death of a Salesman, 3106
Death of an Expert Witness, 2069(F)
Death of an Outsider, 1925(F)

The Death of Ivan Ilyitch: And Other Stories, 319(F)
The Death of Methuselah, 499(F)
The Death of Sleep, 2669(F)
The Death of the Heart, 773(F)
Death on the Nile, 1949(F)
The Death Penalty, 4495
The Death Penalty: A Debate, 4257
Death Roll, 176(F)
Death Squad London, 2021(F)
Death Trance, 1814(F)
Deathbird Stories, 1742(F)
Death's Head Berlin, 2021(F)
Deathtrap, 3097
Deathwatch, 260(F)
Debrett's Kings and Queens of Britain, 7541
The Decade of Destruction: The Crusade to Save the Amazon Rain Forest, 7670
Decade of Disillusionment: The Kennedy-Johnson Years, 8069
December 7, 1941: The Day the Japanese Attacked Pearl Harbor, 7273
Deception Trail, 113(F)
Decision at Delphi, 196(F)
Decision at Doona, 2659(F)
Decisive Battles of the American Revolution, 7855
Decoying the Yanks, 7890
The Dedicated Villain, 1485(F)
Dee Snider's Teenage Survival Guide, 5632
The Deeds of the Disturber, 2129(F)
Deep Blues, 6183
The Deep Range, 2476(F)
Deep Time, 8362
Deep Woods, 8381
The Deerslayer, 393(F)
Definitive Kobbe's Opera Book, 5920
Deliverance, 75(F)
The Deluge Drivers, 2544(F)
Demian, 675(F)
Democracy and Education: An Introduction to the Philosophy of Education, 4002
Democracy in America, 7866
Demon Blues, 1127(F)
Demon Lord of Karanda, 1105(F)
The Demon Lover, 132(F)

Demon of Undoing, 1006(F)
Demystifying Compact Discs: A Guide to Digital Audio, 9053
Depths of Glory: A Biographical Novel of Camille Pissarro, 1475(F)
Dervish Daughter, 1292(F)
The Deryni Archives, 1176(F)
Deryni Checkmate, 1177(F)
Deryni Rising, 1177(F)
The Descent of Anansi, 2699(F)
Desert Exile: The Uprooting of a Japanese American Family, 6963
Desert Warfare: From Its Roman Origins to the Gulf Conflict, 7064
Deserts, 8815
Design for a Livable Planet, 4432
Design with Nature, 4559
The Desperate People, 7701
Destination: Void, 2591(F)
The Destiny Dice, 2411(F)
The Destruction of Pompeii and Herculaneum, 7116
The Detroit Tigers: An Illustrated History, 9642
Devices and Desires, 2065(F)
The Devil and Daniel Webster, 1035(F)
The Devil on Horseback, 134(F)
Devil on Lammas Night, 139(F)
Devil Wind, 1720(F)
Devils, 1711(F)
The Devil's Advocate, 999(F)
The Devil's Alternative, 90(F)
The Devil's Mode: Stories, 2898(F)
Diabetes in the Family, 5169
Dialogue with Darkness, 2343(F)
The Diamond Throne, 1106(F)
Diamonds Are Forever: Artists and Writers on Baseball, 9648
Diana, 1591(F)
Diary of a Medical Nobody, 6684
The Diary of a Young Girl, 6840
The Diary of Anne Frank, 3076
The Diary of Anne Frank: The Critical Edition, 6839

Diaspora: An Inquiry into the Contemporary Jewish World, 7072

Dibs: In Search of Self, 5369

Dicey's Song, 616(F)

Dick Smith's Do-It-Yourself Monster Make-Up Handbook, 9219

Dickens: A Biography, 6239

Dickens: A Life, 6240

Dickens: From Pickwick to Dombey, 3677

Dickens' London: An Imaginative Vision, 7511

Dictionary of American Art, 5790

The Dictionary of Costume, 9174

Dictionary of Food Ingredients, 8416

The Dictionary of Foreign Terms in the English Language, 3910

The Dictionary of Historic Nicknames, 3949

Dictionary of Historical Terms: A Guide to Names and Events of Over 1000 Years of World History, 7033

A Dictionary of Literary Terms, 3572

Dictionary of Misinformation, 9478

Dictionary of Space Technology, 8296

Dictionary of Subjects and Symbols in Art, 5688

The Dictionary of Superstitions, 9479

Did Molly Pitcher Say That? The Men and Women Who Made American History, 7739

Diesel: Fundamentals, Service, Repair, 9044

Different Drummer: Homosexuality in America, 5474

A Different Kind of Christmas, 1525(F)

Different Like Me, 5139

Different Seasons, 1785(F)

A Different Woman, 679(F)

Different Worlds: Interracial and Cross-Cultural Dating, 5598

A Difficulty with Dwarves, 1128(F)

Digging Dinosaurs, 6981

Digital Deli, 8970

Dinner at the Homesick Restaurant, 614(F)

The Dinosaur Heresies, 6974

Dinosaur Planet, 2660(F)

Dinosaur Planet Survivors, 2660(F)

Dinosaur Plots & Other Intrigues in Natural History, 8223

Dinosaurs: An Illustrated History, 6976

Dinosaurs Past and Present, Volume 1, 6978

The Direction of Poetry, 3174

The Director's Voice: Twenty-One Interviews, 6078

Dirk Gently's Holistic Detective Agency, 2332(F)

A Dirty Distant War, 1670(F)

A Disagreement with Death, 1128(F)

Disclosing the Past, 6685

Discontinued, 2195(F)

A Discourse on Method, and Selected Writings, 4001

Discover the Stars, 8247

Discovering Britain and Ireland, 7535

Discovering Great Music, 5821

Discovering Mount St. Helens! A Guide to the National Volcanic Monument, 8189

The Discovery of the Titanic, 8886

Discrimination against Women, 4316

The Disinformer: Two Novellas, 263(F)

The Disney Films, 6100

The Disney Version, 6193

The Disorderly Knights, 1425(F)

Dispatches, 8119

The Dispossessed: An Ambiguous Utopia, 2630(F)

A Distant Mirror: The Calamitous 14th Century, 7140

Distant Neighbors: Portrait of the Mexicans, 7648

Distant Water: The Fate of the North Atlantic Fisherman, 8621

Distortions, 761(F)

The Divide, 2849(F)

The Divided Union: The Story of the Great American War 1861–1865, 7891

The Divination Handbook, 9509

Divine Right, 2468(F)

Dixie Church Interstate Blues, 564(F)

Dizzy Gillespie, 6393

DNA for Beginners, 5265

Do-It-Yourself Automotive Maintenance and Repair, 9079

Do-It-Yourself Car Care, 9083

Do-It-Yourself Video: A Beginner's Guide to Home Video, 6068

Do Lord Remember Me, 472(F)

Do You Like It Here? 766(F)

Do You Love Me, Harvey Burns? 477(F)

Do You Really Love Me? 2296(F)

Do You See What I See? 2167(F)

Doctor Faustus, 3033

Doctor Thorne, 387(F)

Doctor Zhivago, 1456(F)

Doctor's Orders, 2525(F)

A Documentary History of the United States, 7746

Documentary Photography, 9437

Documents of American History, 7722

Dodge Dynasty: The Car and the Family That Rocked Detroit, 6659

Dodger Dogs to Fenway Franks: The Ultimate Guide to America's Top Baseball Parks, 9710

Does God Have a Big Toe? Stories about Stories in the Bible, 4102

The Dog Care Book: All You Need to Know to Keep Your Dog Healthy and Happy, 8719

The Dog for You, 8711

The Dog in Your Life, 8726

A Dog Owner's Guide to Training Your Dog, 8730

Dog Training My Way, 8744

The Dog Who Wouldn't Be, 8729

Dogs, 8732

A Dog's Life: A Year in the Life of a Dog, 8714

The Dogs of March, 673(F)

Dogs of the Conquest, 7632

Dogs of the World, 8718

The Dogs of War, 91(F)

Dogwatching, 8728

Doing Justice: A Trial Judge at Work, 4253

The Doll, 1848(F)

The Dollar Man, 882(F)

Dollars for Scholars: Barron's Complete College Financing Guide, 4776

The Dollmaker, 515(F)

Dollmaking, 9263

Dolphin Island, 2477(F)

A Dolphin Summer, 8649

Dolphins and Porpoises, 8646

Domains of Darkover, 2432(F)

Dome in the Forest, 2841(F)

Domesday: A Search for the Roots of England, 7542

Domestic Revolutions: A Social History of American Family Life, 5670

Domina, 755(F)

Domino, 2216(F)

Don Baylor: Baseball on the Field and in the Clubhouse, 6714

Don Coyote, 8513

The Don Flows Home to the Sea, 1469(F)

Donor: How One Girl's Death Gave Life to Others, 5166

Don't Blame the Music, 537(F)

Don't Explain: A Song of Billie Holiday, 6402

Don't Forget to Fly: A Cycle of Modern Poems, 3280

Don't Know Much about History: Everything You Need to Know about American History but Never Learned, 7730

Don't Panic: The Official Hitchhiker's Guide to the Galaxy Companion, 3664

Don't Worry, You're Normal, 5630

The Doolittle Raid, 7288

Doom of the Darksword, 1315(F)

The Doom That Came to Sarnath, 1807(F)

The Doomed Oasis, 146(F)

Doomstalker, 1076(F)

The Door in the Wall and Other Stories, 2826(F)

A Door into Ocean, 2792(F)

The Door into Summer, 2578(F)

The Door to December, 1818(F)

The Doris Lessing Reader, 2934(F)

Dorothy Hamill On and Off the Ice, 6775

Dorsai! 2509(F)

The Dorsai Companion, 1092(F)

The Dosadi Experiment, 2592(F)

Double Dutch, 9605

Double Header, 9691

The Double Helix: Being a Personal Account of the Discovery of the Structure of DNA, 5268

Double Indemnity, 1939(F)

A Double Life: Newly Discovered Thrillers of Louisa May Alcott, 2184(F)

Double Standard, 2298(F)

Doublespeak, 3936

Doubting Thomas, 2149(F)

Dove, 6142

Down Is Not Out: Teenagers and Depression, 5388

Downbelow Station, 2469(F)

The Downside of Drugs, 5101

Downstream, 613(F)

Dr. Axelrod's Mini-Atlas of Freshwater Aquarium Fishes, 8770

Dr. Dropo's Balloon Sculpturing for Beginners, 9143

Dr. Fischer of Geneva or The Bomb Party, 109(F)

Dr. Jekyll and Mr. Hyde, 382(F)

Dr. Seuss, 6207

Dr. Wildlife: A Northwoods Veterinarian, 6906

Dracula, 1850(F)

The Dracula Book of Great Horror Stories, 1843(F)

Dragon, 66(F)

Dragon Fall, 1153(F)

The Dragon Hoard, 1190(F)

Dragon Prince, 1252(F), 1253(F)

The Dragon Revenant, 1169(F)

Dragon Wing, 1311(F)

The Dragonbone Chair, 1325(F)

Dragondoom, 1205(F)

Dragondrums, 2663(F)

Dragonflight, 2661(F)

Dragonlance Chronicles, 1312(F)

The Dragonlance Legends, 1313(F)

The Dragonlover's Guide to Pern, 3763

Dragonquest, 2661(F)

Dragons, 3371

Dragon's Egg, 2541(F), 2542(F)

Dragons of Autumn Twilight, 1312(F)

The Dragons of Eden: Speculations on the Evolution of Human Intelligence, 5325

Dragons of Spring Dawning, 1312(F)

Dragons of Winter Night, 1312(F)

The Dragon's Village, 7400

Dragonsbane, 1138(F)

Dragonsdawn, 2662(F)

Dragonsinger, 2663(F)

Dragonsong, 2663(F)

Dragonworld, 1250(F)

Drawing: A Studio Guide, 9183

Drawing and Painting from Nature, 9199

Drawing & Painting with Ink, 9195

The Drawing of the Three, 1170(F)

Drawing Portraits, 9192

Drawing the Line: The Korean War, 1950–1953, 8149

Dream Dancer, 1227(F)

The Dream Game, 5534

Dream Jobs: A Guide to Tomorrow's Top Careers, 4821

Dream Makers: Science Fiction and Fantasy Writers at Work, 3629

Dream of Orchids, 2212(F)

A Dream of Passion: The Development of the Method, 6111

Dream West, 1580(F)

The Dream Years, 2270(F)

The Dreaming Jewels, 1281(F)

Dreaming Myself, Dreaming a Town, 5334

Dreams of Dark and Light, 2629(F)

Dreamsnake, 2674(F)

Dreamspeaker, 140(F)

Dreamspy, 1194(F)

The Dreamstone, 1069(F)

Dreemz of the Night, 2045(F)

Dress for Success, 9170

The Dresser, 3031

The Drifters, 886(F)
Drink Down the Moon, 1090(F)
Drive: The Story of My Life, 6741
Driving the Drunk off the Road: A Handbook for Action, 5119
Drug Abuse: Opposing Viewpoints, 5103
Drug Tests and Polygraphs: Essential Tools or Violations of Privacy? 5132
Drug Use around the World, 5135
Drugs and Crime, 5127
Drugs & Pain, 5148
Drugs & Sexual Behavior, 5149
Drugs and Society: Responding to an Epidemic, 5125
Drugs & the Brain, 5113
Drugs & the Family, 5143
The Druid of Shannara, 1059(F)
Druids, 1370(F)
Dubliners, 2927(F)
Duel of Eagles: The Mexican and U.S. Fight for the Alamo, 7964
Duende Meadow, 2489(F)
Duke Ellington, 6343
Dune, 2593(F)
The Dune Encyclopedia, 3757
Dune Messiah, 2593(F)
The Dungeon Master: The Disappearance of James Dallas Egbert III, 5378
The Dunwich Horror and Others, 1804(F), 1806(F)
The Dushau Trilogy, 2646(F)
Dust Bowl: The Southern Plains in the 1930s, 8155
Dust Tracks on a Road, 6269
Dvorak, 6342
Dwarfs, 3371
Dwight D. Eisenhower: Hero & Politician, 6529
Dydeetown World, 2847(F)
The Dying Earth, 2810(F)
Dying Inside, 1269(F)
Dying of the Light, 2684(F)
Dying to Be Thin, 5402
Dying Young, 571(F)
Dylan: A Biography, 6386
Dynamite Kites: 30 Plans to Build and Fly, 9155

E.T. The Book of the Green Planet, 2617(F)
E.T.: The Extra Terrestrial, 2617(F)
Eagle against the Sun, 7295
The Eagle and the Raven, 1578(F)
The Eagle Has Landed, 127(F)
An Ear to the Ground: An Anthology of Contemporary American Poetry, 3277
Early American Dramatists: From the Beginnings to 1900, 3844
The Early Arrival of Dreams: A Year in China, 7423
Earth, 2435(F)
Earth Abides, 2796(F)
Earth, Air, Fire, & Water, 3171
Earth and Fire, 1642(F)
Earth Blood, 2628(F)
The Earth Care Annual 1990, 4448
Earth Descended, 2763(F)
Earth Dreams, 1227(F)
The Earth Report: The Essential Guide to Global Ecological Issues, 4428
Earthquake, 8808
East Africa, 7365
East Asia and the Western Pacific, 7392
East of Eden, 607(F)
East of Midnight, 1190(F)
Easter Island: The Mystery Solved, 7470
Eastern Birds, 8536
Eastern Forests, 8821
Eastern Religions, 4081
Easy Bicycle Maintenance, 9742
Easy Cooking for Today, 9351
Easy Livin' Microwave Cooking: The New Microwave Primer, 9332
Eat Smart for a Healthy Heart, 9325
Eat to Win: The Sports Nutrition Bible, 5414
Eating Disorders: The Facts, 5368
The Ebony Book of Black Achievement, 6487
Ebony Pictorial History of Black Americans, 4361
The Echo of Greece, 7105
Echo of Lions, 1524(F)

Echoes, 2231(F)
Echoes from the Macabre: Selected Stories, 1740(F)
Eclipse Corona, 2781(F)
Ecology, 4430
An Economic Interpretation of the Constitution of the United States, 4183
Economics and the Consumer, 4590
Economics Deciphered: A Layman's Survival Guide, 4576
Economics Explained, 4571
Economics in America: Opposing Viewpoints, 4580
Ecotopia, 2456(F)
Ecotopia Emerging, 2456(F)
Eden Burning, 2309(F)
Edgar Allan Poe, 3706
An Edgar Allan Poe Companion: A Guide to the Short Stories, Romances, and Essays, 3584
The Edge, 2012(F)
Edge of Awareness: Twenty-Five Contemporary Essays, 3536
The Edge of Everest: A Woman Challenges the Mountain, 9554
The Edge of Running Water, 2791(F)
The Edge of the Sea, 8882
Edge of the Sea, 8883
Edisto, 904(F)
Edith Wharton, 3755
The Edith Wharton Reader, 391(F)
Editorial and Political Cartooning, 5748
Editor's Choice: Smithsonian, 3530
Edna St. Vincent Millay's Poems Selected for Young People, 3303
The Education of Henry Adams, 6610
The Education of H*Y*M*A*N K*A*P-*L*A*N, 1899(F)
Edward S. Corwin's The Constitution and What It Means Today, 4187
Eerdman's Handbook to the World's Religions, 4046
The Effect of Gamma Rays on Man-in-the-Moon Marigolds, 3142
Effie's House, 828(F)

Eggs: Nature's Perfect Package, 8533

Eggs and Cheese, 9364

Ego Tripping and Other Poems for Young People, 3271

Egypt after the Pharoahs: 332 B.C.–A.D. 642 from Alexander to the Arab Conquest, 7094

The Egyptian Kingdoms, 7095

Egyptian Life, 7099

Egyptian Mythology, 3459

The Egyptians, 7092

Eichmann in My Hands, 7249

Eiger Dreams: Ventures among Men and Mountains, 9577

Eight Is Enough, 3488

Eight Men Out, 9624

Eight Plays, 3004

Eight Plus One, 793(F) 1876, 1617(F)

1812: The War Nobody Won, 7875

The Eighth Day, 272(F)

80 Years of Yachting, 9934

Einstein, 6660

Einstein: The Life and Times, 6661

Einstein in America, 6662

Einstein's Dream: The Search for a Unified Theory of the Universe, 8913

Einstein's Universe, 8903

Eisenhower, 6526

Eisenhower: A Centennial Life, 6527

Eisenhower and the Cold War, 4136

The Eisenhower Diaries, 6528

The Elderly, 5084

The Elderly: Opposing Viewpoints, 5098

Eleanor: The Years Alone, 6556

Eleanor and Franklin: The Story of Their Relationship Based on Eleanor Roosevelt's Private Papers, 6557

Eleanor Roosevelt: First Lady of American Liberalism, 6561

Eleanor Roosevelt, with Love: A Centenary Remembrance, 6560

Eleanor Roosevelt's My Day: Her Acclaimed Columns 1936–1945, 6555

Eleanor Roosevelt's My Day,

Volume 2: The Post-War Years, 6558

Electra, Antigone, Philoctetes, 3019

Electricity and Basic Electronics, 9039

Electricity and Electronics Today, 9037

Electronic & Experimental Music, 5938

The Electronic Home Advisor, 9034

Electronic Service Careers, 5046

Element of Doubt, 2178(F)

Elementary BASIC, 8995

Elementary PASCAL, 8996

The Elements of Film, 5994

The Elements of Screenwriting: A Guide for Film and Television Writers, 5992

The Elements of Style, 4701

Eleni, 6909

The Elephant & the Tiger: The Full Story of the Vietnam War, 8133

The Elephant Man, 1473(F), 3114

The Elephant Tree, 188(F)

Elf Defense, 1126(F)

Elfquest, 1246(F)

The Elfstones of Shannara, 1061(F)

Elizabeth and Essex: A Tragic History, 6837

Elizabeth Arden: Cosmetics Entrepreneur, 6650

Elizabeth Barrett Browning: A Biography, 6224

Elizabeth Cady Stanton: A Radical for Women's Rights, 6637

The Elizabeth Stories, 844(F)

Elizabeth Tudor: Portrait of a Queen, 6836

Elizabethan Comedy, 3810

Elizabethan Tragedy, 3810

Elkhorn Tavern, 1539(F)

Ellery Queen's Bad Scenes: Stories from Ellery Queen's Mystery Magazine, 2188(F)

Ellis Island: A Pictorial History, 4328

Ellison Wonderland, 2530(F)

The Eloquent Object: The Evolution of American Art in Craft Media since 1945, 5811

Elric at the End of Time, 1223(F)

Elsewhere, Vol. III, 1330(F)

Elven Star, 1314(F)

Elvis: The Final Years, 6431

Elvis World, 6432

The Embattled Farmer, 8587

Embracing the Earth: Choices for Environmentally Sound Living, 4431

Emerald, 2213(F)

Emerald Explosion, 151(F)

Emergency! 5251

Emergency Doctor, 5258

Emerson's Essays, 3531

Emily Dickinson, 3883, 3890, 6241

Emily Dickinson: A Collection of Critical Essays, 3893

Emily Post's Complete Book of Wedding Etiquette, 5576

Emily Post's Etiquette, 5577

Emma, 330(F)

Emma and I, 6919

Emma Chizzit and the Queen Anne Killer, 2036(F)

Emma Goldman, 6589

Emmeline, 1528(F)

Emotional Illness in Your Family: Helping Your Relatives, Helping Yourself, 5382

Emotions & Thoughts, 5116

Empery, 2619(F)

Empire, 1247(F), 1617(F)

Empire in the Dust, 119

Empire of the Sun, 1639(F)

Empires of Time: Calendars, Clocks, and Cultures, 8901

The Enchanted Loom: Mind in the Universe, 5589

The Enchanter, 1142(F)

Enchanters' End Game, 1107(F)

The Enchantress, 248(F)

Enchantress from the Stars, 2531(F)

Encore! More Winning Monologs for Young Actors, 2984

Encounters with Whales and Dolphins, 8644

Encyclopaedia of the Musical Theatre, 5919

The Encyclopedia of American Facts and Dates, 7720

Encyclopedia of American History, 7766

Encyclopedia of American Scandal, 7754

The Encyclopedia of Animal Behavior, 8480

The Encyclopedia of Animal Biology, 8450

The Encyclopedia of Animal Ecology, 8455

The Encyclopedia of Animal Evolution, 6975

The Encyclopedia of Aquatic Life, 8615

The Encyclopedia of Bad Taste, 9534

An Encyclopedia of Battles, 7041

An Encyclopedia of Bible Animals, 4101

The Encyclopedia of Birds, 8541

Encyclopedia of China Today, 7418

Encyclopedia of Dogs and Puppies, 8745

The Encyclopedia of Drug Abuse, 5147

An Encyclopedia of Fairies: Hobgoblins, Brownies, Bogies, and Other Supernatural Creatures, 3360

The Encyclopedia of Ghosts, 9480

The Encyclopedia of Insects, 8600

The Encyclopedia of Jazz, 5862

The Encyclopedia of Jazz in the Seventies, 5862

The Encyclopedia of Jazz in the Sixties, 5862

Encyclopedia of Jewish History: Events and Eras of the Jewish People, 4384

The Encyclopedia of Mammals, 8494

Encyclopedia of Modern Bodybuilding, 5361

The Encyclopedia of Monsters, 9481, 9528

Encyclopedia of Pop, Rock and Soul, 5901

The Encyclopedia of Pottery Techniques, 9162

The Encyclopedia of Reptiles and Amphibians, 8464

The Encyclopedia of Superheroes, 9529

The Encyclopedia of the Strange, 9482

Encyclopedia of Things That Never Were: Creatures, Places, and People, 9521

Encyclopedia of Tropical Fish: With Special Emphasis on the Techniques of Breeding, 8749

The Encyclopedia of World Costume, 9178

An Encyclopedia of World History, 7053

Encyclopedic Dictionary of Electronic Terms, 9042

End as a Hero, 2624(F)

End of Eternity, 2368(F)

The End of My Career, 811(F)

The End of the Line: The Failure of Communism in the Soviet Union and China, 7344

The End of the World That Was: Six Lives in the Atomic Age, 7212

End Zone: A Photographic Celebration of Football, 9844

The Endangered Kingdom: The Struggle to Save America's Wildlife, 8570

Endangered Rivers and the Conservation Movement, 4435

Ender's Game, 2461(F)

Endgame: The Fall of Marcos, 7476

Endgame Enigma, 2598(F)

Endless Life: Selected Poems, 3265

The Endless Steppe, 7216

Endless War, 7652

The Ends of the Circle, 2841(F)

Endurance: The Events, the Athletes, the Attitude, 9571

The Enduring Constitution: A Bicentennial Perspective, 4195

The Enduring Great Lakes, 4455

Enemy at the Gates, 7197

Enemy in Sight, 1440(F)

Enemy Mine/Another Orphan, 2651(F)

An Enemy of the People, 3005

Energy Future, 8919

The Engineer of Beasts, 2770(F)

English and American Folk Music, 5946

English Fairy Tales, 3402

The English-Only Question: An Official Language for Americans? 3904

The English Revolution, 1688–1689, 7536

Enigma, 2619(F)

Enjoying Art: Painting, Sculpture, Architecture and the Decorative Arts, 5719

The Enjoyment of Music: An Introduction to Perceptive Listening, 5825

Enlightening Delilah, 2243(F)

The Enlisted Soldier's Guide, 4861

The Ennead, 2683(F)

Enola Gay, 7309

Enquiry, 2010(F)

Enter Tom, 1894(F)

Enterprise: The First Adventure, 2675(F)

The Enterprising Americans: A Business History of the United States, 7788

Entertaining Satan: Witchcraft and the Culture of Early New England, 7838

The Entrepreneurs: An American Adventure, 4583

Entrepreneurs: The Men and Women behind Famous Brand Names, 6642

The Environmental Crisis: Opposing Viewpoints, 4422

Eon, 2396(F)

The Epic of Latin America, 7626

An Episode of Sparrows, 818(F)

Epitaph for a Spy, 4(F)

Equator: A Journey, 6130

Equus, 3118

The Era of Franklin D. Roosevelt, 8027

The Era of Reform, 1830–1860, 7864

The Era of Theodore Roosevelt, 1900–1912, 8014

Eric, 6926

Eric Hosking's Birds of Prey of the World, 8561

Ernest Hemingway, 3732, 3773

Ernest Hemingway: A Life Story, 6258

Ernest Hemingway: Selected Letters, 1917–1961, 6261

Ernest Hemingway: The Search for Courage, 6260

Ernest Hemingway and His World, 6259

Ernie's War: The Best of Ernie Pyle's World War II Dispatches, 7264

Escalante: The Best Teacher in America, 6904
Escape from Freedom, 4301
Escape from Sobibor, 7276
Escape from Yuma, 63(F)
Escape into Espionage: The True Story of a French Patriot in World War Two, 7280
Escape on Venus, 2450(F)
Escape Plus, 2420(F)
The Eskimos, 7693
Eskimos, Chicanos, Indians, 4359
ESP: Opposing Viewpoints, 9472
Essays, First and Second Series, 3532
Essays of E. B. White, 3559
The Essays of Mark Van Doren (1924–1972), 3555
Essays That Worked: 50 Essays from Successful Applications to the Nation's Top Colleges, 4727
The Essential AIDS Fact Book, 5182
The Essential Cook, 9330
The Essential Darwin, 6992
The Essential Gandhi, 6807
The Essential Guide to Non-Prescription Drugs, 5163
The Essential Immigrant, 4334
The Essential Whole Earth Catalog: Access to Tools and Ideas, 4609
The Essentials of American History, 7729
The Eternal City, 2523(F)
Eternity, 2397(F)
Ethan Frome, 622(F)
Ethel Rosenberg: Beyond the Myths, 6633
Ethnic America, 4341
Ethnic Dilemmas, 1964–1982, 4344
Etiquette: Charlotte Ford's Book of Modern Manners, 5582
Eubie Blake, 6374
Eugene O'Neill, 3833, 3834
Europe 1492: Portrait of a Continent Five Hundred Years Ago, 7126
European Classical Music 1600–1825, 5832
The European Discovery of America: The Northern Voyages, 7832
The European Discovery of

America: The Southern Voyages, 7832
European Mythology, 3411
Euthanasia: Opposing Viewpoints, 5085
Euthanasia: The Moral Issues, 5079
Eva Peron, 6883
The Evening News, 117(F)
Ever Green: The Boston Celtics, 9736
Ever Since Darwin, 8393
Ever the Winds of Change, 6301
Evergreen, 1629(F), 2309(F)
Every Cliché in the Book, 3946
Every Good-bye Ain't Gone: Family Portraits and Personal Escapades, 6935
Every Loving Gift: How a Family's Courage Saved a Special Child, 5399
Everybody Says Freedom: A History of the Civil Rights Movement in Songs and Pictures, 4348
Everybody's Favorite Duck, 2221(F)
Everybody's Guide to the Law, 4232
Everybody's Gymnastics Book, 9883
Everybody's Hockey Book, 9886
Everyday Law for Everyone, 4243
Everyday Life in Ancient Greece, 7110
Everyday Life in Early America, 7841
Everyday Life in New Testament Times, 4096
Everyday Life in Old Testament Times, 4105
Everyday Life in Traditional Japan, 7448
Everyday Life of the North American Indian, 7829
Everyday Things in American Life, 1776–1876, 7873
Everyone's United Nations, 4124
Everything Is Somewhere: The Geography Quiz Book, 7056
Everything That Rises Must Converge, 484(F)
Everything We Had, 8140
Everything You Always

Wanted to Know about Nutrition, 5425
Everything You Always Wanted to Know about Portable Video Tape Recording, 9050
Everything You Need to Know about Date Rape, 5517
Everything You Need to Know about Grammar, 3922
Everything You Need to Know about Sexually Transmitted Disease, 5224
Everything You Need to Know about Teen Motherhood, 5655
Everything You Needed to Learn about Writing in High School—But . . . 4689
Everywoman's Guide to Military Service, 4285
Evidence Not Seen: A Woman's Miraculous Faith in a Japanese Prison Camp during WWII, 7281
Evidence of Things Not Seen, 438(F)
Evil under the Sun, 1950(F)
The Evolution of the Wooden Ship, 9121
Examining the Earthlight Theory: The Yakima UFO Microcosm, 9512
An Excess of Enchantment, 1128(F)
The Excluded Americans: Homelessness and Housing Policies, 4515
Exercise, 5364
Exercise Tiger: The Dramatic True Story of a Hidden Tragedy of World War II, 7240
Exiles at the Well of Souls, 1067(F)
Exile's Gate, 1070(F)
Exiles of the Rynth, 1101(F)
Exiles to Glory, 2744(F)
Exiles to the Stars, 2707(F)
Exodus, 262(F)
Exotic Animals as Pets, 8680
Exotic Plant Manual, 9379
Expanded Universe, 2579(F)
The Experience of World War I, 7166
The Experiment, 2776(F)
The Exploding Suns: The Secrets of the Supernovas, 8359
The Explorers, 9073
Exploring America's Scenic Highways, 7785

Exploring Careers, 4783

Exploring Careers as a Computer Technician, 5057

Exploring Careers as an Electrician, 5021

Exploring Careers in Accounting, 4932

Exploring Careers in Child Care Services, 4996

Exploring Careers in Computer Graphics, 5048

Exploring Careers in Dietetics and Nutrition, 4999

Exploring Careers in Engineering, 5030

Exploring Careers in Nursing, 4995

Exploring Careers in Robotics, 5047

Exploring Careers in Science, 5028

Exploring Careers in the Computer Field, 5060

Exploring Careers in the Military Services, 4972

Exploring Careers in Video, 5033

Exploring Careers Using Foreign Languages, 4831

Exploring Communications, 8951

Exploring Cross-Stitch, 9248

Exploring Earth from Space, 8337

Exploring High Tech Careers, 5056

Exploring Military Service for Women, 4869

Exploring Nontraditional Jobs for Women, 4855

Exploring Our Living Planet, 8785

Exploring Solar Energy: Principles & Projects, 8931

Exploring South America, 7679

Exploring the Deep Frontier: The Adventure of Man in the Sea, 8892

Exploring the Johnson Years, 8056

Exploring the Night Sky with Binoculars, 8274

Exploring with a Telescope, 8252

The Expressmen, 7968

Extinct Birds, 8537

Extinction, 8572

Extra Cash for Kids, 4955

Extremist Groups in America, 4409

The Eye of the Heron, 2631(F)

Eye of the Needle, 85(F)

Eye of the World, 1161(F)

Eye to Eye: How People Interact, 5539

The Eyes of the Dragon, 1171(F)

Eyes on the Prize: America's Civil Rights Years, 1954–1965, 4324

Eyewitness Auschwitz: Three Years in the Gas Chambers, 7263

The Eyewitness History of the Vietnam War: 1961–1975, 8111

Eyewitness to History, 7032

F-15 Eagle, 9126

F-111, 9127

F. Scott Fitzgerald, 3718

F. Scott Fitzgerald: A Collection of Critical Essays, 3761

The Faber Book of Nonsense Verse, 3163

The Faber Book of Northern Folk-Tales, 3395

The Faber Book of Northern Legends, 3395

Fabergé Egg: An Amos McGuffin Mystery, 2202(F)

A Fable, 1165(F)

Fabled Lands, 3366

The Fables of Aesop, 3469

The Fabric of Mind, 5307

The Fabulous Showman: The Lives and Times of P. T. Barnum, 6365

The Face, 2811(F)

Face at the Edge of the World, 635(F)

The Face in the Frost, 1033(F)

The Face of Chaos, 1023(F)

The Face of Death, 2030(F)

Face the Music, 538(F)

Faces of Fear: Encounters with the Creators of Modern Horror, 3791

The Faces of Science Fiction, 3766

Facing Nature: Poems, 3335

Facing Up, 777(F)

The Fact of a Doorframe: Poems Selected and New, 1950–1984, 3319

The Facts on File Dictionary of Archaeology, 7025

The Facts on File Dictionary of First Names, 3916

Fade, 2491(F), 3708

Fadeaway, 2166(F)

Faery! 1329(F)

Fair and Tender Ladies, 604(F)

Fair Land, Fair Land, 1568(F)

Fairies and Elves, 3372

The Faith Healer, 4074

The Falcon and the Snowman, 6893

The Falklands: South Atlantic Islands, 7686

The Fall, 636(F)

Fall of Camelot, 3366

The Fall of Japan, 7320

The Fall of Paris: The Siege and the Commune 1870–71, 7496

A Fall of Princes, 1286(F)

Fall of the Flamingo Circus, 592(F)

The Fall of the House of Usher and Other Tales, 417(F)

The Fall of the Roman Umpire, 9674

Fall of the White Ship Avatar, 2499(F)

Fallen Angels, 1698(F)

Fallen Soldiers: Reshaping the Memory of the World Wars, 7337

Falling Free, 2445(F)

The Falling Woman: A Fantasy, 1228(F)

Falls the Shadow, 1457(F)

Families in Peril: An Agenda for Social Change, 5649

Families of Birds, 8529

Family: Stories from the Interior, 533(F)

Family: The Ties That Bind . . . and Gag! 3487(F)

The Family Book about Sexuality, 5458

Family Closets, 1985(F)

The Family Horse: How to Choose, Care for, Train and Work Your Horse, 8767

Family Installments, 6945

Family Names, 5658

The Family of Man, 5723

Family Resemblances, 898(F)

Family Secrets, 691(F)

Family Trade, 37(F)

Famous All Over Town, 491(F)

Famous American Plays of the 1950s, 3128

Famous American Plays of the 1940s, 3082

Famous American Plays of the 1970s, 3083

Famous American Plays of the 1960s, 3064

Famous American Plays of the 1930s, 3065

Famous American Plays of the 1920s, 3101

Famous American Trademarks, 4605

Famous Firsts of Black Americans, 6473

Famous Ghost Stories, 1722(F)

Famous Political Trials, 7034

Famous Racing Cars: Fifty of the Greatest, from Panhard to Williams-Honda, 9617

Fane, 2337(F)

Fanglith, 2500(F)

The Fannie Farmer Cookbook, 9329

Fantastic Voyage, 2362(F)

Fantastic Voyage II: Destination Brain, 2362(F)

Fantastic Worlds: Myths, Tales and Stories, 1251

The Fantasticks: The Thirtieth Anniversay Edition, 3085

The Fantasy, 967(F)

Fantasy: The 100 Best Books, 3618

Fantasy Annual 4, 1066(F)

Fantasy Art Techniques, 9216

Far As Human Eye Could See, 8208

The Far Dreamer, 1506(F)

Far from Home: Families of the Westward Journey, 7981

Far from the Madding Crowd, 368(F)

Far Frontiers, 2743(F)

Far Harbor, 1221(F)

The Far Pavilions, 1395(F)

The Far Side of Evil, 2532(F)

The Far Side of the Hill, 1442(F), 574(F)

The Far Western Frontier, 1830–1860, 7948

Faraday's Chemical History of a Candle: Twenty-Two Experiments and Six Classic Lectures, 8783

Farenheit 451, 2427(F)

The Farewell Kid, 939(F)

Farewell, My Lovely, 1945(F)

Farewell, Summer, 598(F)

A Farewell to Arms, 1635(F)

Farewell to Manzanar, 7220

Farewell to the Chief: Former Presidents in American Public Life, 6491

The Farm, 1558(F)

Farm: A Year in the Life of an American Farmer, 8585

Farm Journal's Country Cookbook, 9337

Farthest Shore, 2636(F)

Fascinating People and Astounding Events from the History of the Western World, 7074

Fashion in Costume, 1200–1980, 9171

Fashion Sketchbook, 9180

Fast and Easy Home Decorating, 9148

The Fast-Food Guide: What's Good, What's Bad, and How to Tell the Difference, 8417

Fast Lanes, 9781

Fast-Track Careers: A Guide to the Highest-Paying Jobs, 4848

Fasting Girls: The Emergence of Anorexia Nervosa as a Modern Disease, 5176

Fat: A Love Story, 751(F)

A Fatal Advent, 2056(F)

Fatal Affair, 2070(F)

Fatal Fascination: Where Fact Meets Fiction in Police Work, 4248

Fatal Light, 1693(F)

Fate Is the Hunter, 98(F)

The Fate of the Earth, 4161

The Father, 3021

Fathers: Reflections by Daughters, 5671

Fathers and Sons, 323(F)

Fats Waller, 6454

Faulkner's Yoknapatawpha Comedy, 3767

Favorite Folktales from around the World, 3376

Favorite Tales from Shakespeare, 3051

FDR's New Deal, 8034

FDR's Splendid Deception, 6563

Feather on the Moon, 2214(F)

The Federal Courts, 4234

The Federalist, 4186

The Federalist Era, 1789–1801, 7854

Federation, 1247(F)

FEDfind: Your Key to Finding Federal Government Information, 4178

Fedor Dostoevsky, 3803

Feeding the Hungry Heart: The Experience of Compulsive Eating, 5400

Feeding the Rat: Profile of a Climber, 9545

Feel Like Goin' Home, 5866

Feel the Fear and Do It Anyway, 5615

Feelings: Our Vital Signs, 5560

Fell, 156(F)

Fell Back, 156(F)

Fellowship of the Ring, 2808(F)

The Fellowship of the Talisman, 1270(F)

Fell's United States Coin Book, 9441

The Female Animal, 8388

The Female Hero in American and British Literature, 3628

The Feminine Mystique, 4300

Femininity, 4534

Feminism: Opposing Viewpoints, 4306

The Feminist Papers: From Adams to de Beauvoir, 4317

Fences, 3140

Ferrari: The Man and His Machines, 9100

Festival Moon, 2470(F)

Fever Season, 2471(F)

The Fever Tree and Other Stories of Suspense, 2152(F)

A Few Minutes with Andy Rooney, 3508

Fiction Is Folks: How to Create Unforgettable Characters, 4694

Fiction Writer's Handbook, 3958

Fiddler on the Roof: Based on Sholem Aleichem's Stories, 3127

Fidel, 6882

Fiela's Child, 1385(F)

A Field Guide to American Architecture, 5704

A Field Guide to American Houses, 5702

A Field Guide to Animal Tracks, 8487

A Field Guide to Atlantic Coast Fishes of North America, 8627

A Field Guide to Conservation Archaeology in North America, 7019

A Field Guide to Dinosaurs, 6982

The Field Guide to Early Man, 7003

The Field Guide to Geology, 8798

A Field Guide to Hawks: North America, 8558

Field Guide to Medicinal Wild Plants, 8432

A Field Guide to Pacific Coast Fishes of North America: Fish the Gulf of Alaska to Baja California, 8624

A Field Guide to Pacific Coast Shells, Including Shells of Hawaii and the Gulf of California, 8638

A Field Guide to Pacific States Wildflowers, 8439

The Field Guide to Prehistoric Life, 6983, 7003

A Field Guide to Reptiles and Amphibians of Eastern and Central North America, 8462

A Field Guide to Rocks and Minerals, 8828

A Field Guide to Shells of the Atlantic and Gulf Coasts and the West Indies, 8639

A Field Guide to the Beetles of North America, 8605

A Field Guide to the Birds, 8542

Field Guide to the Birds of North America, 8546

A Field Guide to the Butterflies of North America, East of the Great Plains . . . 8606

A Field Guide to the Insects of America North of Mexico, 8592

A Field Guide to the Mammals, 8490

A Field Guide to the Stars and Planets, 8355

A Field Guide to the U.S. Economy, 4564

A Field Guide to Trees and Shrubs, 8429

The Field Guide to U.S. National Forests, 7761

A Field Guide to Western Birds, 8543

A Field Guide to Western Reptiles and Amphibians, 8462, 8468

A Field Guide to Wildflowers of North-Eastern and North-Central North America, 8441

A Field Manual for the Amateur Geologist: Tools and Activities for Exploring Our Planet, 8794

Fieldbook, 9790

Fieldbook of Natural History, 8398

The Fields, 1584(F)

Fields of Fire, 1705(F)

The Fifth Book of Lost Swords: Coinspinner's Story, 1260(F)

Fifth Business, 797(F)

The Fifth Horseman, 50(F)

The Fifth Omni Book of Science Fiction, 2502(F)

The Fifth Profession, 211(FF)

The Fifties: Photographs of America, 8046

Fifty Classic British Films: 1932 to 1982, 6060

Fifty Famous Motor Races, 9615

50 Great American Short Stories, 2907(F)

Fifty Great American Silent Films, 1912–1920, 6060

50 Great Scenes for Student Actors, 2987

Fifty Major Documents of the 19th Century, 7148

Fifty Short Science Fiction Tales, 2382(F)

The Fifty Worst Films of All Time, 6033

50 Years of American Automobiles, 1939–1989, 9089

Fifty Years of American Poetry: Anniversary Volume for the Academy of American Poets, 3266

Fifty Years of the Final Four: Golden Moments of the NCAA Basketball Tournament, 9733

The Fight for a Free Sea, 7878

The Fight for Chattanooga: Chickamauga to Missionary Ridge, 7926

The Fight for Chattanooga, 7890

Fight for Survival, 8571

Fight the Wild Island, 7551

Fighting Back: What Some People Are Doing about AIDS, 5196

Fighting Back, 6751

Fighting for Tony, 5372

Fighting Sail, 7886

Fighting Words: From War, Rebellion, and Other Combative Capers, 3903

Fighting Words: The War Correspondents of World War Two, 7195

Figure Skating with Carlo Fassi, 9889

Film Scenes for Actors, Vol. 2, 3087

Films of Science Fiction and Fantasy, 6055

The Films of Woody Allen, 6058

Final Approach, 213(F)

The Final Days, 8096

Final Flight, 57(F)

The Final Four, 9721

Final Grades, 838(F)

Final Harbor, 7219

Final Harvest: Emily Dickinson's Poems, 3259

Final Payments, 822(F)

Final Warning: The Legacy of Chernobyl, 8922

Financiers and Traders, 4915

Financing a College Education: The Essential Guide for the 90's, 4751

Finder: The True Story of a Private Investigator, 6912

Finding Facts Fast: How to Find Out What You Want and Need to Know, 4653

Finding Your First Job, 4782

Finding Your Roots: How Every American Can Trace His Ancestors, At Home and Abroad, 5678

A Fine and Private Place, 1028(F)

The Fine Art of Ice Skating: An Illustrated History and Portfolio of Stars, 9891

Fine Furniture for the Amateur Cabinetmaker, 9281

A Fine Time to Leave Me, 591(F)

Finger Tips: Professional Manicurists' Techniques for Beautiful Hands and Feet, 5279

Fingers, 1845(F)
The Finishing School, 820(F)
Fire Arrow, 173(F)
Fire from Heaven, 1371(F)
Fire in the Lake: The Vietnamese and the Americans in Vietnam, 8113
Fire in the Valley: The Making of the Personal Computer, 8975
The Fire Next Time, 4352
Fire of Life: The Smithsonian Book of the Sun, 8348
Fire on the Mountain, 1037(F)
Fire! Survival and Prevention, 5441
Fire Time, 2342(F)
The Firebrand, 1051(F)
Firefighters: Their Lives in Their Own Words, 4976
Fireflies, 582(F)
Fireflood and Other Stories, 2676(F)
Fires of Azroth, 1070(F)
The Fires of '88: Yellowstone Park & Montana in Flames, 8158
The Fires of Jubilee: Nat Turner's Fierce Rebellion, 1527(F)
Fireshaper's Doom, 1087(F)
The Fireside Book of Baseball, 9640
Fireside Treasury of Great Humor, 3511
Firestarter, 1786(F)
Firewind, 227(F)
First Affair, 2236(F)
The First Aviators, 9074
First Blood: Fort Sumter to Bull Run, 7909
The First Book of the Lost Swords: Woundhealer's Sword, 1260(F)
The First Eden: The Mediterranean World and Man, 7082
The First Elizabeth, 6835
The First Fig Tree, 552(F)
The First Freedom: The Tumultuous History of Free Speech in America, 4305
First Ladies, 6465
First Lady from Plains, 6525
First Light: The Search for the Edge of the Universe, 8281
First Lines: Poems Written in Youth from Herbert to Heaney, 3176
First Love: A Young People's Guide to Sexual Information, 5497
First Men in the Moon, 2827(F)
The First Rock & Roll Confidential Report, 5886
The First 25 Years in Space: A Symposium, 8312
Fish, 9361
Fish Whistle: Commentaries, Uncommentaries, and Vulgar Excesses, 3507
The Fisherman's Curse, 1104(F)
Fishes, 8628
Fishing, 9827
A Fishkeeper's Guide to Fancy Goldfishes, 8747
A Fishkeeper's Guide to Fish Breeding, 8747
The Fiske Guide to Colleges, 4733
The Fit Swimmer: 120 Workouts & Training Tips, 9958
Fitness through Cycling, 9746
Five Centuries of American Costume, 9175
The 500 Best British and Foreign Films to Buy, Rent, or Videotape, 6039
Five Hundred Fifty-Five Ways to Earn Extra Money, 4847
Five-Hundred-Five Automobile Questions Your Friends Can't Answer, 9106
Five-Hundred-Five Baseball Questions Your Friends Can't Answer, 9670
Five-Hundred-Five Boxing Questions Your Friends Can't Answer, 9787
Five-Hundred-Five Rock and Roll Questions Your Friends Can't Answer, 5898
Five-Hundred-Five Television Questions Your Friends Can't Answer, 5999
Five Hundred Years of English Poetry: Chaucer to Arnold, 3868
Five Patients, 5232
Five Red Herrings, 2170(F)
Five Seasons: A Baseball Companion, 9621
Five Summers, 824(F)
5001 Nights at the Movies, 6022
The Fixer, 1447(F)
The Flame Trees of Thika, 6921
The Flamingo's Smile: Reflections in Natural History, 8393
Flanagan's Version: A Spectator's Guide to Science on the Eve of the Twenty-First Century, 8218
Flashback: A Brief History of Film, 6014
Flashbacks: On Returning to Vietnam, 8138
Flatland: A Romance of Many Dimensions, 8899
Fledger, 281(F)
The Fleet, 2524(F)
Flesh and Blood, 1970(F)
Fletch and the Man Who, 2095(F)
Flight in America, 1900–1983: From the Wrights to the Astronauts, 9059
Flight in Yiktor, 2707(F)
A Flight of Dazzle Angels, 678(F)
The Flight of Flamingo, 69(F)
The Flight of Mavin Manyshaped, 1290(F)
Flight of the Falcon, 2322(F)
The Flight of the Iguana: A Sidelong View of Science and Nature, 8457
Flight to Love, 2290(F)
Flight to Yesterday, 2071(F)
Flights of Fancy? 100 Years of Paranormal Experiences, 9523
Flights of Passage: Reflections of a World War II Aviator, 6148
Floating in My Mother's Palm, 968(F)
The Floating World, 469(F)
Floodgate, 197(F)
The Florentine Table, 1741(F)
Florry of Washington Heights, 851(F)
The Flower Nettle, 6282
Flowering Plants: Magic in Bloom, 8444
Flowers, 8438
The Flowers Around Us: A Photographic Essay on their Reproductive Structures, 8433
Flowers for Algernon, 689(F)
Flowers in the Attic, 1707(F)
Flowers That Last Forever:

Growing, Harvesting, and Preserving, 9144
Flush: A Biography, 6225
The Fly on the Wall, 2053(F)
Flyaway, 557(F)
Flyby: The Interplanetary Odyssey of Voyager 2, 8300
Flying Free, 8562
Flying the Big Jets, 9077
Flying the Mail, 9074
Focus on Families, 5641
The Folded Leaf, 878(F)
Folding Table Napkins, 9154
Folk and Festival Costume of the World, 9176
The Folk of the Air, 1029(F)
The Folk Songs of North America, 5948
Folk Tale Plays round the World, 2986
Folk-Tales of the British Isles, 3396
Folklore in America, 3434
Folktales of India, 3381
Folktales of Mexico, 3447
Folktales Told Around the World, 3364
The Food Additives Dictionary, 8414
Food and Fitness, 5422
The Food Book: The Complete Guide to the Most Popular Brand Name Foods, 5411
Food for Sport, 5427
Food, Nutrition & You, 5423
The Food of the Gods, 2828(F)
The Food Pharmacy: Dramatic New Evidence That Food Is Your Best Medicine, 5410
Fool on the Hill, 1258(F)
Fools Crow, 1512(F), 7816
Fools of Fortune, 1482(F)
Fool's Run, 2677(F)
The Fool's Run, 35(F)
Fool's Sanctuary, 467(F)
Football: A College History, 9858
The Football Book, 9853
Football Dreams, 2877(F)
Football for Women and Men Who Want to Learn the Game, 9842
Football for Young Players and Parents, 9855
The Football Hall of Shame, 9856
Football Made Easy, 9841

Football Register, 9843
Footfall, 2700(F)
Footsteps in the Ocean: Careers in Diving, 5023
For All Mankind, 8303
For All Practical Purposes: Introduction to Contemporary Mathematics, 8834
For Colored Girls Who Have Considered Suicide/When the Rainbow Is Enuf, 3119
For Every Sin, 7171(F)
For Love of Evil, 2352(F)
For Love of Mother-Not, 2545(F)
For Musicians Only, 4900
For Whom the Bell Tolls, 1434(F)
The Forbidden Experiment: The Story of the Wild Boy of Aveyron, 5546
The Forbidden Tower, 1050(F)
Forces of Change: An Unorthodox History, 7047
The Foreign Policy Debate: Human Rights and American Foreign Policy, 4142
Foreigner, 6943
Foreignisms, 3952
Forerunner, 2708(F)
Forerunner: The Second Venture, 2708(F)
Forest, 8820
Forest of the Night, 1278(F)
Forever . . . 770(F)
The Forever Boys, 9647
Forever Nineteen, 1638(F)
The Forever War, 2568(F)
Forever's Team, 9718
The Forge of God, 2398(F)
Forged in Steel: U.S. Marine Corps Aviation, 9128
The Forging of the Union, 1781–1789, 7857
Forging the Darksword, 1315(F)
Forgotten Animals: The Rehabilitation of Laboratory Primates, 8501
The Forsyte Saga, 549(F)
FORTRAN for Beginners, 8990
Fortunate Son: Criticism and Journalism by America's Best-Known Rock Writer, 5887
Fortune-Telling by Playing Cards, 9519
The Forty-Niners, 7958
Forty-one Stories, 403(F)

Forty Thousand in Gehenna, 2472(F)
Forward to Richmond, 7890
Fossils: A Guide to Prehistoric Life, 6985
Foul Play: Drug Abuse in Sports, 5112
Foundation, 2364(F)
Foundation and Earth, 2363(F)
Foundation and Empire, 2364(F)
Foundation Trilogy, 2364(F)
Foundation's Edge, 2364(F)
Foundation's Friends: Stories in Honor of Isaac Asimov, 2566(F)
The Founding: A Dramatic Account of the Writing of the Constitution, 4181
The Founding Fathers, 4198
Founding Mothers: Women in America in the Revolutionary Era, 7850
The Fountainhead, 991(F)
Four from the Witch World, 2709(F)
Four Great Comedies, 3053
Four Great Plays, 3006
Four Great Tragedies, 3054
Four Greek Plays, 2999
Four Major Plays, 3007
The Four-Minute Mile, 6763
Four Moons of Darkover, 2431(F)
Four on the Floor, 2098(F)
Four Past Midnight, 1787(F)
Four Plays, 3008, 3084
The Four Seasons of Shaker Life: An Intimate Portrait of the Community at Sabbathday Lake, 4089
The Fourth Book of the Lost Swords: Farslayer's Story, 1260(F)
Fox Hill, 945(F)
The Foxes of Firstdark, 291(F)
Foxfire, 8197
Fragments of Isabella, 7236
Framers of the Constitution, 4197
France, 7500
The Franchise, 9737
Frank Herbert, 3784
Frank Lloyd Wright, 6210
Frank Lloyd Wright: His Life and His Architecture, 6211
Frank Lloyd Wright: Writings and Buildings, 5706

Frankenstein, 379(F)
The Frankenstein Papers, 2764(F)
Franklin D. Roosevelt: A Rendezvous with Destiny, 6562
Franklin D. Roosevelt and the New Deal, 1932–1940, 8035
Franklin D. Roosevelt, His Life and Times, 8031
Franny and Zooey, 596(F)
Franz Kafka, 3645
Frederic Remington: A Biography, 6204
Frederica in Fashion, 2244(F)
Frederick the Great, 6841
Frederik Pohl, 3710
Free Flight, 2803(F)
Free Money for College, 4773
Free to Choose: A Personal Statement, 4565
Freedom at Midnight, 7439
Freedom Bound: A History of America's Civil Rights Movement, 4382
Freedom in Exile: The Autobiography of the Dalai Lama, 6810
Freedom of Expression, 4236
Freedom Rising, 7379
Freedom Road, 1602(F)
Freedom to Die: Moral and Legal Aspects of Euthanasia, 5097
Freedom's Child, 6939
Freefall, 9065
FreeMaster, 2608(F)
The French Chef Cookbook, 9321
French Folktales, 3391
French Impressionists, 5770
The French Lieutenant's Woman, 1428(F)
French Postcards, 2292(F)
The French Revolution & Napoleon, 7497
Frenchman's Creek, 1423(F)
Freud and Man's Soul, 5529
Friday the Rabbi Slept Late, 2081(F)
The Friendly Persuasion, 1550(F)
Friends You Can Drop: Alcohol and Drugs, 5137
Friendship and Love, 5570
Frigor Mortis, 2099(F)
The Fringe of the Unknown, 8217
Fringes of Reason: A Whole Earth Catalog, 9530

The Frisbee Book, 9575
Fritz Leiber, 3663
From "A" to "Z": The It's Academic Quiz Book, 5983
From A to Z: 200 Contemporary American Poets, 3317
From Alexander to Cleopatra, 7103
From Camelot to Kent State: The Sixties Experience in the Words of Those Who Lived It, 8083
From Cape to Cairo: One Man's Trek across Africa, 7349
From Chocolate to Morphine: Understanding Mind-Active Drugs, 5159
From Front Porch to Back Seat: Courtship in Twentieth-Century America, 5527
From Generation to Generation: How to Trace Your Jewish Genealogy and Personal History, 5663
From Here to Eternity, 1661(F)
From Modern to Contemporary: American Poetry, 1945–1965, 3878
From One Sheet of Plywood, 9285
From One to Zero: A Universal History of Numbers, 8848
From Quarks to Quasars: A Tour of the Universe, 8369
From Quarks to the Cosmos: Tools of Discovery, 8266
From Rockaway, 802(F)
From Satchmo to Miles, 6173
From Set Shot to Slam Dunk, 9735
From Slavery to Freedom: A History of Negro Americans, 4362
From Socrates to Sartre, 4013
From the Country of Eight Islands: An Anthology of Japanese Poetry, 3356
From the Door of the White House, 6896
From the Earth to the Moon, 2814(F)
From the Heart, 6379
From the Kingdom of Memory, 3561
From Versailles to the New Deal, 8028
Frommer's Europe on $30.00 a Day, 7482

The Frontier in American History, 7999
Frontier Living, 7998
Frontiers: New Discoveries about Man and His Planet, Outer Space and the Universe, 8209
The Frontiersmen, 7970
Frost and Fire, 2867(F)
A Frost in the Night, 1637(F)
Frozen Assets, 165(F)
Frozen in Time: Unlocking the Secrets of the Franklin Expedition, 7689
Fruits, 9363
Full Moon, 1803(F)
Fumblerules: A Lighthearted Guide to Grammar and Good Usage, 3948
The Fun House, 3484
The Fun of It: Random Records of My Own Flying and of Women in Aviation, 6138
Fun-to-Make Wooden Toys, 9261
Fundamentals of Contract Bridge, 9809
Funeral in Berlin, 71(F)
Funk & Wagnalls Guide to the World of Stamp Collecting, 9453
Furniture: A Concise History, 5810
The Further Adventures of Sherlock Holmes, after Sir Arthur Conan Doyle, 2031(F)
The Further Adventures of the Joker, 1756(F)
The Future As If It Really Mattered, 4608
Future Magic, 8391
The Future of the Past, 7787
Future Shock, 4419
Futurelife: The Biotechnology Revolution, 5252
Futuretrack 5, 2835(F)
Fuzzies and Other People, 1248(F)
Fuzzy Sapiens, 1248(F)

"G" Is for Gumshoe, 2029(F)
G.I. The American Soldier in World War II, 7230
Gabriela, Clove and Cinnamon, 627(F)
Gaffers, Grips and Best Boys: An Inside Look at Who

Does What in the Making of a Motion Picture, 6065

Gaia: An Atlas of Planet Management, 4416

Gaia: The Growth of an Idea, 8396

Galactic Odyssey, 2625(F)

Galactic Warlord, 2595(F)

Galapagos, 1306(F), 7685

Gallicenae: The King of Ys, Book 2, 1009(F)

Gallowglass, 2205(F)

The Gamblers, 7989

Gambling with History: Ronald Reagan in the White House, 6552

The Game for All America, 9701

The Game of Kings, 1425(F)

Games for the Superintelligent, 8851

Games Mother Never Taught You: Corporate Gamesmanship for Women, 4918

Games Pets Play: Or How Not to be Manipulated by Your Pet, 8671

Gandhi, 6808

Gandhi on Non-Violence, 4407

Gandhi the Man, 6806

Gandhi's Truth: On the Origins of Militant Nonviolence, 4406

Garden of Microbial Delights: A Practical Guide to the Subvisible World, 8660

The Garden of the Finzi-Continis, 1640(F)

The Garden Primer, 9377

The Gardener's Handbook of Edible Plants, 9376

Gardening, 9370

Gardens of Stone, 1701(F)

Gardner's Art Through the Ages, 5737

Gardner's Whys and Wherefores, 8220

Garfield: The Complete Cat Book, 8704

Garibaldi, 6842

Gaston's War, 6165

Gate of Darkness, Circle of Light, 1158(F)

The Gate of Heavenly Peace, 7431

The Gate of Ivory, 2529(F)

The Gate to Women's Country, 2800(F)

Gates of Grace, 449(F)

Gates to the Old City: A Book of Jewish Legends, 4070

Gateway, 2735(F)

Gather Together in My Name, 6212

Gathering Home, 539(F)

A Gathering of Old Men, 459(F)

The Gathering Storm, 7193

The Gauntlet of Malice, 1145(F)

The Gemini Contenders, 187(F)

The Gender Trap: A Closer Look at Sex Roles, 4531

The Gene Business: Who Should Control Biotechnology? 5270

A General's Life, 6577

Generations: A Universal Family Album, 5460

Genethics: The Clash between the New Genetics and Human Values, 5267

Genetic Engineering: Opposing Viewpoints, 5260

Genetic Engineering, 5261, 5266

Genetics, 8241

The Genius of China: 3,000 Years of Science, Discovery, and Invention, 7433

The Gentle Giants of Ganymede, 2599(F)

Gentle Vengeance: An Account of the First Year at Harvard Medical School, 5242

Gentlehands, 854(F)

Geoffrey Chaucer, 3867

Geology, 8789

George Bernard Shaw's Pygmalion, 3652

George C. Marshall: Soldier-Statesman of the "American Century", 6604

George Eliot, 3661

A George Eliot Companion: Literary Achievement and Modern Significance, 3682

George Gershwin: A Biography, 6344

George Orwell: The Political Pen, 6293

A George Orwell Companion: A Guide to the Novels, Documentaries, and Essays, 3666

George Washington: The Making of an American Symbol, 6574

George Washington Laughing, 3519

George Washington, Man and Monument, 6572

Georges Seurat, 6206

Georgia O'Keeffe, 6201

The German-Americans, 4403

The German Lesson, 697(F)

Germany, 7510

Geronimo: His Own Story, 6621

Geronimo: The Man, His Time, His Place, 6622

Get Thee to a Punnery, 3932

Get to the Heart: My Story, 6423

Getting a Job in the Computer Age, 5041

Getting Even, 3482

Getting High in Natural Ways: An Infobook for Young People of All Ages, 5620

Getting In! The First Comprehensive Step-by-Step Strategy Guide to Acceptance at the College of Your Choice, 4728

Getting into College: A Guide for Students and Parents, 4746

Getting into Fashion, 4934

Getting into Film, 4891

Getting into Video: A Career Guide, 4922

Getting It On: The Clothing of Rock & Roll, 5874

Getting Skilled, Getting Ahead, 4806

Getting Started in Bird Watching, 8534

Getting Started in Computer Graphics, 9007

Getting Stronger: Weight Training for Men & Women, 9773

Getting the Most from Your Computer, 9008

Getting to the Right Job: A Guide for College Graduates, 4789

Gettysburg: The Confederate High Tide, 7901

Gettysburg: The Final Fury, 7896

Ghost, 2353(F)

The Ghost Light, 2638(F)

Ghost Stories from the American South, 1812(F)
Ghost Story, 1852(F)
The Ghostly Register, 9518
Ghosts, 1712(F), 9536
The Ghostway, 2051(F)
The Giant Airships, 9060
The Giant Book of More Strange But True Sports Stories, 9579
The Giant Book of Scottish Short Stories, 2937(F)
Giant Steps, 6737
Giants and Ogres, 3371
Giants in the Earth: A Saga of the Prairie, 1587(F)
Giants of Jazz, 6186
Giants' Star, 2599(F)
Gideon's Trumpet, 4246
Gift from the Sea, 3537
The Gift Horse's Mouth, 1943(F)
The Gift of Asher Lev, 486(F)
A Gift of Hope: The Tony Melendez Story, 6425
Gift Wraps, 9221
Gifts and Crafts from the Garden, 9149
Gilbert and Sullivan, 5922
Gin and Daggers: A Murder, She Wrote Mystery, 2007(F)
Giraudoux: Four Plays, 3002
The Girl in the Box, 2173(F)
The Girl in the Grass, 1257(F)
A Girl Named Sooner, 642(F)
The Girl of His Dreams, 880(F)
The Girl Who Wanted a Boy, 947(F)
Girls and Sex, 5489
Girltalk about Guys, 5635
The GI's War: The Story of the American Soldiers in Europe in World War II, 7222
Give and Take, 858(F)
Give Me One Wish, 5186
Glacier, 8809
The Gladstone Bag, 2103(F)
A Glass Face in the Rain: New Poems, 3330
The Glass Key, 2038(F)
The Glass Menagerie, 3138
The Glass Salamander, 1102(F)
Glenn's New Complete Bicycle Manual, 9751
The Global Ecology Handbook: What You Can Do about the Environmental Crisis, 4427
Global Rivals, 4131
Global Warming: Are We Entering the Greenhouse Century? 4439
The Globe Restored: A Study of the Elizabethan Theatre, 6092
The Glorious Fourth: An American Holiday, an American History, 7711
The Glory and the Dream, 7759
Glory Days: Bruce Springsteen in the 1980s, 6445
Glory Road, 2579(F)
A Glossary of Literary Terms, 3563
The Glove of Maiden's Hair, 1124(F)
The Glow, 1849(F)
Gnomes, 3365
Go-Ahead Rider, 51(F)
Go Ask Alice, 5118
Go! Fight! Win! The National Cheerleaders Association Guide for Cheerleaders, 9592
Go Tell It on the Mountain, 439(F)
Go Toward the Light, 5215
Go Well, Stay Well, 468(F)
God and the Astronomers, 8367
God Emperor of Dune, 2593(F)
God Is My Co-Pilot, 7289
The God Letters, 4075
God with Us: The Miracle of Christmas, 4116
Godbond, 1273(F)
Gödel, Escher, Bach: An Eternal Golden Braid, 8222
The Godfather, 233(F)
The Gods, 3372
Gods and Myths of Northern Europe, 3481
Gods & Pharaohs from Egyptian Mythology, 3458
God's Fool: The Life and Times of Francis of Assisi, 6838
God's Grace, 2682(F)
Gods, Graves, and Scholars, 7014
The Gods Laughed, 2344(F)
The Gods of Ancient Egypt, 7100
Gods of Mars, 2453(F)
Gods of Riverworld, 2535(F)
God's Trombones: Seven Negro Sermons in Verse, 3285
Going after Cacciato, 1699(F)
Going Backwards, 567(F)
Going Downtown: The War against Hanoi and Washington, 8104
Going Over to Your Place: Poems for Each Other, 3167
Going Solo, 6237
Going to Extremes, 8183
Going to the Dogs, 710(F)
Going to Work: A Unique Guided Tour through Corporate America, 4585
Gold Buckle Dreams: The Rodeo Life of Chris LeDoux, 6779
The Gold Coast, 908(F)
Gold Dust, 7957
The Gold Ring: Jim Fisk, Jay Gould, and Black Friday, 1869, 8004
The Golden Age of Television: Notes from the Survivors, 6115
The Golden Apples of the Sun, 1045(F)
The Golden Bough: A Study in Magic and Religion, 4048
The Golden Cup, 1629(F)
The Golden Gate, 198(F)
The Golden Horn, 1288(F)
The Golden Thread, 646(F)
The Golden Tore, 1216(F)
The Golden Treasury of the Best Songs & Lyrical Poems in the English Language, 3221
The Golden Turkey Awards, 6033
Golden Unicorns, 2213(F)
Golden Witchbreed, 2555(F)
Golem in the Gears, 1011(F)
Golf for Women, 9880
The Golf Hall of Shame, 9874
Golf Rules in Pictures, 9878
Gone the Dreams and Dancing, 1573(F)
Gone to Soldiers, 899(F)
Gone with the Wind, 1543(F)
Good Behavior, 270(F)
Good Dog, Bad Dog, 8736
The Good Dog Book: Loving Care, 8735
The Good Earth, 1389(F)

Good Grief: The Story of Charles M. Schulz, 6205

The Good Guide for Bad Photographers, 9419

The Good High School: Portraits of Character and Culture, 4631

The Good Housekeeping All-American Cookbook, 9338

The Good Housekeeping Illustrated Cookbook, 9319

The Good Housekeeping Illustrated Microwave Cookbook, 9348

The Good Looks Skin Book, 5339

Good Morning Blues, 6368

The Good Neighbor, 4132

Good Night, Sweet Prince: The Life and Times of John Barrymore, 6367

Good Night, Willie Lee, I'll See You in the Morning, 4379

The Good Old Days—They Were Terrible, 8006

The Good Provider, 1474(F)

Good Sound: An Uncomplicated Guide to Choosing and Using Audio Equipment, 9049

The Good Times, 6215

The Good Times Are Killing Me, 520(F)

"The Good War": An Oral History of World War Two, 7308

Good Woman: Poems and a Memoir, 1969–1980, 3251

Good Words to You: An All-New Dictionary and Native's Guide to the Unknown American Language, 3914

Goodbye, Columbus: And Five Short Stories, 490(F)

Goodbye, Darkness, 7250

Goodbye Gutenberg: The Newspaper Revolution of the 1980's, 3988

Good-bye Mr. Chips, 1435(F)

Goodbye, Paper Doll, 744(F)

Goodbye to All That, 6249

Goodheart-Willcox Automotive Encyclopedia: Fundamental Principles, Operation, Construction, Service, Repair, 9116

Goodnight, Cinderella, 902(F)

Goofbang Value Daze, 2805(F)

Gorbachev: A Biography, 6843

Goren's New Bridge Complete, 9810

The Gorgon—And other Beastly Tales, 1190(F)

Gorilla, My Love, 442(F)

The Gorilla Signs Love, 23(F)

Gorillas in the Mist, 8497

Gorky Park, 1847(F)

Gothic Architecture, 5735

Goya, 5775

Grace in the Wilderness: After the Liberation, 1945–1948, 1679(F)

The Gradual Vegetarian, 9366

The Graduates, 2312(F)

The Grand Adventure, 2536(F)

The Grand Alliance, 7193

Grand Allusions, 3953

The Grand Canyon, 8159

The Grand Failure: The Birth and Death of Communism in the Twentieth Century, 4170

Grand Obsession: Madame Curie and Her World, 6655

Grand Ole Opry: The Official History, 5867

Grand Opening, 562(F)

Grand Prix Greats: A Personal Appreciation of 25 Famous Formula 1 Drivers, 9618

Grandmother Had No Name, 7421

Granny Was a Buffer Girl, 544(F)

Grant and Lee: The Virginia Campaigns, 7915

Grant Moves South, 6530

Grant Takes Command, 6530

The Grapes of Wrath, 1631(F)

Graphic Techniques for Designers and Illustrators, 9202

Graphics and Animation on the Apple II, 8994

Graphics and Animation on the Atari, 8994

Graphics and Animation on the Commodore 64, 8994

Graphics and Animation on the TRS-80, 8994

Grass, 2801(F)

The Grass Is Always Greener over the Septic Tank, 3486

Grass Roots & Schoolyards: A High School Basketball Anthology, 9714

Grasslands, 8811

Grasslands and Tundra, 8823

Grateful Dead Family Album, 5845

A Graveyard for Lunatics, 1042(F)

Gravity's Lens: Views of the New Cosmology, 8361

Gray Victory, 1546(F)

The Great Airship Mystery: A UFO of the 1890s, 9483

The Great American Detective, 2084(F)

Great American Love Stories, 2318(F)

The Great American Magazine, 3989

Great American Short Stories, 2967(F)

A Great & Shining Road: The Epic Story of the Transcontinental Railroad, 8003

Great Baseball Feats, Facts & Firsts, 9686

Great Battlefields of the World, 7057

Great Battles of the Civil War, 7944

Great Battles of World War II, 7248

Great Black Americans, 6489

The Great Book of Dream Cars, 9090

The Great Boy Chase, 2313(F)

The Great British Detective, 2028(F)

The Great Campaigns: Reform and War in America, 1900–1928, 7740

The Great Chiefs, 7797

The Great Chinese Revolution: 1800–1985, 7409

The Great Comic Book Artists, Volume 2, 5796

Great Commanders and Their Battles, 6786

Great Cooking: The Best Recipes from Time-Life Books, 9339

The Great Cosmic Mother, 4084

The Great Crash, 1929, 8029

The Great Depression, 8041

The Great Depression: America, 1929–1941, 8036

The Great Depression and the New Deal: America's Economic Collapse and Recovery, 8040

The Great Depression and World War II: Organizing America, 1933–1945, 8038

The Great Divide: A Walk Through America along the Continental Divide, 7771

The Great Divide: America at This Time, 8091

The Great Escape, 7190

Great Events of Bible Times, 4108

Great Expectations, 355(F)

Great Expectations: A Novel of Friendship, 3669

Great Expectations: America and the Baby Boom, 4459

The Great Explorers: The European Discovery of America, 7833

The Great Gatsby, 1605(F)

The Great Gatsby: The Limits of Wonder, 3748

Great Ghost Stories, 1840(F)

Great Guitarists: The Most Influential Players in Blues, Country Music, Jazz and Rock, 5877

The Great Hunger: Ireland, 1845–1849, 7543

The Great Hunt, 1162(F)

Great Jewish Short Stories, 445(F)

The Great Journey: The Peopling of Ancient America, 7016

Great Journeys, 7044

Great Modern European Short Stories, 2892(F)

Great Modern Police Stories, 2143(F)

Great Modern Short Stories, 2902(F)

Great Moments in Architecture, 5695

Great Ones: NFL Quarterbacks from Baugh to Montana, 9861

The Great Origami Book, 9220

The Great Outdoors, 9549

Great Painters, 5726

The Great Palace: The Story of Parliament, 7524

Great Possessions: An Amish Farmer's Journal, 8584

The Great Psychologists, 5553

The Great Rift: Africa's Changing Valley, 7364

Great Rivers of the World, 7073

Great Rock Musicals, 5927

The Great Santini, 535(F)

Great Scenes from the World Theater, 2989

The Great School Debate: Which Way for American Education? 4628

Great Science Fiction Stories by the World's Great Scientists, 2377(F)

Great Scientific Experiments: Twenty Experiments That Changed Our View of the World, 8242

The Great Scientists, 6643

Great Shape: The First Exercise Guide for Large Women, 5357

The Great Short Works of Joseph Conrad, 343(F)

Great Short Works of Leo Tolstoy, 320(F)

Great Short Works of Willa Cather, 392(F)

Great Singers on Great Singing, 5923

Great Sky River, 2402(F), 2405(F)

Great Slave Narratives, 6464

The Great Song Thesaurus, 5947

Great Southern Mysteries, 9497

The Great Southwest, 8202

Great Sports Humor, 9556

The Great Stage Stars: Distinguished Theatrical Careers of the Past and Present, 6179

Great Stories of Sherlock Holmes, 1989(F)

Great Tales of Action and Adventure, 15(F)

Great Thinkers, Great Ideas: An Introduction to Western Thought, 4005

The Great Thirst, 1384(F)

The Great Train Robbery, 1416(F)

Great True Spy Stories, 4138(F)

Great Voyages of Discovery: Circumnavigators and Scientists, 7142

The Great West, 7961

Greater Nowheres: A Journey through the Australian Bush, 6117

The Greatest Criminals of All Time: An Illustrated Compendium of More Than 600 Great Crooks, 6118

The Greatest-Ever Bank Robbery: The Collapse of the Savings and Loan Industry, 4595

The Greatest First Basemen of All Times, 9654

The Greatest Hunting Stories Ever Told, 9834

Greatest Monsters in the World, 9484

The Greatest Pitchers of All Time, 9655

The Greatest Stories Ever Told (about Baseball), 9685

Greek and Roman Life, 7085

Greek Architecture, 5786

The Greek Gods, 3473

Greek Mythology, 3478

Greek Myths, 3477

The Greek Treasure, 1476(F)

The Greek Way, 7106

The Greek World, 7108

The Greeks and Their Heritages, 7545

Green Berets: Unconventional Warriors, 4284

The Green Berets: U.S. Special Forces from Vietnam to Delta Force, 9124

Green City in the Sun, 1387(F)

The Green Consumer, 4426

Green Grass of Wyoming, 294(F)

The Green Hills of Earth, 2579(F)

The Green Lifestyle Handbook: 1,001 Ways to Heal the Earth, 4436

Green Mansions: A Romance of the Tropical Forest, 1157(F)

The Green Pearl, 1299(F)

Green Politics: The Global Promise, 7503

Greencastle, 866(F)

The Greenpeace Book of Antarctica: A New View of the Seventh Continent, 7699

Greenwich Time and the Discovery of the Longitude, 8860

Greg LeMond's Complete Book of Bicycling, 9758

Greg LeMond's Pocket Guide to Bicycle Maintenance and Repair, 9757

Gremlins Go Home, 2426(F)

Grendel, 1129(F)

Gretzky: An Autobiography, 6774

The Grey Horse, 1200(F)

Grey Seas Under, 8894

Grieg, 6345

Grinding It Out: The Making of McDonalds, 4573

Grizzly Years: In Search of the American Wilderness, 8508

Groucho, Harpo, Chico and Sometimes Zeppo: A History of the Marx Brothers and a Satire on the Rest of the World, 5987

The Ground Zero Club and Other Prize-Winning Plays, 3089

Grounded, 847(F)

The Grounding of Group Six, 256(F)

Grow Up, Cupid, 1895(F)

Growing Minds: On Becoming a Teacher, 4953

Growing Pains, 2314(F)

Growing Season, 785(F)

Growing Up, 6216

Growing Up in Moscow: Memories of a Soviet Girlhood, 1963–1980, 6968

Growing Up Italian, 4398

Growing Up Western, 6167

The Growth of Cities, 4556

Growth of Civilization in East Asia: China, Japan, and Korea before the 14th Century, 7393

The Growth of the American Republic, 7762

Growth of the Soil, 559(F)

Grumbles from the Grave, 3733

Grundberg's Goof-Proof Photography Guide, 9420

Gryphon in Glory, 1232(F)

Gryphon's Eyrie, 1233(F)

The Guaranteed Goof-Proof Microwave Cookbook, 9349

The Guardian Angels, 4479

Guardians of the West, 1108(F)

A Guest of Honour, 961(F)

The Guide, 984(F)

A Guide Book of United States Coins, 9463

Guide to Alternative Education and Training, 4791

Guide to Apprenticeship Programs, 4810

A Guide to Bird Behavior, 8550

A Guide to Bird Behavior: In the Wild and at Your Feeder, 8550

Guide to Careers without College, 4814

A Guide to Enjoying Wildflowers, 8447

Guide to Good Food, 5419

A Guide to Psychologists and Their Concepts, 5540

Guide to Self-Employment, 4929

A Guide to the Behavior of Common Birds, 8550

Guide to the Presidency, 4208

The Guilt-Free Dog Owner's Guide: Caring for a Dog When You're Short on Time and Space, 8716

Guilty or Innocent? 4241

Guinea Pigs: Everything about Purchase, Care, Nutrition, and Diseases, 8758

Guinevere, 1230(F)

Guinness Book of Answers, 9503

The Guinness Book of Astronomy, 8275

The Guinness Book of Music, 5818

Guinness Book of Names, 9492

The Guinness Book of Olympics Records, 9906

Guinness Book of Pet Records, 8686

Guinness Book of Speed Facts and Feats, 8916

The Guinness Book of Stamps, Facts and Feats, 9456

Guinness Book of World Records, 9516

Guinness Book of World Records 1990–91, 9514

Guinness Film Facts and Feats, 6050

The Guinness Guide to Formula One, 9616

Guinness Guide to 20th Century Fashion, 9167

The Guinness Jazz A–Z, 5851

Guinness Sports Record Book, 1989–90, 9572

Guinness Sports Record Book, 1990–91, 9552

The Guitar Book: A Handbook for Electric and Acoustic Guitarists, 5942

The Guitar Greats, 6187

The Guitar Handbook, 5933

The Gulag Archipelago, 1918–1956: An Experiment in Literary Investigation, 7586

The Gulf, 226(F)

The Gulf Breeze Sightings: The Most Astounding Multiple Sightings of UFOs in U.S. History, 9540

Gulliver's Travels, 385(F)

The Gun Control Debate: You Decide, 4527

The Gunfighter: Man or Myth? 7977

The Gunfighters, 7997

Gunga Din, 3214

The Guns of August, 7164

The Guns of Avalon, 1344(F)

The Gunslinger, 1172(F)

Gustave Flaubert, 3635

Guys Like Us, 779(F)

Gypsies, 2850(F)

The Gypsies, 4405

H. G. Wells, 3656

H.M.S. Ulysses, 1664(F)

A Haiku for Hanae, 2109(F)

Hail to the Chiefs: A Guided Tour through the Presidents, 6475

The Haj, 262(F)

Halfbreed, 6898

Halfway Down Paddy Lane, 1215(F)

The Hall of the Mountain King, 1287(F)

Hallapoosa, 587(F)

Halley's Comet: What We've Learned, 8334

Halliwell's Film Guide, 6018

Halloween Horrors, 1830(F)

The Halloween Tree, 1043(F)

Hallucination Orbit: Psychology in Science Fiction, 2378(F)

Hamlet, 3055, 3830

The Hammer and the Horn, 1125(F)

Hand-Me-Down Dreams, 5398

The Hand of Oberon, 1344(F)

The Handbook of Adolescence: A Medical Guide for Parents and Teenagers, 5608

Handbook of Denominations in the United States, 4065

Handbook of Everyday Law, 4252

Handbook of Model Rocketry, 9407

Handbook of Pictorial Symbols: 3,250 Examples from International Sources, 3901

The Handbook of Riding, 8763

Handbook of Russian Literature, 3606

The Handbook of Tennis, 9967

Handbook of Tropical Aquarium Fishes, 8748

A Handbook to Literature, 3588

Handel, 6347

Handel: The Man and His Music, 6346

Handgun, 9134

Handle with Care: Frightening Stories, 2075(F)

The Handmaid's Tale, 2392(F)

Handsome as Anything, 2266(F)

Handsome Man, 2275(F)

The Hanging of Father Miguel, 11(F)

Hank Greenberg: The Story of My Life, 6722

Hannah Senesh—Her Life & Diary, 6873

The Hanukkah Book, 4118

Happy Birthday, Wanda June, 3131

Hard Bodies, 9774

Hard Disk Management with MS-DOS and PC-DOS, 8980

Hard-Hatted Women: Stories of Struggle and Success in the Trades, 4851

Hard Knox: The Life of an NFL Coach, 6753

Hard Lessons: Senior Year at Beverly Hills High School, 5538

Hard Rain, 2(F)

Hard Times, 356(F)

Hard Times: An Oral History of the Great Depression, 8043

Hardball: How Politics Is Played—Told by One Who Knows the Game, 4268

Hardwired, 2844(F)

Harlem Renaissance, 5799

Harmful Intent, 1969(F)

The Harmony Illustrated Encyclopedia of Country Music, 5858

The Harmony Illustrated Encyclopedia of Rock, 5852

Harold Pinter, 3809

The Harp of Imach Thyssel, 1336(F)

The Harper Anthology of Poetry, 3220

Harper's Anthology of 20th Century Native American Poetry, 3307

Harper's Illustrated Handbook of Cats, 8692

Harper's Illustrated Handbook of Dogs, 8715

Harriet Tubman, the Moses of Her People, 6519

The Harrowing of Gwynedd, 1178(F)

Harry, 265(F)

Harry and Hortense at Hormone High., 950(F)

Harry Anderson's Games You Can't Lose: A Guide for Suckers, 9547

Harry Harrison, 3781

Harry S. Truman, 6571

Harry S. Truman: Fair Dealer and Cold Warrior, 6569

Hart's Hope, 1064(F)

The Harvard Book of Contemporary American Poetry, 3336

Harvard Concise Dictionary of Music, 5827

The Harvard Concordance to Shakespeare, 3827

Harvest Home, 1857(F)

Harvesters, 8582

The Harvey Girls: Women Who Opened the West, 7974

Hasidic Tales of the Holocaust, 1650(F)

The Hat of My Mother, 2966(F)

Hatter Fox, 462(F)

Haunted, 1764(F)

The Haunted: One Family's Nightmare, 9489

Haunted Heartland, 9531

Haunted Houses: Tales from 30 American Homes, 9527

Haunted Houses, U.S.A. 9526

The Haunted Mesa, 2623(F)

The Haunted Realm: Ghosts, Spirits and Their Uncanny Abodes, 9517

Haunted Women: The Best Supernatural Tales by American Women Writers, 1715(F)

The Haunting of Hill House, 1769(F)

The Haunting of Willow Dasset, 733(F)

Haunting Women, 1831(F)

Hawaii, 1401(F)

Hawaii for Free: Hundreds of Free Things to Do in Hawaii, 8179

Hawes Guide to Successful Study Skills, 4648

Hawkmistress! 1052(F)

Hawks in Flight: The Flight Identification of North American Migrant Raptors, 8559

The Hawks of Fellheath, 1119(F)

Haydn, 6348

Hazardous Waste in America, 4452

He Freed Britain's Slaves, 6881

Healers, 5236

The Healer's War, 1265(F)

The Healing Rain: Breakthrough Medical Discoveries about How the Brain Manages Health, 5320

The Health Crisis: Opposing Viewpoints, 5253

Health, Medicine, and the Human Body, 5294

The Healthy Body: A Maintenance Manual, 5293

Healthy Microwave Cooking: Better Nutrition in Half the Time! 9346

Hear That Lonesome Whistle Blow: Railroads in the West, 7949

Hearing from Wayne and Other Stories, 1880(F)

The Heart Is a Lonely Hunter, 708(F)

The Heart of a Woman, 6212

Heart of Aztlan, 437(F)

Heart of Darkness, 344(F)

Heart of Darkness: Search for the Unconscious, 3646

Heart of Europe: A Short History of Poland, 7487

Heart of the Comet, 2407(F)

The Heart of the Dragon, 7404

The Heart of the Matter, 669(F)

The Heart of the Order, 9627
Heartbeat, 885(F)
Hearts of Lions: The History of American Bicycle Racing, 9763
Heartstones, 2153(F)
Heaven, 514(F)
Heaven Cent, 2354(F)
Heaven Is a Playground, 9738
The Heavenly Horse from the Outermost West, 1276(F)
Heechee Rendezvous, 2731(F)
Hegel, 6861
The Heir Apparent, 1256(F)
Heir of Rengarth, 1100(F), 2516(F)
The Heirs of Hammerfell, 1053(F)
The Heist, 4496
Helen and Teacher: The Story of Helen Keller & Anne Sullivan Macy, 6627
Helliconia Spring, 2335(F)
Helliconia Summer, 2335(F)
Helliconia Winter, 2335(F)
Hellstar, 2750(F)
Helmet for My Pillow, 7235
HELP! My Parents Are Driving Me Crazy, 5667
Helpers and Aides, 4965
Hemingway, 6263
Hemingway: The Writer as Artist, 3695
Henderson the Rain King, 14(F)
Henry Ford, 6666
Henry James: An American as Modernist, 3740
Hen's Teeth and Horse's Toes, 8393
Her Native Colors, 846(F)
The Herald, 242(F)
Herb Seasoning, 1904(F)
Herbert Rowbarge, 12(F)
Herbs: Their Cultivation and Usage, 8434
Herbs and Spices, 8420
Hercule Poirot's Casebook, 1951(F)
Here Be Demons, 1127(F)
Here Be Dragons, 1458(F)
Here I Stand: A Life of Martin Luther, 6855
Here I Stay, 2113(F)
Here's Looking at You, Kid, 2330(F)
The Heretic's Apprentice, 2133(F)
Heretics of Dune, 2590(F)

Heritage: Civilization and the Jews, 7040
The Heritage of African Poetry: An Anthology of Oral and Written Poetry, 3351
The Heritage of Hastur, 1050(F)
Herman Melville, 3736
Hermann Hesse, 3638
A Hero Ain't Nothin' but a Sandwich, 450(F)
A Hero for Our Time: An Intimate Story of the Kennedy Years, 6540
Heroes: Tales from the Israeli Wars, 7612
Heroes and Monsters of Greek Myth, 3473
Heroes, Gods & Emperors from Roman Mythology, 3479
Heroes, Gods and Monsters of Greek Myths, 3474
Heroes, Villains, and Ghosts: Folklore of Old California, 3438
Heroic Visions, 2768(F)
Heroin: The Street Narcotic, 5162
Herpes, 5214
Herpes Diseases and Your Health, 5171
The Hex Witch of Seldom, 1274(F)
Hexaflexagons and Other Mathematical Diversions, 8853
Hey, Good Looking! 2310(F)
Hey Kid! Does She Love Me? 881(F)
Hey, Mac, Where Ya Been? Living Memories of the U.S. Marines in the Korean War, 8100
Hey, Wait a Minute, I Wrote a Book! 6755
Hi-Tech Babies: Alternative Reproductive Technologies, 5481
Hiawatha, 3291
Hickory Cured, 849(F)
Hidden Longings, 2300(F)
The Hidden Persuaders, 4619
The Hiding Place, 7307
Hiding Places, 889(F)
Hiero's Journey, 1186(F)
High Crimes and Misdemeanors: The Impeachment and Trial of Andrew Johnson, 8020

High-Performance Racquetball, 9573
High Performance Skiing, 9947
High School: A Report on Secondary Education in America, 4623
High School Reunion, 923(F)
High Stakes, 2011(F)
High Tech Holocaust, 4421
A High Wind in Jamaica, 680(F)
Higher Education, 900(F)
Higher Than Hope: A Biography of Nelson Mandela, 6794
Highlights of the Off Season, 920(F)
Highway of Eternity, 2788(F)
The Hiker's Bible, 9793
Hiking Light, 9792
Hiking the Grand Canyon, 8156
The Hinge of Fate, 7193
Hiroshima, 7217
His Eye Is on the Sparrow, 6456
His Last Bow, 1990(F)
His Majesty's U-Boat, 1673(F)
The Hispanic Americans, 4397
Historic Decisions of the Supreme Court, 4204
The Historical Encyclopedia of World War II, 7180
A History of Afro-American Literature, Volume I: The Long Beginning, 1746–1895, 3590
A History of Architecture: Settings and Rituals, 5694
History of Architecture: Stonehenge to Skyscrapers, 5692
History of Art, 5749
A History of Art & Music, 5685
History of Art for Young People, 5749
A History of Christianity, 4058
A History of Civilization: Vol. 1 Pre-History to 1765, 7081
A History of England: Vol. 1: Prehistory to 1714, 7532
A History of English Literature, 3582
A History of Europe 1648–1948: The Arrival, the Rise, the Fall, 7036
A History of Germany, 1815–1945, 7504

The History of Impressionism, 5759

History of Modern Art: Painting, Sculpture, Architecture, Photography, 5730

A History of Modern Poetry: From the Eighteen Nineties to the High Modernist Mode, 3856

A History of Modern Poetry: Modernism and After, 3856

The History of National League Baseball since 1876, 9638

A History of News: From the Drum to the Satellite, 3971

The History of Photography: From 1839 to the Present Day, 5755

A History of Private Life, I: From Pagan Rome to Byzantium, 7120

A History of Russia, 7579, 7581

History of Southern Africa, 7380

A History of the Ancient World, 7088

History of the Arabs, from the Earliest Times to the Present, 7599

History of the House of Representatives, 4220

The History of the Incas, 7681

A History of the Indians of the United States, 7802

History of the Theatre, 6082

A History of the Theatre, 6114

The History of the World Series since 1903, 9639

A History of Their Own: Women in Europe from Prehistory to the Present, Vol. 1, 7481

History of Twentieth Century Fashion, 5278

A History of United States Foreign Policy, 4158

A History of Western Music, 5835

A History of Western Philosophy, 4023

A History of Witchcraft: Sorcerers, Heretics and Pagans, 7071

A History of Women in America, 7750

The History of World Cinema, 6051

Hit and Run: The Jimi Hendrix Story, 6399

Hitchcock in Prime Time, 2120(F)

The Hitchhiker's Guide to the Galaxy, 2331(F)

The Hitchhiker's Quartet, 2331(F)

Hitler, 6845, 6847

Hitler and the Final Solution, 7206

The Hitler Fact Book, 6846

Hitler's Games: The 1936 Olympics, 9907

Hitting Hot, 9969

The HO Model Railroading Handbook, 9405

The Hobbit: Or, There and Back Again, 1295(F)

The Holcroft Covenant, 187(F)

Holding on to the Air: An Autobiography, 6389

Holding Steady, 913(F)

Holiday Tales of Sholom Aleichem, 434(F)

The Hollow Hills, 1279(F)

The Hollow Land, 551(F)

Hollywood Gothic: The Tangled Web of Dracula from Novel to Stage to Screen, 6059

The Hollywood History of the World, 6011

The Hollywood Story, 6010

The Holocaust: A History of the Jews of Europe during the Second World War, 7210

The Holy Bible: Containing the Old and New Testaments, 4107

Holy War: Islam Fights, 4060

Home before Morning: The Story of an Army Nurse in Vietnam, 6965

Home Front: Germany, 7310

The Home Front: U.S.A. 8026

The Home Planet, 8340

Home Sweet Home, 2311(F)

The Home Workshop, 9392

The Homecoming, 2649(F)

Homecoming: When the Soldiers Returned from Vietnam, 8116

The Homefront: America during World War II, 8068

Homegoing, 2736(F)

The Homeless: Opposing Viewpoints, 4512

Homeowner's Complete Outdoor Building Book: Wood and Masonry Construction, 9389

Homesick, My Own Story, 6247

The Homesman, 1593(F)

Homespun, 3441

Homespun, Handknit: Caps, Socks, Mittens, and Gloves, 9244

Homicidal Acts, 230(F)

Honey and Salt, 3322

The Honey Bee, 8603

Honey from the Lion: An African Journey, 6892

The Honorable Barbarian, 1086(F)

Honoré de Balzac, 3637

Hooded Americanism: The History of the Ku Klux Klan, 4342

Hoops! The Official National Basketball Players Association Guide to Playing Basketball, 9720

Hoorah for Yiddish, 3947

Hooray for Hellywood, 1127(F)

Hooray for Peace, Hurrah for War: The United States during World War I, 7157

Hoosier Schoolmaster, 1492(F)

Hoosiers: The Fabulous Basketball Life of Indiana, 9727

The Hopi Way: Tales from a Vanishing Culture, 3427

Horace's Compromise: The Dilemma of the American High School, 4635

Horn Crown, 2703(F)

Horror: 100 Best Books, 3623

Horrors, 1752(F)

The Horse in America, 8759

Horseman, Pass By, 202(F)

Horsemanship, 9885

The Horse's Mouth, 640(F)

Horsewatching, 8765

The Hospice Alternative: A New Context for Death and Dying, 5093

Hostage Bound, Hostage Free, 6967

Hostage One, 84(F)

Hot Money, 2013(F)

Hotel, 116(F)

Hothouse, 2335(F)

Hothouse Earth: The Greenhouse Effect and Gaia, 4429

Hound Dunnit, 1916(F)

The Hound of the Basker-villes, 1991(F)

The Hounds of God, 1288(F)

Hour of Gold, Hour of Lead, 6282

The Hour of the Gate, 1123(F)

The Hour of the Wolf, 34(F)

The House between the Worlds, 1054(F)

A House Divided: America in the Age of Lincoln, 7913

A House for Mr. Biswas, 983(F)

House Made of Dawn, 1509(F)

The House Next Door, 1844(F)

House of a Thousand Lanterns, 134(F)

House of Cards, 910(F)

The House of Doors, 2656(F)

House of Mirth, 1619(F)

The House of the Seven Gables, 400(F)

The House Plant Expert, 9380

How Animals Defend Their Young, 8484

How Can I Keep from Singing: Pete Seeger, 6440

How Congress Works, 4222

How Could I Not Be among You? 5218

How Do They Do That? 8952

How Do You Go to the Bathroom in Space? 8316

How Does a Poem Mean? 3153

How Free Are We? What the Constitution Says We Can and Cannot Do, 4203

How Green Was My Valley, 1443(F)

How I Grew, 6286

How Life Began, 8374

How Life Imitates the World Series, 9628

How Shakespeare Won the West, 6097

How the North Won: A Military History of the Civil War, 7921

How the Other Half Lives: Studies Among the Tenements of New York, 8018

How the World Works: A Guide to Science's Greatest Discoveries, 8229

How Things Work in Your Home: And What to Do When They Don't, 9043

How to Be a Compleat Clown, 4897

How to Be a Waitress (or Waiter), 4961

How to Be a Wildlife Photographer, 9438

How to Be a Working Actor, 4887

How to Bike Better, 9755

How to Break into Modeling, 4925

How to Build Electronic Projects, 9038

How to Build Outdoor Projects, 9267

How to Buy a Car, 1989: A Former Car Salesman Tells All, 9109

How to Buy a Used Car/How to Sell a Used Car, 9102

How to Catch the Action, 9416

How to Choose & Care for Your Cat, 8702

How to Debate: A Textbook for Beginners, 4702

How to Develop a Super-Power Memory, 4650

How to Develop and Write a Research Paper, 4672

How to Dissect: Exploring with Probe and Scalpel, 8453

How to Draw and Paint What You See, 9214

How to Draw and Sell Comic Strips for Newspapers and Comic Books, 9201

How to Draw Comics the Marvel Way, 9200

How to Draw in Pen and Ink, 9204

How to Draw the Human Figure: An Anatomical Approach, 9191

How to Draw What You See, 9188

How to Eat Like a Child, 3495

How to Get an Ivy League Education at a State University, 4753

How to Get and Get Ahead on Your First Job, 4822

How to Get Control of Your Time and Your Life, 5618

How to Get into an Ivy League School, 4750

How to Get into College: A Step-by-Step Manual, 4725

How to Get into the Right College: The Secrets of the College Admissions Officers, 4734

How to Get into U.S. Service Academies, 4824

How to Get Your First Job: A Field Guide for Beginners, 4792

How to Grow Vegetables Organically, 9375

How to Have a Healthier Dog, 8712

How to Identify Birds, 8536

How to Keep Your Car Mechanic Honest, 9096

How to Know the Birds, 8544

How to Land a Better Job, 4800

How to Learn a Foreign Language, 3920

How to Lie with Statistics, 8858

How to Live with a Calculating Cat, 8695

How to Live with a Single Parent, 5652

How to Look Things Up and Find Things Out, 4645

How to Make a Speech, 4668

How to Make Animated Toys, 9264

How to Make More in Music: A Freelance Guide, 4881

How to Make Your Car Last Almost Forever, 9094

How to Paint Living Portraits, 9185

How to Pay for College or Trade School: A Dollars and Sense Guide, 4781

How to Play Guitar: A New Book for Everyone Interested in Guitar, 5935

How to Play Popular Piano in Ten Easy Lessons, 5939

How to Prepare for College, 4729

How to Prepare for the Scholastic Aptitude Test SAT, 4655

How to Protect Yourself from STDs, 5226

How to Publish, Promote, and Sell Your Own Book, 3978

How to Read a Book, 4644

How to Read a Film: The Art,

Technology, Language, History, and Theory of Film and Media, 6038

How to Read and Interpret Poetry, 3852

How to Read and Write about Drama, 3800

How to Read and Write about Fiction, 3624

How to Read Music: For Singing, Guitar, Piano, Organ and Most Instruments, 5820

How to Read the Financial Pages, 5072

How to Read, Write, and Understand Music: A Practical Guide, 5815

How to Rock Climb! 9580

How to Run Better, 9913

How to Speak, How to Listen, 4667

How to Stay Alive in the Woods, 9789

How to Study, 4651

How to Succeed in Show Business by Really Trying, 4892

How to Survive as a Teen: When No One Understands, 5594

How to Survive Medical School, 5001

How to Take the SAT, Scholastic Aptitude Test, 4661

How to Talk Basketball, 9722

How to Talk Football, 9859

How to Talk to Your Cat, 8699

How to Think with Numbers, 8836

How to Understand and Use Design and Layout, 3973

How to Use the Apple II and IIe, 9010

How to Use the Coleco Adam, 9029

How to Use the Vic 20, 9029

How to Watch Baseball: A Fan's Guide to Savoring the Fine Points of the Game, 9643

How to Watch Ice Hockey, 9888

How to Win at Checkers, 9822

How to Win Friends and Influence People, 5601

How to Write, 4690

How to Write a Children's Book and Get It Published, 4898

How to Write a Term Paper, 4683

How to Write a Winning Résumé, 4708

How to Write Better Business Letters, 4638

How to Write Book Reports, 4704

How to Write Book Reports: Analyzing and Evaluating Fiction, Drama, Poetry, and Non-Fiction, 4691

How to Write Irresistible Query Letters, 4673

How to Write, Speak, and Think More Effectively, 4677

How We Choose a Congress, 4264

Hoyle's Modern Encyclopedia of Card Games: Rules of All the Basic Games and Popular Variations, 9808

Hoyle's Rules of Games, 9815

Huckleberry Finn, 4345

Hue and Cry, 476(F)

Huey Long, 6600

The Human Body, 5298

The Human Body: Its Structure and Operations, 5291

The Human Body and Why It Works, 5301

The Human Brain: Its Capacities and Functions, 5305

The Human Brain: Mind and Matter, 5309

The Human Comedy, 599(F)

The Human Factor, 110(F)

The Human Fuel Handbook: Nutrition for Peak Athletic Performance, 5416

The Human Mind: How We Think and Learn, 5318

Human Rights, 4297

Humans in Space: 21st Century Frontiers, 8322

The Humorous Mr. Lincoln: A Profile in Wit, Courage and Compassion, 6545

The Hunchback of Notre Dame, 315(F)

The Hundred Yard Lie: The Corruption of College Football and What We Can Do to Stop It, 9863

Hunger of Memory: The Education of Richard Rodriguez, 6946

Hungry Hill, 1995(F)

The Hunt for Red October, 45(F)

Hunter in the Dark, 141(F)

Hunter's Horn, 516(F)

The Hunters of Prehistory, 7005

Hunter's Stew and Hangtown Fry: What Pioneer America Ate and Why, 7973

Hunting and Fishing from "A" to Zern, 9836

Huysman's Pets, 274(F)

The Hyde Park Murder, 2160(F)

Hypatia's Heritage, 8203

I Always Look Up the Word "Egregious", 3942

I Am England, 1490(F)

I Am Fifteen—And I Don't Want to Die, 7169

I Am Hamlet, 3815

I Am Rosemarie, 7259

I Am the Cheese, 794(F)

I Am the Darker Brother: An Anthology of Modern Poems by Negro Americans, 3234

I Am the Fire of Time: The Voices of Native American Women, 7815

I Been There Before, 1877(F)

"I Can See You Naked": A Fearless Guide to Making Great Presentations, 4680

The I Ching: Or, Book of Changes, 4055

I, Claudius, 1369(F)

I Dare You: How to Use Psychology to Get What You Want Out of Life, 5552

I Didn't Say Goodbye: Interviews with Children of the Holocaust, 7314

I Don't Know What to Say: How to Help and Support Someone Who Is Dying, 5081

I Hate School: How to Hang In & When to Drop Out, 4637

I Heard the Owl Call My Name, 431(F)

I Hope I Shall Arrive Soon, 2506(F)

I Know Why the Caged Bird Sings, 6212

I Lost Everything in the Post-Natal Depression, 3486

I Love Myself When I Am

Laughing . . . and Then Again When I Am Looking Mean and Impressive, 2925

I Love You, Stupid! 882(F)

I Married Adventure: The Lives and Adventures of Martin and Osa Johnson, 6149

I Never Called It Rape, 5522

I Never Loved Your Mind, 948(F)

I Never Met an Animal I Didn't Like, 6906

I Never Promised You a Rose Garden, 667(F)

I Never Said I Love You, 2230(F)

I Never Told Anyone, 5500

I Really Should Be Practicing, 6394

I, Robot, 2365(F)

I Shall Not Be Moved, 3238

I Sing the Body Electric, 1045(F)

I Think I Don't Remember, 3490

I, Tina, 6450

"I Touch the Future . . .": The Story of Christa McAuliffe, 6153

I Want to Grow Hair, I Want to Grow Up, I Want to Go to Boise: Children Surviving Cancer, 5174

The I Was a Teenage Juvenile Delinquent Rock 'n' Roll Horror Beach Party Movie Book, 5991

I Will Fear No Evil, 2579(F)

I Will Fight No More Forever, 7793

I Wonder as I Wander, 6267

I Wonder What College Is Like? 4763

I Wouldn't Have Missed It: Selected Poems of Ogden Nash, 3305

Iacocca: An Autobiography, 6676

Iberia, 1450(F)

IBM PC Introduction, BASIC Programming and Applications, 8979

The Icarus Agenda, 184(F)

Ice Palace, 1604(F)

Ice Station Zebra, 198(F)

Ice Time: Climate, Science, & Life on Earth, 8814

Icebreaker, 2020(F)

The Iceman Cometh, 3112

Icerigger, 2544(F)

Icons: Intimate Portraits, 6075

I'd Rather Be a Yankee, 9703

The Idea of a Theater: A Study of Ten Plays, 3798

Ideas and Men: The Story of Western Thought, 7030

Ideas of the Great Psychologists, 5548

Identifying American Architecture: A Pictorial Guide to Styles and Terms, 1600–1945, 5698

The Idiot, 310(F)

Idle Weeds: The Life of a Sandstone Ridge, 8410

Idylls of the Queen, 1164(F)

If Beale Street Could Talk, 440(F)

If Ever I Return, Pretty Peggy-O, 2092(F)

If I Can Dream: Elvis' Own Story, 6430

If I Were You, 1406(F)

If It Weren't for Sebastian, 749(F)

If Life Is a Bowl of Cherries, What Am I Doing in the Pits? 3486

If Morning Ever Comes, 933(F)

If Only I Could Tell You: Poems for Young Lovers and Dreamers, 3300

If the Stars Are Gods, 2408(F)

If There Be Thorns, 1707(F)

If This Is Love, I'll Take Spaghetti, 2251(F)

If You Could See What I Hear, 6955

The Iguana Killer: Twelve Stories of the Heart, 488(F)

The Iliad, 3183

The Ill-Bred Bride: Or, The Inconvenient Marriage, 2263(F)

I'll Buy That! 4561

I'll Live, 713(F)

I'll Never Walk Alone: The Inspiring Story of a Teenager's Struggle against Cancer, 6951

The Illearth War, 1095(F)

The Illustrated Book of Basic Boating, 9924

The Illustrated Confederate Reader, 7919

Illustrated Dictionary of Natural Health, 5074

The Illustrated Encyclopedia of Helicopters, 9058

An Illustrated Encyclopedia of Traditional Symbols, 3898

The Illustrated Face of Battle: A Study of Agincourt, Waterloo and the Somme, 7051

Illustrated Guide to Gardening, 9381

An Illustrated Guide to Modern Warships, 9131

An Illustrated Guide to the Modern US Navy, 9129

An Illustrated Guide to the U.S. Air Force, 9129

The Illustrated History of Helicopters, 9069

The Illustrated History of the Indianapolis 500, 9614

The Illustrated Man, 1044(F)

The Illustrated Naked Ape: A Zoologist's Study of the Human Animal, 8502

The Illustrated Origin of Species, 7000

The Illustrated Sports Record Book, 9574

The Illustrated Word Processing Dictionary, 9017

The Illustrator in America, 1880–1980: A Century of Illustration, 5758

I'm Christy, 2289(F)

I'm Dancing as Fast as I Can, 5121

The Image and Other Stories, 500(F)

The Image of Chekhov: Forty Stories in the Order in Which They Were Written, 305(F)

Images of America: A Panorama of History in Photographs, 7751

Images of Earth, 8795

Images of the Ice Age, 5732

Images of the World, 7049

Imaginary Lands, 1208(F)

Imagine: John Lennon, 6417

Imaging: Think Your Way to Success in Sports and Classroom Activities, 5625

Immigrant America: A Portrait, 4336

The Immigrant Experience in America, 4329

The Immigrants, 1522(F)

The Impact Zone, 2883(F)

Impeachment: A Handbook, 4205

The Impending Crisis, 1848–1861, 7879

The Imperfect Mirror: Inside Stories of Television News-women, 6044

The Imperfect Paradise, 3309

Imperial Earth, 2478(F)

Imperial Lady: A Fantasy of Han China, 1240(F)

The Imperial Presidency, 4211

Imperial Purple, 1363(F)

Imponderables, 9495

The Importance of Being Earnest, 3045

Impressionism: Selections from Five American Museums, 5739

The Improbable Machine, 5308

Improvisation for the Theatre: A Handbook of Teaching and Directing Techniques, 6108

In a Dark Dream, 1753(F)

In a Place Dark and Secret, 2006(F)

In Advance of the Landing: Folk Concepts of Outer Space, 9488

In Alien Flesh, 2403(F)

In-Between Love, 2291(F)

In Cold Blood: A True Account of a Multiple Murder and Its Consequences, 4470

In Country, 875(F)

In Darkness Born, 8255

In Defense of American Liberties: A History of the ACLU, 4321

In Dreams Begin Responsibilities and Other Stories, 493(F)

In Kindling Flame: The Story of Hannah Senesh, 1921–1944, 6872

In Love and Trouble, 506(F)

In My Father's Court, 1470(F)

In My Father's House, 460(F), 6952

In Our Time, 835(F)

In Praise of Imperfection: My Life and Work, 6687

In Praise of Wolves, 8514

In Print: Text and Type in the Age of Desktop Publishing, 3982

In Search of History: A Personal Adventure, 8094

In Search of Identity: An Autobiography, 6816

In Search of Liberty: The Story of the Statue of Liberty and Ellis Island, 4327

In Search of Our Mothers' Gardens: Womanist Prose, 3557

In Search of Schrodinger's Cat: Quantum Physics and Reality, 8908

In Search of the Big Bang: Quantum Physics and Cosmology, 8909

In Search of the Trojan War, 7112

In Summer Light, 895(F)

In Suspect Terrain, 8170

In the Autumn Wind, 1681(F)

In the Blink of an Eye: Inside a Children's Trauma Center, 5234

In the Combat Zone: An Oral History of American Women in Vietnam, 1966–1975, 8129

In the Company of Animals, 8681

In the Days of the Comet, 2829(F)

In the Drift, 2799(F)

In the Enemy Camp, 80(F)

In the Eye of the Storm: A Memoir of Survival through the Holocaust, 7241

In the Forest at Midnight, 2321(F)

In the Frame, 2016(F)

In the Groove: The Men behind the Music, 5984

In the Heart of the Country, 643(F)

In the Long Run, 1975(F)

In the Middle of a Rainbow, 2269(F)

In the National Interest, 149(F)

In the Ocean of Night, 2404(F)

In the Presence of the Creator: Isaac Newton and His Times, 6696

In the Sea Nymph's Lair, 1136(F)

In the Shadow of a Rainbow, 8516

In the Shadow of FDR: From Harry Truman to Ronald Reagan, 8077

In the Shadow of His Wings, 6948

In the Shadow of Man, 8498

In the Shadow of the Cloud: Photographs & Histories of America's Atomic Veterans, 8927

In the Shadow of the Dome: Chronicles of a Capitol Hill Aide, 4214

In the Shadow of the Poorhouse: A Social History of Welfare in America, 4509

In the Strong Woods, 9797

In the Teeth of the Northeaster: A Solo Voyage on Lake Superior, 6128

In the Wake of the Exxon Valdez: The Devastating Impact of the Alaska Oil Spill, 4451

In Their Own Words: A History of the American Negro, 1619–1865, 7876

In Their Own Words: A History of the American Negro 1865–1916, 7876

In Their Own Words: A History of the American Negro, 1916–1966, 7876

In Their Own Words: Contemporary American Playwrights, 3843

In Vietnam, 8118

Incest: Families in Crisis, 5511

Incident at Badamyâ, 102(F)

Incident at Pishkin Creek, 249(F)

The Incomplete Folksinger, 5953

The Incorporation of Eric Chung, 475(F)

The Incredible Incas and Their Timeless Land, 7680

The Incredible Machine, 5300

The Incredible Voyage, 6151

The Indelible Image: Photographs of War—1846 to the Present, 5717

India, 7442

India: The Challenge of Change, 7443

Indian Country, 7818

Indian Fairy Tales, 3402

The Indian Fan, 2283(F)

Indian Givers: How the Indians of the Americas Transformed the World, 7828

The Indian Heritage of America, 7812

The Indian in America, 7827

Indian Independence, 7438

Indian Mythology, 3460
Indian Place-Names, 8154
Indian Signs and Signals, 7807
The Indians, 7798
Indians of California: The Changing Image, 7820
The Indians of the Great Plains, 7791
Indira Gandhi, 6805
Inferno, 1080(F)
The Infinity Concerto, 1031(F)
The Informer, 1454(F)
Inhalants: The Toxic Fumes, 5117
Inherit the Stars, 2599(F)
Inherit the Wind, 3093
The Inheritors, 1350(F)
The Initiate, 2490(F)
The Initiation, 1721(F)
Inner-City Violence, 4461
Inner Companions, 3538
Innocent Blood, 2066(F)
The Innocents Abroad: Or The New Pilgrims Progress, 3515
Input-Output, 9021
The Insanity Plea, 4259
Insect Pests, 8595
Insects, 8593
Insects: Their Biology and Cultural History, 8596
Insects in Camera: A Photographic Essay on Behaviour, 8601
Insects of the World, 8602
Inside Central America, 7651
Inside Outer Space: Science Fiction Professionals Look at Their Craft, 3741
Inside Pocket Billiards, 9585
Inside Prime Time, 6015
Inside Strategies for the SAT, 4659
Inside the Cell: The New Frontier of Medical Science, 8659
Inside the IBM PC: Access to Advanced Features and Programming, 9006
Inside the Third Reich, 7508
Inside Wrestling, 9788
The Insider's Guide to Modeling: The Pros Tell You How, 4928
The Insider's Guide to the Colleges: 1985–86 Edition, 4771
Instant Replay: The Green Bay Diary of Jerry Kramer, 9852

An Instructional Guide to Amateur Wrestling, 9784
Intangible Evidence, 9500
The Integral Trees, 2694(F)
Intelligence Games, 8850
The Intelligence Men: Makers of the IQ Controversy, 5587
Intelligence—What Is It? 5586
Intensive Scare, 1859(F)
Interactive Fiction and Adventure Games for Microcomputers: An Annotated Directory, 1988, 8967
The Interface Man, 158(F)
The Intern Blues: The Private Ordeals of Three Young Doctors, 5245
The International Cookie Cookbook, 9312
The International Drug Trade, 5140
International Drug Traffic, 5111
International Wildlife Trade: Whose Business Is It Anyway? 8573
Internationalism: Opposing Viewpoints, 4150
Interpretations of American History: Patterns and Perspectives, 7741
Interview with the Vampire, 1828(F)
Interviews with B Science Fiction and Horror Movie Makers, 6071
Into the Darkness, 2111(F)
Into the Heart of the Mind, 9011
Into the Newsroom: An Introduction to Journalism, 4901
Into the Out Of, 1748(F)
Into the Temple of Baseball, 9649
Into the Unknown, 9477
Into the Valley: A Skirmish of the Marines, 7218
Into the Wilderness, 7967
Into the Woods, 5929
Intoxication: Life in Pursuit of Artificial Paradise, 5154
Intrepid's Last Case, 7300
Introducing the Great American Novel, 3775
Introduction to Film, 6074
An Introduction to Haiku: An Anthology of Poems and Poets from Bashó to Shiki, 3348

Introduction to Islam, 4034
An Introduction to Latin American Politics: The Structure of Conflict, 7629
An Introduction to Shakespeare, 3047
Intruder in the Dust, 455(F)
Intruder in the Wind, 36(F)
Intruders: The Incredible Visitations at Copley Woods, 9507
Invasion: Earth, 2574(F)
Inventing a Word: An Anthology of Twentieth Century Puerto Rican Poetry, 3296
The Inventive Yankee: From Rockets to Roller Skates, 200 Years of Yankee Inventors and Inventions, 8954
Inventors and Discoverers: Changing Our World, 8947
Inventors at Work: Interviews, 8942
Investing and Trading, 4599
Investment Banking, 4598
Investments & the Law, 4563
Invid Invasion, 2678(F)
Invincible Summer, 659(F)
The Invisible Alcoholics: Women and Alcohol Abuse in America, 5152
The Invisible Man, 2830(F)
Invisible Man, 453(F)
Invitation to Astronomy, 8272
The Iowa Baseball Confederacy, 2879(F)
The Ipcress File, 71(F)
The Iran-Contra Arms Scandal, 4166
Ireland, 7522
Ireland: A Terrible Beauty, 7537
Irish Folk & Fairy Tales Omnibus, 3410
Irish Folktales, 3398
Iron & Silk, 7427
Iron Destinies, Lost Opportunities: The Arms Race between the U.S.A. and the U.S.S.R., 1945–1987, 4155
Iron Horse: Lou Gehrig in His Time, 6721
The Iron House, 7408
Ironweed, 1626(F)
Is That in the Bible? 4110
Is There a Cow in Moscow? More Beastly Mispronunciations and Sound Advice, 3918

Is There No Place on Earth for Me? 5404

Isaac Asimov: The Foundations of Science Fiction, 3731

Isaac Asimov Presents the Great SF Stories: 17 (1955), 2384(F)

Isaac Asimov Presents the Great SF Stories, 20, 2385(F)

Isaac Asimov's Treasury of Humor, 9464

Isaac Bashevis Singer, 3634

Isaac Bashevis Singer: The Story of a Storyteller, 6309

Isadora Duncan, 6385

Iseult: Dreams That Are Done, 1220(F)

Ishi: Last of His Tribe, 6625

Ishmael, 2572(F)

The Iskra Incident, 33(F)

Islam, 4073

Islam: A Primer, 4080

Island Fighting, 7296

Island in the Sky, 2476(F)

The Island Keeper, 205(F)

Island of Doctor Moreau, 2831(F)

The Island Within, 8186

Islands, 8786

The Isle of Glass, 1288(F)

Isles of the Blest, 1197(F)

Israel, 7604, 7616

The Israel-Arab Reader: A Documentary History of the Middle East Conflict, 7600

It Ain't Cheatin' If You Don't Get Caught, 9650

It All Started with Nudes, 5729

It Did Happen Here: Recollections of Political Repression in America, 4318

It Seemed Like Nothing Happened, 8053

It Was on Fire When I Lay Down on It, 3496

It Won't Happen to Me: Teenagers Talk about Pregnancy, 5514

The Italian Campaign, 7310

Italian Folktales, 3392

The Italians, 7546

Italy, 7550

Italy at War, 7279

It's Always Something, 6433

It's OK If You Don't Love Me, 568(F)

It's Rock 'n' Roll, 5847

It's Your Future! Catalyst's Career Guide for High School Girls, 4788

Ivan the Terrible, 6850

The Ivanhoe Gambit, 1147(F)

Ivory, 2754(F)

Iwo Jima: Legacy of Valor, 7282

J. D. Salinger, 3750

J. D. Salinger: A Writing Life, 6300

J. D. Salinger, Revisited, 6299

J. R. R. Tolkien, 3658, 3684

Jack, 677(F)

Jack London, 3746

Jack London: An American Myth, 6284

Jack of Diamonds, 2965(F)

Jack, the Giant Killer, 1090(F)

Jackie Cochran: An Autobiography, 6131

Jackie Robinson, 6731

Jackie Robinson: A Life Remembered, 6730

The Jacksonian Era, 1828–1848, 7885

Jacob's Ladder, 1391(F)

Jacques Cousteau's Amazon Journey, 7669

Jacques Cousteau's Calypso, 8889

Jaguars Ripped My Flesh, 6129

Jailbird: A Novel, 2820(F)

Jailed for Peace: The History of American Draft Law Violators, 1658–1985, 4408

Jam Plastic, Heavy Metal: Now You Can Play Lead Guitar with a Live Band, 5911

Jam Plastic, Punk, 5911

Jam Plastic, Rock, 5911

Jamaica Inn, 1423(F)

James Baldwin, 3783

James Baldwin: The Legacy, 3607

James Brown: The Godfather of Soul, 6376

James Dickey, 3880

James Herriot's Dog Stories, 8721

James Herriot's Yorkshire, 7521

The James Joyce Murder, 1977(F)

James Russell Lowell, 6285

James Thurber, 3595

James Weldon Johnson, 6272

Jamestown, 1544–1699, 7836

Jan Vermeer, 6209

Jane Addams, 6612

Jane Austen, Feminism and Fiction, 3673

Jane Brody's Nutrition Book, 5409

Jane Brody's The New York Times Guide to Personal Health, 5343

Jane Eyre, 335(F)

Jane Eyre: Portrait of a Life, 3649

Jane Fonda: An Intimate Biography, 6391

Jane's Aerospace Dictionary, 9064

Jane's All the World's Aircraft, 1990–1991, 9068

Janissaries: Clan and Crown, 2746(F)

Japan, 7441, 7455

Japan: From Shogun to Sony, 1543–1984, 7453

Japan: Opposing Viewpoints, 7447

Japan at War, 7311

The Japanese, 7452

The Japanese Mind: The Goliath Explained, 7446

Japanese Mythology, 3465

Japanese Tales, 3386

Japanese Tales & Legends, 3383

A Japanese Touch for the Seasons, 7449

Japan's War: The Great Pacific Conflict, 7450

Jay-Jay and the Peking Monster, 2002(F)

Jazz: America's Classical Music, 5897

Jazz: The Essential Companion, 5849

Jazz Heritage, 5908

Jazz in Its Time, 5909

Jazz Is, 5870

Jazz Portraits: The Lives and Music of the Essential Jazz Musicians, 5882

The Jazz Tradition, 5908

Jean-Paul Sartre, 3567

Jed and Jessie, 2253(F)

Jefferson Davis and His Generals: The Failure of the Confederate Command in the West, 6584

Jeffy's Journal: Raising a Morgan Horse, 8761

Jekyll, Alias Hyde: A Variation, 2194(F)
The Jeopardy! Book, 6067
Jernigan's Egg, 2692(F)
Jesse: The Man Who Outran Hitler, 6766
Jesse Owens: An American Life, 6765
Jessie Benton Fremont: A Biography, 6619
Jesus, 4097
Jesus and His Times, 4056
The Jesus Factor, 1150(F)
The Jewel in the Skull, 1223(F)
The Jewish Americans: A History in Their Own Words, 1650–1950, 4388
Jewish Family Celebrations: Shabbat, Festivals and Traditional Ceremonies, 4114
Jewish Folktales, 3369
Jewish Legends, 4103
Jews, God and History, 4043
Jim Beckwourth, 6614
Jim Fixx's Second Book of Running, 9909
Jim Thorpe: World's Greatest Athlete, 6768
Jimmy's Blues: Selected Poems, 3241
Jinian Footseer, 1291(F)
Jinian Star-Eye, 1292(F)
Job: A Comedy of Justice, 2579(F)
Job Hunting for the Disabled, 4803
Job Resumes: How to Write Them, How to Present Them, Preparing for Interviews, 4785
Jobs for Teenagers, 4843
Jobs of the Future: The 500 Best Jobs—Where They'll Be and How to Get Them, 4826
Jobs! What They Are . . . Where They Are . . . What They Pay, 4870
Joe Gosh, 2503(F)
The Joe Leaphorn Mysteries: Dance Hall of the Dead, Listening Woman, 2052(F)
Joe Louis: 50 Years an American Hero, 6748
Joey and the Girls, 1890(F)
Johann Sebastian Bach, 6336
John Brown's Body, 3242
John Dollar, 1866(F)

John Donne: Life, Mind and Art, 3865
John F. Kennedy, 6541
John F. Kennedy and a New Generation, 6536
John Greenleaf Whittier, 3888
John Hedgecoe's Darkroom Techniques, 9423
John Keats, 3866
John Lennon, My Brother, 6414
John Marino's Bicycling Book, 9760
John Marshall: Defender of the Constitution, 6605
John McGraw, 6728
The John McPhee Reader, 3539
John Muir and His Legacy: The American Conservation Movement, 6695
John Paul Jones: A Sailor's Biography, 6597
John Steinbeck, 3721, 3754
John the Balladeer, 1317(F)
John Updike, 3714
Johnny Miller's Golf for Juniors, 9872
Johnny's Song, 3297
The Johnson & Johnson First Aid Book, 5446
Jomo Kenyatta, 6792
Jonathan Livingston Seagull, 1024(F)
Joni, 6903
Jo's Boys, 389(F)
Joseph Conrad, 3665
Joseph Stalin, 6874
Josie, 1590(F)
The Journals of Sylvia Plath, 6296
Journey, 206(F), 5207
Journey into China, 7416
Journey into Fear, 5(F)
Journey into Space: The First Three Decades of Space Exploration, 8311
Journey into Summer, 8406
Journey of Conscience: Young People Respond to the Holocaust, 7275
Journey to Enchantment, 1486(F)
A Journey to the Center of the Earth, 325(F)
Joy in the Morning, 918(F)
Joy of Cooking, 9356
The Joy of Lex, 3908
The Joy of Music, 5814

The Joy of Running, 9915
Joyce Carol Oates, 3723
Joyce Lain Kennedy's Career Book, 4798
The Joys of Computer Networking: The Personal Connection Handbook, 8959
The Joys of Research, 8234
The Joys of Yiddish, 3947
Jubilee, 1549(F)
Jubilee Jim and the Wizard of Wall Street, 224(F)
The Judas Kiss, 132(F)
Jude the Obscure, 369(F)
Judgement on Janus, 2710(F)
Judging Medicine, 5229
Judo: Beginner to Black Belt, 9900
Juggling, 868(F)
Juggling for All, 9300
Juggling with Finesse, 9306
Julie, 1627(F)
July's People, 965(F)
The Jump-Off Creek, 1566(F)
June Four: A Chronicle of the Chinese Democratic Uprising, 7417
The Jungle, 1614(F)
Jungle Fighters, 7172
A Jungle of Stars, 1068(F)
Junior, 2257(F)
Junior Karate, 9894
Junius Over Far, 558(F)
Jurassic Park, 2494(F)
The Jury in America, 4240
Just a Nurse: The Lives and Experiences of Nurses in America—In Their Own Words, 5241
Just above My Head, 441(F)
The Just and the Unjust, 648(F)
Just Bats, 8525
Just Be Gorgeous, 940(F)
Just Friends, 2293(F)
Just Give Me a Cool Drink of Water 'fore I Die, 3237
Just Hold On, 780(F)
Just Imagine: Ideas in Painting, 5715
Just the Right Age, 2242(F)
Just Too Cool, 2237(F)
Just Wait Till You Have Children of Your Own, 3486
Justaposition, 2356(F)
Justice for Hire: The Fourth Private Eye Writers of America Anthology, 2148(F)

Justice Not Vengeance: Recollections, 6880
Juvenile Justice and Injustice, 4244

Kaffir Boy, 6930
Kaffir Boy in America: An Encounter with Apartheid, 6930
Kafka, 6274
Kant, 4010
Karate: Beginner to Black Belt, 9901
Karate for Young People, 9894
Kareem, 6738
Karen Horney, 6675
Karl Marx, 6860
Kasserine Pass, 7183
Kate: The Life of Katharine Hepburn, 6401
Kate Chopin, 3774
Katherine Anne Porter, 3734
Kathy Sue Loudermilk, I Love You, 3498
Kedrigern and the Charming Couple, 1225(F)
The Keep, 1869(F)
Keep Off the Grass, 5145
Keeper of the Keys, 2855(F)
Keepers of Edanvant, 1099(F), 2516(F)
Keeping a Head in School: A Student's Book about Learning Abilities and Learning Disorders, 5390
Keeping Faith: Memoirs of a President, 6524
Keeping Parrots, 8678
Keeping Score, 869(F)
Keeping Secrets, 6443
Keeping the Faith, 788(F)
The Kennedy Legacy, 6537
The Kennedys: An American Drama, 6598
The Kentish Manor Murders, 2191(F)
Kentucky Derby: The Chance of a Lifetime, 9884
Kerouac, 6275
Kessa, 700(F)
Key Out of Time, 2703(F)
Key to Rebecca, 86(F)
The Keys of the Kingdom, 650(F)
Keys to Racing Success, 9921
KGB: Masters of the Soviet Union, 7567
Khaki Wings, 1633(F)
Kick the Can, 172(F)

Kidnapped, 383(F)
Kids' Games: Traditional Indoor and Outdoor Activities for Children of All Ages, 9608
Kids Who Run Away, 4463
Kill or Cure: Suspense Stories about the World of Medicine, 2118(F)
The Kill Riff, 240(F)
Kill the Tsar: Youth and Terrorism in Old Russia, 7587
Killashandra, 2664(F)
Killdeer Mountain, 1559(F)
Killed in Paradise, 1980(F)
The Killer Angels, 1544(F)
The Killing Ground: Wilderness to Cold Harbor, 7925
Killing the Kudu, 718(F)
Kim, 374(F)
Kind and Unusual Punishment: The Prison Business, 4487
Kindergarten, 594(F)
The Kindly Ones, 2774(F)
King and Joker, 1982(F)
King Arthur, 6826
King Arthur and His Knights, 3405
King David's Spaceship, 2744(F)
King George VI and Queen Elizabeth, 7539
King Herod's Dream: Caesarea on the Sea, 7117
The King Must Die, 1372(F)
King of the Castle, 132(F)
King of the Highbinders, 39(F)
King of the Jews, 6961
King of the Murgos, 1105(F)
King Rat, 1649(F)
King Remembered, 6513
King Solomon's Mines, 114(F)
King Solomon's Ring, 6688
Kingdom in the Sky: A Field Biologist's Adventures in the Jungle Canopy, 8400
Kingdom of Fear: The World of Stephen King, 3785
Kingdoms of Asia, the Middle East, and Africa, 7046
Kings & Queens of England and Great Britain, 7514
King's Blood Four, 1294(F)
The King's Justice, 1179(F)
Kings, Lovers, and Fools, 3049
Kioga of the Wilderness, 40(F)

Kirkland Revels, 134(F)
Kirlian Quest, 2351(F)
A Kiss for Good Luck, 2264(F)
Kiss Mommy Goodbye, 2005(F)
Kisses, 786(F)
Kit Carson's Autobiography, 6618
Kiteworks: Explorations in Kite Building and Flying, 9892
Kitty Collins, 2272(F)
The Kiwi Target, 13(F)
The Klan, 4349
Klass: How Russians Really Live, 7589
The Klondike Fever: The Life and Death of the Last Great Gold Rush, 7633
Knave of Dreams, 2711(F)
Knave of Hearts, 1409(F)
The Knight in History, 7131
Knight Life, 1085(F)
Knight of Shadows, 2868(F)
Knights of the Air, 9074
Knit 4 Seasons, 9235
Knitting by Design: A Step-by-Step Guide to Designing and Knitting Your Own Clothes, 9238
Knock Wood, 6372
The Knot, 2226(F)
Knotted Doughnuts and Other Mathematical Entertainments, 8835
Know Your Sewing Machine, 9236
Knowing Where to Look: The Ultimate Guide to Research, 4681
Knowing Your Trees, 8424
Kobbe's Illustrated Opera Book: Twenty-six of the World's Best-Loved Operas, 5921
Kommando: German Special Forces of World War II, 7246
Kon-Tiki: Across the Pacific by Raft, 6144
Koori: A Will to Win, 7474
The Korean War, 8117
Koviashuvik: A Time and Place of Joy, 8193
Kristallnacht: The Tragedy of the Nazi Night of Terror, 7277
Kristin Lavransdatter, 1383(F)

The Ku Klux Klan: America's Recurring Nightmare, 4519
Kurt Vonnegut, 3745, 3751

The L. L. Bean Guide to the Outdoors, 9803
Labor of Love, Labor of Sorrow: Black Women, Work, and the Family from Slavery to the Present, 4366
The Labyrinth of Dreams: G.O.D., No. 1, 2466(F)
The Ladies of Mandrigyn, 1762(F)
The Ladies of Seneca Falls: The Birth of the Woman's Rights Movement, 4304
The Lady in the Lake, 1945(F)
The Lady of Han-Gilen, 1289(F)
The Lady of the Labyrinth, 175(F)
The Lady or the Tiger and Other Stories, 420(F)
Lady Sings the Blues, 6403
The Lady's Not for Burning, A Phoenix Too Frequent, and an Essay, 3030
The Lais of Marie de France, 2260(F)
The Lake, 1726(F)
The Lake of Fire, 1025(F)
Lakota Woman, 6500
Lamb, 9361
Lame Deer, Seeker of Visions, 6515
Lammas Night, 1180(F)
The Land God Gave to Cain, 146(F)
The Land of Our Dreams, 574(F)
Land of Terror, 2449(F)
Land of the Snow Lion: An Adventure in Tibet, 7456
Landmarks of Modern British Drama, Vol. 1: The Plays of the Sixties, 3812
Landmarks of Modern British Drama, Vol. 2: The Plays of the Seventies, 3812
The Landmarks of Science, 8214
Land's End, 2742(F)
The Landscape of King Arthur, 6825
The Landscape of Memory, 5317
The Landscape of the Brontës, 6220

Landscape Photography, 9440
Landscape Turned Red: The Battle of Antietam, 7934
Langston Hughes, 3578
Langston Hughes: An Introduction to the Poetry, 3887
Langston Hughes: Before and beyond Harlem, 6266
Language in Thought and Action, 3923
The Language of the Night: Essays on Fantasy and Science Fiction, 3626
The Languages of Pao, 2812(F)
The Languages of the World, 3930
A Lantern in Her Hand, 1554(F)
The Laser Book: A New Technology of Light, 8935
Laser Careers, 4992
The Last Algonquin, 6962
The Last Battle, 7284
The Last Catholic in America, 1897(F)
Last Chance Garage, 9111
Last Chance to See, 8568
Last Dance in Redondo Beach, 2077(F)
The Last Days of Socrates, 4020
Last Days of the Sicilians: The New FBI at War with the Mafia, 4468
The Last Defender of Camelot, 1343(F)
The Last Dream, 1093(F)
The Last Enchantment, 1279(F)
Last Flight, 6139
Last Horizons: Hunting, Fishing & Shooting on Five Continents, 9825
The Last Hurrah, 985(F)
The Last Ivory Hunter: The Saga of Wally Johnson, 6150
Last Laugh, 830(F)
Last Laughs: The 1986 Mystery Writers of America Anthology, 2096(F)
The Last of Danu's Children, 1259(F)
The Last of the Just, 494(F)
The Last of the Mohicans, 393(F)
The Last of the Wine, 1373(F)
The Last 100 Days, 7313
The Last Picture Show, 873(F)

Last Places: A Journey in the North, 7552
Last Rights, 1986(F)
The Last Romantic: A Biography of Queen Marie of Roumania, 6858
The Last Ship, 24(F)
The Last Unicorn, 1030(F)
Last Waltz in Vienna, 1648(F)
The Last Wizard, 1159(F)
The Late George Apley, 579(F)
Late Innings, 9622
Late Night with David Letterman: The Book, 6030
The Lathe of Heaven, 2632(F)
Latin America, 7627
Latin America and U.S. Foreign Policy: Opposing Viewpoints, 4163
The Latin American Short Story: A Critical History, 3796
The Latin Riddle Book, 9465
The Latin Tinge: The Impact of Latin American Music on the United States, 5895
Laughing Boy, 695(F)
Laughing Matters: A Celebration of American Humor, 3512
The Laughing Policeman, 2179(F)
Laughing Space, 2386(F)
Laughter in the Dark, 721(F)
Laura: The Life of Laura Ingalls Wilder, 6328
Lauren, 706(F)
Lava—Book III, 2723(F)
The Lavalite World, 1115(F)
Lavender-Green Magic, 1234(F)
Lavondyss, 1155(F)
Law Enforcement Careers: A Complete Guide from Application to Employment, 4977
Law, Medicine, and Social Justice, 5248
The Law of the Land, 4251
Lay Bare the Heart: An Autobiography of the Civil Rights Movement, 6505
Laying the Music to Rest, 2793(F)
The Lazarus Effect, 1150(F)
LBJ: The White House Years, 6535
Lead on Love, 2278(F)
Leaders, 6787

Leaders and Lawyers, 4966
Leaders of the Middle East, 7597
Leading Constitutional Decisions, 4188
The Leading Edge, 9061
Learn to Drive, 9097
Learned Pigs & Fireproof Women, 5980
Learning about Sex: The Contemporary Guide for Young Adults, 5471
Learning by Heart: AIDS and Schoolchildren, 5193
Learning Calligraphy: A Book of Lettering, Design and History, 9161
Learning from Forty Inspiring Business Successes, 4584
Learning How to Fall, 692(F)
Learning IBM BASIC for the Personal Computer, 8997
Learning to Look: A Handbook for the Visual Arts, 5725
Learning to Rock Climb, 9581
The Learning Tree, 485(F)
Leathercrafting: Procedures and Projects, 9141
Leave It to Psmith, 1909(F)
Leaves, 8413
Leaves of Grass, 3341
Leaving Home, 5627
Leaving Home: A Collection of Lake Woebegon Stories, 3499
Leaving Locke Horn, 532(F)
Leaving the Nest: Mom's Guide to Living on Your Own, 5592
Lebanon: Death of a Nation, 7621
The Ledge between the Streams, 6288
Lee and Grant: A Dual Biography, 6490
The Lee Girls, 6466
Lee Takes Command: From Seven Days to Second Bull Run, 7945
The Left Hand of Darkness, 2633(F)
Lefties: The Origins and Consequences of Being Left-Handed, 5312
Lefty, 631(F)
Legacies: A Chinese Mosaic, 7422
Legacy, 980(F)

The Legacy: The Vietnam War in the American Imagination, 8143
The Legacy of Heurot, 2698(F)
The Legacy of Lehr, 2621(F)
Legacy of Silence: Encounters with Children of the Third Reich, 7178
Legal Careers and the Legal System, 4967
The Legend of Dr. J. The Story of Julius Erving, 6743
The Legend of Sleepy Hollow, and Other Stories, 404(F)
Legends, Lies, and Cherished Myths of American History, 7777
Legends of the World, 3361
Legends of Valor, 3366
Lemon Book: Auto Rights, 9105
LeMond: The Incredible Comeback of an American Hero, 6780
Le Morte d'Arthur, 3406
Lena: A Personal and Professional Biography of Lena Horne, 6407
Lenin, 6853
Lennon, 6415
The Lens of Perception: A Field Guide to Inner Resources, 5596
Lens of the World, 1201(F)
Leo Tolstoy, 3643
Leonard Bernstein, 6338
Leonard Maltin's TV Movies, 1991, 6028
Leonardo, 5788
Leonid Breznev, 6831
The Leopard, 1419(F)
Leprechauns, Legends and Irish Tales, 3403
Les Miserables, 316(F)
Leslie Peltier's Guide to the Stars, 8356
Less Than Zero, 803(F)
The Lessons of History, 7038
Let History Judge: The Origins and Consequences of Stalinism, 7578
Let Me Tell You Everything: Memoirs of a Lovesick Intellectual, 772(F)
Let the Lion Eat Straw, 501(F)
Let the Trumpet Sound: The Life of Martin Luther King, Jr. 6511

Let Us Now Praise Famous Men, 8023
Let's Celebrate: Festival Poems, 3160
Let's Go, 1990: The Budget Guide to Britain and Ireland, 7519
Let's Go, 1990: The Budget Guide to California and Hawaii, 8181
Let's Go, 1990: The Budget Guide to Europe, 7483
Let's Go, 1990: The Budget Guide to France, 7494
Let's Go, 1990: The Budget Guide to Greece, 7544
Let's Go, 1990: The Budget Guide to Israel and Egypt, 7596
Let's Go, 1990: The Budget Guide to Italy, 7548
Let's Go, 1990: The Budget Guide to Mexico, 7644
Let's Go, 1990: The Budget Guide to Spain, Portugal, and Morocco, 7555
Let's Go, 1990: The Budget Guide to the Pacific Northwest, Western Canada and Alaska, 8181
Let's Go, 1990: The Budget Guide to the USA, 7744
Letters of a Woman Homesteader, 7983
Letters to Ms. Magazine, 4539
Letting Go with Love: The Grieving Process, 5094
Leviathan, 4009
Levitating Trains and Kamikaze Genes: Technological Literacy for the 1990s, 8941
Lewis Carroll, 3672
Liavek, 1268(F)
Liavek: Spells of Binding, 1268(F)
Liavek: The Players of Luck, 1268(F)
Liavek: Wizard's Row, 1268(F)
Liberation, 7184
Liberties with Liberty: The Fascinating History of America's Proudest Symbol, 8165
Library in America: A Celebration in Words and Pictures, 7732
License Renewed, 99(F)
Licit and Illicit Drugs, 5105
Lie Down in Darkness, 610(F)

A Lie of the Mind: A Play in Three Acts, 3120
Lies, 842(F)
Lieutenant Hornblower, 1427(F)
Life: A Warning, 3489
Life: The First 50 Years, 1936–1986, 8078
Life: The '60s, 8085
Life after High School: A Career Planning Guide, 4801
Life and Death: The Story of a Hospital, 5256
The Life & Death of Stars, 8351
The Life and Times of Chaucer, 6232
The Life and Times of Cotton Mather, 6606
The Life and Times of Frederick Douglass, 6501
The Life and Times of Hercule Poirot, 3668
The Life and Times of Joe McCarthy, 6603
Life and Times of Michael K. 956(F)
The Life and Times of William Shakespeare, 6305
Life Goes to the Movies, 6066
Life Goes to War: A Picture History of World War II, 7242
Life in a Medieval Castle, 7134
Life in a Medieval Village, 7132
A Life in Our Times: Memoirs, 6671
Life in Space, 8325
Life in Sports, 9606
Life in the Universe, 8304
The Life of Benjamin Banneker, 6496
The Life of Charlotte Brontë, 6221
The Life of Greece, 7101
A Life of Gwendolyn Brooks, 6222
The Life of Jane Austen, 6214
The Life of Langston Hughes, Volume II, 1941–1967: I Dream a World, 6268
Life of Python, 6046
The Life of Samuel Johnson, 6273
The Life of the Mind, 3992
Life on Earth: A Natural History, 6988

Life on the Mississippi, 3516
A Life on the Road, 6413
Life Probe, 2670(F)
Life Pulse: Episodes from the Story of the Fossil Record, 6980
Life, the Universe, and Everything, 2331(F)
Lifeguards Only beyond This Point, 2265(F)
Lifetimes under Apartheid, 7373
Light a Penny Candle, 1643(F)
Light and Shadows: A History of Motion Pictures, 5995
Light in August, 456(F)
The Light of Day, 4(F)
Light Raid, 2846(F)
Lightning, 1174(F)
Lightning Bird, 7366
Like It Was: A Complete Guide to Writing Oral History, 4671
The Lilies of the Field, 443(F)
Lillian Hellman, 3840, 6257
Lily, 1863(F)
Lily Pond: Four Years with a Family of Beavers, 8526
Limits, 2695(F)
Lincoln, 1617(F)
Lincoln: A Novel, 1548(F)
The Lincoln-Douglas Debates of 1858, 7874
The Lincoln Murder Conspiracies, 6543
Lincoln Steffens, 6315
Lincoln's Dreams, 1327(F)
Linda Ronstadt: It's So Easy! 6439
Lines of Battle, 7304
Linus Pauling: A Man and His Science, 6452
Lion in the Valley, 2130(F)
A Lion in Winter, 3075
Lion of Ireland: The Legend of Brian Boru, 1444(F)
A Lion on Tharthee, 2457(F)
Lisa and David's Story: Their Healing Journey from Childhood and Pain into Love and Life, 734(F)
Listen to Me, I'm Angry, 5562
Listening for Coyote: A Walk across Oregon's Wilderness, 8190
Listening Woman, 2053(F)
Literary Britain, 3654
The Literary Dog: Great Con-

temporary Dog Stories, 298(F)
Literary Landscape of the British Isles: A Narrative Atlas, 3660
Literature in America: An Illustrated History, 3570
The Literature of Crime & Detection: An Illustrated History from Antiquity to the Present, 3633
Little Big Man, 1556(F)
The Little Drummer Girl, 166(F)
Little Fuzzy, 1248(F)
A Little House Sampler, 8002
Little Men, 389(F)
Little Myth Marker, 1020(F)
The Little Prince, 2767(F)
Little Red Rooster, 877(F)
Little Sister, 2273(F)
Little Women, 389(F)
The Little World of Don Camillo, 1884(F)
Live TV: An Inside Look at Directing and Producing, 6070
The Liveliest Art: A Panoramic History of the Movies, 6096
The Lives and Times of Archy & Mehitabel, 3503
The Lives of a Cell: Notes of a Biology Watcher, 8407
Lives of Courage: Women for a New South Africa, 7383
Lives of Girls and Women, 890(F)
Lives of the Artist, 5741
Lives of the Modern Poets, 3857
The Lives of the Painters, 6169
Lives on the Line: The Testimony of Contemporary Latin American Authors, 3795
Living Buddhism, 4072
Living by the Word: Selected Writings, 1973–1987, 3558
The Living Dock, 8775
Living Dogs and Dead Lions, 681(F)
Living Hungry in America, 4502
Living on the Edge: A Guide to Intervention for Families with Drug and Alcohol Problems, 5134
Living Philosophies: The Re-

flections of Some Eminent Men and Women of Our Time, 4004

The Living Planet: A Portrait of the Earth, 8377

Living Room: New Poems, 3286

The Living U.S. Constitution, 4194

Living Up the Street: Narrative Recollections, 6312

Living with Death and Dying, 5087

Living with Nuclear Weapons, 4144

Living with the Reptiles, 2515(F)

Lloyd on Lloyd, 6769

Lobbying for Freedom in the 1980s: A Grass-Roots Guide to Protecting Your Rights, 4313

Loch Ness Monster, 9491

The Locked Room, 2179(F)

Locked Rooms and Open Doors, 6282

Lodz Ghetto: Inside a Community under Siege, 7168

The Log of Christopher Columbus, 6132

The Loggers, 8430

Logic of the Heart, 2327(F)

LOGO Activites for the Computer, 9012

Lone Tree, 8581

The Loneliness of the Long-Distance Runner, 2960(F)

A Long and Happy Life, 730(F)

The Long Dark Tea-Time of the Soul, 2332(F)

Long Day's Journey into Night, 3113

Long Distance Love, 2261(F)

Long-Haired Cats, 8700

A Long Hard Journey: The Story of the Pullman Porter, 4613

Long Live the Queen, 271(F)

The Long March: Red China under Chairman Mao, 7420

The Long March: The Untold Story, 7425

The Long Night, 2344(F)

Long Night Dance, 1160(F)

The Long Night Watch, 245(F)

The Long Season, 9631

The Long Surrender, 7904

Long Time Passing, 1697(F)

The Longest Tunnel: The True Story of World War II's Great Escape, 7191

The Longest War: Israel in Lebanon, 7617

Longshot, 2014(F)

Look Homeward, Angel: A Story of the Buried Life, 943(F)

Looking After Cage Birds: Keep and Care, 8662

Looking at Law School: A Student Guide from the Society of American Law Teachers, 4969

Looking Backward, 2400(F)

Looking beyond the Ivy League: Finding the College That's Right for You, 4755

Looking Deep, 6752

Looking Forward, 6523

The Loon Feather, 1502(F)

Loony Laws: That You Never Knew You Were Breaking, 9522

Loose Cannons & Red Herrings: A Book of Lost Metaphors, 3915

Lord Darcy Investigates, 1131(F)

Lord Foul's Bane, 1095(F)

The Lord God Made Them All, 6674

Lord Hornblower, 1427(F)

Lord Jim, 345(F)

Lord Kalvan of Otherwhere, 1247(F)

Lord of the Far Islands, 132(F)

Lord of the Flies, 106(F)

The Lord of the Rings, 1296(F)

Lord of Thunder, 2712(F)

Lord Peter, 2169(F)

Lord Valentine's Castle, 2782(F)

The Lords of Discipline, 790(F)

Lords of the Triple Moons, 1217(F)

The Lords of Vaumartin, 1436(F)

Lore of Love, 9536

Loretta Lynn: Coal Miner's Daughter, 6419

Lorna Doone, 334(F)

Lorraine Hansberry: The Collected Last Plays, 3109

Losers and Winners, 2884(F)

Losing Battles, 619(F)

Lost, 1735(F)

The Lost Childhood, 7265

The Lost Cities of Africa, 7345, 7347

Lost City of the Incas: The Story of Machu Picchu and Its Builders, 7668

The Lost Giants, 1589(F)

Lost Highway, 5866

The Lost Honor of Katherina Blum, 632(F)

Lost Horizon, 1152(F)

Lost in Translation: A Life in a New Language, 6920

Lost on Venus, 2450(F)

The Lost Salt Gift of Blood, 576(F)

The Lost Ship of Noah: In Search of the Ark at Ararat, 4094

The Lost World & The Poison Belt, 2517(F)

The Lost Years, 2514(F)

The Lottery, 1770(F)

Lou Dunlop: Private Eye, 2000(F)

Louis Armstrong: An American Genius, 6358

Louis Armstrong: His Life & Times, 6359

Louis D. Brandeis and the Progressive Tradition, 6578

Louis L'Amour, 3725

Love, 5556

Love: First Aid for the Young, 5599

Love Alters Not, 1487(F)

Love Among the Hiccups, 1901(F)

Love and Marriage, 3494

Love and Sex in Plain Language, 5469

Love & Tradition: Marriage between Jews & Christians, 5668

Love Around the Corner, 575(F)

Love by the Book, 2232(F)

Love in the Ruins, 725(F)

Love Is Eternal, 1547(F)

Love Is Like the Lion's Tooth: An Anthology of Love Poems, 3172

Love Is the Crooked Thing, 938(F)

The Love Letters of J. Timothy Owen, 1882(F)

Love Lies Slain, 1929(F)

Love Life: Stories, 876(F)
Love Lines: Poetry in Person, 3278
Love Medicine, 454(F)
Love Not Human, 2510(F)
Love Story, 2320(F)
The Love Talker, 1819(F)
The Love You Make: The Insider's Story of the Beatles, 6168
The Loved One: An Anglo-American Tragedy, 1907(F)
Lovejoy's College Guide for the Learning Disabled, 4767
Lovejoy's Guide to Financial Aid, 4780
Lovejoy's Preparation for the SAT, 4660
Lover Boy, 2259(F)
Lovers and Fugitives, 1667(F)
Lovey: A Very Special Child, 5392
Loving Rachel: A Family's Journey from Grief, 5370
The Lower Depths and Other Plays, 3003
Lucifer's Hammer, 2701(F)
The Luck of Relian Kru, 1304(F)
Luck of the Wheels, 1196(F)
Lucky Jim, 1875(F)
Lucy, 470(F)
Lucy: The Beginnings of Humankind, 7001
Lucy's Child: The Discovery of a Human Ancestor, 7002
Luke Sutton: Lawman, 154(F)
Lunar Activity, 2686(F)
The Lurking Fear, 1807(F)
The Lusitania, 7161
Lust for Life: The Novel of Vincent van Gogh, 1477(F)
Lying: Moral Choice in Public and Private Life, 5572
Lynda Madaras Talks to Teens about AIDS: An Essential Guide for Parents, Teachers, and Young People, 5204
Lyonesse, 1300(F)
Lyonesse, Book I: Suldrun's Garden, 1299(F)
Lyrics, 1962–1985, 5860
Lysistrata, 2990

M.D. Doctors Talk about Themselves, 5249
Mac, 709(F)
Macbeth, 3056

Macbeth: Scotland's Warrior King, 6856
McCampbell's Heroes, 7223
McCampbell's War, 563(F)
McCartney: The Definitive Biography, 6420
Machines, Buildings, Weaponry of Biblical Times, 7087
McKenzie's Boots, 1671(F)
The Macmillan Atlas of the Holocaust, 7211
Macmillan Concise Dictionary of World History, 7080
Macmillan Illustrated Animal Encyclopedia, 8460
The Macmillan Illustrated Encyclopedia of Birds: A Visual Who's Who in the World of Birds, 8553
The Macmillan Illustrated Encyclopedia of Myths & Legends, 3452
The Macmillan Treasury of Herbs, 8415
Mad Blood, 2119(F)
Madame Bovary, 314(F)
Madame Sarah, 6373
Madame Sousatzka, 593(F)
Madbond, 1275(F)
Made in the South Pacific: Arts of the Sea People, 5769
Made in the U.S.A. The History of American Business, 4586
The Madness Season, 2552(F)
Madouc, 1301(F)
Mae West, 6457
Maelstrom, 2748(F)
Maggie: A Girl of the Streets, 394(F)
Maggie Now, 918(F)
Maggie's American Dream: The Life and Times of a Black Family, 6899
Magic and Medicine of Plants, 8443
The Magic Barrel, 2938(F)
The Magic Cup, 1135(F)
The Magic Goes Away, 1231(F)
Magic in Ithkar I, 1239(F)
Magic in Ithkar II, 1239(F)
Magic in Ithkar IV, 1239(F)
Magic in the Dark: A Young Viewer's History of the Movies, 6036
Magic Kingdom for Sale—Sold! 2440(F)
The Magic Labyrinth, 2537(F)

The Magic May Return, 1231(F)
The Magic Mountain, 1449(F)
The Magic of Black-and-White, 9429
The Magic of Holography, 8934
A Magic Summer, 9637
Magic Time, 2227(F)
The Magic We Do Here, 1675(F)
Magic with Everyday Objects, 9401
Magical Beasts, 3373
Magical Justice, 3373
Magician, 1118(F)
Magician's Gambit, 1107(F)
Magic's Pawn, 1184
Magic's Price, 1184
Magic's Promise, 1184
Magic's Touch, 6745
Magnificent Obsession, 1367(F)
The Magus, 1750(F)
Mahler, 6349
The Maid of the North: Feminist Folk Tales from around the World, 3368
Maida Heatter's Best Dessert Book Ever, 9343
Maiden Voyage, 9918
Maiden's End, 1719(F)
Maigret and the Killer, 2177(F)
Main Currents in American Thought, 3597
Main Street, 979(F)
Majestic Island Worlds, 7060
Majipoor Chronicles, 2782(F)
Major Barbara, 3036
The Major Poets: English and American, 3850
Major Soviet Writers, 3568
Major Writers of Early American Literature, 3579
The Majority Finds Its Past: Placing Women in History, 7054
Make Color Work for You, 9430
Make Me a Hero, 1646(F)
The Make-over: A Teen's Guide to Looking & Feeling Beautiful, 5287
Make Your Job Interview a Success: A Guide for the Career-Minded Jobseeker, 4786
Makeba, My Story, 6422

Making a Difference: The Story of an American Family, 5657

Making Birdhouses and Feeders, 9288

Making College Pay Off, 4762

Making Color Work for You, 9416

Making Contact, 5634

Making Fancy Birdhouses & Feeders, 9289

Making Holiday Folk Toys & Figures, 9283

Making It in Video, 4819

Making Money Making Music (No Matter Where You Live), 4877

Making Money with Baseball Cards: A Handbook of Insider Secrets and Strategies, 9447

The Making of a Continent, 8788

The Making of a Gunman, 20(F)

The Making of a Woman Surgeon, 6694

The Making of Britain: The Middle Ages, 7533

The Making of Civilization: History Discovered through Archaeology, 7091

The Making of Mark Twain, 6320

The Making of Modern Drama, 3799

The Making of the Atomic Bomb, 8940

The Making of the Modern Mind: Fiftieth Anniversary Edition, 4022

The Making of the President, 1972, 8095

The Making of the President, 1789: The Unauthorized Campaign Biography, 4276

Making Peace with Your Parents, 5638

Making Small Wooden Boxes, 9276

Makra Choria, 1218(F)

Malaria Dreams: An African Adventure, 7360

Male-Female Roles: Opposing Viewpoints, 4532

The Maltese Falcon, 2038(F)

Mama Day, 483(F)

Mama Poc: An Eyewitness Account of the Extinction of a Species, 8575

Mama's Bank Account, 1623(F)

Mammal Evolution: An Illustrated Guide, 8458

Mammals, 8454

Mammals of the American North, 8491

The Mammoth Book of Great Detective Stories, 2204(F)

The Mammoth Book of Modern Crime Stories, 2041(F)

The Mammoth Book of Private Eye Stories, 2144(F)

The Mammoth Book of Short Horror Novels, 1710(F)

The Mammoth Hunters, 1348(F)

A Man Called Horse, 1571(F)

A Man Called Intrepid: The Secret War, 7300

The Man-Eater of Malgudi, 984(F)

A Man for All Seasons, 3024

The Man from Earth, 2510(F)

Man from Mundania, 2354(F)

The Man from St. Petersburg, 86(F)

The Man in the High Castle, 2507(F)

The Man in the Iron Mask, 312(F)

Man in White, 1365(F)

Man-Made Minds: The Promise of Artificial Intelligence, 9026

The Man of Gold, 1027(F)

Man of La Mancha, 3133

Man of Two Worlds, 2594(F)

A Man Rides Through, 1096(F)

The Man to Send Rain Clouds, 489(F)

The Man Who Fell to Earth, 2804(F)

The Man Who Met the Train, 1911(F)

The Man Who Never Missed, 2727(F)

The Man Who Never Was, 7258

The Man Who Walked through Time, 8390

The Man Who Was Don Quixote: The Story of Miguel de Cervantes, 6231

The Man Who Would Be King, 375(F)

The Man with No Endorphins and Other Reflections on Science, 8392

The Man with the Heart in the Highlands & Other Early Stories, 2959(F)

The Man without a Country and Other Stories, 398(F)

Managing the Student Yearbook: A Resource for Modern Yearbook Management & Design, 3980

Managing Toxic Wastes, 4453

Manchild in the Promised Land, 6223

Manet, 5773

Manhattan Transfer, 396(F)

Manipulating Life: Debating the Genetic Revolution, 5264

Manitou's Daughter, 1507(F)

Manners That Matter: For People under 21, 5580

The Manor, 1471(F)

Man's Fate, 1399(F)

Man's Religions, 4068

Mansfield Park, 330(F)

The Manticore, 797(F)

A Manual for Writers of Term Papers, Theses, and Dissertations, 4705

Manufacturers and Miners, 8944

The Many-Colored Land, 1216(F)

The Many-Forked Branch, 1499(F)

Many Sleepless Nights: The World of Organ Transplantation, 5238

Manzanar, 8045

Mao: A Biography, 6814

Mao Zedong, 6813

The Map Catalog: Every Kind of Map and Chart on Earth and Even Some Above It, 6972

Mapping Our Genes: The Genome Project and the Future of Medicine, 5269

Maps in a Mirror: The Short Fiction of Orson Scott Card, 2458(F)

Marathon Man, 107(F)

The Marauders, 7266

Marc Chagall, 6192

The March of Folly, 7077

The March of the Millennia: A Key to Looking at History, 7029

Marching through Georgia, 1280(F)

Margaret Mead: A Portrait, 6692

Margaret Mead: A Voice for the Century, 6690

Margaret Mead and Samoa: The Making and Unmaking of Anthropological Myth, 6997

Marianne Moore, 3892

Marianne, the Magus, and the Manticore, 1293(F)

Marie Antoinette, 6857

Marine Invertebrates & Plants of the Living Reef, 8617

Marine Mammals of Eastern North Pacific and Arctic Waters, 8651

The Marine Raiders, 7224

Mario Cuomo, 6581

Mark Twain: A Collection of Critical Essays, 3777

Mark Twain: A Writer's Life, 6321

Mark Twain Laughing: Humorous Anecdotes by and about Samuel L. Clemens, 3519

Mark Twain Speaks for Himself, 3553

Marked by Fire, 747(F)

The Marked Man, 2606(F)

Market Guide for Young Writers, 3965

Marketing & Sales Career Directory, 4923

Marry Me Tomorrow, 2267(F)

Marrying Harriet, 2245(F)

Mars Beckons, 8350

Marshall Holman's Bowling Tips and Techniques, 9780

Martha Calhoun, 760(F)

Martha Stewart's Christmas, 4119

The Martial Arts, 9897

The Martian Chronicles, 2428(F)

Martin Chuzzlewit, 357(F)

Martin Eden, 705(F)

Martin Luther King, Jr.: A Documentary . . . Montgomery to Memphis, 6512

Martin Luther King, Jr.: To the Mountaintop, 6514

Martina, 6771

Marty Mann Answers Your Questions about Drinking and Alcoholism, 5142

Marty Stouffer's Wild America, 8580

Marx, 6861

Marx and Marxism, 6859

Marxism: Philosophy and Economics, 4177

Marx's Kapital for Beginners, 4176

Mary Anne, 1423(F)

Mary Jane Harper Cried Last Night, 696(F)

Mary Lou: Creating an Olympic Champion, 6767

Mary, Queen of Scots, 6862

Mary Reilly, 1813(F)

Mary Shelley: Romance and Reality, 6308

Mary Stewart's Merlin Trilogy, 1279(F)

Mary Stuart's Scotland: The Landscape, Life and Legends of Mary, Queen of Scots, 6863

Mas Oyama's Essential Karate, 9895

Masada: Herod's Fortress and the Zealots' Last Stand, 7027

A Mask for the General, 2561(F)

The Mask of Apollo, 1372(F)

Mask of the Wizard, 1079(F)

Maskmaking, 9218

The Masks of Rome, 2088(F)

The Mass Media: Opposing Viewpoints, 3956

The Massacre at Fall Creek, 1596(F)

The Master, 2490(F)

Master Builders: A Guide to Famous American Architects, 5696

"Master Harold" . . . and the Boys, 3143

Master of Ballantrae, 383(F)

Master of the Moor, 2154(F)

Master of the World, 2815(F)

The Master Spy, 6870

The Master Terrorist: The True Story behind Abu Nidal, 4550

Mastering Color Photography, 9416

Mastering Composition and Light, 9429

Mastering Softball, 9711

Masterpiece Paintings from the Museum of Fine Arts, Boston, 5765

Masterpieces of American Painting in the Metropolitan Museum of Art, 5805

Masterpieces of Fantasy and Enchantment, 1146(F)

Masterpieces of Mystery and Suspense, 2032(F)

Masterpieces of Terror and the Supernatural: A Treasury of Spellbinding Tales Old & New, 1775(F)

Masters of Darkness, 1745(F), 1745(F)

Masters of Darkness II, 1746(F)

Masters of Glass, 1104(F)

Masters of Horror, 6002

Masters of Modern Drama, 2978

The Matarese Circle, 181(F), 185(F)

Math and Logic Games, 8849

Math Projects for Young Scientists, 8857

Mathematical Carnival, 8854

Mathematical People: Profiles and Interviews, 8831

The Mathematical Tourist: Snapshots of Modern Mathematics, 8841

Mathematics for the Million, 8838

Mathematics Made Simple, 8842

Matisse, 5774, 5777

The Matlock Paper, 181(F)

A Matter of Feeling, 523(F)

A Matter of Honor, 9(F)

Matters Gray and White: A Neurologist, His Patients, and the Mysteries of the Brain, 5316

Matters of Fact and Fiction: Essays, 1973–1976, 3556

Matters of Life and Death, 5082

Matusow Affair: Memoir of a National Scandal, 8073

Max, the Dog That Refused to Die, 8742

Maximum Sports Performance, 9565

Maya: The Riddle and Rediscovery of a Lost Civilization, 7655

The Mayor of Casterbridge, 370(F)

Mazeway, 2845(F)

Me Me Me Me Me: Not a Novel, 6276

The Meaning of Relativity, 8907

The Measure of the Universe, 8863

Mechanical Drawing, 8945

Mechanter's Luck, 2469(F)

Mediaspeak, 6006

Medical Access, 5225

The Medical Detectives, 5250

Medical Ethics, 5235, 5239

Medical Fakes and Frauds, 5237

Medical School: Getting In, Staying In, Staying Human, 4718

Medicine for Melancholy, 1045(F)

Medicine for the Outdoors: A Guide to Emergency Medical Procedures and First Aid, 5440

Medicine Show, 62(F)

Medieval Art: Painting, Sculpture, Architecture—4th–14th Century, 5766

Medieval Myths, 3455

Medieval Writers and Their Work: Middle English Literature and Its Background, 3569

Meditations at 10,000 Feet: A Scientist in the Mountains, 8790

Meditations from the Breakdown Lane: Running across America, 3549

Meditations in Green, 1706(F)

The Mediterranean, 7330

Mediterranean Cookery, 9355

The Medusa and the Snail, 8408

Meet Me at Jim and Andy's: Jazz Musicians and Their World, 5878

Meeting at Potsdam, 7252

Meeting Rozzy Halfway, 570(F)

Meeting the Winter Bike Rider, 3089

Meeting the Winter Bike Rider and Other Prize Winning Plays, 3090

Megatrends: Ten New Directions Transforming Our Lives, 4417

Megatrends 2000, 7062

Mein Kampf, 4345, 6848

Melusine, 1026(F)

The Member of the Wedding, 871(F)

Memed, My Hawk, 974(F)

The Memoirs of Sherlock Holmes, 1987(F)

Memorable Dogs: An Anthology, 299

The Memorial: A Novel of the Vietnam War, 1691(F)

Memories of a Former Kid, 6890

Memory, 711(F)

Memory and Storage, 9019

A Memory of Dragons, 2609(F)

Memory Wire, 2851(F)

Memphis Blues, 1625(F)

Men from Earth, 8294

Men of the Gambler Bay, 7225

Men to Match My Mountains: The Opening of the Far West, 1840–1900, 7984

The Men Who Ruled India, 7440

Menace from Earth, 2586(F)

Mend It! 9240

Mendocino, 554(F)

Mene, Mene, Tekel, 4099

Menfreya in the Morning, 132(F)

The Mensa Think Smart Book, 9471

Mentally Tough: The Principles of Winning at Sports Applied to Winning in Business, 4578

The Mentor Book of Short Plays, 2982

The Mentor Guide to Writing Term Papers and Reports, 4693

Mercedes Nights, 2824(F)

The Mercenary, 2745(F)

Merchants of Treason: America's Secrets for Sale from the Pueblo to the Present, 4126

Merck Manual of Diagnosis and Therapy, 5208

Mercy Short: A Winter Journal, North Boston, 1692–93, 1515(F)

Mere Mortals, 2315(F)

Meridian, 507(F)

Merlin, 1187(F), 1188(F)

Merlin's Tour of the Universe, 8292

Merry Adventures of Robin Hood, 3409

The Merrymaid, 1432(F)

Meryl Streep: A Critical Biography, 6447

Message from Nam, 1704(F)

Messengers of God: Biblical Portraits and Legends, 4112

The Messiah, 1359(F)

The Messiah Stone, 2455(F)

Metamorphoses, 3185

The Metamorphosis, 1163(F)

Metamorphosis, 2652(F), 2678(F)

The Method, 937(F)

Methuselah's Children, 2586(F)

The Metropolitan Opera Stories of the Great Operas, 5916

MexAmerica: Two Countries, One Future, 4396

Mexican-American Folklore, 3418

Mexican and Central American Mythology, 3445

Mexican Cookery, 9342

Mexican Voices, American Dreams: An Oral History of Mexican Immigration to the United States, 4401

The Mexican War, 7877

Mexico, 7640, 7641

Mexico: A History, 7647

Michael Faraday: Father of Electronics, 6664

The Michael Jackson Story, 6409

Michael Langford's 35mm Handbook, 9428

Michael Strogoff, 1404(F)

Michelangelo, 5776, 5782, 6199

Michelle, 6940

The Mick, 6725

The Micro Millenium, 8972

Microbe Hunters, 6641

Microcomputer Local Area Networks: Network Design and Implementation, 8984

Microwave Cooking, 9320

Microworlds: Writings on Science Fiction and Fantasy, 3627

The Mid-Atlantic States, 8164

Midas World, 2737(F)

The Middle East, 7592

The Middle East: Opposing Viewpoints, 7603

The Middle East and South Asia, 7591

Midnight, 1754(F), 1796(F)

Midnight at the Well of Souls, 1067(F)

A Midnight Clear, 1687(F)
Midnight Express, 6917
Midnight Pleasures, 1717(F)
Midnight Wilderness: Journeys in the Arctic National Wildlife Refuge, 8397
A Midsummer Night's Death, 2137(F)
A Midsummer Night's Dream, 3057
A Midsummer Tempest, 2342(F)
Mies van der Rohe: A Critical Biography, 6461
Mighty Good Road, 2775(F)
The Mighty Rain Forest, 8817
Migraine and Other Headaches, 5198
Migrants, Sharecroppers, Mountaineers, 4359
The Mike King Story, 6777
Mila 18, 1684(F)
Milbourne Christopher's Magic Book, 9394
Milena, 6851
Militarizing Space, 4174
The Military Frontier, 9019
Mill, 8956
The Mill on the Floss, 364(F)
Miller: The Playwright, 3845
Million Selling Records from the 1900s to the 1980s: An Illustrated Directory, 5985
The Millstone, 656(F)
The Milton Cross New Encyclopedia of the Great Composers and Their Music, 6170
The Mime Book, 6095
Mimes on Miming: Writing on the Art of Mime, 6105
The Mind, 5324
Mind and Mood: Understanding and Controlling Your Emotions, 5557
The Mind-Boggling Universe: A Dazzling Scientific Journey through Distant Space and Time, 8269
Mind Children: The Future of Robot and Human Intelligence, 9003
Mind Drugs, 5129
The Mind of South Africa, 7384
Mind over Math, 8839
A Mind to Murder, 2067(F)
Mind Transfer, 2388(F)
Mindsword's Story, 1261(F)
Mine, 1809(F)

Minerals, Rocks and Fossils, 8826
The Miners, 7990
Ministry of Greed: The Inside Story of the Televangelists and Their Holy Wars, 4064
The Minotaur, 58(F)
Minute by Minute, 6020
Miracle at Midway, 7274
Miracle at Philadelphia: The Story of the Constitutional Convention, May to September, 1787, 4185
The Miracle of Dunkirk, 7245
The Miracle Planet, 8793
The Miracle Worker: A Play for Television, 3074
Miracleworker, 1927(F)
Miriam's Tambourine: Jewish Folktales from around the World, 3370
Mirror Image, 2008(F)
Mirror Maze, 2600(F)
A Mirror of Chaucer's World, 7525
The Mirror of Her Dreams, 1097(F)
Mirrorshades: The Cyberpunk Anthology, 2795(F)
The Misanthrope and Other Plays, 3010
The Miser, 3011
The Miser of Mayfair, 2248(F)
Misery, 1788(F)
Misplaced Persons, 1144(F)
Miss 4th of July, Goodbye, 466(F)
Miss Lizzie, 2168(F)
Miss Manners' Guide to Excruciatingly Correct Behavior, 5575
Miss Marple: The Complete Short Stories, 1952(F)
Miss Pym Disposes, 2193(F)
Mission to Moulokin, 2544(F)
Mississippi Writers: Reflections of Childhood and Youth, 2889(F)
Mister God, This Is Anna, 5380
Mister Roberts, 1656(F)
Mistletoe Mysteries, 2104(F)
Mistress Anne, 6829
Mists of Avalon, 1051(F)
Mme Sun Yat-sen, 6817
Mobilizing against AIDS, 5212
Moby Dick, 413(F)
Moby-Dick: Ishmael's Mighty Book, 3758

Model: The Complete Guide to Becoming a Professional Model, 4873
The Modern Age, 3811
Modern American Poetry, 3895
Modern American Scenes for Student Actors, 3078
Modern American Usage, 3905
Modern American Women Poets, 3274
Modern Art: Painting/Sculpture/Architecture, 5721
Modern Black Writers, 3599
Modern Chinese Poetry, 3349
Modern Gymnastics, 9881
Modern Japanese Literature: An Anthology, 2929
Modern Latin America, 7630
Modern Latin American Literature, 3581
Modern Monologues for Young People, 3108
The Modern Poets: A Critical Introduction, 3858
The Modern Researcher, 4669
A Modern Southern Reader, 2916
Modern Soviet Society, 7570
Modern Times: The World from the Twenties to the Eighties, 7151
Modern Women's Gymnastics for Both Teacher and Gymnast, 9882
Mold Making for Ceramics, 9163
Molecules, 8781
Molecules of the Mind: The Brave New Science of Molecular Psychology, 5313
Moll Flanders, 349(F)
Mom, I'm Pregnant, 5499
The Moment of the Magician, 1123(F)
Momentum: Women in American Politics Now, 4269
Momo, 1111(F)
Monday Night Mayhem: The Inside Story of ABC's Monday Night Football, 9846
Monday the Rabbi Took Off, 2081(F)
Money: Its Origin, Development and Modern Use, 4579
The Moneychangers, 118(F)
The Monkey Business: A Scientist Looks at Creationism, 6996

Monkeys on the Interstate and Other Tales from America's Favorite Zookeeper, 8773
Monsieur Pamplemousse Aloft, 19(F)
The Monsters of Loch Ness, 9515
Mont Cant Gold, 1120(F)
Monteverdi, 6350
The Moon and Sixpence, 715(F)
Moon Called, 1234(F)
The Moon in the Water, 1407(F)
The Moon Is a Harsh Mistress, 2580(F)
The Moon Men, 2451(F)
Moon Mirror, 1235(F)
Moon of Three Rings, 2713(F)
Moon Palace, 517(F)
Moonbane, 1834(F)
Moonheart, 091(F)
Moonsinger's Friends, 1266(F)
The Moonstone, 341(F)
Moonwalk, 6410
Moose, 8523
More BASIC Computer Games, 8957
More Celtic Fairy Tales, 3402
More Games for the Superintelligent, 8851
More Joy of Photography, 9432
More Magic, 1231(F)
More Misinformation, 9478
More Murder on Cue: Stage, Screen & Radio Favorites, 2189(F)
More New Games! And Playful Ideas from the New Games Foundation, 9566
A More Perfect Union: The Men and Events That Made the Constitution, 4201
More Than an Average Guy, 6938
More to Life Than Mr. Right: Stories for Young Feminists, 2968(F)
More Wild Westerns, 228(F)
More Wok Cookery, 9334
Moreta: Dragonlady of Pern, 2665(F)
The Mormon Experience: A History of the Latter-Day Saints, 4028
Morning Star, Black Sun: The Northern Cheyenne Indians

and America's Energy Crisis, 7789
Mornings on Horseback, 6564
The Morrow Anthology of Younger American Poets, 3328
Mortal Fear, 53(F)
The Mosquito Coast, 252(F)
The Mossad: Israel's Secret Intelligence Service—Inside Stories, 7610
The Most Common Errors in English Usage and How to Avoid Them, 3926
The Most Dangerous Man in America: Scenes of the Life of Benjamin Franklin, 6586
The Most of Andy Rooney, 3509
Most of My Patients Are Animals, 6886
The Most Popular Plays of the American Theatre: Ten of Broadway's Longest-Running Plays, 3115
Most Valuable Baseball Cards, 9442
Mote in God's Eye, 2700(F)
Motel of the Mysteries, 3501
The Moth, 2254(F)
Mother: A Collective Portrait, 5659
A Mother and Two Daughters, 553(F)
Mother Courage and Her Children, 2992
Mother Earth, Father Sky, 1351(F)
Mother Night, 1305(F)
The Mother Shadow, 2060(F)
The Mother Tongue: English in the World Today, 3909
Motherhood: The Second Oldest Profession, 3487(F)
Mothers: A Celebration in Prose, Poetry, and Photographs of Mothers and Motherhood, 5676
Mothers of Invention, 8236
Motorcycle: The Making of a Harley-Davidson, 9119
Mottled Lizard, 6921
Mount St. Helens: The Eruption and Recovery of a Volcano, 8800
The Mountain Bike Book: Choosing, Riding and Maintaining the Off-Road Bicycle, 9768

The Mountain Bike Repair Handbook, 9749
Mountain Climbing for Beginners, 9548
Mountain People, Mountain Crafts, 5808
Mountains: A Natural History and Hiking Guide, 8812
The Mouse That Roared, 1908(F)
Mouse Traps and Muffling Cups: One Hundred Brilliant and Bizarre United States Patents, 8949
The Mousetrap and Other Plays, 3025
Mouthsounds, 9301
Move Your Shadow: South Africa, Black and White, 7377
A Moveable Feast, 6262
Movie Mastermind: Over 1000 Questions to Addle an Addict and Baffle a Buff, 5990
Movie Monsters: Great Horror Film Stories, 1758(F)
Moviemakers at Work: Interviews, 6000
Moving In, 1896(F)
The Moving Toy Shop, 1976(F)
Mozart, 6351, 6352
Mr. and Mrs. Bo Jo Jones, 834(F)
Mr. Bojangles: The Biography of Bill Robinson, 6437
Mr. Midshipman Hornblower, 1427(F)
Mr. Sammler's Planet, 954(F)
Mrs. Dalloway, 756(F)
Mrs. Mike, 95(F)
Mrs. Pollifax and the Golden Triangle, 103(F)
Mrs. Pollifax and the Hong Kong Buddha, 104(F)
Mrs. Pollifax and the Whirling Dervish, 105(F)
Mrs. Pollifax on the China Station, 104(F)
Mrs. Presumed Dead, 1938(F)
Ms. Architect, 4940
Ms. Engineer, 5019
The Ms. Guide to a Woman's Health, 5345
Ms. Murder, 2181(F)
Ms. Veterinarian, 5024
Much Depends on Dinner: The Extraordinary History and Mythology, Allure and Obsessions, Perils and Ta-

boos, of an Ordinary Meal, 8421
Muhammad, 6815
Muir Among the Animals: The Wildlife Writings of John Muir, 8456
Multilingual Phrase Book, 3940
The Mummy: Or, Ramses the Damned, 1829(F)
The Mummy: Stories of the Living Corpse, 1759(F)
Mummy Stories, 2033(F)
Murder and Magic, 1131(F)
Murder and the First Lady, 2161(F)
Murder at Markham, 2183(F)
Murder at the FBI, 2196(F)
Murder at the Kennedy Center, 2197(F)
Murder at the National Cathedral, 2198(F)
Murder at the Palace, 2162(F)
Murder at the Savoy, 2179(F)
The Murder at the Vicarage, 1953(F)
Murder in a Mummy Case, 1926(F)
Murder in Georgetown, 2199(F)
Murder in the Blue Room, 2163(F)
Murder in the Cathedral, 3029
Murder in the Oval Office, 2164(F)
Murder in the Queen's Armes, 2001(F)
Murder in the Smithsonian, 2200(F)
Murder in the Supreme Court, 2200(F)
Murder in the White House, 2200(F)
Murder in White, 2224(F)
Murder, Murder, Little Star, 1919(F)
The Murder of Roger Ackroyd, 1954(F)
Murder on Capitol Hill, 2201(F)
Murder on Embassy Row, 2201(F)
Murder on the Air, 6037
Murder on the Orient Express, 1955(F)
Murder Will Out, 3615
The Murderous McLaughlins, 545(F)
Murdo's War, 250(F)

The Murkin Conspiracy: An Investigation of the Assassination of Dr. Martin Luther King, Jr. 4372
Murphy, 220(F), 221(F)
Murphy's Gold, 221(F)
Murphy's Herd, 222(F)
Muscle Wars, 9776
Music: An Illustrated Encyclopedia, 5841
Music and Imagination, 5816
Music Festivals in America, 5826
Music from a Blue Well, 1452(F)
Music Is My Mistress, 6388
The Music Men: An Illustrated History of Brass Bands in America, 1800–1920, 5936
The Music of Black Americans: A History, 5839
Music Talks: Conversations with Working Musicians, 5819
Musical Instruments of the World: An Illustrated Encyclopedia, 5934
The Musical Theatre: A Celebration, 5924
Mutation, 1725(F)
Mutiny on Board HMS Bounty, 7466
My Antonia, 1561(F)
My Black Me: A Beginning Book of Black Poetry, 3235
My Brilliant Career, 811(F)
My Cousin Rachel, 1424(F)
My Darling, My Hamburger, 949(F)
My Fair Lady, 3096
My Family & Other Animals, 8387
My Father's Geisha, 522(F)
My Friend Flicka, 294(F)
My House, 3270
My Life and Hard Times, 6318
My Life As a Body, 859(F)
My Life as an Indian, 7823
My Life for the Poor, 6958
My Life in Three Acts, 6398
My Life with the Pros, 9966
My Love, My Love, or the Peasant Girl, 671(F)
My Luke and I, 6720
My Mother Before Me: When Daughters Discover Mothers, 5654
My Mother/My Self: The

Daughter's Search for Identity, 6907
My Name Is Aram, 492(F)
My Name Is Asher Lev, 903(F)
My Name Is Caroline, 5209
My Parents Are Driving Me Crazy, 5677
My People: The Story of the Jews, 7609
My Place, 6934
My Serengeti Years: The Memoirs of an African Game Warden, 6164
My Shadow Ran Fast, 4491
My Sister Clare, 1437(F)
My Small Country Living, 6928
My Son's Story, 962(F)
My Soul Is Rested, 4375
My Wild World, 6663
Myself My Enemy, 1460(F)
Mysteries of the Ancient Americas, 7023
Mysteries of the Ancient World, 7021
Mysteries of the Unexplained, 9525
The Mysterious Island, 326(F)
The Mysterious Maya, 7650
The Mysterious Oceans, 8876
Mysterious Sea Stories, 2126(F)
The Mysterious Stranger and Other Stories, 425(F)
The Mysterious William Shakespeare: The Myth and Reality, 3823
Mystery and Morality, 3810
The Mystery of Comets, 8335
The Mystery of Edwin Drood, 358(F)
The Mystery of the Ancient Maya, 7646
Mystery Train: Images of America in Rock 'n' Roll Music, 5885
Myth Conception, 1021(F)
Myth Information, 9539
Myth-nomers and Impervections, 2390(F)
The Myth of Sisyphus, and Other Essays, 3526
Mythago Wood, 1155(F)
Mythical and Fabulous Creatures: A Sourcebook and Research Guide, 3466
Mythology, 3457
The Mythology of Mexico and Central America, 3448

The Mythology of North America, 3419

The Mythology of South America, 3444

Myths of the Greeks and Romans, 3476

Myths to Live By, 3450

N-Space, 2696(F)

The Naked and the Dead, 1666(F)

The Naked Face, 2174(F)

Naked in Winter, 778(F)

Naked Masks: Five Plays, 3014

Naked Sun, 2361(F)

The Name of the Rose, 1379(F)

A Name to Conjure With, 1000(F)

The Nameless, 1941(F)

Nancy Clark's Sports Nutrition Guidebook, 5344

Napoleon, 6866

Narabedla Ltd. 2738(F)

Narrative of the Life of Frederick Douglass, an American Slave, 6585

Nathaniel, 1837(F)

Nathaniel Hawthorne, 3759, 6254

Nathaniel Hawthorne: The Man, His Tales and Romances, 6255

The Nation Comes of Age: A People's History of the Antebellum Years, 7884

A Nation of Immigrants, 4332

The Nation Reunited, 7901

The Nation Takes Shape, 1789–1837, 7849

The National Air and Space Museum, 9063

National Anthems of the World, 5951

The National Debt, 4225

The National League: An Illustrated History, 9653

Nationalism: Opposing Viewpoints, 4151

The Nations Within: The Past and Future of American Indian Sovereignty, 4392

Native American Literature, 3610

The Native Americans, 7824

Native Son, 512(F)

The Natural, 2882(F)

Natural Acts: A Sidelong View of Science and Nature, 8401

The Natural History of China, 7415

A Natural History of the Senses, 5329

The Natural History of Whales and Dolphins, 8647

The Natural Man, 1892(F)

Natural Obsessions: The Search for the Oncogene, 5228

The Natural Way to Draw: A Working Plan for Art Study, 9206

Natural Weight Loss, 5424

Natural Wonders of the World, 7068

A Naturalist's Guide to the Year, 8172

The Naturalist's Year, 8382

Nature: Poems, 3287

The Nature of Alexander, 6823

Nature of Australia, 7479

The Nature of Human Aggression, 5566

The Nature of Things, 8216

Nature's End: The Consequences of the Twentieth Century, 2797(F)

Nature's Masterpiece: The Brain and How It Works, 5321

Nature's Wonderlands: National Parks of the World, 7065

Navahos Have Five Fingers, 4391

The Navajos, 7825

Nazi Germany, 7509

The Nazis, 7505

Neanderthals: Isaac Asimov's Wonderful World of Science Fiction #6, 1355(F)

Near Eastern Mythology, 3456

Nebula Award Stories Seventeen, 2569(F)

Nebula Awards 24, 2415(F)

A Necessary End: A Novel of World War II, 1641(F)

Necessary Parties, 541(F)

Necessities: Racial Barriers in American Sports, 4365

Necessity, 101(F)

The Neck of the Giraffe: Darwin, Evolution and the New Biology, 6999

Nectar in a Sieve, 1400(F)

The Negotiator, 92(F)

Neil Diamond: Solitary Star, 6384

Neil Simon, 3839

Nell's Quilt, 745(F)

Nelson Mandela: The Man and the Movement, 6793

Nemesis, 1080(F), 2366(F)

Nerilka's Story: A Pern Adventure, 1203(F)

The Net, 2673(F)

Neuromancer, 2558(F)

Never Cry Wolf, 8520

The Never-Ending War: Terrorism in the 80's, 4542

Never Quite Dead, 2175(F)

Never to Forget: The Jews of the Holocaust, 7253

Never Too Young to Die, 6740

The Neverending Story, 1112(F)

The New Address Book: How to Reach Anyone Who's Anyone, 7757

The New Age: Notes of a Fringe-Watcher, 9499

The New Age Music Guide: Profiles and Recordings of 500 Top New Age Musicians, 5843

A New Age Now Begins: A People's History of the American Revolution, 7859

New America, 2345(F)

The New American Computer Dictionary, 9009

The New American Poverty, 4506

New Americans: An Oral History—Immigrants and Refugees in the U.S. Today, 4339

The New Americans: Immigrant Life in Southern California, 4340

New and Collected Poems, 3344

New and Collected Poems, 1917–1982, 3295

New and Improved: The Story of Mass Marketing in America, 4621

New and Old Voices of Wah'kon-tah, 3260

New and Selected Poems, 1923–1985, 3338

The New Assertive Women, 4533

The New Atlas of the Universe, 8276

The New Basics Cookbook, 9358

The New Bedside, Bathtub & Armchair Companion to Agatha Christie, 3683

The New Book of People, 6782

The New Breed: Actors Coming of Age, 6176

New Career Opportunities in Health and Human Services, 4989

New Career Opportunities in the Paralegal Profession, 4956

New Careers in Hospitals, 5005

New Classic Beauty: A Step-by-Step Guide to Naturally Glamorous Makeup, 5285

A New Companion to Shakespeare Studies, 3822

New Destinies, Volume VIII, 2394(F)

The New Diary: How to Use a Journal for Self-Guidance and Expanded Creativity, 5626

New Dictionary of American Family Names, 5673

The New Dinosaurs: An Alternative Evolution, 6979

The New Doubleday Cookbook, 9309

The New Eyes of the Scientist, 8224

The New Fiction: Interviews with Innovative American Writers, 3699

The New Frontier: The Best of Today's Western Fiction, 164(F)

New Frontiers in Genetics, 5259

The New Girl Friend and Other Stories, 1826(F)

The New Good Housekeeping Cookbook, 9368

The New Grove Gospels, Blues and Jazz with Spirituals and Ragtime, 5892

The New Grove Twentieth-Century American Masters, 6181

A New History of India, 7444

A New History of Korea, 7459

New Horizons in Amateur Astronomy, 8260

The New Immigrants, 4331

New Jersey, 581(F)

The New Joy of Photography, 9415

The New Medically Based No-Nonsense Beauty Book, 5275

The New Milton Cross' Complete Stories of the Great Operas, 5913

The New Milton Cross' More Stories of the Great Operas, 5913

The New Music, 1900–1960, 5833

New Native American Drama: Three Plays, 3073

The New Our Bodies, Ourselves, 5342

The New Oxford Book of American Verse, 3263

The New Oxford Book of Canadian Verse in English, 3240

The New Oxford Book of Eighteenth Century Verse, 3217

The New Oxford Book of English Light Verse, 3188

The New Oxford Book of English Verse, 1250–1950, 3202

The New Oxford Book of Irish Verse, 3213

The New Parakeet Handbook, 8668

The New Parrot Handbook: Everything about Purchase, Acclimation, Care, Diet, Disease, and Behavior of Parrots, 8675

The New Pelican Guide to English Literature, 3580

The New Philippines, 7473

A New Pictorial History of the Talkies, 5993

The New Race for Space: The U.S. and Russia Leap to the Challenge for Unlimited Rewards, 8313

The New Real Book: Jazz Classics, Choice Standards, Pop-Fusion Classics for All Instrumentalists and Vocalists, 5891

The New Robert's Rules of Order, 5581

The New Rolling Stone Record Guide, 5888

The New Rules of Golf, 9879

The New Sailboard Book, 9955

New Selected Poems, 3210

New Sounds: A Listener's Guide to New Music, 5828

The New Springtime, 2783(F)

New Stories from the South: The Year's Best, 1986, 2957(F)

The New Teenage Body Book, 5479

The New Terrorism: Politics of Violence, 4544

New Treasures of the Past, 7017

The New Vegetarian: Cooking with Style the Vegetarian Way, 9359

New Women and New Fiction: Short Stories Since the Sixties, 2899(F)

New Words Dictionary, 3933

New Words for Old, 3927

The New World of Philosophy, 4012

New Worlds: In Search of the Planets, 8342

The New York Times Career Planner, 4834

The New York Times Cook Book, 9324

The New York Times International Cook Book, 9324

The New Yorker Album of Drawings, 1925–1975, 5754

The New Young Peoples' Job Power Now, 4837

The News Business, 3983

Newspapers Career Directory, 4856

Newton at the Bat: The Science in Sports, 9594

The Next Century, 8067

The Next Hurrah: The Changing Face of the American Political Process, 4262

The Next One Hundred Years: Shaping the Fate of Our Living Earth, 4447

Next Panda Please! Further Adventures of a Wildlife Vet, 6701

Next-to-Last Things: New Poems and Essays, 3288

Next Year in Jerusalem: A Short History of Zionism, 7611

The NFL All-Pro Workout, 5348

Nibbled to Death by Ducks, 1944(F)

Nicaragua and the United States: Years of Conflict, 7656

Nicholas and Alexandra, 6867

The Nicholas Factor, 212(F)

Nicholas Nickleby, 359(F)

The Nick Adams Stories, 2921(F)

Nigger of the "Narcissus" and Other Stories, 346(F)

Night, 7323

Night Creatures, 3374

Night Flight, 239(F)

Night Kites, 855(F)

The Night Lives On, 8893

Night of Masks, 2714(F)

Night of Reunion, 3(F)

Night of the Claw, 1825(F)

Night of the Fox, 128(F)

Night of the Grizzlies, 8507

The Night of the Moonbow, 261(F)

Night of the Whale, 246(F)

Night Over Day Over Night, 1685(F)

Night Shift, 1789(F)

The Night the Bear Ate Goombaw, 3502

The Night Thoreau Spent in Jail, 3094

A Night to Remember, 7152

Nighteyes, 2751(F)

Nightfall, 2387(F)

Nightfall and Other Stories, 2367(F)

Nightmare Seasons, 1754(F)

Nightmares, 1752(F)

Nightwatch: An Equinox Guide to Viewing the Universe, 8257

Nightwing, 1847(F)

NIK: Now I Know, 787(F)

Nim: A Chimpanzee Who Learned Sign Language, 8504

Nina's Journey: A Memoir of Stalin's Russia and the Second World War, 6929

Nine American Women of the 19th Century: Leaders into the 20th, 6488

The 900 Days: The Siege of Leningrad, 7285

The Nine Nations of North America, 7737

Nine O'Clock Tide, 1998(F)

Nine Princes in Amber, 1344(F)

The Nine Sides of the Diamond: Baseball's Great Glove Men on the Fine Art of Defense, 9641

Nine Stories, 911(F)

The Nine Tailors, 2170(F)

Nine Tomorrows, 2368(F)

1984, 2725(F)

1984 Revisited: Totalitarianism in Our Century, 3670

1941: Our Lives in a World on the Edge, 7231

The 1960s, 7333

1929: The Year of the Great Crash, 8033

19th and 20th Century Art: Painting, Sculpture, Architecture, 5744

The Nineteenth Century, 5761

19th-Century Art, 5763

Nisei Daughter, 6953

No Body, 2138(F)

No, But I Saw the Movie: The Best Short Stories Ever Made into Film, 2975(F)

No Dragons to Slay, 666(F)

No Enemy But Time, 2416(F)

No Exit, and Three Other Plays, 3017

The No-Hit Hall of Fame: No-Hitters of the 20th Century, 9636

No Kidding, 634(F)

No Lady in the House, 2076(F)

No Language but a Cry, 5646

No Man's Land, 7163

No More Saturday Nights, 860(F)

No Name in the Street, 4353

No Time to Wave Goodbye, 7322

No Truce with Kings/Ship of Shadows, 2349(F)

Nobel Costa Rica, 7657

The Nobel Reader: Short Fiction, Poetry, and Prose by Nobel Laureates in Literature, 2910

Noble House, 48(F)

Nobody Knows My Name: More Notes of a Native Son, 4354

Nomads of the World, 7008

Non-Impact Aerobics: Introducing the NIA Technique, 5360

The Nonborn King, 1216(F)

None Died in Vain: The Saga of the American Civil War, 7927

None of the Above: Behind the Myth of Scholastic Aptitude, 4663

Nor Crystal Tears, 2545(F)

Norman Mailer, 3760

The Norse Myths: Introduced and Retold, 3480

North American Indian Art, 5795

North American Indian Mythology, 3421

North and South, 1537(F)

The North Light Illustrated Book of Painting Techniques, 9215

North Star, 171(F)

North to the Pole, 7708

North with the Spring, 8406

Northlight Handbook of Artists' Materials, 9194

Northrop Frye on Shakespeare, 3818

Northshore, 2802(F)

Northwest Passage, 1585(F)

The Norton Anthology of Literature by Women: The Tradition in English, 2918

The Norton Anthology of Modern Poetry, 3157

The Norton Anthology of Poetry, 3148

The Norton Book of Light Verse, 3150

The Norton Book of Nature Writing, 8389

Norwegian Folk Tales, 3390

Not a Stranger, 2004(F)

A Not Entirely Benign Procedure: Four Years as a Medical Student, 5240

Not for Love, 2250(F)

Not Just Another Embroidery Book, 9256

Not That You Asked. . ., 3510

Notes to Myself: My Struggle to Become a Person, 3545

Nothing but the Best: The Struggle for Perfection at the Juilliard School, 5823

Nova: Adventures in Science, 8238

The Novel and the Modern World, 3659

The Novels of Dashiell Hammett, 2039(F)

The Novels of Henry James, 3787

Now and Forever, 2323(F)

Now Sheba Sings the Song, 3875

Now That the Buffalo's Gone, 7813

Nowhere to Run: The Story of Soul Music, 5871

Nuclear Blackmail and Nuclear Balance, 4130

Nuclear Energy at the Crossroads, 8924

Nuclear Power, 8923

Nuclear Power: A Rational Approach, 8921

Nuclear Power for Beginners, 8920

Nuclear War: From Hiroshima to Nuclear Winter, 4159

Nuclear War: Opposing Viewpoints, 4164

Nuclear Waste: The Biggest Clean-Up in History, 8928

The Nuclear Waste Primer: A Handbook for Citizens, 8926

Nuclear Winter, 4157

Nurse, 4985

Nurse Power: New Vistas in Learning, 5003

The Nurse's Story, 6910

The Nurturing Father: A Journey to the Complete Man, 5672

Nutrition and Health Encyclopedia, 5428

Nutrition and the Brain, 5311

Nutrition for Sport, 5429

Nuts and Bolts of the Past: A History of American Technology, 1776–1860, 8946

O Come Ye Back to Ireland, 7540

O Jerusalem! 7606

O Pioneers! 1562(F)

The Oak and the Calf: Sketches of Literary Life in the Soviet Union, 6311

Oath of Fealty, 2701(F)

The Object of My Affection, 1891(F)

Observing the Constellations, 8287

An Ocean Apart, 4135

The Ocean Environment, 8874

Ocean Frontiers, 8891

The Ocean Realm, 8896

The Oceans: A Book of Questions and Answers, 8877

Oceans of Birds, 8548

Oceans of Energy: Reservoir of Power for the Future, 8917

The October Country, 2429(F)

October Dreams: A Harvest of Horror, 1801(F)

The October Revolution, 7582

The Octopus, 416(F)

The Odd Couple, 3125

Oddballs, 9698

The Odessa File, 93(F)

The Odyssey, 3184

Odyssey Book of Houseplants, 9386

The Odyssey of The Bear: The Making of the Film by Jean-Jacques Annaud, 5989

Of Human Bondage, 716(F)

Of Human Bondage: Coming of Age in the Novel, 3675

Of Mice and Men, 1632(F)

Of Plymouth Plantation, 1620–1647, 7835

Of Such Small Differences, 668(F)

Of Time and the River, 943(F)

Of Wolves and Men, 8517

Off Balance: The Real World of Ballet, 5966

Off-Roading: Racing and Riding, 9619

Off the Record: An Oral History of Popular Music, 5900

Offbeat Careers, 4864

The Official Blackbook Price Guide of U.S. Coins, 9451

The Official Kids' Survival Kit: How to Do Things on Your Own, 5602

The Official Pompon Girl's Handbook, 9587

The Official Soccer Book of the United States Soccer Federation, 9949

Ogre Castle, 1137(F)

Oh, Baby, I Love It! 9677

Oh Pray My Wings Are Gonna Fit Me Well, 3237

The Old Curiosity Shop, 360(F)

Old Goriot, 303(F)

Old MacDonald's Factory Farm, 8588

The Old Man and the Sea, 124(F)

Old Possum's Book of Practical Cats, 3200

The Old Regime and the French Revolution, 7492

Old Time Classic Cars, 1885–1940, 9108

The Old West Quiz and Fact Book, 7954

The Old Wives' Tale, 333(F)

Oliver Twist, 361(F)

Oliver Wendell Holmes, Jr. 6593

Olympic Hopeful, 2872(F)

The Omni Book of Computers and Robots, 8965

The Omni Book of Medicine, 5233

The Omni Book of Space, 8299

The Omni Future Almanac, 4420

The Omni Space Almanac: A Complete Guide to the Space Age, 8307

On a Clear Day You Can See General Motors: John Z. De Lorean's Look inside the Automotive Giant, 9118

On a Pale Horse, 1014(F)

On Acting, 6427

On Aggression, 5563

On an Average Day . . . 9505

On and Off the Court, 6739

On Becoming Human, 7012

On Being a Writer, 3605

On Being Gay, 4536

On Children and Death, 5088

On Distant Ground, 1692(F)

On Fiji Islands, 7480

On Golden Pond, 3130

On Her Own: Growing Up in the Shadow of the American Dream, 4538

On Leadership, 7735

On Native Grounds: An Interpretation of Modern American Prose Literature, 3743

On Revolution, 4410

On Stage: Producing Musical Theatre, 5926

On the Brink of Tomorrow: Frontiers of Science, 8227

On the Devil's Court, 2874(F)

On the Edge, 796(F)

On the Edge of the Spotlight, 6885

On the Frontiers of Science: Strange Machines You Can Build, 8245

On the Frontiers of Science, 8215

On the Guard: The YMCA Lifeguard Manual, 9962

On the Lesson Tee: Basic Golf Fundamentals, 9868

On the Loose, 4438

On the Move: American Women in the 1970s, 4323

On the Razzle, 3042

On the Road, 687(F)

On the Road with Charles Kuralt, 7755

On the Streets: The Lives of Adolescent Prostitutes, 5512

On the Third Ward, 653(F)

On the Wing, 8531

On the Wings of Eagles, 86(F)

On the Wrong Side: My Life in the KGB, 6854

On Violence, 4457

On with My Life, 6960

On Writing the College Application Essay, 4720

On Writing the Short Story, 3958

On Writing Well: An Informal Guide to Writing Nonfiction, 4707

On Your Bicycle: An Illustrated History of Cycling, 9759

On Your Own, 5289

Once a Bum, Always a Dodger, 6719

Once a Warrior King: Memories of an Officer in Vietnam, 8107

The Once and Future King, 1320(F)

Once Around the Galaxy, 8262

Once in a Lifetime, 2323(F)

Once in the Saddle: The Cowboy's Frontier, 1866–1896, 7982

Once Upon a Time When We Were Colored, 6956

One Brief Shining Moment: Remembering Kennedy, 6539

One, by One, by One: Facing the Holocaust, 7255

One Child, 5384

One Christmas, 6228

One Day at Kitty Hawk: The Untold Story of the Wright Brothers and the Airplane, 6704

One Day at Teton Marsh, 8383

One Day in the Life of Ivan Denisovich, 995(F)

The One Day Plan for Jobhunters, 4808

One Dead Dean, 1973(F)

One Earth, One Future: Our Changing Global Environment, 4442

One Fat Summer, 704(F)

One Fine Day the Rabbi Bought a Cross, 2082(F)

One Flew over the Cuckoo's Nest, 688(F)

One for the Road: Hitchhiking through the Australian Outback, 6147

The One Hour College Applicant: You Don't Need to Read a 300-Page Book to Apply to College! 4760

One Hundred and One Famous Poems, 3155

142 Ways to Make a Poem: An Anthology of Modern Poetry, 3334

100 Grams of Uranium Equal 290 Tons of Coal, 8929

One Hundred Great Science Fiction Short Short Stories, 2369(F)

100 Great Science Fiction Short Stories, 2379(F)

The 100 Greatest Baseball Players of All Time, 6709

One Hundred Poems from the Chinese, 3355

100 Poems from the Japanese, 3355

One Hundred Problems in Elementary Mathematics, 8843

100 Successful College Application Essays, 4739

100 Years of Negro Freedom, 4357

One Hundred Years of Solitude, 550(F)

The One-Hundred-One Best Jazz Albums, 5881

One-Hundred-One Best Magic Tricks, 9396

101 Soft Toys: Fun to Make Toys for Children & Babies, 9262

101 Stories of the Great Ballets, 5959

110 Selected Poems, 3255

One Knee Equals Two Feet:

(And Everything Else You Need to Know about Football), 9854

One L: An Inside Account of Life in the First Year of Harvard Law School, 4981

One Life: An Autobiography, 6686

One Life at a Time, Please, 3520

One Man's Moon: 50 Haiku, 3353

One More Time! 1651(F)

One More Time, 6378

One Nation under Television: The Rise and Decline of Network TV, 6025

One Size Doesn't Fit All, 6756

One Teenager in Ten: Writings by Gay and Lesbian Youth, 5466

1,001 Things Everyone Should Know about American History, 7736

1066: The Year of the Conquest, 7523

The One Tree, 1098(F)

One Way or Another, 782(F)

One Writer's Beginnings, 6325

O'Neill, 6292

Only Make-Believe, 2328(F)

Only the Lonely: Roy Orbison's Life and Legacy, 6428

Only Yesterday, 8024

The Open Canoe, 9933

The Open Door: When Writers First Learned to Read, 3583

Open Net, 9887

Open Road: A Celebration of the American Highway, 9055

Opening the Space Frontier, 8323

Opera: What's All the Screaming About? 5914

Operation Babylon, 7598

Operation Time Search, 2715(F)

Opportunities for Gerontology Careers, 4982

Opportunities in Accounting Careers, 4931

Opportunities in Acting Careers, 4893

Opportunities in Agriculture Careers, 4872

Opportunities in Airline Careers, 4857

Opportunities in Animal and Pet Care, 4845

Opportunities in Architecture, 4943

Opportunities in Automotive Service Careers, 4945

Opportunities in Banking, 4926

Opportunities in Beauty Culture Careers, 4835

Opportunities in Biological Sciences, 5032

Opportunities in Biotechnology Careers, 5013

Opportunities in Building Construction Trades, 4899

Opportunities in Business Management, 4930

Opportunities in Cable Television, 5037

Opportunities in Carpentry Careers, 4944

Opportunities in Child Care Careers, 4983

Opportunities in Chiropractic Health Care Careers, 5002

Opportunities in Civil Engineering Careers, 5018

Opportunities in Commercial Art and Graphic Design, 4884

Opportunities in Computer Aided Design and Computer Aided Manufacturing, 5036

Opportunities in Computer Science Careers, 5044

Opportunities in Counseling and Development, 4960

Opportunities in Counseling & Development Careers, 4946

Opportunities in Crafts Careers, 4853

Opportunities in Culinary Careers, 4830

Opportunities in Data Processing, 5050

Opportunities in Electrical Trades, 5062

Opportunities in Energy Careers, 5063

Opportunities in Engineering Careers, 5010

Opportunities in Engineering Technology Careers, 5018

Opportunities in Environmental Careers, 4963

Opportunities in Fashion Careers, 4829

Opportunities in Fast Food Careers, 4962

Opportunities in Federal Government Careers, 4817

Opportunities in Film, 5037

Opportunities in Financial Careers, 4938

Opportunities in Foreign Language Careers, 4816

Opportunities in Health and Medical Careers, 5007

Opportunities in High Tech Careers, 5042

Opportunities in Home Economics Careers, 4868

Opportunities in Hospital Administration Careers, 5006

Opportunities in Hotel and Motel Management, 4840

Opportunities in Human Resources Management Careers, 4979

Opportunities in Insurance Careers, 4933

Opportunities in International Business Careers, 4904

Opportunities in Journalism Careers, 4860

Opportunities in Laser Technology Careers, 5011

Opportunities in Law Careers, 4974

Opportunities in Law Enforcement and Criminal Justice, 4978

Opportunities in Library and Information Science, 4951

Opportunities in Marine and Maritime Careers, 5020

Opportunities in Marketing Careers, 4937

Opportunities in Medical Technology Careers, 5000

Opportunities in Microelectronics, 5043

Opportunities in Military Careers, 4858

Opportunities in Modeling Careers, 4880

Opportunities in Newspaper Publishing Careers, 4939

Opportunities in Nursing Careers, 4993

Opportunities in Nutrition Careers, 4987

Opportunities in Occupational Therapy Careers, 4903

Opportunities in Office Occupations, 4912

Opportunities in Paralegal Careers, 4964

Opportunities in Paramedical Careers, 4998

Opportunities in Part-Time and Summer Jobs, 5066

Opportunities in Petroleum Careers, 5045

Opportunities in Pharmacy Careers, 5017

Opportunities in Photography Careers, 4842

Opportunities in Plumbing and Pipe Fitting Careers, 4942

Opportunities in Printing Careers, 5038

Opportunities in Property Management Careers, 4913

Opportunities in Purchasing Careers, 4905

Opportunities in Recreation and Leisure, 4841

Opportunities in Restaurant Careers, 4827

Opportunities in Retailing Careers, 4909

Opportunities in Robotics Careers, 5012

Opportunities in Social Science Careers, 4802

Opportunities in State and Local Government, 4818

Opportunities in Teaching, 4950

Opportunities in Telecommunications, 5037

Opportunities in the Machine Trades, 5035

Opportunities in Transportation Careers, 4859

Opportunities in Travel Careers, 4852

Opportunities in Veterinary Medicine Careers, 5009

Opportunities in Vocational & Technical Careers, 5051

Opportunities in Word Processing, 5049

Opportunities in Writing Careers, 4833

Opportunities in Your Own Service Business, 4849

The Optimist's Daughter, 620(F)

Oral History: An Introduction for Students, 7048

The Oral Report: The Consumer's Common Sense Guide to Better Dental Care, 5340

Orcas of the Gulf: A Natural History, 8650

Ordinary People, 556(F)

The Oregon Trail, 7972
The Organic Gardener, 9378
Oriental Cookbook, 9360
The Origin: A Biographical Novel of Charles Darwin, 1478(F)
The Original Hitchhiker Radio Scripts, 3807
The Original Word Game Dictionary, 3939
Originals: American Women Artists, 6180
Origins: What New Discoveries Reveal about the Emergence of Our Species and Its Possible Future, 7004
The Origins & Sources of Drugs, 5158
The Origins of the Equal Rights Amendment: American Feminism between the Wars, 4293
Origins of Totalitarianism, 4168
Orion, 2421(F)
An Orphan in History, 6901
Orphan Star, 2545(F)
Orsinian Tales, 2634(F)
The Orvis Guide to Outdoor Photography, 9433
Orwell, the Lost Writings, 3542
The Osterman Weekend, 181(F)
Othello, 3058
The Other, 1858(F)
The Other America: Poverty in the United States, 4507
The Other Nuremberg: The Untold Story of the Tokyo War Crimes Trials, 7188
The Other Side of the Fence, 935(F)
The Other Side of the Mirror: And Other Darkover Stories, 2433(F)
The Other Side of the Mountain, 6778
The Other Time, 1255(F)
Other Voices, Other Rooms, 530(F)
Othersyde, 1851(F)
Our Drowning World, 8799
Our Earth, Ourselves, 4423
Our Endangered Atmosphere: Global Warming and the Ozone Layer, 4434
Our Fascinating Earth, 8403
Our Fiery Trial: Abraham Lin-coln, John Brown, and the Civil War Era, 7931
Our Food, Air and Water: How Safe Are They? 4425
Our Future at Stake: A Teenager's Guide to Stopping the Nuclear Arms Race, 4154
Our House in the Last World, 463(F)
Our National Parks: America's Spectacular Wilderness Heritage, 7773
Our Nig: Sketches from the Life of a Free Black, 1533(F)
Our Oriental Heritage, 7391
Our Sacred Honor, 867(F)
Our Threatened Inheritance: National Treasures of the United States, 4433
Our Town, 3135
Ourselves and Other Animals, 8482
Ourselves in Southern Africa: An Anthology of Southern African Writing, 2940
Out of Africa and Shadows on the Grass, 7362
Out of the Blackout, 519(F)
Out of the Bleachers, 9563
Out of the Blue, 6723
Out of the Everywhere, 8210
Out of the Shadows of Night: The Struggle for International Human Rights, 4299
Out of the Silent Planet, 2645(F)
Out of the Sun, 2422(F)
Out on the Marsh, 934(F)
Out on the Rim, 254(F)
Outbreak, 54(F)
The Outcast, 2490(F)
The Outcasts of Poker Flat and Other Stories, 399(F)
The Outdoor Careers Guide, 4839
Outdoor Cooking, 9363
Outdoor Survival Skills, 9801
The Outlaws of Mesquite, 161(F)
The Outlaws of Sherwood, 3404
Outrageous Acts and Everyday Rebellions, 4319
Outside Providence, 805(F)
Outward Leg, 6151
Over Here: The First World War and American Society, 7158
Over the Edge, 2079(F)
Over the Edge: Baseball's Uncensored Exploits from Way Out in Left Field, 9664
Overcoming Computer Illiteracy: A Friendly Introduction to Computers, 8963
Overcoming Math Anxiety, 8844
Overlord: D-Day and the Battle for Normandy, 7214
An Overpraised Season, 952(F)
Owls: An Introduction for the Amateur Naturalist, 8563
Owls: Their Natural & Unnatural History, 8565
Owls of the World: Their Evolution, Structure and Ecology, 8564
The Owl's Song, 461(F)
The Ox-Bow Incident, 1563(F)
The Oxford Anthology of English Literature: Major Authors Edition, 2931
The Oxford Anthology of English Literature, 2930
The Oxford Book of American Light Verse, 3276
The Oxford Book of Ballads, 3168
The Oxford Book of Christmas Poems, 3165
The Oxford Book of English Detective Stories, 1971(F)
The Oxford Book of English Ghost Stories, 1728(F)
The Oxford Book of Humorous Prose: William Caxton to P. G. Wodehouse—A Conducted Tour, 3504
The Oxford Book of Irish Short Stories, 2969(F)
The Oxford Book of Light Verse, 3149
The Oxford Book of Literary Anecdotes, 3691
The Oxford Book of Narrative Verse, 3173
The Oxford Book of Nineteenth-Century English Verse, 3206
The Oxford Book of Satirical Verse, 3164
The Oxford Book of Seventeenth Century Verse, 3204
The Oxford Book of Short Stories, 2954(F)
The Oxford Book of

Twentieth-Century English Verse, 3216
The Oxford Book of Verse in English Translation, 3179
The Oxford Book of War Poetry, 3177
The Oxford Companion to American History, 7753
The Oxford Companion to Classical Literature, 3589
The Oxford Companion to English Literature, 3575
The Oxford Companion to French Literature, 3586
The Oxford Companion to German Literature, 3639
The Oxford Companion to Spanish Literature, 3608
Oxford Guide to Card Games, 9817
The Oxford History of the American People, 7763
The Oxford History of the Classical World, 7083
The Oxford Illustrated History of Britain, 7528
The Oxford Illustrated History of English Literature, 3685
The Oxford Illustrated History of Ireland, 7515
The Oxford Illustrated History of Medieval Europe, 7484
The Oxford Illustrated Literary Guide to the United States, 3576
Ozark Tales and Superstitions, 3442
Ozone Crisis: The 15-Year Evolution of a Sudden Global Emergency, 4437
Ozzy on the Outside, 757(F)

P.S. I Love You, 2252(F)
P.S. You're Not Listening, 5375
Pablo Picasso, 6203
Pablo Picasso: A Retrospective, 5784
Pablo Picasso: The Man and the Image, 6202
Pacewalking: The Balanced Way to Aerobic Health, 5356
Pacific Coast, 8182
Pack Up and Sketch, 9210
Paddle to the Amazon, 9938
Paine and Jefferson on Liberty, 7858
Painless, Perfect Grammar:

Tips from the Grammar Hotline, 3951
The Painted Bird, 1663(F)
The Paladin, 2473(F)
The Paladin of the Night, 1316(F)
Pale Horse, Pale Rider: Three Short Novels, 2953(F)
Pale Kings and Princes, 2124(F)
The Palestine Question, 7605
The Palestinians, 7608
Palm Sunday: An Autobiographical Collage, 6324
Palomino, 2323(F)
Paloverde, 1557(F)
The Panda's Thumb: More Reflections in Natural History, 8394
Panic: Facing Fears, Phobias and Anxiety, 5555
A Panorama of 5000 Years: Korean History, 7462
Papa Was a Farmer, 6931
The Paper Boat, 1036(F)
Paper Capers: An Amazing Array of Games, Puzzles, and Tricks, 9466
Paper Dinosaurs, 9222
Paper Doll, 1677(F), 660(F)
Paper Flight, 9403
Paper Lion, 9860
Paper Money of the United States: A Complete Illustrated Guide with Valuations, 9445
Papillon, 4471
Paralegal Careers, 4968
Pardon Me, You're Stepping on My Eyeball, 950(F)
Parents Book of Baby Names, 3931
Park Lane South, Queens, 2080(F)
A Parrot without a Name: The Search for the Last Unknown Birds on Earth, 8549
The Parsifal Mosaic, 187(F)
The Parson's Daughter, 2255(F)
A Part of My Soul Went with Him, 6796
The Particle Explosion, 8904
Parting the Waters: America in the King Years, 1954–1963, 6510
Partisans, 198(F)
Pass, Set, Crush: Volleyball Illustrated, 9978

Passage at Arms, 2488(F)
Passage Home, 2304(F)
Passage of Arms, 5(F)
A Passage to India, 1392(F)
Passing Shots: Pam Shriver on Tour, 6772
A Passion for Science, 6647
Passion Play, 1930(F)
Passion Play: A Season with the Purdue Boilermakers and Coach Gene Keady, 9731
The Past through Tomorrow, 2581(F)
Past Times, 2346(F)
Pasta, 9363
The Pastel Handbook, 9203
Pasteur and Modern Science, 6698
Pat Widmer's Cat Book, 8708
Pat Widmer's Dog Training Book, 8743
The Patch Boys, 1628(F)
A Patch of Blue, 685(F)
Patchwork Made Easy, 9246
Paterno: By the Book, 6757
The Path between the Seas: The Creation of the Panama Canal, 7663
The Path of No Resistance: The Story of the Revolution in Superconductivity, 9040
Path of the Paddle: An Illustrated Guide to the Art of Canoeing, 9930
The Pathfinder, 393(F)
The Pathfinders, 9073
Pathways to the Universe, 8264
The Patient Has the Floor, 3528
Patriot Games, 45(F)
Patriots, 238(F)
Patterns of Culture, 6989
Patterns of Poetry: An Encyclopedia of Forms, 3860
Patton: Ordeal and Triumph, 6608
Patton: The Man behind the Legend, 1885–1945, 6607
Paul Cézanne, 6191
Paul Revere & the World He Lived In, 6609
Paul Robeson, 6434
Paul Robeson: The Life and Times of a Free Black Man, 6435
Pawn in Frankincense, 1425(F)
The Pawn of Prophecy, 1107(F)

The Pawnbroker, 509(F)

PC Care Manual: Diagnosing and Maintaining Your MS-DOS, CP/M or Macintosh System, 9004

Peace and War, 3166

Peace Breaks Out, 862(F)

Peace Company, 2563(F)

Peace Heroes in Twentieth-Century America, 6467

The Peaceable Kingdom: A Year in the Life of America's Oldest Zoo, 8777

Peacekeepers, 2423(F)

Peak Condition, 5442

The Pearl, 608(F)

Pearl Harbor: Opposing Viewpoints, 7175

The Pearl Pagoda, 1388(F)

Pearl S. Buck, 3715

Pearls of Childhood, 6911

Pebble in the Sky, 2361(F)

The Peculiar Institution: Slavery in the Antebellum South, 4378

Pedaling to the Ends of the World, 7037

Pegasus in Flight, 2666(F)

Peking Story, 7419

Pel and the Bombers, 2048(F)

A Pelican History of Greek Literature, 3594

Pellucidar, 2449(F), 2452(F)

Pembroke, 1608(F)

Pen & Ink, 9182

A Pen Warmed-Up in Hell: Mark Twain in Protest, 3554

Pencil, 9182

The Pendragon, 1410(F)

The Pendragon Chronicles, 1016(F)

The Penguin Atlas of Recent History: Europe since 1815, 7485

The Penguin Book of Ghost Stories, 1730(F)

The Penguin Book of Hebrew Verse, 3346

The Penguin Book of Irish Verse, 3212

The Penguin Dictionary of Art and Artists, 5689

Penguin Dictionary of Saints, 6783

The Penguin Encyclopaedia of Nutrition, 5430

The Penguin Encyclopedia of Horror and the Supernatural, 3631

The Penguin Guide to Medieval Europe, 7122

Penguins, 8566, 8567

The Penitent, 994(F)

Penmarric, 139(F)

Pennsylvania Dutch American Folk Art, 5809

Pentimento, 6256

The People: No Different Flesh, 2588(F)

People and Folks: Gangs, Crime and the Underclass in a Rustbelt City, 5536

People Live Here: Selected Poems, 1949–1983, 3327

People, Love, Sex and Families, 5470

People of Darkness, 2053(F)

The People of Pern, 3793

The People of the Deer, 7701

People of the Totem: Indians of the Pacific Northwest, 7792

People Waging Peace, 4153

People Who Dance: 22 Dancers Tell Their Own Stories, 5968

The People, Yes, 3322

Perelandra, 2645(F)

Perestroika: New Thinking for Our Country and the World, 7568

The Perfect Day, 2644(F)

The Perfect Puppy: How to Choose Your Dog by Its Behavior, 8720

A Perfect Spy, 167(F)

The Perfect 10, 2329(F)

The Perfect Term Paper: Step-by-Step, 4692

Perfecting Fiona, 2243(F)

Performers and Players, 5955

The Perigee Visual Dictionary of Signing, 5431

Peril and Promise: A Commentary on America, 8055

Peril Under the Palms, 1926(F)

The Perilous Gard, 1249(F)

Period Costume for Stage & Screen: Patterns for Women's Dress, 1500–1800, 5282

Perish in July, 2043(F)

Peron, 6884

Perpetual Check, 2047(F)

Perry Mason in the Case of the Burning Bequest, 1946(F)

Perry Mason in the Case of Too Many Murders, 1946(F)

The Persian Boy, 1371(F)

The Personal Computer, 9020

The Personal Computer Book, 9001

Personal Fouls, 9723

Personhood, 5556

Persuasion, 332(F)

Pesticide Alert: A Guide to Pesticides in Fruit and Vegetables, 5421

Pet Sematary, 1790(F)

Petals on the Wind, 1707(F)

Peter Camenzind, 836(F)

Peter the Great, 6869

Peter the Great: His Life and World, 6868

Petersen's Basic How to Tune Your Car, 9107

Peterson First Guide to Fishes of North America, 8625

Peterson First Guide to Insects of North America, 8597

Peterson First Guide to Mammals of North America, 8488

Peterson First Guide to Shells of North America, 8637

Peterson's Guide to College Admissions: Getting into the College of Your Choice, 4772

Peterson's Handbook for College Admissions: A Family Guide, 4741

Phaedra, 3015

Phantoms, 1757(F), 1797(F)

Phenomenon: Forty Years of Flying Saucers, 9532

Philip K. Dick, 3756

Philip Larkin: Collected Poems, 3230

Phoenix Rising: Or, How to Survive Your Life, 665(F)

The Photographer's Bible: An Encyclopedic Reference Manual, 9435

The Photographer's Idea Book: How to See and Take Better Pictures, 9436

Photographing Buildings and Cityscapes, 9434

Photographing Friends and Family, 9434

Photographing the Drama of Daily Life, 9434

Photographs That Changed the World, 5722

Photography and Art: Interactions since 1946, 5743

Photography in Focus, 9426

Photography Until Now, 5724

Photojournalism: The Visual Approach, 9425

Photonics: The New Science of Light, 8932

Phule's Company, 2391(F)

Phyllis Wheatley, 6326

Phylum Monsters, 2726(F)

The Physalia Incident, 2182(F)

Physical Evidence, 215(F)

The Physical World, 8404

Physician Power: New Vistas for Women in Medicine, 5004

The Physics of Baseball, 9620

The Piano: A Pictorial Account of Its Ancestry and Development, 5937

The Piano Bird, 2076(F)

Picasso, 5778

Picnic at Hanging Rock, 2087(F)

Pictorial Guide to the Planets, 8346

A Pictorial History of Science Fiction Films, 6054, 6057

A Pictorial History of the American Theater 1860–1985, 6079

A Pictorial History of the Civil War Years, 7887

Pictorial History of the Jewish People: From Bible Times to Our Own Day Throughout the World, 4385

Pictorial History of the North American Indian, 7830

A Pictorial History of the World War II Years, 7228

Pictor's Metamorphoses and Other Fantasies, 1151(F)

The Picture of Dorian Gray, 1867(F)

Picture Puzzles for the Super Smart, 8856

Pictures from an Institution, 683(F)

Pictures in the Dolphin Mind, 8623

Pieces of My Mind, 3509

Pies and Pastries, 9362

Pigeon Blood, 1912(F)

Pigeon Feathers, 2970(F)

Pigeons, 8683

The Pigman, 951(F)

Pilgrim at Tinker Creek, 8385

The Pilgrim's Progress, 337(F)

The Pillars of the Earth, 1380(F)

The Pimpernel Plot, 1147(F)

The Pink Triangle: The Nazi War against Homosexuals, 7270

Pioneer Women: Voices from the Kansas Frontier, 7985

The Pioneering Image: Celebrating 150 Years of American Photography, 5802

Pioneering Space: Living on the Next Threshold, 8314

The Pioneers, 393(F), 7956

Pioneers of Psychology, 5533

Pitchers Do Get Lonely and Other Sports Stories, 9550

The Place, 1872(F)

A Place among the Fallen, 2487(F)

A Place Called Hiroshima, 7243

A Place for Winter: Paul Tiulana's Story, 7707

The Place I Call Home: Faces and Voices of Homeless Teens, 4514

A Place of Your Own Making: How to Build a One-Room Cabin, Studio, Shack or Shed, 9293

A Place to Hide, 7(F)

The Plague, 637(F)

The Plague Dogs, 1002(F)

Plague Year, 932(F)

Plagues and Politics: The Story of the United States Public Health Service, 5078

Plain Jane, 2248(F)

Plain Speaking: An Oral Biography of Harry S. Truman, 6568

Plains Indian Mythology, 3425

The Plains Indians of the Twentieth Century, 7810

The Plains of Passage, 1349(F)

Planet Earth in Jeopardy: Environmental Consequences of Nuclear War, 4137

Planet of Exile, 2635(F)

Planet of the Apes, 2418(F)

The Planet That Wasn't, 8211

The Planets, 8347

The Planets: Exploring the Solar System, 8345

Planning Your Military Career, 4973

Plant Watching: How Plants Remember, Tell Time, Form Partnerships and More, 8449

The Plantagenet Chronicles, 7518

Plants That Eat Animals, 8442

Plato, 4008

Plato & Augustine, 4011

Platoon Leader, 8127

Play Better Golf: Vol. I, The Swing from A to Z, 9875

Play Better Golf: Vol. II, The Short Game and Scoring, 9875

Play Great Golf: Mastering the Fundamentals of Your Game, 9876

Play It! Over 400 Great Games for Groups, 9593

The Playboy of the Western World, 3044

The Player of Games, 2395(F)

Players' Choice: Major League Baseball Players Vote on the All-Time Greats, 9676

The Playground, 1873(F)

Playing for Pay: How to Be a Working Musician, 4882

Playing in the Band: An Oral and Visual Portrait of the Grateful Dead, 5864

Playing Murder, 2172(F)

Playing the Field: Why Defense Is the Most Fascinating Art in Major League Baseball, 9668

Playmates, 2125(F)

The Plays of Eugene O'Neill, 3837

Plays of Our Time, 3063

Please Don't Eat the Daisies, 3500

The Pleasures of Entomology: Portraits of Insects and the People Who Study Them, 8594

The PLO: The Rise and Fall of the Palestine Liberation Organization, 7590

The Plug-In Drug: Television, Children, and the Family, 6072

The Plumber, 4490

Plutarch's Lives, 6788

PMS: Premenstrual Syndrome and You, 5476

PMS: What Every Woman Should Know about Premenstrual Syndrome, 5498

Pocahontas, 6632

Pocho, 505(F)

The Pocket Book of Ogden Nash, 3306
The Pocket Dictionary of Signing, 5431
Pocket Guide to Astronomy, 8277
A Pocket History of the United States, 7770
Pocket Poems: Selected for a Journey, 3281
The Poem of the Cid, 3181
Poems, 3211
Poems and Sketches of E. B. White, 3560
Poems, 1960–1967, 3289
Poems, 1968–1972, 3290
The Poems of Dylan Thomas, 3229
Poems of Edgar Allan Poe, 3313
The Poems of Gerard Manley Hopkins, 3208
Poems of Lewis Carroll, 3197
Poems of Walt Whitman: Leaves of Grass, 3315
Poems That Live Forever, 3158
Poet in New York, 3182
The Poetical Works of Burns, 3195
The Poetical Works of Byron, 3196
The Poetical Works of Elizabeth Barrett Browning, 3192
The Poetical Works of Longfellow, 3292
The Poetical Works of Shelley, 3224
The Poetical Works of Tennyson, 3226
The Poetical Works of Whittier, 3343
The Poetical Works of Wordsworth, 3231
Poetics, 3846
Poetry Handbook: A Dictionary of Terms, 3851
The Poetry of Black America: Anthology of the 20th Century, 3236
The Poetry of Robert Frost, 3267
Poetry of the World Wars, 3159
The Poet's Dictionary: A Handbook of Prosody and Poetic Devices, 3855
The Poet's Handbook, 3854
Poetspeak: In Their Work, about Their Work, 3282

Point of Departure, 821(F)
Point of Order: A Profile of Senator Joe McCarthy, 6602
Points of View, 2947(F)
The Poison Factory, 1933(F)
The Poison Oracle, 1981(F)
Poland, 1450(F)
Poles Apart: The Natural Worlds of the Arctic and Antarctic, 7694
Police State: Could It Happen Here? 4540
The Policeman's Beard Is Half Constructed, 3849
The Political Spectrum, 4263
Politics, 3994
The Politics of Food: The Decline of Agriculture and the Rise of Agribusiness in America, 8586
The Politics of Recovery: Roosevelt's New Deal, 8039
Politics, Reform and Expansion, 1890–1900, 8008
Polling and the Public: What Every Citizen Should Know, 5590
Poltergeist: A Study in Destructive Haunting, 9543
The Pond, 8620
Pond Life, 8619
Pony Express, 7976
Poodles, 8740
The Pool of St. Branok, 2240(F)
Poor and Minority Health Care, 5077
The Poorhouse Fair, 748(F)
Pop Art, 5751
Pop Culture Mania, 9452
Popcorn Days and Buttermilk Nights, 897(F)
The Popcorn Project, 2232(F)
Pope John XXIII: Shepherd of the Modern World, 6852
The Population Explosion, 4458
Pork, 9361
Pornography and Sexual Violence, 4524
The Portable Arthur Miller, 3107
The Portable Bernard Shaw, 3134
The Portable Blake, 3152
The Portable Chaucer, 340
The Portable Coleridge, 3154
The Portable Conrad, 347
The Portable Curmudgeon, 3518

The Portable D. H. Lawrence, 376
The Portable Dante, 3861
The Portable Emerson, 3533
The Portable Graham Greene, 111
The Portable Greek Reader, 2893
The Portable Milton, 3219
The Portable Nietzsche, 4017
The Portable North American Indian Reader, 3428
The Portable Oscar Wilde, 388
The Portable Roman Reader, 2909
The Portable Saul Bellow, 955(F)
The Portable Sherwood Anderson, 390
The Portable Steinbeck, 419
The Portable Tolstoy, 321
The Portable Twentieth-Century Russian Reader, 2897
The Portable Voltaire, 329
The Portable World Bible, 4032
Portal: A Dataspace Retrieval, 1282(F)
The Portfolios of Ansel Adams, 5789
Portrait Gallery, 5964
The Portrait of a Lady, 406(F)
Portrait of an Artist: A Biography of Georgia O'Keeffe, 6200
Portrait of Jennie, 2307(F)
A Portrait of the Artist as a Young Man, 850(F)
Portrait of the Soviet Union, 7575
Portraits in Silicon, 6646
Possession, 1772(F)
The Possible Human: A Course in Extending Your Physical, Mental, and Creative Abilities, 5353
Post-Impressionism: From Van Gogh to Gauguin, 5760
Post-Impressionists, 5771
Post Mortem, 1816(F)
Postal Service Guide to U.S. Stamps, 9459
The Postman, 2436(F)
The Postman Always Rings Twice, 1940(F)
Postmarked the Stars, 2716(F)
Poultry, 9361
Poverty, 4504

Power: A Political History of the Twentieth Century, 7154

The Power and the Glory, 670(F)

Power Golf, 9869

The Power Hitters, 9656

The Power of Horses and Other Stories, 1500(F)

The Power of One, 957(F)

The Power of the Powerless: A Brother's Legacy of Love, 5433

The Power That Preserves, 1095(F)

Powerlifting: A Scientific Approach, 9771

Powers of Congress, 4228

Powers of Nature, 8787

Powershift: Knowledge, Wealth, and Violence at the Edge of the 21st Century, 7342

The Practical Archaeologist, 7020

Practical Astronomy, 8256

The Practical Fisherman, 9832

The Practical Guide to Calligraphy, 9160

The Practical Guide to Dog and Puppy Care, 8717

A Practical Guide to Selecting a Small Dog, 8731

Practical Things to Do with a Microcomputer, 9018

The Practice Effect, 2437(F)

Practice for the Armed Forces Tests, 4980

The Practice of the Wild, 3550

Practice to Deceive, 1486(F)

Practicing History: Selected Essays, 7078

The Prairie, 393(F)

A Prairie Home Companion Folk Song Book, 5950

Prairie-Town Boy, 6302

The Praise Singer, 1374(F)

The Preacher's Kid, 1898(F)

Precious Bane, 618(F)

Predatory Dinosaurs of the World, 6984

Predicting AIDS and Other Epidemics, 5197

Predicting Nuclear and Other Technological Disasters, 8925

Pregnancy and Birth, 5465

Pregnancy & Childbirth: The Complete Guide for a New Life, 5467

Pregnant and Single: Help for the Tough Choices, 5515

Pregnant Too Soon: Adoption Is an Option, 5478

Prelude to Chaos, 2648(F)

Prelude to Foundation, 2370(F)

Prelude to War, 7167

The Premier Book of Major Poets, 3156

Prentice Alvin, 2459(F)

Preparation for the ACT, 4658

Preparation for the SAT, 4656

Preparing for Power: Oliver Tambo Speaks, 7385

Prescription for Better Home Video Movies: How to Avoid the Most Common Mistakes, 6012

Prescription Narcotics: The Addictive Painkillers, 5151

Presenting Judy Blume, 3789

Presenting M. E. Kerr, 3762

Presenting Norma Fox Mazer, 3739

Presenting Norma Klein, 6277

Presenting Paul Zindel, 6333

Presenting Richard Peck, 3726

Presenting Robert Cormier, 3708

Presenting Rosa Guy, 6251

Presenting S. E. Hinton, 3713

Presenting Sue Ellen Bridgers, 3737

Presenting Walter Dean Myers, 3700

Preserving America's Past, 7768

The Presidency and the Political System, 4209

The Presidency of Dwight D. Eisenhower, 8087

The Presidency of Harry S. Truman, 8079

The Presidency of Lyndon B. Johnson, 8048

The President and the Constitution, 4210

Presidential Anecdotes, 4206

Presidential Campaigns, 4275

The Presidential Contest, 4279

Presidential Elections Since 1789, 4278

Presidential Wives, 6463

The Presidents: A Reference History, 6470

The President's Lady, 1529(F)

The Press and the Presidency: From George Washington to Ronald Reagan, 4213

Press On! Further Adventures in the Good Life, 6166

The Price of the Ticket: Collected Nonfiction, 1948–1985, 3522

Pride, 301(F)

Pride against Prejudice: The Biography of Larry Doby, 6717

Pride and Prejudice, 331(F)

The Pride and the Anguish, 1673(F)

The Pride of Chanur, 2474(F)

Priestesses, 4052

Prime Directive, 2752(F)

The Prime of Miss Jean Brodie, 922(F)

Prime Suspects #1, 2145(F)

A Primer of Fly-Fishing, 9812

Primitive Worlds, 7010

Primitive Worlds: People Lost in Time, 7009

The Prince, 4014

The Prince and the Pauper, 426(F)

Prince of the Blood, 1117(F)

The Prince of Tides, 536(F)

Prince Ombra, 1209(F)

The Princess and the Thorn, 1120(F)

The Princess Bride: S. Morgenstern's Classic Tale of True Love and High Adventure, 1133(F)

The Princess of Celle, 1461(F)

A Princess of Mars, 2453(F)

A Princess of the Chameln, 1322(F)

The Princeton Review: College Admissions—Cracking the System, 4759

The Princeton Review—Cracking the System: The SAT and PSAT, 1990 Edition, 4664

The Princeton Review—Word Smart: Building an Educated Vocabulary, 3945

The Principles of Knitting: Methods and Techniques of Hand Knitting, 9241

The Principles of Technical Analysis, 4603

Print Your Own Pictures, 9429

Prison Life in America, 4482

Prisoner of War, 7070

The Prisoner of Zenda, 136(F)

Prisoner without a Name, Cell without a Number, 7688
Prisoners of Arionn, 2589(F)
Prisoners of War, 7177
Private Domain: The Autobiography of Paul Taylor, 6462
The Private Franklin: The Man and His Family, 6588
Privileged Ones, 4359
Prize Stories: The O. Henry Awards, 2890(F)
Prize Stories of the Seventies, 2891(F)
The Problem of Immigration, 4325
Problem Solving with BASIC, 9014
Problems of Africa: Opposing Viewpoints, 7358
Processes of Manufacturing, 8953
The Professional Baseball Trainers' Fitness Book, 9678
Profiles in Achievement, 6476
Profiles in Courage, 6479
Profiles of Pioneer Women Scientists, 6644
Programming for Microcomputers: Apple II BASIC, 9013
Projects for the Router, 9269
The Promise, 2323(F), 487(F)
The Promised Land, 6613
Promises Are for Keeping, 732(F)
Proof, 2018(F)
Property Of, 841(F)
The Prophet, 3347
The Prophet of Akhran, 1316(F)
Prophet of the Sandlots: Journeys with a Major League Scout, 9709
Prospects for Energy in America, 8918
Protect Your Legal Rights: A Handbook for Teenagers, 4296
Protecting the President: The Inside Story of a Secret Service Agent, 4224
The Proud Tower: A Portrait of the World before the War, 1890–1914, 7155
Proxopera: A Tale of Modern Ireland, 975(F)
Psion, 2817(F)
Psychic Animals: A Fascinating Investigation of Paranormal Behavior, 8473

The Psychic Detectives: The Story of Psychometry and Paranormal Crime Detection, 5328
Psychic Fair, 1815(F)
Psycho House, 1718(F)
The Psychology of Everyday Things, 5541
The Public Speaker's Treasure Chest, 4696
Publicity Stunt! Great Staged Events That Made the News, 3961
Pudd'nhead Wilson, 427(F)
Puerto Rico: A Political and Cultural History, 7664
Pulling Through, 2605(F)
Pumping Up! Super Shaping the Feminine Physique, 9777
Puppet Masters, 2587(F)
Pursuit to Appomattox, 7890
Putting Food By, 9340
Putting Heather Together Again, 701(F)
Putting It Together: Teenagers Talk about Family Breakups, 5666
Puzzles from Other Worlds, 8854
Puzzles of the Black Widowers, 1917(F)
Pygmalion, 3037
Pyramids, 1262(F)
The Pyramids, 5711
The Pyramids: An Enigma Solved, 7096
The Pyramids of Egypt, 7097

The Quade Inheritance, 2220(F)
Quag Keep, 2703(F)
The Quallsford Inheritance, 1928(F)
Quantum Web, 275(F)
Quarks: The Stuff of Matter, 8939
Quarrels That Have Shaped the Constitution, 4190
The Quarterbacks: The Uncensored Truth about Men in the Pocket, 9847
Queen in Waiting, 1462(F)
Queen of Angels, 2399(F)
The Queen of October, 580(F)
Queen of Sorcery, 1107(F)
Queen of the Summer Stars, 1489(F)
Queen Victoria, 6877

Queen Victoria: From Her Birth to the Death of the Prince Consort, 6878
The Queen's Gambit, 929(F)
The Queen's Head, 2108(F)
Queen's Play, 1425(F)
Quest: The Life of Elisabeth Kübler-Ross, 6682
Quest for Apollo, 1185(F)
Quest for Fire, 1354(F)
The Quest for Saint Camber, 1181(F)
Quest for the Past, 7069
Quest for the Well of Souls, 1067(F)
The Question of Max, 1978(F)
Questions & Answers on AIDS, 5184
Quiet Magic, 9555
The Quiet Rebels, 4031
Quilting for Beginners: Patchwork & Appliqué Projects for all Ages, 9239
Quilts! Quilts! Quilts! The Complete Guide to Quiltmaking, 9245
Quit & Win: The War of Cigarette Withdrawal Once and for All, 5133
Quitting Time, 52(F)
Quo Vadis, 1375(F)
Quozl, 2546(F)

R Is for Rocket, 1046(F)
Rabbit at Rest, 615(F)
Rabbit Is Rich, 615(F)
Rabbit Redux, 615(F)
Rabbit, Run, 615(F)
Raccoons: In Folklore, History & Today's Backyards, 8492
Race against Time, 2355(F)
Rachel and Her Children: Homeless Families in America, 4510
Rachel Carson, 6652
Racial Prejudice, 4347
Racing in Her Blood, 2871(F)
Racism: Opposing Viewpoints, 4345
Racquetball, 9544
Radical Departures: Desperate Detours to Growing Up, 4061
The RAF at War, 7179
The Ragged Astronauts, 2778(F)
Rags to Riches, 1618(F)

Ragtime, 1601(F)
Ragtime: Its History, Composers, and Music, 5868
Rail—The Records, 9120
The Railroaders, 7991
Rain or Shine, 6927
Rainbird's Revenge, 2246(F)
Rainbow in the Mist, 2215(F)
Rainbow Jordan, 450(F)
The Rainbow People, 3387
Rainbows Are Made, 3323
Rainsong, 2216(F)
Raise the Titanic, 67(F)
A Raisin in the Sun: A Drama in Three Acts, 3079
Raising Each Other, 5639
Raising Less Corn and More Hell: Midwestern Farmers Speak Out, 8591
Raising Turkeys, Ducks, Geese, Pigeons, and Guineas, 8589
Rakes and Rogues, 3811
Rake's Progress, 2247(F)
Ralph Ellison, 6244
Ralph Ellison: A Collection of Critical Essays, 3735
Ralph Waldo Emerson, 3611
Rama II, 2485(F)
The Ramayana: A Shortened Modern Prose Version of the Indian Epic, 3384(FF)
Ramona, 1503(F)
RAMS, ROMS & Robots: The Inside Story of Computers, 8988
The Ranchers, 7986
Random Harvest, 2280(F)
The Random House Book of Sports Stories, 2886(F)
The Random House Book of Twentieth-Century French Poetry, 3180
Random Winds, 2309(F)
Randy Travis: King of the New Country Traditionalists, 6448
Rape: What Would You Do If . . . ? 5504
Raphael, 1199(F)
Rapid Math without a Calculator, 8833
Raquela: A Woman of Israel, 6941
A Rare Benedictine, 2134(F)
Raspberry One, 1652(F)
Rats, Lice and History, 5227
Ravens in Winter: A Zoological Detective Story, 8556

The Rawhide Knot, and Other Stories, 1583(F)
Ray Bradbury, 6217
The Razor's Edge, 717(F)
Reach for Tomorrow, 2476(F)
Reader's Digest Complete Guide to Needlework, 9233
Reader's Digest Complete Guide to Sewing, 9249
Reader's Digest Crafts & Hobbies, 9150
Reader's Digest Family Safety & First Aid, 5445
Reader's Digest Guide to Creative Gardening, 9385
The Reader's Digest Illustrated Book of Dogs, 8734
Reader's Digest North American Wildlife, 8402
Reader's Digest Strange Stories, Amazing Facts of America's Past, 7774
Reader's Digest Visitor's Guide to the Great Barrier Reef, 7475
The Reader's Encyclopedia of the American West, 7960
A Reader's Guide to Fifty American Novels, 3765
A Reader's Guide to Gerard Manley Hopkins, 3869
Reading the Financial Pages, 4577
Reading the Numbers, 8864
Reading the River: A Voyage Down the Yukon, 6146
Reaganomics: Reagan's Economic Program, 8064
Real Animal Heroes: True Stories of Courage, Devotion and Sacrifice, 8682
Real Food, Fake Food—Everything in Between: The Only Consumer's Guide to Modern Food, 5415
A Real Job for You: An Employment Guide for Teens, 4799
Realm of Numbers, 8847
Reap the Whirlwind, 1073(F)
Reasonable Doubt: An Investigation into the Assassination of John F. Kennedy, 8071
Rebecca, 1995(F)
Rebel in Time, 2574(F)
Rebels & Yankees: The Fighting Men of the Civil War, 7910
Rebel's Choice, 2875(F)

Rebels Resurgent: Fredericksburg to Chancellorsville, 7917
Rebuilding Shakespeare's Globe, 3820
Recollections of a Life, 6592
Reconstruction: After the Civil War, 8009
The Recorder Book, 5943
Recording Your Family History: A Guide to Preserving Oral History, 5650
Recovering from Rape, 5513
Recruiting in Sports, 9589
The Red and the Black, 317(F)
Red Army Resurgent, 7330
The Red Badge of Courage, 3728, 395(F)
Red Branch, 1445(F)
Red Dawn at Lexington: "If They Mean to Have a War, Let It Begin Here!", 7847
Red Dragon, 2046(F)
Red Earth, White Earth, 510(F)
Red Giants and White Dwarfs, 8265
The Red Limit: The Search for the Edge of the Universe, 8364
Red Pandas: A Natural History, 8524
Red Phoenix, 18(F)
Red Planet, 2582(F)
The Red Pony, 300(F)
Red Power, 7814
Red Prophet, 1497(F)
The Red Sabbath, 218(F)
Red Sky at Morning, 775(F)
The Red Smith Reader, 9546
Red Star over China, 7430
Red Storm Rising, 45(F)
Red Sun of Darkover, 2434(F)
The Red Swan: Myths and Tales of the American Indian, 3359
Redcoat, 1520(F)
Redeeming the Time, 8042
Rediscovering America's Values, 4523
Rediscovering the Constitution, 4192
Reefs—Book II, 2723(F)
Reeves: An Autobiography, 6759
Refining Felicity, 2243(F)
Reflections of a Rock Lobster: A Story about Growing Up Gay, 5463

Reflections on a Gift of Watermelon Pickle . . . and Other Modern Verse, 3262

Reflections on Language, 3912

Reflections on the Civil War, 7897

Reflections on the Wall: The Vietnam Veterans Memorial, 8137

The Reformation, 7128

Reggae International, 5857

The Reign of Henry VIII: Personalities and Politics, 6844

Reilly: Ace of Spies, 6157

Reincarnation: Opposing Viewpoints, 9473

The Reivers, 82(F)

Relations: Selected Poems, 1950–1985, 3245

Relatively Speaking: Relativity, Black Holes, and the Fate of the Universe, 8251

The Relativity of Wrong, 8376

Religion and Politics: Issues in Religious Liberty, 4266

Religion in America: Opposing Viewpoints, 4029

Religion in America, 4035

Religions of America: Ferment and Faith in an Age of Crisis, 4079

Religions of Japan: Many Traditions within One Sacred Way, 4045

The Religions of Man, 4085

A Religious History of America, 4051

A Religious History of the American People, 4026

The Religious Right, 4267

Reliving Past Lives, 9541

Remarkable Animals: A Unique Encyclopaedia of Wildlife Wonders, 8479

Rembrandt, 5781

Remember Everything You Read: The Evelyn Wood Seven Day Speed Reading and Learning Program, 4646

Remember Me, 1822(F)

Remember Santiago, 1612(F)

Remember to Remember Me, 2299(F)

Remembering America: A Voice from the Sixties, 8065

Remembering Buddy: The Definitive Biography of Buddy Holly, 6406

Remembrance of Swings Past, 9675

The Renaissance, 7547

A Rendezvous in Averoigne: Best Fantastic Tales of Clark Ashton Smith, 1846(F)

Rendezvous with Rama, 2479(F)

The Renegades of Pern, 1204(F)

Renoir, 5783

Repeal of the Blues, 5957

Representative American Speeches, 1988–1989, 3544

Reptiles and Amphibians, 8467

Reptiles of North America, 8466

The Republic, 4021

A Republic of Rivers: Three Centuries of Nature Writing from Alaska and the Yukon, 8185

Research Shortcuts, 4649

Reserve Officers Training Corps: Campus Pathways to Service Commissions, 4726

The Resistance, 7330

Respect for Acting, 6088

The Response to Industrialism, 1885–1914, 8010

Responsibility, 5573

Rest You Merry, 2105(F)

The Restaurant at the End of the Universe, 2331(F)

Restaurateurs & Innkeepers, 4795

Restless Oceans, 8879

Restoring the Statue of Liberty: Sculpture, Structure, Symbol, 8166

The Resume Kit, 4784

Retakes: Behind the Scenes of 500 Classic Movies, 6007

Retaking the Philippines: America's Return to Corregidor and Bataan, July 1944–March 1945, 7189

Retief: Diplomat at Arms, 2626(F)

Retief to the Rescue, 2626(F)

The Return of Caulfield Blake, 277(F)

The Return of Halley's Comet, 8332

The Return of Nathan Brazil, 1067(F)

The Return of Retief, 2626(F)

The Return of Sherlock Holmes, 1987(F)

The Return of the Gypsy, 2241(F)

Return of the King, 2808(F)

The Return of the Native, 371(F)

Return to Eden, 2575(F)

Return to the Philippines, 7297

Reunion: A Memoir, 6508

Revenge of the Creature Features Movie Guide, 6064

The Revenge of the Hound: The New Sherlock Holmes Novel, 2042(F)

Reviving the Death Penalty, 4484

Revolt in 2100, 2583(F)

Revolution from Rosinante, 2559(F)

Revolution in Central America, 7653

The Revolutionary Age of Andrew Jackson, 7880

The Revolutionary War: America's Fight for Freedom, 7853

The Rhinemann Exchange, 186(F)

Rhinoceros and Other Plays, 3009

Rhinos: Endangered Species, 8578

Rich in Love, 845(F)

Richard Nixon: The Shaping of His Character, 6551

Richard Wright, 3696

Richard Wright: Ordeal of a Native Son, 6331

Richie, 612(F)

Richie Ashburn's Phillies Trivia, 9623

Rickie, 5379

The Riddle of the Dinosaur, 6987

The Riddle of the Sands: A Record of Secret Service, 41(F)

Riddley Walker, 2596(F)

Ride a Tall Horse, 218(F)

A Ride along the Great Wall, 7410

Ride for the High Points: The Real Story of Will James, 6271

Riders of the Monte, 267(F)

Riders of the Purple Sage, 1567(F)

Riders on the Storm: My Life with Jim Morrison and the Doors, 5859

Riding the Dragon's Back: The Race to Raft the Upper Yangtze, 9919
The Right Jewelry for You, 5271
The Right Job, 4811
The Right Moves, 852(F)
The Right On! Book of Hair Care and Beauty, 5284
The Right Place at the Right Time: Finding the Right Job in the New Economy, 4812
The Right Stuff, 8329
Right Stuff for New Hang Glider Pilots, 9612
The Right to Innocence: Healing the Trauma of Childhood Sexual Abuse, 5509
The Right to Privacy, 4309
The Right to Vote, 4295
The Rights of Free Men: An Essential Guide to Civil Liberties, 4292
The Rights of Gay People, 4320
The Rights of Man, 4018
The Rights of Man, the Reign of Terror: The Story of the French Revolution, 7490
The Rights of Racial Minorities, 4308
The Rights of Students: The Basic ACLU Guide to a Student's Rights, 4315
The Rights of Students and Teachers: Resolving Conflicts in the School Community, 4298
The Rights of Young People, 4303
The Ring, 2323(F), 2688(F)
Ring of Bright Water, 8477
A Ring of Endless Light, 572(F)
The Ring of Truth, 8225
The Ringed Castle, 1425(F)
Ringer, 251(F)
Ringmaster! My Year on the Road with "The Greatest Show on Earth", 5976
Ringo, the Robber Raccoon: The True Story of a Northwoods Rogue, 8493
Rings: Discoveries from Galileo to Voyager, 8343
Ringworld, 2697(F)
The Ringworld Engineers, 2697(F)
Ripper! 1751(F)

Rise and Fall of the Shah, 7623
The Rise and Fall of the Third Reich, 7507
The Rise of Industrial America, 8022
The Rise of Life, 7011
The Rise of the Chinese Republic: From the Last Emperor to Deng Xiaoping, 7412
The Rise of the Computer State, 8962
The Rise of the Greeks, 7103
The Rise of Theodore Roosevelt, 6565
Rise Up Singing, 5945
The Rising Sun, 7329
Risk, 2018(F)
A Risky Game, 914(F)
Risky Times: How to Be AIDS-Smart & Stay Healthy, 5173
Ritchie Valens: The First Latino Rocker, 6451
Rites of Passage, 2919(F)
The Rivals, 3040
River of Death, 198(F)
The River of Time, 2438(F)
River Runners: A Tale of Hardship and Bravery, 138(F)
A River Runs through It and Other Stories, 200(F)
River Song, 1508(F)
The River Why, 79(F)
The Rivermen, 7971
Rivers and Lakes, 8897
Road & Track's Used Car Classics: A Guide to Affordable Exciting Cars, 9081
The Road between the Wars: 1918–1941, 8030
The Road from Coorain, 6820
The Road to Gandolfo, 181(F)
The Road to Kitty Hawk, 9073
The Road to Paradise Island, 133(F)
The Road to Pearl Harbor, 7205
The Road to Shiloh: Early Battles in the West, 7929
The Road to Tokyo, 7320
Roadside America, 7715
Roadside Bicycle Repairs: The Simple Guide to Fixing Your Bike, 9767
Roadside Empires: How the

Chains Franchised America, 4617
Roadside Valentine, 2225(F)
Roald Dahl's Tales of the Unexpected, 1731(F)
The Robber Barons: The Great American Capitalists, 1861–1901, 6478
The Robe, 1367(F)
Robert A. Heinlein, 3782
Robert A. Heinlein: America as Science Fiction, 3720
Robert Browning's Poetry: Authoritative Texts, Criticism, 3194
Robert Frost, 3885, 6248
Robert Frost: A Collection of Critical Essays, 3881
Robert Fulton: A Biography, 6670
Robert Kennedy and His Times, 6628
Robert Louis Stevenson, 3688
Robert Louis Stevenson: A Life Study, 6317
Robert Penn Warren, 3778
Robert Silverberg's Worlds of Wonder: Exploring the Craft of Science Fiction, 2784
Robert the Bruce, King of Scots, 6871
Robert's Rules of Order, 5584
Robinson Crusoe, 350(F)
The Robot Builder's Bonanza: 99 Inexpensive Robotics Projects, 9000
Robot Dreams, 2371(F)
Robot Romance, 2643(F)
Robotics, 9019
Robotics Careers, 5059
Robots: Isaac Asimov's Wonderful Worlds of Science Fiction, #9, 2380(F)
Robots and Empire, 2372(F)
Robots at Dawn, 2372(F)
Robots, Machines in Man's Image, 8958
Rock and Roll: 1955–1970, 5848
Rock Facts, 5930
Rock Lives: Profiles and Interviews, 5907
Rock of Ages: The Rolling Stone History of Rock & Roll, 5905
Rock On: The Video Revolution, 5836
Rock On: The Solid Gold Years—Volume I, 5836

Rock On: The Years of Change—Volume II, 5836

The Rock Synthesizer Manual: A Revised Guide for the Electronic Musician, 5910

Rock Voices: The Best Lyrics of an Era, 5856

The Rock Who's Who, 5869

The Rockefeller Century, 6474

Rocket Man: The Roger Clemens Story, 6716

Rocket Ship Galileo, 2584(F)

The Rockies, 7962

Rocking Around the Clock: Music Television, Postmodernism & Consumer Culture, 5876

Rockonomics: The Money behind the Music, 5861

Rocks and Minerals, 8829

Rocks and Minerals: A Guide to Familiar Minerals, Gems, Ores, and Rocks, 8830

Rocks around the World, 9569

Rocks, Minerals & Fossils of the World, 8827

Rod Carew's Art and Science of Hitting, 9634

Rod Serling's Night Gallery Reader, 1842(F)

Rodale's Illustrated Encyclopedia of Herbs, 8418

Roe v. Wade, 4238

Roger Caras' Treasury of Great Cat Stories, 284(F)

Roger Caras' Treasury of Great Dog Stories, 285(F)

Roger Corman: The Best of the Cheap Acts, 6026

Roger Ebert's Home Movie Companion, 6008

Roger Maris: A Man for All Seasons, 6726

Roger Zelazny's Visual Guide to Castle Amber, 3794(F)

Rogue Male, 137(F)

Rogue Powers, 2338(F)

Role of Honor, 99(F)

Roll, Jordan, Roll: The World the Slaves Made, 7738

The Rolling Stone Encyclopedia of Rock & Roll, 5893

The Rolling Stone Illustrated History of Rock & Roll, 5890

The Rolling Stone Interviews: The 1980s, 5896

The Rolling Stone Jazz Record Guide, 5902

The Rolling Stones, 2584(F)

The Rolling Stones Chronicle: The First Thirty Years, 5844

Roman, 1574(F)

Roman Architecture, 5772

Roman Literature and Society, 3596

Roman Mythology, 3464

The Roman Way, 7115

The Roman World, 7121

Romance! Can You Survive It? A Guide to Sticky Dating Situations, 5629

The Romantic Obsessions and Humiliations of Annie Schlmeier, 901(F)

The Romantic Rebellion: Romantic versus Classic Art, 5736

Rome: The Biography of a City, 7549

Romeo and Juliet, 3059

Romeo and Juliet: Plainspoken, 3050

Romeo and Juliet and West Side Story, 2983

The Ron Van Clief Green & Purple Belt Guide Book, 9905

The Ron Van Clief White Belt Guide Book, 9905

Ronald Reagan, 6554

Roofworld, 1749(F)

A Room with a View, 809(F)

Roots, 6472

Rosalind Franklin and DNA, 6669

Rose Cottingham, 1480(F)

Rose Wilder Lane: Her Story, 6278

Roseanne: My Life as a Woman, 6366

Rosemary's Baby, 1802(F)

The Rosen Photo Guide to a Career in Animal Care, 4997

The Rosen Photo Guide to a Career in Health and Fitness, 4994

The Rosen Photo Guide to a Career in Magic, 4902

The Rosen Photo Guide to a Career in the Circus, 4890

The Rosenberg File: A Search for the Truth, 4250

Rosencrantz and Guildenstern Are Dead, 3043

Roughing It, 3517

Rousseau and Revolution, 7145

Row This Boat Ashore, 735(F)

The Rowan, 2667(F)

Rubaiyat of Omar Khayyam, 3352

Rubber Legs and White Tail-Hairs, 1893(F)

Rubber Stamps and How to Make Them, 9151

Ruby in the Smoke, 231(F)

Rudyard Kipling, 3585

Rudyard Kipling's Verse, 3215

The Rule Book, 9558

Ruling Passion, 2049(F)

A Rumor of War, 8052

Rumor Verified, 3339

Rumpole and the Age of Miracles, 2114(F)

Rumpole of the Bailey, 2115(F)

Run, Shelley, Run! 736(F)

Run with the Horsemen, 1630(F)

Runaway Teens, 4462

Runaways: In Their Own Words, 4501

Runes of the Lyre, 1219(F)

The Runner, 616(F)

The Runner's Handbook, 9911

Running Free: A Book for Women Runners and Their Friends, 9916

Running Mates: The Image and Reality of the First Lady Role, 4207

Running MS DOS, 9032

Running the Amazon, 7676

Running Tide, 6764

Running West, 1493(F)

Running with the Fox, 8518

Rupert of Hentzau, 136(F)

Rusalka, 1071(F)

The Rushdie File, 3647

Russia: Broken Idols, Solemn Dreams, 7583

Russia and the Russians: Inside the Closed Society, 7571

Russia Besieged, 7181

Russia from the Inside, 7569

The Russia House, 168(F)

Russian Folk Tales, 3388

Russian Journal, 7574

The Russians, 7585

A Rustle in the Grass, 290(F)

Rusty's Story, 5185

Ryan Rides Back, 1974(F)

Saberhagen: My Best, 2765(F)

Sacajawea, 6635

Sacred Cows . . . and Other Edibles, 3534

The Sacred Path: Spells, Prayers and Power Songs of the American Indians, 3420

Safe at Home: A Baseball Wife's Story, 9651

Safe, Strong, and Streetwise, 5501

Saga of the American Flag: An Illustrated History, 7731

The Sail Magazine Book of Sailing, 9929

Sailing: The Basics, 9925

Sailing for Beginners, 9939

The Sailing Lifestyle: A Guide to Sailing and Cruising for Pleasure, 9936

Sailing School, 9937

Sailing Ships, 9122

Sailing "the Annapolis Way", 9920

Saint Camber, 1175(F)

Saint Joan, 3038

Saint Joan, Major Barbara, Androcles and the Lion, 3039

Saints, Signs and Symbols, 4071

Salads, 9364

Salmagundi, 2258(F)

Saltmaker, 234(F)

Salvation and Suicide, 4042

The Salzburg Connection, 196(F)

Sam Patch: Ballad of a Jumping Man, 287(F)

Samuel Adams's Revolution, 1765–1776, 7848

San Andreas, 1665(F)

San Diego Lightfoot Sue and Other Stories, 2749(F)

The Sandbox and Death of Bessie Smith, 3060

The Sandman's Eyes, 2222(F)

Santa Fe: The Autobiography of a Southwestern Town, 8200

Santiago: A Myth of the Far Future, 2755(F)

Santorini, 199(F)

Sara Will, 633(F)

Sarah Cobb, 2147(F)

Saratoga Trunk, 1565(F)

Sarum: The Novel of England, 1467(F)

Sassinak, 2668(F)

SAT Success, 4665

Saturday Afternoon: College

Football and the Men Who Made the Day, 9864

Saturday Night, 2282(F)

Saturday the Rabbi Went Hungry, 2081(F)

Saturnalia, 2457(F)

Sauces, 9364

Saul Bellow, 3717

Savage Pellucidar, 2449(F), 2452(F)

Save the Birds, 8579

Saving the Earth: A Citizen's Guide to Environmental Action, 4445

Saving the Fragments, 7236

Savings and Loan, 2100(F)

The Savior, 1318(F)

Say Hey: The Autobiography of Willie Mays, 6727

Sayonara, 1402(F)

Scaling the Ivy Wall, 4740

Scandinavia, 7553

Scandinavian Mythology, 3397

The Scapegoat, 1995(F)

The Scarlatti Inheritance, 187(F)

The Scarlet Letter, 401(F)

The Scarlet Letter: A Reading, 3697

The Scarlet Pimpernel, 1455(F)

The Scarlet Thread, 8(F)

Scarne on Card Tricks, 9400

Scarred Man, 2136(F)

Scavenger Hunt, 1822(F)

Scene Design and Stage Lighting, 6104

Scenery for the Theatre, 6083

Scent of Cloves, 1446(F)

Scharansky: Hero of Our Time, 6947

Schindler's List, 1662(F)

The Schirmer Inheritance, 4(F)

Schirra's Space, 6159

Schizophrenia, 5407

Scholars and Priests, 4626

The School, 1874(F)

The School for Scandal, 3041

The School of Visual Arts Guide to Careers, 4889

The Schooling of the Horse, 8769

The Schools We Deserve: Reflections on the Educational Crises of Our Times, 4633

Schumann, 6353

Science: Its History and Development Among the World's Cultures, 8231

Science & Religion: Opposing Viewpoints, 4076

Science Ethics, 4526

Science Fair: Developing a Successful and Fun Project, 8243

Science Fiction: History, Science, Vision, 3630

The Science Fiction Hall of Fame, 2785(F)

The Science Fiction of H. G. Wells, 3676

The Science Fiction of Mark Twain, 428(F)

Science Fiction Writers, 3616

The Science in Science Fiction, 8226

Science Made Stupid: How to Discomprehend the World Around Us, 8237

The Science of Hitting, 9707

Science with Computers, 8239

Scientist at the Seashore, 8884

Scientists and Technologists, 8219

The Scions of Shannara, 1060(F)

Scorpio, 2672(F)

Scorpius, 100(F)

Scott Hamilton, 6776

Scott of the Antarctic, 6160

Scott Standard Postage Stamp Catalogue, 9462

The Scottish Chiefs, 1465(F)

Scoundrel Time, 6256

The Scouts, 8000

The Scramble for Africa, 7359

A Scrap of Time: And Other Stories, 1653(F)

The Screaming Skull, 9542

The Screenplay: A Blending of Film Form and Film Content, 6035

The Screwtape Letters, 4062

Scripts People Live: Transactional Analysis of Life Scripts, 5551

Scroll Saw Puzzle Patterns, 9290

The Sea around Us, 8875

Sea Change, 528(F)

The Sea Hag, 1103(F)

Sea Mammals of the World, 8656

Sea of Glass, 2650(F)

Sea of Slaughter, 8577

The Sea Runners, 1421(F)

Sea Siege, 2717(F)

The Sea-Wolf, 410(F)

Seabirds of the World, 8538

The Search, 8379

The Search for Mavin Manyshaped, 1294(F)

The Search for Meaning: Americans Talk about What They Believe and Why, 4037

The Search for Modern China, 7432

The Searcher, 1581(F)

Searching for Comets: Deciphering the Secrets of Our Cosmic Past, 8331

Searching for Your Ancestors, 5647

Seashells of North America: A Guide to Field Identification, 8635

Seashells of the World, 8636

Seashores, 8885

A Season Inside: One Year in College Basketball, 9719

Season of Glory: The Amazing Saga of the 1961 New York Yankees, 9659

Season of Passion, 2323(F)

Season of Yellow Leaf, 1504(F)

Season Ticket: A Baseball Companion, 9622

Seasons in the Sun, 3294

Seasons of Life: Our Dramatic Journey from Birth to Death, 5525

Seasons of the Seal, 8641

Seawitch, 1665(F)

The Second Black Lizard Anthology of Crime Fiction, 2026(F)

The Second Book of the Lost Swords: Sightbinder's Story, 1260(F)

Second Contact, 2756(F)

The Second Creation: Makers of the Revolution in Twentieth-Century Physics, 8906

A Second Flowering: Works and Days of the Lost Generation, 3711

Second Foundation, 2364(F)

The Second Front, 7186

The Second Self: Computers and the Human Spirit, 9025

The Second Sex, 4535

Second Time Around, 2101(F)

The Second World War: An Illustrated History, 7306

The Secret Arts, 9536

Secret Democracy: Civil Liberties vs. the National Security State, 4310

The Secret Diary of Adrian Mole, Age Thirteen and Three Quarters, 1906(F)

Secret for a Nightingale, 2284(F)

Secret Go the Wolves, 8515

The Secret Government: The Constitution in Crisis, 4525

The Secret House, 8213

The Secret of Van Rink's Cellar, 1523(F)

Secret Scars: A Guide for Survivors of Child Sexual Abuse, 5520

The Secret Sharer, 2786(F)

The Secret War, 7279

Secret Ways, 197(F)

The Secret Worlds of Colin Fletcher, 8390

The Secretary's Quick Reference Handbook, 4640

Secrets Not Meant to Be Kept, 719(F)

Secrets of the Supernatural: Investigating the World's Occult Mysteries, 9520

Secrets of the Temple: How the Federal Reserve Runs the Country, 4221

Secrets, Spies, and Scholars: Blueprint of the Essential CIA, 4215

Secrets Told by Children of Alcoholics, 5131

The Securities and Exchange Commission, 4223

See How They Run: Electing the President in an Age of Mediaocracy, 4212

See You Later Alligator, 29(F)

Seed of Sarah: Memoirs of a Girlhood, 7227

Seeds of Yesterday, 1707(F)

Seeing the Sky: 100 Projects, Activities & Explorations in Astronomy, 8244

The Seekers, 2527(F)

Seekers and Saviors, 3374

The Selected Letters of Mark Twain, 6323

Selected Poems, 3239, 3244, 3246, 3250, 3293, 3314, 3318, 3350, 3354, 3863

Selected Poems of Edwin Arlington Robinson, 3320

Selected Poems of Langston Hughes, 3279

Selected Poems of Rainer Maria Rilke, 3186

Selected Poetry and Prose, 418

Selected Short Stories, 307(F)

Selected Short Stories of William Faulkner, 2913(F)

Selected Stories, 963(F)

Selective Guide to Colleges, 4735

Self-Defense: A Basic Course, 9902

Self-Defense & Assault Prevention for Girls & Women, 9903

Self-Defense for Women: How to Stay Safe and Fight Back, 5444

Self-Made Women, 4572

Sell Your Photographs: The Complete Marketing Strategy for the Freelancer, 9411

Selma, Lord, Selma: Girlhood Memories of the Civil-Rights Days, 4381

A Semester in the Life of a Garbage Bag, 1887(F)

Seminole Skies, 1507(F)

Semites and Anti-Semites: An Inquiry into Conflict and Prejudice, 4387

Sense and Sensibility, 332(F)

Senses and Sensibilities, 5333

Sentience, 2333(F)

The Sentinel, 2476(F)

Sentries, 988(F)

A Separate Peace, 863(F)

Separation of Church and State: Guarantor of Religious Freedoms, 4179

September, 588(F)

Serendipity: Accidental Discoveries in Science, 8230

Serengeti: Natural Order on the African Plain, 7363

The Series, 9658

The Serpent Mage, 1032(F)

Set Up Your Home Studio, 9434

SETI Pioneers: Scientists Talk about Their Search for Extraterrestrial Intelligence, 8324

Setting Limits: Medical Goals in an Aging Society, 4467

The 7-Day Afghan Book, 9243

The Seven Day Circle: The

History and Meaning of the Week, 8862
Seven Days to Petrograd, 144(F)
Seven Famous Greek Plays, 3013
Seven Gothic Tales, 1736(F)
Seven Ideas That Shook the Universe, 8915
The Seven Mountains of Thomas Merton, 6629
Seven of Swords, 1100(F)
Seven Pillars of Wisdom, 7159
Seven Science Fiction Novels, 2832(F)
Seven Suspects, 1947(F)
Seven Tears for Apollo, 2211(F), 2213(F)
Seven Thousand Days in Siberia, 6954
The Seven Towers, 1337(F)
Seven Women: Portraits from the American Radical Tradition, 6483
The Seventh Secret, 266(F)
Seventh Son, 1065(F)
The Seventh Swan, 1134(F)
The Seventies: From Hotpants to Hot Tubs, 8059
73 Poems, 3255
Sew a Beautiful Gift, 9254
Sew It Yourself Home Decorating: Creative Ideas for Beautiful Interiors, 9251
The Sewing Book: A Complete Practical Guide, 9242
Sewing Essentials, 9255
Sewing for Style: Details and Techniques beyond the Basics, 9255
Sex & Birth Control: A Guide for the Young, 5477
Sex, Drugs and AIDS, 5222
Sex Education, 542(F)
Sex in Nature, 8384
Sexual Values: Opposing Viewpoints, 5488
Sexually Transmitted Diseases, 5172, 5199
Sez Who? Sez Me, 3547
Shabano, 7671
Shackles, 2141(F)
Shade of the Tree, 1709(F)
Shadow behind the Curtain, 2072(F)
Shadow Flight, 269(F)
Shadow Hawk, 1362(F)
Shadow in the North, 231(F)
Shadow Lord, 2857(F)

Shadow Man, 2085(F)
Shadow Mountain, 601(F)
Shadow of the Moon, 1395(F)
The Shadow of the Torturer, 1331(F)
The Shadow Warrior, 1347(F)
Shadow World, 2497(F)
Shadowfane, 2855(F)
Shadows, 1752(F)
Shadows across the Sand, 1983(F)
Shadows across the Sun, 870(F)
Shadows 8, 1755(F)
Shadows of the Indian: Stereotypes in American Culture, 4393
Shadows on the Rock, 1491(F)
Shadows on the Tundra: Alaskan Tales of Predators, Prey and Man, 8191
Shahhat: An Egyptian, 6950
Shaker, Why Don't You Sing? 3237
The Shakers and the World's People, 4067
Shakespeare: An Illustrated Dictionary, 3831
Shakespeare: The Globe & The World, 3826
Shakespeare and His Theatre, 3816
A Shakespeare Glossary, 3824
The Shakespeare Handbook, 3817
Shakespeare of London, 6304
Shakespeare Stories, 3819
Shakespeare the Man, 6306
Shakespeare's Comedies, 3829
Shakespeare's English Kings, 3825
Shakespeare's Imagery and What It Tells Us, 3828
Shakespeare's Planet, 2789(F)
Shakespeare's Theatre, 6091
Shall We Tell the President? 10(F)
Shaman, 1222(F)
Shane, 1588(F)
Shanidar, 122(F)
The Shape Changer, 2627(F)
The Shape of Dread, 2117(F)
The Shape of Love, 6412
The Shape of Music: An Introduction to Form in Classical Music, 5830
The Shaping of America: A People's History of the Young Republic, 7860

The Shaping of Black America, 4356
The Shaping of Middle-Earth, 3692
Sharing Traditions: Five Black Artists in Nineteenth-Century America, 5797
Shark: A Photographer's Story, 8632
Sharks, 8634
Sharks: An Introduction for the Amateur Naturalist, 8629
Sharks: Silent Hunters of the Deep, 8630
Sharks in Question: The Smithsonian Answer Book, 8631
Sharks of the World, 8633
Sharpe's Eagle, 1414(F)
Sharpe's Enemy, 1414(F)
Sharpe's Gold, 1414(F)
Sharpe's Regiment, 1414(F)
Sharpe's Revenge, 1414(F)
Sharpe's Siege, 1415(F)
Sharpshod and They Called Him a Killer, 219(F)
Sharra's Exile, 1050(F)
Shattered Silk, 2112(F)
The Shattered World, 1254(F)
Shawnee Dawn, 1507(F)
She, 115(F)
She Who Remembers, 1511(F)
Sheila's Dying, 639(F)
Shellfish, 9361
Shelter for a Seabird, 804(F)
The Shenandoah in Flames, 7943
The Shepherd, 1634(F)
Sheriff Pat Garrett's Last Days, 7881
Sherlock Holmes: The Complete Novels and Stories, 363(F)
Sherlock Holmes and the Case of the Raleigh Legacy, 2034(F)
Sherlock Holmes vs. Dracula: Or, The Adventure of the Sanguinary Count, 1744(F)
Sherlock Holmes's London: Following the Footsteps of London's Master Detective, 3674
Sherman's March, 7905
Sherman's March: Atlanta to the Sea, 7930
The Sherwood Ring, 1249(F)
The Shield of Time, 1007(F)
The Shining, 1791(F)
The Shining Falcon, 1267(F)

A Shining Season, 6762

A Ship Must Die, 1673(F)

Ships and Aircraft of the U.S. Fleet, 9133

Ships of the U.S. Navy, 9130

Shirley Jackson, 3724

Shivering Sands, 134(F)

Shoah, 7233

Shockwave Rider, 2442(F)

Shoeless Joe, 2879(F)

Shoemaker, 6781

Shogun, 1390(F)

Shooting from the Lip, 9582

Shooting War, 9431

Shoplifting: The Crime Everybody Pays For, 4475

A Short Guide to Shakespeare, 3814

A Short History of Africa, 7357

A Short History of Chemistry, 8780

A Short History of Glass, 8955

A Short History of Ireland, 7531

A Short History of Spanish Literature, 3604

A Short History of the Korean War, 8144

A Short History of the Movies, 6031

A Short History of the Vietnam War, 8132

A Short History of World War I, 7162

A Short History of World War II, 7302

Short Season and Other Stories, 2880(F)

The Short Stories of Ernest Hemingway, 2922(F)

The Short Stories of Katherine Mansfield, 2942(F)

The Short Story in English, 3613

Short Story Masterpieces, 2971(F)

Short Story Writers and Their Work, 3622

The Shorter Cambridge Medieval History, 7139

A Shorter History of Greek Art, 5762

Shosha, 1472(F)

Shout! The Beatles in Their Generation, 6356

Show Boat, 1604(F)

Show Me a Hero, 60(F)

Show Me No Mercy, 726(F)

Show Time: Inside the Lakers Breakthrough Season, 6708

Shrapnel in the Heart: Letters and Remembrances from the Vietnam Memorial, 8136

Shroud for a Nightingale, 2068(F)

Shuttle Challenger, 8321

Shy? (You Don't Have to Be), 5609

Shyness, 5636

Siddhartha, 1394(F)

Side by Side, 2286(F)

Sideshow, 2806(F)

Sideshow: Kissinger, Nixon and the Destruction of Cambodia, 7463

The Siege: The Saga of Israel and Zionism, 7614

The Sierra Club Guides to the National Parks of the Desert Southwest, 8198

The Sierra Club Guides to the National Parks of the Pacific Southwest and Hawaii, 8178

The Sierra Club Guides to the National Parks of the Rocky Mountains and the Great Plains, 8157

The Sierra Club Handbook of Whales and Dolphins, 8654

A Sierra Club Naturalist's Guide to the North Atlantic Coast: Cape Cod to Newfoundland, 8378

The Sierra Nevada: A Mountain Journey, 8187

Sight of Proteus, 2779(F)

Sightseeing: A Space Panorama, 8318

The Sign of the Four, 1992(F)

The Sign of the Unicorn, 1344(F)

Signal: Communication Tools for the Information Age—A Whole Earth Catalog, 8991

The Signet Classic Book of American Short Stories, 2956(F)

The Signet Classic Book of Contemporary Short Stories, 2956(F)

Significant Sisters: The Grassroots of Active Feminism, 1839–1939, 6784

Signing: How to Speak with Your Hands, 5432

Signs of Chaos, 2869(F)

The Signs of Our Times: Semiotics, 5549

Silas Marner, 365(F)

The Silent Clowns, 6023

Silent Dancing: A Partial Remembrance of a Puerto Rican Childhood, 2905

Silent Grief: Living in the Wake of Suicide, 5091

Silent Spring, 4424

Silent Spring Revisited, 4424

The Silent Tower, 1139(F)

The Silent Twins, 5571

The Silent World, 8888

The Silicon Mage, 1140(F)

The Silk Road: A History, 7042

The Silk Vendetta, 2285(F)

The Silmarillion, 1297(F)

Silver: The Life Story of an Atlantic Salmon, 8626

The Silver Branch: A Novel of the Keltiad, 2613(F)

The Silver Crown, 1256(F)

The Silver Kiss, 1794(F)

Silver Pigs, 1366(F)

Silver Scream, 1839(F)

Silverlock, 1229(F)

Silversword, 2217(F)

Silverthorn, 1118(F)

Simon and Garfunkel, 5949

The Simon & Schuster Complete Guide to Home Repair and Maintenance, 9390

Simon and Schuster's Guide to Cats, 8701

Simon & Schuster's Guide to Dogs, 8733

Simon & Schuster's Guide to Fossils, 6973

Simon and Schuster's Guide to Garden Flowers, 9383

Simon & Schuster's Guide to House Plants, 9374

Simon and Schuster's Guide to Mammals, 8489

Simon and Schuster's Guide to Pet Birds, 8684

Simon Pure, 1905(F)

Simple Foods for the Pack, 9311

Simple Gifts, 555(F)

Simple Puppets You Can Make, 9146

Since Yesterday: The Nineteen-Thirties in America, 8025

Sinclair Lewis, 3730, 3752

Singin' and Swingin' and

Gettin' Merry Like Christmas, 6212
Singing Sands, 2193(F)
The Singing Stones, 2218(F)
A Single Pebble, 1393(F)
Sinless Season, 812(F)
Sir Gawain and the Green Knight, 3190, 3413
Sister Carrie, 800(F)
Sister Kate, 521(F)
Sister Light, Sister Dark, 1341(F)
The Sisterhood: The True Story of the Women Who Changed the World, 4294
Sisters in Crime, 2208(F)
Sisters in Crime 2, 2208(F)
Sitting Bull, Champion of the Sioux, 6636
The Sivananda Companion to Yoga, 5363
Six Centuries of Verse, 3873
Six Existentialist Thinkers, 3997
Six Great Modern Short Novels, 2962(F)
A Six-Letter Word for Death, 2116(F)
Six Modern American Plays, 3077
Six Modern British Novelists, 3690
Six of Swords, 1101(F)
A Six-Pack and a Fake I.D. 5108
Six Plays, 3102
Six Plays by Lillian Hellman, 3081
Sixteen: Short Stories by Outstanding Writers for Young Adults, 813(F)
The Sixties: Years of Hope, Days of Rage, 8062
60s! 8072
Sixties People, 8089
60 Years of the Oscar: The Official History of the Academy Awards, 6043
Sizing Up: Fashion, Fitness, and Self-Esteem for Full-Figured Women, 5281
Skeeball and the Secret of the Universe, 826(F)
A Skeleton in the Darkroom: Stories of Serendipity in Science, 8233
The Skeleton in the Grass, 1922(F)
Skeleton-in-Waiting, 1982(F)

Ski Tech's Guide to Equipment, Skiwear, and Accessories, 9946
Skills & Strategies for Winning Racquetball, 9972
Skin Care for Teens, 5338
The Skin Diver's Bible, 9961
Skindeep, 972(F)
Skinwalkers, 2054(F)
The Skull beneath the Skin, 2067(F)
The Sky Clears: Poetry of the American Indians, 3256
The Sky Observer's Guide, 8271
Skyguide: A Field Guide for Amateur Astronomers, 8253
Skyscraper, 5710
Skywalker, 296(F)
The Skywatcher's Handbook, 8284
Skywriting by Word of Mouth, 6416
Slade's Glacier, 147(F)
Slaughterhouse-Five: Or, The Children's Crusade, a Duty Dance with Death, 1307(F)
The Slave, 740(F)
Slave and Citizen: The Life of Frederick Douglass, 6502
Slavery and the Slave Trade: A Short Illustrated History, 4322
Slayride, 2011(F)
Sleeping Arrangements, 540(F)
The Sleeping Dragon, 1256(F)
Sleeping Murder, 1956(F)
Sleeping on the Wing: An Anthology of Modern Poetry, 3169
Sleuthing Fossils: The Art of Investigating Past Life, 6977
A Slipping-Down Life, 933(F)
Slow Burn, 982(F)
Small Boat Sailing: The Basic Guide, 9923
Small Comforts: More Comments and Comic Pieces, 3485
Small Computers: Exploring Their Technology and Future, 8968
Small Faces, 6313
Small Felonies: 50 Mini-Masterpieces of Crime & Detection, 2142(F)
Small Quilting Projects, 9253
A Small Sound of the Trum-

pet: Women in the Medieval Life, 7137
Small Victories: The Real World of a Teacher, Her Students & Their High School, 4627
Smart Choices, 5616
Smart Face: A Dermatologist's Guide to Cosmetics and Skin Care, 5336
Smart Like Me: High School-Age Writing from the Sixties to Now, 3889
Smart Moves: How to Succeed in School, Sports, Career, and Life, 5606
Smiley's People, 170(F)
The Smithsonian Book of Flight, 9062
The Smithsonian Book of Inventions, 7075
The Smithsonian Collection of Newspaper Comics, 5791
Smokey: Inside My Life, 6438
Smoking Cigarettes: The Unfiltered Truth—Understanding Why and How to Quit, 5104
Smuggler's Gold, 2249(F)
Snakes of the World, 8470
Snare of Serpents, 2058(F)
Snare of the Hunter, 196(F)
The Snares of Ibex, 1074(F)
Snow Country, 686(F)
The Snow Leopard, 7461
The Snow Queen, 1303(F)
The Snow Walker, 7702
Snow White and Rose Red, 1338(F)
The Snows of Kilimanjaro, and Other Stories, 2923(F)
So Big, 1604(F)
So Far from God: The U.S. War with Mexico, 1846–1848, 7867
So Far from the Bamboo Grove, 1686(F)
So Long at the Fair, 2062(F)
So Long, Senior Year, 831(F)
So Long, Thanks for the Fish, 2331(F)
So You Want to Be a Star: A Teenager's Guide to Breaking into Show Business, 4896
Soaring: Where the Hawks and Eagles Fly, 9610
Soccer Rules in Pictures, 9948
Soccer Skills and Drills, 9952
Social Contract: Essays by Locke, Hume, and Rousseau, 4025

Social Justice: Opposing Viewpoints, 4466
Social Movements of the 1960s, 8051
Social Studies, 2232(F)
Socialism: Opposing Viewpoints, 4593
Sodbuster, 191(F)
Soft and Others, 2847(F)
Softball for Girls & Women, 9680
Software, 9021
The Software Challenge, 9019
Sojourner Truth: A Self-Made Woman, 6518
The Solar System, 8349
Solar Systems, 8344
Soldier Boy, 96(F)
Soldier of Arete, 1332(F)
Soldier of the Mist, 1333(F)
Soldiers: A History of Men in Battle, 7052
The Soldiers, 7969
Soldiers & Civilians: Americans at War and at Home, 971(F)
A Soldier's Embrace, 964(F)
A Soldier's Play, 3066
Sole Survivor, 193(F)
The Solitary, 827(F)
Solitude's Lawman, 131(F)
Solo, 129(F)
Solo Forms of Karate, Tai Chi, Aikido & Kung Fu, 9904
Solo Practice, 6694
Solomon's Seal, 145(F)
The Solution to Pollution: 101 Things You Can Do to Clean Up Your Environment, 4443
Solzhenitsyn, 6310
Some of My Best Friends Are Crazy: Baseball's Favorite Lunatic Goes in Search of His Peers, 9665
Somebody Else's Kids, 5385
Someday the Rabbi Will Leave, 2083(F)
Somehow Tenderness Survives: Stories of Southern Africa, 992(F)
Someone to Love, 2305(F)
Someone Was Here: Profiles in the AIDS Epidemic, 5223
Somerset Homecoming, 6517
Something Beautiful for God: Mother Teresa of Calcutta, 6957
Something Borrowed, Something Blue, 2271(F)

Something for Joey, 9857
Something Happened, 674(F)
Something to Hide, 2159(F)
Something Wicked This Way Comes, 1047(F)
Sometimes I Live in the Country, 781(F)
Somewhere a Child Is Crying: Maltreatment—Causes and Prevention, 5651
Somewheres East of Suez, 6151
Son of a Wanted Man, 162(F)
Son of Golden Turkey Awards: More of Hollywood's Worst Achievements, 6034
Son of Interflux, 1888(F)
Son of the Morning and Other Stories, 2562(F)
Son of the Morning Star, 7951
Son of the Revolution, 6812
A Son of Thunder: Patrick Henry and the American Republic, 6591
The Song of Mavin Manyshaped, 1294(F)
Song of Napalm, 3340
Song of Solomon, 480(F)
The Song of the Meadowlark: The Story of an American Indian and the Nez Percé War, 1510(F)
Songmaster, 2460(F)
Songs from the Alley, 4508
Songs from This Earth on Turtle's Back: Contemporary American Indian Poetry, 3247
Songs from Unsung Worlds: Science in Poetry, 3853
The Songs of Distant Earth, 2480(F)
Sonnets, 3222
The Sonnets, 3223
Sonnets from the Portuguese, 3193
Sons & Lovers: A Novel of Division & Desire, 3678
Sons and Lovers, 569(F)
Sons of the Wolf, 2110(F)
Sooner or Later, 2277(F)
Sophiatown: Coming of Age in South Africa, 6797
Sophie's Choice, 998(F)
Sophocles, 3805
Sorcerer's Legacy, 1340(F)
The Sorcerer's Son, 1110(F)
Sorceress of Darshiva, 1109(F)

Sorceress of the Witch World, 2718(F)
Sorcery and Cecilia, 1339(F)
Soul in Exile, 6818
The Soul of a New Machine, 8992
Soul of America, 7713
The Soul of the Night: An Astronomical Pilgrimage, 8282
The Souls of Black Folk: Essays and Sketches, 4360
The Sound and the Fury, 548
Sound Friendships: The Story of Hearing Ear Dogs, 8746
The Sound of Music, 3098
The Sound of Wings: The Life of Amelia Earhart, 6141
The Sound of Wonder: Interviews from "The Science Fiction Radio Show" Vol. 1, 3747
Sound Off! American Military Women Speak Out, 4866
Sound-Shadows of the New World, 6288
Soups, 9365
The Source, 1451(F), 1808(F)
The Source of Magic, 1012(F)
South Africa: A Different Kind of War, 7372
South Africa: Challenge and Hope, 7369
South Africa: Coming of Age under Apartheid, 7376
South African Dispatches: Letters to My Countrymen, 7389
The South African Quirt, 546(F)
South American Mythology, 3446
South by Java Head, 197(F)
The South Goes North, 4359
South Light: A Journey to the Last Continent, 7704
South to the Pole by Ski, 7703
Southeast Asia, 7394
Southeast Asia: A History, 7396
Southern Black Leaders of the Reconstruction Era, 8017
Southern New England, 8175
A Southern Renaissance: The Cultural Awakening of the American South, 1930–1955, 3592
Southshore, 2802(F)
The Southwest, 8201
Soviet but Not Russian: The "Other" Peoples of the Soviet Union, 7576

The Soviet Colossus: A History of the USSR, 7572
The Soviet Juggernaut, 7330
The Soviet Union, 7565, 7577, 7588
The Soviet Union: Opposing Viewpoints, 7563
The Soviet Union and Eastern Europe 1988, 7584
Soviet Union 2000: Reform or Revolution? 7573
Soweto, My Love, 6799
Sowing the Wind: Reflections on the Earth's Atmosphere, 4449
Space, 207(F)
Space: The Next Twenty-Five Years, 8308
Space and Science Fiction Plays for Young People, 3086
Space Cadet, 2584(F)
Space History, 8315
Space, Inc. Your Guide to Investing in Space Exploration, 8306
The Space Merchants, 2740(F)
The Space Program Quiz and Fact Book, 8297
Space Rocket, 8302
Space Shuttles, 2381(F)
Space Technology, 8328
The Space Telescope: Eyes above the Atmosphere, 8259
Space, Time and Architecture: The Growth of a New Tradition, 5687
Space, Time, Infinity: The Smithsonian Views and Universe, 8290
Space Travel: A History, 8327
Space Wars, 2822(F)
Spacelab: Research in Earth Orbit, 8320
Spacer: Window of the Mind, 2757(F)
Spaceshots: The Beauty of Nature Beyond Earth, 8301
Spacewar, 4160
Spain, 7562
Spain: The Root and the Flower, 7554
Spain in America, 7628
The Spanish American Short Story: A Critical Anthology, 2945(F)
The Spanish Armada, 7558, 7559
The Spanish Civil War, 7561

The Spanish Civil War, 1936–39, 7560
The Spanish Doctor, 1411(F)
The Spanish War: An American Epic—1898, 8015
The Spanish West, 7992
Sparks in the Park and Other Prize-Winning Plays, 3091
Sparky! 6713
Spartacus, 1368(F)
Speak to Me, 5434
Speak to Me: How to Put Confidence in Your Conversation, 5585
Speak Up! A Guide to Public Speaking, 4700
Speaker for the Dead, 2461(F)
Speaking in Chinese, 3911
Speaking Out, Fighting Back, 5510
Speaking with Confidence: A Guide for Public Speakers, 4706
Special Occasions: Holiday Entertaining All Year Round, 9341
A Special Valor, 7321
Speed, 561(F)
A Spell for Chameleon, 1012(F)
Spell Sword, 1054(F)
Spellbound, 2140(F)
The Spellkey, 1102(F)
Spells and Bindings, 3375
Spellsinger, 1123(F)
Sphere, 2495(F)
Sphinx, 55(F)
Spider, 8612
Spiders and Their Kin, 8613
Spies, Scouts, and Raiders: Irregular Operations, 7946
Spike! 6773
Spindrift, 2211(F)
Spinneret, 2862(F)
Spirit Meadow, 217(F)
The Spirit of American Philosophy, 4024
Spirit of Place: Paris, 7489(F)
The Spirit of 1787: The Making of Our Constitution, 4196
The Spirit of '76: The Growth of American Patriotism before Independence, 7837
The Spirit of St. Louis, 9070
Spirit of Survival, 6932
Spirits, Spooks and Other Sinister Creatures, 1766(F)
Spiritual Politics: Religion and

America since World War II, 4082
The Splendid Century, 7498
The Splendid Outcast: Beryl Markham's African Stories, 2943(F)
The Splendid Voyage: An Introduction to New Sciences and New Technologies, 8228
Splendors of the Past: Lost Cities of the Ancient World, 7022
Splinter of the Mind's Eye, 2547(F)
Split Infinity, 2356(F)
Spoon River Anthology, 3298
Sport Speed, 9559
The Sporting News Selects Baseball's 50 Great Games, 9694
The Sporting News Selects Baseball's 50 Greatest Games, 9693
The Sporting News Selects Baseball's 25 Greatest Pennant Races, 9694
The Sporting News Selects Baseball's 25 Greatest Teams, 9694
Sports Classics: American Writers Choose Their Best, 9598
Sports Collector's Digest Baseball Card Price Guide, 9672
Sports Date Book, 9567
Sports Fitness and Training, 5358
The Sports Hall of Shame, 9586
Sports Illustrated Backpacking, 9804
Sports Illustrated Baseball, 9669
Sports Illustrated Basketball, 9728
Sports Illustrated Bowling, 9782
Sports Illustrated Canoeing, 9928
Sports Illustrated Cross-Country Skiing, 9945
Sports Illustrated Figure Skating, 9890
Sports Illustrated Fly Fishing: Learn from a Master, 9814
Sports Illustrated Football: Defense, 9865
Sports Illustrated Football: Offense, 9865
Sports Illustrated Golf, 9873

Sports Illustrated Handball, 9602

Sports Illustrated Pitching, 9666

Sports Illustrated Running for Women, 9912

Sports Illustrated Safe Driving, 9112

Sports Illustrated Scuba Diving, 9956

Sports Illustrated Skiing, 9944

Sports Illustrated Soccer: The Complete Player, 9951

Sports Illustrated Squash, 9603

Sports Illustrated Tennis, 9970

Sports Illustrated Track: Championship Field Events, 9976

Sports Illustrated Track: Championship Running, 9975

Sports Illustrated Training with Weights, 9772

Sports in America, 9584

Sports People, 9576

The Sports Success Book: The Athlete's Guide to Sports Achievement, 9609

Sportsmedicine Book, 5246

Spring Moon: A Novel of China, 1396(F)

A Spy for Freedom: The Story of Sarah Aaronsohn, 6801

Spy in Chancery, 1984(F)

The Spy in the Russian Club: How Glenn Souther Stole America's Nuclear Plans and Escaped to Moscow, 4147

The Spy Master's Handbook, 4149

Spy Story, 72(F)

Spy versus Spy: Stalking Soviet Spies in America, 4148

The Spy Went Dancing: My Further Adventures As an Undercover Agent, 6888

The Spy Who Came in from the Cold, 169(F)

The Spy Wore Red, 6888

Spyclopedia: The Comprehensive Handbook of Espionage, 4134

Square and Folk Dancing: A Complete Guide for Students, Teachers and Callers, 5967

Square One, 6506

Squaring Off, 931(F)

SS-GB: Nazi-Occupied Britain, 72(F)

Stage Makeup, 6084

Stage Scenery: Its Construction and Rigging, 6086

Staggerford, 672(F)

Staging the Musical: Planning, Rehearsing, and Marketing the Amateur Production, 6087

Stalin: A Political Biography, 6875

Stalin: The Glasnost Revelations, 6876

Stalin and the Kirov Murder, 7566

The Stalker, 2121(F)

The Stalking Horse, 2097(F)

The Stand: The Complete and Uncut Edition, 1792(F)

Stand on Zanzibar, 2442(F)

Standard First Aid and Personal Safety, 5439

Standard Handbook for Secretaries, 4639

Standing at Armageddon: The United States, 1877–1919, 8016

Standing Up to the SAT, 4666

Star and Planet Spotting: A Field Guide to the Night Sky, 8249

Star Beast, 2584(F)

Star Born, 2711(F)

A Star for the Latecomer, 626(F)

Star Hunter/Voodoo Planet, 2711(F)

Star of Gypsies, 2787(F)

The Star of Lancaster, 1463(F)

The Star Scroll, 1253(F)

Star Tales, 8283

Star Trek: Rules of Engagement, 2691(F)

Star Trek—Log One, 2548(F)

Star Wars: From the Adventures of Luke Skywalker, 2655(F)

Starbridge 2: Silent Dances, 2498

Stardance, 2762(F)

Starik, 237(F)

Starkadder, 2615(F)

Starman Jones, 2584(F)

Starquake, 2542(F)

The Starry Room: Naked Eye Astronomy in the Intimate Universe, 8288

Stars, 8357

The Stars Are the Styx, 1281(F)

The Stars My Destination, 2409(F)

Stars, Planets and Galaxies, 8352

Stars, Spells, Secrets, and Sorcery: A Do-It-Yourself Book of the Occult, 9504

The Stars, the Snow, the Fire: Twenty-five Years in the Northern Wilderness, 8180

Starship, 2345(F)

Starship Troopers, 2584(F)

Starsilk, 1302(F)

Starspinner, 2393(F)

Startide Rising, 2439(F)

Starting from Scratch, 3957

Starting Pencil Drawing, 9217

The Startling Worlds of Henry Kuttner, 2622(F)

Starving for Attention, 5396

The State of Stony Lonesome, 941(F)

Station Island, 3207

The Statue of Liberty, 8162, 8163

Staying On, 993(F)

Staying Up, 928(F)

Stealing from a Deep Place: Travels in Southeastern Europe, 6143

The Stein and Day Handbook of Magic, 9398

Stengel: His Life and Times, 6734

A Step-by-Step Book about Canaries, 8666

A Step-by-Step Book about Discus, 8755

A Step-by-Step Book about Goldfish, 8753

A Step-by-Step Book about Guinea Pigs, 8756

A Step-by-Step Book about Guppies, 8754

A Step-by-Step Book about Hamsters, 8757

A Step-by-Step Book about Our First Aquarium, 8771

A Step-by-Step Book about Rabbits, 8667

A Step-by-Step Book about Snakes, 8664

A Step-by-Step Book about Tropical Fish, 8751

A Step-by-Step Book about Turtles, 8674

Step by Step to College Success, 4743

Stepfamilies: New Patterns in Harmony, 5644

Stepfather Bank, 2747(F)
Stephen Crane, 3707
Stephen King: The Art of Darkness, 3792
Stephen King: The First Decade, Carrie to Pet Sematary, 3769
The Stephen King Companion, 3698
Stephen King Goes to Hollywood, 6005
Steppenwolf, 837(F)
Stepping Stones, 821(F)
Steve Mizerak's Pocket Billiards: Tips and Trick Shots, 9585
Stevie Wonder, 6459
Still River, 2486(F)
Still Small Voices, 7618
A Stillness at Appomattox, 7898
Stillwatch, 1963(F)
Stilwell and the American Experience in China, 1911–45, 4167
Sting: Every Breath He Takes, 6446
Stitch in Snow, 2302(F)
Stock Options, 4600
Stocks and Bonds, Profits and Losses: A Quick Look at Financial Markets, 4604
Stolen Kisses, 2288(F)
The Stolen Light, 6289
Stolen Moments: Conversations with Contemporary Musicians, 5829
Stolen Years, 7331
The Stone and the Flute, 1034(F)
Stone Bull, 2213(F)
The Stone Giant, 1039(F)
Stone of Farewell, 1325(F)
Stonehenge Decoded, 7520
Stones, Bones, and Ancient Cities, 7024
Stonewall Jackson: Portrait of a Soldier, 6595
Stop in the Name of Love, 2319(F)
Stop the Violence: Overcoming Self-Destruction, 5865
Stopout! Working Ways to Learn, 4805
The Stories and Fables of Ambrose Bierce, 1716(F)
Stories from Shakespeare, 3048
Stories I Ain't Told Nobody Yet: Selections from the People Pieces, 3249(F)
The Stories of Bernard Malamud, 2939(F)
The Stories of F. Scott Fitzgerald, 2915(F)
The Stories of John Cheever, 2904(F)
The Stories of Ray Bradbury, 2430(F)
Stories of the Modern South, 2917(F)
Stories of the Walking Dead, 1760(F)
Storm, 8868
Storm Center: The Supreme Court in American Politics, 4249
The Storm Land, 1190(F)
Storm Rising, 603(F)
Storming Heaven, 1624(F)
Stormswift, 2235(F)
Stormwarden, 2855(F)
The Story of America, 7776
The Story of Art, 5742
The Story of Baseball, 9695
The Story of English, 3937
The Story of Football, 9837
The Story of Henri Tod, 30(F)
The Story of Hollywood, 6040
The Story of Mankind, 7079
The Story of Modern Art, 5752
The Story of My Life, 6626
The Story of Philosophy: The Lives and Opinions of the Greater Philosophers, 4003
The Story of Physics, 8911
Story of the Great American West, 7975
Story of the Von Trapp Family Singers, 6452
The Storybook of Opera, 5912
Straight, 2015(F)
Straight on Till Morning, 6154
Straight Talk about Drinking: Teenagers Speak Out about Alcohol, 5107
Strange and Incredible Sports Happenings, 9557
Strange but True Stories of World War II, 7303
The Strange Career of Jim Crow, 4383
The Strange Case of Dr. Jekyll and Mr. Hyde, 384(F)
Strange Footprints on the Land, 7831
Strange Ground: Americans in Vietnam 1945–1975, 8131
The Strange History of Bonnie and Clyde, 6617
Strange Toys, 814(F)
Strange Waters, 2086(F)
The Stranger, 638(F)
Stranger in a Strange Land, 2585(F)
Stranger in the House, 195(F)
A Stranger Is Watching, 1964(F)
Strangers, 1798(F)
Strangers from a Different Shore: A History of Asian Americans, 4404
Strategic Racquetball, 9971
Street Family, 848(F)
Street Gangs: Yesterday and Today, 4557
A Streetcar Named Desire, 3139
Strength for the Fight: A History of Black Americans in the Military, 4286
Strength to Love, 4367
Strength Training for Baseball, 9633
Stress & Mental Health, 5550
Stress Management, 5381
The Stress of Life, 5568
Stress without Distress, 5568
Strictly Personal, 912(F)
Strictly Speaking, 3941
Stride Toward Freedom: The Montgomery Story, 4368
Strike Three, You're Dead, 2166(F)
Strike Two, 9674
Strikemakers & Strikebreakers, 4517
Strings: A Gathering of Family Poems, 3283
Strokes of Genius, 9867
The Strong Shall Live, 163(F)
Structured COBOL: American National Standard, 8971
Struggle, 7332
The Struggle: A History of the African National Congress, 7374
The Struggle for Black Equality, 1954–1980, 4377
The Struggle for Democracy, 4169
The Struggle for Mastery in Europe, 7149
Struggle for Survival: A History of the Second World War, 7269

The Struggle for Tennessee: Tupelo to Stones River, 7939
Struggles and Triumphs, 6364
The Stuart Age: A History of England, 7513
The Student Body, 1932(F)
The Student Entrepreneur's Guide: How to Start and Run Your Own Business, 5064
The Student Loan Handbook, 4774
A Student's Guide to College Admissions: Everything Your Guidance Counselor Has No Time to Tell You, 4769
The Student's Guide to Good Writing: Building Writing Skills for Success in College, 4674
A Student's Guide to Research and Writing: Literature, 4699
Studies in Starlight: Understanding Our Universe, 8298
Study Abroad, 4717
Study for Success, 4647
A Study in Scarlet, 1993(F)
A Study of History, 7076
Study Smarts: How to Learn More in Less Time, 4649
The Subatomic Monster, 8212
Substance Abuse, 5102
Suburban Geology, 8797
Succeed with Math: Every Student's Guide to Conquering Math Anxiety, 8845
Success to the Brave, 1440(F)
Successful Business Writing, 4670
Sudanna, Sudanna, 1149(F)
Sugar Ray Leonard, 6747
Suicidal Adolescents, 5377
Suicide: The Forever Decision, 5095
Suicide in America, 5386
The Suitcases, 623(F)
Sula, 481(F)
Summaries of Leading Cases on the Constitution, 4182
A Summer Ago, 600(F)
Summer Girls, Love Boys and Other Short Stories, 883(F)
A Summer Life, 6314
Summer Lightning, 907(F)
Summer Nights, 791(F)
Summer of My First Love, 2281(F)
Summer on Campus: College

Experiences for High School Students, 4747
Summer Opportunities for Kids and Teenagers, 9297
Summer Options for Teenagers, 4636
Summer Rules, 704(F)
Summer Show, 702(F)
The Summer Tree, 1166(F)
The Summerboy, 704(F)
Summerhill: A Radical Approach to Child Rearing, 4632
The Summer's King, 1323(F)
Summers of the Wild Rose, 1655(F)
Summertide, 2780(F)
The Sun Also Rises, 1610(F), 3770
Sun Songs: Creation Myths from Around the World, 3467
Sun Up to Sun Down, 8930
Sunday the Rabbi Stayed Home, 2081(F)
Sundown, 280(F)
Sunlight and Health, 5076
The Sunne in Splendour, 1459(F)
Sunrunner's Fire, 1253(F)
Sunshine, 693(F)
Sunspacer, 2865(F)
Super Mafia: Organized Crime Threatens America, 4478
The Super Official NFL Trivia Book, 9839
Superconductivity: The New Alchemy, 8937
Superconductivity: The Threshold of a New Technology, 8938
The Superior Person's Book of Words, 3907
The Supermarket Epicure: The Cookbook for Gourmet Food at Supermarket Prices, 9354
Supermonsters, 9485
Supernova! The Exploding Star of 1987, 8263
The Supernova Story, 8354
The Superpowers: A New Detente, 4162
Superquake! The Last Days of Los Angeles, 8806
Supersense: Perception in the Animal World, 8474
The Supreme Court, 4231
The Supreme Court and Individual Rights, 4256

Surely You're Joking, Mr. Feynman! 6665
Surgeon: The View from Behind the Mask, 5254
The Surrogate Gun, 64(F)
Surrogate Mothers, 4522
A Survey of Historic Costume, 5290
Survival Game, 157(F)
The Survival of Charles Darwin: A Biography of a Man and an Idea, 6656
The Survival of the Bark Canoe, 6964
Survive the Savage Sea, 6158
Surviving, 658(F)
Survivor, 9927
Susan B. Anthony, 6495
Susan B. Anthony: A Biography of a Singular Feminist, 6494
Susan Lee's ABZs of Money & Finance, 4575
Suspect, 2022(F)
Suspicion, 2680(F)
Suspicious Characters, 2146(F)
Swamp Witch, 1720(F)
Swan Song, 1810(F)
Swan's Wing, 1283(F)
Sweet Illusions, 720(F)
Sweet Pain, 729(F)
Sweet Sixteen and Never, 768(F)
Sweet Soul Music: Rhythm and Blues and the Southern Dream of Freedom, 5866
Sweet, Sweet Poison, 2219(F)
Sweet Thursday, 996(F)
Swim Swim: A Complete Handbook for Fitness Swimmers, 9963
Swimming Upstream: A Complete Guide to the College Application Process for the Learning Disabled Student, 4742
A Swinger of Birches, 3268
Sword and Sorceress: An Anthology of Heroic Fantasy, 1055(F)
Sword and Sorceress VII, 1056(F)
Sword and the Chain, 1256(F)
The Sword in the Stone, 1321(F)
The Sword Is Forged, 1377(F)
Sword of Chaos, 1057(F)
The Sword of Shannara, 1061(F)

The Sword of the Prophet, 7595

The Sword, the Jewel and the Mirror, 2757(F)

Swords against Death, 2639(F)

Swords and Deviltry, 2640(F)

The Swordswoman, 2769(F)

Sybil, 5403

Symbol Sourcebook: An Authoritative Guide to International Graphic Symbols, 3899

Symbols of America, 4618

Sympathy and Science: Women Physicians in American Medicine, 5247

Symphony of Light, 2678(F)

The Synthesizer & Electronic Keyboard Handbook, 5931

T. S. Eliot, 3871

T. S. Eliot: An Introduction, 3884

Table of Contents, 3540

The Table Saw Book, 9272

Table Tennis, 9591

The Tachyon Web, 2728(F)

Tai-Pan, 48(F)

Tailchaser's Song, 1326(F)

Taking Better Travel Photos, 9429

Taking Freshwater Game Fish: A Treasury of Expert Advice, 9835

Taking It All In, 6022

Taking Liberties: A Compendium of Hard Cases, Legal Dilemmas, and Bum Raps, 4237

The Taking of Mariasburg, 257(F)

Taking Off: Travel Tips for a Carefree Trip, 5597

The Tale of the Ring: A Kaddish, 7301

Tale of Two Cities, 362(F)

A Talent for War, 2671(F)

Tales and Sketches, 2920(F)

Tales and Stories, 3389(F)

Tales by Moonlight II, 1832(F)

Tales from Alfred Hitchcock's Mystery Magazine, 2074(F)

Tales from Ellery Queen's Mystery Magazine: Short Stories for Young Adults, 2190(F)

Tales from Isaac Asimov's Science Fiction Magazine: Short Stories for Young Adults, 2843(F)

Tales from the Opera, 5928

Tales from the Spaceport Bar, 2773(F)

Tales of Fear and Frightening Phenomena, 1766(F)

The Tales of Henry James, 3788

Tales of King Arthur, 3407

Tales of Pirx the Pilot, 2642(F)

Tales of Terror, 1824(F), 9536

Tales of Terror and Mystery, 1994(F)

Tales of the Cthulhu Mythos, 2654(F)

Tales of the Occult, 1713(F)

Tales of the Quintana Roo, 1855(F)

Tales of the South Pacific, 1668(F)

Tales of the Supernatural, 3896

Tales of the Witch World, 2719(F)

Tales of the Witch World 2, 1236(F)

Taliesin, 1187(F)

The Talisman, 1173(F)

Talk Sex, 5468

Talking God, 2054(F)

Talking in Whispers, 268(F)

Talking Jazz, 6178

Talking Man, 1038(F)

Talking to Strange Men, 2155(F)

Tall Tale America: A Legendary History of Our Humorous Heroes, 3430

Talley's Folly, 3141

Tancy, 1611(F)

The Tanglewood Murders, 2076(F)

The Tar-Aiym Krang, 2545(F)

Tar Baby, 482(F)

Target: Prime Time: Advocacy Groups and Entertainment TV, 3990

Tartuffe, and Other Plays, 3012

Tarzan at the Earth's Core, 2449(F)

Tarzan of the Apes, 32

Taylor's Guide to Ground Covers, Vines & Grasses, 9387

Taylor's Guide to Houseplants, 9387

Taylor's Guide to Shrubs, 9387

Taylor's Guide to Vegetables and Herbs, 9387

Tea with the Black Dragon, 1202(F)

Teach Yourself Fortune Telling: Palmistry, the Crystal Ball, Runes, Tea Leaves, the Tarot, 9524

Teaching as a Conserving Activity, 6048

Teaching Riding: Step-by-Step Schooling for Horses and Rider, 8766

The Teamsters, 4612

Technique in Fiction: Second Edition Revised and Updated for a New Generation, 4687

The Technique of Acting, 6076

The Techniques of Modern Hitting, 9626

Technology, 8943

Technology in the Ancient World, 7084

Tecumseh and the Quest for Indian Leadership, 6639

Teen Angel: And Other Stories of Young Love, 816(F)

Teen Guide to Birth Control, 5486

Teen Guide to Caring for Your Unborn Baby, 5456

Teen Guide to Childbirth, 5457

Teen Guide to Safe Sex, 5487

Teen Guide to Single Parenting, 5518

Teen Pregnancy, 5455

Teenage and Pregnant: What You Can Do, 5493

Teenage Competition: A Survival Guide, 5604

Teenage Depression, 5405

The Teenage Entrepreneur's Guide: 50 Money-Making Business Ideas, 5067

A Teen-age Guide to Healthy Skin and Hair, 5337

Teenage Marriage: Coping with Reality, 5664

Teenage Moneymaking Guide, 5068

The Teenage Parent's Child Support Guide, 5491

Teenage Romance: Or, How to Die of Embarrassment, 5558

Teenage Sexuality: Opposing Viewpoints, 5451

Teenage Stress, 5374

The Teenage Survival Book, 5610

Teenage Survival Manual:

How to Reach 20 in One Piece (and Enjoy Every Step of the Journey), 5605

The Teenager's Guide to Study, Travel, and Adventure Abroad, 1989–1990 Edition, 4709

The Teenager's Guide to Study, Travel, and Adventure Abroad 1990–91, 4710

The Teenager's Guide to the Best Summer Opportunities, 4711

The Teenager's Survival Guide to Moving, 5624

Teenagers Talk about Suicide, 5376

Teens Look at Marriage: Rainbows, Roles and Realities, 5665

Teens Speak Out, 4418

Teepee Neighbors, 7800

Tekwar, 2777(F)

Telecommunications Careers, 4865

Television, 6073

Tell Me a Riddle, 585(F)

Tell Me If the Lovers Are Losers, 936(F)

Tell Me That You Love Me, Junie Moon, 853(F)

The Telling Distance: Conversations with the American Desert, 8810

Telling Secrets, 573(F)

The Temple of My Familiar, 508(F)

Temporary Insanity, 9664

The Ten Grandmothers, 7817

Ten Little Indians, 1957(F)

The Ten Thousand Day War: Vietnam 1945–1975, 8128

10,000 Ideas for Term Papers, Projects and Reports, 4684

Ten Top Stories, 2963(F)

Tender Is the Night, 1606(F)

Tennessee Williams, 3836

Tennis My Way, 6770

Tenting Tonight: The Soldier's Life, 7932

The Terezin Requiem, 1644(F)

Term Paper, 732(F)

The Terminal Man, 2496(F)

Terminating Life: Conflicting Values in Health Care, 5092

Terms of Endearment, 578(F)

Terpin, 915(F)

Terpsichore in Sneakers: Post-Modern Dance, 5960

Terrible Swift Sword, 7899

The Terror Network, 4554

Terrorism: A Special Kind of Violence, 4546

Terrorism: Opposing Viewpoints, 4555

Terrorism: Past, Present, Future, 4553

Terrorism in the 1980s, 4552

The Terrorists, 4551

The Terrorists: Their Weapons, Leaders and Tactics, 4543

Terrors, 1752(F)

Terry Carr's Best Science Fiction of the Year, 2464(F)

The Tery, 2848(F)

Tess of the D'Urbervilles, 372(F)

Test of the Twins, 1313(F)

Test Taking Strategies, 4649

Test-Taking Strategies for the PSAT, 4662

Test Your Movie I.Q. 6003

A Testament of Hope: The Essential Writings of Martin Luther King, Jr. 4380

Testing: Behind the Scenes at Consumer Reports, 1936–1986, 4607

Tevye the Dairyman and the Railroad Stories, 435(F)

Tex! The Man Who Built the Dallas Cowboys, 6760

The Texans, 7993

Texas, 208(F)

Texas: An Album of History, 8195

The Thanksgiving Visitor, 784(F)

That Cheating Sister, 2308(F)

That Hideous Strength, 2645(F)

That Near and Distant Place, 1490(F)

That Night, 872(F)

That Old Time Rock & Roll: A Chronicle of an Era, 1954–1963, 5840

That's Hollywood: A Behind-the-Scenes Look at 60 of the Greatest Films of All Time, 6069

That's My Baby, 861(F)

Theater in America: 200 Years of Plays, Players, and Productions, 6090

The Theater Props Handbook, 6093

Theatre and Playhouse, 6098

The Theban Mysteries, 1978(F)

Their Blood Runs Cold: Adventures with Reptiles and Amphibians, 8463

Their Eyes Are Watching God, 465(F)

Their Finest Hour, 7193

Them, 583(F)

Then and Now: How the World Has Changed since World War II, 7340

Thendara House, 1054(F)

Theo and Me: Growing Up Okay, 6455

Theodore Dreiser, 3753

Theophilus North, 754(F)

The Theory of the Leisure Class, 4465

There Are No Problem Horses—Only Problem Riders, 8768

There Is a River: The Black Struggle for Freedom in America, 7743

There Is No Darkness, 2571(F)

There Is No Zoo in Zoology, 3918

These Good Men: Friendships Forged from War, 8135

These Were the Romans, 7119

The Theta Syndrome, 1856(F)

They Cage the Animals at Night, 6897

They Called Him Wild Bill: The Life and Adventures of James Butler Hickok, 6624

They Have a Word for It: A Lighthearted Lexicon of Untranslatable Words and Phrases, 3944

They Never Said It: A Book of Fake Quotes, Misquotes, and Misleading Attributions, 3525

They Saw the Elephant: Women in the California Gold Rush, 7963

They Shoot Canoes, Don't They? 9798

They're Playing Our Song, 3126

A Thief of Time, 2054(F)

Thieves of Light, 2603(F)

The Thin Man, 2038(F)

Things Invisible to See, 1324(F)

Things That I Do in the Dark, 3286

The Things They Carried, 1700(F)

Thinking about Science: Max Delbruck and the Origins of Molecular Biology, 6658

Thinking Gorillas: Testing and Teaching the Greatest Ape, 8500

Thinking through Writing, 4682

Thinking Under Fire, 4307

The Third Book of the Lost Swords: Stonecutter's Story, 1260(F)

The Third Eagle: Lessons along a Minor String, 2657(F)

The Third Eye, 2061(F)

Third Girl from the Left, 1595(F)

The Third Wave, 4419

The Third World, 7341

The Third World: Opposing Viewpoints, 4464

Thirteen Days: A Memoir of the Cuban Missile Crisis, 8074

The Thirteenth Valley, 1694(F)

Thirty Days to a More Powerful Vocabulary, 3935

Thirty Days to Better English, 3934

Thirty Famous One-Act Plays, 2979

The 39 Steps, 28(F)

Thirty Phone Booths to Boston: Tales of a Wayward Runner, 9914

Thirty Seconds, 5988

33 Fun-and-Easy Weekend Electronics Projects, 9036

Thirty-Six Children, 4629

Thirty-six Exposures, 874(F)

The Thirty-six-Hour Day, 5203

This Boy's Life: A Memoir, 6329

This Fabulous Century, 7782

This Hallowed Ground: The Story of the Union Side of the Civil War, 7900

This I Remember, 6559

This Immortal, 1345(F)

This Is My God, 4090

This Is Your Life, 624(F)

This Land Is Your Land: The Struggle to Save America's Public Lands, 4441

This Life, 6429

This Side of Paradise, 1607(F)

This Sporting Life, 3248

This Strange New Feeling, 473(F)

This Was Harlem, 8160

Thomas Jefferson: An Intimate History, 6533

Thomas More, 6865

Thomas the Rhymer, 1182(F)

Thomas Wolfe, 3719

Thoreau's Method: A Handbook for Nature Study, 8399

The Thorn Birds, 1397(F)

The Thorn in the Starfish: How the Human Immune System Works, 5180

Thornyhold, 2185(F)

Those of My Blood, 2647(F)

Those Other People, 641(F)

Those Who Fall, 7262

Those Who Hunt the Night, 1761(F)

Those Who Love, 1616(F)

Those Who Ride the Night Winds, 3270, 3272

The Thousand-Mile War, 7208

Thousand Pieces of Gold, 1575(F)

Thousandstar, 2351(F)

Thread of Life: The Smithsonian Looks at Evolution, 7006

Three, 6256

Three against the Witch World, 2718(F)

Three Comedies of American Family Life, 3099

Three Days for Emeralds, 1999(F)

Three from Galilee: The Young Man from Nazareth, 1360(F)

Three Hearts and Three Lions, 1008(F)

The Three Musketeers, 313(F)

Three Plays, 3022, 3027, 3034, 3136

Three Plays about Crime and Criminals, 3088

The Three-Pound Universe, 5315

Three Scientists and Their Gods: A Search for Meaning in an Age of Information, 6648

The Three Theban Plays, 3020

3,500 Good Quotes for Speakers, 4686

Three Tragedies, 3000

Three Ways of Asian Wisdom: Hinduism, Buddhism, Zen and Their Significance for the West, 4078

Three Who Made a Revolution: A Biographical History, 6790

Threshold, 1244(F), 2690(F)

Threshold: Straightforward Answers to Teenagers' Questions about Sex, 5482

The Throme of the Erril of Sherill, 1206(F)

The Throne of Scone, 2613(F)

Through a Window: My Thirty Years with the Chimpanzees of Gombe, 8499

Through Gates of Splendor, 4047

The Throwing Season, 2876(F)

Thunder Moon, 21(F)

Thunder Moon Strikes, 21(F)

Thunder Moon's Challenge, 21(F)

Thunder on the Right: The New Right and the Politics of Resentment, 4123

Thunder on the Tennessee, 1552(F)

Thunderhead, Son of Flicka, 294(F)

Thunderstones and Shooting Stars: The Meaning of Meteorites, 8330

The Thurber Carnival, 3514

Thursday the Rabbi Walked Out, 2082(F)

Thursday's Child, 819(F)

Tiananmen Diary: Thirteen Days in June, 7426

Tiananmen Square, 7429

The Tibbets Story, 6959

Tides of Light, 2405(F)

The Tie That Binds, 1569(F)

Tiffany Glassware, 5812

Tiffany's Table Manners for Teenagers, 5583

Tiger: Portrait of a Predator, 8511

The Tiger in the Well, 232(F)

Tiger Moon, 6162

Tim Hartnell's Giant Book of Computer Games, 8982

Tim Hartnell's Second Giant Book of Computer Games, 8982

Time and the Riddle, 2911(F)

Time Bomb: Fermi,

Heisenberg and the Race for the Atomic Bomb, 9132

Time Bomb and Zahndry Others, 2863(F)

A Time for Giants: The Politics of the American High Command in World War II, 7194

A Time for Heroes, 27(F)

Time for the Stars, 2586(F)

Time-Life Complete Fix-It-Yourself Manual, 9307

Time-Life Complete Home Repair Manual, 9308

Time Machine, 2833(F)

The Time of the Dark, 1141(F)

The Time of the Hunter's Moon, 135(F)

Time of the Turtle, 8472

Time of the Twins, 1313(F)

Time Patrolman, 2347(F)

Time Pressure, 2761(F)

A Time to Choose, 2234(F)

A Time to Die, 244(F)

A Time to Stand, 7965

Time Travel, 8861

Time Travel and Other Mathematical Bewilderments, 8855

Time Travelers Strictly Cash, 2759(F)

Time Wars, 2823(F)

The Timekeeper Conspiracy, 1147(F)

Timelines of Sports History: Baseball, 9663

Timelines of Sports History: Football, 9850

Timesaving Sewing, 9257

Timescale: An Atlas of the Fourth Dimension, 8250

Timescape, 2406(F)

The Timetables of History: A Horizontal Linkage of People & Events, 7045

Timetrap, 2528(F)

Timewarps, 8910

The Tin Drum, 966(F)

Tin Woodman, 2412(F)

Tina, 6449

Tina's Chance, 698(F)

Tinker, Tailor, Soldier, Spy, 170(F)

Tirra Lirra by the River, 629(F)

Tisha: The Story of a Young Teacher in the Alaska Wilderness, 6918

Titan, 2813(F)

The Titanic: End of a Dream, 8898

Titanic: The Death and Life of a Legend, 8890

To Appomattox: Nine April Days, 1865, 7906

To Be a Jew: A Guide to Jewish Observance in Contemporary Life, 4044

To Be Young, Gifted and Black, 6252

To Bear Any Burden, 8141

To Destroy You Is No Loss, 7460

To Fight the Wild, 7465

To Have and to Hold, 1517(F)

To Hear a Nightingale, 282(F)

To Keep Them Alive: Wild Animal Breeding, 8779

To Kill a Mockingbird, 471(F)

To Kill and Be Killed: Case Studies from Florida's Death Row, 4486

To Learn and to Teach: Your Life as a Rabbi, 4970

To Life, 6949

To Live in Two Worlds: American Indian Youth Today, 7790

To Live until We Say Good-Bye, 5089

To Mock a Mockingbird, 9468

To Prove a Villain, 1481(F)

To Serve Them All My Days, 1418(F)

To Sir, with Love, 6894

To Space and Back, 8317

To Take a Dare, 798(F)

To the Halls of the Montezumas, 7871

To the Lighthouse, 625(F)

To the Promised Land: The Birth of Israel, 40th Anniversary, 7607

To the Seventh Power, 223(F)

To the Top of Denali: Climbing Adventures on North America's Highest Peak, 9596

To the Vanishing Point, 2549(F)

To Your Scattered Bodies Go, 2537(F)

Today's Handbook of Bible Times & Customs, 4098

Today's Isms: Communism, Fascism, Capitalism, Socialism, 4172

Tokens of Grace: A Novel in Stories, 584(F)

Tokyo Rising: The City since the Great Earthquake, 7454

Tolkien, 6319

Tolkien and the Critics: Essays on J. R. R. Tolkien's The Lord of the Rings, 3671

Tom Jones, 366(F)

Tom Landry: An Autobiography, 6751

Tom Sawyer Abroad and Tom Sawyer, Detective, 429(F)

Tom Stoppard, 3813

Tomas Masaryk, 6864

The Tomb, 1869(F)

The Tomb and Other Tales, 1807(F)

The Tombs of Atuan, 2636(F)

The Tommyknockers, 1793(F)

Tomorrow Will Be Better, 741(F)

Tomorrow's Crimes, 1865(F)

Tomorrow's Rainbow, 1438(F)

The Tongues of Angels, 905(F)

Too Close to the Edge, 1996(F)

Too Fat? Too Thin? Do You Have a Choice? 5408

Too Many Magicians, 1131(F)

Too Many Midnights, 3294

Too Sad to Sing: A Memoir with Postcards, 6895

Tool of the Trade, 120(F)

Toolmaker Koan, 2679(F)

Tools and How to Use Them, 8948

The Toothache Tree, 97(F)

Top of the World, 7705

Topaz, 262(F)

Toposaurus: A Humorous Treasury of Toponyms, 3928

The Torch of Honor, 2339(F)

Torpedo Run, 1673(F)

Tortilla Flat, 997(F)

Tortuga, 628(F)

Toscanini's Fumble: And Other Tales of Clinical Neurology, 5194

The Total Dog Book: The Breeders' and Pet Owners' Complete Guide to Better Dog Care, 8741

Total Recall, 2357(F)

Total Tennis, 9965

The Touch, 1870(F)

A Touch of Chill: Tales for Sleepless Nights, 2334(F)

Touch the Devil, 130(F)

Touch the Stars: Emergence, 2501(F)

Touch Typing Made Simple, 4641

Touched with Fire: The Future of the Vietnam Generation, 8148

Tough Love: How Parents Can Deal with Drug Abuse, 5146

Toughing It Out at Harvard: The Making of a Woman MBA, 4919

Toulouse-Lautrec, 5780

Touring on Two Wheels: The Bicycle Traveler's Handbook, 9750

Tourist Trap, 2180(F)

Toward a Safe and Sane Halloween and Other Tales of Suburbia, 3497

The Town, 1584(F)

A Town Like Alice, 1678(F)

The Town That Started the Civil War, 7893

The Townsmen, 8001

Toxic Threat: How Hazardous Substances Poison Our Lives, 4450

Toy Soldiers, 155(F)

The Toynbee Convector, 1048(F)

Tracey: A Mother's Journal of Teenage Addiction, 5100

Tracing Your Ancestry, 5656

Track of the Grizzly, 8505

The Tracker, 8379

Tracks, 454(F), 7468

Tracks across Alaska: A Dog Sled Journey, 8188

Trading Up, 4588

A Tradition of Victory, 1440(F)

Traditional Samplers, 9237

Trafficking: The Boom and Bust of the Air America Cocaine Ring, 4489

The Tragedy of the Moon, 8211

Trail of Tears: The Rise and Fall of the Cherokee Nation, 7806

The Trail to Honk Ballard's Bones, 26(F)

The Trailblazers, 7994

Traits of a Healthy Family, 5349

The Tranquilizing of America: Pill Popping and the American Way of Life, 5128

Transactions in a Foreign Currency, 801(F)

The Transcendentalists, 4015

Transplants: Today's Medical Miracles, 5165

Trapped: Michael Jackson and the Crossover Dream, 6411

A Traveler on Horseback in Eastern Turkey and Iran, 7619

Travelers, 771(F)

Travels in Mexico and California, 7950

The Travels of Marco Polo, 6156

Travels with Charley: In Search of America, 7778

Travels with My Aunt, 1883(F)

Treason, 2462(F)

Treasure, 68(F)

The Treasure of the Sierra Madre, 258(F)

Treasures from Bible Times, 4109

Treasures from the National Museum of American Art, 5800

Treasures of the Tropic Seas, 8772

Treasury of African Folklore, 3378

A Treasury of Afro-American Folklore, 3435

A Treasury of American Folklore, 3431

A Treasury of Christmas Songs and Carols, 5954

A Treasury of Civil War Tales, 7916

A Treasury of Irish Folklore, 3393

A Treasury of Jewish Folklore, Stories, Traditions, Legends, Humor, Wisdom and Folk Songs of the Jewish People, 3357

A Treasury of New England Folklore: Stories, Ballads, and Traditions of Yankee Folk, 3432

A Treasury of Victorian Detective Stories, 1931(F)

Treating and Overcoming Anorexia Nervosa, 5389

Treblinka, 7298

A Tree Grows in Brooklyn, 1615(F)

Trees, 8431

The Trees, 1584(F)

Trees of North America, 8423

The Trees of Swords and Jewels, 1069(F)

Trekmaster, 2610(F)

The Trembling Earth: Probing & Predicting Quakes, 8802

The Trembling Hills, 2216(F)

Trespass, 83(F)

The Trial, 684(F)

Trial by Fire, 7935

Trial by Jury, 4233

Trial Run, 2016(F)

Triathlon: A Triple Fitness Sport, 9560

Triathloning for Ordinary Mortals, 9974

Tribal Assets: The Rebirth of Native America, 4395

The Tricksters, 1212(F)

Trillion Year Spree, 3612

Trinity, 1483(F)

Trinity and Other Stories, 2618(F)

Triple, 86(F)

Tristram Shandy, 380(F)

Triumph and Tragedy, 7193

Triumph of the Darksword, 1315(F)

Triumph of the Night, 1820(F)

The Triumph of the Novel: Dickens, Dostoevsky, Faulkner, 3621

The Triumph of the Scarlet Pimpernel, 1455(F)

Triumphant Fox: Erwin Rommel and the Rise of the Afrika Korps, 7257

The Trojan War: The Iliad of Homer, 3475

The Troll's Grindstone, 1041(F)

Tropical Fish, 8750

Tropical Fish: A Guide for Setting Up and Maintaining an Aquarium for Tropical Fish and Other Animals, 8752

The Tropical Rainforest: A World Survey of Our Most Valuable Endangered Habitat, 8816

The Trouble with Toni, 2312(F)

Troubled Skies, Troubled Waters: The Story of Acid Rain, 4454

Troubled Waters, 2249(F)

The True Adventures of Grizzly Adams, 6124

The True Believer, 5524
True Grit, 225(F)
True Names and Other Dangers, 2818(F)
True or False? Amazing Art Forgeries, 5727
Truman: A Centenary Remembrance, 6567
Truman Capote, 3768
Trumps of Doom, 1342(F), 1346(F)
Trust Your Heart: An Autobiography, 6381
The Truth about the Ku Klux Klan, 4346
The Truth Trap, 2884(F)
Tuesday the Rabbi Saw Red, 2082(F)
The Tufts University Guide to Total Nutrition, 5413
Tulku, 76(F)
Tumultuous Years: The Presidency of Harry S. Truman, 1949–1953, 8057
Tunnel in the Sky, 2587(F)
The Tunnel of Love, 1878(F)
The Turn of the Screw, 407(F)
Turnabout Children: Overcoming Dyslexia and Other Learning Disabilities, 5393
Turner, 5787
The Turning Place: Stories of a Future Past, 2612(F)
Turning Point: 1968, 8092
Turtles & Tortoises of the World, 8471
Tutu: Voice of the Voiceless, 6800
TV Careers Behind the Screen, 4874
Tweedlioop, 2772(F)
Twentieth-Century Artists on Art, 5731
20th Century China, 7405
Twentieth-Century English Literature, 3566
Twentieth Century Interpretations of Crime and Punishment, 3640
Twentieth Century Interpretations of Gulliver's Travels, 3653
Twentieth Century Interpretations of The Great Gatsby: A Collection of Critical Essays, 3749
Twenty Best European Plays on the American Stage, 2981

Twenty Best Plays of the Modern American Theatre, 3070
Twenty Plays of the Nō Theatre, 3144
A Twenty-fifth Anniversary Album of NASA, 8326
Twenty-Five Best Plays of the Modern American Theatre, 3071
25 Impressionist Masterpieces, 5740
25 Years: The NFL since 1960, 9840
24 Favorite One-Act Plays, 2980
24 Table Saw Projects, 9266
Twenty Million Yankees: The Northern Home Front, 7924
The 29 Most Common Writing Mistakes and How to Avoid Them, 4675
The 26 Letters, 3968
Twenty Thousand Leagues under the Sea, 326(F)
20,000 Years of Fashion: The History of Costume and Personal Adornment, 5273
Twenty Years After, 313(F)
Twenty Years at Hull House, 6611
20 Years of Rolling Stone: What a Long, Strange Trip It's Been, 5906
Twice Shy, 2017(F)
Twice upon a Time, 1015(F)
Twilight at the Well of Souls, 1067(F)
Twilight Eyes, 1799(F)
Twilight World, 2347(F)
Twisted Tales from Shakespeare, 3046
Twistor, 2492(F)
Two against the Ice: Amundsen and Ellsworth, 6125
Two against the Sahara: On Camelback from Nouakchott to the Nile, 7367
Two Corinthians, 2262(F)
Two Cultures: And a Second Look, 8235
Two Fables, 1083(F)
Two from Galilee, 1360(F)
Two Hundred Years of American Art: The Munson-Williams-Proctor Institute, 5792
Two Leggings: The Making of a Crow Warrior, 7819

Two-Park Invention: The Story of a Marriage, 6279
Two Plays, 2993
Two Roads to Sumter, 7863
2001: A Space Odyssey, 2481(F)
2061: Odyssey Three, 2482(F)
2010: Odyssey Two, 2483(F)
Two to Conquer, 1054(F)
The Two Towers, 2808(F)
Two Years Before the Mast, 6137
Typee: A Peep at Polynesian Life, 414(F)
Typhoon and Other Stories, 348(F)
Typing the Easy Way, 4642
The Tyrannosaurus Prescription and 100 Other Essays, 8204

U-Boats Offshore, 7226
U.S. Chess Federation's Official Rules of Chess, 9819
The U.S. Navy Today, Vol. 1, 4287
U.S.A. by Bus and Train, 7745
UFOs: Opposing Viewpoints, 9474
UFOs: The Third Wave, 9486
UFOs Explained, 9510
The Ugly American, 977(F)
Uhura's Song, 2611(F)
Uller Uprising, 2730(F)
The Ultimate Dog Book, 8738
The Ultimate Paper Airplane, 9224
The Ultra Secret, 7325
The Umpire Strikes Back, 9674
Unbeaten Tracks in Japan, 7445
Unbuilding, 5709
Uncanny Tales of Unearthly and Unexpected Horrors, 1767(F)
The Uncivil Wars: Ireland Today, 7530
Uncle Tom's Cabin, 1530(F)
Uncle Whiskers, 8689
Uncollected Stories of William Faulkner, 2914(F)
An Uncommon Man: The Triumph of Herbert Hoover, 6531
Uncovering the Ancient World, 7026

Undefeated: The Life of Hubert H. Humphrey, 6594
Under All Silences: Shades of Love, 3162
Under God: Religion and American Politics, 4273
Under Milk Wood, 3129
Under Siege, 59(F)
Under the Eye of the Clock: The Life Story of Christopher Nolan, 6291
Under the Gun: Mystery Scene Presents the Best Suspense and Mystery, 2027(F)
Under the Gun: Weapons, Crimes, and Violence in America, 4500
Under Two Flags: The American Navy in the Civil War, 7914
Underfoot in Show Business, 6397
Underground Worlds, 8813
Undersea Treasures, 8895
Understanding a Company, 4594, 4602
Understanding Computers, 9015, 9022
Understanding Contemporary American Science Fiction: The Formative Period, 1926–1970, 3619
Understanding Islam: An Introduction to the Moslem World, 4063
Understanding Leukemia, 5205
Understanding Media, 6027
Understanding Modern Architecture, 5686
Understanding Telecommunications, 9045
Understanding Your Immune System, 5217
Understanding Yourself, 5532
Undiscovered Self, 5537
Unearthing Atlantis: An Archaeological Odyssey, 7109
The Uneasy State: The United States from 1915–1945, 8032
Unemployment, 4610
Unexpected Eloquence: The Art in American Folk Art, 5804
The Unfinished Journey: America since World War II, 8054
Unfinished Tales of Númenor and Middle-Earth, 1298(F)
An Unfinished Woman, 6256

The Unfolding Universe, 8310
The Unforgettable Season, 9644
The Unforsaken Hiero, 1186(F)
Unicorn & Dragon, 1001(F)
Unidentified Woman, 1997(F)
Uniforms of the American Civil War in Color, 7922
The Uninvited, 2003(F)
The Uninvited: True Tales of the Unknown, Vol. II, 9508
The United States, 7783
The United States and China, 4139
The United States and World Trade, 4568
The United States in the Spanish-American War, 8011
The United States in the Vietnam War, 8125
The United States in World War I, 7160
The Universal Myths: Heroes, Gods, Tricksters and Others, 3453
The Universe, 8370
The Universe . . . and Beyond, 8363
The Universe from Your Backyard, 8258
The Universe of Dr. Einstein, 8902
The Unlikely Ones, 1062(F)
Unlived Affections, 739(F)
Unnatural Causes, 2068(F)
The Unpleasantness at the Bellona Club, 2170(F)
Unplugging the Plug-in Drug, 6072
Unpuzzling Your Past: A Basic Guide to Genealogy, 5645
Unreliable Sources: A Guide to Detecting Bias in News Media, 3986
Unsafe at Any Meal, 8419
Unsolved: Great Mysteries of the 20th Century, 4499
Unsolved! Classic True Murder Cases, 4480
An Unsuitable Job for a Woman, 2069(F)
Until the Sun Dies, 8368
Unto This Hour, 1551(F)
The Unwritten Chronicles of Robert E. Lee, 1536(F)
Up from Slavery: An Autobiography by Booker T. Washington, 6520

Up from the Cradle of Jazz: New Orleans Music since WWII, 5842
Up in Seth's Room, 884(F)
Up North, 9826
Up the Down Staircase, 1885(F)
Up Your Score: The Underground Guide to Psyching Out the SAT, 4722
The Uplift War, 2439(F)
Upon the Head of a Goat, 1679(F)
Uranus & Neptune: The Distant Giants, 8341
The Urban Nation, 1920–1980, 7767
Ursula K. Le Guin, 3779
The Urth of the New Sun, 2853(F)
Usagi Yojimbo, Book One, 1900(F)
The Used Car Book 1991, 9095
Used Cars: Finding the Best Buy, 9103
The Uses of Enchantment: The Meaning and Importance of Fairy Tales, 3358
Using Calligraphy, 9161
Utopia, 4016
U2: Touch the Flame—An Illustrated Documentary, 5894

V for Victor, 42(F)
V-Mail: Letters of a World War II Combat Medic, 7324
Vacation Fever! 2228(F)
Vale of the Vole, 2354(F)
Valentine Pontifex, 2782(F)
Valiant Friend: The Life of Lucretia Mott, 6630
Valium: The Tranquil Trap, 5161
The Valley of Horses, 1348(F)
Valley of the Broken Cherry Trees, 1403(F)
Van Gogh, 5785, 6194
Van Gogh: His Life and His Art, 6195
Vandalism: The Crime of Immaturity, 4476
The Vanishing Border: A Photographic Journey Along Our Frontier with Mexico, 7712
The Vanishing Hitchhiker: American Urban Legends and Their Meanings, 3433

Vanishing Tracks: Four Years among the Snow Leopards of Nepal, 8510
Vanishing Tribes, 6991
Vanity Fair, 386(F)
Vargr-Moon, 2615(F)
Varieties of Visual Experience, 5683
Vaughan Williams, 6354
VD: The Silent Epidemic, 5190
VD: Venereal Disease and What You Should Do about It, 5192
The VD Story, 5175
Vegetables, 9363
Vegetarian Pleasures: A Menu Cookbook, 9350
The Veiled One, 2156(F)
Velazquez, 6208
The Vendor of Sweets, 984(F)
Venezuela: The Search for Order, the Dream of Progress, 7678
Vengeance of Orion, 2424(F)
Ventriloquism: Magic with Your Voice, 6106
Ventriloquism for the Total Dummy, 9305
Venus of Shadows, 2771(F)
Venus Plus X, 1281(F)
Very Far Away from Anywhere Else, 1192(F)
A Very Touchy Subject, 925(F)
Veteran's Day, 8122
VGM's Handbook of Business and Management Careers, 4924
VGM's Handbook of Scientific and Technical Careers, 5026
The Vicar of Christ, 981(F)
The Vicar of Wakefield, 367(F)
Vicious Circle, 1768(F)
The Victorian Age, 3811
The Victorian Fairy Tale Book, 3401
Victorian Fairy Tales: The Revolt of the Fairies and Elves, 3416
Victorian Ghost Stories by Eminent Women Writers, 1732(F)
Victory in Europe: D-Day to V-E Day, 7215
Victory in Europe, 7293
Victory in the Pacific, 7251
Victory on Janus, 2710(F)

Video: ENG and EFP, 6032
The Video Primer: Equipment, Production, and Concepts, 6052
Video User's Handbook, 9054
Videotape Editing: A Postproduction Primer, 9048
Vietnam: A History, 7458
Vietnam: The Land We Never Knew, 7457
Vietnam: The Valor and the Sorrow, 8101
Vietnam: There and Here, 8126
Vietnam Reconsidered: Lessons from a War, 8139
The Vietnam Veterans Memorial, 8123
The Vietnam War, 8112
The Vietnam War: An Almanac, 8102
The Vietnam War: Opposing Viewpoints, 8109
Vietnam War Almanac, 8145
The View from Rat Lake, 9828
The View from Space: American Astronaut Photography, 1962–1972, 8319
A View from the Bench, 4258
A View from the Square, 259(F)
The Village of Longing and Dancehall Days, 7529
The Vines of Ferrara, 1968(F)
The Vineyard of Liberty, 7719
Violence! Our Fastest-Growing Public Health Problem, 4460
Violence in America: Opposing Viewpoints, 4528
Violent Storms, 8867
The Virgin in the Ice, 2135(F)
Virginia and the Capital Region, 8196
Virginia Woolf and Her World, 6330
The Virginia Woolf Reader, 2977
The Virginian, 1598(F)
A Virtuous Woman, 2268(F)
Virus! The Secret World of Computer Invaders That Breed and Destroy, 8998
Viruses: Agents of Change, 5183
Viscous Circle, 2351(F)
A Vision of Light, 1466(F)
Vision of the Hunter, 1356(F)

The Visit, 2998
The Visitors, 1270(F)
Visual Aid, 5716
Visual Games, 5330
A Visual History of Costume: The Fourteenth & Fifteenth Centuries, 5288
A Visual History of Costume: The Twentieth Century, 5274
Visual Tennis: Mental Imagery and the Quest for the Winning Edge, 9973
Vital Signs, 5211, 56(F)
Viva! Zappa, 6460
Vivienne: The Life and Suicide of an Adolescent Girl, 6925
Vogue Dictionary of Knitting Stitches, 9247
The Vogue Sewing Book, 9259
The Vogue/Butterick Step-by-Step Guide to Sewing Techniques, 9258
A Voice for a Princess, 1226(F)
Voice in the Night, 2073(F)
Voice of the Whirlwind, 2844(F)
Voices & Visions of the American West, 8153
Voices, 1870–1914, 7486
Voices from the Holocaust, 7283
Voices from the Third Reich, 7299
Voices in the Gallery: Poems & Pictures, 3146
Voices in the Mirror: An Autobiography, 6295
Voices of Freedom, 4364
The Voices of Rape, 5503
Voices of the French Revolution, 7491
Voices of the Great War, 7486
Voices of the Wind: Native American Legends, 3422
Volcano, 8807
Volcanoes, 8805
Volcanoes and Earthquakes, 8801
Volcanoes, Earthquakes, and the Formation of Continents, 8804
Volleyball: The Game and How to Play It, 9979
Volpone, 3032
Voltaire, 3601
Volume Three of Clive Barker's Books of Blood, 1714(F)

Volunteer Vacations, 4850
Voorloper, 2720(F)
The Vor Game, 2446(F)
The Vow of the Heron, 1464(F)
VOYA 8/90, 1253(F)
The Voyage of American Promise, 9931
The Voyage of Charles Darwin: His Autobiographical Writings, 6657
The Voyage of the Armada: The Spanish Story, 7556
The Voyage of the Beagle, 6993
Voyage to the Red Planet, 2417(F)
Voyage to the Whales, 8657
A Voyager Out: The Life of Mary Kingsley, 6679
Voyagers III: Star Brothers, 2425(F)
Voyages: Poems by Walt Whitman, 3342
The Voyages of Captain Cook, 6136
The Vulcan Academy Murders, 2653(F)

W. C. Fields: A Life in Film, 6390
W. E. B. Du Bois: Black Radical Democrat, 6504
W. H. Auden, 3872, 3874
W. Somerset Maugham, 3655
Wait for What Will Come, 2113(F)
Wait till Next Year, 9570
Waiting for an Army to Die: The Tragedy of Agent Orange, 8150
Waiting for Godot, 2991
Waiting for the Barbarians, 643(F)
Waiting Spirits, 1727(F)
Waking Dream, 2207(F)
Walden, 3551
Walg: A Novel of Australia, 1405(F)
A Walk across America, 6145
Walk Gently This Good Earth, 1621(F)
Walk in My Soul, 1586(F)
A Walk in the Sun, 1647(F)
A Walk in the Wood, 2023(F)
Walk through Cold Fire, 808(F)

The Walk West: A Walk across America 2, 6145
Walker in the Shadows, 2110(F)
Walking across Egypt, 1879(F)
Walking Hawk, 192(F)
Walking Medicine, 5367
Walking Softly in the Wilderness, 9796
Walks without a Soul, 1582(F)
The Wall, 1659(F)
The Wall Came Tumbling Down: The Berlin Wall and the Fall of Communism, 7502
Wall Street: How It Works, 4601
Wallenberg: Lost Hero, 6879
Walls: Resisting the Third Reich—One Woman's Story, 6969
The Walls of Air, 1141(F)
Walt Frazier: One Magic Season & a Basketball Life, 6744
Walt Whitman, 3891, 6327
Walter Lippmann and the American Century, 6283
Waltz with a Stranger, 2325(F)
Waltz with the Lady, 2301(F)
Waltzing on Water: Poetry by Women, 3299
The Wanderer, 2641(F), 302(F)
The Wandering Fire, 1166(F)
Wandering through Winter, 8406
Wanderings: Chaim Potok's History of the Jews, 7066
The Want Makers: The World of Advertising—How They Make You Buy, 4616
Wanted: The Search for Nazis in America, 17(F)
War, 7039
The War Against the Jews, 1933–1945, 7200
War and Human Nature: Opposing Viewpoints, 4128
War and Peace, 322(F)
War and Peace in the Nuclear Age, 4156
War and Remembrance, 1689(F)
War as I Knew It, 6631
The War Canoe, 447(F)
War Clouds in the West: Indians & Cavalry Men, 1860–1890, 7966

The War Hound and the World's Pain, 1224(F)
War in the Desert, 7196
War in the Outposts, 7279
The War of 1812: A Forgotten Conflict, 7868
War of the Twins, 1313(F)
The War of the Worlds, 2834(F)
The War on Terrorism, 4547
War on the Frontier, 7943
War on the Mississippi, 7943
The War on Villa Street, 880(F)
The War Poets, 3161
A War Remembered, 8147
War under the Pacific, 7320
War within and Without: Diaries and Letters of Anne Morrow Lindbergh, 1939–1944, 6282
War World, 2513(F)
War Year, 1696(F)
The Warden, 387(F)
Ware Hawk, 1237(F)
Warlock Unlocked, 1277(F)
Warlord of Mars, 2453(F)
Warm Hearts & Cold Noses: A Common Sense Guide to Understanding the Family Dog, 8737
A Warmer Season, 894(F)
A Warning to the Curious, 1771(F)
The Warping of Al, 534(F)
Warrior Lives, 1256(F)
The Warrior Queens, 6785
Warriors & Adventurers, 6971
The Warrior's Apprentice, 2444(F)
Warriors, Gods & Spirits from Central & South American Mythology, 3454
Warriors of Arthur, 3462
The Warsaw Ghetto, 7315
The Warsaw Ghetto: A Christian's Testimony, 6891
Wart, Son of Toad, 531(F)
Washington, D.C. 1617(F)
Washington Goes to War, 8049
Washington in Focus: The Photo History of the Nation's Capital, 8161
Washington Irving, 3702
Washington Square, 408(F)
The Washington Square Press Handbook of Good English, 3929

The Waste Land, and Other Poems, 3201
Watch for Me on the Mountain, 1498(F)
Watchers, 1800(F)
Watching Television: A Pantheon Guide to Popular Culture, 6016
Water-Color Painting, 9208
Water Girl, 502(F)
The Water Is Wide, 645(F)
The Water Planet: A Celebration of the Wonder of Water, 8791
Water Spirits, 3371
Water Walker, 3897
Water Witch, 2538(F), 2846(F)
Watercolor: You Can Do It! 9186
Watercolor Day by Day, 9187
Watercolor for Illustration, 9205
Watergate: Scandal in the White House, 8061
Waterlily, 1501(F)
The Waterline, 433(F)
Waterloo, 7146
Watership Down, 1003(F)
The Wave, 1827(F)
Waves and Beaches: The Dynamics of the Ocean Surface, 8880
The Way of All Flesh, 338(F)
A Way of Being, 5545
The Way of the Hunter: The Art and Spirit of Modern Hunting, 9583
Way of the Lawless, 22(F)
Way of the Pilgrim, 2511(F)
The Way of the Scarlet Pimpernel, 1455(F)
The Way of the World, 3026
Way Station, 2790(F)
The Way the Future Was: A Memoir, 6297
The Way Things Work, 8950
The Way to Cook, 9321
Way to Dusty Death, 1664(F)
The Way to Ski! The Official Method, 9943
The Way We Were: 1963—The Year Kennedy Was Shot, 8080
Ways of Indian Magic, 3429
Ways of Seeing, 5712
Wayward Girls & Wicked Women, 448(F)
We, 2864(F)

We Animals: Poems of Our World, 3147
We Are Not Afraid, 4358
We Are Your Sisters: Black Women in the Nineteenth Century, 7779
We Are Your Sons: The Legacy of Julius and Ethel Rosenberg, 6634
"We Have a Donor": The Bold New World of Organ Transplants, 5164
We Have AIDs, 5200
We Have Always Lived in the Castle, 2063(F)
We Have Come a Long Way: The Story of Women's Tennis, 9968
We Hold These Truths: Understanding the Ideas and Ideals of the Constitution, 4180
We Knew Stonewall Jackson, 6596
We Shall Overcome: Martin Luther King, Jr., and the Black Freedom Struggle, 4350
The Weaker Vessel, 7516
Wealth & Poverty: An Economic History of the Twentieth Century, 4581
The Wealth of Nations, 4582
The Wealth of the Nation: An Economic History of the United States, 7718
Weapons, an International Encyclopedia from 5000 BC to 2000 AD, 9125
Weather, 8873
The Weather Companion: An Album of Meteorological History, Science, Legend, & Folklore, 8870
Weather Forecasting: A Young Meteorologist's Guide, 8872
The Weaving, Spinning, and Dyeing Book, 9140
The Web and the Rock, 944(F)
The Web of Life, 8405
Web of Stars, 1050(F)
Web of the Chosen, 1068(F)
Web of the Witch World, 2718(F)
Webster's New World Dictionary of Computer Terms, 8964
Webster's Secretarial Handbook, 4643

Webster's Word Histories, 3954
The Wedding Ghost, 1130(F)
Wednesday the Rabbi Got Wet, 2082(F)
Weeds, 8437
Weekend Mechanic's Handbook: Complete Auto Repairs You Can Make, 9117
Weep No More, My Lady, 1965(F)
Weetzie Bat, 769(F)
Weight Training and Body Building for Young Athletes, 9769
Weight Watchers New International Cookbook, 9352
Weight Watchers Quick Success Program Cookbook, 9353
The Weighting Game: The Truth about Weight Control, 5418
Welcome to Moonbase, 8336
Welcome to the Monkey House: A Collection of Short Works, 2821(F)
Welfare: Helping Hand or Trap? 4516
Well Body, Well Earth: The Sierra Club Environmental Health Sourcebook, 4456
The Well-Tempered Sentence: A Punctuation Handbook for the Innocent, the Eager and the Doomed, 4679
West of Eden, 2575(F)
West of the Moon, 722(F)
West Side Story: A Musical, 3092
Western Birds, 8536
Western Forests, 8824
The Western Intellectual Tradition, from Leonardo to Hegel, 3998
Wetlands, 8818
A Whale for the Killing, 8655
Whale Nation, 8658
Whale Songs and Wasp Maps: The Mystery of Animal Thinking, 8478
The Whale War, 8643
The Whale Watchers' Guide, 8648
The Whale-Watcher's Handbook, 8653
The Whalers, 7886
Whales, Dolphins and Porpoises, 8652

Whales of the World, 8640

What a Way to Go, 9498

What Am I Doing Here? 3527

What Are People For? 3523

What Are the Chances? Risks, Odds, and Likelihood in Everyday Life, 8859

What Can I Write About? 4695

What Color Is Your Parachute? 4787

What Computers Can Do, 9015

What Did Miss Darrington See? An Anthology of Feminist Supernatural Fiction, 1833(F)

What Did You Do in the War, Daddy? Growing Up German, 7506

"What Do You Care What Other People Think?": Further Adventures of a Curious Character, 6665

What Do You Say after You Say Hello? The Psychology of Human Destiny, 5528

What Happens in Hamlet, 3832

What Is a Jew? 4059

What Is a Masterpiece? 5714

What Is a Share of Stock? 4602

What Is the Bible? 4093

What Mad Pursuit, 6654

What Manner of Man: A Biography of Martin Luther King, Jr. 6509

What Should We Do about Davey? 806(F)

What Teenagers Want to Know about Sex: Questions and Answers, 5454

What the Dead Men Say, 108(F)

What the Great Religions Believe, 4049

What They Did for Love: The Untold Story behind the Making of A Chorus Line, 5915

What to Do If You or Someone You Know Is Under 18 and Pregnant, 5490

What to Do with the Rest of Your Life, 4825

What to Know about the Treatment of Cancer, 5170

What to Listen for in Music, 5817

What to Say When You Don't Know What to Say, 4676

What You Can Believe about Drugs: An Honest and Unhysterical Guide for Teens, 5109

What's That Pig Outdoors? A Memoir of Deafness, 6923

What's What: A Visual Glossary of Everyday Objects, 3921

Wheel of Stars, 1234(F)

Wheel of the Winds, 2533(F)

Wheels, 116(F)

When Angels Appear, 9513

When Bad Things Happen to Good People, 5617

When Do Fish Sleep? And Other Imponderables of Everyday Life, 9494

When Eight Bells Toll, 1665(F)

When Food's a Foe: How to Confront and Conquer Eating Disorders, 5387

When Harlem Was in Vogue, 8169

When I Say No, I Feel Guilty, 5569

When Living Hurts, 5611

When Memory Comes, 7207

When No One Was Looking, 2888(F)

When Someone You Know Has AIDS: A Practical Guide, 5206

When Someone You Know Is Gay, 5459

When Summer's in the Meadow, 7540

When the Cheering Stopped: The Last Years of Woodrow Wilson, 6576

When the Legends Die, 446(F)

When the Shooting Stops . . . the Cutting Begins: A Film Editor's Story, 6053

When the World Screamed and Other Stories: The Professor Challenger Adventures, 78(F)

When Time Ran Out: Coming of Age in the Third Reich, 6970

When We First Met, 2306(F)

When Your Parent Drinks Too Much: A Book for Teenagers, 5150

When Your Parents Divorce, 5637

Where Are the Children? 1966(F)

Where Are They Today? Great Sport Stars of Yesteryear, 6705

Where Are You Going, Where Have You Been? Stories of Young America, 893(F)

Where Do We Go from Here: Chaos or Community? 4369

Where Dragons Lie, 1264(F), 1271(F)

Where Dragons Rule, 1271(F)

Where I Live: Selected Essays, 6116

Where Late the Sweet Birds Sang, 2839(F)

Where Silence Reigns: Selected Prose, 3546

Where the Birds Are: A Guide to All 50 States and Canada, 8539

Where the Evil Dwells, 1270(F)

Where the Kissing Never Stops, 1886(F)

Where the River Runs, 1597(F)

Where the Sun Never Shines: A History of America's Bloody Coal Industry, 4518

While My Pretty One Sleeps, 1967(F)

While Reagan Slept, 3491

Whip Hand, 2018(F)

A Whisper in the Night, 2334(F)

Whispers VI, 1838(F)

The Whistleblowers: Exposing Corruption in Government and Industry, 4521

The White Album, 3529

A White Bird Flying, 1554(F)

White Cargo, 279(F)

The White Company, 1422(F)

White Dragon, 2661(F)

White Fang, 411(F)

White Gold Wielder, 1098(F)

The White House, 8174

The White House Pantry Murder, 2165(F)

White House Years, 6599

White-Jacket: Or the World in a Man-of-War, 415(F)

The White Lantern, 7015

The White Man's Indian: Images of the American Indian from Columbus to the Present, 7794
White Out! 159(F)
The White Plague, 125(F)
The White Puma, 292(F)
White Rabbit: A Doctor's Story of Her Addiction and Recovery, 5144
A White Romance, 829(F)
White Silk and Black Tar: A Journal of the Alaska Oil Spill, 4444
White Wolf: Living with an Arctic Legend, 8512
Whitetail Country, 8522
Whitewater, 843(F)
Whitewater Rafting in Eastern America, 9953
Whitney's Star Finder: A Field Guide to the Heavens, 8293
Whittling, 9275
Whittling and Woodcarving, 9292
Who Censored Roger Rabbit? 2223(F)
Who Could Forget the Mayor of Lodi? 776(F)
Who Goes Out in the Midday Sun? An Englishman's Trek through the Amazon Jungle, 7667
Who Is Felix the Great? 566(F)
Who Should Play God? 5262
Who Was When? A Dictionary of Contemporaries, 7035
Who Will Know Us? 3329
Who Will Remember the People . . . 1353(F)
The Whole Baseball Catalogue, 9702
The Whole Film Sourcebook, 6029
The Whole Nine Yards, 712(F)
The Whole World in His Hands, 6436
Who's Afraid of Beowulf? 1156(F)
Who's Afraid of Virginia Woolf? 3060
Who's in Charge? How the Media Shape News and Politicians Win Votes, 4271
Who's Who in New Country Music, 5904

Who's Who in the Ancient World, 7086
Who's Who in the Super Bowls, 9845
Whose Rose Garden Is It Anyway? 3492
Why Am I So Miserable if These Are the Best Years of My Life? 5607
Why Are They Weeping? South Africans under Apartheid, 7387
Why Do Clocks Run Clockwise? and Other Imponderables: Mysteries of Everyday Life Explained by David Feldman, 9495
Why Do Dogs Have Wet Noses? And Other Imponderables of Everyday Life, 9496
Why I Climb: Personal Insights of Top Climbers, 9568
Why I Left Harry's All-Night Hamburgers: And Other Stories from Isaac Asimov's Science Fiction Magazine, 2359(F)
Why Johnny Still Can't Read: A New Look at the Scandal of Our Schools, 4625
Why Me? 2210(F) 6382
Why Me? Coping with Family Illness, 5195
Why Me? Help for Victims of Child Sexual Abuse, 5507
Why Me? The Story of Jenny, 654(F)
Why We Can't Wait, 4370
The Whyte Harte, 1420(F)
The Wicked Day, 1279(F)
The Wicked Godmother, 2248(F)
Wicked Women of the Screen, 6049
The Wide Shore, 2758(F)
Wielding a Red Sword, 1013(F)
Wild Animals of North America, 8496
Wild Child, 5383
Wild Echoes: Encounters with the Most Endangered Species in North America, 8569
The Wild Type, 264(F)
Wild Whales, 8642
The Wild Years (1946–1955), 2564(F)
Wilderness Survival, 9805

Wilderness Survival Handbook, 9795
Wilderness U.S.A., 7786
Wildflowers across America, 8435
Wildflowers of North America, 8448
Wildfowl of the World, 8557
Wildlife in America, 8576
Wildlife of the Deserts, 8409
Wildlife of the Forests, 8822
Wildlife Through the Camera, 8452
The Will of the Wanderer, 1316(F)
Will You Be My Posslq? 527(F)
Willa: The Life of Willa Cather, 6229
Willa Cather, 3727
Willa Cather: A Literary Life, 6230
William Butler Yeats, 3870
William Faulkner, 3722, 3738
William Faulkner: The Yoknapatawpha Country, 3705
William Jennings Bryan: Champion of Democracy, 6579
William Shakespeare: A Compact Documentary Life, 6307
William Shakespeare: The Tragedies, 3821
Willy Brandt, 6830
Win at Chess, 9821
The Wind from the Sun: Stories from the Space Age, 2484(F)
Wind in the Ashtree, 6928
Wind, Sand, and Stars, 9075
Wind Sports, 9611
Windbreak: A Woman Rancher on the Northern Plains, 8583
Windhaven, 1214(F)
The Windjammers, 8005
Windmaster's Bane, 1088(F)
Window on the Square, 2211(F)
Winds of Change, 2729(F)
Winds of Darkover, 1054(F)
The Winds of War, 1689(F)
The Wind's Twelve Quarters, 1193(F)
The Windsor Knot, 2093(F)
Winesburg, Ohio, 630(F)
Winfield: A Player's Life, 6735
The Winged Horse: The Story of Poets and Their Poetry, 3847

The Winged Voice: The Poetic Voice of Henry David Thoreau, 3524

Wingmaster, 2601(F)

Wings and Roots, 746(F)

Wings of the Falcon, 2110(F)

Winners: Women and the Nobel Prize, 6789

Winners and Losers: How Elections Work in America, 4274

Winnie Mandela, 6795

Winning Back the Sky: A Tactical Analysis of Terrorism, 4545

Winning Basketball for Girls, 9739

The Winning Edge: A Complete Guide to Intercollegiate Athletic Programs, 4745

Winning Money for College, 4777

The Winning Pitcher: Baseball's Top Pitchers Demonstrate What It Takes to Be an Ace, 9660

Winning the City, 2887(F)

Winning the War Within: Understanding, Protecting, and Building Your Body's Immunity, 5295

Winning with Science: The Complete Guide to Science Research and Programs for Students, 4712

Winning Wrestling, 9783

Winslow Homer, 6196

Winter Count, 179(F)

Winter Hawk, 253(F)

Winter in Eden, 2575(F)

Winter Season, 6371

Winter Wolves, 1864(F)

Winterkill, 1508(F)

Winter's Tale, 1148(F)

Winters' Tales, 2976(F)

Wired, 6370

The Wisdom of Confucius, 3999

The Wise Child, 2324(F)

The Wise Wound: Eve's Curse and Everywoman, 5492

The Wishsong of Shannara, 1061(F)

The Wit & Wisdom of Mark Twain, 3483

Witch Goddess, 1005(F)

Witch World, 1238(F)

Witchcraft at Salem, 7840

The Witches of Wenshar, 1762(F)

With a Daughter's Eye: A Memoir of Margaret Mead and Gregory Bateson, 6689

With a Single Spell, 1309(F)

With a Tangled Skein, 1014(F)

With All My Might, 6227

With Byrd at the Bottom of the World, 7709

With Justice for None: Destroying an American Myth, 4255

With Malice Toward None: The Life of Abraham Lincoln, 6547

Without Feathers, 3482

Without Honor: Defeat in Vietnam and Cambodia, 8121

Witness at Large, 1997(F)

Witness for the Prosecution, 1958(F)

Witness to the Holocaust: An Oral History, 7239

Witness to War: A Biography of Marguerite Higgins, 6287

Witness to War: An American Doctor in El Salvador, 7654

Witnesses, 1516(F)

Witnesses at the Creation: Hamilton, Madison, Jay and the Constitution, 4200

Wizard, 6733

Wizard at Large, 2440(F)

The Wizard of Earthsea, 2636(F)

The Wizard of Oz, 6024

Wizard of Tizare, 1081(F)

Wizard Spawn, 1072(F)

Wizard World, 2867(F)

Wizardry Compiled, 1078(F)

Wizards, 1019(F)

The Wizards and the Warriors, 1077(F)

The Wizard's Tide, 526(F)

Wizard's Worlds, 2721(F)

Woe to Live On, 1553(F)

Wok Cookery, 9334

Wolf and Iron, 2512(F)

The Wolf Tracker and Other Animal Tales, 288(F)

Wolfbane, 2741(F)

The Wolfen, 1854(F)

A Wolverine Is Eating My Leg, 6129

Wolves, 8521

The Woman Doctor's Diet for Teenage Girls, 5412

The Woman in Black, 1765(F)

Woman in the Dark: A Novel of Dangerous Romance, 2040(F)

The Woman in the Dunes, 953(F)

Woman in the Mists: The Story of Dian Fossey and the Mountain Gorillas of Africa, 6668

The Woman in White, 342(F)

A Woman of Independent Means, 825(F)

A Woman of Substance, 774(F)

The Woman Warrior: Memoirs of a Girlhood among Ghosts, 6922

The Woman Who Knew Too Much, 1959(F)

A Woman's Golf Game, 9870

Women: A World Report, 4312

The Women, 7995

Women Aloft, 9072

Women and Children Last: The Plight of Poor Women in Affluent America, 4513

Women and Fiction, 2900(F)

Women and Medicine: Pioneers Meeting the Challenge! 5243

Women and War, 1682(F)

Women and Wilderness, 6119

Women Artists: An Illustrated History, 5746

Women Artists in History: From Antiquity to the 20th Century, 5764

Women As Healers: A History of Women and Medicine, 5231

Women Expressionists, 5734

Women in American Religion, 4039

Women in Comedy, 5956

Women in Mathematics, 6645

Women in Politics, 4272

Women in Science: Portraits from a World in Transition, 8221

Women in the Middle Ages, 7133

Women in the Resistance and in the Holocaust: The Voices of Eyewitnesses, 7234

Women in War, 7286

Women Making History: Conversations with Fifteen New Yorkers, 4302

Women of the Air, 9071

Women of the Four Winds, 6121
Women of the World: The Great Foreign Correspondents, 3984
Women of Vision, 3716
Women Warlords, 7063
Women Who Changed Things, 6486
Women Who Write: From the Past and the Present to the Future, 3603
Women Working: An Anthology of Stories and Poems, 970(F)
Womenfolks: Growing Up down South, 8194
Women's Diaries of the Westward Journey, 7980
Wonder Boy: Barry Minkow— The Kid Who Swindled Wall Street, 6693
The Wonder Years (1926– 1935), 2564(F)
Wonderful Me, 940(F)
The Wonderful World of Magic and Witchcraft, 9475
The Wonderful World of Superstition, Prophecy and Luck, 9475
Wonder's Child: My Life in Science Fiction, 3790
Wonderworks: Science Fiction & Fantasy Art, 5728
Woodrow Wilson and the Progressive Era, 1910–1917, 8012
Woodrow Wilson and World War I, 1917–1921, 7156
Woodrow Wilson, World Statesman, 6575
Woodstock: The Oral History, 5883
Woodstock: The Summer of Our Lives, 5855
Woodswoman, 6683
The Woodturner's Companion, 9286
Woodturning: A Designer's Notebook, 9278
Woodworker's Handbook, 9270
Woodworking, 9282, 9295
Woodworking Projects for the Home Workshop, 9268
Woody Allen, 6357
Woody Guthrie: A Life, 6395
Word of Honor, 1695(F)
Words by Heart, 495(F)

Words Can Kill, 1979(F)
Words from the Myths, 3470
Words in the Blood: Contemporary Indian Writers of North and South America, 2924
The Words of Peace: Selections from the Speeches of the Winners of the Nobel Peace Prize, 3521
Words of Wisdom: More Good Advice, 3548
Words to Love By, 4088
Wordstruck: A Memoir, 6421
Work, Study, Travel Abroad: The Whole World Handbook, 4713
Work Your Way around the World, 4836
Workfare vs. Welfare, 4505
Working: People Talk about What They Do All Day and How They Feel about What They Do. 4611
Working Cats, 8694
Working in a Very Small Place: The Making of a Neurosurgeon, 6677
Working in Hollywood, 5998
Working in Wood, 9287
Working Out a Painting, 9184
Working Outside: A Career and Self-Employment Handbook, 4838
Working Robots, 8969
Working Trot, 289(F)
Working Wardrobe: Affordable Clothes That Work for You, 9173
Working with Metal, 9152
Working with Wood, 9294
The Workshop of Democracy, 7719
The World According to Garp, 565(F)
The World Almanac Book of World War II, 7328
The World Almanac of First Ladies, 6484
The World at Arms: The Reader's Digest Illustrated History of World War II, 7278
The World at the End of Time, 2739(F)
The World at War, 7173
World Encyclopedia of Civil Aircraft: From Leonardo da Vinci to the Present, 9057

World Folktales, 3362
A World History, 7059
The World History Factfinder, 7058
A World History of the Twentieth Century: Volume 1; Western Dominance, 1900–1945, 7150
World Hunger: Twelve Myths, 4511
The World of Coins and Coin Collecting, 9446
The World of Dance, 5961
The World of Duke Ellington, 6387
The World of Gwendolyn Brooks, 3879
A World of Ideas, 8084
The World of M. C. Escher, 5779
The World of Musical Comedy, 6175
World of Our Fathers: The Jews of Eastern Europe, 4389
World of Our Fathers, 4386
The World of Star Trek, 6085
A World of Strangers, 965(F)
World of the Brain, 5326
The World of UFOs, 9487
World of Wonders, 797(F)
World Power Up Close: Candid Conversations with 31 Key Leaders, 7338
World Religions from Ancient History to the Present, 4069
The World Series: An Illustrated History from 1903 to the Present, 9657
The World since 1945: A Complete History of Global Change from 1945 to the Present, 7343
World War II: A 50th Anniversary History, 7174
World War II Resistance Stories, 7272
World War II Super Facts, 7247
The Worldly Philosophers: The Lives, Times, and Ideas of the Great Economic Thinkers, 4570
Worlds Apart, 2570(F)
The World's Best SF Annual, 2854(F)
World's Fair, 1622(F)
The World's Most Challenging Puzzles, 9469

The Worlds of H. Beam Piper, 2730(F)
The Worst of Everything, 9511
The Wounded Land, 1098(F)
The Wreck of the Mary Deare, 146(F)
Wrestling for Beginners, 9785
Write Your Way into College: Composing a Successful Application Essay, 4731
The Writer on Her Work, 3972
The Writer's Chapbook, 3598
The Writer's Handbook, 4688
The Writer's Handbook, 3975
The Writer's Market 1991, 3979
Writers of the Purple Sage: An Anthology of Recent Western Writing, 204(F)
Writing a Thriller, 3966
Writing Books for Young People, 3962
Writing Down the Bones: Freeing the Writer Within, 3964
Writing for Story: Craft Secrets of Dramatic Nonfiction by a Two-Time Pulitzer Prize Winner, 3960
Writing Music for Hit Songs, 5875
Writing the Research Paper, 4654
Writing Themes about Literature, 4697
Writing with Power: Techniques for Mastering the Writing Process, 3959
Writing Your College Admissions Essay, 4754
Writing Your College Application Essay, 4749
Writings, 7839
Written in My Soul, 5863
The Wrong Stuff, 9671
Wuthering Heights, 336(F)
WW II: Time-Life Books History of the Second World War, 7312
Wyrms, 2463(F)

Yamamoto: The Man Who Planned Pearl Harbor, 6819
Yankee Folk Crafts, 9156
Yarrow, 1734(F)
Yashimoto's Last Dive, 1683(F)
Yaz: Baseball, the Wall, and Me, 6736

Yeager, 6166
The Year before Yesterday, 2336(F)
Year by Year in the Rock Era, 8070
A Year in the Sun: The Life & Times of a Sports Columnist, 9604
The Year It Rained, 657(F)
A Year-Long Night: Tales of a Medical Intern, 6680
The Year of the Gopher, 892(F)
The Year of the Ransom, 2348(F)
Year of the Unicorn, 1238(F), 2718(F)
The Yearling, 297(F)
The Year's Best Fantasy Stories: 14, 1263(F)
The Year's Best Horror Stories: XVIII, 1860(F)
The Year's Best Horror Stories, 1817(F)
The Year's Best Horror Stories, Volume XVII, 1861(F)
The Year's Best Mystery and Suspense Stories, 2055(F)
The Year's Best Science Fiction, 2518(F)
The Year's Best Science Fiction: Second Annual Collection, 2519(F)
The Year's Best Science Fiction: Sixth Annual Collection, 2520(F)
Years of Infamy: The Untold Story of America's Concentration Camps, 7317
Years of Upheaval, 6599
A Yellow Raft in Blue Water, 452(F)
Yellowstone Country: The Enduring Wonder, 8199
Yes Is Better Than No, 444(F)
Yiddish Folktales, 3414
Yogi: It Ain't Over . . . 6715
Yondering, 163(F)
You & Your Aquarium, 8774
You & Your Cat, 8705
You & Your Dog, 8739
You Are Somebody Special, 5530
You Can Fool All of the People All the Time, 3493
You Can Learn Lettering and Calligraphy, 9159
You Can Make It Without a College Degree, 4807

You Can Train Your Cat, 8696
You Can't Get There from Here, 758(F)
You Can't Go Home Again, 944(F)
You Can't Kill the Spirit, 7055
You Don't Have to Be a Genius to Land a Computer Job, 5058
You Know Me Al: A Busher's Letters, 2881(F)
You Never Lose, 926(F)
The Young Actor's Workbook, 6107
Young Alcoholics, 5099
The Young Athlete's Manual, 5351
Young Kate, 6400
The Young Lions, 1676(F)
A Young Man's Guide to Sex, 5464
Young Parents, 5669
The Young People's Yellow Pages: A National Sourcebook for Youth, 5628
The Young United States, 1783 to 1830, 7861
A Young Woman's Guide to Sex, 5496
The Young Writer's Handbook, 4703
The Youngest Science: Notes of a Medicine-Watcher, 6702
Your Career in Nursing, 4984
Your Cat's First Year, 8690
Your College Application, 4738
Your 1st Résumé, 4796
Your Horse: A Step-by-Step Guide to Horse Ownership, 8760
Your IBM PC: A Guide to the IBM Personal Computer, 8981
Your Introduction to Law, 4235
Your Job—Where to Find It, How to Get It, 4790
Your Memory: How It Works and How to Improve It, 5331
Your Parents and Your Self: Alike/Unlike/Agreeing/Disagreeing, 5662
Your Pilot's License, 9085
Your Quick & Easy Car Care and Safe Driving Handbook, 9101
Your United Nations: The Official Guidebook, 4125

You're the Detective! 24 Solve-Them-Yourself Picture Mysteries, 9470

Youth and the Law, 4254

Zarsthor's Bane, 1238(F)
Zelda: A Biography, 6245

Zen: Direct Pointing to Reality, 4033
Zen and the Art of Motorcycle Maintenance: An Inquiry into Values, 4019
Zen in the Art of Writing, 3703

The Zimmerman Telegram, 7165
The Zombies That Ate Pittsburgh: The Films of George A. Romero, 6013
Zora Neale Hurston, 6270
Zorba the Greek, 973(F)

Subject/Grade Level Index

All entries are listed within specific subjects and then according to grade level suitability (see the key at the foot of pages for grade level designations). Subjects are arranged alphabetically and subject heads may be subdivided into nonfiction (e.g., "Adoption") and fiction (e.g., "Adoption–Fiction"). Reference to entries are by entry numbers, not pages.

A

Aaronsohn, Sarah
JS: 6801

Abagnale, Frank
S: 6887

Abdul-Jabbar, Kareem
JS: 6737–38

Abernathy, Ralph David
S: 6493

Abominable snowman–Fiction
S: 1242

Aborigines–Australia
S: 6934, 7474

Aborigines–Fiction
S: 1405

Abortion
JS: 5082, 5508, 5519
S: 4238, 5462, 5521

Abortion–Fiction
JS: 867, 949
S: 857

Abortion–History
S: 5483

Abusive relationships–Fiction
JS: 729, 2319

Academic guidance, 4708–4781

Academic skills, 4638–4707

Academy Awards (Oscars)
JS: 6043

Accidents
S: 9065

Accidents–Fiction
JS: 726, 2139
S: 213

Accounting–Careers
JS: 4932, 4938
S: 4931

Acid rain
S: 4454

Acting
JS: 6076, 6176
S: 6080, 6088, 6099, 6107–9, 6111

Acting–Careers
JS: 4875, 4887, 4892–93, 4896

Acting–Fiction
JS: 2227
S: 758

Actors
JS: 6075, 6176
S: 3815, 5896

Actors–Biography
JS: 6179, 6357, 6429
S: 6367, 6370, 6427

Actors–Fiction
JS: 937

Actresses
JS: 6049

Actresses–Biography
JS: 6400, 6457
S: 6366, 6372–73, 6391, 6397–98, 6401, 6447

Actresses–Fiction
S: 1921

Adams, Abigail
S: 6521–22

Adams, Ansel
JS: 5789
S: 6188

Adams, Grizzly
JS: 6124

Adams, Henry
S: 6610

Adams, Samuel
S: 7848

Addams, Jane
JS: 6612
S: 6611

Adirondacks
S: 6683, 8168

Adirondacks–Fiction
S: 148

Adolescence
JS: 5479, 5607–8, 5610, 5653, 6925
S: 5543, 5558, 5616, 5632

Adolescence–Diet
S: 5423

Adolescence–Fiction
JS: 793, 821, 824, 831, 952, 1308
S: 733, 805, 814, 877, 893, 942

Adolescence–Problems– Fiction, 757–952

Adoption
JS: 5478, 5642

Adoption–Fiction
JS: 727, 804
S: 514, 539, 589, 1878

JS = Junior–Senior High   S = Senior High

Adventure and survival stories–Fiction, 1–280

Adventure stories–Fiction
JS: 12, 15–16, 18–19, 23, 31–34, 40, 42, 49, 62, 76, 78, 80, 83, 89–91, 95–96, 102–3, 105–6, 108, 114, 120–23, 132–34, 139–41, 151, 153, 156–58, 165, 171, 177–78, 182, 188, 194, 197–99, 201, 205, 212, 223, 225, 227, 231–32, 241, 243, 245–47, 250–51, 255–57, 262, 266, 268, 324–26, 350, 373, 383, 410, 420–21, 429, 897, 1364, 1414, 1423, 1439–40, 1667, 1670, 1845, 2285
S: 2–10, 13–14, 17, 24–25, 27–30, 35–37, 39, 41, 43–45, 47–48, 50, 53–60, 65–75, 77, 79, 81–82, 84–88, 92–94, 97–101, 107, 109–12, 115–18, 124–25, 127–30, 136–37, 142, 144–50, 155, 159, 166–70, 172–76, 179–81, 183–87, 189–90, 195–96, 200, 209–11, 213–17, 226, 234, 237–40, 242, 244, 252–54, 258–61, 263–65, 269–70, 272–76, 279, 346, 374–75, 1415–16, 1421, 1427, 1487, 1864, 1866, 1969, 2009, 2019, 2235, 2284, 2287, 2303–4, 2600, 2797

Adventurers
JS: 6124, 6129, 6144, 6149, 6151, 7037, 7044, 7367, 7456, 7676, 7708
S: 3506, 6123, 7552, 7667, 9938

Adventurers–Biography, 6117–6166

Adventurers–History
JS: 6971

Adventures
JS: 6142

Adversity
S: 5617

Advertising
S: 3973, 4616, 4619–20

Advertising–Careers
JS: 4927
S: 4914, 4916, 4920

Aebi, Tania
JS: 9918

Aerobics
JS: 5360
S: 5346–47, 5356

Aeronautics
S: 8270, 9064, 9075

Aeronautics–Careers
JS: 4857

Aeronautics–History
JS: 9062
S: 9059, 9063

Aerospace–Careers
S: 5054

Afghanistan–Fiction
JS: 165

Afghans
JS: 9243

Africa
JS: 6150, 6472, 7196, 7348–49, 7358, 7367, 8509
S: 6679, 6892, 7350, 7352, 7361–62, 7366, 7368, 7390

Africa–Animals
JS: 7353, 8498, 8503
S: 6164, 8499

Africa–Anthropology
S: 7351

Africa–Art
S: 5767

Africa–Atlases
S: 7355

Africa–Cookbooks
S: 9345

Africa–Description and travel
JS: 7360

Africa–East
JS: 7365

Africa–Encyclopedias
S: 7356

Africa–Fiction
JS: 23, 91, 114, 153
S: 14, 88, 115, 152, 244, 344, 669, 960–61, 964, 1384, 1387, 2943

Africa–Folklore
JS: 3377
S: 3378, 3379, 3435, 3463

Africa–Historical fiction, 1384–1387

Africa–History
JS: 7359
S: 7257, 7345–47, 7354, 7357

Africa–History and geography, 7345–7390

Africa–Literature
S: 3593

Africa–Literature–History and criticism
S: 3599

Africa–Music
S: 5813

Africa–Mythology
S: 3463

Africa–Natural history
JS: 7363–64

Africa–Poetry
S: 3351

Africans–Biography, 6791–6800

Africans–Fiction
JS: 2355

Afro-Americans. *See* Black Americans

Agent Orange
S: 8150

Aggressiveness
S: 5563, 5566

Aging, 5079–5098. *See also* Elderly persons

Agriculture–Careers
S: 4872

Agriculture–United States
S: 8586–87

AIDS
JS: 5167–68, 5173, 5187–88, 5191, 5193, 5196–97, 5200, 5204, 5212, 5222
S: 3985, 5177, 5182, 5184, 5201–2, 5206, 5215, 5219–20, 5223

AIDS–Fiction
JS: 855
S: 676

Air Force Academy (U.S.)
S: 4283

Air Force (R.A.F.)
JS: 7176, 7179

Air Force (U.S.)
JS: 7176

Air pollution
S: 4449

Air war
JS: 7260, 7279
S: 7262

Airlines
JS: 9056, 9066

Airlines–Fiction
S: 116

Airplane crashes
JS: 7682
S: 6942, 9065

Airplane crashes–Fiction
S: 213

Airplane pilots
S: 9085

JS = Junior–Senior High   S = Senior High

Airplanes
JS: 9066, 9077, 9127
S: 6131, 6139, 6155, 9068, 9076,
9085, 9133

Airplanes–Fiction
JS: 1690
S: 58, 69, 239, 269, 1633–34, 1677

Airplanes–History
JS: 6138, 6703, 7153, 9057, 9060,
9062, 9072–74, 9126
S: 6704, 7187, 8104, 9061, 9070,
9123

Airplanes–Model
JS: 9403, 9404
S: 9304

Airplanes–Paper
JS: 9224

Airplanes and aeronautics,
9056–9077

Airships
JS: 9060

Alamo (Texas)
JS: 7964–65, 7996

Alaska
JS: 4451, 6918, 8188
S: 4444, 8180, 8183–86, 8193, 8397

Alaska–Animals
S: 8191

Alaska–Fiction
JS: 34, 123, 293
S: 147, 447, 1351, 1513, 1876

Alaska–History
JS: 8192
S: 7633

Alaska–Poetry
JS: 3324–25

Alcohol
JS: 5106–8, 5115, 5129, 5136
S: 5119

Alcohol–Health problems,
5099–5163

Alcoholism
JS: 5099, 5110, 5115, 5122, 5131,
5139, 5141, 5150, 5157
S: 5114, 5120, 5134, 5137, 5142,
5144, 5152, 5155, 6443

Alcoholism–Fiction
JS: 634, 763

Alexander the Great
S: 6821–23

Alexander the Great–Fiction
S: 1371

Alfred the Great
S: 6824

Algonquin Indians
S: 6962

Aliens–Extraterrestrial. *See*
Extraterrestrial persons

Aliens–Illegal
S: 4503

Aline, Countess of Romanones
S: 6888

Allen, Dick
JS: 6712

Allen, Woody
JS: 6058, 6357

Alligators
JS: 8469

Almanacs
JS: 9503

Alphabet
S: 3968

Alphabet–History
S: 3967

Alvarez, Luis W.
S: 6649

Alzheimer's disease
JS: 5178
S: 5203

Alzheimer's disease–Fiction
JS: 567, 711

Amateur radio
S: 9046

Amazon River
JS: 7669, 7676
S: 7667

Amelia Earhart
JS: 6138

American Civil Liberties Union
S: 4321

American College Testing Program
S: 4658

American League (baseball)
JS: 9653

American literature
S: 418–19, 2896, 2916, 3560, 3590,
3764

**American literature–History
and criticism**
JS: 3700, 3708, 3713, 3726, 3737,
3776, 3789
S: 3570, 3577–79, 3584, 3592,
3597, 3611, 3628, 3695–97, 3699,
3701–3, 3705–7, 3709, 3711–12,
3714, 3717–19, 3721–25, 3727,
3729–30, 3734–36, 3738, 3740,
3742–43, 3745–46, 3748–55,

3758–61, 3765, 3767–68, 3770–
73, 3775, 3777–78, 3783, 3787–
88, 3882

American Revolution. *See*
Revolutionary War (U.S.)

Americans–Biography, 6463–
6639

Amish
S: 4054, 8584

Amnesia–Fiction
JS: 182, 2609
S: 1333, 2030, 2280, 2782

Amphibians
JS: 8461–65, 8467

Amundsen, Roald
S: 6125

Amusement parks–Fiction
S: 214

Anatomy
JS: 9191
S: 8453

Ancient cities and places
JS: 7090

Ancient history
JS: 7021–22, 7026, 7110–11
S: 7085–86, 7088, 7091–92, 7094,
7099, 7101, 7103–4, 7107, 7109,
7112, 7545

**Ancient history–Historical fic-
tion,** 1358–1377

Ancient world
See also under Egypt;
Greece; Rome
JS: 7108
S: 7088, 7099, 8248

Ancient world–Fiction
S: 1375

Anderson, Sparky
S: 6713

Angelou, Maya
S: 6212

Anger
JS: 5562

Animal care
JS: 8451, 8501
S: 8588

Animal care–Careers
JS: 4997
S: 4845

Animal stories
JS: 8682

JS = Junior–Senior High   S = Senior High

Animal stories–Fiction, 281–301
JS: 178, 291, 293, 296–97, 411,
1222, 1243
S: 288, 301

Animal tracks–Field guides
JS: 8487

Animals
JS: 5989

Animals–Africa
JS: 7353

Animals–Alaska
S: 8191

Animals–Behavior
JS: 8473–75, 8479–80
S: 8681

Animals–Bible
JS: 4101

Animals–Communication
JS: 8481–82
S: 8483

Animals–Courtship
S: 8486

Animals–Defenses
JS: 8484

Animals–Ecology
JS: 8455

Animals–Encyclopedias
JS: 8460

Animals–Endangered species,
8568–8580

Animals–Exotic–Fiction
JS: 1084

Animals–Extinct
S: 8572

Animals–Female
S: 8388

Animals–Field guides
JS: 8496

Animals–General
JS: 6019, 8474, 8490, 8494–95

Animals–Intelligence
S: 8476, 8478

Animals–Mythology
S: 3466

Animals–Poetry
JS: 3147

Animals–Poisonous
JS: 8485

Animals–Reproduction
S: 8486

Animals–Research
JS: 4526
S: 6688

Animals–Species, 8488–8567

Animals–Wild
JS: 6124

Animals in art
S: 5720

Animals' rights
S: 8574

Annapurna
S: 9551

Anorexia
JS: 5368, 5387, 5395
S: 5176, 5389, 5396–97

Anorexia–Fiction
S: 699–700, 744, 2153

Antarctic
JS: 7699, 7703–04
S: 6160, 7696, 7700

Anthony, Piers
S: 6213

Anthony, Susan B.
S: 6494–95

Anthropology
JS: 7010
S: 5460, 6685–86, 6689–92, 6989–
91, 6997, 7001–2, 7004, 7008–9,
7012, 7015, 7018, 7082, 7351,
7474, 7477, 7671, 8186

Anti-Semitism
JS: 4409
S: 4168, 4387, 7170, 7253

Antietam, Battle of
S: 7934

Antin, Mary
S: 6613

Ants–Fiction
S: 290

Apache Indians
S: 6621–22

Apache Indians–Fiction
S: 1555

Apartheid
JS: 7386
S: 6791, 6800, 6930, 7369–79,
7382, 7385, 7387–89

Apartheid–Fiction
S: 962, 965, 972, 986–87

Apes–Fiction
JS: 2418

Ape family, 8497–8504

Appalachia–Fiction
JS: 1613
S: 560

Appalachian Mountains
S: 8170

**Appalachian Mountains–Folk
Art**
S: 5808

Appleman-Jurman, Alicia
JS: 6889

Appliances–Repair
JS: 9391

Apprenticeships
S: 4809–10

Aqualung
JS: 8888

Aquariums
JS: 8748–49, 8752, 8771–72, 8774
S: 8770

Aquariums–Encyclopedias
S: 8778

Aquatic animals
JS: 8615
S: 8651

Aquino, Corazon
S: 6802, 7473

Arabs
JS: 7604
S: 6818

Arabs–Folklore
S: 3382

Arafat, Yasser
S: 6803

Archaeology
JS: 5031, 7005, 7020–24, 7026,
7108, 9490
S: 3501, 4109, 7014–15, 7017–18,
7027, 7091, 7095, 7117, 7649,
7655

Archaeology–Dictionaries
S: 7025

Archaeology–Fiction
S: 1255, 1451, 2001, 2128–29, 2401

Archaeology–North America
JS: 7019

Archery
JS: 9607

Architects–Biography
S: 6461

Architecture
JS: 5686, 5691, 5709
S: 4559, 5687, 5690, 5696

JS = Junior–Senior High S = Senior High

Architecture—Careers
JS: 4940, 4943

Architecture—Fiction
S: 991

Architecture—Gothic
JS: 5708

Architecture—Greek
S: 5786

Architecture—History
JS: 5695, 5707, 7118, 7124
S: 5692–94, 5697, 5702, 5711,
5735, 5772, 5786, 6098

Architecture—Roman
S: 5772

Architecture—United States
JS: 6210
S: 5698–706, 6211

Architecture and building,
5686–5711

Arctic
JS: 7691–92, 7706, 7708
S: 7697–98, 7702

Arctic National Wildlife Refuge
S: 8397

Arden, Elizabeth
JS: 6650

Argentina
S: 6883–84, 7688

Argentina—History
S: 7683

Aristotle
S: 3991, 3995

Arizona
S: 8156

Arizona—Fiction
JS: 143
S: 444

Arizona—History
S: 8201

Arkansas—Fiction
S: 849

Arlington National Cemetery
S: 8171

Armed forces (U.S.)
S: 6471, 6601, 6604

**Armed forces (U.S.)—Black
Americans**
S: 4286

Armed forces (U.S.)—Careers
JS: 4281, 4858, 4973, 4980

Armed forces (U.S.)—Women
JS: 4869
S: 4285, 4866

Armenian Americans—Fiction
JS: 492

Arms control
S: 4152

Armstrong, Louis
JS: 6359
S: 6358

Army (U.S.)
JS: 96
S: 4284, 4726, 4861, 7230

**Army (U.S.)—Counter Intelli-
gence Corps**
S: 4288

Arson—Fiction
JS: 1786
S: 273, 2123, 2127

Art, 5712–5807

Art—Abstract
S: 5753

Art—African
S: 5767

Art—American
JS: 5805–6, 6193
S: 5758, 5790, 5792, 5794, 5797,
5801, 5803, 6174, 6180

Art—Careers
JS: 4876, 4886
S: 4889

Art—Chinese
S: 5768, 7406

Art—Dictionaries
S: 5688–89

Art—Dutch
S: 5779, 5781, 5785

Art—English
S: 5787

Art—Expressionism
S: 5734

Art—Fiction
S: 55, 1968

Art—Forgeries
JS: 5727

Art—French
JS: 6206
S: 5773–74, 5777, 5780

Art—Greek
S: 5762

Art—History
JS: 5684, 5729–30, 5732, 5737–38,
5742, 5745–46, 5749, 5761,
5764–65, 5805
S: 5682, 5685, 5736, 5740–41,
5744, 5756, 5758–60, 5763, 5766,
5770–71, 5792, 5803, 6195

Art—Italian
S: 5776, 5782, 5788

Art—Modern
JS: 5730, 5738
S: 5721, 5731, 5739–40, 5744,
5747, 5750–52, 5756, 5759–60,
5774

Art—Photography
S: 5743

Art—Poetry
S: 3146

Art—South Pacific
JS: 5769

Art—Spanish
S: 5775, 5778, 5784, 6208

Art appreciation
JS: 5715, 5726
S: 5712, 5714, 5719, 5725

Art deco
S: 5747

Arthur, King
JS: 6825
S: 3405–8, 3412, 3462, 6826

Arthur, King—Fiction
JS: 1279, 1319, 1321
S: 1016, 1085, 1187–88, 1320,
1334, 1408, 1410, 1430, 1489

Arthur, King—Plays
JS: 3095
S: 2985

Arthurian England—Fiction
S: 1230

Artificial intelligence
JS: 5308, 9019
S: 9003, 9011, 9026

Artificial intelligence—Fiction
S: 2818

Artists—American
JS: 5800

Artists—Biography
JS: 6192, 6202–3, 6206
S: 5778, 5783, 6169, 6189, 6194,
6196, 6204

Artists—Career guidance, 4873–
4902

Artists—Dictionaries
S: 5689

Artists—Dutch
JS: 6209

Artists—Fiction
JS: 895
S: 640, 715, 759, 1477, 2103, 2693

JS = Junior–Senior High   S = Senior High

Artists—French
JS: 6191
S: 6190

Artists—Italian
S: 6199

Artists—Women
S: 6180, 6200–1

Artists' materials
S: 9194

Artley, Bob
S: 6890

Arts and entertainment, 5682–6116

Arts and entertainment—Biography, 6167–6462

Asia
JS: 7392
S: 7395

Asia—Biography, 6801–6819

Asia—Fiction
JS: 1670
S: 1912

Asia—Folklore and fairy tales, 3380–3387

Asia—Historical fiction, 1388–1405

Asia—History
JS: 7042
S: 7391, 7393

Asia—History and geography, 7391–7463

Asian Americans
S: 4399, 4404

Asimov, Isaac—Fiction
S: 2566, 3731

Assassination
JS: 6542, 6548
S: 4372, 6538, 6543, 6628, 7566, 8071

Assassination—Fiction
JS: 89
S: 10, 144, 183, 238

Assassins—Fiction
JS: 2794
S: 1304

Assembler (computer language)
S: 8961

Assertiveness
JS: 5621

Astronautics, 8294–8320

Astronauts
JS: 6126, 6153, 8317
S: 6166, 8312–13, 8329

Astronauts—Fiction
S: 1282

Astronomy
JS: 8240, 8244, 8247, 8252–53, 8256–57, 8259–60, 8264, 8268, 8274–77, 8284, 8286, 8289–90, 8292, 8309, 8353, 8355
S: 8248–50, 8254–55, 8258, 8261–63, 8266–67, 8269–73, 8278–83, 8288, 8291, 8352, 8354, 8356, 8358, 8365, 8367, 8915

Astronomy—Field guides
JS: 8293

Astrophysics
JS: 8369
S: 8298

Athletes
JS: 6705

Athletes—Nutrition
JS: 5344

Atlantic Coast U.S.
JS: 8375

Atlantis
JS: 9533

Atlantis—Fiction
JS: 2715

Atmosphere
JS: 4434, 8866
S: 4437

Atomic bomb
JS: 199, 7243, 9132
S: 4156, 6959, 7212, 7217, 7229, 7232, 7267, 7309, 7327, 8940

Atomic bomb—Fiction
S: 1681

Atomic war. *See* Nuclear war

Attlee, Clement
JS: 6827

Auden, W. H.
S: 3872, 3874

Audio equipment
JS: 9049

Auerbach, Red
JS: 6739

Austen, Jane
S: 3673, 6214

Australia
JS: 6117, 6147, 7392, 7465, 7475, 7478
S: 6820, 6934, 7464, 7468, 7471–72, 7477

Australia—Fiction
JS: 1391
S: 265, 521, 811, 1397, 1405, 1671, 1682, 2087, 2240

Australia—History
S: 7474

Australia—Natural history
JS: 7469, 7479

Australia and the Pacific Islands—History and geography, 7464–7480

Austria—Fiction
S: 1648

Austria—History
JS: 7192
S: 7170

Autism
S: 5372, 6913

Authors—Biography, 6212–6333

Autograph collecting
JS: 9303, 9455, 9458

Automation, 8956–8960, 8962–9033

Automobile driving
JS: 9097, 9101, 9112

Automobile industry
S: 6676

Automobile racing
JS: 6711, 9614–16, 9618–19
S: 9617

Automobile racing—Fiction
JS: 2871

Automobiles
JS: 9080–81, 9083, 9086–88, 9090, 9093, 9098–101, 9104–6
S: 6659, 9082, 9111, 9118

Automobiles—Careers
JS: 4945

Automobiles—Encyclopedias
JS: 9116

Automobiles—Fiction
S: 1780

Automobiles—History
JS: 6666, 9089, 9108

Automobiles—Mechanical systems
S: 9113

Automobiles—Poetry
JS: 3178

Automobiles—Purchasing
JS: 9109

Automobiles—Repairs and maintenance
JS: 9078–79, 9084, 9092, 9094, 9096, 9107, 9110, 9117
S: 9091, 9111, 9114–15

JS = Junior–Senior High S = Senior High

Automobiles–Used
JS: 9095, 9102–3

Aviation
JS: 6140, 6161, 9071
S: 7335, 8270, 9128

Aviation–Careers
JS: 5040

Aviation–History
JS: 9074
S: 6141, 6148, 6154, 7289

Aztecs
S: 7643

B

Babies–Fiction
JS: 2239

Baboons
JS: 8503

Baby care
JS: 5518
S: 5365

Baby-sitting
JS: 5069–71

Bach, Johann Sebastian
S: 6334–36

Backgammon
JS: 9813

Backpacking
JS: 9793, 9799–800, 9802, 9804
S: 9794, 9796

Badgers–Fiction
S: 1075

Baez, Joan
S: 6360

Bailey, Pearl
S: 6361

Baker, John
S: 6762

Baker, Russell
S: 6215–16

Balanchine, George
S: 6362

Baldwin, James
S: 3607, 3783

Balkans
S: 6143

Ballet
JS: 5959

S: 5962, 5965–66, 6362, 6371,
6383, 6389, 6412

Ballet–Fiction
S: 743, 819

Ballet–History
S: 5958

Balloon sculpture
JS: 9143

Balloons and ballooning
JS: 9067
S: 9613

Balzac, Honoré de
S: 3637

Band music
JS: 5936

Banks and banking
S: 4221, 4595–98

Banks and banking–Careers
JS: 4926, 4938
S: 4917

Banks and banking–Fiction
S: 118

Banneker, Benjamin
S: 6496

Bannister, Roger
JS: 6763

Barbiturates
JS: 5126

Barnum, P. T.
JS: 6363
S: 6364–65

Barr, Roseanne
S: 6366

Barrymore, John
S: 6367

Bartoszewski, Wladyslaw
S: 6891

Baseball
JS: 6707, 6709, 6712, 6714–24,
6726–27, 6730–34, 6736, 9447,
9626, 9629–37, 9639, 9641, 9643,
9645–46, 9648, 9650, 9654,
9656–59, 9661, 9668–69, 9673–
74, 9676–77, 9681, 9690–91,
9694, 9698, 9703–4, 9706, 9708–
9, 9711, 9737
S: 6713, 6725, 6728–29, 6735,
9620, 9627–28, 9642, 9647, 9651,
9667, 9678–80, 9697

Baseball–Anecdotes
JS: 9664, 9684–88

Baseball–Anthologies
JS: 9640, 9649, 9699
S: 9700

Baseball–Autographs
JS: 9455

Baseball–Batters
JS: 9707

Baseball–Catalogs
JS: 9702

Baseball–Encyclopedias
JS: 9692

Baseball–Fiction
JS: 2885
S: 2873, 2878–82

Baseball–History
JS: 9621, 9624–25, 9638, 9644,
9653, 9663, 9682–83, 9693, 9695
S: 9622

Baseball–Humor
JS: 9705
S: 9675

Baseball–Photography
JS: 9701

Baseball–Pitchers
JS: 9655, 9660, 9666, 9696
S: 9671

Baseball–Stadiums
JS: 9710

Baseball–Statistics
JS: 9652, 9662

Baseball–Trivia
JS: 9623, 9665, 9670

Baseball cards
JS: 9442–43, 9447, 9454, 9672,
9689

BASIC (computer language)
JS: 8957, 8989, 8995, 9014
S: 8979, 8997, 9013, 9023

Basie, Count
S: 6368

Basket making
JS: 9145

Basketball
JS: 6708, 6737–39, 6741–45, 9712,
9717, 9719–23, 9725, 9727–28,
9730–34
S: 6740, 6746, 9713–14, 9716,
9718, 9724, 9726, 9738

Basketball–Fiction
JS: 2874
S: 651, 2166, 2887

Basketball–History
JS: 9736
S: 9735

Basketball–Women
JS: 9729, 9739

JS = Junior–Senior High   S = Senior High

Batik
S: 9147

Baton twirling
JS: 9600

Bats
JS: 8525, 8527

Bats–Fiction
S: 1847

Battles
See also individual battles
(e.g., Britain, Battle of)
JS: 7248, 7282, 7855, 7929
S: 6786, 7041, 7051, 7057, 7274, 7284

Bay of Pigs Affair
S: 7666

Baylor, Don
JS: 6714

Beads
JS: 9142, 9153

Beal, Doug
JS: 6773

Bears
JS: 8506
S: 6122, 8505, 8507–8

Bears–Fiction
JS: 286–87

Beat Generation–Fiction
S: 687

Beat poetry
S: 3269

Beatles
JS: 5879, 6168, 6171, 6356, 6369, 6414, 6417–18
S: 6415, 6420

Beauty care
JS: 5275, 5287

Beauty contests
S: 5272

Beauty culture
JS: 5281

Beauty culture–Careers
JS: 4797, 4835

Beavers
S: 8526

Beckwourth, Jim
S: 6614

Bees
S: 8603–4

Beetles–Field guides
JS: 8605

Behavior
See also Human behavior

JS: 5621
S: 5539, 5563, 5566

Behaviorism
S: 5547

Belcher, Wendy
S: 6892

Bellow, Saul
S: 3717

Belushi, John
S: 6370

Benoit, Joan
JS: 6764

Bentley, Toni
S: 6371

Beowulf–Fiction
S: 1129, 1241

Bergen, Candice
S: 6372

Berlin, Battle of
S: 7284

Berlioz, Hector
S: 6337

Bermuda–Fiction
S: 2182

Bermuda Triangle
JS: 9476

Bernhardt, Sarah
S: 6373

Bernstein, Leonard
S: 6338

Berra, Yogi
JS: 6715

Beverly Hills (California)
S: 5538

Bhutto, Benazir
S: 6804

Bias, Len
S: 6740

Bible
JS: 4091, 4093–95, 4098–99, 4101–2, 4107–8, 4110–11, 9310
S: 4092, 4096–97, 4103, 4105, 4112

Bible–Antiquities
S: 4109

Bible–Fiction
JS: 1360
S: 1359

Bible–History and criticism
S: 4104, 4106

Bicycle motocross
JS: 9715, 9764

Bicycle racing
JS: 9761, 9763

Bicycles
JS: 6780, 9741–42, 9744, 9748–50, 9752–56, 9758, 9760, 9762, 9765, 9768
S: 9740, 9743, 9746, 9751

Bicycles–History
JS: 9759

Bicycles–Repairs
JS: 9757, 9766

Bicycles–Touring
JS: 9767

Bicycles–Women
JS: 9745

Big cats
JS: 5969

Big cats–Fiction
JS: 292

Biko, Steve
S: 6791

Billiards
S: 9585

Billy the Kid–Fiction
S: 1576

Biochemistry
JS: 8374

Biography, 6117–6970

Biological sciences, 8372–8779

Biological warfare
JS: 4165

Biological warfare–Fiction
S: 2648

Biology
JS: 8377
S: 8407

Biology–Careers
S: 5032

Biology–Fiction
JS: 2375

Biology–General
S: 8388, 8396

Bionics and transplants, 5164–5166

Biotechnology
JS: 5252, 5264

Biotechnology–Careers
JS: 5013

Bird, Larry
JS: 6741–42

Bird watching
S: 8534, 8540, 8547

JS = Junior–Senior High S = Senior High

Birdhouses
JS: 8552, 9288
S: 9289

Birds
JS: 8182, 8528, 8530–31, 8538,
  8548, 8552, 8557, 8560, 8579,
  8661–63, 8666, 8669, 8673, 8679,
  8684
S: 8549, 8561, 8665

Birds–Behavior
JS: 8550, 8555
S: 8556

Birds–Encyclopedias
JS: 8541, 8553

Birds–Extinct
JS: 8537

Birds–Feeding
JS: 8551

Birds–Field guides
JS: 8529, 8532, 8535, 8542–46,
  8554, 8558
S: 8536, 8539, 8547, 8559

Birth control
JS: 5450, 5477, 5485–86

Bismarck, Otto von
S: 6828

Black Americans
JS: 4380–81, 5284, 6332, 6469
S: 4350–54, 4360, 4363, 4369,
  4372, 4374, 4382, 6464, 7574

**Black Americans–
  Achievements**
S: 6487

Black Americans–Actors
JS: 6429

**Black Americans–Armed
  forces**
S: 4286, 6471, 8146

Black Americans–Art
S: 5794, 5797, 5799

**Black Americans–
  Autobiography**
S: 6956

Black Americans–Biography
JS: 6223, 6326, 6392, 6435, 6473,
  6513–14, 6516, 6520, 6712, 6727,
  6730–31, 6737–38, 6743, 6745,
  6747–48
S: 6212, 6269, 6343, 6368, 6434,
  6442, 6480, 6482, 6487, 6493,
  6496, 6501–5, 6507, 6509–11,
  6585, 6749–50, 6765, 6933

Black Americans–Children
S: 4359

**Black Americans–Children–
  Fiction**
S: 479, 645

Black Americans–Civil rights,
  4350–4383

Black Americans–Colleges
S: 4721

Black Americans–Dance
JS: 5971, 5975

Black Americans–Education
S: 4630

Black Americans–Entertainers
JS: 3494, 5530, 5957, 6382, 6399,
  6404–5, 6407, 6410, 6437, 6455–
  56, 6459
S: 6173, 6177, 6374, 6387–88,
  6402–3, 6449–50, 6453

**Black Americans–Family struc-
  tures**
S: 4371

Black Americans–Fiction
JS: 440, 443, 450, 458, 471–74,
  495–96, 502, 504, 511, 635, 747,
  829, 891, 1525, 1611, 1698, 2290
S: 427, 438–39, 441–42, 451, 453,
  455–57, 459–60, 464–65, 470,
  476, 478–85, 501, 503, 506–9,
  512, 520, 552, 750, 930, 1526,
  1531, 1533, 1582, 1625

Black Americans–Folklore
JS: 3417, 3439
S: 3435, 3609

**Black Americans–
  Frontiersmen**
S: 6614

Black Americans–Genealogy
S: 6517

Black Americans–History
JS: 4361, 4364, 4368, 4370, 4373,
  6472, 7872, 7876, 7959
S: 4355–57, 4362, 4366–67, 4375,
  4377–78, 4383, 6512, 7738,
  7742–43, 7869–70, 7920, 8013,
  8017, 8160

Black Americans–Leaders
JS: 4376
S: 6489

Black Americans–Literature
S: 2903, 2925, 2935, 3571, 3590,
  3609, 3742

**Black Americans–Motion pic-
  tures**
JS: 6041

Black Americans–Music
JS: 5892
S: 4348, 5831, 5839

Black Americans–Musicians
JS: 6359
S: 6358

**Black Americans–
  Photographers**
S: 6294

Black Americans–Plays
JS: 3079, 6089
S: 3066, 3080, 3109–10, 3119, 3140

Black Americans–Poetry
JS: 3234–35, 3261, 3875
S: 3236–38, 3241, 3246, 3251,
  3270, 3279, 3285–86, 3316, 3331,
  3337, 3879, 3887

Black Americans–Poets
S: 6222

Black Americans–Singers
JS: 6436
S: 6184, 6438

Black Americans–Sports
JS: 6710, 6717, 9704
S: 6766

**Black Americans–War veter-
  ans**
S: 8146

Black Americans–Women
JS: 3875, 6270, 6519, 6899
S: 3119, 3557–58, 4366, 4379,
  6184, 6518, 7779

**Black Americans–World War
  II**
JS: 7213

Black Americans–Writers
JS: 3700, 6244, 6252, 6265, 6272
S: 3578, 3599, 3607, 3696, 3783,
  6185, 6266–68, 6295, 6331

**Black Americans–Writers–
  Fiction**
S: 1533

Black Death
S: 7136

Black Elk (Oglala Indian)
S: 6615

Black holes–Fiction
S: 2435, 2743

Black magic–Fiction
S: 1029

Blackfeet Indians
S: 7823

Blackfeet Indians–Fiction
S: 1512

Blackmail–Fiction
S: 669

JS = Junior–Senior High   S = Senior High

Blacks–Great Britain
JS: 6894

Blake, Eubie
S: 6374

Bleier, Rocky
S: 6751

Blind dates–Fiction
S: 2186

Blindness
JS: 6626–27, 6919, 6944, 6955
S: 6288–89

Blindness–Fiction
S: 668, 685, 721

Blizzards–Fiction
JS: 83

Blues (music)
JS: 5866, 6405
S: 5889, 6183, 6442

Blume, Judy
JS: 3789

Board games, 9806–9823

Body language
S: 3900

Bodybuilding
JS: 5361, 9770, 9773, 9776
S: 9769, 9777–78

Bodybuilding–Women
S: 9774

Boeing 747 (airplane)
S: 9076

Boleyn, Anne, Queen of England
S: 6829

Bolivia–History
S: 7677

Bonney, William
JS: 6616

Bonnie and Clyde
S: 6617

Books and reading
JS: 3977
S: 3583, 3978, 4644

Borden, Lizzie–Fiction
JS: 2168

Borglum, Gutzon
JS: 5807

Borman, Frank
JS: 6126

Boston Celtics
JS: 9734

Boston–Fiction
S: 579

Botany, 8411–8449

Bowie, David
JS: 6375

Bowling
JS: 9779–80, 9782
S: 9781

Boxing
JS: 6747–48, 9786
S: 6749–50

Boxing–Fiction
JS: 474, 931
S: 957

Boxing–Trivia
S: 9787

Boy Scouts of America
JS: 9790

Boyce, Christopher
S: 6893

Boyfriends
JS: 5635

Boyfriends–Fiction
JS: 295, 729, 2176, 2261, 2266, 2269, 2271, 2310, 2312, 2328–29
S: 872, 912

Brace, Ernest C.
JS: 6127

Bradbury, Ray
S: 3703, 6217

Bradley, Omar
S: 6577

Bradshaw, Terry
JS: 6752

Brady, James
S: 8103

Brain
JS: 5113, 5305–6, 5308–9, 5318, 5321–22, 5326
S: 5307, 5310–15, 5319–20, 5323–25, 5327, 5589

Brain teasers
JS: 8851

Braithwaite, E. R.
JS: 6894

Brand names
JS: 4567

Brandeis, Louis
S: 6578

Brandt, Willy
JS: 6830

Brazil
JS: 7687
S: 7670

Brazil–Fiction
S: 627, 2851

Breakdancing
S: 5972

Brecher, Kenneth
S: 6895

Bree, Marlin
JS: 6128

Brezhnev, Leonid
JS: 6831

Bribery–Fiction
JS: 2876

Bridge (game)
JS: 9820
S: 9806, 9809–10

Bridgers, Sue Ellen
JS: 3737

Britain, Battle of
JS: 7260

Britten, Benjamin
S: 6339

Broadcasting–Careers
JS: 4885, 4895

Brontë, Charlotte
S: 3649–50, 6221

Brontë family
JS: 6218, 6220
S: 6219

Brooklyn (N.Y.)
S: 9667

Brooklyn (N.Y.)–Fiction
JS: 1615
S: 486–87, 998, 1910

Brooks, Gwendolyn
S: 6222

Brown, Claude
JS: 6223

Brown, James
JS: 6376

Browning, Elizabeth Barrett
S: 6224–25

Browning, Robert and Elizabeth–Plays
JS: 3023

Bruce, Preston
JS: 6896

Bruckner, Anton
S: 6340

Bryan, William Jennings
S: 6579

Buck, Pearl S.
S: 3715

JS = Junior–Senior High S = Senior High

Buddhism
S: 4033, 4040, 4072, 4077–78, 6810

Buddhism–Fiction
S: 1394

Buffalo Bill
S: 6377

Bugs Bunny cartoons
JS: 5986

Building and construction
S: 9274, 9293

Building and construction–Careers
JS: 4899, 4941

Bulimia
S: 5209, 5373

Burch, Jennings Michael
JS: 6897

Buried treasure
JS: 8895

Burma–Fiction
JS: 102

Burnett, Carol
JS: 6378

Burr, Aaron–Fiction
JS: 1532

Bush, George
JS: 3492
S: 6523

Business
JS: 4561, 4563, 4577, 4594, 4600
S: 4578, 4585, 4598–99, 4602, 8306

Business letters
S: 4638

Business–Careers
JS: 4904–10, 4915, 4924, 4930, 4936
S: 4911–12

Business–Success stories
S: 4584

Business–United States–History
S: 4586, 7788

Businessmen–Biography
S: 4583, 6642, 6693

Butterflies and moths
JS: 8608
S: 8611

Butterflies and moths–Field guides
JS: 8606–7, 8609
S: 8610

Byrd Antarctic Expedition
S: 7709

Byron, Lord
S: 6226

C

Caesarea
S: 7117

Caffeine
JS: 5435

Cahill, Tim
JS: 6129

Cake decorating
JS: 9357

Caldwell, Erskine
S: 6227

Calendar
JS: 8862

California
JS: 4340
S: 4402, 5538, 8187, 8803

California Gold Rush
S: 7963

California–Fiction
JS: 300, 848, 1570, 1965, 2213
S: 39, 461, 491, 554, 607, 908, 996–97, 1503, 1557, 1797, 2036, 2399, 2964

California–Folklore
JS: 3438

California–History
S: 7820, 7957, 8177

California–Travel guides
JS: 8181

Calligraphy
S: 9157–61

Cambodia
S: 6932, 7460, 7463

Cambodia–History
S: 6811

Campbell, Maria
S: 6898

Camping
S: 9791

Camps
S: 5436

Camps–Fiction
JS: 927
S: 261, 905

Camus, Albert
S: 3600

Canada–Animals
JS: 8493

Canada–Fiction
JS: 95, 138, 140–41, 205, 286, 431, 844
S: 576, 797, 1090, 2214

Canada–Geography and history
JS: 7636–38
S: 7635

Canada–Historical fiction
S: 1491–93

Canada–Natural history
JS: 7634

Canada–Poetry
JS: 3240

Canada–Wildlife
JS: 8506

Canaries
JS: 8666

Cancer
JS: 5174, 5189, 6718, 6914, 6940, 6951, 6960
S: 5170, 5210–11, 5228, 6433

Cancer–Fiction
JS: 626, 666, 693, 723, 926, 2252
S: 582, 639

Canning and freezing
S: 9340

Canoes
S: 6964

Canoes and canoeing
JS: 9928, 9930, 9933
S: 9938

Canyons
JS: 7727

Cape Cod–Fiction
JS: 1966, 2167

Capital punishment
JS: 4484, 4495
S: 4239, 4257

Capitalism
JS: 4574, 4591
S: 4565, 4569, 4582, 6478

Capote, Truman
JS: 6228
S: 3768

Cappelletti, John
JS: 9857

Card games
JS: 9807, 9815, 9817, 9820

JS = Junior–Senior High S = Senior High

871

Card games—Encyclopedias
S: 9808

Card tricks
JS: 9400

Careers
JS: 4281, 4791–92, 4794, 4797–98,
4801–2, 4806, 4814–19, 4823,
4827, 4829–31, 4833, 4835,
4839–40, 4842, 4852–53, 4855,
4857–58, 4860, 4862–63, 4865,
4868, 4870–71, 4875–76, 4878–
79, 4882, 4884–87, 4892–93,
4895–96, 4899, 4901, 4903–10,
4913, 4915, 4921–22, 4924,
4926–27, 4930, 4932–34, 4936–
49, 4951–52, 4954, 4957–59,
4961–62, 4966–68, 4972–73,
4975, 4979, 4982–84, 4986, 4988,
4991–96, 4998–99, 5002–3,
5006, 5008–11, 5013–14, 5017–
18, 5020–23, 5025–26, 5028,
5030, 5033–36, 5038–40, 5042–
43, 5047–48, 5051, 5053, 5055–
57, 5060–63
S: 3983, 4280, 4718, 4782, 4788,
4804–5, 4813, 4820–21, 4825–
26, 4828, 4832, 4836, 4844–46,
4851, 4856, 4859, 4867, 4874,
4877, 4880–81, 4883, 4888–89,
4891, 4911–12, 4914, 4916–17,
4920, 4923, 4929, 4931, 4950,
4956, 4960, 4963–64, 4969, 4974,
4977, 4980, 4985, 4989, 5000,
5005, 5007, 5012, 5015–16, 5027,
5032, 5037, 5041, 5044, 5046,
5049–50, 5054, 5058–59, 5998

Careers—Guidance
JS: 4783
S: 4787, 4789, 4834, 4848

Careers—Unusual
S: 4864

Caribbean Islands—Fiction
JS: 558, 671, 856
S: 482, 983, 1494

Caribbean Islands—History
JS: 7661
S: 7662

Caribbean Islands—Writers
S: 3599

Caricature
JS: 5718

Carnegie, Andrew
S: 6651

Carnivorous plants
JS: 8442
S: 8445

Carols
JS: 5954

Carpentry and woodworking,
9265–9295

Carpentry—Careers
JS: 4944

Carroll, Lewis
JS: 3672

Carson, Kit
S: 6618

Carson, Rachel
S: 6652

Carter, Jimmy
S: 6524, 8044

Carter, Rosalynn
S: 6525

Cartoonists
JS: 5796, 6197–98, 6205

Cartoons and cartooning
JS: 5748, 5754, 9189–90, 9197,
9200, 9209, 9211–12

Cash, June Carter
JS: 6379

Castles
JS: 5707, 7124

Castles—Everyday life
S: 7134

Castles—Fiction
JS: 2656

Castro, Fidel
S: 6882

Catamarans
S: 9940

Catastrophes—Fiction
S: 2374, 2796

Cathedrals
JS: 5708

Cathedrals—Fiction
S: 1380

Cather, Willa
S: 3727, 6229–30

Catherine II, Empress of Russia
S: 6832–33

Catholicism—Fiction
S: 1897

Cats
JS: 8672, 8687–95, 8697, 8699,
8702, 8704–5, 8708
S: 8700

Cats—Anecdotes
JS: 8703

Cats—Behavior
JS: 8698

Cats—Breeds
JS: 8701, 8706

Cats—Fiction
JS: 284, 1081, 1934, 1937, 2554,
2722
S: 1326, 1935–36

Cats—Pets, 8687–8708

Cats—Poetry
JS: 8707
S: 3200

Cats—Training
S: 8696

Cattle
S: 8590

Caves
JS: 8813

CD ROMs
JS: 8993

Celebrities
JS: 6782

Cellini, Benvenuto
S: 6189

Cells
S: 8659

Celts—Fiction
S: 1088

Celts—Mythology
JS: 3461

Censorship
JS: 4314
S: 3647

Central America
S: 4132, 7651–53, 7658–59

Central America—Fiction
S: 252, 980, 1855

Central America—Mythology
JS: 3445, 3448

Central Intelligence Agency (U.S.)
S: 4215, 4219, 4226

Ceramics
S: 9163–64

Cerebral palsy
JS: 6938

Cerebral palsy—Fiction
JS: 660

Cervantes, Miguel de
JS: 6231
S: 3636, 3644

Cezanne, Paul
JS: 6191

JS = Junior–Senior High S = Senior High

Chagall, Marc
JS: 6192

Challenger (space shuttle)
JS: 8305, 8321

Chaplin, Charlie
S: 6062

Chaucer, Geoffrey
S: 3867, 6232–33, 7525

Chavez, Cesar
S: 6497

Checkers
JS: 9822

Cheerleaders–Fiction
S: 2140

Cheerleading
JS: 9561, 9587, 9600
S: 9562, 9588, 9592

Chekhov, Anton
S: 3802, 3804

Chemical warfare
JS: 4165
S: 8150

Chemistry
JS: 8783
S: 6655, 6699, 8404, 8781, 8784

Chemistry–History
JS: 8780

Chennault, Claire Lee
S: 6580

Chernobyl
S: 8922

Cherokee Indians
S: 7806

Chesapeake Bay
S: 8622

Chesapeake Bay–Fiction
S: 1514

Chess
JS: 9818, 9821
S: 9816, 9819, 9823

Chess–Fiction
S: 929

Chestnut, J. L.
S: 6498

Cheyenne Indians
JS: 7789

Cheyenne Indians–Fiction
JS: 1505
S: 21

Cheyenne Indians–History
S: 7822

Chicago–Fiction
S: 512, 1614

Chief Joseph–Fiction
S: 1510

Child abuse
JS: 5648, 5651
S: 5380, 5383–84, 5520, 5640, 5646, 5660–61

Child abuse–Fiction
JS: 557, 696, 827
S: 592, 690, 2004

Child care
S: 5365, 5452

Child care–Careers
JS: 4983, 4996

Child development
JS: 5069
S: 5523

Childbirth
JS: 5457, 5465, 5472
S: 5467, 5484

Childhood
S: 5680

Childhood–United States
S: 4359

Children
S: 5460, 5546, 6072

Children–Behavior
JS: 3495

Children–Dress
JS: 9177

Children–Fiction
JS: 61
S: 1873, 2860

Children–Holocaust survivors
S: 7204

Children–Medical care
S: 5234

Children–World War II
S: 7198

Children's books
S: 4898

Children's literature
JS: 3962

Chile–Fiction
JS: 268

Chile–History
S: 7672

Chimpanzees
JS: 8498, 8501
S: 8499

Chimpanzees–Communication
JS: 8504

China
JS: 6246, 7404, 7407, 7426, 7435, 9919
S: 7344, 7398–99, 7410, 7418–19, 7421, 7423, 7427

China–Art
S: 5768

China–Cookbooks
S: 9334

China–Description and travel
JS: 7416
S: 7414, 7434

China–Fiction
S: 48, 248, 1240, 1393, 1396, 1639

China–Folklore
JS: 3387
S: 3385

China–Historical fiction
JS: 1389
S: 1388, 1399

China–History
JS: 6247, 7413, 7417, 7420, 7422
S: 4139, 4167, 6812–14, 6817, 7397, 7400–3, 7405–6, 7408–9, 7411–12, 7424–25, 7429–33, 7436–37

China–Mythology
JS: 3451

China–Natural history
S: 7415

China–Philosophy
S: 3999–4000

China–Poetry
S: 3355

China–Travel guides
S: 7428

Chinese Americans
S: 4402, 6922, 7421

Chinese Americans–Fiction
JS: 449
S: 221, 448, 475, 1575

Chinese Americans–History
S: 4400

Chinese language
S: 3911

Chinese persons–Fiction
S: 193

Chippewa Indians–Fiction
S: 454, 510

Chiropractics–Careers
JS: 5002

Chivalry, Age of
S: 3413

Chivalry, Age of–Fiction
JS: 424

Chopin, Kate
S: 3774

Christianity
JS: 4071, 4116
S: 4030, 4036, 4056, 4058, 6629,
6783, 6855, 6865

Christianity–Fiction
S: 2894

Christianity–Legends
S: 4100

Christianity–Saints
S: 6838

Christie, Agatha
JS: 3693, 6234–35
S: 3668, 3683, 6236

Christmas
JS: 4115–16, 4119–20, 4122, 6228
S: 4117

Christmas–Fiction
JS: 353, 2104
S: 1729

Christmas–Poetry
JS: 3165

Christmas–Songbooks
JS: 5954

Christmas–Wales
S: 3227

**Church and state–United
States**
S: 4179

Cinderella–Fiction
S: 1328

Circus
JS: 4890, 5976–77, 6363
S: 6364–65

Circus–Fiction
JS: 197

Cities
S: 4558

Cities–Folklore
JS: 3433

Cities–History
JS: 4556
S: 4560

Cities–Planning
S: 4559

Cities–Roman Empire
JS: 7118

Cities–Violence
JS: 4461

Citizenship and civil rights,
4290–4409

Civil rights
JS: 4142, 4203, 4290, 4298, 4299,
4305, 4310, 4315–16, 4318, 4320,
4364, 4368, 4370, 4380–81,
6513–14, 6589
S: 4236–37, 4291–92, 4297, 4304,
4307–9, 4311, 4313, 4321, 4324,
4348, 4350, 4358, 4360, 4367,
4369, 4375, 4377, 4382, 4413,
6493, 6497–98, 6503–12, 6518

Civil rights–Fiction
S: 507

Civil rights–Youth
JS: 4296
S: 4254

Civil rights leaders–Biography,
6493–6520

Civil service–Careers
JS: 4817–18
S: 4844

Civil War–Spain
S: 7557

Civil War (U.S.)
JS: 6490, 7888–91, 7894–95, 7900–
1, 7903, 7905, 7907–10, 7912–
13, 7917–19, 7922, 7924–26,
7929–30, 7932, 7937, 7939, 7945,
7947
S: 6466, 6530, 6584, 6595–96,
7863, 7879, 7887, 7892–93,
7896–99, 7902, 7904, 7906, 7911,
7914–15, 7920–21, 7923, 7927–
28, 7931, 7934–35

Civil War (U.S.)–Battlefields
S: 7940

Civil War (U.S.)–Battles
JS: 7944

Civil War (U.S.)–Causes
S: 7933, 7936

Civil War (U.S.)–Eyewitnesses
JS: 7938

Civil War (U.S.)–Fiction
JS: 1524, 1542–43, 1549–50, 1552
S: 395, 1327, 1534–41, 1544–48,
1551, 1553

Civil War (U.S.)–Naval events
JS: 7943

**Civil War (U.S.)–Personal let-
ters**
JS: 7941

Civil War (U.S.)–Poetry
S: 3242

**Civil War (U.S.)–Spies and
scouts**
JS: 7946

Civil War (U.S.)–Stories
JS: 7916

Civil War (U.S.)–Trivia
JS: 7942

Civilization–History
S: 7081

Clapton, Eric
JS: 6380

Clarke, Arthur C.–Fiction
JS: 3620
S: 3681

Clarke, Thurston
S: 6130

**Classical literature–History
and criticism**
S: 3801, 3805–06

Classical mythology, 3468–3479

Classics—Fiction, 302–429

Clemens, Roger
JS: 6716

Clichés
JS: 3946

Climate
S: 8814, 8869

Clipper ships
JS: 7886

Clones–Fiction
S: 2444, 2824, 2839

Clothing and dress
JS: 5274, 5276, 5280–82, 9172
S: 5286, 9170, 9173

Clothing and dress–History
JS: 5273, 5280, 5288

Clowns
JS: 5978–79, 5981
S: 4897

Coal mining–Fiction
S: 1624

COBOL (computer language)
S: 8971

Cocaine
JS: 5130, 5160
S: 5123, 5156

Cochran, Jacqueline
S: 6131

Codes
S: 7300

Codes–World War II
S: 7325

JS = Junior–Senior High S = Senior High

874

Coin collecting
JS: 9441, 9446, 9449–50, 9460

Coins
JS: 9444, 9451, 9457

Coins–Price guides
JS: 9463

Cold fusion
S: 8914

Cold War
S: 4145

Cold War–Fiction
S: 189

Collecting and collections
JS: 9446, 9448–51, 9454, 9457
S: 9452–53

College Level Entrance Program
S: 4657

College sports
JS: 9589

College stories–Fiction
JS: 704, 2232–33, 2311–12, 2314
S: 765, 860, 900, 930, 1293, 1875, 1905, 1932, 1973, 1976–78, 2102, 2105, 2183, 2292, 2305, 2865

Colleges and universities–Academic guidance, 4718–4772

Colleges and universities–Admissions
S: 4725

Collins, Judy
S: 6381

Colombia–Fiction
S: 279, 550

Colonial Period (U.S.)–Crafts
JS: 7845

Colonial Period (U.S.)–Everyday life
JS: 7883

Colonial Period (U.S.)–Fiction
JS: 1515, 1517
S: 401, 1516, 1518–19

Colonial Period (U.S.)–History
JS: 7840–41, 7846
S: 6586–88, 6606, 6609, 6632, 7834–39, 7842–43

Color
S: 8933

Colorado–Fiction
S: 220, 555, 1569

Columbus, Christopher
JS: 6132
S: 6133–34

Comanche Indians–Fiction
S: 1504

Comas–Fiction
JS: 2362

Comedians
JS: 6378
S: 6023, 6081

Comedians–Biography
S: 6433

Comedians–Women
JS: 5956

Comer family
JS: 6899

Comets
JS: 8332–34
S: 8331, 8335

Comets–Fiction
JS: 2482
S: 2407, 2829

Comic books
JS: 9201

Comic books–Collecting
JS: 9448

Comic strips
See also Cartoons and cartooning
JS: 5791

Commandos
JS: 7256

Commercial art
S: 9202

Commercial art–Careers
JS: 4884

Communication–Nonverbal
S: 3900, 5539, 5349

Communication arts
JS: 8951
S: 4667

Communication arts–Careers
JS: 4823

Communication arts–History
JS: 3919
S: 3971

Communism
JS: 4592
S: 4170, 4173, 4175–77, 6603, 6859–61, 7567

Communism–China
S: 7401

Communist Revolution (China)
S: 7419

Compact discs
JS: 9053
S: 9047

Companies
JS: 4594

Compassion
JS: 5574

Competition
JS: 5604

Composers
S: 6175

Composers–Biography
JS: 6182, 6344
S: 6172, 6334–37, 6339–43, 6345–49, 6351–54

Composers–Dictionaries
JS: 6181

Composers–Encyclopedias
JS: 6170

Composers–Italian
S: 6350

Computer crime
S: 9028

Computer games
JS: 8957, 8967, 8982, 8986

Computer graphics
S: 8985, 9007

Computer graphics–Careers
JS: 5048

Computer languages
JS: 8989–90, 8995–96, 9014
S: 8961, 8979, 8997, 9012–13, 9023

Computer programming
JS: 9014
S: 8971, 8977, 8987, 8994, 8997

Computer viruses
S: 8998–99

Computers
JS: 8239, 8960, 8963, 8968, 8970, 8978, 8981, 8988, 8991, 8993, 9001, 9005, 9008, 9010, 9015, 9019–20, 9024, 9027, 9029–32
S: 6678, 8942, 8959, 8962, 8965–66, 8972–73, 8976, 8980, 8984, 8992, 8998–99, 9002, 9004, 9006, 9013, 9016, 9018, 9022, 9025

Computers–Careers
JS: 4910, 4935, 4975, 5034, 5036, 5039, 5056–57, 5060
S: 5041, 5044, 5058

Computers–Dictionaries
JS: 8964, 8974, 9009

Computers–Fiction
JS: 158, 2376, 2481, 2496, 2835

JS = Junior–Senior High S = Senior High

875

Computers–Fiction (*cont.*)
S: 35, 1139, 2403, 2557–59, 2591, 2642, 2644, 2870

Computers–History
JS: 9033
S: 6646, 8975

Computers–Poetry
JS: 3849

Computers–Software
JS: 9021

Confucianism
S: 4055

Congress of Vienna
S: 7147

Congress (U.S.)
S: 4214, 4216, 4218, 4220, 4222, 4227–29

Conrad, Joseph
S: 3665

Conscientious objectors
S: 4408

Conservation
See also Ecology; Environment; Pollution
JS: 4433, 4456, 8580
S: 4438, 6695

Conservatism
JS: 4263, 4267
S: 4123, 4265

Constellations
JS: 8287

Constitution of the United States
JS: 4184, 4192, 4194, 4196–99, 4203, 4305
S: 4180–83, 4185–91, 4193, 4195, 4200–2, 4204, 4256, 7857

Construction–Career guidance, 4940–4945

Consumer credit
S: 4615

Consumer education
S: 4608

Consumerism
JS: 4590, 4607
S: 4606

Contemporary life and problems–Fiction, 430–999

Contests
JS: 9537

Continental Divide
S: 7771

Continental drift
S: 8796

Convents–Fiction
S: 270

Conversation
JS: 5585

Conway, Jill Ker
S: 6820

Cook, Captain James
JS: 6136

Cookbooks
JS: 9309–10, 9312, 9314–20, 9326–32, 9336–39, 9343, 9346, 9348–53, 9356, 9368–69
S: 9311, 9323–24, 9333, 9335, 9340–41, 9344, 9347, 9354, 9359, 9361–67

Cookbooks–Basic
S: 9358

Cookbooks–Christmas
JS: 4115

Cookbooks–Diabetes
S: 9325

Cookbooks–Ethnic
JS: 9360
S: 9313, 9321, 9334, 9342, 9345, 9355

Cookbooks–Heart disease
S: 9325

Cookery
JS: 9322

Copland, Aaron
S: 6341

Corfu–Natural history
S: 8387

Cormier, Robert
JS: 3708

Corporate crime
S: 4521

Corporations
S: 4585

Corruption
S: 4521

Corvette (automobile)
JS: 9088

Cosmetics
JS: 5283, 5285

Cosmetology–Careers
JS: 4835

Costa Rica
S: 7657

Costumes
See also Clothing and dress
JS: 5274, 5874, 9168, 9172

Costumes–Dictionaries
JS: 9174

Costumes–Encyclopedias
JS: 9178

Costumes–Folk
JS: 9176

Costumes–History
JS: 5273, 5278, 5280, 5282, 5288, 5290, 9169, 9175, 9177–78
S: 9171

Cottell, John E.
S: 6900

Counseling–Careers
JS: 4946
S: 4960

Counterfeiting–Fiction
JS: 833

Country music
JS: 5853, 5867, 5884, 5904, 6419, 6423

Country music–Biography
JS: 5858, 6448

Country music–Encyclopedias
JS: 5899

Courage
JS: 6479
S: 7612

Courts (U.S.)
JS: 4241, 4244, 4259, 4494
S: 4234, 4253

Courtship
S: 5527

Cousteau, Jacques
JS: 6653

Cowan, Paul
S: 6901

Cowboys
JS: 7988, 8153
S: 7684, 7952–53, 7979, 7982

Cowboys–Fiction
S: 1, 265

Coyotes
S: 8513

Coyotes–Fiction
JS: 296

Crabs
S: 8622

Crafts
JS: 4119, 8197, 9135, 9149–51, 9156, 9226
S: 6964, 9136–37

Crafts–Careers
JS: 4853

JS = Junior–Senior High S = Senior High

Crane, Stephen
S: 3707, 3712

Crazy Horse
JS: 6499

Creation–Mythology
S: 3467

Credit cards
S: 4615

Creek Indians–Fiction
S: 1496

Crete–Fiction
S: 973

Crick, Francis
S: 6654

Crime and criminals
JS: 4241, 4244, 4474, 4479–80,
4493, 4494, 4496, 5127, 5328,
7997
S: 4233, 4239, 4468–70, 4472,
4477–78, 4481–83, 4486, 4488–
92, 4497–99, 5536, 6118, 6617,
6638, 6693, 6887

Crime and criminals–
Dictionaries
S: 4473

Crime and criminals–
Encyclopedias
S: 6120

Crime and criminals–Fiction
S: 172, 233, 638, 684, 1398, 2079,
2097, 2119

Crime and criminals–Plays
S: 3088

Criminal justice–Careers
S: 4978

Crocheting
JS: 9230, 9243

Crockett, Davy
JS: 6135

Crocodiles
JS: 8469

Cromwell, Oliver
S: 6834

Cronin, A. J.
S: 3687

Cronkite, Kathy
S: 6885

Croquet
JS: 9553

Crossword puzzles–Fiction
S: 2116

Crow Dog, Mary
S: 6500

Crow Indians
S: 7819

Cruise ships–Fiction
S: 1980

Crusades
S: 7123

Crusades–Fiction
S: 1284, 1382

Cryogenics–Fiction
S: 215, 2669

Cuba
S: 6882, 7666

Cuba–Fiction
JS: 251

Cuba–History
S: 7660, 7665, 8074

Cuban Americans–Fiction
S: 463

Cults
JS: 4057
S: 4027, 4050, 4052–53, 4061,
4066, 4074, 4087, 9530

Cults–Fiction
JS: 2195
S: 662

Cultural Revolution (China)
S: 6813, 7431

Cuomo, Mario
S: 6581

Curie, Madame Marie
S: 6655

Curiosities
JS: 7715, 8686, 9477–79, 9482,
9490, 9493–97, 9500, 9504–5,
9511, 9514, 9516, 9523, 9525,
9529, 9539, 9542

Custer, George Armstrong
S: 6582, 7951, 7978

Custer, George Armstrong–
Fiction
S: 1556

Customs
JS: 4541

Cystic fibrosis
S: 5186, 6902

Cytology
S: 8659

Czechoslovakia–History
JS: 6864

Cézanne, Paul
S: 6190

D

Dahl, Roald
JS: 6237

Dalai Lama
S: 6810

Dana, Richard Henry
S: 6137

Dance and dancers
JS: 5961, 5963, 5968, 5969, 5971,
5973, 5975, 6385
S: 5960, 5964, 5970, 5974, 6462

Dancing–Fiction
S: 743

Dante Alighieri
S: 3862

Darrow, Clarence
S: 6583

Darwin, Charles
S: 6656–57, 6993, 7007

Darwin, Charles–Fiction
S: 1478

Data processing–Careers
S: 5050

Dating (social)
JS: 5567, 5599, 5629, 5635
S: 5600

Dating (social)–Interracial
JS: 5598

Davis, Jefferson
S: 6584

Davis, Sammy
JS: 6382

Dead Sea Scrolls
S: 4113

Deafness
JS: 5431–32, 5434, 5438, 6620,
8746
S: 5332, 6923

Deafness–Fiction
JS: 738, 2498
S: 668, 708

Deafness–Plays
JS: 3103

Death
JS: 5080–81, 5085, 5089, 5096,
5166, 6914, 6951
S: 5087–88, 5093–94, 5097, 5215

Death–Fiction
JS: 431, 531, 566, 647, 665, 693,
698, 713, 723, 732, 739, 757,
885, 913, 926, 1087, 2176

JS = Junior–Senior High   S = Senior High

Death–Fiction (*cont.*)
S: 433, 513, 540, 547, 556, 572, 582, 597, 620, 639, 663, 722, 822, 843, 875, 951, 1166, 1742, 1814, 1911, 1933, 2073, 2077, 2101, 2175, 2178, 2187, 2320, 2701, 2811, 2878

Death–True accounts
S: 9498

Death penalty
S: 4486

Debating
JS: 4702

Debs, Eugene–Fiction
S: 1616

Decision making
S: 5596

Decorative arts, 5808–5812

Decorative arts–History
JS: 5684

Deer
JS: 8522

Deer–Fiction
JS: 297

Deford, Alex
S: 6902

Delbruck, Max
S: 6658

De Mille, Agnes
S: 5964, 6383

Democracy
JS: 4169

Demons–Fiction
S: 1719

Denmark–Folklore
JS: 3389

Dental care
JS: 5340

Department of Agriculture (U.S.)
S: 8586

Depression, Great
JS: 8026, 8037, 8040, 8043
S: 6890, 7759, 8023, 8025, 8027, 8029, 8033, 8036, 8038–39, 8041

Depression, Great–Fiction
JS: 526, 1627
S: 478, 485, 505, 600, 623, 1621–22, 1625–26, 1630–32

Depression (mental)
JS: 5388, 5405, 5564, 5611

Desert warfare
S: 7064

Deserts
JS: 8409, 8815, 8819
S: 8810

Deserts–Fiction
JS: 188

Desktop publishing
S: 3982, 8973

Desserts
JS: 9343

Detective stories–Fiction, 1911–2224

Detectives
S: 6912

Detroit Tigers
S: 9642

Detroit–Fiction
S: 583

Developing countries
JS: 4464

Diabetes
S: 5169

Diagnosis (medical)
JS: 5225

Diamond, Neil
S: 6384

Diaries
S: 5626, 6631, 6657, 7928, 7980

Diaries–Fiction
JS: 1906
S: 592

Dick, Philip K.
JS: 3756

Dickens, Charles
JS: 3669, 7511
S: 3677, 3680, 6238–40

Dickey, James
S: 3880

Dickinson, Emily
JS: 3100
S: 3883, 3890, 3893, 6241

Dictionaries
JS: 3933, 3939, 3947, 3952, 5827, 5930, 6181, 8964, 8974, 9009, 9017, 9174
S: 3563, 3572, 3588, 3831, 3851, 3855, 3902, 3910, 3913, 3916, 3949, 4473, 5673, 5689, 5790, 6783, 7025, 7033, 7080, 8296, 8414, 8416, 9323, 9859

Dictionaries–Pictorial
JS: 3921

Diesel engines
S: 9044

Diet
JS: 5412, 5424
S: 5409, 5423, 9335

Dietetics–Careers
JS: 4999

Dillard, Annie
S: 6242

Dinosaurs
JS: 6976, 6978–79, 6982, 6984, 9222
S: 6974, 6981, 6987

Dinosaurs–Fiction
S: 2494

Directories
JS: 7757

Disabilities. *See* individual disabilities, e.g., Dyslexia; Learning disabilities; Physical handicaps

Disabilities–Fiction
S: 561

Discus fish
JS: 8755

Diseases and illness
See also individual diseases
JS: 5195, 5213
S: 5075, 5169–71, 5179, 5205, 5207–08, 5269

Diseases and illness–Children
JS: 5244

Diseases and illness–Fiction
JS: 647, 659, 885
S: 1449

Diseases and illness–Terminal
JS: 5089
S: 5087–88, 5093, 5218

Disney, Walt
JS: 5793, 6100, 6193

Dissection
S: 8453

Divorce
JS: 5637, 5666

Divorce–Fiction
JS: 541, 731
S: 2, 580, 584, 724, 762, 767, 781, 1126

DNA
JS: 5263
S: 5086, 5265, 5268, 6654, 6669

Doby, Larry
JS: 6717

Doctors
JS: 5001, 5004, 5244–45, 6680, 6684

JS = Junior–Senior High S = Senior High

S: 5144, 5211, 5240, 5242, 5254, 6673, 6677, 6682, 6687, 6700, 7654

Doctors–Autobiography
S: 6702

Doctors–Fiction
S: 53–54, 56, 264, 649, 703, 755, 979, 1724, 1859, 1927, 2158, 2837

Doctors–Interviews
S: 5249

Documents–Historical
JS: 7716, 7746
S: 7722, 7801

Dodge family
S: 6659

Dogs
JS: 8672, 8709–12, 8714–15, 8717, 8719–21, 8723–27, 8729, 8734–35, 8737–41, 8743, 8746
S: 8713, 8716, 8722

Dogs–Behavior
JS: 8728

Dogs–Breeds
JS: 8718, 8731, 8733

Dogs–Encyclopedias
JS: 8745

Dogs–Fiction
JS: 178, 283, 285, 293, 298–99, 409, 411, 1916
S: 1002, 1781, 2209

Dogs–History
S: 7632

Dogs–Paintings
JS: 8732

Dogs–Pets, 8709–8746

Dogs–Survival
JS: 8742

Dogs–Training
JS: 8730, 8736
S: 8744

Dollmaking
JS: 9263

Dolls–Fiction
JS: 1835

Dolphins
JS: 6697, 8649, 8652, 8654
S: 8623, 8644, 8646–47

Dolphins–Fiction
S: 2477

Domesday Book
S: 7542

Donne, John
S: 3865

Dostoevsky, Fyodor
S: 3640, 3803

Douglass, Frederick
S: 6501–2, 6585

Doyle, Arthur Conan
JS: 3674, 6243
S: 3657

Dragons
JS: 3763

Dragons–Fiction
JS: 1093, 1271, 2531
S: 1138, 1264, 2789

Dragons–Folklore
JS: 3371

Drama, 6076–6116

Dravecky, Dave
JS: 6718

Drawing and painting
JS: 5793, 9181–82, 9184, 9186–87, 9189–91, 9196, 9198, 9201, 9203–4, 9210, 9212, 9215–17
S: 6200, 9180, 9183, 9185, 9188, 9192–95, 9199, 9205–8, 9213–14

Dreams
S: 5334, 5534

Dreams–Fiction
S: 2632

Dreiser, Theodore
S: 3753

Dress. *See* Clothing and dress

Dressmaking
JS: 9242, 9259
S: 9227

Dropouts
JS: 4637

Drug dealers
JS: 5160

Drug trade
S: 4489

Drugs
JS: 5100–3, 5109–11, 5113, 5116–18, 5124–27, 5129–30, 5132, 5135, 5138–41, 5143, 5148–49, 5151, 5153, 5157, 5160–62, 5306, 5435, 8444
S: 4489, 5105, 5114, 5121, 5123, 5128, 5134, 5137, 5144–46, 5154, 5156, 5159, 6740

Drugs–Encyclopedias
S: 5147

Drugs–Fiction
JS: 382, 644, 869

S: 44, 59, 631, 702, 803, 1388, 2124

Drugs–Health problems, 5099–5163

Drugs–History
JS: 5158

Drugs–Non-narcotic
S: 5163

Drugs–Sports
S: 5112

Druids–Fiction
S: 1370

Drunk driving
S: 5119

Drysdale, Don
JS: 6719

Du Bois, W. E. B.
S: 6503–04

Duncan, David Ewing
JS: 7349

Duncan, Isadora
JS: 6385

Dunkirk, Battle of
S: 7245

Dust Bowl
S: 8155

Dvorak, Antonin
S: 6342

Dwarves–Fiction
S: 966, 1201

Dylan, Bob
JS: 5860, 6386

Dyslexia
See also Learning disabilities
S: 5393

E

Eagles
JS: 8560, 8562

Eareckson, Joni
JS: 6903

Earhart, Amelia
JS: 6140
S: 6138–39, 6141

Earth
JS: 8337, 8340, 8787, 8793, 8795
S: 8338, 8785, 8792

JS = Junior–Senior High   S = Senior High

Earth sciences–Careers
S: 5027

Earthquakes
JS: 8804, 8808
S: 7454, 8801–3, 8806

East (U.S.)–Wildflowers
JS: 8440

Easter Island
S: 7470

Eastern Europe
JS: 7584

Eating disorders
JS: 5368, 5387, 5395, 5402, 6966
S: 5176, 5373, 5389, 5396–97, 5400

Eating disorders–Fiction
S: 699–700, 744

Eccentricity–Fiction
S: 621, 748, 845

Ecology
JS: 4430
S: 4416, 4428, 4438, 4447, 6652, 8405

Ecology–Encyclopedias
JS: 8455

Ecology–Fiction
S: 2544

Economic systems and institutions, 4585–4604

Economics and business
JS: 4223, 4568, 4590
S: 4221, 4565–66, 4569–71, 4575–76, 4582, 4589, 4596, 7718

Economics and business–Careers
JS: 4907
S: 4918–19

Economics and business–History
JS: 4567
S: 4581, 6478, 8010

Economics and business–United States
JS: 4580, 8064

Economics and business–Asia
S: 7441

Economics and business–Fiction
S: 2747

Education
JS: 6476
S: 4002, 4623, 4630–31, 4635, 6915, 6946, 7724

Education–Career guidance, 4946–4954

Education–Careers
JS: 4949

Education–Fiction
S: 969

Education–Handbooks
S: 4713

Education–History
JS: 4626

Education–United States
S: 4628, 4633

Education and the schools, 4622–4707

Edward II, King of England–Fiction
S: 1464

Edward VIII, King of England
S: 7539

Egbert, James Dallas
S: 5378

Eggs
JS: 8533

Eggs–Fiction
S: 2692

Egypt
S: 6950

Egypt–Ancient
S: 7098

Egypt–Ancient–Religion
S: 7100

Egypt–Fiction
JS: 1949, 2130
S: 55, 1262, 1829, 2128–29

Egypt–Historical fiction
JS: 1362
S: 1358

Egypt–History
S: 6816, 7092–99

Egypt–Mythology
JS: 3458
S: 3459

Egypt–Travel guides
JS: 7596

Eichmann, Adolf
S: 7249

Einstein, Albert
JS: 8902
S: 6660–62, 8251

Eisenhower, Dwight D.
JS: 6527
S: 4136, 6526, 6528–29, 8087

El Salvador
S: 7654

Elderly persons
See also Aging
JS: 5084, 5098
S: 4467, 5083

Elderly persons–Careers
JS: 4982

Elderly persons–Fiction
JS: 711, 1983
S: 455, 894, 951

Elderly persons–Illness
S: 5203

Elections
JS: 4274, 4276–79
S: 4264, 4275, 8095

Electric wiring
JS: 9041

Electricians–Careers
JS: 5021, 5062

Electronic music
JS: 5931
S: 5910, 5938

Electronics
S: 9034–39

Electronics–Careers
S: 5046

Electronics–Encyclopedias
JS: 9042

Elephants–Fiction
S: 2754

Eliot, George
S: 3661, 3682

Eliot, T. S.
S: 3871, 3884

Elizabeth I, Queen of England
S: 6835–37

Elizabethan England–Fiction
S: 1338, 2108

Elizabethan plays–History and criticism
S: 3810

Ellington, Duke
S: 6343, 6387–88

Ellis Island
JS: 4328

Ellison, Ralph
JS: 6244
S: 3735

Elves–Fiction
S: 1041, 1054, 1124, 1126

Elves–Folklore
JS: 3372

JS = Junior–Senior High   S = Senior High

Embery, Joan
JS: 6663

Embroidery
S: 9248, 9256

Emerson, Ralph Waldo
S: 3611

Emotional problems, 5368–5407

Emotional problems–Fiction
JS: 701, 2296
S: 585, 725, 1593, 2919

Emotions
JS: 5116, 5557, 5562, 5570, 5574
S: 5323, 5560

Emotions and emotional behavior, 5555–5571

Empire State building
JS: 5709

Encyclopedias
JS: 3452, 4101, 5841, 5893, 5899,
5919, 5934, 6170, 7053, 7720,
7766, 8418, 8450, 8455, 8460,
8464, 8479–80, 8494, 8541, 8553,
8600, 8615, 8745, 9042, 9057–58,
9078, 9116, 9125, 9178, 9250,
9435, 9481, 9521, 9528–29, 9534,
9692
S: 3360, 3631, 3898, 4384, 5147,
5428, 5862, 6120, 7041, 7180,
7356, 7411, 7418, 7517, 7564,
7960, 8778, 9162

Encyclopedias–Fiction
S: 3757

Endangered species
JS: 8570, 8578–79, 8779
S: 8568–69, 8571, 8573, 8575–77

Endangered species–Fiction
JS: 840

Energy
S: 8917–19

Energy–Careers
JS: 5063

Energy and motion, 8916–8931

Energy crisis–Fiction
S: 2737

Engineering, 8941–9134

Engineering–Careers
JS: 5010, 5018–19, 5022, 5030

Engineering–History
S: 7087

England
See also Great Britain
JS: 6684

England–Christmas customs
S: 4117

England–Description and travel
JS: 7521

England–Fairy tales
JS: 3401, 3416

England–Fiction
JS: 121, 133, 518, 544, 928, 1643,
1894, 1948, 1953, 2007, 2023,
2169, 2283, 2288
S: 28, 72, 110, 130, 338, 551, 617,
773, 819, 906, 1437, 1764, 1875,
1881, 1902, 1922, 2025, 2035,
2043, 2064–69, 2114–16, 2154,
2170

England–Folklore
JS: 3394, 3396, 3404
S: 3406–9, 3412–13, 3462

England–Haunted houses
S: 9517

England–Historical fiction
JS: 132, 134–35, 231–32, 355, 381,
1407, 1414, 1417, 1422–24, 1426,
1435, 1439–40, 1462, 2131, 2241,
2243–44, 2325
S: 349, 351–52, 354, 356–57, 359–
61, 364–72, 380, 386–87, 426,
549, 809, 1001, 1004, 1334,
1339, 1366, 1406, 1408, 1410,
1412–13, 1415–16, 1418, 1420,
1427–30, 1432, 1438, 1441–42,
1446, 1457–61, 1463–64, 1466–
67, 1480–81, 1484–85, 1487,
1489–90, 1751, 2108, 2131–35,
2229, 2235, 2238, 2245–47, 2254,
2263, 2327

England–History
JS: 6825, 6827, 6844, 7512, 7538
S: 6824, 6829, 6834–36, 6877,
7132, 7137, 7513–14, 7516, 7518,
7520, 7523–28, 7532–33, 7536,
7542

England–Schools
S: 4632

England–Wit and humor
S: 3504

England–World War II
JS: 7319

English language
JS: 3915, 3936, 3951
S: 3904–5, 3907, 3914, 3922, 3925,
3932, 3941, 3948

English language–Careers
JS: 4947

English language–Clichés
JS: 3946

English language–Dialects
S: 3924

English language–Dictionaries
JS: 3933

English language–Etymology
JS: 3953–54

English language–History
JS: 3937
S: 3909

English language–Pronunciation
JS: 3918

English literature
S: 339–40, 347, 376, 388, 2977,
3151–52, 3154, 3191, 3575

English literature–Anecdotes
S: 3691

English literature–Anthologies
S: 2918, 2930–31

English literature–History and criticism
JS: 3669, 3689
S: 3566, 3569, 3580, 3582, 3585,
3602, 3628, 3650–51, 3655–57,
3659–61, 3665–66, 3673, 3675,
3677–78, 3680, 3682, 3685–88,
3690, 6305

English plays
S: 3129

English poetry–History and criticism
S: 3874

Entertainers–Biography, 6356–
6460

Entertainers–Career guidance,
4873–4902

Entertaining
S: 9341

Environment
JS: 8928

Environment–Alaska
S: 8185

Environment–Careers
S: 4963, 5015

Environmental castastrophes–Fiction
S: 2783

Environmental concerns
S: 4413

Environmental problems
JS: 4422–23, 4425–26, 4431, 4434,
4436, 4440, 4443, 4450
S: 4424, 4427, 4429, 4432, 4437,
4439, 4442, 4445–49, 4454

JS = Junior–Senior High   S = Senior High

Environmental problems—Fiction
S: 2797

Epic poetry
S: 377, 3187

Epics—India—Fiction
JS: 3384

Epidemics
JS: 5197

Epidemics—Fiction
JS: 2665

Epilepsy
JS: 5185

Epilepsy—Fiction
S: 661

Equator
S: 6130

Erving, Julius
JS: 6743

Escalante, Jaime
JS: 6904

Eskimos
JS: 7693, 7707
S: 7695, 7701, 7705, 8193

Eskimos—Fiction
JS: 1453

Eskimos—Literature
S: 3610

Essays
JS: 3508, 3536, 8204
S: 3485, 3498, 3520, 3522–24, 3526–35, 3537–43, 3545–47, 3549–59, 3561–62, 4292, 4448, 6116, 8216, 8407–8, 9598

Essex, Robert Devereux
S: 6837

Ethics
JS: 4411, 5239, 5255, 5488, 8376
S: 4521, 4523

Ethics and ethical behavior,
5572–5578

Ethnic groups. *See* Minorities

Ethnic groups—Names
S: 5658

Ethnic problems
JS: 5598

Etiquette
JS: 5580, 5582–83
S: 5437, 5575–79

Europe—Art, 5770–5788

Europe—Biography, 6821–6881

Europe—Fiction
S: 9, 764

Europe—Fiction classics, 302–388

Europe—Folklore and fairy tales, 3388–3416

Europe—Historical documents
S: 7148

Europe—Historical fiction,
1406–1490

Europe—History
S: 7036, 7120, 7126, 7128–30, 7138, 7143–45, 7147, 7149, 7481, 7484–86

Europe—Literary history and criticism, 3634–3645, 3801–3832, 3861–3874

Europe—Plays, 2990–3059, 3801–3832

Europe—Poetry, 3180–3233

Europe—Travel guides
JS: 7483
S: 7482

Euthanasia
JS: 5082, 5085, 5092
S: 5079, 5097

Evangelism
S: 4064

Evangelists
S: 4083

Evans, Dale
S: 6905

Evolution
JS: 6975, 6988, 6998, 7003, 7006, 7011, 8458
S: 5589, 6656–57, 6992–96, 6999–7000, 7004, 7007, 7012, 8265

Exchange students—Fiction
JS: 2308, 2313

Exercise
JS: 5358, 5360, 5364, 5422, 9633
S: 5341, 5346, 5348, 5352–53, 5357, 5367, 9678, 9775, 9963

Existentialism
S: 3997

Exotic animals—Pets
JS: 8680

Exotic plants
S: 9379

Experiments and projects—Science, 8239–8246

Explorers
JS: 6132, 6136, 7690
S: 6121, 6123, 6125, 6133–34, 6156, 6160, 7142

Extramarital affairs—Fiction
S: 861

Extrasensory perception (ESP)
JS: 5328, 9472, 9500
S: 9499

Extrasensory perception (ESP)—Fiction
JS: 603, 1815, 1845, 2215, 2817
S: 1076, 1196, 1269, 1779, 2024, 2333, 2412, 2586, 2667, 2703, 2806, 2860

Extraterrestrial intelligence
S: 8285, 8324

Extraterrestrial persons
JS: 9535
S: 9488, 9507

Extraterrestrial persons—Fiction
JS: 1103, 2457, 2475, 2500, 2546, 2553, 2589, 2608, 2612, 2617, 2633, 2724, 2728, 2736, 2753, 2761, 3614
S: 1149, 1345, 1748, 2398, 2426, 2439, 2454, 2499, 2511, 2521–22, 2542–43, 2549, 2552, 2555, 2560, 2585, 2588, 2590, 2592–94, 2619, 2628, 2647, 2654, 2659, 2670, 2672, 2700, 2720, 2732, 2734, 2742, 2751, 2756, 2759, 2762, 2772, 2780, 2790, 2804, 2848, 2851

Extraterrestrial persons—Plays
JS: 3086

F

Fables
JS: 3468–69

Face
S: 5297

Failure
JS: 5603

Fairies—Folklore
JS: 3372

JS = Junior–Senior High   S = Senior High

Fairy tales, 3357–3447

Fairy tales–Anthologies
S: 3399

Fairy tales–England
JS: 3401, 3416

Fairy tales–Denmark
JS: 3389

Fairy tales–France
JS: 3415

Fairy tales–History and criticism
S: 3358

Faith healing
S: 4074

Falkland Islands
JS: 7686

Falkland Islands War
S: 7673

Family life
JS: 5657, 5681, 6623
S: 5349, 5650, 5654, 5659, 5670–72, 5680

Family life–Fiction
JS: 525, 3487
S: 943

Family life–Poetry
JS: 3283

Family problems
JS: 5090, 5143, 5153, 5195, 5511, 5637, 5639, 5641, 5643, 5653, 5666–67, 5675, 5677, 6897
S: 4371, 5181, 5638, 5649, 5662, 5674, 5679, 6907, 6935

Family problems–Fiction
JS: 295, 518, 526–28, 531, 534, 538, 541, 546, 557, 567–68, 570, 573, 575, 602–3, 613, 616, 626, 658, 665, 682, 749, 778, 785, 827, 895, 898, 901, 1212, 1385
S: 263, 303, 323, 338, 480, 513, 515, 517, 521–22, 529–30, 535–37, 539, 543, 545, 547–48, 552–54, 556, 559–60, 564, 569, 577–79, 581, 584–85, 592–93, 595–97, 605, 607, 610–12, 614–15, 617–18, 623–25, 633, 655, 657, 691, 722, 733, 760, 781, 921, 1452, 1608, 1630, 1898, 2295

Family stories–Fiction
JS: 389, 449, 544, 558, 562, 574, 598–99, 840, 2234
S: 469, 523, 532–33, 540, 549–50, 555, 561, 565, 572, 583, 586–88, 594, 600, 604, 606, 609, 619–21, 795, 924, 1396, 1412, 1609, 1941, 2309

Family violence
S: 5674

Famines
S: 4511

Fantasy–Fiction
JS: 385, 424, 1000, 1003, 1019, 1026, 1030, 1033, 1040, 1043–44, 1047, 1053, 1055–56, 1061, 1072–73, 1078, 1080–81, 1084, 1087, 1093, 1102–3, 1112–13, 1117, 1130, 1133, 1136, 1146, 1152–53, 1156, 1160, 1171, 1185, 1191–92, 1195, 1197–98, 1203–4, 1207–8, 1211–12, 1215, 1218, 1221–22, 1234, 1239, 1243, 1249, 1271, 1275–76, 1279, 1295–97, 1308–9, 1312, 1319, 1321, 1323, 1335, 1342, 1346, 1900, 2808
S: 337, 1001–2, 1004–6, 1008–15, 1017–18, 1020–25, 1027–29, 1031–32, 1034–39, 1041–42, 1045–46, 1048–52, 1054, 1057–60, 1062–71, 1074–77, 1079, 1082–83, 1085–86, 1088–92, 1094–101, 1104–11, 1114–16, 1118–29, 1131–32, 1134–35, 1137–43, 1145, 1147–51, 1154–55, 1157–59, 1161–70, 1172–84, 1186, 1188–90, 1193–94, 1196, 1199–202, 1205–6, 1209–10, 1213–14, 1216–17, 1219–20, 1223–33, 1235–38, 1240–42, 1244–48, 1250–61, 1263–70, 1272–74, 1277–78, 1280–81, 1283–94, 1298–307, 1310–11, 1313–18, 1320, 1322, 1324–33, 1336–41, 1343–44, 1347, 1762, 1865, 1867, 1871, 2270, 2307, 2415, 2539, 2634, 2858, 2879

Fantasy–History and criticism
JS: 3658, 3672, 3692, 3763, 3766
S: 3618, 3626, 3653, 3662, 3671, 3684

Fantasy–Illustration
JS: 9216

Faraday, Michael
JS: 6664

Farmer, James
S: 6505

Farms and farming
JS: 8581
S: 6928, 8585, 8587–88, 8591

Farms and farming–History
JS: 8582

Farrell, Suzanne
S: 6389

Fashion design
S: 9167, 9179–80

Fashion industry–Careers
JS: 4829, 4934
S: 4832

Fashion retailing–Careers
JS: 4921

Fashion–History
JS: 5278

Fast foods
JS: 4573, 8417

Father–daughter relationships
S: 5671

Father–son relationships
JS: 9708
S: 4019

Father–son relationships–Fiction
JS: 531, 546, 713
S: 323, 612, 613, 781, 1898

Fathers–Changing roles
S: 5672

Faulkner, William
S: 3705, 3722, 3738, 3767

Fear
JS: 5555
S: 5615

Federal Bureau of Investigation (U.S.)–Fiction
S: 2196

Federal Reserve System (U.S.)
S: 4221

Female animals
S: 8388

Feminism
JS: 4306
S: 3673, 4293–94, 4300, 4304, 4317, 4319, 4323, 6784

Feminism–Fiction
JS: 772, 2968
S: 656, 1833

Feminism–Folktales
S: 3368

Ferrari, Enzo
JS: 9100

Fetal Alcohol Syndrome
S: 5181

Feynman, Richard
S: 6665

Fiction, 1–2977

Fiction writing
S: 4678, 4687, 4694

Fiction–Anthologies
S: 390

JS = Junior–Senior High S = Senior High

Fiction–History and criticism
JS: 3624
S: 3617, 3621, 3728

Fiction–Literary history and criticism, 3612–3796

Fields, W. C.
JS: 6390

Fighter planes
S: 9123

Fiji
S: 7480

Filmmaking, 9408–9440

Finance
See also Economics and business
S: 4575

Finances–personal, 5064–5072

Financial aid, 4773–4781

Firefighters
JS: 4230
S: 4976

Fires
JS: 5441

Fires–Fiction
JS: 243

First aid
JS: 5445
S: 5439

First aid manuals
JS: 5440, 5446

First Ladies (U.S.)
JS: 6484, 6560
S: 4207, 6558–59

First Ladies (U.S.)–Biography
JS: 6463
S: 6465, 6525, 6555–57, 6561, 6566

First Ladies (U.S.)–Fiction
S: 1529, 1620, 2160–65

Fish
JS: 8615, 8626, 8747–55, 8771–72, 8774
S: 8770, 8778

Fish–Field guides
JS: 8616, 8624–25, 8627–28

Fish–Pets, 8747–8755

Fisheries
S: 8621

Fishing
JS: 9827, 9830–33, 9835
S: 9812, 9814, 9824–25, 9828–29

Fishing–Fiction
S: 79, 124

Fishing–Humor
JS: 9836

Fitzgerald, F. Scott
S: 3718, 3748–49, 3761, 6245

Fitzgerald, Zelda
S: 6245

Flags–United States
JS: 7731

Flaubert, Gustave
S: 3635

Florida
S: 4469

Florida–Fiction
JS: 247, 297, 2212
S: 235, 465, 907, 1709

Florida–Penal system
S: 4486

Flower arrangement
S: 9298

Flowers
JS: 8438, 8444, 8448, 9144
S: 8433

Flowers–Dried
JS: 9302

Flowers–Field guides
S: 9383

Flying saucers. *See* Unidentified Flying Objects

Folk art
S: 9275

Folk art–United States
S: 5798, 5804, 5808–9

Folk dancing
S: 5967

Folk singers
S: 6395

Folk songs–American
JS: 5948, 5950, 5952–53
S: 5945–47

Folklore–Anthologies
JS: 3363, 3376–77, 3379, 3381, 3388, 3391, 3393–94, 3396, 3398
S: 3361–62, 3378, 3395, 3399–400, 3402, 3423, 3434–36

Folklore–Black Americans
JS: 3417

Folklore–Encyclopedias
JS: 9521

Folklore–General
JS: 3366
S: 3364, 3449

Folklore–Plays
S: 2986

Folklore and fairy tales, 3357–3447

Fonda, Jane
S: 6391

Food
JS: 5411, 5417, 8417
S: 5410, 5415, 5420, 5426, 8416

Food–Artificial
JS: 8419

Food–Dictionaries
S: 9323

Food–History
JS: 7973
S: 8421

Food additives
S: 8414

Food contamination
JS: 8419

Food service–Careers
JS: 4830
S: 4846

Football
JS: 6751–53, 6755, 6757, 6759–61, 9837, 9842–49, 9851, 9855, 9857, 9861, 9863, 9865–66
S: 5348, 6751, 9838, 9841, 9852, 9854, 9860

Football–Careers
JS: 6758

Football–Dictionaries
S: 9859

Football–Encyclopedias
JS: 9853

Football–Fiction
JS: 926, 2877
S: 1836

Football–History
JS: 9840, 9850, 9856, 9858, 9864

Football–Plays
JS: 3062

Football–Records
JS: 9862

Football–Trivia
JS: 9839

Ford, Henry
JS: 6666

Forecasting
JS: 9509

Foreign idioms
S: 3944

Foreign language–Mastery
JS: 3920

JS = Junior–Senior High   S = Senior High

Foreign languages–Careers
JS: 4816, 4831

Foreign languages–Phrase books
S: 3940

Foreign policy (U.S.)
JS: 7656
S: 6485, 6599, 7463, 7624, 7652, 7756, 8066, 8074, 8152

Foreign students
S: 3182, 6288

Foreign study
JS: 4710
S: 4717

Foreign study–Handbooks
JS: 4709

Foreign terms
S: 3910

Foreign words–Dictionaries
JS: 3952

Forest fires
JS: 8158

Forest fires–Fiction
JS: 227

Forestry and trees, 8423–8431

Forests
JS: 7749, 8820, 8822
S: 7761

Forests–United States
JS: 8821, 8824

Forster, Arnold
S: 6506

FORTRAN (computer language)
JS: 8990

Fortune-telling
JS: 9509, 9519, 9524

Fortune-telling–Fiction
S: 1170

Fossey, Dian
S: 6667–68

Fossils
JS: 6985
S: 6983

Fossils–Field guides
JS: 6973, 6986, 8827

Foster, Rory C.
JS: 6906

Foxes
JS: 8518

Foxes–Fiction
JS: 291

Foyt, A. J.
JS: 6711

France
JS: 7500

France–Cathedrals
JS: 5708

France–Cookbooks
S: 9321

France–Fairy tales
JS: 3415

France–Fiction
JS: 1026
S: 126, 210, 328

France–Folklore
JS: 3391

France–Historical fiction
JS: 1436
S: 311–17, 327, 1409

France–History
JS: 6866, 7490
S: 6857, 7140, 7146, 7491, 7493, 7495–96, 7498

France–Travel guides
JS: 7494

Franchises (business)
S: 4617

Francis of Assisi
S: 6838

Franco-Prussian War
S: 7496

Frank, Anne
JS: 6839–40, 7209

Franklin, Aretha
JS: 6392

Franklin, Benjamin
S: 6586–88, 7839

Franklin, Rosalind
S: 6669

Frazier, Walt
JS: 6744

Frederick II, King of Prussia
S: 6841

Freedom
S: 4301

Fremont, Jessie Benton
S: 6619

Fremont, John Charles–Fiction
S: 1580

French language–Poetry
S: 3180

French literature–Fiction
S: 327–29, 2906

French literature–History and criticism
S: 3567, 3586, 3600–1, 3635, 3637, 3641–42

French Revolution
JS: 7490, 7497
S: 4018, 4410, 7491–92, 7495, 7499

French Revolution–Fiction
JS: 362
S: 1455

Freshwater life, 8615–8658

Freud, Sigmund
S: 5529, 5535

Friday, Nancy
S: 6907

Friendship
JS: 5544, 5570
S: 8135

Friendship stories–Fiction
JS: 468, 644, 647, 711, 777, 789, 791, 885, 936, 1702
S: 235, 276, 301, 481, 487, 510, 517, 532, 601, 652, 661, 675, 820, 846, 878, 907, 941, 1680, 1879

Frisbees
JS: 9575

Fritz, Jean
JS: 6246–47

Frontier life (U.S.)
JS: 6097, 6426, 7881, 7949, 7950, 7954, 7956, 7958–59, 7961, 7967–71, 7975, 7976, 7986, 7988–95, 7997, 8000–2
S: 6377, 6619, 6624, 6635, 7948, 7953, 7955, 7957, 7960, 7962–63, 7966, 7972, 7974, 7977, 7979, 7982, 7984, 7999

Frontier life (U.S.)–Biography
JS: 6616
S: 6614, 6618

Frontier life (U.S.)–Family life
JS: 7981, 7998

Frontier life (U.S.)–Fiction
JS: 154, 160, 287, 393, 1554, 1565–66, 1570, 1579, 1590–91, 1595
S: 163, 280, 399, 416, 1539, 1555, 1558–64, 1567–69, 1571–75, 1577, 1580–85, 1587–89, 1592–94, 1596–98

Frontier life (U.S.)–Food
JS: 7973

Frontier life (U.S.)–History
S: 7684, 7952

JS = Junior–Senior High   S = Senior High

Frontier life (U.S.)–Journalism
JS: 7987

Frontier life (U.S.)–Women
S: 7980, 7983, 7985

Frost, Robert
S: 3881, 6248

Fulton, Robert
S: 6670

Furniture–History
S: 5810

Futurism
JS: 4540, 8314
S: 4414, 4417, 4420, 7062

Futurism–Fiction
JS: 223, 2427, 2528, 2726, 2753, 2787
S: 2394, 2400, 2409, 2456, 2507, 2513, 2567, 2650, 2725, 2747, 2847

G

Galapagos
JS: 7685

Galarza, Ernesto
S: 6908

Galbraith, John Kenneth
S: 6671

Gallaudet, T. H.
JS: 6620

Gambling
JS: 7989, 9547

Game hunters–Fiction
S: 244

Game wardens
JS: 6163
S: 6164

Games
JS: 5330, 8851, 9566, 9593, 9608
S: 8850, 9590

Games–Fiction
S: 2395

Gandhi, Indira
JS: 6805

Gandhi, Mahatma
S: 4406-7, 6806-9

Gangs
JS: 4557
S: 4497, 5536

Gangs–Fiction
JS: 808
S: 841, 851

Gardening
JS: 9371-72, 9376-77, 9381, 9385-86
S: 9370, 9375, 9378-80, 9382-84, 9387-88

Garibaldi, Giuseppe
S: 6842

Garvey, Marcus
S: 6507

Gatzoyiannis, Eleni
S: 6909

Gehrig, Lou
JS: 6720-21

Genealogy
JS: 5645, 5656
S: 5647, 5678

Genealogy–Jewish
S: 5663

General Motors
S: 9118

Generals
S: 6786

Genetic diseases
S: 5269

Genetic diseases–Fiction
JS: 698

Genetic engineering
JS: 5260-61, 5266

Genetic engineering–Fiction
JS: 2770
S: 2494

Genetics
JS: 5230, 5259-61, 5263-64, 5266
S: 5228, 5262, 5265, 5267-70

Genetics–Fiction
S: 264, 1725

Genetics–Projects
JS: 8241

Geography, 6971-8202

Geography–General
JS: 7049, 7061, 7068, 7073

Geography–Quiz books
JS: 7056

Geology, 8785-8830

Geology–Careers
S: 5027

Geology–Field guides
JS: 8797, 8826
S: 8794, 8798

Geology–North America
S: 8788

German Americans
S: 4403

German literature–History and criticism
S: 3638-39, 3645

Germany
JS: 7510

Germany–Fiction
S: 30, 632, 697, 966, 968, 2078

Germany–Folklore
S: 3399

Germany–Historical fiction
S: 1448-49, 1636

Germany–History
JS: 6830, 6847, 6916, 6970, 7505, 7509
S: 6828, 6841, 6845-46, 6848-49, 7292, 7299, 7501-2, 7504, 7506-8, 9907

Germany–Plays
S: 2992-93

Germany–Politics
S: 7503

Germany–World War II
JS: 7244

Geronimo
S: 6621-22

Geronimo–Fiction
S: 1498

Gershwin, George
JS: 6344

Gettysburg, Battle of
JS: 7901

Gettysburg, Battle of–Fiction
S: 1544

Ghana
S: 6892

Ghost ships–Fiction
JS: 2126

Ghosts
JS: 3438, 9493, 9536, 9542
S: 9506, 9517, 9526-27, 9531

Ghosts–Encyclopedias
JS: 9480

Ghosts–Fiction
JS: 1130, 1723, 1728, 1730, 1732, 1776, 1803, 1812, 1816, 1820, 1840
S: 407, 1028, 1272, 1708, 1712, 1722, 1729, 1738, 1765, 1771-72, 1862

JS = Junior–Senior High S = Senior High

Gideon, Clarence
S: 4246

Gift wrapping
JS: 9221

Gilbert and Sullivan
S: 5922

Gilbreth family
JS: 6623

Gillespie, Dizzy
S: 6393

Gino, Carol
S: 6910

Girlfriends–Fiction
JS: 96, 477, 810, 2503
S: 571, 879–80

Gissing, Vera
S: 6911

Glacier National Park
S: 8507

Glaciers
JS: 8809

Glass–History
S: 8955

Glassware
S: 5812

Glazes
S: 9164

Gliding and soaring
JS: 9610

Globe Theatre (London)
JS: 3816, 3820, 6091
S: 6092

Gnomes
S: 3365

Gogh, Vincent van
S: 5785, 6194–95

Gogh, Vincent van–Fiction
S: 1477

Gold
JS: 7958

Gold–Fiction
S: 152, 258, 1165

Goldfish
JS: 8747, 8753

Goldman, Emma
JS: 6589

Goldman, Joel
S: 6672

Golf
JS: 9868, 9871–74, 9876–78
S: 9867, 9869–70, 9875, 9879

Golf–Women players
S: 9880

Goodall, Jane
JS: 8498
S: 8499

Gorbachev, Mikhail
S: 6843

Gorillas
JS: 8497, 8500
S: 6667–68

Gorillas–Fiction
JS: 23

Government, 4123–4289

Government–Careers
JS: 4958

Goya, Francisco
S: 5775

Graffman, Gary
S: 6394

Graham, Robin Lee
JS: 6142

Grammar
JS: 3951
S: 3922, 3925–26, 3929, 3934

Grand Canyon
JS: 8159
S: 8156

Grand Ole Opry
JS: 5867

Grand Prix
JS: 9618

Grandparents–Fiction
JS: 558, 567, 575
S: 545, 552, 572, 580, 594, 606, 2110

Grant, Ulysses S.
JS: 6490
S: 6530

Graphic arts
S: 9202

Graphic arts–Careers
JS: 4862, 4884

Grasslands
JS: 8811, 8823

Grateful Dead (rock group)
JS: 5845

Graves, Robert
S: 6249

Great Barrier Reef
JS: 7475

**Great Britain–Description and
travel**
S: 7535

Great Britain–History
JS: 7534, 7541
S: 6878, 7514, 7517, 7528, 7532–33, 7539

**Great Britain–Literary history
and criticism,** 3646–3693,
3807–3832, 3865–3874

Great Britain–Plays, 3023–3045,
3807–3832

Great Britain–Poetry, 3188–3233, 3865–3874

Great Britain–Travel guides
JS: 7519

Great Lakes
S: 4455

Great Rift Valley
JS: 7364

Great Wall (China)
S: 7410

Greece–Ancient
JS: 7108, 7110
S: 7102, 7104, 7107

Greece–Ancient–Biography
S: 6788

Greece–Architecture
S: 5786

Greece–Art
S: 5762

Greece–Fiction
JS: 1361
S: 211, 973, 1332, 1750

Greece–Historical fiction
S: 1371–74, 1377

Greece–History
JS: 7089, 7110–11
S: 4008, 6821–23, 6909, 7083,
7085, 7101–3, 7105–6, 7109,
7545

Greece–Mythology
JS: 3468–69, 3472–76
S: 3457, 3464, 3477–78

Greece–Travel guides
JS: 7544

Greek Americans–Fiction
S: 466

Greek literature
S: 2893, 2990, 3013, 3018–20,
3183–84, 3846, 3864, 3993–95,
4020–21

**Greek literature–History and
criticism**
S: 3573, 3589, 3594, 3801, 3805–6,
7105–6

JS = Junior–Senior High   S = Senior High

Greek poetry—History and criticism
S: 3864

Green Bay Packers
S: 9852

Green Berets
S: 4284, 9124

Greenberg, Hank
JS: 6722

Greene, Marilyn
S: 6912

Greenfield, Noah
S: 6913

Greenhouse effect
S: 4439, 4447, 4449

Greenland—Fiction
JS: 1453
S: 68, 159

Greeting cards
JS: 9223

Gretzky, Wayne
JS: 6774

Grieg, Edvard
S: 6345

Grizzly bears
S: 8505, 8507–8

Grooming
JS: 5279, 5283–85, 5287, 5289

Guardian Angels
JS: 4479

Guidance and personal development, 4622–5681

Guide dogs
JS: 8746

Guilt—Fiction
S: 433

Guinea pigs
JS: 8756, 8758

Guitar
JS: 5933, 5935, 5941–42

Guitarists
JS: 5877, 6187, 6425

Gulf Coast—United States
JS: 8375

Gun control
S: 4527, 4530

Gunfighters—U.S. West
S: 7977

Guns
S: 9134

Gunther, John
JS: 6914

Guppies
JS: 8754

Guthrie, Woody
S: 6250, 6395

Guy, Rosa
JS: 6251

Gyatso, Tenzin
S: 6810

Gymnastics
JS: 6767, 9881
S: 9882–83

Gymnasts—Fiction
JS: 1841

Gypsies
S: 4405

Gypsies—Fiction
S: 1672

H

Haiku
JS: 3348, 3353

Hailey, Kendall
S: 6915

Haing Ngor
S: 6811

Hair
JS: 5277, 5284, 5337

Haley, Bill
S: 6396

Hall, Brian
S: 6143

Halley's Comet
JS: 8332–34
S: 8331

Halloween—Fiction
JS: 1043, 1830

Hallucinogens
JS: 8444

Hamburgers
JS: 9369

Hamill, Dorothy
JS: 6775

Hamilton, Scott
JS: 6776

Hamlet—Fiction
S: 3043

Hamsters
JS: 8757

Handball
JS: 9602

Handel, George Frideric
S: 6346–47

Handguns
S: 9134

Hanff, Helene
S: 6397

Hang gliding
JS: 9612

Hannam, Charles
JS: 6916

Hansberry, Lorraine
JS: 6252

Hanukkah
JS: 4118

Happiness
S: 5554, 5620

Harlem (N.Y.)
JS: 6223, 6251
S: 4629, 5799, 8169

Harlem (N.Y.)—Fiction
JS: 474
S: 478, 509

Harlem (N.Y.)—History
S: 8160

Harps—Fiction
S: 1336

Harrison, Harry
S: 3781

Hart, Moss
S: 6253

Harvard University—Fiction
S: 900

Hasidic Jews—Fiction
S: 486

Hastings, Battle of
JS: 7512

Hatshepsut—Fiction
S: 1358

Haunted houses
JS: 9518
S: 9489, 9517, 9526–27

Haunted houses—Fiction
JS: 1769
S: 1764, 1874

Hawaii—Birds
JS: 8543

Hawaii—Fiction
JS: 2217
S: 1401

JS = Junior–Senior High   S = Senior High

Hawaii–Travel guides
JS: 8181
S: 8179

Hawks–Field guides
JS: 8558

Hawthorne, Nathaniel
S: 3697, 3759, 6254–55

Hayden, Tom
S: 6508

Haydn, Joseph
S: 6348

Hayes, Billy
S: 6917

Hayes, Helen
S: 6398

Hazardous wastes
JS: 4450, 4452–53

Headaches
JS: 5198

Health
JS: 5073, 5343, 5427, 5608
S: 5074–76, 5320, 5345, 5347,
5349, 5353–54, 5410

Health–Encyclopedias
S: 5428

Health care
JS: 5253

Health care–Careers
JS: 4952, 4982, 4991, 5006, 5008,
5055
S: 4989, 5005, 5007

Health clubs–Careers
JS: 4994

Health foods–Fiction
JS: 2195

**Health services–Career guid-
ance,** 4984–5009

Hearst, William Randolph
S: 6590

Hebrew language–Poetry
S: 3346

Heinlein, Robert A.–Fiction
JS: 3733, 3782
S: 3720

Heiser, Victor G.
S: 6673

Helicopters
JS: 9058, 9069
S: 8130

Hellman, Lillian
JS: 6257
S: 3840, 6256

Hemingway, Ernest
JS: 6259, 6263
S: 3695, 3732, 3773, 6258, 6260–62

Hemophilia
S: 5207

Hendrix, Jimi–Biography
JS: 6399

Heng, Liang
S: 6812

**Henry III, King of England–
Fiction**
S: 1457

Henry, Patrick
S: 6591

Henry VIII, King of England
JS: 6844

Hentoff, Nat
JS: 6264

Hepburn, Katharine
JS: 6400
S: 6401

Herbert, Frank
JS: 3784

Herbs
JS: 8418
S: 8415, 8420, 8434, 9373

Heroes–Encyclopedias
JS: 9529

Heroin
JS: 5162

Herpes
JS: 5214
S: 5171

Herriot, James
JS: 6674

Hershiser, Orel
JS: 6723

Hesse, Hermann
S: 3638

Heyerdahl, Thor
JS: 6144

Hickok, Wild Bill
S: 6624

**High school entrance examina-
tions**
JS: 4714–15

High school students
S: 5538

High schools
JS: 4652
S: 4623, 4631, 4635

Highways
JS: 7785

Highways–History
JS: 9055

Hijacking–Fiction
S: 173

Hiking
JS: 9792–93, 9802
S: 9794, 9796

Hildebrand, John
S: 6146

Himes, Chester
JS: 6265

Hinduism
S: 4078

Hindus–Fiction
S: 983

Hinton, S. E.
JS: 3713

Hiroshima
JS: 7243
S: 7212, 7217, 7267, 7309, 7327

Hiroshima–Fiction
JS: 1660

Hispanic Americans
JS: 4397
S: 4396, 4402, 6945

**Hispanic Americans–
Biography**
JS: 6451
S: 6312–14, 6908

Hispanic Americans–Fiction:
488
S: 436, 437, 463

Hispanic Americans–Folklore
JS: 3418

Hiss, Alger
S: 6592

Historical fiction, 1348–1706

History, 6971–8202

History–Dictionaries
S: 7033, 7080

History–Encyclopedias
JS: 7053

History–General
JS: 7028, 7031, 7035, 7043, 7045,
7069, 7079
S: 7030, 7038, 7041, 7046, 7055,
7057–59, 7074, 7076–77, 7081

History–Methodology
S: 7048, 7078

Hit-and-run accidents–Fiction
JS: 2139
S: 195, 2083

JS = Junior–Senior High   S = Senior High

Hitchcock, Alfred
S: 6047

Hitler, Adolf
JS: 6847
S: 6845–46, 6848–49, 7206, 7507–8

Hitler, Adolf–Fiction
JS: 266
S: 187

Hobbes, Anne
JS: 6918

Hobbies and pastimes, 9296–9463

Hocken, Sheila
JS: 6919

Hockey
JS: 6774

Hoffman, Eva
S: 6920

Holiday, Billie
JS: 6404–5
S: 6402–3

Holidays–Poetry
JS: 3160

Holly, Buddy
JS: 6406

Hollywood–Fiction
S: 752, 1042, 1907

Hollywood–History
S: 6040

Holmes, Oliver Wendell
S: 6593

Holmes, Sherlock
JS: 3667

Holmes, Sherlock–Fiction
JS: 2034, 2042

Holocaust
JS: 1654, 6839–40, 6872, 6889, 6949, 7178, 7239, 7241, 7259, 7265, 7275, 7307, 7332, 7505
S: 3561, 6851, 6873, 6879–80, 6891, 6911, 6936, 7168, 7170, 7200, 7202, 7204, 7206–7, 7210–11, 7227, 7233, 7236, 7238, 7249, 7253, 7255, 7263, 7270–71, 7276–77, 7283, 7287, 7290, 7292, 7298, 7301, 7315, 7323

Holocaust–Children
S: 7314, 7331

Holocaust–Fiction
JS: 1655, 1679
S: 430, 1637, 1644, 1650, 1653, 1662, 1672, 1675, 1684, 7171

Holocaust–Plays
JS: 3076

Holography
JS: 8934

Holy books–World religions
S: 4032

Holy war (Islam)
S: 4060

Home economics–Careers
JS: 4868

Home repairs
JS: 9308, 9390

Homeless people
JS: 4512, 4514
S: 4508, 4510, 4515

Homeless people–Fiction
S: 2123

Homer, Winslow
S: 6196

Homosexuality
JS: 4320, 5459, 5466, 5474, 5488
S: 4536, 5453, 5463, 7270

Homosexuality–Fiction
JS: 677, 739, 769, 917, 935
S: 641, 864, 942, 1891

Honduras–Fiction
S: 252

Hong Kong–Fiction
JS: 104

Hoover, Herbert
S: 6531

Hoover, J. Edgar–Fiction
S: 183

Hopi Indians
S: 3427

Hopkins, Gerard Manley
S: 3869

Horne, Lena
JS: 6407

Horney, Karen
JS: 6675

Horror stories–Encyclopedias
S: 3631

Horror stories–Fiction
JS: 382, 384, 417, 1153, 1720–21, 1727, 1733, 1739–40, 1757–59, 1766–68, 1770, 1777, 1794, 1800, 1808, 1813, 1815, 1822, 1824, 1830–32, 1834–35, 1841–42, 1846, 1861, 2075, 2184
S: 190, 407, 1163, 1707, 1709–10, 1712, 1714, 1716–18, 1724–26, 1731, 1734–35, 1737, 1741–47, 1749–56, 1760–61, 1763, 1765, 1772–74, 1778–82, 1785, 1787–91, 1793, 1795–99, 1801–2, 1804–7, 1809–11, 1814, 1817–19, 1821, 1825–28, 1836–39, 1843–44, 1847–54, 1856–60, 1863, 1866–67, 1869–74, 2334, 2647

Horror stories–Films
JS: 6059

Horror stories–History and criticism
JS: 3623, 3698, 3744, 3769
S: 3785, 3791–92

Horse racing
S: 6781, 9884

Horse racing–Fiction
JS: 2875
S: 2010–18

Horseback riding
JS: 9885
S: 8763, 8766, 8768–69

Horses
JS: 6886, 8759, 8762, 8764, 9885
S: 8760–61, 8763, 8765, 8768

Horses–Fiction
JS: 289, 294–95, 300, 1276, 2300
S: 282, 1052, 1274

Horses–Training
S: 8767, 8769

Horwitz, Tony
JS: 6147

Hospices
S: 5093

Hospitals
JS: 5225
S: 5234, 5251

Hospitals–Careers
JS: 5006
S: 5005

Hospitals–Emergency departments
S: 5258

Hospitals–Fiction
JS: 653, 948
S: 1969, 2224, 2315, 2837

Hospitals–Staff persons
S: 5256

Hotels–Careers
JS: 4840

Hotels–Fiction
JS: 946

Hotels–History
JS: 4795

Houdini, Harry
JS: 6408

JS = Junior–Senior High   S = Senior High

Houseplants
JS: 9374, 9386
S: 9380, 9382

Houses
S: 9274

Houston, Sam–Fiction
S: 1586

Hubble Space Telescope
JS: 8259

Hughes, Langston
S: 3578, 3887, 6266–68

Human behavior
S: 5525, 5528

Human beings
JS: 8502

Human body
JS: 5291, 5294, 5298, 5300, 5302, 5304
S: 5293, 5296–97, 5301, 5303, 5342, 5345, 5359

Human body–Photographs
JS: 5299

Human development and behavior, 5523–5681

Human growth
JS: 5526
S: 5525

Human resources management–Careers
JS: 4979

Human rights, 4290–4409

Humanitarians
S: 6957

Humor and satire, 3482–3519

Humorous stories–Fiction
JS: 19, 422, 939, 1882, 1887, 1890, 1893–94, 1900–1, 1903–4, 1906, 1908, 2503, 2643, 2885
S: 172, 565, 591, 806, 1210, 1306, 1875–81, 1883–86, 1888–89, 1891–92, 1895–99, 1902, 1905, 1907, 1909–10, 2223, 2332, 2838, 2881

Humphrey, Hubert H.
S: 6594

Hungary–History
JS: 7488

Hunter, Catfish
JS: 6724

Hunters
S: 6122

Hunting
JS: 6150, 9583
S: 9825, 9834

Hunting–Humor
JS: 9836

Hurston, Zora Neale
JS: 6270
S: 6269

Hutchinson, Anne–Fiction
S: 1516

Huxley, Elspeth
S: 6921

Hygiene, 5341–5367

Hynes, Samuel
S: 6148

I

Iacocca, Lee
S: 6676

Ice hockey
JS: 9886, 9888
S: 9887

Ice skating
JS: 6775–76, 9890
S: 9889, 9891

Iceland
JS: 7551

Illegitimacy–Fiction
S: 460

Illinois–Fiction
S: 1871

Illiteracy–Fiction
S: 673

Illness. *See* Diseases and illnesses

Immigration–Fiction
S: 357, 795

Immigration–United States
JS: 4327–28, 4331, 4335, 4337–38, 4340
S: 4325–26, 4329–30, 4332–34, 4336, 4339, 4341, 4386, 4396, 6939, 7543

Immortality–Fiction
S: 2340

Immunology
JS: 5180, 5213, 5217
S: 5295

Impeachment
S: 4205

Impressionism–Art
S: 5739–40, 5759, 5770, 5783

Incas
S: 7668, 7674, 7680–81

Incest
JS: 5511

Independent living
JS: 5627
S: 5592

India
JS: 7442
S: 6957–58, 7443

India–Animals
JS: 8511

India–Fiction
S: 374, 717, 958, 984, 993, 1392, 1394–95, 1400, 1437, 2321

India–Folklore
JS: 3381, 3384

India–History
JS: 6805, 7438
S: 4407, 6806–9, 7439–40, 7444

India–Mythology
S: 3460

India–Poetry
JS: 3214

India–Writers
S: 6289

Indiana
JS: 9727

Indiana–Fiction
S: 1596

Indianapolis 500
JS: 9614

Indians of Central America
S: 7646, 7650

Indians of North America
JS: 7631, 7789–92, 7797–98, 7826, 7828, 7969, 9512
S: 4242, 4391–92, 4394–95, 6515, 6582, 7794, 7799–800, 7805–6, 7810, 7813, 7816, 7818–20, 7823, 7966, 8186

Indians of North America–Art
S: 5795

Indians of North America–Biography
S: 6477, 6615, 6621–22, 6625, 6635–36, 6639, 6898, 6962

Indians of North America–Chiefs
JS: 6499, 7797
S: 6615, 6621–22, 6639

Indians of North America–Communication
JS: 7807

JS = Junior–Senior High S = Senior High

Indians of North America–
Everyday life
S: 7829

Indians of North America–
Fiction
JS: 138, 171, 192, 431, 462, 695,
1497, 1499, 1505–6, 1579, 2052,
2498
S: 21, 51, 204, 217, 444, 446–47,
452, 454, 461, 489, 497, 510,
1496, 1498, 1500–4, 1507–12,
1555–56, 1568, 1573, 1586, 1596,
1847, 2050–51, 2053–54

Indians of North America–
Folklore
JS: 3419, 3421, 3426, 3429
S: 3359, 3420, 3422–25, 3427–28,
3610, 7809

Indians of North America–
Historical documents
S: 7801

Indians of North America–
Historical fiction, 1496–1512

Indians of North America–
History
JS: 7795, 7821
S: 7655, 7793, 7796, 7802–4, 7808,
7811–12, 7814, 7817, 7822,
7824–25, 7827, 7951, 7978

Indians of North America–
Literature
S: 2924, 3610, 7815

Indians of North America–
Place names
JS: 8154

Indians of North America–
Plays
S: 3073

Indians of North America–
Poetry
JS: 3291
S: 3247, 3256, 3260, 3307

Indians of North America–
Sports
JS: 6768

Indians of North America–
Stereotypes
S: 4393

Indians of North America–
Tribes
JS: 7830

Indians of North America–
Women
S: 6500, 6632

Indians of North America–
Writers–Fiction
S: 489

Indians of South America
JS: 7631, 7828
S: 7675, 7680–81, 7799

Indians of South America–
Folklore
JS: 3454
S: 3359

Indians of South America–
History
S: 7812

Indians of South America–
Literature
S: 2924

Individualism–Fiction
S: 989–91, 2960

Industry–Career guidance,
5033–5063

Influenza–Fiction
JS: 2665

Information science–Careers
JS: 4951

Inhalants
JS: 5117

Insanity–Fiction
JS: 2496
S: 3

Insects
JS: 8601
S: 8594, 8596

Insects–Encyclopedias
JS: 8600

Insects–Field guides
JS: 8592–93, 8595, 8597–99, 8602

Insurance–Careers
JS: 4933

Intelligence
JS: 5586
S: 5325

Intelligence–Fiction
JS: 2341

Intelligence tests
S: 5587

Intergalactic war–Fiction
JS: 2757

Interior decoration
JS: 9251
S: 9148, 9296

International education
S: 4717

International relations
JS: 4141, 4150, 4162
S: 4130, 4133, 4135, 4155–56

Internment camps
S: 6963, 7317

Interpersonal relations
S: 5539

Interracial dating
JS: 5598

Interviews
S: 4698, 4786

Inventions
JS: 4561, 7075, 8947, 8949, 8954

Inventors
S: 4583, 6670, 8942

Inventors–Women
S: 8236

Invertebrates
JS: 8618
S: 8614, 8617

Investments
JS: 4563, 4604
S: 4587–88

Invisibility–Fiction
JS: 2830
S: 2491

Iran
JS: 7619
S: 7622–24

Iran–Fiction
S: 86

Iran–History
S: 7620

Iran-Contra Affair
JS: 4166

Iraq
S: 7598

Ireland
JS: 7537
S: 7529–30, 7540

Ireland–Description and travel
S: 7535

Ireland–Fiction
S: 7, 125, 282, 467, 1135, 2231,
2927, 2951

Ireland–Folklore
JS: 3393, 3398, 3403, 3410
S: 3402

Ireland–Historical fiction
S: 1200, 1444–45, 1454, 1482–83

Ireland–History
JS: 7522
S: 7515, 7517, 7528, 7531, 7543

Ireland–Poetry
S: 3207, 3213

JS = Junior–Senior High S = Senior High

Ireland–Poets
JS: 6291

Ireland–Travel guides
JS: 7519

Irish Americans–Fiction
S: 545, 795, 1609

Irish literature–History and criticism
S: 3648, 3870

Irish literature–Short stories
S: 2969

Irving, Washington
S: 3702

Ishi
S: 6625

Islam
JS: 4080, 7593
S: 4034, 4060, 4063, 4073, 6815, 6943

Islam–History
S: 7595, 7599, 7602

Islands
S: 7060, 8786

Islands–Fiction
JS: 106, 205, 2057
S: 24, 2819

Israel
JS: 7604
S: 6941, 7598, 7609–12, 7614–17

Israel–Fiction
JS: 262, 1488
S: 994, 1451

Israel–History
JS: 7607
S: 4105, 7606

Israel–Travel guides
JS: 7596

Israeli-Arab relations
JS: 7605
S: 6803, 7590, 7600, 7608, 7613, 7617–18

Italian Americans
JS: 4398

Italian literature–History and criticism
S: 3862

Italy
JS: 7550
S: 7546

Italy–Fiction
JS: 198
S: 714, 809, 1647, 1658, 1884, 1968, 2088

Italy–Folklore
JS: 3392

Italy–Historical fiction
S: 916, 1419, 1640

Italy–History
JS: 7313
S: 6842, 7125, 7547, 7549

Italy–Travel guides
JS: 7548

Italy–World War II
S: 7261

Titanic–Fiction
JS: 2793
S: 67

Ivan the Terrible, Czar of Russia
S: 6850

Ivy League schools–Admissions
S: 4750

Iwo Jima, Battle of
JS: 7282

J

Jackson, Andrew
S: 6532, 7880, 7882, 7885

Jackson, Andrew–Fiction
S: 1529

Jackson, Michael
JS: 6409–10
S: 6411

Jackson, Shirley
S: 3724

Jackson, Stonewall
S: 6595–96

Jackson, Stonewall–Fiction
S: 1541

Jamaica
S: 5857

James, Henry
S: 3740, 3787–88

James, Will
S: 6271

Jamestown (Virginia)–History
S: 7836

Jannetta, Peter
S: 6677

Japan
JS: 7447, 7455
S: 7446, 7451–52

Japan–Crafts
S: 7449

Japan–Fiction
JS: 1683, 1900
S: 276, 686, 953, 1390, 1402, 1681, 2109

Japan–Folklore
JS: 3383, 3386

Japan–Historical fiction
JS: 1403, 1660

Japan–History
JS: 7311
S: 6819, 7188, 7205, 7288, 7295, 7441, 7445, 7448, 7450, 7453–54

Japan–Mythology
S: 3465

Japan–Poetry
JS: 3348, 3353

Japan–Religions
S: 4045

Japan–Theater
S: 3145

Japan–World War II
JS: 7326, 7329
S: 7327

Japanese Americans
JS: 6953, 7220
S: 6963, 7185, 7199, 7305, 7317, 8045

Japanese Americans–Fiction
S: 469

Japanese literature–Anthologies
S: 2928–29

Japanese literature–History and criticism
S: 3591

Japanese literature–Science fiction
S: 2358

Jazz
JS: 5849, 5851, 5878, 5891–92, 5909
S: 5842, 5870, 5881, 5897, 5902, 5908, 6178, 6358, 6368, 6374, 6387–88, 6393, 6453–54

Jazz–Biography
JS: 6359
S: 5862, 5882, 6173, 6186

Jefferson, Thomas
S: 6533

JS = Junior–Senior High   S = Senior High

Jenkins, Peter
S: 6145

"Jeopardy" (television program)
JS: 6067

Jerusalem—Fiction
S: 2082

Jesenska, Milena
S: 6851

Jesus Christ
JS: 4095
S: 4056, 4097

Jesus Christ—Fiction
JS: 1360
S: 1367, 1376

Jet planes
JS: 9077, 9126
S: 9076

Jewelry
JS: 5271, 9153

Jewelry making
JS: 9142

Jewels—Fiction
JS: 2673
S: 341, 1074, 1223, 1999

Jewish Americans
S: 4390

Jewish customs
S: 4059

Jewish folklore
JS: 3357, 3369–70, 3414
S: 4103

Jewish history
JS: 3370, 4385, 4388–89, 6801,
6839–40, 6916, 7239, 7241, 7259,
7265, 7275
S: 4070, 4384, 4386, 6879, 6911,
6936, 6961, 7027, 7040, 7066,
7072, 7168, 7200, 7202, 7207,
7210–11, 7227, 7233, 7236, 7238,
7255, 7263, 7271, 7276–77, 7283,
7287, 7290, 7301, 7323, 7331,
7609

Jewish holy days
JS: 4038, 4044, 4114, 4118, 4121

Jewish holy days—Fiction
JS: 434

Jewish humor
JS: 3357

Jews
JS: 4041
S: 4387, 5668, 6931

Jews—Biography
JS: 6309, 6722, 6872
S: 6613, 6901, 6920, 6941, 6947

Jews—Diaspora
S: 7072

Jews—Fiction
JS: 434, 477, 903, 1391, 1488,
1655, 1667
S: 81, 430, 435, 445, 486–87, 490,
493–94, 498–500, 509, 590, 667,
740, 806, 909, 954, 994, 998,
1411, 1431, 1447, 1470–72, 1629,
1637, 1640, 1650, 1653, 1662,
1675, 1899, 1910, 2081–83, 2298,
2961

Jews—Genealogy
S: 5663

Jews—History
S: 4043

Jews—History—Fiction
S: 1659

Jews—Legends
S: 4070

Jews—Literature
S: 3634

Jews—Musicals
S: 3127

Jews—Poetry
S: 3346

Job hunting
JS: 4792–93, 4799, 4811, 4822,
4843, 4870
S: 4708, 4782, 4784–87, 4789–90,
4800, 4804, 4808, 4812, 4836–37,
4847

Job hunting—Disabled persons
S: 4803

Jobs, Steven
S: 6678

John XXIII, Pope
S: 6852

Johnson, Earvin "Magic"
JS: 6745

Johnson, James Weldon
JS: 6272

Johnson, Lyndon B.
JS: 6535
S: 6534, 8048, 8056, 8069

Johnson, Osa
JS: 6149

Johnson, Samuel
S: 6273

Johnson, Wally
JS: 6150

Jokes and riddles
JS: 9464
S: 9465

Jones, Chuck
JS: 6197

Jones, Jim
S: 4042

Jones, John Paul
S: 6597

Jones, Tristan
JS: 6151

Journalism
JS: 3980, 9599
S: 3971, 3981, 3983–84, 3986,
4469, 4536, 6215–16, 6287, 6590,
7195, 9555

Journalism—Careers
JS: 4823, 4860, 4901, 4939
S: 4856

Journalism—Fiction
JS: 2076

Journalists
JS: 7987
S: 6283, 6298, 6315

Journalists—Fiction
S: 2199

Joyce, James
S: 3648

Judaism
JS: 4044, 4114, 4121
S: 4043, 4059, 4070, 4086, 4090

Judo
S: 9896, 9900

Juggling
JS: 9299–300, 9306

Juilliard School
S: 5823

Jujitsu
JS: 9898

July Fourth—History
JS: 7711

Jungles—Fiction
JS: 31–32

Jury system
JS: 4260
S: 4240

Justice
S: 4253, 4255

Juvenile courts
JS: 4244
S: 4254

Juvenile delinquency
JS: 4557, 4624
S: 5398

JS = Junior–Senior High   S = Senior High

K

Kafka, Franz
S: 3645, 6274

Kane, Bob
JS: 6198

Kansas–History
JS: 8154
S: 7985

Karate
JS: 9894–95, 9901
S: 9905

Keats, John
S: 3866

Keller, Helen
JS: 6626–27

Kennedy Center–Fiction
S: 2197

Kennedy family
S: 6598

Kennedy, John F.
JS: 6537, 6539, 6541, 8080
S: 6536, 6538, 6540, 8069

**Kennedy, John F.–
Assassination**
S: 8071

Kennedy, Robert F.
S: 6628

Kenya
JS: 6792
S: 7362

Kenya–Fiction
S: 1387

Kenyatta, Jomo
JS: 6792

Kerouac, Jack
S: 6275

Kerr, M. E.
JS: 3762, 6276

Khmer Rouge
S: 7460

Kidd, William
S: 7844

Kidnapping–Fiction
JS: 49, 102–3, 267, 271, 383, 1964,
2006, 2173, 2714
S: 38, 84, 94, 97, 149, 1809, 2005,
2141, 2205, 2645

Killer whales
JS: 8650

King, Martin Luther, Jr.
JS: 4380, 6513–14
S: 4350, 4372, 6509–12

King, Mike
JS: 6777

King, Stephen
JS: 3698, 3744, 3769, 6005
S: 3785, 3792

Kings and queens–Great Britain
JS: 7541

Kingsley, Mary
S: 6679

Kingston, Maxine Hong
S: 6922

Kinmont, Jill
JS: 6778

Kiowa Indians
S: 7817

Kipling, Rudyard
S: 3585

Kirkland, Gelsey
S: 6412

Kisor, Henry
S: 6923

Kissinger, Henry
S: 6599

Kites
JS: 9155
S: 9892

Klein, Norma
JS: 6277

Klitzman, Robert
JS: 6680

Klondike Gold Rush
S: 7633

Klondike Gold Rush–Fiction
JS: 206

Knight, Bob
S: 6746

Knights
S: 7131, 7141

Knights–Fiction
JS: 1422

Knitting
JS: 9226, 9230, 9238, 9243
S: 9235, 9241, 9244, 9247

Knox, Chuck
JS: 6753

Korea–Fiction
JS: 18, 1686

Korea–History
JS: 7462
S: 7459

Korean War
JS: 8117
S: 8100, 8103, 8144, 8149

Korean War–Fiction
JS: 1690

Kovic, Ron
S: 8124

Kristallnacht
S: 7277

Kritsick, Stephen
JS: 6681

Ku Klux Klan
JS: 4346, 4519
S: 4342, 4349

Kübler-Ross, Elisabeth
S: 6682

Kuralt, Charles
S: 6413

L

LaBastille, Anne
S: 6683

Labor camps
S: 7586

Labor camps–Fiction
S: 995

Labor unions
JS: 4613
S: 4518, 4612

Labor unions–Fiction
S: 1616, 1624

Labor unions–History
JS: 4517, 4614

Laboratories–Fiction
S: 1856

Laboratory animals–Fiction
S: 1986

Laboratory research
JS: 8451

Lake Superior
JS: 6128

Lakes
S: 8897

Lakes–Fiction
S: 1726

JS = Junior–Senior High S = Senior High

Lame Deer, John
S: 6515

L'Amour, Louis
S: 3725

Landers, Ann
JS: 5613

Landry, Tom
JS: 6751

Lane, Kenneth
JS: 6684

Lane, Rose Wilder
JS: 6278

Language
JS: 3928
S: 3912, 3923, 3926–27, 3930

Language–American
S: 3913, 3924, 3938

Language–Foreign
JS: 3920

Language and communication,
3898–3990

Laser technology–Careers
JS: 4992, 5011

Lasers
JS: 8935
S: 8942

Lasers–Fiction
S: 2422

"Late Night with David Letterman" (television pro-
gram)
JS: 6030

Latin
S: 3917, 9465

Latin America
JS: 4163, 7627
S: 7625, 7629–30

Latin America–Fiction
S: 2941

Latin America–History
S: 7626, 7628, 7632

Latin America–Music
S: 5895

Latin America–Poetry
S: 3350, 3354

Latin America–Writers
S: 3795

Latin American literature–
Anthologies
S: 2945, 2948

Latin American literature–
History and criticism
S: 2945, 3581, 3796

Law
JS: 4258
S: 4237, 4243

Law–Careers
JS: 4957, 4966–67
S: 4964, 4969, 4974, 4978

Law–History
S: 4251

Law–United States
JS: 9522
S: 4232, 4235, 4246, 4252

Law enforcement–Careers
JS: 4959
S: 4977

Law school
S: 4981

Lawrence, D. H.
S: 3686

Lawyers
S: 4247, 4307, 6583

Lawyers–Fiction
S: 181, 1961, 2100

Leadership
S: 7735

Leakey, Mary
S: 6685

Leakey, Richard E.
S: 6686

Learning disabilities
JS: 5370, 5390
S: 5393

Learning disabilities–
Universities and colleges
S: 4742, 4767

Learning theories
JS: 5318

Least Heat Moon, William
S: 6152

Leather work
S: 9141

Leaves
JS: 8413

Lebanon
S: 6967, 7621

Lectures
S: 3528

LeDoux, Chris
S: 6779

Lee, Robert E.
JS: 6490

Lee, Robert E.–Family
S: 6466

Left-handedness
S: 5312

Legal rights
JS: 4303

Legends–History and criticism
S: 3361

Le Guin, Ursula K.–Fiction
S: 3779

Leiber, Fritz–Fiction
S: 3663

LeMond, Greg
JS: 6780

L'Engle, Madeleine
S: 6279

Lenin, Vladimir Illich
S: 6853

Leningrad
S: 7285

Lennon, John
JS: 6414, 6417–18
S: 6415–16

Leonard, Sugar Ray
JS: 6747

Leonardo da Vinci
S: 5788

Leonowens, Anna
JS: 6924

Leopards
JS: 8510

Lesbianism
JS: 5459, 5466
S: 5453

Letter writing
S: 3974, 4638, 4673

Leukemia
JS: 6926, 9857
S: 5205, 5216, 5218

Leukemia–Fiction
JS: 659
S: 571

Levchenko, Stanislav
S: 6854

Levi-Montalcini, Rita
S: 6687

Lewis, C. S.–Fiction
S: 3679

Lewis, Clive S.
S: 6280–81

Lewis, Sinclair
S: 3730, 3752

Liberalism
JS: 4263

JS = Junior–Senior High S = Senior High

Libraries
JS: 4645

Libraries–History
S: 7732

Library science–Careers
JS: 4948, 4951

Libya–Fiction
S: 173

Lies and lying
JS: 9501
S: 5572

Lies and lying–Fiction
JS: 842, 915, 2277

Life (magazine)
JS: 5713, 8078
S: 3989

Life–Origin
JS: 8374
S: 8368

Life–Outer space
S: 8285, 8304

Lifeguards
S: 9962

Lincoln, Abraham
JS: 6542, 6545, 6548
S: 6543–44, 6546–47, 6549–50

Lincoln, Abraham–Fiction
S: 1534, 1547–48

Lincoln-Douglas Debates
S: 7874

Lindbergh, Anne Morrow
S: 6282

Lions
JS: 8509

Lippmann, Walter
S: 6283

Literary forms–Fiction, 1–2977

Literary history and criticism,
3563–3897

**Literary landmarks–United
States**
S: 3576

Literature–Dictionaries
S: 3572, 3588

**Literature–History and criti-
cism**
JS: 6244
S: 3587, 3574, 3613, 3646

Literature–Quizzes
S: 3564

Littin, Miguel
S: 7672

Little Bighorn, Battle of
S: 7951, 7978

Lloyd, Chris Evert
JS: 6769

Lobbying
S: 4313

Loch Ness monster
JS: 9491, 9515

LOGO (computer language)
S: 9012

London
JS: 3674, 7511

London–Fiction
JS: 749
S: 519, 818, 1089, 1749, 2021

London–Historical fiction
S: 2037

London, Jack
S: 3746, 6284

Lonetree, Clayton
S: 4242

Long, Huey
S: 6600

Long Island–Fiction
JS: 854
S: 2171

Longitude
S: 8860

Loomis, Vivienne
JS: 6925

Lorenz, Konrad
S: 6688

Los Angeles Dodgers
JS: 9691

Louis, Joe
JS: 6748
S: 6749

Louisiana–Fiction
S: 530, 1737

Love
JS: 5570, 5599
S: 5556, 5558–59

Love–Fiction
JS: 598, 695, 2300, 2318, 2325
S: 734, 816, 870, 882, 890, 919,
1233, 1272–73, 1682, 2295

Love–Poetry
JS: 3162, 3172
S: 3175, 3272, 3278, 3300

Love affairs–Fiction
S: 2178, 2302

Lowell, Amy
S: 3876

Lowell, James Russell
S: 6285

Lucadello, Tony
JS: 9709

Lumber and lumbering
JS: 8430

Lund, Eric
JS: 6926

Lusitania
S: 7161

Luther, Martin
S: 6855

Lynn, Loretta
JS: 6419

M

MacArthur, Douglas
S: 6601

McAuliffe, Christa
JS: 6153

Macbeth, King of Scotland
S: 6856

McCaffrey, Anne–Fiction
JS: 3704, 3793

McCarthy, Joseph
S: 6602–3, 8073

McCarthy, Mary
S: 6286

McCartney, Paul
S: 6420

McDonald's restaurants
JS: 4573

McFadden, Cyra
S: 6927

McGraw, John
S: 6728

Machine trades–Careers
JS: 5035

Machinery
JS: 9043
S: 8245

Machu Picchu
S: 7668

McMullen, Jeanine
S: 6928

MacNeil, Robert
S: 6421

JS = Junior–Senior High   S = Senior High

Macy, Anne Sullivan
JS: 6627

Madden, John
JS: 6755
S: 6756

Mafia
S: 4468, 4477–78, 4490

Mafia–Fiction
S: 8, 233

Magic
JS: 6408, 9393–94, 9396–98, 9402, 9475
S: 9395, 9401

Magic–Careers
JS: 4902

Magic–Fiction
JS: 1000, 1234, 2455
S: 1060, 1063, 1064, 1161, 1231, 1285, 1288

Magic–History
S: 9399

Magic spells–Fiction
JS: 1309, 2185
S: 1299

Magic spells–Folklore
JS: 3375

Magical realism–Fiction
S: 550

Magicians–Fiction
S: 1021

Mahler, Gustav
S: 6349

Mailer, Norman
S: 3760

Maine–Fiction
S: 1518

Makeba, Miriam
S: 6422

Makeup (stage)
JS: 6084, 9219

Malamud, Bernard
S: 3771

Malcolm X
JS: 6516

Mammals
JS: 8454, 8458, 8491

Mammals–Encyclopedias
JS: 8494

Mammals–Field guides
JS: 8488–90, 8495–96

Management–Careers
JS: 4924

Mandela, Nelson
S: 6793–94

Mandela, Winnie
S: 6795–96

Mandrell, Barbara
JS: 6423

Manet, Edouard
S: 5773

Manicures
JS: 5279

Mantle, Mickey
S: 6725

Manufacturing
S: 8953

Manufacturing–History
JS: 8944

Mao Tse-tung
JS: 7420
S: 6813–14, 7425

Maps and globes
JS: 6972

Marcos, Ferdinand
S: 7473, 7476

Marie Antoinette
S: 6857

Marie, Queen of Romania
S: 6858

Marijuana
S: 5145

Marine biology
JS: 8775
S: 8617

Marine biology–Careers
JS: 5020

Marine Corps (U.S.)
JS: 7218
S: 4282, 7224, 7235, 7321, 9128

Marine life, 8615–8658

Marine resources
S: 8874

Marine survival
JS: 9927

Maris, Roger
JS: 6726

Marketing
JS: 4621

Marketing–Careers
JS: 4937
S: 4923

Markham, Beryl
S: 6154

Markovna, Nina
S: 6929

Marley, Bob
S: 6424

Marriage
JS: 3130, 3494, 5664–65
S: 5579, 6279

Marriage–Fiction
JS: 745, 888, 1595, 2271, 2290, 2328, 2704
S: 578, 590–91, 601, 741, 846, 871, 918, 1289, 1568, 2093, 2263, 2268, 2272, 2279, 2317

Marriage–Mixed
S: 5668

Marriage–Plays
S: 3021

Mars
S: 8350

Mars–Fiction
S: 2428

Marshall, George C.
S: 6604

Marshall, John
S: 6605

Martial arts
JS: 9893–95, 9897–99, 9901, 9903–4
S: 9896, 9900, 9902, 9905

Martial arts–Fiction
S: 2473

Martians–Fiction
JS: 2834
S: 2734, 2804

Marx Brothers
S: 5987

Marx, Karl
S: 4176–77, 6859–61

Mary Stuart, Queen of Scotland
JS: 6863
S: 6862

Mary Stuart, Queen of Scots–Fiction
S: 1425

Masada
S: 7027

Masaryk, Tomas
JS: 6864

Masks and maskmaking
JS: 9218–19

Masonry
S: 9389

JS = Junior–Senior High   S = Senior High

Mass media
JS: 3956
S: 3969, 3985, 4212–13, 4271, 6027

Mass media–Careers
JS: 4871

Mathabane, Mark
S: 6930

Mathematical puzzles
JS: 8843, 8849, 8852
S: 8835, 8850, 8853–55

Mathematicians
S: 8831

Mathematics
JS: 8833, 8840, 8843, 8847
S: 6645, 8832, 8834, 8836–39, 8841–42, 8844–45

Mathematics–Careers
JS: 5014

Mathematics–Projects
JS: 8857

Mather, Cotton
S: 6606

Matisse, Henri
S: 5774, 5777

Mattera, Don
S: 6797

Maugham, W. Somerset
S: 3655

May, Antoinette
S: 6287

Mayan Indians
S: 7646, 7650, 7655

Mayan Indians–Fiction
S: 1228, 1855

Mays, Willie
JS: 6727

Mazer, Norma Fox
JS: 3739

Mazes–Fiction
S: 2845

Mead, Margaret
S: 6689–92, 6997

Measurements
S: 8863–65

Mechanical drawing
S: 8945

Meckler, Brenda Weisberg
S: 6931

Media–Writing, 3955–3990

Medical ethics
JS: 4522, 5092, 5165, 5230, 5239, 5255, 5481

S: 5079, 5229, 5235, 5248, 5257, 5267

Medical ethics–Fiction
S: 703

Medical fraud
JS: 5237

Medical school
JS: 5001
S: 4718, 5242

Medical students–Fiction
S: 716

Medical technology–Careers
S: 5000

Medicinal plants
JS: 8443

Medicinal plants–Fiction
S: 1118

Medicine
JS: 5253, 5294, 5343
S: 5179, 5231–33, 5238, 5242–43, 5247–48, 6694, 8432

Medicine–Careers
JS: 4991, 5055
S: 5007

Medicine–Diagnosis
S: 5250

Medicine–Fiction
JS: 2118
S: 215, 1859

Medicine–History
JS: 5236

Mediterranean area
S: 3515

Mediterranean area– Cookbooks
S: 9355

Mediterranean area–Fiction
S: 175, 1657

Mediterranean Sea
S: 7082

Mediterranean Sea–Fiction
JS: 90

Mehta, Ved
S: 6288–89

Melendez, Tony
JS: 6425

Melville, Herman
S: 3736, 3758

Memory
JS: 5317
S: 4650, 5331

Men–Dancers
JS: 5963

Men–Sex roles
S: 4531–32, 5672

Menstruation
JS: 5476
S: 5492

Mental discipline
S: 4578

Mental disorders, 5368–5407

Mental handicaps
JS: 5370
S: 4742, 5372, 5385, 5393

Mental handicaps–Fiction
JS: 726
S: 689

Mental health
JS: 5550

Mental illness
JS: 5382, 5388, 5392, 5407
S: 5369, 5371, 5375, 5379, 5384, 5391, 5394, 5401, 5403–4

Mental illness–Fiction
JS: 602, 745, 749, 2218, 2222
S: 94, 240, 543, 581, 657, 667, 688, 692, 728, 734, 742, 753, 2919

Mental illness–Legal aspects
JS: 4259

Mental problems
S: 5203, 5399

Mental retardation–Fiction
JS: 1378

Merrick, John–Fiction
S: 1473

Merrick, Joseph Carey–Plays
JS: 3114

Merton, Thomas
S: 6629

Metalwork
S: 9152

Meteorites
S: 8330

Meteorology, 8866–8873

Mexican Americans
S: 4396, 4401, 6312–13, 6908

Mexican Americans–Fiction
S: 436–37, 491, 505

Mexican Americans–Folklore
JS: 3418

Mexican War
JS: 7877
S: 7867, 7871

Mexicans–Fiction
S: 628

JS = Junior–Senior High S = Senior High

Mexico
JS: 7641
S: 4503, 7645, 7712

Mexico–Cookbooks
S: 9313, 9342

Mexico–Fiction
JS: 840
S: 258, 608, 670

Mexico–Folklore
JS: 3445, 3448
S: 3447

Mexico–History
JS: 7642
S: 7639–40, 7643, 7647–49, 7867, 7871

Mexico–Travel guides
JS: 7644

Michelangelo Buonarroti
S: 5776, 5782, 6199

Microbiology
S: 6698, 8660

Microcomputers
JS: 8978

Microelectronics–Careers
JS: 5043

Microscopes
JS: 8224

Microwave cooking
JS: 9316, 9320, 9327, 9332, 9346, 9348–49

Middle East
S: 7603

Middle Ages
JS: 7124
S: 7122, 7126–27, 7138, 7140–41, 7533

Middle Ages–Art
S: 5766

Middle Ages–Everyday life
S: 7132, 7134

Middle Ages–Fiction
JS: 1378, 1381, 1984, 2500
S: 1270, 1287, 1379–80, 1382, 1444, 1466, 2131–35, 2337, 2672

Middle Ages–History, 7122–7141

Middle Ages–Poetry
S: 3190

Middle Ages–Women
S: 7133, 7137

Middle Atlantic States (U.S.)
JS: 8164

Middle class–Fiction
S: 978

Middle East
JS: 7591, 7593, 7597
S: 7592, 7594, 7611

Middle East–Fiction
S: 226, 375

Middle East–Folklore and fairy tales, 3380–3387

Middle East–History
JS: 7605
S: 7159, 7595, 7599, 7602

Middle East–Mythology
JS: 3456

Middle East–Travel
S: 7601

Midway, Battle of
S: 7274

Midwest (U.S.)
JS: 6302, 6318

Midwest (U.S.)–Farms
S: 8583, 8585, 8591

Midwest (U.S.)–Fiction
JS: 108, 525, 778, 897, 1565
S: 485, 583, 835, 849, 924, 979, 1305, 1553, 1561–62, 1572, 1574, 1584, 1587, 2100

Midwest (U.S.)–Ghost stories
S: 9531

Midwest (U.S.)–History
S: 6890, 6931, 8155

Midwest (U.S.)–History and geography, 8153–8155

Midwest (U.S.)–Poetry
S: 3298

Mies van der Rohe, Ludwig
S: 6461

Migraine
JS: 5198

Migrant workers
S: 6497

Migrant workers–Fiction
S: 1632

Military education
S: 4824

Military history–United States
JS: 7760

Military service–Careers
JS: 4972

Miller, Arthur
JS: 6290
S: 3835, 3841–42, 3845

Miller, Robert M.
JS: 6886

Mime
JS: 6095
S: 6105

Mind control–Fiction
S: 47, 2624, 2725

Mines and mining–Fiction
S: 1618

Mines and mining–History
JS: 7990, 8944
S: 4518

Minkow, Barry
S: 6693

Minnesota–Fiction
JS: 824
S: 611

Minorities
JS: 4397, 6476
S: 4341, 4343–44

Minorities–Civil rights
S: 4308

Minorities–Fiction
S: 554

Minorities–Health care
JS: 5077

Minorities–Problems–Fiction, 434–512

Missiles–Fiction
S: 2479

Missionaries
S: 4047

Missionaries–Fiction
S: 650

Mississippi–Fiction
S: 2889

Mississippi River
S: 3516

Mississippi River–Fiction
JS: 421, 1604

Model making, 9403–9407

Modeling–Careers
JS: 4873, 4928
S: 4880, 4925

Modeling–Fiction
JS: 891

Modern history
JS: 7167, 7237, 7333, 7336, 7338–39, 7343
S: 7047, 7067, 7150–51, 7154–55, 7334, 7340, 7342

Modisane, Bloke
S: 6798

Mohm, Phat
S: 6932

JS = Junior–Senior High S = Senior High

Molecular biology
S: 6658

Molecules
S: 8781

Money
JS: 4579

Money-making ideas
JS: 4955, 5066–68
S: 5064

Monologues
JS: 2984, 2988, 3108, 6063
S: 3116

Monopoly (game)
JS: 9811

Monsters
JS: 6017, 9219, 9481, 9484–85,
9491, 9515

Monsters–Encyclopedias
JS: 9528

Monsters–Fiction
JS: 1153
S: 1129, 1869, 2764

Monsters–Folklore
JS: 3374

Montana
S: 6981

Montana–Fiction
JS: 249
S: 1564

Montana Territory–Fiction
JS: 192

Monteverdi, Claudio
S: 6350

Moody, Anne
S: 6933

Moon
S: 8336, 8339

Moon–Fiction
JS: 2451, 2584, 2814
S: 65, 2580, 2599, 2827

Moore, Marianne
S: 3892

Moose
S: 8523

Morality–Fiction
S: 2530

Morals–Public, 4519–4530

More, Sir Thomas
S: 6865

More, Sir Thomas–Plays
JS: 3024

Morgan, Elizabeth
S: 6694

Morgan, Sally
S: 6934

Mormons
S: 4028, 6952

Mormons–Fiction
JS: 1993

Morocco–Fiction
JS: 105

Mother–daughter relationships
S: 5542, 5654, 6905, 6907

**Mother–daughter
relationships–Fiction**
JS: 528, 538, 626
S: 578, 584, 586, 624, 657, 2846

Motherhood
S: 5659, 5676

Motion pictures
JS: 5986, 5989, 5991–92, 5995–96,
6000–3, 6005, 6007–8, 6011,
6017, 6019, 6024, 6026, 6028,
6033–34, 6041, 6050, 6058–59,
6063, 6071, 6075, 6085, 6100,
6357, 6390
S: 5987, 5990, 5994, 5997, 6013,
6022, 6035, 6047, 6061, 6094,
6102

Motion pictures–Actresses
JS: 6049

Motion pictures–Careers
S: 4888, 4891, 5998

Motion pictures–Cult status
JS: 6045

Motion pictures–Editing
S: 6053

Motion pictures–Fantasy
S: 6064

Motion pictures–Fiction
JS: 2975
S: 60, 752, 1839

Motion pictures–Guides
JS: 6018, 6039, 6069
S: 6029, 6060

Motion pictures–History
JS: 5993, 6009–10, 6014, 6031,
6036, 6043, 6066
S: 6023, 6038, 6040, 6051, 6062,
6096, 6101

Motion pictures–Production
JS: 6065

Motion pictures–Science fiction
JS: 6054, 6057

Motion pictures–Scripts
S: 3087

Motion pictures–Techniques
S: 6074

Motocross
JS: 9754

Motorcycles
JS: 9119
S: 9747

Motorcycles–Fiction
JS: 121

Mott, Lucretia
S: 6630

Mount Everest
JS: 9554

Mount Rushmore (South Dakota)
JS: 5807

Mount St. Helens
JS: 8800
S: 8189

Mountain bikes
JS: 9768

**Mountain States (U.S.)–
History and geography,**
8156–8159

Mountaineering
JS: 9554, 9577, 9596
S: 8812, 9545, 9548, 9551, 9568,
9581

Mountaineers
JS: 7994

Mountains
JS: 7726
S: 8812

Moving
JS: 5591, 5624

Moving–Fiction
JS: 785, 2278
S: 522

Mozart, Wolfgang Amadeus
S: 6351–52

**Mozart, Wolfgang Amadeus–
Plays**
JS: 3117

Ms. (magazine)
S: 4539

Muhammad
S: 6815

Muir, John
S: 6695

JS = Junior–Senior High   S = Senior High

Mummies–Fiction
JS: 1759
S: 1829

Museum of Fine Arts, Boston
JS: 5765

Museums–United States
JS: 8175

Mushrooms–Field guides
JS: 8422

Music
See also Composers; individual types of music
JS: 5815, 5818–19, 5821, 5830, 5841, 5846, 5854, 5906, 5984, 6386
S: 5824, 5895, 5932, 6172

Music–African
S: 5813

Music–Black American
JS: 5892
S: 5839

Music–Careers
JS: 4878, 4882, 4900
S: 4877, 4881, 5823

Music–Composing
S: 5875

Music–Dictionaries
JS: 5822, 5827

Music–History
JS: 5832, 5834
S: 5685, 5831, 5835, 5838–39

Music–Notation
JS: 5820

Music–Twentieth century
S: 5828, 5833

Music appreciation
S: 5814, 5816–17, 5825, 5833

Music festivals
S: 5826

Music recordings–Guides
JS: 5985
S: 4894

Musical instruments, 5931–5943

Musicals
JS: 5915, 5919, 5924–25, 5927, 5929, 6355
S: 5917–18, 5926, 6087, 6175

Musicals–History
S: 5922

Musicians
JS: 5829, 6168, 6171
S: 6396

Musicians–Biography
S: 6250, 6338, 6393

Musicians–Fiction
JS: 786, 1651

Mutants–Fiction
S: 2445

Mutiny
S: 7466

Myers, Walter Dean
JS: 3700

Mysteries–Unsolved
S: 4499

Mysteries and curiosities, 9472–9543

Mystery and detective stories–Fiction, 1911–2224

Mystery stories–Fiction
JS: 104, 358, 363, 1901, 1914, 1916–18, 1924, 1934, 1937, 1946, 1948–57, 1963–67, 1971, 1983–84, 1987–95, 2000, 2006–7, 2022–23, 2028, 2031–32, 2034, 2042, 2044, 2052, 2057–58, 2061, 2063, 2070, 2072, 2074–76, 2086, 2090, 2094, 2096, 2118, 2121, 2126, 2130, 2137, 2139, 2143, 2167–69, 2172–73, 2176, 2184–85, 2188–89, 2195, 2204, 2206–7, 2211–13, 2215–18, 2220, 2222, 2329, 2621
S: 152, 220, 230, 270, 341–42, 1131, 1366, 1380, 1420, 1737, 1911–13, 1919–23, 1925–33, 1935–36, 1938–45, 1947, 1958–62, 1968–70, 1972–82, 1985–86, 1996–99, 2001–5, 2008–18, 2020–21, 2024–27, 2029–30, 2033, 2035–41, 2043, 2045–51, 2053–56, 2059–60, 2064–69, 2071, 2073, 2077–85, 2087–89, 2091–93, 2095, 2097–103, 2105–17, 2119–20, 2122–25, 2127–29, 2131–36, 2138, 2140–42, 2144–66, 2170–71, 2174–75, 2177–83, 2186–87, 2190, 2190–94, 2196–203, 2205, 2208–10, 2214, 2219, 2221, 2223–24, 2543, 2653

Mystery stories–History and criticism
JS: 3667, 3693, 6243
S: 3615, 3632–33, 3657, 3668, 3683

Mystery stories–Television
JS: 6037

Mystery stories–Writing
S: 3966

Mythical animals–Folklore
JS: 3373

Mythology
JS: 3468–70
S: 3450, 3457, 4048

Mythology–Anthologies
JS: 3397, 3451
S: 3424–25, 3453, 3455, 3480–81

Mythology–Central America
JS: 3445

Mythology–Classical
JS: 3472–76
S: 3464, 3477–78

Mythology–Encyclopedias
JS: 3452, 9521

Mythology–Europe
S: 3411

Mythology–General
S: 3449, 3466–67

Mythology–Greek
JS: 3471

Mythology–Greek–Fiction
JS: 1361
S: 1372

Mythology–Middle East
JS: 3456

Mythology–Roman
JS: 3479

N

Names
JS: 3931, 9492
S: 3916, 3949, 5658

Names–Animal
JS: 8672

Names–Dictionaries
S: 5673

Names–Geographical
JS: 7780

Names–Origins
S: 3950

Napkins
S: 9154

Napoleon I, Emperor of the French
JS: 6866, 7497
S: 7146

Napoleonic Wars–Fiction
S: 1415

National Aeronautics and Space Administration (NASA)
JS: 6159, 8295, 8326

JS = Junior–Senior High   S = Senior High

National Air and Space Museum (U.S.)
S: 9063

National anthems
JS: 5951

National Cathedral–Fiction
S: 2198

National debt
S: 4225

National Forests (U.S.)–Field guides
S: 7761

National Guard (U.S.)
S: 4280

National Museum of American Art (U.S.)
JS: 5800

National parks
JS: 7065

National Parks (U.S.)
JS: 7769, 7773, 8157, 8178, 8198

Nationalism
JS: 4151

Native Americans. *See* Indians of North America

Natural disasters
JS: 8787
S: 8806

Natural history
JS: 8373, 8402, 8580
S: 8172, 8381, 8389, 8395, 8403

Natural history–Essays
S: 8394, 8401

Natural history–Field guides
JS: 8398

Natural history–New England
S: 8378

Natural history–United States
JS: 4433, 8375, 8811, 8815, 8818, 8821, 8824

Natural wonders
JS: 7061, 7068

Nature–Essays
S: 8584

Nature study
S: 8372, 8379–80, 8382–83, 8385–86, 8393, 8399, 8406, 8408, 8410, 8459

Navaho Indians
S: 4391, 7825

Navaho Indians–Fiction
JS: 462, 695, 2052
S: 497, 2050–51, 2053–54

Naval battles
S: 7878

Navratilova, Martina
JS: 6770
S: 6771

Navy (U.S.)
JS: 7223
S: 4287, 7225, 9129–31, 9133

Navy (U.S.)–Fiction
S: 415

Navy (U.S.)–History
S: 6597, 7914, 7923

Nazi Germany
JS: 6970, 7293, 7310, 7313, 7509
S: 6849, 6969, 7270, 7292, 7299

Nazi Germany–Fiction
S: 1174

Nazism–Fiction
S: 17, 72, 93, 107, 174, 2020

Nebraska–Fiction
S: 280

Needlecrafts
JS: 9228, 9231–32, 9234, 9237, 9252
S: 9229, 9233, 9253

Needlecrafts–Encyclopedias
JS: 9250

Nepal
JS: 6162, 8510
S: 7461

Neptune
S: 8341

Nervous system
JS: 5305
S: 5324

Netherlands–History
JS: 7209

Nettles, Graig
S: 6729

Neurology
S: 5194, 5316

Neurosurgeons
S: 6677

New Deal
S: 8039

New England
S: 8378

New England–Crafts
JS: 9156

New England–Fiction
JS: 745, 1215, 1515, 1966
S: 400, 405, 532, 676, 754, 1035,

1608, 1782, 1852, 1857–58, 1864, 2111, 2127, 4089

New England–Folklore
S: 3432

New England–History
JS: 7840, 8175

New England–Plays
S: 3135

New England–Poetry
S: 3245

New Guinea–Fiction
S: 145

New Jersey–Fiction
S: 748

New Mexico–History
S: 8200–1

New Orleans
S: 5842

New York City
S: 6935

New York City–Fiction
JS: 449, 789, 889, 896, 939, 1468
S: 50, 73, 233, 394, 396, 408, 631, 851, 909, 991, 1085, 1124, 1523, 1601, 1619, 1629, 1970, 2045, 2080, 2147

New York City–Fire Department
JS: 4230

New York City–History
S: 8018

New York City–Minorities
S: 4343

New York City–Plays
JS: 3121
S: 3112

New York City–Schools
S: 4627

New York City–Skyscrapers
JS: 5710

New York City–Sports
S: 9570

New York Mets
JS: 9630

New York State
S: 6581, 8168

New York State–Fiction
JS: 546
S: 148, 1626, 2219

New York State–Historical fiction
JS: 404

JS = Junior–Senior High   S = Senior High

New York Yankees
JS: 9691, 9703

New Zealand
S: 7472

New Zealand–Fiction
JS: 1212
S: 13

Newfoundland
S: 8655

Newspapers
S: 3988

Newspapers–Careers
JS: 4901

Newton, Sir Isaac
S: 6696

Nez Percé Indians
S: 7793

Nez Percé Indians–Fiction
S: 1508, 1510

Nicaragua
JS: 7656

Nicaragua–Fiction
S: 980

Nicholas II, Emperor of Russia
S: 6867

Nicknames–Dictionaries
S: 3949

Nidal, Abu
S: 4550

Nigeria
S: 7390

Nile River
S: 7354

Nixon, Richard M.
JS: 8061
S: 6551, 8088, 8096

Njeri, Itabari
S: 6935

Noah's Ark
JS: 4094

Nobel prize
S: 3521, 6789

Nobel prize–Writing
S: 2910

Nolan, Christopher
JS: 6291

Nomads
S: 7008

Nomads–Fiction
S: 1240

Nomberg-Przytyk, Sara
S: 6936

North America
JS: 7726–27, 8402
S: 7737

North America–Ancient peoples
JS: 7023

North America–Animals
JS: 8496

North America–Archaeology
JS: 7019

North America–Art, 5789–5807

North America–Exploration
S: 7831–33

North America–Folklore and fairy tales, 3417–3447

North America–History and geography, 7633–7666

North America–Prehistory
S: 7016

Northeast (U.S.)–History and geography, 8160–8175

Northeast (U.S.)–Natural history
S: 8172

Northern Ireland
S: 7530

Northern Ireland–Fiction
S: 975

Norway–Fiction
JS: 1453
S: 559, 1452

Norway–Folklore
JS: 3390

Norway–Historical Fiction
S: 1383

Norwegian Americans–Fiction
JS: 1623
S: 1587

Nova Scotia–Fiction
JS: 1040, 2761
S: 576

Nuclear accidents
JS: 8925
S: 8922, 8924

Nuclear accidents–Fiction
JS: 90, 2532
S: 2798, 2799

Nuclear devices–Fiction
S: 66

Nuclear energy
S: 8920–24, 8929

Nuclear holocausts–Fiction
S: 2512, 2758

Nuclear physics
S: 8939

Nuclear power
JS: 8925

Nuclear war
JS: 4127, 4157, 4159, 4164
S: 4133, 4137, 4161, 7232

Nuclear war–Fiction
JS: 988, 2423, 2489, 2717
S: 2436, 2596, 2605–6, 2685, 2689, 2841

Nuclear waste
JS: 8928
S: 8926

Nuclear weapons
JS: 4159
S: 4130, 4144, 4152, 4154–55, 8927

Numbers
JS: 8847–48
S: 8846

Nuns–Fiction
S: 646

Nurses
S: 5241, 6910, 6965

Nurses–Fiction
S: 688, 1788

Nursing–Careers
JS: 4984, 4993, 4995, 5003
S: 4985

Nursing homes–Fiction
S: 1944

Nutrition
JS: 5073, 5344, 5355, 5411, 5414, 5416–17, 5419, 5422, 5425, 5427
S: 5074, 5311, 5319, 5409–10, 5413, 5415, 5423, 5426, 5429

Nutrition–Careers
JS: 4987, 4999

Nutrition–Encyclopedias
JS: 5430
S: 5428

O

Oakley, Annie
JS: 6426

Oates, Joyce Carol
S: 3723

JS = Junior–Senior High S = Senior High

O'Barry, Richard
JS: 6697

Obesity–Fiction
JS: 1112

Occult
JS: 9500, 9504

Occupational guidance, 4782–
5063

Occupational schools
JS: 4806

Occupational therapy
JS: 4903

Occupational therapy–Careers
JS: 4986

Occupations
S: 4813, 4826

Occupations–History
JS: 4965

Ocean energy resources
S: 8917

Ocean floor–Fiction
S: 2742

Oceanography
JS: 6653, 8876–77, 8880, 8888–89
S: 8874

Oceans
JS: 8875, 8879, 9476
S: 8799, 8884, 8891

Oceans–Fiction
JS: 2717, 2792

Office management
S: 4640

Office occupations–Careers
S: 4912

Ohio–Fiction
S: 1584

Oil painting
JS: 9196

Oil spills
S: 4444

Oil spills–Alaska
JS: 4451

O'Keefe, Georgia
S: 6200–1

Old age
JS: 5084, 5098
S: 4467, 5083

Olivier, Laurence
S: 6427

Olympic Games
JS: 9906, 9908
S: 6706, 9907

Olympic Games–Fiction
S: 2016

O'Neill, Eugene
S: 3833–34, 3837, 6292

Opera
JS: 5912–14, 5916, 5921, 5928
S: 5920

Opera–Biography
JS: 6441

Optics
JS: 8932, 8934

Options trading
S: 4588

Oral history
JS: 4671
S: 5650, 7048

Orbison, Roy
S: 6428

Orchestras
JS: 5940
S: 5932

Oregon
S: 8513

Oregon–Description and travel
S: 8190

Oregon Trail
S: 7972

Organ transplants
JS: 5165–66
S: 5164, 5238

Organic gardening
S: 9375, 9378

Oriental cookbooks
JS: 9360

Origami
JS: 9220

Orphans–Fiction
JS: 1308

Orwell, George
JS: 6293
S: 3666, 3670

Otters
JS: 8477

Otters–Fiction
JS: 1222

Outdoor cooking
S: 9311

Outdoor life
JS: 3502, 5440, 9753, 9790, 9799–
800, 9802, 9804
S: 6119, 8168, 8180, 9555, 9789,
9795–98, 9801, 9803, 9826

Outdoor life–Careers
JS: 4839
S: 4838

Outdoor recreation
S: 8390, 9549

Owens, Jesse
S: 6765–66

Owls
JS: 8563–65

Ozark Mountains
S: 8395

Ozarks–Folklore
S: 3442

Ozone layer
S: 4437

P

Pacific Northwest–Fiction
S: 2214

Pacific Northwest Indians
JS: 7792

Pacific States
JS: 8178

Pacific States–Ecology
JS: 8182

**Pacific States–History and ge-
ography,** 8176–8193

Pacific States–Travel guides
JS: 8176

Pacific States–Wildflowers
JS: 8439

Pacifists
S: 4520, 6467

Pain
JS: 5148

Paintings–Fiction
S: 1867

Pakistan
S: 6804

Pakistan–History
S: 7439

Paleontology
JS: 6973, 6975, 7685
S: 6977, 6980, 6983, 6987, 8223

Palestine
S: 4550

JS = Junior–Senior High S = Senior High

Palestine Liberation Organization
S: 7590

Palestinian Arabs
S: 7608

Panama Canal–History
S: 7663

Pandas
JS: 8524

Papago Indians–Fiction
S: 444

Papashvily, George
S: 6937

Paper airplanes
JS: 9224

Paper crafts
JS: 9222–23, 9466

Paper money
S: 9445

Papua New Guinea
JS: 7467

Parakeets
JS: 8668

Paralegal careers
JS: 4968
S: 4956

Paramedical careers
JS: 4998

Paraplegia–Fiction
JS: 718
S: 235

Paraplegics
JS: 6777, 6903

Parapsychology
JS: 5328

Parent–teenager relationships
JS: 5653, 5667

Parenting
JS: 5491, 5669

Parents
JS: 5677, 6899
S: 5679

Parents–Fiction
JS: 528, 534, 538, 541, 568, 713, 739, 794, 896
S: 162, 539, 553, 569, 577, 614, 1110, 1886

Parents–Illness
JS: 5221

Parfit, Michael
S: 6155

Paris–Fiction
S: 303, 2270, 7489

Parks, Gordon
S: 6294–95

Parliament
S: 7524

Parliamentary practice
JS: 5581, 5584

Parrots
JS: 8675, 8677
S: 8678

Part-time jobs
JS: 4843, 5066
S: 4847

Particles (physics)
S: 8266, 8904, 8909

PASCAL (computer language)
JS: 8996

Pastel drawing
JS: 9203

Pasteur, Louis
S: 6698

Patents
JS: 8949

Paterno, Joe
JS: 6757

Patton, George S.
S: 6607–8, 6631

Patton, Larry
JS: 6938

Pauling, Linus
S: 6699

Peace
JS: 4153

Pearl Harbor
JS: 7175, 7244, 7251, 7273

Pearl Harbor–Fiction
S: 1661

Peck, Richard
JS: 3726

Peloponnesian Wars–Fiction
S: 1373

Pencil drawing
JS: 9182, 9198, 9217

Penguins
JS: 8566
S: 8567

Pennsylvania Dutch
S: 4054, 5809

Pennsylvania–Fiction
JS: 524, 1627
S: 1628

Performing arts, 5955–6116

Performing arts–Careers
JS: 4896

Performing arts–History
JS: 5955, 5980

Pern series–Handbooks
JS: 3763

Peron, Eva
S: 6883

Peron, Juan Domingo
S: 6884

Persia–Poetry
S: 3352

Persian Gulf–Fiction
S: 226

Persian literature
S: 3347

Personal appearance. *See*
Grooming; Hygiene

Personal development, 4622–5681

Personal finances, 5064–5072

Personal guidance
JS: 4637, 5289, 5561, 5594–95, 5603–5, 5607, 5612–14, 5619, 5621–23, 5625, 5629–30, 5677, 9609
S: 5551–52, 5554, 5565, 5592–93, 5596, 5601–2, 5606, 5615–16, 5618, 5620, 5626, 5631–34, 5662

Personal guidance–Sourcebooks
JS: 5628

Personal letters
S: 7304

Personal problems
JS: 5530, 5627
S: 5617

Personal problems–Fiction
JS: 245, 373, 477, 524, 527, 542, 562, 566, 573, 599, 642, 660, 677, 698, 704, 712, 723, 727, 729, 732, 736, 751, 763, 766, 768–69, 772, 775–76, 778–80, 785–86, 789, 791–94, 796, 798, 804, 807–8, 810, 813, 821, 824, 826, 828–31, 833–34, 836, 838, 844, 854–56, 865, 881, 884, 887–89, 891–92, 895–98, 901–3, 913–15, 923, 925, 927–28, 931, 935, 937, 939–40, 946–49, 952, 988, 1468, 1697, 1904, 1906, 2226, 2257, 2266, 2289, 2299, 2326, 2884
S: 202, 302, 318, 330, 332–34, 344–45, 348, 394, 398, 405, 408,

432–33, 452, 493, 514, 516, 519, 561, 563, 569, 576, 580, 589–90, 601, 615, 622, 624, 629–30, 632, 636–38, 643, 646, 648, 651, 654, 656, 664, 669–70, 672–75, 679–81, 684–87, 690, 692, 697, 699, 705–8, 710, 714, 716–17, 721, 724–25, 730, 737, 740–41, 744, 754, 756, 758–59, 761–62, 764, 771, 773–74, 782–84, 787–88, 790, 797, 799–800, 802–3, 805–6, 809, 811–12, 814–18, 822–23, 825, 835, 837, 839, 841, 843, 845, 847, 850–53, 858, 860–63, 866, 868, 870–80, 882–83, 886, 890, 893–94, 899–900, 904–6, 908, 910–12, 918–20, 930, 933–34, 938, 941, 944–45, 950–51, 954–55, 980, 982, 1398, 1628, 1892, 2272, 2887

Peru
S: 8549

Peru–Fiction
S: 1495

Peru–History
S: 7674, 7680

Pesticides
S: 4424, 5421

Peter I, Emperor of Russia
S: 6868–69

Petroleum industry
JS: 5045

Pets
JS: 8560, 8661–64, 8666–68, 8670–71, 8673, 8675, 8677, 8679–80, 8682, 8685–87, 8692–93, 8710–12, 8715, 8717, 8720, 8723–27, 8750–51, 8756–58, 8776
S: 8665, 8678, 8681, 8713, 8722, 8770

Pets–Breeds
JS: 8719

Pets–Hotels
JS: 8676

Pharaohs
JS: 3458

Pharaohs–Fiction
S: 1358

Pharmacy–Careers
JS: 5017

Philadelphia
S: 4477

Philadelphia Phillies
JS: 9623

Philby, Kim
S: 6870

Philippines
S: 6802, 7473, 7476

Philippines–Fiction
S: 982

Philippines–History
S: 7189

Philippines–World War II
JS: 7297

Philosophy
S: 3991–98, 4001–23, 4025, 4570, 7030

Philosophy–American
S: 4024

Philosophy–China
S: 3999–4000

Phobias
JS: 5555

Photography
JS: 5713, 5716, 5723, 5789, 7049, 7751, 8046, 8060, 8085, 9410, 9412–15, 9418–22, 9428, 9430, 9433–34, 9436
S: 3654, 5717, 5743, 6188, 6294, 8023, 8267, 8561, 9409, 9411, 9416–17, 9423–24, 9426–27, 9432

Photography–Careers
JS: 4842
S: 4883

Photography–Documentary
S: 9437

Photography–Encyclopedias
JS: 9435

Photography–Enlargements
S: 9439

Photography–History
JS: 5722, 5802, 9408, 9429, 9431
S: 5724, 5755

Photography–Landscapes
S: 9440

Photography–Newspapers
S: 9425

Photography–Sports
JS: 9597
S: 9576

Photography–Wildlife
JS: 9438

Photonics
JS: 8932

Physical abuse
JS: 5567

Physical abuse–Fiction
JS: 2319
S: 750

Physical and applied sciences,
8203–9134

Physical disabilities and problems, 5431–5438. *See also* Physical handicaps.

Physical fitness
JS: 5351, 5355
S: 5357, 5366, 9958

Physical geography, 8810–8824

Physical handicaps
JS: 3114, 5029, 6291, 6425, 6626, 6777, 6948, 8670
S: 5433, 5436–37

Physical handicaps–Fiction
JS: 660, 678, 718, 726, 735, 738, 746, 2714
S: 628, 664, 668, 716, 859, 1232, 1473, 1996, 2919

Physically handicapped– Education
JS: 4768

Physically handicapped–Jobs
S: 4803

Physicians. *See* Doctors

Physics
S: 6654, 6660, 6696, 8391, 8404, 8899–900, 8904–5, 8908, 8910–11, 8915, 9620

Physics–General
JS: 8912

Physics–History
S: 8906

Pianists
S: 6394

Pianists–Fiction
S: 593

Piano
JS: 5937
S: 5939

Picasso, Pablo
JS: 6202–3
S: 5778, 5784

Piccolo, Brian
JS: 6758

Picture puzzles
JS: 8856

Pigeons
JS: 8683

Pilgrims (New England)
S: 7835

Pinter, Harold
S: 3809

JS = Junior–Senior High   S = Senior High

Pioneer life (U.S.). *See* Frontier life (U.S.)

Pirates
S: 7844

Pirates–Fiction
S: 2668, 2699

Pirsig, Robert M.
S: 4019

Pissarro, Camille–Fiction
S: 1475

Place names
JS: 8154

Plagues
S: 5227, 7136

Plagues–Fiction
JS: 1203, 2493, 2611, 2801
S: 54, 637, 2693

Plains Indians
JS: 7791, 7807
S: 7810

Planets
JS: 8345, 8347
S: 8342–43, 8346, 8348, 8350

Planets–Fiction
JS: 2357, 2450, 2462, 2526, 2529,
  2582, 2595, 2633, 2635, 2651,
  2660, 2662–64, 2691, 2705, 2712,
  2741, 2752, 2787, 2861–62
S: 1278, 2339, 2356, 2387, 2402,
  2405, 2410, 2417, 2472, 2487,
  2497, 2555, 2601, 2610, 2628,
  2630–31, 2641, 2653, 2658–59,
  2683, 2706, 2708, 2720, 2740,
  2744–46, 2775, 2778, 2789, 2813

Planets–Field guides
JS: 8355

Plants
JS: 9376
S: 8449, 9383

Plants–Fiction
S: 2856

Plants–Field guides
S: 8432

Plants–Medicinal
JS: 8443

Plants–Preservation
JS: 8436

Plate tectonics
S: 8785, 8788, 8802

Plath, Sylvia
S: 6296

Plato
S: 4021

Plays
JS: 3023–24, 3062
S: 2982, 2993

Plays–2-Actor
S: 2987

Plays–American
JS: 3074, 3079, 3081, 3084, 3092,
  3094–98, 3103, 3114–15, 3121–
  26, 3130, 3133, 3138, 3142
S: 2983, 2985, 3060–61, 3063–66,
  3068–72, 3075, 3077, 3080,
  3082–83, 3085, 3088, 3093, 3099,
  3101–2, 3104–7, 3111–13, 3116,
  3120, 3127–28, 3131–32, 3135–
  37, 3139–41, 3833–42, 3844–45,
  6292

Plays–Anthologies
S: 2978–80

Plays–Black American playwrights
S: 3109

Plays–Black Americans
S: 3110

Plays–English
JS: 3045, 3047–48, 3052–54, 3117–
  18, 3812, 6304
S: 2983, 3025–33, 3035–43, 3055–
  59, 3134, 3808, 3813, 3821–23,
  3825, 3829, 6305–7

Plays–English–History and criticism
S: 3811, 3832

Plays–European
S: 2981

Plays–Folktales
S: 2986

Plays–French
JS: 2994
S: 2991, 3001–2, 3008–12, 3015–17

Plays–German
S: 2992, 2998

Plays–Greek
S: 2990, 2999, 3013, 3018–20, 3805

Plays–History and criticism
JS: 3048, 3800, 3819, 6304
S: 2995, 3652, 3797–99, 3809,
  3813, 3821–23, 3825, 3829–30,
  3833–42, 3844, 6307

Plays–Holocaust
JS: 3076

Plays–Humorous
JS: 3482, 5978

Plays–Irish
S: 3034, 3044

Plays–Italian
S: 3014

Plays–Japanese
S: 3144–45

Plays–Literary history and criticism, 3797–3897

Plays–Native American
S: 3073

Plays–Norwegian
S: 3004–7

Plays–One-act
JS: 3067

Plays–Production
S: 6077–78, 6093

Plays–Radio
JS: 3807

Plays–Russian
S: 2995–97, 3003

Plays–Scandinavian
S: 3021–22

Plays–Scenes
JS: 3078
S: 2989, 3116

Plays–Science fiction
JS: 3086

Plays–South Africa
S: 3143

Plays–Spanish
S: 3000

Plays–Teenage playwrights
JS: 3089–91

Plays–Welsh
S: 3129

Plays–Women
JS: 3100

Playwrights–American
S: 3843

Playwrights–Biography
S: 6292

Plumbing
JS: 4942

Pocahontas
S: 6632

Poe, Edgar Allan
S: 3584, 3706

Poetry, 3146–3356

Poetry–American
JS: 3167, 3173, 3262–64, 3268,
  3271, 3273, 3280–83, 3287, 3303,
  3305–6, 3309, 3312–13, 3315,
  3317, 3322–25, 3342–43
S: 397, 3119, 3156–57, 3164, 3220,

JS = Junior–Senior High S = Senior High

3242–43, 3250–55, 3257–59,
3265–67, 3269–70, 3272, 3275–
77, 3284–86, 3288–90, 3292–95,
3297–98, 3301–2, 3304, 3307–8,
3310–11, 3314, 3316, 3318–21,
3326–30, 3332–39, 3341, 3344–
45, 3876–78, 3880–81, 3883–86,
3888, 3890–97, 6222

Poetry–Animals
JS: 3147

Poetry–Anthologies
JS: 3149, 3155, 3158, 3169, 3221,
3234–35
S: 3148, 3150, 3157, 3188–89,
3192–96, 3216, 3220, 3236, 3239,
3244–45, 3247, 3848, 3850, 3868,
3873

Poetry–Black Americans
S: 3241, 3331

Poetry–Canada
JS: 3240

Poetry–Chinese
S: 3349, 3355

Poetry–Computer-generated
JS: 3849

Poetry–Dictionaries
S: 3851

Poetry–English
JS: 3167, 3173, 3214, 3221
S: 3028, 3156–57, 3164, 3168,
3190, 3196, 3198–206, 3208–11,
3215–20, 3222–26, 3230–31,
3865–69, 3871–72

Poetry–Epic
S: 377

Poetry–French
S: 3180

Poetry–German
S: 3186

Poetry–Greek
S: 3183–84

Poetry–Handbooks
S: 3854–55, 3860

Poetry–Hebrew
S: 3346

Poetry–History and criticism
JS: 3852
S: 3153, 3349, 3846–47, 3857–58,
3865–67, 3869, 3871–73, 3876–
78, 3880–81, 3883–88, 3891–95

Poetry–Holidays
JS: 3160

Poetry–Humorous
JS: 3305–6
S: 3150, 3163, 3188

Poetry–Irish
JS: 3221
S: 3207, 3212–13, 3232–33

Poetry–Italian
S: 3861–62

Poetry–Japanese
JS: 3348, 3353
S: 3356

Poetry–Latin American
S: 3350, 3354

Poetry–Love
JS: 3162
S: 3175, 3300

Poetry–Modern
S: 3174, 3858

Poetry–Modern–History and criticism
S: 3856

Poetry–Native American
S: 3307

Poetry–Persian
S: 3352

Poetry–Puerto Rican
S: 3296

Poetry–Roman
S: 3185, 3187

Poetry–Russian
S: 3863

Poetry–Science
JS: 3853

Poetry–Spanish
S: 3181–82

Poetry–Sports
S: 3248

Poetry–Teenage writers
JS: 3889

Poetry–Translations
S: 3179, 3859

Poetry–War
JS: 3159
S: 3161, 3297, 3340

Poetry–Welsh
S: 3227–29

Poetry–Women
S: 3170

Poets–Biography
S: 6285

Poets–Fiction
S: 2858

Poets–Women
JS: 3299
S: 3274

Pohl, Frederik–Fiction
S: 3710, 6297

Poisonous animals
JS: 8485

Poitier, Sidney
JS: 6429

Poland–Fiction
S: 1450, 1470–72, 1659, 1663

Poland–History
S: 6891, 6961, 7168, 7487

Polar bears
JS: 8506

Polar regions
JS: 7690–92, 7694, 7699, 7703–4,
7706, 7708
S: 6125, 7689, 7696–98, 7705, 7709

Polar regions–Fiction
S: 209

Polar regions–Wildlife
S: 8512

Police
JS: 4248

Police–Careers
JS: 4959
S: 4977–78

Police–Fiction
JS: 2143
S: 2179

Polio
JS: 6563

Polio–Fiction
JS: 746

Political science
S: 3994, 4009, 4014, 4016, 4018,
4025

Political science–Careers
JS: 4958

Politicians
JS: 7338
S: 6600, 6602–3

Politics
JS: 7034
S: 4269, 4271

Politics–Fiction
S: 2820

Polls
JS: 5590

Pollution
JS: 4425–26, 4450, 4452–53, 4456
S: 4421, 4432, 4435, 4442, 4445–
46, 4448, 4455

Polo, Marco
S: 6156

Polovchak, Walter
S: 6939

Pompeii
JS: 7116

Ponds
JS: 8620

Ponds–Field guides
JS: 8619

Pony Express
JS: 7976

Pop art
S: 5751

Pop music
JS: 4900, 5900
S: 5843

Popes
S: 6852

Popular culture–Encyclopedias
JS: 9534

Population
S: 4416, 4458–59, 7047

Population control–Fiction
S: 2650

Population problems, 4457–4518

Pornography
JS: 4524

Porpoises
S: 8646

Porter, Katherine Anne
S: 3734

Portrait painting
S: 9185, 9192

Portugal–Travel guides
JS: 7555

Post-Impressionism–Art
S: 5760, 5771

Posters
JS: 5733

Potpourris (floral mixtures)
JS: 9138

Pottery
JS: 9165
S: 9162, 9166

Poultry
S: 8589

Poverty
JS: 4504–5, 4512, 7341
S: 4502, 4506–9, 4513, 8018

Poverty–Fiction
JS: 1615
S: 457, 748, 817, 996–97, 1631

Power boats
JS: 9924

Prairies
JS: 8002

Precocity–Fiction
S: 866

Pregnancy
JS: 5455–56, 5465, 5472–73, 5478,
5480, 5491, 5493–94, 5499,
5514–15, 5669
S: 5452, 5467, 5484, 5490, 5495,
5600

Pregnancy–Fiction
JS: 440, 542, 768, 867
S: 662, 706, 720, 730, 857, 872,
919, 1802, 1891

Prehistoric man
JS: 6998, 7003, 7005
S: 7012–13, 7016–18

Prehistoric man–Art
JS: 5732

Prehistoric man–Fiction
S: 1348–57, 2002

Prehistoric times–Fiction
JS: 1113

Prehistory–Historical fiction,
1348–1357

Prejudice
JS: 4347
S: 4351, 4358

Prejudice–Fiction
JS: 496, 511, 932
S: 438

**Preliminary Scholastic Apti-
tude Test**
S: 4662

Premenstrual syndrome
JS: 5476, 5498

Presidents (U.S.)
JS: 4208, 4224, 6475, 6535, 6537,
6539, 6542, 6548, 6896
S: 4205–6, 4209–11, 4213, 6538,
6543, 6570–71, 8044, 8071, 8077,
8079, 8095–96

Presidents (U.S.)–Biography
JS: 6527, 6541, 6545, 6563, 6575
S: 6468, 6470, 6491, 6523–24,
6526, 6528–29, 6531–34, 6536,
6540, 6544, 6546–47, 6549–54,
6564–65, 6567–69, 6572–74,
6576

Presidents (U.S.)–Fiction
JS: 271
S: 234

Presidents (U.S.)–Profiles
JS: 6492

Presidents (U.S.)–Quotations
JS: 7734

Presidents (U.S.)–Trivia
JS: 6481

Presley, Elvis
JS: 6431–32
S: 6430

Pressed flowers
S: 9139

Price, Michelle
JS: 6940

Priestesses
S: 4052

Priests–Fiction
S: 670, 2098

Primates
JS: 8502

Primitive peoples
JS: 7010
S: 7009

Prince of Wales–Fiction
S: 1458

Printing
S: 3973, 3982

Printing–Careers
JS: 5038

Printmaking
JS: 9225

Prison camps
S: 6954

Prisoners of war
JS: 7070, 7190, 7280, 7326
S: 7281, 8134

Prisons
JS: 4493
S: 4471, 4482, 4487

Prisons–Fiction
JS: 573, 1342, 1645
S: 311, 812, 1649, 2097

Privacy
S: 4309

Private detectives–Fiction
S: 2141, 2144, 2148

Private schools–Fiction
JS: 694, 922, 1435, 1721, 2006,
2261, 2294
S: 805, 852, 862–63, 920, 1418,
1930

Products–Catalogs
S: 4609

JS = Junior–Senior High S = Senior High

910

Professors–Fiction
S: 275, 2149

Prostitution
JS: 5512

Prostitution–Fiction
S: 803

Prywes, Raquela
S: 6941

Psychiatrists–Fiction
S: 725

Psychic abilities–Animals
JS: 8473

Psychoanalysis
S: 5529, 5535

Psychoanalysts
JS: 6675

Psychoanalysts–Fiction
S: 2174

Psychologists–Fiction
S: 2838

Psychology
S: 5313, 5528, 5531–32, 5537,
5540–41, 5543, 5545–46, 5548,
5551–53, 5559–60, 5569, 5571,
8106

Psychology–Careers
JS: 4988

Psychology–Fiction
S: 2378

Psychology–History
S: 5533

Psychology–Sports
JS: 9730

Psychopaths–Fiction
JS: 1964
S: 150, 1735, 1853, 2046, 2186

Public health
JS: 5077

Public Health Service (U.S.)
S: 5078

Public morals, 4519–4530

Public relations
S: 3961

Public relations–Careers
S: 4914

Public speaking
JS: 4676, 4680, 4700, 4702, 4706
S: 4667–68, 4677, 4686, 4696

Public welfare
JS: 4505, 4516
S: 4509

Publishing
JS: 3977
S: 3978–79, 3987

Publishing–Careers
JS: 4935, 4948

Publishing–Fiction
S: 967

Pueblo Indians–Fiction
S: 1511

Pueblo Indians–Legends
JS: 3429

Puerto Ricans–Fiction
S: 2905

Puerto Rico–History
S: 7664

Puerto Rico–Poetry
S: 3296

Puffins–Fiction
JS: 281

Pumas–Fiction
JS: 292

Punctuation
JS: 4679

Puppets
JS: 9146
S: 5982

Purl, Sandy
S: 6942

Puzzles
JS: 8856, 9466, 9468–71
S: 9467

Puzzles–Fiction
JS: 1917

Pyramids
S: 5711, 7096–97

Q

Quadriplegia
JS: 6778

Quakers
JS: 4031

Quakers–Fiction
JS: 1550

Quarks
S: 8939

Quilting
JS: 9228, 9231, 9252
S: 9239, 9245–46, 9253

Quiz books
JS: 7056

Quizzes
JS: 5983, 7954
S: 3564

Quotations
S: 3525, 3548, 4686, 4696

R

Rabbis
S: 4970

Rabbits
JS: 8667

Rabbits–Fiction
JS: 1003, 2546

Raccoons
JS: 8492–93

Rachlin, Nahid
S: 6943

Racing cars
S: 9617

Racism
JS: 4345, 4347, 4409, 4519, 7386
S: 4352–54, 4365, 7384

Racism–Fiction
JS: 495–96, 504
S: 520, 1530

Racquet games, 9964–9973

Racquetball
JS: 9972
S: 9544, 9971

Radiation
S: 8927

Radiation accidents–Fiction
S: 242

Radio
S: 9046

Radner, Gilda
S: 6433

Rafting
JS: 9919
S: 9953

Ragtime music
S: 5868

Railroads
JS: 4613

Railroads–Fiction
S: 224, 416

JS = Junior–Senior High S = Senior High

Railroads—History
JS: 7949, 7991, 9120
S: 7974, 8003

Railroads—Models
JS: 9405–06

Rain forests
S: 8400, 8816–17

Ramusi, Molapatene Collins
S: 6799

Ranches, 7986, 8581–8591

Ranches—Everday life
S: 8583

Ranches—Fiction
S: 277–78, 555, 2138

Rand, Ayn
S: 3729

Rap music
S: 5865

Rape
JS: 5501, 5503–4, 5516–17
S: 4485, 5505, 5513, 5522

Rape—Fiction
JS: 471, 701, 747
S: 112, 641, 654

Raquetball
JS: 9573

Rather, Dan
S: 6298

Rats—Fiction
S: 1856

Ravens
S: 8556

Reading
JS: 4646
S: 4625, 4644

Reading—Fiction
JS: 2427

Reagan, Ronald
S: 3493, 6552–54

Real estate—Careers
JS: 4913

**Reconstruction to World War I
(U.S., 1865–1914)—
Historical fiction,** 1599–1620

**Reconstruction to World War I
(U.S., 1865–1914)—
History,** 8004–8022

Recorders (music)
JS: 5943

Records and recordings
JS: 5984

**Records and recordings—
Guides**
JS: 5985
S: 4894

Recreation—Careers
S: 4841

Recreation and sports, 9135–
9979

Redford, Dorothy
S: 6517

Reeves, Dan
JS: 6759

Refugees—Fiction
S: 1674

Reggae music
S: 5857

Reggae stars—Biography
S: 6424

Reilly, Sidney
S: 6157

Reincarnation
JS: 9473, 9493
S: 9541

Reincarnation—Fiction
S: 1036, 1121

Relationships—Fiction
S: 2938

Relatives—Fiction
JS: 502, 898, 2311
S: 540, 581, 587, 633, 864, 1819,
1883

Relativity theory
JS: 8902
S: 8251, 8903, 8907, 8913

Religion
JS: 4031, 4049, 4076, 4088, 4267,
5595
S: 4026, 4028, 4032, 4034–35,
4042, 4045, 4047–48, 4055, 4062,
4064, 4067, 4075, 4273

Religion—Ancient Egypt
S: 7100

Religion—Comparative
JS: 4081, 4085

Religion—Fiction
JS: 903
S: 646, 787–88, 981, 999

Religion—Handbooks
S: 4046

Religion—History
JS: 4626
S: 4051, 4068–69, 4084

Religion—United States
JS: 4029, 4079

S: 4026, 4030, 4035, 4037, 4039,
4051, 4065, 4082–83

Religious liberty
JS: 4266

Remarriage—Fiction
S: 595, 691

Rembrandt van Rijn
S: 5781

Remington, Frederic
S: 6204

Renaissance
S: 4014, 7125, 7135, 7547

Renoir, Auguste
S: 5783

Repairing
JS: 9307

Report writing
JS: 4684, 4691, 4704–5
S: 4654, 4669, 4692–93, 4695,
4697, 4699

Reproduction
JS: 5481
S: 8384

Reproduction—Human, 5449–
5499

Reptiles and amphibians, 8461–
8471

Reptiles—Encyclopedias
JS: 8464

Reptiles—Field guides
JS: 8461–63, 8466–68

Research—Guides
S: 4681

Research—Methodology
JS: 4645

Research methods
S: 4653

Resnick, Rose
JS: 6944

Responsibility
JS: 5573

Restaurants—Careers
JS: 4827, 4962

Restaurants—History
JS: 4795

Resurrection—Fiction
S: 2535

Retton, Mary Lou
JS: 6767

Reunions—Fiction
JS: 923
S: 2092

JS = Junior–Senior High S = Senior High

Revenge–Fiction
JS: 203

Revere, Paul
S: 6609

Revolution
S: 4171, 4410

Revolution–Fiction
S: 2583

**Revolutionary Period (U.S.)–
History,** 7847–7862
S: 4185, 6521–22

Revolutionary War (U.S.)
JS: 4198, 7851, 7853, 7855
S: 4201, 4410, 6591, 7847–48,
7850, 7852, 7856–59, 7862

**Revolutionary War (U.S.)–
Fiction**
JS: 1521–22
S: 1310, 1520, 1523

Rhinoceros
JS: 8578

**Richard III, King of England–
Fiction**
S: 1189, 1459, 1481, 2193

Rivera, Edward
S: 6945

Rivers
JS: 7073, 7669, 7676, 7728
S: 4435, 7354, 8897, 9953

Rivers–Fiction
JS: 1604

Robberies
JS: 4496

Robbins, Lawrence
JS: 7024

**Robert the Bruce, King of Scot-
land**
S: 6871

Robertson family
JS: 6158

Robeson, Paul
JS: 6435–36
S: 6434

Robin Hood
JS: 3404

Robinson, Bill
JS: 6437

Robinson, Jackie
JS: 6730–31, 9704

Robinson, Smokey
S: 6438

Robotics–Careers
JS: 5025, 5047
S: 5012, 5059

Robots
JS: 8969
S: 8958, 8965, 8983, 9000, 9003

Robots–Fiction
JS: 1103, 1800, 2363, 2371–72,
2643, 2652, 2741
S: 248, 2365, 2388, 2597, 2680,
2737

Rock climbing
JS: 9569, 9580
S: 8812, 9581

Rock music
JS: 5836, 5840, 5844–48, 5850,
5855–56, 5863–64, 5873–74,
5879, 5883, 5886–87, 5894,
5903, 5906, 5927, 6187, 6356,
6460, 8070
S: 5861, 5872, 5876, 5885, 5896,
5910

Rock music–Dictionaries
JS: 5930

Rock music–Encyclopedias
JS: 5852, 5893, 5901

Rock music–Fiction
JS: 810
S: 1213

Rock music–Guides
JS: 5888

Rock music–History
JS: 5890, 5905, 5907

Rock music–Instruction books
JS: 5911

Rock musicians–Biography
JS: 5857, 5864, 5869, 6369, 6375,
6380, 6399, 6406, 6409–10, 6414,
6417, 6418, 6431, 6444, 6451
S: 5859, 6411, 6415–16, 6420,
6428, 6430, 6445–46

Rock musicians–Fiction
JS: 2216, 2237, 2299
S: 815, 933, 1848

Rock videos
S: 5876

Rockefeller family
S: 6474

Rockets
S: 8302

Rockets–Models
S: 9407

Rocks and minerals
JS: 8826

**Rocks and minerals–Field
guides**
JS: 8825, 8827–30

Rocky Mountains–History
S: 7962

Rodeos
S: 6779, 6927

Rodriquez, Richard
S: 6946

Rolling Stones (rock group)
JS: 5844
S: 5872

Roman Empire
JS: 7089, 7116, 7118, 7121
S: 4096, 7083, 7085, 7113, 7115,
7117, 7119

Roman Empire–Biography
S: 6788

Roman Empire–Everyday life
JS: 7114
S: 7120

Roman Empire–Fiction
JS: 1185, 1363–64, 1368
S: 1366–67, 1369–70, 1375–76,
2523

Roman literature
S: 2909, 7115

**Roman literature–History and
criticism**
S: 3596

Romances
S: 5558

Romances–Fiction
JS: 16, 95, 133, 135, 139, 249, 331,
335–36, 603, 659, 671, 735, 779–
80, 834, 842, 881, 947–49, 1417,
1433, 1474, 1590, 1604, 1882,
2023, 2057, 2070, 2207, 2218,
2225–28, 2230, 2232–34, 2236–
37, 2239 2241, 2242–44, 2248,
2250–53, 2256–57, 2259, 2261,
2264–67, 2269, 2271, 2273–75,
2277–78, 2281–83, 2285–86,
2288, 2290–91, 2294, 2296–97,
2299–300, 2308, 2310–14, 2316,
2318–19, 2325–26, 2328–30,
2872
S: 112, 302, 467, 483, 588, 609,
627, 691, 770, 832, 857–59, 874,
906, 960, 1324, 1409, 1432,
1484–85, 1535, 1635, 1704, 1929,
2078, 2111, 2136, 2229, 2231,
2235, 2238, 2240, 2245–46, 2247,
2254–55, 2260, 2262–63, 2268,
2270, 2276, 2279–80, 2284, 2287,
2292–93, 2295, 2298, 2301–07,
2309, 2315, 2317, 2320–24, 2327

Romania
S: 6858

Rome–Historical fiction, 1363–
1377

Rome–History
S: 7549

Rome–Mythology
JS: 3476, 3479
S: 3464

Rome–Poetry
S: 3185

Rommel, Erwin
S: 7257

Ronstadt, Linda
JS: 6439

Roosevelt, Eleanor
JS: 6560
S: 6555–59, 6561

Roosevelt, Eleanor–Fiction
S: 2160–65

Roosevelt, Franklin D.
JS: 6563
S: 6562, 8031, 8035, 8039

Roosevelt, Theodore
S: 6564–65, 8011, 8014

Rope jumping
JS: 9605

Rosenberg, Ethel
S: 4250, 6633, 6634

Rosenberg, Julius
S: 4250, 6634

Rosetta Stone
S: 7093

Rowing
S: 6706

Royalty
JS: 6844, 7541
S: 6837, 6850, 6856, 6869, 6878,
7539

Royalty–Biography
JS: 6863
S: 6829, 6833, 6835, 6858, 6862,
6867–68, 6877

Royalty–Fiction
JS: 1218, 1462
S: 45, 1083, 1201, 1205, 1225,
1457–61, 1463–64, 1481, 1982,
2089, 2193, 2260, 2852

Royalty–Plays
S: 3075

Rubber stamp making
JS: 9151

Runaways
JS: 4462, 4501, 5512
S: 4463

Runaways–Fiction
JS: 575, 736, 848, 889
S: 690, 847

Running
JS: 9912, 9914, 9975
S: 3549, 9909–11, 9913, 9915–16

Running–Fiction
JS: 616, 2884

Rushdie, Salman
S: 3647

Russia. *See also* Soviet Union

Russia–Fiction
JS: 201
S: 43, 74, 144, 168, 170, 253, 260,
305, 318–20, 870

Russia–Folklore
JS: 3388

Russia–Folklore–Fiction
S: 1071

Russia–Historical fiction
S: 308–10, 322–23, 1404, 1421,
1447, 1456, 1469

Russia–History
JS: 7580, 7587
S: 6832–33, 6850, 6867–69, 6929,
7579, 7581

Russia–Plays
S: 3804

Russia–World War II
JS: 7330

Russian literature
S: 321, 2897, 2955

**Russian literature–History and
criticism**
S: 3568, 3606, 3640, 3643, 3802–3

Russian Revolution
S: 6790, 7572, 7582

Russo–Finnish War
JS: 7203

**Ruth, George Herman
("Babe")**
JS: 6732

Résumés
S: 4708, 4784–85, 4796

S

Sabotage–Fiction
S: 2019

Sacajawea
S: 6635

Sadat, Anwar
S: 6816

Sadism–Fiction
S: 412

Safety
S: 5439

Safety, accidents, and first aid,
5439–5448

Sahara Desert
JS: 7367

Sailboarding
JS: 9955, 9957

Sailing and boating
JS: 6128, 9918, 9923, 9925–26,
9929, 9935–37, 9939
S: 9917, 9920–21, 9931–32

Sailing and boating–Fiction
S: 176

Sailing ships–History
JS: 9122

Saint-Exupéry, Antoine de
S: 3642

Saints
S: 4036, 6783

Saints–Christian
JS: 4071

Saints–Fiction
S: 999

Sales–Careers
S: 4923

Salinger, J. D.
S: 3750, 6299–300

Salmon
JS: 8626

Samplers
JS: 9237

Samurai
S: 7451

Samurai–Fiction
JS: 1403

San Francisco–Fiction
JS: 2589
S: 39, 1202, 2117

JS = Junior–Senior High S = Senior High

Sandburg, Carl
JS: 6302
S: 3882, 6301

Santa Fe (New Mexico)
S: 8200

Sartre, Jean-Paul
S: 3567

Satire
See also Humor and satire
S: 4062

Satire–Poetry
S: 3164

SATS. *See* Scholastic Aptitude Tests

Sauk Indians–Fiction
JS: 1506

Savings and loan associations
S: 4595

Scandals
JS: 7754

Scandinavia
JS: 7553

Scandinavia–Folklore
JS: 3390
S: 3395, 3400

Scandinavia–History
JS: 7203

Scandinavia–Mythology
JS: 3397
S: 3480–81

Scandinavia–Travel
S: 7552

Scavenger hunts–Fiction
JS: 1822

Scharansky, Anatoly
S: 6947

Schirra, Walter M.
JS: 6159

Schizophrenia
JS: 5407
S: 5379, 5404

Schizophrenia–Fiction
S: 667

Schliemann, Henry–Fiction
S: 1476

Schoenbrun, David
S: 6303

Scholastic Aptitude Tests
S: 4655–56, 4659–61, 4663–66, 4722

Scholastic Aptitude Tests–Fiction
JS: 2274

School of American Ballet
S: 5965

School stories–Fiction
JS: 156, 256, 511, 694, 709, 766, 772, 791–92, 831, 838, 869, 888, 902, 914, 922–23, 932, 1435, 1887, 1903, 2274, 2330, 2805
S: 683, 790, 852, 862–63, 1827, 1885, 1888, 1895, 1897, 2092

Schools
JS: 4636
S: 4629, 4632

Schools–Poetry
JS: 3273

Schools and education, 4622–4707

Schramm, Tex
JS: 6760

Schuller, Carol
JS: 6948

Schulz, Charles M.
JS: 6205

Schumann, Robert
S: 6353

Science–Careers
JS: 5026, 5028–29
S: 5016

Science–Discoveries
JS: 8230
S: 8914

Science–Education
JS: 4712

Science–Essays
JS: 8209, 8212
S: 8210–11, 8216, 8220, 8372, 8381, 8394, 8401

Science–Ethics
JS: 4526

Science–Experiments
S: 8242

Science–General
JS: 4076, 8204, 8206, 8215, 8226, 8228, 8237–38, 8376
S: 8207–8, 8213, 8217–18, 8222–23, 8225, 8227, 8232, 8235–36, 8389, 8392, 8403

Science–History
JS: 8205, 8214, 8230
S: 6643, 7135, 7433, 8231, 8233, 8242

Science–Methodology
S: 4001, 5314, 8225, 8234

Science–Poetry
JS: 3853

Science–Projects
JS: 4430, 8239–41, 8243–44, 9031
S: 8245–46, 9038

Science–Theories
JS: 8229

Science fiction
JS: 325–26, 379, 428, 634, 1915, 2336, 2341, 2348, 2354–55, 2357, 2359, 2362–63, 2366, 2371–73, 2375–76, 2379–81, 2384–86, 2390, 2414, 2418, 2423–24, 2427, 2429–31, 2434, 2448–53, 2455, 2457, 2462, 2464–66, 2475, 2480–85, 2489–90, 2493, 2495–96, 2498, 2500, 2502–3, 2514, 2517, 2520, 2525–26, 2528–29, 2531–32, 2546–48, 2553–54, 2556, 2564–65, 2572, 2576, 2578, 2582, 2584, 2589, 2595, 2598, 2603, 2608–9, 2611–12, 2616–17, 2621, 2623, 2633, 2635–36, 2639–40, 2643, 2649, 2651–52, 2655–56, 2660–65, 2671, 2673, 2675, 2678, 2688, 2691, 2696, 2702, 2704–5, 2710, 2712–18, 2721–22, 2724, 2726, 2728, 2736, 2741, 2752–53, 2755, 2757, 2761, 2763, 2767, 2770, 2777, 2784, 2787, 2792–94, 2801, 2805, 2814–15, 2817, 2825, 2830–35, 2842–43, 2850, 2857, 2859, 2861–63, 2866
S: 273, 689, 1007, 1046, 1144, 1251, 1282, 1345, 1756, 2249, 2331–33, 2335, 2337–40, 2342–47, 2349–53, 2356, 2358, 2360–61, 2364–65, 2367–70, 2374, 2377–78, 2382–83, 2387–89, 2391–413, 2415–17, 2419–22, 2425–26, 2428, 2432–33, 2435–47, 2454, 2456, 2458–61, 2463, 2467–74, 2476–79, 2486–88, 2491–92, 2494, 2497, 2499, 2501, 2504–13, 2515–16, 2518–19, 2521–24, 2527, 2530, 2533–45, 2549–52, 2555, 2557–63, 2566–71, 2573–75, 2577, 2579–81, 2583, 2585–88, 2590–94, 2596–97, 2599, 2601–2, 2604–7, 2610, 2613–15, 2618–20, 2622, 2624–32, 2637–38, 2641–42, 2644–48, 2650, 2653–54, 2657–59, 2666–70, 2672, 2674, 2676–77, 2679–87, 2689–90, 2692–95, 2697–701, 2703, 2706–9, 2711, 2719–20, 2723, 2725, 2727, 2729, 2730–35, 2737–40, 2742–51, 2754, 2756, 2758–60, 2762, 2764–66, 2768–69, 2771–76, 2778–83, 2785–86, 2788–91, 2795–800, 2802–4, 2806–7, 2809–13, 2816, 2818–24, 2826–

JS = Junior–Senior High   S = Senior High

Science fiction (*cont.*)
29, 2836–41, 2844–49, 2851–56, 2860, 2864–65, 2867–70, 8370

Science fiction–Films
JS: 6054–55, 6057

Science fiction–History and criticism
JS: 2784, 3614, 3620, 3664, 3676, 3694, 3704, 3716, 3733, 3747, 3756, 3766, 3782, 3784, 3790, 3793–94, 8226
S: 3612, 3616, 3619, 3625–27, 3629–30, 3663, 3670, 3679, 3681, 3710, 3720, 3731, 3741, 3757, 3779, 3781, 6213, 6297

Science fiction–Illustration
JS: 5728

Science fiction–Plays
JS: 3086, 3807

Scientific research–Fiction
S: 1002

Scientists
JS: 8219
S: 6641, 6643, 6647–49, 8203

Scientists–Biography
JS: 6640, 6664
S: 6656, 6661–62, 6665, 6688, 6696, 6699, 8906

Scientists–Fiction
JS: 201, 1808, 2830
S: 71, 77, 253, 260, 274, 1725, 1796, 1981, 2486, 2748

Scientists–Physically handicapped
JS: 5029

Scientists–Women
S: 8203, 8221

Scotland
JS: 8477, 9491, 9515
S: 3195

Scotland–Fiction
JS: 158, 922, 1474, 1924, 2061, 2656
S: 85, 588, 609, 1925, 2093, 2324, 2937

Scotland–Historical fiction
JS: 2058
S: 1425, 1465, 1479, 1486

Scotland–History
JS: 6863
S: 6856, 6862, 6871

Scott, Robert Falcon
S: 6160

Scott, Robert Lee
JS: 6161

Scottish Americans–Fiction
S: 1589

Screenwriting
JS: 5992
S: 5997, 6035

Scuba diving
JS: 9956, 9961

Sculptors
JS: 5807

Sculpture–Modern
S: 5757

Sea birds
JS: 8538, 8548

Sea mammals
JS: 8656
S: 8651

Sea monsters–Fiction
JS: 1136
S: 1104

Sea stories–Fiction
JS: 1664–65, 1673, 2126
S: 216, 412–14, 1669

Sea voyages
JS: 7758, 7886
S: 6137, 6993, 7050, 7700

Seacoasts–Fiction
S: 953

Seafarers
JS: 7089
S: 6123, 6134, 7142, 7527

Seafarers–Fiction
S: 346, 1427

Seals
JS: 8641

Seashells–Field guides
JS: 8635–36, 8638–39, 8878

Seashores
JS: 8881–83
S: 8884

Seashores–Fiction
JS: 246

Seashores–Field guides
JS: 8618, 8885

Secret Service (U.S.)
JS: 4224

Secret weapons–Fiction
S: 187

Secretarial careers
S: 5049

Secretarial skills
JS: 4642
S: 4639–40, 4643

Securities and Exchange Commission (U.S.)
JS: 4223

Seeger, Pete
S: 6440

Self-assertiveness
S: 5569

Self-defense
JS: 9899, 9903
S: 5444, 9902

Self-defense–Women
S: 5631

Self-employment
S: 4838, 4929

Self-esteem
JS: 5622–23, 5625

Self-esteem–Fiction
JS: 712, 826

Self-realization–Fiction
JS: 798
S: 802, 1030

Sender, Ruth Minsky
JS: 6949

Senesh, Hannah
JS: 6872
S: 6873

Senses
S: 5329, 5333

Serengeti National Park (Tanzania)
JS: 7363

Sermons
S: 4367

Service academies (U.S.)
S: 4824

Seurat, Georges
JS: 6206

Seuss, Dr.
JS: 6207

Sewing
JS: 9236, 9242, 9249, 9251, 9254, 9258–60
S: 9227, 9240, 9255, 9257

Sex–Fiction
JS: 884, 925, 937, 1890, 2314
S: 770, 868, 874, 877, 882, 894, 912, 1294, 1892, 2883

Sex education
JS: 5149, 5449–51, 5454–55, 5457, 5461, 5464, 5468–70, 5475, 5477, 5479, 5481, 5485–86, 5489, 5496, 5499, 5516
S: 5458, 5471, 5482, 5487, 5495, 5497

JS = Junior–Senior High S = Senior High

Sex roles
JS: 4532, 4537
S: 4531, 4533, 4535, 5542

Sex therapy
S: 5497, 6458

Sexual abuse
JS: 5501, 5506
S: 5500, 5507, 5509–10, 5520

Sexual abuse–Fiction
JS: 682, 709, 719
S: 651, 737

Sexual ethics
JS: 5488

Sexual harassment
JS: 5502

Sexual violence
JS: 4524

Sexuality
S: 5354

Sexuality–Fiction
JS: 865

Sexually transmitted diseases
JS: 5190, 5192, 5199, 5214, 5224
S: 5172, 5175, 5226, 5487

Shahhat
S: 6950

Shakers
S: 4067

Shakers (religion)
S: 4089

Shakespeare, William
JS: 3047, 6304
S: 3815, 6305–7

**Shakespeare, William–
Adaptations**
JS: 3046, 3048–49, 3051
S: 3050

**Shakespeare, William–
Collected works**
JS: 3052–54

Shakespeare, William–Fiction
S: 52

**Shakespeare, William–History
and criticism**
JS: 3816, 3819, 6091
S: 3814, 3817–18, 3821–32, 6092

Shakespeare, William–Plays,
3046–3059

Shakespeare, William–Theater
JS: 3820

Sharks
JS: 8629–31, 8633–34
S: 8632

Sheep–Fiction
JS: 1198

Shelley, Mary
S: 6308

Shells–Field guides
JS: 8637

Shiloh, Battle of–Fiction
JS: 1552

Ships and boats
JS: 7758, 8005, 9922, 9924, 9941
S: 9130

Ships and boats–Fiction
JS: 2086
S: 146, 1688

Ships and boats–History
JS: 9122
S: 9121

Ships and boats–Survival
JS: 9927

Shipwrecks
JS: 6158, 7152, 8886–87, 8893,
8898, 9927
S: 8890, 8894

Shipwrecks–Fiction
JS: 2831
S: 193, 1518, 2774

Shoemaker, Willie
S: 6781

Shoplifting
JS: 4475

Short stories–Fiction: 488
JS: 15, 161, 164, 203, 228–29,
284–85, 298, 300, 306, 363, 417,
420, 423, 428, 473, 492, 524,
793, 813, 821, 830, 844, 952,
992, 1019, 1084, 1208, 1239,
1297, 1542, 1711, 1713, 1723,
1728, 1730, 1732, 1739–40,
1757–59, 1766–67, 1770, 1777,
1812, 1823–24, 1831, 1840, 1846,
1861, 1893, 1914–15, 1917–18,
1951–52, 1987–89, 1994, 2028,
2031–32, 2042, 2074, 2090, 2094,
2096, 2104, 2118, 2143, 2169,
2184, 2188–89, 2204, 2318, 2359,
2375–76, 2379–81, 2384–86,
2414, 2429–31, 2434, 2464, 2484,
2520, 2564–65, 2612, 2696,
2721–22, 2825, 2842–43, 2859,
2863, 2886, 2959, 2963, 2968,
2975
S: 163, 179, 190, 200, 204, 230,
288, 305, 307, 319–20, 343, 346,
348, 378, 392, 399, 402–3, 425,
432, 435, 442, 445, 451, 464,
476, 484, 490, 498–500, 506,
529, 533, 551, 564, 585–86, 630,
707, 714, 720, 765, 782–83, 801,

835, 849, 876, 883, 893, 911,
921, 924, 934, 963, 970–71,
1016, 1018, 1022, 1048, 1057,
1066, 1092, 1094, 1151, 1176,
1193, 1236, 1263, 1266, 1268,
1298, 1317, 1571, 1583, 1650,
1668, 1700, 1710, 1712, 1715–16,
1731, 1736, 1742, 1746–47,
1751–52, 1754–55, 1774–75,
1785, 1789, 1795, 1806–7, 1811,
1817, 1826, 1833, 1839, 1860,
1868, 1880, 1899, 1931, 1947,
1960, 2026–27, 2033, 2041, 2055,
2084, 2091, 2098, 2107, 2114–15,
2120, 2142, 2144–46, 2148,
2151–52, 2181, 2190, 2208, 2249,
2260, 2334, 2342–44, 2346, 2358,
2360–61, 2365, 2367, 2369, 2374,
2377–78, 2382, 2394, 2420, 2438,
2441, 2458, 2468, 2470–71, 2505,
2510, 2518–19, 2523–24, 2530,
2536, 2540, 2550, 2557, 2562,
2569, 2581, 2626, 2634, 2638,
2642, 2654, 2676, 2686–87, 2689,
2695, 2743, 2749, 2765, 2773,
2785, 2795, 2821, 2854, 2867,
2880, 2890–92, 2894–95, 2898–
902, 2904–8, 2911–15, 2917,
2920–23, 2926–27, 2932–34,
2936–39, 2941–47, 2949–58,
2960–62, 2965–67, 2969–74,
2976

**Short stories–History and criti-
cism**
S: 3613, 3622, 3780, 3786, 3796

**Short stories and general
anthologies–Fiction,** 2889–
2977

Shriver, Pam
JS: 6772

Shrubs–Field guides
JS: 8429

Shyness
JS: 5561
S: 5609, 5634, 5636

Siberia–Fiction
JS: 40
S: 1404

Sibling rivalry
JS: 5643

Sibling rivalry–Fiction
JS: 570, 901

Siblings
JS: 5644

Siblings–Fiction
JS: 62, 570, 665, 807, 1646, 1803,
1965, 2063, 2070, 2273, 2884
S: 202, 529, 537, 553, 556, 710,

JS = Junior–Senior High   S = Senior High

917

Siblings–Fiction (*cont.*)
1154, 1227, 1347, 1523, 2008, 2015, 2147, 2262

Sierra Nevada Mountains
S: 8187

Sign language
JS: 5431–32, 7807

Sign language–Dictionaries
S: 3902

Signs and symbols
JS: 3899, 3901, 4071
S: 3898

Sills, Beverly
JS: 6441

Simon and Garfunkel
JS: 5949

Simon, Neil
S: 3839

Simonides, Carol
JS: 6951

Singer, Isaac Bashevis
JS: 6309
S: 3634

Singers–Biography
JS: 6379, 6382, 6386, 6392, 6404, 6407, 6432, 6435–36, 6439, 6444, 6452, 6456, 6459
S: 5923, 6177, 6184, 6360–61, 6381, 6384, 6402–3, 6424, 6438, 6440, 6445, 6449–50

Single parents
JS: 5493, 5515, 5518, 5652

Single parents–Fiction
JS: 881

Single women–Fiction
S: 2972

Sioux Indians
JS: 6499
S: 6515, 6636, 7816

Sioux Indians–Fiction
S: 1501

Sitting Bull, Chief
S: 6636

60 Minutes (television program)
JS: 6020

Skiing
JS: 6778, 6948, 7703, 9943–47
S: 9942

Skiing–Fiction
JS: 2872

Skin care
JS: 5335–39

Skyscrapers
JS: 5710

Slater, Cornelius
S: 6700

Slave trade
S: 7346

Slavery
JS: 6519, 7872, 7876
S: 4378, 6464, 6517, 6881, 7738, 7742–43, 7779, 7869–70, 7893

Slavery–Fiction
JS: 421, 458, 473, 1368, 1524–25
S: 426, 1526–27, 1530–31, 1533.

Slavery–History
JS: 4322
S: 4362

Slugs–Fiction
JS: 2556

Small businesses–Careers
JS: 4849

Smerlas, Fred
JS: 6761

Smith, Bessie
S: 6442

Smith, Ozzie
JS: 6733

Smoking
JS: 5104, 5133

Snakes
JS: 8470, 8664

Snorkeling
JS: 9961

Snowboarding
S: 9942

Soap bubbles
JS: 8912

Soap operas–Fiction
JS: 2297

Soccer
JS: 9948, 9950–51
S: 9949, 9952

Soccer–Fiction
S: 868

Social change
S: 4415, 4417, 4419

Social concerns and conflicts,
4410–4560

Social groups–Personal guidance, 5637–5681

Social problems
JS: 4411
S: 4466, 5371

Social science
S: 4465

Social sciences–Careers
JS: 4802

Social work
JS: 6612
S: 6611

Socialism
JS: 4574, 4593
S: 4172

Society and the individual,
4123–4621

Society-oriented careers–Guidance, 4955–4983

Sociology
S: 5524

Socrates
S: 4020

Softball
S: 9680

Solar energy
JS: 8931
S: 8930

Solar system
JS: 8344, 8347, 8349
S: 8338, 8346

Solar system–Fiction
S: 2732

Soldiers–History
JS: 6971
S: 7052

Solomon, Dorothy A.
S: 6952

Solzhenitsyn, Aleksandr
S: 6310–11

Somers, Suzanne
S: 6443

Sone, Monica
JS: 6953

Song lyrics
JS: 5860

Songbooks
JS: 5891, 5944–45, 5950, 5954

Songs–Thesaurus
JS: 5947

Songs and folk songs, 5944–5954

Songwriting
JS: 5837, 5880

Soto, Gary
S: 6312–14

Soul music
JS: 5871, 6376

JS = Junior–Senior High   S = Senior High

Sound effects
S: 9301

Sound recordings
JS: 5888, 9053

Sound systems
JS: 9049

South Africa
S: 6422, 6791, 6793–800, 6921,
6930, 7369–74, 7376–79, 7381–
83, 7385, 7387–89

South Africa–Fiction
JS: 468, 992, 1385
S: 643, 956–57, 962–63, 965, 972,
986–87, 1386

South Africa–History
JS: 7386
S: 7375, 7380, 7384

**South Africa–Literature collec-
tions**
S: 2940

South Africa–Plays
S: 3143

South America
JS: 7679
S: 7670–71, 7681

South America–Fiction
S: 117, 279, 1157

**South America–History and ge-
ography,** 7667–7688

South America–History
S: 7675, 7677

South America–Mythology
JS: 3444, 3446, 3454

South Asia
JS: 7591

South Dakota
S: 8583

South Pacific
S: 7480

South Pacific–Art
JS: 5769

South Pacific–Fiction
JS: 245
S: 414, 1666, 1668

South Pacific–World War II
JS: 7296, 7320

South Pole
S: 7709

South (U.S.)
S: 3498, 6498, 6933, 8194

South (U.S.)–Civil War
JS: 7939

South (U.S.)–Crafts
JS: 8197

South (U.S.)–Fiction
JS: 471, 1549, 1599, 1812, 2289
S: 82, 457, 483–84, 503, 516, 530,
536, 547–48, 563, 604, 610, 619,
623, 645, 661, 708, 790, 815,
839, 873, 876, 943, 1317, 1530,
1540, 1578, 1602–3, 1625, 1630,
1879, 2004, 2159, 2889, 2912,
2916, 2949–50, 2957, 2973

South (U.S.)–History
JS: 7925, 7930
S: 4378, 4383, 6600, 7879, 8008

South (U.S.)–Literature
S: 3592

South (U.S.)–Plays
S: 3137

South (U.S.)–Poetry
JS: 3249
S: 3243, 3308

Southeast Asia
JS: 7394
S: 8121

Southeast Asia–Fiction
S: 977

Southeast Asia–History
S: 7396

Southwest (U.S.)
JS: 7965, 8198
S: 8810

Southwest (U.S.)–Fiction
JS: 775, 2072
S: 64, 475, 1560

Southwest (U.S.)–Geography
S: 8202

Southwest (U.S.)–History
JS: 7992
S: 7984, 8200–2

**Southwest (U.S.)–Native
Americans**
S: 7805

Soviet Union
See also Russia
JS: 6968, 7563, 7569, 7584, 7588
S: 6311, 6853–54, 6875, 6947,
6954, 7344, 7564–65, 7567–68,
7570–71, 7573–77, 7583, 7585–
86

Soviet Union–Espionage
S: 4147–48, 6870

Soviet Union–Everyday life
S: 7589

Soviet Union–Fiction
JS: 151
S: 237, 976

Soviet Union–Historical fiction
S: 995, 1456

Soviet Union–History
JS: 6831, 6874, 7580
S: 4131, 4170, 6790, 6843, 6876,
7197, 7216, 7566, 7572, 7578–79,
7581–82

Space–Militarization
JS: 4174

Space colonies
S: 8322, 8336

Space colonies–Fiction
JS: 2366
S: 2345, 2559

Space exploration
JS: 6159, 8295, 8297, 8300, 8303,
8307, 8309–10, 8314–18, 8321,
8323, 8337
S: 8294, 8299, 8301, 8306, 8308,
8311–13, 8319–20, 8324, 8328–
29, 8339, 9064

Space exploration–Fiction
S: 207

Space exploration–History
JS: 8325

Space science, 8247–8371

Space shuttles
JS: 8305

Space shuttles–Fiction
JS: 2381

Space stations
JS: 8309

Space stations–Fiction
JS: 2598
S: 2393, 2637, 2666, 2686

Space travel–Fiction
JS: 2603
S: 2560, 2625, 2630, 2847

Space war
JS: 4174
S: 4160

Space war–Fiction
S: 2469, 2822

Spacelab project
S: 8320

Spaceships–Fiction
JS: 2465, 2480, 2483, 2485, 2495,
2621, 2716
S: 2389, 2474, 2488, 2571, 2607,
2699, 2735, 2744, 2766, 2840

JS = Junior–Senior High   S = Senior High

Spain
JS: 6231, 7562

Spain–Fiction
JS: 304
S: 1411, 1610

Spain–Historical fiction
JS: 1433
S: 1429, 1434

Spain–History
JS: 7558
S: 7554, 7556–57, 7559–61, 7628

Spain–Travel guides
JS: 7555

Spain and Portugal–History and geography, 7554–7562

Spanish Armada
JS: 7538, 7558
S: 7526, 7556, 7559

Spanish Armada–Fiction
S: 1429

Spanish Civil War
S: 7560

Spanish language–Poetry
S: 3296

Spanish literature–History and criticism
S: 3604, 3608, 3636, 3644

Spanish-American War
S: 8015

Spanish-American War– Fiction
S: 1612

Speaking skills, 4667–4707

Speeches
S: 3521, 3544

Speeches, essays, and general literary works, 3520–3562

Speed
JS: 8916

Spelling
S: 4685

Spices
S: 8420

Spiders
JS: 8612–13

Spiders–Fiction
JS: 3379

Spiders–Field guides
JS: 8599

Spies and spying
JS: 4149, 7280
S: 4126, 4134, 4147–48, 4215, 4242, 4250, 6157, 6633–34, 6870, 6888, 6893, 6900, 7258, 7300, 7610, 9016

Spies and spying–Fiction
JS: 33, 42, 80, 120, 197, 251, 2609, 4138
S: 4–6, 25, 30, 37, 41, 43–44, 70– 71, 85, 87, 92–93, 110, 142, 167–70, 180, 184–85, 189, 211, 259, 655, 2085

Sports, 9544–9979

Sports–Anthologies
S: 9598

Sports–Biography, 6705–6781

Sports–Careers
JS: 4854
S: 9564

Sports–Disabled persons
JS: 6955

Sports–Drug use
S: 5112, 5366

Sports–Fiction
JS: 2264, 2886

Sports–General
JS: 4745, 4854, 5351, 5358, 6710, 9546, 9550, 9552, 9556–59, 9567, 9572, 9574, 9579, 9586, 9594, 9601, 9609
S: 6756, 9564–65, 9570–71, 9576, 9584, 9590

Sports–History
JS: 9850

Sports–Injuries
JS: 5447–48

Sports–Journalism
JS: 9582, 9599, 9601
S: 9604

Sports–Nutrition
JS: 5344, 5414, 5427
S: 5429

Sports–Photography
JS: 9597, 9606

Sports–Poetry
S: 3248

Sports–Racism
S: 4365

Sports–Recruitment
JS: 9589

Sports–Women
JS: 5362
S: 9563

Sports medicine
JS: 5362, 5443, 5448
S: 5246, 5350, 5442

Sports stories–Fiction, 2871– 2888

Springsteen, Bruce
JS: 6444
S: 6445

Square dancing
S: 5967

Squash
JS: 9603

St. Paul–Fiction
S: 1365

Stage lighting
JS: 6112
S: 6104

Stage props
S: 6086, 6093

Stage sets
S: 6083, 6086, 6104, 6113

Stajner, Karlo
S: 6954

Stalin, Joseph
JS: 6874
S: 6875–76, 7566, 7578

Stamp collecting
JS: 9461–62
S: 9453

Stamps
JS: 9456
S: 9453

Stamps–History
JS: 9459

Stanton, Elizabeth Cady
S: 6637

Starlings
JS: 8669

Starr, Belle
S: 6638

Stars
JS: 8247, 8287, 8351, 8353, 8357
S: 8249, 8273, 8354, 8356

Stars–Fiction
S: 1050, 2541, 2698

Stars–Field guides
JS: 8293, 8355

Starships–Fiction
S: 2786

Statesmen (U.S.)–Biography, 6577–6609

Statistics
S: 8858–59

Statue of Liberty
JS: 4327, 8163, 8165
S: 8162, 8166, 8173

JS = Junior–Senior High   S = Senior High

Steffens, Lincoln
S: 6315

Stein, Gertrude
S: 6316

Steinbeck, John
S: 3721, 3754

Stengel, Casey
JS: 6734

Stepfamilies
JS: 5644

Stepfamilies–Fiction
JS: 2308

Stepparents–Fiction
S: 597, 2883

Stevenson, Robert Louis
S: 3688, 6317

Stilwell, Joseph Warren
S: 4167

Sting (rock star)
S: 6446

Stock exchange
JS: 4601

Stock market
JS: 4603

Stocks
JS: 4577, 4600–1, 4603–4
S: 4598–99, 4602

Stone Age–Fiction
JS: 2449

Stonehenge
S: 7520

Stoppard, Tom
S: 3813

Storms
JS: 8868
S: 8867

Strasberg, Lee
S: 6111

Streep, Meryl
S: 6447

Stress
JS: 5374, 5381, 5550
S: 5323, 5565, 5568

Strikes and strikebreaking
JS: 4517

Student groups–Fiction
JS: 212

Student travel
JS: 4710

Students–Civil rights
JS: 4315

Study skills
JS: 4646–48, 4652, 4672, 4682,
4691, 4703–5, 4729
S: 4649, 4651, 4653–54, 4656,
4669, 4674, 4681, 4683, 4689,
4692–93, 4695, 4697, 4699,
4743–44

Submarines
S: 7219, 7226

Submarines–Fiction
JS: 194, 1665

Subterranean world–Fiction
JS: 2448, 2452, 2705

Suburban life
JS: 3500
S: 3497

Sudan
S: 7368

Suffrage–History
JS: 4295

Suicide
JS: 5090, 5376, 5611, 6925, 8581
S: 5091, 5095, 5377, 5386, 5406

Suicide–Fiction
JS: 635, 658, 727, 731, 887, 1934,
2062
S: 318, 705, 710, 945, 2021, 2158,
2192

Sullivan, Anne–Plays
JS: 3074

Sullivan, Tom
JS: 6955

Summer employment
S: 4711

Summer schools
JS: 4636
S: 4711

Sun
S: 8348

Sung, Ch'ing-ling
S: 6817

Sunlight
S: 5076

Sunquist, Fiona and Mel
JS: 6162

Super Bowl games
JS: 9845

Superconductors
S: 8936–38, 9040

Supernatural
JS: 9508, 9520, 9523, 9543
S: 9489, 9499, 9513

Supernatural–Encyclopedias
S: 3631

Supernatural–Fiction
JS: 1047, 1711, 1713, 1769, 1783–
84, 1786, 1820, 1823, 1845
S: 1708, 1715, 1719, 1736, 1738,
1748, 1764, 1771, 1775, 1792,
1829, 1833, 1855, 1862, 1865,
1868

**Supernatural–Fiction–History
and criticism**
S: 3785

Supernatural–Poetry
S: 3896

Supernovas
JS: 8359
S: 8263

Superstitions
JS: 9479

Supreme Court (U.S.)
JS: 4194
S: 4182, 4191, 4193, 4204, 4231,
4236, 4238, 4245, 4249, 4256,
4261, 4291, 6578, 6593, 6605

Supremes (musical group)
JS: 5903

Surfing–Fiction
S: 2883

Surgeons
S: 5254

Surrogate mothers
JS: 4522

Survival
JS: 7465, 7682
S: 6683, 7468, 8379, 9789, 9795,
9797, 9801, 9805

Survival–Fiction
JS: 83, 206, 350
S: 97, 179, 186, 193, 2551, 2587

Swamps
S: 8383

Swans–Fiction
S: 1134

Swedish Americans–Fiction
S: 1562

Swendsen, David H.
JS: 6163

Swift, Jonathan
S: 3653

Swimming
JS: 9959–60
S: 9958, 9962–63

Switzerland–Fiction
JS: 2294

JS = Junior–Senior High S = Senior High

Synthesizers (music)
JS: 5931
S: 5910

T

Table manners
JS: 5583

Table setting
S: 9154

Table tennis
JS: 9591

Taft, William Howard
S: 8014

Tahiti–Fiction
S: 715

Taillon, Cy
S: 6927

Tap dancing
JS: 6437

Tarot cards
JS: 9524

Tattoos–Fiction
JS: 1044

Taulbert, Clifton L.
S: 6956

Taverns–Fiction
S: 2773

Taylor, David
JS: 6701

Taylor, Paul
S: 6462

Teachers
JS: 4622, 4634, 6918
S: 4625, 4627, 4629–30, 4635, 4953

Teachers–Biography
JS: 6904, 6924

Teachers–Fiction
JS: 135, 732, 776, 838, 940, 1613, 2137
S: 371, 645, 672, 683, 754, 1418, 1492, 1885, 1920

Teaching–Careers
JS: 4949, 4954
S: 4950

Technologists
JS: 8219

Technology
JS: 8943, 8947, 8950, 8954
S: 4421, 5541, 8941, 8946, 8952

Technology–Careers
JS: 5026, 5042, 5051, 5061

Technology–History
S: 7084

Tecumseh
S: 6639

Teenage marriage
JS: 5664–65

Teenage parents
JS: 5491, 5493–94, 5515, 5518, 5655, 5669
S: 5490

Teenage parents–Fiction
JS: 804
S: 860

Teenage pregnancy
JS: 5456–57, 5478, 5480, 5499, 5514

Teenage pregnancy–Fiction
JS: 834, 867
S: 720

Teenage writers–Fiction
JS: 1056

Tennage writers–Plays
JS: 3089–91

Teenage writers–Poetry
JS: 3889

Teenagers–AIDS victims
JS: 5200

Teenagers–Civil rights
JS: 4315

Teenagers–Homeless
JS: 4514

Teenagers–Opinions
JS: 4418

Teeth
JS: 5340

Telecommunications
JS: 8991
S: 9045

Telecommunications–Careers
JS: 4865
S: 5037

Telescopes
JS: 8224, 8252, 8259

Television
JS: 5988, 5999, 6004, 6020–21, 6028, 6030, 6037, 6073, 6085, 6455, 9052
S: 6006, 6015–16, 6032, 6042, 6044, 6046, 6048, 6056, 6072, 6421

Television–Careers
JS: 4819, 4879, 4922, 5052
S: 4828, 4874, 4888

Television–Directors
JS: 6070

Television–Fiction
JS: 1963, 2297
S: 1143

Television–History
S: 6025, 6115

Television–Programming
S: 3990

Television–Programs
JS: 6067

Tenements
S: 8018

Tenements–Fiction
S: 909

Tennessee–Fiction
S: 563

Tennis
JS: 6769–70, 6772, 9964–65, 9967, 9969–70, 9973
S: 6771, 9966

Tennis–Fiction
JS: 2888

Tennis–History
S: 9968

Teresa, Mother
S: 6957–58

Term papers
JS: 4672

Terrorism
JS: 4544, 4546–47, 4551, 4553, 4555, 7587
S: 4542–43, 4545, 4548–50, 4552, 4554, 6803

Terrorism–Fiction
JS: 61, 104, 122
S: 45, 50, 57, 66, 68, 73, 129, 155, 166, 175, 184–85, 238, 975, 2009, 2238

Tests and test taking, 4655–4666

Texas–Fiction
JS: 191, 2121
S: 119, 208, 475, 873, 1578, 1586, 2276

Texas–History
JS: 7964–65, 7993, 7996, 8195

Textiles–History
JS: 8956

Thailand
JS: 6924

Thailand–Fiction
JS: 103

Thanksgiving–Fiction
JS: 1733

Theater
See also Plays
S: 5926, 6078, 6083, 6087, 6093,
6103–4, 6113, 6116

Theater–Biography
JS: 6179

Theater–Careers
JS: 4892

Theater–Fiction
S: 2043

Theater–History
JS: 6079, 6089, 6097
S: 6082, 6098, 6114

Theater–Makeup
JS: 6084

Theater–Musicals
JS: 3126

Theater–Stage sets
S: 6086

Theater–United States
JS: 6090

Third World
JS: 7341

Thirty Years' War–Fiction
S: 1224

Thomas, Lewis
S: 6702

Thoreau, Henry David
S: 3524

Thorpe, Jim
JS: 6768

Thought and thinking
S: 5588

Thurber, James
JS: 6318
S: 3595

Tiananmen Square (Beijing)
JS: 7413, 7426
S: 7408, 7429, 7436

Tibbets, Paul W.
S: 6959

Tibet
JS: 7456
S: 7461

Tibet–Fiction
JS: 76
S: 275

Tie-dyeing
S: 9147

Tigers
JS: 6162, 8511

Tigers–Fiction
S: 1278

Time
S: 8250, 8860, 8901, 8910

Time travel
S: 8861

Time-warp stories–Fiction
JS: 1215, 1904, 2348, 2424, 2572,
2578, 2623, 2715, 2793, 2833
S: 1007–8, 1015, 1017, 1088, 1147–
48, 1174, 1255, 1262, 1340,
2307, 2347, 2353, 2443, 2515,
2540, 2574, 2577, 2690, 2733,
2739, 2760, 2788, 2836, 2853,
2879

Titanic
JS: 7152, 8886, 8893, 8898
S: 8890

Tokyo
S: 7454

Tolkien, J. R. R.
JS: 3658
S: 3671, 3684, 6319

Tolstoy, Leo
S: 3643

Tools
S: 8948

Totalitarianism
S: 4168, 4301

Toulouse-Lautrec, Henri de
S: 5780

Tourists–Fiction
S: 2180

Toy making
JS: 9262, 9264
S: 9261, 9283

Track and field
JS: 6763–64, 6768, 9975–76
S: 6762, 6765–66, 9977

Track and field–Fiction
JS: 2876
S: 880

Trademarks
JS: 4618
S: 4605

Trades–Careers
S: 4851

Trains–Fiction
JS: 241, 1955
S: 1416, 2012

Tranquilizing drugs
JS: 5161
S: 5121, 5128

Transcendentalism
S: 4015

Transplants–Organ, 5164–5166

Transportation, 9055–9134

Transportation–Careers
S: 4859

Transportation–Fiction
S: 2501

Transportation–History
JS: 7968

Transsexuality–Fiction
S: 441

Travel
S: 3527

Travel–Careers
JS: 4852
S: 4836

Travel guides
JS: 4709–10, 7483, 7494, 7519,
7544, 7548, 7555, 7596, 7644,
7725, 7744, 7749, 8181
S: 7482, 7745, 8179

Travel–Handbooks
S: 4713, 5597

Travis, Randy
JS: 6448

Treason–Fiction
S: 234

Treasure–Fiction
JS: 247

Treblinka
S: 7298

Trees
JS: 8426

Trees–Field guides
JS: 8423, 8427–29, 8431
S: 8424–25

Trials
JS: 7034

Trials–Fiction
S: 648, 1958

Trials–Plays
S: 3093

Trials–United States
S: 4233

Triathlon
S: 9560, 9595, 9974

Trinidad–Fiction
S: 983

JS = Junior–Senior High S = Senior High

Tristan and Iseult–Fiction
S: 1220

Trojan War
S: 7112

Trojan War–Fiction
S: 1051

Tropical fish
JS: 8748–52, 8772

Troy
S: 7112

Troy–Fiction
S: 1476

Trucking–Careers
JS: 5053

Trull, Patti
JS: 6960

Truman, Bess W.
S: 6566

Truman, Harry S.
S: 6567–71, 8057, 8079

Trumpelman, I. C.
S: 6961

Truth, Sojourner
S: 6518

Truthfulness–Fiction
S: 1182

Tuberculosis–Fiction
JS: 653

Tubman, Harriet
JS: 6519

Tundra
JS: 8823

Tunisia–Fiction
S: 60, 2303

Turkey
JS: 7619
S: 6917

Turkey–Fiction
S: 974

Turkey–Travel guides
JS: 7544

Turki, Fawaz
S: 6818

Turner, J. M. W.
S: 5787

Turner, Myles
S: 6164

Turner, Tina
S: 6449–50

Turtles
JS: 8471, 8674
S: 8472

Tutu, Desmond
S: 6800

Twain, Mark
JS: 3483, 6321
S: 3519, 3777, 6320, 6322–23

Twain, Mark–Fiction
S: 1877

Twentieth century–History,
7150–7344

Twentieth century–Wars–
Historical fiction, 1633–1706

Twenty-first century
S: 4412

Twins
S: 5571

Twins–Fiction
JS: 12, 518, 1053, 1117, 1803, 2248
S: 248, 1082, 1205, 1313, 1324,
1858, 2586

Two Trees, Joe
S: 6962

Typhus fever
S: 5227

Typing
JS: 4641–42

Tyson, Mike
S: 6750

U

U-boats
S: 7226

Uchida, Yoshiko
S: 6963

Underground Railroad–Fiction
JS: 1525

Underwater exploration
JS: 8886, 8888–89, 8892, 8895–96
S: 8891

Underwater exploration–
Careers
JS: 5023

Underwater exploration–
Fiction
JS: 326, 2495
S: 67

Underwater salvage–Fiction
JS: 199

Unemployment
JS: 4610

Unicorns–Fiction
JS: 1030
S: 1793

Unidentified Flying Objects
JS: 9483, 9487, 9510, 9512, 9538
S: 9486, 9488, 9502, 9507, 9532,
9540

Unidentified Flying Objects–
Fiction
S: 2746

Uniforms
JS: 7922

United Nations
JS: 4124–25

United States (1776–1876)–
Everyday life
JS: 7873

United States (1789–1801)–
History
JS: 7861
S: 7849, 7854, 7860

United States (1789–1861)–
Fiction
JS: 1532

United States (1789–1861)–
History
JS: 7886
S: 7865–66, 7874

United States (1828–1848)–
History
S: 7885

United States (1828–1860)–
History
S: 7884

United States (1865–1914)–
Fiction
JS: 1599, 1611, 1615
S: 406, 1600, 1602–3, 1608–9,
1614, 1617, 1620

United States (1865–1914)–
History
JS: 8005
S: 6610, 8004, 8007–10, 8012–14,
8016–17, 8019–22

United States (1869–1914)–
History
S: 8006

United States (1915–1945)–
History
S: 8030, 8032

JS = Junior–Senior High S = Senior High

United States (1920s)–Fiction
S: 1605–7

United States (1920s)–History
S: 8028

United States (1930s)–History
JS: 8034
S: 8031, 8035

United States Army–Fiction
JS: 96

United States Army–Reserve Officers' Training Corps
S: 4726

United States–Civilization
S: 8084

United States–Costumes and dress
JS: 9175, 9177

United States–Description and travel
JS: 7725, 7728, 7755, 7778, 7783, 7785
S: 6152, 7771

United States–Directories
JS: 7757

United States–Economics
JS: 4562, 4564, 4568
S: 4217, 4225, 4289, 4412, 6651, 6671, 7718

United States–Fiction classics, 389–429

United States–Folklore
JS: 3264, 3431, 3433, 3441, 8492
S: 3430, 3432, 3434, 3436–37, 3440, 3442–43

United States–Foreign policy
JS: 4129, 4140, 4142–43, 4163, 4166
S: 4131–32, 4135–36, 4139, 4146, 4158, 4167, 4297, 4520

United States–Geography
JS: 7715, 8178
S: 6413, 7712, 7962

United States–Government
JS: 4184, 4208
S: 4209, 4211, 4218, 4523, 4525, 6592, 8055

United States–Government–Fiction
S: 959

United States–Government publications
S: 4178

United States–Historic sites
S: 7772

United States–Historical documents
JS: 7713
S: 7722, 7765, 7864

United States–Historical fiction
JS: 495, 1524
S: 400–1, 427, 1514, 1516, 1527–28, 1536, 1545, 1610, 1619

United States–History
JS: 7711, 7713, 7716, 7720, 7730–31, 7736, 7739, 7746, 7751–52, 7754, 7770, 7775–77, 7877, 8026, 8164, 8165
S: 7714, 7717, 7719, 7721, 7723–24, 7729, 7735, 7741, 7748, 7750, 7753, 7762–64, 7768, 7784, 7787–88, 7863, 7867–68, 7871, 7875, 7882, 8042, 8946

United States–History–Anecdotes
JS: 7774

United States–History–Encyclopedias
JS: 7766

United States–History–Spanish-American War
S: 8011

United States–Jacksonian Age
S: 7880

United States–Judicial system
S: 4255

United States–Law and courts, 4231–4261

United States–Literary history and criticism, 3694–3794, 3833–3845, 3875–3897

United States–Military history
JS: 7760

United States–Modern history
JS: 7781–82, 8046–47, 8058–60, 8062, 8070, 8072, 8078, 8080, 8082–83, 8085, 8092
S: 4324, 4459, 6303, 6562, 7337, 7710, 7740, 7747, 7759, 7767, 8024–25, 8050–51, 8053–55, 8057, 8063, 8067–68, 8073, 8075, 8079, 8084, 8086–87, 8089–91, 8093–94

United States–Natural history
JS: 7786

United States–Plays, 3060–3142, 3833–3845

United States–Poetry, 3234–3345, 3875–3897

United States–Politics
JS: 4266, 4274, 4278, 4540
S: 3491, 4123, 4212, 4262, 4264–65, 4268, 4270, 4273, 4275, 6581, 6598, 6628, 8050, 8056, 8065, 8093

United States–Politics–Fiction
S: 959, 985

United States–Presidency, 4205–4213

United States–Predictions
JS: 8058

United States–Public lands
S: 4441

United States–Travel
S: 6145

United States–Travel guides
JS: 7744, 7749
S: 7745

Universe
JS: 8276, 8359, 8369
S: 8265, 8269, 8281, 8304, 8358, 8360–68, 8370–71, 8903, 8909, 8913

Universe–Fiction
S: 2731

Universities and colleges
JS: 4729, 4763
S: 4726, 4730, 4732, 4737, 4743–44, 4748, 4752, 4762

Universities and colleges–Admissions
JS: 4728, 4738, 4741, 4746, 4757, 4766
S: 4655, 4657–58, 4660–61, 4666, 4720, 4724, 4727, 4731, 4734, 4739–40, 4742, 4749–50, 4754–56, 4758–60, 4764, 4769–70, 4772

Universities and colleges–Directories
JS: 4733, 4736, 4761, 4768
S: 4716, 4719, 4721, 4723, 4735, 4753, 4765, 4767, 4771

Universities and colleges–Financial aid
JS: 4776, 4778, 4780–81
S: 4751, 4773–75, 4777, 4779

Universities and colleges–Sports
JS: 4745

Universities and colleges–Summer programs
S: 4747

University of Chicago–Fiction
S: 2183

Updike, John
S: 3714

JS = Junior–Senior High S = Senior High

Uranium
S: 8782

Uranus
JS: 8300
S: 8341

Urban life–History
S: 8006

Used cars
JS: 9095

Utah–Fiction
JS: 1702

Utopias–Fiction
S: 2676

V

Vacations–Fiction
JS: 2228, 2281, 2728

Vaillancourt, Henri
S: 6964

Valens, Ritchie
JS: 6451

Valentine's Day–Fiction
S: 2087

Valium
JS: 5161

Values
S: 4529

Vampires–Fiction
JS: 1794, 1808
S: 1743, 1761, 1821, 1828, 1850

Vampires–Motion pictures
JS: 6059

Vandalism
JS: 4476

Vandermeerssche, Gaston
JS: 6165

Van Devanter, Lynda
S: 6965

Vaudeville
S: 6110

Vaughan Williams, Ralph
S: 6354

Vegetarian cooking
JS: 9331, 9350
S: 9359, 9366

Velazquez, Diego
S: 6208

Venezuela–History
S: 7678

Ventriloquism
JS: 6106, 9305

Verbal abuse
JS: 5612

Vermeer, Jan
JS: 6209

Vermont–Fiction
JS: 289

Veterinarians
JS: 6674, 6681, 6701, 6886, 6906, 8721
S: 6672

Veterinary medicine–Careers
JS: 4990, 5009, 5024

Vice Presidents (U.S.)–Biography
S: 6594

Victoria, Queen of Great Britain
S: 6877–78

Victorian Age–Fiction
JS: 231–32
S: 1442, 1480

Video recordings
JS: 6012, 6052, 6068, 9052
S: 9048, 9050–51

Video recordings–Careers
JS: 4922, 5033

Video recordings–Film guides
JS: 6008

Vietnam
JS: 7457
S: 7458

Vietnam–History
S: 8102

Vietnam Veterans Memorial
JS: 8123, 8137
S: 8136

Vietnam War
JS: 6127, 8101, 8109–12, 8116, 8118, 8125–26, 8145
S: 6965, 7458, 8048, 8052, 8066, 8081, 8097, 8099, 8102, 8104–8, 8113–15, 8119–22, 8124, 8127–36, 8138–43, 8146–48, 8150, 8152, 9124

Vietnam War–Drawings and paintings
S: 8098

Vietnam War–Fiction
JS: 616, 1697–98, 1702
S: 681, 771, 875, 1265, 1680, 1691–96, 1699–701, 1703–6

Vietnam War–Oral history
S: 8151

Vietnam War–Poetry
S: 397, 3290, 3297, 3340

Vikings
S: 7552, 7831

Vikings–Fiction
JS: 1156, 1381

Violence
JS: 4460–61, 4528
S: 4457, 4500, 5865

Violence–Families
S: 5674

Virginia–History
JS: 8196

Viruses
JS: 5183

Viruses–Fiction
S: 2781

Vision
JS: 5330

Vocabulary
S: 3935, 3942–43, 3945

Vocational guidance
JS: 4792–94, 4798–99, 4801, 4806, 4811, 4822, 4843, 4849, 4863
S: 4782, 4788, 4796, 4800, 4804–5, 4807–10, 4812–13, 4820–21, 4825–26, 4837–38, 4841, 4848, 4864, 4867

Volcanoes
JS: 7116, 8800, 8804, 8807
S: 8189, 8801, 8805

Volcanoes–Fiction
JS: 325

Volleyball
JS: 6773, 9978–79

Volleyball–Fiction
JS: 936

Voltaire
S: 3601

Volunteerism
S: 4805, 4850

Vonnegut, Kurt
S: 3745, 3751, 6324

Von Trapp family
JS: 6452

Von Trapp family–Plays
JS: 3098

Voodoo–Fiction
JS: 1720

Voyages and travels
S: 6156

JS = Junior–Senior High S = Senior High

926

W

Waiters and waitresses–
Careers
JS: 4961

Wales
S: 3129, 3227–29, 6928

Wales–Castles
JS: 5707

Wales–Fiction
JS: 1443
S: 1210

Wales–History
S: 7134

Walking
S: 5367, 9578

Wallenberg, Raoul
S: 6879

Waller, Fats
S: 6453–54

War
JS: 4128, 7153
S: 5717, 7051, 7337, 7612, 8015

War–Fiction
JS: 1908
S: 47, 971, 1680, 1696, 1810, 2258,
2551, 2570, 2682, 2803

War–History
S: 7039, 7052, 7057, 7064

War–Photographs
JS: 9431

War–Poetry
JS: 3159, 3166
S: 3177, 3290

War correspondents
S: 7195

War criminals
S: 6880

War games–Fiction
JS: 157

War of 1812
S: 7868, 7875, 7878

War veterans
S: 8148

Warner, Malcolm Jamal
JS: 6455

Warren, Robert Penn
S: 3778

Wars–Twentieth century–
Historical fiction, 1633–1706

Warsaw Ghetto
S: 7315

Warships
S: 9131, 9133

Warships–Fiction
JS: 1664, 1673
S: 415

Washington, Booker T.
JS: 6520

Washington, D.C.
JS: 8161
S: 8049

Washington, D.C.–Fiction
JS: 2256
S: 59, 2112, 2196–201

Washington, D.C.–History
JS: 8196

Washington, George
S: 6572–74

Washington State
S: 8189

Washington State–Fiction
S: 2317

Water
S: 8791

Watercolor painting
JS: 9186
S: 9205, 9207–8

Waterfowl
JS: 8557

Watergate Affair
JS: 8047, 8061
S: 4210, 8081, 8088, 8096

Waterloo, Battle of
S: 7146

Waters, Ethel
JS: 6456

Waves
JS: 8880

Wazeter, Mary
JS: 6966

Wealth–Fiction
S: 982, 1618

Weapons
S: 4500

Weapons–Encyclopedias
JS: 9125

Weapons–Fiction
S: 2819

Weather
JS: 8868, 8873
S: 8867, 8869, 8871

Weather–Folklore
JS: 8870

Weather forecasting
JS: 8872

Weaving
JS: 9145
S: 9140

Webber, Andrew Lloyd
JS: 6355

Wedding etiquette
S: 5576

Weddings–Fiction
JS: 1130
S: 663

Weeds
JS: 8437

Weight control
JS: 5418

Weight lifting
JS: 9773
S: 9769, 9771–72, 9775

Weight problems
JS: 5368, 5408, 5424
S: 5209

Weight problems–Cookbooks
JS: 9352–53

Weight problems–Fiction
JS: 704, 751

Weight training
JS: 9770

Weir, Benjamin
S: 6967

Welfare–United States
S: 4513

Wells, H. G.
JS: 3676
S: 3656

Welty, Eudora
S: 6325

Werewolves–Fiction
JS: 1834
S: 1854

West, Mae
JS: 6457

West (U.S.)
JS: 7986
S: 7955

West (U.S.)–Art
S: 6204

JS = Junior–Senior High S = Senior High

West (U.S.)–Birds
JS: 8543

West (U.S.)–Encyclopedias
S: 7960

West (U.S.)–Fiction
JS: 26, 62, 108, 143, 154, 160–61,
    164, 191–92, 225, 228–29, 236,
    249, 267, 1595, 2623
S: 1, 11, 20–22, 27, 38, 46, 51–52,
    63–64, 113, 119, 131, 162–63,
    200, 202, 204, 217–22, 224, 277–
    78, 280, 416, 1563, 1567, 1571,
    1575, 1577, 1580–81, 1598, 1974,
    2301

West (U.S.)–Frontier life
JS: 7995

West (U.S.)–Frontiersmen
S: 6377

West (U.S.)–History
JS: 6135, 6426, 7881, 7929, 7961,
    7967–71, 7975–76, 7987–92,
    7994, 8000–1, 8153, 8430
S: 7796, 7974, 7979

West (U.S.)–Outlaws
JS: 7997
S: 8177

West (U.S.)–Trees
JS: 8428

West (U.S.)–Wildflowers
JS: 8439

West Virginia–Fiction
S: 466, 1624

Westerns–History and criticism
S: 6167

Westheimer, Ruth
S: 6458

Wetlands
JS: 8818

Whales
JS: 8616, 8640, 8642, 8645, 8648,
    8650, 8652, 8654, 8656–57
S: 8623, 8643–44, 8647, 8653,
    8655, 8658

Whales–Fiction
JS: 246

Whaling–Fiction
S: 413

Wharton, Edith
S: 391, 3755

Wheatley, Phyllis
JS: 6326

Whistling
S: 9301

White House (U.S.)
JS: 6896, 8174

White House (U.S.)–Fiction
S: 2200

White, Theodore H.
S: 8094

Whitman, Walt
JS: 3342
S: 3891, 6327

Whittier, John Greenleaf
S: 3888

Whittling
S: 9275, 9292

Wiesenthal, Simon
S: 6880

Wilberforce, William
S: 6881

Wild animal trade
S: 8573

Wilder, Laura Ingalls
JS: 6328

Wilderness areas
JS: 7786
S: 8184

Wilderness survival
S: 9801, 9805

Wildflowers
JS: 8435

Wildflowers–Field guides
JS: 8439–41, 8446–48

Wildlife
JS: 8452
S: 8397, 8456, 8577

Wildlife–Deserts
JS: 8409

Wildlife–North America
JS: 8402

Wildlife–Photography
JS: 9438

Williams, Tennessee
S: 3836

Wilson, Woodrow
JS: 6575
S: 6576, 7156, 8012

Wind sports
JS: 9611

Windsurfing
JS: 9954

Winfield, Dave
S: 6735

Wit and humor
JS: 3046, 3482–83, 3486, 3488–89,
    3492, 3494–96, 3499–500, 3502,
    3505, 3507–13, 4276, 8237, 9464,
    9836
S: 3484–85, 3490–91, 3493, 3497–
    98, 3501, 3503, 3506, 3514–19

Wit and humor–English
S: 3504

Wit and humor–Fiction
JS: 3487

Wit and humor–History and
criticism
S: 3565, 3595

Wit and humor–Poetry
JS: 3305–6

Witchcraft
JS: 7840, 9475
S: 7838

Witchcraft–Fiction
JS: 1211, 1515
S: 1805

Witchcraft–History
JS: 7071
S: 9399

Witchcraft–Plays
S: 3105

Witches–Fiction
JS: 1093, 1195, 2718
S: 1005, 1062, 1315, 1762, 2840

Wizard of Oz (film)
JS: 6024

Wizards–Fiction
JS: 1019, 1033, 1136, 1309, 2636
S: 1020, 1090, 1137, 1140, 1200,
    1226, 1277, 1313, 1337, 2437

Wok cooking
S: 9334

Wolfe, Thomas
S: 3719

Wolff, Tobias
S: 6329

Wolves
JS: 8515, 8517, 8519, 8521
S: 8512, 8514, 8516, 8520

Wolves–Fiction
JS: 409
S: 1245–46

Women
S: 4312, 4533–35, 5542

Women–Abuse
S: 5500

Women–Activists
JS: 6489, 6589
S: 6483, 6611

JS = Junior–Senior High S = Senior High

928

Women—Alcoholism
S: 5152

Women—American
S: 4323, 4538, 7733

Women—Armed forces (U.S.)
JS: 4869
S: 4866

Women—Artists
JS: 5746, 5764
S: 5734, 6180, 6201

Women—Biography
JS: 6153, 6379, 6385, 6419, 6423,
  6488, 6612, 6675, 6805, 6889,
  7169, 9918
S: 6245, 6360–61, 6366, 6371,
  6373, 6381, 6389, 6391, 6422,
  6447, 6494–95, 6500, 6619, 6630,
  6637, 6689–92, 6795, 6804, 6817,
  6820, 6873, 6915, 6952, 8194

Women—Black Americans
S: 7779

Women—Bodybuilding
S: 9774, 9777

Women—Careers
JS: 4855, 4971, 5019, 5024
S: 4285, 4572, 4825, 4851, 4918

Women—Chinese
S: 7421

Women—Comedians
JS: 3956

Women—Contemporary
S: 4302

Women—Cults
S: 4052

Women—Detectives
S: 6912

Women—Employment
S: 7714

Women—Explorers
JS: 6149
S: 6121, 6679

Women—Fiction
JS: 331, 389, 450, 693, 1055–56,
  1192, 2529, 2968
S: 63, 101, 332–33, 448, 452, 501,
  506–7, 589, 604, 643, 652, 679,
  755–56, 760, 774, 801, 814, 820,
  822, 825, 883, 970, 1214, 1923,
  1959, 2122, 2181, 2208, 2272,
  2392, 2631, 2646, 2800, 2844,
  2900

Women—Health
JS: 5476, 5498
S: 5342, 5345

Women—History
S: 4366, 4539, 7481, 7733, 7963

Women—Humanitarians
JS: 4088
S: 6958

Women—Islamic
S: 6943

Women—Middle Ages
S: 7133, 7137

Women—Military careers
S: 4285

Women—Native American
S: 7815

**Women—Native American—
  Fiction**
JS: 171
S: 1507

Women—Nobel Prize winners
S: 6789

Women—Occupations
S: 4788

Women—Pioneers
JS: 7995
S: 7985

Women—Poets
JS: 3312
S: 3170, 3274, 3311, 3331, 3848,
  3877, 3890, 6296

Women—Poverty
S: 4513

Women—Psychiatrists
S: 6682

Women—Science fiction
S: 2550

Women—Self-defense
JS: 9903
S: 5444, 5631

Women—Sex roles
S: 4531, 5659

Women—Sports
JS: 5362, 6764, 6767, 6769–70,
  6772, 6775, 9729, 9739, 9745,
  9842, 9871, 9881, 9912
S: 6771, 9551, 9563, 9680, 9870,
  9880, 9882, 9916, 9968

Women—Sports—Fiction
JS: 2871

Women—Writers
JS: 3299, 3303, 3603, 3737, 3789,
  6218, 6220, 6234–35, 6246–47,
  6257, 6277–78, 6328
S: 2918, 3301–2, 3304, 3682, 3715,
  3715, 3727, 3729, 3734, 3755,
  3774, 3963, 3972, 6185, 6212,
  6214, 6219, 6221, 6224–25,
  6229–30, 6236, 6241–42, 6256,
  6279, 6282, 6286, 6308, 6316,
  6325, 6330

Women—Writers—Fiction
JS: 1732, 1831
S: 1715, 2899–900, 3779

Women in architecture
JS: 4940

Women in aviation
JS: 6138, 6140, 9071–72
S: 6131, 6139, 6141, 6154

Women in aviation—Fiction
S: 2943

Women in business
JS: 6650
S: 4572, 4588, 4918–19

Women in engineering
JS: 5019

Women in history
JS: 6486
S: 6785, 7054–55, 7516, 7750,
  7850, 7980

Women in journalism
S: 3984

Women in literature
S: 3617, 3628

Women in mathematics
S: 6645

Women in medicine
JS: 5004, 5024
S: 5231, 5240, 5243, 5247, 6687,
  6694

Women in poetry
S: 3170

Women in politics
JS: 4272, 4971
S: 4207, 4269, 7383

Women in religion
S: 4039, 4084

Women in science
JS: 5031
S: 6119, 6644, 6652, 6655, 6669,
  8203, 8221, 8236

Women in television
S: 6044

Women in war
S: 6287, 7063, 7234, 7286, 7291,
  7316, 8129

Women in war—Fiction
JS: 1542

Women's rights
JS: 4295, 4306, 4316
S: 4293–94, 4304, 4312, 4317,
  4323, 6494–95, 6630, 6637, 6784

JS = Junior–Senior High   S = Senior High

929

Women's suffrage–Fiction
S: 2301

Wonder, Stevie
JS: 6459

Woodcarving
JS: 9291
S: 9292

Woodstock Festival
JS: 5855, 5883

Woodworking
JS: 9268, 9270–71, 9276, 9278, 9284, 9288, 9290, 9295
S: 9265–67, 9269, 9272–73, 9277, 9279–83, 9285–87, 9289, 9293–94, 9389

Woolf, Virginia
S: 6330

Word books
JS: 3903, 3906, 3952
S: 3944

Word games–Dictionaries
JS: 3939

Word processing–Careers
JS: 4935
S: 5049

Word processing–Dictionaries
JS: 9017

Words
JS: 3928
S: 3908, 3913, 3927, 3942–43, 3945

Words and languages, 3903–3954

Workers and laboring classes
S: 4611

Workshops
S: 9392

World affairs and contemporary problems–Fiction, 953–999

World figures–Biography, 6782–6884

World history
S: 6787, 7029, 7032, 7054, 7058–59

World history and geography, 7028–8202

World religions, 4026–4090

World Series
JS: 9657

World War I
JS: 7157, 7162
S: 7155–56, 7158–61, 7163–66

World War I–Fiction
JS: 574
S: 1633–36, 2280

World War I–Poetry
S: 3161

World War II
JS: 6165, 6949, 7167, 7169, 7172–79, 7181–84, 7186, 7190–92, 7196, 7203, 7209, 7213, 7215, 7218, 7220, 7223, 7228, 7239–44, 7246–48, 7251, 7256, 7259–60, 7265, 7268, 7272–73, 7278–80, 7282, 7293, 7296–97, 7302, 7307, 7310–13, 7318–20, 7324, 7326, 7329–30, 7509, 8026, 8076, 9132
S: 6148, 6577, 6580, 6607–8, 6631, 6959, 6969, 7180, 7185, 7187–89, 7193–95, 7197–202, 7205–8, 7210–12, 7214, 7216–17, 7219, 7221–22, 7224–27, 7229–36, 7238, 7245, 7250, 7252–53, 7258, 7261–64, 7266–67, 7269, 7271, 7274, 7276, 7281, 7283–86, 7288–91, 7294–95, 7299–301, 7304, 7306, 7308–9, 7314, 7316–17, 7321–23, 7325, 7331, 7335, 7450, 7506, 8038, 8045, 8049, 8068, 8077

World War II–Africa
S: 7257

World War II–Atlases
JS: 7254

World War II–Events and participants
S: 7328

World War II–Fiction
JS: 42, 194, 198, 250, 283, 854, 1638, 1643, 1645–46, 1651, 1664–65, 1667, 1670, 1673, 1679, 1683, 1686, 2336
S: 126–28, 186, 515, 519, 753, 899, 1180, 1280, 1621, 1639, 1641–42, 1644, 1647–49, 1652–53, 1656–59, 1661–63, 1666, 1668–69, 1671, 1674, 1676–78, 1681–82, 1684–85, 1687–89, 7171

World War II–Internment camps
S: 7305

World War II–Personal letters
JS: 7303

Wrestling
JS: 9784
S: 9783, 9785, 9788

Wrestling–Fiction
S: 2077

Wright, Frank Lloyd
JS: 6210
S: 5705–6, 6211

Wright, Richard
JS: 6332
S: 3696, 6331

Wright, Wilbur and Orville
JS: 6703
S: 6704

Writers
JS: 6332
S: 2910, 3583, 3598, 3654, 3703

Writers–African
S: 3593

Writers–American
JS: 3605, 6318
S: 3607, 6167, 6215, 6217, 6241, 6324

Writers–American–Fiction
S: 391

Writers–Biography
JS: 3739, 6207, 6218, 6220, 6231, 6234–35, 6237, 6252, 6257, 6259, 6263–64, 6270, 6276, 6278, 6290, 6293, 6302, 6321
S: 3665, 3732, 6214, 6221, 6224, 6226–27, 6229, 6232–33, 6236, 6238–40, 6242, 6248–49, 6253–56, 6258, 6260–62, 6266–69, 6271, 6274–75, 6280–82, 6284, 6286, 6295, 6299–301, 6306, 6316–17, 6319–20, 6322–23, 6327, 6329–31

Writers–Biography–Fiction
S: 3710, 6213

Writers–Black Americans
S: 6185

Writers–California–Fiction
S: 2964

Writers–English
S: 6273

Writers–Fiction
JS: 757, 836, 2007
S: 705, 967, 1979, 2103, 2302

Writers–Freelance
S: 3979

Writers–Horror stories
S: 3791

Writers–Interviews
S: 3764

Writers–Journals
S: 6296

Writers–Latin America
S: 3795

Writers–Russian
S: 6310–11

Writers–Science fiction
JS: 3766

JS = Junior–Senior High   S = Senior High

Writers–South (U.S.)
S: 2916

Writers–Women. *See* Women–
Writers

Writers–Yiddish
JS: 6309

Writing
JS: 3962, 3965, 4679, 4682, 4690–
91
S: 3929, 3955, 3957–60, 3963–64,
3966, 3968, 3970, 3975–76, 3978,
3987, 4639–40, 4643, 4654, 4670,
4674–75, 4677–78, 4683, 4687,
4689, 4697–98, 5626

Writing–Careers
JS: 4833

Writing–Character delineation
S: 4694

Writing–Children's books
S: 4898

Writing–Composition
S: 4701

Writing–Handbooks
JS: 4703
S: 4688

Writing–History
S: 3967

Writing–Nonfiction
JS: 4707

Writing–School papers
S: 4699

Writing–Study skills
JS: 4684

Writing–Topic selection
S: 4695

Wyoming–History
S: 7983

Y

Yachting
S: 9934

Yachts–Fiction
JS: 2086

Yakima Indians
JS: 9512

Yamamoto, Isoroku
S: 6819

Yangtze River
JS: 9919

Yastrzemski, Carl
JS: 6736

Yeager, Chuck
S: 6166

Yearbooks
JS: 3980

Yeats, W. B.
S: 3870

Yellowstone National Park
JS: 8158, 8199
S: 8505

Yiddish language–American
JS: 3906

Yiddish language–Dictionaries
JS: 3947

Yiddish language–Writers
JS: 6309

Yoga
S: 5292, 5363

Yom Kippur War
S: 7615

Yorkshire
JS: 7521

**Young adult literature–History
and criticism**
JS: 3739, 3762, 6251, 6277, 6333

Young, Cathy
JS: 6968

Young people–Legal rights
JS: 4303

Yukon River
S: 6146

Z

Zappa, Frank
JS: 6460

Zassenhaus, Hiltgunt
S: 6969

Zeller, Frederic
JS: 6970

Zen Buddhism
S: 3550, 4033

Zindel, Paul
JS: 6333

Zionism
S: 7611, 7614

Zola, Émile
S: 3641

Zombies–Fiction
S: 1760

Zoologists
S: 6667–68

Zoology
JS: 6988, 8411, 8450, 8452, 8454,
8460
S: 8456–57, 8576

Zoos
JS: 6663, 8773, 8776, 8779
S: 8777

Zyskind, Elezer
JS: 7332

JS = Junior–Senior High S = Senior High

931